THE
DICTIONARY
OF
PSYCHOLOGY

THE DICTIONARY OF PSYCHOLOGY

Raymond J. Corsini

BRUNNER/MAZEL
· Taylor & Francis Group ·

8.00

USA	Publishing Office:	BRUNNER/MAZEL *A member of the Taylor & Francis Group* 325 Chestnut Street Philadelphia, PA 19106 Tel: (215) 625-8900 Fax: (215) 625-2940
	Distribution Center:	BRUNNER/MAZEL *A member of the Taylor & Francis Group* 47 Runway Road, Suite G Levittown, PA 19057 Tel: (215) 269-0400 Fax: (215) 269-0363
UK		BRUNNER/MAZEL *A member of the Taylor & Francis Group* 1 Gunpowder Square London EC4A 3DE Tel: +44 171 583 0490 Fax: +44 171 583 0581

THE DICTIONARY OF PSYCHOLOGY

1 2 3 4 5 6 7 8 9 0

Printed by Braun-Brumfield, Ann Arbor, MI, 1999.
Cover design by Joan Wendt.

A CIP catalog record for this book is available from the British Library.
⊗ The paper in this publication meets the requirements of the ANSI Standard Z39.48-1984 (Permanence of Paper).

Library of Congress Cataloging-in-Publication Data
Corsini, Raymond J.
   The dictionary of psychology / Raymond J. Corsini.
      p. cm.
   ISBN 1-58391-028-X (alk. paper)
   1. Psychology—Dictionaries. I. Title.
BF31.C72 1999
150' .3—dc21

99-30502
CIP

ISBN 1-58391-028-X (case)

Dedication

To the memory of these lexicographers of psychology:
**James Mark Baldwin, Howard C. Warren,
Horace B. English, and Howard E. Wikening.**

Contents

About The Author

Raymond J. Corsini's career has included professorships at the University of Chicago, the Illinois Institute of Technology, and the University of California, as well as 15 years as a prison psychologist.

As a clinical psychologist for more than 50 years, Dr. Corsini has published over 40 books, including the four-volume *Encyclopedia of Psychology*. Now retired, Dr. Corsini continues to write extensively, including his seven years' work on this dictionary.

How to Use This Dictionary

Knowing how this dictionary works will help users find what they may otherwise be unable to locate.

Two terms separated by five spaces are considered equivalent with the definition found at the latter. For example:

hypophrenia   mental retardation

A term lacking a definition and followed by See... means the concept is defined elsewhere. For example:

age scale   See AGE-EQUIVALENT SCALE, AGE-GRADE SCALING.

Headwords are presented in their natural order rather than in an inverted or reversed manner. For example, **standard deviation**, not **deviation, standard**. Putting them in their natural order reduces the necessity of searching through the dictionary to find definitions.

Many definitions have cross references to related items, and some headwords have long lists of related items following their definition. Check the cross-reference lists under headwords such as **disorder**, **reflex**, and **syndrome** for examples.

In some cases, headwords may have a number of succeeding terms separated by slashes; this means that the concept is known by a similar name. For example:

Korsakoff's disorder/psychosis/syndrome

Some entries may have a name in parentheses. This person either coined the term or is well-known/best-known in relation to the term. For example,

Individual Psychology (A. Adler)...

Some foreign terms as headwords are italicized and usually followed by a literal translation and the name of the language. For example:

jamais vu (never seen—French)...

According to the American Psychological Association, if a term is in the *Merriam-Webster Collegiate Dictionary* it is considered an English term. Thus, in some cases, this dictionary will have déja vu and *jamais vu*.

A headword with two or more distinct definitions identifies them by numbers.

Names of published books are italicized, and, where possible tests are underlined. Abbreviations of the test name and the compiler or person most associated with the test has been given and underlined as well. For example:

Maudsley Personality Inventory (M.P.I.) (H. Eysenck)...

Useful Appendixes to the dictionary can be found at the end:

Appendix A: Refixes, Suffixes, Affixes
Appendix B: DSM-IV Terms
Appendix C: The Greek Alphabet
Appendix D: Medical Prescription Terms
Appendix E: Systems of Treatment
Appendix F: Measuring Instruments
Appendix G: Symbols
Appendix H: Learning Theory Symbols
Appendix I: Rorchach Descriptors
Appendix J: Biographies

Preface

This dictionary was based on interviews with about one hundred psychologists, selected randomly at psychological conventions, asking them what they wanted and did not want in a dictionary of psychology. Every person interviewed wanted as many definitions as possible. More illustrations, biographies, and appendixes were requested by many. They did not want a dictionary that made them move around from page to page to find definitions, nor one that needed another dictionary to understand definitions.

This dictionary attempts to meets these needs in that it has more than three times the number of defined headwords, biographies, illustrations, and appendixes of any other dictionary of psychology ever printed in English. In addition, it is designed to be user-friendly and efficient. See *How To Use This Dictionary* for an understanding of technical aspects of this dictionary as well as how to take advantage of its contents.

In preparation, more than fifty dictionaries of psychology and psychiatry of the more than one hundred published in English since 1892 were examined for ideas regarding how to generate the most effective and efficient reference book possible.

Headwords came from two dozen dictionaries of psychology, psychiatry, and counseling, from the glossaries of about fifty textbooks, and from articles in encyclopedias and reference books, as well as from diverse sources, especially articles in professional journals. Some definitions came directly from three already-published books with permissions; some were written by invited writers and various consulting editors, and others were written by myself.

More than one hundred psychologists as well as a number of physicians participated as consulting editors. They approved headwords and definitions, made corrections, suggested new headwords, revised definitions, and offered suggestions, and when they were not sure of a definition, they so indicated. About six hundred headwords with definitions went to each of these general consultants. A dozen specialist consulting editors were given questioned material to review when either the consulting editors or I were not sure of definitions.

After the manuscript was completed, additional psychologists were hired by the publisher as independent review editors, and every entry was re-examined, re-reviewed and re-approved by at least one additional psychologist. Some of the publisher's review editors suggested additional terms and most of these suggestions were added to this dictionary after approval by additional consulting editors. Entries were reviewed by Alan Auerbach, the American Psychological Association's de facto dictionary expert, who served as the senior consulting editor, and who provided definitions in specialty and current areas of psychology.

I take responsibility for everything in this dictionary since I revised all definitions, whether they came from permitted sources or were supplied by consulting or review editors, and I approved everything.

Even though this dictionary is quite large, a considerable number of terms defined in other dictionaries of psychology are not found in this dictionary. The reasons vary, sometimes because I thought a definition was not necessary since a person with an average vocabulary should know the meaning of the headword; sometimes I thought a term belonged to medicine or some other field entirely.

Definitions were kept short, averaging 31 words. There are no long encyclopedia-type entries as found in some other dictionaries.

Disorders were generally described without speculating about their causes since this is not a textbook. The mini-biographies are of deceased people influential in the history of psychology.

Some slang, obsolete, and foreign terms are included, usually briefly defined, on the argument that this dictionary might be the only convenient source where someone might find definitions of such terms.

Credit has been given, when known, to coiners of headwords as well as to those people believed to be primarily responsible for basic research in various topics. Without a doubt, errors of omission and commission were made despite every effort to be fair and thorough. Individuals mentioned are identified by their last names and initials when known, a practice few dictionaries follow. For example, there are three well-known Cattells in psychology: *J. McKeen*, *Psyche*, and *Raymond B.*, and each one is properly noted. For some individuals whose first names were not to be found, the absence of an initial or first name indicates that fact. In biographies the absence of a birth or death year occurs when all reasonable efforts to find such information failed.

A number of other people assisted in a various of ways, including Patricia Chong, Evelyn Corsini, Millie Evans, Gloria Posner, and Tricia Rigney, as well as two distinguished psychologists who served as consulting editors who asked not to be identified. Van James was the artist of over one hundred illustrations.

The final proofs were read and corrected by Alan Auerbach and Frank Dumont.

Bernadette Capelle, Anthony Wahl, Lisa Tuttle, and Catherine Van Sciver of the publisher's office contributed in producing this dictionary. The devoted efforts of Rebecca (Becky) Wycoff, this dictionary's managing editor, must be acknowledged as well as the efforts of my wife, Kleona, who served as medical advisor as well as my computer maven.

Raymond J. Corsini

Consulting Editors

Abeles, Norman
Albee, George W.
Alcock, James
Allen, Mary
Andreassi, John
Auerbach, Alan
Ault, Ruth
Austad, Carol Shaw
Bandura, Albert
Bass, Bernard
Beins, Barney
Blatner, Adam
Blau, Theodore
Boneau, C. Alan
Borgatta, Edgar
Brown, Sheldon
Brown, R. E.
Brozek, Josef M.
Carroll, John B.
Cattell, Raymond B.
Caudle, Fairfid M.
Chapanis, Alphonse
Child, Irvin L.
Coan, Richard
Coren, Stan
Cox, Richard H.
Cummings, Nicholas
Davis, Stephen F.
Denmark, Florence
Denny, M. Ray
Deutsch, Morton
Diamond, Milton
Diamond, Herb
Dumont, Frank
Eisdorfer, Carl
Elkind, David
Ellis, Albert

Endler, Norman S.
Enfield, Roger E.
Eysenck, Hans
Fisher, Dennis F.
Frederick, Calvin
Gebotys, Robert
Gladding, Samuel T.
Goldberg, Lewis S.
Graham, Stanley
Hatfield, Elaine
Haynes, Steve
Hess, A. K.
Hoover, Michael
Jensen, Arthur
Jones, Russell A.
Kalat, James W.
Kaslow, Florence W.
Kister, Ken
Lamb, Ramdas
Lazarus, Richard
Lazarus, Arnold A.
Leahey, Thomas H.
Lerner, Arthur
Levin, Jerome
Lipsitt, Paul D.
Lipsitt, Lewis P.
Lykken, David T.
Mandler, George
Marvit, Robert
Matarazzo, Joseph
Mazza, Nicholas
McGuire, William
Merenda, Peter
Meyer, Dennis
Millon, Theodore
Miserandino, Marianne
Motet, Dan

Muelleer, Charles
Mussen, Paul
Oscar-Berman, Marlene
Pedersen, Paul
Perloff, Robert
Peyser, Charles
Pribram, Karl
Prilleltensky, Isaac
Rao, K. Ramakrishna
Reuder, Mary E.
Rhoades, George F.
Rigney, Kleona
Robinson, George
Santrock, John
Schaie, K. Warner
Scheuer, Alice D.
Sechrest, Lee
Shneidman, Edwin S.
Silverman, Hirsch L.
Simon, Herbert
Singer, George Milton
Strickland, Bonnie R.
Sundberg, Norman
Tehrani, S. Muhammad
Triandis, Harry
Tsushima, William T.
Urbina, Susana
Vaughan, Frances
Wagner, Edwin
Walsh, Roger
Wedding, Danny
Well, Arnold D.
Wertheimer, Michael
Wiggins, Jack G.
Woodruff, Michael

**THE
DICTIONARY
OF
PSYCHOLOGY**

A

a 1. amplitude (also abbreviated **A, AMP**). 2. Symbol for an incentive substance. See INCENTIVE STIMULI. 3. Regression constant for the y-intercept. 4. Symbol for trials to extinction. 5. ampere (also abbreviated **A**).

A 1. age. 2. albedo. 3. ambitendency. 4. ampere (also abbreviated **a**). 5. amplitude (also abbreviated **a, AMP**). 6. Any number (as a constant). 7. See RESPONSE AMPLITUDE. 8. In Rorschach test scoring, a symbol for animal responses.

Å angstrom unit

AA 1. achievement age. 2. Alcoholics Anonymous (usually **A.A.**).

AAA acute anxiety attack

AAAP American Association of Applied Psychology

AAAPP American Association of Applied and Preventive Psychology

AAASP Association for the Advancement of Applied Sport Psychology

AAC American Association for Counseling

AACP American Association of Clinical Psychologists

AACS American Academy of Clinical Sexology

A-alpha (Aα) fibers One of the three classes of A fibers that have diameters between 13 and 22 microns and conduction velocities as fast as 120 m/sec. They participate in muscle reflexes and are absent from cutaneous nerves. See A FIBER, ALPHA MOTOR NEURON.

AAMR American Association of Mental Retardation

AAP Association of Applied Psychologists

AAR 1. active avoidance reaction. 2. acceptor of action results.

AAS ascending activating system

AASECT American Association of Sex Educators, Counselors and Therapists

AAT Auditory Apperception Test

Ab antibody

aba adrenergic blocking agent

ABAB design An experimental design that compares two independent variables (A and B). Shifting experimental conditions from A to B and then back to A and then back to B to investigate the differing effects of each variable. Also known as ABAB counterbalancing/order/ sequence.

ABA design An experimental design in which a participant's or animal subject's behavior is measured under baseline conditions (A), then an experimental treatment is applied (B) and any changes in behavior are observed, then the original baseline conditions (A) are restored to investigate that the experimental treatment was responsible for changes during the B phase.

abaissement (abasement, humiliation—French) Pierre Janet's term for inability due to exhaustion (whether physical or psychological), to obey the id's demands.

abalienation Obsolete term for mental illness.

abandoned self (W. James) Refers to no longer attempting to model oneself after an ideal self.

abandonment reaction A feeling of emotional deprivation, loss of support, and loneliness experienced by children deserted or neglected by one or both parents. Also experienced by adults who have lost a loved one on whom they have depended. See MARASMUS.

abasement need (H. A. Murray) A desire to submit to aggressive or punishing behavior of others, or to humble or degrade oneself. See MASOCHISM.

abasia 1. Inability to walk because of physiological difficulties. 2. A symptom of conversion hysteria characterized by loss of motor coordination leading to inability to walk or stand; normally assumed to be a psychological rather than physiological condition. See ASTASIA, ASTASIA-ABASIA, HYSTERIA.

ABBA design 1. An experimental design that compares two independent variables (A and B) to one another in the counterbalanced sequence A—B—B—A. Basic is the assumption that a change in the successive positional order of the two independent variables might affect the dependent variable so that the effect of the order in which the former are sequenced becomes apparent. Also known as ABBA order/sequence. 2. A general approach to organism-as-its-own-control (true experiment, within-subjects) research designs, based on works such as Murray Sidman's *Tactics of Scientific Research*, in which the sequence of conditions of a study might be described eventually as A-B-C-B or A-B-A-B-BC-B or any other sequence that will show clearly the impact of conditions A (usually a baseline), B, and C on the dependent variable.

A-B-C-D-E Therapy (A. Ellis) A later formulation of Rational-Emotive Therapy (RET). It is not the Activating experiences that make a person feel bad or behave poorly (ueC, the undesirable emotional Consequences; ubC, undesirable behavioral Consequences) but the Beliefs about these activating experiences. Therapy consists of Disputing or debating the irrational beliefs (iB). Disputing results in three types of Effects: cognitive (cE, similar to rational beliefs), appropriate feelings or emotions (eE), and desirable behaviors (bE). See A-B-C THEORY, RATIONAL-EMOTIVE BEHAVIOR THERAPY.

Abecedarian Project (J. Sparling) A learning-games curriculum for very young children intended to help at-risk children attain their intelligence potentials by being challenged socially and intellectually.

abclution Rejection of the established behavior patterns of the culture.

ABC technique (J. W. Klapman) A group therapy technique used with patients with schizophrenia that includes printing of the alphabet. The therapist at a blackboard prints ABC and then hands the chalk to a patient who is asked to continue, then asks another patient to continue, and in this way promotes cooperation and eventually conversation between the members.

A-B-C Theory (A. Ellis) The basic concept of Rational-Emotive Behavior Therapy (REBT) that Activating events appear to cause Consequences but are actually caused by Beliefs interposed between the event and the consequences.

abderite Obsolete term for a feebleminded person.

abducens nerve Cranial nerve VI. Carries somatic motor (general visceral efferent) fibers for control of the lateral rectus muscle of the eye. Also known as abducent nerve.

abduction Movement of a body part away from the center of the body, such as a fist opening up with fingers showing. Compare ADDUCTION.

abductor A muscle that pulls body parts away from the center of the body. Compare ADDUCTOR.

Aberdeen system A 19th-century industrial-social movement that established a series of schools emphasizing the rights of children, family ties, and meeting the needs of the whole child and his or her family.

aberration Any deviation from the normal or typical, with the implication that the deviation is wrong, unwanted, or abnormal.

aberration (of light) Failure of light rays from a point to form a single-point image on the retina after traversing an optical system. Types of aberration include: CHROMATIC, CURVATURE, LONGITUDINAL, MARGINAL, PERIPHERAL, SPHERICAL.

A-beta ($A\beta$) fibers One of the three classes of A fibers that have diameters between 6 and 12 microns and conduction velocities of 35–75 m/sec. They are sensory and are found in cutaneous nerves. See A FIBER.

abience Movement away from a stimulus. Compare ADIENCE.

abient behavior (E. Holt) Avoidant action that moves an organism away from noxious stimuli. Also known as abient drive/response. Compare ADIENT BEHAVIOR.

ability 1. The physical, mental, or legal competence to function. 2. A present skill, such as being able to spell a certain word, perform arithmetic, ride a bicycle, or recite a poem. Contrasts with capacity, which refers to potential ability. 3. (J. B. Carroll) Refers to the possible variations over individuals in the liminal levels of task difficulty (or in derived measurements based on such liminal levels) at which, on any given occasion in which all conditions appear favorable, individuals perform successfully on a defined class of tasks. See APTITUDE.

ability grouping The assignment of students to levels of classes based on either actual performance, estimated learning potential, or following objective testing.

ability test Any examination designed to measure present skills on any mental or physical dimension (for example, a spelling or driving test). See MEASUREMENT, RELIABILITY OF TESTS, TESTS, VALIDITY OF TESTS.

ability trait A personality characteristic thought to be relatively unchanging and enduring over time.

abiogenesis (T. H. Huxley) A theory of origin of living matter, that life can occur spontaneously from nonorganic material, disproved by Ferdinand Cohn. See SPONTANEOUS GENERATION.

abjection Discouragement, feelings of depression, low self-concept.

Abklingen (to fade away—German) A fading out of a tone or other sensation, involving either an intensive or a qualitative change or both.

ablation Removal of a portion of a body part or the destruction of its function, as by a surgical procedure. See BIOPSY, EXTIRPATION.

ABLE Adult Basic Learning Examination

ableitend German term introduced by Johann Unzer which became "efferent." Compare AUFLEITEND.

ablution 1. Water treatment formerly widely used to quiet restless or violent patients by wrapping them in wet sheets, or immersing them in a tub of warm water. 2. Ritual washing, symbolic of spiritual cleansing. Some systems of psychotherapy, such as Rebirthing, dip clients in water as part of the process of personality change.

ablutomania Morbid preoccupation with cleanliness, exhibited by frequent washing or bathing, as seen in obsessive-compulsive disorder (OCD).

abmodality Not modal. See MODE.

ABMS American Board of Medical Specialties

Abney's effect (W. Abney) An illumination illusion when a large area is lit up. The appearance is that the center lights up first and then the light spreads to other areas. When the area is darkened, the edges appear to darken first and the center last. Named after English chemist and physicist William de Wiveslie Abney (1843–1920). See ABNEY'S LAW.

Abney's law (W. Abney) A principle that the luminance (strength) of a given monochromatic light is proportional to the luminosity (brightness) of the light and the radiance (radiant energy). See ABNEY'S EFFECT.

abnormal 1. Not normal. 2. Differing from the norm to an unusual degree, such as people deviating 20% in weight from the average for their age may be considered statistically abnormal even if perfectly healthy. 3. Refers to behavior or thinking patterns considered different from those of healthy normal people to a gross degree, especially if the deviation is harmful or socially unacceptable. Also known as abnormality.

abnormal behavior 1. Action, reaction, and/or interaction that is not normal because it differs from the usual state, structure, or condition. 2. Behavior differing to an extreme extent from the actions of most people, regarded as evidence of a mental or emotional disturbance ranging from minor adjustment problems to severe a mental disorder. 3. Behavior that is statistically rare, labeled abnormal by society, nonadaptive in particular situations.

abnormal fixation A persistent thought or behavior that is apparently meaningless to others. See TIC.

abnormality See ABNORMAL.

abnormal mental processes Cognitive processes which diverge strikingly from those considered normal.

abnormal psychology A branch of psychology that studies behavior considered unusual, aberrant, deviant, or psychopathological.

aboiement (barking—French) A speech disturbance in which animal sounds such as barking are involuntarily emitted; seen in chronic advanced schizophrenia and de la Tourette's syndrome.

aboral Opposite to or away from the mouth.

aboriginal therapy Psychotherapy practiced in aboriginal societies, including folk healing, sorcery, and the use of a shaman or witch doctor.

abortion The expulsion of an embryo or fetus before it has reached the stage of viability, prior to about 20 weeks of gestation. May be either spontaneous or induced. See MISCARRIAGE.

aboulia abulia

above and below (A. Adler) A tendency to establish a relative, comparative social ranking, consciously or unconsciously, in which those with inferiority feelings place themselves lower in the hierarchy than they merit.

above-down analysis An analysis that proceeds from the whole to the parts, in contrast with an elementistic and summative synthesis from "below-up." See DEDUCTIVE REASONING.

ABPP American Board of Professional Psychology

abreaction (S. Freud, J. Breuer) In Freudian psychoanalysis, a discharge of repressed emotions by bringing into conscious recollection previously repressed or unpleasant experiences that have been buried in the unconscious. See CATHARSIS.

abridgment of response A shortening of the process of a complex behavior following practice.

ABS Adaptive Behavior Scale

abscissa The horizontal reference line on a two-dimensional chart. The X axis. Compare ORDINATE.

absence A brief loss of consciousness usually followed by amnesia for that period.

absenteeism In industrial psychology, a record of the number, duration, and cause of absences from work. Used as one criterion of job performance and job satisfaction.

absentmindedness A form of habitual inattention, marked by preoccupation with thoughts and inattentiveness to environmental stimuli. See ADD, AUTISM.

absent state A vacant, dreamlike state of detachment found in some forms of epilepsy.

Absicht (intention, purpose—German) The aspect of life that motivates and directs behavior. See CONATION, TELEOLOGY.

absolute Free from imperfection; complete; perfect; certain. Refers to totality of reality about something rather than part of the reality.

absolute accommodation 1. The act or state of adjustment or adaptation. 2. In physiology, a change in the shape of the lens of each eye while focusing on objects at various distances. Refers to the accommodation of each eye separately. Compare BINOCULAR ACCOMMODATION.

absolute bliss Complete happiness. See TRANSCENDENTAL MEDITATION.

absolute error The magnitude of the deviation of a score from the true score, without regard to sign.

absolute idealism (G. Hegel) A doctrine positing that the mind is a part of an all-embracing spiritual unity.

absolute impression A judgment based on implied or vague standards, such as "It was a bright day."

absolute inversion 1. Freudian phrase for a kind of homosexuality so well-entrenched that the thought of heterosexual activity evokes repugnance in such a person. 2. Exclusive homosexuality. Compare AMPHIGENOUS INVERSION.

absolute judgment A categorical judgment in which any item is evaluated without respect to previous ones.

absolute-judgment method A procedure for making judgments without respect to any criterion or comparison with anything else.

absolute limen (AL) The statistically determined point at which a stimulus is just barely adequate to elicit a specified sensory response. See ABSOLUTE THRESHOLD.

absolute luminosity 1. The measure of luminosity in standard units of light reflectance, for example, lumens per watt. 2. Variable ability of a surface, such as a mirror, to radiate or reflect light.

absolute measurement A measure made directly and independently of comparison with other variables.

absolute personal equation Deviation between a consistent value obtained by an observer and a standard value accepted as true, as in difference between individuals in simple reaction time.

absolute pitch 1. The frequency of a tone as measured in Hertz (cycles per second). 2. Ability to identify an isolated tone.

absolute rating scale A type of rating instrument in which the given dimensions are evaluated according to absolute values, that is, the dimensions or subjects to be rated are not compared with other dimensions or subjects but are judged according to independent criteria.

absolute reality   Refers to the actual, as opposed to the illusory, that is unaffected by the transient perceptions of fallible humans.

absolute-refractory period/phase   The brief first part of the refractory period following a stimulus during which the nerve or nerve fiber will not respond to any stimulus. Corresponds to the rising phase and the initial falling phase of the action potential and is followed by the relative refractory period.

absolute scale   A scale that is measured in equal intervals from an absolute zero base point. See RATIO SCALE.

absolute sensitivity   1. The minimum stimulus needed to produce a sensation. 2. Degree of sensory acuity based on magnitude of the stimulus needed to evoke a response or the amount of sensation evoked by a standard unit of stimulus. See ABSOLUTE LIMEN, ABSOLUTE THRESHOLD.

absolute temperature scale   Kelvin scale

absolute threshold   The minimum amount of sensory stimulation required to trigger a reaction or produce a sensation. Often taken as the lowest or weakest level of stimulation detectable on 50% of trials. The absolute threshold is relative and fluctuates according to alterations in receptors and environmental conditions. Also known as absolute limen, detection threshold, *Reiz Limen* (German).

absolute true score   The numerical result of a test given to 100% of individuals of a population rather than a result based on examining only a sample of that population. For instance, all recruits in the Marine Corps take a test of military knowledge in any particular year. The average score obtained is therefore absolutely true and not a sampling estimate for this group of cadets for that year. See TRUE SCORE.

absolute value   (A. Cayley) The number of units that a point on a scale would deviate in any direction from the zero point.

absolute zero   The point on any measuring scale on which whatever is being measured cannot go down further. On the Kelvin scale, 0° is the temperature at which all action ceases, at minus 273.16° Celsius. In contrast, a relative score of zero on an intelligence test does not mean total absence of all cognitive ability, only the bottom of that particular scale.

absolutist ethic   An unchanging moral value or point of view about what is right or wrong. See SITUATION ETHICS.

absorbed mania   A mental state in which people have concentrated their attention on inner thoughts so intensely that they have excluded themselves from reality.

absorption   1. In general, the incorporation or taking in of phenomena. 2. In psychology, an extreme involvement or preoccupation with one object, idea, or pursuit with inattention to other aspects of the environment.

absorption curve   A graphic representation that shows the degree to which different wavelengths of light are absorbed or reflected by an object. See ABSOLUTE LUMINOSITY.

abstinence   1. In psychoanalysis, refers to analysands being expected to refrain from activities which might divert the build-up of the requisite tension for their introspective process. See ABSTINENCE RULE. 2. A belief in the field of substance abuse that the only way to control addictive tendencies is to avoid the use of the substances completely, in contrast to those who would tolerate moderate use. 3. Complete avoidance of sexual relationships.

abstinence delirium   A type of delirium that is a part of the withdrawal symptoms of alcoholism or drug dependence. See ALCOHOL-WITHDRAWAL DELIRIUM.

abstinence rule   (S. Freud) In psychoanalytic theory, the primary rule that analysands should not do anything or experience anything during their analysis either pleasurable or unpleasant that could interfere with the course of the psychotherapy. Also known as rule of abstinence.

abstinence syndrome   1. The symptoms of withdrawal from a physiological dependence on a drug. 2. The symptoms of craving and continued residues of addictive cognition that can last for months, if not years, after sobriety has been attained.

abstract   A condensed summary of a report, scientific article, or other writing, summarizing only its major aspects. See ABSTRACT CONCEPTUALIZATION.

abstract ability   1. Ability to interrelate or discern a relationship between ideas, concepts, or theories previously considered disparate. 2. Capacity to operate symbolically to solve problems without doing any physical manipulation. For example, multiplying $8 \times 3 \times 11$ mentally.

abstract attitude   1. A cognitive reaction to a novel situation, not in terms of the objective factors, but rather in terms of a preconception of how to deal with the situation, usually based on a creative solution rather than a stereotyped action. 2. (K. Goldstein) A set of cognitive abilities to perceive as wholes or as general concepts as opposed to perceiving concretely and in terms only of immediate experience. These abilities for abstraction are usually impaired in patients with organic brain syndromes. Also known as categorical attitude. See ABSTRACT THINKING. Compare CONCRETE ATTITUDE.

abstract behavior   (K. Goldstein) Acts in which the person not only perceives and reacts to stimuli but thinks holistically about the meaning, interrelations, and potential usefulness of such stimuli. See QUALE.

abstract conceptualization   The process of forming abstract concepts such as liberty and integrity. See ABSTRACT ATTITUDE, ABSTRACT THINKING.

abstract discourse   Conversation about generalities, such as ideas, ideals, values, concepts, theories, philosophies.

abstract expressionism   Subjective generalizations intended to interpret the meaning intended by an artist of a particular creation.

abstract idea   A generalized concept considered apart from concrete examples, such as discerning that a circle and a square are both shapes, that a table and a chair are both articles of furniture, or Albert Einstein's concept that time varies with the speed of light. See ABSTRACT CONCEPTUALIZATION, DEDUCTIVE LOGIC.

abstracting The act of considering something as a general quality or characteristic, apart from concrete realities, specific objects, or actual instances. Discerning the common elements in situations which are different from one another.

abstract intelligence The intellectual ability to think in terms of more generalized, symbolic concepts and ideas rather than their separate parts. See ABSTRACT THINKING, HOLISM. Compare CONCRETE INTELLIGENCE.

abstraction 1. Absorbed in thoughts, absentmindedness. 2. Removal and study of an element of a whole. 3. Summary of a conclusion. 4. The process through which generalizations are formed from similarities.

abstraction experiment An experiment in which perceptual parts are presented successively to a participant until recognition of the common features from all entities is attained.

abstract learning The intellectual mastering of concepts, relations between concepts, philosophical assumptions, or symbols, as opposed to concrete learning.

abstract modeling (A. Bandura) A high level of observational learning in which people extract the rules governing various actions exhibited by others. Once observers learn the rules, they can use them to create patterns of behavior that go beyond what they have seen or heard. See SOCIAL COGNITIVE THEORY.

abstract perception Unusual, uncanny, and unlocalized experiences in and around the body, such as floating through space, awareness of hazy rotating objects, and sensations of crescendo and decrescendo of sound. Occurs most often in dreams, while falling asleep, or in stress situations. See ISAKOWER PHENOMENON.

abstract thinking A type of thinking characterized by the ability to use generalizations. Specifically, the ability to grasp essentials and common properties, to keep different aspects of a situation in mind and shift from one to another, to predict and plan ahead, to think symbolically, and draw conclusions. See ABSTRACT ATTITUDE, ABSTRACT CONCEPTUALIZATION.

abstract vs representational dimension A system of evaluating the psychological reaction to a work of art based on the amount and pattern of detail referred to or denoted in the art. At the representational end of the dimension, a work of art will be characterized by a great amount of detail. At the abstract end of the scale, a more holistic impression appears and detail and pattern of detail will be highly selective and some details will be excluded.

abstract words Low-imagery words, such as "acquire," "belief," "close," in contrast to concrete words that have high imagery value, such as "acupuncture," "bell," "computer." Note that the latter group are all nouns that can be easily visualized. See CONCRETE WORDS VS ABSTRACT WORDS.

absurdity A blatant contradiction between a conclusion and certain known or accepted truths. An idea or expression that is obviously nonsensical, incoherent, or meaningless.

absurdity test A task in some intelligence tests in which participants are to find or identify inconsistencies or incongruities in a picture, story, or written paragraph. See BINET TEST.

abulia An extreme loss of initiative and will power; inability to make decisions or perform voluntary actions such as speech, movement, thought, or emotional reaction. Found in bilateral frontal-lobe disorder and sometimes in disorders such as schizophrenia and depression. Also spelled aboulia. See HYPOBULIA.

abundancy motive A tendency to want and strive for a greater degree of gratification than that required to fill a particular physical need (for example, eating more food than the amount actually needed to reduce hunger). Compare DEFICIENCY MOTIVE.

abuse 1. Misuse, especially excessive use, as in substance abuse. 2. Injurious or harmful treatment, as in child abuse.

abused children Children who have been physically or psychologically harmed, typically by their parents. ("Normal corrections" in one culture may call for arrest in another.) Psychological abuse can be as harmful to children as physical abuse, but is more difficult to prove. See BATTERED CHILD SYNDROME.

abuse need Refers to the apparent need by some people to be abused, termed so because their actions appear to invite punishment. See ALCOHOLIC'S WIFE/HUSBAND, MASOCHISM.

abuse of substance See SUBSTANCE ABUSE.

abuse potential (of a given drug) A general description or a specific measure of the tendency of a drug to evoke a pattern of chemical dependence or compulsive use of that substance. Generally, this correlates with the degree to which the drug generates euphoria and with the speed at which the substance enters the bloodstream (for example, smoking crack has a far greater abuse potential than, say, drinking a dilute solution of cocaine). Once called abuse liability.

ABX paradigm In research, when a third stimulus is to be matched with the first two. A procedure to establish different sensory thresholds. After exposure to two stimuli, A and B, the participant judges whether stimulus X, a duplicate of A or B, is the same as A or B.

academic 1. Pertaining to any line of inquiry or research intended to expand existing knowledge. 2. Pertaining to formal education.

academic inhibition Not doing as well in school (academically) as might be expected in terms of the student's aptitude for learning academic materials, interest in the topic or subject matter, and amount of time spent studying. See ACADEMIC-UNDERACHIEVEMENT DISORDER, ADJUSTMENT DISORDER IN RELATION TO TASKS.

academic intelligence tasks (U. Neisser) Problems formulated by others, usually of little intrinsic interest, having only one correct answer, and having one method of solution. See PRACTICAL INTELLIGENCE TASKS.

academic journal A periodical that publishes articles that add to knowledge of the discipline covered by the journal. Unlike nonacademic magazines, the authors, editors, and reviewers are generally not paid for their work.

academic overachievement Better performance with school grades or scholastic test scores than is expected or predicted. Causes can be complex, but assumed to be primarily a function of high motivation.

academic problem   1. A behavioral problem associated with children who do not want to, or are afraid to, go to school; who in school will not behave according to normal standards; who are defiant and oppositional, or who behave violently against other children and adults. 2. A problem related to learning characterized by children refusing to learn certain topics or who for reasons unknown to the teacher appear to be unable to learn what the teacher assumes the child could if an effort were made.

academic-underachievement disorder   A problem characterized by a pattern of failing grades or significant underachievement in spite of adequate intellectual capacity and learning opportunity, but without evidence of a specific cognitive or physical disorder to account for the change. See UNDERACHIEVER.

acalculia   A form of aphasia characterized by inability to perform simple arithmetic operations. Associated with lesions of the brain and other forms of dementia or early trauma in learning mathematics. In some cases the person may also be unable to read or write numbers. See ANARITHMIA, DYSCALCULIA.

acanthesthesia   A skin sensation in which the person experiences the feeling of pinpricks in the absence of an external stimulus. May result from disease or abuse of certain drugs. See FORMICATION, PARESTHESIA.

acarophobia   Morbid fear of itching or of skin parasites (mites), ants, worms, and, by extension, small objects such as pins and needles. See FORMICATION, LILLIPUTIAN HALLUCINATION, PARASITOPHOBIA, PEDICULOPHOBIA.

acatalepsia   Inability to comprehend or reason. Formerly used as another name for dementia.

acatamathesia   1. The absence or loss of the ability to comprehend perceptions of objects or situation. 2. Inability to comprehend speech. Also known as acatamathesis, akatamathesia.

acataphasia   1. Inability to correctly form a sentence. 2. The use of inappropriate or grammatically incorrect words and expressions. A speech disturbance found in patients with schizophrenia and patients with aphasia. Also spelled akataphasia. See AGRAMMATIC APHASIA, SYNTACTICAL APHASIA.

acathathis(i)a   akathisia

acathexia   1. An abnormal release of secretions. 2. See ACATHEXIS.

acathexis   1. In psychoanalysis, the absence of feeling ordinarily associated with emotionally charged ideas (for example, the patient is detached or indifferent when told of an event that usually arouses a happy or angry response in others). 2. Flatness of emotions, lack of feelings. Sometimes known as acathexia.

acathisia   akathisia

accelerated interaction   The heightened level of emotional interaction reached for example, by members of a marathon group, due to continuous proximity for an extended period of time. See TIME-EXTENDED THERAPY.

acceleration   1. The act of accelerating. 2. A change in velocity. 3. A change in the speed of motion (such as the rate of growth), usually indicated on a graph by the amount of rise or fall per unit of time. In psychology, a normal curve shows first positive acceleration (upward movement) and then negative acceleration (deceleration). Some curves show constant acceleration such as growth of height at certain ages; some show negative and then positive acceleration as in progress of memorization. See BINOMIAL CURVE, CATENARY CURVE, NEGATIVE LEARNING CURVE, NORMAL CURVE.

accelerator nerve   Any nerve that hastens the performance of a function.

accent   An error in logic when a premise-term has a different meaning from the same term in the conclusion of an argument. See FALLACIES.

accentuation theory   A point of view that there is a tendency to exaggerate the degree of similarities between items placed in the same category and to exaggerate dissimilarities of items placed in different categories.

acceptance   The receptive, approachable, caring quality of people (such as psychotherapists and teachers) who convey respect and regard for their patients and students as individuals. In general, a favorable attitude toward an idea or person.

Acceptance and Commitment Therapy   (S. Hayes) Based on B. F. Skinner's radical behaviorism, the therapist employs behavioral analysis to aid clients accept limitations and potential.

acceptance region   In statistical hypothesis testing, the values of the test statistic for which the null hypothesis is not rejected.

acceptance stage   (E. Kübler-Ross) The fifth and last stage in Kübler-Ross' stages of dying, characterized by a consent and willingness to die. See STAGES OF DYING.

acceptor   A person who has learned to cope with unresolved personality conflicts by accepting them. Compare DENIER.

accessibility   Availability of people to receive services, enter places, receive instructions or information, and to be heard.

accessible   Receptive or responsive to other persons or external influences (for example, a patient who responds to a therapist in a manner that facilitates the development of rapport).

accessory   Contributing to some event but being of secondary importance.

accessory chromosome   An extra X or Y chromosome or a trisomic autosome.

accessory muscle   A muscle that participates with and assists a major muscle.

accessory nerve   (T. Willis) Cranial nerve XI. It has two components. The cranial portion joins the vagus nerve and supplies the muscles of the larynx. Fibers in this portion are classified as special visceral efferent. The spinal portion of the nerve supplies the lateral muscles of the neck and the trapezius muscle. This part is classified as general somatic efferent. It innervates muscles of the neck, shoulder, soft palate, and vocal organs. Some of its fibers join the vagus nerve.

accessory sense-apparatus   All tissues and cells that contribute to the effective functioning of an organ but are not themselves part of the afferent nerves or special receptor cells of the organ.

accessory structure   Any receptor that can either assist or take over specific functions of another receptor.

accessory symptoms   (E. Bleuler) Secondary symptoms that are not fundamental to schizophrenia, such as memory disturbances, neologisms, and disjointed speech.

accident   1. An undesirable or unfortunate happening, unintentionally caused and usually resulting in harm, injury, damage or loss; a casualty of mishap. 2. In logic, an error due to careless use of generalizations. See FALLACIES.

accidental behavior   (S. Freud) Actions that are consciously unintended but unconsciously desired and are likely to generate damage to the person or to others.

accidental chaining   The attachment of a neutral response to a reinforced response due to fortuitous contiguity, such as the neutral response occurring just before the reinforced response so that the stimulus for the reinforced response also produces the previously neutral response.

accidental crisis   In community psychology, one of two major types of crisis, characterized by a period of acute disorganization of behavior or affect precipitated by stressful and unpredictable life experience such as the death of a family member, illness, accident, surgery, loss or change of job, or marital disruption. Also known as situational crisis, unanticipated crisis. See MATURATIONAL CRISIS.

accidental error   1. In research or observation, the unexplained measurement error due to unpredictable, unknown, or uncontrollable factors. 2. A relatively small, variable, unpredictable error by which a single observation differs from the mean of similar observations after all controllable sources of error have been eliminated. See ERROR VARIANCE.

accidental group   A group established by chance, such as passengers on a bus who do not know each other. See ACCIDENTAL SAMPLE, HETEROGENEOUS GROUP, HETEROGENEOUS GROUPING.

accidental property   (Aristotle) A quality added to something that causes superficial changes, for example, in appearance, but not fundamental ones. Also known as contingent property.

accidental reinforcement   The strengthening of responses by some unwanted, unplanned stimulus. Also known as incidental reinforcement.

accidental sample   1. A nonrepresentative sample based on any group available that may not be representative of the population intended. 2. A hit-or-miss sample (for example, interviewing everyone who happens to be at a park). Also known as chunk sample, opportunistic sample, sample of opportunity, sample of convenience. See REPRESENTATIVE SAMPLING.

accidental stimuli   Dream stimuli of an external sensory nature, such as the sound of a telephone ringing or a cramped muscle pain.

accidentally on purpose   Implies that a behavior or act regarded as accidental (such as a server spilling food on a customer) may actually be purposeful.

accident behavior   Unsafe actions that might result in injury to the individual or other persons, or in physical damage to equipment or the environment. Accidents are associated with such situational factors as a risky job, atmospheric conditions, a fatiguing work schedule, and equipment failure; or such personal factors as inattention, perception errors, risk-taking, and decision errors.

accident neurosis   **compensation neurosis**

accident path model   A concept that there are methods of operating that increase the risk of accidents.

accident prevention   In industrial engineering psychology, the application of scientifically tested methods for preventing or reducing the number of accidents.

accident prone behavior   Actions likely to result in injury or damage.

accident prone(ness)   Susceptibility to accidents; a tendency that results in having a greater number of accidents than would be expected of the average person in similar circumstances. See ACCIDENT-PRONE PERSONALITY.

accident-prone personality   (F. Dunbar) A hypothetical type of person who exhibits a chronic susceptibility to accidents; the tendency to be an "accident repeater" marked by characteristics such as impulsiveness, risk-taking, intolerance of authority, emotional instability, a fatalistic outlook. Research in industrial settings has led many (for example, W. K. Kirchner) to question the concept. Beyond chance, accidents seem to be more related either to the setting or to a particular combination of setting and personal characteristics (for example, selective attention, perceptual-motor reaction time). See ACCIDENT PRONE(NESS), PURPOSIVE ACCIDENT, VICTIM RECIDIVISM.

accident reduction   1. Lessening the number and severity of accidents through measures such as safety-education programs, alcohol-detection tests, and the use of safety gear. 2. In industrial engineering psychology, methods to reduce accidents or their consequences. See ACCIDENT PREVENTION.

accident repeater   See ACCIDENT PRONE(NESS), ACCIDENT-PRONE PERSONALITY.

acclimation   1. Adjustment to a climate, whether physical or social. 2. Any emotional or mental adjustment to new circumstances or environmental conditions. See ACCLIMATIZATION.

acclimatization   The alterations in physiological adaptation mechanisms involved in moving to a different climate. Also known as acclimation.

accommodating style   Mode of life in which a person would rather be cooperative than assertive or demanding.

accommodation   1. In general, the act or state of adjustment or adaptation as in adaptation of the body or the whole person to environmental or social situations. 2. In sensorimotor theory, Jean Piaget's term (1950) for the process of modifying existing cognitive structures according to new experience and information. 3. In vision, contraction or relaxation of the ciliary muscles of the eyes to adjust the lens to far or near vision. Also involves changes in convergence and pupil size. Also known as visual accommodation.

accommodation sensation Body sensations accompanying changes of visual accommodation, attributed to changes in tension of the ciliary muscle that controls the shape of the lens.

accommodation time Duration of the period of adjustment of the eyes between near and far vision.

accompanying movement Any movement of other parts of the body which occurs simultaneously with a given response, but is not treated as an integral part of that response.

accomplishment quotient (AQ or A.Q.) Obsolete name for achievement quotient.

accountability The responsibility of an individual or organization for behavior, usually in relation to the welfare of other individuals, such as the responsibility of a supervisor for a trainee psychologist, and the trainee for treatment of a client.

accounts Verbal statements to explain or discuss facts or behavior such as a client might share with or verbalize to a counselor.

accreditation 1. The process by which an institution or program is evaluated to determine if it complies with standards established by an appropriate professional group. 2. A procedure for awarding a person a right or credential to practice a speciality, such as a license or some recognition of special abilities.

accretion 1. In environmental psychology, the accumulation of objects or material in the environment (for example, littering), which may be a measure of the degree of individual responsibility of persons who use the area. 2. In learning theory, the cumulative effect of repeated associations and reinforcements, especially if the learning is not organized, with an individual learning a lot of fragmented bits of information. 3. A growing together.

acculturation 1. The processes by which social and cultural values, ideas, beliefs, and behavioral patterns are inculcated. 2. An attitudinal and behavioral adjustment to conform to a new culture (for example, a new country). Sometimes known as cultural assimilation. 3. In social anthropology, the adoption of alien cultural patterns by a distinct people or group.

acculturation problem 1. Describing a situation where a person is either unable or unwilling to adapt to a new culture. Often such an individual will consider the new culture to be inferior or otherwise undesirable in terms of various standards (for example, cultural or religious) to that he or she has brought from the prior culture. 2. Describing a situation in which a person born and raised in a particular culture apparently rejects such culture or seems unable to adjust to it, even though immediate family members have adjusted. Reasons for inability to tolerate the social environment can vary widely.

accumulation Objects amassed usually without meaning or purpose, unlike a collection. See SOTERIA.

accuracy 1. Absence of error. 2. In testimony, correspondence between statements and objective facts. 3. In behavior, the degree to which actions conform to given conditions.

accuracy compulsion An abnormal need or striving for perfection that in some cases has self-defeating elements in that a person may do nothing in the search for perfection. See PERFECTIONISM.

accuracy progress Measured decrease of time or of number of trials to achieve accuracy to a predetermined criterion level.

accuracy test 1. A task scored for correctness of answers and not for other criteria such as speed. 2. An examination of abilities with the score based on errors made, usually with either no time limits or very long ones. See A TEST.

AC–DC Originally an abbreviation for alternating direct electrical current, now slang for bisexuality (also abbreviated **AC/DC**).

ACE test See AMERICAN COUNCIL ON EDUCATION TEST.

acedia Obsolete term for apathy. A psychological syndrome characterized by listlessness, carelessness, and melancholia.

acenesthesia 1. A loss of the sensation of physical existence; lack of sense of awareness of the body. See DEPERSONALIZATION. 2. Loss of feeling of well-being.

acephaly 1. Congenital absence of a head. Also known as acephalia, acephalism. 2. Being without a normal full-sized head. 3. A headless organism.

acetylcholine (ACh, Ach, or ACH) (H. H. Dale, J. A. von Baeyer) One of the most common neurotransmitters throughout the body, operating at the neuromuscular junctions, in the brain, and especially expressed in the parasympathetic nervous system, where it has cholinergic functions, such as increasing salivation, bowel motility, and bladder function. (These functions are inhibited or countered by anticholinergic drugs.)

acetylcholinesterase (AChE) An enzyme that splits acetylcholine into choline and acetic acid after the neurotransmitter has been utilized by a nerve impulse. Also known as cholinesterase.

ACFE American College of Forensic Examiners

ACh See ACETYLCHOLINE.

AChE See ACETYLCHOLINESTERASE.

acheiria 1. Congenital absence of the hands. 2. Loss of the sense of having one or both hands. Seen in hysteria. 3. Inability to tell on which side of the body a stimulus has been applied. Also spelled achiria.

achieved role/status A social role that has been attained through personal effort. See ASCRIBED GOAL.

achievement 1. (J. B. Carroll) Refers to the degree of learning in some procedure intended to produce learning, such as a formal or informal course of instruction, or a period of self-study of a topic, or practice of a skill. 2. In general psychology, personal accomplishment, or attainment, of goals set by the individual or by society. 3. In educational psychology, a specified level of proficiency in academic work in general or in a specific skill such as reading or arithmetic.

achievement age (AA) The rating of a person on a skill, task, or group of tasks measured in terms of the norm or standard for individuals of a particular chronological age (CA).

achievement battery Any group of coordinated tests that are designed to provide an index of a person's general knowledge or specific aptitudes across a range of specific skills. See ACHIEVEMENT TESTS.

achievement drive   A compelling urge to exert the best effort to achieve a goal and, usually, to gain recognition and approval for attaining it. See ACHIEVEMENT MOTIVATION.

achievement ethic   A cultural standard or ideal embodying a high level of accomplishment. See WORK ETHIC.

achievement level   The score that a person earns on tests measuring any special ability, such as academic achievement. In sports, score in bowling, golf, and other activities.

achievement motivation   1. (H. A. Murray) The need to overcome obstacles and master difficult challenges. 2. (D. C. McClelland) An inferred inherent aspect of humans present from infancy on, to move forward to bigger and better things, to accomplish goals, and to compete with others for first place. Also known as achievement motive/need. See ACHIEVEMENT DRIVE, DRIVE, MOTIVE, NEED FOR ACHIEVEMENT.

achievement-oriented leadership   A management style directed to a specific goal.

achievement quotient (AQ or A.Q.)   The ratio of actual performance or achievement (of an individual or group) to a standard or expected accomplishment or age norm. Once called accomplishment quotient (AQ).

achievement test   A standardized examination intended to measure a participant's present level of skill or knowledge in a given topic such as reading or arithmetic. Often a distinction is made that achievement tests emphasize ability acquired through formal learning or training whereas aptitude tests emphasize innate potential. In addition to usage in academic areas, achievement tests are employed for a variety of vocational, professional, and diagnostic purposes. See ACHIEVEMENT BATTERY.

Achilles (tendon) reflex   An automatic reflexive action of the ankle when the Achilles tendon is lightly tapped. Named after a mythical Greek warrior who was vulnerable only on his heel. Also known as Achilles jerk, ankle jerk.

achiria   acheiria

achloropsia   A form of color blindness with difficulty in perceiving green. See DEUTERANOPIA.

achlu(o)phobia   Morbid fear of darkness. See NYCTOPHOBIA.

achnutshik   In Greenland of old, a male raised as a female who became an adolescent transvestite sexual partner or quasi-legal wife for an older man. See BERDACHE.

achondroplasia   A form of dwarfism in which the bones from cartilage develop at a slower rate than the bones from connective tissue. Also known as achondroplastic dwarfism, achondroplasty, osteosclerosis congenita, Parrot's disease.

achromate   A person who is completely color-blind, seeing everything in shades of grey.

achromatic   (J. Bevis) Colorless. Black and white.

achromatic-chromatic scale   A series of color values ranging through the whole chromatic spectrum of hues and including the achromatic shades of black through gray to white.

achromatic color   A visual quality which belongs to the white-gray-black series, such as one that is colorless and which exhibits no hue or saturation and hence is characterized solely by its intensity. Also spelled achromatic colour. Compare CHROMATIC COLOR.

achromatic color response   In Rorschach testing, responding freely to achromatic (black and white) cards with a lesser number of responses to the chromatic (colored) ones. People who respond more to chromatic than to achromatic cards are considered to have more emotional personalities.

achromatic response   A reaction to a visual task in which color is not a factor, as in responses to the black and white Rorschach cards that involve variations in shading or texture but no colors, or giving noncolor responses to inkblots that do involve color.

achromatic vision   achromatopsia

achromatism   1. Refers to the uncolored state objects. 2. Colorlessness (lacking hue and saturation). 3. Total color blindness. See ACHROMATIC, ACHROMATOPSIA.

achromatopsia   (J. Dollond) A severe congenital deficiency in color vision, hereditary or acquired, in which all colors appear as grays. Often associated with nystagmus and reduced visual acuity. Also known as achromasy, achromatic vision, achromatism, achromatopia, achromatopsy, monochromasia, monochromasy, monochromatism, total color blindness. See NYSTAGMUS.

acid   1. In chemistry, a compound that donates a hydrogen ion in a polar solvent such as water. 2. Sour, sharp to the taste. 3. Slang for lysergic acid (LSD), a hallucinogen. See PSYCHEDELICS.

acid flashback   A repetition of the effect of a drug, particularly lysergic acid diethylamide (LSD), without current ingestion of the drug. See ACID TRIP, HALLUCINOGEN PERSISTING PERCEPTION DISORDER.

acidhead   Slang for a regular user of lysergic acid diethylamide (LSD).

acidosis   A disorder caused by a loss of normal acid-base balance resulting in an increase in the level of acidity in the blood and tissues, depletion of alkaline reserves, and neurologic abnormalities such as muscle twitching, disorientation, coma. See ALKALOSIS.

acid trip   Slang, used more in the late 1960s and early 1970s, to describe the six- to eight-hour duration of psychotropic effects experienced from taking lysergic acid diethylamide (LSD) or related hallucinogen. See PSYCHEDELICS.

ACL   See ADJECTIVE CHECKLIST.

acme   1. A summit; the point of highest pleasure, the ultimate. 2. In psychoanalytic theory, the moment of sexual climax. Also known as summa libido. 3. The period of greatest intensity of any symptom or disorder.

acm(a)esthesia   1. Sensitivity to pinprick. 2. A form of paresthesia in which a sharp cutaneous stimulus that is normally sensed as pain is perceived instead as touch or pressure. Also known as acouesthesia.

ACOAs   Abbreviation for Adult Children of Alcoholics. See AL-A-TEEN, AL-ANON.

acoasm   acousma

aconative   1. Pertaining to purposeless behavior. 2. Lacking desire to act.

aconuresis   Rare term for enuresis.

acoria   A form of polyphagia in which the patient never feels sated; an excessive appetite marked by gluttony or greediness rather than persistent hunger. Also spelled akoria. See BULIMIA.

Acosta's disease/syndrome   (J. de Acosta) A form of altitude sickness resulting from lack of oxygen at high altitudes. Symptoms include dizziness, blue skin, weakness, and impaired mental processes. Also known as D'Acosta's syndrome, mountain-climber's syndrome.

acoumeter   (A. Hartmann, J. Itard) A device used for determining auditory sensitivity; a hearing meter (outmoded term for audiometer). See ACOUMETRY.

acoumetry   Quantitative determination of auditory sensitivity. Also known as audiometric measurement.

acousma   1. An auditory sensation that is perceived in the absence of a stimulus. 2. An annoying self-generated sound, due either to physiological factors or an auditory hallucination, often perceived as a buzzing, crackling, ringing, or roaring sound. Also known as acoasm, acouasm, akoasm, akousma, tinnitus.

acoustic   Pertaining to hearing or the perception of sound.

acoustical resonance   Refers to the reverberant or reflective effect of a person's own vocal sounds contributed by sinuses and other cavities in the skull.

acoustic confusion   Confusing words on the basis of related sound, as in understanding "bad" for "mad."

acoustic encoding   Making sense of sounds, especially the sound of words.

acoustic filter   A device used to screen out unwanted sounds.

acoustic irritability   Hypersensitivity to auditory stimulation.

acoustic nerve   (Erasistratus) The auditory component of cranial nerve VIII. It is classified as special somatic afferent. Transmits impulses for the sense of hearing from the inner ear to the auditory (cochlear) nuclei of the pons from which the information is relayed to other brainstem regions, the cerebellum, midbrain, thalamus, and cortex. Also known as acoustic-vestibular nerve, auditory nerve, statoacoustic nerve, vestibulocochlear nerve.

acousticoamnestic aphasia   A form of aphasia due to lesions in the central portions of the left temporal area or deep portions of the temporal cortex. Marked by difficulties in recalling word lists, comprehension of long sentences, comprehension of words, and naming objects. Also known as acoustic-amnestic aphasia.

acousticophobia   Morbid fear of sound or noise. Also spelled akousticophobia. See PHONOPHOBIA.

acoustic papilla   The organ of Corti.

acoustic pressure   The waves of air pressure of sufficient intensity and frequency to be perceived as sounds. The maximum pressure that the human ear can tolerate is about 280 dynes/cm^2 above atmospheric pressure; the lowest sound audible is about 0.0002 dynes/cm^2 above atmospheric pressure. This ratio is about 1.4 million to one. On the other hand, the ratio of intensities from audible to pain is about 14 log units (leading to the decibel scale ranging from 1 to 140).

acoustic radiation   See AUDITORY RADIATION.

acoustic reflex   An automatic reaction to the intensity of a sound. It frequently is employed in routine hearing tests using sounds of different frequencies. An infant's blinking may be a response to a low-decibel hearing-test sound. See BLINK, CONDITION-ORIENTED, MORO, STRETCH, SUCKING REFLEXES.

acoustics   1. The science of sound. 2. Qualities of any environment regarding the reception of sound, such as an auditorium.

acoustic spectrum   The range of sound frequencies audible to the human ear, from approximately 20 to 20,000 Hertz (cycles per second). Also known as sound spectrum. See AUDITIVE RANGE.

acoustic trauma   A form of sensorineural hearing impairment resulting from exposure to intense noise. Even brief periods of exposure to jet-aircraft engine noise, gunfire, heavy rock music, and heavy drilling may cause damage to the nerve fibers in the cochlea. Damage may be permanent or temporary.

ACPT   Auditory Continuous Performance Test

acquaintance rape   Sexual assault by a person known to the victim. See DATE RAPE.

acquiescence set   1. (J. Block) A tendency to agree at a high rate and to answer "Yes" to questions, even when "No" would be more appropriate. Such yea-sayings distort the results of personality inventories and attitude scales. Also known as acquiescence response set. See YEA-SAYING, NAY-SAYING. 2. In research, the tendency of participants to agree with statements of attitude regardless of their content. Also known as acquiescent-response set.

acquired   Not inherited.

acquired agraphia   Inability to write, or the ability to write single letters but not syllables, words, or phrases due to stroke, head injury, encephalitis, or other events resulting in brain damage.

acquired behavior   Modes of response not inherited but which develop during the individual's lifetime as a result of environmental influences. Also known as acquired reactions/responses.

acquired character   Modification, either structural or functional, which occurs in an organism as a result of the organism's activities or through the influence of the environment.

acquired characteristic   A trait, physical or behavioral, of an individual that was attained by learning or experiences.

acquired color blindness   Partial or complete loss of color sensitivity in a part or the whole of the retina of a person who had normal color vision.

acquired distinctiveness (of cues)   (N. E. Miller & J. Dollard) The learning of the differences of stimuli that are similar.

acquired drive   Any learned rather than inherited predisposition to behave in a certain manner.

acquired dyslexia   Difficulty in reading caused by postnatal damage to the brain. See DEEP DYSLEXIA, PHONOLOGICAL DYSLEXIA, SURFACE DYSLEXIA.

acquired *folie morale* (moral insanity—French) A form of schizophrenia marked by antisocial behavior, the psychotic manifestations appearing as delusions, auditory hallucinations, stupor, or agitation.

Acquired Immune Deficiency Syndrome (AIDS) A disease condition that is caused by the human immunodeficiency virus (HIV-1, HIV-2) which destroys the immune system's ability to fight infection, usually acquired via sexual contact, or contact with contaminated blood. Prior to 1982, known as Gay-Related Immune Deficiency (GRID).

acquired reaction/response Behavior achieved by practice efforts as well as hereditary potential. See ACQUIRED BEHAVIOR.

acquired speech disorder A speech problem or defective speech condition attained after birth, regardless of cause. Compare CONGENITAL SPEECH DISORDER.

acquisition 1. Any new type of response, idea, or information gained by and added to an individual's repertoire. The gain can be either from heredity, as in maturation, or from the environment, as in learning. 2. In conditioning, an increase in strength of the conditioned response in successive trials of pairing the conditioned and unconditioned stimulus.

acquisitive(ness) A behavioral tendency which results in the possession of nutritive or other objects. Sometimes regarded as an instinct or an inherited tendency. Also known as inquisitive instinct. Term is distinguished from hoarding. See ACQUISITIVE SPIRIT.

acquisitive spirit A drive to hoard, by possessing and accumulating money, property, or objects of personal or social value, such as in collecting coins or works of art. See ANAL CHARACTER, ACQUISITIVE(NESS), COLLECTING MANIA, HOARDING CHARACTER.

acrai Arabian term synonymous with nymphomania and satyriasis.

acrasy A pathological absence of self-control; extreme intemperance. Also known as acrasia.

acrescentism Deprivation.

acroagnosia Inability to perceive kinesthetic sensation in a limb. Also known as acroagnosis.

acroanesthesia Loss or absence of sensitivity in the extremities. Compare ACROESTHESIA. See ACROPARESTHESIA.

acrocentric chromosome A chromosome in which the centromere is near one end, making one arm of the replicating chromosome shorter than the other.

acrocephaly oxycephaly

acrocinesia Excessive motion or movement, sometimes observed in hysteria or in the manic phase of bipolar disorder. Also known as acrocinesis.

acrocyanosis A circulatory disorder characterized by bluish coloration of the hands, and less often of the feet, which are persistently cold, seen in patients with Raynaud's phenomenon and less often in patients with schizophrenia.

acroesthesia Abnormal sensitivity to stimuli applied to the extremities. Also known as acroaesthesia, acroesthesis. See HYPERESTHESIA.

acrohypothermy Abnormal coolness of the skin of the extremities found in certain patients with schizophrenia. Also known as acrohypothermia.

acromania Violent incurable insanity.

acromegaloid-hypertelorism-pectus carinatum syndrome A congenital condition of males marked by short stature, mental retardation, hypertelorism, and skeletal anomalies including an enlarged head and a deformed sternum, slow psychomotor development, and intelligence quotients (IQs) estimated in the 20s.

acromegaloid personality A pattern of behavior observed in a large proportion of patients with acromegaly. Features include: frequent mood changes, impulsiveness, temper outbursts, impatience, and in advanced cases, loss of initiative, egocentricity, and somnolence.

acromegaly (N. Saucerotte) Abnormal enlargement of the skeletal extremities, such as the arms, legs, and parts of the skull. Usually occurs in adults whose normal bone growth has already stopped. Caused by a pituitary-gland abnormality that results in hypersecretion of the growth hormone. Also known as Marie's disease. See GIGANTISM.

acromicria A body type with small head and limbs in comparison to the rest of the body; the antithesis of acromegaly.

acronym A combination of first letters of a phrase to generate a word, such as BARS for Behaviorally Anchored Rating Scale.

acroparesthesia Recurrent numbness, tingling, or other abnormal sensation in the extremities. See ACROANESTHESIA, ACROESTHESIA, PARESTHESIA.

acrophobia (A. Verga) Morbid fear of heights. Also known as hyposophobia, hypsophobia.

acrosome A hood-like formation on the front end of a spermatozoon.

acrotomophilia A paraphilia (sexual disorder) directed toward a partner with amputation(s), often to the stump(s) of an amputee. Also spelled acrotophilia.

ACSW Academy of Certified Social Workers

act 1. Behaviorally, an integrated unit of overt behavior having a beginning and continuing to a conclusion. 2. (F. Brentano) Mentation that has at the same time: (a) intention (conation), (b) awareness (cognition), and feeling (affection).

acta Official acts or recorded proceedings of a scientific group or organization.

ACT Assessment See AMERICAN COLLEGE TESTING PROGRAM.

actatic Not coordinated.

actatic speech Uncoordinated verbal communication, filled with "ahs" and "hems," or noticeable gaps between words.

act ending Termination of an act, resulting in relief of tension. See ACT FULFILLMENT.

act frequency approach The use of subjective judgments of a number of people in the naming of any behavior in terms of any standard, such as stating that assertiveness is a basic human trait, then trying to determine from friends whether certain terms fit within the rubric of assertiveness, with words like "pushy," "forward," "demanding" being accepted as part of the concept of assertiveness.

act fulfillment 1. In psychotherapy, reenacting a traumatic situation correctively, producing more satisfactory results. 2. In psychodrama, the reliving of a painful repressed emotional experience. Sometimes called act ending.

act-habit A personality trait acquired from cultural or environmental influences (for example, over-protectiveness, or a scientific attitude).

ACT-HC (S. Hayes) The accepting of limitations and commitment to healthy behavior (health care, or HC) as part of Acceptance and Commitment Therapy.

act psychology 1. Generally, approaches to psychology that emphasize the unity of interactions with the environment. 2. (F. Brentano) Specifically, the act psychology of Franz Brentano, Karl Stumpf, and the Würzburg school contrasted this with the elementarism of Wilhelm Wundt's structural psychology, arguing that the psychological act is intentional, all analytical methodologies destroy the act being studied, and a descriptive treatment of psychology must be empirical while accepting the phenomenological character of psychological acts. Acts (ideations, judgments, emotions), not contents, were considered the proper subject of psychology. See ELEMENTARISM, PHENOMENOLOGY, STRUCTURALISM. Also see AUSTRIAN SCHOOL, IDIOGENETIC THEORY, INTENTIONALITY, WÜRZBURG SCHOOL.

ACT-R (S. Hayes) Behavioral analysis of a client seeking therapy, the starting point of the therapy.

act regression The reappearance of a conditioned response after its extinction.

ACTH adrenocorticotropic hormone

ACT theory The basic concepts of Acceptance and Commitment Therapy (ACT), based on radical behaviorism, and developed by Steven Hayes. ACT-R refers to the patient's therapy seeking behavior, and ACT-HC is the patient's health care seeking behavior in the ACT theoretical model. See ACT-R, ACT-HC.

actin A protein important for muscle contraction. See MYOSIN.

acting in In psychoanalysis, a form of resistance in which the patient discharges repressed wishes during psychotherapy (such as the analytic hour) through actions rather than words, for example, by walking around the room.

acting out A partial release into action of repressed desires; an overt act in daily life that provides an outlet for the expression of unconscious emotional conflicts. See EGO.

acting out behavior A release of impulses often antisocial or delinquent, such as vandalism, torturing animals, attacking defenseless people. See INTERMITTENT EXPLOSIVE DISORDER.

acting out technique (E. Simmel) An early method of group therapy developed during World War I to treat what was then called shell shock. German soldiers were given bayonetted rifles and urged to bayonet straw-filled dummies dressed as German army officers. See BATTLE EXHAUSTION/FATIGUE.

actinic rays Radiant energy of the short-wave visible end of the ultraviolet region of the spectrum, formerly thought to be the only rays capable of producing chemical effects.

action 1. A process associated with performance or the result of the same. 2. In psychotherapy, the behavior of clients in translating insight and understanding into overt energy toward a goal.

action cue Nonverbal communication that consists of body movements, such as nodding the head to indicate "yes."

action current The flow of current across the membrane of an electrically excitable cell such as a neuron or muscle cell that occurs locally in association with an action potential.

action decrement A tendency of an organism not to repeat an identical action just completed.

action group A task-oriented group engaged in achieving goals intended to produce an effect on a group, organization, business, institution, or social unit. Such a group seeks to have a direct impact on and achieve a modification of the environment. See RADICAL THERAPY.

action-instrument In the two-word stage of language development, an expression indicating knowledge of the use of instruments, as in "eat-fork." See ACTION-LOCATION, ACTION-RECIPIENT.

action interpretation A nonverbal reaction of a therapist who communicates with a client by body signs.

action learning The acquisition of knowledge or experience through "doing," as opposed to learning by listening, or other vicarious methods.

action-location In the two-word stage of language development, an expression indicating the location of an action, as in "sleep-bed." See ACTION-INSTRUMENT, ACTION-RECIPIENT.

action-oriented therapies Psychotherapies designed to get group therapy participants to interact. See ABC TECHNIQUE, PSYCHODRAMA.

action painting In art therapy, a procedure in which persons are asked to generate art works without planning or thinking about what they are creating. The paintings are later reviewed, analyzed, and discussed. Also known as tachisme.

action patterns Relatively stable and predictable ways of behaving.

action potential (AP) (E. DuBois-Reymond) The transient change in voltage potential across the membrane of a neuron caused by a stimulus that exceeds threshold intensity. The action potential is not graded in size, but it either occurs if threshold is exceeded or it does not appear. It propagates along an axon as adjacent areas become excited. The initial change in the membrane that causes the action potential is opening of sodium channels and resulting movement of sodium ions into the axon. See ELECTRIC POTENTIAL.

action psychotherapy A group psychotherapy process with its members operating without professional directions, using a variety of techniques for diagnosis, treatment, and training. Goals are openness, self-disclosure, and the giving and receiving of feedback with mutual cooperation. See LEADERLESS GROUP THERAPY.

action-recipient In the two-word stage of language development, an expression indicating the recipient of an action, as "cookie-me." See ACTION-INSTRUMENT, ACTION-LOCATION.

action research   A form of scientific study directed toward a practical goal, usually an improvement in a particular social process or system in contrast to nonapplied research.

action specific energy (hypothesis)   (K. Lorenz) A postulate that organisms have special reserves of energy for instinctive responses.

action stream   Elements in an organism, physiological (such as muscles and nerves) and psychological (such as will and purpose), that are involved in specific behavior. See STREAM OF ACTION.

action system   1. The structural basis of movements of an organism. 2. All physiological elements involved in any behavior including receptors (such as eyes), carriers (such as afferent and efferent nerves), and all effectors (such as glands and muscles).

action theory   (A. Kardiner) A point of view that the body has a mechanism, an action system, for fulfilling a need or desire. The phrase was introduced to explain the cause of traumatic neuroses, which Abram Kardiner assumed was due to damage of an action system.

action therapy   behavior modification/therapy

activated sleep   Describing rapid eye movement (REM) sleep.

activation   Energizing the body for action, particularly arousal of one sensory or organ system by another. See RETICULAR ACTIVATING SYSTEM.

activation-arousal theory   A point of view that every organism has a normal and appropriate level of arousal that it tends to maintain at that level. See HOMEOSTASIS.

activation-elaboration   (G. Mandler) The distinction between the activation of a mental unit and the development of relations between it and other mental contents.

activation pattern   In electroencephalographic (EEG) interpretation, a suppression of alpha waves and a shift to low-voltage rapid activity when participants open eyes to view a displayed object.

activation-synthesis hypothesis   A postulate that dream content reflects a synthesis of the neural activation that occurs during rapid-eye-movement (REM) sleep. See DREAMS.

activation theory of emotion(s)   A point of view that any emotion ranges over a continuum from slight with no overt activity, as in sleep, to maximum, as in violent action.

activator   1. A catalyst. 2. A substance that stimulates the activity of a second substance to become functional. 3. A drug used to increase the activity level of a person who appears depressed or withdrawn.

active aggressive reaction type   A personality trait disturbance characterized by a pattern of overt hostility and resentment, irritability, low frustration tolerance, rebellion against authority, argumentativeness, and in some cases violent behavior.

active algolagnia   sadism (meaning 2)

active analysis   One variation (among many) of Sigmund Freud's basic psychoanalysis, during which the analyst tends to be more active than Freud suggested, giving advice, providing tentative explanations, etc. See WILD PSYCHOANALYSIS.

active analytic psychotherapy   (W. Stekel) A therapeutic approach in which the analyst gives more attention to the intrapsychic conflicts in the patient's present life than to exploring early childhood experiences. Sometimes known as active analysis.

active avoidance   A situation in which an organism must perform a specific action to avoid a noxious (usually painful) stimulus.

active castration complex   (S. Freud) Ideas and behavior, including reaction formation, associated with the fear of losing the penis. Compare PASSIVE CASTRATION COMPLEX.

active concretization   Transforming anxieties into concrete form, as when a paranoid person believes the whole world is hostile and has proof of the delusion in the form of hearing derogatory voices coming from an air conditioner.

active-daydream technique   (C. G. Jung) A form of imagery therapy in which a client is encouraged to allow autonomous images to appear, and then react to them as if they were real, for example by hiding from a threatening figure, or by talking to it. See GESTALT THERAPY.

active euthanasia   Assisted suicide, deliberate action taken to shorten the life of a terminally ill person, to end suffering or to carry out the wishes of the patient. Also known as mercy killing. Compare PASSIVE EUTHANASIA.

active fantasizing   A therapy technique in which clients spontaneously describe their imagery while the therapist listens for clues to sources of the inner conflicts. Also spelled active fantasying/phantasizing.

active imagination   A form of reflection through which people activate and follow imaginative reveries in a purposive manner. See FANTASY.

active inducers   Refers to parents, usually mothers, who make direct efforts to induce symptoms of illness in their children. See MÜNCHAUSEN SYNDROME BY PROXY.

active introversion   Avoidance of contact with others and a preference for being alone. See HERMITISM.

active learning   The mastery or acquisition of skills by doing, trial and error learning, learning on the job.

active listening   (C. R. Rogers) Listening in psychotherapy, during which a therapist attempts to understand a client's cognition and emotion in depth, then these are restated by the therapist to assure clients that they have been understood and their feelings appreciated.

active management   (J. Hater & B. M. Bass) A corrective transaction between the leader and the led. The leader arranges to actively monitor deviances from standards, mistakes and errors in followers' assignments and takes corrective action as necessary when deviations are expected or actually occur. See TRANSACTIONAL LEADERSHIP.

active memory   Short-term memory.

active negativism   Resistance to demands or suggestions, such as a catatonic patient remaining mute when asked a simple question, or continuing to stand up when invited to sit down. See GANSER SYNDROME, PASSIVE AGGRESSION.

active performance   In memorization or learning, the more a person does in an active manner, such as reading aloud, the more likely the learning will be effective in contrast to passive performance during which a person simply reads or memorizes in a silent manner.

active powers   Mental faculties involved in action and emotion.

active recreation   A form of recreational therapy in which the patient is an active participant (for example, dancing). Compare PASSIVE RECREATION.

active scoptophilia   Being sexually aroused by viewing sexual acts, others' genitalia, or both. Compare PASSIVE SCOPTOPHILIA.

active sexual trauma   An eventual psychological trauma resulting from a child's induction into sexual activity, even if the experience was rewarding at the time. Compare PASSIVE SEXUAL TRAUMA.

active therapist   A psychotherapist who does not remain neutral or anonymous, as in orthodox psychoanalysis or person-centered therapy, and who does not hesitate to express opinions and interpretations, make suggestions and recommendations, and even, on occasion, issue injunctions and prohibitions. See ACTIVE ANALYTIC PSYCHOTHERAPY, ACTIVE THERAPY, COGNITIVE-BEHAVIORAL THERAPIST, DIRECTIVE THERAPIST, PASSIVE THERAPIST, WILD PSYCHOANALYSIS.

active therapy   (S. Ferenczi) Any form of therapy in which the therapist plays a more active role then would, for example, an orthodox psychoanalyst or a Rogerian therapist. The active therapist might give the client direct advice or due warning. See ACTIVE ANALYTICAL THERAPY, ACTIVITY THERAPY.

active touch   The perception of objects by touching them, as in reading Braille. Compare PASSIVE TOUCH.

active transport   The movement of ions across a cell membrane by a mechanism other than simple osmosis. Compare PASSIVE TRANSPORT.

active vocabulary   A person's working vocabulary; the vocabulary used in speaking and writing, as opposed to vocabulary used in reading and listening (passive vocabulary). Also known as working vocabulary.

actively aggressive reaction type   A personality trait disturbance characterized by overt hostility and resentment, irritability, low frustration tolerance, rebellion against authority, argumentativeness, and, in some cases, violent behavior.

activeness   The universal aspect of all life based on internal dynamics rather than reactivity to stimuli. The result of voluntary behavior of an individual in search of a goal, rather than a field dependent action. Activeness does not depend on the concept of being mediated by antecedent events but rather that it is essentially autochthonous.

activism   A theory or practice of direct, positive, vigorous action or involvement to achieve an end, in particular, a political goal. See RADICAL THERAPY.

activist movements   Formation of groups in support of or opposition to social or political policies.

activities of daily living (ADL)   Typical routine actions of people, such as getting in and out of bed, dressing, eating, toileting, using chairs. Some persons with disabilities develop new techniques or use aids such as wheelchairs, walkers, and oversized door handles to cope with their disabilities.

activity   1. A change or motion in general. 2. Mental or biological process due to utilization of energy stored within the organism. 3. Organized motion.

activity analysis   A summary of the various behaviors of any organism, or groups of organisms, presented so that even complex behavior can be readily understood, for example, if tracking a cat, a person might learn that daily the cat sleeps 18 hours, feeds 10 times, and grooms itself 12 times.

activity cage   A wheel-shaped cage with recording mechanism that goes through a circular rotation whenever an animal inside moves. See ACTIVITY WHEEL.

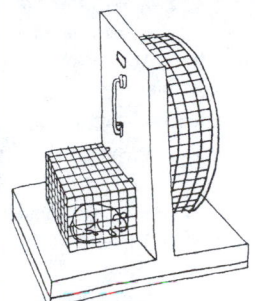

activity cage   An activity wheel. An animal lives in a cage at the left of the apparatus. The animal may enter the revolving drum on the right through a door. Activity in the revolving drum is recorded; since the animal's living quarters are so small, most of the animal's activity is in the drum.

activity catharsis   Doing something physical, such as tearing paper, or punching at something, to reduce negative feelings such as anger, in order to achieve relief of tension. Whether such behavior really succeeds is not established. See DISPLACEMENT, SUBSTITUTION.

activity cycle   Rhythmic fluctuations of activity, as in the two-hour hunger and four-day sex rhythms of rats. See ACTIVITY ANALYSIS.

activity deprivation   Lack of opportunity for physical activity (for example, a prisoner kept in a small cell). Such conditions generate intense need to move about and a high degree of frustration. See ACTIVITY DRIVE, FUNKTIONSLUST.

activity drive   1. An inborn need to be active, to engage in motion. 2. A general urge for bodily activity expressed in a need to move about or keep busy. The satisfaction of being active can be pleasurable in itself. See ACTIVITY DEPRIVATION.

activity-group therapy   (S. R. Slavson) Group therapy developed for children and young adolescents. The youth are given free opportunity to release tensions and feelings of hostility, test out new ways of relating to others, and gradually experience the satisfactions of creative effort and normal give and take.

activity inventory   A list of orders or commands, usually established in some sequence as part of a particular job or task.

activity level   Amount of movement occurring at a given time. In humans, the level tends to be low during a depressive state and high during a manic episode. In animals, activity level increases with hunger, thirst, or prevention of activity and decreases when these needs are satisfied.

activity log   Recording data in an organized fashion such as by a diary kept by a researcher or participants of a study. A method of recording data in an organized fashion, for example, when and where a person smokes during a smoking cessation program. The phrase refers to the act of recording and also to the record of data or the information itself. See ACTIVITY RECORDS.

activity motive   The basic desire of motile organisms to move. Restriction of motion is harmful to simple organisms and may be considered a form of punishment for higher organisms (for example, convicts locked in prison cells).

activity-passivity   Descriptive of modes of reacting to the external environment; for example, some people actively seek to influence and shape events, whereas some people tend to passively allow events to happen.

activity-play therapy   (J. Solomon) A controlled play technique in which a child is given a set of male and female dolls and encouraged to express and explore feelings about them on the assumption that this will cause less fear and repression of the emotions.

activity pleasure   See FUNKTIONSLUST.

activity quotient   A purported measure of a person's emotionality as determined by the ratio of verbs to adjectives the person uses in communications.

activity record   A documentation of certain kinds of behavior that is usually maintained for the purpose of evaluating progress over time (for example, documents about patients in mental hospitals or children in schools). See SCHOLASTIC RECORD.

activity scheduling   The establishment of a written plan or program for completing tasks, regardless of purposes.

activity system   behavior system

activity theory (of aging)   (R. J. Havighurst) A point of view that life satisfaction is maintained by active participation in social roles and diminished if a person is unable to remain active.

activity therapy   Adjunctive therapy in which patients are encouraged to engage in activities such as arts and crafts, exercises, music, and dramatics. Activity programs are designed to maintain interest, increase self-esteem, and prevent patients from lapsing into apathy and passivity. See ACTIVE THERAPY, SOCIAL-BREAKDOWN SYNDROME, TOTAL PUSH THERAPY.

activity vector analysis (AVA)   (W. V. Clarke) A psychological technique consisting of a long list of adjectives used in industrial and other organizations for hiring and promoting personnel. The person is asked to: "Describe yourself by checking all of the adjectives on the first list that anyone has ever used in describing you." Next, to check on a second list containing the same adjectives, "those that you believe are true for you." See Q-SORT.

activity wheel   A vertically oriented cylinder that rotates when an organism such as a rat enters and runs. For research, the wheel has a counter that indicates how many turns of the cylinder the organism executed during the period of observation. See ACTIVITY CAGE for an illustration.

acton(e)   (H. A. Murray) A specific action. See MOTONE, VERBONE.

actor-observer effect   A tendency for actors (the people who perform the behavior) to explain their behavior in terms of situational causes, and for observers to explain the actors' behavior in terms of dispositional causes, for example, "I stole the bread to feed my starving children," "She stole the bread because she is dishonest." Also known as FUNDAMENTAL ATTRIBUTION ERROR.

ACTP   American College Testing Program

actual   Actively present at the given moment, in contrast with potential or latent possibilities.

actual incidence   Phrase used to differentiate correct rates from reported rates, the first through observation, the latter through a survey.

actualization   The process of mobilizing innate potentialities and expressing them in concrete form. See INDIVIDUATION, SELF-ACTUALIZATION.

actualizing counseling   (E. L. Shostrom & L. M. Brammer) A multidimensional theory that emphasizes developmental aspects, perception, and action toward behavioral change as well as the attaining of higher levels of actualization.

actualizing tendency   An innate human predisposition toward growth and fulfillment. Personality theorists including Kurt Goldstein, Abraham Maslow, and Carl Rogers have emphasized this tendency.

actual neurosis   (S. Freud) Maladjustment stemming from current sexual frustrations, such as coitus interruptus, forced abstinence, or incomplete gratification, as contrasted with maladjustment stemming from experiences in infancy or childhood.

actual self   (K. Horney) The totality of self at any instant in time, including unconscious elements.

actuarial   Statistical, as opposed to clinical or intuitive. Paul Meehl raised the issue of whether diagnostic decisions and predictions derived from statistical rules were superior to decisions made by human judgments.

acuity   Perceptual sensitivity.

acuity grate   One of many devices used to measure the visual acuity of a human participant or animal subject. Consists of alternating black and white lines spaced closely together, testing the ability of the individual to determine separations. See VISUAL ACUITY.

aculalia   Nonsensical or jargon speech seen in some patients with Wernicke's type of aphasia and other forms of brain lesions characterized by an impaired comprehension of written or spoken language. See ECHOLALIA, JARGON APHASIA, WERNICKE'S APHASIA.

acupressure   A variation of acupuncture, a method of healing characterized by putting pressure with thumbs (instead of needles) on various points of the body. See UNCONVENTIONAL THERAPIES.

acupuncture   The ancient Chinese practice of inserting needles into specific parts of the body to control pain or cure illness, based on the concept that pathways of energy flow between places on the skin (and perhaps peripheral nerves) and the body's organ systems. See FAITH HEALING, MERIDIAN.

acupuncture anesthesia   Pain relief derived by the insertion and twisting of needles in various parts of the body.

acupuncture theory of pain   (R. Melzack) A point of view that acupuncture can reduce feelings of pain by (a) the needles closing the gate in the pain-signaling system; (b) stimulating the brain stem to generate analgesia in parts of the body; and (c) fibers from the cortex also affecting the "gate" and reducing pain. See GATE CONTROL THEORY OF PAIN.

acutance   In video screens (such as television screens, computer monitors), the relative sharpness between more prominent figures and their background.

acute   1. Sharp, keen, or sensitive (for example, acute pain, acute sense of hearing, acute shyness). 2. Denoting a sudden, short, intense attack of illness.

acute affective reflex   (E. Kretschmer) An initial involuntary emotional reaction (usually tremors) to a severe stress.

acute alcoholic hallucinosis   A psychotic reaction found in heavy drinkers, principally of those with schizoid traits, characterized by auditory hallucinations.

acute alcoholism   A temporary decrease in mental functioning and muscular coordination due to ingestion of alcoholic beverages in toxic amounts.

acute anxiety attack (AAA)   A sudden feeling of morbid dread and apprehension typically stimulated by a threatening situation such as an examination or court hearing. The feeling usually subsides relatively quickly. It is differentiated from fear in which the precipitating stimulus (a verbal threat or a menacing dog) is more obvious. See PERFORMANCE ANXIETY.

acute brain disorder   Organic brain pathology resulting from usually temporary, reversible impairment of brain-tissue functioning, ranging from mild changes in mood to acute delirium. See ORGANIC BRAIN SYNDROMES, ORGANIC MENTAL DISORDERS.

acute cerebrovascular accident   See CEREBROVASCULAR ACCIDENT, STROKE (meaning 2).

acute confusional state   A severe reaction to stresses typically experienced by adolescents required to face an unfamiliar situation such as going away to college. The disorder, usually precipitated by a minor frustration, consists of intense anger followed by inability to concentrate, feelings of alienation and loneliness, depersonalization, and despondency—all of which subside if the person adapts to the situation.

acute delirium   A condition of confusion, disorientation, excitement, frenzy usually of short duration, often as the result of a high fever, alcohol intoxication, etc.

acute delusional psychosis   A reactive psychosis, particularly a schizophrenic episode that has no currently identifiable genetic link, and has a favorable prognosis. See ACUTE SCHIZOPHRENIC EPISODE, CYCLIC ILLNESS.

acute depression   A depression triggered by a life event. A disorder characterized by marked retardation in thought, speech, vegetative functions and general activity along with extreme feelings of guilt, isolation, futility, and unreality as well as loss of interest, utter pessimism, and, on occasion, suicide ideation. See MANIC-DEPRESSIVE REACTION.

acute disorder   A pathological condition with sudden onset and often of short duration.

acute hallucinosis   A sudden onset of hallucinations resulting from alcohol or drug intoxication or a traumatic event. The condition usually subsides.

acute dystonia   An acute form of tension or spasms in the muscles, a lack of normal muscle tone.

acute hallucinatory mania   A disorder during which a person is physically and mentally out of control. Such persons imagine all kinds of threats, are in a frenzy of action, and are often dangerous to others due to their violent unrestrained behavior.

acute intolerance   A strong negative reaction to a negligible amount of some substances, such as the alleged ability of some people to get drunk by just smelling a wine cork. See ALCOHOL IDIOSYNCRATIC INTOXICATION.

acute mania   A symptom in the manic phase of a bipolar (manic depressive) disorder characterized by an extremely unstable, euphoric mood of grandiose optimism with hyperactivity, rapid thought and speech, uninhibited behavior, and flight of ideas. See BIPOLAR REACTIONS, HYPOMANIA, HYPERMANIA, MANIC DEPRESSIVE REACTION.

acute onset   Sudden occurrence of a disorder. See ACUTE DISORDER.

acute paranoid disorder   A pathological condition usually of less than six months' duration, which typically develops suddenly in a person who has experienced drastic environmental changes (such as an immigrant, refugee, prisoner of war, inductee, or a person leaving home for the first time). See PARANOID DISORDERS.

acute preparation   A surgical or other preparation of an animal used in research that is destroyed at the end of a study for humane reasons. See ANIMAL RIGHTS, VIVISECTION.

acute psychotic break   A sudden loss of contact with reality accompanied by symptoms of severe mental disorder, such as hallucinations, delusions, incoherence, and disorganized, violent, or catatonic behavior.

acute schizophrenic episode   A period of sudden onset and usually short duration that may occur in people with no prior history of overt mental disorder. The patient self-isolates, experiences a flight of ideas of extraordinary intensity, and may become confused, disoriented, delusional, and hallucinatory. Symptoms may follow an emotional upheaval due to loss or separation.

acute shock psychosis   A disorder occurring during times of war in which the patient becomes unconscious and lacks sensitivity to pain and external stimuli. The eyeballs are rolled upward and outward and the eyelids flutter. Usually occurs in combat situations and does not last long.

acute stress reaction   A severe emotional response to extreme environmental stress, such as a natural catastrophe, bankruptcy, divorce, or combat experience. Also known as acute situational reaction.

acute tolerance   Rare ability to adjust to chemical substances quickly. See CHRONIC TOLERANCE.

acute traumatic brain disorder   The temporary impairment of brain functions associated with a severe blow to the head. If a concussion with loss of consciousness occurs, the symptoms may include confusion, headache and disorientation, as well as a partial or total amnesia for the event.

acute treatment stage   The first phase of therapeutic intervention, intended to reduce disorganizing symptoms and allow the patient to reestablish some semblance of normality.

AD   1. Alzheimer's disease. 2. average deviation (also abbreviated **A.D.**).

Adam   See ECSTASY.

ADAMHA   Alcohol, Drug Abuse, and Mental Health Administration

Adam plan   The argument that for a fetus to differentiate into a male, the basic "Eve plan" must be overcome through masculinization hormones and the inhibition of an inhibiting hormone.

Adamite   Obsolete term for a nudist, after the Adamite sect which practiced ritual nudity.

adaptability   Capacity to make appropriate responses to changed or changing situations.

adaptation   1. Modification of either a bodily structure or function to adjust to and survive environmental changes. 2. Changes of attitudes toward external situations resulting in better adjustment to these situations. 3. In receptors, modification of sensitivity, to permit optimal functioning, such as a person recently blinded depending more on hearing. 4. In Darwinian theory, survival of the species through natural selection by changing to fit in better with the environment.

adaptational approach/psychodynamics   (S. Rado) A form of psychotherapy that is immediate, directive, and teleological in character, stressing the future rather than the past or present.

adaptation-evoking triggers   Emotionally important interactions, events and situations that activate the human psyche and lead to coping responses.

adaptation in learning   A change in an organism's mode of behavior which results in more effective or more satisfactory adjustment to the situation.

adaptation level (AL)   (H. Helson) A reference point for judging a stimulus value such as loudness or coldness.

adaptation-level phenomenon   A tendency for human judgments (of sounds, of lights, of danger, and so forth) to be in relation to an "adaptation level" set and defined by human prior experience. See ADAPTION-LEVEL THEORY.

adaptation mechanism   (J. Piaget) Biological adaptation through the interplay between the assimilation of data of experience and modification of the organism to accommodate those new data into its mental framework. See ADJUSTMENT PROCESSES.

adaptation period   The period of time during which a participant or animal subject becomes accustomed to instrumentation or research apparatus.

adaptation syndrome   (H. Selye) The physiological changes that may occur in an organism as a result of stress, leading to several stages of greater debility, exhaustion, and, if continued, death. See ADRENAL CORTEX, ALARM REACTION, EXHAUSTION STAGE, GENERAL-ADAPTATION SYNDROME, RESISTANCE STAGE, STRESS.

adaptation time   The time from the start of a stimulus through the end of the effect in the sense organ stimulated. See ADAPTATION PERIOD.

adaptation to reality   Ability to envisage and respond to actual situations of life, without falsifying the self, the environmental conditions, or self-relations thereto by imagination, day-dreaming, rationalization, or other forms of self-deception. See COPING MECHANISM, DENIAL, ESCAPE FROM REALITY.

adapter   1. A connecting part. 2. A person who, stereotypically, constantly moves his or her order own hands or touches various body parts while speaking. Such movement may signal that the person is tense or anxious.

adaption   Rare synonym for the preferred term "adaptation."

adaption-level theory   (H. Helson) A point of view that in sensing any new stimulus such as touch, individuals relate that stimulus to prior ones, and thus a touch of any kind can be interpreted as strong if prior touches were light, or as weak if prior touches were strong. Sometimes known as adaptation-level theory.

adaptive act   (H. Carr) In goal attainment, a behavioral unit that will enable an organism to thrive and reproduce. Such acts depend on both the ability to learn from past experiences and to generate successful behaviors to new situations. See ADAPTATION, ADJUSTMENT.

adaptive act hypothesis   (H. Carr) A postulate that organisms adapt to their environment by three steps: (a) a motivating stimulus that arouses an organism; (b) a sensory stimulus to which the activity is directed; and (c) a response that eventually leads to satisfaction.

adaptive approach   A concept that psychological and behavioral reactions must be viewed in relationship to external reality, emphasizing the principle that humans and society constantly adapt and readapt to each other in the interest of survival.

adaptive behavior   Functions that enable individuals to adjust to the environment appropriately and effectively. See ADAPTIVE ACT, ORIENTATION.

Adaptive Behavior Scale (ABS)   (J. R. Mercer & J. F. Lewis) A questionnaire containing 242 items to be answered by parents and other adults about mental defectives' abilities to take care of themselves. Developed by the American Association on Mental Deficiency for assessing the effectiveness of persons with mental disabilities in coping with the demands of the environment. Respondents provide information in ten behavioral domains, such as independent functioning, language development, physical development, and socialization. The scale is similar to the Vineland Social Maturity Scale.

adaptive delinquency   Actions or conduct considered delinquent by social standards, but, from the individual performing the action's point of view, behavior necessary for survival. See DYSSOCIAL REACTION.

adaptive hypothesis (H. Hartmann) A postulate that the functioning of the primary autonomous ego is to cope with an "average expectable environment" through perception, memory, and motility.

adaptive intelligence The ability of an organism to effectively pursue goals within a changing environment. See INTELLIGENCE.

adaptive nonresponding theory (of sleep) A point of view that sleep is a behavior designed originally to keep early primates out of harm's way during the night.

adaptive processes Any procedures involved in adjusting to environmental demands. Also known as adjustment processes.

adaptive production system (D. A. Waterman, A. Neves, O. Newell, H. A. Simon) In artificial intelligence, a production system that is able to learn by building new productions, which it then adds to its memory. For instance, such a system has learned to solve algebraic equations by being exposed to examples of the solution steps, using means-ends analysis (a) to determine what differences from the goal were removed at each step and what operators were used to remove them, then (b) to connect differences (conditions) to operators (actions) to construct a new production. See ARTIFICIAL INTELLIGENCE, COGNITIVE SIMULATION, PRODUCTION SYSTEM.

adaptive reaction (H. Aubert) The adjustment of eyes to varying intensities of light.

adaptive response Any reaction appropriate to the situation or which promotes the organism's survival.

adaptive skills Activities that require self-management, including controlling impulses, willingness to accept criticism and direction, and an ability to adjust to a new environment and to learn new things. See ACTIVITIES IN DAILY LIVING (ADL).

adaptive testing Evaluation techniques, often computerized, in which correct answers are followed by harder questions or test items, and incorrect ones by easier questions or test items. See BRANCHED FORMAT/PROGRAM.

adaptometer A device for measuring changes in sensory adaptation.

ad baculum (to the stick—Latin) In logic, an error having to do with an inappropriate appeal to force. See FALLACIES.

ADD attention deficit disorder.

ADDH See ATTENTION DEFICIT DISORDER WITH HYPERACTIVITY.

addict A person pathologically habituated to a substance or practice, typically alcohol or narcotic drugs, but also chocolate, reading, or gambling, and unable to desist from engaging in the addiction. A controversial term, used in both a more general and more specific sense. See ADDICTION.

addiction 1. Overdependence on any substance, person, activity, procedure, etc. 2. Physiological dependence, usually on a drug, characterized by increased bodily tolerance and withdrawal symptoms. Acute withdrawal symptoms occur if the substance is sharply reduced or stopped. 3. Psychological dependence, a strong and compelling need for something such as companionship, entertainment, attention, activity, travel, sexual encounters. When such needs are strong and unusual and

continued despite harmful effects to self or others, a person is considered medically or psychologically impaired. See ADDICT, PHYSIOLOGICAL DEPENDENCE, PSYCHOLOGICAL DEPENDENCE, SUBSTANCE DEPENDENCE.

addictive alcoholism Obsolete phrase for chronic alcoholism.

addictive drugs Substances that may create dependency. Examples range from tobacco to Valium to heroin. "Addictive" is problematic, as the recognition of the cocaine or amphetamine "crash" after heavy use can be as dysphoric as a morphine "withdrawal," but its dynamics (psychologically and physiologically) are different, as is withdrawal from alcohol. Meanings of "addiction," "abuse," and "dependence" are still being negotiated; some deny that marijuana is addicting, though dependence and abuse is prevalent.

addictive personality A hypothetical personality pattern characterized by a strong tendency to become psychologically and physically dependent on substances such as alcohol and tobacco. Such persons are purported to easily develop a craving for the substance involved, as well as a tendency to use it in increased amounts. See ADDICT, SUBSTANCE-USE DISORDERS.

Addison-Biermer anemia (T. Addison & A. Biermer) Chronic pernicious anemia due to vitamin-B12 deficiency. Causes neurologic disorders including loss of senses of taste and smell, ataxia, apathy, incoordination, irritability, and psychoses. Also known as Addison's anemia, Biermer's anemia, Biermer-Ehrlich anemia, pernicious anemia. See ADDISON'S DISEASE.

Addison's disease A disorder caused by a deficiency of adrenal hormones. A major symptom is muscle fatigue due in part to inability to maintain a stable level of blood sugar for energy. Mental effects include depression, anxiety, and mood changes. Named after British physician Thomas Addison (1793–1860).

addition In Rorschach test scoring, refers to the ability to first see elements in an inkblot as independent units and later to assemble them into a coherent whole.

addition test An aptitude test of arithmetical addition, performance being scored in terms of speed or accuracy or both.

addition theorem A probability theorem to determine the chances of a complex event occurring when occurrences of simple events are known.

additive color mixture An intermixture of "film color" by either mixing lights or rotating color wheels, resulting in new color perceptions. The mixing of lights results in a hue that is an interaction of the mixed hues, for example, shining yellow and blue spotlights on the same place results in white. Compare SUBTRACTIVE COLOR MIXTURE in which "surface color," such as pigments or paints are mixed. See COLOR MIXTURE.

additive mixture of colors The process and effect of combining colored lights to manifest new, composite colors, such as red and green spotlights blending to form yellow. See COLOR MIXTURE, SUBTRACTIVE COLOR MIXTURE.

additive overlapping clustering See CLUSTER ANALYSIS.

additive scale An equal-unit scale, such as a car's speedometer. See INTERVAL SCALE.

adducted aphonia   Loss of voice as a result of contractions of the muscles that move the vocal cords.

adduction   Movement of a body part toward the center of the body, such as both eyes turning toward the nose, or the fingers closing. Compare ABDUCTION.

adductor   A muscle that pulls body parts toward the center of the body. Compare ABDUCTOR.

adelphogamy   1. Mating among siblings, particularly some insects (such as ants). 2. A form of polygyny in which brothers share one or more wives.

A-delta (Aδ) fibers   One of the three classes of A fibers that have diameters between 1 and 5 microns and conduction velocities of 5–30 m/sec. They are sensory and are found in cutaneous nerves. See A FIBER.

ademonia   Obsolete term for agitated depression.

ademosyne   Obsolete term for nostalgia.

adendritic   Without dendrites.

adenine   (A. Kossel) One of the bases found in both deoxyribonucleic acid (DNA) and ribonucleic acid (RNA). The other two bases found in DNA and RNA are cytosine and guanine. Adenine is a naturally occurring amino purine extractable from a gland. See CHROMOSOME, DEOXYRIBONUCLEIC ACID.

adenine molecule   A purine compound present in the nuclei of plant and animal cells. Adenine and guanine are the essential components of the nucleic acids, deoxyribonucleic acid (DNA) and ribonucleic acid (RNA). When adenine is metabolized, the end product is uric acid.

adenohypophysis   The anterior, larger portion of the pituitary gland that secretes various hormones, including those controlling growth.

adenoid type   Refers to a person whose tonsils or adenoids are pathologically enlarged, a condition associated with constitutional anomalies such as cretinism, deaf-mutism, or oxycephaly.

adenosine (A or Ado)   (P. F. Levene) A naturally occurring chemical of most living cells, consisting of the adenine molecule of the ribonucleic acid (RNA) base and a sugar molecule. It functions as an energy source in metabolic activities at the cellular level. In combination with three phosphate units, adenosine forms a high-energy bond that is easily split when a cell requires quick energy and is associated with nerve-impulse transmissions. See ADENINE, ADENOSINE TRIPHOSPHATE.

adenosine 3′,5′-monophosphate   A natural substance formed from a common cellular chemical, adenosine triphosphate, with a role of mediating many hormonal activities in body tissues. Translates various hormones into specific cellular actions, such as the release of insulin. Also is involved in functions of epinephrine. Also known as cAMP, cyclic AMP.

adenosine triphosphate (ATP)   (F. Lipmann) A nucleotide compound present in all living cells and the source of chemical energy for muscle contractions. See ADENINE MOLECULE, ADENOSINE.

adequately staffed behavior setting   The minimum number of people necessary for normal functioning of an event such as a dance or an awards ceremony. Formerly known as adequately manned behavior setting.

adequate sample   In research, a sample of sufficient size to permit appropriate interpretations of the findings.

adequate stimulus   (C. S. Sherrington) A stimulus of sufficient potential to trigger an impulse that excites a receptor. See ALL-OR-NONE LAW, EFFECTIVE STIMULUS, GRADED POTENTIALS, INADEQUATE STIMULUS, SPIKE POTENTIAL.

ADH   See ANTIDIURETIC HORMONE.

ADHD   attention deficit hyperactivity disorder.

ad hoc   Developed or created for a specific purpose, such as an ad hoc committee. Often used for explaining research results, as in an ad hoc interpretation. Often carries a pejorative connotation.

ad hoc committee   A typically short tenured, task-oriented group created for a specific purpose.

ad hoc hypothesis   An explanation for a phenomenon when no theoretical explanation existed prior to the event or circumstance. A theory or explanation put forth after a fact.

ad hominem   (to the person—Latin) In logic, an error in which criticism is aimed at a person supporting an idea rather than at the merit of the idea or the content of the statement. See AD VERBUM.

adiadochokinesis   (L. Bruns, J. Babinski) Loss of ability to perform rapid alternating movements, such as fanning motions, due to a cerebellar dysfunction. Also known as adiadokokinesis, adiadokokinesia.

adience   Movement toward a stimulus. Compare ABIENCE.

adient behavior   (H. Warren) Approach behavior of an animal toward a particular stimulus. Compare ABIENT BEHAVIOR.

ad ignorantiam   (to ignorance—Latin) In logic, an error in which something is concluded to be true because it cannot be proven false. See APPEAL TO IGNORANCE.

adipocytes   Cells in the body adapted to accept fat. Purportedly, obese people have larger adipocytes than people of normal or typical weight. More commonly known as fat cells.

adipose   Fat in the cells of animal tissues.

adiposis dolorosa   (F. Dercum) A painful condition of obese people, characterized by pendulous masses of fat in various regions of the body. Mental and emotional disorders may be associated with this condition as well as neural-skeletal problems.

adiposogenital dystrophy   A state of obesity that occurs during adolescence due to malfunction of the anterior pituitary. See FROHLICH'S SYNDROME.

adiposogenitalism   (A. Fröhlich) Technical name for Fröhlich's syndrome.

adipsia   1. Absence of thirst. 2. Abnormal avoidance of water or beverages. Compare POLYDIPSIA.

ADJ   See ADJUSTING SCHEDULE OF REINFORCEMENT.

adjacency effect (A. R. Jensen) A number of disconnected words (or nonsense syllables), which far exceeds participants' memory span, are presented one at a time at short intervals, such as every two seconds, in a different random order on each of two (or more) trials. After each presentation, participants are asked to recall as many of the words or syllables as possible. The probability of recalling any given word is related to that word's "adjacency" (that is, whether it precedes, follows or is in-between) words recalled on the previous trial. See MEMORY RETENTION.

Adjective Check List (ACL) (H. G. Gough & A. B. Heilbrun) A self-report personality assessment device in which respondents check adjectives (such as "smart," "quiet," "easy-going") that describe themselves. Can be scored for 37 scales, including 15 Murray needs. Used to gauge self-assessment, how a participant wishes to be, etc.

adjunctive therapist A member of a treatment or rehabilitation team whose functions are ancillary to the core of a therapeutic program, such as a hospital recreation director.

adjusting schedule of reinforcement (ADJ) A complex operant reinforcement schedule in which each successive ratio's size is determined by a prior characteristic. Also known as adjusting reinforcement schedule.

adjustive behavior Actions taken to address changing biological or social conditions.

adjustment Modification of attitudes and behavior to meet the demands of life effectively, such as carrying on constructive interpersonal relations, dealing with stressful or problematic situations, handling responsibilities, fulfilling personal needs and aims, and wearing heavier clothing in colder weather.

adjustment disorder A clinically significant emotional or behavioral disorder occurring within three months after a person is subjected to a specific, identifiable stressor, such as failure in school, divorce, business crisis, family discord, a natural disaster, persecution, death in the family. Such disorders fall into three natural groups: (a) covert, known only to the person involved; (b) overt, evident to others but not to the person; and (c) overt-covert, the person so affected is aware of having an adjustment disorder and it is evident to others. The disorder may manifest itself in ways that are minor such as by a specific phobia (covert), a tic (overt) or ways that are major such as in a full-blown psychopathy (overt-covert).

adjustment disorder in relation to tasks A condition characterized by anxiety about school or occupational performance, including inability to write reports, anxiety about performance, and difficulty in concentrating despite satisfactory intellectual or performance ability.

adjustment disorder with depressed mood A condition characterized by depressed mood, tearfulness, and hopelessness, but etiologically distinguishable from both major depression and uncomplicated bereavement.

adjustment disorder with mixed emotional features A condition characterized by various combinations of depression, anxiety, or other emotions, but distinguishable from depressive and anxiety disorders, for example, reactions of ambivalence, depression, anger, and increased dependency in an adolescent who moves away from home.

adjustment disorder with disturbance of conduct A condition characterized by conduct (for example, vandalism, truancy, reckless driving, fighting, and defaulting on legal responsibilities) that violates the rights of others or major norms and rules of society appropriate to the person's age. See ANTISOCIAL-PERSONALITY DISORDER, CONDUCT DISORDER.

adjustment inventory A survey form used to evaluate a participant's emotional and social adjustment compared with a representative sample of individuals from the same population. See BELL ADJUSTMENT INVENTORY.

adjustment level The degree of successful adaptation of a functioning organism to its social or physical environment.

adjustment mechanism Habitual psychological and behavioral patterns that enable a person to meet the demands of life.

adjustment method/procedure A psychophysical technique in which a participant adjusts a variable stimulus to match a constant standard.

adjustment of measurements A statistical measure by which the effects of differences in the samples being compared have been minimized by accepted statistical procedures.

adjustment of observations Reinterpretation of observed data or weighting of data to correct for atypical information.

adjustment process analysis In the pursuit of complex goals, some individuals attain their goals easily, others fail. In such analyses, reasons for success and failure are searched for. These reasons often have to do with personality factors.

adjustment reaction An often transient situational disorder that is a response to an unusual stressful situation without underlying personality disturbance. See ADJUSTMENT DISORDER, ADJUSTMENT REACTION OF ADOLESCENCE, ADJUSTMENT REACTION OF CHILDHOOD, ADJUSTMENT REACTION OF INFANCY.

adjustment reaction of adolescence A psychological and behavioral disorder associated with desires for freedom from family, school, and other social demands as well as difficulty in controlling impulses. Sometimes known as raging hormones.

adjustment reaction of childhood A psychological and behavioral disorder manifested by symptoms and features such as nail-biting, thumb-sucking, temper tantrums, feeding problems, and behavior problems such as stealing, truancy, and running away from home.

adjustment reaction of infancy A psychological and behavioral disorder related to a difficult birth or to mistreatment by caregivers, manifested by problems in feeding and sleeping, restlessness, and crying.

adjustment reaction of later life A psychological and behavioral disorder often associated with retirement, persistent illness, financial problems, and having to move to unfamiliar quarters.

adjustor The central or ganglionic part of a reflex arc.

adjuvant Accessory or supplementary.

adjuvant therapy/treatment   Secondary or subsidiary methods of treating mental disorders in addition to the main psychotherapy (for example, group therapy may be considered adjuvant therapy to individual psychotherapy). Such methods may include bibliotherapy (suggested readings) and other assignments. The implication is that adjuvant therapy is secondary in importance to primary therapy.

ADL   See ACTIVITIES OF DAILY LIVING.

Adlerian   A follower of the theories of Alfred Adler.

Adlerian psychology   Alternative name for Alfred Adler's Individual Psychology. The following items are important for understanding this theory: ABOVE AND BELOW, ADLER'S DREAM THEORY, ADLER'S PERSONALITY TYPES, ADLERIAN, ADLERIAN PSYCHOLOGY, AGGRESSIVE INSTINCT, AVOIDERS, BASIC MISTAKE, BASIC PERSONALITY, BIRTH ORDER THEORY, COMPENSATION, CREATIVE SELF, EARLY RECOLLECTIONS, FAMILY CONSTELLATION, FICTION, FINAL TENDENCY, GETTERS, GUIDING FICTIONS, INDIVIDUAL PSYCHOLOGY, INFERIORITY COMPLEX, INFERIORITY FEELINGS, JUNCTION, KEY QUESTION, LEBENSLÜGE, LIFE GOAL, LIFE PLAN, LIFESTYLE, MASCULINE PROTEST, MINUS SITUATION, MORPHOLOGIC(AL) INFERIORITY, NEUROTIC CHARACTER, NEUROTIC FICTION, NEUROTIC HUNGER STRIKE, NUCLEAR COMPLEX/CONFLICT, ORGAN INFERIORITY, ORGAN JARGON, OVERAMBITION, OVERCOMPENSATION, PAMPERED STYLE OF LIFE, PLUS-MINUS SITUATION, PRIVATE LOGIC, RULERS, SAFEGUARDING TENDENCY, SLEEPING POSITIONS, SOCIAL INTEREST, SOFT DETERMINISM, SOMATIC COMPLIANCE, STRIVING FOR SUPERIORITY, STYLE OF LIFE, SUPERIORITY, SUPERIORITY COMPLEX, USEFULS, WILL-TO-POWER.

Adler's dream theory   (A. Adler) A point of view that dreams are prodromic; that they foretell the future because the dream is a kind of rehearsal for action. As with Sigmund Freud, Alfred Adler accepted the idea that dreams were symbolized and that in interpreting them, the meanings of the symbols need to be understood.

Adler's personality types   (A. Adler) Alfred Adler purportedly disliked characterizing people as types due to the vast variability between individuals, but for heuristic purposes he proposed four main ones: (a) Usefuls, people who are socially cooperative; (b) Rulers, people who dominate others; (c) Avoiders, people who do as little as possible; and (d) Getters, people who depend on others. See CHARACTER TYPES, HUMORAL THEORY, TYPOLOGY.

ad misericordiam   (toward pity—Latin) In logic, an error based on an appeal for pity from the person to whom the appeal is directed. See FALLACIES.

admission procedure   The process of admitting patients to an institution, which includes such steps as putting them at ease; obtaining necessary information from them, from their family, or from the referral agency; conducting a preliminary interview; and giving them a reassuring account of the type of help they will be offered.

adolescence   The period of life beginning with puberty and ending with completed growth and physical maturity. In humans, the period spans ages 12 to 21 in females and 13 to 22 in males. During this period, major changes occur at varying rates in sexual characteristics, body image, sexual interest, career development, intellectual development, and self-concept. See ADJUSTMENT REACTION OF ADOLESCENCE, ADOLESCENT GROWTH SPURT.

adolescent adjustment reaction   A situational stress disorder associated with emancipatory strivings and inability to control impulses and emotions. See ADAPTIVE PROCESSES, ADJUSTMENT DISORDER, ADJUSTMENT REACTION OF ADOLESCENCE.

adolescent counseling   The professional, academic, or personal guidance of adolescents through interviews, analyzing case-history data, and psychological testing.

adolescent crisis   Refers to the emotional turmoil of adolescence that often accompanies the drive to achieve independence by casting off old emotional ties and developing new relationships, as well as adapting to a changed body. See ADJUSTMENT REACTION OF ADOLESCENCE.

adolescent egocentrism   The belief of some adolescents that they should be the focus of attention in social situations and that their problems are unique. See PERSONAL FABLE.

adolescent growth spurt   A rapid increase in weight and especially height that occurs just after puberty.

adolescent gynecomastia   Breast enlargement in a boy, resulting from hormonal changes. Usually minor and self-limiting.

adolescent homoeroticism   Erotic contacts with or thoughts about members of the same sex (gender) during the pubertal period. Estimates of frequency of occurrence vary in part due to different measurement procedures and variations in definitions of homosexuality.

adolescent homosexuality   See ADOLESCENT HOMOEROTICISM.

adolescent pregnancy   Pregnancy during adolescence.

adolescent rebellion   "Storm and stress" characteristic of some adolescents, encompassing conflict within the family and a general alienation from adult society and its values.

adolescent sex changes   Normal physical and physiological changes that occur in males and females during puberty. Typically includes accelerated development of sex organs and secondary sexual characteristics, such as appearance of pubic hair, and occurrence of first seminal ejaculation by boys and first menstruation by girls.

adolescentilism   Being sexually aroused by imitating an adolescent.

adolor   Inability to feel grief, or, from the point of an observer, to demonstrate grief.

adoptee-family method   An assessment of the degree to which intellectual and personality variables are inherited by comparing biological with adopted children raised in the same home environment. See ADOPTION STUDIES.

adopter categories   In consumer psychology, determination of how various categories of individuals make purchase selections.

adoption studies Estimation of the degree of heritability of a given trait or disorder by methods such as studying the same trait in biologic children in a family and relating it to that of adopted children raised in the same family while controlling for the effects of the trait from the biologic and adoptive parents. See ADOPTEE-FAMILY METHOD.

adoration An attitude of high and intense esteem for a person viewed as incomparably superior to the adorer.

ad populum (to the people—Latin) In logic, an error based on what everyone else assumes, what everyone "knows." See BANDWAGON APPEAL, GROUPTHINK.

ADR adverse drug reaction(s)

adrenal androgens Adrenal cortex hormones that regulate the development of secondary sex characteristics, primarily of the male.

adrenal cortex The outer layer of the adrenal gland and the source of a number of hormones, including the androgens, glucocorticoids, and mineral-corticoids. Its functions are controlled by the adrenocorticotrophic hormone of the pituitary gland.

adrenal gland (Eustachius, T. Addison) An endocrine gland, about the size of a thumb, located above each kidney. The central part (medulla) secretes adrenin and noradrenalin; the outer part (cortex) secretes cortisone, etc.

adrenalin(e) (E. F. Vulpian, J. Takamine, J. J. Abel) A hormone and catecholamine neurotransmitter secreted by the adrenal gland which affects the body by arousing it for action under stress. It has sympathomimetic effects such as increase in alertness, heart and breathing rates as well as shortening the coagulation time of the blood, and regulating metabolism. It later became also known as epinephrine. See ADRENAL GLAND, FIGHT OR FLIGHT RESPONSE.

adrenal medulla The internal portion of adrenal gland that secretes epinephrine (adrenalin) and norepinephrine (noradrenalin), which function as sympathetic nervous system stimulants.

adrenal steroids Hormones secreted into the circulatory system by the adrenal cortex during emotional arousal. Also known as corticosteroids.

adrenarche Premature puberty induced by adrenal gland hyperactivity.

adrenergic (H. H. Dale) A type of nerve cell or neurophysiological function mediated by the neurotransmitter adrenaline, more commonly known as epinephrine, or its even more prevalent form, norepinephrine—both being types of catecholamines—and, in contrast to cholinergic functions, tending to be associated with the sympathetic nervous system.

adrenergic blocking agent (aba or ABA) See ALPHA BLOCKERS, ALPHA RECEPTOR, BETA RECEPTOR, BETA-ADRENERGIC BLOCKERS, BETA-ADRENERGIC RECEPTOR ANTAGONISTS.

adrenergic drug Substance that stimulates the activity of epinephrine or mimics the functions of epinephrine. Such drugs are part of a group of sympathomimetic amines that includes ephedrine, amphetamines, and isoproterenol. Produced naturally in plants and animals or developed synthetically, they include benzphetamine hydrochloride, chlorphentermine hydrochloride, diethylpropion, phendimetrazine, phenmetrazine, phentermine hydrochloride. See ADRENERGIC BLOCKING AGENT, ANALEPTICS.

adrenergic neurons Rarely also known as catecholaminergic neurons. See ADRENERGIC.

adrenergic reaction A response of autonomic nervous-system fibers to stimulation by norepinephrine or epinephrine, the adrenergic hormones.

adrenergic-response state (R. B. Cattell) A physiological reaction pattern of increased pulse, heart rate, and blood-sugar levels due to increased levels of adrenaline.

adrenergic system Part of the autonomic nervous system, including receptor sites influenced by adrenergic drugs.

adrenocorticotrop(h)ic hormone (ACTH) (C. H. Li, H. M. Evans, M. E. Simpson) A hormone released from the pituitary gland which stimulates production of hormones by the adrenal cortex. Also known as corticotrop(h)in.

adrenogenitalism A condition caused by excess androgen secretion from the adrenal glands, resulting in premature puberty in males and masculinization in females. See ADRENARCHE.

adult In law, a person old enough to engage in certain activities or to undertake specific obligations.

adult antisocial behavior See ANTISOCIAL BEHAVIOR.

Adult Basic Learning Examination (ABLE) (B. Karlsen & E. F. Gardner) A test devised to measure adult academic achievement from the first up to the fourth-grade level.

adult-ego state (E. Berne) A component of personality that represents a mature, rational capacity to deal with current reality. See EXTEROPSYCHIC.

adultery Sexual intercourse between a married person and someone other than a legal spouse. The term does not apply in the case of rape.

adult foster home boarding home

adult home rest home

adultomorphism The interpretation of a child's behavior in adult terms. Also known as homuncalism.

adult situational reaction A usually transient personality disorder in which symptoms such as anxiety attacks and insomnia occur as a result of overwhelming stress associated with such stressors as marital discord, pregnancy, premature birth, spontaneous abortion, job difficulties, financial insecurity, menopause, acute illness, or surgery. See TRANSIENT SITUATIONAL PERSONALITY DISORDER.

advanced directives Advice provided by patients on the topic of their future care in the event they are incapacitated. See LIVING WILL.

advanced empathy   A late stage in Carl Rogers's person-centered psychotherapy in which the therapist gradually dares to suggest what might be an underlying theme in the client's overall problem, putting this as a hypothesis, without any attempt to force the insight on the client.

advanced organizers   Material added to assist learned material to be better organized.

advanced placement (AP) examinations   Achievement tests which give high-school students an opportunity to gain admission to college with advanced standing in one or more topics (the College Entrance Examination Board Advanced Placement Program), or to receive credit for college-level education acquired through independent study and other nontraditional procedures (the CEEB College Level Examination Program). Also known as AP exams. See INTERNATIONAL BACCALAUREATE EXAMINATIONS (B EXAMS).

advancing neuroses   A situation characterized by inability to adopt adequate defenses or discharge impulses, which accumulate to cause progressively severe symptoms, for example, becoming increasingly withdrawn and phobic so that a fear of travel gradually evolves into a fear of leaving the house and eventually into a fear of getting out of bed. Some cases of advancing neurosis may stabilize for a period, then advance again.

advantage by illness   A secondary gain. See EPINOSIC GAIN, FLIGHT INTO HEALTH, SECONDARY GAINS.

advantage law   law of advantage

adventitious   Caused by external, often unseen factors. Compare CONGENITAL.

adventitious blindness   Loss of sight due to an external factor such as being poked in the eye or poorly controlled diabetes, rather than due to a congenital or hereditary factor.

adventitious crisis   Accidental, uncommon, and unexpected crisis that may result in multiple losses and gross environmental changes.

adventitious deafness   Loss of hearing due to disease or to an accident (such as being too close to a loud explosion). See ADVENTITIOUS DISABILITIES.

adventitious deficit   Any ability that was lost due to external factors.

adventitious disabilities   Physical and mental disabilities due to factors independent of heredity; accidentally or spontaneously caused by diseases or accidents.

adventitious reinforcement   The conditioning of an operant response in an organism without the response being specified by the researcher. A prime example is B. F. Skinner's experiment on superstitious behavior in pigeons. With reinforcements arriving at regular intervals, each pigeon learns a different response, usually from among typical behaviors such as turning, raising and lowering the head, bowing—whatever occurs immediately prior to the reward several times early in the process. Sometimes called "accidental reinforcement," although this terminology has been criticized as focusing on the behavior of the researcher rather than on the underlying law of effect.

adventure recreation model   In sports psychology, a model of risk participation that includes participant characteristics and behavior patterns to predict the level of engagement.

ad verbum   (to the word—Latin) In logic, refers to the words themselves rather than to the person or persons uttering the words. An "ad verbum" criticism is directed strictly to the thing being criticized. Contrasts with an "ad hominem" criticism which is directed at the person who uttered the words, for example, "This book is incorrect" (ad verbum); "The author of this book is misinformed" (ad hominem).

ad verecundiam   (to modesty—Latin) In logic, an error based on citing as an authority a person who is not really an authority on the topic of discussion. See FALSE AUTHORITY.

adversary model   A method of assigning the approach to truth to two opposing parties. The practice is seen mainly in legal courtrooms where, before a judge, jury, or both, opposing lawyers argue their positions. See DEVIL'S ADVOCATE.

adverse drug reactions (ADR)   Physical and psychological symptoms which are side effects of medicines, such as sleepiness, rashes, itching, nausea, diarrhea, dry mouth. Also commonly called "side effects." An example is the pathogenic effects of the liver of excessive use of acetaminophen, especially in interaction with alcohol.

adverse effects   1. Unpleasant side effects of medicines, which are unpleasant, unhealthy, or interfere with the actions of other medicines. 2. Unpleasant or undesirable effects of treatment.

adverse impact   A negative effect on some individuals following legal guidelines adopted to protect the rights of individuals. A selection procedure has adverse impact on group members if they are generally outperformed on assessment criteria by others, for instance, questions on American issues administered to recent immigrants.

advertising psychology   The study of the techniques and effectiveness of advertising, including motives that prompt consumers to buy, and characteristics of effective ads. See ADVERTISING RESEARCH, MOTIVATION RESEARCH.

advertising research   The study of (a) the selection of effective marketing appeals for specific products or commodities, (b) the creation of product images including trade names and package designs, and (c) the development of methods of measuring the effectiveness of advertising campaigns in different media. May also be applied to generic advertising (for example, advertising of an industry or product category such as cigars or coffee, rather than specific brands). See ADVERTISING PSYCHOLOGY.

advertising response modeling (ARM)   A model to explain how central and peripheral processing cause an advertisement to gain a person's attention.

advice giving   A verbal counseling technique which provides advice, alternatives, or options for the client's consideration.

advice therapy   Counseling intended to get people to change their attitudes on the basis of common sense. Contrasts with Carl Rogers's views. See PERSON-CENTERED THERAPY.

advocacy   Individuals or groups representing clients who do not have the power or the know-how to act for themselves in dealing with the bureaucracy of local governments and related social institutions.

advocacy research   Studies that analyze the impact of specific social institutions on the poor or powerless. Such studies are usually explicitly activist, often combining direct social action with research that seeks to identify social ills and next develops concrete programs for change. See ACTIVISM, ADVOCATE.

advocate   As used in mental health and rehabilitation, a person who represents the "consumer," especially the disadvantaged. Two general types of advocates are (a) those in which a single individual is represented, and (b) those in which a group is represented. Also known as linkage workers, mental-health counselors/ workers. See EXPEDITER, MENTAL-HEALTH WORKER, OMBUDSMAN.

adx   In Rorschach test scoring, a symbol for neurotic traits.

adynamia   1. Lack of strength. 2. Loss of strength for psychological rather than physiological reasons. Also known as neurasthenia. 3. See ASTHENIA.

aedoeomania   Obsolete term for nymphomania.

aelurophobia   ailurophobia

AEq   age equivalent

aerasthenia   Neurotic behavior in airplane pilots characterized by anxiety, restlessness, lack of confidence, headache, and other physical symptoms. Also known as aeroasthenia, aeroneurosis.

aerial perspective   1. A cue used by one eye for perceiving distance, for example, distant objects appearing less distinct than nearby objects. See MONOCULAR DEPTH CUE. 2. The effect of the atmosphere upon perception. From a mountain top a person can see more clearly than at the bottom of the mountain, due to pollutants in the air affecting clarity of perception. See BINOCULAR VISION.

aeroacrophobia   Morbid fear of open (agoraphobia) and high (acrophobic) spaces.

aerobic exercise   Sustained exercise that increases heart and lung fitness; often helps to alleviate depression and anxiety.

aeroneurosis   Neurosis suffered by airmen. Also known as aerosthenia.

aerophagia   The gulping of air as a neurotic symptom, may accompany a rapid-breathing attack during anxiety or panic. Also known as aerophagy, pneumophagia. See HYPERVENTILATION.

aerophobia   Morbid fear of fresh air or moving air, such as wind or drafts. Sometimes known as anemophobia.

aerospace psychology   In human factors engineering, the study of variables such as confinement, disorientation, hypoxia, motion sickness, pressure changes, vertigo, and weightlessness.

aesthesiometer   Infrequent spelling of esthesiometer.

aesthetic appreciation   (D. E. Berlyne) The general finding that, when asked to indicate their liking for various artistic productions, people demonstrate a kind of inverted U-shape pattern of preference with little at either end of the continuum of complexity, for example, if there is too little complexity, the productions are boring; if too much, the productions are confusing. A moderate amount of complexity is best regarded. See CIRCULAR-PATTERN RESPONSES.

aesthetic preference   A liking of artistic elements, such as sculpture, music, poetry, based upon personal reactions of pleasantness or unpleasantness to such endeavors.

aesthetic realism   (E. Siegel) A philosophy and a method of therapy based on three points: (a) a person should learn to like the world; this calls for (b) the understanding of the aesthetic oneness of opposites; and (c) the greatest danger is to have contempt for the world.

affair   Common term for a relationship, presumably sexual, often adulterous.

affect   1. The emotional feeling, tone, and mood attached to a thought, as well as its external manifestations. 2. An early designation of that aspect of the mind that contains emotions and feelings. See AFFECTIVE DISORDERS, COGNITION, CONATION.

affectability   Emotional susceptibility.

affectation   The pretense of possessing a trait or characteristic in the expectation that it will impress others favorably.

affect block   Inability to show strong emotions because of a fear of emotional ties.

affect display   1. A demonstration of feelings by bodily display, for example, a person's hands shaking due to nervousness. 2. An evident indication that an organism is in a specific emotional state (for example, chameleons when startled or frightened may change their body color, dogs may snarl and show their teeth).

affect-energy   Energy that is initiated by a stimulus and that affects the entire human organism (for example, the appearance of a poisonous snake scares a person into running away). See ADRENALINE, FIGHT OR FLIGHT RESPONSE.

affect-fantasy/phantasy   (C. G. Jung) A fantasy or imagined experience laden with strong emotions.

affect fixation   In psychoanalytic theory, remaining attached to feelings and emotions characteristic of (or dominant in) an earlier stage of physical and mental development. Also known as affective fixation, fixation of affect.

affect hunger   Craving for affection and loving care, especially among young children who have been emotionally deprived. See MARASMUS.

affect inversion   A rapid change of feelings toward someone or something from positive to negative or vice versa. See REVERSAL, REVERSAL OF AFFECT.

affection   Feelings and emotions of tenderness and attachment, especially when such feelings are nonsexual. See AFFECTIVE DISORDERS, AFFECTIVE STATE, AMBIVALENCE, ANXIETY, DEPRESSION, ELATION.

affectional attachments   The expressions of affection in infants that begin during the first year of life and are generated by cuddling, kissing, words and acts of endearment, as well as demonstrations of affection between the parents. See AFFECTIONAL BONDS.

affectional bonds   Feelings of positive emotional attachment between humans, animals, and between humans and animals, manifested by such activities as smiling, clinging, cuddling, stroking, and embracing. Evidence of affectional bonds appear in the sense of loss, grief, and anxiety experienced if separation occurs. See AFFECTIONAL ATTACHMENTS, SEPARATION ANXIETY.

affectional drive   The compelling urge to give and to receive affection, possibly innate, since infants respond positively to cuddling and being held from the start of life, possibly due to the need for sensory stimulation. See EMOTIONAL DEPRIVATION, MATERNAL DEPRIVATION.

affectionless psychopathy   (J. Bowlby) The committing of an atrocity (such as murdering and dismembering a human body) without any display of feelings or emotions.

affective   Pertaining to feelings, emotions, and moods. See AFFECTION.

affective ambivalence   Manifestation of co-occurring contradictory feelings toward an object or event such as love and hate, interest and disinterest, affection and revulsion. See AMBIVALENCE.

affective amnesia   Memory loss not related to organic brain conditions and not characterized by patterns of behavior-associated dementia or cortical amnesia. The phrase may be applied in cases of memory defects associated with functional psychological disorders. It must be distinguished from the Ganser syndrome sometimes seen in prisoners feigning mental impairment; for example, when asked to multiply 6 by 4, they may answer 23. See FACTITIOUS DISORDER, FUGUE, MALINGERING.

affective arousal theory   (D. C. McClelland) The (1951) point of view that people learn to seek anticipated pleasure and to avoid anticipated pain. Motives derive from changes in affective states.

affective assessment   A measurement of feeling processes or characteristics such as temperaments, emotions, interests, attitudes, and personality traits.

affective discharge   **cathectic discharge**

affective disharmony   Contradictions between emotional reactions and ideational content, for example, disliking a person (affective reaction) and admiring some aspect of the person such as good character (cognitive reaction). See COGNITIVE DISSONANCE.

affective disorder   A condition of distorted mood, whether "positive" such as elation or happy enthusiasm to an abnormal degree or "negative" such as pathological sorrow and depression. Most mental disorders have either or both of these or a third member of the dispositional triad, "escape" demonstrated by apathy or disinterest. See AFFECTIVE TONE, MIXED BIPOLAR DISORDER, MOOD DISORDERS.

affective domain   Emotion. One of the three areas of the mind originally established by the ancient Greeks, the other two being cognition and conation.

affective education   Instruction that attempts to teach people to control their emotions; also teaching that stresses the value of emotionally involving students in the subject, to go beyond the cognitive. See ANGER MANAGEMENT.

affective equilibrium   A balance of feelings. See ADAPTATION LEVEL, ADAPTION-LEVEL THEORY, HOMEOSTASIS.

affective eudemonia   An explanation for a mental process based on the concept of escape from unacceptable reality. Just as some animals play dead when threatened by a predator, so too when humans are faced with situations that they fear greatly, some may try to escape by utilizing a variety of mental processes or disorders. See ADJUSTMENT DISORDERS, MENTAL ILLNESS.

affective experience   Any feeling of emotion, including pleasure or pain, whether normal, pathological, conscious, or unconscious. See AFFECTION.

affective failure   An extreme deficiency or inadequacy of emotional reactions or adjustment. The person is perceived by others as having no feelings.

affective feeblemindedness   Obsolete phrase describing apparent loss of intellectual ability that is secondary to depression or another emotional state.

affective feedback   The feelings of pleasantness or unpleasantness that follow the execution of a response.

affective hallucination   A strong subjective perception of an object or event when no such stimulus is present, associated with feelings of depression or elation, including grandiose ideas or self-depreciation, or such depressive content as poverty, disease, or guilt.

affective interaction   Interpersonal relationships carried out on an emotionally-charged level, as in group psychotherapy or in the family.

affective logic   A series of apparently logical assertions leading to a conclusion, but actually illogical based on one or more emotional elements. See RATIONALIZATION.

affective meaning   An emotional aspect of a cognitive element, for example, different emotions may be elicited from certain words (such as table, vomit, pencil, butterfly) ranging on a scale from low (abhorrence) through zero (neutrality) to high (pleasurable).

affective monomania   (J. E. Esquirol) Obsolete phrase for the manic phase of bipolar disorder. See MONOMANIA.

affective psychoses   Loose phrase describing any psychotic condition characterized by a severe disturbance of mood, such as extreme depression or elation that dominate the functioning of the person. See AFFECTIVE DISORDERS, BIPOLAR DISORDER, DEPRESSED BIPOLAR DISORDER, MAJOR DEPRESSIVE EPISODE, MANIA, MANIC EPISODE, MIXED BIPOLAR DISORDER, MOOD DISORDER.

affective ratio   In Rorschach test scoring, the total number of responses to the colored cards divided by the total number of responses to the achromatic cards, purported to be an index of emotionality of the participant. See RORSCHACH DETERMINANTS, RORSCHACH TEST.

affective reaction   A mood that is a consequence of a message or behavior. Can range from despair at the death of a loved one, through comfort after eating, to joy from completing a goal. See EMOTIONS.

affective reorganization   The establishment of a new feeling toward something or someone (for example, liking a person on first impression, but disliking the person after spending more time together).

affective rigidity   A condition in which emotions, feelings, or mood remain unchanged through varying situations in which feeling changes normally would occur.

affective separation   A situation in which the mother figure is physically present but not adequately stimulating or responsive to the infant. Also known as masked deprivation. See MARASMUS.

affective slumber   Refers to the middle stage of Alzheimer's disease in which the affected person becomes dull, hard to arouse in terms of attention and emotional response, plus other related symptoms such as disorientation and perplexity.

affective state   The status of having some type of emotional feeling. See AFFECT.

affective suggestion   The effect of the emotional relationship between hypnotist and a person undergoing hypnosis. Also known as hypotaxia.

affective theories   Those points of view of counseling and psychotherapy that emphasize the importance of feelings and emotions in therapeutic change, and that stress the value of affective therapies over cognitive therapies.

affective tone   The feeling associated with any event or stimulus. See AFFECTIVE DISORDER, FEELING TONE.

affectivity   1. Feeling tone. 2. (E. Bleuler) Susceptibility to emotional stimuli to the extent that they affect bodily functions and states.

affectomotor patterns   Refers to a combination of muscular over-activity and emotional excitement. See BIPOLAR DISORDER, INTERMITTENT EXPLOSIVE DISORDER, MANIA.

affectothymia   (R. B. Cattell) The most prominent personality factor, a responsiveness to emotions. See AFFECTION.

affectualization   A defense mechanism in which the emotional repercussions of unwelcome issues confronting the patient are overemphasized to avoid understanding and dealing with the issues.

affectus animi   Obsolete phrase for mental disposition in general.

Affenliebe   German term for monkey love.

afferent   Flowing in: conducting toward a center, denoting certain nerves, veins, arteries, and lymphatics. It is the opposite of efferent. Afferent is also known as esodic. The term afferent is translated from the German *aufleitend*, coined by Johann Unzer. See CENTRIPETAL.

afferent code   A hypothetical entity having to do with trying to explain the "wisdom" of sensory nerve pathways in conveying information to the central nervous system that goes beyond simple increases of information carried.

afferent fibers   **afferent (nerve) fibers**

afferent motor aphasia   A type of motor aphasia caused by a lesion in an afferent part of the nervous system.

afferent (nerve) fibers   Sensory nerves that carry nerve impulses toward the central nervous system from periphery or sense organs. Also known as esodic nerves. See EFFERENT (NERVE) FIBERS.

afferent sensory neurons   Incoming sensory fibers ending at the spinal cord.

afferent stimulus interaction   (C. L. Hull) A concept that afferent neural impulses affect not only target elements but also each other, and so the final effect is more than the summation of the impulses. See GESTALT PSYCHOLOGY, HULL'S THEORY.

afferent synthesis   (P. Anokhin) A combination of material imprinted in memory, information, motivation, and a stimulus that sets the mind in action to a decision. The total integration of aspects of the mind and body in action.

affiliation   Association with others. See AFFILIATIVE DRIVE.

affiliative behavior   Overt actions of a person toward another intended to generate a close, friendly relation.

affiliative bonding   The process of forging close emotional attachments between individuals. Occurs for most people in normal behavior but is absent in some disorders and practically all psychoses. See BONDING.

affiliative drive   (H. A. Murray) The compelling urge to associate, form friendships and attachments, and depend on others; the tendency to join organizations and to enjoy social gatherings. Affiliation appears to be a basic source of emotional security; without it, most individuals feel lost and lonely. See AFFILIATION, AFFILIATIVE NEED, GREGARIOUSNESS.

affiliative need   (H. A. Murray) The fundamental determinant urge, desire, or wish to seek cooperative, friendly association with other individuals. See AFFILIATIVE DRIVE.

affinal   Related by or concerning marriage.

affinity   1. A natural liking for or attraction to a person or thing. 2. A family relationship. 3. Mutual attraction usually based on feelings of similarity. 4. Tendency of a substance to be attracted to or be affected by another substance.

affirmation   In cognitive-behavioral psychology, a short positive statement repeatedly used by a person to establish beliefs and patterns (for example, repeating to oneself "I am a worthwhile person.").

affirmation stage   In autosuggestion, the period during which a person exhibits a positive reaction tendency.

affirmative   A term used in police, military, and aviation communication to mean "yes," "accepted," "agreed."

affirmative action   A process based on legal or social policy that attempts to redress past discrimination effects by adjustments in standards for acceptance in schools and jobs of people in protected groups thought to have been victims of bias.

affirmative postmodernism   (P. M. Rosenau) A movement within postmodernism that uses methods of deconstruction to uncover oppressive messages inherent in social, cultural, and scientific discourses. Adherents of this movement propose to show the oppressive aspects of these discourses to challenge illegitimate structures of domination in society. They embrace a political agenda of empowerment whereby oppressed persons and groups can gain more control over their lives.

affirming the consequent   In logic, a violation of good sense, in assuming that a particular effect is the result of the same cause. For example, if P, then Q; if Rex is a dog (P), then Rex is a mammal (Q); Rex, in fact, is a mammal and therefore is a dog.

affix(es) Prefixes and suffixes. In psychology, there are a large number of affixes, from a- (lacking) as in achromatism to zyg(o)- (union) as in zygote, and a large number of suffixes, as -ad (pertaining to) as in monad to -y (sickness) as in acromegaly. Familiarity with these affixes may help in understanding many terms in psychology. See APPENDIX A.

afflatus (A. Morgan) Overpowering impulse or inspiration, often having religious connotations.

affordance (J. J. Gibson) Intrinsic properties of objects. What is known about something at first glance; its essence regarding usability.

affricate In speech, a sound consisting of a plosive, such as, /t/, followed by a fricative, such as /sh/, as the /ch/ in "chair." Also known as semiplosive.

affusion Pouring of water on the body for therapeutic purposes. An old method of dealing with mental disorders, sometimes using fire hoses.

A fiber Myelinated fiber of the somatic nervous system. A fibers are placed into one of three classes depending on their contribution to the compound action potential evoked in a mixed peripheral nerve. The A-alpha (Aα) fibers have diameters between 13 and 22 microns and conduction velocities as fast as 120 m/sec. They participate in muscle reflexes and are absent from cutaneous nerves. A-beta (Aβ, diameter 6–12 microns, conduction velocity 35–75 m/sec) and A-delta (Aδ, diameter 1-5 microns, conduction velocity 5–30 m/sec) are sensory and are found in cutaneous nerves.

A fortiori For a stronger reason; a conclusion following a prior conclusion that has greater logical necessity than the first conclusion.

afterbrain Medulla oblongata. See MYELEN-CEPHALON.

aftercare 1. An integrated, posthospitalization, continuing program of outpatient treatment and rehabilitation services provided by a hospital or other facility. The program is directed to maintenance of improvement, prevention of relapse, and adjustment to the community. 2. In research, an associated obligation of researchers to continuing responsibility for the health and welfare of participants of research, especially in high stress studies such as those related to issues in social psychology and in drug research.

aftercontraction A muscular contraction occurring after stimulation of the muscle has ceased.

aftercurrent Rare term for action potential.

afterdischarge A nerve impulse that continues to discharge after the stimulus has been removed. Can be sustained by a neuronal circuit made up of interneurons as is the case of a sustained reflex.

aftereffect A sensation that remains or continues after a stimulus ceases or is removed, for example, a weight is lifted off a person's body but the person still feels the weight. Also known as aftersensation. See AFTERIMAGE.

afterexpulsion In psychoanalytic theory, prevention of the return of the repressed idea or impulse. Also known as repression proper, secondary repression. See REPRESSION.

afterglow 1. A feeling of pleasure and relaxation following an enjoyable experience. 2. The above-normal "recovery" metabolism following maximal exercise, usually in the context of its contribution to weight loss (which is minimal).

afterimage (Aristotle) An image that remains after a visual stimulus ceases. A positive afterimage (similar to the original image) occurs rarely, lasts a few seconds, and is caused by a continuation of receptor and neural processes following cessation of the stimulus; it is approximately the color and brightness of the original stimulus. A negative afterimage is more common, and is usually complementary to the original stimulus in color and brightness; for example, if the actual stimulus was bright yellow, the negative afterimage will be perceived as dark blue. The term was translated from the German *Nachbild(er)*. See AFTEREFFECT.

afterimage After looking steadily at the image on the left for one minute, cover it and shift the field of vision to the empty square at the right. The reverse afterimage of a black boat against a white background be seen.

after-nystagmus Jerky movements of the eyes after cessation of rotation of the head in the opposite direction, so that if the body was rotated to the right the eye movements would be to the left. See NYSTAGMUS, ROTATIONAL NYSTAGMUS.

afterplay Affectionate interaction following orgasm or intercourse.

afterpotential The negative afterpotential is a residual depolarization in the declining phase of the action potential (spike) which decreases the rate of decline. The positive afterpotential begins after the negative afterpotential and is a shift to a potential that is more positive than the resting potential.

aftersensation Rare name for aftereffect. See AFTERIMAGE.

aftertest An examination or quiz that is given following the administration of a prior one. May be the same test or a parallel test. Purposes for using an aftertest may vary including testing for reliability, or testing for some kind of change in the person or persons being retested. See BEFORE-AFTER DESIGN.

Ag See ANTIGEN.

agametic Asexual.

agamic Asexual. Reproducing without sexual union, as by fission, budding, etc. Also known as agamous. See PARTHENOGENESIS.

agamogenesis 1. Asexual reproduction. 2. Sometimes used as a synonym for parthenogenesis.

agape Unconditional and unselfish love, a nonsexual feeling of concern for someone else, regardless of gender (sex), age, or any other condition. Love that is absolute, given without restriction. In Christian theologies, the love of God or Christ for humankind. Also known as unconditional love. See LOVE, AFFECTION.

Agapemone　　Group marriage as practiced by the Oneida Community in the 1800s. Also, an association of men and women established at Spaxton in England by the Rev. Henry James Prince in the mid-1800s.

AGCT　　Army General Classification Test

age (A)　　1. Time elapsed since birth. 2. To grow older. 3. A period into which human life is divided, for example, infancy, childhood, adolescence, maturity, middle life, senescence, senility. Types of age include: ACHIEVEMENT, ANATOMICAL, BASAL MENTAL, CEILING, CHRONOLOGICAL, DENTAL, DEVELOPMENTAL, EDUCATIONAL, FUNCTIONAL, GESTATIONAL, MENSTRUAL, MENTAL, OVER-, PHYSIOLOGICAL, TERMINAL MENTAL. See CYBERNETIC THEORY OF AGING, EVERSION THEORY OF AGING, SECONDARY AGING, SIZE-AGE CONFUSION, VINELAND SOCIAL MATURITY SCALE.

age-appropriate maturity　　Psychological maturity, or the ability to deal effectively and resiliently with experience, and to perform developmental tasks (biological, social, cognitive) characteristic of a person's age level.

age avoidance　　A tendency to avoid contact or intimacy with members of certain age groups.

age calibration　　Any process of standardization with reference to chronological age, as in the arrangement of psychological tests by chronological ages, and the adoption of a system of scoring tests so that performance may be scored and expressed in reference to that person's age peers.

age credit　　Adding age-group-specific points before computing the deviation intelligence quotient (IQ) test score of an older person. Doing so provides a more accurate measure of that person's true intelligence level, whose performance on the test is thus judged only against that of age peers and not against that of younger persons, who also are compared against only their own peers. Compare AGE DEBIT.

age crises　　Problems that people have occasioned only by consideration of their ages. Tend to be of two types: (a) varying perceptions between individuals, for example, an adult is not permitted to drive a car by the rest of the family who think that he or she is not capable of safe driving; and (b) blocks by laws or customs; for example, youths are forced to attend an elementary school program because of age, even if capable of doing high school level work; adults dropped from a job because of reaching mandatory retirement age (statutory senility), even though still quite capable of working.

age critique　　(critical age—French) The menopausal years.

age de retour　　(age of return (to childhood)—French) The years of senility.

age debit　　Subtracting intelligence quotient (IQ) points from the scores of younger persons on the assumption that there is an improper age decline of IQs of older people, to equate younger persons' score with that of older persons. Rarely performed. Compare AGE CREDIT.

age discrimination　　Rejections or discriminations for being too young or too old, such as school or job applicants.

age equivalent (AEq)　　Any score or measure of development expressed against chronological age as the standard.

age-equivalent scale　　A system of expressing test scores in terms of age norms or averages. Sometimes known as age scale.

age-grade scaling　　The establishment of norms on tests following the testing of samples of groups of different chronological ages so that by looking at a person's test scores, it can be determined at what age level any child is functioning in that particular subject.

ageism　　1. Stereotyping older persons as debilitated, inadequate, dependent. 2. Discrimination against the middle-aged and older, especially in employment. 3. Negative attitude toward the aged as too powerful, demanding of resources, and controlling. 4. In research, ignoring older persons, especially in view of the fact that there are more changes between the ages of 60 and 80 than between 20 and 60.

agency shop　　In labor relations, an organization in which employees do not have to join the union but must, if they are members of the bargaining unit, pay dues to the union. Compare UNION SHOP. See RAND FORMULA.

agency theory　　Formulations regarding delegation (the engagement of another person or agent to perform tasks). Analyzes costs of delegation, differences in goals between the principal and the agent, and relationships between principal and agent.

agenesis　　1. Absence or malformation of any part. 2. Inability of or failure to reproduce.

agenetic　　Defective in development. See AGENESIS, AGENETIC MODE.

agenetic mode　　A way of acting in which individuals relinquish personal responsibility for their own actions, attributing that responsibility to an external authority (leader, chief, expert, etc.) whose instrument or agent they become. See RESPONSIBILITY FEAR.

agenitalism　　1. Absence or malfunction of ovaries or testes due to inadequate sex hormones. 2. Absence of genital organs.

age norm　　A statistically derived standard used in the standarization of a test to reduce or remove as a factor the effects of chronological age and related confounding variables when that test is administered to individuals of various ages.

agent　　1. In general, that which produces an effect. 2. In biochemistry, a hormone that has a variety of effects. 3. In parapsychology, the person who (a) sends messages for possible telepathy, (b) is to be identified in terms of mental state by the "percipient," or (c) looks at a target object in telepathy, clairvoyance, or both. 4. In individual psychotherapy, a therapist who helps a patient gain self-understanding. 5. In group therapy, a patient who helps another patient achieve a new conception of self or other.

agent action on object　　In the two-word stage of language development, an expression indicating an agent's action on an object, in which only two components of the thought are used, as in "John ball" for "John throw ball." See ACTION-INSTRUMENT.

agent provocateur　　In psychoanalytic theory, the precipitating factor, usually of a psychological character, that bring about symptoms, defensive reactions, dreams, or disorders.

age of consent   In the United States of America, the minimum age required by various states for a legal marriage. With parental consent, in one state people may marry at any age, in another, females may marry at 12 years and males at 14. Without parental consent certain laws may require males be at least 17 and females 15 years. In various countries the age of consent may not exist or may vary considerably.

agerasia   Appearing well-preserved, youthful, especially in reference to older people (for example, a person of 80 who impresses others as being about 60 in appearance and behavior).

age regression   A controversial hypnotic technique in which the hypnotist or therapist helps a client recapture a crucial experience by inducing amnesia for the current date, then suggesting that the client return, sometimes year by year, to the earlier age when the alleged experience took place. See HYPNOTIC REGRESSION.

ager naturae   (nature's field—Latin) The uterus.

age scale   Item arrangement used by the original Binet-Simon Scale and the Stanford-Binet Intelligence Scale until its major revision in 1986. An arrangement by chronological age showing when certain normal functions or abilities may be expected to appear, for example, the age at which certain vocabulary words can be expected to appear in a typical child. See AGE-EQUIVALENT SCALE, AGE-GRADE SCALING.

age score   A person's test score expressed in terms of the relation between that person's own score and the average score derived from a group of persons of the same age.

ageus(t)ia   Loss or impairment of the sense of taste. Also known as ageusis.

agglutination   In language development, the formation of new words by combining old words (for example, "psychological analysis" into "psychoanalysis").

aggregate effects   Group effects.

aggregate idea   A general idea of a group or class, taken collectively rather than discretely.

aggregate score   A summary of individual scores as of tests in a battery.

aggregation   Unorganized or loosely organized group of individuals or similar units; a cluster.

aggregation errors   In evaluation research, not separating individual effects from contextual effects when established groups or institutions are used as the unit of analysis. Evaluators are likely to attribute characteristics of the institution to the individual.

aggregation theory   (J. M. Cattell) A point of view that intelligence is a function of the number of neurons in the brain and the interconnections among them.

aggression   1. Destructive or punitive behavior directed toward people or objects. 2. That aspect of personality that involves treatment of other individuals as if they were simply objects to be used in the attainment of the superiority goal. See SOCIAL FEELING.

aggression-frustration hypothesis   (J. Dollard) A postulate that aggressive behavior is a response to frustration.

aggressive conduct disorder   Repetitive, persistent, domineering, punitive, or assaultive verbal or physical conduct in which the basic rights of others are violated, as manifested by physical violence against persons or property, or thefts with confrontation with the victim; also includes failure to establish a normal degree of affection, empathy, or bond with others. See DELINQUENCY, SOCIOPATHIC DISORDER.

aggressive counseling   (C. Vontress) A procedure for counseling minority youth, employing actively directive counseling techniques, outreach counseling, motivation, personal assistance, and follow-ups.

aggressive cue   Anything that might trigger aggression (for example, reading a book filled with aggressive imagery or seeing a person carrying a weapon).

aggressive erotic   Near violence during sexual behavior.

aggressive instinct   (A. Adler) The idea that humans are instinctively aggressive, a view first promulgated and then retracted by Alfred Adler, and later developed by Sigmund Freud into the thanatos theory. See DEATH INSTINCT, THANATOS.

aggressive mimicry   1. Due to evolutionary selectivity, the appearance of an aggressive animal to look harmless and so prey on other animals by fooling them. 2. Due to evolutionary selectivity, the appearance of harmless animals looking aggressive to keep potential predators away from them. Both are found most in insects and fish. See MIMICRY.

aggressiveness   A behavioral trait consisting of strong self-assertiveness, social dominance, and a tendency toward hostility.

aggressive-predatory type   (B. Karpman) A subgroup of the antisocial personality characterized by predation.

aggressive types   Subgroups of the antisocial personality, according to their characteristic aggressive behavior. See AGGRESSIVE COMPLEX TYPE, AGGRESSIVE-PREDATORY TYPE, AGGRESSIVE SIMPLE TYPE.

aggressive undersocialized disorder   A diagnosis of a condition characterized by lack of social concern for others and others' feelings or property. See AGGRESSIVE CONDUCT DISORDER, SOCIOPATHY.

aggressive undersocialized reaction   Apparent lack of concern for others, their feelings or their property, characterized by antisocial activities such as vandalism, torturing animals, intentionally annoying other people. See AGGRESSIVE CONDUCT DISORDER, SOCIOPATHY.

aging   1. In general, the process of growing older. 2. In humans, the process of life from conception to death involving rapid growth and development during the early stages of life, then a period of relative stability, and finally, a decline physically and in some cases mentally, especially in short-term memory. Physiological aging is distinguished from psychological aging. Although the two may co-exist, some age-young people are psychologically old and some age-old people are psychologically young. See AGING PROCESS.

aging disorder   Brain cell and arterial changes resulting from deterioration felt to be associated with aging, such as from atherosclerosis. May be a consequence of the correlational fallacy, that is, attributing causality to correlated relationships. See SENILE PSYCHOSES.

aging process   The process associated with growing older, with emphasis on changes in mental and physical processes and functioning. It is complex and affected by many biological, psychological, sociological, and environmental factors.

agitated depression   A mental state combining melancholy and hyperactivity. Also known as ademonia.

agitated melancholia   Depression with loss of interest or pleasure in all, or almost all, activities or a loss of reactivity to usually pleasurable stimuli, sometimes with features of anxiety, especially frequent in the later decades of life.

agitation   The subjective feeling of being upset, angry, disturbed, unable to rest. See AGITATED DEPRESSION.

agitographia   Abnormally rapid writing and unconscious omission and distortion of letters, words, or parts of words.

agitolalia   **agitophasia**

agitophasia   Abnormally rapid speech in which sounds, words, or parts of words are unconsciously omitted or distorted. Also known as agitolalia.

aglossia   A peripheral expressive speech disorder resulting from a congenital absence of the tongue.

agnosia   (H. Jackson, H. J. Liepmann) Impairment or inability to recognize objects due to loss of sensory and perceptual abilities. Also known as agnea.

agnosic alexia   A form of word blindness that may occur in the absence of speech disorders. The patient usually is able to write spontaneously or to take written dictation but is unable to copy printed material or to read sentences.

agnosticism   (T. H. Huxley) A doctrine positing that neither the nature nor the ultimate character of God or the universe is knowable. Knowledge is limited only to experience.

agonadal   Absence of gonads.

agonal   Obsolete term for the moment of death.

agonic   A social relationship in which one animal, often a male, dominates the others. Usually applied to nonhuman primates.

agonist   1. A person engaged in contest, conflict, or struggle. 2. A contracting muscle whose action is opposed by another muscle. 3. A substance that acts on a receptor (on the nerve cells in the brain) and produces a strong effect (for example, methadone). A partial agonist has only a moderate effect.

agonist-antagonist   A medicine that acts as an agonist on some of the brain's neuroreceptors, while also acting as an antagonist on other receptor sites.

agonistic behavior   Threatening actions of animals toward conspecifics (members of the same species).

agoraphobia   (K. F. O. Westphal) 1. Morbid fear of leaving the familiar setting of one's own home. Often results in avoidance of many life experiences or situations. 2. An anxiety disorder characterized by fear of being alone or in public places (crowds, subways, elevators) from which escape may be difficult or impossible in case of an emergency. 3. Fear of crowds. See AGYIOPHOBIA, DEMOPHOBIA, OCHLOPHOBIA, TOPOPHOBIA. Compare CLAUSTROPHOBIA.

agrammatism   A form of aphasia characterized by difficulty in understanding or properly using grammatical constructions such as word order and verb endings, a typical symptom of Broca's aphasia. Also known as agrammatica, agrammata(phasia), agramma(to)logia. See SYNTACTICAL APHASIA.

agranulocytosis   A cessation in the production of white blood cells which fight infections; a rare side effect of certain psychotropic medicines, especially clozapine, carbamazepine, and as an idiosyncratic reaction to other drugs.

agraphia   (J. W. Ogle, J. A. Pitres) 1. Total inability to write, or the ability to write single letters but not syllables, words, or phrases. 2. Impairment of the ability to write. Also known as anorthography, logagraphia.

agreement coefficient   (J. Dunlap) A positive correlation of any single item of a scale with the rest of the scale.

agricultural stage   Eras of human culture following the nomadic stage in which the growing of crops and the cultivation of animals constituted the dominant way of life for the people of the community.

agriothymia   Obsolete term for homicidal insanity.

agriothymia hydrophobica   A compelling urge to bite.

agromania   Morbid desire to live alone, especially in rural seclusion. See HERMITISM.

agrypnia   Obsolete term for insomnia.

agrypnotic   1. Inducing wakefulness in any manner. 2. Any substance acting in this manner, such as caffeine.

agyiophobia   1. A form of agoraphobia characterized by a fear of being in the street. 2. Morbid fear of open spaces or places. See AGORAPHOBIA, TOPOPHOBIA.

aha experience/reaction   (K. Bühler, W. Köhler) An emotional response that typically occurs at a moment of sudden insight generally following a long and difficult process of problem-solving. In psychotherapy, the sudden insight into unconscious motives. Also known as ahha(h) experience. See ABREACTION, KAIROS.

aha experience/reaction   A demonstration of insight learning. The chimpanzee knows that the banana is too far away to be reached either by its arms or by a short stick in the cage. The chimpanzee realizes that the short stick can be used to reach a longer stick that may be used to reach the banana. The moment of realization is known as the "Aha" reaction.

AHD   attention-deficit hyperactivity disorder

ahedonia   Inability to enjoy anything. See ANHEDONIA.

ahistorical   Denoting a perspective in terms of contemporary causative factors; emphasis on the here-and-now.

ahistoric therapy   A directive form of psychotherapy that does not focus on the past experiences or history of clients but rather focuses on here-and-now situations and behaviors.

AHP   Allied Health Professional

ahypnia   Pathological insomnia.

AI   1. artificial intelligence. 2. artificial insemination.

aichmophobia   1. Morbid fear of pointed objects such as nails, forks, or knives. 2. Fear of knives. 3. Fear of being touched by slender objects.

aide   A nonprofessional staff member with lesser training, such as a nurse's aide who assists under direction and supervision in the care and rehabilitation and in some cases treatment of patients with physical disabilities, mental retardation, or mental disorders. See PSYCHIATRIC AIDE.

aided recall   1. In trying to recall something, as when being questioned by lawyers in a court of law, a variety of "aids" are used as reminders, for example, when a lawyer aiming to mislead asks pointed questions such as "Did she appear to be intoxicated?" Sometimes this results in false information due to the person doing the remembering being induced to try to give the desired answer rather than the correct answer. 2. In advertising research, the participant who had the opportunity to view the ad (for example, reports watching the television program or reading the magazine issue) is first given the company name and asked to describe the ad. If unable to do so, more and more details are given (exact product, unique advantage of product featured, prominent color) until the ad is recalled. The fewer the cues required, the higher the presumed quality of the ad. See CUED RECALL, FALSIFICATION, MEMORY FALSIFICATION.

aided recognition   After exposure to advertisements, participants in a marketing research study indicate what they recall from a list of possibilities about the ad in question.

aidolomania   A pathological exaggeration of sex behavior. A preoccupation with sexual activities, thoughts, and fantasies; compulsive, insatiable sexual activity with the opposite sex. Also known as erotomania. See DON JUANISM, NYMPHOMANIA, SATYRIASIS.

AIDS   Acquired Immune Deficiency Syndrome

aikido   The Oriental martial art for subduing an opponent through harmony rather than opposition.

ailurophobia   Morbid fear of or aversion to cats. Also known as aelurophobia, galeophobia, gatophobia, geleophobia.

aim   A relatively remote goal to be attained by voluntary activity.

aim inhibition   (S. Freud) Suspending or altering the original activity that gratified an instinctual drive, in favor of another form of gratification (for example, "biting sarcasm" may be an expression of an aim-inhibited wish to bite).

aiming test   A method of evaluating visuomotor coordination, precision, and speed, such as a task requiring the participant to place pencil dots in small circles as rapidly as possible. More elaborate methods using mechanical devices have also been used. Also known as target test.

aim transference   The change of a person's objectives from one life goal to another that appears to be easier to achieve or to be more satisfactory than the first goal.

air blade   In speech, a narrow stream of air passing through the slit formed by placing the inner surface of the lower lip lightly against the tips of the upper teeth, in producing a fricative such as /f/.

Air-Crib   A nursery chamber or "box" developed by B. F. Skinner in which a naked infant can be housed in a temperature-, humidity-, sound-, light-, and germ-controlled environment. As the baby completes the first year the chamber functions increasingly only as a crib. Following a *Ladies Home Journal* article in 1945 several hundred babies were raised in an Air-Crib, but it never became widely used. Sometimes called a Skinner box.

air encephalogram   An X-ray photograph of the skull following the injection of air into areas of the brain normally occupied by cerebrospinal fluid (CSF).

air-conduction testing   An audiological procedure for the purpose of measuring a person's threshold for pure tones in each ear at individual frequencies.

air hunger   (F. Schreiber) Refers to lack of oxygen. About 70% of brain damage leading to mental retardation and paralysis are attributed to lack of oxygen during the birthing process.

air-pollution adaptation   The adjustment of a local population to levels of air pollution through loss of sensitivity to its health and esthetic effects. In industrial communities, air pollution may be regarded as a sign of prosperity, and visitors from less developed countries may find the smog of large cities attractive.

air-pressure effects   Any abnormal mental or physical condition caused by a significant variation from normal atmospheric pressure of 14.7 pounds per square inch, or one atmosphere.

Ajzen-Fishbein model   A theory that choice behavior is most accurately predicted by behavioral intentions, which in turn are a function of attitudinal and normative beliefs. Also known as theory of reasoned action.

Ajzen's theory   A variation of the Ajzen-Fishbein model (theory of reasoned action) which adds "perceived control" as a predictor of behavior and behavioral intentions.

aka   Slang for a false or alternative name, from "also known as."

akathisia   (not sitting—Greek) 1. Inability to sit still, accompanied by extreme restlessness and jitteriness. Also known as acathathisia, acathisia, akatizia. 2. A restless feeling in the legs which may manifest as pacing; one of the extrapyramidal symptoms that are side effects of the use of neuroleptic medicine for schizophrenia and other severe mental disturbances. See RESTLESS-LEG SYNDROME. 3. Inability to sit due to brain pathology affecting the striopallidal area of the brain.

akinesia   Loss of ability to make voluntary movements. Also known as akinesis.

akinesia algera   (P. J. Moebius) A condition in which pain is experienced with any body movement.

akinesthesia   Loss or impairment of the kinesthetic sense.

akinetic   Suffering from akinesia. Also known as akinesic.

akinetic-abulic syndrome   A set of symptoms often resulting from treatment with psychoactive drugs, including slowing of movement (bradykinesia), tremors, hypertonia, and loss of interest.

akinetic apraxia   Loss of the ability to perform spontaneous movements.

akinetic epilepsy   A *petit mal* seizure characterized by a sudden muscular collapse accompanied by head dropping.

akinetic mania   A form of mania accompanied by a lack of movement, may be a symptom of schizophrenia.

akinetic mutism   1. Absence or gross reduction in voluntary movements and speech. 2. Apparent alertness on the part of patients but with no speech or voluntary motor responses.

akinetic psychosis   A form of catatonia in which the patient exhibits stupor, waxy flexibility, and little if any perceptible movement.

akinetic seizure   See AKINETIC EPILEPSY.

akinetic stupor   A disorder characterized by rigidity, postural catatonia, mutism, absence of emotional signs, and lack of movement. Also known as Cairn's stupor.

akoasm   acousma

akoria   acoria

akousticophobia   acousticophobia

AL   1. absolute limen. 2. adaptation level.

alalia   Inability to speak due to the absence or impairment of muscles and sense organs involved in speech. See APHONIA.

Al-Anon   An organization composed of the adult children of alcoholics (ACOAs) and families of alcoholics who belong to Alcoholics Anonymous. It was formed to deal with problems generated by living with an alcoholic. See AL-A-TEEN.

alarm call   A sound made by various social animals that alerts others to danger. A biological puzzle, since it suggests a form of altruism in which the individual appears to endanger its own survival. See ALTRUISM.

alarm reaction/stage   (H. Selye) The first stage of the general adaptation syndrome in which the organism is alerted to cope with stressors. See GENERAL ADAPTATIONAL SYNDROME.

alasia   A gastrointestinal disorder attacks are precipitated or aggravated by anxiety or emotional distress.

Al-A-Teen   An organization composed of the children of alcoholics, aimed at helping them understand their parents' problem, enlisting their cooperation in the parents' efforts to find a solution, and enabling them to face the social and emotional difficulties they experience as a result of their parents' problems. Also known as Alateen. See AL-ANON, ALCOHOLICS ANONYMOUS.

albedo (A)   (J. H. Lambert) The whiteness of a surface, measured by the percentage of light reflected by its surface.

albinism   A condition characterized by the absence of pigment in the skin, hair, feathers, or eyes.

alchemy   A medieval philosophy that combined some knowledge of chemistry with various unscientific procedures, including the belief that gold could be produced from common elements and that a proper mixture of elements would yield an elixir that would cure any disease and prolong life indefinitely.

alcheringa   In aboriginal Australian mythology, an era in which lived supernatural ancestors usually viewed as half-animal, half-human.

alcohol   A class of chemical compounds characterized by a hydroxyl group. The group includes ethyl alcohol in alcoholic beverages. See ETHANOL.

alcohol abuse   A form of substance abuse in which alcoholic beverages are consumed more frequently or in larger amounts than is considered normal, typical, or healthy. See ALCOHOL INTOXICATION, ALCOHOLIC BLACKOUT, ALCOHOLIC BRAIN SYNDROME, ALCOHOLIC HALLUCINATION, ALCOHOLISM.

alcohol addiction   See ALCOHOLISM.

alcohol-amnestic disorder   A syndrome involving both long- and short-term memory, resulting from vitamin deficiency associated with prolonged heavy use of alcohol. The memory impairment often follows an acute episode of Wernicke's disease, and usually persists indefinitely. Also known as Korsakoff's disorder. See AMNESTIC DISORDER.

alcohol derivatives   Drugs obtained from the transformation of alcohol molecules, used because of their sedative and hypnotic effects.

alcohol hallucinosis   A disorder characterized by hallucinations that follows cessation of heavy drinking. Usually does not last more than a few days. Hallucinations are typically auditory, sometimes visual. See ALCOHOLIC HALLUCINOSIS, DELIRIUM TREMENS.

alcoholic   General term for a person whose alcohol consumption extensively interferes with functioning.

alcoholic blackout   1. Amnesia experienced by an alcoholic. 2. A complete loss of memory, variable in time of length, following the consumption of alcoholic beverages.

alcoholic brain syndrome   One of several brain syndromes produced by prolonged heavy use of alcohol, such as alcohol-amnestic disorder and dementia associated with alcoholism. See ALCOHOLIC PSYCHOSES.

alcoholic dementia   alcoholic psychoses

alcoholic epilepsy   Epileptoid attacks exhibited by some alcoholics during withdrawal. Also known as rum fits.

alcoholic hallucinosis   A medical diagnosis referring to an alcohol withdrawal syndrome characterized by auditory hallucinations in the absence of any other psychotic symptoms. See ALCOHOL HALLUCINOSIS.

alcoholic jealousy   A form of jealousy experienced by chronic alcoholics. Not considered an independent syndrome but is diagnosed as "alcohol dependence with an additional diagnosis of paranoid disorder." See ALCOHOL-PARANOID STATE, ALCOHOLIC PARANOIA.

alcoholic neuropathies   A collection of neurologic disorders including numbness, tingling, and tenderness of the extremities, foot drop, and loss of reflexes. In severe cases, vision and hearing may be affected.

alcoholic paranoia   Pathological jealousy in which an alcoholic person is irrationally convinced of the partner's unfaithfulness. Also known as paranoid type alcoholic psychosis. See ALCOHOL-PARANOID STATE, ALCOHOLIC JEALOUSY.

alcoholic pseudoparesis   A periodic paralysis associated with alcoholism characterized by muscular weakness, particularly in the lower limbs, accompanied by numbness and loss of reflexes.

alcoholic psychoses   Mental disorders resulting from excessive use of alcohol. The common denominator of these disorders is an acute or chronic inflammation of the brain which produces psychotic symptoms such as hallucinations, delusions, delirium, clouding of consciousness, memory impairment, confabulation, severely impaired judgment, and, in advanced cases, general mental deterioration. Also known as alcoholic dementia. See ALCOHOL HALLUCINOSIS, ALCOHOLIC DEMENTIA, ALCOHOLISM, ALCOHOL-AMNESTIC DISORDER, ALCOHOL-WITHDRAWAL DELIRIUM.

Alcoholics Anonymous (AA or A.A.)   A voluntary organization of alcoholics and ex-alcohol-ics seeking to control their compulsive urge to drink, through understanding, fellowship, and emotional/social support. The 12-step program includes: (a) individual's admission of an inability to control drinking; (b) recognition of a supreme spiritual power; (c) a searching examination of past errors with the help of a member who serves as "sponsor"; (d) making amends for these errors; (e) development of a new code and style of life; (f) sharing of experiences and problems at meetings; (g) helping other alcoholics in need of support; and (h) other-action steps toward sobriety.

alcoholic's wife/husband   A hypothetical type of person who after marriage unconsciously: (a) arranges for her or his mate to become an alcoholic, (b) arranges for herself or himself to be abused, and (c) accepts her or his condition without complaint. A controversial concept. See MASOCHISM.

alcoholic twilight-state   A condition associated with pathological drunkenness in which twilight states are released, often with illusions, hallucinations, and excessive emotions of rage and anxiety.

alcohol idiosyncratic intoxication   A rare disorder characterized by a marked behavioral change associated with drinking an amount of alcohol that is insufficient to intoxicate most people. The behavior is not typical of the person when not drinking, for example, a shy, quiet person may become belligerent and assaultive, followed by amnesia for the episode.

alcohol intoxication   A temporary condition due to overuse of alcohol, marked by: (a) maladaptive behavior, impaired judgment, defective social and occupational functioning; (b) flushed face, slurred speech, unsteady gait, incoordination, and nystagmus; (c) loquacity, impaired attention, irritability, euphoria, and emotional lability as well as blackouts. See ALCOHOLISM.

alcoholism   Chronic dependence on alcoholic beverages, characterized by compulsive drinking and consumption of alcohol to such a degree that it produces mental disturbance and interferes with social and occupational functioning. Also known as alcohol addiction. See ALPHA ALCOHOLISM and entries beginning with ALCOHOL and ALCOHOLIC.

alcoholophilia   Love of alcohol. See ALCOHOLISM and entries beginning with ALCOHOL.

alcoholophobia   Fear of alcohol, or of becoming an alcoholic.

alcohol-paranoid state   An atypical paranoid disorder in alcoholics, characterized by excessive jealousy, suspiciousness, and delusions of the spouse's infidelity. See ALCOHOLIC JEALOUSY, ALCOHOLIC PARANOIA.

alcohol-withdrawal delirium   A condition developing within a week after cessation or reduction of heavy drinking, and characterized by perceptual disturbances; autonomic hyperactivity such as rapid heartbeat; delusions and hallucinations; and coarse tremors. Also known as delirium tremens (DTs). See ALCOHOLIC PSYCHOSES, ALCOHOLISM.

aleatory theory   A point of view that social changes depend on chance events.

alector   A person afflicted with insomnia.

alert inactivity   A state in infants marked by facial relaxation, calm and even breathing, open, luminous eyes, and considerable visual exploration.

alertness   Being awake, aware, attentive, and ready to act or react. See AROUSAL.

alethia   Inability to forget.

Alexander method/technique   (F. Alexander) A procedure for retraining the body to obtain tension-free movements and well-coordinated musculature, and thereby to generate positive self-awareness. The following are important in understanding Franz Alexander's theory: CORRECTIVE EMOTIONAL EXPERIENCE, DYNAMIC REASONING, PRINCIPLE OF INERTIA, SPECIFIC DYNAMIC PATTERN, ULCER PERSONALITY. Also see DISJUNCTIVE PSYCHOTHERAPIES.

alexia   (K. Wernicke, L. Lichtheim) Inability to comprehend the meaning of words, written or printed. Sometimes known as optical aphasia, sensory aphasia, text blindness, visual aphasia, word blindness. Distinguished from anarthria, inability to read aloud although the meaning of words is understood. See AGNOSIC ALEXIA, DYSLEXIA, MOTOR APHASIA.

alexithymia   1. Difficulty in recognizing, articulating, or conveying one's own emotions. 2. (P. Sifneos) Limited fantasy and emotional life.

alganesthesia   Inability to perceive pain. Also known as alganesthesis.

algebraic summation   The summation of impulses, whether positive or negative and regardless of sources, received simultaneously by an individual, leading to a response affected by the number and strength of the incoming impulses.

algedonic esthetics   A concept that the value of work or art is a function of the degree of pleasure that it provides.

algedonics   The study of the combination of pleasure and pain.

algesimeter   **algesi(o)meter**

algesia   1. Ability to experience pain. Also known as algesis. Compare ANALGESIA. 2. See ALGESTHESIA.

algesi(o)meter   An instrument used to measure the sensitivity of an individual to a painful stimulus. The device consists of a pin with a means of determining how much force must be exerted for a person to experience pain. Used for skin research purposes. Also known as algometer, odynometer. See DOLORIMETER, HEAT DOLORIMETER.

algesthesia   1. Sensitivity to pain. 2. Pain sensibility; the pain senses. Also known as algesthesis. (Algesthesia is the experience of pain, algesthesis is the sense of pain.) 3. Hypersensitivity to pain. Also known as algesia, algesthesis.

algolagnia   (A. Schrenck-Notzing) A paraphilia (sexual perversion) in which sexual excitement or satisfaction is increased by receiving pain (passive algolagnia) or inflicting pain (active algolagnia). Sometimes known as algophilia. See MASOCHISM, SADISM.

algometer   algesi(o)meter

algophilia   1. Love of pain. See MASOCHISM. 2. Pleasure experienced by fantasizing about pain felt by others or self. 3. See ALGOLAGNIA.

algophobia   Morbid fear of pain or abnormal sensitivity to pain. Also known as odynophobia.

algopsychalia   1. Pain recognized by the patient as of mental rather than physical origin. 2. See PSYCHALG(AL)IA (meaning 1).

algorithm   A diagrammatic representation of the sequence of steps, choices, and actions in a process or activity. Also known as flow chart.

ALI   Abbreviation for American Law Institute test. See AMERICAN LAW INSTITUTE GUIDELINES.

alias   In fractionally replicated research designs, aliases are effects that cannot be distinguished from one another.

Alice in Wonderland effect   A visual defect, seeing things as smaller than they really are. See METAMORPHOPSIA.

alien   Strange; foreign. See EGO-ALIEN, TERRESTRIAL KIDNAPPING.

alienation   1. A breakdown of sociological, interpersonal, or experimental relationships. 2. Estrangement from self and others. See SELF-ALIENATION. 3. (J. Falret) In legal terms: Insanity; mental disorder. See ALIENIST, MENTAL ILLNESS.

alienation coefficient (k)   See COEFFICIENT OF ALIENATION.

Alienation Test   (S. Maddi) A 60-item questionnaire designed to measure powerlessness, adventurousness, nihilism, and vegetativeness in the person's relationship to work, persons, social institutions, family, and self.

alien-hand syndrome   (T. Feinberg) A brain disorder characterized by lack of control of one hand. A consequence of surgery to the corpus callosum.

alienist   Old name for a physician (usually but not always a psychiatrist) who serves as an expert witness on mental competence and mental health or illness. Derived from Jean Pierre Falret's (1794–1870) "mental alienation" as a substitute for "imbecility," "dementia," etc.

alimentary orgasm   (S. Rado) In psychoanalytic theory, intense pleasure and satisfaction experienced during satiation of hunger. It is related to breast-feeding and is a prototype of adult orgasm.

alinormal syndrome   (S. Coren) A complex of signs or symptoms, that may include left-handedness, allergies, weakened immune system, sleep disturbance, and slowed physical maturation, resulting from minor birth stress or trauma. See SOFT SIGNS.

alky   Slang for an alcoholic.

allach(a)esthesia   A condition in which tactile (touch) sensations are experienced in a place other than the point of stimulation. See ALLESTHESIA.

allegory   A story with two intentions: (a) to entertain, especially children; and (b) to represent some theoretical, philosophical, political, and religious concepts. Examples include Jonathan Swift's *Gulliver's Travels* and George Orwell's *Animal Farm*.

allele   Alternative forms of a gene. Term is actually allelomorph, but by custom, the shorter form is generally used. See ALLELOMORPH.

allelomimetic behavior   The simultaneous turning in the same direction of many individual animals of the same species (for example, flocks of flying birds and schools of fish), a phenomenon whose mechanism is not yet understood.

allelomorph   Two genes (alleles), one from each parent, found at the same specific locations on chromosomes. If identical, they are homozygous and the offspring will have the same characteristics for that gene as both parents. If different, they are heterozygous and the offspring will have the characteristics of the parent from which the dominant allele came. See ALLELE, HEREDITY.

allergen   A substance capable of producing a sensitivity reaction in an individual. It does not produce an allergic reaction directly, but initiates the immune-response system that produces the antibodies to resist the invading allergen.

allergy   A hypersensitivity of tissues to a physical or chemical agent.

allesthesia   A form of allach(a)esthesia characterized by transference of pain or touch sensations from one limb (such as the right leg) to the opposite limb (the left leg). Also known as alloch(e)iria, alloesthesia, Bamberger's sign. See HYSTEROGENIC ZONES, REFERRED PAIN.

alley maze   An intricate network of pathways, one of which is the shortest route to the goal, and many of which are blind alleys, thus permitting the measurement of animal learning. See Y-MAZE for an illustration.

alley problem   A visual illusion or situation in which a person perceives phenomena as different from existing in reality, but knows that this perception is false (for example, in looking down a street, the street appears to narrow as distance from the observer increases, but the observer knows from direct experience that the street is actually the same width for its whole length). See CONSTANCY.

alliaceous   (H. Zwaardemaker) A quality of olfactory sensations such as those produced by chlorine and garlicky substances, listed in Zwaardemaker's system of odors. See ZWAARDEMAKER'S ODOR CLASSIFICATION.

allied health professional (AHP)   A specialist who contributes to the prevention, treatment, and rehabilitation processes along with psychiatrists and clinical psychologists. For respective fields see ART THERAPY, DANCE THERAPY, EDUCATIONAL THERAPY, INDUSTRIAL THERAPY, MUSIC THERAPY, OCCUPATIONAL THERAPY, PHYSICAL THERAPY, PSYCHIATRIC NURSING, PSYCHIATRIC SOCIAL WORK, REHABILITATION NURSING, REHABILITATION COUNSELING, SPEECH PATHOLOGY.

allied reflexes　　Two or more simultaneous or closely successive reflexes that appear as a single reaction.

allocation decision　　A judgment made about the order in which a number of necessary actions will be performed as well as the amount of time that will be spent on each of them. See DECISION THEORY.

allocative values　　In a zero-sum game situation, for one person to acquire a benefit, another person must lose the equivalent.

allocentered psychotherapy　　(D. Motet) A system of therapy that focuses on others rather than on the self of the patient. To achieve desired results, the therapist must accept this point of view as essential to the patient's overall welfare. See GEMEINSCHAFTSGEFÜHL.

allocentric　　The opposite of egocentric, denoting primary interest in others rather than the self. See ALLO-CENTERED PSYCHOTHERAPY, COLLECTIVISM, GEMEINSCHAFTSGEFÜHL.

allocentrism　　(H. Triandis) A personality variable reflecting attitudes, beliefs, and behaviors usually found in collectivist cultures, such as in East Asia. The self is seen as interdependent with some ingroup, such as a tribe, family, or nation; ingroup goals are given priority over personal goals; norms are important determinants of social behavior; and social behavior reflects paying much attention to the needs of ingroup members. Such individuals are willing to maintain a relationship, out of duty or obligation, even when the costs exceed the benefits.

alloch(e)iria　　**allesthesia**

allochthonous　　Anything coming to the body from the outside. See AUTOCHTHONOUS.

allocortex　　(O. Vogt) The more primitive area of the cerebral cortex, comprising the archipallium (hippocampus) and paleopallium (olfactory cortex). The hippocampus is associated with memory formation; the olfactory cortex is primarily associated with smell. See CORTEX CEREBRI.

alloerot(ic)ism　　The outward extension of erotic feelings toward another person, as opposed to auto-erotism. Also known as heteroerot(ic)ism. See AUTO-EROT(IC)ISM.

allogrooming　　Grooming of one animal by another. See ALLOPREENING.

allolalia　　Any speech defect.

allomone　　A chemical sensed between predators and prey. A predator receiving an olfactory signal searches for the unseen prey, whereas the prey sensing the presence of a predator seeks safety. See PHEROMONE.

allomorphs　　In linguistics, alternate forms of the same morpheme, often used to indicate prefixes and suffixes such as mega-, maxim-, hyper-.

alloparenting　　Caring for the offspring of other mothers. See MATERNAL BEHAVIOR.

allopathy　　A theory and philosophy of treating disease based on clinical and research evidence using agents that produce effects different from those caused by the disease, as opposed to homeopathy. Mainstream medicine is characterized as allopathic. Compare HOMEOPATHY.

allopatric species　　Animal species that do not occur together or occupy the same habitat. Compare SYMPATRIC SPECIES.

allophasis　　Disorganized speech. Also known as allophasia.

allophone　　In linguistics, a variant of the same phoneme. See PHONEME.

alloplastic　　(S. Ferenczi) Pertaining to behavior directed toward the outside of a person, that is, toward others, society, the environment.

alloplasty　　1. In psychoanalytic theory, ability to direct the libido away from the self, and to direct the desire for immediate gratification to other people or activities. 2. (F. Sandor) A method of adapting to stress by trying to change the environment.

allopreening　　1. Behavior of an animal toward another animal, usually of the same species, as in licking it or otherwise rubbing it systematically. See ALLOGROOMING. 2. Preening an animal of the same species prior to copulation. See AROUND THE WORLD, FOREPLAY. 3. In avians, nibbling of another bird's feathers.

allopsyche　　The psyche or mind of another person.

allopsychic　　Refers to the assignment or projection of a person's own thoughts or ideas to people or events in the outside world. See TRANSFERENCE.

allopsychic delusion　　(K. Wernicke) Falsely assigning to other people certain intentions or influences, based on projection of a person's own malice or maladjustment. See ALLOPSYCHOSIS, AUTOPSYCHIC DELUSION, PARANOIA, SOMATOPSYCHIC DELUSION.

allopsychosis　　A delusional or hallucinatory syndrome in which the patient's own feelings or impulses are projected into others, for example, if patients feel hostile, they may become convinced that other people are conspiring to harm them.

all-or-none law/principle　　(H. Bowditch) A theory that a single nerve cell or muscle cell will (a) either respond or not respond at all and (b) if it does respond it responds maximally every time. The intensity of the stimulus does not affect the magnitude of the response. Also known as all-or-nothing law.

all-or-none learning　　Related to Gestalt thinking about mastering complex concepts as when various parts come together in an instant; contrasted with gradual trial-and-error learning emphasized by behaviorists.

all-or-none learning hypothesis　　A postulate that something is learned or is not learned.

allosteric enzyme　　(M. Cohn, J. Monod, M. R. Pollock, S. Spiegelman, R. Y. Stanier) A regulatory enzyme with two specific locations: one for the catalytic site (the enzyme's substrate) and the other for the effector site that may either activate or inhibit actions.

allotriogeus(t)ia　　1. A perverted sense of taste. 2. An abnormal appetite, particularly for nonnutritious or unusual substances. See PICA.

allotriophagy　　1. A desire to eat food offensive to most others. 2. A habit of eating nonnutritious or unusual substances. See PICA.

Allport A-S Reaction Study　　(G. W. Allport & F. H. Allport) A personality test designed to measure the relative strength of ascendance and submission, by presenting standardized life situations and asking participants to choose their own way of meeting such situations.

Allport's personality-trait theory (G. W. Allport) A point of view that the individual's personality traits are the key to the uniqueness and consistency of his or her behavior. The following items are important for understanding this theory: ALLPORT A-S REACTION STUDY, ALLPORT-VERNON-LINDZEY STUDY OF VALUES, A-S SCALE, BODILY SELF, CARDINAL DISPOSITION/TRAIT, CENTRAL DISPOSITION, CENTRAL ORGANIZING TRAIT, CENTRAL TRAIT, CENTRIFUGAL GROUP FACTOR, CHARACTER TRAIT, CHILDHOOD MOTIVATION, COMMON TRAITS, DIRECTEDNESS, EXPRESSIVE BEHAVIOR, FUNCTIONAL AUTONOMY, GROUP-RELATIONS THEORY, HISTORICAL METHOD, NOMOTHETIC RESEARCH, PERSEVERATIVE FUNCTIONAL AUTONOMY, PERSONAL DISPOSITION, PROPRIATE FUNCTIONAL AUTONOMY, PROPRIATE STRIVING, PROPRIUM, SECONDARY DISPOSITION, SECONDARY TRAIT, SELF-EXTENSION, SELF-IDENTITY, SELF-OBJECTIFICATION, TRAITS.

Allport-Vernon-Lindzey Study of Values See THE ALLPORT-VERNON STUDY OF VALUES.

allurement paraphilia A category of paraphilias that involves sexual stimulation by concentrating on the courtship phase that replaces normal sexual intercourse. John Money includes exhibitionism, frottage, voyeurism, telephone scatophilia (obscene phone calls), autoagonistophilia, pictophilia, and scoptophilia in the concept.

allusive thinking Loose cerebration based on inference and suggestion rather than on straightforward logic.

alogia 1. Inability to speak, due to mental deficiency, confusion, or disturbances of the central nervous system. 2. See APHASIA.

alpha The first letter of the Greek alphabet. See APPENDIX C.

alpha alcoholism (E. M. Jellinek) Rare phrase for a type of alcoholism characterized by undisciplined drinking and dependence on the effects of alcohol for the relief of physical or psychological pain, but without losing control or being unable to abstain. Also known as dyssocial drinking, escape drinking, problem drinking, reactive alcoholism, symptomatic alcoholism, thymogenic drinking. See ALCOHOL ABUSE, ALCOHOL DEPENDENCE, ALCOHOLIC, ALCOHOLISM, BETA ALCOHOLISM, BINGE DRINKING, CHRONIC ALCOHOLISM, DELTA ALCOHOLISM, EPSILON ALCOHOLISM, GAMMA ALCOHOLISM.

alpha apparent motion **alpha motion**

Alpha, Beta, Gamma hypotheses (K. Dunlap) Three divergent theories about learning, the Alpha hypothesis states that repetition frequency enhances learning; the Beta hypothesis states that repetition frequency has no effect; the Gamma hypothesis states that repetition frequency hinders learning.

alpha block (E. D. Adrian & B. H. C. Matthews) The suppression of alpha waves by a factor such as a visual stimulus that produces beta waves on EEG (electroencephalographic) tracings. See ACTIVATION PATTERN.

alpha block conditioning Conditioning the alpha block response to a stimulus not ordinarily producing the alpha blocking, resulting in the conditioned stimulus itself producing the alpha blocking response.

alpha block response A process of responding to a desynchronization of the regular 8-13-per-second alpha (wave) rhythm by arousal, concentration, flashing lights, or other alerting stimuli.

alpha blockers Substances that inhibit certain responses to adrenergic nerve activity. The phrase applies particularly to drugs that block the actions of epinephrine and norepinephrine. Also known as adrenergic blocking agents.

alpha blocking Disruption of the alpha rhythm by visual stimulation or by active thought with the eyes closed.

alpha cells Endocrine cells within the pancreas that secrete glucagon. See ISLANDS OF LANGERHANS.

alpha endorphin An endorphin that acts as a mild analgesic and tranquilizer. See BETA ENDORPHIN, ENDORPHIN, ENKEPHALIN, GAMMA ENDORPHIN.

alpha error Rejecting a true null hypothesis. See ALPHA LEVEL, TYPE I ERROR, TYPE II ERROR.

Alpha examination/test **Army Alpha (Intelligence) Test**

alpha feedback The feedback of alpha rhythm to a patient. Standard electrode placement is over the occipital lobes.

alpha female The dominant female in an animal group.

alpha fiber Main motor nerve that supplies contractile muscles.

Alpha hypothesis (K. Dunlap) A postulate that repetition frequency enhances learning. See BETA HYPOTHESIS, GAMMA HYPOTHESIS.

alpha level (α) In hypothesis testing, the probability of rejecting the null hypothesis when the null hypothesis is true. Also known as alpha error/risk. See BETA ERROR.

alpha male The dominant male in an animal group.

alphametric In computers, refers to both alphabetical letters and numbers.

alpha motion/movement A visual illusion in which an object appears to change in size as parts are presented successively. Also known as alpha apparent, alpha movement, apparent motion.

alpha motor neuron 1. A neuron that controls voluntary muscles. 2. A large motor neuron that causes skeletal muscle contractions.

alpha press (H. A. Murray) A force in the objective environment that motivates a person. See BETA PRESS.

alpha receptor An adrenergic nerve receptor stimulated by norepinephrine and blocked by Dibenamine. Alpha receptors represent a part of the autonomic nervous system distinguished from the beta-receptor category. Compare BETA RECEPTOR.

alpha response 1. In conditioning, a response to a stimulus, but not one that indicates learning, such as a startle response on perceiving the stimulus. 2. In classical eyelid conditioning, a response that is most probably due to sensitization rather than to learning. Compare BETA RESPONSE.

alpha rhythm/waves (H. Berger) The most frequently observed impulses or waves seen on an electroencephalogram when a person is awake and relaxed. The waves are large and slow and occur 8 to 12 Hertz (cycles per second) but disappear when a person falls asleep or becomes mentally active. This level of alpha rhythm is sought for in biofeedback training to reduce arousal. See ALPHA STATE, BIOFEEDBACK TRAINING.

alpha risk (α) The probability of making an alpha error (rejecting a true null hypothesis). Preferred name is alpha level. See TYPE I ERROR, TYPE II ERROR.

alpha state Relaxed wakefulness achieved by persons producing alpha brain waves.

Alpha test Army Alpha (Intelligence) Test

alpha waves alpha rhythm

alpha-wave training Biofeedback training in which the participant learns to achieve a state of peaceful wakefulness and relaxation by controlling alpha waves. The technique usually uses a tone that changes pitch or disappears when the alpha state is reached. See ALPHA WAVES.

alpinism General term applied to mental disorders associated with living at high altitudes or other low atmospheric-pressure environments.

alprazolam Generic name for a benzodiazepine used in the treatment of anxiety. Trade name is Xanax. See BENZODIAZEPINE.

ALT See ALTERNATE SCHEDULE OF REINFORCEMENT.

altercasting A problem encountered by people (such as parents, teachers, employers, military leaders) when attempting to lead others. It involves determining how to get subordinates to follow orders or behave as desired.

altered states of consciousness (ASC) Mental states outside of usual experience. Such states can be autochthonous (arising out of inner mental or physical factors) or the result of social or environmental conditions, such as from hallucinogens or other drugs or physical traumas. See CATATONIC STUPOR, COMA, DISSOCIATIVE STATES, DREAMING, FUGUE, HYPNAGOGIC STATES, NIGHTMARES, OUT OF BODY EXPERIENCE, TRANSCENDENTAL MEDITATION.

alter ego 1. Common phrase for an intimate, supportive friend with whom a person can share all types of problems and experiences, as if the friend were "another self." 2. In psychodrama, a therapist's assistant who assumes the inner role of the protagonist. 3. Another side of oneself. See ALTER EGOISM.

alter egoism Altruistic concern or a feeling of empathy for another person in the same situation as oneself. See ALTRUISM, PSYCHODRAMA.

alternate binaural loudness-balance test An examination for abnormal sensitivity to loud sounds. Two tones of the same frequency are played alternately into the two ears, but the intensity of the sound at one ear is set at a level 20 decibels higher than the other. If the participant perceives the two sounds as having the same loudness, it indicates that one ear is more sensitive than the other to loudness.

alternate form A set of test items closely similar to those in another scale, often used for repeat administrations. In some cases each item is considered to be a different version of another item on the same test. See TEST-RETEST RELIABILITY.

alternate-forms reliability An index of consistency determined by correlating the scores of individuals on one form of a test with their scores on another form. See PARALLEL FORMS.

alternate-response test A test form requiring the participant to choose the correct response of two or more alternatives. Usually, "Yes" or "No."

alternate-uses test A quiz or task that requires the person to cite possible uses for a specified object other than its common use, such as that a newspaper may also be used for starting a fire or packing objects in a box. See CREATIVITY.

alternating insanity (J. Falret) Obsolete phrase for manic-depressive psychosis. See BIPOLAR DISORDER.

alternating personality A personality pattern characterized by a person's overt and covert behavior changing considerably, usually rapidly and unpredictably. Often due to alcohol, drugs, or external events. Sometimes known as cyclothymic personality, Dr. Jekyll–Mr. Hyde personality. See DISSOCIATIVE-IDENTITY DISORDER, MULTIPLE PERSONALITY.

alternating perspective A shift in the appearance of things based on internal factors of the observer. See the illustrations associated with these entries: FIGURE-GROUND PERCEPTION, IMPOSSIBLE FIGURE, NECKER CUBE, PENROSE TRIANGLE, RUBIN'S FIGURE, SCHRÖDER'S STAIRCASE ILLUSION, SET.

alternating psychosis Older name for bipolar disorder.

alternating role A periodic shifting from one pattern of behavior to another, such as from an authoritarian to a democratic role and then back to an authoritarian role.

alternating vision The alternate use of only the right or left eye for seeing, one eye usually being dominant.

alternation 1. In animal research, training animals to follow certain patterns of movements to the right (R) or the left (L) as in LRLRLR or RLLRLLRLL in a T-maze or Y-maze. 2. In conflict situations, vacillating between approaching and avoiding a particular stimulus. 3. The replacement of an emotional problem with a physical condition. 4. Training animals in the straight alley to patterns of reward (R) and nonreward (N) as in RNRNRN (single alternation) or RRNNRRNN (double alternation). After many trials rats run faster on R trials than on N trials, thereby demonstrating (in Hull-Spence learning theory) an expectation.

alternation learning Mastering the task of switching from one response to another and back again for many reversals. Serial reversal learning typically shows marked improvement over the series. This may be because the animal learns a win-stay, lose-shift strategy.

alternation method A technique to study complex or rule learning behavior. In double alternation method, the animal subject must learn a pattern of right and left turns (for example, RRLL or LLRR) in a simple maze shaped like the number 8. See DOUBLE-ALTERNATION METHOD/TASK.

alternation problems   A two-choice situation ordinarily studied in a T-maze or Y-maze in which an organism has a choice-point decision to go either right or left. Worms in t-type tubes have been tested for their abilities to learn to make consistent right or left turns. See ANIMAL INTELLIGENCE, INTELLIGENCE, INTELLIGENCE TESTING, MENTAL ABILITIES. See Y-MAZE for an illustration.

alternation response   A tendency to not repeat the same response immediately, even if rewarded.

alternation-of-response theory   A concept based on research evidence that proper division and parsing of a stream of stimuli is an important control mechanism in short-term memory tasks (for example, extending the time interval between right-left alternation-task couplets reduces the rate of errors). See HEARING THEORIES, TELEPHONE THEORY, VOLLEY THEORY.

alternative brain process theory   A point of view that in some cases of damage to a part of the brain, another part will assume the function of the damaged part. Also known as vicarious brain process.

alternative educational systems   Educational systems that differ in their philosophies, structures, and goals from the traditional system. Some alternative systems depend on movement through the academic program in terms of "steps on a ladder" with children placed according to academic ability rather than by age; others, such as the Montessori method, use a gradated system of problems which children attempt to solve alone but have help when needed; whereas other systems forbid outside-of-school assignments including homework.

alternative group session   (G. Bach) The meeting of a therapy group without the presence of the therapist.

alternative hypothesis (H₁ or Hₐ)   1. A secondary hypothesis remaining operable after the null hypothesis has been rejected. 2. A prediction that experimental effects or relationships will be found. The alternative hypothesis is assumed to be true when the null hypothesis is rejected at a predetermined level of significance. See NULL HYPOTHESIS, STATISTICAL HYPOTHESIS.

alternative psychologies   Concepts, theories, conclusions, etc., about animal and human behavior considered unsuitable for scientific publication.

alternative psychotherapies   Modes of therapy not generally considered mainstream. See ALLOCENTERED PSYCHOTHERAPY, AUTOGENIC TRAINING, BIOFEEDBACK THERAPY, COVERT CONDITIONING, DANCE THERAPY, DIRECT PSYCHOANALYSIS, EIDETIC PSYCHOTHERAPY, FEMINIST THERAPY, HOLISTIC EDUCATION, INTEGRITY GROUPS, MORITA PSYCHOTHERAPY, MULTIMODAL (BEHAVIOR) THERAPY, NONDIRECTIVE PSYCHOANALYSIS, ORGONE THERAPY, POETRY THERAPY, REBIRTHING, STRUCTURED LEARNING, TWENTY-FOUR-HOUR THERAPY, VERBAL BEHAVIOR THERAPY, Z-PROCESS ATTACHMENT THERAPY.

alternative schedule of reinforcement (ALT)   A type of reinforcement occurring after the completion of either one of two schedules, as in responses to a fixed-ratio and fixed-interval schedule being reinforced when one is satisfied, whichever comes first. Also known as alternate reinforcement.

alternative test forms   Two or more tests essentially comparable in all respects. Also known as comparable test forms.

alter personality   (R. Kluft) A distinct identity seen in dissociative identity (multiple-personality) disorder, an entity with a firm, persistent and well-founded sense of self and a characteristic consistent pattern of behavior and feelings. See ALTERS.

alters   Within the personality structure of a person diagnosed with dissociative identity disorder (DID), the original identity of the person is seen as having been fractured into different "alters," typically due to trauma at an early age. The alters typically have their own sense of history, emotions, and thoughts. The alter has a purpose within the dissociative system of the DID patient and that patient may or may not be aware (conscious) of the alter's presence. Also known as "parts," "fragments," "identities," "personalities," "personality states," "friends." See DISSOCIATIVE IDENTITY DISORDER, MULTIPLE PERSONALITY DISORDER.

altitude test   A nontimed examination to determine ability in a particular area as indicated by the level of difficulty reached.

altophobia   Morbid fear of high places. Also known as hypsophobia. See ACROPHOBIA, BATOPHOBIA.

altricial species   See ALTRIX.

altrigenderism   A socially approved, nonsexual association between individuals of the opposite sex. See PLATONIC LOVE.

altri   (nourisher—Latin) An ornithological term meaning helplessness, requiring parental care for a period of time after hatching. (Altricial species or young as opposed to precocious birds).

altruism   (A. Comte) Unselfish behavior that favorably affects the survival, comfort, and state of mind of others. Can range from simple avoidance behavior to sacrificing one's own life for another. In some instances, such behavior is instinctive as in the case of an animal warning conspecifics of danger. See ALTRUISTIC BEHAVIOR, ALTRUISTIC SUICIDE.

altruistic behavior   Acting in the interest of others; putting concern for others above concern for the self. Examples cover a wide range, including expressions of interest, support, and sympathy, performing special favors for others, engagement in volunteer activities. See ALTRUISM.

altruistic instincts   Innate behavior that promotes the welfare of others, without regard to the welfare of the individual, seen in bees sacrificing their lives to protect the hive. ("Altruistic" in reference to animal behavior does not suggest any mentation, but only behavior.) Also known as altruistic attitudes/habits.

altruistic suicide   (E. Durkheim) Self-sacrifice associated with excessive integration with a group as exemplified by the suicide of kamikaze pilots, or suicide of people who believe they are a burden to their families. See ALTRUISM, MARTYRDOM.

alveolar   A speech sound made with the tongue touching or near the gum ridge above the upper teeth (alveolar ridge) such as /d/, /t/, /n/, or /s/. Accurate placement of the tongue tip or tongue blade in this area is necessary for precise articulation.

alysosis   Extreme boredom usually associated with the simple form of schizophrenia. Also known as otiumosis.

Alzheimer's disease (AD)/psychosis   (A. Alzheimer) A progressive dementing disorder due to widespread degeneration of brain cells into tangled, thread-like structures and neuritic plaques. Sometimes known as Dementia (of the) Alzheimer type (DAT).

amacrine cell   A unipolar retinal neuron with no axon or long fiber, connects adjacent ganglion cells and the inner processes of bipolar cells.

amastia   Absence of breasts. Also known as amazia.

amative intercourse   Vaginal coitus that does not result in ejaculation, as practiced by selected members of the Oneida Community to express friendship and for contraceptive purposes. See COITUS INTERRUPTUS, WITHDRAWAL METHOD.

amaurosis   1. Blindness. 2. Loss of sight due to defect of the optic nerve, not accompanied by any perceptible change in the eye itself.

amaurotic (familial) idiocy   (A. Stengel) Obsolete phrase (from amaurotic meaning blindness) for Tay-Sachs disease. See TAY-SACHS DISEASE.

amaxophobia   1. Morbid fear of vehicles or riding in a moving vehicle. 2. Fear of carriages. Also known as hamaxophobia, ochophobia.

Amazon   1. Spelled with a capital A, reference to warrior women of Greek mythology. 2. Spelled with a lowercase A, refers to women of extraordinary strength, both physically and socially.

Amazon Feminism   A kind of feminism dedicated to the image of the female hero and athlete in fiction and fact.

ambidexterity   Ability to use either hand with equal or near equal skill. Also known as ambidextral(ity).

ambience   The present surround (for example, the reader is viewing this under ambient light, temperature, and humidity).

ambient conditions   The physical variables in a particular environment, such as temperature and humidity.

ambient situation   (R. B. Cattell) That part of the environment which is other than the focal stimulus. The surround.

ambient temperature   The atmospheric temperature conditions of a particular location, such as inside a person's home or outside the home.

ambiguity   1. In linguistics, the case in which a sentence has two meanings (surface structure and two underlying structures), such as in "These missionaries are ready to eat" overheard in a conversation between two cannibals. 2. The arousal of mutually exclusive concepts by a stimulus pattern. 3. Uncertainty of meaning.

ambiguity and equivocation   In logic, a fallacy by the use of words that have more than one meaning, as in "Chris is only practicing medicine," thus implying Chris has not yet mastered that subject.

ambiguity tolerance   1. The capacity to tolerate generally stressful situations with apparent equanimity. 2. Ability to cope with conflicting situations without undue distress.

ambiguous   1. In general, having more than one interpretation. 2. In anatomy, a problem having more than one interpretation.

ambiguous communications   Verbal or gestural stimuli that are differentially perceived. See PROJECTIVE METHOD, RORSCHACH INKBLOT TEST, THEMATIC APPERCEPTION TEST.

ambiguous figure   (E. Rubin) A figure that may be interpreted in different ways, usually presented as a line drawing. Such a figure appears to change or reverse in perspective to those staring at it, for example, the Necker Cube. See NECKER CUBE and SET for examples of ambiguous figures.

ambiguous genitals   External sexual organs not fully differentiated, and therefore not indicating that organism's sex. May extend to later life, usually at sexual maturity. Such genitals look like both female or male organs. See PSEUDOHERMAPHRODITISM.

ambiguous mediation   Inability of people observing another's unusual behavior to agree on the motivation for that particular act.

ambiguous perspective   Alternating perspective effects observed in a visual figure. See IMPOSSIBLE FIGURE, PENROSE TRIANGLE, NECKER CUBE, RUBIN'S FIGURE, SET for examples of such figures.

ambiguous stimuli   Stimuli that may have more than one meaning or have different meanings for different people. While some stimuli may be identical in meaning to most people, such as → (an arrow). Words and sentences as well as facial grimaces often are differentially understood. Cloud formations are also examples of ambiguous stimuli. See AMBIGUOUS COMMUNICATION, PROJECTIVE METHOD, RORSCHACH INKBLOT TEST, THEMATIC APPERCEPTION TEST.

ambilevous   Clumsiness of the hands. A person lacking normal manual dexterity in both hands. Also known as ambisinister, ambisinistrous.

ambiphilic   Being sexually oriented toward males and females. See SAME-DIFFERENT THEORY.

ambisexual   1. Pertaining to something that has no evident gender or sex dominance. Designating characteristics, traits, etc., which are found equally in both males and females. See ASEXUAL. 2. See BISEXUAL.

ambisexuality   (S. Ferenczi) 1. Erotic interest toward both males and females. See BISEXUALITY. 2. Possession of sexual characteristics identified with both males and females. See HERMAPHRODITISM, TRANS-SEXUALITY.

ambitendency (A)   Simultaneous competing behavioral tendencies.

ambitypic sexuality   The development of sexual dimorphism in the genitals, brain, or behavior, in which both male and female primordia coexist prior to differentiation.

ambivalence   1. The coexistence of contradictory emotions toward a particular thing, person, or situation. 2. Simultaneously having two opposite feelings toward the same object (for example, to love and hate someone at the same time). 3. (E. Bleuler) The presence of two strong opposing tendencies in psychotic patients. Eugen Bleuler introduced the term to psychology. Also known as ambivalence of feelings.

ambivalence of the will   A condition characterized by simultaneously desiring and not desiring to perform an action, as in demanding food but rejecting the food when it is offered. Observed in its most extreme form in schizophrenia. See ABULIA.

ambivalence of the intellect   A condition in which ideas and counter ideas are held at the same time, as when a patient with schizophrenia vehemently denies hearing voices, yet describes what they are saying. See JANUSIAN THINKING.

ambivalent attachment   A pattern of attachment in which an infant demonstrates anxiety before the primary caregiver leaves, appears to be extremely upset during the absence, and both seeks and resists contact upon the caregiver's return. Also known as resistant attachment.

ambivalent depression   (E. Minkowski) Affective disorder characterized by disabling cognitive uncertainty and salient decisional ambivalence. See ABULIA.

ambivalent object   Any object that has conflicting in it negative and positive features.

ambiversion   Defining a personality with approximately equal amounts of introversive and extraversive traits.

ambivert   A person simultaneously described as an introvert and an extravert. (The average person is probably an ambivert.)

amblyacousia   A functional loss of hearing. Also known as amblykusis.

amblyaphia   A defect of the sense of touch.

amblygeustia   A dulled sense of taste.

amblyopia   A functional loss of vision in the absence of organic defect. Signs are blurring and inability to focus. Found in alcohol and substance abusers, cases of nicotine poisoning, and in students suffering from eye fatigue especially when cramming for examinations.

amblystomas   Salamanders, used for research because their larval and adult stages overlap. Also spelled ambystomas.

ambly(o)scope   An instrument consisting of two tubes with accompanying prisms at the ocular end, used to test the fusion-set, either dormant or active, of individuals having various degrees of strabismus or squinting. See HAPLOSCOPE.

ambrosiac   1. Delightful to smell, as perfumes made with musk. 2. Delightful to taste, as a favorite food. 3. Pertaining to "bee-bread" or pollen gathered by the honeybee to provide protein to the larva.

ambrosial   One of Zwaardemaker's classifications of odors, of which musk and sandalwood are typical examples. See ZWAARDEMAKER'S ODOR CLASSIFICATION.

ambulatory care/services   1. Services in an institution such as a hospital, where a person can receive treatment such as psychotherapy or counseling on an out-patient basis (ambulatory psychotherapy). 2. Any kind of treatment provided by a hospital or institution to patients who are not bedridden or otherwise confined (for example, drug rehabilitation programs, alcohol clinics, diet classes, post-operative groups and individual counseling and psychotherapy). See WALK-IN CLINIC.

ambulatory psychotherapy   See AMBULATORY CARE/SERVICES.

ambulatory schizophrenia   1. A form of schizophrenia in which the patient stays out of an institution, but is marginally adjusted and eccentric, for example, wanders aimlessly about, grimacing and talking to self. 2. An early name for what was later called schizotypal personality by Sandor Rado.

ambulatory services   See AMBULATORY CARE, WALK-IN CLINIC.

ambulatory treatment   Any therapy that can be administered to a person on an out-patient basis, such as in a doctor's office, as distinguished from treatment that would be given a patient confined to a hospital.

amelioration (of symptoms)   Improvement of a patient's mental condition, reduction in degree or number of pathological symptoms.

amelostasis   Amputation fetish.

amenomania   (B. Rush) A morbidly elevated affective state, equivalent to the manic phase of a bipolar disorder.

amenorrhea   Absence of the menses; failure to menstruate between menarche and menopause.

amensalism   In biology, the living together of two dissimilar organisms, a relationship that is detrimental to one and has no effect on the other. See SYMBIOSIS.

ament   A person who is mentally deficient.

amentia   1. Literally "lack of mind." Profound, congenital mental retardation. Contrasts with dementia, "disorder of mind." A person who has lack of mind has amentia, and a person who has a sick mind has dementia. 2. (W. Cullen) Imbecility of the intellect, a neurosis. 3. (T. Meynert) Dementia; hallucinatory confusion and functional loss due to cerebral exhaustion, a psychosis.

American Association of Sex Educators, Counselors and Therapists (AASECT)   A national professional association that publishes the *Journal of Sex Education and Therapy*.

American Birth Control League   (M. Sanger) Original name for Planned Parenthood. See PLANNED PARENTHOOD (meaning 3).

American College Testing Program (ACT or ACTP)   A college admission program measuring English Usage, Mathematics Usage, Social Studies Reading, and Natural Science Reading. Also known as ACT Assessment.

American Council on Education Test (ACE Test)   A measuring instrument for testing academic aptitude of upper high-school students and college students, yielding a language score (L), a quantitative score (Q), and a total score (T). See INTELLIGENCE TESTS AND INTELLIGENCE.

American Counseling Association   A national association of counselors.

American Home Scale   (W. A. Keer & H. H. Remmers) An index of the home environment which contains questions on parental status (occupational and educational levels) and such data as size and nature of the home, telephones, refrigerators, vacuum cleaners, books, and magazines, as well as the esthetic and civic involvement of the family.

American Law Institute (ALI) Guidelines   A set of rules adopted in 1962 that combine the M'Naghten rule and irresistible-impulse concept in determining criminal responsibility of a person suspected of a mental disease or defect. States "... a person is not responsible for criminal conduct if at the time of such conduct as a result of mental disease or defect he lacks substantial capacity either to appreciate the wrongfulness of his conduct or to conform his conduct to the requirements of the law." See BRAWNER DECISION, DURHAM RULE, M'NAGHTEN RULE, RESPONSIBILITY.

American Orthopsychiatric Association (AOA)   An association of psychologists, psychiatrists, social workers, educators, sociologists, and other professional people working in a collaborative approach to the analysis, study, and treatment of people in psychological trouble.

American Philosophical Society   The first scientific society in the United States, founded in 1743.

American Psychiatric Association (APA)   The largest professional organization of American psychiatrists. Founded in 1844 as the Association of Medical Superintendents of American Institutions for the Insane, the name was next changed to the American Medico-Psychological Association and in 1921 to its present name.

American Psychoanalytic Association (APsaA)   An association of analytically trained psychiatrists which sets and enforces standards for the training of psychoanalysts, and supervises the program and the individuals-in-training at its affiliated Institutes.

American Psychological Association (APA)   A national association of psychologists in the United States, established in 1892. The preface to the bylaws of the APA reads: "The objects of the American Psychological Association shall be to advance psychology as a science and as a profession and as a means of promoting human welfare by the encouragement of psychology in all its branches in the broadest and most liberal manner." The APA has three levels of membership: fellows, members, and associates. It also has a number of specialized divisions. Members can belong to more than one division.

American Psychological Association Code of Ethics   Known formally as the *American Psychological Association's (APA's) Ethical Principles of Psychologists and Code of Conduct*. Consists of a Preamble, six general principles, and specific examples of ethical behavior. The first edition was published in 1953 and by 1990 there were seven revisions.

American Psychological Society (APS)   A national society in the United States devoted to scientific psychology. Established in 1988. In its early years was the fastest growing scientific society in the world, gaining 15,000 members in five years. Requirements of membership are a doctoral degree and interest in and contributions to scientific psychology.

American Sign Language (ASL or AMESLAN)   The main manual-visual language system of deaf persons in America.

American Society for Psychical Research   Formed in 1885 to investigate spiritualism and related phenomena.

American Standard Code for Information Interchange (ASCII)   The universal eight-bit code in digital systems that allows data to be transmitted from one manufacturer's equipment to another. The code can represent the decimal digits 0–9, the upper- and lower-case alphabet, and such special characters as "," and "$." Each group of eight bits is generally referred to as a byte. See BINARY DIGIT.

Ames demonstrations   (A. Ames Jr.) A series of illusions consisting of distorted rooms used to test depth perception and demonstrate their illusions. See AMES' DISTORTION ROOM for an illustration.

Ames' Distortion Room   (A. Ames Jr.) An experimental room so constructed that sizes and shapes appear distorted even though the room itself appears to be rectilinear when viewed with one eye. Also known as distorted room, distortion room.

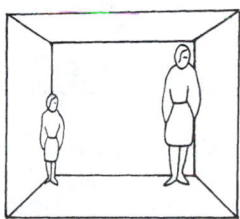

Ames' Distortion Room   This room looks normal from the front, but when a person uses one eye to look through a viewfinder at this distorted room designed by Ames, two people of different sizes are perceived. Actually, the people are of the same size but appear differently because the right corner is quite short, the left corner is quite tall, and the left side slants away from viewers so that the person at the right is much closer to the observer than the person at the left.

Ameslan   Contraction of American Sign Language.

amethystic   A theoretical drug that would counter the intoxicating effects of alcohol. Also known as anti-intoxicant.

ametrometer   An optometric instrument for measuring the kind and degree of refractive error of the eyes.

ametropia   (F. C. Donders) 1. A general term embracing any sort of regular refractive defect in the eye. 2. A disorder of vision or sight caused by the eye not being able to measure correctly the refraction of light rays. Hyperopia is the most frequent form of ametropia, but other varieties are myopia, astigmatism, and presbyopia. 3. A condition in which, with accommodation relaxed, parallel rays do not focus on the retina, usually leading to prescription for eyeglasses, contact lenses, operations on the eye, or eye exercises.

amimia   Inability to convey meaning through appropriate gestures (sensory or receptive) and, in some cases, to interpret the gestures of others. See APHASIA.

amine   (F. Wöhler, B. Liebig, C. A. Wurtz) 1. A chemical complex of one nitrogen atom and two hydrogen atoms commonly found in chemistry. 2. In neurophysiology, the term generally applies to the general class of chemicals called "biogenic amines," which include both the catecholamines (such as epinephrine) and tryptamine derivatives (such as serotonin), as well as related substances. Derivative phrases include amine oxidase, and amino acids.

amine oxidase   An enzyme that neutralizes amines, more specifically in neurophysiology, tending to refer to a substance found at the synapse which prevents an excessive build-up of neurotransmitters. See MONAMINE OXIDASE INHIBITORS.

amine pathways   Outmoded phrase for specific neuroanatomical pathways in the brain as determined by precise histochemical localization of the amines that are sensitive to certain amines only and which allow for transmission of impulses along these paths. More specific pathways, such as GABA pathways, dopamine pathways, and serotonin pathways, are now used.

amino acids   (J. J. Berzelius, E. Fischer) Organic compounds that occur naturally in plant and animal tissues and are the building blocks of protein molecules. Eight of the more than 20 amino acids in the human diet are essential to life and are ordinarily obtained from foods.

amitosis   Cell division in which the nucleus divides by constriction without the formation and splitting of chromosomes. Also known as direct nuclear division, Remak's (nuclear) division.

amixia   1. Demand in some cultures requiring that husband and wife be of different ethnic, religious, caste, or color groups. 2. Restriction of general intercrossing in a species to prevent the deleterious effects of inbreeding. See EUGENICS, MISCEGENATION.

amnemonic   Pertaining to reduction of memory.

amnesia   (P. Broca) Loss of memory. Can be total or partial, temporary or permanent, psychological in origin such as due to psychic shock, repression of traumatic events, or due to organic factors such as blows to the head, stroke, or senility. Types of amnesia include: AFFECTIVE, ALCOHOL AMNESTIC DISORDER, ANTEROGRADE, AUDIOVERBAL, AUDITORY, AUTOHYPNOTIC, CATATHYMIC, CIRCUMSCRIBED, CONTINUOUS, CORTICAL, DISSOCIATIVE, EPISODIC, EPOCHAL, FUGUE, GLOBAL, HYSTERICAL, INFANTILE, LOCALIZED, NEUROLOGIC, ORGANIC, POLYGLOT, POSTENCEPHALITIC, POSTHYPNOTIC, POSTTRAUMATIC, PSYCHOGENIC, RETROGRADE, TACTILE, VERBAL, VISUAL.

amnesic   1. Pertaining to or characterized by amnesia. Also known as amnestic. 2. A condition of being aware of the present but having forgotten the past. See AMNESIA, FUGUE.

amnesic aphasia   **amnestic aphasia**

amnesic apraxia   **amnestic apraxia**

amnesic barriers   **dissociative barriers**

amnesic confabulation   The invention of fanciful tales and experiences unconsciously fabricated to fill gaps in memory, found in Korsakoff's and some other organic disorders. See CONFABULATION.

amnesic-confabulatory syndrome   An alternative name for part of Korsakoff's disorder, based on its two most striking symptoms of memory defect and confabulation.

amnesic misidentification   See MISIDENTIFICATION.

amnesic syndrome   A condition in which the most prominent behavioral symptom is difficulty retaining new information. A second symptom is polyneuritis. Sometimes known as amnestic disorder, axial amnesia, Korsakoff amnesia. See AMNESTIC SYNDROME.

amnestic   1. Pertaining to loss or impairment of memory, as in amnestic aphasia. See AMNESTIC SYNDROME. 2. See AMNESIC (meaning 1). 3. Causing amnesia.

amnestic aphasia   Impaired ability to recognize the meaning of words and to find the correct name for objects. Also known as amnesic aphasia, nominal aphasia.

amnestic apraxia   Inability to remember and therefore carry out a command although there is no loss of ability to perform the task. Also known as amnesic apraxia.

amnestic disorder   Disturbance in short- or long-term memory, which may be due to many different medical conditions as well as the long-term abuse of a drug, especially ones such as alcohol, sedative-hypnotics, inhalants, marijuana, and others. This occurs aside from the immediate intoxication or even a delirium, and may last from several hours or days ("transient") to many years ("chronic"). Also known as amnesic disorder.

amnestic syndrome   An impairment in learning new material and recalling past information, without clouding of consciousness or general loss of intellectual abilities. The patient may be disoriented, and may deny the problem or confabulate to fill memory gaps. See AMNESIC SYNDROME, AMNESTIC DISORDER.

amniocentesis   The extraction and analysis of amniotic fluid from the uterus in the early stages of pregnancy, usually used for the detection of genetic anomalies in the fetus. See CHORIONIC VILLI SAMPLING (CVS), GENETIC COUNSELING.

amobarbital   (I. H. Page) Generic name for a central nervous system depressant. Also known as Amytal, Dexamyl, sodium amytal.

amok   A culture-specific syndrome observed among males in Malay, the Philippines, and parts of Africa. The affected individual experiences a period of brooding and depression, then begins a wild, unprovoked, and indiscriminate attack on any person or animal nearby, usually killing or maiming people before being overpowered, collapsing from exhaustion, killing himself or being killed (hence the term "running amok"). Also known as *amuck*. See FUROR, PSEUDOAMOK SYNDROME, PUERTO RICAN SYNDROME.

amoral   Lacking in a sense of morality. Stage 1 of Jean Piaget's model of moral development.

amorous paranoia   1. Delusions of infidelity. 2. Obsolete phrase for delusional jealousy.

amorphagnosia   Inability to recognize the size and shape of objects.

amorphosynthesis   Inability to perceive a specific form based on tactile sensations. See ASTEREOGNOSIS.

amotivational syndrome   A personality pattern consisting of apathy, passivity, loss of drive for achievement, a tendency to drift, low frustration tolerance, and difficulty in concentrating and following routines.

amour fou   (insane love—French) Obsessive love.

AMP   1. adenosine monophosphate. See ADENOSINE $3',5'$-MONOPHOSPHATE. 2. amplitude (also abbreviated **a, A**).

AMPA receptor   A glutamate receptor that controls a sodium channel.

ampere (A or **a)**   A unit of electrical current applied across a resistance of one ohm. Named after French physicist Andre Ampère (1775–1836). See INTERNATIONAL SYSTEM OF UNITS.

amphetamine (G. Piness, H. Miller, G. Alles) A stimulant synthetic chemical related to the catecholamines in the nervous system. Known since the 1930s, amphetamines have been used to help combat fatigue during World War II, promote alertness, treat hyperactivity in children, and suppress the appetite. "Amphetamine" is an acronym for alphamethylphenylethylamine. See DEXEDRINE, METHAMPHETAMINE, SPEED.

amphetamine dependence A drug dependency in which amphetamines are smoked, snorted, and/or swallowed, characterized by inability to abstain and increased tolerance. Symptoms include restlessness, insomnia, irritability, loss of impulse control, ideas of reference, delusions of persecution, and hallucinosis.

amphetamine-induced psychosis A common form of drug-induced psychosis, arising from the use of large doses of amphetamines over a period of time and characterized by a confused or psychotic state, with loss of reality testing.

amphetamine-related disorders Because of euphoriant effects, amphetamines can be a drug of both dependence and abuse. Amphetamines stimulate and then exhaust the central nervous system of enough of its neurotransmitters so that psychosis can ensue. After a long stretch of use, on cessation a "crash" of depression-like symptoms and other forms of psychopathology may be experienced. See AMPHETAMINE DEPENDENCE, AMPHETAMINE-INDUCED PSYCHOSIS.

amphibole In logic, an error due to the use of loose or ambiguous language. See AMBIGUITY, FALLACIES.

amphierotism 1. Having a bisexual orientation that is predominantly but not exclusively homosexual. 2. (S. Ferenczi) A psychiatric disorder in which a person is able to conceive of himself or herself in erotic terms as a male or a female or both simultaneously.

amphigenesis Ability of a lesbian or gay man to have apparently normal sexual relations with a member of the opposite sex. See BISEXUAL.

amphigenous inversion A form of psychosexual hermaphroditism in which a lesbian or gay man may engage in sexual activity with members of either sex. Compare ABSOLUTE INVERSION.

amphimixis In psychoanalytic theory, the integration of anal and genital erotism in the development of heterosexuality.

amphiphilia Being sexually aroused by bisexual orientation.

amplification 1. A process of making larger. 2. (C. G. Jung) A method of dream analysis in which a person gives multiple, repeated associations to a particular dream element. See JUNG'S DREAM THEORY.

amplitude (a, A, or AMP) The intensity of an acoustic or electric wave.

amplitude distortion A hearing disorder in which loud sounds are distorted or misjudged.

amplitude of light wave (E. Titchener) The distance from the base to the top of a light wave; determines the intensity of visual sensations.

AMPT A drug that interferes with the synthesis of catecholamines by blocking tyrosine hydroxylase.

ampulla osseae (A. Scarpa) Distortion of the bony labyrinth; an enlargement at the base of each semicircular canal of the cochlea of the inner ear.

amputation doll A play-therapy doll that can be taken apart to encourage expression of feelings. The mother doll is the basic member of the "family" but in appropriate situations the therapist can increase members of the family as well as friends, neighbors, doctors, etc.

amputation fetish See ACROTOMOPHILIA, APOTEMNOPHILIA.

amuck 1. See AMOK. 2. Nontechnical term for wild and uncontrolled behavior posing a threat to others.

amulet An ornament, relic, or packet of magic powder which is worn as a charm or preventive against evils, such as diseases or witchcraft. Also known as charm, talisman.

amurakh A culture-specific syndrome occurring among Siberian women. The principal symptom is mimicking other people's words or behavior. See ARCTIC HYSTERIA, COPYING MANIA.

amusia A type of auditory agnosia characterized by inability to recognize melodies or play music. See APHASIA, EXPRESSIVE APHASIA.

amychophobia Morbid fear of being scratched.

amygdala Neural center in the limbic system of the brain affecting emotions. Almond-shaped, it is located immediately below the cerebral cortex of the anterior medial temporal lobe. In humans, it is associated with a variety of behavior patterns including sexuality, aggression, digestion, excretion, arterial blood pressure, and muscle tone. Its connection to the hypothalamus has been observed to be related to rage behavior. Also known as amygdaloid nucleus.

amygdalectomy The removal of a portion of the amygdala as a therapeutic effort to reduce hallucinations or other abnormal reactions. Ablation of various areas of the amygdala can produce a sense of fear, aggressiveness, hypersexuality, and compulsive oral responses, depending upon the area removed. Also known as amygdaloidectomy.

amygdaloid nucleus amygdala

amylase An enzyme found in saliva.

amyostasia A type of muscle tremor frequently observed in locomotor ataxia.

amyosthenia Muscular weakness. See APHORIA.

amyotonia myatonia

Amytal Trade name of sodium amobarbital, a relatively short-acting sedative barbiturate. See AMYTAL INTERVIEW, SEDATIVE BARBITURATE, SEDATIVE-HYPNOTIC DRUGS, SODIUM AMYTAL.

Amytal interview An interview conducted when the interviewee is under the influence of intravenous Amytal, for the purpose of attempting to discover material that the interviewee may have forgotten or knows but is trying to hide. Amytal helps to lower the person's inhibitions, the idea being that the person is more likely to blurt out thoughts and feelings otherwise repressed. For this reason amytal is sometimes called "truth serum." Other short-acting barbiturates have also been used for this purpose, including Pentothal (sodium thiopental). This approach is seldom used today. See PENTOTHAL.

An   In Rorschach test scoring, a symbol for anatomy response.

anabolic system   A constitutional body type in which the abdomen is more prominent than the chest due to the presence of large visceral organs.

anabolism   (Galen) Building up of tissues. A bodily function that synthesizes food elements such as amino acids into complex organic compounds and tissues. The healing process of repair of a wound is an example of anabolism. See CATABOLISM, METABOLISM.

anaclisis   (S. Freud) An extreme dependence on another person for emotional and in some cases physical support. The choice of a love object based on a resemblance to a parent or similar.

anaclitic choice   A preference for anyone resembling adults who were kind to the person in childhood, such as parents. See ANACLITIC OBJECT CHOICE.

anaclitic depression   (R. Spitz) An acute reaction of lethargy and apparent despondency in infants who have been seriously neglected by their caretakers. Such infants will often develop physical illnesses, show no initiative, and may die. Survivors often develop unusual personalities, generally being paradoxically either over-demanding of attention or refusing any contact. See MARASMUS.

anaclitic identification   A tendency of children to identify with a parent or caretaker who shows warmth and acceptance.

anaclitic object choice   (S. Freud) In psychoanalytic theory, the selection by an adult of a mate who is likely to provide the same type of assistance, comfort, and support received from the mother during infancy and early childhood.

anaclitic psychotherapy   A form of therapy in which the patient is encouraged to regress to an infantile state of dependence on the therapist. See PRIMARY RELATIONSHIP THERAPY.

anaclitic relationship   The bond between a child and his or her mother filled with emotions and feelings of safety and trust.

anacusis   Total deafness. Also spelled anacousia, anacusia, anakusis.

Anadenanthera   A genus name for a group of plants indigenous to Latin America used by local populations as a source of a mind-altering snuff. The plants contain bufotenine and dimethyltryptamine, both hallucinogens.

anaerobic exercise   A kind of exercise that does not call for continued effort without rest periods nor excess intake of oxygen, for example, baseball (anaerobic) versus running (aerobic). See AEROBIC EXERCISE.

anaesthesia   British spelling of anesthesia. See ANESTHETICS.

anaglyph   (L. Ducos du Hauron) A three-dimensional depiction achieved by looking through eyeglasses of corresponding colors to two superimposed pictures, usually one red and the other blue. Early 3-D motion pictures used this technique.

anaglyptoscope   A shadow-perspective study instrument that reverses light and dark patterns. It brings the light upon an object in relief from the direction opposite to that from which it would seem to come; the result is to produce an apparent reversal of perspective.

anagogic   Pertaining to an alleged moral, spiritual, or uplifting effect of the unconscious.

anagogic interpretation   (C. G. Jung) The view that dreams and other unconscious material are expressions of ideals and spiritual forces.

anagogic symbolism   (C. G. Jung) The indirect representation of objects associated with moral, spiritual, or idealistic concepts.

anagogic tendency   (W. Stekel) A psychic impulse towards lofty, progressive ideals that tend to aid a person in achieving positive and constructive life goals. Represents the upward-leading, constructive impulses. The opposite of a katagogic tendency.

anal-aggressive character   In psychoanalytic theory, a personality type characterized by obstinacy, obstructionism, defiance, and passive resistance. Such traits are assumed to stem from the anal stage in which children assert themselves by withholding feces. See ANAL CHARACTER.

anal birth   (S. Freud) A symbolic desire to be reborn through the anus as expressed in dreams or fantasies with anal erotic content.

anal castration anxiety   A displacement of the fear of castration by a regressive anal manifestation, for example, various toilet phobias.

anal character/personality   (S. Freud) In psychoanalytic theory, a pattern of personality traits thought to stem from the anal phase of psychosexual development, when defecation was a primary source of pleasure. Such a child is said to develop the anal triad of frugality, obstinacy, and orderliness; and is said to be compulsive, meticulous, rigid, and overconscientious (an anal retentive personality).

analeptic drugs   Rare phrase for central nervous system stimulants that produce subjective effects similar to those caused by amphetamines. Effects may include alertness, elevated mood, increased feeling of energy, decreased appetite, irritability, insomnia. Also known as analeptics. See ANOREXIC DRUGS.

anal erot(ic)ism   (S. Freud) In psychoanalytic theory, pleasurable sensations associated with defecation. Persons fixated at this stage may later derive special gratification from elimination, manipulation of the anal region, or anal intercourse. See ANAL CHARACTER, ANAL PHASE, COPROPHILIA.

anal-erotic traits   In psychoanalytic theory, personality traits considered characteristic of obsessive individuals: Overcautiousness, overmeticulousness, stubbornness, miserliness, overconcern with detail. See ANAL CHARACTER, ANAL EROTICISM.

anal-expulsive personality   In psychoanalytic theory, a personality type characterized by compulsive behavior, especially related to orderliness and cleanliness. Considered derived from toilet training and manifest in ridding the self of disorder or possessions. See ANAL CHARACTER.

anal-expulsive stage   See ANAL STAGE.

anal fantasies   Daydreams or mental images that focus on the anal area, such as anal intercourse or anal pregnancy and birth.

analgesia   Insensitivity to pain regardless of cause. Nociceptive stimuli are perceived but are not interpreted as pain. Also known as analgesthesia, analgia. Compare ALGESIA.

analgesic   A drug or other agent that alleviates sensations of pain. Usually classed as narcotic or nonnarcotic, depending upon their potential for physical dependence. Nonnarcotic analgesics, whether aspirin-like or nonsteroidal anti-inflammatory drugs (NSAIDs) are well established as effective analgesics. Narcotic analgesics (such as morphine or codeine) are often required for more severe types of pain. See SALICYLATES.

anal humor   Jokes that involve the rectal area. According to psychoanalytic theory, the tendency to appreciate such humor harks back to the anal stage when the child derived pleasure from the stimulation of this zone by retention or elimination of feces. Preoccupation with anal humor may be indicative of a fixation at this stage.

anal impotence   Inability to defecate except under certain conditions, for example, absolute privacy.

analingus   Oral sexual stimulation of the anal region. Also spelled anilingus.

anal intercourse   A form of sexual activity in which a penis is inserted into a rectum. See SODOMY.

analist   A person whose erotic fantasies, erotic behavior, or both, are directed to anal sex.

anality   Erotic pleasure associated with the anal region.

anal masturbation   A form of anal erotism in which sexual excitement is achieved through stimulation of the anus.

analog   analog(ue)

analogical thinking   1. The use of analogies, especially verbal analogies, to prove conclusions. 2. The use of analogies to suggest hypotheses. See METAPHOR.

analogies test   A measure of the participant's ability to comprehend the relationship between two items and then extend that relationship to a different situation; for example, "brush" is to "painting" as "pen" is to _____? ("writing"). See MILLER ANALOGIES TEST.

analog(ue)   1. Denoting a continuous or graded representation of information, in contrast to digital or binary representation. 2. A structure that is similar in function to another structure, such as an organ that performs similar functions in different organisms (for example, the ovaries of plants and of mammals). 3. A thing that is similar but not equal to something else. Thus a small photograph of a person and the same photograph blown up are analogues of each other although differing in size.

analogue experiment   A type of experiment in which a phenomenon related to the study objective is created or produced to obtain an improved perspective toward the situation (for example, the use of hypnosis, mind-altering drugs, and sensory deprivation to produce brief periods of abnormal behavior that simulate psychopathological conditions).

analogue research   The evaluation of a particular condition or intervention under conditions that resemble or approximate the situation to which a person wishes to generalize.

analogue study   1. A research method in which a type of treatment is evaluated under well-controlled conditions analogous to those in a clinic. 2. A research method in which the same treatment or procedure is employed and evaluated for two types of people such as males and females or those considered normal and those considered disturbed. 3. A research method, found particularly in the behavior modification literature, in which animals are used in place of humans. See ACTION RESEARCH, APPLIED RESEARCH, EVALUATION RESEARCH, OUTCOME RESEARCH.

analogy   1. An assumed similarity between two things, events, etc., belonging to separate regions of discourse; for example a camel being called a ship of the desert. 2. Similarity in function or structure of an organ in two distantly related organisms.

analogy period   (B. Klopfer) A period of time following the administration of the Rorschach test, during which the examiner asks direct or indirect questions of the participant regarding responses given to the test (for example "You saw a toad here. Can you tell me more about it?").

analogy-principle response   See RESPONSE BY ANALOGY PRINCIPLE.

anal personality   anal character

anal phase   (S. Freud) In psychoanalytic theory, the second stage of psychosexual development, occurring from the age of one to one-and-a-half until about three years, in which the child's interests and sexual pleasures are focused on the expulsion and retention of the feces. See GENITAL PHASE, INFANTILE SEXUALITY, LATENCY PHASE, ORAL PHASE, PHALLIC PHASES.

anal rape   Forced sexual contact via the rectum.

anal-rape fantasy   Fear of being sexually attacked via the anus or fear of so doing.

anal retentive personality   See ANAL CHARACTER.

anal-retentive stage   See ANAL STAGE.

anal sadism   1. In psychoanalytic theory, the expression of destructive and aggressive impulses in the anal stage of psychosexual development. Also, aggressiveness and selfishness expressed later in life as the result of harsh toilet training. 2. Anal intercourse with the intention of hurting and/or humiliating the victim, male or female.

anal-sadistic phase/stage   In psychoanalytic theory, a hypothesized stage during which a person is concerned about anal psychosexuality as well as sadism, thought to be engendered by early harsh toilet training.

anal stage   (K. Abraham) In psychoanalytic theory, a stage of early development of two types: anal-expulsive (pleasure in expelling feces) and anal-retentive (pleasure for retaining feces). Fixation at either stage leads, according to this theory, to differing personalities. See ANAL-CHARACTER, ANAL-EXPULSIVE PERSONALITY, ANAL-RETENTIVE PERSONALITY TYPES.

anal triad   See ANAL CHARACTER.

analysand   The person in psychoanalytic treatment.

analysator   (I. Pavlov) The receptor together with its central nervous connections, by which differential sensitivity to stimulation is produced. Also known as analysor.

analyser   (I. Pavlov) The theoretical part or function of a sensory nerve system responsible for making sensitivity evaluations. Also spelled analyzer.

analysis   1. In general, the division of any complex entity, such as a chemical compound or a personality type, into its component parts. 2. A common abbreviated term for psychoanalysis. 3. The systematic examination of data.

analysis by synthesis   1. A concept of the brain functioning as a kind of computer that takes separate elements via perception or sensation and generates a meaningful concept that then permits proper behavior to the total situation. 2. A theory of perception stating that the perceiver first breaks down (analyzes) a stimulus object into its constituent elements and then assembles (synthesizes) significant components to form a percept in accordance with the object's context and the perceiver's previous experience.

analysis in depth   Any therapeutic approach based on exploration of unconscious processes, especially Sigmund Freud's psychoanalysis and Carl Jung's analytic psychology. See DEPTH PSYCHOLOGY.

analysis of covariance (ANCOVA)   An extension of analysis of variance which adjusts means for the influence of a correlated variable or a covariate. This statistical procedure is appropriate when research groups are known to differ on a background-correlated variable, in addition to differences attributed to the experimental treatment. See ANALYSIS OF VARIANCE.

analysis of resistance   A basic procedure in depth psychotherapy or psychoanalysis, in which the patient's tendency to repress unconscious impulses and experiences is subjected to scrutiny. The process of locating and dealing with resistances is purported to be a major contribution to self-understanding and personality change. See FLIGHT INTO HEALTH, PSYCHOANALYSIS, RESISTANCE.

analysis of transference   In psychoanalytic theory, the interpretation of a patient's early relationships and experiences as expressed in the present relationship to the analyst. See TRANSFERENCE, TRANSFERENCE RESISTANCE.

analysis of variance (ANOVA)   (R. A. Fisher) A statistical procedure that isolates the joint and separate effects of independent variables upon a dependent variable, and tests them for statistical significance. Formula: $F = MS$ among-groups $\div$ MS within-groups.

analysis of variance tests   Tests used in the analysis of variance, such as the F-test.

analysis unit   See ELEMENT.

analyst   1. Anyone who performs analysis of any kind. 2. A common term, short for a psychoanalyst.

analytic   1. Pertaining to analysis. 2. Pertaining to psychoanalysis.

analytical psychodrama   Attempts to determine the truth of certain hypotheses about a person's behavior, thoughts, feelings, etc., that is conducted or tested on the psychodrama stage. The therapist watches the protagonist in psychodramatic interaction with others. Later, perhaps in consultation, a decision is made concerning the probable truth of the matter of concern.

analytical statistics   A branch of statistics concerned with properly drawing inferences from numerical data. See INFERENTIAL STATISTICS.

analytic approach/method   An investigation approach which starts with and emphasizes analysis, that is, which seeks to separate compounds into more elementary units.

analytic group psychotherapy   (S. R. Slavson) A form of group psychotherapy based on the application of psychoanalytic concepts and techniques primarily to preschool children, children in the latency period, as well as adolescents and adults. The groups are selected on the basis of therapeutic balance. Six analytic principles are applied: achievement of insight, catharsis, development of ego strength, reality testing, sublimation, and transference.

analytic impasse   See ANALYTIC STALEMATE, THERAPEUTIC STALEMATE.

analytic insight   In psychoanalytic theory, an awareness of the unconscious origin and meaning of behavior and symptoms, especially as a result of "working through" resistances. See BREAKTHROUGH, INSIGHT, RESISTANCE.

analytic interpretation   In psychoanalytic theory, the therapist's summary of the patient's early experiences, dreams, character defenses, resistances, and other productions in terms meaningful to the patient.

analytic neurosis   Negative consequences of an overextended psychoanalysis, characterized by emotional dependency on analysis and analysts.

analytic patient   (S. Freud) A person receiving analytic treatment. According to Sigmund Freud, psychoanalysis is most effective between the ages of 15 to 50. Ideal analysands are self-motivated, willing to cooperate with the therapist, able to reason and articulate, are not in an acute or dangerous state, and are willing to remain in therapy for a lengthy period. See HOUND, YAVIS.

Analytic Psychology   (C. G. Jung) The theory of personality that includes some of Sigmund Freud's psychoanalysis but minimizes sexual motives and maximizes individual factors. The psyche is interpreted primarily in terms of philosophic values, primordial images and symbols, and a drive for self-fulfillment. The object of life, according to Jungian philosophy, is to achieve a creative balance among all forces. See INDIVIDUAL PSYCHOLOGY, PERSONALITY THEORIES, PSYCHOANALYSIS.

analytic rules   (S. Freud) The three rules proposed by Sigmund Freud for conducting psychoanalytic therapy: (a) the "Fundamental rule" (of free association), gives free reign to the unconscious to bring repressed impulses and experiences to the surface; (b) the rule of abstinence discourages (the analyst's) gratifications (by the client) that might drain off energy that could be used in the therapeutic process; (c) the rule or prohibition against acting out feelings and events, instead of talking them out. See BASIC RULE.

analytic stalemate   A situation that can occur in any form of psychotherapy characterized by no progress being made or the appearance that no progress will ever be made. Causes are diverse. Also known as analytic impasse. See ID RESISTANCE, RESISTANCE.

anamnesis 1. The act of remembering. 2. A written record of a client or patient that is a personal account of his or her history prior to the onset of illness. 3. In psychotherapy, a written record of a client or patient that generally has two parts: (a) In the first interview, recording all relevant factors as stated by the client that led the client into therapy; (b) notes made by the therapist during treatment. Some psychotherapists make no notes. 4. (Plato) Recalling previous experienced concepts of the soul that existed in a previous life. See PSYCHIATRIC HISTORY.

anamnestic analysis (C. G. Jung) A Jungian term for analysis that emphasizes the patient's historical account of the problem of concern with added material from family and friends.

anancasm Repetitious, stereotyped behavior which a person feels impelled to carry out to relieve tension and anxiety (for example, wringing of hands, tapping of fingers). Also spelled anankasm. See COMPULSION.

anancastia An obsession controlling a person who feels forced to act or think against his or her own will. Also spelled anankastia. See ANANCASTIC PERSONALITY.

anancastic personality A pattern of behavior characterized by excessive perfectionism, over-conscientiousness, lack of warmth, preoccupation with form and details, and inability to "loosen up" and enjoy leisure-time activities. Also spelled anankastic personality. See COMPULSIVE CHARACTER, COMPULSIVE PERSONALITY DISORDER, OBSESSION.

anandamide An endogenous lipid that is a ligand for receptors that bind with tetrahydrocannabinol (THC).

anandria Absence of masculinity.

ananke (fate—Greek) External necessity, or fate. In psychoanalytic theory, conceived to be the counterpart of inner necessity arising from Eros, the life instinct, and Thanatos, the death instinct. These two forces, internal and external, are viewed as the sources of human culture.

anaphase A stage of meiotic or mitotic cell division during which the chromosome halves move to the poles of the spindle. In mitosis, a full set of daughter chromosomes (46 in humans) moves toward each pole. In the first division of meiosis, one member of each homologous pair (23 in humans) made up of two chromatids united by a centromere move toward each pole; in the second division, the centromere divides, and the two chromatids separate and move to their respective pole.

anaphia The absence or loss of ability to perceive tactile sensations or stimuli. Also spelled anhaphia.

anaphrodisia Obsolete term for lack of sexual feelings.

anaphrodisiac Any preparation that functions to reduce or suppress sexual desire. Among substances claimed to have such effects are saltpeter, potassium bromide, and camphor. Compare APHRODISIAC.

anaphylaxis 1. Hypersensitivity to the introduction of an allergen into body tissues, resulting from previous exposure to it. A physical allergic reaction to a substance, such as to peanuts, penicillin, or a wasp sting. 2. A negative psychological overreaction to an event identical or similar to a traumatic one in the past.

anaphylactic shock A severe reaction of the entire body due to injections of antibodies to which the person is allergic based on prior contacts. May result in death.

anarchic behavior 1. Lawless, antisocial behavior. 2. Rebellion of children against family and school rules and regulations in an effort to achieve independence or to get attention. 3. Conduct that demonstrates unwillingness to obey normal rules of the family, school, or society. Such behavior when considered to be conscious and responsible usually leads to banishment or to punishment; behavior considered involuntary may be taken as a sign of a mental disorder and may lead to institutionalization or forced treatment.

Anarcho-feminism A kind of feminism that promotes the total restructuring of society.

anarithmia A form of aphasia characterized by inability to count or use numbers. Sometimes used as a synonym for acalculia. See ACALCULIA, DYSCALCULIA.

anarthria Inability to speak due to brain lesions or damage to peripheral nerves that affect the articulatory muscles. See ALEXIA, APHASIA.

anastomoses Alternate pathways formed by branches of main circuits in nerves, blood, and lymphatic tracts. Such pathways in blood vessels help insure a continuing blood flow to the brain in the event one pathway is blocked. Singular is anastomosis.

anatomical age A measure of the state of physical development of an individual, based on an examination of the anatomy, usually by x-rays of the bones of the hands. See CHRONOLOGICAL AGE, MENTAL AGE.

anatomically detailed dolls Dolls of male and female children with secondary sexual elements made explicitly clear, used primarily to determine whether children have been inappropriately touched sexually or otherwise sexually abused.

Anatomy is destiny (S. Freud) The contention that women are defined by their reproductive biology.

anatomy response (**An** or **At**) In Rorschach test scoring, any mention of anatomical elements.

ancestor worship 1. A religion in which the spirits of ancestors are the objects of worship. 2. Extreme respect for the beliefs, customs, and methods of former generations.

ancestral inheritance law See LAW OF ANCESTRAL INHERITANCE.

ancestral spirits In cultures where ancestors are worshipped as protectors and sources of wisdom for the living, it is assumed that they take an active interest in the well-being of living family members, who are expected to show them respect in various ways.

anchor(age) **anchor point**

anchorage effect A tendency of individuals to resist changes, usually in attitudes. The behavior is purportedly strong in older people. See ANCHORING EFFECT.

anchoring 1. Establishing a memory trigger through physical contact connected with a desired feeling or behavior. 2. In hypnosis, generating a conditioning-like method to make certain cues evoke feeling states or desired behaviors.

anchoring bias A tendency to fix on a particular solution to a problem or the evidence for a particular hypothesis and to ignore contradictory information.

anchoring effect   A tendency of clinicians, once they have come to a diagnostic decision, usually early in the therapeutic process, to stick to that diagnoses as time goes on, resisting revisions even in spite of further evidence that the original diagnosis was incorrect. See RIGIDITY, TRADITION.

anchoring of ego   In psychoanalytic theory, how one person identified with another in providing psychological security.

anchor point   An arbitrarily established standard against which a person makes a subjective judgment, for example, someone shown a rectangle with an area of four square inches is asked to indicate which of other rectangles are smaller or larger than this standard; or a person is asked to rate sunsets for beauty on a scale of one to ten based on a subjective scale of beauty. Also known as anchor(age), anchoring point.

anchor test   A scale used to establish comparable norms for new tests.

ancient mariner effect   A tendency of people on meeting strangers with whom they will share some time but most likely will never meet again (such as on an airplane) to tell intimate details of their lives. Name derives from the Samuel Taylor Coleridge poem that begins: "It is an ancient mariner ... Now wherefore stopp'st thou me?" Also known as passing stranger effect.

ancillary   Subservient, auxiliary. A preliminary step to another process.

ANCOVA   analysis of covariance

androgen   androgen(s)

androgenic   1. Pertaining to hereditary factors that generate maleness. 2. Having a masculine effect. 3. A synonym for hermaphroditic. See ANDROGYNY.

androgenic flush   A reddish pigmentation around the neck due to an excess of 17-ketosteroids.

androgen-induced hermaphroditism   A congenital condition causing genital masculinization in a 46,XX female fetus.

androgen insensitivity   A condition in which a genetic male develops female genitals and breasts because of the body's failure to respond to testosterone. Also known as testicular feminization syndrome. See HERMAPHRODITISM.

androgen insensitivity syndrome   In a person with XY chromosomes, a female with testes but no internal genitals, caused by inadequately functioning androgen receptors.

androgenital syndrome   A syndrome affecting some females who at birth appear to have masculine features (the clitoris enlarged, appearing to be a small penis), and do not develop sexual secondary characteristics due to production of androstenedione rather than cortisol in the third to fifth month of their mother's pregnancy. See PSEUDOHERMAPHRODITISM.

androgenization   Transformation of any structure of the body into a masculine rather than a feminine shape.

androgen(s)   1. Generic name for an agent, usually a hormone, that has masculinizing effects. 2. Hormones that produce male sexual characteristics. The main androgens are androsterone and testosterone, manufactured mainly by the testes, partly by the adrenal glands. Androgens contribute to the development of facial hair, masculine voice, as well as growth of bones and muscle that account for the normally greater size and strength of males compared with females. Artificial androgens have been used to build up body mass in athletes and when used in large doses, have resulted also in increased aggression and difficulties in impulse control.

androgyne   Female pseudohermaphroditism. Females with male-like external genitalia. Also known as androgynism.

androgyneity   In anthropology, the cultural assumption that boys and girls require a ritual to acquire a definite gender.

androgynophilia   Being sexually attracted to or aroused by a person with a bisexual orientation.

androgynous personality   A pattern of exhibiting both masculine and feminine behavioral, emotional and cognitive characteristics.

androgynous sex role   A vague phrase indicating confusion or uncertainty about gender identity. A male may play a feminine social role or a female may play a masculine social role. A person considered "androgynous" may be a heterosexual, a bisexual, a gay man, or a lesbian. There may be some hermaphrodism, ostensible females growing facial hair or males developing breasts.

androgyny   A combination of male and female characteristics in one individual, usually applied to a male with feminine traits. See ANDROGYNEITY, ANDROGYNISM, BISEXUALITY, GYNANDROMORPHY, HERMAPHRODISM, PSEUDOHERMAPHRODITISM.

andromania   Obsolete term for nymphomania.

andromimesis   A condition in which a woman impersonates a male and relates sexually only to other women. See LESBIANISM, HOMOSEXUALITY.

andromimetophilia   Being sexually attracted to or aroused by an andromimetic female or preoperative female-to-male transsexual.

androphilia   Attraction toward males.

androphobia   Morbid fear of males. Results in avoidance of situations where men are present.

androsterone   (F. C. Koch, C. R. Moore, T. F. Gallagher) A steroid metabolite having a weak masculinizing effect, somewhat similar to testosterone.

and-summation hypothesis   A postulate that wholes may be constructed by the mere addition of distinct parts, in contrast with the view that elements becoming part of a whole lose their distinct identity. See GESTALT PSYCHOLOGY.

anecdotal evidence   A kind of evidence based on uncontrolled personal observations, as opposed to scientific observations. Although even single cases are sufficient evidence of the validity of the phenomenon for most persons, psychologists are generally suspicious of such evidence and prefer many cases from different observers, if not from controlled studies.

anecdotal method   A technique of presenting data based on personal observation rather than from research with controlled variables. Not likely to reveal causal relationships but can offer clues to areas of investigation that may warrant scientific studies. Also known as method of anecdote.

anecdotal record   A factual, written account containing succinct, cumulative descriptions of a person's behavior. Used in many kinds of institutions or organizations such as schools, athletic groups, reformatories, training sessions, and the military. Such observations highlight given aspects of individuals' personality and development, and may prove useful in later evaluations.

anechoic   Area free of echoes.

anechoic chamber/room   An enclosure scientifically designed to eliminate sound reverberations and echoes, so that the sound within will be pure, without overtones or echoes. Sound waves are absorbed within the chamber walls by structures that muffle echo and standing waves, with negligible sound wave reflection. Typically used in audiological testing centers.

anelectrotonus   (E. F. Pflüger) Rare term for a lessened conductivity and tension of a nerve near an anode as an electrical current passes through it (with consequent increase in cell-membrane polarization). See ELECTROTONUS.

anemomania   Madness incurred by constant wind, such as wind that occurs at times in the Dakotas where it will blow constantly for several weeks at a time. The effect may be the same as that of the purported torture of drops of water dripping at a constant rate for prolonged periods.

anemophobia   Morbid fear of wind or strong drafts. Also known as aerophobia.

anemotropism   Orientation of the body to air currents. See TAXIS, TROPISM.

anencephalic infants   See ANENCEPHALY.

anencephaly   The congenital absence of a brain. May range from complete lack of cerebral hemispheres to the presence of only small masses of cerebral tissue. Anencephalic infants do not live long. Also known as anencephalia.

anergasia   1. Absence of mental activity due to organic brain disease. 2. (A. Meyer) A psychosis or loss of functional activity due to a structural brain disorder.

anergy   Absence of energy, extreme passivity. Also known as anergia. See BURNED-OUT.

anerotic(ism)   Absence of sexual interest or response.

anesthesia   1. A loss or impairment of sensitivity to stimuli due to nerve damage or destruction, narcotic drugs, hypnotic suggestion, or to a conversion disorder. 2. Partial or complete loss of perception, especially pain. Also spelled anaesthesia. See CONVERSION DISORDER, GLOVE ANESTHESIA, HYSTERIA.

anesthetic   1. Agent that produces loss of sensation, unconsciousness, relaxation of skeletal muscles, reduction of motor activity and reflexes, amnesia, or a combination of such effects. 2. Characterized by loss of sensation. See ANESTHETIC GLOVE. 3. Pertaining to a state of anesthesia.

anesthetic glove   Sharply bounded areas of anesthesia that are confined within specific areas, such as those covered by a glove, shoe, or stocking. These areas can be anesthetized through hypnosis to test hypnotizability especially when pain management is the goal. Also known as anesthetic shoe/stocking.

anethopath   A morally uninhibited person.

anethopathy   (B. Karpman) Behavior marked by an absence of ethics or moral inhibitions, accompanied by narcissistic sexual behavior and egocentrism. See ANTISOCIAL PERSONALITY DISORDER.

aneuploidy   Having an irregular number of chromosomes, such as 45 or 49 instead of the normal 46. Frequently associated with neurologic defects, mental retardation, or both. The condition often can be detected before birth through amniocentesis.

angakok   An Eskimo shaman with the ability to enter a trance state and to help tribal members deal with sickness.

angel dust   Slang or street name for phencyclidine (usually abbreviated as PCP), a dissociative drug with some hallucinogenic-like features. See PHENCYCLIDINE.

anger   Reaction of tension and hostility aroused by a wide variety of real or imagined frustrations, hurt, slights, threats, or injustices. May lead to autonomic responses such as increase in blood pressure, respiration, heart rate, perspiration, and increase of blood sugar, all of which serve to put the organism on a "war footing." Anger is ordinarily directed outward. Behavioral reactions may range from avoidance of the cause of the anger to verbal or behavioral violence.

anger and irritability stage   (E. Kübler-Ross) The second stage in Elizabeth Kübler-Ross's process of dying, characterized by a feeling of resentment at having to die. See STAGES OF DYING.

Anger Expression Scale   (C. D. Spielberger) A self-rating scale of 24 items divided into three subscales covering (a) anger toward others, (b) suppressed feelings of anger, and (c) controlled expressions of anger.

anger-in   Hostility turned in, purportedly as a source of depression. See SELF-ACCUSATION.

anger management   Counseling, usually in groups, aimed at helping people deal with anger in constructive ways. People who have demonstrated violent behavior (such as those arrested for domestic violence) are sometimes sent by the judicial system to anger-management centers for retraining. See EMOTIONAL MANAGEMENT, EMOTIONAL STORM.

anginophobia   1. Fear of suffocating. See PNIGOPHOBIA. 2. Fear of having an attack of angina pectoris (constricting pain in the chest, usually caused by coronary disease).

angiotensin   A family of peptides (angiotensin I, II, III) that constrict blood vessels. Causes thirst and the production of aldosterone.

angiotensinogen   A blood protein formed by the liver that the enzyme angiotensinogenase can convert to angiotensin I.

angles of displacement   Angles by which the respective eyes deviate from the direction occupied in the primary position.

angry-woman syndrome A diagnosis of a personality disorder (of men and women, despite its name) marked by obsessive neatness, perfectionism, punctuality, outbursts of unprovoked anger, marital troubles, critical attitude toward others, and a tendency toward drug and alcohol abuse. The patient also may make serious attempts at suicide. See ALCOHOLIC'S WIFE/HUSBAND.

Angst (anxiety, dread—German) (S. Freud, K. Goldstein, S. Kierkegaard) Extreme anxiety about existence; a term used by existentialists to refer to a common human condition of which they assume many are unaware due to denial.

Angstrom unit (Å, Åu, or AU) (A. J. Ångström) A unit of distance equal to 0.1 nm, one ten-thousandth of a micron, one ten-billionth of a meter, $1/100,000,000$ cm. (It is roughly the diameter of an atom.) Usually used in the measurement of light waves. Being supplanted by the nanometer. Named after Swedish physicist Anders Jöns Ångström (1814–1874). Also spelled angstrom, Ångström.

angular gyrus A portion of the cerebral cortex held to be important for comprehension, especially reading. See ALEXIA, DYSLEXIA.

anhedonia Inability to derive pleasure from normally pleasurable experiences; a symptom of depression as well as a sign of schizophrenia. Also known as dystychia.

aniconia An absence of mental imagery; inability to have or to generate mental images.

anililagnia Sexual interest in older women.

anilingus Licking or kissing the anus as a form of sexual activity. Also known as analingus, anilinction, anilinctus.

anima (breath, soul—Latin) 1. The soul. See ANIMUS (meaning 5). 2. (C. G. Jung) The archetype which represents the feminine characteristics of males. See ANIMUS (meaning 4), ARCHETYPE, PERSONA.

animal 1. A living organism that has membranous cell walls, needs oxygen, consumes organic foods, and is capable of voluntary movement. 2. All animal organisms other than humans.

animal aggression Various types of aggression among animals, including: (a) maternal, elicited from a female when offspring are threatened; (b) predatory, observed when prey are sighted; (c) dominance, shown to maintain status or rank; (d) sexual, displayed by a male when trying to find a mate; (e) antipredatory, used for defense of territory; and (f) fear-induced, incited by confinement or threat.

animal-assisted therapy Using pets to help people receive and give affection. Pets can help energize people to activity by the pets' needs for food, water, and attention. Also known as pet-assisted therapy.

animal care and use A set of principles designed to ensure the humane and appropriate treatment of research animals, approved by the American Psychological Association. Principles include: (a) all animals must be lawfully acquired; (b) care shall include humane treatment; (c) avoid unnecessary discomforts; (d) surgical procedures shall be done under appropriate anesthesia and postoperative care of animals must minimize discomfort; and (e) use of animals by students shall be under the supervision of a qualified person. See ANIMAL RIGHTS.

animal care of young The manifestation of parental behavior in animals, usually stimulated by certain hormonal and other physiological changes in the presence of offspring. Influences include the secretion of prolactin which induces broodiness and parental feeding of young and reduced gonadal activity so that reproductive urges are suppressed during care of young.

animal circadian rhythm Daily variations of biological activity and of resulting behavior of animals, such as patterns of sleep.

animal cognition See ANIMAL-HUMAN COMPARISONS, ANIMAL INTELLIGENCE.

animal courtship behavior The varied and sometimes highly unusual actions of different species of animals during the pre-mating period.

animal-cry theory   **bow-wow theory**

animal electricity (S. Hales, J. Walsh, L. Galvani) The electric charges generated by specially adapted organs of some kinds of fish, such as eels, used in localizing prey or obstacles and in attack or defense.

animal fear See AILUROPHOBIA, CYNOPHOBIA, HIPPOPHOBIA, ICHTHYOPHOBIA, TAUROPHOBIA, ZOOPHOBIA.

animal homing Ability of animals to return to their places of origins (as in the case of salmon) or their resting place (as in the case of pigeons).

animal-human comparisons There is a common assumption by many humans that homo sapiens are the most "highly evolved" on the evolutionary scale, in part because there appears to be an enormous difference between humans and the most advanced animals in communication capacity. Some animals may have a dozen or more signals, whereas humans have many thousands of different words that can be assembled in sentences to express highly complex concepts. But for sensitivity to many different stimuli, physical prowess, agility, stamina, etc., many animals are superior to humans. See COMPARATIVE PSYCHOLOGY.

animal hypnosis A "trance" that some animals (for example, rabbits, alligators, sharks) appear to go into when placed on their backs. Also, some animals when in extreme danger may freeze and appear to be unable to escape from present danger (for example, a deer in an automobile's headlights). See CATAPLEXY, DEATH FEIGNING, FREEZING, TONIC IMMOBILITY.

animal intelligence (E. L. Thorndike) Attempts to apply the construct of human intelligence to animals, based on the assumption that the closer the behavior of animals is to that of humans, the higher the animal is on the intellectual scale. In animal research on intelligence, procedures such as delayed responses and alternation problems are frequently used to measure animal intelligence, tasks that presumably have little or no meaning in real life for these animals. There is no accurate measure of animal intelligence.

animalist 1. A hedonist. 2. A person attracted to sexual activity with animals. See BESTIALITY.

animal magnetism (V. Greatrakes, Fr. Hehl, F. A. Mesmer) A hypothetical magnetic fluid which supposedly emanates from the heavenly bodies and pervades the atmosphere. This fluid, Franz Anton Mesmer held, could be focused on ailing parts of the body with curative effect through the use of a magnetized wand, magnetized rods, and magnetized baths. Considered "disproved" in 1840. See BAQUET, HYPNOSIS, TOUCH THERAPY, TOUCHING.

animal mimicry Much imitation-like behavior of young animals may be instinctive behavior that would have occurred regardless of the behavior of others. However, some animals, especially birds, imitate the song of birds of different species. Some birds such as parrots and mynahs mimic sounds made by humans. Apes clearly imitate, and there is increasing evidence that many mammals can learn to imitate or learn through imitation. See COMPARATIVE PSYCHOLOGY, MIMETISM.

animal models The use of animals for the investigation of the effects that drugs or other treatments have on them as a preliminary step in human diagnosis or treatment.

animal mothering See CONTACT COMFORT.

animal phobia Morbid fear of animals in general (zoophobia) or of a particular animal such as snakes (ophidiophobia), cats (ailurophobia), dogs (cynophobia), insects (acarophobia), mice (musophobia), or spiders (arachnephobia).

animal psychology The branch of psychology which investigates animal mind or behavior. See COMPARATIVE PSYCHOLOGY, ETHOLOGY.

animal response (A) In Rorschach test scoring, a respondent's identification of a given part of the stimulus as an animal figure.

animal rights The basic rights of animals to be treated humanely. In psychology, this issue relates to surgery and other painful procedures with living animals, generally for research purposes. There have been numerous protests by animal rights activists about the morality of such procedures. The U.S. federal government established standards for vivisection in 1966, and the American Psychological Association established guidelines for the use of animals in research. See ANIMAL CARE AND USE, VIVISECTION.

animal sexual intercourse 1. Sexual copulation between animals. 2. Sexual intercourse by humans with animals. Sometimes known as sodomy. See BESTIALITY.

animal species cooperation Some animals cooperate, for example, bees; and some animals do not cooperate with others of their kind, for example, tigers. The basic reason appears to be the perpetuation of the species, in that for some animals, such as ants and termites, there is greater chance for individual survival by being part of a larger group, but certain fierce animals such as wolverines fare better alone. A kind of reciprocal altruism exists with certain animals benefiting each other in various ways (for example, a young male Australian songbird assists its parents in feeding new hatchlings). The fighting seen between young animals is primarily training to kill prey. See BEE COMMUNICATION.

animal spirits A vaguely defined substance which Galen in the second century and René Descartes in the 16th pictured as flowing through hollow tubes from the brain to all parts of the body—a precursor of the modern concept of the nerve impulse. Descartes anticipated the modern concept of the peripheral nervous system by maintaining that nerves conduct in either direction between the muscles and sense organs.

animal system (E. Hess) Parts of the nervous system that interact with the outside environment. See VEGETATIVE SYSTEM.

animatism 1. Assigning mental or spiritual qualities to both living and nonliving phenomena. See ANIMISM. 2. A tendency to assign psychological qualities to inanimate objects; personification. A common symptom in schizophrenia. 3. The religious feeling that the reality of existence of all things lies in the supernatural. 4. A tendency to be awed in the presence of nature.

animism (N. S. Bergier, E. B. Tylor) 1. A belief that natural phenomena, such as rivers and clouds, possess souls or spirits. 2. The attribution of soul, spirit, awareness, or consciousness to inanimate objects such as stones or rivers. Seen in young children and as a central concept of some religions of aboriginal people. See ANIMISTIC THINKING, ANTHROPOMORPHISM.

animistic thinking (J. Piaget) A stage in the development of the child's cognitive processes in which friendly or hostile intentions are assigned to inanimate objects such as sticks or stones.

animus (breath, will—Latin) 1. A spirit. 2. An intention to do something. 3. An attitude of hatred, anger, hostility, ill-will. 4. (C. G. Jung) In Jungian analytic psychology, the masculine component of the female personality, an archetype representing the racial experiences of women with men, which are stored in the collective unconscious. Compare ANIMA (meaning 2). 5. The ideal image toward which a human strives.

anion (M. Faraday) A negatively charged ion. See ACTION POTENTIALS, CATIONS.

aniseikonia A difficulty in binocular vision in which the two eyes of a person perceive images of unequal size or shape.

anisocoria Unequal size of eye pupils.

anisometropia Inequality of the refractive power of the two eyes.

anisopia Unequal vision of the eyes.

anisotropy Apparent changes of objects when rotated in space.

ankh Archaic Egyptian symbol of life. Refers to the small door in a larger castle gate, through which individuals must pass one at a time. The term mistranslated as "eye of a needle" in the famous quote attributed to Jesus in reference to the difficulty of the wealthy to go to heaven (Luke 18:25).

ankle clonus A series of rapid calf-muscle contractions and relaxations causing foot tremors.

ankle jerk/reflex The Achilles (tendon) reflex.

ankyloglossia Restricted movement of the tongue due to an abnormal shortness of the membrane on the underside of the tongue (the lingual frenum). Normal speech production may be affected. Commonly known as tonguetie, tongue-tie.

anlage (a beginning arrangement, disposition—German) (C. G. Jung) 1. In psychoanalytic theory, a genetic factor that predisposes a person to a particular personality trait. 2. An individual's hereditary disposition as a whole. See TEMPERAMENT. Plural is anlagen.

Anna O A patient of Joseph Breuer, cured of her neurotic problems by the "talking cure" that eventually led to psychoanalysis. Her real name was Bertha Pappenheim. According to some sources, she created the procedure for her own cure and helped create psychoanalysis. She never had any positive words about the technique.

annihilation anxiety Fear of destroying the self or of being destroyed, sometimes felt by drug users just before or just after taking a heavy dose of a hallucinogenic drug.

anniversary event See ANNIVERSARY EXCITEMENT, ANNIVERSARY REACTION.

anniversary excitement (E. Bleuler) Episodes of elation or mental disturbances that tend to occur on the anniversary of a significant date in the life of the person. See ANNIVERSARY REACTION.

anniversary hypothesis A postulate that the first hospital admission for a mental patient who lost a parent in childhood is likely to occur within a year of the time when the eldest child reaches the age of the patient when the parent died.

anniversary reaction 1. Revival of symptoms, physical or mental, on the anniversary of a disturbing event such as the death of a loved one or of a severe disappointment. 2. A person's expectation that on a certain anniversary, such as the date of the death of a parent, that he or she will also die. See ANNIVERSARY EXCITEMENT.

annoyer 1. Anything that prevents learning. 2. An irritating or unpleasant stimulus which the human participant or animal subject is likely to seek means to terminate. 3. A stimulus that an animal will dislike and avoid.

annulment An attempt to erase disagreeable ideas or events from the conscious mind, whether by self-control or through psychotherapy.

annulospiral ending A type IA sensory nerve the ending of which wraps around the central portion of the muscle spindle and serves as a receptor sensitive to stretch of the muscle.

annunciator 1. In ergonomics, a simplified display, typically in the form of a flashing red "warning" light, a steady green "normal" light, or an orange "caution" light. 2. A sign, usually on a door, to indicate whether entry is allowed.

anodal polarization A condition in which the flow of electrical current is toward the positive pole.

anode (M. Faraday) A positive electrode. Compare CATHODE.

anodimia Lack of olfactory ability. See ANOSMIA.

anodyne A remedy that diminishes pain. Less potent than an anesthetic or narcotic.

anoegenetic (C. E. Spearman) Neither self-evident nor generative of items in the field of cognition. Also known as anoetic.

anoesis A noncognitive consciousness or mere feeling, in which the person lacks knowledge of or reference to objects.

anoetic 1. Lacking capacity for comprehension, as in profound mental retardation. 2. See ANOEGENETIC.

anoetic memory (E. Tulving) A deep level of learning that requires no conscious awareness, such as in riding a bicycle.

anogenital 1. The anatomical region in which the anus and genitalia are located. 2. Refers to the anus and genitalia.

anogenital sex Anal intercourse.

anomaloscope (W. Nagel) An optical instrument for measuring color-vision deficits. Calls for matching one half of a field of color by mixing two other colors.

anomalous color vision (defect) (J. W. Strutt) Color vision characterized by an irregular responsiveness to certain colors; ability to discriminate vivid colors but not poorly saturated ones. Although people with this defect require three-colored lights for spectral vision, as is normal, they demand different proportions to match colors well. Disorders include protanopia, deuteranopia, and tritanopia.

anomalous dichromasy/dichromatism Partial color blindness. See DICHROMATISM.

anomalous differences The differences in the proportion of correct responses when pairs of stimuli are presented to an observer in various time and space orders.

anomalous stimulus A stimulus that provides a sensation, but the stimulus is not the usual or proper one for the sensation (for example, pressure on an eye may result in the person experiencing a flash of light).

anomalous trichromasy/trichromatism 1. Color weakness of red-green. 2. Defective color vision in which more green than typical is required to match yellow with a mixture of red and green (deuteranomalous trichromatism present in 4.9% of males, 0.38% of females) or more red is required (protanomalous trichromatism present in 1.0% of males, 0.02% of females). Those with this sex-linked trait reject matches made by those with normal color vision whereas those with the more severe dichromatism consider them to be close matches. See RAYLEIGH EQUATION.

anomaly 1. In general, anything that is irregular or abnormal, or any deviation from the natural order. See CONGENITAL ANOMALIES. 2. In personality theory, something on the outer fringes of what is considered normal.

anomia 1. See NOMINAL APHASIA (meaning 2). 2. (lawlessness—Latin) Term used by Benjamin Rush for a defective moral sense.

anomic aphasia nominal aphasia (meaning 2)

anomic suicide (E. Durkheim) A type of suicide occurring after an unfavorable change in financial or social situations caused despair about maintaining a former lifestyle.

anomie (E. Durkheim) 1. Social rootlessness. 2. Lawlessness; weakening of social norms, social values, and social cohesion. See ANOMIE SCALE. 3. A personal feeling of not belonging to any social group. 4. A sense of alienation and despair of either an individual or of a whole community, especially during a period of catastrophe such as after a hurricane, war, or depression. Also spelled anomy. See ANOMIC SUICIDE.

anomie scale   Means of evaluating the deviance of an individual from accepted social behavior. Based on responses to questions on such topics as chastity, cheating, bribing, and similar issues. See MORALITY.

anomie theory of crime   (R. Merton) A point of view that people with culturally approved goals of success who cannot achieve them in a normal manner develop innovative (usually criminal) ways of achieving them.

anopia   The congenital absence of one or both eyes, defective vision, blindness.

anopsia   1. Failure to use vision. 2. Upward strabismus. Also spelled anoopsia.

anorexia   (Galen) 1. Absence or loss of appetite. Usually a chronic or continuing condition as opposed to a temporary lack of appetite. See APPETITIVE BEHAVIOR. 2. Loss of appetite as an ongoing state. Can be the result of illness or as a side effect of medicines such as methylphenidate (Ritalin). 3. A shortened term for anorexia nervosa. See ANOREXIA NERVOSA, BULMOREXIA, ELECTIVE ANOREXIA, SOCIAL ANOREXIA.

anorexia nervosa   (W. Gull) Persistent lack of appetite and refusal of food, often accompanied by amenorrhea, vomiting, and severe weight loss. Occurs most frequently in adolescent females. Characteristically, they "feel fat" even when dangerously thin, deny their illness, and some develop disgust for food. Can result in severe malnutrition, semi-starvation, and death. See NEUROTIC HUNGER STRIKE.

anorexiant   1. An appetite suppressant. 2. Anything that leads to diminished appetite or food aversion.

anorexic drugs   Medicines used to reduce the appetite, usually for the treatment of obesity. The earliest of these were of the stimulant type and prone to being abused, and this potential may still be problematical with more current, nonamphetamine formulations. Also known as anorexics. See AMPHETAMINE.

anorgasmy   Inability or unwillingness to experience orgasm. Also known as anorgasmia.

anorthography   agraphia (meaning 2)

anorthopia   A defect of vision in which objects are seen as distorted (for example, straight lines may appear to the patient as crooked).

anorthoscope   A device containing a vertical slit, a drawing moved slowly in front of the slit permits viewers to see successive parts of the drawing.

anorthoscopic visual perception   If an outline drawing is hidden behind an opaque screen that has a narrow vertical slit in it, and if the figure is moved rapidly behind the screen showing only "slices" of the figure, under these conditions, the figure will appear to be foreshortened.

anosmia   (Galen) Lack of olfactory sense. The absence of a sense of smell, which may be general or limited to certain odors. Also known as anosphrasia, anosphresia, olfactory anesthesia, smell blindness. See HYPOSMIA.

anosmia gustatoria   Lack of sense of smell for foods being eaten.

anosognosia   (J. F. Babinski) A form of denial characterized by failure or refusal to recognize the existence of a defect or disease, such as deafness, poor vision, aphasia, disfigurement, or even loss of a limb. See DENIAL.

ANOVA   See ANALYSIS OF VARIANCE.

anoxemia   1. The absence of oxygen in arterial blood. May result in loss of consciousness and brain damage. 2. Former name for hypoxemia.

anoxia   1. Lack of oxygen, especially important during the birth process as it can lead to mental retardation. See CARBON-MONOXIDE POISONING. 2. Former name for hypoxia.

anpsi   (J. P. Rhine) The presumed ability of animals to communicate extrasensorially.

Anschauung   (intuition—German) (I. Kant) 1. Immediate understanding as in sense perception. 2. Intuition, point of view, opinion, contemplation.

ANS   autonomic nervous system

Antabuse   (J. Hald & E. Jacobsen) Trade name for disulfiram, an organic sulfide used in the treatment of alcoholism. See DISULFURAM

antagonist   1. A substance that inhibits another agent by blocking or reducing its functional pathways. Term is often used in neurophysiology to describe certain natural or pharmacological dynamics. See SYNERGISM. 2. In neurochemistry, a substance or medicine that blocks a neuroreceptor in the brain, thus blocking both endogenous and exogenous chemicals from producing an effect. See AGONIST-ANTAGONIST. 3. In psychodrama, a term used to describe the part of anyone who plays the role opposite and against the main player (or protagonist).

antagonist muscles   **antagonist(ic) muscles**

antagonistic colors   See COLOR CIRCLE, COMPLEMENTARY COLORS.

antagonistic cooperation   (W. Sumner) A normally expected condition or conflict that occurs in a competitive society in which groups such as unions cooperate with owners or management but at the same time use their power to derive benefits from that cooperation.

antagonist(ic) muscles   A pair of muscles (or muscle groups) that counteract each other by pulling a structure in opposite directions. Also known as antagonism of muscles.

antagonistic reflexes   A pair of reflexes that terminate in antagonistic muscles.

antagonist-precipitated withdrawal   In substance-abuse treatment, the cessation of a drug's administration plus treatment with an antagonistic drug.

antecedent   A precursor; an event or factor that precedes a situation or outcome and that may be investigated for its effect on that outcome.

antecedent-consequent research   A research strategy of a common type that ordinarily has two or more equated groups measured both at the beginning and at the end of the research. One or more of the groups may be of the control type and one or more of the groups may be of the experimental type. After a period of time, all groups are evaluated to see whether there are differences and of what kind. See BASIC RESEARCH, RESEARCH DESIGNS, RESEARCH TYPES.

antecedent events   Activities preceding emission of a target behavior.

antecedent-to-response analysis The analysis of a brief period of organismic activity as consisting of a sequence. Nearly all behavior theory is based on this pattern.

antedating response 1. A response that occurs earlier than anticipated or scheduled. 2. (C. L. Hull) A response that occurs immediately prior to the main, observable response. See FRACTIONAL ANTEDATING GOAL RESPONSE, HULL'S THEORY.

antenatal **prenatal**

antepartal care Prenatal care.

antepartum Before childbirth. Compare POSTPARTUM.

antergic Exerting force in opposition, applied chiefly to pairs of muscles or muscle-groups which oppose each other in flexing or extending a joint.

anterior 1. First or beginning. 2. Frontal. 3. In front of. In neuroanatomy, especially comparative neuroanatomy, anterior is a directional reference equivalent to ventral (pertaining to the belly, or abdomen side of the body), whereas posterior is equivalent to the dorsal (pertaining to the back, or hind side of the body). See DORSOVENTRAL AXIS. 4. In relation to embryos, the head end. See ANTERIOR-POSTERIOR AXIS, ANTERIOR-POSTERIOR (DEVELOPMENT) GRADIENT. Essentially, in discussing bipeds (animals walking on two-legs), such as human adults, the anterior is the belly side, whereas in discussing embryos and quadrupeds (animals walking on all fours), such as cats and dogs, the anterior refers to the head-end and posterior to the tail-end. To avoid confusion, the term cephalocaudal (head-to-tail) may be used. See CEPHALOCAUDAL, CEPHALOCAUDAL DEVELOPMENT.

anterior commissure A bundle of white fibers in the brain connecting parts of the two cerebral hemispheres, containing fibers of the olfactory tract.

anterior horns The ventral portion of the grey matter in the spinal cord.

anterior pituitary The larger of the two lobes of the pituitary gland, sometimes identified as the adenohypophysis. It secretes hormones affecting body growth, ovaries, mammary glands, and the pancreas, adrenal cortex, and thyroid glands. See ADENOHYPOPHYSIS.

anterior-posterior (development) gradient Rapid growth of the head region as contrasted with lower areas of the body during fetal development. See CEPHALOCAUDAL DEVELOPMENT, CEPHALOCAUDAL SEQUENCE.

anterior-posterior axis In bipeds (humans or other upright species), "front to back," a straight line from the belly or ventral side to the back or dorsal side. In this case also known as ventrodorsal. In quadrupeds, from "head to tail," top to bottom or vice versa. See DORSOVENTRAL.

anterograde 1. Moving forward. Compare ANTEGRADE. 2. Since a particular moment in time, as in amnesia.

anterograde amnesia The loss of memory for events after the psychological or physical trauma that produced the amnesia (for example, a boxer receives a blow to the head and does not remember finishing the fight). Also known as ecmnesia. See RETROGRADE AMNESIA.

anterograde degeneration See WALLERIAN DEGENERATION.

anterophobia 1. Fear of society. 2. Morbid fear of people, of other humans. Sometimes known as androphobia, homophobia.

anthropocentrism Literally, human-centered. The assumption that everything can be evaluated in light of its relationship to humans.

anthropogenesis **anthropogeny**

anthropogenic disturbance The negative effect of humans on animals due to their "invasion" of animals' native territories by encroachments of various kinds such as farming, lumbering, and hiking, that affects the animals' reproductive abilities.

anthropogeny Presumed steps in the evolution of humans from earlier species, particularly hominoids. Also known as anthropogenesis, anthropogony. See EVOLUTION.

anthropoid Human-like. Pertaining to or resembling a human. Term is usually applied to the great apes: gibbon, gorilla, orangutan, and chimpanzee.

anthropology The study of humans (a) from the point of view of their origin, evolution, and adaptation to a changing environment (physical anthropology); (b) from the point of view of the development of their customs, beliefs, and institutions (cultural/social anthropology).

anthropometry 1. The branch of anthropology that studies comparative measurements of the human body. 2. The science of body measurements, with emphasis on ethnic, sexual, cultural and other variables, championed by Francis Galton. 3. The measurement of human bodies for various purposes, such as the Bertillon system formerly used for the identification of criminal suspects or for proper fitting of shoes and garments. 4. In ergonomics, designing equipment for optimal physical fit—by a moving operator (dynamic anthropometry) or a nonmoving one (static anthropometry).

anthropomorphism (H. Moore) 1. The attribution of human characteristics to nonhuman entities such as gods, animals, plants, or inanimate objects. See ANIMISM, THERIOMORPHISM. 2. In comparative psychology, the tendency to interpret the behavior and mental processes of nonhumans in terms of human abilities. In the 19th century, those using this approach were called anthropomorphs. 3. As used by some radical behaviorists, the attribution of any vague or ill-defined characteristic to any human or animal, for example, sad, humorous, wanting. See OPERATIONAL DEFINITION.

anthropomorphizing Attributing emotions or human-like characteristics, such as selfishness, to animals (for example, perceiving dogs as dependable and affectionate). See ANTHROPOPATHY.

anthropomorphs See ANTHROPOMORPHISM (meaning 2).

anthroponomy 1. The study of laws involved in the development of human society and the relation of humans to their environment. 2. (W. Hunter) The investigation of human behavior. Hunter's proposed term to replace psychology never became widely used.

anthropopathy Attributing human sentiments to nonhumans, especially to spiritual entities. See ANTHROPOMORPHIZING.

anthropophobia   1. Fear of people or of human qualities. See ANDROPHOBIA, GYNEPHOBIA, HOMOPHOBIA. 2. Fear of people or human companionship. Also known as phobanthropy.

anthropos   (C. G. Jung) The archetype of the primal human.

anthroposcopy   The practice of judging the body build of an individual by mere inspection, as distinguished from the use of anthropometric techniques of body measurement.

anthrotype   The human phenotype or biological type. See BIOTYPOLOGY.

anti-analytic procedures   In psychoanalytic theory, measures that reduce or block the capacity for insight and understanding by interfering with thinking, remembering, and judging (for example, the administration of certain drugs, facile reassurance, and the assumption by the analyst of the role of a past figure such as a loving parent to make the patient feel better).

antiandrogens   Substances that are antagonistic to androgens.

antiandrogen therapy   Medical treatment directed toward correcting the effects of excessive levels of male sex hormones.

antiandrogenic agent   A substance that reduces the physiological effects of androgenic hormones on tissues normally responsive to the hormones (for example, the female sex hormone estrogen and the synthetic steroid drug cyproterone).

antianxiety drugs/medications   Medicines used to treat generalized anxiety, panic disorders, and acute stress reactions. Also known as anxiolytics, minor tranquilizers, and, in the 1950s, simply tranquilizers. Meprobamate, hydroxyzine, and benzodiazepines have been used for this purpose.

antibody (Ab)   A protein produced in the body to combat antigens.

anticathexis   (S. Freud) 1. In psychoanalysis, shifting of the emotional component of an impulse or action to its opposite; for example, hatred is expressed as love. Also known as counterinvestment. 2. Energy the ego must expend to maintain repression or block the entrance of id derivatives into consciousness. Compare COUNTERCATHEXIS.

anticholinergic   1. Refers to a given medication or substance acting as an antagonist to acetylcholine. 2. In psychiatry, a drug's anticholinergic effects tend to include constipation, dry mouth, difficulties in accommodating visual focus (that is, changing easily from distant to near vision), and difficulty urinating.

anticipation   Appearance before the appointed time.

anticipation error   In serial learning studies, making a response before it is due. Also known as anticipatory error. See ANTICIPATORY REACTION/RESPONSE.

anticipation learning method   Testing rote learning by permitting the scoring of successes and failures throughout the memorization, while providing a running record of the progress. The method, presenting a list of items appearing consecutively in the aperture of a memory drum, is appropriate to either serial memorization or paired-associates learning, whereby the participant learns to anticipate a stimulus item or respond to it with the response item next to appear. See MEMORY DRUM for an example of such an apparatus.

anticipation method   1. Research procedure mostly used in memory studies, wherein a person attempts to predict what will come next of something memorized such as a list of words. 2. A verbal-learning method in which the participant is given the correct answer (prompted) after hesitation or error. Success may be measured by the number of prompts needed to master the material. Also known as prompting method.

anticipatory aggression   Hostile behavior toward another who appears to be a threat, for example, a dog barking at someone passing by its fenced yard is protecting its territory.

anticipatory anxiety   Fear of having a panic attack, often becoming agoraphobia.

anticipatory autocastration   A psychoanalytic explanation for feminine behavior in males as an unconscious symbolic self-castration intended to reduce the fear of actual castration.

anticipatory belief   An expectation of the occurrence of some event whether reasonable such as "Tomorrow the sun will rise" or far-fetched such as "Tomorrow I will win the lottery."

anticipatory grief   Initiating the grieving process before a grave personal loss.

anticipatory guidance   Counseling and educational services provided to individuals or families before they reach a turning point in their lives, as in parental guidance before a child enters school, or counseling of an employee nearing retirement.

anticipatory maturation principle   See PRINCIPLE OF ANTICIPATORY MATURATION.

anticipatory mourning   A series of adaptive processes experienced by survivors during a fatal illness (especially of a child), including acknowledgment of the inevitability of death. See GRIEF.

anticipatory movements   The slight movements that occur when waiting to react to an expected stimulus, such as the prior reactions of runners while waiting for the sound of the starting pistol.

anticipatory reaction/response   1. Any response in research prior to the expected one. 2. A "jumping the gun" response that occurs before the appropriate stimulus.

anticipatory regret   A common feeling after making an important decision, that a mistake has been made, and consequences may be suffered sometime in the future.

anticipatory schema   (U. Neisser) A cognitive cyclic process considered part of perception. It concerns a type of set based on expectations due to prior experiences of outcomes. Behavior therefore is affected by the perceptions, leading to a particular type that is based on the reality and the expectation (for example, given two separate motorists with car trouble, one may stop the car and walk to find help; the other may continue to drive, hoping to get to a service station before the car breaks down).

anti-confirmationism   (T. S. Kuhn) A point of view that proving a hypothesis has little meaning, but disconfirming a hypothesis can be meaningful. See FABILISM.

anticonformity   1. Rejecting the standards of society in general, but accepting the standards of a particular group within that society. 2. In social psychology, behavior that contradicts group standards, specifically behavior motivated by a rebellious need to challenge the power of the group. Compare CONFORMITY.

anticonvulsant drugs/medications   Medicines that act to prevent epileptic seizures or convulsions. Certain members of this class of drugs have come to be called "mood stabilizers" because they have been found to reduce the irritability of the central nervous system and thus be effective in countering mania, reducing the mood-swings of bipolar disorder, and reducing other types of irritability. Also known as anepileptics, anticonvulsants, antiepileptics. See MOOD-STABILIZING DRUGS.

antidepressant drugs/medications   Medicines used originally to relieve depression, but now also used for a wide range of disorders, from hyperactivity and enuresis in children to panic disorder, obsessive-compulsive disorder, and bulimia in teenagers and adults. Common types of antidepressant are the serotonin reuptake inhibitors (SSRIs), while tricyclic antidepressants (TCAs) and monoamine oxidase inhibitors (MAOIs) are also widely used. Also known as antidepressants, antidepressive drugs.

antidiuretic hormone (ADH)   A hormone secreted by the posterior pituitary gland to promote water conservation by the kidney. Helps maintain fluid homeostasis in the body and in the individual cells. Also known as vasopressin.

antidromic activation of nerve impulses   Refers to the conduction of nerve impulses from the distal part of a nerve fiber to the nerve cell body. This is not a normal direction of conduction of the nerve impulse which is orthodromic, that is, from the cell body to the end of the nerve fiber. Compare ORTHODROMIC ACTIVATION OF NERVE IMPULSES.

antidromic phenomenon   The artificially produced passage of a nerve impulse in a reversed direction (from axon to dendrite) rather than the usual way in a neuron, for experimental purposes.

antiepileptics   Rare term for anticonvulsant drugs.

antiestrogens   Substances that are antagonistic to estrogens.

antifetishism   (M. Hirschfeld) A characteristic tendency of latent gay men or lesbians to find aversions to the physical features of members of the opposite sex, as an unconscious protection against recognition of their true sexual interests.

antigen (Ag)   Any agent capable of inducing the production of antibodies in an organism and of reacting with the antibodies. Also known as allergen, immunogen.

antigen-antibody reactions   A part of a natural defense mechanism of the body tissues of humans and animals against the introduction of a foreign substance into the host tissues. The antibody is a protein molecule produced by white cells in the bloodstream with the specific role of neutralizing the foreign substance, which becomes the antigen.

Antigone complex   (B. B. Wolman) The nonsexual love and sacrifice of a person's own life for the sake of a loved person. See ALTRUISM.

anti-intoxicant   See AMETHYSTIC.

anti-intraception   Personality trait marked by denial of the subjective element in life, including the rejection of imaginative, artistic, emotional, and intellectual experiences. This trait has been identified as associated with an authoritarian personality. See AUTHORITARIANISM.

antilibidinal ego   (W. R. Fairbairn) The portion of the ego structure similar to Sigmund Freud's superego in Fairbairn's object-relations theory. Considered to develop out of the unitary ego present at birth when the infantile libidinal ego (similar to the id) experiences deprivation and frustration at the hands of the parent.

antimanic drugs/medicines   Rare name for various medicines used to reduce the symptom of mania or manic-depressive (bipolar) disorder. Also known as antimanics. See LITHIUM.

antimotivational syndrome   A behavior pattern associated with chronic use of cannabis characterized by lethargy, lack of ambition or drive to achieve. Concept is based on observations of the lifestyles of chronic cannabis users in various cultures around the world. See CANNABIS-RELATED DISORDERS, MARIJUANA.

anti-Müllerian hormone   A peptide secreted by fetal testes. Inhibits the development of the Müllerian system, which would otherwise become female internal genitals.

antinodal behavior   The period of quietude that follows nodal peaks of aggressive, disorderly, or excessively active behavior. Compare NODAL BEHAVIOR.

antinode   In therapy, a period of relaxation following a period of tension. See ANTINODAL BEHAVIOR, NODAL BEHAVIOR.

antinomy   In logic, an essential contradiction between two valid inferences, for example, "It was the best of times; it was the worst of times."

antiparkinsonian drugs   Medicines used originally in the treatment of Parkinson's Syndrome but more often to reduce the extrapyramidal symptoms which are side effects of the neuroleptic medicines, especially when used in higher doses or in the higher potency forms.

antipathy   A social attitude characterized by antagonism toward some other individual or groups of individuals. See PREJUDICE.

antipraxia   Antagonistic processes or symptoms.

antipsychiatry   A movement of both mental health professionals and concerned lay persons, beginning in the mid-1960s and continuing, to counter coercion in psychiatric care, especially the practice of involuntary hospitalization, as well as what has been seen as possibly oppressive practices (such as electroconvulsive therapy and the widespread use of medicines). One of the more articulate critics has been Thomas Szasz, who questioned the very idea of mental illness as a social construct. Another early and prominent figure in England was R. D. Laing, who noted that mental illness may be an expression of a dysfunctional family and culture. Also spelled anti-psychiatry.

antipsychotic drugs/medicines   A class of medicines designed to treat the symptoms of psychosis, primarily schizophrenia. Also known as antipsychotics, ataractics, and neuroleptics, as well as major tranquilizers (in contrast to the minor tranquilizers or antianxiety drugs).

antireward system   The administration of a nonrewarding response for an unsatisfactory effort.

anti-Semitism   (W. Marr) Prejudice against Jewish people as a group, frequently expressed in terms of (a) a distorted, unflattering picture of "Jewish" traits; (b) acts of discrimination and persecution; and (c) use of this minority group as a scapegoat for personal frustrations and aggressive drives and the ills of society. A phrase coined by Wilhelm Marr in Germany as a euphemism for *Judenhass* (Jew-hating), based on "semite" from Shem, Noah's son. See PREJUDICE, SCAPEGOATING, STEREOTYPE.

antisocial   1. Opposed to society or to existing social organization and moral codes. Compare ASOCIAL. 2. Being reluctant to meet with people. Reasons may include excessive shyness, feelings of inferiority, or fear of others.

antisocial aggression   Any aggressive act that has socially destructive or undesirable consequences. See AGGRESSION. Compare PROSOCIAL AGGRESSION.

antisocial behavior   Aggressive, impulsive, and sometimes violent actions that flout social and ethical codes such as laws and regulations relating to personal and property rights. See ACTIVE AGGRESSIVE REACTION TYPE, ANTISOCIAL BEHAVIOR TYPE, DELINQUENCY, PROSOCIAL BEHAVIOR.

antisocial compulsion   An irresistible impulse to commit antisocial acts such as stealing. See ANTISOCIAL BEHAVIOR, CONCEALED ANTISOCIAL ACTIVITY, KLEPTOMANIA, PSYCHOPATHY.

antisocial reaction   1. A response marked by lack of responsibility, poor judgment, absence of moral values, inability to learn from experience, or unwillingness to postpone gratifications. 2. Formerly called constitutional psychopath, constitutional psychopathic inferior, psychopathic personality. The disorder was renamed antisocial-personality disorder. See SOCIOPATHY.

antisocial-personality disorder   A diagnosis of a personality disorder characterized by chronic and continuous antisocial or delinquent behavior not due to severe mental retardation, schizophrenia, or manic episodes. This behavior pattern, more common in males than females, starts before age 15 with conduct disorders including lying, stealing, fighting, cruelty, truancy, vandalism, theft, forceful sex, drunkenness, or substance abuse. See DELINQUENCY, PSYCHOPATHIC PERSONALITY, SOCIOPATHIC PERSONALITY.

antispasmodic drugs   Substances that alleviate spasms. See ANTICONVULSANT DRUGS.

antisuggestion   A method of manipulating or influencing a person toward a behavior, by implying that the person should not behave, or is not capable of behaving, in such a manner (for example, by telling a child "You are too young to clean up that mess all by yourself," with the expectation that a child will do just that). Often used by parents to get children to conform. See CONTRASUGGESTIBILITY, LEANING TOWER OF PISA CONCEPT, PARADOXICAL INTERVENTION, REACTANCE THEORY, REVERSE PSYCHOLOGY.

antithesis   1. The dual nature of mind and body. 2. (E. Berne) A counteraction to a transactional game. Example: A child claims to have a headache and refuses to go to school. The parent, assuming that the child is malingering to avoid going to school, tells the child to stay in the bedroom during school hours. See GAMES PEOPLE PLAY, TRANSACTIONAL ANALYSIS.

antithetical behavior   Behavior at opposite ends of any continuum, such as simultaneously laughing and crying, being aggressive and submissive.

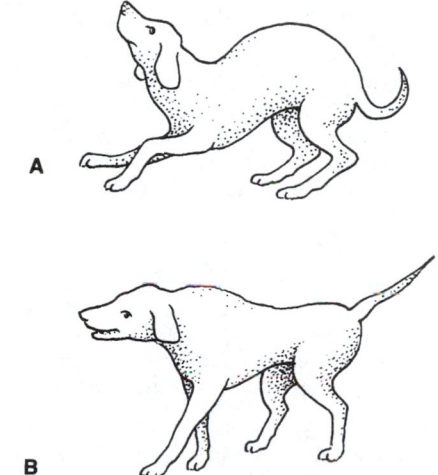

antithetical behavior   In A, a dog is submissive and in B, it is aggressive.

antlophobia   Morbid fear of floods.

Anton's symptom   1. Reduced mental and physical abilities due to brain damage. Unawareness of self or place resulting from brain damage in addition to a general reduction of mental and physical capacities. 2. (G. Anton) A disorder marked by a patient's denial of blindness despite clinical evidence of the loss of vision. May occur in cases of either complete or incomplete blindness. Patients usually confabulate an explanation for the inability to see, claiming it is night or there are no lights in the room. Also known as Anton-Babinski syndrome, denial visual hallucination syndrome, hemiasomatognosia. Named after German neuropsychiatrist Gabriel Anton (1858–1933). See ANOSOGNOSIA, BABINSKI'S SYNDROME, DENIAL, HYSTERICAL BLINDNESS.

antonym test   The type of task in which the participant must identify the opposite of each word in a given series.

antsy   Slang for nervous, impatient, or fidgety.

anuloma   The affiliation of a man with a woman judged socially inferior. See HYPERGAMY.

anuptaphobia   Fear of staying unmarried.

anvil (bone)   A nontechnical name for incus. See EAR.

anxiety   A pervasive and unpleasant feeling of tension, dread, apprehension, and impending disaster. Whereas fear is a response to a clear and present danger, anxiety often is a response to an undefined or unknown threat which may stem from internal conflicts, feelings of insecurity, or forbidden impulses. In both, fear and anxiety, the body mobilizes itself to meet the threat, and muscles become tense, breathing is faster, and the heart beats more rapidly. Types of anxiety include: ACUTE, ANNIHILATION, BASIC, CASTRATION, CASTRATION-THREAT, CATASTROPHIC, CHRONIC, DEATH, DEPRESSIVE, DISCOMFORT, DISEASE, EGO, ELEMENTARY, EMPTY NEST, EROTIC, EROTIZED, EXAMINATION, EXISTENTIAL, FAINTING, FREE-FLOATING, HETEROSEXUAL, ID, INSTINCTUAL, MANIFEST, MORAL, MULTIDIMENSIONAL, NEUROTIC, OBJECTIVE, ORAL, ORGANIC, PAN-, PANIC, PERFORMANCE, PHOBIC, PRIMAL, PRIMARY, REAL, REALITY, SEPARATION, SIGNAL, SOCIAL, STATE, STRANGER, SUPEREGO, TRAIT, TRAUMATIC, TRUE, URETHRAL, VIRGINAL. See ANXIETY VS NEUROSIS.

anxiety attack   A sudden eruption of acute anxiety, which starts with heart pounding, breathing difficulty, excessive perspiration, and dizziness, and in many cases mounts to a full-scale panic in which the patient experiences unbearable tension, fear of suffocation, and a feeling of impending disaster or death. See PANIC ATTACK.

anxiety discharge   Any dread-reducing activity associated with normal daily functions, engaged in repetitive activity for the purpose of suppression of anxiety (for example, a constant cleaning of the house or a wringing of the hands). See COMPULSION, FLIGHT INTO REALITY.

anxiety disorders   A group of disorders in which unpleasant feelings of stress, uneasiness, tension, and worry is either the predominant disturbance or is experienced in confronting a dreaded object or situation, or in resisting obsessions or compulsions. See PHOBIA.

anxiety disorders of childhood and adolescence   A general category of mental disorders seen in children and adolescents in which anxiety is the predominant feature. This category includes: AVOIDANT DISORDER OF CHILDHOOD AND ADOLESCENCE, OVERANXIOUS DISORDER, SEPARATION-ANXIETY DISORDER.

anxiety disturbance   A condition marked by a high level of apprehension and tension, with extreme sensitivity, self-consciousness, and morbid fears.

anxiety equivalent   A neo-psychoanalytic phrase for the physiological reactions due to anxiety but without any subjective feelings of anxiety, for example, profuse sweating but feeling calm and relaxed.

anxiety fixation   The continuation of a feeling of general uneasiness, dread, and tension from one developmental stage to another.

anxiety hierarchy   (J. Wolpe) A list of objects or events that arouse a particular person's uneasiness or dread, ordered according to the degree to which each is tension- or anxiety-provoking. Such hierarchies are constructed for use in desensitization treatments in which the desensitization process proceeds from the least threatening situation and progresses up the hierarchy. See BEHAVIOR THERAPY, COUNTERCONDITIONING, DESENSITIZATION.

anxiety hysteria   (S. Freud) A neurosis in which the dread or uneasiness generated by unconscious conflicts is expressed in phobic symptoms such as an irrational fear of dirt or open spaces, and in physical disturbances known as conversion symptoms. See ANXIETY STATE, CONVERSION DISORDER, PHOBIC DISORDERS.

anxiety matching hypothesis   A postulate that cognitive intervention will be most effective for people with problematic levels of cognitive anxiety, whereas somatic intervention approaches are more effective for those with troublesome levels of somatic anxiety.

anxiety neurosis   Feelings of impending disaster accompanied by such symptoms as difficulty in making decisions, insomnia, loss of appetite, and heart palpitations. Chronic feelings of this kind may occasionally erupt into an acute panic attack. See ACTUAL NEUROSIS, GENERALIZED-ANXIETY DISORDER, OBSESSIVE-COMPULSIVE DISORDER, PANIC DISORDER.

anxiety nightmares   Dreams of danger, embarrassment, failure that usually occur near the end of the sleep period.

anxiety object   Something that represents the original source of fear or tension (for example, a statue resembling a domineering parent). See LITTLE HANS.

anxiety preparedness   The increased state of alertness and motor tension that normally accompanies fear or anxiety.

anxiety reaction   A neurotic disorder characterized by persistent morbid dread with frequent acute attacks of uneasiness.

anxiety-relief responses   In behavior therapy, the use and often repetition of reassuring or relaxing words by self or others (such as "stay calm," "it will pass," "It's OK") in tension-provoking situations. See DESENSITIZATION.

anxiety resolution   Processes that uncover the unconscious roots of a problem so that they can be understood and mastered.

anxiety scale   A test designed to measure manifest anxiety as opposed to assessing hidden sources or effects. See ANXIETY HIERARCHY, BECK'S DEPRESSION INVENTORY, PERFORMANCE ANXIETY.

anxiety state   (S. Freud) Obsolete phrase for a traumatic neurosis precipitated by a war-time experience in which the ego-ideals of war conflict with customary ideals. See ACTUAL NEUROSIS.

anxiety states   See ANXIETY NEUROSIS.

anxiety tolerance   Ability to cope with a high level of anxiety, not display it, and still function relatively normally.

anxiety vs neurosis A neurosis is a general condition of maladjustment; anxiety is one class of neurosis. A person who is neurotic tends to be anxious, often about appearance or performance. *The Diagnostic and Statistical Manual of Mental Disorders* (DSM) has eliminated anxiety and neurosis as nosological categories.

anxiolytic Anxiety reducing. See ANTIANXIETY DRUGS.

anxious depression A form of depression characterized by a high anxiety level.

anxious expectation A sense of apprehension experienced in novel, unexpected, or unusual situations.

anxious intropunitiveness A complex or symptom pattern that consists of self-blame, apprehensiveness, self-depreciation, guilt, remorse, suicidal ideas, morbid fears, and ideas of sinfulness. See NEED FOR PUNISHMENT, SELF-BLAMING DEPRESSION.

AOA American Orthopsychiatric Association

A obj In Rorschach test scoring, a symbol for animal object.

AP 1. action potential. 2. advanced placement. See ADVANCED PLACEMENT EXAMINATIONS.

AP5 2-amino-5-phosphonopentanoate, a drug that blocks NMDA receptors.

APA 1. American Psychiatric Association. 2. American Psychological Association.

APA format The desired format and outline of articles in the various journals published by the American Psychological Association.

apallic syndrome A long period of disturbed consciousness that may follow a head injury, possibly marked by mutism, akinesia, disorders of reflexes, and muscle contractions.

apandria A feeling of aversion toward the male gender.

apareunia Abstinence from or inability to engage in coitus.

apartness The vague feeling of belonging to a vast mass (the human race) without close identification with or ties to any individual or group. See ALIENATION, ANOMIE.

apastia A symptom of a mental disorder manifested by refusing to eat. See ANOREXIA.

apathetic withdrawal A retreat from society with loss of interest and initiative.

apathy The absence of emotional response, or affect, and indifference to surroundings; a common symptom in severe depression and schizophrenia.

apathy syndrome The pattern of emotional insulation (indifference, detachment) adopted by some victims of catastrophes (for example, prisoners-of-war) in an effort to maintain their stability.

apeirophobia Morbid fear of infinity or of endlessness.

A% In Rorschach test scoring, a symbol for percentage of animal responses.

aperiodic reinforcement Irregular, intermittent, or unpredictable rewards intended to achieve desired behaviors.

aperiodic wave A complex wave consisting of various irregular amplitudes and frequencies: The result is known as noise. See NOISE.

apersonal Not relating to any specific individual, such as an event that affects all people.

Apert's syndrome A form of craniosynostosis characterized by acromegaly, eyes spaced far apart, webbed fingers, mental retardation. Named after French pediatrician Eugène C. Apert (1868–1940).

apertural hypothesis A postulate that the psychological representations of the primary instinctual functions center on the apertures of organs that serve primary instincts (mouth, anus, urethra, and vagina). Holds that the phase of a woman's hormonal cycle can be predicted from the analysis of her dreams and fantasies.

aperture color A film color seen in holes or spaces in neutral screens.

apex Uppermost point. Plural is apices.

Apgar scale (V. Apgar) Ratings of newborn infants on five factors (color, respiration, heartbeat, reflexes, muscle tone). Tests are administered one minute and five minutes after birth to assess the degree of physical normality and the ability of the infant to survive independently. Each factor is scored 0, 1, or 2, with a maximum total of ten points. Infants with low scores at five minutes usually have neurologic damage and uncertain survivability.

aphagia 1. A lack of appetite. 2. See DYSPHAGIA. 3. Starvation occurring despite availability of food. See ANOREXIA.

aphanisis 1. Loss of sexuality. 2. (E. Jones) Total extinction of the capacity for sexual enjoyment, the fear of which was assumed by Ernest Jones to be at the root of all neuroses. See ORGASM.

aphasia (J. B. Bouillaud, P. Broca, A. Trousseau, K. Wernicke) The loss or impairment of the ability to understand or express language due to brain injury or disease. Impaired ability to understand words, signs, or gestures is termed sensory, impressive, or receptive aphasia. Impaired ability to speak, write, or make meaningful gestures is termed motor or expressive aphasia. Major causes of the cerebral damage are stroke, brain tumor, encephalitis, and head trauma. Also known as alogia, anepia, logagnosia, logamnesia, logasthenia. Other types of aphasia include: ACALCULIA, ACATAPHASIA, ACOUSTIC-MNESTIC, AFFERENT MOTOR, AMIMIA, AMNESTIC, AMUSIA, ASYMBOLIA, AUDITORY, BROCA'S, CENTRAL, COMBINED TRANSCORTICAL, CONDUCTION, CONGENITAL, DEVELOPMENTAL DYSPHASIA, EFFERENT MOTOR, EXPRESSIVE, ECHOLALIA, MOTOR, RECEPTIVE, SEMANTIC, SENSORIMOTOR, SYNTACTICAL, TRANSCORTICAL, WERNICKE'S, WORD SALAD. See ALEXIA, ANOMIA, DYSPHASIA, EXAMINING FOR APHASIA.

aphemia (P. Broca) The loss of speech ability, usually due to a central nervous system lesion or an emotional disorder. The person knows what to say but cannot say it. Also known as *aphemie* (French). See HYSTERICAL MUTISM.

aphemia pathematic Obsolete name for loss of speech due to fright.

aphemia plastica Obsolete name for voluntary mutism.

aphémie   Paul Broca's term for motor aphasia, the concept was renamed aphasia by Armand Trousseau.

aphephobia   An abnormal fear of being touched.

aphia   The sense of touch.

aphilophrenia   Fear of being unloved.

aphonia   Loss of voice due to organic defect or emotional disorder. Also known as anaudia, aphony. See AKINETIC MUTISM, APHEMIA, APHEMIA PATHEMATIC, APHEMIA PLASTICA, MUTISM.

aphoria   (P. Janet) A condition of general weakness that cannot be improved with changes of diet, exercise, or medication. See AMYOSTHENIA, AMYOTONY.

aphrasia   1. Inability to speak. 2. Inability to understand phrases, even though individual words in the phrases may be used or understood.

aphrodisia   1. A state of sexual excitement. 2. Excessive sexual desire.

aphrodisiac   A substance (for example, oysters, powdered rhinoceros horn) purported to increase sexual desire, performance, pleasure, or all three. Research indicates that such effects may be attributed to placebo or novelty effects. Compare ANAPHRODISIAC.

aphthongia   A spasm of vocal muscles that may affect verbal communication (especially public speaking). May be a variety of occupational neurosis analogous to writers' cramp.

apiphobia   Fear of bees. Also known as melissophobia.

apistia   Marital infidelity.

aplasia   The arrested development or failure of an organ or body tissue to grow. Also known as aplasy.

aplestia   Extreme greediness.

Aplysia   Genus of gastropods used in laboratory studies of neurons. The abdominal ganglion of *Aplysia depilans* contains neurons used in single-cell-conditioning research.

apn(o)ea   1. The temporary cessation of breathing, as in catching a breath. 2. Temporary suspension of respiration during sleep. See SLEEP APNEA, SUDDEN INFANT DEATH SYNDROME.

apocarteresis   Self-destruction by deliberate starvation. See ANOREXIA NERVOSA, NEUROTIC HUNGER STRIKE.

apocleisis   Absence of a desire for food or aversion toward food. See ANOREXIA, APASTIA.

apocrine gland   A gland in the armpit that produces an odor when stimulated by sex hormones. See PHEROMONES.

apodysophilia   Being sexually aroused by exhibitionism.

apoenzyme   The protein component of an enzyme. A second component, a coenzyme, is required to make the enzyme functional.

apolar cell   A nerve cell which lacks processes or projections from the nucleus.

Apollonian attitude   1. Descriptive of a person who emphasizes the intellect rather than the emotions. 2. (F. Nietzsche) A state of mind that is well-ordered, rational, clearly defined, and harmonious (from Apollo, Greco-Roman god of male beauty and wisdom). Compare DIONYSIAN ATTITUDE.

apomorphine   A chemical that first blocks dopamine autoreceptors, then blocks postsynaptic receptors.

apopathetic behavior   Actions influenced by the presence of others although not directed toward them, as in boasting about exploits or showing off.

apoplectic type   (Hippocrates) A body type characterized by a heavyset, rotund physique which roughly corresponds to Ernst Kretschmer's pyknic body type and William Sheldon's endomorphic (body) type. Also known as *habitus apoplecticus*.

apoplexy   1. Obsolete term for a stroke due to intracerebral hemorrhage. 2. A stroke due to cerebral thrombosis. See STROKE.

aporia   1. Doubt, anxiety, uneasiness. 2. Pathological doubt about the self deriving from incompatible views on the same topic. 3. A Greek term, used in rhetoric, to indicate doubt, uncertainty about the best way to proceed. See ABULIA, INFERIORITY FEELINGS.

aposematic   Having conspicuous coloration that advertises unpleasant taste or danger, mainly in invertebrates and their mimics as a warning to would-be predators.

aposognosia   (T. Feinberg) Personal confabulation that is not under the person's control, due to brain impairment.

a posteriori   (from what comes after—Latin) Reasoning from observed facts. See A PRIORI.

a posteriori fallacy   Coming to incorrect conclusions about X causing Y because Y follows X. Both X and Y may come from a common other cause, or the sequence may be temporary. One of many traps that researchers must guard against before coming to conclusions. See POST HOC ERGO PROPER HOC.

apostilb   The luminance measure equal to 0.3183 candela per square meter or 0.1 millilambert.

Apostle to the idiots   Edouard Seguin's appellation because of his advocacy of the welfare of persons with mental retardation.

apotemnophilia   Being sexually aroused by being or fantasizing being an amputee.

apparatus   1. A collection of instruments used for one purpose. 2. One instrument composed of several parts. 3. A group of physiological and anatomical structures involved in the performance of some function. See SYSTEM.

apparatus test   An examination that calls for the participant to construct something or in some other way to manipulate physical objects, for example, screwing nuts onto bolts or stacking blocks. Usually a vocational aptitude test. See PERFORMANCE TEST, WIGGLY BLOCK TEST.

apparent   1. Obvious. See entries beginning with MANIFEST. 2. Appearing or seeming to be. See entries beginning with PSEUDO-.

apparent distance   The subjective distance of an object in comparison to the real, objectively measured physical distance.

apparent magnitude   The perceived size of an object as projected at a set distance from the participant.

apparent motion/movement　　The illusion of movement when stationary stimuli are exposed in brief succession as in "moving pictures." Also known as phi-phenomenon. See ALPHA APPARENT, ALPHA MOTION, BETA MOVEMENT, DELTA MOVEMENT, GAMMA MOVEMENT.

apparition　　1. A visual illusion that results from distortion of a perceived object, often interpreted as threatening. 2. A visual hallucination or illusion, especially when considered to be of a supernatural nature. See GHOST IMAGES, ILLUSION.

appeal　　An effort to arouse a sympathetic response from an individual or group, such as an appeal for blood donations for a dying child.

appeal to ignorance　　In logic, a fallacy based on the argument that something is true because it has not been proven false. Or, that something is not false because it has not been proven to be true, for example, since it is not proven that a faith healer cannot cure cancer, it is assumed the faith healer can do so. Also known as *ad ignorantium* (Latin).

appeasement behavior　　The actions of one organism to a similar organism to communicate that the former acknowledges the superiority of the latter and wants no quarrel with it (for example, two dogs meet, one rolls on its back, communicating to the other dog that it means it no harm). Humans show appeasement behavior in a variety of ways, such as smiling in a friendly manner, and looking down to avoid eye contact with the expected possible aggressor. See ALPHA MALE, HOOK ORDER, PECKING ORDER, SOCIAL HIERARCHY.

appeasers　　1. People who try hard to please others and to avoid giving offense. 2. A descriptive term for parents who avoid exercising authority and avoid confrontation and conflict with their children. 3. (N. Kefir) One of four basic lifestyles characterized by trying to please others and avoid conflict. See MAJOR PRIORITIES, PLEASERS.

apperception　　(G. W. Leibniz) 1. A clear and vivid perception. 2. Awareness of the meaning and significance of a particular sensory stimulus as modified by experiences, knowledge, thoughts, and emotions. 3. The full apprehension of a concept.

apperceptive mass　　(J. Herbart) A group of present ideas, influential in determining what new ideas shall gain admission to consciousness and in what way new objects shall be perceived.

apperceptive visual agnosia　　Inability to perceive objects despite relatively normal visual acuity.

appersonation　　A delusion in which the patient identifies with another person and assumes that person's characteristics. Also known as appersonification.

appestat　　1. The mechanism in the brain that controls appetite and food intake. See SET WEIGHT. 2. A common term among bariatricians (medical experts on dieting) for the ventral medial nucleus of the hypothalamus. Also known as appetitive center. See LOCAL STIMULUS THEORY, VENTROMEDIAL NUCLEUS OF THE HYPOTHALAMUS.

appetence　　A strong desire, a craving.

appetite　　Urge, desire, or bodily need, especially for food, water, sex, and air. Can be specific or general.

appetite control　　The process of increasing or decreasing the rate of food intake by an organism. See ANOREXIA, APPETITE SUPPRESSANT, SELF-SELECTION OF DIET, TONICS.

appetite suppressant　　Any drug or combination of drugs used in the treatment of obesity. See APPETITE CONTROL.

appetition　　A longing for something.

appetitive behavior　　Feeding activity that may be excessive, adequate, or deficient. See APPETITIVE CENTER, VENTROMEDIAL NUCLEUS.

appetitive center　　An area of the hypothalamus. Lesions of the ventromedial nucleus of the hypothalamus result in voracious eating whereas lesions of the lateral hypothalamic nuclei cause anorexia. The ventromedial nucleus has classically been regarded as the satiety center. Also known as appestat. See APPETITIVE BEHAVIOR, SET POINT, VENTROMEDIAL NUCLEUS (OF THE HYPOTHALAMUS).

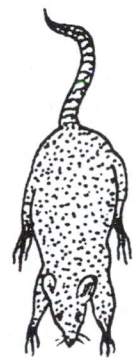

appetitive center

appetitive conditioning　　Respondent conditioning in which the conditioned response is a kind of "seeking," behavior, such as salivation.

applied behavior analysis　　Behavior therapy closely tied to B.F. Skinner's philosophy of radical behaviorism. Stresses observable behavior rather than private events and uses single-subject research designs to determine the relationship between behavior and its antecedents and consequences.

applied linguistics　　Any approach, theoretical or practical, that assists individuals or groups to communicate more satisfactorily.

applied psychoanalysis　　The application of psychoanalytic principles to areas beyond clinical practice, such as to the study of art, religion, anthropology, biography, history, philology, and philosophy.

applied psychology　　The application of the theories, principles, and techniques of psychology to practical problems: political campaigns, consumer affairs, industry, human engineering, education, advertising, military affairs, vocational guidance, and environmental issues.

applied research　　1. The solving of a practical question by objective means rather than by opinions, experiences, or theory. 2. Research designed to solve practical problems rather than to answer theoretical questions. Compare PURE RESEARCH.

applied science　　Research aimed at finding practical applications. Compare PURE SCIENCE.

applied sport psychologist   A sport psychologist who applies principles of psychology to sport settings to enhance the psychological well-being, health, and performance of athletes. See SPORT PSYCHOLOGY.

apport   The alleged supernatural transport of an object from one place to another by poltergeists (spirits) or during a seance. It has been noted that apport tends to occur in families where there are young males.

appraisal   1. An evaluation, often quickly achieved, of the value or extent or character of anything. 2. (M. Arnold) A subjective judgment of other people that usually begins at first meetings and may be modified over time (for example, a person makes a good first impression, but additional exposure to that person results in the opinion of that person changing completely). 3. (R. S. Lazarus) A subjective evaluation, based on both goals and beliefs and environmental factors, of the implications of an encounter for a person's well-being.

apprehension   1. Act or process of becoming aware of presented facts or objects. 2. The formation of a judgment or conclusion. 3. Knowing immediately the essential character of experiences.

apprehension of experience law   law of apprehension of experience

apprehension span   The number of items that a person can perceive in a given time period, for example, the number of dots a person can recall after being shown dots on a screen for one-tenth of a second. See ATTENTION SPAN.

apprehension-span test   A test designed to measure the amount or complexity of perceptual material which a participant is able to grasp at a single brief presentation. Example: A photograph of a number of items is shown briefly to a group, and immediately thereafter each person is asked to list the names of items seen. See APPREHENSION SPAN.

apprehensive expectation   Worry. See GENERALIZED-ANXIETY DISORDER.

apprehensive subjects   Research participants who, often because of coercion to volunteer, approach the study with misgivings.

apprehensiveness   A relatively mild form of anxiety and uneasiness, especially about what might happen in the future.

apprentice complex   A behavior pattern in which a child expresses a desire to follow a parent into a vocational field and is willing to serve as an apprentice to that parent.

approach   1. A technique or method. 2. Refers to how interpersonal relationships are negotiated.

approach-approach conflict   (K. Lewin) A type of conflict situation characterized by a choice between two desirable but incompatible goals. As with students attracted to two divergent career paths or a woman courted by two suitors, this can be a difficult conflict to resolve because of two desirable but conflicting goals. Also known as double-approach conflict, positive-positive conflict.   See APPROACH-AVOIDANCE CONFLICT, AVOIDANCE-AVOIDANCE CONFLICT.

approach-avoidance conflict   (K. Lewin) A type of conflict situation characterized by strong attraction and strong repulsion toward the same goal, such as when a highly desirable job requires long separation from family. Also known as positive-negative conflict. See APPROACH-APPROACH CONFLICT, AVOIDANCE-AVOIDANCE CONFLICT, DOUBLE APPROACH-AVOIDANCE CONFLICT.

approach gradient   Graduated variation in the strength of a drive as an organism approaches its goal. Examples: (a) The nearer a hungry animal gets to a goal such as food, the more motivated it becomes to reach the goal; the stronger it will pull or the faster it will run. (b) Two people agree to get married. As the date for the marriage approaches, one person experiences greater eagerness (positive approach gradient) for the day to arrive, while the other person suffers from misgivings (negative approach gradient). See GOAL GRADIENT for an illustration of example (a).

approaching response   A response characterized by extending a limb (such as an arm) or moving toward the stimulus or situation that induced the activity.

appropriate affect   A feeling-tone in harmony with the accompanying thought, reaction, or verbal expression.

appropriate death   (A. Weismann) The kind of death a person would choose for him- or herself if that were possible, given that the moment of death would not be negotiable.

appropriate maturity   Ability to deal effectively and resiliently with physical and social environmental factors, and to perform biological, social, cognitive tasks at the appropriate age level.

approximation   1. In general, an approach toward, or a close representation of something. 2. In speech and language disorders, the bringing together of the vocal cords.

approximation conditioning   See BEHAVIOR SHAPING, SUCCESSIVE-APPROXIMATION CONDITIONING.

approximation method   See METHOD OF SUCCESSIVE APPROXIMATIONS.

appurtenance   Gestalt term for interaction or mutual influence between parts of a perceptual field.

apractagnosia   Impaired ability to organize movements in space, to remember such movements, or to analyze spatial relationships. Also spelled apractognosia. Sometimes known as spatial apractagnosia.

apragmatism   Indifference to reality or results, mainly concerned with theory, process, or dogmatic belief. Compare PRAGMATISM.

apraxia   (H. Jackson, H. C. Liepmann) 1. A disorder characterized by difficulty or inability to carry out voluntary or purposeful movements. Types of apraxia include: AKINETIC, AMNESTIC, CONSTRUCTIONAL, DYNAMIC, LEFT-SIDED, MOTOR. See APHASIA. 2. A memory disorder, due to brain injury, characterized by inability to remember the performance of skilled movements such as driving a car, getting dressed, or playing baseball. Types of apraxia include: CONSTRUCTIONAL, DRESSING, IDEATIONAL, IDEOKINETIC, IDEOMOTOR. See APRAXIA OF GAIT. 3. Inability to use an object even though the object can be named and its proper uses described. Also known as object blindness. See AGNOSIA, MOTOR APRAXIA.

apraxia of gait Impairment or loss of ability to walk due to lesions in the motor cortex but not involving sensory impairment or paralysis.

apraxic dysarthria Inability to articulate clearly due to spasticity, paralysis, or lack of coordination of the muscles in speaking. See APRAXIA.

a prime The set complement to A or all elements not in A.

a priori (from what comes before—Latin) An adverbial statement that appears to be valid independent of observation or experience (for example, "Two Xs are more than one X.").

a priori method (C. S. Peirce) In research, researchers depending on their own judgments about various elements involved in the research study; accepting their own judgments as valid without need for hard proof.

a priorism A concept that inherent in the formation of the zygote (union of sperm and egg) the new human has potentiality for ideas such as the concept of fairness. This concept differs from John Locke's tabula rasa point of view that humans come into the world with a "blank slate" and learn from experience. See EMPIRICISM, INNATE IDEAS.

a priori test validity An examination that appears to the designer and to users to measure what it intends to measure without research on its validity (for example, a typing test). Most personality type tests offered by mass media are of this type but have unknown empirical validity. See FACE VALIDITY.

a priori theory of probability Ability to state in advance the probability of certain events (for example, that all fourth-grade classes will do better than first-grade classes on the same test of vocabulary in the same school).

a priori validity That which appears valid on its face, not to be questioned. Historically, many assumptions that appeared to be true, such as that the sun circles the earth, were later found to be untrue. See FACE VALIDITY.

aprosexia Loss of the ability to maintain fixed attention, due to a brain lesion or psychiatric disorder, for example, productive mania or marked depression. May be selective for certain subject areas.

aprosody Inability to express oneself in a nuanced, modulated, appropriately emotional way.

APS 1. American Psychological Society. 2. American Pain Society. 3. American Psychosomatic Society.

APsaA See AMERICAN PSYCHOANALYTIC ASSOCIATION.

apsychia Obsolete term for loss of consciousness.

apsychognosia A lack of consciousness about self-behavior or personality, such as an alcoholic's lack of awareness of behavioral inappropriateness and attitudes of others toward the behavior.

aptitude 1. The capacity to acquire competence or skill through training. A specific aptitude is a potential in a particular area, such as mathematical aptitude, whereas a general aptitude is potential in a number of varied fields. 2. (J. B. Carroll) In a relatively narrow sense, any cognitive ability that is possibly predictive of certain kinds of future learning success. See APTITUDE BATTERIES, APTITUDE TESTS.

aptitude batteries/tests A collection of tests of various kinds each considered to be able to predict some future ability, used mainly for vocational counseling or selection of candidates for various kinds of training or programs. Usually such batteries contain mechanical aptitude and clerical aptitude tests. See APTITUDE, TESTS.

AQ 1. accomplishment quotient 2. achievement quotient (also abbreviated **A.Q.**).

Aqua-energetics (P. Bindrim) A system of group psychotherapy involving transformations in a body-temperature pool that allegedly facilitates regression depending on highly emotional sessions with group support.

aquaphobia Morbid fear of water, especially bathing or swimming. Also known as bathing fear. See HYDROPHOBIA.

aqueduct of Sylvius The canal that connects the third and fourth ventricles of the brain.

aqueous (humor) A watery substance between the cornea and the iris of the eye.

Arabic system Rare phrase for the decimal number system.

arachne(o)phobia Morbid fear of spiders. Also spelled arachnaphobia, arachnophobia.

arachnoid 1. A delicate membrane that overlies the pia mater, situated intermediate between the pia mater (next to the brain) and the dura mater (next to the skull). 2. The middle layer of the meningeal membranes covering the surface of the brain and spinal cord. Identified by strands of tissue that resemble spider webs. The meningeal membranes closely follow all of the various contours of the brain and spinal cord.

arachnoid granulation Projections of the arachnoid membrane through the dura mater into the superior sagittal sinus, through which cerebrospinal fluid (CSF) flows.

ARAS ascending reticular activating system

arbitrary constant An assigned quantity that remains fixed for a particular statistical analysis.

arbitrary inference (A. T. Beck) Drawing conclusions without supporting evidence, or even in spite of contrary evidence.

arbitrary origin (o) Any selected point from which all scale values are expressed as deviations; often the midpoint of a class interval.

arbitrary response In Rorschach testing, a response that does not appear to the examiner to relate to the blot or that portion of the block indicated. Such responses may be based (a) on the intention of the participant to fake replies, (b) either extreme youth, as in the case of 3- or 4-year olds, or mental retardation in older participants, or (c) a serious mental disorder.

arbitrary sequence task In testing infant memory, performing two acts that have no direct logical relation to each other, as in an examiner placing a bottle in a box, then putting bottle and box near an infant to determine whether the infant will imitate the examiner's behavior.

arbitrary symbols 1. In general, any term or pictograph or number intended to represent something else. Thus, + means "plus." 2. In language, an arbitrary symbol intended to represent a phoneme re-pronunciation. Thus, the letter "a" indicates that the sound is pronounced as in "that" whereas the symbol "ä" indicates the sound in "father" whereas "â" is to be pronounced as in "late." See PHONEME.

arbitrary weight In statistics, assigning a weight to a factor, usually for convenience in computation.

arbitration A method of settling disputes in which an arbitrator listens to assertions by contending sides and then renders a judgment, agreed in advance to be accepted by both parties. See MEDIATION.

arc de cercle (circular arc—French) A rigid arching of the body concavely or convexly. In psychiatry, the condition has been interpreted as a conversion symptom; Sigmund Freud interpreted this behavior as an invitation to sexual relations.

archaeopsychic See ADULT-EGO STATE, EXTERO-PSYCHIC.

archaic 1. Ancient. 2. In Jungian psychology, refers to the ancestral inheritance of mental processes.

archaic brain The brain structures included in the archipallium (allocortex) containing only 3 cell layers, and the paleopallium or mesocortex, containing 4 or 5 cell layers. The archipallium and paleocortex are present in the human brain and complemented by the neocortex (neopallium), or higher brain areas.

archaic inheritance/residue In Carl Jung's analytic psychology, remnants of inherited primitive mentality in the form of symbolic function-engrams imprinted on the racial unconscious.

archaic thought A type of thinking observed in schizophrenia dominated by concreteness, and lacking abstractness or reasoning.

archaism (C. G. Jung) The unconscious memories purported to be inherited from the prehistoric past as influences on the modern psyche.

arches of Corti Arch-like structures of the internal ear, formed by the fusion of the inner and outer rods of Corti at their upper ends.

archetypal image (C. G. Jung) A theoretical structural component of the mind which derives from the accumulated experience of humankind. These inherited components are stored in the collective unconscious and serve as a frame of reference with which humans view their world, and also serve as one of the major foundations on which the structure of the personality is built. Sometimes known as archetype, archetypical image. See ANIMA, ANIMUS, ANTHROPOS, IMAGO, DEMON, HERO, PERSONA, PHILOSOPHER KING, PRIMORDIAL IMAGE, PUER AETERNUS, REBIRTH, VIRGIN BIRTH.

archetype 1. A primitive or original plan from which others have evolved. 2. In Jungian psychology, manifestation of the collective unconscious in a given symbol or image. See ARCHETYPAL IMAGE.

archetype as such (C. G. Jung) The content of the collective unconscious, the psychological counterpart of instinct; inherited formal property of the human brain to experience typical figures, situations, or behavior patterns. See ARCHETYPAL IMAGE.

archicortex The oldest or most primitive cortical derivative, it includes the hippocampus and dentate gyrus. Sometimes known as archipallium. See ALLOCORTEX, CORTEX CEREBRI.

archipallium (T. Meynert) The original or primitive part of the pallium (the entire cerebral cortex), evolving earlier than the neocortex. Term is generally synonymous with the olfactory cortex, Rudolf von Koelliker's rhinencephalon, or the Vogt's allocortex. See ARCHICORTEX.

architectonic Orderly or systematic, as applied to the arrangement of evidence, etc., in treating a science, or to the hierarchy of principles in some specific branch of science or in nature itself. See CYTOARCHITECTURE.

architectural barriers Building or environmental features that hamper the mobility and functioning of persons with disabilities. The phrase also is applied to designs that hamper persons who lack normal mobility because of pregnancy, childhood, physical size, or old-age frailty. See BARRIER-FREE ENVIRONMENT.

architectural determinism A concept that building design affects behavior, for example, some building designs induce the possibility of people meeting with others, such as private homes with front porches.

architectural psychology The branch of psychology that studies the effects buildings have on behavior; the design of buildings using behavioral principles. See ENVIRONMENTAL PSYCHOLOGY.

archival method The examination of personal papers and official documents for any of a variety of purposes, such as to learn more about a single individual, about a family or group, or historical era. See RESEARCH.

archival records Documents that may be used as unobtrusive measures for a variety of purposes (for example, ticket stubs from various sporting events are counted to determine the preferences of spectators).

archival research 1. The use of books, documents, manuscripts, and other records or cultural artifacts in scientific research. 2. The analysis of records for a variety of purposes including industrial productivity, personality analysis, past research scores, and suicide rates. Records may include school grades, past test scores, old letters, and public documents. 3. The generation or analysis of artifacts usually for understanding individual or group behavior. Examples include: (a) counting the number and kinds of alcoholic drinks bought at a hotel bar to know what kinds of alcoholic beverages to buy in the future; (b) D. C. McClelland's studies relating need achievement in a society to its productivity; (c) research relating increases in suicide rate to a publicized suicide.

arcsin transformation A nonlinear transformation that converts proportions or percentages into corresponding angle values in degrees of arc varying from 0° to 90°. It is often best to transform proportions into angles by: $X' = 2 \arcsin \sqrt{X}$, where X is expressed as a proportion. An arcsin transformation is one of many possible angular transformations. Sometimes known as inverse sine transformation.

Arctic hysteria A culture-specific syndrome occurring among the natives of Northern Siberia, characterized by a high degree of suggestibility and a tendency to imitate the movements and actions of other people. Also known as *amurakh*. See COPYING MANIA.

arcuate nucleus (F. Arnold) 1. A nucleus of the hypothalamus associated with the dorsal part of the median eminence. It functions with the median eminence in control of releasing factors which regulate the adenohypophysis. 2. A cluster of neuron cell bodies located on the anterior surface of the pyramids of the medulla. It is an extension of the pontine nuclei, receives input from the neocortex, and sends output to the cerebellum.

areal Part of a surface, as of an organism, or a zone (as of the cerebral cortex).

area of Wernicke An area of fibers identified by Karl Wernicke as the cortical center for understanding language, forming the extreme posterior segment of the internal capsule, found on the left side in a right-handed person.

area sampling A method of selecting persons for interviews in public-opinion research, in which a specific neighborhood, street, or house is designated in advance as the source of interviewees. Sometimes known as block sampling. See SAMPLING, SURVEY METHODS.

area under the normal curve In fitting a curve to a histogram, it may be assumed that the normal curve has a finite area measurably the same as the area of the histogram to which it was fitted. The area under the entire curve is represented as 1.00, and any portion of it may be indicated in percentage terms.

areal brain stimulation Activation of an extended portion of a sense organ as a means of determining effects on behavior. See BRAIN RESEARCH, BRAIN STIMULATION.

areflexia An absence of reflexes. Absence of a particular reflex indicates a lesion or disease affecting the associated neural pathway.

argot A restricted language used by special groups such as criminals, physicians, lawyers, and psychologists where many common terms have idiosyncratic meanings.

argument In logic, a group of propositions in which the conclusion follows from the premises.

argument against the person See AD HOMINEM.

argumentation In a discussion, explaining a position by giving reasons to show how the conclusion was obtained.

argumentativeness Contentiousness. A persistent urge to dispute and argue.

Argyll-Robertson pupil (D. Argyll-Robertson) A pupil that does not contract when light is shone into the eye, a sign of brain damage often associated with syphilitic and other forms of paralysis.

Arica (O. Ichazo) A system of exercises, verbal and physical, intended to develop the whole person, emotionally, mentally, and physically. The procedures include chanting of mantras, meditation, and dancing.

Aricept Trade name for donepezil.

aristocracy theory A point of view that the social rank of some animals and humans is to some extent determined by their parents' ranks. See PECKING ORDER.

aristogenic Obsolete term referring to persons presumed to be best suited eugenically for parenthood.

Aristogenics Old name for eugenics.

Aristotelian (K. Lewin) A prescientific mode of thinking characterized by the reliance on authorities, sometimes from antiquity. Mistakenly attributed to Aristotle.

Aristotelian method A technique of discovery that employs deductive reasoning, and depends upon deduction as a means of discovering facts.

Aristotle's illusion (Aristotle) The tactile perception that a single object (such as the edge of a ruler) is two objects when touched simultaneously with the crossed index and middle fingers, usually done with eyes closed.

arithmetic disability Rare phrase for a disturbance or deficiency in calculation and reasoning usually associated with neurological impairment.

arithmetic disorder Marked impairment in mathematical skills, characterized by an attitude of dislike and distaste for mathematics, usually noted by inferior performance in grade school arithmetic and later in higher mathematics. Causes may include being forced to perform what may appear to be meaningless tasks before a person is capable of understanding their importance. Also, some people may be easily distracted or careless and do not wish to submit to the rigors of being careful and exact. See DEVELOPMENTAL ARITHMETIC DISORDER.

arithmetic mean (M or X̄) One of several common measure of central tendency of a set of scores obtained by summing the scores then dividing by the number of scores. The deviations of the scores from it sum to zero, allowing it to be considered the balance point of the distribution. Also known as arithmetic average.

arithmetic scale A scale that progresses by simple units, such as 1, 2, 3 or 50, 100, 150 as opposed to logarithmic or geometric scales.

arithmomania A persistent, uncontrollable impulse to count, such as counting the pickets in fences or the steps in stairways—an obsessive-compulsive symptom.

ARM advertising response modeling

armamentarium Materials available to an examiner, such as a variety of tests, standardized and projective.

arm-chair psychology (E. W. Scripture) A general phrase (usually derogatory) for any psychological doctrine not founded upon research or other factual grounds.

Armed Services Vocational Aptitude Battery (ASVAB) A vocational aptitude test used by the American military to help classify inductees.

armor-defended (B. Neugarten) A personality type of late adulthood characterized as either holding on or constricted. Armor-defended people are achievement-oriented, striving, and tightly controlled.

armoring (W. Reich) The body manifestation of a person preparing to resist changes; the total expression of holding back in an individual. Characterized by pulled back shoulders, pulled up thorax, rigidly held chin, shallow respiration, arched lower back, a retracted and "dead" pelvis, and stiffly stretched out legs.

Army Alpha (Intelligence) Test Verbal intelligence examinations used during World War I (1917–1918) for job placement in the Army. Used in combination with the Army Beta (Intelligence) Test. Also known as Alpha examination/test. See ARMY TESTS.

Army Beta (Intelligence) Test See ARMY ALPHA (INTELLIGENCE) TEST, ARMY TESTS.

Army General Classification Test (AGCT)   A group intelligence test developed in World War II to classify inductees according to their ability to learn military duties. Three subtests (vocabulary, arithmetic, block-counting) measure verbal comprehension, quantitative reasoning, and spatial perception. See ARMY TESTS, INTELLIGENCE.

Army tests   Group intelligence tests for classifying inductees, developed during World War I. The Alpha test measured information, reasoning, and ability to follow directions; the Beta test presented nonverbal problems to illiterate and non-English-speaking participants. Also known as Army Alpha, Army Beta, World War I Army Tests. See INTELLIGENCE TESTS.

AromaScan   See ELECTRONIC NOSES.

aromatherapy   1. Inhalation of various scents that purportedly improve physical health, psychological health, or both. 2. (J. Valnet) A type of herbalism that uses aromatic oils of plants that are inhaled, stated to reduce stress and to improve alertness. According to aromatherapists, certain fragrant oils such as substances from flowers and fruit skins, whether inhaled or rubbed on the skin, can have salutary physical and mental consequences, for example, a study indicated that the aroma of vanilla reduced feelings of claustrophobia. Also spelled aroma therapy. See UNCONVENTIONAL THERAPIES.

aromatic   1. A quality of olfactory sensation, of which the odor of nutmeg and anise are typical examples. 2. One of Zwaardemaker's nine classes of odors exemplified by camphor, nutmeg, lemon, anise, and almond. Not equivalent to Hans Henning's spicy class of odors. See HENNING ODOR SYSTEM, STEREOCHEMICAL SMELL THEORY, ZWAARDEMAKER'S ODOR CLASSIFICATION.

around the world   Slang for the sexual licking of a partner's total body. See ALLOPREENING, FOREPLAY.

arousal   A state of alertness or activation.

arousal boost   The measurable increase in the arousal level of a participant or animal subject as a result of a stimulus.

arousal boost-jag   In psychological esthetics, the feeling of pleasure and reward that may accompany activation of both arousal-boost and arousal-reduction mechanisms in succession. The individual experiences a moderate rise in arousal followed by a drop in arousal. See AROUSAL-BOOST MECHANISM, AROUSAL-REDUCTION MECHANISM.

arousal-boost mechanism   (D. E. Berlyne) Any stimulus pattern of responses produced by visual or other contact with a stimulus (such as a work of art) that produces a measurable hedonic or pleasure effect. Berlyne measured the effects using various psychological tests as a participant viewed a selection of paintings by various masters. See AROUSAL BOOST, AROUSAL-REDUCTION MECHANISM.

arousal detection   Discerning of increased arousal by measuring physiological signs such as brain-wave activity, skin-temperature changes, increased heart rate or blood pressure, or galvanic skin response. Arousal signs are associated with environmental factors, such as heat, humidity, crowding, and noise, that may heighten performance or induce aggressive behavior. See AROUSAL, AROUSAL THEORY.

arousal jag   The excitation provided by gambling, sports activities, or adventurous challenges, whether real or imagined. Many individuals appear to have a need or desire for such a jag which may be satisfied by active participation in challenges or vicariously by reading, watching others, seeing films, etc.

arousal level   The extent to which an organism is alert to environmental stimuli.

arousal phase   The excitement phase in the sexual-response cycle.

arousal-reduction mechanism   Any stimulus or inhibitory reaction that decreases the degree of arousal of an individual especially after arousal has reached an uncomfortably high level. D. E. Berlyne proposed that a sharp increase in arousal can have unpleasant or aversive effects, but an arousal-reduction mechanism can produce hedonic value by lowering the arousal curve. See AROUSAL-BOOST MECHANISM, CONCINNITY.

arousal syndrome   Being susceptible to sympathetic nervous system arousal by even minor stimuli.

arousal system   A diffuse network of nerve cells extending from the medulla oblongata through the thalamus, involving organs controlled by both the central nervous system and the autonomic nervous system. The reticular core mediates cortical arousal. Since a well-functioning arousal system keeps the cerebral cortex at a highly alert level, it plays a large role in the intensity level of a drive or motivation. See RETICULAR ACTIVATING SYSTEM.

arousal theory   In environmental psychology, a point of view that arousal increases when personal space is diminished. When personal space becomes inadequate for containment, the level of arousal may become excessive. At that point, arousal may be expressed as aggressive behavior. See AROUSAL, AROUSAL DETECTION.

ARP tests   (J. P. Guilford) Measures of divergent thinking from the Aptitudes Research Project at the University of Southern California. Test items include: (a) word fluency, writing a series of words containing a specified letter; (b) originality, writing titles for short-story plots; (c) associational fluency, writing words similar in meaning to a given word; (c) expressional fluency, writing sentences containing words beginning with given letters; and (d) listing different consequences of a hypothetical situation. See CREATIVITY TESTS, DIVERGENT THINKING, INTELLIGENCE, TORRANCE TESTS OF CREATIVE THINKING.

arpeggio paradox   (G. Humphrey) A tendency for people conditioned to respond to a particular tone, to not respond when that tone is one of a series of tones (as in an arpeggio).

arranged marriage   A marriage negotiated by the partners' parents or group elders. If contracted when the partners are children, "consummation" takes place at puberty or adulthood.

array   A distribution of the measures or scores within any one row or column of a correlation table.

arrectores pilorum   Ribbon-like bundles of smooth muscles connected with the sheaths of hair follicles. Contraction of the muscles causes erection of the hair, "goose-flesh," and a slight discharge of the sebaceous glands. See PILOMOTOR RESPONSE for an illustration of these muscles in action.

arrest   1. To stop. 2. An interference with.

arrested testis   A testis that lies within the inguinal canal but is unable to descend into the scrotum because the normal passage is blocked. Also known as undescended testicle. See CRYPTORCHIDISM.

arrest of development   Cessation of growth of any or all mental of physical faculties.

arrest reaction   The response to stimulation of an inhibitory nerve circuit in an anesthetized animal. The animal may freeze in its tracks as it might when surprised or frightened. See DEATH FEIGNING.

arrhythmia   1. Lack of rhythm. 2. Any deviation from the normal rhythm. 3. An irregularity of the rhythm of the heart beat.

arrhythmokinesis   Inability to perform voluntary movement in a rhythmic pattern, or to maintain a rhythmic sequence of movements.

arteriosclerotic brain disorder   An organic disorder caused by constriction, hardening, or blocking of the cerebral arteries, which reduces the blood flow to the brain, resulting in damage to neural tissue and loss of mental functions. See BRAIN DAMAGE, MULTIINFARCT DEMENTIA.

Arthur Point Scale of Performance Tests   (G. Arthur) The 1930 Form I was a restandardization of 7 historic tests from the Pintner-Paterson (Knox Cube Test, Seguin Formboard, Healy Pictorial Completion I, Casuist Form Board, Mare and Foal Picture Board, Manikin Test, Feature Profile Test) with the Porteus Maze Test and Kohs Block Design Test added. The performance approach to intelligence measurement started around age 6, with instructions mostly by pantomime that made it particularly applicable to the physically handicapped, foreign-born, and—with form II—the deaf. The Two Figure Formboard (form I) and Gwyn Triangle Test (form II) were used for practice. Glueck's Ship Test and the Five-Figure Formboard were part of the original Form II. The 1947 revised Form II retained the Knox, Seguin, Healy Pictorial Completion II, and Porteus Mazes with the newly developed Arthur Stencil Design Test replacing the Kohs Block Design. Also known as Arthur Point Scale.

article nine   Slang for an American federal law permitting drug users convicted of a criminal offense to be sent to a narcotic treatment facility.

articular sensation   A sensation due to excitation of the receptors in or near the joint surfaces by the rubbing or pressure of one bony surface upon another.

articulate speech   Oral language that is meaningful and intelligible.

articulation   1. In speech, utterance, enunciation, or a sound (particularly of a consonant). 2. An aspect of a gestalt based on its characteristic structure (for example, an equilateral triangle is a more simply articulated figure than an irregular triangle and a consonant chord has a simpler articulation than a dissonant one). 3. In anatomy, a joint, usually movable.

articulation disorder   Difficulty in the uttering of words. See DEVELOPMENTAL ARTICULATION DISORDER.

articulation index   1. The relative frequency with which the different sounds of speech occur in speech and the various positions in which they occur within words. 2. A measure of the clarity and purity of sound, such as speech, as obtained by means of acoustical instruments or the judgments of voice experts.

articulation test   The phonetic analysis and recording of the speech of an individual with faulty sound production according to criteria such as developmental sequence, correct placement of the articulators, and intelligibility.

articulatory control process   In memory, a process assumed to control subvocal rehearsal. See PHONOLOGICAL LOOP, WORKING MEMORY.

articulatory suppression   In learning theory, a task in which the participant, during the presentation of a list, is required to say an irrelevant item out loud and continuously. This should prevent a suffix effect because the articulatory suppression should remove any contribution from the precategorical acoustic store. See PRECATEGORICAL ACOUSTIC STORE, SUFFIX EFFECT.

artifact   1. Any person-made object but particularly a product of "primitive" art or craftsmanship. 2. In psychological research, a misleading signal or an erroneous observation. May refer to static, to noise, to electrical interference. 3. In research, an extraneous influence which may threaten validity, usually construct validity.

artificial abortion   **induced abortion**

artificial disorders   See FACTITIOUS DISORDERS.

artificial dream   A dream that appears to be initiated by sensory stimulation, such as dreaming of being caught in a rainstorm when a sprinkler is turned on while the person is sleeping.

artificial hymen   Surgical restoration of the hymen, usually in cultures where bridal virginity is highly valued.

artificial insemination (AI)   The use of medical or surgical techniques to achieve conception by implanting male spermatozoa in the reproductive tract of a female. Often used when the male's sperm count is too low to permit normal pregnancy. Also known as eutelegenesis.

artificial intelligence (AI)   1. The attempted duplication of human thinking by machines. 2. (J. McCarthy) The abstract science of human, animal, and machine cognition in the expectation that it will lead to a unified theory of cognition. 3. (J. McCarthy, A. Newell, H. A. Simon) The art and science of constructing nonliving systems, usually computing systems, that exhibit intelligence (or would be so described if they were thought to be human), and of studying their behavior. See TURING TEST.

artificialism   1. Precausal thinking in which either God or humans are regarded as the maker of all natural things. 2. (J. Piaget) A tendency of children to attribute to individuals the power to control certain natural events such as rain and weather.

artificial neurosis   A state of accumulated tension and anxiety that is produced in an animal during an experiment. Symptoms include stereotyped behavior, compulsivity, disorganized responses, extreme emotional display, and emotional apathy. See EXPERIMENTAL NEUROSIS.

artificial penis See CONSTRUCTED PENIS, DILDO, SEX-CHANGE.

artificial selection The selection of plants or animals that have certain desired characters, and crossing or breeding them, with the aim of changing or enhancing these characters in their offspring.

artificial somnambulism Phrase formerly applied to certain phases of hypnosis, because hypnotized people sometimes manifest behavior resembling that of a sleep-walker.

arts and crafts Creative activities directed by recreational or occupational therapists in rehabilitation programs often including painting, weaving, woodworking, and leatherworking. See ART THERAPY.

art tests Examinations designed to identify special abilities required for painting, architecture, and other arts, to assess creativity in the arts, or to evaluate art productions. Varied techniques are used such as comparing the participant's judgment of pictures with that of experts, reproducing an object from memory, and identifying errors in a drawing.

art therapy The use of artistic activities such as painting, drawing, finger painting, sculpting, and clay-modeling in psychotherapy and rehabilitation to assist individuals in understanding themselves. These activities offer patients a nonthreatening emotional release, a means of restoring confidence and self-esteem, an opportunity for nonverbal communication and expression, and a means of reestablishing social relationships. See ARTS AND CRAFTS, CREATIVITY TESTS, DANCE THERAPY, MUSIC THERAPY.

arugamama In Morita therapy, the concept of accepting oneself and one's own situation, coming to terms with the present. An Asian philosophic concept relating to the importance of accepting life as it is. See MORITA PSYCHOTHERAPY.

asana Yoga postures. There are 84 different postures. From the point of psychology, these different postures are intended to help people achieve effective meditation.

asapholalia A type of speech that is mumbling or indistinct.

ASC See ALTERED STATES OF CONSCIOUSNESS.

A scale A questionnaire used in evaluating tolerance or intolerance for vagueness, ambiguity, and indefiniteness.

ascendance A tendency to assume leadership. Also known as ascendancy, ascendence, ascendant behavior, dominance.

ascendance-submission A behavioral continuum ranging from extreme dominance to extreme subordination. Also known as dominance-submission. See A-S SCALE.

ascending activating system (AAS) reticular activating system

ascending-descending series In psychophysics, the presentation of stimuli, often in threshold-detection research, in both increasing and decreasing intensity levels.

ascending (nerve) tracts Bundles of axons within the central nervous system (CNS) that contain afferent fibers that carry impulses toward the brain. Compare DESCENDING NERVE TRACTS.

ascending paths Nerve fibers rising to the brain from lower levels of the nervous system.

ascending reticular activation system (ARAS) The part of the reticular formation responsible for the waking and arousal processes. Sometimes known as ascending activating system.

asceticism 1. A character trait or lifestyle characterized by renunciation of physical pleasures, sensual experience, and/or bodily needs. Such practices include fasting, keeping silence, solitude, and bodily mortification. 2. Withdrawal from society, and in many cases dedication to unworldly ideals.

Asch conformity effect (S. E. Asch) A classic research situation to test conformity to group opinion. A person is asked to state an opinion after being led to believe that all other members of a viewing group have the same, but incorrect, opinion. Also known as Asch situation.

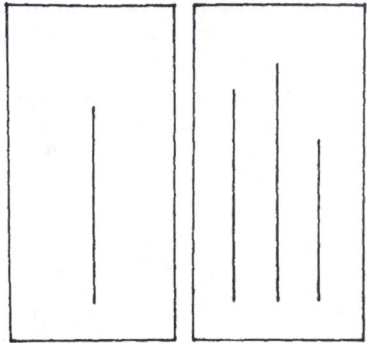

Asch conformity effect An example of a stimulus item in Solomon Asch's experiment on conformity. On a screen, four lines are shown. A group of people who appear to be participants (but who are really confederates of the experiment) are asked in a certain order which of the three lines on the right most resembles the line at the left. All answer "the middle one"; the only person who is not a confederate (the only real participant) is questioned next to last. People who tend to be conformist will say the middle line even though it is evidently incorrect.

ASCII American Standard Code for Information Interchange

ascribed role/status Assigned role, such as age and gender, about which the individual has no choice. See ACHIEVED STATUS.

ascriptive responsibility (T. Szasz) A social judgment that society should inflict punishment on a person found guilty of committing an illegal act. In forensic psychiatry, the phrase is applied in cases in which a criminally responsible person is ascribed legal responsibility. See DESCRIPTIVE RESPONSIBILITY.

ASDC Association of Sleep Disorders Centers

asemasia Loss of the ability to understand or use language; a general communication disorder that includes such conditions as alexia, agraphia, and amimia, which involve the comprehension and use of communicative signs, symbols, or gestures.

asexual 1. Lacking sexual characteristics or drive. 2. Being capable of reproduction without the process of impregnation.

asexual reproduction Any mode of reproduction not involving the union of sex cells or of conjugating organisms; reproduction by nonsexual interchange of genetic material. Also known as agamogenesis, agamogony. Compare SEXUAL REPRODUCTION. See AGAMOGENESIS, PARTHENOGENESIS.

as-if hypothesis (H. Vaihinger) A postulate that human thoughts and actions are guided by unproven or contradictory assumptions that are treated as if they were true. See AS-IF PERSONALITY.

as-if performances (H. Sullivan) The process of adopting various roles to avoid punishment or to obtain sympathy from others. In other words, "putting on an act."

as-if personality A pattern of behavior that appears normal and well-adjusted, but the person is unable to behave in a warm, genuine, spontaneous manner. Compare AS-IF HYPOTHESIS.

asitia Revulsion toward food.

ASL American Sign Language (also abbreviated **Ameslan**)

asocial 1. Not social; withdrawn from society. Compare ANTISOCIAL. 2. Behavior that lacks social sensibility; absence of social customs or values.

asociality A lack of involvement with other people, withdrawal from society, or indifference to social values and customs. Hermits, recluses, and many people with schizophrenia exhibit asociality.

asomatognosia Inability to detect or interpret the environment from body senses.

asonia A form of sensory amusia characterized by inability to distinguish differences of pitch. Also known as tone deafness.

asoticamania A self-destructive squandering of money, frequently manifested in manic episodes. See BIPOLAR DISORDER, MANIA.

aspect ratio In ergonomics, the width divided by the height, generally of a video display unit (VDU). A square would have an aspect ratio of 1.00.

Asperger's disorder A developmental disorder whose essential features include severe and sustained impairment in social interaction as well as restricted, repetitive patterns of interests, behavior and activities. Although it is often considered to be a form of autism, unlike autistic disorder, there are no significant delays in language, cognition, or self-help skills. See AUTISTIC DISORDER, AUTISTIC PSYCHOPATHY.

Asperger's syndrome autistic psychopathy

aspermatism aspermia

aspermia Failure of the male reproductive organs to produce or emit semen. Also known as aspermatism.

asphalgesia False pain. The person reports pain on touching or being touched by nonpainful objects. This can be demonstrated by hypnosis on normal participants.

asphixophilia Being sexually aroused by the idea or act of one's own strangulation. See AUTOEROTIC ASPHYXIATION, EROTIC ASPHYXIATION.

aspiration Striving to reach a certain level of performance or attain a certain goal. See ASPIRATION LEVEL.

aspirational group An aggregate of people that a person wishes to join. May have a formal structure, such as a professional association, or be an informal collection of other individuals with similar interests, economic status, or proximity. See DISSOCIATIVE GROUP.

aspiration level (F. Hoppe, K. Lewin, K. Dembo) The standard used by a person in setting significant goals; the level of performance to which the person aspires. Success tends to raise the aspiration level and failure to lower or restrict it, especially when the judgment of failure reflects group rather than individual standards. Also known as level of aspiration.

A/S ratio See ASSOCIATION-SENSATION RATIO.

assault 1. An attack. 2. In legal terms, a credible threat to attack, usually by words or by gestures.

assaultive behavior Violent attacks on others (child-beating, domestic violence, rape, unprovoked fights) often associated with such conditions as alcoholic intoxication, dyscontrol syndrome, and isolated or intermittent explosive disorder.

A-S Scale (G. W. Allport) A personality scale designed to measure a person's tendency to be dominant or submissive in interpersonal relations; the range is from ascendance to submission.

assembly test A jigsaw-type intelligence task that calls on participants to assemble components to generate a common object. Among such tests are those that when completed depict an ocean liner, a hand, a human head. See FORMBOARD TEST.

assertion-structured therapy (E. Phillips) A systematic cognitive approach to psychotherapy based on the theory that neurotic tendencies can be traced to faulty assumptions and expectations about people and relationships.

assertiveness training (A. Salter, J. Wolpe, A. Lazarus) A behavior-therapy technique intended to reduce interpersonal anxiety and increase interpersonal competence by teaching a person to more honestly express immediate feelings, wishes, ideas, or decisions in nonconfrontational ways. Assertive behavior is thought to differ from both ascendant behavior (which does not sufficiently consider the "rights" of others by being overly aggressive) and submissive behavior (which does not sufficiently consider the "rights" of the self). Also known as assertion training, assertive training.

assessment 1. The appraisal of an individual's traits or accomplishments, more specifically, an evaluation of progress. 2. The appraisal or estimation of the level or magnitude of some attribute of a person. The assessment of human behavior and mental processes involves observations, interviews, rating scales, checklists, inventories, projectives, and psychological tests. See EVALUATION, HOLISTIC ASSESSMENT, PSYCHOLOGICAL EVALUATION.

assessment center An office or department, often in universities, where a person is evaluated with regard to future growth and development, usually for educational and vocational counseling.

assessment-classification model A model applied to certain situations, the core concept being that the best predictor of future behavior is present or past behavior; for example, the best single predictor of college grades are high school grades.

assessment instrument A specific method of acquiring data in psychological assessment, such as a questionnaire, a behavioral observation coding system, and psychophysiological inventory.

assets-discovery   A process of learning and accepting inner resources and strengths, and employing them in everyday life.

assets-liabilities technique   A counseling method in which the client lists personal assets and liabilities as they relate to goals; a counselor or advisor may go over them with the person.

assigned gender/sex   The officially declared sex (male or female) of a neonate. See PSEUDO-HERMAPHRODITISM.

assignment therapy   (A. Ellis) Tasks set by a therapist to patients, usually to be performed outside of the therapy setting, assigned for many reasons, including giving patients experience in testing reality.

assignment worker   contingent employee/worker

assimilation   1. In general, the incorporation of something into something else, for example, new ideas into old ones; new information into knowledge; adoption of others' attitudes. 2. In Jean Piaget's theory, the process of absorbing new information into present cognitive structures. 3. In social psychology, the process by which minority groups lose their distinctiveness within the social mainstream, whether spontaneous, forced, or an outward compliance without inherent conversion. See CULTURAL ASSIMILATION. 4. In linguistics, the change of a sound under the influence of a neighboring sound, by which the articulations of the two sounds become similar.

assimilation contrast change   The relationship between an old and a new point of view, as well as the attitude toward the source of the new attitude. New information that attacks an old view can either lead to a new opinion or strengthen the original position.

assimilation contrast change theory   A point of view, that when keeping everything else constant, a change in attitudes toward anything depends primarily on (a) the distance between prior beliefs and the new beliefs and (b) the amount of confidence a person has in whomever is asserting the validity of the new attitude. For instance, from a religious point of view it may be easier to convert a person from being a Baptist into a Lutheran than it would be to convert a Baptist into a Muslim.

assimilation effect   A shift in judgment toward an anchor (reference standard) after it is introduced in a study. Judgments of relative distance or weight will usually be evenly distributed along a scale before the experimenter provides an anchor. If, once the anchor is introduced, judgments cluster around the anchor, assimilation effects have occurred. See ANCHOR CONTRAST EFFECT.

assimilative illusion   An illusion generated by the environmental context, such as a person walking on a dark street may be perceived as larger and more dangerous than if the person were seen in bright light.

assistant   In psychodrama, a person participating in a scene as an antagonist or a participant, with the protagonist being the main character.

associate   1. An item or person grouped with others by some common factor. See COHORT, PEER. 2. To make an association.

associate visual agnosia   (H. Lissauer) A form of visual agnosia defined by an inability to recognize the meaning of objects seen in outline.

associated movement   A movement using the skeletal muscles of one part of the body in association with muscle activity of another body area, as in kicking and biting an opponent who is restraining the person's arms. See CONJUGATE MOVEMENT.

associated specificity   A theory of psychosomatic illness stating that through learned mediation or accidental conditioning an association between a physiological response and an emotion, thought, or idea may become established.

association   1. A connection between any two things, ideas, or feelings. Associations are established by instruction or by experience. In psychology, associations (conscious or unconscious) may be expressed spontaneously through Sigmund Freud's free-association method, or may be deliberately elicited, as in word-association tests. 2. A learning technique in which verbal items are teamed in a specific order. See ASSOCIATIONISM, FREE ASSOCIATION.

association areas (of the brain)   (P. E. Flechsig) Parts of the cerebral cortex presumed to be involved in complex cortical functions in the integration of sensory and motor areas, as compared to those areas that directly control sensory and motor functions. See INTRINSIC CORTEX.

association by contiguity   See CONTIGUITY OF ASSOCIATIONS, LAW OF CONTIGUITY.

association coefficient   1. A relationship index between discontinuous variables, for example, big-little. 2. A measure of association, such as Pearson's Correlation Coefficient (r). See COEFFICIENT OF ASSOCIATION.

association cortex   Those regions of the neocortex in which complex associations of stimuli are formed or in which sensorimotor integration occurs.

association-deficit pathology   See MINIMAL BRAIN DYSFUNCTION.

association fibers   Axons (or nerve fibers) which connect different regions in the same hemisphere of the brain.

associationism   1. A doctrine positing that neural links, inborn or acquired, bind stimuli and responses. See S-R PSYCHOLOGY. 2. A doctrine positing that human understanding of the environment occurs through ideas associated with sensory experience rather than through innate ideas. See ASSOCIATION OF IDEAS, ASSOCIATION PSYCHOLOGY. 3. A concept that attributes complex mental processes such as thinking, feeling, and desiring to associative links according to specific laws and principles. Aristotle was the first to cite some of these laws (similarity, difference, contiguity in time or space, etc.), but the theory did not come to fruition until the 17th and 18th centuries with the contributions of Thomas Hobbes, who held that all knowledge is compounded from relatively simple sense impressions. Also known as connectionism. See AFFECTION, COGNITION, CONATION, CONTINUITY HYPOTHESIS, MIND.

associationist   Older name for a Stimulus-Response (S-R) psychologist. See ASSOCIATION PSYCHOLOGY, S-O-R PSYCHOLOGY, S-R PSYCHOLOGY.

associationistic theories of learning   Points of view that the process of learning consists of forming associative bonds between stimuli and responses, or among different responses.

association nuclei The nuclei of the thalamus that receive no direct input from ascending sensory systems, connect widely with other thalamic nuclei and send axons to association areas of the frontal, parietal, occipital, and temporal lobes. The dorsomedial nucleus, which projects to the prefrontal cortex, is an example.

association of ideas The process of combining perceptions and ideas into new ideas of varying degrees of complexity and abstractness, such as connecting the relatively simple ideas of four legs, furry coat, a certain shape and size, into the compound concept of cat. See ASSOCIATIONISM, EMPIRICISM.

association psychology A tabula rasa approach to human behavior, in which behavior and mental activity are explained by the building up of associations between experiences and ideas.

association-reaction time The elapsed time between stimulus and response in a word-association test.

association-sensation ratio (D. O. Hebb) A learning-ability index based on the ratio of the weight of the association cortex of the brain to the total sensory cortex. Generally, the larger the ratio, the more the organism is able to learn. Usually identified as A/S ratio.

association test A method of determining reactions to specific stimuli such as colors or words. The participant is required either to say whatever comes to mind or to respond in a specified manner to varied stimuli.

association time The time required to form an association, that is, for the passage from one idea to another suggested by it.

association value The relative ability of anything, such as a word or a smell or a sound or an object, to generate associations (for example, a rose is more likely to generate memories than a daisy).

associative anamnesis (F. Deutsch) An interview technique in which the client in therapy gives an autobiographical report, while the therapist listens for key words and expressions to establish associative linkages to bring the patient closer to the unconscious roots of the causes of the disturbance. Coined by Polish-American psychologist Felix Deutsch (1884–1964). See SECTOR THERAPY, THIRD EAR.

associative chain theory A point of view that in a sequence of acts, each act is caused by the prior act and this act causes the subsequent one.

associative clustering In recalling materials that were presented in irregular order, the tendency to recall or report these in some kind of logical or meaningful order.

associative facilitation The strengthening of one associative connection through the operation of a prior one, such as increased ease in the formation of the association A-B-C, due to the prior association A-B.

associative fluency Ability to generate many answers, responses, or potential solutions; particularly, the ability to generate original responses. See CREATIVITY, DIVERGENT THINKING.

associative illusion A geometric illusion that deceives the viewer because of the influence of some lines of the pattern. A good example of this illusion is the Sander parallelogram. See GEOMETRICAL ILLUSION for an illustration of the Sander parallelogram.

associative inhibition The weakening of an established association such as when a new one is formed, or interference of a former association with a new one.

associative learning 1. A type of learning in which bonds are formed between stimulus-response units. 2. The bringing into relation of elements in learning. The elements may be ideas, or verbal or other stimuli. There is often the implication that one idea may evoke the other, or that one stimulus may call forth the response originally called forth by the other. See S-R PSYCHOLOGY.

associative linkage See ASSOCIATIVE ANAMNESIS.

associative meaning Any words, images, sounds, smells, or ideas that come to mind on hearing a stimulus word such as "horse."

associative memory Revival of the memory of a past event or place by recalling something associated with it.

associative processes A type of learning that occurs as a result of life experiences based on connections made to personal, historical events.

associative shifting law (E. L. Thorndike) A theory that a response to a particular stimulus A may come to be evoked by a rather different stimulus B, provided the organism has been permitted to make that response, with satisfying consequences, to each in a graded series of stimuli created by gradually dropping stimulus elements from A and simultaneously adding elements of B. See LAW OF ASSOCIATIVE SHIFTING, FADING (meaning 1).

associative stimulus A stimulus that elicits a particular response because of a prior association, such as when a young child says "milk" when coming to the breakfast table. See CLASSICAL CONDITIONING, OPERANT CONDITIONING.

associative strength 1. The strength of an S-R (stimulus-response) link as measured by memory persistence. 2. The strength of an S-R association as measured by the frequency with which a given stimulus elicits a particular response (for example, the stimulus word "white" is most likely to bring the response "black").

associative thinking A relatively uncontrolled cognitive activity that takes place during reverie, daydreaming, and free association. Such thinking may express inner needs and desires, and can be the source of deeper understanding and creative ideas. It is the basis of Sigmund Freud's free association procedure in psychoanalysis.

associative visual agnosia Inability to identify seen items that can be nonetheless sketched or matched.

assonance 1. In general, a rough similarity. 2. In linguistics, a similarity of the vowel sounds of words, for example, through and flute, sane and stay.

assortative mating 1. The mating of individuals with similar physical or mental characteristics, or of individuals who are genetically similar but not related. 2. (L. M. Terman) The matings or pairings of individuals who are more alike socially, physically, and psychologically than pure chance would account for, and who tend to be happier in the "marriage" than individuals who differ in these areas. Also known as assortive mating.

assumed mean A judgment of what the mean of any group of numbers is likely to be, made as a step in some methods of calculating the actual mean.

assumed role   1. The act that a person may put on, especially with people that are unknown to the person. 2. A person's usual mode of behavior in a particular situation, such as in an occupation. 3. A role selected or achieved by choice, such as an occupational or marital role.

assumed similarity (bias)   A tendency for people to assume that they are similar to most other people; the degree of apparent correlation between one's self-traits and another person's traits. See IDIOPANIMA, PROJECTION, Q-SORT.

assumption   An underlying often unproved principle, the truth of which is taken for granted in treating or testing some theory.

assurance   A verbal technique that provides support and reduces tension in regards to a client's problems, doubts, or emotional stress; used interchangeably with reassurance.

astasia   1. Inability to stand, due to muscular incoordination. 2. Unsteadiness or tremor of muscular contraction or of posture. See ASTASIA-ABASIA.

astasia-abasia   Inability to stand (astasia) or walk (abasia). Walking with a wobbly, staggering gait, though muscle control is normal while lying down. The cause is usually psychological, rather than neurological. Also known as Blocq's disease.

astereognosis   (P. O. Blocq) A type of amorphosynthesis characterized by the failure of the brain to synthesize an image from neural impressions received by touching an object. The result is a loss or marked impairment of the ability to identify familiar objects or geometrical forms by touch. Also known as astereognosia, stereoagnosis, stereoanesthesia, tactile agnosia. See AMORPHOSYNTHESIS, APHASIA, ASYMBOLIA.

asthenia   (J. C. H. Heinroth) A condition of severe weakness or loss of strength. May be marked by general fatigue, muscle pain, breathlessness, giddiness, and heart palpitations. It is a common symptom in depressive and neurasthenic disorders. Sometimes known as adynamia. See ASTHENIC PERSONALITY, DA COSTA'S SYNDROME, DYSTHYMIC DISORDER, MENTAL ASTHENIA, NEURASTHENIA.

asthenic (body) type   (E. Kretschmer) In Ernst Kretschmer's theory, a frail, narrow-chested individual who tends to be shy, sensitive, and introverted. Also known as asthenic physique, leptosome type. See CONSTITUTIONAL TYPES.

asthenic delusion   (P. Janet) A disorder characterized by apparent lack of intellectual control with the patient expressing delusional thoughts in a frenzied manner.

asthenic reaction   A neurosis characterized by chronic mental and physical fatigue, weakness, and absence of enthusiasm. Also known as neurasthenia.

asthenology   The study of structural or functional disorders characterized by weakness or debility.

asthenophobia   Morbid fear of being weak, or of showing weakness or even in dealing with people perceived to be weak.

asthenopia   (W. Mackenzie) A condition in which the eyes become easily fatigued and function feebly or without strength, often resulting from psychic stress and symptomatized by back pains, neck tension, and headache. Commonly known as eyestrain.

asthma   A disorder in which blocking of the bronchial passages by spasmodic contractions and mucus produce wheezing and gasping. Though the precipitating cause is usually an allergen (dust or pollen) or hypersensitivity to bacteria, psychological factors, such as anxiety and stress, may aggravate or even precipitate an attack. Also known as bronchial asthma.

astigmatism   In an optical system, the failure of light-rays to come to focus properly on the retina due to a cornea that is not evenly curved. The effect is an aberration or distortion of the visual image not unlike the reflection seen in an amusement park mirror.

astigmatometer   An instrument for measuring the extent and variety of astigmatism. Also known as astigmometer, stigmatometer.

astigmatoscope   An instrument for detecting and measuring the extent of astigmatism. Also known as astigmoscope.

astral projection   1. A depersonalization that includes the illusion that the mind has left the body. 2. The hypothetical or purported projection of a person's essence outside of the body as though traveling around an astral plane.

astrapophobia   Morbid fear of thunderstorms; especially fear of lightning. Also known as astraphobia, keraunophobia. See BRONTOPHOBIA.

astrocyte   The most numerous type of glia cell in the brain. Astrocytes regulate the environment of neurons by controlling levels of ions, particularly potassium ions. They have many processes and appear star-shaped. The endfeet of their processes envelop synapses and help keep synaptic activation localized. Their endfeet also surround brain capillaries and induce the endothelial cells of the capillary to form tight junctions between themselves which is the basis of the blood-brain barrier. They react to injury by enlarging, and form scar tissue in the central nervous system.

astrocytoma   A tumor of glial tissue, usually slow growing.

astrology   The belief that the location of planets and stars at the time of conception or of the birth of individuals, or their current location, influences the lives of individuals and determines the course of events. No Western scientific evidence of its validity exists, although it was and still is seen as a science in various traditional Asian cultures, especially in India and China.

A Study of Values   See ALLPORT-VERNON-LINDZEY STUDY OF VALUES.

astyphia   Obsolete term for erectile dysfunction. Also known as impotence.

ASVAB   Armed Services Vocational Aptitude Battery

asyllabia   1. Generally, impaired coherence and incoordination of words. 2. A type of aphasia marked by an inability to form syllables from letters of the alphabet. 3. A form of alexia characterized by an inability to recognize letters arranged into syllables or words, although the person is able to recognize the letters individually.

asylum   1. An institution for the care, protection, and treatment of the mentally ill. 2. Historically, a place of refuge for selected individuals, especially criminals. Term is no longer widely used because of the negative association with criminal behavior and the emphasis on refuge rather than treatment. See INSANE ASYLUM, MENTAL INSTITUTION.

asylum lunacy   Obsolete name for social-breakdown syndrome.

asymbolia   (F. C. M. Finkelnburg) 1. Inability to recognize the form or nature of an object using touch. 2. A form of aphasia characterized by inability to understand or use symbols of any kind, including words, gestures, signals, musical notes, chemical formulae, or signs. Also known as asemasia, asemia, sign blindness. See APHASIA.

asymmetrical confidence levels   See CONFIDENCE LEVEL.

asymmetric(al) contingency   A dyadic interaction in which one person dominates the other by various means such as by being at a superior social level or being the other person's job superior.

asymmetrical distribution   A statistical distribution that is not symmetrical around its center. See SKEWNESS.

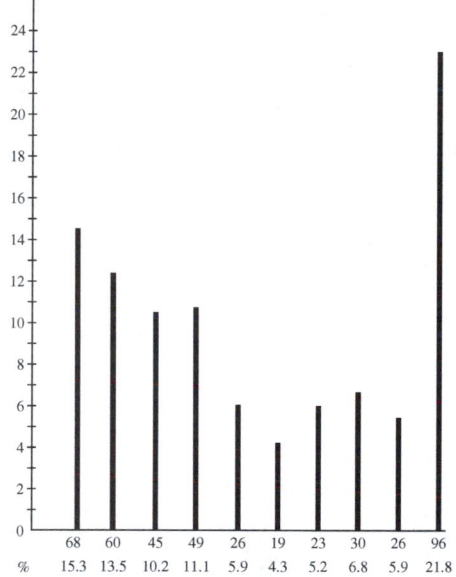

	68	60	45	49	26	19	23	30	26	96
%	15.3	13.5	10.2	11.1	5.9	4.3	5.2	6.8	5.9	21.8

asymmetrical distribution   This example of a statistical distribution shows how statistical data can shatter preconceptions. The ten lines represent the percentages of 442 former students at the Massachusetts Institute of Technology (MIT) who were in *Who's Who in America* in 1936 relative to their grade point averages. Line 1 represents students who were in the top ten percent (decile) in grades (15.3%) at MIT. Line 10 represents the percent in *Who's Who* who had the poorest grades (21.8%). Apparently, for that time period and at that institution, a predictor of success in careers was to do poorly in school.

asymmetric contingency   asymmetric(al) contingency

asymptomatic   Not showing any symptoms. A disease or other disorder may be present but provide no signs for the diagnostician. See PATHOGNOMONIC.

asymptote   1. The extreme position of a curved line on a graph. 2. By extension, the limits of behavior. See LEARNING CURVE for an illustration; the upper-right hand curve approaches the line but never reaches it.

asymptotic curve   A graphic representation of a curve that approaches an axis more and more closely, but never quite touches it. See illustration B at CUMULATIVE RECORD and LEARNING CURVE for examples of an asymptote.

asynchrony   Lack of coincidence in time between different mental and physical processes, for example, the development of different components of the body (arms, legs, breasts, etc.) at different times during puberty, resulting in body asymmetry and, frequently, self-consciousness and transient maladjustment of such individuals.

asyndesis   1. Disjointed speech in which disconnected ideas are thrown together. 2. Inability to put ideas or thoughts in a coherent manner, commonly found in schizophrenia. See THINKING ASIDE.

asyndetic thinking   Thought processes in which ideas and images have no intrinsic connection with each other; fragmented thinking resulting from loosening of association, particularly in schizophrenia.

asynergia   (J. Babinski) A faulty coordination of muscle groups, which may result in difficulty in standing, kneeling, walking, etc. The underlying symptom of cerebellar deficit, that is, an inability to carry out complex motor acts requiring harmonious cooperation of separate muscle groups. Also known as asynergy.

asynesia   1. Obsolete term for severe mental retardation. 2. Lack, whether due to genetic or psychological reasons, of understanding reality or of the ability to use normal common sense. Also spelled asynesis.

At   In Rorschach test scoring, a symbol for anatomy response.

ataque   A culture-specific syndrome observed mainly in Puerto Ricans. Manifested as a convulsive seizure purported to be a conversion defense against aggressive urges. Similar to *ataque de nervios* in the Caribbean.

ataque de nervios   See ATAQUE.

ataractic(s)   (H. D. Fabing) Obsolete term for tranquilizer, both major and minor. See ANTIANXIETY DRUGS, ANTIPSYCHOTIC DRUGS.

ataraxia   A state of mind characterized by perfect peace or detached serenity without loss of mental abilities or clouding of consciousness. Also known as ataraxy.

atavism   1. A genetic trait that is inherited from a remote ancestor but did not appear in nearer ancestors; a throwback, a reversion to an earlier type. 2. (C. Lombroso) The outdated and unsubstantiated concept that some people are more like their distant ancestors than to their parents. See ATAVISTIC HEREDITY.

atavistic heredity   Traits inherited from remote ancestors.

ataxia   (Hippocrates, Galen) A neuromuscular disorder marked by failure of the muscles to perform coordinated movements, voluntary movements, or both, such as walking or reaching for an object. May be due to injury, certain drugs, or disorders affecting muscular coordination, such as cerebral palsy or multiple sclerosis. Also known as ataxy, dyssynergia. Types of ataxia include: CEREBELLAR, FRIEDREICH'S, HYSTERICAL, INTRAPSYCHIC, LOCOMOTOR, MARIE'S, MENTAL, PARATAXIA, PSYCHATAXIA, SENSORY, VOLUNTARY.

ataxiagraph   1. A device for studying ataxia by measuring the degree and nature of muscle coordination. 2. A recording device for measuring involuntary sway while the person is attempting to maintain an erect posture; used in neurological examinations. Such a recording is called an ataxiagram. The device is also known as ataxiameter.

ataxic dysarthria   A speech disorder characterized by slurring, uncontrolled volume, and sudden spastic irregularities of vocal-cord function. Usually associated with cerebral diseases, for example, cerebral palsy.

ataxic gait   A method of walking in which persons must watch their legs and slap their feet on the ground, depending upon sounds and sights to tell where their feet are.

ataxic speech   Verbal communication that is jerky and irregular. See CEREBELLAR SPEECH.

ataxic writing   Uncoordinated or irregular writing caused by a lack of skill or by central nervous system damage.

ataxiophobia   1. Fear of disorder. 2. Dread of messiness.

ataxiophemia   The incoordination of muscles used for speech production.

ATDPS   Attitude Toward Disabled Persons Scale; see ATTITUDE SCALE TOWARD DISABLED PERSONS.

atelesis   Disintegration or splitting, of the contents of consciousness. Term is applied to schizophrenic disjunctions, for example, the lack of integration of the psyche and the environment as manifested in autism.

atelia   1. Incomplete development characterized by the continuation of childish traits into adulthood. 2. Incompatibility of physical or mental traits and the age of a person (such as an adult who has child-like features or one who acts like a juvenile). See ATELIOSIS.

ateliosis   A general term for incomplete development, applied to physical or mental growth (such as infantilism, dwarfism, mental retardation). Also known as atelia.

atelophobia   Fear of imperfection or of being imperfect.

atephobia   Morbid fear of ruin or being ruined.

A test   A quiz for speed of discrimination, in which the participant is required to cancel every A in a long series of capital letters set in page form, in random order, often without spacing between the letters.

athetoid dysarthria   A speech disorder characterized by noisy irregular breathing, hoarseness, and articulatory problems which may result in extreme unintelligibility or slight distortions. Usually associated with cerebral palsy. See ATHETOTIC DYSARTHRIA.

athetoid movements   Involuntary movements of the head and limbs of the body caused by a variety of brain lesions.

athetosis   (W. A. Hammond) A disorder characterized by slow, involuntary, recurrent movements of the fingers, toes, arms, or legs, due to extrapyramidal lesions. A common symptom of cerebral palsy.

athetotic dysarthria   The loss of vocal articulation associated with slow, writhing, involuntary movements of the extremities, as in cerebral palsy. See ATHETOID DYSARTHRIA.

athletic (body) type   (E. Kretschmer) The muscular, well-proportioned, broad-shouldered type of individual who, according to Ernst Kretschmer, tends to be energetic, aggressive, and schizothymic in temperament. Also known as athletic physique. See CONSTITUTIONAL TYPE, SHELDON'S CONSTITUTIONAL THEORY OF PERSONALITY.

athymia   1. (Hippocrates) Melancholia. 2. Absence of affect. 3. Congenital absence of the thymus gland.

atman   (Indian philosophy) The life-force, or soul, of a living being that is seen as an integral part of the ultimate cosmic unity rather than as a separate individual. In Vedantic philosophy, *atman* is said to be the individualized aspect of Brahman, which is the eternal absolute. See PHYLOANALYSIS.

atmosphere effect   A distortion that may occur in reading or writing a message as a function of the conditions of the situation, for example, in finishing a sentence that begins: "I always hate ..." the word "always" might affect some people who believe that there is never an "always." Countering the atmosphere effect is important in planning statements for questionnaires.

atmospheric conditions   The effects of temperature, humidity, air flow, barometric pressure as they affect comfort and performance, for example, heat and humidity may generate conflicts between some people.

atmospheric perspective   One of the several cues that affect perception of depth and distance. See DEPTH PERCEPTION.

atomism   In psychology, a doctrine positing that psychological phenomena can best be understood by analyzing them into elementary units such as sensations, associations, or conditioned reflexes, and by showing how these units combine to form thoughts, images, and perceptions. Also known as atomistic psychology, elementarism, molecularism. See HOLISM, REDUCTIONISM, STRUCTURALISM.

atomistic approach   A point of view that to truly understand any phenomenon, the fundamental elements of that phenomenon must be known. See ATOMISM, ATOMISTIC PSYCHOLOGY, MOLAR APPROACH, MOLECULAR APPROACH.

atomistic psychology   **atomism**

atonement   1. In psychiatry and psychology, acts of apology, repentance, restitution, etc., by which people attempt to relieve anxiety generated by guilty impulses and behavior. 2. Behaviors that attempt to undo harm done to others, demanded by certain religions for divine forgiveness and recommended by certain organizations such as Alcoholics Anonymous. For pathological forms of atonement, see UNDOING.

atony   1. Lack of tension. Also known as atonia, atonicity. 2. A deficiency or absence of normal muscle tone. May be due to a number of diseases. 3. Relaxation or flaccidity of the muscles of the body.

ATP   adenosine triphosphate

atrabilious   Obsolete term denoting depression.

atricocious   Describing nonfunctional organs, such as the eyes and ears of a new-born puppy.

at risk   A state of vulnerability, for example, a fetus of a mother who contracts rubella is at risk for cerebral palsy.

atrophic dementia   General phrase referring to pre-senile organic brain disorders, for example, Alzheimer's disease. Also known as presenile dementia.

atrophy   A degeneration or wasting away of the body or a part it, as from lack of nourishment or from disuse. Also known as atrophia.

atropine   A drug that blocks the action of acetylcholine at some neuronal synapses. Some psychotropic drugs are said to have "atropine-like" side effects. See ANTICHOLINERGIC, BELLADONNA.

attachment   1. In general, connection of one part to another. 2. In socialization, a tendency of young animals to become physically identified with certain older individuals. Infants seek their primary caregivers as a step in establishing a feeling of security. See IMPRINTING.

attachment behavior   1. In animals, behavior demonstrated by one animal of "wanting" to be near another one, whether the animal is of the same or of a different species. A survival need may explain such attachments. See IMPRINTING. 2. In humans, a special relationship that develops between an infant and the primary caregiver (usually the mother). Develops from birth onward and includes the infant trying to be near and calling for the caretaker, and displaying separation anxiety if thwarted. See DEPENDENCY NEEDS. 3. In humans, a tendency of some people to identify with certain older individuals either in actuality or in thought. See CO-DEPENDENCY, DEPENDENCY (meaning 2).

attachment bond   1. A strong emotional relation between two people (such as a pair of twins or best friends). 2. A strong emotional relation between two people, often an inferior one (such as a child) to a superior one (such as an adult). 3. The primary, enduring, and special relationship that gradually develops between an infant and the primary caretaker.

attachment disorder   1. The failure of an infant to thrive because of emotional neglect or social isolation. The disorder is characterized by apathy and unresponsiveness. 2. A disturbance in social relatedness associated with grossly pathological lack of care. See ATTACHMENT THEORY, MARASMUS, REACTIVE ATTACHMENT DISORDER.

attachment theory   (J. Bowlby) A point of view that there is a tendency of humans to make strong affectional bonds to selected others. Separation before adulthood will give rise to a variety of psychological and physical problems. See AFFECTIONAL BONDS, ATTACHMENT, ATTACHMENT DISORDER DEPENDENCY, SOCIALIZATION PROCESS.

attack behavior   The use of force against an adversary, usually with intent to harm. Animals, and some humans, use attack as a form of defense especially when an organism perceived as a threat enters the zone of comfort. See DEFENSE BEHAVIOR.

attainment test   See ACHIEVEMENT TEST.

attendant care   A variety of services provided by some institutions, agencies, and individuals, for persons with disabilities who are able to live somewhat independently but need specific help. See CHALLENGED PERSON, DAILY-LIVING AIDS.

attending   Getting ready to perceive, as in listening or looking, or defining the center of clearness in perception. Focusing of sense organs sometimes involved.

attending behaviors   In counseling, all the verbal, nonverbal, observable, and unobservable behavior engaged in by the counselor while listening and giving attention to the client. Such intense involvement in listening and observing is felt to be a cornerstone of the counselor's general behavior.

attensity   (E. B. Titchener) 1. The clarity of any perception. 2. The sensory clearness or attention-producing effect of a sensation. 3. Clearness of a sensation which varies with attention rather than with the objective characteristics of the stimulus. See DIMENSIONS OF CONSCIOUSNESS.

attention   1. Conscious awareness, accompanied by sensory clearness and central nervous state readiness for response to stimuli such as focusing on specific stimuli or specific aspects of the environment, having concerns for details such as intensity, movement, repetition, contrast, and novelty of stimuli. Types of attention include: CONTROLLED, DIVIDED, DRIFTING, FOCAL, FOCUSED, FREE-FLOATING, IN-, INVOLUNTARY, PRIMARY, SECONDARY, SELECTIVE, SUSTAINED, WANDERING. 2. (R. Dreikurs) A basic need of children that leads them both into "useful" behavior (approved by parents) and "useless" behavior (annoying to parents) depending on parents' reaction to the exploratory behavior of children. See FOUR GOALS OF CHILDREN.

attentional cue words   In sport psychology, words or phrases that remind the athlete of the proper attentional focus for whatever situation ensues.

attention-deficit disorder (ADD)   A neurobiological disorder with onset before age seven, characterized by inconsistent attention and impulsivity. See BLAMING THE VICTIM, BOREDOM.

attention-deficit disorder with hyperactivity (ADDH)   A syndrome characterized by inattention, impulsivity, and considerable activity at inappropriate times and places. See ATTENTION DEFICIT DISORDER, ATTENTION DEFICIT-HYPERACTIVITY DISORDER.

attention-deficit disorder without hyperactivity   A neurobiological disorder with onset before age seven characterized by inconsistent attention and impulsivity but not hyperactivity. See ATTENTION DEFICIT DISORDER.

attention-deficit-hyperactivity disorder (ADHD)   A neurobiological condition characterized by persistent restless overactivity, once thought to occur particularly among persons (especially children) with brain damage, mental retardation, or emotional disturbances. Such persons are overactive, have a short attention span, sleep poorly, and frequently exhibit educational and perceptual deficits. Also known as hyperactive-child syndrome (HACS). See HYPERACTIVITY.

attention disorder   1. A learning disability characterized by a difficulty in maintaining sustained concentration or attention. 2. A phrase once used interchangeably with minimal brain dysfunction. See ATTENTION DEFICIT DISORDER, LEARNING DISABILITIES.

attention fluctuation   Inability of people, especially when young, to attend to anything after a certain period of time has elapsed.

attention-getting (mechanism)   Denoting a type of behavior, often considered inappropriate, that is used to gain attention (for example, childhood tantrums); also, such a behavior itself. See TEMPER TANTRUMS.

attention level   Any one of the several degrees of clarity into which the subject matter of experience (content of consciousness) may be classed. (Certain writers distinguish as many as five degrees or levels: Unconsciousness, subconsciousness, marginal consciousness, general consciousness, and focal consciousness or apperception.) Also known as level of attention.

attention overload   A psychological condition that results from excessive demands for attention to intense, unpredictable, or uncontrollable stimuli. The effect is likely to be temporary depletion of concentration and inability to cope with tasks that demand attention. See INFORMATION OVERLOAD.

attention-placebo condition   A study in which a client receives a believable treatment containing many of the nonspecific aspects of a particular therapy or drug but does not receive what is considered to be the active therapeutic ingredient. The intention is to determine whether outcomes for clients not receiving the active ingredient will differ significantly from those who do. See DOUBLE BLIND, PLACEBO EFFECT.

attention reflex   A change in the size of the pupil upon sudden fixing of attention.

attention span   1. The length of time an individual can concentrate on one topic. 2. The number of objects that can be distinctly perceived in one brief presentation. Also known as apprehension span, span of apprehension, span of attention. See TACHISTOSCOPE.

attention-span test   A test designed to measure the amount or complexity of perceptual material which a participant is able to grasp at a single brief presentation (for example, a photograph is shown briefly, and immediately thereafter the participant is asked to list items seen in the photograph).

attentiveness   1. The state of being alert and actively paying attention. 2. The quality of actively attending to the needs of others.

attenuation   1. A process of reducing strength or quality of anything. 2. In statistics, a reduction of the size of an effect because of errors of measurement.

attenuation theory (of attention)   A point of view that unattended-to stimuli are weaker than information that is attended to, but are not completely blocked from consciousness.

attenuators   The calibrated devices that accurately control the decrease in the intensity of tones, or light, on electronic instruments such as audiometers, stereophonic sound systems, or video equipment.

attic children   Refers to children kept in isolation (in attics, cellars, etc.). Such children usually have physical deformities or mental retardation. Generally, attempts to normalize them have failed, and since experimental research on such issues is unethical, scientists must work with incidents of opportunity, and can never know any child's potentialities prior to any mistreatment. See MARASMUS, SENSORY DEPRIVATION EFFECTS.

attitude   1. A learned predisposition to react to a given situation, person, or other set of cues in a consistent way. Attitudes are generally said to have three components; cognitive, emotive, and behavioral, which combine to convey a positive, negative, or neutral response. 2. A relatively stable predisposition to react in a specific way to something. Attitudes are complex products of learning, experience, and emotional processes and include enduring preferences, aversions, prejudices, superstitions, scientific or religious views, and political predilections.

attitude scale   1. Generally, a list of questions about opinions on any topic or issue. 2. A scale used in attitude surveys to measure the strength of opinions. See LIKERT SCALE, THURSTONE ATTITUDE SCALES.

Attitude Scale Toward Disabled Persons   (H. D. Yuker, J. R. Bloch, & W .J. Campbell) A questionnaire to reveal attitudes toward people with disabilities. Also known as the Attitude Toward Disabled Persons Scale (ATDPS).

attitude survey/test   1. A survey, usually in the form of a questionnaire, used to measure the attitudes or opinions of a group. 2. A series of questions asked of samples of people (such as voters) in an attempt to determine or measure opinions on various issues of interest (such as choosing presidential candidates).

attitude system   A cluster of attitudes having common or similar views leading to a consistent life attitude.

attitude theory   A point of view of psychosomatic medicine that there are specific objective physiological symptoms associated with specific attitudes of patients with a disease condition during a disturbing situation.

attitude therapy   A form of re-educative treatment that emphasizes how current attitudes of people originated, and the purpose these attitudes serve, with the intention of attempting to change them.

attitude tic   A postural position due to tonic rigidity in the limbs, head, or upper body area (for example, torticollis).

attitudinal commitment   1. Apparent devotion to a situation, such as in the case of a job, willingness to work long hours, not to spend useless time talking or reading, etc. 2. The commitment or devotion to the welfare of an organization, project, other person, etc.

attitudinal group   1. Any personal growth or therapy group in which members are given the chance to express and exchange feelings and thoughts in an accepting environment. 2. Any collection of people with the same general set of attitudes toward any particular issue, such as a clique of students in a high school criticizing the way others clothe themselves; a religious group's attitude toward alcohol.

attitudinal reflexes   Kinds of reflexes that ready an organism to make a complex response, as in an animal preparing to attack an adversary.

attitudinal type   (C. G. Jung) Individuals of any personality type (such as Carl Jung's introvert or extravert) that demonstrate their type overtly by appropriate behavior, as in an introvert consistently acting in a shy and self-contained manner.

attonity   Profound stupor. A clinical state of stupor similar to that observed in catatonia but also occurring in cases of severe depression.

attraction 1. The result of elements inherent in objects, animals, or persons that draw attention to them. Elements that generate favorable attention include unusual sizes or shapes, varying colors, erratic movements, appearing and disappearing. 2. In environmental psychology, the act of adjusting proximity relationships between individuals, depending upon factors such as their liking for each other. For instance, male–female and female–female couples or pairs who like each other position themselves closer than pairs not feeling mutual attraction. However, male–male pairs generally do not display attraction as a sign of liking each other. See INTERPERSONAL ATTRACTION.

attribute The essential quality or character of a person, sensation, or object.

attributed risk The absolute incident of a disorder attributable to the risk factor. See EPIDEMIOLOGY.

attribution 1. Assignment of responsibility by the process of inferring underlying conditions and causes regarding behavior of others or self. See CRIMINAL RESPONSIBILITY, IRRESISTIBLE IMPULSE, M'NAGHTEN RULE, PARTIAL INSANITY. 2. Explaining a particular behavior or total personality by considering the history of a person as well as biological factors. See CAUSAL ATTRIBUTION (THEORY), NATURE-NURTURE, SOFT DETERMINISM. 3. In the two-word stage of language development, a noun qualified by an attribute, as in "blue car." See ORIGIN OF LANGUAGE THEORIES.

attributional errors Mistakes about causes. In psychology, many such errors have been debunked by research, such as that personality is determined by hair color, or that people born in February are more intelligent than people born in other months.

attributional style (M. E. Seligman) The habitual way of viewing the causes of good and bad events along three dimensions: internal, stable, and global. See EXPLANATORY STYLE.

attribution of causality See CAUSAL ATTRIBUTION.

attribution theory (F. Heider) The study of the processes by which people ascribe motives to their own and others' behavior, such as the tendency of interpreting others' behavior in internal, psychological terms while interpreting self-behavior in external circumstantial terms. See BLAMING, IDIOPANIMA, RESPONSIBILITY.

attribution theory of leadership A point of view that leaders are affected by their subordinates, with leaders being sensitive to the attitudes of subordinates and consequently adjusting to them.

attribution therapy Efforts made to change a person's views concerning the causes of events or of the basic causes of self-behavior.

attrition In research, loss of participants usually by drop-outs during a study or withdrawal of patients during a clinical trial. Also known as mortality.

A-type personality See TYPE A PERSONALITY.

atypical Not corresponding to the normal type.

atypical affective disorder A category for disorders of mood that do not meet the criteria for a major affective disorder or adjustment disorder. Includes atypical bipolar disorder and atypical depression.

atypical anxiety disorder An anxiety disorder that does not meet the criteria for usual anxiety conditions.

atypical bipolar disorder An atypical affective disorder characterized by having an episode of major depression then followed by an episode of relatively mild manic symptoms. See ATYPICAL DISORDER.

atypical child A child who deviates markedly from the norm in some basic characteristic. See EXCEPTIONAL CHILD, SPECIAL CHILD.

atypical childhood psychosis See CHILDHOOD-ONSET PERVASIVE DEVELOPMENTAL DISORDER.

atypical conduct disorder A pattern of violating either the basic rights of others or social norms and rules, but without conforming to the criteria of other conduct disorders. See CONDUCT DISORDER.

atypical depression An atypical affective disorder characterized by depressive symptoms that do not meet the criteria for other kinds of mood disorders. See ATYPICAL DISORDER.

atypical development Rare phrase identifying any of a wide variety of childhood disorders such as childhood schizophrenia or early infantile autism.

atypical developmental disorder A vague diagnostic category that includes children with multiple disturbances in the development of language and social skill, but not classifiable as infantile autism or childhood-onset pervasive developmental disorder. See ATYPICAL DISORDER.

atypical disorder Any disorder failing to meet full criteria for a more specific disorder, such as atypical depression.

atypical dissociative disorder A category applying to individuals lacking specific dissociative disorders, but who experience trance-like states, a persistent feeling that the external world is unreal (derealization), or dissociative states resulting from prolonged brainwashing, thought reform, or indoctrination during captivity by terrorists or cultists. See ATYPICAL DISORDER, DEREALIZATION.

atypical eating disorder A diagnostic category of unusual or uncharacteristic eating disorders (for example, eating only bananas for one week, then eating only fish for the next week) that cannot be adequately classified among other such variations in eating. See ATYPICAL DISORDER.

atypical factitious disorder with physical symptoms A category for unusual disorders voluntarily adopted by the patient that do not require medical attention or hospitalization, such as voluntary dislocation of a shoulder. See ATYPICAL DISORDER.

atypical gender-identity disorder A category for disorders of gender identity not classifiable as any specific gender-identity disorder. See IDENTITY DISORDER, MALE-FEMALE BEHAVIOR DIFFERENCE.

atypical gender-identity disorder A portrait by an artist of someone who is uncertain of his or her own gender.

atypical impulse-control disorder A category comprising unusual or uncharacteristic disorders of impulse control. The category does not include pathological gambling, kleptomania, pyromania, or explosive disorders. See ATYPICAL DISORDER.

atypical mental disorders A category for cases with unusual symptoms that do not meet the criteria for any specific mental disorder. See ATYPICAL DISORDER.

atypical paranoid disorder A residual category for paranoid conditions that do not qualify as paranoid disorders.

atypical personality disorder A diagnostic category that includes unusual cases of personality disorder in which there is insufficient evidence for a more specific designation; a wastebasket phrase.

atypical psychosexual disorders Psychological sexual disturbances not covered by other categories, such as feelings of inadequacy associated with the size and shape of the sex organs or with sexual performance, confusion about preferred sexual orientation, or distress over repeated sexual conquests or failures. See DON JUAN SYNDROME, NYMPHOMANIA.

atypical psychosexual dysfunctions A category that includes unusual psychosexual behaviors outside the standard categories, such as absence of erotic sensations despite physiologically normal sexual excitement.

atypical psychosis A category that includes cases with psychotic symptoms that do not meet the criteria for any specific mental disorder, such as having as the only symptom, persistent auditory hallucinations that the person knows are not real.

atypical somatoform disorder A category for unusual attitudes regarding a person's own body, such as an imagined defect in physical appearance (dysmorphophobia) or an exaggeration of a minor defect, that cannot be explained organically, but seem to have psychological factors.

atypical stereotyped-movement disorder A childhood condition characterized by behaviors such as repetitive head-banging or rocking which, unlike tics, are voluntary, do not cause apparent distress, and are often associated with mental retardation, pervasive developmental disorder, or inadequate social stimulation, often done as a cry for attention.

atypical tic disorder A diagnostic category for repeated, involuntary contractions of a small group of muscles that cannot be adequately classified among stereotyped-movement disorders.

Åu See ANGSTROM UNIT.

AU Abbreviation for Angstrom unit (also abbreviated Å, Åu).

Aubert diaphragm (H. Aubert) A shutter similar to that of a camera's that opens and closes for precise instants of time, used in studies on visual perception. See TACHISTOSCOPE.

Aubert-Fleishel paradox (H. Aubert & E. von Fleishel) A visual illusion: When fixating on a moving object, it seems to move slower than if fixating on the background.

Aubert-Förster law/phenomenon (H. Aubert & R. Förster) The principle that small-near objects are easier to distinguish than large-distant objects even though the latter subtend the same visual angle.

Aubert illusion/phenomenon (H. Aubert) The illusion that a vertical line tilts in the opposite direction from where the head is tilted when viewing the line.

audibility limits Lowest and highest vibration frequencies which evoke tonal sensation. The range of audibility in the human is 16 to 20,000 Hertz (cycles per second or cps).

audibility range See RANGE OF AUDIBILITY.

audible thought A hallucination in which a person hears self-thoughts as if they were projected by a voice. See AUTOCHTHONOUS.

audience In psychodrama, everyone present at a roleplaying session whether participating or not. The concept is that their very presence, even if they remain silent and do nothing, has an effect on the participants of the psychodrama.

audience analyst In psychodrama, a member of the audience who, after watching a roleplaying demonstration, gives an opinion about the dynamics of a protagonist's behavior.

audience measurement In consumer psychology, evaluations of the characteristics of the people who read a periodical or listen to a particular radio or television program.

audile 1. Pertaining to audition (hearing). 2. Pertaining to a person who learns more easily by listening rather than reading. Also known as auditory type. Compare MOTILE, VISILE. See AUDITIVE.

auding A level of auditory reception that involves hearing, listening, and comprehension of the information.

audio brain stimulation The stimulation of the auditory area of the brain to determine the effect on behavior. See BRAIN STIMULATION.

audiogenic seizure A proxysmal disorder resembling an epileptic episode, produced by auditory stimulation, usually of a high pitch.

audiogram A graphic measure of auditory sensitivity across a range of frequencies, usually graphed as a result of an audiometric examination.

audiogravic illusion (A. Graybiel) An illusion of sound location that can occur when an individual is deprived of visual cues.

audiogyral illusion (B. Clark & A. Graybiel) Relating to an illusion or error in sound localization experienced by a blindfolded person after being rapidly rotated.

audiologist   A person who conducts individual and group examinations for hearing loss, contributes to the diagnosis of hearing disorders and the selection of an appropriate hearing aid, and directs or participates in the retraining and rehabilitation of individuals with hearing defects.

audiology   The study of hearing including the anatomy and function of the ear, impairment of hearing, and habilitation or rehabilitation of persons with hearing loss.

audiometer   (A. Hartmann) An instrument for measuring hearing acuity and range of audibility. Usually designed to measure the ability of the participant to hear frequencies ranging from 500 to 6,000 Hertz (cycles per second or cps) and at intensities of from 0 to 80 decibels. Also known as sonometer. See AUDIOGRAM.

audiometric zero   The level of sound intensity regarded as the normal threshold for human hearing. See BEKESY AUDIOMETER, ELECTROENCEPHALIC AUDIOMETRY.

audiometrician   A person who specializes in measuring hearing levels.

audiometry   The process of measuring hearing, such as determining the absolute threshold of the ear by testing for tone-hearing ability at various frequencies from 125 to 8,000 Hertz (cycles per second). Pure tone threshold measurements can be made by air conduction or bone conduction hearing tests.

audiotape instruction   See COMPUTERIZED THERAPY.

audioverbal amnesia   A type of auditory aphasia in which the person may be able to retain and repeat certain single words presented acoustically but is unable to retain and repeat a series of words. Sometimes known as audioverbal aphasia.

audiovisual aids   Devices such as slides, blackboards, flip charts, computer displays, and television tapes, used to enhance and clarify a presentation or lecture.

audiovisual method/training   The use of audio aids, visual aids, or both, such as films, slides, filmstrips, videotapes, audiotapes, and television in academic education as well as training personnel.

audiovisual sensations   Those sensations involving both hearing and sight.

audit   An evaluation or review, usually of items that can be reduced to numbers such as hours worked by technicians, patients seen in a month, or miles run per day. See PATIENT-CARE AUDIT, MEDICAL AUDIT.

audition   Hearing.

auditive   1. Pertaining to the preference for learning through spoken (listening) as opposed to written (reading) language. 2. A person who recalls most easily stimuli that have been heard, as opposed to those seen. Also known as audile.

auditory   Relating to the sense of hearing or to organs of hearing.

auditory acuity   1. Hearing sensitivity in which a minimum stimulus is detected half of the time. 2. Sensitivity of hearing based usually on the absolute threshold of sounds at various levels.

auditory agnosia   A form of receptive aphasia characterized by defective or loss of ability to understand spoken language. Due to disease, injury, or maldevelopment in the left-hemisphere of the brain. Sometimes known as auditory aphasia, word deafness. See WERNICKE'S APHASIA.

auditory amnesia   Word deafness, the loss of ability to comprehend sounds or speech. Also known as Wernicke's aphasia. See RECEPTIVE APHASIA.

auditory aphasia   Inability to comprehend spoken language due to disease, injury, or maldevelopment in the left hemisphere of the brain. Also known as word deafness. See RECEPTIVE APHASIA, WERNICKE'S APHASIA.

Auditory Apperception Test (AAT)   (D. R. A. Stone) A projective examination designed primarily for people with visual challenges, who respond to a variety of recorded sounds by telling stories with a beginning, a middle, and an ending based on their interpretation of what is heard. See THEMATIC APPERCEPTION TEST.

auditory attribute   **tonal attribute**

auditory blending   Ability to synthesize the individual sounds, or phonemes, of a word so that the whole word can be recognized. See AUDITORY CLOSURE.

auditory canal   A short tube-like structure that extends between the external ear and the tympanic membrane of the middle ear.

auditory closure   Ability to fill in omitted parts in auditory presentation, and to produce a complete word. An automatic process in a normally-functioning person. See AUDITORY BLENDING.

Auditory Continuous Performance Test (ACPT)   (R. W. Keith) An examination to aid in the screening of children ages 6 through 11 years for auditory attention deficits. The child raises a thumb upon hearing the target word in a list of words.

auditory cortex   The sensory area for hearing, located in the superior gyrus of the temporal lobe lining the lateral (Sylvian) fissure. This area is referred to as the transverse gyri of Heschl.

auditory discrimination   1. Ability to tell the difference between sounds of different frequency, intensity, and pressure-pattern components; ability to distinguish one speech sound from another. 2. Ability to identify other auditory qualities, such as timbre, from a spectrum of sound waves. 3. Ability to perceive the separate sound parts of words.

auditory disorder   Any dysfunction in the processes related to hearing, such as frequency gaps, hypersensitivity to sounds, or auditory aphasia.

auditory distance perception   The estimation of distance of the source of a sound depending on cues of intensity, frequency, and complexity of the sound.

auditory fatigue   A form of exposure deafness characterized by a transient loss of hearing due to prolonged exposure to loud sounds, marked by reduced sound threshold sensitivity for several hours. See EXPOSURE DEAFNESS.

auditory feedback   Hearing one's own speech enabling one to adjust its intensity and clarity. Research shows that delaying auditory feedback by using electronic devices (delayed auditory feedback) will cause speech errors such as stuttering, pitch distortion, emotional disturbance in normal people but not in children with schizophrenia, possibly because they do not use auditory feedback in monitoring their speech.

auditory flicker   An auditory experience caused by intermittent stimulation, the beginning and end of each stimulus being sharply defined. Also known as tonal intermittence.

auditory fusion   The combining of two or more sounds into one, a phenomenon that occurs frequently when listening to music.

auditory hallucination   A false auditory perception; hearing sounds without external stimulation, or sounds that do not exist, especially when they convey messages. Examples are accusatory or laudatory voices, muffled or disconnected words, or commands which in some cases appear to emanate from the patient's own body, or from neutral objects such as a photograph.

auditory imagery   1. A type of imagery characterized by the visualization of sounds, for example, some people while listening to music are able to "see" related images such as birds flying and people dancing. 2. The capacity to experience hearing sounds or words that are not real, for example, in extreme stress situations an otherwise normal person may "hear" a voice giving directions to stay calm. In some serious mental disorders patients hear voices abusing and threatening them. In parapsychology, some psychics claim to hear voices of spirits giving them guidance. See DREAM IMAGERY, EIDETIC IMAGERY, IMAGERY TYPES, KINESTHETIC IMAGERY, VISUAL IMAGERY.

auditory labyrinth   A part of inner ear concerned with hearing. An older phrase for cochlea and attachments.

auditory localization   (G. B. Venturi) An ability to name or point to the direction or position from which a sound originated. See AUDITORY SPACE PERCEPTION.

auditory masking   No longer being able to hear a particular tone because another tone or sound overpowers it.

auditory memory   The memory for information obtained by hearing processes. Persons described as "ear-minded" tend to have greater ability to grasp ideas presented through sound than persons who are dependent upon visual stimuli in learning. Auditory memory is particularly important in tonal discrimination. See AUDILE.

auditory memory span   Ability to immediately recall sequences of related or unrelated orally-presented material. See AUDITORY SPAN, MEMORY SPAN, VISUAL MEMORY SPAN.

auditory nerve   **acoustic nerve**

auditory-oculogyric reflex   The automatic turning of eyes in the direction of a sudden sound. Also known as audito-oculogyric reflex.

auditory ossicles   Small bones of the inner ear attached from the ear drum to the cochlea. See INCUS, MALLEUS, STAPES.

auditory pathways   The nerve-fiber pathways and relay nuclei that transmit auditory information from the inner ear to the cortex. Pathways include the cochlear nerve, the dorsal and ventral cochlear nuclei, the acoustic stria including the trapezoid body, superior olivary nucleus, the lateral lemniscus, inferior colliculus, the brachium of the inferior colliculus, the medial geniculate nucleus of thalamus, and the auditory radiations leading to the auditory cortex.

auditory perception   Ability to interpret and organize sensory information received through the ears.

auditory perceptual disorders   A series of language-cognition difficulties associated with lesions in various brain areas. A right-hemisphere lesion may result in acoustic agnosia marked by inability to discriminate among nonverbal sounds. A lesion in the superior temporal gyrus may cause difficulty in phoneme discrimination so that "bike" and "pike" sound the same.

auditory processing   An ability to recognize, remember, organize, and interpret what is heard.

auditory projection area   The terminal point of the primary auditory system in the cortex. Located in the superior temporal lobe, it receives input from the medial geniculate nucleus of the thalamus.

auditory radiations   Nerve fibers originating in the medial geniculate nucleus that terminate in the auditory cortex of Heschl's gyrus and form the last stage of the primary auditory pathway.

auditory range   In humans, normal adult hearing ranges from 20 to 20,000 Hertz (cycles per second or cps) with maximum sensitivity from about 1000 to 4000 Hertz. Newborn infants and many animals respond to sound waves of higher frequency and some to lower frequencies than the adult human. See AUDITORY STIMULI.

auditory sensation   A sensation dependent upon structures in the inner ear and normally upon stimulation by sound waves.

auditory sensation level   The number of decibels (DB) (expressed in units of energy) above a chosen reference level, usually the threshold of the sound in question.

auditory sensation unit (SU)   A logarithmic unit of loudness, corresponding to the physical intensity unit, the decibel.

auditory sequencing   Ability to recall the order of items presented orally, such as a sequence of numbers or a list of nonsense words.

auditory skills   Abilities related to normal hearing, including auditory acuity, auditory memory, comprehension of speech and music, and auditory-feedback control.

auditory space perception   The perception of the direction of the source of sound, dependent on three types of auditory cues: (a) time difference, sounds often reach an individual's two ears at different times; (b) loudness, a sound appears to be more intense to the nearer ear; and (c) phase difference, one ear faces the source of sound more directly than the other. For easier detection, the differences in reception between the two ears of these three cue types can be magnified by movement of the listener's head. In addition, distortion by the sound traveling around the head and pinnae (the long waves of lower Hertz tones bend more) can provide an informative "sound shadow." See HEARING.

auditory span The number of simple items (for example, letters, words, numbers, syllables) that can be repeated by a person immediately after hearing the series one time. The auditory span of a person indicates immediate memory capacity. See AUDITORY MEMORY SPAN.

auditory spectrum See ACOUSTIC SPECTRUM.

auditory stimulus Any sound waves within the normal range of the organism's hearing ability. See AUDITORY RANGE.

auditory system The general organization of the external, middle, and inner ears, including the auditory canal, tympanic membrane, ossicular bones (malleus, incus, stapes), and cochlea. The cochlea converts the sound vibrations to nerve impulses carried by the auditory nerve to the brain.

auditory threshold The minimum level of sound that can be detected by an organism. For most humans the threshold is 6.5 decibels at 1,000 Hertz (cycles per second or cps).

auditory training 1. The instruction of a hearing-impaired person as to the most effective use of remaining hearing. May or may not include the use of a hearing prosthesis. 2. A procedure used by persons with hearing impairments to comprehend what others are saying by attending to key sounds and words in the conversation while watching the speaker's lips move.

auditory type Refers to a person who is especially sensitive to sound and who learns better by listening than by reading. Compare VISUAL TYPE. See AUDILE.

Aufdringlichkeit Hermann Ebbinghaus's term for what Max Meyer called *Eindringlichkeit*.

Aufgabe (purpose, task, homework—German) 1. Refers to what a participant is supposed to do on a test, such as underline the correct answer. 2. A task; a preparation or predisposition which unconsciously determines the way a situation is handled, for example, given the numbers 6 and 4, if the *Aufgabe* is addition then the answer is 10, but if the *Aufgabe* is subtraction, the answer is 2. An *Aufgabe* helps to explain the relation between attitude and meaning. The term was later renamed "determining tendency" by Narziss Ach, and "mental set" by later psychologists. See DETERMINING TENDENCY, MENTAL SET.

aufleitend German term introduced by Johann Unzer which became the term afferent. Compare ABLEITEND.

augmentation 1. An improvement, addition to, or increase in anything. 2. An increase in the amplitude of average-evoked-responses (AER).

augmentation strategies Adding another medicine to a first which then, at times, acts synergistically and effectively. Some cases of "treatment resistance" which do not respond to either ordinary or higher-than-ordinary doses over a reasonable trial period may yet respond if the medicine is given along with some other medication, such as thyroid extract.

augmented communication Assisting individuals in expressing themselves; for example, children with certain disabilities cannot press the letters of a keyboard and are assisted by parents who press the children's fingers on letters that the parents believe the children want to type. In this way it is hoped that others may learn what the child wants to communicate. Critics have suggested that anxious parents actually select the keys themselves.

Augmented Roman Original name for a near-phonemic alphabet of 44 characters, with a single sound for each character. The phrase has been supplanted by Initial Teaching Alphabet (ITA).

augury The art of foretelling the future by means of natural signs, such as the position of the stars, the flight of birds, or the entrails of animals. See ASTROLOGY.

aulophobia Morbid fear of any musical instrument resembling the penis, such as a flute.

aura 1. In medicine, subjective sensations, such as a peculiar odor or weird sounds that precede an epileptic episode or migraine attack. 2. In parapsychology, denoting halos and emanations around the physical body which some individuals claim to see. See EPILEPSY, MIGRAINE, VISUAL HALLUCINATIONS.

aura cursoria (Hippocrates) A condition marked by aimless running, immediately preceding an epileptic episode.

aural 1. Pertaining to the ear. 2. Pertaining to an aura.

aurally challenged Deaf or hearing-impaired.

auricle 1. The ear. 2. Technically, the pinna, the external auditory meatus.

Aussage **test** (declaration, testimony—German) (W. Stern) A social experiment designed to illustrate the limitations of witnesses. In one version, a class is suddenly interrupted by an intruder who berates the instructor and then behaves in an erratic manner. After the incident, students are asked detailed responses to questions about the scene, which usually reveals that their accuracy in remembering events is quite poor.

Austrian school of (act) psychology A group of individuals influenced by Franz Brentano who argued that psychology should be the study of acts (processes) rather than of contents. Also known as Graz school, Würzburg school. See ACT PSYCHOLOGY.

autarchic fever Refers to the belief of some children of their omnipotence. See ADOLESCENT EGOTISM.

autarchy A period of infancy when an infant exerts autocratic power over parents who satisfy all the infant's demands.

authentic counselor/therapist Describing a type of counselor and psychotherapist considered to be the best or most effective; such people are described as genuine, accepting, and caring, in addition to other qualities.

authenticity The quality of being internally genuine and outwardly real. A concept stressed by many philosophers and psychologists, including Søren Kierkegaard, Rollo May, Dan Motet, Carl Rogers, Fritz Perls, and Martin Buber.

authoritarian A type of leadership in group counseling (or groups in general) wherein the processes and decisions of the group rest with the leader.

authoritarian aggression A personality trait marked by hostile, punitive attitudes, and autocratic behavior, usually toward weaker persons or groups who appear to be outside conventional standards, considered one of the traits of the authoritarian personality. See AUTHORITARIAN PERSONALITY, AUTHORITARIAN SUBMISSION, AUTHORITARIANISM.

authoritarian character (structure) See AUTHORITARIAN PERSONALITY.

authoritarian conscience The phrase used by Erich Fromm for the tendency for some people to be guided by fear of an external authority, for example, parents. Compare Fromm's HUMANISTIC CONSCIENCE.

authoritarian ethic (E. Fromm) A value system whose source lies outside of the individual.

authoritarian group One of three groups established by Kurt Lewin to determine efficacy of leadership. See DEMOCRATIC GROUP, LAISSEZ-FAIRE GROUP.

authoritarianism A doctrine positing that people should be controlled by a superior power, whether in the form of a person, state, group, or idea, and that individuals should have no rights of their own apart from such a power. See DIVINE RIGHT OF KINGS.

authoritarian leader A type of leader who imposes his or her own goals and methods on group members, making all decisions, rejecting suggestions, and dominating interactions through frequent criticism and threats of punishment. See DEMOCRATIC LEADER, LAISSEZ-FAIRE LEADER.

authoritarian parent A parent who dominates a child, or tries to control a child's activity according to relatively rigid standards of behavior, stressing obedience without question. Such parents typically punish their children if they fail to obey the rules imposed on them. See AUTHORITATIVE PARENT, PERMISSIVE PARENT, REJECTING-NEGLECTING PARENT.

authoritarian personality (T. Adorno) A personality pattern characterized by preoccupation with power and status, strict adherence to conventional values, identification with authority figures, a demand for subservience or obedience on the part of others, and hostility toward minority or other out-groups. Sometimes known as authoritarian character (structure). See AUTHORITARIAN LEADER, AUTHORITARIAN PARENTING, AUTHORITARIANISM.

authoritarian submission (T. Adorno) A personality trait marked by the need for unquestioning blind submission to a dominant leader or authority. See AUTHORITARIAN AGGRESSION, AUTHORITARIANISM.

authoritative parent (D. Baumrind) A parent who directs the child's activities in a rational, relatively flexible way, encouraging collaboration and dialogue, yet exercising authority when necessary. Obedience is not valued for its own sake, but firm control is used to handle conflicts if a reasoned approach fails. See AUTHORITARIAN PARENT, DEMOCRATIC PARENT, PERMISSIVE PARENT, REJECTING-NEGLECTING PARENT.

authority complex A pattern of emotion-vested concepts of authority that are partially or completely repressed. These concepts may be bipolar, directed to submission or rebellion.

authority diffusion Vacillation between leadership and follower-ship roles, resulting in insecurity.

authority figure A person thought of by others as having power, influence, and proper standards of thought and behavior often invested by others to parents, teachers, and therapists.

authority principle A concept that each member of a social hierarchy is expected to comply with the wishes of those above. See DIVINE RIGHT OF KINGS.

autia (R. B. Cattell) A personality trait characterized by nonconformity, impracticability, dissociative behavior, and an autistic intellectual life. A tendency to believe what one wants to believe.

autism (E. Bleuler) Retreat from reality into a private world of fantasies, thoughts, and, in extreme cases, delusions and hallucinations. The autistic person is turned inward, a "shut-in" personality, apparently completely preoccupied with own needs and wishes, which are gratified largely or wholly in imagination. An autistic person may be indifferent or even hostile to others. See ABSENT-MINDEDNESS, EARLY INFANTILE AUTISM, NORMAL AUTISM.

autisme pauvre (poor autism, impoverished autism—French) (E. Minkowski) Refers to the withdrawal and detachment from reality observed in patients with schizophrenia. Also known as impoverished autism.

autistic child A child who has lost or never achieved contact with other people, demonstrating stereotyped repetitive behavior such as twirling objects or rocking. Other characteristics are indifference to parents or other people, an inability to tolerate change, and defective speech or mutism. The condition is interpreted by some as organically based, by others as a form of schizophrenia. See AUTISM, EARLY INFANTILE AUTISM.

autistic disorder A developmental disorder whose essential features are markedly impaired or abnormal development in communication and social interaction, and a markedly restricted repertoire of activity and interests, with onset before age 3 years. See EARLY INFANTILE AUTISM.

autistic fantasy Bizarre daydreams that may be an attempt to escape from reality.

autistic hostility Withdrawal from and ignoring input from others, usually as a result of being angry, having a defensive attitude, or not being willing to deal with or communicate with others.

autistic phase (M. S. Mahler) The first phase of development of the sense of self, occurring during the first few weeks of life, during which self and object are purportedly not differentiated. Also known as normal autism.

autistic psychopathy A personality disorder that is a combination of autism and psychopathy characterized by a lack of sensitivity and understanding of others and indifference to their rights and feelings. Communications are generally one-sided; patients proclaim rather than interact. Also known as Asperger's syndrome after Austrian physician Hans Asperger (ca. 1844–1954). See DANGEROUSNESS, PSYCHOPATHY, SOCIOPATHY.

autistic psychosis (M. S. Mahler) A form of infantile psychosis in which the child cannot maintain a symbiotic mother-child relationship. The child is thought to develop autism as a defense against both external and internal stimuli.

autistic thinking/thought (E. Bleuler) Narcissistic, egocentric thought processes, such as flights of fancy and daydreaming, which have little or no relation to reality. See AUTISM, DEREISM.

autoaggressive activities Behavior in which individuals hurt or mutilate themselves, as in some cases of chronic schizophrenia or Lesch-Nyhan syndrome. See SELF-MUTILATION.

autoagonistophilia   Being sexually aroused from being observed or on stage while engaged in sexual activity.

autoallergy   A condition in which the body's immune system reacts to and rejects its own cells as if they were foreign proteins. Tends to increase with age as the immune system deteriorates. A primary factor in the development of such diseases as rheumatoid arthritis. See AUTOIMMUNITY.

autoassassinatophilia   Being sexually aroused by the idea of staging one's own masochistic death.

autobiographical memory   Recollections of events of a person's own life. See EARLY RECOLLECTIONS.

autobiography   In counseling and psychotherapy, a technique designed to elicit information regarding a client's behavioral patterns, cognitions, and emotions by means of a life history written or dictated by the client. A structured autobiography is based on topical guidelines supplied by the counselor or therapist. An unstructured autobiography containing no guidelines may uncover more latent content, especially if the client is highly verbal.

autocatharsis   1. A form of therapy in which a person releases disturbing emotions by writing down upsetting experiences or feelings. 2. Essentially, the same concept, but using a voice recorder. Generally, the person speaks into the recorder as though the recorder were another person, and later listens to the recording. The basic premise is that by either method, greater self-knowledge will occur.

autochiria   Obsolete term for suicide.

autochthonous   (from the land itself, from the soil—Greek) 1. Native, indigenous, original. 2. Something that originates from within as from an organ of the body. 3. Coming from within the mind such as an idea, the solution of a problem, a memory, or an invention. 4. Learning on one's own, perhaps by assembling various data into a coherent whole. 5. In therapy, coming to an independent solution to a personal problem, an insight about self, or understanding of others.

autochthonous delusion   A false belief that appears suddenly and without an apparent cause or explanation. Usually involves a disturbance of symbolic meaning (such as the idea that the universe will be twisted out of shape) as opposed to disturbances of perception or intellect. See BIZARRE DELUSION.

autochthonous determinants of perception   Organismic factors or functions that are a direct reflection of the characteristic physiological properties of a sense organ. Compare BEHAVIORAL DETERMINANTS OF PERCEPTION.

autochthonous Gestalt   A perceptual pattern induced by internal factors rather than by an external stimulus.

autochthonous idea   (E. Bleuler) A thought that originates within the mind, usually from an unconscious source, yet appears to arise independently of the person's stream of consciousness, such as fantasies, dreams, delusions, inspirations, insights as well as repetitious thoughts of obsessive-compulsive individuals. See AUTOCHTHONY.

autochthonous laws   Refers to the innate understanding of proper behavior or perceptions that people "obey" without instruction or experience. Some Gestalt laws such as closure, continuity, proximity, and similarity are considered autochthonous. See A POSTERIORI, A PRIORI.

autochthonous variable   A change that develops from internal, as opposed to external, factors.

autochthony   A condition arising from within a person. Term is usually employed to mean autochthonous ideas of a pathological type, such as delusions. See AUTOCHTHONOUS.

autoclitic responses   Verbal responses that incline toward giving a person's thoughts away (for example, "I think that", "I have no doubts about", and "I wonder whether . . ."), which inform listeners as to how a person feels about a forthcoming statement.

autocompetition   Attempts to surpass previous self-performance, self-achievement, etc.

autocorrectivism   See HOMEOSTASIS.

autocorrelation   In statistics, the correlations of elements of a time series with other elements separated by one or more steps or lags. Autocorrelation estimates the amount of serial dependency.

autocorrelation theory   A point of view that groups of individual nerve fibers collaborate to transmit auditory nerve impulses, based on evidence that since a single fiber is unable to transmit impulses faster than 1000 Hertz (cycles per second), fibers must function as a team with one firing at one cycle, another at the next cycle, and so on. See VOLLEY PRINCIPLE.

autocratic leadership   A management style in which decisions and leadership are appropriated by one person or a small group.

autocriticism   Self-criticism.

autodysosmophobia   Morbid fear of smelling bad, or a delusion of having an offensive odor. See AUTOMYSOPHOBIA, BROMIDROSIPHOBIA.

autoecholalia   A type of stereotyped behavior observed especially in catatonic schizophrenia in which the patient continuously repeats the same word or phrase. See CATAPHASIA.

autoechopraxia   A form of stereotyped behavior in which the patient, usually schizophrenic, repeats an action previously experienced, for example, kneeling for hours or days in the same spot.

autoerotic   Sexual arousal or excitement arising through the self, without the participation of another individual.

autoerotic asphyxiation   Being choked or strangled while having sex, usually done during solitary masturbation but also in the presence or with assistance of others.

autoerot(ic)ism   1. Sexual arousal using one's own body, as in masturbation. Also known as autosexualism. 2. See NARCISSISM (meaning 5). 3. Any self-induced sexual excitement, usually through fantasies or through looking at, reading, or listening to erotic material, generally resulting in sexual self-gratification. See ALLOEROTISM. 4. (H. Ellis) A term applied by Havelock Ellis to sexual arousal in the absence of any stimulus, originating autochthonously (within the person), for example, genital excitement during sleep.

autofetishism Narcissism in which the patient's own possessions become an obsessional target of sexual arousal.

autoflagellation Self-inflicted whipping, whether as a form of religious penitence or for erotic arousal (stigmatophilia, automasochism).

autogenic Self-generated; self-created. See AUTO-CHTHONOUS.

autogenic reinforcement The self-induced strengthening of a reaction so that the response to a particular stimulus is more prompt or more intense than would otherwise be exhibited by the same person to the same stimulus.

autogenic standard formulas Suggestions made during hypnotic or semi-hypnotic states intended to induce bodily sensations such as warmth and heaviness.

autogenic therapy/training (J. H. Schultz, O. Vogt) A relaxation technique in which a quasi-hypnotic state is self-induced and relaxation is achieved through deep breathing, muscular relaxation, and abdominal exercises. The method, usually accompanied by a meditative technique or by imagery, is used to correct functional irregularities of organs and for general intellectual and physical invigoration. See BIOFEEDBACK.

autogenic training autogenic therapy

autogenital stimulation The stimulation by a human or animal of own genitals. See MASTURBATION.

autogenous Originating from within, self-generated, self-induced. Also known as autogenetic, autogenic. See AUTOCHTHONOUS.

autognosis Knowledge of self. See INSIGHT.

autohedonia Obsolete term for masturbation.

autohypnosis Self-induced hypnosis. May occur spontaneously, as in looking fixedly at bright lights, listening to monotonously repeated sounds, driving a car at night; or through training in autosuggestion. Also known as autohypnotism, idiohypnotism, statuvolence.

autohypnotic amnesia (C. G. Jung) A Jungian phrase for repression.

autoimmunity A disorder in which the body reacts to some of its own tissues as if they were a foreign substance, as in autoallergy.

autointoxication A form of poisoning caused by toxins generated within the patient's own body. Also known as autotoxicosis, enterotoxication, enterotoxism, endogenic toxicosis, self-poisoning.

autokinesis Voluntary movement. Movement initiated by stimuli within the organism itself. Also known as autokinesia. See PROPRIOCEPTIVE STIMULI.

autokinetic effect The perception of movement in a stationary spot of light on a dark background, associated with a person's own eye movements. Used in research, as in investigating suggestibility to or the establishment of group norms. Also known as autokinetic illusion/phenomenon, Charpentier's illusion.

automasochism Being sexually attracted to or aroused by self-inflicted pain. See APOTEMNOPHILIA, ASPHYXIOPHILIA, AUTOASSASSINATOPHILIA, STIGMATOPHILIA.

automated assessment A system of evaluating psychological information about an individual by the use of computer devices that use data banks of previously acquired information for making comparisons, diagnoses, and prognoses.

automated clinical records A standardized record-keeping system suitable for computerized retrieval of information for purposes such as monitoring patient care, providing data for administrative decisions, and assisting clinicians in understanding and treating patients.

automated desensitization See DEVICE FOR AUTOMATED DESENSITIZATION.

automated learning/training A self-operated type of training (such as computerized flight trainers), which approximates the actual task to be performed, sometimes with token participation (regulating controls, etc.) by an instructor. See LINK TRAINER, PROGRAMMED INSTRUCTION.

automated speech recognition Machine capacity to recognize the speech of humans.

automatic action/behavior (M. Prince) A behavior not under voluntary control. An act performed without conscious awareness such as changing position in bed while sleeping.

automatic decisions Choices made without thought, such as type of item always selected between competing brands.

automatic drawing 1. The act of generating images while in a hypnotic trance or while attention is distracted. 2. An illustration produced without volition, usually said to represent unconscious fantasies or impulses. See AUTOMATIC WRITING, HYPNOSIS, SUGGESTION.

automaticity 1. The establishment of automatic processing on some specific cognitive task. 2. (J. A. Bargh) Cognitive processes or behavioral actions that (a) occur outside of awareness, (b) can be perceived or stopped, (c) do not need volition to begin them, and (c) do not consume additional cognitive processing resources.

automatic memory Rare phrase for a reactivated feeling or emotional complex (for example, déjà vu). Something reexperienced although the person may not be aware of its association to an earlier situation. Usually, the activation is due to one of the senses, often by a smell that brings up a memory of a long-past event, or by hearing a sound such as a song that had meaning in the past or that was associated with the memory.

automatic obedience Pathological behavior in which the person blindly and uncritically or mechanically repeats the speech or actions or commands of others as in deep hypnosis. See COMMAND AUTOMATISM, ECHOLALIA, ECHOPRAXIA, OBEDIENCE.

automatic processes Cognitive processes that can be initiated and run off without the allocation of attentional resources. See HABIT.

automatic processing Effortless encoding of incidental information, such as space, time, and frequency not under conscious control.

automatic promotion A common system of advancing children from one school grade to the next because of their chronological ages rather than because of their knowledge or their potential.

automatic seizures   A form of psychomotor epilepsy in which actions may be carried out automatically, such as continuing to work, with later amnesia for what was performed. See EPILEPSY, AUTOMATIC OBEDIENCE.

automatic speech   1. The mechanical verbal repetition of consecutive words such as days of week, numbers, and various kinds of accessory expressions. 2. Speech that erupts involuntarily, or without conscious control, as in senility or highly emotional states. See TOURETTE SYNDROME.

automatic thought   An idea triggered by a particular stimulus that leads to a specific emotional response.

automatic writing   The act of writing without conscious awareness, as during a hypnotic trance. Purportedly can provide a therapist access to unconscious material. See AUTOMATIC DRAWING.

automation   The allocation of tasks to machines.

automatism   1. Activity without conscious intent. 2. Mechanical, repetitive motor behavior, carried out unconsciously. 3. An activity performed mechanically, without intention, and frequently without awareness. Examples range from reflex responses and habitual acts to complex activities, such as sleepwalking. It is characteristic of various disorders such as psychomotor epilepsy and Pick's disease. Kinds of automatism include confusional, gestural, and verbal. 4. An epileptic episode characterized by performance of mental, sensory, or motor phenomena without full consciousness.

automatization   1. The development of a skill or habit to a point where it becomes routine and requires little if any conscious effort or direction. 2. Obeying compulsive impulses automatically without thought.

automatograph   An instrument intended to measure small automatic movements.

automaton   A machine that simulates human functions, such as a robotic spot-welder or automatic machines that run mazes, take shortcuts, and even "choose" between goals. See CYBERNETICS, FEEDBACK.

automaton conformity   (E. Fromm) A type of behavior in which an individual submissively follows the dictates of a group that establishes the cultural pattern of the individual's environment. Seen in adolescents breaking away from the control of their parents only to be controlled by their friends. See ENCULTURATION, PEER PRESSURE.

automorphic perception   Perceiving others in terms of oneself while ignoring any differences between self and others. See SELF-PERCEPTION.

automutilation   Being sexually aroused by self-inflicted mutilation.

automysophobia   Morbid fear of personal uncleanliness. Fear of being dirty, of being unclean. May inhibit sexual relations.

autonecrophilia   Being sexually aroused by imagining oneself as a corpse.

autonepiophilia   Being sexually aroused by impersonating or being treated as an infant. See AUTOPEDOPHILIA.

autonoetic memory   (E. Tulving) Episodic memory that is dependent on the person's self-awareness.

autonomasia   A type of amnesic aphasia in which the person is unable to recall nouns or names. See AMNESIC APHASIA.

autonomic   1. Pertaining to the autonomic nervous system. 2. Obsolete term for autonomous.

autonomic apparatus   All vital organs, including the ductless glands and viscera, controlled by the autonomic nervous system.

autonomic balance   The complementary interaction between the sympathetic and the parasympathetic branches of the autonomic nervous system that regulate bodily functions.

autonomic conditioning   Gaining conscious control over autonomic processes (such as heart rate) through conditioning. See BIOFEEDBACK.

autonomic disorganization   Overmobilization of the autonomic nervous system occurring during a situation of extreme stress resulting in confusion, with weakness, fright, and behavioral disorganization.

autonomic epilepsy   A type of seizure that may affect an otherwise normal individual, caused by a sudden diffuse discharge of autonomic-nerve impulses. The person may experience fever, chills, tears, and blood pressure changes.

autonomic hyperactivity   Physical signs of anxiety including sweating, pounding heart, dry mouth, frequent urination, and diarrhea.

autonomic motor pools   The motor neurons located in either the brainstem or interomedial lateral portions of the spinal cord that give rise to nerves that supply specific autonomic ganglia.

autonomic nerve   Any nerve that is a part of the autonomic nervous system, such as a nerve involved in regulating activity of the heart muscle or of various glands.

autonomic nervous system (ANS)   A functional division of the nervous system involved primarily in internal, involuntary bodily functions such as those of the circulatory, digestive, and respiratory organs, itself divided into sympathetic and parasympathetic systems. See CENTRAL NERVOUS SYSTEM, SOMATIC NERVOUS SYSTEM.

autonomic reactivity   An individuals reaction tendency that begins in infancy and continues into adult life as manifestations of sensitivity differences to aversive stimuli. Some individuals manifest their reaction by faster pulses, others by stomach pains and others by overall tension.

autonomic responses   Any smooth-muscle or glandular activity that occurs as a result of stimuli received through the autonomic nervous system.

autonomic seizure   A recurrent epileptic episode involving the autonomic nervous system, characterized by heart palpitations, vomiting, sweating, temperature changes, tearing of the eyes, and abdominal distress.

autonomic side effect   A visceral reaction such as increased blood pressure or heart rate and decreased stomach secretions, associated with stress or with ingestion of certain drugs.

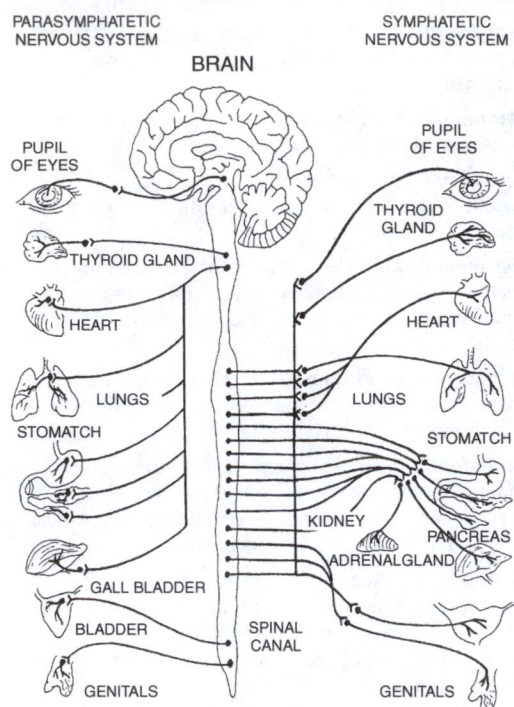

PARASYMPATHETIC NERVOUS SYSTEM

SYMPHATETIC NERVOUS SYSTEM

BRAIN

PUPIL OF EYES

PUPIL OF EYES

THYROID GLAND

THYROID GLAND

HEART

HEART

LUNGS

LUNGS

STOMATCH

STOMATCH

KIDNEY

PANCREAS

ADRENALGLAND

GALL BLADDER

BLADDER

SPINAL CANAL

GENITALS

GENITALS

autonomic nervous system (ANS)

autonomic-sympathomimetic drugs Obsolete phrase for agents that can mimic the actions of natural substances in stimulating functions of the sympathetic nervous system. See SYMPATHOMIMETIC, STIMULANT.

autonomous Independent; not controlled by outside forces. Once called autonomic.

autonomous activity In general systems theory, the view that the human organism is not passive and inert, and not wholly dependent on responses to external stimuli, the reduction of tension, or the reestablishment of equilibrium. Rather, humans are seen as intrinsically active. Spontaneous autonomous processes represent a primitive form of behavior taking many forms, such as play, exploration, and intellectual and esthetic pursuits for their own sake and not merely as a means of reducing tension or satisfying biological drives.

autonomous complex (C. G. Jung) A complex that moved from the unconscious to the conscious level of awareness.

autonomous depression (R. D. Gillespie) A type of depression characterized by restlessness, self-accusation, and more activity than in reactive depression, as well as less hypochondriacal than in certain endogenous depression.

autonomous mode A way of acting characterized by behaving in accordance with needs, wants, and morality and assuming responsibility for self-actions.

autonomous morality 1. The making of a decision that is right because it seems correct at the time of occurrence rather than based on some external standard. The motto "What feels good must be good" expresses this concept. See AUTONOMOUS STAGE.

autonomous stage (J. Piaget) The second stage of Jean Piaget's moral development concept wherein an older child gradually comes to rely less on parental authority and more on individual and independent morality. In this stage the child self-disciplines; in the earlier heteronomous stage, discipline is imposed by parents. Sometimes known as autonomous morality. See AUTONOMOUS MORALITY, FREE WILL.

autonomous therapy Formal self-therapy usually focused on a search for self-identity and critical examination of self-motives, practiced by Sigmund Freud, and considered by Karen Horney and Theodor Reik to be superior to interactive therapy.

autonomous work groups Groups wherein all members work on the basis of equality.

autonomy (law unto oneself—Greek) 1. A state of independence and self-determination, either in a society or an individual. 2. A basic tendency and desire to be free to control the self. See FUNCTIONAL AUTONOMY, HETERONOMY.

autonomy drive (A. Angyal) A basic motivational pattern, the striving toward mastery. Compare HOMONOMY DRIVE.

autonomy-heteronomy The balance between the biological individual and the environment in a world where there are no sharp boundaries but only degrees of ego proximity and ego distance.

autonomy of motives functional autonomy

autonomy vs doubt and shame (E. Erikson) The second of Erik Erikson's eight stages of psychosocial development. During the second and third years, children either develop a degree of independence if allowed to be active at their own pace, or begin to doubt their ability to control themselves and their own world if parents are overcritical, overprotective, or inconsistent. See ERIKSON'S STAGES OF PSYCHOSOCIAL DEVELOPMENT.

autopagnosia autotopagnosia

autopedophilia Being sexually aroused by impersonating an infant and being treated as a baby. See AUTONEPIOPHILIA.

autophagia 1. In psychology, a pathological process characterized by the chewing or eating of one's own flesh. See LESCH-NYHAN SYNDROME, SELF-MUTILATION. 2. In physiology, a normal process characterized by metabolic consumption of some body tissue for maintenance of the whole body. See ANABOLISM, CATABOLISM, METABOLISM.

autophilia 1. Self-love. 2. Literally, love of self. See NARCISSISM (meaning 2).

autophobia Morbid fear of being alone or the fear of oneself. The term erem(i)ophobia is similar and refers to fear of solitude and of desolate, uninhabited places. Also known as monophobia.

autophonic response The echo-like reproduction and vibration of a person's own voice, commonly referred to as "hearing one's own voice." Also known as autophonia, autophony.

autophony 1. Increased resonance of one's own voice, respiratory or circulatory sounds, particularly as the result of disease of the middle ear. See AUTOPHONIC RESPONSE.

autoplastic behavior   Relating to actions that are molded toward fitting oneself to the environment. See AGGRESSION, ALLOPLASTIC.

autoplasty   In psychoanalytic theory, the process of adapting to reality by modifying self-behavioral patterns, particularly those manifested by neurotic behavior. Using libidinous drive to change the self. Compare ALLOPLASTY.

autopsy   A surgical procedure on a corpse usually done to determine the cause of death. Sometimes known as thanatopsy. See PSYCHOLOGICAL AUTOPSY.

autopsy-negative death   Refers to a death that is not explainable by autopsy. Sometimes applied to cases of lethal catatonia among psychiatric patients who suddenly develop fever, hyperactivity, delusions, and hallucinations, then die without other warning. See BELL'S MANIA.

autopsychic   Characterizing ideas and impulses that originate in the self or relate to the individual's personality. See AUTOCHTHONOUS.

autopsychic delusion   (K. Wernicke) A delusion about the patient's own personality, as opposed to one about the patient's body or the external world. See ALLOPSYCHIC DELUSION, SOMATIC DELUSION, SOMATOPSYCHIC DELUSION.

autopsychic orientation   The perception of one's own personality or psychic self, particularly the awareness of changes in self-personality. See IDIOPANIMA.

autopsychosis   A form of paranoid disorder in which patients maintain distorted ideas about themselves, such as being the world's savior, the devil incarnate, or an unrecognized genius. Such ideas are autopsychic in the double sense of pertaining to the self and arising from within the psyche. See AUTOCHTHONOUS.

autoreceptor   A receptor molecule on a neuron that responds to a neurotransmitter released by the neuron.

autorivalry   An endeavor to equal or surpass one's own previous attainment.

autoscopic experiences   Disorders in which people perceive themselves as being projected outside their own bodies.

autoscopic phenomenon/syndrome   A rare delusional disorder in which the patient sees a "double" who looks, talks, acts, and dresses like the patient. The image, which may occur only once or repeatedly, is generally hazy, filmy, and colorless. Also known as autoscopy.

autoscopophilia   Being sexually attracted to or aroused by looking at one's own body and genitals.

autosexualism   1. See AUTOEROT(IC)ISM (meaning 1). 2. See NARCISSISM (meaning 2).

autosexuality   A form of sexual arousal or stimulation that occurs without participation of another as in masturbation, sexual dreams, and sexual fantasies.

autoshaping   A learning process in which a response increases in frequency through self-generated reinforcers rather than being shaped by contingent extrinsic reinforcement.

autosomal   Denoting a genetic characteristic located on or transmitted by an autosome.

autosomal aberrations   Any alterations in the structure of one of the pairs of chromosomes that are not sex chromosomes. May appear as translocations of genetic material from a normal location in a particular chromosome to another, or from deletion of genetic material from a chromosome, or by the rearrangement of genetic material. An example of the effect of an autosomal aberration is Down's syndrome. The abnormality may be dominant as in Huntington's illness or recessive as in Tay-Sachs disease. Also known as autosomal abnormalities/anomalies.

autosomal dominant gene   A gene associated with a nonsex-determining chromosome, that is, one of a pair of alternative alleles present in the same cell that masks the effect of the other allele. See AUTOSOMAL RECESSIVE GENE, PICK'S DISEASE.

autosomal dominant inheritance   Pattern of inheritance in which a specific gene is dominant; if it is inherited, it manifests itself in the organism. Also known as dominant inheritance.

autosomal recessive gene   A gene associated with a nonsex-determining chromosome, that is, one of a pair of alternative alleles present in the same cell whose effect is diluted (masked) by the other allele. See AUTOSOMAL DOMINANT GENE, MICROCEPHALY, PHENYLKETONURIA, TRISOMY.

autosomal recessive inheritance   A pattern of inheritance in which a trait appears only if an organism inherits two genes for it, one from each parent. If offspring inherit only one gene for the trait, it will not appear in those offspring but may be passed on to the next generation.

autosomal trisomy of Group G   Another name for Down's syndrome. See TRISOMY.

autosome   A chromosome, but not an X or Y sex chromosome, that occurs in pairs in somatic cells but singly in gametes. A human normally has 22 pairs, or a total of 44 autosomes in each cell, although irregular numbers may occur through the loss or addition of one or more autosomes. The occurrence of three rather than paired autosomes is identified as a trisomy condition.

autostasis   The perception of an object as stationary when it is moving.

autostereogram   A special type of two-dimensional visual stimulus that may be seen three-dimensionally (stereoscopically) without special devices such as 3-D goggles. Such two-dimensional pictures or patterns may be composed of random dots or shapes that when first apprehended resemble a set of random patterns, but which may be seen by some people as taking on form and depth. Perception of a 3-D picture involves a dissociation of the accommodation response from the convergence response, and some viewers are more successful than others in perceiving depth. However, viewing the picture extremely close-up and then backing away slowly while continuing to stare at it usually helps. See SENSORY MEMORY.

autostereoscopy   The perception of three dimensions from a two-dimensional picture that appears to consist of random patterns. See AUTOSTEREOGRAM.

autostereotype   (H. C. Triandis) The set of attributes that supposedly characterizes a person's own group. See HETEROSTEREOTYPE.

autosuggestibility　　Susceptibility to being influenced by self-ideas, self-attitudes, or by internal commands, as in autohypnosis.

autosuggestion　　Self-suggestion, the process of giving suggestions to oneself to improve morale, induce relaxation, or promote recovery from illness. Autosuggestion has evolved from the crude affirmations of Emile Coué ("Day by Day, in Every Way, I Am Getting Better and Better"), and self "pep talk" approaches to autohypnosis as an adjunct to hypnotherapy and relaxation techniques. See AFFIRMATIONS, AUTOGENIC TRAINING, AUTOHYPNOSIS, SELF-HYPNOSIS, SELF-TALK.

autosymbolism　　The transformation of abstract dream-content into symbolic images that can be seen in dreams. See DREAM ANALYSIS, DREAM CONTENT, DREAM IMAGERY, DREAM STIMULUS.

autotelic　　Behaviors and traits that are central to a person's major goals, such as being self-respecting, or self-protective.

autotomy　　Casting off of a body part, as when a lizard sheds its tail to escape from a predator. May be applied to the acts of some people, almost always considered psychotic, who perform self-mutilation of body parts that may offend or upset them, usually chopping off penises, but occasionally fingers or hands. Also known as autotomia.

autotopagnosia　　Inability to recognize, identify, and locate parts of a person's own body, a result of brain damage. Also spelled autopagnosia. See AGNOSIA, APHASIA, SOMATOTOPAGNOSIS.

auxiliary　　1. Acting as a subsidiary; giving assistance or support, helping. 2. In linguistics, a word that has no complete meaning and function in itself and is used in combination with other words that have independent meaning and function, such as prepositions, conjunctions, and some auxiliary verbs such as "may."

auxiliary ego　　In psychodrama, an assistant to the therapist who helps to advance the therapeutic process by playing the role of a significant figure in the protagonist's life, and in some cases by acting out the protagonist's hallucinations, delusions, and fantasies, or by exchanging roles with the patient.

auxiliary chair technique　　(R. Lippitt) A method of providing inanimate role-players by using a chair. The leader in a therapy group points out that a chair has a back, a seat, legs, and can have arms. The client interacts with the chair as though it were a person.

auxiliary solution　　(K. Horney) A partial or temporary solution to an intrapsychic conflict, as in compartmentalization and externalization.

auxiliary therapist　　A cotherapist in psychotherapy. The cotherapist can play several roles. One role is to remain silent throughout the session until the end, then summarizing and evaluating the session, either with or without the client or clients (as in group therapy) present. See MULTIPLE THERAPY.

AVA　　activity vector analysis

ava　　**kava**

availability　　See READINESS.

availability-assessment data　　In evaluation research, information sought to identify problem areas of program evaluation; a review of expectations for program performance and questions to be answered by evaluation data, followed by a study of program implementation to identify designs, measurements, and possible analyses.

availability heuristic/principle　　1. A cognitive rule of thumb in which the relative probabilities of related events are judged by the ease with which examples of those events can be brought to mind. See SUPPRESSED MEMORIES. 2. The availability of an organism to respond appropriately and easily to a problem or situation.

avalanche conduction　　Neural conduction that affects so many other neurons that the final effect is greatly disproportionate to the size of the original excitation. See LAW OF AVALANCHE.

average　　1. General term referring to a number of procedures for determining the central tendency of a set of numbers or of their results. 2. Arithmetic mean. See MEAN, MEDIAN, MODE, MOVING AVERAGE.

average deviation (AD or A.D.)　　A measure of the dispersion or spread of scores, obtained by finding the average of the absolute differences between each score and the mean. This measure has been supplanted by the standard deviation. In a normal distribution the AD is related to the standard deviation by the $AD = .7979\sigma$. In general, when the mean is allowed to represent every score in the distribution, AD is given by: $AD = \Sigma|X - \bar{X}| \div N$, where: $|X - \bar{X}|$ means the absolute value of the difference between some score, X, and the mean, X $\bar{X}$. Or AD is given by: $AD = \Sigma|D| \div N$, where: $|D|$ is the absolute value of the deviation from the mean. Also known as mean deviation/variation.

average error　　1. The average of deviations from the true measure. 2. See METHOD OF AVERAGE ERROR.

average evoked response technique (AERT)　　Individual electrical responses of parts of the brain to external stimuli are often of quite low magnitudes and hidden in surrounding noise. With the aid of computers, researchers "average out" the electrical noises to expose intrinsic signals not discernible in the raw traces, yielding components of internal cognitive processing.

average score　　1. Any measure of central tendency. 2. Arithmetic mean score.

averages law　　A theory that the arithmetic mean of a group of observations has a probability of occurrence which is greater than that of any single observation for a properly selected population and method of attainment. See LAW OF AVERAGES.

aversion　　The feeling that an individual, object, or situation should be avoided, usually accompanied by physical withdrawal or turning of the face away from it.

aversion conditioning　　Counterconditioning that functions as punishment, used therapeutically, for example, in the treatment of alcoholism and sex deviations. Also known as averse conditioning and aversive conditioning. See AVERSIVE THERAPY, PUNISHMENT.

aversion reaction/response　　Avoiding a distasteful or threatening stimulus or situation, such as refusing to eat certain foods, refusing to enter certain areas, or responding negatively to attempts to obtain participation in an undesired activity. See AVERSIVE THERAPY, AVOIDANCE CONDITIONING.

aversion therapy   A form of behavior therapy in which the patient is conditioned to avoid undesirable behavior or symptoms by associating them with painful or unpleasant experiences, such as a bitter taste (for nail-biting), nausea (for alcoholism), or an electrical shock (for enuresis). Also known as aversive therapy. See THERAPY.

aversive behavior   Actions that remove an organism from some object or other organism considered harmful or dangerous.

aversive center   A nerve center in the brain especially reactive to or involved in noxious stimuli and experiences.

aversive conditioning   Punishing an organism whenever it makes a particular response.

aversive control   The control of an organism through punishment; for example, shocking a rat every time it presses a bar to obtain food suppresses bar-pressing.

aversive event   An unpleasant and undesirable occasion that, when reduced or terminated tends to increase occurrence of responses that preceded the termination. Aversive events elicit reflex motor responses, fear, and newly learned responses. See ESCAPE LEARNING.

aversive learning   A behavior therapy technique intended to inhibit an undesired response to a given stimulus by systematically pairing that stimulus with a painful or unpleasant (aversive) stimulus.

aversive racism   Unconscious racism. A form of racism marked by a dichotomy between conscious attitudes and behavior; specifically, racist behavior coupled with nonracist attitudes, purportedly indicating unconscious denial. Researchers in this area typically check participants' attitudes and then observe their behavior in experimental interracial interactions.

aversive-reinforcement conditioning   A method of getting organisms to either perform or not to perform certain activities by punishing the organism if, depending on what is wanted, it does or does not do what the experimenter desires. See WYATT VS STICKNEY DECISION.

aversive stimulus   Any object or occurrence that tends to produce an avoidance reaction.

aversive therapy   See AVERSION THERAPY.

Aveyron boy   See WILD BOY OF AVEYRON.

aviation psychology   The application of psychological principles to aviation, including selection of personnel (especially pilots), methods of training, effects of time-zone changes, perceptual issues related to landings over water and at night, functioning in fog, and reactions to severe environments and emergencies. See LINK TRAINER.

aviator's neurasthenia   A syndrome of gastrointestinal disorders, irritability, insomnia, emotional stress, and mental fatigue once associated with military aviators in World War I.

aviophobia   Fear of flying.

avocation   A form of self-directed activity which a person pursues in addition to the regular occupation or vocation, either as recreation or as a social (national or religious) obligation.

avoidance   1. Escaping from a noxious stimulus. 2. A defense mechanism in which situations, activities, or objects that recall or represent painful events are avoided, such as in aichmophobia (fear of pointed objects).

avoidance-avoidance conflict   A conflict situation characterized by a choice between two objectionable alternatives, such as a pacifist choosing between going to jail or leaving the country in time of war. Also known as negative-negative conflict. See APPROACH-APPROACH CONFLICT, APPROACH-AVOIDANCE CONFLICT.

avoidance behavior   Any act that enables an organism to prevent the occurrence of a painful stimulus or permits escape from a conditioned aversive stimulus. See AVOIDANCE CONDITIONING.

avoidance conditioning/learning   Training an organism to avoid a noxious stimulus, such as in a shuttlebox situation with animals, a warning buzzer is sounded followed by shock. The animal escapes shock by jumping a barrier to the other side. After several trials the animal jumps as soon as the buzzer sounds and thereby avoids the shock.

avoidance gradient   A graduated variation in the strength of withdrawal as an organism approaches a positive goal which has certain negative elements; the gradient has a steeper slope than the approach gradient. The concept is important in understanding certain types of conflict situations (for example, wanting to avoid an examination usually increases as the day approaches). See APPROACH-AVOIDANCE CONFLICT, GRADIENT.

avoidance reaction/response   A type of response in which the organism moves away from a stimulus, usually because it is sensed as threatening or noxious.

avoidance response   See AVOIDANCE REACTION.

avoidance rituals   (E. Goffman) A variety of procedures that people develop to reduce social contact, for example, not making eye contact with others that a person does not want to relate to. See PRESENTATION RITUALS.

avoidance training   The teaching process in which the organism avoids a painful stimulus by making an appropriate anticipatory response. See ESCAPE TRAINING.

avoidance without warning signal   A phrase sometimes used as a synonym for Sidman avoidance (conditioning).

avoidant attachment   A pattern of attachment in which an infant rarely cries when separated from the primary caregiver and avoids contact with that person upon his or her return.

avoidant disorder of childhood   A disorder lasting at least six months between the ages of 2½ and 18 years, characterized by persistent, excessive shrinking from strangers. May interfere with peer relationships, but satisfying relationships with family members are usually maintained. Also known as avoidant disorder of adolescence.

avoidant paruresis   See BASHFUL BLADDER (SYNDROME).

avoidant personality   A type of personality characterized by seeking to remain anonymous and to not be noticed by others; the individual avoids social interaction but may still desire it, as is the case with some shy people. See AVOIDANT PERSONALITY DISORDER.

avoidant personality disorder   A diagnosis assigned to a person showing a pattern of behavior characterized by hypersensitivity to rejection and criticism, social withdrawal, and low self-esteem. May impair the person's ability to work and maintain relationships.

avoider(s) 1. (N. Kefir) One of four basic lifestyles according to Nira Kefir; the avoider reacts against the possibility of stress, wants a life without problems, and he or she consequently establishes a pattern of finding the easiest way to get along in life. See MAJOR PRIORITIES. 2. (A. Adler) Refers to one of Alfred Adler's four main types of people, those who do as little as possible socially. See ADLER'S PERSONALITY TYPES.

avolition Without volition, having no desires. See ABULIA.

awareness A consciousness of internal or external events or experiences. Types of awareness include: BODY, CHOICE, CONTINGENCY, LINGUISTIC, OBJECTIVE SELF-, REALITY, RESOURCE, SELF-, SENSORY. See CONSCIOUSNESS, SENSORY AWARENESS.

awareness context Knowledge of self and of others about the situational relevance of behavior in any situation.

awareness defect Impaired consciousness or perception; lack of alertness, or inability to be cognizant of internal or external events. Being unaware of what is going on, especially when others are aware.

awareness training institutes Group development sessions for individual growth that usually have up to several hundred people attending, usually for two 12–18 hour sessions. The programs vary with the preferences of the leaders, with members being given instructions for participation in various exercises intended to generate self-understanding and interpersonal trust. See BEHIND THE BACK TECHNIQUE, BLIND WALK, ENCOUNTER EXERCISES.

awareness-training model An approach in psychology and education stressing self-awareness, self-realization, exploration, and interpersonal sensitivity.

awfulizing (A. Ellis) Viewing something inconvenient, unpleasant, or undesirable as terrible or horrible. The basis of much of maladjustment according to Albert Ellis. See RATIONAL-EMOTIVE-BEHAVIOR THERAPY.

Ax See AXIS.

axes of reference Three lines of reference used in describing the location of parts, organs, etc., of the body.

axial 1. Refers to the longitudinal axis of the body. 2. In anatomy, refers to the central portion of the body, not the limbs. 3. Pertaining to an axis.

axial amnesia amnesic syndrome

axial command An order to carry out movements involving the body axis, such as "turn around." Sometimes the only speech to which people with global aphasia respond.

axial gradient A graded difference in the organization of embryonic tissues and physiological capacity along the primary axis of the body. See CEPHALOCAUDAL DEVELOPMENT.

axiodrama Roleplaying of behavior relating to good moral values and ethics. See PSYCHODRAMA, PSYCHODRAMA FORMS.

axiology 1. The science or study of moral values (what is "good" and what is "evil"). 2. The study of values, such as in ethics, religion, and esthetics. See ALLPORT-VERNON-LINDZEY STUDY OF VALUES.

axiom A self-evident truth; a universally accepted principle not capable of proof or disproof, such as Eucledian Postulates.

axis (Ax) 1. A reference line for measuring or defining relationships, such as an organism's head-to-tail (cephalocaudal) placement. 2. The central line of the body or of body parts. 3. The spinal column.

axis cylinder A central or conducting core of an axon, consisting of a plasm (axoplasm) surrounded by a sheath called the axolemma.

axoaxonic synapse A synaptic junction between two nerve cells in which the nerve impulse travels from one axon to the other, rather than between axon and dendrite or axon and cell body. Also known as axo-axonal synapse. See SYNAPSE.

axodendritic synapse A synapse of an axon on a dendrite.

axolemma The plasma membrane of an axon. See AXIS CYLINDER.

axon The cylindrical process of a nerve cell that normally carries an impulse away from its associated cell body and dendrites. Axons range in thickness from 0.25 to 10 microns, and vary in length from a few microns to nearly a meter. Also spelled axone. See NEURON.

axonal bundle A structure made up of a group of axons, also known as a fasciculus.

axonal terminals The ends of axons that convey energy from the terminal ends of the neurons.

axonal transport Rare phrase for axoplasmic transport, the preferred phrase.

axonal varicosities Enlarged areas on an axon containing synaptic vesicles that release a neurotransmitter.

axone axon

axon hillock The region where the axon arises from the neuron cell body.

axon reflex A peripheral-nerve reflex purported to be mediated by collateral afferent neurons.

axoplasmic transport (flow) The mechanism responsible for movement of material such as synaptic vesicles from the cell body to axon terminals (anterograde flow) or, as is the case of nerve growth factor, from the axon terminal to the cell body (retrograde flow).

axosomatic synapse A synaptic junction between an axon and a cell body of a neuron.

Ayurveda An ancient Indian science of health based on the balance between three doschas (mind-body principles): vata (movement), pitta (metabolism), and kappa (structure).

azidothymidine (AZT) A derivative of thymidine used to inhibit the replication of HIV, the AIDS virus. Chemical name is 3-azido-3-deoxythymidine. Trade name is Zidovudine.

azoospermia An absence of viable or any sperm in the semen, usually resulting from a failure of spermatogenesis or following vasectomy.

AZT azidothymidine

B

b 1. Product-moment regression coefficient. 2. Regression constant for the slope of regression line.

B 1. Body. 2. Luminance. 3. Mean number of responses. 4. Body of organism, minus nervous system. 5. Self-actualization needs.

BA Abbreviation for bachelor of arts degree.

babble Prespeech voice sounds such as "dada" sounded by infants around six months of age. Babbling is usually regarded as practice in vocalization, facilitating later speech development. Also known as babbling. See BABY TALK, PRESPEECH DEVELOPMENT.

babble stage (P. Cattell) A period of life of infants during which simple vocalization sounds are made. Typically occurs at about age two months.

Babinski reflex   Babinski('s) sign

Babinski('s) sign (J. Babinski) 1. In infants, a normal reflex characterized by extension of toes upward during plantar stimulation. This response disappears by the time the infant learns to walk. 2. In adults, a reflex characterized by extension of the great toe and abduction of the other toes when the soles of feet are stroked. Considered a sign of pyramidal tract pathology. Also known as Babinski's phenomenon/reflex, great toe reflex, paradoxical extensor reflex, toe reflex.

Babinski's syndrome (J. Babinski) Denial, by a person, that he or she suffers from hemiplegia, despite direct as well as clinical evidence to the contrary. See ANTON'S SYNDROME.

Babkin reflex (B. P. Babkin) Pressing on an infant's palms results in the infant's mouth opening.

baby talk 1. Sounds produced by most children when learning to talk. 2. A disorder of speech articulation, when occurring in older children and adults, where normal speech should occur. Manifested by the substitution of certain letters, sounds, and syllables for others, such as w for r, as in wabbit for rabbit. See BABBLING, INFANTILE SPEECH, PRESPEECH DEVELOPMENT.

bacillary layer A layer of rods and cones in the retina. The ninth of ten retinal layers that light must penetrate, and the layer where the conversion to neural impulse occurs. See JACOB'S MEMBRANE.

bacillophobia Morbid fear of germs, bacilli, and microbes. See MICROBIOPHOBIA.

back-clipping The shortening of a word by omitting the back half of it (for example, "prof" for "professor"). The new word is used with the same meaning and is the same part of speech as the old word, unlike a back-formation. Compare FRONT-CLIPPING.

backcrossing In genetics, the process of crossbreeding a hybrid species with a member of the genetic line from which the hybrid was originally derived. The term is applied to both plants and animals. The offspring of such a mating is known as a backcross.

back-formation In speech, the formation of a word through elimination of a prefix or suffix from an existing word; also, the word formed in this manner (for example, "Enthuse" from "enthusiasm"). Also known as inverse derivation, retrogressive formation. See CLIPPING.

background In visual perception, the less distinct surroundings lying beyond the foreground not perceived as part of the figure or object of concentration and attention. The background is variable and may become part of the figure. See GESTALT PSYCHOLOGY.

background noise See COLORED NOISE, FROZEN NOISE, PINK NOISE, WHITE NOISE.

back solution (M. H. Doolittle) A time-saving computational method for solving normal or first-degree equations in which the desired output is given and adjustments are made in the equation's unknowns until that output is achieved. Compare FRONT SOLUTION. See DOOLITTLE METHOD.

backup reinforcers The additional rewards that clients or patients get as part of behavior modification upon trading in their tokens. See TOKEN ECONOMY.

backward association An association, often found in paired-associate learning, whereby a secondary term evokes a preceding term (for example, a person has learned to follow the word CAT with SPOON and later responds to SPOON with CAT). Compare FORWARD ASSOCIATION.

backward conditioning The presentation of the unconditioned stimulus (US) before the conditioned stimulus (CS). Although this procedure elicits responses that appear conditioned, such responses are not considered genuine learning but rather oversensitization to the conditioned stimulus. Phrase is used in reference to Pavlovian (classical, respondent) conditioning and not for instrumental (operant) conditioning. See PSEUDOCONDITIONING.

backward displacement In parapsychology, extrasensory perception (ESP) responses to targets preceding the intended targets.

backward masking The ability of a stimulus to interfere with the perception of a stimulus presented before it. See MASKING.

backwardness (T. Tredgold) Educational retardation due to extrinsic forces (environmental, social, physical) said to account for approximately one-third of cases of such retardation.

backward pairing A classical conditioning procedure in which a conditioned stimulus (CS) follows the unconditioned stimulus (US). Compare FORWARD PAIRING.

back wards The areas of mental hospitals where long-term, seriously disturbed patients considered "hopelessly insane" were kept.

backward search A heuristic procedure that starts with the end of a problem and working backward to find the starting point.

BACON (P. Langley) A computer program that has been used to simulate human discovery processes in science, and been compared with numerous instances of historically important data-driven discoveries (discoveries where there were only data and no theories to guide the search). Other discovery programs that simulate various human scientific discovery processes include DALTON, STAHL, GLAUBER and KEKADA. Name refers to the British empiricist philosopher Sir Francis Bacon. See COGNITIVE SIMULATION.

Baconian method (F. Bacon) A technique of scientific investigation based on systemic experimentation and inductive logic in contrast to the deductive logic. Bacon's *Novum Organum* (1620) initiated modern scientific inquiry. See DEDUCTIVE REASONING, INDUCTIVE REASONING.

bad-babies Describes newborn infants that are considered "difficult" (those that require a lot of attention). The term is sometimes used in maternity wards of hospitals by nurses and attendants. See BAD-PATIENT.

bad breast (M. Klein) In psychoanalytic theory, the breast or part of the breast experienced by babies as a bad object, reflecting the death instinct, during the first year of life. Compare GOOD BREAST.

bad-me (H. S. Sullivan) A child's rudimentary organization of impulses and behavior disapproved by parents that generates this concept of being not-good within the child and arouses anxiety and guilt. See PERSONIFIED SELF.

bad object In psychoanalytic theory, good refers to "clean" or nonsexual whereas "bad" stands for sexual. Ultimate good is God and ultimate bad is the devil. Compare GOOD OBJECT.

bad-patient A complaining, uncooperative patient from the point of view of caretakers, such as doctors, nurses, aides, and relatives. See BAD-BABIES.

bad self In psychoanalysis, a tendency of both the patient and the therapist to project their guilt feelings upon each other, each making the other a "whipping boy." If the analysis is to be effective, this tendency must be controlled.

bad trip An acute, adversive psychotic-like episode due to use of hallucinogenic drugs such as LSD (lysergic acid diethylamide). Flashbacks may occur at a later date.

Baer's law (K. E. von Baer) A theory that different kinds of organisms are at first similar and develop along similar lines, those of organisms least closely related, diverging first; the others diverging at later periods in proportion to the closeness of relationship. Often confused with the recapitulation theory associated with Ernst Haeckel and G. Stanley Hall. Also known as von Baer's law.

Bahnsen columns If two or more columns of the ragged type are viewed, those symmetrical in nature are likely to be seen as the figure whereas nonsymmetrical columns are seen as the ground. See REGULARITY PERCEPTION for an example.

BAI Beck Anxiety Inventory

bait shyness (J. Garcia) The induced avoidance by animals of certain foods that were ordinarily part of what they usually eat, such as wolves learning to avoid killing sheep after eating a sheep carcass purposely loaded with some substance that later generates gastric distress. Sometimes known as toxicosis.

balance 1. A harmonious relationship of opposing forces, as in emotional equilibrium. See EXPERIENCE BALANCE, MENTAL BALANCE. 2. The maintenance of a harmonious and effective relationship of parts of the body to its kinesthetic and labyrinthine receptors (for example, while walking on a tightrope, making automatic movements of hands and arms to keep from falling off). See AUTONOMIC BALANCE, SALT BALANCE. 3. An apparatus for weighing. See MOSSO BALANCE.

balance control Recreational or physical therapy employed in the rehabilitation of patients who experience difficulty in maintaining balance when standing or walking. Training often uses tricycles with body supports and foot attachments, stilts, pogo-sticks, rocker boards, and trampoline-like rubber bouncing tubes.

balanced design In planning a study, the attempt to nullify all possible sources of errors by controlling selections to nullify the effects of such variables as age, gender, and education level, so that the various research and control groups are equalized as much as possible. See RESEARCH DESIGN.

balanced Latin square A counterbalancing scheme in which every research condition precedes and follows every other condition. See LATIN SQUARE, RESEARCH DESIGN.

balanced replication The repetition of exactly the same experiment, this time with additional safeguards to determine whether any artifacts (spurious factors) affected results. See RESEARCH DESIGN.

balanced scale A type of scale in which half the items have opposing values, such as one in which half of the items are positively and half negatively worded or so that half the items if answered "true" would be scored high for the trait and half would be scored low.

balance of minus judgments In studies on perceptual judgments, the percent of plus and percent of minus judgments subtracted from each other when the comparison stimulus equals the standard stimulus. See RANGE OF MINUS JUDGMENTS.

balance theory 1. (F. Heider) In social psychology, a point of view that people tend to embrace attitudes and opinions they consider compatible with their prior ideas while avoiding or rejecting attitudes they find less acceptable, or contrary to their present views. 2. A point of view that an ideal state exists when all aspects of body and mind are in harmony. All organs work to establish equilibrium when there is an imbalance. 3. In interpersonal relations, identity of social attitudes between people, such as, if A likes B and dislikes C, the situation is in balance if B also dislikes C, and is out of balance if B likes C. See COGNITIVE DISSONANCE THEORY, CONSISTENCY PRINCIPLE, HOMEOSTASIS.

balancing In research, a technique of controlling extraneous variables by assuring they affect members of each group equally.

balancing reaction/response A behavioral act that enables an organism to maintain or reestablish a desired posture with respect to gravity.

balbutier (stuttering—French) Stammering or stuttering. Speech pathologists no longer distinguish between stammering and stuttering, since they are both assumed to emanate from the same learned anxiety-laden conflicts. It is regarded by some as a neurological disorder.

Baldwin's figure (J. M. Baldwin) A bisected line segment with one of the line's ends connected to a large square, and the other to a smaller square. The two halves of the bisected line appear to be unequal in length.

Bales' Category System (R. F. Bales) A list of twelve ratings ranging from positive to negative social–emotional task-oriented behaviors. Used by observers of social interaction, who record the source and recipient of each expressive act and sort these acts into the twelve categories. See CATEGORY-SYSTEM METHOD, INTERACTION PROCESS ANALYSIS.

Balint's syndrome Optic ataxia, ocular apraxia, and simultanagnosia, caused by bilateral damage to the parieto-occipital area. Named after Hungarian neurologist and psychiatrist Rudolph Balint (1874–1929).

ball-and-field test In the Stanford-Binet test prior to the extensive revision of 1986, an excellent example of a culture-fair test. The participant is told that an object of value is lost in a field, represented by a circle, and the participant is asked to trace with a pencil where to look for the object. Any logical path, such as a grid pattern, is considered evidence of intelligence.

ballet technique A structured form of dance therapy considered particularly appropriate for persons unable to handle the emotions aroused by free movement. See KINESICS, KINESIOLOGY.

ballism A bodily disorder characterized by lively jerking movements as in chorea. Also known as ballismus.

ballistic movement A sudden jerky movement over which the person has no control.

ballistophobia 1. Fear of bullets. 2. Morbid fear of thrown objects such as missiles.

balsamic A quality of olfactory sensation or smell, such as jasmine and vanilla. Part of the Zwaardemaker classification of odors.

band chart/diagram A curved surface divided into horizontal groups with the abscissa customarily representing time and the ordinate representing amount of a number of classes, with classes added to one another in some manner, and the groups of classes shaded or colored to make them distinctive.

B & D bondage and discipline

band score In reporting a score on any kind of test, instead of giving an exact number such as percentile 74, giving a range of scores such as percentile 70–79. This is done because more specific ratings would spuriously appear to be exact.

bandwagon appeal In logic, a fallacy based on the concept that "almost everyone thinks so," such as in 15th century Europe when the general populace believed that the sun went around the earth. Also known as ad populum.

bandwagon effect/technique A tendency for people, in social and political situations, to align themselves or their stated opinion with perceived majority opinions (for example, a child roots for a particular baseball team because others do so). See ASCH CONFORMITY EXPERIMENT.

bandwidth 1. Casually, the size of a document transmitted electronically. 2. In ergonomics, the range of frequencies that influence an amplitude-based acceleration/deceleration impulse in goal-directed teleoperation trajectories. 3. (L. J. Cronbach) A range of criteria predictable from a test; the broader the bandwidth of a test, the more that test can predict. See BAND CHART, FIDELITY. Also spelled band width.

bang See BHANG.

Bangungut (nightmare—Filipino) A culture-specific syndrome observed mainly among young Filipino and Laotian males in which the sufferer appears to have been frightened to death by nightmares. Also known as nightmare-death syndrome, oriental nightmare-death syndrome.

banishment An old method of dealing with people considered undesirable, such as convicts. Transporting such people to faraway lands and leaving them there (for example, as was done with English prisoners banished to Australia).

baquet (tub—French) (F. A. Mesmer) A huge tub containing "magnetized" water, with metal rods protruding from all sides. Franz Anton Mesmer's patients placed the rods on ailing parts of their bodies so that they would experience the water's healing power. See ANIMAL MAGNETISM.

bar See BAR(YE).

baragnosis Inability to recognize or compare the weights of objects when held in the hand. Compare BAROGNOSIS.

Bárány chair (R. Bárány) A special chair that revolves as a person is spun around, used for testing labyrinth functions of the ear. See BÁRÁNY METHOD.

Bárány method (R. Bárány) A test designed to reveal whether the semicircular canals of the inner ear are functioning properly by rotating a participant in a special chair such that the participant's head in each of the planes that bring the three canals vertical to the direction of rotation. See INNER EAR, ROTATION CHAIR.

Bárány Pointing Test (R. Bárány) A task in which a participant must point with a finger at an object alternately with eyes open and closed. Repeated failure to return the arm to the original position suggests unilateral cerebellar damage.

barbaralalia The use of the melodic patterns and speech sounds of a speaker's native language when learning to speak a new language. Commonly known as a foreign accent.

barbed-wire psychosis A type of mental disturbance experienced by prisoners of war, with symptoms of irritability and amnesia for events preceding the war. See AMNESIA, COMBAT FATIGUE.

barber's pole effect A tendency for a vertical slit placed in front of a cylinder with diagonal stripes to make the stripes appear to move vertically, but if a horizontal slit is placed in front of the cylinder, the stripes appear to move horizontally. See ILLUSIONS.

barbital The name used in the United States for Veronal, the first clinically useful barbiturate. Known as barbitone in England.

barbitone See BARBITAL.

barbiturate (J. A. von Baeyer) A class of sedative-hypnotic drugs used more in the earlier part of the century, in smaller doses for a myriad of psychosomatic complaints and stress reactions, in larger doses as a sleep aid. Barbiturates were used recreationally as "downers" and sometimes were the object of "prescribed substance abuse." Also used as an anticonvulsant. Different barbiturates have longer or shorter durations of action. The most commonly used long-lasting type was phenobarbital; of the short-acting forms, the more common trade names are Amytal, Pentothal, Seconal, and Nembutal (intermediate-length, often used for sleep). Others are less often or rarely used. Because of the addictive potential and the relative ease of toxic overdose, these medicines have been largely supplanted with other types of tranquilizers, mainly the benzodiazepines. See ANTIEPILEPTICS, HYPNOTICS, SEDATIVE-HYPNOTIC DEPENDENCE, VERONAL.

barbiturate addiction/problems Physical and psychological dependence on barbiturate drugs. See SEDATIVE-HYPNOTIC DRUGS as well as associated items beginning with BARBIT-.

bar chart A type of chart that represents data by showing separate bars of varying heights, arranged either vertically or horizontally with the width of the bars equal to each other. The length of each bar represents the frequency, size, or amount of a variable. Also known as bar diagram/graph. See HISTOGRAM for an illustration.

bar display In ergonomics, a visual display, often computer generated, of bars (usually two), typically showing system input and output.

Bard-Cannon theory Rare name for the Cannon-Bard theory, after Philip Bard who helped to revise the James Lange theory of emotion. See CANNON, CANNON'S THEORY, CANNON-BARD THEORY.

barefoot doctors Medically trained personnel who provide health care in communities or areas not served by modern hospitals or clinics. Personnel may or may not be physicians and the areas served are likely remote rural districts or impoverished urban communities. Phrase is derived from a program established by the People's Republic of China. See PARAPROFESSIONALS.

baresthesia The sensation of weight or pressure. Also known as baresthesis.

baresthesiometer An instrument used to measure pressure usually applied to the skin of a person. See ESTHESIOMETER.

bargaining A process that involves conflict and collaboration in which two parties each attempting to achieve certain levels of goals negotiate, sometimes to mutual satisfaction, but sometimes unable to reconcile differences in demands.

bargaining stage (E. Kübler-Ross) The third stage in the process of dying, characterized by a desire to trade or barter with God in exchange for a longer life; for example, "Save me and I will never bet on the horse races again." See STAGES OF DYING.

bar hustlers See MALE HOMOSEXUAL PROSTITUTION.

bariatrics A medical specialty regarding the causes and treatment of obesity and related conditions.

barking See ABOIEMENT.

Barnum effect 1. In psychology, refers to the perceived applicability, usually to the self, of vague or general statements derived from tests, for example, "more sensitive than he appears to be," or "sometimes has difficulty in controlling anger." 2. In general, a tendency to believe that general and vague predictions or personality descriptions have specific application to individuals, for example, believing the validity of horoscope predictions in daily newspapers. Phrase was inspired by the remark, "There's a sucker born every minute," attributed to the American showman, Phineas T. Barnum (1810–1891).

baroceptor **baroreceptor**

barognosis An ability to detect weight differences of objects held in the hand. Compare BARAGNOSIS.

barophobia Fear of gravity, or of feeling the pull of gravity.

baroreceptor A receptor sensitive to changes in blood pressure. They are found in the blood vessels and in the heart. Also known as baroceptor, pressoreceptor.

barotaxis A simple response or tendency for an organism, such as an animal, to orient itself toward or away from a pressure stimulus, such as a water current. The term barotropism is seldom used and refers to this tendency in plants. See TAXIS, TROPISM.

barotropism See BAROTAXIS.

barrel distortion The departure of optical images from truthful representation of their objects, such that a square is represented in the image with bulging sides. See VISUAL-FIELD DEFECT.

barrier 1. An obstacle, particularly physical. See ARCHITECTURAL BARRIERS, BARRIER-FREE ENVIRONMENT. 2. That which blocks resolving behavior. See DENIAL. 3. A hypothetical "protective envelope" that surrounds an organism, protecting it from overstimulation and traumatic situations. The barrier is both a neural and psychological line of defense. See HERMITISM, PRIVACY.

barrier-free environment   An environment free of obstacles for persons whose normal bodily movements are uncontrolled or unsteady, and who may require the use of prosthetic devices, such as artificial limbs or wheelchairs. Environmental barriers can include street curbs, revolving doors, doors too narrow to admit wheelchairs, inaccessible toilets and washbowls, coin-operated telephones beyond the reach of users, and elevator buttons that cannot be "read" by blind persons.

barrier responses   In Rorschach testing, responses having to do with boundaries; for example, the response "turtle with shell" indicates a body boundary, whereas "a torn coat" and other penetration responses indicate indefinite boundaries. Sometimes known as body boundaries.

Barron-Welsh Art Scale   (F. Barron & G. Welsh) A test in which respondents record liking or disliking each of 86 black and white figures selected to see whether they differentiate between judgments of criterion groups of artists and nonartists. See MAIER ART JUDGMENT TEST, SEASHORE MEASURES OF MUSICAL TALENT.

BARS   behaviorally anchored rating scales

Bartlett technique/tradition   (F. C. Bartlett) A memory research procedure that depends on determination of qualitative changes in the contents of retrieved material, for example, a story is read to X who repeats it from memory to Y, who repeats it to Z, who is to write it down. The original story and the final story are compared to demonstrate any of a variety of memory and communication laws.

Bartlett's test   A statistical test of the hypothesis of homogeneity of variance. Used when there are obvious differences among the variances of the treatment groups. Named after English mathematician Maurice Stevenson Bartlett (b. 1910).

Bartley vs Kremens   A Pennsylvania court decision (1976) that extended due-process protection and provision of legal counsel to children committed to mental facilities by their parents.

bar(ye)   1. A unit of pressure equal to one megadyne (10^6 dyne) per square centimeter or approximately 0.98697 standard atmosphere. 2. The absolute cgs unit of pressure equal to one dyne per square centimeter.

barylalia   1. See BARYPHONIA (meaning 1). 2. Thick, blurred, and indistinct speech, noted in cases of general paresis.

baryphonia   1. A deep voice. Also known as baryglossia, barylalia. 2. A type of dysphasia characterized by a thick, heavy voice quality. Also known as baryphony.

baryphony   baryphonia (meaning 2)

BAS   behavioral approach system

basal   A standard or reference for comparison.

basal age   See BASAL MENTAL AGE.

basal body temperature   The average normal body temperature of an individual as recorded immediately after awakening in the morning and before getting out of bed. Increases by 0.5° to 1.0°F (0.25° to 0.5°C) for a woman on the day she ovulates; the information is used to indicate the peak fertility period in her reproductive cycle.

basal ganglia/nuclei   (R. de Vieussens, S. Ringer) Structures in the forebrain including the caudate nucleus, putamen, and globus pallidus involved in the control of movement. Degeneration or damage to these structures and to structures such as the substantia nigra and subthalamic nucleus cause extrapyramidal diseases such as Parkinson's disease, Huntington's syndrome, and hemiballism.

basal mental age   (A. Binet) In intelligence testing, the highest age at which all items on a standardized age-level test such as the Stanford-Binet are passed by a testee. Also called informally, but incorrectly, basal age. Sometimes known as basal level/year. See MENTAL AGE, TERMINAL MENTAL AGE.

basal metabolic rate (BMR)   The rate of oxygen intake and energy discharge of an organism under certain standardized conditions, including complete physical rest (not sleep), a fasting period, and an ambient temperature that does not require energy expenditure for physiological temperature regulation.

basal metabolism   Minimum energy expenditure, measured in calories, required to maintain the vital functions of the body while at rest. See ANABOLISM, CATABOLISM.

basal nuclei   basal ganglia

basal-reader approach   A method of teaching reading through a series of books of increasing difficulty. A teacher's manual and children's workbooks usually accompany the series.

basal-resistance level   The normal autonomic-response level of a person's emotional state as measured by galvanic skin response and related indices. See GALVANIC SKIN RESPONSE, LIE DETECTOR.

base   1. A fundamental part of anything. 2. The starting point. 3. A fundamental number. 4. (J. Bronsted) A molecule or ion that takes up a proton from an acid.

baseline   A measure of behavior under control conditions before any treatment begins. Later research treatments are expected to modify the baseline. See ABSCISSA.

basement   1. The lower part or bottom. The opposite of apex. 2. The minimum possible, such as the least requirements for a job, or the lowest score needed to pass a test. See BASE, CEILING EFFECT.

basement effect   Inability of measuring instruments or statistical procedures to determine differences at the bottom of data when the difference between data is small. Also known as floor effect. Compare CEILING EFFECT.

base number   The radix or fundamental number of any scale. Ten is the base in the decimal system. Two is the base in the binary system, with eight in the octal notation system, and sixteen in the hexadecimal system.

base rate   The prevalence of a given phenomenon in a given population; the rate of occurrence. See BASELINE.

base-rate fallacy   A tendency to overemphasize exceptional events and to ignore statistical information in making decisions. See ACCURACY, HALO EFFECT, VALIDITY.

bashful bladder (syndrome)   Casual term for difficulty in starting or maintaining urination when it might be seen or heard, especially by a stranger. Sometimes known as avoidant paruresis, public micturition dysfunction.

bashfulness   An attitude characterized by partial inhibition of social responses, usually confined to children. See SHYNESS.

Basic Achievement Skills Individual Screener (BASIS)   An individually-administered test of reading, mathematics, and spelling skills. For use with Grades 1 through 12 and post-high school.

basic act   A component of a complex series of actions; with walking for example, basic acts include lifting up a foot, moving the foot forward, stepping down, and then repeating the same set of basic acts with the other leg. See MOLAR BEHAVIOR, MOLECULAR BEHAVIOR, THERBLIG.

basic anxiety   A feeling of uneasiness, dread, and impending disaster. According to Karen Horney, basic anxiety usually originates in indifference and coldness or excessively high standards and constant criticism on the part of parents that make the child feel isolated, helpless, and insecure in a hostile world. See ANXIETY, HORNEY.

basic concepts   See BOEHM TEST OF BASIC CONCEPTS.

basic conflict   (K. Horney) A description of an internalized state resulting in neurotic behavior characterized by conflicts between two opposing psychic forces, such as the proud self versus the despised self.

basic encounter   The occurrence of a meaningful one-to-one relationship. Often occurs in group therapy, but can occur any time and anywhere when persons develop mutual trust, each having empathy for the other. See HUMANISM, I-THOU RELATIONSHIP, ROGERIAN THEORY.

basic hostility   (K. Horney) A fundamental attitude of expecting harm from other people and thus expecting and being ready to repel attack. See ANXIETY, PARANOIA.

BASIC I.D.   (A. A. Lazarus) An acronym for a grouping of the fundamental concerns in multimodal therapy: Behavior, Affect, Sensation, Imagery, Cognition, Interpersonal relationships, and Drugs (a biological function). See MULTIMODAL THERAPY.

basic intelligence factors   When the concept of intelligence is subdivided, various individuals have arrived at different conclusions as to what its parts consist of, for example, Alfred Binet: comprehension, invention, direction, and self-criticism; E. L. Thorndike: cognitive, mechanical, and social; R. B. Cattell: fluid and crystallized; J. L. Moreno: creative and conserved; C. E. Spearman: general (g) and specific (s); J. P. Guilford: cognition, memory, divergent production, convergent production, and evaluation.

basic-level category   The name most often used for a concept when that concept has the possibility of being called a number of different names, such as the vehicle known also as an automobile is most often called a "car" by most people. See NATURAL CATEGORY.

basic mistake   1. (A. Adler) An early-childhood factor, for example, an attitude or incident, that affects a person's lifestyle in later life and which may need to be corrected to resolve conflicts. 2. (R. Dreikurs) Refers to faulty concepts established in childhood about self, others, and life. In adulthood, these concepts may be the fundamental causes of personal problems, such as feelings of inferiority. Adlerian therapists attempt to determine a person's basic mistakes and to help the person realize such views are incorrect. See ADLERIAN THERAPY, EARLY RECOLLECTIONS, LIFE SCRIPT, LIFESTYLE.

basic mistrust   (E. Erikson) The unsuccessful resolution of the first stage in Erik Erikson's eight stages of psychosocial development in which the baby in the first year of life comes to experience a fundamental distrust of the environment. The acquisition of basic trust or hope is considered essential for the development of self-esteem and normal relatedness. Compare BASIC TRUST. See ERIKSON'S STAGES OF PSYCHOSOCIAL DEVELOPMENT.

basic needs   Human motives arranged in a hierarchy according to their presumed importance. According to Abraham Maslow's concept, the most fundamental level of needs—survival or physiological needs—are located at the bottom of the Maslow pyramid; the highest needs—esthetic needs including self-actualization—are located at the top of the pyramid. Also known as fundamental needs. See ABUNDANCY NEEDS, BASIC PHYSIOLOGICAL NEEDS, DEFICIENCY NEEDS, HIERARCHY OF NEEDS. See MASLOW'S MOTIVATIONAL HIERARCHY for an illustration of such a pyramid.

basic object lesson   See LEVEL OF USUAL UTILITY.

Basic Occupational Literacy Test (BOLT)   A test provided by the United States Employment Service for assessing the literacy skills of educationally deficient adults. Also known as USES test battery.

basic personality   1. (A. Kardiner) The shared behavioral traits of persons raised (as children) in the same culture and subjected to the same type of childrearing practices. 2. (A. Adler) The same idea as Abraham Kardiner's with the proviso that the person has the equivalent of free will to modify personality. See PERSONALITY, DETERMINISM, SOFT DETERMINISM.

basic personality traits   (L. R. Goldberg) An analysis of personality traits identified by factor analytic studies led to the conclusion that the basic traits are agreeableness, extraversion, conscientiousness, emotional stability, and intellect. See SIXTEEN PERSONALITY FACTOR QUESTIONNAIRE, BIG FIVE PERSONALITY FACTORS.

basic physiological needs   Usually refers to basic requirements for physical survival. For adults these are food, water, and shelter; for infants, there is additional need for tactile comfort and nurturances. See MARASMUS.

basic research   Research that has no "intended" immediate value or practical application, but which is intended to clarify, or test, a theory, or to settle fundamental issues.

basic rest-activity cycle (BRAC)   A 90-minute cycle (in humans) of waxing and waning alertness, controlled by the caudal brain stem to regulate REM and slow-wave sleep cycles. See RAPID-EYE-MOVEMENT (REM) SLEEP, NONRAPID-EYE-MOVEMENT (NREM) SLEEP, SLEEP.

basic rule   The fundamental rule of psychoanalysis that the psychoanalyst must assist the patient to put spontaneous thoughts, feelings, and memories into words, and thereby bring unconscious impulses and experiences to the surface, where they can be analyzed.

basic skills   In educational psychology, those abilities (reading, writing, and arithmetic) that traditionally have been viewed as essential for scholastic achievement.

basic technique (BT)   In parapsychology, the clairvoyance technique in which each test card is laid aside by the investigator as it is identified by the participant; the checkup takes place at the end of the trial. See ZENER CARDS.

basic trust   (E. Erikson) The successful resolution of basic trust, the first of Erik Erikson's eight stages of psychosocial development, begins when a child in the first year of life comes to feel that the world is trustworthy. Basic trust leads to the development of self-esteem. Compare BASIC MISTRUST. See ERIKSON'S STAGES OF PSYCHOSOCIAL DEVELOPMENT.

basilar membrane   A flexible band of tissue within the cochlea (of the inner ear) that supports the organ of Corti and vibrates in response to sounds in the environment. See AUDITION, AUDITORY MEMBRANE, AUDITORY SENSATION, PLACE THEORY (OF HEARING).

basiphobia   Morbid fear of walking.

basis   A general designation for whatever underlies and supports a theory, law, procedure, or statement.

BASIS   Basic Achievement Skills Individual Screener

basket case   Slang for a person who is unable to continue within his or her on an acceptable level of daily functioning.

basket cell   A kind of interneuron found in the cerebellum.

basket endings   Specialized structure at the roots of hairs on the body regarded as sense organs for pressure and touch.

basket (nerve) endings   Sensory receptors in the skin that are coiled near the surface. See SKIN, SKIN RECEPTORS.

basking in reflected glory (BIRG-ing)   1. In social psychology, similar to the concept of promotive tension. 2. Seeking direct or indirect associations with prestigious individuals or groups.

basophobia   Morbid fear of standing erect.

batacas   (G. Bach) A pair of pillowlike "encounter-bats" with which opponents can hit each other without hurting or being hurt. Used in Creative Aggression sessions, mostly by spouses, to express their anger and aggression. See CREATIVE AGGRESSION.

bathing fear   See AQUAPHOBIA.

bathmism   Growth force or energy.

bathophobia   (depth—Greek) Morbid fear of depth, of being in high places, or looking down from such places. See ACROPHOBIA, CREMNOPHOBIA.

bath therapy   An early method of dealing with people with mania, by putting them in a tub of warm water. Many years later, variations of this procedure were used, including hosing such persons with streams of cold water, restraining them in tubs, wrapping them in wet sheets. See HYDROTHERAPY.

bathyesthesia   Sensitivity of the deep tissues of the body to pressure, pain, or muscle and joint sensations. Also known as bathyaesthesia, bathyesthesis.

batophobia   Morbid fear of high objects; fear of passing high buildings. See ACROPHOBIA.

bat radar   The use by bats of echolocation, the emission of sound by the bat that reflects off objects in the environment, enabling them to fly in the dark. Bats use sonar rather than real radar, as many believe. See ECHOLOCATION.

Batten-Mayou disease   (F. E. Batten & M. S. Mayou) A juvenile form of amaurotic family mental disability.

battered baby   (C. Kempe) An infant deliberately injured by his or her parents or other caretakers. See FILICIDE, INFANTICIDE, SHAKEN BABY.

battered-child syndrome   The pattern of child abuse by parents or parent surrogates who intentionally and repeatedly injure their children, often to the extent that hospitalization is required. In addition to physical trauma, children may show signs of intellectual retardation and abnormal behavior, such as excessive hostility or submissiveness. Battered children are purported to become battering parents. See CHILD MOLESTATION.

battered people   1. Individuals physically beaten by others, usually children by their parents, and adults by their significant others. 2. By extension, refers to people who have a tendency to be victims of physical abuse. See ALCOHOLIC WIFE/HUSBAND, MASOCHISM, SADOMASOCHISTIC RELATIONSHIP.

battered-wife syndrome (BWS)   A syndrome affecting battered women who are physically abused by their spouses. Such women reluctantly apparently accept abuse for a wide number of reasons, such as cultural acceptance, unwillingness to break up a family, financial considerations, fear of violent consequences for leaving, feelings of unworthiness, and feeling guilty of causing the violence. See BATTERED WOMEN.

battered women   Adult females who are physically abused, usually by lovers or spouses (battered wives). See ALCOHOLIC'S WIFE/HUSBAND, BATTERED PEOPLE, BATTERING MEN'S EXCUSES.

battering men's excuses   Refers to men with a tendency or history of abusing others, usually their spouse, lover, and/or children, taking "excusatory" positions such as being: (a) unable to control themselves because they were tired, tense, nervous, or upset; (b) driven to distraction by crying (of babies), complaining or nagging of spouse; (c) aggravated by circumstances such as a dirty house, food not ready, spouse drunk, absent, or not affectionate; (d) was sick, drunk, or influenced by drugs. See BATTERED BABIES, BATTERED WOMEN.

battery   1. A group of tests administered for analytic or diagnostic purposes. See TEST BATTERY. 2. Physical abuse. See entries beginning with BATTERED.

battle exhaustion/fatigue   A reaction resulting from the stress of participating in a war. Symptoms include the inability to sleep, inability to concentrate, hypersensitivity to noises, hypersensitivity to sudden movements. These reactions may result from the former constant sense of danger, lack of sleep, periodic loud sounds, observations of people dying, etc. Reactions can be short-term or long-term; in the latter cases, the reactions may be frank psychoses. Also known as combat fatigue. See POSTTRAUMATIC STRESS DISORDER (PTSD), SHELL SHOCK.

Bayesian approach   (T. Bayes) In evaluation research, the use of conditional probabilities as an aid in selection or diagnostic procedures. Given some prior information, such conditional probabilities can often be calculated by Bayes' theorem. Although Bayes' theorem is not controversial, the question of its appropriate use has been of some controversy. Also known as decision-theoretic approach. See BAYES' PRINCIPLE/THEOREM.

Bayes' principle/theorem   (T. Bayes) An expression for finding the conditional probability of event A given event B from the opposite conditional probability (the probability of event B given A) and the two marginal probabilities p(A) and p(B): $p(A \mid B) = p(B \mid A)p(A)/p(B)$.

Bayle's disease   (A. L. Bayle) Obsolete name for general paresis.

Bayley Infant Neurodevelopmental Screener (BINS) (G. P. Aylward) An examination that screens infants three months to two years of age for basic neurological functions, auditory and visual receptive functions, verbal and motor expressive functions, and cognitive processes. Developed for use by developmental pediatricians, occupational therapists, school psychologists, etc., in screening for the IDEA mandate. See INDIVIDUALS WITH DISABILITIES EDUCATION ACT (IDEA).

Bayley Scales of Infant Development (BSID)   (N. Bayley) A three-part scale for assessing the developmental status of children between two months and two and a half years. The Mental Scale samples such functions as perception, memory, and vocalization; the Motor Scale measures motor ability; and the Infant Behavior Record assesses aspects of personality development. Revised as the Bayley Scales of Infant Development, Second Edition (BSID-II or Bayley-II).

B-BB   blood-brain barrier

BCD   See BINARY CODED DECIMAL SYSTEM.

B cognition   See BEING COGNITION.

BD   *bouffé délirante*

BDD   body-dysmorphic disorder

BDI   Beck Depression Inventory, also the Beck Depression Inventory-II (BDI-II).

BEAM   brain electrical activity mapping

Beard's disease   (G. M. Beard) Neurasthenia.

beast fetishism   A paraphilia involving contact with animal furs or hides which serve as aphrodisiacs. See PARAPHILIA.

beat   1. A stroke, impulse, or pulsation. 2. Periodic changes in sound intensity produced by two similar tones sounded together. See BEATING FANTASIES/PHANTASIES, BEAT-TONE.

beating fantasies/phantasies   In psychoanalytic theory, when a boy fantasizes being beaten by the father, it is considered an unconscious expression of love; when he daydreams of himself beaten by his mother, it is interpreted as a defense against homosexual impulses. A girl's fantasy that her father is beating another child, means "He loves only me." Her fantasy that he is beating her is interpreted as a masochistic expression of guilt over incestuous feelings toward the father.

beat-tone   A tone of characteristically rough quality, produced by applying simultaneously to the same ear two sound-frequencies that differ by more than 16 to 20 Hertz (cycles per second).

Beauchamp case   (M. Prince) A classic description of a case of multiple personality.

Beaufort wind scale   (F. Beaufort) A system of measuring wind velocities. The scale ranges from 0, for winds of less than one mile per hour, when smoke rises vertically, to 12, for sustained winds of at least 73 miles an hour, as during a hurricane. Purportedly, discomfort generally increases with perceived windiness, as do accident rates immediately before or during the approach of windy weather. See WIND EFFECTS.

beauty   A relationship between elements that appeals to esthetic senses. Beauty has been of constant interest to philosophers who have been unable to decide its final definition. There is a fairly remarkable agreement in judgments of beauty across cultural groups.

Bechtereff   See BEKHTEREV.

Beck Anxiety Inventory (BAI)   (A. T. Beck) A means of measuring anxiety levels in persons 17 through 80 years of age. Twenty-one items are rated by respondents on a scale from 0 to 3.

Beck Depression Inventory (BDI)   (A. T. Beck) A self-report scale of 21 items, aimed at assessing the degree of clinical depression in people over 13 years of age. The items refer mostly to mood states or other internal feeling states and not to external "situations." Revised by Aaron T. Beck, Robert A. Steer, and Gregory K. Brown as the Beck Depression Inventory-II (BDI-II).

Beck Hopelessness Scale (BHS)   (A. T. Beck) A scale of 20 true-false items intended for use with persons 17 through 80 years of age, reflecting three major aspects of hopelessness: feelings about the future, loss of motivation, and expectations. The scale is purportedly a powerful predictor of eventual suicide. See BECK SCALE FOR SUICIDE IDEATION.

Beck Scale for Suicide Ideation (BSS)   (A. T. Beck) A scale of 21 items used to evaluate suicidal thinking.

Beck's Lambda   (S. J. Beck) A ratio between form and no-form replies in the Rorschach. Probably best known as the lambda index.

Beck system   (S. J. Beck) A system for interpreting Rorschach protocols, characterized by empiricism and conservatism in making predictions. The first systematic approach to the Rorschach after Hermann Rorschach's death.

becoming   (L. Binswanger) The process of self-realization and individuation; attempting to fulfill all the possibilities of being-in-the-world.

bedlam   Term derived in the early 16th century from a hospital called St. Mary's of Bethlehem, in London, a "lunatic asylum." Term is synonymous with wild confusion, since many patients there were frenetic. Term became a common name for any mental institution. "Bedlamism" was used for psychotic behavior, and "bedlamite" for a psychotic person.

bed wetter   A person who is enuretic. See BEDWETTING.

bed-wetting   Involuntary discharge of urine, especially during sleep. Termed psychological enuresis if due to psychological causes and treatable by parenting procedures; called functional enuresis when causes are physical. Also known as nocturnal enuresis.

bee communication   (K. von Frisch) Bees, on returning from finding a food source, execute a tail-wagging dance in the dark hive on the (usually) vertical honeycomb. A slow figure-eight dance, such as 3 turns in 15 seconds, means that the nectar source is far away, that is, more than a mile; while a fast dance, such as ten turns in 15 seconds, means that food is perhaps only 500 feet away. The direction of the "wagging run" on the straight line "bar" portion of the figure-eight indicates direction: up means toward the sun; 45° counterclockwise of vertical means 45° to the left of the sun; straight down means opposite to the sun. Understandably, bees rarely gather nectar or pollen from about a half hour before until a half hour after "high noon" since the sun is then directly overhead. The duration of the dance indicates quantity: the more flowers, the longer the dance. Other foragers rarely make more than a 15° error in direction or 20% error in distance when interpreting the "dance." When the food source is within 100 yards of the hive, the simpler "round dance" is used instead, where the speed of the dance indicates distance from the hive but no directional cue is provided. See ANIMAL COMMUNICATION, DANCING LANGUAGE, ROUND DANCE.

bee communication   Dotted lines show the movement of the bee, to indicate to other bees the distance and direction of a food source.

before-after design   1. The administration of a pretest and an aftertest to an experimental group and its control group (if one exists). 2. A research design that depends on the administration of a pretest and an aftertest, for example, participants are (a) given pretests on their knowledge of economics, then (b) are given a course on economics, and later (c) retested with equivalent tests to see how much they had learned about economics. Now called pre-post design. See EXPERIMENTAL DESIGN.

begging the question   In logic, a fallacy based on a circular argument assuming the truth of what is to be proved, in which the premise is the same as the conclusion, for example, saying "Intelligence is important because it makes you smart." Also known as *petitio principii*.

beginning spurt   The increased productivity or gain in performance frequently noted at the start of a job, task, or series of trials. Associated more commonly with new tasks than tasks with which the person is familiar. Also known as initial spurt. Compare END SPURT. See HAWTHORNE EFFECT.

behavior   Actions, reactions, and interactions in response to external or internal stimuli, including objectively observable activities, introspectively observable activities, and unconscious processes. Psychology accepts two types of behavior: (a) covert (internal–phenomenological) and (b) overt (external–observable); for example, in turning this page, the overt behavior is visible to others, but the covert behavior (within the organism) is not. Types of behavior include: ABIENT, ABNORMAL, ABSTRACT, ACCIDENT, ACCIDENT-PRONE, ACCIDENTAL, ACQUIRED, ACTING OUT, ADAPTIVE, ADIENT, AFFILIATIVE, AGGRESSIVE, AGONISTIC, ALTRUISTIC, ANARCHIC, ANIMAL COURTSHIP, ANTINODAL, ANTISOCIAL, ANTITHETICAL, APOPATHETIC, APPEASEMENT, APPETITIVE, ASSAULTIVE, ATTACHMENT, ATTACK, ATTENDING, AUTOMATIC, AUTOPLASTIC, AVERSIVE, AVOIDANCE, BISEXUAL, BIZARRE, CARETAKING, CATASTROPHIC, CHAIN, CHEWING, CIRCULAR, CLINGING, COERCIVE, COLLECTIVE, COMPELLED, COMPLEX, COMPULSIVE, CONCRETE, CONFORMING, CONSUMER, CONTACT, CONTRAPREPARED, COPING, COPULATORY, CORONARY-PRONE, COURTSHIP, CRITERION, CROSS-GENDER, CROWD, CROWDING AND ANIMAL, CUDDLING, CYCLOTHYMIC-DEPRESSIVE, DEFENSIVE, DEFERENCE, DESTRUCTIVE, DETOUR, DIFFERENTIAL INSTINCTIVE, DISORGANIZED, DISPLACEMENT, DISPLAY, DRESSING, DRINKING, DRIVE-SATISFYING, DYSSOCIAL, EATING, EMBRACING, EMITTED, ESCAPE, ESTROUS, EXPLICIT, EXPLOITATIVE-MANIPULATIVE, EXPLORATORY, EXPRESSIVE, EXTRA-INDIVIDUAL, FACE-SAVING, FEEDING, FINGER-BITING, FIRE-SETTING, FOLLOWING, FOOD-GETTING, FREEZING, GOAL-DIRECTED, GREETING, GROUP, GROUP TERRITORIAL, HELPING, HOMICIDAL, HOMOSEXUAL, HUMAN-COURTSHIP, HUNTING, HYPOTHESIS, IMMEDIACY, IMPLICIT, IMPULSIVE, INDIRECT SELF-DESTRUCTIVE, INNATE, INSTINCTIVE, INSTRUMENTAL, INTENTIONAL, INTRAGROUP TERRITORIAL, INTRINSIC, KINESIC, KISSING, LICKING, MALADAPTIVE, MANIPULATIVE, MASS, MATERNAL, MATING, MAZE, MIGRATION, MOBBING, MOLAR, MOLECULAR, MOTOR, MULTIDETERMINED, NATIVE, NODAL, NONVERBAL, NURSING, OBSESSIVE, OPERANT, ORAL, OVERT, PARENTAL, PARTITIVE, PATERNAL, PETTING, PLURALISTIC, PREDATORY, PREFERENCE, PROBLEM, PROBLEM-SOLVING, PROCREATIONAL, PROHIBITED, PROSOCIAL, PSEUDOAFFECTIVE, PURPOSEFUL, RATING, RATIONAL, REGRESSIVE, REGULATORY, REPRODUCTIVE, REQUIRED, RESPONDENT, RETRIEVING, ROLE, SCAVENGING, SELF-DEFEATING, SELF-INJURIOUS, SERIAL, SEXUAL, SHAPING, SISSY, SOCIAL, SOCIOPATHIC, SPECIES-SPECIFIC, SPONTANEOUS, STATE-DEPENDENT, SUPERSTITIOUS, SURVIVAL, TARGET, TERMINAL, TOOL-USING, TRACKING, TYPE A, TYPE B, VISUAL SEARCH, VOLUNTARY, WATER-SEEKING. See BEHAVIOR VS CONDUCT, CONDUCT VS BEHAVIOR and also entries beginning with BEHAVIOR, BEHAVIOR(AL), BEHAVIORAL.

behavioral analysis   1. The complexity and scope of such analytic tasks as discovering controlling stimuli and reinforcements, plus the schedules that relate the two. 2. A variety of methods used in the attempt to understand various aspects of the behavior of organisms in their interaction with the environment, ranging from conditioning to psychoanalysis. It appears that the less complex the organism, the easier it is to analyze behavior, whereas the more complex the organism, the more difficult. See BEHAVIOR, BEHAVIORISM, BEHAVIOR MODIFICATION, EXPERIMENTAL ANALYSIS OF BEHAVIOR, PERSONALITY THEORIES.

behavioral approach system (BAS)   (J. A. Gray) A system theorized to underlie learning and emotions, assumed to guide behavior toward incentives. Persons with a relatively strong BAS are considered likely to be extraverted. Also known as behavioral activating system. See BEHAVIORAL INHIBITION SYSTEM.

behavior(al) assessment/diagnosis   1. A technique of studying behavior by observation, interviews, and other methods of sampling the person's overt behavior. Used in addition to, or instead of, relying on the use of psychological tests and self-reports. 2. An overall evaluation of a person that considers the totality of events that may have affected the person and all aspects of the person's actions.

behavior(al) avoidance test   An examination in which a list of behaviors or tasks are arranged in order of degree of fearfulness and participants are asked for their reactions; for example, given the question "Would you touch a...roach, snake, bear, cow, horse, cat?" the choices may include "Anytime," "Maybe," "Never" for each of the items. See ANXIETY HIERARCHY.

behavior(al) baseline   A stabilized measurable behavior in any organism, subject to operant conditioning techniques under specified conditions, making it possible to compare this baseline with an experimental manipulation.

behavioral cards   A diagnostic set of questions written on cards relating to delinquent behavior in children. The questions are answered by the child by sorting the cards into "Yes" and "No" boxes.

behavior(al) chain   1. The sequence of movements in a complex event, such as the rapidly changing behavior of a tennis player in running, stopping, swinging at balls. 2. A tendency for a person's behavior to elicit a response from others that will stimulate continuation of the original behavior. See BEHAVIOR, BEHAVIOR ANALYSIS, STIMULUS-RESPONSE THEORY.

behavioral checklist   A previously compiled list of observable actions that an investigator may use to keep track of how often the listed behaviors are observed in a particular situation, by particular persons, or both.

behavior(al) clinic   A place such as a school, institution, or hospital, where people go for the express purpose of learning to change their behavior; for example, adults may go to anger-management clinics, parents may go to family education centers, children may go to play therapy.

behavioral congruence   Acting in a usual, consistent, and predictable manner.

behavioral consistency   In industrial psychology, a technique for predicting future job performance on the basis of samples of current and past job behavior.

behavior(al) contagion   (A. Bandura) An imitation effect of watching others, especially those considered to be older, wiser, having greater prestige, etc. There is concern that children's behavior may be thus affected negatively by watching television and movies. See EMOTIONAL CONTAGION, ROLE MODEL.

behavior(al) contingency   The relationship between a specific response and its frequency, regularity, and amount of reinforcement.

behavior(al) contract   See CONTRACT.

behavioral contracting   A common process in behavioral psychotherapy whereby the therapist agrees to work on a specific problem presented by the client.

behavior(al) contrasts   (G. Reynolds) The phenomenon that in certain two-choice discrimination responses, if responses to one of the two choices improves (that is, are faster, more accurate, or both) the responses to the other choice worsens.

behavior(al) control   1. An attempt to affect the behavior of another or others through a variety of means, including by example, coercion, persuasion, and by offers of rewards and threats of punishment. 2. Refers to bringing undesirable behavior under control. See NATURAL AND LOGICAL CONSEQUENCES.

behavioral counseling   A type of counseling in which specific behavior parameters are established by both the counselor and the counselee, both agree to a system of rewards for adherence to the planned program and punishments for deviating from the plan.

behavior(al) criterion   Normal behavior from which deviations are measured. The standard can be of behavior differing from prior behavior in one person, or the standard can be of behavior differing from people in general.

behavior(al) deficit   A lacking or seldom-appearing pattern of responses (such as shallow or no reaction to kissing or other emotional stimuli). See BEHAVIOR DYSFUNCTIONS CLASSIFICATION.

behavioral determinants of perception   (J. Bruner & C. Goodman) The concept that elements of the total personality interact with sense organs to determine perceptions. Cognitions, emotions, desires, as well as past history, present situation, and future intentions affect what a person experiences from the environment. See AUTOCHTHONY.

behavior(al) diagnosis   See BEHAVIOR(AL) ASSESSMENT/DIAGNOSIS.

behavior(al) disorder   1. General phrase for any functional disorder or abnormality. 2. Any form of behavior considered inappropriate by members of the individual's social group. See BEHAVIOR MODIFICATION.

behavior(al) disorders of childhood and adolescence   1. Behavior that is primarily outgoing or activist in nature, usually refers to children having temper tantrums, and adolescents rebelling against parents and teachers. 2. Effects accompanying various areas of behavior: hyperkinesis, withdrawal, anxiety, discomfort with adults, hostile disobedience, destructiveness, group delinquency. See DELINQUENCY.

behavioral dynamics   The motivational patterns, or the causes of behavior. The assumption is that overt behavior is the external aspect of internal factors (such as being motivated by the "little person" inside [homunculus] who directs the body).

behavior(al) ecology   The study of the behavior of organisms within their environment, for example, the axolotl (a type of salamander) of Northwestern United States never grow to full maturity but the axolotl of Mexico do because the two environments differ in the composition of minerals in the water the salamanders drink. See ENVIRONMENTAL ECOLOGY.

behavioral endocrinology　　The study of the effects of endocrine-gland functions on behavior. Gonadal and adrenal functions have a direct effect on behavior patterns as expressed through sexually related and general activity. Animal research shows relationships between the size of endocrine glands and activity states; for example, wild rats that are more physically active than laboratory rats generally have larger adrenal glands.

behavioral environment　　The surroundings of a person, all aspects of the environment, such as people, animals, events, that impinge on a person and to which a person responds. See SURROUND.

behavior(al) experiment　　A procedure used by some psychotherapists in which clients are asked to try out in real life some action that they are convinced will not work, such as getting a shy person to ask someone for a date. Also known as home work. See FIXED ROLE THERAPY.

behavioral facilitation　　In environmental design, the construction of a setting to maximize or optimize the work or activity performed there. Such facilitation includes functional and spatial arrangements. See CONFORMANCE, FUNCTIONAL CONFORMANCE.

behavior(al) field　　1. Any external stimuli or conditions, or accumulation of factors, that produce a behavioral effect. 2. (K. Lewin) Everything from the external environment that affects a person at any given time, such as phenomena that are seen, heard, smelled, tasted, or felt, including temperature, clothing, other people. See BEHAVIOR SPACE, SURROUND.

behavioral genetics　　See BEHAVIOR GENETICS.

behavioral health　　(J. D. Matarazzo) An interdisciplinary field dedicated to promoting a philosophy of health that stresses individual responsibility in the application of behavioral and biomedical science knowledge and techniques to the maintenance of health and the prevention of illness and dysfunction by a variety of self-initiated individual or shared activities.

behavior(al) hierarchy　　A graded list of behavioral segments, beginning with the baseline behavior and gradually moving up to the terminal behavior.

behavior(al) homeostasis　　Balanced behavior that leads to a steady state of equilibrium. Deviations from this balanced state lead to disequilibrium, thus generating responses to return to the balanced condition.

behavior(al) homology　　A concept that in evolution humans have the essential behavioral functions of lower animals.

behavioral immunogen　　(J. D. Matarazzo) A lifestyle activity such as adequate sleep, moderate use of alcohol, no smoking, no overeating, and exercise that inoculates (and thus acts as an immunogen) against future illness and premature death.

behavioral index　　(R. B. Cattell) The loading of a given source trait in the behavioral equation for a given stimulus-response.

behavioral inhibition system (BIS)　　(J. A. Gray) A system theorized to underlie learning and affect, assumed to guide behavior in response to threats and novel stimuli. Persons with a relatively strong BIS are considered likely to be neurotic. See BEHAVIORAL APPROACH SYSTEM.

behavior(al) integration　　Refers to persons described using common jargon as those who "have it all together," are well-adjusted, know themselves, know what they want, and know how to get along.

Behaviorally Anchored Rating Scales (BARS)　　In employee evaluation, a list of specific behaviors such as meeting deadlines and punctuality, to be assigned specific numerical ratings.

behavioral medicine　　The application of behavior therapy techniques such as biofeedback and relaxation for prevention or treatment of various medical and psychophysiological disorders.

behavioral metamorphosis　　A change in behavior patterns, personality, or lifestyle that is significant and usually abrupt, such as the charge of Paul as recorded in the New Testament, of having a dramatic change of attitude while on the road to Damascus (Acts:22). See CONVERSION.

behavioral model　　The systematic description or conceptualization of psychological disorders in terms of overt behavior patterns. See MEDICAL MODEL.

behavioral modeling　　A person serving as an example as to how others should conduct themselves. In some instances, a person is a model for others but does not know it; in other instances a person consciously serves as a model. See BEHAVIOR(AL) MODIFICATION, MODELING.

behavioral neurochemistry　　The study of the relationships between behavior and biochemical influences (such as the effects of drugs) on the brain.

behavior(al) observation　　In research on behavior, observers have different methods of operating, depending on what kind or type of subjects are to be watched (for example, animals or children). Also, one observer may have a preestablished list of behaviors to be noted, and simply checks off preestablished behavioral units (event sampling). Another observer might use a notebook or a tape recorder to record all responses.

behavioral oscillation $(_SO_R)$　　(C. L. Hull) Momentary variations in an organism's reaction potential while performing a test or task. These variations assume over time the pattern of a normal curve. See HULL'S THEORY.

behavioral pathogen　　(J. D. Matarazzo) A lifestyle activity such as chronic inadequate sleep, immoderate use of alcohol, smoking, overeating, and avoidance of exercise that maim, disable, or kill when practiced over a lifetime.

behavior(al) pattern　　Behavioral sequences of stimulus and response that have some kind of recurring regularity, permitting successful prediction from the stimulus to the expected response.

behavior(al) problem　　1. A behavior that is a problem for the person behaving, whether the problem is covert or overt (such as excessive sensitivity, shyness, timidity, fearfulness). 2. Personal conduct that is a problem for others (such as rudeness, social insensitivity, drunkenness, violence, criminality).

behavior(al) procedures (J. B. Watson) Attempts to generate an entire psychological system by avoiding, as much as possible, any mention or consideration of phenomenological aspects such as consideration of the mind. While not rejecting the mind or its attributes of thinking, feeling, and wanting, nevertheless, the aim is to understand, predict, and control behavior by recourse only to observable events. See BEHAVIORISM.

behavioral profiles A means of identifying general and specific patterns of behavior; for example, on the basis of observations of a large number of professors, a series of codable actions can be established such as standing/sitting, lecturing/questioning, class-centered/student-centered behavior, and subject-centered/individual-centered behavior. A norm can be established and later used to identify patterns of behavior for specific professors.

behavioral prostheses Biofeedback devices employed to assist a patient in learning preferred behavior patterns. Examples include portable devices that produce a mild electric shock when the patient's behavior departs from a prescribed course, or a miniature metronome worn like a hearing aid to help stutterers pace their speaking rate.

behavioral psychiatry Psychiatric treatment in which behavior modification and learning-theory techniques are applied.

behavior(al) psychology 1. (J. B. Watson) The systematic investigation of responsive activity in organisms without reference to consciousness. See BEHAVIORISM. 2. Phrase replacing response psychology and reaction psychology.

behavior(al) purpose An intention to act in a certain way prior to the action.

behavioral rehearsal Roleplaying; practicing an act or series of actions, either alone or in the presence of others, such as in giving a speech either before a mirror or in front of family or friends prior to giving the real speech. See ASSERTIVE TRAINING.

behavioral research In industrial psychology, evaluation of job performance that uses criterion and predictor factors as dependent and independent variables, respectively, within a statistical concept.

behavioral risk factors Patterns of, or a specific behavior associated with, breakdowns in physiological functioning. Examples include smoking, overeating. See TYPE A BEHAVIOR.

behavior(al) sampling 1. The evaluation of a person's actions either with the person knowing or not knowing that evaluation is taking place. The data may then be used in appraising personality traits or the consistency or inconsistency of the person's behavior. 2. A method of assessment that observes the behavior of a person in a variety of relevant places, to be contrasted with, for example, shadowing.

behavioral sciences Scientific disciplines in which the actions and reactions of humans and animals are studied through observational and research methods, especially psychology, psychiatry, sociology, psychopharmacology, and anthropology.

behavior(al) segment A descriptive or measurable element of behavior.

behavioral sink An enclosure in which many research animals are crowded together, resulting in disruption of vital modes of normal behavior such as nest building, courting, and care of the young. See CROWDING AND ANIMAL BEHAVIOR.

behavior(al) specification equation A mathematical formula designed to predict behavior on the basis of information about specific traits and situations.

behavioral study of obedience (S. Milgram) Research on the extent to which ordinary volunteers in a research setting would obey a minimally coercive authority figure, even if they believed they were harming or killing another person. Stanley Milgram concluded that obedience to authority is a potent determinant of behavior in American society. See AUTOMATIC OBEDIENCE, DEFERRED OBEDIENCE, DESTRUCTIVE OBEDIENCE, OBEDIENCE.

behavioral teratogens Substances that generate behavioral abnormalities such as mental retardation, extreme sensitivity, and high irritability in newborns. Contrasts with physical teratogens which lead to obvious physical abnormalities such as clubbed feet.

behavior(al) theory (K. Spence) A point of view emphasizing immediate relations to the environment by using stimulus and response variables. Emphasizes the here-and-now, disregarding both the effects of history and the effect of future intentions.

behavior(al) therapy Methods of psychotherapy that focus on modifying faulty behavior rather effectively than basic changes in the personality. Instead of probing the unconscious or exploring the patient's thoughts and feelings, behavior therapists seek to eliminate symptoms and modify ineffective or maladaptive patterns by applying some basic learning techniques, such as aversive therapy, operant conditioning, Pavlovian conditioning, reciprocal inhibition.

behavioral threshold The point or moment in time at which an organism acts as the result of a stimulus.

behavioral toxicity Adverse reactions to drugs resulting in behavioral changes such as insomnia, toxic confusional states, bizarre dreams, tardive dyskinesia, and reduced psychomotor activity.

behavioral variability Diversity of behavior; the fact that the same stimulus or environmental condition evokes dissimilar responses in different persons; the same stimulus situation elicits dissimilar responses in a person at different times. See LENS MODEL.

behavior analysis A method or model, developed by B. F. Skinner based on the experimental analysis of behavior. This model states that include that the subject matter of psychology may be considered the observable interactions between an organism and its environment. Also, that some responses are conditioned by antecedent stimuli (Pavlovian conditioning) and some by consequent stimuli (operant conditioning), which can be used in replacing undesirable behavior with desirable behavior (behavior modification). See BEHAVIORISM and also the entries in parentheses.

behavior chaining In behavioral theory, simple behaviors can be elicited and reinforced in such a way that complex patterns, or chains, of behavior may be produced, for example, the series of behaviors involved in going out to get in the car, start it, back out of the garage, and drive away. Sometimes referred to as chaining.

behavior checklist   1. A system of screening children with learning disabilities at the preschool level by evaluating specified categories of perceptual-motor skills. 2. A printed list of behaviors or acts used to check if, and how often, such behaviors are observed in a particular situation or in a particular person.

behavior consistency   The degree of predictability of behavior; for example, a child may be disruptive only in mathematics classes, or only in the presence of a particular teacher.

behavior-constraint theory   (M. Seligman) A concept that individuals may acquire "learned helplessness" (giving up) when repeated efforts fail to gain control over undesirable environmental stimuli. See GENERAL ADAPTATION SYNDROME, LEARNED HELPLESSNESS.

behavior determinant   1. Any variable factor that produces a behavioral effect. 2. (E. C. Tolman) Any stimulus (S) considered the cause of a response (R) based on statistical frequency of S leading to the appearance of R.

behavior dysfunctions classification   The identification and classification of abnormal behaviors such as those by Thomas Sydenham in the 17th century. The classifications by Emil Kraepelin in the 19th century are still in use. The International Classification of Diseases (ICD) and the Diagnostic and Statistical Manual of Mental Disorders (DSM), both revised at various periods, are the latest such attempts. Such classifications are designed to be practical and descriptive, not theoretical. The DSM-IV has close to 500 separate classifications.

behavior-exchange model   An attempt at developing a unified approach to understanding human behavior by using accumulated research data and information gathered from observing interactions of people. See BEHAVIOR-EXCHANGE THEORY.

behavior-exchange theory   A point of view that human behavior, especially interaction, can be understood as an exchange of rewards and costs. See BEHAVIOR-EXCHANGE MODEL.

behavior genetics   (R. I. Watson) The field of inquiry that investigates the influence of the genes on behavior and personality by studying familial or hereditary behavior patterns. Many studies about genetics and psychological factors indicate that a genetic element exists. See BEHAVIORAL DISORDER, MENTAL DISORDERS.

behaviorism   1. (J. B. Watson) A model positing that a genuinely scientific psychology must be based on objective, observable facts rather than subjective, quantitative processes such as thoughts, feelings, and motives. To make psychology a naturalistic science, John Watson proposed to limit it to quantitative events such as stimulus-response, the effects of conditioning, physiological processes, and a study of animal behavior—all of which can best be investigated through laboratory experiments that yield results that can be analyzed statistically. 2. A branch of psychology that attempts to formulate, through systematic observation and experimentation, laws and principles that underlie the behavior of organisms. Also known as behavioral psychology. See BEHAVIOR METHOD, DESCRIPTIVE BEHAVIORISM, METHODOLOGICAL BEHAVIORISM, NEOBEHAVIORISM, RADICAL BEHAVIORISM.

behaviorist   A person accepting the theoretical position of behaviorism. However, this does not imply that all behaviorists think alike since they do differ among themselves.

behavior language   A type of body language, particularly of persons who cannot or will not speak, including infants and invalids who may express themselves by various ways such as crying, smiling, grimacing, turning. See BODY LANGUAGE.

behavior-mapping   A technique of studying the performance of individuals in different environmental situations, for example, children in a variety of classroom designs. By observing the children in various activities, it may be determined that some of them achieve better performance in an open-structured classroom seating pattern whereas others function better in an old-fashioned classroom setting. Using such observation techniques, conclusions may be drawn for the reasons that people succeed or fail. See SHADOWING.

behavior modification/therapy   The use of operant conditioning, biofeedback, modeling, aversive conditioning, reciprocal inhibition, or other learning techniques as a means of changing human behavior, improving adaptation, and alleviating symptoms. Sometimes known as action therapy.

behavior potential   1. A variable tendency to respond in a special circumstance in terms of expected results, tangible or intangible. 2. (J. Rotter) The strength of a tendency to respond in a particular situation or class of situations in relation to the expectancy of reinforcement and of the reinforcement value of the "reward" expected. See EXPECTANCY, REINFORCEMENT VALUE.

behavior rating   Recording the specific types of behavior such as the number of times a child has a temper tantrum or the number of times an adult drinks an alcoholic beverage in a week. See BEHAVIOR SAMPLING.

behavior-rating schedule   A set of items or questions that are meant to elicit descriptions of overt behavior of participants or subjects.

behavior record   A chronicle of observations intended to provide a complete and accurate account of an organism's behavior in a specified time frame. As a guidance term, behavior record refers to a teacher's written observations regarding a student's behavior and personality. See ANECDOTAL RECORD for an example.

behavior reversal   A behavior-modification method in which the patient practices more desirable responses to interpersonal conflicts under the supervision of a trainer or therapist.

behavior sampling   The recorded observation of an individual's behavior in a designated time frame.

behavior setting   (R. Barker & H. Wright) The geographical and social situation as it affects relationships, ideas, values, and behavior; for example, people in a resettlement community tend to "sort themselves out" according to interests, nationality, background, and social attitudes.

behavior shaping   (B. F. Skinner) A means of changing the behavior of others, especially animals, by establishing a small behavior change via reward and having established that change, going to another behavior change; in many cases a new set of behaviors may be established. In such a manner, animals are trained to do behaviors that are unnatural for them, such as a bear using roller skates. Also known as method of successive approximations. See SHAPING.

behavior space   (K. Lewin) The total situation of all factors affecting a person at any point in time, positive and negative. These include everything from the past inherent in the person at the time, such as memories, fears, attitudes, as well as other people and physical conditions of the environment at the moment. Also known as life space.

behavior-specimen recording   A method of studying behavior of a single person by continuously observing the person for a period of at least one day and recording all details, including conversations, interactions with others, how time was spent. One or more observers may be used.

behavior system   1. Different activities that can be undertaken to reach the same goal or carry out the same function. A system of interrelated actions having the same general purpose but operating in different manners (for example, conveying the same message by speaking, writing, gesturing, or pointing). 2. Important motives expressed in different ways in different cultures, and among different individuals who have been subjected to different training and experiences within the same culture. Also known as activity system.

Behavior Theory   (J. Wolpe) The point of view that maladjustment is a learned process and it can be unlearned. Starting with animal research using behavior modification techniques, Wolpe moved on to human participants and developed the theory of reciprocal inhibition and presented his theories by practical demonstrations of its effects. See ANXIETY HIERARCHY, RECIPROCAL INHIBITION, SYMPTOM SUBSTITUTION, SYSTEMATIC DESENSITIZATION.

behavior theory   See HULL'S THEORY.

behavior therapy   **behavior modification**

behavior types   Personality classifications based upon distinct patterns of behavior, such as Carl Jung's division of personality into extraverts and introverts. See TYPOLOGY.

behavior unit   An element of natural behavior with inherent unity unaffected by outside influences.

behavior vs conduct   Similar terms except that "behavior" is free of judgement whereas "conduct" usually implies an evaluative element.

behind-the-back technique   (R. J. Corsini) A group therapy procedure comprising three phases: (a) Volunteers agree to speak for 30 minutes to the group without interruption; (b) on finishing, they sit outside the group facing outward and hear the rest of the group talking about them; (c) they rejoin the group and engage in a discussion about themselves until the end of the period. See GROUP THERAPY.

Behn-Rorschach Test   (H. Behn & H. Rorschach) A variation on the Rorschach test used for research with people who are excessively familiar with the standard inkblots.

Behrens-Fisher Distribution   (W. U. Behrens & R. A. Fisher) A sampling distribution for sample numbers smaller than 30.

being-beyond-the-world   A concept found in some religions and also in existentialism that there is a greater reality than present existence and that present behavior is inferior to potential behavior.

Being cognition   (A. Maslow) Ability to perceive reality objectively unimpeded by any kind of prejudice or circumstances. A quality ascribed by Abraham Maslow to "self-actualizers." Also known as B cognition.

being cognition   In the existential approach, awareness of the inner core of self-existence, that is, the self, or identity. Distinguished from Abraham Maslow's Being cognition.

being-in-the-world   (L. Binswanger, M. Heidegger) In existentialism, the unique pattern of each person's experience, in a world where humans and the world have no existence apart from each other. Behavior stems from self-existence and not from the attitudes and dictates of others or from circumstances.

Being love   (A. Maslow) A form of love characterized by mutuality, concern for another's welfare, and limited dependency, selfishness, or jealousy. "Self-actualizers" can achieve this state. Also known as B love. Compare DEFICIENCY LOVE.

Being motivation   **metamotivation**

being one's self   (C. R. Rogers) To behave consistently in line with desires, motivations, and feelings. In many situations people act as they think they "should" rather than as they desire. Terms such as civility, courtesy, diplomacy, etiquette, manners, tact, and toleration all have elements of not really being the self.

being there (for . . .)   A concept that a person is always available to another person for support, help, etc., as in "I will always be there for you." See AGAPE.

Being values   **metaneeds**

Békésy audiometer   (G. von Békésy) The first automatic audiometer. Used to measure the absolute threshold of hearing via tracings for continuous and interrupted tones at controlled frequencies.

Békésy's traveling wave theory of hearing   (G. von Békésy) A form of place theory of pitch discrimination.

Bekhterev's nucleus   (V. M. Bekhterev) One of the four major vestibular nuclei in the medulla.

Bekhterev's nystagmus   (V. M. Bekhterev) Nystagmic eye movements observed when the cortex, the cerebellum, or one or both labyrinths are removed.

bel   (A. G. Bell) The common logarithm (that is, $\log_{10}$) of the ratio between two energies, so that an increase of one bel represents a 10-fold increase in energy. A decibel is one-tenth of a bel, so that an increase of 1 decibel represents a ratio of $10^{1/10} = 1.259$. The decibel scale is often used in referring to sound intensity where one energy is the one being measured and the other is a reference intensity. Because energy and pressure are related by the square law, the decibel may also be defined as 1/20 of the common logarithm of the ratio between two pressures. The two common reference intensities are 0.0002 dyne/cm^2 (the absolute threshold for a 1000 Hertz tone in a typical listener), in which case the phrase sound pressure level (SPL) may be used and the threshold of hearing for that specific tone frequency, in which case the phrase sensation level is used. Named after Scottish-American inventor Alexander Graham Bell (1847–1922).

belief An attitude of acceptance about the validity of a doctrine, that may or may not be correct. See EVIDENCE, PROOF, RELIABILITY, VALIDITY.

belief perseverance A tendency for people who have once generated an explanation to maintain this interpretation even when the evidence that gave rise to the explanation is shown to be false.

belief system A set of attitudes, opinions, and convictions that affect personal behavior, interpersonal relationships, and attitudes toward life. See CONCEPTUAL SYSTEM.

belief-value matrix (E. C. Tolman) The set of judgments and values that people use in interfacing with the environment. This matrix represents a person in action, and knowing this about the person, can help predict behavior.

belittling A social behavior reaction in which a person attempts to increase self-esteem by disparaging others or things they have done.

Bell Adjustment Inventory (H. M. Bell) A personality questionnaire that emphasizes home, health, and social and emotional factors. See ADJUSTMENT INVENTORY.

belladonna (beautiful woman—Italian) An extract from the leaves and roots of the nightshade plant *Atropa belladonna* with anticholinergic effects, widely used in the 1920s through the 1960s, often mixed with a small amount of phenobarbital as a counter to what was later called "irritable bowel syndrome" or other chronic gastrointestinal complaints with diarrhea and cramps. The active ingredient is atropine and in large doses can be toxic. See MYDRIASIS.

belladonna delirium An effect on the central nervous system of large doses of belladonna drugs, for example, atropine. Symptoms include delirium, hallucinations, and overactive limb movements. See BELLADONNA, NIGHTSHADE POISONING.

bell and pad system (O. H. Mowrer) A technique for controlling children's bed-wetting. If the sleeping child begins to urinate, an electric circuit is closed via the wetted pad and a bell rings, awakening the child. See ENURESIS.

Bell-Magendie Law (C. Bell, F. Magendie) A theory that cutting the ventral (anterior) spinal roots of the spinal nerves paralyzes muscle contractions, whereas cutting the dorsal (posterior) roots of the spinal nerves eliminates sensory responses.

bell-shaped curve A graphic representation of a symmetrical unimodal curve that has the general profile of a bell. Also known as Gaussian curve, normal curve. The well known Gaussian or normal curve given by the equation $y = (1/\sigma\sqrt{2\pi})\exp(-(x-\mu)^2/2\sigma^2)$ with mean μ, and standard deviation σ. See NORMAL CURVE/DISTRIBUTION for an illustration.

Bell's mania (L. V. Bell) A form of acute maniacal excitement first described in the 1840s as "resembling some advanced stages of mania and fever," which might lead to unexplained death (autopsy-negative death). Also known as deadly catatonia, exhaustion death, lethal catatonia. Named after American physician Luther V. Bell (1806–1862). See DELIRIOUS MANIA, HYPERMANIA.

Bell's palsy (C. Bell) Facial nerve paralysis.

belle indifférence See LA BELLE INDIFFÉRENCE.

Bellevue Scale/Test See WECHSLER-BELLEVUE SCALE(S).

belonephobia 1. Irrational fear of pointed objects, or of sharp-pointed objects, such as knives. 2. Morbid fear of needles, probably generated by earlier hypodermic injections.

belonging The feeling of being accepted and approved, of having a secure place in a certain group or in society as a whole. Some patients with mental disorders (such as schizophrenia) frequently feel they do not belong anywhere. Term is often used interchangeably with belongingness. See ANOMIE, PRINCIPLE OF BELONGINGNESS.

belongingness 1. The feeling of being accepted by another person or group. 2. (E. Fromm) A sense of certainty, security, and rootedness which Fromm contrasted with the anxiety induced by individuality and freedom. 3. (E. L. Thorndike) The argument that some associations naturally belong together and so are easier to connect. See PRINCIPLE OF BELONGINGNESS.

belongingness and love needs See LOVE NEEDS.

belongingness law/principle See PRINCIPLE OF BELONGINGNESS.

beltlines (G. Bach) Tolerance limits set for mutual assaults by which fair and foul fighting behavior ensue during Creative Aggression procedures. See BATACAS.

Bem Sex-Role Inventory (BSRI) (S. Bem) A self-rating scale in which respondents describe themselves by endorsing on a seven point scale statements that describe stereotypically masculine and feminine characteristics.

benchmark job In industry, a job chosen as a reference point for comparison of job evaluations.

Bender Visual-Motor Gestalt Test (BVMGT) (L. Bender) A projective personality test in which the participant copies nine geometrical figures, such as a circle tangent to a diamond and a row of dots. Interpretation of these configurations, and the participant's spontaneous comments, purportedly help examiners in assessing perceptual ability and personality characteristics, and in diagnosing functional and organic disorders. Also known as Bender-Gestalt Test (BGT). See APRAXIA.

bends Decompression sickness.

beneceptor A nerve receptor or sense organ whose stimuli are generally beneficial and produce pleasantness to the organism. Compare NOCICEPTOR.

Benedikt syndrome (M. Benedikt) A pathological condition of the midbrain characterized by palsy of the ipsilateral eye muscles, contralateral involuntary movements, and occasionally, hemiplegia.

beneffectance Nontechnical term of unknown origin composed of the words "beneficial" and "effectance" that refers to the tendency of people to forget unpleasant memories and to emphasize successful events.

benevolent eclecticism An attitude of acceptance in any kind of debate or discussion in which all points of view are accepted at face value with no effort to evaluate or discriminate between the points of view. See BRAINSTORMING, GROUP DECISIONS, PARTISAN ZEALOTRY.

Benham's top   (C. E. Benham) A white disk with a black pattern that, when rotated at the proper speed, produces color sensations of orange and blue.

Benham's top

benign   1. Kind. 2. A disease condition that is relatively mild or transient, as opposed to a malignant disease. 2. In psychiatry, an illness or disorder that is treatable, not serious, and has a favorable prognosis.

benign neurosis   (E. Kempf) A personality disturbance of which the person is aware, even of its origin.

benign senescence   An accepting attitude toward the normal mental and physical disabilities of the aging process on the part of an older person experiencing this process.

benign stupor   Archaic phrase for a state of unresponsiveness, immobility, and indifference to surroundings from which the patient is likely to recover or improve.

benign trend   A tendency toward recovery in any illness.

Bennett Hand-Tool Dexterity Test   (G. K. Bennett) An examination intended to assess proficiency in the use of ordinary mechanical tools. The participant must remove all nuts and bolts from an upright board and install them on another board in a certain order.

Bennett Mechanical Comprehension Test (BMCT) (G. K. Bennett) A combination of pictures and questions used to measure mechanical aptitude in high school students and adults. Also known as Bennett Test of Mechanical Comprehension. See DIFFERENTIAL APTITUDE TEST.

Benommenheit   (benumbing, haze—German) (E. Bleuler) An acute schizophrenic condition in which all mental processes are slowed, and comprehension and ability to deal with complex situations are impaired, although the patient is not dejected or self-deprecatory.

Benton Visual Retention Test (BVRT)   (A. L. Benton) An assessment instrument developed in the 1940s that attempts to measure visual perception, immediate memory, psychomotor reproduction, and possible brain damage. The participant draws ten geometrical designs after each is exposed for ten seconds and removed from view. Purportedly of value in the diagnosis of reading disabilities, attention-deficit disorders, and dementia. See CEREBRAL-DYSFUNCTION TESTS.

Benzedrine   Trade name for a mixture of the active and inactive isomers of amphetamine, a drug rarely used any more. See AMPHETAMINE.

benzodiazepines   A major class of antianxiety drugs which have been widely used: Librium (chlordiazepoxide) in the early 1960s; Valium (diazepam) in the 1970s; Xanax and Ativan in the 1980s. Also some variations have been applied mainly for sleep ("hypnotics"). As with earlier types of antianxiety drugs, these also have been found to be capable of being abused and even addicting. The short-acting types especially are problematical in that efforts to withdraw from their use evokes anxiety which then leads to a vicious cycle of their continuance.

benzothiadiazides   A group of synthetic chemicals widely used as diuretics in the treatment of hypertension. Also known as thiazides.

B = f(POE)   Health status formula. Behavior (B) is a function (f) of Psychosocial (P), Organic (O), and Environmental (E) elements.

berdache   (American Indian) A male who behaved like a female, performed "women's work," and was accepted as such in certain Native American tribes. See TRANSVESTISM.

bereavement   A feeling of deprivation and grief, particularly at the loss of a loved one.

Bereitschaft   (anticipatory mental set or attitude, readiness—German) In psychological laboratory experiments, an organism's readiness to start participating. Similar to *Einstellung* and mental set, but with more of an anticipatory readiness.

Berger rhythms   Named after Hans Berger, another name for brain waves. See ALPHA RHYTHM/WAVES.

beriberi   One of the first discovered nutritional diseases, this Vitamin B_1 (thiamine) deficiency may be present in chronic alcoholics, geriatric patients living on meager and idiosyncratic diets, and other people with undernutrition. Can cause confusion, and therefore in older persons senility should not be assumed. There are other medical problems, ranging from heart failure to painful neuropathies. Also known as endemic neuritis, panneuritis endemica. See WERNICKE'S DISEASE.

Berkeley growth study   A longitudinal study of individuals' growth in intelligence, including measures of stability (reliability) of intelligence test scores, that demonstrated poor reliability between early measures (in infancy) and those obtained at the time children were ready to enter school.

Berkeley Puppet Interview   (J. Ablow & J. Measelle) A diagnostic procedure that uses puppets to elicit responses from young children, for example, Puppet 1 says "I eat what I want to." Puppet 2 says: "I eat what my mama tells me to." Then both puppets turn to the child and say: "How about YOU?"

Bernoulli effect   (D. Bernoulli) A principle that the pressure of a fluid decreases as the velocity increases. This theory has been applied to the effects of air impulses during vocal-cord approximation in speaking. Developed by Swiss mathematician Daniel Bernoulli (1700–1782).

Bernoulli process   (J. Bernoulli) A probability experiment (such as tossing a coin) in which there are only two possible outcomes, which are often referred to as "success" and "failure." If there are a series of *n* independent trials, and if the probability of a "success" is the same on each trial, the probability distribution of the number of "successes" is referred to as the binomial distribution. Demonstrated by Jacques (Jacob) Bernoulli.

Bernreuter Personal Adjustment Inventory (R. G. Bernreuter) A six-trait questionnaire on personality and behavior factors yielding measures of neurotic tendency, introversion-extraversion, self-sufficiency, sociability, self-confidence, and dominance-submission. Used in the 1930s and 1940s, supplanted by longer and more sophisticated questionnaires of this type. Also known as Bernreuter Personality Inventory.

berserk 1. Wild and uncontrolled behavior, a continuous frenzy. 2. Denoting a behavioral disorder marked by violent rage. Term may come from Norse warriors, berserkers, said to howl like animals and foam at the mouth while attacking their enemies.

Bertillon system (A. Bertillon) Obsolete method of identifying individuals by a number of measurements of bodily structures, such as the shape of the ears. See ANTHROPOMETRY.

best-answer test A task in which the participant examines several possible solutions to a problem or reasons for a situation, and chooses the one the participant considers most appropriate. Also known as best-reason test.

best estimate In statistical operations, a judgment of what the mean would most likely be, and using this judgment as the temporary mean from which to measure all findings; later the true value would be substituted for this estimate. See SUFFICIENT ESTIMATE.

best-first search (H. A. Simon) A search through a problem space where each new position is evaluated when it is reached, and the search is continued from that one to the unsearched positions that have the highest value. See HEURISTIC SEARCH, PROBLEM SPACE.

bestiality Legal term for humans having sexual relations with animals. Also known as zooerastia, zooerasty. See SODOMY, ZOOPHILIA.

best-reason test best-answer test

beta The second letter of the Greek alphabet. See APPENDIX C.

beta-adrenergic blockers Medicines that block the effects of certain neurotransmitters mainly associated with the sympathetic nervous system. In psychiatry, a well known example is propanolol (Inderal). Such blockers have been helpful in reducing the frequency of rage attacks in some patients with brain damage or other conditions, and in smaller doses can help with stage fright. Also known as beta blockers. See BETA-ADRENERGIC RECEPTOR ANTAGONISTS, NEUROTRANSMITTERS.

beta-adrenergic receptor antagonists Class of drugs including, most prominently, propanolol, used for certain anxiety and aggressive symptoms; others in this class are used for high blood pressure. See BETA-ADRENERGIC BLOCKERS.

beta alcoholism (E. M. Jellinek) Rare phrase for a type of alcoholism in which drinking has progressed to the point of physical complications such as effects on the stomach, liver, pancreas, or kidneys, but does not yet involve physical or psychological dependence. Patients often exhibit nutritional-deficiency symptoms and diminished job efficiency. Also known as somatopathic drinking. See ALCOHOLISM, CHRONIC ALCOHOLISM.

beta-arc The arousal of higher cortical pathways by the functioning of an alpha-arc, leading to a sensation rather than simple awareness. Beta-arc is roughly the same as a delayed response or implicit behavior, as contrasted with an immediate response. See ALPHA-ARC.

beta blocker(s) beta-adrenergic blockers

beta cells Endocrine cells within the pancreas that secrete insulin. See ISLANDS OF LANGERHANS.

beta coefficient A regression coefficient expressed in comparable units so that its effect on the dependent variable is indicated by its relative size.

beta endorphin A potent endorphin that causes aggressive behavior. See ALPHA ENDORPHIN, ENDORPHIN, ENKEPHALIN, GAMMA ENDORPHIN.

beta error Not rejecting the null hypothesis when it is false. See TYPE I ERROR, TYPE II ERROR.

Beta Examination/Test A set of mental tests used to determine the relative mental ability of military recruits in World War I, designed especially for illiterates and those deficient in knowledge of English, the instructions being given in signs and the material being pictorial in character. Also known as Army Beta. See ARMY TESTS, CULTURE-FAIR TESTS, REVISED BETA EXAMINATION-SECOND EDITION (BETA-II).

Beta hypothesis (K. Dunlap) The postulate that repetition frequency has no effect on learning. See ALPHA, BETA, GAMMA HYPOTHESES.

beta level The probability of making a Type II error (failing to reject a false null hypothesis).

beta motion/movement An illusion in which successive stimuli of different frequencies generate apparent motion, for example, lights on a theater marquee that appear to move when, in fact, the lights simply go on and off in a particular order generating the illusion of movement. See BOW MOTION/MOVEMENT, PHI PHENOMENON.

beta press (H. A. Murray) Interpretations made by a person as to the importance of other people and objects. Compare ALPHA PRESS.

beta receptor One of two basic types of adrenergic nervous-system receptors, the other type being alpha receptors. Beta receptor responses to natural or synthetic biochemical agents are generally inhibitory; an exception is a stimulant effect in heart muscle. Functions include vasodilation, bronchial and intestinal relaxation, and, in some animal species, relaxation of the uterine smooth muscle. Compare ALPHARECEPTOR.

beta-receptor blocking agents See BETA-ADRENERGIC BLOCKERS, BETA-ADRENERGIC RECEPTOR ANTAGONISTS.

beta response The delayed reaction of an eyelid after presentation of a conditioned stimulus. See ALPHA RESPONSE.

beta rhythm/waves (H. Berger) An electroencephalographic (EEG) wave pattern associated with an alert and activated cerebral cortex. The frequency generally is above 12 Hertz (cycles per second) and may range upward of 40 Hertz. Beta activity is recorded during intense mental activity, but it also occurs as a sign of anxiety or apprehension.

beta risk (β)   In hypothesis testing, the probability of making a beta or Type II error, accepting the null hypothesis when it is really false. The beta risk increases as the alpha risk is decreased. See TYPE I ERROR, TYPE II ERROR.

beta testing   1. A concept that something, such as a test, a manuscript, or a body of research, instead of being given immediately to a participant, a publisher, or put into action, is first tested with an intermediate group. 2. Limited preliminary field testing of computer programs, psychological tests, etc., before commercial release.

beta waves   See BETA RHYTHM.

beta weight (β-weight/B-weight)   In multiple correlation, multipliers of predictors to maximize the correlation of all factors. These weights, also referred to as beta coefficients, are relative weights. When expressed in terms of raw units of measurement they are indicated as B-weights and are not comparable. When transformed to standard units of measurement (β-weights) they are comparable.

betel nut   The seed of a palm tree, *areca catechu*, chewed as a stimulant by populations of India and islands of the Indian and Pacific Oceans. Contains a drug (arecoline), which stimulates smooth muscles and glands.

Betts' test of visual imagery   (G. H. Betts, P. W. Sheehan) A test devised to demonstrate differences between individual ability to form mental images upon hearing words such as apple, baby, cart.

between group variance   A statistical measure of the dispersion of scores among groups. See WITHIN-GROUPS VARIANCE.

between-groups variance   A variation in scores attributable to membership in different groups. See WITHIN-GROUPS VARIANCE.

between-subject design   An experimental design in which each participant is tested at only one level for each independent variable. Frequently called an independent groups design. See WITHIN-SUBJECT DESIGN.

between variance   In analysis of variance, given treatment group samples selected from populations that are assumed under the null hypothesis to have equal means and variances, the estimate of the common population variance that is based on the sample means. Distinguished from the "within" variance, the estimate based on the pooled within-group sample variances.

between vs within interactions   (N. S. Endler) "Between" interactions refer to interactions between person-variables (for example, biological and psychological variables) and situational-variables (for example, stressful events and physical environments) in the person-situation interaction model. This is in contrast to "within" interactions which occur between the factors within each class of variables (for example, between biological and psychological variables).

Betz cells   Large pyramidal ganglion cells found in the fifth layer of the cerebral cortex. Betz cells are associated with muscle movement at a low threshold of stimulation. Betz-cell lesions result in convulsive seizures, spasticity, and flaccid paralysis. Named after Russian anatomist Vladimir A. Betz (1834–1894). See MOTOR NEURONS.

bewildered   Appearing lost, dazed, puzzled and apathetic, or confused. See AMBIVALENCE, AUTISTIC THINKING, PREOCCUPATION.

bewilderment   An emotional condition involving a high degree of cognitive confusion, sometimes with rapidly alternating and conflicting impulses.

Bewusstseinslage   (conscious attitude—German) An experience reported as not appearing obviously sensory or affective; for example, doubt, ease, bafflement, sense of approaching the goal. See AUFGABE, EINSTELLUNG, WÜRZBURG SCHOOL.

beyondism   A controversial philosophical doctrine about reproduction and eugenics that recommends reduction of births of individuals considered to be constitutionally inferior. See EUGENICS, EUTHENICS, GENTHANASIA, RACISM.

Bezold-Brücke effect/phenomenon   (W. von Bezold, W. von Brücke) A shift of red and green hues toward yellow and blue hues when illumination increases.

B fiber   A myelinated preganglionic axon of the autonomic nervous system, approximately three microns in diameter. Carries nerve impulses at speeds of between 3 and 15 meters-per-second. See A FIBER, C FIBER.

BGT   Bender-Gestalt Test

bhang   (hemp—Hindi) A variation of cannabis sativa. Bhang is a milder form of the active ingredient of marijuana than charas or ganja. See MARIJUANA.

BHS   Beck Hopelessness Scale

BIA   bioelectric impedance analysis

bi-alphabetism   In linguistics, the availability of two visually distinct alphabets (such as Roman and Cyrillic) that are used interchangeably by readers of that area.

bias   1. An error in a particular direction; a tendency to produce erroneous or misleading conclusions because of the use of data that are incomplete or drawn from a sample not representative of the group studied. 2. A selective preference related to prejudice, placing certain people or groups at an advantage or disadvantage.

biased estimators   Sample statistics that yield estimates consistently larger or smaller than the population parameters.

biased predisposition   (M. Diamond) The belief that a person is born with tendencies toward certain characteristics, based mainly on genetics and prenatal hormonal conditions. A biased predisposition make it more likely that certain behaviors will emerge. These characteristics usually are related to sexuality. For instance this theory holds that males are more likely to adopt certain behaviors or traits and females are more likely to adapt others.

biased sample/sampling   1. Any sample not representative of the total population. 2. The selection of subjects for any purpose, that gives some subjects or classes of subjects a greater chance of being included than others. See RANDOMIZATION, REPRESENTATIVE SAMPLE, SYSTEMATICALLY BIASED SAMPLING.

bias error in sampling   Considerable deviation of obtained findings of a sample from the true statement of a population. Most samples are erroneous to a small degree of error from the true, but when sampling is done incorrectly, the difference can be considerable. A classic example occurred in 1936 in two predictions of the presidential election between Alfred Landon and Franklin D. Roosevelt. A small, correctly-done poll predicted that Roosevelt would win. A much larger, incorrectly-done poll favored Landon. The sampling error was made by the *Literary Digest*, a magazine that polled people selected at random from a telephone book, those owning telephones at that time were not fully representative of the voting population. See REPRESENTATIVE SAMPLING, SAMPLING.

biastophilia   Being sexually aroused by surprise assault on a nonconsenting stranger.

bibliomania   A morbid urge to collect and possess books, particularly rare books.

bibliophobia   Morbid fear of books or of having to read books.

bibliotherapy   The use of literature to promote mental health. A form of supportive therapy in which selected literature is recommended for such purposes as: (a) helping the patient gain insight into personality dynamics; (b) imparting appropriate information on such topics as sex, vocations, and new interests; (c) relieving tensions by stimulating fantasy; and (d) inculcating basic principles of mental health. Some bibliotherapists also use audio-visual aids in addition to literature. See POETRY THERAPY.

BID   *bis in die*, Latin for twice a day (also abbreviated b.i.d., B.I.D.). Term used in the prescribing of medication.

bidirectional influence   A tendency for parties in interaction to affect each other. In considering causation in interaction, especially the effect that parents have on children, usually little attention is given to the possibility that children influence their parents. The ironic statement that "Insanity is hereditary, parents get it from their children," has some validity.

Bidwell's ghost   A second visual afterimage that appears in a hue complementary to the stimulus. Named after English physicist Shelford Bidwell (1848–1909). See PURKINJE AFTERIMAGE.

Bielschowsky-Jansky disease   (M. Bielschowsky & J. Jansky) A condition classified under late infantile cerebral lipoidosis. Occurs in children between 2–4 years of age and differs from Tay-Sachs disease by producing retinal optic atrophy instead of the "cherry-red spot" on the macula, and is found more commonly in non-Jewish families.

bifactorial theory of conditioning   A point of view that attitudes determine probabilities of conditioning while the properties of stimuli affect the magnitude of responses.

bifactor method   In factor analysis, the extraction of a principal factor and then subsidiary factors.

bifactor test   An examination yielding two scores, such as verbal and nonverbal scores of an intelligence test or overall score and time to take the test.

bifunctional therapy   Refers to a construct that concentrates on getting the body to be in proper order, such as correcting slouching and poor posture. Examples include: ALEXANDER TECHNIQUE, BIOENERGETICS, BODY AWARENESS, FELDENKRAIS, PSYCHOMOTOR THERAPY, PSYCHOSOMATICS, ROLFING, TRAGERISM.

bifurcation   Separation into two parts.

bigamy   Being married to two persons at the same time. While bigamy is considered illegal in some cultures, it is accepted in others, as in Muslim communities.

Big Brother Program   An arrangement in which an adult acts as a mentor to a younger person of the same gender. Such arrangements are usually made with the approval of the parent or other members of the family through a social agency that evaluates both parties for suitability and maintains contact with the child. All involved in the program operate on the basis of mutual consent. A variant is Big Sister Program.

bigeminal pregnancy   Being pregnant with twins.

Big Five personality factors   On the basis of examinations of a number of factor analyses, the fundamental dimensions of personality are considered to be: agreeableness, conscientiousness, extraversion, neuroticism, openness.

big lie   A propaganda measure in which a false statement of extreme magnitude is constantly repeated to persuade the public, on the theory that it would be more impressive and less likely to be challenged than a lesser falsehood.

bilabial   A speech sound made with both lips that stop or modify the air stream, for example, /b/, /P/, /m/. Also known as labiolabial. See LABIODENTAL.

bilateral   Having to do with both sides of the body.

bilateral brain lesion   A lesion that begins in one hemisphere but produces dysfunction in the other because of a disruption of blood flow, metabolism, tumor spread, edema, or other complications. See BRAIN.

bilateral descent   In anthropology, ancestry traced through a parent, in contrast to unilateral descent, in which ancestry is traced through either parent. See MATRILINEAL, PATRILINEAL.

bilateral speech   A speech function represented in the left and right hemispheres of the brain in Broca's area. As a general rule, right-handed people have speech representation in the left hemisphere and are more likely to experience speech deficits following a left-hemispheric lesion. See BROCA'S AREA.

bilateral symmetry   1. Correspondence in form of parts on the opposite sides of a body, such as the two halves of a clam shell, or the right and left sides of a human, each having one arm and one leg. 2. When both halves of an organism appear to be alike.

bilateral transfer   The transfer of training from one side of the body to the other. Training of the left hand to perform a task prepares to some degree the right hand to perform the same task. Bilateral transfer is most effective in visual-learning activities.

Bildungsroman   (youth novel—German) Any novel about the psychological growth and developmental of its, usually youthful, main character.

bilingual(ism)   Having approximately equal abilities in two languages.

bilious   Querulous (complaining) personality previously considered due to excess of bile. (A remnant of the humoral theory [Galen, Hippocrates], that stated that an excess of yellow bile generates a choleric [angry] personality).

bill of rights   In psychiatry, the rights of patients, including: (a) to receive suitable treatment; (b) to select the least-restrictive alternative treatment; (c) not to be subject to unusual or hazardous treatment methods without consent; (d) to receive due process, even for children; (e) not to be confined if the patient can survive safely in freedom; (f) to refuse treatment that may be invasive, intrusive, or hazardous; (g) to have a humane environment and adequate staffing. This bill originated out of the landmark case of Wyatt vs Stickney (503 F. 2nd 1305, 1978) and is an example of what has become, via judicial decisions, the law in such matters.

bimbo   Slang and derogatory term for a woman considered sexually promiscuous as well as lacking intelligence.

bimetrology   The employment of two measuring systems simultaneously, such as inches and centimeters.

bimodal (curve)   Refers to a curve with two high values or modes. A graphic representation of a bimodal distribution in which the cases cluster about two relative maxima.

bimodal distribution   A frequency distribution having two modes or peaks. Such distributions often result from two heterogeneous sets of data. Sometimes known as bimodal curve.

bimodal distribution

binary   1. Relating to the integer two. 2. Composed of two things.

binary arithmetic   (G. Leibniz) An arithmetical system developed by Gottfried Leibniz using only 0 and 1. All numbers are represented in terms of powers of 2 (or with a number system to the base 2) as compared to the decimal system in which numbers are represented in terms of powers of 10 (base 10). See BINARY NOTATION, BINARY (NUMBER) SYSTEM.

binary bit   Any binary digit (0 or 1).

binary choice   A situation that requires one of two choices, such as YES–NO.

binary code   A code in which each allowable position has one of two possible states.

binary coded decimal (BCD) system   A coding system using four binary digits that allows for easy representation of a single decimal digit. Each set of four bits represents a numeric digit (for example, $0000 = 0$, $0110 = 6$, $1000 = 8$, $1001 = 9$, etc.), a minimum of four are necessary to represent 10 decimal values (four-bit set having 2^4 or 16 combinations). See BINARY (NUMBER) SYSTEM.

binary digit   A digit in the binary number system with one of two values, a zero (0) or one (1). See BINARY (NUMBER) SYSTEM, BIT.

binary hue   A hue that appears to be a combination of two colors, such as pink appearing to be a combination of red and white.

binary notation   The writing of numbers with base 2. The first twelve numbers with this base are 0, 1, 10, 11, 100, 101, 110, 111, 1000, 1001, 1010, 1011. The 2 does not refer to the number 2 but rather to the fact that the system of notation depends only on two items—a zero and a one. See COMPUTERS.

binary (number) system   (J. Napier) A number system with the base of two rather than ten in the decimal system, with the digits having the values of 0 and 1, and these two digits could express any number. The system used in computers to do millions of calculations per second. See BINARY NOTATION.

binasal hemianopia   The loss of the left visual field of the right eye and the right visual field of the left eye. See HEMIANOPIA.

binaural   Pertaining to both ears. Also known as binotic.

binaural beat   Periodic intensity fluctuations produced when tones of slightly different frequency are perceived separately by the two ears. See BEAT, BINAURAL SHIFT.

binaural cue/difference   The concept that sounds are perceived by their direction by the fact that (for a person facing East) a sound coming from the North will reach a person's left ear first. The minute difference in time for it to also reach the right ear is enough to inform most people in most situations, of the direction of the source of the sound.

binaural fusion   A combination of the effect of stimuli presented to the two ears into a single auditory impression. When two stimuli are presented separately to the ears, as c to the right and e to the left, there is dichotic fusion. When both ears receive the double stimulus (as under normal conditions) there is diotic fusion. See FUSION.

binaural hearing   Listening with the two ears conjointly. Also known as dichotic hearing, diotic hearing.

binaural ratio   The ratio of loudness of sound to each of the two ears.

binaural shift   A periodic shift in the localization or intensity of sound heard when two tones of slightly different frequency are perceived separately by each ear, the rate of fluctuation corresponding to the frequency difference.

Binet-Simon Scale   (A. Binet & T. Simon) A series of graded tests used to rate the relative mental development of children. The test was developed to assess the intellectual ability of French children in 1905 with revisions of 1908 and 1911. Henry Goddard introduced the Binet-Simon type of test to the United States in 1910. Also known as Binet Scale/Test, Binet-Simon Intelligence Test. See STANFORD-BINET TEST.

binge   An unrestrained, excessive indulgence in the consumption of substances.

binge drinking   Periodic drinking bouts interspersed with dry periods lasting weeks or months. During the bouts, the person drinks heavily day after day until collapsing. Similar to dipsomania. Also known as epsilon alcoholism, paroxysmal drinking, periodic drinking.

binge-eating syndrome   A recurrent disorder in which a person ingests large quantities of food, often without great regard for what it is. The condition is most apt to occur after a stressful event. See BULIMIA, EATING DISORDERS.

binocular   Pertaining to the two eyes acting conjointly.

binocular accommodation   The simultaneous accommodation of both eyes. Compare ABSOLUTE ACCOMMODATION. See ACCOMMODATION, VISUAL ACCOMMODATION.

binocular cells   Cortical cells that respond to a stimulus presented to either the left or right eye. Stimulation of both eyes simultaneously results in a summation effect.

binocular color mixture   Using a stereoscope, the presentation of two different colors, one to each eye, at the same time can result in a single fused impression unless the two stimuli are very different in their separate effects.

binocular cue   A visual cue that requires the use of both eyes functioning in parallax. Because of the spacing of human eyes, binocular depth cues are useful over a range of 495 yards. Beyond that, humans use monocular cues.

binocular depth cues   In looking at distant objects, there are a variety of cues that give observers some indication of the actual size of viewed objects. One of these cues is based on binocular disparity; another, the closer the objects are to us, the greater or closer the convergence of the eyes. See DEPTH PERCEPTION.

binocular disparity   (C. Wheatstone) Retinal disparity.

binocular flicker   A flicker evoked by the rapidly alternating presentation of stimuli to the right and left eyes.

binocular fusion/integration   The emergence of a single perception from stimulation of the two eyes. See BINOCULAR PERCEPTION/VISION, RETINAL FUSION.

binocular neurons   Nerve cells in the brain that receive input from both eyes.

binocular parallax   Differences in the two retinal images due to separation of the eyes. To experience this, place a finger about five inches in front of your nose and then look at the finger under three conditions: with both eyes, with left eye closed, and then right eye closed. See RETINAL DISPARITY.

binocular perception/vision   The normal coordinated function of the right and left eyes that permits viewing of the surroundings in three dimensions. The phrase binocular fusion is applied to the merging of the two retinal images such that the perceived object is experienced as a single image. See RETINAL FUSION.

binocular rivalry   The suppression of experience from one eye because of simultaneous experience in the other eye. Sometimes known as binocular suppression.

binocular summation   The concept that if the left and right retina are stimulated at the same time with different degrees of illumination, the apparent degree of illumination will be close to the average of both illuminations.

binocular suppression   See BINOCULAR RIVALRY.

binocular vision   See BINOCULAR PERCEPTION/VISION.

binomial   An algebraic expression consisting of the sum or difference of two terms.

binomial curve   A graphic representation of a curve representing the plot of the successive terms of the expansion $(p + q)^n$ where $p + q = 1$, n having integral value, p = probability of success of an event, q = probability of p's alternative or failure, and n = number of times an event can occur.

binomial distribution   An approximation to the normal probability curve for data in binary form (0–1, YES–NO, etc.). Formula: $p(x) = (N/x)p^x q^{n-x}$, $0 < x < N$. Where: $p(x)$ is probability, X is a random variable, N is the number of independent trials, p is the probability of observing exactly x successes in N independent trials and $0 < X < N$. Sometimes known as Bernoulli distribution. See BERNOULLI PROCESS.

binomial expansion   The expansion of a binomial to a given power that can be used to determine the probability of obtaining a score as large or larger than any given score.

binomial test   A test of the significance of the deviation of binary (two-valued, yes–no, or 0–1) data from their expected or chance frequency.

binomial theorem   (O. Khayyam, I. Newton, N. H. Abel) A general formula, dealing with probabilities, for expanding the power of any binomial $(p + q)^n$ without performing the successive multiplications.

BINS   Bayley Infant Neurodevelopmental Screener

Binswanger's dementia/disease   A progressive neurologic disorder with onset after middle age and characterized by memory disorders, paranoia, emotional instability, speech disorders, and hallucinations. Such changes are associated with demyelination of white matter. Gray matter is not affected. Also known as demyelinating encephalopathy, progressive subcortical encephalopathy, subcortical arteriosclerotic encephalopathy. Named after German psychiatrist Otto Binswanger (1852–1929).

bioacoustics   The study of communications by sounds of animals.

bioanalysis   (R. L. Solomon) An analytic approach that focuses on somatic symptoms as well as psychic phenomena, such as unconscious impulses and conflicts, usually the concern of psychoanalysis.

bioavailability   The readiness of the body to accept a drug.

biocenosis   A relationship between organisms that live in association with each other.

biochemical antagonism   A situation that occurs when two drugs ingested cancel each other out or in any other way interfere with each other.

biochemical approach   1. The use of psychotropic drugs in the treatment of mental disorders. 2. The study of behavioral patterns, including mental disorders, from the standpoint of chemical changes, such as the assumption that schizophrenia can be explained in terms of an excess or deficiency of certain substances in the nervous system, such as dopamine.

biochemical defects   Any of a number of chemical imbalances or aberrations in brain tissue that may be associated with neurological disorders. See MENTAL DISORDERS.

biochemical theories of psychosis   The view that bizarre behaviors are caused by chemical factors. The basics of such ideas are traceable to the early humoral theories.

biochemistry   The investigation of the chemical aspects of vital processes; the chemistry of living organisms.

biocybernetics   The relationship between awareness and physiological conditions, for example, under some conditions people can hear their own pulse. See BIOFEEDBACK.

biodata   Short for biographical data, often used in the context of personnel records.

biodynamics   The vital processes of a living organism; its physiology interacting with the environment.

bioelectric impedance analysis (BIA)   The measurement of electric flow through the body (usually between hands and feet) to estimate the level of body fat.

bioelectric(al) potential   An electric potential of a nerve, muscle, and other living tissue.

bioenergetic analysis   (A. Lowen) An integrated body-mind therapy. A bioenergetic therapist has to do an in-depth and thorough analysis of the patient's history, behavior, dreams, etc. Work on the body is aimed at releasing feelings which are related to the history of the person and which must be understood and expressed if change is to occur on both the body and the psychological level.

bioenergetics   Based on the work of Wilhelm Reich, a way of understanding personality in terms of the body and its energetic processes. Major techniques used for this purpose are respiratory exercises, free expression of feelings, and improvement in the body image, and therefore the self-image, through movement and posture therapy. Because about 50% of the therapeutic time is spent in psychoanalytic work, the preferred name for this therapy is bioenergetic analysis.

bioengineering   The branch of engineering that specializes in the research and design of equipment and environmental features that enhance the performance of human tasks. A bioengineer may develop a bed that enables a person with a physical disability to sit up, turn around, and then be placed in a wheelchair.

bioethics   The issue of what is morally right and wrong in biological matters, especially such controversial issues as assisted suicide, whether to prolong with heroic measures the lives of terminally-ill patients or let them naturally die.

biofeedback   1. The organism's internal regulatory systems that are responsible for control of the organic processes. Impulses are received from muscles, visceral organs, and the nervous system, and control over these organs is maintained at a physiologically desirable level. 2. The use of a monitoring device, such as an electromyograph, psychogalvanometer, or electroencephalograph to provide information to a person regarding certain physiological states such as heartbeat or skin temperature. Also known as sensory feedback.

biofeedback training/use   Procedures that involve a person getting immediate knowledge of an autonomic (physiological) function, such as blood pressure, and then attempting by thought processes such as relaxation to modify that function. This allows self-regulation of body processes related to emotional situations. Considered an adjunctive tool for therapy. See BIOCYBERNETICS, BIOFEEDBACK.

biofunctional therapy   Any form of psychotherapy in which the goal is to correct bodily functioning.

biogen   (E. Coues) A hypothetical unit of living matter postulated as the basis of vital activities.

biogenesis   1. The origin and evolution of living forms. 2. The argument that life comes from other living things rather than from nonliving sources. The concept of spontaneous generation (life arising out of nonliving matter) was accepted as valid up to the 18th century. See ABIOGENESIS, BIOGENETICS, ONTOGENESIS.

biogenetic law   (E. Haeckel) Recapitulation doctrine.

biogenetics   The scientific study of the production of living organisms from other living organisms (biogenesis), especially the mechanisms of heredity.

biogenic   In reference to whatever has a biological origin.

biogenic amine hypothesis   A postulate that imbalances of biogenic amines (such as dopamine, norepinephrine, and serotonin) are a necessary component of major mental disorders. Now superseded by far more highly discriminated theories.

biogenic amines   Organic substances with psychoactive properties. These include epinephrine, norepinephrine, and serotonin. Biogenic amines are neurotransmitters and also are sometimes identified as neurohormones because they can activate the autonomic nervous system during periods of physical or psychic stress. See CATECHOLAMINES.

biogenic law   A theory that every organism begins life, and continues to develop throughout life, from a single fertilized ovum (zygote) to the organism's fullest capacity. See LAW OF RECAPITULATION, RECAPITULATION THEORY.

biogenic psychosis   (E. Kraepelin) Disorders considered to be due to a single major biological cause.

biogram   A pattern of possible events involved in learning a biofeedback experience. May begin as a conscious memory device but through repeated trials eventually becomes subconscious in a manner similar to other learning experiences.

biograms   Short autobiographies by members of a selected group, written with directions as to content, form, and length to be used for research purposes.

biographical data   Information gathered about a person's history and behavioral patterns from various sources. Such data are usually obtained from job candidates from application forms and include such items as age, education, and work experience. Biographical data of professional people are often organized and presented as a curriculum vitae. See AUTOBIOGRAPHY.

biographical method   The use of personal data in studying factors affecting a person's life.

biological   Relating to biology.

biological age   The relative age of individuals' body systems in comparison to others of its kind rather than to time.

biological aging   Aging processes that are governed apparently by inborn and time-related processes but also influenced by stress, trauma, and environment. Distinguished from secondary aging that is accelerated by disabilities resulting from disease. Also known as primary aging.

biological analogy   A description or explanation of society and social relations in biological terms, that is, the transfer of biological concepts to sociology.

biological clock 1. A tendency of an organism to have regular periodic changes or rhythms in physiological and behavioral functions, at approximately the same time each day, each month, or once a year, etc. 2. Refers to a woman's reproductive capacity, with a figurative clock starting at noon at first capacity to reproduce, to final incapacity at midnight. See CIRCADIAN RHYTHMS.

biological determinism A doctrine positing that psychological and behavioral characteristics are entirely the result of constitutional and biological factors. See BEHAVIOR GENETICS.

biological drive 1. A physiological pressure resulting from basic tissue needs, usually directing the organism toward certain types of behavior, such as the drive for sleep when exhausted or the drive to drink when thirsty. 2. An unlearned arousal state resulting from depletion or deprivation of survival necessities, for example, water, oxygen, food, and sleep. Whenever physiological equilibrium is disrupted, the organism is impelled to engage in behavior designed to restore physiological balance. See HOMEOSTASIS.

biological factors in mental disorders Organic or biogenic conditions such as cerebral arteriosclerosis, lead poisoning, hyperthyroidism, syphilitic infection, chromosomal aberrations, or phencyclidine intoxication associated with or actually causing various mental disorders.

biological fallacy The false assumption that the study of the organic, or biogenic, conditions of an organism, species, etc., enables its entire nature to be understood.

biological intelligence 1. (W. Halstead) A level of innate mental ability required primarily for cognitive activity. Halstead introduced the phrase to differentiate forebrain-functioning ability from traditional concepts of intelligence. Biological intelligence is measured with a battery of tests that allegedly give evidence of brain injury and premature senility. 2. (H. Eysenck) Refers to the link between deoxyribonucleic acid (DNA) and psychometric intelligence (IQ), indexed by evoked potentials, glucose uptake, etc. See HALSTEAD-REITAN BATTERY, LURIA-NEBRASKA NEUROPSYCHOLOGICAL BATTERY.

biological life events (C. Bühler) Changes independent of experience declining with age.

biological measures See PRIMARY PREVENTION.

biological memory A concept that humans have inherent in them a memory of the history of the race, a memory not available to them. Carl Jung probably has made the most extensive mention of such an idea. See PAST LIVES/FUTURE LIVES.

biological motion The patterns of movement of living organisms.

biological perspective A view that psychological factors are primarily explained in terms of biology, for example, heredity, physical and/or physiological conditions, such as those affected by diet and disease.

biological psychology See BIOPSYCHOLOGY.

biological psychiatry A point of view in psychiatry that essentially all mental disorders are basically physiological and call for physiological treatments, including drugs. See BIOFUNCTIONAL THERAPY, BIOGENIC AMINE HYPOTHESIS.

biologic(al) rhythms 1. In humans, periodic variations in physiological and psychological functions such as energy level, sexual desire, hunger, sleep, elimination, and menstruation. These rhythms vary considerably from person to person and from one period of life to another, but tend to be a basic characteristic of each individual. Also known as biorhythms, endogenous rhythms, internal rhythms, life rhythms. See CIRCADIAN RHYTHMS, DIURNAL RHYTHM, INFRADIAN RHYTHM, ULTRADIAN RHYTHM. 2. In nonhumans, regular and predictable variations in behavior of plant and animals, for example, some plants which open in the morning and close at night, cicadas which emerge every 17 years, Monarch butterflies that fly to the same location every breeding season.

biological stress Any condition imposing demands on the physical and psychological defenses of the organism, such as acute or chronic diseases, a congenital or acquired disability or defect, exposure to extreme heat or cold, malnutrition or starvation, drugs and toxic substances. See STRESS.

biological symbiosis Mutual cooperation of two organisms that benefits both. Usually the organisms are of unequal size, such as the remora that lives on a shark.

biological taxonomy The science of the classification of plants and animals into categories based on their relationships in nature. Also known as systematics.

biological theories of aging Those concepts of aging that emphasize genetic factors as explanations for aging processes. There appears to be a low positive correlation regarding the life span of individuals and those of their parents and grandparents.

biological therapy Any method that seeks to treat mental disturbance by altering physiological processes, such as through the use of drugs, electric shock, or psychosurgery. Also known as biomedical therapy/treatment. See CLINICAL PSYCHOPHARMACOLOGY, ELECTROCONVULSIVE TREATMENT, PSYCHOSURGERY, PSYCHOTROPIC DRUGS.

biological transducing system A highly specialized and highly ordered biological system that converts energy or information from one form to another, such as the rods and cones of the eye's retina convert light energy into nerve impulses; muscle fibers convert chemical energy into mechanical energy.

biological viewpoint An approach to abnormal psychology based on causative factors that are organic, such as the senile plaques that are an assumed causative factor in Alzheimer's disease. See BIOLOGICAL DETERMINISM, BIOLOGICAL PSYCHIATRY.

biological world English phrase similar to *Umwelt*.

biologism The application of biological method to the whole field of experience, with the implication that knowledge so gained is preeminently valid.

biology The branch of science that deals with life and living organisms, such as plants and animals.

biomechanics The study of the body in its relation to work situations, such as work tolerance, performance effectiveness, and methods of accident prevention.

biomedical engineering   The branch of engineering and medicine specializing in developing equipment for medical treatment, rehabilitation, and special needs, such as devices to monitor the physiological condition of astronauts while in space.

biomedical therapy/treatment   Phrases similar to biological therapy.

biometric method   (F. Galton) A failed attempt to measure intelligence by evaluating certain physiological characteristics, such as reaction time, strength of grip, ability to estimate weights. See INTELLIGENCE, BINET-SIMON SCALE.

biometrics   The mathematical specialty relating to the measurement of living organisms, including measurement of exogenous and endogenous factors that affect optimal functioning and the duration of life. Also known as biometry, which literally means the measurement of life. See PHYSIATRY.

biometry   **biometrics**

bion   1. A living thing. 2. (W. Reich) A hypothetical microscopic vesicle charged with sexual energy, postulated as the ultimate source of the orgasm. See ORGONE, ORGONE THERAPY.

bionegativity   (A. Angyal) The impedance of normal functioning by a part of an organism that is disturbed due to misalignment of functions. The integration of an organism is unbalanced in such a manner that the normal functioning of a part impedes total functioning (as opposed to its normal function that promotes total functioning).

bionics   Combination term based on biology and electronics. The science of simulating the action of biological systems with electronic and mechanical devices.

bionomic factors   Those factors that control or limit the evolution or development of living forms apart from the processes within the organism itself.

bionomics   1. The study of relationships between organisms and environmental influences. 2. The study of the laws of life, such as laws regulating vital functions. Also known as bionomy. See ECOLOGY.

biophore   (A. F. Weismann) An elementary unit postulated as the basis of the structural composition of organisms.

biophysical system   (W. Masters & V. Johnson) The hormonal and genital functions of the sexual response system.

biophysics   1. The interface of biology and physics; the study of biological structures and processes by means of the methods of physics, for example, the application of principles of physics in the study of vision or hearing. See BIONICS. 2. The study of physical or biological processes (for example, electricity) that occur in organisms.

biopsychic   Pertaining to mental phenomena in their relation to the living organism.

biopsychology   A branch of psychology concerned with the effects of biological factors, such as glands, blood pressure, and nervous-system functioning on adaptation and behavior. Sometimes misnamed psychobiology, which is a field of biology. See BIOLOGICAL VIEWPOINT, BIOPHYSICS.

biorhythm   See BIOLOGIC(AL) RHYTHMS (meaning 1).

biosocial   Pertaining to the interplay or mingling of biological and social forces, for example, human behavior influenced simultaneously by complex physiological processes and learned social meanings.

biosocial determinism   A doctrine positing that individual behavior is the result of interaction between biological and social influences. See SOFT DETERMINISM.

biosocial effect   An experimenter bias effect based on possible differential affects made on different participants or subjects by the experimenter's differing moods and attitudes. See EXPERIMENTER BIAS.

biosocial theory   (G. Murphy) A personality theory based on observation of a person's dynamic relations and interactions with the social or ecological environment, as contrasted with theories that view personality as self-contained.

biosphere   The total area of the earth and its atmosphere in which living organisms subsist; the environment in which biological processes take place.

biostatistics   1. Any kind of data kept about living organisms. 2. Data, usually compiled by a government agency or insurance firm, on the rates of birth, death, and disease in a population. 3. A specialty within statistics that is focused on understanding data about living organisms and also on the analysis of data from biomedical research. 4. Analysis of data from biomedical studies. Also known as vital statistics.

biotaxis   The powers of living cells for selecting and arranging themselves with respect to their environment. See NETWORK BIOTAXIS, NEUROBIOTAXIS, TAXIS, TROPISM.

biotechnology   The scientific study of the relation between humans and machines, particularly in the work process, involving the design, use, and placement of mechanical equipment aiming for maximum efficiency and safety. See ENGINEERING PSYCHOLOGY, HUMAN ENGINEERING.

biothesiometer   An instrument used for determining the threshold of vibratory perception.

biotope   1. A physical environment with many different ecological elements. 2. A constant environment, such as a rain forest or a desert, that keeps its conditions reasonably consistent. 3. In relation to animals and plants, descriptive of a particular environment.

biotransformation   The conversion of a biologically active drug into a form that either is inactive or that produces different effects.

biotrope   (E. Boring) A person whose mind is turned toward biological issues, or whose judgment and decision are based upon individual needs. Compare SOCIOTROPE.

biotype   A group of individuals similar in terms of their heredity (genotypically alike) even though they may appear different in their physical appearance (phenotypically varied).

biotypology   The classification of humans according to their constitutional, anatomical, physiological, and psychological characteristics, such as the division into "races" or by genders. See CONSTITUTIONAL TYPE.

biovular twins   A kind of twins that have developed from separate fertilized ova. Also known as dizygotic twins or, more commonly, fraternal twins.

biparental   Having two parents, male and female.

biparental care   The bringing up of young organisms by both the father and the mother, commonly seen in birds with both parents flying out from the nest to bring back food to their hungry offspring.

biparental inheritance   The genetic inheritance from both parents.

biped   1. Two-footed. 2. An animal with only two feet (for example, humans, birds). Compare QUADRUPED.

bipedal locomotion   Walking or running on two feet and in an upright position, as for humans, birds, and, for short periods, four-footed animals such as apes and bears.

biphasic symptom   A symptom of compulsive behavior characterized by two contradictory parts, the second of which is the reverse of the first, such as a compulsion to open a window, followed by a compulsion to close it again.

bipolar   Having two ends, as in a bipolar cell with a cell body at one end and dendrites at the other end; and a bipolar disorder that ranges from pure inertia and lassitude (depression) to extreme excitement and violence (mania).

bipolar (nerve) cell   Nerve cell with two components, an axon and one dendrite. Cells of this type are found mostly in the retina but also appear in the auditory and olfactory systems. They produce graded potentials and not spikes. Also known as bipolar neuron.

bipolar concept/construct   (G. Kelly) A fundamental idea that in human personality, every element has extension and that the extremes contrast with each other, for example, good/bad, mania/depression, introverted/extroverted.

bipolar disorder   An alternating affective condition in which a person experiences both manic and depressive states or moods. Formerly called manic-depressive disorder. Also known as alternating psychosis. See DEPRESSED BIPOLAR DISORDER, MANIC BIPOLAR DISORDER, MIXED BIPOLAR DISORDER.

bipolar electrode   An electrode with a double-poled tip (as opposed to one with a single-poled end, the other pole being the ground).

bipolar factor   Any factor that may be considered to have a neutral aspect near the center of the extension and extremes at either end, such as feelings toward a person ranging from love through being neutral to hate.

bipolar rating scale   A scale usually consisting of a number of lines, with an item at each end such as:

Good . . . . Bad
Cold . . . . Hot
Always . . . . Never

See SEMANTIC DIFFERENTIAL.

bipolar stimulation   A method of electrical stimulation in which a current is passed through the tissue between two closely approximated electrodes.

bird fear   See ORNITHOPHOBIA.

birds of a feather phenomenon   A tendency for people with similar temperaments, interests, values, goals, etc., to find one another and associate with others like themselves. See INTERNAL GROUPING, NICHE PICKING, SIMILARITY AND ATTRACTION.

BIRG-ing   See BASKING IN REFLECTED GLORY.

birth adjustment   The set of major adaptations made by infants within 15 to 30 minutes after birth, including adjustment to a lower temperature, obtaining oxygen by breathing, taking nourishment via the mouth, and eliminating waste products. Usually for several days infants demonstrate signs of behavior disorganization and adjustment, such as gasping, coughing, sneezing, and difficulties in sucking and swallowing. See APGAR SCORE, BIRTH EXPERIENCE.

birth cohorts   1. People born at the same time, usually measured in years, lustrums (five-year periods) or decades. 2. Individuals born within a certain time frame or on a certain date, such as those born in the 19th century; those born in the first decade of the twentieth century; those born from Jan 1, 1939 to July 30, 1939. Researchers may arbitrarily designate certain ages as old, middle-aged, or young, and set arbitrary birth dates for such purposes.

birth control   The voluntary prevention of conception through a variety of methods, including avoidance of vaginal intercourse, the rhythm method (intercourse at periods of low fertility), use of various preparations and devices such as contraceptive pills, spermicides, male (condoms) and female (diaphragms) contraceptive devices, sterilization (salpingectomy for women, vasectomy for men) and termination of pregnancy by abortion. See RHYTHM METHOD, STERILIZATION, VASECTOMY.

birth cry   The first sound produced by a newborn infant upon initial respiration.

birth defect   A physical malformation, sensory or intellectual defect, or disease process present at birth due to such factors as heredity, prenatal conditions, chromosomal aberration, biochemical defect, or birth injury (for example, spina bifida, cleft palate, cerebral palsy, deafness, blindness, Down's syndrome, and brain damage).

birth experience   The abrupt change from a parasitic existence within the womb to independent survival, accompanied by a flood of internal and external stimulation that according to some psychologists, especially Otto Rank, generates basic anxiety. See BIRTH ADJUSTMENT, BIRTH TRAUMA.

birth order   The ordinal position of a child (for example, first-born, second-born, middle, or youngest) in a given family. See BIRTH ORDER THEORY.

birth order effect   (R. Zajonc) Research indicating that firstborn children and only children tend to be high achievers. The larger the family size, the lower the average intelligence quotient (IQ) of the children.

birth order theory   A point of view first maintained by Alfred Adler that the chronological place in the family constellation was an important factor in personality development. Adler held, for example, that the oldest child will generally be conservative, the middle child disgruntled, and the youngest child either will expect lots of attention and help later in life, or will develop a strong impulse to surpass others. Later research indicated that the attitudes of the parents may have a far greater influence than birth order on the child's psychological development and such parental attitudes may bear no relation to the child's ordinal position in the family. See CONFLUENCE MODEL.

birth rate   In population statistics, the number of children born per one thousand people in the population.

birth symbolism   1. A symbolic representation which reproduces the first separation from the first libido object, namely that of the newborn child from the mother. 2. A symbolic metaphor which tends to ignore the libidinal aspect.

birth trauma   1. A physical injury received at birth. 2. (O. Rank) The psychological shock of being born; the sudden transformation from a passive situation of being in the womb to the demands of being in the external world with its myriad demands and stimuli. Otto Rank maintained that "separation anxiety" was a normal result of birth.

bisection   A method of constructing a sensory scale in which the observer sets a stimulus so that it is perceived to be half-way between two other stimuli.

biserial coefficient of correlation (r_{bis} or r_b)   A correlation coefficient that may be obtained when one of the variables is dichotomous and the other continuous. It is an estimate of what the Pearson product-moment correlation coefficient would be if the dichotomized variable was normally distributed.

biserial correlation   An estimate of what the correlation would be if the dichotomous variable were measured continuously.

bisexual   1. A person sexually attracted to others of both sexes, as opposed to a homosexual (attracted only to persons of own sex), or a heterosexual (attracted only to persons of opposite sex). See BISEXUALITY. 2. Descriptive of such a person. 3. Having gonads of both sexes. See HERMAPHRODITISM.

bisexual behavior   Sexual contact by a person with other individuals of both sexes.

bisexuality   Having sexual attraction for both sexes. Also known as amphigenous inversion. Can also be associated with having psychological characteristics of both sexes. See AMBISEXUALITY, BISEXUAL BEHAVIOR, HERMAPHRODITE, INTERSEX.

bisexual libido   Sexual interest toward both sexes.

bisexuals of opportunity hypothesis   A postulate that while a particular person may prefer male–female sexual activity, if circumstances do not permit this (for example, in prison), then the person will engage in male–male or female–female sexual activity. See BISEXUAL BEHAVIOR.

bisexuals of preference   See BISEXUAL, BISEXUAL BEHAVIOR, BISEXUALITY.

bistable   Any device with only two states, such as ON and OFF.

bistable multivibrator   **Eccles-Jordan circuit**

BIS   behavioral inhibition system

bit (H)   Short for binary digit. Used for determining information that can be located or determined by means of a YES–NO reply.

BITCH   See BLACK INTELLIGENCE TEST OF CULTURAL HOMOGENEITY.

bite bar   1. In humans, an object usually attached to an immovable surface that can be put in the mouth and clamped tightly by the teeth, for the purpose of keeping the head in a particular position without possibility of movement as in precise measures of vision. 2. In neurological research on anesthetized animals, a bar placed in the mouth to help hold the head.

bitemporal hemianopia   Loss of half the visual field in both eyes but the affected areas are the left half of the left visual field and the right half of the right visual field.

biting attack   Biting as aggressive behavior, used by young children and animals. In infancy these attacks may be seen as a form of playing or rehearsal for later fighting. See ORAL-BITING PERIOD.

biting mania   A 15th-century epidemic of mass hysteria in which a compulsive urge to bite spread through the convents in Germany, Italy, and Holland. Nuns bit each other, tore out their hair, howled in groups, and indecently exposed themselves. See MASS HYSTERIA.

biting stage   In psychoanalytic theory, the second stage (oral period) of psychosexual development. From the 8th to the 18th month, the child is stated to develop ambivalent attitudes toward the mother and to express hostility by biting her breast. When weaned, the urge to bite may take the form of nail-biting, spitting, sticking out the tongue, or chewing on a pencil or gum.

bitter   1. A quality of gustatory sensation of which the taste of sulphate or quinine is a typical example. 2. One of the four basic classic dimensions of taste. The other three are salty, sweet, and sour. Bartochuk has suggested a fifth (water). See WATER AS TASTE.

bivariate   Characterized by two variables.

bivariate analysis   The analysis of statistical data relating to two variables.

bivariate frequency distribution   The joint distribution of two variables in which the frequencies of each of the combinations of values of the two variables are indicated. See for an illustration BIMODAL DISTRIBUTION.

bivariate method   In research, a common technique using two variables, one variate is manipulated by the experimenter and the changes (if any) in the other variable are noted.

bivariate population   1. A population consisting of elements that are data points, each consisting of paired values of two variables. 2. A population of two variables, both normally distributed. In continuous bivariate populations, the bivariate scales have two coordinate axes, each pair of scores for one individual locating a point in the plane of those axes.

bizarre behavior   1. Actions that are extraordinary from the point of view of observers or in comparison with the individual's usual actions (such as directing traffic at a busy intersection, acting like a traffic officer; or purchasing thousands of dollars worth of useless materials on a limited budget). 2. One of the specific symptoms of consciousness changes in cases of brain damage and psychosis, especially schizophrenia. The precise form of bizarre behavior may depend upon the part of the brain affected.

bizarre delusion   A belief that is patently absurd and fantastic, such as a person asserting to be dead.

black   In perception, this refers to a visual sensation of low brilliance and achromatic character in conjunction with or comparison to a sensation of much greater brilliance.

black art   The alleged practice of magic by witches usually for wicked purposes.

blackboard memory   (H. A. Simon) A memory to which a number of independent processors can provide information and from which a number can access information. In psychological applications, the processors can represent different people or specialized structures in the nervous system of a single person. The "Mind's Eye" can be represented as a blackboard memory.

blackbody   The idealized perfect radiator (opaque to all wavelengths) that absorbs all the radiant energy to which it is exposed and whose surface would appear black if its temperature remained low enough so as not to be self-luminous. Also known as complete radiator.

black box   Anything that works but the functions of which are not understood. A computer is a "black" box to most people. In psychology, mind historically has been considered a black box because it cannot be observed directly. See CONSTRUCTS, LENS MODEL, MIND.

Black English   A dialect of standard English spoken by some African Americans. See EBONICS.

Black Intelligence Test of Cultural Homogeneity (BITCH)   (R. L. Williams) A cross-cultural test in which African American and Caucasian respondents are compared as to their understanding of typical in-group slang used by some African Americans. Using norms of African American people, Caucasian people are shown to be culturally impoverished, not as intelligent as African Americans, etc. See INTELLIGENCE TESTS AND INTELLIGENCE.

blackout   1. A loss of consciousness produced by a variety of physical or social conditions such as sudden lowering of the blood supply to the brain, decreased oxygen supply, alcoholic intoxication, or social shocks leading to fainting. 2. The loss of consciousness experienced by an aviator when gravitational forces lead to a decrease of blood flow to the brain. See ALCOHOLIC BLACKOUT, FAINTING, SYNCOPE.

blackout technique   The turning off of all lights during psychotherapy, individual or group, so that, by speaking in the dark, a person speaking may feel less self-conscious or less threatened.

blackout threshold   The point at which an oxygen-deprived person loses consciousness.

black separatism   A point of view that African Americans, to develop a positive identity, must establish cultural, socioeconomic, and political systems that are distinctively theirs and different from white systems.

Blacky Pictures   (G. S. Blum) A projective personality test consisting of a set of cartoons of dogs with human analogies. Used in discovering social and emotional problems of children, such as family conflicts, Oedipal situations, and sibling rivalry. Also known as Blacky (Picture) Test, The Blacky Pictures.

bladder control   Ability to regulate urination to void at proper places or at proper times. See TOILET TRAINING.

bladder reflex   See MICTURITION REFLEX, TOILET TRAINING, VESICAL REFLEX.

Blake-Mouton managerial grid   See MANAGERIAL GRID.

blame avoidance (need)   (H. A. Murray) The need, desire, or motive to avoid being blamed. See BLAME ESCAPE (NEED).

blame escape (need)   (H. A. Murray) The need, desire, or motive of a person who has acted in a socially unacceptable manner, and who has not succeeded in avoiding blame, to flee the situation. By escaping (physically or psychologically), the person avoids suffering further disapproval or punishment, etc. See BLAME AVOIDANCE (NEED).

blaming others   A common mechanism to avoid blame by attributing the cause of the condition to others, or to events beyond the person's control.

blaming the victim   (M. Lerner) A tendency to blame persons mistreated by others, on the assumption that such people are ultimately responsible for their misfortunes. See RAPE, RAPE COUNSELING, VICTIM PRECIPITATION, VICTIM PSYCHOLOGY, VICTIM RECIDIVISM.

blanket group   A group that has no criteria for membership, one that exists accidentally (such as a group in an elevator in an office building, or people in a shopping mall).

blank experiment   A study that uses irregular or meaningless conditions to prevent the participant from guessing or giving automatic responses.

blank hallucination   A sensation of being in equilibrium and floating in space. Involves rotating or rhythmically moving objects, usually localized in the mouth, hands, or skin, and also in the space immediately surrounding the body, sometimes experienced by people when in a high fever. In psychoanalytic theory, a blank hallucination is associated with primal-scene material.

blank screen   In psychoanalysis, the analyst, who becomes the "screen" on which the patient projects feelings and fantasies during the transference process. The metaphorical screen is blank if the analyst remains passive and neutral, so that the patient will feel free to give voice to innermost ideas and attitudes without interference by the personality of the analyst.

blank trial   In a study, a unit usually consisting of a stimulus and a response that is not recorded, for any of many reasons, such as to give the participant an experience in responding. See BLANK EXPERIMENT.

blastocele   A cavity in the blastula of a developing embryo. Also known as blastocoele. See BLASTULA.

blastocyst   The mammalian embryo at an early stage of development when it consists of an inner mass of cells and a yolk sac forming a tiny sphere enclosed in a thin layer of cells that helped implant the blastocyst in the uterine lining. In humans, this stage occurs at the end of the first week following conception.

blastoderm   A layer of cells on the surface of the yolk from which the embryo develops.

blastogenic   Originating in the germ cell.

blast olfactometer   A device from which a blast of graded amounts of pressurized, odorous gas is released up the nostrils, designed for measuring smell thresholds. See OLFACTOMETER for an illustration of such a device.

blastomere   One of the cells formed by cleavage of the zygote, forming the blastoderm.

blastula   A somewhat spherical group of cells formed by cleavage of the zygote, consisting of a single layer of cells surrounding a fluid-filled cavity (the blastocele).

blend   An experience due to the fusion of sensory elements such as the composite effect of different stimuli (for example, the fusion of the sensations of touch, smell, and taste).

blended family   A type of family that results from the combination of two sets of people, originally from family A and family B, now forming family C. Usually, a father and mother from families A and B, after being divorced, separated, or widowed, form a new family together, each bringing their child or children from the previous marriages or partnerships to the new union. See RECONSTITUTED FAMILY.

blending   1. In visual perception, the gradual or imperceptible change from one color to another as in looking at clouds or at a seascape or landscape. 2. See FUSION.

blending inheritance   The inheritance by offspring of genetic factors intermediate between characteristics of both parents. See LAW OF FILIAL REGRESSION, PARTICULATE INHERITANCE.

Bleuler's theory   The following are important for understanding Eugen Bleuler's theory: ACCESSORY SYMPTOMS, AFFECTIVITY, ANNIVERSARY EXCITEMENT, CATATHYMIC DELUSION, DELUSION OF DOUBLE ORIENTATION, DEREISM, DETERIORATION OF ATTENTION, DIRECTION PROGNOSIS, DISTURBANCES OF ASSOCIATIONS, DOUBLE ORIENTATION, EXPLANATORY DELUSION, FAXENSYNDROM, FOUR A'S, FRAGMENTATION, FUNDAMENTAL SYMPTOMS, MAUDLIN DRUNKENNESS, MORAL IDIOCY, MORAL IMBECILITY, PRIMARY SYMPTOMS, PSEUDOMOTIVATIONS, SECONDARY SYMPTOMS, THYMOPATHIC.

Blickfeld   (fringe area—German) (W. Wundt) Term used in vision for items that are perceivable but not attended to. Similar to William James' "fringe of consciousness."

blind   Unable to see. See BLINDNESS.

blind alley   A pathway or passage in a maze that comes to a dead end. The only way out of the maze is to turn around and exit through the entrance. Also known as cul-de-sac, dead end.

blind-alley job   Work or employment that has no or few opportunities for advancement or self-improvement, such as being a night-watchman. Also known as dead end job.

blind analysis   **blind diagnosis**

blind diagnosis   1. An analysis made by studying test results and data without knowledge about the subject under analysis. 2. Diagnosing a person, or generating a personality description, without ever having direct contact with that person, the conclusion based on information from one or several sources, such as replies to a personality questionnaire, reading past interview notes, examining the person's replies to a projective test, reading that person's diaries, or interviewing acquaintances of the person in question. Sometimes known as blind analysis.

blind experiment   1. An experiment in which the participants are unaware of the experimental condition to which they are assigned. They may be unaware that they are in an experiment. For example, to study the influence (if any) of different kinds of music on rates of healing, classical music is played for the patients in one ward of a hospital, while jazz is played for those in another ward. See DOUBLE BLIND EXPERIMENT. 2. An experiment in which (a) the researcher is unaware of which organisms are receiving which treatment (blind); (b) human participants are unaware of the treatment group to which they are assigned (single blind); (c) neither the researcher nor the human participants knows who is receiving which treatment (double blind); or (d) participants and treatment administrators are unaware that they are participating in a study of treatments (triple blind). In casual or pilot research, (b) is common; the prevailing standards are (a) and (c); and (d) is mostly of theoretical interest with humans because of ethical problems its application would present. See DOUBLE BLIND PROCEDURE/TEST, EXPERIMENT, TRIPLE BLIND.

blind experimental subjects   People in an experimental condition who are not aware that they are in the control of the experimenter or that they are participants in an experiment.

blind(ing) headache   A headache that causes visual disturbances or extreme pain, such as a migraine.

blindism   A mannerism of some blind persons, for example, rubbing the eyes or fanning the fingers before the eyes, as observed in some sighted children, who eventually discontinue the behavior.

blind judgments   1. The evaluation of phenomena on the basis of insufficient evidence. 2. Judgments of the degree of improvement of persons having undergone different forms of treatment, when judges do not know which individuals received which treatments.

blind learning   The mastering of a task through repetition with a minimum understanding of the reason or purpose of the task.

blind-matching technique   A validation procedure undertaken by matching different protocols or sets of diagnostic data to other protocols (for example, given photographs of different people and their handwritten identical sentences, a participant is asked to match the pictures with the sentences). Low positive correlations are usually reported.

blindness   Inability to see; the total inability to receive visual stimuli. However, legal blindness is usually defined as 20/200 vision in the better eye with correction. Organic blindness can be due to sequels of a variety of conditions such as cataracts, glaucoma, and diabetes. Functional (psychogenic) blindness may be a conversion symptom, called hysterical blindness. Also known as typhlosis. Kinds of blindness include: BLUE-YELLOW, COLOR, CORTICAL, DAY, NIGHT, RED-GREEN, SNOW. See AMBLYOPIA, AMAUROSIS.

blind review   A method of review usually done for professional journals, the reviewer gets a manuscript to evaluate, without knowledge of the author, to avoid bias in rating the manuscript.

blind self   The truth or reality about a person that is evident to others but not to the individual in question. It is one quadrant of the Johari Window, a diagrammatic concept of human behavior. See HIDDEN SELF, PUBLIC SELF, UNDEVELOPED POTENTIAL. See JOHARI WINDOW for an illustration.

blindsight   (E. Pöppel) Rare condition resulting from damage to the primary visual cortex in which people who report being blind respond somewhat to visual stimuli as if they can see. For instance, although they cannot see an object in their blind field, they can reach accurately for it while unaware of perceiving it. Blindsight can occur if there is damage to the occipital cortex but not to the superior colliculus, which controls perception of location. Shows that visual information can affect behavior without visual awareness. See BLIND-SIGHTED.

blind-sighted   (L. Weiskrantz) A word used to describe people considered legally blind but who sometimes react as though they can see, for example, by catching a ball suddenly thrown to them. See BLINDSIGHT.

blind spot   1. Phrase mainly used in psychiatry and psychoanalysis for a blind spot in psychological awareness. 2. (E. Mariotte) A small area in the retinal field (where rods and cones converge into the optic nerve) that is insensitive to light-stimulation. See SCOTOMA, SCOTOMIZATION.

blind testing   In consumer psychological evaluation, testing products without knowledge of brand names, such as in serving participants two or more brands of cola, in unmarked containers, then asking them to choose the one they prefer.

blind walk   A technique used in encounter groups to help members experience others and to develop trust. Half of the members close their eyes and so are "blind." Sighted people become their partners and lead the "blind" people to help them experience various events and persons. The partners reverse roles and later the group members discuss their reactions to the blind walk. Also called trust walk. See ENCOUNTER EXERCISES.

blind writing   1. A type of writing produced by persons who have lost their eyesight. 2. A type of writing produced in the dark or under artificial deprivation of eyesight, for example by bandaging.

blink rate   The frequency of shutting/opening the eyelids.

blink reflex/response   Abrupt closing of the eyelids in response to bright light, shifting attention, irritation of the eye or seeing an object coming toward the eyes. Also known as blink(ing) reflex, blinking. See BLEPHAROSPASM.

Bliss symbols   Pictorial symbols for communications either with animals or nonverbal children.

Blix's temperature experiment   (M. Blix) The report of warm and cold spots minutely localized on the skin by the application of cooled or warmed metal points, or droplets of oil.

BLMS   buccolingual masticatory syndrome (also abbreviated **BLM**)

bloating   A feeling of abdominal distention, which may be physical or psychogenic, a common psychophysiologic disorder due to air-swallowing (aerophagia). Also known as abdominal bloating.

Bloch's law   In perception, the threshold for a very short period of illumination is a function of duration multiplied by its brightness. It is called Bloch's law when referring to (human) vision but called Bunsen-Roscoe law when referring to photochemistry (including film in cameras).

block   1. To obstruct. 2. In experimental design, a group of conditions or measures treated as a unit, or pooled.

blockage   Term used by the Horney school for defensive techniques employed by people in and out of psychotherapy to ward off awareness of their inner conflicts and self-hatreds (for example, by minimizing, denying, ignoring, pseudoaccepting, intellectualizing, or attacking interpretations). See DEFENSE MECHANISMS.

block design   An experimental design that divides participants into "blocks" or relatively homogeneous categories. Each block is exposed to experimental conditions and evaluated as a unit. See RESEARCH DESIGNS.

block-design test   (S. Kohs) A generalized task of intelligence consisting of a set of colored blocks that may be assembled to form a pattern. The task, usually timed, is to arrange the blocks so that they will look like the pattern shown. The test is also used in the diagnosis of mental disorders and mental deterioration. See KOHS BLOCK-DESIGN TEST.

block diagram   A histogram.

blocking   An abrupt, involuntary interruption in the flow of thought or speech. Sufferers suddenly cannot recall what they wanted to say or find words to express themselves. Also known as emotional blocking, thought deprivation/obstruction.

blocking effect   The interference by an old stimulus in an attempt to condition a new stimulus.

block maze   A type of maze in which all paths to the goal are equally correct and all are of the same length. Error occurs only when the animal deviates from the direction of the goal or enters a blind alley. Sometimes used for testing cortical damage effects on spatial discrimination.

block randomization   In some research studies, treatment is varied for blocks of subjects who are selected for change by chance.

block sampling   A survey technique for compiling small samples of geographic blocks from each of several larger samples with each block representing different segments of the population. See AREA SAMPLING.

Blocq's disease/syndrome   A fear of standing or walking, or hysterical inability to stand or walk. Named after French physician Paul O. Blocq (1860–1896). Also known as astasia-abasia.

blood-brain barrier (B-BB) (P. Ehrlich, E. E. Gold-mann) A semipermeable membrane surrounding blood vessels of the central nervous system, designed to allow certain nutrients and ions to enter areas of vital brain tissues while screening out substances that might prove harmful.

blood fear See HEMATOPHOBIA, HEMOPHOBIA.

Bloodhound See ELECTRONIC NOSES.

blood-letting Removing blood for therapeutic reasons, usually by cutting into a vein. Also known as phlebotomy, venesection.

blood-pressure phobia Morbid fear of high-blood pressure, which may produce enough tension to aggravate existing hypertension.

blood sacrifices See RELIGIOUS KILLING.

blood sugar The glucose circulating in the blood-stream as immediately available energy for body cell activities. See GLUCAGON, GLUCOSE-TOLERANCE TEST.

blood-sugar level A physiological measurement or standard of sugar content in the blood, below which hypoglycemia results and above which hyperglycemia develops. See GLUCAGON.

blood type A category of a broad spectrum of different inherited red-blood-cell traits. The basic categories are A, B, O, and AB.

B love See BEING LOVE.

bloviate (W. Harding) To talk a lot, but to say nothing of significance. Term was coined by U.S. President, Warren Harding.

blow Slang for cocaine.

blow job Slang for fellatio.

blue-arc phenomenon An effect produced by a stimulus at the center of the visual field against a dark background; it consists of a pair of bluish, luminous arcs seen as connecting the stimulus with the locus of the blind spot.

blue balls Slang for testicular pain after prolonged sexual excitation without orgasm. Also known as hard rocks.

blue-collar therapy A therapeutic approach developed by the William Alanson White Institute for low-income patients who do not relate well to middle-class therapists and their techniques. The emphasis is on external or physical causes, present situations rather than early childhood experiences, alleviation of symptoms, a directive approach, concrete solutions to problems, the use of nonprofessional auxiliaries, and involvement in activity groups. See CLINICAL COUNSELING, COUNSELING.

blue-color blindness See TRITANOPIA.

blue noses Slang for puritanical "killjoys."

blues Slang for depression.

blue-sighted Displaying a heightened color sensitivity (congenital or acquired) for blue.

blue-yellow (color) blindness A rare type of partial color blindness in which the visual system is reduced to reds, greens and grays. See TETARTANOPIA, TRITANOPIA.

blunted affect A disturbance of affectivity in which feeling tone is dulled, cited by Eugen Bleuler as one of the basic symptoms of schizophrenia, also observed in persons considered presenile and senile.

blunting Avoiding unpleasant experiences, such as pain, fear, suffering, boredom, or fatigue, by concentrating on pleasant topics (for example, an important prior experience, a happy occasion), or otherwise mentally protecting the self from the memory of the unpleasant or the prospect of danger.

blunting of affect The reduction of the intensity of feelings often seen in patients with schizophrenia. See LA BELLE INDIFFÉRENCE.

blur Lack of clear outline in an optical image, or in any visual conscious experience.

blur point The distance at which objects become blurred when coming closer to the eye.

blush(ing) An involuntary autonomic rush of blood to the skin (hyperemia) as a normal reaction to embarrassment or self-consciousness, or, if persistent, a conversion symptom stemming from unconscious feelings of guilt, sexual arousal, or shame.

BMCT Bennett Mechanical Comprehension Test

B motivation See METAMOTIVATION.

BMR basal metabolic rate

boarding home A community-living facility which provides food, lodging, general supervision, and personal care to semi-independent or independent persons. Often used for persons with mental retardation or mental illness not requiring intensive programming and who may be able to work. Also known as adult foster home. The phrases, adult foster home and boarding home, are sometimes used interchangeably with halfway house.

boarding-out system A system in which psychotic patients are cared for in private homes. See GHEEL COLONY.

boasting A mode of behavior, characterized by insistent attempts to force others to accept an exaggerated valuation of the boaster's accomplishment or abilities. Often an attempt to conceal some deficiency or inferiority. See SUPERIORITY FEELINGS.

bobo doll A child-size doll with a spherical bottom with the lowest center of gravity possible, that when pushed, punched, or otherwise struck will first fall over but then rebound back to normal vertical status. Used by Albert Bandura and others in research on social learning.

Boder Test of Reading-Spelling Patterns (E. Boder & S. Jarrico) A test used in identifying four subtypes (dyslexic, dysphonetic, dyseidetic, and dysphonetic-dyseidetic) of reading disability on the basis of reading and spelling performance alone.

bodily ego feeling The bodily self or the experienced composite representation of the body that is the core of the ego. See BODY EGO.

bodily self (G. W. Allport) Personal knowledge about one's body and its limits.

body (B) 1. The central part of an organism, that is, the trunk or torso which bears the appendages. 2. A material organism. 3. A coherent unitary object or organ, for example, the pineal body.

body armor (W. Reich) Chronically tense musculature that constricts the flow of life energy, with result that breath is limited and emotions repressed.

body awareness The perception of body structure as a component of the image of self. The body image is derived from internal sensations, movement, and contact with the external world. In emotionally disturbed children, body awareness may be lacking or distorted.

body boundaries A component of body image, consisting of the degree of definiteness of a person knowing where the body ends and the environment begins. In Rorschach testing, barrier responses such as "turtle with shell" may indicate a definite body boundary.

body buffer zone (E. T. Hall) The physical distance between oneself and another, beyond which the participant experiences as uncomfortable. The distance is shorter toward the front than toward the rear, and studies show that the greater the body buffer zone, the more aggressive the individual. See PROXEMICS.

body build A general measure of the body in terms of trunk, limb length, and girth. See SOMATOTYPES.

body-build index (H. J. Eysenck) An index of constitutional types based on measurements of a person's height and the circumference of the chest. Height is divided by the chest circumference to yield an index number. See BODY TYPE.

body cathexis The investment of psychic energy in the person's own body; the emotional attachment to one's body.

body cell Phrase sometimes applied to a tissue cell that is not a germ cell. Also known as somatic cell.

body concept The thoughts, feelings, and perceptions that comprise the way a person views his or her own body; the conceptual image of one's own body. See ANOREXIA, ANOREXIA NERVOSA, BODY EGO, BODY IMAGE, BODY PERCEPT, BODY SCHEMA.

body-contact-exploration maneuver An encounter-group technique in which participants touch or stroke each other to increase awareness of sensations and emotions evoked by this type of experience.

body-dysmorphic disorder (BDD) 1. A preoccupation that an otherwise normal person may have with some aspect of the body thought not to be normal. 2. A condition in which a person's body structure is so unusual that it generates the general opinion that the person is physically abnormal. 3. A psychological state of pathological over-concern with the body, reacting negatively to self-appearance to such an extent that this interferes with the person's social functioning. In many cases, the person may appear normal or typical to others; for example, a person with a barely perceptible scar was so convinced of the ugliness of this perceived deformity that the person would not be seen in public.

body ego The nucleus around which all the perceptions of the self are grouped, that is, individual memories, sensations, ideas, wishes, strivings, and fantasies.

body-ego concept The mental representations of the body as the nucleus of the self, or ego. Derived from sensations, perceptions, fantasies, feelings, and emotions associated with the body image.

body electrode placement In human diagnostic research, the positioning and attachment of usually 16 electrodes to various locations on the scalp, ears, vertex of the skull, and other parts of the body. Used in conducting various bodily tests such as the study of brain waves or sleep apnea (the cessation of breathing while asleep). Usually, the electrode is bonded to the body with a glue-like substance. See ELECTRODE PLACEMENT.

body ideal The body type considered attractive and age-appropriate by the dominant culture.

body identity The concept of one's own body, independently and apart from all other objects in space.

body image (P. Schilder) The mental picture formed of one's body as a whole, including both its physical and functional characteristics (body percept), and attitudes toward these characteristics (body concept). A person's body image stems from both conscious and unconscious sources and is a basic component of the concept of self. See BODY EGO, BODY SCHEMA, BODY-IMAGE DISTORTION.

body-image distortion A perceptual distortion of the body experienced during altered states of consciousness; for example, a person may feel detached from his or her body, or parts of the body may be experienced differently or appear larger or smaller than usual. A beauty-contest winner may think she is hideously ugly and a skeleton-type person with anorexia nervosa may believe she is overweight.

body-image disturbance (P. Schilder) Psychological maladjustments stemming from deformity, disfigurement, or dismemberment. Reactions vary from slight self-consciousness to deep depression and paranoid states, and are relatively mild where the defect is congenital or acquired early in life, since the defect is likely to be incorporated in the body image during the process of development. See BREAST-PHANTOM PHENOMENON, PHANTOM LIMB.

body-image hallucinations False perceptions or fantasies about the body, particularly with respect to size. Some psychotic patients experience body-image hallucinations in which body parts appear to be transplanted to other regions of the body. See LILLIPUTIAN HALLUCINATION.

body language 1. Communications by gestures or signals that are understood by both parties, such as a forefinger of a hand placed vertically over the mouth may mean, "Silence!" 2. The expression of unconscious feelings, impulses, and conflicts through organs of the body, as in conversion symptoms, or through posture, gesture, facial expression, and other forms of nonverbal communication. Physical behavior, whether intended to or not, gives observers information about what the person is trying to convey or hide. Also known as organ language. See POSTURAL ECHO.

body memory A physical sensation or change in functioning without organic illness representing a dissociated aspect of a traumatic or abusive experience. See SENSORY-MOTOR MEMORY.

body-mind dichotomy   The division between the somatic and psychic spheres which raises theoretical questions about the relation between the two sets of factors in the etiology of disease and disorders. Questions include: Why do they covary? Which takes the lead? Is there feedback between them? Where do social and ecological influences fit in? See MIND-BODY PROBLEM.

body-mind problem   See MIND-BODY PROBLEM.

body-monitoring   (B. Neugarten) Close observation of body functions, especially changes in sexual response, vigor, and general health during middle and old age, which leads to various strategies to preserve performance and appearance.

body narcissism   An exaggerated concern with the body especially its erotic zones. According to psychoanalytic theory, this is particularly evident in the phallic-Oedipal years when both boys and girls become preoccupied with body functions, explore their bodies, and dread of any body injury.

body odor   The odor produced by the action of bacteria on skin secretions, such as perspiration.

body percept   A person's mental image of the physical characteristics of the person's own body: whether slim or stocky, strong or weak, attractive or unattractive, tall or short. The body percept may or may not conform to reality since it is influenced by the body concept. See BODY CONCEPT, BODY IMAGE, BODY SCHEMA/ SCHEME.

body protest   (E. L. Richards) Physical disorders that serve as an outlet for frustrations and anxieties.

body schema/scheme   The pattern of one's body as viewed by the person; formed on the basis of touch, movement, posture, and overall structure.

body-sense area   The projection area of the cerebral cortex, lying behind the fissure of Rolando, which helps determine the position of the body in space.

body size (index)   See BODY-BUILD INDEX, HUMAN BODY SIZE.

body therapy   The relief of psychological tensions and other symptoms through body manipulation, relaxation, massage, breathing exercises, and changes in posture and position of body parts, on the theory that the body and its functioning embodies the person's basic personality and way of life. See ALEXANDER TECHNIQUE, AUTOGENIC TRAINING, BIOENERGETICS, RELAXATION THERAPY, ROLFING, TRAGERISM.

body type   A classification of individuals according to body build or physique. A number of people have described the same basic body types with different names, for example, (a) a thin/slender body type is named: asthenic (Ernst Kretschmer), ectomorph (William Sheldon), leptosome (Hans Eysenck), phthisic (Carl Carus), microsplanchnic (Giacinto Viola); (b) an overweight/ heavy body type is named: pyknic (Kretschmer), endomorph (Sheldon), eurymorph (Eysenck), phlegmatic (Carus), macrosplanchnic (Viola); and (c) a well-built body type is named: athletic (Carus, Kretschmer), mesomorph (Sheldon), normosplanchnic (Viola). Theories based on body type have not been shown to be valid. See ASTHENIC TYPE, ATHLETIC TYPE, CONSTITUTIONAL TYPE, CONSTITUTIONAL TYPOLOGY, DYSPLASTIC TYPE, ECTOMORPH, ENDOMORPH, MESOMORPH, PYKNIC TYPE.

body-type theories   Points of view that attempt to relate individuals' body builds to attributes of their personality. See BODY TYPE, CONSTITUTIONAL TYPES, KRETSCHMER'S BODY TYPES, SHELDON'S CONSTITUTIONAL TYPES, SOMATOTYPE THEORY.

Boehm Test of Basic Concepts   (A. E. Boehm) A test designed to assess knowledge of fundamental concepts frequently used but often misunderstood by kindergarten and first-grade children. The concepts are classified under Space, Quantity, Time, and miscellaneous. Revised as the Boehm Test of Basic Concepts-Revised (Boehm-R).

Boehm Test of Basic Concepts-Preschool Version (Boehm-Preschool)   (A. E. Boehm) A downward extension of the Boehm-R for use with children aged 3 to 5 years.

Bogardus Social-Distance Scale   (E. S. Bogardus) A measure of the degree of acceptance or rejection between individuals and members of different ethnic, national, and social groups. Also known as Bogardus Scale.

Bogen Cage   (H. Bogen) A maze test in which a ball is moved with a stick toward the exit by the shortest possible route.

Bogorad's syndrome   (F. A. Bogorad) A disorder characterized by profuse lacrimation (tearing) by the patient when eating or drinking. Sometimes follows an attack of facial palsy. Also known as crocodile tears, gustolacrimal reflex.

bogus erudition   1. Learning without understanding. 2. Memorizing trivial matters or the unnecessary use of technical words intended to generate favorable impressions on others.

bogus pipeline   In social psychology, to enhance the validity of questionnaire responses, participants are led to believe that their answers will be verified by a physiological apparatus that detects falsification.

Bohemian unconcernedness   A group of personality traits consisting of a tendency toward unconventionality, eccentricity, and hysterical upsets. See UNCONCERNEDNESS.

boiler-makers deafness   A high-frequency hearing loss resulting from exposure to high-intensity noise. The condition is relevant today due to the increased noise of highly industrialized society. Acoustic trauma may also be due to the intense sound-level pressures of contemporary music.

Bolgar-Fischer World Test   (H. Bolgar & L. Fischer) A projective examination in which the participant reveals attitudes and orientation to reality by constructing a miniature "world" out of toy houses, animals, cars, and trees, from a chest of more than 200 figurines. Sometimes known as World Test. See MAKE-A-PICTURE-STORY TEST.

bolometer   An instrument used for measuring minute changes in radiant heat.

BOLT   Basic Occupational Literacy Test

bond   A connecting relation between any two items (such as between a piece of iron and a magnet, a stimulus and its usual response, or siblings in a close-knit family) with the implication that they "want to be together." See BONDING, FRIENDSHIP.

bondage   A paraphilia characterized by mock enslavement of one person by another to arouse sexual pleasure in one or both partners. The enslaved person may be immobilized with handcuffs, cords, chains, or other restraining devices. Bondage usually calls for threats and acts of humiliation. See MASOCHISM, SADISM.

bondage and discipline (B & D)   Sexual behavior that includes bondage accompanied by sadomasochism. Because of the potential physical danger, the partners usually agree upon a signal to be used when the erotic activity becomes too painful. See BONDAGE, PARAPHILIA, SADOMASOCHISM.

bonding   1. A process by which a parent and child become emotionally attached to each other. 2. Any close affiliation between individuals, present for most people in normal behavior but absent in some disorders such as sociopathic personality and most psychoses. 3. Used more restrictively by pediatricians to describe a critical period during the first days of life in which parents need to have physical contact with their newborn for optimal development to occur. Also known as affiliative bonding.

bonding theory of criminology   A point of view that career criminals who have disassociated themselves from conventional society no longer accept its legitimacy, and thus establish their own independent norms.

bone age   A measure of the developmental maturity of a person as determined by the degree of ossification of bone structures, usually those of the hands, typically determined by x-rays.

bone conduction   The transmission of sound waves to the inner ear through vibrations of bones in the skull, used by some deaf people (such as Ludwig van Beethoven) to hear.

bone-conduction test   An audiological procedure to determine if hearing loss is due to conductive or to neural factors. Performed at controlled frequencies with a small bone-conduction vibrator, attached to a headband, placed on the temporal bone behind the ear.

bone deafness   Hearing loss due usually to deterioration of the three bones of the inner ear as a result of the aging process.

bone-pointing   In the Australian Aboriginal system, the pointing of a sharpened bone at a person and performing an incantation intending to do that person harm. See VOODOO DEATH.

Bonferroni t test   (O. J. Dunn) A method of testing hypotheses concerning planned contrasts of means. Usually referred to as Dunn's multiple comparison test.

bonking   Slang for sudden fatigue experienced by endurance athletes. Also known as "hitting the wall." See SPORT PSYCHOLOGY.

Bonnet's syndrome   **Charles Bonnet's syndrome**

book fear   See BIBLIOPHOBIA.

books for the blind   See TALKING BOOKS.

Boolean algebra   (G. Boole) A method of representing propositions by means of binary notation. Also known as set algebra.

boomerang effect   The phenomenon where, in effect, the contrary to what one intended to achieve from an action occurs, for example, when B becomes more entrenched in a position when A tries to disuade B. See REACTANCE THEORY.

booster sessions   Arrangements made in counseling or psychotherapy involving the scheduling of occasional further sessions for periodic check-ups, encouragement, consideration of new problems, etc., after the main sessions are officially ended.

bootstrap   A metaphor referring to iterations that become more powerful over time and experience.

bootstrapping   In language and cognition, using experiences as a scaffold for new learning.

borderline   Pertaining to any phenomenon difficult to categorize because it straddles two distinct classes, showing characteristics of both.

borderline cases   Phenomena which fall between two distinguishable classes and are not readily assigned to either.

borderline disorders   Vague phrase for a group of psychological conditions that are characterized between normality and neurosis, between neurosis and psychosis, or between normal intelligence and mental retardation. See BORDERLINE PERSONALITY DISORDER, BORDERLINE INTELLECTUAL FUNCTIONING, BORDERLINE SYNDROME, SCHIZOID-PERSONALITY DISORDER, SCHIZOTYPAL-PERSONALITY DISORDER.

borderline intellectual functioning   A level of tested intelligence between low normal and mentally retarded. Some researchers define it as an intelligence quotient (IQ) between 68 and 83, others as any IQ in the 70s. A research study on the interpretation of the word "borderline" indicated that nonpsychologists thought borderline meant either defective or genius intelligence. To avoid confusion, the phrase borderline mental retardation is used. Also known as borderline intelligence. See BORDERLINE.

borderline mental retardation   An intelligence level between normal and subnormal intelligence.

borderline personality disorder   A diagnosis of a personality disorder characterized by long-standing patterns of instability, poor interpersonal relationships, and inadequate social and occupational functioning.

borderline psychosis   A condition in which a person exhibits psychotic tendencies and employs psychotic mechanisms when under stress, but is still in touch with reality. For specific types, see AMBULATORY SCHIZOPHRENIA, PRESCHIZOPHRENIC EGO, PSEUDONEUROTIC SCHIZOPHRENIA.

borderline schizophrenia   The status of a person appearing to be on the edge of a frank schizophrenic breakdown but has not as yet broken with reality. See BORDERLINE PSYCHOSIS.

borderline state   A pathological condition characterized by fluctuating between normality and abnormality, often with the person no longer feeling in command of self.

borderline syndrome   Loose phrase describing patients showing a combination of characteristics or tendencies associated with a neurosis, psychosis, or character disorder but who lack a specific symptom pattern. See BORDERLINE DISORDERS.

boredom   A general loss of interest in activities accompanied by wandering attention and lack of motivation. Inability to respond to any activity, no matter how meaningful or stimulating it is to others, is considered pathological. See DIVERSIVE EXPLORATION.

Borg Scale (G. A. Borg) A psychophysical scale for assessing perceived exertion.

Borstal system A method of treatment of juvenile delinquents in Britain, that emphasizes close supervision after release from detention, with supportive parole officers.

botany A branch of biology that deals with plants. The behavior of plants has not had much attention from psychologists, but plants appear to have means of communication, of protecting themselves and others from enemies, and other forms of behavior unexpected from these organisms rooted in the ground. See ZOOLOGY.

botryology The intuitive or statistical process of separating objects, such as body types, sounds, or words, into groups of related clusters. See CLUSTER ANALYSIS, FACTOR ANALYSIS.

bottle baby Slang for a habitual alcoholic who has regressed to virtual infancy.

bottom line Slang for the final assessment, the end product.

bottom-up analysis A kind of critical thinking beginning with details or elements and working "upwards" to greater understanding; inductive thinking. Compare TOP-DOWN ANALYSIS.

bottom-up approach In cognitive psychology, an aspect of information processing in which the basis for recognition or categorization of an input is the input itself. Analyzed elements of the input itself when considered as a whole are sufficient for the identification to take place. Compare TOP-DOWN APPROACH.

bottom-up (cognitive) processes See DATA-DRIVEN COGNITIVE PROCESSES.

bottom-up processing Information processing that begins at the receptor level, such as vision, and continues to the higher brain centers. See TOP-DOWN PROCESSING.

bouffées delirantes (BD) An acute delusional disorder marked by confusion and aggression purported to be specific to natives of West Africa and Haiti. See ACUTE DELUSIONAL PSYCHOSIS.

Bouguer-Weber law A rare name for the Weber-Fechner law. Based on the theory that the Weber-Fechner law was anticipated by the work of Pierre Bouguer, a French scientist. See WEBER-FECHNER LAW.

Boulder model (V. Raimy) At an American Psychological Association (APA) conference in Boulder, Colorado in 1949, 71 conferees agreed that psychology practitioners should be trained equally as scientists and as practitioners.

boulimia **bulimia**

boundary 1. A barrier between parts of a system, as in a fence in a yard, or as in a family in which rules are established as to who may participate and who may not participate in certain activities. 2. (K. Lewin) In topological psychology, anything limiting the person as he or she "moves" through the psychological environment or life space.

boundary ambiguity The uncertainty in step-families of who is (or is not) included in the family, and who is performing or is responsible for certain tasks in the family system.

boundary detectors Optic-nerve fibers that respond to a sharp edge in a receptive field, regardless of brightness or contrast on either side of the edge. They are part of the specialized visual system of amphibia. Sometimes referred to as edge detectors.

boundary issues Pertaining to the limits of areas, such as a professional in one area intruding on another area of expertise (for example, a psychologist expressing an opinion to a client about the value of certain pharmaceuticals).

boundary system In general-systems theory, semipermeable boundaries between living systems, permitting information to proceed in either direction; but posing the question of how much interpenetration and interdependence is feasible in a given social system. See EGO BOUNDARIES.

bounded rationality (H. A. Simon) Goal-oriented decision processes that are consistent with the known limits on human knowledge and human abilities to predict and compute the consequences of actions. (In contrast with economics' postulate that the decisions of economic actors maximize utility, as measured objectively in the external world.) See PROCEDURAL RATIONALITY.

bound energy Ego energy used to deal with reality rather than fantasy or repression.

bound flow Body movement that appears tense or restricted because of increased opposition between agonist and antagonist muscles. See BEHAVIORAL HOMEOSTASIS, BODY ARMOR.

bound morpheme A linguistic unit that must be attached to another unit for the combination to make sense; for example, the prefix, pre-, by itself has the general meaning of "prior to," but when attached to other words such as preamble, precession, and precipitate, generates more complete meanings.

Bourdon effect/illusion (B. B. Bourdon) A misperception when two triangles, ABD and BCE, with angles A and C of 90° and angle B of 10°, are placed so that they touch at point B, and the sides AB and BC are colinear, and the line ABC tilts 10°, the line ABC will appear to bend inward toward points E and D.

bouton (terminal) **synaptic knob/swelling**

bouton terminaux French term for synaptic knobs.

bovarism Failure to differentiate between fantasy and reality. A theme of Gustave Flaubert's novel *Madame Bovary*.

Bowditch's law (H. Bowditch) A theory that nerves cannot be fatigued.

bowel control The ability to regulate defecation. On the average, bowel control begins at about six months of age and is fairly complete by age three. Compare BLADDER CONTROL. See TOILET TRAINING.

bowel disorders Disorders of the bowels that frequently occur as responses to stress and anxiety. Major bowel disorders, which may be psychologically caused or aggravated, include chronic constipation, irritable-bowel syndrome, mucus colitis, and ulcerative colitis.

bowel training See BOWEL CONTROL, TOILET TRAINING.

bow motion/movement   A variation of beta motion. If an object is placed between the originating and ending points of an apparent motion, it would appear to bend or bow to avoid the object. See BETA MOTION, PHI PHENOMENON.

bow-wow theory   An origin-of-language theory that assumes language started first by people making sounds following their emotions, such as after accomplishing a task, sounding "OOOOO" in the presence of others, who upon hearing this, repeated "OOOOO" under similar circumstances. See ORIGIN-OF-LANGUAGE THEORIES.

boxer's dementia   A chronic, slowly progressive brain disorder resulting from scattered hemorrhages produced by repeated blows to the head. Common symptoms of being "punchdrunk" are mild mental confusion, uncertain balance, inability to concentrate, and involuntary movements. Also known as dementia pugilistica.

BPRS   Brief Psychiatric Rating Scale

BRAC   basic rest-activity cycle

brachycephalic   Relating to or characterized by brachycephaly.

brachycephaly   A disproportionate shortness of the head, a condition marked by a skull that is abnormally short and wide. Having a cephalic index scale ratio above 80. Also known as brachycephalia, brachycephalism. See CEPHALIC INDEX.

brachymorph(y)   1. Having a shorter form than the norm. 2. A body type characterized by an abnormally short, broad physique. Also known as brachytype, brevitype.

brachyskeletal   Describing a person with abnormally short bones, particularly short leg bones. Also known as brachyskelic.

bradyacusia   Low hearing capacity.

bradyarthria   A form of dysarthria characterized by abnormally slow speech, common in depression, senile brain disorder, general paresis, and emotionally inhibited individuals. Also known as bradyglossia, bradylalia, bradylogia.

bradycardia   Slow heartbeat. Also known as bradyrhythmia. See ARRHYTHMIA.

bradyglossia   1. Slow tongue movement. 2. Slowness of speech due to organic causes, for example, neural lesions or a disease or anomaly of the mouth or tongue. 3. See BRADYARTHRIA.

bradykinesia   Abnormal slowness of movements with a decrease in spontaneous motor activity, due to psychogenic or organic factors. Also known as bradycinesia, bradykinesis.

bradylalia   **bradyarthria**

bradylexia   Extreme slowness in reading.

bradylogia   A functional disorder marked by abnormally slow speech. See BRADYARTHRIA, BRADYGLOSSIA.

bradyphasia   A form of aphasia characterized by extreme slowness of speech. Also known as bradyphemia.

bradyphemia   **bradyphasia**

bradyphrasia   Slowness of speech associated with depression, a complete lack of speech when associated with depression is called hypophrasia.

bradyphrenia   1. Sluggish mental processes associated with severe anxiety or depression, since intense emotional states tend to interfere with thinking. 2. Sometimes used as a synonym for psychomotor retardation, and occasionally used for mental retardation.

bradypragia   Slowness of action due to an organic disorder such as myxedema.

bradypraxia   Slow body movements.

bradyrhythmia   A slow heartbeat. Also known as bradycardia.

bradyscope   A device that presents visual stimuli slowly. See TACHISTOSCOPE.

brahmacharya   The Hindu practice of ascetic self-denial to concentrate the energies toward spiritual attainment.

braid-cutting   A sadistic hair fetish in which a person's hair is cut. In psychoanalytic theory, it is regarded as a symbol of castration in which knowledge that the hair will grow back is a reassurance that castration need not be final.

Braid's strabismus   (J. Braid) A form of strabismus (divergent or convergent eye squint) by means of which hypnosis can be induced by causing the eyes to converge and turn upward.

Braidism   (J. Braid) Old name for hypnotism, named after James Braid who coined the word hypnosis. In France, hypnotism was called Braidism from 1860–1875. See MESMERISM.

Braille   (L. Braille) A system for representing alphanumeric characters with patterns of raised dots that can be read by touch. The basic alphabet consists of six dots organized in two parallel vertical columns.

brain   The mass of central nervous system nerve tissues including the cerebrum and related structures within the skull. Though the human brain weighs only about three pounds, the outer layer (the cortex) alone contains over ten billion nerve cells of two general kinds: association fibers, that connect one part of the brain to another; and projection fibers, that carry messages to and from organs in the rest of the body. The brain is divided into two hemispheres bridged by the corpus callosum, and is divided by deep fissures into four lobes, each with special functions. The brain has been divided and classified by anatomists on the basis of appearance and by researchers on the basis of functions. And there are differences within each of these two approaches. Also known as encephalon. See AMYGDALA, ARCHAIC BRAIN, ARCUATE ZONE OF THE BRAIN STEM, CEREBELLUM, CEREBRUM, CINGULATE GYRUS, CALICULI, CORPUS CALLOSUM, EVOLUTION OF BRAIN, FOREBRAIN, FORNIX, FOREBRAIN, FRONTAL LOBE, HINDBRAIN, HIPPOCAMPUS, HYPOTHYMIAS, LIMBIC SYSTEM, MEDULLA OBLONGATA, MIDBRAIN, OCCIPITAL LOBE, OLFACTORY BULB, PARIETAL LOBE, PINEAL BODY, PITUITARY, PONS, SPLIT BRAIN, TEMPORAL LOBE, THALAMUS.

brain action currents   See ACTION POTENTIAL.

brain atrophy   Degeneration of cerebral nerve fibers occurring in senile dementia and Alzheimer's disease.

brain bank   A parkinsonism-research program to conduct intensive pathological studies into causes and treatments of parkinsonism. The brain bank consists of a registry of parkinsonism patients who have agreed to bequeath their brains for research.

brain barrier systems   Physiological processes that, because of differences in ionic composition and permeability rates between one brain fluid and another, prevent or delay the exchange of fluids, solutes, or ions throughout the brain. See the BLOOD-BRAIN BARRIER for an example.

brain biorhythm   Background electrical activity of the brain indicated by regular or rhythmic activity of a given wave form with insignificant variations over time for certain states of the body.

brain centers   In the brain, certain areas of interconnected neurons that function for various specific purposes, such as vision at the occiput (back area of the brain).

brain comparator   A hypothetical entity that serves to take into account movements of the head and eyes in the perception of motion.

brain control   The manipulation of brain functions by electrical, chemical, or other devices, for experimental or therapeutic purposes.

brain damage   Injury to the brain caused by such conditions as prenatal infection, brain tumors, trauma, stroke, and surgery.

brain-damage language disorders   Any loss of ability to communicate effectively by means of symbolic stimuli due to brain injuries. See ALEXIA, APHASIA.

brain death   The cessation of neurologic signs of life. In 1973, the American Neurological Association adopted a definition of brain death as that of human death; and a 1974 California law states that a person shall be "pronounced dead if it is determined that the person has suffered total and irreversible cessation of brain function."

brain disorders   See ORGANIC BRAIN SYNDROMES (OBS).

Brain Electrical Activity Mapping (BEAM)   Computerized electroencephalography (EEG), mainly used to locate epileptic foci.

brain fag   A condition of nervous irritability and fatiguability, induced by overwork.

brain graft   The transplantation of healthy tissue into a damaged brain.

brain growth (in humans)   (J. Giedd) In humans, the brain continues to grow up to the age of six years, from then until adolescence, the gray matter decreases 10–20% and the white matter increases 10–20%. See BRAIN, GRAY MATTER, WHITE MATTER.

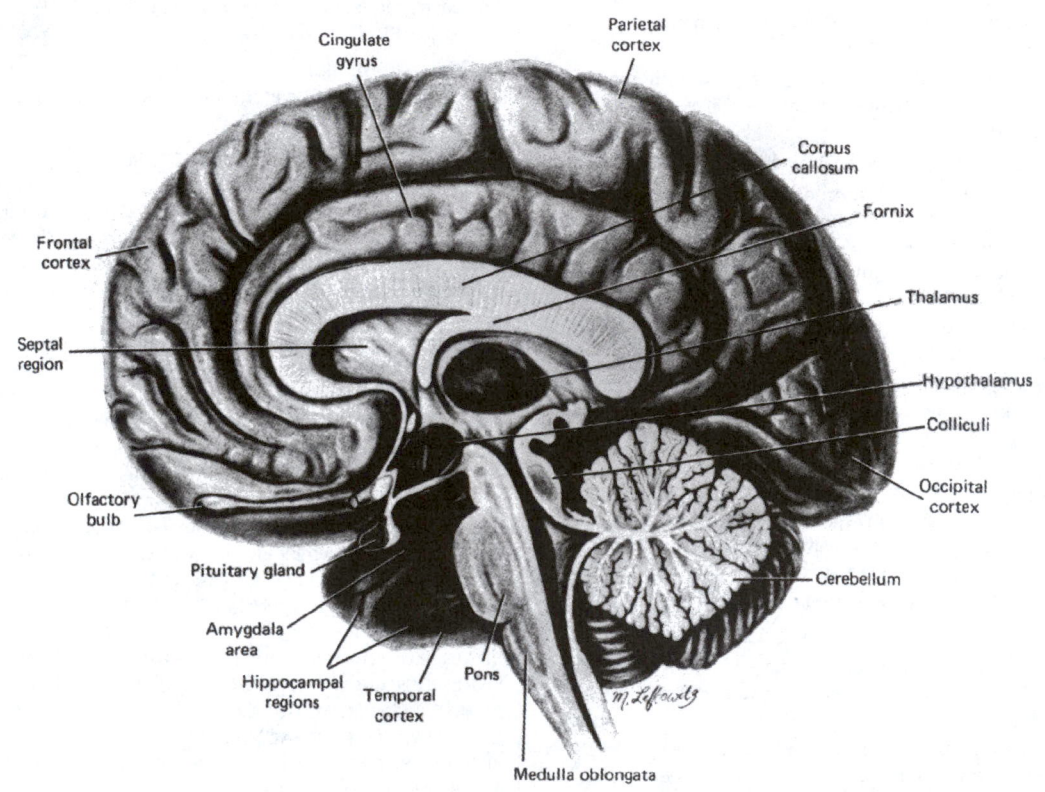

human brain

(Used with the permission of Marlene-Oscar Berman)

brain-imaging　A technique for observing the brain's activity as it performs perceptual, motor, and even cognitive tasks. See BRAIN SCAN.

brain-imaging techniques　The electronic assessment of the structure of brains using noninvasive techniques that are ultimately translated into visual images. See BRAIN SCAN, MAGNETIC RESONANCE IMAGING.

brain-injured child　A child who before, during, or after birth suffered from an infection or injury that damaged the brain. The results of such organic impairment are reflected in communication and learning problems.

brain-injury　Refers to damage to the brain that can affect the personality as well as the physical functioning of an individual. Damage to specific areas can affect specific aspects of functioning, for example, left hemisphere injuries can affect language skills. See AGNOSIA, APHASIA, BOXER'S DEMENTIA, BROCA'S AREA, PHINEAS GAGE, WERNICKE'S APHASIA.

brain lesion　Any damage to an area of brain tissue caused by injury, surgery, tumor, CVA (cerebral-vascular accident), or infection.

brain localization theories　Viewpoints that the brain has different areas for various functions. Galen was one of the first to speculate that the front part of the brain received sensory impressions and the back part had motor functions. Some fifteen centuries later Franz Gall, a phrenologist, resurrected this view and gave the brain a number of specific localized functions, a theory that found no scientific support. Approximately one hundred years later, Paul Broca announced that the left hemisphere of the brain controlled speech. Eventually, a number of different local areas were mapped. See ASSOCIATION AREA, AUDITORY AREAS, BRAIN CENTERS, BRAIN MAPPING, LOCALIZATION OF BRAIN FUNCTIONS, OLFACTORY BRAIN, TOPOGRAPHIC MAPPING.

brain mapping　(M. de Luzzi) A method of laying out the brain's anatomy according to specific functions, assumed or known. See BRAIN, SPEECH AREAS OF BRAIN for illustrations of brain mapping and compare these with the areas seen in PHRENOLOGY.

brain nuclei　Clusters of cells within the cerebrum.

brain pathology　The study of any disorder of the brain due to disease or injury.

brain plasticity　The capacity of the brain to regenerate or compensate for losses in brain cells. See RECOVERY OF FUNCTION.

brain potential　The electrical potential of brain cells. See ELECTROENCEPHALOGRAPH.

brain research　Investigation of the structure and functions of the brain through scientific experimentation and naturalistic observation.

brain scan　A noninvasive procedure to examine the brain by the use of sophisticated machines. See COMPUTERIZED AXIAL TOMOGRAPHY, COMPUTERIZED TOMOGRAPHY, DIGITAL ANGIOGRAPHY, POSITRON EMISSION TOMOGRAPHY, MAGNETIC RESONANCE IMAGING.

brain-splitting　Surgical separation of the cerebral hemispheres. This procedure is performed in humans for therapeutic purposes such as the control of life-threatening epilepsy. See COMMISSUROTOMY, HEMIDECORTICATION.

brain spot hypothesis　(E. Southard) A postulate that emphasizes the role of organic factors in mental disorders.

brainstem　A portion of the central nervous system that includes the hindbrain, midbrain, and the forebrain. Nervous tissues including the pons, medulla oblongata, and midbrain, that connect the cerebral hemispheres of the brain with the spinal cord. Also known as brain-stem.

brain stimulation　The stimulation of the entire brain or activation of specific areas, such as the amygdala, as a means of determining their effects on behavior. Includes: (a) areal stimulation, when an extended portion of a sense organ is stimulated; (b) audio stimulation, when the sense of hearing is stimulated; and (c) cerebral stimulation, when the cerebrum is stimulated, as in learning situations. See BRAIN RESEARCH.

brainstorm　1. Any form of emotional excitement or uncontrolled behavior. 2. A powerful new idea that appears to come out of nowhere generating a strong emotional reaction. 3. A harebrained idea.

brainstorming　A technique of generating ideas among members of a group, characterized by fluency, flexibility, and originality. Involves an initial phase of absolute freedom of expression, and later, a phase of discussion, classification, elimination of options, and targeting of a tentative decision.

brain trauma　Physical injury to the brain produced, for example, by a blow to the head, a gun wound, or a cerebrovascular accident. See ACUTE TRAUMATIC DISORDER, CHRONIC TRAUMATIC DISORDER, HEAD TRAUMA, INTRACRANIAL HEMORRHAGE.

brain tumor　Any abnormal tissue growth within the confines of the skull. As tumors grow larger, patients may experience disturbances of perception in the visual, auditory, and olfactory senses, loss of coordination, weakness, paralysis, and convulsions. Personality changes may take the form of memory lapses, absent-mindedness, loss of initiative, or generally slow reactions to mental stimuli.

brain ventricles　(Galen) Four hollow chambers in the brain. They and the spinal cord are filled with cerebrospinal fluid.

brainwashing　The combination of coercive propaganda techniques presented to political prisoners or prisoners of war under conditions of physical and emotional intimidation. The goal is to produce attitude changes in the prisoners' values and the inculcation of beliefs favorable to the captors. See MIND CONTROL PROGRAMMING, STOCKHOLM SYNDROME.

brain waves　Spontaneous, rhythmic electrical impulses emanating from different areas of the brain. Brain-wave patterns appear to be relatively stable for each individual and are used in diagnosing brain lesions, tumors, and epilepsy, but not neurotic or psychotic disorders. Also known as Berger rhythms (after the German neurologist Hans Berger who gave the first substantial account of brain waves). Wave types include: ALPHA, BETA, DELTA, GAMMA, KAPPA, SAW-TOOTH, SPINDLE, THETA. See ELECTROENCEPHALOGRAPH, SPIKE-WAVE ACTIVITY.

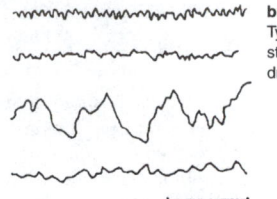

brain waves Brain-wave patterns. Typical brain waves during different states, such as when excited, drowsy, in normal and in deep sleep.

brain-wave therapy The use of alpha or other brain waves for psychotherapeutic purposes.

brain weight The weight of an adult human brain is between 1,200 and 1,500 grams. Brain weight apparently is not related to intellectual ability; one of the smallest brains ever examined belonged to Nobel Prize winner, Anatole France.

branched format/program 1. A mode of evaluation based on items administered on a pass–fail basis, with the next item being of greater difficulty if the prior item was passed, and of lesser difficulty if the prior item was failed. 2. A rapid method used in determining the extent of a person's abilities, such as in using Pascal's triangle to evaluate a person's vocabulary. Also known as branching program. See PROGRAMMED INSTRUCTION.

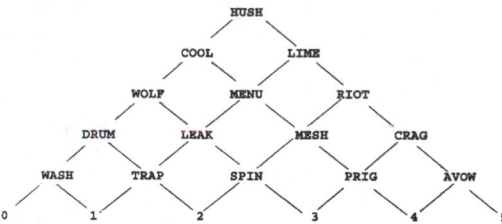

branched format/program A triangle used to obtain a quick estimate of a person's knowledge of vocabulary. For example, an examiner asks the participant to give a definition of HUSH. If defined correctly, the next item is LIME; if answered incorrectly, the next item is COOL, and so on. Scores range from 0 (did not define any of the words along the left side) to 5 (defined all words on the right side). Typically, the first word (HUSH in this case) is of average difficulty, while others are considered to be easier to the left and more difficult to the right.

branching 1. In a programmed learning situation, if a participant, usually a student, does not know the answer to a test item, instead of proceeding to a more difficult test item, the program may move to other items in a parallel manner to prepare the participant for the next level of difficulty. 2. Refers to programmed learning in which a different path is taken depending on which of several alternative responses is selected. While some alternatives indicate lack of understanding, there may be two equally good responses that simply lead to different sets of frames, or there may be a "good" response and an "excellent" response whereby selecting the latter leads to omitting a number of frames deemed "too basic" for the individual.

brand loyalty A tendency of consumers to purchase a particular brand consistently. See BRAND PREFERENCE.

brand preference The preference for a particular brand of cigarette, beer, margarine, or other product. Two types of tests are frequently used to determine if consumers can recognize their own brands: blindfold testing, and submission of unlabeled packages or bottles to a consumer panel for them to taste and compare. See BRAND LOYALTY.

brand-use survey A test of advertising effectiveness in which consumers are interviewed to determine whether they purchased a particular brand of product featured in a specific advertising appeal. The survey sometimes has been accompanied by the pantry-check technique to validate results of the survey.

Brawner decision A 1972 ruling on insanity by the District of Columbia Court of Appeals: "... a person is not responsible for criminal conduct if at the time of such conduct as a result of mental disease or defect he lacks substantial capacity either to appreciate the wrongfulness of his conduct or to conform his conduct to the requirements of the law." Named after Archie W. Brawner, a man suffering from epilepsy and memory disturbances who shot and killed a person after a barroom brawl. He appealed his second-degree murder conviction, resulting in the Brawner decision. See AMERICAN LAW INSTITUTE INSANITY DEFINITION, DURHAM RULE, M'NAGHTEN RULE.

Brazelton Behavioral Assessment Scale (T. B. Brazelton) A measure of a neonate's response to the environment. The scale assesses interactive behaviors, motor behaviors, physiological control, and response to stress. Also known as Brazelton Neonatal Behavioral Assessment Scale, Brazelton Scale. See APGAR SCALE.

break phenomenon The instance at which the more powerful of two rival stimuli suddenly loses its power to call forth responses.

breakdown See NERVOUS BREAKDOWN.

breakthrough 1. A major or significant advance in knowledge, research, or treatment. 2. A sudden forward step in therapy, especially after a plateau.

B-realm (A. Maslow) One of two modes of relating to the world according to Abraham Maslow. In the Being (B) realm, people are concerned with the growth need of self-actualization, that includes such universal needs as truth, goodness, and beauty. See D-REALM, SELF-ACTUALIZATION.

breast complex In psychoanalytic theory, if the mother's breast has been denied or withheld, a breast complex may manifest itself as breast envy in which the penis unconsciously represents the breast.

breast envy In psychoanalytic theory, males having repressed a breast complex as infants may later ignore female breasts and develop overt homosexual traits, or they may deny the importance of the female breasts by becoming sexually excited only if the female partner sucks their breasts. See BREAST COMPLEX.

breastfeeding The transferring of a mother's milk directly to an infant's mouth via the mother's nipple. The physiological effects of breastfeeding babies are well understood, including easily digestible food for the infant, antibodies in the milk that give the child extra protection from diseases, and reduce allergies. From a psychological point of view, breastfeeding tends to generate bonding between mother and child and can generate pleasurable sensations in the mother while in the act of feeding her child. See FEEDING INSTRUCTIONS.

breast-phantom phenomenon The illusion that an amputated breast is still there. The breast is still included in the body image, and in many cases the person feels tingling and, occasionally, painful sensations in the missing organ, and in some instances denies that it has been removed. See PHANTOM LIMB.

breath-holding   A deliberate refusal to respire or breathe, usually by children, to frighten adults in an attempt to get the adults to give the children what they want. See TEMPER TANTRUM.

breathing   The mechanism of respiration, or the cycles of alternate inhalation and exhalation. Term often is accompanied by an adjective to identify a particular type of breathing, such as abdominal breathing or diaphragmatic breathing.

breathy voice   A voice characterized by an excessive emission of breath. When the voice is both weak and breathy, the condition is sometimes described as phonasthenia. Breathy voice may be due to tension, defense against voicing unacceptable feelings, or debility.

breech birth   The delivery of a baby emerging buttocks first, instead of emerging from the mother in the most usual manner (head first).

breed   A group of closely related animals within a species.

breeding behavior   See MATING BEHAVIOR.

Breton's law   (P. Breton) A formula proposed as a substitute for Weber's law; it states that there is a parabolic relation between stimulus and just noticeable difference.

brevitype   See BRACHYMORPH.

bride-price   In some cultures, the parents of a boy are expected to pay the girl's family to obtain her as a wife for their son. See DOWRY.

bridge principle   A means of relating concepts to other concepts, such as transferring part of an idea to a different idea.

bridging   1. (A. A. Lazarus) In multimodal therapy, a method of first focusing on the client's area of discourse (for example, cognitions) before gently moving to another modality (for example, sensations) which more readily allows access to the affective domain that the therapist may wish to pursue. 2. (A. Staats) How disparate bodies can be brought together to form a united science. See UNITED POSITIVISM.

brief group therapy   Group therapy conducted using a crisis-intervention model, as contrasted with long-term group therapy.

brief perseverance   Keeping one's conceptions in the short-term, after the basis on which they were formed has been discredited.

brief psychotherapy   Short-term therapy. Mistakenly thought by some to be less desirable than longer-term psychotherapy.

brief reactive psychosis   Psychotic disorders that develop suddenly following a traumatic event (such as the death of a loved one) and last up to two weeks. Characterized by emotional turmoil and at least one psychotic symptom.

Brief Psychiatric Rating Scale (BPRS)   A system of evaluating clinical psychiatric signs on the basis of 18 factors, such as bizarre thinking, hostility, withdrawal, and anxiety.

brief-stimuli technique/therapy (BST)   Electroconvulsive therapy in which shocks lasting from one-sixth to one-third millisecond are used. Also known as brief-stimulus technique/therapy.

Briggs' law   A Massachusetts law that requires a psychiatric examination for a defendant in a criminal case who has been convicted or indicted previously for an offense. The purpose is to determine if the defendant suffers a mental illness that affects responsibility. Named after American psychiatrist Lloyd Vernon Briggs (1863–1941).

Briggs-Myers Type Indicator   Myers-Briggs Type Indicator

bright adaptation   In vision, changes in the eye to adapt to changing light conditions.

brightness   1. A photometric measure of light emission per unit area of a luminous body or of a translucent or reflecting surface, that is, candle-power per unit area. 2. A dimension of color that correlates with the intensity of the physical stimulus; the dimension of brilliance, ranging from white (the highest value) to black (the lowest value). Bright colors reflect light to a greater extent than dark colors. Compare BRILLIANCE.

brightness adaptation   A decrease in the brilliance of stimuli as general illumination increases.

brightness constancy   A tendency to perceive a familiar object as having the same brightness under different conditions of illumination. A familiar object tends to be seen in the same way even though its stimulus properties have altered. See CONSTANCY, OBJECT CONSTANCY, PERCEPTUAL CONSTANCY.

brightness contrast   The apparent brightness changes resulting from prior stimulations or simultaneous stimulations; for example the same gray disk looks darker on a white background than it does on a black background.

brightness discrimination   Ability of people to distinguish degrees of differences in brightness, which vary according to the wavelength of light.

brightness threshold   The minimum intensity of light of a designated wavelength that can be detected against a surrounding field.

bril   (R. M. Hanes) The perceived brightness of a light equivalent to 1/100 of a millilambert. A bril is a subjective unit of light on the scale of brightness, contrasting with millilamberts, the physical units.

brilliance   That attribute of any color or visual sense-quality in respect to which it may be classed as equivalent to some member of a series of grays ranging from black to white. Compare BRIGHTNESS.

brilliance contrast   A change in brilliance in a given area of the visual field, due to recent stimulation (in respect to brightness) of an adjoining or neighboring area, or of the given area. Also known as brightness contrast.

bril scale   A scale of brightness of surround based on subjective judgments.

bringing up   The care and education of human offspring during the years of immaturity. Usually emphasizing the development of moral character.

Briquet's ataxia   (P. Briquet) A form of hysterical ataxia marked by loss of sensation in the skin and leg muscles. Named after French physician Paul Briquet (1796–1881).

Briquet's syndrome (P. Briquet) 1. Symptoms of apnea and aphonia due to hysterical paralysis of the diaphragm. Characterized by a vague but often dramatic medical history beginning in early adulthood, with numerous visits to many physicians, and a long list of disabling symptoms for which no organic disorder can be found. 2. A somatic disorder based on feelings of vague discomfort and complaints of not feeling well. See BRIQUET'S ATAXIA.

Brissaud's infantilism (E. Brissaud) A developmental anomaly in which infantile mental and physical characteristics continue past puberty. Also known as infantile myxedema. Named after French physician Edouard Brissaud (1852–1909).

British associationism/empiricists A group of 17th century philosophers who asserted that the mind was a blank slate and that knowledge could only come from sensations. Complex thinking was based on associations between simple sensory elements. Leaders in the movement included Thomas Hobbes, David Hartley, John Locke, James Mill, and John Stuart Mill.

British Museum algorithm (H. A. Simon) An unselective, hence inefficient, problem-solving search (named after the hypothetical monkeys in the British Museum who are, by random strokes, able to type out the works of Shakespeare). See HEURISTIC SEARCH.

Broadbent test (W. H. Broadbent) An examination for temporal-lobe-lesion effects. Participants are subjected to different stimuli (sets of digits, words, music) simultaneously played to each ear via headphones. The affected lobe cannot compete effectively with the normal lobe, as measured by the ability of the participant to report the stimuli heard in the ear on the opposite side.

Broadman(n) See BRODMANN'S AREA/CONVOLUTION.

Broad Spectrum Behavior Therapy (A. A. Lazarus) A treatment approach based on learning theory advocated by Arnold Lazarus prior to the development of his multimodal therapy. Also known as broad spectrum therapy.

Broca's aphasia (P. P. Broca) A condition due to a brain lesion in which a person finds it difficult or impossible to communicate by speaking or writing but is able to communicate by gestures. Also known as nonfluent aphasia.

Broca's Area (P. P. Broca) An area of the left cerebral cortex which is located just in front of cortical areas, controlling muscular movements of those organs used during articulation of speech and which is essential to the production of spoken language. Lesions to this area may result in speech that is slow, labored, and grammatically incorrect or which is impossible to carry out. However, comprehension of spoken or written language may be unaffected. Also known as Broca's speech area. See WERNICKE'S AREA.

Brodmann's area/convolution (K. Brodmann) One of several areas of the cerebral cortex characterized by six cell layers. Identified by numbers, they are assumed to be associated with specific brain functions. Brodmann identified 47 different areas. Researchers have identified more than 200 distinctive cortical areas.

broken home A single-parent home resulting from death, divorce, separation, desertion, or institutionalization.

bromide 1. Refers to salts of the element bromine used widely as a sedative around the 1920s, but increasingly rarely sold or used after the 1970s. Gradual build-up of this chemical with prolonged use can lead to a chronic, toxic delirium, sometimes difficult to diagnose unless considered as a possible etiology. 2. In everyday language, any conventional, hackneyed saying, derived from the idea of thinking in a lazy, half-sedated fashion.

bromide hallucinosis An extended hallucinatory state accompanied by marked fear reactions occurring as a result of bromide intoxication. See BROMIDE.

bromide intoxication A toxic reaction to excessive use of bromides, most often employed as sleeping agents. See BROMIDE, BROMIDE HALLUCINOSIS.

bromidrosiphobia Morbid fear of personal body odor; fear of offending others with one's body odors. Also known as bromidrophobia. See AUTODYSOSMOPHOBIA, AUTOMYSOPHOBIA.

bromism A rare chronic, toxic delirium, resulting from the gradual build-up of bromide. Sometimes difficult to diagnose, good for geriatric specialists to watch for. Also known as brominism. See BROMIDE, BROMIDE INTOXICATION.

bronchus Either of the two main branches of the trachea or windpipe. Plural is bronchi.

brontophobia Abnormal fear of thunder. Also known as keraunophobia, tonitrophobia. See ASTRAPHOBIA.

brooding compulsion A compelling drive to ponder persistently and anxiously about trivial details or abstract concepts. A symptom of obsessive-compulsive disorder. See INTELLECTUALIZATION, OBSESSIONAL BROODING.

Brooland experiment (J. Tizard) Research on children with severe retardation that involved removing them from an institution to a small residential nursery school. The children demonstrated considerable improvement in language and behavior. See DEINSTITUTIONALIZATION, INSTITUTIONALIZATION.

brother complex Cain complex

brotherliness (E. Fromm) A feeling of human unity or solidarity as expressed in productive involvement and caring for the well-being of others and society as a whole. See BELONGING, ROOTEDNESS NEED.

brownie points Sarcastic slang for backhanded compliments.

brown noser Slang for a toady. Also known as "ass kisser." See YES MAN/WOMAN.

Brown-Peterson paradigm/technique A memory-research procedure in which a person is asked at Time 1 to memorize something, then from Time 1 to Time 2 the person is distracted in some manner, usually by being asked to count backward from some number by threes, and then at Time 2 asked to recall the items stored at Time 1.

Brown-Séquard syndrome (C. E. Brown-Séquard) A set of symptoms that includes paralysis and hyperesthesia of one side and anesthesia on the other side of the body in the instance of unilateral transection of the spinal cord.

Brown-Spearman formula   See SPEARMAN-BROWN FORMULA.

Bruce effect   Termination of pregnancy due to a pheromone in the urine of a male other than the impregnator; first identified in mice.

Brugsch's index   In anthropometric studies, a method of deciding what kind of body type a person has by multiplying the chest circumference by 100 and dividing the result by the height of the person. See BODY TYPE.

Bruininks-Oseretsky Test of Motor Proficiency   (R. H. Bruininks & N. I. Oseretsky) A measure of fine and gross motor skills. The complete battery contains 46 items grouped into eight subtests. The short form has 14 items. The test yields three scores: Gross Motor Composite, Fine Motor Composite, and a Total Battery Composite.

Bruner's cognitive development stages   (J. S. Bruner) Jerome Bruner's theory of cognitive development that had these modes: enactive (based on movement), iconic (based on stored memory), and symbolic (based on symbols, such as words).

Brunswik faces   (E. Brunswik) A set of crude faces made of lines. Used for studies of perception and classification. See SCHAFER-MURPHY FACES.

Brunswik ratio   (E. Brunswik) A mathematical expression of perceptual constancy as a function of varying environmental factors. The ratio is $(A\text{-}R)/(S\text{-}R)$, where: S is the standard to be matched, A (appearance) is the comparison stimulus chosen as a match, and R is the match that would occur if the standard were judged only in terms of retinal characteristics.

brute force   An inefficient way of solving a problem in comparison to heuristics or algorithms, for example, eleven piles of boxes are each stacked seven boxes high; a person understanding mathematics has an immediate correct answer to the number of boxes, whereas a person using brute force counts them one-by-one to get the answer, and often is incorrect. See HEURISTIC SEARCH.

bruxism   Grinding of teeth without awareness, including during sleep. Also known as stridor dentium.

Bryngelson-Glaspey Test   (B. Bryngelson & E. Glaspey) An examination to evaluate a person's articulation or quality of speech sounds. Pictures are presented to participants who reply using words to identify these visual stimuli.

BS   Abbreviation for bachelor of science degree. Also abbreviated **BSC**.

BSID   See BAYLEY SCALES OF INFANT DEVELOPMENT.

BSRI   Bem Sex-Role Inventory

BSS   See BECK SCALE FOR SUICIDE IDEATION.

BST   brief-stimulus therapy

BT   basic technique

B type   (E. & W. Jaensch) A personality type classified in terms of eidetic imagery. Refers to persons manifesting a tendency to eidetic imagery that is flexible, imaginative, having natural color and generally under voluntary control. Also known as integrate type. Distinguished from Type B personality. See EIDETIC IMAGERY, MARBURG SCHOOL, T TYPE.

B-type personality   See TYPE B PERSONALITY.

bubble concept of personal space   The idea of an imaginary region around a person that serves as a buffer against encroachment by others. Size of the "bubble" varies with different individuals and situations. Distance varies not only for individuals but for different cultures. North Americans may feel uncomfortable with some South Americans who are perceived as standing "too close" during conversations. See COMFORT ZONE, PROXEMICS, TERRITORIALITY.

buccal   Pertaining to or located in the mouth or cheeks.

buccal onanism   fellatio

buccal speech   A rare type of phonation not depending on laryngeal voice generation, produced by shaping of an air bubble at an optimal place in the cheek pouch. Contractions of the buccal musculature force the air through some narrow opening in the posterior buccal area.

buccinator   A muscle that compresses the cheek and retracts the angle of the mouth for eating and speaking. During mastication, it helps hold the food between the teeth. In speech, it compresses air in the mouth and forces it out between the lips.

buccolingual masticatory syndrome (BLM or **BLMS)**   The most common form of tardive dyskinesia, characterized by repeated involuntary movements of the tongue, lips, and mouth. Also known as oral-lingual dyskinesia. See TARDIVE DYSKINESIA.

buccolinguomasticatory triad   A complex of lips, tongue, jaw, and head movements associated with tardive dyskinesia.

buck fever   Refers to a classic situation in which a novice hunter suddenly sees a deer and makes no move to shoot. This type of nonbehavior happens in certain social situations when personal prior intentions and expectations of behavior do not result after meeting an imagined situation in real life.

buddhi   (Hindi) A concept that the capacity for intuitive discernment is innate in humans.

Buddhism   Religion inspired by the life and teachings of Siddhartha Gautama (the Buddha). Its basic philosophy teaches that life's suffering is caused by desire, and that the transcendence of desire and suffering will eventually lead to enlightenment, or nirvana (extinction of desire and consciousness). Any concept of an eternal self is an illusion. See MYSTIC UNION, NIRVANA PRINCIPLE, ZEN BUDDHISM.

budding   An asexual form of reproduction in which a new organism starts as a bud protruding from the parental body, later separating and becoming independent. This occurs with primitive one-celled organisms such as the amoeba.

buddy stage   (H. S. Sullivan) A period of adolescence during which individuals form close personal attachments to others of their own sex.

buddy system   The pairing of two people for any of a variety of purposes, as in two people trying to quit smoking, each agreeing to help the other through a smoking-related problem; two scuba divers swimming together to account for each other; a competent worker training a neophyte.

buffer (items)   Items on a test or in an experiment, that do not really count, given for a variety of reasons, sometimes to prevent participants from knowing the real purpose of the materials.

buffering   In industry, a procedure to make departments of companies more independent of each other, by providing a structure to integrate them.

buffoonery psychosis   A type of hyperkinetic catatonia, or hyperkinetic motor psychosis, characterized by awkward and inept buffoon behavior, for example, pouring water onto the floor instead of into a cup, while otherwise seeming well oriented. Described as a flight into disease to escape reality. Also known as faxen psychosis. See FACTITIOUS DISORDERS, GANSER SYNDROME.

bufotenin(e)   A hallucinogen found in the poison gland of toads as well as in plant sources. Has been reported in the urine of some patients with schizophrenia. Bufotenine is chemically related to lysergic acid diethylamide (LSD), psilocybin, and dimethyltryptamine (DMT). See PSYCHEDELICS.

bug   In computer terminology, an error. Term has become generalized to mean any kind of an error in a procedure or process and in mechanical or electrical instruments.

bugger(y)   Vague term sometimes used in legal documents as a synonym for sodomy, or sexual anilism.

Bühler baby tests   (C. Bühler & H. Hetzer) A series of tests measuring infant development. See BIOLOGICAL LIFE EVENTS, LIFE TENDENCIES.

building-fear   See BATOPHOBIA, DOMATOPHOBIA.

built-in behavior   See INSTINCT.

bulb   1. Any globular structure. 2. Obsolete name for medulla oblongata.

bulbar   Pertaining to a bulb or bulblike structure, for example, the eyeball, but especially the medulla oblongata.

bulbar paralysis   Muscle impairment due to damage in the motor centers of the medulla oblongata.

bulbar retraction reflex   The automatic retraction of the eye with closing of the nictitating membrane (in animals), when the conjunctiva or cornea is touched.

bulbocavernous reflex   See VIRILE REFLEX.

bulbopontine region   That portion of the brain consisting of the pons plus the portion of the medulla oblongata lying dorsad of it.

bulbospongiosus muscle   A urogenital muscle, serving as a urine accelerator in both sexes, as an ejaculation aid in males, and a weak vaginal sphincter in females. Also known as bulbocavernosus muscle, or, if in women, sphincter cunni or constrictor vaginas, or in men, ejaculator seminis.

bulbotegmental reticular formation   A portion of the reticular activating system (RAS) that passes through the medulla oblongata.

bulbourethral glands   Two mucus-secreting glands located on either side of the male urethra, near the urethral sphincter. They are homologous to the Bartholin glands in the female reproductive tract. Also known as Cowper's glands.

bulimarexia   An eating disorder in which periods of bulimia are followed by self-induced vomiting. Also known as bulmorexia. See ANOREXIA NERVOSA, BULIMIA.

bulimia (nervosa)   An eating disorder characterized by repeated episodes of uncontrolled consumption of large quantities of food and drink in a short time (binge eating). The episodes are followed by dieting, vomiting, or the use of cathartics. Also known as binge eating, bulaemia, boulimia, bulimy, eating compulsion, hyperorexia, polyphagia. See ACORIA, ANOREXIA (NERVOSA), APPETITIVE BEHAVIOR, BINGE-EATING SYNDROME, BULMOREXIA, HYPERBULIMIA, HYPERPHAGIA, OBESITY.

bulky color   A transparent, three-dimensional color experience, as observed for example, in looking at a colored liquid.

bumps of the head   See CRANIOMETRY, PHRENOLOGY.

bundle hypothesis   (M. Wertheimer) The study of consciousness and sensory experience as a composite of elements held together by "and-connections," senseless agglutinations (*sinnlose Und Verbindungen*) or hookups (*Kuppelungen*). Other Gestalt psychologists protested against the blind reductionism of this approach. See GESTALT.

bundling   An early American human courting procedure still used in some communities (for example, among some conservative old-school Amish and Mennonites). A man and a woman who were interested in dating one another, or who indicated their intention of marrying each other were permitted to go to bed together by their respective parents. The (fully-dressed) man and woman were commonly separated from each other by a board running down the middle of the bed (a bundling board) and sometimes by each being put into a separate "sack" (a bundling sack) so that only their heads protruded. The intention was for the two to get to know each other better via conversation. See NIGHT CRAWLING.

Bunsan Naikan   The essence of the Naikan treatment process. The Sensei (trainer) visits the client or patient periodically to encourage self-examination, especially of personal history of relations with relatives and friends. See ZEN BUDDHISM.

Bunsen-Roscoe law   A theory that the visual threshold for light is a mathematical function expressed as the product of the stimulus intensity and stimulus duration. Formula: $T \times I = c$, where I is intensity of light, T is a time of 50 milliseconds or less. Also known as the photographic law. In visual science, the relationship is known as Bloch's law. Named after German chemist and physicist Robert W. Bunsen (1811–1899), and British chemist Henry E. Roscoe (1833–1915). See RECIPROCITY LAW.

bureaucracy   (M. Weber) Originally describing a government's organization into separate departments to generate an efficient organization, it has become a pejorative term, implying narrowness, rigidity, formality, and red tape.

bureaucratic leader 1. A leader whose responsibilities and leadership style are largely determined by the position in a hierarchical organization, as in the military. 2. A leader who rigidly "follows the book" or sticks to prescribed routines, making no allowance for extenuating circumstances.

Buridan's Ass (J. Buridan) An illustration of the approach-approach type of conflict that takes the form of an ass (donkey) poised exactly in the middle between two identical haystacks unable to make up his mind which one to eat, and then starving to death. See ABULIA.

Burmese Pyramid **Tower of Hanoi**

burnout 1. Exhaustion or failure, especially in a job or career. Term is mainly applied to middle-aged persons performing at a high level until stress and tension take their toll. 2. A reaction to work stress resulting in such reactions as apathy, emotional exhaustion, withdrawal and refusal to continue this kind of work. See BURNED-OUT. 3. Occupationally-related stress syndrome, found among many in the helping professions, characterized by a triad of symptoms: emotional exhaustion, cynicism, and loss of self-efficacy. The Maslach Burnout Inventory (MBI) assesses individual differences in the extent of burnout in each of these three domains. Also spelled burn-out.

burned See BURNT, ODOR PRISM.

burned-out Phrase applied primarily to chronic patients with schizophrenia who have deteriorated to an apathetic, withdrawn, anergic state. Also known as anergic schizophrenia. See ANERGIA, BURNOUT.

burnt A quality of olfactory sensation of which smoke is a typical example. One of the primary odors in the Henning odor prism, but called empyreumatic in Zwaardemaker's smell theory.

burst Sudden increase in the intensity of any response.

burundanga Colombian name for scopolamine, typically slipped into beverages to induce compliance. Street name is scoop. See DATE-RAPE DRUG.

business game A training method in which teams of employees compete in solving simulated management problems. See BRAINSTORMING.

business psychology The original name of what is now known as industrial/organizational (I/O) psychology.

Buss-Durkee Inventory (A. H. Buss & A. Durkee) A questionnaire that attempts to measure feelings of aggression and active aggression.

butch Slang for a lesbian, especially one taking the aggressive sexual role and who tends to look, act, and dress in a masculine manner. See LESBIAN, SAPPHISM.

butterfly effect See SENSITIVE DEPENDENCE.

buzz group/session A small subdivided group whose purpose is to involve each member in active discussion to ascertain their feelings or opinions. The results are then conveyed to the main group by a spokesperson.

buzz group(s) Phrase intended to indicate the existence of separate coexisting discussion groups at conferences and training sessions due to the sounds of voices co-mingling in the same room.

buzz word Any phrase that calls for a uniform response, for example, in answering the question "How are you?", the usual response, even from someone sick, is "Fine." Or, the obligatory opening statement of a speaker, such as "I am honored to be here tonight . . ."

B values See METANEEDS.

BVMGT Bender-Visual-Motor Gestalt Test

BVRT Benton Visual Retention Test

B wave of electroretinogram A large positive wave pattern that follows a brief negative A wave as part of a complex electrical response to stimulation of an animal's retina by a flash of light. The effect is recorded by microelectrodes placed in either the rods or cones. See ELECTRORETINOGRAM.

BWS battered-wife syndrome

by-idea A secondary thought or symbol that displaces a primary or latent thought. According to Emil Kraepelin, the by-idea is the common feature in dream paraphrasias. Also known as metaphoric paralogia.

bystander apathy (effect) A tendency for people to more likely act in an emergency or come to the aid of others when they are alone. Or conversely, the lesser likelihood of an observer to help people in trouble if other people are present. Also known as bystander effect, bystander intervention (effect), bystander involvement. See DIFFUSION OF RESPONSIBILITY.

C

c̄ An abbreviation used in prescriptions, meaning "with" (Latin *cum*).

c 1. A statistical correction factor. 2. Value of a correction. 3. See C FACTOR.

C 1. Any constant. 2. See CELSIUS SCALE. 3. Class. 4. In Rorschach test scoring, a symbol for color response. 5. The contingency coefficient. 6. A control condition. 7. See CONTROLLED VARIABLE. 8. Slang for cocaine. 9. (C. L. Hull) Larger habit strength. 10. Larger reaction potential. 11. A state of animal neuron activity. 12. In signal detection theory, a measure of response bias. Applied to recognition memory. 13. cathode (also abbreviated **CA**).

CA 1. See CATECHOLAMINE(S). 2. Chronological age or life age (also abbreviated **C.A.**). 3. Cocaine Anonymous. 4. Child abuse. 5. See COEFFICIENT OF ASSOCIATION. 6. See CAUDALITY. 7. See CATHODE.

caapi A powerful hallucinogenic beverage made from the stems of the vine *banisteriopsis caapi*, and the leaves of the shrub *prestonia amazonica*, both Peruvian. The pharmacologically active ingredient is harmaline, a psychotomimetic drug. Also known as *ayahuasca, yagé*.

cabbie position A sitting position in which the weight of the body rests on the pelvis, the arms are laying loosely across the thighs, hands are not touching, the head is slightly forward.

cable properties The decreasing passive conduction of electrical current along an axon.

cable tensiometry In exercise physiology, the measurement of muscular strength through a tensiometer, which shows the tension in a cable (by measuring its resistance to deflection) being pulled by an arm or leg.

cachexia A state of emaciation, extreme weakness, and wasting away due to malnutrition associated with chronic diseases. A similar condition may occur in anorexia nervosa. Also known as Caucasus. See HYPOPHYSEAL CACHEXIA.

cachinnation An unrestrained and inappropriate type of laughter observed in disorganized types of schizophrenia.

cacod(a)emonomania A delusion in which patients believe they are possessed by an evil spirit. Also known as cacod(a)emonia. See EXORCISM, DISORGANIZED TYPE OF SCHIZOPHRENIA, HEBEPHRENIA.

cacogenesis Abnormal growth or development.

cacogenic 1. Pertaining to cacogenesis. 2. Refers to deteriorating factors inherent in heredity, as contrasted with eugenic influences.

cacogeusia A bad taste, particularly the perception of bad taste even when there is nothing in the mouth, sometimes experienced by people with idiopathic epilepsy, somatic delusional states, and those receiving tranquilizer therapy.

cacolalia An uncontrollable impulse to use obscene words and expressions. See COPROLALIA.

cacophoria A generalized feeling of unhappiness; the opposite of euphoria.

cacosmia A kind of parosmia characterized by the persistent experience of displeasing odors, especially nonexistent odors. See PAROSMIA.

cacosomnia Obsolete term for insomnia.

CAD coronary artery disease

caduceus A symbol representing a physician, consisting of a rod with one or two snakes entwining it, and with one or two wings at the top. See SNAKE SYMBOL, SYMBOLISM.

Caesarian section A surgical procedure in which an incision is made through the abdominal and uterine walls to deliver a fetus. The name stems from the belief that Gaius Julius Caesar (100–44 B.C.) was delivered in this manner. Also known as C-section.

cafeteria feeding (experiments) (C. Davis) Research on animals and infants that consists of providing them with dietary choices to see how well they choose balanced life-sustaining nutrition.

cafeteria style A system that allows people to choose alternatives from a selection, typically in the context of employee fringe benefits.

caffeine A xanthine derivative found mainly in coffee, many soft drinks, and some analgesic, cold-relief, or sleep-aid over-the-counter combination drugs. Acts as a psychomotor stimulant and mild diuretic. Effects include quickened respiration and increased pulse rate, and larger doses cause insomnia and jitteriness. This substance has now been recognized in the DSM-IV as a source of potential transient psychiatric problems. See CAFFEINE-INDUCED DISORDERS.

caffeine-induced disorders   Excessive coffee or tea ingestion can lead to an overexcited intoxication, anxiety, sleep loss, gastrointestinal problems, and other symptoms which often need to be differentiated from other psychological conditions. Some people seek treatment for anxiety, for example, not recognizing that their excessive use of coffee or tea can cause these symptoms. "Caffeinism" can also be precipitated by "keep awake" pills. See CAFFEINISM.

caffeinism   A pathological disorder caused by caffeine, characterized by restlessness, nervousness, insomnia, muscle twitching, and gastrointestinal problems. Can progress to cardiac arrhythmia, agitation, and incoherent thinking, and with a dose of 10 grams of caffeine, to seizures, respiratory failure, and death. See CAFFEINE-INDUCED DISORDERS.

cafta   A stimulant herb in Africa. See KAT.

CAGE   See CUT DOWN, ANNOYED, GUILT FEELINGS, EYE-OPENER.

CAH   congenital adrenal hyperplasia

CAI   computer-assisted instruction

Cain complex   A set of attitudes characterized by rivalry, competition, and destructive impulses directed toward a brother. Also known as brother complex.

Cain jealousy   (I. D. Suttie) An older child's hostility to a younger sibling for usurping parental attention.

Cain-Levine Social Competency Scale   (L. F. Cain & S. Levine) An instrument assessing the competence of trainable mentally handicapped children from 5 to 13 years of age, yielding scores on self-help, social skills, initiative, communication, and total social competency.

cainotophobia   An excessive fear of new things, especially new ideas. Also known as cenotophobia. See IDEOPHOBIA, KAINOPHOBIA, NEOPHOBIA.

Cairn's stupor   A condition characterized by stupor, rigidity, postural catatonia, and a lack of spontaneous emotion or movement. Also known as akinetic stupor, diencephalic stupor. See AKINETIC MUTISM.

cajoling   A technique of poking fun at clients used by counselors and psychotherapists to get clients to be more open, by making humorous statements to indicate disbelief, such as "And so, you are the smartest person in the whole family, right?"

CAL   See COMPUTER-ASSISTED INSTRUCTION/LEARNING.

calamitous death   A premature or unexpected death, usually due to accidents or violence.

calamus scriptorius   (writer's pen—Latin) The caudal termination of the floor of the fourth ventricle on the dorsal surface of the medulla oblongata of the brain.

calcarine area   A spur-shaped projection of the occipital lobe that is a part of the visual projection area.

calcarine cortex   Cerebral cortex surrounding the calcarine fissure in the occipital lobe of the human brain, the locus for visual sensations. See VISUAL CORTEX.

calcarine fissure   A fissure on the mesial surface of the cerebral hemisphere, which runs forward from the extreme rear, below the cuneus, to join the parieto-occipital fissure.

calcium-deficiency disorders   Effects of calcium deficiency which commonly include rickets in children, marked by deformed bones and teeth and lax muscles. Lack of vitamin D contributes to inadequate absorption of calcium from food. See OSTEOMALACIA.

calculating geniuses   People, sometimes with subnormal intelligence, who are able to quickly provide answers to complicated numerical computations. Explanations for these abilities are diverse, including: (a) use of a variety of shortcuts such as algorithms; (b) the practice of such computations until ability is outstanding, including storing partial results in short-term memory while calculating the next step; (c) memorization of answers to common problems, such as cube roots of large numbers. However, some such people can do things for reasons that defy explanation. See CALENDAR CALCULATION, LIGHTNING CALCULATORS.

calendar   See CATALOG.

calendar age   **chronological age**

calendar calculation   The rare ability to identify the day of the week for any given date, such as June 1, 1914 in seconds. Calendar calculators are frequently idiot savants with little or no mathematical ability but may be able to perform other feats with the calendar, as in answering the question "In what years did April 16 fall on a Sunday?" No satisfactory explanation has been found for this skill. See CALCULATING GENIUSES, LIGHTNING CALCULATORS.

calendar method of birth control   The restriction of coitus to the least fertile times of a woman's menstrual cycle (the few days before and after the calculated day of ovulation, which is generally 14 days before the onset of menstruation).

calf love   **puppy love**

Calgary General Hospital Aggression Scale   A research instrument intended to identify types of patients who are aggressive. Covers three areas: provocation, aggressive behavior, interactive aggressive behavior.

calibration   1. Standardizing or graduating an instrument or laboratory procedure. 2. The process or result of translating the values given by a certain instrument into terms of a known standard. The relations determined are made permanently available, either by marking the standard values on the instrument itself, or by means of a formula, table, or graph indicating the standard values as related to the corresponding values given by the instrument.

calibration of measures   (L. Sechrest) Establishment of a means for transforming the values of one measure into those of another, including the transformation of scores on scales and other instruments into their behavioral implications.

California Achievement Tests (CAT)   Four batteries of tests of sequential difficulty, each measuring the same general areas of school learning: vocabulary, arithmetic reasoning, reading comprehension, arithmetic fundamentals, spelling, and mechanics of English and grammar.

California F scale   Theodor Adorno's fascism scale (F scale).

California Infant Scale   See BAYLEY SCALES OF INFANT DEVELOPMENT.

California Infant Scale for Motor Development A battery of 76 items to assess motor development from birth to three years, such as sitting without support, walking alone, walking up and down stairs.

California Personality Inventory (CPI) (H. G. Gough) A questionnaire of items related to normal healthy functioning.

California Psychological Inventory Test (CPIT) A self-report inventory that draws about half of its 480 items from the Minnesota Multiphasic Personality Inventory (MMPI), scored for such personality characteristics as self-control, dominance, sociability, self-acceptance, sense of well-being, and achievement-via-independence.

California Tests of Mental Maturity (CTMM) Scales designed to measure various factors, such as memory and logical reasoning, at five different levels of difficulty.

California Tests of Personality (CTP) A type of personality questionnaire intended to yield scores on personal worth, self-reliance, sense of freedom, belongingness, various social skills, and total adjustment.

California Verbal Learning Test-Adult Version (CVLT) (D. C. Delis, J. H. Kramer, E. Kaplan, & B. A. Ober) An examination for use in assessing verbal learning and memory deficits in individuals 17 years and older, including older persons and the neurologically impaired.

California Verbal Learning Test-Children's Version (CVLT-C) (D. C. Delis, J. H. Kramer, E. Kaplan, & B. A. Ober) An examination for individuals 5–16 years of age that assesses verbal learning and memory within the context of everyday memory tasks.

callback 1. In consumer psychology, a second interview, usually done in marketing surveys, to check consistency of reports. 2. In an employment application process, especially in theatrical and musical auditions, seeing an applicant for a second or even a third time during the selection process to find the right person for a specific goal.

call boy/girl A prostitute who books clients by telephone. Originally (and before the telephone), one who was on call. See MALE HOMOSEXUAL PROSTITUTION.

calling cards Professional slang for complaints of clients as they seek psychological help, often avoiding what really is bothering them.

callomania Having delusions of one's own inordinate beauty.

callosal Relating to the corpus callosum.

callosal gyrus **cingulate gyrus**

callosal sulcus A fissure or groove that separates the corpus callosum and the cingulate gyrus along the medial side of the cerebral hemispheres of the brain.

callosum A link between the two cerebral hemispheres composed of white matter. See CORPUS CALLOSUM.

calomel electrodes Electric cell terminals consisting of mercury in contact with mercurous chloride used to record electric potentials of brain cells. Used often as a reference electrode since such electrodes have a constant potential.

caloric intake The consumption of units of energy in food measured in calories. See CALORIE.

caloric nystagmus See NYSTAGMUS.

caloric irrigation The flowing of heated or cooled water into or over a body area for therapy or research, as in the ear canals to stimulate the vestibular system; see NYSTAGMUS.

calorie A unit of heat equivalent to the amount of energy required to raise the temperature of one gram of water by 1° Celsius. Every bodily process requires an expenditure of calories. The brain uses approximately 500 calories per day provided through the metabolism of glucose. Calorie is being replaced by joule (an SI unit equal to 0.24 calorie).

calorimeter A device for directly measuring heat production in the organism.

calorization The application of heat. Specifically, the application of heat to the region of the semicircular canals of the inner ear.

camel-in-the-tent technique The asking for a small allowance, favor, sale, etc., to establish grounds to ask for increases later. See DOOR-IN-THE-FACE EFFECT, FOOT-IN-THE DOOR EFFECT/TECHNIQUE.

camera obscura A darkened box-like enclosure having an aperture and lens through which light enters to form an image on the opposite surface, used for drawing exact pictures or taking photographs.

camisole Infrequently used term for straitjacket.

cAMP See ADENOSINE 3′,5′-CYCLIC PHOSPHATE.

camphoraceous (J. D. Amoore et al.) Of the nature of camphor. One of the seven basic stereochemical smell theory qualities having a sharp odor such as that exuded by the camphor tree (*Cinnamomum camphora*).

campimeter A flat chart used to map out the visual field. Also known as perimeter.

campimetry The measurement of the visual field of a person. The normal field of vision is limited by the area that can be seen peripherally while the eye is fixed on a single point.

camptocormia A hysterical or conversion symptom in which the back is bent forward at a sharp angle, often accompanied by lumbar pain, and impotence. Most frequently observed in soldiers. Also known as prosternation. See WAR NEUROSIS.

campus crisis center A separate unit on some college campuses where usually emergency help is available for a variety of personal problems.

Canadian Psychological Association Formed by Canadian academics in 1938–1939 mainly to insure that the expertise of its members was used maximally in the forthcoming war, it served as a regulatory body until the 10 provincial and one territorial associations/societies took this over. Comprises 23 sections, publishes several journals, holds annual conventions, promotes psychology in terms of science, education, and practice. Also known as *Société Canadienne de Psychologie*.

canal-boat children Refers to children living on English canal boats, who were tested periodically using standard intelligence tests. Children who did not go to school scored increasingly poorly on such tests. Results have been interpreted either as "not going to school lowers intelligence," or "intelligence tests are really scholastic rather than intelligence tests." See PSEUDORETARDATION.

canalization 1. A theory that as certain neural pathways are used, a permanent pathway is often established. 2. (P. Janet) The channeling of needs into specific patterns of gratification. A progressive narrowing of drives that structure perceptions by bringing them into its schema, including the assimilation processes of conceptual organization, and commonality of schema. Related to Sigmund Freud's cathexis and Jean Piaget's sensorimotor scheme of intelligence. 3. In behavior genetics, Waddington's description of the process by which characteristics take a narrow path or developmental course. Apparently, preservative forces help to protect or buffer the individual from environmental extremes. 4. (L. M. Wallack) The channeling of existing attitudes or behavior patterns in a new direction.

cancellation test A task of psychomotor ability, used for measuring clerical aptitude, requiring the participant to cancel out randomly scattered symbols, such as marking every "e" on ten pages of manuscript in a 5 minute time limit. The number correct would be every "e" marked, minus those missed, minus those marked that should not have been.

cancer reactions Emotional responses to the presence or possibility of carcinoma, ranging from acceptance of the inevitable and determination to conquer the disease, to pathological reactions such as interpretation of loss of an organ as punishment for a real or fancied infraction. See PHOBIA.

cancer(o)phobia Excessive fear of cancer. Some psychoanalysts relate this phobia to fear of castration or the dread of being devoured from within. Also known as carcinophobia.

canchasmous Hysterical laughing noted in some forms of mental disorders, notably in hebephrenic (disorganized) schizophrenia.

candela (cd) A standard measure of luminosity, the SI unit of luminous intensity equal to 1 lumen per m^2. Also known as candle. See LUMINOUS FLUX.

candle The unit of luminous intensity of a source of light. The international candle, agreed upon in 1909, is reproduced from any one of a number of carefully intercompared standard incandescent lamps, operated and used under specified conditions. See CANDELA, LUMINOUS INTENSITY.

cannabis General term for plants such as *cannabis indica* or *cannabis sativa* that contain significant amounts of delta-9-tetrahydrocannabinol (THC). Mainly the leaves and buds (flowering tops) are used. Widely used around the world as a recreational drug, offering mild psychedelic effects. When the resin from the buds is condensed, the concentrated substance is called hashish, or "hash." Common slang names include marijuana, dope, grass, pot, bhang (from whence comes the term, "bhang" or "bong" pipe), weed, boo, and pakalolo.

cannabis intoxication Transient behavioral changes while under the effect of cannabis that may include mood lability, impairment of movement and of thinking, acting in an unsocial manner, such as being belligerent or uncommunicative.

cannabis-related disorders A group of symptoms that may develop within a half hour of cannabis use that may include such varied psychological and physical symptoms as rapid heartbeat, dry mouth, inability to concentrate, anxiety, intoxication, an urge to eat ("the munchies"), maladaptive behavior, and persecutory delusions. Cannabis substances can cause psychological dependence, though not physiological dependence to any extent. Their use, like other substances of abuse, can cause a state of intoxication, anxiety, and rarely, short-term psychosis.

cannibalism 1. In psychopathology, a compulsive urge to devour human flesh. A rare symptom observed in schizophrenic and schizophrenia-like psychoses. See KURU. 2. In anthropology, the eating of human flesh is not deemed pathological if it is part of a religious ceremonial or if a dead person is eaten when there is no other food.

cannibalistic fantasy The fantasy of devouring another person which, according to psychoanalytic theory, goes back to the early period of psychosexual development when the infant "incorporates" the mother's breasts during nursing. See INCORPORATION.

cannibalistic fixation In psychoanalytic theory, a libido fixation at the late oral or biting stage, marked by fantasies or impulses of biting, eating, swallowing, and thus eliminating a hated person.

cannibalistic phase/stage The second half of the oral stage in which, according to psychoanalysis, the infant first expresses hostility and aggressiveness by biting mother's breast or the nipple of the bottle during the feeding process. See ORAL-BITING PERIOD.

Cannon-Bard theory (of emotion) (W. B. Cannon, P. A. Bard) A point of view that emotions result from activation of the body's responses to situations of emergencies or threats by body changes such as increased beating of the heart. The thalamus is seen as the seat of emotions, whereas bodily responses come from the hypothalamus. Walter Cannon's modification of the James-Lange theory and modified by Philip Bard; sometimes known as Cannon's theory, hypothalamic theory of Cannon, thalamic theory of Cannon, thalamic theory of emotions. See ACTIVATION THEORY OF EMOTIONS, JAMES-LANGE THEORY, PAPEZ'S THEORY OF EMOTIONS.

Cannon's emergency syndrome (W. B. Cannon) The three Fs of how people will react in situations of great danger and confusion: Flee, Fight, Flight. See EMERGENCY THEORY, GENERAL ADAPTATION SYNDROME.

Cannon-Washburn experiment/technique (W. B. Cannon & A. L. Washburn) A classic study of stomach contractions recorded on a kymograph (via a rubber tube, a manometer, and an inflated balloon in the stomach). The participant (Washburn) pressed a key when he felt hunger pains.

cannula A small hollow tube for either inserting or removing materials, especially to and from the brain.

canon A normative formula or working rule recommended for use in scientific procedure as likely to lead to the discovery of truth. See LAW, METHOD, PRINCIPLE.

canonical Conforming to a general rule. Based on some organizing principle.

canonical correlation   A correlation coefficient describing the degree of relationship between one combination of variables and a second combination of variables.

canon law   The decrees of a church, usually relating to institutional functioning and members' behavior.

canon of ...   See METHOD OF ..., PRINCIPLE OF ...

cantharis   An old folk-substance once considered an aphrodisiac, because one side effect is irritation of the urethra and priapism (sustained erection). (In larger amounts, it can be fatal.) It has a few recognized medical uses, such as being a wart-removal agent or as a counterirritant applied topically for arthritis. It is derived from the dried bodies of a species of a European insect, mainly found in Russia or Spain, whence comes the folk term, "Spanish Fly." Plural is cantharides.

capability   The upper limit of an organism's functional ability at a given stage of its development, with optimal training to function in mental or physical tasks.

capacity   1. Ability to do. See APTITUDE TEST. 2. Potential cubic contents of something, such as a cavity or receptacle. See VITAL CAPACITY.

CAPD   central auditory processing disorder

Capgras' syndrome   (J. M. J. Capgras) A rare psychotic disorder in which the patient insists that other people are not really themselves, but are "doubles" or impostors. Generally considered to be a special symptom of paranoid schizophrenia, organic disorder, or, less often, affective psychoses. See DOPPELGANGER, ILLUSION OF DOUBLES.

capitalism   The economic system of a relatively free market based on the profit motive, associated with Western nations. Term derives from the capital (funding) necessary to build the factories that form the basis of this system.

capitalization on chance   The process of basing a conclusion on data biased in a particular direction by chance factors. Purely random factors often seem to show interpretable patterns, and capitalization on chance involves mistaken inferences from these patterns.

capitation   1. Term used in some private practices of clinical treatment, including in counseling and psychotherapy, where clients or patients are seen with identical fees regardless of the nature of problems. This movement appears to be due to the mounting influence of health management organizations (HMOs) and insurance companies. 2. In health management systems the payment to treatment personnel on the basis of the number of patients they see on the basis of so many dollars per person for a specific period. The intent is to limit costs by having treatment personnel do whatever is necessary to encourage good health to avoid costly treatments.

CAPP   Committee for the Advancement of Professional [psychological] Practice.

capping techniques   Methods used by counselors in directing an interview along less painful or threatening lines for the purpose of lessening the client's anxiety, distress, or resistance.

caprice   Abrupt changes in mode of behavior on the basis of fleeting and unpredictable ideas and feelings.

capricious   Characterizing motions or movements which are free, that is, which lack complete determination.

caprylic   One of nine basic odors according to Zwaardemaker's smell theory, exemplified by cheese or rancid fat. Also known as hircine.

capsaicin   Chemical that makes neurons containing substance P to release it suddenly.

captive products   In consumer psychology, ancillary items required for the operation of products already owned, such as refills that are made only by the same manufacturer.

CAR   conditioned avoidance response

carbachol   A synthetic parasympathomimetic drug, used in the eye for treatment of glaucoma.

carbamazepine (CBZ)   Generic name for an anticonvulsant and also an analgesic used for trigeminal neuralgia. Trade name is Tegretol.

carbohydrate metabolism   Utilization by the body tissues of starch and sugar molecules, which are broken down by various enzymes to simple glucose molecules. The glucose molecule is the ultimate source of cellular energy for the brain and other organs.

carbon-dioxide therapy   (J. Meduna) Inhalation therapy occasionally applied to patients with anxiety, conversion, or psychophysiologic symptoms, sometimes in conjunction with psychotherapy. Rarely used, this approach was introduced by Meduna in the 1940s and used in Europe and to a lesser extent in the United States for a few decades. Patients with neuroses inhale a mixture of this common gas in higher concentrations, blank out, and then recover.

carcinophobia   Excessive fear of cancer, or malignancy. Also known as cancer(o)phobia.

car controls   Special automobile-driving devices for physically challenged persons, such as gearshift extensions, hand controls for brakes, relocated transmission and turn-signal controls, and adjustable seat controls. See DRIVER EDUCATION.

cardiac index   The ratio of cardiac output (heart rate times stroke volume) to surface area.

cardiac muscle   The muscle of the heart, a specialized type of muscle tissue that consists of involuntary striated fibers. See MYOCARDIUM.

cardiac neurosis   1. An anxiety reaction precipitated by a heart condition, the suspicion of having a heart condition, or the fear of developing coronary disease. 2. The overwhelming fear of having a heart attack. Also called cardiophobia.

cardiac pacemakers   See PACEMAKERS.

cardiac psychosis   A disorganization of thought processes associated with an acute state of fear and anxiety following a heart attack.

cardiac reactions   Responses to psychological stimuli that result in abnormal activity of the heart and circulatory system. Anxiety, anger, fear, and excitement are among emotional reactions known to precipitate episodes of angina pectoris.

cardinal disposition/trait   (G. W. Allport) A person's most basic and significant personality characteristic, such as ambitiousness, that influences the person's total behavior.

cardinal number   A number that represents quantity. Compare NOMINAL NUMBERS, ORDINAL NUMBERS.

cardinal point/value (G. Fechner) The point in a quantitative series of sensations at which the difference limen begins to increase according to Weber's law, that is, in proportion to the stimulus.

cardinal virtues (Plato) Leading social virtues, on which all others depend or hinge: prudence, temperance, fortitude, justice.

cardiogram From the word electrocardiogram. A tracing usually on a long narrow slip of paper showing graphically the activity of the heart. The instrument that records such movement is called a cardiograph.

cardiophobia Morbid fear of heart disease or heart problems. See CARDIAC NEUROSIS (meaning 2).

cardiovascular (CV) Pertaining to the heart, arteries, veins and capillaries: the total circulatory system.

cardiovascular reactivity The response of the heart and other parts of the cardiovascular system to mental states due to environmental conditions. See CARDIAC REACTIONS.

card-sorting A test in which the participant is asked to sort randomly mixed cards into specific categories. The test is used to determine learning ability and discriminatory powers, as well as clerical aptitude. Also known as card-sorting task/test.

card-stacking A technique of persuasion by deliberate distortions, suppressing information, overemphasis on selected facts, manipulation of statistics, and quoting rigged research.

CARE Acronym for Communicated Authenticity, Regard, Empathy.

care-and-protection proceedings Intervention by various official agencies including courts on behalf of children's mental, educational and physical care and welfare, especially when parents and relatives are unable or unwilling to be of assistance.

carebaria A form of headache characterized by distressing sensations of pressure or heaviness.

care-based moral reasoning (C. Gilligan) Decisions based on compassion and caring. Usually made by women, in contrast with those based on abstract principles of law and justice, associated more with men.

career 1. The pattern of movements and thoughts in proceeding through life, especially work and social situations. Roughly equivalent to the terms lifestyle and strategies. 2. The pattern of participation in training, experience and events for self-maintenance, social adjustment, and especially work, throughout a person's productive life.

career anchors Perceptions of one's own abilities, motives, and values, leading to efforts to select jobs or careers consistent with these self-perceptions.

career choice Selection of a vocation, often based on parental guidance, vocational counseling, identification with admired figures, trial or part-time jobs, training opportunities, interest, ability, and chance opportunity.

career conference A vocational program provided by some high schools and colleges in which representatives of a given occupational field meet with interested students to provide information and answer questions related to the requirements for and opportunities in the field.

career development Elements of personal experience that contribute to the formation of a "work identity," including life experience, education, career choice, on-the-job experience, level of professional achievement, and degree of satisfaction.

Career Maturity Inventory (J. O. Crites) A series of questionnaires used to determine the extent to which adolescents are prepared for and are realistic about their career decisions. Measures include realism, competence, attitude, decisiveness, and orientation.

career patterns 1. (J. L. Holland) Six dimensions of personal orientation patterns in occupations: realistic, intellectual, social, conventional, enterprising, artistic. 2. (E. H. Schein) Three basic career patterns in organizations: (a) engineering-based (offering opportunities for higher earnings); (b) scientific-professional (providing intrinsic challenges); and (c) pure professional careers (providing service to others.) 3. (D. E. Super & D. T. Hall) Six major stages in choosing an occupation: exploration, reality testing, experimentation, establishment, maintenance, decline.

career pattern theories Approaches that seek to explain lifespan sequences of occupational choices as a function of developmental stages and roles; D. E. Super's work epitomizes this genre.

career planning A vocational-guidance program designed to assist a client in one or more aspects of the decision-making process. An appraisal of desires and abilities is formulated in relation to existing occupational opportunities. Various tests may be administered to aid a counselor in assessing a client's skills and aptitudes.

career workshop A study group in which occupational opportunities and requirements are discussed and explored.

caregiver 1. A person involved in the process of identifying, preventing, or treating an illness or disability; in child psychiatry, a person who attends to the needs of an infant or child. Caregivers include, among others, family physicians, pediatricians, nurses, social workers, and indigenous nonprofessionals. 2. A broad term for whoever takes care of a child or children. Also known as caretaker.

caregiver burden The effect, sometimes tiresome when one person or even several have assumed responsibility for a helpless or near-helpless person, usually a relative such as a child with a disability or a senile parent. The burden may be physical, emotional, financial, or all three. See CARETAKING BEHAVIOR.

care of the body surface (COBS) (P. L. Borchelt) The grooming, bathing, dusting, preening, rubbing, or scratching of the organism's own skin or outer membrane or occasionally that of a conspecific (member of same species). Takes considerable time and energy in many species from marine invertebrates to primates.

care perspective A theory of moral development which describes people in terms of their connectedness with others; more emphasis should be given to relationships and concern for others in understanding what is moral. See SOCIAL INTEREST.

caressa **karezza**

caretaker **caregiver** (meaning 2)

caretaker speech **child-directed speech**

car fear See AMAXOPHOBIA.

cargo cult Any of a variety of native quasi-religious movements in various South Pacific islands which hold that at a chosen time (for example, the millennium), the spirits of the dead or other divinities will return in airplanes, ships, etc., with large cargoes of modern goods, and the believers will be free from having to work or being controlled by foreigners.

caricature A drawing or description of an individual, often someone in authority, in which notable features are exaggerated. Usually to ridicule.

carnal Euphemism for sexual, as in carnal knowledge, carnal congress, carnal appetite. Term derives from the Latin word for flesh.

carousel dynamics In interpersonal relations marked by poor communication, a situation in which one negative experience leads to others.

carpal age A measure of physiological or anatomical age of a child, rather than chronological age, by using x-rays to determine the degree of ossification of the carpals (wrists).

carpal tunnel syndrome (CTS) Pain in the wrist, hand, or thumb following prolonged and repetitive use of the hands, as in keyboarding and playing computer games. Results from compression of the median nerve in the volar area of the wrist. Also seen with acromegaly, myxedema, and pregnancy. See REPETITIVE STRAIN INJURY.

carpentered environment An environment consisting of straight lines, such as buildings of the Bauhaus era, based on the concept of "less is more" with habitations being of the minimalist kind, generating efficient filing-cabinet-like houses.

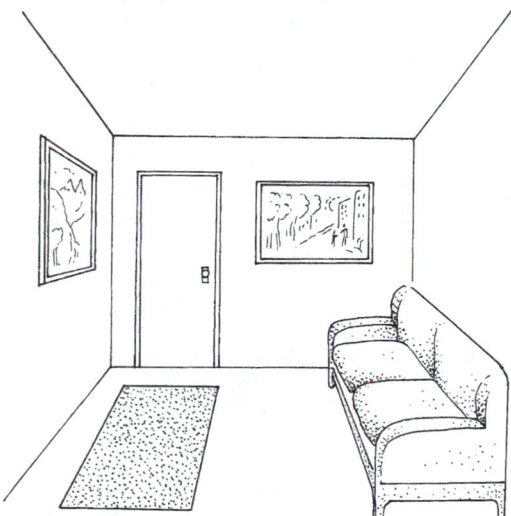

carpentered environment

Carpenter's syndrome (G. Carpenter) Autosomal-recessive hereditary disorder marked by acrocephaly (narrow pointed head), syndactyly (webbing) of the fingers and toes, subnormal intelligence, and usually obesity. Also known as acrocephalopolysyndactyly. Named after British physician George Carpenter (1859–1910).

carphenazine (maleate) Generic name for a phenothiazine tranquilizer of the piperazine group. Used as an antipsychotic medication. Also known as prochlorperazine.

carrier 1. A person or animal with an asymptomatic infection that may be transmitted to others. 2. A person whose chromosomes contain one or more genes for a dominant or recessive trait that can be expressed as a birth defect in an offspring.

carrying task research Research on maximum loads males and females can personally transport under varying conditions of distance, carrying technique, and environmental conditions.

carryover effects Lasting consequences that tested or experimental participants subjects may have following research participation.

Cartesian coordinate system (R. Descartes) A coordinate system that fixes any point in a plane by stating its distance from each of the two intersecting lines called the coordinate axes. If axes intersect at right angles, the Cartesian coordinates are rectangular; if not, they are oblique.

Cartesian dualism (R. Descartes) René Descartes' separation of the mind and body, in which the mind is an incorporeal substance (*res cogitans*) separate and distinct from the body, which is a material substance (*res extensa*). Descartes held that the rational acts of the soul, or mind, and the mechanical activities of the body can be studied independently of each other, but also asserted that mind acts upon the body and body on mind, and proposed that the interaction of mind and body occurred in a part of the pineal body termed the conarium. See DUALISM.

Cartesian(ism) Referring to René Descartes.

Cartesian self (R. Descartes) According to René Descartes, the concept of self is an innate idea, which like the idea of God or of perfection, arises from consciousness alone without need for direct sensory experience.

cartridge weights A set of weights extending in uniform steps over a certain range of intensities and used to determine accuracy of judgment to intensive differences of touch, hefting, etc. The weights were identical in appearance, looked like shotgun shells, and were used in the 1916 Stanford-Binet test.

Carus' typology (C. G. Carus) A classification of individuals by five body types (athletic, phlegmatic, phthisic, cerebral, sterile) proposed by Carl Carus.

CAs See CATECHOLAMINE(S).

Casanova complex Romantic and sexual behavior characterized by many short-term "conquests." Generally considered a disorder of a male who is unsure of himself as a man and continually seeks reassurance of his desirability. See DON JUANISM, EROTOCRAT, NYMPHOMANIA.

case 1. A specific type or example. 2. In research, designating one of a series of observations or trials, or one set of conditions among many that are included in the research. 3. Refers to a person in a particular condition. See following entries. 4. In typography, upper and lower case, meaning capital and small letters.

case advocate See ADVOCATE.

case alternation In research on reading, changing characters in stimulus words between upper and lower case in one of six ways: (1) intact (RIGHTS/rights), (2) changes between pairs (RiGhTs), (3) change after the second letter (RIghts), (4) transition after the third one (RIGhts), (5) change after the fourth (RIGHts), and (6) transition after each pair (RIghTS).

case-finding   In psychiatry, methods of identifying individuals who need treatment by administering screening tests, finding people who had contacted social agencies or mental-health facilities, obtaining referrals from general practitioners, or via triage after a disaster.

case grammar approach   In linguistics, the parsing of sentences based on the semantic, not the syntactic, role of the word in the sentence.

case history   A record of information relating to a person's medical or psychological condition. Usually containing test results, interviews, professional evaluations, as well as sociological, occupational, and educational data used to understand the person's background, relationships, behavior, and adjustment to be able to make recommendations. Also known as case study. See METHODS OF PSYCHOLOGY.

case load   The number of cases or comparative difficulty of cases assigned to a physician, therapist, social worker, or counselor.

case manager   A clinician responsible for all procedures and resources necessary for patients or others unable to take care of themselves, and who coordinates behaviors of others involved in the caring processes.

case method   An industrial training technique in which management or supervisory personnel are presented with an actual or hypothetical business problem in writing, on film, through recordings, or with individuals playing different roles. In any of several ways they indicate how they would handle the problem, and generally their solutions are discussed and evaluated. See SOCIO-DRAMA.

case work   See CASEWORKER, SOCIAL CASE WORK.

caseworker   In most instances, a social worker, a person who usually takes an individual's history, deals with other professionals in various ways during any kind of treatment and usually follows the client or patient to the end of the engagement with the institution, clinic, or hospital. See SOCIAL CASE WORK.

Caspar Hauser experiment   A research procedure that raises animals in total isolation and studies their behavior during and after their confinement. Named after a German boy who had been confined in a cellar his whole life. He had mental retardation, and whether the confinement was the cause of this retardation is not known.

cassina leaves   Foliage of *Ilex cassine*. The leaves contain caffeine and are used in Apalache tea, yaupon, or youpon herbal teas. Members of the Creek nation (Amerinds) roasted the leaves and made a drink that only men were permitted to drink.

caste   A level or rank in a social hierarchy that a person is born into. Complex approved and nonapproved interactions between castes exist in some societies and religions, such as India and some religions, such as Hinduism. See CLASS.

castrate   1. In physiology, to remove from an organism its means of reproduction, testes (geld) or ovaries (spay). 2. Metaphorically, to make a person dependent, weak, or impotent by social attacks.

castrating woman   Unfairly applied to a wife or mother who emasculates a man or men in the psychological sense through domination, derogation, and insistence on making all the decisions unilaterally. An equivalent term does not exist for men who dominate and derogate women. Probably the closest is "macho pig." See MASCULINE SUPERIORITY, PENIS ENVY.

castration   Removal of the male testes or female ovaries by surgery or their inactivation by radiation, parasites, infections, or drugs. It alters the hormonal function of the organism and generally reduces libido. Major behavioral changes seldom result from castration. See CHEMICAL CASTRATION, EUNUCH, ORCHIECTOMY, SKOPTSY.

castration anxiety/fear   See CASTRATION COMPLEX.

castration complex   (S. Freud) According to psychoanalytic theory, boys are afraid of being castrated by their fathers for having sexual feelings for their mothers. In girls, the castration complex takes the form of an unconscious fantasy that the penis has been removed as a punishment, for which they blame their mother. See ACTIVITY CASTRATION COMPLEX, ANAL CASTRATION ANXIETY, ANTICIPATORY AUTOCASTRATION, ELECTRA COMPLEX, OEDIPUS COMPLEX, PENIS ENVY.

castration threat (anxiety)   (S. Freud) In psychoanalytic theory, a reputed concern of young men that their fathers will want to castrate them for having sexual desire for their mothers. See CASTRATION COMPLEX.

casuistry   Reasoning about general principles of religious concepts or ethics on various issues, such as abortion.

CAT   1. See CHOLINE ACETYLASE. 2. Computerized axial tomography. 3. college admission tests. 4. California Achievement Tests. 5. Cognitive Abilities Test. 6. Children's Apperception Test (also abbreviated C.A.T.).

catabolic phase   See CATABOLISM, METABOLISM.

catabolism   The phase of metabolism marked by the breakdown of tissues and expenditure of energy. Also spelled katabolism. See ANABOLISM, METABOLISM.

catagelophobia   Morbid fear of being humiliated, laughed at, or ridiculed. Also spelled katagelophobia.

catalepsy   1. (Hippocrates) A sudden attack of illness. 2. A morbid condition in which the skeletal muscles become semirigid, and will remain in any position in which they are placed, for long periods of time without evidence of discomfort. Also known as catalepsia cerea, cataleptic immobility, cerea flexibilitas, flexibilitas cerea, waxy flexibility. See CATATONIC STATE, EPIDEMIC CATALEPSY.

catalexia   A form of dyslexia characterized by a tendency to reread words and phrases. See DYSLEXIA.

catalog   A listing of items arranged in some systematic manner, such as in universities and colleges, the publication listing programs and courses offered, faculty members, regulations, and financial and other basic information.

catalogia   **verbigeration**

catalysis   The alteration of the velocity of a chemical reaction produced by a substance (a catalyst) which may not itself enter into the reaction, or which may combine with a reactant only during some intermediate phase of the reaction. See CATALYST.

catalyst   A substance producing catalysis which is not itself changed during the reaction.

catalytic agent   1. A member in a psychotherapy group who initiates discussion and activates emotional reactions in other members. 2. See CATALYST.

catalytic variable   A variable (X) necessary for two other variables (A & B) to interact in some manner. The catalytic variable (X) "enables" the change.

catamenia   Obsolete term for menstruation.

catamite   Obsolete term for a male homosexual or a boy subjected to pederasty.

catamnesis   1. The medical history of a patient following the onset of a mental or physical disorder. 2. The medical history after the initial examination or after discharge from treatment. Also known as follow-up history.

cataphasia   1. A disorder of speech characterized by involuntary repetition of the same word. See ECHOLALIA. 2. Loss of the ability to speak in a coherent manner, as in knowing the words of a sentence but being unable to put them together in a meaningful manner. 3. Uncontrollable repetition of apparently meaningless words or phrases. A language disorder that occurs in catatonic schizophrenia and in patients with brain lesions. See VERBIGERATION.

cataphora   A semi-coma, intermittent somnolence and partial consciousness. Also known as coma somnolentium.

cataplexy   1. A complete loss of muscle tone as when in a faint. 2. A sudden loss of muscle tone resulting in immobility or collapse of the entire body. It is a temporary condition usually precipitated by an uncontrollable fit of laughter or an event that produces overwhelming anxiety or anger. See NARCOLEPSY, NARCOLEPSY-CATAPLEXY SYNDROME.

cataract   Loss of transparency of the lens or capsule of the eye. See LENS (OF EYE).

catastrophe model   A paradigm that anxiety affects performance in an inverted-U relationship only with low levels of cognitive anxiety; when moderately highs levels of somatic anxiety are accompanied by high levels of cognitive anxiety, a catastrophic decrease in performance ensues.

catastrophe theory   (S. Ferenczi) A psychoanalytic phrase for the patient's belief that sexual intercourse is destructive to the penis.

catastrophic anxiety   A state of overwhelming anxiety and helplessness in patients with organic brain syndromes and aphasia, who, according to Kurt Goldstein (1939) "become agitated and fearful and more than usually inept when presented with once simple tasks that they can no longer do." See CATASTROPHIC REACTION.

catastrophic behavior   (K. Goldstein) Denoting the efforts of patients with aphasia to adapt to their language defects through such defensive reactions as excessive orderliness, disinterest, and aversion. By these means they seek to avoid embarrassment and agitation arising from ineptness in communicating or carrying out simple tasks.

catastrophic expectation   (F. Perls) The fear of possible consequences that accompanies thoughts, wishes, or behaviors that violate or contradict social standards or an internal moral code, for example, a fantasy of future retribution for personal action. See GESTALT THERAPY.

catastrophic illness   An extremely severe or chronic illness with which patients must cope in their own ways, and come to terms with such reactions as: (a) feelings of being cheated, (b) denial of illness, and (c) hesitation to ventilate feelings of shame, guilt, or fear.

catastrophic reaction   1. A breakdown in the ability to cope with a threatening or traumatic situation characterized by acute feelings of inadequacy, insecurity, anxiety and helplessness as well as signs of pallor, sweating, and incipient collapse, indicating physical and mental shock. See DISASTER SYNDROME. 2. According to Kurt Goldstein, extreme agitation, anger, and resistance demonstrated by patients who have lost such skills as language or arithmetic when they try to solve tasks requiring the use of such lost functions. Also known as Goldstein catastrophic reaction.

catastrophic schizophrenia   schizocaria

catastrophize   To view bad things happening to the self as part of an undermining global pattern of evil and pain.

catastrophizing   (A. Ellis) Exaggerating the consequences of mistakes or of unfortunate events. See PESSIMISTIC OUTLOOK.

catathymia   A condition in which an unconscious complex becomes so affect-laden that it produces changes in conscious functioning.

catathymic amnesia   A loss of memory for a specific event although a clear memory remains for all other events.

catathymic crisis   An emotional explosion accompanied by violent, unusual-for-the-person behavior generated usually by unbearable tension. For example, a person commits suicide after losing the family's life savings through an unwise investment; or a normally loving spouse kills the other spouse when asked for a divorce. See ISOLATED EXPLOSIVE DISORDER.

catathymic delusion   (E. Bleuler) A delusion occasioned by an element in the unconscious.

catatonia   1. A syndrome characterized by periods of muscular rigidity, negativism, excitement, and stupor. 2. (K. L. Kahlbaum) A state of muscular rigidity most frequently observed in catatonic schizophrenia. Also known as catatonic state, catatony, katatonia. See CATALEPSY, CATATONIC SCHIZOPHRENIA, TRAUMATIC PSEUDO-CATATONIA.

catatonia mitis   A relatively mild and transient form of catatonia in which stupor and lack of movement are the main symptoms. See BELL'S MANIA.

catatonic   Pertaining to catatonia.

catatonic dementia praecox   A psychosis with specially marked involvement of motor tension, catalepsy, automatic resistance, and contrary action (negativism, mutism, refusal of food from special persons, echolalia, or echopraxia—in general, reactions of submission, passivity, and withdrawal).

catatonic excitement   1. Psychomotor disturbance characterized by excitement, impulsivity, hyperactivity, and combativeness. 2. A symptom of catatonic schizophrenia consisting of periods of extreme restlessness, and excessive motor activity. See CATATONIC SCHIZOPHRENIA.

catatonic negativism   Schizophrenia marked by thought disorders, mutism, posturing and decreased motor activity. See CATATONIC SCHIZOPHRENIA.

catatonic schizophrenia   A type of schizophrenia marked by mental and psychomotor disturbance in which the patient is mute, immobile, resistant to directions, maintains inappropriate postures for long periods of time and may explode into unexpected violence. Also known as catatonic type schizophrenic disorder.

catatonic stupor   1. Psychomotor disturbance characterized by muteness, and negativity, as well as staring, rigidity, and cataplexy. 2. A symptom of catatonic schizophrenia characterized by inaccessibility to stimuli, waxy flexibility, mutism, extreme negativism, and stereotyped behavior. See CATATONIC SCHIZOPHRENIA. 3. A tonic immobility shown by some animals such as certain birds, usually as a result of being placed on their backs.

catatonoid attitude   Catatonia-like behavior characterized by stereotyped responses, such as a vacant smile, in all personal or social situations.

catatony   Rare term for catatonic state, or catatonia.

catch trials   In tests or studies consisting of several trials, trials in which the independent variable is surreptitiously withheld by the experimenter while the participant's responses are recorded as usual, such as in an experiment in which participants identify auditory signals, catch trials are those in which no signal is given. Used to assist the experimenter in determining the participants' level of accuracy and reliability.

catch 22   A dilemma in which the solution causes another problem. See MORAL DILEMMA.

catch-up growth   A period of relatively rapid growth, usually after a period of physical deprivations, such as a long illness, that permits the child to catch up on expected normal development.

catchment area   In community psychiatry, the geographic area that is served by a particular community mental-health center.

cat-cry syndrome   Phrase similar to the French *cri du chat* syndrome.

catechetical method/procedure   1. A method of instruction or of inducing conviction by means of a skillfully devised series of questions, whose answers lead gradually to acknowledgement of the conclusions desired by the questioner. 2. A method used by Socrates to uncover truth, in which a series of questions are asked intended to lead someone to a logical conclusion. Used frequently by some therapists. See SOCRATIC DIALOG/METHOD.

catecholamine(s) (CA or CAs)   1. A type of neurotransmitter which generally is associated with the actions of the sympathetic nervous system and in addition operates in certain areas of the brain, especially epinephrine (adrenaline); norepinephrine (noradrenaline); and dopamine. 2. Monoamines such as dopamine and epinephrine that act as neurotransmitters, involved in regulating moods. 3. Collective name for the fight-flight hormones secreted by the adrenal medulla (the central part of the small endocrine glands that are located on top of the kidneys). These chemicals, epinephrine and norepinephrine (respectively, adrenaline and noradrenaline) were then manufactured and used to combat shock, overwhelming allergic episodes, and for many other medical uses. More recently, the effects of these chemicals in the brain have become more relevant in the study of the neurophysiology of mental illness, psychosomatic illness, and the like.

catecholamine hypothesis   A postulate to explain affective disorders and the efficacy of antidepressant medications. Assumes that depression is caused by abnormally low concentrations of free catecholamines, as measured in terms of the norepinephrine levels in cerebrospinal fluid. Manic states are marked by excessively high concentrations of free catecholamines. Therapy is directed toward restoring a normal balance of catecholamines. Now superseded by a more discriminated complex of theories.

catecholaminergic neurons   Nerve cells that act by releasing catecholamine, such as norepinephrine. Also known as adrenergic neurons.

categorical   Without conditions or qualifications. See HYPOTHETICAL.

categorical attitude   Phrase similar to Kurt Goldstein's abstract attitude.

categorical differentiation   Exaggerating the differences between individuals or items if they are rated as belonging to two different categories, such as men and women. If individuals were rated one at a time in random or alphabetical order, a certain rating would occur, but if all men were rated first and all women second, and if the rater knew that the two groups were to be compared, a different rating of individuals may occur.

categorical imperative   (I. Kant) An ethical principle obliging individuals to adopt certain courses of conduct and to refrain from others. The unconditional command of conscience (as opposed to the hypothetical imperative, a law of expediency to achieve desired goals). See CONSCIENCE.

categorical intrusions   Inclusion on recall of a memorized list of items, some items that do belong to the category but that were not part of the memorized list.

categorical perception   1. Classification of a perception as a member of a particular grouping rather than as an individual item. For example, a key of a piano is struck, and is identified as middle C by one person, and as the categorical perception of it as a piano note, by another person. 2. Perception in which people have difficulty distinguishing among items from the same category while easily distinguishing among those from different categories.

categorical scale   A systematic categorization of items with general similarities. Not really a scale, despite its name, such as the periodic table of the chemical elements. Also known as nominal scale. See INTERVAL SCALE, ORDINAL SCALE, RATIO SCALE.

categorical series   The grouping of items on the basis of qualitative rather than quantitative criteria, such as works of art arranged according to their relative beauty.

categorical syllogism   See SYLLOGISM.

categorical thought   (J. Piaget) Abstract thinking. Involves the use of general concepts and classifications, and is particularly lacking in some patients with schizophrenia, who tend to think concretely. See ABSTRACT ATTITUDE, ABSTRACT THINKING.

categorical variable   A variable that has been subdivided into classes, such as school children given A, B, C, D, F grades for the variable of learning or of behavior. A finer variable would be using deciles and an even finer one, using percentiles.

categorization   A process of putting concepts, events, people, experiences into general classes or categories such as stereotypes.

categorized list   A list of terms often employed in memory research related to some overarching concept, such as all words referring to some concept such as the law, religion, or vehicles.

categorizing   The process of determining where different items in a particular class or divisions of classes belong in terms of some overriding principle. See CLUSTERING, CONCEPT FORMATION.

category   1. A group of items usually organized by qualitative rather than quantitative factors. 2. The use of numbers, words, etc. to represent separable and identifiable groups, such as sorting things into the following groups: male/female, or wet/dry.

category estimation   See METHODS OF SCALING.

category midpoint   A location exactly between the upper and lower limits of a category.

category-system method   (R. F. Bales) A method describing group interactive behavior by means of which an observer classifies actions of individuals into sets of mutually exclusive categories. See INTERACTION PROCESS ANALYSIS.

Category Test   (W. C. Halstead) An examination intended to measure the ability to achieve conceptual organization of abstract topics for evaluating the capacity to understand, comprehend in depth, and deal with complex problems. See CEREBRAL DYSFUNCTION TESTS.

category width (phenomenon)   A tendency to categorize several related entities into large (inclusive) or small (very few entities included) categories. There are tests that measure this tendency. People who use wide categories have been found to be able to adjust to culturally different environments more easily than people who use narrow categories.

catelectrotonic   Instilling a negative electronic change in a neural element, making it more sensitive for experimental purposes.

catelectrotonus   1. The enhanced excitability and conductivity of a nerve or muscle in the region of the cathode during the passage of a steady direct current. 2. Reduction in a cell membrane's polarization without impulse excitation; nerve depolarization with increased irritability near the cathode area. See ELECTROTONUS.

catenary curve   A graphic representation of a curve of distribution, the opposite of a normal curve, that is high at the ends and low in the middle, resembling a chain held at the ends and sagging at the center. See ETA CURVE for an approximation of this kind of curve.

cat fear   See AILUROPHOBIA.

catharsis   A strong emotional reaction often due to sudden insight of the nature and causes of deeply hidden painful memories. An episode of emotional release and discharge of tension associated with bringing into conscious recollection previously repressed or unpleasant experiences. Also spelled katharsis. See ABREACTION.

cathartic method   (J. Breuer, S. Freud) In psychotherapy, an attempt to generate insight into a client in such a manner that the client will experience strong emotions. See ABREACTION, PRIMAL THERAPY.

cathect(ize)   In psychoanalytic theory, to invest energy in the mental representation of some object (person) or concept. See CATHEXIS.

cathected   Invested with libidinal energy.

cathectic discharge   A release of psychic energy or affect, as in weeping or expressing anger. Also known as affective discharge.

cathexis   (S. Freud) The investment of psychic energy, or drive, in objects of any kind, such as wishes, fantasies, persons, goals, ideas, a social group, or the self. Such objects are cathected when a person attaches emotional significance, or affect (positive or negative), to them. Also known as cathection, investment. See ACATHEXIS, BODY CATHEXIS, COUNTERCATHEXIS, DECATHEXIS, EGO CATHEXIS, ENDOCATHECTION, EXOCATHECTION, FANTASY CATHEXIS, HYPERCATHEXIS, HYPOCATHEXIS, NEGATIVE CATHEXIS, OBJECT CATHEXIS, ORAL-SADISTIC CATHEXIS, POSITIVE CATHEXIS, RECATHEXIS.

cathode (C or Ca)   (M. Faraday, R. Caton) A conductor by which a positive current leaves an electrolyte to pass into a circuit, or to which positively charged ions (cations) are attracted in the electrolytic process. Also known as negative electrode. See ANODE.

cathode-ray oscilloscope   An electrical device which translates a sound wave into lines that can be seen on a monitor.

cation   A positively charged ion. Also spelled kation. See ACTION POTENTIAL, ANIONS.

catoptrics   The branch of optics which deals with the reflection of light. See DIOPTRICS.

catotrophobia   Fear of mirrors, especially of breaking one, may be based in some cases on the superstition that breaking a mirror brings seven years of bad luck. See EISOPTROPHOBIA.

CAT scan   See COMPUTERIZED AXIAL TOMOGRAPHY.

cat's-eye syndrome   A chromosomal disorder caused by additional chromosome material, resulting in birth defects that include a coloboma (cleft-iris) that produces a cat's-eye appearance, downslanting palpebral fissures, an imperforate anus, preauricular fistula and usually retardation. Also known as syndrome of extra-small acrocentric chromosome.

Cattell algometer   (J. M. Cattell) An apparatus for measuring pain sensitivity.

Cattell Infant Intelligence Scale   (P. Cattell) An instrument that measures developmental progress of children from 2 to 30 months, it is essentially a downward extension of the Stanford-Binet test. The scale was first mentioned in Psyche Cattell's 1940 book, *The Measurement of Intelligence in Infants and Young Children*. Sometimes known as Cattell Infant Scale.

Cattell inventories   (R. B. Cattell) Self-report inventories based on a study of personality traits by factor analysis. The best known is the Sixteen Personality Factor (16PF) Questionnaire, which yields 16 scores on such traits as trustful versus suspicious, humble versus assertive, and reserved versus outgoing.

Cattell's factorial theory of personality (R. B. Cattell) An approach to personality description based on the identification of traits, their measurement through factor analysis, and their classification into the surface and source traits which underlie them. See SOURCE TRAITS, SURFACE TRAITS.

Cattell's theory The following items are important for understanding Raymond Cattell's theory: ABOVE-DOWN ANALYSIS, AFFECTOTHYMIA, AMBIENT SITUATION, AUTIA, BEHAVIORAL INDEX, CATTELL INVENTORIES, CATTELL-WHITE FORMULA, COERCION TO THE CULTURAL MEAN, COMENTION, CONFACTOR ANALYSIS, CONFLUENT LEARNING, CONVARKIN DESIGNS, CONVENTION, CORTERIA, COVARIATION CHART, CRYSTALLIZED INTELLIGENCE, CULTURAL PRESSURE FACTOR, DEFLECTION STRAIN, DESURGENCY, DIFFERENTIAL R-TECHNIQUE, DUAL-INTELLIGENCE THEORY, DYNAMIC CALCULUS, DYNAMIC-EFFECT LAW, ECONETICS, ENVIRONMENTAL MOLD TRAIT, ERG, FLUID (GENERAL) INTELLIGENCE, GENDENATHASIA, GENTHANASIA, HARRIA, INDIFFERENCE OF INDICATOR, INSTRUMENT FACTOR, INTEGRATED MOTIVATION COMPONENT, INTEGRATIVE LEARNING, INTERACTIVE SCORE, IPSATIVE SCORING, L-DATA, LAW OF COERCION TO THE BIOSOCIAL MEAN, LIKENESS AND COMPLETENESS THEORIES OF MARITAL SUCCESS, LONG-CIRCUITING, MALERGY, METAERG, METANERG, MOBILIZATION VS REGRESSION, MOTIVATION COMPONENT FACTORS, MULTIPLE ABSTRACT VARIANCE ANALYSIS DESIGN, NEUROTIC-REGRESSIVE DEBILITY, NEUROTICISM, P-TECHNIQUE, PANNORMALIZATION, PARCELLED FACTOR ANALYSIS, PARMIA, PATHEMIA, PERSEVERATION, PERTURBATION THEORY, PRAXERNIA, PREMSIA, PROCRUSTES ROTATION, PROFILE SIMILARITY COEFFICIENT, PROTENSION, Q-DATA, REAL BASE FACTORING, REALBASED FACTOR ANALYSIS, RELATIONAL SIMPLEX SCALING, ROSETTA STONE MATRIX, ROTOPLOT PROGRAM, SCREE TEST, SECOND-ORDER FACTORS, SECONDARY FACTORS, SEM, SIXTEEN PERSONALITY FACTOR QUESTIONNAIRE, SOURCE TRAIT, STAVES, STENS, STRUCTURED LEARNING THEORY, STUB FACTORS, SURFACE TRAITS, SURGENCY, SYNERGY, SYNTALITY, T-DATA, TAXONOME PROGRAM, THRECTIA, TRUE ZERO FACTORING, VISCEROGENIC ERGS, ZEPPIA.

Cattell-White formula (R. B. Cattell) A formula for calculating the effect of higher order factors in lower order performances. See FACTOR ANALYSIS.

Caucasian (J. Blumenbach) Often used to mean white. In 1781, Johann Blumenbach divided humanity into five races on the basis of skull measurements, deeming one skull from the South Caucasus typical of the "white race."

cauda equina Spinal roots at the base of the spinal column.

caudal 1. Pertaining to the tail. Also known as caudalis. 2. Toward the posterior end of the body (tail end in animals) or the base in relation to the brain; opposite of craniad. Also known as caudad. See INFERIOR. 3. Relating to a tail, to that which is tail-shaped, or to the lower or tail end of something.

caudality (CA) A scale on the Minnesota Multiphasic Personality Inventory (MMPI).

caudate nucleus (Avicenna, M. V. G. Malacarne) A long arched mass of gray matter that follows the general curvature of the lateral ventricle and terminates in the amygdaloid nucleus. It is part of the basal ganglia and corpus striatum.

causal Pertaining to physical or logical necessity.

causal ambiguity Inability to determine, if A and B are correlated, whether A caused B or B caused A, or whether they each had a common cause X.

causal attribution (theory) 1. The perceived causes of a behavior. 2. A tendency to devise explanations for other people's behavior. These explanations fall into the basic categories of internal or external factors. See FUNDAMENTAL ATTRIBUTION ERROR.

causal chain A sequence of events regarded as a case of serial causation.

causal explanation An explanation of any phenomenon in terms of its causes, whether simple and direct or complex and multi-stage.

causal explanations of human behaviors Postulates to explain the derivation of various activities. Examples: internal stimuli (pressure on the bladder leads to micturition); external stimuli (an object approaching the eyes causes blinking); old memories (a person who has not ridden a bicycle for years can still ride easily); forgotten memories (a person hearing a dog bark is unaccountably fearful due to a forgotten childhood trauma); future intentions (a person studies what may be useful in an aimed-for occupation); reality (a loud horn blast leads a person to look around); and complex (every one of these factors plus others impinging on a person at any given time).

causalgia A sensation of intense, burning pain, swelling, redness, and sweating resulting from injury to the peripheral nerves. Usually due to a penetrating wound such as one inflicted by a bullet or knife. See THERMALGIA.

causality A mental concept that everything that exists, whether static or dynamic, from stones to ideas, was actualized by some prior event. The causal approach contrasts with the purely descriptive approach of statistical research, and with the introspective method. See CREATIVITY.

causal latency The time period between an event and its response.

causal law 1. A theory that there is a necessary connection between certain events so that A always causes B. 2. An established law based on scientifically secure findings of cause and effect.

causal maps/mapping Diagrammatic representations of individual or group belief structures, sometimes used for studying decision making.

causal mechanism The process through which an effect is produced. It explains why A caused B.

causal nexus A relation between two successive phases of an event, or between two successive phenomena.

causal ordering (H. A. Simon) A partial ordering of the equations and variables of a system of simultaneous equations that specifies which variables bear a causal (asymmetric) relation to specified other variables.

causal paths An assumption that any particular event may be affected differentially by a number of prior events. See LENS MODEL.

causal relations The nature of relationships wherein changes in one element cause another element to change.

causal scheme (G. Kelly) A process for determining causal attributions via three principles: discounting, argumentation, and attributional errors.

causal sequence The performance of two acts that have some direct logical relation to another, such as a child picking up a bottle cap and putting it on a bottle, after seeing this done by an adult. Used in testing infant memory. See ARBITRARY SEQUENCE.

causal texture (E. Brunswik) The environment as composed of mutually dependent events. The dependence is conceived in terms of probability rather than certainty.

causal theory of mental concepts See CAUSALITY.

causal theory See entries beginning with CAUSAL, INTERACTIONISM.

causation 1. An act or process that generates an effect. 2. A process of transition or transformation of phenomena, objects, events, etc., when the earlier stages are regarded as the conditions of the later stages; that is, if in the absence of the earlier phenomena, or their equivalents, the later phenomena never occur. 3. The conditioning of a present event by factors which surround that event both in space and in time. See CAUSATION AND CORRELATION.

causation and correlation A positive correlation between two sets of data does not, of itself, indicate a causal relationship. A causal relationship may be involved in negative or positive correlations, but this cannot be determined merely from the presence of a statistical relationship between the independent variable and the dependent variable. Two or more items can co-vary due to the presence of a third factor. For example, ice and snow in the environment do not create each other although they occur at the same time, but both are due to a third element: cold temperature. Critical elements in determining causation include: (a) factors must be correlated; (b) factors must be temporally related so that the cause precedes the effect; and (c) the potential causal factor remains as the most plausible cause.

cause A phenomenon, object, or group of phenomena or objects so related to a simultaneous or succeeding phenomenon, etc., that in the absence of the former or of some equivalent, the latter never appears. See CAUSATION.

cause and effect An expectation that a certain action will achieve a certain result or, conversely, a certain result is the effect of a certain cause. See CAUSALITY.

cause-and-effect diagram A visual representation of the relationship between some effect, often the problem under study, and its possible or demonstrated causes.

cause-and-effect test An intelligence examination that offers alternative causes for different effects and alternative effects for different causes, requiring the participant to choose the most logical explanations.

cause célèbre An incident that excites great interest. Historical examples include: The Dreyfus case in France, the Sacco and Vanzetti case and the Watergate break-in in the United States.

caution An attitude (either emotional, or intellectual, or both) characterized by partial inhibition of the typical responses to a given situation.

cautious shift A change in opinion of individuals to a more cautious position following group discussion. See CHOICE SHIFT, GROUP POLARIZATION, RISKY SHIFT.

CAVD See COMPLETION, ARITHMETIC, VOCABULARY AND DIRECTIONS TEST.

CBA cost/benefit analysis

CBT cognitive-behavioral therapy

CBZ See CARBAMAZEPINE.

CCK See CHOLECYSTOKININ.

CCT Children's Category Test

CCW child-care worker

cd See CANDELA.

CD 1. conduct disorder 2. communication deviance

CDI Children's Depression Inventory

CDTA Compass Diagnostic Test of Arithmetic

CE constant error

CEA cost-effectiveness analysis

CEEB College Entrance Examination Board

CEFT Children's Embedded Figures Test

ceiling The maximum possible, such as the highest score possible on a test; the opposite of the floor, lower ceiling, or basement. See BASEMENT, CEILING EFFECT.

ceiling age A maximum age level reached on a scaled test such as the Stanford-Binet (S-B): the mental age (MA) level where all tests are failed and the test is discontinued. For example, on a S-B test a student may pass all items at MA-6 (basal mental age) and pass some items at MA-7 and MA-8, but fails all items at MA-9 (ceiling age). Also called terminal mental age.

ceiling effect 1. Inability of measuring instruments or statistical techniques to determine differences at the top of data when the difference between data is large. 2. Inability of a test to measure or discriminate above a certain point, usually because its items are too easy for certain people. See FLOOR EFFECT, SCALE ATTENUATION. Compare BASEMENT EFFECT.

celestial aids to navigation In comparative psychology, the use of stellar or solar cues in traveling and homing to specific destinations by insects, aquatic life, and birds.

celeration Frequency of events per time unit.

celibacy 1. Abstinence from sexual activity, especially coitus, temporarily or permanently. 2. A state of virginity. 3. A term applied to members of religious orders who take a vow of chastity.

cell 1. The basic unit of organized tissue, consisting of an outer membrane, a nucleus, and a mass of protoplasm known as cytoplasm. Some primitive cells may not possess all of these components; for example, certain bacteria lack a specific nuclear entity. 2. The basic microscopic unit of body tissue. Structure and function vary widely. The cell is enclosed in a membrane (also termed plasma membrane) that regulates the flow of chemicals into and out of the cell. The nucleus contains the chromosomes. The cytoplasm may contain other elements, such as ribosomes, lysosomes, and the Golgi complex. 3. In general, a compartment, cavity, or receptacle. 4. In statistics, a set of figures in data tabulation. 5. In social psychology, a small group of people sharing an ideology. 6. In electricity, a compartment in a storage battery.

cell-assembly theory (D. O. Hebb) A point of view that sequences of brain cells upon repeated firings will eventually begin to operate as a single unit. See FRACTIONATION, MARK II CELL ASSEMBLY (THEORY).

cell body 1. The central part of a cell that contains the nucleus. 2. The central, cellular portion of a neuron or nerve-cell, exclusive of the projecting fibers. Also known as soma.

cell differentiation Changes in physical and functional aspects of cells as they become specialized in the embryo to form different body structures.

cell division The steps through which a body or somatic cell produces daughter cells. The stages include prophase, metaphase, anaphase, and telophase.

cellifugal As applied to nerve fibers or impulses, directed away from the cell-body. Also known as cellulifugal.

cellipetal As applied to nerve fibers or impulses, directed toward the cell body. Also known as cellulipetal.

cell nucleus A portion of the cell that controls its metabolic functions, including growth and repair of structures of the cell. Contains the deoxyribonucleic acid (DNA) necessary for cell reproduction.

cell segmentation The splitting of a zygote (a fertilized ovum) into two or more parts with each part becoming a "clone" of the other or others. See IDENTICAL TWINS.

cell theory A point of view that all organisms are composed of one or more cells and of substances produced by these cells.

cellular immunity factors See IMMUNITY FACTORS.

cellular mosaicism **chimerism**

Celsius (C) scale (A. Celsius) The name for what was formerly called centigrade scale. Named after Swedish astronomer Anders Celsius (1701–1744). See TEMPERATURE SCALES.

cementing action In stimulus-response (S-R) connections, the assumption that stimulus and response are bonded together.

cenesthesia A general body feeling including the sense of being alive, and of well-being or discomfort. Purportedly derives from internal sensations often occurring below the level of consciousness. Also known as cenesthesis, coen(a)esthesia.

cenesthopathy A general nonspecific feeling of illness or lack of well-being.

cenogamy A rare type of group marriage of two men and two women. See MARRIAGE.

cenophobia Fear of emptiness; fear of large empty spaces. Also spelled kenophobia.

cenotophobia See CAINOTOPHOBIA.

cenotrope Behavior assumed to be a product of hereditary and environmental forces because it appears in all members of a species in the same environment (for example, most cats groom themselves frequently). Also known as coenotrope.

censor (S. Freud) According to psychoanalysis, a part of the mind that prevents material coming from the unconscious to consciousness. The censor is not quite as vigilant during sleep, but still it operates by not permitting forbidden thoughts to enter awareness, since they are modified during sleep. Also known as endopsychic censor. See CENSORSHIP.

censorship 1. Legal prohibitions against producing, possessing, or distributing proscribed materials, usually those considered pornographic or seditious. 2. In psychoanalytic theory, the exclusion of unacceptable or forbidden thoughts and impulses from consciousness by the process of selection and repression. Sigmund Freud held that this process is governed by the rules and prohibitions imposed by parents or other members of society.

censorship in dreams See FREUD'S THEORY OF DREAMS.

census A complete survey of elements of interest from a specific population.

census tract A small area, comprising 3,500 to 4,000 residents, whose boundaries are established by the Bureau of the Census. Demographic data on such variables as median age, sex ratio, number of children, foreign-born status, labor force, school enrollment, income characteristics, delinquency, suicide rate, and housing characteristics are frequently used in the assessment of area characteristics and needs, including mental health needs.

cent In music and phonology, a unit of pitch; one cent is 1/1200 of an octave.

center 1. In physiology, the center of the body, the point at which the body could be balanced. 2. With regard to attention, the locus of the primary focus.

centered 1. Metaphorically, a state of perfect integration of the organism with its environment. 2. (K. Goldstein) A state of mind characterized by having a firm grip on reality, knowing "who" the self is, "what" is wanted out of life, as well as being prepared to meet all contingencies of life in a mature and competent manner. 3. The body balanced on both feet, crouching forward, ready to defend or to attack.

centering 1. (M. Wertheimer, K. Duncker, W. Köhler) In Gestalt theory, a change in meaning of the parts in accordance with their structural place, role, and function, or a view of the situation in terms of "good structure" so that everything fits the structural requirements. 2. In speech, the opposite of peak clipping. 3. Synonym for Jean Piaget's centration.

center median A large group of nerve cells associated with the thalamus serving as part of the arousal system.

center of rotation A theoretical intersecting point of all possible axes about which the eyeball may rotate in performing its normal movements.

Centigrade (C) See CELSIUS SCALE.

centile One percent of any population, one-tenth of a decile. See PERCENTILE.

centile rank A value which, for a given score, gives the percentage of the entire distribution at or below that score. For example, a score with a centile rank of 43 means that 43% score at or below that score.

centile score A series of scores put in sequence from high to low (usually) or from low to high, and then divided into 100 consecutive groups. Each of the resulting 100 groups is known as a centile or a percentile. A person in the top 1% of a particular population would be in the first centile. See DECILE.

centimeter (cm) A measure of length. Part of the metric system. One hundredth of a meter; equal to 0.39 of an inch.

centimeter-gram-second (CGS, cgs, or **c.g.s.) system** In the centimeter-gram-second system, units represent units of length, weight, and time. Also known as cgs system.

centrad 1. Toward the center. 2. A unit of angular measurement represented by the arc of a circle equal in length to 1/100 of the radius, that is, 1/100 of a radian.

central In linguistics, a sound, usually a vowel, made with the tongue toward the middle of its range of anterior-posterior positions.

central anticholinergic syndrome A condition characterized by anxiety, disorientation, short-term-memory loss, hallucinations, and agitation. Seen in patients receiving combinations of psychotropic drugs, and due to the additive anticholinergic effects of tricyclic depressants, phenothiazines, and antiparkinson agents.

central aphasia (K. Goldstein) Loss of the inner language system.

central auditory processing disorder (CAPD) Malfunction of the hearing sense due to a breakdown of signals between the ear and the brain. Such individuals have trouble interpreting abstract information and remaining focused, especially in distracting environments. See ALEXIA, DYSLEXIA.

central canal The channel in the gray matter of the spinal cord containing cerebrospinal fluid. It is the vestige of the cavity of the embryonic neural tube. Also known as canalis centralis.

central conflict (K. Horney) In Karen Horney's theory, the conflict between the real and the idealized or neurotic self. Intrapsychic struggle between the healthy constructive forces of the real self and the obstructive, neurotic forces of the idealized self; a conflict that leads to neuroses. See OVERAMBITION.

central deafness A hearing impairment caused by dysfunction of the inner ear or damage to the eighth nerve between the inner ear and the brainstem.

central disposition (G. W. Allport) A significant characteristic trait of an individual's personality. See CARDINAL DISPOSITION.

central effector neuron See NEURON.

central fissure fissure of Rolando

central force (C. G. Jung) Carl Jung's primal libido or life force; describing the keystone of a person's total psychic system.

central gray The unmyelinated gray nerve fibers that form a generally H-shaped pattern in the central portion of the spinal cord.

central inhibition A central nervous system (CNS) process that prevents or interrupts the flow of neural impulses that control behavior.

central interval (CI) In the method of a single stimuli, the difference between the upper and lower limens.

centralism A doctrine that focuses on behavior as a function of the higher brain centers, as opposed to peripheralist psychology, which focuses on the effects of receptors, glands, and muscles on behavior. Also known as centralist psychology. See PERIPHERALISM.

centralist A theoretician who considers central neural processes as most important for understanding and controlling behavior.

centralist theories (of emotion) Points of view that consider the brain and neural processes to be central to the emotional experience. See CANNON-BARD THEORY (OF EMOTION), PAPEZ THEORY (OF EMOTION).

centralist theories (of learning) Points of view that learning consists of organizing processes.

centrality of an attitude Refers to the concept that to fully understand behavior, underlying attitudes must be understood since these direct or control thinking and actions.

centralized organization Any organization in which power and decision-making reside at the top.

central-limit theorem (R. la Place, I. Liapounoff) The statistical principle that sample means drawn by chance from a population are normally distributed if the sample size is sufficiently large, even if the population they were drawn from is not normally distributed. See INFERENTIAL STATISTICS.

central lobe A lobe of the cerebral hemisphere that lies deeply within the fissure of Sylvius and is not visible on the cortical surface. Also known as insula of Reil, island of Reil.

central motive state (C. T. Morgan) A theoretical function of the nervous system that accounts for a persistent level of activity in the absence of external stimuli or a continuation of nervous activity when the original motive no longer exists.

central nervous adjustment Readjustment that involves the brain and spinal cord without receptors and effectors participating.

central nervous system (CNS, c.n.s., or **cns)** The brain and spinal cord as well as the peripheral nerves immediately connected with these. Sometimes known as cerebrospinal system, voluntary nervous system. See AUTONOMIC NERVOUS SYSTEM, BRAIN, PERIPHERAL NERVOUS SYSTEM for illustrations.

central nervous system drugs An equivalent phrase for psychotropic or psychoactive drugs. In this context, central nervous system mainly refers to the brain.

central nervous system abnormality Any defect in structure or function of the tissues of the brain and spinal cord.

central neuron Any neuron belonging entirely to the central nervous system.

central organizing trait (G. W. Allport) An aspect of an individual's personality considered key or dominant; for example, using descriptions such as "irascible," "dominating," or "pleasant" in an attempt to create a general impression of the person. See CARDINAL DISPOSITION.

central pain   Pain caused by a disorder of the central nervous system, such as a brain tumor or spinal cord infection or injury.

central process   A process that occurs in the central nervous system.

central-processing dysfunction   A disorder in the analysis, storage, synthesis, and symbolic use of information.

central processing unit (CPU)   The "brain" of computers that controls all operations including the interpretation and execution of instructions.

central processor   Describing part of the brain as equivalent to the processor of a computer: that part of the brain that takes in information, integrates it, and makes decisions.

central reflex time   See REFLEX LATENCY.

central route to persuasion   See ELABORATION-LIKELIHOOD MODEL OF PERSUASION.

central state (identity) theory   A point of view that overt behavior and brain states are identical. Holds that the body does what the brain tells it to do, or if the body is affected by outside forces, such as buffeted by a strong wind, the brain experiences this also. Also known as central state materialism.

central stimulation   The stimulation (electrical or chemical) of an area in the brain by means of implanted electrodes or pipettes.

central sulcus   fissure of Rolando

central tegmental nucleus   A central complex of nuclei in the brainstem with fibers that communicate between the thalamus and the grey nuclei cells of the spinal cord. Also known as nucleus of the raphe.

central tendency   The middle-most location or direction in a set of scores, usually represented by the mean, median, or mode.

central tendency error   A tendency when assessing individuals or things of various kinds (for example, rating works of art, or comparing the beauty of animals) to have a narrow range of judgments all close to the central tendency, such as the mean, rather than having a wide range of evaluations.

central-tendency measure   In obtaining many measurements of individuals or repeated measures of a single individual, if enough samples are obtained, an array of distribution likely occurs that resembles the profile of a bell, high in the middle and sloping down at the sides. There are a number of measures of central tendency, all called "average." The best known and most often used averages in psychology are the mean, median, and mode. See MEASURE OF CENTRAL TENDENCY, MEASURE OF VARIABILITY.

central tendency of judgment   A general tendency for the judgments of a given individual, with respect to a given quality, to gravitate toward the middle portion of the judgment or rating scale which is being used.

central theory   A view of behavior that stresses the importance of central nervous adjustment.

central theory of thinking   A point of view that the center of mentation is a cerebral process. Aristotle had placed thinking in the heart.

central trait   (G. W. Allport) A personality aspect of medium value, below cardinal traits in importance, and more important than peripheral traits. Describes the basic pattern of an individual's personality using adjectives, such as "compassionate," "ambitious," "sociable," or "helpful." See CENTRAL DISPOSITION, GESTALT, PERSONALITY.

central vision   Vision that occurs primarily in the region of the retinal fovea.

centration   (J. Piaget) A tendency to base conclusions on one aspect of a situation neglecting other possibly significant aspects. It is considered usual in preoperational thought. Also known as centering. See DECENTRATION.

centrencephalic   Located near the center of the brain (encephalon).

centrencephalic epilepsy   A form of epilepsy marked by generalized and petit mal seizures that appear to originate near the center of the brain. The electroencephalograph reveals a characteristic three Hertz (cycles per second) spike-and-wave pattern found in petit mal. See CENTRENCEPHALIC SYSTEM.

centrencephalic seizure   An epileptic seizure involving the centrencephalic system located in the central core of the brainstem.

centrencephalic system   (W. Penfield) Identifying a central anatomical brain area in which neurons provide a coherent unity for mental processes. See RETICULAR ACTIVATING SYSTEM.

centrencephalon   (W. Penfield) The center of the encephalon, or brain, a small region of relatively undifferentiated neurons in the subcortical area. Wilder Penfield introduced the term as part of his theory of a centrencephalic system or seat of free-will control over human activities.

centrifugal   1. Direction of the force pulling an object away from an axis of rotation. Compare CENTRIPETAL (meaning 1). 2. Describing any movement away from a center. 3. Conducting or moving away from the central portion of the nervous system. Also known as efferent, exodic.

centrifugal group factor   (G. W. Allport) A tendency to make gestures away from the body, part of Allport's theory of personality.

centrifugal nerve/neuron   A neuron that carries impulses from the central nervous system to the periphery of the body; an efferent or motor nerve.

centrifugal peripheral pathways   The routes followed by certain nerve fibers or impulses that move from the center to the periphery.

centrifugal swing   In maze learning, the tendency of an organism at a choice point in a maze to choose going in the same direction that was the prior successful choice. See Y-MAZE for illustration.

centripetal   1. Direction of the force pulling an object toward an axis of rotation. Also known as axipetal. Compare CENTRIFUGAL (meaning 1). 2. Directing inward, toward the center. 3. See AFFERENT. 4. Treatment focusing inward on small changes in feelings and impulses.

centripetal impulse   An impulse seeking the center. A system of impulses that course from the sense organs toward the brain centers.

centripetal nerve/neuron   A nerve that carries currents from the periphery of the body toward the central nervous system. See AFFERENT NERVE.

centro ritual   A type of folk psychiatry found in Puerto Rico. The "therapist" engages in a variety of rituals such as blowing smoke toward the patient, singing songs, etc., but also asks questions about dreams, sex problems, family concerns, all intended to calm the patient, and provide insight and support. See FOLK PSYCHIATRY.

centroid   An average of a set of data points.

centroid factors   Factors extracted by the centroid method developed by Lewis Thurstone.

centroid method   (L. L. Thurstone) A type of factor analysis used before the advent of computers. The correlation matrix is represented as being on the surface of a sphere.

centromere   A portion of a chromosome attached to the equatorial plane of the mitotic or meiotic spindle during cell division. The centromere of a chromosome occasionally becomes a separate body of genetic material, accounting for certain types of physiological anomalies. See CAT'S-EYE SYNDROME, MONSTER.

centrosome   (W. Flemming) A specialized part of the cell, regarded as the active center during miotic cell division because it divides to form poles of the miotic spindle.

cephal(al)gia   An intense headache, such as occurs in infectious diseases or states of tension. Also known as cephalagra. See HEADACHE.

cephalic   Cranial; pertaining to or located in the head or head-end of an animal.

cephalic index   (A. A. Retzius) A measure of the proportions of an individual head calculated by dividing the maximum width by the maximum height and multiplying the result by 100. Ratios run from below 75 for a long, narrow skull (dolichocephalic), through statistically normal ratios of 76–81 (mesaticephalic), to broad skull with ratios of 81–85 (brachycephalic). Also known as cephalization index.

cephalization   1. Evolutionary tendency for important nervous system functions to move forward in the brain. 2. The concentration of parts toward the head, or their modification so as to become organs of the head.

cephalization index   See CEPHALIC INDEX.

cephalocaudal   1. Pertaining to both head and tail. See CEPHALOCAUDAL AXIS. 2. In the physical development of most organisms the maturational sequence is cephalo (head) to caudal (tail).

cephalocaudal axis   The axis of reference passing from head to tail.

cephalocaudal development   The head-to-tail progression of anatomical and motor development, as determined by the anterior-posterior development gradient. The head and its movements develop first, then the upper trunk, arms and hands, followed by the lower trunk and leg, foot, and toe movements. Also known as cephalocaudad development, cephalocaudal principle/sequence. See PROXIMODISTAL DEVELOPMENT.

cephalogenesis   The stage of embryonic development in which the head begins to form.

cephalometry   The scientific measurement of the dimensions of the head. It is applied in orthodontics to predict and evaluate craniofacial development. See CEPHALIC INDEX.

cephaloskeletal dysplasia   A congenital disorder thought to be hereditary, marked by low birth weight, skeletal anomalies, microcephaly, brain malformations, short lives, and severe retardation.

CER   conditioned emotional response

cerea flexibilitas   (waxy flexibility—Latin) A condition in which a limb remains where placed, found in catatonia. See CATALEPSY.

cerebellar   Pertaining to the cerebellum.

cerebellar ataxia   (M-P. Flourens) Lack of muscular coordination due to damage in the neocerebellum. Patients cannot integrate voluntary movements and therefore find it difficult to stand, walk, feed themselves, or perform complex activities such as playing the piano.

cerebellar cortex   Gray matter, or unmyelinated nerve cells, covering the surface of the cerebellum. Also known as cortex cerebelli.

cerebellar fit   (H. Jackson) A type of seizure associated with a tumor of the vermis and marked by sudden loss of consciousness and collapse, cyanosis, and dilated pupils.

cerebellar folia   The pattern of leaf-like structures that subdivide the cerebellar cortex.

cerebellar gait   An unsteady, wobbly gait due to lack of coordination between the trunk and legs, so that the trunk lags behind or is thrust forward.

cerebellar hemispheres   The cerebellum is divided into two lobes, or hemispheres, on either side of the median plane.

cerebellar rigidity   Increased tone of extensor muscles caused by an injury to the cerebellum. See EXTENSOR RIGIDITY.

cerebellar speech   Verbal expression that is jerky, irregular, explosive, and scanning, due to a cerebellar lesion. Also known as asynergic speech, ataxic speech.

cerebellum   Known as "the little brain" because of its appearance, the cerebellum is located in the hindbrain, and controls muscle coordination and body balance. Modulates muscular contractions to reduce jerking or tremors and helps maintain equilibrium by predicting body positions ahead of actual body movements. See the illustration of the BRAIN.

cerebra   Plural of cerebrum, also cerebrums.

cerebral aqueduct   See AQUEDUCT OF SYLVIUS.

cerebral arteriosclerosis   A hardening of the arteries that provide freshly oxygenated blood to the brain. See ARTERIOSCLEROTIC BRAIN DISORDER.

cerebral beriberi   Wernicke's disease

cerebral blindness   A form of blindness due to damage to specific areas of the cerebrum even though the eyes and the optic nerves are intact. See CORTICAL BLINDNESS.

cerebral brain stimulation   Activation or purposeful stimulation of the cerebrum as a means of determining the effect on behavior. See BRAIN RESEARCH, BRAIN STIMULATION.

cerebral commissure   See COMMISSURE.

cerebral contusion   An injury to the brain that results in damage to blood vessels without a break in the surrounding membranes that would result in a loss of blood for the affected region. The effect is similar to a bruise in which released blood is trapped beneath the skin. A cerebral contusion often results in epilepsy or other neurological disorders. See BOXER'S DEMENTIA, PUNCH DRUNK.

cerebral cortex   1. The most superficial portion of the cerebrum. The cerebral cortex contains a preponderance of cell bodies, which is why it appears gray in fresh brain, but also includes afferent, association and commissural fibers. Three general types of cerebral cortex may be distinguished. The neocortex contains six layers at some point in development if not in the adult. The paleocortex (olfactory) and archicortex (hippocampus and dentate gyrus) contain fewer than six layers. 2. Covering of gray cells several layers in thickness on the outside of the cerebral hemispheres of the human brain. Each hemisphere of the cerebral cortex is divided into an occipital, parietal, frontal, and temporal lobe. The cerebral cortex functions as the source of conscious nervous activity, including reasoning, memory, learning, intelligence, and interpretation of sensory inputs. Also known as cortex cerebri, cortex of the cerebrum, neopallium. See CEREBRAL HEMISPHERES.

cerebral cortex reflex   Haab's pupil (reflex)

cerebral dominance   The control of lower brain centers by the cerebrum or cerebral cortex. See LATERAL DOMINANCE, LATERALITY, SPLIT BRAIN.

cerebral dominance theory   A point of view that cortical activity relating to higher functions, speech, etc., is dominated normally by the cerebral hemisphere which controls the most used hand.

cerebral dynamic imaging   An older name for nuclear imaging. See NUCLEAR MAGNETIC RESONANCE IMAGING (NMRI).

cerebral dysfunctions   Impaired cerebral processes, especially those associated with organic brain syndromes, such as disturbances of memory, verbal ability, numerical ability, psychomotor functioning, and diminished or fluctuating levels of consciousness.

cerebral-dysfunction tests   Clinical procedures for assessing neuropsychological impairment (organicity, brain damage). Examples are the Halstead-Reitan Neuropsychological Battery, and the Luria-Nebraska Neuropsychological Battery.

cerebral dysplasia   Any abnormality in the development of the brain.

cerebral dysrhythmia   Abnormal brain wave rhythms associated with neurologic disease or other pathologic conditions such as a drug overdose. See EPILEPSY.

cerebral eclipse   Brief loss of consciousness, perception, and motor functions due to chronic cerebral circulatory insufficiency, but without cardiac arrest or lowered blood pressure.

cerebral edema   An abnormal accumulation of fluid in the intercellular spaces of the brain tissues. May be a cause of dementia that recedes when the defect is corrected. If not corrected severe permanent damage may occur. Also known as water on the brain, wet brain.

cerebral electrotherapy (C.E.T. or CET)   Application of low voltage pulses of direct electrical current to the brain. Occasionally used in the treatment of depression, anxiety, and insomnia. See ELECTRONARCOSIS.

cerebral gigantism   A growth-hormone disorder marked by excessive physical size and usually a mild degree of mental retardation in childhood, although most such individuals can function adequately as adults. Rarely occurs as a genetic or familial trait.

cerebral hemispheres   The two halves, left and right, of the cerebrum. The hemispheres are separated by a deep longitudinal fissure but the left and right hemispheres are connected by commissural projections. The "great cerebral commissure" is known as the corpus callosum. Fibers of the corpus callosum connect corresponding areas of the two hemispheres except for the inferior temporal lobes which are connected to each other by the anterior commissure.

cerebral hyperplasia   An abnormal increase in the volume of brain tissue, usually due to a proliferation of new, normal cells.

cerebral hypoplasia   The incomplete development of the cerebral hemispheres.

cerebral infarct   The necrosis, or death, of an area of brain tissue due to an interruption of blood flow caused by rupture of a blood vessel, blockage of a blood vessel by a clot, or a narrowing, or stenosis, of a blood vessel. See STROKE.

cerebral infection   The invasion of brain tissues by a pathogenic organism, such as a virus or bacterium. A viral cerebral infection usually is identified as encephalitis; a bacterial cerebral infection usually is called cerebritis.

cerebral integration (hypothesis)   A postulate that all neural functions of the body are integrated through the cerebrum.

cerebral localization   See LOCALIZATION OF BRAIN FUNCTION.

cerebral pacemaker   A hypothetical group of central nervous system tissue cells thought to regulate the rhythms of brain waves in both cerebral hemispheres. Assumed to be located in the diffuse thalamic nuclei, the hypothalamus, or in the reticular formation.

cerebral palsy (CP)   A group of noninherited neuromuscular disorders resulting from damage primarily to the motor region of the brain, causing impairment in control over voluntary muscles. May occur through anoxia (lack of oxygen) during birth. Symptoms include spasticity, uncontrolled movements (athetosis), staggering gait, and guttural speech. See FORCEPS INJURY.

cerebral peduncle   Two bundles on either side of the ventral surface of the midbrain, they include all structures ventral (anterior) to the cerebral aqueduct and contain the tegmentum of the midbrain and the basis pedunculi. The basis pedunculi consists of the substantia nigra and crus cerebri. The crus cerebri contains nerve fibers originating from the neocortex and terminating in the cranial nerve nuclei (corticobulbar fibers), the pontine nuclei (corticopontine fibers) and the spinal cord (corticospinal, or pyramidal tract, fibers).

cerebral specialization   A concept based upon the theory that the two cerebral hemispheres have specialized functions. Speech, writing, and mathematics are the province of the dominant hemisphere, whereas the non-dominant hemisphere controls some aspects of spatial and music perception.

cerebral (telencephalic) vesicles   Structures which develop from the prosencephalic brain vesicle at the anterior end of the neural tube about the end of the fifth week of gestation and give rise to the cerebral cortex, the subcortical white matter, the olfactory bulb and tract, the basal ganglia (including the amygdala) and the hippocampus.

cerebral thrombosis   See THROMBUS.

cerebral trauma   An impairment of brain functions, temporary or permanent, following a blow to the head of sufficient severity to produce a concussion, contusion, or laceration. See ACUTE TRAUMATIC DISORDERS, CEREBRAL CONTUSION, CHRONIC TRAUMATIC DISORDER, HEAD TRAUMA.

cerebral type   (L. Rostan) A body type considered to have a predominance of the nervous system in relation to other body types. See CONSTITUTIONAL TYPES.

cerebral vesicles   cerebral (telencephalic) vesicles

cerebration   1. Mental activity, conscious or unconscious. See MENTATION. 2. Any kind of conscious thinking such as pondering or problem-solving. See UNCONSCIOUS CEREBRATION.

cerebritis   See CEREBRAL INFECTION.

cerebrocranial defect   A deformity or dysfunction of the cerebrum and the eight bones of the skull that form a protective layer around it, such as premature closing of the sutures of the skull resulting in a displacement of cerebral tissues. Hydrocephalus is associated with a cranial deformity. See CRANIAL ANOMALY.

cerebroside   A fatty acid (glycolipid) compound present in the myelin sheath of nerve fibers that are usually identified as white matter.

cerebrospinal fibers   Rare phrase for corticospinal fibers.

cerebrospinal fluid (CSF)   The fluid within the central canal of the spinal cord, the four ventricles of the brain, and the subarachnoid space of the brain. Serves as a watery cushion to protect vital central nervous system (CNS) tissues from damage by shock pressure. Also known as spinal fluid.

cerebrospinal system   Obsolete name for the central nervous system (CNS).

cerebrotonia   (W. Sheldon) A personality type allegedly associated with an ectomorphic (linear, fragile) physique. Characterized by a tendency toward introversion, restraint, inhibition, love of privacy and solitude, and sensitivity. Also known as cerebrotonic type. See SHELDON'S CONSTITUTIONAL THEORY OF PERSONALITY.

cerebrovascular accident (CVA)   Obsolete name for stroke. Also known as cerebral-vascular accident.

cerebrum   The most rostral and largest portion of the brain, it includes the cerebral cortex, diencephalon, and basal ganglia. Also known as telencephalon.

ceremonial language   A special method of speaking used under special circumstances such as in introducing people, or making a speech to a large group on an important topic.

ceremonials   A system of rites and practices, often symbolic in nature, established by law or custom. See RITUALS.

certainty (h)   The highest degree of belief. See CERTAINTY VS CERTITUDE, PROBABILITY.

certainty vs certitude   Certainty is almost synonymous with certitude but certitude is more abstract. Certainty is often ascribed to phenomena, to indicate that their future is assured, that is, without condition. Certitude remains subjective, that is, it is not objectified.

certifiable   A legal designation that an identified individual is not competent and needs either a guardian or institutionalization. Different jurisdictions have various definitions of which and how many experts may be needed for such designations.

certification   1. A designation of competence (achievement of a given level of knowledge and skill) of a professional by a certifying body such as the American Board of Psychiatry and Neurology or the American Board of Professional Psychology. 2. The commitment of a person to a hospital for a mental disorder in a manner legally appropriate for such commitments by so "certifying."

certification laws   1. Legislation governing the admission of patients to mental institutions, including commitment proceedings as well as a review of case records to determine whether health care is necessary and whether the site and type of care are appropriate. 2. Regulations by states governing the rights of individuals to represent themselves as professionals in various areas of mental health care.

certitude   The highest degree of belief. See CERTAINTY, CERTAINTY VS CERTITUDE, PROBABILITY.

ceruloplasmin   A plasma once believed to be a toxic factor in schizophrenia.

cerveau isolé   (isolated brain—French) A detached brain, usually applied to a laboratory animal whose brain has been excised at the level of the mesencephalon for research purposes.

cervical ganglia   The ganglia that innervate blood vessels, sweat glands and the heart. The nerves that supply them arise from the sympathetic intermediolateral cell column of the thoracic cord.

cervical nerves   Eight spinal nerves in the neck area, each with a dorsal root that is sensory in function, and a ventral root that has motor function.

CES-D   Center for Epidemiologic Studies- Depression Scale

CET   See CEREBRAL ELECTROTHERAPY.

cf   Abbreviation for "compare with" from the Latin *confer*—compare. (Does not mean "see" or "refer to" as it is commonly, and erroneously, used.)

C$_f$ See CUMULATIVE (FREQUENCY) DISTRIBUTION.

CF   In Rorschach test scoring, a symbol for color dominant.

C factor 1. General term for group or mass behavior and the characteristic actions and reactions of various kinds of "collectivities," such as audiences, crowds, mobs, clubs, and therapeutic groups. See CROWD BEHAVIOR, MASS HYSTERIA. 2. (C. E. Spearman) The cleverness factor considered independent of the g factor (intelligence). Also known as c factor. See P FACTOR (PERSEVERANCE).

CFF Abbreviation for critical flicker frequency, critical flicker fusion, or critical fusion frequency (also abbreviated **cff**).

C fiber An unmyelinated postganglionic fiber of the autonomic nervous system, which if stimulated generates pain.

CFIDS chronic fatigue immune dysfunction syndrome

CFIT 1. culture-fair intelligence test. 2. culture-free intelligence test.

CFS chronic fatigue syndrome

CGS centimeter-gram-second (also abbreviated **cgs**, **c.g.s.**)

Ch'uan See T'AI CHI CH'UAN.

Chaddock reflex (C. G. Chaddock) 1. In pyramidal tract lesion cases, a reflexive action of extension of the big toe when the external malleolus is stimulated. 2. In hemiplegia, the flexion of the wrist and spreading out of the fingers when the ulna is stimulated. Named after American neurologist Charles G. Chaddock (1861–1936).

chaetophobia See TRICHOPHOBIA.

CHAIN See CHAINED SCHEDULE OF REINFORCEMENT.

chain behavior An integrated series of responses such that each response acts as the discriminative stimulus for the next response in the sequence; for example, in reciting the alphabet, A is the cue for B which is the cue for C. See CHAINED RESPONSES, CHAINING.

chained reinforcement schedule **chained schedule of reinforcement**

chained responses A process in which a complex behavior chain is learned by a subject. The final response is taught first. Once established, it becomes a reinforcer for the next response in the chain. The chain is taught backwards, one response at a time. Circus animals are trained in this manner. Also known as behavior chaining, chaining.

chained schedule of reinforcement (CHAIN) In a schedule of reinforcement the learning of a sequence of responses in a fixed order so that one event serves to elicit the next event, and so on. Also known as chain schedule, chained reinforcement schedule.

chaining 1. Learning the behaviors of a series in which each response is the stimulus for the next response. See CHAIN BEHAVIOR. 2. See CHAINED RESPONSES.

chain reflex 1. A situation when two or more nerves are so related that the action of one always generates the action of another. 2. A group of closely related reflexes which initiate one another in succession. See CHAIN BEHAVIOR.

chain reproduction Relaying material, such as stories from person to person. The final product in the case of a picture when compared with the original might show that a pair of glasses has become a bicycle. Similar distortions occur in rumors through the processes of leveling, sharpening, and assimilation. Chain reproduction occurs in gossiping and other transmissions of information from person to person and group to group.

chakras (wheels—Sanskrit) A spiritual term from India designating cerebrospinal centers of energy. Seven chakras are said to run along the center of the human body from the perineum to the head.

challenged Term suggested as a substitution for "handicapped" with the implication that people with disabilities of various kinds are both motivated to and able to surmount them. See PERSON WITH A DISABILITY.

challenged people Persons with a disability.

challenge(s) 1. In brain research, changes in the environments used to measured evoked brain potentials. 2. In drug research, the administration of a chemical to see what physiological or psychological changes occur. 3. See DISABILITY.

chalone A specific chemical substance formed by one organ and passed into the circulatory fluid to produce an inhibitory effect upon other organs.

CHAMPUS Civilian Health and Medical Program, Uniformed Services

chance The unpredictability of an event. Often used to refer to the likelihood of a random phenomenon, for which individual outcomes are uncertain but there is nevertheless a regular distribution over a large number of repetitions, as in tossing a fair coin.

chance action (S. Freud) An action that appears to have no conscious purpose but may subserve an unconscious intention (for example, forgetting a hat in someone's house, probably meaning that the person wants to return to that house).

chance difference A statistical difference between two measured variables that could have occurred fortuitously and that do not occur reliably. Such differences give no evidence of true difference and cannot be ascribed to error, biased sampling, or other improper experimental procedure.

chance error An unbiased error. See RANDOM ERROR.

chance events (A. Bandura) These are the many chance encounters people experience in their daily lives. These encounters occur fortuitously rather than through deliberate plan. Some chance encounters touch people only lightly, some leave more lasting effects, and others thrust people into new directions of life.

chance-half correlation Rare phrase for split-half correlation.

chance occurrence An occurrence brought about by the conjunction of two or more independent trains of antecedents, this conjunction being usually unpredictable.

chance variations Changes in hereditary traits due to unknown factors.

change An alteration; the advent of a specific difference in the character of a phenomenon in the course of time.

change agent 1. In industry, a person hired to evaluate production processes and to suggest superior methods of operation. 2. A person involved in making changes in social programs, such as school curriculums, social-policy planning, or other ways of meeting people's needs. See ECOLOGICAL-SYSTEMS MODEL.

changed-trace hypothesis A postulate that new information can change old information in memory. Explains the misinformation effect. See MULTIPLE TRACE HYPOTHESIS.

change effect (R. Thouless) A tendency for scores to drop temporarily following the change in experimental conditions in a parapsychological test.

change fear See NEOPHOBIA.

change of environment A technique for eliminating undesirable behavior patterns. A mere change of scene usually produces only temporary results, but if the new environment has different elements from the old one, it is sometimes effective (for example, moving a child from one school to another).

change of life A euphemism for menopause. See CLIMACTERIC, MENOPAUSE.

change-over delay (COD) In reinforcement research, a period of inactivity between changes in the schedule.

change scores A difference of scores between a first and a second equated test.

channel An information transmission system, such as the nervous system that transmits coded messages from sense receptors (input) to effectors (output).

channel capacity In information theory, the maximum amount of information that a given channel or sensory system can accommodate. Usually measured by determining the maximum number of stimulus alternatives among which an individual can discriminate.

channels of communication Channels involved in the source and destination of face-to-face messages, comprising speech (source: vocal tract: destination—ear), kinesics (body movement—eyes; odor (chemical processes—nose); touch (body surface—skin); observation (body surface—eye); and proxemics (body placement—eye).

chaos theory The theory that linear equations cannot predict some complex phenomena such as weather changes, and that relatively minor events at some point in time can have enormous consequences at a later time. This theory put into application can make sense out of complex problems. Practical applications call for computer-generated solutions. Also known as nonlinear dynamical systems theory.

chaotic meditation A nontraditional type of meditation in which participants experience a period of considerable excitement and restlessness followed by a period of quiet contemplation.

chaotic systems Objective systems that cannot be predicted to any degree of certainty.

character 1. An attribute, trait, distinctive feature. 2. The totality of qualities or traits, particularly the characteristic moral, social, and religious attitudes of a person. Character can be said to be what a person actually is and personality what the person appears to be. See IDIOPANIMA, PERSONALITY. 3. In typography, any letter, number, or symbol. 4. In psychoanalytic theory, the attributes that categorize a person into a character type. Types of character include: COMPLIANT, EXPLOITATIVE, GENITAL, HOARDING, NECROPHILOUS, NEUROTIC, PHOBIC, RECEPTIVE.

character analysis 1. (W. Reich) Combination of psychoanalytic and Marxian theories referring to symptoms of individuals as a function of sexual urges (id) and social prohibitions (superego). Reich viewed the task of the analyst, to free the segmented body, section by section to restore life energies. A sign of normality was the ability of people to have powerful "pure" orgasms without fantasies. See CHARACTER-ANALYTIC VEGETOTHERAPY. 2. The psychoanalytic treatment of character disorders. 3. The study of character traits allegedly revealed by external characteristics, such as the length of the fingers or shape of the jaw. See CHARACTEROLOGY, PHYSIOGNOMY.

character-analytic vegetotherapy (W. Reich) Name of Wilhelm Reich's system of character analysis and orgone therapy developed in opposition to Sigmund Freud. See CHARACTER ANALYSIS, CHARACTER ARMO(U)R, ORGONE THERAPY.

character armo(u)r (W. Reich) In Wilhelm Reich's character-analytic approach, the assumption of an impenetrable front by a person to protect the self against intrusions by others. A hypothetical set of character patterns (for example, overaggressiveness, cynicism, passivity, and ingratiation) that serve as defenses against anxiety, standing in the way of attempts to penetrate to the deeper, unconscious levels of the personality. See FLIGHT INTO HEALTH, RESISTANCE.

character defense A defensive pattern, such as humor or escape tendencies, that has become an established personality trait. See CHARACTER ARMO(U)R.

character development The gradual development of moral concepts, conscience, religious values or views, and social attitudes as an essential aspect of personality development.

character disorder A persistent personality pattern characterized by maladaptive behavior with immaturity and rebelliousness as major components, with behaviors generally seen as socially undesirable and personally dangerous; these include promiscuity, compulsive gambling, and substance addictions. Most such individuals are seen as social misfits who have deliberately taken such roles, who see themselves as normal, who tend to have hostility toward their immediate families, who do not establish strong positive relations with others. See SOCIOPATHY.

character displacement The effect of environmental change on a species. See DARWINISM.

characteristic 1. Peculiar to an individual or prominent among the individual's distinctive features. 2. A distinguishing mark. 3. The integral part of a logarithm.

characterization Processes by which personality and character are developed in an individual through interaction with other members of a group.

characterize 1. To be a notable or distinctive feature of an individual, species, disease, etc. 2. To point out such a feature in an individual.

character neurosis (K. Horney) A disorder in which neurotic traits, such as inappropriate shyness, aggressiveness, and avoidance, are dominant parts of the total personality and do not generate intrapsychic conflicts. See CHARACTER DISORDER, PSYCHOTHERAPY, SOCIOPATHY.

characterology 1. A branch of psychology concerned with character and personality. 2. A pseudoscience in which character is "read" by external signs of body characteristics such as hair color. Also called character analysis.

character structure (G. W. Allport) The unique, established pattern of attitudes, traits, and reaction patterns that characterize the individual personality. Also known as personality structure. See ALLPORT'S PERSONALITY-TRAIT THEORY, CATTELL'S FACTORIAL THEORY OF PERSONALITY.

character trait (G. W. Allport) An enduring aspect of the personality associated with ethical or principled aspects. For example, a person may have many faults, but never tells a lie. Truth-telling would be one of that person's character traits.

character types Categories of personality based upon character traits and behavior patterns, for example, anal character, exploitative orientation, oral character, paranoiac character. See PERSONALITY TYPES.

Charas A potent cannabis preparation consumed as hashish. See BHANG, PSYCHEDELICS.

Charcot triad (J-M. Charcot) Three symptoms: Intention tremor, nystagmus, and staccato speech, consequences of brain-stem involvement in multiple sclerosis. See SALPÊATRIÈRE SCHOOL.

charge of affect A form of cathexis in which a part of the instinct is detached from the idea and acquires affective value.

charisma 1. The quality of personal magnetism and the ability to appeal to and win the confidence of a large and diverse group of people. 2. In theology, refers to people believed to have special powers. 3. In psychology and sociology, refers to personal qualities (charm, believability) that enable that person to influence other people, as exemplified in outstanding world political, social, and religious leaders.

charismatic authority A person who generates an aura of superior understanding, knowledge, and ability, and manages to get people to be followers. Such persons can achieve a great deal of good (Mahatma Ghandi) or harm (Adolf Hitler).

charismatic leadership (B. Bass) A management style in which followers endow leaders with extraordinary competence and have complete faith in them. The charismatic leader is confident, determined, and mission-oriented. See IDEALIZED INFLUENCE, INSPIRATIONAL MOTIVATION, TRANSFORMATIONAL LEADERSHIP.

charlatan A person claiming to have expert knowledge and practical skill in some specific area but is actually lacking in such knowledge or skill. Also known as a faker or quack. See PSEUDOSCIENCE.

Charles Bonnet's syndrome A disorder of aging marked by visual hallucinations not related to any other expressions of mental disease. Also known as Bonnet's syndrome.

charley horse Slang for a stiffness, cramping, and muscle spasm after strenuous exercise. Also known as postexertional myalgia.

Charlier's checks (C. W. L. Charlier) A check on the accuracy of computations of certain statistics, such as the standard deviation, when these are performed by hand using grouped data.

charm An ornament or other object, worn for its supposed efficacy either to ward off sickness, disease, or evil, or to secure good fortune.

Charpentier's bands A series of alternating light and dark bands which follow a moving slit-shaped stimulus presented against a dark visual field and which are due to fluctuations of visual excitation similar to those which give rise to afterimages. Named after French physician Pierre Marie A. Charpentier (1852–1916). See FECHNER'S COLORS.

Charpentier's illusion (P. M. A. Charpentier) 1. See AUTOKINETIC ILLUSION. 2. See SIZE-WEIGHT ILLUSION.

Charpentier's law (P. M. A. Charpentier) A visual-perception rule that the product of the foveal image area and the intensity of light is constant for threshold stimuli. See CHARPENTIER'S BANDS.

chart A diagram on a two-dimensional surface, showing the relations between two or more classes, rubrics, or variable quantities.

chastity Generally refers to a person who has never participated in voluntary sexual behavior. Term has various meanings depending on the society or subgroups.

chastity belt A device used in the middle ages, locked on to a woman's pelvic area to prevent her from having sexual relations.

chat *khat*

chatterbox effect A tendency of some hydrocephalus patients to appear fluent in conversation, but be unable to communicate meaningfully, fabricating incidents and events to hold the attention of listeners, but likely later unable to recall what was discussed. Also known as cocktail-party conversationalism.

chauvinism Excessive patriotism, typically with attending a low opinion of other countries and cultures. Derives from Nicolas Chauvin, a military man with an unshakable devotion to Napoleon Bonaparte. See ETHNOCENTRISM, MALE CHAUVINISM, PREJUDICE, RACE.

CHD Abbreviation for coronary heart disease. See CORONARY ARTERY DISEASE.

check 1. To inhibit a self-movement, or to oppose some action in another individual. 2. To test the correctness of an observation or result. Also known as check up, control, verify. 3. To annotate with a checkmark.

checkerboard patterns See SMETS PATTERN RESPONSES.

checklist   1. Examining any kind of list of items and indicating which ones meet certain criteria. 2. A list of varied behaviors to be checked by an observer of behavior of an individual or of members of a group or of the group itself as a unit. 3. The creation of such a list, as in an industrial psychologist interviewing employees to locate problems in an organization. The problems are written down and arranged in some pattern (such as in terms of frequency) and then may either to be used to generate a report or for other purposes with other groups.

check list/sheet   A form for recording the frequency with which certain events are taking place.

checkoff   In labor relations, the process by which union dues are collected by the employer by payroll deduction and remitted to the union.

checkreading   In ergonomics, a systematic inspection of displays to confirm normal values.

cheilophagia   Compulsive biting of one's own lips. Also known as chilophagia.

cheimaphobia   Excessive fear of the cold or of a cold object. Also known as cheimatophobia, psychrophobia.

cheiromancy   palmistry

chelation   The process of binding or attaching chemically, especially bond formation between a metal ion and another molecule through the action of a chelating agent.

chemical antagonism   See DRUG ANTAGONISM.

chemical castration   Hormonal treatment to effect the same result as surgical castration. Typically, a male sex offender is given antiandrogenics such as medroxyprogesterone acetate. The efficacy and ethics of this practice are unclear.

chemical communication   The use of pheromones and location markers for intraspecies communication by many species from invertebrates to nonhuman primates. There is some evidence of this factor in humans.

chemical dependency   Behavior of a compulsive type due to a purported need, whether psychological or physical, for substances such as alcohol, or other drugs over which affected individuals claim they have no control. Such chemical dependency may eventually lead to an early death. The term is a euphemism for drug addiction. See ADDICTIVE ALCOHOLISM, SUBSTANCE DEPENDENCE.

chemical methods of brain study   Methods of studying brain function that use three general types of preparation: (a) the in vivo method, analyzing chemical processes in the alive, functioning, intact brain; (b) the in vitro method, maintaining portions (slices) of brain tissue in nutrient solutions; and (c) the processed tissue method, in which neural tissue is ground up for chemical analysis. See IMMUNOHISTOCHEMISTRY.

chemical reflex   Any reflexive action in which the stimulation is chemical in nature.

chemical senses   The senses of taste and smell activated by contact with chemical substances. Taste depends on electrolytes; olfactory (smell) organs respond to vapors. See CHEMORECEPTORS.

chemical stimulation   An activity change in certain types of nerve receptors caused by contact with specific electrolytes or molecules. The effect usually occurs only in the senses of taste and smell. See CHEMICAL SENSES.

chemical stimulation of brain   In studying brain activity, researchers have been able to inject various neurotransmitters (brain chemicals) to selected parts of the brain to elicit different behaviors (for example, if the ventral medial nucleus of the hypothalamus is affected, an animal's eating behavior can be dramatically changed).

chemical trail   Secretions from an organism's scent glands following its passage over a surface. Such spoors or pheromones provide species information important for survival. See PHEROMONES.

chemical transmission   See ACETYLCHOLINE, SYNAPTIC TRANSMISSION.

chemical transmitter   Any substance that participates in the transmission of a nerve impulse. These include acetylcholine, norepinephrine, dopamine, serotonin, and gamma-aminobutyric acid (GABA).

chemiotaxis   chemotaxis

chemopsychiatry   The use of chemical substances in the treatment of psychiatric disorders. See DRUG THERAPY, PSYCHOPHARMACOLOGY.

chemoreceptor(s)   Sensory nerve endings, such as those in taste buds capable of reacting to certain chemical stimuli. The chemical molecules or the electrolyte generally must be in solution to be detected by chemoreceptors. Some chemoreceptors react only to certain stimuli, such as those producing a bitter taste. Sour taste buds detect the pH of acidic substances. See CHEMICAL TRANSMITTER.

chemoreceptor trigger zone   A cluster of cells in the medulla oblongata sensitive to certain toxic chemicals that cause vomiting. The zone is particularly sensitive to narcotics and responds to their stimulation by producing dizziness, nausea, and vomiting, the precise effects depending upon the agent and the dosage.

chemotaxis   An involuntary change of orientation of a cell or organism toward (positive) or away from (negative) a chemical. Also known as chemiotaxis, chemotropism. See TAXIS, TROPISM.

chemotherapy   (P. Ehrlich) The treatment of physical diseases or behavioral disorders by drugs (chemical substances) to arrest or lessen symptomology. Also known as pharmacotherapy. See DRUG THERAPY.

chemotropism   chemotaxis

Chernoff faces   (H. Chernoff) Cartoon-like schematic faces that vary along 18 dimensions, used to study multidimensional discrimination.

cherophobia   Morbid fear of having a good time; fear of having fun.

chess-board illusion   (H. Helmholtz) A distorted perception of depth that results from looking at a checkered figure in a circle, with the black and white quadrangles shown progressively larger toward the periphery to compensate for the distortion upon the peripheral portion of the retina, and seen as if in perspective.

chest voice   The low register and full tones created by pectoral breathing and chest resonance.

chewing behavior   A reflex process related primarily to the ingestion of food. Animal research shows that chewing behavior is controlled by neurons in the medial nucleus of the lateral hypothalamus and can be produced by electrostimulation. Destruction of the lateral hypothalamic nuclei results in starvation unless the animals are sustained by tube or intravenous feeding. Chewing behavior may also be a manifestation of nervous tension, as in bruxism. See OVERWEIGHT.

chewing method   A nonspecific relaxation method used in the treatment of certain types of functional speech and voice disorders such as stuttering.

Cheyne's disease   A form of hypochondriasis marked by morbid anxiety of patients about their health. Also known as English malady. Named after Scottish physician George Cheyne (1671–1743).

Cheyne-Stokes breathing/respiration   A pattern of breathing with gradually increasing and then decreasing depth and sometimes rate, with periods of apnea in between. Seen often in coma with respiratory-center involvement. Named after physicians John Cheyne (1777–1836) and William Stokes (1804–1878).

Cheyne-Stokes psychosis   (J. Cheyne & W. Stokes) A form of psychosis characterized by anxiety, restlessness, and Cheyne-Stokes breathing. See CHEYNE-STOKES BREATHING/ RESPIRATION.

chi   1. [Chee] The concept of "life force" as found in the phrase *tai chi*. See PRANA. 2. [ky] The twenty-second letter of the Greek alphabet. See APPENDIX C.

chiaroscuro   (bright-dark—Italian) The illusion of depth or distance in a painting produced by the use of light and shade.

chiaroscuro effect   The reactions of people to the differential shadings of the Rorschach cards. Different experts give different interpretations, including that this is evidence of a person's sensitivity to sensuality.

Chicago Institute for Psychoanalysis   An institute founded by Franz Alexander in 1932. See CHICAGO SCHOOL (meaning 2).

Chicago School   1. The Chicago school of functionalism that centered around the University of Chicago's Department of Psychology. Included such psychologists as James Rowland Angell, Harvey Carr, and Edward S. Robinson. Similar to Functional Psychology. See FUNCTIONALISM. 2. The neo-Freudian Chicago school of psychoanalysis that centered around Franz Alexander's Chicago Institute for Psychoanalysis. (Named after the city of Chicago and unrelated to the Chicago school of the University of Chicago.)

Chicago Q-Sort   (R. J. Corsini) A list of 50 adjectives to be distributed in a ten horizontal and five vertical rectangular array: the five words in the high-rated vertical column are rated 9, and the five words in the low-rated vertical column are rated 0. The adjectives can be sorted for self, others, ideal self, how persons think others perceive them, etc. Different sorts can be easily correlated by hand or machine. Constructed at the University of Chicago. See Q-SORT.

chicken game   A conflict situation in which the selection of the worst choice spells disaster for both parties, such as in two automobiles racing toward each other, each having two options—stay in the same lane or turn right. If both turn right, both are "chicken"; if one turns right but not the other, the one who turned right is "chicken" but if both stay in the same lane, both are dead.

chief ray   A light ray from a point focused on the center of the retina. See PRIMARY LINE OF SIGHT.

child   A young boy or girl. It was only with the evolution of the modern concepts of individuality and personality that children were seen apart from adults, and that the reality of child development and the need for child education became recognized. Medieval paintings depicted neonates with adult features and adult head-to-body proportions, and there were essentially no special clothing, institutions, toys, or instructional materials for children.

child abuse (CA)   The harming of a child, usually by parents. Hard to define and especially to prove in a court of law, since in addition to physical abuse (for example, beating or sexual abuse), there exists psychological abuse (for example, name calling, threatening, or criticizing). Also, what may to one parent be a "spanking" or a "reprimand," may appear as a "beating" to someone else. Some authorities, such as Rudolf Dreikurs, view over-protection, over-supervision, and pampering as child abuse. Children at risk have parents with some combination of the following: unrealistic expectations, a history of being abused or ignored as children, immaturity, poor stress-coping skills, unsatisfied needs, and difficulty in forming close relationships. See BATTERED-CHILD SYNDROME, CHILD MOLESTATION, MUNCHAUSEN SYNDROME BY PROXY.

child analysis   The application of psychoanalytic principles to the treatment of children. It became a separate field when Melanie Klein and Anna Freud developed the play technique, in which the child patient acts out feelings and relationships through the use of dolls and toys. See PLAY THERAPY.

child behavior checklist   A list of common problems listed on a form. The usual purpose of such a form is to determine from parents, teachers, or others, major problems presented by children. See FAMILY RELATIONSHIP INDEX for a form intended to evaluate a child in terms of problems in the home.

childbirth fear   See MAIEUSIOPHOBIA, TERATOPHOBIA, TOCOPHOBIA.

child-care aids   Any device or system that enables a parent with a disability to care for an infant or child. Such aids include cribs with adjustable height and swing sides, infant chairs on wheels, prefolded diapers, prepared formula in ready-to-use bottles, and bottle-holder attachments for cribs, baby dishes and other equipment with suction cups, and special carrying devices for moving or transporting an infant or small child.

child-care facilities   1. Day-care centers usually established by government agencies but sometimes by industrial firms, churches, or social agencies, with the prime object of enabling disadvantaged mothers to hold jobs. 2. Special facilities such as developmental schools for physically challenged, delayed, or abused children. See FAMILY CARE.

child-care worker (CCW)   A person trained to work with disturbed or neglected children on a day-to-day basis in collaboration with other members of the treatment team. See FAMILY EDUCATION.

child-centered   An environment in homes, schools, and other places designed to encourage fulfillment of the child's needs and to be maximally safe for toddlers and younger children. May include removing toxic chemicals from sink cabinets near the floor, covering empty electrical sockets, keeping sharp knives in a locked drawer or out of the child's reach.

child-centered family   1. A family in which the children's needs are paramount, sometimes to a point where they dominate the family constellation and the parents' needs become secondary. 2. Refers to a school or a home environment concerned with or dominated by the children's needs or desires. Also known as child-dominated family, child-focused family.

child development   The sequential changes in the child's behavior patterns and physical characteristics as the child matures. See CHILD, DEVELOPMENTAL TASKS, GESELL, DEVELOPMENTAL SCALES/SCHEDULES, PSYCHOSEXUAL DEVELOPMENT.

child-directed speech   The kind that adults, especially mothers, use in addressing babies. Characterized by slow pronunciation, exaggerated and high-pitched intonation, simple vocabulary and syntax, and made-up "baby words." Also known as caretaker speech, motherese.

child find   A diagnostic program in some public schools that screens children between the ages of three and five years to determine the existence of any physical or developmental disorders. Depending on the results of the screening some children may be placed in early-intervention preschool programs.

child find organizations   Social agencies and programs that attempt to locate runaway or throwaway children and also to change any conditions that may contribute to such problems. Such programs often are staffed by volunteers and usually are funded by charitable contributions. Child find organizations work closely with local law enforcement organizations and the National Center for Missing and Exploited Children (NCMEC).

child guidance   A mental health approach focused on the prevention of possible future disorders by offering didactic and therapeutic aid to a child and family at a time when intervention may have a beneficial effect. See FAMILY EDUCATION.

child guidance clinics   See CHILD-GUIDANCE MOVEMENT.

child-guidance movement   A trend toward the establishment of clinics, institutes, and organizations devoted to the prevention or active treatment of mental and emotional disorders in children. Major focus is on the application of mental-health principles to behavior and adjustment problems before they become fixed and hard to modify. See FAMILY EDUCATION.

childhood   In humans, the period of life between infancy and puberty. Definitions of childhood may differ not only between cultures, but also within cultures. Generally, childhood extends from time of the ability of a child to walk to sexual maturity, or from about age one to twelve. See ADOLESCENCE, INFANCY.

childhood adjustment disorders   Persistent maladaptive behavior that may be classified into three groups: habit patterns such as nail-biting, thumb-sucking, enuresis; misbehavior such as disobedience, stealing, destructiveness; neurotic traits such as tics, stuttering, overactivity, fears. Frequently such disorders stem from poor parenting or mistreatment, especially by parents and siblings. Some responsibility for some disorders may be attributed to children in individual cases. See PARENTING.

childhood amnesia   A normal failure to remember events of early childhood. Most people have no memory of their lives before the age of 3 or 4. Some adults claim to remember incidents before the age of one.

childhood depression   Depressive patterns seen in children before the age of 12. Demonstrated by an inability to have fun, display normal emotional reactions, or form and maintain friendships.

childhood disorders   General phrase referring to any of many mental disorders seen in children. See AUTISM, CONDUCT DISORDER, HYPERACTIVITY, MENTAL RETARDATION.

childhood fears   Fears occurring at different stages of childhood. Though no single fear is inevitable, many children tend to fear strangers at about eight months, darkness at about three years, snakes or large animals between three and four, imaginary monsters and ghosts between four and five, and death beginning at nine or ten.

childhood land   See LAND OF CHILDHOOD.

childhood motivation   (G. W. Allport) The search by adolescents for self-identity that usually includes experimentation with various aspects of life, before long-term future planning begins. See PROPRIATE STRIVING.

childhood neuroses   Symptoms in children under 8 years of age that resemble the neurotic symptoms of adults, such as anxiety, sleeplessness, tension, or phobias.

childhood schizophrenia   Abnormal dysfunctional behavior appearing early in life. Symptoms include failure to relate to other people, disturbed language, low frustration tolerance, bizarre postures, and playing endlessly with the same toy. See AUTISM, SCHIZOPHRENIA.

childhood sensorineural lesions   Organic disorders of the auditory system that may be a cause of hearing loss in children. May be congenital and due to a failure of the inner ear to develop normally in the fetal stage or the result of measles, German measles, mumps, and scarlet fever among other causes, as well as direct traumas.

childhood symbiosis   Overdependency in early childhood, shown by overattachment to the mother or mother figure.

child molestation   A form of child abuse characterized by sexual activity. Includes incest with an older member of the family as well as rape, sexual touching, or other erotic behavior between an adult and a child between the periods of infancy and adolescence. Certain social and cultural patterns accepted by one culture may be regarded as child molestation in other societies. See BATTERED-CHILD SYNDROME, PEDOPHILIA.

child neglect   The denial of attention, care, or affection essential for the normal development of a child's physical, emotional, and intellectual qualities, usually due to indifference or disregard.

child-parent fixation   An obsessive child-parent relationship that harms other relationships. Within families all kinds of overly absorbing relations can be established between parents and individual children that in some cases are harmful to all in the family.

child-penis wish   In psychoanalytic theory, the replacement of a little girl's wish for a penis by a wish for a child of her own. The girl may associate her own father with the father of the child she wishes to have, thereby initiating an Electra complex situation.

child-placement counseling   A form of counseling focused on decisions and problems associated with the placement of a child who is considered difficult, unwanted, or has a disability.

child pornography   Pornography in which a child (or a young adult simulating one) is depicted to arouse adults, invariably men. Also known as kiddie porn.

child psychology   The branch of psychology concerned with the systematic study of behavior, adjustment, and growth of a human from birth to maturity. See ANXIETY DISORDERS OF CHILDHOOD OR ADOLESCENCE, ATTENTION-DEFICIT DISORDER, COGNITIVE AND EMOTIONAL PROCESSES, CONDUCT DISORDER, DEVELOPMENTAL TIMETABLE, EATING BEHAVIOR, EMOTIONAL AND BEHAVIORAL DISORDERS, ENCOPRESIS, FAMILY EDUCATION, INFANT PSYCHIATRY, LATCHKEY CHILDREN, MARASMUS, PARENT-CHILD RELATIONS, PEER RELATIONSHIPS, PSYCHOSEXUAL DEVELOPMENT, STUTTERING.

child-rearing practices/styles   Child-raising patterns differ in various societies, cultures, eras and from family to family at any time. Issues such as discipline, affection, and toilet-training are purported to have a profound effect on personality formation, mental and physical health, and interpersonal relationships. See FAMILY EDUCATION.

children in need of supervision (CHINS)   A designation by either a court or a social agency, of children who are considered to require adult attention. Reasons may include being abandoned or neglected by caretakers, being orphaned, or otherwise being abused by caretakers.

Children's Apperception Test (C.A.T. or CAT) (L. Bellak & S. S. Bellak) A projective examination for use with children 3 to 11 years of age, based on the same principles as the Thematic Apperception Test (TAT). Various supplements are available.

Children's Category Test (CCT)   (T. Boll) A nonverbal examination intended to measure complex intellectual functioning in individuals 5 to 16 years of age.

Children's Depression Inventory (CDI)   (M. Kovacs) An inventory of 27 self-rating items used in attempting to determine the level of depression in school-aged children and adolescents (7–17 years of age), based on the Beck Depression Inventory (BDI).

Children's Embedded Figures Test (CEFT)   (S. A. Karp) A verbal and manual examination that attempts to measure perceptual processes including field dependence/independence.

Children's Memory Scale (CMS)   (M. Cohen) A measurement instrument attempting to compare memory and learning to ability, attention, and achievement.

Children's Personality Questionnaire   (R. B. Porter) Paper-and-pencil instrument designed to measure 14 primary personality traits such as emotional stability and self-concept.

Children's Problems Checklist   (J. A. Schinka) Paper-and-pencil test to be completed by a caregiver intended to identify problems in 11 areas such as play, concentration, and habits.

Children's State-Trait Anxiety Inventory   (C. D. Spielberger) An instrument used to assess current anxiety and anxiety proneness in children, grades 4 to 8.

children's thinking   See COGNITIVE DEVELOPMENT.

chill factor   See WIND-CHILL INDEX.

chilophagia   **cheilophagia**

chimera   1. In embryology, the individual produced by grafting part of one animal's embryo on to the embryo of another (whether of same or different species). 2. An organism that has incongruous genetic elements from two different zygotes. See MOSAICISM. 3. See CHIMERISM. Named for the mythical Chimera, a monster with a lion's head, goat's body, and snake's tail.

chimeric stimulation   (R. W. Sperry) A person with a brain split in half by cutting through the corpus callosum, looks through two lenses with both eye simultaneously and sees a face consisting of the left half of one person's face joined to the right half of another person's face. If the participant is unaware of peculiarities about the stimuli, this indicates there are two separate spheres of conscious awareness running parallel to each other in each of the two hemispheres of the brain.

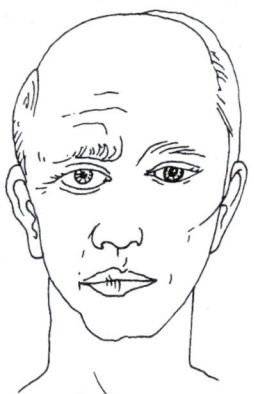

chimeric stimulation

chimerism   A chromosomal anomaly, similar to mosaicism, except that the two different cell populations arise from two different zygotes. The organism is composed of two genetically distinct tissues (such as partly male, partly female); it may also be an artificial organism having tissues consisting of several distinctly different other tissues. Sometimes known as cellular mosaicism.

China syndrome   A form of nuclear-age neurosis in which concern is directed toward a possible catastrophic meltdown of a nuclear reactor core. Name derives from the folk fantasy in which the melting down of a runaway nuclear-reactor core would burn a hole all the way through the earth, and presumably to China on the other side, while producing a massive fallout of radioactive debris on the countryside.

CHINS   See CHILDREN IN NEED OF SUPERVISION.

chionophobia   Morbid fear of snow.

chipping   The controlled, often long-term, use of heroin or other opiates.

chiromancy   palmistry

chirosophy   Ostensible knowledge of a person's character and probable future, derived from the inspection of the lines of the hand and other features.

χ^2 Symbol for Chi-squared. See CHI-SQUARE, CHI-SQUARE DISTRIBUTION.

chi-square (χ^2)   A statistical procedure that enables making inferences about categorical data. For testing goodness of fit, it is possible to determine whether an observed frequency is within or departs from theoretical or empirical expectation. Chi-square compares the frequency of occurrence actually observed with the frequency expected by chance.

chi-square test of goodness of fit   See CHI-SQUARE.

chloral derivatives   A group of sedative-hypnotic drugs first synthesized in the 19th century and introduced as substitutes for alcohol and opium, which were then used to induce sleep.

chloral hydrate   A nonbarbiturate sedative and anticonvulsant. See CHLORAL DERIVATIVES, MICKEY FINN.

chlordiazepoxide hydrochloride   Generic name for one of the first and most widely used of the class of mild tranquilizers of the class of benzodiazepines. Appearing in the mid-1960s under the trade name Librium, it replaced the then fashionable Miltown/Equanil (meprobamate). Librium is used as a mild anxiolytic and in helping alcoholics cope with symptoms of withdrawal. See VALIUM.

chlormezanone   An anxiolytic that resembles meprobamate in its pharmacologic activity and is administered for treatment of anxiety and tension states associated with psychoneurotic disorders. Also known as chlormethazanone.

chlorpromazine (CPZ)   Generic name for a neuroleptic drug of the phenothiazine class. The first major tranquilizer, introduced in the early 1950s and revolutionizing the care of the severely mentally ill. Effects include a slowing of motor activity and reduction in emotionality. It is also an antihistamine, anticholinergic, and antispasmodic agent. Used mainly in the treatment of schizophrenia and natural and drug-induced manic states. In the United States it was marketed under the trade name of Thorazine. See PHENOTHIAZINES.

choc   (shock—French) An uncoordinated response triggered by an unexpected sudden stimulus.

chocolate   A confection rich in phenylethylamine, a chemical that can mimic the "high" associated with feeling in love, possibly explaining the urge to binge on it in periods of stress.

choice   The initiation of a voluntary act, or the attainment of a verdict, after a period of deliberation during which alternative acts have been experienced in thought.

choice awareness   A common procedure in counseling and psychotherapy in which the counselor or therapist introduces the concept of alternative choices to thinking, feeling or behaving.

choice experiment/reaction   A test or situation that requires different responses to different stimuli, as in tapping once when a red light appears and tapping twice at a green light.

choice of a neurosis   A concept that certain conditions tend to lead individuals to generate a neurosis, but what form this neurosis will take depends on the individual, not consciously, but rather in with the individual's propensity (for example, two similar people in similar situations may end up with quite different neurotic traits). See SYMPTOM CHOICE.

choice point   A place in a situation or a test, for example, a maze, where the subject must make a choice of direction or response.

choice reaction   In reaction experiments, the situation of being able to choose between two or more standard responses to stimuli. See CHOICE EXPERIMENT.

choice reaction time   The time taken from the initiation of a signal to a reaction when a choice is involved. Thus, if the choice is between two signals, the reaction time will be relatively short, but were the choice to be among three or more choices, the reaction times would be increasingly longer. As discrimination between stimuli gets more difficult, reaction times (RTs) increase.

choice shift   A change of decision as the result of a group discussion in comparison to individual decisions made prior to the discussions. Some individuals will opt to change to a more radical position than they held originally (risky shifts), and some will decide to take a more conservative position (cautious shifts).

choice shift effect   A purported tendency for groups to make riskier decisions on most problems than the average group member who decides alone; experimental procedures can be of three major types: (a) initial individual decisions by someone who is or who becomes a leader, (b) individual decisions after group discussion and decisions, and (c) individual decisions following group discussion but no group decision. See CAUTIOUS SHIFT, CHOICE SHIFT, RISKY SHIFT.

choice stimuli   In a learning or a decision situation, choosing which one of two simultaneous stimuli to attend to.

choking-fear   See PNIGOPHOBIA.

choking (under pressure)   Sub-optimal performance due to pressure to perform well. See PERFORMANCE ANXIETY.

cholecystokinin (CCK)   A hormone released into the blood when food is absorbed in the intestines that will signal the medial nucleus of the hypothalamus that food has been eaten.

choleric personality/type   A temperament characterized by irritability and quick temper, which Hippocrates and Galen attributed to an excess of yellow bile. See HUMORAL THEORY.

cholesterol   A substance, technically an alcohol, present in fats of some animal tissues. It is a precursor of all steroid hormones and of vitamin D. Cholesterol is associated with circulatory disorders because of the high levels of cholesterol often found in obese individuals and those afflicted by stress, tension, high blood pressure, and atherosclerosis.

choline A water-soluble substance involved in the metabolism of fat and a precursor of the neurotransmitter acetylcholine. Has the same pharmacologic actions as acetylcholine but is much less potent. Choline is converted to acetylcholine by the influence of acetyl-coenzyme A. It has vitamin-like activity and sometimes is included in the vitamin-B complex.

choline acetylase An enzyme involved in the production of the neurotransmitter acetylcholine from choline and acetyl-coenzyme. Also known as choline acetyltransferase (CAT).

cholinergic (H. H. Dale) Pertaining to a type of nerve cell or neurophysiological function mediated by the neurotransmitter acetylcholine and tending to be associated with the parasympathetic nervous system.

cholinergic drug A substance that has a cholinergic function.

cholinergic synapse A synapse that uses acetylcholine as a transmitter substance to mediate a neural activity.

cholinergic system The part of the autonomic nervous system that reacts to cholinergic drugs, such as acetylcholine. Cholinergic system activities are inhibited by cholinergic blocking drugs, such as atropine.

cholinesterase An enzyme that destroys the neurotransmitter acetylcholine; most significantly, at the synapses of nerves, although the enzyme is present in many other places. Less often called specific cholinesterase (as there are other similar enzymes that are less specific) or acetylcholinesterase.

chord keyboard A combination of keys permitting a wide range of characters to be effected by a small numbers of keys (for example, the 23-key stenographic machine).

chorda tympani A branch of the facial nerve which passes downward and in back of the tympanic membrane. Contains taste sensation and sublingual salivary-gland fibers.

chorditis tuberosa A small whitish node on one or both vocal chords caused by vocal abuse and resulting in a low-pitch and hoarse voice.

chorea A motor-nerve disorder that manifests itself by spasms and twitches, primarily of the face but also of the limbs. Kinds of chorea include buttonmaker's, electric, Huntington's, Sydenham's. Various kinds of chorea have also been known historically as Saint Anthony's dance, Saint John's dance, Saint Modestus' disease, Saint Vitus' dance, Saint With's dance. See CHOREA NUTANS, CHOREA OSCILLATORIA, CHOREA SALTATORIA, HUNTINGTON'S CHOREA, VARIABLE CHOREA OF BRISSAUD.

chorea minor Sydenham's chorea

chorea nutans A functional (hysterical) symptom characterized by rhythmic nodding of the head. See CHOREA, CHOREA OSCILLATORIA.

chorea oscillatoria A functional (hysterical) symptom characterized by a rhythmical nodding of the whole body. See CHOREA NUTANS.

chorea saltatoria Chorea marked by involuntary jumping, which may be rhythmical or irregular. See CHOREA.

choreiform **choreoid**

choreiform movements Spasmodic involuntary movements similar to those occurring in chorea, whether due to that disorder or to other conditions. See TIC.

choreoathetosis A form of chorea in which the patient is unable to sustain any group of muscles in a fixed position. The effort is interrupted by slow, sinuous, purposeless movements. It is often found in the hands and fingers but also may occur in such muscles as those of the tongue.

choreoid Resembling chorea. Also known as choreiform.

chor(e)omania 1. A mental disorder characterized by a tendency toward dance-like activities. 2. An uncontrollable impulse to dance, as in the epidemics of frenzied, convulsive dancing that occurred in tenth-century Italy, spreading to Germany and the Flemish countries in the 13th and 14th centuries. Also known as dancing mania. See MASS HYSTERIA, TARANTISM.

chorion The outermost membranes of the sac that surrounds and protects the developing zygote (a fertilized ovum). Also known as chorionic sac.

chorionic villi sampling (CVS) A prenatal diagnostic procedure for fetal defects. A biopsy of fetal membrane villi is performed through the cervix around the ninth week of gestation, which is too early for amniocentesis.

choroid layer One of three coats, or tunics, covering the eyeball. It is located between the retina and sclera layers, covering almost 85% of the globe of the eyeball. The choroid layer contains blood vessels that supply the retina and a pigment that prevents extraneous light from affecting the retina. Also known as chorioid, choroid coat/membrane. See EYE.

choroid plexus A worm-like fringe of blood vessels in the pia mater layer of the meninges of the central nervous system. They are a source of cerebrospinal fluid. They extend through the third, fourth, and lateral ventricles of the brain.

choromania chor(e)omania

chrematisophilia Being sexually aroused by having to pay for sexual services.

chrematophobia Morbid fear of handling money or of the sight of money. Also known as chrometophobia, chronmetophobia.

Christian Science A religion started by Mary Baker Eddy (1821–1910). Primary beliefs include a system of morals according to which pain and disease, as illusions of the mind, are believed to be, and are dealt with as, forms of erroneous interpretations of reality and are to be treated by spiritual healing that sometimes appears to involve denial and assertion.

chroma In the Munsell system, the degree of hue in a color.

chroma-brightness coefficient The chromatic valence of a visual stimulus per unit of photometric intensity, or the ratio of color-producing power to brilliance-producing power. Also known as chroma-brilliance coefficient.

chromaesthesia chromesthesia

chroma scale See SPECTRAL SCALE.

chromatic Refers to color or to variations in visual experiences when some color is present.

chromatic aberration/error   In an optical system, the failure of rays of light from a given point to come to a focus at a point, owing to the fact that the short wavelengths (blue) are bent or refracted more than long wavelengths (red) by uncorrected lenses.

chromatic adaptation   A process by which the visual mechanism achieves equilibrium under the influence of a stimulus of non-daylight chromaticity. Complete chromatic adaptation is the apparent absence of hue in monochromatic light. See ADAPTATION.

chromatic audition   The perception of colors on hearing sounds. Also known as colored hearing. See SYNESTHESIA.

chromatic-brightness coefficient   The ratio of color to brightness of a display, there being a minimum in the yellow sector and a maximum in the violet section of the color spectrum. Also known as chromatic-brilliance coefficient.

chromatic-brilliance coefficient   See CHROMATIC-BRIGHTNESS COEFFICIENT.

chromatic colors   All colors other than black, white, and gray, that is, those colors that possess saturation and hue. See ACHROMATIC COLORS.

chromatic contrast   See COLOR CONTRAST.

chromatic dimming (phenomenon)   An apparent decrease in color saturation when light intensity is suddenly decreased.

chromatic error   See CHROMATIC ABERRATION.

chromatic flicker   A flicker sensation caused by rapid periodic changes in hue or saturation.

chromatic induction   See INDUCED COLOR.

chromaticity   A color-stimulus quality determined by its purity and wavelength. Also known as chromaticness.

chromaticity diagram   A three-dimensional geometrical model that combines the various facts about color mixture so that the viewer can grasp the principle of "color mixing" more readily. See COLOR PYRAMIDfor an illustration.

chromatic response   A category used in the evaluation of certain tests in which one or more colors may be included in addition to shapes or forms, such as in the Rorschach.

chromatics   1. The science of color or of color sensation. 2. See CHROMATIC SCALE.

chromatic scale   The sequence of musical tones in semitone steps through an octave. Also known as chromatics.

chromatic valence   1. A measure of the color-producing power of a visual stimulus, as contrasted with its capacity to evoke brilliance. 2. The strength of a color to affect the total color of a mixture.

chromatic vision   Perception of hues rather than only black and white, as in achromatic vision.

chromatid   In cell division, one of the two spiral filaments which make up a chromosome. Joined at the centromere, they separate, each going to opposite poles of the dividing cell to become new chromosomes in the daughter cells.

chromatin   (W. Flemming) A substance present in chromosomes and cell nuclei which accepts the stains of certain identifying dyes. The substance is composed of deoxyribonucleic acid (DNA) material and proteins.

chromatin-negative   Pertaining to the absence of a substance in the nuclei of human tissue cells that would indicate the presence of an XX, or female complement of sex chromosomes. A chromatin-negative cell, therefore, identifies the tissue as being from a male individual. See CHROMATIN-POSITIVE.

chromatin-positive   Pertaining to the presence in a human tissue cell of a nuclear substance that identifies the cell as being from a female. The substance, sometimes called a Barr body, represents X chromosome material not observed in the tissue cells of normal males. See CHROMATIN-NEGATIVE.

chromatography   A method of chemical analysis in which different molecules in a mixture of chemicals are separated according to their solubility, absorptive properties, or other factors. Kinds of chromatography include column, paper, and gas. Column chromatography and paper chromatography depend upon gravity to move a solvent through a substance as the components separate into predictable zones or areas.

chromatophobia   chromophobia

chromatopseudopsia   1. Color-blindness. 2. A visual aberration due to a variety of situations including being on certain drugs, or environmental stress situations such as being surrounded by snow leading to snow blindness.

chromatopsia   A visual aberration characterized by objects appearing to be abnormally colored or tinged with color, as when colorless substances appear red. Designated according to the color seen, for example, xanthopsia (yellow vision), chloropsia (green vision), and cyanopsia (blue vision). Caused by drugs, intense stimulation, or other abnormal conditions, for example, snow blindness.

chromatotropism   1. A change of color. 2. A simple orienting response, either positive or negative, to a given color or hue. Also known as chromotaxis. See TAXIS, TROPISM.

chromesthesia   A type of synesthesia or crossed perception characterized by experiencing a sensation of color when stimulated by a nonvisual stimulus such as hearing a particular tone (for example, perceiving the color red upon hearing the musical note C). Also known as chromaesthesia, chrom(a)esthesis, color hearing. See SYNESTHESIA.

chromophil substance   tigroid bodies

chromophobia   Morbid fear of color or colors. Also known as chromatophobia.

chromosomal aberration   1. A nonlethal variation in the character of a chromosome. 2. An abnormal chromosome or a congenital defect that can be attributed to an abnormal chromosome. Also known as chromosomal anomaly/defect. See SEX-CHROMOSOME ABERRATION.

chromosomal map   A diagram or photograph showing the number and arrangement of chromosomes for a given individual. See KARYOTYPE.

chromosomal mosaicism   A condition of genetic abnormality in which an individual organism's chromosomes represent two or more different cell lines although derived from a single zygote (fertilized egg). In humans, a person may have one normal cell line and another with an extra chromosome, such as 45,X/46,XX. Cell lines may differ within tissues and organs of the same person. Such mosaicism is associated with Down's syndrome and Turner's syndrome variants. Such individuals or body areas are called mosaic. Also known as chromosome mosaicism. See BARR BODY.

chromosomal sex   genetic sex

chromosome   (W. von Waldeyer-Hartz) A thread-like strand of deoxyribonucleic acid (DNA), ribonucleic acid (RNA), and other molecules that carries the genetic traits of an individual. The normal human complement of chromosomes totals 46 (23 pairs) containing more than 30,000 genes for specific hereditary traits. Types of chromosome include: ACCESSORY, ACROCENTRIC, FRAGILE X, HEMIZYGOUS, HOMOLOGOUS, RING, SEX, X, Y.

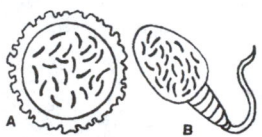

chromosomes   A depicts a human egg with 23 chromosomes, B depicts a human sperm with 23 chromosomes, and C depicts a human somatic (body) cell with two pairs of 23 chromosomes or 46 chromosomes.

chromosome abnormality   Anything in the nucleus of cells that differs from the usual arrangement and structure.

chromosome 18 (deletion of long arm)   A chromosomal disorder characterized by microcephaly, deafness, and mental retardation associated with the absence of part of the long arm of chromosome 18. Hypotonia and nystagmus are other effects. Also known as 46,XX18q-.

chromosome-18 trisomy   A chromosomal disorder of having an extra E-group chromosome (chromosomes 16, 17, or 18), resulting in offspring with a short neck with webbing, congenital heart disease, hernias, and neonatal jaundice. Neurologic effects include deafness, marked psychomotor retardation, jitteriness, seizures, and central nervous system defects. Also known as 47, XX + 18. See PSEUDOTRISOMY 18.

chromosome 5 (deletion of short arm)   See CRI DU CHAT SYNDROME.

chromosome 4 (deletion of short arm)   A chromosomal disorder of lacking a portion of chromosome 4, resulting in microcephaly, visual defects, severe retardation and indifference to painful stimuli. Until 1960, the condition was considered a variation of *cri du chat* syndrome, involving chromosome 5, although the cat-cry effect was rarely noted. Also known as 46XX4p-.

chromosome mosaicism   chromosomal mosaicism

chromosome number   The number of chromosomes present in the tissue cells of an organism. All members of a species normally have the same number of chromosomes. The normal number for humans is 46. The chromosome number of a gamete, or reproductive cell, of a human is half the somatic chromosome number, or 23. See DELETION.

chromosome 13 (deletion of long arm)   A chromosomal disorder of an abnormal chromosome-13 condition, resulting in offspring with microcephaly, microphthalmos, iris colobomas, cataracts, retinoblastomas, pelvic-girdle and lower-spine defects, and missing thumbs. Also known as 46,XX13q- or 46,XX13r or ring-D syndrome.

chromosome-13 trisomy   A chromosomal syndrome of having an extra chromosome 13, resulting in the birth of an infant with a variety of defects including mental retardation, cleft lip and palate, polydactyly, cerebral anomalies, and visual abnormalities such as anophthalmia, microphthalmia, cataracts, and iris colobomas. Also known as 47,XX+13 or Patau's syndrome.

chromosome-21 trisomy   See TRISOMY 21.

chromosomes X and Y   In humans and most animals, the designations for chromosomes that determine sex. Normal females have two X chromosomes whereas normal males have one X and one Y chromosome, and consequently males determine the sex of offspring. Compare CHROMOSOMES W AND Z. See CHROMOSOME.

chromosomes W and Z   In some birds, insects, and fishes, the designations for chromosomes that determine sex. Normal males have two Z chromosomes, normal females may have one Z chromosome and one W chromosome, or one Z and no W. Compare CHROMOSOMES X AND Y.

chromotaxis   Orienting behavior characterized by differential response to different wavelengths of light. Also known as chromotropism. See TAXIS, TROPISM.

chromotherapy   Any form of treatment that depends on the use of colored light. The treatment of mental and physical conditions using colors; a procedure of dubious value. See PHOTOBIOLOGY.

chromotropism   chromotaxis

chronaxia   (L. Lapicque) An index of excitability of a tissue, determined by ascertaining the shortest duration of an electrical current (of double threshold voltage) required to produce an excitation or muscular contraction. Also known as chronaxie, chronaxy.

chronic   A condition that persists over a long period.

chronic affective disorder   See CYCLOTHYMIC DISORDER, DYSTHYMIC DISORDER.

chronic alcoholism   Obsolete phrase for habitual, long-term dependence on alcohol. See ALCOHOL DEPENDENCE, GAMMA ALCOHOLISM.

chronically suicidal   (K. Menninger) Self-destructive behavior, dangerous behavior, or both, done in various subtle ways, such as driving too fast, provoking fights, chronic over-eating, not getting enough sleep, and of course having addictions to dangerous substances. Such behavior may become a coping mechanism for some people. See SUICIDE.

chronic anxiety   A persistent, pervasive state of apprehension not targeted to specific situations or objects. See ANXIETY.

chronic brain disorders   A group of disorders caused by or associated with brain damage, and producing permanent impairment of intellectual and emotional functions. Chronic brain disorders result from such conditions as cranial anomalies, lead or carbon-monoxide poisoning, cerebral arteriosclerosis, head injury, intracranial neoplasm, and senile brain disease. See BRAIN DISORDERS.

chronic brain syndrome   The continuing and progressive pattern of abnormal behaviors, usually of long duration, occurring as the result of brain disease.

chronic conflict   The struggle of opposed id, ego, and superego trends over a considerable period, characteristic of the psychoneuroses.

chronic delusional state of negation   See COTARD'S SYNDROME.

chronic fatigue immune dysfunction syndrome (CFIDS)   Rare phrase for chronic fatigue syndrome.

chronic fatigue syndrome (CFS)   (G. P. Holmes) A condition apparently emerging in the 1980s and characterized by various symptoms. Some of the common symptoms which are often (but not invariably) present include unexplained fatigue, new onset, not substantially alleviated by rest, impairment of short-term memory or concentration, new kinds of headaches, unrefreshing sleep, not the result of on going exertions, substantial reduction of prior levels of activity, postexertional malaise, as well as sore throat, tender lymph node, muscle pain and multi-joint pain. Because its presentation is rather variable and lacks clear etiology, some suspect that it is a psychosomatic condition. Others note that having a difficult-to-diagnose disorder with no clear treatment itself causes psychiatric symptoms of anxiety and depression. Also known as chronic fatigue immune dysfunction syndrome (CFIDS), "yuppie disease." See DEPRESSION, NEURASTHENIA.

chronic illness   Progressive deterioration, with increasing symptoms, functional impairment, and disability over time.

chronicity   See SOCIAL-BREAKDOWN SYNDROME.

chronic mania   A manic state that persists for an indefinite period or permanently.

chronic mental disability   A label that is usually given to any person who has had either one continuous psychiatric hospitalization within the prior 5 years or at least two such hospitalizations in a 12-month period.

chronic motor-tic disorder   A pervasive condition characterized by recurrent, rapid, involuntary movements, such as hitting of the right cheek with the right fist every few minutes.

chronic myopia   See MYOPIA.

chronic or delayed posttraumatic stress disorder   See POSTTRAUMATIC STRESS DISORDER.

chronic preparation   In physiological research studies, a permanent modification of the organism, such as severing a connection in its brain or the implanting of a radio sender in the skin of a dolphin.

chronic psychosis   A pattern of severely disturbed behavior that has existed without change for years.

chronic schizophrenia   Schizophrenia of any type (paranoid, disorganized, catatonic, residual, or undifferentiated) in which the symptoms are persistent but relatively mild, in contrast to acute episodes in which the symptoms are florid and extreme.

chronic simple course   A pattern of mental disorder such as schizophrenia in which the disorder appears gradually and the recovery is slow and incomplete.

chronic tolerance   The repeated ingestions of drugs and low doses of poisons that result in doses having less and less effect over time.

chronic-traumatic disorder   A long-lasting or permanent impairment of brain functions resulting from a blow to the head severe enough to cause brain damage. Common symptoms may include persistent headaches, dizziness, fatigue, impaired memory, anxiety, and difficulty in concentrating. See POSTCONCUSSION SYNDROME, POSTTRAUMATIC PERSONALITY DISORDER.

chronic undifferentiated schizophrenia   A persistent, mixed form of schizophrenia in which symptoms develop insidiously and there is no acute episode. The patient becomes apathetic, poorly adjusted, and develops mild psychotic-like changes in thought and behavior.

chronoamperometry   The measurement of current (such as oxidation/reduction currents), typically in the brain, over time.

chronobiology   1. The branch of biology that studies the timing of biological events, particularly cyclic phenomena in organisms. 2. The study of bodily rhythms, such as the sleep-wake cycle. Practical applications address problems of jet lag, seasonal depressions, disruptions of the sleep cycle in certain psychiatric disorders, and the growing awareness that the timing of medication can significantly determine its effectiveness. See BIORHYTHMS.

chronograph   An accurate time piece that keeps a visual record of time intervals.

chronographic method   The measurement of response time or other duration by some self-registering device, which produces a permanent record.

chronological age (CA or C.A.)   The age from birth; the actual age of an individual in years and months. Also known as calendar age, life age.

chronological complex   Having unusual reactions to a certain period of life rather than to specific incidents or topics, such as an older person who served in the military during a time of war being extremely sensitive to any mention of that period of his life.

chronometer   A carefully constructed mechanism for measuring time, with one or more dials and pointers, which indicate the lapse of time at any instant.

chronometric analysis   Any of a number of techniques used to study the time that certain mental processes take. By using this method it can be determined whether mental processes take place sequentially (serial processing) or simultaneously (parallel processing).

chronometry   Measure of time intervals.

chronophobia   1. Morbid fear of time or duration. 2. Neurotic fear based on preoccupation with time, particularly among prison inmates. Major features of this reaction, which is often called prison neurosis, are feelings of panic, restlessness, dissatisfaction with life, and claustrophobia arising out of contemplation of the length of the sentence and the idea of confinement.

chronoscope   A device used to measure small intervals of time, such as speed of reaction.

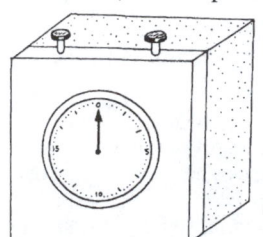

chronoscope

chronotaraxis   A condition of time confusion in which the person tends to underestimate or overestimate the passage of time or expresses confusion about the time of day or day of the week.

chunk   A unit of memory. Normal people have a short-term memory that holds between five and nine chunks. Chunks can range from simple units such as individual letters or numbers to complex chunks of words or phrases. Short-term memory can hold seven words as easily as seven letters, because both types of information are encoded as units.

chunking   The process of combining separate mental units into a single unit, similar to typing a word one letter at a time when first learning the keyboard and later typing the letters quickly and without looking.

churinga   In Australian ethnology, certain ceremonial stones and wooden slabs, two for each individual, kept in secret places, which are supposed to represent a soul or second body of the owner.

chutzpa(h)   A Yiddish-American term meaning colossal nerve, unmitigated gall.

Chvostek reflex/sign   (F. Chvostek) A twitching of the ipsilateral facial muscles elicited by tapping the face in front of the ear. Due to hyperirritability of facial nerves and seen in some anxiety states. Named after Austrian surgeon Franz Chvostek (1834–1884).

CI   1. central interval. 2. confidence interval.

c.i.   class interval

cibophobia   Morbid fear of eating food, or a loathing for food. Also known as sit(i)ophobia. See PHAGOPHOBIA.

cichlid   A family of fish. Often used in research due to their complex reproductive behavior.

CIDS   Comfortable Interpersonal Distance Scale

CIE   *Commission Internationale De L'eclairage* (International Lighting Commission) (also abbreviated **C.I.E.**)

cigarette-smoke reactions   Human responses to tobacco smoke. Studies show that nonsmokers who inhale air polluted by cigarette smoke experience a higher incidence of heart and respiratory disorders than smokers. Nonsmokers tend to increase their "bubble" of personal space when interacting with cigarette smokers. Also called second-hand smoke. See BUBBLE CONCEPT OF PERSONAL SPACE.

cilia   The hairlike outgrowths of certain cells capable of vibratory movement. In mobile cells, cilia are like little oars that move organisms such as the paramecium; cilia on immoble cills move objects along in the respiratory tract. See CILIUM.

ciliary body/muscles   Muscles that change the shape of the lens of the eye automatically to focus on objects near or far. When viewing a near object, the ciliary muscles contract to give the lens a more convex shape, in effect increasing the power of the lens.

cilium   1. An eyelash or eyelid. 2. Any hairlike structure. Plural is cilia.

Cinderella complex   A tendency of women of many cultures to identify themselves in terms of a mated relationship; may involve a hidden fear of independence. Distinguished from the Cinderella syndrome. See DEPENDENCY SYNDROME.

Cinderella syndrome   A form of childhood behavior marked by the child's belief, whether true or false, that the child is a victim of parental rejection or neglect. It is often a cry for help.

cineseismography   A photographic method of recording and measuring abnormal movements of an involuntary nature. The movements remain spontaneous and uninhibited, since no devices are attached to the subject.

cingulate cortex   A portion of the cortex that includes the cingulate gyrus, a component of the brain's limbic system.

cingulate gyrus   A band of association fibers connecting the callosal and hippocampal areas of the brain. Assumed to have a relation to emotions and may also play a role in hunger. Also known as callosal gyrus, gyrus cinguli. See CINGULECTOMY.

cingulate sulcus   A fissure that separates the cingulate gyrus from the superior frontal gyrus.

cingulotomy   A modern form of psychosurgery undergone to relieve pain, in which a small bundle of nerve fibers connecting the frontal lobes with the limbic system is interrupted.

circadian dysrhythmia   Discomfort and inefficiency due to changes in hours of sleeping, typically the result of interrupting normal circadian rhythms, most caused by major changes in hours of work, jet travel, and staying up too late and getting up too early.

circadian rhythms   Biological activities that follow cycles that repeat at approximately 24-hour intervals. See BIOLOGICAL RHYTHM.

circannual rhythm   Occurring once yearly.

circle   1. A ring-shaped structure or a group of structures. See CIRCLE OF WILLIS. 2. A geometric figure having every point equidistant from the center. 3. See WHEEL NETWORK.

circle of Willis   A ring of arteries at the base of the brain. See ARTERIAL CIRCLE.

circuit resistance training   In exercise physiology, usually a set of 8 to 15 exercise stations, at each of which the person lifts a weight, about half the maximum possible repeatedly for 40 seconds, rests for 15 seconds, and moves to the next station for a different exercise.

circular argument   An error in logic when a conclusion is used as a premise. See FALLACIES.

circular behavior   1. A voluntary act or a reflex that generates its own repetition, sometimes without apparent motive or reward, for example, infants may go on sucking after the nipple is withdrawn. Also known as circular response. 2. Any action that stimulates similar behavior or a repetition of the behavior in others (for example, yawning or smiling). Also known as circular reaction. 3. A reflex in which the response serves to renew the original stimulus, leading to a repetition of the same response. Also known as circular reflex.

circular causality   A feedback concept that views any cause as the effect of a prior cause. Some situations such as arguments are of a back and forth nature: Statement A1 leads to statement B1 which leads to statement A2 and so on. See FREE WILL.

circular conditioned response   A response sequence in which each response serves as a stimulus for the next response.

circular definition   Using a word to define itself, as in Gertrude Stein's "A rose is a rose is a rose."

circular discussion(al) group   Any group formed for therapy or problem-solving characterized by approximately 6 to 10 members who sit in a circle. Based on the idea that a circular seating arrangement facilitates communication. See GROUP THERAPY.

circular illness   See CYCLIC ILLNESS.

circular insanity   Obsolete phrase for Falret's disease.

circularity   In logic, resting one element of thinking upon another element that is seen to depend (eventually) on the first. For example, A is true because of B, which is true because of C, which is true because of A. Also known as circular reasoning. See BEGGING THE QUESTION, QUESTION-BEGGING.

circular-pattern responses   (D. E. Berlyne) Responses given by participants viewing circles that contain varying color patterns to determine the degree of aesthetic pleasure. Degrees of appreciation are measured for varying patterns and amounts of circles and colors. An inverted U-shaped curve of appreciation is found in this and similar studies of aesthetic pleasure. See AESTHETIC APPRECIATION.

circular psychosis   Obsolete phrase for manic-depressive (bipolar) psychosis.

circular questioning   A technique used in some methods of family therapy that can yield information about a relationship and personalized meanings within a relationship (for example, one member of a family is asked to comment on who is most hopeful or least hopeful in the family).

circular reasoning   circularity

circulatory psychosis   A confused mental state associated with a disorder of the cardiovascular system, for example, a stroke.

circumcision   The surgical removal of the foreskin of the penis, either for religious or health reasons. See CLITORIDECTOMY, GENITAL MUTILATION.

circumlocution   1. The use of too many unnecessary words to express an idea. 2. A manifestation of aphasia caused by left-sided posterior temporal lesions. The patient perceives an object and recognizes it but has difficulty in finding the correct words to name it. The resulting "roundabout" way of naming is used to prevent others from knowing of one's inability to find the correct word, and serves as a substitute for a lapse of memory. See CIRCUMSTANTIALITY.

circumplex   A circular pattern of correlations. For example, if variables A, B, C, D, and E are correlated, the correlation of A and B might be high, A and C lower, A and D higher than the previous correlation, and A and E may be also high.

circumscribed amnesia   localized amnesia

circumscribed delusions   Unfounded beliefs limited to a specific topic, such as believing that each night one's neighbors enter the house and reorganize food in the refrigerator. See PARANOIA.

circumstantial evidence   In forensic psychology, evidence based on inference or coincidence. Whereas many assume that circumstantial evidence is inferior to direct evidence (reports of witnesses) some legal scholars hold that because of the unreliability of witnesses' memories, circumstantial evidence is superior to direct evidence for the discovery of truth in a court of law.

circumstantiality   Circuitous rambling speech with many irrelevant details, due to disorganized associative processes. Found primarily in patients with schizophrenia, but also occurs in obsessional disorders as well as senile brain disease. See CIRCUMLOCUTION, OVERINCLUSION, TANGENTIAL THINKING.

circumstantial speech   The inclusion of insignificant and unessential details in conversation. See CIRCUMLOCUTION.

circumthanatology   The scholarly study of near-death experience.

circumvallate papillae   Twelve structures in the back of the tongue containing receptors that pick up bitter tastes. See PAPILLA.

CIRCUS   A series of instruments with a circus theme developed by the Educational Testing Service for use by teachers from kindergarten through high school. Among the areas covered (at appropriate levels) are the meaning of words, quantitative concepts, and prereading, reading, mathematics, and writing skills.

circus movements   A forced movement in which the organism tends to move in a circle, or a spiral, due either to one-sided brain injury or to unequal stimulation of the two sides of the organism.

cis-   1. Meaning on this side, on the near side; opposite of trans-. 2. In genetics, two or more genes on the same chromosome of a homologous pair. 3. In chemistry, a form of isomerism in which similar functional groups are attached on the same side of a plane that has two adjacent, fixed carbon atoms.

cissa   A craving for unusual or unwholesome foods; unusual cravings for food often seen in pregnant women. Also known as citta, cittosis. See PICA.

cisterna   A part of the Golgi apparatus that receives part of the presynaptic membrane and recycles it into synaptic vesicles. Plural is cisternae. See PINOCYTOSIS.

cisterna magna   An enlarged subarachnoid space between the lower surface of the cerebellum and the rear surface of the medulla oblongata, serving as a reservoir of cerebrospinal fluid. Also known as cisterna cerebellomedullaris, posterior subarachnoidean space.

cisves(ti)tism   Dressing inappropriately for a particular gender, status, or social situation. See TRANSVESTISM.

citation analysis   Examination of the citations in books and in articles as a measure of the impact and quality of publications. Oft-cited journal articles and books are usually considered within their disciplines as exemplars of high quality.

citric-acid cycle   In biochemistry, the Krebs cycle.

citta   cissa

cittosis   cissa

civil commitment   A legal procedure that permits a person to be certified as mentally ill and to be institutionalized against his or her will, usually by petition of one or two physicians.

civil disobedience   Nonviolent opposition, on the grounds of conscience, to certain laws or policies by such tactics as picketing, boycotting, refusing to obey orders by police, or to pay taxes.

civilian-catastrophe reaction   A transient situational personality disorder resulting from a severely traumatic experience such as being in a fire, an automobile accident, a plane crash, a natural disaster, or being the victim of sexual assault. A typical reaction is a temporary personality disorganization characterized by confusion or disorientation, fearfulness, inability to cope, intense anxiety, and in some cases temporary amnesia for the event and feelings of guilt and depression. See DISASTER SYNDROME, POSTTRAUMATIC STRESS DISORDER.

civilization   1. The most complex and possibly highest level of human development, consisting of the sum total of arts, sciences, laws, religions, moral values, and philosophical concepts. 2. Refers to cultures and societies by various groups, nations, or regions, such as the Neanderthal civilization.

Civil Rights Act   The prime U.S. legislation, passed in 1964, prohibiting employment discrimination based on race, religion, sex, or country of origin.

C-JAM   See COMBINATION JOB ANALYSIS METHOD.

CL   comparison level

cladistics   (J. Huxley) A system of classification of organisms based on their physical appearances.

claiming type of depression   (S. Arieti) Describing a depression in which the anguished patient clings to others and demands their pity and help: "It is in your power to relieve me." See CLASSICAL DEPRESSION, DE-SUBJECTIVIZATION OF THE SELF, DEFORMATION OF THE SELF, LISTENING ATTITUDE, STORMY PERSONALITY, TERTIARY-PROCESS THINKING.

claims review   Evaluation of the appropriateness of a claim for payment for a professional service rendered, including a determination of whether the claimant is eligible for reimbursement, whether the charges are consistent with customary fees or published institutional rates, and whether the service was necessary.

clairaudience   1. In parapsychology, the alleged ability to hear sounds without use of the ears. 2. The supposed power of a medium to hear the voices of the dead.

clairvoyance   (clear sight—French) An alleged sensory ability of psychics in which an assumed supernormal mode of sensibility is said to reveal certain facts (past, present, or future) that lie beyond the range of the sensory receptors.

clairvoyant dream   A dream that is thought to reveal a real scene or event to the sleeper. See PRODROMAL DREAM.

CLAlt   See COMPARISON LEVEL FOR ALTERNATIVES.

clamminess   A complex tactual perception which arises from stimulation by a cool and moist object.

clan   1. A group of families that claims common ancestry. 2. In anthropology, refers to either the unit of tribal society (with descent usually calculated through the maternal line) or to a group concluded to have descended from a common ancestor. See SEPT.

clang   Any musical tone, whether simple or compound, considered from the standpoint of its timbre or character.

clang association   A response in word association tests, in which the person responds with a sound similar to that of the word used as a stimulus, thus: dog—hog, trim—swim. Occurs as a pathological disturbance in some manic states and schizophrenias, and is a normal tendency of young children, expressed in nonsense rhymes. Also known as clanging.

clanging   clang association

clarification   A counselor's formulation of a client's statement or expression of feelings in clearer terms without indicating approval or disapproval. It goes further than restatement and reflection of feeling but stops short of interpretation. See PERSON-CENTERED THERAPY.

Clarke's column   A column, or central group of cell-bodies, in the dorsal horn of gray matter in the spinal cord, whose axons pass up to the cerebellum. Named after English anatomist Jacob Augustus Clarke (1817–1880).

clasp-knife effect   A disorder of the motor nerves controlling the extensor muscles which contract and relax in continuous spasms. Also known as clasp-knife phenomenon/reflex.

clasp-knife phenomenon/reflex   1. In the human, troublesome reflexive spasticity resulting from spinal cord injury or multiple sclerosis. 2. A resistance-relaxation reflex that results from force applied to flex or extend the limb of an animal with decerebrate rigidity.

class   1. A social level or rank based on a societal hierarchy. Variables such as wealth, celebrity, perceived virtue, and political influence determine such ranking. See CLASS SYSTEM, SOCIAL CLASS. 2. In education, a period of study under the direction or supervision of a teacher. 3. (C) A factor or category in research.

class advocate   See ADVOCATE.

class-free test   See CULTURE-FREE TEST.

class frequency   The number of cases or observations in a class interval.

classic(al)   Term with no formal meaning but widely used in psychology (as elsewhere) with implications of old, original, important, esoteric.

classical analysis (S. Freud) Psychoanalysis in which emphasis is placed on the libido, psychosexual development, irrational (id) instincts, rules of free association and abstinence, dream interpretation, and unconscious conflicts. Later developments, such as the dual-instinct theory (Eros vs Thanatos), the transference neurosis, the analysis of the resistance, and ego psychology, are not considered classical. Also known as psychoanalysis (meaning 3). See CLASSICAL PSYCHOANALYSIS, ORTHODOX ANALYSIS, PSYCHOANALYTICALLY-ORIENTED, WILD ANALYSIS.

classical avoidance 1. A Pavlovian process that is the result of pairing of a neutral stimulus with an aversive one. An organism, as a result of this conditioning, may avoid the formerly neutral stimulus despite the fact that it is not intrinsically noxious. Pavlovian and operant conditioning are connected: the pairing is not independent of the animal's response in that the aversive stimulus may occur only if the conditioned stimulus fails to elicit the avoidance response. 2. Another name for free operant avoidance. See SIDMAN AVOIDANCE SCHEDULE.

classical concept (J. Bruner) A logical classification for concepts, refers to particulars found in every member of a certain class, such as the assumption that all people are ambitious, but that not all people use their abilities wisely.

classical conditioning (I. Pavlov) A pattern of learning discovered near the end of the 19th century by Ivan Pavlov in which a neutral stimulus (CS) paired with an unconditioned stimulus (US) develops a learned, or conditioned, response (CR). In the classical conditioning experiment, the ringing of a bell is the CS and food in the mouth of the dog is the US, which results in the CR, when the dog salivates. Also known as Pavlovian conditioning, Type I conditioning, Type S conditioning. Compare RESPONDENT CONDITIONING. See CONDITIONING.

classical conditioning A classical conditioning apparatus used in the laboratory of Ivan Pavlov. The dog salivates on hearing a bell because it has associated the sound of the bell with forthcoming delivery of food. As drops of saliva travel down the tube, tracings are made on the kymograph shown on the left side of the drawing.

classical depression (S. Arieti) In general, a depression characterized by: a pervading feeling of melancholia; disordered thought processes and unusual content; psychomotor retardation; and accessory somatic dysfunctions such as decreased appetite, insomnia, backache, and loss of weight. See DEPRESSION.

classical humours See HUMORAL THEORY.

classical paranoia A rare disorder characterized by elaborate, fixed, systematic delusions usually of a persecutory, grandiose, or erotic character. See PARANOIA.

classical psychoanalysis 1. A personality theory about the nature of the human mind developed by Sigmund Freud. 2. A method of psychological treatment designed by Freud which emphasizes the libido, psychosexual development, irrational instincts, rules of free association, and abstinence, dream interpretation, and unconscious conflicts. Also known as analysis. See CLASSICAL ANALYSIS, ORTHODOX PSYCHOANALYSIS.

classification 1. The orderly arrangement of data in terms of some overall criterion. 2. (J. Piaget) Ability to sort stimuli into categories according to similar characteristics, such as color and shape. 3. The organization of a variety of things into some sensible and easily accessible system so that any single item can be located immediately. 4. In penology, the evaluation of a criminal's prior factors, such as background and crimes, as well as present factors such as age and education, and future factors such as sentence to be served, for the purpose of suggesting programs during incarceration for the betterment of the institution, the society, and the individual, often in that order of importance. See INTERNATIONAL CLASSIFICATION OF DISEASES (ICD-9), PSYCHIATRIC CLASSIFICATION.

classification method In industrial psychology, a system of establishing a table of organization in which job categories are classified along a hypothetical scale, such as The General Schedule system of the United States Civil Service System.

classification of mental disorders/diseases (CMD) Ranges from simple classification in terms of degree of disturbance the person generates, used in deciding which ward to house a patient, to systems that attempt to classify in terms of the essence of the disturbance. Two well-known systems are the International Classification of Diseases (ICD) and the Diagnostic and Statistical Manual of Mental Disorders (DSM). Both have been modified at various times. See entries and also NOSOLOGY.

classification table A table that facilitates classification because of the way the variables are tallied, for example, the rows may refer to tens; the columns to units.

classification test A type of test in which objects or people are sorted into specific categories.

class inclusion (J. Piaget) The operation of assigning an object to the several categories to which it simultaneously belongs (for example, a monkey is a primate, a mammal, and a vertebrate animal). Children progress from classifications based on personal factors, perceptual features, and common function, to classifications based on hierarchical relationships. See CONCRETE OPERATIONS.

class interval (c.i.) 1. An arbitrary division of a continuum of scores to equal parts such as 1–4, 5–8, or 9–12. 2. The range of scores or numerical values that constitute one segment or class in a quantitative series or frequency distribution, for example, weights grouped in class intervals of ten pounds each. Also known as class size, step interval.

class limits/range The limits of a class interval; the lowest and uppermost values that define the boundaries of a particular interval or range, such as intelligence quotient (IQ) interval limits of: 0–19, 20–39. . .120–139.

class method The earliest name given to group therapy. Joseph Pratt discovered that his tuberculosis patients followed directions better when informed in groups than by his doing so individually, and later, others picked this method for treating mental disorders. See DIDACTIC TECHNIQUE, EMMANUEL CHURCH HEALTH CLASS, GROUP BIBLIOTHERAPY, GROUP PSYCHOTHERAPY, GROUP THERAPY, MECHANICAL GROUP THERAPY, MILIEU THERAPY.

Classroom Environment Scale See ENVIRONMENTAL ASSESSMENT.

classroom test A type of test constructed by teachers for use in their own classes, in contrast to a standardized test.

class size 1. In education, the number of students to be taught by a teacher. Research to determine the best class size for optimal learning has yielded inconsistent results. Teachers generally desire smaller class sizes, usually because of the problem of discipline in larger classes. Under optimal conditions, such as students in a class being homogeneous in capacity to learn topic taught, large class sizes may be desirable. 2. See CLASS INTERVAL(meaning 2).

class structure The composition, organization, and interrelationship of social classes within a society. The phrase encompasses the makeup of individual classes as well as their economic role, political power, and social dynamics. See SOCIAL CLASS.

class system 1. Social organization in which certain co-acting groups of individuals having common interests are distinguished from other co-acting groups of individuals having working class, leisure class, military class communality. 2. A synonym for the caste system. The essence of class distinctions is in the attitudes of individuals toward one another and toward others. See CASTE, CORPORATE CLASS, MIDDLE CLASS, SOCIAL CLASS, SOCIOECONOMIC STATUS.

class theory A point of view that objects put into various classes have certain properties in common, as in the Dewey Decimal System for classifying books.

claudication 1. Literally, limping. 2. A certain cramping pain in the muscles. See CEREBRAL INTERMITTENT CLAUDICATION, MENTAL CLAUDICATION.

Claudius' cells (F. M. Claudius) The columnar epithelial cells located at the outer border of the organ of Corti in the internal ear. Named after German anatomist Friedrich M. Claudius (1822–1869).

claustral complex A complex, such as desire for security, attributed to an unconscious effect of prenatal or perinatal events.

claustrophilia The abnormal desire to be enclosed within a small place. See CLAUSTROPHOBIA.

claustrophobia 1. Morbid fear of being confined. A common anxiety symptom that may rise to panic proportions. 2. Fear of enclosed spaces or places. See AGORAPHOBIA, CLAUSTROPHILIA, CLITHROPHOBIA.

claustrophobic flies (A. W. Ewing) A strain of insects that avoided the narrow ends of funnels leading to other compartments.

claustrum A thin layer of gray matter in the white matter of the cerebrum, between the lentiform nucleus and the island of Reil. See BASAL GANGLIA.

clavus A sharp, severe headache, as if a nail were being driven into the head. Usually a conversion symptom.

clawing attacks Aggressive behavior marked by the use of the nails in scratching or clawing an opponent. A normal defensive action taken by some animals but regarded as improper among older children and adults. See BITING ATTACK.

clay-modeling equipment Recreational- and physical-therapy training devices and facilities to aid persons with disabilities in eye-hand coordination and development of neuromuscular abilities of the upper extremities.

clay-modeling therapy A form of therapy for children often used in physical rehabilitation, in stimulating those with mental retardation, and in treating speech disorders. Playing with clay provides substitute satisfactions, the acting out of hostile emotions and "messing" impulses, as well as opportunities for gratification, achievement, and acceptance.

cleaning-fluid inhalation See CARBON TETRACHLORIDE POISONING.

clear sensorium 1. Unimpaired perception of the environment. 2. Normal functioning of all the senses enabling awareness of who and where the self is and what the person is presently doing. Compare CLOUDED SENSORIUM.

clear twilight-state A state of perception and awareness that may occur in an epilepsy patient in lieu of a grand mal episode. Patients may experience a vivid dream state in which they may live briefly in what appears to be another world without cognizance of their true selves.

cleavage 1. A series of cell-divisions occurring in an ovum immediately following fertilization. 2. See SEGMENTATION.

cleft palate A congenital disorder characterized by a fissure or split in the roof of the mouth because of a failure of bones of the head to fuse properly during prenatal development. If not surgically corrected in the first few months of life, the child may develop a speech defect. Also known as uranoschisis.

cleft-palate speech A speech impairment resulting in nasal quality speech caused by a congenital fissure of the soft palate and roof of the mouth which allows air and speech sounds to be emitted through the nose. See CLEFT PALATE.

CLEP College Level Examination Program

Clérambault's syndrome (G. G. de Clérambault) A psychotic form of erotomania, usually in females, consisting of the fixed delusion that a person of high status is in love with them. It has been variously interpreted as a projection of self-love, a narcissistic defense against feeling unloved, and a means of denying homosexual tendencies. Also known as de Clérambault syndrome, *psychose passionnelle*. See EROTOMANIA.

Clérambault-Kandinsky syndrome A delusion in which a person falls in love with an unattainable other who is believed to not only reciprocate the love but also to control the mind or even the life of the person.

cleration The number of occurrences of an event per unit of time, such as the number of arterial pulsations per minute before and after exercise.

clerical aptitude A present ability to perceive, remember, recognize and manipulate printed characters, words and numbers that predicts clerical ability.

clerical-aptitude tests Tasks or quizzes designed to measure specific skills needed in office work. They fall into two major categories: (a) Tests measuring basic visual/perceptual/motor skills, such as separating an ordinary pack of playing cards into four groups by suits and then by ranks, or a test to see how many times a participant can tap a pencil in a certain amount of time. (b) Tests measuring learned skills such as knowledge of the academic basics to estimate the level of clerical competence at which a participant may arrive with further training, as well as general intelligence tests for the same purpose.

clerical test Any of a variety of examinations that usually contain items that involve understanding written directions, doing simple arithmetic, and checking lists of items for identity.

Clever Hans The famous "thinking horse" (Berlin, around 1900) reputed to be able to solve mathematical problems, spell words, distinguish colors, and identify coins by tapping his foot. The psychologist Oskar Pfungst showed that *der Kluge Hans* ("Clever Hans") was responding to "minimal cues" in the form of inadvertent gaze and head movements on the part of its owner and others. See ANIMAL INTELLIGENCE.

Clever Hans phenomenon Animals appearing to perform high-level mental feats may actually be responding to subtle cues given unconsciously by the human trainer. See OSKAR PFUNGST.

cleverness See C FACTOR.

cliché A stereotyped expression that takes the place of genuine thinking or judgment (for example, haste makes waste, Bulgarians are boastful). Many racial, religious, and nationality prejudices are purportedly disseminated by clichés. Also spelled without the accent mark.

client 1. Term frequently used by social workers, counselors, and counseling psychologists to refer to individuals receiving treatment or services. "Patient" is usually employed by psychiatrists, psychoanalysts, and some clinical psychologists. See PATIENT, CLIENT-PATIENT ISSUE. 2. The recipient of services of a counselor or advisor. 3. Euphemism for inmate, welfare recipient, customer, consumer, etc. See also CLIENT-PATIENT ISSUE.

client abuse Inappropriate, exploitive, unprofessional behavior on the part of the psychotherapist or counselor toward the client. Given the prolonged, intense, intimate quality of some therapy sessions, the vulnerability of many clients, and the position of power and trust of the practitioner, abuse often takes the form of sexual involvement between a therapist and client. Generally harmful to the client and grounds for legal and professional sanctions against the practitioner.

client attitudes Points of view towards counseling or therapy by clients that may conflict with the therapist's procedures, especially Carl Rogers's person-centered procedures.

client-centered (psycho)therapy Carl Rogers' former phrase for what he later called person-centered therapy.

client-centered mental health consultation A psychotherapy training process with an expert observing, either in person or indirectly (via audiotapes or videotapes or one-way window) the interaction between a therapist-in-training and a client. Subsequently, the consultant will evaluate the treatment and provide suggestions for improvement.

client lab A means for investigators to determine how participants completing certain tasks using objects, such as to-be-assembled-furniture, behave and feel. Example: In a room, six people are each given the same item to assemble. They may not communicate with each other and are observed through a one-way mirror. When the first person completes the task, all are asked for opinions, attitudes, and difficulties regarding sufficiency of written directions, etc. See FOCUS GROUP.

client-patient issue Confusion over whether a person seen in psychotherapy should be identified as a patient or a client. Many psychologists viewing psychotherapy as a learning experience may use "client." Still many psychotherapists, especially those with a medical background, may prefer "patient." Some health-maintenance organizations use "customer" or "consumer." See CLIENT, PATIENT.

client satisfaction A degree to which persons paying for a service are happy with the result. When professional or other personal services are offered in any field, a major criterion of quality of services is satisfaction expressed by clients. Satisfaction is behaviorally demonstrated by the clients returning for additional sessions and by referrals to other clients. However, client satisfaction is not necessarily evidence of quality of service.

client self-monitoring An assessment procedure to have clients record their own thoughts, feelings, behaviors, or all three. Usually done in a systematic way outside of sessions. Examples include diaries, logs, and checklists.

clients' rights The obligation of a counselor or therapist to inform the client of such matters as the nature of the treatment, diagnostic tests performed, the risks and possible benefits, the length of time expected, and the costs, all in an effort to establish the rights that a client can expect.

climacophobia 1. Morbid fear of stairs or ladders. 2. An excessive fear of climbing.

climacteric The period of life for women during which reproductive capacity declines and finally ceases. Typically lasts two to three years and occurs between 40 and 55 years of age. Also known as change of life, climacterium, menopause. See MALE CLIMACTERIC.

climacteric melancholia A form of depression that develops during menopause. Also known as involutional melancholia.

climacteric psychosis An involutional psychotic reaction. See INVOLUTIONAL MELANCHOLIA.

climacterium **climacteric**

climacterium virile (K. Mendel) The equivalent of a woman's menopause, occurring in men, in their 50s and 60s, with personality alterations, including depression. See CLIMACTERIC.

climate conformance The design and construction of a physical environment to insure comfortable temperature and humidity levels for those who use the area.

climate counseling   A counseling approach in industry whereby both the individual and the organizational climate (consisting of those qualities unique to the organization that are fairly predictable and constant, and that influence people in an organization) are taken into consideration in matching people and jobs.

climatotherapy   The use of climate as a means of therapy, physical or mental.

climax   1. A disease's stage of greatest severity. 2. Orgasm.

clinal difference   (J. Fish) A concept that human physiological differences are clinal, not racial, varying according to cline (morphological variations relative to environment). For example, skin pigmentation darkens in humans from Scandinavia to southern Europe to northern Africa to central Africa. See RACE DIFFERENCES.

cline   See CLINAL DIFFERENCES.

clinging behavior   A form of attachment behavior characterized by clinging to the mother or parent-figure and becoming acutely distressed when left alone. It is first manifested at about six months of age and reaches a maximum in the second and third years, and then slowly subsides. See SEPARATION ANXIETY, STRANGER ANXIETY.

clinic   1. A facility for diagnosing and treating mental and physical problems. 2. A lecture or symposium, especially on topics of disease. 3. A method of teaching using demonstration in a group and typically characterized by "hands-on" learning. 4. Originally a medical treatment facility, now a euphemism to make any type of enterprise as in auto clinic, writers' clinic.

clinical cluster analysis   See CLINICAL FACTOR ANALYSIS.

clinical counseling   A type of counseling that addresses a client's personal or emotional difficulties, encompasses general goals for the client such as greater self-acceptance, improved decision-making ability, and greater effectiveness in interpersonal relationships. The counselor usually gathers and interprets data, identifies the client's major problems, and formulates a treatment plan which may include referral or advice. Such counseling generally takes fewer sessions and does not go into as much depth as psychotherapy, dealing usually with reality and immediate situations. See COUNSELING.

clinical crib   (A. Gesell) An apparatus into which an infant may be placed for the purpose of viewing the infant's behavior through a one-way screen.

clinical diagnosis   The analysis of possible mental disorder through the use of interviews with the patient and relatives, the evaluation of the symptom patterns, investigation of background factors, analysis of significant relationships, and, where indicated, administration of psychological tests, leading to a descriptive label such as neurosis, schizophrenia, Tourette's disorder.

clinical evidence   Information derived from clients and patients whether through direct questions or through observations of behavior such as in obtaining case histories, being told about early recollections or dreams or seeing how the person operates in the clinical setting, or other procedures for gaining information. See CLINICAL DIAGNOSIS.

clinical factor analysis   (B. Rosenberg) A nonmathematical method for generating independent factors. Involves putting either words or phrases on cards, and then seeking other cards that are logically associated; when finished, picking up another card and continuing with a new concept. In analyzing causes of success in group therapy, a study found that the first factor found was altruism. See CLUSTER ANALYSIS, FACTOR ANALYSIS.

clinical grouping   The classification of patients into groups according to their symptoms.

clinical interview   A meeting usually between two people (such as a patient or client and an interrogator, usually a clinical psychologist or psychiatrist) the purpose of which is to obtain meaningful information about the situation. See CLINICAL METHOD, METHODS OF PSYCHOLOGY.

clinical investigation   1. Examination, by any of a variety of methods (for example, interviews, testings, observations of behavior, or analysis of documents), of any individual. 2. An in-depth analysis of life experiences and personal history.

clinical method   The process of a professional person arriving at a conclusion, judgment, or diagnosis about a person (client or patient) in a clinical situation. Involves the use of experience and intuition in deciding on the means by which to acquire data to gain understanding about the person.

clinical neurology   The diagnosis and treatment of diseases of the nervous system.

clinical prediction/procedure   The process of matching such factors as signs and symptoms with personality profiles and case histories to decide on a diagnosis and to predict progress of patients.

clinical psychiatry   The use of medical and psychological procedures concerned primarily with the diagnosis and treatment of organic and psychogenic mental disorders.

clinical psychologist   In psychology, an applied practitioner with a doctorate in psychology and approved training in assessment, diagnosis, and treatment of psychological disorders. In law in most jurisdictions, a person credentialed and registered to so practice and to use the term psychologist. Such clinicians work as independent health care providers or in clinics, organizations, hospitals, the military, etc., in a wide variety of tasks.

clinical psychology   The branch of psychology that specializes in the study, diagnosis, prevention, and treatment of behavior disorders and mental distress.

clinical social worker   A person with a graduate degree in social work, educated and trained to do clinical social work, from a psychosocial perspective. Clinical social workers provide individual, family, and group treatment in a wide range of settings including health, mental health, family and child welfare, and corrections. Credentialing of clinical social workers include Qualified Clinical Social Worker (QCSW), Board Certified Diplomate in Clinical Social Work (BCD), and Licensed Clinical Social Worker (LCSW).

clinical sociology   Phrase sometimes applied to the study of the influence of a culture on the mental health of members of that culture.

clinical sport psychologist   A psychologist trained to deal with athletes' emotional and personality problems. See SPORT PSYCHOLOGY.

clinical study   An in-depth psychological or psychiatric study of an individual or group, utilizing such techniques as diagnostic observation, psychiatric examination, psychological testing, depth interviewing, questionnaires, and a case history approach. See TRIAL.

clinical teaching   A method of teaching geared to the individualized needs of a particular and usually atypical person.

clinical trial   See TRIAL.

clinical type   Anyone diagnosed as falling into a well-established clinical category. Such persons are identified by labels such as "mathematics disorder" or "kidney-stone."

clinical validation   Acquiring evidence to support the accuracy of a theory through successful successive cases via specific procedures for diagnosis or treatment. A clinician may try several methods in the attempt to understand a client, and may eventually find a procedure that meets his or her personal criterion of value, being both fast and efficient. The procedure, although valid in his or her mind, may not, however, be considered valid by others.

clinical vs statistical prediction   (P. Meehl) The issue of whether judgments about individuals for which objective scores are provided are better made on the basis of clinical judgment or by using some statistical operation such as developing a regression equation or weighted average. The evidence supports the position that statistical prediction is more accurate than clinical prediction.

clinodactyly   A permanent deflection or curvature of one or more of the fingers, a rather common physical trait associated with genetic or chromosomal disorders that also may be related to mental retardation.

clinophobia   Morbid fear of going to bed.

cliometrics   Quantitative economic history, usually from the application of statistical techniques such as regression analysis to historical data. Term derives from the muse of history and the word for measure in the United states in the 1950s.

clipping   The shortening of a word in such a way that the new word is used with the same meaning, for example, "exam" from "examination." In general: adults prefer back-clipping—"prof" for "professor," whereas children prefer front-clipping—"fessor" for "professor." See PEAK CLIPPING.

cliques   Usually, but not necessarily, related to adolescent groups which tend to be exclusive, meet frequently, and whose bonding is usually based on shared interests.

clithrophobia   Morbid fear of being enclosed. See CLAUSTROPHOBIA.

clitoral hood   The prepuce that normally covers the clitoris. It is homologous to the foreskin of the male penis.

clitoridectomy   The surgical removal of the clitoris. Performed in various societies, primarily in Africa in the mistaken belief that the absence of a clitoris will prevent women from experiencing orgasms. Incorrectly called female circumcision. See GENITAL MUTILATION.

clitoris   A small body of erectile tissue situated above the vaginal opening. It is homologous to the male penis but much smaller. See PHALLUS.

clitoromania   Obsolete term for what was deemed excessive sexual interest or enjoyment in a female.

cloaca   A common cavity into which the intestinal, urinary, and reproductive canals open during the course of uterine development.

cloaca(l) theory   The false belief sometimes held by children or persons with neuroses that a child is born as a stool is passed, from the rectum of the father or mother.

cloak theory of language   A point of view that the structure of a language is a dependent function of the patterns of thought of the culture.

cloisonnism   Synthetism.

clomipramine hydrochloride   A tricyclic antidepressant noted for its effectiveness in treating obsessive compulsive disorders (OCD). See TRICYCLIC ANTIDEPRESSANT.

clone   An individual organism genetically identical to its "parent," developed from a single cell of the parent organism, common in plants, and also possible in higher organisms. See CLONING.

clonic phase   The phase of a grand mal seizure characterized by rapid bodily movements based on recurrent muscular rigidities and relaxations that usually follows the tonic (rigid) phase of grand-mal epilepsy.

clonic spasm   A sudden involuntary muscle contraction that alternates between contraction and relaxation, as opposed to one that is continuous (tonic spasm). See CLONUS, HICCUP.

cloning   The reproduction of an entire organism from a single cell of the original organism. See CLONE.

clonus   Involuntary contractions and relaxations of the muscles, in alternate rapid succession. Some forms of clonus, such as hiccups or jactitations (extreme restlessness) that may occur when falling asleep, are considered normal. Clonus also may be a part of an epileptic convulsion. See CLONIC PHASE, EPILEPSY.

close-caption(ed) television   Process that allows people with hearing loss to receive televised dialogue as subtitles. Also known as line 21 system, as the caption is inserted into the picture's blank 21st line.

closed call system   A communication system in which every sound has a dedicated, invariable meaning, as in baboon grunts and alarm cries. See OPEN CALL SYSTEM.

closed-class word   function word

closed-ended question   1. In an examination, survey, or interview, a question that provides the respondent with alternative answers from which a response is selected (for example, a multiple-choice item). 2. A question that calls for a specific answer (for example, "How does your neck feel?"). 3. A type of question asked by a test, written form, counselor, therapist, job interviewee, attorney in a court, etc., that calls for a simple answer without elaboration (for example, a question that calls for a "yes" or "no" answer). Compare OPEN-ENDED QUESTION.

closed group   A counseling or therapy group comprised only of those members who constituted the original group. New members may not join during the course of therapy.

closed instinct An instinct highly resistant to modification. For example, a frog will repeatedly extend its tongue if a small object passes in front of it, even if the object is a painful stimulus.

closed-loop control system A compensatory self-regulating system in which feedback regulates the system, as in a household thermostat and in many bodily processes.

closed-loop feedback system A self-contained reflex system in which a physiological need stimulates a neuromuscular portion of the body to satisfy the need, as in the autonomic activity of thirst that induces the organism to seek water to satisfy the desire.

closed-loop model of stress (P. Levine) A theory that views stress in the context of a systems model, suggesting that dynamic feedback patterns govern a variety of behavior and reflect the organism's capacity for order and stability. Contrasts with the open-loop model (such as Hans Selye's), which views stress as a static system in which stressors act cumulatively on a passive organism.

closed-loop system In ergonomics, a system that is continuous, performing an operation that requires continuous control, as in automobile driving. Compare OPEN-LOOP SYSTEM.

closed marriage A marriage based on monogamy. Compare OPEN MARRIAGE.

closed mind See OPEN MINDS VS CLOSED MINDS.

closed-mindedness Being impervious to new ideas, either seen as admirable (having high standards and refusing to lower them) or as deprecatory (not listening to reason).

closed scenario A type of reasoning that occurs when a person is presented with a limited number of options for solving a particular problem.

closed shop See OPEN SHOP VS CLOSED SHOP.

closed skills See OPEN SKILLS VS CLOSED SKILLS.

closed societies See OPEN SOCIETIES VS CLOSED SOCIETIES.

closed swinging The exchanging of sex partners within a limited number of couples.

closed syllable In linguistics, a sound that ends with a consonant.

closed system A self-contained system that has impermeable boundaries and thus is resistant to any new information and change. A common example is the traditional educational system.

closed vowel In linguistics, a sound spoken with the tongue high in the mouth, as in saying "see."

close-sightedness See MYOPIA.

closet homosexual A lesbian or gay man who hides her or his personal sexual preference from most others, generating the impression of being heterosexual.

closing Ending a session in counseling or psychotherapy. Such procedures may vary between and among therapists, for example, some therapists wait for the client to indicate when to finish, others make the decision for the client.

closure 1. A feeling of relief that something pending, such as the solution of a problem or an important decision is finally settled, usually to personal satisfaction or expectation. 2. (M. Wertheimer) A tendency toward perceiving an incomplete or fragmented configuration as if it were closed or complete object. See AUDITORY CLOSURE, GOODNESS OF CONFIGURATION, LAW OF PRÄGNANZ, VISUAL CLOSURE.

closure According to gestalt theory, there is a tendency to generate the perception of a whole when some percept is incomplete. For instance, these three figures are usually perceived as triangle, rectangle, and circle, even though they are incomplete.

closure law See LAW OF CLOSURE.

cloud pictures (W. Stern) An early projective-test by William Stern, similar in purpose to the Rorschach, based on pictures of clouds. Participants were asked to look at the cloud pictures and state what they looked like.

clouded sensorium A state of consciousness in which the ability to perceive and understand the environment is impaired and the patient is confused and disoriented as to time, place, circumstances, and own identity as well as the identity of others. A clouded sensorium occurs most strikingly in toxic psychoses and acute alcoholism, but is also found in schizophrenic and manic-depressive (bipolar) states. Compare CLEAR SENSORIUM.

clouding effect (C. G. Jung) A tendency for people who belong to different types to have problems understanding each other. Purportedly, men and women differ in their communication "styles."

clouding of consciousness A disturbance in mental functioning characterized by impairment of sensory, perceptual, and thought processes to such an extent that patients may be unresponsive.

clo unit A measure of the thermal insulation necessary to maintain comfort in a sitting and resting person in a room of normal temperature and humidity.

cloze In Gestalt psychology, closure; the completing of some kind of gap such as filling in a missing period of memory.

cloze procedure/test (W. Taylor) A technique used in testing and teaching reading and comprehension by deleting words from a text and leaving blank spaces. Measurement is made by rating the number of blanks filled in correctly. The cloze procedure is based on the Gestalt principle of closure.

cloze test **cloze procedure**

club drugs Common name for recreational drugs used in nightclubs to facilitate dancing and the party experience, for example, MDEA, (more commonly known as MDMA Ecstasy) and Ketamine. See DESIGNER DRUGS.

clumsy automation (N. Wiener) The automation of controls, typically in aircraft cockpits, that provides too many options for the operator to understand, choose, and stay aware of.

clumsy-child syndrome Phrase similar to minimal brain dysfunction. See LEARNING DISABILITIES.

cluster analysis　　(R. C. Tryon) Refers to any of a number of multivariate procedures for forming groups of elements that are relatively homogeneous. See CLINICAL FACTOR ANALYSIS, FACTOR ANALYSIS.

cluster approach　　In evaluation research, a strategy for accumulating information concerned with combining and reconciling studies from which conflicting conclusions have been drawn. This approach suggests criteria for determining when data from dissimilar studies can be pooled. See META-ANALYSIS.

clustered random sample　　An area sample. See CLUSTER SAMPLING.

cluster headache　　Brief but severe pain felt in one side of the head that typically recurs for up to three months, followed by a remission for months or years. Usually starts around an eye a few hours after falling asleep. May be a variant of migraine. As with migraine, the cause is unknown. See HEADACHE.

clustering　　1. In cognition, a tendency of the mind to group associated items. 2. In ergonomics, the placement of interrelated displays close to each other in order to facilitate interpreting them.

cluster marriage　　A nontraditional sexual style in which two or three married couples cohabit together.

cluster sampling　　A procedure that divides a population into clusters and then takes a random sample from each cluster or from different clusters. It is considered an integral part of area sampling. See PROBABILITY SAMPLING, STRATIFIED SAMPLING.

cluster suicides　　Multiple suicides, usually committed within a short period of time, usually by adolescents, and usually for the same reasons, often for what may appear to others as silly reasons. Also known as Werther syndrome after a character in Goethe's novel, *The Sorrows of Young Werther.*

cluttering　　A speech disorder characterized by rapid and disorganized speech, often including irrelevant phraseology.

cluttering speech　　A rapid, nervous speech pattern resulting in confused, jumbled, and imprecise speech. Similar to tachyphemia.

Clytemnestra complex　　A triad in which a wife falls in love with her husband's male relative and kills the husband. Term derives from the story in *The Iliad* of the wife of Agamemnon who took his cousin as a lover when he went to war, and killed him upon his return.

cm　　See CENTIMETER.

CM　　cochlear microphonic

CMCHS　　Civilian-Military Contingency Hospital System

CMD　　See CLASSIFICATION OF MENTAL DISORDERS/ DISEASES.

CMHC　　community mental-health center

CMMS　　Columbia Mental Maturity Scale

CMS　　Children's Memory Scale

C(n,r)　　See COMBINATION.

CNS　　central nervous system (also abbreviated **cns, c.n.s.**)

CNV　　contingent negative variation

Co　　comparison stimulus

coaching　　Specialized instruction, training, and practice for a variety of purposes such as to pass a test or to improve or master a skill. In psychological testing, studies indicate that coaching has a more positive effect on students with deficient educational background than on those with superior educational opportunities. The College Entrance Examination Board attempts to choose items not readily amenable to coaching.

coacting group　　A group that works together on a mutual problem or project with minimal interpersonal exchange or communication. The individuals in the group are focused on the work rather than on interpersonal processes (for example, individuals on telephones during an election campaign are co-actors, each calling selected people to find out their election preferences). See TEAMWORK.

coaction　　Any activity done jointly with another person, such as two people pulling on a rope in the same direction at the same time.

coalition　　A relationship of people who join together for any of several purposes, such as companionship or greater efficiency to achieve success or superiority in some project such as a business deal.

coarctation　　(H. Rorschach) Expressive of a personality that is constricted, narrow, limited, unable to generate emotions. A sign of coarctation in the Rorschach test is giving one- or two-word replies.

coarse tremor　　A trembling of the body or a part of the body that involves a large muscle group in slow movements. See INTENTION TREMOR, TREMOR.

coathook strategy　　See ELABORATIVE REHEARSAL.

coats of eyeball　　The three principal layers which compose the wall of the eyeball. These are the sclera or sclerotic coat, choroid or choroid coat, and retina.

COBOL　　See COMMON BUSINESS ORIENTED LANGUAGE.

COBS　　See CARE OF THE BODY SURFACE.

coca　　A tree of the species *Erythroxylon coca* whose leaves have been used for centuries as the source of cocaine.

cocaine　　cocaine (hydrochloride)

cocaine bug　　A symptom occurring among cocaine users, who experience itching and biting sensations and feel as if insects are crawling on or under their skin. See FORMICATION.

cocaine delirium　　A condition of excitement and mental confusion induced by the use of cocaine. Also known as cocaine intoxication delirium, cocainism.

cocaine (hydrochloride)　　A chemical substance that acts as a sympathomimetic and stimulant and is now widely recognized as addictive. Applied locally, it is a topical anesthetic and vasoconstrictor, so it continues to have medicinal applications mainly in ophthalmology and in nose surgery. It is derived from the leaves of the coca tree, grown primarily in areas of South America. May be eaten or drunk in liquids, snorted as a powder, or after being chemically altered slightly, smoked as "free-base" or "crack." In these latter forms it is intensely euphoric and thus intensely addictive. Slang names include blow, C, chit, coke, snow, toot. See ANALEPTICS, COCAINE ABUSE, PSYCHO-STIMULANTS, SYMPATHOMIMETIC.

cocaine intoxication delirium   **cocaine delirium**

cocaine-related disorders   Physiological and psychological conditions that may result from the use of cocaine hydrochloride. Reactions to the ingestion of cocaine may include variations in blood pressure, excitement, intoxication, aggressiveness, poor judgment, mental confusion, loss of consciousness, feelings of grandiosity, euphoria, hypervigilance, anxiety, tension, and delusions of insects crawling over the skin (cocaine bug) may result. Also, psychological dependence on cocaine may result in habitual use. See COCAINE BUG, FORMICATION, SUBSTANCE ABUSE.

coccygeal nerve   The lowest (most caudal) spinal nerve in the human body.

coccyx   The last lower bone of the spinal column. See COCCYGEAL.

cochlea   (G. Fallopius) A bone in the inner ear shaped somewhat like a snail. It is filled with a fluid that transmits sound waves to nerves that carry sound impulses to the brain.

cochleagram   A recording of the electrical activity of the hair cells in the organ of Corti in response to sound stimuli of different frequencies and intensities.

cochlear aplasia   The absence or defective development of the cochlea.

cochlear canal/duct   The central fluid-filled compartment of the cochlea which contains the organ of Corti.

cochlear implant   Microelectrodes positioned by a surgeon at various places on the cochlea to provide audition to those with neural deficiencies for hearing.

cochlear microphonic (CM)   A set of neural potentials generated by cochlear hair cells in the inner ear that have the same wave forms as the sounds producing the stimulus. See COCHLEA.

cochlear nerve   Part of the eighth cranial nerve concerned with the sense of hearing. See AUDITORY NERVE.

cochlear nuclei   Nerve cells located in two groups (dorsal and ventral cochlear nuclei) on each side of the dorsolateral surface of the medulla which receive input from the auditory portion of the vestibulocochlear nerve and give rise to the first stage of the auditory pathway in the central nervous system.

cochlear recruitment   The additional assistance of neurons in the cochlea to aid in the spread of response to a stimulus of prolonged intensity. Needed sometimes to replace the participation of neurons that have dropped out of the response because of fatigue.

cochleopalpebral-reflex test   A hearing test in which a sudden noise is sounded near the ear, leading to the eyelids closing. Also known as cochlearpalpebral-reflex test, cochleo-orbicular reflex.

Cochran Q test   (W. G. Cochran) A nonparametric test of significance for nominally-scaled k related samples.

Cochran Test   (W. G. Cochran) A statistical test of homogeneity of variance that gives the statistic C, the ratio of the largest treatment variance and the sum of all treatment variances.

cocktail   See LYTIC COCKTAIL, SYNANON.

cocktail-party conversationalism   **chatterbox effect**

cocktail-party effect/phenomenon   (C. Cherry) Ability to attend selectively to but one voice among many in crowded situations (such as on a bus). Generally, this effect also includes the notion that, although attention may be directed to a particular conversation, a person also attends at some level to other conversations and can redirect attention when important stimuli occur in the "nonattended" conversations (for example, a familiar name).

cocoa   A product of the cacao plant with pharmacologically active theobromine and caffeine. See CACAO.

co-conscious personality   (M. Prince) A secondary personality split-off and independently acting from the dominant personality as found in cases of multiple-personality (dissociative-identity) disorder.

co-consciousness   (M. Prince) Mental states which coexist with but are dissociated from consciousness; states which are dynamically active and may account for various mental phenomena, both normal (for example, lapses of the pen) and abnormal (for example, visions, hallucinations, and multiple personality). See DISSOCIATION, FREUDIAN SLIP, UNCONSCIOUS.

co-counseling   Leaderless one-on-one or group therapy in which peers discuss their individual problems and matters of common concern, possibly with some direction by an outside person about how the therapy should operate. Also known as peer counseling. See REEVALUATION CO-COUNSELING.

COD   change-over delay

codability   Stimuli easily assigned a language label.

codable actions   Behaviors that can be specified with precision for any kind of purpose to generate a profile of actions, such as obtaining a summary of the operations of a bus driver for a typical day by counting the number of times the bus is started and stopped, and how often the doors are opened and closed, questions are asked and answered, transfers are asked for and given, etc.

code   1. A system of social rules and canons. 2. A system of secret signs, representing letters, words, or phrases. 3. A set of symbols used to represent information items in a convenient form, as for computer use. See ENCODING, DECODING. 4. In hospital and rescue use, a signal for an emergency, often color-named, as in "code red" for fire, "code blue" to summon a resuscitation team. This may lead to further abbreviations, such as "code out" meaning to die, or "no code" on a chart, meaning to not resuscitate.

code capacity   The maximum amount of coded data a channel can transmit in a fixed time period.

codeine   A widely used analgesic and cough suppressant, a slightly less potent opiate drug than morphine. Occasionally abused, though most people find it too nauseating.

code of ethics   A set of standards and principles of professional conduct. The American Psychological Association code includes statements on responsibility, competency, moral and legal standards, assessment techniques, and research with human and animal subjects. The American Psychiatric Association code deals with such issues as confidentiality, soliciting of patients, seeking consultation upon request, and responsibility to society.

codependency   Two or more people who are dependent upon each other to an unhealthy degree.

code test   A task that requires translating one set of symbols into another; for example writing "Cat" in numbers that stand for letters according to the code A = 1, B = 2, C = 3, etc. Also known as coding test, symbol-substitution test.

codes of language   Two different styles of language use identified by Bernstein: elaborated codes (large vocabulary stressing nouns) and restricted codes (small vocabulary stressing pronouns). Bernstein concluded that middle social classes used elaborated codes with complex syntax whereas working class people used restricted codes with simple sentence structure. See GENERATIVE THEORY OF LANGUAGE ACQUISITION.

code-switching   A form of communication most common in European universities when students from different countries communicate with each other by using words in different languages to ensure better communication, such as "Como on dit genug lorsque one hat abastanza dans la lingua Chinese?"

codification   1. The act of classifying items into identifiable categories. 2. The conversion of data or other information into a code that can be translated by others. See CODE TEST. 3. The capacity of the brain to categorize or cluster disparate items. Also known as coding. See ENCODING.

codification-of-rules stage   (J. Piaget) The attitude displayed by many children of ages 11 and 12 toward rules. In this stage, children view rules as binding once they are agreed to, and games are seen as a system of interconnecting laws. Although the awareness of rules emerges at an earlier age, systematic adherence is not manifested until the codification-of-rules stage.

coding scores   Scores that are a linear transformation of the original scale of measurement. One coding method assigns 0 to the arbitrary origin, which is either the midpoint of the lowest class interval or the class interval nearest the middle of the distribution. Intervals above the arbitrary origin are coded 1, 2, 3, ... and those below −1, −2, −3, ... Coding reduces the size of numbers and, hence, the amount of computational labor.

codominance   A sharing of rank or pecking-order positions in certain animal populations, such as wild macaque monkeys that control their colonies through a small group of dominant males, rather than through a linear hierarchy. Studies indicate that codominance is more common among arboreal (tree-dwelling) animals whereas linear dominance is characteristic of ground-living species who are exposed to greater threats from predators.

codpiece   A fabric or leather bag or flap designed to house the male genitals, in fashion in Europe from the Middle Ages to the 1500s.

coefficient   In statistics, a number which can be a numerical index of magnitude, such as degrees of correlation between variables.

coefficient alpha   (L. J. Cronbach) Average split-half reliabilities of a test. A means of measuring the reliability of a test by correlating each item of the test with every other item by the formula: $\alpha = [k \div (k-1)][(S_t^2 - \Sigma S_i^2) \div S_t^2]$ Where: s_i^2 is the variance of the item scores, s_t^2 is the variance of the total scores, and k is the number of items. A high coefficient indicates high internal consistency, each item measuring the same thing.

coefficient law   A statement that alteration in the state of the organ of vision produced by stimulation has approximately the same effect on excitation due to a subsequent stimulus as if the intensity of the latter were diminished by a definite fraction of its amount. Also known as Fechner-Helmholtz law.

coefficient of agreement   See AGREEMENT COEFFICIENT.

coefficient of alienation (k)   (T. L. Kelley) A measure of the amount of unexplained variance or error in prediction applied to the expression $(1 - r^2)^{1/2}$ (wherein r is a product moment correlation coefficient) which measures the lack of relation between two correlated variables. Formula: $\mathbf{k = (1-r^2)^{1/2}}$. Also known as alienation coefficient (k).

coefficient of association (CA)   A relationship index between discontinuous variables, for example, yes–no, males–females.

coefficient of concordance (W)   (M. G. Kendall) A measure of the correlation among three or more sets of ranks. A nonparametric measure of the degree of association among $\underline{k}$ ranked variables. Commonly used for expressing the degree of agreement among rankings given by several judges.

coefficient of contingency (C)   The coefficient of contingency is a measure of degree of association of two or more variables that form the basis of classification for a contingency table. The usual measure is defined in terms of the chi-squared value for the table and the total frequency of items represented in the table. See COEFFICIENT OF MEAN SQUARE CONTINGENCY.

coefficient of correlation (r)   (K. Pearson) An index of the degree of linear relationship between two quantitative variables, such that correlations of +1.0 and −1.0 indicate a perfect positive and a perfect negative relationship, respectively, and a correlation of 0 indicates that there is no overall linear relationship between the two variables. Sometimes known as correlation coefficient. See PRODUCT-MOMENT CORRELATION.

coefficient of correlation calculated from ranks   Another name for coefficient of rank correlation, rho, Spearman-rank difference method.

coefficient of curvilinear correlation (H or η)   An index of the degree of correlation between variables when the distribution is curvilinear. It is often used when two variables stem from interval or ratio scales. Also known as curvilinear correlation coefficient. See ANALYSIS OF VARIANCE, ETA COEFFICIENT.

coefficient of determination (r^2)   A statistic indicating the percentage of variance two variables have in common, equal to r^2. Therefore, a correlation of 0.70 would indicate the two variables have 49% of their variance in common. Formula: $[\mathbf{r^2 = [(S^2y') \div (S^2y)]}$, Where: $S_{y'}^2$ is the variance of the deviation $Y - \bar{Y}$, S_y^2 is the total variance in the predicted variable Y. (r^2 is always positive.) Also known as determination coefficient.

coefficient of dispersion   A means of comparing variabilities of two or more distributions that have different averages. The coefficient is obtained by dividing the standard deviation by the mean of the distribution, and multiplying it by 100.

coefficient of equivalence   The correlation between two equivalent forms of the same test given to the same subjects, indicating the degree of reliability of the test. Also known as equivalence coefficient.

coefficient of intraclass correlation (ρ_I)   A statistic that estimates strength of relationship (linear and nonlinear) between X and Y when the independent variable is qualitative. Intraclass correlation is useful for studying grouped observations from different investigators. With the observations combined into one total sample, rho (ρ) is then used as a means of measuring the extent of the bias existing between subsamples, or classes of the same sample. Formula: $\rho_I = (S_b^2 - S_w^2) \div [S_b^2 + (m-1)S_w^2]$, Where: S_b^2 is the between groups variance estimate, S_w^2 is the within groups variance estimate, m is the number of cases (persons). Also known as intraclass correlation coefficient.

coefficient of mean square contingency (C)   A nonparametric measure of correlation, computed from individuals classified in categories. Formula: $C = [\chi^2 \div (N + \chi^2)]^{1/2}$ Where: C is the coefficient of contingency, N is the number of cases, and χ^2 is the symbol for chi-square. Also known as coefficient of contingency, contingency coefficient (C). See COEFFICIENT OF CORRELATION, RANK-DIFFERENCE CORRELATION.

coefficient of multiple determination (R^2)   An estimate of the proportion of variance in a dependent variable that is related to a set of independent variables. Independent variables other than this defined set also influence obtained variance.

coefficient of nondetermination (k^2)   The proportion of the variance in the dependent variable not accounted for by independent variable(s); the square of the coefficient of alienation. Formula: $k^2 = 1 - r^2$ Where k^2 is the coefficient of nondetermination, and r is correlation. Also known as nondetermination coefficient.

coefficient of partial correlation   A measure of the degree of association between two variables with the effects of one or more other variables partialled out or held constant statistically. Also known as partial correlation coefficient.

coefficient of rank correlation   An index of the degree of relationship between two ranked variables. For example, if the values of each of two variables are ranked and the Pearson correlation is calculated for the ranked variables, the result is the Spearman correlation coefficient.

coefficient of reliability   A number running from +1.00 (perfectly reliable) to 0.00 (not at all reliable) to −1.00 (perfectly negatively reliable) that informs to what degree a test or other means of measurement is consistent. There are a number of ways of obtaining this index. See RELIABILITY INDEX. Types of reliability include: ALTERNATE FORMS, INTER-SCORER, INTER-JUDGE, ODD-EVEN, SPLIT-HALF, TEST-RETEST.

coefficient of reproducibility   1. Index of the proportion of responses to a test that can be predicted on the basis of test difficulty and other scores. 2. An indication of where on a list of items ordered by difficulty a person taking a test twice would most likely end up the second time.

coefficient of stability (W)   A reliability-test measure based on the use of the same type of measuring instrument administered at two points in time to a sample of people. Also known as stability coefficient, test-retest coefficient, test-retest method. See TEST-RETEST RELIABILITY.

coefficient of total determination   The multiple correlation coefficient squared. The result indicates the proportion of the variance of the dependent variable removed by independent variables of the multiple correlation.

coefficient of validity   A number ranging from −1.00 through 0.00 to +1.00 representing the product moment coefficient of correlation between the measure of a test and that which it reputedly measures. Most commercially available "good" tests report validity quotients between about 0.7 to 0.9. Also known as validity coefficient.

coefficient of variation (V)   (K. Pearson) A ratio of the standard deviation of a distribution to the arithmetic mean of that distribution. Formula: $V = (\sigma \div M)100$. Where: M is the mean, σ is the sample standard deviation. V is based on parameters of a frequency distribution. Also known as variation coefficient (V).

coefficient of visibility   A numerical designation of the visibility of a wavelength of radiant energy in relation to a standard maximum visibility of a wavelength of 5540 angstroms. Also known as visibility coefficient. See VISIBLE SPECTRUM.

coenesthesia   A subjective overall feeling of the body as a totality. Also known as cenesthesia, coenaesthesia.

coenotrope   cenotrope

COEPS   See CORTICALLY ORIGINATING EXTRA-PYRAMIDAL SYSTEM.

coercion to the cultural mean   (R. B. Cattell) The finding that cultural pressures tend to move or influence deviant individuals toward the mean.

coercive behavior   A form of behavior designed to force others to comply with personal wishes, often against their will, and often masked as filial devotion or marital or parental concern, and sometimes expressed in undisguised form: "If you don't do what I say, I'll kill myself." See MANIPULATION.

coercive persuasion   Systematic, intensive indoctrination of political or military prisoners who have been "softened up" by such methods as threats, punishments, bribes, isolation, continuous interrogation, and repetitious "instruction." See BRAINWASHING.

coercive power   A leader's ability to punish subordinates for noncompliance.

coercive strategy   A method of achieving goals based on the uses of economic, social, and political power to effect societal change, usually through nonviolent measures, such as organized boycotts, strikes, sit-ins, demonstrations, registration drives, and lobbying. See EMPIRICAL-RATIONAL STRATEGY, NORMATIVE-REEDUCATIVE STRATEGY.

coercive treatment   Treatment of any kind under threat, force, pressure. Psychotherapy is thought to call for voluntary immediate cooperation, but there have been reports of people entering psychotherapy unwillingly but then changing their minds and then gaining value from the process. Sometimes known as forced treatment.

coevolution A process in which species that are mutually dependent for their existence have evolved together, depending on each other for existence. Also spelled co-evolution.

coexistence The presence of two phenomena, objects, etc., at the same instant or during the same period of time.

coexistent cultures Consistent systems of thinking and behavior differing between interacting social groups. The various groups tend to view their ways as correct, morally right, and proper, and may vary in their reactions to other groups from tolerance to hatred.

coexperimenter An experimenter who assists the main experimenter, especially by maintaining double-blind conditions or in some other way keeping the main experimenter uninformed and therefore unbiased.

COEX systems A constellation of memories and fantasies from different life periods of individuals having similar basic themes associated with strong emotional quality. Deepest layers are from infancy whereas more superficial layers come from memories of later life. See EARLY RECOLLECTIONS.

cofigurative culture A society or culture in which children learn chiefly from other children whereas adults learn from other adults. See POSTFIGURATIVE CULTURE, PREFIGURATIVE CULTURE.

CogAT See COGNITIVE ABILITIES TEST.

cogitation Reflection, meditation. Term is not used in precise, scientific discussion.

cognition General term for all forms of knowing and awareness, such as perceiving, conceiving, reasoning, judging, planning, remembering, and imagining. Cognitive processes are often contrasted with conative processes (striving, willing, wanting) and emotive processes (feeling, affect). Types of cognition include: BEING, BEING, DISTRIBUTED, EMOTIONAL, HOT, META-, NEURO-, PRE-, PRIMARY, RETRO-.

cognition disorder Impaired thought processes; inability to know and be aware of people, stimuli, or events, or to perform such cognitive functions as perceiving, conceiving, and reasoning.

cognitive 1. Pertaining to cognition. 2. (R. Descartes) In philosophy, originally a cognate of *cogito* (I think) as used by Descartes. 3. (F. Heider) In social psychology, pertaining to consciousness or awareness. 4. (L. Festinger) In experimental social psychology, refers to what a person knows about self, own behavior, and surroundings. 5. (G. Miller) In information processing, mental. Term used to distinguish some learning paradigms from behaviorism. 6. (U. Neisser) In cognitive psychology, pertaining to and including imagery, perception, problem solving, recall, retention, sensation, and thinking. See COGNITIVE PSYCHOLOGY.

Cognitive Abilities Test (CogAT or CAT) A group of tests for grades kindergarten through 12, that attempt to measure verbal-vocabulary, quantitative-quantitative relations, and nonverbal-figure classifications.

cognitive aids Techniques intended to facilitate awareness and knowledge.

cognitive-appraisal theory See THEORIES OF EMOTION.

cognitive arms race See MACHIAVELLIAN HYPOTHESIS.

cognitive aversion therapy A form of aversion therapy to modify undesirable behavior by linking it to an unpleasant imagined event.

cognitive awareness level (G. A. Kelly) The level at which a diagnostic-therapeutic concept is effective; the degree to which a construct is expressed in effective symbols, has alternatives, but is not contradicted by other constructs. See BIPOLAR CONSTRUCT, CONSTRUCT, CONSTRUCT SYSTEM.

cognitive balance theory (F. Heider) A point of view concerned with the extent, the effect, or both, of logical and illogical concepts on an individual. It states that a balance of these two concepts is necessary for adjustment to life in general, and if an imbalance occurs, a person's cognition tends to reestablish a balance. See COMMUNICATION ARTS, CONGRUITY THEORY, FUNDAMENTAL ATTRIBUTION ERROR, INTERPERSONAL PERCEPTION.

cognitive-behavioral psychology Understanding individuals in depth through exploration of thought processes as well as inferences from behavior, in contrast to the past approaches of either studying the mind through introspection or studying behavior while setting the mind aside. See COGNITIVE-BEHAVIOR THEORY, COGNITIVE SCIENCE.

cognitive-behavioral therapy (CBT) A set of principles and procedures that assume that cognitive processes affect behavior and conversely that behavior affects cognitive processes. Emphasizes a here-and-now process without emphasizing causation.

Cognitive-Behavior Modification/Therapy (D. Meichenbaum) A treatment approach that helps clients examine and change the relationship between their thoughts, feelings, behaviors and resultant consequences. It incorporates a number of diverse interventions (for example, cognitive restructuring procedures, problem-solving, coping skills interventions, stress inoculation training, and self-instructional training). See COGNITIVE THERAPY, RATIONAL-EMOTIVE BEHAVIOR THERAPY.

cognitive-behavior theory A combination of cognition and behaviorism emphasizing the role of perceptions and interpretations of events as determinants of effective behavior. See COGNITIVE-BEHAVIORAL THERAPY.

cognitive capacity Refers to potential ability to learn, to remember, to generalize, to create. Similar to the concept of intelligence that has not as yet been sufficiently defined for general acceptance.

cognitive click (M. J. Mahoney) A dramatic moment in psychotherapy in which the client must face the evidence that his or her thinking is incorrect and must begin a drastic revision of attitudes and beliefs. See ABREACTION, KAIROS.

cognitive complexity 1. The number of categories a person can assign to particular topics, indicating the breadth of the person's interests and concerns. 2. Ability to mentally switch from one topic or task to another and then back to the first one or to a different one. Examples of such complexity are seen in successful sales people, politicians, headwaiters, hotel concierges, and business executives as well as people who are able to play simultaneous chess games.

cognitive conceit (D. Elkind) The belief among some school-age children that they are smarter than adults.

cognitive conditioning (J. R. Cautela) Behavior therapy in which an aversive stimulus is paired with thoughts of the behavior to be modified, for example, a person imagines reaching for a cigarette and gives him or herself an electric shock; the procedure is repeated until the thought of smoking produces the effect of stopping smoking. See COGNITIVE REHEARSAL, COVERT CONDITIONING.

cognitive consistency The degree of agreement or uniformity inherent in a person's ideas, values, beliefs, etc. For example, in politics being consistently or inconsistently liberal or conservative.

cognitive-consistency theories Assumptions that incompatibilities between thoughts and actions cause discomfort, which then lead people to try to reduce the discrepancies. See COGNITIVE DISSONANCE.

cognitive consonance Characteristic of a cognitive system, referring to various cognitions in that system. When congruence exists among the total cognitions, the cognition is considered high in consonance; when contradictory or incongruent elements exist, the cognition is considered low in consonance. See BALANCE THEORY, COGNITIVE DISSONANCE THEORY, COGNITIVE DEVELOPMENT THEORY.

cognitive contiguity The concatenation of events as experienced, which permits them to be memorially associated with one another.

cognitive contour See SUBJECTIVE CONTOUR.

cognitive control The aspect of cognitive style having to do with the extent to which a person differentiates objects or ideas into either a few broad categories or into several smaller, carefully defined categories. As children develop, they tend to progress from general to specific groupings. See COGNITIVE STYLE.

cognitive coping strategies Mental methods for attempting to deal with unpleasant phenomena, events, experiences, or situations; what a person may do in situations that appear dangerous or hopeless. For example, praying, attempting to uncover the cause of the problem, guessing how others might handle the situation, self-distraction by recalling happy moments or by solving mathematical problems. See COGNITIVE BEHAVIOR MODIFICATION, COGNITIVE BEHAVIOR THERAPY, SELF-CONTROL, SELF-HYPNOSIS.

cognitive decline Objective evidence of decline in cognitive ability, as might be expected of otherwise normal persons at any point in their lifespan development, as a function of a degenerative process. Forgetfulness of names and difficulty in solving problems are noted.

cognitive defects Symptoms of difficulty in knowing, understanding, and interpreting reality, including impairment in recognizing and identifying objects or individuals; defects in reasoning and judging; inability in thinking abstractly, remembering, and comprehending, as well as difficulties in using language and performing calculations.

cognitive deficit Inadequacy of the intellectual or knowing aspect of the mind, such as lack of ability to remember or to learn.

cognitive derailment The unpredictable and uncontrolled shifting of thoughts or associations so that they do not follow one another in a logical sequence. Also known as slippage. Similar to cognitive slippage.

cognitive development The growth and extension of thinking processes of all kinds, such as perceiving, remembering, concept formation, problem-solving, imagining, and reasoning.

cognitive development(al) theories Assumptions about the development (and decline) of the human mind from infancy to maturity. This complex topic also concerns itself with the nomenclature of various cognitive factors such as Lewis Thurstone's eight primary mental abilities and Joy P. Guilford's structure of intellect model. From a dynamic point of cognitive growth, the works of Jean Piaget and Jerome Bruner are probably best known. See AUTONOMOUS STAGE, CONCEPT FORMATION STRATEGIES, CONCRETE OPERATIONAL STAGE, CONSERVATION, DECENTRATION, ENACTIVE PERIOD, FORMAL OPERATIONAL STAGE, ICONIC REPRESENTATION, INTENTIONAL BEHAVIOR, MORAL INDEPENDENCE, SYMBOLIC MODE.

cognitive discrimination Ability to make decisions about complex matters on the basis of judgments made about elements from past experiences. See COGNITIVE PROCESS, COGNITIVE PROCESSING THEORY.

cognitive disorder Mild impairment of cognition, the effect of some medical condition, lesion, or trauma.

cognitive dissonance (L. Festinger) Mental discomfort resulting from having two thoughts/attitudes (or a thought/attitude and a behavior) that do not go together comfortably. See COGNITIVE DISSONANCE THEORY.

cognitive dissonance theory (L. Festinger) A point of view that a state of conflict and discomfort occurs when existing beliefs or assumptions are challenged or contradicted by new evidence. Individuals usually seek to relieve the discomfort by denying the existence or importance of the conflict, reconciling differences, altering one of the dissident elements, by demanding more information in an effort to refuse to accept the truth, or seeking others to confirm their beliefs.

cognitive distortion Pervasive, systematic errors in reasoning.

cognitive dysfunctions Disorders of thoughts. There are many examples of such dysfunctions in this dictionary; see entries beginning with: ABNORMAL, DELUSION, MENTAL, SCHIZO-.

cognitive ethology (D. Griffin) Based on the assumption of evolutionary continuity, animals can be viewed as possibly having elements of mental processes similar to that of humans in memory and perception as well as awareness of self and others. See ANIMAL-HUMAN COMPARISON, ANTHROPOMORPHISM.

cognitive evaluation theory (L. Festinger) A point of view that if a person is rewarded for good performance, performance will either get better or worse depending on whether the person sees the reward as the result of improved effectance or as a means for the rewarder to assert control over the performer. See BEHAVIOR SHAPING, BEHAVIORISM, EXTRINSIC REWARDS, INTRINSIC REWARDS.

cognitive faculty A major division or aspect of the mind, usually coordinated with affective and volitional faculties.

cognitive flexibility In educational psychology, refers to the teacher's capacity for objective appraisal of and appropriate, flexible action within the teaching setting. Involves adaptability, objectivity, and fair-mindedness.

cognitive flooding A therapeutic procedure using negative or aversive mental images, usually by means of voice, to generate emotional states intended to achieve positive results to the end that the feared object or situation is no longer feared. Considered especially valuable for treating agoraphobia.

cognitive hypothesis testing Capacity to solve complex problems by establishing rules to check against the problem until one rule satisfies all conditions of that type. See LEARNING.

cognitive inconsistency (R. Cartright) Self-awareness of what the person is and what the person wishes to be.

cognitive intelligence According to E. L. Thorndike, a basic intelligence factor involving the ability to learn symbols. See MECHANICAL INTELLIGENCE, SOCIAL INTELLIGENCE.

cognitive-intensity A degree of consciousness.

cognitive interview A strategy to improve memory of events, especially important in legal issues including criminal investigation. One technique is to ask a witness to report the memory in forward sequence and then again in backward sequence.

cognitive learning Knowledge that goes into the "black box" as available memory; the underlying thought processes involved in learning.

cognitive learning theories Points of view that consider learning as a process of making new discriminations or reorganizing old material into new patterns. Instead of learning responses (as conditioning theorists imply), the person acquires cognitive structures such as knowledge, or ideas. Furthermore, cognitive or sign-learning theorists emphasize the knowledge of location, as in the case of a rat constructing a cognitive map of the maze so that faster trips can be made to the goal. Such cognitive mapping involves changing perceptions and reorganizing knowledge. There also must be understanding, cognitive-feedback, acceptance and rejection, goal-setting, and divergent thinking leading to creative adjustments.

cognitive load A combination of issues in the active conscious mind such as decisions to be made, problems to be solved, conditions to be met, obligations to be performed, that result in mental stress for the overburdened person. See IRONIC MENTAL CONTROL.

cognitive map (E. C. Tolman) A learned pattern of connected behavioral actions to achieve a particular end, be it a rat in a maze who wants to go to a food box, a child who wants to get dressed, or a student who wants to get a college degree. See COGNITIVE PLAN.

cognitive marker (R. Ornstein) The passage of time as experienced subjectively by cognitive activity. Humans can keep track of units of thought and thereby estimate duration of time.

cognitive mediation 1. Thought processes that occur between arrival of the stimulus and initiation of a response. May occur within micro-seconds as when a baseball batter decides to swing at a pitched ball. The process may take days or weeks in struggling with a complex problem. 2. (L. Vygotsky) An experiential method of learning self-regulation in dealing with a problem. See METACOGNITIVE MEDIATION, TRIAL AND ERROR METHOD.

cognitive model of learning A point of view that learning is dependent on behavioral changes based on obtaining information about the environment.

cognitive modification Any procedure intended to change a person's thinking. Counselors and psychotherapists use a wide variety of procedures, such as the betting technique, devil's advocate technique, exegesis, leaning tower-of-Pisa approach, maieutic technique, and role-playing.

cognitive narrowing Undue focusing on part of a situation rather than on the situation as a whole. For example, on the Rorschach, seeing only little parts rather than the whole blot; in examining a large painting of human action, concentrating on a bird in a corner of the painting.

cognitive need A curiosity-exploratory drive to observe and comprehend the environment. Seen most clearly in young children who are usually exploring their environments.

cognitive overload An unpleasant situation when more information is coming in than a person can process.

cognitive penetrability In participating in a task, an individual may have unconscious expectations of results or an expected satisfactory procedure based on past experiences in similar situations. These concepts, not consciously available may in some cases help (if they are correct) or make things worse (if incorrect). See EFFICIENCY EXPECTATIONS.

cognitive perspective A point of view emphasizing the "intellectual" functions of the mind such as memory, thoughts, ideas, and plans.

cognitive-physiological theory A point of view that emotion is a bodily function that interacts with cognition. See JAMES-LANGE THEORY (OF EMOTION).

cognitive plan (E. C. Tolman) A preestablished concept of how to solve problems. When problem-solving individuals developing a kind of mental outline (cognitive map) of how they should proceed, remembered from similar situations.

cognitive play Fun activities such as games that challenge and develop children's intellectual potentialities.

cognitive processes 1. The mental functions assumed to be involved in perception, learning, and thinking. 2. (H. S. Sullivan) A theory that mental advances are made as an individual experiences the world and relates to others. See COGNITION, COGNITIVE MEDIATION.

cognitive processing A general phrase used to describe mental activity (encoding, storing, retrieving, and using information). See COGNITION, COGNITIVE DEVELOPMENT.

cognitive processing therapy (CPT)   A general method of psychotherapy dealing with conceptualizations of self, others, and events, past, present, and future. Used in the treatment of posttraumatic stress disorder due to sexual assault.

cognitive prototype   1. Trait concepts that people use to make inferences about the degree to which a trait is generally present in self and others. 2. (W. Mischel) A person's view of average defining features of a category of behavior.

cognitive psychology   A branch of psychology that explores such functions as perception, memory, learning, thinking, and planning.

cognitive reaction time   The period of time between stimulus presentation and the beginning of a response when understanding is achieved.

cognitive rehabilitation   A process of attempting to restore a person who has suffered injury to cognitive functions, as from a stroke, to prior levels of functioning.

cognitive rehearsal   A technique by means of which a person mentally rehearses expected situations, such as in visualizing delivering a speech. See AFFIRMATIONS, SELF-TALK.

cognitive resource theory   (F. Fiedler) A point of view that leadership performance depends on the leader's control over the group's processes and outcomes.

cognitive resources   Intellectual factors and procedures that process sensory stimulation or elaborate existing cognitive codes.

cognitive restructuring   A process in cognitive-behavioral therapy designed to modify the client's thought processes, away from negative self references and attributions toward positive ones. See REFRAMING.

cognitive schema   An intellectual or perceptual pattern used as a reference for future experiences, usually based on past failure and successful experiences as well as consideration of what made the difference, leading to a general attitude and set to meet new similar situations. See COGNITIVE FLEXIBILITY.

cognitive science   A blend of psychology, philosophy, psychobiology, anthropology, psycholinguistics, and computer science. See COGNITIVE PSYCHOLOGY.

cognitive set   A "self-and-other-and-thing" group of related concepts that determines a person's worldview and influences an ability to succeed in life. It is the covert set of tools needed to get along.

cognitive shift   1. Mental readjustment, sometimes rapid but usually done slowly in intervals. 2. The process of change of thinking, including attitudes and values. Whereas most people are, on a whole, consistent, they tend to change their minds about minor things such as attitudes toward certain foods, books, or television programs. What was important at one time becomes less important and vice versa. See AUTOCHTHONOUS, EPIPHANY, IDIOPANIMA, SELF-CONCEPT.

cognitive sign principle   A theory that true learning involves an awareness that the various steps to the achievement of a goal is a unified pattern, and that every step is a totality, rather than a series of connections. Presumably humans are capable of conceptualizing the overall concepts of the steps, and presumably lower organisms only know connections.

cognitive simulation   (A. Newell & H. A. Simon) A theory of some domain of cognitive processes that takes the form of a symbolic (that is, nonarithmetic) computer program (formally, a system of difference equations). A cognitive simulation has the unusual property that it predicts behavior by carrying out the behavior predicted, that is, it simulates a specific or a "representative" human performing the task. See PHYSICAL SYMBOL SYSTEM.

cognitive slippage   (P. E. Meehl) The disconnected thought processes characteristic of schizophrenia. See COGNITIVE DERAILMENT, LOOSENING OF ASSOCIATIONS, THOUGHT DERAILMENT.

cognitive stage   (P. M. Fitts & M. I. Posner) In the stage model of skill acquisition, the first stage, in which people spend considerable time memorizing and rehearsing essential facts and use general procedures to apply them to the task at hand.

cognitive stimulation   A therapy technique targeted at eliciting cognitive responses new to clients' patterns of thinking.

cognitive structure   (K. Lewin) A mental framework, pattern, or scheme that organizes and retains learned facts. When a need arises for retrieval of stored materials, as in taking a test, a memory search retrieves cognitive material. See COGNITIVE SCHEMA, COGNITIVE SET.

cognitive style   1. The characteristic manner in which a person thinks about a problem and then conceives and implements a solution, for example, an analytical, methodical, cautious style in contrast to intuition and impetuousness. According to some theorists, a person's degree of field dependence or independence is a major component of cognitive style. 2. Refers to field dependence or independence, as studied by H. A. Witkin. Field-dependent people are sensitive to the context of a stimulus, whereas field-independent people ignore the context. There are several tests that measure this attribute, including the embedded figures test and the tilted chair. See COGNITIVE CONTROL, CONCEPTUAL TEMPO, INDIVIDUALITY.

cognitive system   The formation of separate cognitions into a meaningful and functioning complex.

cognitive task   (J. B. Carroll) Any task in which correct or appropriate processing of mental information is critical to successful performance.

cognitive theories   1. Theories of the mind that emphasize the mental or intellectual processes such as thinking, evaluating, and planning, but especially creativity. 2. Emphasizing "knowing" and "understanding" rather than determining S-R relationships as found in behavioral theory.

cognitive theory of developmental behavior   See COGNITIVE GROWTH THEORIES.

cognitive theory of learning   A point of view that learning requires central constructs, innovative perceptions, and reconstructions of events. See COGNITIVE DEVELOPMENT(AL) THEORY, LEARNING THEORY.

cognitive therapy   (P. Dubois) Any of many systems of psychotherapy intended to help people improve themselves by thought, based on the concept that emotional problems are the result of faulty ways of thinking and distorted attitudes toward the self and others. The therapist becomes an active guide who helps clients correct and revise perceptions and attitudes by citing evidence to the contrary or eliciting it from the clients themselves. See COGNITIVE BEHAVIOR MODIFICATION, DIRECT PSYCHOANALYSIS, MORAL THERAPY, RATIONAL-EMOTIVE-BEHAVIOR THERAPY, RECOVERY INC.

cognitive triad   The three basic elements of depression: negative views of self, others, and the future.

cognitive tuning   In forming impressions, a person can "tune" the self in two major ways: restricting information (tuning out) or being open to obtaining information (tuning in).

cognitive vulnerability   The systematic ways of thinking that predispose a person to psychological distress.

cognitivism   A trend in psychology epitomized in the cognitive sciences. It has implications for cognitive psychology, social psychology, personality theory, developmental, psychology, psychotherapy, and other disciplines. Differs from traditional mentalism in that it deals primarily with conscious aspects of mentation.

cognitivists   Theorists primarily concerned with describing intellectual development (for example, Jean Piaget, Jerome Bruner) or early language behavior (Roger Brown).

cognizance need   (H. A. Murray) The drive to acquire knowledge through questions, exploration, and study.

cognize   To think, to consider.

cohabitation   1. The living together by organisms regardless of sex, age, biological connection, or legal relationship. 2. A couple or a group of people of different sexes living together and maintaining a sexual relationship without being married. 3. The act of living together as spouses, regardless of the marital status of the partners. May also apply to a domestic partnership.

coherence   1. One of several criteria for judging the value of conceptualizations based on the internal logical consistency of the statements. 2. A tendency of images to accommodate themselves to perceptual data that are simultaneously present; for example, the blending of the color of an image with the color of the projection ground.

coherence criterion   A means of judging whether a participant's "correct" response is to be accepted as a true or insightful performance of the task set. For example, the correct answer to "What is 7 multiplied by 6?" may yield 42, but a child may respond from memory and not understand the meaning of multiplication.

cohesion   1. A tendency of successive or simultaneous acts to become connected. 2. The overall strength of the attractiveness of a group for its members. 3. The emotional bonds that hold a group together. Such bonds arise out of interactions among the members as well as mutual interests, activities, and purposes. Group cohesion is frequently considered essential to effective group psychotherapy. Also known as cohesiveness, group cohesion.

cohesion law   See LAW OF ASSOCIATION.

cohort   cohort(s)

cohort analysis   Determining for any cohort the reasons for its differing from other cohorts, such as comparing people in their 50s with those in their 20s. If samples of both cohorts were to be equated on other factors such as social level, gender, health, education, or intelligence quotients (IQs), significant differences might exist between the two birth-cohorts in attitudes toward music, art, science, religion, etc., due to time-of-living differences.

cohort effect   The effects attributed to being a member of a group born at a particular time and influenced by pressures and challenges of the era of development. Also known as generation effects.

cohort(s)   1. A statistical group with significant commonality; for example, people born about the same time become part of an age cohort. 2. Members of groups that experience similar treatments, such as students who go through an identical educational process. 3. Group of individuals sharing a common attribute or a common identity, such as a group of students majoring in psychology who attend the same classes for three years. Term often used in epidemiological literature to classify, for example, groups at risk.

cohort sampling   Subsets of a population tested at different times to check the effects of the time factor. See STRATEGIC SAMPLING.

cohort-sequential design   (K. W. Schaie) Samples drawn from two or more birth cohorts are assessed at two or more equivalent ages. Each cohort may be measured repeatedly, or independent random samples can be drawn from each cohort on successive measurement occasions. Design permits simultaneous estimation of age changes and cohort differences, assuming time-of-measurement effects are trivial or of no interest.

cohort-sequential study   A research design that calls for longitudinal and cross-sectional evaluations in which a number of cohorts are recorded over years. See COHORT-SEQUENTIAL DESIGN.

coinage   1. In linguistics, a rare process of word formation from unrelated and meaningless elements. 2. In lexicography, an invented expression.

coincidence   1. A pair of events which belong to two independent causal series, but which bear such a resemblance as to appear attributable to a common cause. 2. In mathematics, a point-to-point correspondence of two geometric figures or certain portions thereof.

coincidence variations   (C. L. Morgan) Congenital variations similar in character to certain acquired modifications, so that the latter seem to be inherited in succeeding generations.

coin test   (J. Bruner and N. Postman) A task in which a participant is to estimate the size of coins. Underestimation has been considered indicative of a lesion in the pyramidal system. However, the test is controversial since 70% of normal individuals are unable to make accurate estimates, and 90% underestimate the size of the coins.

coital anorgasmia   (W. Masters) Inability of a woman to achieve orgasm during intercourse, although she may achieve orgasm under other circumstances. In men, terms like impotence or erectile difficulty (technically different) convey similar meaning.

coital positions   Various postures that may be assumed by sexual partners during intercourse.

coition   Sexual intercourse between a male and a female during which the penis enters the vagina. Also known as intercourse, sexual intercourse. See ANAL INTERCOURSE, COPULATION, FELLATIO, KAREZZA, PAINFUL INTERCOURSE, PRIMAL SCENE, SODOMY.

coitophobia   Morbid fear of sexual intercourse. See CYPRIDOPHOBIA, EROTOPHOBIA, GENOPHOBIA.

coitus   Sexual intercourse. Also known as pareunia. See COITION.

coitus a tergo   Sexual intercourse from the rear position. See COITION.

coitus analis   Anal intercourse.

coitus condomatus   Sexual intercourse performed with the penis enclosed in a condom or sheath.

coitus fear   See COITOPHOBIA.

coitus in ano   Anal intercourse.

coitus in os   Fellatio.

coitus inter femora   See INTERFEMORAL SEX.

coitus interruptus   Sexual intercourse in which the penis is withdrawn from the vagina before ejaculating, mainly done in an attempt to prevent conception. Also known as onanism (meaning 1).

coitus intra mammas   The stimulation of a penis between a woman's breasts.

coitus prolongatus   **karezza**

coitus representation   The symbolic representation of sexual intercourse through symptoms or other mechanisms; for example, the use of the mouth in a manner that allows the tongue to represent the movements of coitus.

coitus reservatus   (H. J. Seymour) 1. Sexual intercourse without ejaculation. 2. Sexual intercourse in which the male intentionally suppresses the ejaculation of semen. See KAREZZA.

coitus sine ejaculatione   Sexual intercourse in which ejaculation does not occur despite adequate erection. Absence of ejaculation is due mainly to involuntary factors, as opposed to coitus reservatus in which ejaculation is deliberately suppressed. Also known as dry orgasm, *ejaculatio deficiens*, ejaculatory incompetence. See COITUS, IMPOTENCE, INHIBITED MALE ORGASM.

coke   Slang for cocaine.

cold-blooded animals   Common name for poikilotherms. Compare HOMEOTHERMS.

cold effects   The effects of cold temperatures on physical and mental health. Research on cold stress indicates that reaction time, tracking proficiency, tactile discrimination, and other types of performance begin to deteriorate at temperatures of 55°F (13°C) or below. Studies of cold effects on social behavior have produced conflicting evidence of both increased and decreased aggression. Criminal activity generally declines in cold weather.

cold emotion   A peculiar reaction to injections of adrenaline. Participants report feeling emotionally moved or shaken but without any specific identifiable reason.

cold-fear   See PSYCHROPHOBIA.

coldness   1. A sensation that occurs when something touches the body that is cooler than the temperature of the skin. The cooler the stimulus the more intense the sensation. 2. An attribute of a person considered self-absorbed, unresponsive to others, and highly controlled. See FRIGIDITY.

cold-pack treatment   The use of ice packs or sheets wrung out in cold water as a sedative in the control of delirious or excited states. Sometimes ice packs are applied to the back of the neck and hot packs to the feet. Also known as cold-wet sheet pack. See PACKS.

cold pressor (pain) test   A standardized technique for measuring pain threshold, pain tolerance, or both, by immersing a body part, usually the hand and forearm, in ice water. The time until the participant reports that the sensation of cold becomes pain is the pain threshold; the time until no further immersion is accepted is the pain tolerance. Compare PAIN DOLORIMETER.

cold sensation   A quality of sensation due normally to stimulation by some object whose temperature is lower than the temperature of the skin or other part stimulated.

cold sense   A specific sense which provides experiences termed cold sensations.

cold spot   Any of the minute, pointlike spots on the skin or mucous membrane which are especially sensitive to stimuli having a temperature lower than the temperature of the body at the point touched.

cold-stimulus   A stimulus which gives rise to a cold sensation.

cold turkey   Slang for the abrupt cessation in the use of addictive substances such as narcotic drugs or tobacco without cushioning the impact with methadone or tranquilizers. Phrase refers to the combination of chills and goose flesh experienced during the withdrawal period.

co-leadership   Installing two equal-status leaders within the same group, often as a group therapy technique.

colic   1. Spasmodic or paroxysmal pains in the abdomen. 2. In infants, may be accompanied by crying and irritability attributable to various causes, such as swallowing air, emotional upset, or overfeeding.

colitis   Inflammation of the large intestine, which may be caused or aggravated by emotional tension. Purportedly is associated with factors such as a strong dependency need and a cold, dominating parent, resulting in feelings of rage and inability to handle stress or failure. See PSYCHOPHYSIOLOGICAL DISORDERS.

collaboration   (H. S. Sullivan) An interpersonal relationship that combines cooperation with sensitivity to the needs of another person.

collaborative empiricism   1. (G. A. Kelly) A point of view in counseling and psychotherapy of seeing the client as a fellow scientist capable of coming to objective logical conclusions. The therapist and client can then proceed to a satisfactory solution by mutual working and communication. 2. Assuming in group therapy that the members can co-counsel and co-diagnose each other.

collaborative filtering   (D. Terry) A means of deriving information from the opinions and experiences of a group. For instance, users read documents, annotate them, and pass them to others, who read (and further annotate) or disregard them, based on the annotations. See BRAINSTORMING, CONCURRENCE SEEKING.

collaborative therapy   1. A form of marriage therapy conducted by two therapists, each seeing one of the spouses and individually, conferring with one another from time to time. See CONJOINT MARITAL THERAPY, MARRIAGE THERAPY. 2. A combination therapy in which a client is in private individual therapy and also a member of a group, either with the same therapist or different therapists. See COMBINED THERAPY, GROUP MARITAL THERAPY. 3. A form of individual therapy in which there are two therapists and one client. The therapists either function as equals, or one is subordinate to the other. Also, the therapists may be seen simultaneously, or one at a time. There can be many possible variations of collaboration depending on the judgement of the therapists. See CONCURRENT THERAPY, FAMILY THERAPY, QUADRANGULAR THERAPY.

collaborative victim   In victimology, a casualty of a crime such as sexual assault or incest who apparently did not resist.

collagen   A fibrous protein present in connective tissue such as ligaments and muscles. See EVERSION THEORY OF AGING.

collapse   An acute pathological condition characterized by a weak, rapid heart; low blood pressure; flaccid muscles; rapid, shallow respiration; cold, perspiring extremities; and extreme prostration.

collapse delirium   A severe and dangerous form of delirium observed most frequently in patients who have suffered prostration and exhaustion during the febrile or postfebrile stage of systemic infectious disease such as pneumonia, diphtheria, or typhoid fever. Delirium is characterized by disorientation, confusion, transient delusions, and emotional lability, and is followed by physical collapse. Similar to hypermania.

collateral   Something secondary to something else, such as a fiber that branches off from the axon or main fiber of the neuron.

collateral fiber   A nerve fiber that issues from the main trunk of an axon. Axon collaterals may return to the vicinity of the parent cell body and synapse on an inhibitory neuron to provide feedback inhibition that limits the firing rate of the parent neuron, or they may synapse on excitatory or inhibitory neurons that influence other parts of the central nervous system.

collateral heredity   Descent along different lines, from a common ancestry.

collateral sulcus   A shallow fissure that runs along the lower medial surface of the hemisphere from approximately the occipital pole to the temporal pole.

collative properties   Structural properties of such stimulus patterns in art forms as complexity and novelty. Studies indicate that mind processes tend to favor these collative properties, which may have hedonic value.

colleague-centered consultation   See PSYCHIATRIC CONSULTATION.

colleague marriage   A type of marriage in which the two partners acknowledge essential equality as well as personal differences, and operate to maintain open communications, as well as accepting responsibility and authority for specific duties and tasks. See COLLEGIAL MARRIAGE.

collecting instinct   1. A tendency to acquire and hoard certain classes of objects, without regard to their usefulness. 2. A tendency on the part of some animals to hoard objects: Squirrels are a prime example. Also known as acquisitive instinct. See HOARDING.

collecting mania   A morbid, compulsive preoccupation with indiscriminate collecting, usually of useless articles or trash. The condition is most frequently found in chronic schizophrenia and senile dementia. Psychoanalytic theory associates it with anal eroticism. See ANAL CHARACTER, HOARDING.

collection-imitation theory   A point of view that the learning of language depends on the memorization of statements of others.

collective   1. All psychic contents that belong not to one individual alone but to the whole group, such as to all of humankind or to all of a family. 2. A group most meaningful to an individual such as a gang, close friends. 3. An enduring community of people united by common goals. 4. A view that the group is more meaningful than the individuals, and that there is a group mind that supersedes individual's minds. In Soviet usage, this term implies an enduring community of persons united by common goals.

collective bargaining   A group effort or action in negotiating various issues including health, safety, and economic issues with employers.

collective behavior   1. General phrase for group or mass conduct and the characteristic actions and reactions of various kinds of "collectivities," such as audiences, crowds, or mobs. 2. Acting as a group when under the direct influence of others or affected by the influence of those who stand out in a group. 3. Having common ideas and behaviors as part of being a member of a particular society or culture.

collective conscience   (E. Durkheim) General and central feelings and beliefs shared by most members of a society.

collective consciousness   A hypothetical aggregation or summation of the conscious processes of the individuals in a given group. See GROUP MIND.

collective experience   (S. R. Slavson) The common body of emotional experience which develops in therapeutic groups out of identification with each other's problems, mutual support and empathy, and putting aside ego defenses.

collective family transference neurosis   Irrational behavior observed in therapy groups when a member projects irrational feelings and thoughts onto other members, transferring childhood attitudes into the group situation.

collective formation   The process of how a heterogenous group becomes a homogenous group via such activities as members engaging in joint activities, establishing interpersonal relations, leading to group cohesion. An important concept in Russian psychology.

collective hypnotization   Mass suggestion: The act of putting a group of people in a hypnotic trance simultaneously.

collective hysteria   mass hysteria

collective induction   Cooperative group problem-solving that includes pooling information, seeking and identifying explanations and generalizations, and testing the latter through discussion and observation.

collective memory   (C. G. Jung) A point of view that memory is installed in individuals based on the common past of all humans. According to Carl Jung, persons have information from past lives and know what they have never learned from direct experience. See ARCHETYPE, RACIAL MEMORY.

collective memory theory   (A. Mahlberg) A point of view that seeks to explain the general rise of intelligence quotient (IQ) scores over time, since the general level of intelligence remains relatively constant for any population. Assumes that intelligence-test items become more familiar over time for popular tests since an increasing number of people learn the answers to questions over time.

collective method   A Soviet Russian view of the almost mystical concept of a group, that it has identity over and beyond the identity of the individuals in it. Related to some extent to the Israeli concept of a kibbutz, and to the concept of nationalism. See COLLECTIVE.

collective mind   Mental activity of the individuals in a group, regarded hypothetically as a unitary process.

collective monologue   See PSEUDOCONVERSATION.

collective neurosis   Neurotic behavior, usually transient, on the part of a group of people, as in disaster syndrome, and mass hysteria.

collective obsessional behavior   mass hysteria

collective psychology   That phase of sociology, anthropology, or social psychology which treats the activities of groups as units, without reference to the specific individuals who compose the groups. See SOCIAL PSYCHOLOGY.

collective psychosis   Grossly distorted reactions of an entire group of people, such as the epidemic of lycanthropy that occurred in 16th-century France and Italy in which hundreds of people experienced the delusion that they had been transformed into wolves. See MASS HYSTERIA.

collective representations   (E. Durkheim) A summary of the elements of systematic knowledge and behavioral expectations developed due to social experiences. Individuals have such social elements superimposed upon their individuality.

collective suicide   1. Phrase sometimes applied to mass-suicidal behavior, as in large numbers of people jumping off a sinking ship to certain death. 2. Historically, cases of mass suicide include that of the Jewish zealots at Masada to evade capture by the Romans and the mass suicide of more than 900 people by poisoning that occurred in Jonestown, Guyana, in 1978 at the request of their leader, Jim Jones.

collective unconscious   (C. G. Jung) The genetically determined part of the unconscious that, according to Carl Jung, is common to all humankind, comprised of the thousands or possibly millions of years of ancestral experiences. See ARCHETYPE, PERSONAL UNCONSCIOUS, RACIAL UNCONSCIOUS.

collectivism   1. (G. Hofstede) A cultural pattern according to which people set a collective (for example, family, tribe, or country) at the center of their perceptual field, give priority to the goals of that collective over their personal goals, behave according to the norms of that collective rather than according to their own attitudes, and pay attention to the needs of others more than to the profit and loss extracted from interpersonal relationships. 2. (H. C. Triandis) Cultural syndrome organized around the theme of the centrality of a collective (for example, family, work group, tribe, religious group, political group, cult, economic group). 3. (G. Hofstede) A close-knit social structure in which all members are prepared to equally protect other members. See INDIVIDUALISM.

college admission tests (CATs)   Tests for admission, placement, and counseling of college applicants. The SAT (Scholastic Aptitude Test), for example, provides separate scores for the verbal and mathematical sections. Also known as college boards. See ACT ASSESSMENT, SCHOLASTIC APTITUDE TEST.

college boards   See COLLEGE ADMISSION TESTS.

college psychiatry/psychology   A form of community psychiatry or psychology in which mental health services are provided in colleges. Provides diagnosis, counseling, short-term psychotherapy, and referral. Typical problems dealt with are depression, anxiety, psychosomatic symptoms, suicidal impulses, drug abuse, alcoholism, apathy, psychosexual problems, student unrest or violence, and dropout prevention.

College Entrance Examination Board Advanced Placement Program   See ADVANCED PLACEMENT EXAMINATIONS.

College Level Examination Program (CLEP)   A series of tests with topics ranging from American History to Western Civilization, which enable students to obtain credit outside of the traditional classroom.

collegiality   1. Professional courtesy. 2. The sharing of authority among colleagues.

collegial marriage   A marriage in which the partners acknowledge essential equality as well as personal differences, maintain open communication, accept responsibility and authority for specific duties and tasks, and respect each other's individuality. Also called colleague marriage. See COMPANIONATE MARRIAGE, OPEN MARRIAGE, TRADITIONAL MARRIAGE.

collegial model   Persons operating as a self-contained group of equals, such as a group of students working cooperatively on a project.

colliculus   Elevated or raised area or prominence on an organ or section of body tissue. In the brain the term colliculus includes the superior and inferior colliculi (corpora quadrigemina) of the dorsal (posterior) surface of the midbrain, and the facial colliculus that protrudes from the floor of the fourth ventricle.

colligation   A collection of units, each retaining its identity rather than forming a group, such as people on a bus.

collusion   A practice in which the therapist joins with the client, or surreptitiously with a significant other of the client, to achieve goals detrimental to the matter. Compromised ethics usually pervade this practice due to therapist incompetence or lack of fully informed consent. See BLAMING THE VICTIM, PERSON-CENTERED PSYCHOTHERAPY, PSYCHOLOGISTS' FALLACY.

collusional marriage   A marriage in which one party male instigates deviant behavior that the partner accepts, covers up, endorses, or participates in, typically while playing the role of a victim. Seen in marriages where the purported victim may actually initiate the deviant activity, such as incest.

collusion relationship   In labor relations, an arrangement in which union and management collude to the detriment of another party.

coloboma   See IRIS COLOBOMA.

colonial nesting   The establishment by some animal species of enclaves in circumscribed areas where they reside.

colony   1. A group of unicellular organisms bound together structurally so that they live and act as a unitary organism, for example the hydromedusae. 2. Any permanent association of animals, for example, a hive of bees. 3. A group of humans living together in a new environment but still holding allegiance to the places from which they came.

color   Quality of light which corresponds to wavelength as perceived through retinal receptors. It is divided into chromatic color (analyzable into hue brightness and saturation) and achromatic color (varying in brightness alone). See ACHROMATIC COLORS, CHROMATIC COLORS, FILM COLOR, FLIGHT OF COLORS, NEUTRAL COLOR, OSWALD COLORS, SPECTRAL COLOR, SUBJECTIVE COLORS, SURFACE COLOR.

color adaptation   In staring at a color for a long time, the sharpness of the color, its degree of saturation, will appear to decrease. See CHROMATIC ADAPTATION.

color anomia   Visual alexia characterized by inability to name colors.

color antagonism   The combination of colors that cancel each other out, resulting in a grey color. See ANTAGONISTIC COLORS, COMPLEMENTARY COLOR.

color attribute   Any of the basic characteristics of color: hue, saturation, brightness.

color blindness/deficiency   Inability to discriminate between certain colors. The most common form involves the green or red receptors of the cone cells in the retina, causing a red-green confusion. About 6% of males and 0.5% of females are affected. Total color blindness is rare, affecting about three out of one million persons. Color blindness may be caused by disease, drugs, or injury, but most often is an inherited trait. Also known as Daltonism. See DEUTAN COLOR BLINDNESS, DEUTERANOMALY, DEUTERANOPIA, PROTANOMALY, PROTANOPIA, TRITANOMALY, TRITANOPIA.

color-blindness tests   Devices used to discover abnormalities of color vision in the individual or to determine their extent. See HOLMGREN TEST, ISHIHARA TEST.

color cells   Three types of cone cells in the retina, each of which is sensitive to one of the visual primary colors: red, green, and blue. Some investigators conclude that there are four types of retinal color cells in humans. The three-color cell, or trichromatic, theory is based on patterns of color blindness. The four-cell, or opponent-process, theory assumes the fourth cell is a luminosity receptor. See COLOR BLINDNESS.

color circle   An array of chromatic colors around the circumference of a circle. Colors are arranged in the order in which they are seen in the spectrum, but nonspectral purples and reds are also included. Complementary colors are opposite each other.

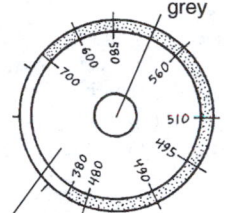

color circle   A color circle with various principal hues around the perimeter. The numbers indicate wavelengths of light in nanometers corresponding to the hues. Hues on opposite sides of the circle are complementary. 580—yellow; 560—yellow-green; 510—green; 495—blue-green; 490—green-blue; 480—blue; 380—blue-purple; 700—red; 600—orange.

color constancy   A tendency to experience a familiar object as having the same color under different conditions of illumination. That is, the object appears the same although its stimulus properties are modified. Color constancy is one of the perceptual constancies. See OBJECT CONSTANCY.

color contrast   The effect of one color upon another when they are perceived in close proximity. In simultaneous contrast, complementary colors such as yellow and blue are enhanced by each other: the yellow appears more yellow and the blue more blue. In successive contrast, the complement of a fixated color is perceived when the fixation is shifted to a neutral surface. Also known as chromatic contrast.

color cycle   The closed, finite system of chromatic colors or hues (including the purples), which is characteristic of trichromatic vision.

color disc/disk   A circular piece of cardboard with a small hole in the center for application to a rotating device, and a slit from center to periphery for fitting together two or more different-colored disks of this kind, so that a section of each disk is exposed and, when rotated, may demonstrate intermediate colors. See COLOR WHEEL and its illustration.

color dominant (CF)   In Rorschach test scoring, any indication that the participant was more strongly affected by the color cards than the achromatic cards.

color dreams   Dream images in color, which purportedly serve definite psychological functions. Though dreaming in color is usually normal, it is also common in epilepsy, migraine, and substance use (especially LSD or other hallucinogens).

colored audition/hearing   A phenomenon characterizing the experience of certain individuals, in which certain auditory sensations (tones, vowels, syllables, or words) are tinged with certain specific colors. See CHROM(A)ESTHESIA, SYNESTHESIA.

colored noise   Cacophony; noise that is irregular. Also known as pink noise. See WHITE NOISE.

colored-shadow experiment An accentuated type of simultaneous contrast observed when two shadows are cast upon the same surface near each other by two lights of different colors; when the shadows are made approximately equal in brilliance, each one tends strongly to appear of a color complementary to that of the light which casts it, the general surface appearing in an indifferent color. Also known as colored-shadow phenomenon/principle.

color fear See CHROMATOPHOBIA.

color formula A scheme for predicting how the primary qualities of vision mix to form secondary qualities.

color fundamental 1. In a given color theory, a color assumed to correspond to a basic color vision response. 2. Any of the three spectral colors (red, green, blue-violet) that are a mixture of light stimuli, not pigments.

color hearing **chromaesthesia**

colorimeter An instrument used to measure or identify colors by comparison with a known mixture.

colorimetry The measurement of color specifications for the purpose of providing standard color information and eliminating as many subjective experiences as possible.

color induction The apparent change of a color when another color is put in sight of the viewer. See INDUCED COLOR, INDUCING COLOR, INDUCTION.

color insistence The attention-demanding power of colors.

color mixer 1. Any apparatus for combining two or more chromatically different visual stimuli upon the same area of the retina. 2. Interlaced colored disks that may be spun, generating various mixtures of colors, including colors that blend and colors that cancel each other. See COLOR WHEEL.

color mixture 1. A fusion effect produced by combining pigments (subtractive mixture), projecting lights simultaneously (additive mixture), or rapid rotation in a color mixer (retinal mixture). 2. The presentation of at least two color stimuli to the same area of the retina at the same time or in close succession, in an attempt to elicit their combined effect. See COLOR DISK.

color-mixture laws Three principal psychological laws of color mixture: (a) For every color or hue there is a complementary color or hue. (b) The mixture of any two uncomplementary colors will produce an intermediate hue which varies with the relative amounts of the two colors and whose saturation varies according to its nearness to grey. (c) If both of two color mixtures arouse a certain visual response, a mixture of them will also arouse the same visual response.

color-mixture primaries The primary colors, usually red, yellow, and blue, which by their additive mixture produce a total range of hues.

color-mixture triangle See CHROMATICITY DIAGRAM, COLOR PYRAMID, COLOR TRIANGLE.

color of tones See TIMBRE.

color preference An order of preferred colors based on results of more than 50 studies of choices made by adults. The order of preference for nearly all humans of both sexes, regardless of ethnic or cultural background, has been found to be blue, red, green, violet, orange, yellow. Infants appear to prefer yellow but shift toward blue and red in later childhood. Exceptions to the rule have been found among Native Americans and Filipinos, whose first choice is red.

color purity The purity of a color depends on its degree of saturation; fully saturated, it is at its purest. See SATURATION.

color pyramid A three-dimensional representation of all dimensions of color, including the various degrees and combinations of hue, brightness, and saturation. The same representation can be shown as a double cone or a double pyramid. Also known as color cone/solid/spindle. See COLOR CIRCLEand its two dimensional representation of colors.

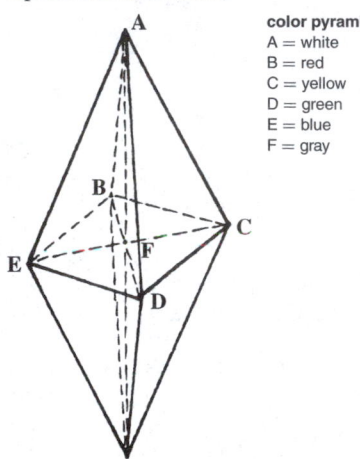

color pyramid
A = white
B = red
C = yellow
D = green
E = blue
F = gray

color response (C) In Rorschach test scoring, notes are often made of responses to the colored cards. A report may indicate a participant reacted negatively to color (color shock) or that a participant responded more often and more vigorously to the color cards—and the report would interpret these reactions and differences. The use of color as a determinant usually receives a special annotation in various Rorschach scoring systems. See COLOR SHOCK.

color saturation The purity of a color. The degree to which it is free of grey.

color scotoma In the visual field, an area of depressed color vision. See ANOMALOUS COLOR VISION, BLUE COLOR BLINDNESS, COLOR WEAKNESS, COLOR BLINDNESS, SCOTOMA.

color sensation 1. Any visual experience which results from stimulation of the retina, as distinguished from the physical considerations descriptive of the stimulus. 2. Those visual experiences which exhibit hue.

color shades Colors of a specified hue and saturation which vary only in brightness.

color shock In Rorschach testing, the reaction of a participant who has shown no problem in replying to achromatic (black and white) cards, finding it difficult to react to the multicolored Rorschach cards or specific card areas that are chromatic. May be a sign of pathology. See COLOR RESPONSE.

color solid   A symbolic figure in three dimensions, which represents the relations of all possible visible colors with respect to their fundamental attributes of brilliance, hue, and saturation. Also known as psychological color solid. See COLOR PYRAMID for an illustration.

color-sorting test   See HOLMGREN TEST.

color square   See COLOR PYRAMID.

color subtraction   The mixture of pigments when illuminated by a white light; the pigments absorb certain colors and reflect others to the observers. See SUBTRACTIVE (COLOR) MIXTURE.

color surface   A plane made by cutting through a color pyramid or color triangle to show all possible hues and saturations at a specific level of brightness.

color system   See RIDGWAY COLOR SYSTEM.

color temperature   The temperature of a blackbody or nonselective incandescent radiator, at which it yields a color matching that of a given sample of radiant energy.

color tint/tone   Any of various shades of any color. See HUE, TINT.

color triangle   1. A triangular representation of the relationships of hues, brightness, and saturation. 2. (J. C. Maxwell) A variation of the color circle. The apexes of the triangle represent the primary colors, red, green, and blue. The center represents white. Also known as Maxwell triangle.

color value   See BRILLIANCE.

color vision in animals   Some animals, ranging from insects to primates, can distinguish colors. Other animals, like most mammals, are in a sense completely color blind but can distinguish shades of brightness of different hues. The quality of color experience for many animals likely differs from that of humans.

color-vision theories   Points of view constructed to explain color phenomena, especially those proposed by Hering, Ladd-Franklin, and Young-Helmholtz. Also known as color theories, theories of color vision. See DOMINATOR-MODULATOR THEORY, DUPLEX THEORY, DUPLICITY THEORY, GRANIT THEORY OF COLOR VISION, HECHT'S THEORY, HERING THEORY, HERING THEORY (OF COLOR VISION), LADD-FRANKLIN THEORY, LAND THEORY OF COLOR VISION, OPPONENT-PROCESS THEORY, YOUNG-HELMHOLTZ THEORY, YOUNG-HELMHOLTZ THEORY (OF COLOR VISION).

color weakness   An impaired ability to perceive hues accurately. Phrase is often used interchangeably with color blindness.

color wheel   An instrument used for color mixture, in which the color stimuli to be mixed are sectors of a rotating disk.

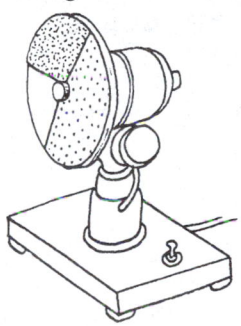

color wheel   A color wheel for mixing colors. Discs of colored paper are assembled overlapping on the wheel, so that different-sized sections of each color are exposed. A mixed color is seen when the wheel is rotated rapidly.

color zones   Retinal areas that respond differently to various colors. All colors are perceived in the fovea: blues, yellows, and grays in the middle zone; and (with some overlap) achromatic colors in the periphery.

colostrum   (foremilk—Latin) The first milk secreted by a mother immediately after giving birth. The milk is thin, opalescent, and different in that it contains important nutrients and antibodies not present in milk secreted during the normal nursing period.

colour-form sorting test   (E. Weigl) A neuropsychological examination which assesses concreteness of behavior.

Columbia Mental Maturity Scale (CMMS)   (B. Burgenmeister, L. H. Blum, I. Lorge) An individually-administered nonverbal test of general ability for children aged 3 to 12. The materials consist of a set of colored cards with several drawings on each, and the child is required to point toward items that do not belong with the others. Judgments are based on dissimilarity of patterns.

column   1. A group of identical or similar neurons that extend together in a longitudinal bundle. 2. In statistics, a vertical row of values.

columnar organization of cortex   The basic functional unit of the neocortex is a vertically oriented group of neurons extending from the white matter to the surface of the cortex with heavy interconnections vertically, and sparse connections horizontally. Neurons in such a column all respond to the same stimulus and not to others, but may respond with differing latencies and patterns as such a column is capable of complex input-output operations.

column chromatography   See CHROMATOGRAPHY.

column diagram   See BAR DIAGRAM, HISTOGRAM.

columns of Goll   (F. G. Goll) Spinobulbar nerve tracts on both sides of the posterior median fissure of the spinal cord that convey impulses from the lower trunk, including the legs, to the brain. Also known as fasciculus gracilis.

coma   A profound state of unconsciousness characterized by little or no response to stimuli, absence of reflexes, and suspension of voluntary activity. Also known as comatose state.

coma therapy   See INSULIN-COMA THERAPY.

coma vigil   Deep sleep that occurs in some people with brain diseases from which they can be easily awakened.

combat exhaustion   A gross mental and physical reaction of exhaustion that can occur in otherwise normal individuals in situations of continuous or intermittent stress and danger, as in battle. Also known as combat fatigue/neurosis. Formerly known as shell shock. See COMBAT HYSTERIA, COMBAT REACTIONS, POSTTRAUMATIC STRESS DISORDER, SHELL SHOCK.

combat fatigue   combat exhaustion

combat hysteria   A functional disorder manifested by some soldiers as a result of exposure to combat, possibly as an unconscious means of avoiding further exposure to danger. See COMBAT EXHAUSTION, COMBAT REACTIONS, SHELL SHOCK.

combat neurosis   combat exhaustion

combat reactions   Traumatic reactions to combat conditions in war. See COMBAT EXHAUSTION, POSTTRAUMATIC STRESS DISORDER (PTSD).

combination   In mathematics and probability theory, the number of ways r items could be chosen from among N items, irrespective of order. Formula: $C(n, r) = n! \div [r!(n-r)!]$, Where: r is things chosen from among N things. The following symbols are also used to represent various combinations: C_r^n is the number of combinations of n things taken r at a time. C_r^N is the number of combinations of N things taken r at a time.

combination (in genetics)   See MIXOVARIATION.

combination job analysis method (C-JAM)   A job analysis technique based on several methods including surveys. See JOB ANALYSIS.

combination motives   The mixed urges or drives, including those acquired and those instinctual, present in an organism at any given time.

combination test   A type of test in which the essential task is to assemble fragments or isolated sections into a meaningful whole, as by putting together a formboard or arranging jumbled words to form a sentence.

combination tone   A third tone produced by simultaneous sounding of two tones of similar timbre.

combinatorial operations   A method of operating by putting together separate elements, usually according to some plan. Thus, in attempting to decipher a secret message, trying to determine whether the letter A in the code actually stands for B, C, D, etc. A chemist tries certain combinations of various substances to see what works best for a particular purpose.

combined tests   Any of a variety of tests assembled to determine the significance of meta-analytic studies.

combined therapy   1. A form of psychotherapy in which the client is engaged in both individual and group treatment with the same or different therapists. 2. Any therapy based on two or more independent systems of therapy, such as the combination of Gestalt therapy with Transactional Analysis. See COLLABORATIVE THERAPY.

combined transcortical aphasia (CTA)   A form of aphasia resulting from lesions in both the anterior speech areas (transcortical motor aphasia—TMA) and the posterior speech areas (transcortical sensory aphasia—TSA), that produces the "isolation" syndrome characterized by echolalia in the context of impaired speech and impaired comprehension. See ECHOLALIA.

combined treatment   A multi-modal treatment program that combines selected drugs with psychotherapy.

comention   (R. B. Cattell) The trait of conformity to cultural standards and obedience to authority.

comfort zone   The temperature and humidity, and sometimes other environmental variables, that are preferred by most people.

Comfortable Interpersonal Distance Scale (CIDS) A measure of the "bubble" of personal space preferred by individuals in various situations with various kinds of people. Not a formally published instrument. See INTERPERSONAL DISTANCE.

comic   A situation or episode which induces laughter. Immanuel Kant emphasized surprise as the essence of the comic. Henri Bergson asserted that people laugh only at others when they do unexpected things, as when they slip and fall. See HUMOR, WIT.

comical nonsense   See EXAGGERATION IN WIT.

coming down   Slang describing the period following the "rush" or "high" produced by taking cocaine intravenously. As euphoria wears off, irritability, depression, or anxiety, along with a strong urge for another dose, occurs. See CRASHING.

coming out (of the closet)   Colloquial phrase for the process by which lesbian women and gay men openly declare their sexual preference to themselves and others. See CLOSET, CLOSET HOMOSEXUAL, OUTING.

command automatism   Mechanical obedience to orders, no matter how inappropriate or dangerous. A form of heightened suggestibility most frequently seen in catatonic schizophrenia.

command style   In education, a highly structured, authoritarian instruction method dominated by the teacher, excluding student participation. See INDIVIDUALIZED EDUCATION.

commensalism   1. In animal behavior, the sharing of the same burrow, hole, nest, cave, etc., of nonsymbiotic creatures, as seen in rats and bats that often share the same quarters. 2. In biology, the living together of two dissimilar organisms, a relationship that is beneficial to one and has no effect on the other. See SYMBIOSIS.

commensurable   Characterizing two or more quantities capable of being measured in terms of a common unit.

commissural fibers   Nerve fibers consisting of myelinated axons of nerve cells that connect the same or equivalent structures in the left and right hemispheres of the brain. Also known as commissure, intercerebral fibers. See ASSOCIATION FIBERS, CORPUS CALLOSUM.

commissure   A body-tissue structure that forms a bridge or junction between two anatomical areas.

commissurotomy   A surgical division of the major commissure of the brain, the corpus callosum, performed in humans to control intractable epileptic seizures. In laboratory animals, commissurotomy may be performed in studies of hemispheric independence or asymmetry.

commitment   1. In general, an agreement or pledge to be obligated to do a particular deed in the future. 2. In psychiatry, confinement to a mental institution by court order following certification by the appropriate authorities. See CERTIFICATION LAWS, CIVIL COMMITMENT, CRIMINAL COMMITMENT, OBSERVATIONAL COMMITMENT, TEMPORARY COMMITMENT, VOLUNTARY ADMISSION.

commitment laws   Regulations governing the involuntary commitment of a patient to a mental hospital usually upon certification by one or more physicians, a physician and some other professional, or both, usually for a limited time. See CERTIFICATION LAWS.

commodity theory   (T. C. Brock) A point of view that products are perceived to have more value when there is a cost associated with them. See COGNITIVE DISSONANCE.

common characters   Characters that are the same in two alphabets. See BI-ALPHABETISM.

common chemical sense   Nonspecialized sensitivity of the body to certain chemicals, an ability considered by some to be an additional (sixth) sense.

common fate   In Gestalt psychology, refers to the tendency of seeing things that move together as belonging together.

common fears   See COMMON PHOBIA, PHOBIA, SIMPLE PHOBIA, UNIVERSAL PHOBIAS.

common-law marriage   A social and legal relationship in which two people are committed to each other and live together as spouses, but are not officially married to each other. Some jurisdictions confer legal recognition after a certain duration of cohabitation. See COHABITATION, MARRIAGE.

common personality   How a person tends to behave in a number of situations at a particular point of life; having a well-established reaction to a variety of situations.

common phobia   A phrase similar to Sigmund Freud's universal phobia or the heightened fear of objects or situations that invoke anxiety in most humans.

common sense   1. In general language usage, similar to reasonableness. 2. Thinking as do others. 3. An attribute that Blaise Pascal claimed everyone has enough of and does not want more of. See SENSUS COMMUNIS.

common sense validity   See A PRIORI VALIDITY.

common sensibility   A diffuse synthetic or integrated experience derived from tactile, organic, and kinesthetic sensations.

common social motive   A motive shared by people of any particular group. Common motives in social groups usually depend on two factors: Common needs and common desires to conform in a specific culture.

common traits   (G. W. Allport) Characteristics shared by all in a specific culture.

Common Business Oriented Language (COBOL)   A computer language for commercial business data processing usage.

common-problem group   A counseling group in which all the participants have the same problem or concern in common. A familiar example is Alcoholics Anonymous (A.A.).

commotional shock   The physical and mental effects of sudden changes in atmospheric pressure.

communal feeling/spirit   A feeling of closeness, neighborliness, and mutual interest directed toward the community, as opposed to individualistic, competitive drives. Also known as community spirit. See GEMEINSCHAFTSGEFÜHL.

communality (h^2)   1. Sum of the proportions of common-factor variances of a test. 2. Common factor variance, as measured by the sum of the squares of factor loadings for a particular test or item. A test with high communality is loaded on several factors. Where: a_{jm}^2 is the square of a test coefficient and is that part of the total variance of test j which is attributable to factor m. h_j^2 is the communality of test j.

commune   A shared living arrangement among individuals of both sexes developed as an alternative to conventional marriage and the nuclear family. Format varies, including central or separate residences; shared or individual property; religious, philosophical, or no commonalities; celibacy or promiscuity; large or small size; established or transitory.

communicata retarda   (retarded communication—Latin) Communication without purpose, speaking just to speak.

communicated psychosis   See FOLIE À DEUX.

Communicated Authenticity, Regard, Empathy (CARE)   Qualities assumed by some theorists to be necessary in a psychotherapist for the therapist to be effective.

communication   1. The process by which one person transmits an idea to another person by means of spoken or written words, pictures, sign language, gestures, and nonverbal communications such as body language. Includes intrapersonal (introspection), face-to-face, group, and extrapersonal communication (for example, with animals or machines). Types of communication include: AUGMENTATIVE, BEE, CONGRUENT, CONSUMMATORY, CORRESPONDENCE, DOUBLE-BIND, DOWNWARD, GESTURAL, HORIZONTAL, INFORMAL, META-, NONVERBAL, PERSUASIVE, PHATIC, POSTURAL, PRIVILEGED, PSEUDO-, THERAPEUTIC. 2. In animals, the sending and receiving of messages through any combination of visual, auditory, tactile, taste, or olfactory channels.

communication analysis   The tracing of messages within an organization.

communication deviance (CD)   Disturbed patterns of expressing thoughts and feelings; thought to be more commonly found in parents of children with dysfunctional personalities.

communication disorder   An impaired ability to transmit thoughts and feelings through speech or writing at a normal rate and without distortion of content or form. See CIRCUMSTANTIALITY, PERSEVERATION, TACHYLOGIA.

communication disorders   Difficulties with speech or language usually first diagnosed in childhood or adolescence.

communication engineering   The application of scientific principles to the development of technical systems for communication, such as telephone, radio, television, and computer programming.

communication ergonomics   A procedure for making messages unambiguous under adverse transmission situations by using a standardized, restricted vocabulary and a phonetic alphabet.

communication interlocks   (G. A. Fine & S. Kleinman) Social structures and mechanisms that provide practical and ideological support beyond the boundaries of specific subcultures. They include overlapping membership in other groups, weak ties among acquaintances, structural roles positioned in intergroup relations, and knowledge diffusion through mass media.

communication magic   The naive assumption that if people tell and share everything, their problems will be solved automatically.

communication multiplex   A situation of confusion when too many people are communicating at the same time or too many channels of information are being fed into the receiving system simultaneously.

communication net   The number of interacting channels of communication in a group.

communication network   Diagrams that represent alternative "communication paths" between individuals in an organization. Among the various official possibilities are the "wheel" with central control of information by the person in the hub. With this pattern, only the central person communicates officially with others.

communication overload   An unpleasant situation when more information is coming in than can be comprehended at once. See COMMUNICATION MULTIPLEX.

communication skills   The abilities making for effective communication; general language proficiency including appropriate vocabulary, syntax, and speech patterns. In public speaking, knowing how to keep the interests of the audience.

communications theory   The study of the interchange of signs and signals that constitutes communication; the branch of science concerned with all aspects of exchange of information.

communications unit   The combination of (a) a sender or encoder, (b) a channel, and (c) receiver or decoder, such as two people communicating by telephone.

communicative acts   (T. Newcomb) The function of communication in establishing a kind of balance between people, especially those in close relationships, exemplified by a marriage. If there is a difference between two people in order for them to move forward and exist in harmony, differences have to be adjusted by communication based on changes of stated position.

communicology   An area of general interest covering the theory and practice of audiology, speech pathology, and improvement in communication by such methods as exchange of ideas, relating experiences, and giving voice to feelings.

communion   In psychoanalytic theory, the unconscious feeling of mystical union with objects or people through the process of incorporation. Also known as magical communion. See MYSTIC UNION.

communion principle   A theory that the first requisite of successful therapy is a sense of unity and mutuality between patient and therapist.

communiscope   A device that gives the participant a brief glimpse of printed material, such as an advertisement. The participant is then questioned about what was seen in the material. A communiscope may be used in readership studies of advertising effectiveness. See MEMORY DRUM and its graphic.

communist theory of criminality   See CONFLICT THEORY OF CRIMINALITY.

communitarian   Refers to a pattern of values that emphasizes both human rights and responsibility toward the community.

communitarianism   1. A social philosophy maintaining that human behavior must be understood in social and cultural contexts, and that the human condition can be improved by enhancing political solidarity and a sense of community. In psychology, the main tenets of this philosophy are espoused by community psychologists. 2. A social theory positing that human behavior is largely determined by the culture and norms of the place where people live. Opposes theories that explain behavior in individualistic and intrapsychic terms that do not take into account the role of the social context in understanding human interactions. 3. A moral philosophy seeking to balance the emphasis on rights and entitlement with an emphasis on social duties and responsibilities.

communitas   (V. Turner) In anthropology, an interpersonal involvement that promotes change in a stable society while solidifying stable structures.

communities for the retarded   Facilities consisting of clusters of houses in which adults with mental challenges who are able to live and work with some degree of independence can function in a dignified setting.

community   1. A territorially organized settlement pattern in which (a) a communication network exists between inhabitants, (b) common facilities and services are shared, (c) the inhabitants have a common symbol, such as the name of the community, (d) there is sharing of work and resources, (e) needs of special individuals are met by not only those connected to the individuals but also by the group, (f) all operate under a system of regulations, and having a sense of overall unity to the concept of the community. 2. By extension, a compound that makes a group sound more formal, established, or respectable, as in defense community, atheist community, or disabled community.

community-action group   A group of citizens specifically organized to attack social problems within the community, such as slum conditions, inadequate delivery of health services, gun control, crime in the streets, or the establishment of residences for persons with mental challenges.

community attitude   General points of view shared by people who live or work together; may become social norms that regulate behavior.

community care   Community-based care of persons with mental or physical disabilities through such services and facilities as halfway houses, adult homes, sheltered workshops, supervised residences for the multichallenged, schools for persons with developmental disabilities, home treatment, cooperative apartments, and satellite clinics.

community-centered approach   A concerted, coordinated attack on the part of agencies and facilities in the local community or catchment area on such problems as mental disorder, delinquency, and alcoholism.

community competence/competency   The use and development of resources, including people, that help the community cope with its problems. See COMPETENCE.

community intervention   Organized efforts by mental-health professionals and others with special interests and competence, to deal with community problems, including influencing legislators, picketing, and public protesting.

community mental health   An approach to mental health based on community resources.

community mental-health center (CMHC)   A facility providing a range of prevention, treatment, and rehabilitation services. Typical services are diagnostic evaluations, individual and group psychotherapy, emergency treatment, specialized clinics, rehabilitation programs, as well as training for all types of mental-health personnel. Also known as comprehensive mental-health center, mental-health clinic.

community mental-health program   An organized, planned approach to the solution of problems relating to mental health. See COMMUNITY-CENTERED APPROACH, COMMUNITY MENTAL-HEALTH CENTER, COMMUNITY PROGRAM, COMMUNITY SERVICES, COMMUNITY-CENTERED APPROACH.

community-of-content theory   A point of view that complex situations have stimuli common to other situations, resulting in consistent responses to different situations based on prior experience with a variety of problems.

community of fate   (R. E. Cole) An organization in which employees feel that they share a common destiny with each other and with management.

Community Outreach Program (COP)   A service that provides health care to persons with mental challenges and their families, sending interdisciplinary health-professional teams to daycare centers, clinics, and public schools where the retarded can be given physical examinations, developmental evaluation and laboratory tests, and specialist consultations. See COMMUNITIES FOR THE RETARDED.

community psychology   The application of psychological methods (in collaboration with psychiatry, sociology, and social work) to problems of mental health, education, group relationships, delinquency, crime, alcoholism, family planning, and social welfare. Often focuses on the empowerment of community members. See COMMUNITY SERVICES, COMMUNITY-CENTERED APPROACH, COMMUNITY MENTAL-HEALTH CENTER, SOCIAL PSYCHIATRY.

community services   A complex of community-based services and facilities designed to maintain health and welfare. See COMMUNITY-CENTERED APPROACH.

community social worker   A person who functions in an advocacy role to maintain liaison between government officials and the public on matters affecting the physical and psychological health of the community. Such a person may inform the community regarding adequate housing, local employment problems, and environmental obstacles to the mobility of those with physical challenges.

community speech-and-hearing centers   Local facilities that provide speech and hearing evaluation and rehabilitation for children and adults.

community spirit   communal feeling

commutative law   In mathematics, a theory that the order in which elements of certain operations are given is unimportant (for example, 3×9 is the same as 9×3).

comorbidity   The simultaneous existence of two or more disorders, whether physical or psychological. In terms of psychiatry, a person can be mentally delayed and be depressed and have psychotic behavioral features. The value of noting different conditions is that each might require a different treatment. See DIAGNOSTIC AND STATISTICAL MANUAL OF MENTAL DISORDERS.

companion animal   Pet—typically a house pet to which the owner is devoted and sometimes emotionally dependent. See ANIMAL ASSISTED THERAPY.

companionate love   (E. Hatfield) Deep friendship felt for those with whom a person's life is intertwined, characterized by affection, attachment, security, intimacy, and commitment which increase with the passage of time. Compare PASSIONATE LOVE. See PLATONIC LOVE.

companionate marriage   A social partnership, typically a marriage, in which the partners do not regard their roles as fixed; each assumes the roles of the other when needed. Each partner has the same rights and obligations of the other, dependent on reality factors such as physical strength, or special education. Also known as companionship marriage.

companion-therapist   A nonprofessional trained to work in an area of community mental health, usually in collaboration with or under the supervision of a professional worker.

comparable forms reliability   The degree of agreement of scores of two tests considered equal to each other in difficulty. Obtained by administering two tests to a sample of people.

comparable groups   Two or more representative samples drawn from the same population for the purpose of observation or experiment.

comparable test forms   Tests that are almost identical, having the same number of items, the same level of difficulty, with scores on one test being nearly equal to scores on the other test. Compare ALTERNATIVE TEST FORMS.

comparable worth   The relative pay-worthiness of jobs.

comparative analysis   The examination of documents or other materials to look for similarities and differences in the content of the texts, with the intention of adjusting matters to provide for further research.

comparative judgment   A judgment by a participant of whether two or more stimuli are similar or different from one another.

comparative method   1. A means of investigation which proceeds by examining individuals or classes that possess certain common characteristics and noting their similarities and differences. See COMPARATIVE PSYCHOLOGY. 2. Comparing or contrasting individuals or species. 3. The study of animal species that resemble the ancestors of present-day species of interest (nonhuman primates for humans, wolves for dogs, bobcats for domestic cats) for understanding the adaptive origin of present behavior. 4. Study of fossils, embryology, genetics, serum proteins, zoogeography, behavior, etc., to determine phylogenetic relationships.

comparative neuropsychology   (M. Oscar-Berman) The study of brain-behavior relationships in disparate human neurobehavioral populations by using experimental paradigms developed in nonhuman primate laboratories to test behavioral dysfunctions resulting from lesions to specific brain structures or systems.

comparative psychology   A branch of psychology that studies animal behavior, conducted in the natural habitat, the laboratory, or both, with the double objective of understanding all organisms in their own right, and of furthering the understanding of human behavior. See ANIMAL-HUMAN COMPARISONS, ANIMAL PSYCHOLOGY.

comparator   An element in some organisms that monitors two variables; if the differences of certain parts of the system are either too small or too large, the comparator either turns the system on or off to have it operate within the desired limits. See VENTROMEDIAL NUCLEUS (OF THE HYPOTHALAMUS).

comparison group   See CONTROL GROUP.

comparison level (CL)   1. A standard that a person establishes based on past experience regarding evaluation of any person, group event, lifestyle, etc. 2. In social exchange theory, a personal standard for determining whether outcomes in a relationship are satisfactory.

comparison level for alternatives (CLAlt)   The examination of present circumstances and changes, with consideration of the personal "price" paid for changes. Important life decisions include when to leave the parental household, whether to stay in an unhappy marriage, whether to stay in a present job or search for a better one.

comparison stimulus (Co)   A stimulus that is compared with a normal or standard stimulus.

compartmentalization   1. Ability to operate in competing circumstances, being secure and certain in two or more situations. For example, a successful executive is (a) the boss on the job, (b) subordinate to the spouse at home, and (c) co-equal with adult children, that is, able to compartmentalize and thus enjoy all three roles. 2. A defense mechanism in which particular types of incompatible thoughts and feelings are isolated from each other in impermeable psychic compartments.

Compass Diagnostic Test of Arithmetic (CDTA)   An examination designed to measure academic deficiencies in mathematics.

compassion   A strong feeling of sympathy for another person's feelings, or a strong feeling of sympathy for others in their sufferings.

compassion fatigue   (C. Figley) The stress experienced by caregivers.

compass reactions   Directed reactions in which the organism moves or adjusts itself so as to be at a specific angle to a stimulus, as in the orientation of some insects to photic stimulation. Also known as transverse orientation.

compatibility   1. A situation in which two or more characteristics may continue to coexist harmoniously in the same individual, organism, or mind. 2. The situation of two people in association who mutually adjust to each other.

Compazine   Trade name for prochlorperazine.

compelled behavior   Conduct that generally is expected of an individual living in any culture. May include covering certain parts of the body, being industrious, obeying others, accepting certain beliefs. Few people are aware of all the cultural imperatives they obey. See PROHIBITED BEHAVIOR, PROSOCIAL BEHAVIOR, SOCIAL DETERMINISM, SOCIAL DYNAMICS, SOCIAL ROLE.

compellingness   The circumstances determining whether a statement will be accepted or rejected may depend on the credibility of the source. A person seen as being a credible source may compel some people to accept nonsense as truth.

compensable job factors   Aspects of a job used to determine its comparable worth, such as training required, responsibility entailed, and working conditions.

compensating error   1. An error that cancels another error. 2. The concept that errors under certain conditions will tend to distribute themselves according to chance and consequently cancel each other out.

compensation   1. The development of strength in one area to offset real or imagined deficiency in another. See COMPENSATORY MECHANISM. 2. (A. Adler) A defense mechanism against feelings of inferiority that motivates a person to attempt to achieve superiority in areas of perceived weakness to gain feelings of social adequacy. These efforts may be "useless" or "useful" according to Alfred Adler. See OVERCOMPENSATION. 3. In the workplace, remuneration for work.

compensation neurosis   A psychoneurotic reaction associated with possible financial compensation for a disability, such as a pedestrian slipping on a sidewalk in front of a store and then reacting disproportionately to the injury or trauma. Such behavior is more likely to develop after slight rather than after obvious and detectable injuries, and tends to clear up with startling rapidity when compensation is won. Also known as accident neurosis, indemnity neurosis. See SECONDARY GAINS.

compensatory education   Educational programs specially designed to enhance the intellectual and social skills of disadvantaged children, such as Head Start, a program initiated in the United States in 1965.

compensatory eye movements   1. The smooth, coordinated eye motion that keeps the eyes fixated on the point of gaze, regardless of the body's movement. 2. A tendency that if one eye is bandaged so that light cannot enter it, and if a light is shown in the other eye, both eyes will change the same way, either opening or closing the iris.

compensatory mechanism   A conscious or often unconscious defense mechanism developed against a real or imagined personal deficit or feelings of inferiority. See COMPENSATION.

compensatory movement   A type of movement to restore parts of the body to normal positions when equilibrium is disturbed, such as moving the arms back and forth to maintain balance while walking on a tightrope. See PROPRIOCEPTION.

compensatory reflex   A response which brings a moving part of the body back to the original position of equilibrium.

compensatory tracking   In ergonomics, a tracking task in which only the difference between the track and the current state is presented; the operator is to move the background to compensate for the movement of the cursor. A more difficult task than pursuit tracking.

compensatory trait   A trait that serves to offset or compensate for another trait possessed in low degree.

competence   1. Ability to exert control over personal life, to cope with specific problems effectively, and to modify the self and environment, as contrasted with the mere ability to adjust or adapt to circumstances as they are. See INTERNAL-EXTERNAL SCALE. 2. In the legal sense, the capacity to comprehend the nature of a transaction and to assume responsibility for personal actions. See COMPETENCY TO STAND TRIAL.

competence knowledge   1. The component of self-image that derives from personal talents and accomplishments. 2. In social psychology, self-esteem and self-worth based on appraisals made by others or as imagined by how others view the person. See IDIOPANIMA, LEGITIMACY KNOWLEDGE, LOOKING GLASS SELF.

competence motivation   A drive to develop personal skill and capability in one or more fields. An inclination to perform high-quality work. See MOTIVATION.

competence motivation theory   A point of view that people are motivated to become competent in a certain domain, and that competence and success in that activity results in a perception of control as well as a feeling of self-worth and positive affect.

competency   Ability to perform certain tasks in a satisfactory manner.

competency-based instruction   A teaching method in which students work at their own pace toward individual goals in a noncompetitive setting. The teacher works with students in identifying appropriate goals and monitoring progress.

competency test   1. In industrial psychology, any kind of test to determine whether a person is able to perform a given task, such as backing up a truck and trailer. 2. In forensic psychology, the evaluation by professionals of individuals (usually the mentally challenged, the presumed insane, or minors) to determine whether they are capable of making choices. The professionals give their conclusions, but decisions about competency are up to a judge or jury. See COMPETENCY TO STAND TRIAL.

competency to stand trial   Capacity to be tried in court, as determined by ability to understand the nature of the charge and the potential consequences of conviction, as well as ability to assist the attorney in mounting a defense. See DURHAM RULE, INCOMPETENCY PLEA, MCNAGHTEN RULES.

competition   1. Contention of two or more individuals for the same object, or for personal superiority. 2. Rivalry between individuals or groups struggling toward the same goal, such as victory on the playing field, advancement in business, or the attainment of academic honors. Psychologically speaking, competition may be healthy or unhealthy, benign or bitter, controlled or uncontrolled, a stimulus for achievement or an expression of hostility. In any case, it is important and realistic to develop a degree of competition tolerance in a highly competitive society. See COMPETITION TOLERANCE, COOPERATION.

competition tolerance   The capacity to compete with another, and to exert effort to win, but to still maintain a favorable attitude toward self and toward competitors in games, sports, business, or social activities. See COMPETITION.

competitive goal structure   In group dynamics, a negative correlation among members' goal attainments. When members perceive it, they can reach their goals only if the other members with whom they are competitively linked fail to obtain their goal. See COMPETITIVE REWARD STRUCTURE. Compare COOPERATIVE GOAL STRUCTURE.

competitive identification   Modeling one's personality, behavior, or both, on that of someone else, usually as a means of outdoing the other.

competitive motive   A drive or urge that influences individuals to advance themselves, may involve the desire to exceed or frustrate the progress of others. Compare COOPERATIVE MOTIVE, INDIVIDUALISTIC MOTIVE.

competitive reward structure   In group situations, a condition that restricts the number of members who can achieve the highest reward such that the success of one member reduces the success of others, for example, an examination graded on a curve. In many cases, this structure reduces group trust, communication, and possibly overall achievement. Compare COOPERATIVE REWARD STRUCTURE, INDIVIDUALISTIC REWARD STRUCTURE.

complementarity   1. In any dyadic relationship, the existence of different personal qualities in each of the partners that contribute a sense of completeness to the other person and provide balance in the relationship. 2. In marriage, a concept that people with dissimilar personalities, who meet each other's needs are attracted to each other, and under proper circumstances will become friends and are likely to get along well if they commit to each other.

complementarity of interaction   A concept that each individual in a dynamic situation plays both a provocation and a responsive role. Emphasizes interaction as opposed to reaction.

complementary classes   In symbolic logic and Boolean algebra, two groups that have no members in common but divide the universe between them (A and -A, X and -X), since each needs the other to complement the universe.

complementary colors   1. Colors such as red-green and yellow-blue, produced by opposing eye processes. 2. Pairs of hues that when mixed in proper proportions, become gray.

complementary distribution   A process of word formation in which two allophones of a phoneme each occurs in a position or positions in which the other does not. See FREE VARIATION.

complementary instinct   1. In psychoanalytic theory, a tendency of infantile sexual instincts with an active aim, to be integrated with antithetical instincts with a passive aim; for example, the childhood wish to beat and to be beaten may be complementary infantile sexual instincts. 2. Hypothetical instincts within any species that oppose each other. If such exist, they might better be called contradictory instincts.

complementary role   A social-behavior pattern that conforms to the expectations and demands of other people. See NONCOMPLEMENTARY ROLE, ROLE.

complementation   In children, the learning of behaviors appropriate to one's assigned gender by adopting those that contradict the behaviors observed in the opposite gender.

complete-learning method   A technique of testing rote-learning in which an individual reviews repeatedly, in a prescribed manner, all the material presented, until it can be reproduced without error. Also known as complete-memorizing method.

completely connected network   A special organization system for groups involved in problem solving, that permits and encourages free communication with all group members, allowing them to decide on their own organizational and communication processing procedures. See GROUP NETWORKS, WHEEL NETWORK.

complete mother   (O. Federn) The ideal mother sought by the patient with schizophrenia in fantasy and real life, that is, a mother who loves the child for him or herself alone and not as a means of gratifying her own needs.

complete Oedipus complex   The presence in a person of both the positive and negative Oedipus complexes at the same time, for example, mother-love with father-fear and father-love with mother-fear.

complete radiator   **blackbody**

complete somnambulism   (P. Janet) An induced trance state during hypnotism, usually forgotten immediately post hypnosis, but may later be recalled. See SOMNAMBULISM.

Completion, Arithmetic, Vocabulary and Directions Test (CAVD/CAVD Test)   (E. L. Thorndike) An intelligence test battery having tests of the four types of items mentioned in the title.

completion test   A task in which the participant inserts the missing part of a sentence, word, or letter in a written text. On a nonverbal version, a missing number, symbol, or representation must be supplied.

completion test item   An objective test item requiring the participant to supply the correct answer. Also known as supply item. See RECALL ITEM.

complex   A group or system of related ideas or impulses that have a common emotional tone and exert a strong but usually unconscious influence on attitudes and behavior. The term was introduced in psychiatry by Carl Jung. Primary examples are Jung's power complex, Sigmund Freud's castration complex and Oedipus complex, and Alfred Adler's inferiority complex. Other complexes include: ACTIVE CASTRATION, ANAL PERSONALITY, ANTIGONE, APPRENTICE, AUTHORITY, AUTONOMOUS, BREAST, BROTHER, CAIN, CASANOVA, CHRONOLOGICAL, CINDERELLA, CLAUSTRAL, CLERAMBAULT-KANDINSKY, CLYTEMNESTRA, COMPLETE OEDIPUS, CONCEPTUAL, CULTURAL, CULTURE, DEMOSTHENES, DIANA, DOMINANT, EGO, ELECTRA, FEMININITY, GIVEN UP, GOD, GRANDFATHER, GRISELDA, HYPER CELL, ICARUS, INFERIORITY, INVERTED ELECTRA, INVERTED OEDIPUS, JEHOVAH, JOCASTA, JONAH, K, MEDEA, MOOD, MOTHER, MOTHER SUPERIOR, NEGATIVE ELECTRA, NEGATIVE OEDIPUS, NUCLEAR, NUCLEAR CONFLICT, OBSCENITY-PURITY, OEDIPAL, ORESTES, PARTICULAR, PASSIVE CASTRATION, PHAEDRA, POLYCRATES, POWER, PURITAN, QUALITY, QUASIMODO, REPRESSED, RESPONSE, SAMSON, SMALL-PENIS, SUBJECT, SUBSTANTIVE, SUPERIOR OLIVARY, SUPERIORITY, SYMPTOM, SYSTEMATIZED, UNIVERSAL, URETHRAL.

complex aggressive type   (S. Arieti) A subgroup of the antisocial personality characterized by careful planning of antisocial or criminal activities, as in bank robbery or embezzlement. Compare SIMPLE AGGRESSIVE TYPE.

complex behavior   An activity (such as juggling oranges) that calls for many decisions and actions, in rapid order or simultaneously.

complex cell   In the visual system, the type that is the most responsive to edges at a specific orientation.

complex function   Complexes according to Carl Jung were a road to understanding the unconscious and bringing the unconscious to awareness. They represent a confluence of emotional traumas and imbalances. See COMPLEX.

complex indicators   (C. G. Jung) In a word association test, unusual reactions such as repeating the stimulus word, taking a long time to react or being unable to reply, that indicate areas of sensitivity (for example, if mother-related items produce such reactions, this finding would be presumptive of a mother complex). See PROJECTIVE TESTS.

complexity-curvilinearity factor   An art-judgment factor that combines simple-complex and curved-angular factors. Phrase is applied to descriptions of paintings that receive high positive ratings for simple-complex, emotions, and surface judgments and high negative ratings for curved-angular, disorderly, orderly, and line judgments from participants asked to evaluate artistic work. See ESTHETICS.

complexity explanation for response theory   A point of view that responses slow with aging due to the greater difficulty that older adults have in responding as tasks become more complex.

complexity factor   In psychological esthetics, a property of a work of art that has variations of light and complexity of composition as principal components of its stylistic ratings. The complexity factor may represent an information overload in a painting, such as Guernica by Picasso. By contrast, a simple work of art may convey a feeling of tranquillity, such as a water lily pond painted by Monet.

complex man   The concept that humans are exceedingly complex and not easily understood, and by implication that psychology is limited by this complexity.

complex motives   Goal-oriented behavior of two types: (a) simultaneously occurring goals; for example, studying because the topic is interesting, and the student is trying to get a good grade and intends to use the knowledge; and (b) simultaneously-occurring opposing tendencies, for example, wanting to go to the movies but also wanting to study to pass an examination. See AUTONOMY OF MOTIVES, COMBINATION MOTIVES, HIERARCHY OF MOTIVES.

complex of ideas   A system of ideas closely associated with emotions so that when one idea is recalled, the associated emotional experience is recalled with it.

complex reaction   In life and in an experiment having to respond properly and in a timely manner to two or more stimuli simultaneously.

complex reinforcement schedule   **complex schedule of reinforcement**

complex schedule of reinforcement   A schedule of reinforcement in which ratio and interval contingencies either: (a) remain constant regardless of the subject's behavior, or (b) vary as a function of the organism's previous behavior. Also known as complex reinforcement schedule.

complex sound-wave   A sound-wave which is not of sine form, and hence may be regarded as the sum of two or more simple periodicities. Also known as compound sound-wave. See NOISE.

complex stepfamily A stepfamily in which both parents bring children from a previous marriage to live in the reconstituted family. Often referred to as a blended family.

complex tone A sound heard in a musical tone that is a mixture of the fundamental tone plus halves, thirds, quarters, fifths, or other frequency overtones.

compliance 1. In general, submission to the wishes or suggestions of others. See SOCIAL COMPLIANCE. 2. Following the suggested treatment plan of a therapist or physician, such as faithfully taking prescribed medicine as directed. See NONCOMPLIANCE. 3. In psychiatry, a compulsion to yield to the desires and demands of other people; neurotic oversubmissiveness. See DEPENDENT PERSONALITY.

compliant character (K. Horney) An overly self-effacing person with a strong tendency to try to please people.

complication 1. The effect of simultaneous stimuli from different senses, for example, the taste and smell of an apple. 2. A second disease that develops during the course of another disease or the worsening of a physical ailment. See COMORBIDITY.

complication experiment 1. An experiment to demonstrate the law of prior entry. See LAW OF PRIOR ENTRY. 2. The attempted perception of two or more events simultaneously, resulting in one being perceived in the focus of attention and the other in the margin.

componential analysis The evaluation of components of any organism or system, usually done to determine what (if anything) has gone wrong.

component impulse In psychoanalytic theory, an impulse derived from a component instinct, for example, sucking, biting, touching, or other libidinal-drive factors, that has become subservient to the adult genital organization.

component instinct 1. Two or more instincts that have united to become one. 2. In psychoanalytic theory, an instinct associated with an organ (mouth or anus), which gave pleasure during the pregenital period and continues to be a source of gratification when these organs become subordinated to the genital zone. Also known as part-instinct, partial instinct. See SEXUALITY.

components-of-variance model An experimental paradigm used in the analysis of variance in which the experimenter randomly samples the independent variables. Also known as random model.

compos mentis (mentally competent—Latin) A forensic phrase meaning mentally competent, legally sane. Considered to have a healthy mind, neither mentally deficient nor legally insane. See COMPETENCE. Compare NON COMPOS MENTIS.

composite figure/person An image- or dream-generated person, the result of combining images of two or more persons. The composite person usually cannot be identified by the dreamer but a therapist's delving may reveal the identities of the individuals formed by condensation in the fantasy or the dream.

composite score An average score derived from several other scores, including weighted scores.

composition of movement A sequence and pattern of neuromuscular activity, as in walking, including the integration of signals in the premotor and cerebellar areas of the brain.

compound action potential A recording of several action potentials in nerve fibers following stimulation of the entire nerve. It is obtained by placing one electrode on a nerve and another somewhere else on the body and recording the results of the nerve's excitations. The compound nature of the response is due to the different amplitude of the action potential and different speeds of conduction of axons of different sizes within the mixed nerve. See EVOKED POTENTIALS.

compound event See EVENT.

compound eye The type of eye found in certain lower forms of animals, such as insects, having multiple separate visual units.

compound F cortisol

compounding In linguistics, word formation from joining words or bases. An old example is "woman" from the original terms for "wife" and "man"; a modern one is "work place" becoming "work-place" and now "workplace."

compound reaction A reaction-time test in which the participant must make a decision before responding, for example, reacting to nouns but not verbs. Also known as disjunctive reaction.

compound reflex A group of associated reflexes that operate together in a single action, the role of the constituent elementary reflexes being coordinate.

compound reinforcement schedule compound schedule of reinforcement

compound schedule of reinforcement A schedule of reinforcement in which several simple schedules are programmed sequentially or concurrently. Also known as compound reinforcement schedule.

compound sound-wave complex sound-wave

compound stimuli In Pavlovian conditioning, compound stimuli are two or more different kinds of stimulus objects or events that occur at the same time. The phrase has acquired currency by virtue of the Rescorla-Wagner theory that makes mathematical predictions about various experimental procedures involving compound stimuli.

compound tones (E. B. Titchener) Tones that an introspectionist can divide into more basic tones and assign mathematical values in relation to other basic tones.

comprehension The understanding of complex signals such as sentences or mathematical symbols.

comprehension test 1. (A. Binet) A mental test requiring participants to state how they would deal with a given practical situation, such as if their house was on fire. 2. A reading-ability test in which understanding is assessed by asking questions about the passages read to determine whether the reader understood what was written.

comprehensive solution (K. Horney) The resolution of an internal conflict by identifying the "real self" with an "idealized self." The coming to grips with reality.

compresence (R. Zajonc) An arousal effect generated by other people being present. Under certain circumstances performance is affected either positively or negatively.

compression The use of a symbol to convey one or more meanings simultaneously, such as a national flag that may evoke many memories, feelings, and attitudes. See CONDENSATION.

compromise distortion (S. Freud) The distortion of a repressed idea into a delusion or hallucination that results from a compromise between ego resistance and the strength of the idea repressed. See COMPROMISE FORMATION.

compromise formation (S. Freud) In psychoanalytic theory, the release of a repressed impulse or conflict in disguised or modified form as a means of avoiding censorship; a balance between expression and repression: a way of gaining expression without giving up ego defenses. See COMPROMISE DISTORTION.

compromiser A group member who, having previously advocated a specific policy, accedes to the opposing or majority point of view even though he or she may still favor the minority point of view. Such people may quit their points of view for a variety of reasons including trusting the judgments of others, willingness to give up their position to permit group action, or an unwillingness to be perceived as rigid and unyielding.

compromise reaction A response to frustration characterized by either giving up, or changing an original goal to other more easily attained goals.

compulsion 1. A persistent, uncontrollable impulse to perform a stereotyped, irrational act, such as washing the hands 250 times a day. The act serves an unconscious purpose, such as warding off anxiety or relieving a sense of guilt. 2. An irresistible command, whether self-induced or at the behest of someone else, that the person may know is wrong or does not want to do, such as to steal, to constantly count windows on buildings. Hypnotic commands may generate silly compulsions, such as to hold the left ear with the right hand. See COUNTERCOMPULSION, OBSESSIVE-COMPULSIVE DISORDER.

compulsion neurosis **compulsive neurosis**

compulsive behavior Inappropriate, irrational actions, such as counting, repeatedly performed as a result of an irresistible impulse. See COMPULSION, OBSESSION.

compulsive ceremonial The ritualistic behavior of an obsessive-compulsive patient. See RITUALS.

compulsive changing A compulsion-neurotic symptom characterized by continuously changing various aspects of life, for example, job, dress, or personal habits, in an effort to make the world conform to one's lifestyle.

compulsive character/personality A personality pattern characterized by rigid, perfectionistic standards, an exaggerated sense of duty, and meticulous, obsessive attention to order and detail. Individuals of this type are usually humorless, parsimonious, stubborn, inhibited, rigid, and unable to relax. See ANANCASTIC PERSONALITY.

compulsive coercion **compulsive restraint**

compulsive disorders Behavioral disorders in which individuals feel forced to perform acts that go against their own conscious wishes or better judgment, such as gambling, drinking, drug-taking. See ALCOHOL ABUSE, OBSESSIVE-COMPULSIVE DISORDER, PATHOLOGICAL GAMBLING, SUBSTANCE ABUSE.

compulsive drinker A person with an apparently uncontrollable urge or drive to consume alcoholic beverages in excessive amounts. For such a person it is said "One drink is too many, a hundred is not enough."

compulsive eating The irresistible urge or drive to overeat, in some cases as a reaction to frustration or disappointment, or as a substitute for denied satisfactions, or as an unconscious attempt to recapture the love and acceptance experienced in infancy when the mother figure provided food and love at the same time. See BULIMIA.

compulsive gambling See COMPULSIVE DISORDERS, PATHOLOGICAL GAMBLING.

compulsive laughter A common symptom of the hebephrenic (disorganized) type of schizophrenia in the form of compulsive, inappropriate laughter. In some cases it appears to be automatic in that even the patient seems unaware of the activity.

compulsive magic An uncontrollable urge to perform a ritual act or utter a prayer or incantation as a means of warding off anxiety or attempting to control events such as the roll of dice or the alleviation of illness.

compulsive masturbation Habitual, obsessive masturbation sometimes performed without pleasure or sexual feeling.

compulsive neurosis A mental disorder marked by an uncontrollable impulse to perform stereotyped, irrational acts. Also known as compulsion neurosis. See OBSESSIVE-COMPULSIVE DISORDER.

compulsive orderliness Overconcern with everyday arrangements, such as a "clean desk" or dust-free house, with discomfort or anxiety regarding variations from desired arrangements. See ANAL PERSONALITY.

compulsive-personality disorder A diagnosis of a long-lasting condition of preoccupation with details, pleasure in dealing with scheduled and structured events, and discomfort with the thought of being imperfect.

compulsive repetition The irresistible need to perform unnecessary acts such as checking and rechecking a door to see whether it has been locked.

compulsive restraint The uncontrollable need to hold the self or others in check by demanding complete devotion to routine or detail. Also known as compulsive coercion (especially when applied to controlling others).

compulsive sexual activity An insatiable, irresistible drive for sexual activity, sometimes without full gratification. See COMPULSIVE MASTURBATION, DON JUANISM, EROTOMANIA, NYMPHOMANIA, SATYRIASIS.

compulsive smoker Describing a person who is aware that he or she should not continue to smoke in terms of adverse effects on health of self and others but who feels unable to quit smoking. Purportedly, some smokers with thromboangiitis (Buerger's disease) have lost fingers, hands and legs as a result of smoking, but continue to smoke; and some smokers who have had their larynxes removed as a result of smoking-related cancer, continue to smoke through holes in the neck. See NICOTINE, TOBACCO DEPENDENCE.

compulsive stealing See KLEPTOMANIA.

compunction A type of anxiety, often based on feelings of guilt, about past, present, or future intended behavior believed to be morally wrong; usually holding back from performing some behavior due to fear or guilt.

computationally equivalent representations (H. A. Simon) A pair of representations of a problem that contain the same information, and in which problems solvable with few and cheap computations in the one are solvable with few and cheap computations in the other, and vice versa. See FUNCTIONAL EQUIVALENCE.

computer address The location in memory for instruction and datum; enables the control unit to find them instantly with a keystroke.

computer-assisted instruction (CAI)/learning (CAL) A sophisticated offshoot of programmed learning, in which memory-storage and retrieval capabilities of the computer are used to provide drill and practice, problem-solving, simulation, and gaming forms of instruction, as well as relatively individualized tutorial instruction. See COMPUTER-MANAGED INSTRUCTION, TEACHING MACHINES.

computer expert system A computer system that can be programmed such a way that inputting specific symptoms (such as fever, runny nose, headache, coughing, depression) will result in a suggestion of one or more likely diagnoses from a possible list of thousands.

computer illiteracy Being culturally handicapped by not knowing how to use a computer. The concept assumes that a person lacking skill with this tool cannot be considered truly literate. It is related to the broader concept of technological illiteracy, referring to inability to function in an increasingly technical society. See KILOBYTOPHOBIA.

computerized axial tomography (CAT or CAT scan) A radiographic technique for producing detailed cross sections of the brain or other organs quickly by feeding X-ray images into a computer rather than projecting them onto a piece of film.

computerized diagnosis The use of computers for cataloging, storing, comparing, and evaluating data as an aid in diagnosing. See DATA BASE, PROBLEM-ORIENTED RECORD.

computerized therapy The use of a specially programmed computer as a therapist or trainer, as in giving audiotape instructions for systematic desensitization, for administering positive or negative reinforcement, or for developing language function in nonspeaking children, and in applying nondirective therapy by having the client converse with a computer.

computer-managed instruction A method of instruction in which a computer is used to assist the teacher in carrying out a plan of individualized instruction.

computer model (H. A. Simon) A computer program designed to simulate psychological functioning. Programs have been designed to enable a computer to simulate the decision-making processes of a human playing a game of chess.

computer of averaged transients If energy from some part of the nervous system is recorded, a series of waves will be found that if seen on a screen or a tape will show variations. This particular instrument is able to find an average of the waves. See AVERAGE EVOKED RESPONSE.

computerphobia Morbid fear of computers, or of using computers. Also known as cyberphobia. See KILOBYTOPHOBIA.

computers Often misperceived as sophisticated typewriters and calculators, they are actually programmable electronic symbol manipulators that can store, retrieve, and process data.

computer slanguage Computer users have developed a language of their own. An example with translation: "My boss is such a propeller head. If she doesn't let me be an open-collar worker, I'm going postal. But a Dilbert was just uninstalled from IS, so I probably shouldn't flame her." Translation: "My boss is such a dope. If she will not let me work from my home, I am going to go crazy. But a friend was fired from the information services department, so maybe I should be careful about what I say."

computer thought See ARTIFICIAL INTELLIGENCE.

Comrey Personality Scales (CPS) (A. L. Comrey) A multitrait personality inventory constructed primarily through factor analysis, yielding scores in eight personality scales. Along paper-and-pencil test for grades 10 and up.

Comte's paradox (A. I. Comte) The paradox: How does the mind function and observe its functioning at the same time?

conarium The hypothetical point of contact between mind (*res cogitans*) and body (*res extensa*) is, according to René Descartes, the centrally located pineal body in the brain. See CARTESIAN DUALISM, DESCARTES.

conation Mental processes concerned with striving and purposive action. Comprises drives, desires, instincts, and motives of all kinds. One of the three aspects of the mind according to early psychologists. The other two are cognition and affection. See REDINTEGRATION.

conatus (attempt—Latin) Self-preservation.

concatenation Sequential interlocking elements in a system that lead components to a desired end.

concaveation The generation of maternal behavior in virgin female animals by putting them in close contact with infant animals.

concave learning curve A graphic representation of a portion or even a whole curve that demonstrates that the rate of learning is decreasing. Compare CONVEX LEARNING CURVE. See item C of CUMULATIVE RECORD, and EBBINGHAUS' CURVE OF RETENTION for illustrations.

concealed antisocial activity Antisocial behavior on the part of people who are not suspected of such behavior. May include making telephone calls to people and hanging up when they answer; making holes in upholstery in theaters, buses, or taxis; investigating a friend's private belongings without permission.

concealed figures Tests of figure-ground discrimination used in neuropsychological assessment. See HIDDEN FIGURES for an illustration. See H-R-R PLATES, PSEUDOISOCHROMATIC PLATES.

conceived values A set of ideal values as conceived by an individual. Such values may be not accepted by others and cause the individual difficulty.

concentration 1. The centering of attention on certain parts of an experience. 2. Term applied to any act of bringing together at a central point several or more components of a process or thing, such as focusing thought processes on the solution of a problem. 3. (I. Pavlov) A mechanism for differentiating conditioned stimuli and specializing conditioned reactions.

concentration camp Originally, a prison established by Lord Kitchener for women and children in the Boer War in South Africa; ultimately, the term for a number of Nazi death facilities.

concentration-camp syndrome Persistent stress symptoms found in survivors of concentration camps, consisting of severe anxiety, defenses against anxiety, an obsessive ruminative state, psychosomatic reactions, depression, and "survival guilt" produced by remaining alive while so many others died. See SURVIVAL GUILT.

concentration difficulty See MENTAL ASTHENIA.

concentration method A traditional yogic method that attempts to achieve intense centering of the mind by silently repeating a cue word (mantra) when exhaling. See TRANSCENDENTAL MEDITATION.

concentrative meditation (R. Walsh) A traditional Asian form of meditation in which a person, with eyes closed, focuses his or her attention on a specific image or repeats a mantra for a period of time (for example, with eyes closed, focuses on the word "love" for a minute without mental movement). Considered difficult for most people. Concentrative meditation, as true for most skills, calls for dedication and practice. Other forms of meditation are easier for the Western mind.

concept 1. A general idea. 2. The end product of conception, an idea that usually relates various elements to one another in a unique manner. Types of concept include DIATHESIS-STRESS, FECES-LOST-PENIS, JUST-WORLD, LEANING TOWER OF PISA, TABULA RASA. 3. A summary of a variety of thought processes, such as an insight into the solution of a problem. Types of concept include: BIPOLAR, BODY, BODY-EGO, CLASSICAL, CONGRUENCE-OF-IMAGES, CONJUNCTIVE, DISJUNCTIVE, EGO, GENDER, MECHANICAL-MAN, PERMANENCE, SELF-. See CREATIVITY.

concept-attainment model Phrase applied to Jerome Bruner's orientation to teaching characterized by an emphasis on developing concepts through inductive reasoning. See CONCEPT-FORMATION STRATEGIES.

concept formation The development of concepts. Ideas generation based on the common properties of objects, events, or qualities. Some concepts, such as love and change, are abstract; some, such as apples and chairs, are concrete; but all tend to be formed by abstraction and generalization. Other processes in forming concepts are discrimination, context clues, definition, and classification. See CONCEPT LEARNING.

concept-formation strategies Jerome Bruner noted that people tend to use four strategies in formulating concepts: (a) simultaneous scanning (testing different hypotheses), (b) successive scanning (testing one hypothesis at a time), (c) conservative focusing (testing hypotheses by elimination of the incorrect guesses one at a time) and (d) focus gambling (by eliminating combinations of guesses.)

concept-formation test A type of test used in studying the process of the formation of concepts and in assessing the level of concept formation achieved by a specific person. See HANFMANN-KASANIN CONCEPT FORMATION TEST, VIGOTSKY TEST, WEIGL-GOLDSTEIN-SCHEERER TEST.

conception 1. The union of a spermatozoon and a ovum (fertilization), which marks the beginning of life of certain organisms. 2. The process of forming an idea (conceptualization), as well as a general concept or group of ideas, such as democracy.

conception ratio The proportion of male to female conception, which is about 150 males to 100 females. (The ratio for live births is about 110 males per 100 females.)

concept learning 1. The attainment of generalizations by comparing elements of learning. 2. The formation of general ideas as a function of experience and classification. For example, a child tasting sugar and honey may have the conception of the similarity of the two substances and eventually learn that they both have a common property: sweetness. See CONCEPT FORMATION, CONCEPTUAL LEARNING.

Concept Mastery Test A measuring instrument that provides sufficient ceiling for the examination of highly gifted adults. Consists of analogies and synonym-antonym items, drawing on mathematics, history, geography, physical and biological sciences, literature, music, and miscellaneous other items.

concept-switching test A projective technique that attempts to measure a person's creativity and mental flexibility. The process involves showing a number of diverse objects to a participant who is asked to give the items a common category, such as "toys," and then asked to give the same items another general category such as "wooden." As in the case of all projective techniques, the materials and the interpretations may vary between examiners.

conceptual bandwagons Common ideas and concepts, whether correct or incorrect, in psychology or other sciences.

conceptual complexity A range of difficulty in understanding ideas, whether in the form of reading, mathematics, music, or physical activity. For example, many people can learn to read a first-grade primer, but few can read and understand Egon Brunswik's *Systematic and Representative Design of Psychological Experiments* with profit. Linked to pauses in speech that appear to be associated with the translation of a thought into a linguistic code.

conceptual dependency (C. R. Schank) The concept of meaning being reduced to a number of semantic primitives.

conceptual disorder A disturbance in the thinking process or in the ability to formulate abstract ideas from generalized concepts for empirical data.

conceptual disorganization A major indication of psychotic thought processes, consisting of irrelevant, rambling, or incoherent verbalizations, frequently including neologisms and stereotyped expressions.

conceptual disturbances   Impaired thought processes comprising such symptoms as difficulty in forming associations, discriminating differences, summoning of images, using words as symbols for meaning, and thinking abstractly. The condition is due to an inability to perceive similarities and to generalize from specific instances, and is characteristic of patients with brain damage and schizophrenia.

conceptual learning   The acquisition of new concepts or modification of existing concepts. Sometimes known as concept learning.

conceptual model   An idea or concept presented in the form of a diagram or other illustration.

conceptual nervous system   A hypothetical model of the neurological and physiological functions of the nervous system that can be manipulated to provide analogies of behavioral activities. Intended primarily for the development of concepts and theories rather than as an accurate representation of the human nervous system.

conceptual replication   See REPLICATION.

conceptual system   Denoting the organization of a person's cognitive achievement, emotional awareness, experience, and philosophical or religious orientation.

conceptual tempo   The pace typical of a person's approach to cognitive tasks, for example, a hasty versus deliberate approach to observing, thinking, and responding. See COGNITIVE STYLE.

conceptualization   The process of using thought processes and verbalization in forming concepts, particularly of an abstract nature, such as hypotheses, theories, and ideologies.

conceptually guided control   A stage of human information-processing controlled by higher-level constructs. Such control functions primarily to direct thinking processes toward well-established goals.

concept validity   1. An accurate reflection or assessment of a specific theoretical concept. 2. A subjective judgment by peers of the probability that a particular concept is valid. Also known as construct validity.

conciliation   A dispute-resolution procedure in which a conciliator attempts to bring disputants together, often by improving communications between them. See ARBITRATION.

concinnity   The quality of an artistic design that features a harmonious arrangement of the various parts to each other and to the whole design to make the total work esthetically pleasing.

conclusion   A judgment formed as a result of reasoning, whether correct or incorrect.

concomitance   The presence together and absence together of two phenomena, or their simultaneous occurrence and disappearance.

concomitant sensation   A sensation that accompanies another sensation, upon the proper stimulation of the latter and in the absence of its own proper stimulus.

concomitant variation   1. (J. S. Mill) The concept that when two phenomena vary together they are causally related. 2. A correlation between variables. See CORRELATION, SCIENTIFIC METHOD.

concordance   1. In twin studies, denoting the degree to which both members of a pair of twins have the same trait or disorder. 2. (W. Schutz) A method of decision-making with three characteristics: (a) inclusion, the decision is made by people who know the most about it (to guarantee quality) and those who are most affected by it (to guarantee implementation), (b) control, everyone has equal power and everyone has a veto, and (c) openness, everyone is totally open (honest) to each other and to themselves.

concordance coefficient   See COEFFICIENT OF CONCORDANCE.

concordance rate/ratio   The percentage of twin pairs or other blood relatives of a person who demonstrate the same trait or disorder as that person, such as the number of blue-eyed individuals in an extended family. See TWIN STUDIES.

concordant twin theory   The theory that identical twins: (a) will be able to communicate via ESP (extrasensory perception) to a higher degree than nonconcordant twins, and (b) even if separated either at birth or soon after, that such twins in years to come will have similar lifestyles and preferences as well as identical physical problems.

concrete attitude   A way of thinking directed to a specific object or immediate situation. A person who exhibits a concrete attitude tends not to make abstract comparisons and will not usually respond to abstract qualities, concepts, or categories. Compare ABSTRACT ATTITUDE.

concrete behavior   (K. Goldstein) Behavior in which a person focuses on some stimulus as it appears at the moment, not concerned or aware of other factors in the environment or with abstractions or generalizations. Compare ABSTRACT BEHAVIOR.

concrete image   A memory image that is recalled in terms of sense qualities such as the taste of a particular kind of cheese or the sound of a ship's bell.

concrete intelligence   1. An ability to handle concrete, practical relationships and situations. 2. The effective management of concrete objects in dealing with novel situations. Compare ABSTRACT INTELLIGENCE.

concreteness   The quality of being specific and particular, as opposed to general and abstract.

concrete operational stage   (J. Piaget) The third stage of cognitive development (from ages 7 to 11 years) during which the child becomes capable of logical thinking and developing conservation concepts, such as the mental representations of time, space, and quantity (concrete operations). During this stage, the growing child begins to deal with physical elements such as pieces of clay or glasses of milk, as contrasted with more abstract entities such as words or mathematical symbols.

concrete peripheral characteristics   The basic, relatively unchanging elements of a personality. These may be considered analogous to atoms in a molecule, the smallest and most stable aspects of overall behavior.

concrete picture   Phrase used to identify primitive thinking and to distinguish it from abstract thoughts. It is assumed that aboriginal humans thought in concrete pictures rather than abstract ideas.

concrete thinking   Thought processes focused on immediate experiences and specific objects or events, as contrasted with thinking that involves abstractions, generalizations, and totalities. It is characteristic of young children, patients with schizophrenia, and brain-injured individuals, especially those with frontal-lobe damage. Also known as concretistic thinking.

concrete words vs abstract words   Words that differ in the extent to which they refer to phenomena, objects, experiences which have a physical, objective basis or are inferred properties and states not directly verifiable. Examples of concrete words: accordion, acrobat, alligator, ambulance, arrow. Abstract ones: adversity, amount, animosity, atrocity, attitude.

concretism   In Carl Jung's analytical psychology, a form of thought and feeling that represents concrete concepts and views related to sensation, as opposed to abstractions.

concretization   1. The process of being specific, or giving an example of a concept or relationship. To the question "What is democracy?" a concrete answer might be: "It's America." 2. In mental disorders, an associative disturbance in which there is an overemphasis on detail and immediate experience, that is, seeing the trees rather than the forest.

concretizing attitude   A symptom of schizophrenia manifested by conversion of an abstract idea into a concrete representation, as in transforming the belief that a spouse is unfaithful into the delusion that the spouse is secretly married to another person.

concurrence-seeking   A situation in which members of a decision-making group inhibit discussion to avoid disagreements or arguments, usually with an emphasis on quick compromise and a lack of disagreement within the group. See BRAINSTORMING, COLLABORATIVE FILTERING, GROUPTHINK.

concurrent audit   The ongoing evaluation of any currently operating project, function, individual, organization, etc., such as a concurrent medical audit evaluates the effectiveness of diagnostic and therapeutic procedures and is conducted while patients are still under treatment. See CONCURRENT REVIEW, TREATMENT AUDITS.

concurrent reinforcement schedule   **concurrent schedule of reinforcement**

concurrent review   An analysis of admission to a hospital or clinic or institution or of a utilization review, carried out while care is being provided, comprising an assessment of the necessity for admission (admission certification), and assessment of the need for care to be continued (continued-stay review). See CONCURRENT AUDIT.

concurrent schedule of reinforcement (CONC)   The simultaneous reinforcements of an organism that operate independently and simultaneously. Also known as concurrent reinforcement schedule. See REINFORCEMENT SCHEDULES.

concurrent therapy   The simultaneous treatment of spouses or other family members in marriage and family therapy, either by the same or different therapists. For example, a husband is seen by therapist A, a wife by therapist B, a child by therapist C. All three therapists report to supervising therapist D who may also independently interview the three patients, and may gather all therapists and family members together at one meeting. See COLLABORATIVE THERAPY, CONJOINT COUNSELING, MULTIPLE THERAPY.

concurrent validity   1. The correlation between test scores given before employment and actual work performance. 2. The extent of correspondence between two variables at about the same time; specifically, the measure of one test's validity by inspection of its correlation with a separate but related test, such as a standardized test. See CONCOMITANT VARIATION, CONTENT VALIDITY, CRITERION VALIDITY, PREDICTIVE VALIDITY.

concussion   1. An injury to soft structures, such as the brain, as the result of a violent shaking or jarring. 2. Disruption of brain function, with spontaneous recovery, that results from an injury to the head, usually through a severe blow. Symptoms may include alteration of consciousness, disturbances of vision, disturbances of equilibrium, paralysis and lasting damage to the brain. See HEAD TRAUMA.

condensation   In psychoanalytic theory, the fusion of several meanings into one image, word, term, or event. It is common in dreams, where several images may fuse into one. For example, a woman dreamt of being chased by a rooster and as she was running, she knew if she reached "Lokonner Bay" she would be safe. Analysis suggested that the rooster was a symbol of the male organ (rooster = cock) and Lokonner Bay was a condensation of "love-honor-obey," and consequently the meaning of the Lokonner Bay was that if she were married then it would be safe to have sex. See COMPRESSION.

condition   1. The antecedent circumstance on which an event is dependent. A phenomenon, force, situation, etc., without which a given event never occurs. 2. The state of body or mind of a person or persons or the combination of these states at any specified time.

conditionability   A capability to acquire and maintain conditioned responses. Research indicates that "introverts" acquire conditioned responses more easily and retain them longer than "extroverts."

conditional assumption   (A. Ellis) An illogical tendency to use "if-then" interpretations based on single incidents or single persons; that is, generating a forest on the basis of one tree. For example, "If she does not like me, then I am unlikable."

conditional discharge   Parole or leave of absence from a psychiatric facility with certain conditions and limitations, such as reporting periodically to a supervisor, or taking certain medications periodically, during which time the patient is still under commitment.

conditionalism   A doctrine positing that an effect can be predicted by knowing the cause, and that an effect can be explained in terms of its cause. See DETERMINISM.

conditional knowledge   (S. Paris) Knowing "when" and "where" to use declarative or procedural knowledge.

conditional positive regard   An attitude of acceptance and esteem which is expressed toward a person by others on a tentative basis, that is, positive regard depends on whether the behavior of the person, rather than the person per se, was perceived as acceptable by a parent or other person seen as an authority figure. Carl Rogers asserted that the need for positive regard, whether conditional or unconditional, was universal. See POSITIVE REGARD, SELF-ESTEEM.

conditional probability   The probability or likelihood of one event taking place, given the occurrence of another event.

conditional reasoning   A cognitive problem with an "if-then" decision.

conditioned avoidance response (CAR)   A conditioned response that anticipates and averts the occurrence of a harmful or unpleasant stimulus. In a CAR, the organism successfully avoids the painful stimulus, whereas in the conditioned escape response, the organism is already exposed but maneuvers away from the stimulus or finds a way to stop it.

conditioned discrimination   Combining of acquisition and extinction procedures for training an organism to respond to a specific conditioned stimulus and not to a generalized one. Performed by pairing the conditioned and unconditioned stimuli and presenting the generalized stimulus alone and then differentially rewarding the organism.

conditioned emotion   A feeling or affective state acquired as a result of conditioning, such that an emotional response (such as fear) elicited by a previously ineffective stimulus (such as a buzzer) has come to be the effective stimulus by virtue of its association with an unconditioned stimulus.

conditioned emotional response (CER)   An affective response, such as fear, elicited by a neutral stimulus as the result of Pavlovian classical conditioning.

conditioned enhancement   A method of strengthening a learned response by presenting a new stimulus that has already been relevantly learned as well as the original stimulus for the first response. See CONDITIONED RESPONSE, CONDITIONING.

conditioned escape response   A conditioned reaction by means of which an organism ends its exposure to a harmful or unpleasant stimulus, resulting in managing to escape or stop the unwanted stimulus. See CONDITIONED AVOIDANCE RESPONSE.

conditioned fear   (J. B. Watson) The induction of fear, usually to some otherwise neutral object or topic via conditioning, likely to wane unless reinforced.

conditioned inhibition ($_S I_R$)   (C. L. Hull) The suppression of a conditioned response by pairing it with a nonreinforced stimulus. See HULL'S THEORY.

conditioned operant   A behavior (response) learned through operant conditioning; a type of behavior with which the organism "operates" in its environment to obtain a desired result.

conditioned reflex/response (CR or R$_C$)   (I. Pavlov) In classical conditioning, the learned or acquired response to a conditioned stimulus; that is, a simple reflex responding to a stimulus that did not elicit the reflex originally.

conditioned-reflex therapy   (A. Salter) A form of behavior therapy based on the writings of the early behaviorists, such as Pavlov, Bekhterev, and Watson; this system of therapy aims to change a patient's psychological tilt from inhibition to excitation. According to this approach, patients are encouraged to act on the basis of feeling rather than thinking.

conditioned reinforcers   Stimuli that require the capacity to reinforce by being paired with primary reinforcers; for example, food may be paired with a token, and eventually the token may become the conditioned reinforcer. See REINFORCEMENT, SECONDARY REINFORCEMENT.

conditioned response   (E. R. Guthrie, I. Pavlov) In classical conditioning, the response that is learned, formed when an indifferent or neutral stimulus is paired with a natural stimulus which elicits a natural or unconditioned response. After repeated presentations, the previously neutral stimulus will evoke the same response as the natural stimulus. Rarely abbreviated R$_c$. Compare UNCONDITIONED RESPONSE.

conditioned stimulus (CS or, rarely, S$_C$)   1. A previously neutral stimulus repeatedly associated with an unconditioned stimulus to the extent that it comes to acquire the power of the unconditioned stimulus to elicit the same response or some aspect of the response; for example, in Ivan Pavlov's classic experiment, the tone associated with the food becomes the CS. 2. In classical conditioning, an originally neutral stimulus, after presentation, simultaneously or nearly simultaneously with an adequate or original stimulus to a given response, becomes capable of arousing this response when presented alone. Also known as conditional stimulus. See CLASSICAL CONDITIONING, UNCONDITIONED STIMULUS, UNCONDITIONING.

conditioned suppression   A temporary decrease in the rate of an operant response because of the presentation of a stimulus that had previously been paired with a painful stimulus.

conditioning   The process by which a response is learned, that is, a response to a stimulus that did not originally evoke it. Types of conditioning include: ALPHA BLOCK, APPETITIVE, AUTONOMIC, AVERSION, AVERSIVE-REINFORCEMENT, AVOIDANCE, BACKWARD, CLASSICAL, COGNITIVE, COUNTER-, COVERT, CROSS, DE-, DECORTICATION, DELAYED, DIFFERENTIAL, ESCAPE, EXCITATORY, EXTEROCEPTIVE, EYELID, FORWARD, GUTHRIE'S CONTIGUOUS, HIGHER-ORDER, INSTRUMENTAL, INTEROCEPTIVE, LONG-DELAY, OPERANT, PAVLOVIAN, PRE-, PSEUDO-, R-R, RATE, RE-, RESPONDENT, SECOND-ORDER, SEMANTIC, SENSORY, SIDMAN AVOIDANCE, SIMULTANEOUS, SKINNERIAN, SPINAL, SUCCESSIVE APPROXIMATION, TEMPORAL AVOIDANCE, TEMPORAL, TRACE, TYPE-R, TYPE-S, VERBAL, VICARIOUS.

conditioning apparatus   Any laboratory device designed to create conditioning, measure conditioning, or both. The earliest was Ivan Pavlov's dog harness, saliva collector, and bell; the most common is the operant conditioning chamber or Skinner box.

conditioning therapy   Descriptive phrase sometimes applied to behavior therapy.

conditions of worth   (C. R. Rogers) Values that other people place on a child's behaviors that become a counterforce to the child's self-actualization tendency or ego-strength. A child comes to believe that his or her own worth is contingent upon behaving in accordance with others' demands. This surrender of integrity may generate problems later on in life. See CONDITIONAL POSITIVE REGARD.

condom   A sheath, usually made of latex, that fits over the penis for use during intercourse, serving both as a contraceptive device and a means of preventing the spread of venereal disease. Sexual intercourse with use of a condom is sometimes called *coitus condomatus*. Also known as prophylactic, rubber, safe.

condonation   In law, an illegal act that is not pursued because the victim forgives the perpetrator.

conduct   1. The behavior of an individual that has ethical or legal considerations. Behavior that conforms to or violates the standards established by the person's social group. 2. Behavior of an individual as determined by foresight. 3. Behavior of the total individual as expressed in psychological as well as physical activity. See CONDUCT VS BEHAVIOR.

conduct disorder (CD)   1. A general term used to describe a pattern of behavior of children and adolescents that violates the basic rights of others, but can apply to any age group. See CRIME, DELINQUENCY, PARENTING. 2. Repetitive behavior that offends people and negatively affects the lives of others psychologically and physically. 3. A grouping of disorders of behavior in the *Diagnositic and Statistical Manual of Mental Disorders*.

conduction   In physiology, transmission of excitation through nerves as well as living tissues. See CONDUCTIVITY, EXCITATION AND CONDUCTION.

conduction aphasia   A form of aphasia associated with lesions in the postcentral cortical area, characterized by difficulty in differentiating speech sounds and repeating them accurately, even though spontaneous articulation may be intact.

conduction deafness   The loss of hearing due to a disorder in the auditory structures associated with the transmission of sound vibrations between the tympanic membrane and the inner ear. There is a uniform loss of sensitivity to all frequencies and an altering of the sound-intensity threshold. Also known as conductive deafness.

conduction time (CT)   The time required for the transmission of a wave of excitation between two determined points.

conduction unit   1. A mechanism for transmitting neural impulses from one place in the body to another place. 2. (E. L. Thorndike) A mechanism inferred when an organism tends to respond in a specific way under given circumstances.

conduction with decrement   The transmission of a wave of excitation in tissue with a gradual loss of the energy of the wave.

conductivity   Capacity of a tissue to transmit a wave of excitation.

conduct vs behavior   Terms often interchanged, but behavior is more neutral; for example, a child's behavior in playing with others while showing rough and unfair conduct.

cones   1. Objects with a circular base and a body that tapers to a point. 2. Cone-shaped receptor cells in the center of the retina that work best in daylight (in comparison to the rods) and are able to receive color and to discern fine details because of the density of their placement.

confabulated response   In Rorschach test scoring, any report of any perception that makes no sense to the examiner, being totally inappropriate to the reality of the inkblot, such as seeing a part of the inkblot as a representation of the Infinite.

confabulation   Falsification of memory in which gaps in recall are filled by fabrications which the patient believes to be facts, often with made-up details that are believable. Occurs frequently in Korsakoff's syndrome, and in other organic psychoses such as senile dementia, general paresis, and head-injury cases.

confact   An overt response between a present situation and certain previously experienced situations of a similar kind.

confactor analysis   (R. B. Cattell) An experimental method using two different samples of people that enables one to reach the underlying determiners. An alternative to simple structure procedures.

confederates   In an experimental situation, the aides of the experimenter who pose as participants but whose behavior is rehearsed prior to the research. The real experimental participants are sometimes termed "naive" participants or subjects. Some experiments in social psychology that involve the use of confederates have been criticized for the possible harm done to naive participants, even though most experimenters debrief these participants after the research situation. See BEHAVIORAL STUDY OF OBEDIENCE.

conference method   A personnel-development technique in which participants develop problem-solving and decision-making abilities, acquire new information, and modify their attitudes by pooling ideas, testing assumptions, discussing new approaches, and drawing inferences and conclusions on business problems and issues. See BRAINSTORMING.

confession   1. A statement of admission of guilt or of having "done wrong." 2. The name given by Carl Jung to the start of analytic therapy, during which the patients describe what is troubling them. 3. A point or stage in psychotherapy, when patients lower their guard and confess the truth about their feelings, thoughts, and behavior and often bring forth material not mentioned in earlier sessions.

confidant   A person with whom another shares intimate secrets, feelings, and thoughts, and who provides emotional support.

confidence course   Euphemism for obstacle course.

confidence game   An elaborate scheme to swindle others. See SCAM.

confidence interval (CI)   See CONFIDENCE (LEVEL) INTERVAL.

confidence level   See CONFIDENCE (LEVEL) INTERVAL, CONFIDENCE LIMITS, FIDUCIAL LIMITS, RISK LEVEL.

confidence (level) interval   A range of values, considering all possible samples, within which a statistical parameter may be expected, or where there is a probability of locating the true population value. See CONFIDENCE LIMITS.

confidence limits 1. For a population parameter, the upper and lower bounds of an interval around the value of a sample statistic (the confidence interval) that estimates the population parameter such that there is a certain degree of confidence that the interval contains the parameter. For example, when the 95% confidence interval for the population mean is obtained, the interval is determined by a procedure such that 95% of the intervals so formed would contain the population mean. 2. The upper and lower boundaries of the confidence level. The usual limits are 95% and 99%, also referred to as confidence interval or fiducial limits. Confidence limits are stated usually at the 95% or the 99% level indicating that in only 5% or 1% of the cases would the results have occurred by chance. This is in contrast to levels of significance which are stated conventionally at the 5%, 10%, or 0.1% level. The former refer to interval estimation, the latter to hypothesis testing. 3. The concept that if observations are repeated, 95% of the time (for example), the estimate of the mean will fall within the interval specified. Refers to the reliability of measurements rather than the validity. See LIKELIHOOD RATIO TEST, TESTS OF SIGNIFICANCE.

confidentiality A principle of ethics requiring people in licensed professions to hold secret all information given by patients, as well as test scores and other research data, except in situations in which the safety of the patient or of other people is threatened by withholding such information. Under some circumstances, confidential or privileged communication must be disclosed, for example when interests of children are paramount.

configural superiority effect A tendency for observers to perceive a difference among integrated stimuli more readily than among simple ones.

configuration An arrangement of elements. The German word Gestalt is best defined as configuration. See GOODNESS OF CONFIGURATION, WORD CONFIGURATION.

configurational learning An organism training to respond to patterns rather than stimuli as such (for example, responding to brightly lit triangles when presented on the left, but not responding to other bright objects, other triangles, or other objects on the left).

confinement effects The results of restricting an organism's freedom of action. In humans, it generally results in a higher-than-usual incidence of maladaptive behavior, even though most prison inmates and nursing home or mental hospital patients find ways to adapt to their restricted environments. See REACTANCE THEORY.

confinement fear See CLAUSTROPHOBIA.

confirmation (E. C. Tolman) The fulfillment of an expectancy. That is, the behavior in question leads to the expected goal, which tends to reinforce the process.

confirmation bias 1. A tendency to seek evidence to confirm a hypothesis, for example, a researcher searches for information that confirms preconceptions and neglects or discounts information that denies expectations. 2. A tendency of participants who know the hypothesis of any experiment to act in manners that provide unwanted evidence supporting the hypothesis. See CONTAMINATION, YEASAYING.

confirmatory factor analysis A factor analysis that confirms the existence of specific factors.

confirmed negativity condition (P. Claude-Pierre) A disorder of thinking on the part of some emotionally sensitive people who believe they are helpless to solve the world's problems and collapse into self-loathing. Considered to be an essential cause of anorexia. See SELF-CONCEPT.

confirming reaction A presumed pleasant reaction that occurs in a person when an objective is reached.

conflation 1. The combination of two or more elements into one. The generation of a single entity by merging related entities to form a new united and meaningful entity, for example, a dictionary is a conflation of terms from many sources brought together to form a single reference book. 2. The mixing of two or more points of view to make a single united one. No implication of the value of the conflation is implied.

conflict The clash of opposing or incompatible emotional or motivational forces, such as drives, impulses, or wishes. In psychoanalytic terms, conflict is a struggle taking place between conscious and unconscious forces. Types of conflict include: APPROACH-APPROACH, APPROACH-AVOIDANCE, AVOIDANCE-AVOIDANCE, BASIC, CENTRAL, CHRONIC, CULTURE, DOUBLE-APPROACH AVOIDANCE, EMOTIONAL, ETHICAL, EXTRAPSYCHIC, INTERGROUP CULTURE, INTERNAL CULTURE, INTERPERSONAL, INTERROLE, INTRAPERSONAL, INTRAPSYCHIC, INTRAROLE, MARITAL, MOTIVATIONAL, NEUROTIC, NUCLEAR, OEDIPAL, ROLE, ROOT.

conflict-free area An aspect of the personality so well-integrated that it does not give rise to internal conflict, maladjustment, or neurotic symptoms.

conflict-free sphere (H. Hartmann) A period of functioning during which neither the id nor superego are in conflict with the ego.

conflict of interest 1. In general, an inability to act without threat of self-serving bias. 2. In counseling or psychotherapy, competing interests that may affect therapist-client relationships. 3. In industrial psychology, being asked to make decisions that may affect the interests of the employer, one's own interests, or those of others. Ethical dilemmas sometimes can be solved in such cases by refusing to participate in such decisions. 4. In group dynamics, the actions of an individual attempted to maximize personal needs and benefits by blocking, interfering with, or damaging the actions of another person with similar objectives.

Conflict Resolution Inventory A questionnaire designed to measure self-assertiveness, by presenting 35 situations and asking participants to consider whether or not they would perform unreasonable actions, such as letting a casual acquaintance interrupt last-minute study for an examination. Sometimes used in assessing the effects of assertiveness training.

conflict theory In large-group social psychology, the interpretation of "race" and ethnic relations as an interplay of groups that compete for resources in contexts that differentially favor some groups over others.

conflict theory of criminality A point of view that the rich and the powerful make laws to maintain the status quo and repress the poor and powerless. Also known as communist theory of criminality.

confluence The fusion of several instincts, motives, or perceptual elements into a single motivating factor. The combined influence of heredity and environment.

confluence approach A point of view that for creativity to occur, multiple components must converge.

confluence model 1. A theory correlating the intelligence of siblings to family size, which holds that average intelligence declines as the number of children in a family increases. Thus, the greater the number of children, the less intelligent they would be expected to be. Intelligence is also held to decline with birth order. 2. (R. B. Zajonc) A point of view that children in a family are exposed to different levels of experience in sequence from first child to later children. A first child who initially interacts only with adults (the parents) has a different linguistic experience than the third child in a family of five children. See BIRTH ORDER, INTELLIGENCE.

confluence theory A point of view that intelligence quotients (IQs) decrease from first-borns to later-borns. See BIRTH-ORDER THEORY, CONFLUENCE MODEL.

confluent learning (R. B. Cattell) 1. Learning of a single response in substitution of two former responses. 2. A group of responses that serve originally conflicting goals.

conformance 1. To agree in pattern with the general type: thus a particular duck will quack and walk like other ducks. 2. In the social behavior of humans, to act according to certain standards. 3. In environmental psychology, design of a living or working area in terms of functional, spatial, climatic, and sensory goals (for example, sensory conformance would require lighting to meet needs for specific visual tasks). See BEHAVIORAL FACILITATION.

conforming behavior Human actions that are similar to those of other people in similar situations (for example, most people will apologize when bumping into others).

conforming stage The period, especially during adolescence, when children want to look and act like their peers. Deviation from the "accepted codes" is frowned upon and may lead to rejection by others.

conformism A tendency of some people to agree with local standards, to go along with others without consideration of whether or not others think is correct. See GOAT, SHEEP.

conformity 1. Social behavior that follows conventional patterns. 2. A tendency, often unwitting, to adopt the opinions, norms, or behavior of a particular social group such as a peer group or religious group. May be demanded in certain situations, or it may represent an inner need of the individual. See ANTICONFORMITY, MOVEMENT CONFORMITY.

confounding The presence of one or more extraneous variables that occur at the same time as the experimental variable, that will affect the findings in unaccountable ways, so that the effect of the experimental treatment is distorted or cannot be accurately assessed. See EXPERIMENTAL CONTROLS.

confounding variable A type of variable not controlled by the experimenter, that influences the results of an experiment. Extraneous variables may enter into an experiment unintentionally and become so difficult to define, measure, or separate, as to render the study results doubtful or invalid. Such undesired variables weaken a research and question its findings. Also known as confounds.

confounds confounding variables

confrontation 1. The act of directly facing or being required to face personal attitudes or shortcomings, as well as how a person is perceived by others or the possible consequences of personal behavior. 2. In psychoanalytic theory, the first step in therapy in which the patient must recognize the psychiatric phenomena to be analyzed. 3. In Adlerian therapy, a statement or question calculated to motivate the patient to make a decision or face the reality of a situation. 4. A direct, overt, and often hostile encounter involving a challenge or complaint by a person or a group of people, to another individual or group (such as a bully on a playground picking on a smaller child or employees going on strike against the owners of a business). See AGGRESSIVE BEHAVIOR, CONFLICT, HOSTILITY.

confrontational meeting 1. Ordinarily, a face-to-face interaction between two or more people in disagreement with each other. See CONFRONTATION. 2. In organizational development, a meeting of disputants called by the change agent to articulate the problem, expose the attitudes to it, and facilitate a solution, usually by establishing priorities, setting targets, and eliciting commitments to action.

confrontational methods 1. Direct, here-and-now treatment techniques considered helpful in certain programs, such as those drug treatment programs usually staffed by ex-addicts in which members "grill" a person suspected of a violation. 2. In therapy, confrontation is used selectively to force a person to admit reality. See BEHIND-THE-BACK TECHNIQUE.

confrontive coping Aggressive efforts to improve a situation, usually including risk-taking. See COPING.

Confucian Analects (Lun Ye) The most reliable source of the teachings of Confucius. Includes such concepts as *jen* (benevolence), *li* (proper conduct), and *Hsaio* (providing for parents and animals). See Confucius in APPENDIX J.

confusion 1. A pervasive disturbance of consciousness characterized by bewilderment, inappropriate decisions, inability to think clearly, inability to function normally, and disorientation for time, place, and person. 2. The mingling of items of any sort, but particularly of ideas or concepts, so that clear discrimination is impossible. 3. The mixing of ideas which have no logical associations, so that the conclusion reached does not follow from the premises. Also known as mental confusion.

confusional automatism See AUTOMATISM.

confusional psychosis An atypical psychosis in which the patient is in a state of confusion together with other symptoms.

confusion of responsibility (J. T. Cacioppo) In social psychology, reluctance to come to a victim's aid for fear that onlookers will assume that the helper caused the problem; an additional explanation of bystander apathy.

congenial transcendency   According to Adrian Van Kaam, the modulation and integration of a person's nuclear life form in a way that fosters increasing disclosure and realization of uniqueness as a person in the light of the foundation of chosen formation tradition. See CONGRUENT TRANSCENDENCY, CONSCIENTIZATION, CONSISTENCY MODEL, CURRENT LIFE FORM.

congenital   Actually or potentially present in the individual at birth, whether as a consequence of heredity, environmental factors, or both. Also known as connate.

congenital adrenal hyperplasia (CAH)   Hypersecretion of adrenal cortex androgens, causing masculinization of external genitals in females. Also known as adrenogenital syndrome. See PSEUDOHERMAPHRODITISM.

congenital alexia   A form of word blindness due to organic brain damage present at birth, as distinguished from acquired alexia which represents the loss of a skill previously established.

congenital anomalies   Any deformity or abnormal function of the body present at birth. Phrase may be applied regardless of the cause: hereditary, injury during labor, viral infection, or of noxious substances such as tobacco, alcohol, or drugs used by the mother during pregnancy. Some inborn defects, for example, Huntington's chorea, do not present symptoms until after the patient has reached adulthood.

congenital aphasia   Any disorder of written or spoken communication ability due to a defect present at birth.

congenital character   A character present at birth, or one which develops later owing to hereditary factors.

congenital cytomegalovirus infection   A viral infection that affects approximately 3% of pregnant mothers. Infants born with signs of this virus may show subsequent deafness, cerebral palsy, mental retardation, motor retardation, hyperactivity, seizures, or other abnormalities involving the nervous system.

congenital deafness   An inability to hear that existed at birth, regardless of the cause. Compare ADVENTITIOUS DEAFNESS.

congenital defects   Any deformity present at birth regardless of the cause, for example, genetic or teratogenic. Sometimes known as congenital anomalies.

congenital hypothyroidism   A condition of motor and mental retardation associated with a deficiency of thyroid hormone. See CRETINISM.

congenital malformation   Any deformity or abnormal function of the body that was present at birth. Phrase may be applied regardless of the cause. Sometimes known as congenital anomalies.

congenital-rubella syndrome   A complex of congenital defects in infants whose mothers were infected by the rubella virus in early pregnancy. May include low brain weight, deaf-mutism, cataracts, heart disease, cerebral palsy, microcephaly, mental retardation, and psychomotor retardation marked by general lack of response to stimuli. Neurologic abnormalities occur in about 80% of such cases. See GERMAN MEASLES.

congenital sensory neuropathy with anhidrosis   A disorder marked by the absence of pain perception and suppression of perspiration. Patients may have severe injuries such as multiple fractures and feel no pain. All such people studied had intelligence quotients (IQs) below 80. Skin biopsies show structurally normal but nonfunctional sweat glands.

congenital speech disorder   A speech defect that was acquired before birth, such as one due to a deformed mouth cavity. Compare ACQUIRED SPEECH DISORDER.

congenital syphilis   Infection with the syphilitic *treponema* organism passed by a pregnant mother to the fetus through the placenta. Neurologic effects in a surviving infant include seizures, organic dementia, and abnormal behavior such as delusions or hallucinations.

congenital toxoplasmosis   An infectious disease caused by a protozoan parasite, *toxoplasma gondii*, which may be transmitted through the placenta to the fetus by a pregnant mother's contact with infected cat feces or undercooked meat. A fetus that survives the intrauterine infection may suffer brain damage such as hydrocephalus or microcephaly, seizures, deafness, and mental retardation.

congeries   Collections of any kind without any organizing principle.

congruence   1. In general, mutual agreement or point-by-point conformity, as with two matching geometrical figures or a well-matched couple. 2. (C. R. Rogers) The need for the therapist to act in accordance with her or his true feelings rather than a stylized image ("genuineness"). 3. A therapist making a conscious effort to empathize with or see life through the eyes of the patient. 4. (C. R. Rogers) The conscious integration of an experience into the self.

congruence coefficients   A statistic used in factor analyses to indicate the similarity of two patterns of factor loadings.

congruence conformity   See CONFORMITY.

congruence-of-images concept   The idea that in any social system, people have images of themselves and others and all interact in manners to confirm these images. See IDIOPANIMA, LOOKING GLASS CONCEPT.

congruence principle/theory   A point of view that it takes less time to find items that are similar than to find items that are different from each other. See CONGRUITY THEORY.

congruent attitude change   A modification of a specific attitude in line with a person's general attitude; such as being biased toward a particular social group but having an otherwise humanistic attitude and then changing the biased attitude to one of acceptance.

congruent communication   A pattern of information transfer in which the sender is conveying the same message on both verbal and nonverbal levels. For example, nodding one's head while saying "yes." For the importance of such communications see DOUBLE BIND.

congruent externals   A tendency to perceive outcomes as not being under the control of the person involved, so that the person operates as though these outcomes did not exist. See DEFENSIVE EXTERNALS.

congruent points   Points on the two retinas that normally are involved in perception of the same stimulus or the same point in space.

congruent transcendency　(A. Van Kaam) According to Adrian Van Kaam, a highly theoretical position about life form (fundamental personality) which assumes that a kind of master plan permits integration of present status with the ultimate life form. See CONGENIAL TRANSCENDENCY, CONSCIENTIZATION, CONSISTENCY MODEL, CURRENT LIFE FORM.

congruent validity　Comparing a test with another test that is considered to be the criterion for the property under evaluation. In psychology, a method of evaluating group intelligence tests is to correlate their results with those of individual tests such as the Binet and the Wechsler.

congruity theory　(R. B. Zajonc) A point of view that when changes in attitudes occur, they tend to be congruous with individuals' prevailing frames of reference. See COGNITIVE DISSONANCE.

congruous　Harmonious, capable of existing together or of being thought of together.

CONJ　See CONJUNCTIVE SCHEDULE OF REINFORCEMENT.

conjoint counseling　A therapeutic technique commonly applied in solving marital disputes with the spouses meeting together with the therapist or a team of therapists as opposed to counseling the individuals separately. May be used also in resolving disputes involving multigenerational family problems. Compare CONCURRENT THERAPY.

conjoint decisions　1. Decisions of a sequential nature in which two or more minor decisions are made to arrive at a final decision. 2. A determination arrived at after consideration agreed upon by two or more individuals.

conjoint family therapy　(V. Satir) A method of therapy in which an entire family is counseled to help just one of its members.

conjoint interview　In marital and sex therapy, an interview with both partners together, to observe their reactions to each other through facial expressions, body movements, and expressions of feeling as well as the content of their statements.

conjoint marital therapy　A type of marriage therapy in which the two partners meet with the therapist in joint sessions. Also known as triadic therapy, triangular therapy. See CONJOINT INTERVIEWING, MARRIAGE THERAPY.

conjoint measurement　An overall measurement based on a number of specific factors, each of them having differential weight, as in the judgment of other people.

conjoint sessions　Counseling or psychotherapy in which two or more people are treated simultaneously by the same therapist or therapists. See CONCURRENT THERAPY, GROUP THERAPY, MULTIPLE THERAPY.

conjugal　Sometimes used as a euphemism for sexual, as in conjugal visits to prison inmates by their spouses.

conjugal delusion/paranoia　The unfounded conviction that a person's spouse is being unfaithful. See OTHELLO DELUSION, PARANOID DISORDERS.

conjugal duties　1. Commonly, the obligation of the wife to submit to coitus; occasionally, the obligation of the husband to perform it. 2. In law, obligations accepted by (or imposed by statute upon) marriage partners, such as financial support. See CONJUGAL RIGHTS.

conjugal paranoia　Irrational jealousy over the supposed or actual unfaithfulness of a sexual partner. See PARANOID DISORDERS.

conjugal rights　Obligations and entitlements of husbands and wives. These differ in various societies and times. Generally, in the developed Western World, both partners are expected to maintain themselves, raise any children they may have, have sexual intercourse with each other, keep old friendships, make new independent friendships, maintain relationships with their families, as well as to behave in an appropriate manner including being sexually faithful to each other. The reciprocal of conjugal duties. See OPEN MARRIAGE.

conjugate eye movements　Coordinated movements of the two eyes functioning together. This ensures that the image of an object falls on the same portions of both retinas.

conjunction　1. In biology, the reproductive union of single-celled organisms during which genetic material is exchanged. 2. In Boolean algebra, the "and" function.

conjunctival reflex　The immediate closing of the eyelids when the cornea of the eye is touched or appears to be touched.

conjunctive concept　The general notion based on the joint presence of a group of parts working together, for example, the human body that consists of such attributes as eyes, limbs (overt features) and heart, lungs, liver, kidneys (covert features) working in a coordinated fashion.

conjunctive motivation　The drive to achieve true and lasting, not temporary or substitute, satisfactions.

conjunctive reinforcement schedule　**conjunctive schedule of reinforcement**

conjunctive schedule of reinforcement (CONJ)　A conditioning schedule that calls for both a prescribed ratio and interval period to be met in order for reinforcement to occur (for example, a rat may be rewarded if it has learned to push a bar only after having waited for one minute after it has pushed the bar twice). Also known as conjunctive reinforcement schedule. See COMPLEX REINFORCEMENT SCHEDULE.

conjunctive tasks　Work being done by a group with each member being of equal status.

conjunctivity　The coordination of motives with actions.

conjuncture of events　A combination of apparently disconnected circumstances which brings about some important result.

conjure　To produce phenomena that appear to violate physical or mental laws, by means of sleight of hand, skillfully arranged or concealed devices, and the misdirection of the observer's attention.

conjuring　magic (meaning 1)

connate　Present at birth, congenital.

connected　Refers to an awareness of personal thoughts, emotions, and bodily reactions in response to relations with others, resulting in feelings of security and meaningful involvement. See CENTERING.

connected discourse A series of utterances related to each other produced in a conversation, as in one person asking, "How are you feeling? You look tired." The other person answers, "Oh, I'm okay but I was up all night with my sick daughter." First person replies, "Well, I hope she gets well soon."

connected region (K. Lewin) Within a boundary of activity, the concept that all aspects are interconnected, each affecting the others. See FIELD THEORY.

connection 1. A link. 2. A logical sequential relationship such as a series of ideas. 3. A relationship in which a person experiences a meaningful bond with someone else. See CONNECTED.

connectionism 1. The interactive relationship of the neural system to both phenomenology and overt behavior. 2. (E. L. Thorndike) Another name for associationism; the connections between stimuli and responses. See PARALLEL DISTRIBUTED PROCESSING.

connectionist model In cognition, a theory that information is stored as connections between "nodes" that represent cognitive or neural structures.

connector neuron A neuron that unites other neurons. See GOLGI TYPE I NEURON, INTERNUNCIAL NEURON.

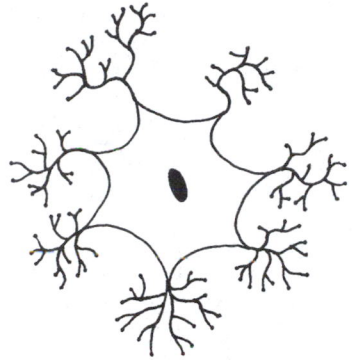

connector neuron A local circuit neuron; the nucleus is the dark spot in the middle and from the cell body branch a number of dendrites.

connotation In communication, implications rather than literal meanings, often understood from a phrase, statement, or gesture. For instance, in the novel *The Virginian*, when the Virginian is called a name, he says: "When you call me that, smile." The implication being that the name would be an insult if no smile accompanied the word. Also known as connotative meaning. See COMMUNICOLOGY.

conquering-hero daydream A typical waking fantasy in which the wish for recognition is fulfilled in the imagination. Individuals who may believe that they are inferior console themselves by imagining doing great things in the face of adversity. See DAYDREAM, FANTASY, SUFFERING-HERO DAYDREAM.

consanguineous matings Marriage or sexual intercourse between persons who are closely related or descended from the same ancestor, forbidden by custom or law. See INCEST.

consanguinity 1. Having the same "blood" due to common ancestors. 2. A biological relationship or degree of relationship between two or more individuals who are descended from a common ancestor. See AFFINITY.

conscience 1. Awareness of the moral or social implications of personal behavior. 2. A person's pattern of moral values and sense of right and wrong in terms of a judgment of value. 3. In psychoanalytic theory, the superego, or ethical component of personality, that acts as judge and critic of personal actions and attitudes. See AUTHORITARIAN CONSCIENCE, HUMANISTIC CONSCIENCE, SUPEREGO.

conscientization The bringing to focused awareness of formation directives that shape behavior, be it on a pre-, infra-, or supra-conscious level. See CONGENIAL TRANSCENDENCY, CONGRUENT TRANSCENDENCY, CONSISTENCY MODEL, CURRENT LIFE FORM, TRANSCENDENCE.

conscious 1. Being aware, or being able to respond to stimulation. 2. (Cs) The portion of the mind immediately aware of the environment at any given time, synonymous with consciousness. See CONSCIOUSNESS, PRECONSCIOUS, SUBCONSCIOUS, UNCONSCIOUS.

consciousness The distinguishing feature of mental life, variously characterized as the: (a) state of awareness as well as the content of the mind, that is, the ever-changing stream of immediate experience, comprising perceptions, feelings, sensations, images, and ideas; (b) central effect of neural reception; (c) capacity of having experiences; (d) subjective aspect of brain activity; (e) relation of self to environment; and (f) totality of an individual's experiences at any given moment. Types of consciousness include: COSMIC, CROWD, DIVIDED, DOUBLE, EXPENDED, GROUP, HEAD, MARGINAL, PERCEPTUAL, SOCIAL, SUBLIMINAL. See ALTERED STATES OF CONSCIOUSNESS, CLOUDING OF CONSCIOUSNESS, FIELD OF CONSCIOUSNESS, SELF-CONSCIOUS, STREAM OF CONSCIOUSNESS.

consciousness disturbances 1. Disorders of awareness symptomatic of mental illness, including clouding, confusion, delirium, fugue states, dream states, and hallucinations. 2. Disturbances produced by hallucinogens or other consciousness-altering drugs.

consciousness expansion Attempts to help individuals modify their thinking, especially to be more open to new ideas, usually done in group exercises. See CONSCIOUSNESS RAISING, EXPANDED CONSCIOUSNESS.

consciousness of action The experiencing of self-activity.

consciousness of effort The experience of striving, derived from kinesthetic and organic sensations.

consciousness of freedom The awareness or conscious experience that personal decisions are or may be made by the self, regardless of external influences and mental predisposition.

consciousness of kind The awareness of characteristics in other individuals that are similar to one's characteristics, especially in respect to factors such as ethnic background, nationality, caste, class, and religion.

consciousness-raising 1. A group-discussion process directed toward greater awareness of: (a) personal condition, needs, values, and goals as a means of achieving full self-potential as a person; or (b) behavior and relations with others, such as discrimination against a particular group of people. See GROUP THERAPY, RAP GROUP. 2. A term popularized in the late 1960s and early 1970s by the women's movement to draw attention to its objectives and concerns, which has since also become a euphemism for changing attitudes, including, in some totalitarian regimes, group indoctrination and "brainwashing." See CONSCIOUSNESS EXPANSION.

consciousness span The amount of information that a person can obtain at a glance. Also known as span of consciousness. See SHORT-TERM MEMORY.

conscious processes The combination of active and passive mental activities. An active mode of consciousness may include planning and carrying out an activity. A passive mode of consciousness is represented by watching a sports event on television or reading a newspaper or a novel.

conscious resistance 1. A deliberate refusal to cooperate. 2. A Freudian phrase for the deliberate withholding of information by a patient because of shame, fear of rejection, or distrust of the analyst.

conscious state Being mentally aware and mentally active, as opposed to being asleep, unconscious, under hypnosis, or under the influence of certain substances (drugs).

conscious vs unconscious mentalism (R. I. Watson) A prescriptive dimension of the philosophical underpinnings of psychology, namely, awareness of mental operations or activity versus unawareness of them. See OPPONENT-PAIRS DIMENSION.

consensual eye reflex A phenomenon in which the pupil of a shaded eye contracts when the other eye is stimulated by a bright light.

consensual validation 1. The establishment of a definition, fact, or truth by prevailing agreement. 2. (H. S. Sullivan) The determination that a given phenomenon is real, not illusory, by general agreement. An example of reliability, not validity. See PARATAXIC DISTORTION.

consensual validity Determining the validity of a notion, test, or perception through agreement of experts. See DEFINITIONAL VALIDITY.

consensus An agreement by the majority or the whole group, usually following a discussion.

consensus information The degree to which people are affected by a particular stimulus.

consensus trance A view of the waking state as dreamlike, for example, "I dreamt I was a chicken. Am I a chicken dreaming that I am a human or am I a human dreaming that I am a chicken?" The view that the immediate present is not ordinarily the most important state of consciousness.

consent 1. Generally, permission or agreement. 2. In law, the voluntary, noncoerced acceptance by a competent adult. See INFORMED CONSENT.

consentience (M. Jahoda) Sensuous impressions apart from all intellectual processes.

consequence 1. The resultant in a sequence, considered as directly related to certain earlier occurrence in a series. 2. An event following a behavior that strengthens or weakens the tendency to repeat the behavior. Consequences are either reinforcers or punishers. See LOGICAL CONSEQUENCES, NATURAL CONSEQUENCES.

conservation conservation (theory)

conservation of energy/of force first law of thermodynamics

conservation of number An ability to recognize that rearrangement of items does not change the quantity of items involved in the processing.

conservation (theory) (J. Piaget) The awareness that physical quantities do not change in amount when altered in appearance, for example, the water in a short, wide glass beaker is poured into a tall, thin glass beaker, whereupon a child is asked whether the amount of water has changed. See CONSTANCY, MEMORY RETENTION, PERCEPTUAL CONSTANCY, REVERSIBILITY.

conservation-withdrawal A tendency to withdraw from family and friends and to want to be left alone after undergoing surgery, as a means of recouping psychological and physical strength.

conservative focusing 1. (J. Bruner) One of the four strategies used in formulating concepts, involving the testing of hypotheses by eliminating incorrect guesses one at a time. 2. A strategy useful in solving complex problems by changing a single element of a set and then noting resulting changes. See CONCEPT-FORMATION STRATEGIES.

conservator An individual appointed by a court to protect the interests and property of mentally competent persons who are too infirm by reason of a physical condition to manage their affairs. See CONSERVATORSHIP.

conservatorship A legal arrangement in which one person (the conservator) assumes control over another person's (the conservatee's) rights and responsibilities on the grounds of that person's incompetence to make good decisions. This control is usually limited to fiscal aspects and not to matters of life and death, and ordinarily occurs with older persons who are both mentally and physically debilitated. Also frequently arranged by the court for children who have independent wealth and parents not available or appropriate to manage the children's fiscal needs.

conserve (J. L. Moreno) The accumulated habits, wisdom, knowledge, skills that a person has; the sum of retained past experiences. See CRYSTALLIZED ABILITIES.

conserved intelligence (J. L. Moreno) Knowledge based on past learning, as evidence of general intelligence based on the assumption that the more intelligent a person, the more that person will have learned from the environment. See CRYSTALLIZED INTELLIGENCE.

consideration 1. Careful thought about a decision. 2. An attitude of concern for others, thought by some therapists to be an essential element for successful counseling or psychotherapy. 3. In social psychology, an important component of a group leader's role, the ability to foster and sustain productive group spirit and cooperation through even-handed and sympathetic interaction with group members. 4. (A. W. Halpin & B. J. Winer) The nature and extent of the leader's response to subordinates' need for warmth, trust, and respect.

consilience (E. O. Wilson) An attempt to generate one unified science, combining the natural sciences and the social sciences.

consistency index A measure of reliability of responses by any group, to the same stimulus under identical conditions within a specified time. Formula: $i = [(1 \div N)\Sigma\{(\cos \pi) - (BC)^{1/2}/(AD)^{1/2}(BC)^{1/2}\}]^{1/2}$, Where i is the index of consistency, N is the number of subjects, A is the number of responses both times; B and C responses present one time and not the other; D responses denied or omitted both times.

consistency model Theoretical conception that emphasizes the formative influence of individuals' response to the external world. Life is to be understood as an extended attempt to maintain consistency. See CONGENIAL TRANSCENDENCY, CONSCIENTIZATION, CONGRUENT TRANSCENDENCY, CURRENT LIFE FORM, FORMATION, FORMATIVE DIRECTIVE.

consistency paradox In social perception, the gap between (a) the belief that people have stable personality traits and ways of perceiving and responding, and (b) the observation that an individual's responses are not necessarily consistent across situations.

consistency principle A theory that people strive to be constant in their overt and covert behavior. A stable and secure person has attitudes that do not conflict with each other and these attitudes are consonant with that person's behavior. See COGNITIVE DISSONANCE.

consistency theory (A. Korman) Work behavior based on a two-point premise: a balance concept and a self-image standard. The view that workers will engage in and find satisfying behaviors that maximize their sense of cognitive balance and will be motivated to perform in a manner consistent with their self-image.

consistent mapping condition (W. Schneider & R. M. Shiffrin) In human information processing studies, a research condition in which the same stimulus is always mapped onto the same response. Compare VARIED MAPPING CONDITION.

consistent missing A tendency to make a consistent inappropriate response to an ESP (extrasensory perception) target, such as calling "square" when the target is a "cross."

consolidation The process of storing short-term memories into long-term memory.

consolation dream A dream that contains an expression of encouragement or reassurance to the dreamer.

consolidation hypothesis The theoretical process by which each experience sets up a circuit in the brain that must be allowed to solidify or strengthen in order for the experience to be stored permanently in long-term memory. Thought to occur during rest periods. See ENGRAM.

consolidation period The period of time that it takes for experiences, events, or other stimuli to be stored in long-term memory.

consonance 1. An effect produced by two or more tones heard simultaneously that blend or fuse, characterized by smoothness and (usually) pleasantness. 2. In communication, harmony between content (denotative meaning) and intent (connotative meaning), as when a speech on peace is spoken in soft tones, content and intent agree and the communication possesses consonance. 3. In cognitive dissonance theory, the resolution of dissonant cognitions.

consonantal weakening See WEAKENING.

consonant trigram A combination of three consonants, such as KBM, used in various kinds of research, especially for memory. See NONSENSE SYLLABLES.

conspecific A member of the same species.

conspicuity The attention-attracting ability of a display or an object. Examples: daytime running lights on cars, fluorescent garb for skiers and cyclists, "zebra shirts" for coal miners, and fluorescent orange for a "black box."

Constable Reaction Apparatus See MASHBURN COMPLEX COORDINATOR.

constancy A tendency of perceptions to remain unchanged despite variations in the external conditions of observation. Types of constancy include: BRIGHTNESS, COLOR, OBJECT, PERCEPTUAL, SHAPE, SIZE, THING, WHITENESS. See CONSERVATION.

constancy hypothesis 1. The assumption of a formal, one-to-one correspondence between a local stimulus and a percept. Étienne Bonnot de Condillac formulated this idea in his 1754 book *Treatise on the Sensations* and it was implicit in the psychology of the nineteenth century. Gestalt psychologists viewed this position as untenable. 2. A postulate that a reaction to a stimulus will maintain itself regardless of the situation.

constancy of internal environment A tendency of the internal state of an organism to remain in equilibrium. See HOMEOSTASIS.

constancy of the IQ A tendency for IQ (intelligence quotient) results for an individual to remain approximately the same when the same or similar tests are administered over time.

constancy principle A point of view that what is alive will some day be dead; or organic matter will return to inorganic matter.

constancy scaling An automatic process whereby, in looking at the same object by some people close to it and some far-away, the object is much larger on the retina for those near it than for those who are far-away, and yet all perceive it as being the same size. See PONZO ILLUSION.

constant 1. In an experiment, an absence of changes of the environment. 2. In mathematics, an expression whose value is fixed, the opposite of a variable. 3. In personality, an attitude that remains unchanged despite environmental changes. (In definition 1, "constant" is an adjective, in definitions 2 and 3, "constant" is a noun.)

constant error (CE) 1. A deviation of results from the true value, or from an established standard, due to some unwanted factor which affects all observations. 2. A persistent mistake. See RANDOM ERROR, SYSTEMATIC ERROR.

constant object of love (M. Mahler) A belief that someone exists, usually the mother, who has and will always love the person forever. See AGAPE, UNCONDITIONAL POSITIVE REGARD, Urpsychology.

constellation A group of separate ideas with a common theme or association.

constellatory construct (G. A. Kelly) A concept that binds together a group of other concepts, such as the concept of a just-world. See PREEMPTIVE CONSTRUCT, PROPOSITIONAL CONSTRUCT.

constellatory power (C. G. Jung) The power of a complex to accept new ideas into itself.

constipation See PSYCHOGENIC CONSTIPATION.

constitution An organism's innate, genetically determined characteristics, or endowments.

constitutional depressive disposition (E. Bleuler) An ingrained "melancholic mood" characterized by appearing consistently depressed and pessimistic, lacking self-confidence, and difficulty in making decisions.

constitutional disorders A disturbance of function, structure, or both, inherent in the make-up of the individual, inherited or at least ingrained, and not situationally or accidentally determined.

constitutional factors Basic physiological tendencies purported to contribute to personality, temperament, and the etiology of specific mental and physical disorders. These factors include body build, hereditary predispositions, and physiological characteristics (for example, circulatory, musculoskeletal, glandular). See CONSTITUTIONAL TYPOLOGY.

constitutional insanity Describing mental disorders caused by genetic factors. The original 19th-century meaning suggested congenital, hereditary, or constitutional defects and deviant trends.

constitutional manic disposition (E. Bleuler) A personality type characterized by impulsive and thoughtless manners representative of the manic temperament. According to Bleuler, the "manic mood" may also be expressed by a sunny disposition and tireless energy as well as in snobbish, inconsiderate, or quarrelsome manners.

constitutional medicine A branch of medicine that deals with hereditary factors involved in resistance or susceptibility to disease and the possible associations between susceptibility factors and body builds. See CONSTITUTIONAL TYPOLOGY.

constitutional psychology An ancient idea developed before Aristotle that there is a relationship between body type and personality traits. Of those who accepted this idea in modern times were Ernst Kretschmer and William Sheldon. See BODY BUILD, BODY TYPE, BODY TYPE THEORIES, CONSTITUTIONAL DISORDERS, CONSTITUTIONAL FACTORS, CONSTITUTIONAL TYPE.

constitutional psychopath Archaic phrase for antisocial personality disorders, based on the idea that the condition is congenital. See CONDUCT DISORDERS.

constitutional psychopathic inferiority Obsolete phrase for conduct disorders. See ANTISOCIAL PERSONALITY DISORDER.

constitutional type (theories) A classification of individuals based on their body structure. These structures are stated to have a relationship with temperament, personality, and tendencies to develop specific mental disorders. Some examples of such typologies: Giacinto Viola: microsplanchnic, macrosplanchnic, normosplanchnic; Ernst Kretschmer: asthenic, athletic, dysplastic, pyknic; William Sheldon: ectomorph, endomorph, mesomorph. Also known as constitutional typology. See CARUS' TYPOLOGY, HIPPOCRATES, HUMORS, KRETSCHMER'S TYPOLOGY, SHELDON'S CONSTITUTIONAL THEORY OF PERSONALITY.

constrain To compel another individual to adopt a certain course of action.

constrained association See CONTROLLED ASSOCIATION.

constraint of movement See CONSTRAINT OF THOUGHT.

constraint of thought A belief, particularly among patients with schizophrenia, that their thoughts are controlled or influenced by other persons. A related effect is constraint of movement, in which patients believe their movements are controlled by others.

constraint questions Questions that narrow the field of inquiry, especially in counseling and psychotherapy. Examples of some questions (and answers) in probable order: "What kind of people have you had difficulty with?" (All kinds.) "More so with those in the family or those outside the family?" (Outside my family.) "Young or old?" (My age.).

constriction of thinking 1. A process that occurs to otherwise normal people in emergency situations such as when they are in pain, being attacked, terrorized, or when people they love are in danger, in that their attention is frozen and limited and frequently they are unable to act. 2. A narrowing focus of the mind symptomatic of acute suicidal tendencies. 3. A situation in which a person involved in a project of great interest or importance simply does not pay attention to matters considered of less interest or importance.

construal Interpretation of facts.

construct 1. A hypothetical entity that describes differences between individuals (for example, spatial ability) or differences in individuals' behaviors from time to time (for example, anxious actions). See HYPOTHETICAL CONSTRUCT, INTERVENING VARIABLE. 2. (G. A. Kelly) A tendency of individuals to develop certain unique interpretations of events. Many constructs are attempts to explain behaviors such as acts of willpower, appetence, patriotism, and love. See FUNDAMENTAL POSTULATE. 3. Any psychological entity that does not exist in physical reality but is created by the mind. For instance, intelligence cannot be directly observed; it is a construct whose nature and extent is inferred from test performance or other behavior that is consistent with a theory of intelligence.

constructed penis In sex change surgery, an artificial penis.

constructional apraxia 1. Difficulty in drawing pictures or manipulating simple building materials, caused by damage to the right parietal lobe. 2. Inability because of brain damage to assemble parts of an object so that it becomes a complete structure or device. Tests of this condition include drawing from a model, reconstructions of puzzles, and building with wooden sticks or blocks toward the formation of a particular structure. Also known as constructive apraxia. See APRAXIA.

constructional praxis Ability to draw, copy, or manipulate spatial patterns or designs.

constructionism (J. Piaget) A theory that children construct their understanding of reality out of their actions on objects in the environment, which produce both a knowledge of the effects of their behavior and the properties of the objects.

construction need (H. A. Murray) The urge or drive to create and build.

constructive alternativism   (G. A. Kelly) A point of view that any event is open to a variety of interpretations.

constructive approach   See PSYCHOSYNTHESIS.

constructive conflict resolution   (M. Deutsch) A sustainable resolution of a conflict which is beneficial to the parties involved in the conflict.

constructive conflict resolution process   (M. Deutsch) A cooperative problem-solving process which takes the conflict as the mutual problem to be solved.

constructive confrontation   A procedure employed by supervisors to help employees deal with poor work or personal habits. The process usually calls for documenting problems and specifying their consequences to the employees.

constructive memory   The use of general knowledge stored in memory to construct a more complete and detailed account of an event or experience. Includes elements not present in the original event. These elements reflect the culture and context of the individual.

constructive play   Recreational and creative activity during which time materials used are arranged or modified in some purposeful manner.

constructive process   The modification of material memorized that is done at the time of the memorization. See RECONSTRUCTIVE PROCESS.

constructive reverie   (H. S. Sullivan) A mental exploration of intended future steps of some project, that may later be followed by appropriate behavior.

constructive thinking   That form of the thinking process that results in the production of new judgments or conclusions, and which underlies invention, scientific discoveries, etc.

constructivism   Emphasizing the subjective ways in which each individual creates a perception of reality. See CONSTRUCTIONISM.

constructivist (theory of) perception   A point of view that perception is not solely based on what is seen, heard, felt, tasted, or smelled, but in a sense is compared with elements in a memory bank rather than being solely pure reactions to stimuli. See DIRECT PERCEPTION.

construct system   1. An orderly conceptual plan that integrates multiple variables and relationships for the purpose of making predictions, explaining behavior, or guiding interventions. The concept of "habit" is an example of a construct. Experimental facts without the glue of a construct can remain as only isolated and relatively meaningless facts. Constructs enable investigators to articulate what they are attempting to describe and make possible a certain degree of prediction. 2. (G. A. Kelly) The sum total of an individual's system of conclusions about self and others, practically equivalent to the concept of personality. See CONSTRUCT, FUNDAMENTAL POSTULATE.

construct validation   The subjective process of establishing the construct validity of a test.

construct validity   The extent to which any test measures the underlying hypothetical qualities or factors of whatever it is intended to measure. Construct validity may vary (as measured, for example, by factor loadings of tests on a factor that represents a construct).

consultancy   See POLICY RESEARCH.

consultant   1. A person regarded as especially knowledgeable in some area of specialization, who may be asked to give an opinion or suggestion about an issue. 2. By extension, an elevated term for various occupations, such as educational toy consultant for toy seller, mortuary consultant for funeral director, transportation investment consultant for car salesperson, and faculty consultant for the teacher who grades exams for the Educational Testing Service.

consultation   A situation in which a person who has special experience and knowledge meets with another person or other persons to offer advice or give an opinion, for example, a psychologist advising a school teacher on how to deal with behavioral problems in the classroom.

consulting psychologist   1. A psychologist who gives professional advice or services for a fee. 2. A psychologist who provides professional services for therapy on emotional, vocational, marital, or educational problems either on a private basis or an organizational basis, as in a business organization or health agency.

consulting psychology   Provision of psychological services to business and industry, governmental agencies, armed forces, or educational and scientific groups. Among the kind of services provided is selecting key personnel, discovering causes of disharmony of personnel, evaluating current personnel, counseling executives and other problems relating to human behavior.

consumer   Term that tends to be used by HMOs instead of client; a term generally resented by most psychologists.

consumer characteristics   The personality traits of consumers that can be used in planning advertising campaigns. Most sophisticated studies of consumer characteristics go beyond area, sex, income, and neighborhood of residence, using established psychological theories and techniques in analyzing motives behind buying decisions, which may be psychosexual or emotional rather than practical or sensible. The theory is that often it is the "sizzle" and not the "steak" that leads to purchasing decisions.

consumer counseling   A type of counseling that focuses on effective money management and good decision-making in the purchase of products and services.

consumer education   Educational programs directed primarily to (a) teach consumers to evaluate complex technical products and services, (b) sharpen decision-making skills, (c) increase their knowledge of the workings of business, government, and the marketplace, (d) generate techniques for judging advertising and selling claims, and (e) provide insight into money-saving buying strategies.

consumer innovator   A person who is first in buying and trying new products.

consumerism   1. A movement to protect the rights of consumers with regard to the quality and safety of products and services in the marketplace, including medical care. Has resulted in the legally enforced rights of mental patients, as well as other patients, to have access to treatment or to refuse treatment. 2. Extensive indulgence in buying and consuming commercial goods. See PATIENT'S RIGHTS.

consumer-jury technique   Usually the advance testing of a marketing campaign. Generally, typical buyers of the product category are shown various advertisements and probed for their reactions. See CONTINUOUS PANEL.

consumer psychology   The study of variables such as motivations, advertising responses, and demographic characteristics of potential buyers.

consumer research   The application of clinical, scientific, and statistical research techniques in the study of consumer behavior. May include studies of tastes and preferences, package designs, and personality traits of a target audience. Also known as market research. See MOTIVATION RESEARCH.

consumer surveys   In consumer psychology, surveys of consumer likes and dislikes in certain product categories that may yield information used to design and package products in ways that consumers will find attractive. May be conducted by questionnaires, in-depth interviews, group interviews, and similar techniques.

consumer unit   In governmental statistics, a household.

consummate love   (R. Sternberg) The most complete form of love, according to Robert Sternberg, having the components of intimacy, passion, decision, and/or commitment.

consummatory act/response   The final stage of a complex response to a stimulus or learning experience, for example, the fertilization of the eggs of a female fish by the male, after the innate sequence of nest establishment and courtship, to entice the female to the nest.

consummatory communication   A message that conveys the sender's ideas or feelings adequately and does not require feedback.

consummatory events   1. The ultimate purpose of common motivational sequences, behavioral sequences, or both. 2. The final reason for the chain of prior events. The initial cause, for example, a feeling of thirst, generates a variety of logically concatenated incidents that lead to the final desired event of getting a drink. See TELEOLOGY.

contact   1. A relationship with another person. 2. The basic unit of relationship between "me" and "not me." 3. (E. Berne) The validational feedback protection and strokes that come from a mutual support group.

contact-analogy displays   A gauge or pictorial representation inside a moving vehicle that gives the operator, such as an airplane pilot or submarine captain, an understanding of where the vehicle is in relation to surroundings so that the operator need not depend on external visual cues.

contact behavior   Actions and interactions occurring during an intimate, personal relationship (for example, sexual contact) or a relatively impersonal relationship (for example, buying or selling).

contact comfort   (H. Harlow) The satisfaction obtained from clinging to a soft, warm object. Harry Harlow's phrase to explain why infant monkeys when frightened would cling to a soft surrogate mother rather than to a hard one that had been feeding them. See MARASMUS, MOTHERING.

contact desensitization   In psychotherapy, a physical contact between therapist and patient intended to have the effect of desensitizing a patient, such as one in awe or fear of the therapist. A handshake may achieve the desired result, although some therapists will use hugs for this purpose. Discretion is called for on the part of the therapist as to what actions to take.

contact hypothesis   1. A postulate that increased contact between members of different social or ethnic groups will reduce prejudice between them. 2. In group dynamics, the prediction that equal-status contact between members of different groups will reduce intergroup conflict.

contact sensation   A feeling stimulated by an impact of low intensity with little or no dermal deformity, such as might be experienced by touching a piece of ice or a piece of fur.

contact sense   A sense whose receptors detect an external stimulus only through touching it, as in senses of taste and touch. Smell is technically a contact sense, but resembles the distance senses of vision and hearing.

contact species   Organisms that spend a lot of time touching each other, for example bees. Compare DISTANT SPECIES.

contagion   The transmission of ideas, feelings, or mental disorders from person to person or group to group by suggestion, propaganda, rumor, imitation, or sympathy. See BITING MANIA, CHOREOMANIA, FOLIE A DEUX, LYCANTHROPY, MASS HYSTERIA, SHARED PARANOID DISORDER.

containment-aggression relationship   In labor relations, an arrangement in which the union and management tolerate each other, but just barely. Typically legalistic and militant, with frequent recourse to strikes and arbitration.

contaminated response   In Rorschach testing, a report by the participant of some aspect of an inkblot that is in the examiner's opinion incongrous, such as a fox wearing a dress. If the examiner can also see that incongruent element, then the response is considered within the bounds of normality. However, if the examiner cannot by any stretch of the imagination see that combination, the response is considered a sign of abnormality. The examiner becomes the criterion for whether a contaminated response is or is not normal.

contamination   1. In research, some kind of error, conscious or unconscious, in the selection of participants or subjects, the procedures, the handling of data, intrusion of unwanted elements, interpretation, receiving of unwarranted information, etc., that results in partial or complete invalidation of results. See CONFOUNDING. 2. The creation of neologisms by amalgamating a part of one word with a part of another, usually resulting in an unintelligible word or the joining of two incompatible concepts. 3. In employee selection or evaluation, ratings that are based on irrelevant factors.

contamination fear   See COPROPHOBIA, MOLYSMOPHOBIA, MYSOPHOBIA, SCATOPHOBIA.

contamination obsession   Morbid and unusual interest about or concern with disease, dirt, germs, mud, excrement, sputum, and the like, based on a feeling that the world is disgusting, decaying, and dying. An extreme contamination obsession of this kind is regarded as a symptom of schizophrenia. See MYSOPHOBIA, PICA.

contemplation   See MEDITATION.

contemporal thought   (M. K. Johnson & C. L. Raye) In memory, processes that enhance, join, or clarify one's perceptual experience but that possibly are not part of the true representation of the perceptual experience.

contemporaneous-explanation principle   (K. Lewin) A theory that only present or current events can influence behavior and should be studied. Also known as billiard ball theory.

contempt for others   The basis of all mental illnesses and evil behavior according to Eli Siegel: The attitude of disdain and general lack of concern for others. See GEMEINSCHAFTSGEFÜHL.

content   The constituents of any composite totality, whether of experience, or of material phenomena.

content addressability   Ability of a person's memory system to access or reinstate particular memories given specific probes. In other words, it is not necessary to sort through an entire set of material to discover whether or not a particular fact is known, it can be recalled directly. See ENGRAMS.

content analysis   A systematic, quantitative procedure of analyzing conceptual material (articles, speeches, films) by determining the frequency of specific ideas, concepts, or terms. There are two types of such analysis: (a) manifest content calls for counting certain words such as "me" or "you"; (b) latent content is what the person is really saying "between the lines" and is much more difficult to establish reliably. Called quantitative semantics by H. D. Lasswell.

contentiousness   Quarrelsomeness observed in manic syndromes and the early stages of paranoid reactions when patients feel they are being treated unfairly.

contentment   An attitude characterized by a mild degree of pleasantness, induced by the total life situation which confronts the individual.

content morpheme   A minimum distinctive unit of grammar (morpheme) that carries the main burden of the meaning of words. Contrasted with function morphemes that add details to a meaning and also serve various grammatical purposes.

content of consciousness   The totality of an individual's experiences at a given time, that is, the constituents of experience.

content psychology   A branch of psychology concerned with the role of conscious experience. See PHENOMENOLOGY, STRUCTURALISM.

content response   In Rorschach test scoring, *what* is seen rather than *how* it is seen; for example, the usual response to Card One is "bat," the content response. If the participant mentions the color of the bat, or that the bat appears to be flying, these responses are considered independent elements for the examiners' evaluations.

content scores   In Rorschach testing, listing the type of reply by a letter, such as "A" for an animal reply, "An" for an anatomical reply, or "V" for a vista response. A preponderance of various contents may have diagnostic meanings; for example, too many reports of animals by an adult may be considered a sign of immaturity, depending on the adult's background.

content-thought disorder   A thought disturbance typically found in schizophrenia, characterized by multiple, fragmented, bizarre delusions.

contentual objectivism vs contentual subjectivism (R. I. Watson) A prescriptive dimension of the philosophical underpinnings of psychology, namely, psychological activity viewed as observable, such as behavior versus nonobservable mental activity. See OPPONENT-PAIRS DIMENSION.

content validity   1. Degree to which the elements of an assessment instrument are relevant to and representative of the targeted construct, for a particular assessment purpose. 2. Extent to which a test measures a representative sample of the subject matter or behavior in question. If a test is designed to survey arithmetic skills on a third-grade level, to the degree that it covers the range of arithmetic operations at that level determines its content validity. Also known as content validation.

content variables   (N. S. Endler & D. Magnusson) Within the context of the interactional model of personality, a type of mediating variable that resides within the situation, such as situationally determined or stored information (for example, the content of an aggression-arousing situation).

content word   1. A word (noun, verb, adjective, or adverb) that conveys meaning. 2. A word that has a full lexical or semantic meaning, such as a noun, verb, or adjective (in contrast to a function word such as a preposition or conjunction). Also known as autonomous word, contentive, full word, lexical word, notional word, open-class word, semanteme, vocabulary word. Compare FUNCTION WORD.

context   1. The totality of conditions which affect an individual at a given time, and form the setting of some particular fact or partial experience. 2. Information surrounding stimuli or phenomena being recognized, categorized, or searched for.

context Alpha (effect)   (D. D. Wickens) An effect of context on information processing in which the environment or situation surrounding an event does not influence it. Compare CONTEXT BETA (EFFECT). See CONTEXT-DEPENDENT MEMORY EFFECT.

context Beta (effect)   (D. D. Wickens) An effect of context on information processing in which the environment or situation surrounding an event combines with another situation or event to determine the correct response to it. Also known as interactive context, integrated context. Compare CONTEXT ALPHA. See CONTEXT-DEPENDENT MEMORY EFFECT.

context-bound   1. Behavior dependent on the circumstances, such as how a person eats in various social situations, or how a person acts on meeting a long-time friend not seen for years versus how the person acts on meeting a business associate. 2. (B. Bernstein) In verbal communications, people in certain groups communicate differently with each other in comparison with internal communications of other groups; for example, some people in lower socio-economic levels or particular geographic areas may use a different vocabulary, and may tend to vary the sounds of words more than people in other socio-economic levels or geographic locales. See RESTRICTED CODES OF LANGUAGE.

context clues   Information permitting the understanding of new words in the context of the sentence or paragraph in which they appear.

context-dependent memory effect   The finding that memory can be worse when tested in a new or different context relative to performance in conditions where the context remains the same.

context effect   A tendency or ability of the surroundings to affect learning, and the idea that the more similar the recall context is to the learning context, the better recall will be.

context-shifting   A tendency of patients with schizophrenia to change the subject or topic abruptly and irrelevantly to avoid an anxiety-laden idea, for example, asking "Do you feel that other people do not like you?" and the reply is "The fly is on the window."

context theory of meaning   (E. B. Titchener) A point of view that meaning depends upon the mental images associated with a specific body of sensations, as in the concept of fire.

contextual element   (R. J. Sternberg) The practical aspect of intelligence, which determines how people deal with their environment, for example, adaptation, selection and shaping (changing the environment).

contextual interference effect   The improvement in retention but decrement in acquisition of new information as a function of heightened similarity in items to be learned. Increasing the processing demands between trials has a similar effect.

contextualism   A doctrine positing that the memory of experiences is not the result merely of linkages between events, as in the associationist doctrine, but is due to meanings of the psychological space in which they occur.

contiguity   1. The interconnectedness of two or more objects, experiences, etc., in time, or space, usually without the interposition of anything else between them. 2. Two or more items such as ideas coming together or events occurring simultaneously or close together. See LAW OF CONTIGUITY.

contiguity learning   (E. R. Guthrie) The acquiring of an association between two stimuli presented close together in time.

contiguity mediational model   (A. Bandura) The theory that observational learning depends on verbal and imaginal coding of modeled actions and their effects.

contiguity of associations   The concept that an internal connection, or association, is usually established between two objects, experiences, or behaviors that are close together in space or time. See LAW OF CONTIGUITY.

contiguity theory   See LAW OF CONTIGUITY.

contiguity theory of learning   (E. R. Guthrie) A point of view that acquisition of knowledge, mastery of tasks, etc., depends only on the proximity in time or space of stimulus and response.

contiguous-motor technique   (A. Luria) A method for evaluating emotional reactions to various stimuli (for example, words or pictures). Participants are instructed to press a telegraph key or to turn a knob when stimuli are shown on a screen. The stimuli shown are expected to evoke different emotional reactions from the individual participants. These emotional reactions are supposedly demonstrated by, for example, pressing the telegraph key harder, and by holding it down longer. See ASSOCIATION TEST, JUNG ASSOCIATION TEST, KEELER POLYGRAPH.

continence   1. Ability to control bodily functions such as defecation and urination. 2. Sexual abstinence or restraint.

contingency   1. In statistics, describing the degree of association between two variables or two sets of attributes in which a researcher has only categorical information about one or both sets of these attributes, and in which the actual frequencies of association are compared with the frequencies expected if there is no association between the variables. 2. A dependency relationship between events, as between response and reward. See CONTINGENCY CONTRACT.

contingency analysis   Statistical examination of the relationship between two variables that is aimed at determining the degree to which they are associated with or depend on one another.

contingency awareness   The knowledge of a relationship or connection between two occurrences; awareness of the dependence of one variable upon another.

contingency coefficient (C)   A measure of the association of categorical variables based on chi-square. The coefficient C is the square root of the quantity chi-square divided by (N + chi-square).

contingency contract   An agreement on the part of either the therapist, the client, or both, to abide by certain rules during the course of therapy. Clients may agree to arrive on time for appointments, disclose all secrets to the therapist, refrain from telephoning the therapist at home, and to pay for therapy promptly. Therapists may agree to be available on time for appointments, explain or clarify that which the client does not understand, and refuse to receive telephone calls from the client while at home. Some therapists do not establish rules, some pre-establish rules, others establish rules as needed. Sometimes known as contract. See CONTRACT (IN THERAPY), CONTRACT MANAGEMENT, CONTRACTUAL PSYCHOTHERAPY.

contingency contrast   See BEHAVIOR CONTRAST.

contingency management   The regulation of management of reinforcement with reference to such questions as: Who does the reinforcing? How much reinforcement for how much work? When is reinforcement to be delivered? Of what does it consist?

contingency model   (R. Blake) In industrial psychology, a leadership concept based on the generalization that management or supervisory personnel tend to be either task-oriented or person-oriented and that the ideal model would be for them to be maximally capable of both orientations. See CONTINGENCY MODEL OF LEADER EFFECTIVENESS.

contingency model of leader effectiveness (F. Fiedler) A point of view that a leader's efficacy is dependent not only on the leader's own qualities, but also by (a) personal relationships with group members, (b) the extent of the leader's actual authority or power, and (c) the nature of the task for the group. Also known as contingency theory of leadership.

contingency reinforcement A behavior-therapy technique in which a reinforcement, or reward, is given each time the desired behavior is performed, that is, the reward is contingent, or dependent, on the behavior.

contingency table A table of data showing relationships among variables.

contingent Dependent upon special associated circumstances, such as the presence of some other phenomenon or event.

contingent aftereffect A visual anomaly. If a person looks at two objects of different colors until adaptation occurs and then looks at two neutral (grey) objects, the person will tend to see the complementary color of the original colors if the original objects differed in form and if the grey objects were of the same form as the colored ones.

contingent employee/worker Euphemism for a temporary, disposable, low-paid employee. Also known as assignment worker, contract worker, flexible worker.

contingent negative variation (CNV) If an organism, connected to an electroencephalograph (EEG), is waiting for a particular stimulus to respond to, and if an earlier warning stimulus is given, the EEG will show a long negative deflection, a sign that the organism is waiting for the other stimulus.

contingent pacing The adjustment of personal behavior with respect to, or in accordance with, another person's behavior.

contingent probability An event likely to occur dependent on preceding events; for example, in a crossword puzzle, a four-letter word beginning "TH-" probably has a vowel following the "H." In complex behavioral situations, how a person may react to various situations can be predicted fairly well if the person and relevant prior behavior are known.

contingent reinforcement (in leadership) A transactional type of leadership in which the leader promises and provides rewards for follower compliance or corrects or disciplines the followers for failure to carry out assignments as agreed upon. See CONTINGENT REWARD, TRANSFORMATIONAL LEADERSHIP.

contingent relationship A milieu in which two or more persons work in such a manner that what one does influences the other. May be contrasted to a superior–subordinate relationship. See CIRCULAR CAUSALITY.

contingent reward (B. Bass) In leadership, a constructive transaction in which the leader promises and provides rewards for agreed-upon followers' enactments of their roles. See CONTINGENT REINFORCEMENT, TRANSACTIONAL LEADERSHIP.

continual distractor task In memory research, a task in which participants are continuously distracted from rehearsing the items that are to be remembered. Also known as continuous distractor task.

continuation The Gestalt concept that there is a tendency to perceive randomly placed similar objects as having a shape or pattern. See GROUPING.

continuing-care unit A hospital unit to which a patient with a catastrophic or chronic illness is transferred for additional care after the acute hospitalization period.

continuing valuing process An ongoing evaluation made by individuals about their specific situations and skills as well as in making decisions in terms of experience and the probability of certain anticipated behaviors.

continuity A perceptual tendency to group stimuli into smooth, consistent patterns. See GESTALTQUALITÄT.

continuity hypothesis 1. The associationist position that discrimination learning or problem-solving results from a progressive, incremental, continuous process of trial and error. Responses that prove unproductive are extinguished; those that yield results are strengthened. Problem-solving is conceived as a step-by-step learning process in which the correct response is discovered, practiced, and reinforced. Compare DISCONTINUITY HYPOTHESIS. 2. In concept formation, a postulate that people gradually learn concepts by forming stimulus-response associations between what they encounter and the categories in which these items are placed. Compare NONCONTINUITY HYPOTHESIS.

continuity law See AUTOCHTHONOUS LAWS.

continuity of germ-plasm theory A point of view that all germ cells are derived from other germ cells, and not from other tissues.

continuity principle A theory that the more a skil!, task, etc., is practiced or rehearsed, the better it is being learned. See ALL-OR-NOTHING LEARNING.

continuity theory A point of view that human speech was originally based on the signalling cries of animals. Sometimes known as the bow-wow theory. See ORIGIN-OF-LANGUAGE THEORIES.

continuity theory of learning A point of view that in discrimination learning, every reinforced response results in an increase.

continuous action theory (J. Loeb) A point of view that the operation of tropisms, the orienting responses of animals (for example to light) depends upon the continuous application of the stimulus and not upon mere changes in intensity. See TAXIS, TROPISM.

continuous amnesia See PSYCHOGENIC AMNESIA.

continuous-bath treatment A method of calming excited, delirious, or agitated patients by placing them in a tub of continuously-flowing water kept at 98.6°. See HYDROTHERAPY.

continuous controls Controls that can be set at any value along a continuum.

continuous-discrimination reaction/response A technique for reaction-time experiments consisting of an apparatus which provides two or more stimuli in an order unknown to the observer, so arranged that when the correct response is made to one stimulus the next stimulus is automatically presented, so that one stimulus-response pair immediately succeeds another. Also known as serial reaction.

continuous distractor task   **continual distractor task**

continuous group   See OPEN GROUP.

continuous narcosis   A type of therapy used to treat mania introduced in the 1920s that prescribed 20 hours of sleep daily under sedation for up to three weeks. See CONTINUOUS-SLEEP THERAPY, DAUERSCHLAF, SLEEP TREATMENT.

continuous panel   A consumer jury in which members participate long-term so that consumer psychologists can detect shifts in attitudes, values, or behavior. The members are carefully selected to represent the demographic or psychographic characteristics of a population, and they are tested periodically for signs of psychic mobility that may also represent attitude changes in the general population.

continuous rating scale   Some rating scales are based on numbers, for example from one to ten. But a continuous rating scale has a near infinity of ratings, when based on pencil marks on a line. However, in the latter case, a ruler is placed over the location on the line to be changed into numbers.

continuous recognition task   A task in which the participant sees or hears a word and is asked to decide if it is old or new.

continuous reinforcement schedule   **continuous schedule of reinforcement**

continuous scale   A type of scale in which increments are assumed or known to be continuous.

continuous schedule of reinforcement (CRF)   An experimental schedule in which every occurrence of a response is reinforced by providing a reward for each correct response, as compared with partial reinforcement in which the behavior is reinforced intermittently rather than continuously. Also known as continuous reinforcement schedule. See MAINTENANCE SCHEDULE, MIXED SCHEDULE, REINFORCEMENT SCHEDULE.

continuous-sleep therapy/treatment   The use of prolonged sleep as treatment for certain psychiatric disorders. Also known as prolonged-sleep treatment. See SLEEP TREATMENT.

continuous variable   A variable that can assume any value, for example, in length or weight. Compare DISCRETE VARIABLE.

continuous variations   Any variations connected by numerous intergradations.

continuum   Any scale, series, or graph that extends continuously without gaps or other interruptions.

continuum approach   Conceptualizing behavior as ranging from effective functioning to severe personality disorganization. A scale can be established to judge the severity of behavioral abnormality.

contour   1. The outline of a visual figure, such as the defining difference between a shadow and the rest of a visual perception. 2. The demarcation between adjacent areas, as when a spot of black ink spreads over a white sheet of paper, indicating where the black stops and the white begins. See SUBJECTIVE CONTOUR.

contour   A demarcation of a visual object dependant on the contrast between different textures, or colors, black and white in this case.

contourogram   A compressed graphic record of signals such as those produced by an electroencephalograph (EEG) or electrocardiograph (EKG), used to show cycle-by-cycle variations.

contraception   The planned prevention of the natural fertilization of the female ovum by the male spermatozoa (conception) by physical, medicinal, or chemical means. See BIRTH CONTROL.

contractibility   The capacity of living tissue, particularly muscle, to contract in response to a stimulus. Also known as contractility (of cells).

contract (in therapy)   A mutually agreed-upon statement of the change a person wants to accomplish in therapy as well as what the patient and the therapist are to do. Also known as a behavioral contract, contingency contract. See CONTINGENCY CONTRACT, CONTRACT MANAGEMENT, CONTRACTUAL PSYCHOTHERAPY.

contract plan (for schools)   The establishment of a curriculum based on units of instructions. Students are individually evaluated as to learning ability and they agree to study to the point of success a certain number of these units in a prescribed time.

contract session   The first meeting between a psychotherapist and a client. Usually it is for the exchange of expectations and giving of information including topics such as frequency of visits, expectation of results, or payment of fees. See CONTINGENCY CONTRACT, CONTRACTUAL PSYCHOTHERAPY.

contractual norms   Statements that specify the rules to be observed and the penalties for violating them.

contractual psychotherapy   Agreement between therapist and patient about the goals to be sought as well as the role of each in the therapeutic situation. See CONTINGENCY CONTRACT, CONTRACT MANAGEMENT, CONTRACT (IN THERAPY).

contractures   Usually the flexing of the fingers or toes, or rigidity of large joints such as elbows and knees.

contract worker   **contingent employee/worker**

contradiction principle   In formal logic, one of the three laws of thought that states no statement can be simultaneously true and false. See LAWS OF THOUGHT.

contradictory representation   A relationship between two images, ideas, or thoughts, such that the presence of the one by its very nature inhibits the presence of the other; for example the representation of an object as cold inhibits its representation as warm. Also known as inconsistent representation.

contralateral   1. The other side of the body. 2. Refers to something on the other side. 3. In neurology, identifying a physical effect, such as paralysis, that occurs on the side of the body opposite to the side on which a brain lesion is found. See IPSILATERAL.

contralateral control   The motor cortex of each of the left and right hemispheres of the brain control movements on the opposite sides of the body.

contralateral hearing aid   An electronic device that detects sounds for persons who have suffered a hearing loss in one ear. It transmits signals from the deaf ear to an earphone placed near the good ear, thus producing a normal stereophonic effect that is important in determining sound orientation. See HEARING AID.

contralateral hemisphere   See IPSILATERAL HEMISPHERE.

contraprepared   1. Pertaining to an organism to which is difficult or impossible to teach a new skill or action because of its evolutionary history (instinct). 2. Having an attitude or a personal history incompatible with a particular learning task, making it particularly difficult (if not impossible) for the person to learn the task. Sometimes known as contrapreparedness.

contraprepared behaviors   Feats that are impossible or almost impossible for certain animals to achieve, such as dogs walking exclusively on their front feet. See PREPARED BEHAVIORS, UNPREPARED BEHAVIORS.

contrarian   (F. Dumont) A person who dissents for the purpose of dissenting, independently of the topic's apparent, even demonstrated, validity. See NAY-SAYING, YEA-SAYING.

contrasexual   (Y. Jacobi) Describing the repressed sides of male–female elements assumed by Carl Jung to be present in all individuals, regardless of their sex. See ANIMA, ANIMUS.

contrast   1. An intensification of differences between stimuli caused by contiguous presentations, either simultaneous or successive. 2. See PRINCIPLE OF MAXIMUM CONTRAST. 3. In the effect of illumination on performance, the extent to which the figure stands out from the ground; the lower the illumination intensity, the more the contrast needed to maintain performance on a visual task.

contrast detectors   Sensors in the visual system that respond to contrast variations in visual perception. See LATERAL INHIBITION.

contrasted-groups design   A type of research design in which group membership is the independent variable; for example, male and female students are studied in terms of some experimental condition, with the intention of seeing whether there is a gender difference.

contrast effect   1. A heightened difference between two contrasting stimuli or sensations when they are juxtaposed (simultaneous contrast) or when one immediately follows the other (successive contrast), for example, when a trombone precedes a violin (successive contrast) and when a yellow and a red spot are viewed at the same time (simultaneous contrast). 2. In social psychology, contrast effects occur when there is a shift in judgment away from an anchor attitude, concept, or judgment. See ASSIMILATION EFFECT.

contrast effects in interviewing   A tendency to rate an interviewee relative to the previous one(s). Closely related to contrast error.

contrast error   In interviewing or rating, a tendency to judge some phenomena (for example, a person, animal, object) higher than proper if the preceding one was viewed negatively, or to judge a thing more negatively than justified when a preceding one was viewed positively. See CONTRAST EFFECTS IN INTERVIEWING.

contrast illusion   Describing a certain optical illusion in which the value of an angle, curve, distance, etc., is altered by the presence of some adjacent angle, curve, etc., through the contrasting effect of size, direction, or position of the adjacent figure.

contrastives   Differences of cognitive elements, such as that knowledge recently acquired is different from what was previously thought, or information told by others differs from what has been gleaned from personal experience.

contrastive stress   In speaking, stressing a word to indicate its importance, such as "one must NEVER do anything to endanger self or others."

contrast polarity   In monitor displays, dark-on-light versus light-on-dark.

contrast procedures   In consumer psychology, checking product performance against predictions.

contrast sensitivity   In perception research, the minimum amount of contrast needed to perceive a grating pattern. Contrast sensitivity plotted as a function of stimulus spatial frequency is the contrast sensitivity function (CSF). See SPATIAL FREQUENCY.

contrast sensitivity function (CSF)   In ergonomics, as well as perceptual research, a graph showing sensitivity to contrast as a function of the spatial frequency of a sinewave grating. See CONTRAST SENSITIVITY.

contrast sensitivity test   Measures the minimum contrast at which an object can be detected (usually visually) as a function of its size or spatial frequency.

contrast theory   The view that an object can be judged or known when other objects are available for comparison, as, for example, in judging brightness constancy of an object.

contrasuggestibility   A tendency to do or say the opposite of what someone else has suggested or ordered. Also known as antisuggestion, negative suggestibility. See REVERSE PSYCHOLOGY.

contrasuggestion technique   A suggestion presented by one individual to another, to take advantage of his or her known negativistic attitude. See REACTANCE THEORY.

contravolitional   Refers to movements or thoughts that occur in opposition to the person's voluntary attempts to suppress or direct them.

contrecoup   (reciprocal blow—French) An effect in which an external injury to an area on one side of the head causes a brain injury on the opposite side, caused by pressure waves traveling to the right and left around the skull from the point of impact and producing a summation of force 180° away. Thus an injury to the left side of the head may disrupt motor functions on the right side of the body rather than the left side.

contrection   Touching or fondling another person, usually with genital stimulation.

contributing cause   One of two or more antecedents which condition an effect.

contrient interdependence   (M. Deutsch) A situation in which the link between the goals of two or more people are such that if one person obtains his or her goal, the others cannot.

contrived situations In psychodrama, the establishment by the therapist of a situation in which the client is to participate for a specific purpose, for example, to test assertiveness; a situation causing frustration may be established to see how long the client will persist in attempting to achieve a social goal.

control 1. In psychoanalytic theory, the process of restraining or regulating impulses, which Sigmund Freud assumed to be the major function of the ego. 2. The regulation of the conditions of an experiment in such a way that the effects will be due solely to the experimental or independent variable and not to any extraneous factor. 3. (J. Rodin) An ability to cause an influence in the intended direction. 4. In ergonomics, the apparatus with which an operator communicates with a machine. 5. In social psychology, power or influence.

control adoptees Offspring of normal parents reared by normal adopting parents, selected for comparison with index adoptees. See CROSS FOSTERING.

control analysis Psychoanalysis conducted by a trainee under the supervision of a qualified analyst. Also known as controlled analysis. See THERAPY SUPERVISION.

control condition In research, the way in which a control group is treated: the same as the experimental group except for one aspect, that being the treatment given to the experimental group, such as two classes studying the same subject, but in the experimental class soft background music is played.

control-devices research The study of devices used to operate and control machines, in terms of (a) correct identification through shape, size, color, or texture coding, to reduce errors; (b) specific design features of knobs, levers, or push buttons most suitable for different purposes; and (c) location, as in the relative location of the brake and accelerator in motor vehicles.

control-devices Examples of some hand control-devices designed for tactile discriminability.

control discriminability The differentiation of controls (as in an aircraft) by variables such as size, shape, texture, color, and movement required, so that one will not be confused with another. See CONTROL DEVICES for illustrations.

control-display ratio The ratio of the extent of control movement to the magnitude of the display response.

control experiment In research, the replication of an experiment for the purpose of gathering additional information about or increasing the validity of the original experiment. The experimental conditions may be duplicated exactly to provide another measure of the dependent variable, or to assess the impact of a variable that experimenters suspect was not previously controlled. See ANALOGUE EXPERIMENT, CRITICAL EXPERIMENT, CRUCIAL EXPERIMENT, EXPERIMENTAL PLAN, REPLICATION.

control freak Slang for a person who "needs" to be the leader, in control of others, and who cannot tolerate taking orders from anyone else.

control function logic In engineering psychology, an intuitively obvious connection between control input and output, for example, an automobile window switch that is moved up to raise a window and down to lower it.

control group In research, an aggregate of organisms reasonably similar in characteristics to an experimental group before the start of the research procedures that is subjected to the same research conditions as the experimental group except for one aspect or variable being tested. Put simply, a part of the sample to which nothing is done, so that any differences in the experimental group can be attributed to the treatment. See BASIC RESEARCH, EXPERIMENTAL GROUP, PURE RESEARCH.

controlled analysis control analysis

controlled association In an association experiment, a constraint imposed on the participant's responses; for example, the association response must be a synonym of the submitted word. Also known as constrained association. See FREE ASSOCIATION.

controlled attention Ability to attend selectively to what is significant in the environment; the capacity to distinguish important stimuli from peripheral, incidental stimuli. Also known as selective attention.

controlled drinking Consumption of alcoholic beverages in moderation, avoiding the extremes of abuse or abstinence. Strong opinions exist, pro and con, as to whether people diagnosed as alcoholics can ever learn to drink in moderation.

controlled-drinking therapy A type of behavioral therapy designed to reduce a patient's tendency to excessive consumption of alcoholic beverages by self-control techniques. See CONTROLLED DRINKING.

controlled experiment 1. An experiment in which special attention is paid to eliminate all possible sources of errors. 2. An experiment with at least two groups of sample members, a control group and at least one experimental group.

controlled-exposure method/technique A procedure employed in testing the effectiveness of advertisements or the reactions to a movie, by using suitable participants who may (a) have electrodes attached to their bodies, (b) be photographed while attending to the ads or the movies, (c) respond to questionnaires after the exposure, or (d) be interviewed. A combination of these methods may be used in an attempt to determine, in effect, which advertisements are best or how the audience reacted to the film. See CONSUMER CHARACTERISTICS, CONSUMER PSYCHOLOGY, CONSUMER-JURY TECHNIQUE, EVALUATION INTERVIEW.

controlled observation The study or observation of a phenomenon, such as an object, person, or situation, under special conditions delimited in some manner, for example, watching children on a playground to see how often and in what manner they initiate aggressive behavior. Such observation yields better results when those being observed are not aware they are being watched. See ONE-WAY MIRROR.

controlled processing task A task that requires slow processing and conscious attention.

controlled sampling A type of sampling technique in which the known risk of chance effects is eliminated.

controlled therapy   Therapy performed by a person in training who is closely supervised by a more experienced therapist. Also known as controlled analysis when the trainer is a psychoanalyst. See CONTROL ANALYSIS.

controlled variable (C)   1. A variable manipulated by the experimenter; the independent variable. 2. A variable that is constant in an experiment or is not systematically biased by other variables or factors.

controller   One of four basic lifestyles according to Nira Kefir. Controllers, according to this view, fear being ridiculed and for this reason keep tight control over themselves, being careful to avoid doing that which could be potentially criticized by others, being as perfect as possible, and otherwise being obedient and subservient. See MAJOR PRIORITIES.

control order   The relation between the position of a machine control and the position, velocity, or acceleration of a display or machine system.

control orientation   A world-view that recognizes the human need to be able to predict and influence events important in their lives. See ATTRIBUTION THEORY.

control procedure   See WITHIN-SUBJECTS DESIGN.

control processes   In information-processing, memory material is transferred from one part of the brain to another.

control series   In research, a set of observations or measurements designed to check up on the conditions of the experiment proper.

control theory   A point of view that there are self-monitory functioning systems in living organisms similar to governors on motors that prevent them from going too fast. The control protects the organism from itself (for example, having the ability to eat a delicious food, feel satiated, and then stop).

control variable   The independent variable in an experiment, always under the control of the experimenter. See CONTROLLED VARIABLE.

contusion   A diffuse disturbance, with edema and multiple intracerebral hemorrhages, usually from a severe blow to the head. See ACUTE TRAUMATIC DISORDER, CEREBRAL CONTUSION, HEAD TRAUMA.

convalescent centers   Extended care facilities for patients whose recovery from disease or injury has reached a stage where full-time hospital inpatient services are no longer required.

convarkin designs   (R. B. Cattell) The investigation of the magnitude of hereditary and environmental effects by comparisons of variance among related family and other groups.

convenience dreams   A Freudian phrase for dreams that appear to solve a practical problem, for example, a dream that the person has started the day's routine, while the dreamer is sleeping later than usual.

convenience sampling   A type of sampling that selects individuals as subjects or participants for research because they are easily available. College sophomores serve this purpose well. See STRATEGIC SAMPLING.

convenience shoppers   1. People who purchase what they need when they need it without being influenced by advertising. 2. People who favor products that are prepared and packaged for convenient and simple use.

convention   A rule of social conduct generally accepted as proper by the members of a social group, but not regarded as rigidly binding. See FOLKWAYS, MORES.

conventional crowd   A group that deliberately gathers in a particular location, such as the audience at an event.

conventionalism   1. A personality trait marked by excessive concern with and inflexible adherence to social customs and mainstream values and standards of behavior. 2. Refers to one of the traits associated with the authoritarian personality. See AUTHORITARIANISM.

conventionality   1. A characteristic of an individual of adhering closely to recognized social usage. 2. The character of a course of action that follows stereotyped lines of social procedure. 3. The entire body of conventions or recognized social usages.

conventional level of moral reasoning   (L. Kohlberg) Kohlberg's second and intermediate level of moral reasoning characterized by identification with and conformity to the moral rules of family and society. See PRECONVENTIONAL LEVEL, POSTCONVENTIONAL LEVEL.

convergence in binocular vision   Turning inward of the eyes to fixate the gaze on a near object. The rotation of the two eyes inward toward the source of light so that the image will fall on corresponding points in the foveae. Convergence enables the slightly different images of an object seen by each eye to come together and form a single tridimensional image.

convergence theory   A point of view that individuals begin with hereditary givens that are then modified by environmental stimuli.

convergent evolution   1. The development of similarities, not based on community of descent, in two or more groups of organisms. 2. A tendency of unrelated animals in a particular environment to acquire similar body structures that enable them to adapt effectively to the habitat, for example, aquatic animals generally acquire external features that include smooth surfaces and streamlined bodies for rapid movement through a watery medium. See ANALOGOUS STRUCTURES, HOMOLOGY, HOMOLOGOUS STRUCTURES.

convergent external validity   Empirical evidence of the amount of overlap between two separate and independent measures of the same construct or of constructs that are supposed to overlap; phrase is used mostly in reference to psychological tests.

convergent hierarchy   A hierarchy of varied stimuli each eliciting identical responses, leading to the formation of concepts. See LENS THEORY.

convergent operation   A superior method of research to demonstrate the validity of a theory by testing two or more hypotheses or aspects of the theory, rather than only one; the common sense theory that two independent proofs are more convincing than one. See RESEARCH DESIGN, RESEARCH TYPES, REPLICATION.

convergent production   (J. B. Guilford) An ability or capacity to take from a store of knowledge a specific bit of information needed quickly, as when asked, "What is the French term for *to run*?" and replying immediately "*courir*." See CRYSTALLIZED INTELLIGENCE, DIVERGENT PRODUCTION.

convergent series   In mathematics, a series of terms whose sum, as the number of terms added is increased, approaches more and more closely to a fixed value.

convergent strabismus   Cross-eye.

convergent thinking   An aspect of critical thinking characterized by the search for a problem's best answer. Possible solutions are considered and the task is one of analyzing all alternatives to determine the most logical answer. See DEDUCTIVE THINKING, DIVERGENT THINKING.

convergent validity   1. A statistical demonstration showing a correlation between two measures of the same theoretical construct. 2. A subset of construct validity in which the results from a measurement are consistent with the theory. 3. A means of establishing the validity of a test by using other tests as criteria (for example, the Immediate Test was validated against the Stanford Binet Test and the Wechsler-Bellevue Test, on the argument that since the correlation with both of these other tests was high, this short test measured whatever the other two tests measured). See CONCURRENT VALIDITY.

converging operations   In research, several independent investigations coming to the same results or conclusions. See CONVERGENT VALIDITY.

conversational catharsis   1. In general, the reduction of tension, anger, and other negative feelings as the result of talking with others (for example, friends, relatives, even strangers). 2. A formal means of release of repressed or suppressed thoughts and feelings through verbal interchange via counseling or psychotherapy.

conversational maxims   (H. Grice) The well-understood rules for communication regarding: (a) quantity (neither too much nor too little); (b) quality (tell the truth); relation (stick to the topic); and manner (be brief and well organized). See CONVERSATIONAL RULES.

conversational rules   In discussions, the assumption that normal people will obey the general rules of conversation: well-timed turn-taking, reacting normally to questions by answering them, making statements that can be taken at face value, and keeping to the topic under discussion. Variations from these rules may lead to the suspicion that a person is trying to hide something, has a private agenda, or has a mental disorder. See CONVERSATIONAL MAXIMS.

converse accident   An error in logic caused by hasty generalizations. See FALLACIES.

conversion   1. A sudden, often inexplicable change from one point of view, or one concept, or relationship to another, often the exact opposite of the prior one. See INTRAINDIVIDUAL CHANGE. 2. An unconscious psychological process in which repressed material (impulses, memories, fantasies) are transformed into bodily (somatic) symptoms. See CONVERSION DISORDER. 3. See PRIVATE ACCEPTANCE (meaning 1).

conversion disorder   A loss or alteration in physical functioning for which there is evidence of psychological involvement. Symptoms may include paralysis, loss of voice, seizures, blindness, and disturbance in coordination or balance. See CONVERSION HYSTERIA, HYSTERICAL AMNESIA, MOTOR CONVERSION SYMPTOMS, SENSORY CONVERSION SYMPTOMS.

conversion hysteria   A psychoneurosis in which a physical disability is due to psychological causes. The lines of demarcation of the disability are usually logical rather than physiological, one of the signs of this form of hysteria. See CONVERSION DISORDER.

conversion paralysis   Hysterical paralysis.

conversion reaction   The DSM-I phrase for what was later called conversion disorder, or conversion type hysterical neurosis. See CONVERSION DISORDER.

conversion seizure   A seizure of unknown origin with no explanation available for its occurrence. See HYSTERICAL CONVULSIONS, IDIOPATHIC EPILEPSY.

conversion symptoms   Among reported deficits of individuals suffering from sensory conversions are anesthesias of various parts of the body, blindness, impairment of taste or smell, and tunnel vision. Each of these specific symptoms can be traced to specific experiences. Also known as sensory conversion symptoms. See CONVERSION DISORDER, MOTOR CONVERSION SYMPTOMS.

conversion therapy   (J. Nicolosi) A psychotherapeutic technique based on the idea that some gay men or lesbians are not comfortable with their sexual orientation and would like to become heterosexual.

convex learning curve   A graphic representation of a portion of a curve or even a whole curve that demonstrates that the rate of learning is increasing. See item B of CUMULATIVE RECORD for an example.

conviction   Certitude of belief. Often, people believe or put their faith in certain concepts that can never be proven. Many religious, political, and philosophical issues exist on which various people of intelligence and good will can take diverse and often contradictory positions.

convince   To induce belief in another individual by suggestion, argument, etc.

convolution   A gyrus of the cerebral cortex.

convoy   The network of friends and family members who accompany a person throughout his or her life-cycle.

convulsant   Rare name for a substance that causes convulsions. Historically, substances such as camphor or metrazol or, via hypoglycemia, insulin, were used to provoke convulsions in chemical convulsant therapy in the 1930s before electroconvulsive therapy became more widespread.

convulsion   An involuntary, generalized, violent muscular contraction, in some cases tonic (contractions without relaxation), in others clonic (alternating contractions and relaxations of skeletal muscles). For epileptic convulsions "seizure" is preferred. See PSEUDOCONVULSION, SPASM.

convulsive disorders   Disturbances of function, structure, or both, involving generalized seizures, as in grand mal and petit mal, or focal seizures, as in Jacksonian and psychomotor epilepsy. Also known as epileptic disorders, seizure disorders.

convulsive seizures   See EPILEPSY.

convulsive therapy   A form of psychiatric therapy based on the induction of a generalized seizure by electrical or chemical means. See ELECTROCONVULSIVE TREATMENT, METRAZOL SHOCK TREATMENT.

cooing   Describing the sounds made by an infant from about one to six months of age, characterized by repeated vowel sounds.

Coolidge effect   Renewed interest in a new partner by a male sexually sated with a previous one. Based on an unverified quip about the sexual abilities of hens and roosters, attributed to U.S. President Calvin Coolidge to the effect that males can exhibit extraordinary sexual potency if a large number of attractive females are available.

cooling of affect   A tendency to become emotionally cold, a disturbance of affectivity occurring in schizophrenia and in presenile and senile brain disorders.

cooperation   The working together of two or more units of a group in such manner as to jointly produce a common result. Many animals, such as deer, cooperate against common enemies. Human infants begin cooperative play at about three years of age; cooperative group activities begin at about age six or seven.

cooperative education   A school-administered program that combines study with employment. Periods of full-time study alternate with periods of full-time employment usually at intervals of three or six months. See COOPERATIVE TRAINING.

cooperative goal structure   A positive correlation among group members' goal attainments in a situation in which members perceive that they can attain their goal only if the other members with whom they are cooperatively linked also obtain their goal. See COOPERATIVE REWARD STRUCTURE.

cooperative learning   1. Attempts made by students to teach themselves and others. Fostered in some schools that believe in the value of peer teaching. 2. What occurs in study groups of various kinds, often using a book such as an encyclopedia or the Bible.

cooperative motive   A type of motivation that influences individuals to advance themselves as well as all members of their group through behavior that favorably affects everyone involved and is neither competitive nor individualistic. See COMPETITIVE MOTIVE, INDIVIDUALISTIC MOTIVE.

cooperative play   A form of play that has rules or goals, whether or not they are expressed.

cooperative reward structure   In group situations, a condition in which rewards are assigned on the basis of group, rather than individual, achievement. In most cases, the cooperative reward structure improves group trust, communication, and achievement. See COMPETITIVE REWARD STRUCTURE, INDIVIDUALISTIC REWARD STRUCTURE.

cooperative training   A vocational program for high-school students placed in jobs related to the occupational fields of their choice. A program coordinator provides classroom instruction that supplements the job experience while monitoring the students' progress on the job by consulting with employers. See COOPERATIVE EDUCATION.

cooperative urban house   A type of halfway house in the form of a small residence for 10 to 30 ex-psychiatric patients, inmates of an institution for the retarded, or prisoners who are being readied for outside living. The residents assume certain responsibilities, such as household chores, and participate in group meetings to discuss personal and vocational problems. See HALFWAY HOUSES.

cooperative therapy   multiple therapy

cooperators   Parents who try to work out a relationship with their children based on mutual respect, favoring the use of logic and reason, avoiding authoritarianism to achieve obedience. See APPEASERS, DEMOCRATIC PARENTING, DICTATORS, FAMILY COUNCIL TEMPORIZERS.

Cooper-Harper Scale   (G. Cooper & R. Harper) A 1969 subjective measure of mental workload.

Cooper Test   (K. Cooper) A test of aerobic fitness in which the participant runs as far as possible in the allotted time. In the original version for American military personnel, the time was 15 minutes; for civilian use it was shortened in 1968 to 12 minutes. The test is easily-administered and highly correlated with more sophisticated measures, but does not take into consideration factors such as motivation and running technique and strategy.

co-optation   (P. Selznik) A political process that manages opposition by "co-opting" (electing) outsiders who could otherwise threaten or disturb the group by giving them status within the group.

coordinated leisure   The free selection of various kinds of work viewed as hobbies, for example, making a table in a home workshop.

coordinates   The values, X (the abscissa) and Y (the ordinate), of a point. The positions of points on planes usually refer to the Cartesian coordinate system in which the three basic dimensions are designated x, y, and z.

coordination   1. The fitting together or the moving together of elements in a system. 2. The relation between two or more data or classes such that both bear the same relation to a certain genus, or higher class. 3. Organisms operating in sequential relation, as when people are dancing.

coordination of secondary schemes   According to Jean Piaget, the increasingly adept and purposeful combination of repetitive reactions to achieve a desired aim, such as picking up a pillow to get a toy placed underneath. This behavior usually emerges near the end of an infant's first year and occurs in the latter part of the sensorimotor stage. See PRIMARY CIRCULAR REACTION.

COP   Community Outreach Program

cope   To endure, struggle, confront, etc., always in terms of unfavorable situations in which achievement or survival is involved.

COPE model   In sports psychology, a cognitive-behavioral strategy for handling anxiety that focuses on controlling emotions, organizing input, planning the next response, and executing the response.

coping   (R. S. Lazarus) Constantly changing cognitive and behavioral efforts to manage specific external demands, internal demands, or both, appraised as taxing or exceeding the resources of the person.

coping behavior   Positive, striving behavior rather than avoiding or defensive actions in dealing with difficult or threatening situations, for example, a simple detour around a crowded city street, or the elaborate defense mechanisms employed to ward off anxiety. See COPING MECHANISM.

coping imagery (J. Cautela) A technique of covert desensitization that pairs relaxation with images of successful self-control in situations that previously generated anxiety in an attempt to alleviate experienced tensions. See BEHAVIOR(AL) THERAPY, FLOODING.

coping mechanism Any conscious or unconscious adaptation that lowers tension in a stressful experience or situation. See COPING BEHAVIOR.

coping skills training (J. Wolpe) The use of relaxation as a means of therapy. A person is asked to imagine a situation that is anxiety producing and then to relax. A graded list of anxiety-producing items is generated and relaxation is used at all points.

Coping Strategies Questionnaire (CSQ) An instrument designed to measure the frequency with which individuals use a variety of mental and behavioral strategies to cope with pain.

coping strategy An action, series of actions, or thought processes used in meeting a stressful or unpleasant situation or in modifying a personal reaction to such a situation. Usually, the phrase implies a conscious and direct approach to problems, in contrast to defense mechanisms. See COPING BEHAVIOR, COPING MECHANISM.

coping style The general method that an individual tends to employ in dealing with emergency situations.

cop-out Slang for quitting or refusing to take responsibility. Used in transactional analysis for a pattern of exonerating the self, as in saying "But I couldn't help it."

coprography Being sexually aroused by creating graffiti about excrement.

coprolagnia A paraphilia in which the sight, or even the thought, of excrement may result in sexual pleasure. Also known as coprophemia, koprolagnia. See COPROLALIC, SCATOLOGY.

coprolalia 1. (G. Gilles de la Tourette) Original name for Tourette's disorder. See TOURETTE'S SYNDROME. 2. The obsessive-compulsive, uncontrollable utterance of obscene words observed in some patients with chronic schizophrenia, and in patients with Tourette's disorder or latah. Also known as cacolalia, coprophrasia, koprolalia.

coprolalic A person who obtains sexual pleasure from using scatalogical language.

coprophagy The eating of feces. Also known as coprophagia. See PICA.

coprophemia The use of obscenities as a paraphilia, for example, to stimulate sexual excitement. Also spelled koprophemia. See COPROLALIC, SCATOLOGY.

coprophilia 1. A tendency, characteristic of infancy, to be attracted by the excreta, particularly the feces. 2. An excessive or pathological preoccupation with excreta or filth, or with objects and words that represent feces. 3. Being sexually aroused by feces: smelling, tasting, or seeing their production. Also known as koprophilia. See ANAL EROTISM, HOARDING, SCATOPHILIA.

coprophobia Morbid fear of excrement, often symbolically expressed as fear of dirt or contamination. In psychoanalytic theory, it is interpreted as a defense against anal erotism (coprophilia). Also known as koprophobia, scatophobia.

coprophrasia coprolalia

copula carnalis In law, marital coitus.

copula fornicatoris In law, coitus other than marital.

copulation Coitus sexual intercourse.

copulation fantasy sexual fantasy

copulatory behavior Behavior patterns associated with sexual intercourse. Such patterns may include species-specific courting activities with pecking order or dominance playing a significant role in some animals.

copy 1. To imitate. 2. The printed, as opposed to pictorial, part of an advertisement. 3. In aviation/police/military communication, to understand.

copying mania Morbid, obsessive impulse to imitate the speech or actions of other people, observed in catatonic schizophrenia (echolalia, echopraxia) and certain culture-specific disorders such as *amurakh*.

copyright In law, the protection of certain materials from plagiarism.

copy theory A point of view that what is perceived is a replica of real objects and that memory is an accurate repository of reality. Sometimes known as passive registration theory.

core (S. Maddi) Central overriding ideas or assumptions about personality.

core construct (G. A. Kelly) A concept that determines the way individuals maintain themselves in their environments.

core gender identity 1. Physical identity as male or female, a sense of maleness or femaleness resulting from a combination of biologic and psychological influences, including family and cultural attitudes. See GENDER IDENTITY, GENDER ROLE, ROLE CONFUSION, SEXUAL IDENTITY. 2. In psychoanalytic theory, an infant's sense of self as a female or male in the second year of life. 3. Physical characteristics, sex chromosomes and hormones, and fetal gonads, that together determine the development of the external genitals.

co-regulation A stage in parent-child relationships between complete supervision and control of parent (as in infancy) and complete independence of the child (as following marriage), in which parents give children (or children assume) various rights and privileges of independence.

core hours Time during which flextime employees must be on the job.

core of personality That aspect of human nature common to all people, such as the desire to survive, to grow and develop, to be noticed, to belong to a group, and to be accepted. Personality theorists have suggested various configurations of this universal core which humans all share. See PERSONALITY THEORY.

core relational themes (R. S. Lazarus) The basic meanings of person-environment relationships, as synthesized from several separate components of an appraisal, which differ for each of the emotions.

core temperature Deep body temperature.

core tendency A point of view that all humans have common goals and methods that shape their operations, such as wanting to do well and improve their abilities. See INSTINCT.

Coriolis illusion   Pilot disorientation or dizziness plus the illusion of rolling when, during a prolonged turn, the head is tilted in a plane other than the aircraft's. Also known as cross-coupling effect.

cornea   A transparent portion of the outer coat of the eyeball (anatomically continuous with the sclera), situated in front of the iris and constituting the first of the refractive media of the eye.

corneal-reflection method/technique   A method of studying eye movements with light reflected from the cornea.

corneal reflex   Closure of the eyelids, elicited by touching the cornea. Also known as conjunctival reflex, eyelid closure reflex, lid closure reflex.

Cornelia de Lange's syndrome   de Lange's syndrome

Cornell Selective Index   (A. Weider) A 92-item questionnaire designed during World War II for screening potentially mentally unstable military personnel. Later adapted for diagnosing psychosomatic disorders as the Cornell Index (Revised) with 101 items.

Cornell Word Form (CWF)   A modified word-association instrument used primarily in industrial psychology to reveal disorders. Each stimulus word is followed by two response words from which the participant is required to select the one that seems to be most closely related to the stimulus, for example, "parent" (followed by) "boss/friend."

coronal plane   A plane that shows structures as they would be seen from the front; in the brain, the "hat brim" plane. Also known as frontal plane.

coronal section   A cut or slice on the coronal plane.

coronary artery disease (CAD)   Cardiovascular disorder characterized by restricted flow of blood through the coronary arteries supplying the heart muscle. Usually caused by atherosclerosis of the coronary arteries and often leads to myocardial infarction. Behavioral (overeating and lack of exercise) and psychosocial factors (Type A behavior) frequently are involved in the development and prognosis of the disease. Subsequent heart damage is known as coronary heart disease (CHD).

coronary-prone behavior   Behavior that generally has a high degree of competitiveness, work-orientation, impatience, drive for perfection, and general tension. See TYPE A BEHAVIOR.

corpora   Plural of corpus.

corporal   Pertaining to the body.

corporal punishment   The infliction of physical pain upon the body.

corpora quadrigemina   Two pairs of midbrain nuclei known as the superior and inferior colliculi that control visual and auditory functions. See COLLICULUS.

corporeal   Having a body.

corpse fear   See NECROPHOBIA.

corpus   A body or distinct organ. Singular is corpora.

corpus callosum   A thick band of nerve fibers connecting the cerebral hemispheres; the principal connection between the two sides of the brain. Also known as callosum. See COMMISSURAL FIBERS.

corpusculum   1. A small body or mass. 2. A blood cell. Also known as corpuscle.

corpus luteum   A yellowish glandular mass in the ovary that remains after a follicle releases an ovum. The development of the corpus luteum is stimulated by secretions of the luteinizing hormone of the pituitary gland. The corpus luteum in turn becomes a transient endocrine gland, secreting estrogen and progesterone.

corpus mamillare   **mammillary bodies**

corpus striatum   (striated body—Latin) A mass of fibers beneath the cortex and in front of the thalamus. Contains projection fibers passing in both directions between the thalamus and cortex, as well as cell bodies, giving it a striped appearance. Composed of the caudate nucleus and lenticular nucleus, they are separated from each other by the internal capsule.

correct detection   One of the four possible replies in a signal detection trial, in which the participant correctly states that there was a signal. See SIGNAL-DETECTION THEORY.

correction   1. In statistics, the elimination or reduction of chance or observational errors. 2. In optometry, the rectification of visual defects through the use of lenses.

correctional facility   A euphemistic or professional term, in use since the early 1800s, for prison.

correctional mechanism   In a regulatory process, a mechanism that can alter the value of a system variable.

correctional psychologist   A psychologist who works within the correctional system. Generally, duties include measurement of intelligence and academic knowledge, interviews with entering inmates usually with the intent of helping to decide the study or work program suggested or assigned to the inmate, counseling and (rarely) psychotherapy, reports written for administrators and parole board on inmates for a variety of reasons, and participation in psychiatric conferences.

correctional psychology   A branch of psychology concerned with the application of diagnostic and counseling techniques to inmates in correctional institutions (reformatories, training schools, penitentiaries). Correctional psychologists also may participate in courts, parole boards, prison administration, and programs for the rehabilitation of offenders. See FORENSIC PSYCHOLOGY.

correction for attenuation   A statistical formula to estimate what the validity coefficient for a test would be if both the test and criterion were perfectly reliable. Formula: $r_c = (r_{xy}) \div [(r_{xx}r_{yy})^{1/2}]$ Where: r_c is the correlation between X and Y corrected for attenuation, r_{xx}, r_{yy} is the reliability coefficient of test X and criterion Y, respectively, r_{xy} is the computed validity coefficient.

correction for chance guessing   A procedure for adjusting scores on a true-false or multiple choice test because subjects can get some items correct even if they simply guess at the answers. Although it has some technical limitations, the usual formula score (as it is called) is obtained by subtracting from the number of correct answers the number of incorrect answers (divided by the number of alternative choices minus one). For instance, if a person got 30 items correct, 24 items incorrect, and 26 items were omitted, on an 80-item test in which each item had 4 alternative choices, the formula score would be $30 - 24/3 = 22$. For two-choice (true-false) items, the formula score becomes simply the number of correct answers minus the number of incorrect answers. Sometimes the number of items omitted are counted with the number incorrect, but this procedure is generally not to be favored.

correction for continuity   A statistical adjustment in computing chi-square from small samples, in which the differences between observed and expected frequencies are decreased by 0.5. It helps bring the distribution (based on a discontinuous frequency) nearer to the continuous chi-square distribution from which published tables for testing chi-square are derived. Also known as Yates correction.

correction for guessing   See CORRECTION FOR CHANCE GUESSING.

correction method   In training, given permission to make a different choice, for example, in working on a finger maze with a blindfold on, arriving at a dead end and retracing with a finger to go in a different direction. Otherwise, if a noncorrection method is used, the participant would have to start all over again. See MAZE TEST.

corrective emotional experience   (F. Alexander) Short-term psychotherapy consisting of reviving the memory of an experience the patient could not handle in the past, with the therapist playing a significant role in discussing that experience in a secure environment to facilitate insight and change.

corrective therapist   An adjunctive health professional who directs therapeutic exercises and physical-education activities in the treatment of mentally or physically ill patients. In addition to improving coordination, strength, and agility, exercise routines are intended to build morale, self-confidence, and socialization interests of the patient.

correct rejection   One of the four possible replies in a signal detection trial, in which the participant correctly states that there was no signal. See SIGNAL-DETECTION THEORY.

correlate   A variable related to another variable.

correlated axes   Nonorthogonal axes. See ORTHOGONAL.

correlated t-test   Statistical procedure that tests for mean differences between two groups in a within- or matched-subjects design.

correlated vectors method   Correlating factor loadings with correlations between factor-analyzed tests and an outside criterion to examine the relationship between a factor and the criterion.

correlation   1. A tendency of certain paired measures to vary concomitantly, so that knowledge of the value of one gives information as to the mean value of all measures paired with this one. 2. A number of different mathematical methods used to establish relationships between two or more variables. Types of correlation include: BISERIAL, FIRST-ORDER, FOUR POINT, INDIRECT, KENDALL RANK, LINEAR, MULTIPLE, PARTIAL, NEGATIVE, PERFECT, INDIRECT, POINT-BISERIAL, PRODUCT-MOMENT, RANK DIFFERENCE, RANK ORDER, SIMPLE, SPLIT-HALF. See CORRELATION RATIO, SPURIOUS CORRELATION.

correlational method   A statistical method used to establish noncausal relationships between two or more variables.

correlational redundancy   See DISTRIBUTIONAL REDUNDANCY.

correlational statistics   correlational studies

correlational study   Research on acts or processes in which two or more variables covary, usually with the objective of establishing an orderly relationship between the variables or of considering them together to find relationships. Also known as correlational statistics.

correlation barrier   (F. Galton) In the history of intelligence testing, early attempts were made to evaluate intelligence by physiological measures such as ability to discriminate between lengths of lines presented in extremely short intervals. However, correlations between such measures and intelligence tests of the Binet type typically did not exceed a correlation of 0.30. See INSPECTION TIME.

correlation center   A region or area in the nervous system where two or more afferent pathways unite to exercise a combined influence on neural functions.

correlation cluster   Variables that tend to have high correlations between them, indicative that they have something in common. See CLUSTER ANALYSIS, FACTOR ANALYSIS.

correlation coefficient   See COEFFICIENT OF CORRELATION.

correlation matrix   An intercorrelation table, showing all possible relationships among a set of variables; for example, correlations between Variable A and Variables B, C, and D are given, then the correlations between Variable B with C, and D, etc. In the table below, the correlation of A and B is 0.37 while A and D is 0.77.

	A	B	C	D
A		.37	.58	.77
B			.89	.04
C				.53
D				

correlation matrix   An example of intercorrelations of arrays ABCD. A and D correlate best with each other; B and D least.

correlation ratio (η_{yx})   A measure of the magnitude of a curvilinear or nonlinear relationship. Formula: $\sqrt{\eta_{yx}^2}$. Where Σn_k is the sum of the squares between groups, $\Sigma(Y - \bar{Y})^2$ is the total sum of squares, n_k is the number of sample observations in the treatment group k.

correlation table   A representation of the quantitative relationship of two variables. Values of one variable are represented by horizontal rows, those of the other by vertical columns. In the square formed by the intersection of a row with a column are recorded the cases whose scores are represented by row and whose scores are represented by row and column respectively. Thus, a person scoring 10 on one test, 20 on another, would be recorded in the square formed by the intersection of row 10 with column 20. Also known as double-entry table, double-frequency table, two-way table.

correspondence   The extent to which an observed behavior, such as cutting in on a line of people waiting to enter a theatre, is attributed to a general personality trait, such as rudeness or aggressiveness.

correspondence bias   A tendency to draw inferences about a person's unique and enduring dispositions from behaviors that can be entirely explained by the situations in which they occur.

correspondence communications   1. The reporting of information by one person to another so that such information will be properly interpreted by the recipient. 2. A means of reporting data by a scientist in one field in such a manner that the data may be understood by scientists in other fields.

correspondent inference theory   (E. E. Jones) A point of view that people make meaningful attributions when they believe that other peoples' actions correspond to their disposition.

corridor illusion   A distorted perception seen when looking at two or more identical figures placed along a continuum, such that the farther away they appear to be from the point of origin, the larger they appear. See GEOMETRICAL ILLUSION, ILLUSIONS.

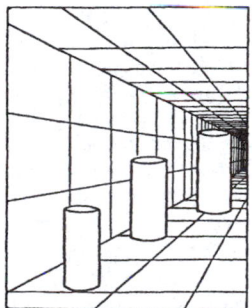

corridor illusion   The three cylinders are the same size.

corrigendum   An error to be corrected. Plural is corrigenda.

corteria   (R. B. Cattell) The factor of cortical alertness and arousal as displayed on objective tests such as reaction time and flicker-fusion speed.

cortex   (bark, rind—Latin) 1. A shortened form for the cerebral cortex of the brain. 2. The outer layer or layers of any organ. 3. The outer or superficial layer of a structure, as distinguished from the central core. The cortex of a structure is almost always identified with the name of the gland or organ, as adrenal cortex, cerebellar cortex, cerebral cortex, or renal cortex. Types of cortex include: ADRENAL, AGRANULAR, ARCHAIC, ASSOCIATION, AUDITORY, CEREBELLAR, CEREBRAL, CINGULATE, EXTRINSIC, GRANULAR, INFEROTEMPORAL, INTRINSIC, LIMBIC, NONSTRIATED VISUAL, ORBITOFRONTAL, PERIAMYGDALOID, PREMOTOR, PRESTRIATE, PRIMARY, SENSORY, STRIATE, TERTIARY, TRANSITIONAL, VISUAL. See ALLOCORTEX, CELLULAR LAYERS OF CORTEX, COLUMNAR ORGANIZATION OF CORTEX, ENTORHINAL-CORTEX LESION, HEMIDECORTICATION, NEOCORTEX, PALEOCORTEX, SOMATIC SENSORY AREAS.

cortex cerebelli   The layer of gray neural substance which forms the outer coating of the cerebellum. Also known as cerebellar cortex.

cortex cerebri   Obsolete phrase for cerebral cortex.

cortical activation   Refers to activation of the cerebral cortex.

cortical apraxia   motor apraxia (meaning 1)

cortical area   See BRODMANN'S AREA, CEREBRAL CORTEX.

cortical-arousal factor   (D. Berlyne) Ratings related to drowsy-alert and weak-powerful scales, as judged by participants asked to respond to random adjective-noun combinations.

cortical barrel   In rodents' cortex, a group of neurons that receives input from a whisker.

cortical blindness   Complete or partial blindness caused by ischemia (inadequate blood flow to occipital lobes, in the posterior areas of the cerebrum). Most cases of cortical blindness are accompanied by other neurological deficits usually associated with strokes. Also known as cerebral blindness.

cortical center   1. Areas of the cortex where sensory fibers terminate or motor fibers originate. 2. Any group of nerve-cells in the cortex which act as an integrated unit in the performance of some specific function.

cortical deafness   Permanent inability to hear (deafness) caused by damage to the cortex of the brain, which is involved in auditory functions.

cortical-evoked potential   See EVOKED RESPONSE.

cortical-evoked response   evoked potentials

cortical excitation level   The degree of electrical activity in the brain's cortex. See ELECTROENCEPHALOGRAM.

cortical inhibition   Nerve inhibition occurring in the cortex.

corticalization   The increased cerebral control of neural functions in higher animals. See ENCEPHALIZATION.

cortical lamina   Six layers may be defined in the neocortex according to distribution of neurons. The layers, identified by Roman numerals, are: I molecular layer (or plexiform layer), contains terminal ramifications of the deeper pyramidal cells and thin myelinated axons of the horizontal cells of Cajal; II external granular layer, containing stellate (granular) cells and apical dendrites of pyramidal cells; III external pyramidal-cell layer, with medium-size pyramidal cells in the outer zone and larger pyramidal cells in the inner zone; IV internal granular layer, which contains stellate neurons and is the terminal zone of projections from the specific nuclei of the thalamus. This layer is expanded in the primary sensory regions of the cortex such as the somatosensory cortex of the postcentral gyrus; V internal pyramidal layer which contains large pyramidal cells. This layer is expanded in the motor areas of the cortex and is thickest in the primary motor cortex of the precentral gyrus where the pyramidal cells giving rise to the pyramidal tract are known as the giant cells of Betz; and VI multiform layer (or fusiform layer), which contains cells of various shapes but mainly spindle-shaped cells. The thickness of the various layers varies from one cortical region to another. This variation in cytoarchitecture is the basis of the cortical mapping schemes of Brodmann and others.

cortical layers   Refers to patterns of cells or fibers in the cerebral cortex. See CORTICAL LAMINA.

cortical lesions   Pathological changes in tissues of the cortex of the brain. The sites of cortical lesions generally determine the types of functional deficits, for example, causing altered sensory effects, motor-function effects, or cognitive changes.

cortical localization of function   See LOCALIZATION OF BRAIN FUNCTION.

cortically originating extrapyramidal system (COEPS)   Neurons of the extrapyramidal system that originate in the cerebral cortex and descend the brainstem and spinal cord to motor neurons.

cortical maps   See LOCALIZATION OF BRAIN FUNCTION.

cortical neuron   See NEURON.

cortical potentials   Effects of firing small electrical currents across cortical cells. The procedure generally has been limited to experiments in enhancing consolidation or reinforcing learning experiences or recall of memorized information.

cortical satiation theory   A point of view that certain aspects of the brain can be overfatigued and its functions impaired by an overabundance of signals to that area.

cortical undercutting   A type of prefrontal lobotomy used to control severe emotional and mental disturbance. The skull is opened and long association fibers are severed. Designed to prevent purported frontal-lobe damage, which affects thinking processes.

cortical zones   Three types of cortical regions behind the central sulcus defined by function. They include: (a) the primary, consisting of specific primary sensory projection areas, (b) the secondary, concerned with perception, and (c) the tertiary, with cells that integrate information areas.

corticifugal nerve fibers   Nerve fibers conveying impulses away from the cerebral cortex. Also spelled corticofugal. See AROUSAL.

corticobulbar fibers   corticonuclear fibers

corticobulbar nucleus   Nerve-cell bodies in the medulla that link neurons of the cortex and lower motor system. Associated with the corticoreticular fibers that terminate in the reticular formation of the rhombencephalon and corticonuclear fibers that innervate muscles of the face, tongue, and jaws.

corticofusimotor system   Nerve pathways that involve gamma motoneurons extending from the cerebral cortex to the intrafusal fibers of the muscle spindles. It is part of a feedback loop of the body's motor-control system. Dysfunction of the corticofusimotor system results in movement disorders.

corticonuclear fibers   Longitudinal-pyramidal-tract fibers that extend from the cerebral cortex to the mesencephalon, pons, and medulla oblongata to terminate in the nuclei of the cranial nerves. Also known as corticobulbar fibers.

corticopontine nucleus   A neural-cell body in the pathway connecting the cerebral cortex and the pons. A collecting point for numerous fibers from all parts of the cerebral cortex. The individual fibers usually are further labeled as to their origin in the cortex, for example, frontopontines or occipitopontines.

corticoreticular nucleus   A nerve-cell body of fibers extending from the cerebral cortex to the reticular formation of the mesencephalon and rhombencephalon.

corticospinal fibers   Motor nerve fibers (axons) originating from pyramidal neurons of the cortex that extend through the internal capsule, the crus cerebri, the pyramids of the medulla, and cross in the caudal medulla to terminate in the spinal cord.

corticospinal tract   Nerve fibers that connect the cerebral cortex with the spinal cord. The corticospinal tract contains motor-control fibers that are excitatory for flexor action. The rubrospinal tract duplicates much of the corticospinal tract pathway except that it passes through the red nucleus.

corticosteroid(s)   A general term for the steroid hormones produced by the adrenal cortex, sometimes simply called (with some imprecision) "steroids." These include three main subtypes: those which affect the chemical balance of salts (also known as "mineralocorticoids"), those which are similar to and affect the sex hormones, and those which help the body cope with stress, immunological reactions, and many other functions (also known as "glucocorticoids"). The latter group is the most relevant to the reactions relating to psychiatric and psychosomatic illness. See CORTICOSTEROID THERAPY, CORTISOL, CORTISONE.

corticosteroid therapy   Treatment with hormones usually produced in the adrenal cortex for conditions of adrenal insufficiency or inflammatory or autoimmune disorders. Therapy when prolonged may lead to osteoporosis, diabetes mellitus, electrolyte imbalance, obesity, and hypertension (Cushing's syndrome). Whereas these substances have many uses in medical treatment, they often also are accompanied by significant and rather variable psychiatric side-effects, such as irritability, a hypomanic state, significant dysphoria, depression, and even psychosis. See CORTISOL, CORTISONE.

corticotropic releasing factor (CRF)   A peptide generated by the hypothalamus that stimulates the release from the nearby pituitary gland of the regulating hormone, corticotropin (also known as ACTH), which in turn then stimulates the growth and function of the adrenal gland. Also known as corticotropic releasing hormone (CRH).

corticotropin   adrenocorticotropic hormone (ACTH)

corticovisceral control mechanisms   The brain centers that regulate autonomic and hormonal body functions, for example, the lateral-hypothalamic control of the desire to eat.

cortin   An acetone extract of the cells of the adrenal cortex containing several steroid hormones.

Corti's membrane   See TECTORIAL MEMBRANE.

cortisol   One of the glucocorticoid hormones secreted by the adrenal cortex. Blood levels of cortisol in humans vary according to wake–sleep cycles, being highest around 9 a.m. and lowest at midnight. Also known as hydrocortisone, compound F.

cortisone 17-hydroxy-11-dehydrocorticosterone, a hormone produced by the adrenal cortex, or synthetically, it influences carbohydrate metabolism and blocks inflammation.

Corti('s) organ See ORGAN OF CORTI.

coruscation A subjective sensation of a flash of light before the eyes.

Corybantic rites In classical mythology, the rites performed in celebration of Cybele, a nature goddess of Phrygia and Asia Minor. The rites included frenzied dancing, which was purported to have a therapeutic effect. See CHOREOMANIA.

cosatiation Satisfaction of a need by meeting the needs of something else. See SUBLIMATION.

cosmic consciousness A sense of awareness of the universe as a whole, which appears to be achieved, in at least some cases, through hallucinogenic drugs, "peak" experiences, religious ecstasy, or metaphysical disciplines such as yoga exercises and various forms of meditation. See MYSTIC UNION.

cosmic identification The feeling of identification with the universe: "I am the whole world." In some Eastern religious traditions, cosmic identification is seen as a spiritual goal, in which an individual transcends the dualistic world and reaches realization. In the West, similar expressions are most frequently observed in disorganized (hebephrenic) schizophrenia, and are explained psychoanalytically in terms of regression to the stage of infantile incorporation, when there was no distinction between the self and the outside world. See MYSTIC UNION.

cosmic narcissism (H. Kohut) A higher and rare form of narcissism in which the libido is transferred from the self to self-transcending ideals, leading to a timeless cosmic perspective that makes personal mortality acceptable.

cosmic shadow Concern, expressed by Carl Jung in his later years, that God relies on the individuation of humans for the energy necessary for divine completion.

cosmogony A theory of the origin and early history of the world or universe. Most religious traditions have their own cosmogony, or even cosmogonies, which includes the religious beliefs surrounding the origins of their tradition.

cosmology The science of the structure of the universe and of its evolution.

cosmos The universe regarded as an orderly system. See CHAOS.

costal stigma Stiller's sign

cost containment See REVIEW.

cost-benefit analysis (CBA) 1. In evaluation research, an attempt to compare costs and benefits of a program by translating these into currency amounts and comparing them. Institutional review boards that approve (or disapprove) research projects use a CBA to assess whether the potential benefits of research outweigh the potential (ethical) costs. 2. An explanation for altruistic behavior which asserts that people help others when the reward for the giver is greater than the cost. See COST-REWARD ANALYSIS.

cost-benefit ratio The value of a solution compared to the cost of the investment to reach it.

cost-effectiveness analysis (CEA) In evaluation research, an attempt to compare the costs of various programs for attaining a goal or objective assumed to be worthwhile.

cost of concurrence The difference between the performance level on a task performed alone and when performed with another task, usually one to which no attention is paid.

cost-reward analysis In social psychology, a model that attempts to explain helping behavior according to the reinforcements and costs associated with any specific helping action. A helping act that possesses either high reinforcement value or low cost value is more likely to be performed than a low-reinforcement, high-cost act.

cost-reward model In environmental psychology, an approach based on an analysis of the potential costs and benefits of different environments. Individuals and companies are likely to choose the environment with the highest reward-to-cost ratio.

cost-reward model (of helping) A point of view that people consider the costs and rewards of helping or not helping. An extension of the Latané-Darley decision model of helping.

cot death A common name for sudden infant death syndrome (SIDS). Also called crib death.

Cotard's syndrome A psychotic disorder in which patients insist that their bodies, and in some cases the whole of reality, has ceased to exist. This symptom pattern most often occurs in women of involutional age. Also known as chronic delusional state of negation, *délire de négation*. Named after French neurologist Jules Cotard (1840–1887).

cotherapy Psychotherapy with two therapists at any one time, whether in dealing with a single client or a group of clients. Done for various reasons with many arrangements possible. See COLLABORATIVE THERAPY, MULTIPLE THERAPY.

cottage plan Decentralized organization of a mental institution or training school, with the patients living in separate, supervised units according to their symptomatology or level of mental retardation.

co-twin control A method of using one twin as a control for the other "experimental" twin; for example, differential training in a specific function is given to one of a pair of identical twins whose overall level in that function is identical before training. A comparison between twins at the end of the training period can show what effect training has had upon modifying the natural behavior of the experimental twin. A later comparison may show that both twins are again equal in that respect and that special training was ineffective in the long run.

couch In psychoanalysis, the couch on which the patient reclines, recommended on the theory that this posture will facilitate free association, encourage the patient to direct attention to his or her inward world of feeling and fantasy, and enable the patient to recall childhood experiences. Also known as analytic couch.

Coué method A procedure developed by Emile Coué, a French pharmacist, of self-improvement as well as a cure of physical diseases, initiated by periodically saying: "Day by Day in Every Way, I am getting Better and Better." See AFFIRMATION, SELF-THERAPY.

coulomb (Q) The quantity of electricity carried in one second by one current of one ampere.

counseling 1. A process of defining, understanding, and addressing a specific problem, as well as advice and suggestions given by a person acknowledged as being an expert in one or more areas, such as in marriage, dependency on substances (drugs), vocations, or child rearing. 2. Professional assistance in coping with emotional, vocational, marital, educational, rehabilitation, retirement, and other personal problems. The counselor makes use of such techniques as guidance, advice, discussion, and the administration and interpretation of tests. Spelled counselling in countries such as England and Canada. See PSYCHOTHERAPY.

counseling interview An interview for the purpose of providing guidance or counseling.

counseling ladder A succession of steps of advice, suggestions, or exercises, each representing a step closer to the desired conclusion, as employed by a counselor while guiding a course of treatment.

counseling psychologist A psychologist who has received professional education and training in one or more counseling areas such as educational, vocational, employee, old age, personal, marriage, or rehabilitation counseling. In contrast to a clinical psychologist who usually emphasizes underlying motivation and unconscious factors, a counseling psychologist emphasizes adaptation, adjustment, and more efficient use of the individual's available resources.

counseling relationship The interaction between counselor and client. An affective, personal yet professional relationship in which the counselor brings professional training, experience, and personal insight to bear on the problems revealed by the client. The relationship in and of itself is considered to be of central importance in effecting desired modifications in the client.

counseling services Assistance with advice, suggestions, and related services from an agency that provides counseling to families with problems associated with social conflicts, for example, drug addiction or alcoholism.

counselling counseling

counselor A professionally trained person who specializes in one or more counseling areas such as geriatrics, sex, careers, rehabilitation, education, marriage, family, or substance abuse, who provides evaluations, information, and suggestions designed to enhance the client's ability to make decisions and effect desired changes.

counselor-centered therapy See DIRECTIVE COUNSELING.

counteraction need (H. A. Murray) A drive to overcome difficult challenges rather than accept defeat. A tendency to persist after defeat, denial, or rejection, to strive to achieve personal goals. See SELF-CONFIDENCE, SELF-EFFICIENCY, SELF-MAXIMATION.

counterattitudinal advocacy In experimental social psychology, asking a participant in an experiment to advocate a position opposite to the one believed by the participant. Research indicates such participant's own beliefs tend to be modified thereby toward the position advocated. The implications of this research may explain how dictators are able to mold public opinions.

counterattitudinal roleplaying A situation in which people engaging in psychodrama or similar situations are directed to express opinions contrary to those in which that they believe, for example, using derogatory terms for people they regard highly. See DEVIL'S ADVOCATE.

counterbalanced research design The systematic variation of conditions in experiments of repeated measures design in order to balance extraneous factors to minimize the effect of possible confounding factors. A simple form of counterbalancing would be to administer experimental conditions in the order ABBA. Also known as counterbalancing. See ABAB DESIGN, ABBA DESIGN.

countercathexis In psychoanalytic theory, the psychic energy used by the unconscious to block the entrance of id impulses into consciousness. For instance, an obsessive impulse to wash may block the desire to play with feces; philanthropy may neutralize a concealed tendency to hoard (reaction formation). Also known as anticathexis, counterinvestment. See CATHEXIS.

countercompulsion A compulsion secondarily developed to resist the original compulsion when it cannot be continued. The new compulsion then replaces the original so that compulsive behavior can continue.

counterconditioning The extinction of a particular response, such as a fear, through conditioning an incompatible response to the same stimulus. It is a behaviortherapy technique used in eliminating unwanted behavior, replacing it with a more desirable response. See SYSTEMATIC DESENSITIZATION.

counterconformist A person who deliberately adopts views that run counter to the prevailing views.

counterconformity A behavioral pattern in conflict with socially approved or group standards.

counterculture A social movement, such as the hippie or drug "cultures," that maintains its own mores, procedures, concepts, and values in opposition to prevailing cultural norms. See COUNTERNORM, YOUTH CULTURE.

counterego (W. Stekel) The part of the unconscious self which is antagonistic to the ego.

counterfactual Pertaining to what has not happened but what could have happened had circumstances been different.

counterfactual thinking Thought processes in which individuals imagine events or outcomes different from those that actually occurred.

counterfeit role Playing a false role, such as generating the impression of being single and available when actually married. See MASKING, ROLEPLAYING.

counteridentification A form of countertransference in which the analyst identifies with the patient.

counterimitation Avoiding the kind of behavior that a person has seen a model perform. See INDIRECT IMITATION.

counterinvestment See ANTICATHEXIS, COUNTERCATHEXIS.

counterirritant An agent that produces an irritation to relieve the symptoms of another irritation. The effect may be explained by the gate-control theory of sensory receptor stimulation.

countermeasure-intervention programs Social-reform programs.

counternorm   An alternative standard of behavioral appropriateness; an alternative to prevailing social norms. See COUNTERCULTURE.

counterphobia   The attempt of some phobic individuals to overcome their anxiety and terror by facing and defying the feared object or situation.

counterscript   In transactional analysis, a new role that the client may temporarily take in life which is the opposite of his or her chosen life script. A person may take on a new role because of a conflict between two ego states, such as parent and child.

countershock   Mild electrical stimulation administered to an electroconvulsive-shock patient for one minute after the convulsive shock. The purpose of the countershock is to relieve some of the common after-effects of the electroconvulsive shock treatment (ECT), namely, postconvulsion confusion or amnesia.

countersuggestion   A suggestion presented to an individual to inhibit the effect of some previous suggestion or to counteract the influence of some fixed idea. Often used in hypnosis.

countertransference   1. A transference reaction on the part of the therapist toward the patient. 2. The analyst's use of empathy to understand the conscious and unconscious communications and experiences of the patient. See COUNTERIDENTIFICATION, DIDACTIC ANALYSIS, TRANSFERENCE.

countertransference neurosis   In psychoanalysis, neurotic reactions in the analyst precipitated by the patient's reactions to the analyst or by an unconscious reaction to the patient's neurotic tendencies if the analyst's repressed paranoid or masochistic tendencies are aroused.

counterwill   See WILL THERAPY.

counterwish dream   A Freudian phrase for a dream in which the content is the opposite of what the dreamer wants, concealing a wish that the dreamer is unwilling to express openly, for example, a person may dream of losing a wallet but the real wish is to have a lot of money.

counting obsession   An obsessive-compulsive impulse to count. See ARITHMOMANIA.

couples counseling   See COUPLES THERAPY, MARITAL COUNSELING.

couples therapy   1. Husbands and wives in therapy aimed at understanding each spouse as a separate individual. Differs from couples counseling in which advice is given to improve the marriage. 2. Both partners in a committed relationship in therapy at the same time with the same therapist. Based on the idea that both partners have deep-seated problems that affect not only both individuals and their relationship but also their relationships with others. Also called marital therapy, marriage therapy, and relationship therapy. See MARITAL COUNSELING, MARRIAGE THERAPY.

coupling   In genetics, the association, or linkage, of different hereditary characteristics for several generations, in contrast to the Mendelian principle of independent assortment.

coupon-return technique   A method of testing advertising effectiveness in a printed medium, for example, magazine or newspaper, by inducing consumers to mail in coupons. Can be done on a split-run basis with two different messages, and used only in selected marketing areas.

courage   The willingness to take risks without being sure of the consequences; necessary for effective living.

courtesan   1. Originally a woman of the (royal) court. 2. A refined prostitute. 3. Almost synonymous with "working girl."

courtesan fantasy   hetaeral fantasy

courtroom psychology   The study of courtroom procedure such as jury selection, presentation of testimony, methods of interrogation, examination of defendants, guilt-detection techniques, and the functions of expert witnesses in commitment, adoption, or criminal proceedings. See FORENSIC PSYCHOLOGY.

courtship behavior   The behavior of different species of animals and humans in different environments, societies, or social strata during the courtship period. See ANIMAL COURTSHIP BEHAVIOR, BUNDLING, HUMAN COURTSHIP BEHAVIOR, MATE SELECTION IN ANIMALS, MATE SELECTION IN HUMANS, NIGHT CRAWLING.

couvade   (to brood or hatch—French) 1. Pregnancy symptoms experienced by a male. Interpretations include cultural ritual, neurosis, and developmental crisis. 2. A custom in some aboriginal cultures that when a child is born, the father takes to bed as if he is suffering the pangs of childbirth. Often he will enact the birth experience in detail, usually subjecting himself to elaborate taboos.

covariance   An expected value of the product of the deviations of two random variables from their respective means. Formula: covariance $= (\Sigma XY) \div N$. Where: X and Y are deviations from the mean of the two variables in the series, N is the number of cases.

covariate   A correlated variable controlled or held constant through analysis of covariance. An apparently significant difference in means across groups might need to be adjusted for the effects of a covariate, which could be any variable systematically related to the means.

covariation chart   (R. B. Cattell) The possible covariation of persons, responses, stimuli, and occasions.

covariation theory   A point of view that when people try to determine the locus of causality for a behavior, they try to acquire information about consistency, distinctiveness, and consensus.

covenant   In Jewish and Christian theology, a solemn agreement binding a people and a divinity.

coverant   (L. Homme) Internal, private events seen by Homme (a student of B. F. Skinner) to be, in effect, operants of the mind that can be objectively analyzed. A neologism from covert operant, also known as coverant behaviorism. See BEHAVIORISM.

cover memory   screen memory

cover story A false explanation given to participants who are about to participate in an experiment to deceive them as to the purpose of the experiment. Usually used in social psychology research and usually retracted when the experiment is over. The classic example is the Aussage situation. See AUSSAGE TEST, DEMAND CHARACTERISTICS, EXPERIMENTER BIAS, EXPERIMENTER BIAS EFFECTS.

covert Denoting that which is not directly observable, often because it is disguised or concealed. From one point of view, psychology itself is a covert science, if defined as the science of the mind. This view is still shared by some people who assume the old view of psychology as taught in the United States in the structuralist tradition. The counter movement of behaviorism denied the importance of the mind to psychology but, as the saying went, psychology did not lose its mind, since psychology eventually was accepted as being both a covert and an overt science. See SOFT DETERMINISM.

covert behavioral reinforcement A behavioral-therapy technique in which a desired reinforcement is imagined. It is ironic that such procedures that are entirely covert are labeled "behavioral."

covert conditioning (J. Cautela) A form of therapy depending on the use of imagination that has three main theoretical assumptions: (a) correspondence of overt and covert behavior, (b) the hypothesis that each of these domains affects the other, and (c) that both overt and covert behavior depend on the laws of learning. Essentially, a person mentally rehearses certain behavior, and mentally rewards the self for such, thus leading to behavioral changes. See COVERT EXTINCTION.

covert desensitization The linking of an anxiety-producing stimulus with imagined punishment.

covert extinction (J. Cautela) Imagining an unwanted habit, etc., to be decreased, and then imagining a reward being given for the imagined success. See COVERT REINFORCEMENT.

covert homosexual See CLOSET HOMOSEXUAL.

covert modeling (J. Cautela) Visualizing a role model, then fantasizing acting as this person might, and then imagining particular favorable consequences. See ACTIVE DAY-DREAMING TECHNIQUE, COVERT REINFORCEMENT.

covert negative reinforcement (J. Cautela) Imagining pairing of behavior that the client wants to adopt afterwards, such as smoking, and then imagining horrible consequences, such as dying of cancer, in the expectation that this will assist in breaking the undesired habit. See COVERT REINFORCEMENT.

covert positive reinforcement (J. Cautela) Imagining participation in an action or behavior that the person wants to adopt, and then mentally rehearsing such behavior in the expectation that it will eventually become an overt pattern of activity. See COVERT REINFORCEMENT.

covert processes See COVERT DESENSITIZATION, COVERT EXTINCTION, COVERT NEGATIVE REINFORCEMENT, COVERT POSITIVE REINFORCEMENT, COVERT REINFORCEMENT.

covert reinforcement (J. Cautela) The strengthening of a desired behavior by imagining a pleasant outcome.

covert response Any unobservable response such as a thought, image, emotion, or internal physiological reaction. There are, however, instruments designed to measure covert responses such as polygraphs. See OVERT RESPONSE.

covert self A person's estimate of his or her true self; what a person thinks he or she really is. See OVERT SELF, IDEAL SELF.

covert sensitization 1. (J. Cautela) Therapeutic aversive conditioning in which noxious mental images are associated in the patient's mind with an undesirable behavior that needs to be eliminated. 2. The linking of a rewarding stimulus with imagined punishment.

covert speech subvocalization

covert trial and error Mentally taking a series of alternative positions for the solution of a problem, without physically externalizing the process. Trial-and-error work that is mental only.

coverture In law, the requirement of a bride to turn over her present and future assets (including any children) to the ownership of her husband.

Cowper's glands Small paired glands at the base of the penis that secrete alkaline fluid into the urethra during sexual arousal.

COYOTE Acronym for Call Off Your Old Tired Ethics, a California prostitutes' labor union.

CP cerebral palsy

c personality See HISTRIONIC PERSONALITY DISORDER.

CPI California Personality Inventory

CPIT California Psychological Inventory Test

cps 1. centimeters per second 2. cycles per second

CPS Comrey Personality Scales

CPT Cognitive Processing Therapy

CPU central processing unit

CPZ See CHLORPROMAZINE.

CR 1. conditioned reflex or response. 2. critical ratio (also abbreviated **C.R.**)

C.R. critical ratio (also abbreviated **CR**)

cracking facades (W. Schutz) Refers to penetrating the personal "mask" or getting others to open up and reveal their true selves; associated with Carl Rogers' encounter group work.

crackpot Pejorative term for people who have certain fixed ideas of no apparent value, in the opinion of the majority of professionals in that area of specialization.

craft Skill or dexterity in planning or executing (especially a manual performance).

Craig's Wife (compulsion) See HOUSEWIFE'S NEUROSIS.

Cramer's V coefficient A measure of the correlation between two nominal variables whose values are cross-classifiable in a 2×3 or larger contingency table. Based on chi-square.

cramp A painful, involuntary contraction of a muscle or muscle group, sometimes prolonged and violent. Causes are usually physiological, occasionally psychological. Types include: MUSICAL, OCCUPATIONAL, SEAMSTRESS, TELEGRAPHIC, VIOLINIST, WERNICKE'S, WRITER'S. See CONVULSION.

cramp neurosis See WERNICKE'S CRAMP.

cranial anomaly An abnormal head due to a congenital defect often related to a chromosomal error. May be abnormally large, as in hydrocephalus, or abnormally small, as in microcephaly.

cranial bifida A congenital disorder manifested by a horseshoe-shaped depression of the medial plane of the forehead. Because of a failure of the two sides of the head to fuse normally during prenatal development, the corpus callosum may be defective. Mental retardation is common.

cranial capacity The cubic area of the cranium of a given individual.

cranial diameter A measure of the maximal distance across the skull.

cranial index A measure of the skull. See CEPHALIC INDEX.

cranial nerve (N) 1. A nerve that originates or terminates within the cranium. 2. One of twelve nerves that arise out of, or terminate in, the brains of mammals, birds, and reptiles going directly to various parts of the body, bypassing the spinal cord. They are: I olfactory, II optic, III oculomotor, IV trochlear, V trigeminal, VI abducens, VII facial, VIII statoacoustic, IX glossopharyngeal, X vagus, XI accessory, XII hypoglossal.

cranial reflex Any reflexive action whose path is mediated by cranial nerves and the brain stem.

cranial senses The four modalities of vision (sight), audition (hearing), gustation (taste), olfaction (smell).

craniofacial anomalies Structural deformities, usually congenital, of the face and cranium. Seen in Treacher Collins' syndrome, hypertelorism, Crouzon's disease, microcephaly, and Hurler's syndrome. See CRANIAL ANOMALY.

craniograph A chart or photograph of the skull; also, an instrument for measuring skulls.

craniography Investigation of the skull by means of photographs, charts, etc.

craniology 1. The scientific study of size, shape, and other characteristics of the human skull. See CRANIOSCOPY. 2. (F. J. Gall) The pseudoscience of phrenology. See PHRENOLOGY.

craniometry The systematic measurement of the (human) skull. Also known as cephalometry. See CRANIOLOGY.

craniosacral division The parasympathetic division of the autonomic nervous system. See AUTONOMIC NERVOUS SYSTEM.

craniosacral system The parasympathetic nerve network that runs through the spinal cord and extends branches through four cranial and three spinal nerves. The cranial nerves of the system are the oculomotor, facial, glossopharyngeal, and vagus nerves. The spinal nerves are those of the pelvic plexus.

cranioscopy A systematic description of the structural and functional characteristics of the skull and its contents. See PHRENOLOGY.

craniostenosis A skull deformity caused by premature closing of cranial sutures. Restricts normal development of brain structures, usually resulting in mental retardation. See CRANIAL ANOMALY.

cranium The bony structure situated at the anterior or cephalic end of the vertebrate body and enclosing the brain. Also known as skull.

crank 1. A person with insistent fixed ungrounded, obtrusive ideas. 2. Slang for a form of methamphetamine, usually snorted. See ICE.

crashing Slang for withdrawal symptoms, usually dominated by severe feelings of depression, that occur at the end of a run with a stimulant drug, usually cocaine or amphetamines. During the crashing phase, the user may sleep on-and-off for several days, displaying signs of exhaustion and irritation during waking periods. Also known as crash period.

Crawford Small Parts Dexterity Test (CSPDT) (J. E. Crawford & D. M. Crawford) A psychomotor examination involving several manipulative skills, such as the use of tweezers in (a) inserting pins in holes, (b) placing a collar over each pin, (c) placing small screws in threaded holes and then (d) screwing them down with a screwdriver. See VOCATIONAL APTITUDE TESTS.

craze The rapid adoption of some new mode of behavior, style of dress, sport, etc., by a given community, usually in an uncritical manner or to an exaggerated degree. See FAD.

craze of why Phrase similar to the French *folie du pourquoi*. A person who always demands an explanation for everything.

crazy Slang for mentally disordered.

creaming Providing an unfair amount of favorable attention or services to selected individuals. Metaphor is based on cream rising to the top of milk.

creation The act of bringing into existence phenomena essentially or absolutely new.

creationism A doctrine that maintains that all living organisms were created separately and immediately by a supreme spiritual power, a view maintained by a number of religious and cultural groups including African tribes, Native Americans, Aztecs, Hindus, Buddhists, Christians, and ancient Egyptians, Greeks, and Romans. See DARWINISM, EVOLUTION.

creative aggression (G. Bach) A process sometimes used in marriage counseling in which spouses are asked to express and discharge their anger physically by hitting each other with batacas (soft pillow-like bats) in the expectation that by so doing, they will become more relaxed and able to discuss their differences in a reasonable manner. See GROUP THERAPY, MARRIAGE COUNSELING.

creative arts therapy Forms of therapy that use creative processes and media, most often used with children but also used for adults. Types of (psycho)therapy include: ART, CLAY-MODELING, DANCE, DRAMA, EMOTIVE, EVOCATIVE, IMAGERY, MUSIC, POETRY, PUPPETRY, RHYTHMIC-SENSORY, SAND.

creative imagination A process whereby dormant unconscious elements are organized with conscious thoughts to produce new ideas.

creative power of the self The force that, together with heredity and environment, determines innovative human behavior; a person's unique way of interpreting and making use of heredity and experience.

creative regression   The behavior of a therapist in attempting to re-create a psychotic state in a patient to facilitate reintegration of the disordered personality.

creative self   (A. Adler) The dynamic aspects of human development. The creative self was never fully defined by Alfred Adler, but was described as the "first cause" of all behavior and the "active principle of life," comparable to the concept of soul. Its function was to guide all in their quest for experiences that would enable them to realize their unique style of life.

creative self-direction   Learning controlled by the learner involving the formulation or creation of new interpretations from previous associations or conceptualizations.

creative synthesis   (W. Wundt) The fusion of various concepts into a united whole. See MENTAL CHEMISTRY.

creative thinking   Mental processes leading to a new invention, solution, or synthesis in any area. A creative solution may use preexisting objects or ideas but creates a new relationship between the elements it uses, such as new mechanical inventions, social techniques, scientific theories, and artistic creations. See FUNCTIONAL FIXEDNESS.

creativity   Ability to apply original ideas to the solution of problems; the development of theories, techniques, or devices; or the production of novel forms of art, literature, philosophy, or science. See CREATIVE THINKING, CREATIVITY TEST.

creativity cycle   (G. A. Kelly) Moving from a loose system of constructs to a tighter, more validated one.

creativity-tapping techniques   Any technique that assists anyone in reassessing a familiar situation in new ways or in actualizing latent creative potentials.

creativity test   A psychological instrument designed to identify creative ability, or "divergent thinking," assumed to be as essential in the sciences as in the arts. Such tests focus on a variety of factors, such as word and ideational fluency, original associations, solutions to practical problems, suggesting different endings to stories, and listing unusual uses for objects.

crèche   (cradle—French) A child-care facility.

credulity   A tendency to accept statements or hypotheses on slight evidence. See INCREDULITY.

credulous argument   In sports psychology, holds that personality predicts athletic performance.

cremasteric reflex   Reflexive retraction of the testis due to cold temperature or to stimulation of the skin on the front inner surface of the thigh, due to contraction of the cremasteric or cremaster muscle.

cremnophobia   Morbid fear of precipices. See BATHOPHOBIA.

Creole   A new language ordinarily made up of words from two or more well established languages, often with various terms pronounced differently from the original language, that often becomes the language of choice of people in some lower social and economic groups. See PIDGIN ENGLISH.

crepitation   1. Repeated sharp crackling sounds, particularly those made by male crickets and other insects as a communication signal. 2. Flatulation.

crepuscular animals   Organisms that are most active in a dimly lighted environment, such as bats at twilight.

Crespi Effect   (L. Crespi) A tendency for there to be an increase in learning or response strength disproportionate to the reinforcement when the amount of reward changes from high to low or low to high.

cretin   1. Technically, a person with cretinism, but in English as well as in some other languages, the term refers unfairly to persons with mental retardation, especially those who are vulgar and brutal. 2. Derogatory slang for a disliked person (also moron, idiot, and imbecile have become so used).

cretinism   (W. Hoefer) A condition appearing in early childhood, due to congenital thyroid insufficiency, characterized by anatomical and mental retardation. Also known as Brissaud's infantilism, congenital myxedema, hypothyroid dwarfism, infantile hypothyroidism. See ATHYREOSIS, CONGENITAL HYPOTHYROIDISM.

crew resource management research   A study of cooperating groups such as airplane flight crews or surgical teams to determine difficulties in working efficiently as a unit, including human error, machine failure, climactic conditions or combinations thereof. See HUMAN FACTOR ENGINEERS.

CRF   1. corticotropic releasing factor 2. See CONTINUOUS SCHEDULE OF REINFORCEMENT.

crib death   Common phrase for the sudden, unanticipated death of an infant with no apparent reason. Also known as cot death, sudden infant death syndrome (SIDS).

cribriform plate   A bone in the roof of the nasal cavity where receptor cells for olfaction are located. An opening in this plate permits the passage of the olfactory nerve.

cri du chat **syndrome**   (cat's cry—French) A chromosomal disorder of deletion of the short arm of chromosome 5 resulting in microcephaly, epicanthic folds, palmar simian crease, severe mental retardation, walking and talking difficulty or inability, and an anomaly of the epiglottis and larynx that causes a high pitched wailing cry. Possibly hereditary although sporadic incidence has been noted. Also known as cat-cry syndrome, or chromosome 5, deletion of short arm, or crying-cat syndrome, or 46,XX5p-.

crime against nature   In law, this and similar phrases usually refer to activities such as homosexuality and anal or oral copulation.

crime from sense of guilt   The commission of a crime by an individual with an unconscious need for punishment.

crime of passion   In law, an offense that is partly forgivable because of circumstances, such as a husband killing his wife's lover in a fit of jealousy.

crime prevention   Refers to efforts made by individuals, communities, or social agencies of various kinds to generate attitudes of personal responsibility on the part of young people to conform to the values of society.

criminal anthropology   The study of the physical, mental, cultural, social, and genetic aspects of the maladjusted human. See PENOLOGY.

criminal conversation   In law, fornication, especially between a married woman and a man other than her husband.

criminal intent   A legal phrase indicating a conscious disregard of the law, presumed to be known by defendants. See SCOFFLAW.

criminal investigative psychology   The development and application of psychological theory and practice to (a) studying information collected as part of a court-related investigation, (b) the decision process involved in investigations, including the social psychological and emotional implications of involvement in investigations and the computer-aided decision support possibilities, both formed by (c) empirically validated hypotheses that can be made about offenders' motives and personalities.

criminality   A fixed pattern of illegal antisocial behavior such as stealing, rape, or assault.

criminally insane   Characterizing a defendant judged to be not responsible for the criminal act he or she is alleged to have committed due to a mental state that in psychological terms, psychiatric terms, or both, is either amentia or dementia but in legal terms is insanity. Different jurisdictions have different standards for declaring people insane. "Insane" and "insanity" are purely legal terms.

criminal (mental hospital) commitment   Confinement in mental institutions of people found not guilty of crimes by reason of insanity or to establish their competency to be tried as responsible individuals for the crimes they committed.

criminal operation   Formely used euphemism for abortion.

criminal psychiatry   1. The branch of psychiatry dealing with individuals who were either charged with committing a crime or convicted thereof, with the primary intent of diagnosing the individual according to some nosological standard, to help determine the individual's sanity and to predict dangerousness of individuals, as well as to make recommendations of various kinds, usually related to control of the individuals by means of medications. 2. A branch of criminology that studies the psychological aspects of crime and the criminal personality, such as personality factors, social environment, and heredity. See CRIMINAL PSYCHOLOGY, CRIMINAL RESPONSIBILITY.

criminal psychology   1. A branch of psychology that specializes in criminal behavior. Within the judicial system a criminal psychologist gives opinions about the mental status of people charged with crimes, serving time for crimes, or those considered for parole. Such psychologists will within institutions do individual and group therapy, and will also conduct idiographic and nomothetic research in the area of criminology. 2. A branch of psychology that specializes in criminal behavior, and research into the mentality and social behavior of criminals. See CRIMINAL PSYCHIATRY, CRIMINAL RESPONSIBILITY, FORENSIC PSYCHOLOGY.

criminal responsibility   Legal phrase meaning that before persons charged with a crime can be convicted, it must be proved that they possessed the ability to formulate a criminal intent. The court may appoint experts (usually psychiatrists or psychologists) to help determine this issue. See COMPETENCY TO STAND TRIAL, DURHAM RULE, INSANITY DEFENSE, IRRESISTIBLE IMPULSE, M'NAGHTEN RULES.

criminology   A social science covering all areas of criminality including causes of criminal behavior and the prevention of such behavior, as well as the functions of the legislature, the police, the courts, and correctional institutions, in terms of crime prevention and control.

crisis   1. A stress-producing situation that can precipitate personal disorganization. 2. A decision or turning point in which an immediate decision must be made about an important change in life. See CRITICAL PERIOD, IMPRINTING. 3. (F. A. Mesmer) The term used by Franz Anton Mesmer to refer to the convulsions induced by hypnotism that he considered to be evidence of the moment of improvement.

crisis center   A facility established for emergency therapy or referral.

crisis counseling   Immediate emergency counseling for drop-in, phone-in, or on-site clients, as when social workers aid police in mediating family crises where some amount of battering or threatening has taken place. See HOTLINE.

crisis effect   The after-consequences of crises. Direct action to study and prevent future crises and disasters tends to be undertaken only during or immediately after a crisis (for example, a drought may induce officials to enact water-conservation measures whereas potential of drought in the future is far less likely to stimulate action).

crisis group   A group organized by a mental-health facility, a government agency, or both, to explore and resolve crisis situations, such as loss of a job, arrest of a child for shoplifting, a bad LSD trip, or withdrawal of financial support for a patient. See COMMUNITY SERVICES.

crisis intervention   1. Services provided by mental-health practitioners and others during a period of community disaster or personal crisis. Intervention includes such approaches as short-term psychotherapy, psychological first aid, and telephone crisis (hotline) service. 2. In psychotherapy, active efforts to ameliorate patients' conditions through prescribing drugs, manipulating the environment or committing to an institution. By crisis intervention, serious consequences are sometimes avoided. See CRISIS COUNSELING, HOTLINE.

crisis-intervention group   See CRISIS TEAM.

crisis-intervention group psychotherapy   A therapeutic group directed to alleviating emotional disturbances resulting from situational crises, such as disasters, or other situations of overwhelming stress, usually to a community. See CRISIS TEAM.

crisis-intervention theory   A point of view that people are most responsive to helping others when the helpees are in a state of crisis, such as when contemplating suicide or under other great stress.

crisis management   The responses of people in authority to disasters and serious threats. Principles include having operational preparations in place, resolving the issue first and assigning responsibility later, reaching out by communicating facts and concerns, and sharing solutions with all those who share the problem.

crisis team   A group of professionals and paraprofessionals trained and prepared to handle emergencies such as suicide threats or attempts, situations of danger to the individual or others, or mass tragedies such as the crash of an airplane with fatalities.

crisis theory (G. Kaplan) A body of concepts that deals with the nature of a crisis: behavior, precipitants, prevention, intervention, and resolution.

crisis therapy Psychosocial interventions provided on an emergency, "drop in," basis for such crises as psychotic break, suicidal threats, acute alcoholism, drug intoxication, continuous seizures, or family crises. See CRISIS COUNSELING.

crispation A sensation of creepiness of the skin based on muscular contractions. See DYSPHORIA NERVOSA.

crista ampullaris An enlargement at the end of each semicircular canal of the inner ear in which sensory-hair cells are embedded in a gelatinous material. Due to head movements these hairs also move, signalling to the brain the position of the head in the external environment. Also spelled *crysta*.

criterial dispute A difference of opinion based on differences of definitions of terms rather than on reality.

criteria of the psychic (R. Yerkes) Refers to whether or not an organism has a "mind," structural criteria (an animal could be said to have a mind if it possessed a sufficiently sophisticated nervous system), and functional criteria (behaviors that indicate the existence of a mind).

criterion A standard by means of which a judgment can be made; a test or score against which other tests, scores, or items are compared.

criterion analysis A special type of factor analysis of a deductive (hypothesis-testing) rather than inductive (exploratory) kind. See CLINICAL FACTOR ANALYSIS, FACTOR ANALYSIS.

criterion-based content analysis See STATEMENT VALIDITY ANALYSIS.

criterion behavior A response, aspect of behavior, score, or value that represents the standard or model used to evaluate other responses, types of behavior, scores, or values.

criterion contamination The effect of any element in a criterion that negatively affects the criterion as a valid measure; for example, if teachers use intelligence test scores in assigning grades, then grades are not a valid criterion for validating a new intelligence test since the criterion has been contaminated.

criterion cutoff The level of workplace performance above which the employee is considered satisfactory, below which, unsatisfactory.

criterion data Information obtained from a logical source to be used for generating a criterion that can be used for a variety of purposes such as evaluating job behavior (for example, in a large company with many secretaries, a standard of productivity may be established against which secretaries are evaluated).

criterion dimensions In industry, multiple criteria are used for evaluating employees' overall job performance. However, in fairness, criteria should be differentially weighted, for example, if servicing customers is more important than initial sales, then servicing should be weighted more highly than initial sales. See CRITERION INDEX.

criterion group A group tested for traits it is already known to possess, usually for the purpose of validating a test.

criterion index The summation of a number of scores for various elements of a job, some weighted differently from others, the sum indicating total satisfaction with a person's performance. See CRITERION DIMENSIONS.

criterion-referenced test An examination that uses an established score to judge performance, for example, a passing mark on a particular test might be 80% correct answers. Civil service tests are usually of this type. See NORM-REFERENCED TEST.

criterion score 1. A numerical index of quality or quantity that can be used for comparisons with other entities. 2. A predicted score based on some theory. Example: In learning to read by Method A, a particular level of reading ability is achieved, if another method, B, is said to be superior to Method A, the intended or expected score is the criterion score.

criterion validity An index of how well a test predicts a criterion; the ability of a test to predict behavior accurately. Also known as predictive validity.

critical 1. Characterizing a judgment that involves careful and unbiased examination of a literary, artistic, or scientific work. 2. Important, defining.

critical common sense The understanding and formulation of the experience of an unbiased intelligent person, who lacks technical knowledge or use of terms and concepts except those familiar to reasonably informed and inquiring individuals. See DISTRIBUTIVE ANALYSIS AND SYNTHESIS.

critical experiment A unitary research project intended to provide evidence for the validity of more than one theory or hypothesis.

critical flicker frequency (CFF or cff) The rate at which a periodic change, or flicker, of a visual stimulus fuses into a smooth, continuous stimulus. A similar phenomenon occurs with rapidly changing auditory stimuli. Also known as critical flicker fusion, critical fusion frequency.

critical-illumination level An optimal level of lighting above which no improvement in viewing occurs.

critical incidents (J. Flanagan) In industrial psychology, anecdotal reports of job behaviors that exemplify successful and unsuccessful work behavior.

critical level/score A score used as a dividing line between groups or categories: a passing score. Critical scores are often arbitrary, for example, in some jobs height and weight limits are established, thus someone 5 foot 5 1/2 inches might be rejected whereas someone 1/2 inch taller would be accepted. Also known as cut-off point/score, cutting score. See CRITERION-REFERENCED TEST.

critical path method In group dynamics, identifying the final goal and working backward to detail what must take place before it is achieved, what resources must be allocated, the timetable, and the allocation of responsibilities.

critical period A span of time during development in which the organism is sensitive to certain stimuli; for example, embryos are easily affected by harmful agents. Imprinting occurs usually during a short period after hatching for certain species of birds such as geese. Young humans appear to have a critical period for learning two or more languages simultaneously perfectly and without accents. See IMPRINTING, SENSITIVE PERIOD.

critical period hypothesis   A postulate that certain abilities, such as learning languages, are confined or maximized at certain time periods either for individuals or all members of a species. See IMPRINTING, SENSITIVE PERIOD.

critical point   A point in life, especially in reference to psychotherapy when people see the causes of their problems clearly and must decide on appropriate courses of action to deal with them.

critical ratio (CR or C.R.)   1. A measure to determine if the observed deviation is significantly greater than the random fluctuation about the average. Obtained by dividing the observed deviation by the standard deviation. 2. The difference between two statistics divided by their standard error. The critical ratio is used in tests of significance (for example, the difference between two means divided by the standard error of that difference). Formula for a critical ratio (CR) for uncorrelated means: $CR = (M_1 - M_2) \div (\sigma_{\mu 1}^2 + \sigma_{\mu 2}^2)^{1/2}$. Where M is the mean, σ is the standard error of the mean. [The difference is not regarded as significant unless the critical ratio is at least 3.] Also known as the standard error difference $\sigma_{diff} = (\sigma_{\mu i}^2 + \sigma_{\mu j}^2)^{1/2}$ where: μ is the mean, σ is the standard error of the mean. See STUDENT'S T TEST, T-DISTRIBUTIONS.

critical region   The area under a portion of a statistical curve within which the null hypothesis will be rejected.

critical thinking   1. Ability and willingness to assess claims critically and to make judgments on the basis of objective and supported reasons. 2. Directed mentation that includes such purposeful mental activities as examining the validity of a hypothesis, interpreting the meaning of a poem, or deciding whether a book is worth publishing.

critical value   A number above or below which a statistic is significant. In hypothesis testing, the value of the statistic that marks off the region of rejection of the null hypothesis.

critical variable   A variable that has powerful effects especially during a sensitive period.

criticism trap   An increase in the frequency of a negative behavior that often follows the use of criticism instead of a decrease in frequency as expected by the critic. See PUNISHMENT, SELF-CONFIDENCE.

criticizing faculty   (S. Freud) Self-criticisms inherent in individuals. An expression used by Sigmund Freud to characterize conscience, or the superego. Freud pointed out that healthy individuals may at times be severe with themselves, but that in depressives, the superego may become overcritical, abusive, reproachful, and humiliating toward the ego, or self.

critique   The systematic statement of a detailed criticism, that is, of an impartial examination of some theory.

Crocker-Henderson (odor) system   (E. Crocker) A classification of odors into four categories: acid, burnt, fragrant and caprylic or goaty (smelling like a goat). See HENNING ODOR PRISM, STEREOCHEMICAL SMELL SYSTEM, ZWAARDEMAKER SMELL SYSTEM.

Crocodile Man   Phrase applied to the forensically intriguing Charles Decker whose sudden murderous assaults had no apparent reason and did not seem to be in keeping with his personality. The defense argued that Decker suffered from a dysfunction or lesion of the limbic system that released impulses comparable to those of a crocodile. See ISOLATED EXPLOSIVE DISORDER.

crocodile tears   Refers to a false display of emotions. See BOGORAD'S SYNDROME.

Crô-Magnons   Possible precursor of *Homo sapiens*. Primitive humans represented by skulls found in various parts of western Europe, regarded as a representative of homo sapiens as contrasted with Neanderthals. Named for a hill in France where skulls were found in 1868.

Cronbach's alpha   (L. J. Cronbach) A measure of internal consistency test such that all the items elicit comparable responses.

crop milk   A fluid secreted in the crops of male and female doves, fed to offspring until they can feed independently.

cross adaptation   After repeated exposure to a particular stimulus, the adapted organism becomes less sensitive than ordinarily to other stimuli of a similar type. Sometimes known as cross-adaption.

cross addiction/tolerance   Ability of one drug to produce effects of another when the body has developed a tissue tolerance for effects of the first substance, for example, a person who has developed a dependence upon alcohol can substitute barbiturates to prevent withdrawal symptoms, and vice versa. Similarly, a cross tolerance can develop between mescaline and lysergic acid diethylamide (LSD) even though they have different molecular characteristics. See CROSS-DEPENDENCE OF HALLUCINOGENS.

cross breaks   In data analysis, display of dichotomous data in tables to show trends or to highlight similarities and differences. Also spelled crossbreaks.

cross-breeding   In plant and nonhuman animal propagation, a hybrid mating (one that mixes strains, as between a German Shepherd dog and a Chihuahua).

cross-categorical definitions   Clinical classification of people with learning and behavior disabilities on the basis of the problem's severity (such as mild, moderate, severe), rather than by traditional categories (mental retardation, learning disability, behavior disorder, etc.).

cross classification   Schema that uses more than one basis for grouping, so that an item may belong in more than one class, such as classifying subjects by gender and by age.

crosscoding   In psychosexual development, a conflict between any two aspects of sex or gender.

cross conditioning   Conditioning to a stimulus that is coincidental to an unconditioned stimulus, for example, a dog has been conditioned to salivate on hearing a bell ring. But on seeing someone approach the bell, the dog may start salivating. In cognitive human terms, the dog learns that the arrival of the person signals that the bell will be rung and food will follow next. However, if the person were continually present whether or not a bell rang, the arrival of the person would not lead to cross conditioning.

cross-correlation mechanism   The auditory mechanism that permits sound localization by an individual through the brief time difference required by sound to reach auditory nerves in both ears and summate effectively.

cross correspondence   In psychic research, messages in automatic writing by one medium interpreted by another medium.

cross-coupling effect   Corliolis illusion

cross-cousin   The offspring of a father's sister or mother's brother.

cross cuing   In split-brain patients, the use by one hemisphere of cues to detect information supposedly available only to the other, as in the use of auditory cues to identify an object not registering visually.

cross-cultural approach/method   The observation, study, or comparison of specific practices or behavioral patterns in different cultures, for example, the comparison of diverse sexual patterns, child-rearing practices, or working relationships in different cultures. Such comparison may show the specific dynamic effects upon behavior of particular environmental stimuli.

cross-cultural counseling   A process of understanding and advising people of a particular culture about a different culture they are either going into or are already in. Also called multicultural counseling. See CROSS-CULTURAL PSYCHIATRY, CROSS-CULTURAL PSYCHOLOGY, CROSS-CULTURAL TREATMENT.

cross-cultural psychiatry   The comparative study of mental illness and mental health among various societies around the world, including data on the incidence of disorders and variations in symptomatology. Also known as comparative psychiatry, cultural psychiatry, ethnopsychiatry, transcultural psychiatry. See CULTURE-SPECIFIC SYNDROMES.

cross-cultural psychology   The study of overt (behavioral) and covert (cognitive, affective, and conative) differences between different cultures. Usually the culture studied is compared with the culture from which the researchers came from, for example, few if any such researchers come from Indonesia to research in the United States or other cultures, but many go to Borneo from other countries. See ANTHROPOLOGY.

cross-cultural research   Systematic analysis, description and comparisons of various societies in an attempt to identify significant principles that may account for their similarities and differences.

cross-cultural testing   Evaluations of individuals with diverse cultural backgrounds in relation to a dominant culture. Culture-fair tests are nonverbal in instructions and content, avoid objects indigenous to a particular culture, and usually deemphasize speed. Examples include: Goodenough-Harris Drawing Test, Leiter International Performance Test, Porteus Maze Test, Raven Progressive Matrices Test. See CULTURE-FAIR TESTS, CULTURE-FREE TESTS.

cross-cultural treatment   (P. Pedersen) The attempts at counseling, advise-giving, information, and even therapy transacted by individuals of different cultures. Special difficulties may occur due to different value systems of the counselor and the counselee. See TRIANGULAR COUNSELING.

cross-dependence of hallucinogens   A temporary tolerance effect that develops in the use of alkylamine-derived psychedelic drugs, for example, a user of lysergic acid diethylamide (LSD), a substituted indole alkylamine, tends to have tolerance for mescaline, a substituted phenyl alkylamine. A similar kind of cross-dependence occurs in users of barbiturates and other sedatives. See HALLUCINOGENS.

cross-dressing   The process or habit of putting on the clothes of the opposite sex: (a) by males or females in using clothes of the opposite sex with the purpose of achieving sexual excitement (fetishistic cross dressing); (b) as part of a performance in which men or women are mimicked by members of the opposite sex; (c) as an attempt at transformation (transsexualism). See TRANSVESTISM, TRANSVESTITISM.

crossed aphasia   Aphasia whether to right- or left-handed people, with the injury on the right side of the brain rather than in the usual left side (Broca's area) of the brain.

crossed dominance   A tendency for some right-handed persons to have a dominant left eye, and vice versa for the left-handed.

crossed-extension reflex   A reflexive action by a contralateral limb to compensate for loss of support by an injured limb. The reflex, which helps shift the burden of body weight, also is associated with the coordination of legs in walking by flexing muscles on the left side when those on the right are extending, and vice versa.

crossed-nerve experiments   Research on the transfer of nerves in mammals to different muscles, the muscles then acting as would those to which the nerves were originally connected, for example, when nerves to leg muscles are crossed, the animal extends its leg when it should flex it, and vice versa.

crossed perception   See SYNESTHESIA.

crossed reflex   A response which occurs on the opposite side of the body from that on which the stimulus is applied.

crossed transactions   In transactional analysis, interactions that result in interpersonal conflict or a breakdown in interpersonal communication.

cross education   The positive transfer of a skill acquired by one part of the body to another part (usually from practices from the preferred hand to the unpracticed hand).

cross-elasticity of demand   In consumer psychology, the situation of products that consumers switch between, depending on the relative prices.

cross-eye   Slang for a squint or strabismus in which there is a deviation of one or both eyes toward the center. Also known as convergent strabismus, esotropia.

cross-fostering   In comparative psychology, a technique for investigating the effect of genetic factors in the development of a disorder by having offspring of biological parents considered "normal" reared by adopting parents who manifest the disorder being studied, or having offspring of parents with the disorder reared by "normal" adopting parents. Offspring cross-fostered in this manner are called index adoptees. See CONTROL ADOPTEES.

cross-gender behavior The process or habit of assuming the role of the opposite gender by adopting the clothes, hair design, manner of speaking and gesturing that society considers characteristic of the opposite sex. See CROSS-DRESSING.

crossing See SPONTANEOUS VARIATION.

crossing over 1. In meiosis, the twisting of a pair of chromosomes during which individual genes in a chromosome cross over to the opposite chromosome. Two homologous chromosomes interchange parts with a corresponding interchange of genes. As a result of this exchange of genes, the final cell division that produces reproductive cells may contain genes from both chromosomes of a pair, increasing the random assortment of genes in offspring. See RECOMBINATION. 2. Assuming the racial or naturalization identity of another kind, such as an Albanian claiming to be an Italian.

cross-lagged panel correlation Testing the same group of subjects a number of times at varying periods, such as following a group of students from the first grade to the end of high school, checking annually for the correlation between tests of general intelligence and school grades. This technique attempts to let researchers draw tentative conclusions about causality within the framework of correlational data. See PARTIAL CORRELATIONS, STRUCTURAL MODELING.

cross-lagged panel design A research design to determine the causal relationship between two variables through collecting correlational data on the variables at two separate times.

cross-linkage theory of aging See EVERSION THEORY OF AGING.

cross-modal association The coordination of sensory inputs involving both cerebral hemispheres. Usually required in matching tasks that involve auditory and visual, tactual and visual, or a similar combination of cognitive functions. Lesions in temporal, parietal, or occipital lobes may be diagnosed by means of cross-modal association testing.

cross-modal perception/transfer The transfer of information from one sensory source into an association area where it can be integrated with information from another sensory source. Such transfer is required in tasks that coordinate two or more sensory-motor activities, such as playing a musical instrument according to the pattern of notes on a page of sheet music. Also known as intersensory perception.

cross-modality matching (S. S. Stevens) In psychophysics, a method of scaling stimuli in which the magnitude of a given stimulus is matched to the magnitude of another well-established stimulus. See SCALING TECHNIQUE.

cross modality transfer The exchange of information from one sense to another, for example, feeling an object by touch, and then selecting the same object from among others by sight.

cross-out tests A method of test construction in which the participant responds by crossing out an extra, incorrect, irrelevant or undesirable element in a series of elements.

crossover (in genetics) See CROSSING OVER (meaning 1).

crossover design An experimental procedure in which a treatment is introduced and withdrawn, and often introduced and withdrawn again, with assessment of behavior before and after each of these treatments. Also known as reversal design.

crossover effect The phenomenon of two entities growing or developing with one being faster or larger than the other and then the slower or smaller one passing the first, such as in a set of twins, one is taller up to a certain age, and then the shorter surpasses the other in height.

cross-parental identification A strong emotional attachment for a parent of the opposite sex. See ELECTRA COMPLEX, OEDIPUS COMPLEX.

cross-sectional (analysis) method A research approach to the relationship between variables, such as age and intelligence, using two or more groups available simultaneously or a systematic investigation of samples of behavior at different ages, comparing one sample with another.

cross-sectional design A research design in which groups of individuals differing in age, sex, etc., are compared at the same moment in time.

cross-sectional method/study A research design that studies groups that differ in age. The groups are seen usually at the same time. Differences between the groups are attributed to age differences. This method does not study development or changes over time. Compare LONGITUDINAL STUDY.

cross-sectional sampling Samples selected from different groups, such as age or location. See STRATEGIC SAMPLING.

cross-sectional sequences (P. Baltes) A bifactorial model design in which at least two independent cross-sectional age samples are drawn at each cohort level.

cross sequential A design in developmental research that separates the time of measurement and cohort effects, where age is confounded.

cross-sequential design (K. W. Schaie) Samples drawn from two or more birth cohorts are assessed at two or more equivalent times of measurement. Each cohort may be measured repeatedly, or independent random samples can be drawn from each cohort on successive measurement occasions. Design permits simultaneous estimation of time-of-measurement changes and cohort differences, assuming chronological age effects are trivial or of no interest.

cross-sequential method/technique A study design or procedure in research that combines cross-sectional and longitudinal techniques by assessing people in a cross-sectional sample more than once.

cross-sequential study The testing of different age groups (or other groups) at different time periods.

cross-situation consistency The extent to which an individual behaves in a similar fashion across different contexts or situations.

cross tabulations Arrangement of data in tables to show the influence of one or more variables.

cross-transfer   A tendency to have an easier time at a task using a particular limb (for example, the left arm) when the task has already been performed using the opposite limb (the right arm), in comparison with learning to perform a task that has never been attempted before. Thus, it will take less time to learn to swing a tennis racquet proficiently with the left hand if the person already knows how to swing the racquet with the right hand than if the person had never swung a racquet before. See CROSS EDUCATION.

cross-validate   The computation of a validity statistic with two random halves of the data.

cross validation   The process of reestablishing a test's validity on a new sample, to check the correctness of the initial validation. Cross validation is necessary because chance and other factors may have inflated or biased the original validation.

crowd   A temporary aggregation of individuals all attending and responding in a similar manner to some object of common attraction, their responses being simple, prepotent, and often emotional in nature.

crowd behavior   The characteristic behavior of an unorganized group of people who congregate temporarily when their attention is focused on the same object or event. Typically, an audience may smile, laugh, or applaud; a crowd on New Year's Eve is likely to shout and sing; and a mob may perform violent actions such as rioting and lynching. See COLLECTIVE BEHAVIOR, CROWD CONSCIOUSNESS, MASS HYSTERIA, MOB, MOB PSYCHOLOGY.

crowd consciousness   (G. Le Bon) The mentality of a crowd or mob. Mobs are usually distinguished from crowds by their activity, irrationality, and potential for violence. See CROWD BEHAVIOR.

crowd fear   See DEMOPHOBIA.

crowding   Tension produced in environments of high population density. See CROWDING AND ANIMAL BEHAVIOR.

crowding (in testing or learning)   A situation in testing or learning assignments when too many items or tasks exist for the time allowed, such as an exam requiring the student to respond to 20 in-depth essay questions in one hour.

crowding and animal behavior   (J. B. Calhoun) A small group of rats was established in a delimited area. Although the animals had unlimited food and water, when the population came to a certain point, it remained stable. Females did not conceive, young rats were killed by adults, etc. In short, the rats themselves adjusted for the number of rats in the given area.

crowd mind (hypothesis)   A postulate that all individuals will be of the same mind when as a group they experience a certain event.

crowd psychology   1. That branch of social psychology or sociology which treats crowds or mobs as agents, behaving units, or phenomena. 2. The psychology of individuals acting in crowd situations.

crucial experiment   An empirical experiment intended to settle a disputed hypothesis. There have been few such experiments in psychology, since most results raise new questions. Also known as crucial research/test.

crude range   range

crude score   A raw score.

CRUMBS   An acronym for Continuous, Remote, Unobtrusive Monitor of Behavior used for evaluation of degree of improvement in rehabilitation efforts.

crura cerebri   Left and right nerve tracts constituting the ventral portion of the midbrain; they lie below the corpora quadrigemina and extend from the medulla beneath the pons to the hemispheres. Also known as crus cerebri, pedunculi cerebri. See CEREBRAL PEDUNCLES.

crus communes   Part of the superior semicircular canal of the inner ear that joins with the posterior semicircular canal to form a common passageway into the vestibule of the bony labyrinths.

crux   In scientific theory and methodology, a factual situation whereby competing hypotheses may be so brought into opposition that a decision between them may be reached.

crying   Weeping, shedding tears, sobbing, a behavior elicited by a variety of experiences and needs: loss, frustration, defeat, pain, shame, or a need for help. Crying may also be employed consciously or unconsciously, for secondary gain (sympathy, power over others). Some people may cry for joy or while laughing.

crying-cat syndrome   A phrase synonymous with the French *cri du chat* syndrome.

cryophobia   Fear of ice or frost. See PSYCHROPHOBIA.

cryotherapy   An experimental method used to try to "shock" people with mental disorders into normality. The reduction of body temperature to about 15 degrees lower than normal, usually by wrapping up a person in a sheet with ice cubes around the body, has been attempted with uncertain results. See EXPERIMENTAL TREATMENTS.

crypsis   Animal protection through camouflage. Cryptic animals blend in with the background (especially when stationary) through their shape, color, or patterning.

crypt(a)esthesia   The experience of clairvoyance, clairaudience, or similar forms of paranormal cognition that cannot be associated with any known sensory stimulus. Also known as cryptesthesia. See CLAIRVOYANCE, EXTRA SENSORY PERCEPTION, PSYCHICS.

cryptarithmetic   (F. C. Bartlett, A. Newell & H. A. Simon) A much-studied problem-solving task that substitutes digits for letters in an array in such a way that when the substitution is complete the resulting digit array is an arithmetic problem and its solution.

cryptogenic epilepsy   Epilepsy with no known causes. See IDIOPATHIC EPILEPSY.

cryptogram   A coded, enciphered, secret arrangement of words or letters in a message.

cryptomnesia   1. The unconscious production of information read, heard, or seen at any earlier period of time and then forgotten. 2. A trick played by the mind, thinking of a concept that appears to be new, such as an idea, but actually it is a forgotten memory. See CREATIVITY.

cryptophoric symbolism   (R. Kopp) Indirect or hidden representation; a pictorial representation based on a metaphor, such as "He is like a stone wall." (Indicating someone who cannot be swayed by words). "They are like lambs." (Referring to people who are easily led.) See METAPHOR THERAPY.

cryptorch(id)ism A condition of males characterized by one or both testes failing to descend into the scrotum.

crysta See CRISTA AMPULLARIS.

crystal See ICE, METHAMPHETAMINE.

crystal gazing A technique in which a person, sometimes hypnotized, is instructed to visualize significant experiences, or produce associations, while staring into a glass ball, light bulb, or mirror. Used also by mediums to produce what they claim to be extrasensory perception of events in the lives of their clients. Also known as scrying.

crystal healing A method of healing based on the concept that natural quartz crystals retain energy and provide vibrations that are transferred to the body and help a patient to relax, heal illness, and attain higher levels of consciousness. The patient either looks at the crystals or they are placed on the patient's body. See UNCONVENTIONAL THERAPIES.

crystallization 1. The process of assuming definite form, in personal attitudes, values, or goals. 2. The emergence of a career direction or the decision to enter a given field. Typically occurs during adolescence, based on a realistic examination of career options dependent on individual interest, abilities, and educational opportunities. See EXPLORATION, FANTASY PERIOD.

crystallized abilities Competence or capacity in mental acts such as vocabulary, mechanical knowledge, and logical reasoning, due to learning and experience. See FLUID ABILITIES.

crystallized intelligence (R. B. Cattell) The second general factor in primary abilities, acquired from investment of fluid intelligence in experience.

crystallophobia Morbid fear of glass. Also known as hyalophobia.

Cs See CONSCIOUS (meaning 2).

CS conditioned stimulus

CSAT Center for Substance Abuse Treatment

C scale (J. P. Guilford) A scale of eleven units. The mean is 5.0 and the standard deviation is 2.0. See T SCORE.

CSE Certificate of Secondary Education

CSF 1. contrast sensitivity function 2. cerebrospinal fluid

CSPDT Crawford Small Parts Dexterity Test

CSQ Coping Strategies Questionnaire

CT conduction time

CTA combined transcortical aphasia

C Test See RCAF CLASSIFICATION TEST.

CTMM California Test of Mental Maturity

CTP See CALIFORNIA TEST OF PERSONALITY.

CTS carpal tunnel syndrome

C type One of the two personality types differentiated by Hermann Rorschach, based on the ratio of human movement responses (M) to color responses (C). According to Rorschach, color responses are more numerous than movement responses, and indicate among other things a personality with lower imaginative intelligence, and greater instability of emotions than the M type.

cube model (H. H. Kelley) In social psychology, a three-dimensional theory holding that people formulate attributions by considering the covariation of an effect and its possible causes across objects (distinctiveness), time (consistency), and people (consensus).

cubic difference tone A subjective tone perceived when two tones are presented to the ear that differ in frequency by 20% or less.

cuckoo theory See ORIGIN-OF-LANGUAGE.

cuddling behavior Attachment behavior initiated by the primary caretaker or sometimes by the child as a means of allaying feelings of fear, fatigue, or strangeness. "Noncuddlers" are not necessarily detached, but may be so active that they resist close and confining physical contact. May connote a genetic deficiency, such as autism.

cue 1. A signal received by an organism that leads it to respond in a particular manner. 2. A stimulus that provides information concerning an appropriate response.

cue-dependent forgetting Inability to remember information because appropriate retrieval cues are lacking; cues present during learning are not present during recall.

cued recall Operations or prompting by a person to help another person remember something, as in drama rehearsals: an actor forgets the dialog, and the director begins the forgotten statement to help the actor recall the dialog. See CUE, RECALL.

cued speech Communication by persons with hearing loss combining hand gestures with lipreading.

cued speech technique A method of teaching lip reading to the deaf and hearing-impaired by use of eight hand signals in four positions close to the mouth that signal phonetic signs.

cue overload principle (D. D. Watkins) A theory that there are a limited number of items that can be associated with a cue before it starts to lose its effectiveness; the more items that are connected with a cue, the less effective the cue will be in eliciting the item sought.

cue reduction The ability of a portion of a stimulus to elicit a total response, for example, a hungry person may salivate when smelling the odor of roasting meat or seeing the chef going into the kitchen—knowing that food will soon be on the table. See MINIMAL CUE, REDUCED CUE.

cue reversal A stimulus that has changed from a response to a nonresponse for any organism, or vice versa.

cues to localization In audition, cues that indicate the source of a sound. They may include intensity (greater in the ear nearer the source), phase (more easily detectable at frequencies below 800 Hertz), and the delay between the arrival of the sound at one ear and the other.

cul-de-sac A dead end, as in a maze. Also known as blind alley.

culminating incident In labor relations, an employee's error or fault that would not ordinarily justify a severe penalty, but that does, in light of the past poor record of the employee.

culpability A judgment of moral delinquency formulated with respect to one individual by another or by the social group.

cult   cult(us)

cult of personality   A group of individuals bound together by devotion to a charismatic political, religious, literary, or other leader. Also known as personality cult.

cult of the aged   Refers to the Colonial period in America during which it was considered acceptable and positive to be old. The aged were viewed with respect and occupied places of honor, prestige, and leadership in both business and society. This point of view has a long history in many traditional societies, where the old are honored and respected.

cult of the young   Refers to the period of the 1960s in America when being young was considered good and positive, and being old was considered bad and negative. Such a view is still somewhat prevalent in the United States and has gained influence in many westernized societies.

cultural absolutism   The primarily Western secular belief that values, concepts, and achievements of diverse cultures can be understood and judged according to a universal standard. This idea was promoted by 19th century anthropologists, such as Clyde Levi-Strauss. In psychology, this is the belief that a theory developed in one culture has equal validity in a different cultural setting. See CATEGORICAL IMPERATIVE, CULTURAL RELATIVISM, MALUM IN SE, MALUM IN RES.

cultural adaptability   An ability of individuals or groups to adapt to the culture of a new community to which they have migrated.

cultural anthropology   The study of societies, their ways of thinking and acting; their beliefs, values, ceremonies, customs and whatever else that differentiates them from other societies. See ANTHROPOLOGY.

cultural area   A geographical region in which all tribes have similar patterns of culture. Also known as culture area, diffusion area.

cultural assimilation   1. The learning and adoption of customs of another culture to merge with that culture. 2. See ACCULTURATION.

cultural test bias   The effect of culture on test-taking ability that will unfairly either lower or raise scores of respondents from particular populations relative to the test norms.

cultural competency   (S. Sue) Ability of people to appreciate and recognize differences in values and behavioral schemas among cultural groups and to adaptively moderate their behavior when interacting with members of such cultures. See PREJUDICE.

cultural complexity   (H. Triandis) A culture whose constituent elements, such as social structure, political stratification, educational, aesthetic, religious and economic institutions (for example, 2500 instead of 20 job definitions) are numerous, diverse, and organized into complex patterns (for example, as found in information societies).

cultural conserve   (J. L. Moreno) That which maintains and preserves cultural memories, findings, ideas, inventions, concepts, for example, folk tales, traditions, histories.

cultural content   See PSYCHOCULTURAL STRESS.

cultural deprivation   Lack of opportunity to participate in the culture of the larger society due to such factors as economic deprivation, substandard living conditions, or discrimination. See CULTURALLY DEPRIVED, PSEUDORETARDATION.

cultural determinism   (A. Marsella) A doctrine positing that character is largely influenced by culture, the combined features of a given society's economic, social, political, and religious organization. Suggests that environment influences personality to a greater extent than do hereditary factors. See DETERMINISM, SOCIAL DETERMINISM, SOFT DETERMINISM.

cultural disorganization   Changes within a particular cultural group due to any of a variety of situations. The dissolution of certain cultural values and practices as a result of various interfering factors such as introduction of new ideas from outside the culture, especially those brought in by younger members of the culture who may have the most contact with different values.

cultural drift   Changes in folkways of society over time, often due to factors such as the effect of art and technology on the society.

cultural epoch theory   A point of view that due to universal causes, groups of humans tend to pass through the same type of culture (that is, organized social behavior) in the same order, such as hunting, pastoral, agricultural, industrial, and informational cultures. Also known as culture epoch theory, monotypic evolution theory, unilinear theory of cultural evolution. See RECAPITULATION THEORY.

cultural ergonomics   (M. Kaplan) Cultural influences on human factors research and practice, such as social determinants of risk perception, crew training, and safety standards.

cultural ethics   Prevailing attitudes and values of a society at any point in time that determine how individuals view what is morally right and wrong and their relationships with others and society. See POLITICAL CORRECTNESS.

cultural-familial mental retardation   Pertaining to mental retardation that develops in the absence of any determinable organic cause and is thus attributed to hereditary or environmental factors.

cultural feminism   A version of feminism that works to build a woman-centered culture.

cultural genocide   genocide (meaning 3)

cultural heritage   1. The corpus of concepts, beliefs, myths, values, knowledge, formal and functional behaviors that newborns find awaiting them in the environment. 2. A society's continually evolving reservoir of accumulated knowledge that each subsequent generation uses and extends. What any individual entering life finds waiting. What a person has to deal with in relating to a new culture.

cultural homicide   The destruction of a culture.

cultural island   A cohort group within another larger group having customs, traditions, values, and language distinct from the larger group. Such groups are generally found within first and second generation immigrant populations of most large cities. See COHORT(S).

culturalists   Theoretical therapists who are not content with primary emphasis on the individual, who prefer instead to look at the overall social context in dealing with personality, for example, Alfred Adler, Karen Horney, Paul Pedersen, and Erich Fromm. See NEO-FREUDIAN, RADICAL PSYCHOTHERAPY.

cultural items   Test questions that cannot be correctly answered unless the participant is sufficiently familiar with their cultural or subcultural meanings. They constitute bias in favor of the group or social class from whose experience they are drawn. See BITCH TEST, CULTURE-FAIR TESTS.

cultural lag   A tendency of some aspects of a culture to change at a slower rate than others, resulting in a retention of dated or obsolete beliefs, customs, and values mixed with newer ones. The persistence of slavery in the United States for more than 80 years after the Declaration of Independence is an example.

culturally deprived   Refers usually to immigrants and members of minority groups whose early family and social environment amount to inadequate preparation for successful social adjustment, especially academically. Such deprivation may have physical, social, intellectual, and emotional consequences. See CULTURAL DEPRIVATION, CULTURALLY DISADVANTAGED.

culturally different   Members of immigrant families, minority groups or subcultures that differ substantially from the larger society and who are frequently economically disadvantaged. See CULTURALLY DEPRIVED.

culturally disadvantaged children   Children whose parents (such as some immigrants) either do not know or who reject the tenets of the dominant culture, and thus their children are deprived of experiences that can affect their social and intellectual development. Overall, they have problems of allegiances to their parents' cultural values and to those of the greater society. See CULTURALLY DEPRIVED, SIX-HOUR RETARDED CHILD.

cultural parallelism   In anthropology, the development of analogous cultural patterns, such as sun worship, in geographically separate groups assumed to have had no communication with each other.

cultural pluralism   The intermixture of members of various cultural subgroups, each maintaining its own identity and traditions. Compare MULTICULTURALISM.

cultural pressure factor   (R. B. Cattell) The impact of cultural complexity upon unchanging genetic populations. It increased in the United States, Britain, and Australia uniformly through the nineteenth century.

cultural process   The vertical process by which ethnic and social values are transmitted through subsequent generations and modified by prevailing influences in each generation. See CULTURAL TRANSMISSION.

cultural relativism   A doctrine positing that attitudes, beliefs, values, concepts, and achievements must be understood in light of specific cultural milieux and social contexts and not judged according to another culture's standards. In psychology, this position questions the universal application of psychological techniques or insights since theories developed in one culture may not apply to another. Proponents hold that no culture should be typified as primitive or inferior; critics contend that practices such as human sacrifice, cannibalism, genocide, and genital mutilation, whether sanctioned by sacred writings or secular tradition, are inherently wrong. See CULTURAL ABSOLUTISM.

cultural residue   The existence of customs long after they have lost their value and meaning; the results of cultural lag.

cultural sadism   The acceptance of male aggression, violence, and sadism as normal or biologically driven.

cultural science psychology   Psychology that is interpretive rather than explanatory, more like literature than chemistry.

cultural sensitivity   Realization of the importance of concepts, traditions, and ways of living of people of different cultures.

cultural shock   Mental stress associated with assimilation into a new culture vastly different from that in which the person was brought up, stress that many immigrants experience. See CULTURE SHOCK.

cultural simplicity   (H. Triandis) A culture whose constituent elements, such as social structures, political stratification, educational, aesthetic, religious and economic institutions, are simply organized (for example, as found among hunter/gatherer societies).

cultural syndrome   (H. Triandis) A pattern of attitudes, beliefs, self-definitions, role definitions, norms, and values organized around a central theme, that is shared among those who live in a geographic region, who speak a particular language, during a historic period. See CULTURE.

cultural transmission   The processes by which customs, beliefs, rites, and knowledge are imparted to successive generations as well as to people moving into new cultures. It is vertical in nature when the customs, etc., are passed on by older individuals to younger ones and horizontal in nature when information is taught by an established majority group to a minority immigrant group. See CULTURAL PROCESS.

cultural universal theory   A point of view that all children, regardless of culture, develop in an identical manner up to a certain point in their development.

culture   1. The distinctive customs, manners, values, religious behavior, and other social and intellectual aspects of a society. 2. A shared pattern of attitudes, beliefs, self-definitions, role definitions, norms, and values that can be found in a geographic region among those who speak a particular language, or during a particular historic period. See CONFIGURATIVE CULTURE, COUNTERCULTURE, POSTFIGURATIVE CULTURE, PREFIGURATIVE CULTURE, YOUTH CULTURE.

culture-bias theory   A point of view that certain tests, especially intelligence tests, favor various cultural groups and so are biased against persons from cultures other than the culture on which the tests were standardized.

culture bound   The acceptance of only one's own customs as natural and normal.

culture-bound syndromes   Old phrase for culture-specific syndromes.

culture change   The observed tendency of culture traits to alter, in both form and content, in the course of time.

culture clash   A conflict between two sets of beliefs, values, and traditions; for example, in culture A, physicians inform patients when their condition is fatal; in culture B this is never done. A family of culture B would be distressed if a member of their family were being treated by a doctor of culture A who wanted to inform the patient of impending death.

culture complex   In a specific culture, the activities, beliefs, rites, and traditions that distinguish life in that culture, for example, the ceremonies, folklore, songs, and stories associated with the hunting and use of the buffalo by Native Americans.

culture conflict   1. Clashing or opposing loyalties experienced by immigrants. 2. Competition or antagonism between neighboring but different cultures. Problems arising when social groups of varying cultures live in close contact as in "melting pots," when the practices of one group infringe on or interfere with the values of another group. See CULTURALLY DISADVANTAGED CHILDREN, INTERGROUP CULTURE CONFLICT, INTERNAL CULTURE CONFLICT.

culture determination   The process by which culture directs and limits the development of behavior patterns in the individual.

culture epochs   The successive stages in the growth of culture in the history of a given human group.

culture-epochs theory   1. An outmoded assumption that there is a typical evolution in human culture which all societies follow, for example, evolving from hunting and gathering to pastoral to agricultural. 2. An outmoded idea that all children pass through cultural stages, phases, or levels of mental development typical of their "race," and so education should be organized around such phases. See PHYLOGENETIC THEORY, RECAPITULATION THEORY.

culture-fair intelligence test (CFIT)   A mental-ability test designed to be "free" of cultural influences. Unlike the standard intelligence tests, which reflect predominantly middle-class experience, such tests are designed to apply across social lines and to permit fair comparisons between people from different cultures. Studies have shown, however, that even these items may be culture bound. See CROSS-CULTURAL TESTING, INTELLIGENCE QUOTIENT, SIX-HOUR RETARDED CHILD.

culture-fair test   An examination relatively free of special cultural influences, especially those of the test designer and administrator. Often nonverbal, as culture is connected with language. Some are designed for participants with impairments of hearing, vision, or body control, and for speakers of various languages. Compare CULTURAL ITEMS. See CROSS-CULTURAL TESTING, CULTURE-FAIR INTELLIGENCE TESTS, INTELLIGENCE QUOTIENT, KOHS BLOCK DESIGN TEST, O'CONNOR WIGGLY BLOCK.

culture-free intelligence test (CFIT)   A mental-ability test designed to eliminate cultural biases by constructing items that contain no factors or elements that favor any specific culture. (The creation of such a test is probably impossible.) See CULTURE-FAIR TESTS, PORTEUS MAZE TEST.

culture-free tests   1. (F. Galton) Tests that attempt to measure innate abilities not affected by culture. Tests measuring physiological factors, such as hand-grip strength, acuity of hearing or vision, have traditionally not correlated well with psychological factors such as intelligence or personality. 2. Examinations designed to eliminate cultural biases. Test items avoid factors or elements that favor any specific culture. Such tests probably do not exist except in theory, although examples of tests that appear to come close to the idea are maze tests and block design tests. See CULTURE-FAIR TESTS.

culture hero   A legendary superior human, revered for deeds, the subject of hero-worship and myths. Carl Jung saw similar patterns in which these heroes exist in most cultures. He referred to such figures as "archetypes." Examples include Hercules, Joan of Arc, William Tell, Sitting Bull, Robin Hood, Muhammad Ali, and Martin Luther King.

culture set   An established attitudinal propensity that leads a person to accept as valid certain cultural forms and to reject others.

culture shock   Feelings of inner tension or conflict experienced by an individual or group who has been suddenly thrust into an alien culture or who experiences divided loyalties to two different cultures. See CULTURAL SHOCK.

culture-specific psychological motives   See PSYCHOLOGICAL MOTIVES.

culture-specific syndromes   (A. Marsella) Mental disorders peculiar to an ethnic or cultural population. It has been suggested that all disorders are "culture-specific" since it may be impossible for any disorder to escape cultural influence and determination. Because there are hundreds of "culture-specific" disorders that are not part of the DSM-IV, some Western nosologists and researchers have suggested that these disorders can be grouped according to (a) fear reactions, (b) rage reactions, (c) phobic reactions, and (d) dissociation states and reactions. It should be remembered that all disorders may ultimately reflect the standards of normality–abnormality for a cultural group. What is abnormal in one society may not be abnormal in another. Also known as culture-bound syndromes. See AMOK, AMURAKH, ARCTIC HYSTERIA, BANGUNGUT, BERSERK, BUFFÉE DÉLIRANTE, DELAHARA, ECHUL, IMU, HSIEH-PING, JUMPING FRENCHMEN OF MAINE SYNDROME, JURAMENTADO, KIMILUE, KORO, LATAH, MALGRI, MENERIK, MIRYACHIT, NEGI-NEGI, PA-LING, PIBLOKTOQ, PIBLOKTO, PSEUDOAMOK SYNDROME, PUERTO RICAN SYNDROME, SHINKEISHITSU, SUSTO, TOURETTE'S DISORDER, TROPENKOLLER, VOODOO DEATH, WINDIGO.

culture trait   A relatively indivisible unit of tribal culture or tradition, such as fire-making procedures, forms of marriage, specific customs, or taboos.

cult(us)   1. A specific complex of beliefs, rites, and ceremonies held by a social group in association with some person (usually considered charismatic) or object (usually considered magical). 2. The group of persons associated with such beliefs, usually not considered mainstream, and often the term is used derogatorily for groups of persons (fanatically) committed to a certain belief. 3. A group of people who view some individual, usually a charismatic leader, or object with feelings of veneration and who operate in some ritual manner with each other and toward the object of their devotion. The groups usually call for the separation from or abandonment of family and friends, generating a condition of social isolation so that the cult may become "everything" to the person. See DOGMA.

cum   1. Slang for semen. 2. Slang for orgasm, alternately spelled "come."

cumulative   Pertaining to progressive increase by successive additions of new data, more terms, etc.

cumulative curve   cumulative (response) curve

cumulative distribution   cumulative (frequency) distribution

cumulative educational advantage   (J. Stanley) Positively accelerated learning within educational settings augmented by tutoring and apprenticeships with mentors.

cumulative (frequency) distribution   A distribution in which each score value, X, is plotted against the frequency of all the scores having a value less than or equal to X. A cumulative frequency is sometimes abbreviated C_f. See CONVERGENT PRODUCTION, GROWTH CURVE, LEARNING CURVE, OGIVE, PRACTICE CURVE, S CURVE.

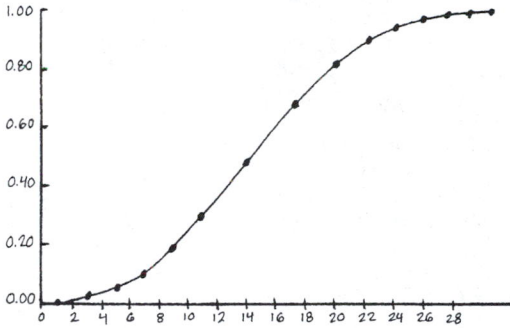

cumulative (frequency) distribution

cumulative probability distribution   A distribution that denotes the probability of a random sample being less or equal to any given possible value.

cumulative record   A chart whose horizontal plane refers to passage of time and whose vertical plane is the total number of responses up to particular times. The slope of the record indicates the rate of responding. See CONCAVE LEARNING CURVE, CONVEX LEARNING CURVE, STRAIGHT LINE LEARNING CURVE for explanations.

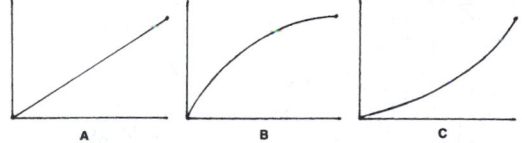

cumulative record   Cumulative record A, a straight curve shows a steady and predictable gain over time. Record B, a convex curve shows an initial rapid gain over time, but slows down as it approaches its limit (asymptote) while Record C, a concave curve shows that it is also reaching its limit.

cumulative recorder   An electrically driven roller with a pen that records each response (lever press or key peck) by moving a short distance at right angles to the movement of the paper. The steeper the slope of the record the higher the rate of responding. See REINFORCEMENT SCHEDULES for an illustration of what such records look like.

cumulative (response) curve   A method of measuring responses, widely used in operant conditioning, in which each response raises a pen up one unit along a moving sheet of paper. Lack of response, therefore, is indicated graphically by a flat horizontal line, while faster responses are indicated by steeper slopes away from the horizontal. See CUMULATIVE RECORD for an illustration of three different types of curves.

cumulative scale   An attitude scale in which a positive response to one item indicates agreement with all items lower in the scale. Also known as Guttman scale, scalogram.

cumulative test   A type of test that measures abilities and traits that can be expected to increase with age. Scoring is usually done by establishing a criterion and determining the subject's deviation from it.

cuneate funiculus   Dorsal-column tract that carries epicritic touch (A) fibers from the skin and deep tissues to the cuneate nuclei. See A FIBER.

cuneate nuclei   Dorsal-column nuclei located in the medulla and are the terminal point for tracts carrying fibers from the skin and deep tissues of the upper body and arms. See DORSAL COLUMNS, FASCICULUS CUNEATUS, GRACILE NUCLEUS.

cuneus   The triangular lobe on the inner surface of the cerebral hemisphere (at the extreme back of the head) behind the parieto-occipital and above the calcarine fissure. Plural is cunei.

cunnilinctus   cunnilingus

cunnilingus   Stimulation of the external female genital organs (vulva, clitoris) with the mouth or tongue. Also known as cunnilinctus.

cupula cristae ampullaris   A gelatinous flap that fits over the ampulla at the end of a semicircular canal. Contains the crysta, with hair cells that monitor the sense of balance. See AMPULLA, CRISTA AMPULLARIS.

curative-factors model (in groups)   (I. Yalom) Elements in group settings that facilitate personal growth and adjustment. These include imparting information, imitation, interpersonal learning, and group cohesiveness.

curiosity   The impulse to investigate, observe, or gather information, particularly when the material is novel or interesting. It appears spontaneously in animals and in young children, who inspect, bite, handle, taste, or smell practically everything in the immediate environment (sensory exploration and motor manipulation). Curiosity is a prime method for learning and takes the form of asking myriad questions from the nursery-school period onward. Because of its early appearance, many psychologists conclude it is an inborn, unlearned drive. Also known as investigatory tendency. See EXPLORATION DRIVE, MANIPULATORY DRIVE, QUESTION STAGE, SEXUAL CURIOSITY.

curiosity instinct   A tendency for many organisms to explore their surroundings. In humans, a tendency for young children to want to touch and taste things, the attraction to new sights and sounds. The existence of instincts, however, especially in humans, has been questioned by many psychologists. See EPISTEMOPHILIA.

Currens formula   A 1961 ruling by the Third Circuit Court of Appeals of the United States that to be held responsible for a crime a person must have "adequate capacity to conform his conduct to the requirements of the law." It is applied only in certain federal courts. See CRIMINAL RESPONSIBILITY.

current life form   (A. Van Kaam) The transitional form that life assumes in reaction and response to a life situation, to a new disclosure of a person's uniqueness, or both. See CONGENIAL TRANSCENDENCY, CONGRUENT TRANSCENDENCY, CONSCIENTIZATION, CONSISTENCY MODEL.

current material   Data from present feelings and interpersonal relationships used in understanding individual psychodynamics, as contrasted with data from past experience. See GENETIC MATERIAL.

cursing magic   The idea that a person can bring misfortune to another by reciting a formula or uttering an imprecation. Based upon a belief in magical thinking. See VOODOO DEATH, WITCHCRAFT.

cursive writing   A form of writing in which the letters are connected by running strokes formed without raising the pen, as in writing signatures. Also known as script.

Curtis Classification Form   (J. W. Curtis) A projective sentence-completion test designed for use with children aged eleven and older.

curve of equal returns   See CURVES OF RETURNS.

curve of increasing returns   See CURVES OF RETURNS.

curves of returns   Graphic representations of learning situations in which: (a) early trials yield the same amount of improvement as later trials (equal returns); (b) the greatest improvement in performance occurs during the early trials with a consequent trailing off (decreasing returns); and (c) improvement is small at first but greater as time goes on (increasing returns). See CUMULATIVE RECORD for a graphic illustration of these types of learning.

curvilinear correlation   A measure of how close the data fit a curvilinear model. See COEFFICIENT OF CURVILINEAR CORRELATION, MULTIPLE R.

curvilinear regression/relationship   A systematic relationship between two variables that is described by a curve rather than a straight line.

Cushing's Syndrome   See CORTICOSTEROID THERAPY.

custodial care   Minimal maintenance care for institutionalized patients; hospitalization without treatment, for example, the periodical feeding and cleaning of senile and bedridden patients whose conditions are not expected to improve.

custodial case   A person who, through mental defect, mental disorder, or criminality, requires organized supervision or exclusion from society.

custody of children   A legal determination in cases of divorce, death of parents, etc., specifying which parent, adult or other guardian will be in charge of any children. This determination is usually made by a judge when there is conflict between potential caretakers, is based on what is considered to be in the best interests of the children; for example, joint custody may be awarded so that responsibility is shared between both parents, or children will be assigned to grandparents. Typically, in joint custody after a divorce, the child lives with each parent for fixed periods. See CUSTODIAL PARENT.

custom(s)   1. Unwritten laws of behavior. 2. Certain behaviors generally representative of a person, often repeated. 3. A complex mode of behavior prevalent in any given social group over a comparatively long period of time, due not to biological inheritance but to the formation of habits by training early in the lives of the individuals concerned. See MORES.

Cut down, Annoyed, Guilt Feelings, Eye-opener (CAGE)   A four-question screening instrument used in detecting alcoholism: (a) Have you ever felt you should cut down on your drinking? (b) Have people annoyed you by criticizing your drinking? (c) Have you ever felt bad or guilty about your drinking? (d) Have you ever used a drink as an eye-opener?

cut off   Stopping contact with some source of stimulus by moving away, closing the eyes, repositioning of the body, etc. One organism no longer attending to another. See COMMUNICATIONS, COMMUNICATIONS OVERLOAD.

cut-off point   See CRITICAL LEVEL.

cutaneous anesthesia   Impairment or loss of sensitivity in an area of the skin, resulting from medications, nerve damage, or psychogenic factors, as in conversion disorder. In the latter, the anesthesia does not correspond to the distribution of the nerve fibers, or dermatomes. Although occasionally in peripheral neuropathy, glove and stocking distributions may occur.

cutaneous experience   Sensations resulting from stimulation of receptors in the skin. Kinds of cutaneous experience include warmth, cold, tickle, itch, pin prick, sharp pain, and dull pain.

cutaneous perception   Touch and pressure, the perception of any of the receptors in the skin.

cutaneous-pupillary reflex   Dilation of the pupil caused by scratching the skin on cheek or chin. Mediated by V cranial (sensory) to 1st thoracic nerves and sympathetic efferent to eye. Also known as ciliospinal reflex, platysma reflex, pupillary skin reflex.

cutaneous receptors   Nerve endings that terminate at various levels of the skin that report such elements as being touched, hurt, stroked; feeling heat or cold, or pressure. See TOUCH SENSE.

cutaneous-secretory reflex   Activity of the sweat glands elicited by any stimulation of the skin, mediated by cutaneous sensory nerve and sympathetic fibers.

cutaneous senses   In the old concept, the only cutaneous sense was touch, but since then, pulling, warmth, cold, and pain have been added. See SENSES, TOUCH SENSE.

cutting Self-mutilation by repeatedly cutting the wrists or body. Some "slashers" feel little pain. May be a strategy employed by persons with abusive backgrounds to keep painful feelings at bay by replacing emotional pain with physical pain, or to stop dissociative episodes of derealization or depersonalization, for example to persuade the person he or she is real. More common in women; often associated with depression.

CV 1. coefficient of variation 2. See CARDIOVASCULAR.

CVA cerebrovascular accident

CVLT See CALIFORNIA VERBAL LEARNING TEST-ADULT VERSION.

CVLT-C See CALIFORNIA VERBAL LEARNING TEST-CHILDREN'S VERSION.

CVS chorionic villus sampling

CWF Cornell Word Form

cyanopsin A bluish retinal pigment composed of photopsin and retinene, important for vision. See IODOPSIN, OPSIN, PHOTOPSIN, RHODOPSIN, SCOTOPSIN.

cyanotic syndrome of Scheid A theory to explain sudden death in manic or catatonic patients in terms of a feverish or toxic condition resulting from the psychosis. Has been challenged by those who hold that the sudden deaths are related to physiologic exhaustion resulting from pathologic hyperactivity.

cybernetic epistemology A framework for conceptualizing and analyzing what is being observed in terms of the information moving through a system. The conceptualizing and understanding of events as they occur in a dispassionate and neutral scientific manner.

cybernetics (steersman—Greek) The scientific study of communication and control as applied to machines and living organisms. Includes the concept of self-regulation mechanisms, as in thermostats or feedback circuits in the nervous system, as well as transmission and self-correction of information not only in computers but in persons who are communicating with each other. Introduced by mathematician Norbert Wiener in the late 1940s.

cybernetic system The study of methods of feedback control within a system.

cybernetic theory of aging A point of view that aging is related to a loss of ability to handle information-transfer functions from environmental inputs. Holds that the loss is related to the rate at which neurons and neural activity gradually decrease with advancing age. See EVERSION THEORY OF AGING.

cyborg The cybernetic organization or fusion of human and machine; machines embodying biological components and humans incorporating sensors and mechanical organs as part of their symbiotic selves.

cycle of violence A tendency for people who were battered by their parents as children to batter their own children, who will allegedly then batter their children, etc. Or, violence begets violence. Such cycles of behavior purportedly can be broken via some type of counseling or therapy.

cyclencephaly A birth defect marked by the partial or complete fusion of the two cerebral hemispheres during the fetal stage of development. Also known as cyclencephalia.

cycles per second (cps) The number of times a wave of air alternates between maximal positive and negative values in a single second. The preferred designation for this unit of frequency is Hertz (hz or Hz).

cyclic A repetitive pattern, going from step 1 to step X. Some abnormal cyclic stages are seen in alcoholics who may go from being depressed, starting drinking, becoming ebullient at the start of a drinking bout, then becoming talkative, then aggressive, and finally, passing out. Similar patterns are also seen in individuals with mental disorders.

cyclic AMP adenosine 3′, 5′-monophosphate

cyclic illness Any mental disorder characterized by alternating phases. Phrase is most frequently applied to the minority of cases of manic depressive, or bipolar, disorder in which alternation between manic and depressive phases occurs. Also known as circular illness. See CYCLOTHYMIC DISORDER.

cyclic insanity Obsolete phrase for manic-depressive (bipolar) psychosis. See FALRET'S DISEASE.

cyclic nucleotides Substances in physiological systems that function as "second-messenger" hormonal accessories to translate the original hormone code into specific activity within a cell.

cyclical depression Obsolete phrase for recurrent episodes of depression that may alternate with normal periods or alternate with periods of excitement. Replaced by "cyclothymia" for its milder forms and "bipolar disorder" in its more severe form.

cycloid 1. A ring-shaped object or process, such as an organic molecule. 2. A personality type characterized by alternating states of psychic and motor activity and well-being on the one hand and diminished activity and malaise on the other. Similar to manic-depressive (bipolar) psychosis except that the symptoms occur in an otherwise normal person. (Term is used as noun or adjective.)

cycloid psychoses See ACUTE DELUSIONAL PSYCHOSIS.

cyclophoria An eye-muscle imbalance in which one eye deviates when not focused on an object.

cyclopia A birth defect characterized by the merging of the two eye orbits into a single cavity that contains one eye. The anomaly sometimes is a part of a pattern that includes cyclencephaly. The pituitary gland usually is absent. Occurs with chromosome-13 trisomy, monosomy G, and 18p- syndromes. Term is based on the Greek myth of a race of giant humans with a single eye in the middle of their foreheads.

cycloplegia Paralysis of the muscles of accommodation in the eye.

cyclostat An apparatus consisting of a glass cylinder in which an animal is rotated uniformly at various speeds about the vertical axis. Usually provided with a dial from which the number of rotations per unit of time can be read. Used for various research purposes.

cyclothymia (K. L. Kahlbaum) A tendency to experience relatively mild and uneven fluctuations of mood, from periods of elation and excitement to periods of depression and underactivity. See BIPOLAR DISORDER.

cyclothymic-depressive behavior　Refers to the actions of patients with manic-depressive (bipolar) disorder who experience periods of mildly increased activity or euphoria, frequently at the end of a depressive episode or during treatment with antidepressants or electroconvulsive treatment.

cyclothymic disorder　A chronic mood disturbance lasting at least two years, characterized by many periods of depression and hypomania in which symptoms are severe. The periods may be separated by intervals of normal mood lasting for months, and may be intermixed or alternate. A milder variant of the bipolar disorder. See MAJOR DEPRESSIVE EPISODE, MANIC EPISODE.

cyclothymic personality　Another name for alternating personality, or a Dr. Jekyll–Mr. Hyde personality. See CYCLOTHYMIC-PERSONALITY DISORDER.

cyclothymic-personality disorder　A diagnosis for a personality-pattern disturbance characterized by frequently alternating moods of elation and dejection, usually occurring spontaneously and not related to external circumstances.

cyclothymic type　(E. Kretschmer) A personality type that, according to Ernst Kretschmer, is likely to have a bipolar disorder, said to be associated with the pyknic (body) type. See TYPOLOGY.

cyesis　Obsolete term for pregnancy.

cymophobia　Fear of waves.

cynanthropy　A delusion in which the patient believes he or she is a dog. A rare symptom sometimes found in schizophrenia.

cynic　A person who doubts the sincerity of almost everything, including altruistic motivation, viewing it as essentially selfish. Distinguished from a skeptic, whose doubts are focused on matters of the intellect. See GEMEINSCHAFTSGEFÜHL, SKEPTIC.

cynophobia　1. Morbid fear of dogs. 2. Fear of rabies. Also known as pseudohydrophobia. See HYDROPHOBIA, HYDROPHOBOPHOBIA.

cypridophobia　Morbid fear of sexual activity, including sexual intercourse. Also known as cypriphobia. See COITOPHOBIA, EROTOPHOBIA, GENOPHOBIA, VENEREOPHOBIA.

Cyt　See CYTOSINE.

cytoarchitectonics　A system of organizing information about the structure of cells, their occurrence and arrangement, as in an organ such as the brain. Various neuron maps dividing the cerebral cortex into from 20 to 200 areas have been drawn.

cytoarchitecture　The arrangement of the various cells of the cerebral cortex, particularly those in the neocortex. The different types of cells are organized in layers and cortical zones. The number of layers varies in different brain areas, but a typical section of cortex shows six rather distinct layers. See CORTICAL LAYERS (LAMINA), CORTICAL ZONES.

cytochrome oxidase (CO) blob　The central area of a primary visual cortex module in the parvicellular system, shown by a stain for CO.

cytogenics　The study of the cellular units of heredity. See CHROMOSOMES, DEOXYRIBONUCLEIC ACID, GENETIC MATERIAL, GENETICS, GENES, HERITABILITY RATIO, RIBONUCLEIC ACID.

cytokines　Chemicals released by the immune system that cross the blood-brain barrier and can affect neuronal activity.

cytology　The subdivision of biology that deals with cells. See CYTOTECHNOLOGIST.

cytoplasm　The protoplasm of a cell, excluding the material within the nucleus.

cytosine (Cyt)　One of the bases found in both deoxyribonucleic acid (DNA) and ribonucleic acid (RNA). The other two bases found in DNA and RNA are adenine and guanine. Thymine is found only in DNA, and uracil is found only in RNA. Cytosine, thymine, and uracil are pyrimidines, that is they have only one carbon ring, whereas adenine and guanine are purines having two carbon rings. In the DNA molecule, the four bases form complementary pairs across each strand of the double helix, with cytosine joined to guanine and adenine to thymine. See CHROMOSOME, DEOXYRIBONUCLEIC ACID.

d 1. drive (also abbreviated **D**). 2. In statistics, deviation. 3. diopter. 4. In Rorschach test scoring, a symbol for a response involving small details of a usual kind.

D 1. drive (also abbreviated **d**). 2. In Rorschach test scoring, a symbol for responses of a usual sort to the large portions of the inkblot. 3. (C. L. Hull) The strength of a primary drive to action after formation of the habit involved (also abbreviated **D**). See DRIVE STRENGTH. 4. See DRIVE STIMULI.

DA 1. developmental age. 2. See DOPAMINE.

dabbler In the black arts, typically an adolescent experimenting in Satanism, witchcraft, or both, who gets involved in the use of black candles, incantations, and the forming of a coven (a band of witches).

DaCosta's syndrome (J. M. DaCosta) A condition observed in soldiers during the stress of combat and marked by fatigue, heart palpitations, chest pain, and breathing difficulty. A form of cardiac neurosis. Also known as neurocirculatory asthenia, soldier's heart. See EFFORT SYNDROME, IRRITABLE HEART OF SOLDIERS.

dactylology A technique of communicating using manual signals, used by persons who are deaf, mute, or both, as well as in an abbreviated form by other people. Also known as cheirology, chirology.

DAD 1. Depression After Delivery. 2. See DEVICE FOR AUTOMATED DESENSITIZATION.

daedaleum See STROBOSCOPE.

daemon(ic) **demon(ic)**

daemonophobia **demonophobia**

daily-living aids Objects, techniques, or animals that enable a person with a disability to function more "normally." Can include electronic communication equipment and household cleaning devices. Pets have been trained to perform special tasks, such as opening doors. See ACTIVITIES OF DAILY LIVING.

daimon Demon.

Dale's law/principle (H. Dale) A theory that only one kind of neurotransmitter substance is produced by a given neuron.

Dallenbach stimulator (K. M. Dallenbach) A hollow metal device applied to the skin whose temperature can be changed due to change of temperature of the water in the stimulator.

Daltonism Obsolete term for red-green color blindness. Named after British chemist John Dalton, who was himself color blind and gave the first known accurate description of this visual condition.

dammed-up libido A Freudian concept of what occurs when erotic forces are inhibited by superego prohibitions, or lack of opportunity for sexual expression. The "damming" of these urges, especially during the latency period.

damming up See FRUSTRATION.

damping The opposition to vibratory movement imposed by frictional forces, both internal and external to the vibrating body, whereby such movement is reduced in amplitude or is brought to an end.

damping constant A value expressing the rate of decrease in amplitude of a vibratory body. Formula: $dc = \sigma \div T$, where: dc is the damping constant, σ is the amplitude, T is the time.

damping effect The diminution of the amplitude of vibrations because of the absorption of energy by the surrounding medium.

danazol A synthetic androgen that relieves endometriosis by suppressing pituitary gonadotropins.

dance education Professional training in dance and rhythmic movement done for therapeutic and rehabilitative purposes. See DANCE THERAPY.

dance epidemics The rapid spread of "dancing madness" among the masses during the period of the Black Death (bubonic plague) in 14th and 15th century Europe. See CHOREOMANIA.

dance therapy (M. Chase) The use of various forms of rhythmic movements in treatment and rehabilitation, generally combined with in depth discussions.

dancing eyes Nontechnical phrase for opsoclonus.

dancing language (K. Von Frisch) Movements of bees in or near their hive to inform other bees of direction and distance of suitable food (waggle dance). See BEE COMMUNICATION for an illustration of such a dance.

dancing madness See DANCE EPIDEMICS, TARANT-(UL)ISM.

dancing mania Choreomania. Also known as *Danse de St. Guy*, epidemic chorea, St. Vitus' dance. See CHOREA.

dancing mouse A genetic strain of mouse whose behavior consists of constant rotations, used with other varieties of genetically pure mice in psychological research. Also known as waltzers.

danger build-up model   In accident theory, proposes two phases in which a hazard develops and leads to an accident; emphasizes decision points for intervention.

dangerousness   An unpleasant state characterized by agitation and hostility, either toward the self, or toward others, including harmful impulses to harm self or others. Chemical restraints (tranquilizing or sedative drugs) are often effective in such cases.

dangerous tendencies   Mental traits or predispositions that are judged likely to result in acts entailing injury to others or to the self.

danger recognition   The perception of potential danger in unfamiliar situations. Animals exposed to novel stimuli generally show initial signs of fear and will freeze, call out, giving way to exploratory behavior in the absence of real threat. Human children will cry on being approached by strangers, hearing sudden loud noises, and being surprised by bright lights.

danger situation   A situation which elicits typical fear in the psychoneuroses. See DREAD.

DAP Test   See DRAW-A-PERSON TEST, MACHOVER DRAW-A-PERSON TEST.

daring   A type of suggestion characteristic of childhood, in which one person challenges another to undertake some dangerous or discountenanced performance. See BOASTING, SHOWING OFF.

dark   Absence of light, low brilliance, low illumination, or low brightness.

dark adaptation   The reflex adjustment of the eye to dim light or darkness. The three mechanisms are pupillary enlargement, increased sensitivity of the photoreceptors, and a change from cone to rod activity. In general, the amount of time required to be able to achieve dark adaptation varies inversely with the amount of light exposure during a previous light adaptation. A fully light-adapted eye placed in darkness becomes about half dark-adapted in seven minutes, fully in 40 to 60 minutes. Maximum time for full adaptation to total darkness from full lighting is also 40 to 60 minutes. Also known as darkness adaptation.

dark-adaptation curve   A graph showing the increasing sensitivity to light of a light-adapted eye placed in darkness. The curve shows two downward swoops, the first representing the increased sensitivity of the cones, and the second the increased sensitivity of the rods, while both also show the result of pupil dilation. See DARK ADAPTION.

dark and light adaptation   Due to photochemical process in the rod cells of the retina characterized by progressive adjustment of the building up and breaking down of rhodopsin. A parallel process occurs in the cones with iodopsin as the photosensitive chemical.

dark-field illumination   A type of illumination in optical instruments (especially the microscope), in which objects are seen by reflected or diffracted light (usually derived from a laterally directed beam) against an unilluminated background.

dark light   In absolute darkness a faint light may appear to be seen by people due to the activity of the photoreceptors in the retinas.

darkness fear   See ACHLUOPHOBIA, NYCTOPHOBIA.

dark-side hypothesis   The postulate that humans have inherent in them an evil aspect of personality, often unknown to them, or if suspected, minimized. See ID.

dart and dome   Describing the spike and wave EEG (electroencephalographic) pattern recorded in cases of petit mal epilepsy. Consists of a sharp spike followed by a low amplitude slow wave that occurs at a frequency of three per second and indicates a thalamic lesion. Also known as spike-and-dome discharge.

Darwinian fitness   (C. R. Darwin) The extent to which an organism can produce viable offspring. Sometimes known as fitness.

Darwinian reflex   (C. R. Darwin) A grasping response of the newborn infant.

Darwinism   A theory of evolution based on Charles Darwin's investigations and conclusions, especially the use of the principle of natural selection, to explain the origin of species. See SOCIAL DARWINISM. Also see EVOLUTION THEORY, EVOLUTIONARY STRATEGY, FACIAL DISPLAY, NATURAL SELECTION, PANGENESIS, STRUGGLE FOR EXISTENCE, TRANSFORMISM.

DAS   Differential Ability Scales

Das Es   (the it—German) The id.

Dasein   (being here—German) A sensation of existence and a complete awareness of being here and now, which implies knowledge of existence.

Daseinanalyse   (existence—German) A philosophic and psychological approach that emphasizes the need for recognizing not only where humans are but what they can become. Its objective is to help people to accept themselves and realize their potentials. See EXISTENTIALISM, INSIGHT THERAPY.

Dashiell maze   (J. Dashiell) A maze that has several correct paths to the goal.

DAT   1. See ALZHEIMER'S DISEASE. 2. Differential Aptitude Test.

data   Generally, summaries of observations, results of tests, etc., indicated by numbers. Any information (measurements, observations, or estimates) that can be collected, stored for review, analyzed, evaluated, and interpreted. The singular of data is datum. See QUALITATIVE DATA, QUANTITATIVE DATA.

data analysis   Phase of research in which the obtained numbers are analyzed, usually through statistical procedures.

data bank   1. Informally, any mass of data, usually on a specific topic. 2. Formally, a facility for the storage, preservation, and retrieval of information, usually scientific social data. Exemplified by the International Federation of Data Organizations for the Social Sciences, which in 1977 combined four North American and seven European archives. Also known as data archive.

data base   A centralized word bank or data file common to a group of applications, systems or users, such that all have access to the centralized data. Also spelled database. See COMPUTERIZED DIAGNOSIS, PROBLEM-ORIENTED RECORD.

data collection 1. Common phrase for "running the study," that is, the systematic gathering of research results. 2. Systematic gathering of facts for research or practical purposes, as by consumer surveys, consumer panels, psychology experiments, rating methods, structured interviews, and preference-recording devices in market research.

data-driven cognitive processes Inferential processes that rely more on incoming perceptual data than the perceiver's existing cognitive structures. Also known as bottom-up processes.

data driven processing Information conveyed to the brain directly from sense organs.

data handling system A coordinated method for automatically sorting, decoding, or storing information. Also known as data reduction system.

data snooping 1. A secondary analysis of data, usually to generate hypotheses for further research. 2. Looking for unpredicted, post hoc effects in a body of data. 3. Examining data before an experiment or study is over, sometimes resulting in premature conclusions.

date rape A type of acquaintance rape, sexual assault by a person the victim had agreed to meet with socially. See ACQUAINTANCE RAPE, DATE-RAPE DRUGS.

date-rape drugs Slang for drugs usually slipped into alcoholic beverages to render the drinker compliant and amnesic. See BURUNDANGA, GAMMA-HYDROXYBU-TYRATE, KETAMINE, MIDAZOLAM HYDROCHLORIDE, ROHYPNOL, SCOPOLAMINE.

Dauerschlaf (perpetual sleep—German) A type of therapy in which prolonged sleep is induced with drugs in the treatment of chemical dependence, status epilepticus, and acute psychotic episodes. See CONTINUOUS NARCOSIS, PROLONGED-SLEEP TREATMENT.

Davis-Eells games (A. Davis & K. W. Eells) A test of general intelligence for children in grades one to six. All instructions are given orally.

DAWN Drug Abuse Warning Network

day blindness Abnormal sensitivity of the retinal fovea to bright light.

day camps Facilities that provide educational, recreational, and rehabilitative services for physically challenged or disturbed persons, mainly children, on a day-by-day basis, as opposed to long-term camp experiences that require overnight accommodations.

day-care program A daytime activity and treatment program for persons with mental illness, physical challenges, or mental retardation. The persons may engage in games, vocational training, adjustment programs, and, where possible, gainful work in sheltered workshops. For mental patient programs, see DAY HOSPITAL.

daydream A waking fantasy, or reverie, in which wishes are fulfilled in imagination. Among these are the wish for recognition (the "conquering hero"daydream), the wish for pity and compassion (the "suffering-hero" daydream), and daydreams that express financial, social, romantic, and vocational interests. See FANTASY.

day hospital (D. A. Cameroon) A community-based mental institution to which patients go during the day to receive a full range of treatment services, returning to their homes in the evening. The concept may be used in rehabilitation as well as psychiatric care. See COMMUNITY PSYCHIATRY, DAY-CARE PROGRAM, NIGHT HOSPITAL.

daylight fear See PHENGOPHOBIA.

daylight vision See PHOTOPIC VISION.

daymare An attack of acute anxiety precipitated by waking state fantasies.

day residues Elements of life events that appear in dreams.

dazzle reflex of children (A. Peiper) When a bright light is applied to an infant's eyes, the eyelids close immediately and remain closed as long as the stimulus lasts. Also known as dazzle reflex of Peiper.

db See DECIBEL.

DBI diazepam-binding inhibitor

dc Abbreviation for discontinue, as in discontinue medication.

DC amplifier Direct current devices used to amplify the potential difference across a neural membrane so that the cortical current can be recorded and studied.

DC potentials Direct current electrical sources used to sensitize or stimulate the cortex. In research with animals, small DC potentials of a few microamperes have been used to polarize areas of the cortex so that any stimulus, for example, visual or auditory, might result in a motor response such as a limb movement.

dd In Rorschach test scoring, a symbol for small unusual detail.

Dd In Rorschach test scoring, a symbol for a rarely selected detail.

Dds In Rorschach test scoring, a symbol for a response to a small unusual detail having a small white space.

DdW In Rorschach test scoring, a symbol for a small unusual detail.

de In Rorschach test scoring, a symbol for a small, unusual edge detail.

DEA (United States federal) Drug Enforcement Agency

dead end A cul-de-sac or blind alley. See MAZE.

deadline 1. In testing, usually either of intelligence or of academic knowledge, a time limit in which participants must complete a self-administered test. 2. In research, a prescribed time period after which research participants' performance is stopped if there has not been a response.

deadline mechanism (J. M. Henderson) In research on eye movements and gaze fixation in reading, the signal presented for the eyes to move when a certain amount of time has elapsed since the beginning of the fixation (if no prior signal to move the eyes is given).

deadly catatonia Bell's mania.

deadman Mechanical safety device, usually a switch that stops a machine when the operator lets go or leaves the seat. Originally a pedal on New York subway trains, which, if released, would stop the train.

deaf-blind   Having neither vision nor hearing. Such a person encounters special communication and learning difficulties; a deaf person usually learns by depending upon vision, and a blind person depends heavily upon the sense of hearing. Persons who are deaf and blind sometimes are educated in special sheltered workshops or facilities with professional personnel prepared to assist such persons. Helen Keller is a special case of such a person.

deaf-mute   A person who can neither hear nor speak, usually one who was born deaf.

deafferentation   The cutting of sensory nerves to the spinal cord to study nerves no longer connected to the brain.

deafness   Partial or complete loss of hearing. Major kinds are conduction deafness, due to a disruption in sound vibrations before they reach the nerve endings of the inner ear, and nerve deafness, caused by a failure of the nerves or brain centers to transmit or interpret properly the impulses from the inner ear. Types of deafness include: ADVENTITIOUS, BOILERMAKERS, CENTRAL, CONDUCTION, CONGENITAL, CORTICAL, EXPOSURE, FUNCTIONAL, HYSTERICAL, PERCEPTION, TONE, TRANSMISSION, WORD. See SENSORINEURAL HEARING LOSS.

de-aggressivization   The neutralization of the aggressive drive so that its energy can be diverted to various tasks and wishes of the ego.

deamination   A catabolic process in which protein is degraded into its amino acid components and nitrogen is removed in the liver and excreted as urea.

de-analize   In psychoanalytic theory, the transference of sexual impulses from the anal area to other excretory or "dirty" locations or activities, whether mud smearing, finger painting, or telling dirty jokes.

death   1. The cessation of physical and mental processes. Sometimes determined in humans by two flat encephalograph readings taken 24 hours apart. 2. In patients with schizophrenia, "death" may signify the end of the patient's life in a particular environment as a step toward rebirth in another, without actual cessation of physical or mental functions. 3. Some view the end stages of certain brain diseases, such as Alzheimer's as death of the spirit if not of the body. See AUTOPSY-NEGATIVE DEATH, BELL'S MANIA, BRAIN DEATH, CRIB DEATH, DYING PROCESS, PHENOTHIAZINE DEATH, THANATOLOGY, VOODOO DEATH.

death and transformation workshops   Didactic-experiential groups, focusing on the ultimate death of participants and their significant others. Exercises revolve around action therapy, active imagination, art and music therapy. See AWARENESS TRAINING INSTITUTES.

death anxiety   A depressive state in which tension and apprehension over dying and fear of death (thanatophobia) are the salient symptoms.

death expectation   (E. Kübler-Ross) The psychological response to the expectation of death. See STAGES OF DYING.

death fantasy   Imagining that the self is already dead, as in children daydreaming about how sad their parents will feel for having mistreated them.

death fear   See THANATOPHOBIA.

death feigning   The act of becoming immobile, or "playing dead," when threatened, found in some animal species such as the opossum. Also known as playing possum. See TONIC IMMOBILITY.

death instinct   (S. Freud) The universal impulse for death, destruction, and self-destruction, seen in aggression. Sigmund Freud pictured human life as a theater of operations in which two ultimate forces, the life instinct (Eros) and the death instinct (Thanatos) battle for supremacy. See DESTRUDO, THANATOS.

death neurosis   (E. M. Pattison) Neurotic defenses against awareness of death and depression arising out of unresolved grief.

death-qualified jury   Jurors who have passed the process of "death qualification": during jury selection in capital cases, candidates are asked whether they are so opposed to capital punishment that they would not consider voting for such if the defendant is convicted. Those who answer yes may be disqualified from service. Such juries are considered by some to be unrepresentative of the general population and conviction-prone.

death-trance   A state of apparent suspended animation of a patient during an episode of hysteria or catatonia.

death wish   A conscious or unconscious wish that another person, particularly a parent, will die. Guilt and depression are two common reactions for those with death wishes for others.

debauchery   Loose term denoting a tendency to indulge excessively in sexual intercourse or the drinking of alcoholic beverages.

debility   Abnormal lack of force or vigor in the vital functions.

debriefing   A process at the conclusion of a study in which participants are informed about the research: its actual purpose, its rationale, any deception involved, where results can be located, and questions answered. This is an ethical responsibility of researchers.

debug   To isolate and remove malfunctions or mistakes from a control system or data input program.

decadence   The deterioration of an individual or group as a result of social changes rather than physical or biological factors.

decadent   A person who has regressed morally, or whose personality has become disintegrated.

décalage   (irregularity—French) Term used by Jean Piaget for achievement of various mental or physical abilities at various times during cognitive development. See HORIZONTAL DÉCALAGE, VERTICAL DÉCALAGE, OBLIQUE DÉCALAGE.

decarceration   (A. Scull) The process of removing people from institutions such as prisons and mental hospitals, often to community facilities. See DEINSTITU-TIONALIZATION.

decatastrophizing   A "what if" technique designed to explore actual, rather than feared, events and consequences.

decathexis   1. In psychoanalytic theory, withdrawal of libido from objects in the external world. 2. Retreat from reality in patients with schizophrenia, usually resulting in delusions and hallucinations as an attempt to recover the lost objects. ("Objects" refers to "other people" in psychoanalytic terminology.)

decay theory (of memory)   1. A point of view that material learned leaves traces in the brain that eventually disappear unless practiced and used. 2. A point of view that memories are kept alive by review otherwise they will disappear. Also known as trace decay theory.

deceit tests   Procedures to determine whether people will cheat, and under what conditions. Example: After taking an examination, children are given an opportunity to see the correct answers, and observed to see who will change their answers if they think no one is looking.

deceleration   1. Negative acceleration; a lessening of speed of motion per unit of time. 2. Reduction in the rate of change or development in a given activity or function. 3. The characteristic of a curve that is steep at its beginning but becomes increasingly flat as it approaches its end. Learning curves are typically of this shape. See ACCELERATION, POSITIVE ACCELERATION.

decenter   See DECENTRATION.

decentering   1. Moving the focus of attention away from the self. 2. Recognizing another person's thoughts and feelings even if they differ from a person's own. See EMPATHY.

decentralization   (T. Kirkbride) The trend toward modifying the centralization of living conditions, care, and administration inherent in massive mental hospitals. As a result of the Kirkbride plan, most patients now live and are treated in smaller units with a more intimate and homelike atmosphere. Each unit has a semiautonomous administrative status. See COTTAGE PLAN, KIRKBRIDE.

decentralized organization   An organization in which many decisions are made by lower level managers and employees.

decentration   A child's gradual progress from egocentrism toward a reality shared with others. According to Jean Piaget, the capacity to decenter develops as the child moves away from a predominantly egocentric mode of thinking at around seven or eight years of age, characteristic of operational thought. See EGOCENTRIC.

deception experiment   A research design in which participants either are totally unaware that they are participating in an experiment, or they are aware that they are participating in an experiment but not of the purpose of the research. Usually deception is used in cases when awareness of an experiment would defeat the purpose of the experiment. See AUSSAGE TEST.

decerebrate   Deprived of the cerebrum. An animal whose cerebrum has been removed. See DECEREBRATION.

decerebrate plasticity   A form of motor-function reaction in which the limbs of a decerebrate animal can be "molded" in various positions by lengthening or shortening the degree of contraction of the extensor muscles. Depending upon location of the lesion, plasticity may be controlled by stimulation of appropriate reflexes.

decerebrate posture   decerebrate rigidity

decerebrate rigidity   Marked exaggeration of the postural reflexes which appears in the extensor muscles of the limbs of animals after decerebration. Also known as decerebrate posture. See DECEREBRATION.

decerebration   The surgical removal of the cerebrum, the largest part of the brain, resulting in loss of ability to discriminate, learn, and control movements. Decerebrate rigidity or decerebrate posture is the condition following removal of the cerebrum in which the four limbs are spastic. See DECEREBRATE, DECEREBRATE RIGIDITY, DECORTICATE CONDITIONING.

decibel (db or Db)   The smallest difference in loudness that can be detected by a person of normal hearing ability. It is a quantitative unit equal to the logarithm of the ratio of two levels of intensity. Thus, increasing the sound level by 10 dB is an increase of 10 times in sound intensity; an extra 20 dB is a 100-fold increase. Ten decibels equal one bel, named in honor of Alexander Graham Bell.

decile   The result of dividing a series of numbers into ten equal parts.

Decile maze   (J. Decile) A maze with several correct paths to the goal, in contrast to the Porteus maze that had only one correct path. Compare PORTEUS MAZE.

decimal number system   A number system with real numbers in terms of place values for multiples of ten including digits 0 through 9. Also known as Arabic system.

decision   1. The formulation of a course of action with a firm intention of carrying it out. 2. An attitude characterized by firm adherence to some line of conduct.

decision making   Ability to make independent and intelligent choices, a process which counselors seek to enhance.

decision-premotor time   In a perceptual-motor-reaction-time task, time from the onset of the stimulus to the initiation of the response.

decision-rules   One of the predetermined rules (derived from decision theory in mathematics) for making a decision in the face of uncertainty. Criteria for choosing decision-rules are the extent to which expected loss is minimized, and the extent to which subjective loss is minimized. See BAYESIAN APPROACH.

decision-theoretic approach   The Bayesian approach.

decision theory   1. A point of view that people identify and then weigh the possible positive and negative aspects of any course of action before arriving at what appears to be the best decision. 2. In psychometrics, a mathematical procedure for determining the optimum success ratio as a function of the selection ratio adopted.

decision tree   A flowchart model in which answers to specific questions lead to branching to a new set of questions or procedures. Can be applied to troubleshooting faulty equipment, deciding the appropriate statistical test, diagnosing illness, etc.

decisive moment   The instant of making a decision; the "knife edge" of change, as in a patient in psychotherapy deciding to tell the therapist a long-held secret.

declarative knowledge   The understanding of a phenomenon, such as why an airplane flies, rather than procedural knowledge, knowing how to fly an airplane.

declarative memory   Knowledge about facts. The capacity for intentionally recovering specific facts and events. Compare PROCEDURAL MEMORY.

de Clérambault syndrome   Clérambault's syndrome

decline effect A tendency for scores on "psi" (parapsychological) tests to decline within a run, a session or an experiment.

decode To translate signals so that they convey a message. For example, the cerebral cortex "decodes" nerve impulses that reach it and gives these impulses meaning. Also, in Morse code the dots and dashes are translated into words.

decoded Converted back to an original form (for example, if a series of numbers were coded into letters and later the letters were changed back to their numbers, they would be decoded).

decoding 1. The understanding of spoken language. 2. To transform information given in one modality that is not understandable to the receiver to a different understood modality. 3. In information theory, the process in which a receiver (the brain, or a device such as a teletype machine) translates signals (electrical impulses, sounds, writing, gestures) into readable or audible messages. 4. The returning of a coded message back to its original form (for example, if A is M in a coded message, when decoded, M becomes A).

decompensation A breakdown in psychological defenses, resulting in a variety of symptoms, neurotic or psychotic, such as depression and thought disorders.

decompensative neurosis A psychological or behavioral disorder in which psychological defense systems break down and the person experiences incapacitating anxiety.

decomposition A tendency of patients with paranoid schizophrenia to split both themselves or their persecutors into separate personalities.

decompression sickness An adverse effect of exposure of the body to extremely high air pressure, resulting in the formation of nitrogen bubbles in the body tissues. When decompression sickness affects mainly the bones and joints, the disorder is called the bends. See RAPTURE-OF-THE-DEEP SYNDROME.

De Condillac See CONDILLAC.

deconditioning A behavior-therapy technique in which learned responses such as phobias are "unlearned," or deconditioned. See DESENSITIZATION, EXTINCTION.

deconstruction 1. (J. Derrida) The undoing or the exposing of assumptions or of internal contradictions of any system of thought, such as a theory. The critical process of rejecting claims for concepts, researches, ideas, works of art, etc., by finding other meanings or explanations. It can involve "taking apart" the whole, examining elements in details to determine whether everything fits with everything else. This procedure may be used for almost any complex system with interacting parts. 2. A method used to elucidate the role that personal power, subjectivity, and political interests play in the way people explain social and psychological phenomena. Based on the postmodern assumption that claims about morality and knowledge cannot be fully objective or detached from the personal motives and social circumstances of the person making those claims. As a method, deconstruction consists of a critical examination of the values and assumptions implicit in theory, research, and practice. See OCCAM'S RAZOR, MORGAN'S CANON.

decontextualization 1. Interpretation of material without regard to its context. 2. (R. Sears) Avoidance of objects and persons associated with unpleasant experiences.

decorticate conditioning (F. L. Goltz, P. Zelinii) 1. A conditioned reflex learned without involvement of the cerebrum. 2. Conditioning that takes place in a decorticated animal, one whose entire cerebral cortex has been destroyed or removed. Such conditioning or learning occurs readily in the cat. Also known as decortication conditioning.

decortication 1. The surgical removal of the outer layer of the brain while allowing brain tissues below that level to remain functional. 2. The removal of the cerebral cortex from an animal for experimental purposes.

decorum Conformity to social standards of conduct, especially as regards dignity of manner in public gatherings.

decreasing returns A learning situation in which the greatest improvement in performance occurs during the early trials with a consequent trailing off during later trials. See CURVES OF RETURNS.

decrement A measure of the rate of decrease in amplitude of a partially damped vibration, obtained as the ratio of the (maximum) amplitudes in two successive periods.

Decroly method of schooling (O. Decroly) An innovative system of formal education based on the concept that children's natural instincts and interests should be determined and given free reign rather than trying to regiment rigid preconceptions of what should and should not be learned, while also stressing the importance of social participation and high standards of behavior. Academics played a relatively small role in this kind of school. See SCHOOL PSYCHOLOGY.

deculturation (B. Wolman) A regression to more primitive states on the part of a social entity, as in a group isolated from society reverting to jungle law.

decussation 1. A crossing over, such as the crossing over of nerve fibers from one side of the nervous system to the other. 2. An intercrossing of structures or parts of structures, as in the decussation of pyramids of the medulla oblongata and of fibers of optic nerves from the right and left eyes in the optic chiasm. See MEDULLA OBLONGATA, OPTIC CHIASM, OPTIC NERVE.

decussation of pyramids The oblique crossing of the motor fibers from each side of the medulla to the other, over the anterior median fissure.

dedaleum See STROBOSCOPE.

dedifferentiation A process in which ordinarily differentiated psychic contents are confused, as in the obliteration of the difference between concrete and abstract concepts. A form of thought disorganization characteristically occurring in patients with schizophrenia. Compare DIFFERENTIATION.

deduction 1. A conclusion or inference derived by reasoning from formal premises or propositions. 2. The act or process of leading down or away; tracing the derivation of; deducing. Compare INDUCTION.

deductive reasoning 1. A fundamental process for discovering truth by making assertions (theoretical statements) and then establishing hypotheses to be checked to obtain evidence to support the validity for the assertions. 2. Reasoning from the general to the specific. Also known as hypothetico-deductive. See DEDUCTION, INDUCTION, INDUCTIVE REASONING.

deductive thought A form of logical reasoning based on rules that lead to logical conclusions.

deep body temperature The body's internal temperature. Also known as core temperature.

deep depression A feeling of dejection that has progressed to the point where initiative is lost, the patient is preoccupied with ideas of guilt and unworthiness, refuses to move, wants to be in bed, and acts in a sluggish manner. Delusions of sin and suicidal thoughts are common and are likely to be acted out.

deep dyslexia Almost total inability to read despite personal efforts and assistance from others. It is an acquired dyslexia, as distinguished from a developed dyslexia, characterized by the reading of nonsense syllables or making substitutions of familiar words for somewhat unusual words. See ACQUIRED DYSLEXIA, DEVELOPMENTAL DYSLEXIA.

deep kiss **French kiss**

deep phase structure 1. In physiology, any organ within the body. 2. In linguistics, the true meaning of a sentence, often not immediately apparent from the words alone. 3. Mental contents of what a person is about to say or do; the personal intention preceding behavior. Also known as deep structure.

deep-pressure sensitivity A system of sensibility depending on deep-lying cutaneous and subcutaneous receptors.

deep reflex A reflexive action of one of the tendon systems, for example, the knee-jerk or jaw-jerk reflexes.

deep sensibility Sensitivity from body structure not on the surface of the body, such as receptors near the joints of the body.

deep sleep The characteristic sleep of children in which heart rate, blood pressure, and brain activity decrease. Leads to less sensitivity to external stimuli, which explains children's capacity to sleep in noisy situations, while being carried, etc. Sometimes known as slow-wave sleep. See RHOMBENCEPHALIC SLEEP.

deep structure In linguistics, the meaning of a sentence, this is, the grammatical relationship inherent in the words of a sentence that is not immediately apparent from the formal order of the words alone, in contrast to the surface structure. See DEEP PHASE STRUCTURE.

deep tones Tones of relatively slow rate of vibration.

deep trance See TRANCE.

de-erotization In psychoanalytic theory, the reduction, elimination, or sublimation of the libido by eliminating the sexual emotional investment from the psychic representation of an object. Also termed delibidinalization, desexualization.

Deese paradigm (J. Deese) A procedure used to test for true and false memories using words that have something in common with a "lure." Example: An original list of words including "wheel," "motor," "seat," "gas," and "drive" is memorized. Later, participants are given another list, now including the lure "automobile," and asked to indicate words recalled from the original list. Those who incorrectly recall "automobile" as one of the original words were induced by the arrangement of words that relate to an automobile to falsely recall it. See FALSE MEMORIES, LURE.

de facto In reality, actually.

defaulter 1. Any person who does not perform an act as promised. See NONCOMPLIANCE. 2. See PATIENT IN NONCOMPLIANCE.

defecation reflex An action that causes emptying of the rectum and lower portion of the colon by movement or pressure of fecal material. The voluntary nervous system can override the reflex and, under normal conditions, prevent automatic defecation. See ANAL PHASE, TOILET TRAINING.

defect Failure to conform to a given standard, either through some lack, or by misarrangement of parts. Applied in many fields, for example anatomy, personality, experimentation, and statistics. See DEFICIENCY.

defective Refers to anything, person or object, that is incomplete or lacking a significant quality, as in "mentally defective."

defective children Obsolete phrase applied to children who were physically or mentally impaired due to hereditary or congenital disorder, severe illness, or trauma. Phrase was sometimes limited to persons with mental retardation, who were termed "mentally defective."

defective delinquent A person who is both a criminal and a mental defective, especially a person who is predisposed to commit crime owing to some mental deficiency.

defective stimulus control of behavior See BEHAVIORAL DYSFUNCTIONS CLASSIFICATION.

defectology The study of defects. A broad term in Russian psychology referring to any behavioral or physiological defects, especially to aberrations in children.

defect orientation The argument that all persons with mental retardation are also in some manner physically defective.

defect theory A point of view that cognitive processes of persons with mental retardation are qualitatively different from those of persons considered "normal." See DEVELOPMENTAL THEORIST.

defeminizing effect The result of hormonal interference with the development of female anatomical or behavioral characteristics.

defendance (H. A. Murray) The need to defend personal actions or to respond to blame or criticism.

defender strategy In industrial psychology, attempts by a business to protect its market share.

defense A type of behavior that tends to protect an organism from psychological or physical injury. Also rarely spelled defence. Types of defense include: CHARACTER, EGO, INSANITY, MANIC, PERCEPTUAL, SCREEN.

defense hysteria (S. Freud) The dissociation that may occur after traumatic experiences due to unacceptable ideas and affects being expelled from consciousness.

defense interpretation An understanding of the ego and superego that helps the psychoanalyst understand the defensive resistances of the patient.

defense mechanism/strategy A reaction pattern, usually unconscious, that protects a person from anxiety, guilt, unacceptable impulses, internal conflicts, or other threats to the ego. Defensive behavior is a common, normal means of coping with problems, but excessive use of any mechanism, such as displacement or repression, is considered pathological. P. L. Giovacchini proposed a hierarchy of defense mechanisms from the most to the least sophisticated: Rationalization, Repression, Displacement, Identification, Conversion, Isolation (intellectualization), Reaction formation (overcompensation), Undoing, Introjection, Projection, Denial. Also known as ego-defense mechanism, safeguarding tendencies. Individual defense mechanisms include: AGGRESSION, AVOIDANCE, COMPENSATION, DENIAL, DISPLACEMENT, EMOTIONAL INSULATION, FANTASY, FLIGHT INTO REALITY, IDEALIZATION, IDENTIFICATION, INCORPORATION, INTELLECTUALIZATION, INTROJECTION, ISOLATION, PROJECTION, RATIONALIZATION, REACTION FORMATION, REGRESSION, REPRESSION, SUBSTITUTION, SYMPATHISM, UNDOING. See DYNAMISM.

defense-mechanism inventory An evaluative procedure that asks participants to respond to stories, yielding scores on five sets of defenses (turning against object, projection, turning against self, and reversal). See PROJECTIVE TESTS.

defense-oriented reaction Behavior in terms of personal feelings rather than on the objective facts of the situation.

defense psychoneurosis A psychoanalytic phrase for reactions to a painful experience that may have been repressed to become an unconscious source of a mental disorder.

defense reaction In psychoanalytic theory, the outward manifestation (in behavior) of a defense mechanism.

defense reflex A sudden body or limb movement (usually flexion, and interpreted as primitive) elicited by an unexpected stimulus. Also known as defensive reflex.

defense response A basic unlearned reaction occurring when there is an evident threat to the organism. See REFLEX.

defensible space 1. Phrase primarily used in connection with large multiple-family dwellings whose design permits residents to closely observe movements of nonresidents on the premises. 2. Semipublic areas around private dwellings that residents can territorialize.

defensive attribution 1. Blaming something else for a mistake made by oneself. Refusal to assume responsibility for errors. See BLAME AVOIDANCE, SCAPEGOATING. 2. Blaming individuals for actions that result in negative outcomes by those who are themselves putatively responsible, even when the former could not predict the outcomes nor have intended them to happen.

defensive avoidance reaction An apparently illogical response of a person engaged in behavior considered undesirable. Upon being told of the possible consequences of such behavior, the person may tune out the message, refuse to believe the consequences, minimize the consequences, or dismiss the information as "only statistics." See COPING STRATEGIES, FEAR APPEAL.

defensive behavior A form of behavior characterized by the overuse of defense mechanisms operating on an unconscious level; a pattern of responses to real or imagined threats of bodily harm or ego damage. See DEFENSE MECHANISM. Compare ATTACK BEHAVIOR.

defensive coping Adjusting to an unpleasant situation by doing nothing, by moving away from the problem situation, or by refusing to consider the matter. See DENIAL, ESCAPE BEHAVIOR.

defensive emotion An expression of an intense emotion, such as anger, to block a more threatening or anxiety-provoking feeling, such as fear.

defensive emotional reaction A response to advice, criticism, or other information given by one person about another's behavior, that is not the intended response (for example, advising an obese person to go on a reducing diet may result in the person gaining more weight). See DEFENSIVE AVOIDANCE REACTION, REACTANCE THEORY.

defensive externals A tendency for persons to excuse their behavior by claiming their actions were unintentional when it suits them to make this claim; a frequent assertion by criminals. See CONGRUENT EXTERNALS.

defensive identification A protective process of joining with or becoming like a threatening person. The apparent rationale is "If you cannot beat them, join them." See BLAMING THE VICTIM, IDENTIFICATION WITH THE AGGRESSOR, STOCKHOLM SYNDROME.

defensiveness A behavioral trait of being overly sensitive to criticism or about perceived personal deficiencies.

defensive reaction Behavior, such as over-aggressiveness, adopted either consciously or unconsciously to protect the self against blame, threat, embarrassment, or anxiety.

defensive strategies (G. M. Gilbert) Complex ways of operating to protect the self especially in socialization processes. See DEFENSIVE BEHAVIOR, DEFENSIVE REACTION.

deference (H. A. Murray) A need to follow and serve a leader.

deference behavior (E. Goffman) Unwritten rules for social interactions that convey respect and value for others that lead to successful group behavior.

deferred character/instinct A trait or aspect of personality derived by inheritance, but not manifested till some time after birth.

deferred imitation (J. Piaget, A. Bandura) Behaviors reproduced by the child after having earlier observed them. The modeled events are retained in symbolic representations of modeled events.

deferred instinct See DEFERRED CHARACTER.

deferred obedience   (S. Freud) A command to right a wrong repressed for a period extending into years before finally being obeyed, usually after the onset of a neurotic illness. Examples include commands or prohibitions by parents made early in life. A self-command is made to repay a debt or return a stolen or broken object years after the event even when the person owed or mistreated is unaware of the sin or crime.

deferred reaction   A later response to an experience that had little effect at the time of its occurrence. Sigmund Freud cites the case of the Wolf Man, who viewed the "primal scene" (parental intercourse) when he was a year and a half old, but reacted to it in disguised form in a dream about a wolf at age four.

deficiency   Lack of something, or inadequacy, as compared with some accepted standard. See DEFECT.

deficiency cravings   Desires for certain specific foods based on nutritional needs, said to be common in pregnant women. Also known as the "Willies."

deficiency love   (A. Maslow) Love characterized by dependency, possessiveness, lack of concern for mutuality, and diminished caring for another's welfare, where one person depends on another to fulfill various needs. Also known as D love. See LOVE.

deficiency motivation   (A. Maslow) Motivation operating on the lowest level of the hierarchy of needs, usually characterized by the striving to correct a physiological deficit. See META-MOTIVATION, NEED-HIERARCHY THEORY.

deficiency motive   A tendency to strive only for the degree of gratification required to fill a particular need. Compare ABUNDANCE MOTIVE.

deficit measurement paradigm   (M. Lezak) A strategy for assessing the presence and extent of behavioral symptoms of neurological impairment; consists of comparing a patient's current level of performance either with a normative standard or with the level expected for the patient on the basis of history or prior performance.

definiendum   A term to be defined or in need of definition.

definition   1. A statement of what something is. A nominal definition is a consensus to use a specific term or name; a real definition attempts to describe the essence of a phenomenon in a way that represents a basic truth. See OPERATIONAL DEFINITION. 2. A boundary separating percepts; with a good definition, one item stands out clearly from another or from the background. See FIGURE-GROUND.

definitional validity   A test that consists of items identified by the title of the test.

definition research   Performing research on a particular problem to generate a true finding but a false conclusion. For example, "100% of drug users began by drinking milk," or "One out of eight women will have breast cancer," when the sample is based on women up to 85 years of age. It is an example of the statement "There are lies, damn lies and statistics."

deflection   A defensive act in which attention is diverted from an unpleasant thought or idea, typified in "I'll think about it tomorrow."

deflection strain   (R. B. Cattell) Resistance to novel learning. Tension generated by operating in unfamiliar life-enhancing or life-saving ways in emergencies.

defloration   The rupture of a virgin's hymen (membrane that covers the opening of the vagina), usually during the woman's initial coital experience. The concept that a female is thus deflowered, or deprived of her "bloom," is not found in all cultures. See HYMEN, JUS PRIMAE NOCTIS, VIRGINITY, WEDDING NIGHT.

deformation fear   See DYSMORPHOPHOBIA, TERATOPHOBIA.

deformation of the self   (S. Arieti) A negative effect upon the self due to science and technology, as exemplified by mass production, consumerism, emphasis on numbers rather than feelings, and advertising and publicity.

deformative attachment   A clinging to worn out directives that are no longer relevant or congenial. See DETERMINING TENDENCY.

deformity   1. A marked deviation from the standard. 2. Any malformation, distortion, or disfiguration of any part of the body. See ANOMALY.

degeneracy   A state characterized by an absence of moral and social standards. Degeneracy is often commonly used with special reference to sexual offenses. See DEGENERATION.

degeneracy theory   1. (C. Lombroso) The physiognomic theory that criminals could be identified by certain "stigmata of degeneracy," such as low foreheads, closely set eyes, and small, pointed ears. The famous chess player Charles Goring who used modern statistical methods decisively disproved Lombroso's theory. 2. The dogma, common in Europe of the Middle Ages, that all disease is caused by loss of semen or other "vital fluids."

degenerating axons   Axons that have been injured or destroyed, leaving a residue that absorbs a particular dye. A degenerating myelinated nerve fiber releases myelin which absorbs osmium, producing a black trail where the live or healthy fiber had been.

degeneration   General term denoting deterioration or decline in any of a number of contexts, for example, in the quality of organic, intellectual, emotional, or moral functioning.

degenerative psychoses   1. Rare phrase for psychoses in which patients regress to earlier, sometimes infantile, behavior. 2. Psychoses characterized by irreversible intellectual deterioration.

degenerative status   A constitutional body type marked by an accumulation of deviations from what is considered normal, although a single deviant feature would have no particular pathological significance.

degree   Relative amount or quantity (for example degree of temperature [°], and degree of information).

degree of probability   A number between 0 and 1 that indicates the likelihood of occurrence of an event, such that 1 indicates that the event will occur, 0 indicates that it will not occur, and 0.5 indicates that it is as likely to occur as not to occur.

degrees of freedom (df, d.f., D.F., or DF)   1. The number of elements free to vary in a statistical calculation, or the number of scores less the number of mathematical restrictions. If the mean of a set of scores is fixed, then degrees of freedom is one less than the number of scores. 2. A value required in ascertaining the computed probability of the results of a statistical test (such as the t test). There are different equations for each statistical test. The phrase specifies the number of independent observations possible for a source of variation minus the number of independent parameters used in estimating that variation computation. One df is lost each time a population parameter is estimated on the basis of a sample of data from the population.

degree specifier   In linguistics, a category whose members combine with an adjective or adverb to describe the extent to which the property designated by the modifier is present, such as "very" and "quite."

dehoaxing   Following an experiment, the disclosure of deceptions carried out during the experiment, for the purpose of informing naive participants as to the precise nature of the research. See DEBRIEFING.

dehumanization   The process of reducing humans, particularly in institutions, to an animal-like existence by depriving them of freedom of choice. See OPEN HOSPITAL, THERAPEUTIC COMMUNITY.

dehydration reactions   Metabolic and psychological disturbances occurring when the body's water supply falls far below its normal quota. May progress to delirium and death if more than 10% of body weight is lost. See HYDRATION.

dehypnosis   Eliminating the assumption that hypnotic fantasies are real; viewing thoughts as images and not as reality.

deification   The attribution (usually by aboriginal peoples) of supernatural characteristics to animate or inanimate objects.

deindividuation   1. The condition of comparative anonymity in a group, characterized by the lessening of members' feelings of individuality, reduction of self-consciousness, and the weakening of group members' internal restraints. Considered to be a general goal in the training of military recruits. 2. (L. Festinger, A. Pepitone, & T. M. Newcomb) In social psychology, the process whereby inhibitions are weakened as a person loses personal identity, resultant behavior being impulsive, aggressive, or regressive. See BRAINWASHING, MIND CONTROL.

deinstinctualization   See NEUTRALIZATION.

deinstitutionalization   The process of transferring care of persons with mental retardation or mental illness from the structured institutional facilities to homes and workplaces that are part of the social mainstream of the community. See COMMUNITIES FOR THE RETARDED.

deintegration   A maturational process beginning with birth, when a primary self or state of original wholeness and integration is disrupted in the service of growth.

deism   A doctrine positing that a divinity, formed the universe, including the earth and all its inhabitants, but subsequently did not get involved.

Deiters' cells   Elongated cells which support the outer hair cells of the organ of Corti in the internal ear.

Deiters' nucleus   (O. F. Dieters) The lateral vestibular nucleus of the brain.

deity fear   See THEOPHOBIA.

déjà entendu   (previously heard—French) The feeling that what is now being heard has a familiar ring, even though it has not been heard before. It is a distortion of memory, or false recognition. See DÉJÀ VU, PARAMNESIA.

déjà pensé   (previously thought–French) The feeling of having had the exact same thoughts at a previous time, when this is not the case. A distortion of memory, or false recognition. See PARAMNESIA.

déjà raconté   (previously said—French) A feeling that a long forgotten event which is now recalled has been heard before. The illusion is assumed to arise from the need for reassurance that a threatening experience was previously mastered and could therefore be mastered again. See PARAMNESIA.

déjà vécu   (previously lived—French) A paramnesia characterized by a feeling of having lived previously, a déjà vu experience in which feelings of familiarity in novel situations are attributed to recollection of experiences from another life. See EPILEPSY, PARAMNESIA, PSEUDOMNESIA.

déjà vu   (previously seen—French) An illusive feeling of familiarity; the uncanny conviction that a newly experienced event has already been experienced or that the same scene has been witnessed before. The feeling of familiarity may be due to resemblance between the present and the past scenes, or to the fact that a similar scene has been pictured in a daydream or night dream. See PARAMNESIA, PSEUDOMNESIA and terms beginning with DÉJÀ.

delahara   A culture-specific syndrome occurring among Philippine women and occasionally among men. Similar to *amok*, but less violent.

delamination   The splitting off of one cell-layer from another in the embryo.

de Lange's syndrome   A congenital disorder characterized by moderate-to-severe mental retardation. Occurs in two forms: a Bruck-de Lange type (afflicted persons have short broad necks, broad shoulders, short and thick extremities, muscular hypertrophy) and a Brachman-de Lange type (afflicted persons have delayed bone maturation, visual problems, microbrachycephaly, syndactyly, and short arms and fingers). Also known as Amsterdam dwarf disease, and Amsterdam type of retardation, because the disorder was identified among patients in the Amsterdam area. Also known as Cornelia de Lange's syndrome.

delay of gratification   1. (W. Mischel) The ability to forgo immediate reward for the sake of greater, future reward. 2. An aspect of frustration tolerance involving dealing with tension arising from an unsatisfied urge, desire, or drive. See DELAYED GRATIFICATION.

delay of reinforcement   The time between the moment of occurrence of a stimulus and the time of reinforcement (thus establishing the amount of delay). Ivan Pavlov found that the amount of delay dictated how quickly the conditioned animals would later react, and how quickly their conditioning was established. B. F. Skinner later determined that the sooner the reinforcement occurred, the quicker the learning. See DELAY OF REWARD GRADIENT.

delay path   A neurological entity assumed to take part in the prolongation of a response.

delay therapy   A form of behavior therapy employed in treating obsessive-compulsive patients by placing them in situations that ordinarily would provoke their rituals, but preventing them from carrying out the compulsive behavior. Also known as response prevention.

delay-of-reward gradient   The greater the time between a response and its reinforcement or reward the poorer the learning of that response. Consequences, natural or logical, should follow target behaviors as soon as possible. See DELAY OF REINFORCEMENT.

delayed alternation   A variation on the alternation method in which an experimental organism is required to wait for an interval between each response in a series of alternations. See ALTERNATION METHOD, DELAYED REACTION.

delayed-alternation test   A variation of the delayed-response test in which the reward is alternated from side to side with a delay between trials. The subject, often a laboratory mouse, must learn that a cup containing food is always on the opposite side from the previous trial. The delayed-alternation test is used in the study of lesions in various brain areas and their effects on memory or related functions.

delayed conditioned response   A conditioned response that was established through delayed conditioning in which the prior conditioned stimulus (CS) typically overlaps the unconditioned stimulus (UCS) to some extent.

delayed conditioning   A variation in classical conditioning in which the unconditioned stimulus (UCS) is delayed for a period of time (generally five seconds or longer) during which the conditioned stimulus (CS) is continually present.

delayed discharge   A major function of the ego, consisting of postponement of immediate gratification of instinctual drives, such as sex or hostility. The delay gives the person time to master any danger that may be involved, especially by trying different ways of dealing with the situation in thought rather than action.

delayed effect   The consequence of some precipitating cause, not occurring at the time of the intervention but at a later time.

delayed gratification   An ability or willingness to wait for a desired goal rather than having to meet it now. For example, a married couple saves a percentage of their income to buy a new car instead of obtaining a loan to buy the car immediately. See DELAY OF GRATIFICATION. Compare IMMEDIATE GRATIFICATION.

delayed instinct   Unlearned forms of behavior which, owing to immaturity of the organism, cannot be elicited in the period just after birth.

delayed-matching test   A task in which the participant is rewarded for pressing an illuminated colored panel that matches the color of a sample. Scoring is based on the amount of time required to match the color. Participants with frontal-lobe lesions often have difficulty in making the proper choices in normal time.

delayed matching-to-sample task   A situation in which an organism, usually a human infant or an animal, is shown an object that is next hidden, and after a delay is supposed to find it.

delayed nonmatching-to-sample task   A task in which a subject is shown an object, and after a delay must choose the alternative that does not match the object.

delayed reaction/response   An appropriate response to a cue that has been absent for a period of time. Under most circumstances a rat can delay a response for only 3-4 seconds. See ALTERNATION METHOD.

delayed-reaction experiment   A complication of the signal experiment, in which the organism, a child or animal, is not allowed to react until a given time has elapsed after the signal, the typical aim of the research being to determine how long the response can be delayed without failing to occur altogether. Also known as delayed-reaction method/problem/procedure. See DELAYED-RESPONSE PROBLEM.

delayed-reaction method/problem/procedure delayed-reaction experiment

delayed recall   The ability to recollect information acquired earlier. Used sometimes in neuropsychological examinations at the end of sessions to determine the rate of loss of information presented earlier, compared with persons thought to be normal.

delayed reflex   A reflexive response which occurs after an abnormal interval following stimulation.

delayed reinforcement   An adaptation mechanism whereby an organism may acquire a new behavior pattern through discriminative conditioning (for example, bait shyness). The reward or punishment may occur after a delay following introduction of a new stimulus. Delayed reinforcement usually is demonstrated with relatively simple neural circuits, such as taste or smell sensations, in which new information can be stored for long periods of time. Also known as delayed reinforcement procedure.

delayed response   See DELAY OF REINFORCEMENT.

delayed-response problem/procedure   A method of research used with infants and animals in which a desired item is shown to the subject, put in one of several containers and then hidden from the subject. After a delay period, the subject is allowed to choose one of the containers, to see whether the correct one was remembered. Also known as the delayed-reaction method, delayed-response task.

delayed reward   A reward not given immediately after the required response but administered following a designated interval. Usually done during research on learning.

delayed speech   The failure of speech to develop at the expected age. May be due to lags in maturation, hearing impairment, brain injury, mental retardation, social insufficiency, or emotional disturbance.

Delboeuf disk   (J. J. Delboeuf) An apparatus for the determination of difference thresholds for brilliance by the method of equal sense distances.

Delboeuf('s) illusion   (J.J. Delboeuf) A false visual perception of the apparent change of size in one of two identical circles if a larger circle surrounds it. See UZNADZE ILLUSION.

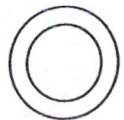

Delboeuf('s) illusion   The inner of the larger circles is the same size as the outer of the smaller circles.

deletion   In genetics, the loss of genetic material from a chromosome. Usually associated with physical and mental retardation, as in cri-du-chat syndrome. See DELETION SYNDROME, GENETICS.

deletion syndrome   A complex of disorders resulting from the loss of genetic material from a chromosome. Usually identified with a chromosome number and a minus sign, such as 46,xx13q-, the q denoting a deletion of the long arm of chromosome number 13. A deleted arm of a chromosome may become reorganized in a small circle known as a ring chromosome. If the deletion does result in a ring, its symbol is 46,XX13r. See GENETICS.

deliberate discourse   In group dynamics, a discussion of the pros and cons of proposed action to resolve controversy.

delibidinization   In psychoanalytic theory, elimination, neutralization, or diversion of a sexual goal, as in diverting sexual voyeurism to curiosity about intellectual matters. Also known as desexualization.

Delilah syndrome   A behavior pattern in which a woman is motivated by a wish to control and manipulate men, and seeks multiple partners to do so. Purportedly associated with an unsatisfactory relationship with a dominating and exploitative father. She assumes the role of Delilah, and renders men (representing the father) weak and helpless by seducing them (as in the story of Samson and Delilah). See SAMSON COMPLEX.

delimination   To establish limits or boundaries. See PROBLEM-SOLVING BEHAVIOR.

delinquency   1. Behavior, especially of youths, unacceptable to adults or disappointing to parents. 2. Violating of special legal codes by juveniles, such as curfew laws.

delinquent   A criminal or social offender, viewed as a social type. Term is usually limited to minors.

délire d'emblée   (delirium at one blow—French) (E. Bleuler) A delusion that is fully developed when it first appears. See AUTOCHTHONOUS DELUSION.

délire de négation   French phrase similar to Cotard's syndrome.

délire du toucher   (morbid desire to touch—French) A compulsion to touch objects.

délire tremblant   French phrase similar to alcohol withdrawal delirium or delirium tremens (DTs).

delirious mania   The most severe type of manic reaction in which the patient becomes totally disoriented and incoherent, may have vivid auditory and visual hallucinations, and engage in constant over-activity that includes screaming, gesticulating, shouting, and pacing up and down. See BELL'S MANIA, HYPERMANIA.

delirious rage   A violent emotional disturbance approaching utter disorganization. See FRENZY.

delirious states   Clinical states exhibiting the essential features of delirium. Develop during amphetamine, barbiturate, phencyclidine intoxication, alcohol withdrawal, or as a result of other toxic conditions, systemic infections, head trauma, thiamine deficiency, postoperative conditions, or seizures. See DELIRIUM.

delirium   A state of clouded consciousness in which attention cannot be sustained, the environment is misperceived, and the stream of thought is disordered. The patient experiences hallucinations, illusions, and misinterpretation of sounds or sights and may become incoherent, disoriented, agitated, and extremely restless. Episodes are usually brief. Types of delirium include: ABSTINENCE, ACUTE, ALCOHOL-WITHDRAWAL, BELLADONNA, COCAINE, COLLAPSE, EXHAUSTION, FEBRILE, MUTTERING, RHYMING, SENILE, SUBSTANCE-ABUSE, SUBSTANCE-WITHDRAWAL, TOXIC, TRAUMATIC. See SUBDELIRIOUS STATE.

delirium abstinence   A state of mental confusion caused by the sudden cessation of intake of intoxicants, including drugs and alcohol.

delirium of metamorphosis   The belief that a person can transform self or others into a wolf or other animal. This delusion was not uncommon during the medieval period. See LYCANTHROPY.

delirium tremens (DTs, dts, or **d.t.s)**   (T. Sutton, J. Ware) A condition generated by serious alcoholism, characterized by physical unsteadiness, hallucinations, delusions, clouding of consciousness, disorientation, sweating, rapid heartbeat, and course irregular tremors. Also known as *délire tremblant* (French). See ALCOHOL-WITHDRAWAL DELIRIUM.

delirium verborum   (delirium of words—Latin) A delirious state in which the patient is excessively loquacious. See WORD SALAD.

Delphi method/technique   A technique in evaluation research for group decision making in which experts are individually presented with as much information as possible about the problem. Their recommendations are collected by a facilitator who discloses them and seeks consensus about what is likely to occur in the future of the topic. Developed by the Rand Corporation, named after the Delphic oracles in ancient Greece who prophesied the future. See META-ANALYSIS.

delta   The fourth letter of the Greek alphabet. See APPENDIX C.

delta alcoholism   (E. M. Jellinek) A type of alcoholism characterized by daily consumption, increased tolerance, cellular adaptation, leading to withdrawal symptoms if the patient goes "on the wagon" for even one or two days. There is, however, no compulsive craving, and control over intake is not completely lost. Also known as inveterate drinking.

delta mean-square successive differences method   A technique that indicates the presence but not necessarily the degree of relationship between successive observations in the same series of data. Can detect both linear and nonlinear serial correlations.

delta motion/movement   A form of apparent movement in which a brighter stimulus appears to move toward a darker stimulus, provided certain conditions of stimulus size, distance, and time between stimuli obtain. See GESTALT.

delta-9-tetrahydrocannabinol (THC)   See CANNABIS, HASHISH.

delta rhythm/wave   A slow, large, regular-shaped brain wave with a frequency of one to three Hertz (cycles per second). Associated with deep sleep, a delta wave indicates a synchronization of cells of the cerebral cortex. Also known as slow wave. See ELECTROENCEPHALOGRAPH, PARADOXICAL SLEEP, SLEEP STAGES.

delta-wave sleep   Periods of deep, usually dreamless, sleep in which delta waves (one to three Hertz) predominate. These periods occur at irregular intervals. The waves appear to arise from the deeper regions of the brain. See DELTA WAVES, RAPID-EYE-MOVEMENT (REM) SLEEP, SLEEP STAGES.

deltoid   Pertaining to or located in the muscle or region just below the acromial region and forming the uppermost outer part of the arm.

delusion   An erroneous belief impervious to reason, maintained in spite of irrationality or evidence to the contrary. Delusions, though absurd and a symptom of psychosis, appear to serve such purposes and needs as emotional support, relief of anxiety or guilt, counteracting feelings of inferiority or insecurity. Types of delusion include: ALLOPSYCHIC, ASTHENIC, AUTOCHTHONOUS, AUTOPSYCHIC, BIZARRE, CATATHYMIC, CIRCUMSCRIBED, CONJUGAL, ENCAPSULATED, EROTIC, EXPANSIVE, EXPLANATORY, FRAGMENTARY, FRENOLI, GRANDIOSE, HYPOCHONDRIACAL, MIGNON, MULTIPLE, RELIGIOUS, RESIDUAL, SEXUAL, SOMATIC, SYSTEMATIZED. See ACUTE DELUSIONAL PSYCHOSIS, COTARD'S SYNDROME, DEMENTIA PRAECOX, DOUBLE ORIENTATION, HALLUCINOGEN-DELUSIONAL DISORDER, NIHILISM, ORGANIC-DELUSIONAL SYNDROME, REFORMISM AS DELUSION.

delusional jealousy   A paranoid jealousy reaction characterized by a fixed delusion that the spouse or sexual partner is unfaithful. The person may constantly watch for indications that this suspicion is justified, may manufacture evidence, and is blind to facts that contravene the conviction. Once called amorous paranoia.

delusional loving   1. Infatuation and emotional attachment to an extreme degree on the part of a person who "falls in love" with another person who usually possesses superior characteristics, in politics, the arts, and sciences. The emotions are usually intense but transient in nature. 2. Refers to patients, typically women, who believe falsely that they are loved by a particular person, in many cases that person may not even know that the patient exists; a kind of phantom lover. See DE CLÉRAMBAULT SYNDROME, DON JUANISM, EROTOMANIA.

delusional mania   (E. Kraepelin) A subtype of acute mania characterized by grandiose delusions similar to those in the expansive type of general paresis.

delusional misidentification   Inability of a patient to identify a known person or object because of a delusion that the person or object has been changed or transformed. See CAPGRAS SYNDROME, MISIDENTIFICATION.

delusional system   A pattern of false beliefs that is internally coherent and systematized. Also known as delusion system.

delusion classification   (K. Wernicke) A tripartite classification of delusions of self (autopsychic delusion); of the world (allopsychic delusion); and of the body (somatopsychic delusion).

delusion of being controlled   A false belief that machines or other people are manipulating a patient's thoughts or actions. The reaction is one type of delusion of influence, and is often associated with delusions of persecution.

delusion of grandeur   A grossly exaggerated belief of self-importance, power, wealth, or personal mission in life. The misconception that oneself is more important than one actually is, frequently manifested in the belief that one is famous. Also known as expansive delusion, grandiose delusion, grandiose idea, megalomania.

delusion of impoverishment   A false belief, usually of an older person with sufficient financial resources, who insists that personal finances have run out or will soon run out. See POOR MOUTH.

delusion of individualism   A belief that (a) individuals are separate and distinct from other people, and (b) others' frustration, unhappiness, and despair have no bearing on their own well-being.

delusion of influence   The false belief, often associated with delusions of persecution, that other people are exerting secret control over the patient's thoughts and behavior, or that the patient is being subjected to harmful radio waves, or that enemies are "pouring filth" into the patient's mind. Also known as ideas of influence.

delusion of negation   A nihilistic delusion, the false conviction that the world and everything in it have ceased to exist. See NIHILISM.

delusion of observation   delusion of reference

delusion of orientation   (E. Bleuler) A condition in which a person with a serious mental disturbance functions quite normally in some circumstances despite having fixed false convictions or fantastic notions (for example, an employee appears to be normal, but confides to the supervisor that Martians nightly move shoes from one shelf to another). Also known as double orientation.

delusion of persecution   A false belief, common in paranoia, in which patients believe that people, such as the CIA, FBI, or neighbors are conspiring against them. Also known as persecutory delusion.

delusion of poverty   A false belief of lacking finances, of being destitute, financially ruined. See DELUSION OF IMPOVERISHMENT, POOR MOUTH.

delusion of reference   A pathological misinterpretation in which patients feel that others are referring to them, that is, whispering, or talking about them, referring to them in newspapers or via television and that outside worldwide events relate to them in some way. Also known as delusion of observation, idea of reference.

delusion of sin   A false belief of having committed an unpardonable sin, such as believing that the self is responsible for war, economic depression, drought, and other catastrophes. Thought to be exaggerations of guilt feelings generated by hostile attitudes and wishes. They are frequently accompanied by intense fear of punishment. Sometimes such people after hearing of a murder, confess to it even though they usually know nothing about the details of the crime. Also known as delusion of sin and guilt.

demand   Any internal or external condition that arouses a drive in an organism.

demand character   The inherent aspect of any signal that attracts attention. For example, LARGE TYPE, *UNUSUAL TYPE,* variations, moving letters as on a theatre marquee, and colored print.

demand characteristics   1. The effect of particular environments on behavior, for example, a dimly lit church with people silently praying may encourage a person to be subdued. 2. Cues available to participants in a study that may enable them to determine the purpose of the study, or what is expected by the researcher. See AFFORDANCE, COVER STORY, EXPERIMENTER EFFECT.

demand feeding   See SELF-DEMAND SCHEDULE.

demandingness   Insistence upon attention from others. A common symptom found in hypomania and young children.

demandments   (A. Ellis) Internalized sentences, often unconscious, having an arbitrary, "must" quality that often lead to discouragement.

demasculinization   The prenatal developmental process in which anatomical/neurological masculinization is inhibited. The female fetus is normally demasculinized due to the absence of threshold levels of androgens.

demented type general paresis   The most common psychosis occurring in advanced general paresis, characterized by mental deterioration, masklike facies, loss of interest, apathy, and withdrawal. Also known as simple type general paresis.

dementia   (W. Cullen) 1. A lasting deterioration of memory, judgment, and emotions generating erratic behavior, with the dementia based on some type of objective brain damage, such as destruction of the cerebral cortex; or through somatic poisoning such as heavy doses of lead, or due to functional causes. 2. One of Jean Esquirol's five classes of mental disorders. Types of dementia include: ALCOHOLIC, ATROPHIC, BOXER'S, DEPRESSIVE, EPILEPTIC, FALSE, MULTIINFARCT, MYOCLONIC, ORGANIC, PARALYTIC, POSTTRAUMATIC, PRESENILIS, PRIMARY DEGENERATIVE, SEMANTIC, SENILE, SUBCORTICAL, TRAUMATIC, WERNICKE'S. See ALZHEIMER'S DISEASE, BINSWANGER'S DISEASE, CATATONIC DEMENTIA PRAECOX, EPILEPTIC DETERIORATION, HYSTERICAL PSEUDODEMENTIA, IDIOTISM, INFANTILIS, PREDEMENTIA PRAECOX, PRESBYOPHRENIA, PSEUDODEMENTIA, SENILE DEMENTIA OF THE ALZHEIMER TYPE (SDAT).

dementia associated with alcoholism   Disorder associated with prolonged heavy use of alcohol, rarely occurring before age 35. Diagnosis is made only if all other causes of dementia have been excluded. The disorder takes three forms: Mild, moderate, and severe, depending on the degree of social, occupational, and personality impairment. Also known as Korsakoff's Disease, Wernicke's encephalopathy.

dementia due to Huntington's disease   Huntington's disease

dementia praecox   (early madness—Latin) Phrase coined by Thomas Willis for a mental disorder of early madness, characterized primarily by withdrawal from reality with associated delusions of grandeur and persecution. Emil Kraepelin also used the phrase, noting that the condition worsened in late adolescence. Eugen Bleuler later substituted the term schizophrenia. See PREDEMENTIA PRAECOX.

Demerol   Trade name for meperidine.

Deming Management Method   (W. E. Deming) A set of 14 guidelines for optimal organizational behavior and quality management.

demivierge   (half virgin—French) A "technical virgin"; a woman who may have engaged in various sexual activities but not penile–vaginal intercourse.

democratic atmosphere   A nonauthoritarian situation in which group members participate in planning and are encouraged to give their opinions.

democratic leader   (K. Lewin) The type of leader who participates with group members in developing goals and procedures. Stimulates group participation by making but not imposing suggestions. Research has shown that groups with democratic leaders showed greater originality and higher morale, and less anxiety, aggression, and apathy than groups with authoritarian leaders or leaderless groups. See LAISSEZ-FAIRE LEADER.

democratic parent   A parent who establishes an egalitarian tone in the family, allowing children to participate to various degrees in family decisions. Adlerians are likely to run family councils, and in which major family decisions are discussed and some settled by either majority vote or by consensus.

democratic parenting   (R. Dreikurs) A child-rearing style based on natural and logical consequences, featuring periodic democratic family councils, and in which there is no punishment. See AUTOCRATIC PARENTING, FAMILY COUNCIL, PERMISSIVE PARENTING.

demographic analysis   See DEMOGRAPHIC PATTERNS, DEMOGRAPHY.

demographic patterns   Statistical information on trends in population variables, such as marriages, births, infant mortality, income, as well as in some instances geographical distribution of mental retardation or mental illness.

demographics   Statistics about populations in established areas, such as numbers of births, marriages, deaths, houses with bathrooms, or divisions of ethnic or racial populations.

demographic variables   Characteristics of people, such as age, sex, marital status, and the like, that often are related statistically to differential incidence or prevalence of disorders.

demography   The statistical study of human populations in regard to various factors including geographical distribution, sex and age distribution, size, and population-growth trends. Demographic analyses are used in epidemiological studies. See DEMOGRAPHIC PATTERNS.

demon   An evil spirit. Also spelled daemon, daimon.

demon fear   See DEMONOPHOBIA, SATANOPHOBIA.

demonic   (R. May) A powerful obsessive urge. Also spelled daemonic, daimonic.

demonic character   A self-destructive trait characterized by repetition of actions that are damaging to self or others.

demonic possession   The belief that humans can become possessed by or under the control of evil spirits or demons. The concept of the invasion of the body by an evil spirit who controls the mind and produces madness, disease, or criminal behavior. Also known as demon possession. See DEMONOLOGY.

demonizing   1. Generating the impression that there are unnatural evil forces at work that have negatively influenced or caused events in life that have not gone as desired. 2. To view or cause others to view a person or entity as bad, evil, or demonic.

demonolatry   The worship of devils or demons. See SATANISM.

demonologic concept of illness   A belief that mental and physical diseases are caused by an evil spirit that has gained possession of the soul and must be exorcised if the patient is to recover. Aspects of this belief are found in various indigenous religious traditions.

demonology   The systematic study of the belief in invisible demons and evil spirits, frequently pictured in folklore and mythology as invading the mind, gaining possession of the soul, and producing disordered behavior. See EXORCISM, INCUBUS, SUCCUBUS, WITCHCRAFT.

demonomania   Morbid preoccupation with demons and demonic possession.

demonophobia   Morbid fear of spirits, ghosts, devils, and the like. Also known as daemonophobia, entheomania, phasmophobia. See SATANOPHOBIA.

demonstration   An attempt to induce belief or understanding in another person, either by a careful train of reasoning or by presenting empirical evidence, whether experimental or observational.

demonstration experiment   Policy research based loosely on the experimental research design. New policies are introduced in one school, factory, etc., and the results are compared with control settings.

demophobia   Fear of crowds. See AGORAPHOBIA, OCHLOPHOBIA.

demoralization   A breakdown of values, standards, and mores in individuals or groups, such as occur in periods of rapid social change, wars and economic depressions, or personal traumas. A demoralized person is disorganized and feels lost, weak and helpless, and has lost confidence in self and others.

demoralization hypothesis   (J. Frank) A postulate that behind all functional mental disorders is personal demoralization, and that the purpose of psychotherapy is encouragement.

demorphinization   Obsolete term for the gradual diminution of the doses of morphine in the treatment of morphine habit.

Demosthenes complex   The use of language to compensate for feelings of inferiority, by such techniques as using unusual words and complex sentences and speaking at great length.

demyelination   The loss of the myelin sheath that covers the nerve fibers. It is associated with several kinds of diseases and inborn errors of lipid metabolism.

denarcism   A movement of thoughts and attitudes away from the self and consequently having greater concern for others. See DEREFLECTION.

denasality   The voice quality associated with obstructed nasal passages that prevent adequate nasal resonance during speech.

dendrite   (W. His) Bushy extensions of a neuron that receive impulses from other neurons. The number and length of dendrite processes may vary with the specific function of the neuron.

dendritic potential   The electric charge constituting the constant state of excitation of the dendrite.

dendritic zone   Any part of a receptive surface of a neuron. For some neurons, the dendritic zone may extend several feet from the perikaryon (cell body).

dendrodendritic synapse   Meeting of the dendrites of two neurons.

dendron   Part of the neuron stem before the cell body.

dendrophilia   A paraphilia of sexual attraction to trees. The person may have sexual contact with trees, venerate them as phallic symbols, or both. Also known as dendrophily.

denervation   Loss of functioning of nerves by disease, trauma or surgery.

denervation hypersensitivity   A condition in which neurons that have been denervated (deprived of afferent input) become hypersensitive and require less stimulation to fire. Spinal shock is an example of denervation hypersensitivity.

denial   A defense mechanism that consists of an unconscious, selective "blindness" that protects the person from facing intolerable deeds, and situations, observed in parents who insist their child is innocent of a crime despite overwhelming evidence of guilt. Also known as denial of reality, disavowal, negation. See HYSTERICAL BLINDNESS, MENTAL BLIND SPOT, REPRESSION.

denial and shock   (E. Kübler-Ross) The first stage of Kübler-Ross' five stages of dying, characterized by an inability to accept the inevitable. See STAGES OF DYING.

denier   A person who copes with unresolved personality conflicts by denying rather than accepting them.

denotation   The objects or phenomena to which a given term is applied and which are included in its meaning. A direct and clear message or communication, such as an arrow indicating a direction to follow. Also known as denotative meaning. See CONNOTATION.

denotational meaning   The meaning of words as found in a dictionary. These differ from connotational meaning, the effect that words have on others.

density   1. A stimulus quality, for example, a tonal characteristic of solidity distinct from pitch, volume, or timbre. 2. The amount of some characteristic per volume.

density function   1. The probability of a continuous variable where the area under the curve is equal to one and the function is zero or greater. 2. A statistical or mathematical derivative in which the frequency of a random variable, as a function of x, represents the proportion of the total frequency or unity. Used to determine the probability of cases falling within a certain interval under the curve: Also known as frequency function, probability density function.

dental   A speech sound loosely used as an alternative term for alveolar.

dental age   A measure of childhood dental development based on the number of permanent teeth. See CARPAL AGE.

dental pattern   The species-specific arrangement of teeth by types. In the human it is 2,1,2,3, the number of incisors, canines, bicuspids, and molars in each quadrant of the mouth from front to back. Also known as dentition pattern.

dental-patient reactions   Responses of individuals with differing behavioral patterns to dental care. Studies show pleasure, pain, and sexuality associations with the oral cavity and some transference to the dentist in the form of sexual attraction by certain patients. Other dental-patient reactions may be manifested by ambivalence and an association of pain and money with dental care.

dental phobia   Morbid fear of dental treatment usually traceable to a traumatic dental experience in childhood, but also associated in many cases with a lower-than-normal pain threshold and in some cases with a neurotic predisposition.

dentate gyrus   A brain convolution that interlocks with Ammon's horn in the hippocampal system. It is a narrow strip of cortical tissue that lies in the hippocampal sulcus and is named for its surface which resembles a set of teeth.

dentate nucleus   A semicircle of cerebellar cell bodies assumed to be associated with emotions.

dentilabial   labiodental

dentition pattern   dental pattern

de-orality   The transfer of instinctual drives from the oral region to some other region or agency. In psychoanalytic theory, de-orality may be interpreted as a transfer of breast-feeding pleasure to dependency on a maternal person.

deoxyribonucleic acid (DNA)   A complex molecule that occurs in all body-cell nuclei as a pair of helix-shaped strands of smaller molecules called bases, or basic nucleotides. Which bases (adenine, thymine, cytosine, or guanine) follow which in a DNA gene sets the position of the amino acids. The DNA molecule is the primary structural unit of genetic material for all living organisms, including viruses. DNA material is inherited half from the father's sperm and half from the mother's egg. The basic (double-helix) structure of the DNA molecule was discovered by James D. Watson, Francis H. C. Crick and Maurice H. F. Wilkins. See DNA ANALYSIS, RECOMBINANT DNA.

dependence   1. A causal relation between two variables. See DEPENDENT VARIABLE. 2. Wanting or needing help from others. Also known as dependency. See CODEPENDENCE. 3. Reliance on some substance for feeling good. See DRUG DEPENDENCE.

dependence on therapy   The conviction on the part of some people that they cannot survive without psychotherapy.

Dependency Court   A court of law in some U.S. states, to which Child Protective Services can file a petition alleging child abuse. If the court accepts the case, it can deem the child to be a "dependent of the court" and determine the child's living arrangements and supervision until final disposition.

dependency needs   Compelling urges that must be satisfied by others, including the need for affection and security. Such needs are considered universal and normal for both sexes and at all ages, but it is also recognized that dependence can be excessive, and over-encouraged. See MORBID DEPENDENCY.

dependency syndrome   A tendency of women of many cultures to identify themselves in terms of a mated relationship.

dependency theory   A point of view that the failure of Third World nations to achieve adequate development results from their dependence on advanced capitalist countries.

dependent mentally retarded   Describing persons with mental disabilities who require supervision for daily living.

dependent organizational model   In an organizational hierarchy, the relationship between an administrator and subordinate leaders. See INTEGRATED MODEL.

dependent part   A component which derives its properties from the whole of which it belongs. See DEPENDENT-PART QUALITY.

dependent-part quality   In Gestalt theory, the structural character of a part derived from its relation to and its role in the total configuration.

dependent-personality disorder   A diagnosis for a pattern of allowing other people to take responsibility for major decisions in the person's life and agreeing with or following others with more dominant personalities. Marked by low self-confidence, fear of self-reliance, and an inability to function effectively without the help of others.

dependent variable (DV)   The response predicted to change as a result of manipulations of the independent variable. Compare INDEPENDENT VARIABLE.

depersonalization   (M. Prince) A state of mind in which the self appears unreal. A person feels estranged from the self and from the world of people and things. Thoughts and experiences have a dreamlike character. Sometimes interpreted as an unconscious attempt to escape from threatening situations. The extreme form is known as depersonalization syndrome.

depersonalization disorder/neurosis   A dissociative condition characterized by a sense of unreality of self, objects and others, severe enough to impair social and occupational functioning. See NEUROSIS, PSYCHASTHENIA.

depersonalization neurosis   depersonalization disorder

depersonalization syndrome   See DEPERSONALIZATION.

depersonification   Inability to achieve independence and individuality, as in a failure to separate from parents and venture out into the world.

depletive treatment   A treatment of mental disorders based on the concept of weakening the organism through such means as bleeding, purging, blistering, and making the patient vomit. Originated in the time of Hippocrates, and held sway for one thousand years.

depolarization   The electrical activity within the neuron as a nerve impulse is transmitted. Before the impulse, the cell is in equilibrium. When stimulated, the membrane's barrier permits the positive ions to enter, thereby depolarizing the cell in a wavelike movement lasting a few milliseconds.

depraved appetite   See CISSA, PICA.

depressant(s)   Agents that diminish or retard any function or activity of a body system or organ such as alcohol, barbiturates, and tranquilizers.

depressed parents   (G. Painter) Parents who are discouraged by their inability to deal effectively with their children. In some cases, the children are essentially normal, but the problem is that the parents had unrealistic expectations of the children, and as a result the parents feel they are failures, taking blame on themselves.

depressed type general paresis   A psychosis occurring in advanced general paresis, consisting of discouragement due to failing powers, followed by loss of insight, deep despondency, and, in some cases, nihilistic delusions (such as "My body is a hollow shell").

depression   An emotional state of persistent dejection, ranging from relatively mild discouragement and gloominess to feelings of extreme despondency and despair. These feelings are usually accompanied by loss of initiative, listlessness, insomnia, loss of appetite, and difficulty in concentrating and making decisions. Types of depression include: ACUTE, AGITATED, AMBIVALENT, ANACLITIC, ANXIOUS, AUTONOMOUS, CHILDHOOD, CLAIMING TYPE OF, CLASSICAL, CYCLICAL, DEEP, ENDOGENOUS, INVOLUTIONAL, MAJOR, MASKED, MENOPAUSAL, MILD, MODERATE, MONOPOLAR, NEUROTIC, POSTICTAL, POSTPARTUM, POSTSCHIZOPHRENIC, PRIMAL, REACTIVE, RECURRENT, RETARDED, SELF-BLAMING, SOMATIC, UNIPOLAR. See BECK DEPRESSION INVENTORY, BIPOLAR DISORDER, CHILDREN'S DEPRESSION INVENTORY, CONSTITUTIONAL DEPRESSIVE DISPOSITION, EXCITEMENT-DEPRESSION, HYPODEPRESSION, MAJOR DEPRESSIVE EPISODE, MANIC-DEPRESSIVE ILLNESS, MANIC-DEPRESSIVE REACTION, PSYCHOTIC-DEPRESSIVE REACTION, RESPIRATORY DEPRESSION, SPREADING DEPRESSION, UNIPOLAR MANIC-DEPRESSIVE PSYCHOSIS.

depression and acceptance   (E. Kübler-Ross) The fourth stage of Kübler-Ross' five stages of dying, characterized by a giving in to a sense of weakness and hopelessness in accepting the inevitable. See STAGES OF DYING.

Depression After Delivery (DAD)   A national support group of mothers, established after increased awareness of instances of infanticides (killing of infants) and filicides (killing of own children) by mothers who were depressed. See POSTPARTUM DEPRESSION.

depressive anxiety   (M. Klein) A state of tension and apprehension derived from the fear of a person's own wishes and capacity to destroy, harm, or damage an ambivalently loved object.

depressive character   See MELANCHOLIC PERSONALITY.

depressive dementia   See CATATONIC SCHIZOPHRENIA.

depressive equivalent   Symptoms that are not overtly depressive but that express an underlying depression.

depressive hebephrenia   Depression usually associated with manic-depressive (bipolar) psychosis but observed periodically in patients with hebephrenic (disorganized) schizophrenia.

depressive mania   A mixed state described by Emil Kraepelin, characterized by a combination of manic and depressive symptoms.

depressive neurosis   Old name for dysthymic disorder.

depressive position   Phrase applied by Melanie Klein and her school to the stage of development that reaches its peak at about the sixth month of life. The infant begins a process of individuation and separation from the mother figure resulting in the capacity to tolerate ambivalent feelings of love and hate simultaneously. See PARANOID-SCHIZOID POSITION.

depressive psychosis   A type of psychosis in which there is a severe depressive component. See DEPRESSED BIPOLAR DISORDER, DEPRESSIVE STUPOR, INVOLUTIONAL PSYCHOTIC REACTION, MAJOR DEPRESSIVE EPISODE, MANIC-DEPRESSIVE REACTION, PSYCHOTIC-DEPRESSIVE REACTION.

depressive stupor   The most severe form of the depressive phase of manic-depressive (bipolar) disorder. The patient usually is mute, disoriented, wears an anxious or masklike expression, is constipated, refuses food, is preoccupied with hallucinations, delusions, and fantasies that may involve sin, death, and rebirth.

depressor nerve   A nerve that depresses motor or glandular activity when stimulated.

deprivation   1. An involuntary lack of something desired, as of food or human associates. 2. Denial of access to certain stimuli or needed substances, such as attention or food. 3. The unpleasant conscious experience of such lack.

deprivational homosexuality   See FACULTATIVE HOMOSEXUALITY.

deprivation discipline   A form of punishment frequently used by parents, of depriving children of certain privileges such as being allowed to go out to play with other children. Also known as grounding.

deprivation dwarfism   A state of delayed physical growth in children thought to be the result of insufficient emotional nurturance. Children from emotionally aloof homes recorded increases in weight and height when temporarily withdrawn from home environments; however, these children failed to thrive when restored to their homes. Studies of infant rats provide evidence for a link between maternal deprivation and suppression of growth hormones. See MARASMUS.

deprivation experiments   Research techniques in which subjects are deprived of something desired to study their reactions; for example, will rats deprived of food run a maze faster than usual?

deprivation index   A measure of the degree of inadequacy of a child's intellectual environment with respect to such variables as achievement expectations by significant adults, possibilities of exploring the environment, provisions for learning, and interaction with significant adult role models.

deprivation schedule   A pattern of withholding nutrients, such as water, from animals for research purposes.

deprivative amentia   Obsolete phrase for a form of mental retardation due to a lack of social stimuli or due to an organic disorder such as cretinism.

deprogramming   The use of reason, persuasion, coercion, and re-indoctrination, in the effort to "win back" a person who has adopted a new system of beliefs displeasing to family or friends, especially if they believe that the indoctrination was coerced (for example, in a cult, a person may have been indoctrinated by performing ritualized behaviors). If the deprogramming is successful, the person will ordinarily repudiate the new values and reaccept the original belief system. See BRAINWASHING, CULT(US).

depth   1. In perception, the distance from a viewer based on visual or auditory receptor stimulation. 2. In cognition, the extent of understanding of a concept, from superficial to complete comprehension. 3. In psychotherapy, the degree of relationship between patient and therapist and the extent of the patient's exploration of personality structure and history. See PSYCHOTHERAPY.

depth criteria   The visual means used in judging the distance of objects from the viewer. See BINOCULAR, UNIOCULAR.

depth cue   Any single indicator, or a combination of indicators, as to how far away a phenomenon seen is actually located. Among the cues are: What is seen before the object (interposition); how the size of the phenomenon looks near and far (linear perspective); how that object and other objects appear to move when the person viewing it moves, with objects that are close appearing to move more than distant objects (motion parallax); how the elements of a similar kind appear to be closer together as distance increases (texture gradient); and for those who can see with both eyes, the differences viewed by each eye (stereopsis). See DEPTH PERCEPTION, MONOCULAR DEPTH CUES.

depth fear   See ACROPHOBIA, BATHOPHOBIA.

depth from motion   Obtaining at first the impression of a phenomenon as two-dimensional, but on the object or person moving, realizing that the phenomenon is really three-dimensional.

depth from shading   A perception of distance due to light that reaches an object bouncing off in various directions and amounts, generating graduations of shades, that generates the impression of three dimensions.

depth interviewing   1. In consumer psychology, a motivation-research-oriented technique in which participants are encouraged to express themselves freely rather than answer a structured questionnaire. The purpose is to get the know the applicant in depth. One of the elements searched for is whether the interviewee remains guarded and not open. 2. In counseling or employment interviewing, interviewing a person for a long time, going into details, looking for opportunities to explore the person's areas of privacy. See QUALITATIVE INTERVIEW.

depth of processing   1. Understanding and feelings about others may go from superficial to deep and vice versa. In a good relationship, depth of understanding will increase; in others, an early flash feeling may disappear on further acquaintance. 2. (G. Craik, E. Tulving) The extent of association for an item to be remembered. The greater the depth of processing, the more readily the person can recall the item under varying circumstances.

depth perception   Ability to estimate distances from information from the sensory system. Awareness of three-dimensionality, solidity, and the distance between observer and observed objects based to some degree on the fact that human eyes are set apart and see any object from different angles (retinal disparity). Depth perception is also achieved through such cues as linear perspective, atmospheric perspective, degrees of grayness, and visual accommodation. Also known as stereoscopic vision, stereopsis. See BINOCULAR DEPTH CUES, DEPTH CUES, MONOCULAR DEPTH CUES, RETINAL DISPARITY, VISUAL CLIFF.

depth-perception apparatus   A device used to determine the participant's spatial relationships or perception of object in terms of distance and angle away from the observer. See HOWARD-DOHLMAN APPARATUS.

depth psychology   1. A school of thought that assumes that people operate in terms of unconscious forces. 2. Psychotherapy that focuses on unconscious mental processes as the source of emotional disturbance and symptoms, as well as personality, attitudes, creativity, and lifestyle. See ANALYTICAL PSYCHOTHERAPY, PSYCHOANALYSIS.

derailment   (E. Kraepelin) A type of thought disorder in which patients, usually schizophrenics, constantly interrupt themselves and jump from one idea to a totally unrelated and irrelevant idea. See COGNITIVE DERAILMENT, DERAILMENT OF VOLITION, SPEECH DERAILMENT, THOUGHT DERAILMENT.

derailment of volition   (E. Kraepelin) A type of indecisiveness in which consistency of goals and purposes is replaced by tangential and irrelevant impulses, contradictory wishes, and short-lived causes.

derangement   A mental disturbance meaning about the same as dementia, but with the implication that the condition is either temporary or relatively minor. See DEMENTIA, INSANITY, PSYCHOSIS.

derealization   1. A feeling of the unreality of the environment. 2. The situation when family surroundings appear different from expectation or experience. 3. A defense mechanism in which people, events, and surroundings appear changed and unreal. In its extreme form derealization may be a symptom of schizophrenia. See ATYPICAL DISSOCIATIVE DISORDER, DEPERSONALIZATION, DEPERSONALIZATION DISORDER, DEREISM.

de-reflection   1. (V. Frankl) Shift of attention away from the self, reduction in self-examination. Used as a therapeutic tool for reducing excessive self-concern, shyness, and worry about how others perceive the person. A central component of Japanese Morita therapy. See MORITA THERAPY. 2. A common technique of attempting to allay anxiety, avoid provocation, or stop misbehavior by diverting a person's attention to some different topic or issue. See DECENTERING, PARENTAL BEHAVIOR, THOUGHT-STOPPING.

dereism Mental activity that is not in accord with reality or logic, such as an irrational belief that a person can cure any disease with a glance. Normal daydreams are somewhat dereistic but the person knows that they are fantasies. Dereism is similar to autistic thinking. See DEREISTIC THINKING.

dereistic thinking (E. Bleuler) Cognitive behavior that is imaginative, illogical and is not in accord with reality or experience, found in daydreams and delusions. See DEREISM.

derepressor A substance that reacts with operator genes to influence a deoxyribonucleic acid (DNA) molecule to develop a particular type of tissue cell. A derepressor probably removes a mask from part of a DNA molecule so it can serve as an ribonucleic acid (RNA) pattern to direct a basic cell toward becoming a neuron or bone cell or some other kind of specialized cell.

derivative 1. A conclusion based on a number of accepted logical premises. 2. In psychoanalytic theory, behavior disguised by the ego to permit expression without anxiety. 3. In psychoanalytic theory, expressions of the id in ways acceptable to the superego. 4. In mathematics, a coefficient that indicates the rate of change from one state to a different state.

derivative insight An insight into a problem achieved by the patient without interpretation by the therapist. See AUTOCHTHONOUS.

derived emotion (W. McDougall) Feelings generated by news of a forthcoming event, such as joy for a desired event and sorrow for an unwanted event.

derived ideas (R. Descartes) The product of experiences of the senses. For example, an idea of the sound of a buzzer follows the experience one has of it. See INNATE IDEAS.

derived measure/score The transformation of a raw or observed score into a different score that has meaning such as a percentile rank or standardized score. See RAW DATA, Z SCORES.

derived property Gestalt phrase for parts of a perception derived from the whole.

derma The skin; specifically, the true skin, which lies beneath the superficial epidermis. Also known as dermis.

dermal sensation A sensation due to stimulation of one of the receptors situated in the skin. Also known as cutaneous sensation, skin sensation.

dermal sensitivity Cutaneous sensations detected by nerve receptors in the skin.

dermal-sweating response See PSYCHOGALVANIC SKIN-RESISTANCE.

dermatoglyphics A procedure for diagnosing certain chromosomal abnormalities. The method is based on the observation that patterns of finger, palm, and footprints are associated with certain types of birth defects, for example, Down's syndrome patients have a simian crease across the palm and a single crease on the skin of the fifth, or smallest, finger.

dermatographism A form of urticaria (hives), a vascular phenomenon due to unusual irritability of the capillaries in the skin, characterized by the appearance of wheals in the form of words or pictures on the skin after they have been lightly traced. Also known as autographism, dermagraphy, dermatographia, dermatography, dermography, dermographia, dermographism, dermography, Ebbecke's reaction, factitious urticaria, skin writing.

dermatome 1. An area of the skin connected to a particular spinal nerve. 2. An instrument for cutting thin slices of skin or excising small lesions. 3. In embryonic development, the part of the mesodermal layer that develops into the dermal layers of the skin.

dermatoneurosis A skin condition due to psychological causes.

dermatopathophobia See DERMATOSIOPHOBIA.

dermatophobia Morbid fear of suffering an injury to the skin, such as a lesion. See DERMATOSIOPHOBIA.

dermatosiophobia Morbid fear of contracting a skin disease. Also known as dermatopathophobia.

dermatothlasia An urgent and maddening desire to scratch, pinch, and/or bruise one's skin.

dermatozoic Pertaining to the sensation that some form of insect or animal life has invaded the skin, as in cases of formication due to toxic substances. See COCAINE BUG.

dermo-optical perception (DOP) (R. P. Youtz) An alleged ability to identify the color of objects through sensors in the skin. Youtz hypothesized that participants detect colors by means of temperature differences due to reflection of hand heat or other heat from the object.

DES Department of Education and Science

de Sade See SADE.

descending nerve tract Bundles of axons within the central nervous system (CNS) that contain efferent fibers that carry impulses from the brain to the spinal cord. Compare ASCENDING NERVE TRACTS. See NERVE TRACT.

descending pathways Sensory nerves that appear to carry impulses away from the central nervous system rather than from sense organs to the brain or spinal cord. Efferent sensory fibers function as inhibitors or suppressors and have an effect of improving transmission of signals from a receptor. See EFFERENT.

descending reticular activating system (DRAS) A part of a closed-loop reticular-transmission mechanism in which signals are sent downward from the cortex to the spinal cord as well as along ascending pathways from the spinal cord to the cortex. See BRAINSTEM, RETICULAR ACTIVATING SYSTEM.

descensus 1. The descent of the testes into the scrotum, usually around the time of birth. 2. The descent of the uterus from the false into the true pelvic cavity at the termination of sexual stimulation.

descent group A group in which membership depends on common descent from a real or mythic ancestor.

deschooling (I. Illich) A movement influential in the 1970s holding that learning permeates all life experiences and social relationships, and should not be considered the monopoly of the formal education system, which is exclusive and creates dependence on institutions.

descriptive approach   systematic approach

descriptive average   An approximate, rough estimate of the average calculated on the basis of imprecise or partial data.

descriptive behaviorism   An early characterization of behaviorism when Burrhus Skinner was experimenting with reinforcement on learning. Skinner's behaviorism was always considered descriptive; the phrase distinguished it from J. B. Watson's behaviorism, and E. C. Tolman's purposive behaviorism.

descriptive research   A type of research that calls for careful study of certain phenomenon by observation, using techniques to ensure that findings are as objective as possible. Example: To find out what people tend to discuss between acts in a theatre, first an exploratory category of topics is established, such as: other people, clothing, business matters, political topics, material objects, current events. Later, trained, independent observers listen to actual conversations during intermission at the theatre and take notes checking what is discussed against the list of topics. See OBSERVATIONAL RESEARCH.

descriptive responsibility   In forensic psychology, the judgment that a defendant has performed a criminal act, without consideration of blame or punishment. Compare ASCRIPTIVE RESPONSIBILITY.

descriptive statistics   Statistical measures that summarize data such as a frequency distribution or a correlation. See INFERENTIAL STATISTICS, INTERPRETATIVE STATISTICS.

descriptive study   A written statement that attempts to summarize some event or finding in such manner to make the reader understand it as completely as possible.

Desegregation Scale   (J. G. Kelly, J. E. Ferson, & W. H. Holtzman) A type of scale that was designed to measure the attitudes of Caucasians toward African Americans and school integration. The scale provides a rough measure of racial prejudice. Sometimes known as Kelly Desegregation Scale.

desensitization   1. The weakening of a response, usually due to repeated exposure to a situation; a method used in psychotherapy to enable a person to reduce anxiety for certain situations. 2. A reduction of the emotional effect of disturbing experiences or thoughts through such means as gaining insight into their nature or origin, catharsis, or deconditioning techniques. See CONTACT DESENSITIZATION, DECONDITIONING, DEVICE FOR AUTOMATED DESENSITIZATION, FLOODING, RECIPROCAL INHIBITION, SYSTEMATIC DESENSITIZATION.

desexualization   1. Removing sexual significance from an object or activity. 2. In psychoanalytic theory, the sublimation of the libido. Also known as deerotization. See DELIBIDINIZATION. 3. Removing sexual capacity, as through drugs or surgery.

designatory scale   Not really a scale, but rather the assignment of numbers in an arbitrary manner to a number of items.

design cycle   (J. Zeisel) A concept for the improvement of structures such as buildings by utilizing information gained from existing models. The concept includes five steps: analysis, synthesis, realization, reality testing, review.

designer drugs   1. In the illegal recreational "drug culture," certain chemicals, some of which are reputed to have long-term toxic effects on the nervous system. 2. In legal drug usage, medicines that have been designed in hopes that they will have pleasurable or beneficial effects. Chemical technology has allowed medicines to be created with slight changes in structure to address different effects.

design for the average   In ergonomics, an equipment design strategy based on the characteristics (usually dimensional) of the average operator.

design-judgment test   See GRAVES DESIGN JUDGMENT TEST.

design notation   In factorial research designs, a means of indicating the number of factors and the number of levels of each. For instance a $2 \times 4 \times 3$ design has three factors, the first of which has two levels, the second 4, and the third 3, for a total of 24 combinations.

design of research   See RESEARCH DESIGN.

desire phase   (H. S. Kaplan) Suggested as the prelude to the four stages of the physiological sexual response cycle proposed by Masters and Johnson. See SEXUAL-RESPONSE CYCLE.

de-skilling   The change from skilled craftspersons to unskilled assembly-line workers, a result of the factory system.

desocialization   Gradual withdrawal from social contacts and interpersonal communication, with absorption in private thought processes and adoption of idiosyncratic and often bizarre behavior, as frequently observed in the developmental processes of patients with schizophrenia. See AUTISM.

despeciation   Modifications of a species, such as attempts to breed dogs to meet certain desired standards of appearance. The result of the inbreeding led to attractive but less healthy dogs.

Despert fables   (L. Despert) A type of projective test. Stories presented to children that call for the children to make choices or decisions.

despondency   A complex emotional attitude constituted of sorrow and sense of failure.

destination   In information theory, the place where messages arrive; the recipient of messages.

destiny neurosis   A compulsive unconscious need to arrange life experiences in such a way that failure and defeat are bound to occur. Such persons blame others or an unkind fate for their reverses and are unaware that they themselves are responsible or that they are "paying the piper" for guilty impulses or behavior. Also known as fate neurosis, neurosis of destiny. See MASOCHISM.

destruction method   A procedure in physiological research in which part of an organism, such as a brain region, gland or nerve, is removed or rendered nonfunctional, usually to determine its function.

destructive behavior   A tendency to express anger, hostility, or aggression by damaging or destroying external objects or other people. Such behavior, regardless of the victims, may be based on self-destructiveness. See SCAPEGOATING.

destructive-conflict resolution   (M. Deutsch) A resolution of the conflict which is harmful to one or more of the parties involved in the conflict.

destructive conflict resolution process (M. Deutsch) A competitive process in which the parties engage in a struggle to see who will win or lose the conflict.

destructive drive/instinct The impulse to destroy; in psychoanalytic theory, the death instinct, or Thanatos. See DESTRUDO.

destructiveness The expression of aggressive behavior by destroying or defacing objects.

destructive obedience Extreme compliance behavior that violates moral standards when associated with submission to or identification with an authority figure. See AUTHORITARIANISM, BEHAVIORAL STUDY OF OBEDIENCE, OBEDIENCE.

destrudo Term coined by psychoanalyst Edoardo Weiss for the energy associated with Sigmund Freud's death or destructive instinct (Thanatos). Contrasts with libido, the energy of Eros, the life instinct. See EROS, THANATOS.

de-subjectivization of the self (S. Arieti) The process of diminishing the intensity or minimizing the content of subjective experiences by blunting of affect, denial, undoing, reaction formation, suppression, and repression.

desurgency (R. B. Cattell) A personality trait characterized by anxiety, brooding, and seclusion.

de-symbolization The process of depriving symbols, especially words, of their accepted meaning and substituting distorted, neologistic, autistic, or concrete ideas for them. It is a prominent symptom of schizophrenia.

desynchronization 1. A blocking or disruption of a brain-wave pattern, or EEG (electroencephalographic) recording, usually because of a stimulus that alters the rhythm. 2. A stimulus that disrupts a normal alpha wave pattern of EEG tracings sometimes called alpha block. The stimulus usually alerts or arouses or otherwise changes the cortical activity of the organism.

desynchronized sleep (DS or Ds) Sleep stages characterized by interruption or deprivation of periods of slow wave EEGs (electroencephalographs) that are associated with restoration of the body's physical resources, by bursts of disorganized rapid-eye-movement (REM) activity. Repeated desynchronized sleep results in psychological disturbances. Research with cats indicates that adverse physiological effects also occur when such treatment is done. See RAPID-EYE-MOVEMENT (REM) SLEEP, SLEEP STAGES.

detached affect In psychoanalytic theory, an emotion that has separated itself from its original source and attached itself to another source.

detached retina Separation of the inner layer of the retina, or neural retina, from the pigment epithelium layer of the choroid portion. Symptoms may include flashes of light followed by clouding of vision, appearance of floaters (spots or visual artifacts before the eye), sudden and complete loss of vision.

detachment 1. A lack of feelings for others, unconcern about the condition of others. See ESTRANGEMENT. 2. (J. Bowlby) Nonreactivity in children deprived of mothering. Also known as hospitalism. See MARASMUS. 3. A separation from others or from situations with the implication that such separation is voluntary, as expressed by the sentiment, "Go your way, I don't care

what happens, keep me out of it. " 4. Lack of social or emotional involvement with ability to consider a problem on its merits alone (that is, with intellectual detachment). 5. A defense mechanism of emotional insulation. See EMOTIONAL INSULATION. 6. (K. Horney) A neurotic need demonstrated by extreme self-sufficiency and lack of feeling for others. 7. In developmental psychology, a child's desire to have new experiences and develop new skills when beginning to outgrow dependence on adults.

detachment level The extent to which an immigrant group has been detached (separated from) its prior association to its original group and associated with a new organization or cultural group.

detail perspective The perception of an object's depth or distance that results from the details seen; the farther from the viewer, the hazier the details.

detail response (H. Rorschach) In Rorschach test scoring, responses can be to the blot as a whole (W), or to details (d). There is usually only one response to the blot as a whole but there can be many detail responses. Detailed responses are symbolized with the letter d first and then additional letters to indicate special characteristics, for example, rare detail (dr). See RORSCHACH TEST.

detailed inquiry (H. S. Sullivan) A phase of the clinical interview, during which period the therapist checks original hypotheses about the patient.

detection task In research, being able to state that a particular stimulus is sensed but cannot be identified. Thus, a person may detect a spot but is unable to identify its shape.

detection theory See SIGNAL DETECTION THEORY.

detection threshold 1. The degree to which a stimulus must be varied to be discriminated from another stimulus. 2. A more modern phrase for absolute threshold. Sometimes known as difference-limen, differential limen/threshold, just-noticeable difference.

deterioration Progressive impairment or loss of physical or psychological functions. "Going downhill" would be a common phrase for this condition.

deterioration effect In abnormal psychology, an adverse effect attributed to the psychotherapeutic technique applied in a particular case. See IATROGENICS.

deterioration index/quotient (D. Wechsler) Indicating the degree of reduced intellectual performance that could be attributed to aging. The "don't hold" functions that usually show loss with age are digit span, digit symbol, block design, and similarities; the "hold" functions are vocabulary, information, object assembly, and picture completion.

deterioration of attention (E. Bleuler) A primary symptom of schizophrenia marked by inconstant shifting attention and impaired ability to concentrate on external reality.

deteriorative psychosis Severe mental illness characterized by increased impairment of such psychological functions as memory, emotional and social response, judgment, and reality testing.

determinant An internal or external condition antecedent to and viewed as the cause of an event.

determinant evolution   A theory according to which the direction taken by organic variations is not random, but that variations of the same sort tend to appear preponderantly and cumulatively.

determinant reflex   Response at the same place where the stimulus was applied.

determination   A mental attitude characterized by thought of some course of action and a strong commitment to accomplishing that action.

determination coefficient   See COEFFICIENT OF DETERMINATION.

determinative idea   The objective of a thought system achieved by focusing attention toward the end result.

determined-creative   A personality pattern characterized by striving, strong-willed, creative behavior. It is hypothesized that such people had equally strong-willed parents, against whom the person rebelled.

determining quality   (S. Freud) Freudian phrase for evaluating factors in the etiology of a case of hysteria. A disturbing memory and the traumatic power of a disturbing event are considered the two conditions needed to explain hysteria.

determining set   A tendency to behave in a certain manner (for example, during an earthquake, finding a doorway to stand under).

determining tendency   1. A general thought of doing something that leads to the performance of a specific behavior or to the consideration of an appropriate idea. For example, thinking about exercise leads to taking a walk that happens to end up at the park. 2. The role of a goal or set in arousing and maintaining a behavior sequence. For example, wanting to see the new flowers at the park and taking a walk to get to the park. It is the thought of the end product (seeing the flowers) that leads to the behavior sequence (taking a walk). 3. Phrase similar to "set" but having a broader implication, referring to philosophical and moral aspects of total behavior of intact, fully functioning humans. Also known as directive tendency. See AUFGABE, MENTAL DETERMINISM, WÜRZBURG SCHOOL.

determinism   A doctrine positing that all events, physical or mental, including all forms of behavior, are the result of prior causal factors. In psychology, these factors may be either external or internal to the self. Hard determinism allows no freedom of choice; in contrast indeterminism and soft determinism, hold that within the limitations of self-constitution and past experience, it is possible to determine personal goals, type of life, and future. Types of determinism include: ARCHITECTURAL, BIOLOGICAL, BIOSOCIAL, CULTURAL, ENVIRONMENTAL, ETHICAL, MORAL, PSYCHIC, PHYSICAL, PSYCHOLOGICAL, RECIPROCAL, SOCIAL. See FREE WILL.

determinism vs indeterminism   (R. I. Watson) A prescriptive dimension of the philosophical underpinnings of psychology, namely, that psychological activity is explained by antecedent events versus it is not explained by such events. See OPPONENT-PAIRS DIMENSION.

deterministic categories   In concept formation, the categorization procedure used in early studies (from Clark Hull's in 1920) in which certain stimulus features always belonged to a specific one of the categories involved. Compare PROBABALISTIC CATEGORIES.

deterministic psychology   See DETERMINISM.

deterrence theory   1. In forensic psychology, the assumption that punishing a criminal will deter potential offenders from perpetrating criminal acts in the future. 2. A point of view that the knowledge of assured retaliatory consequences that will occur following hostile actions will lead to a reduction of aggressive actions by individuals or groups and that the stronger and more certain the punishment, the fewer violations will occur.

deterrent therapy   Techniques aimed at actively discouraging and preventing undesired behavior, as in the administration of Antabuse (disulfuram) for alcoholism, painting fingernails with bitter substances to curb nail-biting, and ringing a bell to awaken a child who wets the bed to discourage enuresis. See AVERSIVE THERAPY.

detour behavior   Alternative actions to achieve a desired goal when an obstacle is placed between the organism and the goal (for example, an animal on one side of a U-shaped fence, where it can see food on the other side, may walk away from the food to find the end of the fence to get to the food). See DETOUR PROBLEM.

detour problem   (W. Köhler) Any problem that must be solved indirectly or circuitously; any goal that requires an indirect approach because direct access is blocked. Also known as Umweg problem.

detoxification   Procedures designed for the reduction or elimination of toxic substances in the body. Also known as detox. See DETOXIFICATION CENTER, WITHDRAWAL.

detoxification center   A clinic or hospital unit organized to treat acute withdrawal symptoms from drugs or alcohol. See ALCOHOL WITHDRAWAL, ALCOHOLICS ANONYMOUS, METHADONE CENTER.

detoxification effects   Rare phrase for the subjective and objective effects experienced by some alcoholics after abrupt cessation of heavy drinking, including irritability, confusion, tremors, and nausea. See WITHDRAWAL.

detraction   Reduction of attention.

detumescence   The subsidence of a swelling, especially in the genital organs of either gender, following sexual excitement. Compare TUMESCENCE.

deuteranomaly   Color blindness in which the green part of the spectrum is perceived inadequately. In testing for deuteranomaly, an unusual amount of green would be required in a red-green mixture to match a given yellow.

deuteranope   One of the three groups of dichromats. A person who is not able to recognize or see the second primary color (green); a form of dichromatism. The person has no difficulty in making brightness discriminations, but is unable to distinguish red and green hues, confusing them with bluish and yellowish grays. Possibly due to insensitivity toward blue-green light. Compare PROTANOPE, TRITANOPE.

deuteranope(s)ia   Red-green color blindness in which the color-perception deficiency is due to a fusion of red and green receptor processes with green-sensitivity loss. May be unilateral in that a person may have normal color vision in one eye. See PROTANOPIA.

deuteranopia   Color blindness in which green hues are perceived imperfectly or green is confused with red. In some cases, it results from an ability to perceive only two distinct hues, blue and yellow. See DALTONISM.

deuterolearning   Acquiring knowledge about the learning process; studying how to be more efficient in learning.

deuterophallic phase   (E. Jones) According to Ernest Jones, the second stage of the phallic phase (between ages three and seven), when the child first suspects that the world of people is divided into male and female, each with a different type of genital organ. See PROTOPHALLIC PHASE.

deutoplasm   The yolk or nutritive material contained in the egg. The part of cytoplasm that is not alive, usually either protecting the living part or serving as food for the rest of the cell.

Deutsch's crude law of social resolutions (M. Deutsch) A point of view that the typical effects of a given social relationship (for example, either cooperative or competitive) will tend to induce that relationship in a social situation which is not yet strongly determined (that is, the typical effects of cooperation, for example, trust, perception of similarity, honest communication, and sharing of resources) will tend to induce cooperation when such effects are introduced into a conflict situation whose character is not yet strongly determined.

development   The progressive changes in shape, organization, and functioning of an organism from birth to death. Types of development and some relevant scales include: ARREST OF, ATYPICAL, CAREER, CEPHALO-CAUDAL, CHARACTER, CHILD, COGNITIVE, EGO, EMOTIONAL, MAL-, MASS-TO-SPECIFIC, MENTAL, MORAL, MOTOR, ORGANIZATIONAL, PERSONALITY, PRESPEECH, PROXIMODISTAL, PSYCHOSEXUAL, PSYCHOSOCIAL, QUALITATIVE, QUANTITATIVE, REASONING, SELF-, SEXUAL, SOCIAL, SPEECH. See ANTERIOR-POSTERIOR (DEVELOPMENT) GRADIENT, ATYPICAL DEVELOPMENTAL DISORDER, BAYLEY SCALES OF INFANT DEVELOPMENT, CALIFORNIA INFANT SCALE FOR MOTOR DEVELOPMENT, COGNITIVE DEVELOPMENTAL THEORIES, ERIKSON'S STAGES OF PSYCHOSOCIAL DEVELOPMENT, FROSTIG DEVELOPMENTAL TEST OF VISUAL PERCEPTION, GESELL DEVELOPMENT SCALES, GESELL DEVELOPMENTAL SCHEDULES, GRIFFITHS MENTAL DEVELOPMENT SCALE, IDENTIFICATION (IN LANGUAGE DEVELOPMENT), INCREMENTAL THEORY OF DEVELOPMENT, INSTRUCTIONAL THEORY OF DEVELOPMENT, KOHLBERG'S THEORY OF MORAL DEVELOPMENT, LINCOLN-OSERETSKY MOTOR DEVELOPMENT SCALE, MIXED-SPECIFIC DEVELOPMENTAL DISORDER, MOTOR DEVELOPMENT LEVELS/STAGES, PERVASIVE DEVELOPMENTAL DISORDERS, PRENATAL DEVELOPMENT ANOMALY, PSYCHOANALYTIC DEVELOPMENT PSYCHOLOGY, STAGE THEORIES OF DEVELOPMENT, STAGES OF HUMAN COGNITIVE DEVELOPMENT, TWO-WORD STAGE (OF LANGUAGE DEVELOPMENT).

developmental acceleration   An abnormal amount of precocious growth in one or more functions, as in a two-year-old child having a vocabulary of a typical four-year-old.

developmental age (DA)   A measure of development expressed in an age unit or age equivalent, such as a four-year-old having a developmental age of six in verbal skills. Phrase is also used to mean an average measure of maturation derived from several tests in several developmental areas. Can refer to social, mental, behavioral, or mechanical functioning, but ordinarily it refers to social and intellectual ages.

developmental amentia   Obsolete phrase for mental retardation purported to be associated with a combination of heredity and environmental factors.

developmental aphasia   A condition found in children who are unable to use language normally. See DEVELOPMENTAL DYSPHASIA.

developmental arithmetic disorder   Marked impairment in arithmetic skills not due to mental retardation or inadequate schooling. The diagnosis is formed usually only by individual intelligence tests and academic mathematics achievement tests.

developmental articulation disorder   Failure to develop consistent pronunciation of speech sounds. Though grammar and vocabulary and intelligence may be normal, baby-talk persists and is characterized by lisping or lalling.

developmental assessment   The evaluation of a child's level of development in terms of such factors as developmental tasks, maturity tests, observation of peer relationships, activities, intellectual status, and academic adjustment. There are two major types of developmental assessments, both made against certain standards: (a) objective evaluations such as height and weight, carpal and dental age; and (b) subjective evaluations based on short-term observations, as in a clinician seeing a child for a limited time or based on long-term observations as by parents or teachers. See APGAR SCALE, INTELLIGENCE TESTS, VINELAND SOCIAL MATURITY SCALE.

developmental counseling   A counseling approach directed to helping clients develop more effective behavior in personal and social relationships through learning about the self and testing out new patterns of behavior. Emphasis is placed on the client's mastery of social and emotional goals that were not achieved in earlier stages.

developmental crisis   maturational crisis

developmental disability/disorder   A mental or physical disorder originating before the age of 18, and in some cases continuing throughout life as a substantial challenge to normal functioning (for example, cerebral palsy, epilepsy, autism, blindness, deafness, mutism, muscular dystrophy, and mental retardation).

developmental dyslexia   Reading problems in a person whose intelligence and perceptual abilities are normal. May be caused by genetic, prenatal, or perinatal influences.

developmental dysphasia   Language retardation purported to be associated with brain damage or cerebral maturation lag, characterized by defects in expressive language and articulation (expressive dysphasia) and in more severe cases by defects in comprehension of language (receptive dysphasia). Sometimes known as developmental aphasia.

developmental factors   In child psychology, the conditions that influence emotional, intellectual, social, and physical development from conception to maturity, such as parental attitudes and stimulation, peer relationships, learning experiences, recreational activities, and hereditary predispositions.

developmental hyperactivity   Phrase applied to children who are within or above the normal range intellectually but show higher than normal activity levels.

developmental imbalance A disparity in the normal developmental patterns of cognitive and perceptual skills.

developmental language disorder A diagnostic category of two types: (a) failure to develop vocal expression (vocabulary restricted and immature articulation) despite relatively normal comprehension; and (b) defective recognition of sounds and pictures, defective recall of auditory and visual sequences, and reading and spelling difficulties.

developmental levels A chronological division of the life span. Eleven arbitrary levels are indicated below:
(a) Neonatal, from birth to one month.
(b) Infancy, from birth to one year.
(c) Preschool childhood, from one to six years.
(d) Mid-childhood, from 6 to 11 years.
(e) Late childhood or preadolescence, from 10 to 12 years.
(f) Adolescence, from 13 to 21 years.
(g) Adulthood or maturity, from 22 to 39 years.
(h) Middle age, from 40 to 64.
(i) Young-old age, from 65 to 74 years.
(j) Old-old age, from 75 to 84 years.
(k) Very-old age, from 85 years of age and above.

developmental mechanics A study of the mechanical principles involved in the development of organisms, undertaken experimentally by removing parts, by transplanting parts, and by controlling the environmental factors.

developmental norms Typical skills and expected levels of achievement associated with the successive stages of development. Such norms are derived from extensive testing and observation, reflecting average growth trends of people, young and old, in many areas of development, for example, perception, motor skills, and communication abilities.

developmental parallelism A theory that different animals in related species, as well as predators and prey develop over time in a parallel relationship to each other.

developmental perspective 1. The attitude or point of view held as a person progresses through life. Generally, attitudes toward individuals, groups, occupations, concepts, ideas, etc., as a person grows older. What was valued at one time may lose importance at another time. 2. Viewing structures, functions, etc., in terms of developmental stages.

developmental pharmacokinetics The specialized study of the way medicines are chemically processed by the body (metabolized) and how this varies according to age. Children, for example, in part because of their relatively active liver metabolism, generally require higher doses in some cases lower dosages per unit weight than adults, whereas adults can tolerate doses of some drugs which in older persons tend to build up to toxic levels.

developmental psycholinguistics An area of psycholinguistics that concentrates on the development of language ability in children. Observations are made of young children learning to speak to discover the steps by which they progress in their ability to communicate.

developmental psychology A field of psychology that deals with change over time (growth processes and decay), mental or physical, of an individual or individuals from conception to death.

developmental quotient (DQ) The developmental age is divided by chronological age to yield a developmental quotient. See INTELLIGENCE QUOTIENT (IQ).

developmental readiness In education, the student's state of psychological and intellectual preparedness for a given task, subject (topic), or grade level. See READINESS.

developmental reading The acquisition and growth of skills in a child normally learning the sequential stages of the reading process.

developmental reading disorder Failure to reach age appropriate reading skill levels.

developmental retardation Abnormally slow growth in any or all areas (intellectual, motor, perceptual, linguistic, social).

developmental scale An inventory of developmental norms used to evaluate an individual's developmental stage. See DEVELOPMENTAL NORMS.

developmental schedules A series of perceptual motor growth progressions in normal children, primarily dating from birth. See DEVELOPMENTAL ASSESSMENT.

developmental school An educational facility for children with developmental delays. A typical developmental school may be sponsored by local voluntary organizations to provide early growth and learning experiences, helping the child participate in and adjust as much as possible to the mainstream of society at an early age. Known by a variety of other names.

developmental sensitivity Responsiveness of various capacities or processes to disruption or enhancement at specific developmental stages (psychobiology, ethology). See DEVELOPMENTAL SEQUENCE, IMPRINTING.

developmental sequence The order in which changes in structure or function occur during the process of development of an organism. See CEPHALOCAUDAL DEVELOPMENT, COGNITIVE DEVELOPMENT, MOTOR MILESTONES, PSYCHOSEXUAL DEVELOPMENT.

developmental stage A period or phase of life in which specific traits or behavior patterns usually appear.

developmental tasks The fundamental physical, social, intellectual, and emotional achievements and abilities that need to be acquired at each stage of life for normal and healthy development, such as talking in early childhood and achieving independence during adolescence. Since development is largely cumulative, inability to master developmental tasks at one stage is likely to inhibit development in later stages. See DEVELOPMENTAL SEQUENCE.

developmental teaching model A general approach in education. Cognitive, social, and moral developments are considered to advance in discrete stages. In the area of cognitive development, the emphasis is on logical reasoning and the enhancement of knowledge. See KOHLBERG'S THEORY OF MORAL DEVELOPMENT, PIAGETIAN THEORY.

developmental test of visual perception See FROSTIG'S DEVELOPMENTAL TEST OF VISUAL PERCEPTION.

developmental theories   Varying points of view about the continuity of human development and the importance of early experiences in shaping personality, as in Sigmund Freud's psychoanalytic theory of psychosexual development, Erik Erikson's stages of personality development, Jean Piaget's development theories, learning theories that stress early conditioning, role theories that focus on the gradual acquisition of different roles in life, and moral developmental views such as those of Lawrence Kohlberg.

developmental theorist   (E. F. Zigler) A person who assumes that mental retardation is due to a slower-than-normal development of cognitive processes and is not qualitatively different from the cognitive processes of normal persons. Compare DEFECT THEORIST.

developmental therapy   A general method of attempting to treat children with emotional problems by planning a series of graded experiences intended to move such children forward to their proper levels of functioning in a variety of desired modalities such as social functioning.

developmental toxicology   The study of medicines having certain effects on patients who are younger, but not older. Thus, for example, aspirin may rarely trigger a severe illness, Reye's syndrome, when given for fever in younger children; tetracycline can discolor young children's teeth and affect other organs; valproic acid can be toxic to the livers of young children, but not of older children. Similarly, some medicines can be more toxic in older persons than they are in younger or mid-life adults. See DEVELOPMENTAL PHARMACOKINETICS.

developmental units   Mathematical expressions used for indicating levels of development that ideally should be based on equal intervals and have a zero point. For example, the units for height and weight are based on equal intervals, but not the units for intellectual development or social development. Consequently, it may be said that a child is twice as heavy as another but not twice as intelligent.

developmental zero   The starting point or base line; the moment when a new organism begins to develop, usually considered to be the time of union between ovum and sperm cell. Also known as ontogenetic zero. See CONCEPTION, FERTILIZATION.

deviance   1. Operating in other than what is considered a proper manner, outside the range of standards of socially accepted behavior. 2. Any behavior that deviates significantly from what is considered normal for the group with which the individual or subgroup is to be compared. Also known as deviant behavior. 3. In statistics, the concept of anything being away from its norm. See DEVIATION, SECONDARY DEVIANCE, SEXUAL DEVIANCY.

deviance amplification   (L. Wilkins) Phrase borrowed from cybernetics to note how a small initial social deviation my grow in significance through labelling and over-reacting.

deviance disavowal   A special role interaction between a person with physical challenges or one stigmatized in some manner (such as an ex-convict) and a person considered normal or typical in which the latter person avoids any reference to the former person's situation.

deviant case analysis   Examination and consideration of why individuals expected to react similarly either in research or in life, differ from one another in relation to the dependent variable (the response to the stimulus or stimuli in research), or considerably from the mean of the responses of others. See INDIVIDUAL DIFFERENCES, OUTLIERS.

deviant filter theory   A point of view that patients with schizophrenia are unable to ignore unimportant stimuli and consequently cannot attend to matters of greater importance.

deviant sexuality   Modes of sexuality considered unusual or improper in a given society at any particular time.

deviate   An individual whose behavior differs markedly from normal (typical) or standard conduct.

deviation (d)   1. The difference between an item of data and some measure of the average of the whole data. 2. The interval between a point in a distribution and some other point.

deviation-amplification feedback   A method in which output fed back into a system increases or decreases further output, small variations may lead to major changes, as seems to occur frequently in psychotherapy. See PERSON-CENTERED PSYCHOTHERAPY.

deviation IQ   (D. Wechsler) A standard score on an intelligence test that has a mean of 100 and a standard deviation specific to that of the test administered. The Wechsler tests were based on a deviation intelligence quotient (IQ) with the average score for any age set at 100 and the standard deviation at 15 IQ points.

deviation score   The difference between a specified score and the mean of the scores, demonstrating the extent to which that score departs from the mean.

device for automated desensitization (DAD)   A computerized system for applying desensitization therapy to the treatment of focused-phobic behavior. The device administers audiotape instructions for muscle relaxation and visualization of fear stimuli arranged in a hierarchical order. See SYSTEMATIC DESENSITIZATION.

devil fear   See DEMONOPHOBIA, SATANOPHOBIA.

devil's advocate   A person who argues for an unpopular position, often only to help prove the popular position. See ADVERSARY MODEL.

devil's contract technique   (E. E. Landy) A procedure used in counseling in which the counselor asks a client to make a promise before the client is told what it is. Only after such a promise is obtained, is the client told what to do. For example, a person lacking self-confidence has promised to ask someone out on a date. The intent is to test the client's beliefs, in this case that the person asked will not accept. See BETTING TECHNIQUE, LEANING TOWER-OF-PISA APPROACH, PARADOXICAL INTENTION.

devil's pitchfork   An example of a two-dimensional representation of an impossible three-dimensional figure. Also known as three-pronged clevis. See PENROSE TRIANGLE.

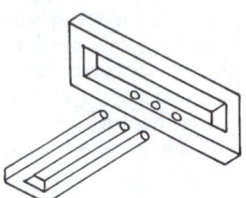

Devil's pitchfork This illustration demonstrates that seeing is not believing; the more closely it is examined, the more it appears to change.

devoids   Slang, sometimes used in law enforcement, for people who apparently commit crimes without conscience or emotion. Similar to psychopath or sociopath.

devolution   Degeneration, backward development, reversal of evolution.

dexamethasone suppression test (DST)   A test of the responsiveness of the nervous system to a dose of a steroid medicine. Used to test for endogenous depression.

Dexedrine   Trade name for dextroamphetamine sulphate.

dexterity test   A manual examination of speed and accuracy. See CRAWFORD SMALL PARTS DEXTERITY TEST for an example.

dextrad   Toward the right side, pertaining to the right side of the body. Also known as dextral. See SINISTRAL.

dextrality   A tendency or preference to be right-handed or to use the right side of the body in motor activities. See RIGHT-HANDEDNESS, DEXTRALITY-SINISTRALITY.

dextrality–sinistrality   The phenomenon by which an uninfluenced child will spontaneously develop right-handedness (dextrality) or left-handedness (sinistrality).

dextroamphetamine sulfate   Generic name for the isomer of amphetamine that rotates chemically to the right. A stimulant of the central nervous system, causes hyperexcitability; also serves as an antidepressant. Trade name is Dexedrine.

dextrophobia   Morbid fear of anything situated to the right. Compare LEVOPHOBIA.

dextrosinistral   1. A direction from right to left. 2. Refers to a person who was originally left-handed but was re-trained to be right-handed.

dextrosinistral axis   Pertaining to a line which extends from the right (dextro) to the left (sinistro) side of the body. Also known as lateral axis. See ANATOMICAL DIRECTIONS.

dextroversion   Toward the right. See ANATOMICAL DIRECTIONS.

df   See DEGREES OF FREEDOM.

dharma   (Asian philosophy, primarily Buddhist and Hindu) Codes and rules that define goodness, maturity, and appropriate behavior; also defined as "truth," "righteousness," or "spirituality."

dhat   A culture-specific syndrome of males in India that centers on excessive concern about semen. Affected persons are stated to be listless and apathetic.

DHHS   Department of Health and Human Services

di   In Rorschach test scoring, a symbol for inside detail.

d$_i$ Symbol for difference between ranks of paired scores.

D$_i$ Symbol for difference between pairs of scores.

diabetic reactions   Psychophysical symptoms occurring in diabetics, associated with inadequate blood insulin and characterized by a rise in blood-sugar level during periods of emotional stress, a state of keto-acidosis or insulin coma precipitated by a life crisis, and the tendency of some depressed and suicidal patients to give up their diet or neglect to take their insulin.

diabolism   A dehumanizing process of attributing the nature of the devil to despised others. Often done during times of war to demonize the enemy. See DEMONIZING, PROPAGANDA.

diachronic linguistics   The study of the historical development of languages or a language over long periods.

diacoustics   A branch of physics which investigates the principles governing the transmission of sounds through media of varying densities. Also known as diaphonics.

diad   dyad

diadochokinesia   Ability to rapidly perform repetitive alternating muscular movements such as finger-tapping, pursing, and retracting lips. Also known as diadokokinesis.

diagnosis (Dx)   1. The determination of the type of disorder, on the basis of symptoms and signs, or tests and examinations. 2. The classification of individuals, societies, cultures, etc., on the basis of a disease, abnormality, or set of characteristics. See PATHOGNOMONIC SIGNS.

Diagnostic and Statistical Manual of Mental Disorders   (currently, DSM-IV) A manual published by the American Psychiatric Association that attempts to classify and define a wide variety of mental and behavioral disorders. Widely used, especially by insurance companies and HMOs. See APPENDIX B for some DSM-IV classifications. See INTERNATIONAL CLASSIFICATION OF DISEASES.

diagnostic baseline   Measures of various parameters obtained under normal or abnormal conditions to be compared later after treatments.

diagnostic center   A facility designed and equipped with skilled personnel and appropriate laboratory and other equipment for evaluating the condition of a patient and determining the cause of the patient's physical or psychological disorder.

diagnostic educational test   A type of examination designed to identify and measure academic deficiencies, such as the Durrell Analysis of Reading Difficulty, the Gray Oral Reading Test, the Iowa Tests of Basic Skills, and the Stanford Diagnostic Arithmetic Test.

diagnostic formulation   A comprehensive evaluation of a patient, including a summary of behavioral, emotional, and psychophysiological factors often include a treatment plan.

diagnostic interview   An interview in which an examiner explores a patient's presenting problem, current situation, and background, with the aim of formulating a diagnosis and prognosis, as well as developing a treatment program.

Diagnostic Interview Schedule (DIS)   (L. Robins, J. Heizer, J. Crougham, & K. Ratcliff) An interview format for psychiatric disorders that can be used by both lay people and professionals. Diagnoses can be developed therefrom by clerical or computerized procedures.

diagnostic-prescriptive educational approach   The concept that effectiveness of classroom teaching of children with disabilities depends to a large extent upon the teacher's understanding of the medical model of the disability. For example, the more the teacher and educational administrators know about hydrocephalus, the more effectively they can diagnose and prescribe an appropriate educational program for the students who have it.

diagnostic test   Any criterion that may help reveal the nature and source of a person's problems, physical or mental or both.

dialectic   1. A systematic course of reasoning or a system of logic. 2. A tension generated by opposing ideas. See SOCRATIC METHOD.

dialectic(al) logic/process   1. A method of coming to conclusions through generating contrasting arguments known as the thesis (statement) and antithesis (opposing statement) that leads to synthesis, a new proposition based on the integration of the two divergent positions. 2. A general process in individuals, societies, etc., of development via thesis, antithesis and synthesis.

dialectical materialism   (K. Marx) A philosophical doctrine that the ultimate reality is matter, existing objectively and independently of mind or perception.

dialectical method/teaching   A method that engages students in a critical examination of their reasoning through repeated questioning of their answers, much as Socrates is portrayed doing in the Platonic dialogues. See SOCRATIC METHOD.

dialectical operations   1. (K. F. Riegel) Ability to understand that a thing can be right and wrong at the same time. 2. The view that internal factors such as traits and character and external factors such as the social environment are influenced by each other.

dialectical psychology   The view that in the mind there is an interaction between thoughts (cognition) and feelings (affection) such as cognitions being in conflict with emotions, as in "I was going to do that but I felt that it was wrong."

dialectical reasoning   A logical process in which a series of deductions leading to a conclusion. Also known as dialectic.

dialectology   A branch of linguistics dealing with the analysis and description of regional varieties of a language.

dialects   Variations in speaking the same standard (written) language.

dialogic method   See SOCRATIC METHOD.

dialog(ue)   1. Generally, a conversation. 2. A genuine, open, equal, honest communication between two people, an I-thou relationship as advocated by Martin Buber. Dialogue also has a more general meaning of simply dialectical communication.

dialogue technique   (F. Perls) In Gestalt therapy, engaging in an imaginary dialogue: (a) with a body part from which the patient feels alienated; (b) with a person such as a parent, imagined as sitting in an empty chair; or (c) with an object associated with a dream.

Diana complex   In psychoanalytic theory, the repressed desire of a woman to be a man. (In Greek mythology, Diana was a goddess of hunting and protectress of women.)

Dianetics   A controversial system of philosophy and psychological theories and psychotherapies introduced by L. Ron Hubbard that uses concepts from psychoanalysis, cybernetics, and other disciplines.

dianoetic   Obsolete term pertaining to the intellectual functions in general, especially reasoning.

diaperism   See AUTONEPIOPHILIA, NEPIOPHILIA.

diaphragm   1. A large sheet of muscle that separates the chest cavity from the abdomen. 2. A dome-shaped cup, usually of latex with a flexible metal rim, for insertion into the vagina to cover the cervix as a barrier contraceptive. See BIRTH CONTROL.

diary method   1. A technique for compiling child-development data by recording daily observations. 2. Part of research methods in general, recording daily or periodic events.

diaschisis   1. A functional deficiency that occurs in a part of the nervous system distant from the site of a lesion. 2. The temporary lowering of excitability of a nerve center due to the withdrawal of normally exciting impulses from other centers. 3. A sudden inhibition of function following an acute focal disturbance in a portion of the brain physically separate from the original seat of injury, but anatomically connected with it through fiber tracts.

diastole   The period in the cardiac cycle during which the ventricle is filled with blood. Compare SYSTOLE.

diastolic blood pressure   The pressure of blood in a major artery when the blood is flowing into the ventricles while the heart rests briefly between contractions. On blood-pressure recordings, the diastolic blood pressure is the smaller number, usually noted to the right side of the systolic blood pressure. See BLOOD PRESSURE.

diathesis   An inherited susceptibility to certain diseases, for example, arthritic diathesis.

diathesis-stress conception   (J. Zubin & B. Spring) A theory that disorders, mental and physical, arise from a physical predisposition for that illness and from psychological factors relating to the nature of environmental stresses. Also known as diathesis-stress hypothesis/paradigm/position/theory.

diatonic scale   See SCALE.

diazepam   Generic name for Valium.

diazepam-binding inhibitor (DBI)   Brain protein that blocks the behavioral effects of diazepam and other benzodiazepines.

dibit   Any pair of bit or binary signals (00, 01, 10, etc.), understood to be part of a more complex signal. Derived by analogy from digraph (any pair of written characters extracted from a sequence of characters).

dichoglottic   (H. Henning) A taste sensation due to stimulation on two separate areas of the tongue of two different substances. Also known as diglottic.

dichoptic   Stimulating each eye at the same time with different stimuli. See DICHOTIC.

dichorial twins   Dizygotic twins, each with its own chorionic sac.

dichorhinic   (H. Henning) Characterizing olfactory stimulation of both nostrils simultaneously with a different stimulus for each nostril. See DIRHINIC, MONORHINIC.

dichotic Pertaining to the stimulation of the two ears simultaneously but with a different stimulus for each ear.

dichotic listening A form of perception in the absence of sustained attention. A participant can hear and retrieve information from different but simultaneous inputs of material in the left and right ears. In dichotic listening, attention is shifted alternately from left to right for a few seconds, and vice versa.

dichotomism (F. Dumont) The cognitive propensity to impose a bipartite structure on continuous variables. This reaches dysfunctional levels in primitive religious, philosophical, political, psychometric, and legal schemas.

dichotomizing Categorizing experiences, ideas, concepts, people, etc., on equivalent but different bases such as black/white, usually in extreme terms such as all-good/all-bad with no middle ground. Examples of dichotomizing in psychology include: Abstract/Concrete, Analytic/Synthetic, Behaviorism/Phenomenalism, Clinical/Statistical, Cross-sectional/Longitudinal, Deductive/Inductive, Determinism/Indeterminism, Differential/Existential, Empiricistic/Scientific, Explicit/Tacit, Heredity/Environmentalism, Historical/Ahistorical, Idiographic/Nomothetic, Monism/Dualism, Normal/Abnormal, Objective/Subjective, Positivism/Teleology, Rational/Intuitive, Reductionism/Holism.

dichotomous qualitative variable A variable that has two categories, for example, in a survey people can be listed by age and by sex. See MULTINOMINAL QUALITATIVE VARIABLE.

dichotomous thinking Either-Or pondering; the tendency to think in terms of polar opposites, especially common in some religions and moral systems. See DICHOTOMIZING.

dichotomy The separation of any set of items into two groups on the basis of existence or nonexistence of certain qualities, such as dividing a pack of playing cards into a black group and a red group; or the division of scores into those above and those below the mean.

dichromasy Defective color vision, hereditary or acquired, in which the colors seen are reducible to two hues and their variants. Also spelled dichromacy. See ACHROMATISM, ANOMALOUS TRICHROMATISM, DICHROMATISM.

dichromat A person exhibiting dichromatism. The three groups of dichromats are: deuteranopes, protanopes, tritanopes.

dichromatism Partial color blindness in which the observer is satisfied in matching any hue with two other wavelengths, rather than the three required by those with normal color vision. Those for whom bluish-red, green, and gray appear the same have deuteranopia (1.1% of males, 0.01% of females); those for whom red, bluish-green, and gray are indistinguishable have protanopia (1.0% of males, 0.02% of females). Both forms are sex-linked traits inherited in simple Mendelian fashion. The rare tritanopia (0.0001% males) in which purplish-blue, greenish-yellow, and gray appear the same, is caused by direct injuries to the retina, disease, or prolonged exposure to toxic agents such as carbon disulfide. Also known as dichromatic vision, dichromatopsia. See ACHROMATISM, ANOMALOUS TRICHROMATISM, DICHROMASY.

dichromic 1. Having or pertaining to two colors. 2. Able to distinguish only two colors.

dictators In child psychology, parents who stress obedience and assume authority in their relationships with their children. See APPEASERS, COOPERATORS, AUTHORITARIAN PARENTING, DEMOCRATIC PARENTING, ECLECTIC PARENTING, LAISSEZ-FAIRE PARENTING.

Dictionary of Occupational Titles (DOT) A reference book that describes and classifies a wide variety of jobs. Updated every 5 to 10 years by the U.S. government. Used in vocational counseling and personnel matters. Sample of contents: "Rheostat Assembler (elec. equip) 729.684-026; Rhinestone Setter (jewelry-silver.) 735-687-034; Rhinologist (medical serv.) 070.101.062; Rib Bender (musical inst.) 569.685.104; Ribber (meat products) 525.684-104; Ribbon Blocker (narrow fabrics) 699.885-014; Ribbon Cutter (garment) 699-685-014."

didactic analysis A treatment and training program that some organizations of psychotherapy require, especially Freudian and Jungian psychoanalysis, before certification of competency is conferred. Also known as training analysis.

didactic group psychotherapy (J. Pratt) A form of group psychotherapy based on the theory that some patients will respond most effectively to active teaching by a professional leader. The didactic approach is used in therapeutic social clubs, such as Recovery, Inc. See GROUP COUNSELING.

didactic therapy 1. Therapy undertaken by people who must go through therapy as part of their training in that particular system. 2. Therapy of a teaching type by the therapist doing a lot of active counseling. In some circles it is assumed that every psychotherapist has had personal therapy. This is definitely not so. See DIDACTIVE ANALYSIS, DIDACTIC GROUP PSYCHOTHERAPY.

didactogeny A negative reaction of children to school due to inappropriate teaching methods, or due to the placement of the child in an inappropriate grade level. See SCHOOL PHOBIA.

diencephalon An interbrain group of neural structures that include the thalamus and hypothalamus, the geniculate bodies, and the pineal gland. Also known as betweenbrain. See POSTERIOR DIENCEPHALON.

diestrus A short interval of quiescence separating the estrous cycles of polyestrous animals.

diet 1. The type or types of food habitually taken in by an organism. 2. The restriction of nutrition to certain specified types of food. See DIETING, SELF-SELECTION OF DIET.

dieting Efforts to lose weight by: (a) changing the diet from foods high in fat to foods low in fat; (b) reducing the number of calories in food and drink eaten; (c) exercising combined with at least one of the other efforts. See MORBID OBESITY, OBESITY, WEIGHT REGULATION, YO-YO DIETING.

difference between means The application of inferential statistics to differences between means of samples representing two populations to determine whether the differences are statistically significant. See STATISTICS.

difference canon (J. S. Mill) The theory that differences in otherwise identical results are due to changes in preceding events.

difference detector (G. Mandler) A hypothetical mechanism that detects states of the world different from what is expected, and initiates sympathetic nervous system discharge.

difference hypothesis In dealing with people who are mentally challenged and their learning, a postulate that their differences from those people considered normal are not only quantitative but also qualitative. See DEFECT THEORY, DEVELOPMENTAL THEORIST.

difference judgment A judgment based on the perception that two stimuli are not equal, but that one is louder, brighter, heavier, etc., than the other or that there is no apparent difference.

difference limen (DL) Minimum change in a stimulus that can be detected as a change. See ABSOLUTE THRESHOLD, LEAST-NOTICEABLE DIFFERENCE.

difference sensation (DS) The simultaneous perception of two nearly similar objects, but discriminating that one is different from the other.

difference threshold The smallest perceptible difference between two stimuli that can be consistently and accurately detected on 75% of trials. Also known as differential threshold, just-noticeable difference (jnd), least-noticeable difference. See ABSOLUTE THRESHOLD, DETECTION THRESHOLD, WEBER'S LAW.

difference tone A third tone heard when two tones of similar timbre and pitch are sounded together. Its frequency is the difference between the frequencies of the two tones. Also known as Tartini's tone.

differentia (E. Weber) The objective difference between objects in terms of units, such as inches, seconds, or amounts of pressure.

differentiable abilities 1. Distinct abilities in a given individual for performance of different specific activities. 2. Comparison of such abilities among different individuals.

differential 1. Ability of individuals to distinguish similar but not equivalent items. 2. Refers to changes of related measures: Affecting one affects the other, for example, increasing the diameter of a circle also increases both the area of the circle and its circumference.

Differential Ability Scales (DAS) (C. D. Elliott) A battery of individually administered tests for cognitive assessment at both the preschool level (ages 2 1/2–6 years) and school-aged level (ages 7–17 years), as well as screening for academic achievement.

differential accuracy Ability to determine accurately in what way a person's traits differ from a stereotype associated with equivalent groups, for example, to determine in what way an adolescent differs from the stereotype of teenage groups. See STEREOTYPE ACCURACY.

differential amplifier An electrical device that amplifies the voltage difference between two input leads. In neural research, potential changes may be as small as one microvolt, and electrical resistances and sources of interference may be greater than the voltages being studied. Thus, complex electronic equipment, such as a differential amplifier, is required.

Differential Aptitude Test (DAT) (G. K. Bennett) A battery of tests designed for grades 8 to 12, to measure Abstract Reasoning, Language Usage, Numerical Reasoning, Mechanical Reasoning, Perceptual Speed and Accuracy, Space Relations, Spelling, Verbal Reasoning. The fifth edition has two levels for Grades 7–9 and 10–12. See MULTIPLE-APTITUDE TEST.

differential association (E. Sutherland) A concept that behavior of an individual is affected as a function of the type of people associated with. Sutherland, a criminologist, referred specifically to delinquency being the result of living in high-delinquency neighborhoods.

differential conditioning A conditioning program in which two stimuli are employed, one positive and one negative. An animal may thus be conditioned to lift a leg in response to the positive stimulus and not to lift its leg as a response to the negative stimulus.

differential diagnosis 1. The process of determining which of two or more diseases or disorders with overlapping symptoms applies to a particular patient. 2. The distinction between two similar diseases by identifying critical symptoms that are present in one but not the other. 3. Refers to the list of possible diagnoses from which a final diagnosis will be determined by further testing, examination, etc.

differential effect (K. Rao) In parapsychology, a tendency to score positively (psi-hitting) and negatively (psi-missing) in the same test when the participant is presented with two sets of contrasting conditions.

differential extinction The elimination of one or more responses established through conditioning whereas other related conditioned responses are not eliminated.

differential fertility Essentially, the fertility rate of any group versus another. Usually, in humans, it is made in comparison to ethnic, racial or economic groups.

differential growth The growth rate of any organ at a rate different from other organs in the body.

differential inhibition (I. Pavlov) 1. A conditioning procedure in which on some trials one stimulus (S1) is paired with the unconditioned stimulus and on other trials another stimulus (S2) is presented without the unconditioned stimulus. S1 tends to elicit a conditioned response and S2 to inhibit it. 2. A decreased tendency to respond to stimuli resembling the original conditioning stimulus.

differential instinctive behaviors Certain animal behaviors are considered instinctive, such as the hunting behavior of cats. However, within the instinct there may be variations of behavior; for example, in the hunting behavior of cats there are three distinct variations: (a) for prey on land, such as a mouse: a short pounce; (b) for flying prey, such as a bird: a leap into the air swiping at the prey with both front feet; and (c) for water prey, such as fish: putting paw(s) in the water to flip the fish out of the water. See INSTINCTIVE ACTIONS.

differential K theory (J. P. Rushton) Two scales of reproductive strategy of different species or human "races"; the "r" strategy has high rates of increase of populations in comparison to the "K" strategy. Whereas r-selected individuals reproduce at an early age, individuals in K-strategic groups produce fewer children and nurture them more carefully. Purportedly, warmer climates are associated with the r-strategy, harsher climates with the K-strategy.

differential level of constraint   Research in which two or more groups defined on the basis of some preexisting organismic variable(s) are compared on a dependent measure.

differential limen   See DIFFERENCE LIMEN.

differential mortality   A confounding situation in research when there are two balanced groups and more members drop out of one group to a greater extent than the other.

differential opportunity hypothesis   In sports psychology, a postulate that athletes select positions on teams based on the number of opportunities to play.

differential psychology   1. A branch of psychology that studies the nature, magnitude, cause, and consequences of psychological differences among individuals of the same type. 2. The study of differences between organisms of different types, such as between chimpanzees and humans, or cats and dogs. See VARIATIONAL PSYCHOLOGY.

differential R technique   (R. B. Cattell) A variation of factor analysis for determining personality changes over time. See FACTOR ANALYSIS, P TECHNIQUE.

differential rate reinforcement   In some learning experiments reinforcement is based on rate of responding by the organism. There are generally two types of such reinforcements: differential reinforcement of high rate, differential reinforcement of low rate.

differential reaction/response   A response limited to a specific stimulus among a variety of stimuli.

differential reinforcement   In conditioning, the rewarding of responses to certain stimuli while either not rewarding or punishing responses to other stimuli.

differential reinforcement of high rate (DRH or drh)   (B. F. Skinner) A schedule in which responding faster than a specified rate leads to reinforcement. Compare DIFFERENTIAL REINFORCEMENT OF LOW RATE.

differential reinforcement of low rate (DRL or drl)   (B. F. Skinner) A schedule in which slower responses than a specified rate brings on reinforcements. Compare DIFFERENTIAL REINFORCEMENT OF HIGH RATE.

differential relaxation   A technique characterized by reducing the contraction of muscles directly employed in an activity while fully relaxing muscles that are not involved, for example, relaxing the left hand while writing with the right.

differential response   A response by an organism to a specific stimulus, as in a test in which one presses a button only if a word is a noun. See DIFFERENTIAL REACTION.

differential scoring   A method of scoring tests in more than one way to obtain different data, as in scoring an interest test for different occupations.

differential sensibility   Responsiveness to differences in the intensity or quality of stimuli.

differential threshold   See DIFFERENCE THRESHOLD.

differential validity   An indication of the value of a test or test battery for decision-making. It is a function of the test and the criterion to be predicted. Selection is best when the differential validity is highest.

differentiation   1. In psychology: (a) sensory discrimination between stimuli; (b) a conditioning process in which discrimination is achieved through selective reinforcement of successive approximations; and (c) a change from homogeneity to heterogeneity in the psychological field. 2. In Kurt Lewin's social psychology, refers to the application of intelligence to learning experiences, which invariable leads to better personality development. 3. A social process in which a culture becomes more complex, more specific, and more specialized in its functions. 4. In mathematics, the process of obtaining a differential coefficient. 5. In biology, the transformation of cells from an undifferentiated mass into specialized tissue.

differentiation of cells   A process whereby daughter cells of a developing embryo undergo the changes necessary to become specialized in structure and function, such as heart-muscle tissue, a neuron, or a part of a bone. See DEREPRESSOR.

differentiation of self   The psychological separation of an individual from a primary group, such as a family, gaining independence thereby.

differentiation test   A method aimed at assessing whether in a blind testing procedure a rater can differentiate between two similar samples; for example, in consumer psychology the testing of various kinds of cola drinks to see whether tasters can distinguish between different brands of these drinks.

differentiation theory   A point of view that perception can be understood as an incremental sifting or filtering process whereby environmental "noise" (dispensable, incidental, peripheral information) is screened out while an individual learns to distinguish the hallmarks or essential characteristics of sensory patterns.

difficult child   1. Describing a child who generates problems for others, especially parents and teachers. 2. Describing a child who does not get along socially with others, especially with other children. See EASY CHILD, SLOW-TO-WARMUP CHILD.

difficulty scale   Any collection of things, such as tests, organized with items in order of increasing difficulty.

difficulty value   The ranking of an item, such as a question on a test, as measured by the percentage of participants or students in a designated class, age level, or experimental group, who reply to the item correctly.

diffraction   1. The deflection of light rays when passing the edge of an opaque body. 2. A phenomenon connected with the propagation of waves (sound, light, etc.), which consists in the bending of a portion of the wave-front due to an edge of an object of different refractive index.

diffraction grating   A highly polished surface ruled with a large number of parallel, finely-cut lines, used instead of a prism to produce a spectrum.

diffuse sclerosis   A group of neurological disorders involving extensive demyelination in the cerebral hemispheres. Symptoms may include hemianopsia, optic atrophy, various motor and sensory disturbances, headache, vertigo, convulsions, memory defect, confusion, disorientation, dementia, and paralysis of all limbs.

diffuse thalamic projection system (DTPS)   A set of thalamic nuclei that project diffusely into the cerebral cortex. The DTPS has arousal and activation functions similar to those of the reticular activating system but with less intensity in most instances and with more transient effects.

diffused expression/response   A responsive activity which is not definite and specific as in the reflex, but which involves widespread and uncoordinated responsive reactions in the organism.

diffused responsibility   See DIFFUSION OF RESPONSIBILITY.

diffusion   1. A stage of identity formation that has no sharp focus, possibly due to one having an easy life without too many problems or concerns. 2. In psychoanalytic theory, the separation of instincts that usually operate together. Best illustrated by the separation of the aggressive instinct from constructive, sexual instincts. 3. The spread of cultural aspects from one group to another as a result of contact between two cultures.

diffusion circle   A cutaneous area of the skin in which an extensive pressure sensation is aroused by a stimulus applied to a single point.

diffusion of responsibility   The observation that an individual's acknowledgment of personal responsibility diminishes in a group. Apparently, willingness to accept responsibility decreases as group size increases. See BYSTANDER EFFECT, CROWD BEHAVIOR.

diffusion of treatment   Potential confounding variable that occurs when participants in one treatment condition communicate biasing information to those in another.

diffusion process   In consumer psychology, the technique employed in gaining general acceptance by the public, of a new concept or product. Phrase is based on the analogy of a stone dropped in the water, producing waves that spread outward to reach the entire pond. The diffusion process depends upon acceptance by an initial core of people who influence those around them, the effect rippling outward through the entire population.

diffusion response   In Rorschach testing, comments made about shading on the cards.

digestion sensations   A group of organic sensations resulting at least in part from stimulation of receptors in the alimentary canal. Also known as digestive sensations.

digestive type   (L. Rostan) A constitutional body type in which the alimentary system dominates other systems. Corresponds to Ernst Kretschmer's pyknic type.

digital   1. Pertaining to or located in the fingers or toes. 2. Representing information in binary form (yes-no, 0-1), in contrast to analog representation, which is graded or continuous.

digitalograph   See STEADINESS APPARATUS.

digit-span test   An examination of short-term memory as found in a number of individual intelligence tests. A series of numbers are read out loud at the rate of one per second and the participant is asked to repeat them.

diglossia   (C. Ferguson) The simultaneous existence of two versions of the same languages such as Low German and High German, the first ordinarily spoken by illiterate people and the other by educated people. See DIALECT.

digraph   A combination of two letters or symbols representing a single speech sound, for example, "ph" in "digraph" or "ou" in "house," also the phonetic transcription /ks/ for the "x" in "explain." The corresponding term "trigraph" refers to three letters or symbols, for example, "tth" in "Matthew."

dihydroxyphenylalanine   A biogenic amine precursor for dopamine and noradrenalin that can cross the blood-brain barrier (B-BB), whereas dopamine cannot. Also known as dopa.

dikephobia   Morbid fear of justice, of seeing justice applied.

Dilantin   (T. J. Putnam & H. H. Merritt) Trade name for diphenylhydantoin sodium.

dilapidation   Deterioration of chronic mental patients to a point where they cannot feed themselves, may not control eliminative processes, and completely lose interest in their appearance. Most frequently observed in patients with regressed schizophrenia and patients with senile-brain-disease. See VEGETATIVE STATE.

dilation   1. The act of stretching or enlarging something, such as a hollow physiological structure. 2. (G. A. Kelly) The expansion of the meaning of any construct. See CORE CONSTRUCT.

dilator muscles and nerves   Mechanisms for causing active enlargement of various bodily structures.

dildo(e)   An artificial penis often made of rubber or plastic, used in masturbation and other sexual activity. Also known as godemiche, lingam, olisbos. See VIBRATOR.

dilemma   A situation in which a choice between two alternatives must be made, both of which may be undesirable. See MORAL DILEMMA.

dilemma of honesty and openness   In negotiation, the risk of either being exploited for disclosing too much too soon, or damaging the proceedings by refusing to disclose information and thereby seeming to be distrustful or deceptive.

dilemma of trust   In negotiation, the choice between believing the other negotiator and risking being exploited, or disbelieving the other and risking a failure to agree.

dimensions of consciousness   According to Edwin Boring, consciousness has these attributes: attensity (clearness), extensity (spaciality), intensity (force, strength), protensity (duration), and quality (goodness).

dimethyltryptamine (DMT)   A chemical substance that is said to foster introspection and intense distortion of the senses, but can also precipitate anxiety, panic attack, paranoia, possibly a heart attack.

diminished responsibility   See LIMITED RESPONSIBILITY.

diminishing-returns law   Another name for the law of diminishing returns. Distinguished from the diminishing-returns principle.

diminishing-returns principle   The perceived value of anything lessens the more a person has of that item. Thus, were a person to have only one dollar, another dollar would be a big difference, but if one had a hundred dollars, that same dollar would not seem so important or valuable. Compare LAW OF DIMINISHING RETURNS.

diminutive visual hallucination   **Lilliputian hallucination**

dimming effect   An enhancement or rejuvenation of either a chromatic or an achromatic adaptation effect (that is, an afterimage) due to reduction in the intensity of the stimulating field upon which it is seen.

dimorphism   1. The capacity of an organism to produce two different forms, such as a male and a female. See SEXUAL DIMORPHISM. 2. Two radically different structures of the same organism such as a caterpillar that changes into a butterfly.

DIMS   disorders of initiating and maintaining sleep

dingbat   Slang for a fool, an incompetent person.

ding-dong theory   **nativistic theory**

diode   A device for sending electrical current flow into two paths, one path facilitating the current to flow through it in one direction while inhibiting its flow in the other direction.

Dionysian   (F. Nietzsche) A state of mind that is sensuous, frenzied, and disordered (from Dionysus, Greek god of wine, orgiastic religion, and fertility). Nietzsche, in 1872, introduced the term Dionysian with the meaning of creative-passionate in contrast to Apollonian, or critical-rational. Compare APOLLONIAN ATTITUDE.

diopter (d)   A unit of convergence power applied to spectacle lenses, represented by a convex lens whose focal distance is 1.0 meter.

dioptrics   That branch of optics which deals with the refraction of light.

diotic   The stimulation of both ears with the same sound.

diphenylhydantoin (sodium)   Generic name for a substance used as an anticonvulsant and antiepileptic in the treatment of epilepsy. Related to barbiturates. Trade name is Dilantin.

diplacusis   An auditory disorder in which a given sound produces different pitch effects in each ear.

diplegia   A paralysis that affects similar parts on both sides of the body, for example, facial diplegia.

diplogenesis   A theory that whatever modifies a body tissue generates a corresponding change on the germ plasm. See LAMARCKISM.

diploid   Pertaining to the normal chromosome complement in human somatic cells (46). There are 22 pairs of homologous chromosomes plus the male (XY) or female set (XX) of sex chromosomes. See HAPLOID.

diploma disease   (R. Dore) Nontechnical name for excessive reliance on and the ritualization of educational credentials, especially in the job market.

diplopia   Double vision, usually due to weak or paralyzed eye muscles resulting in a failure of coordination and focus. May also be a conversion symptom.

dippoldism   The flogging of children, particularly school children. Term is named after a German schoolteacher, Dippold, who was convicted of manslaughter in the fatal flagellation of a schoolchild.

dipsomania   1. An enduring desire to drink alcohol to an excessive degree. May be indicative of a more serious underlying disorder. 2. An alcoholic mental disorder characterized by periodic drinking bouts or "binges." See ALCOHOLISM.

direct action   1. Generally, corrective action that is forceful, focused, immediate. 2. Euphemism adopted by terrorist groups in the 1970s to mean assassinations, bombings, etc. See PROPAGANDA.

direct aggression   Aggressive behavior directed toward the source of the frustration or anger. See DISPLACED AGGRESSION.

direct analysis   See DIRECT PSYCHOANALYSIS.

direct apprehension   Partial recognition in which objects are identified without being fully recognized.

direct association   Connections between items of a series which are related by immediate succession; for example in the alphabet, AB, BC, CD, or DE.

direct-contact group   A face-to-face group.

direct coping   Ways of dealing with problem situations by confronting them and acting in aggressive manners to contain or solve them.

direct cortical response   A response activated by direct electrical stimulation of cortical nerve tissue.

direct differences t-test   See CORRELATED T-TEST.

direct dyslexia   A language disorder in which the person reads common words aloud without understanding them. Caused by brain damage.

directed movement   Any movement of an organism definitely related to a specific stimulus.

directedness   (G. W. Allport) Describing the sense of unified purpose that provides the mature individual with enduring motivation, continuity, and orientation to the future.

directed reverie therapy   A procedure in therapy where the client is instructed to imagine having a dream or to imagine that something happened in early life and to report it to the therapist and, if in a group, to the other members.

directed thinking   Cerebration focused on a specific goal and guided by the requirements of that goal, such as attempting to solve a crossword puzzle. See CREATIVE THINKING, CRITICAL THINKING.

direct glare   Glare due to a light source in the field of vision.

direct inquiry   (H. Rorschach) A procedure in administering the Rorschach where, in addition to the relatively nondirective question: "Tell me what you see in these cards," an examiner later asks specific questions to clarify responses, such as "Did the color of this picture have any affect on your reply?"

directional confusion   Difficulty in distinguishing left from right and in some cases other directions as well, such as uptown from downtown. Some directional confusion is to be expected up to age six or seven, especially during the beginning stages of reading, writing, and spelling and in cases of mixed dominance. Persistent directional confusion may involve minimal brain damage or may be due to forced conversion from the left to the right hand. See HARRIS TESTS OF LATERAL DOMINANCE.

directional hypothesis   A prediction that a change in the independent variable will result in a change in the dependent variable.

directionality problem   In correlational studies, a problem in which it is known that two variables are related but it is not known which is the cause and which is the effect.

directional test of hypothesis   A statistical test that specifies direction of an effect. The null hypothesis is rejected only if statistical significance is achieved in the hypothesized direction. Compare NONDIRECTIONAL TEST OF HYPOTHESIS.

direction prognosis   (E. Bleuler) The predicted course of the development of a single person in a particular direction to an expected conclusion (for example, parents spoil their child, others predict that the child will turn out to be a helpless adult). Direction prognosis is distinguished from extent prognosis, which predicts the progress of the case.

direction sense   See LOCATION RESPONSE.

directions test   An intelligence examination or test item which concerns the participant's ability to follow verbal instructions on a series of tasks. See THREE PAPER TEST.

direction theory of tropisms   A point of view that the tropic orientation of an organism is determined by the direction or point in space from which the stimulus acts, rather than its duration or intensity. See TAXIS, TROPISM.

directive   An authoritative command by a superior body or instrument (for example, the Ten Commandments); something must be either performed or avoided. Examples include: LAWS, MORES, ORDINANCES, TABOOS.

directive counseling   (E. Williamson) A trait-and-factor type of counseling, based on interviews, testing, and direct educational and vocational advice. Also known as counselor-centered therapy. See TRAIT-AND-FACTOR COUNSELING.

directive disciplines   Fields of human philosophical concerns such as history, ethics, religion, and literature that provide people with directions for proper or superior behavior.

directive fiction   1. A conceptualization about self, others and the future that is established early in life and directs self-behavior toward indefinite goals. 2. Adlerian phrase for a concept of superiority, fantasized as an absolute truth, to compensate for a feeling of inferiority.

directive group   An aggregate of people in search of answers of various kinds, personal and impersonal, that features free discussions and mutual guidance (clients to clients, group leader to clients, and clients to leader), having elements of both psychotherapy and counseling. See ECLECTIC COUNSELING, ECLECTIC PSYCHOTHERAPY.

directive group psychotherapy   (S. R. Slavson) A type of therapy designed to help members adjust to their environment through didactic educational tasks, group guidance, group counseling, and therapeutic recreation.

directive leadership   A management style in which the leader knows what is to be done, and directs subordinates in their various duties in proper sequence. See LEADERSHIP.

directive-play therapy   An approach in which the therapist structures the child's activities by providing selected dolls or figurines meant to represent significant persons in the child's life, and by encouraging the child to use them in enacting "pretend" situations.

directive psychotherapist   A therapist who directs the course of the patient's therapy, as contrasted with nondirective psychotherapy. See RATIONAL EMOTIVE BEHAVIOR THERAPY.

directive tendency   See DETERMINING TENDENCY.

directive therapy   An approach that uses active advice-giving along lines considered relevant by the therapist based on the assumption that the therapist is equipped by his or her training and experience to understand the patient's behavior. Also known as counselor-centered therapy. See DIDACTIC THERAPY, TRAIT-AND-FACTOR COUNSELING.

direct measurement   A measurement that can be made with some instrument that provides meaningful information, without conversion to another scale, for example, using a ruler to get a length in inches.

director   In psychodrama, the therapist who sets the scene to be enacted and who supervises the interactions. See PSYCHODRAMA.

direct psychoanalysis   (J. Rosen) A modification of psychoanalytic techniques based on attempts to communicate directly with a psychotic patient's unconscious. In this process, the therapist interprets bizarre behavior, and encourages reliving early traumatic experiences. John Rosen's approach is a continuation of a tradition originally started by Paul Dubois. See PSYCHOANALYSIS.

direct realism   (J. Gibson) Viewing perception as a passive pickup of information based on patterns of light that land on the retina, in contrast to other theories, such as that of Wilhelm Wundt, that bring in central processes. See PERCEPTION, ECOLOGICAL VALIDITY.

direct reflex   An automatic action involving a receptor and effector on the same side of the body.

direct relationship   In statistics, a relationship between variables on two sets of scores such that knowing any one of the scores of one set predicts the other score.

direct replication   Repeating a research process as closely as possible to a prior research process, covering every single step by every single person with as close an attention to topics and participants of the original group, or even with the same group.

direct scaling   (S. S. Stevens) A subjective scaling method in which participants not only indicate rank order of items to be scaled but also the degree of difference between the item and others directly above and below.

direct scaling of psychophysical factors   Scaling accomplished by determining participants' estimates of relative differences on a scale. See METHOD OF MAGNITUDE ESTIMATION, PSYCHOPHYSICAL SCALING METHODS.

direct suggestion   Clear-cut advice intended to achieve a specific result, as in advising a parent whose child has frequent temper tantrums to not respond to the child, but to walk away from the child until the child is done having a tantrum.

direct theory of perception   A point of view that what is experienced via human senses is what actually exists.

dirhinic   (H. Henning) Characterizing olfactory stimulation of both nostrils simultaneously with the same scent. See MONORHINIC.

dirt phobia   Morbid fear of dirt often accompanied by a fear of contamination (mysophobia) and a hand-washing compulsion (ablutomania). Also known as rhypophobia, rupophobia.

dirty dozens   Prison slang for one inmate's testing another's emotional limits by making insulting and insinuating public remarks, usually about the members of the inmate's family, such as "How often have you had sex with your mother?"

DIS   Diagnostic Interview Schedule.

dis(a)esthesia   A sensation of discomfort, such as "pins and needles," located in cutaneous and subcutaneous areas.

disability   A lasting physical or mental impairment which significantly interferes with functioning in major areas of life, such as self-care, ambulation, communication, social intercourse, sexual expression, or ability to work inside the home or to engage in substantial gainful activity outside. See CHALLENGED, HANDICAPPED.

disability glare   See DISCOMFORT GLARE.

disability syndrome   An institutional neurosis consisting primarily of apathy, withdrawal, and resignation, occurring in long-term institutionalized patients with physical or psychiatric disabilities. See SOCIAL-BREAK-DOWN SYNDROME.

disabled   See CHALLENGED, PERSON WITH A DISABILITY.

disadvantaged   Individuals or families who lack the advantages of economic or cultural assets. See CULTURALLY DISADVANTAGED.

disaggregation   The dissolution of a social group into individual units.

disappearing-differences method   A procedure in psychophysics of determining limits of perception by presenting two stimuli that at first differ considerably in size (for example circles) and as the participant advances in making judgments (which is the larger or the smaller) in successive presentations, the differences become smaller and smaller until the participant no longer can make reliable judgements.

disarranged-sentence test   A task or test item in which the object is to put a scrambled sentence in proper order (for example, IF—VERY—BE—DICTIONARY—THIS—USEFUL—PROPERLY—CAN—USED). Such sentences are found in the Stanford Binet Intelligence Test.

disaster adaptation   Adaptive behavior assumed by most of the population of a community following earthquakes, floods, hurricanes, tornadoes, or other natural cataclysms. Disaster adaptation activities include establishment of communications and organization of the survivors into self-help work units. A common disaster adaptation phenomenon is rejection of assistance from outside the community except in extreme cases as well as the intention to rebuild and to remain in the same area.

disaster syndrome   A three-stage symptom pattern observed in civilian catastrophes: (a) shock stage: persons are so stunned by overpowering anxiety that they do little to help themselves or others; (b) suggestible stage: persons regress to a state of dependence and passively accept directions from others; (c) recovery stage: persons gradually regain control, but remain apprehensive, talking incessantly about the disaster, and may relive the experience in nightmares. See POSTDISASTER ADAPTATION.

disavowal   Denial.

discarnate   Having no body, characterizing a person considered to exist after death. Also known as disembodied, ghost.

discernment   1. The perception of the characteristics of an object or situation, including observation of differences. 2. A tendency to note social processes and values.

discharge   1. In neurophysiology, the firing or excitation of a neuron or group of neurons. 2. In psychiatry, the abrupt reduction in psychic tension that occurs in symptomatic acts, dreams, or fantasies. 3. In hospital administration, the dismissal of a patient from treatment or other services. 4. In industrial psychology, dismissal (of an employee).

discharge of affect   (S. Freud) The reduction of an emotion by giving it active expression, for example, by crying.

discharge rate   The number of patients released from a hospital or other institution in a given period.

dischronation   Confusion about time, part of the triad of orientation: Location, Persons, Time.

disciple   A person in the process of learning from a teacher, to become like the teacher.

discipline   1. A branch of knowledge. 2. A set of teachings. 3. Providing rewards and punishments to achieve desired patterns of behavior. See PARENTING. 4. Punishment, and by extension, slang for sadism. See BONDAGE AND DISCIPLINE.

disclosure of deceptions   Refers to the ethical principle in certain kinds of research in which deception is involved, that participants be informed later on of the true nature of the research. See DEHOAXING.

discomfort anxiety   (A. Ellis) Feelings of anxiety that largely result from unpleasant experiences but also from wishing that such does not exist, and worrying about the fact that they did.

discomfort disturbance   (A. Ellis) Anxiety, depression, anger, or low frustration tolerance which are caused by a person demanding that discomfort and hassles absolutely must not occur in his or her life.

discomfort glare   Annoyance or pain due to high or non-uniform distribution of light in the field of view. Variables include glare properties (size, luminance, number, location) and background luminance. When reading performance is reduced, the effect is termed disability glare.

discomfort-relief quotient (DRQ or drq) In communication, usually verbal, and especially in terms of research, the degree of statements that indicate unhappiness, criticism, or dissatisfaction, as compared to those statements indicating happiness, improvement, or satisfaction. In counseling or psychotherapy, if used in two interviews, the initial and the final, it may serve as a measure of a change of attitude toward self and others. Sometimes known as distress-relief quotient.

disconfirming the consequent In logic, the reasoning that if X implies Y, then if there is no Y there must be no X.

disconnection syndrome The neurologic condition resulting from a break in the transmission of impulses required to complete a response. Term is usually applied to the separation of the two cerebral hemispheres as a consequence of lesions in the corpus callosum, resulting in a failure of communication between the hemispheres.

discontinuity A break or gap in a series of any sort.

discontinuity hypothesis A Gestalt view that emphasizes the role of sudden insight and perceptual reorganization in discrimination learning and problem-solving. Holds that a correct answer is recognized when its relation to the issue as a whole is discovered. Contrasts with the associationist emphasis on step-by-step, trial-and-error learning. Compare CONTINUITY HYPOTHESIS.

discontinuity theory (of learning) (K. Lashley) A point of view that animal learning takes place discontinuously, in an all-or-none fashion, rather than gradually and continuously. See AHA EXPERIENCE.

discontinuous variable A variable whose values do not change in an orderly manner but which demonstrate abrupt changes. See DISCRETE DATA, DISCRETE VARIABLE.

discordance 1. Any situation where there is lack of agreement. 2. Research term used in twin studies to indicate dissimilarity between twins with respect to a particular trait or disease. The occurrence of a trait in only one member of a twin pair. See TWIN STUDIES.

discount To invalidate something, such as refusing to accept the truth of a statement.

discounting clue Some kind of indicator while receiving a string of information that indicates the accuracy, meaningfulness, or truth of the overall message is compromised. The message should not be accepted as valid.

discounting principle A theory that people tend not to attribute causes to proper events when other events seem more plausible, such as upholding the seemingly plausible reason that "He stopped smoking because he realized it was unhealthy" when the less plausible, but real reason was learning that a role model had stopped smoking, or that he could no longer afford to smoke. See ATTRIBUTION.

discourse analysis The study of interactive communication, back-and-forth speaking and writing.

discourse routine In linguistics, a complex set of interrelated rules for speech acts, roles, and status, repairs by speaker or listener, sequences, etc., that are learned as part of the language acquisition process and generally followed without awareness.

discovery learning A process whereby individuals learn a task or acquire knowledge on their own, usually with little or no help from books or other people.

discovery method A teaching method that seeks to provide students with experience of the processes of operations that will result in understanding, done through inductive reasoning and active experimentation with minimal teacher supervision. See MONTESSORI METHOD.

discovery risk See ETHICAL-RISK HYPOTHESIS.

discrepancy evaluation In evaluation research, the search for discrepancies or differences between two or more elements or variables of a program that should be in agreement. Reconciling differences may then become a major objective.

discrepancy evaluation theory A point of view that arousal is produced by discrepancies between expected and actual events.

discrepancy hypothesis In industrial psychology, a postulate that job satisfaction depends on the difference between what is desired and what is experienced on the job.

discrepancy principle A proposed preference on the part of infants and young children for experiences that are moderately novel to them.

discrepant stimulus In studies of perception in childhood, a stimulus that varies moderately from a known stimulus, for example, a stranger's face is a discrepant stimulus for an infant.

discrete data Data derived from a variable that can only take on a limited set of values, for example the whole numbers between one and ten, or the number of questions on a test. Related to discrete measure/unit/variable. See CONTINUOUS VARIABLE, DISCONTINUOUS VARIABLE.

discrete stimulus Some tangible phenomenon which is separate, distinct, or disjunct in space or time from other phenomena that are acting concomitantly or in temporal sequence with it.

discrete variable A variable that has separate numerical values that differ by clearly defined steps with no intermediate values possible, such as 1–2–3...n. See DISCONTINUOUS VARIABLE.

discretion Being cautious and reserved. Characterized by a tendency to avoid unsolicited intervention in the affairs of others and to refrain from action in a given issue until its merits have been carefully examined.

discretionary task In group dynamics, a relatively unstructured problem that can be solved cooperatively.

discrimen (division, distinction—Latin) (E. H. Weber) A sensory difference which may or may not be noticed or perceived.

discriminability 1. In testing, the extent to which overall high scorers answer an item on a test correctly and low scorers incorrectly. 2. In creating tests, finding which items correlate best with the criterion measures or with the total test.

discriminanda 1. (E. C. Tolman) Sensory capacity of organisms. 2. A stimulus a subject can differentiate from others. Singular is discriminandum.

discriminant analysis/function   A statistical technique for classifying individuals based on a combination of predictors; for example, a number of independent signs are combined into a regression equation and used to predict the probability of a person having organic brain damage.

discriminant evidence   Data obtained when a measure taps something unique when compared with other similar measures in assembling convergent evidence.

discriminant external validity   Empirical evidence of divergences or lack of correspondence between two separate and independent measures (usually psychological tests) of constructs which are supposed to differ from one another.

discriminant validation   1. Concurrent validity in which test scores of different groups are compared; for example, if mechanics score higher on a test of mechanical ability than clerks, then this provides additional discriminant validation for the test. 2. A subset of construct validation, in which a measurement does not significantly correlate with variables that are not consistent with the given theory.

discriminant validity   Two conceptually similar measurements are empirically discriminably different.

discriminated operant   (B.F. Skinner) The effect of behavior of an organism on the environment dependent on the situation in which the organism is located. The operant is defined in terms of the conditions it typically occurs under and the response or effects it has on the environment.

discriminating power   Ability of a test to discriminate between two groups.

discriminating range   **discrimination range**

discrimination   1. Ability to make judgments between similar but different items, such as in size, amount, brightness, sound. In this sense, types of discrimination include: AUDITORY, BRIGHTNESS, CONDITIONED, DRIVE, FINENESS OF, FLICKER, FORM, FREQUENCY, INDEX OF, PATTERN, PITCH, ROUGHNESS, SENSE, SENSIBLE, SIZE, STIMULUS, TACTUAL SHAPE, TACTUAL SIZE, TEMPORAL-FREQUENCY, THERMAL, TWO-POINT, VISUAL, WEIGHT. See CONTINUOUS-DISCRIMINATION REACTION/RESPONSE, TEST DISCRIMINATION INDEX, WEPMAN TEST OF AUDITORY DISCRIMINATION. 2. Treating some people favorably or unfavorably on the basis of arbitrary criteria, such as ethnicity, gender, "race," political ideology, religion. In this sense, types of discrimination include: AGE, GENDER, RACIAL, SEX.

discrimination experiment   A series of trials in which the animal subject or human participant is presented, simultaneously or successively, with slightly differing stimuli, and is motivated to discriminate between the stimuli, and to give proof of this discrimination by a prescribed differential response.

discrimination learning   A conditioning or learning experience in which the human participant or animal subject must learn to make choices between seemingly identical or similar alternatives to reach a goal, for example, a cat learns to find food under a white cup on the left side of an area in which there are white and black cups on both sides. Also known as discriminative learning.

discrimination method   In a research procedure, giving an organism a choice of one of two (or one of several) objects simultaneously. Choice of the positive one is rewarded; for example, an animal may be rewarded if it selects a symbol such as a square, a circle, or an oval, but not any other symbol.

discrimination of cues   The ability of an organism to recognize and react differentially to stimuli that are perceptually close or similar to each other. For instance, in research on responses to visual cues, animals learn to discriminate between figures with straight lines, such as a square and a hexagon, and those with curved lines, such as a circle. Animals may also learn to discriminate between figures with only five straight lines and all others or to discriminate between circles and ovals; the second step calls for discrimination of near cues.

discrimination range   The range of scores within which a test has discriminating power.

discrimination reaction/response   1. A response to one of two or more stimuli that may be presented. 2. A specific response for each of two or more stimuli that may be presented.

discrimination-reaction time   The amount of time measured between the display of two or more stimuli and the reaction to a pre-selected stimulus.

discrimination value   See D VALUE.

discriminative responses   In operant conditioning, the process of getting organisms to associate the functional meaning of a particular stimulus in that a particular response to the stimulus leads to a particular reaction. In this manner, animals can be taught to do various things or not to do various things depending on the association that has been made between stimuli and consequences of their behaviors.

discriminative stimulus (SD or SΔ)   In operant conditioning, the stimulus that an organism learns to associate with a specific response and reinforcer, for example, the ringing of a bell that conditions a person to answer the telephone. Also known as discriminatory stimulus. See REINFORCEMENT.

discussion groups   A range of groups, formal and informal, that explore many problems, issues, and matters of common interest, in a variety of vocational, educational, guidance, therapeutic, and community settings.

discussion leader   The member of a small group who is responsible for stimulating and guiding discussions.

discussion method   A teaching method in which both teacher and students actively contribute to the instructional process through classroom dialogue.

disease   A definite pathological process marked by a characteristic set of symptoms, dysfunctions, or both, which may affect the entire body or a part of the body. Types of disease include: ADDISON'S, ALZHEIMER'S, CHEYNE'S, CORONARY ARTERY, CORONARY HEART, ECONOMO'S, GENETOTROPHIC, GENOTROPHIC, HUNTINGTON'S, JANET'S, KANNER'S, KEMPF'S, KRAEPELIN'S, KUFS', LANGDON DOWN'S, MARIE'S, MOTOR-NEURON, NEUROMUSCULAR, NIEMANN-PICK, ORGANIC, PARKINSON'S, PICK'S, SACRED, SAINT DYMPHNA'S, SAINT

MATHURIN'S, SENILE BRAIN, SEXUALLY TRANS-MITTED, STERN'S, STUDENT'S, TAY-SACHS, VENE-REAL, WERNER'S, WERNICKE'S, YUPPIE. See CLAS-SIFICATION OF MENTAL DISEASES, FLIGHT INTO DISEASE, INTERNATIONAL CLASSIFICATION OF DIS-EASES (ICD-9).

disease fear   See NOSOPHOBIA.

disease model   Alternative phrase for medical model, the physiological paradigm of abnormal behavior.

disease narcissism   A reaction to disease or injury in which an unaffected body area is overvalued, perhaps as compensation for the defect.

diseases of adaptation   Describing the psychosomatic disorders, such as tension headaches, that are associated with stress-adaptation patterns. See GENERAL ADAPTA-TION SYNDROME.

disembedded thought   Thinking in general, not in terms of specifics, without context, for example, "How much is seven plus eight?" versus "Harry had seven dollars and he earned eight more dollars. How many dollars does Harry have now?" See DISEMBODIED THOUGHT.

disembodied   Freed from body. Discarnate.

disembodied thought   (J. Piaget) Thinking without context.

disengaged family   A family whose members are psychologically isolated from each other due to overrigid boundaries of communication or distant relationships between the members. See BOUNDARY.

disengagement   A psychological or social process of withdrawing from attachments with others.

disengagement theory   A point of view about aging that social withdrawal in old age is to a great degree due to reduction of social roles. See ACTIVITY THEORY, RETIREMENT NEUROSIS.

disequilibrium   1. Absence of equilibrium. 2. A loss of physical balance, as in Parkinson's disease and ataxias due to cerebellar disorder or injury. 3. Denoting emotional imbalance, as in patients with extreme mood swings. 4. In developmental psychology, disequilibrium is a state of tension between cognitive processes competing against each other. Some theorists assume, in contrast to Jean Piaget, that disequilibrium is the optimal state for significant cognitive advances to occur. See EQUILIBRATION.

disfigurement   A blemish or deformity that mars the appearance of the body. The psychological effects of dis-figurement, especially of the face, are often devastat-ing, since disfigurements often repel people in a soci-ety that places a high value on physical attractiveness. See ACROCEPHALY, APERT'S SYNDROME, CRETINISM, CROUZON'S DISEASE, DOWN'S SYNDROME, FACIAL DISFIGUREMENT, GARGOYLISM, HYDROCEPHALUS, HYPERTELORISM, MACROCEPHALY, MICROCEPHALY, MICROGNATHIA, PORT-WINE STAIN (SUPERFICIAL HE-MANGIOMA), MAROMBERG'S DISEASE, TREACHER COLLINS' SYNDROME.

disfluency   Difficulty in speaking clearly.

disgenic pressure   (R. J. Herrnstein, C. Murray) A controversial view of the downward pressure of intelligence quotient (IQ) to selected portions of a population are due to differential fertility rates of racial entities.

disguised wage-workers   A workforce that is appar-ently self employed but is contracted on a piecework or commission basis. Term can imply social criticism of capitalism.

dishabituation   1. An increased responding to a new stimulus following decreased attention to an earlier stimulus. 2. The elimination of a response to which an animal or human has become habituated.

disillusioning process   (K. Horney) Phrase used by Karen Horney to describe the first stage of therapy, which consists of undermining two pervasive illusions of a neurotic patient, the idealized self and despised self.

disincentive   As used primarily in industrial psychol-ogy, an obstacle to productivity or worker motivation, such as excessive overtime or unpleasant working con-ditions. In business, high taxes may also act as a disin-centive to entrepreneurs.

disinhibition   1. (I. Pavlov) After a response has been extinguished or otherwise inhibited, the presentation of a novel stimulus can restore the response. 2. A loss of cortical control; unrestrained emotions or actions often due to alcohol, drugs, or brain injuries.

disintegration of personality   Fragmentation of a person's self-concept and social behavior to such an extent that the person no longer presents a unified, predictable set of beliefs, attitudes, traits, and behavioral responses. The most extreme examples of disintegrated, disorganized personality are found in the schizophrenias.

disjoint sets   Describing two sets that have no elements in common. The intersection of the sets is empty, and they are mutually exclusive.

disjunction   The act of separation. In genetics, the normal separation of both chromosomes during the reduction division in meiosis.

disjunctive concept   1. A concept possessing some but not necessarily all the elements of a particular category, for example, a car can be described as a four-wheeled vehicle, a self-propelled vehicle, or an automobile. 2. Refers to one of two essential elements of anything. 3. A concept of the unity or combination of differences, for example, when faced with a large number of objects varying in sizes, shapes, materials, colors, etc., being asked to pick all items that are round and black. See CONJUNCTIVE CONCEPT.

disjunctive   Consisting of two antithetical parts.

disjunctive psychotherapies   (E. E. Landy) Behav-ioral techniques in psychotherapy that result in cognitive changes. See TWENTY-FOUR HOUR THERAPY.

dismantling-treatment strategy   In behavior therapy, the identification of the effective components of a treatment package by comparing groups that receive the entire package with groups that receive the package minus one or another component.

disorder   1. A situation in which a group of phenom-ena exhibit no intelligible relationship with one another. 2. Synonym for mental disease. Types of disorders in-clude: ACADEMIC UNDERACHIEVEMENT, ACQUIRED SPEECH, ACUTE, ACUTE BRAIN, ACUTE PARANOID,

ACUTE TRAUMATIC BRAIN, AFFECTIVE, AGGRESSIVE CONDUCT, AGING, ALCOHOL-AMNESTIC, AMNESIC, AMNESTIC, AMPHETAMINE-RELATED, ANTISOCIAL-PERSONALITY, ANXIETY, ARITHMETIC, ARTERIOSCLEROTIC BRAIN, ARTIFICIAL, ASPERGER'S, ATTACHMENT, ATTENTION, AUDITORY, AUDITORY PERCEPTUAL, AUTISTIC, AVOIDANT PERSONALITY, BEHAVIOR(AL), BIPOLAR, BODY DYSMORPHIC, BORDERLINE, BORDERLINE PERSONALITY, BOWEL, BRAIN-DAMAGE LANGUAGE, CAFFEINE-INDUCED, CALCIUM-DEFICIENCY, CANNABIS-RELATED, CATATONIC TYPE SCHIZOPHRENIA, CENTRAL AUDITORY PROCESSING, CHARACTER, CHILDHOOD ADJUSTMENT, CHILDHOOD, CHRONIC MOTOR-TIC, CHRONIC-TRAUMATIC, COCAINE-RELATED, COGNITION, COMMUNICATION, COMPULSIVE, COMPULSIVE-PERSONALITY, CONCEPTUAL, CONDUCT, CONGENITAL SPEECH, CONSTITUTIONAL, CONTENT-THOUGHT, CONVERSION, CONVULSIVE, CYCLOTHYMIC, CYCLOTHYMIC-PERSONALITY, DEPENDENT-PERSONALITY, DEPERSONALIZATION, DEVELOPMENTAL ARITHMETIC, DEVELOPMENTAL ARTICULATION, DEVELOPMENTAL LANGUAGE, DEVELOPMENTAL READING, DISRUPTIVE BEHAVIOR, DISSOCIATIVE, DYSTHYMIC, EATING, EJACULATORY, EMANCIPATION, EMOTIONAL, EPISODIC-BEHAVIOR, EXPRESSIVE, FACTITIOUS, FEMALE ORGASMIC, FEMALE SEXUAL AROUSAL, FORMAL-THOUGHT, FRONTAL PERCEPTUAL, FUNCTIONAL, FUNCTIONAL HEARING, FUNCTIONAL VOICE, GENDER-IDENTITY, GENERALIZED-ANXIETY, HABIT, HALLUCINOGEN PERSISTING PERCEPTION, HALLUCINOGEN-INDUCED MOOD, HEARING, HEREDITARY, HISTRIONIC-PERSONALITY, HYPERKINETIC-IMPULSE, HYSTERICAL, IDENTITY, IMPULSE-CONTROL, INHALANT-RELATED, INHERITED, INTERACTIONAL PSYCHOTIC, INTERMITTENT EXPLOSIVE, INTERSENSORY, ISOLATED EXPLOSIVE, LANGUAGE, LOGICOGRAMMATICAL, MALE ORGASMIC, MALE SEXUAL, MANIC BIPOLAR, MANIC-DEPRESSIVE, MASKED, MEDICATION-INDUCED MOVEMENT, MEMORY, MENSTRUAL, MENTAL, METABOLIC AND ENDOCRINOLOGICAL, MIXED BIPOLAR, MIXED SPECIFIC DEVELOPMENTAL, MOOD, MOOD-CYCLIC, MOTILITY, MOTOR, MOVEMENT, NARCISSISTIC PERSONALITY, NEUROTIC, NONAGGRESSIVE CONDUCT, NUTRITIONAL, OBSESSIVE-COMPULSIVE, OPIOID RELATED, OPPOSITIONAL, ORGANIC, ORGANIC MENTAL, ORIENTATION, ORTHOPEDIC, OVERANXIOUS, PANIC, PARANOID TYPE SCHIZOPHRENIA, PASSIVE-AGGRESSIVE PERSONALITY, PERCEPTUAL, PERSONALITY, PERVASIVE DEVELOPMENTAL, PHOBIC, PHONEMIC, POSSESSION TRANCE, POSTOPERATIVE, POSTPARTUM, POSTTRAUMATIC, POSTTRAUMATIC STRESS, PREMENSTRUAL, PRIMARY AFFECTIVE, PRIMARY BEHAVIOR, PRIMARY THOUGHT, PSYCHOGENIC, PSYCHOGENIC PAIN, PSYCHOMOTOR, PSYCHOSEXUAL, PSYCHOSOMATIC, PUERPERAL, REACTIVE ATTACHMENT, REACTIVE, REACTIVE DEPRESSIVE, REM BEHAVIOR, RESIDUAL ATTENTION-DEFICIT, RESIDUAL SCHIZOPHRENIA, RHYTHM, RUMINATION, SCHIZOAFFECTIVE, SCHIZOID-PERSONALITY, SCHIZOPHRENIFORM, SCHIZOTYPAL-PERSONALITY, SEASONAL AFFECTIVE, SECONDARY AFFECTIVE, SEDATIVE AMNESTIC, SEIZURE, SEMANTOGENIC, SENSORY, SEPARATION-ANXIETY, SEXUAL AVERSION, SEXUAL, SHAM, SHARED PARANOID, SHARED PSYCHOTIC, SHYNESS, SKIN, SLEEP, SLEEPWALKING, SOCIALIZED CONDUCT, SOCIOPATHIC, SOMATIC, SOMATIZATION, SOMATOFORM, SOMATOPSYCHIC, SOMESTHETIC, SPATIAL, SPEECH, STEREOTYPIC-MOVEMENT, STRUCTURAL, SUBSTANCE-USE, TACTILE-PERCEPTUAL, TEMPORAL-PERCEPTUAL, THOUGHT, TIC, TIME AND RHYTHM, TOURETTE'S, TOXIC, TRANCE, TRANSIENT SITUATIONAL PERSONALITY, TRAUMATIC, UNDIFFERENTIATED TYPE SCHIZOPHRENIA, UNIPOLAR, VARIED PSYCHOSEXUAL, VISUAL-SEARCH PERCEPTUAL, VOICE. See entries beginning with ATYPICAL and also DISTURBANCE VS DISORDER, REACTION VS DISORDER.

disorders of initiating and maintaining sleep (DIMS) See INSOMNIA.

disorders of the self 1. Any of a variety of disorders that refer to a person's self-concept, such as feelings of inferiority, of social inequality, or of fearfulness. 2. (H. Kohut) Phrase similar to narcissistic problems.

disorder vs reaction See REACTION VS DISORDER.

disorganization In psychiatry, an inability to integrate thought processes, emotions, and volition in meeting the demands of life. Disorganization, in extreme form, is a fragmentation or disintegration of the personality such as occurs in advanced schizophrenia. See DISINTEGRATION, DISORGANIZED SCHIZOPHRENIA.

disorganized behavior Inconsistent nonpurposive action which does not achieve a desired goal, includes self-contradictory actions and inappropriate behavior such as laughing after a catastrophe.

disorganized schizophrenia A condition marked by inappropriate affect, silly behavior, shallow relationships, and childish actions. Once termed hebephrenia because it originally was considered to occur around puberty. Also known as disorganized type of schizophrenia. See HEBEPHRENIC SCHIZOPHRENIA, SCHIZOPHRENIA.

disorganized serial-killer A type of serial killer who impulsively or spontaneously murders, often using as the weapon an object that is convenient and at hand. May show signs of deteriorating mental health. Compare ORGANIZED SERIAL-KILLER.

disorientation Inability to correctly identify the self in relation to time, place, or person. Not being able to answer these questions: (Place) "Where are you right now?", (Person) "Who are you?" and (Time) "What is today's date?" See ORIENTATION, TIME DISORIENTATION, TOPOGRAPHICAL DISORIENTATION.

disparate retinal points Points on the two retinas whose sensory representations fail to yield identical space impressions.

disparate sensations Sensations which belong to different senses, or which lack mediating (that is, transitional) forms though belonging to the same sensory field.

disparation A double visual image seen when the object is behind or in front of the fixation point.

disparition The disappearance of items from the cognitive field.

disparity Short for binocular disparity.

dispersion analysis The study of the distribution of data. See KURTOSIS and SKEWNESS for examples of various kinds of dispersion.

dispersion measure   Summary information about the spread or variability of a distribution of scores. Scores that cluster closely around a measure of central tendency represent a low degree of dispersion; widely scattered scores indicate a high degree of dispersion. Measures of dispersion most widely used are range and the standard deviation. Also known as variability. See BINOMIAL DISTRIBUTION, RANGE.

dispersion of scores   The extent to which points vary from a reference point or among themselves.

displaceability of libido   In psychoanalytic theory, the substitution or replacement of partial impulses related to the four libidinal phases (oral, anal, phallic, genital) for each other in sexual arousal, particularly in foreplay or purported perversions.

displaced aggression   The direction of hostility away from the source of frustration and toward either the self or a different person or object, usually someone or something weaker that is unable to strike back. Also known as displacement of aggression. See DIRECT AGGRESSION, DISPLACEMENT, SCAPEGOATING.

displaced-child syndrome   A pattern consisting of sibling jealousy, irritability, discouragement, and feelings of rejection that may be precipitated by the birth of another child in the family.

displaced homemakers   Generally, women who no longer have a home "job" and no longer receive income from other family members, usually their husbands, as a result of a divorce or death of a provider, and who now are required to work to support themselves.

displaced speech   Characterizing the speech of young children that transcends the here-and-now and the single word stages, to refer to past or future concepts.

displacement   1. In psychoanalytic theory, a defense mechanism in which an aggressive impulse (usually anger) is shifted from dangerous and powerful objects or persons to safer ones, such as those less threatening or neutral (for example, an angry child might hurt a sibling instead of attacking the parent, or a frustrated employee might criticize the secretary instead of the boss). See DISPLACED AGGRESSION, DISPLACEMENT ACTIVITY, DRIVE DISPLACEMENT, SUBSTITUTION. 2. In dreams, shifting the emphasis from an important element to a minor one. See DISPLACEMENT DREAMS. 3. In Rorschach testing, deliberately faking the test by picking on insignificant elements. 4. Changing a usual way of behaving under abnormal conditions. 5. In parapsychology, extrasensory perception (ESP) responses to targets other than those for which the calls were intended. See BACKWARD DISPLACEMENT, FORWARD DISPLACEMENT.

displacement activity/behavior   A form of behavior in which an organism substitutes one type of action for another when the first fails to answer a need. For instance, an animal frustrated by small servings of food may express displacement behavior by drinking instead of eating.

displacement dreams   The contents of dreams may appear obvious and understandable to the dreamer, but according to dream theory, things are frequently not what they appear to be; for example, objects may have certain symbolic meanings, such that a certain person in a dream may in fact represent an entirely different person, including the self.

displacement of affect   Movement of feelings for something or someone to another thing or person. Also known as transposition of affect. See TRANSFER, TRANSFERENCE.

displacement of aggression   See DISPLACED AGGRESSION.

displacement theory   A point of view that the mind's capacity is limited for learning or memory and that when this limit is reached, new learning or new memories are possible only if older learning is lost. In short, that the mind is limited.

displasia   (W. Sheldon) The three primary components of physique according to William Sheldon's theory of body types, appearing in an irregular manner, for example, physical appearance that is inconsistent, such as a burly person with slender legs. Also known as dysplasia. See SOMATOTYPE.

display   1. In ergonomics, a presentation of information, usually by a machine to an operator or monitor. Generally visual or auditory, rarely tactile or olfactory; may be graphical, numerical, pictorial, or symbolic. See DISPLAY DESIGN. 2. In ethology, an animal behavior pattern and/or appearance change that communicates emotion, sexual receptiveness, dominance/submission, etc. Sometimes applied to "flirting" behavior in humans. See DISPLAY RULES. 3. In experimental psychology, the presentation of a stimulus to the subject.

display behavior   Actions that are intended to effect a response by another animal or individual. May be verbal or nonverbal, usually with stimulation of the visual or auditory senses. Display behavior may include body language that would convey a message of courtship to a member of the opposite sex (such as a show of plumage or color) or a suggestion that would be interpreted by an opponent as threatening (such as bared teeth or hissing noises). See DISPLAY RULES.

display design   In industrial psychology, the design of displays for communicating information efficiently, safely, and unambiguously to the person(s) intended. See DISPLAY (meaning 1).

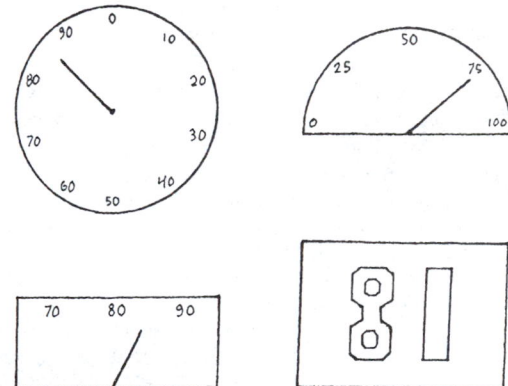

display design   To make a quick judgment of amounts, which of these four designs would be the most useful?

display rules   The socially learned standards or guidelines that control and inhibit the expression of emotion. Vary from culture to culture; for example, direct expression of anger may be socially appropriate in one culture but unacceptable in another, or crying may be considered appropriate for women but not for men. See DISPLAY BEHAVIOR.

disposition 1. A tendency to behave in a similar manner at different times and places. 2. The sum total of an individual's characteristic tendencies, such as basic temperament, attitudes, inclinations, and drives. 3. The total attitude of a person at any one time. See MOOD, TEMPERAMENT, TRAIT.

dispositional attribution Explaining any behavior as due to underlying psychological factors. Also known as personal attribution. See ATTRIBUTION THEORY, ATTRIBUTIONAL ERROR, AUTOCHTHONOUS VARIABLE, SITUATIONAL ATTRIBUTION.

dispositional inference In observing the overt behavior of a person, the assumption that a second person can make valid inferences about covert and inner behavior of the first person.

dispositional sets Based on Karen Horney's triangle, Nira Kefir has constructed a map of personality dispositions. At the top corner is democratic equality relationships; at the bottom left is aggressive behavior; and at the bottom right is escape-avoidance. In the middle is indifference. Any person's conduct at any moment (or overall) can be located on this map. This map can be useful in marriage and family counseling by finding out where people think they are and where others see them. See DISPOSITIONAL TRIAD for diagram.

dispositional theory (V. Yadov) A point of view that the readiness of a person to operate selectively in social situations depends primarily upon how that person has operated in the past in a similar situation. According to Yadov, such dispositions are based on a hierarchy depending on interests, values, and generalized attitudes. See DISPOSITIONS, DISPOSITIONAL ATTRIBUTION, SET.

dispositional triad (K. Horney) A triad of personality best illustrated by a triangular map whose corners are appropriately named; for example, for mood, the corners might be happy–sad–indifferent; for relationships (with any particular person or in general), they might be labeled democratic–bossy–laissez faire. The center of the triangle represents an equal distance from the three corners, and so generally represents normality. See HORNEY TRIANGLE for an illustration.

disruption 1. A sudden loss of personality organization that is similar to disintegration but which occurs at a more rapid pace. 2. Interference in the normal progression of some event.

disruptive behavior disorder A pattern of misbehavior marked by inattention, making careless mistakes, lacking interest in matters considered serious. Typically begins in children at about age six when they enter school. Disruption can be either passive (not doing what is reasonably to be expected) or active (doing what is not permitted) in social situations, such as shouting in a theatre, going through another's private things, taking the property of others. See ATTENTION DEFICIT DISORDER, AUTISM, SOCIOPATHY.

dissembling Feigning.

dissent Refusal by one person to accept as valid a statement or conclusion put forward by another person or adopted by the social group to which the person belongs.

dissimilation A change in one or more adjacent sounds that serves to make a string of similar sounds less similar.

dissimulation The process of deliberately generating a false impression on others by actions or words, often by means other than actually lying. See HIDDEN AGENDA.

dissipation 1. The spreading of a definite group or mass of units into a larger area or space which results in their becoming a less prominent portion of the total contents of the given locality (for example dissipation of gases, of energy, of a social group). 2. A mode of life characterized by persistent overindulgence in intoxicants or drugs or other excesses which undermine the person's physical constitution, mental constitution, or both.

dissipative behavior (T. Burrow) Processes that instead of increasing a person's energy, growth, or development do the opposite, leading the person to reduction, dissolution, and eventually to uselessness as in psychoses. See PARTITIVE BEHAVIOR, PHYLOANALYSIS, PHYLOBIOLOGY.

dissipative structures An open nonequilibrium system with a high degree of energy exchange within the environment, which creates instabilities that drive such a system toward high entropy productions within a new, dynamic system that creates a new state of complexity.

dissociated learning See STATE-DEPENDENT LEARNING.

dissociated states Reactions to overwhelming or extreme stress which develop as a way of coping. Involves the splitting apart of components of the personality that are usually integrated and manifests itself in the form of alterations or subtractions of the personality, especially in the areas of memory, identity, perception of self, and/or environment. See AMNESIA, DEPERSONALIZATION, FUGUE, MULTIPLE PERSONALITY.

dissociation (M. Prince) An unconscious process in which one or more parts of mental functioning become split off from others and appear to operate outside of consciousness. Its origin is thought by some Freudians to be the result of conflicting impulses that are repressed and kept apart from each other by compartmentalization, or threatening ideas and feelings which are separated from the rest of the psyche. See DISSOCIATIVE DISORDERS.

dissociative amnesia A sudden failure to recall self-identity and, in some cases, one's past, but without forgetting basic habits and skills. Recovery of memory often occurs spontaneously within a few hours, but in resistant cases hypnosis or sodium amytal may be used to bring about recall or remembering. See FUGUE, PSYCHOGENIC AMNESIA.

dissociative anesthetic A drug that prevents pain from being felt, separating the mind from the body.

dissociative barriers (G. Rhoades) Reversible memory impairment in which a specific memory or groups of memories (typically relating to traumas) are not available for recall. Also known as amnesic barriers.

dissociative disorder A pathological condition in which dissociation occurs as a way of coping with overwhelming or extreme stress. Manifests symptoms in the areas of memory, identity, perception of self, and/or environment. DSM-IV lists the major types as dissociative amnesia, dissociative fugue, dissociative identity disorder, depersonalization disorder. See AMNESIA, DEPERSONALIZATION, FUGUE, MULTIPLE PERSONALITY.

dissociative group   A group with which the person wishes not to be associated. Compare ASPIRATIONAL GROUP.

dissociative hysteria   See DISSOCIATIVE DISORDERS.

dissociative identity disorder   A psychiatric disorder as defined by the American Psychiatric Association's Diagnostic and Statistical Manual of Mental Disorders, Fourth Edition. The disorder (not attributable to a general medical condition or substance abuse) is characterized as a person having at least two distinct identities or personality states that recurrently take control of the person's behavior. The person also has an inability to recall extensive important personal information, that would not be accounted for by normal forgetfulness. See MULTIPLE PERSONALITY.

dissociative patterns   Abnormal functioning of consciousness and behavior characterized by separation of cognitive functions and personality. The person may perform apparently normal operations while having no consciousness of the behavior, as though there were two independent entities operating at the same time. See AMNESIA, DISSOCIATIVE DISORDERS, FUGUE, MULTIPLE PERSONALITY.

dissociative process   The dynamics of the splitting off of the psyche from its central core, ranging from "spacing out" while engaged in boring tasks to dividing the self into multiple personalities. See DISSOCIATIVE-IDENTITY DISORDER (MULTIPLE-PERSONALITY DISORDER).

dissociative reaction   See DISSOCIATED STATES, DISSOCIATION, DISSOCIATIVE IDENTITY DISORDER, DISSOCIATIVE PATTERNS.

dissolution   (H. Spencer) The reversal of the process of evolution.

dissonance   1. In music, a usually unpleasant effect due to two or more tones within the same octave, which do not blend or fuse, played simultaneously. 2. A clash between anticipated and actual events, between theory and fact, etc. 3. Lack of harmony, such as incongruity between two perceptions or concepts. See COGNITIVE DISSONANCE.

dissonance reduction (theory)   1. (L. Festinger) A view that when indecisive, confused or uncertain about two conflicting concepts, a person will seek more information so that one view or the other may be taken with greater confidence. 2. A view that when faced with two dissonant cognitions, a person will reduce the dissonance by changing one (the one that is easier to modify) to make it consonant with the other. See COGNITIVE DISSONANCE.

distal   Farther away from an area such as a body organ, or from the center of the area; for example, the toe is distal from the hip. Compare PROXIMAL.

distal anticipatory stress   Emotional response induced by a consideration of events that are not of immediate concern but that may arise in the future.

distal criteria   In judgment formation, standards used to make long-term decisions. Compare PROXIMAL CRITERIA.

distal effects   (E. Brunswik) The resultant behavior of an organism in terms of events at a distance, for example, a person flinches due to a noise heard in the distance.

distal poststress interventions   Procedures designed to help people cope effectively with the long-term aftereffects of exposure to stressors.

distal response   A response that occurs away from the body or boundaries of an organism and produces an effect in the environment. A distal response is related to a proximal response. In playing the piano, the proximal stimulus is the action of the fingers on the keyboard whereas the distal response is the chord produced. See DISTAL EFFECTS, ECOLOGICAL VALIDITY, PROXIMAL STIMULUS, REPRESENTATIVE DESIGN.

distal stimulus   (E. Brunswik) The actual object or physical energy occurring in the environment some distance away that stimulates or acts on a sense organ. A sound or a light that impinges on an individual is a distal stimulus. Compare PROXIMAL STIMULI/STIMULUS.

distal urethra   Skene's glands

distal variable   A stimulus source (for example the ringing of a telephone) that acts on a receptor through a proximal variable (the sound waves striking the ear).

distance cue   An auditory or visual stimulus that acts as a signal enabling a person to judge the distance to the source. Auditory distance cues include the time difference, however brief, between the arrival of a sound at the left and at the right ears. See BINOCULAR CUE, MONOCULAR CUE.

distance paradox   (K. Dunker) If a dot is in a rectangle, and if the rectangle is moved, the impression is that both the dot and the rectangle moved to a greater distance, when summed, than the actual movement.

distance perception   See DEPTH CUES, DEPTH PERCEPTION.

distance receptor   A sense organ or receptor that can detect stimuli from a distance, for example, visual and auditory receptors. See TELEORECEPTOR.

distance sense   1. A sense whose receptor is stimulated by energies the immediate source of which may be at a distance from the organism, notably vision and hearing. 2. An ability to correctly identify the point of origin of a stimulus whose source is at a distance from the receptors of the organism. Also known as distant sense.

distance vision   Visual perception that permits discrimination of objects more than 6 meters (20 feet) away.

distance zones   Areas of interpersonal physical distance most commonly adopted between persons. Distances usually increase in proportion to the formality of the relationship, the setting, and the interaction's function. Also, preferred distance zones vary from culture to culture. See PROXIMITY.

distant point   A point in the visual field arbitrarily set at more than 10.0 meters from the observer's eye, about 33 feet away.

distant receptor   Refers to the specific organs or elements of the body of the various senses that are able to receive "messages" from objects at a distance. This would include vision, hearing, smelling, and even cells in the skin that detect heat. Also known as teleoreceptor.

distant species   Organisms that are generally solitary, for example tigers. Compare CONTACT SPECIES.

distinction   The basis of discrimination between two data of any sort.

distinctness An aspect of perception during attending, in that what humans focus on tends to be well defined and easy to differentiate. Also known as clearness. See ATTENDING.

distinguish To discriminate various sensations in terms of perceptual capacities, such as differentiating between various odors.

distoceptor A biological receptor such as those for vision and audition used to estimate distances. See DISTANCE RECEPTOR, TELEORECEPTOR.

distorted room See AMES' DISTORTION ROOM.

distortion 1. In psychoanalytic theory, the modification of forbidden thoughts, impulses, or experiences to make them more acceptable to the ego. In dreams, forbidden wishes are frequently expressed in disguised or symbolic form: The innocent act of walking upstairs is more likely to pass the superego that acts like a censor rather than the act of sexual intercourse which such a dream allegedly represents. 2. In social relations, a tendency for people to give a warped account of experiences that would otherwise put them in a bad light, often without realizing they are doing so. 3. Regarding pathology, many abnormal conditions such as delusions, hallucinations, feelings of unreality, flattened affect, and neologisms are distortions of mental or emotional processes.

distortion by transference A misperception of the analytic situation or the analyst due to transference.

distortion of form See FORM DISTORTION.

distractibility Susceptibility to attentional variability, the tendency to give attention to peripheral items and not to stick to a desired or mandated topic or concern. Excessive distractibility is frequently found in children with learning disorders, and in manic patients who shift rapidly from topic to topic. See FLIGHT OF IDEAS.

distractible speech A communication pattern in which the patient shifts rapidly from topic to topic in response to external or internal stimuli. A common symptom in mania. See FLIGHT OF IDEAS.

distracting task A test for evaluating a task requiring close attention conducted in an environment that features sudden loud noises at irregular times, bumps that affect the seating of the participant, interruptions when the participant is about to answer questions, etc. Used to gauge how well a job candidate can perform under suboptimal conditions.

distraction 1. Withdrawal of attention from a given focus, either perceptual or imaginal, by irrelevant stimuli. 2. A condition in which the attention is not concentrated, but is divided among various parts of the experience.

distractor(s) 1. Generally, anything that takes attention away from the task at hand. 2. On psychological tests, items designed to conceal the purpose of the instrument, also termed filler items. 3. In memory tests, a task that interrupts the information processing. 4. In theatrical performances (especially by illusionists), something that attracts the audience's attention to where the performer wants it.

distress-relief quotient (drq)/ratio The ratio of verbal expressions of distress to those of relief, used as an index of improvement in counseling and psychotherapy. Also known as discomfort-relief quotient.

distributed-actions theory of leadership The performance of acts that help the group to complete its task and to maintain effective working relationships among its members.

distributed cognition The argument that several agents sharing information between themselves can accomplish tasks that could not otherwise be done.

distributed learning A learning procedure in which practice periods of something too long to be learned in one session, such as a long poem, are separated by timed intervals of rest. In many learning situations, distributed practice (in separate time periods) is found more effective than massed practice (in one time period). Also known as spaced learning. Compare MASSED PRACTICE.

distributed memory storage (theory) A point of view that mental activity is due to the integrated activity of various brain components; Karl Lashley concluded that memories are not stored "anywhere" but rather, everywhere. Memory is widely distributed, but different aspects of it are stored in different locations. Compare LOCALIZED MEMORY STORAGE (THEORY).

distributed practice See DISTRIBUTED LEARNING.

distribution Any set of data that is presented according to its magnitude in a systematic or tabular summary form, as in a frequency distribution.

distributional redundancy In psychological esthetics, the development of uncertainty in an artistic pattern by some kinds of elements occurring more frequently than others.

distribution curve A graphic representation showing values on the base line and frequency on the vertical axis. See NORMAL CURVE.

distribution-free statistics Statistics that make no a priori assumption about the shape of the frequency distribution under study; statistics applicable even in the absence of a normal distribution. See NONPARAMETRIC STATISTICS.

distribution-free tests Tests of statistical significance that make relatively few assumptions about the underlying distribution of scores, such as the chi-square test that does not assume that observations are normally distributed.

distributive analysis and synthesis (A. Meyer) A common-sense approach to psychotherapy, in which a systematic analysis is made of the patient's past and present experience, including symptoms and complaints, assets and liabilities, and pathological or immature reactions. This analysis is used as a prelude to a constructive synthesis built on the client's or patient's own strengths, goals, and abilities. See PSYCHOBIOLOGY.

distributive bargaining Negotiations between two parties, with each side attempting to achieve its own gains. Compare INTEGRATIVE BARGAINING.

distributive justice According to Jean Piaget, children's beliefs that rewards and punishments should accord to equality and equity. In the equality stage (ages eight to ten), children demand that everyone be treated in the same way. In the equity stage (age 11 and older), children make allowances for subjective considerations, personal circumstances, and motive. Compare IMMANENT JUSTICE.

distributive law   A theory that an operation performed upon a complex whole affects each part of this complex in the same way, as if performed upon each part separately.

distributive practice   A process of learning by practicing in small units over time. See DISTRIBUTED LEARNING, MASSED PRACTICE.

distributive synthesis   (A. Meyer) A form of guidance based on a close evaluation of an individual by means of extensive verbal questions, leading to conclusions and specific recommendations. See COUNSELING, REALITY THERAPY.

disturbances of associations   According to Eugen Bleuler, a basic symptom of schizophrenia, in which interruptions of thought associations lead to haphazard, confused, bizarre thinking.

disturbance vs disorder   A "disturbance" may be transient, whereas "disorder" implies greater permanence, and a disorder is biologically-based, whereas a disturbance may be due to psychological factors.

disturbed neurotic delinquency hypothesis   A postulate that some delinquent behaviors may have causes or purposes related to personal or family problems, and that the delinquent is acting out some symbolic personal problem, for example, a child may steal not necessarily to get a stolen object, but perhaps to get caught and thus perhaps escape from the family or punish the family through disgracing it.

disulfiram   The generic name for an organic sulfide used for deterring the consumption of alcohol. Causes an accumulation of aldehyde in the blood that results in nausea and vomiting. The drug interferes with normal metabolism of alcohol, so that if taken regularly, drinking even small amounts of alcohol makes the person feel nauseated, flushed, and toxic. If much alcohol is ingested, the results may include collapse and psychosis. Trade name is Antabuse.

disuse supersensitivity   Increased responsiveness in a post-synaptic cell after a period of decreased input by incoming axons.

disuse theory of aging   A point of view that age-related declines are analogous to muscles that atrophy if not exercised.

disynaptic arc   A nerve circuit in which there is a neuron between a motor neuron and a sensory neuron, requiring a nerve impulse to cross two synapses to complete the arc.

diurnal cycles   Patterns of activity or behavior that follow the day-night cycles. Most humans and many other species, such as wild birds, often follow predictable patterns of daylight activity. Other animals may be crepuscular (active in the twilight) or nocturnal in their 24-hour activity cycles. A number of species undergo diurnal color changes that persist even in a controlled environment of continuous light or darkness. See CIRCADIAN RHYTHMS.

diurnality   The daily repetition of an activity, such as the opening of a flower each morning. See DIURNAL CYCLES, DIURNAL RHYTHM.

diurnal mood variation   Changes in affect related to the time of day. See SEASONAL-AFFECTIVE DISORDERS (SADS).

diurnal rhythm   An activity or series of activities occurring each day during the day, such as getting up at about the same time daily, or eating meals at fairly regular intervals. See BIOLOGICAL RHYTHM, DIURNAL CYCLES.

divagation   1. Meaningless speech. 2. Rambling, digressive speech and thought.

divergence   Turning outward of the eyes. A tendency for the eyes to turn outward when shifting from near to far fixation. A permanent divergence of one eye is termed exotropia.

divergent conduction   Simultaneous conduction by two or more neurons from a single point to two or more different locations. See PARALLEL CONDUCTION.

divergent production   (J. B. Guilford) The capacity to recall from memory information needed to solve a particular problem. See FUNCTIONAL KNOWLEDGE.

divergent thinking   1. An aspect of creative thought characterized by the formulation of alternative solutions to problems. The task is to generate answers, whereas in convergent thinking the task is to analyze already formulated solutions. 2. In the solving of problems, creative cognition in which at least one person mulls over possible answers and solutions. See BRAINSTORMING, CONVERGENT THINKING, GROUPTHINK.

divergent validity   An aspect of construct validity in which a test of a construct give results that differ from a test measuring a different construct.

diversion of sex energy   See SUBLIMATION.

diversity   Unlikeness or dissimilarity among data. Also cultural dissimilarity, as in multiculturalism.

diversive exploration   Behavior that seeks stimulation in the environment, such as a bored adolescent seeking excitement in street-gang activities if life at home provides inadequate stimulation. See BOREDOM, RESTLESSNESS.

divided attention   Concentration on more than one activity at the same time, often with a reduction in performance.

divided brain   See SPLIT BRAIN.

divided consciousness   The disputed view that a state of consciousness can exist in which two or more mental activities are carried out at the same time, as in simultaneously listening, planning questions, and taking notes during an interview. Parallel processing theory supports such a view. Serial processing theory, however, holds that the ability to attend to two things at once is not possible, and that there is only a rapid shifting between information sources.

divination   The use of a paranormal practice to obtain extrasensory information; a paranormal process by means of which future events are alleged to be foretold, or hidden knowledge is discovered. The process may entail a spiritualistic medium's supernatural powers (as in crystal-gazing, or crystallomancy), or by augury (the interpretation of omens or portents such as: aeromancy (divination from the air) to zoomancy (the examination of the entrails of a sacrificed animal) as well as by a variety of other methods. See EXTRASENSORY PERCEPTION, PARAPSYCHOLOGY.

divine right of kings   A concept, notably expressed by James I of England, that all power comes from God, who gives it to kings, who distribute it to lords, who grant power downward as they see fit, with males ruling females and parents having power over children. See CASTE SYSTEM, JUS PRIMAE NOCTIS, POLITICAL SYSTEM.

diviner   A person, also known as a dowser, who employs a device (usually a forked stick) to find phenomena located underground (usually water, but also oil, or precious metals). When the diviner walks holding the stick, its end will allegedly point down (on its own) when the person is over the substance sought. See DIVINING ROD, DOUSING ROD.

divining rod   1. A magic wand, staff, or rod used for divination. 2. A dousing rod, a forked rod used for indicating the location of objects or substances, usually underground.

divisibility   The property of certain magnitudes, bodies, processes, or acts, such that they can be broken up into parts.

divorce counseling   Advice applied to divorced or divorcing spouses, usually on a group basis, to provide group support and to encourage a sense of belonging and identity during the transitional period. Members are encouraged to let go of the past, to learn through the experiences of others what types of behavior contributed to the breakup, and to learn to deal with mood swings and thoughts of vindictiveness.

dizygotic twins   Fraternal twins, produced by two ova conceived about the same time. The children can be from different fathers. Three-fourths of all twins are dizygotic, or fraternal, and they may be of the same or different sexes. Also known as biovular twins, dizygote twins, DZ twins, fraternal twins. See MONOZYGOTIC (MZ) TWINS, TWIN STUDIES.

dizziness   A whirling sensation, often with nausea and a fear of fainting. See VERTIGO.

DL   difference limen

D-love   (A. Maslow) Deficiency love.

DMH   1. Department of Mental Health. 2. Department of Mental Hygiene.

DMT   See DIMETHYLTRYPTAMINE.

DNA   See DEOXYRIBONUCLEIC ACID.

DNA analysis   In forensic psychology, an analysis of the structure and inheritance components of cellular components for individual identification insofar as population genetics allows.

D-needs   (A. Maslow) Deficiency needs.

Do   In Rorschach test scoring, a symbol for oligophrenic (mentally retarded) responses.

do age   Defining the age of older persons in terms of what they can do. Some people at 80 can do more than some people at 60.

docility   1. Characterizing an organism which is easily managed. 2. (E. C. Tolman) The quality of being easily taught. 3. Term adapted by Herbert Simon from earlier usage by E. C. Tolman to mean teachability, especially the tendency to accept instruction and advice from sources regarded as "legitimate" or reliable without complete empirical re-examination of their validity. (For an organism with bounded rationality, docility is an important contributor to evolutionary fitness.) See BOUNDED RATIONALITY.

doctor   1. A physician. 2. A holder of a doctorate degree, usually a Ph.D. 3. A title applied to some professions in some countries; for instance, in some Spanish-speaking jurisdictions, lawyers are addressed as Doctor. 4. To tamper with, alter.

doctor game   Play characterized by touching and examining the genitals, usually of the opposite sex. Generally a child plays "doctor" or "nurse."

doctor of psychology (Psy.D.)   A degree earned by those who wish to become professional clinical psychologists. Their interest lies less in research, per se, than the applied psychology.

doctor-patient relationship   The interpersonal relationship that develops between doctor and patient. A relationship characterized by warmth, cooperation, patience, and mutual esteem can have a positive effect on the outcome of both physical and psychological treatment.

doctrine   1. A theory affirmed dogmatically, that is, without presentation of evidence. 2. A thesis put forward by a person of authority upon a controversial issue.

doctrine of formal discipline   A point of view that mental faculties can be exercised and strengthened, as muscles are, such as the memorization of Latin verbs to strengthen the faculty of memory generally. Also known as formal-discipline theory.

Dodge mirror tachistoscope   (R. Dodge) An early tachistoscope (device for the brief presentation of visual stimuli). Involved positioning a half-silvered mirror at 45° to the line of sight, and the turning on and off of two light bulbs.

Doerfler-Stewart test   (R. Doerfler & J. P. Stewart) An examination originated for screening for functional hearing loss during World War II. Used to examine a person's ability to respond to selected two-syllable words in the presence of a masking noise.

dog fear   See CYNOPHOBIA.

Dogiel corpuscle   (A. S. Dogiel) A transitional type of nerve end-organ located in the mucous membranes of mouth, nose, eyes, and genitals.

dogma   A theory or tenet promulgated or asserted by authority. Often in the absence of conclusive evidence.

dogmatic   The behavior of those who seek to impose their ideas upon others by reason of personal authority and not by evidence.

dogmatism   Strong opinions usually based on unsubstantiated assumptions.

dogmatism scale   (M. Rokeach) A questionnaire, devised to measure inflexibility in thinking.

dol   A subjective unit of pain, from the Latin *dolor* meaning pain.

dolichocephaly   Having a long and narrow skull. A cephalic index below 75 is considered dolichocephalic.

dolichomorphic   Characterizing a tall thin body.

doll fear   See PEDIOPHOBIA.

Dollinger-Bielschowsky syndrome   A form of amaurotic familial idiocy in which the onset of symptoms occurs between the ages of three and four years. Effects include cerebroretinal degeneration with cerebellar ataxia, defective hearing, convulsions, ocular disorders, and mental deterioration. See TAY-SACHS DISEASE.

doll play   In therapy with young children, the use of dolls which represent familiar individuals, for playing out such feelings as anger, rejection, and anxiety. Dolls are used in telling or enacting "stories" to reveal significant family relationship dynamics. See PLAY THERAPY.

Dolophine   Trade name for methadone.

dolorimeter   An apparatus for measuring pain perception. In a heat dolorimeter, a light is shone on a blackened spot on a participant's forehead under standardized conditions. The time for the participant to report a change from heat to pain is taken as the pain threshold; the time at which no further stimulation is voluntarily endured is the pain tolerance.

dolorimetry   The measurement of the intensity of pain.

dolorology   The study of the causes and treatment of pain.

domain   1. A demarcated area. In psychology, various specific areas that can be established such as comparative physiological, social, etc. 2. In a causal relationship, the conditions under which a particular form or strength of the causal relationship is operational. May involve developmental stages, environmental settings and contexts, physiological states, parameter values, time, persons, or the presence or absence of particular variables.

domain-free problem   A problem that does not require any special expertise for its solution.

domain identification   (C. M. Steele) Achievement barriers experienced by people, especially women and African Americans. See PREJUDICE, GLASS CEILING, STEREOTYPE THREAT.

domal sampling   1. A survey in which a specific member of a predetermined household is interviewed, such as divorced or widowed women with children. 2. Probability sampling in which a preselected sample is used, for example, alphabetically listing all members and then selecting every "nth" name. The "nth" depends on the size of the original group. So, if the original group contained 200 then every second name might be selected, if 2000, then every 5th name, and if 20,000, every tenth name. Also known as systematic sampling.

Doman-Delacato patterning therapy   (R. J. Doman & C. H. Delacato) A procedure for dealing with children with central nervous system lesions, conducted by several adults holding a child who is in a prone position; the adults then move the child's head, arms, and legs in the hope of helping to improve body functioning.

domatophobia   1. Morbid fear of being home. 2. Morbid fear of being inside a building. Also known as ecophobia, oik(i)ophobia. See OIKOPHOBIA.

domesticated drug   A psychotropic substance that is socially accepted, such as caffeine.

domesticated pride   (S. Rado) An overvaluation of the self in obsessive people, which Rado interpreted as a reaction to guilt, fear, and repressed feelings of humiliation. This type of pride has been distinguished from real pride or brute pride based on self-assertive rage. See MORAL PRIDE, PENIS PRIDE, PRIDE.

domestic partnership   A relationship between two people, either of the same sex or different sexes, who live together as a couple. See INTENTIONAL FAMILY, FAMILY, SAME-SEX MARRIAGE.

domestic violence   1. Term popularized by the feminist movement in the 1970s to refer to the physical and psychological abuse of women by men. 2. Generally, any violence within the family (usually excepting children, where it's termed child abuse).

domicile   A residential setting in which continued care is given to deinstitutionalized patients according to need. These settings usually include chronic-care hospitals, skilled-nursing facilities, health-related facilities, intermediate-care facilities, halfway houses, residential facilities or homes, social-rehabilitation facilities, and satellite housing. See ADULT FOSTER HOME, HALFWAY HOUSE.

dominance   1. Ascendance, or assertion of control over others. 2. A tendency for one hemisphere of the brain to exert greater influence than the other over certain functions, such as language and handedness. 3. Prepotency of one response over another; for example, flexion is dominant over extension in withdrawing the hand from a hot stove. 4. In genetics, a tendency for one trait to predominate over another, such as a gene for brown eyes over a gene for blue eyes. See HANDEDNESS, LATERAL DOMINANCE.

dominance aggression   A type of aggression among animals used to maintain status or rank. See ALPHA MALE, ANIMAL AGGRESSION.

dominance hierarchy   1. In behavior, the ordering of responses in terms of their priority or importance, for example, a sneeze takes precedence over making the bed. 2. In social psychology, dominance hierarchy denotes the classification of group members as a function of their power or prestige, for example, a captain takes precedence over a corporal, a cardinal over a bishop.

dominance need   (H. A. Murray) The drive to dominate, lead, direct, or otherwise control others.

dominance-submission   ascendance-submission

dominance-subordination relationships   A tendency of many animal and human communities to organize in social patterns with a dominant member who imposes its will on subordinate members; for example, in baboon troops, dominant males and subordinate females and offspring that form affectionate but protective clusters.

dominant character   A character which suppresses or prevents the appearance of the corresponding recessive character, when the factors of the two are associated. The "stronger" of two competing hereditary characteristics to be seen in the phenotype. See DOMINANT GENE.

dominant complex   An associated emotional disturbance that dominates or controls self-conduct.

dominant eye   A tendency for one eye to be dominant for viewing objects in the distance and the other eye for viewing objects that are close, or for one eye to be dominant in all cases.

dominant gene   A gene or hereditary trait that manifests itself in the offspring. A dominant gene will be expressed even when it occurs on only one of the two inherited chromosomes. See DOMINANT CHARACTER, GENE, RECESSIVE GENE.

dominant genotype   See GENOTYPE.

dominant hemisphere   A tendency for one hemisphere of the brain to exert greater influence than the other in certain functions, such as language and handedness as well as controlling generally the opposite side of the body. See DOMINANCE, LATERAL DOMINANCE, LATERALITY, SPLIT BRAIN.

dominant ideology thesis   A theory that in class-stratified societies, the ruling class controls both ideas and goods, thus shaping working-class thought in the interests of the status quo.

dominant inheritance   (G. Mendel) A pattern of inheritance in which only the dominant trait of two competing traits is apparent in an individual. See COMBINATION (IN GENETICS), CROSSOVER (IN GENETICS, DOMINANT CHARACTER, GENETIC CODE, PHYLOGENETIC.

dominant-recessive relationship   An ability of a dominant gene to manifest its characteristics in the body (such as brown eyes) instead of its paired recessive gene (such as blue eyes).

dominant trait   In genetics, the member of a gene (allele) pair that is expressed and produces an observable effect (phenotype) in the organism. See DOMINANT CHARACTER, DOMINANT GENE.

dominant wavelength   A color wavelength which when mixed with white will match a given hue.

domination   The act or state of controlling the lives or behavior of others, especially by an ascendent person.

dominator-modulator theory (of color vision)   (E. Q. Adams, R. Granit) A theory based on electrical stimulation of extremely small areas of the retina, revealing three types of receptors: (a) scotopic dominators, rods that are most sensitive at 500 millimicrons; (b) photopic dominators, cones that are most sensitive at 560 millimicrons; and (c) photopic modulators, other cones sensitive to very narrow frequency ranges. Hue is attributed to the activity of the modulators, brightness to the dominators, and color blindness to a defect in particular modulator cells. The theory was first expressed by E. Q. Adams but the phrase dominator-modulator was later applied by Ragnar Granit. Also known as Granit theory (of color vision). See COLOR VISION, VISION.

dominators   Visual receptors that react to peaks of brightness at certain color frequencies and they also respond to a broad band of the spectrum and produce ganglion-cell responses.

dominatrix   A female who plays the dominating role in sadomasochistic sexual activities sometimes specialized in by prostitutes. See SEXUAL MASOCHISM.

Donald Green syndrome   (F. Dumont) A condition characterized by fantasizing negative possible consequences and living in constant apprehension of events that may never occur.

Donahue's syndrome   leprechaunism

Donatism   1. An early phase of the hypnotic state in which the participant follows the hypnotist's suggestions but is aware of them and is able to remember them later. 2. A form of hypnosis in which imitation plays an important role. Term is derived from Donato, the professional name of Alfred d'Hout who first demonstrated this phenomenon.

Donato   See D'HOUT.

Donders' law   (F. C. Donders) A theory that the position of the eyes in looking at an object is independent of their movement to that position.

Donders' method   (F. C. Donders) A procedure in which discrimination reaction time is subtracted from choice reaction time to measure the time required for a choice decision and simple reaction time is subtracted from discrimination reaction time to measure the time taken to make a discrimination.

donepezil   Generic name for a medicine used to counter mild to moderate symptoms of Alzheimer's disease. Functions as a cholinesterase inhibitor, theoretically allowing more of the neurotransmitter acetylcholine to operate in the brain, retaining memory and alertness. It does not cure, but may delay the progress of the disease. Trade name is Aricept.

Don Juanism   In men, a condition characterized by promiscuity, philandering, ruthless seduction, concern with sexual conquest, and abrupt loss of interest in conquests after the sexual act. A Don Juan thinks of women as prey, is considered to be insecure as a man, and therefore obsessed with the need to prove his masculinity or his desirability to women. Named after a legendary Spanish libertine, Don Juan, whose escapades are themes in literature and Mozart's opera *Don Giovanni*. Also known as Don Juan syndrome. See CASANOVA, EROTOMANIA, SATYRIASIS.

don't hold functions   (D. Wechsler) On the Wechsler Intelligence Scale for Adults (WAIS), those items that show a decline in performance as a result of aging. These are usually items that call for hand manipulation or dexterity. See DETERIORATION INDEX, HOLD FUNCTIONS.

Doolittle method   (M. H. Doolittle) In mathematics, a procedure for locating a number of unknowns simultaneously in a set of equations. Useful in multiple correlational studies and in curve fitting. See BACK SOLUTION, FRONT SOLUTION.

door-in-the-face effect   In social psychology experiments, a tendency for a person who denies a substantial request to be more likely to accede later to a lesser request. See FOOT-IN-THE-DOOR EFFECT.

DOP   dermo-optical perception

dopa   See DIHYDROXYPHENYLALANINE.

dopamine (DA)   An important catecholamine neurotransmitter in the brain, and also the precursor of epinephrine and norepinephrine. It is derived from dopa and is a primary form in which catecholamines are stored in tissues outside the nervous system. See CATECHOLAMINE, NEUROTRANSMITTER.

dopamine hypothesis   A theory that schizophrenia is caused by an excessive activity of the nerve cells in the brain which produce dopamine, one of the neurotransmitters (other brain cells produce other types of neurotransmitters).

dopamine receptor antagonists   A certain type of antipsychotic medicine, referring to its function in the brain. Generally equivalent to the other term, neuroleptic.

dopamine receptors   1. Molecular sites on the membranes of neurons at the synapses which are especially sensitive to dopamine. 2. Receptors sensitive to dopamine and chemically related compounds.

dopaminergic neurons   1. Cells that secrete or are affected by dopamine as the main neurotransmitter. 2. Nerve cells in the central nervous system which have been found to be depleted in Parkinson's disease and which may be involved in the pathological processes of schizophrenia and other mental disorders. 3. Nerve cells in the peripheral, sympathetic system and ganglia influenced by the adrenergic drug dopamine.

dopaminergic pathways   Specific neuroanatomical pathways in the brain that carry the nerves that discharge dopamine at the synapse.

Doppelganger phenomenon   (double—German) 1. The fantasy or delusion that an exact double, twin, or alter ego exists, who looks and acts the same as the patient. See AUTOSCOPIC SYNDROME. 2. Used to indicate a person similar to the self in ideas, values, and goals. See ALTER EGOISM.

Doppler effect/shift   (J. Doppler) The increase or decrease in wavelength when a source of light or sound recedes or approaches the observer, producing a change in hue or pitch. Also known as Doppler phenomenon/principle.

Dora (case)   One of Sigmund Freud's earliest and most celebrated cases, reported in Fragment of an Analysis of a Case of Hysteria (1905). The study of this woman's multiple symptoms (headaches, aphonia, suicidal ideation, amnesic episodes) contributed to Freud's theory of repression and the use of dream interpretation as an analytic tool.

doraphobia   Morbid fear of fur; of touching or seeing the skin of animals.

Dorian love   Obsolete phrase for male homosexuality, particularly pederasty (allegedly practiced by the Dorians, a Greek tribe of the twelfth century B.C.).

Dorpat school   Researchers under K. Girgensohn at Dorpat University in Estonia (and later at Greifswald and Leipzig) who applied the Würzburg method of experimental introspection to religious experience.

dorsal   Pertaining to the posterior (back) side. Compare VENTRAL.

dorsal columns   Tracts of nerve fibers that run through the spinal cord on its dorsal side. See A FIBER, LEMNISCAL SYSTEM.

dorsal column system   Old name for the lemniscal system.

dorsal reflex   See SACROSPINAL REFLEX.

dorsal roots   The bundles of sensory-nerve fibers that enter the spinal cord on the back sides of the spinal cord.

dorsolateral   Pertaining to a straight line running through the back to the sides of the body in humans.

dorsolateral pathway   A neural bundle traveling from the brain stem to the spine that controls the forearm muscles.

dorsomedial nucleus   A cluster of neuronal cell bodies in the thalamus having connections with the frontal lobes.

dorsoventral   Pertaining to a straight line from the back to the stomach in humans; sagittal direction.

dose-response functions   The concept that the amount of a drug will affect the reaction to the drug. Physicians typically suggest doses appropriate to each patient, but empirical verification may mean that the dose should be reduced, increased or abandoned. See DRUG ABUSE.

dose-response relationship   A principle that the pharmacological effect of a drug is generally dependent upon the size of the dose. It is modified in practice to accommodate a number of variables, for example, the body weight, skin surface area, and rate of metabolic activity, of individual organisms. With variables adjusted, the dose-response relationship of a drug usually plots as a straight-line curve.

DOT   See DICTIONARY OF OCCUPATIONAL TITLES.

dotage   Senility or second childhood.

dot figure   A figure consisting of a number of dots, arranged either regularly or irregularly, used to illustrate visual geometrical illusions.

dotting test   A paper-and-pencil motor task in which the participant makes as many dots as possible in a given time period, either randomly (tapping test) or in small circles (aiming test). Measures speed and accuracy of small movements of the hand.

double   A psychodrama procedure of acting out another person's private thoughts, such as expressing to a group what a person imagines that another person is thinking and feeling. See DOUBLES, DOPPELGANGER.

double-agentry   A conflict of interest that may exist when a therapist deals with a patient while employed or paid by a third party.

double alternation   In a temporal maze, an animal may learn to make two responses to the left and two responses to the right (LLRR) or the opposite pattern (RRLL) at the same choice point. In the early stages the animal is prevented from making errors and reinforced for partial responses. Mammals like the raccoon and cat can learn only one double alternation.

double-alternation method/task   A required response of the character AABB, for example, an animal entering a maze must turn right twice (RR) and then left twice (LL) to be rewarded. Also known as Double Alternation Test. See DELAYED REACTION METHOD, DOUBLE ALTERNATION.

double approach-avoidance conflict   A situation that requires an individual to choose between alternatives when each choice contains positive and negative consequences. See APPROACH-AVOIDANCE CONFLICT.

double-aspect theory/view   1. A view that two incompatible assumptions about a topic are actually both accurate, for example in physics, the view that light is at the same time based on waves and on particles. See JANUSIAN THINKING. 2. In psychology, a view that the mind is matter (the brain) or operations (functions). 3. (B. Spinoza) A philosophical doctrine of the reality of both the mind and the body. Conscious experiences and brain processes are considered to be fundamentally identical, the two groups of phenomena being two manifestations or aspects of a single set of events. See BODY-MIND DICHOTOMY, MIND-BODY PROBLEM.

double bind 1. A situational trap in which individuals are "damned if they do and damned if they don't"; receiving equal disapproval for doing something or not doing it. 2. (G. Bateson) A situation in which a child receives simultaneous contradictory messages usually from parents, and is therefore torn between conflicting feelings and demands. The parent may complain that the child is not affectionate, yet turn a cold shoulder when the child seeks a hug. Anthropologist Gregory Bateson claimed this type of situation is a major cause of schizophrenia. See CONGRUENT COMMUNICATION, DILEMMA.

double-bind communication (G. Bateson) A message with at least two elements in contradiction with each other, putting the recipient of the message in an untenable position, as in saying "I love you" but using body language to say "Keep away from me." See DOUBLE BIND.

double-blind control **double-blind procedure/test**

double-blind crossover A double-blind procedure, usually used in drug research. During the trial, the placebo and the experimental drug are switched, and only the principal investigator or a third party knows when the switching occurs. See BLIND EXPERIMENT, DOUBLE-BLIND, DOUBLE-BLIND PROCEDURE/TEST.

double-blind procedure/test In a research design, a standardized method of concealing some treatment information both from a participant and the person administering the treatment. Example: Pills identical in appearance and taste are given to participants by an assistant. Half the pills are placebos, half are active. Only the experimenter (who has no contact with either the participants or the assistants) knows who received which pill. Also known as double-blind control. See BLIND EXPERIMENT, SINGLE-BLIND PROCEDURE, TRIPLE-BLIND PROCEDURE.

double consciousness Describing the state of mind of a dual or alternating personality. Also known as dual consciousness. See BOREDOM, MULTIPLE PERSONALITY.

double dissociation (of function) (H. Teuber) The association between anatomical lesions and behavioral disturbances. Involves processes for demonstrating that possible multiple sites of brain lesions account for multiple symptoms in syndromes of neurologic defects. For instance, one lesion impairs behavior A more than B, while a second lesion impairs B more than A.

double entendre A statement that has a double meaning. Usually an evident meaning (for example, what would be understood by a person newly learning the language) and a hidden meaning (for example, what is understood by a person who knows the language well). The hidden meaning is often of a sexually suggestive or threatening nature, for example, "I'll take care of you" may mean that the speaker will not let harm come to the person spoken to, or it may mean that the speaker is threatening the person. Also known as double meaning. Compare PUN.

double helix The formal arrangements of deoxyribonucleic acid (DNA) chemical components. See ADENINE, CYTOSINE, GUANINE, THYMINE.

double heterozygousness A situation in which an individual has both dominant and recessive alleles for two linked genes.

double images 1. Duplicate retinal images that occur as a result of eye defects. 2. Doubling of images in the distance when fixating on near objects, and of near images when fixating on far objects.

double insanity Phrase similar to *folie à deux*.

double-interpretation illusion A false visual perception in which one and the same figure may appear successively as two quite different patterns or objects. See NECKER CUBE, SCHROEDER STAIRCASE ILLUSION.

double jeopardy A theory that some people, such as older African Americans, suffer a dual cultural disadvantage because they are both old and African American.

double meaning See DOUBLE ENTENDRE, PUN.

double orientation (E. Bleuler) An ability of some patients with schizophrenia to function normally in the real world while maintaining a fantastic delusion, such as a satisfactory restaurant worker falsely believing herself to be Joan of Arc. Also known as delusion of orientation.

double personality See DISSOCIATIVE IDENTITY DISORDER, MULTIPLE PERSONALITY.

double representation The perception of two hues or brightnesses when an object is illuminated by light of a different color.

doubles In psychodrama, those who attempt to speak out the presumed thoughts of others.

double sampling The use of two or more methods of selecting samples for surveys or studies of a population.

double-simultaneous stimulation (DSS) A test used in studies of parietal-lobe lesions by presenting two stimuli simultaneously. Various types of inattention are seen visually and tactually. See DOUBLE-SIMULTANEOUS TACTILE SENSATION.

double-simultaneous tactile sensation An ability to perceive two tactile sensations in different areas at the same time. In one test of the ability, the Fink-Green-Bender Test, the person is touched on the face and hand at the same time. See ARISTOTLE'S ILLUSION, FACE-HAND TEST.

double standard 1. The general concept that a code of behavior is permissible for one group or one individual but not for another; in particular, the concept that free sexual expression is acceptable for males but not for females. 2. A sexual norm in which behavior is socially sanctioned for one sex and not for the other, for example, a parent condones a son's sexual escapades, but wants a daughter to keep her virginity. See MASCULINE PROTEST.

double superego A concept of the existence of two consciences in cases of psychic dualism. One conscience is masculine and the other feminine, and each is antagonistic toward the other.

double-take effect The experience of not understanding something that is said, but upon "replaying" what the person was told, the person can understand it.

double technique A procedure used mostly in psychodrama in which a person, such as the therapist or another member of a therapy group sits next to the client, or behind the client, and speaks for the client, saying what the person believes the client is thinking but not saying. Also known as priming the pump technique.

double vision   Perception of a single object as a separate image by each eye. May be caused by strabismus in which the image perceived by the right eye may appear to the left of the image perceived by the left eye, as a binocular effect of two separate parallel images, or in vertical displacement in which one image appears above the other. Double vision may occur only in certain visual fields, for example, when looking to the left rather than straight ahead. Similar to diplopia.

double-Y condition   A genetic disorder involving an abnormality of the male sex chromosome. Individuals born with this condition have an XYY complement of sex chromosomes rather than the normal male set of XY. XYY chromosomes were once considered incorrectly to be related to tendencies toward violence. See CHROMO-SOMAL ABERRATION.

doubling   A procedure in psychodrama by means of which a member of the viewing group reenacts a demonstrated role behavior of another member, so that the latter (as well as others) may understand, and thereby correct the error of his or her behavior.

doubling time   The time required for a population to double in numbers.

doubt   Alternation of belief with disbelief, or the experience of both at once with absence of complete conviction. See AUTONOMY VS DOUBT.

doubtful judgments   Answers given by the observer or participants during an experiment, of the correctness of which judgments they are not fully convinced, such as "I think the color is purple, but I am not sure."

doubting madness/mania   Extreme and obsessive doubting; a feeling of uncertainty about even the most obvious matters, such as the name of a spouse. The patient may feel compelled to check and double-check to see whether the gas has been turned off, the door has been locked, or a column of figures has been added up correctly. See ABULIA, OBSESSIVE-COMPULSIVE DISORDER.

doula   From the Greek, a woman who helps other women. Usually doulas assist women giving birth, providing advice and encouragement. During the birthing process, a doctor or midwife takes care of the forthcoming child, while the partner and the doula are on either side of the mother-to-be.

downers   Slang for drugs, usually of the sedative-hypnotic class, which are sometimes used recreationally like alcohol, to get a kind of drunk "high." Compare UPPERS.

Downey's Will-Temperament Tests   See WILL-TEM-PERAMENT TESTS.

Down's syndrome   Disorder characterized by moderate to severe retardation; docile, agreeable disposition; "mongoloid" appearance (round flat face, eyes that seem to slant); and other physical signs; usually recognizable at birth. Chromosome abnormality is three instead of two copies of chromosome 21. Such persons can live outside institutions, hold jobs, and maintain social relationships. Named after English physician John Langdon Down (1828–1896), who first described the "Mongolian Idiot." From the early 1960s the condition was renamed Down's syndrome (or, especially in North America, Down syndrome). Also known as autosomal trisomy of Group G, congenital acromicria, mongolism, trisomy 21. Has been called Down's anomaly, Langdon-Down anomaly, Langdon Down's disease. See TRISOMY, TRISOMY 21.

down through   In parapsychology, the clairvoyance technique in which the cards are called down through the pack before any of them are removed or checked. See ZENER CARDS.

downward communication   Information or commands from higher-status persons to inferiors or subordinates.

downward drift hypothesis   A postulate that disturbed individuals are mobile downward and drift eventually to lower standards of socialization, ending up in pitiful circumstances. See DRIFT HYPOTHESIS.

downward mobility   The movement of a person or group from one social class or level to a lower social class or level. See SOCIAL MOBILITY, UPWARD MOBILITY.

dowry   1. Money or property payment, usually by the bride's family to the groom or his family, at the time of betrothal or marriage. May be based on the concept that the groom's family will take care of the bride for her lifetime. Still practiced in some societies. In societies that have shed this practice, it continues in a modified way, that is, the parents of the bride traditionally pay for the wedding costs. See BRIDE-PRICE. 2. Informally, the collected household goods and financial savings accumulated by a woman to contribute to the marriage.

dowsing   A practice to attempt to locate water, minerals, oil or any hidden things by using a device such as a divining rod. See DIVINING, DOWSING ROD.

dowsing rod   A divining rod or forked stick used to allegedly locate underground water or minerals. See DIVINING ROD, RHABDOMANCY.

d prime (d′)   In a signal detection experiment, the difference between the signal and noise.

DPT   Slang for analog of dimethyltryptamine.

DQ   developmental quotient

dr   In Rorschach test scoring, a symbol for rare detail.

Dr   1. Deviation from the mean. 2. Rank difference between two sets of values. 3. Statistic for group differences assessed by Student's t test. 4. In Rorschach test scoring, a symbol for small detail. 5. See DRIVE.

DR   1. An increment of response. 2. Reaction of degeneration. 3. A change in response (also symbolized ΔR).

drainage   The drawing off of nerve impulses or nerve energy from a neural arc by some external agency, such as an adjacent activated arc.

drainage hypothesis   (W. McDougall) A postulate that facilitation of neural conduction over certain neurons and its inhibition over others is due to a drainage of energy (on analogy with principles of hydraulics) from paths of higher resistance into those of lower.

drama therapy   The use of theater techniques to gain self-awareness or increase self-expression in groups. See PSYCHODRAMA.

dramatic personality   See HISTRIONIC PERSONALITY DISORDER.

dramatics   The use of drama as a rehabilitation technique, using published or original scripts with patients as performers. Therapists may use special puppet-show scripts in the rehabilitation of children with disabilities. See PSYCHODRAMA.

dramatization 1. The use of attention-getting behavior as a defense against anxiety, for example, the exaggeration of the symptoms of an illness to make it appear more important than it actually is. 2. In psychoanalytic theory, dramatization is the expression (as in dreams) of repressed wishes or impulses.

dramaturgical perspective (E. Goffman) A theoretical perspective that uses the theater as its organizing metaphor. It was expressed by Goffman as a study of the micro order of interaction highlighting the ways people engage in "impression management." Related to symbolic interactionism and role theory. See ROLEPLAYING.

dramaturgy (E. Goffman) A tendency when directly interacting with others to behave in such manner as to favorably influence the impression given. In a sense, being "on stage" when in the presence of others. See IMPRESSION MANAGEMENT, MASK.

DRAS descending reticular activating system

Draw-a-Man Test (F. Goodenough) A task of intelligence for children that asks the child to "Please draw a picture of a man. Draw the very best man that you can." This examination is considered relatively culture-free. It is scored for various elements, such as fingers, eyes, ears, hair. The test was renamed the Goodenough-Harris Drawing Test, and also revised by Karen Machover as Machover's Draw-A-Person Test.

Draw-a-Man Test An example of a response to the Goodenough Draw-a-Man Test.

draw-a-person test Refers to several tests requiring the drawing of a person such as Florence Goodenough's original Draw-a-Man Test (1926), revised by D. B. Harris in 1963, and Karen Machover's Machover Draw-a-Person Test (1946). Goodenough's original test was considered to measure a child's intelligence based not on artistic ability but on details portrayed by children. Machover's test, and other versions, extended the value of the test to elements of personality such as self-concept.

drawing disability See DYSGRAPHIA (meaning 1).

drawing test A task in which the participant is asked to draw certain familiar objects such as people, trees, and houses. Attitudes and feelings are often revealed in the way that the participant depicts these objects. See DRAW-A-MAN TEST, DRAW-A-PERSON TEST.

dread Anxiety elicited by a specific threat, such as going out on a dark night in a strange neighborhood, as contrasted to anxiety that does not have a specific object. See FREE-FLOATING ANXIETY.

dream See DREAMS.

dream analysis (S. Freud, C. G. Jung) The attempt to explain the meaning of a dream by a therapist. Some therapists specialize in dream analysis, some rarely or never perform it (dream analysis).

dream anxiety attacks See NIGHTMARE.

dream censorship The disguise of unconscious impulses in dreams. According to Sigmund Freud, the thoroughness of dream disguise varies directly with the strictness of the censorship.

dream content In psychoanalytic theory, the images, ideas, and impulses expressed in dreams. See LATENT CONTENT, MANIFEST CONTENT.

dream deprivation research (W. Dement) Studies made of reactions of animals and humans deprived of rapid-eye-movement (REM) sleep; the sleepers are awakened as soon as they show REM (start to dream). Research attributed various pathological disturbances to the deprivation of the normal amount of dreaming.

dream ego (C. G. Jung) Identifying a fragment of the conscious ego active during the dream state. See LUCID DREAM.

dream function The purpose of dreaming is not known. Theories about what dreams do, include:
(a) Early cultures: foretell the future if properly interpreted.
(b) Sigmund Freud: preserve sanity by allowing people to gratify forbidden or unrealistic wishes; the latent content is a wish that is fulfilled in hallucinatory form in the dream. See FREUD'S DREAM THEORY.
(c) Carl Jung: reflect fundamental personality tendencies with either a transient or continuous importance. See JUNG'S DREAM THEORY.
(d) Alfred Adler: rehearse expected future behavior. See ADLER'S DREAM THEORY.
(e) Information-processing: assimilate new data into memory and jettison irrelevant material.
(f) Activation-synthesis: result from the brain trying to make sense of random neural activity that occurs during sleep.
(g) Hans Berger: exercise the eyes by periodically exercising the complex neuromusculature of vision, allowing a suddenly-woken primate to see.
(h) Wilson: allow the reprocessing or remembering of information important for survival.
(i) R. Cartright: allow the exploration of the emotional components of a tension area.
(j) F. Crick & G. Murchison: clear the mind of the useless, bizarre, redundant.

dream imagery The sequence of presentations, usually visual, which make up a dream story.

dream induction The production of a dream through hypnosis, either by command or as a posthypnotic suggestion. Dream induction is a technique used in hypnoanalysis.

dream instigator See DAY RESIDUES.

dream interpretation In psychotherapy, the deciphering and understanding of the unconscious meanings of dreams and dream symbols, primarily through free association. Sigmund Freud thought dreams indicated desires, Alfred Adler thought they indicated intentions, Carl Jung saw dreams as having compensatory functions or regulating purposes. See DREAM FUNCTION, PRODROMAL.

dream material   The succession of experiences which occur during a single dream, together with the underlying meaning or significance of the dream.

dream pain   See HYPNALGIA.

dreams   1. Coherent imagery sequences, which (ordinarily) occur during sleep. 2. A fleeting sequence of images, often structured, occurring spontaneously and with a sense of reality during sleep. Dreams appear to serve many functions, such as being outlets for tension, guardians of sleep, or safety valves in preventing emotional disorder. Types of dreams include: ARTIFICIAL, COLOR, CONSOLATION, CONVENIENCE, COUNTERWISH, EMBARRASSMENT, EXAMINATION, INSOMNIUM, PARALLEL, PERENNIAL, PRODROMIC, PROPHETIC, RECURRENT, TELEPATHIC, WET. See MASOCHISTIC WISH-DREAM.

dream screen   (K. Lewin) A surface, or screen, on which dreams sometimes seem to be projected. A patient is quoted as saying, "While lying here looking at my dream, it turned over and away from me, rolled up and away from me, over and over like two tumblers." See ISAKOWER PHENOMENON.

dream series method   A procedure for studying dreams. The participant is asked to write any dreams recalled immediately upon waking and after a considerable number have been accumulated, they are read by the analyst, who will then come to a conclusion, such as, "X reports 20 dreams and in most of them there is frustration." See DREAM CONTENT ANALYSIS.

dream state   The state in sleeping during which dreaming takes place. Dreaming usually occurs four or five times during the night. The dream state is physiologically different from ordinary sleep and waking. During dreaming, rapid eye movements (REM) can be detected and electroencephalographic (EEG) patterns resemble those of wakefulness. About 20% of sleeping time is spent in the dream state and there is probably a basic need for dreaming. The pons appears to be the area most involved in the dream state. Also known as D-state. See TWILIGHT STATE.

dream stimulus   Any stimulus that may initiate a dream, such as external events, internal sensations, or psychological elements, such as worry, memory, and stress.

dream suggestion   A hypnotic technique in which the participant is instructed to dream about personal problems or the source of the problems either during the hypnotic state or posthypnotically, during natural sleep. See DREAM INDUCTION.

dream wish   Representation of the fulfillment of an egocentric and ungratified wish in a dream.

dream within a dream   See LUCID DREAMING.

dream work   In some forms of psychotherapy, the interpretation of dreams. Different theoretical systems advocate different ideas about how to interpret dreams. Freudians tend to see dreams as wishes; Adlerians see them as rehearsals. See CONDENSATION, DISPLACEMENT, DRAMATIZATION, DREAM FUNCTION, DREAM STATE, SECONDARY ELABORATION, SYMBOLIZATION.

dreamy state   A brief altered state of consciousness similar to a dream, during which the patient experiences visual, olfactory, or auditory hallucinations. Marijuana and other drugs can produce such a state in some people.

Dreikurs theory   The following are important in understanding Rudolf Dreikurs' theory: ATTENTION, BETTING TECHNIQUE, DEMOCRATIC PARENTING, FAMILY COUNCIL, FOUR GOALS OF CHILDREN, LIFESTYLE ANALYSIS, LOGICAL CONSEQUENCES, MIDDLE-CHILD SYNDROME, MULTIPLE THERAPY, NATURAL CONSEQUENCES, PARENTING TRAINING, THE QUESTION.

dressing aid   Help in the form of training and special design of equipment to minimize daily-living problems experienced by some persons with physical disabilities. Example: Training in the use of special clothing fasteners, such as Velcro shoe closures, zippers that close or open by pulling on a ring, or devices to aid in pulling up stockings or pants.

dressing apraxia   A brain-damage disorder manifested by an inability to clothe the self properly (for example, a patient may put clothes on in a manner so that only the right side of the body is covered, neglecting the left side). Possibly caused by a parietal lesion of the nondominant hemisphere.

dressing behavior   Wearing clothes in accordance with social expectation for the person's sex as an important factor in gender identity. Studies of transvestites and transsexuals indicate they usually cross-dressed (or were cross-dressed) in childhood. See CROSS-DRESSING.

dressing ring   Mainly in Victorian England, a metal ring that was inserted through the glans of the penis to increase sexual stimulation, also to secure the penis so as to prevent it showing through the pants, hence also known as Prince Albert.

DRH   See DIFFERENTIAL REINFORCEMENT OF HIGH RATE.

Dr. Habil.   A second doctorate degree in Germany, roughly equivalent to the French *Docteur d'état* and the Russian *Federal Doctorate*.

drift hypothesis   A sociological concept attempting to explain the higher incidence of schizophrenia in the center of an urban area than in the outskirts, suggesting that during the preclinical phase, people tend to drift into the anonymous environment of the central city. See DOWNWARD DRIFT HYPOTHESIS.

drifting attention   A tendency to maintain focused attention for a few moments, when alerted, but to drift back to a somnolent state. It is a disorder of the subcortical alerting system which usually indicates pathological involvement of the midbrain or thalamic portion of the reticular activating system. See WANDERING ATTENTION.

drill   The methodical repetition or systematic practice of a physical or mental response or response sequence for the purpose of learning.

drinking aids   Daily-living aids that permit a person with a disability to ingest liquids without the aid of another person. May include terry-cloth tumbler jackets, wooden or metal glass holders, various built-in and flexible sipping straws, coasters with suction cup attachments, and cups designed for drinking when the patient is in a supine position.

drinking behavior   (E. M. Jellinek's categories) See ALPHA ALCOHOLISM, BETA ALCOHOLISM, DELTA ALCOHOLISM, EPSILON ALCOHOLISM, GAMMA ALCOHOLISM.

drinking bouts   See BINGE DRINKING, DIPSOMANIA.

drinkometer   A laboratory device that provides a signal for recording an animal's physical contact with various aspects of the experimental environment that involves ingestion of liquids (such as its rate of ingestion of food, or the occurrence of licking the fluid in a liquid dispenser).

drive (d, D or Dr)   A state of organic tension, as in hunger, sex, or pain, that motivates organisms to perform actions assumed to alleviate the tension. The distinction is sometimes made between primary drives, which are directly based on physiological needs, and secondary or acquired drives, such as competition, which are indirectly based on these needs. See INSTINCT, MOTIVATION.

drive arousal   The activation of a drive by any stimulus, internal or external, or a combination of both.

drive attributes   (S. Freud) A psychoanalytic theory that contains three aspects: (a) source, what originated the drive; (b) aim, goals such as pleasure seeking; (c) object, a result or consequence that leads to the goal.

drive discrimination   The capacity of organisms to react differently in similar situations depending on their particular physiological needs. Thus, an animal will drink when thirsty, eat when hungry.

drive displacement   The replacement of a frustrated drive by one more easily gratified, such as "raiding the refrigerator" when disappointed or smoking a cigarette when tense.

drive gate filter system   See RESPONSE-HOLD MECHANISM.

drive reduction   A fundamental concept about behavior of organisms that the primary motive of organisms is to reduce drives. Apparent in basic physiological drives such as hunger and thirst, but may be more difficult to understand when the drives are of a social nature, such as the drive to be important, to be admired, to be successful.

drive-reduction theory   (E. L. Thorndike, C. L. Hull) A point of view that life consists of a series of drives that motivate animals and people to activity. Were there to be no drives, all sentient organisms would die since they would have no feelings of hunger, no sense of importance, no desire for sex. Drives are of various types: physiological, social, psychological. See DRIVE, HULL'S THEORY and these sample drives: ACHIEVEMENT, BIOLOGICAL, ESTEEM, MATERNAL, SLEEP.

drive satisfying behavior   A fundamental concept in psychology to explain animal behavior. Animals tend to sleep or rest when in a state of equilibrium, but behave in specific ways when they become aware of needs that then become drives that require appropriate action. See DRIVE-REDUCTION THEORY, DYNAMIC APPROACH.

drive state (P)   (P. Teitelbaum) An internal condition of disequilibrium or perceived need, such as hunger pangs, that activates drive behavior.

drive stimuli (d or S$_D$)   (C. L. Hull) Stimuli considered to regulate reinforcement.

drive strength (*D*)   (C. L. Hull) The intensity of any drive. See HULL'S THEORY.

driver education   1. In schools, training of youths in safe operations of motor vehicles. 2. In rehabilitation, training of a person with a physical disability previously capable of operating an automobile to learn to operate a vehicle with hand-operated accelerator and brakes, or a gearshift extension for left-hand rather than right-hand use. See CAR CONTROLS.

Dr. Jekyll–Mr. Hyde personality   Rare name for alternating (cyclothymic) personality, based on Robert Louis Stevenson's short story.

DRL   See DIFFERENTIAL REINFORCEMENT OF LOW RATE.

Dr. Mises   The pseudonym of Gustav Fechner when he wrote articles relating to philosophy or the occult.

droit du seigneur   *Jus primae noctis*

dromolepsy   A short spurt of running that may precede an epileptic seizure and usually ends in the seizure. Also known as procursive epilepsy.

dromomania   An abnormal drive or desire to travel. Also known as vagabond neurosis.

dromophobia   A morbid fear of crossing a street or road; also, a morbid fear of traveling. See AGYROPHOBIA, HODOPHOBIA.

drop-in center   A mental health facility, such as a methadone clinic, in which treatment can be obtained without an advance appointment.

dropout   1. In education, a student who leaves school before graduating. 2. In psychotherapy, a patient who terminates treatment before completion.

dropping out of movements   An aspect of the learning process, in which certain elements included at the start in a complex act are gradually eliminated with successive repetitions, the elements so eliminated being those which are irrelevant.

Drosophila   Fruit flies, often used for research in genetics.

drowsiness   Sleepiness. See SOMNOLENCE, TWILIGHT SLEEP.

dr. phil.   Abbreviation of *doctor philosophiae* (Ph.D.)

drq   distress-relief quotient

DRQ   discomfort-relief quotient (also abbreviated **drq**)

dr. rer. nat.   Abbreviation of *doctor rerum naturalium* (Dr.Sc. or Sc.D.)

drug   1. A substance introduced into the body for the purpose of counteracting the effect of disease, of restoring normal function to tissues which have been pathologically altered. Narcotic drugs, by reason of their depressant action on the nervous system, diminish or abolish nervous and mental activity. 2. Another name for a medicine or a chemical (rarely now, though hundred years ago more commonly), a compound of plants, other substances, or both. However, the "war against drugs" has contaminated the term, so that all medicines which are called "drugs" become suspect as being addicting or in other ways toxic to the nervous system. Thus, as the meanings of words and language in general continues to evolve, great care must be taken in how the term, "drug" is used. Explicit differentiation between drugs of abuse and medicines must be made.

drug abuse   See SUBSTANCE ABUSE, SUBSTANCE-USE DISORDER.

drug addiction   The pathological use of drugs.

drug culture   Former phrase for a social subgroup whose members used illicit drugs such as marijuana, hashish, cocaine, heroin, LSD, or other agents known to produce altered states of consciousness or states of exaltation (highs). Phrase usually was not applied to cultural or religious groups, such as members of the Native American Church, who use mind-altering drugs in their ceremonies and rituals. (Those who use drugs no longer constitute so identifiable a subculture. Marijuana use is widespread, as are other drugs, and used in so many different ways that the phrase is misleading in suggesting a specific countercultural trend.)

drug defaulter   patient in noncompliance

drug dependence   A continuation of substance use despite significant substance-related problems. It is not the intensity of the needs, which cannot be objectively noted, but rather the degree to which there are problems related to the use. Also known as substance dependence.

drug-drug interactions   How more than one drug modifies the effects of another drug. See DRUG INTER-ACTIONS.

drug education   Formal information offered to individuals or groups about the effects of various chemical agents on the human body, usually with special emphasis on effects of mind-altering substances.

drug holiday   Discontinuance of a psychoactive drug for a limited period to control dosage and side effects, and to evaluate the patient's behavior with and without it.

drug-induced Parkinsonism   A side effect of neuroleptic medicines. See EXTRAPYRAMIDAL SYMPTOMS, PARKINSONISM.

drug-induced psychosis   1. A psychotic state resulting from heavy doses of therapeutic drugs (for example, corticosteroids). 2. A psychotic state resulting from substance abuse or substance use (for example, amphetamines, PCP, cocaine, LSD). See ALCOHOL ABUSE, AMPHETAMINE-INDUCED PSYCHOSIS, BARBITURATE DEPENDENCE, COCAINE ABUSE, HALLUCINOGEN ABUSE, OPIOID ABUSE, PHENCYCLIDINE, SEDATIVE-HYPNOTIC DEPENDENCE, COCAINE ABUSE, HALLU-CINOGEN ABUSE, OPIOID ABUSE.

drug interactions   The effect of a drug combination that differs from the components' additive effect. A significant percentage of the thousands of medicines used interact with certain others in different ways: Two medicines may have similar actions so the effect may be increased, doubled, or more than doubled. Or they may counter each other's effects. Some compete for the action of the enzymes that neutralize the medicines, so that if two drugs are used, one or both may be raised to excessively high levels and effects. On the other hand, the enzymes that neutralize the medicines may be activated so that they work more efficiently, so that one medicine given along with another tends to have different levels than might be ordinarily expected. Certain blood-serum proteins tend to bind various medicines, and when two of a kind are being given, one might be displaced from off its binding site and act as if the dose were much higher than what its effects would be if given alone. All these and many more reactions can occur also in the use of psychotropic medicines.

drug of choice   The most appropriate drug for a given situation. See FIRST LINE MEDICINES.

drug synergism   See DRUG INTERACTIONS.

drug therapy   Not a preferred term, see BIOLOGICAL PSYCHIATRY, CHEMOTHERAPY, PHARMACOTHERAPY, PSYCHOPHARMACOTHERAPY.

drug tolerance   See TOLERANCE.

drunken sailor's walk   Statistical ant. See STATRAT.

dry humping   Colloquial phrase for simulated coitus. See INTRAFEMORAL SEX, INTRACRURAL SEX, VESTURED GENITAL APPOSITION.

dry mouth   1. An autonomic system effect associated with intense emotions such as fear. Caused by sympathetic system changes that restrict or inhibit salivation. 2. Inadequate saliva secretion as a symptom of thirst, the result of the effects of cholinergic drugs, or environmental effects such as heat and dry air.

dry orgasm   Male orgasm without emission of semen. Inevitable prior to adolescence, common as a result of sexual fatigue, may be experienced by older men.

DS   1. desynchronized sleep (also abbreviated **Ds**) 2. difference sensation.

D sleep   See RAPID-EYE-MOVEMENT (REM) SLEEP.

DSM   Diagnostic and Statistical Manual of Mental Disorders. Editions: I (1952), II (1968), III (1980), IV (1994).

DSM III-IV changes   In DSM-III and in DSM-IV 17 major categories of disorders were listed. However, the following six categories in DSM III were not in DSM IV: (1) Organic mental disorders, (2) Paranoid disorders, (3) Psychotic disorders not otherwise classified, (4) Affective disorders, (5) Psychosexual disorders, (6) Psychological Factors affecting Physical Conditions and Conditions not Attributable to a Mental disorder that are a focus of Attention or Treatment. In DSM IV six new categories were added: (1) Delirium, Dementia and Amnestic and other Cognitive disorders, (2) Mental Disorders Due to a General Medical Condition, (3) Mood Disorders (4) Sexual and Gender Identify Disorders, (5) Eating Disorders, (6) Sleep Disorders.

DSS   double-simultaneous stimulation

DST   dexamethasone suppression test

D-state   A sleep period when the individual appears to be dreaming. The dream state, as contrasted with the S-state (sleep state) and W-state (waking state). See CONSCIOUSNESS, SLEEP, WAKEFULNESS.

D system   A serotonergic system of neurons originating in the dorsal raphe nucleus, with thin axons that do not form synapses.

DT ⟶ PI model   (J. C. Stanley) Diagnostic testing of students' knowledge of a specific subject (topic) such as the first year of high school algebra followed by prescribed instruction to help them master the points, concepts, or facts not yet known.

DTPS   diffuse thalamic projection system

D trisomy   See CHROMOSOME-13 TRISOMY.

DT's   See DELIRIUM TREMENS.

dual   In linguistics, a special form of a word to show that two persons or items are referred to, as opposed to singular and plural.

dual ambivalence   The conflicting emotions of adolescents and parents that characterize their changing relationship as the adolescent strives for independence while still wanting and needing guidance and support, and the parents also wanting the adolescent to become more self-sufficient and still wanting to protect the adolescent from making mistakes.

dual-arousal model   An explanation of the physiological relationships between sleep and wakefulness based on evidence that the arousal function involves two nerve pathways, the diffuse thalamic system and the reticular activating system. Holds that the two systems allow the brain to operate in two modes, one a stimulus-processing and the other a response-executing function.

dual-career family   A type of family characterized by both parents holding jobs outside the home. Some people conclude that children are thereby deprived of a "normal" life.

dual-coding theory   1. A point of view that thinking is a result of two interacting systems of information processing, one perceptual (primarily visual) the other verbal. 2. (A. Pavio) A point of view that concrete words can be encoded in two ways, abstract words in only one. For instance, "tooth" can be encoded as a word and as a visual image, whereas "truth" can be encoded only as a word.

dual diagnosis   The combination of serious emotional problems and mental retardation.

dual division   In anthropology, one of two approximately equal divisions of a tribe.

dual impression   Two experiences from a single stimulus.

dual-instinct theory   (S. Freud) A point of view that humans operate primarily in terms of pervasive instinctive drives toward both love (eros) and aggression (thanatos). Sigmund Freud held "The interaction of the two basic instincts with or against each other gives rise to the whole variegation of the phenomena of life."

dual-intelligence theory   (R. B. Cattell) The opinion that there are two kinds of intelligence, fluid and crystallized.

dualism   1. A doctrine positing that there is a real difference between physical and mental states and between ideas and the results of ideas. 2. A theory or point of view common to many sciences of the dual nature of reality. In psychology, the concept of the mind and the body as independent realities. 3. René Descartes' assumption that humans were comprised of two independent elements: the mechanistic body and brain, and the spiritualistic soul and ephemeral mind. See CARTESIAN DUALISM, DOUBLE CONSCIOUSNESS, MONISM, BODY-MIND DICHOTOMY, MIND-BODY PROBLEM.

dualistic view of genders   Masculinity and femininity seen as two separate clusters of traits, whether based on genetic or social factors or the combination. See ASSIGNED GENDER, CORE GENDER IDENTITY, CROSS OVER GENDER BEHAVIOR, TRANSGENDERISM.

duality of consciousness   A concept that the two hemispheres of the brain are really two brains, each having separate functions related to consciousness.

dual labor market   The division of employment that reflects relative advantages/disadvantages, particularly along racial lines in urban settings.

dual-leadership therapy   See MULTIPLE THERAPY.

dual masturbation   1. Tactile stimulation of each partner's genitals by the other. 2. Self-masturbation in which each partner observes the other(s). See MUTUAL MASTURBATION (meaning 2).

dual-memory theory   (W. James) A point of view that memory is a two stage process; short-term memory, which allows retention of certain information for a few seconds to a few hours, and long-term memory, which permits the retention of information for hours to many years. See MEMORY.

dual orgasm   In psychoanalytic theory, now discredited, the labeling of a clitoris-based orgasm in mature women as an arrested form of psychosexual development. Compare to VAGINAL ORGASM.

dual personality   A dissociative disorder in which the personality is divided into two relatively independent and generally contrasting systems. The primary personality is usually unaware of the existence of the secondary, or "coconscious," personality. Also known as double personality. See MULTIPLE PERSONALITY.

dual-process theory   A point of view that a response by an individual to a stimulus that permits behavioral control has two stages: A decision as to whether or not to respond and a decision as to the choice of alternative methods of response.

dual relationships   A situation that exists when people have two different relationships with each other. In psychology, it is considered unwise for a researcher to have a dual relationship with participants; and unethical for psychotherapists to have certain relationships with clients, especially financial and sexual. Some psychologists have lost their licenses to practice and have been expelled from psychological organizations for such violations.

dual-sex therapy   (W. Masters & V. Johnson) Behavioral therapy for sexual disorders developed by William Masters and Virginia Johnson. Treatment is focused on a specific sexual problem, and consists largely of a round-table session with a couple in which the male and female therapy team suggest special exercises that will improve sexual performance, alleviate inhibitions and anxieties, and facilitate communication both in sexual and nonsexual areas.

dual thresholds   The apparent ability to sense stimuli, such as a dim light in the distance, but to be unsure of its existence until by moving toward the light being certain that it indeed exists.

dual-transference therapy   Treatment of the same patient by two therapists, used primarily when the patient needs both support and confrontation with reality and cannot accept both from the same therapist. See MULTIPLE THERAPY.

duct   A tube that provides means for the flow of some specialized secretion or liquid (for example tears or saliva), or for the restricted circulation of lymph in the body.

duct gland   See EXOCRINE GLAND.

ductless gland   See ENDOCRINE GLAND.

DUI   An American abbreviation for driving under the influence (of alcohol, etc.), synonymous with DWI (driving while intoxicated).

dull normal   Pertaining to a person whose intelligence is just below normal, roughly between 80 and 90 on the intelligence quotient (IQ) scale. See MILD MENTAL RETARDATION.

dumbness   Mutism.

dummy   Placebo.

dummy variables   Variables that are limited to 0 and 1, often used in simulation modeling procedures.

Duncan new multiple-range test   (D. B. Duncan) A sequential procedure for testing a series of pairwise posteriori comparisons that attempts to control for Type 1 error. Also known as Duncan test.

Duncker candle problem   (K. Duncker) A task to be solved using creativity, for example, participants receive a cardboard box, a number of pins, matches, and candles, and must use these materials to construct a lamp to light up a room.

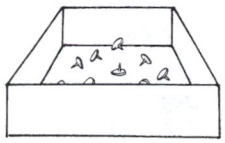
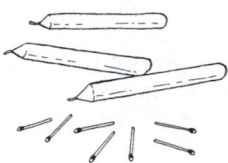

Duncker candle problem
How could a candle be mounted on a wooden wall using only these components?

Dunlap chronoscope   A time measuring instrument using a clockwork system to stop when each time interval has been measured. Named after Knight Dunlap. Also known as Johns Hopkins chronoscope.

Dunn's multiple comparison test   (O. J. Dunn) A procedure for holding the probability of Type 1 error for a set of k statistical tests to a value no larger than α by using an error rate of α/k for each test. Also known as the Bonferroni test since it is based on the Bonferroni inequality.

Dunnett's multiple comparison test   (C. W. Dunnett) A procedure which controls the probability of Type 1 error for a set of comparisons between k treatment groups and a single control group. Also known as Dunnett's t statistic.

duos   Word pairs uttered by children, usually by 24 months or earlier. Duos express children's ideas of cause and action as well as their understanding of relationships between people and objects; for example, recurrence may be verbalized as "more milk," possession as "my milk," and quantity as "little milk." See ACTION-INSTRUMENT, ACTION-LOCATION, ACTION-RECIPIENT; AGENT, ACTION AND OBJECT; ATTRIBUTION, HOLOPHRASES, IDENTIFICATION, NEGATION, POSSESSION, QUESTION STAGE, RECURRENCE, TELEGRAPHIC SPEECH.

duo-stage   (R. W. Brown) Children's verbal developmental achievement between 18 to 30 months when they tend to use two-word expressions.

duplex inheritance   The inheritance by an organism of characters from its two parents.

duplex theory (of color vision)   (J. von Kries) A point of view that color vision is duplex in that the cones mediate color and daylight vision, the rods achromatic and twilight vision. Rods are sensitive primarily to intensity of light waves and cones to differences in wave length. Also known as duplicity theory (of color vision), duplicity theory of vision, von Kries theory of vision. See COLOR BLINDNESS, COLOR CELLS, VISION.

duplicative reaction   A perceptual manifestation observed in some children with schizophrenia who encounter the same person at different times or places and believe they are seeing different persons.

duplicity theory (of color vision)   duplex theory (of color vision)

dura (mater)   The outermost of the three layers of membranes covering the brain and spinal cord, extending as far down the body as the second sacral vertebra. It is the thickest and strongest of the three membranes. Also known as pachymeninx. See MENINGES.

durance   (H. A. Murray) A unit of time within which a life activity occurs.

duration estimates   Subjective judgments of the length of time taken for some phenomenon to occur. Such time-judgments can be prospective (judging how much time will elapse before some coming event) or retrospective (judging how much time elapsed during a past event).

Durham decision   A 1954 United States Court of Appeals ruling that states a person should not be held criminally responsible if an unlawful act was the product of a mental disease or mental defect. This rule has since been modified by the American Law Institute formulation of insanity. Also known as Durham rule/test. See AMERICAN LAW INSTITUTE GUIDELINES, McNAUGHTEN RULE.

DUSO program   (D. Dinkmeyer) An educational program developed by the American Guidance Services to provide therapy for emotionally disturbed children. The program is one of several similar methods of providing a curriculum milieu in which children can explore and understand their own feelings, and how they affect friends and family.

dustbowl empiricism   The opportunistic collecting and analyzing of data without a theoretical framework.

dust figure   See KUNDT TUBE.

duty fear   See HYPENGYOPHOBIA, PARALIPOPHOBIA.

duty to protect   A concept that mental health professionals are legally obligated to protect the public from actions of their clients/patients. An early precedent was 1943's Jones vs State of New York, which established that a mental hospital is responsible for injuries caused by escaped patients; a 1977 decision of the Supreme Court of Canada found a Toronto hospital similarly liable. See TARASOFF DECISION.

DV   dependent variable

D value   A discrimination value of test results displayed in a statistical index that shows the relationship of individual items to the total scores.

Dvorak keyboard   (A. Dvorak) A typewriter keyboard designed to conform to ergonomic principles, giving the most commonly used keys to the strongest fingers.

dwarfism   A condition of underdeveloped body structure due to a development defect, a hereditary trait, hormonal or nutritional deficiencies, or diseases. The proportions of the body to the head and limbs may be normal or abnormal. See ACHONDROPLASIA, BONE DISEASE, MIDGET, NANISM, PSEUDOACHONDROPLASTIC SPONDYLOEPIPHYSIAL DYSPLASIA, PYGMYISM, PSYCHOSOCIAL DWARFISM.

DWI   Driving while intoxicated, synonomous with **DUI**.

Dx   See DIAGNOSIS.

dyacusia   A distressing sensation of tones or noises of peripheral origin, for example, tinnitus. Also known as dysacousia, dysacusis.

dyad   1. A pair of any kind, be it two dice, or a horse and buggy. 2. In psychology it refers to two interacting people such as spouses, twins, two friends, coworkers, and most often, a therapist and a patient. Also spelled diad. See SOCIAL DYAD.

dyadic   Pertaining to a relationship between two persons.

dyadic effect   A tendency if two people are interacting, that the more one person self-discloses, the more the other will do the same.

dyadic psychotherapy   A form of psychotherapy conducted on a one-to-one basis, as contrasted with group therapies, in which there is more than one patient and in some instances more than one therapist. Also known as dyadic therapy, individual (psycho)therapy.

dyadic relationship   In psychotherapy or counseling, the working relationship between therapist and patient, or counselor and client.

dyadic session   A psychotherapeutic meeting of only the therapist and patient.

dyadic therapy   See DYADIC PSYCHOTHERAPY.

dying fear   See THANATOPHOBIA.

dying process   Psychological processes occurring in a dying patient, usually feelings of fear, anger, shame, and sadness. Psychotherapy includes an opportunity to ventilate these feelings, to grieve for lost functions, and if possible to plan or delegate responsibility for the care of others left behind, and to regress to a more dependent state without feeling guilty. See DEATH EXPECTATION, STAGES OF DYING.

dynaception   The combined awareness and movement of an organism in terms of satisfaction of its needs.

dynamic   Pertaining to the causes and effects of behavior and mental activities, often with special emphasis on motivation.

dynamical-system theory   The interpretation of events and relationships including homeostasis, personality, and psychopathology in terms of mutual interactions and feedback mechanisms.

dynamic anthropometry   In ergonomics, the measurement of the body in motion in the context of operating equipment, usually focusing on reach. See ANTHROPOMETRY.

dynamic approach   In relation to personality theories of psychotherapy, human behavior considered from the standpoint of underlying and often unconscious forces that mold the personality, influence attitudes, and produce emotional disorder. See DYNAMIC PSYCHOLOGY, NOSOLOGICAL APPROACH, SYSTEMATIC APPROACH.

dynamic apraxia   Impairment of the ability to perform purposeful, continuous movements due to lesions in the premotor cortex.

dynamic calculus   (R. B. Cattell) Growth of dynamic prediction (conflict, choice, etc.) through use of objectively measured ergs and sems.

dynamic data   See DYNAMIC ANTHROPOMETRY.

dynamic-effect law   (R. B. Cattell) The theory that goal-directed behaviors become habitualized as they effectively attain the goal desired.

dynamic equilibrium   A concept of energy stabilization in which an energy-level change at one point results in redistribution of total energy.

dynamic formulation   The integration of diverse and seemingly conflicting pieces of information about a person's behavior, traits, attitudes, and symptoms into a consistent and meaningful picture.

dynamic interactionism   (N. S. Endler & D. Magnusson) A model which focuses on the reciprocal interaction between situational (or stimulus or environmental) events and behaviors.

dynamic psychiatry   A system of psychiatry that deals with internal, unconscious drives associated with behavior patterns, as opposed to the observable, objective factors of descriptive psychiatry.

dynamic psychology   (J. Dewey, W. James, R. S. Woodworth) A psychological approach based on the study of motivation and causation; in particular, an approach that focuses on inner forces (drives, needs, purposes, emotions, wishes) that motivate behavior. Woodworth changed the then traditional SR (stimulus-response) formula to SOR (stimulus-organism-response). See ABC THEORY, DRIVE REDUCTION, DRIVE-SATISFYING BEHAVIOR.

dynamic psychotherapy   Any form or technique of psychotherapy that focuses on the underlying, often unconscious, factors (drives, experiences) that determine human behavior and adjustment. See DEPTH THERAPY, DYNAMIC APPROACH, DYNAMIC PSYCHIATRY, PSYCHOTHERAPY.

dynamic reasoning   (F. Alexander) The process of reconstructing a patient's developmental history based on clinical evidence gathered from the patient's own account (anamnesis).

dynamic resignation   See RESIGNATION.

dynamics   (Heraclitus) The concept of forces acting on an individual, for example, environmental (the wind blowing against a person), physiological (needing to urinate), psychological (wanting to be the best at something). See PSYCHODYNAMICS.

dynamic self-distribution (W. Köhler) In Gestalt psychology, the idea that the dynamics of the whole determine where and with what function each part of the whole must occur (for example, the parts of the film of a soap bubble distribute themselves so as to produce relative uniformity in the thickness of the film throughout the entire bubble). Gestalten tend toward optimal forms because of forces inherent in the gestalten themselves, not because of arbitrary forces imposed from without. See GESTALT.

dynamic-situations principle (V. W. Voecks) A point of view that any stimulus pattern undergoes continuous changes due to such factors as uncontrolled variables, visceral changes, and varied responses. Therefore, a person may react differently to a certain stimulus (such as the smell of food) when hungry and when not hungry; a dog that has been recently abused by a small boy might avoid a different small boy.

dynamic subsidization See SUBSIDIZATION.

dynamic system A system in which a change in one part influences all interrelated parts.

dynamic theory (W. Köhler) A point of view that brain activity is determined by constant energy changes which do not correspond point-for-point with environmental stimuli. Also known as psychic dynamism.

dynamic visual display Machine displays such as dials and scales through which changing information is shown.

dynamism (H. S. Sullivan) A psychological device employed to protect the ego. Term was preferred by Harry Sullivan to defense mechanism, since it implies an active, adaptive process rather than an automatic reaction. The specific dynamisms are, however, basically the same as defense mechanisms. See SAFEGUARDING TENDENCIES.

dynamogenesis A principle that initiation or increase of muscular activity or tension is due to sensory activity. Also known as dynamogen, dynamogeny.

dynamograph A recording dynamometer; commonly a dynamometer equipped either with a direct mechanical marker or with an air piston connected with a tambour marker, which makes a continuous record on a kymographic drum or other moving surface.

dynamometer An instrument used to register the strength of muscular exertion.

dynamometric test A measure of physical strength or endurance in which the participant is required to exert a maximal muscular effort against a stiff coiled spring, commonly of a hand dynamometer (strength of grip test) or of a back-and-leg dynamometer.

dyne The unit of force in the centimeter-gram-second system equal to the force that would give a free mass of one gram an acceleration of one centimeter per second per second. See ERG, JOULE.

dynorphin A potent opioid peptide.

dysarthria Inability to use the voice effectively in speaking because of an emotional or organic disorder affecting the muscles used for speech. See APRAXIC DYSARTHRIA, ATAXIC DYSARTHRIA, ATHETOID DYSARTHRIA, ATHETOTIC-DYSARTHRIA.

dysautonomia Malfunctioning of the autonomic nervous system. See FAMILIAL DYSAUTONOMIA.

dysbasia Difficulty in walking normally.

dysbulia A difficulty in thinking or maintaining attention or a train of thought, a disturbance of will. See ABULIA.

dyscalculia Difficulty in performing simple mathematical functions or problems such as $2 + 2 = 4$. Seen in parietal lobe lesions. See ACALCULIA, ANARITHMIA.

dyscontrol The state of being out of control in any of many ways, in a rage, in fear, in sorrow.

dyscousia Discomfort due to hearing sounds.

dysdiadochokinesia(s) An impairment in the ability to perform rapid alternating movements, as in fanning the self, due to cerebellar disorder. See ADIADOCHOKINESIS.

dyseidetic dyslexia (E. Boder) Dyslexia with primarily visual or phonological deficits, respectively. Also known as dysphonetic dyslexia.

dyseneia A deafness-caused articulation difficulty.

dysergasia (A. Meyer) Psychiatric syndromes caused by toxic psychoses or similar brain dysfunctions. Delirium is a common symptom.

dysesthesia Diminished sensitivity to pain.

dysexecutive syndrome (A. Baddeley) A group of disorders typically seen in patients with bilateral frontal-lobe damage, manifesting attention and control problems, and ability to recall the past in detail but unreliably.

dysfluency Any of a variety of difficulties in speaking. See PRIMARY STUTTERING, SECONDARY STUTTERING, STUTTERING.

dysfunction Describing any impairment, disturbance, or deficiency in the functioning of an organ or body system.

dysfunctional Abnormal; impaired in the ability to cope with stress.

dysgenic Describing influences that may be detrimental to heredity. The opposite of eugenic.

dysgenics (W. Shockley) The argument that people considered genetically disadvantaged should not be permitted to reproduce, a concept based on fundamentally flawed reasoning that usually does not take into consideration the effects of social factors on specific ethnic and racial groups. See EUGENICS, EUTHENICS.

dysgenic trends in intelligence The claim that the general level of intelligence is falling.

dysgeusia An impairment or perversion of the sense of taste. Occasionally, hysterical patients eat such substances as ashes, salt, or vinegar; schizophrenia patients sometimes complain of peculiar tastes in their mouths; and strange tastes may be experienced as an aura, or warning signal, before an epileptic episode. See CISSA, PICA.

dysgrammatism A persistent use of incorrect grammar not due to educational impoverishment; a symptom of aphasia. See AGRAMMATISM.

dysgraphia 1. Inability to perform certain motor movements from oral instructions or directions. The affected person is able to copy a drawing of an object but is unable to draw the same object, such as a clock. The auditory input fails to evoke the visual image needed to carry out the task. 2. Difficulty in writing. 3. See WRITER'S CRAMP (meaning 1).

dysidentity A characteristic of childhood schizophrenia in which the patient is unable to perceive boundaries or limits.

dyskinesia (G. Huntington) 1. Dysfunctional movement. 2. A distortion of voluntary movement, as in cerebral palsy; also, involuntary muscular activities such as tics, spasms, or sudden "myoclonic" contractions of the limbs, body, or face that frequently occur in petit mal or grand mal. Dyskinesia is a undesired side effect of some psychoactive drugs. Also known as dyskinesis. See EXTRAPYRAMIDAL DYSKINESIA, OROFACIAL DYSKINESIA, TARDIVE DYSKINESIA.

dyslalia Errors of articulation due to functional causes, especially errors of omission, distortion, and substitution that often accompany delayed speech in children. See DYSFLUENCIES.

dyslexia (R. Berlin) Impaired ability to understand written or printed words due to brain dysfunctions or brain damage, usually unrelated to disorders of speech and vision. In some cases, there is an inversion of letters or numbers (reads GOD as DOG or dials 727 rather than 272 on a telephone). Term was introduced to replace word-blindness. Types include: ACQUIRED, DEEP, DEVELOPMENTAL, DIRECT, DYSEIDETIC, NEGLECT. See ALEXIA, CONGENITAL ALEXIA, PARALEXIA, READING DISABILITY, STREPHOSYMBOLIA.

Dyslexia Screening Instrument (K. B. Coon, M. J. Polk & M. McCoy Waguespack) A tool used by classroom teachers for measuring a cluster of characteristics associated with dyslexia. Developed to aid in the identification of Individuals with Disabilities Education Act (IDEA).

dyslogia A speech defect associated with mental retardation, manifested as inability to express the self clearly. See DYSFLUENCY.

dysmenorrhea Difficult or painful menstruation.

dysmentia 1. A temporary disturbance of mind. 2. Pseudoretardation in which the patient shows impaired performance due to psychological factors rather than true mental retardation. See IDIOT SAVANT.

dysmetria An impaired ability to gauge distance of body movements.

dysmnesia Impairment of memory. See MEMORY LOSS.

dysmnesic syndrome A disorder that frequently develops after an acute delirious episode. Characterized by amnesia for the episode, with faulty orientation and difficulty in retaining recent events. The condition usually clears up within a few days.

dysmorphophobia Morbid fear of being or appearing physically deformed; also, the illusion of being thus deformed.

dysnisophrenia General term for psychopathic disorders including antisocial personality. See SOCIOPATHY.

dysnomia A deficiency of ability to recall names of objects. See MEMORY DEFECT, MEMORY DISORDERS.

dysorexia An impaired or perverted appetite. See PICA.

dysostosis The defective development of the skeleton of an individual.

dyspareunia Painful or difficult sexual intercourse, especially for women, due to physical factors. Can be due to aversion to having sexual relations or fear of pregnancy or disease. Term is sometimes used for an inability to enjoy intercourse, by people who are otherwise normal. See FUNCTIONAL DYSPAREUNIA.

dysperception Any impairment or abnormality in perceptual functions.

dyspermia Old term for difficult or painful orgasm in a man.

dysphagia 1. Difficulty in swallowing. Also known as aphagia. 2. Impaired ability to swallow, usually due to a physical condition. But also as a hysterical symptom involving spasms of the throat muscles. See DYSPHAGIA SPASTICA.

dysphagia spastica A somatic or functional symptom in which the act of swallowing is painful or difficult because of throat muscle spasms. In functional cases, it is classified as a hysterical symptom.

dysphasia Impairment of the power of language in any of its forms, usually because of cortical damage. The dysphasic (person with dysphasia) has difficulty in arranging a series of spoken words in a meaningful or understandable pattern. The disorder is not as severe as aphasia. See DYSARTHRIA.

dysphemia A disorder of speech associated with psychological disturbance and, frequently, a neurological predisposition. Includes such disorders as stuttering and tachyphemia. See DYSFLUENCIES.

dysphemic speech Poor speech quality due to imperfections of the voice apparatus. See DYSPHEMIA, STUTTERING, TACHYPHEMIA.

dysphemism 1. Communications, verbal or expressive by gestures or facial expressions, that hurt another person's self-esteem. 2. An unpleasant replacement term such as "scab" for replacement worker; the opposite of euphemism.

dysphonetic dyslexia **dyseidetic dyslexia**

dysphonia A defect in phonation or vocalization. See FUNCTIONAL VOICE DISORDER, SPASTIC DYSPHONIA.

dysphoria A feeling of unpleasure, often an inarticulate mixture of anxiety, doubt, bewilderment, and irritability. Compare EUPHORIA.

dysphoria nervosa Fidgets; mild convulsive or spasmodic muscle contractions. Also known as crispation. See TIC.

dysphoric mood An unpleasant feeling state characterized by discontent, depression, anxiety, and restlessness. See DYSPHORIA, EUPHORIA.

dysphrasia Difficulty in speaking or writing due to a central nervous system or intellectual defect.

dysplastic (body) type (E. Kretschmer) A disproportioned body type, an impaired form or shape. One of Ernst Kretschmer's body types, representing incompatible mixtures of his other three types: pyknic, athletic, leptosome. Also known as dysplastic type (of body build). See CONSTITUTIONAL TYPE.

dyspn(o)ea Shortness of breath or difficult breathing that often has subjective overtones. The patient has an awareness of increased breathing efforts or a feeling of inadequate breathing. Dyspnea may be a hysterical symptom, or associated with heart or lung disease.

dysponesis 1. A faulty or misdirected effort. 2. In biofeedback, describes a state of unconscious and habitual tension that generates hypertension, migraine headaches, bruxism, or related disorders.

dyspraxia An impaired ability to perform skilled, coordinated movements. Usually due to cerebral lesions and not to muscular defect. See SYMPATHETIC DYSPRAXIA.

dysprosody An altered melodic speech pattern often associated with brain injury.

dysraphic Pertaining to a developmental disorder, particularly one involving the central nervous system. Also known as dysontogenetic. See BOREDOM.

dysrhythmia 1. An abnormality in speech rhythm due to defects in breathing, inflection, and placement of stress. 2. Irregular or chaotic brain-wave sequences.

dyssocial behavior Delinquent or criminal activities such as gangsterism, racketeering, prostitution, or illegal gambling. Usually attributed to distorted moral and social influences, frequently aggravated by a broken home or a deprived environment. Formerly termed sociopathic behavior. See ANTISOCIAL-PERSONALITY DISORDER.

dyssocial drinking Phrase similar to Elvin M. Jellinek's alpha alcoholism.

dyssocial personality Describing a criminal with a good self-concept.

dyssocial reactions Disorders of behavior characterized by strong loyalties to subgroup values that conflict with the larger societal values, such as observed in gang loyalties and in hippie revolts against the "establishment." See ADAPTIVE DELINQUENCY.

dyssomnia A form of insomnia characterized by wide fluctuations in depth of sleep, and such disturbances as nightmares, teeth-grinding, and sleepwalking.

dysstasia Difficulty in standing upright.

dyssymbiosis A pathological mutually dependent relationship between mother and child. See CODEPENDENCY.

dyssymbolia Inability to discriminate among gradations of personal emotions in language that can be comprehended by others. Also known as dyssymboly.

dystaxia A mild degree of ataxia; difficulty in performing coordinated muscular movements.

dysteleology The lack of purposiveness sometimes exhibited in the structure of organisms, especially the possession of useless rudimentary organs.

dysthymia 1. Any mood disorder. 2. Morbid depression with obsessions. 3. A depressive mood less severe than observed in cases of manic-depressive (bipolar) psychosis or major depression. The depression may be accompanied by neurasthenic-hypochondriacal symptoms. 4. (H. J. Eysenck) A personality description combining neuroticism and introversion. 5. Persistent sadness.

dysthymic disorder A chronic mood disturbance characterized by persistent, recurrent, depressed mood. Mild, chronic depression. Also known as depressive neurosis.

dystocia Difficult labor.

dystonia An abnormal tension of muscles resulting in spasmodic body movements such as twisting of the neck. See EXTRAPYRAMIDAL SYMPTOMS, TARDIVE DYSKINESIA, TORTICOLLIS.

dystrophy Changes in a tissue or organ resulting from defective or faulty nutrition. Also known as dystrophia.

dystropy Eccentric behavior.

dystychia See ANHEDONIA.

dysuria Painful or difficult urination.

DZ dizygotic twins

DZa dizygotic twins raised apart (also abbreviated DZA)

DZt dizygotic twins raised together (also abbreviated DZT)

DZw In Rorschach test scoring, a symbol for a large white space.

e   1. error. 2. The base of Napierian logarithms.

E   1. Energy. 2. Environment. 3. Excitatory tendency. 4. See EXPERIMENTAL GROUP. 5. Experimenter. 6. See ILLUMINANCE. 7. See ECSTASY.

E.A.   educational age (also abbreviated **EA**)

eager beaver   Slang for an excessively ambitious and active person.

EAHCA   See EDUCATION FOR ALL HANDICAPPED CHILDREN ACT.

EAP   employee assistance program

ear   The receptor for sound-wave stimuli; that is, the organ of hearing. The human ear has three main divisions: external, middle, and inner ear.

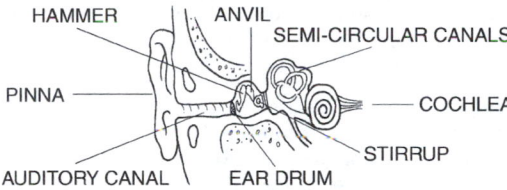

ear   A cross-sectional diagram of the human ear.

ear bones   See AUDITORY OSSICLES.

eardrum   A membrane at the end of the auditory canal that conveys vibrations of sound to the bones of the inner ear. Also known as tympanic membrane.

early and periodic screening—diagnosis and treatment (EPSDT)   A general recommendation for managing physical and mental conditions.

early infantile autism   (A. Kanner) Original name for what was later called infantile autism, and regarded as the earliest appearing form of childhood schizophrenia. See AUTISM.

early intervention   Actions taken for infants and young children who appear to be at risk for developing some aversive condition. Action is aimed at minimizing or modifying the effects, preventing the condition from developing, or both.

early recollections   (A. Adler) Salient memories of single incidents from childhood; used as a projective technique by Adlerian therapists. Clients are asked to report in chronological sequence their earliest memories and these are written down. The therapist goes over each memory trying to discover the element or aspect most clearly remembered, and the feelings that were involved with each. The group of memories are then examined, looking for common elements. The theory is that these early memories tell a great deal about the recaller's self- and other's concepts. See PROJECTIVE TECHNIQUES.

ear-mindedness   A tendency for some people to depend more on learning by using their hearing than by using their vision (eye-mindedness).

earphone   See HEARING AID.

ear pulling   A habit of tugging at the ear. In psychoanalytic theory, it has been interpreted variously as a substitute for thumb-sucking or masturbation.

ear reflex   See PINNA REFLEX.

Easterbrook hypothesis   A postulate that emotional arousal narrows the focus of attention.

easy child   A child considered by adults such as nurses, teachers, and parents to be agreeable and easy to live with. See DIFFICULT CHILD, SLOW-TO-WARM-UP CHILD.

eating aids   Daily-living aids used by persons with disabilities who might not otherwise be able to feed themselves, including devices for holding food, nonslip place mats, dishes with suction cups attached to the bottom, handles designed at angles or with extensions, and combination eating devices such as knife-fork.

eating behaviors   Normal social eating behaviors vary within any culture in terms of a variety of situations. Usually, one will eat in one manner at home, but differently at a picnic, or a banquet. See EATING DISORDERS, FEEDING BEHAVIOR, KLÜVER-BUCY SYNDROME.

eating compulsion   See BULIMIA.

eating disorders   Pathological behavior patterns in relation to the consumption of nutritive, or in some cases, nonnutritive substances. Kinds of eating disorders include: ANOREXIA NERVOSA, ATYPICAL EATING DISORDER, BULIMIA, HYPERPHAGIA, PICA, RUMINATION DISORDER OF INFANCY, VOMITING.

eating-fear   See CIBOPHOBIA, PHAGOPHOBIA.

Ebbinghaus test   (H. Ebbinghaus) An evaluation procedure in which the participant is to complete sentences from which several words have been omitted.

Ebbinghaus' curve of retention   (H. Ebbinghaus) A graphic representation of a curve that represents the rate of loss of memorized material (such as nonsense material) after learning. The curve of forgetting shows a sudden drop followed by a gradual decline and is in a sense similar to the process of extinction, recalling increasingly less of what has been learned over time. See AUFDRINGLICHKEIT, IMPLICIT MEMORY, NONSENSE SYLLABLES, SAVINGS (METHOD), SERIAL-LEARNING TASK, SERIAL MEMORY.

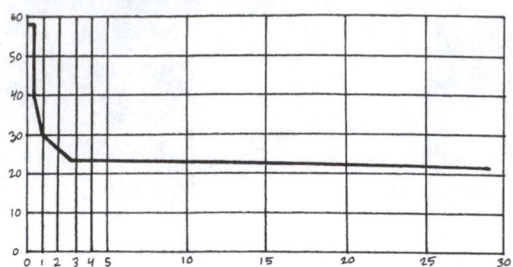

Ebbinghaus' curve of retention   A well-known curve in psychology. Imagine that a long poem has been memorized and is represented by the number 60 at the upper left of the chart. The following day, according to the curve, half of the poem is forgotten (represented by the 30); the loss continues slowly until the end of the month when the person remembers about as much of the poem as was remembered at the end of the fifth day.

Ebbinghaus' savings method   See SAVINGS METHOD.

Ebonics   Described as the language content, structure, and process associated with African American inner city culture. It reflects and perpetuates the cultural context of its speakers. Its promotion in schools has been based on the need to educate African American inner-city youth within a sociolinguistic framework that is culturally familiar and supportive rather than alienating. Incorrectly spelled Ibonics. See CREOLE, PIDGIN ENGLISH.

EBS   electrical brain stimulation

E/C intervening variable   (M. H. Marx) Difference between E (experimental) and C (control) conditions.

eccentric   General behavior considered unusual but not necessarily abnormal, as in eating ice cream with ketchup.

eccentricity   Notable oddness in an individual's habitual behavior.

eccentric projection   The location of a sensation as an object in space rather than in the sense organ at the point of stimulation.

Eccles-Jordan circuit   A monostable or bistable electronic circuit and trigger that maintains one of two stable states enabling the storage of one bit of information. Also known as bistable multivibrator, flip-flop.

ecclesiophobia   Fear of church(es). Also known as euclosephobia.

ecdemo(no)mania   Morbid desire to wander or travel.

ecdysiasm   (H. L. Mencken) Morbid impulse to disrobe to arouse sexual excitement in a member of the opposite sex. Term coined by Mencken from a zoological term for molting. A person with this impulse is called an ecdysiast.

ecdysiast   (H. L Mencken) A "strip-teaser" or "exotic dancer."

ECG   See ELECTROCARDIOGRAM.

echatic   Pertaining to random behavior without any goal. See TELIC.

echo   A sound that after reflection is received by the ear at an appreciably later time than the unreflected sound.

echo des pensées   (an echo of thoughts—French) An auditory hallucination characterized by hearing one's own thoughts repeated in spoken form. Also known as thought-echoing.

echoencephalogram   See ECHOENCEPHALOGRAPH.

echoencephalograph   A method of mapping the inside of the head for diagnostic purposes by using ultrasonic waves. Waves are beamed through the head from both sides, and echoes of the waves from midline structures are recorded as visual images. Any variation in reflections from the midline may indicate an abnormality in the brain structure. The recording is called an echoencephalogram.

echoic memory   A momentary sensory memory of sound. Music and words can still be "heard" for several seconds after the sound has ceased.

echoic store   A concept that sounds are held in an unprocessed state for a short time before entering cognition. Compare ICONIC STORE.

echolalia   (Gilles de la Tourette) 1. Mechanical repetition of the words and phrases uttered by another person; a symptom of a number of personality disorders such as catatonic schizophrenia and Alzheimer's disease. 2. One of Jean Piaget's three types of egocentric speech in which words and syllables are repeated for the pleasure of reciting them. Also known as echophrasia, echo-speech.

echolocation   (M. H. Romberg) An ability to judge the direction and distance of large objects or obstacles from reflected echoes such as those made by footsteps, the tapping of a cane, or traffic noises. The phenomenon, often highly developed in blind people, is similar to a dolphin or bat's ability to locate objects by emitting high-pitched sounds that bounce back to them. Echolocation was once described as FACIAL VISION.

echopathy   A pathological, automatic copying and repetition of another's speech, gestures, or actions. A common symptom of catatonic schizophrenia. See ECHOPRAXIA, ECHO PHENOMENON.

echo phenomenon   (E. Kraepelin) Phrase suggested for both echolalia and echopraxia. See ECHOPATHY.

echophrasia   echolalia

echopraxia   A pathological, automatic copying and repetition of another's movements, a common symptom of catatonic schizophrenia. Also known as echokinesis, echomatism, echomimia. See AUTOMATIC OBEDIENCE, ECHOPATHY.

echo principle   1. An observation that one animal will imitate the behavior of another if it has been involved in the same act. 2. A tendency of children to imitate the behavior or linguistic patterns of their parents.

echo sign   A speech disorder in which single words are repeated.

echo-speech   See ECHOLALIA.

echul   A culture-specific syndrome observed among the native American Indians of southern California, characterized by sexual anxiety and convulsions that reach a peak during severe crises such as divorce or death of a spouse or child.

eclamptic amentia   Old phrase for cases of mental retardation associated with a brief period of epilepsy-like seizures during infancy.

eclectic behaviorism   A behavior-therapy approach that does not adhere to one theoretical model, but applies, as needed, any of several techniques, including classical conditioning, modeling, operant conditioning, self-control mechanisms, cognitive restructuring, and psychodynamic concepts of personality. See ABC METHOD, MULTIMODAL THERAPY, PERSON-CENTERED THERAPY.

eclectic counseling   Any counseling theory or practice that incorporates and combines doctrines, findings, and techniques selected from diverse theoretical systems. See ECLECTIC THERAPY.

eclecticism   1. The blending of diverse conceptual formulations or techniques into an integrated approach. 2. In psychotherapy, the practice of drawing from diverse sources in formulating client problems and devising treatment plans.

eclectic parenting   A common parenting style based on the parent's own concepts of correct child-raising.

eclectic therapy   Any therapy based on either a combination of theories or formats, such as the combination of transactional analysis and Gestalt therapy, or using procedures and concepts from a number of different sources, including dependence on some unique personal views.

eclima   1. A large increase in appetite and eating due to insatiable hunger. 2. Insatiable hunger. See BULIMIA.

ecmnesia   1. Loss of memory for recent events. 2. Rare term for anterograde amnesia.

ecnoia   A fear reaction in children provoked as a normal fright event but continuing for days or weeks with adverse effects on sleep and appetite.

eco-feminism   1. The argument that women generally take a conciliatory, nonaggressive attitude toward the environment rather than the hostile, dominating attitude representative of men. 2. A spiritual, anti-patriarchal movement opposed to male values that foster the destruction of the planet.

ecofeminist   Within a lesbian relationship, the domestic partner who stays home to do the domestic chores.

ecological assessment   An evaluation method that relates to how an individual interacts in a natural environmental setting.

ecological fallacy   The incorrect inference of an individual's characteristics from group ones of the category or group that the individual in question belongs or seems to belong.

ecological perception   (J. J. Gibson) The individual's view of the environment in terms of reciprocal adjustments between physical, social, and individual influences. It is holistic in that environmental properties are perceived as meaningful entities, and that perceptual patterns may be direct rather than concepts that require interpretation by higher brain centers from visual or other cues. Ecological perception is a reaction of any organism that may interpret environmental features in terms of affordances. See AFFORDANCE.

ecological perspective   In community psychology, the viewing of any social entity in terms of the interrelations among persons, roles, organizations, local events, resources, and problems to be handled.

ecological psychology   A branch of psychology concerned with the study of its relationships to the environment. Ecological psychology embraces the molar behavior of humans in relation to all possible factors that might affect them. See ECOLOGICAL-SYSTEMS MODEL, ENVIRONMENTAL PSYCHOLOGY.

ecological studies   Research on the mutual relations between organisms and their environment. In animal behavior, studies of eating habits, formation of groups, and building of shelters. In human behavior, studies of occupants of trailer camps, geographical and social class distribution of mental disorders, voting patterns in different areas or among different social groups, and the comparative incidence of criminal behavior in urban versus rural areas. See ECOLOGICAL-SYSTEMS MODEL.

ecological-systems model   A point of view that mental disorders are reflections not merely of personal imbalance but of environmental disequilibrium, and can be effectively prevented and treated only by studying and modifying the environmental forces that impinge on the individual. See ECOLOGICAL STUDIES, RADICAL PSYCHOTHERAPY.

ecological validity   1. Representativeness in research. 2. (E. Brunswik) Sampling of the typical environment in consideration of the degree of exactness of the conditions of a research to real life conditions. 3. The reflection in a person's daily cognitive, behavioral, and emotional functioning of deficits found in tests, particularly neuropsychological ones.

ecology   The science of interactions (especially regarding population and distribution) between organisms and their physical environments. First used scientifically by German biologist E. H. Haeckel regarding plants, later included the social environment. See BIONOMICS.

ecomania   Irritable, domineering behavior directed toward members of one's own family. Also known as oikomania.

econetics   (R. B. Cattell) The study of cultural patterns and their effects on individual satisfactions.

economic   1. Pertaining to the production, distribution, and consumption of energy, according to the principle of the greatest advantage with the least effort. 2. In psychoanalytic theory, economic concepts refer to the distribution of energy, libido, and cathexes.

economically disadvantaged   1. Persons deprived of opportunities due to poverty. 2. Individuals or groups lacking the same opportunities as others in the particular culture for potential economic attainment, as in some children who, because of where they live or the cost of good schooling, go to inadequate schools, thereby not learning the skills needed to climb the socio-economic ladder. See CULTURALLY DIFFERENT.

economic approach   The study of the amount and distribution of psychic energy used in maintaining the mental economy, the force exerted by human drives, both unconscious and conscious.

economic-efficiency index   A ratio, with the numerator being a number representing the total prior "cost" of an operation in industry and the denominator being the present cost after efficiency-based changes. A ratio of 1.0 would mean that the new way costs as much as the old way. Ratios above 1.0 indicate improvement with a ratio of 2.0 being 100% better than the prior way. See COST EFFICIENCY-EFFECTIVENESS RATIO.

economic motive   A motive of behavior or social conduct that is concerned with the gaining of livelihood, or with increasing wealth or the potentiality for gaining wealth.

economics   The science that deals with wealth and its relations to the individual and the community; the study of the efforts of humans to provide themselves with the means of satisfying their material wants.

economic type   (E. Spranger) A personality type centered about practical issues having to do with economic security. See TYPOLOGY.

Economo's disease   encephalitis lethargica

economy   The arrangement of any system whereby waste is avoided or eliminated.

economy of effort   A tendency of an organism in repeated performances to minimize the expenditure of energy by eliminating useless movements.

economy principle   See OCCAM'S RAZOR, PARSIMONY PRINCIPLE, PRINCIPLE OF ECONOMY.

eco-pathology   The identification of people as abnormal as influenced by the attitudes of community members. In some locations, certain behavior may be seen as normal, in other locations as eccentric, and in still other locations as psychotic. See COMMUNITY SPIRIT.

eco-pharmacology   Rare phrase for a branch of pharmacology concerned with the relationships between drugs and the external environment, including the role of the individual patient in the patient's ecological background.

ecophobia   Morbid fear of being in one's own house or home. Also known as oikophobia. See DOMATOPHOBIA.

ecopsychology   See ECOLOGICAL-SYSTEMS MODEL.

ecosystem   A continuing balance maintained among competing and mixed components within a group or society, requiring that a change in any one component be followed by commensurate changes in other components.

écouteur   (one who listens—French) A person who gets sexual gratification from listening to sexual accounts or from sounds produced during sexual encounters.

ecouteurism   Being sexually attracted to or aroused by listening to sexual encounters or accounts of them.

ecphoria   (R. Semon) A memory trace. Also known as ecphory, ekphorie.

ecphorize   To reexperience a particular emotional experience, as in recalling a past moment of terror and thereby once again feeling terrified. Also spelled ekphorize. See POSTTRAUMATIC STRESS DISORDER.

ecphory   (E. Tulving) Describing the process of encoding. See ENCODING SPECIFICITY PRINCIPLE.

ecplexis   (C. Galen) A stupor.

ecstasy   1. Excessive and overmastering joy or rapture. 2. In sexology, the peak of sexual excitement and pleasure at the moment of sexual climax with a partner. 3. In religion, the rapturous, mystical union with the cosmos. 4. In psychiatry, a state of exaltation or extreme euphoria sometimes experienced in epileptic or hypomanic states.

Ecstasy   Street name for MDMA, a substance with the chemical formulation 3,4-methylenedioxymethamphetamine, said to evoke exhilaration, increased libido, sensory distortion, and a desire to dance; toxicity includes dehydration, hyperthermia, loss of appetite, and possibly neurotoxicity to serotoninergic neurons, depression, and anxiety. Introduced in the late 1970s, it is the precursor to many other synthetic, recreational drugs. Some psychiatrists have found it a useful adjunct to therapy, in a way similar to how LSD was used in an experimental fashion a decade earlier, but it is not now an approved treatment. A similar substance is MDEA or "Eve." Also known as Adam, E.

ecstatic trance   A state of pure joy, a high moment of ecstasy, often occurring in religious revival meetings in which among other manifestations people will speak in "tongues" (regarded by skeptics as gibberish).

ECT   See ELECTROCONVULSIVE   (SHOCK) THERAPY.

ectoderm   (K. E. von Baer, R. Remak) The outer germ layer of the embryo that eventually evolves into the skin and nails, hair, glands, the mucous membranes, the nervous system, and external sense organs such as the ears and eyes. See EMBRYONIC PERIOD.

ectomorphic (body) type   (W. H. Sheldon) A constitutional type, or somatotype, characterized by a thin, long, fragile physique, which William Sheldon (but few others) found to be highly correlated with a cerebrotonic temperament (tendencies toward introversion, inhibition, and love of solitude). Such a person is referred to as an ectomorph. Also known as ectomorphy. See BODY TYPES, CEREBROTONIA, SHELDON'S CONSTITUTIONAL TYPOLOGY.

ectopic pregnancy   A pregnancy that develops outside the uterus. Also known as eccyesis, extrauterine pregnancy, paracyesis.

ectoplasm   1. The outer layer of a cell or of a one-cell organism. See ECTOSARC. 2. The outer layer of cytoplasm in cells. Compare ENDOPLASM. 3. In parapsychology, a tenuous substance (also known as teleplasm) said to emanate from a medium's body. Purportedly represents rematerialized dead people. See EFFLUVIUM.

ectosarc   Outer layer of cytoplasm of unicellular organisms.

Ed.D.   Abbreviation for doctor of education degree.

Edinger-Westphal nucleus   A collection of small nerve cells comprising the parasympathetic pathway to the ciliary muscle and the pupillary sphincter of the eye, which play a role in visual accommodation.

Edipism   Rare spelling of Oedipism (meaning 1).

Edipus complex   Oedipus complex

EDR   See ELECTRODERMAL RESPONSE.

educability   Potential for learning.

educable-mentally-retarded (EMR) child   A child who scores enough below the norm on intelligence tests to be considered mentally-challenged, but who is able to benefit from an education. Typically, such a child has an intelligence quotient (IQ) between 50 and the low 70s, and can be educated in the three R's (Reading, Riting, Rithmetic) at elementary school levels. Also known as special-needs child. Compare TRAINABLE-MENTALLY-RETARDED CHILD. See EDUCATIONALLY SUBNORMAL.

educare   To lead forth.

education   The development of abilities, attitudes, or forms of behavior and the acquisition of knowledge as a result of teaching or training. Types of education include: COMPENSATORY, CONSUMER, COOPERATIVE, CROSS, DANCE, DRIVER, DRUG, EMOTIONAL RE-, ENVIRONMENTAL, HOLISTIC, HYPNOTIC RE-, INDIVIDUAL, MIS-, MOVEMENT, PHYSICAL, PROGRESSIVE, RE-, SAFETY AND HEALTH, SEX, SPECIAL, VALUES, VOCATIONAL. See ALTERNATIVE EDUCATIONAL SYSTEMS, AMERICAN COUNCIL ON EDUCATION TEST, CUMULATIVE EDUCATIONAL ADVANTAGE, DIAGNOSTIC EDUCATIONAL TESTS, DIAGNOSTIC-PRESCRIPTIVE EDUCATIONAL APPROACH, FOUR GOALS OF EDUCATION, GRADING IN EDUCATION, INDIVIDUALIZED-EDUCATION PROGRAM, MAINSTREAMING IN EDUCATION, PSYCHOEDUCATIONAL DIAGNOSTICIAN, SPECIAL EDUCATIONAL PROGRAMS, TAXONOMY OF EDUCATIONAL OBJECTIVES, TRACKING IN EDUCATION.

educational acceleration   Educational progress at a rate faster than usual through a variety of measures, such as strengthening curriculum, combining two years' work into one, or grade-skipping. These measures are designed to provide the intellectually gifted with academic work better suited to their abilities. Also known as scholastic acceleration.

educational age (EA or E.A.)   The level of a child's performance on school subjects (topics) as measured by academic achievement tests scored in terms of age. See DEVELOPMENTAL AGE.

educational counseling   A counseling specialty concerned with guiding students in their choice of educational programs and choice of college or technical school. Such information and advice-giving is also concerned with school-related problems that interfere with performance, such as learning disabilities. See COUNSELING PSYCHOLOGIST, VOCATIONAL COUNSELING.

educational diagnosis   Identification of all factors affecting academic performance, including attitudes, interests, intelligence, cultural, and other relevant factors.

educational guidance   The process of assisting people, by the use of standardized procedures and ascertained facts, to plan and pursue their education, in the light of past achievements, difficulties, present abilities, attitudes, and vocational interests.

educationally subnormal (ESN)   Phrase introduced in Great Britain designed to authorize special education programs outside the standard school curriculum for the benefit of children regarded as consistently retarded in scholastic progress. See EDUCABLE-MENTALLY-RETARDED CHILD.

educational measurement   The development and application of tests used to measure student academic abilities. Generally measured are language arts, mathematics, physical science, and social science.

educational pacing   Arranging the introduction of new learning material in accordance with a student's interests and abilities. Also known as pacing.

educational placement   Assignment to a particular entry level of schooling, usually by age for children, through interviewing and testing for adults.

educational psychologist   A researcher in epistemic and learning issues who evaluates students in terms of their potentials, constructs academic tests, counsels students, teachers and parents, relative to further academic pursuits. See EDUCATIONAL COUNSELING.

educational psychology   A branch of psychology that deals with the principles and theories that can be applied to methods of learning and psychological problems arising in the educational system. Also known as pedagogical psychology. See SCHOOL PSYCHOLOGIST.

educational quotient (EQ)   The result of dividing a child's educational age by chronological age times 100. A child of 6 who scores an educational age of 8, has an EQ of 133. Essentially, The EQ is an indicator of how a child compares academically with other children of the same age. Formula: $EQ = (EA \div CA) \times 100$ where EA is the educational age, CA is the chronological age, and EQ is the educational quotient.

educational rehabilitative programs   Services for children with disabilities that adapt standard teaching materials and methods to the child's type of challenge to achieve the optimum level of training for the individual. Similar services are occasionally available for adults who are educationally disadvantaged, especially those who are illiterate.

educational retardation   Consistently scoring lower than normally expected for a person's chronological age and possibly mental age on academic achievement tests.

educational sports psychologist   A sports psychologist who teaches the principles of sports psychology to athletes and coaches. See SPORTS PSYCHOLOGY.

educational tests   Instruments used in educational measurements. See DIAGNOSTIC EDUCATIONAL TESTS.

educational therapist   A rehabilitation professional who specializes in enhancing learning with persons with emotional or physical challenges. A major objective of educational therapy is helping to build self-esteem and confidence in people as well as giving them greater academic abilities.

educational therapy   See EDUCATIONAL THERAPIST.

Education for All Handicapped Children Act (EHA or EAHCA)   The EHA act of 1975 (also EAHCA, "142"); Public Law 94-142. Mandates a publicly financed education to all handicapped children (ages 3–18), an individually tailored education plan for each child with periodic reassessment (IEP), and that any tests used be reliable, valid, and nondiscriminatory with regard to the nonEnglish speaking, the poor, members of minority groups and the bilingual. See INDIVIDUALS WITH DISABILITIES EDUCATION ACT.

education stage   (C. G. Jung) In analytic therapy, the stage in which the patient achieves a more effective adaptation to environmental and social demands.

eduction   (C. E. Spearman) Creative thinking, especially new concepts about relationships of events.

eduction of relations and correlates   The cognitive, noegenetic process of applying relations between, or evoking correlates of, two (or more) fundaments (that is, ideas, characters, concepts, etc.). Noegenetic is a neologism by Charles Spearman, a conflation of noetic (intellectual) and genetic (hereditary).

Edwards Personal Preference Schedule (EPPS)
(A. L. Edwards) A self-report personality inventory for college students and adults with 210 items, based on H. A. Murray's personality theory. See MURRAY'S NEEDS, PERSONALITY TESTS, SELF-ANALYSIS, SELF-CONCEPT.

EEG   See ELECTROENCEPHALOGRAM, ELECTROEN-CEPHALOGRAPH.

EEG biofeedback   neurofeedback

effect   1. The specific result of a particular action. 2. A phenomenon, object, or group of phenomena or objects so related to certain preceding or simultaneous phenomena, etc., that in the absence of these phenomena or of their equivalents the phenomenon in question (that is, the effect) never appears. Types of effect include: ABNEY'S, ACTOR-OBSERVER, ADJACENCY, AD-VERSE, AFTER, AGGREGATE, AIR-PRESSURE, AL-ICE IN WONDERLAND, ANCHORAGE, ANCHOR-ING, ANCIENT MARINER, ASCH CONFORMITY, AS-SIMILATION, ATMOSPHERE, AUTOKINETIC, AUTO-NOMIC SIDE, BANDWAGON, BARBER'S POLE, BAR-NUM, BASEMENT, BERNOULLI, BEZOLD-BRÜCKE, BIOSOCIAL, BIRDS OF A FEATHER, BIRTH OR-DER, BLOCKING, BOOMERANG, BOURDON, BUTTER-FLY, BYSTANDER, CARRYOVER, CAUSE AND, CEIL-ING, CHANGE, CHATTERBOX, CHIAROSCURO, CHOICE SHIFT, CLASP-KNIFE, CLOUDING, COCKTAIL-PARTY, COHORT, COLD, CONFINEMENT, CONTEXT, CONTIN-GENT AFTER, CONTRAST, COOLIDGE, CRESPI, CRI-SIS, CROSSOVER, DAMPING, DECLINE, DELAYED, DETERIORATION, DETOXIFICATION, DIFFERENTIAL, DIMMING, DISTAL, DOOR-IN-THE-FACE, DOPPLER, DYADIC, EINSTELLUNG, ELATION, EMPIRICAL LAW OF, EXPECTANCY, EXPERIMENTAL BIAS, EXPERI-MENTER, EXPERIMENTER-EXPECTANCY, EXPRESSED EMOTIONS, FATIGUE, FETAL-ALCOHOL, FIGURAL AF-TER-, FIGURE-GROUND, FLOOR, FLYNN, FOCUSING, FOOT-IN-THE-DOOR, FORCED COMPLIANCE, FUNC-TIONAL NEAR, GARCIA, GIBSON, GRADIENT OF, GREENSPOON, HALO, HAWTHORNE, HEAT, HONI, HORNS, HUMIDITY, INFANT OR NEONATE FEEDING PROCEDURE, INTERACTION, INTERFERENCE, INTER-MEDIATE GENE, INTERPRETER, INTERVIEW CON-TRAST, INTERVIEWER, INVESTIGATOR PARADIGM, ISOLATION, KAMIN, KAPPA, KINETIC AFTER-, KI-NETIC DEPTH, KOHLER-VON RESTORFF, LAND, LEFT-RIGHT, LESS-LEADS-TO-MORE, LEVEE, LEVELING, LIEBMAN, LOCAL NEAR, LONG-HOT-SUMMER, MAG-NITUDE OF, MAIN, MAJOR EVENTS, MCCOLLOUGH, MERE-EXPOSURE, MODALITY, MODELING, MOTION AFTER-, NEAR, NEGATIVE HALO, NEGATIVE RE-CENCY, NETWORK, NOISE, NONSPECIFIC, OBJECT-SUPERIORITY, OPTOKINETIC, ORDER, ORGANIZING, ORNE, OVERJUSTIFICATION, OVERLEARNING REVER-SAL, PARTIAL REINFORCEMENT, PASSING STRANGER, PERKY, PERLOCUTIONARY, PHONEMIC RESTORA-TION, PILOMOTOR, PLACEBO, POSITION, POSITIVE RECENCY, POSTURAL AFTER-, PÖTZL, PRACTICE, PREFERENTIAL, PRIMACY, PRIMING, PSYCHOSO-CIAL, PULFRICH, PYGMALION, RAMAN, RANGE, RANSCHBURG, REBOUND, RECENCY, REGRESSION, REICHER-WHEELER, REMOTE, RESTORFF, ROMEO AND JULIET, ROSENTHAL, ROTATIONAL AFTER-, SAUCE BÉARNAISE, SCALE ATTENUATION, SEN-SORY DEPRIVATION, SEQUENCE, SERIAL-POSITION,

SHAFER-MURPHY, SHEEP-GOAT, SIDE, SITUATIONAL, SLEEPER, SPECTATOR, SPILLMAN-REDIES, STILES-CRAWFORD, STIMULATION, STROBOSCOPIC, STROOP, SUMMATION, TAU, TEMPERATURE, TESTING, THETA, TRANSYLVANIA, TROXLER, TUTORING, UNACCOM-PLISHED ACTION, VALIDITY, VERBAL CONTEXT, VON RESTORFF, WEDENSKY, WIND, WORD SUPERIORITY, ZEIGARNIK, ZUBER.

effectance   An inherent disposition to make things happen, found in people who are doers.

effectance motivation   1. A general tendency of people to do as well as possible in any situation. 2. The desire to develop competence, to initiate projects, and to find effective ways of coping with the environment. Several major theorists (for example, Alfred Adler and Erik Erikson) assumed that children's need to master inferiority feelings contributes to the desire to develop competence. See GROWTH PRINCIPLE.

effect gradient   See GRADIENT OF EFFECT.

effective group   A group whose members commit themselves to the common purpose of maximizing both their own and each other's success.

effective-habit strength   (C. L. Hull) The strength of a learned reaction established by a reinforcement process determined by the number of reinforcements. See HULL'S THEORY.

effective range   A crude, rough-and-ready method of establishing a spread of scores (range) by eliminating the extremes (top 1% and bottom 1%) on either end of obtained scores. Example: Test results for a population of one hundred people range from 2 (the lowest score) to 90 (the highest score). If the second lowest score is 12 and the next to highest score is 72, the effective range is set from 12–72 or 60 points. See OUTLIERS.

effective-reaction potential   The reaction-potential strength of an organism minus any inhibitory tendencies.

effective stimulus   Any stimulus that produces a response. Stimuli may have different meanings for any organism. Thus, if the stimulus is of a mixed type, for example a sound and a light, one organism may respond only to the sound and the other only to the light.

effective temperature   An index of ambient temper-ature obtained by considering both the temperature and humidity levels. Human comfort depends on both factors.

effect laws   See LAW OF EFFECT, LAW OF RELATIVE EFFECT, STRONG LAW OF EFFECT.

effector   1. Any agent that produces a result or effect. 2. (C. S. Sherrington) A motor-nerve ending that triggers activity in neighboring tissue cells, such as causing a muscle to contract or a gland to secrete.

effector cells   Specialized cells that trigger activity in muscles and glands.

effect size   1. An indication of how strongly an inde-pendent variable affects a dependent variable. For exam-ple, if a correlation between an independent variable and a dependent variable is 0.80, the 0.80 is squared and be-comes omega 64. This indicates that 64% of the variation of the effect is due to the independent variable. 2. An in-dication of the strength or power of a particular treatment, often used in meta-analysis, especially if sample sizes are considered in proportion to their number.

effects of punishment on extinction   An observation regarding the extinguishing of learned behavior by punishing an organism that generally is not effective in the long run. For an example, examine the accompanying illustration. Note that although both the solid line and the dotted line begin and end at the same place, the two curves differ. Each line represents a different way to achieve extinction of specific undesired behaviors: the solid one by nonreward and punishment and the dotted line solely by nonreward. This graph depicts that punishment does not stop undesired behavior. Adlerians specializing in family counseling have demonstrated (before knowledge about B. F. Skinner's research on rats) that using logical and natural consequences (nonreward methods of dealing with undesired behavior) works as well in reducing undesired behaviors as does the additional punishment of children. Nonpunitive ways of dealing with children are purported to have enormous effects in mental health, delinquency, and other social problems. See AUTHORITARIAN PARENTING, AUTHORITATIVE PARENTING, DEMOCRATIC PARENTING, EXPERIMENTAL EXTINCTION, EXTINCTION, LOGICAL CONSEQUENCES, NATURAL CONSEQUENCES, PARENTING, PARENTING METHODS, PERMISSIVE PARENTING.

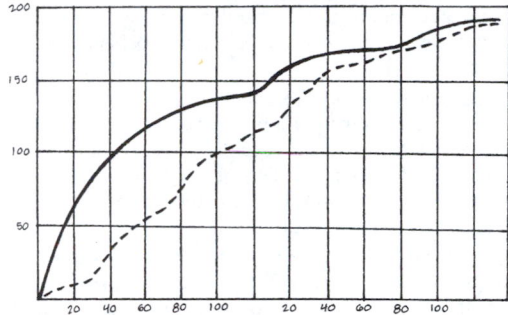

effects of punishment on extinction

effect spread   See SPREAD OF EFFECT.

effeminacy   1. Pronounced feminine characteristics in males or females. 2. The presence of feminine structural characters, or the manifestation of characteristically feminine modes of behavior, in the male of any species. See EFFEMINATION.

effeminate homosexuality   Exhibited in gay men who cross-dress, act, and talk in a feminine manner. See CROSS-DRESSING, TRANSSEXUALISM.

effemination   1. Extreme femininity in a man. 2. Homosexuality characterized by a gay man having sexual feelings and mental characteristics resembling those of a typical female. Improperly known as androgyny. See EFFEMINACY, TRANSSEXUALISM.

efferent   1. Leading out from. 2. Conducting or conveying from a central region of the body toward a more peripheral region, that is, proximal-distally. 3. Conducting or conveying nervous system impulses away from the central nervous system and toward peripheral effector units in muscles or glands. The opposite of afferent. See EFFECTOR.

efferent motor aphasia   A form of expressive aphasia marked by difficulty in articulating sound and speech sequences due to lesions in the lower part of the left premotor area. See INTERMEDIATE PRECENTRAL AREA.

efferent nerve fiber   A kind of nerve fiber that conducts impulses outward from the central nervous system to peripheral muscles and other effector mechanisms. Compare AFFERENT NERVE FIBER. See EFFERENT.

efferent neuron   A neuron that carries an impulse that terminates in a muscle or a gland.

efficacy   A sense of personal worth, competence that confers.

efficacy expectations   See PERCEIVED SELF-EFFICACY.

efficacy study   A comparison between two or more procedures or conditions to see which one produces the desired results to better satisfaction, with "better" usually meaning quicker, easier, less work, more convenient, or best liked. The usual conditions for research of this type are used, such as control groups, equated comparison groups, identical standards with results. See EFFECTIVENESS STUDY.

efficiency   The ratio of the work obtained from a mechanism to the energy consumed by that mechanism.

efficient cause   The total of antecedent (prior) factors leading to a given effect or event.

effluvium   In parapsychology, emanations in a cloud-like formation, usually issuing from the body of a medium in a spiritualism session. Since the debunking efforts of Harry Houdini, such sessions have been rare. See ECTOPLASM.

effort   1. Activity in the presence of some task. 2. A subjective experience of strain that accompanies voluntary action, especially impeded action. See CONSCIOUS OF EFFORT, ECONOMY OF EFFORT, LAW OF LEAST EFFORT, MENTAL EFFORT, PRINCIPLE OF LEAST EFFORT, REPRODUCTIVE EFFORT.

effort after meaning   (F. C. Bartlett) Refers to the concept that memory is rarely clean, pure, or exact. People organize and modify their memories to make them consistent and meaningful. See ANSCHAUUNG.

effort experience   The kinesthetic sensations that accompany the contraction or tension of muscles against resistance.

effortful processing   Encoding that requires considerable attention and effort to generate understanding.

effort justification   A tendency to justify effort invested in tasks or activities by raising evaluations of the importance of the tasks.

effort-shape technique   A method used in dance and movement therapies (as well as systematic observation of human movement in general), based on an analysis of the flow of muscular tension between stasis and freedom, movements flowing toward or away from the body, attitudes toward space, time, and force, and relationships between gestures and postures. See LABANANALYSIS.

effort syndrome   An anxiety reaction associated with excessive exertion or tension, characterized by such somatic symptoms as heart palpitations, fatigue, shortness of breath, and neurocirculatory weakness, all out of proportion to the exertion. See DA COSTA'S SYNDROME.

E-F scale   Thirty items from the <u>Minnesota Multiphasic Personality Inventory</u> (MMPI) that measure authoritarianism. See F-SCALE.

EFT   Embedded Figures Test

egersis   1. Inability to sleep. 2. Abnormal wakefulness. See INSOMNIA.

egg   The female germ cell. See OVUM.

ego   1. A person's self-concept. 2. (S. Freud) In psychoanalytic theory, the part of the mind that is aware of reality mediating between the id and the superego. Term was used in philosophy by Descartes in referring to the whole human, body and mind, but was adapted into psychology by Sigmund Freud. Types of ego include: ALTER, ANTILIBIDINAL, AUXILIARY, COUNTER-, DOUBLE SUPER-, DREAM, GROUP SUPER-, HETERONOMOUS SUPER-, ID-, INTER-, PLEASURE, SCHIZOPHRENIC, PRIMITIVE SUPER-, RATIONAL, REALITY, SUPER-, SUPPORTIVE, WEAK. See ADOLESCENT EGOCENTRISM, ADULT-EGO STATE, ANCHORING OF EGO, BODILY EGO FEELING, BODY-EGO CONCEPT, EXISTENTIAL EGO FUNCTION, EXTINCTION OF EGO, MULTIPLE EGO STATES, NAIVE EGOTISTIC ORIENTATION, PRESUPEREGO PHASE, REACTIVE EGO ALTERATION, REGRESSION IN THE SERVICE OF THE EGO, REWARD BY THE SUPEREGO, TRANSIENT EGO IDEAL.

ego-alien   A thought or idea foreign to or incompatible with the person's self-concept (values, standards, ethics, ideals, etc.). If the ego-alien item is presented from the outside, for example by some other person, the tendency is to get away from the source. If it comes autochthonously (from the person experiencing the thought), it tends to be rejected and upset the person harboring the forbidden thought. See EGO-DYSTONIC, EGO-SYNTONIC.

ego-alter theory   1. (H. Witkin) A point of view that social interaction is controlled by the individual's self-perception in relation to others (alters). 2. A point of view that social institutions are based on self-interest.

ego analysis   Psychoanalytic techniques directed toward discovering the ego's strengths and weaknesses and uncovering defenses against unacceptable impulses. Ego analysis is a short form of psychoanalysis; it does not attempt to penetrate to the ultimate origin of impulses and repressions. See EGO STRENGTH.

ego anxiety   The anxiety caused by conflicting demands of the ego, id, and superego.

ego block   Any event that inhibits the growth and development of the ego.

ego boundary   One of two flexible boundaries that, according to the psychoanalyst Paul Federn, exist between the ego and the unconscious (inner boundary) and between the ego and the outside world (outer boundary). If the inner boundary is blurred, as in falling asleep, repressed material may enter consciousness; if the outer boundary is blurred, a feeling of unreality may be experienced. See EGO PSYCHOTHERAPY, INNER BOUNDARY, INNER ESTRANGEMENT, MORTIDO, ORTHRIOGENESIS.

ego-boundary loss   An explanation of schizophrenia that the parameters of the ego are lost as the ego is unable to test reality and merges with the nonego or the cosmic identity of the entire world.

ego cathexis/libido   (S. Freud) In psychoanalytic theory, concentration of psychic energy in the conscious ego and its executive function of integrating the id, ego, and superego in the process of adjusting to reality. Considered to be a form of narcissism. See OBJECT CATHEXIS.

egocentric   1. Self-centered; overconcerned with personal needs, wishes, and feelings, and usually insensitive to the rights or interests of others. 2. Generally, concerned only or mostly with the self. 3. Describing a person disposed to dwell on the self and to view every situation from a personal angle. 4. In Piagetian theory, characterizing a type of thinking that is directed by the needs and concerns of the self. Also known as egotropic. See DECENTRATION, EGOCENTRISM, EGOMANIA.

egocentricity   Excessive concern with self and, as a result, less concern with others. Also known as egocentrism.

egocentric predicament   Phrase signifying that the human observer is always tied to his or her own personality and is unable to directly share the experiences of others or to experience a stimulus directly. See EMPATHY, I-THOU RELATIONSHIP.

egocentric response   A reaction to some stimuli, such as in association tests, characterized by a tendency toward responses that are distinctly personal to the reactor.

egocentric speech   Verbal expression that does not take into account the point of view of the listener, makes no attempt to exchange thoughts or take into account another person's point of view. According to Jean Piaget, egocentric speech prevails until the seventh or eighth year. See BABBLING, ECHOLALIA.

egocentrism   A tendency to think that others see things from the same point of view as the self, and that these views elicit the same thoughts, feelings, and behavior in others as they do in the self. See EGOCENTRIC, GROUPTHINK, MULTIPLE IGNORANCE, PSYCHOLOGIST'S FALLACY.

ego complex   (C. G. Jung) Concentration of psychic energy in the ego or self.

ego concept   A person's idea or belief of himself or herself and sense of self-worth.

ego constrictions   Denying true feelings and modifying self-behavior to attempt to gain power or favor, as in a politician having a particular position on an issue, but then changing the position to get elected to a higher office.

ego-coping skills   Adaptive techniques developed by a person to deal with personal problems and environmental stresses.

ego decomposition   In psychoanalytic theory, the division of the ego within dreams into various tendencies represented by different events, localities, individuals, or objects. See DREAM, DREAM CONTENT.

ego defect   In psychoanalytic theory, the absence of an ego function.

ego defense   In psychoanalytic theory, protection of the ego from the anxiety of threatening impulses and conflicts through the use of defense mechanisms by means of unconsciously rejecting, denying, or otherwise neutralizing unpleasant aspects of life. See DEFENSE MECHANISM, DENIAL.

ego development/formation (S. Freud) In psychoanalytic theory, the gradual transformation of a part of the id into the ego as a result of environmental demands. Ego development goes through a preconscious stage, in which ego cathexis is partly developed, to the conscious stage, in which ego functions such as reasoning, judging, and reality-testing come to fruition and help to protect the person from internal and external threats.

ego disintegration See PERSONALITY BREAKDOWN.

ego drive A motive to draw positive attention to the self.

ego dystonia A state of experiencing wishes, thoughts, or impulses unacceptable or repugnant to the self. See CONSCIENCE, GUILT.

ego-dystonic 1. Describing impulses, wishes, or thoughts that are unacceptable or repugnant to the ego. 2. Undesired wishes or ideas that appear to come from the outside the person. See EGO-ALIEN, EGO-SYNTONIC.

ego-dystonic homosexuality A psychosexual disorder characterized by a complaint that the person cannot be fully aroused by members of the other sex. Often, unwanted homosexual arousal causes unhappiness and discomfort. See SEXUAL-ORIENTATION DISTURBANCE.

ego eroticism (S. Freud) Self-love. Directing sexual impulses to the self. See MASTURBATION, NARCISSISM.

ego failure In psychoanalytic theory, a concept of the inadequacy of the superego and reality to keep id impulses in check.

ego functions In psychoanalytic theory, the various activities of the ego, including perception of the external world, self-awareness, problem-solving, control of motor functions, adaptation to reality, memory, and reconciliation of conflicting impulses and ideas. The ego is frequently described as the executive agency of the personality, working in the interest of the reality principle.

egogram In transactional analysis (TA), a diagram that represents estimates of time and energy spent in each ego state (parent, adult, or child ego state).

ego ideal (S. Freud) In psychoanalytic theory, the part of the ego that is the repository of introjected positive identifications with parental goals and values the child genuinely admires and wants to emulate, such as integrity and loyalty. The ego ideal acts as a model of how a person wishes to be. Also known as self-ideal. See INTROJECTION, SUPEREGO.

ego identity 1. In psychoanalytic theory, the experience of the self as a recognizable, persistent entity resulting from the integration of a person's unique ego ideal, life roles, and ways of adjusting to reality. 2. (E. Erikson) The gradual acquisition of a sense of continuity, worth, and integration thought to be the essential process in personality development.

ego instincts In psychoanalytic theory, the nonsexual instincts, such as eating, defecating, and urinating, directed toward self-preservation. These instincts may, however, become eroticized. See EROTIZATION.

ego integration The process of organizing the various aspects of the personality (drives, attitudes, aims) into a balanced whole.

ego-integrative Moving toward a harmonious and balanced existence.

ego integrity (E. Erikson) A personality factor characterized by a wise and understanding attitude and acceptance of the self, usually develops late in life. See INTEGRITY VS DESPAIR.

ego involvement A subjective personal reaction rather than an objective impersonal reaction to anything or any person. A personal identification with a concept, task, or cause. Some people figuratively go overboard with their enthusiasms and this may lead to poor judgments and personal stress.

egoism A personality characteristic marked by selfishness and behavior based on self-interest with disregard for the needs of others. See EGOTISM.

egoistic suicide (E. Durkheim) The killing of oneself due to feelings of extreme alienation from others and general society, with overtones of punishing others in this manner. "Goodbye, cruel world!" is the essential message. See ANOMIC SUICIDE.

egoistic theory of dreams A fundamental hypothesis of psychoanalysis, which assumes that dreams are egoistic. Any major player in a dream is likely to be the dreamer.

ego-libido Attachment of libido to the ego. See EGO CATHEXIS.

egology (S. Rado) The scientific analysis of egos.

egomania Extreme pathological self-preoccupation; a tendency to be totally self-centered, selfish, callous to the needs of others, and interested only in the gratification of personal impulses and desires.

ego model A person on whom an individual patterns his or her ideal; a person the individual admires, identifies with, and tries to emulate.

egomorphism The interpretation of the behavior of others in terms of self motives, needs, and desires.

ego needs See NEED-HIERARCHY THEORY.

ego noise In psychoanalytic theory, putting the psyche or oneself above or below others for the purpose of gaining interpersonal power and ego-esteem.

ego nuclei (M. Klein) The first components of the ego, arising during the oral and anal stages.

ego nucleus (functions) Eduardo Weiss held that the ego nucleus integrates new experiences with old ones by relating them to already acquired knowledge.

egopathy Hostile attitudes and actions stemming from an exaggerated sense of self-importance, often manifested by a compulsion to deprecate others. See PARANOIA.

ego perception (P. Schilder) Self-reflection: the ego examining itself.

ego polarity The spread of the awareness of what is "self" and what is "not-self."

ego-psychoanalytic theory (H. Hartmann) The point of view in which emphasis is on the nature and functions of the ego within psychoanalytic theory rather than on the superego or the id.

ego psychology (H. Hartmann, E. Kris, R. Loewenstein, E. Erikson) 1. In psychoanalytic theory, an emphasis on the functions of the ego in controlling impulses and dealing with the external environment, in contrast to id psychology, which focuses on the primitive instincts of sex and hostility. See ADAPTIVE HYPOTHESIS, CONFLICT-FREE SPHERE, NEUTRALIZATION, SOCIAL COMPLIANCE. 2. In Alfred Adler's theory, characterizing the view that humans are governed by a conscious drive to express and create a unique style of life, instead of being controlled by "blind," irrational impulses acting on an unconscious level.

ego psychotherapy (P. Federn, E. Weiss) An approach based on the concept that mental disturbance involves a weakening of the integrating capacity of the ego, a blurring of the boundaries between the ego and the outer reality. Therapy is largely a question of redirecting the ego cathexis (an integrating force), repressing id impulses, increasing reality-testing ability, and solving current problems of adjustment. See DIRECT PSYCHOANALYSIS, EGO BOUNDARY, INNER BOUNDARY, INNER ESTRANGEMENT, MORTIDO, ORTHRIOGENESIS.

ego regression Operating "like an infant," particularly in new and risky situations. For example, if frustrated, throwing a temper tantrum, screaming, and hitting things.

ego resistance The reaction displayed by the ego to repress unacceptable impulses. Also known as repression-resistance.

ego-splitting 1. A pathological coexistence of different personality systems such as occurs in multiple (dissociative) personality. 2. (M. Klein) A mechanism in which infants defend their egos against the death instinct by making a distinction between good and bad objects (people). (Objects in Kleinian theory refers to people.)

ego state 1. An integrated state of mind that determines relationships to the environment and to other people. 2. In Eduardo Weiss and Paul Federn's ego psychotherapy, there are two basic ego states: one that establishes boundaries separating the ego from the id, and the other that separates the ego from external reality. 3. (E. Berne) In transactional analysis, behavior patterns based on the interactions between three ego states: parent, adult, and child. See EGO PSYCHOTHERAPY, TRANSACTIONAL ANALYSIS.

Ego-State Therapy (J. Watkins & H. Watkins) A system of treatment in which the ego is seen as a confederation of states, with the total ego having parts, each having local autonomy. When the boundaries of these separate states become rigid, multiple personalities may emerge. The treatment uses techniques for resolving conflicts between the various ego states inherent within an individual.

ego strength (ES) The ability of the conscious self to maintain an effective balance between inner impulses and outer reality. A person with a strong ego can tolerate frustration and stress, postpone gratification, modify selfish desires when necessary, and resolve internal conflicts and emotional problems before they lead to neurosis. See SELF-CONFIDENCE.

ego stress Any situation, external or internal, producing stress that requires adaptation by the ego, often expressed as unusual defensive reactions, such as dissociation, somatization, or panic.

ego structure A continuing pattern of personality traits that influence ego processes.

ego suffering In psychoanalytic theory, the guilt feelings produced in the ego by the aggressive forces in the superego when it disapproves of the ego.

ego-syntonic 1. Describing thoughts, wishes, impulses, and behavior that form no threat to the ego and can be acted upon without interference from the superego. 2. A thought or idea compatible with the person's sense of values. See EGO-ALIEN, EGO-DYSTONIC.

egotism Excessive conceit or excessive preoccupation with self-importance. The tendency to overvalue, in a rather obvious manner, personal actions, qualities, possessions, or achievements. See EGOISM.

ego transcendence Refers to the feeling, experienced mainly during altered states of consciousness, that a person is beyond a concern with self and thus able to perceive reality with less bias and greater objectivity.

ego trip Refers to the presentation of an undue sense of self-confidence and self-importance to others.

egotropy (A. Meyer) An exaggerated self-conception. See NARCISSISM.

ego weakness Inability to control impulses and tolerate frustration, disappointment, or stress. A person with a weak ego suffers from anxiety and conflicts, makes excessive use of defense mechanisms, and is likely to develop character defects or neurotic symptoms.

EGY test See KENT SERIES OF EMERGENCY SKILLS.

EHA See EDUCATION FOR ALL HANDICAPPED CHILDREN ACT.

eidetic Characterizing such psychic phenomena as depend upon (or are otherwise related to) the capacity for clear projected images.

eidetic disposition An ability of certain individuals (especially children) to project images of an unusually lively, pseudoperceptual character. See EIDETIC IMAGERY.

eidetic image An unusually vivid and detailed memory image. Also known as primary memory image.

eidetic imagery (E. and W. Jaensch) Detailed imagery in memory. Such imagery is usually visual but occasionally auditory, and closely resembles actual perception. More common in children than in adults and greater in some individuals than in others. Most children tend to lose this ability as they get older. Roughly 10% of children demonstrate strong eidetic imagery, and perhaps 50% or more show some degree of it. In adults, it is usually known as photographic memory.

eidetic individual A person possessing the ability to visualize unusually life-like (eidetic) images after visual exposure. For example, if 100 items arrayed on a desk are shown to participants for one second, a true eidetic will probably be able to reproduce many of them at a later time, whereas most participants might remember perhaps only a dozen such items. Also known as *Eidetiker*.

eidetic psychotherapy (A. A. Sheikh) A system of psychotherapy based on the elicitation and manipulation of eidetic images posited as acting as self-organizing nuclei in the psyche to direct personality development and to restore mind-body-wholeness. Eidetic therapists aim to uncover appropriate healthful experiences through eidetic progression. When the original wholeness of the psyche has been mobilized, therapy is achieved.

eidetic type (E. Jaensch) A constitutional body type in which a major feature is eidetic imagery. See EIDETIC IMAGERY.

eidotropic Refers to the tendency of people to see things as more regular or perfect than they really are. See GESTALT LAWS OF ORGANIZATION.

Eigenwelt (own world—German) In existential psychology, the aspect of the personal world that is constituted by a person's relationship to the self, as contrasted to *Umwelt* and *Mitwelt*.

eightfold path A way of living to attempt to achieve bliss (nirvana) according to Buddhist tradition that incorporates eight concepts: right views, right intentions, right speech, right action, right livelihood, right effort, right mindfulness, and right concentration. See ZEN BUDDHISM.

eighth cranial nerve See ACOUSTIC NERVE.

eikonometer A device to test stereoscopic vision. See SPACE EIKONOMETER.

Eindringlichkeit (forcefulness—German) 1. A specific characteristic or quality of a perceived sensory dimension (such as color, brightness, or size) that forcefully attracts a person's attention. 2. (D. Katz) Describing the awareness an observer has about the brightness and stimulus intensity of a color. 3. (M. Meyer) Describing the intense nature of the stimulation that held a person's attention. A concept that Hermann Ebbinghaus had termed *Aufdringlichkeit*.

Einfühlung German term meaning empathy.

Einhorn-Hogarth ambiguity model A model that explores how ambiguity affects choices through its effect on decision weights.

Einstellung (attitude, mindset—German) A mental set or relatively inflexible attitude; a propensity to react to or perceive a situation in an expected way, for example, the tendency to apply formerly successful techniques to the solution of a new problem.

Einstellung effect (A. Luchins) In Gestalt psychology, a mental set or tendency to solve a series of similar problems all in the same way. Sometimes results in a person arriving at the correct answer in an inefficient manner or not seeing an obvious way to deal with the problem simply. See WATER-JUG PROBLEM for an illustration.

eisoptrophobia Morbid fear of mirrors or of seeing self-reflection. Also known as spectrophobia.

either-or fallacy A logical fallacy of providing only two alternatives when there are actually more, as in the expression "You can either agree with my proposal or disagree with me." Implying that there are no other alternatives, such as agreeing with some aspects of the proposal and disagreeing with others. Also known as false dilemma. See ARISTOTELIANISM.

either-or situation A condition of doubt and vacillation, usually manifested in an inability to make a choice between two different things desired at the same time. Frequently is expressed in the dreams of a person with a neurosis. See ABULIA.

either-or thinking See DICHOTOMOUS THINKING.

ejaculatio deficiens/retardata Difficulty or inability of a man to ejaculate during sexual intercourse, perhaps due to psychogenic factors, aging, or the use of drugs. Such individuals may be able to ejaculate via masturbation. Purportedly, a condition difficult to treat. Also known as *coitus sine ejaculatione*, male continence. See EJACULATORY DISORDERS.

ejaculation The automatic expulsion or discharge of semen through the penis resulting from involuntary and voluntary contractions of various muscle groups. See FEMALE EJACULATION, ORGASM, PREMATURE EJACULATION, RETROGRADE EJACULATION.

ejaculatio praecox Latin for premature ejaculation.

ejaculator seminis In men, another name for the bulbospongiosus muscle. In women, it is called sphincter cunni or constrictor vaginae. See BULBOSPONGIOSUS MUSCLE.

ejaculatory disorders Male sexual dysfunctions such as inability to ejaculate sperm during sexual intercourse, or ejaculating sooner than desired by either party.

ejaculatory duct A passageway on either side of the prostate gland, formed by a union of the ductus deferens and the seminal-vesicle duct. The ejaculatory ducts on either side converge in the prostate and empty into the urethra at a point below the urinary bladder.

ejaculatory incompetence The inability of a man to ejaculate within the vagina, or during sexual activity with a partner, or (more rarely) in masturbation. See EJACULATORY DISORDERS, INHIBITED ORGASM, INHIBITED SEXUAL EXCITEMENT.

eject To expel or throw out.

E_{jk} The expected frequency for the jkth cell.

Ekbom's syndrome A sense of uneasiness, twitching, or restlessness that occurs in the legs after retiring for the night. Possibly caused by a circulation impairment but also appears to be more common in persons with neuroses. Also known as Jimmy-legs syndrome, restless-legs syndrome, tachyathetosis, Wittmaack-Ekbom syndrome. See HYPNIC JERK.

EKG See ELECTROCARDIOGRAM, ELECTROCARDIOGRAPH.

ekphorize ecphorize

elaborating symbols See KEY SYMBOLS.

elaboration 1. A period of intense, systematic work to clarify the gist of a creative insight called for and often achieved. 2. The process (conscious or unconscious) of developing an idea and incorporating details or relationships that amplify the original concept. See SECONDARY ELABORATION.

elaboration-likelihood model (ELM) (R. E. Petty & J. T. Cacioppo) A theory that how much analysis people do of a message depends on their motivation level, so that there are multiple paths to persuasion.

elaborative choice (G. Kelly) People tend to make decisions in such manner to enable them to improve their predictions.

elaborative code (B. Bernstein) In communicating with a stranger, verbal communication is likely to differ from speaking with people a person knows or knows about, characterized by slow speaking, careful pronunciation, avoidance of difficult words, etc.

elaborative faculty Mental faculty or power to which the process of thinking out problems is ascribed. A concept used chiefly by the faculty psychologists.

elaborative rehearsal 1. An encoding process used when placing an item into long-term storage by forming associations between new information and items already in long-term memory, often by constructing stories that link items together. Also known as coathook strategy. 2. The rehearsal or practicing of verbal information by actively constructing stories intended to enhance the total effect of the information.

élan vital (life force or spurt—French) (H. Bergson) The force that gives impulse to life, the creative principle responsible for evolution. See GROWTH PRINCIPLE, LIBIDO, VITALISM.

elasticity The capacity of a body to recover its original shape or position after deformation by a force.

elation A state of extreme joy, exaggerated optimism, and restless excitement.

elation effect A tendency for an animal administered a larger than usual reward, to respond more strongly than usual.

Elavil A trade name for the antidepressant, amitriptyline, used widely in the 1970s. See IMIPRAMINE HYDROCHLORIDE.

Elberfeld horses Horses trained around 1900 in Elberfeld, Germany, who reacted to trainer cues and thus appeared to be able to solve mathematical problems. The trainer and many others were convinced that the horses could solve mathematical problems. See CLEVER HANS, UNCONSCIOUS CUES.

elbow reflex See TRICEPS REFLEX.

elder abuse Neglect and harming of dependent older persons, often by relatives including their own children.

elective affinity (M. Weber) Originally the coherence between the teachings of Protestantism and those of capitalism, later the connections between beliefs, actions, and the unintended consequences of actions.

elective anorexia Loss of appetite associated with a conscious effort to limit the amount of food consumed accompanied by a revulsion to food. See ANOREXIA.

elective mutism Rare childhood disorder wherein a child refuses to talk in some situations despite the ability to speak and understand language.

electives School courses that students voluntarily select.

Electra complex (C. Jung) The female counterpart of the Oedipus complex characterized by a daughter's love for her father, jealousy toward the mother, and blaming the mother for depriving her of a penis. Name derives from the Greek myth of Electra, who induced her brother Orestes to kill their mother Clytemnestra who had murdered their father. This Jungian construct was repudiated by Freud.

electrical activity of brain Spontaneous electrical discharges observed in the brain cells of humans and lower animals. Such oscillations may vary from one to more than 50 Hertz (cycles per second) in frequency and from 50 to 200 microvolts in amplitude. See BRAIN WAVES, ELECTROENCEPHALOGRAPH.

electrical brain stimulation (EBS) By means of implanted electrodes in the brain, organisms can be directed positively or negatively relative to certain behaviors. Sometimes known as electrical intracranial stimulation. See ELECTRICAL STIMULATION OF CORTEX, INTRACRANIAL STIMULATION, SELF-STIMULATION for an illustration.

electrical habituation In an evoked response experiment, the amplitude of the response diminishes with repetition of the stimulus.

electrical intracranial stimulation The stimulation of the brain cells of a human or other animal by direct application of an electric current. Has been used in research and diagnostic purposes since the 1930s.

electrical self-stimulation of the brain (ESSB) See SELF-STIMULATION OF THE BRAIN.

electrical stimulation The use of electrical or electronic devices to initiate sensations and responses of various sensory and motor neurons. Has been used to study brain areas associated with memory traces and to follow pathways of impulses through various brain structures.

electrical stimulation of cortex (W. Penfield) Electrical charges delivered through electrodes implanted in the brain cells have been used to produce varied effects. In animal studies, they can have a reward or punishment effect depending upon the site of the electrodes and the intensity of the stimulation. See SELF-STIMULATION for an illustration.

electrical transcranial stimulation (ETS) See ELECTRO-SLEEP THERAPY.

electric organ Modified muscle tissue of such nature that it forms an electric generator that, on excitation through its nerve supply, produces an electric shock, found chiefly in primitive fish. At one time certain types of eels were used to deliver electric shocks to patients with mental disorders.

electric senses Nervous-system receptors or other organs in certain animals that enable them to detect or generate electric currents.

electric shock method 1. A variety of the method of punishment in animal training whereby a habit is broken or a new habit formed by applying an electric shock at some point in the behavior series. 2. Use of electricity in treating humans. See ELECTRO-SLEEP THERAPY, ELECTROCONVULSIVE THERAPY.

electric sink A device that collects or dissipates electric energy. See EXCITATION AND CONDUCTION.

electric skin response See ELECTRODERMAL RESPONSE.

electro(a)esthesiometer A highly sensitive meter that measures the electrical potential or resistance across two points on the surface of the skin of a participant used to various research purposes such as spatial thresholds. See GALVANIC SKIN RESPONSE, LIE DETECTOR.

electrocardiogram (EKG or ECG)   The tracing or graphic record of the heart's action potential as shown by an electrocardiograph.

electrocardiograph (EKG or ECG)   (W. Einthoven) An apparatus that records changes in the electrical potential of the heartbeat, enabling interpretations to be made of irregularities of heart action. See STRING GALVANOMETER.

electroconvulsive (shock) therapy (EST)   (G. B. A. Duchenne, U. Cerletti, & L. Bini) The induction of a seizure by passing a controlled electrical current through electrodes applied to one or both temples. The seizure is attenuated by administration of a muscle relaxant medication. EST seems to be primarily helpful for depressed patients. There is controversy as to whether this procedure's benefits outweigh its risks. Historically, electric eels were used for the same purpose. Also known as electroconvulsive treatment (ECT), electroshock therapy (EST). See CONVULSIVE THERAPY, METRAZOL SHOCK TREATMENT, REGRESSIVE ELECTROSHOCK THERAPY, SHOCK TREATMENT.

electroconvulsive treatment (ECT)   **electroconvulsive (shock) therapy**

electrocorticogram (ECoG)   An electronic tracing of the signals of the brain's activity, obtained from electrodes placed directly on the cortex rather than on the scalp, as is usually done with the ELECTROENCEPHALOGRAPH.

electrode   1. (M. Faraday) A device used to join an electric circuit to some substance or object that is usually regarded as non-electrical in nature. The positive pole is the anode, and the negative, the cathode. 2. A device, usually metallic, for applying electrical current (stimulating electrode) or for recording (recording electrode) electrical activity.

electrode placement   The positioning of electrodes on the surface of the body, usually the scalp, or in neurons, to record changes of electrical potential caused by neural activity. In animal research studies, and certain human studies, needlelike microelectrodes are placed in specific brain cells. See also BODY ELECTRODE PLACEMENT.

electrodermal changes   Modifications of the skin that affect its electric conductivity.

electrodermal response (EDR)   A change in the skin's electrical conductance, used as an indicator of ongoing cognitive processing. See GALVANIC SKIN RESPONSE.

electrodiagnosis   The use of electrical instruments, such as the electroencephalograph and electromyograph, as diagnostic tools. Term also denotes application of electric current to nerves and muscles for diagnostic purposes.

electroencephalogram (EEG)   (H. Berger) The visual recordings of an electroencephalograph. See BRAIN-WAVES for examples of such tracings.

electroencephalograph (EEG)   An instrument that amplifies and records the electrical activity of the cerebral cortex through electrodes placed at various points on the skull (scalp). See ALPHA WAVES, BERBER RHYTHMS, ELECTRICAL ACTIVITY OF BRAIN.

electroencephalographic audiometry   The measurement of hearing sensitivity with use of electroencephalography. Gross measures are obtained from changes in brain-wave patterns when above threshold sound stimuli are introduced.

electroencephalographic (EEG) examination   A method of diagnosing the functioning of the brain by evaluating recording electroencephalograph (EEG) fluctuations. The examiner can determine whether there are any variations from normality in waking or sleeping brain-wave patterns that could be due to tumors, epileptic foci, or other types of brain lesions. See BRAIN WAVES, ELECTROENCEPHALOGRAPH.

electrolysis   1. A process of chemical decomposition produced by passing an electric current through a solution of ionizable substance. 2. Destroying hair roots by electric currents.

electrolyte   See ELECTROLYTES.

electrolyte imbalance   Abnormal levels of one or more electrolytes (ions) that play a vital role in fluid balance, acid-base balance, and other functions of body cells. Electrolytes involved in electrolyte imbalance include sodium, needed for water regulation and normal nerve and muscle function; potassium, necessary for acid-base balance; chloride, necessary for control of acid-base balance; magnesium and calcium, essential for normal blood clotting, cardiac rhythm, and muscle functions. See THIRST.

electrolytes   1. Compounds that in solution dissociates into positively and negatively charged particles called ions. 2. The major chemical components of the body fluids, mainly sodium (abbreviated Na), potassium (abbreviated K), chloride (abbreviated Cl), and bicarbonate (abbreviated HCO_3). When out of balance, they can cause mental confusion and other serious medical dysfunctions—and if extreme, electrolyte imbalance can be fatal.

electrolytic stimulus   An inadequate or abnormal stimulus by means of which sensory experiences are aroused by electrochemical action. Noted especially in the sense of taste.

electromagnetic senses   Capacities to receive and respond to magnetic sensations. Certain birds appear to be able to fly in the dark or over water based on their sensitivity to the earth's magnetic field.

electromagnetic spectrum   See VISUAL SPECTRUM.

electromyograph (EMG)   An instrument that records the electrical potential of the muscles through electrodes placed in or on different muscle groups when they are relaxed or during various activities. Results are an electromyogram. See ELECTROENCEPHALOGRAPH.

electron-proton theory   (A. P. Weiss) A point of view that everything about a living organism, overt and covert, is nothing more in the final analysis than a grouping of electrons and protons in a dynamic structure. The ultimate example of atomism. See BLACK BOX, GESTALT PSYCHOLOGY, MOLAR APPROACH, REDUCTIONISM.

electronarcosis   A form of electrotherapy in which the amount of electricity, duration of electricity, or both, is sufficient to generate the tonic but not the clonic phase of convulsion. See ELECTROCONVULSIVE SHOCK THERAPY.

electronic aids   Electronic devices that enable a person with a physical disability to achieve independent living, including tape recorders, portable intercom equipment, walkie-talkie radios, computers, and devices that turn on lights, open doors, and operate wheelchairs.

electronic noses   Any of several electronic devices such as AromaScan, Bloodhound, and Neotronics Olfactory Sensing Equipment, designed to identify and measure odors. Vapors of test substances are processed to end up as "smell fingerprints."

electronic yoga   See BIOFEEDBACK TRAINING/USE.

electrooculogram (EOG)   Graphic representation of the movements of the eyes over a constant distance between two fixation points. Measured by an electrooculograph.

electrooculograph (EOG)   An instrument that measures eye movements.

electroolfactogram (EOG)   A recording of the response of olfactory-nerve endings to various stimulating odors. Can be used to diagnose disorders such as anosmia (loss of the sense of smell) after injury or disease affecting the olfactory receptors.

electrophobia   Morbid fear of electricity.

electrophysiology   The study of the role of electricity in the physiology of organism functions. The classical concept of electrophysiology assumes that a nerve impulse is a traveling wave of depolarization, moving at a constant velocity along a nerve pathway, with an accompanying pattern of circulating currents around and outside the pathway. See ANIMAL ELECTRICITY, NERVE IMPULSE.

electroretinogram (ERG)   A recording of the electrical activity of retinal-nerve endings when stimulated by a pulse of light. The response is detected by a galvanometer attached to leads placed on the surface of the eyeball.

electrosane   See ELECTRO-SLEEP THERAPY.

electroshock therapy   **electroconvulsive shock therapy**

electrosleep   A method of treatment of serious mental disorders accomplished by putting a person to sleep by application of low frequency electricity to the brain in experimental treatments of mental disorders. See ELECTRIC SHOCK THERAPY.

electro-sleep therapy (EST)   Treatment of depression, chronic anxiety, and insomnia by inducing a state of relaxation or sleep through low voltage electrical transcranial stimulation (ETS), a technique developed in Russia in the 1940s, in which an instrument termed an electrosane was used.

electrostimulation   A negative reinforcement technique involving administration of an electric shock by an electrostimulator. See AVERSIVE THERAPY.

electrostimulation of the brain (ESB)   The application of electrical current through an electrode, usually in an attempt to simulate normal brain activity, sometimes to destroy the area stimulated.

electrostimulator   Any special apparatus devised or used for the purpose of delivering a current for shock stimulation.

electrotaxis   The involuntary positioning or movement of an organism in relation to an electric force. The attraction or repulsion effects on an organism to electrical stimulation. See GALVANOTAXIS, GALVANOTROPISM, TAXIS, TROPISM.

electrotherapy   General term for the use of an electrical current on the central nervous system as a therapeutic measure. See ELECTROCONVULSIVE TREATMENT.

electrotonic conduction   Nerve-impulse transmission that may occur in some nerve and muscle fibers over short distances in addition to or instead of the usual core-conduction properties of fibers.

electrotonus   Altered physiological condition of a nerve or muscle during the passage of a (steady direct) galvanic current, as exhibited in altered excitability in the neighborhood of the electrodes. Described and named in 1843 by Emil du Bois-Reymond.

electrotropism   Old term for electrotaxis. See GALVANOTAXIS, GALVANOTROPISM, TAXIS, TROPISM.

elegant solution   Solutions to any kind of problem that has a mini-max quality: minimum effort and maximum return.

element   1. The simplest unit of analysis; the basic subunit of a sensation, image, or affective state; that which cannot be reduced further. 2. In set theory, an element is anything that belongs to a set.

elementarism   1. A system of psychology such as Wilhelm Wundt's, which describes the mind in terms of mental elements and their compounds. 2. A doctrine positing that to really understand something, one should go into details, studying constituent components.

elementary anxiety   **primordial panic**

elementary event   In probability theory, every possible outcome of an experiment. Also known as simple event. See EVENT.

elementary hallucination   Simple sensations without direct external stimuli, usually involving the visual or auditory senses, consisting of sparks or amorphous darkenings, murmurs, or knocks.

elementary information processes   (A. Newell, J. C. Shaw, H. A. Simon) The lowest-level (primitive) processes of an information-processing language, comparable to the machine instruction code for a computer.

Elementary Perceiver and Memorizer (EPAM)   (E. A. Feigenbaum, H. A. Simon) A computer simulation of human perceptual, recognition, and memory processes and the symbolic structures that support them, which has been successful in fitting and predicting a large range of experimental findings about human perception, verbal and concept learning, and short-term and long-term memory. See COGNITIVE SIMULATION, INTUITION.

elementerism   **atomism**

eleutherophobia   Morbid fear of freedom.

elevated maze   A maze on stilts. Another variation of a maze is one in water in which subject animals have to swim to get to the proper goal.

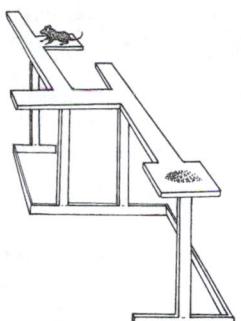

elevated maze Many different kinds of mazes have been developed for laboratory research. Note the path that a mouse must take to get to the food. A real maze of this type would have barriers over the runways to prevent the mouse from seeing the final goal.

elevation The overall level or trend of an individual's test profile. See PLATEAU, SCATTER.

elevator phobia Morbid fear of elevators, which may represent fear of height (acrophobia), fear of the sensations of speed (tachophobia), or most likely, a fear of being shut in (claustrophobia).

eleventh cranial nerve See ACCESSORY NERVE.

Elgin checklist A list of behavior patterns associated with psychotic individuals.

elicited behavior respondent behavior

eligibility paraphilias A category of paraphilias in which self-abandonment to the lustful act can be achieved only if the partners have some quality that places them beyond the limits of being conventional and undefiled. For example, the distancing of lust in an extramarital affair and seeking partners from socially unacceptable classes or ages (gerontophilia, infantophilia, pedophilia). Eligibility paraphilias include stigmatophilia (the partner is tattooed, body-pierced), apotemnophilia and acrotomophilia (the partner is an amputee), zoophilia (the sexual partner is an animal), and necrophilia (the partner is dead).

elimination drive The urge to expel feces and urine from the body. Psychological factors have considerable effects on these drives: in small children, defecation can be stimulated by cuddling, and if emotional warmth is lacking, as in institutions, children usually become constipated. Tension and fright may precipitate involuntary voiding of both the bladder and intestines. See ANAL CHARACTER, ANAL EROTISM, BLADDER CONTROL, BOWEL CONTROL, DEFECATION REFLEX, FUNCTIONAL ENCOPRESIS, FUNCTIONAL ENURESIS, MICTURITION REFLEXES, TOILET TRAINING.

eliminativism Attempts to discard certain concepts completely. A prominent example is the mind-matter controversy. Some materialists such as behaviorists will admit they and others do have minds, but take the position it is better to eliminate the mind as an explanation in human or animal research.

elision The omission or partial omission of initial or final sounds of words. For example, as found in very young children, and people who are learning a new language. See CREOLE.

ellipsis The omission of words in writing or speaking, or of significant ideas in free association or dreams. In psychoanalysis, efforts are made to recover these ideas.

elopement 1. The departure of a patient from a psychiatric hospital or unit without permission. 2. Secretly leaving home to marry, without parental consent. 3. In law enforcement, slang for an inmate escaping.

elucidation (stage) The second stage of Carl Jung's analytic approach in which the therapist focuses on interpretation of the patient's individual and collective unconscious.

elusion (R. D. Laing) The use of self-impersonation by which persons can avoid confrontation with themselves and others.

emancipated minors Legal term for minors who have asserted independence from the family and exercise general control over their own lives, and hence may claim the legal rights of an adult.

emancipation disorder A problem of early adulthood in which the person experiences conflicts between a desire for freedom from parental control and from the responsibilities of independence. Symptoms may include indecisiveness, homesickness, excessive dependence on peers, and paradoxical overdependence on parental advice.

emancipatory communitarianism (I. Prilleltensky) A proposed psychological approach that seeks to improve human welfare through the removal of interpersonal and social oppression and the enhancement of mutuality and social obligations. Interventions suggested in this approach seek to change individuals as well as social systems of domination.

emancipatory strivings Attempts to free the self from the influence or domination of parents and to achieve a sense of independence and self-dependence.

emasculation See CASTRATING WOMAN.

embarrassment An emotional condition marked by unpleasant self-consciousness, and by some degree of confusion and impulsion conflict.

embarrassment dream 1. A dream in which the person feels shame or embarrassment. 2. In psychoanalytic theory, a dream of being naked in public, resulting from such an experience or fear in childhood.

Embedded Figures Test (EFT) A task consisting of identifying a simple form in a complex figure. Used to demonstrate a relationship between personality characteristics and a perceptual task. See GOTTSCHALDT FIGURES for an example of a test item.

emblem 1. An object with a symbol on it. 2. A body gesture that can be readily comprehended by most individuals in a given culture, as in turning the head back and forth sideways to indicate negation. See GESTURAL COMMUNICATION, ILLUSTRATOR.

embol(ol)alia A speech disorder characterized by the insertion of inappropriate or meaningless words when speaking.

embolophrasia The unnecessary repetition of phrases in speaking.

embracing behavior Cuddling, contact-seeking actions in children, adults, and animals (such as chimpanzees) in stressful or frightening situations. Embracing of this kind (as contrasted with embracing as a form of sexual or affectional expression) is a primary means of seeking comfort and relief from anxiety.

embryo An organism in an early stage of development; an intermediate state of an organism. See EMBRYONIC PERIOD, FETUS.

embryology The branch of biology that deals with eggs, their fertilization, and development into adult organisms.

embryonic period In human prenatal development, the roughly six-week period in which the endoderm, mesoderm, and ectoderm develop. During this time, the embryo is purported to increase in size by approximately 2,000,000%. The embryonic period follows the two-week germinal period and precedes the fetal period beginning in the third month.

EMDR eye-movement desensitization and reprocessing

emergence epigenetic theory

emergency See entries beginning with EMERGENCY and also CANNON'S EMERGENCY SYNDROME, KENT'S SERIES OF EMERGENCY SKILLS, PSYCHIATRIC EMERGENCY.

emergency contagion The process whereby emotional reactions by one individual to a presumed emergency stimulates similar reactions in other individuals who sense or observe the emergency function but not the precipitating cause. See MASS CONTAGION.

emergency dyscontrol (S. Rado) A tendency to overreact emotionally in emergency situations, and an inability to use available means of handling the emergency effectively.

emergency intervention An action taken on behalf of another person or persons, under stressful and possibly dangerous conditions with little or no expectation of reward. See BYSTANDER EFFECT.

emergency psychotherapy Psychological treatment of persons occurring as soon as possible for people who have undergone a traumatic experience (for example, survived a plane crash) and are in a state of anxiety, panic, shock, or suicidal ideation.

emergency reaction A physiological correlate of intense emotional excitement interpreted by Walter Cannon and others as an adaptive preparation of the organism to meet emergencies; the alarm reaction state of the GENERAL-ADAPTATION SYNDROME.

emergency services Aid provided by a community mental-health center or other facility such as a clinic or general hospital, in emergency situations, as in disasters affecting the entire population or crises affecting individuals or families. For details, see CRISIS INTERVENTION, PSYCHIATRIC EMERGENCY, TRAUMA PSYCHOLOGY.

emergency theory (H. Selye) A point of view that the body goes through three phases in long-lasting emergencies: alarm, resistance, and exhaustion. See GENERAL ADAPTATION SYNDROME.

emergency theory (of the emotions) (W. B. Cannon) A point of view that animal and human organisms respond to emergency situations with increased sympathetic nervous system activity that leads to increases in blood pressure, heart and respiratory rates, and skeletal muscle blood flow. Also known as Cannon's theory. See GENERAL ADAPTATION SYNDROME, RELAXATION RESPONSE.

emergent The result of a clash of ideas or as a result of pondering of a problem: a solution, usually sudden, complete and satisfactory. See GESTALT, INSPIRATION.

emergent evolution A theory that new or unpredictable phenomena evolve from an interaction of simpler factors.

emergentism A doctrine positing that new and unpredictable elements or events may appear mysteriously, without explanation, or in defiance of scientific expectation. For example, a genius or a prodigy.

emergent leader A person in a situation with others who takes over leadership of the group.

emergent pole (G. A. Kelly) A pole of a construct used to interpret an event by noting its similarity to other events. See IMPLICIT POLE, PERSONAL CONSTRUCT THERAPY.

emergent vitalism A theory that life originated from nonliving materials. See ABIOGENESIS, EMERGENTISM, SPONTANEOUS GENERATION.

emetomania Morbid desire to vomit, usually a symptom of hysteria.

emetophobia Morbid fear of vomiting. A common hysterical (conversion) reaction.

EMG See ELECTROMYOGRAPH.

emic Pertaining to concepts or constructs that possess meaning only in a designated cultural context; pertaining to concepts that are not universal, for example, future shock. Compare ETIC.

emissive centers/functions Those functions (or centers) that deal with efferent nerve impulses resulting in movement or some other effector response.

emitted behavior Responses or response sequences that do not depend for their arousal on external stimuli but arise as a result of the organism's internal state. See RESPONDENT BEHAVIOR.

Emmanuel Church Health Class (E. Worcester) A group healing process for the treatment of physical conditions started in the early 1900s in Boston. An early attempt to join together religion and psychiatry by use of the class method of Joseph Pratt in the treatment of mental disorders. See CLASS METHOD, FAITH HEALING, HEALING GROUPS, MENTAL HEALING.

Emmert's law/phenomenon A theory that the size of an afterimage or eidetic image increases with the distance between the image and the ground on which it is projected. Formulated by German physiologist Emil Emmert (1844–1913).

emmetropis(m) A normal condition of the ocular refractive system, in which rays from distant objects are focused sharply on the retina of the eye, while the accommodation muscle is relaxed. Also known as emmetropia.

emotion Any mental state characterized by various degrees of feeling and usually accompanied by motor expressions, often quite intense. The subjective state may be pleasurable, threatening, frightening, or of some other nature. Emotions are usually directed toward a specific person or event and involve widespread physiological changes, such as increased heart rate and inhibition of peristalsis. Common emotions are anger, elation, fear, horror, love. Types of emotion include: COLD, CONDITIONED, DEFENSIVE, DERIVED, ESTHETIC, ICTAL, PRIMARY, SECONDARY, UNCANNY. See AFFECTION, CORRECTIVE EMOTIONAL EXPERIENCE, FEELINGS, GENE CORRELATES OF EMOTION, HEART RATE IN EMOTION.

emotional adjustment   An ability to maintain a balance in the affective aspects of life, to exert reasonable control over emotions, and to express emotions that are appropriate to the situation.

emotional anesthesia   (E. Minkowski) One of the self-protective responses as experienced by young survivors of concentration camps, featuring lack of affective response toward those who died, including close relatives. See SURVIVAL GUILT, SURVIVOR SYNDROME.

emotional beggar   Describing a person whose lifestyle includes constantly asking for approval but never feeling it has been given.

emotional bias   Prejudice based on emotional factors.

emotional blockage/blocking   A situation that can occur in emergencies when, because of terror, a person is without feelings, has become an emotional zero, and is unable to think or act.

emotional charge   A concept of early psychology of strong emotion such as anger being bottled up, under pressure, and ready to "blow" or explode.

emotional cognition   The means by which, both consciously and unconsciously, humans perceive and process emotionally-charged information and meaning in the service of satisfaction or adaptation.

emotional conflict   A clash between intense emotions or affect-laden impulses of approximately equal strength, for example, ambivalent feelings such as love and hate, affection and hostility, or the conflict between a strong desire for success and a fear of failure.

emotional contagion   The process whereby emotional reactions are experienced in one person because the person is observing the experience of the same emotion in others, as in becoming frightened in a thunderstorm, not because the person is afraid of thunderstorms, but because someone else is frightened. See BEHAVIOR(AL) CONTAGION, EMERGENCY CONTAGION, MASS CONTAGION.

emotional content   Themes or situations, as in books or movies, that tend to elicit strong feelings from readers or viewers.

emotional decompensation   A violent emotional outburst, due most likely to an accumulation of incidents of anger, that finally occurs due to a minor incident. Also known in slang as "blowing one's lid" in reference to a pot on a hot stove generating enough steam to move its lid. See EMOTIONAL CHARGE.

emotional dependence   Reliance on others for support, comfort, and nurturing. See EMOTIONAL BEGGAR.

emotional deprivation   Lack of adequate warmth, affection, and interest, especially from the primary caregiver during a child's developmental years. Also known as emotional acrescentism. See MARASMUS, MATERNAL DEPRIVATION.

emotional deterioration   An emotional state observed in chronic institutionalized patients with schizophrenia, characterized by carelessness toward themselves, indifference to their surroundings, including other people, and inappropriate emotional reactions.

emotional development   A gradual increase in the capacity to experience and express the full gamut of emotions, beginning with the diffuse excitement of the infant in response to intense stimulation to expressions of rage in the form of temper tantrums a year or so later. Cortical control, imitation of others, glandular influences, home atmosphere, and conditioning play a major role in emotional development throughout life.

emotional disorder/illness   A psychological disorder characterized by maladjustive emotional reactions such as irrational or uncontrollable fears, persistent anxiety, or extreme hostility.

emotional disposition   A state in which emotional factors, distinctive feeling-tones, or affective reactions predominate.

emotional divorce   A marital relationship characterized by the spouses living in "separate worlds," with an absence of normal interaction between them even though they live together.

emotional expansiveness   A characteristic of those people who are easily moved in terms of their feelings. See EMOTIONAL DISPOSITION.

emotional expression   1. The behavioral display of emotions by such means as smiling, laughing, and gesturing. 2. The somatic changes, such as rapid heartbeat and muscular tension, that constitute an integral aspect of emotional reactions.

emotional flatness   **flat affect**

emotional flooding   Uncontrolled and uncontrollable emotional expression, such as continuous weeping, sometimes used by hysterical patients as an appeal for sympathy or help in escaping a distasteful situation.

emotional handicap   In educational psychology, a learning or behavioral disorder based on fears or anxieties (for example, a child is afraid of a schoolyard bully or is devastated because parents are contemplating divorce) that prevents children from functioning normally in a regular classroom either socially or academically.

emotional illness   Lay phrase often used euphemistically for any type of mental disorder, neurotic or psychotic. See EMOTIONAL DISORDER/ILLNESS.

emotional immaturity   1. A tendency to express emotions without restraint or in ways that are characteristic of children. 2. Common phrase for maladjustment.

emotional incest   Parental use of an offspring as a surrogate spouse emotionally or affectionally (not sexually).

emotional inferiority   See INFERIORITY FEELINGS.

emotional inoculation   The imagining (cognitive rehearsal) of unpleasant emotional experiences (for example, anger, anxiety, fear) that may increase such unpleasant states temporarily but eventually reduces them. See FLOODING, COGNITIVE REHEARSAL TECHNIQUE.

emotional insight   1. An awareness and understanding of the emotional reactions of self or others. 2. In psychotherapy, refers to the patients' comprehension of the meaning of the emotional forces, such as internal conflicts or traumatic experiences, that underlie their symptoms. Some therapists consider this form of insight a prerequisite to therapeutic change.

emotional instability   A tendency to exhibit unpredictable and rapid changes in emotions.

emotional insulation   A defense mechanism consisting of indifference and detachment in response to frustrating situations or disappointing events. The extreme of emotional insulation is found in states of complete apathy and catatonic stupor. See EMOTIONAL ANESTHESIA.

emotional intelligence   1. (D. Goleman) Social competence, the ability to deal effectively with other people that involves empathy for others, control of impulses, and conflict resolution. 2. A kind of intelligence purportedly comprised of five basic qualities: the ability to recognize one's own emotions, competency to manage these emotions, self-motivation, accurate recognition of emotions in others, and capacity to handle relationships. 3. An ability of people to identify their own and others' emotions accurately, to use their emotions to motivate themselves and others, to spur creativity, and to deal empathetically with others. Similar to H. Gardner's intrapersonal and interpersonal domains of intelligence and to E. L. Thorndike's social intelligence.

emotional leader   A person in any group who tends to maintain the morale of the group, operates to help anyone in trouble. See RED CROSS NURSE.

emotional loneliness   Feelings of isolation and depression that occur when people desire, but cannot achieve, a meaningful and intimate relationship with another.

emotionally-unstable character disorder (EUCD)   A diagnosis of a pathological condition characterized by extremes of behavior. People with this disorder may exhibit wide fluctuations in affect and behavior, such as changing rapidly from normal to aggressive and vice versa or becoming violent following apparently minor provocations.

emotionally unstable personality   Designating a personality-trait disturbance characterized by immaturity and lack of control over emotions, resulting in such reactions as frequent outbursts of anger over minor irritations, poor tolerance for frustration and stress, sulking, quarrelsomeness, and stubbornness.

emotional maturity   Having achieved a high or mature and appropriate level of emotional control and expression as opposed to childish emotional behavior.

emotional nutriment   See DIRECT ANALYSIS.

emotional pattern   A definite grouping of bodily changes of any sort occurring either simultaneously or in a fixed temporal sequence, characteristic of some reactions to strong emotions, such as the face turning white or red; inability to talk, feeling faint, wringing of hands.

emotional re-education   Training, usually in groups, using various modalities of cognitive change, including psychodrama, lecturing, reading, watching films, flooding, as well as cross discussions, etc., focused on the modification of attitudes and behavioral reactions to help people gain greater insight into their emotional conflicts, self-defeating behavior, and possibly violence. See ANGER MANAGEMENT, COUNSELING.

emotional release   The catharsis or sudden outpouring of emotions that have been pent up or suppressed.

emotional response   (R. Spitz) An emotional reaction to people or events. Research has shown that evidence of emotional responses appear in the first few weeks of life when signs of anxiety occur and the primary caregiver seeks to alleviate them by holding or caressing the child. If the child is placed in an institution, emotional response is usually curtailed and the child tends to become apathetic. See EMOTIONAL ANESTHESIA.

emotional security   The feeling of safety, confidence, and freedom from apprehension. In Karen Horney's approach, the need for emotional security is the underlying determinant of behavior, and in H. S. Sullivan's approach, emotional security is determined primarily by interpersonal relations. See SECURITY OPERATIONS.

emotional storm   A sudden, intense, uncontrolled flood of emotion, sometimes experienced by persons with explosive disorders. Lies somewhere between anger and mania in terms of strength. See INTERMITTENT EXPLOSIVE DISORDER.

emotional stress/tension   The feeling of psychological strain and uneasiness produced by facing situations of danger, threat, and loss of personal security, as well as stresses produced by internal conflicts, frustrations, loss of self-esteem, and grief.

emotional stupor   A form of affective stupor marked by depression or intense anxiety, usually accompanied by mutism.

emotional superiority   See SUPERIORITY FEELINGS.

emotional supplies   See PRIMAL DEPRESSION.

emotional support   Reassurance, encouragement, and approval received from an individual or group. A major factor in maintaining morale, found in inspirational groups (for example, Alcoholics Anonymous) as well as in solo activities, such as meditation, reading, and prayer.

emotion theories   See ACTIVATION THEORY OF EMOTION(S), CANNON-BARD THEORY (OF EMOTION), EMERGENCY THEORY OF THE EMOTIONS, JAMES-LANGE THEORY (OF EMOTION), OPPONENT-PROCESS THEORY OF EMOTION, PAPEZ'S THEORY OF EMOTIONS, THALAMIC THEORY OF EMOTION, TWO-FACTOR THEORY OF EMOTIONS, WUNDT'S PRINCIPLES OF EMOTIONAL EXPRESSION, WUNDT'S TRIDIMENSIONAL THEORY OF EMOTION.

emotiovascular   Pertaining to effects of emotions, such as shame, embarrassment, or fear, due to underlying sympathetic blood shifts noted by appearance of the skin, primarily of the face, such as loss of color when in fear or flushing of face when embarrassed. See EMOTIONAL PATTERN.

emotive imagery   (J. Wolpe) A variation of systematic desensitization used with phobic children. The child's fears are listed in order of severity, and the therapist tells one of the child's favorite stories, but centers the account on the least feared characters and events. The therapist then progresses step by step to the most fearful in further story variations.

emotive techniques   Therapy techniques that are vigorous, vivid, and dramatic.

emotive therapy   A psychotherapeutic approach based on the evocation and dilution of the patient's habitual and often self-defeating attitudes and emotional reactions. See RATIONAL PSYCHOTHERAPY.

empathic concerns   Feelings of caring and sympathy for another with whom the person identifies.

empathic understanding   Insight into the feelings, thoughts, or attitudes of persons achieved by projecting themselves into situations of others, that is, by "putting oneself into someone else's shoes." Commonly done by most counselors and psychotherapists as well as salespeople.

empathy   The objective awareness of another person's thoughts and feelings and their possible meanings. Identity of feeling and thought with another person exemplified by the statement "I know how you feel."

empathy training   1. Generally, a procedure designed to improve empathetic communications. 2. Specifically, an intervention often offered to convicted abusers to help them envision their victims' feelings, making them sensitive to the harm and pain they've caused.

empirical   1. Pertaining to observation, measurement, or experimentation, in contrast to theoretical or explanatory. 2. Based on experience, observation, measurement, or experimentation, in contrast to theory, tradition, or speculation. See DEDUCTION, EMPIRICISM, INDUCTION.

empirical classification   The process of grouping elements on objective criteria to generate a nosological categorization.

empirical-criterion keying   A method employed in selecting and scoring questions for personality inventories, in which the items are selected and weighted according to an external criterion, such as the responses of mental patients or ratings made by a large standardization sample.

empirical determinism   **psychological determinism**

empirical knowledge   Information derived from either extensive observations or replicated research.

empirical law   A principle expressing a general relationship between variables based on replicated observations and research.

empirical law of effect   Based on Edward Thorndike's early experiments, the pre-1930 conclusion that rewarded behaviors tend to re-occur and that punishment tends to stamp out behavior. In 1930, Thorndike truncated the law of effect and de-emphasized annoyers. This law has been superseded by more specific statements. See LEARNING, REINFORCEMENT.

empirically derived test   A personal inventory such as the Edwards Personal Preference Schedule developed by generating and evaluating a pool of items and then selecting those that differentiate groups of interest.

empirically keyed test   An examination in which items do not necessarily reflect what they seem to be asking. Norms are established by tabulating responses from a known criterion group. The correct answer is the one that most of the criterion group selects. See EMPIRICAL SCORING.

empirical method   The scientific method that proceeds by observation and experiment.

empirical psychology   1. The investigation of mental phenomena by observation and experiment, as contrasted with rational psychology, which proceeds by deduction. 2. (E. B. Titchener) The investigation of what the mind does, as contrasted with what it is. 3. Phrase introduced and defined by Christian Wolff, who considered empirical and rational psychology to be equivalent.

empirical-rational strategy   In social psychology, the idea that societal and institutional change can be brought about if the public receives enough convincing factual evidence. The concept holds that reason alone can motivate people to change their attitudes. See NORMATIVE-REEDUCATIVE STRATEGY, POWER-COERCIVE STRATEGY.

empirical scoring   A test based on the "correct" answers coming from criterion groups. Thus, the correct answer to the question "which of two practically-identical works of art is superior?" may be based on the replies of a majority of artists. See EMPIRICALLY KEYED TEST.

empirical self   (W. James) The equivalent of "me."

empirical test   The test of a hypothesis through experiments or observational data. See HULL'S HYPOTHETICO-DEDUCTIVE THEORY.

empirical validity   Accurate measurement or prediction of performance, as demonstrated by research. Refers to a test that has more than mere face validity.

empiricism   A doctrine positing that all knowledge comes through experience. Different versions of empiricism exist; for example, John Locke held that new-born children have no innate ideas; other philosophers assume innate ideas such as justice preexist.

empiricism vs rationalism   (R. I. Watson) A prescriptive dimension of the philosophical underpinnings of psychology, namely, emphasis on experience as the source of knowledge versus reason as the source. See OPPONENT-PAIRS DIMENSION.

empiric-risk figure   In genetic counseling, a percentage representing the risk for common disorders such as schizophrenia and depression where there is evidence of genetic factors of unknown mechanism. The figure is based upon reports of frequency of occurrence in large series of families (in addition to the approximate 3% risk of mental retardation or birth defects that every couple takes when having a child).

employee appraisal/evaluation   The judgment of employee behavior and certain related personal characteristics exhibited by their work; a judgmental process whereby a superior or consultant evaluates the job behavior of a subordinate.

employee assistance program (EAP)   A provision of some companies that provides confidential counseling or other forms of help to employees and their immediate families on issues that relate only indirectly to work performance, such as financial management, domestic discord, and substance abuse.

employee comparison technique   Any formal method of placing employees, whether they are doing equal work or different kinds of work, at the same level of compensation, based on some kind of rating scale or rank order.

employee selection   There are a wide variety of methods for selecting employees, ranging from a short interview to an extensive and expensive evaluation that might include intense interviews; examination of a person's written credentials and letters of recommendations (checking them by telephone when seriously considering hiring) with permission, of course; physical examinations; tests to evaluate an applicant's intelligence, personality; special evaluations by experts in a specialized field; as well as job tests. As a general rule, the simpler jobs, such as sorting tasks, call for little evaluation, but jobs in scientific fields, upper management, etc., call for more intense evaluations.

employment discrimination   Prejudicial treatment of people seeking work, based on irrelevant factors.

employment interview   A meeting with a job seeker and a prospective employer or an agent such as a personnel director, in which the "employer" (a) imparts information and answers questions about the company, (b) describes jobs in which the applicant shows an interest and appears qualified, and (c) obtains information about the applicant to make a judgment of that person's suitability for a particular job or jobs. Also known as job interview.

employment psychology   The study and application of psychological principles and techniques used in selecting from applicants those who show the greatest probability of success. Mistakes can happen by hiring people who are overqualified and underqualified or those who are just qualified who have personality or behavioral problems, such as any kind of addiction.

employment test   A quiz or task administered to job applicants, either before or after their interviews, that are of two major types: those used to try to predict successful employment (aptitude tests) and those used to determine existing skills or capabilities (performance tests). An example of the first type would test for whether a person has a good vocabulary, which might serve as an indicator of learning a difficult task; an example of the second type would be a typing test.

empowerment   The granting of authority to individuals. See AUTONOMY.

emptiness fear   See KENOPHOBIA.

empty-chair technique   A Gestalt-therapy "exercise" in which a person conducts an emotional dialogue with some aspect of self or a significant person, such as a parent, who is imagined to sit in an empty chair; the person then exchanges chairs and "becomes" that aspect or person. See HOT-SEAT TECHNIQUE.

empty nest (phase)   The transitional period of parenting when the last child leaves the parents' home. This usually generates an emotional vacuum for the parents.

empty organism (approach)   The pure stimulus-response approach in psychology (S-R), which, it is charged, has neglected conscious thought and feelings and the internal drives and activities of the organism. This approach has since been replaced by the stimulus-organism-response (S-O-R) view with the O representing the organism. See STIMULUS-ORGANISM-RESPONSE.

empty organism psychology   Having knowledge of external behavior without having an understanding of internal processes. Refers to an observation that organisms respond predictably to various stimuli, without knowing various constructs such as intelligence, feeling, or desires. They know that stimulus A leads to response Z without knowing about possible intervening steps from B to Y. See S-O-R PSYCHOLOGY.

empty set   A set with no elements; a null set.

empyreumatic   One of Zwaardemaker's classifications of odors, of which coffee, tar, and tobacco smoke are typical examples. Also known as burned, burnt, smoky.

EMR   See   EDUCABLE-MENTALLY-RETARDED (CHILD).

emulation   1. Imitative rivalry. 2. Ambition to excel in achievement.

enabler   1. A member of the community who assists in the deinstitutionalization of mental patients by helping them adjust to normal daily-living routines. 2. The role frequently assumed by significant others and, at times, closely allied family and friends of substance abusers, characterized by covert support of (enabling) the substance-abusing behavior.

enaction   Preliminary plans to guide actual performance.

enactive mode   (J. Bruner) The way a child first comes to know the environment through physical interactions, for example crawling. It is learning through doing; the iconic mode is knowing through mental images; the symbolic mode is knowing through language and logic. See ICONIC MODE, SYMBOLIC MODE.

enactive representation   (J. Bruner) The forming of meaning by young children, using a kind of muscle memory based on kinesthetic sensations. See ICONIC CONTENT, SYMBOLIC MODE.

enactive stage   (J. Bruner) A stage of cognitive development from birth to about age two during which the infant gains control over the environment and when physical actions are the main ingredient of the child's understanding of the world. See MODES OF LEARNING.

enactment   Showing (rather than verbalizing) an important life event. See PSYCHODRAMA.

enantiobiosis   A mutually antagonistic relationship between organisms, the opposite of symbiosis.

enantiodromia   1. Heraclitus' conception that all things eventually turn into their opposites. 2. (G. Hegel) A view of the importance of conflicts between opposites leading to the emergence of new ideas. 3. (C. G. Jung) Refers to the "necessary opposition" that governs psychic life, as in the interplay between conscious and unconscious, introversive and extroversive tendencies, or ego and shadow. 4. In analytical psychology, the eventual emergence of the unconscious opposite of some conscious psychic tendency.

encapsulated delusion   A delusional system sealed off from the rest of life so that it does not have any significant effect on everyday behavior, as in a person claiming to receive advice from somewhere/nowhere but living an otherwise normal life.

encapsulated end organ   The terminal portion of a sensory nerve fiber, usually located in peripheral tissue such as the skin, and enclosed in a membranous sheath.

encapsulation In psychiatry, a tendency of some people with serious mental disorders (for example, patients with schizophrenia) to keep their delusions separated from the routine of the real world. See ENCAPSULATED DELUSION.

encéphale isolé (isolated brain—French) (F. Bremer) A midbrain that has been transected so that the organism is alive but permanently in an unconscious or sleep state. The condition is sometimes produced experimentally in laboratory animals. See SPINAL ANIMAL.

encephalitis An inflammation of the brain caused by agents, including viruses and heavy metals, as in lead encephalitis. Symptoms may be mild, with influenza-like characteristics, or very serious, with fever, delirium, convulsions, coma, and death. See ECONOMO'S DISEASE, HYPERSOMNIA.

encephalitis lethargica Inflammation of the brain caused by infection with *trypanosoma gambiense* through the bite of the tse-tse fly. Residual psychological and physical symptoms are often noted. Also known as African sleeping sickness, Economo's disease, epidemic encephalitis, human trypanosomiasis, hypersomnic encephalitis, sleeping sickness.

encephalization Corticalization or transfer of mental functions from phylogenetically primitive brain areas to cerebral centers as steps in the evolution of the mind.

encephalography The examination of the brain by X-ray, etc., and possibly mapping of its various areas.

encephalomyelitis Encephalitis (inflammation of the brain) that also includes the spinal cord. Usually caused by a virus.

encephalon The brain.

encephalopathy A disease of the brain. See BINSWANGER'S ENCEPHALOPATHY, HYPERKINETIC ENCEPHALOPATHY, LEAD ENCEPHALOPATHY, MERCURY ENCEPHALOPATHY, SCHISTOSOMIASIS, TRAUMATIC ENCEPHALOPATHY.

encephalopsy The association of words, numbers, or both, with particular colors. Some children may visualize the number 8 as green, others as blue, etc. See SHORT-TERM MEMORY, SYNESTHESIA.

encode To transform information from one form to another so that it is available for storage and retrieval.

encoded message A communication that has two simultaneous meanings, one direct and conscious and the other disguised and hidden. See ENCRYPTION.

encoding 1. The conversion of a sensory input into a form capable of being processed and deposited in memory. 2. In communication, conversion of data into codes or signals capable of being conveyed by a communication channel into meaningful categories, units, or terms (for example, words changed to dots and dashes in Morse code, and then again being re-coded into words).

encoding specificity principle 1. (E. Tulving) In learning theory, a theory that the recollection of an event depends on an interaction between the properties of the encoded event and those of the retrieval information. 2. A theory that a person can more easily recognize something when placed in a familiar context, as in being unable to recall the name of an acquaintance when seen in an unfamiliar situation, although being able to easily recall the name in the usual place.

encoding strategy A tactic for memorization such as transmuting the names of people into pictures. See MNENOMICS.

encopresis Persistent fecal soiling of self by children over three years of age. Psychologically, it may be the expression of a child consciously or unconsciously rebelling against a powerful restrictive parent. Also known as functional encopresis.

encounter In psychotherapy, a stressful interaction of a client and a therapist or in group therapy between group members, sometimes leading to adaptive cognitions and new insights.

encounter exercises Any of a wide variety of planned procedures used in growth groups for giving individuals unusual experiences of various kinds. See BLIND WALK.

encounter group A group designed to provide an interactive experience between members featuring sometimes brutal honesty, complete self-disclosure, and strong emotional expression. A main intention is to shed all inhibitions with the expectation that the experience will have positive lasting effects. Such groups tend to be noisy and emotional, and often call for physical touching. See GROUP THERAPY, INTENSIVE GROUP EXPERIENCE, SENSITIVITY TRAINING.

encounter movement A trend toward the formation of small groups in which various techniques, such as confrontation, games, "stroking," and reenactment, are used to stimulate awareness, personality growth, and productive interactions.

encouragement therapy (L. Losoncy) A system of psychotherapy that takes the position that all who come for psychotherapy are discouraged, and therapy depends on encouraging clients to achieve needed reorganization. See PROVOCATIVE THERAPY for a system that apparently is the opposite in procedure but works toward the same goal.

encryption The generation of a coded message, usually by some prearranged method. Also known as encoding.

enculturation 1. The processes that infants begin to go through wherein they learn the rules of the society they are entering. 2. Usually a period of stress for immigrants who enter a new society where some of their culture's beliefs and folkways are not accepted, and where new and often unacceptable behaviors are expected.

end brain telencephalon

end brush/plate The finely branched terminal of an axon; the area where excitation is transferred from nerve to muscle cells. Also known as telodendron.

end button See SYNAPTIC KNOB.

endemic Prevalent in or peculiar to a specific region, nation, or people. Term denotes usually a disease, but is also applied to customs or folkways. See EPIDEMIC, PANDEMIC.

endergonic Any physical or chemical process that absorbs energy. See EXERGONIC.

end feet Axon terminals.

endocathection (H. A. Murray) Inward focusing of psychic energy and withdrawal from external pursuits. See EXOCATHECTION.

endocept   In the cognitive-volitional school, a nonrepresentational, preverbal mental construct occurring between the fantasy stage of inner reality toward the end of the first year of life, and later stages when mental constructs are representational and lead to action. Endocepts are feeling states, forerunners of esthetic and empathic states. See OCEANIC FEELING.

endocratic power   In the cognitive-volitional school, transformation of the commands of parents and other authorities into an inner power over personal actions and thoughts. If this introjection is excessive (endocratic surplus), it may lead to blind obedience and acceptance of tyranny.

endocrine gland   A gland that secretes a hormone substance directly, or without a duct, into the bloodstream, such as the pituitary or thyroid. Also known as ductless gland.

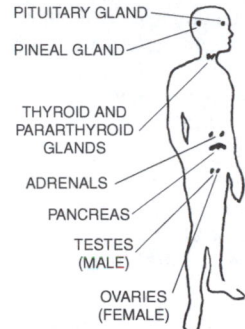

PITUITARY GLAND

PINEAL GLAND

THYROID AND PARARTHYROID GLANDS

ADRENALS

PANCREAS

TESTES (MALE)

OVARIES (FEMALE)

endocrine glands   Location of some endocrine glands in the human male and female.

endocrine system   The whole set of ductless glands that secrete and distribute hormones through the bloodstream.

endocrinology   The branch of science dealing with morphology, physiology, chemistry, and pathology of the endocrine glands.

endoderm   (K. E. von Baer, R. Remak) The embryo's innermost layer of cells from which the gastrointestinal tract, liver, lungs, and other vital organs, and some glands develop. The other two layers are the ectoderm and mesoderm. See EMBRYONIC PERIOD.

end-of-line question   A query by the interviewer at the end of an interview or a line of questions, for instance, "Is there something you'd like to add, change, or delete?"

endogamy   1. The practice of limiting marriage to members of a kinship, caste, or religious, local (regional), or social group. 2. The prohibition of marrying outside of a social group common to some aboriginal groups. Compare EXOGAMY. See MARRIAGE.

endogenesis   Originating from within. See AUTOCHTHONOUS.

endogenetic factors   Causal factors that arise within the organism, including hereditary factors that give rise to some cases of mental retardation, constitutional factors that many investigators assume to be at the root of schizophrenia and manic-depressive (bipolar) disorders, and psychological factors such as intrapsychic conflicts. Also known as endogenic factors, endogenous factors.

endogenetic   Pertaining to an event or effect that originates within the organism, such as genetically determined mental retardation. Smiles seen during the sleep of newborns are considered endogenous because they are caused by internal physiological factors. Also known as endogenic, endogenous. See AUTOCHTHONOUS, EXOGENOUS.

endogenic   See ENDOGENETIC, ENDOGENOUS.

endogenous   Being generated in the body, as differentiated from exogenous. May refer not only to certain chemical substances, like estrogen, but even some disorders are viewed as not being triggered by external stresses so much as internal bodily rhythms or as yet unknown processes. Certain depressions, manic episodes, and psychotic outbreaks are considered endogenous, whereas others are more clearly evoked by environmental events. See ENDORPHIN.

endogenous depression   Somatogenic rather than a psychogenic depression based on the idea that the condition was actually present in strong potentiality in the original zygote or during fetal development. Determining the truth of this concept is difficult because of the environmental effects experienced by every individual. Compare REACTIVE DEPRESSION.

endogenous drive   A compelling urge that comes from an internal factor. Compare EXOGENOUS DRIVE.

endogenous factor   Any substance, object, or determiner originating from within or caused by heredity.

endogenous mental retardation   Mental impairment attributed to developmental defects, especially in the central nervous system. Compare EXOGENOUS MENTAL RETARDATION.

endogenous rhythm   See BIOLOGICAL RHYTHM.

endogenous stimulation   Stimulation that originates within the organism, as in arousal during rapid-eye-movement (REM) sleep. See AUTOCHTHONOUS, EXOGENOUS STIMULATION.

endolymph   A fluid contained in the membranous labyrinth of the inner ear that helps translate sound vibrations transmitted through the middle ear into the nerve impulses carried to the sense of hearing by the auditory, or acoustic, nerve.

endolymphatic potential   One of several electric potentials measured by electrodes inserted into the cochlear region of the ear.

endometrial cycle   The pattern of proliferation and loss of endometrial tissue during the female reproductive cycle.

endometrium   The layer of cells lining the uterus. The endometrium varies in thickness during the menstrual cycle, reaching a peak of cellular proliferation approximately one week after ovulation, sloughing off as menstrual flow two weeks after ovulation if the ovum is not fertilized. See ENDOMETRIAL CYCLE.

endomorphic (body) type   (W. H. Sheldon) A constitutional type, or somatotype, characterized by a soft, round physique, which William Sheldon found to be highly correlated with a viscerotonic temperament (tendencies toward love of comfort, love of food, relaxation, and sociability). Such a person is referred to as an endomorph. Also known as endomorphy. See SHELDON'S CONSTITUTIONAL TYPES, SOMATOTYPE, VISCEROTONIA.

endomusia   The implicit or silent reproduction of a song.

endomysium   A fine layer of connective tissue that wraps and separates voluntary muscle fibre.

endophasia   The implicit or silent reproduction of a word or of phrases and sentences.

endoplasm   The central portion of a cell. Distinguished from ectoplasm, which is located near the peripheral portion of the cell.

endoplasmic reticulum (ER)   A network of tubular and vesicular structures extending from the nucleus to the outer membrane of a typical body cell. Functions include secretion of proteins and lipids, release of glucose, and transport of substances. Exists in different forms in different types of cells.

endopsychic   Pertaining to unconscious material or intrapsychic processes. Compare EXOPSYCHIC.

endopsychic perception   Insight or perception arising from within the mind, particularly from unconscious sources.

endopsychic structure   The internal structure of the mind. There have been many such topographies of the psyche by different theorists, starting with Hippocrates' humoral theory going to the structuralists' concept of cognition, affection, and conation. Later examples include conscious, preconscious, and unconscious; the id, ego, and superego; the transactional theory of parent, child, adult.

endoradiosonde   A sounding line or miniature radio transmitter capsule implanted or ingested into an organism for studying internal reactions. In physiological psychology, this biotelemetric device is important for obtaining information about the internal behavior of animals. Named by R. Stuart Mackay in 1968.

end organ   The fine branching of fibrils at the end of the axon of a neuron. See ENCAPSULATED END ORGAN.

endorphins   1. Opiate-like substances released by the brain that prevent pain signals from being perceived. 2. A short chain of amino acids that has the chemical structure of a portion of a pituitary-gland hormone. Several kinds of endorphins are known, each of which has a neurological effect. Alpha-endorphin acts as a mild analgesic and tranquilizer, beta-endorphin causes aggressive behavior, and gamma-endorphin causes a catatonia-like state. The effects are blocked by morphine-antagonist drugs, indicating they are a natural form of analgesic. The term "endorphin" is a portmanteau word for "endogenous morphine-like substance." See ACUPUNCTURE, ENKEPHALIN.

endosomatic currents   Electric currents or potentials set up within a living organism.

endotherm   Refers to a living organism that can maintain a constant body temperature regardless of external temperature, such as a mammal, as opposed to a reptile. See HOMEOTHERM.

endowment   A natural capacity for development and activity, both mental and physical, so far as determined by heredity. See CONSTITUTION.

end path   The final neuron (or nerve) of a reflex path.

end plate   A specialized motor-nerve fiber terminal that forms a junction with a muscle cell. See END BRUSH.

end-plate potential (EPP)   The firing of muscle fibers by the depolarization of the end plate of a neuron via release of acetylcholine.

end pleasure   The pleasurable release of tension during an orgasm.

end spurt   The increased productivity or gain in performance frequently noted near the end of a task, series of trials, or day's work. Also commonly observed in athletic endeavors, for example, in long-distance running. Compare INITIAL SPURT.

end state   (M. S. Mahler) The goal or culmination of progressive stages of development. Once a given end state is defined, interest then centers on precise description of the stages that lead to it.

endurance   1. Generally, the capacity to bear pain or hardship or to put forth effort especially in the face of difficulties. 2. In physiology, the time limit of a person's ability to maintain either a specific isometric force or a specific amount of power in concentric or eccentric muscle contracting.

enelicomorphism   The attribution of adult traits or motives to children; the interpretation of children's behavior in terms appropriate to adults. Also known as adultomorphism or humuncularism.

enema addiction   The medically unnecessary use of enemas that may develop through the repeated use of laxatives, and possibly occurs most frequently among binge-purge bulimics and persons with obsessive-compulsive personalities who feel "unclean." See KLISMAPHILIA, LAXATIVE ADDICTION.

energization theory   A point of view that the strength of an incentive's valence varies with the level of energy mobilized to obtain or avoid the incentive; the higher the energization, the greater the subjective desirability of a positive outcome and the subjective awareness of a negative outcome.

energizer   Rare term for an antidepressant drug which has the effect of restoring or producing a flow of psychic energy in a patient. See PSYCHOTROPIC DRUG.

energy   1. (E) The capacity for doing work. Measured in joules. 2. The degree of activity displayed in behavior.

energy flow systems   The Asian concept of electro-magnetic vital energy such as *chi, ki,* and *prana* thought to run along meridian patterns.

enervation   1. Loss of energy. 2. Literally, the removal of a nerve. 3. Figuratively, a feeling of weakness.

engendering psychology   (F. L. Denmark) Cultivating a psychology that is sensitive to issues of gender and diversity.

engineering anthropometry   The application of knowledge of body structures and functions in equipment design.

engineering model   A theory that views living organisms, including humans, as machines. See MEDICAL MODEL.

engineering psychologist   A psychologist who specializes in the design of the equipment and environment of the workplace so that humans can function more effectively at their tasks. See HUMAN-FACTORS ENGINEER.

engineering psychology A field of psychology concerned with research, development, application, and evaluation of psychological principles relating human behavior to the characteristics, design, and use of the environments and systems within which humans work and live. The design of space capsules for astronauts is a responsibility of engineering psychologists. See EQUIPMENT DESIGN, HUMAN ENGINEERING, HUMAN FACTORS, HUMAN-FACTORS ENGINEERING, SAFETY PSYCHOLOGY.

engram 1. A hypothetical physical trace of pathways in the nervous system made by certain stimuli or new experiences information, based on the assumption that retention and recall processes require an electrical, chemical, or other unit of information storage in the brain or central nervous system. Also known as memory trace, mneme, mnemonic trace. 2. (J. M. Nielsen) A previously existing set of cells, axons, and dendrites used through practice to form a kind of "pathway," over which impulses can travel with greater ease than over those pathways not practiced upon; sometimes called a neurogram.

engraphia 1. The formation of records of experience, or engrams. 2. The property of organisms whereby they may become impressed with engrams.

engrossment A state of being absorbed or preoccupied.

engulfment (R. Laing) A type of anxiety in which a person feels totally helpless, at the mercy of others.

enissophobia Fear of criticism.

enkephalin An endorphin that serves as a powerful painkiller. Any of several peptide molecules found in the brain that produce a narcoticlike analgesic effect. Purportedly, enkephalins interact with a brain peptide, substance P, to switch on and off neurons involved in pain control. See ENDORPHIN.

Enlightenment A period of history of the 1700s that ushered in the scientific revolution as well as humanism. Rationality overthrew superstition. Psychology as a science, rather than pure philosophy, emerged after this historical period. Also known as The Enlightenment and The Age of Reason.

enmeshed family Describing a family in which the individual members are overly involved in each other's lives, making individual autonomy impossible.

ennui An experience characterized by an unpleasant hedonic tone, induced by prolongation of an uninteresting situation. Similar to being bored.

enosimania The obsessive belief of having committed an unpardonable offense.

enosiophobia Morbid fear of having committed an unpardonable sin. See HAMARTOPHOBIA, PECCATIPHOBIA.

enriched environment See ENVIRONMENTAL ENRICHMENT.

enriched perception Enhancement of a perception as influenced by any of a variety of circumstances or conditions, such as extreme needs.

enrichment See ENVIRONMENTAL ENRICHMENT, JOB ENRICHMENT, SENSORY ENRICHMENT.

enrichment program 1. The provision of additional experiences rather than only concentration on academic subjects (topics). Cultural activities, programs in art and music, attending public events are often used in enrichment programs. 2. An educational program designed to develop the potential and forestall the boredom of bright or gifted children by providing them with an expanded curriculum. An enrichment program may be individually applied to students in regular classes or applied to an entire class of gifted students.

enrichment theory A point of view that during early development, the more stimuli that an infant experiences, the more likely the child is to develop full potentialities.

entelechy 1. Activity of self-realization (Aristotle). 2. The autonomous, nonmechanical, natural activity essential for the maintenance of life. 3. The thought that physical forms, such as human bodies, are controlled by a hypothetical immaterial entity. See VITALISM.

enteroceptor See INTEROCEPTOR.

Enthorn maze A paper-and-pencil maze which requires that the participant trace a path along a pattern made of dotted lines that form a mosaic of diamond shapes. Considered valuable in detecting signs of brain damage.

entitativity (D. T. Campbell) In group dynamics, the quality of being an entity, that is, perceived groupness.

entitlement programs Governmental programs that provide financial assistance benefits to persons who are mentally or physically challenged, senior citizens, or persons below the poverty level. For example, pensions are given to governmental retirees and people entitled to social security insurance. Federal entitlement programs are administered through Medicare, Medicaid, Social Security disability insurance, and similar sources.

entity A portion of reality that maintains its identity.

entomology The branch of biology that studies insects.

entomophobia Morbid fear of insects. Sometimes known as acarophobia. See PARASITOPHOBIA.

entoperipheral feelings Any sensory experience whose source of stimulation is localized within the body.

entoptic Occurring within the eye.

entoptic phenomena Visual experiences due to stimuli or conditions within the eye itself. See FLOATING BODIES.

entrainment 1. Reaction to a person in a manner similar to theirs, for example, infants stick out their own tongues in response to parents doing the same thing. See MIMICRY. 2. Synchronous movements of two or more people as when walking in step. A couple dancing side by side would be an example of synchronous entrainment.

entrance requirements The establishment of standards for permitting people to apply for various schools, jobs, etc., often based on what is considered to be reasonable (for example, a minimum visual requirement to get a license to drive a car). May change from year to year and vary between jurisdictions.

entropy   (R. J. Clausius) 1. In thermodynamics, the amount of energy that cannot be converted into work; the tendency of the energy in the universe to reach a state of inertia. 2. In psychology, inability to convert psychic energy into active adjustment to reality, for example, the tendency of some older persons to "turn inward" and become rigid and stodgy. 3. In information theory, a measure of the number of possible outcomes a given event might have. 4. Eventual disintegration and dissolution of a living system such as a society. See EROSION.

entry behavior   See READINESS.

enumeration   The counting of items whether or not they are logically related. The classification a number of items by number in some sort of logical order. See RANK ORDER.

enuresis   Involuntary urination; usually refers to "nocturnal" enuresis, nighttime bed-wetting; occasionally patients have "diurnal" or daytime wetting their pants. See FUNCTIONAL ENURESIS, NOCTURNAL ENURESIS.

environment (E)   The sum total of all external phenomena that impinge on organisms. For humans, the environment includes the family and all other people, books and other objects made by other humans, physical geographical elements, natural conditions such as storms, invisible items such as germs and viruses, and social, cultural, legal conditions. Types of environment include: BARRIER-FREE, BEHAVIORAL, CARPENTERED, FREE-ACCESS, IMPOVERISHED, INTERNAL, NEUTRAL, PERMISSIVE, PRIMARY, PSYCHOLOGICAL, RURAL, SECONDARY, SIMULATED, SOCIAL, TASK. See CHANGE OF ENVIRONMENT, CONSTANCY OF INTERNAL ENVIRONMENT, ECOLOGY, SURROUND.

environmental approach   A therapeutic approach directed toward reducing external pressures, such as employment or financial problems, that contribute to emotional conflicts (for example, enrolling a child in a different school to meet the special child's needs). See ENVIRONMENTAL MANIPULATION.

environmental assessment   The evaluation of the environment on the theory that disordered functioning is rooted to some degree in the social system rather than solely in individuals. Examples of assessment tools: the Classroom Environment Scale (measuring teacher support and teacher control) and in hospitals, the Ward Atmosphere Scale (measuring such factors as staff support, patient autonomy, and patient involvement).

environmental deprivation   An absence of conditions that stimulate personality growth and development, such as educational, recreational, and social opportunities. Usually associated with social isolation, poverty, and slums, and may be so severe that it causes pseudoretardation. See CANAL BOAT CHILDREN.

environmental design   The creative planning of living and working areas to enhance their habitability. Environmental design also may be applied to recreational areas. Habitability factors range from simple shelter needs to complex and sophisticated environmental esthetics and conformance factors, such as selection of paint colors or specific wavelengths of illumination.

environmental determinism   A doctrine positing that human thinking and acting is decided by the surround, that is to say, the environment they grew up in. A refutation of the theory of instincts and biological givens, or it may be considered an adjunction to innate factors.

environmental education   The study of the physical environment in its relation to natural resources, energy, economics, social organization, and basic ecology.

environmental enrichment   Denoting an environment enriched by social contacts, play materials, and stimulating activities. Such environments have been shown to enhance normal emotional, cerebral, sexual, and activity development in both animals and children.

environmental esthetics   A factor contributing to the quality of the environment, including visual attractiveness of the landscape, reduction of noise, rerouting of traffic, diminution of air pollution, and proper maintenance of the environment.

environmental factors   Elements in the surround that affect the organism from without and influence its structure or its behavior. See INTERNAL FACTORS.

environmental field   In Gestalt psychology, the overall context in which an object, an organism, or the ego is embedded.

environmental hazards   External physical factors that pose some danger for an organism or community. See EROSION.

environmentalist   In psychology, a person who assumes that behavior is largely modifiable by changes in outward circumstances, in contrast to a hereditarian, who emphasizes the role of genetic inheritance in determining ability, intelligence, and personality. See EUGENICS, EUTHENICS, NATURE-NURTURE CONTROVERSY, SOFT DETERMINISM.

environmental-load theory   A point of view that humans have a limited ability to handle environmental-stress factors. The capacity is determined by the amount of information inputs that can be processed by the central nervous system. When the environmental load exceeds the person's capacity for processing, the central nervous system reacts by ignoring some inputs. See INFORMATION OVERLOAD.

environmental manipulation   A method of improving the well-being of mental patients by changing their living conditions, as by placing a child in a foster home when the child's family situation is intolerable, or transferring an adult patient to an adult home or halfway house. See ENVIRONMENTAL APPROACH, ENVIRONMENTAL EDUCATION, ENVIRONMENTAL-CENTERED SERVICES.

environmental mold trait   (R. B. Cattell) A personality factor found in individuals that is clearly due to the impress of a cultural institution.

environmental press   (H. A. Murray) An external situation or circumstance ("press") that arouses a need, for example, a person cornered by a snake feels the need to escape; a child whose sibling has just been born needs to adjust to the newcomer.

environmental psychology   A branch of psychology that emphasizes the effects of external influences on overt and covert behavior. Also known as ecological psychology.

environmental stress   A condition of tension and strain provoked by external situations that puts special burdens on a person's adaptive mechanisms, such as being in a Prisoner of War camp. See EROSION.

environmental-stress theory   A point of view that autonomic and cognitive factors combine to form a person's appraisal of environmental stress factors as threatening or nonthreatening; for example, a native Alaskan and a Bedouin would have similar autonomic body responses to a blizzard or a heat wave, but their perception and interpretation as well as their experience in the environmental situations would result in different adaptive behaviors. See ENVIRONMENTAL STRESS.

environmental therapy   Organization of the patient's entire surroundings, especially in a mental hospital, as a means of promoting recovery. See MILIEU THERAPY, THERAPEUTIC COMMUNITY.

environment-centered services   Efforts made to maximize the mental and physical health of people through improving physical environments by reducing noise, toxicity, or air pollution in the working and living environments. See PATIENT-CENTERED SERVICES.

enzygotic twins   Monozygotic twins. Twins resulting from a single fertilized ovum. Commonly known as identical twins.

enzyme genes   Hereditary units that affect enzyme systems. An enzyme deficiency caused by a genetic defect often results in mental retardation.

enzymes   Catalytic agents found in living organisms promoting chemical reactions. They cause chemical activity in other substances without becoming a part of the end product. Enzymes are, with a few exceptions, identified by their role in physiology, such as acetyl-cholinesterase, which splits the acetylcholine molecule as soon as it has completed a neurotransmitter task. Term was coined by German physiologist Wilhelm Kühne (1837–1900) to replace the word "ferment."

Eoanthropus   The alleged hominid known as the Piltdown or Sussex man. Literally: "dawn man."

EOG   See ELECTROOCULOGRAM, ELECTROOCULO-GRAPH.

eonism   (H. Ellis) Assuming the dress and the manners of the other gender. Named for a French transvestite, Chevalier d'Eon (1728–1810). See BERDACHE, CROSS-DRESSING, TRANSVESTISM.

eosophobia   Morbid fear of dawn and sunrise.

EP   evoked potential

EPAM   elementary perceiver and memorizer

epena   Hallucinogenic snuff prepared from a red resinous bark of *Virola* trees that grow in South America. Also known as *nyakwana, parica, yakee*. See HAL-LUCINOGENS, PSYCHEDELICS.

ephebophilia   Being sexually attracted to or aroused by a postpubertal or adolescent partner. See PE-DOPHILIA.

ephedrine   The plant of the genus *Ephedra*, a sympathomimetic agent that acts similarly to epinephrine. A chemical found in over-the-counter drugs for asthma, weight loss, with sympathicomimetic or amphetamine-like qualities. See HERBAL ECSTASY, PSYCHOSTIMU-LANTS.

ephialtes   Upsetting dreams or "nightmares" during the day.

EPI   1. See EXTRAPYRAMIDAL INVOLVEMENT. 2. Eysenck's Personality Inventory. 3. See EPINEPHRIN.

epicritic sensation   (H. Head) A cutaneous sensation, such as pressure or temperature, which an organism detects at a extremely low threshold of sensitivity. Henry Head held that "lower animals" were less sensitive than humans to cutaneous stimuli. See PROTOPATHIC SYSTEM.

epicritic sensibility   (H. Head) A system of cutaneous sensibility by which faint pressure, cool, and warm stimulations are appreciated, finely discriminated, and localized. Also known as gnostic function.

epicritic system   One of the two subsystems (the other is the protopathic system) of the sensory-nerve network. The epicritic system has receptors sensitive to joint movement, light touch, and deep pressure. Impulses from the receptors feed into the somatosensory cortex of the brain.

epideictic behavior   Phrase used by V. C. Wynne-Edwards to refer to collective displays, especially in birds, and by others for a lack of reproductive displays in mammals presumably to control population.

epidemic   1. A disease not usually found in a population and introduced from outside, attacking many people in a community simultaneously. 2. A new folkway, such as a fad, affecting many people in a community simultaneously. See DANCE EPIDEMIC, ENDEMIC, PANDEMIC.

epidemic catalepsy   A condition in which catalepsy occurs in a number of people at the same time as a result of identification or imitation. See MASS HYSTERIA.

epidemic chorea   See CHOREOMANIA.

epidemic hysteria   Mass hysteria.

epidemiology   The study of patterns of occurrence of disease and disorders, especially pertaining to causation. Epidemiology is concerned with the incidence of various pathological conditions and their distribution or other relationship to such factors as heredity, environment, nutrition, or age at onset. Epidemiologists are detectives seeking to find clues to determine causes. See RELATIVE RISK IN EPIDEMIOLOGY.

epidermis   The outer or epithelial layer of the vertebrate skin.

epigamic   Tending to attract the other sex.

epigastric reflex   Drawing in of the abdominal wall, elicited by stroking the skin from a nipple downward.

epigenesis   A theory that new characteristics not determined by the original fertilized egg (zygote) can emerge in the process of embryonic development, as in the concept that a woman will favorably affect her unborn child intellectually if she listens to classical music during her pregnancy. See EPIGENETIC THEORY.

epigenetic theory   A point of view that mind and consciousness developed unpredictably from living matter and in the course of evolution have reached a high level of complexity. Also known as emergence.

epilepsy (Hippocrates) Term for a group of disorders associated with disturbances in the electrical discharges of brain cells, characterized by transient, recurrent episodes of clouding or loss of consciousness, often accompanied by convulsive seizures or automatic behavior. Many forms and several classifications have been proposed. Also known as convulsive seizures, cerebral dysrhythmia, falling disease/sickness, seizure disorder, the royal disease, Saint Valentine's disease. Types of epilepsy include: ABDOMINAL, AKINETIC, ALCOHOLIC, AUTONOMIC, CENTRENCEPHALIC, CRYPTOGENIC, DIGESTIVE, FOCAL, HALLUCINATORY, HYSTERO-, IDIOPATHIC, JACKSONIAN, MAJOR, MASKED, MINOR, MUSICOGENIC, MYOCLONIC, MYOCLONUS, PHOTOGENIC, POSTTRAUMATIC, PRECURSIVE, PSEUDO-, PSYCHOMOTOR, PYKNO-, REACTIVE, READING, REFLEX, RESIDUAL, RETROPULSIVE, SENSORY, SHORTSTARE, SLEEP, SUBICTAL, SYMPTOMATIC, TEMPORAL-LOBE, TONIC, VISCERAL. Also see AKINETIC SEIZURE, ANTIEPILEPTICS, AUTONOMIC SEIZURE, CATAPLEXY, DROMOLEPSY, EPILEPSIA CURSIVA, FUROR, GRAND MAL, LAUGHTER, NARCOLEPSY, ORTHOSTATIC EPILEPTOID, PETIT MAL, PYKNOLEPSY, RUM FITS, SACRED DISEASE, STATUS EPILEPTICUS.

epileptic absence A type of *petit mal* episode in which the patient experiences a brief lapse of mental functions with occasional twitching of the face and has retrograde amnesia for the event.

epileptic aura Various experiences, felt as the initial stage of an epileptic episode, typically recurring as warning according to the individual case (such as gastric aura, visual aura). See MIGRAINE AURA.

epileptic character/personality A personality pattern observed in a minority of individuals with epilepsy, possibly due to a reaction to the frustrations and anxieties this disease engenders rather than to constitutional tendencies. These individuals are described as irritable, stubborn, egocentric, uncooperative, and aggressive.

epileptic clouded states A condition in which psychotic symptoms, such as hallucinations and bewilderment, occur before or after a convulsive episode.

epileptic cry A momentary cry produced by sudden contraction of the chest and laryngeal muscles during the tonic phase of a *grand mal* seizure. Also known as initial cry.

epileptic dementia A pathological mental state as a result of the insults to the body of repeated and long-lasting epileptic episodes, the succumbing of body and mind into complete deterioration. See EPILEPTIC DETERIORATION.

epileptic deterioration A progressive mental deterioration occurring in no more than 5% of patients with epilepsy, especially those who have had seizures all their lives. Possibly due to nerve-cell degeneration caused by circulatory disturbances during the episodes.

epileptic equivalent A disorder that resembles epilepsy with similar behavioral patterns resulting in exhaustion and sleep.

epileptic focus See EPILEPTOGENIC FOCI.

epileptic furor An accompaniment of epileptic fits, consisting of acts of blind, often brutal violence, for which the patient has no memory. See FUROR.

epileptic stupor A period of near unconsciousness or insensibility following epileptic convulsions.

epileptiform seizures An epileptic-like convulsion due to specific causes such as hysteria, brain injury, or disease. See HYSTERICAL CONVULSIONS.

epileptogenic 1. Causing epilepsy. 2. Circumstances that lead to epileptic seizures.

epileptogenic foci Sites within the brain that are the sources of abnormal electrical discharges associated with epileptic seizures, for example, *petit mal* seizures are associated with a focus in the thalamus, whereas psychomotor-epilepsy behavior is accompanied by an abnormal focus in the temporal lobe. Hallucinatory seizures are related to foci in the visual or auditory cortex.

epileptogenic lesion An area of tissue damage in the brain that results in epileptic seizures.

epileptoid 1. Resembling epilepsy. 2. Denoting various conditions displaying convulsions, especially those coming from functional rather than physiological causes. Also known as epileptiform.

epileptoidism In persons without epilepsy, traits similar to those in some patients with epilepsy: stubborn, aggressive, self-centered. Also known as epileptoid personality. See EPILEPTIC CHARACTER/PERSONALITY.

epimeletic behavior (J. P. Scott) Care-giving.

epinephrine (EPI) (J. Takamine, T. B. Aldrich) A catecholamine hormone secreted by the medullary portion of the adrenal gland. Secreted in large amounts when an individual is stimulated by fear, anger, or a similar stressful situation. Epinephrine is the primary stimulant of both alpha and beta receptors of the adrenergic nerves. It increases the heart rate and force of heart contractions, relaxes bronchiolar and intestinal smooth muscle, and produces varying effects on blood pressure as it acts both as a vasodilator and vasoconstrictor. Epinephrine is a catecholamine and technically an alcohol. Occasionally spelled epinephrin in the United States. Also known as adrenaline. See ADRENAL GLAND, CATECHOLAMINES.

epinosic gain In psychoanalytic theory, indirect advantages obtained from illness or injury, such as extra sympathy, pity, or power over others. See ADVANTAGE BY ILLNESS, SECONDARY GAINS for details.

epinosis Feeling ill (when actually well) after a period of illness. A kind of hypochondriasis. See EPINOSIC GAIN, MALINGERING, SECONDARY GAINS.

epiperipheral feeling Any experience whose source of stimulation is localized outside the body.

epiphany A feeling of ecstasy following a sudden understanding of an element of self, others, or of the essential nature of reality. See ABREACTION, CONVERSION.

epiphenomenalism (T. Hobbes, S. Hodgson, T. H. Huxley) A doctrine of the mind-body relation, or a corollary to certain such theories, according to which conscious processes are not in any sense causal agents, even with respect to one another, but are merely concomitants of certain causally effective physiological processes. Compare INTERACTIONISM. See BODY-MIND DICHOTOMY, MIND-BODY PROBLEM.

epiphenomenon An event that accompanies another event but has no causal or dependent relationship with it.

epiphora A profusion of tears.

epiphysis cerebri   The corpus pineale or pineal body.

episcotis(t)er   A disk that can revolve at a desired speed, providing the participant with brief views of target material behind the device. Used in early research on vision. See CRITICAL FLICKER FREQUENCY, TALBOT-PLATEAU LAW.

episcotis(t)er   Episcotister; Device that can probably still be seen only in a museum of psychological instruments.

episode   Any transitory phase in a disorder or disease. See ACUTE SCHIZOPHRENIC EPISODE, INTERACTIVE EPISODE, MAJOR DEPRESSIVE EPISODE.

episodic amnesia   A loss of memory only for certain significant events.

episodic-behavior disorder   A mental disorder characterized by sudden, usually brief, periods of behavior out of character for the individual and inappropriate for the situation, such as periods of impulsive and uncontrolled behavior. May be due to psychological factors or, in some cases, to an undetected brain syndrome. Also known as episodic disorder.

episodic disorder   See EPISODIC-BEHAVIOR DISORDER.

episodic drive   A bodily urge that does not occur with normal regularity, such as for normal hunger, but for unusual conditions such as wanting a piece of cherry pie, or for alleviation of a new pain, such as a toothache.

episodic dyscontrol syndrome   Periodic violent outbursts with no cause, or insufficient cause. See IMPULSE NEUROSIS.

episodic memory   Past experiences or specific events that may be as far back as early life available for reminiscences. Also known as autobiographical memory. See EARLY RECOLLECTIONS, SEMANTIC MEMORY.

epistasis   Suppression of the effect of a gene by a nonallelic gene.

epistemic   Pertaining to the need to know, often considered to be a fundamental drive. Seen chiefly in young children who touch everything, want to know everything, and are constantly exploring any new environment.

epistemological loneliness   Feeling apart from others in terms of the futility of trying to discover the meaning of life and where the self fits into the universe. See EXISTENTIAL NEUROSIS, WELTSCHMERTZ.

epistemology   The study of knowledge or understanding. One of the basic and enduring topics of philosophy asking and attempting to answer such questions as: What do humans really know? How do humans learn? What is truth? What is reality?

epistemophilia   The love of knowledge; the impulse to investigate and inquire. See CURIOSITY INSTINCT.

epistemophobia   Fear of knowledge.

epithalamus   The area of brain tissue immediately above and behind the thalamus. Includes the pineal gland and the posterior commissure. The epithalamus contains fibers of cranial nerves and the superior colliculi, but its functions are uncertain.

epithelium   The cellular covering of surfaces of the body exposed externally, or the lining of any of its natural cavities.

epitonos   A state of extreme tension.

epochal amnesia   The loss of memory for a certain epoch of personal past, covering a period of days to years, usually after a severe shock.

epochal psychoses   See CLIMACTERIC PSYCHOSES.

EPP   end-plate potential

EPPP   See EXAMINATION FOR PROFESSIONAL PSYCHOLOGY PROGRAMS.

EPPS   Edwards Personal Preference Schedule

EPS   See EXTRAPYRAMIDAL SYMPTOMS.

EPSDT   See EARLY AND PERIODIC SCREENING–DIAGNOSIS AND TREATMENT.

epsilon   The fifth letter of the Greek alphabet. See APPENDIX C.

epsilon alcoholism   (E. M. Jellinek) Rare phrase for periodic drinking bouts interspersed with dry periods lasting weeks or months. Commonly called binge drinking. Also known as paroxysmal drinking, periodic drinking. Similar to dipsomania.

epsilon motion/movement   A visual illusion of movement when a white line on a black background is instantly changed to a black line on a white background. See APPARENT MOTION.

EPSP   See EXCITATORY POSTSYNAPTIC POTENTIAL.

EQ   educational quotient

equal   See EQUALITY.

equal-appearing-intervals method   (L. L. Thurstone) In psychophysics, a technique in which magnitudes between pairs of stimuli are adjusted so that the sensed differences are equal. Also known as equal-and-unequal-cases method, mean-gradation method.

equal distribution of ignorance   The fallacy that when the relative probabilities of two or more events are unknown, the chances of their occurrences are equal.

equal-interval scale   A scale marked in equivalent intervals from a zero-base point. An older name that has been replaced by interval scale.

equality   The absence of discernible or discoverable difference in magnitude between two or more data.

equality of outcome   1. The relative goodness of a response in terms of some standard. Often quality is measurable by quantity; otherwise it is a subjective evaluation. See DIALECTICAL MATERIALISM. 2. See SUBSTANTIVE EQUALITY.

equality stage   See DISTRIBUTIVE JUSTICE.

equalization of excitation   (K. Goldstein) A tendency for nervous excitation to spread evenly throughout a functional system.

equal judgment   The judgment or report, upon comparison of two given stimuli: (a) that no difference is observed between, or (b) that they are subjectively equal.

equally-noticeable differences   In perception research, the point when differences are noted about half the time.

equal opportunity   In any situation, such as formal education or work, giving all individuals the same chances to succeed without any bias. See EQUALITY OF OUTCOME.

equal returns   A learning situation in which early trials yield the same amount of improvement as later trials. See CURVES OF RETURNS.

equal rights amendment (ERA)   An amendment to the U.S. Constitution proposed by the National Women's Party in 1923: "Equality of rights under the law shall not be denied or abridged by the United States or by any State on account of sex." Accepted by most states.

equal sense-difference method   A psychophysical procedure for attempting to equalize two sensory modalities by manipulating one of them until they both seem identical.

equal steps   A series of stimuli that differ in intensity or other quantitative character, such that the difference between any contiguous pair is judged equal to the difference between any other contiguous pair.

Equanil   Trade name for meprobamate.

equanimity   Ability to experience stimuli that could be expected to generate strong emotions without demonstrating any evidence of emotions, such as being unfairly criticized but maintaining normal composure.

equated scores   Scores from two tests that have been weighted to form a common basis for comparison. See EQUIPERCENTILE METHOD.

equatorial plane   See METAPHASE.

equilibration   (J. Piaget) Theory of development, the principle that an organism constantly tends to strive for an ideal stage of psychological and biological balance, to be in harmony with all psychological aspects of self as well as with the environment. See DISEQUILIBRIUM.

equilibratory senses   Organs that regulate equilibrium are the semicircular canals and the vestibular sacs in the inner ear. They regulate orientation of the body in space and are responsible for body position and the adjustment of parts of the body to each other.

equilibrium hypothesis   A postulate that there is a tendency of people to situate themselves a particular distance from other people, and, if too close, to move away and, if too far apart, to come closer. If people cannot move physically (as in public transportation), they tend to adjust their eye contact to compensate.

equilibrium   Maintenance of balance in posture, body processes, or psychological adjustment. See DYNAMIC EQUILIBRIUM, EQUILIBRATION, SENSE OF EQUILIBRIUM.

equilibrium latency   The time required for an organism to reach a stable state following any disturbance of tranquility.

equilibrium state   A state of rest and repose, that is, not needing or wanting anything.

equipercentile method   A technique for comparing two different scores from two different tests by changing both scores to percentiles, for example, a raw score of 43 on test A and 117 on test B when changed into percentiles gives a 93 percentile on test A, but only a 27 percentile on test B. Therefore, the score of 43 on test A is better than the score of 117 on test B. See EQUATED SCORES.

equipment automation   The extent to which tasks are performed by machines. See WORK-FLOW INTEGRATION.

equipment design   An area of human factors concerned with the efficient arrangement of the work space and design of tools. The psychologist serves as a "human engineer" whose major function is to see that the equipment is designed with human factors in mind, such as safety, fatigue, convenience, comfort, and efficiency. See ENGINEERING PSYCHOLOGY, HUMAN-FACTORS ENGINEERING, TIME-MOTION STUDY, TOOL DESIGN.

equipotentiality   1. (K. S. Lashley) Equal potential, or the ability to develop or achieve equal powers, such as the capacity of one part of the brain to be trained or conditioned to perform a function previously performed by another part of the brain. 2. The capacity of any part of the egg or embryonic tissue (at an early stage) to produce any or all parts of the developed organism. See CLONING, LAW OF EQUIPOTENTIALITY.

equipotentiality in memory   A point of view that as far as memory is concerned, all cortex areas are equally important.

equiproportional table   A table of correlation coefficients satisfying the tetrad criterion.

equity   (E. Hatfield) A relationship in which all persons benefit in proportion to their efforts or contribution. An equitable relationship is one in which all participants feel that they are getting just what they deserve from the relationship, that is, no more and surely no less. See DISTRIBUTIVE JUSTICE.

equity stage   See DISTRIBUTIVE JUSTICE.

equity theory   1. (G. C. Homans) A point of view that people strive to generate conditions in which there are a fair distribution of rewards and costs and that they will attempt to achieve equity when there are perceived imbalances. 2. (J. S. Adams) In industrial psychology, the subjective judgment of employees that their incomes will compare fairly to those of others doing equivalent work.

equivalence   A relationship between stimuli or variables that permits one to replace another.

equivalence belief   (E. C. Tolman) A hypothesis that an organism reacts to a subgoal as it would to a goal. See TELEOLOGY.

equivalence coefficient   coefficient of equivalence

equivalence test   The process used to determine that a new stimulus is equivalent to a prior one.

equivalency test   An examination intended to determine the degree of knowledge of a particular topic that an individual can demonstrate, usually for the purpose of getting academic credit. For example, a test may be administered to a student to demonstrate knowledge of calculus; if passed, the student receives proper credit.

equivalent form   An alternate form of a test, with similar items, for use in retesting or used to test individuals who have some knowledge of the prior test. See RELIABILITY.

equivalent groups   Two or more groups matched for all significant variables.

equivalents method   An average-error technique in which a participant adjusts a variable stimulus until it appears equivalent to a standard.

equivalent stimulus   A new stimulus that produces the same effect as a prior stimulus, for example, an organism is conditioned to respond to a circle but not to a triangle or a square. The organism may now respond to an oval, and if so the oval is considered equivalent to a circle in these circumstances.

equivocal   (H. Rorschach) The style of a person in approaching or dealing with a projective test.

ERA   Equal Rights Amendment

erg   1. A metric unit of energy equal to the work done by force of one dyne over a distance of one centimeter. One erg equals 10^{-7} joules. See JOULE. 2. (R. B. Cattell) An innate psychophysical disposition that predisposes a person to respond readily and intensely to certain events.

ERG   See ELECTRORETINOGRAM.

ergasia   (A. Meyer) Comprehensive term for psychobiological functioning or behavior. The totality of activities (psychological, biological, social) that constitute the human personality. See PSYCHOBIOLOGY, THYMERGASIA.

ergasiatry   Adolf Meyer's term for psychiatry.

ergasiology   Adolf Meyer's term for psychology. He conceived ergasiology as a study of the functioning of the personality as a whole. See PSYCHOBIOLOGY.

ergasiomania   Excessive desire to be busy at work.

ergasiophobia   Morbid fear of functioning or moving, with the illusion that personal movements would disastrously affect the surrounding world. See ERGOPHOBIA.

ergic   Pertaining to purposeful work.

ergogram   A graph showing work output.

ergograph   A recording device for muscular action, usually employed in fatigue studies. Compare DYNAMOMETER.

ergometry   The measurement of strength, endurance, or work.

ergonomics   1. The study of the relationship between expended energy and work accomplished. 2. (K. Murrell) The study of the relationship between humans and machines. Including such matters as maximum efficiency, safety, comfort, and accuracy as well as selection and training of individuals for operations. Similar to human engineering. See ENGINEERING PSYCHOLOGY, HUMAN FACTORS.

ergonomist   A human factors specialist.

ergophobia   Morbid fear of work or working. Sometimes called ergasiophobia. See PONOPHOBIA.

ergot   A fungus, *Claviceps purpurea*, that infests rye and other grain plants, and that gives off a toxic by-product chemically related to a number of drugs, including LSD.

ergotherapy   1. Treatment of disease or disorder through muscular exercise. 2. Therapy through working, used extensively in Asian countries. Similar to what is called occupational therapy in other countries.

ergotism   A disorder caused by eating ergot-contaminated bread or other grain products. Mentioned in the Middle Ages as "Saint Anthony's Fire," the symptoms including a burning sensation of the skin, weakness, drowsiness, hallucinations, and convulsions.

ergotropic   (W. R. Hess) Having the effect of producing action or excitement by stimulating the brain cells, as when an ergotropic agent such as amphetamine increases brain activity. Compare TROPHOTROPIC.

ergotropic activity   Relating to an activity system that centers or turns around work, preparing the body for interaction with the environment.

ergotropic arousal   Increased sympathetic nervous system activity and emotional excitement following various ecstatic practices.

ergotropic process   (W. R. Hess) The mechanism whereby the sympathetic division of the autonomic nervous system performs functions related to the expenditure of energy, for example, the increased physiologic activity that follows intake of stimulants. Compare TROPHOTROPIC PROCESS.

ergotropic system   Any system marked by a strong drive or arousal factor.

ERG theory   See EXISTENCE, RELATEDNESS, AND GROWTH THEORY.

Erhard Seminar Training (EST)   (W. Erhard) A form of group therapy based on a mixture of theories popular in the 1960s. A controversial training system, supposedly consciousness-expanding, borrowing from business-world motivation techniques and assorted theories of psychology. Processes included long lectures on a variety of topics, as well as the use of directed meditation and a number of other techniques. Promoters of EST insisted that this procedure was not psychotherapy. See CONSCIOUSNESS EXPANSION, GROUP THERAPY.

eric trait   A dynamic trait that motivates someone to achieve an objective.

Ericksonian Psychotherapy   (J. Zeig) A form of psychotherapy developed by Milton Erickson based on eliciting previously dormant intrapsychic resources by using injunctive techniques such as hypnosis and suggestive metaphors; the therapist creates a "symbol drama" to enable the client to cope more effectively.

Erikson's stages of psychosocial development   Theory by Erik Erikson based on the concept of psychosocial development, in which human "ego identity" is gradually achieved by facing positive and negative risks at each of eight stages of life: (a) infancy: trust vs mistrust, (b) toddler: autonomy vs shame and doubt, (c) preschool age: initiative vs guilt, (d) school age: industry vs inferiority, (e) adolescence: identity vs role confusion, (f) young adulthood: intimacy vs isolation, (g) middle age: generativity vs self-absorption or stagnation, (h) mature age: integrity vs despair. Also known as Erikson's eight stages of man. Erikson's psychosocial development stages, ages, and crises:

Stage	Age	Crisis
I	Oral-sensory	1	Trust vs Mistrust

II	Muscular-anal	1–3	Autonomy vs Doubt and Shame
III	Locomotor-genital	3–5	Initiative vs Guilt
IV	Latency	6–12	Industry vs Inferiority
V	Puberty	13–18	Identity vs Role Confusion
VI	Early adulthood	19–22	Intimacy vs Isolation
VII	Young and middle age	23–45	Generativity vs Stagnation
VIII	Mature adult	46+	Integrity vs Despair

See above entries and also BASIC MISTRUST, BASIC TRUST, EGO IDENTITY, EGO INTEGRITY, GENERATIVITY, IDENTITY, INTIMACY, MORATORIUM, MUTUALITY, ROLE CONFUSION, ROLE DIFFUSION, STAGE THEORY OF DEVELOPMENT.

ermitophobia   **monophobia**

erogenous   Pertaining to that which will excite people sexually. Also known as erotogenetic.

erogenous zones   Parts of the body especially sexually sensitive to caressing, often used to start the sexual response. Also known as erotogenic zone.

Eros   1. Term used by Sigmund Freud as a poetic metaphor to personify the life-force and sexual instinct. 2. In later psychoanalytic theory, the drive that comprises the instinct for self-preservation, that aims for individual survival; containing also the sexual instinct, whose goal is the survival of the species. Named for the Greek god of sexual love (responsible for permitting and harmonizing life, secret lover of Psyche). Also known as life instinct. Compare THANATOS.

erosion   In environmental psychology, the deterioration or corrosion of a physical setting from climatic effects and use by all organisms including humans. The amount of wear evident in footpaths in an otherwise pristine area is an indication of the degree of erosion of the natural environment, as well as the pollution of rivers and oceans. The physical environment affects humans. See ACCRETION, ECOLOGY, ENVIRONMENT, ENVIRONMENTAL DEPRIVATION, ENVIRONMENTAL ENRICHMENT, ENVIRONMENTAL-LOAD THEORY, ENVIRONMENTAL STRESS, ENVIRONMENTAL STRESS THEORY.

erotic   Invested with sexual sensations, or feelings of love; also, pertaining to stimuli that give rise to sexual excitement.

erotica   Literature, illustrations, motion-picture films, or other material likely to arouse sexual response. Term is sometimes used interchangeably with pornography.

erotic-arousal pattern in animals   The sequence of actions or stimuli that produce sexual response in animals differs with various species; for example, female cheetahs must run fast for a period of time before they will ovulate, as they do in the wild when pursued by ardent suitors. For this reason cheetahs are difficult to breed in captivity, but when given opportunity for this behavior, they will breed.

erotic asphyxiation   A dangerous sexual practice of being choked or strangulated during sex, usually done during solitary masturbation (autoerotic asphyxiation) but also in the presence or with assistance of others. See EROTIZED HANGING.

erotic character   General sexual attractiveness aside from a person's actual physical body is a function of factors, such as how the person dresses, behaves socially, and feels about himself or herself.

erotic code   (W. H. Davenport) In anthropology, culture-specific signs and actions that convey sexual interest and arousal, from penile extenders to dancing.

erotic delusion   The false perception of being secretly loved by or having had a sexual affair with a public figure or other important individual the patient has never met. See CLÉRAMBAULT'S SYNDROME, EROTIC PARANOIA.

Erotic Feminism   A kind of feminism that started as a rebellion to the "blood and iron" policies of Otto von Bismarck, fostering eroticism as a philosophical and metaphorical value; often includes Goddess worship and vegetarianism.

erotic inertia   A form of hypophilia in which the person cannot make any sexual initiatives or maintain sexual activities in normally conducive situations.

erotic instinct   In psychoanalytic theory, the sex drive or libido; also, the equivalent of Eros, the life instinct.

erot(ic)ism   1. A condition of sexual excitement. 2. Preoccupation with sexual excitement, explicit photographs, and written material with sexual themes. Types of eroticism include: ADOLESCENT HOMO-, ALLO-, ANAL, AN-, AUTO-, EGO, GENITAL, HETERO-, HOMO-, LIP, OLFACTORY, ORAL, ORGAN, PARANOID, PHASE, RESPIRATORY, SECONDARY AUTO-, SKIN, TEMPERATURE, URETHRAL. See AGGRESSIVE EROTIC, AMPHIEROTISM, ANAL-EROTIC TRAITS, DE-EROT(IC)IZE.

eroticization   The investment of bodily organs and biological functions or other activities with sexual pleasure and gratification. Also known as erotization, libidinization.

erotic love   (E. Fromm) A craving for mental and physical unity with another person.

erotic paranoia   A paranoid disorder in which the patient experiences erotic delusions, such as claiming that other people of great wealth or high status are in love with the patient, finding evidence of this delusion in newspaper photographs or even in the flight path of birds. See EROTIC DELUSION.

erotic pyromania   Being sexually aroused by arson; pyrolagnia.

erotic revulsion   The experience of erotic activity as repulsive, either generally or in relation to a specific partner.

erotic self-strangulation   See ASPHIXOPHILIA, EROTIC ASPHYXIATION.

erotic transference   The process of taking erotic feelings associated with one person and attaching those feelings to another, for example, from a lover in the past to a lover in the person's present life.

erotic type   (S. Freud) A type of individual whose main interest is applied to the libido or the love life. One of Sigmund Freud's three libidinal types in which the libido remains largely in the id, the main interest is in loving and being loved, and if decompensation occurs, a hysterical disorder is said to develop. See LIBIDINAL TYPES, NARCISSISTIC TYPE, OBSESSIONAL TYPE.

erotism   **erot(ic)ism**

erotization 1. In psychoanalytic theory, the process by which a mental process becomes part of the self. 2. See EROTICIZATION.

erotized anxiety A method of dealing with anxiety by moving toward its source and apparently enjoying it.

erotized hanging A dangerous sexual practice in which persons literally hang themselves or have a sexual partner help to produce neck constriction and cerebral hypoxia as a means of sexual arousal. See AUTOEROTIC ASPHYXIATION.

erotocrat A man with great sexual ability, a natural sense of his virility, and who attracts many women. See CASANOVA.

erotogenesis In psychoanalytic theory, the origin of erotic impulses whose sources may include anal, oral, and phallic zones.

erotogenic Arousing sexual sensations.

erotogenic masochism **primary masochism**

erotographomania Pathological urge to write love letters, usually anonymously.

erotolalia 1. Obscene talk. 2. Speech that contains sexual obscenities, particularly as used to enhance gratification during sexual intercourse.

erotomania 1. An extreme exaggeration of or preoccupation with sexual matters. 2. Compulsive, insatiable activity with the opposite sex. Sometimes known as aidolomania. See DON JUANISM, NYMPHOMANIA, SATYRIASIS.

erotopathy An abnormality of the sexual impulse.

erotophobia Morbid aversion to sexual love or any sexual matters. See COITOPHOBIA, CYPRIDOPHOBIA, GENOPHOBIA.

erotophonophilia See HOMOCIDOPHILIA.

ERP event-related potential

error (e) 1. A deviation from true or accurate information; an incorrect response, a mistaken belief. 2. In experimental psychology, any change in a dependent variable not attributable to the independent variable. 3. In statistics, deviation from a true score. Types of error include: ABSOLUTE, ACCIDENTAL, AGGREGATION, ALPHA, ANTICIPATION, ATTRIBUTION, ATTRIBUTIONAL, AVERAGE, BETA, CENTRAL TENDENCY, CHANCE, CHROMATIC, COMPENSATING, CONSTANT, CONTRAST, EXPERIMENTAL, FUNDAMENTAL ATTRIBUTION, GENETIC, GROUPING, HUMAN, ILLOGICAL, INSTRUMENTAL, INTRUSION, KUNDGABE, LENIENCY, LOGICAL, MEASUREMENT, METHOD OF AVERAGE, MOTIVATED, OBSERVATIONAL, PROCESSING, RANDOM, RATING, REFRACTION, RELATIVE, REVERSAL, SAMPLING, SIMILAR-TO-ME, SPACE, SPHERICAL, STANDARD, STATISTICAL, STIMULUS, SUBJECTIVE, SURVEY, SYSTEMATIC, TIME, TYPE I, TYPE II, UNBIASED.

error analysis The study of human factors and engineering-design factors that may result in production errors.

error judgment A judgment or decision that does not truly represent the stimulus conditions, for example, reporting a judgment of two points on the skin, given in the two-point limen experiment when only one point was stimulated. See ESTHESIOMETER for an illustration of such an experiment.

error methods Phrase commonly applied, since Gustav Fechner, to two psychophysical methods, average error and right and wrong cases. See METHOD OF JUST NOTICEABLE DIFFERENCES.

error of anticipation In psychophysical measurements, a tendency to anticipate a stimulus and respond too soon.

error of estimate The variance expected in an individual's predicted score as a result of the imperfect validity of the test. See STANDARD ERROR OF ESTIMATE.

error of expectation In psychological experiments, an error in (a) perception or (b) response, due to the observer's preconceived idea of what is to be presented or of when the presentation will occur. In (a), the observer may report images as being actual perceptions; in (b), the observer may react to the wrong stimulus.

error of habituation In psychophysics, the error resulting from habit or from resistance to changing a response. See EINSTELLUNG, SET.

error of judgment Mistakes made that on further consideration tend to diminish and move to truer value as more information occurs. Error in judging tends to be "averaged out" toward greater reliability and validity as more judges are used.

error of measurement/observation Deviation of any measurement from its true value due to the unreliability of the measuring instrument, the person doing the measuring, or both.

error of recognition The recognition as familiar of an item not previously experienced, as in mistakenly identifying a suspect in a police lineup.

error of refraction Failure of the optical image to focus normally upon the retina, due to imperfection in the shape of the eyeball. Also known as refraction error.

error phenomenon (K. R. Rao) Psi-mediated error. A procedural error in an experiment, for example, may trigger a psi response or a psi response may be masked by the error. It is hypothesized that error phenomena provide evidence for the self-evasive aspect of psi.

error rate The expected number of errors per experiment, the rate usually being defined in terms of the probability of its being falsely declared significant. See TYPE A ERROR, TYPE B ERROR.

errors of reference Describing errors or deviations that occur (a) in the method of limits, according as the variable approaches the standard stimulus from above or below, and (b) in the method of average error due to the fact that only the variable (and not the standard) is subject to change.

errors of sampling See SAMPLING ERROR.

error variance 1. Score variability not systematic or controlled, nor produced by the independent variable. 2. That part of the variance not accounted for by known factors, sometimes due to poor measurement and other experimental errors. See EXPERIMENTAL ERROR, NOISE, RESIDUAL ERROR.

erythrogenic radiations Long-wave light stimuli that normally give rise to the experience of red. Suggested by Christine Ladd-Franklin to replace the physicist's equivocal term red.

erythrophobia 1. Persistent, pathological fear of the color red in general, and of blood in particular. 2. Fear of objects or activities associated with red, such as red flags or blushing. Also known as ereuth(r)ophobia. See BLUSHING, HEMATOPHOBIA, HEMOPHOBIA.

erythropsia A type of chromatopsia (colored vision) usually following over-exposure to intense light, in which all objects appear tinged with red. Occurs in snow blindness.

Es German term for the id. Translated, literally, as the "it."

ES ego strength

Esalen Institute (M. Murphy) A growth center, located in the Big Sur area of Northern California, a hub of the human potential movement. A basic goal of this institute was to unite the traditions of the East with the technical innovations of the West. Among those who have shared their theories and procedures at Esalen have been Frederick Perls, William Schutz, and Milton Trager.

Esalen massage A massage taught and practiced at the Esalen Institute in California that lasts from one to three and a half hours, intended to be a type of warm, loving, nonverbal communication between the receiver of the massage and the masseur or masseurs, since a group may participate in the massage. See TRAGERISM.

ESB See ELECTROSTIMULATION OF THE BRAIN.

escalation of aggression A step in the sequence of aggression following an initial perceived provocation, in which the person who may eventually become violent will first react with some form of minor aggression, possibly verbal, and if there is further perceived aggression, will react with excess counter-violence.

escalation of commitment A tendency to become increasingly committed to bad decisions even as losses associated with them increase, exemplified by the behavior of some compulsive gamblers.

E scale An attitude scale used in ethnocentrism measurement.

escape behavior Any behavior directed toward freedom from a restricted, painful, or otherwise unpleasant situation, for example, mental escape through fantasy or daydreams, physical escape by avoiding a noxious stimulus by providing a conditioned response, or taking some action to retreat from a perceived threat. See ESCAPE LEARNING.

escape conditioning The training of an organism to terminate an aversive stimulus.

Escape from Freedom The title of a book by Erich Fromm, stressing loneliness. In moving away from nature, a person becomes isolated, and in combating loneliness, two possible solutions facing the person are love or conformance to social demands. See IDENTITY NEED.

escape into illness flight into illness

escape learning A conditioning experience in which an organism is exposed to a painful or threatening situation and acquires a successful or proper response behavior for avoiding the noxious stimulus; for example, by accidently pressing a lever that terminates continuous electric shock, a rat may come to acquire a lever-pressing response as a learned escape mechanism. See CONDITIONING, ESCAPE BEHAVIOR, NEGATIVE-REINFORCEMENT.

escape mechanism A behavioral pattern or device unconsciously adopted for avoidance or freedom from a threatening or anxiety-laden situation, for example, flight into illness, daydreaming, detachment, or amnesia. Also known as escape from reality.

escape training A learning process in which an organism is trained to avoid an unpleasant stimulus, for example, a shock. See ESCAPE LEARNING.

escapism In psychoanalytic theory, a tendency to free the self from the pressures of the real world by returning to the security of childhood by regressive thinking, feeling, and behavior, ordinarily accompanied by symptoms of neurosis. Usually a form of resistance. The person may also engage in substance abuse to escape from responsibility, anxiety.

escutcheon The shieldlike pattern of pubic-hair distribution that develops after puberty.

ESN See EDUCATIONALLY SUBNORMAL.

esodic Afferent. See CENTRIPETAL.

esodic nerves afferent nerves

esophageal voice The low-frequency vibrations produced by the narrow upper portion of the esophagus when swallowed air is belched out.

esophoria 1. A tendency for the eyes to turn inward. 2. An inward deviation of one eye due to muscular imbalance, interfering with binocular vision. Esophoria is a form of heterophoria. Also known as cross-eye. Compare WALL EYE.

esoteric Pertaining to the inner, hidden, or mystical meaning of a theory or system. Nearly all religious traditions have such beliefs, practices, or both, as an integral part of their makeup.

ESP See EXTRASENSORY PERCEPTION.

ESP forced-choice test A research procedure for testing extrasensory perception (ESP) in which a participant is aware of the target alternatives. See ZENER CARDS for an example of materials used in such tests.

ESP free-response test A research procedure for testing extrasensory perception (ESP) where the target range is unknown to the participant.

esprit de corps (feeling of solidarity—French) The feelings of confidence by individuals of shared loyalty of other members of the group, expressed by the motto of The Three Musketeers: "All for one and one for all."

Esquirol's classification of mental disorders (J. Esquirol) Five classes of pathological conditions of the mind: dementia, imbecility, lypemania (melancholia), mania, (affective) monomania. See AFFECTIVE MONOMANIA, LYPEMANIA.

essay test An examination in which a participant answers a question, whether written or delivered orally, by writing an essay. See OBJECTIVE EXAMINATION.

ESSB See ELECTRICAL SELF-STIMULATION OF THE BRAIN.

essence 1. The real character or nature of a phenomenon. 2. A concentrated substance that has the characteristics of the original substance. 3. The contributions made by individuals in determining their own fates in their own given existence.

essential alcoholism See GAMMA ALCOHOLISM.

essential hypertension   High blood pressure due to a variety of causes, including obesity, cigarette-smoking, and psychologic influences, such as a stressful environment. See TYPE A PERSONALITY.

essential memory trace circuit   (R. F. Thompson) That brain circuit necessary and sufficient for the learning, memory, and behavioral expression of a given type or instance of memory.

EST   1. Erhard Seminar Training. 2. See ELECTRO-CONVULSIVE (SHOCK) THERAPY. 3. Electro-sleep therapy.

established pair   **pairmates**

establishment   (H. A. Murray) The combination of ego, id, and superego factors modified along functional lines to serve as basic components, or "establishments," of personality.

esteem drives   (A. Maslow) Drives, motives, and urges that depend on a need for status and respect.

esteem from self   (A. Maslow) Self-esteem arising out of a person's feelings of accomplishment of desired goals independently of attitudes of others. See SELF-ESTEEM.

esteem needs   (A. Maslow) The fourth level in Abraham Maslow's hierarchy of needs, characterized by the striving for a sense of personal value as derived from achievement, reputation, or prestige. See MASLOW'S HIERARCHY OF NEEDS THEORY, NEED-HIERARCHY THEORY.

esthes(i)odic   Conveying sensory impressions. Also known as aesthesodic.

esthesiogenic   Producing sensation.

esthesiometer   (E. H. Weber) A device for measuring tactual acuity by determining the two-point limen; there are several forms, the essential feature being a pair of slightly rounded points that may be adjusted at various distances from each other and applied simultaneously to the participant's skin.

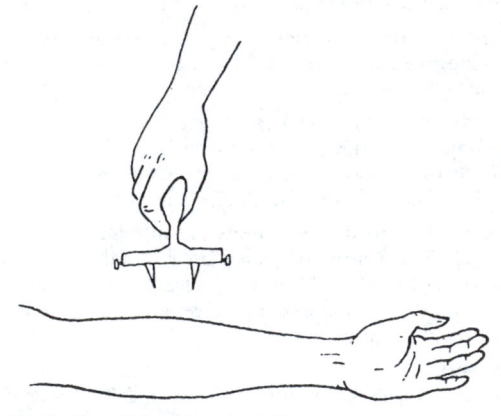

esthesiometer   Determining a 2-point limen.

esthesiometry   The branch of psychophysics that deals with the measure of touch and pressure sensations and thresholds.

esthete   A person who attaches great importance to the place of beauty in human experience.

esthetic emotion   A pleasant feeling experienced during the perception of a work of art or of a natural object that looks beautiful.

esthetic expression   Manifestation of any esthetic emotion or sentiment in any of the fine arts.

esthetic pleasure   (S. Freud) Denoting the enjoyment of an experience, such as a joke or a painting of a nude, for its own sake, without instinctual gratification (sexual excitement).

esthetics   The study of the psychological or philosophical components and aspects of beauty, in nature and art. The scientific investigation of beauty and ugliness, or (more precisely) of the pleasant-unpleasant feelings aroused for their own sake by various composite (or simple) stimuli. See ENVIRONMENTAL ESTHETICS, EXPERIMENTAL ESTHETICS, PSYCHOLOGICAL ESTHETICS.

esthetic type   (E. Spranger) Descriptive of a person strongly attracted to what is beautiful and harmonious. Also spelled aesthetic type. See TYPOLOGY.

esthetic value   The emotional and uplifting value imparted to an observer or participant by the beauty of a work of art or nature.

estimation   Inference from sample statistics to population parameters, for example, determining of the size of an effect from its occurrence in one or more samples.

estimation difference   (W. Wundt) Designating half the difference between the upper and lower limens. See LIMEN, THRESHOLD.

estimators   (R. Gelman) The mental processes involved in judging quantity, as in the child's ability to recognize that a given set contains six elements rather than five or seven. See OPERATORS.

estradiol   One of the two most active of the estrogens (the other being estrone) produced by follicular fluid of the ovaries and by the placenta. Used to treat menopausal conditions and other human female disorders.

estrangement   See ALIENATION.

estrin   (C. W. Bellergy) Generic term for any ovarian secretion that affects female sexual development and response.

estrogen   Generic name for a group of hormones that have a general effect of inducing estrus in female animals and secondary female sexual characteristics in humans. Forms occurring in humans are estradiol, estrone, and estriol (secreted by the ovarian follicle), corpus luteum, placenta, testes, and adrenal cortex. Estrogen may also be produced synthetically or obtained from other biological sources. Also known as estrin.

estrone   (B. Zondek, S. Ascheim, A. Butenandt, E. Doisy) A female hormone that stimulates physiological changes characteristic of estrus and induces growth of the female sex organs. See ESTRADIOL.

estrous behavior   A behavior pattern observed in primates during the phase of their sexual cycle when the female expresses a willingness to mate. Estrous cycles range from as short as two weeks in sheep to as long as six months in dogs, whereas the period of estrous behavior may last only 12 hours in sheep to a week or more in dogs. Also known as heat, rut.

estrus (cycle)   1. The period of recurrent estrum, or heat, in animals. 2. The reproductive cycle of animals as manifested by periods of sexual desire or mating, particularly in the female of the species. Also known as estral cycle. See ESTROUS BEHAVIOR, MONESTROUS, POLYESTROUS.

et See ETIOLOGY.

eta The seventh letter of the Greek alphabet. See APPENDIX C.

eta coefficient (η) A measure of association between two variables when the regression line is curvilinear. See ASYMMETRICAL DISTRIBUTION for an illustration of an irregular distribution.

et al Abbreviation for and others.

eternal suckling Freudian phrase for the type of individual who expects to be cared for, supported, and protected throughout life by somebody else.

ethanol A depressant and a narcotic, ethanol (alcohol) has been used as an anesthetic. It has been mistakenly identified as a stimulant but the stimulating effect is an illusion associated with loss of cortical inhibition. The depressant effect begins in the cortex and gradually spreads to lower centers as dosage increases. Also known as ethyl alcohol. See ALCOHOLISM.

ethanolism Alcoholism.

ethereal 1. Relating to ether or the air. 2. (J. D. Amoore et al.) In the stereochemical smell theory, one of the seven primary small qualities. A quality of olfactory sensation of which beeswax and sulfuric ether are typical examples. 3. In Zwaardemaker's smell theory, one of his nine smell qualities of which fruits and wine are typical examples. 4. In Henning's smell prism, one of the six primary smells. 5. Pertaining to regions beyond the earth. Lacking material substance.

ethical approach (S. Freud) Denoting the therapeutic goal of helping the patient to achieve personal high individual standards without blind conformity to the conventional demands of society.

ethical conflict See CONFLICT OF INTEREST.

ethical determinism (Socrates) A philosophical doctrine espoused by Socrates but opposed by Aristotle, that humans will automatically seek out the good if they know what is "good." See DETERMINISM.

ethical dilemma An issue in which moral claims conflict with one another. A difficult value-oriented problem that seems to have no satisfactory solution; a choice between equally unsatisfactory alternatives. Also known as a catch-22 situation.

ethical freedom Psychological ability to make and act upon decisions that conform to widely accepted principles of justice and fair conduct. See FREE WILL, SOFT DETERMINISM.

ethical imperative The commanding influence of moral principles on mental life and behavior; the moral consciousness of the individual. See CONSCIENCE, CATEGORICAL IMPERATIVE.

ethical intuition Assumption that certain moral concepts such as fairness, justice, and correct and incorrect behavior are part of human genetic inheritance, as in a child indicating disapproval after seeing a bigger person hitting a smaller person without provocation. See CONSCIENCE, ETHICAL RELATIVISM, KOHLBERG'S THEORY OF MORAL DEVELOPMENT, PIAGETIAN THEORY.

ethicality Internally based emphasis on moral or principled behavior.

ethical judgment An appraisal given to acts of conduct in terms of their conformity or nonconformity to some implied standard of fairness, justice, or kindness to fellow humans.

ethical relativism A doctrine positing that ethical behavior is a function of the environment (specifically the culture). What is morally correct in one culture (for example, genital mutilation, or males and female in a state of equality) may be considered unjust in other cultures. See ETHICAL INTUITION.

ethical-risk hypothesis A postulate that moral or immoral behavior depends on a child's evaluation of the risk involved (getting caught). That is, as the possibility of discovery increases, the occurrence of the behavior diminishes. Some early social-learning theorists viewed this theory as essential in understanding the process of moral judgment in children.

ethical sense The capacity to discriminate between human actions upon the basis of their conformity to a standard of fairness, justice, or kindness to those affected.

ethics 1. A branch of philosophy that deals with moral values and systems of beliefs focused on the differences between right and wrong. 2. In general, a person's or group's principles of morally correct conduct. See CATEGORICAL IMPERATIVE, CODE OF ETHICS.

ethnic In casual use, short for ethnic group or minority.

ethnic cleansing A 1990s euphemism for the killing or deportation of a people.

ethnic drift (J. Lefkowitz) In personnel management, a tendency to assign employees to supervisors of the same ethnicity.

ethnic factors The common traits and customs that form the basis of a division of people who are biologically, socially, or politically related.

ethnic group A social group that possesses a common history, culture, language, and, often, religion. Members are likely to be biologically related. An ethnic group may be of any size and is a subset of a racial grouping, each of which contain many ethnic groups, for example, Gypsies, Hawaiians, Hopis.

ethnic surge In social psychology, the recent growth of ethnic issues, particularly the assertiveness of minorities who use cultural or racial symbols as resources in the competition over resources.

ethnobotany The field that explores how plants are used in particular cultures. Especially relevant is the growing exploration of plants for healing or for their psychological effects. See ETHNOPSYCHOPHARMACOLOGY.

ethnocentricity An attitude of members of a tribe, clan, or nation that they are superior by reason of natural selection or divine predeliction to others. See PREJUDICE, RELIGOCENTRISM, SOCIOCENTRISM.

ethnocentrism scale See E SCALE.

ethnographic approach A strategy for studying the history, culture, social structure, and lifestyle of a community to gain insight into its total culture. Various 19th and 20th century ethnographers have developed differing ethnographic theories and methodologies for understanding and interpreting cultures. See ETHNOGRAPHY.

ethnography   The division of anthropology that studies the origin, history, geography, distribution, culture, and social institutions and relationships within and between ethnic groups.

ethnology   The branch of anthropology that investigates human culture, customs, and social relations from the genetic standpoint.

ethnomethodology   (B. Malinowski) An anthropological procedure aimed at understanding the thoughts and behaviors of aboriginal people by living with them, learning their languages, rituals, traditions, and concepts, and generally getting in tune with their views.

ethnopsychology   The study of mental processes of a natural human group, a community, or a tribe, sometimes restricted to the psychology of "primitive peoples." Also known as cross-cultural psychology.

ethnopsychopharmacology   The branch of pharmacology, related to ethnobotany, that deals with the use of psychotropic drugs in ethnic or subcultural populations, such as research on the use of hallucinogenic agents as part of shamanistic or visionary rituals in indigenous tribes, that has opened significant awareness of the nature of myth and altered states of consciousness in culture. See ETHNOBOTANY, PSYCHEDELICS, SORCERY DRUGS.

ethnoscience   The study of the rules of society, including laws, traditions, morals, ethics, etiquette, standards, etc.

ethogram   An account or chronicle of the behavior of an animal in its natural habitat. See ETHOLOGY.

ethological models of personal space   Personal space "bubbles" (the proximity within which creatures of one species will not comfortably allow other members of the same species to venture near them) have been used by various species throughout evolutionary history to protect individual organisms against intraspecies aggression. People living near the equator have relatively small such person-space limits, whereas those in the northern areas need to have relatively larger limits. See BUBBLE CONCEPT OF PERSONAL SPACE, PROXEMICS.

ethologist   A student of the natural behavior of animals in their normal environment. Such a person conducts studies in the field rather than in the laboratory.

ethology   (J. S. Mill) The study of animals under their normal conditions in their native habitats.

ethos   The character or spirit of an individual, ethnic group, culture, or nation.

ethyl alcohol   Ethanol.

etic   Pertaining to studies of a people or institution conducted from the outside that tend to be comparative and cross-cultural in an attempt to locate universal patterns of thought and behavior existing in all cultures. Compare EMIC.

etiological equation   An attempt to explain any behavioral disorder by generating a kind of equation of causative factors, each weighted in terms of presumed importance; for example, $2A + 3B + 6C =$ depression score, if A is ethnic background, B is gender, and C is socio-economic level (socio-economic levels considered twice as important as gender and three times as important as ethnic background).

etiological validity   Truth and accuracy in terms of causation of an disorder, determining if the prior facts of that particular case were similar to historical antecedents that caused other instances of the phenomenon, such as a mental disorder.

etiology (et)   1. The investigation of the causes or significant antecedents of a given phenomenon. 2. In a broader sense, the study of causal relations. The investigation and assignment of causes and their mode of operation. 3. The systematic study of the causes of mental and physical disorders, or the causal factors that account for a particular disorder and their interactions. Also spelled aetiology.

etiquette   The prescribed ceremonial procedure in any given ethnic or social group, with regard to definite events in social intercourse; for example, meeting or eating.

E trisomy   Another name for trisomy 17–18.

ETS   Educational Testing Service

etymology   The history of words: how they originated, changed, and were affected by other languages.

EUCD   emotionally-unstable character disorder

eudaemonism   A doctrine positing that the chief end of living is happiness. Also spelled eudemonism. See HEDONISM, PLEASURE PRINCIPLE, REALITY PRINCIPLE.

eudemonia   (Aristotle) 1. A feeling of well-being or happiness. 2. Refers to a life governed chiefly by reason.

euergasia   (A. Meyer) Denoting normal mental functioning.

eufunction   Working well and harmoniously. Compare DYSFUNCTION.

eugenics   (F. Galton) 1. Denoting processes and methods aimed at improving the qualities of humans through better mate selection, sterilization, etc. 2. The study of genetic practices, processes, and policies, especially in connection with improvement of innate human qualities through selection. Positive eugenics would promote reproduction by individuals with superior traits, whereas negative eugenics would prevent reproduction by individuals with undesirable traits. See KALLIKAK.

Euglena   A genus of flagellate protozoan. The species *euglena viridis* is particularly of interest on account of its pigment spot, a primitive type of visual receptor.

Euler diagrams   A diagram of concentric circles or some variation of them designed to show relationship between sets and subsets. A set within a larger set is represented as a circle within a larger circle. Independent sets are shown by separate circles. Named after Leonhard Euler, they set the stage for Venn diagrams. See VENN DIAGRAMS.

eumorphic   Pertaining to a constitutional body type characterized by normal shape and structure, and roughly equivalent to the normosplanchnic type. Also known as normotype.

eunoia   Rare term for a healthy mind.

eunuch   A castrated male who develops some secondary sex characteristics of a female, such as a higher voice and absence of a beard, likely to be deficient in sexual desire or ability, especially if the castration was done before puberty. See CASTRATION, SECONDARY SEX CHARACTERISTICS.

eupareunia   Sexual intercourse resulting in orgasm. Compare DYSPAREUNIA.

euphemism   An acceptable or pleasant-sounding word or phrase that is substituted for one that might annoy, upset, or irritate, such as saying "The dog was put to sleep" instead of "The dog died." Compare DYSPHEMISM.

euphenics   Treatment of a physiological or anatomical irregularity to permit a relatively normal life.

euphonia   A pleasant sound, including voices.

euphoria   A sublime mood of well-being. If a person experiences feelings of boundless strength, happiness, and optimism that do not correspond to the reality of the situation, then euphoria is possibly due to a disorder.

euphoriant   A drug that has as a major effect the capacity to cause a feeling of pleasure, a "high." Cocaine, heroin, and other drugs with a strong abuse potential tend to be euphoriants.

euphoric apathy   (C. G. Jung) A state of happy indifference. See LA BELLE INDIFFERENCE.

euphorogenic   (F. Dumont) Quality of an event, often unexpected, that changes a person's attitude from a prior state, whether neutral or depressed, to excited, happy, optimistic.

euphorohallucinogen   Obsolete term for a substance, such as mescaline, capable of producing euphoric hallucinations.

eupsychia   (A. Maslow) A society of fully realized people.

eureka task   A problem with a solution that, once suggested, seems obviously correct.

European mandrake   mandragora

eurotophobia   Morbid fear of the female genitals.

eurymorph   (H. Eysenck) A broad-body typology. See BODY-BUILD INDEX.

euryplastic (body) type   Pertaining to a constitutional body type roughly equivalent to Ernst Kretschmer's pyknic (body) type and William Sheldon's endomorphic (body) type.

eustachian tube   (B. Eustachio) A slender tube extending from the middle ear to the pharynx, with the primary function of equalizing air pressure on both sides of the ear drum.

eusthenia   Normal strength.

eusthenic body type   Pertaining to a constitutional body type roughly equivalent to Ernst Kretschmer's athletic (body) type and William Sheldon's mesomorphic (body) type.

euthenics   Evironmental changes to provide the best possible conditions for those with deficiencies.

eusthesia   A sense of well-being.

eustress   (H. Selye) A type of stress that has a beneficial or stimulating effect, for example, the stress of a job promotion. The concept is similar to "No pain, no gain."

euthanasia   1. Alleviation of pain associated with impending death. 2. Mercy killing, in which death is deliberately brought about by painless means.

euthenics   1. A branch of applied science that aims at the improvement of humans or other species by regulating their environment. 2. A belief that improvement of the human race can be achieved by proper treatment of present individuals, rather than via eugenics. Term implies that the human condition can be bettered by improving the environment. See EUGENICS.

euthymia   A mood of well-being and tranquillity. Also known as euthymic mood.

eutychia   A state of general satisfaction.

evaluability-assessment data   In evaluation research, information sought to identify problem areas of program evaluation; a review of expectations for program performance and questions to be answered by evaluation data, followed by a study of program implementation to identify designs, measurements, and possible analyses.

evaluation   1. Determination of the relative value of phenomena such as therapeutic techniques, hypotheses, and observations. 2. Overall appraisal of the progress of a client, patient, student, team, or other persons in a designated task. 3. Interpretation of test results and experimental data. 4. Finding the value of a dependent variable by assignment of a specific value or values to the independent variable or variables. Types of evaluation include: DISCREPANCY, EMPLOYEE, FEEDBACK, FORMATIVE, IN-HOUSE, JOB, META-, NETWORK-ANALYSIS, NEUROLOGICAL, NONSTATISTICAL, OPERATIONAL, outcome, process, program, program-impact, secondary, self-, sensory, sucking, summative, systematic, time and motion, training, transactional, vocational, work. See COGNITIVE EVALUATION THEORY, GOAL MODEL OF EVALUATION, LOCUS-OF-EVALUATION, MODEL OF EVALUATION, SYSTEM MODEL OF EVALUATION, TREATMENT-EVALUATION STRATEGIES.

evaluation apprehension   1. Feelings of inadequacy, degrees of uncertainty on the part of people who are or expect to be evaluated. 2. A worried, uneasy feeling on the part of a participant in a study who desires a favorable evaluation by the experimenter. 3. Concern over being evaluated by others. May increase arousal and facilitate social interaction.

evaluation contract   A commitment by an evaluator to produce a specified product or result by a specified date.

evaluation interview   1. An interview conducted as part of a personnel-evaluation program: a routine or periodic discussion of a subordinate's job performance. 2. An attempt to learn more about a person by asking questions, specific or general, usually to determine, for example, suitability for a job, admission to a particular school, or, in forensic procedures, to determine guilt.

evaluation of training   A review of training programs with emphasis on motivation, reinforcement, stimuli, orientation, safety, and special skills involved. Such training is conducted in schools, industry, the military, and other agencies and organizations.

evaluation research   The application of scientific principles, methods, and theories to identify, describe, measure, predict, change, and control factors in the assessment of persons or topics.

evaluation utilization   Using the findings of an evaluation program. Involves the managing of different assessment outcomes as well as generalizing solutions to problems discovered through this process.

evaluative ratings Orderings (ranking) of judgments of the estimated value (wealth, beauty, power) or other qualities of a group of objects. These may be based on hedonic values, such as the relative pleasantness of a series of paintings, or on the relative complexity of a series of problems, or other factors.

evaluative reasoning Critical thinking that involves appraisal of the effectiveness, validity, meaning, or relevance or other qualities of any act, idea, feeling, technique, or object.

evaluator A person, usually acknowledged to be an expert on some topic, whose role is to oversee a person, a group, an institution, etc., to present unitary and global evaluations, and to make suggestions for improvements.

evasion 1. An attempt to conceal information from others and thus change perceptions and attributions that would work to the person's advantage, for example, to escape trouble or to keep a secret. 2. A communication disorder in which an idea logically next in a chain of thought is replaced by another idea that is closely but not appropriately related to it. A form of paralogical thinking frequently observed in schizophrenia. See PARALOGIA.

Eve See MDEA.

evening people Individuals who may become lively and active late in the day and during the night but who are lethargic in the mornings and early afternoons. See MORNING PEOPLE, SUNDOWNER, SUNDOWN SYNDROME.

event In probability theory, a fundamental concept where every possible outcome of an experiment is called an elementary or simple event. Compound events are constructed from simple events, the outcome of the elements of the experiment. See INTERBEHAVIORAL PSYCHOLOGY.

event system (F. H. Allport) Common actions by individuals who have the same goal; the combination of two or more persons cooperating in the same endeavor.

event-related potential (ERP) In specific contexts, an electric potential change evoked by a specific stimulus.

event-triggered saccades Saccades (rapid, jerky eye movements) induced by external events such as a pulsating peripheral field, as opposed to reading saccades, which are typically the result of voluntary attentional changes.

Eve plan/principle The tendency for sexual differentiation as a female to occur spontaneously, whereas differentiation into a male (the Adam plan) requires hormonal events to occur at the critical prenatal period.

eversion theory of aging A point of view that aging results from functional deterioration of body tissues due to changes in the structure of the collagen molecules. (Collagen is the major protein of the white fibers of connective tissue, cartilage, and bone.) Also known as cross-linkage theory. See CYBERNETIC THEORY OF AGING.

everyday intelligence Refers to cognitive processes used daily in life and usually not measurable or reflected on intelligence tests; for example, a person may perform poorly on such a test and be labeled as having a low intelligence quotient (IQ) but nevertheless may be able to function well in life and achieve much more than someone with a high IQ. Sometimes known as common sense, street smarts.

everyday racism Bigotry expressed and reinforced in common, routine incidents.

evidence Empirically valid data that support a specific conclusion or tend to resolve a conflict.

evidence law Codified principles of behavior in trying facts to insure that the facts are weighted properly.

evidence report The summarized results of an empirical study used in the confirmation process for a hypothesis.

evil What is morally reprehensible. "Evil," as is true of "sin," are terms that do not belong to psychology proper, but to moral philosophy/theology. Generally, when psychologists examine "evil" or horrible human behaviors, causal explanations are found that have the tendency to exculpate offenders.

evil eye A superstition found in many indigenous cultures, according to which certain individuals, either consciously or unconsciously, cause harm to those upon whom they fix their gaze. Also known as *mal occhio* in Italian, and *mal de ojo* in Spanish. See FASCINUM.

eviration 1. Emasculation of a male by castration. 2. The delusion of a male that he has been emasculated and turned into a female.

evocative therapy (J. Frank) A treatment method or procedure based on the concept that behavior is evoked by underlying factors. It is directed first to finding what generates behavioral dysfunctions and then making appropriate changes, both dispositional and environmental. See PSYCHOTHERAPY.

evoked potential (EP) An electric activity in a particular part of the brain that occurs when a specific sense organ or peripheral-nerve ending is stimulated. Differs from ordinary brain waves in that the activity occurs at the time of stimulation rather than spontaneously, and occurs in a sensory area associated with the appropriate nerve tract. The evoked potential is predictable and reproducible. Also known as cortically-evoked response (ER).

evoked response (ER) A response in the nervous system brought forth usually by some sensory stimulus.

evolution The series of phylogenetic changes in the structure or behavior of organisms. In the broadest sense, it includes consideration of all factors that may be involved and embraces all changes whether in the direction of decrease or of increase in complexity.

evolutionary epistemology (M. Mahoney, D. T. Campbell) The argument that the growth of knowledge is a product of both biological and social evolution independent of the knowledge that flows from the social environment.

evolutionary psychology 1. The study of psychology in terms of the development of the species, theoretically from the earliest forms to the most complex contemporary forms, trying to understand the continuity between the latter and the more primitive. 2. A new branch of psychological inquiry that derives its principles from Darwinian and sociobiological concepts and then applies them to the study of social development, personality styles of adaptation, as well as interactions between humans and their ecological habitat.

evolutionary strategy   (C. Darwin) The concept that an individual organism of any species may try a variety of strategies to survive in times of danger or in terms of competition with others of the same species. Those who succeed may pass on their traits to the next generation, whereas those who fail usually do not. Over time (sometimes millions of years), successful strategies that can vary tremendously become dominant in the species; for example, the giraffe with a long neck may have evolved due to long-dead ancestors that survived by being able to reach the leaves of trees during a food shortage at the ground level. See NATURAL SELECTION.

evolution of brain   The concept that the human brain has evolved over a period of many millions of years from a set of simple nerve fibers, as found in primitive multicellular animals, to the highly convoluted cerebral cortex of modern humans.

evolution theory   (C. Darwin) A principle that present organisms developed from preexisting organisms through genetic adaptations to the environment. Evolution theories are quite old: Aristotle stated that the ancients believed humans descended from animals. See CONVERGENT EVOLUTION, DARWIN.

exacerbation   An increasing degree of power in the symptoms or manifestations of a disorder as a function of impact on an environmental or other agent.

exafference   See REAFFERENCE PRINCIPLE.

exaggeration   A reaction, presumably defensive, in which the person justifies questionable attitudes or behavior through overstatement, such as by magnifying hatred for a parent, or by expanding on the faults of an employer.

exaggeration in wit   The use of caricature, parody, and exaggeration to achieve pleasurable "comical nonsense."

exaltation   1. A sense of supreme happiness, especially in achieving a highly desired goal. 2. A state of joyous excitement during which patients may dance, sing, laugh, or declaim in an unrestrained and uninhibited manner; a symptom that frequently occurs in acute mania.

exalted paranoia   A type of paranoid disorder in which the person experiences great elation and makes extravagant claims, such as claiming to have invented a system that will bring peace to the world, or claiming to have access to divine powers. See EXPANSIVE DELUSION.

examination   1. A formal evaluation. 2. A search, especially for a cause of some pathological element. Types of examination include: ADULT BASIC LEARNING, ADVANCED PLACEMENT, ALPHA, BETA, ELECTROENCEPHALOGRAPHIC, GRADUATE RECORD, MENTAL, MENTAL STATUS, NEUROLOGICAL, OBJECTIVE, POSTMORTEM, PRESENT STATE, PSYCHIATRIC, PSYCHOLOGICAL, PSYCHOMETRIC, SEXOLOGICAL, SHORT-ANSWER, SUBJECTIVE.

examination anxiety   Tension and apprehension associated with taking a test.

examination dream   A dream associated with test or examination anxiety. Also known as matriculation dream.

Examination for Professional Psychology Programs (EPPP)   An examination given to graduates of Ph.D. programs to assess knowledge of the field of clinical psychology. Schools are rated as well as individuals.

Examining for Aphasia (EFA)   (J. Eisenson) A series of tests consisting of subtests for identifying objects by (a) sight, sound, and touch, (b) answering questions posed in auditory and silent reading comprehension tasks to identify receptive disturbances, and (c) tests using action, speech, word-finding, and writing tasks to identify predominantly expressive disturbances.

exaptation   1. The use of a certain bodily structure for a new, unusual, often culture-specific purpose, such as using teeth to hold something. See ADAPTATION. 2. (S. J. Gould) A feature, now useful for an organism, that did not arise as an adaptation for its present role but was subsequently co-opted for its current function. For instance, feathers may have originally served as a cooling mechanism but now aid in flying. See ADAPTATION, DARWINISM, EMERGENT EVOLUTION, SPANDREL.

exceptional child   Comprehensive phrase denoting a child who is substantially above or below normal in some significant respect. See GIFTEDNESS, MENTAL RETARDATION, SLOW LEARNER.

exceptional student   In educational circles, frequently meaning a person who is retarded in relation to some cognitive function. See GIFTEDNESS, MENTAL RETARDATION, SLOW LEARNER.

exchange theory   A point of view that explains social interactions in terms of their consequences. People, according to Jeremy Bentham, engage in transactions where perceived rewards will be the same as or exceed personal costs.

excitability   1. The property of living tissue whereby it responds variously to varied stimulations. 2. A property of some people marked by varying levels of reactivity to irritating stimuli with resulting varied behavioral and emotional displays.

excitability of neurons   The property of neurons reacting to irritation, marked by an electric or chemical response. Whereas all living cells display some irritability, some neurons and muscle cells show irritability characterized by a sudden, transient increase in their ionic permeability, and change in the electric potential of the neural membrane.

excitant   An agent capable of eliciting a response.

excitation   The activity elicited in a nerve when stimulated.

excitation and conduction   A two-stage process in which (a) excitation first occurs in a neuron as a response to the irritation of a stimulus, and the potential difference across the membrane becomes an electric sink (a device that collects or dissipates energy), causing in turn a flow of current from neighboring areas, and (b) the neighboring areas also become electric sinks and a wave of excitation spreads in a manner as conduction. See EXCITABILITY OF NEURON.

excitation gradient   A principle that the closer the similarity of, for example, stimulus A to stimulus B, the closer will be the similarity of the response to B in intensity and character, to that normally evoked by stimulus A. Also known as generalization gradient.

excitation therapy   Therapeutic methods based on a concept of Pierre Janet that people who are depressed may be restored to a normal affective state by treatment that would invigorate and generate psychic energy. The means would vary with the therapist.

excitation transfer theory   A point of view that residual arousal from one setting can be mistakenly attributed to a subsequent emotional setting, thereby increasing the emotional response.

excitatory conditioning   A form of classical conditioning in which the conditioned stimulus becomes a signal for presentation of the unconditioned stimulus.

excitatory field   An area of the brain near the termination of an excited sensory neuron.

excitatory-inhibitory processes   1. Processes whereby the transmission of neuronal signals is inhibited or enabled by the action of inhibitory or excitatory neurotransmitters on the postsynaptic membrane. 2. In Ivan Pavlov's early theories, antagonistic functions of the nervous system: excitation and inhibition. 3. (H. Eysenck) A theory that predominance of the excitatory process predisposes the person to hysterical neurosis, and a predominance of the inhibitory process is associated with obsessive-compulsive or phobic reactions.

excitatory irradiation   The spread of excitation outward from an active neural center.

excitatory-postsynaptic potential (EPSP)   (J. S. Coombs, J. C. Eccles & P. Fatt) 1. The temporary reduction of the negative potential in a postsynaptic cell. 2. The reduction of the potential difference (depolarization) in a postsynaptic dendrite leading to postsynaptic excitation.

excitatory potential ($_SE_R$)   (C. L. Hull) The hypothesized strength of a tendency to respond in a certain way; a hypothetical variable combining the effects of drive and habit strength. Formula: $_SE_R = D \times _SH_R$ where: $_SH_R$ is the habit strength and D is drive. See GENERALIZED REACTION POTENTIAL, HULL'S THEORY.

excitatory synapse   1. A junction at which a neuron releases a chemical that causes depolarization of an adjacent cell. 2. The location for a postsynaptic excitatory potential (EPSP), which is a graded local polarization across a synaptic cleft at the end of an axon. Transmitter-chemical changes at the terminal button change the permeability of the receiving neuron that makes possible the activation of the excitatory synapse.

excitatory tendency (E)   An ability of a certain stimulus to generate a particular response.

excitement   An emotional state marked by impulsive behavior, tense anticipation, and general arousal. Kinds of excitement include: ANNIVERSARY, CATATONIC, INHIBITED SEXUAL, MANIC, PSYCHOMOTOR, SCHIZOPHRENIC.

excitement-calmness   (W. Wundt) Dimensions or attributes of Wilhelm Wundt's tridimensional theory of emotion in which people differ in being generally highly alert to being totally inert. Also known as excitement-depression/-inhibition, feeling of excitement-depression. See PLEASANTNESS-UNPLEASANTNESS FEELING, TENSION-RELAXATION FEELING, WUNDT'S TRIDIMENSIONAL THEORY OF EMOTION.

excitement phase   (W. Masters & V. Johnson) The first phase of the sexual-response cycle, in the genital areas become engorged with blood. Also known as arousal phase. See SEXUAL-RESPONSE CYCLE.

exciting cause   A specific stimulus that, taken in conjunction with existing conditions, produces a given effect.

exclamation theory   See ORIGIN-OF-LANGUAGE THEORIES.

excluded middle principle   In formal logic, one of the three laws of normal thought that states something is either true or false. See LAWS OF THOUGHT.

exclusion (designs)   In ergonomics, workplace designs that prevent accidents.

excrement   Feces. Also known as scat.

excrement fear   See COPROPHOBIA, SCATOPHOBIA.

executive area (of the brain)   A cortical area that integrates the functioning of other parts of the cortex.

executive organ   The body organ that plays the major role in responding to a stimulus. When the stimulus leads a person to touch an object, the hand becomes the executive organ. Other organs often play subsidiary roles, such as eyes that help direct the executive organ serve as auxiliary organs.

executive program   A permanently stored computer program that provides a master control over all the system's functions.

executive stage   (K.W. Schaie) The fourth of Schaie's cognitive stages, in which the middle-aged person responsible for societal systems integrates complex relationships on several levels.

executive stress   Strain experienced by management personnel who are responsible for major decisions, the effectiveness of subordinates, and the success of the company as a competitive organization.

exegesis   Explanations intended to make material understandable, whether of difficult-to-understand literature or of research findings. See DECONSTRUCTION.

exemplar theory   A point of view that certain desirable traits may be personified by single individuals, such as braveness by Richard the Lion Hearted; patience by Griselda; saintly by Mother Theresa; handsomeness by Adonis. See PERSONIFICATION, STEREOTYPE.

exercise high   Feeling of exhilaration or euphoria following strenuous activity, possibly due to endorphin secretion. Also known as runners' high.

exergonic   Any physical or chemical process that results in a release of energy to its surroundings. See ENDERGONIC.

exhaustion   The limiting case of muscular fatigue in which a stimulus or excitation ceases to elicit any overt motor response.

exhaustion delirium/psychosis   A clouded state of consciousness and confusion with disordered thinking and defective perception occurring among some mountain climbers, long-distance swimmers, explorers, and individuals lost in the wilderness, as well as patients suffering from advanced cancer or other debilitating diseases. Particularly apt to occur when extreme overexertion is coupled with other forms of stress, such as prolonged insomnia, starvation, loneliness, or excessive heat or cold. See DELIRIUM.

exhaustion stage (H. Selye) The third and final stage of the general adaptation syndrome in which the organism is no longer able to endure continuing stress, and should the stress continues, the organism dies. Also known as stage of exhaustion. See ALARM REACTION, GENERAL ADAPTATION SYNDROME, STAGE OF RESISTANCE.

exhaustive search A systematic, comprehensive, and multifactorial scanning of items in a domain of inquiry to locate a specific item.

exhaustive stupor A coma-like reaction resulting from a severe infection or toxic condition, sometimes due to exceptionally strenuous and long-term efforts.

exhibitionism Acting in a manner to generate attention from others, including: (a) female exhibitionism by baring parts of the body, such as breasts, where this is not culturally sanctioned, (b) male exhibitionism by exposing genitalia or buttocks for purposes of shocking.

exhibitionist A person who has a pattern of behavior exposing self to others.

existence (C. P. Alderter) The condition of being. Often referred to in contradistinction to essence. In Aristotelian philosophy, it refers to the actualization of essence.

Existence, Relatedness, and Growth theory (ERG theory) A variation of Abraham Maslow's hierarchy of needs as applied in industrial psychology. The categories include existence needs, related to physical needs of the organism (food, clothing, shelter); relatedness needs that involve interpersonal relations with others on and off the job; and growth needs in the form of personal development and improvement.

existential analysis A phase in existential psychotherapy in which analysands explore their own being: values, relationships, and commitments. The object, however, is not to accept things as they are but to develop new and more fulfilling modes of existence. Being is not seen as static and fixed; rather, it is the process of becoming.

existential anxiety A profound sense of apprehension associated with the feeling that life is ultimately meaningless and futile, and that a person is alienated not only from other people but from the self. Also known as existential angst/anguish. See ANGST.

existential crisis (V. Frankl) The basic crisis faced by humankind consisting in finding or developing meaning and purpose in life.

existential dilemma (E. Fromm) A conflict between limited abilities and unlimited goals. See FEELINGS OF INFERIORITY.

existential ego function The activities of the ego in dealing with the problem of existence: increased awareness of the self and of the meaning and possibilities of human lives.

existential-humanistic therapy A form of therapy that addresses the entire person rather than one aspect, such as behavior or unconscious dynamics. Emphasis is placed on patients' subjective experiences, freedom, ability to decide their own life course, and realization of their potential. Also known as humanistic-existential therapy.

existentialism A school of philosophical thought that focuses on the meaning of present experiences and holds that the essential problem of existence is to fully understand, be, and actualize the self. See BEING-IN-THE-WORLD, EXISTENTIAL PHENOMENOLOGY, EXISTENTIAL PSYCHOTHERAPY, ZEN THERAPY.

existential isolation The profound sense that, as in birth and in death, throughout life a person is fundamentally alone, and that there is an unbridgeable abyss between the person and the rest of the world.

existential judgment Any set of postulates or definitions that implies the actual existence of the subject or topic. It is a generally recognized canon of modern logic that an existential judgment, to be valid, must depend upon empirical evidence, that is, it cannot be deduced from any set of mere assumptions or definitions.

existential living (C. R. Rogers) The capacity to live fully in the present and respond freely and flexibly to new experience without fear. Carl Rogers considered the capacity for existential living a central feature of the fully functioning person.

existential neurosis (V. Frankl) The inability to perceive meaning in life as expressed in feelings of emptiness, alienation, futility, aimlessness. In accord with other existentialists, Viktor Frankl considers meaninglessness to be the quintessential illness of the modern age. Sometimes known as existential vacuum. See EXISTENTIAL PSYCHOTHERAPY, EXISTENTIAL VACUUM, LOGOTHERAPY, WILL TO MEANING.

existential phenomenology The direct, immediate awareness of the self and unique experience, putting aside all preconceptions, hypotheses, and analyses. Existential phenomenology means knowing the self instead of knowing about the self. See EXISTENTIALISM, PHENOMENOLOGY.

existential psychology (R. May) 1. The view that psychology is concerned with observing and understanding personal inner experience. Humans are viewed as responsible, feeling people concerned with fears and doubts. 2. (E. G. Titchener) An archaic point of view that limited psychology to the sensory aspects of experience. See EXISTENTIALISM, PHENOMENOLOGY, STRUCTURAL PSYCHOLOGY.

existential (psycho)therapy (L. Binswanger, R. May) A form of therapy that places an emphasis on exploring present life and values and working toward the development of a more meaningful, integrated, fulfilling existence. See LOGOTHERAPY.

existential questioning Exploring such constructs as meaninglessness, death, isolation, freedom, and other elemental issues of human existence.

existential school See EXISTENTIALISM.

existential therapy See EXISTENTIAL (PSYCHO)-THERAPY.

existential vacuum Existential neurosis characterized by feelings of emptiness, isolation, and meaninglessness.

exit interview 1. A meeting between two or more persons, one of whom is being severed from an organization, and the other(s) representing that organization. Its purpose is to facilitate the separation and give the departing person counseling and information. 2. An interview conducted by a personnel officer or manager with an employee who is leaving the organization permanently to invite feedback.

exitotoxic lesion   A brain lesion produced by an intracerebral injection of an excitatory amino acid.

exocathection   (H. A. Murray) Preoccupation with practical, worldly affairs rather than personal matters. Compare ENDOCATHECTION.

exocrine gland   A gland that secretes its product through ducts either onto the surface of the body (tear gland) or into the body cavities (salivary gland), but not directly into the bloodstream. Also known as duct gland.

exogamy   1. The practice of marrying outside the tribe, clan, or social unit. 2. The prohibition of marrying within one's own social group. Compare ENDOGAMY.

exogenic   Relates to factors produced or generated by external events or the environment. Distinguished from endogenous.

exogenous   1. Originating outside of the body. 2. Refers to a condition caused by a foreign object, such as an injury caused by a bullet, or a bit of dust in the eye. 3. Having its origins external to the body, in contrast to endogenous, generally referring to either certain hormones, medicines, or occasionally even certain conditions. A person might be administered exogenous corticosteroids to reduce the body's occasional tendency to over-react in its immune response.

exogenous depression   See REACTIVE DEPRESSION.

exogenous drive   A motive or urge that comes from a source external to the organism. Compare ENDOGENOUS DRIVE.

exogenous factors   Causes from the surround that contribute to healthful or pathological mental and physical conditions, for example, variations in the weather, economic conditions, neighbors.

exogenous mental retardation   Mental impairment largely attributable to environmental insults. Compare ENDOGENOUS MENTAL RETARDATION.

exogenous stimulation   Stimulation from sources outside the body that impinge on an organism, such as sound waves, air pressure, or physical objects. Compare ENDOGENOUS STIMULATION.

exogenous stress   Mental stress arising from external situations, such as natural catastrophes, excessive competition on the job, or climbing a precipice.

exolinguistics   The science of verbal communication as it relates to characteristics of the sender, receiver, and the message itself. Also known as metalinguistics. See DISTRIBUTED COGNITIONS LINGUISTICS, LINGUISTIC APPROACH, METALANGUAGE.

exonerative moral reasoning   A process by which a person consciously formulates moral justification for an act that would normally be considered immoral or unacceptable. Refers to a process of self-serving reasoning designed to achieve vindication in the eyes of self or others. See RATIONALIZATION.

exopsychic   Characterizing mental activity that purportedly produces effects on the world outside the individual. See ENDOPSYCHIC.

exorcism   Religious or superstitious rite, usually performed by a shaman or priest, that attempts to expel purported demons from possessed individuals and sometimes objects. The rite includes prayers, incantations, threats to the demon, and various ritual gestures.

exosomatic current   Electrical current or potential delivered by agencies external to the organism. Mesmerists believed in flow of magnetic fluid by which healing communications were transmitted. See MESMERISM.

exosomatic method/technique   A technique that uses electrical resistance of the skin in psychogalvanic-response studies. See GALVANIC SKIN RESPONSE.

exosystem   (U. Bronfenbrenner) The society in which individuals are born but which exists and functions largely independently of them.

exoteric   Pertaining to the superficial or apparent meaning of a system or theory, as opposed to the hidden or mystical meaning.

exotic bias   A tendency of social scientists to overemphasize features of a culture that contrast sharply with the investigator's own culture while overlooking features that are the same or similar.

exotic psychosis   See CULTURE-SPECIFIC SYNDROMES.

exotropia   A form of strabismus in which the visual axes diverge; imbalance of the muscles of the eyes so that one of the eyes points outward. Also known as wall-eye. See DIVERGENCE, STRABISMUS.

expanded consciousness   A subjective reaction to psychedelic drugs (of the class of hallucinogens) such as mescaline or LSD in which people claim to gain new insights, often of a mystical, philosophical, or spiritual type, see things more clearly, and have a greater understanding of themselves and others.

expanded personality   The totality of external objects felt by a person to be parts or extensions of the self; that which the person views as "me" in addition to the self. May include clothing, material possessions, friends, etc.

expansion ad   In consumer psychology, an advertisement designed to increase a brand's or general product's usage by encouraging consumers to use it in a wider range of situations. For example: "Florida Grapefruit— You don't just have to halve it in the morning."

expansive delusion   delusion of grandeur

expansive mood   1. A mood or affective state that reflects feelings of grandiosity. 2. A state in which the individual projects self with energy and high spirits.

expansiveness   A personality trait or state manifested by loquaciousness, overfriendliness, hyperactivity, and lack of restraint.

expansive type general paresis   A psychosis occurring in advanced general paresis, marked by euphoria, grandiose schemes, and delusions ("I am the richest person in the world"; "I know how we can have an unlimited supply of energy").

ex-patient club   An ongoing group organized as part of an aftercare program of people who have been cured of some disorder or other pathological condition. The objective is to provide social and recreational experience, to promote readjustment and rehabilitation, and to maintain improvement through group support and, in some cases, group therapy. See GROW, RECOVERY INC.

expectancy   1. An attitude of anticipation of a given stimulus or event based upon previous experience with related stimuli or events. 2. In statistics, expectancy is the probability of an occurrence based on mathematical calculation. 3. (J. Rotter) The belief that in a certain psychological situation, a particular behavior will lead to success in moving to a personal goal.

expectancy charts   The graphic representation of performance expected on the basis of tests of ability. These may be individual when predicting performance of a single person or institutional when based on expected performance of a group of individuals who have been tested, such as a cohort of job applicants.

expectancy effect   A tendency for an expectation to cloud a person's ability to observe or reason that may lead to an error or bias in the direction in which the person expected the results to go. See EXPECTANCY.

expectancy theory   1. (E. C. Tolman) A purposive-behaviorism point of view that cognitive learning involves acquired expectancies and a tendency to react to certain objects as signs of certain further objects previously associated with them. See ANTICIPATION PURPOSIVENESS, TELEOLOGY. 2. See VALENCE-INSTRUMENTALITY-EXPECTANCY THEORY.

expectancy-value model   A concept that motivation for any particular end is a combination of the importance of the goal and the possibility of achieving it.

expectant analysis   See FOCUSED ANALYSIS.

expectation   An attentive state of anticipation, sometimes suffused with emotion and tension.

expectation-states theory   (J. Berger) In group dynamics, explains status differentiation in groups, emphasizing the individual's standing on positively and negatively valued status characteristics. Holds that status differences are more likely to develop when members work together on a task that is important to them.

expected frequency   1. A frequency predicted from a theoretical model, to be contrasted with an observed frequency. 2. A frequency that would occur on the basis of chance alone.

expected payoff   In game theory, how much a person will win or not win by playing a game according to a consistent theory. In gaming houses, even a small advantage in favor of the house will always lead to winning everything eventually if play goes on forever.

expected value   The mean value of a random variable over an infinite number of samplings. The expected value E(X) of a discrete random variable X is given by $E(X) = \Sigma X p(X) = $ **mean of X**, the sum being taken over any value of X. If the expected value of a measure corresponds to the parameter (population value), the measure is an unbiased estimate. The two most common applications are formulas for the population variance and population mean.

expedient   An experimental device used to overcome some difficulty in either the apparatus, the general conditions, or the make-up of the observer.

expediter   A person who helps patients obtain the treatment or rehabilitation services needed by contacting various agencies and facilities and by making recommendations and referrals. See ADVOCATE.

experience   1. An event that is lived through, or undergone, as opposed to one imagined or thought about. 2. Knowledge or skill resulting from instructive events and practice.

experience balance (Exp)   In Rorschach test scoring, the ratio of movement (M) to color (C) responses or of movement to total responses to the ink-blots. See EXPERIENCE TYPE.

experience inventory   A questionnaire that measures various aspects of openness to experience. Examples suggested by factor analysis: aesthetic sensitivity, openness to ideas, unconventional ideas, fantasy utilization, and unusual perceptions.

experiencing   Idiosyncratic sensing and a becoming aware of self and others in interaction with the world. This process admits degrees of flexibility and rigidity.

experience type   In Rorschach test scoring, relating to introversion-extraversion categorization, assessed in Rorschach test scoring by the ratio of movement (m) responses (revealing introverted tendency) to color (c) responses (extroverted tendency).

experiential   The "lived," sensed, and felt aspect of a person's presence.

experiential avoidance   A conscious attempt to be freed of certain private experiences such as thoughts, desires, goal, memories. Research indicates such attempts do not succeed and actually generate pathogenic effects. See IRONIC MENTAL CONTROL, PARADOXICAL INTENTION, PHENOMENOLOGY.

experiential element   (R. J. Sternberg) The creative aspect of intelligence that determines how effectively people approach both new as well as usual tasks.

experiential family therapists   Therapists who project themselves clinically as authentic and self-disclosing persons and use that self instrumentally in their interactions with families.

experiential group   A group of persons who come together to share feelings and experiences (for example, an Alcoholics Anonymous group), as contrasted with a task-oriented group.

experiential history   (A. Anastasi) Features of a person's environment, including both physical properties and human behavior, that have actually affected (that is, reached) the particular individual from conception to death.

experiential psychotherapy   (E. Gendlin) A system of treatment that depends on interpersonal encounters stressing heightened feelings, immediate reactions to present sensations, and immediate concreteness. See DIRECT PSYCHOANALYSIS, FOCUSING, LOGOTHERAPY.

experiment   The manipulation of one or more independent variables conducted under controlled conditions to test one or more hypotheses, especially for making inferences of a cause-and-effect character. Involves the measurement of one or more dependent variables. Types of experiment include: ABSTRACTION, ANALOGUE, ARISTOTLE'S, ASCH CONFORMITY, ASSOCIATION, BEHAVIOR(AL), BLANK, BLIND, BLIX'S TEMPERATURE, CANNON-WASHBURN, CASPAR HAUSER, CHOICE, COLORED-SHADOW, COMPLICATION, CONTROL, CONTROLLED, CRITICAL, CROSSED-NERVE,

CRUCIAL, DECEPTION, DELAYED-REACTION, DEPRIVATION, DISCRIMINATION, EXPLORATORY, FALSIFYING, FERRIER'S, FIELD, FRANKLIN, GROUP, ISOLATION, MEYER'S CONTRAST, MICHELSON-MORLEY, MULTIPLE-CHOICE, NATURAL, NEWTON'S COLOR, RAGONA SCINÀ, REACTION TIME, SCHEINER'S, SIGNAL, SPLIT-BRAIN, STRATTON'S, THOUGHT, TRANSPOSITION, TRUE, WEBER'S, WEIGHT, WEIGHT-LIFTING, WUNDT'S PERCEPTION.

experimental analysis of behavior (B. F. Skinner) The study of the shaping, maintenance, and extinction of behavior by environmental contingencies. This approach uses experimental manipulation rather than statistical averaging, emphasizes an engineering rather than a theoretical orientation, and analyzes the effects of schedules of reinforcement on rate of response. See BEHAVIOR ANALYSIS.

experimental attrition A reduction of number of participants or animal subjects often found in any experimental group over time.

experimental control The control of contaminants, that is, extraneous conditions and variables in an experiment, usually through randomization procedures so that any change in the dependent variable can be attributed solely to the independent variable.

experimental design/plan An outline or plan of the procedures to be followed in scientific research, including how participants are assigned to treatments.

experimental error 1. A deviation or false value in experimental data, usually due to a design error. 2. The sum of all uncontrolled sources of variation that affect a dependent variable measure. 3. The denominator of statistical tests such as the t test and the F test.

experimental esthetics The use of experimental-psychology techniques in the study of art forms and qualities; for example, the use of Gestalt concepts in analyzing emotional effects and preferences for colors and patterns.

experimental extinction The weakening or abolition of a conditioned reflex by repeated excitation without reinforcement by an unconditioned stimulus.

experimental group (E) A group of participants exposed to one or more independent variables or to a set of treatment conditions for purposes of scientific study. See CONTROL GROUP.

experimental hypothesis A premise, the basis for a scientific study that describes what the researcher hopes to demonstrate or disconfirm if certain experimental conditions are met. Hypotheses are testable aspects of research based on general theories.

experimental introspection The process of discussing personal phenomenology (internal experiences) as part of a laboratory-type research, sometimes done because experimenters may thereby find errors in the procedures or other information of value.

experimental marriage An agreement between two people to live together as spouses for a period of time to determine their compatibility and desire to formalize the marriage. Also known as trial marriage.

experimental method A system of scientific investigation, usually based on a design and carried out under controlled conditions with the aim of testing a hypothesis and establishing a causal relationship between independent and dependent variables. See EXPERIMENT.

experimental neurosis (I. P. Pavlov) A psychological disorder characterized by anxiety that is produced in animals or humans when forced or induced to make decisions or solve problems beyond their abilities. Such procedures are unequivocally unethical with human participants. Also known as artificial neurosis. See TRANSFERENCE NEUROSES.

experimental philosophy Historically, in academics, the first true experimentalists were not called psychologists but rather experimental philosophers. Both William James and Wilhelm Wundt were so labeled. Such individuals differed from arm chair philosophers by experimenting to find out the truth about their views relative to the speed of nerve impulse transmission.

experimental plan See EXPERIMENTAL DESIGN.

experimental psychology (A. von Haller) The scientific study of behavior, motives, or cognition normally in a laboratory setting for the purpose of predicting, explaining, or controlling behavior. Experimental psychology aims at establishing lawful, quantified relationships and explanatory theory through comparison of responses under various controlled conditions. See EXPERIMENT.

experimental realism An experiment, particularly in the social-psychological area that is realistic from the point of view of participants who usually are unaware that they are in an experiment. Deception is often employed to achieve experimental realism. It is ethical after such an experiment to inform all persons of the facts and purposes of the experiment. Some people think that all such experiments should be outlawed. See ASCH EFFECT, AUSSAGE TEST, MUNDANE REALISM, OBEDIENCE.

experimental series The successive trials in an experiment that are fully implemented, as distinguished from theoretical and interpretive phrases.

experimental study Research where independent variables will be manipulated and behavior changes (dependent variables) recorded.

experimental treatment(s) Special interventions whose effect on behavior is to be evaluated.

experimental variable See DEPENDENT VARIABLE, INDEPENDENT VARIABLE.

experimentation The art of designing and conducting systematic trials for measuring the influence of an independent variable on behavior, psychological impressions, expressions, and functions.

experimentee (S. Rosenzweig) The individual working in cooperation with but in a complementary relation to the experimenter. See PARTICIPANT, SUBJECT.

experimenter (E) A person who attempts systematically to control, repeat, or vary conditions or stimuli to produce or modify psychological responses.

experimenter bias effect   The distortion of findings due to experimenters giving participants improper information or making other errors; for example, a psychologist, asked to evaluate a hospital diagnostic program for screening executives for premature senility, entered as a patient, and went through the total procedure. An important part of the procedure was the administration of an individual intelligence test, with which he was familiar. The test was administered incorrectly. The report pointed this out and all prior findings of the diagnostic program were invalidated. See EXPERIMENTER BIAS.

experimenter bias   Proclivity of experimenters to unconsciously shape their perception of the data to fit the research results hypothesized. Bias takes effect when the experimenter is engaged in a non-blind condition in the rating, especially of subjective data. BIOSOCIAL, EXPERIMENTER-EXPECTANCY, INTENTIONAL, INTERPRETER, MODELING, OBSERVER, PSYCHOSOCIAL, SITUATIONAL.

experimenter drift   A common error in research that occurs when experimenters, over time, change the nature of their relationships with participants. Can be due to such factors as boredom, fatigue, or loss of interest. See EXPERIMENTER EFFECT.

experimenter effect   Distortion in experimental findings caused by mistakes made by the experimenter in handling and interpreting the data, or due to the experimenter's behavior toward the participants; for example, a harsh and impersonal experimenter may compromise external validity by intimidating all the participants and thus altering their experimental behaviors.

experimenter-expectancy effect   A distortion in experimental findings caused by the impact of an experimenter's expectations on a participant's responses, a type of experimenter effect. The experimenter's body gestures, expressions, and tone of voice have all been found to influence a participant's responses. See EXPERIMENTER BIAS, EXPERIMENTER EFFECT.

experiment of nature   Any event or development that occurs without human prearrangement, in a manner analogous to an experiment. As the consequences of the causal events are often deleterious to the humans involved, ethical considerations prevent the confection of such an experiment. Such ex post facto studies are the norm where intentional experimentation is prohibited.

experimentum crusis   German phrase for crucial experiment.

experts   Persons who have had special training or expertise in any given branch of science, art, or industry, such that their statements or judgments or activities in that field are entitled to special consideration and credence. See EXPERT WITNESS.

expert-novice differences   (W. G. Chase, H. A. Simon) Differences in knowledge and cognitive processes between persons who are expert performers in a domain and persons who are novices in that domain. Such differences are measured, and the mechanisms underlying them studied through experiments in which the level of expertise of subjects serves as the principal independent variable. See STRONG METHODS, WEAK METHODS.

expert system   In artificial intelligence, certain programs designed to solve problems, typically medical diagnoses, by presenting questions, situations, descriptions, instances, etc., that can be answered YES or NO. The answers given eventually lead to diagnoses that persons answering the specific questions would not have come to independently.

expert testimony   In courts of law, in civil or criminal trials, specialists in any given relevant area (for example, psychology) may be hired by the court itself, a district attorney, or by an attorney representing someone to testify as an expert. The expert, after being sworn in, is usually questioned in a critical manner by an attorney who represents either the state or an individual to challenge the person's expertness. A judge will decide whether the person is indeed an expert. See EXPERT WITNESS.

expert witness   1. A person with the training, experience, and credentials to offer credible opinion in a court of law. 2. In forensic psychiatry and psychology, a professional who is considered qualified by a judge (after possible objections by attorneys) by reason of training and experience to serve as a consultant in legal proceedings. Expert witnesses are asked for opinions within the narrow aspects of their specialty. Psychologists might be asked questions about the value of certain tests, opinions as to whether a person was responsible at the time of committing a crime, and whether a person is likely to be violent in the future.

expiation   An action performed for the purpose of reducing feelings of guilt or wrong done to others, often suggested by counselors and clergy.

expiatory punishment   (J. Piaget) The type of punishment preferred by children up to about age 8 in which the child is made to suffer in proportion to the severity of the misbehavior. The punishment should match the misbehavior in kind and strength. See LOGICAL CONSEQUENCES, RECIPROCAL PUNISHMENT.

explanation   1. The setting forth of a principle or the description of an event or procedure in such terms that the average hearer or reader will understand the operation. 2. The description of a complex event plus evaluation of the factors involved, with the aim of showing how or by what processes the antecedent situation was transformed into the later situation. 3. An attempt to link an event with its cause or causes that may go through a number of steps, an early one being the proximal cause and the final one being the distal cause.

explanatory delusion   (E. Bleuler) A compound delusion in which mental patients give explanations, logical only to them, to justify the correctness of their delusions.

explanatory research   Research aimed at determining the causes of a phenomenon, for example, to determine why a certain couple are both seeking a divorce.

explanatory style   (M. E. P. Seligman) A person's idiosyncratic way of explaining personal historical events.

explicit behavior   Any overt, observable action.

explicit memory   The conscious recollection of facts and events. Also known as declarative memory.

explicit response   See OVERT RESPONSE.

exploitative character   (E. Fromm) Describing a person who enjoys using or exploiting others to gain what he or she wants without concern for those others. Also known as exploitive character. See EXPLOITATIVE ORIENTATION.

exploitative orientation   (E. Fromm) An exploitative character type, denoting a behavior pattern marked by stealth, deceit, power, or violence to obtain what the person wants.

exploitative-manipulative behavior   The use of other people to attain personal ends without regard for their needs or feelings. In industrial or business situations, exploitative-manipulative behavior means treating workers as commodities rather than persons. In slave-based economics, many workers were threatened in this manner.

exploration   (E. Ginzberg) The "realistic period" of adolescence when existing job opportunities are actively explored in light of the adolescent's interests and abilities. See CRYSTALLIZATION.

exploration drive   The motivation that impels an organism to examine its environment out of desire for, among other things, security, food, or sex. Highly developed in humans and other vertebrates and appears to be intrinsically satisfying. Also known as exploratory drive. See CURIOSITY.

exploratory behavior   1. Random or systematic searching behavior in a relatively novel environment, often with no apparent particular purpose except to satisfy curiosity. See CURIOSITY, EXPLORATION DRIVE. 2. Trial and error attempts to find solutions to situations of discomfort or need.

exploratory drive   exploration drive

exploratory experiments   Given a hypothesis that seems to call for extraordinarily long, detailed, and expensive research, an exploratory experiment is an attempt to obtain some evidence about one aspect of the hypothesis. It has the character of a pilot study. See EXPLORATORY RESEARCH/STUDY.

exploratory movements   Behavioral actions made by an organism in new situations that serve to orient the organism and yield information regarding the elements and spatial relations of the situation. Applies especially to behavior of children in connection with learning processes.

exploratory research/study   Preparation for research by gathering relevant facts and opinions. The first step is data-based research and the study of the literature on the topic. A second step is consulting experts in the domain. A facultative third step is doing a pilot study; this permits checking out equipment, accessing reactions of participants, and getting a 'feel' for the project.

explosive diathesis   (A. Meyer) The potentiality for extreme violence by individuals who are intoxicated or who also have basic personality difficulties. These two factors, among others, can have a synergistic effect.

explosive personality   A personality exemplified by a pattern of frequent outbursts of uncontrolled anger and hostility that are out of proportion to any provocation. Sometimes known as epileptoid personality disorder. See INTERMITTENT EXPLOSIVE DISORDER, ISOLATED EXPLOSIVE DISORDER.

exponent   1. In mathematics, a number denoting the power to which a given number or expression is to be raised. 2. A person who exemplifies or teaches authoritatively a specific doctrine.

exponential curve   A graphic representation of a curve for which the general formula $y = AC^t$ is often used to represent physical growth, where C and A are positive numbers, time t takes only positive values, C is the rate of exponential increase or decrease, and A is the starting value of the variable y.

exposition attitude/need   (H. A. Murray) A tendency to explain, demonstrate, lecture, and define relationships.

ex post facto   (after the fact—Latin) Phrase that can precede a number of other terms, such as design, experiment, findings, explanation, or research, and always refers to an event or phenomenon that followed one that happened earlier.

ex post facto research   A type of research that begins with data already collected, or research technologies applied to events not originally intended for research purposes. The experimenter does not directly manipulate the independent variable in ex post facto research.

exposure deafness   A loss of hearing due to prolonged exposure to loud sounds. The condition may be temporary or permanent, depending upon the loudness, length of exposure, and sound frequencies. A transient form marked by reduced auditory acuity for several hours is called auditory fatigue.

exposure factor   An objective determination of the risk factor in possible accidents.

exposure therapies   Various psychotherapeutic techniques based on classical conditioning theory to diminish conditioned fears by exposing the client repeatedly, in the absence of any aversive experience, to a stimulus that has become associated with stress. An example is implosive therapy.

expressed emotions effect   (R. W. Brown) A tendency for a high relapse rate in schizophrenia to be associated with critical emotions expressed toward mental patients by their families, indicating that schizophrenia may in some measure be a protective device to escape from unpleasant social situations.

expression   1. Any observable response, simple or complex, of an organism. 2. The subsidiary accompaniments of a response (for example, trembling, blushing, or adjustment of facial muscles) that serve to indicate the effect of the situation upon an individual when the gross responses are inhibited or distorted. 3. Modulations of the voice in speaking or singing, which accentuate the meaning or emotional value of the words or music. 4. A word, phrase, or formula, considered as a unit.

expression method   The technique of measuring and describing emotions in terms of bodily changes.

expressionism factor   (D. E. Berlyne) In psychological esthetics, the components of artistic style that emphasize the artist's emotional experience and intensity of feeling. The factor is based on stylistic ratings that vary along continua of intensity–tranquillity and artistic feelings, as well as on the balance between objective ideas and inner feelings. See ABSTRACT EXPRESSIONISM.

expressive aphasia (P. Broca) A language disorder in which the ability to speak, write, or use gestures is lost or impaired. The condition is often associated with a lesion in Broca's area of the brain. Also known as cortical motor aphasia, expressive dysphasia, verbal aphasia, word dumbness. See RECEPTIVE APHASIA.

expressive babble/jargon Human vocal sounds characterized by tones and inflections similar to those of speech.

expressive behavior (G. W. Allport) Conduct of a general and routine character as it becomes manifest and apparent to others.

expressive disorder Any behavioral abnormality or malfunction of a psychomotor character that a person was formerly capable of, usually evidencing neurological impairment. Common examples are speaking and reading disorders. See RECEPTIVE DISORDER.

expressive emotions See AMUSIA.

expressive functions The adaptive motor and glandular capabilities of an organism in the broadest sense, including the autonomic functions as well as those of the striped muscles.

expressive jargon **expressive babble**

expressive language Normal communication procedures, including speaking, writing, and gesturing. See EXPRESSIVE LANGUAGE SKILLS.

expressive language skills Abilities in using language effectively for communicating with other individuals. Speaking, writing, or gesturing are forms of expressive language.

expressive movements Body language, particularly posture, gesture, and facial expression. Can be clues to personality and emotions.

expressive therapy A generic process occurring in many forms of psychotherapy in which patients are encouraged to express feelings openly and without restraint. See PRIMAL THERAPY, SCREAM THERAPY, SUPPRESSIVE THERAPY.

expressive vocabulary types (K. Nelson) Classification of earliest vocabularies of children; they are dominated by words describing people and feelings.

expressivity The degree to which a gene gets expressed phenotypically. In psychology, this can be manifested as a trait or disorder. See PENETRANCE.

ext. extinction

extended care A health-care service provided to patients who have completed a period of hospitalization but require rehabilitation, skilled nursing, or other convalescent care.

extended family A number of nuclear families, related by blood, who live in one household or in close quarters.

extended-family therapy A kind of group psychotherapy with the nuclear family and other family members as well, such as aunts and uncles, grandparents, and cousins.

extended-stay review The review of a continuous hospital stay that equals or exceeds a period defined in the hospital's utilization review plan. See CONTINUED-STAY REVIEW.

extended suicide (G. B. Palermo) Murder-suicides in which one person kills another or others and then kills himself or herself.

extension 1. The spatial characteristic of physical phenomena. 2. The objects, for example, denoted by a given concept. 3. The straightening of a jointed member of the body, brought about by rotation of the portion which lies beyond the joint. See EXTENSION REFLEX.

extensional meaning Cognitive or emotional significance that can be established by pointing to persons, objects, or incidents. Also known as extensive meaning; distinguished from intentional meaning. See EXTENSIONALIZATION.

extensionalization Determination of meanings of words or sentences. Various kinds of problems regarding personality and relations with others that are due to words either alone or in groups, having different meanings to different people. Example: Jazz may be defined as loud, vulgar music by one person and soulful, creative improvisation by another. The process is sometimes used in psychotherapy, based on the hypothesis that some emotional problems are due to semantic confusion. See HERMENEUTICS.

extension reflex Any reflexive action that causes a limb or part of a limb to move away from the body. Kinds of extension reflex include extensor thrust, stretch or myotatic reflex, and crossed extension reaction.

extensity The spatial characteristic or attribute of mental phenomena. See DIMENSIONS OF CONSCIOUSNESS.

extensor motoneurons Efferent-nerve cells with fibers that connect with extensor effectors or to muscles that extend a part of the body by contracting. See EXTENSOR MUSCLE.

extensor (muscles) Muscles that via their contraction extend limbs. Also known as extensors. Contrasts with flexors. Together an extensor and a flexor form a pair of antagonistic muscles.

extensor rigidity Rigid contractions of extensor muscles. The kind of rigidity sometimes indicates the site of the motoneuron lesion associated with the disorder; for example, an injury to the cerebellum produces increased tone of extensor muscles known as cerebellar rigidity.

extensor thrust (reflex) A reflex extension of the leg caused by applying a stimulus to the sole of the foot. The reflex normally occurs each time a person takes a step in walking or running, signaling a need for body support and providing the thrust for taking the next step. See STRETCH REFLEXES.

extent The one or two dimensional aspect of experience found in the visual and tactual sensory modalities.

extent prognosis See DIRECTION PROGNOSIS.

exteriorization The outward expression of private and personal ideas. The act or process of relating personal interior affects, thoughts, and attitudes to external, objective reality in the form of words and deeds.

external acoustic meatus The opening in the outer ear. See EAR, EXTERNAL EAR, PINNA.

external auditory canal The tube connecting the pinna (external ear) to the middle ear.

external boundary See EGO BOUNDARIES.

external capsule   A thin flat layer of tissue separating the claustrum from the putamen, near the center of the human brain. Consists of white fibers from the anterior white commissure and subthalamic region and is continuous with the internal capsule. Also known as capsula externa. See BASAL GANGLIA.

external chemical messenger (ECM)   A pheromone, a hormonal substance secreted and released by an organism that may stimulate a physiological or behavioral response in another individual of the same species. Can have excitatory or inhibitory effects.

external controls   Factors exterior to the organism that direct that organism's behavior, such as traffic signals that influence driving behavior in humans.

external disinhibition   Recovery of a response that had been previously extinguished by an unrelated event.

external ear   The pinna, that part of the ear that extends beyond the surface of the head. Includes the auricle and the external or auditory opening (meatus). The external ear is connected by the auditory canal with the tympanic membrane of the middle ear. A part of the auditory apparatus that serves for the collection of sound-waves and their conduction through the temporal bone. Also known as outer ear.

external experimental validity (threats to)   See THREATS TO EXTERNAL EXPERIMENTAL VALIDITY.

external frustration   The inhibition or defeat of an organism's attempts to achieve a goal by external forces. The state of being thwarted, normally accompanied by a negative emotion.

external hair cells (of ear)   Sensory epithelial cells arranged in three or four successive rows on the organ of Corti. There are about 12,000 hair cells per cochlea. They contain tiny projections that are receptors of physical stimulation that transduce into electrical impulses. These hair cells are in the auditory and the vestibular systems. They control various functions such as hearing sounds and maintaining physical balance. Also known as outer hair cells. Compare INTERNAL HAIR CELLS (OF EAR). See HAIR CELLS.

external inequity   The unfair allocations of rewards to members of one organization in comparison to their counterparts at a comparable organization. Compare INTERNAL INEQUITY.

external inhibition   A reduction in a conditioned response that occurs when an extraneous external stimulus accompanies the conditioning stimulus.

externality–internality   (J. Rotter) A psychological construct that characterizes individuals by positions they may take on a bipolar continuum, suggesting the relative strength of agents that control reinforcements in their lives. At one end are people who assume that they are responsible in a neutral world, and at the other end are those who see themselves as manipulated by circumstances and powerful others. See SOCIAL LEARNING THEORY.

externalization   1. The paranoid projection of thoughts into the external world, as in ideas of reference. 2. The process of distinguishing between the self and the environment. 3. The process by which a drive comes to be aroused by external stimuli instead of internal stimuli; for example, hunger may be aroused by the sight of tempting food even when an organism is sated.

externalizers   (J. Rotter) Describing people who accept as fact that they react to conditions or situations around them and that things beyond their control are destined to happen. Characterized by lack of desire to compete or struggle. Compare INTERNALIZERS.

externalizing–internalizing   (T. M. Achenbach) A classification of reasons for rejected child referrals by adoptive parents, based on the children' unpleasant externalizing behavior (acting out, antisocial behavior, and hostility) or by undesirable internalizing behavior (anxiety, excessive inhibition, somatization, and depression).

external locus of control   See LOCUS OF CONTROL.

external memory   In computers, a storage medium outside the computer system.

external rectus   An extrinsic eye muscle that rotates the eyeball outward.

external reward   Generally, an award received in recognition of an accomplishment or the performance of an activity, often in the form of a token. Compare INTERNAL REWARD. See PRIMARY REINFORCEMENT.

external sense   A sense-organ system that depends upon external stimulation, for example, vision.

external validity   1. (D. T. Campbell) Representativeness of the sample of subjects studied as in relation to the population or universe of discourse to which research findings purport to apply. There are threats to external validity such as the reactive effects of testing. 2. (D. R. Krathwohl) An overall judgment of a study's power to support the generality of a causal relationship beyond the study's conditions—its generalizing power (GP). It combines five judgments: the generality claimed in the explanation, the extent claimed generality is operationalized, the appearance of the relationship within the generality operationalized, the elimination of conditions restricting generality, and the result's judged replicability with alternative operationalizations. Compare INTERNAL VALIDITY.

external world   1. The totality of physical phenomena outside the body of a given organism. 2. The totality of spatial-temporal phenomena, distinguished from the ego or self but including the body of the percipient.

exteroception   The process of an organism reacting to outside-the-body stimuli.

exteroceptive conditioning   A type of conditioning that depends primarily upon external stimuli such as auditory, visual, or somatic cues. See INTEROCEPTIVE CONDITIONING.

exteroceptive stimulus   A stimulus that impinges on an organism from outside the organism. See PROPRIOCEPTIVE STIMULUS.

exteroceptor   (C. S. Sherrington) A sense organ that receives stimulation from outside the body. Compare INTEROCEPTOR, PROPRIOCEPTOR.

exteropsychic   (E. Berne) Pertaining to personality tendencies that come from outside the individual, such as borrowed from friends or parents, as contrasted with neopsychic tendencies that represent the individual's own views or archaeopsychic tendencies that are relics from childhood. See ADULT-EGO STATE.

exterosystem   (R. Monroe) Constitutional equipment relating the organism to the external world, including sensorimotor elements, memory systems.

extinction   1. The disappearance of a conditioned response to a particular stimulus that previously elicited the response, due to the stimulus no longer being reinforced. 2. The gradual diminution in the strength or rate of a conditioned response when the unconditioned stimulus (that is, reinforcement) is withheld. See PRIMARY REINFORCEMENT. 3. In neurophysiology, a progressive decrease in excitability of a nerve to a previously adequate stimulus until it becomes completely inexcitable. Extinction for visual and tactile stimuli occurs in occipital-parietal lesions. See SENSORY EXTINCTION. 4. See EXTINCTION OF EGO. See INATTENTION.

extinction of ego   In psychoanalytic theory, the impulse to annihilate the ego due to primitive feelings of guilt and repressed hostility toward the self generated by a punitive superego. Obsessive attempts to protect loved objects by magical rituals. When these fail, feelings of dejection, apathy, and unworthiness are overwhelming. Can eventuate in a state of mind called extinction of the ego.

extinction ratio   The proportion of unreinforced responses to reinforced responses emitted by a participant in a period of reinforcement reconditioning.

extirpation   The surgical removal of some organ or part of the body for research or curative purposes. Sometimes known as ablation. See VIVISECTION.

extraception   (H. A. Murray) A personality trait of people who are outwardly constrained, limited in imagination, and inclined to deal with objective matters. Compare INTRACEPTION.

extrachance   In parapsychology, not due to chance alone.

extradimensional shift   A process that calls for an organism first to be conditioned by one type of stimulus (for example, sound) and then further conditioned by another type of stimulus (for example, touch).

extra-individual behavior   Conduct influenced by situational variables rather than dispositional variables of individuals. The concept assumes that otherwise normal people will adapt behavior to their surroundings. Thus, individual behavior and styles of self-projection will vary as a function of whether a person is in a church, casino, court of law, or funeral parlor. See SITUATED IDENTITIES.

extrajection   The act of attributing personal feelings or characteristics to another person. See EMPATHY, PARANOIA, PROJECTION.

extraneous variables   Variables that are not pertinent to the purposes of an experiment but that, if not controlled, may contaminate the results by having a systematic but unknown influence on the dependent variables.

extrapolate   To estimate the value of a variable beyond its known range by making projections from past performance.

extrapsychic conflict   A conflict arising between the individual and the environment, as contrasted to internal or intrapsychic conflict. See CONFLICT, EXTERNALITY-INTERNALITY.

extrapunitive   (S. Rosenzweig) A reaction to frustration or distress in which anger or aggression is directed at the person or situation perceived to be the source of the frustration.

extrapunitive personality   A personality type that tends to view difficult situations as products of outside factors rather than on internal factors. Such persons blame others and things rather than themselves. See PARANOIA.

extrapyramidal dyskinesia   1. Distortions of voluntary movement, such as tremors, spasms, tics, rigidity, gait disturbance, that derive from organic disorders. 2. A side effect of some antipsychotic drugs that can produce such conditions as acute dystonia and tardive dyskinesia.

extrapyramidal involvement (EPI)   Refers primarily to symptoms such as tremors and other parkinsonian side effects induced by phenothiazine compounds. See EXTRAPYRAMIDAL SYMPTOMS.

extrapyramidal motor system   **extrapyramidal system**

extrapyramidal symptoms (EPS)   A common side effect of the use of the stronger types or higher doses of neuroleptics, characterized by stiffening of the body's muscles, a flattened facial expression, stilted walk, slightly bent arms, and sometimes a painful twisting of the neck, back, or eye muscles.

extrapyramidal system   (S. A. Wilson) A portion of the central nervous system that includes parts of the spinal cord, basal ganglia, and mesencephalon. Its functions are the regulation of muscle tone, body posture, and coordination of opposing sets of skeletal muscles and movement of their associated skeletal parts. All cortical descending neural pathways outside the pyramidal system (consisting of cortical motor neurons destined for the brainstem and spinal cord). See PYRAMIDAL SYSTEM.

extrasensory perception (ESP)   (J. B. Rhine) Acquisition of information presumably shielded from bodily senses. The alleged awareness of external events by means other than the sensory channels. ESP includes telepathy, clairvoyance, precognition, and, more loosely, psychokinesis. There is considerable divergence of opinion as to the existence of any of these modalities. Also known as paranormal cognition. See ESP FORCED-CHOICE TEST, ESP FREE-RESPONSE TEST.

extraspective perspective   A methodological approach based on objective, empirical observation of actions and reactions, as contrasted with an introspective, first-person account of experience. The natural-science approach of behaviorism is based on an extraspective perspective. See OVERT BEHAVIOR.

extraspectral hue   A hue, such as purple, that is not found within the series of spectral colors.

extrastriate cortex   Part of the visual association cortex that receives fibers from the striate cortex and superior colliculi and projects to the inferior temporal cortex.

extratensive   In Rorschach test scoring, refers to a strong need for emotional contact with the environment, a need to be with and to be like others and having social interest.

extraterrestrial kidnapping (S. Kingsbury) A mounting number of people claim they were kidnapped by extraterrestrial beings. Support groups have started for those who claim to be traumatized by the experience. Such people are described as sincere, not psychotic, and some have evidence of posttraumatic stress disorder. There is no physical evidence to prove the authenticity of their experiences. See FALSE MEMORIES, INCUBUS, PAST LIVES, SATANIC CULTS, SUCCUBUS.

extraversion A tendency to direct interests and energies toward the outer world of people and things rather than the inner world of subjective experience. Compare INTROVERSION.

extraverted type Jungian phrase for a person who is considered to be habitually socially oriented and whose attitudes, values, and interests are directed toward the physical and social environment. Compare INTROVERTED TYPE.

extravertive mystical experience The vivid perception of an ultimate unity shining through material objects. Usually spontaneous and uncontrollable.

extrinsic Characterizing a value attached to a given object or datum due to its relation with other data or to its general setting.

extrinsic cortex (K. H. Pribram) The portion of the cortex innervated by fibers that receive impulses from stimuli originating in the environment. Another name for sensory area. Compare INTRINSIC CORTEX.

extrinsic eye muscles The muscles attached to the outside of the eyeball that control its movements.

extrinsic interest Interest in a topic developed usually by social factors, for example, going to operas because it is a trendy thing to do, and thereby developing a true interest in this art form. Compare INTRINSIC INTEREST.

extrinsic motivation An externally imposed reward or reinforcement, as contrasted with intrinsic reward, in which the reward is inherent in an activity itself (for example, a child studies to get good grades to please a parent, or someone works at a disliked job to get a paycheck). Compare EXTRINSIC REWARD.

extrinsic reward A positive reinforcement not necessarily related to the performance or the behavior itself.

extrinsic thalamus A part of the thalamus containing nuclei that relay incoming impulses.

extroversion   extraversion

eye See the following types of eye: COMPOUND, CROSS-, DARK-ADAPTED, DOMINANT, EVIL, LAZY, LEADING, MIND'S, NAUTILUS, PINEAL, REDUCED, SCHEMATIC, SIMPLE, THIRD, WALL-. See also ACCOMMODATION (OF THE EYE), COMPENSATORY EYE MOVEMENTS, CONJUGATE EYE MOVEMENTS, CONSENSUAL EYE REFLEX, EXTRINSIC EYE MUSCLES, INTRINSIC EYE MUSCLES, LENS, PUPIL OF EYE, SMOOTH PURSUIT EYE MOVEMENTS, VISUAL SYSTEM.

eyeball-to-eyeball exercise A nonverbal exercise in growth groups in which two persons stare into each others' eyes for a preestablished period as set by the group leader, and later discuss their reactions to this exercise.

eyebrow flash On meeting a person who is recognized, the eyebrows are raised for a brief instant. See FACIAL EXPRESSION.

eye contact Engaging in an interpersonal relation by looking into another person's eyes. Maintaining appropriate levels of eye contact is considered important in communication between therapist and client. Eye contact is used as a variable in some social-psychological studies to represent the degree of interpersonal intimacy.

eyedness See EYE DOMINANCE, LATERALIZATION.

eye dominance The preference for the use of one eye over the other. Eye preference is more often right-sided than left-sided, and the main influence of preference is based on a differential acuity of the two eyes. There is no valid relationship between eye dominance and learning to read. Also known as ocular dominance.

eye fear See OMMATOPHOBIA.

eye-hand coordination The harmonious functioning of eyes and hands in grasping and exploring objects. By six months, eye-hand coordination develops so that most infants can grasp an object within reach, although full use of the thumb develops later, between 8–12 months.

eyelash sign A reaction of eyelid movement to the stimulus of stroking the eyelashes. It is part of a diagnostic test for loss of consciousness due to a functional disorder, such as hysteria. If the loss of consciousness is due to an organic central nervous system disease or injury, the reflex will not occur.

eyelid conditioning A common method of demonstrating conditioning with humans by associating some extraneous stimulus with a puff of air to the eyes.

eye-mindedness A tendency for some people to depend more on learning by using their vision than by using their hearing (ear-mindedness).

eye-movement camera (J. Tiffin) A research device amounting to a camera that photographs eye movement, thus indicating what the person is looking at various times, usually in sequence. Used in determining appropriate visual sequences in performing complex operations.

eye-movement desensitization and reprocessing (EMDR) (F. Shapiro) A controversial therapeutic process used primarily for treating posttraumatic stress disorders that involves simultaneous visualization of a traumatic event while concentrating on the lateral movements of a therapist's finger.

eye preference See EYE DOMINANCE.

eye-roll sign (H. Spiegel) An index of susceptibility to hypnosis. Participants are directed to roll their eyes upward as far as possible and at the same time lower their eyelids slowly. If little or no white space shows under the cornea, they are considered not hypnotizable. These low scorers, on a scale of 0 to 5, tend to be critical and to favor thinking over feeling, whereas high scorers, who are readily hypnotizable, tend to be uncritical and suggestible and to favor feeling over thinking.

eye span See READING SPAN.

eye structure The three-layer structure of the eye, consisting of: (a) The fibrous outer coating, which forms the cornea in front and continues as the sclera over the rest of the globe. (b) The middle layer, called the uveal tract, which includes the iris. (c) The innermost, or retinal layer, which is composed of nerve tissue. The anterior chamber, between the cornea and lens, is filled with a fluid, the aqueous humor, and the space behind the crystalline lens, a cavity occupying about four-fifths of the globe or eyeball, is filled with the jellylike vitreous humor. The humors serve as refracting media. See AQUEOUS HUMOR, VISUAL SYSTEM.

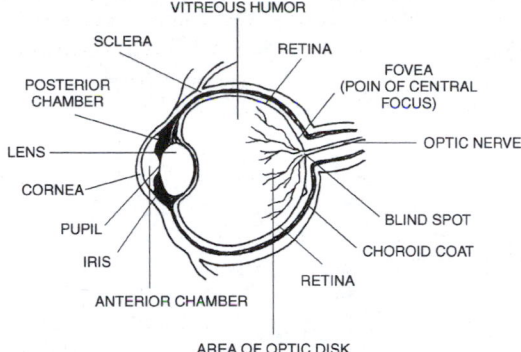

VITREOUS HUMOR

SCLERA

RETINA

FOVEA (POIN OF CENTRAL FOCUS)

POSTERIOR CHAMBER

OPTIC NERVE

LENS

CORNEA

BLIND SPOT

PUPIL

CHOROID COAT

IRIS

RETINA

ANTERIOR CHAMBER

AREA OF OPTIC DISK

eye structure   Human eye in cross section.

eye-switch   A device developed by the National Aeronautics and Space Administration (NASA) that permits quadriplegics to control wheelchairs, computers, and other appliances by their eye movements.

eye tracker   A device that measures the location of a person's fixation point while observing visual displays.

See EYE CAMERA, EYE-MOVEMENT CAMERA.

eye-voice span   The distance in terms of letters between the word being spoken and the word focused on in oral reading.

eye-wink reflex   See BLINKING, WINKING.

eyewitness testimony   Reports by people who have perceived a particular phenomenon or activity. It is commonly but mistakenly accepted that eyewitness testimony is better than circumstantial evidence. Aussage tests indicate how untrustworthy such testimony can be.

Eysenck Personality Inventory (EPI)   (H. J. & S. Eysenck) A self-report personality test of the questionnaire variety, designed to measure two major personality dimensions derived by factor analysis: Extraversion-introversion, and neuroticism.

Eysenck's typology   (H. J. Eysenck) Based on his analysis of personality tests, Hans Eysenck declared that humans have two major dimensions of personality: Introversion-Extraversion and Stability-Instability. These can be arranged to make a fourfold table compatible with the humoral theory of Hippocrates. See BIOLOGICAL INTELLIGENCE, BODY-BUILD INDEX, EURYMORPH, MESOSOMATIC, NEUROTICISM, PSYCHOTICISM, SYMPTOMATIC TREATMENT, TOUGH-MINDEDNESS.

F

f 1. fluency. 2. frequency. 3. Symbol for frequency in a sample. 4. factor. 5. See FUNCTION (meaning 2). 6. See LUMINOUS FLUX.

F 1. See F RATIO. 2. Fahrenheit. 3. force. 4. In Rorschach test scoring, a symbol for form response. 5. See LUMINOUS FLUX. 6. farad. 7. See FOCAL LENGTH. 8. See FUNCTION (meaning 2).

fables test The interpretation of fables, often as part of an individual examination of intelligence.

fabrication See CONFABULATION, FABULATION.

fabulation 1. The recounting of an imaginary event, intended to entertain or to deceive. 2. (A. Meyer) Random and meaningless talk including imaginary incidents, by a person who believes they are real. See CONFABULATION.

fabulism Accepting something as true without sufficient evidence, such as ESP, touch therapy, or the Roswell incident. See ANTI-CONFIRMATION.

face In social psychology, the impression a person makes on others. Having a "face" means being accepted. When "out of face," a person has not behaved according to social expectations and is not recognized or accepted by certain others. In some societies, losing face can lead to suicide. See FACE-SAVING RITUAL, PERSONA.

face-hand test An examination of cerebral dysfunction in which the examiner touches the patient's face and the back of the patient's hand at the same time (double-simultaneous tactile sensation). According to Lauretta Bender, the inability to perceive both sensations is indicative of minimal brain damage or schizophrenic tendencies in children, and of diffuse brain damage in adults. See DOUBLE-SIMULTANEOUS TACTILE SENSATION.

face-ism 1. Slang for the unfair advantages accorded to a person with an attractive face. 2. Slang for the featuring of men's faces in advertisements whereas their female counterparts are shown full-body. Term is derived from "sexism."

face-saving behavior An act intended to redress a social blunder or compensate for a perceived "wrong impression." See FACE, IMPRESSION MANAGEMENT.

face-saving ritual A procedure that differs in various cultures. If X offends Y in some manner, Y or others will in some manner let X know that the offense is noted and that some kind of retribution is called for. X will now perform an action to alleviate the hurt and to re-establish a relationship. If the apology or atonement is accepted by Y, face is saved. See FACE.

facet An aspect or part of a person or entity.

face time Time spent dealing with a person face-to-face, as opposed to by mail, telephone, email, etc.

face-to-face group 1. A group in which the individuals react mainly to one another, for example a family or a committee. 2. Any group whose members are in personal contact and are thus able to perceive each others' needs and responses and carry on direct interaction, for example, in a T-group or psychotherapy group. Also known as direct-contact group.

face-to-face interaction (E. Goffman) The reciprocal process in which people who are together influence each other.

facet theory (L. Guttman) A model designed to help the conceptualization of complex problems. It precisely relates a research domain to empirical observations; used mostly in applied areas.

face validity 1. The extent to which a test appears to measure what it is designed to measure. Generally assessed by asking psycho-metricians to guess the test's purpose. 2. The impression of greater or lesser validity that a prima facie examination of a test or measuring instrument generates on a psychometrician. Many "personality tests" found in magazines have face validity but may in reality have no validity at all. An example of a test that has both face validity and validity is a typing test.

facework 1. A common social phenomenon in which people alter their facial and body expressions in the presence of others to communicate a more congenial social impression, for example, spouses in a heated argument may, as they are approached by others, change their "faces" to look as though they are on good terms. 2. Social rituals intended to protect others' feelings and help them save "face." See FACE, FACE SAVING RITUAL.

facial action coding system (FACS) (P. Ekman) A breakdown of facial expressions into 46 component parts that can express facial characteristics of anger, contempt, disgust, happiness, sadness, and surprise.

facial-affect program (P. Ekman) A computer-like program, universally present at birth, that patterns the facial musculature to some primary emotions. For instance, happiness causes the zygomatic major muscle to contract, raising the corners of the mouth.

facial angle The angle of projection of the forehead from the basal or horizontal plane of the skull, measuring the amount of prognathism (projection of the upper jaw).

facial blends   A fusion or combination of features belonging to different faces or different halves of the same face.

facial disfigurement   Distortion, malformation, or abnormality of the facial features due to injury, disease, or congenital anomaly. Because many people assign traits to others on the basis of facial features, the patient with facial disfigurement is vulnerable to social, psychological, and economic discrimination. See DISFIGUREMENT.

facial display   (C. Darwin) Nonverbal behavior consisting of facial movements and set positions of the face, such as smiles or scowls. Darwin assumed that facial expressions were innate reactions that possessed survival value; for example, an infant's smile evokes nurturing responses in parents. Cross-cultural research reveals that certain facial expressions are universally correlated with such primary emotions as surprise, fear, anger, sadness, pleasure.

facial electromyography   A physiological device that records the activity of facial muscles, usually in research on facial reactions to positive and negative stimuli. See FACIAL MUSCLES.

facial expressions   A facial pattern indicative of an emotional response. The face can also reflect emotional disorder, as seen in the anguished look of some people who are depressed or the exalted expression of some patients who are paranoid. Though there are local patterns of facial expressions, the more fundamental ones appear to be common to all humans, even those born blind. See EYEBROW FLASH, EYELASH SIGN.

facial-feedback hypothesis   A postulate that facial muscles generate emotions by sending messages to the brain (supported by findings that when people are asked to smile or frown they report emotions consistent with their expression). Thus, a person feels happy because the person smiles and not vice-versa. Compare JAMES-LANGE THEORY OF EMOTION.

facial muscles   The set of 80 muscles in the human face that not only control functional movements of the eye and mouth areas, but can also display an estimated 7,000 expressions. Generally, activity of the cheek muscles reflect positive emotions, whereas negative ones increase activity in the forehead and brow areas.

facial nerve   (H. Mayo) Cranial nerve VII. The motor nerve of all muscles involved in facial expressions. Its branches serve parts of the ear and its sensory branch supplies the taste organs. The facial nerve is more vulnerable to paralytic disorders than any other cranial nerve.

facial talk   See CONDITIONED-REFLEX THERAPY.

facial vision   1. A mistaken theory that blind people have a special sense due to unusual facial sensitivity to air currents. This ability is a form of echolocation and can be learned by sighted people. 2. Old phrase for echolocation.

facies   1. Face. 2. Facial expression, often a guide to a person's state of health or emotions. See FACIAL DISPLAY.

facile aments   (A. F. Tredgold) Persons with mental retardation who are considered particularly suggestible.

facilitation   1. In environmental psychology, a user-benefit effect of environmental design such as physical facilitation, as measured by how well a design helps a user of space and materials accomplish performance tasks. See BEHAVIORAL FACILITATION. 2. In social psychology, adequacy of an environmental setting in providing personal space that permits communication with others without threats of crowding. See SOCIAL FACILITATION. 3. In learning theory, the helpful effect of one task upon another.

facilitator   1. A group member, usually professionally trained, who fulfills some or all of the functions of a group leader; for example, a psychotherapist in training who co-leads a therapy group. 2. A person who helps a group to function better, come to agreements, settle differences. See ARBITRATION.

FACM   functional analytic causal model

FACS   facial action coding system

fact   An actual occurrence or state of affairs, empirically established and usually consensually validated, distinguished from fictive, confabulated events. The latter may be held as opinion, belief, or theory.

fact-giver   A person who provides factual information during a group discussion.

facticity   1. Factualness of data. 2. Actuality of the properties of an individual deriving from nature and personal experience. What exemplifies facticity is, for example, gender, body type, parents, and personal history.

factitious   1. Created and artificial; not natural or spontaneous. 2. An assumed or self-induced mental or physical condition. See FABULATION.

factitious disorder   A pathological condition characterized by severe psychological (often psychotic) symptoms that appear to have no unitary explanation. The symptoms are not feigned, as in malingering, but usually make up a hodgepodge of elements that does not conform to any standard mental disorder. See GANSER SYNDROME, PSEUDODEMENTIA.

fact memory   Having readily available for recall a fact such as date or an event or the definition of a word. See SOURCE MEMORY.

factor (f)   An underlying, unitary variable or construct that accounts in part for variations in individual behavior and is relatively distinct from other variables. Types of factor include: BASIC INTELLIGENCE, BEHAVIORAL RISK, BIG FIVE PERSONALITY, BIOLOGICAL, BIONOMIC, BIPOLAR, C, CENTRIFUGAL GROUP, CENTROID, CLASSICISM, COMPENSABLE JOB, COMPLEXITY, COMPLEXITY-CURVILINEARITY, CONSTITUTIONAL, CORTICAL-AROUSAL, CORTICOTROPHIC RELEASING, CULTURAL PRESSURE, DEVELOPMENTAL, ENDOGENETIC, ENVIRONMENTAL, ETHNIC, EXOGENOUS, EXPOSURE, EXPRESSIONISM, FAMILIAL, FIRST ORDER, GENERAL, GERMINAL, GESTALT, GROUP, HEDONIC-TONE, HIGHER-ORDER, IMPRESSIONISM, INSTRUMENT, INTEREST, MOTIVATION COMPONENT, MOTIVATIONAL, MULTIPLE-, NUMBER, NUTRITIONAL, O, P OR PERSEVERATION, POWER, PSYCHOBIOLOGICAL, PSYCHOLOGICAL, PSYCHOSOCIAL, RANDOM, REALISM, REPRESENTATIVE, RH, RISK, SECOND-ORDER, SECONDARY, SOCIAL, SOCIOCULTURAL, SOCIOLOGICAL, SOMATOPSYCHOLOGICAL, SPACE, SPECIAL,

SPECIFIC, SPIRITUAL, STUB, SUBJECTIVISM, TERMINAL, THORNDIKE'S BASIC INTELLIGENCE, UNCERTAINTY, UNCERTAINTY-AROUSAL, UNCONSCIOUS, VULNERABILITY, WILL, WISDOM.

factor analysis (C. E. Spearman, L. L. Thurstone) A collection of techniques designed to uncover possible underlying variables that might have in part accounted for the relationships observed among a set of variables. Distinction is made between confirmatory factor analysis, which tests whether a set of hypotheses about underlying variables of factor can be rejected on the basis of the data, and exploratory factor analysis, which attempts to extract possible factors that are consistent with the relationships among the observed variables. See CLINICAL FACTOR ANALYSIS, CLUSTER ANALYSIS, CRITERION ANALYSIS, DIFFERENTIAL R-TECHNIQUE, P-TECHNIQUE, Q-TECHNIQUE, T-TECHNIQUE.

factor-comparison method In industrial psychology, a system of comparing key jobs in terms of factors common to all jobs. The factors include requirements of a cognitive, psychomotor, and physical nature.

factorial (! or n!) A mathematical concept identified by the symbol ! (exclamation mark) put at the end of a number. This asks for the product of multiplying 1 by 2 (= 2) and then the 2 by 3 (= 6) and so on to the final number. So, for 5! the product would be 30, and for 6! it would be 180. Used in probability theory and for other purposes.

factorial design A research design in which two or more independent variables are simultaneously manipulated. Allows both the separate and joint effects of the factors to be studied. Also known as factorial type experiments.

factorial invariance The identity or similarity of factors across different samples.

factor(ial) theory of personality An approach to the discovery and measurement of personality components through factor analysis. The components are identified primarily through a statistical study of performance on personality tests, as contrasted with an intuitive or clinical approach. Examples include Hans Eysenck's three-dimensional typology (introversion-extraversion, neuroticism, psychoticism); R.B. Cattell's 16 traits and states (including ego strength, harria, surgency, arousal, zeppia); Robert McCrae's five-factor model (neuroticism, extraversion, openness, agreeableness, conscientiousness). See FACTOR ANALYSIS, PERSONALITY THEORIES.

factorial validity See VALIDITY.

fact-oriented acquisition Encoding material so as to emphasize factual knowledge rather than applications.

factoring In psychology and other social sciences, the process of performing a factor analysis.

factor-loading In factor analysis, a measure of the correlation between an item and a factor. For instance, in a factor analysis of Rorschach scores, the number of anatomy responses might have a high factor-loading on a neuroticism factor.

factor loadings In factor analysis, meaningful correlations between the observed variables and the factors.

factor matrix A table of factor loadings arrayed into several columns of factors. See FACTOR ANALYSIS.

factor method In factor analysis, the extraction first of a general factor and subsequently of group factors.

factor of uniform density See LAW OF COMMON FATE.

factor reflection A change of the signs of a set of factor-loadings from positive to negative or vice-versa. See FACTOR ANALYSIS.

factor resolution See FACTOR STRUCTURE.

factor rotation In factor analysis, a rotation of the factors in the factor space, usually with the intention of making the rotated factors more interpretable in terms of the observed variables.

factors of enlightenment Seven mental qualities considered important for enlightenment and psychological well-being in some denominations of Buddhism: mindfulness, effort, investigation, rapture, concentration, calmness, equanimity.

factor structure (L. L. Thurstone) The spatial relation of test vectors after factor analysis.

factor theory A point of view that any complex living unit or complex concept can be divided into X number of simpler unitary elements either by logic or by factor analysis.

factor theory of learning A point of view that there are two or more processes or factors involved in learning, especially a conditioning factor, a comprehension factor, an attention factor.

factor theory of intelligence Points of view based on empirical and statistically treated data that seek to explain intelligence, as a measurable phenomenon, in terms of relations among capacities that vary in number, extensity, and organization. See C FACTOR, G FACTOR, S FACTOR, STRUCTURE OF INTELLECT MODEL, W FACTOR.

factor theory of personality **factor(ial) theory of personality**

factor trait An independent trait cluster derived from commonalities exhibited in behavior or test performance.

Factor X **unlearned factor (in forgetting)**

fact-seeker A person who takes the role of seeking information about specific topics, especially during a group discussion.

facts of life Usually refers to parents or teachers explaining reproduction to children. See SEX OFFENDERS.

factual knowledge The knowing of discrete facts, sometimes without much understanding of the meaning of the facts or how they relate to other facts.

facultative 1. Able to adapt to more than one condition. 2. Not obligatory.

facultative homosexuality Male–male or female–female sexual acts performed by heterosexuals only in situations where partners of the other sex are not available (as in prisons). Sometimes known as functional homosexuality.

facultative mutualism See MUTUALISM.

faculty 1. A power or agency of the mind (for example, intellect, feeling, will, and memory) through the action and interaction of which all mental phenomena were at one time supposed to be explained. 2. In English and American colleges and universities, the teaching personnel. 3. Especially in Canada and Europe, a major division in a university, such as Faculty of Arts.

faculty psychology (St. Augustine) A theory that mental faculties can be separated into specialized abilities or powers (such as will power, memory, intelligence) that can be developed by mental exercises in the same way that muscles can be strengthened by physical exercises. This theory and other variations of faculty psychology have not been supported by research.

fad Transient interest, custom, or fashion usually of a trivial nature (hula hoop, pet rock, Rubik's cube), which sweeps rapidly throughout a population. Such fads rarely last more than a year, but while they exist, they are testimony to the power of mass suggestion, conformity, and publicity. See FOOD FADDISM.

fading 1. In operant conditioning, a process of shifting one kind of reinforcement or discriminative stimulus to other, different stimuli by "mixing" the new stimuli with the old, and progressively increasing or heightening the presence of new stimuli and reducing the old. 2. In behavior therapy, the gradual removal of prompts so that the clients perform desired responses on their own without any prior stimulation.

FAE 1. figural aftereffect. 2. fetal alcohol effects.

FAGR fractional antedating (or anticipatory) goal response (also abbreviated **rg-sg**)

Fahrenheit (F) scale A method of measuring temperature usually by a liquid in a glass tube so arranged that it reads 32° in ice water and 212° in boiling water. Named after German physicist Gabriel Fahrenheit (1686–1736). Compare CELSIUS SCALE. See TEMPERATURE SCALES.

fail-safe 1. Generally, a design that prevents a failure. 2. In ergonomics, a workplace design that reduces the consequence of a mishap.

failure 1. In research, not achieving the expected or desired result. 2. In social psychology, said of persons who did not achieve their own or socially expected goals. 3. In psychometrics, describing a person who did not achieve a minimally accepted score. 4. In computers, inability of a system to operate properly, such as through a loss of power, inadequate software or hardware, or operator error.

failure through success A self-injuring trait characterized by striving to achieve a goal but renouncing it when the goal is within reach. One explanation is that there is covert satisfaction in rejecting potential success in that the person may not feel worthy of the success. Another explanation is to punish others, usually parents, by failing when success was possible and expected.

failure-to-grow syndrome Failure to grow at a normal rate due to inadequate release of growth hormone. A childhood condition that appears to be related, in some cases at least, to parental neglect and emotional deprivation. Secretion of the hormone often returns to normal after a period of emotionally supportive caregiving and interpersonal bonding. See DIFFERENTIAL GROWTH, FAILURE-TO-THRIVE SYNDROME, GROWTH SPURTS.

failure-to-thrive (FTT) syndrome A progressive decline (marasmus) in responsiveness, accompanied by loss of weight (poor appetite) and retardation in physical and emotional development among infants who have been neglected, ignored, or institutionalized. See FAILURE-TO-GROW SYNDROME, MARASMUS, REACTIVE ATTACHMENT DISORDER OF INFANCY.

fainting Temporary loss of consciousness due to physical or psychological factors. See SYNCOPE.

faintness 1. A relatively low degree of intensity. 2. An organic condition characterized by dizziness or muscular weakness. 3. A partial loss of conscious integration.

fair-fight exercises (G. Bach) Simulated verbal and physical fighting under supervision for the purpose of ventilating feelings and eventually leading to rational discussions. See BATACAS, MARRIAGE COUNSELING.

fairness 1. Generally, equality or equity. 2. On an achievement test, the extent to which the test items represent what the participant can reasonably be expected to have learned in relation to others with whom he or she is being compared. 3. On an aptitude test, the extent to which test scores do not misrepresent capability of future performance on some criterion measure by virtue of past socio-educational deprivations or special training.

faith Belief in a phenomenon without empirical evidence. In psychology, there are two main kinds of hypotheses or questions in this matter: (a) those that may be confirmed or disconfirmed, such as whether extrasensory perception exists, and (b) metaphysical issues that can never be definitively answered. See RELIGIOUS FAITH.

faith cure/healing The process of alleviating or curing physical or mental illnesses through belief in divine intervention or the services of a faith healer. See HEADSHRINKING, HEX DOCTORS, MAGICAL THINKING, PLACEBO, SUPERSTITIOUS CONTROL, VOODOO.

faithful subject Old name for a participant who fits the particular research criteria and who behaves according to instructions. Also known as good subject.

faker charlatan

faking Trying to appear particularly good or, occasionally, bad. The usual context is in tests, for instance, to win acceptance, or to be exempted from military service.

fallacious reasoning More than one hundred systematic errors in reasoning have been identified, many of them variations on the thirteen that Aristotle identified. To the degree that psychology is a science, it observes the rules of logic, which some logicians regard in large part as common sense codified. To examine some fallacies in reasoning, see AMBIGUITY & EQUIVOCATION, APPEAL TO IGNORANCE, ARGUMENT AGAINST THE PERSON, BANDWAGON APPEAL, CARD-STACKING, CIRCULAR ARGUMENT, EITHER-OR FALLACY, FALSE ANALOGY, FALSE AUTHORITY, FALSE CAUSE, GUILT BY ASSOCIATION, HASTY GENERALIZATIONS, IRRELEVANT ARGUMENT, RED HERRING, SELF CONTRADICTION, TAKING SOMETHING OUT OF CONTEXT. See FALLACY for the classical Latin and still widely used equivalents for these terms.

fallacy 1. An error in reasoning that leads to a conclusion that appears true but is actually false; the result of such reasoning. 2. Mistakes in logic common in ordinary discourse. See ACCENT, ACCIDENT, AD BACULUM (APPEAL TO FORCE); AD HOMINEM (ATTACK ON A PERSON RATHER THAN ON THE SUBSTANCE OF AN ARGUMENT); AD IGNORANTIA (ARGUMENT FROM IGNORANCE); AD MISERICORDIAM (APPEAL TO PITY); AD POPULUM (APPEAL TO EMOTION); AD VERECUNDIAM (APPEAL TO AN INAPPROPRIATE AUTHORITY);

AMPHIBOLY, IGNORATIO ELENCHI (IRRELEVANT CONCLUSION); NON CAUSA PRO CAUSA (FALSE CAUSE); PETITIO PRINCIPI (BEGGING THE QUESTION).

fallacy of composition The mistaken assumption that if an action is in the collective interest of a group of rational members, the group must be collectively rational and will therefore act in its best interest.

fallacy of misplaced concreteness reification (meaning 1)

fall chronometer An instrument used in the early days of psychophysical research for measuring time intervals by means of the fall of a heavy weight when a person pressed a button on completion of a task.

falling sickness Archaic phrase for epilepsy.

Fallopian tube (G. Fallopius) Either of two slender fleshy tubes that extend from either side of the uterus up to an ovary. During ovulation, an egg drops into the open end of the Fallopian tube and migrates downward toward the uterus.

Fallopian-tube pregnancy Implantation of a fertilized ovum (zygote) in the wall of a Fallopian tube rather than in the lining of the uterus. Also known as tubal pregnancy.

Falret's disease (J-P. Falret) Old name for a form of manic-depressive (bipolar) psychosis marked by a range of emotional oscillation from hyperactivity, excitement, and violence to depression with suicidal tendencies in a recurrent pattern. Also known as circular insanity, cyclic insanity, *folie circulaire* (French).

false alarm 1. Incorrectly reporting the presence of a signal on a trial where only "noise" occurred. 2. Giving a signal indicating that a condition in an experiment has been seen or experienced when no stimulus or evidence of the condition was provided. See SIGNAL-DETECTION THEORY.

false analogy An argument about one situation or event by reference to a comparable situation or event such that the bases of comparison have little in common.

false association (W. Stekel) The identification by a dreamer of several persons in the dream who may actually represent the same single love object (person). The concluded association may be partial and misleading.

false authority An inadequate person or source as a purported expert.

false belief task A measure of children's ability to take another person's perspective when it is different from their own. In one such task children are shown a milk carton and asked to predict what is in it. They are then shown that the carton contains water rather than milk, and asked to predict what other people think is in the carton. Children who take the other person's point of view appreciate that he or she does not have the information they do, and predict the person will guess that milk is in the carton. Children who behave in this way are at a higher level of cognitive maturity than those who predict the other person will guess water.

false cause An event or thing to which is attributed erroneously the power of bringing another event or thing to pass.

false consciousness The Marxist concept of thinking that fosters servitude rather than emancipation.

false consensus Falsely believing that some concept is shared by the majority of people. This mistake is usually made because a person tends to connect with others of similar status who tend to have opinions in common. See SUBJECTIVE ERROR.

false-consensus effect A tendency to assume that personal traits are common in others. See ASSUMED SIMILARITY BIAS.

false dementia A psychological condition that gives the appearance of dementia but that is a normal response to, for example, institutionalization with extensive medication, a dependency-inducing environment, and restricted movement.

false detection One of the four possible replies in a signal-detection experiment, when the participant incorrectly states that there was a signal. See SIGNAL-DETECTION THEORY.

false frame effect (L. Jacoby) The assumption that if a name is familiar, it must be of a famous person.

false gastropaths (J. Dejerine) People who claim to have food phobias but do not.

false knowledge Incorrect belief structures about reality.

false memory Having a clear recollection of some person, place, event, situation, etc., that never occurred; for example, remembering a meeting with a relative who died before the person was born, or a trip to a foreign country that a person has never visited. See IATROGENIC PATHOLOGIES, PARAMNESIA.

false memory syndrome Typically, the controversial "recollection" usually by women, through a therapist's or counselor's prompting, of having been sexually abused in their early years, often by a close and trusted relative.

false-negative cases Individuals who have been erroneously judged to be unqualified to engage in an activity for a variety of reasons, such as candidates who would have been successful in a program but were excluded because they fell below a criterion score on an entrance examination. Compare FALSE-POSITIVE CASES.

false-positive cases Individuals who are mistakenly admitted into a program by satisfying the criteria, and then fail the program because the culling instruments and their interpretation were flawed. Compare FALSE-NEGATIVE CASES.

false pregnancy 1. A psychosomatic condition in which a woman shows all the usual external signs of pregnancy even though conception has not taken place. There can be absence of menstruation, distended abdomen, breast changes, and morning sickness. Usually occurs in immature women who experience intense unconscious conflicts over child-bearing. Also known as hysterical pregnancy, phantom pregnancy, pseudocyesis, spurious pregnancy. See COUVADE, PREGNANCY, PREGNANCY FANTASY. 2. See PSEUDOPREGNANCY.

false recognition See MISTAKEN IDENTITY.

false rejection One of the four possible replies in a signal-detection experiment, when the participant incorrectly states that there was no signal. See SIGNAL-DETECTION THEORY.

falsetto A thin, high-pitched voice that occurs when the reduced surface of the vocal cords is activated by the airstream. In the male, this quality of vocal resonance may represent some voice abnormality.

false twins　Misnomer for dizygotic twins.

falsifiability　The quality of a theory or hypothesis that permits it to be subjected to disconfirmatory tests.

falsifiability position　(K. Popper) A point of view that any theory can never be proven to be true, but can be demonstrated to be false. Consequently, a good theory is one that can be refuted. See FALSIFICATIONISM.

falsifiable hypothesis　A predictive statement whose outcome can be observed and can therefore be either confirmed or refuted.

falsification　1. A deliberate attempt to deceive. 2. Distortion, to achieve some goal whether knowingly or unconsciously.

falsificationism　The fundamental position of Karl Popper that it is more important to attempt to disconfirm than to confirm hypotheses and theories, as risky predictions are called for in research. This principle affirms that *modus tollens* is the only appropriate procedure for approximating positions of truth in science. Hypotheses must be subjected to serious risk of disconfirmation. See CRUCIAL EXPERIMENT, EVOLUTIONARY EPISTEMOLOGY, MODUS TOLLENS.

falsifying experiments　According to Karl Popper, hypotheses should be formulated in such a manner as to be easily tested for falsification and consequently abandoned immediately. Under this theory, a crucial falsifying experiment would demonstrate lack of validity for a given concept, and science would thereby be advanced. See CRUCIAL EXPERIMENT, EVOLUTIONARY EPISTEMOLOGY.

falsity　General term for what is characterized by lack of correspondence between a report, a conclusion, etc., and the objective facts or situation on which these are based.

familect　See IDIOLECT.

familial amaurotic idiocy　See TAY-SACHS DISEASE.

familial factors　Any factors in the family that account for a certain disease or trait. The exact nature, or even existence, of these factors is often a matter of conjecture.

familialism　A tendency to maintain strong intrafamilial relationships, culturally transmitted and inherited. This leads to a state of strong family solidarity.

familial mental deficiency　Mental retardation assumed to be of genetic origins, probably involving several as yet undetermined genes. See FAMILIAL RETARDATION.

familial psychosis　A psychosis that appears to "run in the family" because it occurs in many or all of its members. This occurrence does not necessarily indicate that the condition is hereditary, since psychoses can have multiple causes, including heredity and environment. Possibly one or both parents created conditions that led to generating psychoses in the children. See SCHIZOPHRENOGENIC MOTHER.

familial retardation　Any type of abnormally slow or limiting mental or physical development pattern that tends to occur in certain families at a frequency greater than in the general population. The familial retardation trait usually is inherited although a genetic link often is difficult to document. Consanguineous marriages have an increased rate of familial retardation cases. The term "retardation" is usually replaced by "challenged."

familial unconscious　(L. Szondi) A hypothetical domain of the mind that contains genetic tendencies through which human "repressed ancestors" direct human behavior, choice of friends, occupation, and relationships with the opposite sex. See ANALYTIC PSYCHOLOGY, FATE ANALYSIS, SCHICKSAL.

familiar　familiar (spirit)

familiarity　Acquaintance with a person, object, or action that permits quickness of response and ease of performance.

familiarity feeling　A specific feeling or experiential datum that serves as a basis for judgment and recognition when faced with pressure to problem solve or make decisions.

familiar (spirit)　A supernatural spirit that supposedly lives in the body of an animal, or those such as the mythical genii of Muslim demonology thought to be at the service of the individual who controls them.

family　1. A group of blood relatives. See JUKE FAMILY, KALLIKAK FAMILY. 2. In humans, a group of individuals typically represented by father, mother, and children, but also including groups lacking one parent, or groups embracing other relatives, adopted children, and in some cultures, slaves and servants. Types of family include: BLENDED, CHILD-CENTERED, COMPLEX STEP-, DISENGAGED, DUAL-CAREER, ENMESHED, EXTENDED, FOSTER, INADEQUATE, INTENTIONAL, MATRIFOCAL, MATRILINEAL, MATRILOCAL, NEOLOCAL, NUCLEAR, OCCUPATIONAL, PATHOGENIC, PATRIARCHAL, PATRILOCAL, PATTERN, PERMEABLE, PSEUDO-, RECONSTITUTED, RIGID, SCHIZMATIC, SCHIZOGENIC, SIMULATED, SKEWED. See DOMESTIC PARTNERSHIP. 3. In taxonomy, a division between the order and the genus.

family care　A type of aftercare in which older persons, former mental patients, the cognitively impaired, and abused or delinquent children live with foster families on a temporary or permanent basis. Caregivers usually receive instruction about the special needs of the foster person, such as maintenance medication. Rationale is to provide an opportunity to live as normal a life as possible. Also known as foster-family care, foster placement. See GHEEL COLONY.

family-centered therapy　family therapy

family constellation　(A. Adler) The position of all members of a family in relation to each other as a function of age and role. Alfred Adler held that personality characteristics are related to the individual's location in the family constellation.

family council　(R. Dreikurs) A periodic meeting of all family members able to communicate (thus excluding infants) for a variety of purposes, such as discussing chores, allowances, special events, handling various problems. See DEMOCRATIC PARENT, HOUSE ENCOUNTER.

family counseling　Advising parents or other family members by professionals, psychiatrists, psychologists, social workers, etc., who provide information, emotional support, and guidance on problems faced by the family, such as raising a physically challenged child, as well such issues as adoption, public assistance, family planning, abortion, delinquency, substance abuse, and mental disorders of family members. See GENETIC COUNSELING.

family group psychotherapy (N. Ackerman) A process, involving all family members, intended to improve relationships and to attenuate harmful home influences. See CONJOINT THERAPY.

family incubus A family member who because of physical or mental disability creates a burdensome problem or is depressing to the other members of the family.

family-interaction method A study technique for investigating family behavior by observing the interaction of its members in a controlled situation, such as a structured laboratory. See FAMILY STRUCTURE, INTRAFAMILY DYNAMICS.

family limitation Any procedure designed to restrict the number of children, including abortion, contraception, sterilization, and limitation of sexual intercourse. See FAMILY PLANNING.

family method In behavior genetics, the study of the frequency of a trait or a form of a disorder by determining its occurrence in relatives who share the same genetic background.

family neurosis Maladaptive patterns that pervade an entire family; also, a family member's neurotic reactions that are interrelated with the psychopathology of other members of the family on an unconscious level.

family pattern The characteristic quality of the relationship among all members of a family. Family patterns vary widely in emotional tone and in attitudes of the members toward each other. See INTRAFAMILY DYNAMICS.

family planning 1. Controlling the number and spacing of children in the family, and ultimately the size of the population, especially through the use of birth-control measures. See POPULATION RESEARCH. 2. Colloquial term for contraception.

Family Relationship Index A form used in parenting counseling. An interviewer asks parents which of the 24 problems on the sheet are of concern; the problems are rated by the parent from (0) "No problem" to (3) "Serious." The counselor later advises the parent(s) on how to deal with the concerns. Later, using the reverse of the sheet, a new set of ratings is obtained, thus indicating any improvement.

family romance A fantasy in which children picture themselves as born of distinguished parents or as saving the life of illustrious persons. Such fantasies are purported to arise out of the child's need for independence and recognition and possibly rejection of their parents. See FANTASY.

family sculpting A technique used by family therapists for observing how members of the family position themselves when they meet in a conference room. Therapists can note the position of the children and adults and comment on the meaning of these relative positions.

family social work A branch of social work that specializes in helping individuals deal effectively with problems involving relationships with family and community. See SOCIAL AGENCIES, SOCIAL WORKERS.

family-systems model 1. A paradigm that families can best be understood in terms of systems theory. Traits and disorders emerge as a function of the healthfulness and functionality of the family as a whole. 2. See FAMILY SYSTEMS THEORY.

Family Relationship Index

family systems theory (M. Bowen) An approach to understanding and treating families that includes conceptualizing the family as a complex of interrelating individuals. Also known as family systems model. See FAMILY-SYSTEMS MODEL.

family therapy (J. Bell, C. Oberndorf, N. Ackerman) The treatment of an entire family, usually with the understanding that the "identified client" may be a scapegoat for the systematic "illness" of the family itself. The treatment, favored by some psychotherapists and social workers, usually includes the analysis of observed intra-family dynamics. Criticized by some feminists as ignoring power differences between the sexes. Also known as family-centered therapy.

family values Coded term for a value system that upholds conventional, marital, heterosexual relationships.

fanaticism Blind, rigid devotion to a set of extreme beliefs, or an overzealous crusade for a cause.

fancy 1. To prefer. 2. The mental representation of a scene or occurrence that is recognized as unreal but is either expected or hoped for. 3. Moderate liking.

fan effect A tendency for the greater the number of links to a concept, the more the time necessary to verify any one link.

fantasm A vivid image of a person or thing perceived as a disembodied spirit. Also spelled phantasm.

fantastic Weird, whimsical, or distorted in shape.

fantastica melancholia (E. Kraepelin) A personality disorder featuring a complex of depression with fantastic hallucinations.

fantasy A figment of the imagination; a mental image, night dream, or daydream in which human conscious or unconscious wishes and impulses are fulfilled. Also spelled phantasy. Kinds of fantasy include: AFFECT-, ANAL, ANAL-RAPE, AUTISTIC, BEATING, CANNIBALISTIC, COURTESAN, DAYDREAM, DEATH,

FELLATIO, FORCED, FOSTER-CHILD, HETAERAL, INCEST, KING–SLAVE, MASOCHISTIC, NECROPHILIC, NIGHT, OBSESSIVE, POMPADOUR, PREGNANCY, PRIMAL, PROCREATION, REBIRTH, RESCUE, SPIDER, UNCONSCIOUS, WOMB. See ACTIVE FANTASIZING, FLIGHT INTO FANTASY.

fantasy cathexis In psychoanalytic theory, the investment of psychic energy in images or wishes, or in their sources within the unconscious.

fantasy life A collective reference to the generality of daydreams in which coveted experiences are played out in pleasurable ruminations. Distinguished from logical and realistic thinking. Some authors conclude that fantasies provide a psychic safety valve for the abreaction of strong affects.

fantasy period (E. Ginzberg) The phase of early adolescence when future occupations and career are envisioned in fantasies that express inner needs. So named because its formulations occur in the absence of realistic judgments of interests, abilities, and opportunities. See CRYSTALLIZATION.

fantasy proneness (S. C. Wilson & T. X. Barber) Differential abilities of individuals to generate mental images.

FAP fixed action pattern

FAR fetus at risk

far point The farthest, most remote point at which an object can be seen clearly under conditions of relaxed accommodation.

Farad (F) (M. Faraday) The SI (metric system) unit of electrical capacitance; the capacitance of a condenser that retains one coulomb of charge with one volt difference of potential. See INTERNATIONAL SYSTEM OF UNITS.

farsightedness Deficient visual acuity in which distant objects are seen more clearly than near ones. Two types include hyperopia and presbyopia. It is commonly believed that people who are visually farsighted can see distant objects better than others. The truth is that farsighted refers to the fact that a person's near point is farther from the eye than normal; thus farsighted people can see nearby objects less well than nearsighted people can. At the same time, distance vision for farsighted people is no better than for emmetropes. Compare NEARSIGHTEDNESS. See NEAR POINT.

fartlek training (speed play—Swedish) In sports psychology, a combination of interval and continuous exercise training, as in alternately running fast and slow over level and hilly ground.

FAS fetal alcohol(ic) syndrome

fascial tissue A collagenous, protective, connective tissue that surrounds muscles and muscle groups.

fasciculus A small bundle of muscle or nerve fibers. Plural is fasciculi. See AXONAL BUNDLE.

fasciculus cuneatus The lateral component of the dorsal columns. It carries two-point tactile discriminatory, vibratory, and proprioceptive senses from the upper body and arms to the cuneate nucleus of the medulla oblongata. See CUNEATE NUCLEI, MEDULLA OBLONGATA.

fasciculus gracilis The medial component of the dorsal columns. It carries two-point tactile discriminatory, vibratory, and proprioceptive senses from the lower body and legs to the gracilic nucleus of the medulla oblongata. Also known as columns of Goll.

fasciculus gyrus Brain convolution, part of the hippocampal system, a delicate band of tissue that communicates with the indusium griseum, on the surface of the corpus callosum. Also known as gyrus fasciolaris.

fasciculus proprius A bundle of nerve fibers in the spinal cord that connects a series of nearby segments.

fascinating gaze The intense gaze of some hypnotists toward their participants.

fascination Enchantment with a person, object, or activity; enraptured attraction.

fascinum (evil eye—Latin) A superstition that certain individuals possess an "evil eye" that can be used to control, injure, or destroy others simply by staring at them and wishing them evil.

fascism Originally, the ideology of the Fascist party, a political party founded by Benito Mussolini following World War I; currently any authoritarian ideology, political party, or jurisdiction.

fascism scale (T. Adorno) A scale designed to measure antidemocratic ideology and authoritarianism. Also known as F scale.

fashion The style of art, literature, garments, manners, and customs, which may be transient and irrational but often reflects the mood of the social period. See FAD.

fashioning effect The influence of a self-determined social role upon own self-perception and behavior.

fast mapping A process through which children attach a new word to an underlying concept on the basis of a single encounter with it.

fatal familial insomnia An inherited and fatal disorder characterized by progressive insomnia.

fatalism A belief in predestiny, a doctrine holding that all the acts of humans and all events of history have and will be predetermined, and individuals have no free will. In Christianity, this notion can be traced back to the philosophy of Augustine.

fat cells Common name for adipocytes.

fate analysis (L. Szondi) A theory that the life of every individual is governed by a hidden plan determined by latent recessive genes. These genes are said to stem from the familial unconscious through which human repressed ancestors direct human behavior, choice of friends, occupation, and the type of diseases to which humans are subject. See FAMILIAL UNCONSCIOUS, KARMA, SCHICKSAL.

fate neurosis destiny neurosis

father See all citations beginning with FATHER and NEW-FATHER BLUES, PRIMAL FATHER, VAGINAL FATHER.

father-daughter incest Erotic activities between father and daughter.

father figure A substitute father, either real or imagined; a person who takes, if only subjectively, the place of the biological father, performing typical paternal functions and serving as an object of identification and attachment. Also known as father surrogate, surrogate father.

father fixation   1. An abnormally strong emotional attachment to the father or father figure. Purportedly due to dependency or some personality deficit as in the case of mother fixation. 2. In psychoanalytic theory, a child's irrational attachment to the father, likely to prevent the child from establishing normal attachments with the opposite sex. See ELECTRA COMPLEX, OEDIPAL COMPLEX.

father hypnosis   (S. Ferenczi) Refers to hypnotic submission derived from blind obedience, a transference of father fixation. It is associated with fear and mother hypnosis with coaxing. Compare MOTHER HYPNOSIS.

father ideal   In psychoanalytic theory, the father component of the ego ideal, the other component representing the self. See PARENT FIGURES.

father's movements   See MEN'S MOVEMENTS.

father surrogate   A person, usually a male, who serves someone else as a substitute for a father. See FATHER FIGURE.

fatiguability   The relative rate at which fatigue increases in an organ, or in an individual, as compared with other organs or individuals.

fatigue   A usually transient state of discomfort and loss of efficiency as a normal reaction to emotional strain, physical exertion, boredom, or lack of rest. Abnormal precipitating factors may include emotional stress, improper diet, or a debilitating disease. A sensory system, such as hearing, may experience fatigue from overexposure to a stimulus. Fatigue may be localized, involving only certain muscles. Kinds of fatigue include: BATTLE, INTRINSIC, RELATIVE. See CHRONIC FATIGUE IMMUNE DYSFUNCTION SYNDROME, CHRONIC FATIGUE SYNDROME.

fatigue effect   In research, a contamination error that may occur due to tiredness or boredom. See RESEARCH METHODS.

fatigue fear   See KOPOPHOBIA, PONOPHOBIA.

fatigue studies   Research on factors that cause both mental and physical fatigue. Fatigue studies by E. S. Robinson indicated that some signs of physical fatigue, for example, by visitors to museums, actually represented mental stress due to attention overload.

fatiguing vigil   Sleep deprivation during which an experimental participant performs mental work.

fatuity   Stupidity, dullness, foolishness, dementia.

fault   1. A moral defect, usually minor. 2. A defect in apparatus, method, or procedure that interferes with the reliability or validity of the results.

fausse reconnaissance   (false recognition—French) Phrase similar to paramnesia. See DÉJÀ VU.

faute de mieux   (for lack of something better—French) 1. Second choice. 2. The choice of a sexual partner of the same sex as the person's own when no partner of the other sex is available. See ACCIDENTAL HOMOSEXUALITY, FACULTATIVE HOMOSEXUALITY, SITUATIONAL HOMOSEXUALITY.

Faxensyndrom   (E. Bleuler) Denoting a prison psychosis characterized by irrelevant "clownish" behavior. See GANSER SYNDROME.

FDA   Food and Drug Administration

F distribution   (R. A. Fisher) A distribution of random variables. Suppose there are two distinct populations, each normally distributed with the same variance σ^2. Two independent samples are drawn: the first from population 1 of n_1 scores and the second from population 2 of n_2 scores to find the ratio of the sample variances, s_1^2/s_2^2. The sampling distribution of this ratio is the F distribution with $n_1 - 1$ and $n_2 - 1$ degrees of freedom. The F distribution is used in many statistical tests, notably Analysis of Variance (ANOVA). Also known as Fisher's distribution.

FDMD   Foundation for Depression and Manic Depression

FDTVP   See FROSTIG DEVELOPMENTAL TEST OF VISUAL PERCEPTION.

fear   A common emotion with many variations, running from slight anxiety to terror and panic. It is aroused not only by direct danger but by situations or objects that are cues to danger. See ANXIETY, PHOBIA.

fear appeal   An attempt to influence actions and attitudes by arousing fear, for example, fear of cancer, body odor, or embarrassment. Studies show that fear appeals frequently backfire by arousing a "defensive avoidance reaction."

fear drive   (O. H. Mowrer & N. E. Miller) The theory of avoidance learning that posits that an unpleasant feeling can motivate organisms to avoid a particular situation.

feared item   An object that causes concern or anxiety to people. Some intrinsically innocuous things or events can form part of a phobic syndrome. See PHOBIA.

fear-induced aggression   See ANIMAL AGGRESSION.

fear of ...   See PHOBIA.

fear of darkness   Normal or pathological trepidation when faced with darkness or night. This fear is neither universal nor inevitable, but when it occurs, it appears to be associated with feelings of danger and helplessness, inability to see, and a sense of unfamiliarity because things look different in the dark. The fear first becomes manifest at about three years of age but may develop into a phobia in which darkness has unconscious symbolic significance. Also known as achluophobia, darkness fear, nictophobia, nyctophobia.

fear of dismemberment   A psychiatric disorder in which the person expects or fears the loss of a body part. Symptoms are associated with strong feelings of persecution and occur in cases of schizophrenia and the involutional psychoses. Also known as dismemberment complex.

fear of everything   See PANPHOBIA.

fear of failure   Dread of failing to measure up to standards and goals set by oneself or by others, including anxiety over academic standing, job performance, sexual inadequacy, or loss of face and self-esteem. Also known as kakorrhaphiophobia.

fear of flying   See AVIOPHOBIA.

fear of rejection   1. Dread of being socially excluded or ostracized. 2. Fear of sexual rejection, sometimes associated with paraphilias such as pedophilia. See REJECTION.

fear of strangers   See STRANGER ANXIETY, XENOPHOBIA.

fear of success (M. Horner) A negative emotion due to achievement and success. Such a fear can deter realistic efforts to reach goals. Underlying reasons may vary, for example, the belief that if the person succeeds this time, expectations will occur that the person cannot meet, or that the person does not deserve such success.

fear response A reaction to a perceived threat, either manifest or covert, that entails changes in behavior.

Fear Survey Schedule II (FSS II) An instrument with statements about 51 stressful situations to which participants respond.

feasibility tests 1. In evaluation research, investigations conducted prior to a main evaluation to establish properties of response measures and to determine the probable success of evaluation designs. 2. Generally, a preliminary evaluation to determine if a product or process is practical. See PILOT STUDY, RESEARCH, RESEARCH METHODS.

Featherman-Jones-Hauser hypothesis (D. L. Featherman, F. L. Jones, R. M. Hauser) A controversial postulate that there is a cross-national similarity of social mobility rates such that in all societies with a nuclear family system and a market economy, the mobility pattern will be similar.

feature An aspect of an object that gives a phenomenon individuality and character. Examples of kinds of feature include: high-frustration tolerance, invariant, mood-congruent, mood-incongruent psychotic, and paralinguistic.

feature abstraction Capacity to understand complex matters and being able to order or summarize them in a simple but adequate manner.

feature analyzers/detectors 1. Generally, any perceptual sensitivity to a specific type of stimulus, usually visual or auditory, sometimes hypothesized. 2. Neurons in the brain sensitive to specific features, such as movement or shapes.

feature detection theory A point of view that pattern recognition is accomplished via the abstraction and reassembly of specific aspects of sensory stimulation.

feature indicator Design factors of objects that provide visual cues to feature detectors in the visual cortex; for example, boundaries between dark and light regions, straight or curved edges or surfaces, and connecting features such as crossbars.

feature model (J. S. Nairne) In memory, a model designed to account for the effects of immediate serial recall, such as recency, the modality effect, and the suffix effect, so named because items are assumed to be represented as a set of features.

feature-profile test A combination examination in which the task is to assemble seven pieces to complete the profile (three pieces) and the ear (four pieces) of a person's head. See FORMBOARD TEST.

febrile delirium Abnormal behavior and thinking associated with various diseases such as malaria that involve a rise in body temperature.

febriphobia Morbid fear of fever. Also known as pyrexeophobia, pyrexiophobia.

feces Waste matter expelled from the bowels. In psychoanalytic theory, interest in feces is an early expression of curiosity; withholding feces is an early expression of the drive for aggression and independence. Also known as excrement, faeces, fecal matter. See ANAL-RETENTION STAGE, ANAL SADISM, SCAT.

feces-lost-penis concept In psychoanalytic theory, the complex of anal-stage factors that influence the Oedipal and castration conflicts; for example, the infantile association between feces as a part of the body that has been lost and the later concern about loss of the penis. Also known as feces-child-penis concept.

Fechner-Helmholtz law See COEFFICIENT LAW.

Fechner's colors (G. T. Fechner) Colors perceived when a black and white disk is rotated at specific speeds. See BENHAM'S TOP for an illustration of such a disk.

Fechner's law (G. T. Fechner) 1. A psychophysical formula proposing that changes in the intensity of the sensation experienced is proportional to the logarithm of the stimulus magnitude. 2. An extension of Weber's law. The relation between changes of stimulus intensity and changes in sensation. Sensation varies arithmetically as the stimulus ratio varies geometrically. The formula is $S = K \log R$, when S equals magnitude of sensory intensity measured from the absolute threshold as zero, R is the magnitude of the stimulus measured with the absolute threshold as a unit, and K is an appropriate constant. See STEVENS' LAW, WEBER'S LAW, WEBER-FECHNER LAW.

Fechner's paradox (G. T. Fechner) An apparent increase in brightness of a figure caused by closing one eye after viewing the figure with both eyes open.

Fechner weight holders (G. T. Fechner) An apparatus devised for the presentation of stimuli in lifted weight experiments; each holder was an identical-looking square-bottomed receptacle covered with a lid and lifted by a handle in the act of comparing weights. See WEIGHT COMPARISON INSTRUMENTS.

fecundity The relative variability in the biological capacity of populations of females to have offspring. If that capacity has been reduced, the term subfecundity is used, and if totally lacking, it is termed sterility. In contrast, fertility can refer to the number of offspring actually had by an individual or a population. The meanings of these terms are sometimes reversed, with fecundity referring to the number of offspring, and fertility referring to the capacity to have offspring. See NET FERTILITY.

feebleminded(ness) Obsolete term describing persons with various degrees of mental retardation or severe cognitive impairment. See AFFECTIVE FEEBLEMINDEDNESS.

feedback 1. Knowledge of results. 2. A direct response by an individual or group to another person's behavior, such as the reactions of an audience to a speaker's remarks. 3. The process of receiving afferent impulses from proprioceptors, which enable humans to make accurate movements such as reaching for a pencil. 4. The reception of appropriate signals by a regulator, such as a thermostat. Varieties of feedback include: AFFECTIVE, ALPHA, AUDITORY, BIO-, CLOSED-LOOP, CYBERNETICS, DEVIATION-AMPLIFYING, FEEDFORWARD

MECHANISMS, HORMONAL, INFORMATION, INFOR-MATIONAL, INTERNAL, NEGATIVE, PHYSIOLOGICAL, POSITIVE, SOCIAL, THETA. See CLOSED-LOOP FEED-BACK SYSTEM, FACIAL-FEEDBACK HYPOTHESIS, PRO-PRIOCEPTION, PROPRIOCEPTOR.

feedback evaluation   See FORMATIVE EVALUATION.

feedback system   Nerve circuits that in sending their messages via the afferent path also send messages along an efferent path to the input receptors, thus modulating their activity and acting as a control (governor) of the system. See FEEDBACK.

feed-forward   The command for any activity posed either by others or the self about how to operate to achieve any particular goal, including modes of attaining goals and restrictions on certain behaviors. See ETHICS, MANAGEMENT BY OBJECTIVES.

feeding behavior   In humans, the sequential develop-ment of a child's need and skills in taking nourishment, including stimulation and coordination of the sucking and swallowing reflexes in early infancy, adaptation to breast or bottle and to scheduled or self-demand feeding, biting at about the fourth month, anticipatory chewing movements, chewing when the teeth are developed, and transferring from finger feeding to the use of utensils. See SELF-DEMAND SCHEDULE.

feeding center/system   Once considered to include only restricted regions (centers) of the hypothalamus be-cause destruction of the lateral hypothalamus produced a cessation of food and water intake (aphagia and adipsia) whereas lesions of the ventromedial hypothalamus pro-duced overeating (hyperphagia). Now recognized to in-clude many structures in the brain as a distributed system, including the lateral and medial hypothalamus, globus pallidus, frontal cortex, and especially structures associ-ated with distribution of the dopaminergic and noradren-ergic transmitter systems. See PALLIDOHYPOTHALAMIC TRACT.

feeding disorder   See FEEDING DISTURBANCE/PROB-LEM.

feeding disturbance/problem   A form of behavior disorder among children characterized by refusal to eat at all, by eating an inadequate amount or type of food, or by failure to hold down the food. Problems of this kind may be indicative of emotional maladjustment. See EATING BEHAVIOR, RUMINATION DISORDER OF INFANCY.

feeding system   See FEEDING CENTER.

fee-for-service plan   A system of charging a patient for each professional procedure authorized, with differ-ent fees based on the length of time, treatment difficulty, and degree of specialization and expertise required.

feel(ing)   1. An affective or emotional state, or an in-tuitive awareness. 2. A tactile or temperature sensation. 3. The word "feel" (affection) is sometimes misused when the word "think" (cognition) is meant; for example, saying "I feel that will do," when "I think that will do" is meant. Types of feeling(s) include: BODILY EGO, COM-MUNAL, ENTOPERIPHERAL, EPIPERIPHERAL, FAMIL-IARITY, GROUP, GUILT, HOLIDAY SYNDROME, INFERI-ORITY, MIXED, OCEANIC, RACKET, REALITY, SELF-, SENSE, SEX, SOCIAL, STHENIC, SUPERIORITY. See AM-BIVALENCE OF FEELINGS, EMOTION, REFLECTION OF FEELINGS, SENSATION, TRIDIMENSIONAL THEORY OF FEELING.

feeling apperception   (C. G. Jung) Jungian phrase for an active or passive feeling apperception or awareness; the passive undirected form (termed feeling intuition) is elicited by an external stimulus, whereas the active form is initiated from within and is occasioned by an act of will.

feeling of activity   An essential qualitative dimension of a person's experience during a volitional act; this feeling follows a course, increasing and decreasing with and parallel to volitional experience.

feeling of excitement-inhibition   (W. Wundt) Dimen-sions or attributes of Wilhelm Wundt's tridimensional theory of feeling in which a person alternates from being highly alert to being inert. See FEELING OF PLEASANT-NESS-UNPLEASANTNESS, FEELING OF TENSION-RE-LAXATION, WUNDT'S TRIDIMENSIONAL THEORY OF FEELING.

feeling of fitness   A feeling or appreciation of the eth-ical worth of a certain course of conduct—the harmony, for example, of an object or artistic composition with cer-tain esthetic standards.

feeling of pleasantness-unpleasantness   Dimensions or attributes of Wilhelm Wundt's tridimensional theory of feeling in which a person alternates from being in a state of relaxed harmony to being in a state of high discomfort. See FEELING OF EXCITEMENT-DEPRESSION, FEELING OF TENSION-RELAXATION, WUNDT'S TRIDIMENSIONAL THEORY OF FEELING.

feeling of reality   (W. James) 1. The sense of being, of the actuality of things and events, awareness of the self and others. 2. A feeling *sui generis* that constitutes the essential factor in belief.

feeling of responsibility   Awareness on the part of mainstream adult humans of any given culture that they are bound to act according to its prevailing standards and are subject to proportionate sanctions for violating them. See CATEGORICAL IMPERATIVE.

feeling of tension-relaxation   Dimensions or attributes of Wilhelm Wundt's tridimensional theory of feeling in which a person alternates from being calm to being tense. Also known as tension-relaxation feeling. See FEELING OF EXCITEMENT-DEPRESSION, FEELING OF PLEASANTNESS-UNPLEASANTNESS, WUNDT'S TRIDIMENSIONAL THEORY OF FEELING.

feeling of unreality   A feeling of greater or lesser in-tensity attached to a perceptual experience, especially in pathological conditions, such that the experience appears to lack objectivity or reality. See DEPERSONALIZATION, FEELING OF REALITY.

feeling rules   (A. Hochschild) Rules about what emotion is and is not appropriate to a given social setting.

feelings   The emotional aspects of an experience.

feelings of guilt   Self-criticism based on actions or thoughts the person had or did in opposition to what that person believes should have been done. May be rational remorse or irrational and self-punitive. Also known as guilt feelings.

feelings of inferiority   See INFERIORITY FEELINGS.

feelings of superiority   See SUPERIORITY FEELINGS.

feeling states   See AFFECTIVE STATES.

feeling-talk   See CONDITIONED-REFLEX THERAPY.

feeling tone   Affective quality of an experience or object, or situation, such as its level of pleasurableness; also the affect it arouses. Also known as affective tone, affectivity, emotional tone.

feeling type   One of Carl Jung's basic functional personality types, characterized by a dominance of feeling or affect. The feeling type is included in the rational class of functional personality types.

feigning   1. Pretending, faking. 2. A behavior attitude that conveys information about the person that is unauthentic and deceptive.

Feldenkrais Functional Integration   (M. Feldenkrais) A body movement process intending to lead to psychological wholeness. Related to *judo*, *tai chi*, and other Eastern psychophysical disciplines.

felicitation   Behavior intended to generate happiness.

fellatio   The use of the mouth in sexual stimulation of the penis. In psychoanalytic theory, the child's gratification from sucking the nipple (and later the finger) is transferred to the penis. Also known as buccal onanism, fellation, fellatorism, oral coitus, oral sex, penilingus.

fellator   A person who performs fellatio.

Fels Parent Behavior Rating Scales   Means of assessing a preschool child's home environment on such factors as child-centered versus child-subordinate, close rapport versus isolation, approval versus disapproval, harmony versus conflict, freedom versus restriction, mild versus severe penalties, uncritical versus critical. Also known as Fels Scales of Parent Behavior.

felt need   1. Awareness of a need. 2. The open and authentic expression to others of a need.

felt sense   (E. Gendlin) A sense of being, comprising affect, intuition, kinesthesia, and imagination.

female circumcision   Incorrect phrase for clitoridectomy. Female circumcision is also known as female genital mutilation.

female ejaculation   1. Release from the Skene's glands of a liquid analogous to male prostatic fluid. Occurs in a small percentage of women at orgasm; the quantity ranges from a few drops to a stream. 2. Inaccurate phrase for the transudation of lubricating plasma fluids from blood vessels in the vaginal wall during sexual arousal. This oozing normally peaks prior to orgasm, increases when preorgasmic stimulation is prolonged, is higher prior to menstruation, and inhibited in cocaine users. See GRAEFENBERG SPOT (G-SPOT).

female-genitals fear   See EROTOPHOBIA.

female impersonator   A male, regardless of sexual orientation, who adopts female clothing and mannerisms, often as part of a stage act.

femaleness   In humans, the quality of being female in the anatomical or physiological sense; the possession of sexual characteristics derived from the XX (sex) chromosomes. Other psychological and sociological definitions of femaleness are culture bound. See FEMININITY, SUPER-FEMALE.

female Oedipus complex   Electra complex

female orgasmic disorder   Inhibition of the capacity to participate in normal sexual relations, or inability to enjoy sexual activity with a chosen partner or alone. The main feature is the incapacity to achieve orgasm. Often related to early attitudes, feelings of insecurity, and embarrassment. Compare MALE ORGASMIC DISORDER.

female sexual arousal disorder   1. Chronic failure in achieving physiological readiness for sexual intercourse. 2. Lack of sexual desire or pleasure prior to or during sexual activity.

female sperm   In humans, the female-determining sperm, with 24 autosomes and an X chromosome.

Feminazis   (R. Limbaugh) Slur term for pro-abortion feminists, in which the victims are fetuses.

feminine identification   In humans, a tendency of certain males to adopt feminine characteristics, and in some cases feminine roles, although this psychological trait may be covert. Feminine traits and roles are largely but not exclusively culture-specific. See BERDACHE.

feminine identity   A person's inner sense of affiliation with the female gender.

feminine masochism   A form of masochism found in male patients who gratify their need to be punished and humiliated by playing the role of a woman in fantasy. In these cases the woman (in the male's fantasy) may be pictured as suffering birth pangs or serving as a prostitute against her will.

femininity   1. Possession of the secondary sex characteristics of a woman, as contrasted with femaleness, determined in part by the XX chromosomes. 2. A "typically feminine" personality pattern, whether in a female or male. Stereotypes of femininity vary from culture to culture. However, there is little agreement in certain societies on the description of these patterns, or even whether they exist at all. See MASCULINITY-FEMININITY TESTS.

femininity complex   A psychoanalytic concept that proposes that the male child unconsciously defends himself against maternal castration by identifying with her and wishing for a vagina and breasts, an expression of "vaginal envy." According to Melanie Klein, the boy actually dreads the feminine role and may respond to this dread by becoming aggressive. See VAGINAL ENVY.

feminism   1. A social and political movement with activities directed toward the aim of females achieving political and economic equality with men. A frequent quotation is Rebecca West's 1913 "I myself have never been able to find out precisely what feminism is: I only know that people call me a feminist whenever I express sentiments that differentiate me from a doormat, or a prostitute." See FEMINISM MOVEMENT (TYPES), FEMINIST PSYCHOLOGY, FEMINIST THERAPY, WOMEN'S LIBERATION MOVEMENT. 2. Female physiological characteristics in males, such as enlarged breasts due to undersecretion of androgens or oversecretion of estrogens. See FEMINIZATION. 3. A social pattern of gender-specific behaviors independent of female biological functions. See BERDACHE, TRANSSEXUALITY. 4. A body of philosophical writing, usually by female scholars, that encourages strategies for achieving feminist goals.

feminism movement (types)   Various kinds of feminism have developed since the 1960s, especially in the United States, and definitions are fluid. Kinds of feminism include: AMAZON, ANARCHO, CULTURAL, EROTIC, ECO-, INDIVIDUALIST, MARXIST, MATERIAL, MODERATE, RADICAL. See FEMINAZIS.

feminist   1. A person, usually a woman, who furthers the goals of feminism either personally or in the context of social, cultural, and intellectual areas. 2. A person, usually a woman, who actively supports feminist organizations.

feminist psychology   A school of psychology influenced by the feminist movement, started in the 1970s, that analyzes gender relationships, challenges the traditionally male-oriented bias in psychological research and therapy, and studies the social consequences of the above. Seen by proponents as the "foremother" of other psychological approaches that seek to reduce bias in the study of, for instance, ethnic and cultural minorities, gay men, lesbians, older people, people with disabilities, and the socially disadvantaged.

feminist therapy   A philosophical and practical approach with certain assumptions; for example, therapy is political, sexism limits options, nontraditional strategies are needed, and therapists must be aware of personal, gender-biased value systems in relation to appropriate behavior. Feminist therapists promote self-awareness, self-affirmation, and personal integration, outcomes that may conflict with the societal norms that were the original source of dysfunctional behavior patterns of women.

feminization   1. The process of becoming more feminine, regardless of the gender (sex) of the individual. 2. The anatomical and neurological differentiation of the fetus as a female.

feminization of poverty   The economic disadvantaging of women.

feminizing-testes syndrome   Pseudohermaphroditism associated with a defective trait for testosterone response. Typical patients have normal female external genitalia and breasts, a blind vaginal pouch, no uterus, and male gonads. In some treatments, the gonads are removed and estrogen therapy is administered to enhance the female appearance.

femme sole   (woman alone—French) In law, a single, divorced, widowed, or separated woman. Also spelled *feme sole*.

femto   One-quadrillionth.

FEN   See FENFLURAMINE.

fenestra   (window—Latin) In anatomy, an aperture or opening. Plural is fenestrae. See FENESTRA COCHLEAE, FENESTRA OVALIS.

fenestra cochleae/rotunda   (C. Folli) The round membranous window of the cochlea of the inner ear that equalizes pressures of sounds. Also known as round window.

fenestra ovalis/vestibuli   (C. Folli) The oval membranous window, that separates the middle and inner ears. Also known as oval window.

fenfluramine (FEN)   A pharmaceutical that decreases appetite by releasing serotonin. See ANOREXIANT.

fensternl   (window courting—German) A rural German courtship custom designed to ensure a fiancée's fertility. The young woman signals in her window an invitation for a boy to spend the night and leave before dawn. When she becomes pregnant and is thus proven capable of bearing children to help with the farm work, she announces her choice of husband (who may or may not be the father). See BUNDLING.

feral children   Human children who have reportedly been raised by wild animals and isolated from human contact. See WILD BOY OF AVEYRON.

Ferberizing   Common name given to a procedure recommended by pediatrician Richard Ferber to deal with sleeping situations of infants. A crying infant is ignored for a period of time, and then parents are advised to pat and talk to the baby for a short time and then retreat. If the infant reawakes and cries again, the parents are to wait five additional minutes before returning with additional reassurance. The parents are to continue in this manner with increasingly longer waiting periods each time for the purpose of teaching the infant nocturnal self-reliance.

Féré phenomenon   (C. S. Féré) The galvanic skin response. The changes in the amount of direct (galvanic) current that is passed between two points on the skin surface brought about by arousal or activation of the nervous system, as in emotional arousal. The electrical conductance of the skin changes during emotional arousal were first called the psychogalvanic reflex and later renamed the galvanic skin response. Compare TARCHANOFF PHENOMENON.

Féré rotary campimeter   (C. S. Féré) An instrument for mapping visual perceptions up to 92° from center vision. The stimulus object is fixed while the fixation point is movable.

Fernald method   (G. Fernald) A multisensory teaching-of-reading method using Visual, Auditory, Kinesthetic, and Tactile (VAKT) modalities. Also known as VAKT (method).

Ferree-Rand double broken circles   (C. E. Ferree & G. Rand) A chart used to test visual acuity consisting of circles of varying size, with two gaps in each instead of one, as in the Landolt circle.

Ferree rotary campimeter   (C. E. Ferree) A device for mapping the visual field up to 92° of excentricity. In this device, the fixation point is movable while the stimulus is fixed, distinguishing it from other devices of this type and allowing for the use of bulky apparatus for stimulus presentation.

Ferrier's experiment   (D. Ferrier) Research in which participants are asked to imagine pressing a button but are not actually pressing one. Any sensations can be attributed to central nervous system processes but not to local afferent or efferent nerve impulses.

Ferry-Porter law   (E. Ferry & T. Porter) A theory that the apparent fusing of a flickering light is related to the amount of illumination: The more illumination the sooner the light appears as a steady glow. Ervin Ferry originally presented the law, but Thomas Porter presented a broader range of measurements to support the relationship between critical fusion frequency and luminance as stated by Ferry.

FERS square   The front face of the Henning odor prism, representing these smells: Fragrant, Etherial, Resinous, Spicy.

fertility   See FECUNDITY.

fertility rate   1. The theoretical maximum or actual rate of reproduction of any individual, couple, or set of organisms. 2. The number of pregnancies per year per 1,000 women of childbearing years in a given population.

fertilization   The penetration of the ovum by a spermatozoon and the fusion of the nuclei of the male and female gametes. See IMPREGNATION, ONTOGENETIC ZERO.

fertilization age fetal age

festinating gait An involuntary gait of Parkinson patients in which their body leans stiffly forward and the walk becomes a half run.

fetal activity Motor activities of the fetus that have low positive correlations with performance on the Gesell Maturity Tests administered six months after birth. Correlations with performance at more advanced ages appear inconclusive.

fetal age The age of the fetus calculated from the time of fertilization. Also known as fertilization age.

fetal-alcohol effect (FAE) Relatively serious teratogenic effects on fetuses by alcohol ingested by the mother during pregnancy. See FETAL ALCOHOL SYNDROME, TERATOGEN.

fetal-alcohol(ic) syndrome (FAS) Three effects observed in some children born to mothers who have been abusing alcohol heavily during their pregnancy (growth retardation, facial anomalies, central nervous system dysfunction). Possibly the leading nongenetic cause of mental retardation. See TERATOGEN.

fetal distress The condition of a fetus whose life or health is threatened by effects of a disease or other disorder originating in the mother. May be due, for example, to toxemia, an infectious disease transmitted through the placenta or hypoxia due to umbilical cord involvement. See FETUS AT RISK.

fetal infant A child born during the late fetal period, about 7 months after conception.

fetal infection Any disease that may affect a fetus as a result of the infectious agent being transmitted from the mother via the placenta. A fetal infection usually is caused by a virus, but other agents are tuberculosis bacteria, the syphilis spirochete, or the toxoplasmosis protozoa. See RUBELLA, TOXOPLASMOSIS.

fetal-maternal exchange Transfer across the placental barrier of substances required for the maintenance of fetal life (oxygen, water, electrolytes) and the elimination of its waste products (urea). In addition to such substances, other, undesirable substances including alcohol, opiates, and other drugs, as well as disease organisms such as viruses and syphilis spirochetes may cross the placental barrier to produce congenital defects.

fetal period The postembryonic stage of human prenatal development from the eighth or ninth week after conception to birth.

fetal presentation The position of the fetus prior to childbirth. The vertex position is the most common, easiest, and safest, with the head emerging first. Varying levels of difficulty and danger to mother and infant are associated with other presentations.

fetal response The reaction of the unborn child to environmental stimulation. Fetuses react to noxious noises such as low-flying overhead aircraft or high-decibel amplifiers. Stress hormones and tobacco toxins entering the fetus through the placental "barrier" provoke responses as well as morphological anomalies. See PRENATAL INFLUENCE.

fetal-tobacco syndrome A controversial attribution of growth retardation, and possibly mental retardation, of some infants born of women who smoked tobacco regularly during pregnancy. Infants appear to suffer from neurological impairment, reduced weight, and other anomalies. Possibly caused by the capacity for nicotine to reduce blood flow to the placenta.

feticide Rare term for abortion.

fetish (magic—Portuguese) 1. (A. Binet) In sexology, nonsexual objects (such as gloves, shoes, handkerchiefs) or parts of the body (feet, locks of hair, ears) that arouse sexual interest or excitement. See FETISHISM. 2. In anthropology, an object, such as a talisman or amulet, that embodies a supernatural spirit or exerts magical force, usually intended to protect the owner or wearer. 3. An idea, goal, or mode of behavior that elicits special devotion, such as when a person makes a fetish of success.

fetishism (A. Binet) 1. A pathological condition characterized by an erotic attachment to certain parts of the body, or (more generally) to certain articles of clothing worn by the object of attachment. Gratification is usually achieved by fondling, kissing, or licking the objects. 2. Being sexually attracted to or aroused by any nonsexual inanimate object or nongenital body part. Types of fetish(ism) include: AMPUTATION, ANTI-, AUTO-, BEAST, FOOT, OBJECT, SHOE. See FETISH, PARTIALISM.

fetishistic cross dressing See CROSS-DRESSING.

fetish paraphilias A category of paraphilias in which a fetish or token is the object of erotic excitement and sexual satisfaction. Includes autonepiophilia or diaperism, coprophilia (feces), hyphephilia (fabrics, especially rubber and leather), mysophilia (filth), klismaphilia (enemas), urophilia or undinism (urine), olfactophilia (smell), and foot fetish.

fetus The human organism in the postembryonic period prior to birth. The fetal period begins with the ninth week when the major organs have been developed and hardening of the bones has begun. Also spelled foetus. See EMBRYO, FETAL PERIOD.

fetus at risk (FAR) A fetus with a significant risk of being born with a mental or physical disorder because of known influences (such as diabetes or hypertension) from parents or other family members. The risk of a mental disease in a child born in a family with no history of mental disease is less than 3%, but the risk may range up to 50% in certain cases, such as a defect that is a sex-linked recessive trait inherited from the mother's side of the family and the parents are related. See FETAL DISTRESS.

fever fear See FEBRIPHOBIA.

fever therapy Induction of fever by malaria or other means, formerly used for treating general paresis (syphilis of the brain).

FFDE fit(ness) for duty evaluation

FG Abbreviation for foreground. See FOREGROUNDING.

F-G Abbreviation for figure-ground. See FIGURE-GROUND DISTORTION.

FI fixed interval

Fiamberti hypothesis   Obsolete theory that schizophrenia results from a nervous-tissue deficiency of acetylcholine, which may be secondary to a toxic or infectious condition.

fiat   1. A conscious arbitrary decision that amounts to an order to the self or others. 2. (W. James) A distinctive determinative experience that sometimes attends an act of volition or choice between alternatives.

fiber   An elongated threadlike structure, which in a living organism is usually the smallest part of a nerve, muscle, bone, skin, or other organ system. Also spelled fibre. See FIBRIL.

fiber tract   A group of nerves close to one another resembling a bundle.

fibril   A component of a fiber. In the body, the general term fibril is defined as a collagenous component of a fiber. There is no collagen in the central nervous system, but structural proteins known as fibrils are found in the cytoskeleton of neurons and glia. See GLIOFIBRIL, NEUROFIBRIL, NEUROFILAMENT NEUROTUBULE.

fibrillary tremor   A trembling of the body or a part of the body caused by a small bundle of muscle fibers that produce a fine tremor. See INTENTION TREMOR, TREMOR.

fibrillation   1. The rapid movements of fibers, such as the movements of the tails of sperm. 2. Rapid uncoordinated, chaotic heart beats. 3. The process of fibril formation.

fiction   1. (A. Adler) The complex set of lifestyle guidelines that may resolve inferiority feelings or that provide a person with a set of imagined satisfying results. This can help the person to actively pursue desired goals. See FICTIONAL FINALISM. 2. A complex set of imagined beliefs regarding the self and others that become the basis for self-actions; they serve as guidelines for behavior. See VAIHINGER'S PHILOSOPHY OF THE AS IF.

fictional finalism   (A. Adler) Alfred Adler's doctrine that humans are more strongly motivated by "fictions" (goals and ideals they create for themselves) and more influenced by future possibilities than by past events such as childhood experiences. The goal itself is also known as fictional final goal, fictional future/goal, fictive goal. See ADLERIAN PSYCHOLOGY, INDIVIDUAL PSYCHOLOGY, TELEOLOGY.

fidelity   In psychometrics, the combination of reliability and validity of a measuring instrument such as a test. A test with high fidelity is a good predictor of what it measures. See BANDWIDTH, TEST CONSTRUCTION.

fidelity check   A method for ensuring that an activity has been performed correctly, for example, after administering a test, reviewing the steps to determine that proper protocol was followed.

fidgetiness   A state of increased motor activity associated with anxiety, tics, chorea, or boredom.

fiducial   Pertaining to that which is trustworthy, faithful, and reliable.

fiducial interval   The space of any statistical finding that includes a percentage of expectation that the finding is to be accepted as probable.

fiducial limit(s)   Confidence limits.

field   (K. Lewin) In field theory, a complex of personal, physical, and social factors within which psychological events takes place. See FIELD THEORY.

field-cognition mode   1. A combination of perception, memory, and thought that directs the behavior of a person within his or her environment. 2. (E. C. Tolman) The totality of experience of an organism, including its memory, cognitive aspects, and perception that serves the organism in an environment, such as to find the goal in a maze.

field defect   An abnormality in the normal curvature of a visual field, including tunnel vision and partial or total blindness.

field dependence   (H. Witkin) A tendency to uncritically rely on environmental cues, particularly deceptive ones, in tasks requiring the performance of simple actions or the identification of familiar elements in unfamiliar contexts. Passivity, as well as cognitive complexity, is associated with field dependence, and women tested tended to be more field-dependent than men. However, in societies where women are more self-reliant, such sex differences diminish sharply; for example, in Eskimo society, no differences were found between men and women. See COGNITIVE STYLE, FIELD INDEPENDENCE, FIELD DEPENDENCE-INDEPENDENCE.

field dependence-independence   1. (H. Witkin) In personality theory, susceptibility to or immunity from the influence of "field" (environmental) cues, particularly in tasks requiring the performance of simple actions or the identification of familiar elements in unfamiliar contexts. First quantified with the rod-and-frame test as perception research, then with other tests to measure "locus of control." See COGNITIVE STYLE, ROD-AND-FRAME TEST, LOCUS OF CONTROL. 2. A learning style in which the learner operates holistically, perceiving the entire field as a whole rather than its component parts (dependence), or in which the learner operates analytically, perceiving the field in terms of its components (independence).

field expectation   A set established in an organism that makes it responsive to an external stimulus and that elicits a particular reaction or response; for example, a trained dog on hearing a particular whistle may run either to or away from its owner depending on how it was trained.

field experiment   An experiment carried out in a natural or "real-world" setting in which participants are stimulated or manipulated (traditionally without their awareness) in some manner and observed for their reactions. See OBSERVATIONAL METHOD.

field force   (K. Lewin) In field theory, a manifestation of drive or energy inherent in a person in relation to the entire psychological field in which the person is located. See FIELD THEORY.

field independence   (H. Witkin) A component of a person's cognitive style. The general capacity to orient the self correctly despite deceptive environmental cues (for example, not being distracted by incidental elements in making a decision). Field independence is highly correlated with analytic ability, high achievement motivation, and an active coping style. See COGNITIVE STYLE, FIELD DEPENDENCE, FIELD DEPENDENCE-INDEPENDENCE.

field investigation/observation 1. The investigation by interviews and observations in natural settings of social conditions of humans. 2. The observation of animal behavior in the natural habitat. See FIELD STUDY.

field observation field investigation

field of consciousness The total awareness of a person at a given time.

field of regard The total space and all the objects within that space that can be seen at one time by the moving eye.

field of touch Generic phrase embracing all aspects of tactual sensibility.

field properties The environmental factors that surround and influence a living organism.

field research field study

fields See the following types of field(s): BEHAVIOR(AL), ENVIRONMENTAL, EXCITATORY, FORCE, LEAVING THE, MINIMAL AUDIBLE, PERCEPTUAL, PHENOMENAL, POWER, PSYCHOLOGICAL, RECEPTIVE, REGARD, RETINAL, SEMANTIC, SENSORY, SHARED, SUBJECTIVE VISUAL, VISUAL.

fields of forel See SUBTHALAMUS.

fields of psychology Subdivisions of psychology into specialty or theoretical topics, such as rational and empirical (Howard Warren); theoretical and applied (Howard Wilkening); objective, subjective, and personalistic (Horace English); idiographic and nomothetic (Wilhelm Wildelbrand); and biological and social (Wilhelm Dilthey). Other divisions include basic and applied, social and physiological, clinical/professional, and experimental. Most introductory textbooks divide psychology into 15 to 20 chapters, each covering a different field. Some coalesce several fields, for instance, emotion/motivation/sexuality, clinical/abnormal/personality/psychometrics, comparative/physiological, and educational/developmental/adolescence/adulthood; others separate them. Currently, the American Psychological Association recognizes more than fifty divisions of psychology.

field space See FIELD THEORY.

field structure (K. Lewin) In field theory, the pattern, distribution, or hierarchy of parts of a psychological field, or life space. See FIELD THEORY.

field study 1. Research performed in a natural, rather than a laboratory setting. Also known as field research. See FIELD INVESTIGATION/OBSERVATION. 2. See NATURALISTIC OBSERVATION (meaning 3).

field theory (K. Lewin) A systematic approach to psychology that describes behavior in terms of patterns of dynamic interrelationships between the individual and the total situation (psychological, social, and physical) in which the individual is embedded. The situation is termed the field space or life space, and the dynamic interactions are conceived as forces with positive or negative valences, represented diagrammatically as vector lines. See CONFLICT, LIFE SPACE, VALENCE.

field theory of personality A point of view that humans are what they do and what they do is dependent on a series of immediate forces acting on them, with humans programmed at birth (constitutionally) and from birth (socially) to react, in particular ways. See FREE WILL, PERSONALITY THEORIES, SITUATIONISM, SPONTANEITY THEORY.

field verification Testing, often of documentation, by a representative sample of end users.

field work 1. In topics such as clinical psychology and social work, a practicum in which students supplement and apply classroom theory by taking responsibility for actual cases in agencies under the tutelage of qualified supervisors. 2. In disciplines such as social psychology, sociology, and anthropology, research on people in their, rather than the researcher's, environment. Ranges from large-scale surveys or observations to a single case study. 3. In such areas as ethology and biology, research conducted in the animals' natural habitat. 4. Loosely, any study that takes the researcher out of the office or laboratory and into a natural setting.

fifth cranial nerve See TRIGEMINAL NERVE.

fight See FAIR-FIGHT EXERCISES.

fighting instinct See PUGNACITY.

fight-or-flight reaction/response (W. B. Cannon) A reaction to a stressful situation in which the sympathetic nervous system mobilizes the organism and puts it on a "war footing," either to fight back or to flee. Also known as fight-flight reaction.

figural aftereffect (FAE) A gestalt-perceptual phenomenon in which a shift of vision from a first figure superimposes its image on a second figure. May be classified as kinesthetic aftereffects or rotational aftereffects.

figural cohesion A gestalt-perceptual tendency for parts of a figure to be perceived as a whole figure even if the parts are disjointed. See CLOSURE, STREET FIGURES for illustrations.

figurative knowledge (J. Piaget) Knowledge acquired by attending to and remembering specific perceptual features, words, or facts; for example, the ability to recall vocabulary, dates, colors, shapes, impressions, and other details. Many followers of Jean Piaget hold that figurative knowledge is overemphasized in schools and intelligence tests. See OPERATIVE KNOWLEDGE.

figurative language The use of similes and metaphors to make communication clearer, for example, "He is as stubborn as a mule." See COMMUNICATION SKILLS, COMMUNICATIONS THEORY.

figure A group of impressions derived from a single sense, perceived as a unit or object. Types of figures include: AMBIGUOUS, AUTHORITY, BALDWIN'S, COMPOSITE, CONCEALED, DOT, EMPIRIC-RISK, FATHER, GOBLET, GOTTSCHALDT, HELPFUL, IDENTIFICATION, IMPOSSIBLE, KANIZSA, KEY, LISSAJOU, MOTHER, NONSENSE, PARENT, POWER, PURKINJE, RABBIT-DUCK, REFLEX, REVERSIBLE, RUBIN'S, RYBAKOFF'S, STREET. See EMBEDDED FIGURES TEST, HIDDEN-FIGURES TEST, RECURRING-FIGURES TEST.

figure-drawing test An examination in which the participant draws a human figure. Used as a measure of intellectual development or as a projective technique. See GOODENOUGH DRAW-A-MAN TEST, HOUSE-TREE-PERSON TEST, LEVY DRAW-AND-TELL-A-STORY TECHNIQUE, MACHOVER DRAW-A-PERSON TEST, ROSENBERG DRAW-A-PERSON TECHNIQUE.

figure-8 maze 377 *final common path(way)*

figure-8 maze　　(W. Hunter) A maze resembling a figure-8 lying on its side. An animal subject enters the maze in the middle and immediately must decide to go right (R) or left (L); when returning to the starting point, the subject again makes a decision. Used to study the human concepts of reasoning, memory and intelligence in animals, assumed to be demonstrated by how many LR decisions the subject makes to achieve its goal, usually of being fed. See ALTERNATION PROBLEMS.

figure-ground distortion　　Inability to focus on an object without having its setting interfere with its perception. See FIGURE-GROUND PERCEPTION.

figure-ground effect　　(R. Ruben) The principle that perceptions have two parts: a figure that stands out in good contour and an indistinct, homogeneous ground. See REVERSIBLE FIGURE-GROUND.

figure-ground effect　Either a white cross on a black background or four black triangles in front of a white background are seen. Sustained examination will lead to changes of foreground and background.

figure-ground perception　　Ability to attend to and discriminate properly between figure and ground in a visual field presentation. An impairment in this perceptual skill can seriously affect a child's ability to learn.

figure-ground relationship　　1. In Gestalt psychology, the tendency of one part of a complex perceptual input (figure) to stand out as separate from and in front of its field (ground). 2. The Gestalt concept that visual perception is divided into two parts, figure and ground. The figure or object attended to is seen "in focus" and as a whole, while the rest of the visual field, less clearly seen, is the ground or background. By a shift in attention or perception, different objects in the field may become figure and the former figure may become part of the ground. See FIGURE-GROUND EFFECT, RUBIN'S FIGURE for examples of this phenomenon.

file-drawer problem　　The fact that nonsignificant research findings tend to remain unpublished in private files.

filial　　Pertaining to the offspring.

filial generations　　The successive generations from a given parent or pair.

filial maturity　　A stage in life when adults regard their aged parents as dependent people who need their help.

filial psychotherapy　　(B. G. Guerney) Therapy in which parents under direction of a psychotherapist play with their own children to achieve beneficial therapeutic results.

filial regression　　Refers to regression of a son or daughter. Francis Galton stated that offspring generally tend to approach the average of their parents' general group, and that offspring of gifted parents tend to regress to the average. See LAW OF FILIAL REGRESSION.

filial responsibility　　The obligation that members of a family are expected to feel, in most cultures, toward the other members of their family, especially their elders.

filiate　　1. To establish a relationship similar to that between a parent and child. 2. In groups, relationships similar to those of a family tree with parents, children, uncles, etc.

filicide　　The killing of children by their parents. See DEPRESSION AFTER DELIVERY (DAD).

filiform papilla　　See PAPILLA.

filled pause　　Sounds made by a speaker between words, usually to keep the attention of the listeners, such sounds as "err" or "mmmm" or clearing of the throat.

filled-space illusion　　The impression that, of two identical spaces, if one is filled and the other unfilled, the filled space will seem larger.

filled-time interval　　A time period during which a person is occupied: performing an action, thinking, daydreaming. Such time subjectively goes much faster than its counterpart, unfilled-time, when a person is unoccupied.

filler material　　Items in a test or questionnaire that will not be scored. They are inserted for various reasons, such as to disguise the purpose of the instrument or to reassure the respondent.

fill-in questions　　A test item in which the usual instructions are to write in a missing word in a sentence, for example, "The brain lobe at the back of a person's head is called the _____." Sometimes the number of letters of the desired word is indicated.

film color　　A film-like, texture-free soft color that lacks localization, as contrasted with the color of a surface.

filter　　1. A device that is interposed between a source of some kind and a receptacle (or the equivalent) with the intention of letting some items through but not others. 2. In physiology, any device that will restrict stimuli from reaching the brain. Many stimuli such as light and sound can be filtered. 3. An initial hurdle (such as a test score or some credential) used for the preliminary screening of candidates.

filter theory　　(D. E. Broadbent) A point of view that although a tremendous number of potential stimuli impinge on organisms, only a small fraction of them at a given time are received and dealt with because the processing capacity of any organism is limited and many stimuli are kept from coming to awareness. See FLUCTUATION OF PERCEPTION, SELECTIVE ATTENTION, SET, SUBLIMINAL PERCEPTION.

filter theory (of mate selection)　　A point of view that in search for mates, people establish (sometimes without conscious intent) a series of standards in a hierarchy; the one who passes the final filter is selected. Filters may include age, appearance, education, vocation, nationality, personality, family, friends, and resources.

filth fear　　See COPROPHOBIA, DIRT PHOBIA, SCATOPHOBIA.

fimbria hippocampi　　Part of the hippocampal-system of the brain, consisting of a flattened band of fibers along the surface of the hippocampus. The fimbria continues as the crura of the fornix passing beneath the corpus callosum.

final cause　　Those motivations for which a goal, a complex of actions, is undertaken, such as wanting to be an accountant, and pursuing this goal for years.

final common path(way)　　(C. Sherrington) A motor neuron that serves as a funnel for the routing of a variety of different nerve impulses from many reflex arcs. Motor neurons in general carry impulses from two or more arcs rather than serving one reflex arc exclusively.

final free recall (test) In memory, asking the participant to recall all the words from all the lists that have been presented, as a measure of long-term store.

finalism A doctrine positing that human behavior can best be explained in terms of expectations about the future, with individuals seeking to achieve goals. See FICTIONAL FINALISM, TELEOLOGY.

finality See FINALISM, PURPOSE.

final-offer arbitration total package arbitration

final offer selection In negotiation, a procedure in which each side makes a final proposal, one of which is selected by an arbitrator.

final tendency (W. Stekel & A. Adler) The ultimate objective of a neurosis. According to Wilhelm Stekel and Alfred Adler, every neurosis has a central idea around which motives group themselves. It is the objective of the therapist to uncover the final tendency as early as possible. Both theorists emphasized the importance of fictional finalism. See TELEOLOGY.

fine motor activities 1. Selected activities used to develop effective usage of the small muscles needed for eye-hand coordination, speaking, and eye movements. 2. Generally, the activities of the fingers and hands.

fine motor composite A score on the Bruininks-Oseretsky Test of Motor Proficiency based on performance of small muscles of fingers, hands, and arms. See GROSS MOTOR COMPOSITE, TOTAL BATTERY COMPOSITE.

fine motor skills Ability to coordinate precise movements necessary for such activities as writing, tracing, catching, throwing, cutting, and visual tracking.

fineness of discrimination The variable ability of an individual or an instrument to make judgments of differences, for example, a jeweler's scale can judge differences of hundredths of an ounce whereas a household scale can discriminate only between pounds.

finger agnosia A body-image disorder in which the patient has difficulty in discriminating between different kinds of tactual stimuli applied to the fingers. If the patient's fingers are touched in two places, for example, the patient may be unable to judge without visual clues whether the sensations come from the same finger or from two different fingers.

finger-biting behavior A compulsive self-mutilation observed particularly in children with Lesch-Nyhan syndrome, in which the fingerbiting is usually accompanied by lip-biting.

finger maze A maze, often used to test blindfolded human participants, in which the path to the goal is traced by finger-touch.

finger-nose test A neurological examination used to observe a person's facility in alternating movements by having the person repeatedly touch a finger to its nose and then to the examiner's finger.

Finger Oscillation Test A neuropsychological examination intended to assess possible damage to either side of the brain.

finger painting 1. A type of projective test in which participants paint on a surface with their fingers. 2. A children's play activity which gives them a chance to "mess" and express themselves freely.

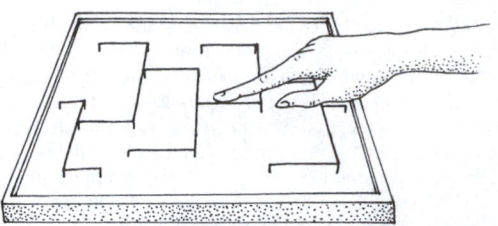

finger maze Partial schematic of a maze used with blindfolded participants who start at the bottom and, using their fingers, move upward until they reach a point where a decision must be made to continue either right or left. In the example shown, the first correct decision would be to the right (under the person's hand) and the next correct decision would be to the left. The correct pattern to get to the endpoint would then be R-L-R-L-R, a pattern that most humans can easily learn.

finger spelling 1. A form of symbolized language; a manual alphabet used by people who are deaf or have auditory impairments to spell out words. See BRAILLE. 2. Sign system of communication that incorporates all letters of the alphabet, signed independently to form words. Also spelled as one word.

Fink-Green-Bender Test See DOUBLE-SIMULTANEOUS TACTILE SENSATION.

fire fear See PYROPHOBIA.

fire-setting behavior A tendency to set fires as an expression of aggressiveness, defiance, or revenge by a person with an antisocial personality disorder or conduct disorder, by a patient with schizophrenia responding to delusions or hallucinations, or by a person with a mental disorder who fails to appreciate the consequences of the act. In some cases, fire setting appears to have sexual implications, as in pyrolagnia. See PYROMANIA.

fire-worship An element in various indigenous religious cultures in which adoration of fire is a central concept. The most elaborate expression is found in early Brahmanical Hinduism.

firing The initiating of a nervous impulse.

FIRO See FUNDAMENTAL INTERPERSONAL RELATIONS ORIENTATION (THEORY).

first admission A patient admitted for the first time to a hospital or institution for the mentally disturbed or the retarded.

first cause The reason for the beginning of any phenomenon, such as an idea that is acted on; the initial meeting of two people who later start a family; or the creation of the universe either due to the big bang theory, infinity, or by a divine presence. See CREATIVE SELF.

first cranial nerve See OLFACTORY NERVE.

first impressions The primacy effect in social relationships; a tendency to regard early perceptions of a person as more valid than later information, which, if contradicting first impressions, may be discounted or rationalized away. See PRIMACY EFFECT.

first law of thermodynamics A principle of physics and biology that in a closed system (one not receiving energy from or sending energy to the outside), the total energy remains constant despite transformations from one form of energy into another; that is, energy is neither destroyed nor created. Also known as conservation of energy/force.

first line medicines   Drugs considered the most effective and least likely to generate side effects, and therefore to be tried first in treatment. Phrase is relevant because a certain percentage of patients are treatment resistant and do not respond to the ordinary dosage of medicine. Also known as drugs of choice.

first moment   The first moment about a mean is zero. See MOMENTS.

first negative phase   The period generally occurring during the second and third years of some children's lives when they go through a period of saying "No" to reasonable requests and are in rebellion against parents. Compare SECOND NEGATIVE PHASE.

first-order factors   The factors that directly emerge from the original set of intercorrelations while doing factor analysis. Compare SECOND-ORDER FACTORS.

first order neuron   A myelinated preganglionic neuron whose cell body lies in the central nervous system. Their axons (preganglionic fibers) pass through cranial or spinal nerves to ganglia, where they terminate.

first-order partial correlation coefficient   A partial correlation in which only a single variable has been held constant.

first phase of repression   See PRIMARY REPRESSION.

first-rank symptoms (FRS)   (K. Schneider) A system of differential diagnosis of schizophrenia based on the division of symptoms into five categories. The categories include hallucinations, changes in thought process, delusional perceptions, somatic passivity, and external impositions. The system has been tested in nine countries, where nearly 60% of schizophrenia patients were found to show first-rank symptoms.

first signaling system   (I. P. Pavlov) Immediate environmental stimuli of a physical nature responsible for evoking animal and human behavior. According to Ivan Pavlov, it forms the basis of the second signaling system. Also known as primary signal(ing) system, sensory-conditioning system. See SECOND SIGNALLING SYSTEM, SIGNALING SYSTEM.

first signal (system) stimulus   Any or all stimuli that are basically nonverbal in nature.

fish   Slang for a newly entered prison inmate.

fishbowl technique   A procedure used in growth groups in which two subgroups are arranged in concentric circles. The outer group observes the inner group in process and provides information and evaluations of the operations of the inner group as a whole as well as of the individuals. Later, the two groups may shift patterns and repeat the process. See PHILLIPS 66 TECHNIQUE.

Fisher Exact (Probability) Test   (R. A. Fisher) A nonparametric test of statistical significance of the difference between two small independent samples when the scores belong to one or the other of two mutually exclusive classes. In a four-fold table $p = [(A + B)!$ $(C + D)!(A + C)!(B + D)!] \div (N!A!B!C!D!)$ $z = 1.1513 \log_{10} [(1 + r) \div (1 - r)]$ or the standard error of z; $\sigma_z = 1 \div (N - 3)^{1/2}$

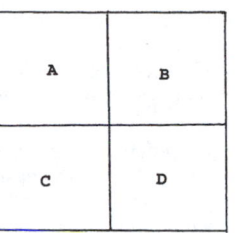

Fisher exact probability test   A 2×2 contingency table for data presentation.

Fisher's distribution   (R. A. Fisher) A mathematical sampling distribution that can be used for testing the significance of variance ratios, that is, one variance divided by another. Used for comparing between-groups variance and within-groups variance in the analysis of variance, as well as for assessing variability differences within any two samples.

Fisher's F Test   A test developed by R.A. Fisher and based on the F distribution. The use of the symbol F was introduced later by G.G. Snedcor. See FISHER'S DISTRIBUTION.

Fisher's r to z transformation   (R. A. Fisher) A nonlinear transformation of the correlation coefficient that, under the assumption of bivariate normality, makes the sampling distribution of r normal. Also known as Fisher's z-transformation. The transformation is $Z_r = 1/ 2\log_e\{(1+r)/(1-r)\}$.

Fisher's *z* statistic   (R. A. Fisher) A logarithmic transformation of the correlation coefficient r that has a normal distribution. This makes it possible to test the statistical significance of an r or a difference between two r's.

Fisher's z-transformation   Fisher's r to z transformation

fish fear   See ICHTHYOPHOBIA.

fission   The reproduction of a cell or one-celled animal by splitting into two independent parts.

fissure   A large cleft or indentation in a surface. The cerebral cortex of the brain contains numerous fissures, which have the effect of increasing the actual surface of the brain. A small fissure is called a sulcus. Types of fissures include: CALCARINE, CENTRAL, LATERAL, LONGITUDINAL, PALPEBRAL, ROLANDIC, SAGITTAL, SYLVIAN.

fissure of Rolando   sulcus centralis

fissure of Sylvius   sulcus lateralis cerebri

fistula   1. A small tube or pipe. 2. An abnormal hollow passage from an abscess or cavity to the exterior. 3. In physiology and psychology, a surgical canal not permitted to heal, for instance, as created in the cheeks of Ivan Pavlov's dogs to collect and measure saliva flow during his classic research. Plural is fistulae, fistulas.

fit   1. Common term for seizure or convulsion(s), hence by extension, manifest anger or upset. See SEIZURE. 2. In a graph, establishing a line or curve that best represents the data. See LINE OF BEST FIT. 3. The connection between data and some standard. 4. Adjusting data to match some standard.

fitness   1. In individual animals, their reproductive success, in consideration of competition for mates. 2. Adaptation to the conditions of the environment; that is, capability of an organism, due to its structural organization, to meet the general conditions of life.

fit(ness) for duty evaluation (FFDE) An examination, usually psychological, of a worker such as a police officer (often following a stressful experience, a serious complaint, or aberrant behavior) to judge competence to continue work.

fitness for trial In forensic psychology, competence to stand trial, as determined by the judge on the basis of a defendant's ability to understand the nature of the proceedings, and to cooperate with counsel and plead to the charges. If the question of mental illness is raised, the determination is usually based on a psychiatric examination, psychological examination, or both; the judge makes the final decision.

Fitt's law A theory that in sensory motor processes, the more precise results must be, the more movements must be made and the longer it will take to get to the best approximation; for example, in tuning a radio, more time must be spent adjusting the dial to tune in weak stations. Formula: $MT = a+[b \log_2(2D \div W)]$, where a and b are constants, M is movement, T is time, D is the distance moved and W is the width of the target moved toward. See HICK'S LAW.

Fitts' movement task (P.M. Fitts) A tracking task in which the targets are usually much larger in a direction perpendicular to the direction of motion.

five-day hospital A program of partial hospitalization in which mental patients are treated on an in-patient basis during the week but return to their families on weekends. It is a transitional arrangement designed to bridge the gap between hospital and community life for patients who are not acutely ill.

five-factor model (of personality) (R. McCrae) A model of personality including neuroticism, extraversion, openness, agreeableness, and conscientiousness. See FACTOR ANALYSIS.

five-hydroxytryptamine (5HT) Chemical name of serotonin.

five-hydroxytryptophan (5HTP) The chemical precursor to serotonin.

five-to-seven shift Considerable progress in all aspects of children's cognitive and social development that occur between ages five and seven. Among the changes are a decline in egocentrism, the ability to adopt the perspective of others, and a vastly improved competence in communication.

fixated response 1. A reaction from an organism that continues despite all efforts to extinguish it. 2. A strongly established reaction pattern, difficult to change.

fixation 1. In general, an obsessive preoccupation with a single idea, impulse or aim, as in an "idée fixe." 2. In psychoanalytic theory, failure to resolve an early psychosexual stage or inappropriate attachment to an early psychosexual object or mode of gratification, such as anal or oral activity, so that the concerns of that stage dominate the adult personality. 3. The focusing of both eyes on a single object, or looking quickly and accurately from one object, or word, to another, as in reading. 4. The process of strengthening a habit until it becomes established. 5. In learning theory, refers to a well-conditioned response. Types of fixation include: ABNORMAL, AFFECT, ANXIETY, CANNIBALISTIC, CHILD-PARENT, FATHER, LAW OF, NARCISSISTIC ORAL-, NEGATIVE, ORAL, RE-, VESTIBULAR-OCULAR, VISUAL.

fixation hysteria A form of conversion hysteria in which the area or function affected is one that is or has been injured or diseased. See SECONDARY GAIN, MÜNCHAUSEN SYNDROME.

fixation line A straight line between the object of visual focus and the retinal fovea. Also known as line of fixation.

fixation of affect 1. The retention of a feeling or affect after it is no longer appropriate. 2. See AFFECT FIXATION.

fixation pause A period during which the eyes are focused directly on an object. See SACCADE.

fixation-point 1. The point in space upon which one or both eyes are fixated. 2. The point on the retina upon which the image of the fixated point or object falls.

fixation reflex/response The response of the eye in turning to fixate an extrafoveal light stimulus.

fixation response time The interval between the onset of an extrafoveal stimulus and the beginning of movement of the eye to fixate that stimulus. Also known as eye reaction time.

fixed action pattern (FAP) A response pattern that is part of a near-instinctive sequence, done in a stereotyped manner. See SPECIES-SPECIFIC BEHAVIOR.

fixed alternative question A question that is to be answered by choosing one of two or more given alternative answers. In surveys, asking questions that can be answered by a "yes" or "no," or perhaps by simple ranking. See MULTIPLE-CHOICE TEST.

fixed belief (R. Bertisch) Repetitive or automatic thoughts that controls peoples behavior.

fixed-class society A society in which membership in class or caste is fixed by heredity, and mobility is not possible. See HINDU CASTE SYSTEM, CLASS STRUCTURE, CLASS SYSTEM, SOCIAL CLASS, SOCIAL STRUCTURE. Compare OPEN-CLASS SOCIETY.

fixed effects fallacy Making generalizations based on too small a sample of the normal range of organisms or of elements tested, as in interviewing college graduates and coming to conclusions about people in general.

fixed effects model A research design in which generalizations are made only to the conditions actually studied. See RANDOM EFFECTS MODEL.

fixed factor A variable factor that has a limited number of values of independent variables. For example, there are only two genders.

fixed idea An idea or trend of thought that tends to dominate the mental life of a person. See INCESSANT IDEA.

fixed interval (FI) A reinforcement schedule by means of which the first response after a set interval has elapsed is reinforced. FI = 3 minutes means that reinforcement is given to the first response occurring three minutes after a previous reinforcement. See FIXED INTERVAL SCHEDULE.

fixed-interval (FI) reinforcement An operant conditioning technique characterized by the provision of reward to an organism at a fixed rate. The duration (time) of the interval depends on the organism's first response to the stimulus. If the interval were three minutes, the rate would be listed as FI3. See SCHEDULE OF REINFORCEMENT.

fixed-interval scallop   The pattern of gradually increasing rates of responding between successive reinforcements on a fixed-interval schedule.

fixed-interval (FI) schedule   In operant conditioning, interval reinforcement in which the reinforcement or reward is presented at the end of regular, consecutive intervals; for example, every 30 seconds. See INTERVAL REINFORCEMENT, VARIABLE-INTERVAL REINFORCEMENT SCHEDULE.

fixed model   An experimental paradigm used in the analysis of variance in which the experimenter sets or fixes levels of the independent variables, instead of sampling them at random. See MIXED MODEL, RANDOM MODEL.

fixedness   See FUNCTIONAL FIXEDNESS.

fixed-ratio reinforcement schedule   **fixed-ratio schedule of reinforcement**

fixed-ratio schedule of reinforcement (FR)   An operant conditioning technique characterized by the provision of reward to an organism only after a predetermined number of correct responses have been given since the preceding reinforcement. If the ratio is FR25, the reinforcement schedule is such that the 25th response after the preceding reinforcement is reinforced. Also known as fixed-ratio reinforcement schedule, ratio reinforcement. See SCHEDULE OF REINFORCEMENT.

fixed-role sketch   (G. A. Kelly) A detailed description of a fixed role that the person is to display during fixed-role therapy.

Fixed Role Therapy   (G. A. Kelly) Psychotherapy based on an agreement between a therapist and client that the client will play a particular role in real life for a specific period with the intention of determining whether certain new patterns of behavior are superior to prior well-established ones. Periodic discussions continue throughout the therapy. See PSYCHODRAMA.

fixed schedule   Unchanging schedules of reinforcement.

FK   In Rorschach test scoring, a symbol for vista response.

flaccid   Soft or flabby, usually applied to an absence of muscle tone, as in muscular atrophy.

flaccid paralysis   A form of paralysis with loss of tonus and absence of reflexes producing a weak, flabby condition in the affected areas.

flagellation   1. Verbal "whipping": sharp criticism or self-criticism. 2. Whipping another person or oneself, or submitting to whipping as a religious ritual. In medieval Christianity, flagellation was a form of penitence, purification, or religious austerity. 3. A means of achieving sexual excitement (a common form of sexual sadism and masochism). See MASOCHISM, SADISM, S & M.

flapping   A phonetic process in which an alveolar stop is pronounced as a voiced flap between vowels, the first of which is usually stressed.

flashback   1. Vivid memories of traumatic situations, reported occasionally by war veterans with posttraumatic-stress disorder (PTSD), for example. 2. A phenomenon experienced by users of hallucinogenic drugs during which they suddenly reexperience the effects of the drug, usually a recall of events of a previous time. See HALLUCINOGEN PERSISTING PERCEPTION DISORDER.

flashback hallucinosis   Spontaneous recurrence, after a drug-free period, of predominantly visual hallucinations similar to those experienced during an acute toxic episode. Flashbacks are most common after repeated ingestion of LSD, and may occur months after the last use. See FLASHBACK.

flashbulb events   Singular, unusual events remembered in considerable detail with complete confidence in their accuracy. In some cases, such memories turn out to be false.

flashbulb memory   (R. W. Brown & J. Kalik) A specially vivid and long-lasting memory for the circumstances in which (where, what a person was doing, from whom) a person learned of an emotionally charged (or personally consequential) event; for example the assassination of John F. Kennedy.

flash card   Ordinarily, in schools, a card that is shown (for any length of time) to students for them to call out the answer to a question; or for studying, a card with a question or term on one side and a definition or answer on the back.

flash device   A device or apparatus for exposing something for a brief period. See EPISCOTISTER, FLASH CARD, TACHISTOSCOPE.

flat   A tone whose pitch is slightly lower than a given standard.

flatness of affect   Impaired ability to react emotionally; extreme apathy and indifference even in situations that usually arouse intense feeling. A common symptom of schizophrenia. Also known as emotional flatness, flat, shallowness of affect.

flat organizational structure   Any organization with few or no supervision levels.

flavor   A sensation produced by a combination of aroma, taste, and texture, involving olfactory, gustatory, and tactile sense organs.

flehmening   A courtship behavior of some male mammals characterized by approaching a female and sampling her odors by tasting or smelling. More common in social and herd species. Also known as lipping in horses and domestic barnyard animals, from the conspicuous turning up of the upper lip. Males that flehmen or flehm have a Jacobson's organ. See JACOBSON'S ORGAN.

Flesch Index   (R. F. Flesch) A measure of the difficulty level of written English. Its "readability formula" computes syllables per word and words per sentence in 100-word samples, leading to an index number from zero (very hard) to 100 (very easy). Published in 1951, revised in 1974 (calibrated on a measure of reading comprehension validated in 1926).

Flesch (Readability) Formula   See FLESCH INDEX.

flexibilitas cerea   (waxy flexibility—Latin) Rigidity of catalepsy that can be temporarily overcome by someone else moving a patient's limb, but which returns immediately, with the patient holding the limb in the new position. Also known as cerea flexibilitas. See CATALEPSY, WAXY FLEXIBILITY.

flexibility   (J. P. Guilford) The mental ability to attempt as different possible ways of organizing and planning future steps for the solution of a problem.

flexible careers   Occupations that permit individual flexibility (for example, a graphic artist).

flexible worker   contingent employee/worker

flexible work hours   A work schedule that permits employees to determine the hours worked per day, as long as they work during certain core hours, and for a specified number of hours per week. The purpose is to enable them to adjust their schedule to commuting, family, school, or shopping demands. Also known as flex schedule/time, flexitime, flextime.

flexion   The bending inward of a jointed member of the body, such as an elbow.

flexion reflex   Any reflexive response by a limb or part of a limb in which the movement is toward the body. Often a reaction to a painful or intense stimulus. See EXTENSION REFLEX.

flexitime   flexible work hours

flexor (muscle)   A muscle that contracts producing bending of limbs. A muscle that makes a limb move, such as the bicep muscles of the upper arms. Compare EXTENSOR (MUSCLE).

flicker   A rapid periodic change perceived in a visual impression due to a corresponding rapid periodic change in the intensity or some other character of the stimulus. Types of flicker include: AUDITORY, BINOCULAR, CHROMATIC.

flicker discrimination   Ability to perceive a change in brightness of a light source. Ability varies with the frequency of alternating changes in brightness until a point called critical flicker frequency, or fusion frequency, is reached, when the observer sees only an apparently steady level of brightness.

flicker fusion   An illusion produced by a flickering light source when the rate of the light going on and off is so rapid that the light pulses seem to fuse into a continuous illumination. See CRITICAL FLICKER FREQUENCY.

flicker photometry   A method of photometry in which two different-colored and congruent light-fields are alternately presented to the eye at a suitable rate; the fields are considered equal in brightness when the appearance of flicker is at a minimum.

flicker stimulus   A rapidly alternating visual (sometimes auditory, where the term should be "flutter") stimulus. See CRITICAL FLICKER FUSION.

flight   A mode of response characterized by rapid locomotion away from the source of stimulation.

flight from reality   Withdrawal into inactivity, detachment, or fantasy as an unconscious defense against anxiety. A retreat into psychotic behavior as a means of escaping real or fancied problems.

flight into disease   A tendency to exaggerate minor physical complaints (usually without organic pathology), as an unconscious means of avoiding stressful situations and feelings. Also known as flight into illness, flight into sickness. See CONVERSION DISORDER, FLIGHT INTO HEALTH, SECONDARY GAIN.

flight into fantasy   A defensive behavior in which a person, fearing an impulse, withdraws and becomes hypoactive going into prolonged daydreaming.

flight into health   A defense process, considered common in psychotherapy, by means of which a client states that symptoms have disappeared and there is no further need for therapy. May be a conscious or unconscious escape from an expectation of disclosures. Also known as transference cure/remission. See FLIGHT INTO ILLNESS, RED-CROSS NURSING.

flight into illness/sickness   See FLIGHT INTO DISEASE.

flight into reality   A defensive reaction in which a person becomes over-involved in activity and "busywork" as an unconscious means of avoiding threatening situations or painful thoughts and feelings. See ANXIETY DISCHARGE.

flight of colors   1. Different colors in some sequential order as an afterimage of a bright light. 2. The afterimage response to fixation on white.

flight of ideas   Rapid joining of disconnected ideas in thought or speech. Observed in the manic phase of bipolar disorder. Also known as topical flight. See PRESSURE OF ACTIVITY, PRESSURE OF SPEECH.

flip-flop   Eccles-Jordan circuit

flippancy   A defensive attitude in which serious problems are avoided or glossed over by taking them lightly.

flirtation   Superficially seductive behavior engaged in for the enjoyment of the experience itself, without serious intention.

floaters   floating bodies (meaning 2)

floating affect   1. Feelings moved from their original object to some other object; for example, a person loved a parent who was a pipe smoker and, in adulthood, because of this, has a favorable attitude toward smoking pipes. 2. In psychoanalytic theory, an emotion that has separated from its original referent, and may become "free floating."

floating bodies   1. Describing particles or specks sometimes observed floating in own eyeball. 2. Slow-moving "spots" seen in the field of vision individually or in strings, more noticeable against a white background. Due to vitreous debris from the membrane attachment of the vitreous body to the optic nerve and retina. Also known as floaters, flying flies, *mouches volantes* (French), *muscae volitantes* (Latin), spots. See DETACHED RETINA.

floating limb response   The apparently self-propelled behavior of arms that seem to rise out of their own volition.

floating transference   In psychotherapy, the positive feelings of the patient toward the therapist and to the therapeutic situation that generally occur at the beginning of the process following initial anxiety.

floccillation   Aimless plucking at clothing or bed clothes common in senile dementia, delirium, and high fever. Also known as carphologia, carphology.

flocking   Animals forming compact defensive groups, as in some species of ruminants forming a circle with horns outside when threatened by a predator.

flogging a dead horse   1. A metaphor for continuing activities to make an argument, already won. 2. Assailing a discredited proposition.

flogging fear   See MASTIGOPHOBIA.

flood fear   See ANTLOPHOBIA.

flooding   In psychotherapy, a technique in which a client, usually with a phobia, is exposed directly to ("flooded" with) a maximum-intensity fear-producing situation for a considerable period of time with the intention that the client will realize that the fear was unnecessary. Also known as emotional flooding. See IMPLOSION THERAPY, SYSTEMATIC DESENSITIZATION.

floor effect   Inability of a test to measure or discriminate below a certain point; for example, a scholastic achievement test (SAT) for ninth to twelfth graders is unsuitable for fourth grade students. See BASEMENT EFFECT, CEILING EFFECT.

floor of a test   A level beneath which a test ceases to distinguish between differences in the variable being tested.

floral   (J. D. Amoore et al.) Relating to flowers. A flowery smell, one of the seven primary qualities of the stereochemical smell theory. See ETHEREAL, FLOWERY.

Flourens' theory   (M-P. Flourens) A point of view that thinking depends on the action of the cerebrum as a whole.

flow   (M. Csikszentmihalyi) The feeling of optimal experience achieved primarily by creative people, especially artists and scientists, featuring the excitement of deep concentration and the joy of discovery. Creative people with flow are considered to be well-adjusted.

flow chart   A step-by-step, chronological description of research procedures or, in computers, of information-processing; a diagram that presents a visual outline of the orderly progression or sequence of an activity that has been broken down into component features. A flow chart may include possible options and indicate consequences. Also known as flowchart, Gantt chart.

flower-spray ending   A type of nerve-fiber ending in a muscle spindle in which the fiber spreads into numerous endings among various muscle fibers. See ANNULOSPIRAL ENDING.

flowery   An odor typically emitted by flowers. Also known as fragrant. See HENNING'S SMELL PRISM.

flowing consciousness   Drifting, unconcentrated awareness.

fluctuation   Variation or difference in some character exhibited by the members of a species, whose values are distributed uniformly about the mean value of the group.

fluctuation of attention   Sensory clearness that waxes and wanes despite constant stimulation.

fluctuation of perception   Periodic changes of vision when figure changes to ground and ground to figure, as in the case of the Rubin's figure that either resembles a vase or the profiles of two people. See FIGURE-GROUND EFFECT, RUBIN'S FIGURE for examples of this phenomenon.

fluctuations of sampling   The changes in value that a statistical constant takes when determined from successive (but otherwise similar) samples.

fluency (f)   Ability to rapidly think of and easily produce words and their associations.

fluid abilities   Capacities, such as memory span and mental quickness, functionally related to physiological condition and maturation. Fluid abilities improve during childhood and deteriorate in old age. See CRYSTALLIZED ABILITIES.

fluid general intelligence   (R. B. Cattell) The second order factor among primary abilities that is free of cultural effects, is more innate than crystallized intelligence, and has a totally different curve of age decline. See CRYSTALLIZED INTELLIGENCE.

fluid intelligence   Concept formation, reasoning, and the identification of similarities.

flunitrazepam   Generic name of a recognized drug in Europe, Rohypnol, used by physicians and veterinarians as a pre-anesthetic, and as a "downer", similar to the way the Quaalude was, as a sedative-hypnotic. A person under the influence of this medication "feels drunk." The drug causes memory loss, and has therefore been used to spike a person's drink for the purpose of "date rape." In excess, can cause coma. Slang names include R, roofies, roachies. Commonly known as the date-rape drug. See CLUB DRUGS, DATE RAPE, DATE-RAPE DRUGS, ROHYPNOL.

fluoxetine (hydrochloride)   Generic name for a medication used as an oral antidepressant. Trade name is Prozac.

fluttering hearts   An illusion observed with colored figures (for example of red, heart-shaped components against a blue background), moved to-and-fro, the illusion consisting in the apparent springing of the figures suddenly from side to side.

flutter stimulus   See FLICKER STIMULUS.

fluvoxamine   Generic name for a medication used in treating obsessive-compulsive disorder (OCD). Trade name is Luvox.

flux   See LUMINOUS FLUX, RADIANT FLUX.

fly agaric   Common name for the mushroom *Amanita muscaria*. Effects on humans range from euphoria through hallucinations to violent behavior. Identified as the drug taken by Norse berserkers before battle and as the mushroom supposedly eaten by Alice (of *Alice in Wonderland*) before she experienced hallucinations of size change. The active ingredient is muscarine. Also known as soma.

flying flies   English phrase for *mouches volantes* (French), *muscae volitantes* (Latin). See FLOATING BODIES.

flying saucers   Slang for alleged disk-shaped objects that come from "outer space" into the atmosphere of the earth. See UNIDENTIFIED FLYING OBJECTS (UFOs).

Flynn effect   (J. Flynn) A tendency for a world-wide gain in intelligence test scores found occurring over time in various populations, estimated at three intelligence quotient (IQ) points per decade, noted on both cultural and culture-fair tests, about 15 points in 50 years. No acceptable explanation has been found for this effect. Corresponding gains have not been found in scholastic achievement tests.

Fmax statistic   A test designed by Herman O. Hartley and also known as Hartley's test. **Fmax = largest of k treatment variances ÷ smallest of k treatment variances. Fmax = s^2 largest ÷ s^2 smallest**. In looking up Fmax in a regular F table, significance level is to be doubled because placing the largest s^2 in the numerator is arbitrary. Not generally used because of its extreme sensitivity to violations of the normality assumption.

F-   In Rorschach test scoring, a symbol for inaccurate or poor form response.

fMRI   See FUNCTIONAL MRI.

FMSTB   Frostig Movement Skills Test Battery

focal attention   (E. B. Titchener) The strongest degree of attention a person can generate.

focal-conflict theory   (T. French) A point of view that the current behavior of a person in meeting current problems is based on that person's technique of meeting conflicts early in life.

focal degeneration   Development of a lesion in a specific area of the brain leading to a specific dysfunction, as in a degeneration in Broca's area generating aphasia.

focal epilepsy   An epileptic seizure involving an isolated disturbance of cerebral function, somatosensory phenomenon, or temporary impairment of higher mental function. See EPILEPSY.

focal length (F)   A characteristic of a lens or other focusing optical system, being the focal distance for parallel entering rays.

focal lesion   A physical deficit due to a specific defect, usually located in the brain.

focal motor seizure   A convulsive movement that occurs only in the part of the body controlled by a damaged part of the brain.

focal pathology   The study of changes in body tissues and organs involved in a disease at the focal point of the diseased area.

focal person   In research, a participant who often is not aware of his or her status, being naive regarding the experiment. See SUBJECT, SUBJECT VS PARTICIPANT.

focal psychotherapy   1. Brief therapy aimed at the relief of a single symptom, such as anxiety or feelings of guilt, and not involving a depth approach. 2. Treatment by psychological methods of one symptom or problem, such as a tic, drug addiction, sexual orientation, pedophilia, or fear of public speaking. Preferred procedures are psychodrama, behavior modification techniques, concentrating in one way or another on the specific problem.

focal stress   In speech, the effect made by stressing words (for example, actress Ethel Barrymore would say "Yes" in many different ways, each time conveying a different meaning by changing the stress of the word).

focal symptoms   The abnormal phenomena, functions, or sensations that pertain to the principal seat of a disease.

focus   The concentration or centering of attention on a stimulus. See PARABOLA.

focused analysis   A form of psychoanalysis in which interpretations are focused on a specific area of the patient's problem, as opposed to expectant analysis, in which there may be a gradual free-floating unfolding of the patient's psyche. Also known as directed analysis.

focused attention   Concentrating on one aspect of a stimulus while ignoring all other parts.

focus gambling   (J. Bruner) According to Jerome Bruner, one of the four strategies used in formulating concepts, by eliminating combinations of guesses. The strategy, used in artificial concept attainment tasks, includes simultaneously changing more than one element of the problem array and then observing the outcome. See CONCEPT-FORMATION STRATEGIES.

focus group   A small group selected to discuss a particular topic with the leader keeping the group focused on the particular topic.

focusing   Paying close attention to a particular object, person, condition, emotion.

Focusing   (E. Gendlin) A system of experiential psychotherapy in which the client (and sometimes the therapist) periodically remain silent for a period of time to experience an entire problem globally and to get in touch with deeper feelings about it. See EXPERIENTIAL PSYCHOTHERAPY.

focusing effect   (J. G. Pratt) A tendency on the part of some participants to concentrate extrasensory perception (ESP) on some targets and not to others in an ESP test.

focusing mechanism   A system of ciliary muscles, lens elasticity, and ocular-fluid pressure that enables the eye to focus an image sharply on the retina. The natural shape of the lens is spherical, but it is partly flattened by the fluid pressure when the ciliary muscles are relaxed to observe distant objects.

focusing strategy   The argument that concepts occur by first having a global perception of the whole and later examining relevant characteristics to come to a new understanding.

focus of attention   The upper level of attention; that is, the clearest portion of a perceptual or ideational experience.

focus of convenience   (G. A. Kelly) Events that a particular construct is best able to predict.

fog fear   See HOMICHLOPHOBIA.

fog index   A measure of readability. High scores on this index mean low readability. See FLESCH FORMULA.

folie   (madness—French) 1. Insanity, madness, psychosis. 2. The eighth class of a special class of nervous disorders as classified by François Boissier de Sauvages in the 1700s.

folie à cinq   (insanity of five—French) A rare paranoid disorder in which five people, usually members of the same family, share the same delusional system. See FOLIE À DEUX, SHARED PARANOID DISORDER.

folie à deux   (insanity of two—French) (J. Falret & E. C. Lasègue) A psychosis of association in which two intimately related persons simultaneously share identical delusions. The usual pattern reveals a dominant partner who transfers the paranoid delusions to the submissive, suggestible partner. The pair commonly comprises either two spouses, two sisters, or a parent and child. Also known as communicated psychosis, double insanity, induced psychosis. See FOLIE DE PLUS, SHARED PARANOID DISORDER.

folie à double forme   Obsolete French phrase for manic-depressive (bipolar) disorder.

folie à trois   (insanity of three—French) A rare disorder or psychosis of association in which three intimately related persons simultaneously share identical delusions. Also known as triple insanity. See FOLIE À DEUX, FOLIE À CINQ, SHARED PARANOID DISORDER.

folie circulaire   French for circular insanity or Falret's disease.

folie de plus   (insanity of many—French) A rare psychotic disorder or psychosis of association in which three or more intimately related persons simultaneously share identical delusions. See FOLIE À DEUX.

folie des grandeurs   French phrase similar to megalomania.

folie des persécutions   French for paranoid psychosis.

folie du doute   (J. P. Falret) French for doubting mania.

folie du pourquoi   (insanity of why—French) A form of obsessive-compulsive behavior in which a patient has an abnormal urge to ask questions.

folie en famille   (foolishness in the family—French) A delusion fostered within the family that certain family abnormalities are normal; for example, children do not speak unless addressed. The parents generate the impression that this is how other families operate.

folie morale   French phrase similar to moral insanity. See ACQUIRED FOLIE MORALE.

folk devils   (S. Cohen) Groups seen as deviant and disapproved of by society, and that remind others what they should not be.

folk drugs   Traditional substances usually employed by members of nonliterate societies for a variety of purposes such as to cure maladies, reduce pain, or get intoxicated. Medicinal substances include lichen, liverwort, orchid, and willow. Intoxicating substances or those used for the reduction of pain include cannabis, cacti, poppies, and mushrooms, and their derivatives such as hashish, mescal buttons, and opium. See ETHNOBOTANY, RECREATIONAL DRUGS, SORCERY DRUGS.

folklore   The traditions, beliefs, myths, legends, customs, tales, and songs that endure in a specific culture because they are transmitted from generation to generation.

folk psychology   1. The investigation of the mental processes peculiar to any ethnic group or people, especially the study of "primitive" (primary) societies. 2. A branch of psychology that deals with nonliterate or aboriginal societies, studying their customs, beliefs, legends, religious behavior, folk remedies, and the activities of folk healers. 3. Wilhelm Wundt's *Volkerpsychologie* (Folk Psychology).

folk soul   Identifying a transcendental group mind or collective consciousness that influences the behavior of individuals within the group.

folkways   (W. G. Sumner) The conventional or traditional modes of behavior in a culture, group, or society. According to William Sumner, societies develop by trial and error those ways of behaving that are suited to their milieu, producing individuals' habits and societies' customs, and these customs and mores become the folkways.

follicle   (C. Linnaeus) Any small sac-like gland producing a secretion or excretion.

follicle-stimulating hormone (FSH)   One of the three gonadotrophic hormones, it is produced by the adenohypophysis (anterior pituitary gland) that stimulates appropriate follicles to produce sperm cells and ova.

follow along   The establishment of a life-long relationship with specified individuals for the purpose of feeling assured of continuance of relationships throughout life.

following behavior/reaction   A species-specific trait of certain young animals that run or swim after a parent or surrogate parent. The characteristic is a manifestation of imprinting.

following the flow   The attitude and behavior of a therapist who follows along with the patient not attempting to direct the content of the sessions. See PERSON-CENTERED THERAPY.

follow-through   A research technique in which the investigator examines experimental and control subjects in childhood and again at intervals until they reach the age at which outcomes are measured.

follow-up counseling   1. The measures taken by a counselor or clinician in helping the student or client with on-going problems or new manifestations of the original problems. 2. Evaluation of the client's progress and the effectiveness of counseling to date.

follow-up history   An account of a patient's history following discharge from treatment. See CATAMNESIS.

follow-up study   1. A general procedure of getting information about individuals or groups for various purposes such as finding how a patient is doing after an operation or treatment. 2. A study of discharged patients during an extended period, for such purposes as determining if rehabilitation efforts are continuing, assessing the effectiveness of treatment, gauging the patient's adjustment to the community, and detecting indications of relapse. 3. Long-term study of research participants or subjects to determine whether the effects of the experimental conditions are lasting.

F_1 In biology, a symbol for the offspring of any two parents.

F_1, (F_2, F_3, ... F_n)   In biology, symbols for the first (second, third, ...nth) filial generations.

fontanel(le)   A soft, membrane-covered area in the incompletely ossified skull of an infant. The "soft spot" in an infant's skull, where the bones have not yet fully joined.

food as therapy   A behavior-training technique in which food is used as reinforcement; for example, children who fear doctors are given a candy each time they pretend to have a doll stay at a doctor's office. Similarly, a person with a psychosis who insists on wearing all of his or her clothing at once may be denied access to the dining room until dressed appropriately.

food aversion   1. Avoidance of certain edible foods by humans due to cultural, personal, historical or religious reasons. 2. Avoidance of certain edible foods by animals because the animals have been conditioned by humans to avoid such foods. See LEARNED TASTE AVERSION.

food faddism   Strange or inappropriate food patterns and habits resulting from pathological modes of thinking. Individuals exhibiting food faddism are convinced that certain foods are beneficial and others harmful, and give bizarre or complex theories to back up their beliefs.

food fear　See CIBOPHOBIA, SITOPHOBIA.

food-getting behavior　The complex functioning of an organism in the presence of food stimuli, which normally results in the ingestion of the food substance. Also known as food-response.

food-intake regulation　Ability of organisms to adjust their intake of calories according to the temperature of the environment, energy expended at various tasks, and other factors, so that calorie intake and calorie expenditure are constantly in balance.

food preferences　A behavior pattern in which organisms prefer the foods they need for normal body functions. However, studies usually show that participating organisms tend to develop habits that override preferences based on bodily requirements, such as the habit of preferring sugar although it is not required by the body to function normally. See CAFETERIA FEEDING, SELF-SELECTION OF DIET.

food self-selection　See CAFETERIA FEEDING, SELF-SELECTION OF DIET.

food-satiation theory　A point of view that cells in the ventromedial nucleus of the hypothalamus induce an animal to stop eating after a predetermined amount of food has been consumed. Injury to the satiety center is associated with an urge to continue eating beyond the normal point of satiety. See DIETING.

foot-candle　One illumination unit; the amount of light falling upon an area of one square foot placed at a distance of one foot from a light of the intensity of one international candle. Was replaced in the SI system by the candela.

foot-dragging　The abnormal-gait pattern of a patient suffering from paretic leg muscles. The patient may walk in a shuffling manner or appear to literally haul or push the defective leg forward while walking.

foot fetishism　Common name for retifism.

foot-in-the-door effect/technique　Inducing people to make large changes by first getting them to make small changes. See CAMEL-IN-THE-TENT TECHNIQUE, DOOR-IN-THE-FACE EFFECT.

foot-lambert (ftl)　A unit of measurable brightness; the brightness of a perfect reflection of a standard candle from the distance of one foot. See FOOTCANDLE, INTERNATIONAL CANDLE.

footrule correlation　(C. E. Spearman) A relatively crude method of obtaining a coefficient of correlation based on gain in ranks. Best used for few cases. See SPEARMAN'S FOOTRULE CORRELATION.

foot-writing　A method of writing or drawing in which the writing or drawing implement is held between the toes. See CHALLENGED, PARAPLEGIC.

foramen　(hole—Latin) A small opening of the body such as a tear duct or the holes in the skull through which the cranial nerves run, as in the foramen magnum through which the spinal cord enters the skull to become the brainstem. Plural is foramina.

foramen magnum　A large opening at the base of the skull through which the spinal cord and the left and right vertebral arteries, as well as other tissues, pass between the neck and the interior of the skull.

force (F)　Any condition or set of conditions effective in bringing about changes or maintaining equilibrium among mental or social phenomena. See NEWTON.

forced-choice format　A test or survey reply format in which a respondent must choose between or among alternatives for each item. Also known as forced-choice method/test, forced-response test. See FREE-RESPONSE TEST, QUESTIONNAIRE.

forced-choice test　1. A test on which a person is asked to answer every item. An example is a True-False test. Such tests are usually attitude or other personality measures. See FORCED-CHOICE TESTING. 2. An experimental procedure for testing extrasensory perception (ESP) in which the participant is aware of the target alternatives such as the five symbols in ESP cards. See ZENER CARDS.

forced-choice testing　Being required in a test to make a decision, such as between two terms referring to personality.

forced compliance effect　A tendency for a person induced to change an opinion by means of a reward, to be more likely to truly change the opinion if the reward is small than if the reward were large. See COGNITIVE DISSONANCE.

forced counseling/psychotherapy　A process only possible in institutions such as prisons. Whereas such forced counseling is generally ineffective, some involuntary clients begin to see the value of the process, and it can be helpful. Generally, such people are forced to attend five sessions, individual or group, after which further attendance depends on the judgment and decision by the therapist and the individual. See FORCED TREATMENT.

forced distribution　A rating technique in which the rater must place a given proportion of individuals in each predetermined category, such as "above average" and "below average." In certain circumstances some raters will rate everyone as either below or above average.

forced fantasy　A figment of the imagination that has been brought to awareness and exposure by efforts of the analyst.

forced movement　External pressure on an organism to move, this being regulated by internal mechanisms.

forced psychotherapy　See FORCED COUNSELING.

forced-response test　See FORCED-CHOICE FORMAT.

forced restudying　A requirement to learn a topic a person already knows. Forced restudying is a problem for approximately 25% of school children, such as Hilda Doolittle, who published poetry before she was six years old, but was made to study the ABCs in the first grade when she entered school. See HETEROSCEDASTICITY, USELESS STUDYING, XYZ GROUPING.

forced treatment　Therapy administered to patients against their will or without their consent, particularly unusual or hazardous treatment, such as lobotomy, electroconvulsive therapy, and aversive-reinforcement conditioning. In Western countries in particular, patients have the right to refuse such treatments. Also known as coercive treatment, enforced treatment. See CONSUMERISM, RIGHT TO REFUSE TREATMENT.

forced vital capacity　vital capacity

force field   (K. Lewin) In field theory, all factors occurring at any instant on an organism that impels either no movement or movement. See FIELD THEORY.

force field analysis   A portrayal of a problem as a balance between forces working in opposite directions, some helping the movement toward the desired outcome, and others restraining such movement.

force of habit   Routine behaviors that are so well established that a person seems to be "in a rut." Such patterns are difficult to change.

forceps injury   A congenital defect, temporary or permanent, induced by the use of forceps to extract a newborn infant from the mother's uterus during labor. It is one cause of cerebral palsy, a disorder in which 85% of the cases are due to neurologic damage during gestation or delivery.

FORCE typology   (L. Mann) A classification of audience or spectator aggression, comprising frustration, outlawry, remonstrance, confrontation, and expressive.

fordism   (A. Gramsci) According to Antonio Gramsci, a form of productive organization typical of advanced capitalism and exemplified by Henry Ford's assembly lines and F. W. Taylor's concepts of "scientific management." See TAYLORISM.

forebrain   The part of the brain that includes the cerebral hemispheres plus the basal ganglia, olfactory bulb and olfactory tracts, third ventricle, thalamus, hypothalamus, pituitary bodies, mammillary bodies, optic tracts, and retinas. Collectively, those tissues control virtually all sensation and perception, emotion, motivation, language, learning, and thinking. Also known as prosencephalon. See BRAIN.

foreclosure   (J. E. Marcia) A situation in which a person who has not been able to prepare for alternatives in life situations, must depend on other people in emergency situations and go along with them. See IDENTITY FORECLOSURE.

foreconscious   Memories not presently in awareness that can be evoked periodically from time to time. An unconscious mental process that enters awareness under specified conditions. Also known as preconscious.

fore-exercise   In work-experiments, repeated reaction of the participant to the experimental situation prior to introduction of the experimental variable, the purpose being to establish a base line against which to measure the effect of the variable, or to discover variations in the base line from one experimental session to another.

foregrounding   A procedure for getting people to concentrate on a certain aspect of a complex stimulus. Examples include an ability of artists to direct the eye to a particular part of a painting, of composers to compel attention to certain aspects of a musical composition, or orators to bring people's attention to an important concept.

foreign accent   See BARBARALALIA.

foreign hull   (K. Lewin) In field theory, the objective world, the area beyond the life space. See FIELD THEORY.

forensic   (forum—Latin) Refers to the law and courts.

forensic psychology   The application of psychological principles and techniques in law, including the evaluation of testimony, functions of the expert witness, methods of interrogation, guilt detection, legal policies, diagnosis and therapy, and general assistance in a variety of problems. Also known as legal psychology. See CORRECTIONAL PSYCHOLOGY, COURTROOM PSYCHOLOGY, CRIMINAL PSYCHOLOGY.

forensic social work   Social work practice that connects the legal system with mental health, for instance, in providing specialized knowledge to courts on issues of family dynamics, social and community support networks, and the fit between an individual before the court and the environment.

foreperiod   In reaction-time experiments, the pause between the ready signal and the presentation of the stimulus.

foreplay   The "first stage" of sexual arousal, marked by psychological and physical stimulation. Can last from minutes to hours; includes kissing, stroking, fantasy, and related activities. Usually results in engorgement of sex-linked tissues. Term has been criticized as male-centered. See FOREPLEASURE.

forepleasure   A psychoanalytic term for preliminary sexual play that focuses on any of the erogenous zones and leads to sexual intercourse and end pleasure. See FOREPLAY.

foreshortening   The illusion that the length of a line appears shorter when viewed lengthwise (horizontally) than it does when viewed vertically or diagonally.

foresight   Mental picturing of events as likely to occur, particularly of situations that may affect a person.

forest fear   See HYLEPHOBIA.

forethought   A thought (or thinking) of some event as one that will probably occur.

fore-unpleasure   (A. Freud) Term suggested by Anna Freud to denote a child's anticipation of punishment and the suffering it will produce.

forgetfulness   A recurring tendency to be unable to recall events on appropriate occasion.

forgetting   The loss, temporary or permanent, of an earlier acquisition. See DECAY THEORY, MOTIVATED FORGETTING.

forgetting rate   The speed with which material, once learned, is forgotten during a period of no recall or review. See EBBINGHAUS' CURVE OF RETENTION.

form   According to Adrian Van Kaam, a kind of blueprint of life for any individual's current psychological situation; that is, where a person is at any moment in terms of present and future behavior, subjective and objective, and where the person is likely to go.

formal academic knowledge   The understanding of a concept with or without practical ability. Example: a person who has studied about flying an airplane but has never operated one has formal academic knowledge. This contrasts with a person who has never been educated about airplanes or the theory of flight, but who can fly safely; the latter is said to have practical knowledge.

formal discipline   1. The educational tenet that studying difficult topics such as Greek, Latin, and mathematics improves the intellect. Although once generally accepted, it has not been substantiated and is no longer deemed credible. See FACULTY PSYCHOLOGY. 2. An approach to education requiring the teaching of certain topics for their value in basic schooling or in "training the mind." See MENTAL-FACULTY THEORY.

formal exercises   Drills based on one type of material or situation, used with a view to develop some general mental process or faculty or a character trait.

formal experimentation   A research procedure that has a hypothesis, a properly selected sample, closely monitored procedures involving manipulation of the independent variable, and correct assessment of dependent responses. See HULL'S HYPOTHETICAL DEDUCTIVE THEORY.

formal group   A hierarchy in which each level is associated with specific obligations and privileges.

formal inception   (H. S. Sullivan) That part of interviews, especially those of a clinical nature that occurs before any words are spoken, including first impression of the person, hand-shaking, etc. See PSYCHIATRIC INTERVIEW.

formalism   Theories of art that view beauty as a matter of form rather than of content.

formal operational stage   According to Jean Piaget, the fourth stage of cognitive development that appears during adolescence and is characterized by the ability to entertain contrary to fact propositions, to construct ideals, and to grasp possibilities and probabilities as well as higher order abstractions such as milliseconds. Also known as formal stage.

formal parallelism   (H. Werner) A comparative approach to the concept of development based on relating multiple modes of functioning to different levels of organization and integration, rather than relating them to a single line of chronological development, as in the law of recapitulation. See RECAPITULATION THEORY.

formal reasoning   Employment of logical inference rules in special situations when common sense is not conducive to answers.

formal stage   formal operational stage

formal structure   Phrase coined by the Human Relations Movement for the organizational chart, chain of authority, and communication in an organization, or the "managerial blueprint."

formal-thought disorder   A thought disturbance most commonly observed in schizophrenia in which the patient fails to follow semantic and syntactic rules in speech or writing in spite of adequate education, intelligence, and cultural background.

formants   Frequency bands of sounds produced by the vocal cords and other physical features of the head and throat in speaking. A simple sound like the vowel /ä/ may span several kilohertz of frequencies when recorded on a sound spectrogram.

formation   According to Adrian Van Kaam, the process of an organism developing in accordance with its ideal form in accordance with extraneous factors in its environment.

formative directive   Adrian Van Kaam's theory that there is an ideal life form that operates preconsciously in all people as one of the guiding principles of the unique formation of a person's life. Essentially, it is a kind of predesign inherent in the zygote (fertilized egg) of an organism that directs the development of an individual toward individual fulfillment.

formative evaluation   In evaluation research, a process to help developers of programs. Ideally, an evaluator will work along with the developer from the outset so that while planning is taking place, problems related to personnel, cost, and procedures of formative evaluation can be solved. Also known as feedback evaluation. See SUMMATIVE EVALUATION.

Formative Spirituality   See TRANSCENDENCE THERAPY.

formative tendency   A generalized inclination in life for individuals and groups to move toward order, complexity, and interrelatedness.

formboard   (E. Seguin) Usually a wooden board with cut out recesses into which identically shaped blocks are to be placed. Usually considered a test of intelligence of young children, who are told "Pick up these blocks and place them where they belong." See FORMBOARD TEST.

formboard test   A performance task in which the participant fits blocks or cutouts of various shapes into depressions in a board. Used for testing young children who are informed to put the correct boards in the correct holes. The score being expressed in terms of time, errors, or both. See FORMBOARD.

form constancy   See CONSTANCY, OBJECT CONSTANCY.

form discrimination   An ability to use the senses to judge the weight, shape, size, texture, and other features of an object. Form discrimination tests usually are performed visually but, in some instances, as in testing a person with a visual challenge, may be done by tactile sensations alone.

form distortion   Any change in the image of an object, due to the spherical nature of the retina or to imperfections of the eye, which gives the image a character different from that of the object itself.

formes frustes   (coarse forms—French) Indefinite or atypical symptoms or types of a disease. See ATYPICAL DISORDERS.

formication   A distressing subjective sensation (and sometimes delusion) that one's own skin is "crawling" with ants or bugs (the term deriving from the formic acid present in the bodies of ants). It is a haptic (tactile) hallucination that sometimes occurs in cocaine abuse, delirium tremens (DTs), and delirious states associated with meningitis, rheumatic fever, scarlet fever, diphtheria, and other infectious disorders. See ACAROPHOBIA.

formicophilia   Being sexually attracted to or aroused from small creatures, for example, ants, crawling on the genitalia.

form psychology   Common name for Gestalt psychology.

form quality   (C. von Ehrenfels) A positive content of consciousness that appears, according to Christian von Ehrenfels, in complexes over and above their separable elements (sensations), and is responsible for the peculiar properties attaching to such complexes as wholes.

form response (F) In Rorschach test scoring, responses that are judged to be either signs of normality or abnormality depending on whether the examiner can see them or not.

forms See the following types of form(s): ALTERNATE, ALTERNATE TEST, COMPARABLE TEST, CURRENT LIFE, CURTIS CLASSIFICATION, EQUIVALENT, PARALLEL, PSYCHODRAMA, ROTTER INCOMPLETE SENTENCE, SLOW-RELEASE, TRANSCENDENCE LIFE, VISUAL, WARTEGG DRAWING COMPLETION.

formula A concise (generally abstract) statement of fact, whether of principle, structure, method, or relationship, conventionally accepted or intended for acceptance as a fixed statement. Types of formula(s) include: AUTOGENIC STANDARD, CATTELL-WHITE, COLOR, CURRENS, FLESCH READABILITY, HOYT, KUDER-RICHARDSON, PROPHECY, RANK-DIFFERENCE, RUMOR-INTENSITY, SPEARMAN-BROWN, SPEARMAN-BROWN PROPHECY.

formula score See CORRECTION FOR CHANCE GUESSING.

formula translator See FORTRAN.

formulation The expression of a principle in words or symbols, whether mathematical or not.

formulation aphasia Loss of ability to formulate sentences.

fornicate gyrus An arched or horseshoe-shaped prominence on the cerebral cortex between the hippocampal and cingulate gyri. Also known as gyrus fornicatus.

fornication Sexual intercourse between partners who are not married to each other. The legal definition varies. Term derives from the Latin *fornix* (arch), after Roman prostitutes who worked in archways of buildings or viaducts.

fornix 1. A long tract of nerve fibers that forms an arch between the hippocampus and the hypothalamus. Animals develop hyperphagia after lesions of the fornix. 2. The arched upper space of the vaginal canal.

FORTRAN A portmanteau word for formula translator. An artificial programming language of the algebraic procedure-oriented type. It translates, through a compiler, standard algebraic and arithmetic equations into machine language for solving scientific problems.

fortuitous Pertaining to chance. Usually implies absence of known or intended antecedents. Applied in statistics to extreme values; improperly used as a synonym for random.

45,X See TURNER'S SYNDROME.

47,XXX See TRIPLE-X SYNDROME.

47,XXY See KLINEFELTER'S SYNDROME.

forward association The forming of an associative link between one item and its successor in a series or sequence. Compare BACKWARD ASSOCIATION.

forward conditioning Normal or classical conditioning during which the conditioned stimulus (a ringing bell) occurs before the unconditioned stimulus (food), as in Ivan Pavlov's experiment with dogs.

forward-conduction law See LAW OF FORWARD CONDUCTION.

forward displacement In parapsychology, extrasensory perception (ESP) responses to targets coming later than the intended targets. Compare BACKWARD DISPLACEMENT.

forward masking See MASKING.

forward pairing In conditioning, the unconditioned stimulus (US), such as food, may be paired with an conditioned stimulus (CS), such as a bell, either at the same time (simultaneous pairing) or the more usual way, forward pairing, in which the CS is presented first and then the US.

forward reference The directional character of growth processes whereby the growth of organisms is accounted for in terms of a remote future stage or a remote end.

forward solution (M. H. Doolittle) A rapid and systematic tabular arrangement for solving the unknowns in a first-degree equation by successively eliminating one unknown after another until a value is found for one of the unknowns. Compare BACK SOLUTION. See DOOLITTLE METHOD.

fossa of Sylvius Fossa lateralis cerebri. See SYLVIAN FISSURE.

foster-child fantasy A common childhood belief or daydream that a child's parents actually are foster parents. A form of wishful thinking, such fantasies are especially strong in bright children who are unhappy with their parents' status in life. See FAMILY ROMANCE, FANTASY.

foster family A temporary placement of children when their own parents no longer are able to take care of them, for any reason. Foster families may be biologically based, for example grandparents, or may be established by a social work agency.

foster-family care See FAMILY CARE, FOSTER CARE.

Foster Grandparents Program A program developed by the United States federal government in which senior citizens are trained to provide care, companionship, and emotional support to children with developmental disabilities in residential institutions such as training schools.

foster home 1. A home for the temporary placement of children whose family are unavailable or incapable of proper care. 2. A home in which a mentally- or physically-challenged person is placed by a social agency for purposes of family care and sustenance. The foster family is usually paid by the agency, and the placement may be temporary or permanent. See FAMILY CARE.

fostering Giving sustenance or care to others, as to a family, even though not related to these others. See ALTRUISTIC BEHAVIOR.

foster placement See FAMILY CARE, FOSTER CARE, FOSTER HOME.

founding process (A. Meinong) Denoting an intellectual activity by which conscious contents are consolidated to form objects of higher order, termed complexes.

Four A's The four fundamental symptoms of schizophrenia according to Eugen Bleuler include autism, inappropriate affect, ambivalence, and loosening of associations.

four-card selection problem   A reasoning task requiring the decision of which of four cards should be turned over to evaluate a conditional rule. Has been used to demonstrate confirmation bias. See CONFIRMATION BIAS.

four-day week   In industrial psychology, a work schedule that arranges, for example, a standard 40-hour employment week into four 10-hour days. See FLEXITIME.

fourfold table   A 2×2 contingency table for data presentation. See FISHER EXACT PROBABILITY TEST for an example of a four-fold table.

four goals of children   (R. Dreikurs) A theoretical explanation for the sometimes puzzling or unusual behavior of children, especially misbehavior. Holds that children want to attract attention (Goal 1), to be powerful (Goal 2), to achieve revenge (Goal 3), and to assume inadequacy (Goal 4). See PARENTAL TRAINING.

four goals of education   1. (E. Hunt) According to Hunt, the objectives of education are to motivate students to solve problems, to challenge them with impasses, and to teach learning from problem solving, and metacognition. 2. According to Raymond Corsini, education should produce responsibility, self-and-other respect, resourcefulness, and responsiveness.

Fourier analysis   (J-B. Fourier) The analysis of complex sound or light waves into simple sine waves. See FOURIER'S LAW for the principle on which this analysis is based.

Fourier series   (J-B. Fourier) A Fourier series for a function is a sum of periodic sine and cosine terms with appropriate coefficients that can represent the function within a given interval.

Fourier's law   (J-B. Fourier) A mathematical principle, according to which any complex periodic vibration may be resolved into a harmonic series of sine (or cosine) functions.

Four Noble Truths   The initial teachings said to be presented by Siddhartha Gautama (the Buddha) shortly after his enlightenment: (a) All life is suffering; (b) Desire, or more specifically attachment of desires, is the cause of suffering; (c) Only the cessation of desires can release one from suffering; and (d) The way to transcend desires is through the eightfold path.

four phases of medical practice   See REHABILITATION.

Four Pictures Test   (D. Van Lennep) A projective examination consisting of four ambiguous illustrations to which participants are to make up stories. See PROJECTIVE TESTS, THEMATIC APPERCEPTION TEST.

Fournier tests   (A. F. Fournier) A series of tests for signs of ataxia in a patient who lacks an ataxic gait in normal walking. The patient is commanded to rise quickly from a seated position, walk, stop, turn quickly, or perform other movements. Named after French scientist Jean A. Fournier (1832–1914).

fourth cranial nerve   See TROCHLEAR NERVE.

fourth ventricle (of the brain)   One of four hollow chambers in the brain, the lowermost ventricle. Located where the central canal of the spinal cord merges with the brain. See BRAIN VENTRICLES.

fovea centralis   A small depression in the retina where the lens normally focuses an image most clearly. It is also the portion of the retina in which cone cells are concentrated with the greatest density.

foveal vision   Visual experiences due to stimulation of the fovea centralis, or center of the retina.

fox people   (A. Simpkins) People who tend to change throughout life, as in frequently having different living quarters, vocational specialties, relationships, and social circles. See HEDGEHOG PEOPLE.

F+   In Rorschach test scoring, a symbol for accurate or good form response.

F+%   In Rorschach test scoring, a symbol for good form response percentage of total responses. The percent of good form response. A low F+% is usually interpreted as poor reality testing.

F'   F prime, a symbol for the F ratio.

FR   fixed ratio

fractional analysis   A technique in which therapy is interrupted at various intervals while the patient works through insights of previous therapy periods.

fractional antedating goal response (rg-sg, r_G, or FAGR)   (C. L. Hull) That portion of the goal response that can readily come forward in a behavior chain because of conditioning. An expectancy or anticipatory response that could be a verbal response in humans. Example: The salivation of an animal well experienced in a particular maze while en route to its goal (food). Also known as fractional anticipatory goal response (FAGR). See HULL'S THEORY.

fractional anticipatory goal response   fractional antedating goal response

fractional goal stimulus (S_g or S_G)   A proprioceptive stimulus following a fractional antedating goal response (r_G).

fractional replication designs   An experimental design that includes only a fraction of treatment combinations possible. Reduces time, labor, and cost and makes possible other replicative studies because of saving of total effort. The theory of fractional replication was developed by D. J. Finney and extended by O. Kempthorne.

fractionation   1. A psychophysical procedure to scale the magnitude of sensations. A participant might be asked to adjust a light so that it seems half as bright as a comparison light, that is, to bisect it. 2. (D. O. Hebb) A concept that certain cells will no longer function in often-repeated neural sequences. See CELL-ASSEMBLY THEORY.

fragile X chromosome   See FRAGILE X SYNDROME.

fragile X syndrome   An abnormal, inherited constriction near the end of the long arm of the X chromosome. The second most prevalent cause, after Down's syndrome, of mental retardation among males due to a genetic defect. Named from the tendency of the long arms of the X-shaped chromosome to break when the defect is present.

fragmentary delusion   An unsystematized, undeveloped delusion or series of disconnected delusions. Especially common in delirium.

fragmentary seizures   Brief, partial phases of a generalized seizure, such as auras alone or abortive movements and disturbances of consciousness. May occur in patients under anticonvulsant drugs that have not attained complete control.

fragmentation   1. A concept that as a science, psychology takes no universal notice of its psychological orientation. 2. (G. Bower) A point of view that psychology is a collection of disciplines rather than a coherent science.

fragmentation (of thinking)   A psychological disturbance in which thoughts or actions that are normally integrated are split apart, as in loosening of associations, vagueness of ideas, or bizarre actions. Thinking processes become confused to the point that complete actions or ideas are not possible. Eugen Bleuler considered fragmentation to be a primary symptom of schizophrenia (which literally means "splitting of the mind").

fragrant   Describing odors that are distinctly pleasant. A quality of olfactory sensation of which violet, hyacinth, and heliotrope are typical examples. Also known as flowery. See HENNING'S ODOR PRISM, ZWAARDE-MAKER SMELL SYSTEM.

frame   The therapeutic contract, physical setting, and interpersonal boundaries between patient and therapist; as such, these aspects of therapy have powerful effects on both parties to therapy. See GROUND RULES, LINEAR PROGRAM, PROGRAMMED INSTRUCTION.

framing (effect)   1. The way an issue is posed when a decision is called for. For instance, a client's statements are often "reframed" by the therapist to enable the client to see the issue from another point of view. 2. The effect of the wording of a problem on the proposed solution. If the wording is positive (leading to gain), risk-aversive outcomes are induced; if negative (indicating losses), more risk-seeking responses ensue. 3. Magnifying or shrinking elements of a story, for instance, in news reports.

Framingham Study   A large-scale, long-range (over 20 years) study of over 5,000 residents of Framingham, Massachusetts, representing a cross section of the American population. Main finding was that primary factors associated with heart disease are cigarette-smoking, physical inactivity, high cholesterol levels, and hypertension.

frame-of-orientation need   (E. Fromm) A compelling urge to develop or synthesize major assumptions, ideas, and values into a coherent world view. Erich Fromm distinguished between frames of reference based on reason and those based on subjective distortions, superstition, or myth.

frame of reference   A standard against which ideas, actions, and results are judged; the set of reality, ethical, and other parameters that form a person's "cognitive map" for evaluating and coping with the real world. See COGNITIVE MAP.

frame-of-reference training   Usually in an industrial context, defining performance dimensions, listing a sample of behavioral incidents, and matching present performance to the samples for feedback and evaluation.

framework analysis   Reviewing available data within the framework of psychological analysis to develop a theory regarding the predisposing, precipitating, and maintenance factors of a given behavior.

Franck Drawing Completion Test   (K. Franck) A projective examination for older children who are asked to complete various partial drawings. Intended to measure masculinity-femininity variables.

Franklin experiment   Benjamin Franklin's demonstration that a visual afterimage may be positive when seen against a light background but positive when the background is darkened.

frankness   The personal characteristic or trait of dealing with others openly and without reserve or inhibition, especially in speech.

fraternal twins   Siblings that have developed from separate simultaneously fertilized eggs. A common name for dizygotic twins.

F ratio (F)   1. Term often applied to a test statistic, such as the between mean square divided by the within mean square that should be distributed as the F distribution if the null hypothesis is true. 2. (R. A. Fisher) The ratio of the variances of two samples. Determined by dividing the larger variance by the smaller, and consulting a table (of significance or critical values of F) to see the likelihood of the obtained results having been due to chance. See F TEST.

Fraunhofer's lines   Certain dark lines seen in the solar spectrum, due to the absorption of light from the denser central portion of the sun while passing through its atmosphere of gases and vapors.

freak   In genetics, an organism considerably different from others of its kind, usually oddly-shaped or having extra parts, such as a two-headed frog. See SPORT.

free   Not subject to an arbitrary external power, compulsion, or determination but still not exempt from all restraints. See FREE WILL.

free-access environment   An open, unrestricted environment to which most individuals have easy access.

free association   1. An association of ideas formed in the absence of limiting instruction or predisposing conditions. 2. (S. Freud) A technique in psychotherapy in which a client is asked to speak freely, avoiding omittance, censorship, or making modifications while the therapist listens. See ASSOCIATION, PSYCHOANALYSIS.

free-association test   (C. G. Jung) An evaluative procedure similar to a projective test in which the participant is offered a stimulus word and is expected to respond as quickly as possible with a word he or she associates with the stimulus. Variations in responses such as slower reaction times to specific topics, or unusual replies to some of the stimulus words, may be important indicators in evaluating the participant.

freebase   A highly concentrated and chemically altered form of cocaine prepared by treating cocaine with ether. It is ingested by smoking the substance.

freedom   1. The state or quality of exercising one's own choices or decisions without external or internal constraint. 2. (C. Rogers) According to Rogers, freedom is the quality of courage that enables a person to venture into the unknown when the person chooses. The burden of being responsible for the self that person chooses to be.

freedom and independence   An innate need, drive and source of human behavior. Leads people to make choices and to function on their own without being excessively reliant on the approval of others.

freedom of will   Conscious volition, the capacity to freely choose an attitude or course of action. In Viktor Frankl's Logotherapy, freedom of will is not considered to be significantly compromised by unconscious factors or environmental conditions. See FREE WILL.

freedom to withdraw   An ethical issue in certain research studies in which participants are permitted by the experimenter to discontinue participation if they object to the research.

free-floating anger   A chronic reaction pattern in which hostility becomes so generalized that even neutral situations are met with anger.

free-floating anxiety   1. A state of experienced discomfort of unattributable anxiety. 2. A state of diffuse and pervasive tension and apprehension not attached to specific ideas, situations, or activities of the individual. The outstanding symptom of anxiety neurosis is the constant background of uneasiness in all aspects of awakedness, and on awakening, it is there.

free-floating attention   In certain systems of psychotherapy, but especially in classical psychoanalysis and client-centered therapy, the therapist's state of mind during the time in which attention is focused on patients. During this period therapists are impervious to distractions, and typically will not permit phone calls or visitors to interrupt their mental operations.

free-floating fear   A generalized sense of fear not directed to a particular object or situation. A more extreme form of free-floating anxiety.

free flow   An attitude characterized by relaxation, taking it easy, meeting things as they come, not focused or in a hurry, and with attendant bodily positions and movements that tend to be smooth and gentle.

free form   In linguistics, a language element that can meaningfully occur in isolation and/or whose position related to neighboring elements is not strictly fixed. See WORD.

free love   An American philosophical movement in the late 19th and early 20th centuries that promoted the abolition of marriage, the right to live without government regulation (especially regarding marriage), and sexual freedom for women.

free morpheme   A morpheme that constitutes a word by itself, such as "eat." See MORPHEME.

free nerve ending   A branched afferent neuron ending found in the skin and assumed to be a pain or temperature receptor.

free operant   An operant by which an organism re-emits a response immediately following reinforcement, to be reinforced again.

free operant avoidance   (M. Sidman) The behavior of an organism that is in a situation (termed a free-operant shock-delay procedure) where it will be given brief shocks preprogrammed in relation to intervals between the shocks. If the animal responds appropriately in the intervals between the shocks, the next shock is delayed. S-S is the preprogrammed shock-shock interval; R-S is the response-shock interval. Organisms that learn how to perform the appropriate behavior such as pressing a bar or lifting a leg may avoid the shock. Also known as classical avoidance, Sidman avoidance schedule.

free-operant shock-delay procedure   See FREE OPERANT AVOIDANCE, SIDMAN AVOIDANCE CONDITIONING.

free play   A form of play not controlled or directed by a group leader, teacher, or play therapist.

free recall   A memory trial in which a list of words is presented singly and participants attempt to remember them in any order. The first and last words presented are best remembered; proponents of the dual-memory theory attribute this finding to the fact that the last words are still in short-term memory, whereas the first words received the most rehearsal and were transferred to long-term memory. See DUAL-MEMORY THEORY.

free-recall learning   A means of measuring memory by presenting a participant with a list of items (visually, orally, etc.) and at a later period determining how many of the items are recalled.

free-response method   A way of evaluating the meanings of concepts by asking for definitions and examples of the concept.

free-response test   1. An examination in which students construct answers in their own words, such as a short-answer or essay test. This type of test is sometimes termed "subjective." 2. A research procedure for testing ESP (extrasensory perception) where the target range is unknown to the participant. Compare FORCED-RESPONSE TEST.

free rider   A person in a group project who does not contribute a fair share of time and energy to the project. See SOCIAL LOAFING.

free-running rhythms   The natural rhythms that, in the absence of time cues, determine cycles for sleep and waking. See CIRCADIAN RHYTHMS.

free variation   A situation in which two or more allophones of a phoneme can occur in a particular position. See COMPLEMENTARY DISTRIBUTION.

free-will   A philosophic concept that humans are not ruled by cause and effect but have the capacity to make their own independent choices and decisions. Both laws and religions accept free will as basic to the responsibility of individuals (excepting some—such as persons who are young, are cognitively impaired or are insane—from responsibility). See DETERMINISM, SOFT DETERMINISM.

freezing behavior   A form of passive avoidance in which an organism remains motionless and makes no effort to run or hide. Most often observed as a severe reaction to a threatening situation. See CATAPLEXY, DEATH FEIGNING, TONIC IMMOBILITY.

Fregoli's phenomenon   Misidentification of people known to the patient. The patient may claim they have undergone changes in appearance and intend to persecute the patient. Also known as illusion of negative doubles.

French kiss   Kissing with open mouths, usually focusing on tongue contact. Also known as deep kiss, soul kiss, tongue kiss.

Frenoli delusion   The mistaken belief that a malicious demon has taken over the identity of a person that the patient knows and that the demon intends to harm the patient having the delusion. See CAPGRAS SYNDROME, ILLUSION OF DOUBLES, PARANOIA.

frenzy   1. A state of wild emotionalism and out-of-control movement. 2. A violent emotional disturbance approaching utter disorganization. Also known as delirious rage.

frequency (f)   1. The number of times a phenomenon occurs within a defined period of time, such as urinations per day or heart beats per minute. 2. In acoustics, a measure of the number of Hertz (cycles per second) of air vibrations perceived or recorded. 3. In electromagnetic radiation, the rate of vibration. Types of frequency include: CLASS, CRITICAL FLICKER, EXPECTED, OBTAINED, POSITIVE, RESPONSE, SOUND, WAVE. Term is also applicable to other psychological phenomena.

frequency analysis   Ability of the auditory senses to distinguish specific desired sounds in the midst of noises. See COCKTAIL-PARTY PHENOMENON, SIGNAL DETECTION THEORY.

frequency curve   1. A plot of the frequency of occurrence of scores of various sizes, arranged from lowest to highest score. 2. A graph depicting a statistical distribution, made up of lines connecting the peaks of adjacent intervals. It is a smoothed frequency polygon, that is, a curve fitted mathematically to the polygon $[y = f(x)]$. Also known as frequency polygon.

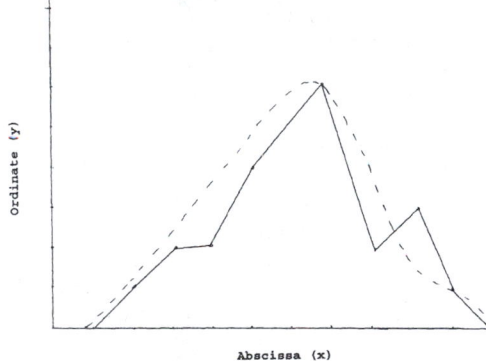

frequency curve

frequency discrimination   Ability to detect variations in sound frequencies. Generally, the test involves gradually narrowing the difference between frequencies until they become so close that differences cannot be perceived.

frequency distribution   See FREQUENCY CURVE, FREQUENCY TABLE.

frequency functions   Density functions.

frequency of cycles   Number of cycles per time period (for example, rate of vibration of sounds).

frequency of response   The number of responses within a particular period that serves as a measure of the strength of the response; for example, how often will a rat press a particular bar within the first 10 minutes after not eating for 6 hours if pressing the bar results in food for the rat.

frequency polygon   **frequency curve** (meaning 2)

frequency principle   1. A theory that the greater the number of impulses along nerve fibers, the greater the stimulation and the more intense the response of the organism. This holds for perceptions of vision, sound, odors, etc. 2. (F. Ruch) A theory that the more often a response is repeated, the greater the tendency for that response to take place the next time the individual is put in a situation calling for it.

frequency table   A tabulation of data showing the number of cases found at each successive score, grade, age, or other class interval. A frequency curve is a graphic representation of such a distribution. A frequency table is also known as frequency distribution.

frequency theory (of hearing)   (W. Rutherford) A point of view that the cochlea functions like a microphone and pitch is determined by the frequency of impulses traveling up the auditory nerve.

Freudian   A follower of Sigmund Freud.

Freudian approach   General phrase sometimes applied to Sigmund Freud's emphasis on clinical cases and the view that humans are driven by unconscious, especially psychosexual, impulses. Also known as Freudianism. See PSYCHOANALYSIS.

Freudian slip   A slip of the tongue. A person saying what was really meant but not what was meant to be said, such as telling someone "Glad you are going" instead of "Glad you are coming" (with the implication that the person would rather see the other go).

Freudian theory of personality   The general psychoanalytic proposition that character and personality are the product of experiences and fixations stemming from the early stages of psychosexual development.

Freud's dream theory   (S. Freud) Sigmund Freud's view that dreams are disguised wishes, or fears censored and revised. Those dreams that would be easily understood are heavily charged with all kinds of symbolism.

Freud's theory   The following are important in understanding Sigmund Freud's theory: ABSTINENCE RULE, ACTIVE CASTRATION COMPLEX, ACTUAL NEUROSIS, AIM INHIBITION, ANACLISIS, ANACLITIC OBJECT CHOICE, ANAL BIRTH, ANAL CHARACTER, ANAL EROT(IC)ISM, ANAL PHASE, ANAL TRIAD, ANAL-SADISTIC PHASE/STAGE, ANALYTIC PATIENT, ANALYTIC RULES, ANATOMY IS DESTINY, ANTICATHEXIS, ANXIETY HYSTERIA, CASTRATION COMPLEX, CASTRATION THREAT (ANXIETY), CENSOR, COMPROMISE FORMATION, CONTROL, CRITICIZING FACULTY, DEATH INSTINCT, DEFENSE HYSTERIA, DEFERRED OBEDIENCE, DETERMINING QUALITY, DISCHARGE OF AFFECT, DORA (CASE), DREAM ANALYSIS, DRIVE ATTRIBUTES, DUAL-INSTINCT THEORY, EGO CATHEXIS/LIBIDO, EGO DEVELOPMENT/FORMATION, EGO IDEAL, ELECTRA COMPLEX, EROS, EROTIC TYPE, ESTHETIC PLEASURE, ETHICAL APPROACH, FREUD'S DREAM THEORY, FREUDIAN, FUNDAMENTAL RULE, GENITAL CHARACTER, ID, IDENTIFICATION, INSTINCTUAL ANXIETY, INTRAPSYCHIC CENSOR, ISOLATION (OF AFFECT), LATENCY PERIOD/STAGE, LATENT DREAM, LATENT STAGE, LIBIDINAL TYPES, LIBIDO, LITTLE HANS, METAPSYCHOLOGICAL PROFILE, MOURNING WORK, NARCISSISTIC TYPE, NEO-FREUDIAN, NEUROPSYCHOSIS OF DEFENSE, NIGHT FANTASY, NIRVANA PRINCIPLE, NUCLEAR COMPLEX/CONFLICT, OBSESSIONAL TYPE, OCCASIONAL INVERSION, OEDIPAL

COMPLEX, ORAL-AGGRESSIVE TYPE, ORAL-PASSIVE TYPE, OVERDETERMINATION, PENIS ENVY, PERCEPTUAL CONSCIOUSNESS, PHALLIC PHASE/STAGE, PHOBIC ANXIETY, PLEASURE EGO, PLEASURE-PAIN PRINCIPLE, POLYMORPHOUS PERVERSE, PRECONSCIOUS, PRIMAL FATHER, PRIMAL SADISM, PRIMAL-HORDE THEORY, PRIMARY ANXIETY, PSI SYSTEM, PSYCHIC APPARATUS, PSYCHIC TRIUMVIRATE, PSYCHOANALYSIS, RETENTION HYSTERIA, SCHREBER CASE, SECONDARY ELABORATION, SLIPS OF TONGUE, STRANGULATED AFFECT, SUBLIMATION, SYSTEMATIC APPROACH, TALKING CURE, THANATOS, TOPOGRAPHIC HYPOTHESIS/THEORY, UNCONSCIOUS GUILT, UNIVERSAL PHOBIA, VAGINAL PHASE, WILD PSYCHOANALYSIS, WIT WORK.

Frey esthesiometer (M. von Frey) A stiff bristle used in experiments on cutaneous sensitivity. The hairs in the bristle, usually from humans or horses, are known as von Frey hairs. Also known as von Frey esthesiometer.

fricative A speech sound made by forcing a stream of air through a narrow opening of the vocal tract. A fricative has high-frequency vibrations. May be voiced, for example, /v/, /z/, /zh/, /th/, or voiceless, for example, /f/, /s/, /sh/, /th/. See LABIAL.

friction-conformity model The concept that a pedestrian's rate of walking is influenced by the number of obstacles met and by conformity to the pace set by adjacent pedestrians.

Friedman test for J matched groups (M. Friedman) A test similar to the Wilcoxon Signed Ranks Test serving as an alternative to matched groups analysis of variance; it is appropriate when each of r sets of matched individuals contains j individuals assigned at random to experimental treatments or when each of r individuals is observed under each of j treatments in random order.

Friedreich's ataxia (N. Friedreich) A form of ataxia that may be accompanied by abnormal deep-tendon reflexes in the legs, foot deformity, spine curvature (kyphoscoliosis), visual and speech defects, as well as nystagmus and mental retardation. Ataxic symptoms begin in childhood, involving the legs first, followed by the arms. Eventually, the patient becomes bedridden. Different genetic factors have been established, of both dominant and recessive genes. Named after German physician Nikolaus Friedreich (1826–1882). Also known as hereditary ataxia.

friendship A social relationship between two individuals, characterized by mutual attraction and cooperation, in which the factor of sexual attraction is not present or is not emphasized. However, some authorities claim that friendship is more important than love for a successful marriage.

friendship network Varied patterns of relations with friends and the friends of friends. See KINSHIP NETWORK.

fright An acute manifestation of fear that develops in reaction to an unexpected danger. It develops rapidly, is not restrained, and is short-lived, but it may have long-term effects.

frightened to death See VOODOO DEATH.

frigidity 1. Outdated and pejorative term for lack of sexual response in women, now more specifically termed anorgasmia, preorgasmia, orgasmic dysfunction, or desire phase dysfunction. Ranges from disinterest in sexual relations to sexual activity without orgasm to active aversion. Possible causes include attitudes of fear or distaste usually acquired from parents, conflict, or abuse, distasteful early sex experiences, a clumsy or inept partner, unrealistic performance demands or expectations, and unconscious hostility toward the partner's gender (sex). Such a woman is said to be frigid. See DYSPAREUNIA, SEXUAL ANESTHESIA, VAGINAL HYPOESTHESIA, VAGINISMUS. 2. A female sexual disorder consisting of impairment of desire or inability to achieve full gratification from sexual activity.

fringe (W. James) The unobtrusive but functionally important feelings of meaning and relationship which accompany the perception or image of an object; for example the suggestion of meaning carried by a heard or seen word.

fringe of consciousness 1. Concept similar to Wilhelm Wundt's "*Blickfeld*," the area in visual consciousness that falls outside of focal attention, that is, those items that are registered as present but which cannot be precisely identified. 2. (W. James) A point of view that people operate in certain situations with the assistance of mental states that they are not conscious of. Also known as marginal consciousness. See HABIT, SUBCONSCIOUS.

fringer A person on the fringe, not genuinely accepted in a social group (though not clearly or obviously rejected).

Fröbelism (F. Fröbel) The educational philosophy of Friedrich Fröbel that the educational process in schools should follow the natural law of human physical and mental development.

Froehlich's syndrome **Fröhlich's syndrome**

frog fear See BATRACHOPHOBIA.

Fröhlich's syndrome (A. Fröhlich) An endocrine disturbance associated with deficiency of the anterior lobe of the pituitary gland and the hypothalamus resulting in short and obese individuals with maldeveloped physiques and social and mental disabilities without mental retardation. Also spelled Froehlich's syndrome. Also known as adiposogenitalism.

from above down See ABOVE-DOWN ANALYSIS.

Fromm's theory The following items are important in understanding Erich Fromm's theory: AUTHORITARIAN CONSCIENCE, AUTHORITARIAN ETHIC, AUTOMATON CONFORMITY, BELONGINGNESS, BROTHERLINESS, EROTIC LOVE, EXISTENTIAL DILEMMA, EXPLOITATIVE CHARACTER, EXPLOITATIVE ORIENTATION, FRAME-OF-ORIENTATION NEED, HAVING MODE, HISTORICAL DICHOTOMY, HOARDING CHARACTER, HOARDING ORIENTATION, HUMANISTIC COMMUNITARIAN SOCIALISM, HUMANISTIC CONSCIENCE, HUMANISTIC ETHIC, IDENTITY NEED, INCESTUOUS TIES, IRRATIONALITY, LOVE OF GOD, MAGIC HELPER, MARKETING ORIENTATION, NECROPHILOUS CHARACTER, NEED, NONPRODUCTIVENESS, PRODUCTIVE LOVE, PRODUCTIVE ORIENTATION, PRODUCTIVE THINKING, RECEIVING TYPE, RECEPTIVE CHARACTER, ROOTEDNESS (NEED), SENSE OF IDENTITY, SYMBIOTIC RELATEDNESS, TRANSCENDENCE NEED, UNCONDITIONAL LOVE, WITHDRAWAL-DESTRUCTIVENESS.

frontal   Pertaining to the front, or anterior, side of the body or an organ such as the brain.

frontal association area   Part of the frontal lobe of the brain that lies in front of the motor and premotor areas. It functions in attention, planning, and expressive aspects of memory. Also known as prefrontal area.

frontal cortex   An area of the cortex of the brain in the front wall of the brain. See BRAIN for illustration.

frontal eye-field lesion   A lesion, produced surgically or by injury, in a region of the brain anterior to the motor area involved in head and eye movements. Such a lesion may result in unilateral blindness with the effect observed on the side opposite the lesion.

frontalis muscle   A muscle layer that covers the scalp immediately beneath the skin of the forehead. Because the frontalis muscle is closely associated with stress reactions of muscles from the cranium to the shoulders, it is used in biofeedback training for the treatment of a variety of postural and nervous-tension disorders.

frontal lobe   The part of the cerebral cortex lying in front of the central sulcus, containing areas involved in motor functions, attention, and planning. It is associated with personality factors in humans such as initiative and tact; intelligence apparently is not affected by frontal lobe lesions. See BRAIN, PHINEAS GAGE for some illustrations.

frontal lobotomy   (A. E. Moniz & A. Lima, W. Freeman & J. Watts) The severing of nerve fibers linking the frontal lobes of the brain (which were thought to control emotion) to the thalamic areas, to cure depression, aggression, anxiety, and schizophrenia. Thoroughly discredited as a therapeutic procedure since the mid-1950s. Also known as lobotomy, prefrontal lobotomy. See LEUCOTOMY, LOBECTOMY, PSYCHOSURGERY, THALECTOMY, TRANSORBITAL LOBOTOMY.

frontal-lobe syndrome   An organic mental disorder due to lesions in the frontal lobe, characterized by such symptoms as impairment of purposeful behavior, emotional stability, impaired social judgment and impulse control, and marked apathy. Symptoms vary with the size and location of the lesion. See ORGANIC PERSONALITY SYNDROME.

frontal perceptual disorders   A condition observed in some patients with tumors or other lesions of the frontal lobes who have difficulty in performing certain problem-solving tasks, such as following a moving target, finding matching numbers, letters, or other symbols, or evaluating thematic pictures.

frontal plane   1. In bilaterally symmetrical animals, any plane which is perpendicular to the dorsoventral axis. 2. See CORONAL PLANE.

front-clipping   Shortening of a word in such a way that the new word is used with the same meaning, for example, "fessor" from "professor." In general, children prefer front-clipping, whereas adults prefer back-clipping. See CLIPPING, PEAK CLIPPING.

front (sound)   A sound, usually a vowel, articulated with the body of the tongue positioned relatively forward, in the palatal region.

Frostig Developmental Test of Visual Perception (FDTVP)   (M. B. Frostig) A group of tests of visual perceptual skills used as a diagnostic procedure in the rehabilitation of children with learning disabilities. The tests include eye-motor coordination, figure ground, form consistency, position in space, and spatial relations. Also known as Marianne Frostig Developmental Test of Visual Perception. See VISUAL-SPATIAL ABILITY.

Frostig-Horne training program   (M. B. Frostig) A learning program developed to remedy deficiencies in visual perception revealed by the Frostig Developmental Test of Visual Perception.

Frostig Movement Skills Test Battery (FMSTB)   (M. B. Frostig) A series of sensorimotor tests used in evaluating learning problems in children. Sensorimotor skills may include the stringing of beads, and the transferring of blocks or other objects from one side of the body to the other.

frottage   (rubbing—French) Rubbing or pressing against another person (usually a stranger in a crowded place). Term implies a mild offense committed against another without consent. See FROTTEURISM.

frotteur   See FROTTEURISM.

frotteurism   A sexual disorder, or paraphilia, in which a person deliberately and persistently seeks sexual excitement by rubbing against other people, possibly because the person is unable to face the challenge of mature sexual relations. A person displaying this behavior is called a frotteur or a rubber.

frozen noise   White noise presented in a regular repeated manner to ensure equivalent background sound settings in research studies.

FRS   first-rank symptoms

fruity   A quality of olfactory sensation of which nutmeg and pineapple are typical examples. See HENNING'S ODOR PRISM, ODOR, STEREOCHEMICAL SMELL THEORY, ZWAARDEMAKER'S SMELL SYSTEM.

frustration   1. Generally, the thwarting of impulses or actions by external or internal forces. Typical internal forces are intrapsychic conflicts and inhibitions; typical external forces are the admonitions of parents and the rules of society. According to psychoanalysis, frustration "dams up" psychic energy, which then seeks an outlet in wish-fulfilling fantasies and dreams, or in various neurotic symptoms. In Adlerian theory, the essence of frustration is not the situation per se but how a person responds to situations that generate frustrations. 2. The emotional state presumed to result from the thwarting and to provide motivational energy. See AGGRESSION-FRUSTRATION HYPOTHESIS, EXTERNAL FRUSTRATION, FRUSTRATION TOLERANCE, INTERNAL FRUSTRATION, ROSENZWEIG PICTURE FRUSTRATION STUDY.

frustration-aggression hypothesis/theory   (J. Dollard) A point of view that frustration nearly always produces aggression and, conversely, aggression is nearly always an expression of frustration. See AGGRESSION-FRUSTRATION HYPOTHESIS, FRUSTRATION-REGRESSION HYPOTHESIS, LEARNING DILEMMA, MEDIATED GENERALIZATION, PERFORMANCE PHASE.

frustration-regression hypothesis   A postulate that frustration does not always lead to aggressive acts (as the frustration-aggression hypothesis is often interpreted) but may lead to regressive behavior, as in children who become infantile, dependent, and unable to cope with problems on their own if they are repeatedly thwarted.

frustration response   Usually anger, temper tantrums, and depression due to unsuccessful efforts to achieve a goal.

frustration tolerance   (S. Rosenzweig) The degree to which an individual is able to withstand frustration without resorting to inadequate modes of reaction. See FRUSTRATION RESPONSE, STRESS TOLERANCE.

F scale   Fascism scale, a measure of authoritarianism.

FSH   follicle-stimulating hormone

FSS II   Fear Survey Schedule II

F test   A test of statistical inference that compares between-group variability to within-group variability for two or more groups and leads to determination of significance of differences. Involves the F-ratio to statistically test hypotheses concerning two variance estimates under the assumption that $\sigma_1^2 = \sigma_2^2$. Sometimes called analysis of variance test. See F RATIO.

ftl   foot-lambert

FTT   See FAILURE TO THRIVE SYNDROME.

F_2   In biology, a symbol for the offspring of two F_1 parents. See CONSANGUINEOUS MARRIAGE, EUGENICS, INBREEDING.

Fuchs phenomenon   (W. Fuchs) When viewing an object through a transparent filter against a homogeneous background, if the object's contours are inside the contours of the filter and the contours of the filter are inside the contours of the background, the filter will be perceived as transparent both on the background and the object. However, if the object is displaced completely outside the contours of the filter, the filter will appear opaque.

fucosidosis   A rare metabolic disorder involving a deficiency of the sugar enzyme, fucosidase, and marked by progressive neurologic deterioration. After developing normally for the first few months, children begin to show mental developmental regression by about one year of age. Spasticity and dementia develop in the third and fourth years. Also known as mucopolysaccharidosis fucosidosis.

fugue (state)   (flight—French) An amnesic, dissociated state in which a person suddenly flees from home, forgets the entire past but not basic skills, and starts a new life with a new name. After recovery, the earlier events of life can be recalled, but not the fugue period. Brief fugues may also occur due to extreme stress, in epilepsy, or states of catatonic excitement. Also known as partial amnesia, temporary amnesia.

fulfillment   The satisfaction of needs and desires, or attainment of aspirations, sometimes more in fantasy than in reality. See WISH FULFILLMENT.

fulfillment model   A philosophical assumption that each human as an individual has potential in all directions and that humans are fulfilled to the extent that all of their abilities, talents, and other aspects have been used to the utmost. See CONFLICT MODEL, CONSISTENCY MODEL.

Fullerton-Cattell law   (G. S. Fullerton, J. M. Cattell) An 1892 theory that errors of observation and of just-noticeable differences are proportional to the square root of the magnitude of the stimulus. Has been proposed as a replacement for Weber's law.

full organism point of view   A theory that emphasizes the differentiating and determining role of the organism in behavior events, in contrast with the point of view that organisms are recipients of outside energy. See EMPTY ORGANISM, INTERNAL-EXTERNAL SCALE.

fully functioning person   (C. R. Rogers) A person guided by internal processes, in voluntary control of self, in good health psychologically, creative, and who exhibits the qualities of existential living. See FULFILLMENT MODEL.

fun and enjoyment   A possibly innate human need, drive, and source of human behavior. Leads people to want to learn, to laugh, to relax, and to see humor.

function   1. The typical activity of an organ directed toward a purpose or goal; for example, secretion of a hormone by a gland, or the control of balance by the cerebellum. 2. (**f** or **F**) In algebra, two sets of elements with an element of the first set x being so related to an element of the second set y that for each element x there corresponds one and only one element y. Types of function(s) include: COMPLEX, DENSITY, DISCRIMINANT ANALYSIS/, DON'T HOLD, DOSE-RESPONSE, DREAM, EGO, EGO NUCLEUS, EMISSIVE CENTERS/, EU-, EXISTENTIAL EGO, EXPRESSIVE, GENERATIVE, GNOSTIC, HÖFFDING, HOLD, HYPER-, HYPO-, INTELLECTUAL, INVERTED-U, LINEAR, LOCALIZATION (OF BRAIN), MAINTENANCE, MAND, MENTAL, MOTOR BEHAVIOR/, PHASIC, PHI-GAMMA, PHYLOGENETIC, POWER, PSI, PSYCHOMETRIC, PSYCHOPHYSICAL, RECOVERY OF, REPRODUCTIVE, RESPONSE, RESTITUTION OF PSYCHOLOGICAL, SECONDARY, SOMATIC, SPEECH, STEP, STEVEN'S POWER, STIMULUS, STRUCTURE-, SUPERIOR, SYMBOLIC, T, TRANSCENDENT(AL), TROPHIC, TROPHOTROPIC, VEGETATIVE, VICARIOUS.

functional   1. Pertaining to a disorder, one in which the normal action is impaired, generally with no apparent organic (physical) cause. See PSYCHOGENIC. 2. Pertaining to an object, one that is serviceable, useful, effective. 3. In biology, carrying out a purpose.

functional ability   Capacity to care for oneself, to cope in general.

functional activities   Actions associated with basic daily home and work requirements, for example, eating, grooming, dressing, and operating simple equipment such as can openers. The required skills sometimes must be trained or improved in persons who have experienced stroke or other neurologic damage.

functional age (industrial)   In industrial psychology, the age at which a person functions.

functional aids   Devices designed and developed by biomedical engineers to assist persons with disabilities in basic daily activities such as eating, grooming, or driving.

functional ailment   A mild, temporary symptom resulting from disturbed physiological functioning, such as a visceral expression of an emotional disturbance.

functional analysis 1. Breakdown of any behavior in terms of its beginning; the unit action itself; and the consequences. 2. A synthesis of a client's behavior problems and the variables that are correlated with and hypothesized to cause those behavior programs. Strongly affects treatment design because it is a working model of problem behaviors, behavior goals, maintaining and mediating factors, and the interrelationships among these variables.

functional analysis of behavior An analysis of an individual's performance on an assigned task. Usually done in industrial counseling, pointing out a person's strengths and weaknesses, often based on some kind of chart.

functional analytic causal model (FACM) (S. N. Haynes) A vector diagram of a functional analysis of an individual client. The purpose of a FACM is to symbolize, organize and clarify several types of variables, and relationships among those variables, that influence the design of intervention programs. It is a visual model of the clinician's hypothesizes about a client's behavior problems and goals and the variables that affect them. A FACM is an alternative language or representation of a clinical case conceptualization.

functional aphonia The absence of voiced speech due to a psychogenic rather than organic disorder.

functional approach to attitudes Examination of the psychological needs or purposes that attitudes serve for individuals in different contexts. Functions that attitudes serve include knowledge (understanding the world), utility (obtaining rewards and avoiding punishment), so- cial-adjustive (relating to reference groups), ego-defen- sive (protection from having to acknowledge unpleasant truths), and value-expressive (satisfaction from express- ing central values).

functional articulation disorder Articulation prob- lem not due to structural or neurological defects.

functional asymmetry hypothesis A postulate that there is perceptual superiority of eyes or ears on one side of the body for certain kinds of stimuli. For instance, the right ear usually is better for receiving verbal sounds; the left ear is superior for environmental sounds. The right half-field of the eyes has superiority for reading; the left half-field is better for face recognition. Not well documented.

functional autonomy (G. W. Allport) According to Gordon Allport, a tendency for patterns of behavior originally motivated by drives or instinctual forces to develop derivative motives that eventually supersede the primary drives and operate autonomously, for example, studying motivated by the need for approval is gradually replaced by love of scholarship. Also known as autonomy of motives, functional autonomy of motives, functional autonomy principle.

functional conformance In environmental design, the provision of the objects and equipment required to adapt an environment to a given set of functional uses, for example, providing a study with desk, lights, and comfortable chair.

functional deafness A loss of hearing not associated with organic damage or defect to the ear. May be a conversion symptom.

functional disorder 1. A personality disorder with no apparent physical cause. 2. Disorders without known alteration of structure. Also known as psychogenic disorder.

functional distance In environmental psychology, the distance between two living quarters. In studies of the impact of physical environment on interpersonal behavior, functional distance represents the possibility for interaction between persons in any two residences.

functional dyspareunia A psychosexual (and not caused by physiological factors) disorder in which there is persistent pain during (or before or after) coitus, in either male or female.

functional encopresis Involuntary or apparently in- voluntary passage of feces after the age of four, not due to physiological causes. Among the various psychological causes might be fear, shock, great excitement. However, sometimes this condition represents rebellion of a child against a dominating parent.

functional engram (C. G. Jung) A hypothetical neurological entity, the physiological basis of archetypes.

functional enuresis Inability to control leakage of urine, due often to fear, excitement, anxiety, or other situations having strong emotional elements. See ACONURESIS.

functional equivalence (H. A. Simon) The relation between two or more problem-solving processes or strategies that are equally, or nearly equally, effective over some range of problem situations. See COMPUTA- TIONALLY EQUIVALENT REPRESENTATIONS.

functional experiment Old name for controlled ex- periment.

functional fixedness (K. Duncker & A. Luchins) A tendency to have rigid thinking; an inability to adopt a new perspective or productive solution for a problem; a tendency toward the reproduction of a previous solution; a tendency to cling to set patterns and overlook new approaches. The opposite of functional fixedness is creative thinking. Also known as functional fixity.

functional hearing disorders Disorders that reflect an inability to understand the human voice at certain levels of loudness. See HEARING DISORDERS.

functional homosexuality facultative homosexual- ity

functional invariants (J. Piaget) Basic modes of interactions with the environment leading to appropriate behavior based on prior experience. Assimilation and accommodation are a person's fundamental modes of interaction with the environment during the entire life course.

functionalism (J. R. Angell, W. James, J. Dewey) An approach to psychology that views behavior in terms of active adaptation to the environment, emphasizing the causes and consequences of human behavior, union of the physiological with the psychological, a need for the objective testing of theories, and the applications of psy- chological knowledge to the solution of practical prob- lems and the improvement of human life. Functionalism is practically an expanded definition of psychology as it is generally understood. See STRUCTURALISM.

functionalism vs structuralism   (R. I. Watson) A prescriptive dimension of the philosophical underpinnings of psychology, namely, psychological events described as activities versus as contents. See OPPONENT-PAIRS DIMENSION.

functional job analysis   A quantitative approach to a job analysis based on compiling an inventory of the various functions that are performed. See JOB ANALYSIS, WORK FUNCTION SCALE.

functional leadership   A management style that advances a group's progress toward fulfilling its goal or function.

functional load   In linguistics, the amount of work that some item in a language has to perform. For instance, there is a small load between the voiced and voiceless "th" sound (as in thy and thigh), whereas the center vowel in the word "b-d" has a high load.

functionally specific state   A state of consciousness in which particular abilities such as introspection, are increased, while other abilities are reduced; found mostly in Asian mental exercises.

functional MRI (fMRI)   A magnetic-resonance-imaging (MRI) variant that shows metabolism in brain regions.

functional near effect   The degree of excitation as a function of the greater or less appropriateness of the stimulus for the neural component in question.

functional pain   Pain without an organic cause.

functional plasticity   Ability of one of the cerebral hemispheres to adapt to the absence of the other hemisphere by carrying on most of the mental functions of both. Observed in cases of infantile hemiplegia when it has become necessary to remove by surgery one of the hemispheres to control the symptoms of the disorder. See SPLIT BRAIN.

functional plateau   A special case of causal discontinuity in which a variable may have no causal relationship to another variable (for example, a behavior disorder) while its values remain within a particular range, but significant causal relationships if its values fall below or above that range.

functional psychology   See FUNCTIONALISM.

functional psychosis   A mental disorder, such as schizophrenia and bipolar conditions, assumed to originate primarily from psychogenic factors, since no specific organic pathology can be demonstrated. However, there may be a hereditary or constitutional predisposition in some cases.

functional reasoning   The cognitive process of arriving at a valid conclusion using knowledge about the matter in question.

functional relationships   (J. Mill) A fundamental attribute of philosophy that if A changes and then B changes and this occurs often enough, it can be concluded that A affects B. This concept is basic to science. See ATTRIBUTION, CAUSATION AND CORRELATION.

functional satisfaction   See FUNCTIONSLUST.

functional selection   A mode of biological selection whose distinctive feature is the survival of certain functions or motor capacities that are more useful to the individual or social group, and the disappearance of other functions that are not so useful. See EVOLUTION.

functional shift   A process of word formation in English in which a word is shifted from one part of speech to another in the same form, made possible by the gradual loss of most inflectional affixes.

functional skills   Activities that develop from aptitudes, for example, mechanical ability, artistic talent, salesmanship, and writing.

functional stimulus   In information processing, what was actually encoded, likely to include many elements of the context as well as idiosyncratic associations. Compare EFFECTIVE STIMULUS, NOMINAL STIMULUS.

functional systems theory   (P. Anokhin) A point of view that given an intact organism, interactions with its environment lead to adjustments in the organism's internal or physiological processes due to the effect of the invariant environment. These processes become more complex over the evolution of organisms. See GENERAL-SYSTEMS THEORY.

functional theory   See FUNCTIONAL SYSTEMS THEORY, GENERAL-SYSTEMS THEORY, SCIENTIFIC THEORIES (IN PSYCHOLOGY).

functional type   Phrase used in classifying personality types from a functional point of view. The four basic functional types according to Carl Jung are: feeling, thinking, sensation(al), and intuitive.

functional unity   The combination of various parts, traits, or processes working as an integrated unit.

functional universal   (W. J. Lonner) A correlation between two variables that is consistent across cultures and organizations (for example, in leadership, everywhere, the assigned leader who frequently avoids responsibilities and shirks duties is dissatisfying to followers).

functional vaginismus   Spasms of the muscles surrounding the vaginal entrance due to psychological factors, impeding vaginal penetration. Also known as vaginismus.

functional variable   Any variable that demonstrates a mathematical relationship with another variable of interest.

functional voice disorder   Abnormality of pitch or melodic patterns, absence of voice, spasticity, or hoarseness associated with psychogenic disturbances in the absence of organic factors. Also known as functional dysphonia.

function engram   A memory imprint, or "archaic residue," that constitutes a functional inheritance in Carl Jung's concept of racial memory. The archetypal symbols are function engrams.

function morphemes   Parts of words such as prefixes, suffixes, and final endings such as "s," "ing," and "ed," that add details to the meaning of words. See CONTENT MORPHEMES.

function of dreams (theory)   (R. Cartright) A point of view that people dream to explore the emotional components of a tension area. See DREAM FUNCTION, MENTAL HOUSECLEANING HYPOTHESIS.

function pleasure   The pleasure of activity for its own sake. See FUNKTIONSLUST.

functions   Four sets of processes according to Carl Jung by means of which humans acknowledge and react to the environment: (a) cognition serves understanding and solutions; (b) affection (emotions) provides the spice of life: pain and pleasure; (c) sensations yield perceptions of self and of the environment; and (d) intuition gives deep understanding of the unconscious and inner resources.

function word   A word that has no independent lexical meaning and expresses primarily a grammatical relationship or function of other words, such as prepositions, conjunctions, articles, and certain pronouns. Also known as closed-class word, empty word, form word, functional moneme, functor, grammatical word, relational word, structure word. Compare CONTENT WORD.

functor   Any entity that performs a function or an operation.

fundament   (C. E. Spearman) An immediately recognizable elementary percept or a basic mental entity, such as a character or idea.

fundamental attribution error   1. (F. Heider) A general tendency to interpret someone else's behavior as caused by internal dispositions rather than by external causes, while tending to see self-behavior as caused by external causes. The tendency to undervalue the importance of the situation and to overvalue the power of the individual in specific behaviors, such as in assuming that a person's behavior is due to attitudes or beliefs while disregarding influences such as financial or social pressures. Also known as causal attribution, fundamental attribution bias. See ATTRIBUTION, FREE WILL, RESPONSIBILITY. 2. (L. Ross) In attribution theory, the pervasive tendency to emphasize the influence of dispositional (personality) factors while underestimating situational explanations. For instance, a speeding driver is seen as a "lead foot" rather than as someone called to an emergency. Also known as overattribution bias. See BLAMING THE VICTIM, SELF-SERVING BIAS.

fundamental color   General phrase used to designate certain hues assumed to be original or of more importance than other hues.

fundamental definition   A definition that encompasses specific definitions of a concept, avoiding ambiguity. See OPERATIONAL DEFINITION.

Fundamental Interpersonal Relations Orientation (FIRO) theory   (W. C. Schultz) A philosophical-psychotherapy point of view referring to the necessity for honesty and openness in human relations. Based on the interpersonal needs of inclusion, control, and affection. A teaching-learning-experiencing group interaction that has been employed as a form of group therapy.

fundamental needs   See BASIC NEEDS.

fundamental postulate   (G. A. Kelly) A hypothesis that behavior is directed by how people construe their worlds; for example, a glass is seen by one person as half-empty (pessimistic view) while thought of by another person as half-full (optimistic view). Both are correct in fact, but from George Kelly's point of view, the two people construe reality differently, and this makes all the difference.

fundamental question of psychology   Refers to the issue of essential differences between people, why they behave as they do in terms of internal mechanisms of thinking, feeling, and wanting, and externally in terms of behavior.

fundamental-response processes   The several physiological activities thought to produce color vision.

fundamental rule   (S. Freud) In psychoanalysis, the rule of free association, that an analysand is to be given complete freedom to self-expression, to say whatever comes to mind without self-censorship or comment by the analyst. See ANALYTIC RULES.

fundamental skill   An ability that is required for further progress.

fundamental symptoms   (E. Bleuler) Phrase introduced by Eugen Bleuler to distinguish primary from secondary symptoms of schizophrenia. Includes autism, schizophrenic dementia, ambivalence of emotions, intellect or will, or disturbances of attention, activity, behavior, and associations. See SECONDARY SYMPTOMS.

fundamental tone   The lowest tone in a complex tone or simple clang.

fundaments   The mental elements between which a relation such as a thought or idea mediates.

fundus oculi   Part of the interior of the eye structure around the posterior pole. May be viewed with an ophthalmoscope. See EYEGROUND.

Funktionslust   (pleasure of action, functional satisfaction—German) (K. Bühler) Related to the concept of "play," refers to activity pursued for the pleasure it gives the person rather than being done for an ulterior purpose, such as earning a living. This explains to some extent why some children keep repeating certain behaviors. Some activities, especially those that have a creative element, are of this type but they may also have a utilitarian value. Also known as functional satisfaction.

funneling   A neural process by which auditory sensations are sharpened, primarily by inhibition of excited fibers. Peripheral fibers intensify the sensation without altering the frequency (being that of the tone conducted by the central fibers).

funnel procedure/sequence   In surveys and interviewing, starting with general questions and gradually narrowing down to specifics.

funny farm   Slang for a mental hospital.

furlough psychosis   A period of acute schizophrenic behavior, characterized by delusions, suicidal tendencies, and inappropriate feelings, that affects some soldiers soon after they begin military leave. May subside within a few months, possibly due to the sudden release of a vulnerable person from military life on which the person has become dependent. See PRERELEASE ANXIETY STATE.

furor   A sudden outburst of rage or excitement during which an irrational act of violence may be committed. The term furor epilepticus (or epileptic furor) is applied to the rare cases of grand mal or psychomotor epilepsy in which this occurs. See ISOLATED EXPLOSIVE DISORDER.

furor therapeuticus   Disparaging phrase for a psychotherapist's enjoying the process. Sigmund Freud felt it was against the interests of analysands; D. H. Malan considered it to be useful in short-term therapy.

furthest-neighbor analysis   In psychological esthetics, a hierarchical-grouping method for classifying judgments of dissimilarity. Used in evaluating how well selected participants rate differences between works of art when given no specific criteria for making judgments.

fusiform gyrus   A long convolution of brain tissue that extends lengthwise along the medial surface of the cerebral hemisphere across the ventral sides of the temporal and occipital lobes.

fusion   1. A process of melting together; a blending. 2. The combination of the effects of two or more stimuli in any given sense-mode, so as to yield a single, unanalyzed sensation. 3. In psychoanalytic theory, a merging of different instincts, as in the union of sexual and hostility drives in sadism. 4. The blending of two colors into one (color fusion), of sounds received by the two ears (binaural fusion), or of images falling on the two retinas (binocular fusion). See UNITY AND FUSION.

fusion state   The experience of merging with a particular person, with all of humankind, or with the whole of reality. It is a state of mind that may be induced by drugs, such as LSD or opiates, but also by religious or mystical experiences.

future lives   See PAST LIVES—FUTURE LIVES.

future projection   An attempt to look into the future to visualize the self or others at a later point in time.

future shock   (A. Toffler) The personal confusion and social disorientation that accompany rapid technological and social change.

futurism   The art or science of predicting future or forthcoming trends. Also known as futurology.

futuristics   An area of inquiry into expected forthcoming patterns of technological, economic, and social organization. Futuristics aims to identify and propose solutions to significant problems that may occur at a later time.

futurology futurism

fuzzy logic   A form of algebra employed to come to conclusions from imprecise, conflicting, and insufficient data. It is stated to operate the way the brain comes to conclusions. Constructs who see boundaries are fluid, imprecisely defined, and permeable. See ARTIFICIAL INTELLIGENCE.

fuzzy set   A concept in mathematics dealing with topics that do not have sharply defined edges, such as numbers, but rather general topics such as good and bad, high and low.

G

g 1. See GENERAL FACTOR. 2. The force of gravity (also abbreviated **G**). See GRAVITY (meaning 1). 3. gram.

G 1. General ability (also abbreviated **G**). 2. Goal. 3. Abbreviation for a general intellectual factor or ability. See GENERAL ABILITY, GENERAL INTELLIGENCE. 4. gravity (meaning 1).

GA 1. Gamblers Anonymous (frequently, G.A.). 2. guessed average.

GABA See GAMMA-AMINOBUTYRIC-ACID.

GAD Generalized-anxiety disorder

Gage See PHINEAS GAGE.

GAI Guided affective imagery

Gaia hypothesis A postulate that the earth is a single functioning organism (Mother Earth) with all flora and fauna regulating the health of the planet in interaction with the atmosphere and oceans to maintain its existence. In this hypothesis, the earth is neutral about the concerns of its inhabitants in the same sense that humans are not concerned with many microscopic organisms that live on or them. See DEISM.

gain-loss hypothesis (W. Aronson & D. Linder) In social psychology, holds that "A gain in esteem is a more potent reward than invariant esteem . . . the loss of esteem is a more potent "punishment" than invariant negative esteem." Thus, if one alternately likes and dislikes certain others, the intensity of these feelings will be stronger over time for people liked or disliked consistently; and in some cases people can increase their interpersonal attractiveness by disliking others. See HARD-TO-GET PHENOMENON.

gain-loss theory (of attraction) A point of view that if a person alternately likes and dislikes certain other people, the intensity of these feelings will be stronger over time for people liked or disliked consistently.

gainsharing A performance-based bonus plan in which the financial rewards of employees are linked to the performance of the entire unit. Programs include Scanlon (which emphasizes labor cost savings), Rucker (uses a value-added formula for bonuses), and Improshare (de-emphasizes employee participation and measures hours saved to determine the bonus level).

gait 1. A manner of performing a function, usually applied to the pattern of muscle activity of an organism while walking. In humans, kinds of walking gait include waddling, spastic, tabetic, hemiplegic, and marche à petits pas. 2. Refers to speech mannerisms (for example, a stuttering gait).

galactosemia (A. von Reuss) A recessively-inherited inborn error of metabolism marked by an abnormal accumulation of milk sugar (galactose) in the blood. Infants with this condition rarely survive, but survivors may suffer from jaundice, edema, poor appetite, and physical and mental retardation. Sometimes known as galactose diabetes.

galeophobia Fear of cats. Also known as ailurophobia, gatophobia.

Galilean (K. Lewin) In reference to scientific thinking, explaining individual cases, analyzing dynamic causal interaction in the present, and predicting well. Word is based on the philosophical-scientific views of Galileo rather than those of Aristotle. Compare ARISTOTELIAN.

gallows humor A macabre or comical type of behavior that is inappropriate at a time of death or disaster. Often observed in cases of organic psychosis and delirium tremens. See JOKE, SCHADENFREUDE.

Gall's craniology phrenology

Gall's personality areas (F. J. Gall) Sites on a human head as mapped by Franz J. Gall that he alleged identified particular personality traits. Gall's map consisted of labeled areas for bumps or projections of the skull, for example, the bump at the extreme end of the skull was called philoprogenitiveness (love of children). See PHRENOLOGY.

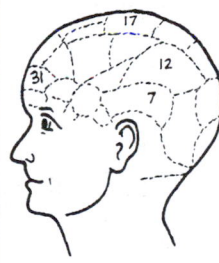

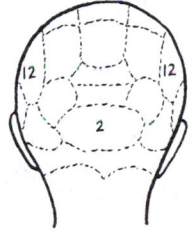

Gall's personality areas A phrenology chart such as used by Franz Gall and other phrenologists, who claimed to interpret personality according to the size and shape of regions of the skull. For example, a prominent occiput (back bump of the head) was supposed to indicate a love of children called *philoprogenitiveness*.

Galton bar (F. Galton) A rod with gradations, an instrument for measuring the jnd (just-noticeable difference) for visual linear distances.

Galton's laws See ANCESTRAL INHERITANCE, FILIAL REGRESSION.

Galton's questionary An inquiry about mental imagery. Applied in the early 1880s, it is the first known use of a questionnaire for psychological investigation.

Galton whistle (F. Galton) A high-pitched whistle used to determine the upper threshold for pitch.

galvanic skin response (GSR) (L. Galvani) 1. A measurement of electrical conductance of the skin, which provides a gauge of sympathetic nervous system activity. 2. A measurement of the impedance of the skin, which reflects its electrical conductance, providing a gauge of autonomic nervous system activity; high conductance reflecting sweating due to sympathetic nervous system arousal, and low indicating parasympathetic activity. 3. An electrical manifestation of increased conductivity of the skin (perhaps due to insensible perspiration). Also known as electrodermal response, psychogalvanic reflex. See FÉRÉ PHENOMENON. 4. The GSR is sometimes known as Tarchanoff phenomenon, after Ivan R. Tarchanoff's early work. See TARCHANOFF PHENOMENON.

galvanometer (J. C. Schweiger) An instrument that indicates strength of an electric current. The meter also aids in determining direction of a current by showing the movement of a magnetic needle in a magnetic field. See PSYCHOGALVANIC REFLEX, PSYCHOGALVANOMETER.

galvanotaxis   electrotaxis

Gamblers Anonymous (G.A. or GA) An organization of compulsive gamblers with the objective of controlling the impulse to gamble through mutual understanding, sharing of experiences, and emotional support. Modeled after Alcoholics Anonymous (A.A.). See PATHOLOGICAL GAMBLING.

gambler's fallacy 1. A mistaken belief that a person has the capacity to predict correctly in a random situation. For example, if a flipped coin shows "heads" nine times, a gambler might think it will come up "tails" the tenth time, although the probability of either occurring is still 0.5 (or pure chance) because prior events do not affect the chance of a current event. 2. The belief of some gamblers after successive losses that their luck is about to change.

game(s) 1. A contest conducted according to rules. 2. An interaction, or transaction, in which one person tries to get the better of others or make her or his mark in society. 3. In transactional analysis theory, repetitive sets of transactions that are psychologically gratifying. 4. In Gestalt therapy theory, "exercises" or "experiments" designed to increase self-awareness. 5. (G. H. Mead) The second stage in the development of the self, in which the child adopts various roles to be "part of the game." Types of game include: BUSINESS, CHICKEN, CONFIDENCE, DAVIS-EELLS, DOCTOR, HALLUCINATORY, MILLION-DOLLAR, MIXED-MOTIVE, NONZERO-SUM, PLUS-SUM, PRISONER'S DILEMMA, SQUIGGLE, TEACHING, ZERO-SUM. See RULES OF THE GAME, SYNANON.

games people play (E. Berne) A concept that people constantly play games with others to motivate them, to punish them, and to achieve secret goals. See ANTITHESIS, TRANSACTIONAL ANALYSIS.

gamete 1. Any germ cell, includes ovum, spermatozoon, pollen. 2. (G. J. Mendel) A sex cell, male (sperm) or female (ovum), that can combine with the cell of the other gender to form a zygote, the beginning of another individual. See GERM CELL.

game theory 1. (J. von Neumann & O. Morganstern) A branch of mathematics applied to competitive situations (for example, social behavior, business management) in which one strategy is chosen from among several available strategies, the strategy resulting in maximum gain, minimum loss, or both. 2. A model for understanding the dynamics of interpersonal conflict. This theory likens conflict situations to the relationship of two players in a game that employs offensive and defensive maneuvers. See MAXIMIN STRATEGY, MINIMAX STRATEGY, ZERO-SUM GAME.

gametogenesis The process of generating gametes in the sex cells.

gametophobia   gamophobia

gamma The third letter of the Greek alphabet. See APPENDIX C.

gamma alcoholism (E. M. Jellinek) Rare name for a form of alcoholism characterized by increased tolerance, physiological adaptation, loss of control, and, if drinking is suspended, a withdrawal or abstinence syndrome consisting of craving for alcohol, convulsions, and delirium tremens. Also known as addictive alcoholism, essential alcoholism, malignant alcoholism, regressive alcoholism. See CHRONIC ALCOHOLISM.

gamma-aminobutyric acid (GABA) A substance present in the central nervous system of mammals and assumed to be a neurotransmitter inhibitor. In studies with cats, GABA levels were found to be three times as high during sleep as during the waking state.

gammacism 1. A speech pattern, typical of the baby talk of small children, in which dental consonants, for example, /d/ and /t/, are used to replace velars, such as /g/ and /k/. 2. Difficulty in pronouncing the "g" sound.

gamma efferent fiber A motor nerve fiber connecting with the muscle spindle and affecting the receptor's sensitivity so as to provide a feedback loop regulating the input of kinesthetic information.

gamma endorphin An endorphin that causes a catatonia-like state. See ALPHA ENDORPHIN, BETA ENDORPHIN, ENDORPHIN, ENKEPHALIN.

gamma-hydroxybutyrate (GHB) A dose-specific central nervous system depressant, it can also cause memory loss, seizures, nausea, coma, and death. Its effects of disorientation, confusion, and anterograde amnesia have led to its use as a "date-rape" drug. Street names include Easy Lay, Energy Drink Gamma 10, Georgia Home Boy, Grievous Bodily Harm, Liquid X, Liquid Ecstasy. See DATE-RAPE DRUG.

gamma motion/movement A form of apparent, or illusory, perceptual movement in which an object appears to expand when it is suddenly presented, or to contract when it is withdrawn. When the intensity of a light is suddenly increased, the object appears to grow larger and to approach, and when its intensity is suddenly decreased, it appears to shrink and recede. Also known as gamma phenomenon. See APPARENT MOTION/MOVEMENT.

gamma motoneurons   A category of motor neurons usually found in muscle spindles and originally identified as A-gamma fibers because their conduction rate is slower than that of A-alpha and A-beta nerve fibers. Some muscle-spindle motor neurons are large with fast conduction rates and technically are not gamma motoneurons. Also known as intrafusal motoneurons.

gamma phenomenon   **gamma motion/movement**

gamma rhythm/waves   Brain waves with the highest frequency of any as recorded on the electroencephalograph (EEG), reaching 40 to 50 Hertz (cycles per second) at peak amplitude. Gamma waves are found primarily in the forward part of the cortex and appear to reflect thinking and reasoning.

Gamma hypothesis   (K. Dunlap) In learning theory, the postulate that repetition frequency hinders learning. See ALPHA, BETA, GAMMA HYPOTHESES.

gamogenesis   Sexual reproduction; the union of two gametes, the beginning of reproduction. See ONTOGENETIC ZERO.

gamone   A hormonelike substance possibly produced by male and female gametes to attract the opposite-sex germ sells to facilitate fertilization.

gamonomania   An abnormally strong urge to marry.

gamophobia   Morbid fear of marriage. Also known as gametephobia, gametophobia.

gang   1. A social group composed of members with a high degree of personal contact who share common interests and standards of behavior, which in some instances are antisocial. 2. Refers to loosely organized groups of teenagers, some of whom from a social point of view are of the useful type and others of the dangerous category.

ganglia   Clusters of nerves usually close to various organs of the body. The plural of ganglion. See GANGLION.

gangliated nerve   A nerve on some part of which there is an enlargement containing cell bodies, the axons of which run in the nerve.

ganglioblast   An embryonic cell from which ganglion cells develop.

gangliocyte   A ganglion cell.

ganglion   1. A collection of the cell bodies of neurons. 2. Historically, any group of nerve cell bodies in the central or peripheral nervous system. 3. Specifically, a collection of nerve cell bodies in the peripheral nervous system. See GANGLIA. 4. (Hippocrates) A tumor under the skin. 5. (Galen) A nerve swelling. Whereas Hippocrates and Galen both used the term, French anatomist, Raymond Vieussens, first used "ganglion" in the neurological sense. Plural is ganglia.

ganglion cells   Cells in the retinas of the eyes that carry visual information to the brain.

ganglionic blocking agents   Substances antagonistic to drugs that stimulate the autonomic ganglia.

ganglioplexus   A loosely aggregated ganglion embedded in a network or nerve fibers.

ganglioside   A complex chemical agent found ordinarily in trace amounts in nerve tissues.

gang rape   Slang for sexual assault or rape of a victim by two or more assailants.

ganja(h)   A potent form of hashish or cannabis sativa. Has been used in studies to determine if cannabis may increase the incidence of chromosome damage among marijuana smokers. Ganja smokers reportedly experience respiratory disorders at a rate twice that of the average for cannabis smokers. See BHANG.

Ganser('s) syndrome   (S. J. Ganser) 1. A pseudodementia assumed by people under severe stress, such as being interrogated by law enforcement personnel, that includes symptoms such as apparent memory deficits, and an inability to follow simple commands or answer questions properly. 2. A relatively rare disorder in which a prisoner awaiting trial or a patient under examination for commitment gives absurd, approximate, or inappropriate answers to simple questions. Considered to be an unconscious attempt to avoid a distasteful situation rather than a deliberate attempt to malinger. Also known as acute hallucinatory mania, nonsense syndrome, prison syndrome, syndrome of approximate answers.

Ganzfeld   (entire field—German) A featureless, evenly illuminated visual environment, used in research, especially in sensory deprivation and parapsychology.

Ganzheit **psychology**   (F. Krueger) A theory that stressed psychological totality to be studied by the phenomenological method. A competitor to Gestalt and American operationalism, this point of view was started by Felix Krueger when he succeeded to Wilhelm Wundt's chair at Leipzig.

gap   1. An opening. 2. A discontinuity in a series of events. 3. (M. Wertheimer) In Gestalt psychology, a structural disturbance or trouble in a percept or in reasoning that may be productively resolved by recentering the problem (for example, Albert Einstein recognized a "gap in real understanding" in the Michelson experiment).

Garbage in–Garbage out (GIGO)   In computerspeak, the principle that if input is inaccurate, unsatisfactory, or unrealistic, then output will be equally valueless.

Garcia effect   (J. Garcia) Learned taste aversion.

garden path sentence   A sentence that suggests at first one thing and then abruptly changes the expected message, for example, "You just won nothing."

gargalanesthesia   Absence of tickle sensitivity.

gargalesthesia   Sensitivity to tickling.

gargoylism   Obsolete term for the facial features associated with Hurler's syndrome and Hunter's syndrome. Features include an abnormally long and narrow skull, broad nose bridge, open mouth with a large tongue protruding, thick lips, and clouded corneas. See HURLER'S SYNDROME.

GAS   general-adaptation syndrome (also abbreviated **G.A.S.**)

gasoline intoxication   A euphoric reaction induced by gasoline-vapor inhalation. Also results in headache, weakness, central nervous system depression, confusion, nausea, and respiratory disorders. Nasal inhalation of volatile hydrocarbons is extremely rapid and more toxic than oral ingestion of the same substance. See INHALANT ABUSE.

Gasserian ganglion   A nerve complex at the point in the trigeminal nerve where three branches join. Also known as ganglion trigeminale. Named after Viennese anatomist Johann L. Gasser (1723–1765). See TIC DOULOUREUX, TRIGEMINAL NERVE.

gastric motility   Movements of the stomach muscles, particularly those caused by digestive processes. Also may occur in the absence of food in the stomach, as in the reaction of a patient to stress. See STOMACH REACTOR.

gastrocolic reflex   An automatic reaction in the colon due to introduction of food in an empty stomach.

gastroenteritis   Inflammation of the mucous lining of the stomach and intestines. Causes include food poisoning, infectious disease, allergic reaction, as well as psychological factors, such as fear, anger, or other emotional disturbance. Symptoms may include headache, nausea and vomiting, diarrhea, and gas pain. Also known as enterogastritis.

gastrula   A two layered stage of early embryonic development that follows the blastula stage.

gastrulation   A stage of embryonic development in which the blastula, or clump of undifferentiated cells, begins to evolve into the shape of a primitive organism.

GATB   General Aptitude Test Battery

gate   1. A device, circuit, or module of switches and relays providing one output signal dependent upon one or more (past or present) input channel states; it controls flow of a signal through a system. 2. A special nerve fiber blocking transmission of nerve impulses through a synapse. See GATE-CONTROL THEORY (OF PAIN).

gate-control theory (of pain)   (R. Melzack & P. D. Wall) 1. A point of view that the experience of pain depends partly on whether the pain impulses pass a "gate" in the spinal cord and thus reach the brain; a mechanism in cells of the substantia gelatinosa in the dorsal horn of the spinal cord regulates the pain reaching the brain by opening or closing gates for the flow of pain impulses. Normally the gate is closed by impulses into the cord from larger fibers that respond to pressure or by signals from the brain; chronic pain occurs when disease, infection, or injury damages the fibers that ordinarily close the gate. Suggests that pain may be relieved by interrupting excitatory fibers or stimulating inhibitory pain fibers. See GATING, PHANTOM PAIN, SPINAL GATE. 2. A point of view that the spinal cord regulates the amount of perceived pain reaching the brain by opening or closing "gates" in lacuna of dorsal horn of spinal cord for the flow of pain impulses. See GATING, SPINAL GATE.

gated channels   Refers to the permeability of neuron membranes controlled by a number of channels that can be opened and closed.

gatekeeper   1. A person designated to judge whether a person or group is eligible for specified services. 2. A functionary who decides access to a superior. 3. A person whose position permits screening, filtering, or controlling communication and information.

Gates-MacGinitie Reading Tests   (A. I. Gates & W. H. MacGinitie) A series of tests (replacing the Gates Reading Tests) designed to assess vocabulary, comprehension, reading speed, and reading accuracy at the primary level.

gate theory   A point of view that it is possible to block pain via the spinal cord by stimulating axons in the brain or in the skin. See GATE-CONTROL THEORY (OF PAIN).

gating   1. (J. S. Bruner) The process by means of which the central nervous system "tunes" peripheral sense organs for stimuli they will receive. See DEFENSIVENESS. 2. Refers to brain processes inhibiting some portions of the brain's functioning while allowing other parts to operate. Also known as sensory gating. See GATE-CONTROL THEORY OF PAIN, SPINAL GATE. 3. Canadian slang for the national parole board's canceling prisoners' "mandatory supervision" because of concerns about their reoffending. On the day of normal parole, or as they exit the gate (literally or figuratively) of a federal penitentiary, they are re-incarcerated to complete their full sentence. See PAROLE.

gating mechanism   The spinal gate.

gatophobia   ailurophobia

Gatti illusion   (A. Gatti) Given a number of equally spaced, concentric equilateral triangles upon which is superimposed a square, the false visual perception that the side of the square facing one of the apexes of the triangle appears longer than the side of the square that is parallel with one of the sides of the triangle.

Gauss   (K. F. Gauss) In electricity, a unit of measurement of magnetic induction. One Gauss is equal to one line of magnetic force per cm^2.

Gaussian curve   A normal curve. Also known as Gauss's curve. See NORMAL CURVE OF DISTRIBUTION.

gay   Common, nonpejorative term for a homosexual (originally male, now including female) or pertaining to homosexuality.

gay liberation   1. The movement for legal recognition of the rights of homosexuals, commonly traced to the 1969 Stonewall Inn riot in Greenwich Village, New York City. 2. Refers to militant gay men and lesbians seeking recognition of their lifestyle as normal and to achieve civil rights they feel are denied because of their sexual orientation. See FEMINISM.

Gay-Related Immune Deficiency (GRID)   Phrase that after 1982 became Acquired Immune Deficiency Syndrome (AIDS).

gaze   1. Fixation of the eyes toward a point, a characteristic of primate vision. 2. (M. Buber) A small but significant unit of interpersonal interaction that may affect another considerably, such as saying "thank you" with eye contact that conveys sincerity.

gaze duration   Refers to the total amount of time a reader has spent attending to a particular point of text; if there has been only fixation on that particular point, then gaze duration is equal to fixation.

GCE   general certificate of education

GED   general education degree

Gedanken experience   (thought—German) The process of thinking about some kind of problem during which the person mulls over what should be done and what could happen; may establish a kind of scenario of consequences of various actions.

GEFT   Group Embedded Figures Test

Gegenhalten   German phrase for resistance to the movement of limbs (by someone other than the person), the resistance apparently not under the voluntary control of the person to whom the limbs belong.

Gegenstandstheorie   (A. Meinong) A theory about the reality of the essence of objects in terms of what effects they have on perception and cognitions.

geisha   (arts person—Japanese) In Japanese culture, an honored woman trained as a professional hostess, entertainer, and companion of men. She may provide sexual relations, although geishas are not considered prostitutes.

Geist Picture Interest Inventory   See INTEREST TESTS.

Geisteswissenschaftliche Psychologie   (social science psychology—German) (W. Dilthey) One of two major divisions of psychology as established by some German thinkers, variously translated into English as "moral science" and "human studies" but generally as "human sciences." Between the 1880s and the 1910s, German academics debated the separation of, and differences between, the above (the human, cultural, moral, spiritual, and historical approaches to behavior), and *Naturwissenschaftliche Psychologie* (natural science psychology). Wilhelm Windelband argued that reality is indivisible and only the methodology may differ, whereas Wilhelm Dilthey separated *Geisteswissenschaften* and *Naturwissenchaften* in terms of their subject-matter. This debate later influenced the writings of Max Weber.

geleophobia   ailurophobia

Gellerman series   A series of the letters Rs and Ls, some obtained randomly with various constraints used in two-choice discrimination learning.

gematria   The pseudoscience of turning words into numbers and then interpreting them.

Gemeinschaft   (F. Tönnies) German term referring to a relationship characterized by the sharing of advantages and disadvantages such as of a parent and child, as opposed to a relationship that is formal or contractual in nature. Compare GESELLSCHAFT.

Gemeinschaftsgefühl   (feeling for community—German) Translated by Heinz Ansbacher as "social interest," by others as "community spirit." A spirit of equality and belonging that unites the entire community. Emphasizes the importance of individuals feeling they are an equal part of their community, whereupon feelings of inferiority disappear (since they now feel that they belong regardless of what they have to offer, how they look, etc). See SOCIAL INTEREST.

gemellology   The study of twins.

gemmation   Asexual reproduction by budding from the body of an organism. Also known as budding, bud fission.

gemmule   1. A bud from a parent cell that detaches to form a new generation. See GEMMATION. 2. An ultramicroscopic particle assumed by Charles Darwin to be given off at times by each cell in the body and to serve as the basis for the reproduction of similar cells in the offspring.

Gemütsbewegung   (emotions or feelings—German) Affective or affective-conative processes or their underlying and accompanying conditions. Also known as *Gemüt*.

gendenathasia   (R. B. Cattell) Raymond Cattell's term for the argument of euthanasia for "unsuccessful" groups (groups considered genetically unfit). See EUGENICS.

gender   1. Social or societal aspects of sex. "Boy" and "girl" are social (gender) terms for biological qualities associated with male and female. Although "sex" and "gender" are often used interchangeably, "sex" is the biological division into male and female; "gender" refers to masculinity and femininity, with cultural, symbolic, stereotypic, and self-identity overtones. A male transvestite knows he is a male but prefers, at least occasionally, to live in the female gender. See ASSIGNED GENDER, DUALISTIC VIEW OF GENDERS, NEGATIVE NUCLEAR GENDER, PSYCHO-, SEX VS GENDER. 2. A classification of nouns based primarily on sex distinctions.

gender assignment   The public or official classification of an infant at birth as either male or female. In some cases, an incorrect classification (due to sexual anomalies) becomes apparent at puberty. See PSEUDO-HERMAPHRODITISM, SEX REASSIGNMENT.

gender coding   The designation of characteristics (usually biological) or behavior as appropriate for males, females, or both. Sex adjunctive gender coding is based on the anatomical consequences of prenatal hormonal differences, and can be applied to, for instance, the division of labor between males and females. Sex adventitious gender coding is sex-coded behavior that extends the former though social scripting; includes clothing, cosmetics, and etiquette. Sex derivative gender coding refers to male and female distinctions related to reproduction, such as secondary sexual characteristics, bone structure, and musculature. Sex irreducible gender coding refers to differences that are immutable because of biology, such as pregnancy, menstruation, and lactation. Sex-shared gender coding covers characteristics that may be long-term consequences of prenatal brain coding, such as roaming, assertiveness, visual erotic threshold, and positioning in sexual play.

gender concept   The understanding of what it means to be a boy or a girl, usually achieved by most children by the age of six.

gender constancy   The final step in comprehending gender, when a child understands that a person's gender (sex) doesn't change even though there are external changes, as in behavior or clothing. See GENDER STABILITY.

gender constancy (theory)   A point of view that a person's core gender identity or role identity, once established in childhood, does not normally or easily change.

gender differences in attainment   Historically, there have been evident differences in quality and quantity of important contributions by the two sexes in the fields of art, music, literature and science in favor of males. This disparity may be attributed to biological, environmental, or social-cultural factors or a combination thereof. Different expectations and opportunities for different classes of people prevent accurate claims of basic psychological differences between the genders.

gender discrimination   Bias against one sex (usually female) in hiring practices, work roles, and wage levels, and the nonacceptance of that sex in work previously done only by the other sex. Also called sex discrimination. See GLASS CEILING.

gender dysphoria   Displeasure or unhappiness associated with a person's assigned gender role, and with reactions of others who have certain expectations about gender-appropriate behavior. See GENDER ROLE DYSPHORIA, PSEUDOHERMAPHRODISM.

gender identity   Awareness of how well persons see themselves as outwardly matching societal stereotypes or expectations of boys and men or girls and women. See GENDER ROLE, ROLE CONFUSION, SEXUAL IDENTITY.

gender-identity disorder   A psychosexual disorder consisting of a persistent feeling of inappropriateness concerning a person's anatomic sexual status, includes the desire to be the other gender with persistent repudiation of the anatomy and activities typical of own gender. See TRANSVESTISM, TRANSSEXUALITY.

gender identity disorder of childhood   A clinical condition in which a child experiences a strong discontent with or rejection of own sexual anatomy and a prevailing wish to change sex. See GENDER DYSPHORIA.

gender identity (G-I)   (J. Money) Phrase that emphasizes the connection between a person's gender identity and gender role as a lifelong interaction, especially at critical developmental periods. Also known as gender role (G-R).

gender nonconformity   Not behaving in accordance with others of the same sex or with cultural expectations of proper male and female behavior, such as girls who are called "tomboys" or boys who are called "sissies."

gender orientation   Psychosexual identity, focusing on own sexual orientation as evidenced in preferences, fantasies, etc.

gender reassignment   The changing of gender identification. This occurs: (a) due to original incorrect gender assignment because of anomalous genitalia at birth; (b) by surgical intervention, in that some males and some females wish to change their gender and manage to do so by having appropriate surgical changes; (c) by hormone therapy.

gender role (G-R)   1. Acting out of social norms and expectations associated with being a male or female (gender patterns). 2. The pattern of masculine or feminine behavior that characterizes a person, defining masculine and feminine in terms accepted by the particular culture. The role is largely determined by socialization and may or may not conform to the person's biologically determined sexual identity. See PSEUDOHERMAPHRODITISM, ROLE CONFUSION. 3. See GENDER IDENTITY.

Gender role differences   Male and female ways of carrying books.

gender role dysphoria   A behavior pattern characterized by adopting the gender role of the opposite sex, either chronically, as in transgenderism, or episodically, as in transvestitism. See GENDER DYSPHORIA.

gender role socialization   The training of children in the culture-specific behavior, expectations, and attitudes associated with the child's gender.

gender schema theory   1. An explanation for gender-typing; it states that concepts of maleness and femaleness are established by social learning and cultural definitions. 2. (S. Bem) A point of view about how the socialization of gender impacts a child's perception of self and place in the world. Sandra Bem holds that at an early age children learn the cultural expectations for gender norms, and this knowledge affects their self-concept, behaviors, and aspirations.

gender stability   A step in gender concept development in which the child understands that a person's gender continues to be stable throughout the person's lifetime. See GENDER CONSTANCY.

gender stereotypes   Behaviors or expectations about behaviors of individuals based on culturally determined definitions of appropriate expected or demanded behavior for males and females. See GENDER SCHEMA THEORY.

gender-typing   The degree or extent that a person operates as per expectation regarding that person's gender. An example of negative gender typing are girls considered to be tomboys.

gene   (W. L. Johannsen, T. H. Morgan) The essential unit of hereditary transmission. A substance in the chromosomes of the sex cells that controls the development of characters in organisms. Element in chromosomes composed of chemicals (DNA) that contain specific hereditary instructions for the development of specific bodily elements, such as hair color, size of body, and gender. A gene carries a particular trait from one generation of the species to the next. The trait may be expressed in the organism if the gene inherited is dominant or if chromosomes inherited from both parents, in the case of higher organisms, are both recessive for that trait. Also known as determiner, factor. Types of genes include: AUTOSOMAL DOMINANT, AUTOSOMAL RECESSIVE, DOMINANT, ENZYME, INTERMEDIATE, RECESSIVE, SELFISH.

genealogy   The study of the ancestry of a person with emphasis on family history and relationships rather than hereditary traits.

gene correlates of emotions   The subdiscipline that examines the genetic or biological correlates of emotional experience and expression.

gene fertility rate   The number of live births per 1,000 women of childbearing age in a given year.

gene flow   The gradual diffusion of genes between or among populations as they interbreed.

gene knockout (approach)   Biochemical research method to direct a mutation to a particular gene.

gene linkage   A tendency for all the genes (DNA molecules) in the same chromosome to be inherited together, except for crossing-over (exchanging of homologous segments of chromatids).

gene mapping   See GENETIC MAP.

gene mosaicism   1. A condition in which an organism has genetically different tissues side-by-side, resulting from somatic mutation. 2. Partial expression of a chromosomal disorder.

gene mutation A sudden alteration in a genetic trait that results in an advantage abnormality that may or may not be transmitted to the individual's offspring. Can be caused by radioactive energy, a chemical in the environment, or unknown factors; for example, achondroplastic dwarfs occur about 80% of the time in families that have no record of the abnormality. According to Darwinian theory, most mutations that last are beneficial. See MUTATION, SPORT.

genephobia   gynephobia

gene pool The total number of genetic traits distributed within the population of a species. In populations that favor random sexual selection, the genes are distributed along a normal, or bell-shaped, curve. Each gene adds slightly to or subtracts slightly from a given trait. See MULTIFACTORIAL INHERITANCE.

general ability (*G*) (C. E. Spearman) A measurable ability to handle all types of intellectual tasks. See GENERAL FACTOR.

general ability tests Mental tests designed to measure general all-round intellectual capacity, as distinguished from special ability tests (for example, the Binet-Simon Scale is considered a general intelligence test, whereas the Wiggly Block Test is viewed as a mechanical aptitude test).

general-adaptation syndrome (GAS or G.A.S.) (H. Selye) The mobilization of an organism's resources and defense systems to meet situations of stress. Hans Selye posited three levels of defense, each determined largely by endocrine secretions. In Stage One (alarm reaction), pituitary-adrenal secretions produce an increase in heart rate, blood sugar, muscle tone, and general alertness. In Stage Two (resistance), secretions from the adrenal cortex help the organism to repair damage and sustain continued stress. In Stage Three (exhaustion), the hormone defenses break down, and continued exposure to stress may lead to disintegration, diseases of adaptation (hypertension, arthritis, peptic ulcer), and even death. The abilities of an individual to survive depends on the length and severity of the stress condition and the body's ability to cope and endure. Also known as adaptation system, stress-adaption theory. See CONCENTRATION-CAMP SYNDROME.

general adaption theory   emergency theory

General Aptitude Test Battery (GATB) A test battery published by the U.S. Department of Labor in 1965 for job counseling. Not available commercially. Seven of the subtests are multiple-choice paper-and-pencil; five measure motor speed and coordination. They cover verbal, numerical, and spatial aptitude as well as manual dexterity, form perception, and clerical perception. Usually given in federal agencies for evaluations of skills, often for selection purposes.

general arousal   orienting response

general certificate of education (GCE)   general education degree (GED)

general consciousness Experiences common to two or more individuals, usually to all members of a given social group.

general developmental model (K. Warner Schaie) A paradigm defining the interrelationship of cross-sectional, longitudinal, and time-lag strategies for collecting developmental data, and explicates the confounds in each attributable to the components of age, time, and cohort.

general drives Refers to those self-motivational influences or desires to accomplish or acquire something that may be strong but if left unsatisfied will not lead to death. Most people have them and some such drives may be innate, for example, the desire for companionship.

general education degree (GED) A high school equivalency degree, determined by testing.

general extrasensory perception (GESP) In parapsychology, extrasensory perception (ESP) that could be due to telepathy, clairvoyance, or both.

general factor (g) 1. (C. E. Spearman) A mathematical quantity for the basic ability underlying the performance of different varieties of intellectual tasks in contrast to specific abilities unique to special tasks. 2. (L. L. Thurstone) The ability with which each of the primary factors of intelligence is correlated. See SPECIAL FACTOR, STRUCTURE OF INTELLECT MODEL.

general gender identity disorder A persistent condition characterized by having a strong cross-dressing penchant and profound conviction that one is of a gender other than the one to which one has been socially assigned.

general habit Learned acts that are a result of stability of actions between situations serving as stimuli and behavior as responses.

general idea An idea or concept that includes the likenesses and excludes the differences common to a number of individual or particular ideas. A special form of abstract idea.

general image An image representing any one of a class of objects.

general intelligence A concept with no universally accepted definition, it is variously described as the ability to deal with abstractions; the capacity to learn; the ability to survive; or as being represented by success in achieving reasonable goals. It was called *g* by Charles Spearman. Joy P. Guilford viewed intelligence as composed of separate and independent elements, known as *s*. E. L. Thorndike thought there were three separate forms of intelligence: symbolic, mechanical, social. See INTELLIGENCE TESTS, MECHANICAL INTELLIGENCE, NONVERBAL INTELLIGENCE.

general intelligence factor See GENERAL FACTOR, GENERAL INTELLIGENCE.

generalizability The accuracy with which results or findings can be generalized or transferred to situations other than those originally studied.

generalization 1. The application of a concept, judgment, principle, test result, or theory derived from a limited number of cases to an entire class of objects, events, or people. The common statement that generalizations (about people) cannot be made is untrue; psychologists do generalize about animals and people. What cannot be done is universalize. See IDIOGRAPHICS, NOMOTHETICS, UNIVERSALIZATION. 2. In therapy, the ability of the client or patient to transfer what has been learned in the therapeutic environment to external reality. See RESPONSE GENERALIZATION PRINCIPLE, STIMULUS GENERALIZATION. 3. Becoming widespread. See EPIDEMIOLOGY.

generalization decrement (C. L. Hull) Response strength loss due to differences between the reinforced stimulus and the present stimulus. It is the reverse of stimulus generalization. See HULL'S THEORY.

generalization gradient The degree to which responses to a given stimulus become weaker and fewer as the stimulus changes from its original form. For example, if an organism has been conditioned to respond to a square, the more that the lines of the square deviate in proportion, the less and fewer responses can be expected. Sometimes known as excitation gradient.

generalization of response A principle of conditioning that once a conditioned response has been established, similar stimuli may evoke the same response: the more similar the stimuli, the greater the generalization or degree of response. See TRANSFER.

generalization of stimulus In learning, elicitation of responses by stimuli (or general classes of stimuli) similar to the specific stimulus. It is common in early stages of learning, and lessens as discrimination improves.

generalized amnesia See MOTIVATED FORGETTING, PSYCHOGENIC AMNESIA.

generalized-anxiety disorder (GAD) An unpleasant feeling of tension, dread, apprehension, and impending disaster lasting at least a month, and manifested in such symptoms as motor tension, autonomic hyperactivity, apprehensive expectation or vigilance, and scanning that may involve difficulties in concentrating and sleeping.

generalized conditioned reinforcers (B. F. Skinner) Learned reinforcers that can affect a wide variety of behaviors.

generalized curve A graphic representation of growth, learning, or similar developmental functions in relation to time, with other factors being kept constant by either experimental or statistical control.

generalized expectancies (J. Rotter) Expectations that apply across a range of situations. A kind of philosophical view of life generating a readiness for any situation that comes along.

generalized habit strength (C. L. Hull) The strength of a habit after the effect of the generalization decrement has been eliminated. See HULL'S THEORY.

generalized inhibitory potential ($_SI_R$) (C. L. Hull) A conditioned inhibition that results from a stimulus generalization. See HULL'S THEORY.

generalized other 1. (G. H. Mead) The values, norms, and views of a group or community. Parallels Sigmund Freud's superego, except that the latter develops unconsciously whereas the development of the generalized other is conscious. 2. The concept of people other than the self such as "the average man" or "old people."

generalized reaction potential ($_SE_R$) (C. L. Hull) The strength of reaction potential considering generalized decrement made up of drive strength and generalized habit strength plus other variables. See HULL'S THEORY.

generalized reinforcer A rewarding factor that will reinforce a wide range of behavior. For humans, money is a generalized reinforcer; for laboratory animals, food is a generalized reinforcer.

generalizing 1. The process of perceiving or conceiving a general characteristic, fact, or meaning in single or in complex situations or things. 2. Responding to the common aspects (from any point of view) of the specific elements in a complex situation.

generalizing assimilation (J. Piaget) Refers to how new concepts are formed by children through generalizations based on experiences.

general language disability A wide-ranging language disorder in children characterized by delayed speech, prolonged use of infantile speech and grammar, and reading and spelling difficulty. May stem from minimal brain damage.

general motive A category of motives that have in common an ultimate goal, sometimes not known to the individual. Such goals may be as diverse as success-in-life and failure-in-life. See FAILURE THROUGH SUCCESS.

general norms Average scores according to age or grade that are obtained by means of mental or educational tests based upon a supposedly random sampling of school children, and that presumably represent the attainment of the entire population.

general paralysis/paresis The neurologic manifestation of tertiary syphilis, caused by the destructive action of the spirochete on brain tissue. A variety of physical signs (such as unsteady gait) and personality aberrations (such as various psychotic reactions) that may occur usually many years after the original infection of syphilis. Types of general paresis include: DEMENTED, DEPRESSED, EXPANSIVE, PARANOID. See ORGANIC PSYCHOSIS, PARESIS.

General Problem Solver (GPS) (A. Newell, J. C. Shaw & H. A. Simon) A computer simulation of human problem-solving processes that uses means-ends analysis as its principal heuristic method. See COGNITIVE SIMULATION, MEANS-ENDS ANALYSIS.

general psychology The study of the basic principles, problems, and methods underlying the science of psychology, including physiology, human growth and development, emotions, motivation, learning, sensations, perception, thinking processes, remembering and forgetting, intelligence, personality theory, psychological testing, behavior disorders, social behavior, and mental health.

general psychotherapy An eclectic psychotherapeutic approach using a variety of techniques, such as reassurance, relaxation, ventilation, and play therapy.

general semantics (A. Korzybski) A philosophical-psychological theory referring particularly to the study of symbols, including the meaning of words, signals and gestures. See SEMANTIC THERAPY, SEMANTICS.

general somatic efferent fibers See ACCESSORY NERVE.

general systems theory (GST) 1. A concept that there exist interrelations and interconnections between parts of entities that work together harmoniously. 2. A point of view about living organisms taken from three points of view: (a) large systems, such as organizations, schools, government impact on individuals; (b) individuals as entities in these systems; and (c) individuals being composed of sub-systems such as their organs and ultimately their cells. Compare GENERAL-SYSTEMS THEORY.

general-systems theory   (L. von Bertalanffy) An attempt to integrate the fragmented approaches and different classes of phenomena studied by contemporary science into an organized whole. In this theory, human behavior is viewed as a subsystem of the whole, to be investigated by a holistic approach that draws upon many disciplines and specialties. Compare GENERAL SYSTEMS THEORY.

general-to-specific-sequence   The maturational development of responses from undifferentiated general movements to specific and detailed movements. See INDIVIDUATION.

general transfer   An ability to apply skills and knowledge acquired in one field to problems in another field, such as using Jungian theory to analyze a Shakespearian play. Compare SPECIFIC TRANSFER.

general will   A hypothetical entity representing the desires of the majority of a group that directs the entire group.

generating tone   One of the two or more tones that when sounded together produce a combination tone. Also known as generator.

generation   1. The act of procreating or the production of a new individual. See REPRODUCTION (meaning 1). 2. The offspring of a pair of parents. See FILIAL GENERATION. 3. The average length of life between birth and the beginning of reproduction in a given species.

generation effect   The finding that when participants are asked to read aloud an item on some lists and to generate an item on other trials, memory is often better for items that are generated. See COHORT EFFECT.

generation gap   A communication and understanding void between generations, a gulf (sometimes incorrectly assumed) between the values, attitudes, and expectations of adolescents and their parents and grandparents. May exist due to rapid technological, social, and moral changes. See COHORT EFFECT.

generative function   The operations involved in the bringing into being of a new organism, insofar as these operations are activities of the parent organism or organisms.

generative grammar   A system of rules that lead to forming sentences.

generativeness   In psychometrics, the generation or invention by a computer of new test items appropriate to the ongoing performance of the participant.

generative theory of language acquisition   (N. A. Chomsky) A linguistic proposal claiming that children gain language comprehension by intuitively generating meaning out of experience with proper word sequences, while the brain assimilates and organizes the material like a computer. Continuous environmental feedback (such as learning grammar rules in school) is considered not essential.

generative transformational grammar   Rules that generate grammatically correct sentences resulting in satisfactory communications.

generativity   (E. Erikson) A drive toward showing concern for and interest in others, especially guiding and encouraging those in rewer generations. The term includes the concepts of productivity and creativity, and is roughly equivalent to social interest. See GENERATIVITY VS STAGNATION.

generativity vs stagnation   (E. Erikson) The seventh of Erikson's eight stages of psychosocial development, during which the person either develops a sense of responsibility toward the next generation or remains with a narrow interest in the self. Generativity is seen as the positive goal of adulthood. Also known as generativity vs self-absorption. See ERIKSON'S EIGHT STAGES OF PSYCHOSOCIAL DEVELOPMENT.

generator potential   1. The specific electrical impulse that triggers a nerve to react. 2. A change in the electrical charge of a receptor as a result of a stimulus. Usually is important in visual studies in which the potential may be roughly proportional to the stimulus triggering the effect.

generic   Applying to all instances in a class or to all the subgroups in a class.

generic memory knowledge   (J. Cavanaugh, J. Feldman, C. Hertzog) A set of propositions about how memory functions, such as which intentionally activated cognitive processes are more or less.

generic name   Common name of a medicine, in contrast to the trade name, the name by which the medicine was first or most commonly marketed (for example, fluoxetine, the generic name, is most widely known by its trade name, Prozac, and similarly, Ritalin is the trade name for the generic chemical methylphenidate). It is important to be acquainted with some of the generic names of medicines because after the patent has run out, other companies often manufacture almost the same medicine at a lower price. To save the patient money, a number of states have passed laws that the pharmacist, unless specifically instructed on a prescription, should then dispense the medicine under its generic (chemical) name. Knowing the generic name of a medicine, the therapist might be able to clarify the resulting confusion to the patient.

generic service system   A full range of services available to people in the areas of health, education, social service, rehabilitation, employment, legal services, and housing. See SOCIAL SERVICES.

generic skills   Phrase introduced by the Canadian Employment and Immigration Commission to identify work behaviors fundamental to the performance of a wide range of occupations (for example, a manipulative skill, which requires eye-hand coordination; the use of the body for lifting and carrying). Generic skills are matched in a matrix with jobs requiring one or more such skills.

genesis   The origin of anything.

gene-splicing   A technique of removing deoxyribonucleic acid (DNA) genetic material from one organism and inserting it into another organism, usually of a different species. The purpose is to develop new sources of drugs or similar organic substances from microorganisms or to correct genetic defects in organisms. Gene-splicing is the basic method of recombinant-DNA efforts. See GENETIC ENGINEERING, RECOMBINANT DNA.

genetic   1. Pertaining to genetics. 2. Pertaining to ontogeny.

genetic balance theory   An explanation for how sex chromosomes and autosomes together determine sex at the molecular level, cellular level, and organ level in the embryo.

genetic blueprint   Instructions in the genes that fore-tell an individual organism's potential to develop physi-cal factors.

genetic code   The arrangement of genetic factors in a chain-like fashion in a chromosome that determines the transmission of hereditary information, such as the sequence of amino acids needed to form the protein of a body tissue.

genetic counseling/guidance   The provision of infor-mation and advice to individuals and couples of the prob-able risk of having children with specific hereditary de-fects. See AMNIOCENTESIS, CONGENITAL DEFECT, FAMILY COUNSELING, GENE.

genetic counselor   A health professional with special training in genetics who provides counseling and advice to prospective parents in matters of birth defects and inherited diseases. Many such counselors have an M.D. or Ph.D. degree, or both.

genetic defect   Any physical or mental deformity or abnormality due to a faulty gene or genes. Generally, a genetic defect expresses itself in a failure to synthesize a normally functioning enzyme required for a specific step in building a certain body cell or for a vital stage in the metabolism of a food element. In addition to single-gene defects, this phrase may be applied to chromosomal aberrations, such as Klinefelter's syndrome.

genetic dominance   The overt characteristics (pheno-type) of the dominant gene of the two genes in the allele. For example, an allele for brown eyes is inherited from one parent, and a gene for blue eyes is inherited from the other parent; as genes for brown eyes are dominant over genes for blue eyes, the children will have brown eyes.

genetic drift   The chance variation in gene frequency in a population from one generation to the next. The smaller the population, the greater the random variations.

genetic engineering   Selective alterations of the ge-netic contents of living cells or viruses, by methods such as enzymatic transfer of genes between genomes, for pur-poses such as basic research on genetic mechanisms and bacterial production of medically helpful gene products. See GENE-SPLICING, GENETIC MAP.

genetic epistemology   (J. Piaget) Jean Piaget's concep-tualization of how children come to conceptualize self and the environment.

genetic error   A hereditary trait associated with a single-gene defect. May be due to a spontaneous mutation or an environmental hazard such as radiation. A genetic error that becomes hereditary is usually not lethal since the individual is able to become a fertile adult and thus able to transmit the genetic error to another generation of individuals. Some genetic errors, however, may result in fetal death or mortality for the individual before maturity. More than 2,000 different genetic errors have been cataloged.

genetic inheritance   The blueprint of a child's physical characteristics carried in genes, consisting of molecules of DNA (deoxyribonucleic acid) and RNA (ribonucleic acid). Genes normally are in pairs, one from each parent in linear sequence in twenty-three pairs of chromosomes. One of these pairs of chromosomes, known as the sex chromosome, decides the gender of the child. See GENETIC MAP, GENETIC PSYCHOLOGY.

geneticism   A doctrine positing that behavior is inborn, as found in Freud's theory of instincts and psychosexual development.

geneticist   A health professional who specializes in the study of genetics. May be a member of the staff of a medical-services department of a hospital, medical college, or research institution.

genetic lethal   A genetically determined characteristic causing infertility or death prior to sexual maturity.

genetic map   A genetic map shows the location of each gene and is developed retrospectively by analyzing the chromosome patterns in tissue cells of an individual organism with hereditary abnormalities and comparing the patterns with those from organisms considered normal.

genetic marker   Any gene identified as related to a specific genetic trait.

genetic material   Data from the developmental history and previous experiences or relationships of patients that may "shed light" on their present adaptation, problems, and psychodynamics. See CURRENT MATERIAL.

genetic memory   A theory that information based on experience or learning may be stored in a deoxyribonu-cleic acid (DNA) or ribonucleic acid (RNA) molecule, which might in turn be inherited as part of a chromo-some. See GENETIC STORAGE.

genetic method   The study of behavior in terms of hereditary origins and developmental history.

genetic predisposition   A tendency for certain physi-cal or mental traits to be inherited. Schizophrenia seems to be a genetic predisposed mental trait affecting approx-imately (some estimates are higher) 1% of the general population, but 4% of distant relatives of patients, 12% of siblings of patients, and 82% of identical twins when one of the pair has schizophrenia.

genetic psychology   The study of genetic and early environmental factors that influence the development of a child's personality.

genetics   (W. Bateson) The branch of biology con-cerned with the phenomena of heredity, variation, evo-lution, and the laws that determine inherited traits. See BEHAVIOR GENETICS, BIOGENETICS, POLITICAL GE-NETICS, SOCIOGENETICS.

genetic sequences   The order in which genetically determined structures or functions develop.

genetic sex   The sex determined by the chromosomes at fertilization. In most humans, the sex-linked pair XX is female, the XY is male. Also known as chromosomal sex.

genetic storage   A theory that learned information, such as a fear of poisonous snakes or an ability to recognize family members, may be stored by the nervous system at the synaptic or metabolic level. See GENETIC MEMORY.

genetic technology   The study of the biochemical constitution of genes and chromosomes, including the manipulation of genes of organisms so that they produce substances beyond their natural functions, such as drugs or hormones needed by humans. Genetic technology also permits predicting by amniocentesis that a fetus may be born with a certain specific congenital defect.

genetic theory   A point of view that psychological traits can be explained by hereditary and developmental factors.

genetotrophic diseases   Diseases or pathological conditions due to an inherited enzyme defect or deficiency, such as the inborn errors of metabolism. See PHENYLKE-TONURIA (PKU).

Geneva school of genetic psychology   (J. Piaget) An orientation to the study of the cognitive development of children. The main tools of this "school" are observation of behavior and clinical interviews. Research gave evidence that children moved from a position of egocentrism to one of decentration. See PIAGETIAN THEORY.

geniculate bodies   Small masses on the surface of the thalamus containing nuclei that relay impulses to the cortex. The lateral geniculate body processes visual impulses, and the medial geniculate body processes auditory information.

genital   1. Pertaining to reproduction. 2. Pertaining to the genitals.

genital arousal in sleep   See MORNING ERECTION, VAGINAL LUBRICATION.

genital character   (S. Freud) The adult stage of psychosexual development that has evolved from the pregenital levels (anal and oral) to serve the interest of genitality.

genital eroticism   The arousal of sexual excitement by stimulation of the genital organs.

genitality   1. Capacity to experience erotic sensation in the genital organs, starting with childhood masturbation and culminating in adult sexuality. 2. In psychoanalytic theory, the penis and vagina's relationship to sexuality.

genitalization   The focusing of pleasure from the sex organs to nonsexual objects that resemble or symbolize them, such as shoes or locks of hair. See FETISH.

genital level   (S. Freud) In psychoanalytic theory, the final stage of psychosexual development, reached in puberty, when a mature pattern of traits are developed, including erotic interest and activity focused on a (hetero)sexual partner. Also known as genital phase/stage. See GENITAL PERIOD.

genital love   1. A positive emotional attachment to the genitals during the period of object love. 2. In psychoanalytic theory, mature sexual love of another person.

genital mutilation   The destruction or physical alteration of the external genitals. May be (a) ritual or cultural, as in clitoridectomy, (b) self-inflicted, as in males who cut off their penises (as a psychotic act or as part of a cultural ritual), (c) inflicted on others, as in the castration of enemy soldiers or sexual predators, or (d) in the form of rings, bells, or jewelry inserted into the genitals. When performed as a cultural dictate on infants or children, some perceive penile circumcision as genital mutilation; others consider infibulation and clitoridectomy as merely akin to circumcision. See CLITORIDECTOMY, INFIBULATION, ORCHIECTOMY, SKOPTSY, TRANSSEXUALISM, VULVECTOMY.

genital penetration phobia   Irrational, disabling fear that prevents a female, and sometimes a male, from performing penis-vagina intercourse. See DYSPAREUNIA, VAGINA CAPTIVA, VAGINA DENTATA.

genital period   Sigmund Freud's original 1905 concept of the genital stage, described as the third stage in libidinal development (from 3 to 5 years). He later altered this concept in 1933 to the fourth and final stage of libidinal development, representing the unification and maturation of all erotic functions. See GENITAL LEVEL.

genital phase/stage   genital level

genital primacy   In psychoanalytic theory, an assumption that genitally-based eroticism is the final normal level of sexual development.

genitals   The reproductive organs of the male and female of the species. The male genitals include the penis, testes and related structures, prostate, seminal vesicles, and bulbourethral glands. The female consist of the vagina, labia, clitoris, uterus, ovaries, fallopian tubes, and related structures. Also known as genitals, private parts. See AMBIGUOUS GENITALS.

genital stimulation   A complex set of factors associated with sexual arousal in mammals, including integration of male and female genital reflexes, odors, hormone secretions, sights, sounds, and tactual and kinesthetic cues. Each factor contributes to genital stimulation, which still may occur in the absence of one or more of the cues.

genital zones of the nose   Olfactory receptors sensitive to body odors of certain kinds that cause sexual arousal.

genital zones   The external reproductive organs and adjacent areas capable of producing genital sensations. See EROTOGENIC ZONE.

genius   1. A person with extraordinary powers of creativity. 2. A person with exceptional skill or ability, usually in the arts. 3. A person who does extremely well on a test of intelligence. See TALENT.

genius and pathology   "Geniuses" are reputed to experience above-average psychological disorders. However, biographical research by Catherine Cox, Francis Galton, Havelock Ellis, and James McKeen Cattell (according to Leona Tyler) concluded otherwise. Later longitudinal studies by Lewis Terman and others of children with intelligence quotients over 135, including seven follow-up studies, found them physically, temperamentally, and socially superior.

genocide   1. The killing of a people. Term coined during World War II by R. Lemkin in the context of the Holocaust, adopted by the United Nations in 1948. 2. The systematic, impersonal destruction of a defined group of innocent people by a state. What manner of large-scale killing constitutes a "genocide" has become controversial; some include events such as the purging of "witches," persecution of Native Americans, and the bombing of Hiroshima. 3. By extension, major and pervasive persecution of an outgroup, sometimes termed cultural genocide.

genocopy   An individual whose genotype appears to be identical to that of another. See GENOTYPE.

genogram   A schematic diagram of a family's relationship system used to trace recurring family patterns of genes and behavior through generations.

genome   A complete set of hereditary factors in the chromosomes of a single organism; either of the two sets of chromosomes in a zygote. Term is a contraction of gene and chromosome. See GENETIC ENGINEERING.

genomic imprinting   A mechanism that permits a gene contributed by either parent to differ functionally from an identical gene from the other parent. Also known as genomic inactivation.

genophobia   Morbid fear of anything having to do with sex. Also known as aeratephobia. See COITOPHO-BIA, CYPRIDOPHOBIA, EROTOPHOBIA.

genotrophic disease   A disease that tends to be transmitted by a genetic defect, such as an inborn error of metabolism.

genotrophism   (L. Szondi) An explanation to account for a person's instinctive choices. Argues that a person acquires through recessive genes mental traits that determine certain spontaneous actions, such as the choice of male or female companions with a similar genetic background.

genotype   (W. L. Johannsen) The genetic characteristics or mold directly inherited by an individual or group that is transmitted to descendants despite acquired characteristics. The genetic constitution of an individual; a set of genes within every cell of an organism's body, some dominant, some recessive, comprising somewhere between 30,000 and 100,000 traits or trait components acquired through myriad generations of ancestors. The genotype is not necessarily observable, as contrasted with the characteristics manifested by an organism, the phenotype.

genotypic continuity   The argument that persons with certain clusters of traits change physically and mentally in pre-established predictable ways.

gens   In anthropology, the concept that familial descent comes through the males. Also known as patrilineal clan. See MATRILINEAGE.

genthanasia   Raymond Cattell's term for a nonviolent but intentional phasing out of particular biological groups on the basis of their presumed lack of social utility. See BEYONDISM, EUGENICS, EUTHENICS, RACISM.

gentrification   (R. Glass) The upgrading of decaying, usually inner-city housing, generally including physical renovation, the displacement of low-income residents by wealthy ones, and the change from property rental to ownership.

gentry   Originally, the societal stratum immediately below the aristocracy in medieval Britain.

genu   1. The knee, or any anatomical structure resembling it. 2. Denoting the anterior portion of the corpus callosum as it bends forward and downward; this portion contains nerve fibers that radiate from the anterior forceps to the frontal lobe on either side. Plural is genua.

genuineness   See CONGRUENCE.

genus   A division of taxonomy between family and species. A class or group of closely related species that share certain physical characteristics, usually referring to animals or plants. Example: Ocelots, tigers, and domestic housecats are members of the genus *felis* with common characteristics such as rounded head, retractable claws, teeth suitable for a carnivorous style of life. Plural is genera.

geographic mobility   Physical movements from one geographic location to another.

geographic segmentation   In consumer psychology, dividing a potential market by geographical subunits.

geometric(al) mean   The geometric average of all the observations. Algebraically, it is the Nth root of the product of N observations or values of a variable. Useful for averaging ratios.

geometrical illusions   Misinterpretations of simple straight and curve-line figures.

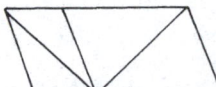

geometrical illusions   The two angled lines are equal in length.

geon   (I. Biederman) An elementary shape that can serve as a prototype in recognizing more complex shapes that can be perceived as constructions of one or more individual geons. See NONSENSE FIGURE for an illustration.

geophagy   Earth-eating, a form of pica frequently associated with iron deficiency anemia. Also known as geophagia, geophagism.

geotaxis   1. A form of positive barotaxis characterized by a tendency to grow toward or into the earth. Movement in terms of effects of gravity, for example, if a seed is placed on a damp surface, part of it (the roots) will grow down and part of it (stems and leaves) will grow up. Jacques Loeb's "geotropism" is passé or obsolete for fauna but is still employed for flora. Also known as geotropism. See TAXIS, TROPISM. 2. Involuntary movement of an organism that helps it maintain a postural orientation that relates to the force of gravity. Most animals have statocysts, or gravity detectors, as part of their nervous system. The human statocyst is a part of the labyrinth apparatus of the cochlea of the inner ear.

geotropism   geotaxis (meaning 1)

gephyrophobia   Morbid fear of bridges, or of crossing a bridge, river, or walking along a river bank. Also known as gephrophobia.

Gerbrand's memory drum   One of several types of memory drums, the earliest having been devised by C. E. Muller. See MEMORY DRUM for an illustration of Gerbrand's memory drum.

geriatric delinquency   Delinquency among older persons, from misdemeanors such as shoplifting to serious "crimes of passion." The main motivating factors include neediness and boredom. As a pattern, geriatric delinquency was first observed in the 1980s when a higher average-age level of crime began in the United States.

geriatric disorders   Chronic diseases that occur commonly, but not exclusively, among older persons.

geriatrician   A physician who specializes in treating older patients.

geriatric psychopharmacology   The branch of pharmacology that deals with the diagnosis and treatment of mental disorders associated with the aging process, such as disturbances of sleep patterns, cognitive functioning, mood, and behavior. Because of metabolic changes of aging, drugs may have different biologic activity, and central nervous system sensitivity to drugs may be increased.

geriatric rehabilitation   The restoration of ambulation and independent-living ability to persons afflicted with a geriatric disorders. Gerontologists (physicians specializing in aging) generally agree that many of the diseases associated with aging are preventable and controllable when the patients seek early treatment and do not regard infirmities of aging as inevitable.

geriatrics (I. L. Nascher) The branch of science that deals with old age and the treatment of physical and mental disorders that arise in this period.

geriatric screening and evaluation centers Agencies that are staffed and equipped to provide physical examinations and care, as well as psychological and financial counseling, to older persons.

geriopsychosis General term for manifestations of brain deterioration and serious mental disorders associated with aging.

German measles **Rubella**

germ cell The gametes, or reproductive cells, of an organism. In humans, the germ cells are the ova and spermatozoa, each containing the haploid (unpaired) chromosomes, as distinguished from the somatic cells.

germ fear See BACILLOPHOBIA.

germinal factors The structures and their interrelations in the reproductive cell, which determine the inheritance of characteristics.

germinal period/stage In humans, after conception, the first one to two weeks of prenatal life in which the fertilized egg (zygote) travels down the Fallopian tube to the uterus, where it is implanted. It is followed by the embryonic stage.

germinal selection (A. F. Weismann) The hypothetical elimination of the weaker or less adapted vital units in the struggle which August Weismann assumed to occur between these units in the germ plasm. See WEISMANNISM.

germinal vesicle The nucleus of the ovum before the polar bodies are formed.

germinally affected A person who carries a homozygous recessive pair of genes for a disorder not expressed in that person's own body.

germ layer A layer of cells formed early in embryonic development that gives rise to the fundamental organ systems of the body.

germ plasm Reproductive tissue from which the male and female gametes develop, as distinguished from the somatoplasm, or tissues that form the rest of the body.

germ theory A point of view that infectious diseases are caused by the invasion of the body tissues by microorganisms such as bacteria, viruses, rickettsials, protozoa, or fungi.

gerocomy The care of aging patients.

geromorphism Obsolete term for premature senility.

Gerontological Apperception Test (R. B. Wolk & R. L. Wolk) A variant of the Thematic Apperception Test designed for the older persons.

gerontological psychology **geropsychology**

gerontological psychiatry **geropsychiatry**

gerontology 1. The scientific study of old age and the aging process. 2. The study of the general problems of old age. See GERIATRICS, SOCIAL GERONTOLOGY.

gerontophilia 1. A love of old people. 2. Being sexually attracted to or aroused by a much older sex partner. Also known as gerophilia.

gerontophobia 1. Fear of old people. 2. Morbid fear of growing old or of old age. See AGEISM.

geropsychiatry A branch of psychiatry concerned with diagnosis, treatment, and management of mental disorders that first emerge in old age, or first become significant in old age. Treatment is generally holistic and multidisciplined, taking into account the patient's mental and emotional condition, social and recreational life, and living conditions. Also known as geriatric psychiatry, gerontological psychiatry, psychogeriatrics (in Great Britain).

geropsychology The study of old age and the psychological aspects of the aging process. Also known as geriatric psychology, gerontological psychology.

Gerstmann's syndrome A condition characterized by acalculia, agraphia, left-right spatial disorientation, and finger agnosia. Likely due to lesion in the left parieto-occipital area. Named after Austrian neurologist Josef L. Gerstmann.

Geschwind's theory (N. Geschwind) In physiological psychology, the contention that excessive intrauterine exposure to androgens inhibits thymus and left-hemisphere development, explaining why learning disabilities (including dyslexia) and left-handedness are associated with autoimmune disorders, and are more prevalent in men than in women.

Gesell Development Scales (A. Gesell) Scales developed at the Yale Clinic of Child Development for assessing the linguistic, motor, adaptive, and social development of infants and preschool children.

Gesell Developmental Schedules (GSCH) (A. Gesell) A clinical method for the study of sensorimotor growth of preschool children. Qualitative measurements in the form of normative tables of motor development, adaptive behavior, language development, and personal-social behavior are provided. Named after Arnold Gesell. Also known as Gesell Developmental Norms.

Gesellschaft (F. Tönnies) German term referring to a relationship characterized by pacts or contracts; utilitarian in nature. Compare GEMEINSCHAFT.

GESP See GENERAL EXTRASENSORY PERCEPTION.

Gestalt (configuration; good form—German) 1. A unitary, integrated, articulated perceptual structure or system whose parts are in dynamic interrelation with each other and with the whole. 2. A tendency when perceiving a variety of elements to make sense out of them by distorting reality, that is, not seeing them as they actually are, but mentally "improving" what is seen, organizing them, or otherwise making them better or more nearly complete or perfect. Max Wertheimer adopted the term for application to his concepts.

gestalt completion test An examination consisting of incomplete pictures so designed that the missing parts can be replaced but only if the picture is perceived as a unified whole. See CLOSURE, STREET FIGURES for examples. See FIGURAL COHESION.

gestalten Plural of gestalt.

gestalt factor A condition, such as proximity, that favors perception of a gestalt figure.

gestalt homology A principle that parts of a whole are comparable with parts of another whole in terms of their function (for example, the middle C key of any musical instrument is homologous to the C of any other instrument, regardless of differences in pitch or loudness). See GESTALT.

gestaltism   A doctrine positing that the objects of mind are complete configurations that cannot be broken down into parts, for example, a triangle is perceived as a geometric shape rather than as three separate lines. See GESTALT.

gestalt laws   Principles that govern how structures and integrated systems in nature and in cognition are organized and comprehended.

gestalt laws of organization   Gestalt psychology refers mostly to the organization of natural phenomena, including cognitive or perceptual structures; for example, three equally long, randomly arranged straight lines look like what they are, but if each end of each line touches an end of another line, the new perception is a triangle. From such observations came the expression that the whole is more than and different from the sum of the parts. See LAW OF GOOD CONTINUATION, LAW OF GOOD SHAPE, LAW OF PRECISION, LAW OF PROXIMITY, LAW OF SIMILARITY, PRINCIPLE OF PRÄGNANZ.

gestalt logic   (M. Wertheimer) In Gestalt psychology, an approach to thinking "from above" based on deductive logic with emphasis on the operations of centering, grouping, and structural transposability of the rho-nature or essential features of events as opposed to the structure-blind associations of traditional logic.

Gestalt psychology   A psychological approach that focuses on the dynamic organization of experience into patterns or configurations. This point of view came into prominence as a revolt against structuralism and behaviorism. Gestalt psychology holds that the whole is greater than the sum of its parts, as shown by Max Wertheimer's crucial experiment with successively flashed lights, which gave the illusion of motion, and by later experiments that gave rise to principles of perceptual organization (proximity, closure, similarity, Prägnanz), which were then applied to the study of learning, insight memory, social psychology, and art. Gestalt psychology was developed in the early 1900s by German psychologists Max Wertheimer, Wolfgang Köhler, and Kurt Koffka. See AUTOCHTHONOUS GESTALT, PRINCIPLE OF PRÄGNANZ.

Gestaltqualität   (quality of configuration—German) (C. Ehrenfels) An added element, the "form quality," of a configuration over and above the elements composing a whole (for example, a melody played in a given key is not just the sum of the notes but is, in addition, the theme itself; a square is four equal lines plus four 90° angles, plus the form quality of "squareness"). *Gestaltqualität* held that the experiencing person always adds an extra "quality" to sensory entities resulting in perception.

Gestalttheorie   The holistic system of psychology developed by Max Wertheimer, Kurt Koffka, and Wolfgang Köhler in the early twentieth century as a protest against atomistic psychology. Although grounded mostly in investigations of thinking and perception, *Gestalttheorie* was conceived as a *Weltanschauung*, an all-encompassing world view. The core of it was a faith that the world is a sensible coherent whole, that reality is organized into meaningful components, and that natural units have their own structures. See GESTALT PSYCHOLOGY.

Gestalt therapy   (F. R. Perls) 1. A therapeutic procedure that uses Gestalt concepts in perceiving human life processes and the attempts by humans to adjust to problems. Emphasis is on the "here and now" and the person in therapy must be made aware of the "what" and "how" of behavior rather than the "why." 2. A form of psychotherapy that focuses on the immediate presence as opposed to the investigation of past experiences and history. Gestalt therapy openly admits to the use of game playing as part of its existential continuum. See GAME(S).

gestation period   The period of intrauterine development from conception to birth. In humans the normal gestation period is about 280 days, 40 weeks, or nine calendar months. See PREGNANCY.

gestural communication   Nonverbal transmission and reception of messages (ideas, feelings, signals) by means of body movements.

gestural language   A system of communication, generally among humans and apes, through conventional visual symbols that consist in movements or position of the hands or other members of the body. Also known as gesture language, sign language.

gestural-postural language   A nonverbal language in which communication is limited to gestures and postures.

gesture   1. A movement or position of the hands or other members of the body used in communicating with other beings. 2. (G. H. Mead) In G. H. Mead's theory of the self, the act of an organism that stimulates a response by others, as a growling dog incites other dogs to growl. In humans, the process relies upon symbols and words, which call up more complex and reflective responses.

getters   (A. Adler) Refers to one of four main types of people according to Alfred Adler: those who depend on others socially. See ADLER'S PERSONALITY TYPES.

getting partner   In sex therapy, the partner who receives the activity (usually a sensate focus exercise) from the giving partner, and is expected to provide verbal feedback or instructions.

geumaphobia   Morbid fear of taste or tasting. Also known as geumatophobia.

GG   goal gradient

GH   growth hormone

GHAA   Group Health Association of America

GHB   See GAMMA-HYDROXYBUTYRATE.

Gheel colony   A group of homes in Gheel, Belgium, in which psychotic patients reside with families. This practice dates from the 13th century and can be traced, in legend at least, to Saint Dymphna, who is said to have dedicated her life to the care of the insane. See FAMILY CARE, SAINT DYMPHNA'S DISEASE.

ghetto   (town square—Italian) 1. Areas in Eastern European cities to which Jews were confined. 2. A disadvantaged inner-urban area, often densely populated by ethnic groups.

ghost   Visual appearance attributed to the presence of a disembodied personality. Also known as apparition. See DISCARNATE, GHOST IMAGES.

ghost fear   See DEMONOPHOBIA, PHASMOPHOBIA.

ghost image   Apparition of a disembodied individual that retains some general bodily characteristics of the living person. Tend to occur in periods of emotional crisis. A ghost image often includes implausible physical factors.

ghost theory   A point of view that religions originated from aboriginal peoples' beliefs in ghosts (disembodied spirits).

G-I   gender identity

giantism   gigantism

gibberish   Incoherent and unintelligible language of a type observed in some schizophrenia patients who use a language that appears to be representative of a primitive mentality.

Gibson effect   (J. J. Gibson) A tendency for vertical lines to appear curved when viewed through a wedge prism. When the prism is removed, the vertical lines appear to be curved in the opposite direction.

Gibson's perception theory   (J. J. Gibson) A point of view that perception is a process of reduction of sensory input, filtering out essential signal phenomena from the abundance of stimulus "noise." See AFFORDANCE, DIRECT REALISM, ECOLOGICAL PERCEPTION, GIBSON EFFECT.

gifted   1. Possessing one or more special talents or abilities of a high order (for example, gifted musicians, painters, and mathematicians). 2. Possessing a high degree of intellectual brightness. See GENIUS.

giftedness   In children, the possession of outstanding intelligence, ability, or creative talent. Frequently calculated as the half-percent of children who score 140 or higher on intelligence quotient (IQ) tests. As a group, the gifted generally receive less attention and fewer special services than children with learning disabilities.

gift relationship   In cultural anthropology, customs regarding gift-giving.

gigantism   An abnormal increase in stature due to hyperactivity of the anterior lobe of the pituitary gland, resulting in an excess of growth hormone. Term sometimes is applied to persons more than 205 cm (6 feet, 9 inches) in height. Also known as giantism. See ACROMEGALY, CEREBRAL GIGANTISM.

GIGO   See GARBAGE IN–GARBAGE OUT.

gigolo   1. A man who provides social or sexual companionship to women for compensation. See PROSTITUTE. 2. By extension, a womanizer. See DON JUANISM.

Gilles de la Tourette's syndrome   A disorder named after Georges Gilles de la Tourette who originally called it coprolalia. It was next called Tourette's Syndrome (TS), and later referred to as Tourette's Disorder or simply, Tourette's. See TOURETTE'S DISORDER/SYNDROME.

Gindler method   (E. Gindler) A procedure intended to help people to get in touch with themselves that includes relaxation exercises, breathing practices, self-massage, and massage by others during group sessions. All these are in the interests of developing proper posture, smooth movements, and good muscle tone, as well as greater self-knowledge.

ginseng (root)   The roots of several species of the Genus *Panax*, reputed, originally in the Orient, to serve as a tonic, stimulant, aphrodisiac.

girdle sensation   A painful sensation like that caused by a tight belt, that occurs in certain diseases such as tabes dorsalis.

girl fear   See PARTHENOPHOBIA.

give-and-take process   Refers to the mutual accommodations between people, as in bargaining or compromising. See INTERPERSONAL ACCOMMODATION.

given(s)   1. Refers to that which is obtained from heredity. 2. The material available to the investigator, upon which generalizations and explanations are based. Also known as data.

given-up complex   (G. Enget) A pattern occurring in depression and bereavement: feelings of helplessness or hopelessness, depreciated self-image, inability to experience gratification from roles and relationships, lack of continuity between past, present, and future, and recurrent memories of previous periods of giving up. Also known as giving up. See GIVE-UP-ITIS.

give-up-itis   Refers to the condition in which a prisoner of war (POW) or patient with a malignant illness loses hope, relinquishes all interest in survival, and eventually dies. See THANATOS.

giving partner   See GETTING PARTNER.

Gjessing's syndrome   (L. R. Gjessing) A disorder of recurring catatonic and manic episodes in patients with schizophrenia, related to levels of nitrogen in the patient's body caused by deficient protein metabolism. Named after Norwegian physician Leiv R. Gjessing (b. 1918).

glabrous   Refers to hairless skin, as on the palms, soles, and eyelids. Also known as glabrate.

gland   (acorn—Latin) An organ that secretes substances needed for some bodily functions or that are to be discharged from the body. Endocrine glands discharge products into the bloodstream; exocrine glands discharge substances (such as tears and sweat) outside the body, or into the gastrointestinal tract (such as insulin). Exocrine glands generally release their products into a duct whereas endocrine glands are ductless. Types of glands include: ADRENAL, APOCRINE, BULBOURETHRAL, ENDOCRINE, EXOCRINE, LACRIMAL, LINGUAL, PINEAL, PITUITARY, SALIVARY, THYROID.

glandular response   A type of response to stimulation, usually mediated by autonomic nerve fibers or chemicals in the blood stream and characterized by increased or decreased activity of one or more glands.

glans   Any small rounded mass of tissue, whether or not erectile. Plural is glandes.

glans clitor(id)is   A small mass of erectile tissue at the distal end of the clitoris.

glans penis   The head of the penis, normally covered with the foreskin prior to and in the absence of circumcision. The urinary meatus is at the distal end.

glare   A quality of intense brightness, due either to a reflection from a glass or metallic surface or to any strong and harsh light that hinders visual acuity (for example, high-beam headlights).

glare sensitivity   Discomfort due to bright light that results in undue interference with vision.

glass ceiling   Metaphor for discriminatory barriers to employees, usually women managers, attaining top-level promotions. A world-wide phenomenon. The concept of glass has been ascribed to the barriers being invisible, their being so subtle as to be transparent, and to the victims' ability to see the rewards and responsibilities of upper management. See GENDER DISCRIMINATION, GLASS ESCALATOR.

Glass Ceiling Commission   A body that counters discrimination, primarily against working women. Created by the U.S. Civil Rights Act of 1991, which entitles women to sue on the basis of discrimination.

glass escalator   The subtle and pervasive form of sex discrimination resulting in men attaining the top positions in female-dominated fields. Barriers to job promotion at all levels, an extension of the "glass ceiling" concept. See GLASS CEILING.

glass fear   See CRYSTALLOPHOBIA, HYALOPHOBIA.

glass sensation   (F. Schumann) A subjective visual effect, according to which transparent solids appear different from empty space, that is, as if filled by a colorless substance.

glia (cells)   neuroglia

glial insufficiency   A lack of neuroglia cells that provide structural support and aid in the excitation and conduction of nerve impulses in the central nervous system. Some glial cells also serve as a provider of nutrients for the neurons, collecting substances from the blood supply or manufacturing some from materials in the blood and storing the nutrients for use as needed by the central nervous system neurons.

glial RNA   A form of ribonucleic acid (RNA) presumed to be associated with short-term memory, on the basis of animal research that indicated that RNA levels increased in areas associated with learning tasks, following training periods.

glide   In linguistics, a sound produced with an articulation like a vowel's but that quickly terminates or moves to another articulation. Types include glottal, palatal, velar.

gliding   In child language acquisition, the replacement of a liquid by a glide, as in "wayd" for "rayd."

gliding time   In industrial psychology, a system that allows flextime employees to choose their work hours without having to ask permission or give advance notice. See FLEXITIME.

gliofibrils   Filaments of about 60 Å diameter that run the length of the processes of glial cells and serve as part of the cytoskeleton.

glioma   A tumor of glia cells. See NEUROGLIA.

glittering generalities   Vague but catchy phrases and slogans frequently used in propaganda and political campaigns to elicit favorable reactions (for example, "good, clean government" or "our noble heritage"). See GARDEN PATH SENTENCE, PROPAGANDA.

global amnesia   A type of memory disorder so severe that the patient is incapable of effective thought processes. The condition is associated with diffuse cerebral lesions.

global aphasia   Impairment or loss of ability to perceive and understand as well as to use language. Also known as sensorimotor aphasia, total aphasia.

global focusing strategy   A procedure for solving a complex problem by establishing a number of theories and testing them in some manner, such as by ratiocination (the process of exact reasoning) until the answer is obtained. Example: Consider all possibilities, discard those that do not belong or fit, and whatever remains is the answer.

global intelligence   (D. Wechsler) Refers to intelligence as measured by tests that contain both verbal and nonverbal material. See BINET-SIMON SCALE.

globalization   1. In industrial psychology, the cohesive network of manufacturing and commerce throughout various parts of the world. 2. In sociology and social psychology, a theory examining the emergence of a global cultural system seen in international athletic competitions, world political bodies, world-wide health problems, global political movements, etc.

global memory models   Explanations about memory processes. See MINERVA 2, SEARCH OF ASSOCIATIVE MEMORY, THEORY OF DISTRIBUTED ASSOCIATIVE MEMORY.

global perception   A perception based on a response to the stimulus perceived as a whole rather than to separate parts of the stimulus.

global rating   A generalized and often ill-defined rating of personality, intelligence, or improvement (such as "improved," or "markedly improved"), as contrasted with more specific ratings based on observations or tests of specific behaviors.

global style   In R. J. Sternberg's theory of mental self-government, a preference for dealing with relatively large and abstract issues coupled with a tendency to ignore or dislike details. See THEORY OF MENTAL SELF-GOVERNMENT.

globus hystericus   A psychosomatic "lump in the throat." A hysterical (conversion) symptom in which a person feels a lump in the throat, sometimes accompanied by choking sensations. Also known as spheresthesia. See ESOPHAGEAL NEUROSIS.

globus pallidus   (K. F. Burdach) The pallidum. One of the two parts (the other being the putamen) of the lentiform nucleus of the brain. The output component of the basal ganglia. See PALEOSTRIATUM.

glomeruli   Complex but spatially restricted synaptic units found within the autonomic ganglia, lateral geniculate nucleus of the thalamus, the cerebellum, and the olfactory bulb.

glossal   Pertaining to or located in the tongue.

glossalgia   glossodynia

glossodynia   A feeling of pain or burning in the tongue, or in the tongue and buccal mucous membranes, without any observable cause. Also known as glossalgia, glossopyrosis.

glossolalia   Speaking in tongues, most commonly found in religious ecstasy, or hypnotic or mediumistic trances. In Christianity, justification for its practice is found in The New Testament (Mark 16:17). An apparently similar phenomenon, the babbling of nonsense material, is occasionally found in schizophrenia. See CONFABULATION, FABULATION, LOGORRHEA, NEOLOGISM, WORD SALAD.

glossopharyngeal nerve　　(G. Fallopius) Cranial nerve IX. This cranial nerve serves the pharynx, soft palate, and posterior third of the tongue including the taste buds of that portion. It is responsible for the swallowing reflex, stimulation of parotid-gland secretions, and reflex control of the heart through innervation of the carotid sinus.

glossophobia　　Excessive fear of speaking. See LALIO-PHOBIA, LALOPHOBIA, PHONOPHOBIA.

glossosynthesis　　The creation of nonsense words.

glottis　　The vocal portion of the larynx. Plural is glottides.

glove anesthesia　　A hypnotic effect or conversion disorder in which there is a functional loss of sensitivity in the hand and part of the forearm, or areas that would be covered by a glove. Phrases "shoe anesthesia" and "stocking anesthesia" are applied to similar effects experienced in the foot or leg.

glow　　A mode of appearance characteristically seen in self-luminous bodies (for example, the appearance of an incandescent lamp filament or a flame).

Glu　　See GLUTAMIC ACID.

glucagon　　A hormone secreted by the alpha cells of the islets of Langerhans that activates the muscles and liver to release stored blood sugar into the blood supply. By increasing blood sugar (glucose) its action is opposed by insulin, thereby operating with insulin to provide a balanced blood-sugar level. When blood sugar falls, glucagon secretion increases whereas insulin decreases.

glucocorticoids　　1. Steroid-like compounds that influence metabolism. 2. A set of adrenal hormones that have an important role in stress situations in providing energy to the body.

glucoreceptors　　Special cells in the hypothalamus that react to the rate at which glucose passes through them.

glucose　　A sugar found in the blood that provides energy for body functions and the only nutrient of the central nervous system.

glucostatic theory　　1. A point of view relating to the stabilizing of blood sugar in the hypothalamic regulatory mechanism. 2. A centralist position, maintaining that the homeostatic balance in the brain, arteries, and veins primarily provides the signals to the hypothalamus for the starting and ending of feedings; that is, animals eat because of a low rate of glucose utilization and stop eating because of a high rate. Compare LIPOSTATIC THEORY, THERMOSTATIC THEORY.

Glueck prediction table　　(E. Glueck & S. Glueck) Based on histories of delinquents, a method of making predictions about the likelihood of any person or any group becoming delinquent (for example, males from low income areas are more likely to become delinquent than females from middle class neighborhoods.)

glue-sniffing　　A dangerous practice engaged in primarily by adolescents, leading to addiction to toluene obtained by inhaling model airplane cement. Effects include erratic behavior and stupor. A related juvenile addiction is sniffing paints. Also called huffing. See INHALANT ABUSE.

glutamate　　A salt or ester of glutamic acid that acts as a neurotransmitter, generally an excitatory one. Common in the mammalian brain. See GLUTAMIC ACID.

glutamate hypothesis (of schizophrenia)　　A postulate that schizophrenia is caused by deficient activity at some glutamate synapses.

glutamic acid (Glu)　　An amino acid regarded as essential in diets and important for normal brain function. It is converted by pyridoxine, or vitamin B6, into gamma-amino-butyric-acid (GABA). Has been studied to determine if its administration might increase brain-cell function, thereby enhancing learning ability and intelligence. Results have been inconclusive. Also known as glutamine. See GAMMA-AMINO-BUTYRIC ACID.

glutethimide　　Generic name for a substance used as a hypnotic, sedative, and depressant. Trade name is Doriden. See PIPERIDINEDIONES.

Gly　　See GLYCINE.

glycine (Gly)　　(J. J. Berzelius) The simplest amino acid in proteins, used as a dietary supplement or nutrient. See SYNAPTIC TRANSMISSION.

glycogen　　(C. Bernard) A polysaccharide found throughout the body but mostly stored in the liver and muscles that is readily converted into glucose (blood sugar) for energy needs. Also known as animal dextran, animal starch, hepatin, liver starch, zoamylin.

GM　　guessed mean

gnostic function/sensation　　The process of discriminating light touch sensations that stimulate the cutaneous receptors. Also known as epicritic sensibility. See PHOTOPATHIC SYSTEM.

gnothi seauton　　(know thyself—Greek) A maxim on the walls of Apollo's temple at Delphi, attributed to various Greek philosophers, mainly Socrates, but more appropriately attributed to Thales.

G.O.　　See GOAL-ORIENTATION.

goal (G)　　The objective or end result toward which an organism strives. Types of goals include: LATENT, LIFE, MANIFEST, SEXUAL, SUB-, SUPERORDINATE, TRANSCENDENT.

goal-attaining response (*Rg*)　　(C. L. Hull) **goal consummatory response**

goal-attainment model　　In evaluation research, a process that focuses on the achievement of a particular time-limited goal and measures the degree to which a program has achieved its objectives.

goal-directed behavior　　Action that appears to be related to an organism's efforts to reach a specific attainment.

goal gradient (*GG*)　　(C. L. Hull) The principle that an organism makes greater efforts the closer it gets to its goal (for example, a mouse is attached to a leash which in turn is attached to an ergometer; the pull of the mouse on the leash increases as the mouse gets closer to the goal, usually food.) Sometimes known as gradient of reinforcement. See HULL'S THEORY.

goal gradient　　The closer the mouse gets to the food, the more strongly it will pull on the rope to get to the food.

goal-limited therapy   Brief or short-term psychotherapy in which the objective is to treat specific emotional problems and maladjustments in cases in which a long-range approach is considered unnecessary, undesirable, or impractical. The focus is usually on the modification of behavior and the removal of symptoms. Also known as goal-limited adjustment therapy. See SECTOR THERAPY, SHORT-TERM THERAPY.

goal model of evaluation   In evaluation research, a system of assessing organizational effectiveness in terms of meeting public goals or expectations rather than assessing the private goals of the organization.

goal orientation (G.O.)   1. A tendency of organisms to aim at their goals. 2. Descriptive of humans who operate frequently in terms of long-distance goals, in that they think and operate to achieve these goals.

goal response (r_G)   (C. L. Hull) In instrumental conditioning a response directed to achieving a goal. See HULL'S THEORY.

goal-setting   The process of establishing specific future objectives or end-results that provide (a) a basis for motivation, (b) an estimation of the amount of effort to expend, and (c) guidelines or cues to determine if one is moving toward the desired end-result. Such a process is effective only if the person is aware of what is to be accomplished and what has to be done to achieve the objective.

goal stimulus (S_G)   (C. L. Hull) An object or event acting as the goal. See HULL'S THEORY.

go-around   1. (H. Mosak) A technique used in certain therapy groups in which the leader or therapist asks that each member of the group participate in sequence. See BEHIND-THE BACK TECHNIQUE, GROUP THERAPY. 2. A balk at one aspect of a procedure, and a re-approach. Most commonly applied to aircraft landings, as part of training or because of a problem.

goblet figure   Rubin('s) Figure

GOCL-II   Gordon Occupational Check List II

God   The prime deity believed in, often devoutly, in Christianity, Islam, Judaism, and other religions. Concepts of God permeated philosophy, the forerunner of psychology.

God complex   (E. Jones) An attitude of some psychotherapists that they can accomplish more than is humanly possible, that their word should be accepted as the final truth, or that they are the best in their field; a kind of benign paranoia, but possibly necessary for some therapists to be effective. See MOTHER SUPERIOR COMPLEX.

Gödel's Proof   (K. Gödel) "All consistent axiomatic formulations of number theory include undecidable propositions." This means that all mathematics is based on a set of axioms; some mathematical truths cannot be derived from these axioms, and the set of axioms is therefore incomplete. Gödel's proof has a bearing not only on formal logic and mathematics but also on psychology and artificial intelligence. For example, computers must be programmed but there is only a finite number of programs. Humans, however, are capable of an unlimited variety of behaviors. It follows that any set of existing computer programs will be incomplete, and, hence it will be impossible to construct a machine that will behave like a human.

God's flesh   teonanacatal

Goethe-Hering opponent-process theory   See HERING THEORY (OF COLOR VISION).

Golden Rule   The philosophic-moral maxim "Do unto others as you would want them to do unto you." The basis of many religions and ethical systems, found in different words in early Chinese, Jewish, and Christian writings. See EQUITY, RECIPROCITY.

golden section   The most pleasing division of a line or an area into two parts, x and y, proportioned so that x is to y as y is to either the whole line or the entire area.

Goldstein-Scheerer Tests   (K. Goldstein & M. Scheerer) A group of tests that require copying color designs, sorting objects into categories (color, form, material), and reproducing designs from memory with sticks. Assess ability to abstract and form concepts, and are often used in diagnosing brain damage. See WEIGL-GOLDSTEIN-SCHEERER TEST.

Goldstein's theory   The following are important in understanding Kurt Goldstein's theory: ABSTRACT ATTITUDE, ABSTRACT BEHAVIOR, CATASTROPHIC BEHAVIOR, CATASTROPHIC REACTION, CENTERING, CENTRAL APHASIA, CONCRETE BEHAVIOR, EQUALIZATION OF EXCITATION, GOLDSTEIN-SCHEERER TESTS, HOLISTIC THEORIES, NEAR EFFECT, ORGANISMIC PERSONALITY THEORY I, WEIGL-GOLDSTEIN-SCHEERER TEST.

golem   (embryo, shapelessness—Hebrew) In Jewish legend, a man supernaturally created from a clay figure through cabalistic rites; by extension, robot, automaton, monster.

Golgi apparatus   (C. Golgi) A network of threadlike substances in a nerve cell.

Golgi corpuscles   (C. Golgi) Receptors in muscle tendons with relatively high firing thresholds compared to muscle spindles. Increased tension on the tendon, usually caused by muscle contraction, increasing firing rate of the Golgi tendon organ sensory afferents and inhibition (via an interneuron) of the alpha motor neuron supplying the muscle of the stretched tendon. Also known as Golgi tendon organs.

Golgi-Mazzoni corpuscles   (C. Golgi & V. Mazzoni) A type of encapsulated nerve ending found in the skin.

Golgi reflex   (C. Golgi) A simple polysynaptic reflex. The origin is in a tendon. Increased pressure on the tendon is the stimulus for activity that ends in an interneuron that slows down action in the efferent axon.

Golgi tendon organ   (C. Golgi) A type of nerve ending found near the point of attachment of tendon and muscle.

Golgi Type I neuron   A neuron that extends its axon out of the region of the central nervous system in which its cell body resides. Examples are the pyramidal neurons of the neocortex and the Purkinje cells of the cerebellum. Also known as principal neuron, projection neuron, relay neuron.

Golgi Type II neuron   A neuron, the axon of which stays in the vicinity of the cell body. Stellate cells of the neocortex are examples. Also known as interneuron, local circuit neuron.

Gompertz curve   (B. Gompertz) A formula intended to indicate the number of people likely to be living at various ages, based on a number of constants, later used for a variety of related purposes.

Gompertz hypothesis (B. Gompertz) A postulate that the probability of mortality increases in a geometrical progression as function of length of time one has lived.

gonad 1. The primary organ of reproduction, in the female the ovary and in the male the testis, both of which produce gametes (the testes make spermatozoa, the ovaries produce ova) and appropriate sex hormones. 2. The undifferentiated embryonic gland that develops into an ovary or testis.

gonadal cycle The ebb and flow of sexual behavior. Kinds of gonadal cycles include life, seasonal, and estrous, each of which is related in turn to the activity of certain sex hormones.

gonadal hormones The primary male and female sex hormones, including the androgens and estrogens, which generally require the presence of other hormones to perform effectively.

gonadocentric In psychoanalytic theory, a stage of psychosexual development, normally reached at puberty, in which the libido becomes focused on the genitals. See MASTURBATION.

gonadopause Reduction or cessation of sexual activity associated with aging.

gonadostat theory A hypothetical mechanism in which ovarian or testicular hormones regulate hypothalamic and pituitary secretions.

gonadotropic 1. Describing the actions of a gonadotropin. 2. Promoting growth or function of the gonads. See GONADOTROPIN. Also spelled gonadotrophic.

gonadotropin A hormone that can promote gonadal growth and function. Secreted by the anterior pituitary gland to promote the activity of the gonads. Examples include follicle-stimulating hormone (FSH), luteinizing hormone (LH). Also known as gonadotrophic hormone (GTH), gonadotrophin.

goniometer An instrument for measuring angles. In psychology, a device that measures the degree of sway of person while standing upright.

go no-go test A form of delayed-alternation test, used mainly in animal research, in which the subject is trained to respond to cues or signals that are the equivalent of "go" and "no-go" or "stay."

gonosome A sex chromosome. In humans, the X or Y chromosome. See SEX CHROMOSOME.

good-and-evil test A variation of the right-and-wrong examination employed in criminal-responsibility evaluations to determine whether the person accused was cognizant of the differences between morally right and wrong behaviors. See M'NAGHTEN RULES.

good-boy-nice-girl orientation/stage (L. Kohlberg) An earlier stage (stage 3) of Lawrence Kohlberg's conventional level of moral reasoning. At this stage, the idea of motive and underlying intention emerge, and moral behavior is that which wins approval. Also known as good-boy-good-girl stage, interpersonal concordance. See CONVENTIONAL LEVEL.

good breast (M. Klein) In Melanie Klein's variation of psychoanalytic theory, the concept of the introjection of a part of the mother's breasts seen as a good object by babies during the first year of life. Compare BAD BREAST.

good continuation In Gestalt theory, the tendency of a line to maintain its direction even when interrupted. An example may be seen in the bottom horizontal line of the illustration of hidden figures that forms a fish and maintains its continuity although crossing a number of other lines. See LAW OF PRÄGNANZ.

good-cop/bad-cop approach Mutt and Jeff approach

Goodenough Draw-a-Man Test See DRAW-A-MAN TEST, GOODENOUGH-HARRIS DRAWING TEST.

Goodenough-Harris Drawing Test (F. L. Goodenough & D. B. Harris) An elaboration by Dale B. Harris of the Goodenough Draw-A-Man Test in which the participant is required to draw a picture of a man, a woman, and him- or herself. An estimate of intelligence is made on the basis of 73 items such as individual body parts, clothing details, proportion, and perspective. See INTELLIGENCE TESTS, NONVERBAL INTELLIGENCE TESTS.

good faith bargaining In labor relations, an elusive concept meaning that both sides make an honest, effortful, meaningful attempt at reaching a negotiated settlement. For instance, if one side makes an offer and the other responds only with "No," that could comprise bad faith bargaining, which is impermissible in some jurisdictions.

good Gestalt 1. A configuration that appears complete, orderly, or clear, such as a triangle or a circle. 2. A pattern or system logically arranged, such as a coherent, consistent series of ideas (for example, the Declaration of Independence.) See GOODNESS OF CONFIGURATION, LAW OF PRÄGNANZ.

good-me (H. S. Sullivan) The personification of behavior and impulses that meet with parental approval. The good-me develops as a part of the socialization process, and serves to protect children from anxiety about themselves. See PERSONIFIED SELF.

good-me self (H. S. Sullivan) The self-awareness of being worthwhile and consequently acceptable to the self.

goodness of configuration Qualities of shapes or forms that emphasize simplicity, regularity, symmetry, and continuity. Wolfgang Köhler speculated that the mind tends to perceive more goodness of configuration than may actually exist in a shape. See CLOSURE, GESTALT, LAW OF PRÄGNANZ.

goodness of fit The accuracy with which a set of predictions based on theory matches the corresponding observed values. See CHI-SQUARE, FITNESS (meaning 2).

good object Phrase used by Melanie Klein to identify the introjected object that supports the ego in its binding of the death instinct by libido during early infant life. Compare BAD OBJECT.

good patient A cooperative, noncomplaining patient.

good-patient role Behavior of a sick person who conforms to doctors' and nurses' expectations. Even newborn infants are labeled as good and bad patients in terms of the amount of trouble they cause their caretakers. See BAD-BABIES.

good structures Gestalten that tend to remain stable, vivid and distinct, as opposed to structures characterized by confusion and instability. See GROUPING.

goose pimples   Common name for piloerection.

Gordon Holmes rebound phenomenon   See RE-BOUND PHENOMENON (OF GORDON HOLMES).

Gordon Occupational Check List II (GOCL-II) (L. V. Gordon) A checklist of 240 descriptions of activities related to occupations that do not require a college degree. Used in identifying the career interests of noncollege-bound individuals grade 8 through adult in six categories: business, outdoor, arts, mechanical technology, industrial technology, and service. See INTEREST TESTS.

Gordon-Overstreet syndrome   A form of Turner syndrome with partial virilization. See TURNER SYNDROME, X-O SYNDROME.

Gordon Personal Profile Inventory (L. V. Gordon) An inventory intended to measure eight aspects of personality (ascendancy, responsibility, emotional stability, sociability, cautiousness, original thinking, personal relations, vigor). A combination of the Gordon Personal Profile and the Gordon Personal Inventory.

Gordon reflex/sign   (A. Gordon) 1. A variation of the Babinski reflex/sign: as the calf muscle is compressed, the big toe or all toes extend, seen in patients with lesions of the pyramidal tract. Also known as Gordon leg sign. 2. As the forearm muscle is compressed, the thumb and index finger or all fingers flex, seen in patients with damage to the pyramidal tract. Also known as Gordon's finger sign. Named after American neurologist Alfred Gordon (1874–1953).

gossip   Chatty talk, usually between equals; spreading of rumor. See INFORMAL COMMUNICATION.

gossypol   A cotton-seed extract that suppresses spermatogenesis. Used in China as an oral male contraceptive.

Gottschaldt figures   (K. Gottschaldt) Simple geometric figures concealed in complex figures for the purpose of testing form perception. See EMBEDDED FIGURES TEST.

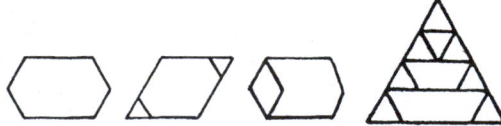

Gottschaldt figures   Which one of the first three figures will fit into the fourth?

Gp   group

GPA   See GRADE POINTS.

GPS   general problem solver

G-R   gender role

Graafian follicle   A pouchlike cavity in an ovary in which an ovum develops and matures. At ovulation, one of the follicles ruptures and releases a mature ovum, which travels into a Fallopian tube to be fertilized. Named after Dutch physiologist and histologist Reijnier de Graaf (1641–1673).

graceful degradation   Describing cognitive systems that remain relatively efficient up to a certain point under some adverse condition induced either by processing overloads or by impoverishment of incoming stimuli.

gracile nucleus   A slender nucleus along the dorsal aspect of the medulla which, with the cuneate nucleus, contains synapses between first- and second-order neurons. Both gracile and cuneate nuclei are involved in relaying proprioceptive impulses destined for the thalamus.

gradation changes   Refers to making changes by tiny and even imperceptible units.

grade   The position of a given person, organism, or datum of any sort in a series or scale in which values determined on the basis of some character or group of characters or items, are assigned to all the individuals included in the series.

graded activities   1. Behaviors that have been put in some kind of sequence (for example, in gymnastics, a list of activities on parallel bars, ranging from simple to difficult). 2. A system of grading handicrafts and other occupational-therapy activities according to increments of mental or physical skills.

graded approach   A series of small movements in searching for the limen in any perceptual study.

graded potential(s)   1. Neural potential that is not self-propagating as is the action potential, but that decays in amplitude with distance from its origin and with time. Kinds of graded potentials include receptor or generator potentials, postsynaptic potentials, and subthreshold potentials. 2. Action potentials with continuously varying magnitude that occur in local neurons that interact only with neurons in their own vicinity. Thus, they do not respond in an all-or-none fashion in which the action potential has only one magnitude transmitted the length of the axon without diminishing.

graded-task assignment   Dealing with behavioral changes by starting with a simple task and moving step by step to problems of greater complexity and difficulty.

grade equivalent   A test score expressed in terms of a grade norm; for example, if a third-grader's score of 47 is equivalent to fifth-grade norms, a score of 47 is expressed as grade 5 functioning for that child. See GRADE NORM.

grade inflation   The upward movement of average grades, often attributed to lowered standards related to (a) students' feelings of entitlement that intimidate teachers, and (b) teachers' concerns about student self-esteem, and sympathy for students' lack of readiness and sociocultural disadvantages.

grade norm   The standard score or range of scores that represent the average achievement level of a particular school grade; for example, the mean achievement of a test of history by all fifth-graders in Wisconsin might be taken to constitute a fifth-grade norm. See GRADE EQUIVALENT.

grade points   Conversion of school grades to points. Usually, A = 4, A− and B+ = 3.5, B = 3, B− and C+ = 2.5, C = 2, C− and D+ = 1.5, D = 1. School grades are obtained and assigned in various ways, such as from the subjective ratings of teachers, from test results of tests the teachers have devised, and rarely from well-established objective tests. In some schools, grade points overall are averaged for the student's career in decimals (a grade point average or GPA), so that a total grade point such as 3.28 can be obtained and these in turn might be translated into academic deciles. See GRADES, ETA COEFFICIENT.

grade scale   A standardized scale with scores expressed in terms of grade norms. Consequently, on a test of 140 items, a score of 57 correct may be equivalent to third grade; 64 correct, fourth grade; and 72 correct, fifth grade. See GRADE EQUIVALENT.

grade-skipping   The promoting of a student from a particular grade to another grade, such as from the fourth grade to the sixth grade, passing over the fifth grade. It is based on the argument that the student already knows the material to be learned in the grade that has been omitted. See EDUCATIONAL ACCELERATION.

gradient   In the psychology of motivation, a graduated change in the strength of drives in situations of conflict and ambivalence, that is, the degree to which a person feels pulled in different directions. See APPROACH GRADIENT, AVOIDANCE GRADIENT for examples. Types of gradient include: ANTERIOR-POSTERIOR (DEVELOPMENT), AXIAL, DELAY-OF-REWARD, EXCITATION, GENERALIZATION, GOAL, MUSCLE-TENSION, PHYSIOLOGICAL, PRESSURE, REINFORCEMENT, RESPONSE GENERALIZATION, STIMULUS, STIMULUS-GENERALIZATION, TEXTURE.

gradient of avoidance   The changing strength of the tendency to avoid a negative incentive, dependent upon distance from the unpleasant event, among other factors. The closer an organism is to a perceived danger, the stronger will be its efforts to escape. See GOAL GRADIENT.

gradient of color   A monocular depth cue involving color, for example, in watching a field of corn, the corn rows in the distance tend to appear grayer than identical colored corn nearby, thus informing the brain as to which corn is growing further away and which corn is closer to the viewer. See GRADIENT OF TEXTURE.

gradient of effect   The principle that S-R (stimulus-response) sequences closely preceding reinforcement are more likely to occur than remote ones.

gradient of generalization   The greater a test stimulus is different from the original one, the less the tendency to make the original response; often plotted as a curve.

gradient of reinforcement   1. The generalization that the closer a response is to the reinforcement, the stronger it will be. 2. In conditioning experiments, there are two primary time gradients to consider: (a) those based on time elapsed between the conditioned stimulus (found mainly in classical conditioning), and (b) those based on time elapsed between the response to be strengthened and the reinforcement (found principally in instrumental conditioning). Sometimes known as goal gradient.

gradient of response generalization   See RESPONSE GENERALIZATION GRADIENT.

gradient of stimulus generalization   An organism that has been conditioned to respond to a particular stimulus is likely to respond to similar stimuli, and the more similar the other stimuli are to the original one, the more likely the organism is to respond. See RESPONSE GENERALIZATION GRADIENT.

gradient of texture   The observation that textures and surface grains of objects appear progressively finer as the viewer moves away from them. Compare DISTANCE CUES.

grading in education   The rating of a student by a letter or a number. Because teachers use different grading criteria, grades may not be uniformly meaningful or an indication of how much a student has learned (one teacher may grade for effort, another for cooperation, another to indicate improvement). Consequently, intelligent children may receive poor grades because they are disruptive; children of lesser intelligence may receive good grades because of their effort. Number grades, as opposed to letter grades, tend to be based more on objective test scores than on teachers' subjective judgments. See GRADE POINTS.

Graduated and Reciprocated Initiatives in Tension Reduction (GRIT strategy)   (C. Osgood) In group dynamics, a ten-step program for reducing intergroup conflict by increasing trust and cooperation. A suggested process for reducing international tensions through unilateral de-weaponizing.

graduate dissertation/thesis   A demonstration of scholarly maturity required by most schools that offer graduate degrees. Usually termed a thesis at the M.A. level and a dissertation for the Ph.D.

Graduate Record Examination (GRE)   An aptitude-achievement test of verbal and mathematical ability used to select candidates for graduate schools. Includes an Aptitude Test and an Advanced Test in various specializations, including psychology. Results are reported as a single standard score with a mean of 500 and an SD of 100. Available in versions for the visually challenged.

graduate theses procedures   Generally, a student submits a research proposal to test a theory-based hypothesis with a plan detailing the variables to be manipulated, the instruments to be used, measurement techniques, individuals to be studied, etc. Upon approval, the student further reviews the relevant academic literature, then begins the research under supervision. See GRADUATE DISSERTATION/THESIS.

Graefenberg spot (G-spot)   An erotically sensitive area presumably located in the anterior wall of the vagina, the stimulation of which is supposedly a contributor toward female ejaculation. Named for German gynecologist Ernst Graefenberg (1881–1957), who wrote of the spot originally reported by Reijnier de Graaf in the 1600s.

gram (g)   A unit of weight, originally equal to one cubic centimeter of water at 4 degrees centigrade, later 1/1000 of a metal cylinder located in France.

grammar   The distinctive features and structural principles of a language, involving the construction of words (morphology) and sentences (syntax). See LINGUISTICS, TRANSFORMATIONAL GRAMMAR.

grammar translation (method)   A procedure for teaching a second language, emphasizing reading, writing, translation, and the learning of grammatical rules. Objective is literary mastery of the language.

grammatical structure   See DEEP STRUCTURE, SURFACE STRUCTURE.

grammatical word   A word such as a preposition or article that conveys little meaning of a sentence but structures its grammar.

gramophone symptom A disorder seen in Pick's disease, in which the patient tells an elaborate anecdote with precise expression and diction from start to finish, ignoring attempts to interrupt the story. After completing the anecdote, the patient may repeat it exactly, as if it had never been told before.

grande crise (great crisis—French) An apparently convulsive seizure experienced by Franz Anton Mesmer's patients, which he thought to be a major factor in his "animal magnetism" therapy. Similar to Mesmeric crisis.

grande hystérie French phrase for hysteroepilepsy.

grandeur See DELUSIONS OF GRANDEUR.

grandfather complex The desire of small children to become their parents's parent.

grandiose delusions/ideas See DELUSIONS OF GRANDEUR.

grandiose expansiveness A delusional feeling of vast power, importance, or wealth, accompanied by a state of euphoria. See DELUSIONS OF GRANDEUR.

grandiosity An extreme, totally unrealistic feeling of greatness, importance, or ability, apparently stemming from feelings of inferiority, insecurity, or guilt. See DELUSIONS OF GRANDEUR.

grand mal A major epileptic seizure pattern consisting of a generalized convulsion with tonic and clonic phases, sudden loss of consciousness, often with frothing at the mouth and urinary incontinence, followed often by a period of confusion, and deep sleep. Also known as major epilepsy, tonic-clonic epilepsy. See AURA, EPILEPSY, PETIT MAL, STATUS EPILEPTICUS.

grand mean The average of a group of averages.

grandmother cells Feature-detector cells in the visual cortex stimulated by only certain objects in the visual field, such as a moving insect or the outline of a hand. The grandmother cells refer to hypothetical cells that would be stimulated only by the features of a person's grandmother.

grand theory (W. W. Mills) The form of highly abstract theorizing in which the formal organization and arrangement of concepts take priority over understanding the social world.

Granit theory of color vision (R. Granit) A point of view that chromatic vision depends upon a modulator that mediates the dominant receptor for brightness. See DOMINATOR-MODULATOR THEORY (OF COLOR VISION).

granular cortex Portions of the cerebral cortex dominated by the presence of granule (stellate) cells. In granular cortex the granule cells occur not only in layers II and IV, which are very much expanded, but in other layers, especially layer III. There is a corresponding reduction in pyramidal cells. The sensory areas of the cortex, such as the calcarine cortex (primary visual cortex) are the most granular.

granular layers Layers II and IV of the neocortex.

granular pressure A specific pressure quality that results from moderately intense blunt stimulation of the skin.

grapevine Informal communications, sometimes through secret channels. Used in organizations such as prisons where open communication is difficult or not allowed. See GOSSIP, INFORMAL COMMUNICATIONS.

graph A means of illustrating the relationship between two or more variables. Generally, the independent variable is plotted on the x-axis (abscissa), and the dependent variable on the y-axis (ordinate) with values increasing as they move from a point of intersection.

graphanesthesia Tactual inability to recognize figures written on the skin, found in some organic brain diseases. Compare GRAPHESTHESIA.

grapheme 1. A basic structural unit of written speech. 2. A letter or combination of letters that represents one sound (for example, the g or the ph [f sound] in "grapheme"). 3. A minimum distinctive unit of meaning in a writing system. See CORRESPONDENCE, MORPHEME, PHONEME, PHONEME-GRAPHEME.

graphesthesia The ability to recognize figures written on the skin; the inability to do so is called graphanesthesia.

graphic alignment The degree of deviation from a straight vertical line in writing. It is claimed by some graphologists that the degree of variation from the vertical has significance in diagnosing people through their handwriting.

graphic-arts therapy The use of drawing, writing, painting, or printmaking as a therapeutic tool in the treatment of disturbed children and adults. See ART, CREATIVE ARTS THERAPIES, THERAPY.

graphic individuality A pattern or combination of many specific writing characteristics, which by its uniqueness furnishes the basis for handwriting identification.

graphic language 1. Communication or permanent recording of ideas by means of symbols perceived by the visual sense. 2. Coarse, profane, or sexually explicit language.

graphic method A technique of recording responses by means of some device that registers the response or successive responses on a moving sheet of paper or other material.

graphic rating scale A graph in the form of a line with gradations used to chart degrees of traits or characteristics of subjects.

graphic size The height of letters in handwritten words, thought by some graphologists to have diagnostic value.

graphic variability 1. The range of variation in the handwriting characteristic of any individual person (intra-individual variability). 2. The range of variation in handwriting characteristics within groups (inter-individual variability).

graphodyne A mechanism that transmits handwriting pressure to a recording device.

graphokinesthetic sensations Feelings in the fingers, hands, and arms while writing. In some cases, people report feeling that these parts have a "life of their own."

graphological elements The phases of handwriting upon which graphologists largely rely for their characterological analyses. These include graphic dimensions, slant, alignment, line quality and pressure, continuity, proportions, and spacing.

graphological portrait The interpretation of graphic signs in their relation to one another and to the totality that comprises them.

graphology   The analysis of the physical characteristics and patterns of handwriting as a means of identifying the writer, indicating psychological states at the time of writing, or evaluating personality characteristics. The value of this method depends on the examiner and not on the procedure. Also known as handwriting analysis.

graphomania   A pathological, inordinate impulse to write (for example, the tendency of some paranoid patients to write letter after letter to the authorities or to the press as an expression of their persecutory or grandiose delusions).

graphometry   A projective test in which a participant draws a figure blindfolded, then describes the drawing while blindfolded and without the blindfold.

graphomotor technique   A projective method in which a participant makes a free drawing while blindfolded, after which the clinician attempts to interpret the drawing.

graphopathology   1. Changes in handwriting as a result of mental or physical disorder. 2. The interpretation of personality disorders from an analysis of handwriting. See GRAPHOLOGY.

graphophobia   Morbid fear of writing.

graphorrh(o)ea   The writing of long lists of meaningless words, a trait of certain patients (among them, manics) who also may have similar speech habits. See LOGORRHEA.

graphospasm   writer's cramp (meaning 1)

graph theory   A branch of mathematics that represents relations and networks, using theorems and algorithms used to obtain information. Applied to sociometric analyses. See SOCIOMETRY.

grasp(ing) reflex   An involuntary reaction in which the person automatically grasps whatever touches the palm. In infants this reaction is normal; later, it may be a sign of frontal-lobe lesion. The grasp reflex is observed mainly in infant humans and monkeys before the cerebral cortex has matured. A similar response occurs when the sole is stimulated. Also known as grasping and groping reflex.

Grassi Block Substitution Test   (J. R. Grassi) A 1953 variant of the Kohs test, designed to detect brain damage. See KOHS BLOCK DESIGN TEST.

gratification   The satisfaction of a need or desire, or the pleasant state following such satisfaction. See DELAY OF GRATIFICATION.

Graves Design Judgment Test   (M. Graves) An artistic aptitude examination designed to evaluate a participant's concepts of unity, dominance, variety, balance, continuity, symmetry, proportion, and rhythm.

graviceptor   Bodily detectors of gravity or "G" forces, some of which are likely located in the trunk, limbs, skin, and vestibular apparatus.

gravida   A pregnant woman. In medical terminology, gravida I designates a woman in her first pregnancy, gravida II in her second pregnancy, etc.). See PRIMIPAROUS.

gravidity   The number of pregnancies.

gravity   1. (**g** or **G**) The attraction toward the earth that causes a mass to exert downward force or have weight. 2. An enduring disposition, marked by dignity or seriousness. 3. A transient posture or attitude marked by dignity or seriousness.

gray   Visual sensation of a color that possesses zero saturation and (hence) no hue. Also known as achromatic color, grey.

gray commissure   The gray matter surrounding the central canal of the spinal cord connecting the gray matter of the two sides of the cord.

gray market   An unauthorized source of drugs, particularly of controlled substances. It sometimes is identified as an informal source to differentiate it from an illegal, or black-market, source.

gray matter   1. Cell bodies of neural tissue. Gray matter occurs in masses of cell bodies in the spinal cord, the cerebral cortex, and subcortical nuclei. 2. Those parts of the brain and spinal cord composed primarily of the cell bodies of neurons, in contrast with those areas composed primarily of myelinated axons of neurons, which by contrast appear nearly white. Also known as grey matter. See WHITE MATTER.

Gray Oral Reading Tests   (W. S. Gray) Originally developed by William S. Gray (1885–1960) and subsequently revised several times, the tests attempt to assess oral reading speed, comprehension, and accuracy of pronunciation, and to identify various defects such as word-for-word reading. Tests consist of a graded set of standardized passages that are administered individually to pupils in grades 1 to 12.

gray out (syndrome)   1. Loss of peripheral vision due to positive G forces. 2. Partial loss of consciousness due to anoxemia (deficiency of oxygen in the blood). May occur in mountain-climbing or in pilots flying in high-altitudes without supplementary oxygen. Symptoms include a dulling of sensory, motor, and mental capacities, and impairment in judgment, memory, and time sense. 3. Light-headedness and instability on standing, due to orthostatic hypertension.

gray ramus   A collection of unmyelinated axonal fibers of the autonomic system. The gray rami originate in the sympathetic trunk and enter each spinal nerve to supply the blood vessels, arrector pili muscles, and glands of the body wall.

Graz school of psychology   The Austrian school of (act) psychology.

GRE   Graduate Record Examination

great imitator   1. Former term for syphilis, whose symptoms, considered separately, could suggest other infections. 2. Phrase is also applied to chlamydia, which can be taken for gonorrhea. See SEXUALLY-TRANSMITTED DISEASE.

great man theory (of leadership/of history)   great person theory

Great Mother   English phrase for *Magna Mater*.

great person theory   A point of view that historical progress or leadership is determined by "great persons," typically those who intervene with commanding positions of influence, power, and authority. Contrasts with the idea that events are more determined by economics, technological development, a broad spectrum of social influences, and the *Zeitgeist*. Also known as great man theory (of leadership/of history).

Greco-Latin square design   A research design in which a composite square obtained by combining two orthogonal Latin squares is used to balance the levels of two factors over the levels of other factors.

A α	B β	C γ
C β	A γ	B α
B γ	C α	A β

Greco-Latin square design

Greek love   Rare name for male homosexuality.

Greenspoon effect   (J. Greenspoon) A tendency of speakers to use certain words with greater frequency if listeners appear to give approval to these words, such as by nodding, smiling, or making sounds indicating acceptance of the words.

green revolution   1. The use of advanced technology in Third World agriculture. 2. Public concern with environmental preservation.

greeting behavior   Attachment behavior of babies to their caregiver that begins to manifest itself clearly at about six months of age, with babies showing delight at the sight of their caregiver, usually the mother.

gregariousness   A tendency, manifested within certain species, to congregate or to live in groups. For humans, the drive is probably not instinctual but develops slowly out of the child's helplessness and dependence; gregariousness gives children security, companionship, acceptance, and a sense of belonging. See AFFILIATIVE DRIVE, SOCIAL INSTINCT.

Gregory's cognitive styles   Patterns of perceiving, thinking, learning, and problem-solving that result from various combinations of the concrete-versus-abstract and sequential-versus-random dimensions.

Greig syndrome   (D. M. Greig) Ocular hypertelorism (abnormal distance between the eyes) associated with mental retardation. Also known as ocular hypertelorism. Named after Scottish physician David M. Greig (1864–1936).

grey   gray

grey matter   Phrase used to mean basic intelligence. See GRAY MATTER.

GRID   Gay-Related Immune Deficiency

grid organizational development (grid OD)   A formal, seven-stage, long-term process for managers throughout an organization to adopt an ideal style. A variant of the Blake-Mouton managerial grid.

grief   A distressing state of sadness in response to a significant loss, usually of a cherished person. Includes a period of mourning in which the bereaved individual may weep, sigh, and become preoccupied with thoughts of the deceased. Where neurotic tendencies or feelings of guilt are minimal or nonexistent, this period is self-limiting for most people. See MOURNING, PATHOLOGICAL GRIEF REACTION.

grievance   1. Generally, a complaint. 2. In labor relations, a formal, written accusation (usually by the designated representative of the employee union against management) of an infraction of the union contract or collective agreement, which invariably specifies the procedures to be followed in resolving it.

Griffiths Mental Development Scale   (R. Griffiths) A scale used to assess the level of development of infants up to two years of age in five areas: locomotor, personal-social, hearing-speech, hand and eye development, and performance. The scale yields a general quotient derived by dividing the mental age by the chronological age. Also known as Griffiths' Scale. See APGAR SCALE, CATTELL INFANT SCALE.

grimace   A distorted facial expression, sometimes appearing as an involuntary facial tic, often observed in catatonic patients and patients with organic neurologic disorders.

Griselda complex   The reluctance of a father to allow his daughter to marry because of the father's desire to keep the daughter himself.

GRIT   See GRADUATED AND RECIPROCATED INITIATIVES IN TENSION REDUCTION.

grooming   1. Behavior of certain animals in cleaning themselves and others of their kind. Particularly in nonhuman primates, communicates social connections and dominance-submission. See LICKING BEHAVIOR. 2. A basic function of self-care and an important part of the responsibility of rehabilitation of persons with mental disabilities, physical disabilities, or both. See ACTIVITIES OF DAILY LIVING.

gross indecency   Old legal phrase for behavior that was not only illegal but considered unmentionable (generally anal or oral sex, depending on the jurisdiction).

gross motor activities   The involvement of the total musculature of the body and the ability to control body movements in relation to such elements as gravity, sidedness, and body midline.

gross motor composite   A score on the Bruininks-Oseretsky Test of Motor Proficiency based on the performance of large muscles, shoulders, trunk, legs. See FINE MOTOR COMPOSITE, TOTAL BATTERY COMPOSITE.

gross motor coordinations   Coordinated bodily movements in which strength is the primary factor. See FINE MOTOR SKILLS.

gross motor skills   The smoothly functioning and effective body movements required for walking, running, hopping, and awareness of a person's own body image, as well as for athletic events and tasks as simple as changing a tire on an automobile. Compare FINE MOTOR SKILLS.

gross stress reaction   A transient situational personality disorder in which such symptoms as nightmares, tremors, and anxiety attacks occur as a result of exposure to severe physical demands and extreme emotional stress experienced in military situations or civilian disasters (fire, earthquake, tornados, explosions). See CIVILIAN-CATASTROPHE REACTION, COMBAT REACTIONS, POSTTRAUMATIC STRESS DISORDER, PRISONER-OF-WAR REACTIONS.

ground   The relatively homogeneous and indistinct background of figure-ground perceptions.

grounded theory　　(B. Glaser & A. Strauss) A systematic strategy for theory development based on close observation of the world, without a prior theoretical bias of framework. Grounded theories are developed through the use of conceptualization to bind facts together, rather than through inferences and hypothesis testing. They begin with no *a priori* hypotheses and use inductive generation of categories and associations as the analysis proceeds. This freedom from the verification approach allows researchers to address complex meanings and create theory on topics that are not amenable to laboratory experimentation.

grounding　　1. The use of body positions, especially when standing, to generate a body posture leading to greater self-awareness, self-regard and courage. 2. A phenomenological feeling of being secure, safe, and in control. 3. Slang for a form of deprivation discipline used by parents on children, depriving them of freedom, such as making the children stay home when they wish to go out and play with other children.

ground of existence　　(M. Boss) The circumstances in which a person is born. Also known as throwness.

ground rules　　The elements of the analytic or therapeutic contract and setting, including the fee, time, place, and frequency of sessions, free association, total privacy and confidentiality, and the therapist's non-judgmental and neutral use of neutral interventions. The therapist's management of the ground rules has strong effects on the client or patient. See FRAME.

group (Gp)　　1. Any collection of objects, beings, or data that may be treated as a unitary whole. 2. A collection of organisms that associate or live together or that respond to one another or to a common stimulus. 3. A pattern or configuration of items, of which the existence and properties of each depend upon the nature of the pattern or configuration of the whole. Also known as class, social group. Types of group include: ACCIDENTAL, ACTION, ASPIRATIONAL, ATTITUDINAL, AUTHORITARIAN, AUTONOMOUS WORK, BLANKET, BLOOD, BUZZ, CIRCULAR DISCUSSIONAL, CLOSED, CO-ACTING, COMMON-PROBLEM, COMMUNITY-ACTION, COMPARABLE, CONTINUOUS, CONTROL, CRISIS, CRITERION, DIRECTIVE, DISCUSSION, DISSOCIATIVE, ENCOUNTER, EQUIVALENT, ETHNIC, EXPERIENTIAL, EXPERIMENTAL, FACE-TO-FACE, FOCUS, FORMAL, GROWTH, HEALING, HETEROGENEOUS, HOMOSOCIAL PEER, HORIZONTAL, IN-, INFORMAL, INTEGRITY, INTENSIVE, LAISSEZ-FAIRE, LARGE, LEADERLESS, MARATHON, MARGINAL, MATCHED, MEDIAN, MEMBERSHIP, MINORITY, NATURAL, NEGATIVE REFERENCE, OPEN, OUT-, PATCHED-UP CONTROL, PEER, PERSONAL-GROWTH, PRIMARY, QUASI, RANDOM, RAP, REFERENCE, SECONDARY, SELECTED, SELF-HELP, SENSORY-AWARENESS, SMALL, SOCIAL, STRUCTURAL, STRUCTURED, T-, TASK-ORIENTED, THERAPEUTIC, TRAINING, TRANSIENT, VERTICAL, WAITING-LIST CONTROL, WE-, YOKED-CONTROL.

group abilities/factors　　Phrases used interchangeably with primary mental abilities.

group absolutism　　The argument that the particular group a person belongs to has proper views and positions on all issues. See ETHNOCENTRISM.

group acceptance　　The degree to which group members approve of a new or potential member and that person's perceived relative status.

group analysis　　1. The study of the behavior of groups, normal and pathological. 2. Another name for group psychotherapy, especially if it is based on psychoanalytic principles. 3. (T. Burrow) Trigant Burrow's early name for what later became phyloanalysis.

group-analytic psychotherapy　　(S. H. Foulkes) A type of group therapy that focuses on the communication and interaction processes taking place in the total group. Interventions make use of group rather than individual forces as the principal therapeutic agent. Also known as therapeutic group analysis. See GROUP PSYCHOTHERAPY.

group behavior　　1. The actions of a group as a whole. 2. The unique behavior of an individual in a group. See HELP-REJECTING COMPLAINER, THERAPIST'S ASSISTANT.

group bibliotherapy　　A therapy procedure used by Jacob W. Klapman with lobotomized patients with schizophrenia. Each was given a copy of the same issue of the *Reader's Digest*, the therapist began reading aloud as patients followed, then a patient would continue reading aloud until some kind of conversation was started. See BIBLIOTHERAPY, POETRY THERAPY.

group boundary　　Rules, formal and informal, that govern group membership and activities. In the case of formal groups with a constitution and bylaws, boundaries are made explicit. In other groups, limits are generally commonly understood, and those who go beyond the boundaries suffer a variety of consequences, from mild correction to complete rejection.

group-centered leader　　The type of leader who views his or her function in relation to the desires and potential of the group; a nonauthoritarian leader concerned with the group's needs, abilities, development, independence, and responsibility.

group climate　　The relative degree of acceptance, tolerance, and freedom of expression that characterizes the relationships within a counseling or therapy group. A distinction is drawn between temporary behavior of any member in the group and the individual as a whole while the meaning of the behavior is probed. See GROUP BEHAVIOR.

group cohesion　　1. The emotional bonds that hold an aggregate of persons together. See COHESION. 2. Bonds formed by people as a result of common efforts to a goal.

group cohesiveness　　An index of the overall solidarity, unity, or attractiveness of a group to its members. A multidimensional composite index characterizing a group's structure and symbolizing all the forces acting together to hold each member within the group.

group consciousness　　1. An awareness by each group member of the group as a whole. 2. An awareness that pervades the group of its cohesiveness and purpose.

group contagion　　Outmoded phrase denoting the communication or transmission of emotion through a group or crowd (for example, the rapid spread of fear). See CROWD CONSCIOUSNESS, MASS HYSTERIA.

group counseling (J. H. Pratt) A method of providing guidance and support for people organized as a group, as opposed to individual counseling. The difference between group counseling and group therapy is based on whether the leader is seen as the expert on some topic, such as parenting skills, or whether the leader assumes the role of a facilitator rather than an expert. See GROUP THERAPY.

group curve A graphic representation based on the performance of two or more organisms.

group differences The calculated variations between two or more groups on one or more variables; for example, the variation between men and women in reaction-time studies constitutes a group difference.

group dimension Any group trait constituting a variable that can be measured and used to characterize a particular group (for example, average age, size, or homogeneity of religion).

group distribution The distribution grouped as a result of numerical values, within a certain range, to form a single class interval.

group dynamics/process (K. Lewin et al.) Phrase applied to the study of the interactions and interrelationships within as well as between groups and the surrounding social field. This topic includes investigations of group cohesiveness, interdependence of group members, collective problem-solving and decision-making, types of leadership, group conformity, subgroups, and the social climate of different groups.

grouped measures Numerical observations recorded as falling within statistical classes, such as 6–10, 11–15, rather than being recorded separately.

group experience In group counseling, the interactions that afford the client an opportunity to gain insight into personal problems by sharing with and learning from other members. See CLINICAL CLUSTER ANALYSIS, GROUP THERAPY, IDIOPANIMA.

group experiment A research technique in which several participants or subjects are observed or tested either simultaneously or within a given experimental session.

group factors in intelligence (C. E. Spearman) Factors (or determiners) that underlie efficiencies and occur in more than one but less than all of any given set of abilities.

group fallacy 1. The assumption, generally regarded as fallacious, of a collective mind. 2. Any assumption of the existence of a group mind separate from the minds of individuals, as in the statement "The United States takes the position that. . ." when perhaps only a minority may affirmatively take that particular position.

group feeling A desire to be associated with members of a group and to participate in the group's activities.

group harmony The status of any group when all of its members are in agreement about the functions or purpose of the group. See GROUPTHINK.

group home A small residence for persons with emotional disturbances, severe mental impairment, or physical disabilities, as well as recovering addicted persons, where they can live in a noninstitutional, family-like setting, maintain healthy relationships, and achieve a measure of independence and integration with the community.

group hysteria Mass hysteria.

group identification The awareness by persons that they are members of a group; also, the process of sharing or internalizing the group's objectives.

grouping 1. In education, the process of assigning pupils to grades, classes, or subgroups in terms of some standard, such as age, size, intelligence quotient (IQ) scores, or academic levels. 2. In statistics, the process of arranging scores in categories, intervals, classes, or ranks. 3. A scheme or method of compressing distributions (especially those with wide ranges) by clustering several measurement units into intervals. 4. (M. Wertheimer) In Gestalt theory, the organizing tendency of a person "to perceive consistent whole-qualities, reasonable groupings with features belonging to the inner structure nature of the situation—the so-called factor of the 'good Gestalt'."

grouping error An error made by the grouping of the data. If data are in single units, no such errors can be made, but the size of grouping may establish an error, since the grouping may not be useful to the purpose of the research.

group interview 1. An interview of more than one person at a time. 2. A conference or meeting in which one or more questioners elicit information from two or more respondents in an experimental or real-life situation.

group justification A tendency to support and favor an ingroup a person belongs to.

group marriage A family pattern in which several men and women live together, share the burdens of the household, the rearing of children, and a common sexual life. Such marriages have been practiced among various indigenous groups often as an insurance against "dying childless." The Oneida community practiced a form of group marriage called stirpiculture.

group mind (G. LeBon) Outmoded phrase for the overall character and behavioral pattern of a group. The concept implies the existence of a group consciousness that exceeds or is qualitatively different from individual consciousness and assumes that a group's behavior cannot be understood in terms of individual psychology. See SYNTALITY.

group morale The spirit of the group, marked by confidence and willingness to pursue common goals.

group networks In social psychology, a specialized organizational system devised for use with groups involved in problem-solving. See COMPLETELY CONNECTED NETWORK, WHEEL NETWORK.

group norms Social norms.

group polarization The splitting of a group into two or more groups after discussions, each going in different directions, having opposite views. See CAUTIOUS SHIFT, RISKY SHIFT.

group pressure Psychological pressure exerted by a group to induce individual members to conform to group standards, attitudes, or behavior, by pointing out the importance of teamwork or majority rule, by threatening expulsion or ostracism, or by rewarding conformity with approval or special benefits or many other means. See SOCIAL NORMS.

group problem-solving   The collective effort of two or more persons to perform a task or solve a problem. When the nature of the problem is objective and has a single definite solution, groups generate more and better answers than individuals working alone. However, individuals work faster than groups. When the nature of the problem is subjective, as in questions requiring moral judgment, groups may not be superior to individuals. See BRAINSTORMING, GROUPTHINK.

group process   **group dynamics**

group (psycho)therapy   Collective treatment of psychological problems in which two or more members of a therapy group interact with each other in the presence of one or more psychotherapists who serve as catalysts, facilitators, or interpreters. A common element in all groups has to do with the importance of communications across members, with the concept that each person is simultaneously a patient and a therapist for others. Jacob Moreno labeled group treatment methods as "group psychotherapy." For individual types of group therapy, see ACTIVITY, ACTIVITY-INTERVIEW, DIDACTIC, DIRECTIVE, INSPIRATIONAL, INTERVIEW, MECHANICAL, NONDIRECTIVE PLAY, PSYCHOANALYTIC, ROUND TABLE. See also ABC THERAPY, ACTING OUT THERAPY, CIRCULAR DISCUSSION GROUPS, CLASS METHOD, FAMILY THERAPY, GROUP-ANALYTIC PSYCHOTHERAPY, GROUP BIBLIOTHERAPY, PSYCHODRAMA.

group-relations theory   (G. W. Allport) Gordon W. Allport's assumption that behavior is influenced not only by a person's unique pattern of traits, but by the person's need to conform to social demands and expectations. Social determinants become particularly evident in group therapy, since this type of therapy tends to challenge attitudes, such as prejudices based on conformity and restricted thinking.

group residence   A home-like setting for a small population of patients or ex-patients who require a certain amount of supervision and care although they no longer need the facilities of a hospital or nursing home. See GROUP HOME.

group rigidity   A tendency of a given social group to oppose or thwart structural change; also, the group's resistance to internal or environmental pressures. Many factors, including group size, history, cohesiveness, physical environment, and relationship to other groups, may affect group rigidity.

group risk-taking   The willingness of a group to make a decision that may have potential hazards or negative results. In contrast to the traditional belief that groups always tend to make more conservative decisions than individuals, studies indicate that group decisions tend toward greater extremity or risk than individual decisions.

group roles   The behavior patterns carried out by the members of a group. Members may adopt different roles at different times. Some members may take on multiple roles whereas other members fill no definable roles.

group scores   Separate values of individual scores put in a distribution grouped into a number of equal intervals, classes, or steps along a scale to form a frequency distribution.

group selection   A process of natural selection in which the group, instead of the individual as such, operates as a unit in the struggle for existence.

group sex   1. Three or more people engaged simultaneously in interactive sexual activities. 2. Sexual activity among any group of people who may meet with the express purpose of obtaining maximum sexual satisfaction through such means as observing each other, experimenting with different techniques, and exchanging partners.

group solidarity   A common bond among a group of people such as a team, combat unit, or therapy group, arising from shared feelings, activities, and objectives. When group solidarity is high, the morale of the group is also likely to be high.

group space   A "bubble" of personal space that may be established and defended by two or more persons who share the space. Research shows that members of a group tend to stand or walk closer together when an individual who is not a member of the group approaches. Group space defense is most aggressive when the group consists of a male-female pair. See GROUP TERRITORIAL BEHAVIOR, INTERACTION TERRITORY, PROXEMICS.

group structure   The characteristics of a social group in relation to size, purpose, attitudes, and relationships between individuals, subgroups, leaders, and other members, as well as the relations of the group as a whole to other groups.

group superego   The portion of the superego acquired from peer groups, as opposed to the part derived from parental influence.

group territorial behavior   A tendency for ethnic and other human groups to establish and defend areas as separate or shared territories. The behavior is observed in some neighborhoods of large cities and in city street gangs. A form of intragroup territorial behavior is seen in family settings where spouses regard bedroom areas or dining-table seating patterns as personal territory.

group test   A type of test that can be administered to several persons simultaneously. Examples include the ARMY GENERAL CLASSIFICATION TEST, GENERAL RECORD EXAMINATION, HARROWER-ERICKSON'S GROUP RORSCHACH, SCHOLASTIC APTITUDE TESTS.

group therapy   **group (psycho)therapy**

groupthink   (I. Janis) The phenomenon of people in a group reinforcing one another, seeking concurrence and group cohesiveness rather than pursuing a realistic appraisal of alternatives in open discussion. Usually, such a situation occurs if a small group becomes so bound up with emotional ties that individuals tend no longer to think for themselves but to accept the opinion of the majority, forming a unity of concepts.

GROW   (C. Keogh) An international community mental health movement originally started in Australia that provides round-the-clock caring of and sharing with people recovering from mental disorders. GROW has more than 650 self-help groups. See ALCOHOLICS ANONYMOUS, RECOVERY INC.

growing edge   The point in a continuum considered the optimal situation for a student to learn; for example, a child has just learned addition and is considered ready to learn multiplication (which uses addition). Another child has not mastered addition and so is not on the growing edge of multiplication. Another child already knows multiplication, and so has gone past that growing edge. See HETEROSCEDASTICITY.

growth 1. Enlargement of the individual organism or its parts. 2. Any kind of increase such as growth in complexity, efficiency, or value. Term is applied to species and societies as well as to individuals. Types of growth include: CATCH-UP, DIFFERENTIAL, MEMBRANE, MENTAL, SOCIAL, VOCABULARY, ZERO-POPULATION.

growth center A facility established specifically for the application of group techniques directed toward personal change. The common purpose of most of these centers appears to be self-development, or fulfillment of "human potential," in various ways. Also known as human-potential growth center. See BIOENERGETICS, ENCOUNTER GROUP, EST, FIRO, SENSORY-AWARENESS GROUPS, TRANSACTIONAL ANALYSIS, T-GROUP.

growth cones Projections from the tips of immature neurons with tiny knobs at the end of the filaments.

growth curve A graphic representation of the growth rate of an organism or a function such as learning. See LEARNING CURVE for an example of such a curve.

growth function The relation between growth and another factor, such as age.

growth group A group established for the purpose of focusing on the personal growth of members. See T-GROUP, ENCOUNTER GROUP, MARATHON GROUP.

growth hormone (GH) Common name for the pituitary growth hormone (somatotropin).

growth motive The fundamental desire of most humans to be better than they are at any given time: stronger, wealthier, more attractive or more intelligent, etc. This concept is inherent in almost all personality theories. Whereas animals may be content as long as their existence is in harmony with their needs, humans will intentionally practice all kinds of artifices to achieve their goals in attaining superiority. See INFERIORITY FEELINGS, METAMOTIVATION.

growth needs See EXISTENCE-RELATEDNESS-GROWTH THEORY.

growth principle (C. R. Rogers) The basic view of Carl Rogers that in an atmosphere free of coercion and distortion, a person's creative and integrative forces will lead to fuller adaptation, insight, self-esteem, and realization of potential.

growth spurt The rapid growth in height during adolescence.

grumbling mania A state of restlessness marked by feelings of dissatisfaction, complaining, and capriciousness.

GSCH See GESELL DEVELOPMENTAL SCHEDULES.

G spot See GRAEFENBERG SPOT.

G.S.R. galvanic skin response or reflex (also abbreviated **GSR**)

GST general systems theory

guanine (J. A. Unzer) A purine with two carbon rings, one of the bases found in both deoxyribonucleic acid (DNA) and ribonucleic acid (RNA). The other two bases found in DNA and RNA are adenine and cytosine. See ADENINE, CHROMOSOME, CYTOSINE DEOXYRIBONUCLEIC ACID (DNA), RIBONUCLEIC ACID (RNA), THYMINE, URACIL.

guarded In describing a patient's medical condition, sometimes a euphemism for hopeless.

guardianship In law, the placing of a person deemed by a court to be incompetent (due to immaturity, mental illness, etc.) under the control of a designated guardian who will make appropriate personal and/or property decisions for that person.

Gudden's law (B. A. von Gudden) A theory that lesions of the cerebral cortex do not cause an atrophying of peripheral nerves.

guerrilla (little war—Spanish) 1. Low-level or irregular warfare, often by indigenous peoples against technological superior adversaries. 2. A person so engaged.

guessed average (GA) See ASSUMED MEAN.

guessed mean (GM) See ASSUMED MEAN.

guessing bias A characteristic way a person responds to situations that call for guessing, such as always picking the last of several alternatives, or choosing the one that appears to be the least likely.

Guess-Who technique A type of personality-rating device used chiefly in school settings. Uses short word-pictures of diverse personality types. Students are directed to identify classmates whose personalities seem to correspond most closely to these descriptions.

guidance The use of personal interviews and tests in providing educational or vocational direction in cooperation with the client.

guidance program The cumulative resources, staff, and techniques used by a school, usually at the high-school level to assist students in resolving a range of scholastic or social problems.

guidance specialist A person trained in a counselor-education program or who has sufficient credentials and experience to function in one or more guidance capacities.

guided affective imagery (GAI) The excitation of emotional fantasies, or waking dreams, in psychotherapy, a technique used primarily in brief psychotherapy and group therapy.

guide dog A dog specially trained to aid in the mobility of a blind person. Such dogs are raised as normal puppies until the age of three months, when they are tested for their aptitude. In their 13th week, dogs that qualify are placed in private hands and trained as guides until after they are one year old. About 90% of dogs tested initially and selected for training pass the final test after one year's training. Many jurisdictions require such dogs to be admitted to, for instance, restaurants, public transportation, and apartments that ban animals. Also known as Seeing-Eye dog.

guided performance A means of helping organisms learn by giving them various kinds of information and assistance.

guiding fictions (A. Adler) Personal principles and goals about the self and others that serve as guidelines by which individuals can understand and evaluate their experiences and determine their future lifestyles.

guiding idea An idea that persists or constantly recurs and determines the course and direction of associated trains of thought.

Guilford dimensions of intelligence (J. P. Guilford) A point of view in which intelligence is viewed as having three dimensions: (a) content, concerned with concept; (b) operations, dealing with utilization of content; and (c) products, the final results. See STRUCTURE OF INTELLECT MODEL/THEORY for an illustrative model. Also see ARP TESTS, C SCALE, CONVERGENT PRODUCTION, DIVERGENT PRODUCTION, GUILFORD-ZIMMERMAN TEMPERAMENT SURVEY, IMPLICATIONS.

Guilford-Zimmerman Temperament Survey (GZTS) (J. P. Guilford & J. M. Zimmerman) A personality inventory for use in grades 9 through 16 and with adults, measuring ten factorially analyzed traits: Ascendance, sociability, friendliness, thoughtfulness, personal relations, masculinity, objectivity, general activity, restraint, and emotional stability.

guilt In its normal expression, a feeling of remorse in proportion to actual violations of responsibility or ethical codes. Pathological guilt is a highly exaggerated reaction to real or fancied transgressions. In most instances, guilt includes loss of self-esteem and a need to make amends. Often, when a serious crime occurs, people will confess to it who had nothing to do with the crime. Also known as feelings of guilt, guilt feelings, sense of guilt. Kinds of guilt include: NEUROTIC, PATHOLOGICAL, SURVIVOR, UNCONSCIOUS. See CRIME FROM SENSE OF GUILT, INITIATIVE VS GUILT.

guilt by association A logical fallacy based on irrelevant elements about a person (for example, "Chris hangs out with a bad crowd and therefore Chris is also no good."). See PREJUDICE.

guilt culture A culture relying mostly on individual consciences as a means of social control. See GUILT, GUILT SENSE, GUILT FEAR.

guilt feelings See GUILT.

guilt psychoanalysis Psychoanalysis focusing on neurotic guilty feelings, generally the result of conflict between the superego and infantile sexual and aggressive impulses.

guilt sense An unpleasant emotional state in which a person is dominated by the belief or knowledge that he or she has contravened some social custom, ethical principle, or legal regulation. Also known as sense of guilt.

guilty fear The fear of severe consequences resulting from a forbidden impulse or action. See GUILT SENSE.

guilty knowledge test A procedure in lie detection that evaluates responses of a suspect to details of a crime known only to the guilty person. If 50 dollars are stolen, and if a polygraph of a suspect shows a strong reaction to questions mentioning only that number, this may be presumptive evidence of guilt.

guru 1. A Hindu religious teacher or spiritual guide. 2. Colloquially, any spiritual or intellectual leader or counselor.

guru stage (L. Kohlberg) Descriptive phrase sometimes applied to Lawrence Kohlberg's speculative concept of a stage beyond the highest (postconventional) level of moral reasoning. The guru stage represents an understanding of the basis of a person's own moral principles, possibly through a philosophical or religious framework. See POSTCONVENTIONAL LEVEL.

gust A standard unit of taste produced by a 1% solution of sucrose. See GUSTOMETER.

gustation Act or process of tasting. The sense of taste, based on receptor taste buds distributed on the surface of the tongue, palate, and oral cavity and activated by substances soluble in saliva. Contemporary investigators usually limit gustatory qualities to four: sweet, sour, bitter, and saline. Henning lists these as primary tastes (like primary colors) with simple intermediate tastes connecting them. The senses of taste and smell are often combined. See TASTE, WATER AS TASTE.

gustatory hallucination A taste sensation for which there seems to be no basis, as in a person "tasting" poison in the food or acid in the mouth.

gustatory nerve lingual nerve

gustatory qualities The several qualities of taste sensation. See GUSTATION.

gustatory seizure A type of epileptic episode accompanied by distortions of taste and smell sensations, that is, by peculiar tastes and odors.

gustatory stimulus An aqueous solution of a substance that acts chemically upon some material in the receptor-cells of the lingual papillae.

gustometer A tube so constructed as to deliver a measured amount of a solution. The device is put on a person's tongue and a small amount of the solution is released. The purpose is to determine the quality and strength of taste of the dissolved substance. See GYMNEMIC ACID.

gustometer

Guthrie's contiguous conditioning theory (E. R. Guthrie) A learning concept based on the premise that each response becomes linked with stimuli present at the time; that is, the theory emphasizes contiguity rather than reinforcement or the law of effect. See CONDITIONED RESPONSE, CONTIGUITY LEARNING, CONTIGUITY THEORY OF LEARNING, LAW OF CONTIGUITY, POSTREMITY PRINCIPLE.

Guttman scale (L. Guttman) A scale, usually an attitude scale, in which items are arranged so that a response to any item may be considered to be indicative of the kind of response that will be given to all the items of lower rank. See SCALOGRAM ANALYSIS.

Guttman scaling (method) (L. Guttman) A procedure that orders both items and participants with respect to an underlying cumulative dimension. Also known as cumulative scaling, Guttman's scalogram analysis, scalogram analysis. See GUTTMAN SCALE, SCALE REPRODUCIBILITY.

guttural General lay term for a velar or a pharyngeal speech sound made behind the hard palate (for example, the /l/ in "all," the /kh/ in Scottish "loch" or German "Bach," and the near-/kh/ in French "Paris" or Spanish "Juan").

gutturophonia Dysphonia characterized by a throaty voice.

gymnemic acid   A substance obtained from leaves of a southern Asiatic shrub used in taste-tests. It abolishes the sense of taste for sweet and bitter but does not affect sensitivity for sour, astringent, or pungent substances.

gymnophobia   Morbid fear of nudity; fear of being naked or of being among naked bodies. Also known as nudophobia.

gynander   An organism with both male and female characteristics. In most instances, male characteristics occur on one side of the body and female on the other, and in a few cases the head is female and the rest of the body male. Also known as gynandromorph. See ANDROGYNY, CHIMERIC STIMULATION.

gynandromorphism   1. The union of both male and female characters in the same organism. 2. An abnormal combination of male and female characteristics in the same organism. See GYNANDER, GYNANDRY.

gynandromorphy   (W. Sheldon) The degree to which body parts exhibit both male and female characteristics. Also called androgeny. See CHIMERIC STIMULATION, GYNANDER.

gynandry   1. A tendency of some females to have male physical components. 2. A tendency of a female body to approach the shape of a male body; a masculine-looking woman.

gynecology   Branch of medicine that studies endocrinology and reproductive physiology, as well as diseases of the reproductive organs of females.

gyn/ecology   (M. Daly) The concept of women rediscovering and redeveloping the complex web of living/loving relations of their own kind.

gynecomastia   Breast development in the male.

gynecomimesis   A male appearing female in body form, dress, and behavior.

gynecophilic   Having a preference for women.

gynemimetophilia   Being sexually attracted to or aroused by a transvestite, gynemimetic, or preoperative male-to-female transsexual as a sex partner.

gynephilia   See GYNOPHILIA.

gynephilic   Being sexually oriented toward females. See SAME-DIFFERENT THEORY.

gynephobia   Morbid fear of women. Also known as genephobia, gynophobia, horror feminae.

gynetresia   A congenital anomaly of a female with no vagina or a rudimentary one.

gynomastia-aspermatogenesis syndrome   A variant of Klinefelter's syndrome, characterized by breast development, gynecomastia, and the absence of spermatogenesis.

gynomonoecism   Capability a person who is genetically a female to produce spermatozoa in the ovaries. See CHROMOSOME ABERRATIONS, SECONDARY SEX CHARACTERISTICS, SEX DETERMINATION, SEXUAL ANOMALY.

gynophilia   Being sexually attracted to a woman sex partner.

gynophobia   **gynephobia**

gynosperm   In humans, the X-carrying sperm that will, following conception, result in a female child.

gyri   Plural of gyrus.

gyrus   1. A circle. 2. Any of the elevations or convolutions of the surface of the brain caused by folds and clefts of the cortex. Each gyrus is identified by its location or some other feature, such as the cingulate gyrus, an arch-shaped convolution. Also known as convolution. Various gyri include: ANGULAR, CINGULATE, DENTATE, FASCIOLAS, FORNICATE, FUSIFORM, HESCHL'S, LATERAL, LINGUAL, ORBITAL, SUBCALLOSAL. Plural is gyri.

GZTS   Guilford-Zimmerman Temperament Survey

h 1. A measure of precision in a normal psychometric function, it bears an inverse relation to the probable error. 2. Symbol for certainty.

H 1. See HARMONIC MEAN. 2. A test statistic for the Kruskal-Wallis test. 3. See ENTROPY. 4. In Rorschach test scoring, a symbol for human figure. 5. Slang for heroin. 6. henry. 7. hyperopia.

Haab's pupil (reflex) The normal contraction of both pupils when the eyes focus on a bright object in a darkened room. Also known as cerebral cortex reflex, Haab's pupillary reflex. Named after Swiss ophthalmologist Otto Haab (1850–1931).

habeas corpus (you may have the body—Latin) A writ requiring a person to be brought before a judge or court to determine whether confinement in any kind of institution has been undertaken with due process of law.

habilitation The process of bringing an individual to a state of fitness through treatment or training. Term usually is applied to cases of congenital disorders or those acquired during infancy. See REHABILITATION.

habit Any systematically repeated behavior pattern performed automatically. These patterns help people to adjust to life by permitting them to meet various situations with little attention, but if they become too rigid, they may hinder adaptation to new situations. Kinds of habit include: ACT-, GENERAL, MOTOR, NERVOUS, PREPOTENT, READING, SOCIAL, VICIOUS. See EFFECTIVE-HABIT STRENGTH, FORCE OF HABIT, GENERALIZED HABIT STRENGTH.

habitability The degree to which a specific environment fills the functional and esthetic requirements of its occupants. See ENVIRONMENTAL DESIGN.

habitat The usual environment of individuals, groups, varieties, or species of plants and animals; generally refers to type of location rather than a specific locale, as do terms such as territory or home range.

habit complaint A hypochondriacal tendency in certain children who react to emotional or other problems with health complaints.

habit deterioration/disorganization A tendency of patients to regress in social behavior to less integrated patterns as a result of mental or physical illnesses.

habit disorders Repeated maladaptive actions that interfere with biological and social functioning.

habit disturbance of children Repetitive, maladaptive behaviors of children, such as nail biting, thumb sucking, or head banging. Often these habits are indicators that children are seeking attention. See TRANSIENT SITUATIONAL PERSONALITY DISORDERS.

habit-family hierarchy (C. L. Hull) In Hull's behavior system, habits integrated by a common goal-stimulus, organized by strength of conditioning; under normal conditions, the most strongly reinforced will occur, but when it is blocked, the next alternative habit in the hierarchy that will reach the goal will occur in its place the most likely response is the one that, with the least effort, will most rapidly produce reinforcement. See HULL'S THEORY.

habit formation The process, usually assumed to come about through repetition, whereby a response becomes gradually fixed in a relatively invariable and automatic form. See HABIT TRAINING, LEARNING.

habit-forming drug Common phrase for a drug that produces a craving for continuing its use. See ABUSE POTENTIAL.

habit hierarchy 1. An arrangement of habits in terms of their strength, with long-held habits having generally the greatest force. 2. An arrangement of habits in terms of their complexity.

habit interference The weakening of one or both incompatible habitual responses due to their conflicting with each other, often leading to the domination of one over the other.

habit progression A tendency of established habits to give way to new ones as the organism matures.

habit regression A return to an earlier habit, especially likely to occur in an emotional state such as when angry or frustrated.

habit reversal A behavior process in which the individual must learn a new correct response to a stimulus and stop responding to a previously learned cue. Employed in behavioral conditioning to control obesity or smoking.

habit spasm A persistent, involuntary mannerism resembling a tic, such as repeatedly shrugging the shoulders or nodding the head regardless of the situation. Also known as *maladie des tics*, mimic spasm. See SPASM, TIC.

habit strength ($_SH_R$)   (C. L. Hull) Learned strength of a habit that varies with the number of reinforcements, amount of reinforcement, and interval between stimulus and response and between response and reinforcement (one of the most important intervening variables in his 1943 theory). In Hull's final system of 1952, habit strength varied only with number of reinforcements, with the other listed factors handled in some other fashion, such as amount of reinforcement affecting the new intervening variable Incentive Motivation (K). See HULL'S THEORY.

habit tic   Phrase sometimes applied to a brief, recurrent movement of a psychogenic nature as contrasted with tics of organic origin. See TIC.

habit training   Instruction, guidance, and practice aimed at inculcating specific habit patterns in animals or humans, especially the training of children in such functions as eating, dressing, sleeping, and elimination.

habituation   1. The process of growing accustomed to a situation or pattern of behavior. 2. Becoming psychologically dependent on the use of a particular drug but without the increasing tolerance and physiological dependence characteristic of addiction. 3. Decreased attention to a stimulus as a result of repeated presentations.

habituation technique/test   A procedure in which infants are repeatedly shown a stimulus until their response to it declines.

habitus   1. The general appearance of the body. 2. Susceptibility to certain types of physical disorders associated with particular somatotypes. See APOPLECTIC TYPE, HABITUS PHTHISICUS.

habitus apoplecticus   (Hippocrates) A constitutional body type characterized by a stout physique, and considered likely to suffer a stroke (cerebrovascular accident).

habitus phthisicus   (Hippocrates) A constitutional body type characterized by a slender, flat-chested physique reminiscent of a person with tuberculosis.

hacker   1. Originally, a clumsy hobbyist. 2. Later, a person engrossed in technology, usually telephones or computers, who may apply ingenuity to solving a problem or use expertise illicitly, as in breaking into and tampering with private systems (known as hacking).

HACS   See HYPERACTIVE-CHILD SYNDROME.

hadephobia   Morbid fear of hell. Also known as stygiophobia.

hair cells   Sensory cells located in the organ of corti of the inner ear that act as sound receptors as well as similar cells in the semicircular canals that act as motion detectors. At the bottom of the hair cells are endings that form the auditory nerve, a part of the eighth cranial nerve. See HAPTOMETER, EXTERNAL HAIR CELLS (OF EAR), INTERNAL HAIR CELLS (OF EAR).

haircut   Term employed in some long-term, self-improvement groups, such as Synanon, for a kind of hazing by members of the group applied to a member who has broken a rule. For an agreed period, the client must listen to a tirade on faults and errors without any attempt at a defense. In some communities, the culprit is literally given a haircut, always with the permission of the guilty one; otherwise that person will be ejected from the group.

hair esthesiometer   A pencil-shaped device with a hair at its end to test pressure sensitivity of the skin at various points on the skin. A spring can be attached to indicate amount of pressure used; pressure can be manipulated by varying the diameter of the hair used. See ESTHESIOMETER for an illustration demonstrating the use of one.

hair fear   See TRICHOPHOBIA.

hair follicle   The protective casing of a root of a hair. The basket-shaped ending about the shaft of hair is surrounded by a flower-spray type of nerve ending, one of the six basic types of somatosensory receptors. In defensive behavior, the follicular nerve ending stimulates muscle fibers that contract and make the hair shaft stand erect. See PILOERECTION, SKIN RECEPTORS.

hair-pulling   A compulsion to pull out strands of hair from the head (sometimes from the pubic area). Variously interpreted as a substitute for masturbation, an aggressive act, and a denial of castration. Onset usually prior to young adulthood. Also known as trichotillomania.

half-life (of drugs)   The time taken for the activity of the drug in the body to decrease by half, due to its being metabolized and later excreted.

half-show   A form of child therapy in which a psychological problem is presented as a puppet show drama that is stopped at a crucial moment, when the child is asked to suggest how the story should end.

halfway house   A transitional facility, such as a group residence, for previously institutionalized persons to help them prepare for independent living. See BOARDING HOUSE, COOPERATIVE URBAN HOUSE.

hallucination   1. An imaginary perception; seeing, hearing, tasting, smelling, touching, or feeling something that is not there. Persistent hallucinations that the perceiver insists are real may be primary signs of a serious mental disorder. 2. A perceptual misreport of something occurring external to the person when the appropriate sense organ has not been stimulated. Distinguished from perceptual misreport of genuine external stimulation by virtually all observers (illusion) and misinterpretation of external stimulation by a few observers (delusion). Kinds of hallucinations include: ACUTE, AFFECTIVE, AUDITORY, ALCOHOL, BLANK, BODY-IMAGE, BROMIDE, ELEMENTARY, FLASHBACK, GUSTATORY, HAPTIC, HYPNAGOGIC, HYPNOPOMPIC, INDUCED, KINESTHETIC, LILLIPUTIAN, MICROPTIC, NEGATIVE, NONAFFECTIVE, OLFACTORY, ORGANIC, PEDUNCULAR, POSITIVE, PSEUDO-, PSYCHOGENIC, PSYCHOMOTOR, SOMATIC, STUMP, TACTILE, TELEOLOGIC, TEMPORAL, TEMPORAL-LOBE, VERIDICAL, VESTIBULAR, VISUAL. See ANTON'S SYNDROME, TEMPORAL-LOBE ILLUSIONS.

hallucinatory epilepsy   A form of focal epilepsy in which the patient experiences transient paroxysmal hallucinations.

hallucinatory game   A childhood game in which fantasy objects are created by children for their amusement, and differ from true hallucinations in that the children are aware the imagined objects do not really exist.

hallucinatory image   A mental image accepted as real. Can be achieved in some people via hypnosis.

hallucinatory verbigeration   A type of hallucination in which people hear the same meaningless sentences echoing through their minds in endless repetition with few if any changes.

hallucinogen   (H. Osmond) A substance (drug) that produces visual, auditory, or other sensory distortions that may be interpreted as hallucinations. Examples include ANADENANTHERA, ANGEL DUST, BUFOTENINE, CAAPI, DIMETHYLTRYPTAMINE (DMT), EPENA, FLY AGARIC, HENBANE, IBOGAINE, LYSERGIC ACID DIETHYLAMIDE (LSD), MAGIC MUSHROOM, MANDRAGORA, MESCALINE, PEYOTE, PHENCYCLIDINE (PCP), PSILOCYBIN, TEONANACATL, VIROLA. See CROSS-DEPENDENCE OF HALLUCINOGENS, MIND-ALTERING DRUGS, PSYCHEDELICS, PSYCHOLEPTICS, PSYCHOTOMIMETIC DRUG.

hallucinogen-affective disorder   See HALLUCINO-GEN-INDUCED MOOD DISORDER.

hallucinogen-delusional disorder   Old phrase for hallucinogen persisting perception disorder (flashbacks).

hallucinogen hallucinosis   Syndrome characterized by brief or extended hallucinations (usually visual) produced by hallucinogens, such as alcohol (usually auditory hallucinations), and in some cases, sensory deprivation (blindness, deafness) or seizures. Does not involve clouding of consciousness, significant loss of intellectual abilities, predominant delusions, or mood disturbances.

hallucinogen-induced mood disorder   A brief-to-long-lasting organic-affective syndrome persisting beyond the period of direct effect of hallucinogen use, characterized by depression or anxiety, self-reproach, guilt feelings, tension, and concern over brain damage or "going crazy." Previously known as hallucinogen-affective disorder.

hallucinogen intoxication   A disorder that usually develops within an hour of oral use of LSD, DMT, or mescaline, consisting of (a) perceptual changes during wakefulness, (b) two or more physical symptoms, such as pupil dilation, tachycardia, blurring of vision, or tremors, or (c) varied behavioral effects, such as marked anxiety or depression. These effects last about six hours for LSD and from an hour to two days for other hallucinogens.

hallucinogen persisting perception disorder   An organic delusional syndrome, transient or long-lasting, that persists beyond the period of direct effect of a hallucinogen. The user experiences all the perceptual changes that occur in hallucinogen hallucinosis, plus the conviction that they correspond to reality. Previously known as hallucinogen-delusional disorder. Commonly known as flashbacks.

hallucinosis   A mental disorder in which recurrent hallucinations are experienced. Types of hallucinosis include: ACUTE, ALCOHOL, BROMIDE, FLASHBACK, HALLUCINOGEN, ORGANIC, PEDUNCULAR. See HALLUCINATION.

halo   1. A narrow bright band observed surrounding the dark afterimage of a bright stimulus. 2. A circle of light surrounding a luminous body, such as the sun or moon, due to light refraction. 3. A bright surround effect in photographic portraits due to strong back-lighting.

halo effect   A tendency when estimating or rating a person with respect to a certain trait, to be influenced by an estimate of some other trait or by the general impression of the person. Impact may be favorable or unfavorable. Compare HORNS EFFECT.

Halstead Impairment Index   (W. Halstead) A measure of biological intelligence computed from results of a battery of tests that include time-sense memory, tactual form-board, critical fusion-frequency, auditory flutter-fusion frequency, speech-perception, and rate-of-tapping tests.

Halstead-Reitan Neuropsychological Test Battery (HRNTB)   (W. Halstead & R. Reitan) A series of tests, including part of the Wechsler tests and the Minnesota Multiphasic Personality Inventory (MMPI), intended to measure brain functioning. There are forms for children and adults. The adult battery commonly has eleven tests. Developed to measure "biological intelligence." Also known as Halstead-Reitan Neuropsychological Scale, Halstead-Reitan Battery (HRB), Halstead-Reitan Test Battery. See CEREBRAL DYSFUNCTION TESTS.

halving method   In psychophysics, adjusting a perception to one-half of some standard.

hamartia   1. A defect of character. 2. The making of a serious error of judgment, usually due to ignorance of a pertinent fact rather than malevolence.

hamartophobia   Morbid fear of making an error. See ENOSIOPHOBIA, PECCATIPHOBIA.

hamaxophobia   Fear of vehicles, seeing or being in them. Also known as amaxophobia.

hammer   A bone in the middle ear, one of the three ossicles that convey sound from the ear drum to the oval window of the inner ear. Also known as malleus.

Hampstead index   A procedure for examining psychoanalytic protocols for the purpose of using the data for research investigations. Developed by employees at the Hampstead Child Therapy Clinic in London.

Hampton Court maze   A well-known maze in England built in 1690 at a palace of William III made of patchwork-hedges. Early mazes (1901) by Willard Small to study learning in the white rat imitated this maze's contour.

Hamsa mantra   (I am that—Indian) The natural vibration of the Inner Being or Self, which occurs spontaneously with inhalation and exhalation of the breath.

hand controls   Devices for persons with disabilities that enable them to operate automobiles or other machinery with only the use of the hands. A car may be equipped with hand controls for the accelerator and brakes, which normally are operated with the feet. See CAR CONTROLS.

hand dominance   See HANDEDNESS, HARRIS TESTS OF LATERAL DOMINANCE.

hand dynamometer   A device used to measure strength of hand grip. Indicates degree of pressure exerted by closing the hand and usually records maximum pressure exerted.

handedness   A tendency to prefer either the right or left hand for performing certain tasks. Usually is related to a dominance effect of the motor cortex on the opposite side of the body. Some investigators have found an association between hemispheric dominance for speech and motor activity. See CEREBRAL DOMINANCE, DOMINANCE, LATERALITY, LEFT-HANDEDNESS, MANUAL DOMINANCE, RIGHT-HANDEDNESS.

handicap   A disability that interferes with normal daily-living activities. See CHALLENGED.

handi-capable   Term sometimes used for handicapped or challenged to indicate that the person has both abilities and feelings.

handicapped   Unable to participate freely in activities typical for the person's age and gender because of a mental or physical abnormality. "Disabled" refers to an impairment that may not be a handicap, depending on the degree to which it is overcome and the specific situation with which the person has to cope. "Challenged" has been suggested to replace handicap because of the negative connotations of that term. See CHALLENGED, DISABILITY, EMOTIONAL HANDICAP.

handicapped child   A child with physical or mental abilities below the level of those of a typical child that impair functioning to some degree, also sometimes used to indicate social deficiencies. See ALEXIA, CHALLENGED, DYSLEXIA, EMOTIONAL HANDICAP.

handicapping strategy   See SELF-HANDICAPPING STRATEGY.

handshake   In electronics, a signal exchange acknowledging that communication can take place between or among devices. A hardware handshake takes place over wires not used for data; in a software one, the signals go through the lines that transmit data.

hands-on (learning)   Training in which the learner participates actively and realistically in the activity being learned.

Hand Test (HT)   See THE HAND TEST.

hand-to-mouth reaction   A tendency of infants to bring all objects within reach of the hand to the mouth.

hand-tool dexterity test   See BENNETT HAND-TOOL DEXTERITY TEST.

hand-washing obsession   A morbid preoccupation with washing the hands, possibly the result of an unconscious feeling of guilt ("Out, damned spot! out, I say!" Act V, Scene 1, *Macbeth*). See ABLUTOMANIA.

handwriting analysis   1. A reputedly unscientific practice that purported to analyze personality from handwriting. Also known as graphology. 2. A science used largely for signature and document identification.

handwriting scale   A scale consisting of the same sentence written by ten or more individuals with handwriting ranging from illegible to exceptionally clear. A person is asked to write the same sentence as on the scale, and the rater compares the person's written sentence with the sentences on the scale; rating the person's handwriting from 1 (very poor) to 10 (excellent).

handwriting system   Any conventional style of writing that involves standardization of design of letters, slant, size, and proportion of parts (such as relative height and width of letters), and organization of one, two, and three space letters into a scale of thirds, fourths, or fifths. Well-known systems of English include roundhand, Spencerian, and vertical writing. See CURSIVE WRITING.

Hanfmann-Kasanin Concept Formation Test (E. Hanfmann & J. S. Kasanin) A task used to assess conceptual thinking as well as mental impairment. The participant classifies 22 blocks of various colors, shapes, heights, and width into four categories: tall-wide, flat-wide, tall-narrow, flat-narrow. See VYGOTSKY TEST.

hanging-arousal   See EROTIZED HANGING.

Hans   See LITTLE HANS, CLEVER HANS.

haphalgesia   1. Abnormal sensitivity of the skin. 2. An extreme sensitivity of cutaneous pain receptors, usually of psychogenic origin, as observed by reactions to specific substances, such as certain fluids that have special significance for the person. Also known as aphalgesia. See HAPTIC.

haphazard sampling   In research, selecting subjects or participants in an inconsistent and unsystematic manner so that the sample is probably not representative of the population under study. See these forms of sampling: ACCIDENTAL, ADEQUATE, BIASED, CONVENIENCE, JUDGMENT, REPRESENTATIVE.

haphephobia   Excessive dislike or morbid fear of being touched. Also known as aphephobia, haptephobia.

haploid   Pertaining to cells or similar structures that have a single set of unpaired chromosomes. Also known as monoploid.

haploid cell   A cell that contains half the normal number of chromosomes needed for a complete genetic complement. For humans, the haploid number is 23 chromosomes. Haploid cells are gametes, or the cells of ova or spermatozoa, which, when combined in a zygote (fertilized ovum), contain the normal diploid number, or full set of genetic traits (46 chromosomes for humans).

haploid number   In humans there are 23 chromosomes in the sex cells (collectively, gametes; specifically, sperm and ova). The diploid number found in somatic cells is 46.

haploidy   1. The state or condition of haploid. 2. The process of meiosis in which the diploid number of chromosomes in a germ cell is reduced by half, during a stage of cell division in which each daughter cell receives one rather than two of each chromosome in a diploid set.

haplology   Speech so rapid that syllables are omitted, common in manic states in which there is pressure of speech.

haploscope   An instrument in which figures are presented separately to the two eyes in such manner as to force compensatory displacement or rolling movements of the eyes to maintain binocular fusion.

haptephobia   1. Morbid fear of being touched by another person, or of touching another person. 2. See HAPHEPHOBIA.

haptic   1. Pertaining to the sense of touch or contact and the cutaneous sensory system in general. 2. Refers to skin sensitivity.

haptic hallucination   tactile hallucination

haptic illusion   A distorted perception of touching or of being touched. See ARISTOTLE'S ILLUSION for an example.

haptic perception   The detection of stimuli through tactile-nerve endings in the skin. See TOUCH SENSE.

haptometer   A device for measuring differential sensitivity to touch. See ESTHESIOMETER, HAIR ESTHESIOMETER.

haptophobia   Excessive fear of touching another person. Also known as haphophobia, thixophobia. See HAPTEPHOBIA.

hara-kari   seppuko

hard colors   Phrase applied to red and yellow.

hard data   Information obtained from objective sources, such as blood pressure, weight, and multiple choice tests, in which no discretion or judgment is needed to get numeric results. Compare SOFT DATA.

hard determinism   In psychoanalytic theory, a kind of determinism that allows no room for freedom of choice or indeterminism. See DETERMINISM, SOFT DETERMINISM.

hardheaded   hard-nosed

hardiness   (S. Kobasa) The capacity to survive physically and mentally in conditions of extreme environmental stress.

hard-nosed   Slang, possibly used mostly by graduate students in psychology, referring to a psychology based on experimentation, especially of physiological factors, and in turn those students so designated refer to psychology students in other areas as "soft-headed" or Paul Meehl's "muddleheaded." Also known as hardheaded. See TOUGH-MINDED.

hard-of-hearing   Refers to a person with mild deafness that usually can be corrected with the use of a hearing aid. See HYPACUSIA.

hard sell   An attempt to get people to buy merchandise by powerful stimuli, such as visual or verbal announcements that are compelling to listen to, or that repeat themselves strongly. Often implies overly-aggressive selling.

hard-to-get phenomenon   (E. Hatfield) In social psychology, the finding that, contrary to popular assumption, remaining aloof and showing no interest do not inspire attraction.

hard-wired   Slang for well-established genetic behaviors, resistant to modification.

Hardy-Rand-Rittler Pseudoisochromatic Plates (H-R-R Plates)   (L. H. Hardy, G. Rand, & J. M. Rittler) A test for color blindness that can indicate tritanopia (blue deficiency where yellow, yellow-orange, and yellow-green are not distinguished; rarest form of dichromatism) and tetartanopia (hypothesized color anomaly with difficulty discriminating between yellow and blue). Also known as American Optical Corporation Pseudoisochromatic Plates for Testing Color Vision.

Hardy-Weinberg law   (G. H. Hardy & W. Weinberg) A principle of genetic stability in a large, geographically stable population in which random mating occurs. States that, with respect to a particular pair of alleles, the frequency of the genes or alleles remains the same, providing there is no mutation, selective advantage, or differential mating.

harm-avoidance need   The need to avoid harm, illness, or injury.

harmonic   An overtone whose frequency is an exact multiple of the lowest, or fundamental, tone.

harmonic analysis   The use of Fourier's series analysis (1822) or a harmonic analyzer to resolve complex wave forms into simple sine components. Ohm's Acoustic Law (1843) asserted that the mathematical technique actually occurred psychophysiologically as part of hearing.

harmonic mean (HM or **H)**   A method of obtaining an average of differing rates, depending on the reciprocal of the arithmetic mean of the reciprocals of a series of values.

harmonics   Components of complex tones that are multiples or partials of the fundamental frequency. Each partial has its own pitch, known as a harmonic or overtone. The harmonics heard with the fundamental tone give a distinct timbre to the sound of a musical instrument and permit, for example, distinguishing a clarinet and saxophone playing the same note.

harmonizer   A group member who plays the role of diplomat and facilitates group unity by mediating between opposing points of view and reducing interpersonal tension.

harmony   1. In music, an arrangement of parts such as lines or musical tones into balanced and pleasing patterns. 2. Friendly relations among people.

harm reduction   The argument that since it is impossible to get some people to give up harmful or undesirable behavior, measures should be taken to minimize the adverse effects or results of such behavior. For instance, intravenous drug users should be given clean needles to prevent the spread of disease from sharing needles. Some see such efforts as encouraging criminal or sinful behavior. See LOGICAL CONSEQUENCES, NATURAL CONSEQUENCES.

harpaxophobia   Morbid fear of robbers, or of becoming a victim of robbery.

harp theory (of hearing)   place theory (of hearing)

harria   (R. B. Cattell) A personality factor trait marked by assertiveness, decisiveness, and realism in behavior.

Harris Tests of Lateral Dominance   (D. B. Harris) Tests designed to determine predominance of one side of the body over the other, and, in some cases, crossed dominance. Hand dominance is determined by such activities as hammering and cutting with scissors; eye dominance, by looking through a tube; foot dominance, by kicking or pretending to stamp out a fire.

Harrower-Erickson Group Rorschach   (M. R. Harrower-Erickson, M. E. Steiner) The Rorschach technique administered in a group. Usually, the cards are flashed on a screen and participants write their responses, later to be read and summarized. Also known as Harrower's Group Rorschach, Harrower's Multiple Choice Test. See PROJECTIVE PSYCHOTHERAPY.

Harrower Rorschach Inkblots   (M. R. Harrower-Erickson) Inkblots that may be either projected or shown one at a time by means of large posters. Participants write what they see. Various ways of evaluating replies are used, depending on specific needs of the examiners. See HARROWER-ERIKSON GROUP RORSCHACH, PROJECTIVE PSYCHOTHERAPY.

Hartley oscillator   (R. V. Hartley) A bio-telemetric technique in which an encapsulated, ingestible tiny transmitter is swallowed for purposes of determining pressure changes within the viscera.

Hartley statistical test   (H. O. Hartley) A test for detecting homogeneity of variance that uses the F_{max} statistic. Test is not generally used because of extreme sensitivity to violations of the normality assumption. Also known as Hartley's Test. See F_{MAX} STATISTIC.

hashish   A form of cannabis sativa made of resin obtained from the flowering tops of the marijuana plant. Generally is several times as potent as marijuana made from the leaves and stems of the same plant. The active ingredient in all forms of cannabis is delta-9-tetrahydrocannabinol, metabolized in the liver to a related substance that produces intoxicating effects. Hashish oil is an even more potent form. See HALLUCINOGENS, PSYCHEDELICS.

hassles   (R. Lazarus) Little stressors that include irritating demands and troubled relationships that impact on a person daily.

hasty generalizations   In logic, a fallacy committed by concluding or generalizing on the basis of insufficient evidence, as in "All Italians are romantic."

haunted swing illusion   A distorted perception experienced when a participant is placed in a swing that apparently oscillates in the usual manner, whereas in reality the swing is motionless and the participant is in a special room that, with its entire contents, is in motion.

haunting   The supposed return of the spirit or ghost of someone who met an untimely death, for the purpose of attending to "unfinished" business, which may include tormenting the guilty.

having mode   (E. Fromm) An attitude to life that overvalues possessions.

Hawthorne effect   (F. I. Roetheisonberg, W. J. Dickson) In research, the tendency of the participants to behave differently than they normally would because they know they are taking part in a study. In the Hawthorne study, a reduction of illumination did not reduce production as expected because, it was concluded, the participants knowing they were part of a study, strove to do better when illumination was reduced. The Hawthorne effect may threaten the validity of some experiments. A second Hawthorne effect was that of social pressure to make personal output level conform to the prevailing norm. Named after the Hawthorne Works of the Western Electric Company, a site of famous experiments and studies performed around 1930 by Elton Mayo and others on the effects of social organization and productivity. Compare NOVELTY EFFECT. See EXPERIMENTAL ERRORS.

Hay Aptitude Test Battery   (E. N. Hay) Five brief paper-and-pencil tests for measuring various types of office and clerical ability.

Hay method (of job evaluation)   Using employee questionnaires to measure the knowledge and skill required; the thinking or problem-solving needed; accountability and influence; and the physical, sensory, and stress-related working conditions. A widely used proprietary system of the Hay Group, an international management consultant firm founded in 1943 in Philadelphia by Edward N. Hay. See JOB EVALUATION.

Hb   See HEMOGLOBIN.

H.C.   hypothetical construct

HCFA   Health Care Finance Administration

Hd   In Rorschach test scoring, a symbol for human (H) and detail (d), parts of human figures visible in a living body such as head or foot; not anatomical.

HD   Huntington's disease

head   1. In electronics, the read/write mechanism in a disk or tape drive. 2. Slang for oral sex.

headache   Pain often originating from some other part of the body but experienced in the head. Types include: CLUSTER, LEAD-CAP, MIGRAINE, ORGANIC, POST-TRAUMATIC, TENSION. See CAREBARIA, CLAVUS, NEURASTHENIC HELMET.

head-banging   The act or habit of repeatedly striking the head on a crib, wall, or floor during a temper tantrum. Considered to be one of the many expressions of rage in a young child who feels frustrated or neglected. See HEAD-KNOCKING.

head consciousness   Over-awareness of the head, with a fear that it might suffer injury. It is a posttraumatic symptom that sometimes develops after a severe head injury.

headhunter   A job recruiter, usually one looking for scarce-to-find specialists or senior executives in high demand, often without public advertisement.

head-knocking   A habit of bumping the head against a wall, crib side, or other solid object, observed in infants but differentiated from the temper-tantrum type of head-banging by being more persistent but less powerful than head-banging. Considered by some as an attempt to get attention.

head nystagmus   The oscillatory movement of the head that occurs when an animal is rotated; the head is slowly turned in the opposite direction to that of the rotation and then brought quickly back; this is repeated, with the rapid component of the action always in the direction of rotation.

head retraction   A reflex withdrawal of the head when the nares (nasal cavity) are sharply irritated.

head-rolling   Repeated movements of the head from side to side as manifested by some infants prior to going to sleep. Has been attributed to inhibition of movement in the crib, lack of stimulating play, and possibly to intrauterine passivity. Also known as *jactatio capitis nocturna*.

Head's areas/zones   (H. Head) Areas of the skin showing lack of sensitivity or excessive sensitivity due to visceral disease.

head-shrinking   The shrinking of severed heads, usually human, through the application of heat or herbal liquids, practiced among headhunters and other societies mainly in Asia and South America, who use such heads for mental healing and other ritual purposes. The "power" or strength of the individual is often said to reside in the head and be available to its possessor. Probably derived from this practice is "headshrinker," or simply "shrink," as a slang word for a psychotherapist. See FAITH HEALING, HEX DOCTOR, MAGICAL THINKING, VOODOO DEATH.

head-slaved   In ergonomics, output directed by the position of the operator's head/helmet. Also known as neurocontrol.

Head Start   A federally funded program offering early life compensatory education to preschoolers in families below the poverty level.

head trauma   An injury to the head, usually through a severe blow. Results may range from concussion to chronic head trauma, in which impairment is permanent. See BRAIN TRAUMA, CEREBRAL TRAUMA.

healing groups   (M. A. Lieberman) Such groups have been divided into four classes: (a) group therapy, using such methods as psychodrama and round table therapy; (b) self-help organizations, such as Alcoholics Anonymous, GROW, Recovery, THEOS; (c) sensitivity groups, encounter groups connected with the human potential movement; and (d) consciousness raising groups that stress nonprofessional control.

health   See ALLIED HEALTH PROFESSIONALS, CLIENT-CENTERED MENTAL HEALTH CONSULTATION, COMMUNITY MENTAL HEALTH, EMMANUEL CHURCH HEALTH CLASS, FLIGHT INTO HEALTH, HOME HEALTH AIDE, INDIAN HEALTH SERVICE, MENTAL HEALTH, MENTAL-HEALTH CLINIC, MENTAL-HEALTH WORKER, MILLON BEHAVIORAL HEALTH INVENTORY, PUBLIC-HEALTH APPROACH, PUBLIC-HEALTH NURSE, SAFETY AND HEALTH EDUCATION.

health belief model   A theory that whether a person practices a particular health-related behavior depends on the degree to which the person fears a personal health threat and believes that practicing the behavior will reduce the threat.

health-maintenance organization (HMO)   A form of multidisciplinary medical care in which physicians, often including psychiatrists and psychologists as well as paramedical personnel, provide comprehensive health services to subscribers for a fixed fee. The health-maintenance organization then may assume financial responsibility for subsequent hospitalization, if required. The United States Public Health Service Act of 1973 recognized the health-maintenance organization program and provides subsidies. Also known as health-management organization.

health professionals   Persons who have received advanced training that equips them to work in the field of physical or mental health (for example, as a psychiatrist, psychologist, neurologist, physiatrist, orthopedist, rehabilitation counselor, speech pathologist, physical therapist, occupational therapist, social worker, psychiatric nurse, and biomedical engineer).

health psychology   (J. D. Matarazzo) An aggregate of specific educational, scientific, and professional contributions of scientific psychology to the promotion and maintenance of health, the prevention and treatment of illness, and the identification of etiologic and diagnostic correlations of health, illness, and related dysfunctions.

health-related facilities   See COMMUNITY-MENTAL HEALTH CENTER, PSYCHIATRIC SERVICES, PSYCHOTHERAPY.

health sweep imagery   Conjured mental pictures of a liquid or other substance flowing through the person's body, usually starting from the head and going to the toes. Imagined as cleansing the body of disease and pathology.

health visitor   A health professional, usually employed by a local agency, who visits families where health supervision is needed.

healthy identification   Modeling personal attitudes or behavior, consciously or unconsciously, after another person who has sound values, attitudes, and reactions.

Healy Picture Completion Test   (W. Healy & G. Fernald) An early intelligence task consisting of a large board showing an outdoor scene. The board has ten square "holes." Typically, there are 50 squares that can be put into the "holes," all of the same size with different pictures on them. The task of the participant is to put the correct squares in the proper places to complete the scene. Also known as Healy Completion Test, a part of the Healy-Fernald Test series. See PINTNER-PATERSON SCALE OF PERFORMANCE TESTS.

hearing   The perception of sounds through the auditory sensory mechanism in the inner ear and brain. Sound waves enter the external ear (pinna), cause the eardrum (tympanum) to vibrate, and then are transmitted by the ossicles to the fluid-filled cochlea in the inner ear. The vibrations are transformed into electrical impulses, carried by the auditory nerve to the cortex, where they are registered and interpreted. Also known as audition. Types of hearing include binaural and colored. See COMMUNITY SPEECH-AND-HEARING CENTERS, CONTRALATERAL HEARING AID, FUNCTIONAL HEARING DISORDERS, NONORGANIC HEARING LOSS, RANGE OF AUDIBILITY/OF HEARING, SENSORINEURAL DEAFNESS/HEARING LOSS.

hearing aid   An electronic device that amplifies sounds for persons with a hearing deficiency. Useful with conduction deafness but does not compensate for nerve deafness.

hearing disorders   Diseases, injuries, or congenital defects that are the cause of some degree of deafness. Congenital deafness may include persons who were born with normal hearing but suffered a loss of that ability before sounds became meaningful. Deafness acquired after sounds became meaningful is called adventitious deafness. "Functional hearing disorders" refers to inability to understand the human voice at certain levels of loudness.

hearing loss   Inability to hear a normal range of tone frequencies or a normally perceived level of sound intensity, or both. The degree of loss is usually recorded as a percentage of the normal level. See SENSORINEURAL DEAFNESS.

hearing meter   Outmoded phrase for audiometer.

hearing mute   Common phrase for a person who, from birth or from an early age, has been unable to speak and who behaves as though deaf, but who nevertheless possess ability to hear.

hearing theories   Several theories of hearing have been advanced to explain auditory phenomena, but no single one is completely satisfactory. Theories of hearing include: BÉKÉSY'S TRAVELING WAVE, FREQUENCY, HELMHOLTZ, HYDRAULIC, PLACE, RESONANCE, TELEPHONE, VOLLEY, WEVER-BRAY. See WEVER-BRAY EFFECT.

heart-lung machine   A mechanical device that maintains functions of the heart and lungs during surgery. Being on such a machine may result in depression and memory deficits, such as vocabulary reduction.

heart rate in emotion   Strong emotions can increase the rate of the heartbeat through sympathetic impulses. Parasympathetic reflexes resulting from increased blood pressure during emotion also can have an effect of altering the heart rate. A strong parasympathetic reflex can slow the heart rate to a point at which it may appear on the verge of stopping. See CARDIAC REACTIONS.

heat dolorimeter   An instrument used to measure pain. Under standardized conditions a light is shone on a black-painted spot on the participant's forehead until reported that the sensation of heat becomes pain (the time is taken as the pain threshold) or until no further stimulation is accepted (pain tolerance). Compare COLD PRESSOR TEST. See DOLORIMETER.

heat effects   Changes in mental or physical conditions due to temperatures above the normal comfort range. Performance appears optimal up to temperatures of around 90° F (32° C), after which performance declines. See ACCLIMATIZATION, HEAT-INDUCED ASTHENIA, HEAT STRESS, OVERHEATING.

heat fear   See THERMOPHOBIA.

heat grill   A device for simultaneously arousing warmth and cold sensations in adjacent skin areas. Consists of glass or metal tubes that can be filled with water of different temperatures that can be simultaneously applied to an area of the skin. See PARADOXICAL COLD.

hot   cold   heat grill

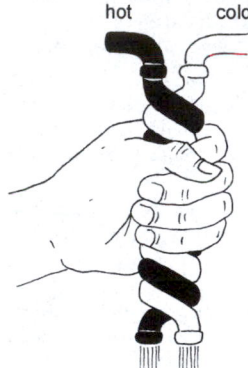

heat-induced asthenia   A condition associated with extended exposure to heat and characterized by general physical and mental impairment, fatigue, lethargy, irritability, insomnia, headache, and possible loss of appetite. See HEAT EFFECTS, HEAT STRESS.

heat spot   See WARM(TH) SPOT.

heat stress   Any stress effect on an organism that results from exposure to excessive ambient temperatures, particularly the physiological disorders that include heat-induced asthenia, heat exhaustion, and heat stroke.

Hebb rule   (D. O. Hebb) A theory that the cellular basis of learning is due to strengthening of synapses that are repeatedly active when the postsynaptic neuron fires. See ASSOCIATION-SENSATION RATIO, AUTOCORRELATION THEORY, FRACTIONATION, HEBB'S THEORY OF PERCEPTUAL LEARNING, PHASE SEQUENCE.

Hebb's Theory of Perceptual Learning   (D. O. Hebb) A point of view that impulses are stored in cell assemblies in the cerebral cortex, and separate assemblies can become coordinated to form a sequence or totality. See ASSOCIATION-SENSATION RATIO, AUTOCORRELATION THEORY, CELL ASSEMBLY THEORY, FRACTIONATION, HEBB RULE, PHASE SEQUENCE.

hebephilia   1. The loving of a youth by an older person, usually much older. 2. Sexual activity by an adult with an adolescent. See PEDOPHILIA.

hebephrenia   (K. L. Kahlbaum, E. Hecker) Schizophrenia marked by inappropriate affect, silly behavior, shallow relationships, and childish actions; so named because it originally was considered to occur around puberty. Also known as disorganized type of schizophrenia, hebephrenic schizophrenia. See SCHIZOPHRENIA.

hebetic   Pertaining to youth or adolescence.

hebetude   A state of severe emotional dullness or disinterest observed in some schizophrenia patients who withdraw from the environment and also from themselves, becoming apathetic and listless.

heboid   Pertaining to youth, and particularly to puberty. See HEBETIC.

heboidophrenia   (K. Kahlbaum) Obsolete name for the simple form of schizophrenia.

Hecht-Shlaer anomaloscope   (S. Hecht & S. Shlaer) An instrument used to screen for color blindness by measuring the amounts of green and red needed to match a given yellow (the Rayleigh equation). Narrowband color filters generate lights of the appropriate wavelengths.

Hecht's theory (of vision)   A theory of retinal excitation consistent with knowledge of neural action. Selig Hecht assumed that light as a stimulus decomposes retinal photosensitive substances, and that recomposition takes place immediately but quickens after the stimulus ceases. Aided by catalytic action, the decomposition and recombination excite the neural impulse. Also known as Hecht's photochemical theory, Hecht theory of color vision.

hedgehog people   (A. Simpkins) People who tend to remain in the same place throughout life, as in the same geographic area, vocational specialty, marriage, and social circle. See FOX PEOPLE.

hedging   In communications, generally verbal, indicating not being sure, with statements such as "It could be . . .", "perhaps . . .", "it is possible . . .", "one hears . . .".

hedonic enjoyment   (A. S. Waterman) The positive effect that accompanies the satisfaction of needs.

hedonic level/value   The level of pleasure.

hedonic relativity   The degree of pleasantness of a reinforcer in relation to other reinforcers. See REINFORCEMENT.

hedonics   The branch of psychology that investigates pleasurable and unpleasurable feelings.

hedonic theory   (J. Bentham) A point of view that behavior can be explained quite simply: moving toward pleasurable stimuli and away from unpleasant ones.

hedonic tone   The simple pleasantness-unpleasantness dimension (quality) accompanying certain sensory experiences.

hedonic-tone factor   (D. E. Berlyne) The quality of an experience in terms of its position on a scale ranging from pleasant to unpleasant. Proposed to identify artistic evaluation variables manifested by verbal expressions of pleasure.

hedonism   1. (Epicures) In philosophy, a doctrine positing that pleasure is the prime goal of life. 2. Orientation toward need gratification and pleasure. 3. (H. Spencer) In psychology, a theory that activities are selected by resulting in pleasure or removing pain, the major motivating forces in human behavior. Ideas permit humans to prefer greater future pleasure combined with lesser present pleasure. See LAW OF EFFECT, PLEASURE PRINCIPLE.

hedonistic calculus   (J. Bentham) A general explanation of behavior as dependent on the calculation of anticipated pain and pleasure (the "two sovereign masters") as the consequence of considered actions.

hedonistic orientation   Phrase sometimes applied to stage 2 of Lawrence Kohlberg's preconventional level of moral reasoning. In stage 2, an act is appraised for its potential for self-gratification, although awareness of the needs of others does exist.

hedonophobia   Morbid fear of feeling pleasure. Also known as hedenophobia.

heel-to-knee test   An examination for physical ataxia in which the patient, from a reclining position, must raise a foot, then touch the knee with the opposite heel and move the heel along the leg to the shin, with eyes open or closed.

heft   1. To lift. 2. To experience the weight of an object as judged by the kinesthetic sensations aroused by holding or lifting it.

hegemony   Overriding influence or control over others, especially as established by law or custom. In some cultures males have social control over females; parents over their children. See EMPOWERMENT.

Heidbreder test   Alternative name for the Minnesota Mechanical Ability Tests, named for Edna Heidbreder, who helped develop the technique.

Heidelberg man   An extinct race of humans represented by a fossil jaw found in 1907 near Heidelberg, Germany, regarded as an early type of human being. Thought to have lived between the second and third glacial periods. Also known as *Homo heidelbergensis*.

height fear   See ACROPHOBIA, ALTOPHOBIA, BATOPHOBIA.

Heinis constant   A measure of mental-growth rates by converting mental-age units into theoretically equal mental-growth units and dividing the result by the chronological age. Also known as personal constant. Named after Swiss psychologist Hugo Heinis (b. 1883).

Heisenberg indeterminacy principle   (W. Heisenberg) A basic concept in the general field of measurement. Developed in the field of physics (that it is impossible to measure simultaneously the location and the velocity of an atomic particle), the principle states that the act of measuring a process changes that process. Also known as the uncertainty principle.

Hejna test   An instrument used to measure speech articulation by presenting pictures designed to elicit verbal responses that contain specific sounds. Named after 20th century American speech pathologist Robert F. Hejna.

helicotrema   A small opening at the apex of the cochlea of the inner ear connecting the scala tympani and the scala vestibuli.

heliocentric theory   The Copernican understanding of the solar system; the universe is no longer seen to revolve about humans on the earth. From the mid-16th century an increasing awareness that the earth is but one planet circling a medium-sized star in one corner of the known universe. The new thinking even depreciates the importance of humans, and it raises the possibilities of many other people on a large number of other inhabitable planets.

heliophobia   Morbid fear of the sun or sunlight. See PHENGOPHOBIA.

heliotropism   Orienting of an organism in relation to a light source, especially the sun. There is positive heliotropism and negative heliotropism, bending toward or away from light. See PHOTOTROPISM, TAXIS, TROPISM.

helix   A spiral or spiral in form. Plural is helices. See CYTOSINE.

Hellenic love   Old name for homosexual love based on the concept that such love was common in ancient Greece. See LOVE.

helleno(logo)mania   A tendency to use obscure Greek or Latin terms instead of English words in writing.

hellenologophobia   Morbid fear of Greek terms (such as this one) or, generally, fear of complex scientific or pseudoscientific terminology.

Heller's dementia/syndrome   (T. Heller) A degenerative disease of the neurons of the cerebral cortex. Typically occurring around the age of three and leading to loss of speech, as well as motor impairment.

hell fear   See HADEPHOBIA, STYGIOPHOBIA.

Hellin's law   A theory that as the number of infants in a multiple birth increases, the relative frequency of occurrence compared to total births in a population decreases geometrically. (Twins occur once in 89 births, triplets in 89^2, and quadruplets once in 89^3.) Named after Polish pathologist Dyonizy Hellin (1867–1935).

Helmholtz chessboard   (H. von Helmholtz) A hyperbolic chessboard used to demonstrate the curving of ocular direction lines in vision.

Helmholtz color mixer   (H. von Helmholtz) A device that permits viewing two complete spectra, superimposed at right angles to each other.

Helmholtz color triangle   (H. von Helmholtz) An early representation of the color diagram, depicting the spectral colors located at different distances from the inside of the triangle which represents white.

Helmholtz ligament   (H. von Helmholtz) In the middle ear, the part of the anterior ligament of the malleus attached to the greater tympanic spine.

Helmholtz resonators   (H. von Helmholtz) Spherical brass bottles of different sizes used to produce tones by blowing air across the tops of the bottles.

Helmholtz theory (of hearing)   (H. von Helmholtz) In 1863, the point of view that the ear is a resonating organ, the resonators being the rods of Corti. In 1869, Helmholtz changed what he thought were the resonators from the rods of Corti to the transverse fibers of the basilar membrane. Each basilar membrane fiber was thought to resonate to a particular frequency of sound. See PLACE THEORY (OF HEARING).

Helmholtz theory (of accommodation) (H. von Helmholtz) A point of view that the shape of the lens of the eye becomes convex as the ciliary muscle relaxes and flattens as the ciliary muscle contracts. The concept of the lens changing shape originated with Descartes, with important data support from Young and Purkinje, but it was Helmholtz who suggested the physiological mechanism and vehemently argued for the theory.

Helmholtz theory (of vision) See YOUNG-HELMHOLTZ THEORY.

helminthophobia Morbid fear of worms or of having worms. Also known as vermi(ni)phobia.

helpful figure A child's make-believe fairylike person, which may be male or female, to which the child can turn for help or sympathy. See IMAGINARY COMPANION, URPSYCHOLOGY.

helping behavior Prosocial actions, typically in response to a small request that involves no personal risk.

helping model (R. R. Kerchief) A broad-based educational helping model concerned with the learner's motor development, perceptual skills, cognitive development, emotional maturity, interpersonal skills, expression, creativity, and ethical values.

helping professions Fields of physical or mental health. Sometimes also referred to as allied helping professions. See HEALTH PROFESSIONAL.

helping relationship A "relationship in which at least one of the parties has the intent of promoting the growth, development, maturity, improved functioning, improved coping with life of the other. The other . . . may be one individual or a group" (From Carl Rogers' *On Becoming a Person*).

helplessness See LEARNED HELPLESSNESS, HELPLESSNESS THEORY, PSYCHIC HELPLESSNESS.

helplessness theory 1. (M. Seligman) The point of view that in humans a feeling of being dispirited and helpless is due to continued frustrations and failures, becoming depressed, giving up, and simply surviving as, for example, is seen in some homeless street people. 2. The phenomenon of an animal giving up when faced with an impossible-to-solve problem. See ATTRIBUTION, LEARNED HELPLESSNESS.

help-rejecting complainer A person who seeks assistance, counseling, psychotherapy etc., then rejects assistance, advice, counsel, but still continues rather than quitting.

hematophobia Morbid fear of blood or, more specifically, the sight of blood. Also known as hemophobia. See ERYTHROPHOBIA, HEMOPHOBIA.

hemeralopia A form of day blindness in which the person has difficulty seeing in bright light but has good vision in dim light. Also known as day blindness, hemeralopsia, hemeranopia, night sight. See DAY BLINDNESS.

hemeraphonia A speech disorder in which the person is unable to vocalize during the day but able to speak normally at night.

hemian(a)esthesia Insensibility to touch stimuli on one side of the body. Also known as unilateral anesthesia.

hemianacusia Loss of hearing in one ear.

hemianalgesia Insensitivity to pain on one side of the body.

hemianopsia An ocular disorder marked by the loss of vision of one half the visual field in one or both eyes. Also known as hemianopia, hemiopia. See VISION THEORIES.

hemiasomatognosia Anton's symptom/syndrome

hemiballism(us) A type of involuntary movement characterized by flailing of the arms and legs on one half of the body. Often is associated with extrapyramidal lesions.

hemichorea (S. W. Mitchell) Silas Mitchell's term for athetosis, or slow chorea-like movements on one-half side of the body.

hemicrania A disorder (such as pain experienced during a migraine headache) in only one side of the head. See MIGRAINE.

hemiopia hemianopia

hemiparesis Paralysis of one side of the body. See SPASTIC HEMIPARESIS.

hemiplegia A type of paralysis that affects one side of the body. See HYSTERICAL PARALYSIS, NOCTURNAL HEMIPLEGIA.

hemiplegia alternans A type of contralateral paralysis involving cranial nerves and the limbs on the opposite side of the body.

hemiplegia alternans hypoglossica A form of hemiplegia due to a lesion of the hypoglossal nerve on the opposite side of the paralyzed area.

hemisphere Half of a spherical structure, particularly the brain. Kinds of hemisphere include: CEREBELLAR, CEREBRAL, CONTRALATERAL, DOMINANT, IPSILATERAL, LEADING, LEFT, MINOR, RIGHT.

hemispherectomy Sometimes refers to a surgical removal of half of the cerebral hemisphere of the brain but more often to cutting it in half, usually done in the case of malignant brain tumors or intractable epilepsy. Despite expectations of mental deterioration following this radical surgery, some patients show improvement on many tests after removal of the affected portion of the brain. The removal is also known as hemidecortication.

hemispheres The symmetrical halves of the cerebrum and cerebellum.

hemispheric communications The study of interhemispheric and intracerebral communications. Various disciplines and sophisticated measurement techniques are employed in conducting research aimed at understanding the coordination of mental activity involving both hemispheres of the brain.

hemispheric lateralization The separate functions of the two hemispheres of the brain.

hemispherical dominance lateral dominance

hemizygote An organism with only one of a possible pair of chromosomes. It is normal for human males with respect to the X chromosome since males possess only one, the matching chromosome being a Y. Males with the XY complement are hemizygous in the matter of X-linked genes. See ZYGOTE.

hemizygous Having unpaired genes in an otherwise diploid cell. See HEMIZYGOTE.

hemizygous chromosome A chromosome having a genetic deficiency or without allelic counterparts. See HOMOLOGOUS CHROMOSOME.

hemlock   See SORCERY DRUGS.

hemoglobin (Hb)   An iron-rich pigment of red blood cells that has a powerful attraction for oxygen molecules. Allows the blood to carry 60 times as much oxygen per fluid volume as blood plasma without hemoglobin. The pigment, when saturated with oxygen, produces the red color of blood.

hemophilia   An X-linked hereditary tendency to hemorrhage caused by a congenital deficiency or total absence of factor 8. See BLOOD DISORDER.

hemophobia   Morbid fear of blood or, more specifically, of bleeding. See HEMATOPHOBIA.

hemorrhage   Bleeding. Any loss of blood from an artery or vein, but especially when copious.

hemorrhage and thirst (hypothesis)   A postulate that loss of blood increases thirst. Various animal experiments have produced conflicting evidence regarding an association between blood loss and thirst.

hemothymia   Morbid desire to murder. Almost literally, a lust for blood.

hemp (plant)   Common name for cannabis sativa, the source of marijuana, hashish, bhang, charas, and ganja. Hemp is also used to make products such as clothing, rope, and paper, even American paper currency. The breed of hemp that makes the best clothing is tall and stringy and has little psychoactive potency; and contrariwise, the breeds used for the cannabinoid resins tend to be short and make poor fiber products.

henbane   Folk name for the plant, *hyoscyamus niger*, a source of an anticholinergic substance that in small doses functions as a sedative and mild hallucinogen, but in concentrated form can cause delirium and death. One component chemical, hyoscine, is a drug sometimes associated with twilight sleep, administered in the 1950s to women in labor. In the Middle Ages, henbane was administered to people believed to be possessed by a demon. Henbane is identified in Shakespeare's Hamlet as the poison poured into the ear of Hamlet's father.

Henmon-Nelson Test of Mental Ability   (V. Henmon & M. J. Nelson) A group test to assess mental ability for persons from the third through 14th grades. A verbal test of the spiral omnibus variety, used mostly as a scholastic aptitude test.

Henning odor prism   (H. Henning) A classification scheme for smells in which the six primary smells are located at the six corners of a prism: spicy, resinous, and burned at one end of the prism, and fragrant, ethereal, and putrid in corresponding positions at the other. Intermediate smells are represented along the edges of the prism or on the surfaces, but not inside. Also known as Henning's smell prism. See ODOR PRISM.

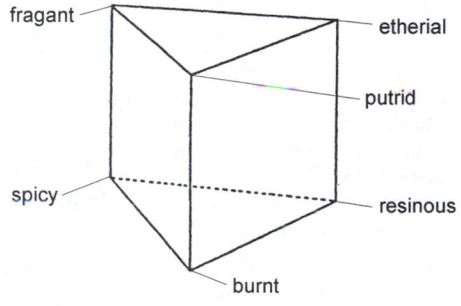

Henning odor prism

Henning's taste tetrahedron   (H. Henning) A four-sided solid with the primary tastes: sweet, sour, salty, and bitter located at its apexes. Other tastes located on the edges, surfaces, or inside the solid were considered to be made up of two, three, and all four primaries respectively. See WATER AS TASTE.

henry (H)   The SI (metric system) unit of inductance, equal to the inductance of a closed circuit in which an electromotive force of 1 volt is produced by a current in the circuit which varies uniformly at a rate of 1 ampere per second. Named after American physicist Joseph Henry (1797–1878).

Hensen's cells   (V. Hensen) Supporting cells of triangular shape that form the outer rounded border of the organ of Corti in the inner ear. Named after German anatomist and physiologist Victor Hensen (1835–1924).

hepatic   Pertaining to or located in the liver.

herbal ecstasy   A street drug using ephedrine, promising euphoria and enhanced sexual performance, basically a mild stimulant. Can cause heart attack. See ECSTASY.

Herbartianism   (J. F. Herbart) A 19th-century psychological system built around the idea that a new sense perception, to be recognized, must be related to an apperceptive mass of previously acquired ideas. Also known as Herbartian psychology.

herd   A group of animals, human or otherwise, that manifests a low degree of social organization.

herd instinct   (W. Trotter) A drive in animals to congregate in flocks and herds, and for humans to belong to groups and participate in social activities. No longer considered either universal or instinctual. See GREGARIOUSNESS.

here and now   In group dynamics, a therapeutic technique that requires the processing of events within rather than outside the group.

here-and-now approach   An emphasis on understanding present feelings and interpersonal reactions as they occur in an ongoing psychotherapy, with little or no emphasis on past experience or the basic reasons underlying behavior. See BEHAVIOR THERAPY, ENCOUNTER GROUP, GESTALT THERAPY, PSYCHODRAMA, THERE-AND-THEN APPROACH.

hereditarian   A person assuming that genetic inheritance is the major influence on behavior.

hereditarianism   A doctrine emphasizing the influence of heredity on behavioral traits.

hereditary color-blindness   See HORNER'S LAW.

hereditary disorder   Any disease or defect that may be transmitted from one generation to another through genes or chromosomal aberrations.

hereditary potential   An organism's biological limits of abilities.

hereditary predisposition   A genetic susceptibility to a disorder whose appearance is determined by environmental factors.

heredity 1. The transmission of genetic characteristics to descendants. Depends upon the union of sperm and ovum during conception, upon the character of the genes contained in the chromosomes of these cells, and upon the particular genetic code contained in the deoxyribonucleic acid (DNA) of which the chromosomes are composed. 2. Also refers to the transmitted characteristics themselves. Types of heredity include: ATAVISTIC, COLLATERAL, SOCIAL. See CHROMOSOME, GENE, ZYGOTE.

heredity-environment issue See NATURE-NURTURE CONTROVERSY.

heredity fear See PANOPHOBIA.

Hering-Breuer reflex An automatic mechanism involved in normal breathing, with stimuli from sensory endings in lung tissue limiting inspiration and expiration. Named after German physiologist Heinrich Ewald Hering (1866–1948).

Hering grays (K. E. C. Hering) A set of 50 papers ranging in subjectively equal steps from extreme white to extreme black.

Hering illusion (H. E. Hering) Given two parallel lines placed on two groups of lines radiating from the same point but in opposite directions, the false visual perception that the two lines appear curved with the direction of the curvature being away from the point from which the lines radiate.

Hering('s) afterimage (K. E. C. Hering) The first, brief (0.05 sec.) positive afterimage phase occurring about 0.05 seconds after looking at a bright visual image. In contrast with the second or Purkinje image (Bidwell's ghost) and third or Hess image.

Hering theory (of color vision) Ewald Hering suggested that there were three receptors in the retina of the eyes for these antagonistic color pairs: red-green, blue-yellow and black-white. Also known as Goethe-Hering opponent-process theory, opponent theory of color vision. See COLOR VISION, VISION THEORIES.

Hering window (K. E. C. Hering) An apparatus used for determining color contrast effects.

heritability (h^2) 1. The capacity to be inherited. 2. An estimate, based on a sample of individuals, of the relative contribution of genetics to a given trait or function. 3. The proportion of the total variation of a trait due to genetic factors. A heritability ratio is expressed as $h^2 = V_g/V_t$, where h^2 is the heritability ratio, V_g is the variance in a trait due to hereditary factors, and V_t is the total variance.

heritability estimate A measure of the effect of genes on development. Arthur Jensen concluded that intelligence is based primarily on the effect of heredity.

heritage The sum total of traits and characteristics derived from hereditary transmission.

hermaphrodite 1. An organism possessing both male and female sex organs, such as earthworms. Also known as hermaphroditic organism. 2. Humans with ambiguous genitalia or semi-hermaphroditic elements. The four types are (a) a true hermaphrodite with ovariotestes, (b) a male hermaphrodite with testes and female genitalia, (c) a female hermaphrodite with ovaries and male external genitals, and (d) agonadal hermaphroditism, where the discordance is among the chromosomal sex, the anatomical sex, and the gender identity. See AMBISEXUALITY, PSEUDOHERMAPHRODITISM.

hermaphroditic dreams (I. Coriat) Dreams bisexual in their blurring or blending, indicating the bipolarity of the sexual impulse.

hermaphroditic organism **hermaphrodite**

hermaphroditism Presence of both the male and female reproductive organs in a single organism, such as earthworms.

hermeneutics Originally referring to interpretations of the Bible, the term now often refers to a method of interpretation of texts as well as experiences.

hermetics Any system or school of secret lore such as the Rosicrucians.

hermit A reclusive who escapes from contact with others by living some distance away from other people.

hermitism Morbid desire to live alone, especially in rural seclusion, an occasional symptom of schizophrenia. This phenomenon also has been seen in prisons, with some inmates preferring to be in solitary confinement. Also known as agromania.

hero 1. A human, real or legendary, distinguished for valor, fortitude, or bold enterprises, revered by contemporaries or by posterity; in classic form, the hero is of humble birth, rapidly rises to prominence or power, shows fallibility to the sin of pride, yet is triumphant in a struggle with the forces of evil. 2. The central character in psychodrama, the person who is presenting a problem.

heroin (H. Dreser) Diacetylmorphine, an addictive substance of abuse, once the paradigmatic "narcotic." Easily processed from the resin derived from the opium poppy, raised especially in Southern Asia, it is a pervasive substance of abuse worldwide. Because heroin is more euphoric and less likely to cause nausea than morphine and other opioids, it is favored as an illicit drug. Heroin addicts have been called "junkies," and, since users of the substance tend to develop physiological dependence, with tolerance and significant withdrawal symptoms as features, heroin abuse and dependence is a widespread problem. Sharing needles has led to a spread of HIV (human-immunodeficiency virus) among heroin addicts. Like other opioids, it depresses respiration, constipates, causes pinpoint pupils (miosis), as well as a kind of drunk "high" and sleepiness. May be injected intravenously, smoked, or snorted. Slang names include dope, H, horse, shit, stuff.

heroin dependence Strong physiological and psychological reliance or dependence on heroin characterized by tolerance and, when discontinued, withdrawal symptoms. The term "dependence" is preferred over "addiction." Formerly known as heroin addiction. See OPIOID DEPENDENCE, OPIOID WITHDRAWAL.

heroin overdose Use of an amount of heroin sufficient to produce opioid intoxication (apathy, psychomotor retardation, drowsiness, slurred speech, impairment of attention or memory) and opioid poisoning (shock, coma, pinpoint pupils, and depressed respiration with the possibility of death from respiratory arrest).

hero-traitor dynamic In negotiation theory, the situation in which the winner is seen as a hero, and the loser appears as a traitor.

hero worship   A need of many people for an authority figure they can admire, submit to, or both, as a representative of an idealized parent or leader. Helps explain the willingness of the masses to be dominated by a "great" person.

herpes zoster   A condition of spreading skin eruptions caused by the herpes varicella-zoster virus that also causes chicken pox. Characterized by pain and lesions of the skin usually in the area of the dorsal nerve roots, for example, in a girdle formation around the waist. Herpes zoster is purportedly precipitated or exacerbated by emotional stress. More commonly known as shingles.

herpetophobia   Excessive fear of reptiles, especially snakes. See BATRACHOPHOBIA, OPHIDIOPHOBIA.

Herring-Binet Test   (J. P. Herring) A version of the original Binet Test based on a point count rather than as in the Stanford version on mental levels of difficulty. Contained thirty-eight tests, taken mainly from Binet. See INTELLIGENCE TESTS.

herstory   A feminist term for history from the perspective of women, as opposed to the traditional male orientation.

Heschl's gyrus   One of several transverse temporal convolutions of the cerebral cortex associated with the sense of hearing. Named after Austrian pathologist Richard L. Heschl (1824–1881), who first traced the auditory nerve fibers of humans to this convolution.

Hertz (Hz)   1. A unit of frequency equal to one cycle per second. 2. Cycles per second of energy waves, usually used in reference to sound, named after German physicist Heinrich Hertz (1857–1894).

Hess image   (W. R. Hess) A faint, third phase, positive afterimage sometimes seen after a second negative afterimage. See HERING AFTERIMAGE, PURKINJE IMAGE.

hetaeral fantasy   A fantasy in which women play the role of courtesan. In the male version of the fantasy, the man possesses a courtesan. Also known as courtesan fantasy.

heterochrony   A time and speed difference between two processes such as nerve impulses or the development of organs. Also known as heterochronia.

heterodox   In science, characterizing fundamental beliefs contrary to the generally accepted scientific principles of the time; or, characterizing the person holding such beliefs.

heterodoxy   Fundamental beliefs about science contrary to current beliefs, such as proclaiming the heliocentric theory in the 14th century or of psychics presently. See ORTHODOXY.

heteroerotic(ism)   Sexual interest in persons of the other gender (sex).

heterogamous   Refers to the structural and functional differences between female and male gametes of organisms.

heterogeneity   Difference in quality, kind, or sort among the constituents of any group or class.

heterogeneous   Varied, not homogeneous.

heterogeneous group   Generally, any group not based on any selection criteria, such as people in a bus, in an elevator, those listed on a certain page of a telephone book. See ACCIDENTAL GROUP, ACCIDENTAL SAMPLE, HETEROGENEOUS GROUPING.

heterogeneous grouping   1. The identification of or the establishment of a group based on no particular prior criterion or rationale, but the members become aware of their having something in common, such as being isolated from the rest of society, even temporarily. 2. In group therapy, individuals with different problems assembled together with the intention of demonstrating that people with different problems and diagnoses have certain elements in common, such as lack of self-confidence. Compare HOMOGENEOUS GROUPING.

heterohypnosis   A state of hypnosis induced in one person by another, as opposed to autohypnosis.

heterokinesia   On being told to make some movement, making the opposite movement. See GANSER'S SYNDROME.

heterolalia   A form of aphasia characterized by the substitution of meaningless or inappropriate words for the intended words in speech or writing. Also known as heterophasia, heterophemia, heterophemy. See HETEROPHEMY.

heteromorphic   1. Deviating from the normal type. 2. Unusual in shape. 3. Differing in size or form; for example, X and Y chromosome pairs in human males.

heteromorphosis   The development of an organ in a position in which it does not normally occur, such as the formation of an antenna in place of an eye in the crayfish.

heteronomous   Subject to outside controls. Compare AUTONOMY.

heteronomous psychotherapy   Any type of psychotherapy that fosters dependence on others, especially on the therapist. See AUTONOMOUS PSYCHOTHERAPY.

heteronomous stage   Jean Piaget's first stage of moral development wherein the young child equates morality with the rules and principles of parents and other authority figures. In the heteronomous stage, discipline is imposed by parents. In the autonomous stage, children learn to discipline themselves. See MORAL REALISM.

heteronomous superego   An opportunistic type of superego controlled by an ego demand to behave in whatever manner is expected at the moment to secure the approval of others.

heteronomy   (A. Angyal) A state characteristic of childhood when children are unable to evaluate or regulate their own behavior. Inability to make independent moral judgments. See AUTONOMY, AUTONOMY DRIVE, HETERONOMOUS STAGE, HOMONOMY DRIVE.

heteronymous hemianopia   A visual field defect in which vision in either the left or right half of both eyes is absent, due to a lesion between the optic chiasma and the visual cortex. See HEMIANOPIA.

heteronymous reflex   A reflexive action that begins with stimulation in one muscle of a synergistic group but results in contraction of another muscle in the same group. See HOMONYMOUS REFLEX, SYNERGISTIC MUSCLES.

heterophemy   heterolalia

heterophilia　Being sexually attracted to the opposite sex.

heterophilic　Refers to people interested in close personal relations with members of the other gender.

heterophily　See HOMOPHILY.

heterophoria　The deviation of an eye because of an extrinsic muscular imbalance when the eye is covered and fusion prevented.

heteroscedasticity　The absence of homoscedasticity, or homogeneity of variance. See SCEDASTICITY for an illustration.

heterosexism　An argument that male-female sexuality is the only correct, natural, proper, or moral mode of sexual activity. Also known as heterosexualism.

heterosexist language usage　According to standards set by the American Psychological Association, there should be an avoidance of terms that indicate that homosexuality is abnormal.

heterosexual　A person sexually attracted only to others of the other gender, as opposed to a bisexual (attracted to persons of both genders), or a homosexual (attracted only to persons of own gender). See HETEROSEXUALITY.

heterosexual anxiety　Apprehensiveness about male-female sexual relationships. May include feelings of being unattractive to the other gender either in appearance or behavior, resulting in expectations of rejection, avoidance of social situations. See INFERIORITY FEELINGS, SELF-ASSESSMENT, SELF-ESTEEM.

heterosexual impulses　Positive sexual attitudes and feelings toward people of the opposite gender (even if there are no overt sexual acts). See HETEROSEXUALITY.

heterosexuality　Sexual attraction to members of the other gender. Compare BISEXUALITY, HOMOSEXUALITY.

heterosexual love　Romantic feelings for a person of the opposite gender.

heterosexual rape　Forcible sexual assault by a person upon another of the opposite gender. See RAPE.

heterosexual stage　The developmental period in which sexual attraction to members of the other gender occurs.

heterosis　The resultant of cross breeding within any species leading to individuals with greater vigor in comparison to breeding close relatives. In animal management of endangered species, animal conservationists remove some animals from a particular environment to a new one far away for breeding purposes to preserve the species.

heterosociality　Relationships on a social level between members of the opposite sex.

heterosome　An X or Y sex chromosome, as distinguished from an autosome.

heterostasis　A tendency to seek new stimuli and challenges that will further growth. A desire to grow, to learn, to satisfy curiosity. This element is found in many personality theories and also in views of animal and even plant behavior. See HYBRID VIGOR.

heterostereotype　(H. C. Triandis) The set of attributes that supposedly characterize an outgroup.

heterosuggestion　The inducing of an idea or action in one person by another.

heterotopia　1. The presence of a tissue in an abnormal location such as the congenital development of gray matter in the white-matter area of the spinal cord. 2. A mispronunciation of words in which the syllables are all present but out of sequence.

heterotropia　Crossed eyes. Also known as heterotropy, strabismus.

heterozygosity　Possessing one or more pairs of heterozygous genes as a result of crossbreeding. Also known as heterozygosis, heterozygousness. See DOUBLE HETEROZYGOUSNESS.

heterozygote　An organism with two different alleles for the genetic positions on a pair of matching chromosomes. Compare HOMOZYGOTE.

heterozygous　Possessing different forms of a genetic trait on each of a pair of otherwise normal chromosomes (for example, a gene for blue eyes on one chromosome and a gene for brown eyes on the matching chromosome of the pair); the dominant allele will determine the phenotype of the organism. Compare HOMOZYGOUS.

heterozygousness　heterozygosity

heuristic　1. Leading to new discoveries or promoting new conclusions. 2. A problem solving technique or one that is intended to lead to discovery. 3. A special mode of study or investigation.

heuristic search　1. A nonrigorous method, mostly trial and error, related to the discovery of answers to problems by approximations to the correct answers using short cuts, rules of thumb, analogies, etc., without exploring more scientific possibilities. 2. (A. Newell & H. A. Simon) Solving problems by search through a problem space using various fallible principles (rules of thumb) to guide the search, making it highly selective hence computationally feasible for systems (like human brains) with limited computational capabilities. Also known as heuristic method. Compare ALGORITHM. See BOUNDED RATIONALITY.

heuristic thinking　Mental processes involved in problem solving or invention.

HEW　Health, Education and Welfare (U.S. Department of)

hex doctors　Medicine men or women who attempt to alleviate mental or physical conditions by the use of spells, incantations, or charms. See FAITH HEALING, HEADSHRINKING, SHAMAN, WITCHCRAFT.

hexenmilch　witch's milk

Heymans' law　(C. Heymans) A theory that the threshold level of one stimulus is increased in proportion to the intensity of a second inhibitory stimulus.

hey-nonny-nonny theory　See ORIGIN-OF-LANGUAGE THEORIES.

HHS　Health and Human Services (U.S. Department of)

hibernation　A sleep-like period of inactivity accompanied by a significant decrease in body temperature that occurs in certain homoiothermic (warm-blooded) vertebrates. Poikilothermic (cold-blooded) animals such as frogs become dormant, like plants, in cold temperatures.

hiccups Acute spasms of the diaphragm resulting in rapid inhalation interrupted by spasmodic closure of the glottis. Often caused by increased abdominal pressure or diaphragmatic irritation. See SINGULTUS, SPASM.

Hick's law A theory that in a choice reaction situation, the more information given that is related to making a choice, the more time it will take to make the choice. Also, the more choices available, the longer it will take to make a decision. See FITT'S LAW.

hidden agenda The real goal of a person different from the apparent one. Behavior thought quite common in advertising and in politics as well as scams and confidence games. Also known as private agenda.

hidden-clue situation/test An examination in which the participant must discover a particular feature of the stimulus situation that is the clue to a reward.

hidden-figures test An examination of visual-field defects in which the participant is required to find hidden figures embedded in complex figures of interlocking contours. Poor performance on the test often indicates a lesion or injury in the cerebral cortex. See EMBEDDED-FIGURES TEST.

hidden-figures test

hidden observer (E. R. Hilgard) A phenomenon in hypnosis that demonstrates the existence of two levels of consciousness, one of which is typically concealed.

hidden reasons The elements in thinking that are used to justify personal inappropriate behavior.

hidden variable In research, a variable that is undetected by a researcher. Such a variable may cause a researcher to infer that a variable A and a variable B are correlated and that one causes the other, when in fact, a third factor X that A and B both correlate with may be the important factor. Also known as lurking variable.

hierarchical order The arrangement of phenomena (people, objects, experiences, needs) in presumed order of importance or value; for example, the rankings of individuals in a business organization or of faculty in a university.

hierarchical style In R. J. Sternberg's theory of mental self-government, a tendency to be systematic in the approach to solving problems, along with a preference for dealing with many goals and the ability to prioritize them. See THEORY OF MENTAL SELF-GOVERNMENT.

hierarchical theory of instinct The point of view that patterns of specific behavioral responses are generated through the hypothalamic, sensory, and cortical systems. In Niko Tinbergen's model, motivational energy accumulates in the neural centers, is released by an appropriate stimulus, and flows through motor-system pathways to produce the behavior most likely to achieve a goal object or reward.

hierarchy 1. Any system of organisms, objects, things, etc., ranked one above the other. 2. In behavior therapy, the rank order of issues, stimuli, or situations associated with anxiety. Types of hierarchies include: ANXIETY, BEHAVIOR(AL), CONVERGENT, DOMINANCE, HABIT, HABIT-FAMILY, MASLOW'S MOTIVATIONAL, OCCUPATIONAL, RESPONSE.

hierarchy of needs A ranking of needs. See BASIC NEEDS, MASLOW'S HIERARCHY OF NEEDS THEORY, NEED-HIERARCHY THEORY.

hierarchy of response (N. Miller) A tendency for specific responses to occur before other responses.

hieroglyphic writing A graphic system in which pictures are used to represent objects, words, syllables, or occasionally phonetic elements.

hierophobia 1. Morbid fear of religion, religious rites, sacred objects. 2. Fear of priests. 3. Intense concern or fear about things believed to be holy or sacred.

high 1. Slang for euphoria, particularly as it results from illicit use of drugs. See NATURAL HIGH. 2. Slang for being under the influence of alcohol or other drugs.

high blood pressure A circulatory disorder characterized by persistent systolic blood pressure that is equal to or exceeds 140, a diastolic pressure equal to or exceeding 90, or both. Blood pressure depends on many physiological and psychological factors. Also known as hypertension.

high dream An experience in dreaming of being "high" as though on hallucinogenic drugs.

high-end Refers to an apparatus that uses the latest technology.

higher brain centers The parts of the cerebrum associated with functions such as learning, memory, intelligence, and language.

higher level skills The work methods and skills that can be applied in many tasks rather than one particular task.

higher mental processes (L. Vygotsky) Intelligence, judgment, imagination, and thinking, complex mental processes that over time fuse into a kind of unity or totality that enables people to make judgments of complex issues with all elements in coordination. See HUMANISM, INTERIORIZATION, JUDGMENT, MIND.

higher moments See MOMENT (meaning 4).

higher order conditioning A classical-conditioning method utilizing the conditioned stimulus of one series as the unconditioned stimulus of a second. See CONDITIONED REINFORCERS.

higher order constructs The organization of information into coherent constructs that enhance the integration of the information into general knowledge. Higher order constructs are composed of multiple lower order constructs.

higher order factor Additional factors extracted from the intercorrelations of second-order factors. See FACTOR ANALYSIS.

higher order interaction Interaction of more than two independent variables in analysis of variance with multifactorial experiments. In complex factorial experiments, problems arise regarding the interpretation of statistically significant higher order interactions; for example, 3-way and 4-way or higher.

higher order invariance   Regularity in patterns of stimuli that are available to be perceived as organisms move through their environment.

higher order reinforcement   Reward provided by value-rewarding stimuli through association with secondary reinforcing stimuli or with a reinforcement even further removed from the primary reinforcement.

higher response unit   An integrated response comprising a group of simple responses.

higher states of consciousness   (Asian) States of consciousness that extend beyond normal levels of awareness and open the doors of perception to greater sensitivity and understanding of the world and reality. One of the goals of many Buddhist and Hindu meditation practices. See TRANSPERSONAL PSYCHOLOGY.

higher units of response   Complex unitary responses (for example, a word in typewriting) that are integrations of simpler acts. They may in turn function as integral parts of still higher units.

highest audible tone   The upper limit of the tonal continuum at which hearing occurs without pain, corresponding to the relatively high stimulus-frequencies. For the normal human ear, the limit is 18,000–23,000 Hertz (cycles per second).

high involvement management   A management philosophy that encourages decision participation by subordinates.

high machs   See MACH SCALE.

high pass filter   A device intended to inhibit waves below a certain point from passing through.

high resolution   In vision, able to see fine details.

high-risk approach   A research method in which vulnerable or "high-risk" individuals are studied over a period of time to identify factors that differentiate between those who ultimately develop certain disorders and those who do not. See HIGH-RISK STUDIES for details.

high-risk studies   Research on individuals or groups who may be predisposed to (at risk for) social, physical, or psychiatric pathology by reason of genetic, constitutional, or environmental factors. The object is to identify specific factors and establish the statistical probability of different types of pathology, such as congenital deformity, mental illness, mental retardation, delinquency, or drug abuse that may actually result.

highway hypnosis   Common phrase sometimes applied to accident proneness resulting from a state of drowsy inattention experienced during long-distance driving on monotonous roads.

Hill-interaction matrix   A format designed to indicate content and process of groups, containing four criteria for content and five for process.

hindbrain   The posterior of three bulges that appear in the embryonic brain as it develops beyond the neural tube stage. The bulge eventually becomes the medulla oblongata, pons, and cerebellum in humans. Also known as rhombencephalon.

hindsight bias   **I-knew-it-all-along phenomenon**

Hindu caste system   The orthodox Hindu social-religious system. It was developed over two thousand years ago by the priestly caste as a means of promoting and maintaining a social and religious hierarchy in which the priests are the determinants and controllers of right and wrong, purity and pollution, etc. See SOCIAL IMMOBILITY.

Hindu Tantrism   A religious movement developed in early medieval India, both in Buddhism and Hinduism, that challenged the existing orthodox value systems. Among the values and rules challenged were prevalent restrictions on and views surrounding sexuality and sexual relations. See TANTRIC FUSION, TANTRIC SEX.

hippanthropy   The delusion of being a horse; a delusion occasionally observed in disorganized (hebephrenic) schizophrenia.

Hipp chronoscope   (C. Wheatstone, M. Hipp) An electrically operated clock used to measure small fractions in time (in 1/1000 of a second), formerly used in reaction-time experiments. Also known as Wheatstone-Hipp chronoscope.

hippie   A representative of an American subculture starting in the 1960s composed of young people who were in revolt against conventionality in all forms, and developed their own "relaxed," "loose," or "cool" way of dressing, hairstyle, and living arrangements, such as communes. They frequently used, or were assumed to use, psychedelics or other drugs, especially marijuana and LSD. See HALLUCINOGENS.

hippocampal commissure   A body-tissue structure that joins the posterior columns of the fornix.

hippocampal region of the brain   Area of the brain below the pituitary gland in front of the pons. See HIPPOCAMPUS. See also BRAIN for an illustration.

hippocampus   (G. Aranzai) (seahorse—Greek) A part of the limbic system of the brain associated with memory and emotional functions.

hippophobia   Morbid fear of horses. Also known as equinophobia. See LITTLE HANS.

hircine   A quality of olfactory sensation of which cheese and goats are typical examples. Called caprylic in the Zwaardemaker smell system.

Hiskey-Nebraska Test of Learning Aptitude   (M. S. Hiskey) An individually administered intelligence test developed and standardized on deaf and hearing-impaired children, with pantomime and practice exercises to communicate instructions for the twelve subtests. Named after 20th century American psychologist Marshall S. Hiskey.

histogenesis   The origin, differentiation, and growth of tissues in the body.

histogram   A statistical chart of bars of equal widths but unequal vertical lengths, each touching its neighbor. They can also be arranged horizontally. The varying lengths indicate the degree of magnitude of the different statistics. Also known as bar chart/graph.

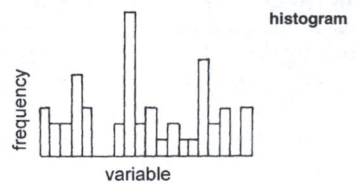

histogram

histology   A branch of biology or medicine concerned with (primarily) microscopic structures of animal and plant tissue and their functions.

historical dichotomy   (E. Fromm) A conflict that arose in human history and between societies.

historical fallacy   The assumption that the study of the history of a person, species, "race," etc., enables its entire nature to be understood.

historical method   (G. W. Allport) The technique of studying clients by tracing their personal history.

historical semantics   **semasiology**

history-taking   The process of compiling a history of anyone, especially people who become participants, counselees, patients, etc. Usually based on an interview, and the interview is often based on a form that the interviewers follow. History-taking can be focused (for example, "Tell me the history of this problem . . .") or unfocused ("Tell me everything about yourself.") In psychology, history-taking is routinely done in some types of research, counseling, and psychotherapy, but not in others.

histrionic-personality disorder   A diagnosis of a pervasive personality disturbance characterized by excessive, extensive attention-seeking in a highly emotional fashion usually beginning in early adulthood. Characterized by constantly seeking or demanding reassurance, approval, or praise from others and being uncomfortable in situations when not the center of attention. Upon close examination, such individuals are often superficial, shallow, and possibly suggestible, and show little tolerance for frustration and delay of gratification. Formerly called hysterical-personality disorder.

hit   The correct detection of a presented signal in communication over any background "noise."

HIT   Holtzman Inkblot Technique

hives   Common name for temporary raised wheals in the skin that itch considerably and appear to be associated with strong emotions as well as definite allergic and other physiological causes. Also known as urticaria.

HM   harmonic mean

HMO   health-maintenance organization.

H$_0$ Symbol for the null hypothesis.

hoarding   The carrying and storing of food or other items believed necessary for survival. Various authors have identified hoarding as instinctive or learned behavior, or both, and as part of a manipulative drive. For humans, see ANAL CHARACTER, HOARDING CHARACTER, SORTERIA.

hoarding character   (E. Fromm) A personality type characterized by self-protecting from dangers in the world by establishing a reservoir of money or things.

hoarding orientation   (E. Fromm) In Fromm's theory, a nonproductive personality type who bases a sense of security on what can be saved and owned. The attitude toward other people is to possess them, and any form of personal intimacy is threatening to this type of person. In addition, there is a tendency toward rigidity, stubbornness, and obsessive orderliness. See ANAL CHARACTER.

hobo syndrome   Slang for the tendency to "job hop."

hodological space   (K. Lewin) The dynamic "space" based on positive and negative vectors that any organism is in according to Gestalt theory. In Kurt Lewin's theory, an indicator of strength of attractions or repulsions within the life space of a person. See HODOLOGY.

hodology   (K. Lewin) The study of pathways of behavior. A tridimensional concept that uses depth to help explain the paths of various forces acting either toward or away from an object.

hodometer   (R. Bechtel) An instrument to map the standing and movement patterns of individuals. Pressure-sensitive pads extend over a floor space with a counting device connected to all of the pads, and the counting mechanism records each time an individual moves on one of the pads.

hodophobia   Morbid fear of traveling. See AGORA-PHOBIA, DROMOPHOBIA.

Höffding function   The mediating cognitive step assumed to be necessary for connecting an experience with a corresponding memory trace. This early model of pattern recognition, in which similarity is viewed as crucial, was developed by Harald Höffding and later adopted by Köhler and Koffka in the construction of a Gestalt model of memory.

Höffding step   (H. Höffding) A mediating mental step thought to connect current perceptions to memory traces.

hold functions   On the Wechsler intelligence tests for adults, those items that do not show a decline in performance for people as they grow older. Vocabulary is one such item. "Don't hold" functions are those that do show a decline in performance with age; such items call for motor abilities such as the digit-substitution test. See DETERIORATION INDEX.

holergasia   (A. Meyer) A major psychosis of the entire socially organized personality.

holiday syndrome   Diffuse anxiety, dejection, psychic pain, and other symptoms that tend to occur prior to and during major holiday periods, especially those (for Western societies) that start in the fall about Thanksgiving and end after the New Year. The feelings are purportedly a result of nostalgic reminiscence and presently unmet dependency needs. Serious injuries, suicides, and fatal accidents tend to increase significantly during these seasons. See SUNDAY NEUROSIS.

holism   (J. C. Smuts) A Gestalt-like concept that the whole is more than the sum of its parts, that a complex organism cannot be understood by examination of its separate parts. In contrast with reductionism, atomistic psychology. Also spelled wholism.

holistic   Overall or global.

holistic assessment   An overall evaluation of the entire person in social situations.

Holistic Education   (W. Schutz) A form of psychotherapy in which the therapist is viewed as a teacher and the patient a student. The therapist/teacher's task is to create conditions within which the "student" may choose to learn. Responsibility for learning is up to the "student." For maximum growth, all aspects of a person should be developed to the fullest in harmony with each other to generate a person of integrity.

holistic formation   (A. Van Kaam) The unique ability of humans to rise above past experiences to a new direction in their lives, based on the concept of free will.

holistic healing   A health-care concept based on the premise that body, mind, and spirit function as a harmonious unit and an adverse effect on one also affects the others. Holistic healers seek to treat the whole person to restore a harmonious balance, that is, a state of mental and physical health.

holistic individuality   (A. Maslow) A point of view that healthy and normal development consists of actualizing the self and fulfilling self-potentialities, with needs and motives presented in a hierarchical order, beginning with primary physiological needs and culminating in an integration of the biological, psychological, and socio-cultural aspects of life and the attainment of personal highest and most creative goals.

holistic medicine   A branch of medicine that approaches diagnosis and therapy based on the assumption that an illness may affect the total being, the mind as well as the body.

holistic strategy   Moving ahead on the basis of maximum information available in terms of some plan or theory rather than moving with only partial evidence. In essence, playing it as safe as possible. Compare PARTIST STRATEGY.

holistic theories   (K. Goldstein) Points of view that emphasize the importance of the wholeness of the individual, the unity and organization of behavior in shaping the parts of the whole. They assume that all properties of a living organism must be described in terms of its totality and not in isolated parts.

holistic theory of intelligence   A point of view that the brain operates as an entity in matters of intelligence.

Holland Vocational Preference Inventory   (J. L. Holland) A test with pictures showing people performing various work tasks, participants indicate their attitudes about the tasks. Classifies people according to 6 factors. Used to help make decisions about selecting a vocation. See INTEREST TESTS.

hollow-square puzzle   An industrial personnel and organizational development procedure in which members of different parts of an organization meet to plan how to handle a particular problem or intention (real or contrived). The major benefit is expected to be better understanding between individuals and better coordination in the future on the part of different departments. See REALITY ROLEPLAYING, PSYCHODRAMA.

Holmes phenomenon/sign   **rebound phenomenon of Gordon Holmes**

Holmgren's test   (F. A. Holmgren) A color-blindness examination requiring participants to match skeins of colored yarns (Holmgren wools) with standard colored skeins.

hologeistic method   A technique used when data from the Human Relations Area Files are used with cultures located all over the earth to compute relationships between attributes of the cultures.

hologram   The film used in holography, usually made by photographically recording wave-fronts of laser light reflected from a real object.

holograph   A document in the handwriting of its author.

holographic memory   (K. Pribram) The hypothetical concept of the neurophysiological aspects of memory being somewhat like a hologram, having a three-dimensional aspect.

holography   1. A method of producing three-dimensional images by using light-wave-interference patterns. The technique is used in photography and has been suggested as an explanation for the process whereby images may be formed in the mind. 2. Writing a document by hand.

holoism   In education, a doctrine calling for the training of the whole individual as a unit rather than installing disparate elements in an individual's mind. See HOLISM.

holophrase   1. A single word being a sentence, such as "Coming?" Also known as word sentence. See HOLOPHRASTIC SPEECH. 2. A single-word expression spoken by children, usually by 18 months or earlier, such as "Mama", "milk", or "no." See DUOS.

holophrastic speech   The expression of several ideas or words in a single word or phrase, as in "Jeet?" meaning "Did you eat?"

Holtzman Inkblot Technique (HIT)   (W. H. Holtzman) A projective test with two parallel sets of 45 inkblots producing 22 scored responses. Unlike the Rorschach, some blots are asymmetric and technical standards of psychometric instruments were largely met before publication.

Holzinger-Crowder Uni-factor Test   (K. J. Holzinger & N. A. Crowder) A group examination intended to measure intelligence based on factor-analytical findings. Designed for vocational and educational counseling for grades seven through twelve, the test attempts to measure verbal, spatial, numerical, and reasoning factors. Scores may be translated into intelligence quotients (IQs).

home   See the following kinds of homes: ADULT FOSTER, BOARDING, BROKEN, FOSTER, GROUP, NURSING, REST.

home-care (program)   Patient care in the home for persons with disabilities; an alternative to institutionalization, enabling the patient to live in familiar surroundings and preserve family ties. See HALFWAY HOUSES, HOMEMAKER PROGRAM, HOSPICES.

home health aide   A specially trained person who provides certain personal-care needs (such as bathing) for persons with physical disabilities. See CAREGIVER.

homemaker program   A service provided for persons with disabilities who prefer independent living but require assistance in cleaning the home, preparing meals, handling the laundry, and similar tasks.

homeopathy   (S. Hahnemann) 1. A school of thought regarding the physical treatment of disease based on the idea that "like cures like" and "less is more." 2. A method of treating disease by administering minute doses of extracts of natural substances (herbs, minerals, etc.) that would produce, in a healthy person, symptoms similar to those of the disease. This system of treatment was developed nearly 300 years ago and was the inspiration for the concept of vaccinations. See ALLOPATHY, OSTEOPATHY, UNCONVENTIONAL THERAPIES.

homeostasis (W. B. Cannon) 1. The balance between living cells and their surrounding environment, including such factors as constant temperature, salt-and-water balance, and steady blood-sugar levels of the body. The body may be seen as a complex regulator or thermostat. 2. The same concept applied to psychological aspects of the individual, with the psyche in balanced equilibrium. Dreams are sometimes considered as the ultimate mechanism for generating psychological homeostasis.

homeostatic model A point of view that all people are motivated by the need to maintain or restore their optimal level of environmental, interpersonal, and psychological stimulation. Insufficient or excessive stimulation automatically causes tension and sets in motion the motive and usually the behavior required to achieve equilibrium.

homeostatic principle Systems, especially biological or physiological ones, tend to strive to maintain a state of optimal balance. See HOMEOSTATIC MODEL.

homeotherm A warm-blooded animal, such as a mammal or avian, that has developed mechanisms for maintaining a fairly constant body temperature thus permitting survival over a wide spectrum of environmental conditions. Also known as hom(o)iotherms, warm-blooded animals. See HIBERNATION, POIKILOTHERMS.

home range For any organism, the area in which it ordinarily resides. In contrast with territoriality, the organism does not drive away members of its own and similar species but peacefully shares its home range with those outside the immediate family group (if one exists). In some mid-size East African antelope, the males are territorial and the females home ranging.

home-schooling The teaching of children of academic subjects (topics) in their own homes by their parents, rather than sending the children to schools. Various school districts have different standards for permitting such teaching and for evaluating parents and children. Also spelled homeschooling.

home-service agency A group that provides homemaker or home health aides for mentally or physically challenged persons.

homesickness See NOSTALGIA.

home visits 1. Short visits by institutionalized people to their homes in preparation for discharge to their homes. 2. Visits to patients at home by professional personnel for crisis intervention, aftercare, and assistance in solving personal problems. See HOME-CARE PROGRAM.

homework 1. (A. Ellis) In therapy, assignments by the therapist for the client to carry out between counseling sessions, such as trying out new behaviors that the client has been reluctant to do. 2. In school, assignments by teachers to students of school work they should do outside normal school hours. 3. Permitting an employee to work at home rather than in an office.

homichlophobia Morbid fear of fog.

homicidal behavior/tendency Attempts at or actual killing of other persons. The majority of persons with homicidal tendencies do not have a mental disorder, although many have antisocial personalities. Among factors associated with homicidal potential are parental brutality, parental seduction, arson, arrest for assault, and alcoholism.

homicidal mania Obsolete phrase for a form of "partial insanity" in which the person is preoccupied with ideas of killing. Also known as homicidomania, homicidal monomania.

homicide The illegal killing of one human by another.

homicidophilia Being sexually aroused by a lust murder.

homilophobia 1. Morbid fear of sermons. 2. Fear that a group of people will criticize one's appearance or manners.

homing (instinct) The capacity of some animals to return to their homes. Formerly thought that some form of extrasensory perception was involved, research indicates that physiological cues are involved. In a homing study, banded Manx shearwaters (birds) transported to North America, 3,050 miles away, were released separately and returned within 13 days to their burrows on an island off the west coast of England. See LOCALITY ATTACHMENT.

hominids Bipedal primate mammals of the family Hominidae, including Homo Sapiens (humans).

hominology (T. C. Kahn) The study of bipedal primate mammals, including humans.

homiotherm **homeotherm**

homo 1. The genus to which humans belong, the only existing living species of which is homo sapiens. 2. Slang for a homosexual, usually male.

homoerotic Homosexual.

homoerot(ic)ism An erotic desire for persons of own gender (sex).

homogamy The interbreeding of an isolated population group of members with similar hereditary traits, resulting in the reinforcement of such traits in future generations. See HOMOPLASTY.

homogeneity Similarity of the constituents of any group in respect to quality, kind, or sort. Compare HETEROGENEITY.

homogeneity of variance An assumption underlying some parametric tests of statistical significance that the samples being compared do not differ in variability (spread of scores). See HOMOSCEDASTICITY.

homogeneous 1. Having similarity of elements, not heterogenous. 2. A quality of a group of class in which elements are consistent, the opposite of heterogenous.

homogeneous grouping 1. The practice of putting people of equal ability together; for example, an entire class or a smaller group formed within a class based on ability in a specific area, such as mathematics. 2. The arrangement of variables of similar value in categories. Compare HETEROGENEOUS GROUPING.

homogeneous reinforcement The presentation at the same time of two stimuli that elicit the same or a similar response.

homogenesis The production of offspring similar to the parents. Also known as homogeny. Compare HETEROGENESIS.

homogenitality An abnormal interest in the genitalia of a person's own gender (sex).

homoiotherm Older name for homeotherm.

homolateral   Refers to that which is on the same side. A lobe is homolateral to another structure, for example in the brain, if it is on the same cerebral hemisphere.

homologous   1. In genetics, pertaining to chromosomes identical in their genetic loci. 2. In biology or zoology, denoting physiologically different bodily organs or parts that were identical at one time during embryonic development, such as the penis and clitoris. 3. Refers to organisms with identical genes as found in clones or identical twins. 4. See HOMOLOGY.

homologous chromosome   A chromosome that is genetically normal, with alleles in the same order.

homologue   One member of a homologous pair.

homology   In biology or zoology, the correspondence or similarity of anatomical structures in different animals, regardless of a relationship in function (for example, the flippers of whales and the arms of humans). Homology suggests evolution of different species from a common remote ancestor. See DARWINISM, EVOLUTION, ICONICITY.

homonomy drive   (A. Angyal) One of two basic motivational patterns, the striving toward love or to fit into social groups; for example, trying to fit into a family or the community. The other affect force in his personality theory is the autonomy drive, or striving toward mastery.

homonymous hemianop(s)ia   The loss of sight in the same half of the visual field of each eye (for example, the left half of the visual field of both the left and right eyes) caused by a lesion in the optic tract or striations. See BINASAL HEMIANOPIA, BITEMPORAL HEMIANOPIA, HEMIANOPIA.

homonymous quadrantic field defect   A loss of vision in one quadrant of the visual field of both eyes.

homonymous reflex   A reflexive action in which a stimulus in a muscle produces a contraction of the same muscle. Compare HETERONYMOUS REFLEX. See SYNERGISTIC MUSCLES.

homophilia   Being sexually attracted to or aroused by a sex partner of the same sex.

homophily   The principle of communication that quality of information between the source and the receiver of information is greater when both have similar or shared attitudes, interpretations of language, belief structures, and other similar attributes. Opposite of heterophily.

homophobia   Fear of, or prejudice against, homosexuals, including gay men and lesbians.

homoplasty   Similarity of corresponding organs in different species that are not due to inheritance from a common ancestry. See HOMOLOGY.

homoscedasticity   Indicating that two or more frequency distributions are equal in variance; that is, neither is significantly more spread out than the other (for example, individuals in a group progressing over time at about the same rate). See SCEDASTICITY for an illustration.

homosexual   A person sexually attracted only to others of own sex, as opposed to a bisexual (attracted to persons of both sexes) or a heterosexual (attracted only to persons of opposite sex). Often a man is referred to as a gay; a woman as a lesbian. Also known as homophile. See HOMOSEXUALITY.

homosexual community   A homosexual culture that has its own meeting places, customs, social demands, linguistic expressions, organizations, and, in some areas, its own bars, beaches, and shops.

homosexual fear   See HOMOPHOBIA.

homosexual impulses   Positive sexual attitudes and feelings toward people of the same gender as self (even if there are no overt sexual acts). See HOMOSEXUALITY.

homosexuality   Sexual attraction to members of the same sex. Old names for types of homosexuality include: ACCIDENTAL, ADOLESCENT, EGO-DYSTONIC, EGO-SYNTONIC, IATROGENIC, INVERSION, LATENT, MASKED, OVERT, SITUATIONAL. Compare BISEXUALITY, HETEROSEXUALITY. See ABSOLUTE INVERSION, AMPHIGENOUS INVERSION, FAUTE DE MIEUX, LESBIANISM, NATURAL HOMOSEXUAL PERIOD, PSEUDO-HOMOSEXUALITY.

homosexual love   Romantic feelings for another person of own gender.

homosexual marriage   A committed relationship between gay men or lesbians, whether or not legitimized by law. See DOMESTIC PARTNERSHIP.

homosexual neurosis   Phrase applied to a group of anxiety disorders resulting from repressed homosexual thoughts and feelings.

homosexual panic   A sudden, acute anxiety attack precipitated by (a) the fear of being a gay man or lesbian or of acting out homosexual impulses, (b) the fear of being sexually attacked by a person of own sex, or (c) loss, or separation from, a homosexual partner. See KEMPF'S DISEASE.

homosexual rape   Forcible sexual assault by a person (invariably a man) upon another of the same sex. Legally termed "sodomy" or "buggery" in most jurisdictions of the United States. See RAPE.

homosocial peer group   A group of individuals, usually children or adolescents, of similar age and the same sex.

homotype   (M. Wertheimer) In Gestalt psychology, objects or properties that serve the same function in a whole or are otherwise intrinsically, functionally related are homotypic and have the same properties. Homotypic relations are concretely and functionally related with respect to some whole or goal.

homozygote   An organism with identical alleles at the same genetic positions of each of a matching pair of chromosomes. Compare HETEROZYGOTE.

homozygous   Having two alleles for the same trait.

homunculus   1. A completely formed "minute human" figure thought by some 16th- and 17th-century theorists to exist in the spermatozoon and to simply expand in size in the transition from zygote to embryo to infant to adult. This idea is an illustration of preformism, and is in opposition to the epigenetic principle of cumulative development and successive differentiation. 2. A drawing of the human in an arc with body parts in proportion to number of muscle connections to the precentral gyrus (motor control center of cerebral cortex) or to number of tactile sense connections to the postcentral gyrus. 3. A dwarf with typical proportion of body parts. 4. View held by early Egyptians (among others) that a little person resided inside each person's skull. After looking out through the eyes and listening through the ears, the homunculus reacts by pulling strings to operate the muscles.

H₁   Symbol for alternative hypothesis.

honesty   1. In general, truthfulness, uprightness, integrity. 2. In psychotherapy, ability to express true feelings and communicate immediate experience, including conflicting, ambivalent, or guilt-ridden attitudes.

Honi effect/phenomenon   The failure of a familiar person (such as sibling or spouse) to be perceived as abnormal in size when viewed in the Ames distorted room. Named after the family name of the first woman who reported this phenomenon. See AMES DEMONSTRATIONS.

honor   The fact of being regarded by others, and of regarding the self, as conforming to commonly accepted standards of honesty, truthfulness, rectitude, etc; a condition accompanied by a feeling of self-esteem. Also spelled honour.

honorarium   A payment. Term is sometimes preferred by payers to imply that the amount is smaller than deserved, and by recipients to imply that they are not in it for the money.

hooker   Slang for prostitute.

hook order   A hierarchy of social dominance in which any one member within a herd of cattle may hook one of lower status with its horns and will allow another one of higher status to do the same to her. See PECKING ORDER.

hope   1. An attitude or sentiment having a mixed hedonic quality, characterized by expectation of a favorable outcome of future events. 2. One of the three heavenly graces (I Corinthians 13:13, the other two being faith and charity).

hopelessness   An unpleasant subjective sense of being physically, mentally, or socially beyond repair. Feelings of hopelessness are particularly strong in children and adolescents who attempt suicide, as well as in states of alienation and demoralization, and in the grief-stricken.

Hopkins Symptom Checklist (HSCL)   A 58-item self-report inventory designed to identify symptom patterns commonly found in out-patients, such as obsessive-compulsive behavior, anxiety, depressive tendencies, and somatization.

hopping reaction   A complex series of neuromuscular actions requiring a flexion of the leg followed by a lateral movement, then an extension. Cats, rats, and monkeys may move in hopping patterns but with different cortical-control mechanisms.

horde   1. Any social group having a low degree of organization. 2. In humans, usually refers to a group of nomads. 3. In anthropology, a loosely-knit unit of some 35 individuals from perhaps 5 families.

horizontal career move   A move from one career to another at the same level of functioning, at the same level as compared with the CEO in the company organization chart.

horizontal cell   A type of association cell found in the retina. Horizontal cell functions include collection of impulses from some receptor cells and carrying the impulses to other retinal cells, much as association cells within the brain relay impulses between cells.

horizontal communication   Messages sent among people in the same general status level in an organization.

horizontal décalage   (J. Piaget) A child's ability to transfer learning from one type of problem to another type, for example, length to area, while remaining in the same developmental stage. Compare VERTICAL DÉCALAGE.

horizontal group   A group composed of and restricted to one social class. Horizontal mobility refers to a shift of roles within the same social class, such as moving from a position on the school board to a position on the chamber of commerce. See SOCIAL MOBILITY, VERTICAL GROUP.

horizontal job enlargement   The expansion of responsibilities associated with a particular job by increasing the number of subtasks at the same level of complexity and by performing different duties at different times. Compare VERTICAL JOB ENLARGEMENT.

horizontal loading   In relation to jobs, starting and finishing the whole task, such as making a shoe (beginning with raw material to completion). Compare VERTICAL LOADING.

horizontal location   Refers to placement of a person (such as a student in a class or a job applicant on a task) depending on ability. See PLACEMENT, VERTICAL LOCATION.

horizontal mobility   See HORIZONTAL GROUP.

horizontal (occupational) segregation   See OCCUPATIONAL SEGREGATION.

horizontal plane   Any plane of the body parallel to the horizon and at right angles to the vertical.

horizontal sample   Considering a particular stratum as a sample, such as interviewing only homeless people or only bankers on some issue.

horizontal section   A theoretical or actual slice of a body or organ, such as the brain, which has been cut at a right angle to the vertical, for example, a slice from the tip of the nose to the back of the head. See SAGITTAL.

horizontal transmission   Host-to-host transmission of infection, as contrasted with vertical transmission (transplacental transmission) of infection.

horizontal-vertical illusion   A visual phenomenon in which a vertical line or dimension appears longer than the horizontal line or dimension of the same length, as in the figure of the opera hat.

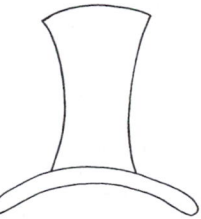

horizontal-vertical illusion   Which is greater, the height of the "hat" or the length of the "brim"?

hormephobia   Morbid fear of experiencing a shock.

Hormic psychology   (W. McDougall) A school of psychology that emphasizes goal-seeking, striving, and foresight, with human instincts serving as a primary motivation for behavior. Also known as purposive psychology. See INDIVIDUAL PSYCHOLOGY, TELEOLOGY.

Hormic theory   (W. McDougall) A point of view that organic phenomena are largely determined by purposive factors (for example, native dispositions, tendencies, urges) that transcend the realm of physics and chemistry.

hormism   (W. McDougall) A doctrine of goals or purpose.

hormonal feedback   A control mechanism in which the internal release of a chemical, usually a product of metabolism, regulates the amount of the end product (for example, gonadotropic-releasing factors activate gonadotropin production in the pituitary, which then activates estrogen/androgen production, whereupon the latter inhibit the production of the releasing factors).

hormones   (W. M. Bayliss & E. H. Starling) Secretions from certain ductless glands introduced directly into the bloodstream and carried to other organs of the body where they stimulate functional activity. The best-known hormones are from the thyroid, gonads, adrenal, parathyroid, and pituitary glands, as well as those special cells in the pancreas which secrete insulin. Types of hormones include: ADRENOCORTICOTROPIC, ANTIDIURETIC, GONADAL, GONADOTROP(H)IC, GROWTH, INTERSTITIAL CELL-STIMULATING, LUTEINIZING, MAMMOTROPHIC, NEURO-, SEX, SOMATOTROPHIC, THYROTROPIC.

Horn Art Aptitude Inventory/Test   (C. C. Horn) A task designed to assess artistic aptitude or achievement for use in grades 12 to 16, and with art-school applicants. Includes an imagery exercise, a scribble exercise and a doodle exercise.

Horner's Law   A principle that red-green color blindness is a genetic disorder transmitted indirectly from male to male through mothers. Named after Swiss ophthalmologist Johann F. Horner (1831–1886).

Horney's theory   The following items are important for understanding Karen Horney's theory: CENTRAL CONFLICT, CHARACTER NEUROSIS, COMPLIANT CHARACTER, COMPREHENSIVE SOLUTION, DETACHMENT, DISILLUSIONING PROCESS, DISPOSITIONAL TRIAD, HORNEY TRIANGLE, IDEALIZED IMAGE, IDEALIZED SELF, INTROSPECTIVE ANALYSIS, MAJOR SOLUTION, MOTIVE TO AVOID SUCCESS, MOVING AGAINST, MOVING AWAY, MOVING TOWARD, NEUROTIC CLAIM, NEUROTIC CONFLICT, NEUROTIC DEFENSE SYSTEM, NEUROTIC NEEDS, NEUROTIC RESIGNATION, NEUROTIC SOLUTION, NEUROTIC TREND, PRIDE SYSTEM, REAL SELF, RESIGNATION, SAFETY DEVICE, SAFETY MOTIVE, SEARCH FOR GLORY, SELF-EFFACEMENT, SELF-EFFACING SOLUTION, SELF-EXPANSIVE SOLUTION, SELF-EXTINCTION, SELF-IMAGE, SHOULDS, VICIOUS CIRCLE, WOMB ENVY.

Horney triangle   (K. Horney) A map of human behavior and attitudes on an isosceles triangle. The apex (arrows going in the same direction) indicates harmony, and equality. The lower left corner (arrows pointing at each other) represent conflict. The lower right (arrows moving away from each other) represents avoidance. The center represents laissez-faire, indifference, unconcern.

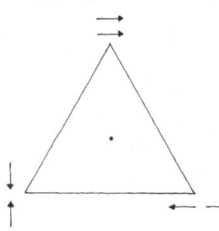

Horney triangle   Karen Horney's representation of human behavior, overt and covert. Used for various purposes. Note the three extremes: *going along with* (top corner), *moving against* (lower left corner) and *moving away from* (lower right corner). The middle point represents eclecticism, a mixture of all three, and is interpreted to mean *indifference* or *laissez faire*.

Horn-Hellersberg Test   (C. C. Horn & E. F. Hellersberg) A projective technique for children in which the child is required to make complete drawings based on a series of stimulus patterns. C. C. Horn adapted the test from the Horn Art Aptitude Test. Sometimes known as Horn-Hellersberg Drawing Completion Test.

horns effect   (A. Simpkins) The converse of the halo effect. (Simpkins understood the halo effect as only being positive.) This is an illegitimate extension of an overall negative impression of a person based on specific attributes, such as seeing a person who is poorly or inappropriately dressed and making negative judgments about that person's intelligence and other personal aspects as a result.

horopter   The focus of points of the visual field area where all points in space fall in corresponding positions on the two retinas.

horoscope   A graph or map of the positions of the stars, planets, and constellations at the time of a person's birth, on the basis of which astrologers attempt to read character, interpret past actions, and predict the person's fate. See ASTROLOGY.

horrific temptation   (S. Rado) A compulsion to kill or injure another person, especially one who may be closely related, while at the same time shrinking in horror from the temptation.

horror feminae   Obsolete phrase for gynophobia.

horse fear   See HIPPOPHOBIA.

horse-shoe crab   limulus

Horsley-Clarke stereotaxic instrument   (V. Horsley & R. H. Clarke) Apparatus used for precise localization of points inside the brain. Used in electrical stimulation or ablation of focal points with the brain.

horticultural therapy   Gardening programs to help rehabilitate children and adults with disabilities. Main association is the American Horticultural Therapy Association.

hospice   A department within a hospital or a stand-alone institution based on caring for the terminally ill and usually providing counseling for their family members. The intention is to make the last days of such people as happy and as pain-free as possible.

hospital design   The basic plan of a hospital building and facilities. Traditional hospitals were designed for the benefit of the staff. Newer designs are based on behavior-oriented environmental factors that offer more personal control and privacy for the patients.

hospital phobia   Fear of a hospital or being hospitalized, sometimes unrealistically. Such people may feel they are treated as inferiors, resent normal hospital procedures, find strangers invading what they consider their territories without asking for permission. May result from early unpleasant and painful experience, or the belief that many people are damaged or even killed by hospital personnel.

hospitalism   1. (R. Spitz) A syndrome observed in infants who have been institutionalized and receive little "mothering." Such children may be listless, emaciated, unresponsive to smiles, and have poor appetite. 2. A neurotic tendency of constantly seeking medical treatment; Münchausen syndrome. See ANACLITIC DEPRESSION, FAILURE TO THRIVE, INFANTILE ATROPHY, MARASMUS, MATERNAL DEPRIVATION.

hospitalitis   The states of mind of patients so dependent psychologically upon hospital life that their symptoms suddenly recur when they learn they are about to be discharged.

hostile aggression   Any form of aggression explicitly intended to cause suffering or injury, in contrast to instrumental aggression.

hostility   Persistent resentment combined with an intense urge to retaliate for real or imagined hurts and humiliations. Though hostile impulses may be normal when a person feels frustrated, deprived, or discriminated against, these impulses may be a factor in anxiety attacks, obsessive-compulsive behavior, depression, antisocial personality, paranoid reactions, and physical assaults. See ANGER.

hot cognition   1. An exciting new idea, insight, or understanding. 2. Insightful understandings of self, others, and events that produce strong emotional reactions. See ABREACTION.

hot flashes/flushes   Sudden sensations of warmth, sweating, or chilliness experienced by many women during menopause.

hotline   A telephone service maintained by trained personnel for providing crisis intervention service and in some cases recorded information about topics relating to emergency situations, advice about a series of health related issues, and related topics. Also known as telephone support service.

hot-seat technique   A technique developed by Rosemary Lippitt in which participants interact with empty chairs who represent imagined people. The technique is said to generate a new awareness, leading participants to find their own new solutions. Used by Gestalt therapists. See BEHIND THE BACK TECHNIQUE, PSYCHODRAMA.

hot spot   See WARM(TH) SPOT.

hot stove   A metaphor derived from the experience of touching a hot stove that refers to immediate unpleasant consequence of misbehavior.

hottentotism   An exaggerated form of stuttering. Term apparently was derived from the name "Hottentot," a South African tribe whose native speech, to Europeans, sounded like stuttering.

HOUND   Acronym for (allegedly) the least desirable type of client for counseling and psychotherapy: those who are considered by the therapist to be Humble, Old, Unattractive, Nonverbal, and Dumb. Compare YAVIS.

house encounter   A group meeting of all members of a treatment facility, such as a halfway house, to discuss and attempt to solve problems within the organization, to make plans for future developments, and to generate a feeling of unity on the part of all involved. See FAMILY COUNCIL.

house fear   See DOMATOPHOBIA, OIKOPHOBIA.

House-Tree-Person (HTP) Test   (J. N. Buck) A projective technique based on the Goodenough Draw-a-Man Test but (a) used as a measure of personality rather than of intelligence and (b) asks for a drawing of a house, a tree, and a person rather than of a man followed by someone of the other gender. The test is intended to reveal personality dynamics and emotional tone through interpretation of the drawings. As in the case of all projective techniques, interpretations are based on the judgment of the examiner. At the same period, the Goodenough technique was also being adapted to measure personality as the Machover Draw-A-Person Test.

housewife's syndrome   A state of frustration and resentment among women who feel trapped and isolated by household chores and child-rearing responsibilities, without sufficient outlets for their energies and aspirations. As they grow older, such women are stated to become increasingly frigid and suffer from fatigue, backaches, and other somatoform symptoms. Phrase has also been applied to a "Craig's wife" (from the play of that name) compulsion, characterized by spending the majority of their time keeping the house spotlessly clean. Also known as housebound housewife's syndrome.

Howard-Dolman apparatus   A depth perception box in a window of which appear two upright black rods against a uniform light background; after being set markedly unequal by the researcher, the rods are to be adjusted by the use of strings or other device so they are equally distant from the observer. Used in evaluating airplane pilot candidates.

Hoyt formula   A formula for computing the reliability coefficient (r) using analysis of variance: $r = 1 - (V_r \div V_t) = [(V_t - V_r) \div V_t]$ where V_r is the variance of the remainder sum of squares and V_t is the variance for participants.

HRAF   human relations area files

HRB   See HALSTEAD-REITAN NEUROPSYCHOLOGICAL TEST BATTERY.

HRNTB   Halstead-Reitan Neuropsychological Test Battery

H-R-R Plates   See HARDY-RAND-RITTLER PSEUDOISOCHROMATIC PLATES.

hsaio   The importance of providing for parents and animals for the good life according to Confucius. See CONFUCIAN ANALECTS.

H scaling   A means of increasing the reliability of certain kinds of questionnaires, such as personality or attitudinal scales, by putting in a number of items that are differently worded but mean about the same thing.

HSCL   See HOPKINS SYMPTOM CHECKLIST.

HSD test   See TUKEY'S HONESTLY SIGNIFICANT DIFFERENCE TEST.

Hsieh-Ping   A culture-specific condition observed in Taiwan, characterized by ancestor identification and temporary trancelike states accompanied by tremors, disorientation, delirium, and visual or auditory hallucinations.

h²   Symbol for heritability.

HT   See THE HAND TEST.

HTP   See HOUSE-TREE-PERSON TEST.

hubris   (insolence, pride—Greek) Overweening pride and smugness that leads a person to make poor judgments.

hue   The aspect of a color determined by the dominant wavelength that permits identification of different colors even though they have the same brightness and saturation.

huffer   Slang for a person who inhales solvents for their euphoric effects. See HUFFING.

huffing   Deliberate inhalation of organic solvents, such as in glue, or volatile gases, such as butane, to achieve a euphoric state or "high"; the procedure is typically repeated at intervals (for example, every 5, 10, or 15 minutes) for hours. See GLUE-SNIFFING.

Hughlings Jackson's syndrome   Jackson's syndrome

Hull's behavior system   Hull's hypothetico-deductive theory of learning

Hull's hypothetico-deductive theory of learning (C. L. Hull) A complex concept of learning based on classical S-R conditioning with 34 postulates and corollaries (1952) to explain various behaviors. Major emphases are on need reduction as a condition of learning, the building up of habit strength by contiguous reinforcement, extinction brought about by nonreinforced repetition of responses, and forgetting as a process of decay with the passage of time. Also known as Hull's behavior system, Hull's mathematico-deductive theory of learning. See BEHAVIORISM, HABIT-FAMILY HIERARCHY, INTERVENING VARIABLE, MONAD, REACTIVE INHIBITION.

Hull's theory   A complex mathematical theory of learning developed by Clark L. Hull based on Sigmund Freud and Ivan Pavlov's teachings and using the hypothetical-deductive method. Essentially, Hull was concerned with intervening variables that he thought could be precisely defined and could be added and subtracted. The following items are important for understanding Clark Hull's theory: EFFECTIVE-HABIT STRENGTH, EFFECTIVE-REACTION POTENTIAL, EXCITATORY POTENTIAL, GENERALIZATION DECREMENT, GENERALIZED HABIT STRENGTH, GENERALIZED INHIBITORY POTENTIAL, GENERALIZED REACTION POTENTIAL, GOAL GRADIENT, HABIT STRENGTH, HABIT-FAMILY HIERARCHY, HULL'S HYPOTHETICO-DEDUCTIVE THEORY OF LEARNING, HULL'S THEORY, INHIBITORY POTENTIAL, INITIAL JOB INTERVIEW, INTERVIEW, J, K, K PRIME, NEOBEHAVIORISM, PURE-STIMULUS ACT, REACTIVE INHIBITION, STIMULUS TRACE, TRACE PERSEVERATIVE, WAT.

human   See HUMAN(KIND).

human body size   Physical measurements of groups of people (for instance, height times chest diameter) typically expressed as means and standard deviations above and below the mean. See ANTHROPOMETRY, BODY-BUILD INDEX, REFERENCE MAN/WOMAN.

human courtship behavior   In technologically developed societies, courtship is generally regarded as a testing period during which time two people have an opportunity to test their suitability in relation to marriage to each other. Such proceedings are unknown in some societies where some couples are married without ever having met one another before. An example of differential behavior in Western societies may be the courtships between some religious conservatives (who generally refrain from having sex before marriage and probably maintain separate domiciles) versus the courtships of some "liberals" (who generally engage in sex with each other before marriage and possibly live together).

human ecology   The study of society in its distributive aspect; that is, the migrations of humans and the relocations of their institutions.

human engineering   A branch of psychology concerned with the design of environments and equipment to promote optimum use of human capabilities and optimum efficiency, safety, and comfort. See ENGINEERING PSYCHOLOGY.

human error   The mistakes made in the operation of complex technology, whether it be as small and as insignificant as mis-operating a home computer and erasing the hard drive, or as enormous as the mis-handling of an airplane with 500 passengers, thereby causing a crash and the death of all. Purportedly, more such major disasters are caused by human error (including mistakes in equipment design) than by physical failure of the system technology. See SUSTAINED ATTENTION.

human factors   A broad field concerned with the study of relationships between humans and their work, equipment, and home environments with the objective of enhancing habitability by redesigning buildings and equipment to fit human abilities and characteristics and also to enhance efficiency of work and work satisfaction. See HUMAN ENGINEERING, HUMAN-FACTORS ENGINEERING

human-factors engineering   The study of interactions of machines and people to enhance the efficiency and safety of all concerned.

human-factors engineer   An expert in the possible causes of errors, problems, dangers, or disasters in relation to humans and their relationship to machines and their environment. Such people attempt to prevent the occurrence or recurrence of any problems through the proper training of personnel, redesigning of equipment, changing conditions of operation (including which tasks are assigned to humans and which to machines), or combinations thereof.

human-factors psychology   A branch of psychology that studies relationships between humans and their work and home environments with the objective of enhancing habitability by redesigning buildings and equipment to fit human abilities and characteristics.

human figure (H)   In Rorschach test scoring, designation for subject response that an inkblot looks like a person.

human figure-drawing test   See MACHOVER DRAW-A-PERSON TEST.

human genome   A normal haploid set of 23 chromosomes from one parent as found in a sperm cell and in an unfertilized ovum. See CHROMOSOMES, GENES, HEREDITY.

human-growth movement   human potential movement (meaning 1)

humanics   (S. Rosenzweig) A suggested synonym for psychology implying that psychology is a composite discipline of coordinated members, elements, or both, all needing to be engaged.

humanism   (R. May) 1. Any mode of thought or action in which human interests and dignity are valued and which takes an individualistic, critical, and secular perspective (in the tradition of the Humanists of the Renaissance.) 2. A doctrine that values the human spirit but at the same time rejects spirituality. See HUMANISTIC THEORY.

humanist theories 1. Perceptions about human behavior that emphasize optimistic and idealistic human values and potentials. 2. Assumptions that humans have free will and both the right and potential for self-determination based on purposes and values. Contrasts with Sigmund Freud's emphasis on unconscious forces.

humanistic communitarian socialism (E. Fromm) An ideal society in which humane values underlie the socioeconomic structure; a nonexploitive society in which all members develop to maximum ability, are self-regulating, and contribute fully as individuals and citizens. See WALDEN II.

humanistic conscience (E. Fromm) According to Erich Fromm, a feature of the healthy person in which behavior is regulated by individual standards and not by fear of external authority. See AUTHORITARIAN CONSCIENCE, CONSCIENCE, PRODUCTIVE ORIENTATION.

humanistic ethic (E. Fromm) A value system based on the argument that people act in accord with the essence of human nature with individuals assuming full responsibility for their behavior.

humanistic perspective A point of view that people are essentially good and constructive, that the tendency to self-actualize is inherent, and that, given proper environment, humans will develop to maximum potential. This perspective is inherent in the theories of Alfred Adler, Gordon Allport, Abraham Maslow, Carl Rogers, and others, who advocated the study of individuals who are healthy as opposed to individuals who are neurotic or pathological. See HUMANISM, HUMANISTIC PSYCHOLOGY, NEED-HIERARCHY THEORY, SELF-ACTUALIZATION.

humanistic psychology An outgrowth of existentialism and phenomenology that focuses on individuals' capacity to make their own choices, create their own style of life, and actualize themselves. Its approach is holistic, and its emphasis is on spontaneity and the development of the human potential through experiential means rather than analysis of the unconscious or behavior modification. See ENCOUNTER GROUP, ENCOUNTER MOVEMENT, EXISTENTIAL PSYCHOLOGY, HUMAN-POTENTIAL MOVEMENT, HUMANISTIC PERSPECTIVE, INDIVIDUAL PSYCHOLOGY, PHENOMENONALISM, SENSITIVITY TRAINING, SOFT DETERMINISM.

humanistic theory A general approach to human behavior and human life that emphasizes the uniqueness, worth, and dignity of each individual, and the development of personal values and goals that reflect the interplay of physical, psychological, and sociocultural factors. Among those who pioneered or contributed to these ideas were Alfred Adler, Erik Erikson, Eric Fromm, Abraham Maslow, and Carl Rogers.

humanistic therapy Third-force therapy aimed at treating the person as a whole.

humanistic-existential therapy An integration of existential and humanistic approaches in which treatment is focused on subjectivity (J. Bugental), the courage to be (R. May), and the confrontation with freedom, death and isolation (I. Yalom). Also known as existential-humanistic therapy.

human(kind) The human species. Preferred over man/mankind as more specifically including women. Term derives from the Latin *humanus* (person).

human nature The innate characteristics of humankind as a whole.

human pheromones See PHEROMONES.

human-potential growth center growth center

human potential movement 1. (F. Perls) A point of view that people have greater abilities than they display, and that by certain interactions with others, such as in growth-oriented groups, they may be able to achieve superior-to-prior results in their lives. Also known as human-growth movement. See GESTALT THERAPY, GROUP THERAPY, T GROUPS. 2. (A. Maslow) A general attempt to achieve a better world through personal improvement and cooperation with others using group methods such as assertiveness training and other humanistic methods.

human relations Relationships and interactions between two or more persons, especially socially and emotionally significant relations. See INTERPERSONAL RELATIONS.

human relations area files (HRAF) A classification of ethnographic data on a number of aboriginal tribes, coded in such a way that it is possible to compare the same topic across a number of tribes. Such files are useful for cross-cultural research.

human-relations theory A point of view that the most important aspect of organizational functioning is interpersonal relations.

human-relations training Programs designed to train personnel to deal effectively with interpersonal relations through various forms of interaction, such as sensitivity training programs and communication and interaction groups. See INTENSIVE-GROUP EXPERIENCE, SENSITIVITY TRAINING, T-GROUP.

human resources Phrase that is increasingly replacing "personnel" because it implies that employees are a valued resource, and it sounds more prestigious.

human sexual contact Any person-to-person contact that involves touching or connection of genital or erogenous skin or membrane surfaces, as in fondling, kissing, coitus.

human therapeutic experience Reactions to new situations in real life that have the same effects as psychotherapy is supposed to have, such as through meeting people who value and encourage a person, seeing potentials that others do not; such contacts in general have a strong positive effect on the individual's self-concept.

humidity effects A principal factor affecting the experience of ambient temperature. High humidity in hot weather is uncomfortable because it diminishes the capacity of the air to absorb water vapor from sweat. Both short-term and long-term humidity can affect feelings of comfort and behavior.

humidity fear See HYGROPHOBIA.

humiliation A feeling of shame due to being embarrassed, disgraced, or depreciated. Some individuals invite humiliation as punishment for real or fancied wrongdoing; others lose so much self-esteem through humiliation that they become depressed. Humiliation of the partner is frequently desired in sexual sadism and sexual masochism. See FACE.

humor 1. The capacity to perceive or express the amusing aspects of situations. There is little agreement on the essence of what is funny and a number of theories abound. Plato and Thomas Hobbes held that situations that make the observer feel superior, such as an elegant person slipping and falling, lead to laughter. Max Eastman took the position that triumphing over adversity was humorous. Sigmund Freud assumed that fear turned around was humorous, such as making jokes about people who were dangerous. Many jokes depend on "punch lines" in which the story preceding ends with an unexpected twist, suggesting delight in being fooled. Humor that degrades some group, such as racial or ethnic jokes, may be based on feelings of superiority, such that a person feels he or she can disparage others with impunity. Humor may also come from disparaging the self. See GALLOWS HUMOR. 2. (fluid, moisture—Latin) Bodily fluids, especially the semifluid substances that occupy the spaces in the eyeball: aqueous humor, and vitreous humor. See HUMORAL DOCTRINE OF DISEASES, HUMORAL THEORY.

humoral reflex A vital response caused by a hormone.

humoral theory (Hippocrates, Galen) The point of view that temperaments or personality characteristics can be attributed to the effects of four primary body fluids, or "humors." These temperaments were allegedly related to these humors: Sanguine (blood), Melancholy (black bile), Choleric (yellow bile) and Phlegmatic (phlegm).

Humphrey's law (G. Humphrey) A principle that if a person performing a complex behavioral action (for example, flying an airplane or having sexual intercourse) thinks about what he or she is doing, performance is likely to be negatively affected.

Humphrey's paradox **arpeggio paradox**

hunger drive An urge or arousal state induced by food deprivation. It is regulated in large measure by the hypothalamus. Psychological influences play a major role in determining the intensity of the hunger drive and in determining individual modes of hunger-related behavior, such as types of food preferred or avoided. See NERVOUS HUNGER, SOCIAL HUNGER, SPECIFIC HUNGER.

hunger pains/pangs A feeling of emptiness in the stomach, at one time attributed to contractions of the stomach muscles in the absence of food. However, persons without stomachs also experience hunger pains.

hunger strike See ANOREXIA NERVOSA, NEUROTIC HUNGER STRIKE.

hunting (behavior) An instinctive activity of most animals that pursue other animals for food. Includes stalking, chasing moving objects, or use of concealment or camouflage to wait for prey to come sufficiently close to be caught, as well as cooperative efforts with other predators of the same species.

hunting stage The stage of human culture in which hunting provided most of the food, clothing, and materials needed for the good life.

Huntington's chorea/disease (HD) (G. Huntington) A hereditary progressive disease marked by involuntary movements and dementia (cognitive and emotional). Both childhood and adult forms occur in the same family, but most cases have an average onset age of 35 years. Also known as Dementia Due to Huntington's Disease.

Hunt-Minnesota Test for Organic Brain Damage An examination for organic brain damage intended for use with persons 16 years of age and older. Consists of three parts: (a) the vocabulary subtest of the 1937 Stanford-Binet Scale, (b) six memory and recall tests, and (c) nine tests used to predict validity. Named after American psychologist Howard Francis Hunt (b. 1918).

Hurler's syndrome (G. Hurler) Genetic disorder marked by mental deficiency and physical abnormalities giving rise to calling it gargoylism. Named after 20th century Austrian pediatrician Gertrude Hurler.

hurried child syndrome (D. Elkind) Refers to children who exhibit stress symptoms as a result of being overprogrammed.

hurry sickness An obsessive time consciousness, it is considered to be a key trait of the heart-attack-prone Type A personality.

hustling theory A point of view that activities and behaviors involved in the use of drugs reinforce drug use.

hyaline membrane disease **respiratory distress syndrome**

hyalophagia The eating of glass. Also known as hyalophagy. See PICA.

hyalophobia Morbid fear of glass. Also known as crystallophobia.

hybrid The offspring of two parents of different varieties or species, such as a mule whose parents were a horse and a donkey.

hybrid vigor Increased vitality resulting from outbreeding.

hybristophilia Being sexually attracted to a sex partner who is a criminal.

hydration The act or process of accumulating or combining with water. Body cells undergo hydration when sodium intake is increased. See DEHYDRATION.

hydraulic model An erroneous concept of the nervous system introduced by René Descartes, who assumed that nerves were tubes through which "vital spirits" flowed from the sense organs to the brain and from the brain to the muscles. Habits were formed, according to the hydraulic model concept, when repeated use of the nerve tubes caused them to become distended or blocked.

hydraulic theory A point of view that depicts the mind as operating like a fluid in a closed system. Seen most notably in Sigmund Freud's contention that if a symptom is alleviated without curing the underlying causes, the pressures will surface in a new symptom. See PSYCHOANALYSIS.

hydraulic theory (of hearing) (M. Meyer) A point of view that different tones are produced by differential responses of different lengths of the basilar membrane. See HEARING THEORIES.

hydrocephalus (A. C. Celsus, J. Cheyne) A physical condition in which excess fluid in the brain cavity causes enlargement of the ventricles with increased intracranial pressure and subsequent brain damage. Also known as hydrocephaly.

hydrodipsomania An uncontrollable thirst for water that occurs periodically, especially in patients with epilepsy.

hydrophobia   1. Morbid fear of water. Also known as Saint Hubert's disease. See AQUAPHOBIA. 2. Rabies, in which water aversion is a major symptom due to a reflex irritation that prevents a patient from drinking water regardless of thirst. See RABIES.

hydrophobophobia   Morbid fear of rabies. Also known as hydrophobiaphobia. See CYNOPHOBIA, HYDROPHOBIA.

hydrotherapy   Any kind of treatment using water. See CONTINUOUS-BATH TREATMENT, WET PACKS.

hydrotropism   A simple orienting response of an organism or of certain organs to stimulation by water or moisture. See TAXIS, TROPISM.

hygiene   The science or systematic practice concerned with the maintenance of health in the individual or community.

hygienic needs   (F. Herzberg) Denoting those facets of a job, such as salary, working conditions, hours, and benefits, that produce discontent if lacking but which do not motivate employees to improve their job performance if present.

hygrophobia   Fear of dampness, humidity, moisture.

hylephobia   1. Morbid fear of forests. 2. Morbid fear of materialism.

hylopsychism   hylozoism

hylozoism   A doctrine positing that all matter has life, sensation, consciousness. Also known as hylopsychism. See ANIMISM, VITALISM.

hymen   A thin membrane that normally covers a part of the opening to the vagina before the first coitus. In certain women, the hymen may be completely absent or remain unruptured after coitus, so the presence or absence of the hymen is not a reliable sign of virginity.

hyoscine   scopolamine

hypacusis   A state of partial deafness. Such persons may have difficulty following ordinary conversations. Also known as hypacousis, hypac(o)usia, hypoacusia, hypoacusis.

hypengyophobia   Morbid fear of assuming responsibility. See ERGOPHOBIA, PARALIPOPHOBIA.

hyperactive-child syndrome (HACS)   Old name for attention deficit hyperactivity disorder. See HYPERACTIVITY.

hyperactivity   A condition characterized by excessively vigorous responses, or motor restlessness. See DEVELOPMENTAL HYPERACTIVITY, HYPERKINETIC SYNDROME, MINIMAL BRAIN DYSFUNCTION, PURPOSELESS HYPERACTIVITY.

hyperacusia   Abnormally acute hearing and a lowered tolerance for loud sounds. Also known as hyperacusis. See COCHLEAR RECRUITMENT.

hyperadrenal constitution   A body and personality type associated with overactivity of the adrenal gland and characterized by muscular strength and development, a tendency toward hypertension, and a personality marked by euphoria and moral and intellectual energy.

hyperaggressivity   An extreme tendency to express anger and hostility in action, as in assaulting and maiming other people. It is a major symptom of intermittent or isolated explosive disorder and epileptic furor.

hyperalg(es)ia   Abnormal sensitivity to pain. Occasionally results from development of new nerve endings in skin areas that have been severely injured. In auditory hyperalgesia even slight noises cause pain.

hyperbulimia   Inordinate appetite and excessive intake of food, observed in some patients with schizophrenia, in cases of diabetes mellitus, and in patients with hypothalamic lesions. See BINGE EATING, BULIMIA, HYPERPHAGIA.

hypercathexis   An excess of psychic energy invested in an object (person, activity, goal).

hyperc(o)enesthesia   An extreme state of well-being. See COENESTHESIA.

hypercompensatory type   A constitutional type characterized by overdevelopment of blood and lymph vessels, digestive tract, and ductless glands. The hypercompensatory characteristic is expressed in the form of symptoms of paranoid or bipolar (manic-depressive) reactions.

hypercomplex cell   A cell that receives information from complex cells, which in turn receive information from simple cells in vision. See VISUAL CORTEX.

hypercritical   Indulging in too much or too minute criticism.

hyperemia   An involuntary autonomic rush of blood to the skin. See BLUSHING.

hyperergasia   1. (A. Meyer) Obsolete name for the manic phase of manic-depressive (bipolar) psychosis. 2. Excessive activity.

hyperesthesia   Extreme sensitivity to sound, light, heat, cold, and, particularly, tactile stimuli. It is a common hysterical (conversion) symptom as well as a symptom of some organic conditions such as alcoholic polyneuritis and menopause.

hyperesthetic memory   A memory that is abnormally sensitive to past associations, a condition that Freud and Breuer regarded as a causative factor in hysteria.

hyperexcitability   An extreme tendency to emotional arousal; a tendency to overreact to the slightest stimulus.

hyperfeminization   Exaggerated feminization of structure and behavior, which is reported as appearing in certain cases of castrated male animals in which female sex gland elements have been implanted. See HYPERMASCULINIZATION.

hyperfunction   The functioning of an organ or system at more than its normal level.

hypergamy   Marrying upwards. Marriage to a spouse in better financial or social circumstances than self. See HYPOGAMY, SOCIAL MOBILITY.

hypergargalesthesia   An extreme sensitivity to tickling.

hypergasia   Diminished ability to function.

hypergenital type   (N. Pende) A constitutional type characterized by premature and exaggerated development of sexual characteristics, relatively short extremities, and a large chest and skull. The female version also has extremely sensitive breasts and genitalia, and experiences an unusually early menarche.

hypergenitalism   An excessive development of the genital system.

hypergeusia   An excessive sensitivity of taste. May be due to either a neurological or a hysterical disorder. Also known as hypergeusesthesia.

hyperglycemia   A metabolic state of abnormally high levels of glucose in the blood, usually resulting from a lack of insulin needed to remove the excess glucose.

hypergnosis   A perception that is exaggerated to the point of being expanded into a philosophical system or concept, as observed in certain types of paranoid behavior.

hyper-Greco-Latin square   See GRECO-LATIN SQUARE DESIGN, LATIN SQUARE DESIGN.

hyperhedonia   1. Abnormal reactions of pleasure from almost any act or event. 2. See SEXUAL ERETHISM.

hyper(h)idrosis   Abnormal production of perspiration by the sweat glands. Although the exact nature of the excessive production is unknown, it commonly occurs in otherwise normal individuals during periods of anxiety or stress.

hyperingestion   Excessive or abnormally high rates of intake of food, fluid, or drugs through the mouth, particularly when intake is greater than the maximum safe level. See BULIMIA.

hyperkinesis   Hyperactivity.

hyperkinetic   Pertaining to excessive motions, especially of the body.

hyperkinetic-impulse disorder   A childhood condition characterized by extreme impulsiveness, overactivity, restlessness, distractibility, and a short attention span. May also include dyslexia, perceptual-motor deficits, defective coordination, and negativism. See HYPERKINETIC SYNDROME.

hyperkinetic syndrome   Pathological energy found in some children with brain injuries or mental defect. Hypermobility and restlessness are main behavioral symptoms, as well as concurrent emotional instability and personality deficits ranging from social aggressiveness to shyness. See ATTENTION-DEFICIT HYPERACTIVITY DISORDER, HYPERACTIVITY.

hyperlexia   Learning to read at an unusually early age.

hyperlogia   Excessive loquacity. See LOGORRHEA.

hypermania   The highest degree of mania. Characterized by incessant pressure of activity, disorientation, and incoherent speech. Such people exhibit wild behavior and often are put in strait-jackets or sedated. Also known as delirium grave, typhomania. Similar to collapse delirium. See BELL'S MANIA, DELIRIOUS MANIA, HYPOMANIA, MANIA.

hypermasculinization   An exaggerated masculinization of structure and behavior that is reported as appearing in certain cases of castrated female animals in which male sex gland elements have been implanted. Compare HYPERFEMINIZATION.

hypermetamorphosis   A form of hyperresponsiveness observed in animals after temporal-lobe ablation. The new behavior is regarded as exploratory or manipulatory. The animal may spend an hour exploring a strange cage whereas a normal animal might devote only a few minutes to this activity.

hypermetropia   hyperopia

hypermnesia   An extreme degree of retentiveness and recall; unusual clarity of memory images. Found in some persons with mental disabilities in relation to particular events, such as the date of first meeting someone; also found in patients with schizophrenia, mania, and those intoxicated by certain drugs such as amphetamines, hallucinogens. See CIRCUMSTANTIALITY, PANORAMIC MEMORY.

hyperobesity   Being extremely overweight, sometimes defined as weighing in excess of 100 pounds above the accepted ideal body weight for a standard for height, age, and body build. An unusual case of hyperobesity is recounted in an autobiography, *Diet or Die* of a circus fat lady who initially weighed approximately 700 pounds and subsequently shed 555 pounds over a two-year period to achieve a more normal weight; she maintained her new weight for over ten years.

hyperopia (H)   (F. Donders) Far-sightedness, being able to see well at far distances. It is a refractive error due to a defect in the lens of the eye. Focusing occurs behind the retina of the eye. Also known as far sight, farsightedness, hypermetropia, long sight, longsightedness.

hyperosmia   An abnormally acute sensitivity to odors. Also known as hyperesthesia olfactoria, hyperosphresia, hyperosphresis, olfactory hyperesthesia, oxyosmia.

hyperparesthesia   Oversensitivity to pressure or touch.

hyperphagia   Gluttony; a tendency to overeat characterized by eating abnormally large quantities of food. See BINGE EATING, HYPERBULIMIA.

hyperphilia   Refers to a proceptive sexual response, acceptive sexual response, or both, above the normal range. Don Juanism, nymphomania, premature ejaculation, and satyriasis fit in this category.

hyperphoria   Deviation of one eye in an upward direction when covered and fusion is prevented. Compare HYPOPHORIA.

hyperphrasia   logorrhea

hyperphrenia   1. A form of mania characterized by excessive intellectual activity. 2. Mental activity far above normal and in pathologic states may be a manifestation of the manic phase of bipolar (manic-depressive) disorder or psychoneurotic preoccupations. 3. Formerly, high intellectual ability. Compare HYPOPHRENIA.

hyperpituitary constitution   A body and personality type associated with overactivity of the pituitary gland near or after the end of the normal growth period. Physical characteristics resemble those of Ernst Kretschmer's athletic type, with a hypervigilant attitude and a tendency to control emotions through intellectualization.

hyperplane   A subspace U of dimension r is a hyperplane of dimension r through the origin a geometric space in which vectors are points and the zero vector $\emptyset$ is the origin. A straight line is a hyperplane of dimension 1 and a plane is a hyperplane of dimension 2.

hyperplasia   An abnormal increase in the size of an organ or tissue caused by the growth of an excessive number of new normal cells.

hyperpolarization   An increase in the internal charge of a neuron after activation of an inhibitory synapse.

hyperpragia Excessive mental activity, generally associated with the manic phase of bipolar disorder.

hyperpraxia Rapid, jerky, and exaggerated bodily movements observed in some people during manic states.

hyperprosexia 1. Dwelling on a single idea. 2. Inability to refrain from dwelling on a particular thought or from attending to a particular stimulus, such as the creaking of a door.

hypersensitivity reactions Severe allergy-like reactions experienced after exposure to certain types of drugs. See REVERSE TOLERANCE.

hypersexuality Extreme frequency of sexual activity, or an inordinate desire for sexual activity. See NYMPHO-MANIA, SATYRIASIS.

hypersomnia Abnormal desire to sleep. Excessive sleepiness or sleep of excessive duration, as in Economo's disease, and, commonly, sleeping sickness. People in solitary confinement, purportedly can learn to sleep for 16 hours at a time. See PSYCHOGENIC HYPERSOMNIA.

hypersthenia In constitutional medicine, a condition of excessive strength and tension associated with hyperactivity of the lymphatic system. Also known as hypersthenic.

hypersynchrony The massed simultaneous discharge of electrical energy from the brain as noted by an electroencephalogram.

hypertelorism (D. M. Grieg) An abnormally great distance between two body organs or areas, as when the eyes of a person are separated farther from each other than a normal distance. Often associated with mental retardation or other neurologic deficits where cranial anomalies are involved. Also known as Grieg's disease. See DISFIGUREMENT.

hypertension Technical term for high blood pressure. See ESSENTIAL HYPERTENSION.

hypertensive 1. Marked by increased blood pressure. Compare HYPOTENSIVE. 2. Refers to a person who generally has high blood pressure. See NORMOTENSIVE INDIVIDUAL.

hypertensive crisis Sudden extreme rise in blood pressure that may result in intracranial hemorrhage, due in some cases to overwhelming emotional stress and occasionally to certain antidepressant drugs.

hyperthymia 1. An excessive emotional response. 2. Overactivity that is almost manic.

hyperthyroid constitution A constitutional type associated with overactivity of the thyroid gland, characterized by youthfulness and well developed sexual characteristics, hypermotility and instability, roughly corresponding to Ernst Kretschmer's asthenic type.

hyperthyroidism A pathological condition resulting from excessive production of the internal secretion of the thyroid gland. No impairments of cognition are noted but a tendency to hypersensitivity, excitability, and general activity as well as insomnia. Also known as hyperthyreosis. Compare HYPOTHYROIDISM. See EXOPHTHALMIC GOITER.

hypertonia Abnormally high body tension.

hypertonic type (N. Pende) A constitutional (body) type characterized by a high degree of muscle tone. Corresponds to Ernst Kretschmer's athletic type.

hypertrichophobia Fear of growing bodily hair, especially in excessive amounts. See TRICHOPATHOPHOBIA, TRICHOPHOBIA.

hypertrophy A condition of excessive increase in the size of an organ or part because of growth in the size of its individual cells. Also known as hypertrophia. Compare HYPERPLASIA.

hypertropia A form of strabismus in which one eye fixes on an object and the other eye deviates upward. Also known as strabismus sursum vergens.

hypertychia A state of elation with excitement and accelerated physical and mental activity.

hypervegetative type A constitutional (body) type that corresponds roughly to the pyknic type and more closely to the megalosplanchnic (large viscera and belly) and brachymorphic (short, heavy set) types.

hyperventilation Prolonged deep breathing that, due to excess carbon dioxide output, causes respiratory alkalosis, producing symptoms such as numbness and tingling in fingers, light-headedness, and perhaps blurring of vision. Particularly if anxiety has caused the individual to pant in terror, the alkalosis symptoms serve to exaggerate the situation. Hyperventilation may precipitate a seizure in patients with epilepsy. Emergency treatment calls for a person to breathe or rebreathe into a container or a paper bag. Also known as hyperventilation syndrome, overbreathing.

hypervigilance A state of heightened alertness, usually with continual scanning of the environment for signs of danger or for particular classes of stimuli.

hyphedonia A state of diminished pleasure during an experience that normally would produce pleasure.

hyphenophilia Being sexually attracted to or aroused by touching or feeling skin, fur, hair, leather, or fabric.

hypnagogic hallucination A hallucination experienced while falling asleep; false perceptions occurring between sleeping and full wakefulness, analogous to hypnagogic imagery. Such hallucinations are ordinarily not considered pathological; some do not even use "hallucination," preferring "dream imagery."

hypnagogic image Imagery in any sense modality of an almost hallucinatory quality experience in the drowsy state preceding deep sleep.

hypnagogic imagery Vivid imagery occurring during the drowsy state between wakefulness and full sleep, or while falling asleep. See HYPNOPOMPIC IMAGERY, WAKING DREAM.

hypnagogic reverie Fantasies occurring between sleeping and waking. Induction of hypnagogic reverie by hypnosis is sometimes used as a means of encouraging patients to free-associate and bring unconscious material to the surface.

hypnagogic state The drowsy, trancelike period between waking and sleep during which transient, dreamlike fantasies and hallucinations may appear. During a hypnagogic state suggestibility is high and the person will usually raise an arm or perform some other action on command.

hypnalgia Literally, dream pain: pain experienced during sleep or in a dream.

hypnic Relating to sleep.

hypnic jolts   A phenomenon consisting of a sudden single jerk of the body that occurs to most people when they are just about to fall asleep. Neither its cause nor its cure are known, and there appears to be no explanation for its unwelcome arrival.

hypnoanalysis   A form of psychotherapy that includes hypnosis as all or part of the treatment process, especially to tap the unconscious.

hypnocatharsis   A recapturing and reliving of memories through free association while in a hypnotic state.

hypnodelic therapy   The combined use of hypnosis and LSD. A controversial form of brief therapy that has not lived up to early claims. See LSD PSYCHOTHERAPY.

hypnodontics   The use of hypnotic suggestion in dentistry as a means of relaxing tense patients, relieving anxiety, reinforcing or replacing anesthesia, and correcting such habits as bruxism and nail-biting. See DENTAL PHOBIA.

hypnodrama   (J. L. Moreno) A psychodramatic technique in which a hypnotic state is induced. The object is to eliminate the patient's resistance to dramatizing problems, and to stimulate the revival of past incidents and emotional scenes in their full intensity.

hypnogenic   Sleep-producing.

hypnogenic spot   A point on the body that when touched may induce hypnosis if the person is highly susceptible.

hypnograph   An instrument used to measure sleep and physiological activities that occur during sleep; for example, motor activity, pulse, and reflexes.

hypnoid(al) state   Characterizing a state that resembles to a certain extent the milder hypnotic conditions but is usually brought about by means other than those used in hypnosis.

hypnoidization   A hypnotic induction technique in which participants are asked to recline, close their eyes, and attend to a stimulus such as the beat of a metronome as a means of reaching a hypnagogic state in which they experience a vivid flow of free associations that frequently evoke memories of early emotional events.

hypnolepsy   Obsolete term for narcolepsy.

hypnology   The scientific study of sleep and hypnotism.

hypnonarcosis   A deep sleep state induced by hypnosis.

hypnopedia   Alleged learning during sleep.

hypnophobia   Morbid fear of sleeping or falling asleep. See INSOMNIA.

hypnophrenosis   (C. H. Schutze) General term applied to any of a variety of sleep disturbances.

hypnoplasty   A hypnotic technique in which participants are put into a light trance and given a claylike substance with which they are asked to give plastic expression to repressed feelings and then are asked to discuss conflicts with the encouragement of the therapist.

hypnopompic   1. Characterizing the drowsy state following deep sleep and preceding awakening. 2. Refers to visions or dreams just before or after sleeping during a semi-sleeping period. See HYPNAGOGIC, HYPNAGOGIC IMAGE, LUCID DREAMING.

hypnopompic hallucination   A false sensory perception occurring in the period between sleeping and full wakefulness. See HYPNAGOGIC HALLUCINATION.

hypnosedatives   Obsolete term for drugs that are both sleep-inducing and relaxing, such as the barbiturates. See SEDATIVE-HYPNOTIC DRUGS.

hypnosigenesis   The induction of hypnosis.

hypnosis   (J. Braid) A process in which a distinct focusing of attention is induced, resulting in a trance-like state probably due to demand characteristics. Responses to stimuli of sight, sound, and touch are customarily employed in the induction. Varying degrees of hypnosis may occur at different times, often depending upon the skill of the hypnotist and the stimuli used. It is probable that most persons can be hypnotized to some extent if the ability to concentrate is intact. Many health professionals take the view that hypnosis should not be used for entertainment purposes but used solely for the treatment of health problems. The power of suggestion in some hypnotic states may be quite profound. Hypnosis has been employed in a variety of situations, including smoking cessation, functional memory loss, weight problems, pain control, childbirth and some surgical procedures. Formerly known as Mesmerism, neurohypnotism.

hypnosuggestion   The application of direct hypnotic suggestion to such problems as insomnia, intractable pain, uncontrolled hiccuping, functional sterility, cigarette smoking, malnutrition resulting from psychogenic vomiting or anorexia nervosa, and various types of crises, including combat situations, panic, and hysterical amnesia.

hypnotherapy   The controversal use of hypnosis in psychological treatment. See ABREACTION, AGE REGRESSION, AUTOMATIC DRAWING, DIRECT SUGGESTION, DREAM SUGGESTION, HYPNOANALYSIS, HYPNODRAMA, HYPNOSIS, HYPOPLASTY.

hypnotic   1. A drug that helps induce and sustain sleep by increasing drowsiness and reducing motor activity. Such drugs (barbiturates, methaqualone, antihistamines, minor tranquilizers) often are employed in small doses to produce sedation and may be used in larger doses to produce anesthesia. See SEDATIVE-HYPNOTICS. 2. Pertaining to hypnosis, as in "hypnotic state."

hypnotic amnesia   Forgetting that occurs either as a result of undergoing hypnosis or due to suggestions to forget what happened. Usually such forgotten memories return to the hypnotized person.

hypnotic amnestic disorder   Temporary impairment in long-term and short-term memory without clouding of consciousness, following prolonged heavy use of a barbiturate or similarly acting sedative or hypnotic. Also known as sedative amnestic disorder. See AMNESTIC SYNDROME.

hypnotic analgesia   A participant's unresponsiveness or substantially reduced sensitivity to pain under hypnotic suggestion.

hypnotic induction   The process by which a person is hypnotized by verbal suggestion, mechanical aids, or drugs. The process depends upon the participant's susceptibility and needs and the hypnotist's skills and experience, but all methods generally involve the participant's fixation of attention and reduction of sensory and motor activities through relaxation while the hypnotist in one way or another makes suggestions to go into a trance-like state.

hypnotic re-education   Hypnotic suggestion combined with increased awareness of the emotional basis of the symptom.

hypnotic regression   The process whereby a person under hypnosis is induced to relive a past experience. The experience often is forgotten. Term is often used interchangeably with age regression. The validity of this phenomenon has been criticized. See HYPNOSIS.

hypnotic rigidity   A condition of muscular rigidity sometimes induced during hypnosis.

hypnotic set   A posthypnotic command obeyed without the person understanding the reason for so behaving.

hypnotic susceptibility   Hypnotizability, or hypnotic suggestibility or responsiveness.

hypnotic trance   The dreamlike state of intensified suggestibility induced in a hypnotized person; later, what occurred during the trance may or may not be recalled.

hypnotism   The study of the nature of hypnosis and its diagnostic and therapeutic applications. See BRAIDISM, COLLECTIVE HYPNOTIZATION.

hypnotizable   People able to be hypnotized. These can be further classified as low, medium, or high, depending on their degree of hypnotizability. One research study of some 200 people showed that about 25% were hypnotized at the first session; about 50% by the second session, but one person did not become hypnotized until after 100 sessions. Thus practically anyone who volunteers to be hypnotized can be.

hypnotization   See HYPNOIDIZATION, HYPNOSIS.

hypoactivity   Underactivity, as in the state of psychomotor retardation experienced in depression. See HYPERACTIVITY.

hypoacusis   hypacusis

hypoadrenal constitution   (N. Pende) A constitutional type associated with underactivity of the adrenal gland. According to Nicola Pende, such individuals are lean with slender bones, show a tendency toward melancholia with intelligence that is normal or superior.

hypoaffective type   (N. Pende) A constitutional body type distinguished by an absence of emotional reactivity. It corresponds roughly to the schizothymic type.

hypoageusia   Diminished sensitivity to taste that sometimes occurs in depression or depersonalization states, and as a neurologic disease symptom. See HYPOGEUSIA.

hypoalgesia   A reduced sensitivity to pain.

hypoallergenic   Low allergic potential (but without formal or scientific meaning).

hypob(o)ulia   Diminished will power, loss of initiative, and impaired ability to make decisions. A common symptom in schizophrenia and depression.

hypocathexis   An abnormally low investment of psychic energy.

hypochondria   (B. de Mondeville) Excessive concern about personal health, especially in the absence of related organic pathology.

hypochondriac   A person who obsessively complains of feeling ill, usually with a variety of ailments and pains, without any evidence of physical dysfunction. Such people usually enjoy informing others of their condition and seem to seek attention and pity.

hypochondriacal neurosis   A somatoform disorder characterized by unrealistic interpretation of normal physical signs or sensations as abnormal, leading to the fear or conviction that the person has a serious disease. Also known as nosomania. See HYPOCHONDRIA, HYPOCHONDRIASIS.

hypochondriasis   Exaggerated concern about personal health and often involving complaints to others as well as seeking out doctors who will be sympathetic to self-concerns.

hypochondrophthisis   Obsolete term for the wasting away of the body in hypochondriasis.

hypocrisy theory   (E. Aronson) A point of view that if one person attempts to convince another person to refrain from some activity or behavior that the first person engages in, the attempt will not succeed (for example, preaching to children that smoking is dangerous, yet continuing to smoke cigarettes). What is really meant is: "Do as I say and not as I do."

hypodepression   A state of simple or mild depression, similar to grief or mourning but with the added factors of self-accusation, self-depreciation, and reduced self-esteem.

hypoergasia   (A. Meyer) Obsolete term for the depressive phase of manic-depressive (bipolar) psychosis.

hypoesthesia   Diminished sensitivity to one or more types of sensory stimuli, such as heat, cold, light, or touch. Hypoesthesia is a common hysterical (conversion) symptom. Also known as hypesthesia, hypoesthesis.

hypoevolutism   An inadequate or deficient development of the morphological, physiological, and psychological aspects of the entire body, or of a body system, body part, or body function.

hypofunction   Reduced function or activity, especially of an organ, such as a gland.

hypogamy   Marrying downwards. Marriage to a spouse in poorer financial or social circumstances than self. See HYPERGAMY, MOBILITY.

hypogastric nerve   A part of the nervous system that may run as a single large nerve or as several smaller parallel nerves extending into the pelvic region. Postganglionic fibers innervate the bladder, rectum, and genitalia.

hypogenital type   (N. Pende) A constitutional body type in which the lower extremities are abnormally long and the individual shows delayed development of genitalia and other sexual characteristics.

hypogeusia   Diminution of the sense of taste.

hypoglossal nerve   Cranial nerve XII. It originates in a gray-matter nucleus on the floor of the fourth ventricle and controls (innervates) the tongue, lower jaw, and areas of the neck and chest.

hypoglycemia   A condition of low blood-sugar levels. In infants, symptoms may include tremors, seizures, weakness, and failure to develop intellectually. In adults, major symptoms may include debility, profuse sweating, nervousness, and dizziness.

hypognathous   Having a constitutionally deformed lower jaw.

hypogonadalism   A condition of reduction in the amount of testosterone produced by the testes.

hypokinesia   A pathological reduction in movement, as in depression and certain organic conditions such as Pick's disease and cerebral arteriosclerosis. Also known as hypokinesis.

hypokinesthesia   A diminished sensitivity to the motion and position of the body, involving reduction in proprioceptive sensation. See PROPRIOCEPTION.

hypolepsiomania   Denoting the various forms of monomania.

hypologia   1. An abnormal reduction in the capacity to speak, due to mental retardation or a cerebral disorder. 2. Speech deficit.

hypomania   The mildest degree of mania characterized by a sense of exhilaration, euphoria, and optimism, also by tireless activity, loquacity, uninhibited behavior and preoccupation with unrealistic schemes and solutions to problems. Disturbance is not sufficient to interfere with occupational functioning or to require hospitalization; delusions are never present. Term was suggested by English physician Henry Johnson as a replacement for Jean Esquirol's term monomania. Also known as hypomanic state. See BIPOLAR DISORDER, HYPERMANIA, MANIA, MANIC, MANIC EPISODE.

hypomanic personality   Refers to a high-strung, fast-moving and fast-talking person, halfway between normal and manic. See HYPOMANIA.

hypomanic state   **hypomania**

hypomelancholia   A mild episode of the depressed form of bipolar (manic-depressive) disorder.

hypomenorrhea   Reduction of normal production of menstrual flow.

hypomnesia   Poor or inadequate memory.

hypomotility   A reduced or abnormally slow rate of movement.

hyponoia   Deficient or sluggish mental activity.

hyponoic   (E. Kretschmer) Hysterical reactions stemming from deep within the mind. From the Greek, for underlying meaning.

hypoparathyroid constitution   A constitutional type associated with deficient parathyroid gland activity, marked by hyperflexia and hyperkinesis of the skeletal and smooth muscles and a tendency toward rickets or other disorders of calcium metabolism.

hypophagia   An abnormally small appetite, as in anorexia nervosa.

hypophilia   Refers to a proceptive sexual response, acceptive sexual response, or both, below the normal range. Includes sexual dysfunctions such as desire phase dysfunctions, inhibited arousal, and orgasm.

hypophonia   1. A form of dysphonia characterized by a whispered voice. 2. A very weak or barely audible voice. Due to incoordination of vocal muscles. Also known as microphonia, microphony.

hypophoria   Deviation of one eye in a downward direction when it is covered and fusion is prevented. See HYPERPHORIA.

hypophrasia   A lack of speech or slowness of speech associated with depression or a psychotic condition. Also known as bradyphrasia.

hypophrenia   Obsolete term for lack of (or deficiency in) mental or intellectual ability.

hypophrenosis   (E. E. Southard) Obsolete term for feeblemindedness (mental retardation).

hypophysectomy   Excision or destruction of the pituitary gland.

hypophysis (cerebri)   (B. G. Wilder) Alternative name for the pituitary (gland).

hypoplasia   An underdeveloped organ or tissue, usually due to an inadequate number of cells or diminished size of cells forming the structure.

hypoprosexia   Abnormal lack of attentive ability. Also known as hypoprosessis.

hypopsychosis   Obsolete term for a state of diminished mental activity.

hyposexuality   An abnormally low level of sexual behavior. Hyposexual individuals may show no capacity for sex drive or interest in sexual activity.

hyposmia   Olfactory hypesthesia; impaired ability to smell.

hyposomnia   A state of reduced total sleep.

hypostatization   The generating of entities out of abstract concepts, as in considering honesty or kindness as a unitary trait.

hypostenia   Physical weakness.

hypotaxia   A condition of weak coordination. See AFFECTIVE SUGGESTION.

hypotensive   Refers to a person with abnormally low blood pressure, the opposite of hypertensive. See NORMOTENSIVE.

hypothalamic sulcus   A groove in the lateral wall of the third ventricle, on either side, dividing the structure into upper and lower parts, the thalamus and the subthalamus.

hypothalamic theory of Cannon   **Cannon-Bard theory (of emotion)**

hypothalamus   (B. Bramwell, J. P. Karplus, & A. Kreidl) The ventral and medial region of the diencephalon forming the walls of the ventral half of the third ventricle, which contains the nuclei with primary control of the autonomic functions of the body. The hypothalamus integrates autonomic activity into appropriate responses to internal and external stimuli and also has a major role in endocrine function. Lesions in metabolic centers of the hypothalamus cause increased or decreased appetites, depending upon the hypothalamic area affected. See LATERAL HYPOTHALAMUS.

hypothermesthesia   An abnormally diminished sensitivity to heat or heat stimuli. Also known as thermohypesthesia.

hypothesis   A testable proposition based on theory, stating an expected empirical outcome resulting from specific observable conditions.

hypothesis behavior   (I. Krechevsky) A pattern of performance by experimental animals in which one particular cue or response is chosen consistently from a number of alternatives. Krechevsky analyzed patterns followed by rats in running mazes with alternate pathways, according to visual or spatial cues, or both.

hypothesis testing   Choosing, on the basis of sample data and a set of decision rules, between two mutually exclusive and exhaustive statistical hypotheses: the null hypothesis and the alternative hypothesis. The null hypothesis is rejected if empirical results are extremely unlikely if it were true.

hypothetical   Unproved conjecture.

hypothetical construct (H.C.)   An explanatory concept using terms far removed from observation, or terms with much surplus meaning. For instance, many psychodynamic structures and processes are hypothetical constructs. See INTERVENING VARIABLE.

hypothetical imperative   (I. Kant) Behavior based on necessity rather than on ethics, dependent on realistic conditions that must be met, such as stealing a loaf of bread to feed starving children. See CATEGORICAL IMPERATIVE.

hypothetical proposition   A statement consisting of two parts: (a) an antecedent clause, introduced usually by "if," stating the condition under which a certain result will occur or under which a certain conclusion will be reached, and (b) a consequent stating the occurrence or the conclusion.

hypothetical reasoning   Formal reasoning that begins with an antecedent and a consequent, such as "If I behave myself, everyone will like me." There are four possible premises: (a) I do behave myself (affirming the antecedent), (b) I do not behave myself (denying the antecedent), (c) everyone likes me (affirming the consequent), and (d) everyone does not like me (denying the consequent).

hypothetico-deductive method   (C. L. Hull) A general research method that involves formulation of hypotheses from empirical data (induction) as well as the formulation of larger-scale postulates from which new predictions can be made (deduction) and can then be tested against empirical data. Predictions that are confirmed support the theory; those that are not confirmed suggest that the theory should be revised. See HULL'S THEORY.

hypothetico-deductive reasoning   The abstract, logical reasoning that, according to Jean Piaget, emerges in early adolescence and marks the period of formal operations. Distinguished by the capacity for abstract thinking and hypothesis-testing, which frees the adolescent from total reliance on concrete thinking and immediate perception.

hypothymia   A subnormal level of emotional tone, as observed in cases of depression.

hypothyroid constitution   A constitutional body type associated with a deficiency of thyroid gland activity. Corresponds roughly to Ernst Kretschmer's pyknic category but with the added features of fatty deposits about the face and neck, short, stubby hands, low basal metabolism, and mental torpor. See CONGENITAL HYPOTHYROIDISM.

hypothyroidism   A pathological condition resulting from insufficient production of the internal secretion of the thyroid gland. Cretinism, myxedema and endemic goiter are consequences. Also known as hypothyreosis. Compare HYPERTHYROIDISM.

hypotonia   Poor, flaccid muscle tone.

hypovegetative (type)   A constitutional type in which the body features correspond to Ernst Kretschmer's asthenic type.

hypovigility   Subnormal awareness or response to external stimuli, as observed in many patients with schizophrenia.

hypovolemia   A state of reduced extracellular-fluid volume that is associated with the urge to increase water consumption. See HYPERVOLEMIA.

hypoxemia   Less than adequate presence of oxygen in arterial blood. Not as serious as anoxia, connoting total oxygen deprivation. Once included under the term "anoxemia."

hypoxia   Less than adequate provision of oxygen to organism. Distinguished from anoxia, connoting total oxygen deprivation.

hypoxyphilia   See ASPHIXOPHILIA.

hypsarrhythmia   An abnormal and chaotic electroencephalographic (EEG) pattern characteristically observed in certain infants in the first year of life who exhibit epilepsy-like spasms. Also known as major dysrhythmia, myoclonic encephalitis.

hypsophobia   Excessive fear of high places. Also known as acrophobia.

hysterectomy   The surgical removal of the uterus.

hysteresis   1. The time lag (especially an unduly long one) between an event in the body and perception of its effect, as from being pinched to feeling it. 2. Tendency of an organic system to behave differently, depending on the direction of change of an input parameter. 3. The time lag between a cause and its effect in a living body that may be due to a variety of conditions, including new learning.

hysteria   1. A neurotic disorder characterized by suggestibility, emotional outbursts, histrionic behavior, repressed anxiety. 2. In psychoanalytic theory, transformation of unconscious conflicts into physical symptoms, such as paralysis, blindness, and loss of sensation. Types of hysteria include: ANXIETY, ARCTIC, COMBAT, CONVERSION, DEFENSE, MASS, RETENTION. See CONVERSION DISORDER, DISSOCIATIVE DISORDERS, DISSOCIATIVE FIXATION, GLOBUS HYSTERICUS, HISTRIONIC-PERSONALITY DISORDER, "LA BELLE INDIFFERENCE."

hysterical amaurosis/blindness Loss of sight, or partial blindness, in eyes that are organically intact. It is a hysterical (conversion) symptom frequently due to an unconscious attempt to screen out a threatening or guilt-laden situation. Despite the "blindness," the pupils continue to react to light and the patient automatically avoids objects that would result in injury. See ANTON'S SYNDROME, BLINDSIGHT.

hysterical amnesia A dissociative reaction characterized by inability to recall anxiety-provoking events, such as experiences associated with guilt, failure, or rejection.

hysterical anesthesia The absence of sensation in certain areas of the body (such as the hands or genital organs) not due to organic pathology or defect. It is interpreted as an unconsciously adopted conversion symptom resulting from anxiety, internal conflict, or other emotional disturbance.

hysterical aphonia A sudden loss of voice due to emotional conflicts.

hysterical arc An arcane physical position that some people with mental disorders of various kinds assume, with the head and feet on a surface but not the rest of the body, forming a convex shape. Illustrations of this phenomenon were often found in old texts on mental disorders, but are not found in newer ones.

hysterical ataxia astasia-abasia

hysterical blindness hysterical amaurosis

hysterical convulsions Seizures precipitated by psychological rather than organic factors, usually distinguishable from epileptic seizures by the presence of emotional conflict or stress and the fact that patients do not injure themselves, lose pupillary reflexes, or become incontinent during the episode. Also known as conversion seizures.

hysterical deafness A loss of hearing developed unconsciously, usually due to intolerable emotional stress.

hysterical disorder Any pervasive disturbance characterized by involuntary psychogenic dysfunction of the sensory, motor, or visceral activities of the body, such as loss of the ability to speak normally after an emotional trauma.

hysterical hiccup A myoclonic spasm of the diaphragm due to emotional causes. Rarely also spelled hysterical hiccough.

hysterical hypalgia A decrease in the normal sensitivity to pain in various parts of the body due to psychogenic influences.

hysterical imitation The imitation of symptoms observed in a person with whom the patient identifies; for example, one student faints and other students then also faint though hysterical identification.

hysterical materialization The symbolic expression of a repressed fantasy in somatic terms.

hysterical mutism A state during which a person cannot talk even though there is nothing wrong with the physical apparatus of speech.

hysterical paralysis A conversion symptom affecting one limb (monoplegia), the lower part of the body (paraplegia), or one side of the body (hemiplegia). It is functional and psychogenic, and, in contrast to organic paralysis, deep reflexes are not lost and there is little or no wasting. Also known as conversion paralysis.

hysterical-personality disorder Older name for histrionic-personality disorder.

hysterical pregnancy A false pregnancy.

hysterical pseudodementia (C. Wernicke) A conversion syndrome in which a person of normal intelligence acts as if mentally retarded. See GANSER SYNDROME.

hysterical psychosis 1. An acute psychosis occurring in hysterical personalities and usually lasting three weeks or less without residual symptoms. An hysterical psychosis is characterized by the sudden onset of hallucinations, delusions, and bizarre and sometimes violent behavior. 2. A brief reactive psychotic-like state usually following a stressful precipitating event. See AMOK, LATAH, MIRYACHIT, PIBLOKTO, WINDIGO.

hysterical puerilism A psychogenic condition in which an adult patient reverts to behavior characteristic of infancy or early childhood. See HYSTERICAL PSEUDODEMENTIA.

hysterical seizure See HYSTERICAL CONVULSIONS.

hysterical stupor A conversion reaction in which the patient is mute, unresponsive, and immobile. See CONVERSION DISORDER.

hysterical twilight states Mental episodes of hysteria in which the patients imagine themselves in an entirely different environment or are the subjects of remarkable adventures.

hysteriform Pertaining to a condition characterized by symptoms that resemble those associated with hysteria.

hysteriform seizures Convulsions or other episodic motor disturbances that appear to be of hysterical origin, usually with only partial unconsciousness and partial amnesia.

hysterogenic zones Areas of the body in which stimulation produces a hysterical reaction, such as anesthesia, pain, or tenderness, usually in the breasts, spine, head, or ovarian region. Allochiria sometimes occurs in these cases.

hysteroneurasthenia Neurasthenia with evidences of the mechanism of hysteria.

hysterosyntonic A personality type that combines hysterical and syntonic types of personalities. (A syntone is a normal person who is in emotional harmony with the environment).

Hz See HERTZ.

I

i. The class interval in a frequency distribution (also abbreviated **I**).

I 1. See INDEX NUMBER. 2. Induction. 3. See LUMINOUS INTENSITY. 4. Intensity. 5. Intelligence. 6. The class interval in a frequency distribution (also abbreviated **i.**).

iatrochemical school of thought One of two major 17th century, materialistic beliefs about neural physiology, which treated physiological phenomena as resulting from chemical changes. Compare IATROPHYSICAL SCHOOL OF THOUGHT.

iatrogenesis A process in which the treatment exacerbates the disorder that it is designed to ameliorate, such as a treatment for depression that results in greater subjective mood disturbance, or creates a new problem, as in undesired side effects of a medication or other form of intervention.

iatrogenic 1. Refers to an unintended negative condition produced by treatment. 2. Literally, caused by the physician, refers to any condition that is largely caused by some medical intervention.

iatrogenic addiction Physiological drug addiction due to the prescribing of narcotic drugs by a physician or others (such as military corps attendants during war) for a legitimate purpose, often overprescribed. See MORPHINE TOLERANCE, SOLDIER'S SICKNESS.

iatrogenic conditions (D. Motet) The assumption that some environments are "crazy making" and the cause of behavioral deviations. For example, a child with low academic potential is placed in classes where the child does not understand what is going on, is criticized for not paying attention, and is punished at home for not doing well in school.

iatrogenic homosexuality Male-male (or female-female) sexual feelings or behavior either initiated or encouraged by the attitude of professionals, such as physicians, psychologists, social workers, counselors or others while treating or counseling people.

iatrogenic illness A disease caused by a physician's advice or treatment.

iatrogenic neurosis A behavior disorder induced or aggravated by health professionals, especially by incautious comments. Particularly affects suggestible people or those with hypochondriacal tendencies.

iatrogenic pathologies Any medically-induced problem, for example, false memories implanted in a client by a "professional" such as a counselor, clinical psychologist, psychiatrist, or social worker, regarding the client being sexually abused as a child, through suggestions made by the professional. See FALSE MEMORIES.

iatrophysical school of thought A point of view that medicine and the healing arts can be understood from knowledge of the physical sciences. René Descartes accepted this point of view. Compare IATROCHEMICAL SCHOOL OF THOUGHT.

iatropic stimulus A bodily sensation that indicates the body is sick. Such sensations can be imagined or real. Conflicts may arise with a doctor, the patient, and family members if no organic signs of illness are found, since the patient may be accused of being a hypochondriac.

IB exams See INTERNATIONAL BACCALAUREATE EXAMINATIONS.

ibogaine A hallucinogenic agent found in the root of the African plant *Tabernanthe iboga*, used mainly in rituals by members of the Bwiti (Bouiti) cult of Gabon. Hallucinations reportedly include visitations with specific ancestors and verbalizations related to the history of the people. If death occurs during use of the drug, the event is regarded as divine intervention.

Ibonics See EBONICS.

IBT See INKBLOT TEST.

Icarus complex (H. A. Murray) According to Henry Murray, a desire to be important and gain fame and fortune but paired with a tendency to not succeed, in part because of refusing to try or giving up too quickly.

ICD See INTERNATIONAL CLASSIFICATION OF DISEASES.

ice 1. Slang for crystal methamphetamine. Its purity has been developed so that it can be smoked, thus making it a highly attractive and intensely addicting substance. See CRANK, METHAMPHETAMINE. 2. Slang for killing someone. See HOMICIDE.

iceberg principle (E. Dichter) A theory that people purchasing merchandise make some decisions based on unconscious goals. See UNCONSCIOUS MOTIVATION.

iceberg profile In sport psychology, a psychological profile of successful athletes marked by depression, anger, fatigue, confusion, high vigor, and low tension.

iceblock theory (K. Lewin) A concept of behavior change in group dynamics of T-groups or sensitivity training in which existing attitudes and behavior are to be unfrozen, and new attitudes and behavior are to be first explored and then frozen into new habit patterns.

icebreaker In any new interactive group situation, a procedure to get individuals in the proper mood for future interactions.

ichthyophobia Morbid fear or strong dislike of fish.

icon 1. A pictorial representation. Also spelled ikon. 2. (U. Neisser) The visual contents of sensory storage.

iconic 1. Pertaining to an image, or representation of a phenomenon. 2. Sensation of a light that lasts after the light is turned off. 3. A symbol that has many of the properties of that which it symbolizes. See ICONIC SIGN.

iconic content (J. Bruner) Mental images of a particular aspect of reality, as for example, a child's mental representation of a tricycle. Also known as icon mode.

iconic gesture A gesture that conveys meaning, as in rubbing the belly to indicate hunger.

iconicity 1. In psychological esthetics, denotes the tendency for visual impressions to remain as short-term images in the mind. It is associated with whole-word reading methods and subliminal advertising. 2. The resemblance between two objects or images despite structural differences, such as the superficial similarity between birds and bats. See HOMOLOGY.

iconic memory An instantaneous memory of a visual stimulus. An image that flashes into memory for a second or so.

iconic mode Representation of reality through mental images based on sensory impressions, as in the conversion of experience or perceptions of a table into a mental picture based on those perceptions. Characteristic of the iconic stage. Jerome Bruner's other two modes of representation are the enactive mode and the symbolic mode. See ICON.

iconic representation (J. Bruner) Memories categorized by sensory images. According to Jerome Bruner this is the second mode of representation, preceded by enactive representation and followed by symbolic representation. See ICONIC MODE.

iconic sign (C. Morris) A representation of an image, such as a photograph or caricature of a person. A sign similar in appearance to what it signifies. See ICON.

iconic stage Jerome Bruner's second stage of cognitive development, when internal images (icons) become important. Occurs between the ages of two and seven, beginning to develop in early infancy and becoming dominant in the preschool years. A period between the enactive and symbolic stages during which a child develops mental images or perceptual representations of objects and events. Also spelled ikonic stage. See ICONIC MODE.

iconic store The concept that visual memory is kept in an unprocessed state for a short time before entering cognition. Compare ECHOIC STORE.

iconoclast (breaker of images—Greek) A radical thinker, a person who "attacks" established beliefs and institutions.

iconolatry The worship of images; or more specifically, the worship of pictures.

iconomania A morbid urge to collect and worship images.

iconophobia 1. Morbid fear of images, idols, or works of art, often stemming from religious doctrines. 2. Fear of idols.

ICS See INTRACRANIAL STIMULATION.

ICSH Interstitial-cell-stimulating hormone

ICSS Abbreviation for intracranial self-stimulation. See INTRACRANIAL STIMULATION, SELF-STIMULATION.

ICT Insulin-coma therapy

ictal emotions Affective states that occur and disappear suddenly or rapidly, particularly anxiety and depression.

ictus 1. A sudden epileptic seizure without an aura. 2. An apoplectic stroke. 3. The characteristic of a particular tone or syllable in a series more prominent than those before or after it.

id (it—Latin) 1. (A. Weismann) In August Weismann's (1834–1914) evolutionary theory, a unit of germ plasm. 2. (S. Freud) One of the three main divisions of the mind in psychoanalytic theory (the other two are ego and superego). The id, *Das Es*, consists of basic, instinctual drives, concerned with selfish pleasure, pure hedonism. The id is unconscious, and in Freudian theory, the id, ego, and the superego will be in an ongoing dynamic tension. See ID PSYCHOLOGY, PRIMARY PROCESS, STRUCTURAL HYPOTHESIS.

id anxiety A Freudian concept of a type of anxiety derived from instinctual drives.

IDEA See INDIVIDUALS WITH DISABILITIES EDUCATION ACT.

idea 1. A mental image or cognition that may occur without direct reference to perception or sensory processes. 2. In classical associationist doctrine (for example, Hume), the residue of a sensory perceptual process. Types of idea include: ABSTRACT, AGGREGATE, AUTOCHTHONOUS, DETERMINATIVE, FIXED, FLIGHT OF, GENERAL, GRANDIOSE DELUSIONS/, GUIDING, INNATE, INSISTENT, OBTRUSIVE, OVERCHARGED, POVERTY OF, PRESSURE OF, RATIONAL ELABORATION OF, TRAIN OF.

ideal The conception of something in its most perfect form, or the thing or person that embodies such a standard. In classical philosophy (for example, Plato), a true prototype of which actual instances are imperfect examples.

idealism 1. A doctrine that insists that the world is most adequately conceived of in terms of ideas or thought rather than in terms of matter (for example, Plato). See MIND-BODY PROBLEM. 2. Being guided by ideals which one places before practical consideration.

idealistic monism A doctrine positing that all of reality, including the physical world, can be reduced to the world of the mind or of ideas.

idealization The exaggeration of another person's positive attributes. In psychoanalytic theory, idealization is a defense mechanism that protects the person doing the exaggerating from conscious feelings of ambivalence toward the idealized person.

idealized image (K. Horney) Phrase introduced by Karen Horney for a neurotic defense consisting of an exaggerated, unrealistic picture of own (or another's) abilities and potentialities, derived from wishful thinking rather than from fact.

idealized influence in leadership (B. Bass & B. Avolio) Leaders demonstrate their determined commitment to particular beliefs, values, and aspirations. The leaders are admired, respected, and trusted by their subordinates or followers. These leaders serve as role models for their followers who identify with the leaders and want to emulate them. It is said to be the single most important factor in transformational leadership. See CHARISMATIC LEADERSHIP.

idealized self (K. Horney) The self that a person believes he or she should be.

ideal masochism Freudian phrase for psychic or moral masochism in which the injury is mental rather than physical (that is, ideational rather than material). Also known as mental masochism. See MORAL MASOCHISM.

ideal observer 1. A person who, or a theoretical function that, receives information and records it properly. The observer is between input and output and represents the input accurately in the output. 2. In psychophysics, a theoretical error-free observing function.

ideal self According to Carl Rogers, the person one would like to be. A desired personality, both in terms of covert self and overt self; that is, how a person wants to be and how a person wants to be seen by others. In Rogers' later writing referred to as the "emerging person."

ideal self-image (C. R. Rogers) High standards a person wishes to live up to in terms of self. Not meeting these standards may result in feelings of inadequacy, as seen in some persons with neuroses who raise the standards for themselves and consequently never feel satisfied with themselves.

idea of reference A belief that a certain issue relates to the person although in reality it does not; neutral stimuli or phenomena may be interpreted as having special meaning. In extreme cases, this becomes delusion of reference.

ideation 1. (J. Locke) The process of forming ideas and images, which might include sense impressions. 2. (D. Hume, J. Mill) The process of forming ideas and images; an alternative form of consciousness to, and distinct from, sensations. 3. Reflective thinking based on organization of thoughts and experiences throughout personal history (for example, Fritz Perls) leading to a here-and-now approach to any new situation.

ideational apraxia A condition marked by loss or impairment of the ability to know how to perform a complex series of actions, such as tying shoelaces; inability to conceive a sequence of steps. Also known as ideomotor apraxia, sensory apraxia.

ideational learning A form of learning based on cognitive analysis and reflection with a minimum of involvement of overt movement; contrasts with motor learning.

ideational shield A defense reaction in which individuals fearing rejection or criticism by others protect themselves against anxiety by generating intellectual reasons for not criticizing others who wrongly criticize them.

ideational sociocultural systems (P. Sorokin) In social systems thinking, beliefs based on mysticism, tradition, faith, and authority. See SENSTATE SOCIOCULTURAL SYSTEMS.

ideational stimulus A stimulus that produces a reaction through the mediation of associated ideas.

idée fixe (fixed idea—French) (P. Janet) An idea so rigidly held that every effort to change it is resisted. Such ideas may become obsessions that govern a person's mental life and may take the form of delusions maintained despite evidence to the contrary. Phrase was used by Pierre Janet for dissociative ideas that split off from the rest of consciousness and develop an autonomous system or even "personality" of their own.

idée-force (strength of an idea—French) (A. Fouillée) An idea possessing dynamic properties and acting as a force leading to actions.

id-ego Prototypic psychic function in the newborn from which psychoanalytic theory proposes that the id and ego functions develop.

identical-components theory (E. L. Thorndike) Part of the theory of transfer of training that asserts that new tasks are easier to learn to the extent that they contain some of the stimulus elements to which appropriate responses have already been learned. Also known as identical-elements theory.

identical points Sites on the retinas of the left and right eyes that receive identical sensory input from the same object at a specified distance.

identical twins A common name for monozygotic twins.

identifiability principle A theory that it is easier to learn to make responses to situations when the situation or its elements are readily identified separately or distinguished from others.

identification 1. The process of associating the self closely with other persons and assuming their characteristics or views. In psychoanalytic theory, such identification operates largely on an unconscious or semi-conscious level. 2. (H. A. Simon) A tendency to make decisions in terms of the goals of a particular group or organization to which the person belongs. Identification has both motivational (the member's well-being may be associated with that of the group) and cognitive (the member's representation of the situation is influenced by position in the group or organization) foundations. Whatever its psychological roots, identification is an important determinant of organizational and group behavior. 3. (S. Freud) Assuming the characteristics of some ideal person; becoming as much as possible similar to this perceived paragon. Kinds of identification include: ANACLITIC, COSMIC, COUNTER-, CROSS-PARENTAL, DEFENSIVE, DOMAIN, FEMININE, GROUP, HEALTHY, MIS-, MULTIPLE, ORGANIZATIONAL, PRIMARY, PROJECTIVE, PSEUDO-, SECONDARY, SELF-, SEX, TRIAL. See FIXED-ROLE THERAPY.

identification figures 1. Parents, caretakers, or other significant adults who provide role models for a child. 2. Individuals, real or imagined, with whom the person consciously or unconsciously identifies. See IDENTIFICATION.

identification (in language development) A verbal extension of a simple pointing response, as in "see kitty."

identification of bodily elements The assignment of names or numbers to bodily elements. The simplest examples are numbers used for measuring height or weight of the whole body and parts of the body upon autopsies. However, some bodily elements are classified by colors such as eyes or by description such as bald, hairy, solid. The parts of the brain have had a number of competing and complex names and numbers.

identification test A verbal or nonverbal subtest of an intelligence test in which the participant identifies objects or parts of objects in a picture.

identification transference (S. R. Slavson) In group therapy, the patient's identification with other members of the group and a desire to emulate them. See LIBIDINAL TRANSFERENCE, SIBLING TRANSFERENCE.

identification with prohibitions See IDENTIFICATION WITH THE AGGRESSOR.

identification with the aggressor A presumably unconscious mechanism characterized by identification with a hostile, punitive opponent who cannot be mastered. The person avoids punishment by acceding to the demands of the authority figure; in psychoanalytic contexts, sometimes called identification with prohibitions. The classic example occurs as part of the resolution of a boy's Oedipal complex. The father, a powerful rival for the affection of the mother (who has been the boy's main source of gratification), is a threatening figure. Since the boy is no match for his father, and he cannot leave the situation, the only way to reduce anxiety is to identify with the father, thereby strengthening the superego. This syndrome apparently occasionally occurred with inmates in concentration camps and prisons as well as with hostages in close contact with their captors. See STOCKHOLM SYNDROME.

identified patient A member of a family for whom treatment is sought because of the hurt, damage, or pain this person has caused to the family and others. Such a person is occasionally a scapegoat blamed for misbehavior that only reflects the family's pathology. Also known as symptom bearer/wearer. See FAMILY THERAPY THEORY.

identity 1. A person's social role and his or her perception of it. 2. In cognitive development, refers to the awareness that an object remains the same even though it may undergo a transformation; for example, a piece of clay may be made to assume various forms, but is still the same piece of clay. 3. (E. Erikson) A feeling of being the same person as yesterday and last year; a sense of continuity derived from body sensations (coenaesthesia), body image, and the conviction that memories, purposes, values, and experiences belong to a person; a sense of uniqueness and independence ("I am my own person"). Also known as personal identity. Types of identity include: BODY, CORE GENDER, DYS-, EGO, FEMININE, GENDER, LATENT SOCIAL, MASCULINE, MISTAKEN, OBJECT, SELF-, SEX, SEXUAL, SOCIAL. See LAW OF THOUGHT, LOSS OF PERSONAL IDENTITY, SENSE OF IDENTITY, UNCONSCIOUS IDENTITY WITH THE AGGRESSOR.

identity achievement (J. E. Marcia) A commitment to choices made following a crisis of self-analysis.

identity confusion (E. Erikson) A stage in life, usually during adolescence, when a person must decide who he or she is and what role to play in life. See ROLE CONFUSION.

identity crisis A period of confusion, usually as the result of a transition, that occurs autochthonously (from within) or is due to outside factors (such as an accident, death of a person, economic events, a move to a new environment), during which the support for personal previous identity is lost and the person must in a sense redefine the self.

identity diffusion (J. E. Marcia) An absence of commitment that may or may not follow a period of considering alternatives, especially during crises. Also known as role confusion.

identity disorder 1. A chronic disturbance, usually of late adolescence, in which the patient suffers uncertainty and stress due to issues about long-term goals, career choice, group loyalty, moral values, religious identification, and sexual orientation and behavior. 2. Being uncertain of "what" the self is, usually referring to a gender disorder. Whether a person self-identifies as male if a male or female if a female. See ATYPICAL GENDER-IDENTITY DISORDER.

identity foreclosure (J. E. Marcia) The premature imposition of an identity, usually occupational, before young people have had a chance to experiment and select an identity of their own.

identity formation The process of achieving a consistent, well-integrated, and mature personality based on earlier positive influences.

identity need According to Erich Fromm, the need to achieve a sense of uniqueness, individuality, selfhood, and psychological autonomy; the severing of infantile familial ties considered essential for healthy individuality. Unhealthy, spurious individuality is expressed in conformity, a manifestation of what Fromm called escape from freedom.

identity politics In social psychology, the acknowledgment that different groups want their identities to be respected on their own terms, or the belief that some issues regarding disadvantaged minorities are the exclusive jurisdiction of those members; for instance, that only an African American person can deal with color-based racism. Also known as politics of recognition.

identity position The view that mental processes are the same as certain types of brain process but described in different terms. See MONISM (meaning 2).

identity principle In formal logic, one of the three laws of normal thought that states if any statement is true, it is true. See LAWS OF THOUGHT.

identity status (J. E. Marcia) The four levels of Marcia's identity process: identity achievement, identity foreclosure, identity diffusion, moratorium.

identity theory A point of view of the mind-body relation holding that whereas the mind and physical reality appear to be fundamentally different, they are never the less ultimately identical.

identity vs role confusion　　(E. Erikson) The fifth of Erikson's stages of psychosocial development, approximately between the ages of 12 and 18, the years of adolescence during which the person either develops a stable identity or remains unable to escape from being confused about personal roles. See ERIKSON'S STAGES OF PSYCHOSOCIAL DEVELOPMENT.

Identity, Negation, Reciprocal, and Correlative transformations (INRC)　　(J. Piaget) Cognitive capacities that characterize the intellectual stage of development of bright adolescents: these transformations in their symbolic logic system lead them to form structural groups that permit the operation of the highest, most abstract intellectual thought.

ideoglandular　　Pertaining to glandular functions initiated by mental processes, such as the production of adrenaline by the perception of a frightening object.

ideogram　　A pictograph or figure that symbolizes an object or idea (for example, ♡ for love). Some written languages, such as the Chinese, are based on ideograms. Also known as ideograph.

ideographs　　Symbols representing ideas; for example, the symbols + and × have special meanings in mathematics.

ideokinesis　　Muscular motions of an automatic type that occur without conscious intent due to a dominant idea. See IDEOMOTION.

ideokinetic　　See IDEOMOTOR.

ideokinetic apraxia　　A condition in which a person can perform individual motor responses but is unable to perform a motor-response sequence composed of these same responses. See IDEATIONAL APRAXIA.

ideological attitude　　The basic philosophy underlying all attitudes of a person. The essence of a person, from which all voluntary behaviors stem.

ideology　　1. A systematic ordering of ideas with associated doctrines, attitudes, beliefs, and symbols that together form a coherent philosophy or *Weltanschauung* (world-view) for a person, group, or sociopolitical movement, as in being a Jungian or a Democrat. 2. The system of de Condillac in which all ideas are derived from sensory stimulation.

ideomotion　　Movement responses that follow thought processes. (May be of a fleeting character.) Refers to muscular activity that is directed by an idea rather than by an intention; may be performed without awareness of the person (for example, someone thinks of something pleasant and smiles).

ideomotor　　Pertaining to movements that follow upon and are initiated by ideas. See SENSORIMOTOR.

ideomotor act　　(D. Hartley) An action that reveals a thought; an involuntary behavior based on thought.

ideomotor action　　(W. James) An action initiated by an idea. Normally, an idea will lead to behavior unless the idea is inhibited by other ideas.

ideomotor activity　　Actions that are generated by thought processes; such responses may be of a fleeting character. See SENSORIMOTOR ACTIVITY.

ideomotor apraxia　　Inability to perform a complex series of actions, such as riding a bicycle, because of failure to conceive the sequence as a whole. The preferred phrase is ideational apraxia.

ideomotor center　　A hypothetical command center in the brain, a site that makes the decision to perform some action that the person has been thinking of doing, such as finally saying "Yes" in a bargaining situation.

ideophobia　　Morbid fear of having or being confronted with ideas. See CAINOTOPHOBIA.

ideophrenia　　(J. Guislain) A form of delirium characterized by ideational disorders. Distinguished from ideophrenic and idiophrenic.

ideophrenic　　(W. Tuke) Insanity caused by inflammation of the brain. Mistakenly spelled idiophrenic. Distinguished from ideophrenia and idiophrenic.

ideoplasty　　1. The operation of ideas upon physiological processes. 2. The process of molding a person's mental events by the verbal suggestions of a hypnotist. Also known as ideoplastia. Sometimes spelled ideoplasy. See SUGGESTIBILITY, VERBAL SUGGESTION.

id interpretation　　In psychoanalytic therapy, an interpretation that penetrates defenses and permits painful thoughts to be released into consciousness. Also known as impulse interpretation.

idiocentric　　See IDIOCENTRISM.

idiocentrism　　(H. Triandis) A personality variable reflecting attitudes, beliefs, and behaviors usually found in individualistic cultures, such as in Northwestern Europe and North America. The self is autonomous from ingroups, personal goals have priority of ingroup goals, attitudes and personal needs determine social behavior much more than norms, and people compute the advantages and disadvantages of behavior for themselves, without much consideration of the needs of ingroup members. Such idiocentric individuals stay in relationships only if the benefits exceed the costs. A personality attribute parallel to individualism at the cultural level. Compare ALLOCENTRISM.

idiocy　　Obsolete term for the lowest level of mental deficiency, characterized by an IQ (intelligence quotient) of less than 20 and a maximum social and intellectual level of a three-year-old. "Idiot" has been replaced by "profoundly retarded." See AMAUROTIC IDIOCY, IDIOT, JUVENILE AMAUROTIC IDIOCY, KALMUK IDIOCY, MORAL IDIOCY, PROFOUNDLY RETARDED, TAY-SACHS DISEASE, XERODERMIC IDIOCY.

idiodynamics　　1. (S. Rosenzweig) A concept that decisions about behavior are complex and compound functions of a number of interacting factors such as goals, situations, or needs. See IDIOVERSE. 2. A doctrine positing that a person attends to the environmental aspects considered relevant. An individual selects stimuli and organizes responses, thus in charge of his or her life even at the level of habit.

idiogamist　　A person capable of full sexual response with a spouse but who is sexually incapable or inadequate with other partners. May refer to a man impotent with any partner other than his wife or perhaps only with women who resemble his wife.

idiogamy　　The ability of some men to have successful sexual relations with only a single woman or, at most, only with women who resemble their wives.

idiogenesis　　Origin without apparent cause.

idiogenetic　　Pertaining to mental processes that arise from images of sense impressions rather than from ideas that can be expressed verbally.

idiogenetic theory (F. Brentano) A point of view that the function of judgment is an original or primordial mental capacity. See ACT PSYCHOLOGY.

idioglossia 1. An extreme form of lalling or vowel or consonant substitution resulting in unintelligible speech. Seen in some children. See LALLATION. 2. Unintelligible speech, characteristic of some persons of low mentality. 3. See IDIOLALIA (meaning 1).

idiographic (W. Windelband) Pertaining to an individual or individual case. Refers to assessment procedures and observed relationships and results that are not necessarily generalizable across persons or groups. Sometimes called idiothetic and incorrectly spelled ideographic. See MORPHOGENIC.

idiographic approach 1. The study of individuality, the uniqueness of an individual's behavior and adjustment, as contrasted with a study of the universal, or nomothetic, aspects of experience or behavior. 2. Focus on individual subjects in research. Preferring a report showing that six participants each responded identically after a particular manipulation to a report that the mean performance of one treatment group was significantly superior to the mean performance of two other groups following different manipulations. See ALLPORT'S PERSONALITY-TRAIT THEORY, NOMOTHETIC.

idiographic psychology (J. M. Cattell) The study of a single person as undertaken by a diagnostician or a psychotherapist concentrating on a particular client. Contrasted with nomothetic psychology wherein examiners or therapists look for principles that apply to people in general or to groups of people, such as newborns. Sometimes called idiothetic psychology.

idiolalia 1. Self-generated language; use of a language invented by the person. 2. The omission, substitution, and distortion of so many sounds that speech is rendered unintelligible. It is often associated with mental retardation. See IDIOGLOSSIA.

idiolect The unique mode of speech used by a particular person; the dialect spoken by any single person. Different people tend to use the "same" dialect somewhat differently, and many families develop a unique mode of speech within the family, a "familect."

idiom In linguistics, a peculiar or unusual form of language, not ordinarily understood by those who study the classical language; for example, "Beat it" does not mean "Strike it" but, to those who have an understanding of American idiom, "Go away." See PERSONAL IDIOM.

idiopanima The concept that a person has of how others view the person on how people think others view them. See LOOKING-GLASS SELF.

idiopathic Arising spontaneously or from an unknown origin. Relating to diseases of unknown etiology. See AUTOCHTHONOUS.

idiopathic autoscopy A rare delusional disorder in which patients see "doubles" who look, talk, act, and dress like them that probably has a psychogenic, as opposed to organic basis (symptomatic autoscopy). See AUTOSCOPIC SYNDROME.

idiopathic epilepsy Epilepsy of unknown origin or due to nonspecific brain defect. Genetic predisposition to this condition can be found in many but not all cases. Compare SYMPTOMATIC EPILEPSY.

idiophrenic Relating to, or originating in, the mind or brain. Distinguished from ideophrenia, ideophrenic.

idioretinal light An illusion of shades of gray observed in a dark environment. The effect is caused by chemical changes in the retina or brain cells rather than the wavelength of visible light.

idiosyncrasy 1. An unusual or peculiar mental, physical, or behavioral aspect of an individual, such as refusing to eat fruit unless wearing gloves. 2. An unusual physical reaction to some substances, foods, medications, or environments.

idiosyncrasy credit (E. P. Hollander) Refers to the reputation that a leader has in relation to how the leader's thinking differs from the expectations of the subordinates; for example, if leaders vary too much from what is expected of them, they lose credit until eventually all credit is lost and the leaders are no longer effective.

idiosyncrasy-credit model (E. P. Hollander) The theory that a leader is able to diverge from group standards to the extent that the leader has built up "credits" or prestige over time by conformity to group norms.

idiosyncratic Relating to, or marked by an idiosyncrasy.

idiosyncratic intoxication An acute psychotic state precipitated by a moderate amount of alcohol; characterized by confusion, disorientation, hallucinations, and impulsive violence with complete amnesia for the episode. Also known as *mania à potu*, pathological intoxication.

idiosyncratic reaction 1. An unexpected reaction to some stimulus, whether it be a single word, a sentence, or a comment, that is totally unrelated to the stimulus as expected by others. 2. An unexpected reaction to a drug resulting in effects that may be contrary to the anticipated results; for example, a barbiturate may have a stimulating rather than a sedative effect for some people.

idiot 1. Legal term dating to the 1300s for a person congenitally deficient in reasoning; also referred to as a "sot" or "natural idiot" in contrast with a lunatic. 2. In psychology, an obsolete term for an older person with a mental age of less than three years and an intelligence quotient (IQ) of less than 20. "Idiot" has been replaced by "profoundly retarded." See IDIOCY, IMBECILE, MENTAL RETARDATION, MONGOLIAN IDIOT, PROFOUND MENTAL RETARDATION.

idiothetic psychology idiographic psychology

idiotic 1. Ridiculous. 2. See IDIOCY, PROFOUNDLY RETARDED.

idiotism (P. Pinel) One of Philippe Pinel's four categories of insanity, the others being mania, melancholia, dementia.

idiot-prodigy *idiot savant*

idiotropic (turned toward the self—Greek) Egocentric, introspective, introverted.

idiot savant (learned idiot—French) A person with mental deficiency who possesses a remarkable, highly developed ability or talent in a single area such as rapid calculation, skill in music, or feats of memory. Such cases are rare and usually occur in persons with only mild or moderate deficiency. Also known as idiot-prodigy. See CALENDAR CALCULATION.

idiovariation   A phenomenon of genetic mutation in which genotypical structures are undergoing continual mutation and new groups of species are constantly being formed. See MUTATION.

idioverse   A universe of experiential events representing a given individual at a particular time. According to Saul Rosenzweig, three milieus, the organic, the cultural, and the idiodynamic, blend through a matrix that produces experiential uniqueness.

id psychology   Part of psychoanalytic theory that focuses on unorganized, instinctual impulses that seek immediate pleasurable gratification of primitive needs. The id is thought to dominate the life of the infant and possibly the schizophrenic. It is frequently described as blind and irrational until it is counteracted by the other two major components of the personality, the ego and the superego. See EGO PSYCHOLOGY, EXPERIENTIAL PSYCHOTHERAPY.

id resistance   A type of resistance in psychoanalysis that takes the form of a repetition compulsion; that is, the same material continues to recur regardless of the number or validity of interpretations offered by the analyst. See ANALYTIC STALEMATE.

id sadism   The primitive instinctual destructive urges of the early years of infancy associated with the desire for omnipotent gratification and security; usually provoked by frustration, a psychoanalytic concept. See INFANTILE SADISM.

id wish   Instinctual desires that psychoanalytic theory claims arise from the repressed, unconscious, infantile, and primitive reaches of the mind. Such urges generally are erotic or aggressive.

IE   1. Individual Education. 2. Introversion-extraversion. 3. Internal–External, the directionality of a score on a measure of locus of control; a personality construct of Julian Rotter. See INTERNAL-EXTERNAL SCALE.

IEM   See INBORN ERROR OF METABOLISM.

IEP   Individualized Education Program, required by United States federal law (Individuals with Disabilities Education Act or IDEA).

I/E ratio   See INSPIRATION-EXPIRATION RATIO.

I-E Scale   See INTERNAL-EXTERNAL LOCUS OF CONTROL SCALE.

IFD   in flagrant delict

ignoratio elenchi   (irrelevant conclusion—Latin) A fallacy of logic when the premises of an argument purported to establish a conclusion, in reality establish a different conclusion.

I-It   (M. Buber) A relationship in which people treat themselves or other people as objects. The philosopher Martin Buber, who originated the term, maintained this type of relationship stands in the way of human warmth, mutuality, trust, and group cohesiveness. See I-THOU.

I-knew-it-all-along phenomenon   Claiming to have foreseen how an event or situation turned out, after learning the outcome. Also known as hindsight bias.

ikonic   iconic

ikota   A culture-specific syndrome that affects some married women among the Samoyeds of Siberia, a neurosis similar to *latah*.

illegitimacy   A term usually applied when a child is born out of wedlock or the mother is not recognized as such with respect to laws governing inheritances. A denigrating term, unfair to children, no longer so commonly used, though it still has legal implications.

illiata   Things inferred but not able to be proven, such as existence of a human soul, another person's thoughts.

illicit   Not permitted. Contrary to law or to logic, particularly pertaining to drugs (such as heroin) not considered to have any legitimate use.

Illinois Test of Psycholinguistic Abilities (ITPA) (S. Kirk et al.) An examination designed to measure linguistic abilities considered important in communications and learning disorders, such as the ability to understand spoken words.

illiteracy   Inability to read or write. Provides no explanation of the fact, a person may be illiterate for many reasons, lack of opportunity to learn, functional inability, etc.

illness   Disease. See the following types of illness: CATASTROPHIC, CHRONIC, CYCLIC, EMOTIONAL, IATROGENIC, MANIC-DEPRESSIVE, MENTAL DISORDER/, PSYCHOSOMATIC, REFRACTORY MENTAL, UNITARY.

illness as self-punishment   A form of superego resistance in which guilt feelings and masochistic behavior produce symptoms that are a barrier to their own resolution through psychoanalysis.

illogical error   See LOGICAL ERROR.

illogicality   A tendency to draw unwarranted or faulty inferences. It is characteristic of delusional thinking and speech.

illuminance (E)   The intensity of light energy falling on a surface. Formerly called illumination. Three common measures are foot-candles, meter-candles and lamberts.

illuminant color   A color perceived as belonging to a self-luminous object, a glowing color (not reflected).

illumination   1. The aha experience when there is a flash of insight into the solution of a problem or the understanding of the meaning of an event. See AHA EXPERIENCE. 2. A former term for illuminance.

illumination conditions   The type of illumination, including such factors as intensity and absence of glare, most suitable for performance of different tasks, and for the comfort of the worker. A loosely-defined phrase used generally to refer to the kind and amount of illumination provided in a particular environment.

illumination standards   The amount of illumination recommended for effective performance of certain tasks, as specified by the Illuminating Engineering Society. The illumination standards, when expressed in footcandles, range from ten for a hotel lobby to 2,500 for a surgical-operating table.

illumination unit   The amount of light produced by a single footcandle. See CANDELA, FOOTCANDLE.

illuminism   A hallucinatory state in which a patient carries on conversations with imaginary, usually supernatural, beings.

illusion 1. Seeing one thing but interpreting it as something else (for example, in the dark, a coat is mistaken for a dog). 2. A misinterpretation of sensory stimuli (for example, the impression that railroad tracks come together in the distance). 3. A positive idea or belief, often shared by others or other groups, which is false. Types of illusion include: ARISTOTLE'S, ASSIMILATIVE, ASSOCIATIVE, AUBERT'S, AUDIO-GRAVIC, AUDIOGYRAL, AUTOKINETIC, BOURDON, CHARPENTIER'S, CHESS-BOARD, CONTRAST, CORRIDOR, DOUBLE-INTERPRETATION, FILLED-SPACE, GATTI, HAPTIC, HAUNTED SWING, HERING, HIGH-HAT, LIPPS, MACH-DVORAK STEREO-, MEMORY, MOON, MOVEMENT, NEGATIVE DOUBLES, OCULO-GRAVIC, OCULOGYRAL, OPTICAL, ORBISON, PERCEPTUAL, POGGENDORF, PONZO, PROOFREADER'S, RAILROAD, RAILWAY, REBOUND, REID'S MOVEMENT, SIZE-WEIGHT, SPILLMAN'S, STAIRCASE, STROBOSCOPIC, TACTILE, TEMPERATURE, TEMPORAL-LOBE, UZNADZE, VERTICAL-HORIZONTAL, WATERFALL, WINDMILL, WUNDT'S, ZÖLLNER'S. For illustrations, see DELBOEUF'S ILLUSION, GEOMETRIC ILLUSION, HORIZONTAL-VERTICAL, KANISZA FIGURE, LINEAR-PERSPECTIVE, MÜLLER-LYER ILLUSION, OPPEL-KÜNDT, SIZE-DISTANCE. See also APPARENT MOVEMENT.

illusionary correlation 1. A perceived or assumed association between two unrelated variables, such as being hard-working and being wealthy, often generating stereotypes. 2. Overestimation of the strength of the relationship between unrelated characteristics, especially as possessed by the members of a given group.

illusion des sosies French phrase for a delusion characterized by seeing others who look exactly like the person having the delusion. Also known as the illusion of doubles. See CAPGRAS SYNDROME, FREGOLI'S PHENOMENON, FRENOLI DELUSION.

illusion of control A mistaken belief of having more control over events than in actuality.

illusion of cyclorama An effect produced on an observer in a room or other confined place in which a foreground of solid objects on all sides melts into a painted background, so that the observer seems to be in the midst of a great open area.

illusion of doubles A delusion that other people are not themselves, but are really someone else. See CAPGRAS SYNDROME, FREGOLI'S PHENOMENON.

illusion of equilibrium A false perception of bodily position or orientation produced through continuous rotation in any one direction with the head held in various positions, leading to such phenomena as past-pointing and nystagmus, which are the reflex responses arising from the semicircular canals.

illusion of movement While at rest, a sudden feeling of being in motion or of perceiving a stationary object as moving. See APPARENT MOTION.

illusion of orientation The misidentification of a stimulus because of a clouding of consciousness, as during a febrile or toxic delirium. Hospitalized patients may be confused about where they are and about the identity of people seen in the hospital.

illusory contours An illusion of the perception of edges that do not exist. See KANIZSA FIGURE for an illustration.

illusory correlation The perception of a relationship where none exists; or the perception of a stronger relationship than actually exists. Two variables may be correlated by pure chance or because they are both related to a third variable.

illusory motion/movement The perception of motion in a motionless stimulus. Compare APPARENT MOVEMENT.

illustrator A nonverbal body gesture clearly associated with a spoken word or phrase, for example, pointing to a light switch while saying, "It's in front of your nose." Companions of words in contrast to emblems, which are substitutes for words. See EMBLEM.

image A likeness or copy of an earlier sensory or perceptual experience recalled without external stimulation. Kinds of images include: AFTER-, ARCHETYPAL, BODY CONCEPT, CONCRETE, DOUBLE, EIDETIC, GENERAL, GHOST, HALLUCINATORY, HESS, HYPNAGOGIC, IDEALIZED, MEMORY, PARENT, PERCEPT, PERSONAL, PRIMORDIAL, PRODUCT, PURKINJE-SANSON, RECURRENT, RETINAL, SCHEMATIC, SELF-, SOCIAL, SOUL, STABILIZED RETINAL, TIED.

image agglutinations (E. Kretschmer) Dream images formed from conglomerations of discrete images influenced by affects and representing day residues. Image agglutinations may be in the form of several objects or faces seen as one. See CONDENSATION.

image envy An unpleasant feeling of jealousy experienced when appraising another's potential or actual image as more desirable than the person's own.

image inversion See INVERSION.

imageless thought (O. Külpe, R. S. Woodworth) Cognition that occurs without the aid of images or sensory content. The Würzburg School upheld the existence of imageless thought on the basis of experimental studies of the "directedness" of thought, such as in naming a piece of fruit without picturing it. E. B. Titchener and others in the structural school opposed this view.

imagery 1. Mental images considered collectively. 2. The particular type of imagery characteristic of an individual person, such as visual, auditory, or kinesthetic imagery.

imagery code The encoding of an object, idea, or impression in terms of its visual appearance. If the item "computer" is stored in memory via a mental picture of a computer, an imagery code is said to have been employed in the memory-storage process. See SEMANTIC CODE.

imagery reactor A person who responds to the environment predominantly in terms of images, usually auditory or visual.

imagery therapy (J. E. Shorr) The use of mental images as a therapeutic technique; for example, to induce relaxation, a client may be asked to imagine lying on a beach and to visualize associated imagery, such as sun, sand, ocean, gentle breezes. See GUIDED AFFECTIVE IMAGERY, PSYCHO-IMAGINATION THERAPY.

imagery types Based on a questionnaire, Francis Galton concluded that people fell into one of these six types of perception of mental images: AUDITORY, GUSTATORY, MOTOR, OLFACTORY, TACTUAL, VISUAL.

imaginal flooding   A type of semi-hypnotic trance in which a person is treated for some obsessive, hypochondrial or phobic condition by imagining, via vivid speech of the therapist, matters of crucial importance to the specific disorder (for example, someone with a snake phobia imagines that a snake is coming closer and that it begins to ascend the legs while the person is unable to move).

imaginary audience   (D. Elkind) Refers to the strong belief among early adolescents that everyone is thinking about them and observing their behavior. See DAY DREAMING, FANTASY, PARANOIA.

imaginary chromaticity   Relating to the hue of a color that does not exist naturally in the spectrum.

imaginary companion   A fictitious person, animal, or object created by a child. The imaginary companion is given a name, and the child talks to it, shares feelings, and plays with it. May use it as a scapegoat for the child's misdeeds ("Topo did it, he is bad. . .Topo made me do it"). Also known as invisible playmate. See HELPFUL FIGURE, SOCIAL OBJECT.

imagination   The creation of ideas and images in the absence of direct sensory data, frequently combining fragments of previous sensory experiences into new syntheses. Types of imagination include: ACTIVE, CREATIVE, REPRODUCTIVE.

imaging   1. The use of suggested mental images to control bodily processes, including the easing of pain. 2. In radioisotopic encephalography, the process of scanning the brain after injection of a radioisotope and recording the patterns in graphic form. The imaging may be either static or dynamic. See NUCLEAR IMAGING.

imago   (image—Latin) 1. In Carl Jung's analytic psychology, the idealized image of a key person in the patient's early life, especially the mother (mother-imago). See ARCHETYPE. 2. (E. Jones) In psychoanalytic theory, the image of such a person is preserved indefinitely in the unconscious and often identified with persons other than the original one.

Imago Relations in Therapy   (H. Hendrix) A form of relationship therapy based on the idea that marriage selection is determined in large part by individual unconscious impulse to heal the wounds of childhood with a partner who, psychologically, is a composite of early caretakers. The goal is mutual conscious intentionality in communication and behavior. Uses diverse psychoeducational processes, especially that of dialogue.

imbecile   Obsolete term for a person of low intelligence. See IMBECILITY, MENTAL RETARDATE.

imbecility   (J. Esquirol) Obsolete term for a low-to-moderate level of mental deficiency characterized by an intelligence quotient (IQ) between 20 and 50 and a social and intellectual age of a three-to-seven-year-old child. "Imbecility" has been replaced by "severely retarded" (IQ 20–35) and "moderately retarded." See MENTAL RETARDATION, MODERATE MENTAL RETARDATION, SEVERE MENTAL RETARDATION.

imipramine (hydrochloride)   (R. Kühn) The generic name for Tofranil, the first antidepressant medication, released in 1957. Also known under the trade name Elavil.

imitation   1. Copying the behavior of another. It is a basic form of learning that accounts for many human skills, gestures, interests, attitudes, role behaviors, social customs, and verbal expressions. Though ordinarily normal, imitation can take pathological forms, as in echolalia and echopraxia. 2. An important early life process for most animals that learn how to survive by imitating their parents. See MIMETISM. 3. A tendency of people to pattern their behavior after the actions of others. Some theorists, such as Albert Bandura, adopt a broader conception of the process as modeling rather than the narrow conception of imitation as specific behavioral mimicry. See ABSTRACT MODELING, MODELING.

imitation of models   A tendency of people to imitate the behavior and thinking of those people whom they admire. This phenomenon is usually strong in young people who are searching for a meaningful identity.

imitative speech   The sounds and words that are normally acquired by children between 12 and 18 months of age.

immanent justice   (J. Piaget) A young child's belief that rules are fixed and immutable and that punishment automatically follows misdeeds regardless of extenuating circumstances. See DISTRIBUTIVE JUSTICE, MORAL REALISM.

immanent objectivity   A major tenet of Franz Brentano's act psychology, to the effect that the object of any psychical process (for example, judging, perceiving, desiring) is immanent in, or implied by, that process, function, or act.

immaterialism   A doctrine positing that the existence of matter cannot be confidently affirmed since all perceptual experiences are items of consciousness. See MATERIALISM, SPIRITUALISM.

immature personality   A personality-trait disturbance characterized by an inability to tolerate frustration or stress, lack of emotional control, and, when the person is opposed or under pressure, reversion to infantile and childish behavior, such as sulking, pouting, or temper outbursts. Also known as infantile personality.

immediacy   In social psychology, a spontaneous, attentive response to social interaction initiated or continued by another.

immediacy behavior   Any action, movement, or physical stance that indicates intimacy or a close relationship between two people, such as eye contact or touching.

immediate experience   Raw subjective impressions, without analysis into preconceived "elements." See PHENOMENOLOGY.

immediate gratification   Focus on getting what a person wants at present, not waiting for gratification regardless of consequences; for example, paying high interest annually by purchasing merchandise on credit rather than waiting until enough money has been saved.

immediate memory   A type or stage of the memory process in which a person recalls information recently acquired, such as a street address or telephone number, the information being forgotten after its use. Immediate memory is frequently tested in assessing intelligence or cerebral impairment. See DIGIT-SPAN TEST, SHORT-TERM MEMORY.

immediate recall test   A memory evaluation examination that asks a participant to state material just previously presented; for example, the examiner says "nine-five-seven-three-nine-six" and asks the participant to repeat these numbers. Such items are found in both the Stanford-Binet Scale and the Wechsler-Bellevue Intelligence Tests. Also known as recall method/test.

immediate reinforcer   (B. F. Skinner) A reinforcement that directly follows a desired behavior.

Immediate Test   (R. J. Corsini) A vocabulary examination consisting of eleven sets of six nouns each based on the Binet-type format, with mental ages from 10 to 20. The test is aimed at providing a three-minute estimate of mental age (intelligence quotient for adults). See BASAL MENTAL AGE, TERMINAL MENTAL AGE.

immediate therapy   A "single-shot" psychotherapy procedure intended to involve both the mind and the body; it stresses strong emotions and is usually performed in a situation that will last a fairly long time. See BEHIND-THE-BACK THERAPY, PRIMAL THERAPY, PSYCHODRAMA.

immobility   Showing no signs of motion, as in death-feigning or being "rooted to the spot" by a sudden fright. Called "playing possum" because opossums exhibit such behavior. See DEATH FEIGNING, TONIC IMMOBILITY.

immobilization paralysis   A functional, sometimes hysterical type of paralysis, such as an inability to move a limb that had been splinted because of injury. The limb is functionally mobile but the patient fails to recognize that it is now capable of motion.

immoral imperative   An impulsive rebellion against moral principles, or a compulsion to act against the rules of society, often seen in persons with compulsive neuroses.

immunohistochemistry   A chemical method of cell research. For instance, to study acetylcholine receptors in the rat brain, a purified protein or peptide is injected into a mouse, whose immune system forms antibodies to it. The antibodies in the blood are dyed and placed on a slice of rat brain, where they gradually attach to acetylcholine receptors.

immunology   A branch of medicine that specializes in the study of immunity and immune reactions; for example, allergies and hypersensitivities.

impact analysis   An analytic procedure used to assess the effectiveness of an evaluation program on participant outcomes; a quantitative approach to evaluating the success or failure of a program. See PROGRAM-IMPACT EVALUATION.

impaired professionals   People no longer able to function in their specialty occupations due to physical and psychological disorders.

impairment index   The product of a system of measuring impairment of mental functions and relating the results to some standard of normality. See HALSTEAD-REITAN IMPAIRMENT INDEX.

impasse-priority theory   (N. Kefir) A personality theory based on four "impasses" (or efforts to avoid certain conditions): controller (to avoid ridicule); pleaser (to avoid insignificance); morally superior (to avoid rejection); and avoider (to escape stress).

imperative   In psychoanalytic theory, a demand of the superego that represents the commanding voice of parental or social rule and operates on an unconscious level to direct the behavior of the person. Types of imperative include: CATEGORICAL, ETHICAL, IMMORAL.

imperative attitude   A subjective feeling of being about to perform an undesirable action against the person's wishes (for example, a strong craving to smoke a cigarette although the person does not want to smoke). See ENDOCRATIC POWER.

imperceptible difference   A difference between two stimuli that is too small (in respect to intensity, extent, or duration) to be detected. See JUST-NOTICEABLE DIFFERENCE (JND).

impersonal projection   A process of attributing unobjectionable or neutral qualities found in the self to another person, as opposed to the projection of objectionable impulses or ideas.

impersonal relationship   A distant nonemotional contact with another person. See CONTACT BEHAVIOR.

impersonation   Deliberate assumption of another person's identity, usually as a means of gaining status or other advantage. See IMPOSTOR SYNDROME.

impetus   In psychoanalytic theory, the force or energy behind an instinct or drive.

impingements   (A. Ames) Energies that reach sense organs.

implantation   Attachment of a fertilized ovum (blastocyst) to the endometrium, occurring 6 to 7 days after fertilization of the ovum.

implanted memories   A concept that one person can convince another person that an event happened in the past that actually did not. There have been allegations that some psychotherapists have in effect done this by pointed questioning of their clients. See RECOVERED MEMORIES.

implementation stage   In group dynamics, the final stage of decision-making, during which the group's decision is carried out and (usually) its effectiveness is appraised.

implications   An understanding of the reason(s) for the logical consequences of an event or proposition. See INSIGHT.

implicit behavior   1. Any activity that is neither observable nor measurable. 2. Behavior that cannot be observed directly without the aid of instruments. See BETA-ARC.

implicit causality in verbs   (R. Brown & D. Fish) Verbs relating two persons either imply that primary causality is either in the "Agent" (for example, astonish, please) or in the "Patient" (for example, admire, detest). Thus "Sue admires Peg because of the kind of person she is." Who is "she"? Peg. But "Sue astonishes Peg because of the kind of person she is." In this case who is "she"? Sue.

implicit cognition   How unidentified past experiences affect cognitions. See PHENOMENOLOGY.

implicit learning   (A. S. Reber) Knowledge or skills acquired unintentionally and unconsciously and that usually remain unknown or unexamined by the person, such as the processes of socialization or language acquisition. See LEARNING.

implicit memory   Memory that cannot be intentionally retrieved but that nevertheless persists. Hermann Ebbinghaus demonstrated this by showing that people could learn long-forgotten materials such as poems much more quickly than new poems of equal length and difficulty. See UNCONSCIOUS.

implicit movement   A faint muscular contraction that can be detected only by sensitive recording or measuring instruments. Also known as covert movement.

implicit personality theories   1. Assumptions about people based on superficial characteristics, such as age, size, gender, ethnicity. 2. A point of view that if a person has a particular behavioral characteristic, then this same person has other related characteristics, for example, "All smokers are self-centered."

implicit personality theory   The perceiver's personal assumptions about the naturally occurring relationships among various traits.

implicit pole   (G. A. Kelly) In making some kind of evaluation of the self or other, there is a standard against which the person makes the evaluation. Thus to consider a person "good," the evaluator has compared this personally developed construct of "good vs evil" or "good vs weak" to the person.

implicit reaction   1. A response in people that may have been predictable but usually is not verifiable (for example, a psychological reaction involving anxiety, happiness, fear, hate) 2. A covert reaction such as an increase in pulse rate. Used as a measure in lie-detection, the premise of which is that a liar may not show any overt signs, such as blushing or stammering, but will show various implicit reactions, such as palmar sweating or changes in breathing rhythms. See IMPLICIT RESPONSE.

implicit response   1. A response assumed to occur although it cannot be observed directly. 2. A minute muscle movement detectable only by special recording or measuring instruments. See IMPLICIT REACTION.

implicit speech response   See SUBVOCALIZATION.

implicit trial and error   In the solution of problems, mental operations engaged in prior to action.

implied answer question   A query worded so as to imply the correct or expected answer.

implosion   1. A bursting inward such as may happen to an electric light bulb or television screen. 2. In phonetics, the process of building air pressure in the air tract just before its explosive release in the production of speech sounds. See PLOSIVE.

implosion therapy   (T. Stampfl) A behavior-therapy technique in which the client is repeatedly encouraged to imagine an anxiety-arousing situation, and to experience anxiety as intensely as possible while doing so. Since there is no actual danger in the situation, the anxiety response is not reinforced and therefore is gradually extinguished. Also known as implosive therapy. See FLOODING, IN VIVO DESENSITIZATION.

impossible figure   A contrived two-dimensional figure designed to confuse correct perception by presenting clearly incompatible information to the eyes. See DEVIL'S PITCHFORK, PENROSE TRIANGLE for examples.

impossible objects   A pictorial representation of an object that cannot exist in reality. See THREE-PRONGED CLEVIS.

impostor syndrome   (P. Greenacre) A personality pattern characterized by pathological lying that takes the form of fabricating an identity or a series of identities (doctor, lawyer, war hero) and playing a role designed to bring recognition and status. The dynamics of this pattern are obscure. See IMPERSONATION, MÜNCHAUSEN SYNDROME.

impotence   The inability of a man to achieve or maintain a penile erection. If it occurs, regardless of cause (age, medications, surgery), it is called erectile dysfunction. Those who can achieve erection only about 25% of the time are considered to have secondary impotence, which is usually psychogenic and may take the form of premature ejaculation, limited interest in sex, orgasm without experiencing pleasure, coitus without ejaculation, and sexual ability only with prostitutes. Also known as impotency. See ANAL IMPOTENCE, COITUS SINE EJACULATIONE, ERECTION, INHIBITED SEXUAL EXCITEMENT, ORGASTIC IMPOTENCE, PRIMARY ERECTILE DYSFUNCTION, PSYCHIC IMPOTENCE, SECONDARY ERECTILE DYSFUNCTION.

impoverished autism   See AUTISM PAUVRE.

impoverished environment   Any situation, including school, family, or social environment that lacks advantages or its advantages are distinctly less than the norm. See ENVIRONMENTAL ENRICHMENT, SENSORY DEPRIVATION.

impoverishment   See DELUSION OF IMPOVERISHMENT, INTELLECTUAL IMPOVERISHMENT, POVERTY OF IDEAS.

impregnation   The process of initiating pregnancy by the penetration of the ovum by a spermatozoon and the fusion of the nuclei of the male and female gametes. Also refers to the implantation of a fertilized ovum to the uterine wall. Also known as fertilization, fecundation, ingravidation.

impression   A vague or unanalyzed cognition, judgment or reaction. See ABSOLUTE IMPRESSION, DUAL IMPRESSION, FIRST IMPRESSIONS.

impressional tendency   (T. Brown) A tendency of certain ideas or conscious contents to recur in mind because of the strength or vividness of their original impression. See ASSOCIATIVE TENDENCY.

impression formation   1. The process of generating an attitude, mostly occurring by a combination of prior views plus indications from the subject of the impression. 2. Similar to the concepts of person perception, person cognition, and social perception.

impressionism factor   The designation for an art style characterized by blurred outlines and an emphasis on surface qualities and textures. The style was popular with impressionist painters of the 19th century.

impression management   1. Behavior designed to elicit particular responses or reactions from another, such as stratagems to portray the self in a positive manner. See IDIOPANIMA. 2. A display of social behaviors that establish, maintain, or refine the impression that others (often termed the "target") have about the person. Common strategies include defensive tactics (such as excuses, apologies, self-handicapping), self-presentation (an attempt to appear more appealing), and other-enhancement (flattery of, favorable evaluation of, or agreement with, the target). Also known as self-presentation.

impression method   A procedure in which observers make an introspective report about a stimulus pattern in terms of their feelings; for example, pleasant or unpleasant.

impression of universality   A belief that numerous other persons are responding in a similar manner as the self in a given situation, thereby justifying the acceptance of an idea or facilitating own personal behavior or course of action. See MOB PSYCHOLOGY.

impressive aphasia   A loss or impairment of the ability to understand words, signs, or gestures. See RECEPTIVE APHASIA, SENSORY APHASIA.

imprinting   A term coined by Konrad Lorenz for a form of highly effective, long-lasting learning that typically occurs during a short critical period early in an organism's development. A well known case is that of ducklings that shortly after hatching will learn to follow movement, whether it be a toy, their mother, a human, or other animal. A type of attachment that takes many forms and can influence adult sexual behavior. This learning process was first described by Sir Thomas More. See CRITICAL PERIOD, RESTRICTED LEARNING.

imprinting   The young birds follow the person because they are genetically predisposed follow the first moving organism (usually the mother) during a critical period following their hatching.

improbable-achievement technique   A procedure used to determine if a person has cheated on a test. The person is given opportunity to cheat and if a level of excellence is attained that is highly improbable for that person by honest means, the conclusion is that cheating has occurred.

Improshare   See GAINSHARING.

improvement rate   The ratio of the number of patients discharged as improved from an institution within a given period of time in relation to the total number in the original group. The improvement rate is usually expressed as a percentage.

improvisation   In psychodrama, the spontaneous acting out of problems and situations without prior preparation.

impuberism   A state of not having reached puberty because of age or delayed development.

impuberty   The persistence of childhood characteristics into adolescence or adulthood.

impulse   1. A strong, sometimes irresistible, urge; a sudden inclination to act without deliberation. Kinds of impulse include: COMPONENT, HOMOSEXUAL, IRRESISTIBLE, OBSESSIVE, PRIMORDIAL, THOUGHT, UNCONSCIOUS, WANDERING. 2. The wave of electrical energy that passes along a nerve fiber when it discharges. Kinds of impulse include: ANTIDROMIC, CENTRIPETAL, NERVE.

impulse control   Ability to resist an impulse, desire, or temptation, as in restraining an urge to gamble heavily, drink to excess, or give vent to anger.

impulse-control disorder   A chronic mental disturbance characterized by a tendency to gratify immediate desires or express immediate impulses to act, without regard to consequences. Characteristically, people displaying the disorder interrupt their typical lifestyles to "act out," obeying irresistible impulses, as in choking a sister or brother or marrying an almost unknown person. See ATYPICAL IMPULSE-CONTROL DISORDER, EPISODIC-BEHAVIOR DISORDER, INTERMITTENT EXPLOSIVE DISORDER, ISOLATED EXPLOSIVE DISORDER, KLEPTOMANIA, PATHOLOGICAL GAMBLING, PYROMANIA, SUBSTANCE-USE DISORDERS.

impulse fear   A fear that arises in the absence of a real threat, that according to psychodynamic theory is usually due to a factor such as a fear of sudden death in the absence of signs or symptoms of disease.

impulsion   1. A sudden, forced, thrusting movement of the body or of a limb. 2. An abnormal or compelling urge to perform a certain activity. Occurs primarily in young children and in obsessive-compulsive or antisocial adults, who, according to psychodynamic theory, have not developed adequate defenses against their impulses. See IMPULSIVE BEHAVIOR.

impulsive behavior   Activity abruptly engaged in without forethought, reflection, or consideration of consequences. Also known as impulsiveness, impulsivity. See IMPULSION.

impulsive character   A personality pattern marked by a tendency to act hastily and without reflection.

impulsive raptus   Rare phrase for a sudden attack of agitation that may occur in cases of catatonic schizophrenia.

impunitive aggression   (S. Rosenzweig) Aggression turned off or avoided in overt expression because the person views a frustrating situation as unavoidable. See ROSENZWEIG PICTURE-FRUSTRATION STUDY.

impunitive response   A reaction to a frustrating experience in which a problem is minimized or denied to avoid placing blame on self or others. Also, a situation wherein a person modifies the goal to an obtainable goal, thus avoiding frustration. See ROSENZWEIG PICTURE-FRUSTRATION STUDY.

imu   A culture-specific syndrome resembling *latah*, observed among the Ainu women of Japan, and characterized by automatic movements, imitative behavior, and infantile reactions. See CULTURE-SPECIFIC SYNDROME.

in absentia   Refers to an action by, or affecting, a person who is not present (such as voting). In forensic psychology, relating to a legal proceeding against a person conducted in that person's absence. Courts prefer that persons be able to participate meaningfully and personally in their own case and not be tried in absentia, such as because of a mental disorder.

inaccessible   Unreceptive and unresponsive to external stimuli. A withdrawn state characteristic of autism, schizophrenia, and depression. A patient who does not react or respond to the therapist in a way that facilitates the development of rapport is considered inaccessible. See WITHDRAWAL REACTION.

inaccessible memory   A memory not available to consciousness at a particular time. It may suddenly come to mind at a later time.

inadequate family   A family unable to cope with ordinary problems of family living.

inadequate personality   A diagnosis of a personality disturbance characterized by failure to adapt to the social, emotional, occupational, and intellectual demands of life. Though lacking in effectiveness, stability, judgment, and foresight, such as individual tests in the normal intellectual range, but frequently becomes a vagrant, a substance abuser. See PERSONALITY DISORDERS.

inadequate stimulus   An ineffective stimulus, one not strong enough to achieve an expected or usual response. See INEFFECTIVE STIMULUS.

inappetence   Lack of appetite or desire.

inappropriate affect   An emotional response not in keeping with the situation, or incompatible with expressed thoughts or wishes, as in smiling upon hearing of the death of a friend. Inappropriate affect is a common symptom of schizophrenia. Also known as inappropriateness of affect.

inappropriate stimulus   A type of stimulus that is unusual for a given receptor but that elicits a response, such as an electric current producing visual sensations.

inattention   A state characterized by a lack of concentrated or focused attention, or in which attention drifts back and forth. See SELECTIVE INATTENTION, SENSORY INATTENTION.

in-basket test   A work-sample task used in management training and selection. The trainee is given an assortment of items (letters, memos, reports) that might be found in an in-basket, and must take action on them while under observation as if the trainee were actually on the job.

inborn error of metabolism (IEM)   (A. Garrod) Any biochemical disorder caused by a genetic defect, often a defect or deficiency in the structure or enzymatic function of a protein molecule or in the transport of a vital substance across a cell membrane. These errors may have severe adverse mental and behavioral effects, including mental retardation, seizures, and motor dysfunction. Examples include diabetes mellitus, gout, phenylketonuria, and Tay-Sachs disease. Also known as metabolic anomaly.

inbreeding   The mating of closely-related individuals (humans or animals), usually for preserving certain preferred traits or characteristics while preventing the acquisition of unwanted traits of other genetic stock in the offspring. Inbreeding increases the risk of perpetuating certain genetic defects in the family, as in consanguineous marriages.

incantation   A ritualistic verbal procedure, usually a kind of chant, used by shamans and priests to achieve a particular goal, which may include curing an illness, exorcising a hurtful spirit, or injuring an enemy.

incendiarism   Setting fires compulsively or for a criminal purpose. See PYROLAGNIA, PYROMANIA.

incentive   The reward that an organism expects to obtain for engaging in certain behaviors. The incentive may be immediate, such as water when thirsty, or long range, such as the probability of getting a college degree.

incentive motivation (*K*)   (C. L. Hull) The use of promises of rewards or threats of punishment to get organisms to behave in a desired manner. See CONDITIONING, HULL'S THEORY.

incentive stimuli   Desired objects or incidents that act as incentives.

incentive systems   In industry, a set of rewards designed to motivate better job performance. Incentives vary in motivating power from group to group and include such items as bonuses, vacation packages, and gifts. Such systems sometimes have an unintended effect: they may make other workers feel discouraged and tend to make winners unpopular. See BEHAVIORISM, EXTRINSIC REWARD, INTRINSIC REWARD.

incentive theory   A point of view that the motivation to act depends on the interaction between stimulus objects and an organism's state. Positive and negative incentives arouse the organism and instigate or prevent specific behavior. See DRIVE-REDUCTION THEORY.

incentive value   The subjective or objective importance of a stimulus that may differ considerably across individuals; for example, a plastic object that has no value to one person may be strongly desired by another person who has never seen anything like it. Value varies with deprivation and quantity or quality of incentive stimulus.

inception   (H. S. Sullivan) The first phase of an interview in which patients describe the problems that brought them to the session.

incest   Sexual activity between persons of closer genetic relationships than permitted by law or custom. See FATHER-DAUGHTER INCEST, INCEST TABOO, MOTHER-SON INCEST.

incest barrier   In psychoanalytic theory, an ego defense erected during the latency period against incestuous impulses and fantasies. The barrier is due to the introjection of social laws and customs. These internal and external prohibitions are considered to help free the libido to make an external object choice.

incest fantasy   In psychoanalytic theory, a young child's wish to have sexual relations with the parent of the opposite sex, as expressed in fantasies and dreams. Incest fantasies directed toward the mother are considered to be particularly prominent among boys during the act of masturbation and to feed into castration fears; incest fantasies toward the father may be a source of severe conflict in girls.

incest taboo   Social prohibition against sexual intercourse between persons of closer relationship than the culture allows. In some societies, sexual intercourse between cousins or between uncles and nieces, aunts and nephews, is prohibited; in others it is permitted. See INCEST.

incestuous desire   Wanting to engage in sexual activity with a relative.

incestuous ties   (E. Fromm) Emotions that keep a person psychologically dependent on the parent (especially the mother), family, or a symbolic substitute to the extent that healthy involvement with others and with society is inhibited or precluded. According to Fromm, incestuous ties represent the negative resolution of the search for rootedness. See BROTHERLINESS, ROOTEDNESS NEED.

incidence rate   The number of new cases of a given condition (usually a disease) in a particular population in a given period of time. The rate is often expressed as the number per 100,000 population per year.

incidental cues   Refers to stimuli that occur occasionally in connection with a given or intended stimulus that influence the character of the response to the given stimulus.

incidental learning   Nonintentional or unpremeditated learning acquired as a result of some other, possibly unrelated, activity. Some theorists assume that unmotivated learning takes place; however, others maintain that no learning occurs in the absence of a motive. Also known as passive learning. See LATENT LEARNING.

incidental memory   A memory that occurs without conscious effort or intention, such as recalling a particular play in a football game while reading an unrelated book.

incidental reinforcement   **accidental reinforcement**

incidental stimulus   An unintended stimulus that may occur during an experiment or in another situation and that may result in a response; such stimuli, if not detected, can distort research results.

incident causation model (of accidents)   The identification of causal factors in serious accidents.

incident process   Focusing on a single incident as a training procedure; for example, a life-like dummy is identified as having heart failure and a trainee is asked to resuscitate it. See CRITICAL INCIDENT.

incidents of opportunity   Unplanned events, whether favorable or unfavorable, that can be taken advantage of for useful purposes. See SERENDIPITY.

incipient   1. Latent. 2. In an initial stage.

incipient movement   A bare beginning of a movement that is not carried out.

incipient psychosis   **latent psychosis**

incitogram   The neural organization of afferent impulses that leads to a response.

inclusive fitness   Ability or tendency of an individual to ensure the survival of its genes in future generations.

inclusiveness   (W. Köhler) A tendency to perceive the entire figure when a smaller figure is embedded in a larger figure. See GOTTSCHALDT FIGURES for an example of this perception.

incoherence   Lack of organization; especially, disjointed or incomprehensible speech.

incommensurable   Pertaining to two or more characteristics or variables that are not measured in the same units and thus cannot be compared in terms of the same scale or standard; for example, comparing apples to oranges.

incompatibility   1. An inability of people to be or remain together, especially in marriages. 2. Factors that cannot coexist. 3. The relation between two judgments that if one is correct, the other must be false.

incompatible response   A response or action that conflicts with another when they occur at the same time, such as trying to contract antagonistic muscles (flexor and extensor muscles) at the same time.

incompatible response method   1. A habit-breaking technique in which a different, more desirable response is substituted for a prior undesired one with which the latter cannot exist. 2. A response incapable of being elicited simultaneously with another response.

incompetence   Inability to perform a task adequately.

incompetency   In forensic psychology, the lack of the capacity to make sound judgments regarding transactions and to assume responsibility for own life.

incompetency plea   The plea, in a court of law, that defendants were not legally responsible for the action in question due to lack of capacity to comprehend the nature or consequences of the action (this condition may be because of mental disease, defect, or other reasons) and that the persons do not understand the nature and object of the proceedings pending against them and are unable to assist an attorney in the defense. See COMPETENCY TO STAND TRIAL.

incomplete-pictures test   A task of visual recognition and interpretation in which drawings in varying degrees of completion are presented, and the person being tested attempts to identify the missing part or object. See PICTURE-COMPLETION TEST.

Incomplete Sentences Blank (ISB)   A psychological instrument that elicits information about wishes, fears, or attitudes by asking participants to complete sentences, usually by adding one word or a short phrase, for example, "When I feel good, I like to_____."

incomplete-sentence test   See SENTENCE-COMPLETION TEST.

incomplete trial   A course of treatment, usually medical, that may not have been sufficient in dose or time to evoke an optimal effect. Many psychotropic medicines work gradually, beginning to effect improvement in symptoms only after several weeks of not seeming to have any effect, and the improvement may then continue gradually for several more weeks. See SUBTHERAPEUTIC DOSE.

incomprehensible   The property of a statement or position that is self-contradictory, confused, or that cannot be understood.

incongruence   1. (C. R. Rogers) A state in which a difference exists between the actual self and the demands of the organismic valuing process. 2. Lack of harmony that results when personal symbolized experiences or expectations do not realistically represent actual experiences.

incongruity   The quality of being inconsistent, incompatible, not harmonious, or otherwise in disagreement with an accepted mode or standard. Perception experiments on incongruity, for example, may use a deck of playing cards with mismatched colors and suits, such as black hearts and red spades. See PRESS TEST.

incongruity theory (of humor)   A point of view that the essence of humor is putting together apparently incompatible concepts in an unexpected manner, leading to a surprising but logical conclusion.

incontinence   1. An inability to restrain sexual impulses. 2. An inability to retain urine or feces. Often due to spinal-cord injury or brain damage in the motor region, as in severe cerebral palsy or grand mal epilepsy. See FUNCTIONAL ENURESIS.

incoordination   A lack of harmony or balance in the action of muscle groups.

incorporation   The assimilation of the attitudes or attributes of others as part of the self. In psychodynamic theory, incorporation is the earliest form of identification and introjection and the most primitive recognition of external reality.

incorporation dream   A dream that includes a sensation, often auditory, that the dreamer is actually experiencing while asleep (for example, dreaming of being in school and hearing the dismissal bell ring when the alarm clock sounded and was incorporated into the dream). Also known as reconstruction dream.

incorrigibility   An apparently inherent inability to conform to reasonable standards of social behavior. See DELINQUENCY.

increasing returns   A graphic representation of a learning situation in which early trials yield small improvements in performance, but the amount of improvement is greater as time goes on. See CURVES OF RETURNS.

incremental learning   The acquisition of knowledge or skill in a series of steps. Such learning tends to be irregular, each step requiring a different amount of time or practice, depending on the individual's ability to cope with each phase of an assignment.

incremental reflex   The increase of a reflexive action following a sudden intensification of the provoking stimulus.

incremental theory of development   (F. Dumont) A point of view that mental and physical development occurs seamlessly and constantly and that the establishment of developmental stages is an artificial although useful way of conceptualizing development. An analogy might be the difference between a watch with a sweep second hand and a watch with digital characters.

incremental validity   1. (L. Sechrest) The increase in accuracy of a prediction or in the measurement of a construct that can be expected from the addition of a measure (scale, instrument, test) to an already existing predictor or set of predictors. 2. The amount of additional validity that evaluation method B adds to method A and that evaluation method C adds to methods A and B; for example, a sanity evaluation might include (a) an interview, (b) an intelligence test, and (c) a projective test. The judgment of the examiner is affected by these three separate sources of information, and each may add an increment toward the final diagnosis. See MULTIPLE CORRELATION.

incubation   See INCUBATION PERIOD.

incubation of anxiety   The increased impairment of ongoing behavior that occurs following a period of time away from an anxiety-inducing setting. Reported both in animals and humans, the impact of anxiety is often greater after a rest period; hence the common advice to "get right back on the horse" after taking a spill from the saddle.

incubation of avoidance theory   A point of view that avoidance learning requires a period of consolidation or incubation before it becomes established in memory. Based on evidence of a delayed appearance of conditioning in experimental animals exposed to electroconvulsive shock.

incubation period   (G. Wallas) A major stage of creativity when, at a level unavailable to consciousness, the mind is working on a problem and that eventually results in a period of comprehension, which may lead to actual creative activity. The incubation period may operate for minutes, hours, days, or even years, and the answer or explanation may occur in a flash. See CREATIVITY, CREATIVE IMAGINATION, GESTALT.

incubus   (to lie upon—Latin) 1. Medieval term for a male demon or evil spirit who is believed to have sexual relations with sleeping women. See FAMILY INCUBUS, SUCCUBUS. 2. A nightmare.

inculcation   Teaching by repeated admonitions such as nagging.

incus   (Vesalius) A small bone in the middle ear (located between the malleus or hammer and the stapes or stirrup) that helps pass vibrations to the inner ear. Also known as anvil (bone).

indemnity neurosis   **compensation neurosis**

independence (statistical assumption)   1. For all tests of inferential statistics, parametric or nonparametric, the error effects are assumed to be unrelated; that is, the precision of the observations of one participant has no impact on the precision of any other participant's data. With proper experimental control, for example, Moe is not permitted to copy answers from Curly's paper, and with appropriate (that is, independently drawn) sampling of subjects, the assumption can usually be met. When this assumption is violated, the probability statements (α-levels) concerning type-I and type-II errors are spurious. 2. Some inferential statistics also require that each dependent variable is independent of every other dependent variable. When such is not the case (for example, a matched-pairs design or pretest-posttest control-group design), appropriate techniques must be selected; for example, the *t*-test for correlated (nonindependent) observations.

independent assortment principle   See MENDELIAN MODES OF INHERITANCE.

independent events   Two or more unrelated or noncontingent events. Many statistical tests assume that the observations being compared or added together are independent events. More formally, two events A and B are independent if the probability of A, p(A), is the same as the probability of A given B, p(A | B).

independent influence   The effect a message has on the attitudes or thoughts of those who receive it when the message is not attributed to any specific origin (for example, an individual or a group). The message in and of itself may lead to any effect.

independent invention   The unrelated creation of physical, social, or conceptual novelties (such as the wheel or the calculus) by two or more people or cultures. See CULTURAL PARALLELISM.

independent living   Ability to perform all or most of the normal daily functions required in maintaining a home and job, and mobility between home and job, as a self-sufficient person. Independent living is a primary objective of habilitation and rehabilitation, which can be achieved by many persons with disabilities with a variety of special devices and equipment designed to compensate for challenges.

independent-living aids   Any objects, mechanisms, or techniques that enable a person with a disability to function as a more typical individual. Also known as daily living aids.

independent phenomena   In parapsychological research, any phenomena that occur independently of the medium or of any other person; for example, levitation.

independent segregation principle   See MENDELIAN MODES OF INHERITANCE.

independent variable (IV or I.V.)   In an experiment, the variable systematically manipulated by the experimenter. Contrasts with the dependent variable (DV) in the experiment, which is measured to determine whether its value is systematically affected by the value of the independent variable.

indeterminism   A doctrine positing that humans have free will and are able to act independently of antecedent or current situations, as in making choices. See DETERMINISM, FREE WILL, SOFT DETERMINISM.

index   A number, such as a ratio, used as an indicator or standard. Types of index include: ARTICULATION, BEHAVIORAL, BODY-BUILD, BRUGSCH'S, CAREER MATURITY, CEPHALIC, CONSISTENCY, CORNELL SELECTIVE, CRANIAL, CRITERION, DEPRIVATION, DETERIORATION, ECONOMIC EFFICIENCY, FAMILY RELATIONSHIP, FLESCH, FOG, HALSTEAD IMPAIRMENT, HAMPSTEAD, IMPAIRMENT, JOB DESCRIPTION, LAMBDA, MORPHOLOGICAL, PONDERAL, PRECISION, REACTION, REFRACTIVE, SELECTION, SKELIC, SOCIABILITY, SOCIAL-ADEQUACY, TEST DISCRIMINATION, WIND-CHILL.

index adoptees   Refers to offspring of normal biological parents that are reared by adopting parents who manifest a disorder being studied, or offspring of parents with a certain disorder reared by normal adopting parents. See CONTROL ADOPTEES, CROSS FOSTERING.

index cases   Members of a population of related persons whose clinical behavior pattern meets predetermined criteria and who serve as a standard. Also known as proband cases.

index number (I)   A number used for comparison purposes; for example, the Consumer Price Index number for oranges is the price as a percentage of the average price for oranges in 1967 (1967 = 100).

Index of Adjustment and Values   A personality test based on the participant's reactions to trait words designed to measure self-concept, self-acceptance, concept of the ideal self, self-esteem, or personal adjustment.

index of autonomic stability   A measure of autonomic functioning based on composite measures of blood pressure, heart rate, respiration, and galvanic skin status. See LIE DETECTOR, KEELER POLYGRAPH, MARSTON DECEPTION TEST.

index of change   (W. Stern) The blurred perceptual experience that occurs when one distinct experience changes into another, which serves as the basis for the judgment that a change has occurred.

index of consistency   A formula that indicates the degree to which individuals give the same response within a given time period to identical stimuli.

index of co-relation   An older name for coefficient of correlation.

index of differentiation   A measure representing the discrepancy between a personal attitude (expressed in a projective questionnaire) and an overt attitude (as revealed in direct responses to questions).

index of discrimination   An index of the sensitivity of a test or test item to actual differences in subjects tested.

index offenses   Specific crimes considered by the Federal Bureau of Investigation (FBI) as serious, about which records are kept. These include aggravated assault, larceny, burglary, motor vehicle theft, arson, robbery, forcible rape, murder.

index of forecasting efficiency (E)   A measure of the amount of improvement over chance in prediction given by the correlation coefficient. It is equal to $E = 100(1-k)$, where E is the index of forecasting efficiency and k is the square root of $(1 - r^2)$, or the coefficient of alienation.

index of refraction   A number indicating the degree to which a light ray is bent in passing from one transparent medium to another. See REFRACTIVE INDEX.

index of reliability   An estimate of the degree to which two different administrations of the same test yield comparable scores on the test, or to which different parts of a test provide similar scores.

index of selection   A formula to determine the discriminatory (D) value of a test for selection purposes. See SELECTION INDEX.

index of validity   An estimate of the correlation between actual test scores and corresponding theoretical true scores.

index of variability   A measure of dispersion of data, such as the range, the average deviation, or the standard deviation.

index variable   A variable that is not a determinant or true causal factor but represents or symbolizes the complex process or processes under study.

indexical signs   Symbols or signs that have a semantic connection with what they signify, such as a sign showing a dog on a leash, indicating that dogs are permitted but that they must be leashed.

Indian Health Service   An agency of the United States Department of Health and Human Services that provides care for Native Americans and Alaskans. The Indian Health Service operates hospitals and health centers, some of which, such as in Navaho tribal areas, encourage the use of native faith healers for the psychological benefits that the ceremonies provide.

Indian science of health   See AYURVEDA.

indicant   1. Indicating. 2. A sign of the presence of another phenomenon, particularly a symptom indicating the proper line of treatment. 3. A sign of impending activity, as in clearing the throat prior to speaking.

indifference of indicator (R. B. Cattell) The finding that the same personality factors emerge despite differences of instrument factor measurement.

indifference point/zone The intermediate region between experiential opposites; for example, on the pleasure-pain dimension, a degree of stimulation that provokes an indifferent or neutral response.

indifferent stimulus A stimulus that has not yet elicited the reaction being studied.

indigenous nonprofessional In blue-collar therapy, a nonprofessional auxiliary used as a helper in the therapeutic process. See BLUE-COLLAR THERAPY.

indigenous worker An auxiliary worker in the field of mental health, drawn from the same background as low-income clients so as to help bridge the gap between these clients and the therapists (who are usually from the middle class). See BLUE-COLLAR THERAPY.

indirect agonist A drug that attaches to a receptor's binding site and facilitates the receptor's action. Compare inverse agonist.

indirect association A symptom of schizophrenic logic in which an association between ideas is not clearly expressed, so that an observer may fail to see the connection and the association therefore seems bizarre and incoherent.

indirect counterimitation Avoiding the general kind or class of behavior that a person has seen a model perform. Compare INDIRECT IMITATION.

indirect imitation Performing the general type or class of behavior, but not the same action, that a person has seen a model perform. See DEFERRED IMITATION, IMITATION OF MODELS, INDIRECT COUNTERIMITATION.

indirect measurement 1. Measurement of a variable different from, but related to, a variable a person wishes to measure; for example, measuring pulse rate to indicate anxiety. 2. A measurement that must be transformed or converted to a different scale to become meaningful; for example, transforming a measurement in inches to millimeters (or vice versa) or z-scores to percentiles.

indirect method of therapy 1. A form of therapy in which the therapist does not attempt to direct the patient's communication or evaluate the patient's remarks, although the therapist may refer back to the patient's remarks or restate them. See PERSON-CENTERED THERAPY. 2. A therapeutic procedure for which (for some reason or other) the client is unaware of its purpose; for example, a person meets with a therapist under the pretense of a friendly chat when really the person needs therapy but would never consent to it willingly. See TWENTY-FOUR HOUR THERAPY.

indirect scaling of psychophysical factors A type of scaling in which observers estimate numerically where particular sensations produced by particular stimuli belong on a subjective continuum. See METHOD OF BISECTION, METHOD OF CROSS-MODALITY MATCHING, METHOD OF EQUAL APPEARING INTERVALS, METHOD OF PRODUCTION.

indirect self-destructive behavior (ISDB) Injuring oneself or committing suicide covertly or indirectly, as by intentionally drinking many alcoholic beverages before driving an automobile. See SUICIDALITY.

indirect vision Vision induced by stimulation of any part of the retina outside the fovea centralis.

indissociation (J. Piaget) A Piagetian term for a process in an early child-development stage in which perceptions of physical-world phenomena are not clearly distinguished from each other or from the self.

individual accountability In group dynamics, assessing each member's contributions and disclosing the results to the group.

individual difference Deviations or variations along a variable or dimension that occur among members of any particular group; for example, scores on an arithmetic test of a class of fourth grade students, or scores on an intelligence test.

Individual Education (IE) (R. J. Corsini) A system of formal education based on the theories of Alfred Adler that stresses the achievement of the four R's of Responsibility, Respect, Resourcefulness, and Responsiveness (social interest).

individualism 1. (H. C. Triandis) An approach to life emphasizing the right to be oneself and to have personal aims, interests, and idiosyncrasies, as contrasted with conformity to group standards or conventional lifestyles. 2. (G. Hofstede) A cultural pattern according to which people set themselves at the center of the perceptual field, give priority to personal goals when they are competing with the goals of collectives, behave according to their attitudes rather than the norms of their collectives, and pay attention to the profit and loss extracted from interpersonal relationships. See COLLECTIVISM.

Individualist Feminism A kind of feminism that promotes philosophies of individual autonomy, independence, minimum government, and diversity. Also known as Libertarian Feminism.

individualistic motives Motivations that influence individuals to advance their own objectives through behavior in which they neither cooperate nor compete with others. See COMPETITIVE MOTIVE, COOPERATIVE MOTIVE.

individualistic reward structure A situation in which the success of one person has no bearing on the success of others; for example, an examination graded not on a curve but on an absolute scale so that all students could potentially receive an A or all an F. See COMPETITIVE REWARD STRUCTURE, COOPERATIVE REWARD STRUCTURE.

individuality Having become differentiated as a unique person.

individualization The process whereby an individual becomes distinguished from one or more others of the same species, sex, age, or other category, either by outward signs such as appearance or behavior or by covert variations of thinking, feeling, and wanting.

individualized consideration (B. Bass) In transformational leadership, paying special attention to each individual's needs for achievement and growth by serving as coach or mentor. Such leaders continuously create new learning opportunities along with a supportive climate. Individual differences in terms of needs and desires are recognized, addressed, and raised to higher levels through continuous development. Two-way exchanges in communications are encouraged, and "leadership by involvement" is practiced. Interactions with followers are personalized (for example, the leader remembers previous conversations, and sees the individual as a whole person rather than as just part of the organization). Individually considerate leaders listen actively and reflectively. They assume that what they have said is not always what others have heard. The leaders delegate tasks as a means of developing followers. See TRANSFORMATIONAL LEADERSHIP.

individualized-education program (IEP)   1. Individually tailored objectives and procedures to enable a child to achieve, usually based on an evaluation of a particular child's potential. 2. A federally mandated procedure to achieve the same goals as above.

individualized instruction   An instructional method that permits students to work separately at their own pace. Teachers assist students in identifying skills that need development or knowledge that needs to be acquired. Group projects are often incorporated in the program as well.

individualized reading   A method of teaching reading that uses a variety of books geared to the child's interests and level of skills.

individual man   Carl Jung's phrase for a person who identifies with deeper aspects of the self in contrast to the personal man. See PERSONA.

individual program   An instructional method in which students are responsible for developing and carrying out their own learning. An individual program may, for example, be designed for children who possess a high level of motivation and of cognitive development. See COMMAND STYLE, INDIVIDUAL TEST, INDIVIDUAL EDUCATION.

Individual Psychology   The personality theory of Alfred Adler. Its tenets include: (a) the organism moves from a perceived "minus" to a perceived "plus" situation; (b) each individual has a unique goal; (c) the final goal is unknown; (d) goals are the ultimate cause of behavior; (e) individuals operate in a consistent manner; (f) people are unified wholes; (g) objective conditions only provide possibilities, not certainties; (h) an apperceptive schema determines all motivational processes; (i) social conditions determine individuality; (j) all problems are social problems; (k) social interest is a human potential to be developed; and (l) maladjustment is due to an exaggerated and uncooperative goal of personal superiority. See COMPENSATION, FICTIONAL FINALISM, INFERIORITY COMPLEX, OVERCOMPENSATION, STRIVING FOR SUPERIORITY.

individual psychotherapy   individual therapy

individual response   A type of response peculiar to an individual and distinct from the modal response of the community of which the person is a member; human creativity is sometimes considered to be such a response, and an argument for differentiating humans from animals, which are sometimes considered to have a much narrower capacity for individuality.

Individuals with Disabilities Education Act (IDEA)
Public Law 101-476 enacted in 1990 that amended Education for All Handicapped Children Act (EHA) of 1975. Mandates a free, appropriate public education for ages 3 to 21 regardless of the nature or severity of the disability.

Requires that the education take place in the least restrictive environment (LRE) and that an individualized education program (IEP) be developed that considers both long- and short-term goals. Extends the right of individuals with disabilities to nondiscriminatory treatment in aspects of their lives beyond education.

individual symbol   A psychoanalytic concept that certain objects or persons dreamed about may represent something unique for the dreamer; for example, in a dream, a polar bear might represent a parent, whom the dreamer considers to be at the same time both powerful and cold. See SYMBOL, UNIVERSAL SYMBOL.

individual test   A type of test intended for administration to one person at a time (as distinct from a test that can be administered simultaneously to a group of people), usually administered by a trained tester, such as the Wechsler and Binet intelligence tests.

individual therapy   Psychotherapy conducted on a one-to-one basis (one therapist and one client). Also known as individual psychotherapy, dyadic therapy. Compare GROUP THERAPY. See DYADIC PSYCHOTHERAPY, INDIVIDUAL RESPONSE, INDIVIDUAL SYMBOL.

individuation   1. (C. G. Jung) The process in human development that leads toward a stable, unique, and unitary personality. See ACTUALIZATION, TRANSCENDENT(AL) FUNCTION. 2. (M. S. Mahler) A phase of development, occurring between the 18th and 36th month, in which infants become less dependent on the mother or mother figure and begin to satisfy their own wishes and fend for themselves. See AUTONOMY.

indolamines   Biogenic amines due to combinations of indoles with amines that become neurotransmitters.

induced abortion   The deliberate premature removal of the embryo or fetus prior to the stage of viability, by artificial means such as drugs or mechanical interventions. Contrasts with spontaneous abortion, or the expulsion of a fetus without artificial means. Also known as artificial abortion. See THERAPEUTIC ABORTION.

induced aggression   Generating aggression in an organism by frustrating it; for example, an animal that has been starved and then placed near other well-fed animals will likely attack them.

induced color   The changed perceived color of an object produced by placing other colors near it.

induced goal   An objective that originates from external factors as opposed to intrinsic factors.

induced hallucination   A hallucination evoked in one person by another. This phenomenon may occur during hypnosis.

induced hypothermia   A severe loss of body temperature that is caused and employed in surgery and for treatment of neurological diseases causing fever.

induced motion/movement   (K. Duncker) In Gestalt psychology, the tendency to perceive motion in an enclosed or surrounded body, physically at rest, when an enclosing or surrounding object in the field, or the entire field itself, is in motion (for example, if a person on a train looks out, and sees another train move on the track next to his or hers, perceiving his or her train as moving when it actually is not).

induced psychosis   A psychotic condition generated in one person by another person, whether deliberate or accidental. See FOLIE À DEUX, FOLIE À TROIS.

induced tonus   A muscle tonus (muscle contraction) brought about by movement of other body parts.

inducibility   Openness to influence.

induction (I)   1. The formulation of general rules or explanations from specific cases or observations; reasoning from particulars to the general. Compare DEDUCTION. 2. The end result of such reasoning. 3. Facilitation between neural paths, usually occurring when the regions showing facilitation are close together. 4. The process that induces seemingly identical cells in the neural plate to develop into neurons, skin, hair, etc. 5. (I. P. Pavlov) In Pavlovian or classical conditioning, when an excitatory conditioned stimulus (CS) occurs in a neighboring area immediately prior to an inhibitory CS, the inhibitory effect of the CS increases in strength (that is, negative induction). When an inhibitory CS occurs in a neighboring area immediately prior to an excitatory CS, the impact of that excitatory CS is enhanced (that is, positive induction).

induction test   1. A test item or series of test items in which a student or participant must derive or formulate a general law, rule, or principle based on several relevant facts or cases. 2. An examination given on a person's entrance to a military or to other institutional status.

inductive logic   Reasoning from particular instances to general conclusions, from experiences to broad generalizations. Compare DEDUCTIVE LOGIC.

inductive problem-solving   A learning situation in which students are presented with particular facts and events from which they must infer relationships and explain the general principles that underlie the relationships.

inductive reasoning   The reasoning process whereby inferences and general principles are derived from particular observations and cases; reasoning from the specific to the general. Inductive reasoning is a cornerstone of the scientific method in that it underlies the process of developing hypotheses from particular facts and observations. Compare DEDUCTIVE REASONING.

inductive schema   A complex, interactive, articulated process of scientific reasoning involving inductive thinking, generalizations, explanation, and prediction. See RESEARCH.

inductive statistics   Techniques for determining whether or not obtained descriptive data could be due to chance. Also known as inferential statistics.

inductive teaching model   An approach in education that emphasizes the role of inductive reasoning in cognitive development: presenting specific instances of a phenomenon to students and requiring them to discover the broad generalization implied by the instances. See INQUIRY TRAINING MODEL.

inductive thinking   A process of considering a number of related matters and attempting to come to a conclusion, such as a general rule that applies to all. Compare DEDUCTIVE THINKING.

inductive vs deductive   (R. I. Watson) A prescriptive dimension of the philosophical underpinnings of psychology, namely, an approach from the particular to the general versus the other way around. See OPPONENT-PAIRS DIMENSION.

industrial action   job action

industrial democracy   The granting of partial or complete participation by the workforce in a firm's operation, especially regarding job design. Variants include the drafting of a collective agreement, the appointment of employee or union representatives to company boards, an emphasis on communication and consultation, and employee control over the organization through ownership plans.

industrial efficiency   Generally, the ratio of input, usually measured by cost, effort, or both, to output.

industrial-organizational psychology   The application of psychological theory and methods to industrial and organizational problems having to do with a person's self, others, jobs, machines, operations, etc., as well as to improving selection of personnel and work procedures, all in the interest of establishing a productive and happy climate in a variety of shops, agencies, and organizations, as well as enhancing profit.

industrial psychology   See INDUSTRIAL-ORGANIZATIONAL PSYCHOLOGY.

industrial psychopath   A psychopathic individual in an occupational setting.

industrial rehabilitation counselor   1. A person who works with industry by providing information on available community services as well as assistance for persons with disabilities in the company. 2. A company counselor provided for persons whose jobs have been eliminated.

industrial relations   Labor relations.

industrial therapy   Work activities carried out by persons with mental or physical challenges in a hospital or sheltered workshop for such purposes as morale building and preparation for outside employment.

industry vs inferiority   The fourth of Erik Erikson's stages of psychosocial development, covering the "latency" period of ages 6 to 11 years, during which the child learns to obey the rules of society and is interested in how things work and how to make things. If the child is not encouraged to be industrious, a feeling of inferiority may result. Also known as Robinson Crusoe age. See ERIKSON'S STAGES OF PSYCHOSOCIAL DEVELOPMENT.

ineffability   The property of an ecstatic state that a person finds indescribable, not able to convey its essence to anyone else unless the other has already also experienced it. See ECSTASY, EXALTATION.

ineffective stimulus   A stimulus that fails to evoke a response, usually because the stimulus is not capable of affecting a receptor or is below threshold.

inequalities   The relation between two quantities, usually expressed by a sign of inequality, indicating that the quantities are not equal, for example, $5 < 9$ indicates that 5 is less than 9; $9 > 5$ shows that 9 is greater than 5; and $a \neq b$ indicates that whatever the quantity a symbolizes it does not equal that of b. The symbols used for inequality indicate only position and do not tell "how much" or to what degree there is a difference. See NULL HYPOTHESIS.

inertia   1. A property of a moving object, such that the motion tends to persist unless there is an external force that changes the motion. 2. A process in the nervous system consisting of a delay between stimulus and response. 3. See PSYCHIC INERTIA.

infancy The earliest period of postnatal life, roughly the first year, during which the child is relatively helpless and dependent upon a caretaker.

infant adjustment reaction A situational stress disorder in early human development that may be due to the birth experience, feeding problems, sleeping disturbances, maternal rejection, or overprotection.

infant and preschool tests Individually administered tests intended to assess the development of infants (from birth to 18 months) and preschool children (from 18 to 60 months). Among the better known scales are the Gesell Developmental Schedules, which determine the level of linguistic, motor, and social behavior for both groups; the California First-Year Mental Scale, which assesses postural adjustment, motor activity, perception, attention, and manipulation; the Merrill-Palmer Scale of Mental Tests, comprised of verbal and performance items standardized for children from 24 to 63 months of age; and other tests such as the Bayley Scales of Infant Development, the Cattell Infant Intelligence Scale, the Griffiths Mental Development Scales, the McCarthy Scales of Children's Abilities, and the Wechsler Preschool and Primary Scale of Intelligence (WPPSI). See INFANT SCALE/ TEST.

infant at risk A newborn child whose development may be threatened by complications at the time of birth, such as conditions that reduce the supply of oxygen to the brain.

Infant Behavior Record The third part of the Bayley Scales of Infant Development that assesses aspects of personality development, such as social behavior, attention span, and persistence. See BAYLEY SCALES OF INFANT DEVELOPMENT, MENTAL SCALE, MOTOR SCALE.

infant development program A program for children born at risk for developmental delay due to disorders such as Down syndrome or sometimes environmental factors. A family-oriented program in which parents receive special instruction for developing their infant's mental and communication capacities. Formerly known as infant learning, infant stimulation program.

infant feeding procedure effects Refers to the controversy over whether neonates (newborn infants) should be fed by either bottle or breast, and the pros and cons related to each technique. Possibly the most important factor is an accepting, warm attitude on the part of the caretaker evidenced by direct, caressing bodily contact during the feeding, regardless of the chosen method.

infanticide 1. The killing of an infant. Has been practiced in a number of societies, notably Sparta, as a means of eliminating the unfit, and in some cultures on the basis of gender (usually killing female infants). See DEPRESSION AFTER DELIVERY (DAD). 2. The person who murders an infant.

infantile 1. Pertaining to infants or infancy. 2. Denoting childish behavior.

infantile amnesia Inability to remember events from the first years of life.

infantile atrophy marasmus

infantile autism Atypical behavior of infants characterized by unresponsiveness to people, and not manifesting normal awareness and responsiveness. Also known as Kanner's disease/syndrome. See AUTISM, CHILDHOOD SCHIZOPHRENIA, ECHOLALIA, RITUALS.

infantile dynamics Psychological processes, such as oral sexuality, that according to psychoanalytic theory originate in early childhood but continue to exert an unconscious influence on the personality during adulthood.

infantile masturbation In psychoanalytic theory, self-stimulation during infancy and early childhood, including genital play as well as stimulation of other erogenous zones and parts of the body, as in smacking the lips and sucking the fingers.

infantile personality immature personality

infantile sadism In psychoanalytic theory, aggressive and destructive behavior during the early years of life. See ANAL SADISM, ID SADISM, ORAL SADISM.

infantile seduction A mature person persuading an immature person, particularly a young child, to participate in sexual activities.

infantile sexuality (S. Freud) A psychoanalytic theory that humans have the capacity for sexual feeling during the first months of life and throughout the early childhood years, as manifested in the oral, anal, and phallic stages of development; that is, obtaining sexual gratification from sucking the mother's breast, defecating, and masturbatory activities. See SEXUAL INFANTILISM.

infantile speech Human verbal expression using the sounds and forms characteristic of young children (baby talk) beyond the stage in which such speech is normal. Immature speech may be encouraged by parents who find it cute, or it may be an expression of general emotional immaturity. See BABY TALK.

infantilism 1. Abnormally slow development of mind and body. 2. Childishness. Regressive behavior of people who are no longer children, such as demanding things, wanting attention, or throwing fits. 3. Being sexually attracted to or aroused by impersonating an infant and being treated as one; autonepiophilia.

infantilization The active encouragement of infantile behavior such as extreme dependence on the mother or primary caretaker; the process of deliberately keeping the child in an infantile state. Chronically ill children, challenged children, as well as youngest, only, and adopted children, are especially likely to be infantilized by their parents.

infant learning Developing an infant's mental and communication capacities through activities using pictures, sounds, objects, games, and later letters and numbers. See INFANT-STIMULATION PROGRAM.

infant massage therapy (T. Field) A procedure recommended for mothers with depression who might otherwise neglect their newborn children; infants are to be rubbed by their mothers, over all parts of their bodies for about fifteen minutes a day, at least twice a week, for six weeks. See POSTPARTUM DEPRESSION.

infant narcotic withdrawal A syndrome in some neonates born to a mother addicted to narcotics, consisting of vomiting, trembling, hyperactivity, shrill crying, and rapid respiration, which may be fatal if untreated.

infant scale/test A behavior examination measuring infantile development, usually through the performance of sensorimotor tasks that use coordination and manipulation. Examples include the California First-Year Mental Scale, the Gesell Developmental Schedules, and the Cattell Infant Intelligence Scale.

infant stimulation program   infant development program

infant test   See INFANT AND PRESCHOOL TESTS, INFANT BEHAVIOR SCALE, INFANT SCALE.

infatuation   Love that usually is short-lived, extravagant, or shallow, and based on a superficial reason, such as the sheer physical attractiveness of the love object.

infavoidance need   The need to avoid failure or humiliation, often characteristic of people who do not undertake tasks that they are likely to fail.

infection theory   (W. Sahakian) A point of view that personal contacts among scientists tend to spread information about theories and research findings, and some worthy results may be neglected if they are not disseminated in this manner. It is in effect a version of "It is not necessarily what you know but who you know that counts."

infecundity   Female sterility.

inference   A process of reaching conclusions or generalizations by deduction or induction from sampling evidence rather than from direct observation of all the potential population or data.

inference statistics   inferential statistics

inference strategies   In psychology, the mental processes whereby on the basis of one or more previous judgments, the individual reaches still other judgments.

inferential statistics   Statistical procedures for making inferences about the characteristics of a population on the basis of results found from a sample selected from it. These procedures generally involve estimating population parameters, such as the mean and variance, finding confidence intervals for the parameters, or testing hypotheses about them. Also known as inductive statistics, inference statistics. See DESCRIPTIVE STATISTICS.

inferior   An anatomical direction referring to a lower part of the human body; away from the head.

inferior colliculi   Paired nuclei that form eminences on the dorsal midbrain and constitute the caudal part of the tectum. They serve as relays for auditory nerve impulses. See CORPORA QUADRIGEMINA.

inferior functions   See SUPERIOR FUNCTIONS.

inferiority   Perception of deficiency or inadequacy. A person who feels inferior believes his or her worth is less than that of others. See INDUSTRY VS INFERIORITY.

inferiority complex   (A. Adler) Abnormal and usually exaggerated feelings of being worthless, hopeless, incompetent, or not lovable; a type of depressive feeling. See INDIVIDUAL PSYCHOLOGY, INFERIORITY FEELINGS, ORGAN INFERIORITY.

inferiority feelings   (A. Adler) Normal feelings of being less valuable than others and less than what a person wants to be. Such feelings are usually unpleasant but tend to motivate people to improve themselves, in contrast to the inferiority complex that leads to no action for self-improvement.

inferior longitudinal fasciculus   A bundle of association fibers in the brain that extends from the occipital to the temporal poles of the cerebral hemispheres.

inferior oblique   One of the six muscles used in controlling eye movements, for looking upward and inward. The superior and inferior oblique muscles also control rotation movements of the eyeball. See INFERIOR RECTUS, LATERAL RECTUS, MEDIAL RECTUS, SUPERIOR OBLIQUE, SUPERIOR RECTUS.

inferior rectus   One of the six muscles used in controlling eye movements, for looking downward. See INFERIOR OBLIQUE, LATERAL RECTUS, MEDIAL RECTUS, SUPERIOR OBLIQUE, SUPERIOR RECTUS.

inferotemporal area/cortex   A region of the brain immediately beneath the temporal cortex that contains nerve fibers associated with visual perception. Lesions of the inferotemporal cortex impair visual learning related to either object or form discrimination.

infertility   1. Diminished or absent fertility. Does not imply sterility. 2. Inability to produce offspring due to low fertility on the part of the woman (in about 60% of cases) or the man (in nearly 40% of cases), or both. Physical causes predominate, but the condition may be due to psychological factors. In contrast to sterility, many cases can be remedied. See FECUNDITY, STERILITY.

infibulation   Stitching that closes the vulva or the penile prepuce, a component of some cultural *rites de passage*. Sometimes done to prevent premature unions among children. See GENITAL MUTILATION.

infinite-valued logic   The logical system that assumes that between "completely true" and "completely false" lie an indefinitely large number of possible partial truths.

infinity fear   See APEIROPHOBIA.

infinity neurosis   Abnormal preoccupation with the concepts of the infinity of space and the eternity of time. Occurs during adolescence or among persons with autism.

in flagrant delict   Caught "red-handed" as in the act of committing a crime. Also known as *in flagrante delicto* (Latin).

inflection   A change of quality of voice, as in its timbre and register, such as speaking with a different tone of voice to emphasize a point.

influence   Impact of the behavior of one person on another. See DELUSION OF INFLUENCE.

influencing machine   A machine as part of a paranoid delusion; the patient feels controlled by a machine that serves as an instrument of persecution (for example, believing that a radio tower broadcasts malignant signals about the patient to others).

informal communications   In any organization, communications outside of official channels, as in executives' personal assistants exchanging information not known to the executives. See GOSSIP, GRAPE VINE.

informal groups   Associations among individuals in an organization that form spontaneously and often without the knowledge of the higher officials of the organization.

informal test   A nonstandardized examination of knowledge or abilities, usually constructed and graded intuitively; for example, a test made up by a teacher given to students to determine whether they have learned a particular lesson.

informant 1. A person who provides information. 2. A person who provides information in a survey or a research project. Also, a research participant who before, during, or after participating voices opinions, attitudes and conclusions about the procedures; such observations can add to the value of the objective results.

informational feedback Indicators of behavior presented in such a manner as to permit the person to become aware of the behavior (for example, a meter activated by a pulse that visually displays the heart rate). Also, information about the correctness of a person's responses, their social effect, etc. See BIOFEEDBACK.

informational social influence Refers to conformity resulting from the acceptance of others' opinions about reality.

informationally equivalent representations (H. A. Simon) Two or more representations of the same problem or problem domain that contain the same information, hence are mutually translatable. See COMPUTATIONALLY EQUIVALENT REPRESENTATIONS.

information dependence Reliance on others for information, usually in the context of their preferences, expectations, and needs, in the formation of a group agreement.

information feedback Information provided to individuals about the correctness or physical effect of their responses, or about the social or emotional impact of their behavior on others. See KNOWLEDGE OF RESULTS.

information-input process The process whereby sensory data from the environment are received and transmitted to centers of the brain for generating percepts, judgments or evaluations that can lead to responses. Also, the process of providing input to a computer.

information-optimization position The theory that the organism as an information-processing system has an optimal or preferred level of stimulation. Negative affect and avoidance behavior tend to be generated by small and large variations in the stimulus, whereas moderate degrees of stimulus variation tend to generate a positive affect.

information overload A state occurring when the amount or intensity of environmental stimuli that needs to be processed exceeds a person's stress and capacity, potentially leading to disregard of some important information. The demands of everyday life in large urban centers can generate information overload, contributing to the degeneration of social life in these areas. See OVERLOADING.

information processing (IP) (W. R. Garner) In cognitive science, the encoding, performance of operations on, and output transmission of, informational input. This model of cognitive processes is based upon the assumption that the human mind works with information provided to it, much as a high-speed computer operates on input it receives.

information processing language (A. Newell & H. A. Simon) A symbolic (as distinguished from algebraic) computer programming language whose instructions commonly take the form of productions and whose data structures are symbols connected by links. Thus, the symbol "black" may be linked with "white," or "red" linked with "apple" as its "color." In the latter case, "color" is called the "label" of the link between "red" and "apple." The links are pointers that enable the second symbol to be found when the first is known. Such languages, especially LISP, OPS-5, and Prolog, are commonly used in cognitive simulation.

Information Processing Language V (IPL-V) (A. Newell, J. C. Shaw & H. A. Simon) The first list-processing or information-processing computer programming language, used extensively as a language for cognitive simulation, later replaced by LISP and Prolog. See ARTIFICIAL INTELLIGENCE, COGNITIVE STIMULATION, INFORMATION PROCESSING LANGUAGE.

information processing level (A. Newell & H. A. Simon) A level in the modeling of cognitive phenomena in which the elementary information processes are symbolic. The level represents events in less detail than the neural level but in more detail than the level of complex tasks. See INFORMATION PROCESSING SYSTEM.

information processing psychology (A. Newell & H. A. Simon) A psychological theory (usually focused on cognition) based on the physical symbol system hypothesis and the use of cognitive simulation as the language of theory. See COGNITIVE SIMULATION.

information processing system (A. Newell & H. A. Simon) A cognitive system that operates on symbols stored in one or more memories, such as short-term or long-term memory, by bringing them into working memory and performing operations on them there. A physical symbol system. See PHYSICAL SYMBOL SYSTEM.

information-rich world (H. A. Simon) An environment in which the amount of information available is large in comparison with the capacity of people and of computers to process it. See BOUNDED RATIONALITY.

information science A system for studying and describing communicative processes, usually involving mathematical analysis of the encoding, transmission, and decoding of signals without concern for the specific semantic content of the message itself. See INFORMATION THEORY.

Information Test A verbal subtest of the Wechsler Intelligence Scales that measures the participant's fund of general knowledge in different areas and at different levels of complexity.

information theory The study of communication processes involved in the transmission of knowledge involving sender and receiver characteristics, physiological, and mechanical modes of sending and receiving data. See BAYESIAN APPROACH, COMMUNICATION UNIT, CYBERNETICS, INFORMATION SCIENCE, LINGUISTICS.

informed consent Permission by a participant given without coercion to a researcher or practitioner to perform a procedure after receiving clear information about it, including knowing that the procedure is voluntary and that the participant may withdraw at any time, what the procedure entails (including its risks, possible benefits, and alternatives), and any consequences of withholding consent. Ethical practice requires that such consent be obtained from the participant (or a responsible representative) in all psychological research and medical or other therapeutic procedures.

infradian Occurring periodically, but less frequently than daily (for example, the full moon).

infradian rhythm   A biological rhythm with a cycle longer than one day. See BIOLOGICAL RHYTHM, CIRCADIAN RHYTHM.

infrahuman   Literally, below human; characterizing all species "below" the human level, such as felines or canines.

infraprimate   Below the level of primates. Refers to behavior, traits, or functions characteristic of animals "below" the primate level such as crustaceans, insects, etc.

infrapsychic   Cognitions or other psychological processes that occur below the level of consciousness.

infra reality   (J. L. Moreno) The "reduced" level of "reality" typical in psychotherapy. The contact between doctor and patient or client is not a genuine encounter between equals but a controlled or contrived situation.

infrared   Portions of the light spectrum that include wavelengths just longer than those that produce the sensation of red in the visible spectrum.

infrared theory of smell   The point of view that the olfactory sense organ functions at least in part through the filtering or absorption of infrared radiation from substances that produce odors. See RAMAN SHIFT, SMELL MECHANISM, ULTRAVIOLET ABSORPTION.

infundibulum hypothalami/hypothalamus   The stalk of the pituitary gland.

ingratiation   The intentional effort to win the liking and approval of others through conformance, flattery, and other measures designed to create a good impression. Ingratiation is an example of impression management. See IMPRESSION MANAGEMENT.

ingroup   1. The group to which a person belongs, such as family, school, nationality, clique, political party, friends, professional colleagues. Also known as we group. 2. An exclusive group (for example, an adolescent clique) characterized by intense bonds of cohesion or affiliation such that each member feels a sense of kinship and loyalty to other members by virtue of their common group membership. Also known as we-group. Compare OUT-GROUP.

ingroup bias   A tendency to favor the group to which a person belongs. See INGROUP FAVORITISM.

ingroup extremity effect   A tendency for those strongly identifying with a group to evaluate members of their group more extremely than those in other groups. Compare OUTGROUP EXTREMITY EFFECT.

ingroup favoritism   A tendency of members of groups to maintain favorable attitudes toward all others in the group and to give them favored treatment over those not in the group. Individuals in these groups need not even know each other; for example, an American may be likely to give preference to another American over others who are not so identified. See ETHNOCENTRISM, RACISM.

inguinal   The region of the groin.

inhabitance   Haunting, as by a ghost or spirit.

inhalant(s)   A group of substances, the fumes of which are purposely breathed in because they are intoxicating, such as model airplane glue (glue sniffing, huffing), lighter fluid, typewriter correction fluid, fabric protector sprays, fingernail polish, aerosol propellants, paints, paint thinners, gasoline, or freon. See INHALANT-RELATED DISORDERS.

inhalant-related disorders   Breathing in the vapors of gasoline, airplane glue, cleaners, spray-paint propellants, correction fluid, and other volatile compounds gives a kind of mild euphoriant, drunk high. These substances can damage the liver and nervous system—both the brain and the peripheral nerves and in large doses can cause a delirium and occasionally death. Other problems are similar to the effects of being drunk. This kind of use and abuse is common, especially among youngsters in underdeveloped communities and countries around the world. See GLUE-SNIFFING, HUFFING, VOLATILE CHEMICAL INHALATION.

inhalation of drugs   A means of injesting and absorbing a substance into the body tissues rapidly when the substance is in the form of a gas or aerosol. Anesthetics for major surgery are often administered through the lungs, which permits almost instant contact with the bloodstream flowing through the alveoli. Inhalation of drugs also is employed in self-administration of other volatile substances and (through smoking) of cannabis, nicotine, cocaine, crystal methamphetamine. See VOLATILE-CHEMICAL INHALATION.

in heat   See ESTROUS BEHAVIOR.

inheritance   1. Psychological or physical traits that have been transmitted. 2. The process of transmission of genes from parents to offspring. See MENDELIAN MODES OF INHERITANCE, MULTIFACTORIAL INHERITANCE.

inherited disorder   Any pathological condition in an offspring that was received from its ancestors. See GENETIC DEFECT, INBORN ERRORS OF METABOLISM, METABOLIC ANOMALY.

inherited releasing mechanism (IRM)   **innate releasing mechanism**

inhibited mania   (E. Kraepelin) A manic state characterized by psychomotor inactivity together with a cheerful and even exultant mood, flight of ideas, and occasionally irritable and even violent behavior.

inhibited orgasm   A condition in which sexually-aroused people either intentionally abort an orgasmic climax or are unable to reach orgasm.

inhibited sexual desire (ISD)   Persistent lack of sexual interest.

inhibited sexual excitement   General lack of interest in sexual matters that usually results in a lack of penile or vaginal readiness for sexual intercourse.

inhibition   1. In general, the blocking of one process by another. 2. Restraint of impulses or behavior, either consciously or unconsciously, due to lack of confidence, fear of consequences, or moral qualms. A tendency to suppress impulses or desires, or suppress certain modes of expression that would subject an individual to social or self-censure. 3. A response reduction caused by an incompatible response being activated. 4. In learning, a process thought to occur during extinction. 5. In Freudian theory, the expression of a functional limitation of the ego. 6. In conditioning, the active blocking or delay of a response by the subject, as when a dog is trained to salivate only after the bell has rung for several seconds. Types of inhibition include: INTERNAL, OCCUPATIONAL, PROACTIVE, REACTIVE, RECIPROCAL, RETROACTIVE, SPECIFIC. See DISINHIBITION, INHIBITORY POSTSYNAPTIC POTENTIAL, REPRESSION.

inhibition mechanism   A series of biochemical mechanisms within the nervous system that restrict the flow of excitatory impulses. The devices include presynaptic and postsynaptic influences and depolarization and hyperpolarization of cells. See HYPERPOLARIZATION.

inhibition of delay   A reduction in the amount of time that elapses between the onset of a stimulus and a response or between the onset of a conditioned stimulus and a conditioned response.

inhibitor   A stimulus that suppresses potential behavior.

inhibitory-postsynaptic potential (IPSP)   (J. S. Coombs, J. C. Eccles & P. Fatt) A brief hyperpolarization of a neuron's postsynaptic membrane, with resulting heightened threshold for the depolarization that initiates neuron excitatory response. See ACTION POTENTIAL.

inhibitory potential ($_sI_R$)   (C. L. Hull) An hypothesized temporary state in which conditioned inhibition results from making a response and reduces the potential of recurrence of that response. See HULL'S THEORY.

inhibitory process   Any physiological function that retards growth, movement, activity. See EXCITATORY-INHIBITORY PROCESS.

inhibitory reflex   A negative reflexive action effect that may become established during differential conditioning of an animal. The negative conditioned reflex is not reinforced, does not result in a positive conditioned effect, and hence represents an inhibition of the conditioned reflex. See REFLEX INHIBITION.

inhibitory synapse   A connection between neurons, the action of which reduces the probability of an action potential being produced in the postsynaptic cell, usually by hyperpolarizing the postsynaptic membrane.

in-house evaluation   An organization's internal assessment program, as opposed to evaluation conducted by outside evaluators.

initial clinical interview   The first interview with a client. In psychotherapy, its purpose typically is to establish a positive relationship, listen to the client's problem described in the client's own words, make a tentative diagnosis, and formulate a plan for diagnostic tests, possible treatment, or referral.

initial cry   epileptic cry

initial delay   The pausing or slowing down process immediately before the execution of a patterned movement.

initial insomnia   Persistent difficulty in falling asleep, usually thought to be due to tension, anxiety, or depression. Some anxiety insomniacs may become so worried about failing asleep or about the effects of loss of sleep that they are unable to relax sufficiently to fall asleep.

initial job interview   The first interview with a job applicant. The purposes for the interview are, according to Clark Hull, to generate good feelings for the interviewees and to establish satisfactory communications. See EMPLOYMENT INTERVIEW, HULL'S THEORY.

initial reflex   The earliest reflexive action evoked by a series of stimuli of increasing strength when the first stimulus is below the threshold level.

initial spurt   The increased productivity or gain in performance frequently noted at the start of a job, task, or series of trials. The initial spurt occurs more commonly in new tasks than in tasks with which the individual is familiar. Also known as beginning spurt. Compare END SPURT, NOVELTY EFFECT.

Initial Teaching Alphabet (ITA)   (J. Pitman) A near-phonemic alphabet of 44 characters, with a single sound for each character. Used since the early 1960s in teaching English-speaking children to read, with varying success. The system originally was called Augmented Roman.

initiating structure   1. (J. K. Hemphill) A component of a group leader's role, consisting of the ability to identify group objectives and to create an effective organization aimed at achieving those objectives. 2. Leadership behavior that consists of getting the group organized and preparing it to start functioning.

initiation   1. A ritual that represents dedication to a specific goal or group. 2. In psychoanalytic terms, the redirecting of the infantile libido into mature objectives through ceremonies of initiation of an adult male into manhood or, less common, an adult female into womanhood. 3. A ritual employed in the process of accepting a person as a member of an organization, such as social clubs, fraternities and sororities.

initiative vs guilt   The third of Erik Erikson's eight stages typically occurring in the child's fourth and fifth years. Central to this stage is the child's feeling of freedom in planning, launching, and initiating all forms of fantasy, play, and other activity. If resolution of the two earlier stages was unsuccessful or if the child is consistently criticized or humiliated, guilt and a feeling of not belonging develop in place of a feeling of initiative. See ERIKSON'S PSYCHOSOCIAL DEVELOPMENT STAGES.

initiator   A person who introduces new ideas or helps to launch specific courses of action.

injury fear   See TRAUMATOPHOBIA.

injury feigning   Instinctive actions of certain animals, such as birds that by flapping their wings in a certain manner, can generate the impression that they are hurt to draw attention to themselves (and away from their offspring) to lead a predator away (from their offspring). See DEATH FEIGNING.

ink blot (masking) technique   (P. H. Lindsay & D. A. Norman) In information processing, masking parts of letters with what looks like a blob of ink, as in covering the bottom horizontal line of the letter E to see if it is read as an occluded E or as an F, as a function of adjoining letters.

inkblot test (IBT)   See HOLTZMAN INKBLOT TECHNIQUE, PROJECTIVE METHOD, RORSCHACH TEST.

innate   An inborn (rather than acquired) property, attribute, or trait.

innate behavior   A kind of behavior controlled by inborn factors, rather than by learning experiences (for example, limb buds of amphibia that are transplanted to opposite sides of the body and, when they become fully developed, function according to the way in which they would have moved in their original anatomic sites).

innate hierarchies of response   (N. Miller) A tendency in infants for certain responses to occur in a particular temporal order that is genetically determined.

innate ideas   Fundamental or general ideas assumed to be universal and inborn, and present in all individuals prior to experience, such as the concept of fairness or the idea of God (R. Descartes).

innate patterns   Instincts.

innate releasing mechanism (IRM)   (N. Tinbergen) An action pattern in animals triggered by specific environmental signals or stimuli because of an inborn rather than a conditioned response to the stimuli, such as the zigzag dance performed by male stickleback fish when they see another fish with a swollen abdomen and respond appropriately to a pregnant female stickleback, even though they have never seen a pregnant female of their own species. Also known as inherited releasing mechanism. See RELEASER.

innate response system   The unlearned motor responses with which an organism is endowed at birth, such as infants turning their heads toward a light source.

inner boundary   (P. Federn) A flexible boundary that exists between the ego and the unconscious. If the inner boundary is blurred, as in falling asleep, repressed material may enter consciousness. See EGO BOUNDARY, EGO PSYCHOTHERAPY, OUTER BOUNDARY.

inner conflict   intrapsychic conflict

inner controls   Inhibitory factors, such as reality and values, that psychodynamic and other theories propose as preventing dangerous or undesirable behavior.

inner dialog   Internal mental debate engaged in about any issue, be it as simple as whether to eat or as complex as contemplating suicide. In some systems of psychotherapy, the client is encouraged to express the inner dialog by verbalizing the thoughts. See INTERNALIZED PSYCHODRAMA.

inner-directed   (D. Riesman) The characterization of a person who is self-motivated and not easily influenced by the opinions, values, or pressures of other people. Compare OUTER-DIRECTED.

inner ear   The internal part of the ear consisting of the cochlea, the semicircular canals, and the vestibule. Some divide the labyrinth (entire inner ear) into the cochlear apparatus (containing the hair cells on the organ of Corti, involved with hearing) and the vestibular apparatus (three semicircular canals and the otolith organs, utricle and saccule, involved with balance). Also known as auditory labyrinth, internal ear.

inner estrangement   (P. Federn) An unfamiliar and unreal feeling about external objects, a characteristic of some depressive psychoses. See EGO PSYCHOTHERAPY.

inner granular layer   The seventh layer in the retina of the human eye. Also known as inner molecular layer. See INNER NUCLEAR LAYER.

inner hair cells   internal hair cells (of ear)

inner harmony   A pleasant condition of being at peace with self and others, free of tensions and emotions. See NIRVANA.

inner language   1. (J. B. Watson) The "language" of the mind, considered by early behaviorists as equivalent to intelligence, exemplified by a person's inner private self-talk. 2. (L. Vygotsky) The mental image of words and concepts in terms of visual, auditory, and kinesthetic sensations; speech spoken mentally, without vocalization. See EGOCENTRIC SPEECH, INTERNALIZED SPEECH, PURE MEANING, VERBAL THOUGHT.

inner nuclear layer   The sixth layer of the retina of the human eye (counted from the outside, Polyak's identification) that contains mostly rod and cone bipolar cells, which join the ganglionic or "optic nerve cells" of layers 8 and 9 to the rod and cone granules of layer 4, which in turn connect to the rods and cones. In addition the layer contains horizontal cells, amacrine cells, and blood vessels.

inner personal region   An individual within Kurt Lewin's field theory of personality. See FIELD THEORY.

inner psychophysics   (G. T. Fechner) The relation of sensory experience (mind) to the neural events upon which it is dependent.

inner speech   See INNER DIALOGUE.

innervation   The distribution of nerve fiber endings in muscles, glands, or other tissues. See INNERVATION RATIO.

innervation apraxia   motor apraxia (meaning 1)

innervation ratio   The proportion of muscle fibers to motor-neuron axons. The innervation ratio may vary from three muscle fibers per axon for small muscles to as many as 150 muscle fibers per axon for the large muscle bundles of the arms and legs. See INNERVATION.

inoculation theory   (W. J. McGuire) A point of view that attitudes can be made resistant to change by desensitizing a person by "inoculation" with a series of weaker arguments that can gradually be built up.

inoculative hypothesis   A postulate that if a person's belief is refuted in a weak manner or by another not accepted as an authority on the topic, the person becomes more strongly attached to the point of view.

in-patient services   Diagnostic and treatment services available to hospitalized patients and usually unavailable or not completely available in out-patient facilities. In the case of mental patients, may include continuous supervision, nursing care, and specialized treatment techniques, such as electroshock therapy, occupational therapy, movement therapy, as well as medical treatment, recreation therapy, social-work services, and frequent group therapy.

input   1. Signals fed into a communication channel. 2. Energy put into a system. 3. Any contribution.

input-output (IO) mechanism   A function of the human information-processing system involved in getting information into and out of the system. May involve acquiring the information needed to accomplish a task (input), such as studying a diagram and then assembling a bicycle on the basis of the information (output).

inquiry   A period of questioning following the administration of a test. With respect to Rorschach testing, a period of review and questioning about responses to the inkblots to refine the understanding of what determined a respondent's perceptions and responses.

INRC   See IDENTITY, NEGATION, RECIPROCAL AND CORRELATIVE TRANSFORMATIONS.

INS   involuntary nervous system

insane asylum   Old name for an institution for the care, protection, and treatment of the mentally ill. Sometimes called asylum.

insanity   1. (Celsus) Outmoded term for a severe mental illness or psychosis. In this sense, kinds of insanity include: ALTERNATING, CIRCULAR, CONSTITUTIONAL, CYCLIC, DOUBLE, MORAL, NEGATION, NORMAL, REASONING, TRIPLE. 2. Legal term whose definition and legal implications vary among jurisdictions and may involve such concepts as guardianship, lack of responsibility for contracts or crimes, inability to distinguish between moral right and wrong, and necessity for commitment. Whereas psychologists and psychiatrists may testify as experts about the mental state of a person, the judge or jury decide whether the person is sane or insane. See CRIMINALLY INSANE, INSANITY DEFENSE, PARTIAL INSANITY, PSYCHOSIS.

insanity defense   The criminal-law defense plea that the accused person lacks criminal responsibility by reason of insanity. See M'NAGHTEN RULES/TEST.

insanity fear   See LYSSOPHOBIA, MANIAPHOBIA.

insanity of negation   A psychosis characterized by delusions of nihilism. See COTARD'S SYNDROME.

insect fear   A phobia about insects; entomophobia. See ACAROPHOBIA.

insecure attachment   (M. Ainsworth, J. Bowlby) Ambivalent or insecure patterns of bonding between children and their parents or other caretakers when the children are not sure they are accepted.

insecurity   A feeling of inadequacy, lack of self-confidence, or inability to cope, sometimes accompanied by general uncertainty and anxiety about personal goals, abilities, or relationships to others.

insemination   The deposit of seminal fluid within the vagina, usually during coitus. If the semen is introduced by means other than coitus, the process is called artificial insemination.

insensible   1. Unable to experience sensations occurring, for example, while asleep, drugged, unconscious, in a coma, or delirious. 2. Descriptive of people who are uncaring of the feelings of others, described as insensitive.

inside density   1. The number of persons per room within a residence. 2. The number of rooms per residence. A significant relationship has been found in the United States between persons-per-room density and various kinds of social pathology, including crimes of homicide and rape. Explanations for the relationship given by proxemicists vary. Compare OUTSIDE DENSITY.

insight   1. A grasp or understanding of the self or of relationships that illuminate past experiences or help to solve a problem. The phenomenological reaction is sometimes called the "aha experience" of self-realization. See AHA EXPERIENCE, INTUITION. 2. In psychotherapy, the awareness of underlying, often unconscious, sources of emotional difficulty. Most therapists distinguish between intellectual insight (cognitive awareness that may, on occasion, lead to a change in the maladaptive behavior) and visceral or affect insight (considered by many, especially experimental psychotherapists, to be essential in a successful therapeutic process). See INTELLECTUALIZATION. 3. In psychoanalytic theory, recognition of the unconscious origins of pathological symptoms. See ABREACTION. 4. In Gestalt theory, understanding the essential features of the solution to a problem. 5. (H. A. Simon) In information processing psychology, discovery of a new problem representation (problem space) that permits rapid solution, by intuition or heuristic search, of a previously intractable problem.

insightful learning   In contrast with rote memorization, discriminating between the superficial aspects and the core features of a problem or issue in a way that leads to an understanding of the fundamental essence of the problem or issue, thus permitting transfer of the insight to new problems or issues that are structurally similar but superficially different. A Gestalt concept.

insight therapy   A school of psychotherapy that advocates that deep and lasting personality changes cannot be brought about unless patients cognitively understand the origin of their distorted attitudes and defensive measures. This approach contrasts with methods of psychotherapy that emphasize affect, the removal of symptoms or behavior modification. See DASEIN ANALYSIS.

insistence   An attribute of color perception that concerns a color's impressiveness and that is strongly associated with the luminance of the stimulus. Sometimes considered to be synonymous with brightness.

insistent idea   An idea or trend of thought that tends to recur and dominate a person's mental life. Also known as fixed idea, *idée fixe* (French), obsession.

in situ   A manner of actual being in a single place, the local position, the site; situated in its natural position.

insomnia   1. Inability to sleep, usually caused by transient physical or emotional conditions. 2. Chronic sleeplessness resulting from persistent physical disorders or deep-seated psychological disturbances. Also known as agrypnia, ahypnia, ahypnosia, aypnia. See DYSSOMNIA, INITIAL INSOMNIA, INTERMITTENT INSOMNIA, MIDDLE INSOMNIA, PSEUDOINSOMNIA, SLEEP CHARACTERISTICS, TERMINAL INSOMNIA.

insomnium dream   A type of dream that reflects the current state of a person's psyche and body (according to Artemidorus, who lived in the second century A.D. and wrote an important work on dreams in ancient times, *The Oneirocritica*). Insomnium dreams differ from somnium dreams, which arise from deeper, more obscure sources, a distinction made by Carl Jung.

inspection interval   In a paired associates task, the lapse of time taken to cognize the item pair.

inspection technique   (R. Monroe) A method of evaluating a person taking the Rorschach, looking only for specific patterns deemed to be significant signs of personality characteristics; for example, if the concern is immaturity in an adult, looking for more than the usual number of animal responses (purportedly indicating immaturity).

inspection time (IT)   1. The shortest interval of time between the presentation of a target stimulus and of a backward-masking stimulus for which an individual can correctly make a dichotomous (usually visual or auditory) discrimination on a criterial percentage of test trials. This interval defines an individual's IT. 2. The minimum time that a stimulus must be exposed for individuals to make an accurate judgment about it.

inspiration   1. Inhalation. See INSPIRATION-EXPIRA-TION RATIO. 2. A moment of creative insight, a kind of mental leap, that calls for an effort to follow its implications and may result in a global understanding mixed with excitement, as when suddenly "seeing" a solution to a complex problem or the possibility of a personal advance in a new direction. See CREATIVITY. 3. Motivation.

inspirational group therapy   (F. Cody Marsh) A group approach in which a dynamic leader uses a wide variety of supportive measures to arouse and encourage a group (such as a group of patients in a mental hospital). Among the measures are testimonials, acceptance by the group, esprit de corps, group identification, the realization that others are "in the same boat," sharing of experiences, reassurance, and, in the case of Alcoholics Anonymous, recognition of a higher spiritual power. See CLASS METHOD, GROUP THERAPY.

inspirational motivation   (B. Bass) A factor in transformational leadership involving enthusiasm, optimism, and inspiration as a result of providing meaning and challenge to work. Team spirit is aroused. The leaders get others involved in envisioning future scenarios that are attractive, exciting, and shared. See CHARISMATIC LEADERSHIP, TRANSFORMATIONAL LEADERSHIP.

inspiration-expiration ratio (I/E ratio)   The rate of inspiration of breath divided by the rate of expiration, sometimes used as an index of emotionality and as a test of lying.

instability   A tendency toward lack of self-control, erratic behavior, and rapidly changing or excessive emotions. See EMOTIONALLY UNSTABLE PERSONALITY.

instigation therapy   Behavior therapy in which the therapist serves as a positive model and reinforces the client's progress toward self-regulation and self-evaluation.

instinct   1. An inborn behavior pattern that appears in every physiologically normal, like-sexed member of a species at a given point in its development (for example, nest-building by ants and some fishes, and the mating behaviors of various birds). Such patterns are more readily found in animals other than humans. In humans, the two most likely candidates for being labeled instincts, sex drives and maternal drives, are questioned as they vary greatly in intensity and form of expression and are greatly influenced by learning. Sometimes known as a fixed-action pattern. Kinds of instinct include: AGGRESSIVE, ALTRUISTIC, CLOSED, COLLECTING (MEANING 2), COMPLEMENTARY (MEANING 2), COMPONENT (MEANING 1), DELAYED, HOMING, MOTHER, REPRODUCTIVE, SELF-PRESERVATION, SEXUAL. See ACQUISITIVENESS, IMPRINTING, INSTINCTIVE DRIFT, INSTINCTUAL DRIFT, INSTINCTUAL, SATISFACTION OF INSTINCTS. 2. An impulse to perform an action without immediate awareness of the outcome to which the action may lead. Also known as instinctual drive/impulse. Kinds of instinct include: COLLECTING (MEANING 1), CURIOSITY, DEFERRED, HERD, MASTERY, OPEN, RELIGIOUS, SELF-PRESERVATION, SOCIAL. 3. In psychoanalytic theory, forces behind the tension resulting from needs of the id. Kinds of instinct include: COMPLEMENTARY (MEANING 1), COMPONENT (MEANING 2), DEATH, EGO, EROTIC, LIFE, SELF-PRESERVATION, SEX. See ACQUISITIVE SPIRIT, DESTRUCTIVE DRIVE, DESTRUDO, EROS, LIBIDO.

instinctive action/behavior   Innate activity patterns that develop through maturation and that are released by specific types of stimuli, usually of a species-specific nature. William McDougall saw instinctive behavior as a predisposition to notice certain stimuli, to make movements toward a goal, and to experience an emotional core after completion of the instinctive act. See IMPRINTING, INSTINCT.

instinctive drift   (K. & M. Breland) A tendency of an animal that has been trained with food reward to "misbehave" by "disregarding" the reinforced behavior to "return" to a more basic, instinctive behavior, as in a pig rewarded with food for picking up large wooden coins and placing them in a piggy bank repeatedly drops and roots the coins. Also known as instinctual drift.

instinctive monomania   Obsolete 19th-century phrase for what was later called obsessive-compulsive disorder (OCD).

instinctive stimulus   (W. James) A stimulus the perception of which arouses some normal, congenital mode of behavior.

instinctive tendency   (W. James) A tendency to act so as to produce some generic type of result (usually having biological utility) due to inherited factors, while the specific mode of behavior may be learned. The general drive is inherited (instinctive) but the specific action to satisfy the instinct may be shaped by social or other factors.

instinctoid   A concept that Abraham Maslow's hierarchy of human needs is essentially basic human nature.

instinctoid needs   1. (A. Maslow) Biologically based human needs, the highest of which is striving toward self-actualization. 2. Universal human urges that must be met if humans are to develop to maximum potential.

instinctual   Having to do with an instinct, such as an innate or built-in response pattern.

instinctual aim   An activity that gratifies an instinct and discharges it, restoring the organism to a state of equilibrium; for example, eating food fulfills the aim of the hunger instinct. See AIM INHIBITION.

instinctual anxiety   (S. Freud) Freudian phrase for anxiety based on an unknown or instinctual danger, as opposed to realistic anxiety caused by a known and actual threat from an external source. See FREE-FLOATING ANXIETY.

instinctual diffusion   Separation of the mixture of the death instincts and the life instincts, normally mobilized in the unconscious.

instinctual drift   instinctive drift

instinctual dyscontrol   A dysfunctional lack of control in which a person makes an explosive response to a situation on an impulse, whim, or sudden urge, and tends to have no explanation for the response: "I just did it, I don't know why." See IMPULSE-CONTROL DISORDER.

instinctual fusion   In psychoanalytic theory, a balanced union of life and death instincts.

instinctualization of smell   Olfaction plays a part in coprophilia and in anal fixations, and is an instinctual component in sexual foreplay. In some societies, genital odors are considered a potent sexual stimulant; in the United States and some other cultures, body odors of all kinds are taboo, as indicated by the wide use of perfumes and deodorants. See COMPONENT INSTINCT, COPROPHILIA, SMELL.

instinctual renunciation   In psychoanalytic theory, a refusal of the ego to satisfy a demand of the id. Reasons for instinctual renunciation include the concern that satisfying the instinct would result in a threat to the ego from the outside world or would require disobedience to the superego.

institutional accommodation   A concept that mainstream institutions should make room for the historically disadvantaged.

institutional care   Any type of psychiatric, medical, nursing, or other care or treatment received by a patient in a mental hospital, training school, or other residential institution.

institutionalization   1. Placement of an individual in an institution for therapeutic or correctional purposes. 2. A person's gradual adaptation to institutional life. Cases have been known of people in prisons or mental hospitals who refuse to accept parole or release, having been so institutionalized that they are afraid to venture out into an unknown world.

institutionalized racism   Social practices that support social-political-economic prejudicial attitudes against people because of their "race" or ethnicity. This phenomenon has existed in some form in most cultures throughout history. In the United States, the treatment of African Americans from slave-holding days prior to the Civil War up to relatively recent times has been a continuing example of institutionalized racism. In such cases, it is often the silent majority, who while not necessarily agreeing with the attitude do little or nothing to change it, who allow prejudice to continue.

institutional peonage   The practice of using patients in mental hospitals and inmates of prisons as indentured labor for the maintenance of the institution or even for the production of products (usually sold within the jurisdiction). Peons are deprived of the therapeutic value of financial incentives, and if they are compensated, the compensations or benefits are usually as minor as to be no more than symbolic. See RIGHTS OF DISABLED.

institutional review board (IRB)   A group appointed by an agency or institution to review research proposals originating within the agency to assure compliance with scientific and ethical standards.

institutional sales promotion   Effort designed to promote a favorable attitude toward an entire industry, commodity, or service, not concerned with any particular firm or brand.

institutional transference   In psychodynamics, denoting emotional dependence upon an institution, such as a hospital, rather than upon a health professional on the staff of the institution.

instructional set   An orientation established in participants in an experiment to prepare them for coming events; for example, if a picture of a fish is seen, the participants are to press a particular button, but if the picture does not contain a fish, a different button is to be pressed.

instructional theory of development   A point of view that the environment shapes the development of an unorganized population of neural elements from the moment of ontogenetic zero (the creation of the zygote.) See NEURAL DARWINISM.

instrument   Any tool or device used in measuring, recording, testing, or similar functions; in general, an implement used in performing specific operations, such as cutting, displacing, printing.

instrumental act   Any activity directed toward a specific objective or toward meeting certain needs. Operant acts as distinguished from the reflexive responses that are conditioned through classical (respondent, Pavlovian) techniques.

instrumental activity   1. Any activity directed toward a specific objective or toward satisfying certain needs. 2. An activity that precedes and makes possible consummatory activity, not only persisting but even increasing in intensity over time if not satisfied (such as the persistence of a person in searching for water in a desert).

instrumental aggression   Hostile action directed at acquiring or retrieving an object, territory, or privilege. See HOSTILE AGGRESSION.

instrumental behavior   Any performance used to accomplish a purpose or satisfy a need. The consequence of the behavior reinforces the individual by positive reward or by providing removal of aversive stimuli.

instrumental behavior of animals   Utilization by animals of objects, as in birds making nests from twigs, or beavers constructing dams from trees. Unusual animal behaviors can also be generated by conditioning, such as seals playing musical instruments, or bears riding bicycles. Animals have been taught various behaviors that are useful to humans, such as dogs to bring in the newspaper, and monkeys to do a variety of simple tasks such as turning lights on and off for quadriplegics. See ANIMAL IMITATION, COMPARATIVE PSYCHOLOGY.

instrumental conditioning/learning   Any form of conditioning in which the subject's response is instrumental in reaching a goal, as when a rat is trained to run a maze or push a lever to obtain food. The immediate consequences of the response, whether pleasant or obnoxious, determine the likelihood that the response will be repeated. Also known as Skinnerian conditioning, Type II conditioning, Type R conditioning. The concept markedly differs from classical conditioning (also known as Pavlovian learning, respondent conditioning). Similar to operant conditioning.

instrumental dependence   A tendency to depend on others for accomplishing a task while engaging in other activities.

instrumental error   Constant error in research data due to some defect in the measuring instrument (for example, a measuring instrument that is poorly calibrated such as a weighing scale that always over- or underestimates weight). See INSTRUMENT DRIFT.

instrumentalism   1. (J. Dewey) Translation of theory into practice: the solution of problems by a scientific application of intelligence and critical inquiry and the evaluation of ideas by testing them in actual situations. 2. A tendency to exploit other persons for pleasure or profit.

instrumentality theory A point of view that a person's attitude about an event depends upon the perception of the event's function as an instrument in bringing about desirable or undesirable consequences. Two prominent examples of this cognitive approach to work motivation are Vroom's Valence-Instrumentality-Expectancy theory and the Porter-Lawler model.

instrumental learning See INSTRUMENTAL CONDITIONING, OPERANT CONDITIONING.

instrumental orientation Stereotypical attitudes of workers about task orientation, such as feelings of independence and maintaining emotional control. See EXPRESSIVE ORIENTATION.

instrumental-relativist orientation Phrase sometimes applied to the second stage of Lawrence Kohlberg's preconventional level of moral reasoning, when seemingly "unselfish" acts are performed only if they benefit the actor in the long run.

instrumental response Any response that achieves a goal or contributes to its achievement; a response effective in gaining a reward or avoiding pain (for example, a rat pressing a bar to obtain food). See INSTRUMENTAL BEHAVIOR.

instrumentation 1. The apparatus used in a study. 2. Learning that involves the invention or use of instruments; for example, a chimpanzee uses a small stick to get a big stick that will in turn help to achieve a goal such as retrieving a banana. See AHA REACTION for an illustration of the example.

instrument drift In research, instruments may go out of adjustment and may threaten the validity of results if they are not recalibrated or adjusted; for example, in psychophysical experiments, a device that generates stimuli must remain calibrated. In one study on human sexuality, vaginal plethysmographs had to be frequently recalibrated for accuracy. By extension, applied to gradual changes over time in the subjective standards used by researchers in scoring tests and questionnaires.

instrument factor (R. B. Cattell) A factor appearing among similar instruments or devices of measurement when the same personality factors are measured by a different array of devices.

insufficient deterrence hypothesis (L. Festinger) A postulate that the severity of a minimally sufficient deterrent is inversely related to the degree of internalization of the prohibition. The milder the threatened punishment, assuming the individual refrains from the forbidden behavior, the more likely that the prohibitions will be internalized.

insula of Reil   island of Reil

insulation See EMOTIONAL INSULATION.

insulin (A. Sharpey-Schäfer, F. Banting, C. H. Best) A hormone from the islands of Langerhans in the pancreas that controls glucose utilization.

insulin-coma therapy (ICT) (M. Sakel) A now repudiated treatment for schizophrenia developed in the 1930s, in which insulin is used to produce a coma. Also known as insulin-shock therapy.

intake interview/process The initial interview between a potential client and a member of the therapeutic team that usually begins the diagnostic interview process. Phrase is particularly used in reference to admission to a mental health facility.

intake process   intake interview

integral phenomenology Attempting to understand people in depth by examining personal documents, such as letters, diaries, speeches. Also known as psychological autopsy.

integrate type Another name for the B type of the Marburg School. See B TYPE.

integrated context   context Beta (effect)

integrated model In industrial/organizational psychology, an administrative relationship used in evaluation between the program director and at least two production units to determine the quality of collaboration. Also known as dependent model. See SEGREGATED MODEL.

integrated motivation component (R. B. Cattell) One of the two main second-order factors found in the pattern of intercorrelations among objective tests of motivation strength. It represents a conscious, integrated source of motivation. The other main second-order factor is the unintegrated motivation component.

integrated personalities (B. Neugarten) Characteristics of people who know themselves, who can enjoy themselves and live a full life.

integrated therapy A form of treatment that combines two or more systems of thought; for example, Transactional Analysis and Gestalt Therapy are often combined. See ECLECTIC THERAPY.

integration In general, the unification of parts into a totality. The developmental process in which separate drives, experiences, abilities, values, and personality characteristics are gradually brought together into an organized whole. See PERSONALITY INTEGRATION, PRIMARY INTEGRATION, SECONDARY INTEGRATION.

integrative bargaining Negotiating that searches for "win-win" solutions that benefit both sides.

integrative learning 1. The process of learning tasks that involve simultaneous or successive functioning of several modalities, as in reading and writing. 2. (R. B. Cattell) The learning of a new course of action which performs the services of several earlier, unintegrated responses.

integrative properties The characteristic tendencies of living organisms to maintain functional integrity.

integrative therapy (W. A. Urban) A combination of techniques from different therapeutic modalities based on the therapist's judgment of which particular techniques will provide the greatest benefit for the client at any given moment. See ECLECTIC THERAPY.

integrity 1. Completeness of structure; an unimpaired condition. 2. The quality of moral consistency, honesty, and truthfulness. See EGO INTEGRITY VERSUS DESPAIR.

integrity group (O. H. Mower) An aggregate of people that has a strong explicit moral component. A therapy group with experienced members serving as models of honesty, responsibility, and involvement. The requirements of a successful psychotherapeutic group include openness and honesty on the part of everyone involved. See GROUP THERAPY, INTEGRITY THERAPY THEORY, INTERPERSONAL MORALITY.

integrity test   An instrument such as a questionnaire intended to measure honesty.

integrity testing   Generally the use of written or physiological tests to assess honesty. The concept was supported by the American Psychological Association's *The Prediction of Trustworthiness in Pre-Employment Selection Decisions.*

integrity therapy theory   (O. H. Mower) A point of view in which neuroses are considered to be a form of moral failure (sins). The sufferer should be focused on taking responsibility for misdeeds committed and live up to an acceptable code of ethics. See INTEGRITY GROUPS.

integrity vs despair   (E. Erikson) The eighth and final of Erik Erikson's stages of psychosocial development; in old age the person looks back at the past and either concludes that he or she has made a "contribution" and has had a meaningful existence, or that life has been meaningless. See ERIKSON'S STAGES OF PSYCHOSOCIAL DEVELOPMENT.

intellect   The cognitive functions of the mind, including such capacities as reasoning, conceiving, judging, and relating.

intellection   The process of forming concepts or judgments.

intellective soul   See SENSITIVE SOUL.

intellectual functions/operations   Mental functions involving the acquisition, development, and application of ideas, and the formulation of hypotheses and theories in efforts to achieve the solution of problems. These functions include such processes as cognition, memory, judgment, evaluation, and creative thinking.

intellectual impoverishment   Depletion or diminution of intellectual resources in individuals or groups of individuals. Produced by the absence of sufficient intellectual stimulation. See INTELLIGENCE TESTS AND INTELLIGENCE.

intellectual inadequacy   See MENTAL RETARDATION, MILD MENTAL RETARDATION.

intellectual insight   In psychotherapy, objective, rational awareness of experiences or relationships that provide the basis for better understanding of self and others and may lead to still further discoveries about self at a deeper level. See ABREACTION, INSIGHT.

intellectualism   1. In metaphysics, the position that ultimate reality is based on ideas or on reason. 2. A doctrine positing that all mental processes, including emotions, can be explained in terms of cognitive functions.

intellectualization   A defense mechanism in which emotional problems are attacked abstractly or concealed by excessive intellectual activity (for example, a diffident person may avoid the hazards of social intercourse by "keeping his or her head in books").

intellectual maturity   1. Generally, a high level of good judgment, often combined with wisdom. 2. The young-adulthood or fully-adult stage of intellectual development.

intellectual monomania   A 19th-century phrase for a type of "partial insanity" characterized by concentration on a certain single false idea, roughly equivalent to paranoia.

intellectual plasticity   A capacity to change ideas; openness to new and different concepts.

intellectual rigidity   A tendency to be inflexible on cognitive matters or to be unable to change past patterns of thinking. As a disorder, it is evidenced by inability to deal with new situations that could be potentially beneficial to that person. See CATASTROPHIC REACTION, INTELLIGENCE TESTS AND INTELLIGENCE.

intellectual stimulation   (B. Bass) A factor of transformational leadership involving the stimulation of subordinates' efforts to be innovative and creative by questioning assumptions, reframing problems, and approaching old situations in new ways. When a mistake is made, the attention is on "what" happened and "what" can be learned instead of "who" was responsible. Creativity is encouraged. Followers' ideas are not criticized simply because they differ from the leaders' ideas. Constructive conflict over perspective is viewed as resulting in better solutions to difficult problems. See TRANSFORMATIONAL LEADERSHIP.

intellectual subaverage functioning   Generally denoting an intelligence quotient (IQ) more than one standard deviation below the mean score obtained on an intelligence test. However, people with above-average IQs may function well below their potential for many reasons. See ACADEMIC ACHIEVEMENT DISORDER, ACADEMIC INHIBITION, INTELLIGENCE TESTS AND INTELLIGENCE, UNDERACHIEVEMENT.

intelligence (I)   1. Originally, information. The 1905 Binet-Simon Scale was designed to measure level of information acquired by children of different ages. The later Stanford-Binet Scale used a formula (devised by Stern in 1914) for computing the "intelligence quotient." See INTELLIGENCE QUOTIENT. 2. Generally, wisdom, cognitive capability, intellectual acumen, ability to profit from experience. 3. Statistically, intelligence is divided in two basic ways: First *g* (for general intelligence) and *s* for special intelligence. 4. (L. M. Terman) An ability to carry on abstract thinking. See ABSTRACT INTELLIGENCE. 5. (S. S. Colvin) An ability to learn to adjust oneself to the environment. 6. (R. Pintner) An ability to adapt oneself in positive ways to new situations in life. 7. (W. Woodrow) A capacity to learn or to profit from experience. 8. (C. S. Spearman) The eduction of relationships and correlates. 9. (H. English) A person's problem-solving and discriminating responses that are typical for a given age level. 10. (G. Stoddard) An ability to effectively attempt activities that are characterized by difficulty. 11. (A. Binet) An ability to judge, comprehend and reason. 12. (D. Wechsler) A person's capacity to act purposefully, to think rationally, and to respond effectively to the environment. 13. (F. Galton) The speed at which a person can respond to various physiological cues. 14. (V. Henmon) A capacity for knowledge and the knowledge possessed. Other kinds of intelligence include: ANIMAL, ARTIFICIAL, BIOLOGICAL, BORDERLINE INTELLECTUAL, COGNITIVE, CONCRETE, CONSERVED, CONTEXTUAL, CRYSTALLIZED, EMOTIONAL, EVERYDAY, FLUID (GENERAL), GENERAL, MARGINAL, MECHANICAL, MULTIPLE, NONVERBAL, REPRESENTATIVE, SENSORIMOTOR, SOCIAL, SPATIAL, VERBAL. Also see INTELLIGENCE TESTS AND INTELLIGENCE.

intelligence quotient (IQ or I.Q.)   (W. Stern, L. Terman, D. Wechsler) A rating of intelligence based on psychological tests, originally calculated by dividing the mental age (MA) by the chronological age (CA), and multiplying by 100 to eliminate the decimal. Later IQs were determined by administering tests to large groups of age peers assumed to be representative of a population group, assigning 100 IQ to the mean score, and using the normal curve with standard deviation 15 for others (for example, the 25th percentile became IQ 90 and the 75th percentile IQ 110). Some critics consider the concept of IQ deeply flawed, reflecting a purported biological determinism that often serves racist purposes. They point out that such tests measure prior academic learning and are not a valid measure of underlying inherent ability. See CONSTANCY OF THE IQ, CULTURE-FAIR TESTS, CULTURE-FREE TESTS, DEVIATION IQ, GLOBAL INTELLIGENCE, MULTIPLE INTELLIGENCE, SIX-HOUR RETARDED CHILD.

intelligence quotient (IQ) stability   Consistency of IQ over time. Whereas measurements of intelligence using IQ-type tests indicate fair stability after the age of six, measurements of intelligence of infants show low correlation with measures taken later. See BERKELEY GROWTH STUDY, INTELLIGENCE TESTS AND INTELLIGENCE.

intelligence scale/test   An examination composed of mental tasks of graded difficulty standardized by use on a representative sample of the general age-peer population; for example, the Stanford-Binet Intelligence Test, the Wechsler Adult Intelligence Scale (WAIS), and the Wechsler Intelligence Scale for Children (WISC). Specific intelligence scales and tests include: ARMY ALPHA, ARMY BETA, ARMY GENERAL CLASSIFICATION TEST, ARTHUR POINT OF PERFORMANCE TESTS SCALE, BLACK INTELLIGENCE TEST OF CULTURAL HOMOGENEITY, CALIFORNIA TESTS OF MENTAL MATURITY, CATTELL INFANT INTELLIGENCE SCALE, CAVD, COGNITIVE ABILITIES TEST, DRAW-A-MAN TEST, DRAW-A-PERSON TEST, HERING BINET TEST, HISKEY-NEBRASKA TEST OF LEARNING APTITUDE, IMMEDIATE TEST, KENT EGY TEST, KUHLMANN-ANDERSON TESTS, MANNIKIN TEST, MILLER ANALOGIES TEST, NATIONAL INTELLIGENCE TEST, OTIS QUICK SCORING MENTAL ABILITY TEST, PEABODY PICTURE VOCABULARY TEST, PINTNER PATERSON SCALE OF PERFORMANCE TESTS, PORTEUS MAZE, PRIMARY MENTAL ABILITIES TEST, PROGRESSIVE MATRICES TEST, QUICK TEST, SCHOLASTIC APTITUDE TEST, STERNBERG TRIARCHIC ABILITIES TEST, TERMAN GROUP TEST OF MENTAL ABILITIES, THREE PAPER TEST, WECHSLER-BELLEVUE SCALES. See INTELLIGENCE TESTS AND INTELLIGENCE.

intelligence test   See INTELLIGENCE SCALE.

intelligence test item types   Below are examples of items on individual intelligence tests. The first seven are verbal; the next six are nonverbal items.

(a) Information: Who was the second president of the United States?

(b) Arithmetic: If you had seven dollars and spent a dollar and a quarter, how much money would you have left?

(c) Similarities: In what ways are a bicycle and a motorcycle similar?

(d) Differences: What is the difference between stinginess and poverty?

(e) Vocabulary: What is a bunion?

(f) Sentence rearrangement: Showing the participant a card with the following printed words and instructing him or her to rearrange them to make a sentence: do do you when do to not nothing know what.

(g) Proverbs: What does this saying mean? "A stitch in time saves nine."?

(h) Bridge-making: The examiner makes a bridge out of three blocks and then asks a child to do the same with three different blocks.

(i) Block Design: Given nine blocks, the participant is asked to arrange them so that when assembled, the top of the blocks will form a specific picture.

(j) Planning: Showing the participant a map of a park with the instructions "If you lost your purse in this triangular park at night, trace with this pencil the path you would choose to try to find the purse."

(k) Object assembly: Giving the participant a Jigsaw puzzle of a bird and the instructions "Put these pieces together as quickly as possible."

(l) Object identification: Showing the participant a tea cup. "What is this called?"

(m) Block tapping: Putting three small blocks in front of a participant, and saying: "Do what I do," then tapping them in the order of 1-3-2-1 with another block, and then giving the tapping block to the participant who must try to follow the order.

(n) Cartoon arrangement: Showing five cartoons that originally were in the order 1-2-3-4-5, but are now placed in the order of 3-1-4-2-5 and saying: "Place these in the correct order."

intelligence tests and intelligence   Instruments which, when properly used on individuals of a proper population, provide a rough indication primarily of academic potential. Every test given has to be determined as to appropriateness for the person, checked for proper administration, and interpreted by a trained examiner. No test has yet been developed which measures "intelligence" as that concept is commonly conceived.

intemperance   Behavior that is extreme. Lacking self-control, especially in consumption of alcohol.

intensity (I)   1. The quantitative value of a stimulus. 2. The strength of any process or tendency, such as an impulse or emotion. See DIMENSIONS OF CONSCIOUSNESS.

intensity theory of tropisms   A point of view that tropismic orientation of an organism is due to unequal intensity of stimulation of symmetrical points on the organism; for example, newly-spawned salmon orient themselves in response to the sun shining differentially on their sun-sensitive bodies. To avoid the sun's intensity they increase their depth in the water by heading downstream (to deeper water) and continue until they reach the open ocean. See TAXIS, TROPISM.

intensive   Marked by intensity, particularly forms of treatment in terms of exposure or those using large doses of substances. See INTENSIVE PSYCHOTHERAPY.

intensive-care syndrome   A type of unfavorable reaction observed in certain intensive-care patients who are immobilized in an isolated, unfamiliar environment, similar to the effect of sensory deprivation or of being confined in an isolated cell.

intensive group experience   (K. Lewin) Any of a variety of group interactions that have as their purpose helping individuals to be more aware of themselves in relating to others, rather than as in therapy. The interactions tend to be of an "here-and-now" and an "in-your-face" orientation, with members often being critical of other members' behaviors in the group. See ENCOUNTER GROUPS, INTENSIVE GROUP, SENSITIVITY TRAINING, T GROUPS.

intensive group   Generally a small group of people who come together periodically with or without a therapist or leader to engage in interpersonal experiences designed to expand awareness of self and of others.

intensive psychotherapy   An extensive and prolonged investigation and treatment of a person's concerns and problems. The intensive quality stems from both the psychodynamic nature of the discussions and the length or number of sessions. Contrasts with "counseling," which tends to remain focused on relatively benign real-life issues.

intent analysis   The assignment of verbal statements into various categories done for research purposes; for example, statements made by a client at the beginning and at the end of therapy are checked for percentages of optimistic and pessimistic statements.

intention   A decision to act in a certain way, or an impulse for purposeful action, whether conscious or not.

intentional accident   A purposive accident. See PURPOSEFUL ACCIDENT.

intentional behavior   (J. Piaget) Goal-oriented activity emerging between eight and 12 months in which the child employs a number of strategies to achieve various ends or effects.

intentional family   A family neither based on blood relations nor marriage. A familial grouping of people who either live together as though they were a traditional family or consider themselves as part of a family even though having separate domiciles. See DOMESTIC PARTNERSHIPS.

intentional forgetting   Not remembering due to repression or to an unconscious or conscious wish to forget.

intentional inexistence   A basic principle in Franz Brentano's act psychology that maintains that the object of a psychological act or process exists inherently in the act or process itself. For instance, in leaning over and smelling a rose, the rose and its smell are captured as the core objects of the intentional act of trying to smell the flower. Also known as intentionality.

intentionality   A characteristic of psychic acts that always refer to, or intend, something outside themselves. See ACT PSYCHOLOGY, INTENTIONAL INEXISTENCE.

intentional learning   Acquisition of knowledge or mastery of a skill that depends on attention or voluntary concentration. Compare INCIDENTAL LEARNING.

intentional operating process   (D. M. Wegner) Conscious attempts to control cognition sometimes blocked by monitoring processes.

intentional response   An explicit movement, such as one requested by the experimenter; for example the pressing of a button by an experimental participant after the occurrence of an expected stimulus in a controlled laboratory experiment.

intention movements   Behavior that precedes other behavior; signs of forthcoming action (for example, a cat arching its back and puffing out its tail before it attacks).

intention tremor   A tremor associated with voluntary movement, as when the hand trembles while about to perform a delicate task. Also known as kinetic tremor.

INTER   1. See INTERLOCKING SCHEDULE OF REINFORCEMENT. 2. See INTERPOLATED SCHEDULE OF REINFORCEMENT.

interaction   Relationship between two or more systems, persons or groups resulting in reciprocal influences.

interactional model of anxiety   (N. S. Endler & D. Magnusson) The assumption that state anxiety and trait anxiety are both multidimensional and that the person and the situation must be considered in predicting anxiety responses.

interactional psychotic disorder   A psychotic-like reaction in children between ages two and five who had previously demonstrated normal behavior, characterized by an abnormal symbiotic co-dependency type of relationship usually between the child and the mother or mother figure.

interactional synchrony   In dance therapy, movement of a listener in synchronicity with the speech and movements of the speaker.

interaction analysis   Assessment of the stimulus and response patterns of participants in a group. A major concern is the degree to which any person's behavior or responses are modified by the opinions and attitudes of others.

interaction effect   In the analysis of variance, indicates the joint effect of two or more independent variables upon the dependent variable (for example, the relation between X and dependent variable Y is positive when Z is high, but negative when Z is low).

interactionism   1. Belief in the existence of a body and a mind, each affecting the other (for example, the philosophy of René Descartes). See MIND-BODY PROBLEM. 2. (N. S. Endler & D. Magnusson) A model of personality stating that actual behavior is a function of a continuous process of multidirectional interaction (feedback) between individuals and the situations they encounter. It posits a continuous and ongoing process whereby situations affect persons, who in turn affect situations. 3. In social psychology, point of view that personal traits interact with social variables to determine a person's social behavior.

interaction-process analysis (IPA)   (R. F. Bales) A format for recording the behavior of individuals interacting in groups. The format is of the checklist variety. Rows list the names of individuals and columns specify particular behaviors. Thus, if in a measured period of time participant A does behavior "smile" four times, after A and under "smile" a 4 will appear.

interaction territory   A space around two people or a small group of persons while they converse. Outsiders are aware that the interaction territory should not be invaded as long as the interaction is in progress. Also known as bubble. See GROUP SPACE, INTERPERSONAL DISTANCE, PROXEMICS.

interaction variance   The proportion of the variance due to the interactions between the independent variables.

interactive context   context Beta (effect)

interactive dualism   A doctrine positing that mind and body are different but affect each other.

interactive episode   An event that occurs during psychotherapy, characterized by a client making a sudden and often unexpected deviation from a prepared script to a new level of communication.

interactive explanation   (J. L. Moreno) Explanatory descriptions of behavior based on in situ situations that call for immediate reactions to social stimuli. Behind all such responses are to be found persons' philosophies of life, histories of experiences, as well as their values, intentions, and immediate goals. See PSYCHODRAMA.

interactive score   (R. B. Cattell) A measure indicating the effect of a person on the physical environment.

interaural difference   The difference in the sound perceived by each ear. The detection of the location of sound depends on two aspects in relation to the two ears: (a) the relative intensity, and (b) the time difference.

interaural rivalry   Competition within the auditory system to comprehend conflicting inputs received simultaneously in both ears. Such stimulation may be employed diagnostically in the study of temporal-lobe lesions or surgical effects on brains. Patients recall less of the information heard in the left ear if a lesion is on the right side, and vice versa. See COCKTAIL-PARTY EFFECT.

interbehavioral psychology   **interbehaviorism**

interbehaviorism   A behavioral system of psychology created by J. R. Kantor (1888–1984), a logician, historian, and critic of psychology, who developed interbehaviorism as an example of the appropriate way of handling difficult concepts. Rejecting "mental fictions" that result from human dualistic culture, he focused on the interbehavioral field, the constantly evolving interaction between the "response functions" of the organism and the "stimulus functions" of the environment. Also known as interbehavioral psychology. See MATERIALISM as a solution to the mind-body problem.

intercalation   The automatic, illogical insertion of irrelevant words or sound between words or phrases.

intercerebral fibers   commissural fibers

intercorrelations   The correlations between each variable and every other variable in a group of variables.

interdental sigmatism   In speech disorders, the substitution of /th/ for /s/ and /z/, a form of lisping. Also known as signation. See LISPING.

interdependency   In Gestalt psychology, configurations are interdependent wholes with parts that cannot be changed without altering the whole.

interdisciplinary approach   Cooperative behavior by members of various professions to assess and treat individuals or groups or to undertake research projects that transcend traditional disciplinary borders. Also known as multidisciplinary approach.

interdisciplinary environmental design   The design of buildings, houses, and other facilities with contributions from experts in many areas of environmental expertise, such as architecture, psychology, ecology, engineering and social sciences.

interego   Wilhelm Stekel's suggested term for Sigmund Freud's superego, based on the point of view that the part of the superego associated with moral standards serves as a mediator or compromiser rather than as a vigilant authority.

interest   An attitude characterized by a desire to give selective attention to something significant to the individual. Likes and dislikes for activities and objects.

interest factors   In industrial psychology, the vocational likes, dislikes, desires, and goals of persons combined with personality factors in predicting probable success in an employment assignment. May include such information as hobbies, recreation, leisure-time activities, and previous jobs.

interestingness   A scale sometimes used in the evaluation of art. On a scale of uninteresting–interesting, the judged interestingness of items tends to increase with growth in the item's complexity and uncertainty.

interest inventories/tests   Self-report descriptions in which respondents express likes or dislikes for activities and attitudes, especially as associated with different types of work. These are typically compared with the interest patterns of successful members of different occupations. Other interest tests include the Brainard Occupational Preference Inventory, the Minnesota Vocational Interest Inventory, the Gordon Occupational Check List, the Thurstone Interest Schedule, the Forer Vocational Survey, the Geist Picture Interest Inventory, the Holland Vocational Preference Inventory, and the Guilford-Zimmerman Interest Inventory. See KUDER PREFERENCE RECORD-VOCATIONAL, STRONG-CAMPBELL INTEREST INVENTORY.

interface   The point at which two systems or components of a system meet and interconnect. Term is used as a noun, verb, or adjective.

interfemoral sex   Literally, sex between the thighs. Sexual relations characterized by moving the male genitals on or between the partner's thighs with contact stopping short of penetration.

interference   1. In perception, the reduction of the strength of a sensation due to separate sources of physical waves, be it in light or sound, occurring at the same time as the stimulus and leading to diminution of the effect. 2. In learning, negative transfer. The learning of a new habit or response may take longer or require more trials if a similar but somewhat different habit or response has already been learned than if the earlier learning had not occurred. Also, trying to learn two similar activities at the same time may result in the rate of improvement of both being reduced. 3. In learning, proactive inhibition or retroactive inhibition. The recall of material that has been learned is reduced due to other learning that occurred either before (proactive) or after (retroactive) the material in question. Kinds of interference include: ARBITRARY, HABIT, INTRASERIAL, PROACTIVE, RECIPROCAL, REPRODUCTIVE, RETROACTIVE, SOCIAL, THEME.

interference effects   1. Inhibition due to opposing response tendencies as in the explanation of experimental extinction. 2. Interference with learning by overloading neural activity in the brain. The effects have been demonstrated experimentally by introducing electrical stimulation of certain brain centers in animals during training in visual discrimination, bar-pressing, or similar activities.

interference method A technique for the study of memory in which the memory of one learned task is measured by the degree to which it interferes with the learning of a second task that involves new relations between the material of the first task and the responses in the second task.

interference theory (of forgetting) (J. A. McGeoch, B. J. Underwood, L. Postman) In learning, a point of view based on the idea that information is destroyed or forgotten when new, incoming information conflicts or interferes with it rather than by the mere passage of time. See DECAY THEORY.

interference tube A device consisting of a tube that can be modified so that new tones of any degree of purity can be produced from other tones.

interflection Ambient light bouncing against the sides of a room and its contents.

intergluteal sex 1. Pressing the penis against or between the partner's buttocks. 2. See ANAL SEX.

intergroup-contact hypothesis A postulate that the prejudice between two hostile groups can be diminished and positive attitudes fostered by mere social contact.

intergroup culture conflict Problems between two or more cultural groups who live in close proximity, when the practices of one of the groups negatively affect another or others, as when one group makes a great deal of noise (such as shooting fire crackers) in celebration on a particular day when another group practices meditation on that same day.

intergroup problem-solving The attempt to solve problems by discussions between all members of the group.

interhemispheric transfer The transfer of memory traces or learning experiences from one cerebral hemisphere to the other. It can be demonstrated with experiments using laboratory animals and can be observed in humans who transfer handedness from the right to the left hand, or vice versa, following an injury to or loss of a hand.

interindividual differences Variations between persons on one or more traits; for example, variations in intelligence. See INTRAINDIVIDUAL DIFFERENCES.

interiority (B. Neugarten) A tendency to become preoccupied with inner experiences with increasing age.

interiorized imitation Phrase used by Jean Piaget to describe a child's ability to form a mental image during the period of sensorimotor intelligence. This period starts during the second year of life when the child begins to manipulate representations as contrasted with direct, objective action. From there on, images can be combined and organized, and even imitated on their own, as in make-believe play.

interitem consistency (A. Anastasi) A process in the construction of a single test in which every item of the test is examined for its relationship to the test as a whole. Items are discarded that do not correlate highly with the test as a whole for the purpose of generating a test of high internal reliability. The test itself becomes the criterion for including or excluding an item. See TEST CONSTRUCTION.

interitem interval The time-spacing between the presentation of successive items in a learning experiment. Spacing-times usually are identical. In some intelligence tests, a series of numbers are to be repeated back, and the numbers are to be presented to the participant at the rate of one per second.

interjectional theory A point of view that spoken language arose from the automatic utterance of exclamations or ejaculations. See ORIGIN-OF-LANGUAGE THEORIES.

interjudge reliability The degree of consistency of measurement obtained when different judges independently evaluate the same individual or material.

interkinesis Interphase; the period between two mitoses (cell divisions) of a nucleus.

interlocking items Test items on which a participant's response to any item is affected by a preceding item or by responses to it.

interlocking pathologies (N. Ackerman) Multiple dysfunctions in a family that are interdependent as expressed and maintained; for example one quasi-psychotic parent can generate a situation where other members become quasi-psychotic in different ways.

interlocking schedule of reinforcement (INTER) An intermittent-reinforcement schedule characterized by a decreasing ratio of required responses per reinforcement. Also known as interlocking reinforcement schedule.

interlocking triangles Basic units of family relations of three-person sets, such as three generations of women, a parent and two children.

intermale aggression In animals, a tendency of especially adolescent males of some species to compete with older males for supremacy, especially during mating season. There appears to be evidence that male children are more aggressive than female children and their aggression is mostly directed to other males. See ANIMAL AGGRESSION.

intermarriage 1. Marriage between individuals belonging to different racial, ethnic, or religious groups. 2. A marriage between two closely related persons, as in a consanguineous marriage.

intermediate-care facilities Hospital-care services for moderately ill patients. Patients may be incapable of fully independent living and usually require routine medication and nursing care. Intermediate care generally is second to intensive care in a hospital's progressive patient-care priorities.

intermediate gene A dominant gene modified by a recessive gene so that the offspring resembles a blend of the parental traits; for example, genetic traits for red and white flowers may blend to effect an intermediate expression for pink flowers.

intermediate gene effects The capacity of some genes to "work together" with other genes, rather than one being dominant over the other, so that each get expressed in some aspect of the organism.

intermediate precentral area A region in the frontal lobes lying anterior to the precentral motor area. Involved in motor functions. Also known as Brodmann's area 6, premotor area.

intermission   The interval between episodes of a mental disorder, when the symptoms temporarily subside or disappear, as frequently occurs between episodes of manic depressive disorders.

intermittence tone   A tone produced by interrupting a tone of uniform pitch and renewing it. When interruptions and renewals succeed each other at a rapid rate, a secondary tone is produced whose pitch is determined by the rate of succession.

intermittent explosive disorder   A pathological condition of impulse control, the diagnosis depending on several episodes in which aggressive impulses are suddenly released and expressed in serious assaults or destruction of property. The outburst is often called an "attack" or "spell," and usually is grossly out of proportion to any precipitating stress. There are no signs of generalized impulsive or aggressive behavior between episodes, nor is the condition caused by any other mental disorder.

intermittent insomnia   Periods of insomnia occurring several times a night, followed by difficulty in falling asleep. Occurs primarily in middle-aged and older persons suffering from such disorders as hypertension and stress.

intermittent processing   serial processing

intermittent psychosis   Phrase applied primarily in Europe to manic-depressive (bipolar) psychosis to indicate that the episodes are recurrent.

intermittent reinforcement   In operant conditioning, any pattern of reinforcement that is not continuous; periodic or aperiodic reinforcement. See PARTIAL REINFORCEMENT.

internal boundary   See EGO BOUNDARY.

internal capsule   (Vesalius, T. Willis) A large tract of nerve fibers that penetrates the corpus striatum. Contains afferent and efferent fibers from all parts of the cerebral cortex as they converge near the brainstem.

internal conflict   intrapsychic conflict

internal consistency   The degree to which all of the items on a test measure the same thing.

internal control   Essentially, the same as self-control, obeying rules or following orders even though no one else is monitoring or watching (for example, a motorist, stopping a car for a red traffic light and not proceeding until the light turns green even though there is no other vehicle or person in sight).

internal culture conflict   Problems generated by a small group that "resides" within a larger group, when certain values or practices of the smaller inner group conflict with the values of the larger group.

internal dialogue   (D. Meichenbaum) Mental self-discourse, talking back and forth with the self internally as if in two-sided conversation, such as "If I do, some will be angry with me." "If I don't, some will be disappointed with me." See SELF-TALK.

internal environment   (C. Bernard) The metabolic, hormonal, homeostasis, and those chemical, thermal, or other influences that affect the normal functioning of the body organs, excluding factors that are external to the body.

internal equity   A situation where everyone gets privileges equally and all are treated fairly in terms of their capacities and abilities.

internal experimental validity (threats to)   See THREATS TO INTERNAL EXPERIMENTAL VALIDITY.

internal-external scale   (J. Rotter) A scale assessing locus of control, the degree to which a person feels controlled by either internal factors (the self) or external factors (the environment). Also known as the I-E Locus of Control Scale, Internal-External Locus of Control Scale (I-E Scale).

internal feedback   A form of conditioning in which the response of an organ or organ system of the body influences the nervous system. Sometimes known as physiological feedback. See BIOFEEDBACK.

internal frame of reference   A person's subjective view of the world.

internal frustration   Negative subjective reactions to goals based on deficiencies acknowledged by the person rather than from outside barriers. Essentially, the person is aware that it is lack of capacity that is the cause of the frustration.

internal granular layer   Layer IV of the cerebral cortex. See CORTICAL LAMINA for more information.

internal grouping   A tendency of people to form subgroups within any larger group based on some conception of similarity. The grouping may be based on criteria such as gender (sex), "race," nationality, physical size, geographical factors, educational levels. Sometimes known as the birds of a feather phenomenon.

internal hair cells (of ear)   One of the two types of hair cells in the organ of Corti (of the inner ear or cochlea). These cells form a single row of auditory hairs, separated from four rows of outer hair cells by other tissue structures. Also known as inner hair cells. Compare EXTERNAL HAIR CELLS (OF EAR). See HAIR CELLS.

internal inequity   1. The unfair distribution of rewards within an organization. Compare EXTERNAL INEQUITY. 2. A group situation in which there is uneven distribution of privileges or treatment in terms of personal capacities and abilities; for example, the boss's relative getting special privileges.

internal inhibition   (I. P. Pavlov) Any neural inhibitory process that reduces a conditioned-response magnitude despite the use of reinforcement.

internalization   Incorporation of attitudes, standards, and opinions of others, and particularly those of parents, into the personality. In psychoanalytic theory, internalization is considered a major process involved in the formation of the superego.

internalized psychodrama   A guided-by-a-therapist fantasy in which clients pretend to interact with important persons in their lives, usually speaking both parts, but sometimes with the therapist or an assistant playing the part of the absent person. See FANTASY, PSYCHODRAMA.

internalized speech   Silent self-conversation in which the person for example, argues a course of action, rehearses an act, or reassures the self when feeling threatened. See INNER LANGUAGE, INTERNAL DIALOGUE, SELF-TALK.

internalizers (J. Rotter) People who believe that they are in charge of their behavior, that they control what they do. Compare EXTERNALIZERS.

internal locus of control According to Julian Rotter, the belief that a person is in control of own destiny, and that humans get out of life what they put into life. See EXTERNAL LOCUS OF CONTROL, FREE WILL, SOFT DETERMINISM.

internal rectus The medial extrinsic eye muscle that turns the eyeball inward.

internal rewards Feelings of satisfaction as a consequent of achievements. Compare EXTERNAL REWARDS.

internal rhythm Biological rhythm.

internal senses The interoceptive and proprioceptive systems within the body that convey information to the brain. See INTEROCEPTOR, PROPRIOCEPTOR.

internal speech Covert speech. See INTERNALIZED SPEECH, SUBVOCALIZATION.

internal-state ratings In psychological esthetics, one of several methods of evaluating a person's reactions to a work of art. Based on a person's mood while exposed to a pattern. Other types of esthetic rating scales include descriptive ratings and evaluative ratings. See STYLISTIC RATINGS.

internal validation The validity of experimental results assured by manipulation of the independent variable by a variety of methods such as using control groups.

internal validity (D. R. Krathwohl) An overall judgment of the power of a study to link independent and dependent variables in a causal relationship—its linking power (LP). It combines five judgments: credibility of the explanation, congruence of each variable's operationalized with its conceptual definition, appearance of the hypothesized relationship in data, elimination of any rival explanations, and justifiability of this result considering previous studies. Compare EXTERNAL VALIDITY.

international baccalaureate examinations (IB exams) Achievement tests that give high-school students an opportunity to gain admission to college with advanced standing in one or more subjects. In contrast with the advanced placement (AP) exams of the CEEB, the International Baccalaureate system is more than achievement testing; each school offering IB courses must submit detailed plans as well as pass periodic inspection by IB staff. See ADVANCED PLACEMENT EXAMINATIONS.

international candle An arbitrary amount of light intensity equivalent to the total light emitted by an ordinary candle having a flame one inch in height. See FOOTCANDLE.

International Classification of Diseases (ICD) A system of categories of disease conditions developed by the World Health Organization and based on principles similar to the system of classifications used in biology. Basic disease categories are assigned a three-digit code number with optional additional digits and other codes for specific disease entities. The system was initiated in 1946 and is revised periodically. See DIAGNOSTIC AND STATISTICAL MANUAL OF MENTAL DISORDERS (DSM).

International Phonetic Alphabet (IPA) (O. Jespersen) A listing of unique speech sounds found in various languages, each unique sound having a special symbol.

International System of Units The SI (Le Système International d'Unités) system of measurement consists of six base units (meter, kilogram, second, ampere, kelvin, candela), two supplementary units (radian, steradian), a series of derived units (meter per second squared, radian per second squared, volt, ohm, etc.) consistent with the base and supplementary units, and a series of approved prefixes for the formation of multiples and submultiples of the various units. Adopted as the metrication standard by American Psychological Association (APA) journals as well as many others in all fields of science. Also known as metric system, SI units and symbols.

internecine Mutual destruction; war; fighting to the death; bitter conflict.

interneurons Golgi Type II neurons

interneurosensory learning A process of learning that occurs when two or more sensory systems function together, such as the auditory and visual modalities.

intern's disease student's disease

internuncial neurons Classically defined as neurons with short axons that do not leave gray matter and branch extensively in the vicinity of the cell body. However, some interneurons do send axons into white matter and in the spinal cord participate in crossed and intersegmental reflexes. Also known as interneurons, Golgi Type II neurons, local circuit neurons.

interoception Internal sensation such as thirst or hunger or pain from some interior part of the body.

interoceptive conditioning (K. M. Bykov) Conditioning that employs techniques requiring direct access to internal organs, through fistulas, balloons inserted into the digestive tract, implanted electrical devices, etc. Compare EXTEROCEPTIVE CONDITIONING.

interoceptive system The totality of nerves and receptors found in the internal organs of the body.

interoceptor (C. S. Sherrington) A form of small sensory end organs (receptors) located within the walls of viscera. Any receptor consisting of sensory nerve cells that respond to changes within the body, such as blood acidity or the stretching of muscles. Compare EXTEROCEPTOR, PROPRIOCEPTOR.

interorgan generality (G. Murphy) Common property of an organism as a unit, or of related organs within an organism such as common sensitivity.

interosystem (R. Monroe) Any of several physiological systems that function wholly within the body, controlled by the autonomic nervous system, for example, the respiratory system.

interpersonal accommodation The "give-and-take" process involved in developing satisfactory interpersonal relationships.

interpersonal attraction Having a positive feeling for another person without knowing the person or knowing little. The maximum degree of such attraction would be love at first sight.

interpersonal circumplex   1. A circumplex (term found in facet theory) consisting of a pattern of correlations among interpersonal variables. 2. A visual format for organizing eight or more major traits of emotion or personality in a circle such that each trait becomes a pie-shaped segment. Interpersonal traits are common to such circumplexes. Those traits that are highly similar to one another are aligned close together, whereas those that are dissimilar appear at distant or opposite sides of the circle.

interpersonal conflict   A clash, disagreement, or difference of opinion between persons who differ with respect to goals, values, or attitudes. See EXTRAPSYCHIC CONFLICT.

interpersonal distance   The distance that individuals choose to separate their "bubble" of personal space from one or more other individuals. Studies show that most individuals maintain a smaller interpersonal distance for friends than for strangers. A Comfortable Interpersonal Distance Scale (CIDS) measures the interpersonal distance preferred by individuals. See PROXEMICS.

interpersonal morality   (N. Haan) A form of standards which emphasizes the interpersonal aspect of moral reasoning, in contrast to the cognitive, abstract qualities of moral judgment which are emphasized in most major theories. Moral judgment occurs within a social context as a process of discussion, dialogue, compromise, and negotiation.

interpersonal perception   An involved process of perceiving, evaluating, and interacting directly with another in terms of the situation-background. Perceptual constancy, imbeddedness, closure, and causality all play a prominent part in such interrelationships.

interpersonal process   1. The interaction of a person or persons with various continuums of communication, expressions of liking or disliking, competitive elements, bonding or separating. 2. In psychoanalysis, the transference and countertransference between patient and therapist, with the additional exchange of overt feelings of like or dislike for each other.

Interpersonal Process Recall   (N. Kagan) A method for understanding the processes of psychotherapy and the training of therapists. Involves videotaping psychotherapy sessions where, later, either the patient or the therapist view and hear what went on and question their thinking and feelings related to their actions and responses.

interpersonal psychiatry   (H. S. Sullivan) A treatment philosophy and procedure based on the study of the interpersonal relationships of patients, both in and out of the therapeutic situation. The therapist functions as a "participant observer" who identifies with the patient's anxiety, anger, or delusions to discover and modify the faulty "security operations" and "parataxic distortions" which he or she is attempting to screen out by "selective inattention" or dissociation. See PARATAXIC DISTORTION.

interpersonal psychotherapy (IPT)   (H. S. Sullivan) A psychotherapeutic approach (using communications as a major focus); a theory that stresses interpersonal interactions in conjunction with environmental impact.

interpersonal relations   (H. S. Sullivan) Interactions among individuals; the patterns of personal dealings with other people, which Harry Stack Sullivan regarded as the most crucial aspect of personality and the basic source of emotional security or insecurity. See INTERPERSONAL PROCESS.

interpersonal skill   Aptitude to carry on effective relationships with others, such as cooperating, communicating thought and feeling, assuming appropriate social responsibilities, and exhibiting adequate flexibility.

interpersonal theory   (H. S. Sullivan) A theory of personality, based on the relatively enduring pattern of recurrent interpersonal situations which characterize human life. Interactions with other people, particularly "significant others," determine not only a personal sense of security and sense of self, but also the "dynamism" that motivates behavior.

interpersonal trust   (J. Rotter) A generalized expectancy that other people's words can be relied on; a belief in the honesty and integrity of others.

interphase   The interval between one stage and another stage in the development of meiosis or mitosis. Also known as interkinesis.

interphase analyzer   A means of analyzing and scoring electroencephalographs and correlating results with various phases of brain activity.

interpolated schedule of reinforcement (INTER)   The temporary insertion of one reinforcement schedule into another. Also known as interpolated reinforcement schedule.

interpolated task   An assigned activity used to fill the interval between the study of material and its recall in memory experiments.

interpolation   The placement of an intermediate value ascertained by calculation that uses known values, between those previously known values in a system.

interposition   A monocular cue to depth perception occurring when two objects are in the same line of vision and a closer object partly conceals a farther object. Also known as relative position.

interpretation   1. In general, elucidation of the meaning of a play, musical composition, work of art or other material not easily understood. 2. In psychoanalysis, it is the attempt to explain the inner significance of the patient's attitudes, impulses, dreams, memories, and characteristic behavior. See CLARIFICATION.

interpreter effect   1. In communication, refers to the misunderstanding that may occur between people due to each of them "using" a different definition of some term that was mentioned. Whether within the same language or with an intermediary acting as a go-between for foreign languages, it is possible that what is meant and what is understood are two different things even if all parties are fluent in the language. 2. In research, an experimenter bias effect that is due to a misunderstanding of the language used between the participant(s) and the experimenter. Misunderstandings may lead to incorrect conclusions. See AMBIGUOUS COMMUNICATION STIMULI, COMMUNICATION DEVIANCE, CONGRUENT COMMUNICATION, EXPERIMENTER BIAS, LEVELS OF COMMUNICATION.

interpretive response (C. R. Rogers) A response that seeks to capture the underlying meaning or motive of a statement made by a client in therapy.

interpretive therapy Active, directive psychotherapy in which the therapist elicits patient's conflicts, repressions, dreams, and resistances, which he or she interprets and teaches the patient to interpret in the light of the patient's experience. Also known as interpretative psychiatry.

interquartile range (IQR) The middle 50% of a frequency distribution; that is, the distance between the first and fourth quartiles or the 25th and 75th percentiles. It is a measure of dispersion or spread of scores.

interrater agreement The correlation between several ratings by independent evaluators of a variable (for example, participant's performance), that is, the extent of agreement among the evaluators. See INTERSCORER RELIABILITY, RELIABLE.

interresponse time (IRT) The time between responses.

interrole conflict A state of tension or conflict that arises in the clash between two different roles, for example, that of parent and that of employee. See INTRAROLE CONFLICT, ROLE CONFLICT.

interrupted-time-series design A method that uses multiple measures taken both before and after the event of interest; the event may either be manipulated by the researcher or occur naturally. Example: To determine the effects of a police department's effort to prevent rapes, the number of rape crimes brought to trial each month might be examined starting 12 months before the new policy and for 18 or 24 months following its inception, ensuring, that no other change occurred at the same time (for example, when public concerns lead to the installation of improved lighting in high crime areas, prosecutors begin settling fewer cases by plea bargaining). If these other changes occur at least two or three months away from the change in police procedure it may still be possible to identify the procedure's effects apart from the other changes.

interruption tone A beat or tone heard when a constant-pitch tone is interrupted. If the interruption is slow, a beat is heard; if fast, a tone.

interscorer reliability 1. A measure of the degree of agreement between two people independently scoring or rating the same material. 2. The degree of consistency or concordance of ratings by different people usually expressed by a number. See INTERRATER AGREEMENT.

intersegmental arc reflex A reflex arc formed by interneuron fibers that travel up or down the spinal cord to communicate with motoneurons. In some instances, the pathways may cross from one side of the spinal cord to the other, creating a crossed intersegmental arc reflex.

intersensory disorder A pathological condition associated with damage to brain tissues involved in association or integration functions. The areas can be in the temporal, parietal, or occipital lobes and are usually in the dominant hemisphere. Intersensory disorders are characterized by difficulty in performing crossmodal matching tasks, such as tactual-visual or auditory-visual tests. See BRAIN DAMAGE.

intersensory perception *cross-modal perception*

intersex A person exhibiting sexual characteristics of both male and female. A true intersex human is a pseudo-hermaphrodite who possesses one or more contradictory sex features such as has both male and female gonadal tissue. See BISEXUALITY, HERMAPHRODITE, PSEUDO-HERMAPHRODITISM.

intersexualism Possession of the sexual characteristics of both sexes, particularly secondary characteristics and in some cases partial development of the internal or external sex organs. Also known as intersexuality. See AMBIGUOUS GENITALIA, PSEUDOHERMAPHRODITE, TESTICULAR-FEMINIZATION SYNDROME.

interstimulation The modification of behavior by the presence of others, such as the presence of peer-group members resulting in either increases or decreases in interest, activity, or anxiety.

interstimulus interval (ISI) In experiments, the time measured between two successive stimuli, usually determined from the onset of the first to onset of the second. See LATENCY OF THE CONDITIONED RESPONSE.

interstitial cells The cells in spaces or between parts of a tissue. In the testis, interstitial cells produce the male hormone testosterone. Also known as Leydig cells, after German anatomist Franz von Leydig (1821–1908).

interstitial-cell-stimulating hormone (ICSH) A hormone, or chemical messenger, that stimulates the interstitial cells, or Leydig's cells, of the testes.

intersubjective validation (L. Binswanger) A phenomenological research technique that establishes validity by comparing several investigators' observations of the same phenomenon. See INTRASUBJECTIVE VALIDATION.

intertrial interval (ITI) In a series of trials, the amount of time that intervenes between each initial presentation of the stimulus.

interval See the following kinds of intervals: CENTRAL, CLASS, CONFIDENCE (LEVEL), FIDUCIAL, FILLED-TIME, FIXED, INSPECTION, INTERITEM, INTERSTIMULUS, INTERTRIAL, MEDIAN, PHOTOCHROMATIC, PREPARATORY, RESPONSE SHOCK, S-S, STEP, UNFILLED-TIME.

interval estimation/estimate An estimate of a parameter placing it somewhere between upper and lower limits. See POINT ESTIMATE.

interval of uncertainty (IU) The area between the lower and upper thresholds of observation in the determination of a difference threshold.

interval reinforcement schedule *interval schedule of reinforcement*

interval scale A class of order-preserving scales that has equal units between its values but an arbitrary rather than a "true" zero. While arithmetic operations of addition and subtraction are meaningful on such data, results from multiplication or division are uninterpretable. An example of an interval scale is the Celsius temperature system. See NOMINAL SCALE, ORDINAL SCALE, RATIO SCALE.

interval schedule of reinforcement   Reinforcement delivered on the basis of a predetermined time schedule regardless of the number of responses per interval, in contrast to ratio reinforcement which is contingent on the number of responses. Interval reinforcement may be delivered at uniform, consecutive intervals or at variable intervals. Also known as interval reinforcement schedule. See FIXED-INTERVAL SCHEDULE OF REINFORCEMENT, VARIABLE-INTERVAL SCHEDULE OF REINFORCEMENT.

interval timer   A device that automatically provides an audible or visible signal at the end of the period for which it is set, making it especially convenient for timing group tests, or any tests that have time limits.

intervening   1. Refers to events or time periods that occur between the start and end of a series of events. 2. The interval between the start and end of a series.

intervening variable (IV or I.V.)   (C. L. Hull, E. C. Tolman) An unseen process inferred to occur within the organism between the stimulus event and the response. A neural response or a psychological expectation that influences the eventual response. Also known as mediating variable. See HULL'S THEORY, HYPOTHETICAL CONSTRUCT.

intervention   1. In emergency situations, services provided by mental-health practitioners and others during a period of community disaster, including short-term counseling, psychological first aid, telephone-calls to relatives. 2. In counseling and psychotherapy, stepping from a "hands-off" attitude to one of making active efforts to ameliorate clients' conditions including referrals to a hospital, manipulating the environment, or recommending institutional commitment.

interventionists   1. Persons who provide emergency services, especially during times of crisis. 2. Refers to people who are aware of certain improper, unhealthy, and/or dangerous circumstances and who call attention to the problem so that it may be solved, or who in some other way directly interfere. Such individuals put themselves between people and events usually intending to improve relations, provide aid, reduce suffering. 3. People who assume that research should be done in laboratory circumstances with complete control over experimental organisms even if the research only slightly resembles natural situations.

intervention programs for children   Programs, such as Head Start, intended to make up for deficits in children's environments of the home and the community, to enrich their environments.

intervention research   In evaluation research, methods or procedures designed to measure the effect a systematic modification has when it is imposed between two points in time, or the effect one type of intervention program has in comparison with the effects of an alternative program.

interventricular foramen of Monro   Bilateral openings that connect the third ventricle of the brain with the lateral ventricles and through which cerebral spinal fluid flows.

interview   1. (C. L. Hull) A meeting with another to achieve a specified goal. 2. Generally, a meeting at which the interviewer(s) evaluate or receive information from the interviewee (as in certain selection and exit interviews); sometimes the purpose is primarily to impart information. 3. In personnel psychology, a means of obtaining information during the hiring process; also used to gather information on employee progress as in performance review. Types of interviews include: AMYTAL, BERKELEY PUPPET, CLINICAL, COGNITIVE, COUNSELING, DEPTH, DIAGNOSTIC, EMPLOYMENT, EVALUATION, EXIT, GROUP, IN-TAKE, INITIAL CLINICAL, INITIAL JOB, JOB, PATTERNED, PROBLEM-SOLVING, PSYCHIATRIC, RENARD DIAGNOSTIC, SODIUM-AMYTAL, STRESS, STRUCTURED, UNSTRUCTURED.

interview contrast effect   A tendency for an interviewer's judgment of a person to be affected by a previous interview of another person. See CONTRAST EFFECTS IN INTERVIEWING, INTERWIEVER BIAS/EFFECT.

interviewer bias/effect   The effect upon the interview process of interviewer attitudes, expectations, preconceptions, training, demographics, and behavior.

interviewer stereotype   In industrial psychology, the interviewer's concept of an ideal job candidate, which becomes the standard for actual job applicants.

interviewer training   Instructional methods employed in training a person to be an effective interviewer. The various techniques include the use of videotapes of interviews and group discussions in addition to instructions in basic principles of interviewing.

interview group psychotherapy   A type of group therapy developed by Samuel Slavson for adolescents and adults in which a therapeutically balanced group is selected on the basis of common problems and general intelligence level, and a therapeutic atmosphere is created in which the participants are encouraged to reveal their attitudes, symptoms, and feelings. See ANALYTIC GROUP PSYCHOTHERAPY.

interview therapy   General phrase for a therapeutic dialogue in which the objectives are to discover the roots of clients' problems, and help them resolve their conflicts and achieve a better emotional adjustment.

in the closet   A metaphor for gay men and lesbians who maintain secrecy about their sexual preference.

intimacy   1. In general, a feeling or attitude characterized by a complete emotional sharing with another. 2. (E. Erikson) According to Erik Erikson, one of the steps in normal personality development when one person's personality fuses with the personality of another who is not from the person's own family of origin (for example, sharing ideas, feelings and concerns with a best friend).

intimacy problem   Difficulty of a person in trusting another or forming close bonds, whether physically or psychologically.

intimacy vs isolation   The sixth of Erik Erikson's eight stages of psychosocial development, extending between adolescence through courtship and early family life to early middle age. During this period, persons either learn to share and care without losing themselves or fail and feel alone and isolated. See ERIKSON'S STAGES OF PSYCHOSOCIAL DEVELOPMENT.

intimate zone   An area of physical distance adopted by persons in close relationships such as that of mother and infant. The intimate zone is defined as an distance of no more than 0.5 meter or (1.5 feet). See PROXEMICS.

intimidation   The act or habit of threatening and inspiring fear in other people. According to some psychoanalysts, such as R. P. Knight, this behavior may be used as a defense against anxiety associated with unconscious passive homosexual impulses.

intonation   1. Being in pitch or in harmony with others in choral speaking, singing, etc. 2. The sound pattern, melody, accent, and pauses of a language or an individual speaker. See PROSODY.

intoxication   A transient mental disorder characterized by impaired judgment, inappropriate emotionalism, impulsive behavior, and language and movement difficulties due to recent intake of certain substances, such as alcohol, or illicit drugs.

intraception   (H. A. Murray) An outlook that is warm, humanistic, and dominated by aspirations and feelings. A primary subjective attitude, that is internalized in terms of motivation, values, and concerns. Compare EXTRACEPTION.

intraceptive signaling   (H. A. Murray) Impulses generated and transmitted internally as stimuli for imaginative thinking.

intraclass correlation coefficient   See COEFFICIENT OF INTRACLASS CORRELATION.

intraconscious personality   A phenomenon of dissociative identity (multiple personality) disorder, in which one personality is aware of the thoughts and outer world of another personality. See ALTERS, DISSOCIATIVE IDENTITY DISORDER, MULTIPLE PERSONALITY.

intracranial stimulation (ICS)   Activation of the brain cells of a human or other animal by direct application of an electric current or other types of innervation. Electrical intracranial stimulation has been used for research and diagnostic purposes. Other types of ICS include the use of chemicals, such as hormones and neurotransmitter substances. See SELF-STIMULATION.

intractable   Not changeable, determined, obstinate.

intrafamily dynamics   The relationships and interactions among members of a family. In a family, subsystems are likely to occur, for example, parent pairs versus the children. Also special dyadic relationships may exist such as parent–son, parent–daughter, as well as pairing between children. See FAMILY CONSTELLATION, FAMILY PATTERN, FAMILY SYSTEM, PARENTAL PREFERENCES.

intrafusal fibers   Muscle cells that are located within muscle spindles and have a specialized function of setting the length of the muscle spindle and therefore its sensitivity to stretch.

intragroup territorial behavior   A form of territorial behavior seen in family settings where housemates regard bedroom areas, a particular living room chair or dining-table seating patterns as their personal territory. See GROUP TERRITORIAL BEHAVIOR.

intra-individual changes   Modifications within an individual over time regarding any aspect of personality.

intra-individual differences   Variations between two or more traits of a single person, such as being kind and generous in some situations and mean and stingy in other situations. Compare INTERINDIVIDUAL DIFFERENCES.

intralaminar nuclei   The nuclei located in the internal medullary laminae (layer of fibers) of the thalamus. Purported to have an inhibitory function since stimulation of the cells can cause moving laboratory animals to freeze in their tracks.

intralaminar system   A diffuse system of thalamic nuclei associated with sleep and wakefulness and assumed to be strongly influenced by the reticular activating system. Also known as recruiting system.

intramaze cues   The cues leading to the goal within a maze.

intraneurosensory learning   A process of learning via one single system. Most likely, learning is never purely an intraneurosensory function. Compare INTERNEUROSENSORY LEARNING.

intra-organizational bargaining   Negotiations that occur among members of each side by themselves, usually to establish the position they present to the other side.

intrapersonal conflict   intrapsychic conflict

intrapsychic   Pertaining to impulses, ideas, conflicts, or other psychological phenomena that arise or occur within the psyche or mind.

intrapsychic ataxia   Lack of coordination between feelings, thoughts and volition. Intrapsychic ataxia is a common symptom of schizophrenia. Also known as mental ataxia. See INAPPROPRIATE AFFECT.

intrapsychic censor   (S. Freud) Repression of threatening ideas or feelings.

intrapsychic conflict   The clash of opposing forces within the self, such as conflicting drives, wishes, or goals. Also known as inner conflict, internal conflict, intrapersonal conflict.

intrapsychic events   Processes that occur in a person's mind: thoughts, ideas, feelings, emotions, wishes.

intrarole conflict   A state of tension or conflict that arises within one role, for example, the parental role when two children have incompatible needs. See INTERROLE CONFLICT, ROLE CONFLICT.

intraselection   Natural selection arising from competition in growth between elementary units such as cells and organs of the body, resulting in the survival of the most viable. Also known as histonal selection.

intraserial interference   Difficulty in learning any item in a series as a consequence of other items.

intraserial learning   The learning of the relationships among items within a series or sequence as opposed to learning relationships between material in separate sequences.

intrasubject replication design   single-case experimental design

intrasubjective validation   (M. Boss) A phenomenological research technique that establishes validity on the basis of consistency of judgments of a single investigator who observes several examples of similar behavior of another person in a variety of situations. See INTERSUBJECTIVE VALIDATION.

intrauterine device (IUD)   A device inserted in the uterus to prevent conception. See BIRTH CONTROL, CONTRACEPTION.

intravenor   A person in an organization who has the power to settle a dispute between two parties, and who is not an uninterested party. See ARBITRATION.

intraverbal function   (B. F. Skinner) Verbal behavior controlled by "past associations" and only serving to keep the conversation going: no information is conveyed, for example, "How's it going?" "Fine, thank you. How are you?" "Can't complain." Also known as intraverbal behavior. Compare MAND, TACT.

intrinsic   Inherent, an activity that has value in and of itself, is its own reward.

intrinsic behavior   An act or movement by a single group of muscles (for example, a smile).

intrinsic cortex   (K. H. Pribram) Area of the cerebral cortex that receives impulses from nonsensory thalamic neurons. Also known as association area. See EXTRINSIC CORTEX.

intrinsic eye muscles   Muscles, such as the iris and ciliary muscles, located within the eyeball, that control the size of the pupil. Compare EXTRINSIC EYE MUSCLES.

intrinsic fatigue   **synaptic depression**

intrinsic force   Influence on behavior originating in the biological system (such as organic disturbance, homeostatic imbalance), as opposed to environmental or extrinsic forces.

intrinsic motivation   1. Behavior done for its own sake rather than for some kind of reward or payoff, for example, fishing for the pleasure of doing so versus fishing to make a living. 2. The intellectual satisfaction derived from the understanding of a meaningful solution; engaging in an activity for its own sake. Compare EXTRINSIC MOTIVATION.

intrinsic religion   A set of principles that a person has about self, others, and the cosmos that may resemble the tenets of organized religions but are the person's own values. See AGNOSTICISM, GEMEINSCHAFTSGEFÜHL, GOLDEN RULE, VALUE SYSTEM.

intrinsic reward   A reward implicit in an activity, for example, the pleasure or satisfaction of developing a special skill.

intrinsically motivating behavior   See INTRINSIC MOTIVATION.

introception   The adoption of social standards (morals, habits, conventions, and values) from outside sources (family, friends, teachers) into a personal system of motives and behavior.

introitus   An opening or entrance, for example, the anus is the introitus of the rectum.

introjection   (S. Ferenczi) A process of incorporating external social standards and values into the personality, as in a child adopting parental attitudes, or an adolescent adopting the behavior of the peer group. See IDENTIFICATION, INCORPORATION, STOCKHOLM SYNDROME.

introjects   Persons who have served any individual as role models. Many youths, male and female, pick role models from various sources, such as family, friends, teachers, actors, and attempt to be like them.

intromission   The act of sending or putting in something; insertion.

intropunitive   Being overcritical of oneself. A type of aggression in which the arousal is turned inward on the self. Common in depression. See PSYCHOSOMATIC REACTION.

intropunitive response   A tendency to take undue responsibility for events and assume blame unnecessarily. See ROSENZWEIG PICTURE-FRUSTRATION STUDY, SELF-ACCUSATION.

intropunitiveness   A tendency to blame oneself. Also known as self-accusation.

introspection   Looking inward. The examination of one's own thoughts and feelings, sometimes for the purpose of reporting on them in the introspective method of study. See PHENOMENOLOGY.

introspectionism   (W. Wundt) A doctrine positing that the basic method of psychological investigation is self-examination.

introspectionist   (W. Wundt, E. B. Titchener) Persons trained to examine their own cognitive, emotional and perceptive elements and to report them to an experimenter. See STRUCTURALISM.

introspective analysis   (K. Horney) Careful systematic self-observation with the intent to learn more about the self. This is a method equivalent or superior to traditional psychoanalysis, according to Karen Horney and Theodor Reik.

introspective method   (W. Wundt & E. B. Titchner) A study approach in which participants describe the fundamental qualities and characteristics but not the analyzed or interpreted contents of their conscious experiences. See STRUCTURALISM.

introspective psychology   1. Psychological investigation by the introspective method. 2. The body of knowledge whose facts are obtained by the introspective method.

introversion   (a turning inward—Latin) Preoccupation with the self and personal thoughts, feelings, and fantasies rather than with the outer world of people and things. Carl Jung considered this orientation to be the basis of a distinct personality type which he characterized as contemplative, reserved, sensitive, and somewhat aloof. Hans Eysenck has found that anxiety states, obsessive reactions, and depressive disorders tend to be associated with this pattern. See PASSIVE INTROVERSION.

introversion-extraversion (IE)   (C. G. Jung) A distinction made by Carl Jung to describe the range of self-orientation from introversion (preoccupation with own "thoughts," to extraversion (characterized by outward-directed concerns). See EYSENCK'S TYPOLOGY, STABILITY-INSTABILITY.

introversion-extraversion continuum   A concept that most normal individuals are neither true (extreme) introverts or extraverts but possess traits of both types.

introversive   (H. Rorschach) Describing people who live in a world of daydreams allegedly manifested by many responses of seeing movement in the Rorschach cards.

introvert   A person whose mind, attention, emotions, etc., have strong reference to him- or herself.

introverted   Turned inward.

introverted type (C. G. Jung) Jungian phrase describing a person whose attitudes and feelings are habitually directed inward.

intrusion error/response An inappropriately substituted response in serial learning that was either not in the original learning list or that was in the original list but placed incorrectly, for example, responding with the sixth item instead of the fifth in repeating a string of learned responses.

intrusive treatment 1. A treatment, presumably therapeutic, that is relatively invasive. For instance, flooding is more intrusive than biofeedback. 2. The imposition of a treatment or therapeutic procedure against the will of the patient. See INVOLUNTARY HOSPITALIZATION.

intuition 1. Immediate insight or perception as contrasted with reasoning or reflection. Intuitions appear to be products of feeling, minimal sense impressions, or unconscious forces rather than deliberate judgment. 2. Herbert Simon adapted the term from traditional usage to mean a belief, judgment or decision arrived at by the process of recognizing cues in the surrounding situation, and using them to access information already stored in long-term memory. Intuition permits problems to be solved, or steps taken toward solution with no awareness or incomplete awareness of the solution process (the nature of the cues recognized). See ELEMENTARY PERCEIVER AND ORGANIZER.

intuitive judgment A decision made without thinking, without focusing on relevant data, on the basis of "just knowing." It is possible that "intuition" is based on a good deal of forgotten knowledge based on early experiences.

intuitive knowledge A feeling of certainty about matters upon which a person may have no real knowledge or experience, a mysterious assurance of reality, such as the certainty of knowing a particular person that has never been met before.

intuitive period A stage in the mental development of children during which they can solve problems but not be able to explain how they were able to do so.

intuitive sociogram (J. Moreno) In sociometry, a diagram depicting the interactions and interrelationships between a certain group of people (such as class, team, work group) that is based on relationships noted by the therapist in the first session. See SOCIOGRAM.

intuitive stage (J. Piaget) A part of the preoperational period of cognitive development, from ages four to seven.

intuitive type One of Carl Jung's four functional personality types, characterized by an ability to adapt "by means of unconscious indications" and "a fine and sharpened perception and interpretation of faintly conscious stimuli." It is one of Jung's two nonrational (irrational) types, that is, knowledge is obtained by unspecifiable perception (a "sixth sense") rather than through a process of reason or judgment.

in utero (inside the uterus—Latin) While in the uterus, unborn.

invalid 1. Weak; sick. 2. A person with a disabling, but not necessarily incapacitating condition. See INVALIDISM. 3. Being without foundation, illogical. See INVALID CONVERSION.

invalid conversion An error in logic giving more or less meaning than proper to a premise.

invalidism 1. The state of being an invalid. 2. Accepting the role of a chronic invalid, characterized by preoccupation with personal health or refusal to recognize that the illness or disabling condition has been remedied. The motivation, usually unconscious but sometimes conscious, is to enjoy the benefits and "secondary gains" of illness such as attention and concern, being excused from responsibilities, or achieving power over others. See HYPOCHONDRIASIS, MÜNCHAUSEN SYNDROME.

invariable color A color that does not change its appearance when illumination changes.

invariable hues Three hues at spectrums 474, 506, 571 millimicrons that do not change when the luminance changes as in the BEZOLD-BRÜCKE PHENOMENON.

invariance 1. Remaining constant although the surrounding conditions may change. 2. The tendency of an image or afterimage to retain its size despite variations in the distance of the surface upon which it is projected.

invariant That which does not change.

invariant dynamics (W. Köhler) In Gestalt psychology, identical dynamic properties or relations in superficially different configurations, as in isomorphism.

invariant features In the visual field, information that does not change regardless of an individual's movement through it.

invariant sequence (J. Piaget) An unchanging pattern of units or variables. In Jean Piaget's view, the growth sequence is sensorimotor development, then preoperational thought, then concrete operational thought.

inventory A list of items, often in question form, used in diagnosing behavior, interests, and attitudes.

inventory test A type of test that measures more than one dimension in an attempt to evaluate simultaneously two or more aspects of individuals, such as knowledge and interests.

inverse agonist A drug that attaches to a receptor's binding site and interferes with the receptor's action. Compare INDIRECT AGONIST.

inverse derivation A word formed through elimination of a prefix or suffix from an existing word. Also known as back-formation, retrogressive formation. See CLIPPING.

inverse factor analysis The original name for what was later called Q-technique by William Stephenson.

inverse relationship A negative relationship, meaning that as one variable increases, the other variable decreases. A negative correlation.

inverse square law 1. A law of physics stating that energy decreases in proportion to the square of the distance from its source, thus sound at a point one foot away from the source may be x in volume but at two feet away it will be .25x. 2. The principle true for many inferential statistics; the sampling error tends to be inversely proportional to the square root of the size of the sample.

inversion 1. Homosexuality. 2. The assumption of the role of the opposite sex. See OCCASIONAL INVERSION. 3. Images on the retina are a reversal of the external object, due to passing through the lens. Distinguish image inversion from inverted retina.

inversion of affect   In psychoanalytic theory, the change in the aim of an instinct into its opposite. Also known as reversal, reversal of affect.

inversion relationship   A change in the usual roles of members of a family or group, as when a child replaces the prior family breadwinner.

invert   Rarely used term for a homosexual (gay man or lesbian).

invertebrate   1. A multicellular animal that does not possess a spinal or vertebral column. 2. Any animal other than the craniate members of the phylum Chordata.

inverted Electra complex   In psychoanalytic theory, a reversed Electra complex in which the daughter is erotically attached to the mother and regards the father as competition. Also known as negative Electra complex. See HOMOSEXUALITY.

inverted factor analysis   (W. Stephenson) A factor-analysis technique for investigating persons and their traits by correlating their scores on a series of tests. Stephenson developed Q methodology by interchanging the persons and test spaces in R-methodology. Also known as Q technique. See Q METHODOLOGY.

inverted Oedipus complex   In psychoanalytic theory, a reversed Oedipus complex in which the son desires the father sexually and regards the mother as a rival. Also known as negative Oedipus complex. See HOMOSEXUALITY.

inverted retina   Characteristic of vertebrates, the rods and cones of the retina are in the layers farthest from the entering light, that is, light must pass through eight layers of membranes, neurons and blood vessels in humans before it reaches the photosensitive receptor cells. Due to the inverted retina, in humans only about 10% of the light that strikes the cornea breaks down the photochemical in the rods and cones. Compare IMAGE INVERSION (meaning 3).

inverted-U function   A relationship between two variables X and Y such that as X increases, Y first increases, then levels off, then decreases. This type of relationship exists between arousal level and performance, for which as arousal continues to increase, performance first improves then declines after an optimal point has been reached.

investigative process management   (M. Godwin) A procedure for profiling violent crimes and criminals.

investigative psychology   A branch of forensic psychology that applies psychology to the study of criminals and criminality.

investigator paradigm effect   (T. X. Barber) A tendency at any one time and place for researchers to be affected by conceptual bandwagons (popular fads) that determine what questions are asked, what kind of data are obtained and what conclusions will be reached.

investigatory reflex   (I. Pavlov) A highly adaptive tendency in mammals to orient the appropriate sense organs to the slightest change in surroundings.

investment   In psychoanalytic theory, the psychic charge (cathexis) invested in an object (person).

inveterate drinking   Chronic drinking, similar to Elvin M. Jellinek's delta alcoholism.

inviolacy motive   (H. A. Murray) The need to defend the self and prevent self-depreciation.

invisible playmate   An imaginary person "created" by a child with whom the child talks with and plays. Also known as imaginary companion.

in vitro   (in glass—Latin) Refers to biological conditions or processes that occur or are made to occur outside the living body, usually in a test tube.

in vivo   (in live conditions—Latin) Refers to biological conditions or processes that occur or are observed within or in the presence of the living organism.

in vivo desensitization   (M. Jones) The process of exposing a client to the actual stimuli in an anxiety hierarchy, instead of just imagining them; for example, after preliminary methods of desensitization, showing a cat to a client who fears cats, asking the client to come as close to the cat as the client dares, hoping eventually to have the client touch the cat to conquer the fear).

invocational psychosis   A psychotic reaction to some religious rituals, such as prayers or incantations in revivalist meetings or in voodoo ceremonies.

involuntary   1. Not volitional. 2. Contrary to the will.

involuntary attention   Stimuli of such character that demand attention, such as flashes of light, loud noises, sudden silence.

involuntary civil commitment   A legal right of specified individuals, often two physicians, or a physician and a psychologist, to place a person considered by them to be a danger to self or others in a hospital. Upon certifying that such a person should be checked into a mental hospital or into a ward in a general hospital, the person is brought to the hospital usually by the police. In some cases, the patient may be required to remain hospitalized for a specific period (for example, 72 hours), whereupon the individual after an evaluation may be released, or may be further retained if treatment is deemed necessary.

involuntary hospitalization   The commitment of a person to a mental hospital against the wishes of the person and perhaps of others.

involuntary movements   1. Movements occurring without intention or volition, such as tics and mannerisms. 2. Movements carried out in spite of an effort to suppress them, as in athetosis.

involuntary muscles   smooth muscles

involuntary nervous system (INS)   (W. H. Gaskell) Those nerve pathways which are involved in most automatic behavior. Named by Italian-English physiologist Walter H. Gaskell (1847–1914). See AUTONOMIC NERVOUS SYSTEM.

involuntary response   A reaction not under conscious control; an automatic, unlearned response or reflex (for example, the contraction of the pupils of the eyes to bright light).

involution   A retrograde change in development, marked by physical and psychological deterioration, commonly occurring as the natural result of aging, but also occurring in some unusual genetic conditions or as a result of trauma.

involutional   1. The state of deterioration of a person. Any change after achieving the maximum level of ability or function, mental or physical. 2. Occurring in the years of menopause; menopausal. See INVOLUTIONAL MELANCHOLIA.

involutional depression   (D. R. Meyer) Archaic phrase for depression that tends to occur in older people. Tends to be quite common among persons who have had major surgery, especially arterial bypass and heart surgery.

involutional melancholia   Refers to guilt feelings that were once widely thought to occur mostly to women after their menopause. Characterized by oppressive thoughts and sadness about earlier misdeeds, such as having had an abortion or giving up a child for adoption. The existence of this subtype of depression has since been challenged (M. Weissmann). See CLIMACTERIC, DEPRESSION.

involutional paranoid state   A psychosis occurring in the climacteric period characterized by delusions of sin, guilt, poverty, nihilism, or persecution in addition to depressive symptoms. See INVOLUTIONAL MELANCHOLIA, INVOLUTIONAL PSYCHOTIC REACTION.

involutional paraphrenia   Obsolete phrase for a paranoid state occurring during the involutional period. See INVOLUTIONAL PSYCHOTIC REACTION.

involutional psychotic reaction   A mental disorder occurring in late middle life or the menopausal period, characterized by severe depression, and less often by paranoid thinking. Salient symptoms of the depressed type are agitation, apprehensiveness, feelings of despair and worthlessness, persistent insomnia, chronic fatigue, and loss of appetite. Symptoms are purportedly psychological reactions to physical changes and external stresses. Also known as climacteric psychosis. See MAJOR DEPRESSION, MELANCHOLIA.

involved shoppers   Purchasers who prefer a particular store or product.

invulnerability   An attitude, typically found in male adolescents, that they cannot be hurt mentally or physically.

inward picture   Internally perceived images such as those in dreams and fantasies. Carl Jung emphasized that the inward picture not only occurs inwardly but is a picture of the inner, true self.

I/O   Industrial/Organizational (also abbreviated IO).

IO   1. See INPUT-OUTPUT MECHANISM. 2. Industrial-Organizational.

iodopsin   A photosensitive violet-colored, neutral chemical pigment in the eye, located specifically in the cones of the retina of mammals. It breaks down upon exposure to light into retinene and photopsin, a protein. This chemical decomposition (and recombination) stimulates the neural network, thus serving as the transition point from light energy to the electrochemical nerve impulse. Considered important in adjustments in daylight vision. Chemically, reactions are similar to rhodopsin.

ion   (M. Faraday) A charged particle. An atom with an electric charge, acquired by having gained or lost one or more valence electrons. An atom that gains an electron is negative (cation), an atom that loses an electron is positive (anion).

ionotropic receptor   A receptor that contains a binding site for a neurotransmitter. An ion channel opens when the latter attaches to the site.

iophobia   toxi(co)phobia

iota   The ninth letter of the Greek alphabet. See APPENDIX C.

Iowa Scale of Stuttering Severity   A series of 39 recorded samples of stuttering ranked according to the equal appearing-intervals method. The object is to assign a scale value (from 0 for no stuttering to 7 indicating severe stuttering) to the person's speech.

Iowa Tests of Basic Skills   (A. Hieronymus) An achievement battery providing tests for reading, vocabulary, language, arithmetic, and work-study skills for each grade from grades 3 to 9, with norms for the beginning, middle, and end of each year.

IP   information processing

IPA   1. interaction-process analysis. 2. International Phonetic Alphabet.

IPAT   Abbreviation for Institute for Personality and Ability Testing, a company that publishes a variety of tests including the IPAT Anxiety Scale and the Sixteen Personality Factor Questionnaire.

IPAT Anxiety Scale   (R.B. Cattell) A self-report anxiety scale of 40 items that yields five subscores. Half of the items manifestly refer to anxiety the other 20 are "more covert hidden-purpose cryptic probes." The booklet title is "Self Analysis Form." See SIXTEEN PERSONALITY FACTOR QUESTIONNAIRE.

I-persona   (T. Burrow) Representing a synthesis of the individual's cortical, social, and symbolic functions in the personality.

IPL-V   Information Processing Language V

ipsation   Seldom used term for autoerotism.

ipsative-normative research strategy   (R. S. Lazarus) The study of a number of individuals in depth, over time and across circumstances, to develop the fullest portrait possible of the personality makeup of those individuals.

ipsative scale   A scale in which the individual's characteristic behavior is used as the standard. See IPSATIVE SCORE.

ipsative score   A person's score in relation to own baseline, rather than compared with other individuals. Thus an individual with generally low ability will still have relative strength in certain areas, and an ipsative score will emphasize this. Example: The Allport-Vernon-Lindzey Study of Values reports 240 points total for six scales ipsatively. For a participant to score 55 on, say, Theoretical, the scores on the other five scales must be a total of 15 points below the scale mean of 40, perhaps 30 on Political and 35 on Economic. See NORMATIVE SCORE.

ipsative scoring   (R. B. Cattell) Scoring a trait in an individual in terms of the normal distribution of scores "within" the individual, hence free of inter-individual comparisons.

ipsilateral   Existing on the same side. Also known as ipsolateral. Compare CONTRALATERAL.

ipsilateral deficit   A loss of ability to perform a learned task on one side of the body following an injury or induced lesion to a cortical area on the same side of the body. A cortical lesion usually results in a contralateral deficit, or loss of a normal function on the opposite side of the body.

ipsilateral hemisphere   Whichever one of the two brain hemispheres is on the same side as another part of the body being used as a reference point; its opposite is the contralateral hemisphere.

ipsolateral   See IPSILATERAL.

IPT   See INTERPERSONAL PSYCHOTHERAPY.

IQ   intelligence quotient (also abbreviated I.Q.)

IQ stability   See INTELLIGENCE QUOTIENT (IQ) STABILITY.

IQR   See INTERQUARTILE RANGE.

IR   See REACTIVE INHIBITION.

IRB   institutional review board

iridology   The assumption that the iris of the eye provides information to practitioners that enables them to make diagnoses of nutritional imbalances. Widely considered a pseudoscience. See REFLEXOLOGY, UNCONVENTIONAL THERAPIES.

iris   A muscular disk that surrounds the pupil of the eye and controls the amount of light entering the eye by constricting or dilating. Contains a pigment that gives the eye its coloration, determined by hereditary factors. Plural are irides or irises.

iritic reflex   The action of the iris in adjusting the diameter of the pupil as the intensity of the light in the environment changes.

IRM   innate (or inherited) releasing mechanism

ironed-out facies   A flattened facial expression observed in general-paresis patients, due to atonicity of the facial muscles.

ironic mental control   (D. M. Wegner) René Descartes' third maxim included the statement that there is nothing absolutely under human control except the ability to control own thoughts. Wegner gave evidence that this is not true; the more a person tries to control his or her mind, the paradoxical fact is that thought tends to resist being eliminated because of the reciprocal actions of intentional operating processes and ironic monitoring processes. See PARADOXICAL INTENTION, PHENOMENOLOGY.

ironic monitoring process   (D. M. Wegner) An aspect of the conscious mind that balances or blocks the actions of the intentional operating process in mental control. See IRONIC MENTAL CONTROL.

irradiation   1. An outward diffusion of energy, such as nerve impulses, light, or diffusion of conditioned responses. 2. (I. P. Pavlov) In general, whether it be neurological or cognitive, the concept that any process that involves the brain tends to spread and have effects on associated nerves.

irradiation theory (of learning)   1. A theory that learning involves selective reinforcement of one of many responses within a response hierarchy. 2. A hypothesis, advanced in explaining learning, which assumes that excitation spreads into neighboring structures, such as nerves.

irrational   Not reasonable in thinking or behavior; a symptom of obsessive compulsive disorder.

irrational belief   (A. Ellis) The unreasonable conviction that the world should be different than what it is.

irrationality   As used by Erich Fromm, a distorted perception of reality; a highly subjective world view or "frame of orientation."

irrational number   A number that cannot be expressed as the quotient of two numbers, for example $1 \div 3 = 0.3333333333$ to infinity. Compare REAL NUMBER.

irrational types   A category of functional types established by Carl Jung for persons whose functions seem to be determined by the intensity of perceptions rather than reasoned judgment. The category includes intuitive and sensational (sensing) types. See TYPOLOGY.

irreal   In Kurt Lewin's theory, describing an unreal aspect of a person's psychological environment (life space). Irreal behavior obtains gratifications considered unrealistic by the society of which the individual is a member. Includes daydreaming, fantasying, and fabricating.

irreality level   (K. Lewin) A part of a person's life space dominated by fantasy, desire, prejudices, and needs.

irrelevant argument   A logical fallacy based on conclusions that do not follow from premises, for example, "Evelyn will be a good mother when she grows up because she loves to play with dolls." Also known as Non sequitur.

irrelevant language   A language composed of sounds, phrases, or words that are possibly understood only by the speaker, as observed in cases of schizophrenia and autistic children.

irresistible apprehension   Emil Kraepelin's phrase for obsessive-compulsive disorder (OCD).

irresistible impulse   In forensics, an uncontrollable urge, particularly the urge to perform a criminal act. The irresistible impulse test is accepted in some states (as well as the M'Naghten rule) to the effect that a person is exempt from criminal responsibility if at the time of the crime he or she was acting under an impulse which he or she was powerless to resist by reason of mental disease. See M'NAGHTEN RULES, PRINCIPLE OF IRRESISTIBLE IMPULSE.

irresistible impulse rule   A test of insanity that supplements the M'Naghten rule. Where and when the rule of an irresistible impulse is accepted as an explanation for criminal behavior, an offender is not considered criminally responsible.

irresponsibility   A legal term used in claiming a person is not responsible for his or her conduct because of mental impairment.

irreversible decrement model   A view of aging as a decline in relevant abilities, both physically and mentally.

irritability   1. A state of excessive, easily provoked anger, annoyance, or impatience. 2. Capacity of living matter, and particularly nervous tissue, to respond to stimulation.

irritability of cell   A loss of equilibrium in a cell because of a mechanical, chemical, electrical, or other stimulus that alters the status of ions or ion charges on or near the cell membrane. Irritability of cell usually causes an expression of cell activity, such as transmission of a nerve impulse.

irritable heart of soldiers   An American Civil War term for what was known in World War I as shell shock, and during World War II as combat reaction or battle fatigue. According to some authorities, it corresponds most closely to Da Costa's syndrome, an anxiety reaction experienced by soldiers in active combat.

irrumation   Fellatio.

IRT   1. See INTERRESPONSE TIME. 2. item response theory.

Isakower phenomenon   (O. Isakower) Strange sensations in the mouth, skin, hands, and the border region around the body, including vaguely perceived advancing or receding objects. The phenomenon occurs primarily while falling asleep, but may also occur in high fever and stress situations. Otto Isakower compared these sensations to déjà vu and the epileptic aura, and attributed them to a revival of traumatic experiences involving oral deprivation early in life. See ABSTRACT PERCEPTIONS, BLANK HALLUCINATION, DREAM SCREEN.

ISB   1. Incomplete Sentences Blank. 2. See ROTTER INCOMPLETE SENTENCES BLANK.

isch(n)ophonia   (to keep back, stop—Greek) Stuttering or stammering.

ISD   inhibited sexual desire

ISDB   indirect self-destructive behavior

Ishihara Color Test   (S. Ishihara) An examination for color blindness (hue sensitivity) using a series of plates in which numbers or letters are formed by dots of different colors against a background of dots in varying degrees of brightness and saturation. The test diagnoses specific types of color blindness. See HARDY-RAND-RITTLER PSEUDOISOCHROMATIC PLATES, REUSS'S COLOR CHARTS/TABLES, STILLING TEST.

Ishihara plates   See ISHIHARA COLOR TEST.

ISI   See INTERSTIMULUS INTERVAL.

island deafness   A range of normal pitches to which a person may be totally insensitive although able to perceive pitches on either side of the range. See TONAL GAP, TONAL ISLAND.

island of Reil   A part of the cortex buried in the depths of the lateral (Sylvian) sulcus. Sensory information about the viscera is relayed to the island of Reil. Named after German physician Johann Reil (1759–1813). Also known as central lobe, insula of Reil.

islands of Langerhans   Clusters of endocrine cells within the pancreas that secrete two hormones, insulin and glucagon. Cells that secrete glucagon are called alpha cells, those that secrete insulin are called beta cells. Named after German physician and anatomist Paul Langerhans (1847–1888). Also known as islets of Langerhans.

isogloss   In linguistics, a line drawn on a map showing the geographical limit of some feature or usage.

ISO 9000   A set of quality standards for systems and processes established by the International Organization for Standardization. Industrial firms that meet these standards can be listed on the ISO's register.

isochron   A 1% unit of growth from birth to full adult development.

isochronal   Equal in rate, frequency, or time of occurrence to some other timed item.

isochronia   The correspondence between two or more processes with respect to time, rate or frequency of occurrence. See CHRONAXIE.

isocortex   (O. & C. Vogt) The Vogt's term for the larger part of the mammalian cerebral cortex. Also known as homogenetic cortex, homotypic cortex, neocortex, neopallium. Compare ALLOCORTEX.

isokurtic   In reference to a distribution that is normal in shape, not skewed.

isohippocampal rhythm   A theta-wave electrical rhythm detected in the hippocampal region of the limbic system in response to arousal stimuli. It is demonstrated in laboratory animals during performance of learning tasks.

isolate   1. Any person who maintains no, few, or exceedingly shallow personal relationships. 2. On a sociometric test, the person chosen least often or not at all; the group member who is psychologically isolated. Also known as outsider, social island. See SOCIOMETRY, STAR.

isolated explosive disorder   An acute disturbance of impulse control characterized by an unexpected display of violence, a single discrete episode in which a person commits a violent and undisciplined act. The episode is triggered by an apparently minor incident or by no apparent cause. Theorized to be due to long-held feelings of repressed anger that suddenly surface. Puzzling acts of violence against individuals, families, co-workers or innocent bystanders are reported, caused often by people generally regarded as quiet, friendly and even peaceful. See CATATHYMIC CRISIS, CROCODILE MAN.

isolate monkey   (H. Harlow) In animal research, a monkey (usually rhesus) artificially raised in total isolation. See MONKEY THERAPIST, SOCIAL-ISOLATION SYNDROME.

isolation   See ALIENATION, EXISTENTIAL ISOLATION, PSYCHIC ISOLATION, SENSORY ISOLATION.

isolation amentia   Mental deficiency due to extreme childhood isolation from social stimuli. See WILD BOY OF AVEYRON.

isolation aphasia   A form of aphasia due to isolation of the brain's speech areas.

isolation defense   In psychoanalytic theory, a defense mechanism that isolates an unpleasant event (or its affect), especially one that relates to a neurosis, from the person. The person interpolates a time interval of neutrality during which the connections to the event are interrupted or suppressed.

isolation effect   Köhler–von Restorff effect

isolation experiments   Removal of an organism from social or other contact with other members of its group to observe behavioral or other effects. Rats reared in isolation show brain-cell deficits ranging from 11% in the medulla to 59% in the neocortex, when compared with litter mates raised together.

isolation mechanism   See ISOLATION DEFENSE.

isolation (of affect)   (S. Freud) An unconscious defense mechanism characterized by screening out painful anxiety-provoking feelings by such methods as recalling traumatic events without experiencing emotion or adopting a stoical attitude. See COMPARTMENTALIZATION, INTIMACY VERSUS ISOLATION, SENSORY ISOLATION, SOCIAL-ISOLATION SYNDROME.

isometric contraction/twitch   A muscle contraction in which tension develops although the muscle's length does not change (there is no movement). Compare ISOTONIC CONTRACTION/TWITCH.

isometric controls The controls on a machine that respond to force. See ISOTONIC MOVEMENT.

isometric myograph A device for measuring muscle contractions, or other push-and-pull-type forces, against a strong resistance. The other type of myograph is an isotonic myograph.

isometric twitch **isometric contraction**

isomorph A formal identity, point-for-point, between two conceptual systems. See HOMOLOGY.

isomorphic attributions (H. C. Triandis) Assigning causes to the behavior of another person that are similar to the causes that persons assign in thinking about their own behavior. See PSYCHOLOGISTS' FALLACY.

isomorphism 1. In general, a one-to-one relationship. 2. The relationship between a perceived stimulus and the resulting verbal process, such as pronunciation of a printed word. 3. The point-to-point relationship of the excitatory fields of the brain to the perceived stimulus. 4. (M. Wertheimer & W. Köhler) A Gestalt position on the mind-body problem, namely that there is a functional and structural correspondence between the form of experience (percepts) and the form of underlying neurological processes. See MIND-BODY PROBLEM.

isopathic principle (E. Jones) A point of view that a symptom can be relieved by the simple expression of the emotion that has been repressed, for example, guilt caused by hate can be relieved by an exhibition of hate. Also known as homeopathic principle.

isophilia (H. S. Sullivan) Feelings of affection or affectionate behavior between members of the same sex (gender), with no genital component.

isophonic contour Visual demonstration on a monitor of the interaction of different attributes of tone, such as loudness as a function of both frequency and intensity. See PHONATOGRAPH.

isoprinciple Correspondence between a person's mood and an artistic stimulus, such as feeling happy and creating joyful music or feeling sad and reading a tragedy.

isoscope (F. Donders) An instrument by means of which one eye sees a pair of vertical wires and the other eye a single wire. Used for testing rotation perception.

isotonic contraction/twitch A muscle contraction in which the muscle bundle shortens and thickens, as when a person flexes the biceps muscle of the upper arm. Compare ISOMETRIC CONTRACTION/TWITCH.

isotonic controls The controls on a machine that result in movements. Compare ISOMETRIC CONTROLS.

isotonic myograph A device for measuring muscle contractions, or other push-and-pull-type forces, against a relatively minor resistance. The other type of myograph is an isometric myograph.

isotope A subspecies of a chemical element characterized by the number of neutrons in the nucleus.

isotropic Being uniform in all directions.

IS Unit See INTERNATIONAL SYSTEM OF UNITS.

IT inspection time

ITA initial teaching alphabet

itch A cutaneous sensory experience related to pain. The nerve endings associated with itch are the same as those sensitive to the prick-pain sensation produced by a needle or electric stimulus. A rapidly repeated prick-pain sensation produces the itch reaction.

item In tests, a single element to which the participant is to respond.

item analysis 1. A statistical comparison of the items in a test against a particular criterion, usually done to select the most valid items. 2. The evaluation of test items, externally and qualitatively in terms of their content and form, and quantitatively by internal statistics. The latter measures difficulty, validity, reliability, internal consistency, distribution, and discriminability (the extent to which overall high scorers answer the item correctly and low scorers incorrectly). See ITEM VALIDITY.

item difficulty The difficulty of a test item for a particular group as determined by the proportion of individuals who pass or fail the item.

item response theory (IRT) A theory guiding the construction of tests controlling for both their difficulty and their discriminative power. For instance, when tests are administered to people of various languages, IRT is used to determine whether the translated items have the same meanings as the original.

items See the following kinds of item(s): BUFFER, COMPLETION TEST, CULTURAL, FEARED, INTER-LOCKING, RECALL, RECOGNITION, SUPPLY, TEST, WEIGHTED.

item scaling The assignment of a test item to a rank-order position according to its difficulty.

item selection The selection of a test item on the basis of factors such as validity, reliability, discriminability and freedom from ambiguity.

item test Any question, task, problem, etc., the response to which can be measured as a single item or unit and related to what the test is measuring as a whole.

item validity The degree to which a test item actually expresses a question's meaning or a problem's essence, usually by measuring item-criterion relationships, or externally by cross-validation, as by testing a different sample of respondents. See ITEM ANALYSIS, TEST CONSTRUCTION, VALIDITY.

item weighting Assigning a numerical value to a test or a test item that expresses a percentage of the sum total of the final score; for example, an essay question may be assigned a value of 40, representing 40 out of 100 possible points of an examination, with the other 60% to three other essays, each having a weight of 20%.

iteration 1. A research technique in which investigators gradually refine a concept by repeatedly gathering and reassessing data. 2. (A. Maslow) A process of starting over again from the beginning.

iteration method The use of successive approximations as in the solving of equations.

I-Thou relationship (M. Buber) Existential phrase relating to the importance of real (honest, intense, complete) meetings between people. See EXISTENTIALISM, FORMATIVE DIRECTIVE, HUMANISM, I-IT.

ithyphallic Possessing an erect penis, associated with representations of gods such as Priapus and Shiva.

ITI See INTERTRIAL INTERVAL.

itinerant teacher An educationally trained person who travels to several schools providing specialized instruction to children in many classrooms.

ITPA See ILLINOIS TEST OF PSYCHOLINGUISTIC ABILITIES.

IU See INTERVAL OF UNCERTAINTY.

IUD See INTRAUTERINE DEVICE.

I.V. 1. independent variable (also abbreviated IV). 2. intervening variable (also abbreviated IV).

Ivanov-Smolensky technique (A. Ivanov-Smolensky) An operant conditioning technique involving a child, a rubber ball, and a piece of chocolate. If a child squeezes the rubber ball at a correct time, chocolate is delivered via a chute. Pairing a conditioned stimulus with the event results in the child's response anticipating the delivery of the chocolate.

J

j   The number of standard deviations from the mean.

J   (C. L. Hull) In Hull's theory, the abbreviation for delay in reinforcement. See HULL'S THEORY.

Jacksonian epilepsy   (J. H. Jackson) A type of epilepsy characterized by convulsions on the side of the body contralateral to the cortical locus of the disturbance. Typically the convulsions spread from central to secondary muscle groups, and may eventually affect one whole side of the body in a progressing movement known as a Jacksonian march. Also known as hemiplegic epilepsy.

Jackson's law/principle   (J. H. Jackson) A point of view that when there is a loss of a mental function due to disease or natural deterioration, the higher and the more recently developed functions are lost first.

Jacob's membrane   (A. Jacob) A stratum of the retina along the posterior wall of the eye, consisting of the rods and cones, the outer parts of the neuroepithelial cells constituting the end-organs (or receptors) for the sense of vision. Also known as bacillary layer, layer of rods and cones, rods and cones layer.

Jacobson's organ   In snakes and many mammals, an olfactory receptor located in the top part of the mouth. In snakes, a basic chemoreceptor; in mammals, a pheromone detector. Also known as vomeronasal system. See FLEHMENING.

Jacobson relaxation method   Based on the maxim "Contract and then Relax," a treatment procedure for people in stressful situations and who cannot sleep or are on the verge of behaving rashly. Also known as progressive relaxation; often used as one component of systematic desensitization. Named after American physician Edmund Jacobson (b. 1888).

Jacquet chronometer   An instrument designed to measure and record seconds and fifths of seconds, indicating, by hands on two dials, the total period elapsed.

jactatio capitis nocturna   Latin phrase for head-rolling at night.

jactitation   Extreme restlessness marked by convulsive movements, changing from one posture to another, and tossing about. Also known as jactation.

jamais vu   (never seen—French) A falsification of memory in which a situation that has actually been previously experienced appears to be completely unfamiliar. It is an example of denial. See PARAMNESIA.

James-Lange theory (of emotion)   (W. James, C. G. Lange) A combination of postulates of William James (1884), who assumed that emotions consist of experiences of muscular and visceral reactions to provoking stimuli, and Carl Georg Lange (1885), who contended that emotions coincide with vascular changes. James argued that humans do not run because they are afraid but are afraid because they run, and that "a disembodied emotion is a sheer nonentity." Compare CANNON-BARD THEORY (OF EMOTION).

James's theory   The following items are important for understanding William James' theory: DUAL-MEMORY THEORY, FRINGE OF CONSCIOUSNESS, FUNCTIONALISM, IDEOMOTOR ACTION, INSTINCTIVE STIMULUS, INSTINCTIVE TENDENCY, JAMES-LANGE THEORY, ME, PRAGMATISM, QUANTITY OBJECTION, RADICAL EMPIRICISM, SPLIT-OFF CONSCIOUSNESS, STREAM OF CONSCIOUSNESS, SUBSTANTIVE STATES, TENDER-MINDED, TOUGH-MINDED.

Janet's disease   (P. M. F. Janet) Psychasthenia, characterized by stages of pathologic fear or anxiety, obsessions, fixed ideas, feelings of inadequacy, self-accusation, and feelings of strangeness and depersonalization.

Janet's test   (P. M. F. Janet) A tactile-sensibility examination for distinguishing between functional and organic anesthesia in which the patient simply answers in the affirmative or negative when asked if he or she feels the touch of the examiner's fingers.

jangle fallacy   In research, assuming that measures with different names measure different things. Compare JINGLE FALLACY. See THREATS TO EXTERNAL EXPERIMENTAL VALIDITY.

Janis-Feyerabend hypothesis   (I. L. Janis) A postulate that it is better to rebut positive arguments before defending negative ones.

Janusian thinking   The capacity to simultaneously conceive or maintain contradictory ideas or images. Name derives from a Roman god, Janus, who faced in opposite directions simultaneously. Also known as oppositional thinking. See ATYPICAL GENDER.

Japanese management   In industry, typical components include using work teams, quality circles, just-in-time inventory; encouraging loyalty, collective values, the putting of organizational interests ahead of individual ones, hard work; and offering job security, minimal direct supervision.

Japanese psychology Introduced from the West in the late 1800s. Has concentrated on educational and experimental psychology. Main journal is *Japanese Journal of Psychology*, founded in 1926.

jargon 1. A specialized language of a group or profession that is understood within that group but may be meaningless to others. 2. Unintelligible speech such as the babbling of children in prelanguage stages and speech of persons with brain damage; in either case, the speakers may think that they are communicating, but they are not understood.

jargon aphasia A form of aphasia in which a person's speech is incoherent. See WORD SALAD.

Jastrow automatograph (J. Jastrow) An early instrument for recording automatic movements. See AUTOMATOGRAPH.

Jastrow's cylinders (J. Jastrow) A series of weights for measuring the limen of intensity and of discrimination for pressure and kinesthesis. The cylinders are set on the palm for pressure and for kinesthesis experiments.

Java man *Pithecanthropus erectus.* An extinct race of hominids with apelike skull but modern human's skeleton. See ANTHROPOLOGY, PHRENOLOGY.

jaw-grinding An unconscious habit of grinding or gnashing the teeth, often associated with intense mental or physical strain. See BRUXISM, TEMPOROMANDIBULAR JOINT (TMJ) SYNDROME.

JCAHO Joint Commission for Accreditation of Healthcare Organizations

J coefficient (E. S. Primoff) An estimate of the predictive usefulness of each of the subtests of a battery-type test. The technique calls for obtaining a correlation between each subtest and the test as a whole. In a more advanced design, different beta weights can be given to the various subtests. See TEST CONSTRUCTION.

J-curve (F. Allport) A strongly skewed graphic representation in the shape of a J or a reversed J with many cases falling at the mode and others clustered at one side and close to the mode. Frequency distribution of scores (of institutional behavior are greatly influenced toward conformity by social pressure) and tend toward a J-type of curve or its reversal. Also known as J-Curve, J-shaped curve.

JDI Job Description Index

jealousy A state of psychic distress centered on hostility toward a real or imagined rival who enjoys some real or imagined advantage. It is characterized by intense psychic pain, overvigilance regarding the rivalry situation, and envy. See ALCOHOLIC JEALOUSY.

Jehovah complex A megalomaniac fantasy of identification with God.

jen The importance of benevolence for the good life according to Confucius. See CONFUCIAN ANALECTS.

Jena method (K. Brauckmann) A technique for teaching deaf children to speak by having them touch the lips of a speaker to feel how the lips vibrate while forming different words and making different sounds.

Jendrassik maneuver/reinforcement (E. Jendrassik) A technique of reinforcing the patellar reflex response by having the participant grasp his or her hands and pull on them while the reflex is tested. Also known as Jendrassik's reinforcement of reflexes.

Jenkins Activity Survey (C. D. Jenkins, R. H. Rosenman, & M. Friedman) A 1968 questionnaire to assess Type-A behavior.

Jennifer fever (B. Gordon) A man's compulsion to marry a much younger woman to cope with his midlife crisis.

Jensenism (D. P. Moynihan) Arthur Jensen's theory that a person's intelligence are quotient (IQ) and, consequently, basic intelligence, are mostly due to heredity, especially racial origins; often used pejoratively. See BIOLOGICAL INTELLIGENCE, BLACK INTELLIGENCE TEST OF CULTURAL HOMOGENEITY, INTELLECTUAL IMPOVERISHMENT, INTELLIGENCE, INTELLIGENCE TESTS AND INTELLIGENCE.

jet lag A maladjustment of circadian rhythms that results from being transported through several global time zones within a short span of time. Rest, work, eating, body temperature, and adrenocortical-secretion cycles may require days to adjust to local time.

jidoka Japanese term for a system that stops an assembly line (controlled by a "smart machine" or manually by a workstation "and on cord") whenever production or quality problems are detected.

jiggle cage A spring-mounted cage that can contain an animal. The activity level of the animal within it can be recorded. Similar to activity cage with the addition of springs to each corner and a device to record all movements of the animal and of the wheel. See JIGGLE CHAIR.

jiggle chair A chair used to measure attention levels in movie and television viewers by detecting and recording the viewer's movements, purportedly reflecting anxiety, restlessness, and boredom. See JIGGLE CAGE.

jigsaw method (E. Aronson, C. Stephan, J. Sikes, N. Blaney, & M. Snapp) In social psychology, the setting of a problem to be solved or a task to be accomplished by a group (often children of different skin color), each member of which is provided with a "piece of the puzzle" that must be cooperatively contributed for the group to succeed. Designed to reduce prejudice.

jigsaw technique In group dynamics, a learning technique in which topics are assigned to members, after which those with the same topics work together, and finally teach theirs to the other members.

jimsonweed Common name of *datura stramonium*, an anodyne. Grows wild, contains an intoxicating agent. Ingestion produces hallucinations, loss of motor coordination, and amnesia for the period of intoxication.

jingle fallacy In research, assuming that measures of the same name measure the same thing. Compare JANGLE FALLACY. See THREATS TO EXTERNAL EXPERIMENTAL VALIDITY.

jinjinia bemar Assam name for *koro*.

JIT just-in-time

JND just-noticeable difference (also abbreviated **jnd**, **j.n.d.**)

jnnd just not-noticeable difference

job action Euphemism for job inaction or strike. Known as industrial action in Britain.

job analysis   1. A list of every minute element performed as part of a given job. Used in personnel decisions, job redesign, and research. 2. Casually, an examination of work.

job analyst   A specialist (usually an industrial/organizational psychologist) in performing job analyses.

job autonomy   The authority to work without much direct supervision.

job-characteristics model   (J. R. Hackman & G. R. Oldham) A theory that specific employee needs (autonomy, feedback, task variety, identity, and significance) affect job satisfaction and other employee outcomes. See JOB DIAGNOSTIC SURVEY.

job classification   For the employee, the title and level of the position. For the employer, the structural and functional organization of tasks and their division among employees.

job-component method   A job-evaluation technique based on the assumption that similarities in job content impose similar job demands on the employees and should therefore warrant corresponding pay scales. This method may be applied through a statistical analysis of data obtained from the Position Analysis Questionnaire that covers 194 different job components.

job component validity   The ability of a test to predict performance of a specific component of the job.

job context   The social and physical aspects that comprise the milieu of a job, such as personnel and quality of the surroundings.

job creation   The development of new opportunities for paid employment, typically as government policy.

job criterion   The measure of job performance, often in terms of quantity and quality of productivity. Typical contexts are in psychometrics (where the predictive validity of a test administered to job applicants is the correlation of test scores with the later job criterion) and in employee evaluation (where the criterion on which the employee is measured must be established). See JOB PERFORMANCE.

job description   A compact outline of a specific job, including the experience and ability of the successful applicant, as well as the hours, work conditions, pay, and benefits of the job.

Job Description Index (JDI)   A questionnaire that measures job satisfaction by asking the employee to describe the job.

job design   In industrial psychology, systematic efforts to improve work methods, equipment, and the working environment through such approaches as: (a) methods analysis, or industrial engineering, focused on the development of efficient work methods; (b) human factors, an approach primarily concerned with the design of physical equipment and facilities as well as the environment in which people work; and (c) job enlargement or enrichment, aimed at expanding the complexity and responsibility of jobs. See ENGINEERING PSYCHOLOGY, HUMAN ENGINEERING, HUMAN-FACTORS PSYCHOLOGY, JOB ENLARGEMENT.

Job Diagnostic Survey   Test that measures the work aspects described in the Job Characteristics Model.

job dimensions   The basic features of jobs, such as operating machines or equipment, performing clerical or related activities, or having decision-making or communicating responsibilities, as well as the work schedules and environment.

job dissatisfaction   1. Generally, unhappiness with the situation at work. 2. In F. Herzberg's model of work motivation, the result of problems with "hygiene needs" such as salary, management practices, and working conditions. Compare JOB SATISFACTION.

job enlargement   The expansion of responsibilities associated with a particular job, either "horizontally," by increasing the number of subtasks at the same level of complexity and performing different duties at different times, or "vertically," by requiring the employee to perform more complex tasks and undertake increased responsibility and autonomy.

job enrichment   The enhancement of employees, interest and attitude toward work tasks by improving the "quality of life" on the job. Methods include reducing boredom by giving employees a variety of different tasks during a work schedule and allowing employees freedom to design their own ways of doing work if it improves their effectiveness on the job.

job entitlement   The conviction that an employee is, usually by virtue of precedent, entitled to certain remuneration and other benefits.

job evaluation   Determination of the grading structures and pay scales for jobs by such methods as: (a) comparison with other jobs and with the going rate; (b) assigning jobs to specific classifications on the basis of overall worth; (c) assigning point values to jobs according to such factors as education, experience, and the initiative or effort needed; (d) comparison with rankings and ratings of key jobs according to skill and responsibility requirements; and (e) weighting of the various components of the job.

job-hopping   Changing employers or type of work, particularly frequently and suddenly.

job information   The data relating to jobs and workers used in job-analysis studies. The data may include work activities, such as weaving or welding, human behaviors required, such as communicating or making decisions, personnel requirements, and types of materials processed and equipment used.

job interview   An employment interview.

job inventory   task inventory

job involvement   The extent to which an employee internalizes or is absorbed by the work.

job family   A group of related jobs.

job performance   A criterion of job-related behavior, usually measured in terms of quantity or quality of output, or both. The performance of, say, clock assemblers can be quantified directly and objectively; that of artists, admirals, managers, or mothers might have to be assessed more subjectively. See JOB CRITERION.

job placement   The assignment of employees on the basis of the employees' abilities, interests, and job availability.

job-placement stage A level of rehabilitation training and work readiness training where the person undergoing treatment is presumed ready to move into the competitive job market. Transition assistance is usually offered by rehabilitation personnel with tasks such as filling out job applications and handling job interviews.

job preview In employee hiring, an accurate presentation by the interviewer about the position, especially including the negative aspects, so that the applicant does not have unreasonable expectations. Also known as realistic job preview.

job requirements Personnel requirements reasonably judged necessary for performing a work task effectively. May include good eyesight, ability to drive a truck, or ability to perform mathematical calculations quickly.

job research Evaluation of job performance that uses criterion and predictor factors as dependent and independent variables respectively within a statistical concept.

job rights Employee entitlement, often prescribed by statute and collective agreements. R. Walton lists these: adequate and fair compensation; safe and healthy work environment; opportunity to use and develop capacities; opportunity for growth and security; social integration in the organization; organizational fairness, reasonableness, and democracy; and social relevance.

job rotation Systematic movement of personnel to different tasks to, for instance, promote greater understanding of the work being done, to generate greater flexibility, to reduce boredom, etc.

job-sample experiences A type of vocational training in which clients obtain training in a sheltered environment for jobs that are samples of those typically available in the community workforce.

job sample test **work sample test** (meaning 1)

job satisfaction 1. The attitude of an employee toward a job, sometimes expressed as a hedonic response of liking or disliking the work itself, the rewards (pay, promotions, recognition), or the context (working conditions, benefits). 2. In F. Herzberg's model of work motivation, the result of satisfying "motivator needs," such as opportunity for advancement. Compare JOB DISSATISFACTION.

JobScope A multimethod procedure used in the insurance industry for performing job evaluations, using computer technology and sophisticated quantitative analysis.

job shadowing A learning program in which a novice follows a mentor around, closely observing the work.

job sharing An employment arrangement in which two or more people are employed part time to perform work that otherwise would be assigned to one person full time.

job-specific test A task of the particular abilities required for a given job, such as typing or welding. Used primarily in personnel selection and placement and in measuring performance in a training program.

job specifications Personnel specifications.

job tenure 1. How long an employee has remained at the same firm or at the same job. See TURNOVER. 2. In academia, tenure is a privilege granted to faculty members who have proven themselves to the extent that they no longer need apply for periodic renewals of their teaching contracts. 3. Generally, security of employment.

job transfer Relocation of an employee to another job or organizational unit.

Jocasta complex An abnormal sexual attachment of a mother for her son, named for Jocasta, the mother and wife of Oedipus.

Johari Window A management training exercise in which behavior is analyzed as being part of one of four panes demonstrated by a square divided into four smaller squares. Each quadrant refers to an area of knowledge of behaviors: I, public behavior known both to the self and to others; II, behavior known to others but not to the self; III, private behavior known to the self but not to others; and IV, behavior known neither to the self nor to others. The concept is used in human relations training with the intention of developing self-awareness by increasing the size of I and reducing the sizes of quadrants II and III.

Johari window

John's Hopkins chronoscope **Dunlap chronoscope**

Johnny and Jimmy Twin boys studied by Myrtle McGraw. If one child was given training in particular body movements such as climbing a ladder, the child had superior skills over the other at that time, but eventually the untrained one came to have the same abilities as his brother.

joie de vivre (joy of living—French) A combination of a joyous ebullient mood and high energy level, when a person feels "on top of the world."

joining up process A workshop or similar meeting designed to integrate a new member of an organization.

joint marital role relationship A marital relationship in which each spouse is the other's empathetic friend, companion, confidante, etc.

joint probability The chances that two or more events will occur simultaneously.

joke Anything said or done to provoke laughter, and thus contributing to the potential power of laughter to improve physical and mental health. See GALLOWS HUMOR, HUMOR, PUN, WIT.

joking mania Compulsive wisecracking. A morbid tendency to pun, tell pointless stories and poor jokes, and thereby entertain oneself. See MORIA, WITZELSUCHT.

joking relationship   1. A social relationship that allows people to comment on members of a particular group in a fashion that would otherwise be considered offensive (for example, racist or sexist) if performed by persons outside the relationship. 2. The recognized right among some aboriginal peoples, of certain relatives by marriage to jocularize, defame, and deride one another in public with impunity, regardless of differences in age, sex, or rank.

Jonah complex   (A. Maslow) Fear of self-potential and of the possibility of being a failure.

Jordan curve   (C. Jordan, K. Lewin) A closed plane graphic representation that does not intersect itself and divides the plane into two regions for which it is the common boundary. Used by Kurt Lewin to define regions in life space.

Jost's law (of associates)   (A. Jost) A theory that given two associations of equal strength but unequal age, practice is of greater benefit to the older association; also more recently learned material is more likely to be forgotten than material acquired earlier. See LAW OF DIMINISHING RETURNS, PRINCIPLE OF DISTRIBUTED REPETITIONS.

joule (J)   The SI (metric system) unit of work or energy; a standard for measuring work equal to 10,000,000 ergs. Named after English physicist James P. Joule (1818–1889).

joy   A sentiment or emotional attitude characterized by a pleasant feeling tone, related to events or experiences of the immediate present.

J-type   In the perceptual typology of E. R. Jaensch in the 1930s, the "integrated," reality-based person, whose perceptions are systematic, logical, and realistic. Compare S-TYPE.

judg(e)ment   1. An opinion or conclusion drawn from evidence, and from the critical, discerning evaluation of events and people. 2. The opinion regarding the presence or intensity of a signal in relation to other stimuli.

judgment distortions   Situational construals, often maladaptive, based on faulty motives due in some cases to peer pressures or infantile wishes.

judgment sampling   A sampling procedure characterized by attempting to select a sample that is "representative" of a population according to personal opinion, rather than attempting to select by random methods. See NONPROBABILITY SAMPLING, PURPOSIVE SAMPLING.

Jukes (family)   (R. L. Dugdale, A. H. Estabrook) The pseudonym given to an American family studied by psychologists in the 1870s and early 1900s because most members were considered demented or social misfits. See KALLIKAK.

Julesz's stereogram   A stereogram of computer-generated square arrays of sequences of black and white dots arranged in two identical matrices of rows and columns. In one of the matrices, some dots are shifted laterally. These displaced dots viewed through a stereoscope are seen as an object either in front of or behind the stereogram. A person with deficient stereopsis can only see random arrays of dots.

jumping apparatus/stand   See LASHLEY JUMPING STAND.

Jumping Frenchmen of Maine syndrome   A culture-specific syndrome occurring among members of a religious sect that originated in Wales—the United Society of Believers in the Second Appearing of Christ. Their rites include jumping, rolling on the ground, and uttering barking sounds until a state of ecstasy is achieved.

jumping power tests   Part of a physical fitness assessment battery, mainly the Sargent jump-and-reach test (the difference between the standing reach and the maximum jump-and-touch height) and the standing broad jump (the horizontal distance covered in a leap from a semi-crouched position).

jump movements   Eye movements made when looking at motionless objects. See SACCADE.

junction   1. Where two parts join. 2. (A. Adler) An agreement or bargain a person with a neurosis makes in which the person justifies and accepts the neurosis as a means of preventing a personal tragedy (for example, the death of a parent). Also known as neurotic proviso, parapathetic proviso.

Jung association test   (C. G. Jung) The original word-association test in which the person is asked to give immediate verbal associations to a list of common words as they are spoken. The aim is to discover complexes through examining verbal and nonverbal responses.

Jungian   An adherent of the psychological theories of Carl Jung or any theory or technique related to Jung.

Jungian typology   A system of characterizing people based on the four functions of thinking, feeling, sensation, and intuition. In addition, a person may be introverted (predominantly aware of internal states) or extraverted (predominantly aware of others and the outside world). Also known as Jung's typology. See EXTRAVERSION, INTROVERSION, JUNG'S FUNCTIONAL TYPES.

Jung's theory   The following items are important for understanding Carl Jung's theory: ACTIVE-DAYDREAM TECHNIQUE, AFFECT-FANTASY, AMBIVERSION, AMPLIFICATION, ANAGOGIC INTERPRETATION, ANAGOGIC SYMBOLISM, ANALYTIC PSYCHOLOGY, ANAMNESTIC ANALYSIS, ANIMA, ANIMUS, ANTHROPOS, ARCHAISM, ARCHETYPAL IMAGE, ARCHETYPE AS SUCH, ATTITUDINAL TYPE, AUTOHYPNOTIC AMNESIA, AUTONOMOUS COMPLEX, CENTRAL FORCE, CLOUDING EFFECT, COLLECTIVE UNCONSCIOUS, COMPLEX FUNCTION, COMPLEX INDICATORS, CONCRETISM, CONDITIONALISM, CONFESSION, CONSTELLATORY POWER, COSMIC SHADOW, DREAM ANALYSIS, DREAM EGO, EDUCATION STAGE, EGO COMPLEX, ELUCIDATION, ENANTIODROMIA, EUPHORIC APATHY, EXTRAVERTED TYPE, FEELING APPERCEPTION, FEELING TYPE, FREE-ASSOCIATION TEST, FUNCTIONAL ENGRAM, FUNCTIONAL TYPE, FUNCTIONS, INDIVIDUAL MAN, INDIVIDUATION, INTROVERSION-EXTRAVERSION, INTROVERTED TYPE, INTUITIVE TYPE, INWARD PICTURE, IRRATIONAL TYPE, LAND OF CHILDHOOD, LIBIDO, MEDIUMISTIC HYPOTHESIS, MENTAL LEVELS, MIDLIFE CRISIS, MIDLIFE TRANSITION, MYTHOLOGICAL THEMES, OBJECT-RELATIONS THEORY, PARALLEL DREAM, PERSONA, PERSONAL MAN, PERSONAL UNCONSCIOUS, PRIMORDIAL IMAGE, PSYCHIC ISOLATION, QUATERNITY, RACIAL MEMORY, RACIAL UNCONSCIOUS, RATIONAL TYPE, REDUCTIVE INTERPRETATION/METHOD, SENSATION

TYPE, SHADOW, SOUL IMAGE, SUPERIOR FUNCTION, SYNCHRONISM, THEORY OF COMPLEXES, THINKING TYPE, TRANSENDENT(AL) FUNCTION, TRANSFORMATION STAGE, WORD-ASSOCIATION TEST.

jungle law (R. Kipling) "The red claws and teeth of the jungle; the strongest is the one who is right." Refers to a type of intra- or intergroup interaction characterized by the principle that might makes right.

Jung's dream theory Carl Jung distinguished two types of dreams, namely, little dreams and big dreams: the former, Jung held, were mere continuations of a person's daily preoccupations, whereas the latter were viewed as valuable messages from the collective unconscious concerning neglected aspects of a person's mental life.

Jung's functional types Serving the ego, according to Carl Jung, were four functions of thinking, feeling, sensing, intuiting. Thinking and feeling were considered evaluation functions, whereas sensing and intuition were considered perceptual functions. Jung held that people with different typologies had trouble understanding each other. See JUNGIAN TYPOLOGY.

Jung's functional types A diagram of Carl Jung's functional types: thinking, feeling, intuiting, sensing, and also Hans Eysenck's two bipolar scales intersecting with Galen's four temperaments: sanguine, phlegmatic, choleric, and melancholic.

junk box classification Pejorative name for personality classifications that are loose and vague, into which all manner of individual cases are thrown due to superficial similarities, because the diagnostician is uncertain how else to classify them, or both. See WASTEBASKET CLASSIFICATION.

junkie 1. Slang for a person addicted to drugs, particularly opioids. 2. A heroin addict. See HEROIN. 3. Slang for a person addicted to a behavior or any specific substance.

juramentado (cursed person—Spanish) A culture-specific syndrome seen in some Malays and Moros with animistic beliefs. Victims are suddenly overwhelmed by frenzy, rush about stabbing everyone they encounter, after which they lapse into a stuporous sleep from which they awaken with complete amnesia for the episode. The seizures are often preceded by exciting religious rites or by a devastating emotional experience such as the death of a loved one. See AMOK, CULTURE SPECIFIC SYNDROMES.

jurisprudence The science of law. See FORENSIC PSYCHOLOGY.

jurisprudential teaching model A type of teaching model that emphasizes the role of social interaction and uses the model of law and the system of laws as an information-processing model and paradigm for evaluating social issues.

Jus primae noctis (law of the first night—Latin) Historically, a concept that permitted feudal lords, as a symbol of their authority, to take to bed the bride of a serf to "deflower" her. This reflected the medieval European attitude that regarded women as sexual property. Modern scholarship suggests this possibly occurred briefly in the early medieval period in France, Britain, and Italy, but never existed elsewhere in Europe; rather, this was one more way for the lord to tax the vassal (to avoid enforcement of the "right"). Also known as *droit du seigneur* (right of the lord—French), right of the first night, virginal tribute. See DOWRY, WIFE-SWAPPING.

justice 1. A situation in which a certain reward or deprivation is meted out to a person as a fitting and equal exchange or exaction for the results of that person's conduct. Also called retributive justice. 2. A subjective feeling or experience that fairness in reward or punishment has been accomplished. 3. Social or distributive justice speaks to the fair apportioning of resources to all members of the community. 4. (Plato) A trait predisposing a person to fairness in the bestowal of rewards or punishments upon others.

justice perspective Any theory of moral development that focuses on the rights of the individual person; individuals stand alone and independently in making moral decisions. See KOHLBERG'S THEORY OF MORAL DEVELOPMENT.

justification A type of rationalization, finding excuses for behavior that the person knows is wrong.

justification of effort (E. Aronson & J. Mills) Following work to reach a goal, a mental re-evaluation of either the amount invested or the value of the result to make the two consistent. See COGNITIVE DISSONANCE.

justification theory A point of view that rewards given by others will reduce motivation if the person being rewarded views the rewards as bribes.

just intonation The production of tones in their true, mathematically exact vibration ratios, as in the untempered scale.

just-in-time (system) 1. Manufacturing procedure that schedules raw materials and components to arrive from suppliers exactly as needed. The lack of stockpiling lowers costs by eliminating warehousing and by reducing the capital tied up in materials. Originated in Japanese car assembly plants. Also known as JIT, JiT, jit. 2. By extension, the use of temporary employees from a contracting service on an as-needed basis rather than "warehousing" permanent employees.

justitia pectoralis stenophylia Botanical name for an herb that grows wild in Brazil and Venezuela and is a source of a hallucinogenic snuff used by local populations. See HALLUCINOGEN.

just-noticeable difference (JND, jnd, or **j.n.d.)**   (E. H. Weber) An objective measure of difference between two sensory data, such that if this difference be decreased, the two can no longer be distinguished. Also known as difference limen/threshold, differential threshold, just-perceptible difference, least noticeable difference, least-perceptible difference (lpd or l.p.d.), limen of difference, threshold of differences. See ABSOLUTE THRESHOLD, WEBER'S LAW.

just-noticeable-differences method   A psychophysical technique in which a standard stimulus is presented along with a variable stimulus whose magnitude is increased in some trials and decreased in others until a just-perceptible difference is reported. The average of the two series is taken, and the threshold is calculated at the point where the difference can be recognized 50% of the time.

just-noticeable duration   The least-perceptible duration.

just-perceptible difference   **just-noticeable difference**

just-world hypothesis   (M. J. Lerner) A postulate that the world is just, logical, and fair, and whatever happens to a person is just what that person deserves. May lead to blaming victims for their misfortunes. Also known as just-world bias/concept/phenomenon/theory. See PANGLOSSIAN ATTITUDE.

juvenile amaurotic idiocy   A type of familial disease marked by dementia, impaired vision and lipid defect, occurring between ages six and 14 years. Characterized by deposits of pigment around macula of the eye and progressive blindness, mental deterioration, loss of motor control, and finally death. Also known as Batten-Mayou disease and Spielmeyer-Vogt disease. When occurring in infants between the ages of one and 12 months, it is infantile amaurotic idiocy or Tay-Sachs disease; the late infantile form is Bielschowsky-Jansky disease; the late juvenile to adult is Kufs' disease.

juvenile delinquency   Illegal behavior by a minor, including behavior that would be considered criminal if committed by an adult, such as vandalism, truancy, petty thievery, auto theft, forcible rape, arson, drug abuse, and aggravated assault. Major causes appear to be home environment (broken homes, low family standards of behavior, sociopathic parent) and community influences (gangs, criminal subculture, drug subculture), among both the privileged and underprivileged.

juvenile period   The time span extending from the start of puberty to the end of adolescence. Adolescence may be said to end when the law declares individuals to be adults. In some American states it may be as young as 18 or as old as 21 years of age.

juvenilism   A paraphilia in which sexual arousal, orgasm, or both, requires the actual or fantasized impersonation of a juvenile and being treated as such by a sexual partner. A stigmatic-eligible paraphilia in John Money's classification.

juxtallocortex   Oskar Vogt's term for regions of the cerebral cortex situated between the isocortex and the allocortex.

k 1. Any nonzero constant. 2. Symbol for the coefficient of alienation.

K 1. (C. L. Hull) In Hull's theory, the abbreviation for incentive motivation. 2. (C. E. Spearman) Aptitude for remembering structure on a spatial test, such as the Kohs Block Design Test. Sometimes a lower case k; essentially the same as L. L. Thurstone's S factor.

KAE kinesthetic aftereffect

Kahn Test of Symbol Arrangement A standardized diagnostic test in which a participant arranges 16 plastic objects (heart, anchor, etc.) as a means of identifying the participant's cultural-symbolic thinking. Arrangements are compared with typical patterns of normal and clinical groups. Also known as Kahn Test. Named after German psychologist Eugen Kahn (b. 1887).

kainophobia Excessive fear of new things, especially experiences and situations. Also known as kainotophobia. See CAINOTOPHOBIA, NEOPHOBIA.

kairos (fitness, opportunity, time—Greek) In existential psychology, the moment when a person gains insight into the meaning of an important event, past or future. A moment of heightened awareness, an aha experience. See ABREACTION, INSIGHT, OUTSIGHT.

kaisha Japanese for large business organization.

KAIT Kaufman Adolescent and Adult Intelligence Test

kaizen (continuous improvement—Japanese) Striving toward constant improvement in, and taking personal, team, and organizational responsibility for, task performance, equipment, and work design. Used in the singular and plural, with and without definite and indefinite articles.

kakorrhap(h)iophobia Morbid fear of failure. Also spelled kakorrhaphiaphobia. See FEAR OF FAILURE.

Kallikak (family) (H. H. Goddard) The pseudonym for an American family that included one line of continuing distinguished citizens and one of social misfits, mental defectives, alcoholics, criminals, and mentally disturbed individuals. Henry Goddard, who studied the family in the early 1900s, concluded that his "pedigree method" established heredity as the prime factor in mental defect, since the "eminent branch" derived from a normal woman, whereas the "degenerate branch" derived from a retarded one (ignoring the squalid conditions in which she raised them).

Kallmann's syndrome (F. J. Kallmann) A rare condition of insufficient gonadotropic pituitary hormones to stimulate maturation of the testes or ovaries, resulting in infertility. Also known as hypogonadism with anosmia.

Kalmuk idiocy Obsolete name for Down syndrome or Trisomy 21. Name derives from the name of a nomadic Mongol tribe, reflecting the "Mongoloid" appearance of people with Down syndrome.

kalotropic Characterizing the influence exerted by observers' esthetic tastes upon the content of their images, especially eidetic images.

Kama Sutra A sex manual written in India by Vatsyayana in the second century B.C. Discusses techniques, positions, and spiritual aspects. First English translation and publication by Sir Richard Burton in 1883. See TANTRIC FUSION, TANTRIC SEX.

kamikaze (divine wind—Japanese) Self-description of Japanese soldiers in World War II who engaged in suicide missions. See ALTRUISTIC SUICIDE, MARTYRDOM.

Kamin effect (L. J. Kamin) A tendency for animals that have been conditioned in avoidance behavior to later demonstrate a U-shaped curve of performance, first avoiding, then not avoiding, and then avoiding.

kanban Japanese term for a physical system of inventory control and production regulation. A procedure used to realize just-in-time manufacturing. See JUST-IN-TIME.

Kanizsa figure The generation of a clear-cut figure that is outlined by the absence of a contour, for example, three triangles or three black balls, each with a V-shaped cut form another triangle that stands out and tends to be seen as lighter than the surrounding white in contrast to the black lines and the semi-balls that shape the contour.

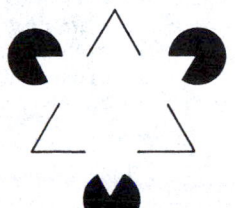

Kanizsa figure An example of apparent perception; perceiving something that does not exist. Most people not only "see" a triangle, but see the "triangle" as being whiter than the surrounding background.

Kanner's disease/syndrome (L. Kanner) Rare names for infantile autism. See INFANTILE AUTISM, AUTOAGGRESSIVE ACTIVITIES, CHILD PSYCHIATRY, EARLY INFANTILE AUTISM, REFRIGERATOR PARENTS.

Kantner and Zelnik surveys   Landmark surveys of "The Sexual Experience of Young Unmarried Women in the United States" conducted in 1971 and 1976 by J. Kantner and M. Zelnik.

Kaposi's sarcoma (KS)   An opportunistic cancer of the skin capillaries and connective tissue, once rare, recently associated mostly with AIDS. Also known as multiple idiopathic hemorrhagic sarcoma, Kaposi's hemorrhagic sarcoma. Named after Austrian dermatologist Moritz K. Kaposi (1837–1902). See ACQUIRED IMMUNE DEFICIENCY SYNDROME.

kappa   The tenth letter of the Greek alphabet. See APPENDIX C.

kappa effect   (J. Cohen) A tendency that if three unequally spaced lights in a straight line (A–B–C) are flashed at equal time intervals, the perceived time interval will appear to be longer between the two lights (B–C) that are further apart from each other, than the perceived time interval for the two lights (A–C) that are closer together. See TAU EFFECT.

kappa waves   Brain waves with a frequency similar to that of alpha waves (ten Hertz or cycles per second) but with a much weaker amplitude. They normally occur while a person is reading, thinking, or dreaming.

kapu   Polynesian term meaning sacred or forbidden. See TABOO.

karass   (K. Vonnegut) A group of people with common interests.

karate-chop exercise   In encounter groups, a exercise used to elicit aggression, considered especially valuable for fearful people. Pairs are matched in any of various ways; one person suddenly makes a quick threatening "karate chop" move toward the other, yelling "Hai!" After, the members discuss their reactions.

karezza   (A. B. Stockham) Coitus in which orgasm is not to be achieved, practiced for contraception and to concentrate and retain the sexual energies released by intercourse. The techniques are derived from principles of Hindu Tantrism. Rarely spelled caressa, carezza, karessa, also known as coitus prolongatus, coitus reservatus. See ONEIDA COMMUNITY, TANTRIC FUSION, TANTRIC SEX.

karma   (Sanskrit) A force believed to be generated by the ethical quality of personal actions, personal intentions, or both, that subsequently influences, either positively or negatively, that person. This force is also purported to propel a person to a particular status in a later incarnation.

Karpman Triangle   (B. Karpman) A roleplaying technique used in encounter groups. There are three roles: the "persecutor" (who assumes a superior attitude), the "rescuer" (who assumes superior understanding and caring), and the "victim" (who assumes helplessness).

karyokinesis   Nuclear activity during mitosis.

karyoplasm   nucleoplasm

karyotype   The chromosomal constitution of a cell; the chromosomes of an individual cell arranged in graphic form. See TRIPLOID KARYOTYPE.

Kasanin-Hanfmann Concept Formation Test   See HANFMANN-KASANIN CONCEPT FORMATION TEST.

kat   A mild hallucinogen and stimulant derived from the perennial shrub *catha edulis* that grows in tropical Africa. Active ingredients include ephedrine and amphetamine-type drugs. Kat herbs have been exported from Africa for centuries and were the source of a tea before the development of coffee as a beverage. Also known as *cafta, chat, khat, qat, quatt.*

katagelophobia   Excessive fear of being humiliated, laughed at or ridiculed. Also spelled catagelophobia.

katagogic tendency   (W. Stekel) A psychic impulse that tends to prevent a person from achieving a positive and constructive life goal. The opposite of the anagogic tendency, which represents upward-leading, constructive impulses.

katasexual(ity)   A sexual preference for dead persons or humans with animal-like characteristics. See NECROPHILIA.

katatonia   Obsolete spelling of catatonia.

Katch test   (V. L. Katch) An intense, short-duration test on an exercise bicycle to estimate the power and capacity of the anaerobic energy system.

katharsis   catharsis

kathisophobia   Morbid fear of sitting down. See THAASSOPHOBIA.

Katz Index of Activities of Daily Living   (S. Katz) A rating chart used to measure persons' ability to bathe, dress, toilet, transfer, and feed themselves and remain continent. Sometimes referred to as Katz Index of ADL.

Kaufman Adolescent and Adult Intelligence test (KAIT)   (A. S. Kaufman & N. L. Kaufman) An examination used with persons from ages 11 to 85. Based on the theory of crystallized and fluid intelligence of John Horn and Raymond Cattell, there are three subtests of each type in the core battery. An expanded battery for estimating neurological damage and a mental status test also exist.

kava   Hawaiian name for an aromatic resin derived from the crushed roots of a Polynesian shrub, *Piper methysticum.* Active ingredients produce sedation without clouding of consciousness. Also known as *ava, cava, kaava, kavakava, kawa, keu, yaqona.*

K complex   A generalized cortical response elicited by an auditory stimulus during sleep and recorded in electroencephalographic changes. See SLEEP STAGES.

Keeler polygraph   (L. Keeler) A lie-detector device that simultaneously records pulse, respiration, blood pressure, and the electrodermal response while the participant is asked questions and generally instructed always to answer no. Rationale is that when the answer is untruthful, the resulting autonomic arousal will indicate the lie. First used as evidence in a court of law in the 1930s, later considered controversial and not usually accepted as legal evidence. See KEELER, LIE DETECTOR.

keep-awake pills   Common name for stimulant pills that contain caffeine as their active ingredient and can be obtained without a prescription. Such pills usually contain approximately 100 milligrams of caffeine, the equivalent of the amount of caffeine in one cup of regular coffee or two cups of strong tea. See CAFFEINISM.

Kegel exercises (A. H. Kegel) A regimen of voluntary isometric exercises for a woman to strengthen the pubococcygeus muscles, performed by tightening and relaxing these muscles several times daily. Originally designed as a nonsurgical treatment for urinary incontinence following childbirth, the exercises purportedly aid in postpartum recovery, deter prolapse of the uterus and bladder, improve urine retention, and add extra control and may increase mutual pleasure during intercourse. Have been used by men to increase sexual response and pleasure. Also known as pubococcygeal (PC) muscle exercises.

Keller plan (F. S. Keller) A college-level system of instruction based on giving a student a small amount of information to learn through individual study, with each student deciding when to take a test to demonstrate complete mastery of that material. Usually only 9 out of 10 multiple-choice questions correct is required to proceed to the next unit, as there might be a defective question. Lecture/demonstrations are used as rewards for students who have completed the specified number of lessons by that date.

Kelley's constant process (T. L. Kelley) A method of fitting psychophysical data obtained by the constant stimuli method to the normal by converting the data to z-scores.

Kelly desegregation scale See DESEGREGATION SCALE.

Kelly's Fundamental Postulate (G. A. Kelly) Of a dozen postulates dealing with personality formation and operations, George Kelly's most basic one was: A person's behavior is explained by how he or she anticipates events. See TELEOLOGY.

Kelly's theory The following items are important for understanding George A. Kelly's theory: CAUSAL SCHEME, COGNITIVE AWARENESS LEVEL, COLLABORATIVE EMPIRICISM, CONSTELLATORY CONSTRUCT, CONSTRUCT SYSTEM, CONSTRUCTIVE ALTERNATIVISM, CORE CONSTRUCT, CREATIVITY CYCLE, DILATION, ELABORATIVE CHOICE, EMERGENT POLE, FIXED ROLE THERAPY, FIXED-ROLE SKETCH, FOCUS OF CONVENIENCE, FUNDAMENTAL POSTULATE, IMPLICIT ROLE, NONCORE ROLE, OPTIMAL MAN, PERSONAL CONSTRUCT THERAPY, PERSONAL CONSTRUCT THEORY, POLAR PROFILES, PREDICTIVE EFFICIENCY, PREEMPTIVE CONSTRUCT, PREVERBAL CONSTRUCT, RANGE OF CONVENIENCE, REGNANT CONSTRUCT, REPERTORY GRID, ROLE THERAPY, ROLE CONSTRUCT REPERTORY TEST, THREAT.

Kelvin (K) scale (W. Thompson) A temperature scale on which the unit of measurement equals the centigrade degree so that absolute zero ($0°K$) is equal to $-273.16°C$. On the Kelvin scale, water freezes at $-273.16°C$, and boils at $373.16°C$. Kelvin is the SI unit of thermodynamic temperature. See CELSIUS SCALE, FAHRENHEIT SCALE, TEMPERATURE SCALES.

Kempf's disease An acute anxiety episode based on the fear of being attacked by a homosexual or that other people may believe one to be a homosexual. Named after American psychiatrist Edward J. Kempf (1885–1971). Similar to homosexual panic.

Kendall coefficient of concordance (W) **coefficient of concordance**

Kendall's rank-correlation coefficient (τ or **Tau**) Kendall's tau.

Kendall's tau (τ) (M. G. Kendall) A measure of the correlation between two sets of ranks. Unlike the Spearman rho, which is based on the numerical differences between paired ranks, the tau coefficient is based on the number of disagreements in orderings. Both tau and rho have equal power since they will reject a false null hypothesis at the same level of significance. The formula for tau uses the statistic S, which symbolizes the disarray in a set of ranks; measures the relationship between pairs of variables in the form of ranks. When there are no tied ranks Tau is calculated by: $\tau = [(4n_{agree}) \div n(n-1)] - 1$ or $\tau = 4n_{disagree} \div n(n-1)$ where n is the number of persons or objects ranked. When there are tied ranks, the two rankings must be rearranged in a two-way frequency table with columns representing ranks assigned by one judge and rows those assigned by the other. Or: $\tau = S \div [1/2N(N-1)]$ where S is the disarray in a set of ranks and N is the number of individuals on both x and y. [Note: The statistic $S = n_{agree} - n_{disagree}$ is restricted to the case in which there are no ties; $n \geq 10$; and a table showing the critical values of s for testing H_o is available.] Tau can be adjusted to measure partial correlation. Also known as Kendall's rank-correlation coefficient.

Kennard principle (C. Kennard) A theory that it is easier to recover from brain damage when young than later in life.

kenophobia Morbid fear of emptiness, barren or wide empty spaces. Fear of the void. Also spelled cenophobia.

kenson (humility, modesty—Japanese) A subtle informal ritual of highlighting some ability or achievement, then discounting it, acknowledging it indirectly or implicitly, and finally interacting to maintain the status quo of the social relationship.

Kent E-G-Y Test Kent Series of Emergency Scales

Kent-Rosanoff Free Association Test (G. H. Kent & A. J. Rosanoff) A standardized, 100-word, free-association examination, with tables of relative frequency of responses that can be used in determining whether the participant's associations tend to be common and normal, unusual and eccentric, or somewhere in between. Also known as Kent-Rosanoff List/Series/Test.

Kent Series of Emergency Scales (G. H. Kent) A brief intelligence test for children ages 5 to 14 designed to provide a quick, preliminary estimate of general intelligence. Also known as E-G-Y Test, Kent E-G-Y Test. See IMMEDIATE TEST.

Kent-Shakow Industrial Formboards (G. H. Kent & D. Shakow) A form board with five spaces that may be fitted using sets of blocks of the same shape. Eight sets of blocks constitute tasks of differing degrees of difficulty.

keraunoneurosis A traumatic neurosis associated with the experience of fear of lightning, thunder, or other forms of intense electric shock.

keraunophobia Fear of lightning. See ASTRAPHOBIA, BRONTOPHOBIA.

kernel (sentence) 1. A simple, active, affirmative, declarative sentence (SAAD). 2. An elementary sentence composed of a noun phrase and a verb phrase. Kernels are the foundation for longer and more intricate constructions.

kernel of truth hypothesis   A postulate that at one time a prejudice might have had a factual basis, whether for a specific prejudiced individual or for groups. See PREJUDICE, POSTJUDICE.

ketamine hydrochloride   A short-term anesthetic that has become a street drug of abuse, causing hallucinations, disorientation, and in excess, high blood pressure, respiratory depression, amnesia. Related to phencyclidine. Street names include "Special K," "Vitamin K," "Kit-kat." See DATE-RAPE DRUG.

ketosis   (F. M. Allen) The excessive formation of ketones in the body or high concentrations of ketoacids in the extracellular fluid, a potentially dangerous medical condition. Can result from low-calorie (ketogenic) weight-loss diets or starvation, poorly controlled diabetes mellitus, and incomplete fat metabolism.

keu kava

key   1. A set of symbols or concepts used in coding or decoding. 2. A set of answers used in scoring a test. 3. The legend on a figure that explains the symbols used in it. 4. The manipulandum (sometimes also serving as a discriminandum) used for subjects, such as pigeons, that peck. 5. A control that the user presses or touches to operate.

keyboard   The fingertip-operated control device, originally for typewriters, then for calculators and the like, and especially for computers. Increasingly used as a verb, meaning to operate the board.

key figure   In every organization, large or small, the person who emerges as a de facto leader, the person relied upon more than any other. See LEADERSHIP, SOCIOMETRY.

key question   (A. Adler) A question designed to reveal the patient's purpose in being ill and his or her personal feelings associated with the symptoms. The examiner asks: "What will you do if you were cured of this condition?" or a similar question and the reply may indicate whether the condition is real, imagined, or assumed.

key symbols   In organizational psychology, symbols that express and evoke the substance of an organization's culture (as pumpkins and black cats are key symbols of Halloween in North America). They include summarizing symbols (undifferentiated and emotionally strong, for instance, a crucifix) and elaborating symbols (more specific and leading to orderly action, such as uniforms, signs, photos, furniture).

key word   In linguistics, nouns and verbs (usually) that determine the choice of syntax.

key-word-in-context   An index or concordance in which designated terms are listed alphabetically and preceded/followed by associated material.

key-word method   A mnemonic technique used in learning foreign-language vocabulary. If the native language is English, the key word would consist of an English word associated with the sound of a foreign word and linked to the foreign word's meaning in a mental image; for example, the French word *livre* (book) may remind a person of the sound of "leaf"; the key word "leaf" can be connected to "book" in a mental image-visualizing a leaf in a book as a bookmark. See MNEMONIC STRATEGY.

khat kat

Ki   Japanese term for "life force" as found in the term *aikido*. See PRANA.

kibbutz   A cooperative or collective settlement in Israel based on the principles of idealistic socialism. Child-rearing is shared by the parents and professional caretakers. See MULTIPLE MOTHERING.

Kiddie Mach Test   An examination intended to measure Machiavellianism in children. See MACH SCALE.

kiddie porn   child pornography

Kiesow's area   (F. Kiesow) A small area located in the inner cheek that is insensitive to pain.

Kilner goggles/screen   An apparatus for viewing the human "aura" or etheric body consisting of a liquid or solid light filter containing a special dye. When a person or other object is viewed through the screen it appears to be surrounded by cloudy emanations, said to represent the "aura." Purportedly, various states of mind and health can be gauged from changing luminosity and colors of the aura. Named after English medical electrician Walter J. Kilner (1847–1920). See KIRLIAN PHOTOGRAPHY.

kilobytophobia   Jocular term for fear of computers. See COMPUTER ILLITERACY.

kilogram (Kg)   The SI (metric system) unit of mass, equal to 1000 grams (about 1000 cubic centimeters of water and about 2.2 pounds).

KIM   A visual learning test in the memory test battery of J. Barbizet and E. Cany. Requires the naming of familiar objects presented to the participant.

kimilue   A culture-specific syndrome found among the Native American Diegueno Indians of lower California. Characteristically, those affected lose all interest in daily life, are generally apathetic, suffer a loss of appetite, and experience vivid sexual dreams.

kindling   A tendency of the nervous system to become more irritable with each episode of seizures, mania, depression, or psychosis. Research suggests that each episode or relapse becomes harder to treat and less likely to achieve full remission.

kindness   A type of behavior characterized by the promotion of another's welfare, without expectation of personal benefit or gain. See ALTRUISM.

kinematics   The science of motion. Also spelled cinematics.

kinephantom   An illusion of mismovement, often seen in movies as wheels moving in an opposite direction to reality.

kinephantoscope   An instrument for projecting shadows or other stimuli that lend themselves to various movement pattern interpretations. See PROJECTIVE TECHNIQUES.

kinesalgia   kinesialgia

kinescope   Obsolete instrument for measuring refraction of the eyes.

kinesia   Motion sickness, such as seasickness.

kinesialgia   Pain caused by muscular movement. Also known as kinesalgia.

kinesic behavior   Communication by the use of body motions rather than formal language, as in winking, shrugging, changing of facial expressions.

kinesics   The study of movement of the body, particularly as in communication through gestures, posture, and facial expressions. Some bodily motions, such as leaning forward with the mouth hanging open or dancing upon hearing some good news, may have universal meaning. See BODY LANGUAGE, SIGN, SIGNAL, SYMBOL. See POSTURAL COMMUNICATION for an illustration.

kinesics technique (of interviewing)   The analysis of the body language (including facial expressions) of a person, particularly a suspect, under the assumption that all body signals have some meaning.

kinesimeter   An instrument used for measuring thresholds of sensations of movement. Also known as kinesiometer.

kinesiology   The study of muscles and muscular movement in relation to the principles of mechanics and anatomy.

kinesiometer   kinesimeter

kinesis   1. Movement of some member of the body resulting from muscular contraction. 2. The process of moving from place to place, tends to be random behavior. Compare TAXIS, TROPISM.

kinesophobia   Morbid fear of motion or of making movements. Also spelled kinetophobia. See DROMOPHOBIA, ERGASIOPHOBIA.

kinesphere   The area of space around a human body in which a person can move a body part or (hypothetically) move the whole body while remaining in one place.

kinesthesia   Sensations arising from movements of any part of the body and arising from stimulation of receptors in the muscles, joints, and tendons. Sensory information from the semicircular canals of the ear also contribute to the sensation of bodily movement. While "kinesthesia" overlaps in meaning with "somesthesia," the former relates more to the perception of movement and position of the body, whereas the latter relates more to the perception of the weight and position of the body. See SOMESTHESIA.

kinesthetic aftereffect (KAE)   An illusion involving the muscle sense, where apparent weight or width, for example, is influenced by shifting from accustomed weight or width to a heavier or wider one, to create the experience of comparative lightness or narrowness in the previous object (as in a batter who picks up two bats and swings them so that a single bat will feel lighter). A type of figural aftereffect.

kinesthetic hallucination   A false perception of body movement, as in patients with schizophrenia "feeling" their heads are enlarging, or an amputee feeling movement in a missing limb. See PHANTOM LIMB for an illustration and also ARISTOTLE'S ILLUSION.

kinesthetic method   A technique for improving speech and writing disorders in which attention is focused on the muscle sensations involved in correct and incorrect performance.

kinesthetic receptor   A sense organ located in the tendons, muscles, and most importantly, in the joints of the body. See PROPRIOCEPTOR.

kinesthetics   Refers to perceptions of movements of a person's own body parts. See EQUILIBRIUM, PROPRIOCEPTION.

kinesthetic sense   The sense that provides information through receptors in the muscles, tendons, and joints, that enables humans to control and coordinate their movements, including walking, talking, facial expression, gestures, and posture. Also known as movement sense. See PROPRIOCEPTION.

kinetic   Pertaining to physical movement, as in the term hyperkinetic.

kinetic aftereffect   An illusion of motion in the reverse direction after stopping a prolonged motion; for example, spinning clockwise and, after stopping, feeling that one is rotating counterclock-wise.

kinetic depth effect   A tendency for a two-dimensional visual pattern to appear to be three-dimensional when the viewer is in motion.

kinetic energy   The energy of motion; the capacity for doing work that a body possesses due to its motion.

kinetic information   The observed gestures, postures, and other behavioral clues used in making an evaluation of any person. See BODY LANGUAGE, GESTURE.

kinetogenesis   The production of evolutionary changes through activity or functioning.

kinetoscope   An apparatus that uses the projecting photographic record of motion in such a way as to produce perceived motion on a screen. The viewer is shown a series of slides in sequence to generate the sense of motion; a precursor of the cinema.

king-slave fantasy   A type of fantasy in which the person plays a role of king or slave or, alternating between the roles, plays both parts.

Kinney's law   (R. Kinney) A theory that in cases of acquired deafness, the length of time over which changes in speech develop is directly proportional to the length of time during which normal speech has been present.

kinocilia   Sensory hairs in the semicircular canals of the inner ear.

kinohapt   A type of esthesiometer used for presenting one or more tactual stimulations at precise temporal and spatial intervals.

Kinsey Institute for Research in Sex, Gender, and Reproduction   A major center at Indiana University for research into all aspects of sexuality. Originally established by Alfred Kinsey as the Institute for Sex Research.

Kinsey reports   The original reports were the results and interpretations of 18,500 interviews (about half of which were conducted by Alfred Kinsey) concerning human sexual behavior published in 1948 (*Sexual Behavior of the Human Male*) and 1953 (*Sexual Behavior of the Human Female*). The first large-scale empirical research on human sexual behavior.

Kinsey (Six) Scale   A discontinuous scale from 0 to 6 that rates the proportion of heterosexual and homosexual activity and fantasy, with 0 being exclusively heterosexual, 3 indicating bisexuality, and 6 meaning totally homosexual in orientation.

kinship   A relationship between two or more persons based upon common descent, often including relationships by marriage or adoption. A prime organizing principle of human society.

kinship network/system 1. The system of blood relationships recognized by a given culture or society. 2. The general communication and interactional behavioral standards established in various societies as well as by individual family conglomerates. Sometimes known as kinship.

KIPS knowledge information processing systems

Kirlian photography (S. D. Kirlian & V. K. Kirlian) A method of photography in which the image of an object is obtained by placing the object in contact with photographic film and sandwiching them between metal plates subjected to high-voltage and high-frequency electricity. The resulting photograph is alleged to be that of the "aura" of the object. See KILNER SCREEN.

Kirschmann's law of contrast (A. Kirschmann) A theory that the saturation of a color induced by simultaneous chromatic contrast is proportional to the logarithm of the saturation of the contrast-inducing color. Named after German psychologist August Kirschmann (1860–1932).

Kish grid (L. Kish) A survey technique designed in 1949 in which interviewers supplied with a sample of household addresses follow rules for selecting one interviewee in each household. Also known as Kish selection table.

kissing (behavior) The activity of making contact with the lips, usually as a sign of friendship or affection. The kiss may involve lip contact with any part of the body and with varying degrees of pressure. Possibly related to licking behavior manifested by other animals. Not observed in all cultures. See FRENCH KISS.

Kjersted-Robinson law (C. L. Kjerstad & E. S. Robinson) A theory that the amount of material learned in a given time is relatively constant and does not depend on the length of the material.

Klebedenken (sticky thinking—German) A schizophrenic association disturbance in which thinking is sticky or adhesive and perseverative.

Kleine-Levin syndrome (W. Kleine & M. Levin) A condition of excessive sleepiness that afflicts persons, usually teenagers, periodically. May be accompanied by inability to remember the episodes and by irritability and confusion.

kleptolagnia Stealing, usually associated with sexual excitement.

kleptomania Impulsive stealing in which the intrinsic value of the article to the person is of little importance.

kleptophilia Being sexually attracted to or aroused by stealing. See KLEPTOPHOBIA.

kleptophobia Morbid fear of becoming a thief or of stealing.

Klinefelter's disease/syndrome (H. F. Klinefelter, E. C. Reifenstein Jr., & F. Albright) A chromosomal disorder affecting males born with a karyotype of 47,XXY, resulting in such symptoms as small testes, absence of sperm, enlarged breasts, excretion of FSH (follicle-stimulating hormone), mental retardation, and behavioral problems.

klinotaxis A tendency for a motile organism such as an animal to pause when orienting itself toward or away from a stimulus to evaluate stimuli sources. See TAXIS, TROPISM.

klismaphilia A psychosexual disorder characterized by the dependence on enemas to obtain sexual stimulation. See PARAPHILIAS.

Klopfer system (B. Klopfer) A technique for interpreting protocols of the Rorschach using a phenomenological and structural approach. See BECK SYSTEM.

Klüver-Bucy syndrome (H. Klüver & P. C. Bucy) A condition resulting from temporal lobectomy or certain atrophic changes in the cerebral cortex, and marked by a tendency to examine all objects by touch or by placing them in the mouth. Other effects include increased sexual activity of all kinds, lack of concentration, and development of a special appetite for meat. The syndrome is observed in both humans and laboratory animals following temporal lobectomy.

knee A sudden operant response-rate change which, on a graph, resembles a knee.

knee-jerk reflex Involuntary contraction of the quadriceps muscle of the leg, following a sharp tap on the patellar ligament. It provides a test of the integrity of the nervous system as the tap on the tendon stretches the muscle and causes a volley of impulses from the spindle receptors to travel to the spinal cord. This in turn triggers a motoneuron response that travels back to the muscle, causing its contraction. See PATELLAR REFLEX, PENDULAR KNEE JERK.

kneejerk response Commonly used to mean any predictable reaction to a message, as in "Opposing taxation is a kneejerk response." See CLASSICAL CONDITIONING.

knismolagnia Being sexually gratified by tickling.

knock-it-off (treatment) Slang for direct, unsympathetic responses to patient excuses. If a client says, "I beat my spouse because I suffer from intermittent explosive syndrome," the therapist might reply, "You, not a syndrome, are responsible for your behavior; make better choices; knock it off."

knockout drops Slang for drugs that are added to alcohol to produce compliance, vulnerability, loss of consciousness. See DATE-RAPE DRUGS, MICKEY FINN.

Know thyself. "Gnothi seauton" a maxim on the walls of Apollo's temple at Delphi, attributed to various Greek philosophers, mainly Socrates, but more appropriately attributed to Thales.

knowledge A type of experience that includes a vivid representation of a fact, formula, or complex condition, together with strong belief in its truth.

knowledge engineer A computer programmer or the like who has or acquires the requisite expertise to design a program.

knowledge information processing system (KIPS) A computer capable of 10^8 logical inferences per second.

knowledge of results (KR) A principle of learning that states that the learner profits from immediate information about his or her progress, such as the accuracy of responses on a test or quiz. Holds that prompt feedback is more effective than delayed feedback in reinforcing correct responses and helping the learner to focus on problem areas. Sometimes known as performance review.

knowledge representation Usually in computer programming or artificial-intelligence designs, the procedures that form the basis for the decision-making structure, usually in the form of "if-then" rules.

knowledge-rich domains   **semantically rich domains**

known-group validity   A method of testing the validity of a test by giving the same test to two groups known to differ in a particular ability (for example, administering a vocabulary test to all fourth grade and sixth grade students in a large school and finding significant group differences).

Knox Cube Imitation Test   (H. A. Knox) An apparently culture-fair performance task in which the participant taps a series of four numbered cubes in various sequences determined by the examiner, such as 2–4–2–1–3. Became part of the Arthur Performance Scale. Named after American psychiatrist Howard A. Knox (b. 1885).

ko ham   (Sanskrit, Vedantic philosophy) "Who am I?" A question some meta-philosophic seekers ask throughout their lives.

koan   In Zen Buddhism, issuing a paradoxical statement or question that has no intellectual solution, such as "What is the sound of one hand clapping?" The purpose of such questions is to generate greater reliance on intuition and less on reason. The stress of such meditation is stated to increase insight into the nature of being.

Koenig cylinders   A set of cylinders tuned to emit high-pitch tones for use in determining the upper absolute threshold of hearing. Also known as König cylinders. Named after German-French physicist Karl Rudolph (1832–1901).

Kohlberg's theory of moral development   (L. Kohlberg) A point of view that there are three levels in moral development with two stages in every level: 1. Preconventional morality: (a) punishment oriented, (b) hedonistically oriented; 2. Conventional morality: (a) interpersonal concordance, (b) social order; 3. Postconventional morality: (a) contractual orientation, (b) personal principles. The following items are important for understanding Lawrence Kohlberg's theory: GURU STAGE, INSTRUMENTAL-RELATIVIST ORIENTATION, LAW-AND-ORDER ORIENTATION, LEGALISTIC ORIENTATION, MORAL DEVELOPMENT, MORAL JUDGMENT, NAIVE EGOTISTIC ORIENTATION, PERSONAL COMMITMENT, POSTCONVENTIONAL LEVEL, PRECONVENTIONAL LEVEL, PREMORAL LEVEL, PREMORBID STAGE, PRINCIPLED MORAL REASONING. See MORALITY.

Köhler-von Restorff effect   (W. Köhler, H. von Restorff) In Gestalt psychology, the superiority of recall for isolated or perceptually distinctive items over items that are more similar to, and easily confused with, others that are known. Also known as isolation effect. See RESTORFF EFFECT.

Kohnstamm maneuver/test   A demonstration frequently used in preparing a person for hypnosis: the person is asked to stand next to a wall and press an arm tightly against it for two minutes; after stepping away, the arm spontaneously rises-showing the person how it feels to yield automatically to an external force, as in hypnosis. Also known as Kohnstamm's phenomenon. Named after German physician Oskar Kohnstamm (1871–1917).

Kohs Block Design Test   (S. C. Kohs) A timed performance task of intelligence consisting of a set of colored cubes that the participant must arrange (4, 9, or 16 at a time) so that the upper surfaces match designs presented on test cards. In the original version, the blocks had sides of red, white, blue, yellow, red-and-white, and yellow-and-blue. Used for differentiating psychiatric from brain-injured participants. With modifications, became part of the Arthur Performance Scale Form I, the Goldstein-Scheerer Tests, and the Wechsler-Bellevue Scale. Further modified by limiting the colors to red and white and the number of blocks used to 4 or 9, it is part of the Wechsler Adult Intelligence Scale (WAIS) and Wechsler Intelligence Scale for Children (WISC). To reduce the distraction of the side patterns, the cubes became 1/8-inch tiles for the Wechsler Preschool and Primary Scale of Intelligence (WPPSI).

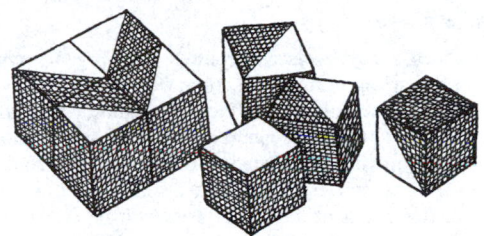

Kohs' Block Design Test   Kohs blocks. In the Kohs' Block Design Test, the examiner shows a participant four scattered blocks and an illustration of a certain (for example, V-shaped) figure. The task is to assemble the blocks so that on the top of the combination they form the V-shaped picture. The score is the amount of time taken to finish the arrangement correctly.

koinonia   (association, communion—Greek) A special relation and sharing in a common commitment, earlier in a religious sense but later used in terms of existential commitments.

KOIS   Kuder Occupational Interest Survey

kola nut   A seed of the trees *cola acuminata* or *cola nitida* whose active ingredient is caffeine. A Congo missionary in the 1660s observed that local tribesmen chewed this nut before meals. Also known as cola nut, colia, goora nut, gura nut, kolia.

Kolmogorov-Smirnoff Tests (K-S Test)   (A. N. Kolmogorov & N. V. Smirnoff, also spelled Smirnov) Two related nonparametric tests sensitive to differences between cumulative distributions. The K-S one-sample test is a test of goodness of fit between the distribution of a set of observed scores and a specified theoretical distribution. The K-S two-sample test, an extension of the K-S one-sample test, is concerned with the degree of agreement between two observed cumulative distributions.

kolytic   Having an inhibitory effect.

König bars   Stimuli used to measure visual acuity.

koniophobia   Fear of dust. Also known as amathophobia, coniophobia.

Kopfermann cubes   A series of line drawings that can be perceived tridimensionally (in a different viewing angle) as well as bidimensionally. Devised and reported by the German physicist and experimental psychologist Hans Kopfermann (b. 1895).

kopophobia   Morbid fear of being fatigued. See PONOPHOBIA.

koprophobia   **coprophobia**

koro   A mental state affecting males and females found in China and the Malay archipelago. Males so affected believe their penis is shrinking and will disappear in their abdomen; women feel their breasts are shrinking and that their labia are entering their vagina. Also spelled *kora*. Also known as *jinjinia bemar, rok-joo, shook yong, shuk yang, suk-yeong, suo yang*. See CULTURE-SPECIFIC SYNDROMES.

Korsakoff amnesia   (S. S. Korsakoff) A type of amnesia in which the person has difficulty retaining new information. Sometimes known as amnestic disorder, axial amnesia.

Korsakoff's psychosis/syndrome   An organic syndrome occurring primarily in chronic alcoholics and occasionally in patients with severe head trauma, prolonged infections, metallic poisoning, pellagra, or brain tumor. Symptoms include anterograde amnesia with confabulation (invented stories), confusion, disorientation, and in some cases polyneuritis. Sergei Korsakoff described the condition only as it affected alcoholics. Also known as Korsakov's psychosis, Korsakow's psychosis. See ALCOHOL-AMNESTIC DISORDER, AMNESTIC SYNDROME.

Korte's laws   (A. Korte) A group of laws for the perception of apparent movement when two stationary visual stimuli are given in succession. The laws cover the relationship between the phenomenon of apparent movement and interstimulus interval, spatial separation of the successively presented stimuli, exposure times, and intensity of the stimuli.

Kpelle   African tribe visited by cultural anthropologists.

KPR   Kuder Preference Record

KPR-V   Kuder Preference Record-Vocational

K prime (K')   (C. L. Hull) In Hull's theory, the symbol for the size of an objective reward in incentive motivation. See HULL'S THEORY.

KR 20/21   See KUDER-RICHARDSON FORMULAS.

K-R 20/21   See KUDER-RICHARDSON FORMULAS.

Kraepelin's disease   (E. Kraepelin) A form of atypical depressive psychosis, a category of persons whose symptoms do not satisfy the criteria for a major affective disorder.

Kraepelin's theory   The following items are important for understanding Emil Kraepelin's theory: DERAILMENT, DERAILMENT OF VOLITION, ECHO PHENOMENON, FANTASTICA MELANCHOLIA, INHIBITED MANIA, IRRESISTIBLE APPREHENSION, KRAEPELIN'S DISEASE, PARABULIA, SIMPLE SCHIZOPHRENIA.

Krantz Health Opinion Survey   (D. Krantz, A. Baum, & M. Wideman) A 1980 questionnaire that assesses the extent to which respondents in stressful medical situations prefer to have information concerning, or to be actively involved in, their own treatment.

Krause's corpuscles/ending   (W. Krause) A specialized sensory nerve ending enclosed in a capsule. It is associated with temperature sensations. Also known as Krause('s) end bulb.

Krebs cycle   A complex metabolic mechanism in which carbohydrates, fatty acids, and amino acids from ingested foods are oxidized to yield carbon dioxide, water, and high-energy phosphate compounds. This mechanism is the principal source of energy for mammals. Also known as citric-acid cycle, tricarboxylic acid cycle. Named after German-British biochemist Hans A. Krebs (1900–1981). See GABA SHUNT.

Kretschmer's (constitutional) typology   (E. Kretschmer) A controversial classification system based on a "clear biological affinity" between specific physiques and specific personality tendencies. Holds that a short, stocky pyknic type tends to be jovial and subject to mood swings; the frail asthenic type is likely to be introversive and sensitive; the muscular athletic type is usually energetic and aggressive; and the disproportioned dysplastic type presents a combination of traits but tends toward the asthenic. Also known as Kretschmer's types. See HUMORAL THEORY, NOSOLOGY.

Kretschmer's theory   The following items are important for understanding Ernst Kretschmer's theory: AFFECTIVE REFLEX, CYCLOTHYMIC TYPE, EUSTHENIC, IMAGE AGGLUTINATIONS, KRETSCHMER'S (CONSTITUTIONAL) TYPOLOGY, LINEAR TYPE, PHTHINOID, PSYCHOBIOGRAM, SCHIZOTHYMIC TYPE.

K-R formulas   See KUDER-RICHARDSON FORMULAS.

Kries theory of vision   duplex theory (of color vision)

Kruskal-Shepard scaling   (W. H. Kruskal & R. Shepard) A psychophysics procedure for determining the processes that participants use in judging the similarity of stimuli.

Kruskal-Wallis ranks test   (W. H. Kruskal & W. A. Wallis) A nonparametric method for determining statistical significance with ranked data. It is analogous to one-way analysis of variance. It is a generalized version of the Mann-Whitney U Test.

KR   See KNOWLEDGE OF RESULTS.

KS   Kaposi's sarcoma

K scale   1. One of the four original control keys on the Minnesota Multiphasic Personality Inventory (MMPI). K score is raised by answers that show a bland "all is well" facade, defensiveness, or "faking good"; a low K suggests excessive frankness and self-criticism or "faking bad." Designed empirically and used in a regression formula to correct the other scales for test-taking attitude. 2. For the meaning in genetics, see DIFFERENTIAL K THEORY.

KSAs   Knowledges, skills, abilities (usually in the context of job requirements).

K-S Test   See KOLMOGOROV-SMIRNOFF TESTS.

kteis   Representation of the female external genitals, usually as a symbol in cult worship.

Ku   See KURTOSIS.

Kübler-Ross's stages of dying   See STAGES OF DYING.

Kuder Occupational Interest Survey (KOIS) (G. F. Kuder) A revision of the original Kuder Preference Record-Vocational (KPR-V) that expresses the score as a type of point-biserial correlation between the respondent's interest pattern and the interest pattern of 126 occupational groups (truck driver to lawyer) and 48 college majors. Some groups include only men, some only women, some both. In addition, ten broad, homogeneous Vocational Interest Estimates similar to the KPR-V are provided.

Kuder Preference Record-Vocational (KPR-V) (G. F. Kuder) An interest inventory based on triads of activities to be marked most and least liked, and yielding percentile scores in ten vocational areas: clerical, computational, art, music, social service, outdoor, science, persuasive, literary, and mechanical.

Kuder-Richardson formulas (K-R 20, KR20, K-R 21, KR21) (G. F. Kuder & M. W. Richardson) In item-analysis of group responses to pass-fail test questions, an internal (inter-item) consistency measure that is the mean of all possible split-half reliability coefficients. K-R 21 assumes equal difficulty of each item; K-R 20 uses the mean item difficulty instead. Coefficient alpha is a generalized version of the K-R technique. Also known as Kuder-Richardson coefficients (of equivalence).

Kufs' disease A late juvenile or adult form of amaurotic family idiocy. It differs from other forms, such as Tay-Sachs disease, in that the incidence is not related to an ethnic group and there is an absence of ocular lesions. The onset of symptoms is from 15 to 26 years of age, and it is diagnosed by the development of dementia, myoclonic jerks in a young adult, and associated with blindness and retinitis pigmentosa. Named after German psychiatrist H. Kufs (1871–1955).

Kuhlmann-Anderson Test (F. Kuhlmann & R. G. Anderson) A series of tests used to measure general intelligence of those ranging from kindergarten to grade 12. Some editions were titled the Kuhlmann-Anderson Intelligence Tests.

Kuhlmann-Binet Test (F. Kuhlmann & A. Binet) A 1912 revision of Henry Goddard's translation of the Binet Test. This revision is usable with those as young as three months of age. It was adapted for American culture. It was the first revision that extended the scale down to the age level of three months.

kundalini (circular, coited—Sanskrit, yogic philosophy) A concept of latent spirituality, in the form of a coiled serpent (♀), who sleeps at the base of the spine, until a person begins to do spiritual practices to awaken her. With the beginning of enlightenment, the snake gradually moves up the spinal canal to the head to merge with Shiva (♂), at which point there is enlightenment. Various Buddhist schools, such as those in Tibet, have adopted the metaphor and the belief and have incorporated practices geared toward such awakening. Some psychologists relate the concept to near death and other transcendental experiences.

Kundgabe (commentary—German) A statement about a mental process or event, contrasted with a direct description of it (*Beschreibung*).

kundgabe error (E. B. Titchener) A misleading report of introspection by experimental participants who,

instead of reporting "what comes" (*Beschreibung*), report what is inferred from what comes. Adding interpretation rather than sticking to scientific description. In contrast, Gestalt psychology insisted that this distinction of Structuralism was impossible to make.

Kundt tube An apparatus for determining the wavelength of sound from which the velocity of sound is calculated; it consists of a resonator tube containing a small amount of fine dust or powder; the tube is completely closed at one end and partially closed by a vibrating disk at the other end. Named after German physicist August A. Kundt (1839–1894).

Kundt's rules (of perception) (A. A. Kundt) Two theories about vision: (a) A distance divided by regular gradation marks appears greater than an unfilled distance. (b) In bisecting a line with one eye closed, the person is likely to put the dividing point closer to the nasal side. See Kundt tube.

kung-fu (boxing principles—Chinese) A Chinese system now known as a martial arts procedure that was originally viewed as a religious and cultural expression toward maximum self-development. Also spelled kung fu.

kurtosis (Ku) A descriptive statistic that describes the degree of peakedness in a set of data. The normal curve is mesokurtic, a tall thin distribution is leptokurtic, a low flat distribution is platykurtic.

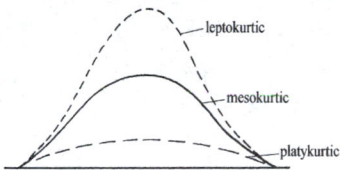

kurtosis

kuru A culture-specific central nervous system disease that afflicts some natives of the New Guinea highlands and is associated with cannibalism. Symptoms include ataxia, tremors, difficulty in walking, and strabismus. Purportedly transmitted by eating the brains of persons previously infected with a kuru virus.

Kurzweil Personal Reader (R. Kurzweil) A device that converts printed matter into synthetic speech.

kwashiorkor Infantile pellagra, a protein-deficiency disease observed in infants and small children who are deprived of essential nutrients during breast-feeding. Symptoms include fluid accumulation in the tissues, liver disorders, impaired growth, distention of the abdomen, and pigment changes in the skin and hair. Normal cerebral development also may be impaired. The condition is found mainly in Third World countries.

kymogram Graphic curve made by a kymograph.

kymograph (J. M. Poiseville, K. F. W. Ludwig, E. Delabarre) An electrically controlled recording instrument essentially consisting of a sensitized, paper-covered rotating drum on which a tracing point (stylus) or pen draws a record, indicating changes in intensity or frequency of response. Used for recording temporal data in psychological or physiological research, it measures heartbeat, body sway, tremors, etc. See illustration at CLASSICAL CONDITIONING for a kymograph (the apparatus at the far left).

L

L 1. See LAMBDA INDEX. 2. lambert. 3. limen. 4. luminance. 5. Symbol indicating the lower limit of the class interval containing the median. 6. Lumen (also abbreviated **lm**).

Labananalysis (R. Laban) Objective analysis of movement as an expression of the individual developed by the Hungarian-born choreographer, together with a system of graphic representation known as Labanotation. See EFFORT-SHAPE TECHNIQUE.

Labanotation See LABANANALYSIS.

labeling 1. Classifying a patient according to a certain diagnostic category. Patient labeling may be misleading since not all cases conform to the sharply defined characteristics of the standard diagnostic categories and some patients may display many traits associated with normal individuals. See DIAGNOSTIC AND STATISTICAL MANUAL. 2. Giving names, usually critical, to social behavior of an undesirable sort, thereby often making that behavior deviant by definition. 3. A mediated response in cognitive thinking, specifically in problem-solving and categorizing.

labeling theory (E. Lemert) A point of view that a label attached to a person may have a significant effect on behavior. Describing a person as "deviant" tends to generate an automatic, self-fulfilling prophecy that may result in the person eventually having a mental disorder or becoming delinquent. Also known as societal-reaction theory. See SELF-FULFILLING PROPHECY.

la belle indifférence (beautiful indifference—French) Phrase originally used for a lack of concern for a person's own physical disability. Seen in persons with hysteria who seem indifferent to the usual ideas associated with the neurotic state. Also manifested by patients with conversion disorders, possibly because the symptoms help to relieve anxiety and bring secondary gains in the form of sympathy and attention. See SECONDARY GAINS.

labia Relating to lips. Though occasionally used in other senses (labia cerebri, edge of cerebral hemisphere overlapping the callosum; labia oris, lips of the mouth), more commonly refers to labia pudendi, the lips of the vulva, consisting of the labia majora (labia externa) or larger, more prominent outer lips and the labia minora (labia interna) or thinner inner lips.

labial A speech sound made with the lips, for example, /b/, /p/, /m/, /w/, /f/, or /v/. If the sound is made with both lips, it is called a bilabial, or labiolabial; if the sound is made with the lower lip and the upper teeth, it is called a labiodental, or dentolabial. See BILABIAL, FRICATIVE, LABIODENTAL, PLOSIVE.

labile Emotionally expressive in a rapidly changing fashion. Describing a person who seems flighty, talks a lot, and demonstrates inappropriate range of emotions.

labile affect An unstable, changeable, uncontrolled expression of feelings and emotions. Common in histrionic individuals and in early schizophrenia and organic brain syndromes.

lability 1. (N. Vvedensky) The maximum number of impulses that a nerve or other body structure can pass on without distortion in any unit of time. 2. Unstable emotions, alternating somber and euphoric moods, common in bipolar disorder and some organic brain syndromes.

labio-alveolar (speech) A kind of speech dependent on both lips rounded as in pronouncing "when."

labio-dental 1. Relating to the lips and the teeth. 2. A speech sound made with the lower lip touching or near the upper teeth, for example, /f/ or /v/. Also known as dentolabial, labiodental. See BILABIAL, FRICATIVE.

laboratory-method model An educational approach in which the role of social interaction is emphasized. The development of personal awareness and interpersonal skills is a major area of concern.

laboratory training A process directed to the improvement of interpersonal relations, group functioning, and organizational behavior under the general guidance of a leader. See GROUP DYNAMICS, SENSITIVITY TRAINING, T-GROUP.

labor motility 1. The rate of workforce movement in and out of an industry, including replacements (labor turnover) but also increases and decreases in overall working force. 2. The ease with which employees either move from one company to another, or from one geographic location to another, or even internally from one position to another.

labor turnover Assuming a stable company, the number of people who leave and who are replaced in a year, for example, a company has 100 salespeople and during a particular year, 23 leave and 23 are hired, the turnover rate is 0.23 or 23%.

labyrinth (G. Fallopius) The fluid-filled, bony chamber of the inner ear containing the receptors for the sense of hearing and the sense of balance. See COCHLEA, SEMICIRCULAR CANALS.

labyrinthine 1. Characterizing speech that is hard or impossible to follow because it wanders from topic to topic with no apparent associative connections, observed primarily in schizophrenia. 2. Less common in psychology, pertaining to the labyrinth.

labyrinthine sense The sense of equilibrium.

lacing agent A chemical used as filler or substitute for portions of the active ingredient in drug products, particularly illicit drugs, for example, caffeine may be used as a lacing agent for cocaine.

laconic speech 1. Excessively brief, unelaborated verbal expression. 2. Verbal communication lacking spontaneity, frequently found in major depression, schizophrenia, and organic brain syndromes. Also known as poverty of speech.

lacrimal Pertaining to the secretion of tears. Etymologically incorrect spelling is lachrymal.

lacrimal glands Structures of the body that secrete tears, located in depressions of the frontal bones of the face near the eyes. Incorrectly spelled lachrymal.

lacrimal reflex Increased secretion of tears following irritation of the conjunctiva (mucous membrane of the inner surface of the eyelid and related areas of the eye). Sometimes incorrectly spelled lachrymal.

lacrimation Secretion of tears, especially in excess. Excessive tearing; crying.

lactation 1. Production of milk by the mammary glands of mammals. 2. The period following birth during which milk is secreted from the mammary glands of mammals.

lactogenic hormone A substance released by the anterior pituitary gland that stimulates ovarian progesterone and the production of milk; also helps in the maturation process of the corpus luteum. See FOLLICLE-STIMULATING HORMONE (FSH).

lacuna A gap or break, such as a gap in memory. Plural is lacunae.

lacunar amnesia   localized amnesia

LAD language-acquisition device

L   add-Franklin theory (of color vision) (C. Ladd-Franklin) An explanation of color vision based on gradual evolution of color-sensitive visual receptors from a normal state of color blindness in primitive animals. Proposes that yellow and blue receptors evolved first, then red and green receptors developed out of yellow-sensitive cones. Regression to a more primitive stage would account for absence of certain receptors in color-blind humans. See COLOR VISION, THEORIES OF COLOR VISION.

ladder fear See CLIMACOPHOBIA.

la folie circulaire French phrase used by Jean Falret, similar to Emil Kraepelin's manic-depressive insanity, or what was later called bipolar disorder.

lag 1. Continuation of a sensation after the stimulus excitation has ceased. 2. The elapsed time between stimulus presentation and resulting response. See REACTION TIME. 3. See CULTURAL LAG.

lagena A portion of the auditory labyrinth of lower vertebrates that is probably the specific receptor organ of hearing. The corresponding organ in humans is the cochlea. Plural is lagenae.

laissez-faire (let it be—French) Phrase used primarily to indicate a type of nonleadership in which the authority (such as teacher, parent, employer) basically allows subordinates to do as they wish.

laissez-faire group (K. Lewin) In social psychology, a group with passive leadership and a minimum of control.

laissez-faire leader A type of leader who is minimally directive and authoritarian, providing minimal or no structure for group activities. Goals and procedures are determined by members. In studies by Kurt Lewin, Ronald Lippitt, and R. K. White, laissez-faire leaders were passive, providing information or guidance only if directly asked; their groups showed low productivity, low cohesiveness, and apathy. See AUTHORITARIAN LEADER, DEMOCRATIC LEADER.

laissez-faire leadership 1. (B. Bass) The absence or avoidance of leadership, which may be appropriate on occasion, but is highly ineffective if it becomes a steady way that the leader works with subordinates. This avoidance or absence of leadership is, by definition, most inactive. 2. (K. Lewin) A style of leadership that calls for giving people more leeway and freedom of action than necessary to achieve optimal results. It is the other side of the ineffective supervision coin from autocratic leadership, with democratic leadership best. See PASSIVE MANAGEMENT BY EXCEPTION.

laissez-faire parenting A parenting style characterized by parents taking a "hands off" approach in the upbringing of their children, allowing children considerable freedom of action.

Laius jealousy (I. D. Suttie) The father's regressive jealousy of the child's nurturance from the mother, based on the myth of Oedipus' father.

Lake vs Cameron See LEAST-RESTRICTIVE ALTERNATIVE.

laliophobia Morbid fear of speaking or talking, especially the fear that stammering or stuttering will occur while speaking. Also known as lalophobia.

lallation 1. Infantile speech that persists beyond the age at which precise speech sounds should have been acquired. Characterized by sound omission, or substitutions, such as saying "lellow" instead of "yellow" or "wed" instead of "red." 2. See LALLING.

lalling Stuttering in which speech is almost unintelligible.

lalopathy Any form of speech disorder.

laloplegia Inability to speak due to paralysis of the speech muscles, not including the muscles of the tongue.

Lamarckian (evolution) theory Jean Lamarck's view that acquired characteristics may be transmitted via genetic changes to their descendants, for example, giraffes stretching their necks to eat leaves from trees imparting this tendency to their offspring. Also known as Lamarckian transmission, Lamarck(ian)ism. Compare DARWIN'S THEORY.

Lamaze method (F. Lamaze, D. Reed) A variation of the natural-childbirth technique, developed in the 1950s. The woman learns about childbirth anatomy and physiology, controlled breathing, muscular relaxation, and concentration. She is active during labor, and there is emphasis on the father sharing in the birth experience. The Lamaze method evolved indirectly from work of Ivan Pavlov. See NATURAL CHILDBIRTH.

lambda The eleventh letter of the Greek alphabet. See APPENDIX C.

lambda index (L) In Rorschach test scoring, an indicator based on the ratio of all non-F to F scores. Indicates responsiveness to objective features or environment, from inadequate emphasis through normal realism to over-emphasis.

lambert (L) (J. H. Lambert) A measure of luminance; the amount of light reflected from a perfectly diffusing and reflecting surface emitting one lumen per square centimeter.

Lambert's law (J. H. Lambert) A theory that the incidence, emission, and reflection of light vary directly as the cosines of the angle of the rays perpendicular to the surface.

Lambert's method (J. H. Lambert) A method for mixing colors using two pieces of clear glass and patches of color.

lamella 1. A thin sheet or layer. 2. Thin metal plate, usually set in vibration at a known rate. Used in research on audition. See APPUNN'S LAMELLA.

lamina terminalis Anterior boundary of the third ventricle of the brain.

Landau reflex A normal reaction observed in infants when the child is supported horizontally in the prone position; the head raises and the back arches. An absence of the reflex is a sign of a neurologic disorder such as cerebral palsy or motor-neuron disease.

Land effect The perception of color in black-and-white photographs. A demonstration by Edwin Land that full-color effects can occur using only red and white light and a green filter. See YOUNG-HELMHOLTZ THEORY OF COLOR VISION.

landmarks Sensory cues that assist an organism in orientation or providing cues to a goal location.

land of childhood (C. G. Jung) Describing the period in which the rational consciousness has not yet separated from the collective unconscious. Mythological images and associations predominate.

Landolt circles/rings A set of printed circles with gaps of varying size that the participant is asked to locate, used to test visual acuity. Named after French ophthalmologist Edmund Landolt (1846–1926).

Land theory of color vision A point of view that color is perceived because of relationships or ratios between different light frequencies. Thus, red is in relation to orange, orange is in relation to yellow, etc. Edwin Land discovered that varied colors could be produced by mixing black and white. (The neurochemistry and neurophysiology of this mechanism is not well documented.) See YOUNG-HELMHOLTZ THEORY OF COLOR VISION.

Langdon Down's disease *Down's syndrome*

Langerhans cells Free nerve endings that terminate in the epithelium. Named after German anatomist Paul Langerhans (1847–1888). See GLUCAGON, INSULIN.

language Any means, vocal or other, of expressing or communicating thought or feeling. Types of language include: AMERICAN SIGN, ARTICULATE, BEHAVIOR(AL), BODY, CEREMONIAL, COMMON BUSINESS ORIENTED, DANCING, EXPRESSIVE, FIGURATIVE, GESTURAL, GESTURAL-POSTURAL, GRAPHIC, INFORMATION PROCESSING, INNER, IRRELEVANT, META-, METAPHORIC, ORGAN, PARA-, RECEPTIVE, SECOND-ORDER, SIGN, SOURCE, SYNTHETIC, TARGET.

language-acquisition device (LAD) 1. (B. Whorf) The innate mechanism of children in developing a language structure to use linguistic data from parents. 2. (N. Chomsky) An inherited ability of children to learn rules of language.

language acquisition theory A point of view that the capacity to employ language to send and receive depends on the capacity of the organism to decode and reorganize a complex of sounds.

language arts In education, part of the school curriculum that incorporates the language skills of listening, speaking, reading, spelling, and handwriting.

language centers Areas of the cerebral cortex, such as Broca's area, involved in spoken or written language functions as well as music.

language deficit A delay, or deviance, in the normal speech and language development of a child due to some neurological dysfunction.

language development See ORIGIN-OF-LANGUAGE THEORIES.

language disability See GENERAL LANGUAGE DISABILITY, LANGUAGE DISORDER.

language disorder/dysfunction Disturbance of speech or writing characterized by failure to follow the rules that govern meaning (semantics) or structure (syntax). See AGRAMMATISM, APHASIA, CLANG ASSOCIATION, INCOHERENCE, NEOLOGISM, WORD APPROXIMATION, WORD SALAD.

language ESP (K. Rao) Ability to use extrasensory perception (ESP) in tests where the targets are words in languages unfamiliar to the participant.

language-experience approach to reading A method of teaching language skills based on children's experiences. Experience-based materials may be dictated by the child to the teacher, then used as material for teaching reading.

language localization Areas of the brain in which various functions of written and spoken words and music are centered. Broca's original discovery found language localization near the third frontal convolution of the left hemisphere. Later research has identified numerous cortical centers associated with visual and auditory language processing as well as neural pathways linking the areas. See SPEECH LOCALIZATION.

language origin See ORIGIN-OF-LANGUAGE THEORIES.

language pathology The study of the causes and treatment of symbolic behavior disorders.

language retardation   Delayed language skills manifested by lisping, lallation, baby talk, congenital auditory agnosia, and word deafness.

language score (L)   See AMERICAN COUNCIL ON EDUCATION TEST.

language theories   See CLOAK THEORY OF LANGUAGE, GENERATIVE THEORY OF LANGUAGE ACQUISITION, ORIGIN-OF-LANGUAGE THEORIES, TWO-WORD STAGE (OF LANGUAGE DEVELOPMENT).

language universal   1. Features purportedly found in all natural languages. 2. (N. Chomsky) The innate capacity of humans to understand basic grammar of language, considered a refutation of fundamental behavioral theories. 3. The assumption that all human infants have the capacity for easily learning any language's rules of syntax, implying of negation, indicating plurals, putting in questions, since all languages have these basic elements in common.

lap dancing   A method of sexual stimulation in which a person, usually naked, squirms on a seated person's lap, stimulating the latter by movements of the body. There is no direct contact between sexual organs. See INTERFEMORAL SEX, PROSTITUTION.

lapsus calami   (slip of the pen—Latin) Mistakes dictated by unconscious feelings or impulses. See FREUDIAN SLIP, PARAPRAXIS, SYMPTOMATIC ACT.

lapsus linguae   (slip of the tongue—Latin) An unconscious, unintentional error that alters the surface meaning of what a person is saying while revealing an unconscious association, motivation, or wish. See FREUDIAN SLIP, SYMPTOMATIC ACT.

lapsus memoriae   (memory lapse—Latin) A temporary inaccuracy in memory or a temporary inability to remember a common fact, especially when the lapse has unconscious significance, as in forgetting the name of a person who is disliked. See FREUDIAN SLIP, SYMPTOMATIC ACT.

large group   In general terms, a group too large for all members to get to know each other.

large-object fear   See MEGALOPHOBIA.

larval sadism   Masked or concealed sadism.

larval schizophrenia   Latent or incipient schizophrenia. Schizophrenia assumed to be present but not overtly advanced to the level of psychosis.

laryngeal reflex   Coughing due to irritation of the larynx or the throat.

larynx   A muscular and cartilaginous structure at the top of the trachea and below the tongue roots; the organ of voice consisting of nine cartilages connected by ligaments, and containing the vocal cords. Plural is larynges.

Lashley's jumping stand   (K. S. Lashley) A photographer's tripod with a small horizontal platform on which a small animal is placed. The animal is induced to jump toward a screen by various methods, including a low frequency electric shock. The screen may have two symbols, for example + and 0. The animal learns that if it jumps toward the 0 it breaks through the screen and lands on a feeding platform, but if it jumps toward the + it strikes a hard surface and falls below to a basket.

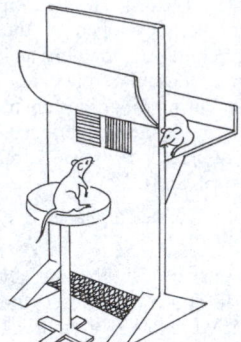

Lashley's jumping stand   Invented by Karl Lashley, an apparatus used in experiments on animal learning. In the example shown, the rat may jump towards the screen with vertical lines and land on a surface where there is food. Making an incorrect jump toward the screen with the horizontal lines results in the rat falling to the net below.

Lashley-Wade hypothesis   A postulate (in opposition to Hull-Spence theory of 1943) stating that in learning experiments with animals, stimulus generalizations will require that animals get differential training with several values presented of the stimulus material. Karl Lashley and Marjorie Wade described the stimulus generalization hypothesis in 1946. See ANIMAL LEARNING. Also see ENGRAM, LASHLEY'S JUMPING STAND, LAW OF EQUIPOTENTIALITY, LAW OF MASS ACTION, MASS ACTION THEORY.

lata   *latah*

latah   (ticklish—Malaysian) A culture-specific syndrome seen in Malaysia, Thailand, Siberia, the Congo, and the Philippines, manifested mainly in dull, submissive women who have been subjected to a sudden fright. Major symptoms include overwhelming fearfulness, imitative behavior, and a compulsion to utter obscenities. Also known as latah syndrome. See CULTURE-SPECIFIC SYNDROME, JUMPING FRENCHMEN OF MAINE SYNDROME.

latch-key children   School-age children who come home from school to an empty house usually because either there is only one parent (who works), or both parents are at work or otherwise absent. Also known as latch-key kids.

late adolescence   (H. S. Sullivan) The last stage of adolescence before adulthood.

late-adult transition   (D. Levinson) A transition period between mid-life and late adulthood.

latency   1. See LATENCY PERIOD/STAGE. 2. The time period between the stimulus and the response.

latency of response   The amount of time between the onset of a stimulus and the beginning of the response. Also known as latency of reply, response latency. See REACTION TIME, RESPONSE TIME.

latency of the conditioned response   The amount of time between presentation of the conditioned stimulus and occurrence of the conditioned response. See INTERSTIMULUS INTERVAL.

latency period/stage   In psychoanalytic theory, the stage of psychosexual development when overt sexual interest is purposefully repressed and sublimated. This stage lasts from the resolution of the Oedipal phase (fifth or sixth year) to the onset of puberty (eleventh to thirteenth year). Also known as latency, latent period.

latent   1. Hidden, not known to anyone, but eventually a potent or effective element. 2. Not evident but in existence. Compare MANIFEST.

latent addition period   A brief time span when a second stimulus may add to the effects of a first stimulus. Varies with the size of the nerve and synaptic factors and lasts approximately one-half millisecond.

latent causal variable   A causal variable that does not act until triggered by other variables. Compare TRIGGERED CAUSAL VARIABLE.

latent content   In psychoanalytic theory, concealed or disguised impulses and ideas that lie beneath symbolic images, or manifest content, of dreams or fantasies. According to Sigmund Freud, unconscious wishes and impulses seeking expression in dreams encounter "censorship" and are distorted into symbolic representations, that is, the manifest content or dream as experienced. Through free association and interpretation, the latent content can be uncovered. See CONTENT ANALYSIS, DREAMWORK, MANIFEST CONTENT.

latent dream   (S. Freud) The real meaning of a dream rather than the overt meaning.

latent fat   A situation in which a high number of adipocytes (fat cells) provide the potential for obesity, even though they may be presently thin due to dieting.

latent goals   1. In evaluation research, objectives of a program or organization that are not publicly stated. Functions that result from the attempt to obtain manifest goals that are not obvious, apparent, or planned by the program director. 2. Program objectives known to the staff considered unacceptable for public statement.

latent homosexuality   Homosexual tendencies never expressed overtly, usually not recognized by the person experiencing them.

latent learning   Knowledge acquired unintentionally and remaining subconscious or latent until a specific need for it arises, for example, a student writing an exam may be able to cite a quotation subconsciously memorized. A form of incidental learning. See SIGN LEARNING.

latent need   A need evident neither to the person nor to others, for example, a child may have a need for social interaction but this need is neither capable of being expressed by the child nor considered by adults. Compare MANIFEST NEED.

latent process   A subliminal neural or mental process intervening between two supraliminal events or preceding such an event.

latent psychosis   An underlying psychotic disorder, such as schizophrenia, that has not reached a full-blown, or florid stage. Also known as incipient psychosis, prepsychotic psychosis.

latent schizophrenia   A diagnosis of a person who appears likely to develop schizophrenia, having shown prodromic (predictive) signs.

latent social identity   In social situations, a person's behavior is to some degree based on that person's perception of what is proper for him or her in that specific situation.

latent stage   (S. Freud) A period of life in pre-adolescence in which there is purportedly relatively little conscious sexual interest. See LATENCY PERIOD.

latent structure analysis   (P. F. Lazarsfeld) A method of evaluating replies to an attitude questionnaire based on the assumption that contradictory or partially inconsistent replies can be explained in terms of the latent distance found in deeper underlying attitudes.

latent trait theory   The point of view that performance on a personality test is predictive of some trait that will eventually be manifested.

lateral   Pertaining to the side, or away from the midline of the body.

lateral axis   In anatomical direction, the axis that lies away from the medial plane of the body, and is identical to the dextrosinistral axis.

lateral bundle   A bundle of nerve fibers in the spinal cord that carry impulses from pain- and temperature-sensory end organs.

lateral cervical nucleus   Part of the lemniscal system, appearing as a small mass of gray matter beneath the medulla. Axons of the lateral cervical nucleus communicate with the medial lemniscus.

lateral confusion   See MIXED LATERALITY.

lateral corticospinal tract   One of the two primary motoneuron pathways in the spinal cord, consisting of crossed fibers running between the spinal motor mechanisms and the direct sensory fibers.

lateral difference   General phrase referring to differences between the two hemispheres of the brain in relation to covert and overt behavior.

lateral dominance   A tendency for one hemisphere of the brain to be dominant over the other for most functions, leading to preferential use of one side of the body. Also known as hemispherical dominance. See HARRIS TESTS OF LATERAL DOMINANCE, LATERALITY.

lateral fissure   A groove on the surface of the brain that is below the frontal and parietal lobes and above the temporal lobe. Sometimes known as Sylvian fissure. See BRAIN for an illustration.

lateral geniculate   An area where ganglion cell axons terminate.

lateral geniculate body (LGB)   An oval swelling on the rear of the thalamus toward the outer (right or left) side, connected to the superior colliculus through the superior brachium. Most of the fibers of the optic nerve end in the lateral geniculate body and are relayed to the visual cortex. Also known as external geniculate body.

lateral geniculate nucleus (LGN)   A nerve cell located on the lateral surface of the thalamus and serving as a relay neuron for visual impulses being transmitted to the cortex.

lateral gyrus   A convolution in the surface of the brain located in the area of the cingulate gyrus above the corpus callosum.

lateral horns   A lateral portion of gray matter located between the dorsal and ventral horns of the spinal cord. Lateral horns contain the autonomic-motor fibers that innervate the smooth muscles, heart, and glands.

lateral hypothalamic syndrome   A pattern of recovery from lateral hypothalamic lesions, marked by aphagia and adipsia, during which period an experimental animal is kept alive by tube feeding, followed by a period of adipsia-anorexia when only wet, palatable foods are accepted. In the third stage, the animal will eat hydrated dry food but continue to avoid water intake and may suffer dehydration. Recovery is the fourth stage.

lateral hypothalamus (LH)   A portion of the hypothalamus that regulates appetite. Lesions of the lateral hypothalamus in animal experiments result in a loss of interest in food. Stimulation of that part of the brain increases the animal's appetite. See VENTROMEDIAL NUCLEUS OF THE HYPOTHALAMUS.

lateral inhibition   A theory that discrimination between various sensory inputs, such as taste sensations, involves a feedback mechanism of second-order cells and collaterals relaying impulses into an inhibitory network which in turn raises the threshold for the sensation.

laterality   The preferential use of one side of the body for certain functions such as eating, writing, sighting, and kicking. The trait is associated with cerebral dominance. See DIRECTIONAL CONFUSION, FUNCTIONAL PLASTICITY, HANDEDNESS, LANGUAGE LOCALIZATION, LATERALIZATION, MIXED LATERALITY, RIGHT-LEFT DISORIENTATION, SPEECH LATERALIZATION, SPLIT BRAIN.

lateralization   Relationship between handedness, eyedness, footedness, and cerebral dominance as manifested by learning tasks and also signs of localized brain damage. Right-left confusion and dyslexia are among disorders diagnosed through lateralization tests. Lateralization is observed more frequently in humans than in primates. See SPEECH LATERALIZATION.

lateralization of functions   See CEREBRAL SPECIALIZATION.

lateral lemniscus   A bundle of nerve fibers running longitudinally upward through the pons, terminating in the medial geniculate body and inferior colliculus. It carries auditory-nerve fibers from one side of the body to the other. Compare MEDIAL LEMNISCUS. See LEMNISCAL SYSTEM.

lateral masking   See MASKING.

lateral olfactory tract   A bundle of axons of mitral cells which forms the primary communication between the olfactory system and portions of the brain. See OLFACTORY TRACT.

lateral orbital gyrus   See ORBITAL GYRI.

lateral rectus   A muscle used in controlling eye movements, for turning the eye away from the nose. Also known as internal rectus. The other five eye muscles are INFERIOR OBLIQUE, INFERIOR RECTUS, MEDIAL RECTUS, SUPERIOR OBLIQUE, SUPERIOR RECTUS.

lateral section   A portion of a body or organ located on or toward a side and away from the medial, or middle, section. See CONTRALATERAL, IPSILATERAL.

lateral specialization   Special abilities in the right or left hemisphere of the brain, such as the general tendency for speech, writing, calculation, and language to be controlled by the left hemisphere and nonverbal ideation and spatial construction to be controlled by the right hemisphere. See LATERALITY.

lateral spinothalamic tract   One of the long sensory-nerve bundles that runs through the lateral, or outer, areas of the spinal cord. It contains second-order neurons and fibers that ascend all the way to the thalamus without synapses. See SPINOTHALAMIC TRACT.

lateral sulcus   See SYLVIAN FISSURE.

lateral thalamic nucleus   A large mass of cell bodies on the lateral side of the thalamus which relay incoming sensory impulses.

lateral thinking   (E. de Bono) A way of solving problems by attacking them in an unusual manner, usually tried after the usual direct manner has failed. A restatement of the problem may lead to a satisfactory answer.

lateral ventricle   A reservoir of cerebrospinal fluid found in each of the cerebral hemispheres of the brain. The lateral ventricles on each side communicate with each other and with the third ventricle at a point near the thalamus. See BRAIN VENTRICLES.

later life adjustment   Reactions of older people stemming from stress situations including physiological changes, moving from a long-term home, retirement from work, loss of family members and friends, illness, decline in attractiveness, financial problems, dependency on others or the prospect of disabling conditions and imminent death.

lateropulsion   An involuntary sidewise movement, a symptom of certain central nervous system disorders, for example, parkinsonism, in which the patient makes rapid, short steps sidewise.

lateroventral nucleus of hypothalamus   One of a group of relay nuclei located in the thalamus where it transmits impulses from the cerebellum to the frontal lobe. Its function is related to coordination of muscular movements.

late selection theory   A point of view that most incoming stimuli are sent to working memory before any screening out is done.

Latin square (design)   A research design in which treatments are administered in orders systematically varied, denoted by Latin letters. Latin squares permit an experimenter to isolate variations due to two nuisance variables in evaluating treatment effects.

latitude effect   The further from the equator, the higher the incidence of schizophrenia.

laudanum   (Paracelsus, T. Sydenham) A mixture of alcohol and opium once commonly used as an analgesic and anesthetic. The mixture was introduced around 1530 by Paracelsus and was used as an intoxicating beverage in 18th-century England. Laudanum was also a common component of patent medicines in the 19th century.

laughing spells   Unrestrained or paroxysmal laughter. Such spells have been found to: (a) precipitate cataplectic attacks; (b) be a common manifestation in manias, and a symptom of the Angelman or "happy-puppet" syndrome; (c) be an occasional symptom of psychomotor seizure among children (termed gelastic epilepsy).

laughter   Pleasurable convulsive sounds which serve to release tension built up when people listen to an amusing story or watch or recall an amusing event.

launching   The departure of children from their homes to establish themselves as independent entities, such as by attending college, getting married, starting a career, or joining the armed forces. See EMPTY NEST SYNDROME.

law   A theory accepted as correct, that has no significant rivals in accounting for the facts within its domain.

law-and-order orientation (L. Kohlberg) The stage of Lawrence Kohlberg's conventional level of moral reasoning in which the emphasis is on authority, established rules, performing "one's duty," and maintaining the social order. See CONVENTIONAL LEVEL.

law of advantage (R. S. Woodworth) A theory that, given two or more inconsistent responses to the same situation, one has an advantage over the others, and is more dependable than the others. Also known as advantage law/principle, principle of advantage.

law of ancestral inheritance (F. Galton) A theory by Sir Francis Galton that on the average, one-fourth of an organism's characters are derived from each parent, one-sixteenth from each grandparent, etc. Also known as ancestral inheritance law.

law of assimilation A theory that organisms respond to new situations in a manner similar to their reactions to familiar situations. Also known as assimilation law.

law of association (Aristotle) A theory that acts or ideas (or stimuli and responses) that occur simultaneously or in close succession tend to become combined or unified, thus forming an integrated act or idea of more complex character (or a stimulus-response connection). Also known as cohesion law, combination law, law of cohesion, law of combination.

law of associative shifting (E. L. Thorndike) A theory that stimuli associated with an original S-R bond will in time initiate a response to a somewhat similar stimulus in the absence of the original stimulus. Also known as law of shifting. See CONDITIONING.

law of avalanche (R. Cajal) A theory that neural impulses spread from a stimulus receptor to a number of other neurons, resulting in an effect disproportionate to the initial stimulus, as in an epileptic seizure. Also known as avalanche law.

law of averages 1. A theory that, given a measurement far from the mean, the later measurements even for the same individual are likely to be closer to the mean. See REGRESSION TO THE MEAN. 2. The statement that a large sample is better than a small sample for estimating a population parameter. A common-sense intuition rather than a mathematical theorem such as the law of large numbers.

law of belongingness (E. L. Thorndike) A principle that items organized or sorted into groups (that is, that are seen as belonging together) are better remembered than the same items in an isolated conformation. Also known as belongingness law, principle of belongingness.

Law of Bichat An early concept (18th century) that the vegetative body system provides for anabolism whereas the animal body system provides for catabolism, the two systems being in inverse ratio in the development of ontogenetic evolution.

law of biogenesis See ONTOGENESIS.

law of biogenetics See RECAPITULATION THEORY.

law of closure 1. In Gestalt psychology, a tendency to complete or close an incomplete part or whole so as to attain maximum simplicity or stability in the entire configuration. 2. A theory that parts of a whole that forms a closed figure are perceived or cognized as belonging together (one of the Gestalt laws of organization).

law of coercion to the biosocial mean (R. B. Cattell) A theory that genetic factors are held in check by environmental ones, for example, boisterous children are restrained; shy children are encouraged to express themselves.

law of coexistence A theory that if two mental events occur at the same time, the recurrence of one tends to call forth the idea corresponding to the other. Also known as coexistence law.

law of cohesion A Gestalt concept that parts of a meaningful visual perception tend to generate a sense of wholeness of an object. See STREET FIGURES for an example.

law of combination A theory that two stimuli or two responses both occurring either simultaneously or in close proximity may act as either one stimulus or one response. See LAW OF ASSOCIATION.

law of common direction See LAW OF GOOD CONTINUATION.

law of common fate (M. Wertheimer) A Gestalt principle that objects functioning or moving in the same way (that is, are undergoing a "common fate") appear to belong together. Also known as common fate law.

law of configuration See LAW OF GROUPING.

law of constancy A theory that there is a one-to-one correspondence between a stimulus and a perception. Also known as constancy hypothesis, constancy law, constancy principle, principle of constancy.

law of contiguity (E. R. Guthrie) A theory that if a stimulus and response occur together in time and space, the later presentation of the stimulus will generate the response. Holds that, contiguity, not reinforcement or drive reduction, explains learning. Also known as contiguity law, contiguity principle, contiguity theory.

law of contrast A theory that thinking about any item, idea, or special quality tends to remind the person of its opposite. In later associationist doctrine, this principle was considered a special case of contiguity. Also known as contrast law.

law of degradation (J. Delboeuf) A theory that sensation is always strongest as it enters consciousness and from then on becomes less intense. Also known as degradation law.

law of diminishing returns 1. A theory that each later practice session produces a smaller gain than earlier ones. The more a person learns at first, the less the person will learn per unit of time or energy spent subsequently. 2. (C. E. Spearman) A theory that the size of correlations among diverse cognitive tests decreases for any class of persons as a function of increasing values for general cognitive ability (g). Theorized to be due to the increasing differentiation of mental ability with increasingly higher levels of intelligence quotient (IQ). Also known as diminishing-returns law.

law of disuse 1. A theory that responses not practiced will weaken and disappear. 2. (E. L. Thorndike) A theory that a learned association is weakened by disuse. Also known as disuse law/principle.

law of du Bois-Reymond   A theory that the excitatory efficiency of an electric current which passes through neural or muscular tissue is dependent upon the rate of change of the current density (that is, is not dependent upon the latter's absolute value). Also known as du Bois Reymond law.

law of dynamogenesis   A theory that changes in sensory stimulation have a corresponding effect in altering muscular activity. Also known as principle of dynamogenesis.

law of effect   (E. L. Thorndike) A theory that a successful or satisfying outcome of a response tends to "stamp in" its association with the antecedent stimuli, and an unsuccessful or unsatisfying outcome tends to "stamp out" such an association. After 1930, Thorndike dropped the second part of the law of effect, stating, in essence, that punishment had no effect on the strength of associations. Sometimes known as effect law, law of psychological hedonism, law of selection. See REINFORCEMENT, THORNDIKE'S PUZZLE BOX.

law of eidotropics   See LAW OF PRÄGNANZ.

law of equipotentiality   (K. S. Lashley) A theory that intact areas of the cortex of the brain can take over some functions of areas that have been destroyed. Based on studies of rats with cortical lesions running a maze. Also known as principle of equipotentiality. See LAW OF MASS ACTION.

law of exercise   (E. L. Thorndike) A theory that the connection between a stimulus and a response is strengthened by repetition. Also known as exercise law.

law of extinction   A theory that a conditioned response to a stimulus will eventually diminish and then disappear if reinforcement is discontinued. In Ivan Pavlov's approach, reinforcement meant presenting the conditioned and the unconditioned stimulus in close temporal proximity; in C. L. Hull's it meant a reward following the response. See HULL'S THEORY.

law of filial regression   (F. Galton) A theory that inherited traits tend to revert toward the mean for the species, for example, "tall" parents tend to have children shorter than themselves. Also known as filial regression law, regression toward the mean.

law of fixation   A theory that in learning anything, the more it is practiced and rehearsed, the more likely it is to become automatic, for example, most people can effortlessly recite the whole alphabet in less than ten seconds even though they have not recited it for many years. Also known as overlearning.

law of forward conduction   A theory that nerve impulses always travel from the postsynaptic membrane of the dendrites to the terminal knob of the axon. The law of forward conduction prevails in nature, but the direction can be reversed under experimental laboratory conditions. Also known as forward-conduction law.

law of frequency   A theory that the rate of learning increases with the rate of practice. Also known as frequency law, law of repetition, law of use.

law of good continuation   (M. Wertheimer) A theory that items tend to be grouped together based on continuity in direction, trajectory, or curvature; items that are natural successors in a series will be viewed as belonging to that series. Also known as law of common direction.

law of grouping   In Gestalt theory, the observation that items in a field tend to be grouped in a manner that appears logical. Also known as law of configuration. See LAW OF PROXIMITY for an illustration.

law of identical direction   A theory that in normal binocular vision the images focused on the retinas of the left and right eyes become fused to appear as a single image focused onto the median plane of the head. A line seen in the left eye and a line in the same direction seen in the right eye are perceived as a single line. Also known as identical-direction law.

law of inclusiveness   (W. Köhler) In Gestalt psychology, a theory that there is a tendency to perceive only the larger figure and not the smaller figure when a smaller figure is embedded in a larger figure.

law of independent assortment   Gregor Mendel's second law of modes of inheritance that states there is no tendency for genes of one parent to stay together in offspring. The average distribution of two traits in the F_2 generation (grandchildren of the original mating) will show a ratio of 9:3:3:1 representing the dominant genes of both traits. See MENDELIAN LAWS OF INHERITANCE.

law of independent segregation   Gregor Mendel's first law of heredity stating that recessive traits are neither modified nor lost in further generations since both dominant and recessive genes are independently transmitted and are able to propagate independently through future generations. See MENDELIAN LAWS OF INHERITANCE.

law of inertia   (C. E. Spearman) A theory that (a) those who are slow in starting a mental process take a long time to finish; (b) such people have trouble going back and forth between two ideas; (c) such people have difficulty adjusting a prior learned skill to new ideas.

law of initial values   A theory that the initial level of a physiological response is a major determinant of a later response in that system. Thus, if a person's pulse rate is high, cardiovascular response to an emotion-provoking stimulus will be smaller than if the initial pulse rate had been low. Also known as initial values law, Wilder's law of initial values after American neuropsychiatrist, Joseph Wilder (b. 1895).

law of large numbers   (J. Bernoulli) A mathematical principle indicating that as the sample size increases, the theoretical expectations of its statistical properties will be more and more closely realized. Also known as large-numbers law.

law of least effort   A theory that an organism tends to choose the means or course of action that appears to require the smallest amount of effort or the least resistance. Also known as law of least action, law of least energy, least-effort law/principle. See LAW OF PARSIMONY.

law of mass action   A theory that large areas of brain tissue function as a whole in learned or intelligent action. The theory evolved from experiments by Karl Lashley on the effects of different amounts of destruction of brain tissue on the ability of rats to relearn a maze. Also known as mass action law, principle of mass action. See LAW OF EQUIPOTENTIALITY.

law of neurobiotaxis   (A. Kappers) A theory that dendrites of developing nerve cells grow in the direction of the axons of nearby active neurons.

law of parsimony An important concept in science that the simplest explanation is the best, everything else being equal. It is an adaptation by William Hamilton of "Occam's razor," a concept first formulated by William of Occam, a 14th-century Franciscan. Also known as economy principle, Okham's razor, parsimony law, principle of economy, simplicity law. See LAW OF LEAST EFFORT, MORGAN'S CANON.

law of participation (L. Lèvy-Brühl) A theory about primitive thinking that things that are similar are identical. See MYSTICAL PARTICIPATION.

law of piecemeal activity (E. L. Thorndike) A theory that part of a complex stimulus can become so potent that it alone will evoke the response to the original stimulus.

law of Prägnanz (M. Wertheimer) A Gestalt principle that the organization of any structure in nature or in cognition will be as "good" (regular, complete, balanced, or symmetrical) as the prevailing conditions allow. Also known as law of eidotropics, principle of Prägnanz.

law of primacy See PRIMACY EFFECT.

law of prior entry A theory that of two simultaneous stimuli, one attended to and the other not, the attended stimulus will be perceived as having been introduced sooner than the other. Also known as prior-entry law.

law of progression (J. Delboeuf) A principle that if stimuli increase in geometric increments, resulting sensations increase only in arithmetic increments.

law of proximity (M. Wertheimer) A Gestalt principle that objects or stimuli that are viewed as being close together will tend to be perceived as a unit, for example, trees growing close together will be seen as a copse, and a series of unconnected lines in a neon sign become a word. Also known as Gestalt law of proximity, law of nearness, principle of proximity, proximity law/principle.

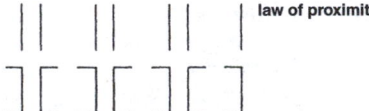

law of proximity

law of psychic resultants 1. (W. Wundt) A principle that as a result of consideration of a set of diverse elements of a problem, a creative resultant is likely to occur. 2. A theory that the mind is capable of generating creative conclusions from observations. See AUTOCHTHONOUS, DIALECTICAL MATERIALISM.

law of psychological hedonism Rare name for law of effect.

law of readiness (E. L. Thorndike) A theory that when some aspect of the body is ready to achieve some function, such as conduction of an impulse by the nervous system, the process will be satisfying. Also known as readiness law. See THORNDIKE'S LAWS OF LEARNING.

law of recapitulation (G. S. Hall) A theory that an organism reenacts the whole history of its species both physically and psychologically, such that "ontogeny recapitulates phylogeny." Also known as law of biogenetics. See RECAPITULATION THEORY.

law of recency A theory that the arousal of any previously learned response varies in ease or readiness inversely with the length of time since it was last learned or practiced. Also more recently presented material (for example, nearer the end than the middle of a list of items) are retained better than those presented more remotely in the past. Also known as principle of recency, recency effect, recency law. See PRIMACY EFFECT, SERIAL POSITION EFFECT.

law of relative effect A theory that the frequency of occurrence of a response depends on the reinforcers that followed that response in relation to reinforcers that followed other possible responses. Also known as relative effect law.

law of repetition A theory that an activity or function is facilitated by being exercised and weakened by not being used. In common parlance: Use it or lose it. See LAW OF FREQUENCY.

law of segregation A theory of the independent inheritance of genes on different chromosomes. That is, which genes an organism inherits from each parent on chromosome #1 do not affect which genes will be inherited on chromosome #2, and so forth. Also known as segregation law.

law of shifting law of associative shifting

law of similarity 1. A principle that a thought or present experience recalls another thought which resembles it in some respect. 2. (M. Wertheimer) In Gestalt psychology, the perceptual tendency to group together items that are similar in some respect such as shape or color, so that they are perceived as parts of a single whole. Also known as similarity law. 3. In Gestalt psychology, things that appear to have the same attributes are usually perceived as being a whole. See LAW OF PROXIMITY for an illustration.

law of simplest path A theory that organisms over time will find the simplest way to achieve any goal. See LAW OF LEAST EFFORT.

law of span An outmoded theory by Charles Spearman that, "Every mind tends to keep its total simultaneous cognitive output constant in quantity, however varying in quality."

law of specific nerve energies A principle that nerves are specialized in that they always deliver the same kind of message to the brain when stimulated. Thus, nerves that would report a touch on the hand, when stimulated after amputation still produce the sensation of the missing hand being touched (as in phantom limb). Although described more than a decade earlier by Sir Charles Bell, it was Johannes Müller who named and popularized the concept.

law of sufficient reason (G. Leibnitz) A principle that given sufficient knowledge and time, it should be possible to discover why any specific occurrence took place, and not a different occurrence. Also known as sufficient reason law.

law of surroundingness In Gestalt psychology, a theory of perception stating that whatever surrounds something tends to be perceived as the background, and what is surrounded tends to be perceived as the figure. See FIGURE-GROUND PERCEPTION.

law of symmetry A Gestalt principle that a set of elements will tend to be grouped in some symmetrical manner, if that is an option given the configuration of those elements.

law of the first night See JUS PRIMAE NOCTIS.

law of unreadiness (E. L. Thorndike) A theory that if an organism is not ready for a learning change, the organism is "disturbed."

law of use **law of frequency**

law of vividness A classical principle of associationism: vivid stimuli or experiences tend to be better retained than less vivid ones. Also, in applied mnemonics, generating a powerful image to aid in remembering (for example, to remember to buy a loaf of bread, imagine it in the mouth of a charging lion).

laws of association Hypotheses to explain mechanisms of association. For the major laws of association, see entries for LAW OF: CONTIGUITY, CONTINGENCY, CONTRAST, FREQUENCY, REPETITION, SIMILARITY.

laws of learning Principles that state the conditions under which learning occurs. Also known as learning laws. For the major laws of learning, see entries for LAW OF: BELONGINGNESS, CONTIGUITY, DIMINISHING RETURNS, EFFECT, EXERCISE, FREQUENCY, READINESS. See also PRIMACY EFFECT, RECENCY EFFECT. For other principles and practices that enhance learning, see ASSOCIATIVE LEARNING, MEANINGFUL LEARNING, OVERLEARNING, PROGRESSIVE EDUCATION, ROTE LEARNING, SPACED PRACTICE.

laws of thought In logic, three principles, identity, contradiction, and excluded middle, which are considered to be the fundamental principles of all reasoning.

laxative addiction Dependence upon the use of laxatives to induce bowel movements. It evolves as a vicious cycle in which the laxative use itself gradually reduces normal bowel activity so that laxatives or enemas become increasingly necessary to prevent constipation problems. See ENEMA ADDICTION, KLISMAPHILIA.

lay analysis Psychoanalysis performed by a person not trained or not credentialed by a psychoanalytic training institute nor accepted by a recognized psychoanalytic association. Originally in the United States (but not in Europe), acceptance for training required holding a M.D. degree.

lay analyst Refers to a person without a medical license who practices psychoanalysis. Phrase is no longer widely used since nonphysicians have been accepted in psychoanalytic associations.

layer of ganglion cells The eighth stratum of the retina from without inward (Polyak); it contains the cell bodies of the third set of neurons in the visual path or the ganglion cells whose axons eventuate from the optic nerve.

layer of rods and cones **Jacob's membrane**

layman A person who has not received formal training or enough formal training to qualify for membership in a profession, or who, generally, is not a member of the said profession or does not have the special knowledge or skills. Also known as layperson.

lazy eye Refers to the weaker eye when the other eye principally is used for vision. Compare LEADING EYE.

LCU life-change units

LD 1. learning disability. 2. learning disorder. 3. See LETHAL DOSE OF A DRUG.

L-data 1. (R. B. Cattell) Abbreviation for life-record data (information from life records of individuals), compiled as the person reacts to life situations. 2. Life data. The summary of autobiographical information in a convenient form. 3. See LIFE DATA.

LD50 See LETHAL DOSE OF A DRUG.

lead-cap headache A sensation of a heavy weight or a severe constriction about the head, sometimes described as skull-lifting headache or splitting headache, occasionally associated with hypertension.

lead encephalopathy A brain disorder most commonly found in children who eat paint that contains lead. Symptoms include convulsions, cortical blindness, mania, delirium, coma. Also occurs in people who, accidentally, or purposefully, inhale gasoline fumes that contain tetraethyl lead. Also called lead poisoning.

leader A person who directs others, such as the person who is literally first, or the person who has been appointed or selected as the person in charge of a group of people, who are to follow that person literally and figuratively. Types of leader include: AUTHORITARIAN, BUREAUCRATIC, DEMOCRATIC, DISCUSSION, GROUP-CENTERED, LAISSEZ-FAIRE. See CONTINGENCY THEORY OF LEADERSHIP, FUNCTIONAL LEADERSHIP, GREAT-MAN THEORY OF LEADERSHIP.

leaderless group Any aggregate of people that meets with intention and expectation of being and remaining leaderless. Such groups are established sometimes by eventual members of the groups and sometimes by others for research, or for practical reasons, etc.

leaderless group discussion (LGD) 1. Interaction in groups formally started as therapy groups on the assumption that self-analysis and discussions between members will have personal beneficial effects. 2. A test for, or demonstration of, leadership and other interactional qualities. A group of similar-status individuals is asked to discuss a problem or issue. Observers monitor the participants for their leadership behavior.

leaderless-group therapy Group psychotherapy in which leaderless meetings are held either on: (a) an occasional or regularly scheduled basis as an adjunct to the traditional therapist-led process. (b) an entirely self-directed basis, in which a group meets for its entire life span without a designated leader.

leader match (F. E. Fiedler) A concept of leadership training in which it is assumed that leaders' styles tend to resist change but that leaders can be trained to diagnose a situation and alter it to fit their own style. See CONTINGENCY MODEL OF LEADERSHIP, LEAST-PREFERRED COWORKERS SCALE.

leadership The capacity to influence the actions and attitudes of individuals or groups through such means as organizational skill, superior knowledge and expertise, the power of personality, and, in general, the ability to evoke the cooperation and commitment of others. See entries beginning with LEADERSHIP and also the following types of leadership: ACHIEVEMENT ORIENTED, AUTOCRATIC, CHARISMATIC, DIRECTIVE, FUNCTIONAL, LAISSEZ-FAIRE, PARTICIPATIVE, SITUATIONAL, SUPPORTIVE, TRANSACTIONAL, TRANSFORMATIONAL.

leadership models (Z. M. Wong) According to Wong, three leadership types: (a) trait, based on the personality of the leader, (b) behavioral, dependent on the relationship between the leader and subordinates, and (c) contingency, emphasizing compatibilities of leaders, subordinates and situation. See LEADERSHIP, LEADERSHIP STYLES, LEADERSHIP THEORIES.

leadership role The specific functions and activities of a person who heads a group, serving as director, guide, catalyst, or mobilizer. Some leaders play an authoritarian, others a democratic or a laissez-faire role. Some are rule-centered ("going by the book") and some are individual-centered (dealing with problems on a case-by-case manner). See LEADERSHIP THEORIES.

leadership simple universal The contention by General Norman Schwartzkoff that whenever there is a group of two or more persons, one of them is the leader.

leadership styles Three styles of leadership according to Kurt Lewin: authoritarian, laissez-faire, and democratic. Lewin's research with youths indicated that democratic leadership worked the best and laissez-faire the worst for them.

leadership theories Competing theories advanced to explain leader effectiveness, particularly: (a) trait theories, which focus on such characteristics as supervisory ability, intelligence, self-assurance, and decisiveness; (b) behavior theories, which focus on a combination of employee-centered supervision (characterized by friendliness, treating others as equals, eliciting suggestions) with production-centered supervision (assigning tasks, scheduling the work); (c) situational-moderator theories, which attempt to describe what works best in different situations, since no single leader or leadership style is equally effective in all settings. See ATTRIBUTION THEORY OF LEADERSHIP, GREAT-MAN THEORY OF LEADERSHIP, LEADERSHIP, TRAIT THEORY OF LEADERSHIP.

leading eye The eye that is the first to turn toward a visual stimulus. Compare LAZY EYE.

leading hemisphere (J. Jackson) The dominant hemisphere of the brain, usually considered the one that controls language.

lead-pipe rigidity A plastic type of muscle hypertonus involving opposing muscle groups. Occurs in some cases of parkinsonism and cerebral palsy.

lead poisoning See LEAD ENCEPHALOPATHY.

leakage Any discussion by a person undergoing therapy with a person other than the therapist about topics discussed in the therapy.

leaning-tower-of-Pisa approach/concept A counselor advises certain actions intended to induce a person making a mistake to make an even bigger mistake. Example: Parents want a child to go to bed at 7:00 pm, the child wants to stay up until 11:00 pm. Counselor asks "Why 7?" Answer: "The child needs lots of sleep." Counselor: "Then why not have the child go to bed at 4? In that way the child will get a lot more sleep." The intent of using this technique is to demonstrate to the clients the nonsense of their thinking. See PARADOXICAL INTENTION.

leapfrogging whipsawing

leaping ague Dancing mania sometimes called choreomania.

learned autonomic control A person's capacity to learn to regulate visceral functions such as blood pressure and temperature, which are ordinarily under the control of the autonomic nervous system (ANS). Such learning is accomplished primarily by using biofeedback techniques, and in some cases by hypnosis. Also known as visceral learning. See BIOFEEDBACK, HYPNOTHERAPY.

learned helplessness (M. Seligman) The passive reaction induced in animals and humans by exposure to noncontingent aversive events.

learned motives Goals shaped by social and other environmental factors rather than genetic inheritance.

learned optimism (M. Seligman) Habitually viewing aversive events as unstable, specific and to a lesser extent, external.

learned taste aversion (J. Garcia) A generalized reaction of an animal after tasting a certain food that has made that animal ill, to no longer eat that food. Also known as Garcia effect.

learning The process of acquiring new and relatively enduring information, behavior patterns, or abilities; modification of behavior as a result of practice, study, or experience. See entries beginning with LEARNING and also these types of learning: ABSTRACT, ACTION, ACTIVE, ALL-OR-NONE, ALTERNATION, ASSOCIATIVE, AUTOMATED, AVERSIVE, AVOIDANCE, BLIND, COGNITIVE, COMPUTER-ASSISTED, CONCEPT, CONCEPTUAL, CONFIGURATIONAL, CONFLUENT, CONTIGUITY, COOPERATIVE, DEUTERO-, DISCOVERY, DISCRIMINATION, DISSOCIATED, DISTRIBUTED, ESCAPE, FREE-RECALL, IDEATIONAL, IMPLICIT, INCIDENTAL, INCREMENTAL, INFANT, INSIGHTFUL, INSTRUMENTAL, INTEGRATIVE, INTENTIONAL, INTERNEUROSENSORY, INTRANEUROSENSORY, INTRASERIAL, LATENT, MASSED, MASTERY, MAZE, MEANINGFUL, MEDIATIONAL, MOTOR, MOVEMENT, MULTISENSORY, NONINTENTIONAL, OBSERVATIONAL, ONE-TRIAL, OPERANT, OVER-, PAIRED ASSOCIATE, PASSIVE, PASSIVE-AVOIDANCE, PATTERN, PERCEPTUAL, PERCEPTUAL-MOTOR, PLACE, PRINCIPLE-, PROBABILITY, PROGRAMMED, RATIONAL, RELATION, RE-, RESPONSE, RESTRICTED, REVERSAL, REWARD, ROTE, RULE, S-S, SELECTIVE, SENSELESS, SERIAL, SIGN GESTALT, SIGN, SIGNAL, SLEEP, SOLUTION, SPACED, STATE-DEPENDENT, STIMULUS-STIMULUS, STRUCTURED, SUBCORTICAL, SUBLIMINAL, SUBSTITUTION, THORNDIKE'S TRIAL-AND-ERROR, UN-, VERBAL, VICARIOUS, VISCERAL, VISUAL, WHOLE AND PART.

learning activities Processes occurring while learning, such as attending, comparing, memorizing, visualizing.

learning by doing See PROGRESSIVE EDUCATION.

learning capacity The relative and absolute ability of a person to learn.

learning curve A graphic representation that reflects the course of learning. A measure of performance (for example, gains, errors) represented along the vertical axis. The horizontal axis plots trials or time. The learning of a group or individual may be represented by the curve. See CUMULATIVE (FREQUENCY) DISTRIBUTION for an example of a learning curve.

learning dilemma (J. Dollard) A situation in which any response an organism makes is unsuccessful or in which a response that has been successful is no longer reinforced, for example, in the past, a hungry rat pressed a lever and always obtained food from a little tube. The experimenter decides no longer to feed the rat in this manner. When the rat presses the lever, and nothing comes out, this generates a learning dilemma. Should the rat try again? And if so, how many times before giving up? Similar situations occur with humans. See AGGRESSION-FRUSTRATION HYPOTHESIS, EXTINCTION, FRUSTRATION-AGGRESSION HYPOTHESIS, PERFORMANCE PHASE.

learning disability (LD) A disorder in one or more of the basic psychological processes involved in understanding or using spoken or written language. Phrase includes reading problems attributed to minimal brain dysfunction and developmental aphasia; not, however, visual or hearing disabilities, mental retardation, or emotional disturbance as the primary challenging conditions.

learning-disabilities specialist A person trained to identify and remedy the problems associated with learning disabilities. Often acts as a school's team coordinator in an interdisciplinary approach to the child.

learning disorder (LD) Not learning as much or as quickly as can normally be expected of a person of the same age and educational level. Reasons may include disinterest, hyperactivity, unspecified brain damage, rebellion, as well as social impediments to learning process.

learning laws See LAWS OF LEARNING.

learning machines See TEACHING MACHINES.

learning model (H. Gardner) An orientation to the study of human development and behavior that stresses the critical influence of environmental conditions on the physical, cognitive, interpersonal, and emotional functioning of the individual. It primarily regards children as absorbing the relevant features of the environment in a continuous line of development in contrast to the cognitivist emphasis on development as an active construction of knowledge in several specific stages characterized by distinct modes of organization and expression. Also known as environmental-learning theory. See COGNITIVE STRUCTURE.

learning paradigm In abnormal psychology, a theory that abnormal behavior is learned through the same processes as other forms of behavior. Holds that humans learn to "be crazy." It is a refutation of mental disorders as physiologically based. See BIOSOCIAL DETERMINISM, SOCIAL CONTAGION, SOCIAL DETERMINISM, COLLECTIVE FAMILY TRANSFERENCE NEUROSIS, PATHOGENIC FAMILY PATTERNS, SCHIZOGENIC FAMILY.

learning session See PRACTICE PERIOD.

learning set 1. The establishment of a strategy of responding during testing or learning in choosing responses (for example, in a multiple-choice test never choosing the first of five answers but usually selecting the fourth out of five choices when guessing for the correct answer). 2. A tendency to respond in a particular way. See SET. 3. See POSITIVE TRANSFER.

learning sets (H. F. Harlow) Discriminative learning in which the organism is given a number of different problems and each problem is offered for a fixed number of trials. The number of trials is repeated for each problem regardless of whether it is solved the first or second time. The purpose is to improve the learning ability of the organism.

learning strategy A tendency of any organism to have some kind of systematic manner of attempting to achieve mastery of any problem or situation (for example, a worm faced with the choice of turning either right or left in a Y-shaped tube may at first always go in one direction; a student studying a topic may at first go through the material rapidly but then return to various elements to study slowly).

learning theory A body of concepts and principles rather than a single theory, which seek to explain the learning process. For major approaches, see CLASSICAL CONDITIONING, COGNITIVE THEORY OF LEARNING, CONDITIONING, CONTINUITY THEORY OF LEARNING, DISCONTINUITY THEORY OF LEARNING, FACTOR THEORY OF LEARNING, GUTHRIE'S CONTIGUOUS CONDITIONING, HABIT, HEBB'S THEORY OF PERCEPTUAL LEARNING, HULL'S MATHEMATICO-DEDUCTIVE THEORY OF LEARNING, INSIGHT, IRRADIATION THEORY (OF LEARNING), LAWS OF LEARNING, LINEATOR-OPERATOR MODEL OF LEARNING, OPERANT CONDITIONING, THORNDIKE'S LAWS OF LEARNING, THORNDIKE'S TRIAL-AND-ERROR-LEARNING, TOLMAN'S PURPOSIVE BEHAVIORISM.

learning types 1. Humans tend to have different methods of acquiring knowledge or mastering skills. Some people approach a learning task with a totalistic set to apprehend what is to be learned all at once, others will learn by steps. Some people prefer to read, some to listen, some to observe others, some to proceed by trial and error, etc. 2. See TYPE I CONDITIONING, TYPE II CONDITIONING, TYPE-R CONDITIONING, TYPE-S CONDITIONING. 3. See COGNITIVE LEARNING THEORIES.

learning without awareness A controversial issue that depends on what learning and awareness mean in this context. Some assert that the acquiring of knowledge or mastering of a skill occurs only with conscious attention; others assume that learning may occur incidentally without conscious attention or effort. See UNINTENTIONAL LEARNING, SLEEP LEARNING.

learn-to-learn concept See LEARNING SETS.

least-effort law/principle See LAW OF LEAST EFFORT.

least group size In learning, the optimal size of a group is the smallest group in which all included have the abilities required for the learning activities involved.

least-noticeable difference just-noticeable difference (jnd)

least-perceptible difference (lpd or l.p.d.) just-noticeable difference

least-perceptible duration The least or shortest elapse of time between two successive events that can be distinguished from simultaneity. Also known as just-noticeable duration.

Least-Preferred Coworkers (LPC) Scale   (F. E. Fiedler) A measure of leadership style. The leader is asked to rate a least preferred coworker from 1 to 8 on a set of 16 bipolar dimensions. The ratings are used to distinguish between task-oriented and relationship-oriented leaders. Also known as Least-Preferred Coworkers Test.

least resistance   See LAW OF LEAST EFFORT, LINE OF LEAST RESISTANCE.

least-restrictive alternative   A concept that less treatment, rather than more treatment, is the most desirable objective in any kind of treatment, with the minimum level of restrictions on the patient's freedom. This position was emphasized in two 1996 decisions of David Bazelon, Chief Judge of the U.S. Circuit Court of Appeals for the District of Columbia: Rouse vs Cameron, and Lake vs Cameron.

Least Restrictive Environment (LRE)   Required by federal law (IDEA) as the setting for the appropriate public education of those with disability. See INDIVIDUALS WITH DISABILITIES EDUCATION ACT (IDEA).

least-squares criterion   One generally accepted way of deciding which of many possible lines best fit the data: the sum of the squared deviation of each point from the regression line is less than from any other straight line. The Pearson product-moment correlation is a function of the slope of this best fit line.

least-squares method/principle   (G. E. Müller, F. M. Urban) A technique for obtaining the regression coefficients (unknown parameters of A and B in fitting a regression equation) such that the sum of squares of the deviations from the regression line is less than from any other straight line fitted to the data points. See MÜLLER-URBAN METHOD.

leaving the field   (K. Lewin) Reacting to frustration or conflict by removing oneself from the situation or escaping into psychogenic illness.

Lebenslüge   (life lie—German) The false conviction of some persons with neuroses that their life plan is bound to fail due to other people or circumstances beyond their control. Alfred Adler interpreted this conviction as a method of freeing themselves from personal responsibility. The term was also used for a false belief around which the person's life is built.

Lebenswelt   German term for lifeword.

Leboyer technique   (F. Leboyer) A psychological approach to childbirth that focuses on the feelings and sensations of the baby, and advocates peace and quiet, dim lights, delay in severing the umbilical cord, body contact between the newborn and the parents, and an immediate warm bath that approximates the conditions within the womb. See LAMAZE METHOD.

lecanomancy   A system of divination in which a person (known as a medium) looks into a basin of water and sees visions. Has been used in psychoanalytic studies to show relationships between the mediums' supposed visions and their dreams and complexes.

lécheur   (licker—French) A person who touches genitals with his or her mouth, performing cunnilingus or fellatio. If the person doing this is female, she is more properly called a *lécheuse*. See OROGENITAL ACTIVITY.

lecture method   In industrial psychology, personnel-training procedure used primarily to present new material to large groups, especially when classroom time is limited. It is also used to introduce other instructional methods, such as films, or to summarize material developed by other instructional methods.

Lee-Boot effect   A tendency toward false pregnancies in mice housed together, due to a pheromone in the urine.

left-handedness   The preferential use of the left hand for major activities, such as eating, writing, and throwing. It is a component of sinistrality. See CEREBRAL DOMINANCE, DEXTRALITY-SINISTRALITY, HANDEDNESS, LATERALITY.

left hemisphere   The left side of the brain (separated from the right side of the brain by a fissure). It appears that the hemispheres may have different functions, for example, in most people the left hemisphere appears to control language. See BRAIN, DOMINANT HEMISPHERE, RIGHT HEMISPHERE.

left lateral ventricle (of the brain)   One of four hollow chambers in the brain, located in the cerebrum above the third ventricle and to the left side of the midline, opposite the right lateral ventricle. See BRAIN VENTRICLES.

left-right effect   A tendency for children to learn easily the concepts of up/down, but to have difficulty learning the concepts of left/right.

left-side fear   See LEVOPHOBIA.

left-sided apraxia   A form of apraxia marked by the inability of right-handed persons to carry out actions with their left hand that they are able to carry out with their right hand. See RIGHT-HANDEDNESS.

left temporal lobectomy   See TEMPORAL LOBECTOMY.

legal capacity   Mental capacity to manage legal affairs, that is, to make and understand a contract, make a will, and to stand trial and understand the nature of the proceedings.

legalistic orientation   The lower stage of Lawrence Kohlberg's postconventional or principled level of moral development, in which the emphasis is on rights and standards that have been agreed upon by the whole society. See POSTCONVENTIONAL LEVEL.

legal psychology   Forensic psychology.

legal responsibility   The obligation to be knowledgeable about and to conform to existing laws. Legally, only those considered insane are not responsible for their behavior.

legal testimony   Statement formally presented in a court of law, usually oral and given by a witness.

legasthenia   Difficulty in analyzing a given word into its component letters despite adequate intellectual and perceptual ability. Also known as dyslexia with dysorthographia.

legend   A traditional story about a person or group or place that has the effect of unifying the group to whom the story is told.

legerdemain   (light of hand—French) A term translated as "sleight of hand" and applied to displays of skill or adroitness, particularly as practiced by magicians or "sleight of hand" artists.

legitimacy knowledge   A person's perception of the culture's degree of acceptance of that person's social, vocational, ethnic, or religious group-belonging. See IDIOPANIMA.

Lehmann's acoumeter   (A. G. L. Lehmann) An early form of acoumeter to measure sound thresholds. The intensity of the sound was changed by dropping a small metal ball on a wooden board from varying heights. See HEARING. For a variation of this acoumeter see SOUND HAMMER.

Leipzig school of Gestalt psychology   A point of view in Gestalt psychology that differs from that of the Berlin School. The Berlin school emphasized the phenomenology of experience, primarily perception, but the mentors of the Leipzig school wanted to include all factors of mentation including affective and conative elements.

leisure   The industrial psychologist Thomas Gilbert points out that leisure does not imply laziness or frivolity; rather it is derived from an old French word meaning "permission." Humans are permitted a break from arduous labor so that later they are capable of accomplishing; leisure is an opportunity afforded by freedom from occupations. If people watch television for an hour and get up wondering why they sat there, it was time wasted; if people get up refreshed and better able to accomplish their goals, it was leisure.

leisure lifestyles   Patterns of activity among retirees, for example, some retirees continue the activities they did before retirement; some retirees cease participation in such activities.

Leiter International Performance Scale (LIPS) (R. G. Leiter) A nonverbal intelligence task primarily for cross-cultural administration, consisting of number series, concealed figures, picture-completion tasks, and matching wooden blocks according to colors, forms, and pictures.

lek   Land area (sometimes "owned" by a single male) used for lek displays. Also known as arena. See LEK DISPLAY.

lek display   In animals, especially some birds, a courtship display in which males band together to present communal displays to females (thereby increasing the attractiveness and the strength of the signals, usually auditory plus visual). See MATING BEHAVIOR.

lemniscal system   A part of the somatosensory network of nerve fibers, composed mainly of large diameter myelinated A fibers. It includes the dorsal columns, the tract of Morin, and the neospinothalamic tract of nerve fibers, extending from the spinal cord to the thalamus and cortex. See LATERAL LEMNISCUS, MEDIAL LEMNISCUS.

lemon-juice therapy   (T. Sajwaj) The preferred method of dealing with infant rumination (regurgitating food or drink, which can be life-threatening) by squirting lemon juice into the infant's mouth while he or she is regurgitating.

leniency error   A tendency to rate a person higher on a positive characteristic and less severely on a negative characteristic than he or she actually should be rated. See BIAS.

lens (of eye)   The transparent crystalline structure near the front of the eye whose change in shape permits a range of accommodation (that is, sharp focus) for objects from around 4 inches to about 10 feet in front of the eye. When the lens becomes relatively opaque either through normal aging (which also reduces the degree of plasticity) or some environmental impact it is known as a cataract; even in the young it absorbs about 8% of the light that reaches it.

lens model   (E. Brunswik) A model for general psychology based on the concept of a lens in that a single distal stimulus can have a variety of consequences and that a number of different distal stimuli can have the identical effects, exemplifying the statement that "the same fire that softens the butter hardens the egg." This model is the O in the S-O-R model.

lenticular-fasciculus stimulation   Self-stimulation that occurs in rats when an electrode is inserted in a subthalamic pathway near the lenticular nucleus of the brain and wired to a lever that the animals can press. When the level is pressed, a mild electric current flows to the electrode. Because rats tend to press the lever repeatedly when wired to the electrode, it is assumed that lenticular-fasciculus stimulation has a pleasurable effect. See SELF-STIMULATION for an illustration.

lenticular nucleus   1. A nucleus shaped like a lens. 2. The lens-shaped portion of the corpus striatum and the outermost of the large nuclei located near the thalamus, as a result of pressure from the developing fore-brain about midway through a human pregnancy. It consists of a wedge of gray matter with fibers associated in motor-neuron activity. Also known as lentiform nucleus. See BASAL GANGLIA, CAUDATE NUCLEUS.

Leonardo's paradox   Leonardo da Vinci stated that it is not possible to reproduce by means of a painting what a person can see with two eyes. Because in binocular vision, each eye sees something that the other eye cannot see.

leprechaunism   A familial disorder characterized by a large head with small, emaciated body, large, wide-set eyes, long, low-set ears, and an abundance of hair at birth. Affected persons have poor psychomotor development and muscular hypotonia. The syndrome is purportedly due to an autosomal-recessive gene which becomes manifested through consanguinity. Also known as Donahue's syndrome.

leptokurtic   Describing a frequency distribution that is more peaked than a comparison distribution, such as the normal curve. See KURTOSIS for an illustration of the three types of kurtosis.

leptomorph   (H. Eysenck) A thin body type. See BODY-BUILD INDEX.

leptosome type   (E. Kretschmer) Describing a person having a slender or asthenic physique. See ASTHENIC TYPE.

lerema   Mumbled rapid speech seen in some persons who are retarded, psychotic, senile. Also known as leresis.

leresis   **lerema**

LES   local excitatory state

lesbian   1. A person who practices lesbianism. 2. Characteristic of or pertaining to lesbianism.

lesbian feminism A point of view of some lesbians that women who are heterosexual harm the feminist cause, some stating that only lesbians can be feminists. Also known as radical lesbian feminism. See LESBIAN SEPARATISM.

lesbianism Homosexual desires and sexual relations between women. Named for the Aegean Island, Lesbos, where the poetess Sappho (ca. 600 B.C.) wrote accounts of erotic activities between women. Also known as Sapphism. See HOMOSEXUALITY.

lesbian separatism A doctrine that rejects patriarchy in favor of an autonomous woman-centered culture.

Lesch-Nyhan syndrome (M. Lesch & W. L. Nyhan) An X-linked recessive disease, mainly in boys, associated with a hypoxanthine-guanine enzyme deficiency, and overproduction of uric acid. Distinctive features are severe chronic self-mutilation, particularly self-biting of fingers and mouth area. All reported patients have mental retardation, with intelligence quotients (IQs) below 50. Motor development deteriorates after the first six to eight months of life, marked by spasticity, chorea, and athetosis. Also known as hereditary choreoathetosis/hyperuricemia.

less-leads-to-more effect A tendency for rewards minimally sufficient to induce people to state positions contrary to their own views to generate more attitude change than do larger rewards. See COGNITIVE DISSONANCE.

lethal catatonia Bell's mania.

lethal dose (LD) of a drug Lethal dose; LD50 or LD_{50} followed by a mg/kg indicates that 50% of a group of test organisms, usually animals, were killed by that particular dose.

lethality 1. The quality of being lethal. 2. (E. Shneidman) According to Edwin Shneidman, a measure of how "lethal" a person is, that is, how likely to commit suicide in the near future. See SUICIDALITY. 3. (V. Frankl) An estimation of the probability that a person who is threatening suicide will succeed based on the method described, the specificity of the plan, and the availability of the means. Also known as self-lethality. 4. Ratio of deaths, including suicide, from a disorder to the number of diagnosed cases of that disorder.

lethality scale A set of criteria used in predicting the probability of a person to attempt or commit suicide.

lethargy A listless, drowsy, apathetic state usually accompanied by a low energy level and lack of motivation. Observed in various degrees in depressive disorders, and in an extreme degree in lethargic encephalitis (sleeping sickness).

lethologica Temporary inability to recall an appropriate noun or name.

letter square A group of letters placed in rows and columns in the form of a square, used as a memory test. The square is exposed for a brief period and participants are then asked to reproduce the contents of the square from memory.

letting go A concept that dying persons can decide to give up trying to stay alive and will in this manner terminate their existence. See APPROPRIATE DEATH, DEATH EXPECTATION, SUB-INTENTIONAL DEATH.

letting off steam Expressing emotions strongly or even violently such as, in extreme cases, by screaming, hitting things, or otherwise losing normal control. The analogy is to a kettle that blows steam when the liquid reaches a boiling point. See TALKING IT OUT.

leucotomy Psychosurgery in which the prefrontal lobes of the brain are separated from the rest of the brain by cutting the connecting nerve fibers; the purpose is to sever the brain areas associated with emotion in an effort to reduce anxiety or violent behavior. Also known as leukotomy, prefrontal lobotomy. See LOBECTOMY, TRANSORBITAL LOBOTOMY.

levee effect A reaction to disaster or to the threat of disaster characterized by the acquisition of devices believed to protect the individual or group. Phrase derives from the belief that a home or workplace in a flood plain is safe from floods if a levee or dike forms a boundary between the people and the water. The levee may not protect against the next flood, but its presence provides a sense of security.

leveling A family-therapy technique in which verbal aggression is encouraged on the assumption that it will reduce tensions that may otherwise lead to physical aggression. See BATACA.

leveling effect A tendency for repeated measurements to cluster about the mean due to practice effects.

leveling-sharpening A tendency to perceive and remember any object or event in a way that minimizes or omits small features, details, and irregularities (leveling) while emphasizing or exaggerating the highlights (sharpening). Leveling and sharpening occur simultaneously; for example, as a rumor is retold, the insignificant details are dropped but the outstanding aspects are heightened.

level of aspiration (K. Lewin & K. Dembo) The degree of expectation that a person may have for future achievements. Also known as aspiration level, level of anticipation.

level of confidence See CONFIDENCE LEVEL.

level of significance The likelihood of rejecting the null hypothesis when it is true. More commonly known as alpha level. See SIGNIFICANCE.

level of usual utility (R. Brown) If the various possible names for a referent are conceived of in a rank order of usage there will be a level at which the referent usually functions, and the name at that level of usual utility will be thought of as the referent's "real" name (for example, a "dime" is also known as a "coin," a "jit," "ten cents," and "currency," but its level of usual utility is "dime.") This concept was later somewhat reformulated by Eleanor Rosch.

Level I-Level II tests (A. R. Jensen) Level I tests require of the subject little or no transformation of the stimulus input to arrive at the correct output (for example, tests of recognition memory, and various forms of rote learning). Level II tests require transformation or mental manipulation of the stimulus input to arrive at a correct response, such as tests highly loaded on Spearman's *g*, involving reasoning, abstraction, inference, and problem-solving. See CONSERVE, CRYSTALLIZED INTELLIGENCE, GENERAL INTELLIGENCE.

levels of communication   Three levels of communication as suggested by R. T. Lakoff: (a) statements that are unambiguous ("Hello."); (b) those that are not fully intelligible ("Eat, your grandmother said."); (c) those transactions that defy logic, seen for example, in people who have been "inseparable" for a long period of time (such as identical twins, long-married couples) and who understand what the other person is conveying, although it makes no sense to anyone else.

levels of consciousness   A hierarchical arrangement of states of consciousness, stages of consciousness, or both, based on capacities, in which higher states or stages have greater or additional capacities than lower states. Examples of levels of consciousness include Ken Wilber's spectrum of consciousness (nine levels); Yogic psychology (seven levels associated with the *chakras*, or psychic energy centers); Buddhist stages of insight; and transcendental meditations states of consciousness scale. Levels of consciousness familiar to many include waking, dreaming, dreamless sleep, and intoxication. Also known as levels of awareness.

levels of intelligence   Historically, before intelligence testing was developed, it was evident to people that there were distinct levels of intelligence and terms such as "genius" and "idiot" were generally used. With mental testing, it was determined that people tested fell somewhere along the base of a normal distribution, a variety of names were suggested for various segments of the distribution such as "idiot" at the bottom level, "normal" for the middle group and "genius" for the top level of intelligence quotient (IQ). Later, different segments were suggested such as "dull-normal," "borderline," and "high-average." Over time, terms such as "imbecile," "feebleminded," and "moron" were dropped and less pejorative terms such as "academically limited," "learning disabled," "intellectually challenged," "mental retardation," and "trainable" were used.

levels-of-mind therapies   See SPECTRUM OF CONSCIOUSNESS.

levels of processing model (of memory)   (F. Craik) A paradigm of memory suggesting that the ability to remember is dependent on how deeply a person processes information. The greater the effort expended in processing information, the more readily it can be later recalled.

levirate   Marriage of a widow to her deceased husband's brother or other next of kin. Compare SORORATE.

levitation   1. The illusion of ascending into the air without support. Term is mainly used in referring to dreams and parapsychological phenomena. 2. The presumed actual raising of objects or persons into the air by nonphysical means. See PSYCHOKINESIS, TELEKINESIS.

levophobia   Morbid fear of phenomena situated to the left. Also known as sinistrophobia. See DEXTROPHOBIA.

levorotatory (L- or l-)   In organic chemistry, rotating the plane of polarized light counterclockwise or to the left side.

Levy Draw-and-Tell-a-Story Technique   (S. Levy) A projective test in which participants draw two figures of their own gender and one of the opposite gender, and tell a story about them. Purportedly reveals Oedipal and sibling-rivalry reactions.

Lewin's theory   The following items are important for understanding Kurt Lewin's theory: ASPIRATION LEVEL, AUTHORITARIAN GROUP, BEHAVIOR SPACE, COGNITIVE STRUCTURE, CONTEMPORANEOUS-EXPLANATION PRINCIPLE, DEMOCRATIC LEADER, DREAM SCREEN, FIELD FORCE, FIELD STRUCTURE, FIELD THEORY OF PERSONALITY, FORCE FIELD, FOREIGN HULL, GALILEAN, GROUP DYNAMICS/PROCESS, HODOLOGICAL SPACE, HODOLOGY, ICEBLOCK THEORY, INNER PERSONAL REGION, INTENSIVE GROUP EXPERIENCE, IRREAL, IRREALITY LEVEL, JORDAN CURVE, LAISSEZ-FAIRE GROUP, LAISSEZ-FAIRE LEADERSHIP, LEADERSHIP STYLES, LEAVING THE FIELD, LEVEL OF ASPIRATION, LIFE SPACE, LOCOMOTION, MOTORIC REGION, ORAL TRIAD, POWER FIELD, PSYCHOLOGICAL FIELD, QUASI NEED, REGIONS OF LIFE SPACE, SENSITIVITY TRAINING, SITUATION(AL)ISM, SITUATIONAL UNIT, T-GROUP, TASK SUBSTITUTION, TOPOLOGICAL PSYCHOLOGY, TRAINING GROUP, VALENCE, VECTOR ANALYSIS/PSYCHOLOGY, ZEIGARNIK EFFECT/PHENOMENON.

lexical   Relating to words.

lexical access   The process of recognizing a word (such as the word "lexical"), which if a person has learned its meaning, can later recall what it means as though he or she had access to a dictionary.

lexical ambiguity   The same word seen outside of context may have multiple meanings, for example, the various meanings of "run" in any general dictionary.

lexical-decision procedure/task   Making immediate decisions about whether sets of letters shown briefly are or are not real words. See LEXICAL MEMORY.

lexical memory   Words that are known by a person and identified as such when briefly shown. See LEXICAL-DECISION PROCEDURE, PASSIVE VOCABULARY.

lexical uncertainty   Being unsure of unusual or unfamiliar words, noted by pauses in the stream of speech occurring just prior to the appearance of such words.

lexical word   content word

lexicographic sort   An arrangement that places items alphabetically. With written numbers (for example, 7 and 3), such a sort places them where they would be if they were spelled out (alphabetized under S and T respectively).

lexicography   The science and art of compiling dictionaries. See LEXICOLOGY.

lexicology   The study of the meaning of words and their idiomatic combinations. Applied lexicology is called lexicography.

lexicon   1. In general parlance, the words that a person knows. 2. The vocabulary of a field, such as psychology or medicine.

lexicostatistics   A method of deciding how much of a parent language a particular language has or which of two languages is closer to a parent language (for example, a basic set of common words from a parent language is established, and then an examination of how many of these common words are found in the other languages is performed).

lexis ratio   A statistic to determine the normality of a distribution. The formula calls for the obtained standard deviation to be divided by the theoretically expected standard deviation.

Leydig's cells   interstitial cells

LGB   lateral geniculate body

LGD   leaderless group discussion

LGN   lateral geniculate nucleus

LH   1. lateral hypothalamus. 2. luteinizing hormone.

li   The importance of proper conduct for the good life according to Confucius. See CONFUCIAN ANALECTS.

liberal pluralism   A doctrine positing that the individual is, and should be, at the center of efforts to improve human welfare. Unlike communitarians, who are concerned with the welfare of the community as a whole, and with ways to improve social structures for the benefit of everyone, liberals prefer to look for ways to let individuals worry about their own welfare. Liberal pluralism strives to create societies in which people of varied backgrounds can pursue their personal welfare, and in which they can all co-exist with minimum conflict.

liberated woman   1. Casual phrase for a woman who feels free of the demands and limitations of the culture in which she lives. 2. A woman who takes the position of having the same rights and freedoms as men.

liberation psychology   1. Originally developed by Latin American psychologists in the 1970s, this movement seeks to use psychology for the liberation of oppressed persons and communities. This school of thought claims that, although psychology has been used mainly to support structures of social inequality, the profession can help in the empowerment and emancipation of subjugated and disadvantaged people. Also known as emancipatory psychology. 2. An approach to psychological theory, research, and social action, originated in the late 1980s by El Salvador psychologist/priest Ignacio Martin Baro, that promotes the emancipation of oppressed individuals and groups. Goal is to empower people in overcoming psychological, social, and political forces that limit their potential and humanity. Relevant journal is *Critical Psychologist.*

Libertarian Feminism   Individualist Feminism

libidinal development   psychosexual development

libidinal object   A person or thing toward which sexual attention and energy is directed.

libidinal phases   (S. Freud) In psychoanalytic theory, the four stages in the development and expression of the sexual instinct, each of which is focused on a single erotogenic zone (the mouth, the anus, the phallus, the genitals). See PSYCHOSEXUAL DEVELOPMENT.

libidinal transference   According to psychoanalytic theory, a patient having moved sexual drives once directed toward parents to the therapist.

libidinal types   (S. Freud) A psychoanalytic personality classification based on a three-fold distribution of libidinal (sexual) energy in the psyche. In the erotic type the main interest is in loving and being loved. In the obsessional type the person is dominated by conscience and may develop an obsessive-compulsive neurosis. In the narcissistic type the main interest is in self-preservation, with little concern for others.

libidinization   erot(ic)ization

libidinous   Pertaining to the libido, but implying an excessive amount of thinking and behavior (sexual in nature).

libido   (desire, lust—Latin) 1. (S. Freud) The energy of the sexual instinct in all its manifestations. 2. (C. G. Jung) The general life force which provides energy for biological, sexual, social, cultural, and creative activities. See LIBIDO THEORY.

libido analog(ue)   An object that substitutes for the libidinal object. Carl Jung cites fetishes, figures of the gods, and churingas (sacred objects of wood or stone).

libido-binding activity   (S. R. Slavson) Describing an activity in which members of a group concentrate libidinal energies on a specific interest or occupation, as contrasted to activities that stimulate the libido. Also known as immobilizing activity.

libido damming   Attempts to block the development or expression of sexual feelings.

libido organization   (S. Freud) In psychoanalytic theory, the hierarchical system in which weaker or residual erotogenic areas are subordinate to the dominating or primacy zone: oral, anal, phallic, or genital zones.

libido theory   (S. Freud) In psychoanalytic theory, the impetus for psychosexual development and expression stems from a single instinctual energy source, the libido.

library design   In environmental psychology, planning a library to provide optimum space for users, including those who use libraries as quiet, comfortable areas for reading or study and are not particularly concerned about methods of classifying and displaying books and periodicals. See ENVIRONMENTAL DESIGN.

Librium   Trade name for chlordiazepoxide hydrochloride. See VALIUM.

Lichtheim's test (for aphasia)   (L. Lichtheim) An inner-language test for persons with serious speech disturbances or expressive aphasia. If a person cannot say a particular word, the test attempts to determine the possibility of inner speech or mental knowledge of the word, by asking the person to indicate the number of syllables in the word.

licking behavior   The act of an animal tongueing itself or another animal, particularly an offspring. Such behavior appears to be part of the maternal instinct of many mammals; the pregnant female licks itself before giving birth, then licks the offspring, thereby establishing a means of identifying her own young. Some animal mothers lick their young before licking themselves; others lick themselves first.

Liebmann effect   A tendency for luminosity differences to mark off an area more sharply than hue differences. As the luminosity of a colored figure increases, the contrast between figure and ground decreases. The point at which the luminosities of figure and ground are equal, the figure cannot be distinguished from the ground. Named after German psychologist Susanne E. Liebmann (b. 1897).

lie detector   (W. M. Marston, L. Keeler) A device that purportedly determines the truthfulness of a person by detecting galvanic skin responses, changes in heart rates, respiration, or other physiological signs of anxiety or similar emotions associated with stress. See DECEPTION, KEELER POLYGRAPH.

lie scale   On some questionnaires, a number of items that contradict each other to check whether the respondent is consistent. Can also consist of items that, if checked consistently, indicate that the respondent is trying to generate a false favorable impression. Also known as L scale. See MALINGERING SCALE.

lifeboat situation   A group therapy or sensitivity-training technique in which members of a group are to imagine being on a lifeboat and the group is to discuss who to throw overboard to save the rest. A vote prevails after the discussion. After a person is "thrown out" the reasons are discussed. The intention is to help those "thrown out" learn more about themselves.

life chances   Opportunities presented to people in life.

life-change rating scale   A scale used in measuring the relative impact of diverse stress-producing life experiences, changes, and crises. See LIFE CRISIS, LIFE-CHANGE UNITS.

life-change units (LCU)   Measured units of life experiences in accordance with their stress-generating potential. See LIFE CRISIS, LIFE-CHANGE RATING SCALE.

life crisis   A serious or significant life experience that produces stress and necessitates major adjustment, for example, divorce, marriage, career change, and death of a close family member. See LIFE-CHANGE RATING SCALE, LIFE-CHANGE UNITS.

life cycle   The entire progression from birth to maturity to death which characterizes a particular species, group, institution, or culture. Also, life cycle is the average time this process takes, that is, its life span or life expectancy.

life data (L-data)   Information of a direct or primary type about a person. Such information may be obtained by such methods as observing or shadowing the person or by asking people considered to be the person's primary sources (such as close friends or relatives). See SHADOWING.

life energy   (W. Reich) Refers to the "orgone," or cosmic energy, which Wilhelm Reich assumed to be emitted by energy vesicles called bions. See ELAN VITAL, ORGONE.

life events   Prominent occurrences in life that are easily recalled, whether pleasant, such as getting a college degree, or unpleasant, such as a death in the family. T. H. Holmes & R. H. Rahe located 43 unpleasant life events running from "Death of a Spouse" to "Minor Violation of a Law."

life expectancy   The number of years that a human neonate can expect to live. The life expectancy of an average person is influenced by such factors as the situations surrounding their birth and early childhood and the development of new medical techniques, for example, drugs or surgical procedures, that may extend the life expectancy.

Life Experiences Survey   (I. G. Sarason & B. R. Sarason) A questionnaire in which respondents are asked to the evaluate the favorable and unfavorable experiences of a lifetime.

life fear   According to Otto Rank, a pervasive feeling of terror experienced during the birth process, which generates a lasting urge to return to the safety of the womb and live a dependent life.

life force   English phrase similar to the French *élan vital*.

life goal   According to Alfred Adler, the continuous strivings of persons based on their concepts of what they can expect to attain in life and how they might compensate for real or imagined inferiority. See FICTIONAL FINALISM.

life history   A longitudinal account of the meaningful aspects of a person's emotional, social, and intellectual development, used by some therapists in their treatments.

life-history method   A procedure for understanding a person. The three components are the interview, examination of relevant-for-the-person historical records, and obtaining information from knowledgeable others.

life instinct   In psychoanalytic theory, Eros.

life lie   See LEBENSLÜGE.

life line   A group technique in which members are asked to draw lines representing their lives, beginning with birth and ending with death, marking past and expected events with angles indicating even, upward or lower progressions of functioning. Comparison and discussion usually reveal that the shape and slope of the lines are based on a variety of personality meaningful parameters, such as maturity and academic achievement.

life-organization pattern   A generally consistent mode of behavior involving role, attitudes, standards, practices for various situations throughout life. See LIFESTYLE.

life plan   According to Alfred Adler, a person's style of life and guiding fictions as the person strives to realize life goals. See LIFE SCRIPT.

life review   1. The integration of a person's, usually older, whole life experience, such as by gathering memorabilia in an album for easy reference or by writing an autobiography. Sometimes an adjunct to psychotherapy. 2. An internal process by which a person comes to terms with crises, problems, conflicts, etc., in an effort to make sense out of personal life experiences via reminiscence. Usually in old age or near death.

life rhythm   See BIOLOGICAL RHYTHM, CIRCADIAN RHYTHM.

life satisfaction   An overall positive perception or feeling about the quality of own life.

life script   The scenario which a person uses in "performing" his or her roles and in playing interpersonal games throughout life. According to Eric Berne, it is an unconscious plan based largely on fantasies derived from early experience. See LIFE GOAL, LIFE PLAN, SCRIPT ANALYSIS.

life space   The fundamental concept of Kurt Lewin's field theory comprising the "totality of possible events" for one person at a particular time. Contained within the life space are positive and negative valences, forces or pressures on the person to approach a goal or move away from a perceived danger. See FIELD THEORY.

life-space interviewing   (F. Redl) A technique in which children in residential treatment are interviewed by staff members during moments of stress. Efforts are made to convert these events into therapeutic experiences by attempting to restore the children's belief in themselves and to strengthen their self-concepts.

life span (LSp) The precise length of an organism's life or the typical duration of an average member of a species. See LIFE EXPECTANCY.

life stress Events or experiences that produce strain, such as failure on the job, marital separation, loss of a love object (particularly the death of a spouse).

lifestyle The unique pattern of peoples' total behavior including their thinking, feeling, and acting. See LIFE SCRIPT, PERSONALITY, STYLE OF LIFE.

lifestyle analysis (R. Dreikurs) Based on Alfred Adler's theories, a method of discovering the degree of mental health of an individual and understanding clients' self-concepts, prior to psychotherapy. It has three parts: (a) structured interview about family and early life, thoughts, and feelings; (b) elicitation of early memories; (c) summary of findings with tentative suggestions about the client's basic mistakes and present positive aspects. See ADLER'S THEORY, FICTIVE GOALS, MULTIPLE THERAPY, PSYCHOTHERAPY.

life table A tabulation showing the life expectancy of persons at each life age, usually for males and females.

life tasks According to Alfred Adler the basic challenges and obligations of life are society, work, and family.

life tendencies (C. Bühler) A set of motivating forces that organize behavior at various points in development.

lifetime personality (H.A. Murray) The pattern of behavior that dominates a person's lifestyle between birth and death. See LIFESTYLE, LIFE SCRIPT.

Lifwynn Foundation (H. Zys) An organization established as a social community to study personal interactions based on the phyloanalytic concepts of Trigant Burrow.

ligand A chemical that locks onto a receptor's binding site.

light adaptation 1. Decline in the sensitivity of cone cells in the retina during exposure to light so that more light over time is required to obtain the same degree of visual acuity as in the beginning. 2. Compensation for changes in ambient light from low to high intensity, characterized by pupils of the eye constricting, scotopic (rod) vision changing to photopic (cone) vision, and the cones becoming more tolerant of bright light and less functional in moderate light.

light fear See PHOTOPHOBIA.

light induction A light shining on one part of the retina can affect other parts of the retina and even the retina of the other eye.

lightness constancy A tendency for an object to appear to have the same degree of light under different amounts of illumination.

lightning calculator Nontechnical phrase for a person who is able to rapidly (almost instantly) perform a complex mathematical process such as squaring a five digit number or determining what day of the week any date in history took place. See CALCULATING GENIUSES.

light reflex See PUPILLARY REFLEX.

light therapy 1. Treatment for seasonal-affective disorder (SAD), in which the depressed person is exposed to special fluorescent lights, usually for several hours before dawn and after dusk. 2. Medical treatment, for instance, for hyperbilirubinemia (excess amount of bilirubin in circulating blood). Usually termed phototherapy.

light trance See TRANCE.

light valence The effectiveness of a given light stimulus, which varies with its frequency and intensity as well as with the constitution of the retina, in evoking a given light or color quality.

likelihood ratio (test) (R. A. Fisher, J. Neyman, E. S. Pearson) An approach to analyzing categorical data based on evaluating the null hypothesis on the basis of the ratio of two likelihoods, the likelihood that the data would occur if the null hypothesis is true and the likelihood that the data would occur under the hypothesis for which the data are most probable.

likeness and completeness theories of marital success (R. B. Cattell) The finding that likeness and group completeness of responses are characteristic of more successful marriages.

Likert procedure/scale **Likert Summated Scale**

Likert Summated Scale (R. Likert) A measure of attitudes in which a participant responds to a series of statements on a continuum from "strongly agree" to "strongly disagree" (for example, strongly agree—agree—undecided—disagree—strongly disagree) that would form a five-point Likert scale). The scaling procedure has been used in many studies since its introduction in the 1930s. Also known as Likert procedure/scale, Likert-type Scale. See ATTITUDE SCALE, RATING SCALE, SUMMATED RATING SCALE, THURSTONE ATTITUDE SCALES.

Lilliputian hallucination A false visual perception or hallucination (more properly, an illusion) of objects, animals, or people greatly reduced in size. Vivid examples are found in delirium tremens (alcohol withdrawal delirium) in which tiny animals appear to dart around the room and terrify the patient. Named after Lilliput, an imaginary country in Jonathan Swift's *Gulliver's Travels* (1726) whose inhabitants were 6 inches tall. Also known as diminutive visual hallucination, microptic hallucination. See MICROPSIA.

l'illusion des sosies French phrase for the illusion of doubles. See CAPGRAS' SYNDROME, FREGOLI'S PHENOMENON.

limbic cortex Portions of the brain associated with the limbic system, a part of the brain that is relatively old in terms of evolution.

limbic lobe A part of the brain that includes the hippocampal formation and the cingulate, dentate, parahippocampal, and subcallosal gyri. The limbic lobe forms a ring of neural tissue about the brainstem and is a part of the limbic system. It is associated with emotional function and memory.

limbic system   The designation first used by Paul Maclean for the hippocampus, the amygdala, the septal nuclei, portions of the hypothalamus especially the mammillary bodies, the anterior thalamic nuclei, the cingulate gyrus, and the pathways that connect these structures. The components of the limbic system are essential for normal expression of emotion, motivated behavior, and memory. Psychopharmacological interventions are often aimed at reducing overexcitability of these structures. See PAPEZ('S) THEORY OF EMOTION.

limb-kinetic apraxia   motor apraxia (meaning 1)

limen (L)   A point at which a certain effect takes place, usually referring to the threshold level below which nothing happens and above which the effect occurs. See THRESHOLD.

limen gauge   (M. von Frey) An instrument for providing varied pressure stimulations to the skin.

limen of difference   just-noticeable difference

limerance   (D. Tennov) Describing being in love.

liminal   The threshold of perception. See THRESHOLD.

liminal sensitivity (LS)   The degree of sensory acuity expressed as the lowest value of a given stimulus that gives rise to a sensation (for example, a participant instructed to press a button upon hearing the first tone in a series, does so, though several tones have already been sounded that the participant could not hear). See LIMEN, LIMITS, PSYCHOPHYSICS.

liminal stimulus   A threshold-level stimulus that elicits a response half the time.

limited-capacity retrieval hypothesis   A postulate that short-term memory is of finite capacity and can store relatively few impressions or facts at one time. Its limited capacity would appear to restrict the number of ideas, feelings, or cognitive functions that can be considered or carried out at one time.

limited hold   A restriction on how long reinforcement remains available. In order for a response to be reinforced, it has to occur during the limited-hold period.

limited responsibility   (H. Weihofen) In forensic psychology, a phrase applied to cases of "partial insanity," or diminished responsibility, which means a mental impairment that is not total and so does not render the person free from blame for any criminal acts. See PARTIAL INSANITY.

limited term psychotherapy   Treatment with preestablished limits regarding number of hours, sessions, or both. May be due to research considerations or limits established by third parties, such as insurance companies.

limits   A psychophysical method for determining just-noticeable-differences (JNDs) and other constants. Participants are presented with varying amplitudes or intensities of stimuli and asked to compare these with standard stimuli, or to report absence or presence of same.

limophoitas   A psychotic episode induced by starvation.

limophthisis   The physical and mental signs of emaciation caused by severe undernourishment.

limulus   A species of *arachnida merostomata* used in animal vision experiments. Also known as horseshoe crab.

Lincoln-Oseretsky Motor Development Scale   (W. Sloan) A test designed to assess general motor ability of children between 6 and 14 years of age through their performance on 36 sensorimotor items. The Lincoln adaptation of the Oseretsky tests were constructed by William Sloan, who at the time was at Lincoln State School and Colony at Lincoln, Illinois.

lineae albicantes   stria atrophica

linear   Having to do with a straight line, such as a linear relationship between Y and X described by the equation for a straight line $Y = a + bx$.

linear causation   A point of view that one event causes another event in direct sequence of a phenomenon (for example, A causes B causes C, etc.). See SIMPLE CAUSATION.

linear correlation   A measure of relationship between two variables where the deviations of the data points from a straight line are minimized. See CORRELATION, LINEAR REGRESSION.

linear discriminant technique   Fisher's discriminant function technique employed when a score is used to assign a person or object to one of two classifications. Related to Hotelling's T^2 and to Mahalanobis's D^2. Also known as multiple-regression pattern analysis.

linear equation   See LINEAR FUNCTION.

linear function   A mathematical function of the first degree whose mean rate of increase is constant and which can be combined only by addition and subtraction. Formula: $y = a + bx$. Where: a and b are constants, a is the y-intercept (the value of y when $x = 0$), and b is the slope (the amount y changes when x increases 1 unit).

linear-operator model of learning   (B. Bush & F. Mosteller) The view that learning is based on an organism responding to part of the total stimulus and that responses then occur due to fractional elements of the total stimulus. Learning is enhanced by reinforcement but reduced by the effort required by the process of learning.

linear perspective   The knowledge of the actual size of faraway objects based on the principle that the size of an object's visual image is a function of its distance from the eye. Thus, the same object up close looks smaller when removed to a distance. Two objects appear closer together when viewed at a distance, for example, the tracks of a railroad appear to converge on the horizon but it is generally known that they are in reality identically parallel all the way.

linear program   Programmed learning in which information is presented in small, discrete, step-by-step frames that usually are progressively more complex. Correct answers are given after each frame, providing immediate feedback and continuous reinforcement. See BRANCHING PROGRAM, PROGRAMMED INSTRUCTION, TEACHING MACHINES.

linear regression   A statistical procedure in which a linear equation is developed which optimally predicts a criterion variable from one or more predictor variables. Most commonly using the least-squares criterion.

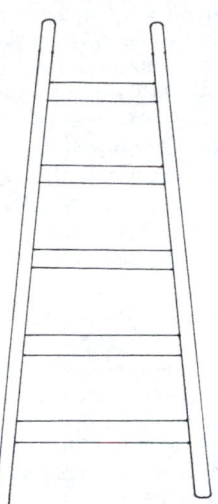

linear perspective   This figure shows how a ladder might appear smaller at the top than at the bottom. Such a common illusion is observed when looking upwards at a tall building in which the top appears smaller than the base.

linear system   1. A system in which the units of input summate in a straight line manner. 2. System in which the response to a complex stimulus is a simple summation of individual responses. Sometimes known as linear model.

linear type   Phrase occasionally applied to Ernst Kretschmer's asthenic body type, characterized by a slender, narrow-chested, long-necked, long-nosed physique.

line authority   Power in an organization that flows down the chain of command, whereas accountability flows upward.

line of beauty   (W. Hogarth) A serpentine line regarded as the most beautiful shape.

line of best fit   A line drawn on a scatter diagram that minimizes variance around the line. See LEAST-SQUARES CRITERION.

line of least resistance   A course of action on the part of an individual that meets with the fewest social objections or environmental obstacles. Also known as least resistance line.

line of regard   A straight line between an object being viewed and the center of rotation of the eye.

line of unbearability   A personal equation governing suicide as an end to life where life's quality is emphasized over its quantity.

lingam   Dildo.

linguadental   A speech sound made with the tongue placed against the teeth (for example, /th/).

lingual   Pertaining to the tongue or, by way of extension, to speech.

lingual gland   A gland located on the tongue that probably serves to wash out the taste buds.

lingual gyrus   A relatively short convolution of the brain, running horizontally from the occipital to temporal lobes immediately above the fusiform gyrus.

lingual nerve   A branch of the fifth cranial nerve that supplies fibers to the anterior two-thirds of the tongue, including the taste-bud papillae and mucous membrane. Also known as gustatory nerve.

lingual papilla   Any of the four types of papillae (nipple-like projections on the surface of the tongue): circumvallate (in back), filiform (largely tactile), foliate (taste buds on back and edges), and fungiform (taste buds in front).

linguistic approach   A method of teaching reading which assumes that children have mastery of oral language. Letters and sound equivalents taught in reading are embedded in meaningful words with regular spelling patterns.

linguistic awareness   1. The ability of a child to understand two different meanings of the same word. 2. Refers to the awareness of grammatical structures.

linguistic categories   The morphology, syntax, and lexicon used in the creation of computer languages.

linguistic-kinesic (L-K) method   The objective study of disordered behavior in terms of language and movement involved in interactions between people. See RECOVERY, INC.

linguistic-relativity hypothesis   (B. Whorf) A postulate that language determines how a person thinks, it affects perception and thought. Also known as Sapir-Whorf hypothesis, Whorfian hypothesis.

linguistics   The study of languages and their structure and origins including phonology, grammar (morphology, syntax), lexicology, and, in a wider sense, phonetics and semantics. See ORIGIN-OF-LANGUAGE THEORIES, PSYCHOLOGICAL LINGUISTICS, PSYCHO-LINGUISTICS.

linguistic universals   1. Aspects of language (for example, grammar) that hold for all languages. 2. Rules for the use of language, such as how to transform singulars into plurals, and the proper order of adverbs to verbs. See LANGUAGE-ACQUISITION DEVICE.

linkage   In genetics, a tendency for two or more genetic traits to be inherited together, so that an offspring may show the combination of traits or none of them.

linkage worker   See ADVOCATE.

link analysis   The study of any system with the intention of generating maximal efficiency in terms of connections between parts.

Link Trainer   (E. A. Link & G. Link) The original commercially successful cockpit simulator. A device used in airplane pilot training and human engineering research in which the conditions of piloting an airplane are closely simulated without leaving the ground. Superseded by computerized variants from dozens of firms. Also known as Link Instrument Trainer.

linonophobia   Irrational fear of string.

lip-biting   See FINGER-BITING BEHAVIOR.

lip eroticism   The use of the lips to obtain sexual arousal or satisfaction.

lipidhistiocytosis   Technical name for Niemann-Pick disease.

lip-key   A response key to measure reaction time when a person opens the lips to respond to some stimulus with a word or a sound.

lipostatic hypothesis/theory   A proposition relating to control of long-term feeding patterns through processes in a hypothalamic regulatory mechanism involving the circulation of blood metabolites (foodstuffs or wastes in the blood) concerned with the storage of fat in the system. Compare GLUCOSTATIC THEORY.

lipping   See FLEHMENING.

Lipps illusion (T. Lipps) Given a figure consisting of a circle, with the apices of short-sided right angles tangent to the circle at 12, 3, 6, and 9 o'clock points, such that at these points the circle falsely appears flattened.

lip-reading A procedure used by persons with hearing-impairment to comprehend what others are saying by watching their mouths and expressions. Also known as speech-reading, which is generally preferred because lip-readers get cues from not only the lips but the whole body of the speaker.

LIPS Leiter International Performance Scale

liquidation of attachment (P. Janet) The freeing of a patient from a socially painful situation by unraveling the attachments in which she or he is embedded. See PSYCHOTHERAPY.

LISP An acronym for List Processing, an information processing language.

lisping In speech, the defective production of sibilant sounds caused by improper tongue placement or abnormalities of the speech mechanism. Lisping may be lateral or frontal, emitting different sounds depending upon the placement of the jaw and tongue. See INTERDENTAL SIGMATISM, SIGMATISM.

Lissajou's figures (J. A. Lissajou) Revolving figures produced by reflection from a mirror of a beam of light from two tuning forks vibrating in parallel planes perpendicular to each other.

Lissauer('s) tract (H. Lissauer) An area near the tip of the dorsal horn of the spinal cord where unmyelinated and lightly myelinated dorsal root fibers enter the cord and propriospinal fibers travel to interconnect different levels of the cord.

Lissauer type paralysis (H. Lissauer) An uncommon form of general paresis in which the patient may experience severe focal symptoms, such as hemiplegia and aphasia, but retain most intellectual functions. Also known as Lissauer's dementia paralytica.

lissencephaly agyria

lissophobia lyssophobia

listening attitude A behavior set in which persons prepare themselves to receive a message. Silvano Arieti claimed that a patient with schizophrenia who habitually prepares to experience a hallucination may learn to avoid it.

listening strategies Patterns of attention established by people during lectures, such as listening intently at the beginning and at the end but not in the middle of any long talk.

listening with the third ear Empathy in which a therapist develops a special sensitivity to the unspoken thoughts and feelings behind the patient's spoken words. Phrase was originally used by Friedreich Nietzsche, and adopted by Theodore Reik as the title of one of his books.

Listing's law (J. B. Listing) A principle in vision which states that when the eye moves from sighting one object to another, the eyeball rotation to the new location is the same as if the eye had moved on an axis at right angles from the first to the second sighting spot.

listwise deletion The elimination of all cases with any amount of missing data from a calculation such as a correlation matrix.

literacy test Any test that examines the ability to read and write. Such examinations generally provide comparative scholastic grade levels of such abilities.

literal alexia/dyslexia A form of alexia in which individual letters or numerals are not recognized and letters like "d" and "b" are confused. See ALEXIA.

literalism See OBJECTIVE ORIENTATION.

literal paraphasia A form of aphasia in which phonemes are substituted in speech, making it difficult to comprehend what the person is trying to say, as in saying "lar" for "car." See PARAPHASIA.

literary psychoanalysis See APPLIED PSYCHO-ANALYSIS.

lithium A medication used in the treatment of bipolar disorders (what used to be called manic-depressive illness). It seems to work by altering the irritability of the neurons in the central nervous system. Lithium has also been used for other conditions in which the person suffers from chronic irritability or agitation.

lithium therapy Using lithium, usually in the form of lithium carbonate, as a therapeutic agent in manic states and in preventing the recurrence of both manic and depressive episodes in bipolar disorder. Dosage must be carefully regulated and blood-level tests must be regularly administered because of possible toxicity.

litigious paranoia A type of paranoid reaction in which persons are constantly quarreling, claiming persecution, and insisting that their rights have been breached. Such individuals usually threaten to go to court, and frequently do to seek redress for exaggerated or fancied wrongs. Also known as paranoia querulans, paranoid litigious state.

litigiousness A personality characteristic consisting of contentiousness, quarrelsomeness, and readiness to threaten a lawsuit.

Little Albert (J. B. Watson & R. Rayner) A child who was an experimental subject of Watson and Rayner. He developed a phobia of white rats via classical conditioning with a loud noise as the unconditioned stimulus, though instrumental components of Albert's reaching for the rat were also involved. He showed generalized response to other white fur objects.

Little Hans (S. Freud) A controversial case in which a child's phobia for horses was traced by the father, with Sigmund Freud's help, to castration anxiety stemming from masturbation, to repressed death wishes toward the father due to the son's rivalry over the mother, and to fear of retaliation, with displacement of that fear onto horses. The case was reported in "Analysis of a Phobia in a Five-Year-Old Boy."

live modeling The observation of the behavior of models "in the flesh," that is, models who are physically present.

living will Usually, a written document specifying a person's wishes about resuscitation during the dying process. See MERCY KILLING, PHYSICIAN-ASSISTED SUICIDE.

L-K See LINGUISTIC-KINESIC METHOD.

Lloyd Morgan's canon The original name for a principle proposed in 1894 by Lloyd Morgan. Also known as Morgan's canon/principle.

lm See LUMEN.

L method A short-cut method for selecting a small number of items or variables that, when weighted equally, will predict a criterion almost as well as or better than the entire pool of items or variables, based on optimally selected regression weights from which the sample is drawn.

l- See LEVOROTATORY.

ln See LOG$_e$.

L- The levorotatory form of a chemical compound; a substance that rotates the plane of polarized light to the left (for example, L-dopa). See LEVOROTATORY.

LNNB Luria-Nebraska Neuropsychological Battery

loading 1. The weight or relative significance given to a statistic. 2. The degree to which a test is correlated with a factor.

load theory See ENVIRONMENTAL-LOAD THEORY.

lobar divisions Major topographic regions of the cerebral hemisphere separated generally by principal sulci of the cerebrum. Comprise the frontal, parietal, temporal, and occipital lobes. There also may be subdivisions, for example, the inferior, middle, and superior temporal lobes.

lobe A curved division of an organ, separated from each other by a fissure or sulcus. See LOBAR DIVISIONS.

lobectomy A psychosurgical technique in which the prefrontal region of the frontal lobes is surgically removed. Once held to be a treatment for severe psychoses. No longer performed in the United States of America. See LEUCOTOMY.

lobotomy 1. Incision into a lobe. 2. (E. Moniz) A frontal lobotomy.

local circuit neuron A neuron that has synapses only with immediately adjacent neurons; no long axon. Another name for Golgi Type II neuron.

local excitatory state (LES) The localized increase in negative potential on the surface of a neuron as an initial response to a stimulus. Also known as local excitatory potential.

local-global distinction In problem solving, there are two possibilities of movements: (a) local, seeking the next logical step in the process; (b) global, having an understanding of the big picture, that is, the final goal.

locality attachment Ability of an organism to detect its position in space with reference to other points, such as the home or nest of the individual animal. Locality attachment may be associated with the ability of domestic animals to return to their place of birth or a former home after being removed to another locality many miles away. See HOMING.

locality memory Ability of organisms to identify a certain region by means of certain landmarks.

locality survey Exploring a given locality by an organism, either when it is newly born and able to move about or in entering a strange environment. See CURIOSITY.

localization The assignment of mental functions to nervous-system tissues involved in specific activities, for example, visual functions are associated with specific nerve tracts, projection and association neurons of the cortex, receptor neurons, and other cells that mark localization of the function. See LOCALIZATION OF FUNCTION, VICARIOUS FUNCTION.

localization of (brain) function The assignment of different mental functions, such as vision and speech, to specific areas of the cortex. Also known as cortical localization of function. See PHRENOLOGY.

localization of symptoms Psychoanalytic phrase for the unconscious selection of a particular bodily function or part of the body to express a neurotic impulse (for example, a person developing constipation as a defense against the wish to engage in anal intercourse). See SYMPTOM CHOICE.

localization theory A point of view that all receptive, motor as well as some associative functions (such as language) have their neural locus in a specific region or area of the brain. See LOCAL SIGN, LOCALIZATION OF (BRAIN).

localized amnesia Memory loss for specific or isolated experiences, usually restricted to events connected with a certain time, place, or some other special incident. Also known as circumscribed amnesia, lacunar amnesia.

localized functions See LOCALIZATION OF FUNCTION, LOCALIZATION THEORY.

localized memory storage (theory) A point of view derived from early research showing specialized memory structures in the brain, such as Broca's area for speech production. Compare DISTRIBUTED MEMORY STORAGE (THEORY).

local near effect The degree of excitation of a neural component as a function of its distance from the point where the stimulus is applied.

local potential/response A phase of a graded or generator potential that precedes the spike potential, if the localized stimulation is above threshold level.

local sign (R. Loize) An explanation of how the nervous system is able to localize a stimulus, visual or tactual, by an association between experience and one or more cortical cells. A local sign helps the body determine the specific area of the skin that has been stimulated and the type of stimulation. Also known as locality sign.

local static reaction A static reflex which is confined to one limb or part of body.

local stimulus theory (W. B. Cannon) A point of view that hunger is a sensation produced by an empty stomach. The theory was discredited by research demonstrating that people without stomachs experienced hunger due to a lack of nutrients in the blood supply that triggered the "appestat" (the ventral medial nucleus of the hypothalamus) to signal that it was time to eat.

local style In R. J. Sternberg's theory of mental self-government, a pragmatic orientation along with a preference for concrete problems and detail work.

local theory of thirst A concept introduced by Walter Cannon to explain the association between thirst and dryness of the mouth. The theory asserted that dryness of the mouth represented the general state of body-tissue hydration. Later studies found hormonal, neural, and other factors of greater significance in the control of water intake.

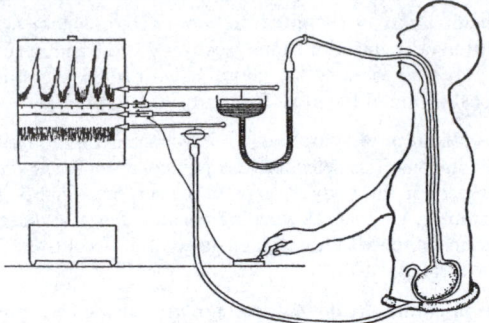

local stimulus theory The Cannon-Washburn apparatus used to test whether feelings of hunger and movements of the stomach were correlated. The participant presses a button when feeling hunger pangs. Both hunger pangs and movements of the stomach were found to be affected by the brain, and the brain was affected by nutrients in the blood.

location In early language development, the stage in which such words as "here" and "there" are first used in identifying the location of objects.

location constancy A tendency for a resting object and its setting to appear to have the same position even if the relationship between setting and observer is altered as the observer shifts position. See OBJECT CONSTANCY.

location response/sense The element in a person's spatial experience which allocates each point in external space to some definite point in the visual field, or to some point on the surface of the person's body. Also known as sense of direction.

loci Plural of locus.

loci method of memorization A technique of committing to memory a sequence of items by first thinking of a series of locations and then associating the items to be remembered with the locations, for example, to remember items on a grocery list, visualize a door next to a carton of milk; a key stuck into a loaf of bread; and a doorknob with bananas hanging from it. See METHOD OF LOCI, MNEMONIC TECHNIQUE.

lock and key theory A point of view that different odor receptors can only be stimulated by molecules of a specific size and shape that fit them like a key in a lock.

locked ward A hospital unit in which mentally disturbed patients are kept under lock-and-key. There is a trend away from locked wards, since some patients feel they are being incarcerated and punished for being ill. Other factors responsible for eliminating locked rooms and units are the concept of the mental hospital as a treatment rather than custodial institution, the effectiveness of psychoactive drugs, and the concepts of the open hospital and therapeutic community.

lockout In labor relations, the opposite of a strike; management bars employees from the workplace.

locomotion Movement of an organism from one place to another. Kurt Lewin used the term for psychological movement in a person's life space due to a change in the valence of a region or regions. See LIFE SPACE.

locomotor activity General bodily activity in movement from one area to another, as when an animal explores or chases. See RESTLESSNESS.

locomotor arrest Inhibition of movement, an effect that can be produced in experimental animals by electrical stimulation of the hippocampus.

locomotor ataxia (J. Cruveilhier) 1. Motor ataxia; inability to perform coordinated muscle movements in walking, producing an unsteady gait. 2. Old name for tabes dorsalis, a condition of muscular incoordination in walking, resulting from a degeneration of the posterior columns of the spinal cord due to progressive syphilitic disease. Robert Remak changed the name from locomotor ataxia to tabes dorsalis to more appropriately describe the wasting away of the spinal cord's dorsal column. See GENERAL PARESIS.

locomotor maze A maze that requires bodily movement to reach a goal. See ELEVATED MAZE, HAMPTON COURT MAZE.

loco-plant/-weed (crazy—Spanish) 1. Any of a number of species of *Astragalus* or *Oxytropis* that grow wild in western North America, particularly in the Rocky Mountain region. Loco identifies the effects the plant has on humans and animals that ingest them. The loco toxin produces irreversible changes in the central nervous system, including brain lesions and eventual paralysis. 2. See MARIJUANA.

locus (place—Latin) The place or position of an anatomical entity, for example, a rash on the skin, or a gene on a chromosome. Plural is loci.

locus caeruleus (blue place—Latin) Bluish-tinted nuclei found on the floor of the fourth ventricle of the brain. The area cells contain large amounts of catecholamines, primarily norepinephrine. Lesions of the locus caeruleus in experimental animals have resulted in disturbances in normal sleep patterns. Also spelled locus cerleus/coeruleus.

locus of control (J. Rotter) A point of view that a person holds or maintains about self-independence and control by others. An internal locus of control refers to the conviction that a person can use self-behavior to achieve desired goals; an external locus of control refers to the belief that real power resides outside the person, and that forces outside the self determine a person's life. See DETERMINISM, FREE WILL, INDETERMINISM, SOFT DETERMINISM.

locus-of-evaluation The place of a judgment's origin, its source; whether the appraisal of an experience comes more from within the individual (internal) or from outside sources (external).

log Short for logarithm, where the logarithm of a number N to a base b is the power to which b must be raised to give the number N. Because, for example, $10^2 = 100$ is the logarithm of 100 to the base 10, $\log_{10} 100$ equals 2.

logagnosia A form of aphasia characterized by the ability to read or call off words but without comprehension. See RECEPTIVE APHASIA.

logamnesia A form of aphasia characterized by inability to recognize words, spoken or written. See RECEPTIVE APHASIA.

logaphasia A form of aphasia characterized by inability or impaired ability to articulate in speech.

logarithm See LOG.

logasthenia aphasia

$\log_e$ The natural or Napierian logarithm, e = 2.7183. Also known as ln.

logic   1. The branch of philosophy that deals with the principles that distinguish rational from irrational reasoning procedures. Includes the use of syllogisms, and inductive and deductive thinking processes. 2. A series of rules for coming to the correct conclusion based on premises.

logical atomism   A doctrine positing that any whole can be derived from, or explained in terms of, pre-existing parts. See ELEMENTARISM, HOLISM, REDUCTIONISM.

logical consequences   (R. Dreikurs) A parent's training of children by means of a prior agreement with the child for particular circumstances, such as going shopping. A parent tells the children that if they are ready to go to the store at 3:30, they can go, but if they are not ready, they cannot go. The parent makes it clear that the children will not be reminded and will be left behind if late. The intent is to teach the children a sense of responsibility. Compare NATURAL CONSEQUENCES. See PUNISHMENT.

logical construct   See HYPOTHETICAL CONSTRUCT.

logical deduction   A conclusion reached by proceeding from premises according to the rules of logic.

logical error   Making a decision or drawing a conclusion not based on facts or proper thinking, or based on a single case or on tradition. An example is the belief that certain physical traits go with certain personality traits, such as the wearing of glasses and intelligence, or red hair and a fiery temperament. Phrase is somewhat self-contradictory and perhaps should be called illogical error.

logical inference   A necessary deduction from a premise, such as if Mike is older than Roberta, and if Roberta is older than Jon, then logically Jon is younger than Mike.

logical method of instruction   The arrangement and presentation of instructional materials in a sequence according to their inherent relationships, such as addition being taught before multiplication.

logical positivism   (M. Schlick) A doctrine positing that verifiable, factual, experiential knowledge and intersubjective scientific language must be employed in philosophy and psychology, rather than metaphysical concepts and theories. This view influenced P. W. Bridgman's concepts of operationalism and operational definition. See PHYSICALISM, VIENNA CIRCLE.

logical thinking   See LOGICAL DEDUCTION.

logicogrammatical disorder   A manifestation of semantic aphasia, which affects patients with lesions of the dominant parietal region. The patient uses the correct words, but they are arranged in a sequence that gives a different meaning, for example, "the garage is in the car" vs "the car is in the garage." See LANGUAGE DISORDERS.

logic-tight compartments   A form of intellectualization (defense mechanism) in which sets of ideas or schemas that are mutually inconsistent or contradictory are kept separated. Sometimes the person is vaguely aware that a logical analysis would lead to discomfort.

logistic curve   An S-shaped graphic representation showing the growth of a population dependent upon fixed resources. Growth is initially slow because of the small number of individuals, then picks up speed, then slows again at a saturation point as the limited resources become constraining. See LEARNING CURVE for an example.

log-log coordinate paper   Graph paper in which both ordinate and abscissa are in logarithmic form, used especially for plotting psychophysical data.

Logo   (word, reason—Greek) A trademark for a computer-programming language designed to encourage the development of problem-solving skills. Logo is based on Jean Piaget's research in the development of thinking in children.

logoclonia   A speech characteristic in which parts of words are repeated in a manner similar to that of stuttering. Often a symptom of senile or presenile disorders such as Alzheimer's disease. Also spelled logoklony. See LANGUAGE DISORDERS.

logodiarrhea   logorrh(o)ea

logoklony   logoclonia

logomania   logorrh(o)ea

logopathy   General term for a speech disorder of any kind.

logopedics   The study and treatment of speech disorders. Includes the study of the physiology and pathology of the organs of speech.

logophobia   The fear of words.

logorrh(o)ea   1. Compulsive behavior in speech; inability to stop talking. 2. Excessive and incessant flow of words. 3. Rapid, jumbled speech. 4. A rush of rapid, uncontrollable, and incoherent talking typically observed in the manic phase of bipolar (manic-depressive) disorder. Also known as hyperlogia, hyperphrasia, lalorrhea, logodiarrhea, logomania, polylogia, polyphrasia, tachylalia, tachylogia, tachyphrasia, verbomania. See AUTOECHOLALIA, CLUTTERING, CONFABULATION, GLOSSOLALIA, PRESSURE OF SPEECH, TACHYPHEMIA.

logospasm   A speech disorder marked by explosive utterances or stuttering, similar to logoclonia. See LANGUAGE DISORDERS.

logotherapy   (V. Frankl) A philosophical-theoretical approach to psychotherapy based on meaning. The therapeutic process consists of examining three types of values: creative (work, achievement); experiential (art, science); and attitudinal (loss, suffering).

log_{10}   Logarithm to the base 10; also written without subscript. See LOG.

Lokian personality   A hypothetical personality characterized by a need to cause distress to others. Named after Loki, the Norse god of turmoil, mischief, and destruction. See PSYCHOPATHY.

Lombroso's theory   (C. Lombroso) A point of view that over-development of certain capacities or traits in individuals accompanied by certain physiological traits or features indicate an instability of organization pointing toward degeneration and criminalism. See ATAVISM, DEGENERACY THEORY, PHYSIOGNOMY, STIGMATA OF DEGENERACY.

loneliness fear   See AUTOPHOBIA.

loner   Slang for a person who has no friends. See AFFECTIVE SEPARATION, FRIENDSHIP NETWORKS, HERMITISM.

long-circuiting   (R. B. Cattell) Renunciation of immediate satisfactions in favor of attaining remote, long-term goals. See SHORT-CIRCUITING.

long-delay conditioning   A classical-conditioning procedure in which the conditioned stimulus is presented a long time before the unconditioned stimulus on each conditioning trial.

longevity   Length of life.

long-hot-summer effect   A theory that incessant heat conditions can cause or contribute to increased aggression and violence. Often associated with crowded slum-type areas of major cities.

longilineal   Denoting a constitutional type of body that is long rather than broad and roughly equivalent to Ernst Kretschmer's asthenic type. See BODY TYPE.

longitudinal   1. In anatomy, running lengthwise in the direction of the long axis of the body. 2. In research, refers to length in terms of time. See LONGITUDINAL METHOD/STUDY.

longitudinal fissure   longitudinal sulcus

longitudinal method/study   Research on the same population of individuals at different points in time, such as a comparative study of the same group of children in an urban and a suburban school over several years for measuring their cognitive development. See CROSS-SECTIONAL STUDY.

longitudinal sampling   Repeated sampling of the same group over time. See STRATEGIC SAMPLING.

longitudinal sulcus   A fissure that runs along the top of the cerebral cortex and marks the division between the left and right hemispheres of the brain. The fissure is quite prominent at the frontal and occipital poles. At the bottom of the longitudinal sulcus the hemispheres are connected by the corpus callosum. Also known as longitudinal fissure.

longitudinal study   1. Research concerned with changes occurring in individuals over extended periods of time. 2. Research in which samples of a population are selected and then studied as age and related activity increases. See LONGITUDINAL METHOD STUDY.

long-term care facilities   Extended-care institutions, such as nursing homes, that provide medical and personal services for patients who are unable to live independently but do not require hospitalization. Patients utilizing long-term care facilities are generally over the age of 65 and suffer from disorders such as Alzheimer's disease, parkinsonism, and stroke.

long-term depression   A prolonged decrease in the excitability of a neuron to a specific synaptic input.

long-term memory (LTM)   1. Memory that can be recalled for long periods of time. 2. The ability to practice a skill, recall events, or reproduce names and numbers long after they were originally learned, characterized by the organization (mostly but not entirely semantic) of knowledge. See EARLY RECOLLECTIONS, SHORT-TERM MEMORY.

long-term (memory) store   See SHORT-TERM VS LONG-TERM (MEMORY) STORE.

long-term potentiation (LTP)   A prolonged increase in the excitability of a neuron to a specific synaptic input, caused by repeated activity of that input.

long-term psychotherapy   Psychological treatment requiring a number of sessions per week over a period of many months. The most extended technique, psychoanalysis, takes on the average two to three years since it seeks to evoke unconscious material stemming from the patient's earliest experiences and is directed toward the reorganization of the patient's entire emotional life.

long-term storage   See LONG-TERM MEMORY.

long-term storage theory   An information-processing theory of memory suggesting that long-term storage is organized through meaning, has an infinite capacity, and produces retrieval failures by interference. Compare SHORT-TERM STORAGE THEORY.

look angle   In ergonomics, the direction of the operator's gaze.

looking-glass self   (C. H. Cooley) A concept of the self obtained upon reflection of other people's reactions and opinions. See IDIOPANIMA.

looming   Space perception in which the retinal image of an object is magnified as it approaches. Reactions to looming vary; for example, chicks run away, kittens avert their heads, monkeys leap backward and make alarm cries, human infants attempt to withdraw their heads at two weeks and blink at three weeks.

loop   1. A reverberatory circuit. 2. A series of instructions that predictably repeat a set of computations, modifying some variable each time. 3. A closed path or circuit over which a signal can circulate, as in a feedback control system, that provides a flow of information back to a source, thereby allowing a comparison with an input command signal. 4. In industrial psychology, closed-loop processes are self-contained, such as something that will start, operate, and close on its own. Open-loop processes include those such as driving a bus that has a particular route repeated over and over, but controlled by the driver. See ITERATION METHOD.

loose cultures   (H. C. Triandis) A cultural syndrome organized around the theme of great tolerance for even major deviations from the norms of a collective. Compare TIGHT CULTURES.

loosening of associations   A mental disturbance in which thought and speech processes are disconnected and fragmented, and the patient (usually a schizophrenic) jumps from one idea to a totally unrelated and irrelevant idea instead of following the usual lines of association. Also known as loose association. See COGNITIVE SLIPPAGE.

lordosis   1. In humans, a backward curvature of the spine, usually lumbar, resulting in a saddle back. See CAMPTOCORMIA. 2. In animals, the "presenting" posture of female mammals to invite and facilitate copulation.

Lorge-Thorndike Intelligence Tests   (I. D. Lorge & E. L. Thorndike) A test intending to measure intelligence, designed to be given in groups for grades kindergarten through high school. Consists of a verbal and nonverbal battery at each level from ages three to five. There are five age levels and raw scores are translated into intelligence quotient (IQ) equivalents. See THORNDIKE-LORGE TEST.

Lorr Scale Common name for the Multidimensional Scale for Rating Psychiatric Patients (MSRPP).

loss of access theory A point of view that forgetting is a process of losing accessibility to the information because of inadequate retrieval cues.

loss of affect Inability to respond emotionally; apathy, emotional flatness. A common symptom of schizophrenia, also found in presenile and senile brain disorders.

loss of personal identity Failure to recall self-identity and past life. It is a major symptom in dissociative, or psychogenic, amnesia. See AMNESIA, FUGUE.

loss resolution The final and concluding stage of grieving.

lost in thought See PREOCCUPATION.

lost letter procedure/technique (S. Milgram) A technique for determining attitudes. A number of stamped envelopes addressed to specific organizations are left in various localities to see how many are helpfully mailed (for example, letters addressed to a smokers-rights group and to an anti-smoking group are left in different types of neighborhoods).

loudness A partly subjective measure of the amplitude of sound waves, the perception of intensity varying with the individual listener. Loudness also varies slightly with the wavelength of the sound, with human sensitivity being greatest for sounds in the middle range of sound-wave lengths. Loudness is measured in decibels. See MOST COMFORTABLE LOUDNESS, PITCH, SOUND, TIMBRE.

love A complex yet basically integrated emotion comprising strong affection, feelings of tenderness, pleasurable sensations in the presence of the love object, and devotion to the well-being of the loved one. This emotion takes many forms including concern for fellow humans (brotherly love); responsibility for the welfare of a child (parental love); sexual attraction and excitement (erotic love); self-esteem and self-acceptance (self-love); and identification with the totality of being (love of God). Other types of love include: BEING, COMPANIONATE, DORIAN, GENITAL, HELLENIC, HOMOSEXUAL, MONKEY, MOTHER, OBJECT, PHALLIC, PLATONIC, PREGENITAL, PRODUCTIVE, PUPPY. See POSTAMBIVALENT PHASE, SELF-LOVE, TRANSFERENCE-LOVE.

lovemap (J. Money) The private conception of any person about love, especially how others who love that person are supposed to act (for example, two people get married, each with different expectations of how the other should behave afterward).

love needs (A. Maslow) The next level in Abraham Maslow's hierarchy of needs beyond physiological and safety needs, characterized by the striving for affiliation and acceptance. Also known as belongingness and love needs. See NEED-HIERARCHY THEORY.

love object A person in whom another invests the emotions of affection, devotion, and, usually, sexual interest.

love of God According to Erich Fromm, a form of love of the highest value and most desired good. See AGAPE.

love scale (Z. Rubin) A scale allegedly measuring romantic love that consists of three elements: affiliative/dependent needs, predisposition to help, and exclusiveness.

love schemas According to Elaine Hatfield, people's cognitive models as to what it is appropriate to expect from themselves, those they love, and from their love relationships.

love slob (A. Ellis) A person who has a dire need for love and approval from others and will go to great lengths to achieve it. Also known as love junkie.

love varieties (J. Lee) According to John A. Lee there are six varieties of love: (listed alphabetically) agape (other-centered, considerate), eros (romantic and sexual), ludic (self-centered and playful), mania (obsessive, demanding), pragma (practical and logical), and storge (compassionate and caring).

love-withdrawal A form of discipline based on threatened loss of love (showing anger or hurt, isolating children, threatening to leave them or institutionalize them.) Excessive use may lead to anxiety, dependency, and inhibitedness.

low-ball phenomenon A way of getting people to comply with a request, such as to make a purchase, by offering some kind of bargain, in the expectation that the person will want the object or to obtain the benefits even if the "price" increases.

low ceiling Refers to the highest level of measurement of a test being below the functioning level of a particular individual, as if a college student were given a scholastic achievement test designed to measure up to grade six.

Lowenfield Mosaic Test (M. F. J. Lowenfield) A projective task composed of 456 differently shaped colored tiles that a participant is asked to assemble. Interpretations depend on the clinical insights of the examiner. Persons with mental retardation might be expected to make simple designs, patients with schizophrenia to make disorderly patterns, and people considered imaginative to generate complex designs.

lower category In the psychophysical method of single stimuli, reports that will surpass other reports in frequency if the stimulus-magnitude is sufficiently decreased.

low Machs See MACH SCALE.

LPC See LEAST-PREFERRED COWORKERS SCALE.

l.p.d. least perceptible difference (also abbreviated **lpd**)

LS liminal sensitivity

L scale See LIE SCALE.

LSD (A. Hoffman, M. Rinkel) Abbreviation for the psychedelic or hallucinogenic chemical lysergic acid diethylamide. It alters consciousness, evokes predominantly visual hallucinations, and distorts the sense of reality. Used widely in the drug subculture of the late 1960s and has continued as a recreational drug. Some users suffer from negative acute reactions ("bad trips") and a few seem to have significant aftereffects, especially after many episodes. Also known as "acid," LSD-25. See HALLUCINOGEN.

LSD psychotherapy   An experimental technique in which LSD (lysergic acid diethylamide) was administered to patients with chronic alcoholism or character disorders during the 1960s as a means of facilitating the process of uncovering and reliving repressed memories, and increasing the ability to communicate thoughts and feelings. According to some reports, the method was moderately successful, but has been abandoned due to the risks involved, particularly that of releasing latent psychotic tendencies. See HALLUCINOGENS, PSYCHEDELICS, PSYCHOLYTIC THERAPY, PSYCHIC DRIVING.

LSD-25   Abbreviation for d-lysergic acid diethylamide tartrate 25. See LSD.

LSp   See LIFE SPAN.

LTM   long-term memory

LTP   long-term potentiation

lucid   Clear; not confused.

lucid dream   A dream experience in which the dreamers are aware that they are dreaming. Also known as dream within a dream.

lucidity   A mental state or interval in which persons may not have complete ability to reason or comprehend complex matters but have adequate mental powers to be legally responsible for behavior.

'lude   Street name for Quaalude, a brand of methaqualone. Also spelled 'ludes.

ludic activity   Play.

lues   A plague; specifically syphilis.

Lüscher Color Test   (M. Lüscher) A personality examination used to infer personality traits from a participant's performance on a forced-choice color preference test. Based on the concept that the color red evokes tension and anxiety. Sometimes also spelled Luescher.

lumbar nerves   See SPINAL NERVES.

lumen (L or lm)   (light—Latin) (A. E. Blondel) The SI (metric system) unit of luminous flux, the amount of illumination shed by a light of one candlepower over an area of one square meter. See LUMINOUS FLUX.

Luminal   Trade name for phenobarbital.

luminance (L)   The amount of light reflected from an object as measured in millilamberts.

luminance formula   Lux multiplied by r (lux × R) when illuminance is measured in lux and R is the reflectance of a surface.

luminance ratio   A measure of the brightness of an object divided by the brightness of the surround.

luminosity   The relative brightness of a light source as measured in terms of reflectance of surfaces in the environment and other factors that may influence the perceived light intensity. A light will appear brighter in a room with white walls than in a room with dark walls.

luminosity coefficients   Numbers by which color mixture data are to be multiplied for every color so that the sum of the three numbers equals the desired luminance of the specified sample.

luminosity curve   A graphic representation of the brightness values of visible wave lengths as plotted with the wave length on the abscissa and luminosity on the ordinate.

luminous flux (f, ƒ, or F)   The flow of bright (luminous) light. That part of radiant flux visible to the unaided eye as viewed from directly overhead. The luminous flux of the standard light under such conditions is one lumen per steradian (the solid angle subtended by one meter-squared of the surface of a sphere one meter in radius.) The luminous intensity of the standard source of light, therefore, is one candela. The lumen is the unit of light flux. A lux is equal to one lumen per square meter.

luminous intensity (I)   See CANDELA, LUMINOUS FLUX.

lump in the throat   See GLOBUS HYSTERICUS.

lunacy   1. Obsolete term for legal insanity but still in widespread use. 2. Mental derangement or insanity. Term is a legacy of the belief that the stars and especially the moon are somehow associated with madness. 3. A concept that intermittent mental disorders are in some manner correlated with the phases of the moon. See ASYLUM LUNACY, MENTAL DISORDERS, MOON-PHASE STUDIES.

lunacy commission   An ad hoc group of experts in mental disorders appointed by judicial order to evaluate the mental state of a person whose case is being considered by the court.

lunatic   Obsolete term describing a person who is legally insane or psychotic.

lunatismus   (D. Tuke) A term applied by David Tuke to somnambulists who walk in their sleep only when the moon shines. See MOON-PHASE STUDIES.

lure   A word (for example, "heat") used to test for false memories using the Deese paradigm. "Heat" (the lure) is not on a list of words to be memorized that includes words such as "warm," "hot," "burn," and "scorch." Later, participants are given the lure ("heat") in addition to the original list of memorized words and instructed to indicate which words were on the original list. Those who recall that the lure was in the original list are considered to have a false memory.

Luria-Nebraska Neuropsychological Battery (LNNB)   A standardized version of tests based on the neuropsychological theories of the Russian neuropsychologist Alexander (or Aleksandr) Luria for the purpose of diagnosing neurological conditions. The battery of tests are named Luria-Nebraska after Luria and the University of Nebraska where one of the principal three developers, Charles J. Golden, was working at the time of the battery's publishing. See HALSTEAD-REITAN NEUROPSYCHOLOGICAL TEST BATTERY.

Luria's Neuropsychological Investigation   (A. L. Christensen) The first English version (1975) of Aleksandr Luria's procedure for neuropsychological assessment.

Luria technique   (A. Luria) A method of measuring emotional tension, in which participants hold their fingers on a tremor recorder during a free-association test.

lurking variable   hidden variable

lust   An intense desire, usually associated with erotic excitement or arousal.

lust dynamism   (H. S. Sullivan) Overtly expressed sexual desires and abilities.

lust murder   Extreme sexual sadism in which a rapist murders the victim and then often mutilates the body.

luteal phase   A stage of the menstrual cycle beginning immediately after ovulation, when the ruptured follicle becomes the corpus luteum, a temporary endocrine gland that secretes the hormone progesterone. If fertilization of the ovum does not occur, the luteal phase ends with menstruation.

luteinizing hormone (LH)   A gonadotrophic hormone secreted by the pituitary gland that causes the rapid growth of a follicle in the ovary until it ruptures and releases an ovum. The same hormone is secreted by the pituitary in males, where it is called the interstitial cell-stimulating hormone (ICSH).

lux   (light—Latin) A measure of illuminance on a surface of one square meter receiving a uniformly distributed flux of one lumen from a light source. See LUMINOUS FLUX.

lycanthropy   (wolf—Greek) 1. The false belief by a person that he or she is a wolf. 2. The belief that some individuals can change themselves or others into wolves or other animals. The delusion reached epidemic proportions in Europe during the 16th century; one judge sentenced 600 lycanthropes to death, since many "werewolves" were accused of violent crimes. Lycanthropy is still occasionally reported, as in the mountainous villages of Italy. Also known as lycomania, zoanthropy.

lycomania   See LYCANTHROPY.

lygophilia   (twilight—Greek) Abnormal desire to be in dark or gloomy places.

lying   Making false statements with conscious intent to deceive. Nonpathological lying is often found in children or adults seeking to avoid punishment or to save others from distress ("white lies"). Pathological lying is a major characteristic of the antisocial personality. See CONFABULATION, MALINGERING.

lynching   Murder, often by hanging, by a number of others, usually in a mob, whose members are convinced that the person or persons involved are guilty of a crime that deserves immediate death. See COLLECTIVE BEHAVIOR, CROWD BEHAVIOR.

lypemania   Jean Esquirol's term for melancholia.

lysergic acid diethylamide (LSD)   (A. Hoffman, M. Rinkel) Full generic name of the hallucinogen better known as LSD. Also known as lysergide.

lysine   (E. Drechsel) An amino acid essential for the nutrition of humans and animals.

lyssophobia   Morbid fear of becoming insane. Also spelled lissophobia. See MANIAPHOBIA.

lytic cocktail   (V. P. Dole, M. Nyswander) A mixture of antipsychotic (neuroleptic) drugs, such as chlorpromazine, promethazine, and Hydergine, formerly used in treating acute or impending delirium that produces a state called artificial hibernation.

M

m 1. millimicron. 2. meter. 3. mean. 4. In prescriptions, minim.

M 1. See ARITHMETIC MEAN. 2. In Rorschach test scoring, a symbol for movement response. 3. Slang for morphine. 4. memory. 5. myopia.

MA 1. mental age (also abbreviated **M.A.**) 2. See MASTER OF ARTS.

mace An aromatic spice made from the fibrous seed coat of the nutmeg. It has been associated with the euphoric effects produced by nutmeg intoxication. See NUTMEG.

Mach bands/rings (E. Mach) An illusion produced during the ramp-stimulus-visual test when a dark line is observed at the dark transition zone and a bright line at the light end of the ramp.

Mach-Breuer-Brown theory of labyrinthine functioning (E. Mach, J. Breuer, A. C. Brown) A point of view that information about rotary acceleration and deceleration is sent to the brain via sensory cells in the crista.

Mach card (E. Mach) A drawing of a folded sheet of paper that upon examination gives the illusion of either looking into an open book or looking at a book from the back side. See ILLUSION.

Mach-Dvorak stereoillusion (V. Dvorak, E. Mach) Apparent shifts in depth when the left and right eyes alternately see a moving target.

Machian positivism (E. Mach) A doctrine positing that immediate experience provides all the basic information of science.

Machiavellian Hypothesis A postulate that the main selective force in the evolution of intelligence was social competitiveness. Also known as the "cognitive arms race."

Machiavellianism A personality trait characterized by expediency and a belief that ends justify means. A Machiavellian views other people as objects to be manipulated and dominated through deception and dishonesty if necessary to achieve own goals.

machina docilis (docile machine—Latin) A hypothetical automated device capable of motility, problem-solving, avoiding obstacles, and obeying sounds. See AUTOMATON.

machine fear See MECHANOPHOBIA.

machine intelligence (MI) See ARTIFICIAL INTELLIGENCE.

machine pacing In industrial psychology, tasks in which a machine determines when the employee must make a response. Long exemplified by assembly-line work, now introduced to nonfactory work by computer technology that requires operators to respond to the screen at a pace determined by the machine.

machine theory A point of view that mind and behavior, or both, are determined by static neural localization rather than by the distribution of energy within a system. See DYNAMIC PSYCHOLOGY, FIELD THEORY.

macho Slang describing a masculine stereotype, based upon aggressive, assertive behavior and a lack of warmth.

Machover Draw-A-Person Test (MDAP, D-A-P, or **DAP Test)** (K. Machover) A projective technique based on the interpretation of drawings of human figures of both sexes. The examiner notes the sequence of the drawings, verbalizations, and attitudes and comes to conclusions depending on analysis of the drawings and the comments made by the participants. Sometimes known as the Machover Figure Drawing Test.

Mach rotation frame (E. Mach) A large rectangular frame pivoted on the top and bottom on a vertical axis with a chair suspended off the ground. The chair can be made to tilt or rotate horizontally and move up and down. Used in the study of body movement.

Mach Scale (R. Christie) A measurement of the degree to which a person uses manipulation and deceit in pursuit of material or other aims. Low Machs affirm high ethical standards; high Machs reveal relative, shifting standards of behavior. (Mach is an abbreviation of Machiavelli or Machiavellianism). See MACHIAVELLIANISM.

MACI Millon Adolescent Clinical Inventory

Mackworth Clock Test (N. H. Mackworth) A vigilance task in which participants watch a hand on a special clock; the clock's hand is programmed to usually cycle in one second, but occasionally to cycle in two seconds. The participant's task is to press a button when the latter happens.

MacQuarrie Test for Mechanical Ability (T. W. Macquarrie) A paper-and-pencil test focusing on spatial relations and eye-hand coordination as a predictor of mechanical aptitude. The items include tracing a twisting line through other lines, tapping, block analysis, and counting, and pursuit. See APTITUDE TESTS.

macrobiotics (G. Ohsawa) Diets based on ratios of foods considered "Yin" or "Yang." The dieter progresses through a series of six restrictive diets, each more severe than the preceding one, ultimately reaching a "perfect diet" of brown rice and tea. The diets are claimed to cure epilepsy and various other disorders. Not considered safe by mainstream dieticians.

macrocephaly   megacephaly

macrocosm The outer environment of an individual. Compare MICROCOSM.

macro-expectations See STORE IMAGE.

macroglossia An abnormally large-sized tongue, associated with hypothyroidism, affecting production of lingual (of the tongue) sounds in speech. Also known as megaloglossia.

macromania 1. The delusion that everyone and everything is huge. Compare MICROMANIA. 2. Rare term for megalomania.

macrophobia Morbid fear of anything large. Also known as megalophobia.

macropsia A false perception that objects are larger than they actually are, usually due to disease of the retina or hysterical (conversion) disorder. Also known as megalop(s)ia. Compare MICROPSIA.

macroskelic A constitutional type of body build in which the most prominent characteristic is abnormally long legs. Such a person would be classified as asthenic in Ernst Kretschmer's system. See BODY TYPE.

macrosomatic animals Creatures with body sizes statistically (more than one standard deviation) larger than the mean for the species. Compare MICROSOMATIC ANIMALS.

macrosomatognosia Misperception of one's own body or its parts as abnormally large. See MICROSOMATOGNOSIA, SOMATOGNOSIA.

macrosplanchnic build/type (G. Viola) A body type in which the trunk is disproportionately large compared with the limbs. See BODY TYPE, MICROSPLANCHNIC TYPE.

macrosystem (U. Bronfenbrenner) The overall social structure of any society that also interacts with other social entities. See EXOSYSTEM, MESOSYSTEM.

macula Refers to anatomical sensory structures, especially of the eyes and ears. Plural is maculae. Derives from latin for spot, stain.

macula lutea (E. Mariotte, S. T. von Soemmering) A yellowish-pigmented disk-shaped area of the retina that overlays the fovea and the region of the retina that has the best visual acuity and color vision. See RETINAL MACULA.

mad 1. Colloquial term for rabid. 2. Nontechnical term for mentally ill; insane. Madness is considered not quite equivalent to insanity (a legal term), but rather to rashness. See INSANITY, RAVING MADNESS.

Maddox Rod Test (E. E. Maddox) A test of eye-muscle balance in which the participant views a candle flame through glass rods that convert it into a line of light; the differential images perceived by the two eyes indicate the degree of heterophoria.

made shaunda (intoxicating fruit—Hindi) Nutmeg. See MACE.

madness See MAD (meaning 2).

MAE 1. See MOTION AFTEREFFECT. 2. See MULTILINGUAL APHASIA EXAMINATION—THIRD EDITION.

MAF minimal audible field

magazine A food delivery device used in operant conditioning apparatus to provide reinforcements, such as pellets of food, to the organisms being trained. See MAGAZINE TRAINING.

magazine training A means of familiarizing an animal subject with the food magazine in a Skinner box. Typically, the sound of the food-delivery device is repeatedly paired with food so that the animal will learn to go to the food cup when the food is delivered.

magic 1. An illusory demonstration of supernatural or paranormal powers, as in tricks using sleight of hand. Also known as conjuring, prestidigitation. 2. The attempt to control natural events through incantations, dances, or gestures, or efforts to allay anxiety by invoking certain numbers, performing certain rituals, or repeating long lists of feared persons or objects. See COMMUNICATION MAGIC, COMPULSIVE MAGIC, CURSING MAGIC.

magical number seven plus or minus two (G. A. Miller) Humans can process or keep approximately five to nine separate pieces of information (or chunks) in their working memories, with the average being seven. Also, seven appeared to be the optimal number of divisions of ratings, or in making sensory judgments. Later research indicated six rather than seven items. See MNEMONIC DEVICE.

magical thinking A primitive cognitive process based on the illusion that thought or rituals can influence events, fulfill wishes, or ward off evil. Originates in early childhood and is manifested in superstitions, dreams, fantasies, obsessive thoughts, ritual acts, as well as the belief found in some patients with schizophrenia that they can "think" an enemy to death or right the world's wrongs through the power of thought. See CURSING MAGIC, FAITH HEALING, OMNIPOTENCE OF THOUGHT, PALEOLOGIC THINKING, PRELOGICAL THINKING, PRIMARY PROCESS, VOODOO DEATH.

magic bone See VOODOO DEATH.

magic circle A group therapy process, usually involving children who gather in a circle and discuss personal issues and concerns. Because such groups are usually conducted in schools, the term therapeutic is not attributed to such processes. See GROUP THERAPY.

magic helper (E. Fromm) 1. A person in whom another person places considerable trust and who is seen as able to take care of the latter under any circumstances. 2. A person on whom a person with a neurosis has bestowed a sort of magical omnipotence to solve all the patient's problems. See COSMIC IDENTIFICATION, URPSYCHOLOGY.

magic mushroom Nontechnical name for psilocybin, a fungus with mild to moderate hallucinogenic properties when ingested. See TEONANACATL.

magic omnipotence See COSMIC IDENTIFICATION.

magic phase/stage A period during child development when merely imagining an object seems equivalent to having created it. Characteristically observed in young children and patients with schizophrenia. See MAGICAL THINKING.

magic shop technique   A procedure that can be used in counseling as a projective technique. Clients meet the magic shop "proprietor" (usually played by the counselor) and are told they may have three wishes. After making choices, there is a discussion of the meaning of the choices.

Magna Mater   (Great Mother—Latin) 1. An Eastern religion appearing in Western civilization in Hellenistic times. 2. In psychology, Carl Jung's archetype of the primordial mother image and the Great Mother of the Roman Gods, Cybele, including magnesium. See MOTHER ARCHETYPE.

magnesium   An electrolyte and mineral in the diet necessary for nutrition; an important component in the treatment of delirium tremens, because chronic alcoholics often have developed a variety of nutritional deficiencies, including magnesium. See ELECTROLYTE.

magnesium deprivation in rats   Research on rats deprived of magnesium show that they develop an aversion to the mineral when it is returned to their diet, whereas deprivation of other minerals results in a preference for these chemicals. The effect is thought to be due to adverse reactions such as gastric distress when magnesium is first restored to the diet.

magnetic apraxia   Rare form of apraxia in which a person stops in the process of a complex action, as in picking up a hat to put it on, but holding the position, hat in hand, for an unusually long time before completing the action. See CATATONIA.

magnetic crisis/pass   Other names for Mesmeric crisis.

magnetic flux   The total number of lines of induction through a given cross section of a surface. Measured in Webers (Wb).

magnetic resonance imaging (MRI)   A noninvasive, risk-free procedure capable of high resolution in imaging soft as well as hard bodily structures, including the brain. Used in medical diagnosis and neuroscientific research. Linked to a computer, an MRI device can create moving images of the brain in action. Compare COMPUTERIZED AXIAL TOMOGRAPHY (CAT SCAN).

magnetic sense   Ability of an organism to orient itself according to the lines of force of a magnet or the magnetic fields of the earth. Roots of certain plants have been found to align themselves with magnetic fields, and it has been postulated that migrating birds tend to follow magnetic fields of the earth with the aid of sensory apparatus that detects the force of magnetism.

magnetoencephalography (MEG)   The measurement of the brain's magnetic fields. Produces results similar to those obtained by electroencephalography.

magnetotropism   Automatic movement (tropism) to one or the other pole in a magnetic field. See TAXIS, TROPISM.

magnet reflex   Response of some animals to the sensation of touch on the plantar surface (sole) of the foot. Rather than withdraw the foot, the animal extends its foot toward the source of the sensation as it normally would extend its foot in making contact with the ground.

magnification   1. In general, enlarging the size of an image. 2. In psychology, exaggerating something's significance.

magnitude estimation   A procedure in which a series of stimuli that vary on some physical dimension are presented and the participant assigns to each stimulus a number to represent the intensity of the sensation produced by the stimulus. See METHOD OF CONSTANT STIMULI, METHOD OF LIMITS, SCALE, PSYCHOPHYSICS.

magnitude of effect   In research, a measure of the strength of the experimental effect, or the magnitude of the contribution of the independent variable to performance on the dependent variable.

magnitude of response   See RESPONSE AMPLITUDE.

magnitude production   A psychophysical procedure in which a standard stimulus is assigned a number representing the intensity of the sensation produced by that stimulus, and then the participant is asked to produce stimuli of appropriate intensity for a series of numbers in relation to the standard stimulus and its number.

maiden fear   See PARTHENOPHOBIA.

Maier's law   (N. R. F. Maier) A cynical recommendation to dispose of facts that do not fit the theory.

Maier's (three-table) reasoning problem   (N. R. F. Maier) An elevated structure comprising three equidistant platforms interconnected by runways that intersect at a central choice point. Each day, a rat is fed on a different platform, then placed at the choice point. The 90% correct return to the rewarded table provided evidence in the 1920s of reasoning in rats.

maieusiophobia   1. Morbid fear of childbirth. 2. Fear of pregnancy, of being pregnant. Also known as parturiphobia, tocophobia.

maieutic technique   (Socrates) Asking pertinent questions to achieve understanding on the part of the questioned person, usually done when the questioner already knows the answers. Commonly used in psychotherapy.

main effect   In the analysis of variance, a phrase that estimates the effect of an independent variable acting alone, contrasted with interaction effects.

main score   The original scoring of the Rorschach, not considering material obtained subsequent to the testing (such as following the test, a participant remarking "I knew these were all sex pictures") that might also be considered important.

main sensory trigeminal nucleus   See TRIGEMINAL NUCLEUS.

Main's syndrome   (T. Main) A condition in which psychotic patients (usually female) who have been health professionals exploit their background to obtain therapeutic privileges and special sympathy from physicians, nurses, and attendants.

mainliner   Slang for a drug abuser who takes illicit drugs by intravenous injection (mainlining). See SKIN-POPPING.

mainstreaming   1. In education, the formal education of children with learning-disabilities within regular schools, usually attending the same classes as other children of their age, but getting special assistance where needed. 2. In mental health, the de-institutionalizing of mental hospital patients. As a result of advances in psychopharmacology, many mental institutions were either abandoned or downsized, and institutionalized patients were released to the community with the expectation that they would be able to make social adjustments if they continued their medication. They were to be supervised periodically by aides. Many such individuals did not report for periodic checks, medications, etc., and became street people. See DE-INSTITUTIONALIZATION.

maintaining conditions in maladjustment   Influences in a person's environment that tend to maintain and reinforce maladaptive behavior.

maintaining stimulus   An object similar in appearance to a particular stimulus that will elicit a learned response by its presence; for example, a replica of an owl that will keep certain other birds away from that area.

maintenance   1. A plan to keep patients on medication for a prolonged period of time to prevent relapse (for example, many people diagnosed with recurrent depression, bipolar disorder, and schizophrenia need to continue taking medication indefinitely). 2. A special program of treating opiate addicts with supervised, legal methadone.

maintenance dose   An amount of medicine used in longer-term treatment; it is often somewhat lower than the amount used during treatment of the acute phase of an illness.

maintenance functions   Bodily activities that keep the organism's physiological activities in homeostasis.

maintenance level   A stage of maturity when physiological development has progressed as far as it can, as in size and weight remaining at a constant level.

maintenance minimum   1. The least number of persons needed to maintain a behavior unit or setting. 2. In a hospital or clinic, the smallest number of staff members required to provide adequate service for the patients.

maintenance rehearsal   Mental practice, usually accompanied by subvocalization, aimed at retaining information in working memory. See REHEARSAL.

maintenance schedule   1. Maintaining a particular organism or organisms at a specified level of health for a specific period of time. 2. In Skinnerian work, denoting the schedule of reinforcement that maintains a particular rate of responding. 3. Establishment of a particular level of food, water, temperature, humidity, etc., for an organism, kept for research purposes in a specified environment.

maintenance strivings   Needs and motives directed toward retaining a biological and psychological steady state. May include such basic needs as food, water, sleep, sexual gratification, psychological stimulation, and physical and mental activity. See HOMEOSTASIS.

major affective disorders   See DEPRESSED BIPOLAR DISORDER, MAJOR DEPRESSION, MAJOR DEPRESSIVE EPISODE, MANIC BIPOLAR DISORDER, MIXED BIPOLAR DISORDER.

major depressive disorder (MDD)   An affective disorder characterized by (a) a persistent unhappy mood, general loss of interest in almost everything, (b) feelings of hopelessness, as well as (c) some of the following: appetite and sleep changes, decrease of sexual drive, loss of energy, feelings of worthlessness, reduced ability to think and recurrent thoughts of death or suicide. See BIPOLAR DISORDER.

major epilepsy   Old phrase for Grand Mal (epilepsy).

major events effect   A tendency for personal emergencies, such as suicides, to be reduced in rate of occurrences prior to "major events" (for example, sporting events or hotly contested elections) and for the rate of occurrence of such conditions to increase following major catastrophes.

major priorities   (N. Kefir) Conceptualization of four major personality types in terms of behavioral characterization: avoider, controller, morally superior, pleaser.

major-role therapy   Vocational counseling focused on the selection of occupational goals and vocational retraining to enable individuals in need of rehabilitation to work at maximal capacity and satisfaction as useful members of society.

major solution   (K. Horney) A neurotic tendency to repress or deny trends that conflict with the idealized self, as in abandoning an unrealistic or difficult goal to reduce anxiety.

major tranquilizer   1. Refers to the antipsychotic agents, slightly misleading because sedation or tranquilization is not their basic goal or essential effect, although it is sometimes a side effect. 2. A medication that calms agitated or psychotic patients and lessens or eliminates psychotic symptoms, including hallucinations and delusions, with little overall effect on consciousness, as compared with a sedative-hypnotic drug. Used mainly in the treatment of schizophrenias and manic states. Major tranquilizers include the phenothiazines, thioxanthenes, and some opiates. See ANTIPSYCHOTIC MEDICATIONS, NEUROLEPTICS.

majority influenced people   Individuals driven to conform to the majority and who may appear to have no volition or mind of their own. Research by Solomon Asch showed that some people will make ridiculous statements, overruling their own perceptions and common sense to agree with the majority's opinion. See ASCH CONFORMITY EFFECT, CONFORMISM.

Make A Picture Story (MAPS)   (E. S. Shneidman) The projective technique is a variation of the Thematic Apperception Test (TAT) in which the participant (usually a child) is given a background setting and selects the figures, mostly human in a wide variety of costumes but including a few animals, before telling a story about the scene. Number, selection, and placement of figures are scored with the emphasis on interpersonal relationships in fantasy. See PROJECTIVE TESTS, THEMATIC APPERCEPTION TEST (TAT).

make-believe   Dramatic play in which a child pretends to be another person, real or imaginary, and imitates activities involved in such situations as preparing a dinner or putting an infant to bed. Jean Piaget describes such activities as "symbolic play." Playing house is one common make-believe situation in which children put on the clothes of adults and act out such roles. See IMAGINARY COMPANION, PSYCHODRAMA.

maladaptation   Failure of an organism to acquire biological traits, psychological traits, or both, needed to interact effectively with an environment.

maladaptation reinforcing cause   Behavior of caretakers that tends to maintain maladaptive behavior, especially unnecessary special attention given persons who are ill or sickly, which can contribute to a delayed recovery. See EPINOSIC GAIN, IATROGENIC.

maladaptive behavior   Actions detrimental to a person, group, or society; ineffective or self-defeating behavior. Phrase is often preferred by social-learning theorists as a substitute for mental illness, particularly when emphasizing the fact that detrimental patterns represent learned behavior and are thus modifiable. See MENTAL DISORDER.

maladaptive mechanisms   Behavioral elements that interfere with capacity to adjust to the demands of life; for example, overmobilization under stress, a "workaholic" pattern, self-defeating behavior, retreat from reality, and use of certain defense mechanisms, such as denial.

maladie   (illness—French) A disease or illness, especially a chronic one.

maladie des tics   French phrase for Tourette's disorder. See HABIT SPASM.

maladie du doute   French phrase for doubting mania.

maladjustment   1. Inability to maintain effective relationships and meet the demands of life satisfactorily. 2. Broad term for any emotional disturbance of a relatively minor nature.

malaise   (discomfort, not feeling well—French) A slight feeling of illness, a vague feeling of discomfort and uneasiness.

malapropism   Humorous misuse of a word. Name derives from a character, Mrs. Malaprop in a play by Richard Sheridan, who would unintentionally say a word that resembled the word she wanted to use that revealed her lack of understanding of the word, as in saying "irreverent" when meaning "irrelevant."

maldevelopment   Defective development of an individual because of genetic, dietary, or external factors that interfere with the normal rate of growth of tissues and bodily functions.

male chauvinism   The conviction (or related behavior indicating the belief) that men are superior to women. See CHAUVINISM.

male climacterium   "Male menopause" said to occur in men, about ten years later than in women. Unlike menopause, it appears to be the result of psychological reactions to aging including anxiety over diminished sexual potency. There is controversy over whether such a thing exists.

male homosexual prostitution   Sexual contact by a male with another male for financial or other personal gain. Studies indicate that a social hierarchy exists, as is true for female prostitutes. Lowest in status are "street hustlers," usually teenage boys and not necessarily gay themselves; next are "bar hustlers"; and highest in prestige are "call boys," who do not solicit in public. See HOMOSEXUALITY, PROSTITUTION.

male menopause   See MALE CLIMACTERIUM.

maleness   Male anatomical structures and physiological functions associated with the male sexual and reproductive role as well as related psychological aspects, such as interests and attitudes considered to be typical of men. See MASCULINE SUPERIORITY, PENIS ENVY, SUPERMALE.

male orgasmic disorder   Inability to achieve orgasm after sexual excitement and an erection. Many such males can achieve orgasm by masturbation or even by manipulation by a partner, but not during coitus. Causes vary. Compare FEMALE ORGASMIC DISORDER.

malergy   (R. B. Cattell) A condition of subnormal or inefficient functioning.

male sexual disorders   Inability of males to achieve normal sexual satisfaction, whether due to physiological or psychological reasons or both. See ERECTILE DISORDER, IMPOTENCE, PRIMARY ERECTILE DISORDERS.

malevolent personality theory   (C. Goldberg) A point of view that evil personalities are neither explained by mental illness nor the devil, but rather by choices between good and bad behavior starting early in life. People considered to exhibit malevolent personalities tend to have six personality characteristics: (a) shame, (b) contempt for others, (c) rationalization, (d) justification, (e) unwillingness to examine the self's dark side, and (f) magical thinking. See PSYCHOPATHOLOGY.

malevolent transformation   (H. S. Sullivan) An unpleasant subjective feeling of living among enemies and that nobody can be trusted. This attitude purportedly results from harsh or unfair treatment during childhood, and may be the basis for social withdrawal and, in some cases, mental disorder of a paranoid nature.

malformation   Abnormality of structure, generally genetic in nature.

malignant   A condition likely to cause disfigurement or death. Compare BENIGN.

malignant alcoholism   A form of alcoholism characterized by increased tolerance, physiological adaptation, loss of control, and, if drinking is suspended, a withdrawal or abstinence syndrome consisting of craving for alcohol, convulsions, and delirium tremens. Similar to E. M. Jellinek's gamma alcoholism.

malignant neurosis   A progressive neurosis in which symptoms become increasingly severe until the person withdraws into a room or bed, fails to perform any activity, and may become literally paralyzed by doubts and indecision. See BIPOLAR DISORDER, DEPRESSION.

malignant psychosis   (O. Fenichel) Progressive schizophrenia that terminates in permanent dementia. See NUCLEAR SCHIZOPHRENIA, PROCESS PSYCHOSIS.

malignant stupor   A psychogenic stupor from which there is little or no chance of recovery.

malingering   Deliberate feigning of an illness or disability for financial gain or to escape responsibility, as in faking mental illness as a defense in a trial, faking physical illness to win compensation, or faking a defect to avoid military service. Such a person is called a malingerer.

Malin syndrome   A symptom pattern occasionally occurring as a side effect of major tranquilizers, in which the outstanding symptoms are dehydration, hyperhidrosis (excessive sweating), hypersalivation, hyperthermia (high temperature), and mental confusion. See TARDIVE DYSKINESIA.

malleation   A spasmodic activity of the hands that resembles the movements of hitting or hammering; a tic that usually involves striking the thighs.

malleus (hammer—Latin) (A. Achellini, Berengarius, Vesalius) The largest of the three ossicles (bones) in the middle ear, attached to the upper part of the tympanic membrane (eardrum). The malleus transmits vibrations of the eardrum to the incus. Also known as hammer, mallet. See OSSICLES.

Malleus Maleficarum (The Witch's Hammer) (J. Sprenger & H. Kramer) A book c.1486 by two Dominican monks, that acquired special importance due to the famous 1484 Bull of Pope Innocent VIII designating its authors as inquisitors in Northern Germany. After a proof that witchcraft exists, *The Witch's Hammer* describes in detail the various signs and behaviors denoting demonic possession—in which a person can recognize accurate descriptions of many clinical syndromes of today. Intended as a guide for inquisitors, it is the premier textbook of psychopathology of its era.

malnutrition A state of health characterized by an improper balance of carbohydrates, fats, proteins, vitamins, and minerals in the diet. May be due to excessive intakes of food categories as well as inadequate levels, as in examples of obesity or hypervitaminoses (excessive intake of vitamins). Dietary deficiencies are associated with many physical and psychological disorders. See BERI-BERI, KWASHIORKOR, MACROBIOTIC DIETS, MAGNESIUM.

malpractice Unethical or negligent behavior on the part of a professional person, such as an attorney, physician, psychologist or other therapist, which may lead to legal action.

Malthusian theory (T. R. Malthus) A prediction that whereas population increases on a geometric scale, food production increases only on an arithmetic scale, and for this reason, humanity is destined to live in hunger and poverty. Also known as Malthusianism, Malthus' theory.

malum (an evil—Latin) A disease.

malum in res (evil in the law—Latin) Refers to behavior that is considered evil only because a law says that this behavior is wrong. See MALUM IN SE.

malum in se (evil in itself—Latin) Refers to certain behaviors that are considered intrinsically evil for all people in all cultures at all times. See MALUM IN RES.

malum prohibitum (evil forbidden behavior—Latin) Refers to behavior forbidden by various legal, social, and religious groups. See MALUM IN SE.

mammalingus (E. Jones) The act of suckling the breast during coitus, particularly in terms of Ernest Jones' concept that the act represents a type of fellatio.

mammillary bodies A pair of small spherical masses located on the underside of the brain, forming a part of the hypothalamus. Purportedly involved with emotion and sexual desire. Also known as buila of fornix, corpus mamillare.

mammillary body Obsolete name for the olfactory bulb.

mammotrophic hormone Prolactin.

mana 1. In ancient India, according to *Mahabharata*, it was taught that in addition to the five senses, there is an intermediate faculty (*mana*) that transmits information to *buddhi* (intellect) before reaching the soul. 2. In Hawaii and Maori cultures, the power of the elemental forces of nature embodied in a person.

managed care See HEALTH-MAINTENANCE ORGANIZATION.

management by objectives (MBO) The establishment of goals, often by executives of an organization and often with the agreement of subordinates to achieve specified goals, usually by a certain date. May include frequent feedback as to the progress in attaining the goals.

management fashion (E. Abrahamson) Transitory collective beliefs that certain management techniques are at the forefront of management progress.

managerial psychology The study of the relationships between leaders and those led, especially in business and industry, with special concern about attitudes on both sides and effectiveness of leadership.

mandala (circle—Sanskrit) A geometric design thought to represent various deities, forces, or powers in the cosmos. Carl Jung used the concept as an archetypal symbol of the union of conflicting conscious and unconscious forces in the self. In both Hindu and Buddhist traditions, mandalas have long been used to help meditation. Also known as *yantra*. See SYMBOL, UNIDENTIFIED FLYING OBJECTS.

mandate To make obligatory, usually by some authority, such as by law.

mand function (B. F. Skinner) A function of certain words or utterances that specify how the listener can reward the speaker; derived from "demand," for example, "Please pass the salt," "Say yes!" Sometimes a person has to know the speaker to determine whether the statement is a mand or a tact, for example, "My, that cake is beautifully decorated" may be a subtle request for a piece (mand) or merely a compliment (tact). Compare INTRAVERBAL, TACT.

mandragora The European mandrake, *Mandragora officinalis*, or *Atropa mandragora* the roots, leaves, bark, or berries have been used for millennia as anesthetic, aphrodisiac, hallucinogen, and folk remedies. One of the active ingredients is hyoscyamine, a form of atropine. Also known as European mandrake.

mania (frenzy—Greek) 1. One of Jean Esquirol's five classes of mental disorders. 2. A state of excitement characterized by frenzied and uncontrollable impulses, uncoordinated movements, logorrhea, quick changes of emotions, tearing own clothing, inability to keep attention, or a morbid preoccupation with an activity or idea. Can range from persons appearing normal to requiring either a straight-jacket or sedatives to control them. Types of mania include: ABLUTO-, ABSORBED, ACRO-, ACUTE, AFFECTIVE MONO-, AGRO-, AKINETIC, AMENO-, ANDROPHONO-, ARITHMO-, APHRODISIO-, ASOTICA-, BELL'S, BITING, CHOREO-, CHRONIC, COLLECTING, COPYING, DELIRIOUS, DELUSIONAL, DEPRESSIVE, DIPSO-, DROMO-, DOUBTING, ECDOMO-, ECO-, EGO-, EMETO-, EROTOGRAPHO-, EROTO-, GAMONO-, GRAPHO-, GRUMBLING, HELLENO-, HYDRODIPSO-, HYPER-, HYPO-, ICONO-, INHIBITED, INSTINCTIVE MONO-, INTELLECTUAL MONO-, LYPE-, MACRO-, MEGALO-, METRO-, MICRO-, MONO-, MONOMANIE BOULIMIQUE, MYTHO-, NARCO-, NAUTO-, NECRO-, NYMPHO-, OIKIO-, OINO-, ONIO-, ONOMATO-, OPIO-, PARATERESIO-, PHAGO-, PHANERO-, PHARMACO-, PHONO-, PHOTO-, PLUTO-, POLYTOXICO-, PORIO-,

PORNOGRAPHO-, PSEUDO-, PSEUDONO-, PYRO-, RE-ACTIVE, RELIGIOUS, THANATO-, TOXICO-, TRICHOR-RHEXO-, TUBERCULO-, UTERO-. See ALCOHOL-OPHILIA, AMURAKH, ANTIMANICS, CONSTITUTIONAL MANIC DISPOSITION, HYPOCHONDRIASIS, HYPO-MANIC PERSONALITY, MANIC EPISODE, MONOMANIE BOULIMIQUE, MONOMANIE DU VOL, MONOMANIE FROTIQUE, MONOMANIE INCENDIÈRE, SCHIZOID-MANIC STATE, UNIPOLAR MANIC-DEPRESSIVE PSY-CHOSIS, WITZELSUCHT. (Some terms listed above are not defined in this dictionary when the meaning is obvi-ous. As with phobias, manias can be established for any-thing; someone who loves cats could be labeled as having ailuromania.)

mania à potu (drinking mania—Latin) Similar to idiosyncratic intoxication.

maniac 1. A person exhibiting the excited disturbed phase of bipolar (manic-depressive) disorder. Also known as manic (meaning 2). 2. Lay term for a mentally dis-turbed person, especially one considered deranged and likely to be dangerous to others.

mania phantastica infantilis (childhood disorder—Latin) Rare childhood mental condition characterized by exaltation, fugues, confabulations, fantasies, and retar-dation. Symptoms may be a spontaneous autochthonous event or may occur during a delirious state following a febrile disease.

maniaphobia Morbid fear of becoming insane, or of dealing with insanity. Also known as lyssophobia.

mania transitoria (transitory mania—Latin) (T. S. Clouston) Obsolete phrase for an acute, transient form of maniacal exaltation that develops suddenly, character-ized by incoherence, partial or complete unconsciousness of familiar surroundings, and sleeplessness. Also known as ephemeral mania.

manic 1. Relating to or characterized by mania. Also known as maniacal. 2. A maniac (meaning 1), the adjective serving as a noun, as in "He's a manic" commonly used as a short hand term in mental hospitals.

manic bipolar disorder An abnormal affective con-dition in which a manic episode alternates with periods of depression, with the manic phase being most evident, occurring longer, or being most prominent. See MANIC EPISODE.

manic defense (M. Klein) In psychoanalytic theory, a position achieved to protect reaction of the ego against experiencing feelings of guilt and loss that go with depressive anxiety.

manic-depressive (MD) disorder (Aretaeus, A. Piquer, J. Baillarger) Old phrase for a severe affective disorder characterized by a predominant mood of elation or depression, and in some cases, an alternation between the two states. Also known as manic-depressive illness (MDI)/psychosis. Called *la folie circulaire* by Jean Falret. The condition was renamed bipolar disorder. See DEPRESSED BIPOLAR DISORDER, MAJOR DEPRESSIVE DISORDER, MANIC BIPOLAR DISORDER, MANIC EPISODE, MIXED BIPOLAR DISORDER, UNIPOLAR MANIC-DEPRESSIVE PSYCHOSIS.

manic-depressive insanity Phrase coined by Emil Kraepelin in the 1890s for what later was called manic-depressive disorder or bipolar disorder.

manic excitement A state of elation with hyperactiv-ity occurring in manic episodes.

manic hebephrenia Old name for a manic phase sim-ilar to that of manic-depressive (bipolar) psychosis that occurs in some patients with hebephrenic (disorganized) schizophrenia.

manic state A mental state characterized by apparent pressure of activity and speech, flight of ideas, and elation, ranging from relatively mild hypomania to the extreme of delirious mania. Some people in the manic state tear off their clothing and walk rapidly talking loudly to themselves and continue to exhaustion.

manic stupor A mixture of manic and depressive reactions, in which the patient is elated but inactive, unresponsive, and unproductive of ideas. Occasionally found in bipolar (manic-depressive) disorder, and has been cited as one of the "mixed" types. Also known as stuporous mania, unproductive mania.

manie de recommencement (repetition compulsion—French) Pierre Janet's concept similar to repetition compulsion/pattern.

manifest Evident, on the surface. Compare LATENT.

manifest anxiety Overt symptoms indicating anxiety, such as agitation, restlessness, reduced attention, wring-ing hands. In psychoanalytic theory, such anxiety is con-sidered a symptom of a basic but repressed conflict.

Manifest Anxiety Scale (MAS) (J. Taylor-Spence) A scale made up of selected items of the Minnesota Multi-phasic Personality Inventory (MMPI) that have elements related to anxiety. See ANXIETY SCALES.

manifestation Objective evidence of a physical or psychological condition, such as high temperature of the body (indicative of fever), pinpoint pupils after ingestion of drugs, pallor of the skin due to fear, reddening of the face caused by embarrassment. See PILOERECTION.

manifest content of a dream In Freudian dream theory, the experienced content or overt story of a dream. Compare LATENT CONTENT.

manifest dream What a person is conscious of in a dream. May include awareness that a person is dreaming (lucid dream), which is different from the manifest content of a dream, which refers to the images and figures in the dream. See LUCID DREAM.

manifest goals In evaluation research, objectively de-fined goals of an organization or program; goals speci-fied by indicators of success and assessed in an evalua-tion program. See MANAGEMENT BY OBJECTIVES.

manifest need A need that is obvious and important. Compare LATENT NEED.

manifest personality The impression that a person makes on others, as in being perceived as a "lamb," a "lion," and a "turtle," depending on the situation. In a sense, people have as many personalities as they manifest to others. See ROLE.

Manikin Test (R. Pintner & D. Paterson) A perfor-mance task in which wooden pieces must be fitted to-gether to form a man. A subtest on the Pintner-Paterson and other performance scales. Also known as Pintner's Manikin Test.

manipulandum In operant psychology, any object whose operation constitutes a response and therefore results in a consequence (reinforcing or punishing event). To be satisfactory as the operational definition of a response, the device must provide a clear indication that it has been operated, such as the flow of electrical current through the microswitch component of a rat lever or the ringing of a chime when the front door button is pressed sufficiently far.

manipulation check In an experiment, questioning designed to help the researcher evaluate the efficacy of the experimental manipulation and to verify that participants perceive the manipulation as the researcher intended. See RESEARCH.

manipulative behavior Actions designed to exploit or control others, such as weeping, throwing a tantrum, threatening suicide, and lying or scheming to gain special consideration.

manipulative drive Motivations that have no direct relationship to food or other survival needs. May be directed toward a learning experience that exposes the organism to new stimuli, which may in turn contribute to survival; for example, a monkey may perform tasks merely for the reward of watching a mechanical toy move. Young children usually go through a phase in which they want to touch or taste everything they can. Also known as manipulatory drive.

manipulative techniques Various devices used in the attempt to get clients to "open up," used particularly in brief psychotherapy, such as exhortation, suggestion, advice, and environmental modifications.

man-machine system See PERSON-MACHINE SYSTEM.

mannerism A gesture, facial expression, or verbal habit peculiar to the individual.

manners Rules of deportment. In various societies are found many ways of dealing with others. One of the oldest books on the subject is *On Duties* by Cicero that takes up many topics still observed today.

Mann-Whitney U test (H. B. Mann & D. R. Whitney) A nonparametric statistical test of whether two independent samples have been drawn from the same population. The data must be at least on the ordinal scale of measurement. It is the most powerful non-parametric alternative to the parametric t test. Formula: $U = n_1n_2 + [n_1(n_1+1) \div 2] - R_1$ or $U = n_1n_2 + [n_2(n_2+1) \div 2] - R_2$, where $R_1 = \sum$ ranks to group of size n, $R_2 = \sum$ ranks to group of size n_2.

manoptoscope An instrument for measuring eye dominance. It is a hollow cone-shaped tube that the participant looks through; the participant can only use one eye and will ordinarily use the preferred eye.

MANOVA See MULTIVARIATE ANALYSIS OF VARIANCE.

mantle layer The middle layer of the embryonic neural plate that develops into cerebral gray matter.

man-to-man rating/scale A method of evaluating people by having informed judges compare individuals two at a time and rate one as better than the other. By doing this for a group of individuals, the result is a rank order array, especially if the instructions specifically state that no two people are to be considered equal. A variation of the method of paired comparisons. See RATING ERROR.

mantra 1. A syllable, word, or phrase, repeated audibly or silently, that a person can use for the purpose of concentration in meditation. 2. A word or phrase (often in Sanskrit) repeated over and over to block out extraneous thoughts and induce a state of relaxation that enables the person to reach a deeper level of consciousness. Traditionally, a mantra is assigned by a guru, or teacher, and is kept secret by the devotee. See TRANSCENDENTAL MEDITATION.

manual alphabet See FINGER SPELLING, MANUALISM, SIGNING.

manual aphasia Inability to write words. See AGRAPHIA.

manual-arts therapist A health professional who assists in rehabilitation by training persons with mental or physical disabilities in creative projects requiring the use of the limbs, such as woodworking, metalworking, animal care, gardening, and printing. The purpose is to build self-esteem, confidence, and a sense of achievement while also preparing the patient for outside employment. See OCCUPATIONAL THERAPIST, PHYSICAL THERAPIST.

manual dominance Favoring one hand over the other and using it more frequently in acts that require only one hand. See HANDEDNESS, LATERAL DOMINANCE.

manualism A method of instruction for the deaf consisting of communication by means of finger spelling and sign language. Also known as manual method. See BRAILLE.

MAO See MONOAMINE OXIDASE.

MAOI See MONOAMINE OXIDASE INHIBITOR.

MAP 1. See MILLER ASSESSMENT FOR PRE-SCHOOLERS. 2. minimal audible pressure.

mapping of genes See GENETIC MAP.

map-reading test An examination of the ability of persons to orient themselves in space. May require using a map to follow a path while holding the map in a position other than in the direction of movement. Thus, the direction of the path on the map would be different from that of the person following the path. See MISORIENTATION EFFECT.

MAPS Make A Picture Story

marasmus (withering, wasting away—Greek) Progressive wasting away of infants because of nutritional disease, inadequacy of diet, by maternal deprivation, or anaclitic depression. Also known as infantile atrophy.

marathon group (therapy) (F. Stoller) An encounter group that meets in seclusion for a period varying from eight hours to a week, running continuously. Based on the theory that a single extended session will encourage a freer expression of feelings than a series of shorter, interrupted sessions. See TIME-EXTENDED THERAPY.

Marbe's law (K. Marbe) The observation that in a word-association test, response latency (time taken to respond to a word) will be less for common words than for uncommon words.

Marburg school (E. R. Jaensch) A group of students of personality who attempted to classify personality types in terms of eidetic imagery. See B TYPE, T TYPE.

Marey tambour (E. J. Marey) An apparatus used for recording physiological processes, such as breathing. Consists of a shallow pan covered with a membrane, levers, and a stylus for recording movement on a kymograph. The membrane moves up and down depending on air pressure changes within the tambour. Changes are produced by a similar tambour, attached to the participant's body part and connected to the recording tambour via a rubber hose.

Marfan's syndrome In humans, a genetic variation characterized by a tall thin body, excessively long extremities, and a variety of minor physical abnormalities. Abraham Lincoln is thought by some to have had this condition. Named after French pediatrician Antoine Bernard-Jean Marfan (1858–1942).

marginal consciousness Those contents of consciousness that, while above the threshold of awareness, are not the center or direct focus of attention. (Marginal stimuli are not equivalent to subliminal stimuli.) Similar to William James' fringe of consciousness.

marginal group In a relatively homogeneous country or community, a distinct group not absorbed into the social mainstream because it differs in one or more significant dimensions, for example, a specific religious, national, or racial group.

marginal individuals Persons who live on the fringe of their sociocultural group, and who do not accept nor are fully accepted by the dominant group, such as some immigrants and street people.

marginal intelligence A mental ability level between normal and mentally deficient, with intelligence quotients (IQs) between 70 and 80.

marginalization The denial to groups or individuals of access to positions and symbols of economic, religious, or political power. See PREJUDICE, GLASS CEILING.

marginal man See MARGINAL INDIVIDUALS.

marginal mental state A state of mind that is borderline between evident normality and overt pathology. Some marginal-mental-state individuals purportedly function quite well in appropriate environments.

marginal numbers The row and column totals in a bivariate frequency distribution. Also known as marginals.

marginals marginal numbers

marginal sulcus A branch of the cingulate sulcus of the brain that turns upward between the paracentral lobule and superior frontal gyrus. Also known as marginal branch of the cingulate sulcus.

marianismo The belief that women have an affinity and connection to the Virgin Mary that make them morally superior to most men. Associated with Latin America.

Marie's ataxia (P. Marie) A form of ataxia, or failure of muscular coordination, that affects mainly adults. Progressive and disabling, symptoms may include gait disturbances, tremors, slurred speech, and difficulty in swallowing.

marihuana marijuana

marijuana Popular name for a substance derived from the *cannabis sativa* plant, controversial because of purported medicinal value. Slang names include dope, ganja, grass, Loco weed, Mary Jane, pakalolo, pot, weed. Also spelled marihuana, marouana. The most psychoactive chemical in marijuana is tetrahydrocannabinol (THC). See CANNABIS, HASHISH.

Mariotte's (blind) spot (E. Mariotte) An area of the ocular fundus that lacks light receptors (rods and cones) due to the exit of the optic nerve (inverted retina). Also simply known as the blind spot.

marital adjustment Ability to meet the demands of marriage, especially (a) the sharing of thoughts, (b) respect for the partner's individuality, (c) open expression of feelings, (d) clarifying roles, (e) cooperation in living-together decisions, and (f) attainment of mutual sexual satisfaction.

marital aids Colloquial euphemism for sexual devices such as vibrators and erotic clothing. Also known as toys.

marital conflict Discord between marriage partners. Problems often include differences in attitudes related to sex, child-rearing, and relatives, as well as struggles for supremacy, and, to a lesser extent, differences about religion, values, interests, and money management.

marital counseling Advice provided by marriage counselors to individuals or couples without necessarily going into causes of marital unhappiness (for example, asking each party to indicate common annoying behaviors of the other party and then trying to negotiate agreements to stop some or all of these annoyances). See MARRIAGE THERAPY.

marital opportunity ratio (MOR) The ratio of marriage-minded men to suitable woman.

marital rape The forcing of a spouse, almost always the wife, to engage in unwanted sexual relations. Formerly a self-contradiction in that husbands were assumed to be entitled to sexual relations; a felony in the majority of American states since 1980.

marital schism 1. A condition of open discord between spouses that puts a strain on the marriage. 2. A situation occurring when two unstable people live together in a partnership, each one contributing to the other's maladjustment.

marital skew 1. An unbalanced family situation characterized by the domination of one spouse by another; generally, the dominant spouse makes all major decisions, and that spouse's opinions are imposed on the other. 2. A defective family pattern in which the pathological behavior of the dominant partner is accepted by the other.

marital subsystem (S. Minuchin) The nature of a marital relationship within context of overall family structure. See STRUCTURAL FAMILY THERAPY.

markedness hypothesis 1. In psycholinguistics, a phrase applied to one member of some polar opposite adjective pairs, such as good-bad or tall-short. In pairs showing marking, one member refers to the semantic dimension to which the pairs refer. Thus, asking "How tall is Bob?" refers only to his relative height. However, asking "How short is Bob?" refers to the dimension of height and also implies that Bob is, in fact, short. Adjectives that refer to a dimension and suggest a particular position on that dimension are said to be "marked;" those that refer neutrally to the dimension as a whole are "unmarked." 2. In linguistics, a postulate that oppositional terms or antonym pairs are learned by children piecemeal. Holds that children first concentrate on the more obvious or salient term; for example, a child will learn to use the word "big" before learning to use "little" and will, in the early stages, employ "big" to designate small as well as large objects.

marker Any item or article used to indicate territorial possession in a public setting, such as a coat or briefcase left on a seat in a waiting room.

marker variable A variable whose value is correlated with another variable of interest or the magnitude of covariance between variables; for example, a parental history of hypertension may serve as a marker variable for an increased probability of developing hypertension (the variable of interest) or a heightened cardiovascular response to laboratory stressors (the relationship between environmental stressors and cardiovascular response).

marketing orientation (E. Fromm) Denoting an attitude in which an individual evaluates personal worth in terms of commercial value. Attributes perceived as leading to business or social success are valued more than knowledge, creativity, integrity, or dedication.

market research Research applied to purchase patterns, marketing techniques, consumer motivation, etc. Often in the form of surveys conducted in much the same manner as public-opinion polls with the purpose of measuring attitudes concerning specific commercial products, the effectiveness of advertising, and the relative preferences of consumers for different brands. Also known as consumer research.

Markoff chain (A. A. Markoff) 1. A stochastic process consists of a set of states along with the probabilities of passing from one state to another. A Markoff process is a stochastic process in which the probability of moving from one state to another does not depend on the past history of the system. The states, together with their transition probabilities, constitute a Markoff chain. 2. A mathematical description of a chain of events in which a given event may give rise, with different probabilities, to one of several subsequent events. Used extensively in the psychological study of language in which words follow one another with different frequencies. Developed by later theorists into more powerful augmented transition networks.

Markoff chaining (A. A. Markoff) A theory that central motor mechanisms involve a chain reaction in which each movement depends upon a preceding movement which sends a feedback signal. It has been challenged on several points, including the fact that a chain of movements may not be repeated in exactly the same manner each time a task is performed. Also known as Markov chaining.

Markov See MARKOFF.

Mark II cell assembly (theory) Adds to cell-assembly theory a model of inhibitory mechanisms and sensitization to account for the association of ideas.

marriage A social commitment between two or more people usually for the purpose of being recognized by society or by various others as a stable unit, partnership, family. Often a marriage occurs via some kind of ceremony with legal approval, religious approval, social approval, or combination thereof. Kinds of marriages include: CLUSTER, COMMON LAW, HOMOSEXUAL, OPEN, SYMBIOTIC, SYNERGIC, TRADITIONAL, TRIAL. See EXPERIMENTAL MARRIAGE GROUP, INTERMARRIAGE.

marriage encounter A marriage enrichment movement with lay leadership, often with a religious orientation.

marriage-enrichment group A support and mutual therapy group in which couples meet with a leader to discuss and resolve marriage-related problems. See MARRIAGE THERAPY.

marriage fear See GAMOPHOBIA.

marriage therapy A form of psychotherapy directed to improving a disturbed marital relationship that may center on the psychodynamics and behavior of one or both of the partners. Usually such therapy is one-on-one with a therapist who may see both partners independently, or each partner may be seen by a different therapist. In some cases, especially in group practice, a third therapist may meet with the two primary therapists and even both spouses, to help reconciliation. The basic assumption of marriage therapy is that something in either or both persons exists that prevents them from having a good marriage, and that marriage counseling is not sufficient to achieve desired results. Also known as couples therapy, marital therapy, and relationship therapy. See CONJOINT THERAPY, MARRIAGE COUNSELING, TANDEM THERAPY.

Marston Deception Test (W. M. Marston) An early form of a lie detector based on variations of systolic blood pressure. See LIE DETECTOR.

Martinotti cells Spindle-shaped cells in the inner stellate (bottom) layer of the cortex of the brain, with axons that extend to the surface and communicate with the pyramidal cells of the cortex. Named after Italian physician Giovanni Martinotti (1857–1928).

Martius disk A disk consisting of concentric circular areas of varying shades of gray. Has been used to determine the values of shades of gray. Named after German psychologist Gotz Martius (1853–1927).

Marxist Feminism A kind of feminism holding that women are oppressed due to capitalism. Sometimes known as Socialist Feminism.

Marxist theory of psychology Refers to the influence of Karl Marx's socialist doctrines of materialism and class struggle on psychological theorizing, especially in the Soviet Union from the 1920s to the 1980s.

masculine identity A well-developed sense of affiliation with males, or identification with what are conceived to be masculine attitudes and values.

masculine protest According to Alfred Adler, attempts by males and females to deny feminine qualities and wish for the qualities and privileges regarded in Western culture as male, such as strength, courage, independence, success. See PENIS ENVY.

masculinity   1. Social-role behaviors, as distinguished from reproductive functions, that identify an individual as a boy or man. See MALENESS, SEX ROLES, VIRILITY. 2. (G. Hofstede) Describing a society in which there is a sharp distinction between men's and women's roles, with men associated with profit making, women with providing services.

masculinity-femininity scale (MF scale)   Any scale on a psychological test that assesses the relative masculinity or femininity of an individual; scales vary and may focus, for example, on basic identification with either gender or preference for a particular sex role.

masculinity-femininity tests   Questionnaires designed to measure the degree of masculinity or femininity in individual respondents. The earliest was the Attitude-Interest Analysis Test of Terman and Miles. In addition to being included as one scale of the Minnesota Multiphasic Personality Inventory (MMPI), California Personality Inventory (CPI), Guilford-Zimmerman Temperament Survey, and Personal Relationship Inventory, there is the separate Bem Sex-Role Inventory.

masculinization   1. A normal condition marked by attainment of male characteristics, such as deepening of voice, growth of facial hair. 2. Rare term for virilism.

masculist movement men's movements

Mashburn Complex Coordinator   (N.C. Mashburn) An instrument for measuring eye-hand and eye-foot coordination by lining up rows of red and green lights with a stick and rudder bar. Used for evaluating physiological coordination in the selection of pilot trainees. Superseded by the Constable Reaction Apparatus. Also known as the Mashburn apparatus, Mashburn Automatic Serial Action Apparatus.

mask   1. An expressionless facial appearance seen in certain diseases. 2. (W. Stekel) A character disguise, putting on different-from-usual behavior to make false impressions; for example, acting with civility to others with whom the person has close relationships, such as spouse, children, and employee, but only when in the presence of others. See HYPOCRISY THEORY, PERSONA. 3. A shield that covers the nose and mouth, used to maintain antiseptic conditions or to administer inhalants (such as anesthetics, oxygen).

masked affection   (W. Stekel) Expressions of love, tenderness, affection, or friendship toward others that actually mask feelings of dislike or hatred for these people.

masked depression   A condition in which psychosomatic symptoms occur episodically and in association with some degree of depressed mood with the person able to hide evidence of these feelings (for example, acting jolly when feeling sad).

masked deprivation   **affective separation**

masked disorder   An emotional disturbance concealed by abnormal behavior that appears to be unrelated to the cause of the disturbance. May represent an unconscious effort to treat a real problem as if it did not exist.

masked epilepsy   An epileptic equivalent, such as a sudden act of violence, rather than convulsions. See EPILEPTIC EQUIVALENT.

masked homosexuality   An unconscious form of homosexuality characterized by the seeking in male-female sexual activities the pleasures usually obtained in male-male or female-female sexual acts.

masked obsession   A strong but blocked desire that manifests itself in the form of a physical symptom, such as organic pain. The organic symptom may represent a pleasurable but tabooed memory and can defy both physical diagnosis and relief through medication. See HYPOCHONDRIASIS.

masked recall test   An examination of the recall of a print advertisement by covering various areas.

masking   1. Diminishing acuity of perception of one stimulus by another. Partial or total obliteration of one sensation by another. Example is background conversation screening out speech addressed to listener. 2. The effective diminution of the ability to hear one sound by another that occurs simultaneously. In general, low pitched tones have a greater masking effect than those that are high pitched. 3. In audiology, deliberately applying a noise to one ear while testing the hearing acuity of the other. Types of audial masking include (a) simultaneous: the stimulus and the masker are presented together; (b) backward: the masking occurs right after the target stimulus; (c) forward: the order in item (b) is reversed; screen memories are also a form of masking. See SCREEN MEMORY.

Maslach Burnout Inventory   (C. Maslach & S. E. Jackson) A method for evaluation of the "burnout" type of stress reaction.

Maslow's motivational hierarchy   (A. Maslow) A hierarchy of human motives, or needs, as described by Abraham Maslow: physiological needs at the base, followed by safety and security; then love, affection, and gregariousness; then prestige, competence, and power; and, at the highest level, esthetic needs, the need for knowing, and self-actualization. See MASLOW'S THEORY OF HUMAN MOTIVATION.

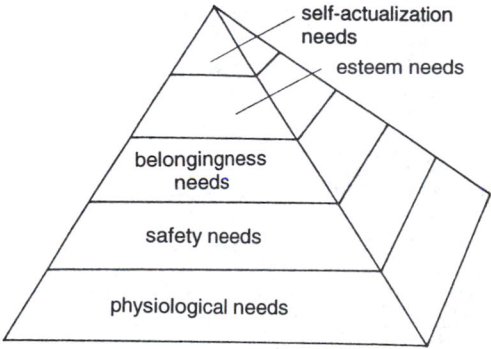

Maslow's motivational hierarchy   This pyramid represents Abraham Maslow's generalized concept of the primacy of classes of needs. Most important at the broad base are physiological needs such as water, food, shelter; when these needs are satisfied other needs can be fulfilled in indicated sequence.

Maslow's theory of human motivation   (A. Maslow) A humanistic view proposed by Abraham Maslow, advocating an emphasis on the higher human motives for understanding, esthetic values, self-realization, and peak experiences. Maslow called them abundancy needs, which contrast with the usual emphasis on deficiency needs that stem from physical needs, insecurity, and alienation. The following items are important for understanding Abraham Maslow's theory: BEING COGNITION, BEING LOVE, DEFICIENCY LOVE, DEFICIENCY MOTIVE, ESTEEM DRIVES, ESTEEM FROM OTHERS, ESTEEM NEEDS, EUPSYCHIA, HOLISTIC INDIVIDUALITY, INSTINCTOID, INSTINCTOID NEEDS, ITERATION, JONAH COMPLEX, LOVE NEEDS, MASLOW'S MOTIVATIONAL HIERARCHY, MASLOW'S THEORY OF HUMAN MOTIVATION, METAMOTIVATION, METANEEDS, METAPATHOLOGY, NEED, PEAK EXPERIENCES, PHYSIOLOGICAL NEEDS, SAFETY NEEDS, SELF-ACTUALIZATION, SELF-ESTEEM, THIRD FORCE IN PSYCHOLOGY.

Masoch See SACHER-MASOCH.

masochism 1. See SEXUAL MASOCHISM. 2. Term also applies to experiences that do not involve sex (or in which it may exist in disguised form), such as martyrdom, humiliation, religious flagellation, or asceticism. 3. In psychoanalytic theory, a perverse attitude in that a person expects and wants to be mistreated for many reasons having to do with conscious and unconscious rewards. Named by Richard von Krafft-Ebbing for L. von Sacher-Masoch, who described the behavior in a novel. See PASSIVE ALGOLAGNIA, SACHER-MASOCH.

masochistic character A type of personality that persistently and characteristically obtains gratification or freedom from guilt feelings as a consequence of humiliation, self-derogation, self-sacrifice, wallowing in misery, and submitting to physically painful acts under sexual excitement. See ABASEMENT NEED, MASOCHISM.

masochistic fantasies Daydreams of being whipped, choked, or otherwise abused as an expression of masochistic tendencies, particularly as a means of achieving sexual excitement.

masochistic sabotage Behavior that tends unconsciously to provoke punishment, scorn, or other adverse reactions. In psychoanalytic theory, people who are clumsy or who have repeated accidents may be practicing masochistic sabotage. Self-defeating behavior may also be manifested by a patient's uncooperative attitude or insulting remarks to the therapist while in therapy.

masochistic wish-dream In sleep, having dreams in which injury is inflicted upon the dreamer.

mass action hypothesis A concept that although the brain has specific sensory- and motor-function centers, the cortex is relatively nonspecific in learning and the general mass of the cortex is involved in cognitive functions. See LAW OF MASS ACTION, LOCALIZATION OF BRAIN FUNCTION.

mass action principle/theory (K. Lashley) A point of view that quantity equals quality in relation to learning; the more neurons involved in the process, the more learning. See LAW OF MASS ACTION.

massage The systematic stroking or kneading of a body area by hand or a mechanical or electrical device, such as a vibrator. Manual massage usually is administered for therapeutic and rehabilitative purposes because the hands can detect abnormalities, such as swellings or muscle spasms. Massage may be performed in a fluid environment, as in a whirlpool bath. Used for relaxation and pain relief.

mass behavior Common conduct of large groups of people who do not have direct communication between them, seen in fads that seem to arise spontaneously, often mentioned in the media after the fad has started, which may extend the fad.

mass contagion/hysteria An epidemic of extreme suggestibility and irrational behavior among an entire group of people, such as the dancing manias, werewolf delusions, and biting manias that swept through Europe between the 13th and 16th centuries, the tulip craze of 17th-century Holland, the Florida real-estate boom of the 1920s, bank runs during the 1929–1939 Depression, and mass reactions to the Orson Welles broadcast based on H. G. Wells' *War of the Worlds* in 1938. Also known as collective hysteria, epidemic hysteria. See COLLECTIVE PSYCHOSIS, LYCANTHROPY, TARANTISM.

massed learning/practice The learning of verbal material or motor skills by constant, uninterrupted practice for long periods. It is inferior to spaced learning, in which rehearsal or practice sessions are brief and interrupted by other activities. The memorizing of relatively long verbal series, or the formation of a complicated motor habit, by repetition without interruption. Massed is usually more effective when the learner is intelligent, and the material is cognitive as opposed to sensorimotor. Compare SPACED LEARNING. See DISTRIBUTED LEARNING.

Massformel (measuring formula—German) Gustav Fechner's final revision of the Weber formula: $S = C \log R/R_0$.

mass masochism (T. Reik) Willingness of a population to endure sacrifices and suffering as demanded by a dictatorial leader to whom people have surrendered their own power (for example, the mass suicide of Jim Jones' cult members in Guyana in 1978).

mass media Large-scale, influential communication organizations, generally divided into print media (such as newspapers and magazines) and electronic media (including television, radio, and computers). Except for the latter to some degree, the communication is basically one-way. Generally regulated by authorities, from mild controls to comprehensive censorship.

mass methods Experimental, testing, or measurement procedures administered simultaneously to a large number of participants, as in giving reading tests to all school children in a certain city. See GROUP TESTING, GROUP TESTS.

mass movement Concerted effort by a large number of people to bring about social changes as found in a political revolution.

mass observation A survey technique in which a large number of people are interviewed, as in a public-opinion poll.

Masson disk (A. P. Masson) A device for measuring the threshold of brightness vision by observing a rotating disk with concentric rings of diminishing grayness.

mass polarization The focusing of attention of an entire population on a single message or propaganda theme as when a nation prepares for war.

mass psychology The study of the characteristic actions and reactions of crowds, mobs, gangs, audiences, or the public at large, including such phenomena as mass hysteria, fads, rioting, lynching, group revelry, group conformity, political movements, and relationships to leaders. See MOB PSYCHOLOGY.

mass reflex   An indiscriminate response of many body effectors to a single stimulus, as in "freezing" with fear.

mass suicide   See COLLECTIVE SUICIDE, MASS MASOCHISM.

mass-to-specific development   In fetal and infantile development, progression from gross random movements of the whole body to more refined movements of body parts.

MAST   Multilevel Academic Survey Tests

masterful inactivity   A technique in eclectic counseling employed to delay client action by use of explanation and justification for inactivity at the moment; it facilitates the postponement of action until a later or more appropriate time.

Mastermind   A game in which the participant must logically deduce the color and location of hidden buttons using only the feedback provided.

master of arts (MA or **M.A.)**   A degree earned following the award of a university baccalaureate. Usually requires two years of study in a specialized field.

mastery instinct/motive   1. The impetus to master or control outer demands and inner drives. 2. The drive to achieve and be successful. 3. Urge to be assertive, to stand out in the crowd, to be dominant.

mastery learning   A fundamental concept that learning some topics, such as mathematics, requires a step-by-step approach. Only when the person has completed a particular step can he or she move to the next step. See KELLER PLAN, PROGRAM FOR LEARNING IN ACCORDANCE WITH NEEDS (PLAN), TEACHING MACHINES.

mastery play   Fun, voluntary activity that teaches children new ways of dealing with people, of testing their capacities and in general learning how to achieve self-control and control over others.

mastery tests   Examinations that help determine whether a person has mastered a certain trade, profession, level of education, etc. (for example, tests given to assess whether a person has the equivalent of a master's degree before acceptance to study for a doctorate in psychology). See KELLER PLAN, PROGRAM FOR LEARNING IN ACCORDANCE WITH NEEDS (PLAN).

mastery training   Experimental or "real-world" training that prepares participants for aversive situations or conflict by teaching methods of assertion and constructive control over environmental conditions. See SOCIO-DRAMA, STRESS-INOCULATION TRAINING.

mastigophobia   Morbid fear of receiving a flogging, also of witnessing a flogging. See RHABDOPHOBIA.

masturbation   Erotic self-stimulation of one's own body, usually the genital organs, occassionally performed by a partner, with the intention in most cases of achieving orgasm. The act is usually accompanied by sexual fantasies. Possibly the most common form of human sexual behavior. Kinsey reported that about 95% of men and 85% of women reported that they masturbate at least occasionally. See ANAL MASTURBATION, AUTOEROTISM, COMPULSIVE MASTURBATION, INFANTILE MASTURBATION, MUTUAL MASTURBATION, ONANISM, PSYCHIC MASTURBATION, SYMBOLIC MASTURBATION.

masturbation equivalents   Activities that have been identified by psychoanalysts as psychological substitutes for masturbation, such as gambling, nail-biting, pulling on one's earlobe, twisting strands of one's hair. See PREPHALLIC MASTURBATION EQUIVALENTS.

MAT   1. Metropolitan Achievement Test. 2. Miller Analogies Test. 3. multiple-aptitude test.

matched-dependent behavior   See IMITATION.

matched-group design   Experimental design in which experimental and control groups are equated or matched on a background variable before being exposed to the experimental procedure. See RANDOMIZED-GROUP DESIGN.

matched groups   Refers to individuals in groups being matched by pairs, by trios, by quartets, etc., for experimental purposes. Thus, each group in the experiment is equated in as many respects as are considered important for the problem. Typically, members of each pair/trio/quartet are assigned randomly to the specific group. See MATCHING OF SUBJECTS, RESEARCH.

matched sample   Two or more individuals considered equivalent with respect to a relevant variable (such as weight, blood pressure). See MATCHED GROUPS, MATCHED-GROUP DESIGN.

matching   1. A research technique for assuring comparability of research participants by equating them on background variables. 2. The assumption that an individual organism will tend to operate in a decision process depending on the alternatives in the same manner that groups of that type do. See IMITATION, PROBABILITY MATCHING, RESEARCH DESIGNS, RESEARCH METHODS.

matching hypothesis   In social psychology, a postulate that people tend to be attracted to and interact with individuals who are roughly equal to themselves in certain factors, such as age, intelligence, ethnicity, and physical beauty. Appears to be true for both opposite-sex and same-sex relationships. See COMMUNAL FEELINGS, FRIENDSHIP.

matching law   (R. Herrnstein) In operant psychology, a law of operant choice behavior. When an organism in an experiment can make more than one response for some reward, it must allocate its behaviors across the possible responses, and it does so on the basis of magnitude, quality, and frequency of reward (see SCHEDULES OF REINFORCEMENT). The matching law has been found to govern choice behavior across all these variables. Roughly, the organism matches its rate of response to the prevailing magnitude, quality, or frequency of reward (for example, if one response yields two food pellets per response and another yields only one pellet, the subject will make the first response twice as frequently as the second).

matching of subjects   In any experiment with a control and experimental groups, establishing any of various sets of criteria for individuals and then locating participants on a one-to-one basis, for each of the two (or more) groups. Ordinarily, once two (or more) equated individuals are located, a toss of a coin determines in which group the individual goes. See MATCHED GROUPS.

matching test   An examination based on selection of items from one list and assigning them to the appropriate items on another list.

matching to sample   A procedure for studying learning in which a human or animal is shown a stimulus and is then required to pick out an example of it from an array of alternatives. Comes in a variety of forms, such as delayed matching to sample (used to study memory), in which a waiting period of some length comes between the initial presented stimulus and the choice stimuli.

material   In psychoanalytic theory, the utterances of clients, comprising material for interpretation.

Material Feminism   A kind of feminism that seeks to liberate women by improving their material condition, as by removing the burdens of housework and cooking.

materialism   1. A prevailing desire for physical possessions or comforts at the expense of higher moral or spiritual values. 2. In philosophy, the doctrine that matter is the only ultimate reality. See MIND-BODY PROBLEM, MONISM. 3. In social-political theory, national values of production, distribution, and consumption. 4. In physiological psychology, the belief that the brain is a machine and that consciousness is irrelevant to its functioning. See MONISM.

materialistic monism   A doctrine positing that nothing exists except matter and space. In psychology, materialist monists conclude that mind is a set of brain processes. See IDEALIST MONISM.

materialization   The alleged production of a body or its parts or objects by supernormal or spiritualistic methods.

maternal aggression   A hostile reaction of most females to strange or threatening others, when in the presence of their young. See ANIMAL AGGRESSION.

maternal attitudes   Mothers' feelings about their children, particularly those attitudes that play an important role in character formation, emotional adjustment, and self-image. Negative examples include overly permissive, indulgent, overprotective, rigidly disciplinary, neglectful, and abusive attitudes. Positive examples include caring, accepting, and recognition of the child's need for independence and self-esteem. See PARENTING, LOGICAL CONSEQUENCES, NATURAL CONSEQUENCES.

maternal behavior   Actions of mothers associated with caring for offspring and in some cases, caring for the young of other mothers (alloparenting). Males of some animal species exhibit maternal behavior after receiving injections of prolactin, the lactogenic hormone.

maternal deprivation   Lack of adequate affection, care, and stimulation from the mother or mother substitute, particularly during infancy. Occurs in disturbed families and institutions and likely has a negative effect on all aspects of the child's personality (emotional reactions, intellectual development, self-concept, interpersonal relations, and physical well-being). In some cases this type of deprivation may lay the basis for severe mental disorder. See FAILURE TO THRIVE, MARASMUS.

maternal drive   A strong tendency in female animals to feed and otherwise care for their offspring. Some male animals such as birds also show this kind of behavior.

maternal nondisjunction   Unequal distribution of a homologous chromosome pair during oogenesis.

maternity blues   Common expression for transient feelings of dejection on the part of a new mother and sometimes of a new father, that occur after giving birth to a child. Also known as postpartum blues. See POSTPARTUM DISORDERS, POSTPARTUM EMOTIONAL DISTURBANCES.

mate selection   1. In humans, decisions regarding the selection of mates in modern advanced societies are generally done within relatively narrow limits of social levels, based on that elusive concept called love. Research indicates that whereas differences between people may generate interest, committing to a person of the same age, ethnicity, interests, values, and education (homogamy) is the best predictor of a happy relationship. 2. In animals, the selection process of sexual partners for reproduction. Members of sexually reproducing animal species rarely mate indiscriminately but choose their mates on the basis of criteria suggesting relative Darwinian fitness. Typically, the sex that must make the higher parental investment, usually the female, is choosier than the other. See PARENTAL INVESTMENT.

Mateson Multistimulus Olfactometer   (J. Mateson) An odorant-mixing olfactometer designed to yield "information about and control of temperature, pressure, and humidity of the odorivector (odorant vapor)." See OLFACTOMETER for an illustration of a primitive instrument for determining odors.

mathematical biology   The branch of biology that deals with the development of mathematical models of biological phenomena, such as evolution or nerve conduction.

mathematical model   Representation of a psychological or physiological function in the form of a mathematical formula or equation, as in Fechner's law. See HULL'S THEORY.

mathematical psychology   A general attempt to express psychological theories by mathematical expression, formulations, operators, etc. In general, precisely formulated theories of the psychophysical type seem amenable to such procedures, but those of the verbal or sociological type do not. See CHOICE THEORIES, DECISION THEORIES, LOGICAL POSITIVISM.

mathematico-deductive method   (C. L. Hull) The use of postulates and corollaries in mathematical form to develop a deductive system based on mathematically formulated premises to give rigor to a theory so as to be able to produce precise, testable predictions. See HULL'S THEORY.

mating behavior   The physical union of male and female for reproduction of their species. See ANIMAL COURTSHIP BEHAVIOR, ANIMAL INTERCOURSE, FILTER THEORY OF MATE SELECTION, MATE SELECTION, NATURAL SELECTION, REPRODUCTIVE SELECTION, SEX SELECTION, SEXUAL REPRODUCTION.

matriarchy   A society ruled by women, who are symbols of power or of love and motherhood. Some theorists assume the matriarchal society preceded the patriarchal because the first relationship of infants of both sexes is to the mother. Others conclude the patriarchal came first because of the superior strength of the male.

matrices   1. Plural of matrix. 2. See RAVEN'S PROGRESSIVE MATRICES TEST.

matricide 1. The killing of a person's own mother. 2. The person who committed such an act. Compare PATRICIDE.

matriculation dream **examination dream**

matrifocal family Those families in which women are considered heads of the family by virtue of family tradition or the prevailing mores of a society.

matrilineage Familial descent being considered through the female members. Compare GENS, PATRILINEAGE.

matrilineal Pertaining to a society in which lineage is traced through the mother and the female line. See MATRIARCHY.

matrilineal family A family in which the female members pass on their names or the traditions to the children.

matrilineality In anthropology, refers to ancestry being traced through the mother.

matrilocal family A family system in which a husband goes to live with his wife's family (matrilocality); contrasted to patrilocality, in which the wife joins the husband's family, and neolocality, in which husband and wife live in a new location.

matrilocality See MATRILOCAL FAMILY, NEOLOCAL FAMILY.

matrimonial rights In legal usage, the responsibilities and expectations spouses have to each other's society, comfort, and affection. See CONJUGAL RIGHTS.

matrix A two-dimensional array of elements. Matrix notation and matrix algebra constitute a convenient method for representing and manipulating systems of linear equations. Plural is matrices.

Matrix Analogies Test-Expanded Form (MAT-Expanded Form) (J. A. Naglieri) An examination for children and young adults (ages 5–17 years) intended to provide individual assessment of nonverbal reasoning abilities.

matrix organization In industrial/organizational psychology, a management structure in which specialists belong to project teams and report to more than one supervisor. Common in organizations with continuous special projects, such as research and development organizations.

maturation 1. Achievement of optimal development or growth potential. 2. The process of "unfolding from within," the biological and personality development from infancy through adulthood. Biological development is governed primarily by heredity, and personality is a product of both constitutional tendencies, environmental influences and individual creativity. See SOFT DETERMINISM.

maturational crisis In community psychology, one of two major types of crisis, characterized by a period of time of acute disorganization of behavior or affect precipitated by a transition from one developmental phase to another, such as entering kindergarten, becoming engaged, getting married, becoming a parent, and retiring. Also known as developmental crisis, normative crisis. See ACCIDENTAL CRISIS.

maturational hypothesis/theory A point of view that maturing people have available to them certain mental and physiological abilities that they do not use until they need them.

maturational lag Slowness or delay in some aspects of neurological development that affects learning but does not involve specific brain damage.

maturation-degeneration hypothesis A postulate that functions and abilities between birth and death can be plotted as a trajectory curve that reaches a peak in the early years and then gradually declines.

maturation hypothesis/theory A point of view that some behaviors are solely (or heavily) hereditary but do not appear until appropriate organs and neural systems have matured.

mature 1. Fully developed. 2. The process of becoming fully developed.

mature facial features General characteristics of adult versus infantile facial proportions, such as relatively smaller eyes and longer nose. Observed in various mammalian species.

maturity A state characterized by completed growth or development. See DEVELOPMENTAL LEVELS.

maturity rating An evaluation of adult behavior on a particular trait in comparison with a relevant peer-group norm; for example, "He acts like a teenager rather than a man of 35," "She is four, going on forty."

matutinal insomnia Waking up too early; not getting enough sleep. Also known as terminal insomnia.

maudlin drunkenness Eugen Bleuler's phrase for the silly, blissful, unpleasant sentimental type of behavior observed in some intoxicated people.

Maudsley Personality Inventory (M.P.I. or MPI) (H. J. Eysenck) A personality test containing 24 items characteristic of neuroticism (N) and 24 of extraversion (E). Named after the hospital where Hans Eysenck, the author of the inventory, once worked as a research psychologist. Superseded by the Eysenck Personality Inventory (EPI).

MAVA See MULTIPLE ABSTRACT VARIANCE ANALYSIS DESIGN.

mavericks **wild ducks**

maximal age A designation similar to terminal mental age.

maximin strategy In game theory, a strategy chosen by a player that maximizes the amount the player can win. Compare MINIMAX STRATEGY.

maximizing hypothesis A postulate that people act so as to gain as much utility (in money, happiness, or some other measure) as possible; also known as optimizing. Contrast with H.A. Simon's satisficing hypothesis, which claims that people act to gain only a certain satisfactory level of utility. See BOUNDED RATIONALITY, RATIONALITY, SATISFICE, UTILITY THEORY.

maximum contrast principle See PRINCIPLE OF MAXIMUM CONTRAST.

maximum likelihood principle 1. In making a subjective judgment, basing a prediction on what appears to be the most reasonable estimate. 2. In statistics, having any population estimate as the basis of predicting the total parameter.

maximum-security unit   1. A section of an institution for the mentally ill reserved for patients who are dangerous to themselves or others. 2. A prison (section or entire facility) that houses criminals who either have committed violent crimes against the person, have a history of escape attempts, or have been adjudged criminally insane.

Maxwell (color) triangle   (J. C. Maxwell) A triangular diagram (for testing the chromatic aspects of perception as related to daylight adaptation) in which the apexes of the triangle represent the primary colors. Also, the base of the color pyramid, showing certain color relationships. Also known as Maxwell chromaticity diagram. See COLOR TRIANGLE.

Maxwell disks   (J. C. Maxwell) A series of slotted color disks on a rotating spindle used to produce mixed hues. See BENHAM'S TOP for an example of such a disk.

Maxwellian view   (J. C. Maxwell) The elimination of fluctuations in the amount of light entering the eye due to fluctuations in pupil size by concentrating light coming off an object via a spherical (fish-eye) lens to focus light in the plane of the pupil.

Maxwell's demon   (J. C. Maxwell) Refers to considering the molecules on either side of a semipermeable barrier as minute humanlike agents, as a construct to try to disprove the Second Law of Thermodynamics by regulating the movement of the molecules.

Maxwell triangle   Maxwell (color) triangle

maya   (Sanskrit) An illusion or a delusion. An integral part of the concept found originally in Vedantic philosophy (Hindu), in which the material world and its accompanying dualities are seen to be no more than projections of a limited consciousness that cannot perceive reality as its actually is. The goal of this belief system is to transcend maya, an attachment to which is held to be the cause of suffering.

maze   A puzzle labyrinth of the type known since antiquity, traditionally used to study learning and memory (especially in lab rats) because it allows for clear measurement of time from start box to goal box and of error pattern; the first such use was by W. S. Small in 1899. Single-choice (Y- or T-shaped) mazes are used with invertebrates, and varied forms are designed for studying intellectual and emotional reaction of people, as with a printed paper pattern on which the participant traces the correct pathway with a pencil. See ELITHORN MAZE, ELEVATED MAZE, FINGER MAZE, HAMPTON COURT MAZE, LOCOMOTOR MAZE, PORTEUS MAZE, Y-MAZE.

maze behavior   Manifestation of ability to perform intelligent planning and to have good memory.

maze-bright/dull (rats)   (W. T. Heron, R. C. Tryon) The best maze-runners in an F-1 generation of rats were interbred, also the worst maze-runners were interbred, and this pattern of breeding was repeated for successive generations. By F-8, there was little overlap between the two groups, showing that specific kinds of mental ability can be inherited (the maze-bright rats excelled only in maze-running).

maze learning   Finding how to reach a certain location by starting from a designated point and following a circuitous pathway that has randomly or systematically located obstacles or blind alleys. Usually involves multiple trials, and regarded as successful when the subject reaches the goal in the most direct way and without errors on two or more successive trials. See CULTURE-FAIR INTELLIGENCE TESTS, CULTURE-FREE INTELLIGENCE TESTS.

MBD   minimal brain dysfunction

MBHI   Millon Behavioral Health Inventory

MBO   management by objectives

MBTI   Myers-Briggs Type Indicator.

M-C   See MULTIPLE-CHOICE EXPERIMENT/PROBLEM.

McAdory Art Test   (M. McAdory) An examination to measure artistic potential. See ART TESTS.

McCarthy Scales of Children's Abilities (MSCA)   (D. McCarthy) A comprehensive instrument for children between 2½ and 8½ years of age, consisting of six overlapping scales: Verbal, Perceptual-Performance, Quantitative, General Cognitive, Memory, and Motor. Yields a traditional intelligence quotient (IQ).

McCarthy Screening Test (MST)   (D. McCarthy) A short form of the McCarthy Scales of Children's Abilities intended to diagnose academic potentials and disabilities for children ages 4 to 6. It has six scales: verbal memory, right-left orientation, leg coordination, draw a design, numeric memory, conceptual grouping.

McCarthy's reflex   A contraction of the eyelid muscle when the supraorbital foramen is tapped. Better known as the supraorbital reflex. Named after American neurologist Daniel J. McCarthy (1874–1958).

McCollough effect   In perception, a contingent aftereffect. Celeste McCollough showed that after looking at horizontal stripes of one color and vertical ones of another, then looking at black and white horizontal and vertical stripes, the horizontal stripes seem tinged with the complementary colors of the original horizontal ones and the vertical stripes appear tinged with the complementary color of the vertical ones. The effect can last for hours and can be elicited when using one eye for stimulation and the other for the aftereffect, showing that the mechanism is not solely retinal.

MCD   Minimal cerebral dysfunction.

McDougall's theory   The following are important in understanding William McDougall's theory: DERIVED EMOTION, DRAINAGE HYPOTHESIS, FACTOR THEORY OF LEARNING, HORMIC PSYCHOLOGY, HORMIC THEORY, HORMISM, INSTINCTIVE ACTION/BEHAVIOR, PRIMARY EMOTION, SELF-FEELING, SELF-SENTIMENT.

MCL   Most comfortable loudness.

MCMI   Millon Clinical Multiaxial Inventory.

MCMI-III   Millon Clinical Multiaxial Inventory-III.

McNaghten   M'Naghten

McNemar test   (Q. NcNemar) A statistical test of the nonparametric type for determining the significance of change for repeated measurements on a nominal or ordinal scale. See TERMAN-MCNEMAR TEST OF MENTAL ABILITY.

MCO   Managed Care Organization.

MCT   Minnesota Clerical Test

M.D.   Mean deviation.

Md D   See MEDIAN DEVIATION.

Md   See MEDIAN.

MD   1. See MANIC-DEPRESSIVE DISORDER. 2. mental deficiency.

MDA   Abbreviation for 3,4,-methylenedioxyamphetamine. See MDMA.

MDAP   See MACHOVER DRAW-A-PERSON TEST.

MDD   Major depressive disorder.

MDEA   A recreational synthetic drug available in the 1990s, similar effects to MDMA (Ecstasy). Also called Eve. See ECSTASY.

MDI   See MANIC-DEPRESSIVE DISORDER.

MDMA   3,4,-methylenedioxymethamphetamine, more commonly known as the designer drug Ecstasy. Also called Adam. See ECSTASY.

MDS   See MULTIDIMENSIONAL SCALING.

me   (W. James) A concept, "I know me," with "I" being the knower and "me" being the known; "I" being a watcher and evaluator of "me" and both being part of "self."

mean (m, M, or X̄)   Arithmetic average or mean, the most widely used statistic for describing central tendency. Formula: $M = (\Sigma X) \div N$, where M is the mean, X is any score, and N is the number of cases. See GEOMETRIC MEAN, HARMONIC MEAN.

mean deviation (M.D., m.d., or m.v.)   Average deviation.

mean-gradation method   **equal-appearing-intervals method**

meaning   The cognitive or emotional significance of a word, theory, signal, or symbolic act. See CONTEXT THEORY OF MEANING, WILL TO MEANING.

meaningful learning   1. Acquisition of material that relates to the learner's experience, that enriches his or her life in an interesting or challenging way, as contrasted with material learned that has little or no relevance. 2. (G. Katona) In Gestalt psychology, a form of learning based upon insight and meaningful organization. See READINESS.

meaninglessness   Absence of meaning, particularly when associated with a pervasive feeling that life in general, or the entire world, lacks significance, purpose, or direction. The perception or feeling of meaninglessness poses the major problem that the existential approach attempts to solve. See EXISTENTIALISM, LOGOTHERAPY, WILL TO MEANING.

meaningfulness   Presence of meaning, especially as relates to a person's life; for example, a person's existence is generally considered meaningful if it is perceived as having significance, purpose, direction, or all three.

mean length of utterance (MLU)   In linguistics, the average number of morphemes spoken at a time; gradually increases from the age of two onward.

means   Any object, process, or activity used by an organism in its movement toward a goal or toward solution of a problem.

means-end capacity   (E. C. Tolman) Ability to perceive and respond to the linkages between means-objects and goals, such as the ability to judge cues to distance, depth, and direction on the way to a goal.

means-end(s) expectation/readiness   (E. C. Tolman) Capacity or responsiveness established through experience and inheritance to judge stimuli in a certain way or to prefer one behavior over another potentially effective behavior in pursuit of a specific goal. Animals in a maze or similar situation attain their goals by making decisions at various points in terms of their expectancies of achieving success. Expectancy of what leads to what. See MAXIMIZING PRINCIPLE, SIGN-GESTALT EXPECTATION OR READINESS.

means-end relations   (E. C. Tolman) All aspects of direction and distance broadly defined that provide the basis for exhibiting sign-significance relations (sign Gestalts). Factors like direction, distance, similarity, and final common pathness that intervene between the start and a given end or final goal, as perceived by organisms. See MEANS-END(S) EXPECTATION/READINESS.

means-ends analysis   1. (A. Newell & H. A. Simon) A heuristic process used in problem-solving search that: (a) compares the goal situation with the current situation to find one or more differences; (b) finds an operator relevant for reducing differences of this kind; (c) applies the operator to reduce the difference; (d) repeats the process until the goal is reached. 2. A general method of problem-solving involving looking for differences between the current state and the goal state and seeking ways to reduce the differences. See GENERAL PROBLEM SOLVER, HEURISTIC SEARCH.

means-object/situation   Any object, response, event, or condition that contributes to an organism's progress toward a goal. Refers not only to objects as such but to environmental cues that alert the organism to the correct route or response.

mean square (MS)   In the analysis of variance, the sum of squares divided by the degrees of freedom. The mean square between groups divided by the mean square within groups yield an F ratio. The mean square is a variance estimate.

mean square contingency coefficient (ϕ^2)   A statistic to determine whether entries in a contingency table could have occurred by chance. See CHI SQUARE.

measurement by fiat   Quantifying data by assigning numbers on the basis of arbitrary units, intuition, or face validity.

measurement error   An error generated by an inadequate instrument, incorrect statistic, or human error that if constant generates consistent erroneous findings. See STANDARD ERROR OF MEASUREMENT.

measurement levels   Refers to the four levels of measurement that are nominal, ordinal, interval, and ratio, in order of increasing accuracy and meaningfulness. See NOMINAL SCALE, ORDINAL SCALE, INTERVAL SCALE, RATIO SCALE, SCALE TYPE.

measure of central tendency   The value of scores used to represent the total distribution; the average or typical value. The mean, median, and mode are several measures of central tendency. All measures of central tendency are measures of the center, though different ones for different purposes. Also known as central-tendency measure. See MEASURE OF VARIATION.

measure of dispersion   A measure of the spread of a distribution of scores. An indication of "how typical" the "typical measure" (for example, central tendency, mean) is. Common measures include the standard deviation and variance as well as the interquartile range. Also known as measure of variability, measure of variation. See AVERAGE DEVIATION, MEAN, BIMODAL DISTRIBUTION, KURTOSIS, MEASURE OF CENTRAL TENDENCY, NORMAL CURVE, RANGE, STANDARD DEVIATION.

measure of meaningfulness   An attempt to measure a word's meaning by presenting a word and counting how many associations a participant can make to that particular word. Or by determining likely word familiarity, as by frequency counts in typical English prose.

measure of variability/variation   Other names for measure of dispersion.

mechanical aptitude   A potential ability to comprehend and deal with machines or mechanical objects. See MECHANICAL-APTITUDE TESTS.

mechanical-aptitude tests   Procedures designed to measure various abilities related to mechanical work, such as mechanical information, mechanical reasoning, spatial relations, perceptual skills, understanding of mechanical principles, mechanical assembly, and manual dexterity. See MECHANICAL APTITUDE.

mechanical causality   A theory that all behavior involves direct physical connection between interacting objects. Championed by René Descartes, mechanical causality was rejected by Isaac Newton and later physicists, who postulated field theories of causality (for example gravitational and electromagnetic fields). At the quantum level, causation is never mechanical.

mechanical-comprehension test   An examination designed to measure familiarity with and understanding of mechanical facts and principles. See BENNETT MECHANICAL COMPREHENSION TEST.

mechanical group therapy   (E. Schmidhoffer) A method of therapy in an institution by the medium of having taped announcements periodically heard by all patients such as: "Pay attention. Pay attention. You can get rid of all symptoms immediately if you want to."

mechanical intelligence   (E. L. Thorndike) The mental ability to understand concrete objects and mechanical relationships. See COGNITIVE INTELLIGENCE, SOCIAL INTELLIGENCE.

mechanical-man concept   (D. E. Woodridge) A point of view that humans and life itself can be understood as forms of machinery subject only to physical processes and not subject to nonphysical phenomena such as consciousness. See MACHINE THEORY, MECHANISTIC APPROACH.

mechanical problem-solving   (K. Duncker) Analysis from below. In Gestalt psychology, a problem-solving strategy characterized by habit and by a blindness to the inner nature of the problem situation. Compare ORGANIC PROBLEM-SOLVING.

mechanism   1. (J. de La Mettrie) A classic position that asserts a mechanical model for understanding behavior. Organisms thus behave according to the principles of physics. See MACHINE THEORY, VITALISM. 2. (R. S. Woodworth) A purposive response or set of responses. 3. See MENTAL MECHANISM.

mechanism vs vitalism   (R. I. Watson) A prescriptive dimension of the philosophical underpinnings of psychology, namely, explaining psychological events physiologically versus in other ways.

mechanistic approach   A point of view that complex psychological processes can ultimately be understood as the outcome of underlying physiological processes; for example, perception is explained by recourse to the scientific principles (especially chemical and electrical) that govern the nervous system. See MECHANISM, REDUCTIONISM.

mechanistic interactionism   (N. S. Endler & D. Magnusson) A model that describes and discusses the interdependency of determinants of behavior, such as persons, situations, and modes of response. It is primarily concerned with the "structure" of interaction and not the continuous process of interaction.

mechanistic theory   (R. Descartes) A point of view that all organisms except humans lack minds. Infrahuman behaviors are considered to be based on primitive reflexes and instincts. A more modern version would add that other organisms' learning is strictly of the reward-punish association type without the capacity to make generalizations.

mechanomorphism   The use of physical and mechanistic terms to refer to psychic activities. See BEHAVIORISM.

mechanophobia   Morbid fear of machinery.

mechanoreceptors   Receptors sensitive to mechanical forms of stimuli, such as receptors in the ears that translate sound waves into nerve impulses as well as receptors in joints and muscles that inform humans of the location of their limbs. See CHEMORECEPTORS.

Medea complex   The compulsion of a mother to kill her children as revenge against their father, named for Medea of Greek myth, who killed her children fathered by Jason after he deserted her in favor of another woman. See INFANTICIDE.

medial   Pertaining to the middle or center of a body area or organ.

medial bundle   A group of sensory fibers located between the dorsal ganglion and the spinal cord, composed mainly of large myelinated nerves including pressure-receptor fibers. The medial bundle fibers communicate with the dorsal column of white matter.

medial canal   See SCALA MEDIA.

medial geniculate body (MGB)   A swelling on the rear end of the thalamus between the lateral geniculate and pulvinar bodies. Contains the auditory relay nucleus and functions as a relay point for auditory impulses between the inferior colliculus and the auditory cortex. Sometimes known as internal geniculate body.

medial lemniscus/lemnisci   Sensory tract(s) from the spinal cord that transmit impulses from the medulla through the pons and midbrain to the thalamus.

medial olfactory stria   Nerve tract that connects the olfactory bulbs through the anterior commissure.

medial orbital gyrus   See ORBITAL GYRI.

medial rectus   One of the six muscles used in controlling eye movements for turning the eye toward the nose. See INFERIOR OBLIQUE, INFERIOR RECTUS, LATERAL RECTUS, SUPERIOR OBLIQUE, SUPERIOR RECTUS.

medial temporal lobe The middle part of the temporal or lateral region of the brain.

median (Md or Mdn) A measure of central tendency, specifically the middle item of a series of items arranged in order of magnitude. Thus, the median of 1-3-4-5-8 and of 1-3-4-9-12 are both 4. Whereas the mean is the most frequently used measure of central tendency, sometimes the median is more appropriate, especially when there are either small or large outliers.

median class An interval or class of a frequency distribution in which the median or middle value of a distribution is found. Also known as median group/interval, midinterval.

median deviation (Md D) The median value of the deviations of a set of measures (usually) from the median of the whole set.

median gray A gray halfway between pure white and pure black.

median group/interval **median class**

median test A nonparametric test for significance of difference between two or more distributions determined by finding the median for the combined samples and then by using chi-square to check the values above and below the combined median.

mediate(d) association A connection between two ideas formed by means of an intermediate, or intervening, idea, as in remembering a chemical formula by making a word out of the symbols.

mediated generalization (N. E. Miller & J. Dollard) Conditioning in which a generalized response follows a stimulus dissimilar to the original stimulus, but having some resemblance; for example, in a study by Riess, 8-year-olds tended to respond (GSR) strongly to homonyms (won-one, ate-eight) of conditioned words but the effect decreased markedly by age 11. Synonyms (won-beat, ate-fed) showed increased response from age 11 to 18. Antonyms (won-lost, ate-starved) decreased through age 14 but then increased at age 18. The generalization with the original conditioned stimulus (CS) is mediated through the meaning of words learned in another context.

mediating variables (N. S. Endler & D. Magnusson) Intervening variables and hypothetical constructs of various kinds inferred from observations of behavior and from own inner experiences. They enable people to understand, explain, and predict the process by which both situational and stored information is selected, interpreted, and transformed into reactions. See INTERVENING VARIABLES.

mediation In dispute resolution, the use of a mutually acceptable outside party to help the contending factions communicate and compromise. Compare ARBITRATION.

mediational learning A concept of learning that assumes the presence of mediators to bridge the association between two or more events that are not directly contiguous in space or time. The mediators are events or processes that serve as cue-producing responses. See MEDIATION THEORY, MEDIATOR.

mediational processes Cognitive processes through which environmental influences affect behavior.

mediational stimulus-response model A behavioral model that posits internal events, such as thoughts and images, as links between perceiving a stimulus and making a response. See MEDIATION LEARNING, MEDIATION THEORY.

mediation theory Offspring of Hullian S-R theory, the point of view that in sophisticated organisms, external stimuli provoke internal, covert responses, which in turn provoke internal, covert stimuli, which in turn cause an overt behavior (S-r-s-R). The covert s-r links thus mediate between stimulus (S) and response (R). See HULL'S THEORY.

mediator 1. A person who functions as a "bridge" between disputants to help them settle their differences or agree on a solution. 2. An effector, such as a process, object, or system, found between a stimulus and a response, between the source and destination of a neural impulse, or between the transmitter and receiver of communications that serves to connect both the source and the result.

medicalization 1. (I. Illich) The spread of the medical profession's influence and activities, as in its increased involvement in the processes of birth and death. 2. The attachment of medical diagnoses to, and the medical treatment of, socially or culturally unacceptable behaviors (as was once the case with homosexuality).

medical model (of mental disorders) 1. A point of view that mental disorders are physical diseases that have physical causes that can be treated and, in most cases, cured by purely medical techniques. Disorders are to be diagnosed on the basis of their symptoms and cured through appropriate treatment of medications as well as hospital stays that include rest, recreation, and occupational therapy. 2. Phrase is used metaphorically to hold that maladaptive behaviors are symptoms of a hidden mental disorder in the same way that the signs of a physical disease are symptoms of that medical disorder. Since a "germ" has infected the mind, the "sick ideas" show up as disordered or maladaptive behavior. The cure, obviously, is to heal the mind of the "sick ideas."

medical psychology An area of applied psychology devoted to psychological questions arising in the practice of medicine, such as emotional reactions to illness, attitudes toward terminal illness and impending death, psychological means of relieving pain (for example, hypnotic suggestion, relaxation), reactions to disability, studies of iatrogenic factors, development of techniques for testing drug side effects on psychological functions (behavioral toxicity), and application of personality tests to patients with migraine, ulcers, and other stress-related disorders. Sometimes includes teaching self-control techniques so the person will take the medications as prescribed.

medical psychotherapy A treatment procedure utilizing medicines and medical techniques in the treatment of mental illness. See MEDICAL MODEL, PSYCHIATRY.

medical social worker A health professional educated (generally with an appropriate graduate degree, a doctorate for administrative posts) and trained to help individuals and families with problems mainly associated with disabling diseases and injuries. Expertise includes social life, employment, finances, living arrangements, marriage, child care, and emotional reactions. See CLINI-CAL SOCIAL WORKER, PSYCHIATRIC SOCIAL WORKER, SOCIAL WORKER.

medication-induced movement disorders   A general category that includes the kinds of tremors that arise as a side effect of lithium and other medicines, as well as tardive dyskinesia, pseudoparkinsonism, neuroleptic malignant syndrome, akathisia, and acute dystonia.

medicine fear   See PHARMACOPHOBIA.

meditation   1. Quiet and deep self-reflection about the self, aims, relationships, or the meaning of life. 2. Tension reduction in various ways, such as closing of the eyes and relaxing major muscle groups. See TRANSCENDENTAL MEDITATION.

medium   1. In parapsychology, a person credited with the ability to receive communications ostensibly from the deceased or to manifest physical effects attributed to an alleged discarnate entity, usually in a dissociated state of trance. See PSYCHIC. 2. Any agency through which something is achieved, including the air or a wire through which messages are transmitted.

mediumistic hypothesis   (C. G. Jung) In Jungian theory, a postulate that patients with schizophrenia are close to the collective unconscious and therefore in a position to see and accept the trend of events and signs of their disintegration.

medulla   The inner portion of an organ or gland, surrounded by the cortex.

medulla oblongata   A portion of the spinal cord that becomes enlarged at the base of the brain. It contains many nerve tracts that conduct impulses between the spinal cord and higher brain centers. The medulla oblongata, or "bulb," also contains autonomic nuclei involved in the control of breathing, heartbeat, and blood pressure. It is one of the three structures of the hindbrain, the most primitive part of the brain, the others being the pons and cerebellum. Also known as myelencephalon.

medullary sheath   A fatty insulating sheath that covers peripheral sensory and motor neurons. See MYELIN.

medullation   The covering of a nerve fiber with a sheath of medullary substance, or myelin.

MEG   See MAGNETOENCEPHALOGRAPHY.

megacephaly   1. A condition in which the head is abnormally large. May be congenital or acquired. Also known as macrocephalia, macrocephaly, megacephalia, megalencephaly, megalocephalia, megalocephaly. 2. A rare congenital defect characterized by gross enlargement of the head due to abnormal growth of the supporting tissue of the brain, resulting in moderate-to-severe mental retardation, frequently with impaired vision and seizures.

megadose pharmacotherapy   Using very high doses of pharmacologic agents to treat certain disorders, as in prescribing high doses of neuroleptic medicines to control schizophrenia. This approach became fashionable in the late 1970s but was not found to be effective in the long run. See MEGAVITAMIN THERAPY, ORTHOMOLEC-ULAR PSYCHIATRY, ORTHOMOLECULAR TREATMENT.

megalocephaly   megacephaly

megalomania   A delusion of greatness or importance. A highly inflated, overvaluation of self-power and capabilities, bordering on delusions of grandeur. Rarely known as macromania.

megalophobia   Morbid fear of anything large. See MACROPHOBIA.

megalop(s)ia   macropsia

megavitamin therapy   Using very high doses of vitamins to treat certain disorders, as in giving high doses of nicotinic acid to control schizophrenia. See MEGADOSE PHARMACOTHERAPY, ORTHOMOLECULAR PSYCHIATRY.

Meier Art Tests   (N. C. Meier) Two tests that attempt to determine artistic abilities of participants by asking them to express a preference for either a masterpiece or that same masterpiece rendered esthetically inferior by subtle changes; the nature of the modification is specified on the answer sheet. Part I. Art Judgment consists of 100 pairs of pictures, the original and one variation. Part II. Aesthetic Perception consists of 50 sets of 4 pictures, the original and three variations; the observer must rank order the quality from high to low. Revised when it replaced the Meier-Seashore Art Judgment Test (N. C. Meier & C. E. Seashore). These tests have been among the most widely used tests of artistic appreciation.

Meier-Seashore Art Judgment Test   See MEIER ART TESTS.

meiosis   Cell division leading to the production of gametes. In the production of ova and spermatozoa, each daughter cell is haploid (containing one of each pair of chromosomes from the original diploid set in the parental gonads). During fertilization, the ova and spermatozoa undergo a fusion that restores the double set of chromosomes within the nucleus of the zygote thus formed. Incorrectly spelled miosis.

Meissner's corpuscles   (G. Meissner) Small, oval sensory nerve receptors sensitive to touch. They are located in the skin and mucous membranes of the mammary papilla, the lips, and the tip of the tongue.

mel   A unit of pitch measurement in which a tone of 1,000 Hertz (cycles per second) is equivalent to 1,000 mels. Term is an abbreviation of melody.

melancholia   1. Old term for feelings of dejection, loss of interest and initiative, inability to feel pleasure, low self-esteem, and preoccupation with self-reproaches and regrets. More commonly known as depression. See DEPRESSION. 2. A severe form of depression characterized by insomnia, inability to feel pleasure, psychomotor changes, and guilt. See CLIMACTERIC MELANCHOLIA, DEPRESSION. 3. A symptom found in some conditions, marked by depression, lethargy, and slowness of thought processes. Also known as melancholy. See HYPOCHONDRIASIS.

melancholia agitata   (agitated melancholy—Latin) 1. 19th-century phrase for the excited phase of catatonic schizophrenia. 2. Phrase is occasionally used for agitated depression, especially when associated with senile psychosis.

melancholic mood   See CONSTITUTIONAL DEPRESSIVE DISPOSITION.

melancholic personality   A pattern of emotional disturbance characterized by a subdued emotional tone, persistent mild depression, inability to enjoy life, self-depreciation, insecurity, and fear of disapproval, and a tendency to develop a severe depressive disorder under stress. See DEPRESSION.

melancholic type   A personality pattern characterized by general depression, which Hippocrates attributed to an excess of black bile. See CONSTITUTIONAL TYPE. Compare HOMORAL THEORY.

melanocortin-4 receptor (MC4-R)   A receptor that responds to melanocortin, causes production of melanin, and affects appetite.

melanocyte-stimulating hormone (MSH)   A hormone produced by the anterior lobe, the adenohypophysis, of the pituitary gland. See PITUITARY.

melatonin   A neurohormone secreted into the blood by the pineal gland that affects circadian rhythms. In humans, production is affected by light, with more production during the night than during the day and more during dark months than light months. Also thought to affect sexual development, sleep and appetite.

melioristic   Having a tendency to make things better.

melissophobia   (honey fly—Greek) Morbid fear of bees. More commonly known as apiphobia.

melodic intonation therapy   In speech pathology, since patients with Broca's aphasia can often sing well and because musical functions are associated with the right hemisphere, patients are trained to sing simple phrases, then to delete the melody, leaving only the words.

membership character   1. A Gestalt theory of relationship such that a change in a member of a group influences the whole and a change in the whole influences the members. 2. A character of an element derived from the totality.

membership group   Any social group to which an individual belongs as a accepted member. See REFERENCE GROUPS.

membrane growth   Development of a neuron, which presumably releases a substance that enhances the building of membrane tissue from available protein and lipoid molecules under genetic control. The membrane gradually advances toward a target organ or a synaptic communication with another neuron. Each neuron has its own membrane growth pattern and is not influenced by neighboring neurons growing in different and even opposite directions to other targets.

membrane potential   The electrical charge within a neuron. See ACTION POTENTIAL.

memory (M)   1. Ability to revive past experience, based on the mental processes of learning or registration, retention, recall or retrieval, and recognition; the total body of remembered experience. 2. A specific past experience recalled. Types of memory include: ASSOCIATIVE, AUTOMATIC, CONSTRUCTIVE, GENETIC STORAGE, HYPERESTHETIC, IMMEDIATE, INCIDENTAL, LONG-TERM, MINUTE, MOTOR, PANORAMIC, PARAMNESIA, PHOTOGRAPHIC, PHYSIOLOGICAL, PRODUCTIVE, RACIAL, REDUPLICATIVE, REMOTE, REPLACEMENT, SHORT-TERM, UNCONSCIOUS, VERBAL, VISUAL, VISUAL-SEQUENTIAL. Also see AUDITORY MEMORY SPAN, DUAL-MEMORY THEORY, EIDETIC IMAGE, GENETIC STORAGE, PSEUDOMEMORY, RECALL, RECOGNITION, RELEARNING METHOD, REPRODUCTION, RETENTION, PRIMARY ABILITIES, DECEPTION, REMEMBERING, SERIAL MEMORY SEARCH, TWO-STEP MEMORY THEORY, VON RESTORFF EFFECT.

memory afterimage   A clear and strikingly intense memory of an experience shortly after it has occurred, for example, after hearing the closing notes of Beethoven's Ninth Symphony, it may be possible to "hear" them again distinctly and vividly in memory. See MEMORY IMAGE.

memory aids   See MNEMONIC DEVICE.

memory apparatus   A device for presenting successively at a desired rate a series of stimuli to be memorized. See MEMORY DRUM for an example of such an apparatus.

memory beliefs   A memory about an event that the person doubts happened. Seen often in attempts to search for early memories. See EARLY RECOLLECTIONS.

memory color   Any object's color as modified in memory. Phrase emphasizes the fact that the quality of remembered color often differs substantially from the actual hue.

memory consolidation   A process of changing short-term memory into long-term memory. Psychologically, the most common means of promoting consolidation is by rehearsal, although mnemonic strategies are more powerful. At the neural level, consolidation is a prolonged process not fully understood, although the hippocampus is the crucial brain structure involved. See HIPPOCAMPUS, MNEMONIC DEVICE.

memory cramp   The constant mental recurrence of certain melodies or lines of poetry or similar usually irrelevant material. Sometimes memory cramps persist for days.

memory curve   A graphic representation of the relative amounts of memorized material that can be recalled, or that are forgotten, after various intervals of time. Also known as retention curve. See EBBINGHAUS CURVE OF EXTINCTION for an illustration of such a curve.

memory defect   An impairment of the ability to recall, usually due to the effect of an organic condition on brain functioning, as in stroke or senile brain disease, as well as operations such as arterial bypasses, when the patient is on a heart-lung machine. See MEMORY DISTORTION.

memory disorders   General phrase for both organic and psychogenic disorders of memory, including amnesia, long-term and short-term memory defects, and pseudoreminiscence. A memory disorder may be partial or total, mild or severe, permanent or transitory, anterograde or retrograde. See AMNESIA, GLOBAL AMNESIA.

memory distortion   Inaccurate or illusory recall or recognition. See CONFABULATION, DÉJÀ VÉCU, DÉJÀ VU, DÉJÀ RACONTÉ, JAMAIS VU, PARAMNESIA, RETROSPECTIVE FALSIFICATION.

memory drum   (G. E. Müller & F. Schumann) A rotating drum designed to expose, one unit at a time and for a controlled interval, what is to be memorized. It is particularly suited to the methods of paired-associate learning and serial anticipation. The device has been replaced by computers. See GERBRAND'S MEMORY DRUM.

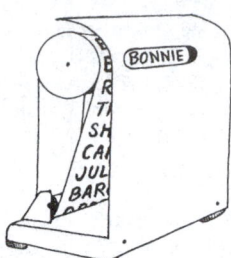

memory drum

memory falsification A symptom of Korsakoff's psychosis in which the patient fills in memory gaps with detailed fabrications. Similar to confabulation.

Memory-for-Designs Test (MFD) (F. K. Graham & B. S. Kendall) A perceptual-motor task used for assessing brain damage in which 15 geometric figures are presented for five seconds each, then removed and drawn from memory.

memory illusion (H. L. Roediger) Describing another person's experiences as a personal one, often believing implicitly that the event was experienced and "recalling" the details quite accurately. Includes verbal overshadowing (the effect of a verbal label), reality monitoring (separating memories of perceived events from those of imagined ones), misattributions of memory, and remembering more than is seen.

memory image A mental reconstruction of an object or event with an awareness that it originated in the past. See MEMORY AFTERIMAGE.

memory impairment See MEMORY DEFECT.

memory loss Not being able to recall events that occurred at some time prior. Normal memory loss occurs for events in the first several years of life, and for many of the vast number of things that a person has experienced throughout life. Also, abnormal memory loss may result from various traumatic events, psychological and physiological, and may be general or for specific incidents. See ANTEROGRADE AMNESIA, MEMORY DEFECT, MEMORY STORAGE, RETROGRADE AMNESIA.

memory-operating characteristic curve (MOCC) A process for analyzing data from memory experiments using a receiver-operating characteristic curve that indicates hits and misses.

memory retention See CONSERVATION.

memory self-efficacy (A. Bandura) A set of beliefs of personal capacity to use memory capably in various situations.

memory span The number of items that can be recalled immediately after one presentation. Usually, the items consist of letters, words, numbers, or syllables that the participant must reproduce in order. The distinction may be drawn between visual memory span and auditory memory span depending on the nature of the presentation. See IMMEDIATE MEMORY, SHORT-TERM MEMORY.

memory span test (J. Jacobs) A task to determine the maximal number of related or unrelated elements that a participant can reproduce exactly after (usually) a single presentation.

memory storage Retention of memories in the organism. Explanations of this process include reverberations of loops of neurons; growth of new nerve endings grouped in "synaptic knobs"; the recording of messages similar to the operation of a digital computer; encoding of information in complex molecules, such as ribonucleic acid (RNA); and number and type of neural connections where the memory is not "in a location" but "is" the connection network widely distributed throughout the brain and nervous system.

memory system One of various learnable techniques used to improve memory; for example, when trying to associate faces with names, using mental imagery to make both face and name more vivid or meaningfully related. See MNEMONIC DEVICE.

memory trace (K. Koffka & W. Köhler) In Gestalt psychology, the remnant of a memory that remains in the brain as a result of any given former experience. A network of traces may be consolidated into a "trace system." Sometimes known as engram.

memory transfer (J. V. McConnell) The transfer of acquired information from one individual to another, presumably via ribonucleic acid (RNA). While planaria (flatworm) research using the Pavlovian learned contraction response to light CS is tenuous due to subjectivity in detecting the response, studies with planaria in a Y-maze provide reasonably clear, albeit controversial evidence that the cannibal planarian "remembers" what the trained planarian learned. Attempts to transfer brain RNA extractions between mice and gerbils via brain injection have failed. (Unlike flatworms, the digestive system of mammals destroys RNA.)

menacme The period in a woman's life between puberty and menopause.

ménage à trois (household of three—French) 1. A domestic relationship, often sexual, of three persons, frequently two women and a man. See CISCISBEISM. 2. A three-person sexual encounter, usually including both sexes.

menarche A female's first menstruation, usually occurring between the 11th and 17th year, marking the onset of puberty.

mendacity Pathological lying.

Mendelian laws of inheritance Principles of genetics as developed around 1865 by Gregor Mendel. The first law, the principle of independent segregation, states that recessive traits are neither modified nor lost in future generations since both dominant and recessive genes are independently transmitted during the formation of sex cells. The second law, the principle of independent assortment, states that there is no tendency for genes of one parent to stay together in future offspring. As a result, the average distribution of two traits in the F2 generation, the grandchildren of the original mating, will show a ratio of 9:3:3:1, with 9 of 16 grandchildren expressing the dominant genes of both traits, 3 expressing one dominant and one recessive gene for each of the traits, and one expressing only the recessive traits. Not all genes express only a dominant or recessive trait, as can be demonstrated in human skin colors in which the genes are expressed as a trait intermediate between the dominant and the recessive. The third, the law of genetic dominance, states that some genes, when matched with other genes, will be subordinate to the them. See HEREDITY, PRINCIPLE OF INDEPENDENT ASSORTMENT, PRINCIPLE OF INDEPENDENT SEGREGATION, GENETIC DOMINANCE.

Mendelian ratio The varying amounts in which dominant and recessive heredity traits are likely to occur in the offspring of a specific type of mating. See MENDELIAN LAWS OF INHERITANCE.

Mendelism (G. Mendel) A doctrine of genetic principles of heredity as established in the 19th century. See DOMINANT INHERITANCE, LAW OF INDEPENDENT SEGREGATION, LAW OF INDEPENDENT ASSORTMENT, MENDELIAN LAWS OF INHERITANCE, MENDELIAN RATIO.

menerik A culture-specific syndrome, mainly among Eskimos of both sexes, manifested in paroxysms of wild screaming and dancing, often culminating in epileptiform seizures.

meninges Three layers of membranes that provide a protective cover for the surfaces of the brain and spinal cord. They consist of a tough outer layer, the dura mater, the arachnoid tissues that also serve as a reservoir of cerebrospinal fluid, and a thin pia-mater layer that fits over the various contours and fissures of the cerebral cortex. The meninges vary somewhat in structure from the cortical areas to the end of the spinal cord. Singular is meninx.

meninx Singular of meninges.

menopausal depression A state of despondency occurring during the feminine climacteric, or menopause, particularly among women who have had a prior tendency toward depression or feelings of inadequacy and dissatisfaction with life or come from a culture which places great emphasis on the role of woman as mother. See INVOLUTIONAL PSYCHOTIC REACTION, MIDLIFE CRISIS.

menopause A period during which menstruation ceases; the end of the reproductive cycle in women. See CHANGE OF LIFE, CLIMACTERIC.

menotaxis The involuntary movement of an organism either to or from some stimulus at an angle rather than the usual direct line of movement. See TAXIS, TROPISM.

Mensa An organization of individuals who, by Mensa's intelligence tests, are in the top 2% of the adult population with intelligence quotients (IQs) of about 130 or above.

menses **menstruation**

Men's Liberation Movement A reaction to the Women's Liberation Movement of the 1960s in which some men in the United States and Britain attempted by consciousness-raising techniques and other means to reduce the harm done to them by the existing sex roles. See MASCULINE PROTEST.

men's movements Political or social movements started in the United States around 1970, sometimes inspired by and in support of feminism, sometimes in opposition to it. One catalyst was M. Fasteau's 1975 *The Male Machine*. Goals are usually similar to some feminist movements, but generally do not hold that men oppress women. Also known as masculist movement, men's rights movement. Fathers' movements promote reform of divorce and support-payments and access to and custody of children.

mens rea (guilty mind, intent to harm—Latin) In forensic psychology, a phrase used to contend that a person had a guilty intention or motivation when the crime was committed, as opposed to being insane at the time.

men's rights movement **men's movements**

menstrual age The age of the fetus calculated from the beginning of the mother's last menstruation.

menstrual cycle A period of time, lasting approximately 5–7 days, occurring usually every 28 days in a typical human female, during which the endometrial lining of the uterus proliferates and sheds. It is repeated continuously, except for periods of pregnancy, between puberty and menopause. Ovulation normally occurs about midway in the menstrual cycle. The mean length of cycle in infrahuman primates varies from 20 to 30 days, with large individual differences. The four-and-a-half to five-and-a-half day cycle of the albino laboratory rat changes the female activity to such a pronounced degree that most experiments are conducted only with males.

menstrual disorders Psychophysiologic conditions associated with menstruation, including premenstrual tension, dysmenorrhea (painful menstruation), menorrhagia (profuse and persistent bleeding), and oligomenorrhea (scanty menstruation). Whereas these conditions may have organic causes, they may also be due to emotional factors. See PREMENSTRUAL DISORDERS, PREMENSTRUAL SYNDROME.

menstrual synchrony The gradual harmonizing of menstrual cycles in women living close together.

menstrual taboo Culture-specific customs or rituals regarding menstruating women, in which generally they are not to engage in food-preparation or other work, or family duties and coitus.

menstruation The cyclic discharge of blood and uterine cells that occurs in females of child-bearing age. Also known as catamenia, menses, monthly period, period. See MENSTRUAL CYCLE.

mental aberration 1. Mental unsoundness, as evidenced by abnormal behavior. 2. A pathological deviation from normal thinking. 3. General phrase for a mental or emotional disorder of any kind; it is also applied to individual symptoms, for example, a delusion of persecution. See MENTAL ILLNESS.

mental abilities Capacities as measured by tests in areas such as spatial visualization, perceptual speed, number facility, verbal comprehension, word fluency, memory, or inductive reasoning. See ABSTRACT INTELLIGENCE, BASIC INTELLIGENCE FACTORS.

mental age (MA or M.A.) (A. Binet) Performance on an intelligence test reported as a number of years and months, such as VI-3 (six years and three months). With Binet's second test (1908), it was equivalent to saying "overall, this individual performed intellectually the same way as the typical child of six years and 3 months." See INTELLIGENCE, INTELLIGENCE TESTS.

mental alienation Legal phrase for mental disorders that estrange the personality and character to such a degree as to constitute legal insanity. See PSYCHOSIS.

mental apparatus **psychic apparatus**

mental asthenia A disorder of subjective loss of mental strength, physical strength, or both; lack of energy or motivation for mental tasks, often expressed as concentration difficulty. See CHRONIC FATIGUE SYNDROME, PERSONALITY DISORDERS.

mental asymmetry An unbalanced relationship between different mental processes, seen in a person performing considerably better on a vocabulary test than on a test of immediate recall.

mental ataxia intrapsychic ataxia

mental balance Integration of mental processes, indicated by absence of eccentricity or of maladjustments of behavior.

mental blind spot A persistent and continuous lack of insight or awareness about self-thinking or motives with refusal to admit them upon being questioned. May be partly unconscious. Sometimes known as a blind spot. See DENIAL.

mental capacity Potential mental ability, however determined.

mental chemistry (J. S. Mill) 1. An assumption that simple associations can combine to create an idea in the same sense that hydrogen and oxygen can create water. 2. The process that enables a synthesis of ideas or various sensations, such as disparate sounds to be organized into meaningful units. See CREATIVE SYNTHESIS.

mental chronometry The systematic investigation of the duration of mental processes and phenomena.

mental claudication Temporary interruption of blood flow to a portion of the brain that results in brief episodes of mental confusion. In this context, it means not thinking clearly.

mental coaching (R. Zimmerman) Techniques intended to sharpen cognitive abilities such as memory, learning, and reasoning.

mental defective Old phrase for a person with intellectual subnormality. At one time an intelligence quotient (IQ) of 70 or below so established this diagnosis, with the range 70–80 labeled "borderline deficiency." In contrast, "feebleminded" often included IQs as high as 80. More recently, this appellation is predicated on Alfred Binet's original suggestions and is based on a medical examination and achievement testing (possibly including social development) in addition to intelligence test performance. See MENTAL DEFICIENCY.

mental deficiency (MD) 1. Formerly known as mental retardation. 2. Lack of some mental functions present in an otherwise normal individual. Also known as feeblemindedness, mental defectiveness.

mental derangement See MENTAL ABERRATION.

mental development Changes that occur in cognitive functioning over time with increasing capacity for thinking, planning, reflecting, and creativity occurring at a relatively steady rate from birth to about the age of 12 to 15, and then moving slowly upward to about age 25 when it appears to level off. See LEARNING CURVE for a graphic picture of the general development of intelligence up to about age 25.

mental diplopia Having illusions, hallucinations, or both but realizing at the same time that they are not real but abnormal manifestations.

mental discipline 1. Structured approach to study and research. 2. An idea that specific areas or fields of study strengthen mental ability in such a way as to generalize or transfer to all other subjects (topics) and intellectual pursuits and to enhance learning in those areas. The study of mathematics, Greek, Latin, and classic literature were once thought to promote such improvement. Disproved by studies of transfer of learning.

mental disease See MENTAL DISORDER.

mental disorder General phrase for a serious mental problem of an organic or psychogenic nature. Phrase is preferred to "mental disease" or "mental illness," since the terms disease and illness are primarily associated with organic conditions and many mental disorders can be purely psychogenic as well as mixed psychogenic and physiological in origin. Also known as mental disease/illness, psychiatric disorder/illness. See MALADAPTIVE BEHAVIOR.

Mental Disorders of the International Classification of Diseases (ICD-9) A classification system of mental and physical diseases adopted by the World Health Organization in 1978 for use in gathering health statistics worldwide. The *Diagnostic and Statistical Manual of Mental Disorders, Fourth Edition* (DSM-IV) is a revision and expansion of ICD-9 by the American Psychiatric Association. Mental disorders are gathered in four groups.

MENTAL DISORDERS (290–319)

Organic psychotic conditions (290–294)

290 Senile and presenile organic psychotic conditions

291 Alcoholic psychoses

292 Drug psychoses

293 Transient organic psychotic conditions

294 Other organic psychotic conditions (chronic)

Other psychoses (295–299)

295 Schizophrenic psychoses

296 Affective psychoses

297 Paranoid states

298 Other nonorganic psychoses

299 Psychoses with origin specific to childhood

Neurotic disorders, Personality disorders, and other Nonpsychotic mental disorders (300–316)

300 Neurotic disorders

301 Personality disorders

302 Sexual deviations and disorders

303 Alcohol dependence syndrome

304 Drug dependence

305 Nondependent abuse of drugs

306 Physiological malfunction arising from mental factors

307 Special symptoms or syndromes not elsewhere classified

308 Acute reaction to stress

309 Adjustment reaction

310 Specific nonpsychotic mental disorders following organic brain damage

311 Depressive disorder not elsewhere classified

312 Disturbance of conduct not elsewhere classified

313 Disturbance of emotions specific to childhood and adolescence

314 Hyperkinetic syndrome of childhood

315 Specific delays in development

316 Psychic factors associated with diseases classified elsewhere

Mental retardation (317–319)
317 Mild mental retardation
318 Other specified mental retardation
319 Unspecified mental retardation

mental dumbness   Aphasia characterized by inability to utter appropriate words or sentences.

mental dynamism   See DYNAMISM.

mental eclipse   Rare phrase for a delusion that someone else is stealing a person's ideas.

mental effort   Intensification of mental activity to overcome resistance to the flow of ideas or thoughts.

mental energy   **psychic energy**

mental evolution   An increase in the complexity of brain structure and function that follows the phylogenetic pattern of evolution.

mental examination   A comprehensive evaluation of a person's behavior, attitudes, and intellectual abilities, usually for the purpose of establishing or ruling out pathology or for deciding legal responsibility or competence. Also known as psychological examination.

mental faculties   Certain powers supposed to be inherent in the mind at all times, whether active or not, such as memory. See FACULTY PSYCHOLOGY.

mental-faculty theory   A point of view that formal education and study helps to develop mental faculties so that students become better able to solve all sorts of problems. See DOCTRINE OF FORMAL DISCIPLINE, FORMAL-DISCIPLINE THEORY.

mental fog   See CLOUDING OF CONSCIOUSNESS.

mental functions   Mental processes or activities such as thinking, sensing, and reasoning.

mental growth   Gradual increment in a mental function with increasing age, usually applied to intelligence.

mental healing   Diseases and disorders cured by suggestion, usually supported by the faith of the patient in their cure. Also known as faith healing.

mental health   A state of mind characterized by emotional well-being, relative freedom from anxiety and disabling symptoms, and a capacity to establish constructive relationships and cope with the ordinary demands and stresses of life. See LIFE TASKS.

mental-health clinic   An out-patient facility for the diagnosis and treatment of mental disorders. It is usually operated by a mental hospital but is sometimes free-standing. Usually operated by a group of psychiatrists, clinical psychologists, psychiatric social workers as well as other professionals, mental health workers of various kinds as well as support staffs, paid and volunteers. Also known as community-mental health center (CMHC), mental-hygiene clinic.

mental-health worker   A staff member who assists core mental-health professionals in handling the social and psychological problems of patients. Usually has special training either in supportive therapy or as an expediter. See ADVOCATE.

mental history   The background, history, and past factors concerning a person's mental health. This information can be taken by a single person or by a number of people. A form may be used or the interviews can be free-floating. Questions usually cover a past mental history of the client and family members. Medical history, employment history, and educational histories are gathered separately.

mental hospital   A public or private institution providing a wide range of diagnostic techniques and treatment modalities to disturbed individuals on an in-patient basis. Treatment modalities may include psychotherapy (group and individual), pharmacotherapy, occupational therapy, sociotherapy, and recreational therapy. Also known as psychiatric hospital. See MILIEU THERAPY, PRIVATE MENTAL HOSPITAL, PUBLIC MENTAL HOSPITAL, THERAPEUTIC COMMUNITY.

mental housecleaning hypothesis   (F. Crick & G. Murchison) A postulate that dreams clean the mind of what is useless, bizarre, or redundant. See DREAM FUNCTION.

mental hygiene   A general approach aimed at maintaining mental health and preventing mental disorder through such means as educational programs, promotion of a stable emotional and family life, prophylactic and early treatment services, and public-health measures.

mental-hygiene clinic   Old phrase that has been replaced by community-mental health center and mental-health clinic.

mental illness (MI)   **mental disorder**

mental illness and family causation   (R. D. Laing) The concept that mental illness may be an expression of individuals being in a dysfunctional family culture.

mental imagery   Phenomenological productions such as pictures, fantasies, hallucinations, or representations of objects, people, or events.

mental image (types)   (I. Richardson) Four types of images, in terms of clarity and completeness of detail: afterimages, eidetic images, memory images, and imagination images.

mental institution   A treatment-oriented facility in which persons who are mentally challenged or disturbed are provided supervised general care and therapy by trained professionals and an auxiliary staff. Patients are generally those unable to function independently as out-patients even if supported by psychoactive drugs. A mental institution is required by most but not all jurisdictions to be licensed by a government agency. Also known as psychiatric hospital.

mentalism   1. A doctrine positing that mental phenomena cannot be reduced to physical or physiological phenomena. See HOLISM, MONISM. 2. See ANIMISM. 3. A type of illusionist's act that simulates extrasensory perception (ESP). 4. Term often used to denigrate findings that cannot be reproducted. See STRUCTURALISM.

mentalist position   (G. Berkeley) A philosophical point of view that reality does not exist but is a function of perception.

mentality   Mental capacity or the use of the mind. Denoting intellectual powers, as in rating mental ability as superior, inferior, or average. See MIND, PHENOMENOLOGY.

mentally handicapped   Old phrase for a condition of being unable to function independently in the community because of arrested or incomplete development of the mind or any severe and disabling mental disorder. See CHALLENGED, DEFECTIVE CHILDREN, PERSON WITH A DISABILITY.

mentally retarded persons' rights   See RIGHTS OF THE MENTALLY RETARDED.

mental levels   1. According to Carl Jung, mental activity may be divided into the three categories of consciousness, personal unconscious, and collective unconscious. 2. (S. Freud) Refers to the psychoanalytic division of the mind into the conscious, preconscious, and unconscious. 3. In relation to intelligence, the use of such dated words as genius, superior, average, borderline, retarded, or moron, to describe various levels of intelligence either by means of conversion from intelligence quotients (IQs) or from estimated levels of mental ability.

mental masochism   Seeking to be punished emotionally and mentally rather than physically.

mental maturity   Achievement of an adult level of intelligence and behavior.

mental measurement/testing   The use of quantitative scales and methods in measuring psychological processes and abilities. See PSYCHOMETRY.

mental mechanics   A doctrine of James Mill that a complex idea is no more than its simpler components that always maintain their individual identity.

mental mechanism   General phrase applied to a large number of psychological functions that help humans meet environmental demands, protect the ego, satisfy inner needs, and alleviate internal and external conflicts and tensions. Among them are (a) language, which enables the retention and expression of thoughts; (b) memory, which stores the information needed in solving problems; (c) perception, which involves recognition and interpretation of events; and (d) thought processes involved in overcoming difficulties. In addition, various defense mechanisms such as rationalization and compensation help to ward off anxiety and protect the loss of self-esteem. Also known as mechanism. See DEFENSE MECHANISMS, MACHINE THEORY, MECHANISM, SAFEGUARDING TENDENCIES, VITALISM.

mental metabolism   The rate of energy exchange between an individual and the environment as a result of mental processes. Certain individuals, such as manics, are thought to have a higher rate of mental metabolism than others.

mental-patient organization   (J. Bierer) A club or other organization established to provide social and recreational activities to former mental patients, to help them maintain their morale, and to readjust to community life. Many mental-patient organizations are independent, but others are affiliated with clinics, hospitals, and mental-health associations or centers.

mental philosophy   **rational psychology**

mental process   A psychological process; any activity of an organism that uses the mind.

mental razzle   (D. Katz) Slang for irrelevant elements that demand attention but make problem-solving difficult.

mental rehabilitation   The process of restoring mentally challenged patients to acceptable participation in the community. In a hospital organized as a therapeutic community, this process consists of activity programs, patient government, and discussion groups aimed at preparing them for a constructive, independent life, often including stay in a transitional home. After discharge, readjustment to the community is achieved with the aid of vocational counselors, employment specialists, and social workers. See ADJUSTMENT METHOD, HALFWAY HOUSE, LATER LIFE ADJUSTMENT.

mental retardation (MR)   Vague and obsolete phrase for any of various degrees of low intellectual levels, from mild to profound. Levels of impairment include: MILD, MODERATE, PROFOUND, SEVERE, UNSPECIFIED.

mental scale   A series of standard values of mental development or mental age, based upon the person's ability to answer or solve a set of graded tests. See INTELLIGENCE QUOTIENT (IQ), INTELLIGENCE TESTS, MENTAL AGE.

Mental Scale   The first part of the <u>Bayley Scales of Infant Development</u>, which samples such functions as perception, memory, and vocalization. See BAYLEY SCALES OF INFANT DEVELOPMENT, INFANT BEHAVIOR RECORD, MOTOR SCALE.

mental scotoma   Nontechnical phrase for lack of insight or stubborn denial of reality.

mental set   Readiness to make a particular response or to perform a psychological function, such as solving a problem in a particular way, usually determined by instructions. See SET.

mental size   The amount of mental space hypothetically taken up by an image.

mental status   The psychological state of a patient as revealed by a mental examination that covers such factors as appearance, mood, speech, cooperativeness, facial expression, motor activity, emotional state, awareness, orientation, memory, general intelligence level, and judgment. See PSYCHIATRIC EXAMINATION, PSYCHOLOGICAL EXAMINATION.

Mental Status Examination (MSE)   1. In psychology, structured inquiry into a person's mental health. May be obtained through the use of interviews, examination of documents, accounts by people who know the person. Also, the results of objective tests of knowledge (such as intelligence tests) and projective personality tests. 2. In psychiatry, generally a more subjective estimation of a person's mood, appearance, behavior, memory, and ability to communicate, as well as knowledge of present date, location, and persons present. 3. In jurisprudence, inquiry into the person's condition relevant to a court case, such as legal insanity at the time of an offense and likelihood of reoffending.

Mental Status Examination Report (MSER)   A component part of the Multi-State Information System consisting of an optical scan form made up of structured, multiple-choice items covering the usual mental-status categories. Also included is a Periodic Evaluation Record (PER) administered at frequent intervals to provide a running narrative of the patient's progress.

mental structure   A stable organization of the mind or the personality, composed of complex but interrelated traits. Also known as psychological structure.

mental subnormality   A diagnosis of below-normal intelligence, usually considered to be intelligence quotients (IQs) below 90, or about the bottom quartile of the population. Can result from any of a variety of causes, including environmental effects and possibly improper testing. See BITCH TEST, INTELLIGENCE TESTING.

mental synthesis   (J. S. Mill) Compounding elementary mental phenomena in which the product manifests characteristics not found in the elementary constituents, as seen in the color wheel.

mental telepathy   Alleged ability of people to communicate without sensory contact. See EXTRASENSORY PERCEPTION.

mental tension   The level of psychic activity in a person as a relative state of emotional charge. The manic phase of manic-depressive (bipolar) psychosis represents a state of high mental tension.

mental test   1. Any examination that measures one or more psychological traits. 2. See INTELLIGENCE TEST.

mental testing   See MENTAL MEASUREMENT.

mental vs psychological   "Mental" refers to behaviors of the mind that can be categorized as cognitive (thinking), affective (emotions), and conative (willing). "Psychological" refers to all behaviors except maintenance behaviors (for example, the heart operating while the person sleeps). Consequently, "psychological" refers to covert behaviors (mental), such as planning, feeling, or wanting, and to overt behaviors (visible actions), such as reading or a reflex of the eye. Some behavioral psychologists divide "psychological" into affect (emotions), behavior (actions), and cognitions (thoughts).

mental workload   An estimate of how much thinking is involved in a particular operation. Some routine jobs such as running an elevator call for practically no thinking most of the time. Some jobs, such as being an executive calls for constant thinking, planning, deciding, remembering.

mentastics   See TRAGER MENTASTICS.

mentation   Any mental activity (for example, thinking, planning, recalling, day-dreaming).

menticide   The deliberate and systematic effort to brainwash or otherwise alter allegiances, beliefs, standards, or values in favor of a different set of attitudes and ideas. See BRAINWASHING.

mentoring   The advising of novices by those with experience.

mercantile paraphilias   Forms of sexual behavior, usually considered abnormal, characterized by a saintly person assuming the role of a sinner such as a whore. Examples include narratophilia, troilism.

mercy killing   See EUTHANASIA.

mere exposure   The formation of an attitude (generally positive) to a concept or object through repeated exposure to it.

mere-exposure effect   A tendency to have positive feelings for what is familiar. Helps explain why people vote for familiar politicians and buy familiar products.

mere presence theory (of arousal)   A point of view that the mere presence of another person is enough to trigger an arousal response.

merergasia   Adolf Meyer's term for a diagnosis of partial personality disorganization, as in cases of psychoneurosis in which the patient has ability, sometimes impaired, to work or function.

merger state   A feeling of fusion with an idealized object, with reality as a whole, or with other people. Sometimes sought through gang memberships or with drug users as a means of overcoming feelings of alienation and emptiness. See BELONGINGNESS, COSMIC CONSCIOUSNESS, FUSION STATE.

meridian   In acupuncture, a purported pathway of a "force" or electromagnetic energy flow in the body.

merit   An ethical concept denoting a positive evaluation or a belief in the worth of some act of an individual or of general conduct.

meritocracy   A society or social group in which status depends on individual merit rather than on family background, inherited money, or other incidental elements.

merit ranking   Arrangement of people, data, or objects in order of size, value, or other characteristics. Also known as order of merit.

merit rating   Evaluation of an individual's performance at a particular task usually based on some arbitrary scale, sometimes based on objective data such as production, and often based either entirely or partially on subjective impressions.

Merkel's corpuscles   (F. S. Merkel) In the skin, tiny knobs at the ends of nerve fibers. See MERKEL'S TACTILE DISK.

Merkel's law   A theory that equal differences between stimuli at above-threshold strength have corresponding equal differences in sensation. Named after German psychologist Julius Merkel.

Merkel's tactile disk   (F.S. Merkel) A sensory-nerve ending in the mucous membranes of the mouth and tongue. Also known as Grandy-Merkel corpuscles, Merkel's corpuscles.

merogony   Reproduction in which an enucleated egg of one species is fertilized with the sperm of another, producing an embryo with the characteristics of the species from which the sperm was obtained. It is generally a research procedure used to demonstrate the dominance of the genetic contents of the nucleus in determining the traits of the embryo.

Merrill-Palmer Scale of Mental Tests   (R. Stutsman) A series of 93 verbal and performance items designed to measure the intellectual ability of children between 24 and 63 months of age. The scale was developed by Rachel Stutsman at the Merrill-Palmer School. See INTELLIGENCE TESTS.

merycism   (chewing the cud—Greek) The voluntary regurgitation of food from the stomach to the mouth, where it is masticated and swallowed a second time. Occassionally found in persons with severe retardation, although some think the delayed development may be due, in part at least, to the disorder. See RUMINATION DISORDER OF INFANCY.

mesaticephaly   A skull that approximates statistical normal. A cephalic index of 76 to 81 is considered mesaticephalic. Also known as mesaticephalism, mesocephaly.

mescal buttons   See MESCAL(INE), PEYOTE.

mescal(ine)   One of the earliest popular hallucinogens, a crystalline alkaloid substance obtained from the Mexican peyote cactus, *Lophophora williamsii*. Eating a few dried slices (in the shape of disks) of the "mescal buttons" usually causes nausea and vomiting, followed by a psychedelic experience. See PEYOTE, PSYCHEDELIC.

mesencephalic nucleus   One of the three nuclei of the trigeminal nerve. Extends through the pons into the lower part of the mesencephalon. Its fibers innervate the muscles and joints of the head.

mesencephalic tegmentum   A region of the midbrain behind the substantia nigra with neural connections between the cerebrum, spinal cord, thalamus, and subthalamus, forming an indirect corticospinal tract. Lesions in the tegmentum affect the eating habits of laboratory animals, producing in some cases participants that feed voraciously and indiscriminately. See APPETITE, APPESTAT, VENTRAL MEDIAL NUCLEUS OF THE HYPOTHALAMUS.

mesencephalon   (F. Chaussier) A relatively small mass of neural tissue lying between the forebrain and hindbrain. Contains the inferior and superior colliculi, a portion of the reticular formation, sensory tracts, and motor tracts and reflex centers. Also known as midbrain. See PROSENCEPHALON, RHOMBENCEPHALON.

Mesmeric crisis   A therapeutic reaction produced by Franz Anton Mesmer. One of his techniques was the "magnetic pass" in which he clasped the patient's knees between his own and repeatedly drew his hands down the patient's body until the patient lost consciousness and experienced an apparent seizure which was supposed to eliminate or alleviate "hysterical" symptoms. Also known as magnetic crisis. See GRAND CRISIS, MESMERISM.

Mesmerism   (F. A. Mesmer) Obsolete name for hypnotism. Originally a doctrine that attempted to reconcile old ideas of astrology with the then new discoveries in electricity and magnetism. See MESMERIC CRISIS.

mesmerize   Obsolete term for hypnotize. See MESMERISM.

mesocephalic   Describing a relatively normal-size head. Also known as mesaticephalic. See CEPHALIC INDEX.

mesoderm   (K. E. von Baer, R. Remak) The middle of the three primary germ layers of the developing embryo. Mesodermal cells evolve into cartilage and bone, connective tissue, muscle, blood vessels and blood cells, the lymphatic system, notochord, gonads, kidneys, and pleural membranes. See EMBRYONIC PERIOD.

mesokurtic   Describing a curve of distribution that tends to have a normal bell-shaped curve appearance. See LEPTOKURTIC, PLATYKURTIC. See KURTOSIS for an illustration of three classes of distributions.

mesomorph   See MESOMORPHIC (BODY) TYPE.

mesomorphic (body) type   A constitutional type, or somatotype, characterized by a muscular, athletic physique that William Sheldon found to be correlated with a "somatotonic" temperament (tendencies toward energetic activity, assertiveness, physical courage, and love of power). Such a person is a mesomorph. See SHELDON'S CONSTITUTION TYPES.

meso-ontomorph   A constitutional body type characterized by a broad, stocky body, roughly equivalent to William Sheldon's mesomorph.

mesopic luminosity   The brightness of a color of a designated wavelength at an intermediate level of adaptation of both rods and cones.

mesopic vision   Ability to see during daylight and twilight, representing a joint function of rods and cones.

mesoskelic   (L. P. Manouvrier) A constitutional body type identified as intermediate between brachyskelic and macroskelic and roughly equivalent to Ernst Kretschmer's athletic type and William Sheldon's mesomorphic (body) type.

mesosomatic   (H. J. Eysenck) Denoting a person whose body build is within one standard deviation of the mean after scores for height and chest measurements have been multiplied. See BODY-BUILD INDEX, EYSENCK TYPOLOGY.

mesosystem   (U. Bronfenbrenner) What constitutes society for an individual in terms of social interaction.

message   1. Any symbolic or other communication between individuals or groups. 2. Output of a transmitter that is fed into a receiver. 3. Content and ideas that are communicated; a variable in the study of attitude change.

Messalina complex/syndrome   Archaic name for nymphomania, from the purportedly promiscuous Valeria Messalina, wife of Roman Emperor Claudius.

messenger RNA (mRNA)   Ribonucleic acid (RNA) molecules that carry genetic-code instructions from the inherited gene to the subcellular mechanisms responsible for building protein or other molecules from chemicals present in the cell's cytoplasm.

messianic   Possessing a crusading inspiration to effect some supposedly predestined ideal.

meta-analysis   (O. Jesperson) Integration of the findings of a number of research studies by means of statistical techniques focusing on the same research question leading to meaningful quantitative data. For instance, a hypothesis states there is a relationship between body structure and personality. Each of a dozen independent studies show a low positive correlation. Whereas none of the studies by themselves offer convincing evidence for the hypothesis, together they do. See COMBINED TESTS, RESEARCH METHODS.

metabolic and endocrinological disorders   Many forms of mental retardation or neurological deficits are due to inborn errors of metabolism. Endocrine disorders are due to abnormally high or low levels of pituitary, thyroid, adrenal, or sex hormones. See BEHAVIORAL ENDOCRINOLOGY.

metabolic anomaly   inborn error of metabolism

metabolic defect   Any deficiency in the structure or enzymatic function of protein molecules or in the transport of substances across cell membranes due to inborn errors or derangements caused by toxic agents or dietary excesses; for example, alcohol or cholesterol-rich foods. A metabolic defect may manifest its effects in the kidney functions as well as in the gastrointestinal system.

metabolic dysperception   (B. Kowalson) Phrase for schizophrenia suggested by Bella Kowalson to emphasize the variety of perceptual changes in patients with schizophrenia as well as the probable metabolic origin for these changes.

metabolic equivalent   A method of determining the amount of work a person is doing (metabolic energy cost—MET) at any time. Examples:

Activities	Mets per Minute
awake, lying down, resting	1
slow level walk	2

fast level walk	3
median speed bicycling	4
jogging	7
normal running	10
heavy exercises	up to 25

metabolic-nutritional model   A system of study of mental disorders in which the emphasis in on long-term assessments of influences of such factors as toxins and deprivations in populations.

metabolism   (S. Sanctorius) 1. The general building and destroying of cells that provides energy and continuity in organisms. 2. Biochemical processes by which chemical substances in the environment are ingested as sources of energy and structural materials. The breaking down of large complex molecules in the body is the catabolic phase of metabolism; the synthesis of new molecules in the body is anabolism. The human body can synthesize most substances required for normal functioning from basic molecules in a variety of common foods. See ANABOLISM, BASAL METABOLISM, CARBOHYDRATE METABOLISM, FAT METABOLISM, INBORN ERROR OF METABOLISM, MENTAL METABOLISM.

metabolite   The chemical product of the transformation or neutralization of a substance in the body; e.g., the metabolite for serotonin is a chemical abbreviated as 5HIAA. Some metabolites of certain medicines are medicinally active themselves. There may be more than one or two metabolites of a given chemical. Both endogenous and exogenous substances are metabolized, often by breaking down a chemical, or linking it with some other molecular components so that it can then be excreted in the bile (and from thence, the feces) or the urine. See METABOLISM.

metabotropic effect   A neurological event at a synapse in which neurotransmitters produce a prolonged, slow effect through metabolic instead of ionic reactions.

metacognition   Awareness, thought, or knowledge of own cognitive activity. See COGNITION.

metacognitive mediation   (L. Vygotsky) Acquisition of semiotic tools of self-regulation through the ideas of others; for example, a child learns to say "No" to the same activity that a parent has said "No" to. See COGNITIVE MEDIATION.

metacommunication   Auxiliary or covert messages, usually in the form of nonverbal subtle gestures, movements, and facial expressions that suggest how a communication should be understood.

metacontrast   A situation in which two stimuli are presented within a short time interval and the second stimulus affects the perception of the first.

metacriterion   Superordinate criterion used to evaluate the adequacy of epistemological theories, moral discourses, and social and ethical practices; for example, a metacriterion for evaluating the morality of a psychological practice is that its proponents articulate their values and key assumptions.

metaerg   (R. B. Cattell) An underlying motivational trait acquired through environmental rather than constitutional influences.

metaevaluation   The systematic evaluation of evaluation procedures including methodological rigor, utility, cost, relevance, scope, importance, credibility, and timeliness.

metagnomy   A concept that a person can obtain superior knowledge from superior spiritual beings. See PSYCHIC, RELIGIOUS DELUSIONS.

metalanguage   1. A language or set of symbols used to describe another language or set of symbols, such as English words in a French-English dictionary. 2. In a dictionary, the definitions of headwords. Also known as second-order language. See SOURCE LANGUAGE, TARGET LANGUAGE.

metalinguistics   The study of the practical use of language and its various forms in social groups. Also known as exolinguistics.

metallophobia   Morbid fear of metals or of metal objects.

metamemory   Self-memory for what is in a person's memory, including self-assessment or self-estimates of memory capacity or efficiency.

metamers   1. Phenomena that are similar to, but discernible from, other phenomena. 2. Refers to two colors that appear to be identical to the eye but actually have different physical spectrums.

metamorphopsia   A visual disorder in which objects appear to be distorted. In migraine and temporal-lobe epilepsy, it can be a symptom characterized by the illusion that the relative sizes of parts of objects are deformed. Also known as Alice in Wonderland effect. See MACROPSIA, MICROPSIA.

metamorphosis   Transformation; a change in form, structure, or function. See BEHAVIORAL METAMORPHOSIS, DELIRIUM OF METAMORPHOSIS.

metamorphosis sexualis paranoica   Rare phrase for a relatively common delusion in paranoid patients who believe their gender has been changed. See GENDER-IDENTITY DISORDER.

metamotivation   According to Abraham Maslow, growth tendencies that impel a person to develop self-actualization and transcendence in the hierarchy of the metaneeds. Also known as Being motivation, B motivation, growth motivation. See DEFICIENCY MOTIVATION, NEED-HIERARCHY THEORY.

metaneeds   According to Abraham Maslow, the highest level of needs that come into play primarily after the lower-level needs have been met. Metaneeds include the need for knowledge and various creative pursuits. In Maslow's view, inability to fulfill metaneeds results in metapathology. Also known as Being values, B-values. See NEED-HIERARCHY THEORY.

metanerg   (R. B. Cattell) Any environmentally developed structure from an ergic basis. See ERGIC.

metapathology   (A. Maslow) A state of frustration or discontent due to inability to satisfy higher level needs. See METANEEDS.

metapelet   Surrogate mother. Term for women who assume maternal responsibility for others' children in an Israeli kibbutz.

metaphase   The second stage (following prophase and preceding anaphase) of mitotic cell division characterized by the flow of nuclear material through the cytoplasm to a hypothetical line in the center, called the equatorial plane. There, the chromosomes form a line in pairs but begin to separate into matched sets of individual chromosomes about to be divided.

metaphor A figure of speech in which one object is likened to another by speaking of it as if it were that object. Metaphor is recognized as an important aspect of creative thought.

metaphor therapy (R. R. Kopp) A system of psychotherapy that focuses on the hidden meaning of language; for example, a person complains of being a "tunnel" for a spouse that is a "locomotive." The therapist changes the imagery from "tunnel" to "railroad switch," to enable the person to change self-perception and tactics in dealing with the marriage.

metaphoric language The use of metaphors to express feelings and experiences, such as "Straining at the leash," to indicate tension or pent-up energy, or a bow-and-arrow image to express a fear of "letting go." See METAPHOR, PRIMARY PROCESS.

metaphoric symbolism cryptophoric symbolism

metaphrenia A condition marked by libidinal withdrawal from the family or group while psychic energy is directed toward personal material gains.

metaphysics 1. A branch of philosophy which attempts to explain the nature of being and reality. 2. Disciplines, especially those of classical philosophy and religion, that pose questions some of which are empirically unsolvable, such as What is goodness, justice, beauty? Metaphysics includes such disciplines as cosmology, ontology, and epistemology.

metapsychics The study of physical or psychical phenomena apparently dependent upon (a) an undetermined intelligence, (b) unknown but intelligent forces, (c) unknown powers latent in the human mind, or (d) subconscious or unconscious processes. See OCCULT, PARAPSYCHOLOGY, PSYCHIC REALITY.

metapsychoanalysis Any variation of psychoanalysis that derives from Sigmund Freud's classic system, representing a historical but not necessarily a theoretical advance. See PSYCHOANALYTICALLY-ORIENTED.

metapsychological Indicating the fullest possible description of psychic processes.

metapsychological profile (A. Freud) The systematic classification of signs and symptoms of patients.

metapsychology 1. A speculative, theoretical approach to philosophical problems relating to human behavior (literally, "beyond psychology"), such as the relation between mind and body and the place of mind in the universe. 2. (S. Freud) Describing general theory, or statements at the highest level of abstraction. Freud's metapsychological formulations include the psychic apparatus (such as the id and ego) and the distribution of energy within it.

metathalamus The thalamic nuclei bodies associated with the senses of hearing and vision, respectively. It is located immediately below the posterior extremity of the thalamus.

metatheory 1. The science of theories. 2. A set of general rules governing the construction of a theory. 3. A theory about a theory.

metathetic In relation to changes in amount of stimulus and perception of the stimulus. Changes result in subjective differences in the quality of the sensation (for example, changes of wavelengths of light change the quality of the perception). See PROTHETIC.

metempirical Pertaining to phenomena that lie beyond empirical investigation and are considered speculatively. See METAPSYCHOLOGY.

metempsychosis A belief in transmigration of a soul to another human or animal body following death, often carrying its memories with it. The concept is found in some Hindu religions.

metencephalon A portion of the brain that includes the pons and cerebellum. With the medulla oblongata, the metencephalon forms the hindbrain. In the 1870s, Thomas Huxley suggested the rhombencephalon be descriptively divided into metencephalon and myelencephalon. Also known as epencephalon.

meteorophobia Morbid fear of meteors.

meter (m) The basic SI (metric system) unit of length, equal to 39.37 inches. The square meter (m^2) is the SI unit of area; the cubic meter (m^3) is the SI unit of volume. See INTERNATIONAL SYSTEM OF UNITS, METRIC SYSTEM.

meterology The science of measurement.

meth Slang for methamphetamine, used widely as a drug of abuse.

methadone (hydrochloride) (M. Nyswander & V. Dole) A relatively long-acting, orally-taken opioid used primarily as an alternative, legally-prescribed drug in the treatment of chronic heroin addiction. See SYNTHETIC NARCOTICS.

methadone clinic A drug abuse treatment center where methadone maintenance therapy is provided for chronic heroin addiction. These clinics also may provide medical treatment for addiction complications, legal aid, psychotherapy, family counseling, and welfare assistance, depending upon local funding and laws.

methadone maintenance Treatment for chronic addiction, mainly to heroin, in which, instead of trying to foster abstinence, patients are given a prescribed, free dose of an opiate that can be taken orally (thus having fewer problems, such as local or cardiac infections from dirty needles, AIDS, or overdose). Such treatment also prevents the need to engage in crime to get the money to obtain illicit drugs. See MAINTENANCE DRUGS.

methamphetamine (hydrochloride) Generic name for a sympathomimetic drug marketed in the 1960s under the trade name Desoxyn, used as an appetite suppressant. It soon became a prevalent street drug because it can be prepared in a purified crystalline form called "ice" or "crystal," inhaled, and it gives similar effects to cocaine with greater duration, and correspondingly similar problems of psychosis, overdose, crime, etc. Methamphetamine produces increased alertness, an energy burst, loss of appetite, but in overdose, cardiovascular collapse, extreme anxiety, nausea, and respiratory distress. Used for prolonged periods, it can result in paranoia, violence, psychosis, and occasionally a chronic and treatment-resistant condition that is indistinguishable from schizophrenia. Street names include crank, crystal meth, ice, meth, speed. See AMPHETAMINES.

methaqualone (hydrochloride)   A habit-forming sleep medicine with the trade name Quaalude that became somewhat prevalent as a "downer" street drug called "ludes" in the 1970s. See QUAALUDE.

methectic   Characterizing communications between one stratum of an individual's personality and another, as when a person writes messages, the origin of which is the subconscious activity of the person's own mind.

meth monster   Slang for a person demonstrating bizarre and uncontrollable behavior resulting from methamphetamine abuse. See AMPHETAMINE-RELATED DISORDERS, ICE, PUNDING.

method of absolute judgment   A psychophysical method in which no standard stimulus is used. Each member of the series of variables is judged by absolute impression, being related to a subjective impression of the range of the series as a whole that had been built up by experience.

method of adjustment   1. In psychophysics research, the participant is to manipulate a stimulus to match it to equal a standard measure. Also known as method of average error. 2. See METHOD OF PRODUCTION.

method of agreement   (J. S. Mill) In logic, if event A is followed by event B to some predetermined level of occurrence, then A is considered the cause of B. Also known as canon of agreement. See SIGNIFICANCE, SIGNIFICANCE LEVEL.

method of agreement and differences   A process of inductive inference in which agreement and difference are used in combination to determine truth. Also known as canon of agreement and differences. See DIALECTICAL MATERIALISM.

method of amplification   In Jungian therapy, an analytical method whereby a person focuses repeatedly on an element and gives multiple associations to it.

method of approximations   method of successive approximations

method of average error   (G. T. Fechner) A procedure devised for psychological measurement in which a constant (standard) stimulus is presented and the observer is required to adjust a variable stimulus until the two are subjectively equal. Also known as Herstellung's Methode, method of adjustment, method of equation, method of mean error, method of reproduction.

method of bisection   A procedure for scaling psychophysical sensations whereby participants attend to a particular stimulus and attempt to put the one they experienced half-way between two other stimuli.

method of choice   In psychophysics research, any method based on rank ordering of items, for example, method of ranking.

method of co-twin control   A method of control (or checking results) with which one member of a pair or pairs of identical twins is subjected to a certain experimental condition in the other, the second twin, serving as a control or standard.

method of constant stimuli   A psychophysical procedure for determining the sensory threshold by repeatedly presenting several constant stimuli known to be close to the threshold. Also known as method of frequency, method of right and wrong cases. See MAGNITUDE ESTIMATION, METHOD OF LIMITS, RIGHT-AND-WRONG CASES METHOD.

method of correlated vectors   (A. R. Jensen) A method in which the column vector consisting of a number of different tests' factor loadings on a particular factor (for example, *g*) is correlated with a corresponding column vector consisting of each of the same tests' correlations with some variable external to the factor analysis (for example, each test's correlation with the latency of the average evoked potential) as a means of testing a hypothesized relationship of the particular factor to the external variable.

method of cross-modality matching   A psychophysical method for scaling sensations by matching them with another sensation (for example, a line on a piece of paper is to be separated into two parts by the ratio of two lines rubbed with a stick on the participant's back).

method of difference   (J. S. Mill) A general working principle or canon used in reaching inductive conclusions, according to which any difference among effects that are otherwise similar is to be attributed to differences in their antecedents. Also known as canon of difference.

method of disappearing differences   (P. Bouguer) A psychophysical method in which two sensibly different stimuli are presented to the observer, and the lesser is gradually increased or the greater diminished until the original difference becomes unnoticeable.

method of equal sense differences   method of equal-appearing intervals

method of equal sense distances   method of halving

method of equal and unequal cases   (J. Merkel) A modified form of the method of right-and-wrong cases in which a difference limen between two stimuli is first determined by the method of minimal changes, and then these two stimuli are presented to the observer, who is required to judge whether the two are equal or unequal.

method of equal-appearing intervals   A psychophysical measurement method in which the observer is required to adjust a stimulus R_3, so that the difference between R_3 and a stimulus R_2 will appear to be the same as the difference between R_2 and a third stimulus R_1. Also known as method of equal sense distances, method of mean gradations, method of supraliminal differences, method of equal-appearing intervals.

method of equation   method of average error

method of equivalents   (E. H. Weber) A procedure devised as a form of the method of average error in which the observer is required to adjust a variable stimulus to the point of subjective equality with a constant stimulus.

method of exclusion   The systematic elimination of nonessential material in the process of inductive reasoning.

method of fractionation   method of production

method of frequency   method of constant stimuli

method of halving   In psychophysical research, a participant is to separate into two equal parts any stimulus, be it visual, auditory, olfactory, etc. Also known as method of equal sense distances.

method of just-not-noticeable differences   The general procedure in psychophysics for determining difference thresholds. The experimenter has a standard of some kind; for example, the shotgun shell used by Alfred Binet and others, and x number of identically appearing shells. The method calls for the participant to pick up the standard shell, then other shells (that become progressively lighter), and then move back up to and beyond the weight of the standard shotgun shell as long as no difference is noted in relation to standard weight. This can be done with a variety of modalities, such as differences in sizes, magnitudes, darkness, or colors. Compare METHOD OF JUST-NOTICEABLE-DIFFERENCES.

method of just-noticeable-differences   (G. E. Müller) An experimental procedure of gradually decreasing the quantitative difference between two stimuli until the two resulting sensations are not distinguished, or of gradually increasing the difference, starting with equality, until the two resulting sensations are just distinguished. Also known as method of just discernible differences, method of least-differences, method of limits, method of minimal changes, method of serial exploration.

method of least-differences   **method of just noticeable differences**

method of limits   A psychophysical procedure for determining the sensory threshold by gradually increasing or decreasing the magnitude of the stimulus presented until the stimulus is either no longer apprehended or finally apprehended. Also known as method of just-noticeable-differences, method of minimal changes, method of serial exploration. See MAGNITUDE ESTIMATION, METHOD OF CONSTANT STIMULI.

method of loci   A mnemonic strategy (memory aid) in which the items to be remembered are converted into mental images and associated with specific positions or locations; for example, to remember the name of each person sitting around a table, the table might be envisioned as a clock and the faces of each person associated with an hour position and the hour to a name. This method was used by orators during the Roman Empire. See MNEMONIC DEVICE.

method of magnitude estimation   A procedure for obtaining a ratio scale for estimating levels of psychophysical sensations. A certain stimulus is given a number (for example, 5.00) that becomes the standard base of the scale. Other stimuli of the same type are presented to the raters who are asked to indicate by other numbers how much more or less the new stimulus is in proportion to the standard base. See PSYCHOPHYSICAL SCALING METHODS.

method of paired comparisons   In psychophysics, a systematic procedure for comparing sets of stimuli in which the participant ranks the members of all pairs of items with every other item.

method of polar profiles   Any of several procedures in research that depend on establishing sets of antithetical terms at either end of a continuum where participants are to make judgments at various points on the continuum. See SEMANTIC DIFFERENTIAL, ROLE CONSTRUCTS REPERTORY TEST.

method of probits   **probit analysis**

method of production   A psychophysical experimental procedure in which a person is shown a standard stimulus and then is to produce one that differs from the standard by a particular ratio (for example, a circle is shown and the participant is to draw a new circle with twice the area of the first circle). Also known as method of adjustment, method of fractionation.

method of rank correlation   See COEFFICIENT OF RANK CORRELATION, RHO, SPEARMAN-RANK DIFFERENCE METHOD.

method of rank differences   See COEFFICIENT OF RANK CORRELATION, RHO, SPEARMAN-RANK DIFFERENCE METHOD.

method of ranking   A common procedure for a variety of purposes in which people are asked to rank various stimuli in some order; for example, ranking crimes from minor to serious. In contrast, rating would require the participant to choose a given number (for example 1 to 5) for the severity of each crime. (Students often confuse ranking and rating.)

method of rating   In psychophysics, any scaling method that calls for participants to rate items to be scaled.

method of ratio estimation   In psychophysics, a scaling procedure in which participants estimate the ratio of two presented stimuli to each other.

method of reproduction   1. A procedure in studying memory, for example, by asking a person to reproduce certain material, such as to draw the QWERTY keyboard with letters in the correct positions. 2. In psychophysics, a synonym for method of adjustment. 3. In psychophysics, a synonym for method of production.

method of residues   (J. S. Mill) What is not explained in an antecedent condition remains unexplained in subsequent events. Or, in Mill's own words: "Subduct from any phenomenon such part as is known by previous inductions to be the effect of certain antecedents, and the residue of the phenomenon is effect the remaining antecedents." See MILL'S CANONS.

method of right and wrong cases   **method of constant stimuli**

method of right associates   Also known as Jost's law (of associates), invented by Georg Müller but published by Adolph Jost.

method of selection   A procedure used in certain experiments in which the observer picks out from a series that object, figure, etc., judged as equal to a previously presented standard object. Also known as selection method.

method of serial exploration   **method of limits**

method of shaping   **method of successive approximations**

method of single stimuli   Any psychophysical method in which a report follows the presentation of one stimulus only.

method of successive intervals   A procedure in which stimuli are presented to a person who is to indicate where on a horizontal line each item belongs; for example, the terms "average," "high," "medium," "low," "borderline," "genius," "delayed" are to be placed on an axis relative to how each term is an ordered assessment of intelligence. Also known as successive-intervals method.

method of successive approximations 1. A procedure in mathematics and in research in which a person gets closer to the correct answer by a number of trials. 2. The technique of reinforcing each operant response that approximates a response desired by the experimenter. At first, all responses that roughly approximate the desired behavior are reinforced. Later, only responses that more closely approximate the desired behavior are reinforced. The rewarding of these successive responses gradually leads to the desired behavior. The process is known as shaping or response differentiation. Also known as approximation method, method of approximations, successive-approximations method.

method of successive-practice A technique for assessing transfer of learning by measuring the saving in time or trials when B is learned after A has been learned, in comparison with a control group that learns B without learning A. Also known as successive-practice method.

method of triads In psychophysics, any research procedure in which a participant is shown three stimuli, of which the participant must make a decision based on some instruction such as "choose the one thing that is not like the others."

methodolical behaviorism A version of behaviorism that concedes that mental aspects are real, but holds that they cannot be studied scientifically. Consequently, only overt measurable behavior can be studied in humans. See BEHAVIORISM, NEOBEHAVIORISM, RADICAL BEHAVIORISM.

methodological objectivism vs subjectivism (R. I. Watson) A prescriptive dimension of the philosophical underpinnings of psychology, namely, methods that can be replicated versus those that cannot be.

methodology The analysis and systematic application of procedures used in scientific investigation or in a particular research project.

methods analysis (F. Gilbreth & L. Gilbreth) Development of improved ways of performing a job through analysis of the particular operation, process charts, micromotion studies, and application of the principles of motion economy. See MOTION ECONOMY, THERBLIG, TIME AND MOTION EVALUATION.

methyl pemolines A class of street drugs that purportedly causes distortion of the senses, intense hallucinations, feelings of harmony, but occasional "bad trips" evoking anxiety, paranoia, panic, or heart attack. Slang names include 2C-B, U4Euh (euphoria), Nexus.

methylphenidate (hydrochloride) Generic name for a central-nervous system stimulant used primarily as a first-line treatment for hyperactivity in children (more precisely termed attention-deficit hyperactivity disorder or ADHD). In higher doses, it is occasionally used as a recreational drug, because its effects are similar to the amphetamines. Trade name is Ritalin.

metonymic distortion A cognitive disturbance found in patients with schizophrenia, characterized by using related but inappropriate verbal expressions in place of the proper expression, such as "I eat three menus a day" instead of "three meals a day." See METONYMY.

metonymy 1. A figure of speech in which not the literal word but one associated with it is used, such as "the sword" for "war," "sails" for "boats." 2. In speech pathology, a disturbance in which imprecise or inappropriate words and expressions are used that may be unintelligible to others. See METONYMIC DISTORTION.

Metrazol Trade name for pentylenetetrazol. See METRAZOL SHOCK THERAPY.

Metrazol shock therapy (L. J. Meduna) Obsolete treatment of psychotic illness in the 1930s, preceding the use of electroconvulsive treatment. Ladislas Meduna had observed that patients with schizophrenia who were also epileptics tended to have a remission of their psychotic symptoms following a seizure. Other substances that provoked seizures were used, via intramuscular or intravenous injections, but Metrazol for a time had fewer negative features, such as the evocation of intense feelings of dread.

metric methods 1. Procedures that include measurements. 2. Measuring in the metric system.

metric system The measurement conventions (including length, area, volume, mass/weight) adopted by most scientific workers and organizations. Formal name is the International System of Units or SI (*Système Internationale d' Unités*).

metromania Rare term for a compulsion to write continuously in verse form.

metron A unit of metrical information: a measure of the degree of confidence merited by a descriptive statement. See INFORMATION THEORY.

metronome An instrument for marking off short periods of time by sharp sounds. Often used in learning to play music.

metronoscope A device that exposes printed material at a given rate for use in measuring and increasing reading speed. See MEMORY DRUM for a drawing of such an instrument.

Metropolitan Achievement Test (MAT) Batteries of scholastic tests consisting of items that measure vocabulary, reading, arithmetic skills, and language usage at the elementary levels, and social studies, science, and study skills at the higher levels.

Metropolitan Readiness Tests-Sixth Edition (MRT 6) (J. R. Nurss) An individually-administered examination for children of prekindergarten and kindergarten ages to identify those with special needs.

Meyer's (contrast) experiment (H. Meyer) A means of demonstrating simultaneous color contrast. A piece of gray paper is placed on a larger background of the inducing color, and both are covered with tissue paper. A color complementary to the color of the background is induced in the gray piece. Also known as Meyer's contrast pattern.

Meyer's theory The following items are important for understanding Adolf Meyer's theory: ANERGASIA, DISTRIBUTIVE ANALYSIS, DISTRIBUTIVE SYNTHESIS, DYSERGASIA, EGOTROPY, ERGASIA, ERGASIATRY, ERGASIOLOGY, EUERGASIA, EXPLOSIVE DIATHESIS, HOLERGASIA, HYPERERGASIA, HYPOERGASIA, MERERGASIA, OBSESSIVE-RUMINATIVE TENSION STATE, OLIGERGASIA, ORTHERGASIA, PAREROGSIS, PATHERGASIA, PSYCHOBIOLOGICAL FACTORS, PSYCHOBIOLOGY, SYNTROPY, THYMERGASIA, VICIOUS HABIT.

MF   See MULTIFACTORIAL MODEL OF INHERITANCE.

MF scale   See MASCULINITY-FEMININITY SCALE.

MFD   See MEMORY-FOR-DESIGNS TEST.

mg   See MILLIGRAM.

Mg   See MILLIGRAM.

mg/kg   Milligram (of drug) per kilogram (of body weight); a common way of adjusting drug dosage to body size.

MHA   mental health association

MI   1. machine intelligence. 2. mental illness.

Michelson-Morley experiment   A test of Isaac Newton's theory of ether, presumably at rest while the earth and other bodies moved through it. In 1887, the time it took for a beam of light to be reflected directly back from a straight-ahead mirror was compared to the time it took for reflection from a beam traveling the same distance at right angles to the first beam. There was no difference in any direction, and, hence, no ether. Led to Albert Einstein's theory of relativity.

Mickey Finn   Slang for "knockout drops" (originally, and still occasionally, chloral hydrate) usually put into alcoholic beverages with the intention of heavily sedating (or rendering unconscious) the person drinking the beverage. See DATE-RAPE DRUGS, KNOCKOUT DROPS.

microanalytic approach   (A. Bandura) A finegrain analysis of the relation between thoughts and actions. Used extensively in the analysis of how beliefs of personal efficacy give rise to actions and emotional reactions. See SELF-EFFICACY.

microbiophobia   Fear of small animals, such as microbes, microorganisms. See ACAROPHOBIA, BACILLOPHOBIA, MICROPHOBIA.

microcephaly   (B. Metlinger) Having a small head in relation to the rest of the body. There are numerous causes and manifestations of this condition, including familial microcephaly. Mental retardation ranging from moderate to profound often accompanies the condition. Also known as microcephalia. See PRIMARY MICROCEPHALY, PURE MICROCEPHALY.

microcosm   The inner world of the individual, as opposed to the macrocosm, the environment.

microcounseling   1. A method of training counselors through the use of videotapes. 2. Counseling on one narrowly focused issue.

microdialysis   In physiological psychology, a technique for measuring the concentration of chemicals in a small area of the brain by enabling them to pass through a membrane into an implanted tube.

microelectrode   An electrode so small that it can record electrical activity in, or electrostimulate, a single neuron or sensory cell.

microelectrode technique   The use of intracellular microelectrodes that are able to record activity within a single nerve cell; several working together can be used to study behavior patterns. Microelectrode technique in therapy may be used to locate specific foci of brain damage associated with parkinsonism, epilepsy, or other disorders. See MICROELECTRODE.

micro-expectations   See STORE IMAGE.

microfarad (μf)   One-millionth of a farad.

microgeny   A series of small steps that lead up to a patient's symptoms, or to an individual's specific behavior or mental processes.

microglia   (Pio del Rio Hortega) Small glial cells of the central nervous system. Also known as Hortega cells, microglial cells.

microglossia   An abnormally small-sized tongue, resulting in a disturbance in the speech production of lingual sounds.

micrognathia   Facial disfigurement characterized by an abnormally small jaw, or jaws. Usually affects the lower jaw.

microgram (μg)   One-millionth of a gram.

microiontophoresis   The use of electricity to eject a chemical from a micropipette to measure the chemical's effects on the electrical activity of a cell.

micromania   A psychiatric state in which people believe their bodies have diminished to a minute size. See MICROPSIA.

micromastia   Abnormally small female breasts. Also known as micromazia.

micromelia   A developmental defect marked by abnormal shortness or smallness of the limbs, a condition sometimes associated with delayed mental development. Also known as nanomelia. See ACHONDROPLASIA.

micrometer   1. One-millionth of a meter. Also known as micro-meter, micron. 2. A device for measuring objects in a precise manner, such as a lens accurately marked for measuring microscopic forms.

micromicron (mu-mu, μμ, or mμ)   Former term for picometer.

micron (μ)   Former term for micrometer (meaning 1).

micro-orchidism   Abnormal smallness of one or both testicles. Also known as microrchidia.

microphobia   1. Morbid fear of small things. 2. Fear of germs. See ACAROPHOBIA, MICROBIOPHOBIA.

microphonia   **hypophonia**

micropsia   A visual disorder in which objects appear to be much smaller than they actually are. May be due to retinal defect or disease, but is often a conversion symptom or hallucination, and possibly an unconscious attempt to shrink the world to a less threatening size. Also known as micropsias. See LILLIPUTIAN HALLUCINATION, MACROPSIA.

micropsychophysiology   The study of psychological processes, such as the formation of a delusion or obsession, in minute detail, paralleling the microscopic investigations conducted by physiologists.

micropsychoses   See PSEUDONEUROTIC SCHIZOPHRENIA.

microptic hallucination   **Lilliputian hallucination**

microsaccades   Very small saccadic movements. See SACCADES.

microscopic level   A psychological approach that focuses on the smallest recognizable units of analysis; for example, components of cells. Usually associated with physiological psychology.

microsecond (Nsec. or μsec)   One-millionth of a second. Also known as μ-second.

microsleep   Brief intervals of dozing or sleeping that occur during periods when a participant presumably is awake. May be an effect of sleep deprivation, which also may result in a shift of some desynchronized sleep signs, as normally observed on electroencephalographic (EEG) tracings, to appear during slow-wave sleep, when they usually are absent. See APNEA.

microsocial engineering   Descriptive phrase applied to behavioral contracting, or contract therapy, in which a technique of conflict resolution among family members is established through a specific schedule of responsibilities, privileges, sanctions for violations, and bonuses for compliance. See BEHAVIOR MODIFICATION, CONTRACT.

microsomatic animals   Abnormally small animals calculated in terms of general body size. Sizes one or more standard deviations smaller are classified as microsomatic. Compare MACROSOMATIC ANIMALS.

microsomatognosia   Misperception of one's own body or its parts as abnormally small. See MACROSOMATOGNOSIA, SOMATOGNOSIA.

microspectrophotometer   A spectrophotometer enabling the study of light transmitted by small specimens (as in obtaining spectral-absorption of light through a single human retinal cone and computer-analyzing the energy transmitted).

microsplanchnic build/type   (G. Viola) A constitutional type characterized by a small abdomen and an elongated body, according to Giacinto Viola's classification. See BODY TYPES, MACROSPLANCHNIC TYPE.

microvolt (μV)   One-millionth of a volt.

micturition   1. Urination. 2. The urge to urinate. 3. Frequency of urination.

micturition reflexes   A series of nerve signals organized along the spinal cord by the autonomic nervous system as the need arises to empty the urinary bladder. Through training, cerebral control of these reflexes is developed, as in toilet-training a child or "house-breaking" a dog.

MID   See MULTIINFARCT DEMENTIA.

Midas punishment/syndrome   (G. W. Bruyn & U. J. DeJong) Compulsive masturbation interpreted as a type of self-punishment, reflecting the punishment of King Midas in Greek mythology who was ruined through the fulfillment of his wishes.

midazolam (hydrochloride)   Generic name for a benzodiazepine central nervous system depressant and memory inhibitor, used medically prior to invasive procedures, and illicitly as a date-rape drug. See DATE-RAPE DRUG.

midbrain   The middle of three divisions of the brain. Contains reflex centers for hearing and vision, pathways to and from the forebrain, and several other centers. Also known as mesencephalon. See FOREBRAIN, HINDBRAIN.

midchildhood   See DEVELOPMENTAL LEVELS.

middle cerebral artery   The largest branch of the internal carotid artery, running first through the Sylvian fissure, then upward on the surface of the insula where it divides into several branches that spread over the lateral surface of the cerebral hemispheres, including the anterior choroidal branch.

middle-child syndrome   According to Rudolf Dreikurs, the tendency of children who have both an older sibling and a younger sibling to harbor paranoid ideas. The middle child sees the benefits of being an older child (who is given more freedom and has fewer restrictions) and the benefits of being a younger child (who is babied and is seldom punished for the same deeds that when performed by the middle child are punished). See INDIVIDUAL PSYCHOLOGY, PARENTING.

middle class   The middle part of a classification system pertaining to status stratification found in most societies. Social scientists often define 3 to 7 classes based on such variables as occupation, income, education, and prestige. For instance, the middle class may be between the upper one-third and the bottom one-third in income, or between professional and managerial occupations and the unskilled and unemployed. Popularly defined as white-collar work.

middle commissure   A body-tissue structure that joins the optic thalami.

middle ear   A membrane-lined cavity in the bone of the skull, adjacent to the mastoid cells that contains the ossicles. It is filled with air and communicates with the nasopharynx through the Eustachian tube. Also known as tympanic cavity.

middle insomnia   A period of sleeplessness occurring after falling asleep normally, with difficulty in falling asleep again.

"middle man" hormones   Pituitary gland secretion that acts on other glands to stimulate their functioning.

middle path   A Buddhist concept of balance, being in the neutral center of opposites, such as being between self-enhancement and self-acceptance.

midget   A perfectly formed but undersized dwarf. See NANISM, NANOSOMIA BODY TYPE, PRIMORDIAL NANOSOMIA, PYGMYISM.

midinterval   median class

midlife crisis   1. (C. G. Jung) Crises that occur when people in their 30s or 40s come to certain realizations, such as that they will never be successful or that they have been doing what others wanted them to do, and have not followed their dreams. 2. (B. Neugarten) Crises occurring during the middle years, including for women menopause, and for men the threat of younger workers on the job. See EMPTY NEST, MENOPAUSAL DEPRESSION.

midlife transition   (C. G. Jung) A time for reevaluating life that generally occurs in the late 30s or the early 40s that calls for decisions about whether to continue in whatever a person has been doing, or the making of major changes.

midparent   A measure used to indicate parental "contribution" to offspring that is calculated by taking the mean of the measures of the father and of the mother in such characteristics as intelligence and height. See FILIAL REGRESSION.

midpoint (MP)   A point or value halfway between the highest and lowest values in a frequency distribution or class interval.

midpontine wakefulness   An effect of a lesion in the brainstem at the level of the middle of the pons marked by loss of signals associated with drowsiness or sleep. Animals subjected to midpontine sectioning remain permanently awake.

midrange value   A rough measure of central tendency gained by averaging the highest and lowest scores in a frequency distribution.

midscore   The median.

Midtown Manhattan Study   (L. Strole) An interview study of the Yorkville area of New York City conducted in 1962. It revealed that 9% of the social upper class, 18% of the middle class, and 28% of the lower class were afflicted with severe mental and emotional disturbances. Of the total group impaired by mental illness, less than one-third had any professional psychotherapeutic contact. These findings indicated that those who come to the attention of psychiatric facilities do not constitute the majority of those who need help, and may be a nonrepresentative sample of the mentally ill.

midwife   A trained birth attendant or assistant.

Mignon delusion   A variation of the family-romance fantasy in which children believe that their parents actually are foster parents and the "real" family is one of distinguished lineage. (Phrase is derived from a character in Goethe's *Wilhelm Meister's Apprenticeship*.)

migraine (headache)   Severe headache, often recurring, lasting for hours or days, sometimes preceded by prodromal symptoms. Of vascular origin but unknown cause. The pain is usually generalized but sometimes unilateral, beginning in or around the eyes, throbbing, and accompanied by any combination of anorexia, nausea, vomiting, irritability, fatigue, and vision sensitivity and distortion. Also known as blind headache, vascular headache.

migraine personality   A pattern of behavior found in many migraine sufferers, who tend to be perfectionistic, overambitious, highly competitive, and overcritical. When disappointed or frustrated, they "hold everything in," and may nurse resentments for long periods, thus keeping themselves under constant emotional tension.

migration   In physiological psychology, the movement of neurons toward their eventual destinations in the brain.

migration adaptation   Adjustment to a new community or area involving contact with unfamiliar people, surroundings, and customs. See UPROOTING NEUROSIS.

migration behavior   1. Instinctive activity marked by travel to or from breeding areas. In some animal species it is seasonal; in others, such as the salmon, it occurs once in their lifetime. Factors influencing migration behavior include sensitivity to chemical or magnetic cues, pituitary or other hormones, daylight, and temperature. 2. The relatively permanent relocation of people across symbolic, political, or geographical boundaries, as from rural to urban areas.

mild depression   The lowest degree of depression, characterized by dejection, loss of interest and enthusiasm, inertia, and vague aches and pains without an organic basis. Also known as simple depression.

mild mental retardation   Obsolete phrase for people having slightly below average in intelligence. Many such individuals identified as having delayed development in schools succeed in life in terms of work, society and family. See SIX-HOUR RETARDED CHILD.

milieu   1. In general, surroundings. Also known as environment, surround. 2. In psychology, the particular climate of the home and character of the neighborhood as they affect the personality and adjustment of the individual. 3. In psychiatry, the social setting of the patient. Plural of milieu is milieux.

milieu therapy   (M. Jones) Maxwell Jones' approach to the treatment of mental disorders whereby an institution as a whole is made a therapeutic community, with everyone (janitors, doctors, nurses, clerks, spouses) being made aware of the role they should play in the therapeutic process. Also known as environmental therapy. See THERAPEUTIC COMMUNITY.

militancy   Concerted verbal or behavioral opposition. Also known as militance.

military psychology   The application of psychology to armed services, including the evaluation, selection, assignment, and training of military personnel; the design of equipment; the application of clinical and counseling techniques to the maintenance of morale and mental health; and evaluation of propaganda directed to their enemies as well as to the military and civilians of their side.

millenarianism   A religious movement that prophesizes the coming of the end of the physical world at the millenium. Millennial movements occur within and outside of diverse religions, and take many forms. They can be expected to intensify prior to a calendar millenium, and to dissipate thereafter (whether or not the prophecy is vindicated). See CARGO CULT.

Miller Analogies Test (MAT)   An examination used for selecting candidates for graduate schools. Consists of 100 verbal analogy items of the type "A is to B as C is to _" from diverse academic topics. The participant supplies the appropriate term for the blank space from a choice of words or symbols. Named after American psychologist Wilford S. Miller (b. 1883).

Miller Assessment for Preschoolers (MAPS)   (L. J. Miller) A short but comprehensive assessment instrument for evaluating children at the preschool age for mild to moderate developmental delays.

Miller-Mowrer shuttlebox   (N. E. Miller, O. H. Mowrer) In avoidance learning, a box with a grid floor through which electric shocks can be administered to the subject, usually a rat or dog. The subject must learn to avoid the aversive stimulus on schedule, such as moving to the opposite end of the box (where there is no shock) within a given time limit after the warning buzzer is sounded.

Mill Hill Vocabulary Scales   (J. C. Raven, J. Raven, J. H. Court) A scale with a Junior Level (ages 6½–16½) and Senior Level (ages 18–adult) that attempts to provide a measure of acquired verbal knowledge that supplements nonverbal reasoning ability measures yielded by the Ravens' Progressive Matrices. The participant is asked to supply synonyms and definitions for specific words.

milligram (Mg or mg)   One-thousandth of a gram. See GRAM.

millilambert (ml.)   (J. H. Lambert) One-thousandth (0.001) of a lambert, which is a measure of the luminance (amplitude) of a radiation. A unit of brightness equal to 0.929 lumen per square foot.

milliliter (ml. or mL)   One-thousandth of a liter.

millimeter (mm)   One-thousandth of a meter.

millimicron (m, mμ, mu, or μ)   One-billionth of a meter. Under SI the term has been replaced by nanometer (nm).

milling around   The initial stage in an encounter group in which members engage in superficial talk and exploration as a sign of resistance to opening up to new persons and to a new process of relating.

million-dollar game   A group game designed to explore the psychological meaning of money and to encourage free, creative thinking. The group is told that it has a million dollars, which is to be used productively in any way, as long as the endeavor actively involves all members of the group.

milliphot   One-thousandth of a phot, the unit of illuminance equal to 1/000th of a lumen per square centimeter, or 1.000th of a centimeter-candle.

millisecond (ms, σ, or msec)   One-thousandth of a second.

millivolt (mW, mV, or mv)   One-thousandth of a volt.

Millon Adolescent Clinical Inventory (MACI)   (T. Millon) A 160-item multiaxial self-report inventory co-ordinated with the structure of DSM-IV, which assesses common syndromes of psychopathology and the adolescent parallels of the personality disorders for use with troubled youth.

Millon Behavioral Health Inventory (MBHI)   (T. Millon) A 150-item adult self-report inventory that assesses the interaction of personality and disease-prone attitudes in producing and mediating the course of disease in a variety of medical populations and conditions.

Millon Clinical Multiaxial Inventory (MCMI)   A 175-item, forced-choice (true-false) test to measure 11 personality disorders and clinical symptoms. Widely used on clinical populations in the United States, based on Theodore Millon's theory of personality, uses base-rate rather than T scores. Not linked to the Diagnostic and Statistical Manual of Mental Disorders (DSM), but compatible with it. Versions include MCMI2 and MCMI3.

Millon Clinical Multiaxial Inventory-III (MCMI-III) (T. Millon) A theoretically based 175-item multiaxial self-report inventory closely coordinated with the structure and criteria of DSM-IV, used frequently to assess common syndromes of Axis I adult psychopathology and the fourteen Axis II personality disorders.

Millon Index of Personality Styles (MIPS)   (T. Millon) A 180-item adult and college-level normal personality self-report inventory assessing not only the personality constructs derived from Millon's evolutionary theory, but also the Jungian constructs of Extroversing-Introversing, Sensing-Intuiting, Thinking-Feeling and Systematizing-Innovating.

Mill's canons   (J. S. Mill) Principles intended to guide the use of induction. They consist of the principles of (a) agreement, (b) difference, (c) joint agreement and difference, (d) residues, (e) functional relations, and (f) concomitant variation.

mimesis   1. Imitation. 2. The process of copying the appearance or behavior of another member of the species in the absence of teaching or previous learning or without awareness.

mimetic   Pertaining to imitation, as in a young chimpanzee copying its mother's actions. Term is often applied to species-specific behavior, that is, behavior that appears spontaneously and in identical or nearly the same form in all members of a species. See INSTINCT, INSTINCTIVE BEHAVIOR.

mimetic response   1. Copying or imitative response. 2. A responsive act that is stimulated by some act of another creature, and that tends to resemble this act in character and form. See POSTURAL ECHO.

mimetism   Assumption by one creature of the color, shape, attitude movements, etc., of another, serving as a protection against enemies or for concealment from prey. Some insects resemble other insects that are poisonous, presumably to avoid being eating by predators.

mimicry   1. In humans, making fun of others by acting as they do but in an exaggerated manner. See HUMOR. 2. In animals, evolutionary changes whereby one organism looks like another organism. See MIMESIS, MIMETISM.

mimpathy   A type of thinking and presentation necessary for a novelist or historian to recreate the feeling-tone of an historical event or for anyone to make real to others a personal experience. See EMPATHY.

mind   1. The organized totality of mental and psychic processes of an organism, and the structural and functional components on which they depend. 2. A tri-partite dimensional system of the mind developed by structural psychologists, including (a) cognition: the "knowing" aspects of the mind including perceptions, sensations, memory, intelligence, creativity; (b) affection: "emotions" such as fear, anger, hatred, boredom, fatigue; and (c) conation: "motivation" such as needs, wants, desires, goals, ambition. 3. J. Strachey's translation of Sigmund Freud's term *Seele*, criticized by Bruno Bettelheim who felt it should have been translated as soul.

mind-altering drugs   Substances such as mescaline or LSD that produce altered states of consciousness through pharmacological activity. The state of mind may become hallucinogenic, euphoric, excited, depressed, anxious, or a combination of such responses. See HALLUCINOGENS, MOOD-ALTERING DRUGS, PSYCHEDELICS.

mind-body problem   (Plato, R. Descartes) A question of the relationship between mental and physical processes, between psyche and soma. The major concepts are: (a) Interactionism, or mutual influence (see ISOMORPHISM); (b) Parallelism, or separate processes with a point-to-point correspondence; (c) Idealism, only mind exists, and the soma is a function of the psyche; (d) Double aspect theory, body and mind are simply two different ways of looking at the same thing, similar to the differences in looking at an apple sliced in half vertically and horizontally; (e) Epiphenomenalism, mind is a by-product of bodily processes; (f) Materialism, body is the only reality and the psyche is a nonexistent construct.

mind control   Physical activities of the body, particularly autonomic functions affected by mental processes. See AUTOGENIC TRAINING, BIOFEEDBACK, MEDITATION, YOGA.

mind control programming   Techniques used to indoctrinate persons in social, religious and political attitudes and beliefs, thereby giving up previously held beliefs. May be accompanied by forceful incarceration and sleep deprivation, hypnosis, and mind-altering drugs. Often called brain-washing.

mind-cure   See FAITH CURE/HEALING, MENTAL HEALING.

mind-dust theory   A point of view that atoms or particles of mind or mental substance pervade the universe and combine to form actual minds.

mindfulness   (Asian) Clear objective awareness of an ongoing experience. Often associated with Buddhist or Hindu training in turning the thoughts fully to what is going on at the moment.

minding system   (S. S. Tomkins) The stressing of both the cognitive processing and the caring about others in thought.

mindlessness   (E. Langer) Thoughtlessness or inattention to an ongoing experience; for example, most behavior is considered "mindless," that is, occurring without much thought, as the result of habit, such as exhaling when speaking. See PROCEDURAL MEMORY.

mind-reading   Purported paranormal perception in which it is alleged that a person can have access to the thoughts in the mind of another person by extrasensory means. See EXTRASENSORY PERCEPTION.

mind's eye   (S. Kosslyn) The location in the brain where visual information obtained from the eyes or from long-term memory is stored temporarily while being processed as a visual image. Phrase is a metaphor for an as-yet-unidentified neurological structure whose existence and properties are established empirically by experiments on the abilities of humans to gain information from and reason from visual images, perceptual or remembered.

mind stuff   (W. K. Clifford) Denoting the elemental material that constitutes reality, consisting internally of the constituent substance of mind, and appearing externally in the form of matter.

mineral regulation   A relationship between mineral metabolism and behavior. Loss of parathyroid glands in animals, for example, disrupts calcium-phosphate balance and results in convulsions. Animals may show food preferences for items rich in calcium, sodium, or potassium when such minerals are lacking in their diets. See SELF-FEEDING.

MINERVA 2   (D. L. Hintzman) Named after the Greek goddess of wisdom, a memory model that explains memory for individual experiences (episodic) and generic or semantic memory; 2 refers to double aspect.

miniature end-plate potentials   Very small variations in postsynaptic end-plate potential due to random release of acetylcholine at axonal end-plates.

miniature mind   The mind possessed by a psychoinfantile person; a mentality that is developmentally delayed in all aspects. See PSYCHOINFANTILISM.

miniature system   Organized knowledge, including facts and assumptions, relating to a restricted area of study; for example, psychological theories of perception.

minimal audible field (MAF)   An auditory threshold test in which participants face a sound source while the intensity is measured at the midpoint of their heads.

minimal audible pressure (MAP)   An auditory-threshold measuring technique in which the pressure on the participant's eardrum is measured.

minimal brain damage   The presumption of a mild degree of organicity based upon "soft signs" such as overactivity, restlessness, short attention span, and poor coordination. See IATROGENIC ILLNESS, IATROGENIC CONDITIONS.

minimal brain dysfunction (MBD)   A relatively mild impairment of brain function that affects perception, behavior, and academic ability. These deviations may manifest by various combinations of impairment in perception, language, memory, and motor function. The effects include hyperactivity, emotional lability, untidiness, short attention span, and speech disorders. See ATTENTION DEFICIT HYPERACTIVITY DISORDER, MENTAL RETARDATION.

minimal cerebral dysfunction (MCD)   Phrase previously used for attention deficit disorders or other behavioral abnormalities of children when they act in manners different from others and where there is no other explanation for the behavior. Formerly attributed to hypothesized minimal brain damage.

minimal-change method/procedure   An experimental technique in which a variable stimulus is presented in very small ascending and descending steps.

minimal cue   The smallest measurable stimulus that will evoke a response. The participant usually is not aware of the stimulus; emotional responses can often be detected by slight changes in expression or posture. See CUE REDUCTION, REDUCED CUE.

mini-max   Refers to achieving maximal goals using minimal effort. See EFFICIENCY, MINIMAX PRINCIPLE.

minimax principle   1. A theory of minimizing risk and maximizing gain. See MAXIMIN STRATEGY, MINIMAX STRATEGY. 2. A strategy in which the minimum number of procedures are used to find the maximum value of a function of one or more variables.

minimax strategy   In game theory, a strategy chosen by a player that minimizes the amount the player can lose. Compare MAXIMIN STRATEGY.

minimization   1. Making an event seem far less important than it actually is. 2. A cognitive style consisting of a habitual tendency to play down the significance of disturbing events, for example, serious medical conditions. See DENIAL.

minimum   The least amount of whatever is measurable.

minimum-change therapy   (L. Tyler) A type of counseling with limited goals using existing strengths. The basic assumption of the value of small step-by-step positive changes in thinking and acting in comparison with comprehensive all-inclusive immediate personality change as the result of an overall insight. See ABREACTION, CONVERSION.

minimum distinguishable acuity   The smallest stationary detail that a person reports seeing.

minimum-power theory (D. E. Shapley) In group dynamics, an explanation of coalitions that form, in relation to individuals' prior resources, payoffs and power types and amounts.

minimum-resource theory (W. A. Gamson) In group dynamics, a point of view that group members will form coalitions that maximize their control over the others, and that the most likely grouping is that which is sufficient to prevail but whose members own the minimal resources for the purpose.

minimum separable method A technique used to measure the clarity or sharpness of visual perception in which the participant attempts to detect very small gaps between two parts of a figure. See ACUITY GRATING, VISUAL ACUITY.

Minnesota Assembly Test An individual mechanical-aptitude task in which the participant is given a time limit within which to put together 33 common objects such as a bicycle bell and a mousetrap. Also known as Minnesota Mechanical Assembly Test.

Minnesota Clerical Test (MCT) An examination designed to predict clerical aptitude by attempting to measure a person's perception of detail, accuracy, and speed in comparing pairs of names and numbers, to determine which are identical and which nonidentical.

Minnesota Mechanical Assembly Test Minnesota Assembly Test

Minnesota Multiphasic Personality Inventory (MMPI) A self-report questionnaire that has undergone revisions originally designed as a substitute for a psychiatric interview consisting of 550 true-false items with nine scales such as hypochondria, depression, hysteria, psychopathic deviation, masculine-feminine interest, paranoia, psychasthenia, schizophrenia, and hypomania. In addition, there are four attitude scales, such as L (Lie), and additional scales developed for other purposes. Named after the University of Minnesota by its developers Starke Hathaway and J. Charnley McKinley.

Minnesota Multiphasic Personality Inventory-Adolescent (MMPI-A) A new form of the MMPI designed for ages 14–18 with only 478 true-false items that yield 10 basic Clinical Scales; 6 validity scales; 28 Harris-Lingoes subscales such as Psychomotor Retardation, Brooding and Familial Discord; 3 Si subscales; 15 Adolescent Content scales such as Obsessiveness, Alienation, and Conduct Problems; and 6 supplementary scales.

Minnesota Multiphasic Personality Inventory-2 (MMPI-2) A revision of the MMPI consisting of 567 true-false items that yield 7 validity indicators, the 10 basic Clinical Scales, 12 supplementary scales such as Anxiety and revised MacAndrew Alcoholism Scale, 2 Posttraumatic Stress Disorder scales, 15 content scales, such as Health Concerns and Bizarre Mentation, 3 Si subscales, and 28 Harris-Lingoes subscales, such as Lassitude-Malaise and Authority Problems.

Minnesota Paper Formboard Test (R. Likert & W. H. Quasha) A nonverbal mechanical-aptitude task consisting of 64 geometric diagrams. The participant is required to select printed parts of geometric figures which, when correctly assembled, will make one of five figures shown. Designed to test the capacity to visualize how cut-up pieces would look like when assembled.

Minnesota Rate of Manipulation A task of manual dexterity as a measure of mechanical aptitude in which multicolored disks are fitted into a pegboard in a prescribed order, first with one hand and then with the other after turning them over.

Minnesota Spatial Relations Test (MSRT) A mechanical-aptitude task designed to measure speed and accuracy in fitting 58 cutouts of different shapes and sizes into the proper spaces on four boards.

Minnesota Test for Aphasia (H. Schuell & J. J. Jenkins) An examination used for diagnosing aphasia. Consists of linguistic tasks that a participant is to respond to orally and in writing.

Minnesota Test for Differential Diagnosis of Aphasia (H. Schuell) An examination used to gather information so that patients may be classified into one of seven diagnostic categories. An objective method, the clinician asks questions of and makes observations about the patient with aphasia.

minor 1. In academics, a field of study, not a person's main field. 2. A person who is not yet considered an adult (for example, an adolescent) and who has yet to achieve full civil rights and responsibility. See EMANCIPATED MINOR. 3. Considered not as large, important, etc., as something else, the opposite of major.

minor analysis Psychoanalysis of short duration, limited to the important aspects of a patient's problem, as opposed to a deeper, more exhaustive orthodox analysis. See COUNSELING, GOAL-LIMITED THERAPY, LIMITED-TIME THERAPY.

minor epilepsy See PETIT MAL.

minor hemisphere A cerebral hemisphere nondominant for an individual or a particular function such as language or handedness. The minor and dominant hemispheres usually have complementary or supporting roles. Functions of the minor hemisphere can be demonstrated in many visual tests that involve embedded figures, depth perception, or other visual-spatial functions, and functions of the dominant hemisphere can be demonstrated with tests of linguistic abilities.

minority group 1. A population subgroup with unique social, religious, or other interests that differ from those of the majority of the population (for example, Gypsies). 2. Also sometimes employed to refer to any group (whether a minority or not) that is subjected to discrimination by more powerful groups (for example, women).

minor tranquilizers See ANTIANXIETY MEDICATIONS.

minty (J. D. Amoore et al.) One of the seven basic stereochemical smell theory qualities that has the odor of plants of the genus *mentha*, a sharp generally pleasant odor found in the alcoholic drink; mint julip, for example.

minus situation According to Alfred Adler, an unpleasant subjective state of feeling inferior to or less than others. Such a conclusion may lead the person to either give up, or to make an effort to improve to a plus (positive) situation. See INFERIORITY FEELINGS, PLUS-MINUS SITUATION.

minute memory Short-term memory, or immediate recall.

miosis   1. An extreme contraction of the pupil, usually due to drugs or disease. 2. Rare term for the period in a disease process when intensity of symptoms diminish. Also spelled myosis. 3. Incorrect spelling for meiosis.

MIPS   See MILLON INDEX OF PERSONALITY STYLES.

mirror drawing   A motor-skill test in which a participant traces an image while looking into a mirror that shows only the image and the pencil. The object is to test ability to alter a manual-habit pattern.

mirror-image perceptions   Distinct but similar views of one another often held by parties in conflict; all individuals tend to view themselves as moral and peace-loving and their opponents as evil and aggressive.

mirror-image thinking   In group dynamics, a tendency for groups in conflict to adopt the same misconceptions about each other.

mirror-imaging   Reversed asymmetry of characteristics often found in sets of twins, particularly monozygotic twins. Examples include handedness, fingerprints, hair whorls, and certain inherited pathological traits.

mirroring   mirror technique

mirror reading   Employing a pattern of reading the reverse of the pattern generally followed by another language, such as in English reading by lines left to right and in Hebrew reading right to left. Thus, each is mirror reading from the other's point of view. See PALINLEXIA.

mirror reversal   Refers to the reflection seen in a mirror; a left/right shift, as when the letter "p" looks like "q."

mirror script   mirror writing

mirror sign   A symptom of autistic withdrawal observed in some patients with schizophrenia who tend to stand in front of a mirror or other reflecting surface for a long period. Also, advanced Alzheimer's patients may not only look at their image but talk to it, not realizing it is their own.

mirror technique   1. In psychotherapy, active, reflective listening. 2. A procedure used in psychodrama whereby one person imitates another's behavior in the expectation that the person being portrayed can see how own behavior looks to others. Also known as mirroring.

mirror transference   (H. Kohut) A concept in the treatment of narcissistic-personality disorders that patients' grandiosities are reactivated in transference as a replica of the early phase of their lives when their mothers established their sense of personal perfection.

mirror writing   1. A mirror-like inversion of letters and words often noted in children with severe reading disability. It is related to strephosymbolia, a perception reversal of left and right. Also known as mirror script, palingraphia. 2. See RETROGRAPHY.

miryachit   (to play the fool—Russian) A culture-specific syndrome marked by indiscriminate, apparently uncontrolled, imitation of the actions of other people encountered by the patient. Sometimes accompanied by involuntary jumping motions. Similar to *latah*, but observed in Siberia. Also spelled *myriachit*. See LATAH.

misala   A culture-specific disorder similar to *Tropenkoller* in which victims start quarrels and rapidly work themselves up to a frenzy of speech and wild gesticulation without apparent purpose or cause. The episode lasts from a few minutes to a few hours, after which the victim collapses in exhaustion.

misandriast   A person who hates men. Compare MISOGYNIST.

misandry   Hatred of men by women. Compare GYNANDRY.

misanthropy   Hatred, aversion, or distrust of all humans.

misattribution theory   A point of view that due to favorable emotional outcomes, phenomena that happen to be present may gain value they would not otherwise have.

miscarriage   A spontaneous abortion of a fetus before it is able to survive outside the womb, usually before the 28th week of pregnancy. See SPONTANEOUS ABORTION.

miscegenation   Marriage, interbreeding, or cohabitation of two individuals of different "races." Historically, miscegenation has been a common result of invasions and wars. Some jurisdictions have, or have had, laws against interracial marriage.

miseducation   According to David Elkind, developmentally inappropriate education that puts children at risk for no purpose. A common feature of schools that promote children due to their age rather than to their abilities.

Mises   See DR. MISES.

misidentification   1. Failure to identify other individuals correctly due to impaired memory or a confused state. 2. Failure to recognize people due to a delusion that they have been transformed. 3. Calling a person by someone else's name. See DELUSIONAL MISIDENTIFICATION.

misinformation acceptance   Believing that a memory suggested or planted by another person is true.

misinformation effect   In learning theory, a tendency for a certain type of misleading information presented after the original event to cause disruption to or biasing of memory. For instance, after viewing a traffic collision, people are asked to estimate the cars' speed; the estimate varies according to whether the verb used in the description of the event was neutral ("contacted") or dramatic ("smashed").

misocainea   Abnormal hatred of new concepts.

misogamist   A person who hates marriage.

misogynist   A person who hates women. Compare MISANDRIAST.

misogyny   Hatred of women. According to psychoanalytic theory, in men this condition may be due to many factors, such as homosexual conflicts or a frustrated desire to become a woman. In women, misogyny may be due to desire to have been born a male or because of parents who were disappointed when a daughter rather than a desired son was born.

misologia   An aversion to speaking or arguing, which in patients with catatonic schizophrenia may be related to a fear that speaking may have destructive effects. Also known as misology.

misoneism   1. An extreme resistance to change; intolerance of anything new. A common symptom in presenile patients. Also known as misocainea. 2. A pathological reaction to changes or anything new.

misopedia   1. Aversion to or hatred of children, which in some cases may be associated with a morbid compulsion to kill them. 2. A neurotic dislike for one's own children for any of many reasons. Also known as misopedy. See PEDOPHILIA.

misorientation effect   In ergonomics, difficulty in recognizing an object in an orientation different from that presented during the initial familiarity, as in reading a map rotated after being studied.

miss   In signal detection theory, not getting the message.

missile fear   See BALLISTOPHOBIA.

missing-parts test   Any task requiring the participant to point out what is missing in a picture, for example, given a drawing of a person with only one arm, and asking "What is missing from this picture?" Frequently used as an observation test in intelligence scales such as the Wechsler.

Missionaries & Cannibals   (A. Newell & H. A. Simon) A traditional problem much used in problem-solving research that involves transporting some missionaries and cannibals across a river, with certain restrictive rules about boatloads and numbers of missionaries and cannibals on each bank. Also sometimes called "Hobbits and Orcs."

missionary position   Sexual intercourse with partners prone and (in heterosexual relations) the man on top. The name is commonly attributed to Christian missionaries in Hawaii, the South Pacific, and Africa, who advocated the use of this position only.

mistaken identity   Seeming to recognize or to remember somebody or something that in reality has a different identity than the person thinks. May or may not be the first time the person has seen the mistaken object. Also known as false recognition. See DÉJÀ VU.

mistress   1. A woman who provides compensated sexual and companionship services over an extended period to a man who is often married to another. Also called "the other woman." 2. Originally a term of rank, still seen is usages such as mistress of the house. 3. In sadomasochistic culture, a code word for a woman who role-plays being a "dominant" partner (sometimes refusing overt sexual activity and thereby denying being a prostitute as defined in law). See SEXUAL MASOCHISM.

mistrust   See BASIC MISTRUST, TRUST VS MISTRUST.

mistuned fork   A tuning fork intentionally tuned slightly above or below the pitch of a standard, to measure pitch discrimination or differences of sensitivity between the ears. When sounded with the standard, beats are produced.

Mitchell Rest Cure   rest-cure technique

mitochondrion   (R. Altmann, C. Benda, M. R. Lewis & W. H. Lewis) A minute, folded, granular, thread-like, self-perpetuating organelle found in the cytoplasm of cells of animal and plant organisms. It functions in cellular metabolism, secretion, and respiration, creating biological energy (through reactions of oxidative phosphorylation) to help run the body. Plural is mitochondria.

mitosis   (W. Flemming, E. A. Strasburger) A cell division process by which a body cell reproduces by dividing into two daughter cells, each having the same number and kinds of chromosomes. Mitotic cell division usually requires that a cell possess enough deoxyribonucleic acid (DNA) to permit doubling of its chromosomal material. Also known as nuclear division. See CELL DIVISION, MEIOSIS HAPLOID CELLS.

mitral cells   Pyramidal cells that form a layer of the olfactory bulb. Each mitral cell may receive signals from hundreds of olfactory filaments embedded in the nasal epithelium.

mitten pattern   Unusual, slow, spike-and-wave electroencephalographic (EEG) pattern that resembles the thumb and hand outline of a mitten. Occurs mainly in EEGs of adult patients with schizophrenia and epileptic patients with psychosis, was also claimed to be found in EEGs of some criminals.

Mitwelt   (contemporary world—German) The way each individual relates to the world as it is now in relation to others; the age presently lived in, present times, the present generation, contemporaries. See EIGENWELT, UMWELT.

MIX   See MIXED SCHEDULE OF REINFORCEMENT.

mixed bipolar disorder   A pathological affective condition marked by manic and depressive episodes, intermixed or alternating every few days. Depressive symptoms are usually most prominent and last at least a full day. See MAJOR DEPRESSIVE EPISODE, MANIC EPISODE.

mixed cerebral dominance   1. A condition in which neither cerebral hemisphere is clearly dominant in motor control, causing speech disorders or conflicts in handedness. 2. A theory of brain function stating that instead of one or the other of the cerebral hemispheres having a clear role over some function, that there may be some unusual distribution of control between the two hemispheres. Sometimes known as mixed dominance.

mixed design   1. An experimental method in which some treatment comparisons are inter-subject and some are intra-subject comparisons; a mixture of simple-randomized and the treatments-by-subjects designs. An example of a Lindquist Type I mixed design randomly assigns subjects to one of three stimulus intensities with each subject being placed in turn under each of the four magnitudes of reinforcement. 2. An experimental study method in which participants who can be divided into two or more discrete and typically overlapping population groups are assigned to different experimental conditions, such as types of therapies, to reveal the relative effectiveness of the therapies.

mixed feelings   Having antithetical emotions simultaneously, such as hate and love for a particular person. See AMBIVALENCE, AMBIVALENT FEELINGS.

mixed laterality   A tendency to shift from right to left side for some activities, or perform some acts with a preference for the right side and others with a preference for the left. Also known as lateral confusion.

mixed model   In factorial designs when one or more bases of classification involve random sampling and the other(s) involve fixed constants.

mixed-motive game   A situation that contains elements of both a cooperative and a competitive reward structure. See COMPETITIVE REWARD STRUCTURE, CO-OPERATIVE REWARD STRUCTURE.

mixed neurosis   Old Freudian phrase for a condition in which the patient showed symptoms of two or more neuroses.

mixed organic brain syndrome   Organic syndromes, such as Addison's disease, in which the clinical picture does not meet the criteria of other organic brain syndromes.

mixed reinforcement   An intermittent reinforcement in which the reinforcement pattern changes randomly or by design, such as from intervals of 4 minutes to 40 minutes. See MIXED SCHEDULE.

mixed sampling   double sampling

mixed schedule of reinforcement (MIX)   A combination of two or more simple schedules of reinforcement, programmed so that no cues are given as to which schedule is in effect at any given time but usually alternating at random. See MIXED REINFORCEMENT.

mixed schizophrenia   A form of schizophrenia manifested by symptoms of two or more of the basic categories of schizophrenia: simple, paranoid, catatonic, and hebephrenic (disorganized).

mixed specific developmental disorder   A diagnosis in which no single developmental disorder predominates, as when a child's arithmetic level is well below expectation but language skills are above expectation; the child is much smaller for his or her age than normal but is above average for social abilities.

mixoscopia   A form of voyeurism in which sexual satisfaction is achieved by observing sexual intercourse, particularly between the voyeur's lover and another person. See PEEPING TOM, PERVERSION, SCOTOPHILIA.

mixoscopia bestialis   A paraphilia in which a person achieves excitement by watching another person have coitus with an animal. See BESTIALITY, VOYEURISM, ZOOERASTY.

mixovariation   In genetics, the combination of multiple hereditary factors over several generations, due to the union of individuals with unlike hereditary elements (hybridization). Also known as combination.

mL   See MILLILITER.

ml   1. See MILLILITER. 2. See MILLILAMBERT.

MLU   See MEAN LENGTH OF UTTERANCE.

mm   See MILLIMETER.

MMECT   See MULTIPLE MONITORED ELECTRO-CONVULSIVE THERAPY.

MMPI   Minnesota Multiphasic Personality Inventory.

MMPI–A   Minnesota Multiphasic Personality Inventory–Adolescent.

MMT   See MULTIMODAL THERAPY.

M'Naghten rules/test   A set of rules established by the Judges of England in 1843 stating that to plead insanity as a defense, the accused must be "laboring under such a defect of reason, from disease of the mind, as not to know the nature and quality of the act he was doing, or if he did know it, he did not know that what he was doing was wrong." The name has no firm spelling, also spelled McNaghten, McNaughten. See AMERICAN LAW INSTITUTE GUIDELINES, COMPETENCY TO STAND TRIAL, CRIMINAL RESPONSIBILITY, GOOD-AND-EVIL TEST, IRRESISTIBLE IMPULSE, PARTIAL INSANITY.

mneme   1. (R. Semon, E. Hering) Refers to the capability of all living cells to remember; the basic memory in the individual or human race. 2. That which accounts for memory; the engram of a specific experience. See ENGRAM.

mnemic theory   A point of view that heredity is a form of memory based on inherited engrams. See COLLECTIVE UNCONSCIOUS, PRIMORDIAL IMAGE.

mnemometer   (J. P. Ranschburg) Obsolete instrument for timed exposure of visual stimuli, used in perception, association, and memory experiments.

mnemonic device   Any device or technique employed to assist memory, usually by forging a link or association between the new information to be remembered and information previously encoded (for example, remembering the numbers to a combination lock by associating them with familiar birth dates or phone numbers). Also known as mnemonic strategy/system. See KEY-WORD METHOD, MEDIATE ASSOCIATION, METHOD OF LOCI, PEG-WORD MNEMONIC SYSTEM.

mnemonics   1. Systems for aiding recall. See MNEMONIC DEVICE. 2. See MNEMOTECHNICS.

mnemonic trace   An engram. See MNEME.

mnemonist   A person who knows a variety of methods or techniques to aid in memorization, such as of a list of objects, or numbers. May seem to have an extraordinary memory whether or not he or she actually does.

mnemotechnics   The art of improving memory.

Mo   Old abbreviation for the mode.

MO   modus operandi.

mob   A disorderly crowd of people characterized by (a) unruly action; (b) heightened emotional response and irrationality, (c) a sense of anonymity, and (d) a loss of a sense of responsibility among its members. See CROWD BEHAVIOR, CROWD CONSCIOUSNESS, MOB PSYCHOLOGY.

mobbing behavior   Activity often observed in animals such as birds or deer that join together to drive away a predator.

mobile type   According to June Downey, a temperament characterized by a flexibility in shifting from one type of task to another, and by a tendency to proceed rapidly in a task with little attention on accuracy. See WILL TEMPERAMENT TEST.

mobility   1. Literally, movement, usually applied to the ability to transport self between home and work or community facilities, etc. For an infant, mobility is the ability to creep; for an adult with a disability, mobility may be the capability of traveling by wheelchair or public transportation. 2. A state or quality of movability. See MOTILITY. 3. Figuratively, changing position or status, as in upward mobility.

mobility of libido   In psychoanalytic theory, the transfer of libidinal energy from one subject to another, that is, from one part of the body, or one person, to another.

mobilization reaction   A response to acute or prolonged stress in which the individual becomes emotionally aroused, tense, and alert, and calls upon all available psychological and physical resources to meet the threat. See GENERAL ADAPTATION SYNDROME.

mobilization vs regression   (R. B. Cattell) A personality factor that marks psychological regression versus capacity to mobilize.

mob psychology   The force of group pressure that sweeps individuals into action, as in lynchings, riots, and demonstrations. Reasons given for the fact that ordinarily law-abiding citizens commit violent acts include the anonymity of the crowd, the "impression of universality" (everybody's doing it), and the tendency to release feelings of frustration stemming from other areas in their lives. See COLLECTIVE BEHAVIOR, CROWD BEHAVIOR, CROWD CONSCIOUSNESS, MASS HYSTERIA, MASS PSYCHOLOGY, MOB.

MOCC   memory-operating characteristic curve.

modal   Referring to the mode.

modality   (I. Kant, H. Helmholtz) 1. A therapeutic technique or process. 2. A type of sensation, for example, vision. See SENSE MODALITY.

modality effect   Different effects on retention often produced by visual and auditory presentation; auditory presentation usually produces better memory for the last few items in a series than does visual presentation.

modality profile   According to Arnold Lazarus, a list of problems and proposed treatments across seven discrete but interactive dimensions known as the BASIC I.D.

mode (M_o)   A statistic describing the central tendency of a set of data. It is the highest point or peak in a bar graph or frequency polygon, since it is the most frequently occurring score (for example, if a shoe store has more 10½ size shoes in its inventory than any other size, then 10½ is the modal size in that store). See BIMODAL DISTRIBUTION, MEAN, MEDIAN, UNIMODAL. For an example of a mode see BAR CHART. Of the 17 bars, the tallest one (seventh from the left) is the mode of that distribution.

model   1. A copy or representation of how a system functions. 2. A representation (verbal, quantitative, or graphic) of principles or hypotheses proposed to explain a condition or process, usually showing correlational or cause-effect relationships. For instance, a model of a psychological disorder might show epidemiological patterns as they relate to different diagnoses. The model may be a computer program.

model psychosis   In the 1950s and 1960s it was thought that the use of the hallucinogen lysergic acid diethylamide (LSD) offered a fair model of psychotic process. This idea has been largely discarded as more complex theories have evolved. See PSYCHOTOMIMETIC, HALLUCINOGEN.

modeling   1. (A. Bandura) A process in which people expand their knowledge and skills by observing people's behavior and its consequences for them. Modeling influences can promote development of competencies, alter behavioral restraints, create emotional disposition and shape images of social realities. See SOCIAL COGNITIVE THEORY. 2. In behavior modification, treatment in which a therapist performs the target behavior which the client is to imitate and adopt as the client's own. See MODELING THERAPY.

modeling effect   An experimenter bias effect based on giving participants improper information or showing improper observer effect. See EXPERIMENTER BIAS.

modeling theory   A point of view that observing actual or depicted activity (or fantasizing it) leads to performing it. Often applied to pornography and violence.

modeling therapy   A behavior therapy procedure in which a person imitates others in various social relationships. See FIXED ROLE THERAPY, PSYCHODRAMA.

mode of appearance   A characteristic way in which a sensory phenomenon (such as visual sensation, including glow, bulk, volume, surface) is presented.

mode pleasure   Satisfaction obtained by the learning itself; performance for its own sake rather than for goal-achievement. See FUNKTIONSLUST.

moderate depression   A degree of depression marked by (a) persistent feelings of anguish; (b) despondent ruminations; (c) periods of silence; (d) a dispirited manner; (e) constant complaints about being unwanted and unappreciated; (f) difficulties in thinking and concentrating; (g) various somatic disturbances. See DEPRESSION.

Moderate Feminism   A kind of feminism that espouses feminist ideas but opposes those of radical feminism; those who fit this description are said to often deny being feminists.

moderate mental retardation (MMR)   A poorly defined diagnostic category for persons with below average intelligence quotients (IQs). The range of IQs for this category are given variously as: 35–49; 36–51 by the World Health Organization and American Psychiatric Association; and 40–54 by the American Association on Mental Deficiency. Persons with MMR are considered "trainable" although they rarely achieve education beyond the second grade and may have poor coordination. See INTELLIGENCE, MILD MENTAL RETARDATION, RETARDATION.

moderation   Behavior within reasonable limits, as exemplified by the Greek philosophy of "nothing to excess." See ABSTINENCE.

moderator variable   A variable unrelated to a criterion variable, but still retained as useful in a regression equation because of its significant relationship to other predictor variables. In consumer psychology, a moderator variable is an influence by an individual factor (for example, a personality trait) that may alter, or moderate, a prediction of product choice. Studies found that personality variables in consumer groups may account for about a quarter of brand-choice decisions. The self-confidence of the purchaser was given as an example of a moderator variable.

modernism 1. A philosophical-scientific point of view of attempting to adjust ancient concepts to modern events. 2. A doctrine that demands a deliberate separation from ideas and values of the past and the search for new expressions without constraints from tradition. 3. Related to modernization in international development, a term which many critics see as demeaning existing and traditional cultures. 4. A point of view stressing up-to-date ideas, values, and conceptualizations. 5. Nontraditional innovative forms of expression characteristic of the 20th century.

modern racism A subtle form of prejudice in which people superficially appear to be impartial but in fact harbor racist attitudes.

modes of learning (J. Bruner) According to Jerome Bruner, three main ways that people acquire knowledge: enactive (by action), iconic (by mental images) and by symbols (as by reading).

modified replication See REPLICATION.

modified (union) shop In labor relations, an establishment in which employees who are currently union members must maintain their membership and all new employees must join the union, but current employees who are not members do not have to join.

modifier In genetics, a gene that appears to have an effect of modifying other hereditary factors and that has no significant effect when the main factor is absent.

modularity theories Assumptions that the human mind is composed of various independent units or modules that can be made to operate in various ways and that over time these modules relate to one another in various ways to achieve a kind of integrative synthesis. See FACULTY PSYCHOLOGY, STRUCTURE-OF-INTELLECT.

modulation transfer function (MTF) The process of changing a physical input modality to an output modality. For instance, in hearing, sound waves are transferred in modulated form to the brain by the inner ear.

modulation transfer function area (MTFA) An electronic measure of the resolution of a screen display; the higher the MTFA, the better the image quality. Correlates highly with task performance (especially reading time) and user preference.

modulator (in retina) 1. A nerve fiber that carries impulses from single retinal cones assumed responsible for transmission of color sensations. 2. A set of horizontal and amacrine cells that respond to narrow ranges of light wavelengths with peaks corresponding to different colors. See DOMINATORS.

modus operandi (MO) A specific form of behavior pattern typical of a particular individual, often in the context of criminal behavior. See HABIT.

modus ponens A valid form of conditional argument that has the following steps: If P, then Q; P therefore Q.

modus tollens A valid form of conditional argument which has three steps: If P, then Q; Not Q; Therefore, not P.

mogigraphia **writer's cramp** (meaning 1)

mogilalia Difficulty or hesitancy in speaking (including stuttering) frequently associated with resistance to psychotherapy. Also known as molilalia.

mogiphonia Difficulty in speaking because of overuse of the voice, as from speaking loudly for a long time.

molar Level of analysis or conceptualization focusing on large components or divisions, without considering (fine grain) elements of a phenomenon.

molar approach 1. An approach that stresses comprehensive concepts and problems, avoiding highly structured, detailed prescriptions for achievement of stated goals. 2. A level of analysis focusing on a few large components or divisions, without reduction to a number of small elements. 3. An approach stressing that behavior is a transaction of an individual, not merely of some part of the body. Compare HOLISM, MOLECULAR APPROACH, PHENOMENOLOGY.

molar behavior A large but unified segment, or holistic unit, of a person's total behavior. Compare MOLECULAR BEHAVIOR.

molecular approach Stressing particular elements of a problem, focusing on systematically detailed concepts. Compare MOLAR APPROACH.

molecular behavior Any action that can be analyzed into smaller units such as reflexes, as opposed to gross overall behavior. Compare MOLAR BEHAVIOR, HOLISM.

molecularism **atomism**

molecularism vs molarism (R. I. Watson) A prescriptive dimension of the philosophical underpinnings of psychology, namely, the description of psychological data in small versus large units. See OPPONENT-PAIRS DIMENSION.

molecular model of memory A theory that permanent memory recall is through self-regeneration via a sensory stimulus that triggers an electrical impulse code to produce a specific ribonucleic acid (RNA), and then a protein.

molecular study A study that stresses the analysis of larger units of behavior and experience into minute details (habits into constituent reflexes and neural concomitants, perceptions into sensations, or receptor and neural processes). Contrasts with molar studies in this respect, although the line cannot always be sharply drawn. See MOLAR STUDY.

molestation An assault, generally sexual touching of an individual, particularly a child or a person who is mentally challenged or comatose, "without lawful consent." See PEDOPHILIA, SEX OFFENSES.

molimen Unpleasant symptoms experienced by some women during the premenstrual or menstrual periods. Also known as molimina. See PREMENSTRUAL TENSION.

Molyneux's question A 17th-century problem posed to John Locke in a letter from William Molyneux: If a blind person is taught by touch to distinguish between a cube and a sphere ... and if the cube and sphere are placed on a table and the blind person miraculously made to see: before touching the object, can the person now distinguish which is the sphere and which the cube? The answer is no; research with people born blind who regained their sight has shown that they cannot tell the difference between the cube and the sphere by sight.

molysmophobia Fear of infection.

molysophobia Morbid fear of contamination. See MYSOPHOBIA.

moment (μ)   1. In relation to time, a short period. (A court of law once decided that a moment is 20 seconds.) 2. In mathematics, the mean of powers of the deviations of the observed values in a set of statistical data from a fixed value which may be either the mean or some arbitrary origin. 3. In statistics, the descriptive consonant of a frequency distribution that measures its average value, relative scatter of observations, symmetry, etc. **Higher moments** $= \Sigma(x_i - M)^r/N$, where x_i is the individual values, M is the mean of the individual values. In the second moment, $r = 2$, in the third moment $r = 3$, and in the fourth moment $r = 4$. Statistical moments were originated by Karl Pearson who was initially a physicist. 4. In mechanics, the moment of a force on a lever is the force times its distance from the fulcrum; hence, various meanings in mathematics in which the frequency distribution is analogous to the fulcrum, and the frequencies are analogous to forces operating at various distances from it. Mu is also the statistical symbol for population mean.

momism   1. (P. Wylie) Common term for excessive giving of maternal care; acceptance of maternal dominance, resulting in lack of independence and maturity on the part of the child. See MONKEY LOVE, SPOONFED. 2. Derisive term for women's behavior in general.

mommy track   1. Slang for the choice of a woman to have children and stay home. 2. Refers to the practice in some organizations and institutions of setting a ceiling for promotions of women who have young children.

monad   (C. von Wolff) 1. (G. Bruno) An independent unit having the characteristics of both mind and matter. A Pythagorean concept, revived by Giordano Bruno; adopted by Gottfried von Leibnitz as a means of overcoming both the dualism of René Descartes and the monism of Baruch Spinoza. See MONADOLOGY. 2. A spiritual substance from which material objects develop.

monadology   The philosophy of Gottfried von Leibnitz, who postulated the existence of "monads," life-giving entities that are the ultimate units of life and that include the human soul. As an early figure in German psychology, Leibnitz influenced the assumption that mental activity is dynamic and self-generating.

monaural   1. Pertaining to one ear. 2. Hearing with only one ear, whether the other ear is deaf or blocked from hearing. Also known as monoaural, uniaural.

mondo   A procedure in Zen Buddhism in which a Zen master forces students or monks to answer rapidly any question put to them. Spontaneity of response is emphasized, to lead the learner beyond the limits of ordinary conceptual thinking, which is usually logical and organized. See FREE ASSOCIATION, WORD ASSOCIATION.

monestrous   Describes animals that experience one estrus cycle per year. See ESTROUS BEHAVIOR, ESTRUS.

money dreams   In psychoanalytic theory, the meaning of such dreams, including gratification of anal impulses to hold back (hoard), evacuate (spend), or handle coins.

mongolian idiot   (L. Down) Obsolete phrase for a person of moderate to severe mental subnormality, with facial characteristics of alleged mongolian cast, as a result of chromosomal anomaly. See DOWN SYNDROME.

mongolism   Obsolete name for Down syndrome.

monism   1. (Shankara) A philosophical doctrine that mind and matter are the same, that the apparent duality is only maya (illusion), and that there is only one eternal reality. See NATURAL MONISM. 2. The belief that the universe comprises only one kind of existence. Includes materialism (the view that only the physical world exists and that mental processes are a mere by-product of physical ones), mentalism (holds that only the mind exists, and that the physical world is only imagined), and identity position (the view that mental processes are the same as certain types of brain process but described in different terms). Compare DUALISM, PLURALISM.

monism vs dualism   (R. I. Watson) A prescriptive dimension of the philosophical underpinnings of psychology, namely, the assumption that the basic principle of life is of one type versus two kinds.

monitor   1. To observe carefully with intention to diagnose or evaluate what is happening and to be ready to interfere in the ongoing process if considered necessary. 2. A television-type screen as found on computers.

monitoring   Observing phenomena such as patients in a hospital, experimental participants, participants, machines while operating, and checking them at intervals.

monitrice   A childbirth coach, usually a nurse or midwife, trained in the Lamaze method.

monkey love   Rare phrase from the German term *Affenliebe* (monkey love), refers to the attitudes of some parents, usually mothers, who take an unusually overprotective attitude toward their children and who thereby may eventually harm their children's emotional and social behavior. See MOMISM, PAMPERING, REACTION FORMATION.

monkey therapist   (H. Harlow) In primate-behavior studies, a normally-raised monkey provided as a companion to an isolation-reared one. Reduced the isolate's socialization and behavioral deficits; led to speculation about the applicability of equivalent therapy for human children with disorders such as autism.

monoamine hypothesis   A postulate that clinical depression is due to inactivity in monoaminergic synapses.

monoamine oxidase (MAO)   An enzyme that breaks down biogenic amines, referring in neurophysiology especially to the function of this substance at the synapse (the space between the axon and the dendrite of two nerve cells). Enzyme is the focus of medicines that can interfere with its function. See MONOAMINE OXIDASE INHIBITOR.

monoamine oxidase inhibitor (MAOI)   A class of psychotropic drugs which counter or inhibit the monoamine oxidases (MAOs). In so doing, they effectively allow more of a presence of the monoamines, such as norepinephrine, acetylcholine, dopamine and serotonin, which in turn tends to have an anti-depressant effect. See MONOAMINE OXIDASE.

monoaural   **monaural**

monoblepsia   A situation when a person can see better with one eye than with two.

monochorionic twins   A set of twins that shared the same chorionic membrane as embryos. See DIZYGOTIC TWINS, FRATERNAL TWINS, IDENTICAL TWINS, MONOZYGOTIC TWINS.

monochromasy   A form of color blindness in which only a single color can be seen.

monochromatism   1. An abnormal visual condition in which all colors are seen as matching a single primary color. See ACHROMATISM, COLOR BLINDNESS. 2. See ACHROMATOPSIA.

monochronic task   (E. T. Hall) Work that involves doing only one task (for example, in a garment factory, a worker who only makes button holes). Compare POLYCHROMIC TASK.

monocular   Pertaining to a single eye. Also known as uniocular.

monocular (depth) cues   The cues to the perception of distance and depth that involve only one eye such as linear perspective, relative position, relative movement, chiaroscuro or light and shadow, accommodation, and atmospheric perspective. Compare BINOCULAR CUES.

monocular suppression   A tendency of one eye to be dominant while the other is suppressed, resulting in a deficit or failure of binocular vision.

monocular vision   The use of only one eye.

monodrama   A roleplaying situation in which a person acts out a scene alone, such as simulating a conversation on a telephone. Usually done in the presence of others who evaluate the person's behavior.

monogamy   A pairing of mates as in a human marriage. Implies exclusive commitment of each to the other.

monogenic   Characterizing hereditary variation due to a single major gene. Also known as Mendelian inheritance, simple inheritance.

monogenism   A theory that all humans developed from a single ancestral human stock. Many anthropologists conclude that human life started in what is now Africa.

monoideic somnambulism   Ideational content related to a single idea that occurs in a state of somnambulism (sleepwalking). When more than one idea is involved, the appropriate phrase is polyideic somnambulism.

monoideism   Obsessive preoccupation with a single idea, and inability to think of anything else. Found in its most extreme form in senile patients. See MONOMANIA.

monomania   (J. Esquirol) 1. Obsolete term for "partial insanity," in which a person is preoccupied with one topic and is assumed to be pathological only with reference to that topic. Examples of monomanias include kleptomania, erotomania and pyromania. See MONOIDEISM. 2. One of Jean Esquirol's five classes of mental disorders.

monomatric   Having one mother. Pertains to a family or household in which all or most of the child-rearing responsibilities are fulfilled by one person. Compare POLYMATRIC.

monopathophobia   Morbid fear of acquiring a specific illness or disease; for example, fear of brain disease (meningitophobia), fear of pellagra (pellagraphobia). See NOSOPHOBIA.

monopediomania   Being sexually attracted to a one-legged person or sex partner.

monophagism   1. Eating of only one kind of food. 2. Eating only one meal a day.

monophasic sleep rhythm   A sleep pattern in which sleeping occurs in bits of subphases once a day. Associated with canaries, snakes, and human adults. See POLYPHASIC SLEEP RHYTHM, SLEEP-WAKE CYCLE.

monophobia   1. Fear of being alone, of loneliness. 2. Fear of one thing. See AUTOPHOBIA, EREMOPHOBIA.

monoplegia   The paralysis of a single part of the body; for example, one arm, one leg, or one digit. See HYSTERICAL PARALYSIS.

monopolar depression   An affective disorder consisting of one or more depressive episodes with no manic episodes. See BIPOLAR DISORDER.

monopolist   A person in social situations or in group therapy who seeks to capture exclusive attention of the group. See GROUP THERAPY, HELP REJECTING COMPLAINER, THERAPIST'S ASSISTANT.

monorchid   A male with only one testis in the scrotum. The second testis may be undescended. See CRYPTORCHID, ECTOPIC TESTIS.

monosomy   Missing one chromosome of a pair of homologous chromosome. See GROUP MONOSOMY.

monosymptomatic   Denoting a disorder characterized by a single marked symptom.

monosymptomatic circumscription   A mental disorder characterized by a single symptom.

monosymptomatic neurosis   The exhibition of a single symptom of a neurotic disorder, such as an obsessive thought.

monosymptomatic psychosis   Phrase sometimes applied to a rare type of dysmorphophobia in which an obsession or delusion of physical deformity is the patient's single symptom or complaint.

monosynaptic arc   A simple synaptic communication between two neurons, such as a synapse between a sensory fiber and a motor neuron in the spinal cord.

monosynaptic stretch reflex   Muscle contraction in response to a sudden stretching, due to a sensory and a motor neuron communicating over a single synapse.

monosynaptic transmission   Synaptic transmission in which nerve activity is relayed only once from presynaptic to postsynaptic neurons.

monotherapy   A technique in which the counselor requests the client to write or create a dramatic scene and roleplay all characters involved; the client is encouraged to roleplay personal fantasies or repressed wishes for the purpose of facilitating awareness and therapeutic discussion. See PSYCHODRAMA.

monothetic similarity   A system for classifying species based on their sharing one important characteristic. Compare POLYTHETIC TAXONOMY.

monotonic   Describes a variable that progressively either increases or decreases; it may temporarily remain constant but does not change its direction, such as the height of a growing child.

monotonic relationship   Variables in which an increase on one is accompanied by a consistent increase or decrease in the other although there may be sections of no change.

monovular twins   monozygotic twins

monozygotic   Refers to or developed from one zygote (fertilized ovum); said of identical twins.

monozygotic twins (MZ) Twins that develop from a single ovum fertilized by a single sperm. Approximately 25% of human twins are monozygotic. They are identical in genetic composition, having inherited the same sets of genes from both parents. Also known as enzygotic twins, identical twins, monovular twins, uniovular twins. See CLONE, DIZYGOTIC TWINS, TWIN STUDIES.

Monroe Diagnostic Reading Test (M. Monroe) An examination used to diagnose factors other than intelligence which interfere with a child's ability to read. Designed for use with children in grades one to five. Consists of nine parts aimed at pinpointing visual and auditory difficulties.

monster 1. Obsolete term for a newborn child, usually born dead, who is severely disfigured, for example, not having a brain, or without arms or legs or both. 2. Rare term for individuals with congenital defects or acquired injuries that have severely disfigured their appearance. See TERATOGEN.

monster fear See TERATOPHOBIA.

Monte Carlo fallacy A (false) belief that after a run of "bad luck" or successive losses that there must be a change to "good luck" or successive wins. See GAMBLER'S FALLACY.

Monte Carlo method A mathematical simulation in which the values of random variables are repeatedly sampled.

Monte Carlo study A study that uses random values (usually generated by a computer) instead of real data, to test a statistical model or theory.

Montessori method (M. Montessori) An educational system developed in Italy in the early 1900s that focuses on self-education of preschool children through the development of initiative by means of freedom of action. Involves sense-perception training with objects of different shapes and colors; and development of coordination through games and exercises. See ALTERNATIVE EDUCATIONAL SYSTEMS.

mood 1. A mild, usually transient, emotional state such as euphoria or irritability. 2. A predisposition or receptivity toward an emotional reaction, such as excited. See ADJUSTMENT DISORDER WITH DEPRESSED MOOD, DIURNAL MOOD VARIATION, EXPANSIVE MOOD, HALLUCINOGEN-INDUCED MOOD DISORDER, MELANCHOLIC MOOD.

mood-altering drugs Outmoded phrase for medicines used in treating affective disorders. See MOOD-STABILIZING DRUGS.

mood complex (M. Prince) The suppression of desires, inclinations, feelings, etc. Becoming a kind of living robot.

mood-congruent psychotic features Delusions that reflect a depressed mood (themes: inadequacy, guilt, disease, death) or a manic mood (themes: great personal worth, absolute power, or a special relationship to a deity or famous person).

mood-cyclic disorders A category of Sandor Rado's adaptational approach/psychodynamics in which the person may show any of a variety of cycles of depression, elation, or both.

mood-dependent memory A recollection due to being in a particular emotional state similar to the state that a person was originally in when the event recalled happened.

mood disorder A pathological condition in which a person's mood is inappropriate to the situation, such as smiling or laughing when the person should be sad, or becoming violent with little provocation; may involve sudden mood changes with no apparent cause. See MOOD SWINGS.

mood-incongruent psychotic features Delusions or hallucinations, the content of which does not involve the characteristic themes found among mood-congruent psychotic features (for example, persecutory delusions, thought broadcasting, delusions of being controlled, found in a person with catatonic-like symptoms of stupor, mutism, negativism, and posturing).

moodiness Affective state characterized by ill humor, sullenness, and sulking. Usually a response to disappointment or frustration, and generally subsides over time.

mood-stabilizing drugs Medicines particularly useful in treating affective disorders, especially bipolar (manic-depressive) disorder and related conditions. Lithium, approved around 1970, was a major breakthrough. In the late 1980s, the anticonvulsant drugs carbamazepine and later valproic acid were added to this category. Antidepressants may also be considered part of this class of drugs.

mood swings Periodic alternation between feelings of well-being and dejection. If mild and occasional, these changes are normal; but if severe, they may be a neurotic reaction; and if they are intense and persistent, they may be symptomatic of bipolar (manic-depressive) disorder. See BIPOLAR DISORDER.

Mooney Problem Check List (R. L. Mooney & L. Gordon) A personality inventory containing statements of problems compiled from students, case records, and counseling interviews. The respondent checks personal problems. Designed to facilitate interviews and counseling.

moon illusion A common illusion in which the moon appears larger on the horizon than at the zenith.

moon-phase studies Research on the possible relationship between the phases of the moon and episodes of violence or mental disorder. The relationship has long been expressed in folklore, folk medicine, and language itself ("lunacy," "lunatic"). David Tuke used the archaic term "lunatismus" for somnambulists who walk in their sleep only when the moon shines.

MOR marital opportunity ratio

moral Describing persons or groups whose conduct is ethical or proper.

moral absolutism The total unquestioning acceptance of rules as established by others.

moral anxiety 1. A fear of retribution based on a person's guilty conscience. 2. In psychoanalytic theory, the anxiety experienced by the ego in terms of guilt or shame, usually as an expression of fear of punishment by the superego for a failure to maintain proper standards of conduct.

moral code A set of rules of conduct accepted by a society or group as binding on all members.

moral conduct   Behavior that conforms to the accepted set of values, customs, or rules of a given society or religious group.

moral consistency   Stable, predictable pattern of moral attitudes and character throughout the years. According to a longitudinal study, children tended to maintain a consistent pattern of moral standards. However, some studies raise questions about consistency from situation to situation of such characteristics as honesty.

moral determinism   (B. Spinoza, G. W. Leibnitz) A doctrine developed from human interest in the goodness of God; the idea that the world is basically good because God made it so.

moral development   (J. Piaget, L. Kohlberg) The gradual development of a person's concepts of right and wrong, conscience, ethical and religious values, social attitudes, and behavior. See KOHLBERG'S THEORY OF MORAL DEVELOPMENT, PIAGETIAN THEORY.

moral dilemma   A situation where a choice must be made, and whatever choice is made will have undesirable consequences ("Damned if you do and dammed if you don't"). Sometimes known as a Catch-22 situation.

moral hazard   In sociology, the danger that providing benefits such as welfare will increase the number of people seeking or depending on them.

moral idiocy   (E. Bleuler) Obsolete phrase for a total incapacity to feel sympathy or to be concerned with the welfare and woes of other people, though capable of other emotions. See MORAL IMBECILITY, PSYCHOPATHY, SOCIOPATHY.

moral imbecility   Obsolete phrase used by Eugen Bleuler to refer to a person who is intellectually and emotionally sound but ethically defective and lacking in appreciation for the feelings and rights of others. See ANTISOCIAL REACTION, MORAL IDIOCY, PSYCHOPATHY, SOCIOPATHY.

moral independence   Phrase used by Jean Piaget for an older child's recognition that an act's morality may be substantially determined by its motive and other subjective considerations. Moral independence is a principle of the autonomous stage. See KOHLBERG, MORAL REALISM, MORAL RELATIVISM.

moral insanity   Obsolete phrase used by James Prichard for an intellectually normal person in whom "the moral and active principles of the mind are strongly perverted and depraved," making them "incapable . . . of conducting themselves with decency and propriety in the business of life." See ANTISOCIAL REACTION.

morality   A system of social beliefs, and a set of values relating to right conduct usually codified in various religions, for example, the Ten Commandments, against which certain behaviors can be judged acceptable or unacceptable.

morality of constraint   According to Jean Piaget, the young child's attitude toward morality which consists of an unquestioning, unchallenging obedience to the rules laid down by parents. Obedience is based on fear and on the perception that rules established by parents are fixed, eternal, and eternally valid. Piaget believed morality of constraint to be characteristic of children until roughly age ten. See MORALITY OF COOPERATION, RULES OF THE GAME.

morality of cooperation   According to Jean Piaget, the ten-to-eleven-year-old child's attitude toward morality characterized by the perception that rules are social conventions that can be challenged and modified when concerned parties agree. See MORALITY OF CONSTRAINT, RULES OF THE GAME.

moral judgment   Decisions as to which actions are right and which are wrong. May vary between people, for example, one person considers it acceptable behavior to take a brand-new pencil from the office to use at home; a second person thinks it is acceptable behavior to take a much-used pencil, but not a new pencil home; a third person believes that taking anything home is stealing.

morally superior   One of four basic lifestyles according to Nira Kefir. Such persons are most afraid of being rejected, and to prevent this, act on the highest level of morality and distinguish themselves by having high standards of behavior. See ETHICS, MAJOR PRIORITIES.

Moral Majority   A coalition of American evangelical fundamentalists generally opposed to school sex education, permissiveness, secular humanism, among other less traditional positions.

moral masochism   A desire, generally unconscious, for self-punishment. A self-defeating mechanism often evident in clients in psychotherapy. The realization of this unconscious desire often leads to a strong abreaction. It is generally assumed that such people have deeply hidden guilt feelings and act to be punished for their past sins, real or imagined. See ABREACTION.

moral model   An explanation of mental illness, common during the middle ages, that insanity was the result of sin and possession by the devil. See EXORCISM.

moral nihilism   (M. de Sade) A doctrine that there are no reasons for morals and that absolute pleasure at anyone else's expense is justified.

moral realism   (J. Piaget) A type of thinking characteristic of younger children who equate good behavior with obedience just as they equate the morality of an act only with its consequences. See HETERONOMOUS MORALITY.

moral relativism   (J. Piaget) In Piagetian theory, the developed ability to consider intention behind an act along with possible extenuating circumstances when judging its rightness or wrongness. See MORAL REALISM.

moral therapy   (P. Dubois) A psychotherapy based on the concept that a person considered insane could be reached by taking the position that listening to a person talking rationally and being kind could help deliver the person from the mental disorder. See DIRECT PSYCHOANALYSIS.

moral treatment   Humane treatment of mental patients championed by such people as Philippe Pinel and Jean Esquirol in France, William Tuke in England, and Benjamin Rush, Isaac Ray, and Thomas Kirkbride in America. Prior treatment was based on the assumption that the devil inhabited those with mental disorders and that punishment of the body would drive the devil out of such people. See WITCHCRAFT.

moratorium   (E. Erikson) An experimental stage in adolescence when youths try out alternative roles before making permanent commitments. An extended moratorium is not a universal feature of adolescence; it is more likely to occur in economically advantaged classes. See ERIKSON'S STAGES OF PSYCHOSOCIAL DEVELOPMENT, IDENTITY CRISIS.

morbid   1. Diseased. 2. In psychology, deviant or abnormal.

morbid dependency   (K. Horney) Having excessive needs, overencouraged needs, or both, that must be satisfied by others. Sometimes seen in persons who are immature, disabled, or those exhibiting a compulsive need to efface themselves and surrender to a stronger person. See DEPENDENCY NEEDS.

morbidity   1. A pathological condition, whether organic or functional. 2. See COMORBIDITY, MORBIDITY RATE.

morbidity rate   1. The ratio of sick individuals to well individuals in a population. 2. In descriptive statistics, information about the number of cases per thousand or multiple of a thousand per a certain time period of cases of disorders or diseases.

morbidity risk   In epidemiology, the statistical chance that any individual of certain status in a particular environment will develop a certain disease or disorder. The probability often is expressed in terms of risk factors, using 1.0 as a base; the larger the number, the greater the morbidity risk.

morbid obesity   Being 100 pounds over the "ideal" body weight for height, age, and body frame type.

morbid perplexity   A maladjustment symptom associated with loss of ego boundaries, characterized by profound confusion about personal identity and the meaning of existence. It is associated with schizophrenia.

Moreno's theory   The following items are important for understanding Jacob Moreno's theory: CONSERVE, ENCOUNTER, HYPNODRAMA, INFRA REALITY, INTERACTIVE EXPLANATION, INTUITIVE SOCIOGRAM, NETWORK, PERCEPTUAL SOCIOGRAM, PSYCHODRAMA, PSYCHODRAMA FORMS, PSYCHOLOGICAL GEOGRAPHY, SOCIAL ATOM, SOCIATRY, SOCIO-GROUP STAR, SOCIODRAMA, SOCIOGRAM, SOCIOGRAM ANALYSIS, SOCIOMETRY, SPONTANEITY TEST, SPONTANEITY THERAPY/TRAINING, STRUCTURAL GROUP, TELE, THEATER OF SPONTANEITY, THERAPEUTIC SOLILOQUY.

mores   Social customs accepted by members of a culture or population even though the standards of behavior may lack legal sanction. Singular is mos.

Morgan's Canon/principle   (C. L. Morgan) A theory that the action of an animal "cannot be interpreted as an exercise of a higher psychical faculty if it can instead be interpreted in terms of a faculty that stands lower in the psychological scale." Proposed in 1894, it helped reduce the older practice of anthropomorphism, the endowment of animals with human traits. Also known as Lloyd Morgan's canon. See COINCIDENCE VARIATIONS, LAW OF PARSIMONY, OCCAM'S RAZOR.

moria   1. Rare term for slowness of comprehension. 2. Rare term for an obsessive or morbid desire to joke, particularly when the humor is inappropriate. See GALLOWS HUMOR, WITZELSUCHT.

Morita therapy   (S. Morita) Therapy for hypochondriasis introduced in the early 20th century in Japan. Treatment consists of a period of absolute bed rest, during which the patient is allowed only to sleep and suffer, followed by a period of increasingly difficult and tiring work in a communal setting, with the objective of teaching the patient to accept life as it is at the moment, a process called *arugamama*. See REST-CURE TECHNIQUE.

morning-after pill   Colloquial term for an estrogenic drug such as diethystilbesterol (DES) that prevents pregnancy when taken 24 to 72 hours after sexual intercourse.

morning erection   Genital arousal of men during the last rapid-eye-movement (REM) period of sleep, lasting up to an hour, not necessarily connected with sexual dreaming, occurring even in some men with erectile dysfunction. Compare PRIAPISM.

morning people   Refers to individuals who wake up bright and cheery and ready to start the day, but who later in the day become lethargic, as opposed to "evening people" who, in the morning, wake up tired and possibly in a bad mood, but who as the day progresses become more active and alert. It is speculated that morning people should not marry evening people.

morning sickness   Episodes of nausea and vomiting experienced by some women during the first months of or throughout the pregnancy. Usually occurs soon after arising, although some women have the symptoms throughout the day. Causes appear to be both physiological and psychological. Medical term is *nausea gravidarum*.

moron   (foolish—Greek) 1. Obsolete subclass of mental retardation. 2. (H. Goddard) Obsolete term applied by Henry Goddard to persons with mild mental retardation (intelligence quotients of 50 to 70), capable of performing simple tasks under supervision in spite of limited academic ability. An adult said to function at the 8-to-12-year-old level. Term has practically disappeared from professional language but is commonly used as a disparaging remark to people who act in manners indicating stupidity. See TRAINABLE-MENTALLY RETARDED. 3. Has been used incorrectly as equivalent to pederasty.

Moro reflex/response   (E. Moro) A reflexive action in which newborn infants, when startled, throw out arms, extend fingers, and often quickly bring the arms back together as if clutching or embracing, in response to loud noises or unexpected events. Most infants lose this reflex at about the age of six months. See STARTLE REACTION.

morpheme   The minimum distinctive unit of spoken words, for example, in the word "cats," "s" is a morpheme (indicating the plural) and "cat" is a morpheme (because in speech, it cannot be divided into its parts "c," "a," and "t" without losing its meaning). Any word is composed of one or several morphemes. See GRAPHEME, PHONEME.

morphine   (F. Sertürner) The most well-established strong narcotic and analgesic in medical use for a century. Found in raw opium, it can be synthesized. Like other opiates, it is susceptible to dependence and abuse. Also known as M, morphine sulfate (M.S.). See OPIOID-RELATED DISORDERS.

morphine tolerance   A condition that develops as a result of continued use of morphine so that increasingly larger doses are required to relieve a given degree of pain. Can be rapid, developing in a normal individual in three weeks as a result of a daily therapeutic dose. See HEROIN DEPENDENCE, OPIOID-RELATED DISORDERS, SOLDIERS' SICKNESS.

morphine withdrawal   See OPIOID WITHDRAWAL SYMPTOMS.

morphodite   Colloquial term for both a hermaphrodite and a lesbian.

morphogenesis   The development of the form and structure of an organism.

morphogenic method   A technique relating to the normal development of the human's form, particularly concerning the formation of personality.

morphogenotype   (W. Sheldon) A hypothetical biological structure that underlies the observable structure, or physique, of the human.

morphologic(al) inferiority   Phrase introduced by Alfred Adler to describe a subgroup of organ inferiority, characterized by a deficiency in the shape, size, or strength of an organ or a part of it.

morphological index   The index or relationship among body proportions that describes a particular body build. See BODY BUILD, BODY-BUILD INDEX, BODY BUILD THEORIES, TYPOLOGY.

morphology   1. (J. W. von Goethe) The branch of science that deals with body structure and form; the study of personality as related to body build. 2. In grammar, the study of the inflection, derivation, and composition of words, as distinct from syntax.

morphophilia   Being sexually attracted to a partner whose body characteristics are selectively particularized, prominent, or different from the person's own. See PARAPHILIA.

morsicatio buccarum   (cheek biting—Latin) A form of compulsive self-mutilation characterized by the chewing of the inside of the cheeks. See FINGER-BITING BEHAVIOR, SELF-MUTILATION.

morsicatio labiorum   (lip biting—Latin) A form of compulsive self-mutilation characterized by the chewing of the lips. See FINGER-BITING BEHAVIOR, SELF-MUTILATION.

Mosher Forced-Choice Guilt Inventory   (D. Mosher) A test that elicits a respondent's level of sex guilt, hostility guilt, and morality-conscience guilt. Conceptualizes guilt as an expectancy for self-monitored punishment for violating socially acceptable behavior.

mort douce   (sweet death—French) 1. Bliss following sexual orgasm. 2. Euthanasia. 3. Death occurring during sexual intercourse.

mortality   1. A fatality. 2. In research, attrition of subjects.

mortido   The death instinct. Coined by Paul Federn as the counterpart of Sigmund Freud's libido (life instinct). Similar to Freud's Thanatos. See EGO PSYCHOTHERAPY.

morula   An early stage of embryology, extending from the first cleavage of the zygote until the blastula is formed by further divisions of daughter cells.

mos   A specific custom. Singular of mores.

mosaic   Refers to an organism having genetically different tissues side-by-side, resulting from cellular mosaicism, chromosomal mosaicism, or gene mosaicism. See CHIMERISM.

mosaicism   The condition of being mosaic.

mosaic test   A projective technique in which the participant, usually a child, is asked to "make anything you like" out of approximately 400 tiles of different colors and shapes. Interpretations, as in the case of all projective tests, depend on the insight and experience of the examiner. See LOWENFIELD MOSAIC TEST.

mosaic theory of perception   A point of view that each nerve fiber of a peripheral organ, such as the ear, communicates directly with a specific neuron in the brain, complex sensations being produced by combinations of sensory-fiber impulses.

Mosso balance   (A. Mosso) A device for measuring changes in blood supply; it consists of a large platform balance (tilting board) movable in a vertical plane; the reactor lies flat on the balance, any disturbance of which, due to increased blood supply in legs or head, is recorded directly on a kymograph.

Mosso ergograph   (A. Mosso) A device to measure finger muscle contractions and changes during prolonged work.

most comfortable loudness (MCL)   The level of hearing at which speech is most comfortable for the listener. This has important implications for a hearing-impaired child in school.

most-likely law   A theory that in predicting or in diagnosing any organism's behavior that what has occurred most frequently in the past is probably what will happen in the future.

mote-beam mechanism   Identifying a personality characteristic in individuals who express concern about an undesirable trait in others, especially in members of a minority group, but ignore the presence of the same trait in themselves. See IDIOPANIMA, INSIGHT, OUTSIGHT.

mother archetype   (C. G. Jung) The primordial image of the mother figure that occurs repeatedly in various cultural concepts and myths since ancient times. See MAGNA MATER.

mother complex   An abnormally strong emotional attachment to the mother, usually accompanied by sexual desire. See MOTHER FIXATION.

motherese   Term used by linguists to describe the special form of language used by adults when speaking to young children, including simplification of sentence structure and high-pitched intonational patterns. See CHILD-DIRECTED SPEECH.

mother figure   A mother substitute (sister, father, friend, teacher, foster mother) who assumes the basic functions of the biological mother. Also known as mother substitute/surrogate, surrogate mother. See TRANSFERENCE.

mother fixation   An abnormally strong emotional attachment to the mother, especially by an adult. See MOTHER COMPLEX.

mother hypnosis   (S. Ferenczi) A type of hypnotic submission purported to originate in transference of mother fixation, an obedient response to the coaxing of the mother. Compare FATHER HYPNOSIS.

mothering   (H. S. Sullivan) A relationship in which the mother or mother surrogate provides an infant or child with adequate emotional warmth, personal care, and sensory stimulation, all of which are purportedly essential to the development of a sense of security, feelings of self-worth, and the capacity to deal with the environment. See COMPLETE MOTHER, MOTHERING ONE, MULTIPLE MOTHERING, SCHIZOPHRENOGENIC MOTHER.

mothering instinct   See MOTHER INSTINCT.

mothering one   A mother surrogate. See MOTHER SURROGATE (meaning 1).

mother instinct   The mother's drive to protect and care for offspring, usually but not always her own offspring. Appears to be unlearned and instinctive in animals, but its instinctual character is questionable among humans. Usually called mothering instinct when applied to an organism other than the biological mother. Also called maternal instinct. See INFANTICIDE.

mother love   The natural protective and possessive affection a mother displays toward her children. The feeling, sometimes called instinctive, usually is reinforced by pressures of the social group which expects human mothers to show tender feelings toward their offspring.

mother-son incest   Sexual activity between mother and son. Much rarer than father-daughter incest, and is associated with such factors as absence of the father, an ethically defective home, disturbed marital relations, alcoholism, and psychosis or other emotional disturbances on the part of one or both partners. See PHAEDRA COMPLEX.

mother substitute   1. See MOTHER FIGURE. 2. See MOTHER SURROGATE.

Mother Superior complex   A tendency of some therapists to play a maternal role in relations with patients, often to the detriment of the therapy. Also known as Red Cross nursing. See PRIMARY RELATIONSHIP THERAPY.

mother surrogate   1. A substitute for a mother, such as wet-nurse, or grandmother. Also known as mothering one. 2. An object such as a wire or cloth model, devised and used by Harry Harlow in experiments on affectional responses in the infant monkey. See LOVE, MOTHER FIGURE.

motility   1. Movement or activity; an essential principle in working with the body. Parts of the body have their own inherent motility; for example, the motility of the scrotum, or gut. 2. The capacity to move either voluntarily or involuntarily (as in sleepwalking). 3. The style and speed of movement. Motility may be inhibited for physical reasons or for psychological reasons, as in hysterical paralysis. See MOBILITY.

motility disorder   Any abnormality of posture, gesture, or other motion or movement. See HYSTERICAL PARALYSIS.

motility psychosis   Atypical cycloid psychosis in which behavior ranges from hyperkinetic to akinetic.

motion aftereffect (MAE)   A reversal perceptual reaction to observing certain classes of motion, in that the original perception, such as looking at a series of lights that blink from right to left for a while, then glancing at a neutral surface and "seeing" lights moving from left to right. See ILLUSION.

motion detection   An ability of the eye to observe motion even under conditions of cortical blindness.

motion economy   (H. & L. Gilbreth) Principles developed for efficient performance of industrial operations. Motion economy recommends: simultaneous use of both hands moving in opposite directions; arrangement of work to permit an easy, natural rhythm; fixed, convenient location of tools; adequate illumination and workplace height, etc. See METHODS ANALYSIS, THERBLIG, TIME AND MOTION EVALUATION.

motion fear   See ERGASIOPHOBIA, KINESOPHOBIA.

motion parallax   A monocular cue to depth perception conveyed by the image of a closer object moving more rapidly across the retina than that of a farther object when both objects are actually traveling at the same rate. The nearer the object, the larger the change of position.

motion perspective   (J. J. Gibson) Any perception in which visual factors such as eye movements produce or create motion that is apparent rather than actual, as in apparent motion, or induced motion. See MOTION PARALLAX.

motion sickness   Discomfort marked by nausea, dizziness, headache, pallor, cold sweats, and in some cases, vomiting and prostration, caused by irregular or abnormal motion (such as being on a rocking boat) that disturbs the normal sense of balance maintained by the semicircular canals of the inner ear (resulting in "seasickness"). Motion sickness may also occur due to an organic brain lesion, usually within the fourth ventricle.

motion study   Analysis of industrial operations into their component movements. See TIME-MOTION STUDY.

motivated error   1. A mistake or miscue that reveals a hidden motive, for example, a "Freudian slip." 2. Interference with an intended act by an "accidental" one, resulting from the deeper mechanisms of an unconscious wish whose primary purpose it is to carry out this "accidental" performance. See UNCONSCIOUS.

motivated forgetting   Over time people tend to recall pleasant and to forget unpleasant events. An explanation for this is that there is a general tendency of people to avoid unpleasantness in all forms, including memories.

motivated skepticism   A tendency to require more information to make a decision contrary to initial preference than a decision consistent with initial preference.

motivation   The process of initiating, sustaining, and directing psychological or physical activities, including internal forces such as impulses, drives, and desires involved in this process. Motives may operate on a conscious or unconscious level, and are frequently divided into physiological (primary, or organic, such as hunger and elimination) and psychological (secondary, or personal/social, such as affiliation, competition, and individual interests and goals). See CONATION, DESIRE, WANT.

motivational conflict Two or more motives in conflict with each other resulting in frustration, as in an animal desiring food but wanting to avoid a fight with a predator. Some motivational conflicts involve acquired motives.

motivational disposition A persistent and potential tendency of a diffused motive to become specific and aroused.

motivational factors Any factor—conscious or unconscious, physiological or psychological—that stimulates, maintains, and directs behavior. Among these factors are basic or immediate needs, interests, incentives and rewards, social drives, and personal drives for security, self-esteem, or superiority. See DESIRE, MOTIVATION.

motivational hierarchy See MASLOW'S MOTIVATIONAL HIERARCHY.

motivational research (MR) (E. Dichter) In consumer psychology, market research programs using modified projective techniques, carried out usually by advertising agencies. Their purposes are to unearth hidden or unexpected motives as to why people buy or do not buy certain products.

motivational selectivity Phrase indicating the influence of individual motives on cognitive processes as an explanation for the differences in ways that an event or object may be perceived by different persons.

motivational sequence A series of events beginning with a motive and proceeding through goal-directed behavior to the goal itself. See GOAL DIRECTED BEHAVIOR for an illustration of such a sequence.

motivational variables (N. S. Endler & D. Magnusson) Within the context of the interactional model of personality, variables that are involved in the arousal, maintenance, and direction of behavior (for example, attitudes, drives, motives, needs).

motivation component factors (R. B. Cattell) Seven factors found in a wide variety of objective measures of motivation.

motivators (F. Herzberg) In industrial motivation, opportunities for professional growth and personal satisfaction.

motive A conscious or unconscious reason for behavior that directs a person's energies toward a goal. Term has various loose as well as specific meanings, especially as used by motivational theorists. See DESIRE, DRIVE.

motive to avoid success (K. Horney) Anxiety about the negative consequences of success resulting in avoidance of success to lessen the anxiety. Seen, for example, in a salesperson selling a lot of merchandise. Instead of being elated, the salesperson suspects that at least such selling performance will be expected the following year, fears that this may not be possible, and consequently decides to lessen the amount of sales (and therefore also the anxiety).

motives hierarchy See NEED-HIERARCHY THEORY.

motokinesthetic method A technique for developing or improving speech whereby the speech pathologist manually manipulates the speech muscles of the person, or touches specific areas to suggest movement at that point. The therapist simultaneously emits the correct sound. Also known as motor-kinesthetic method.

motone (H. A. Murray) A unit of muscular action. See ACTONE, VERBONE.

motoneuron motor neuron

motoneuron axon motor neuron axon

motoneuron pool motor neuron pool

motor Characterizing muscular or glandular body functions.

motor agraphia A disorder characterized by an inability to write because of motor incoordination. Also known as anorthography.

motor amimia A communication disorder characterized by an inability to convey meaning through appropriate gestures. Also known as expressive amimia. See AMIMIA, RECEPTIVE AMIMIA, SENSORY AMIMIA.

motor amusia Loss of the ability to reproduce melodies, resulting from cortical lesion. A person may be able to recognize melodies but can no longer sing or play them correctly. See AMUSIA.

motor aphasia Disturbance in the ability to express language as a result of brain damage. Also known as expressive aphasia. See BROCA'S APHASIA.

motor apraxia 1. An inability to make purposeful movements or to use objects for the purpose intended. Also known as cortical apraxia, innervation apraxia, limb-kinetic apraxia. 2. A disorder marked by loss of ability to perform certain skilled motor tasks involving the arm and hand on one side of the body. Tasks may include typing or such simple movements as manipulating buttons on clothing or safety pins. The condition is associated with a lesion of the precentral gyrus on the side of the body opposite that of the affected limb. May also be due to a cerebellar lesion. See APRAXIA.

motor area One of three areas of the frontal lobes of the brain which, when stimulated, produces movements of skeletal muscles in various parts of the body. Also known as Brodmann's area 4, precentral area.

motor behavior General phrase for any activity resulting from stimulation of muscles or glands. Similar to motor function.

motor-cognitive rigidity The degree to which an individual can shift without difficulty from one activity to another.

motor compliance A motor response observed in many children with schizophrenia with motility disturbances. Such children will change positions or turn toward the examiner as an automatic reaction to light palm contact.

motor conversion reactions Hysterical reactions resulting in a nonorganic impairment of some motor process.

motor conversion symptoms One of two major categories of conversion symptoms that includes paralysis, tics, and unsteady gait, as well as headaches, loss of appetite, coughing spells, and false pregnancy. Thought to alleviate feelings of anxiety, and also may help patients to obtain sympathy, attention, and services from others. The other major category is sensory conversion symptoms. See EPINOSIC GAIN.

motor coordination　　The cooperative action of reflexive or involuntary and voluntary movements of the body, requiring accuracy, timing, and manipulation of cortical and subcortical controls to carry out complex activities. It is a main function of the cerebellum.

motor development　　The development of muscular coordination and control required for physical activities and skills. Follows predictable maturational patterns associated with the development of muscles, nerves, skeleton, cerebellum, and cerebrum. For some attainment ages, see MOTOR MILESTONES.

motor development levels/stages　　The average physical expectations of human infants at various ages in months; for example, lifts head while lying on the back (3 months); when helped, maintains sitting position (6 months); stands when held (9 months); walks with some help (12 months). See MOTOR MILESTONES.

motor disorder　　Loss of ability to perform simple or complex acts or skills because of permanent damage to the motor or premotor areas of the central nervous system. Damage may be due to a congenital or inherited defect, injury or surgical excision, or a psychochemical factor.

motor disturbance　　A disturbance of motor behavior, such as hyperactivity, retarded activity, automatism, repetitive movements, rigid posture, grimacing, and tics. See DISTURBANCE VS DISORDER, MOTOR DISORDER.

motor dominance　　Controlling influence of one cerebral hemisphere over another, shown in motor activity (preferential handedness in writing, or throwing a ball). Also known as cerebral dominance.

motor end plate　　The junction between the terminal of a motor neuron and a group of muscle fibers.

motor equivalence　　A muscle-feedback mechanism that permits higher animals to perform various complex acts, such as eating meals, repeatedly without using the same combinations of nerve and muscle fibers in exactly the same way each time. The feedback function permits other nerve and muscle fibers in the same body area to perform equivalent body movements.

motor-function homunculus　　Figural, cartoon-like representation of the brain that displays the motor areas of humans or other mammals in proportion to bodily function. Motoneurons associated with hand functions, for example, occupy a larger proportion of brain area than those required for the trunk or legs, and hence the figure's hands are larger than its trunk or legs.

motor habit　　A habit described in terms of the same movement responses.

motoric region　　(K. Lewin) The experience aspect of personality manifested in terms of motor responses and outward appearance. See FIELD THEORY.

motoric reproduction process hypothesis　　A postulate that the reproduction of motoric processes calls for capacities that will permit an individual to translate what is learned through observation into actual behavior, as in reproducing the motions of a tennis serve following a demonstration.

motor incapacitation　　Incoordination of striate muscular activity, refers usually to gross behavioral and motor changes. See ATAXIA.

motor inhibition　　See PSYCHOMOTOR RETARDATION.

motorium　　Brain areas that control the voluntary or skeletal muscles; the motor cortex.

motor learning　　A type of learning in which muscular and glandular functions are emphasized, as in acquiring new skills and habit patterns.

motor manipulation　　A kind of behavior that appears spontaneously in animals and young children who inspect, play with, bite, or handle practically everything in their immediate environment. See CURIOSITY.

motor memory　　Capacity to remember previously learned movements or series of movements; for example, the sequential elements of an exercise or dance. See MOTOR EQUIVALENCE VERBAL MEMORY, VISUAL MEMORY.

motor milestones　　The significant achievements in motor development during an infant's first two years. Although individual children vary, typically a normal child will lift the head while prone at three months; support head in other positions at four months; sit with props at five months; reach with one hand at six months; pick up small items and stand when holding on to support at eight months; creep, take side steps while holding on to support at ten months; walk backwards, sideways, upstairs, and downstairs with assistance at 16 months; and run and walk up and down steps 24 months. See DEVELOPMENTAL SEQUENCE, MOTOR DEVELOPMENT.

motor modalities　　In reaction-time experiments, a particular reaction-response type of motor set or readiness. The other two types are sensory and mixed. See MOTOR-REACTION TYPE, REACTION RESPONSE TYPE.

motor nerve　　An efferent nerve that terminates in a muscle or gland.

motor neuron　　Any nerve that innervates a muscle or a gland. Their cell bodies are in the medulla or in the spinal column. See ALPHA MOTOR NEURON, DISYNAPTIC ARC, FINAL COMMON PATH, MOTOR END PLATE.

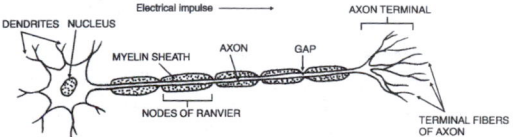

motor neuron　　Motor neurons activate effectors. Their axons extend outward to generate functional connections with a gland or a muscle.

motor neuron axon　　A projection from the cell body of a neuron that allows the central nervous system to innervate a muscle, gland or other effector. Also known as motoneuron axon.

motor-neuron disease　　Any disease that involves neurons of the motor functions of the nervous system. However, the phrase often is applied specifically to amyotrophic lateral sclerosis (ALS).

motor-neuron lesion　　Any damage to a motor nerve, particularly if the disease or injury is to the cell body.

motor neuron pool　　A collection of motor neurons that may be scattered over several segments of the spinal cord, although all members of a motor neuron pool terminate in a single muscle. Also known as motoneuron pool.

motor neurons   Spinal neurons with a cell body in the ventral horn of the spinal cord and numerous synaptic connections with fibers communicating to the cerebral cortex and peripheral body areas. Also motor neurons from cranial nerves associated with movement or glandular activity. Also known as motoneurons.

motor neurosis   Abnormality of motor function, for example, tremors, tics, or hyperactivity.

motor pathways   Nerves from the brain to muscles.

motor-primacy theory   1. A point of view that body mechanisms associated with motor-nerve functions develop before sensory-nerve mechanisms. 2. A concept that neuromuscular mechanisms for movement mature before sensory mechanisms and that their degree of maturation dictates their capability of responding to stimulation.

motor-reaction type   The type of person whose attention is focused on the motor response rather than the stimulus in a situation (such as a reaction-time experiment or the start of a race) that calls for rapid action.

motor root   1. A nerve emerging from the ventral side of the spine (front) that controls motor functions. 2. A motor root from mixed cranial nerves associated with movement or glandular activity; for example, the trigeminal nerve (cranial nerve V) has both a sensory and a motor root. See MOTOR NEURONS, SENSORY ROOT.

Motor Scale   The second part of the Bayley Scales of Infant Development that measures motor ability, such as sitting, stairclimbing, and manual manipulation. See INFANT BEHAVIOR RECORD, MENTAL SCALE.

motor set   Preparatory adjustments or readiness to make a certain response or begin an activity, as in "Ready, Set, Go!" at the start of a foot race.

motor system   The complex of skeletal muscles, neural connections with muscle tissues, and the central nervous system structures associated with motor functions. Also known as neuromuscular system.

motor tension   Symptoms of an anxiety state or a neurosis that include jitteriness, muscle aches, fatigue, inability to relax, and a furrowed brow. See GENERALIZED-ANXIETY DISORDER.

motor tests   Means designed to measure manipulative skills such as finger dexterity or the use of hand tools.

motor theory of thinking   A point of view in which the process of thinking is examined as a succession of implicit stimulus-response relations; that is, muscular activity occurs simultaneously with the thinking process. An opposing argument stresses that motor action is not essential for all thinking, since people who are paralyzed are not handicapped in their thinking.

motor theory of consciousness   (J. B. Watson) A point of view popularized by behaviorists in the 1920s that motor-system responses are controlled by conditioned-reflex links between the motor-cortex and sensory-cortex areas. Also known as motor theory of thought.

motor tract   Any motor pathway from the brain to the spinal cord.

motor unit   A group of muscle fibers that respond collectively and simultaneously because they are innervated by nerve endings from a single motoneuron.

mouches volantes   (flying flies—French) Subjective seeing of specks in one's own eyes. See FLOATING BODIES, MUSCAE VOLATES.

mountain sickness   Discomfort (headache, dizziness, nausea, dimmed vision, insomnia) often experienced during the first few days above 3,000 meters.

mourning   Grief reactions due to loss of a loved one, includes feelings of dejection, loss of interest in the outside world, feelings of guilt about the dead person, and diminution in activity and initiative. Similar to depression and melancholia, but are less persistent and are not considered pathological unless continued past several months. See ANTICIPATORY MOURNING, GRIEF, WIDOWHOOD CRISIS.

mourning work   (S. Freud) A stage of mourning during which mourners can separate themselves from the identity of the deceased person while recalling memories of the deceased. Follows the period of introjection in which the mourner identifies with the deceased.

mouse fear   See MUSOPHOBIA.

mouthing   Explorations of objects via the mouth, usually by infants and young children.

movement conformity   Social behavior where a group standard is established. Seen in animals, such as birds that fly in V-shaped groups, fish that swim and turn as a group, also marching of military groups as well as in dance groups.

movement disorders   Physiological conditions that result in unintended movements as in epilepsy, Parkinsonism, tics, etc.

movement education   A technique designed to help students or patients develop motor skills, creative expression, and self-awareness through physical movement. See MOVEMENT THERAPY.

movement illusion   1. (T. Reid) If a person is asked to move an object sideways a certain distance and then asked to move the same object up or down the same distance, the horizontal distance will usually be less than the vertical distance. 2. Misperception of motion in a part or all of one's body.

movement learning   response learning

movement perspective   A visual illusion produced by the relative distance of moving objects, for example, a nearby bird flying at 30 miles an hour may appear to be traveling faster than a jet airliner in the distant sky moving at 600 miles an hour.

movement response (M)   In Rorschach test scoring, any report of movements of humans, or movements of an humanoid animal.

movement sense   kinesthetic sense

movement-sensitive retinal cells   Cells in the retinas of lower animals that respond to various specific movements across the visual field, such as bug-detector cells of amphibia that respond best to small dark spots that move. Such cells seem to be absent in higher animals with binocular vision.

movement therapy   A therapeutic modality in which persons with disabilities are encouraged to express emotion, work off tensions, develop an improved body image, and achieve greater body awareness and social interaction through rhythmic exercises and responses to music. It is carried out under the supervision of a movement or dance therapist. See DANCE THERAPY.

moving against   According to Karen Horney, one of the three primary modes of relating to other people, in which a person seeks to protect him- or herself by revenge or controlling others. See HORNEY'S TRIANGLE.

moving average   moving total

moving away   According to Karen Horney, one of three primary ways of relating to other people, in which a person self-isolates and keeps apart. See HORNEY'S TRIANGLE.

moving edge detectors   Sensors in the visual network which respond to the edges of moving objects.

moving total   The mean of statistical data computed over progressively shifting intervals. Example: Given the numbers 37, 41, 44, 45, 48, 52, the moving-total method would begin with 37 and add the next two numbers to get 122, then divide by 3 to get 41.77. Then, start with 41 and add the next two numbers to get 130, divide by 3 to get 43.3. Continue with 44, 45, etc. The resulting four numbers 41.7 43.3, 45.66, 48.3 show generalized growth or decline more regularly than the prior six. Also known as moving average. See AVERAGE.

moving toward   According to Karen Horney, one of three primary modes of relating to other people, in which persons accept their own helplessness and become compliant and dependent on others. See HORNEY'S TRIANGLE.

moving-total method   See MOVING TOTAL.

moving window technique   (G. W. McConkie & K. Rayner) In research on reading (especially in terms of gaze fixation and perceptual span limits), a participant reads (and reports) text from an electronic screen display while the eye position is automatically recorded. On each fixation, a window of normal text around the fixation point is presented, and the text outside the window is altered. Each time the eye moves, the window is changed.

Mowat sensor   Hand-held, flashlight-sized, ultrasonic walking guide, used by the visually impaired as an alternative to a cane for warning (by vibrating) of physical obstructions.

Mowrer's theory   The following are important in understanding O. Hobart Mowrer's theory: BEHAVIOR MODIFICATION, BELL AND PAD SYSTEM, ENURESIS, FEAR DRIVE, INTEGRITY THERAPY, MILLER-MOWRER SHUTTLEBOX, NEUROTIC PARADOX, RESPONSE INHIBITION, SOLUTION LEARNING, TWO-FACTOR THEORY OF AVOIDANCE.

MP   See MIDPOINT.

MPD   multiple-personality disorder.

M.P.I.   Maudsley Personality Inventory (also abbreviated **MPI**)

MPI   Maudsley Personality Inventory (also abbreviated **M.P.I.**)

MPPP   A recreational, synthesized street drug, a meperidine derivative, causing an opiate-like euphoria, analgesia, and dulling of the senses, but can be overdosed like heroin, leading to coma and respiratory distress. Another street drug, MPTP is similar.

MR   1. mental retardation. 2. motivational research.

MRI   magnetic resonance imaging.

mRNA   See MESSENGER RNA.

MRT 6   See METROPOLITAN READINESS TESTS-SIXTH EDITION.

ms   See MILLISECOND.

MS   1. Mean square or estimate in the analysis of variance. 2. multiple sclerosis.

M.S.   See MORPHINE.

Ms   A form of addressing a woman, especially in letters, rather than either Mrs. or Miss (equivalent to Mr., in not signalling marital status). Began in the 1960s, sometimes spelled Ms., pronounced miz. See WOMEN'S LIBERATION MOVEMENT.

MSCA   See MCCARTHY SCALES OF CHILDREN'S ABILITIES.

MSE   mental status examination.

msec   See MILLISECOND.

MSER   Mental Status Examination Report.

MSH   melanocyte-stimulating hormone.

MSIS   Multi-State Information System.

MSP   See MÜNCHAUSEN SYNDROME BY PROXY.

MSRPP   See MULTIDIMENSIONAL SCALE FOR RATING PSYCHIATRIC PATIENTS.

MSRT   Minnesota Spatial Relations Test.

MST   McCarthy Screening Test.

MTF   modulation transfer function.

MTFA   modulation transfer function area.

M type   One of the two personality types differentiated by Hermann Rorschach, based on the ratio of human movement responses (M) to color responses (C). According to Rorschach, movement responses are more numerous than color responses, and the M personality includes among other things imaginative and discriminating intelligence, and stability of emotion. Compare C TYPE.

mu   1. The twelfth letter of the Greek alphabet. See APPENDIX C. 2. (μ) An abbreviation for population mean. 3. Symbol for micron (also abbreviated μ).

mμ   See MICROMICRON.

μ   See MICRON.

μ-second   See MICROSECOND.

$\mu\mu$ See MICROMICRON.

μf   See MICROFARAD.

μsec   See microsecond.

muliebrity   1. Womanhood, womanliness, femininity. 2. Strength and self-possession in a woman. Compare VIRILITY.

Müllerian   Pertaining to Johannes P. Müller.

Müller-Lyer illusion   (F. K. Müller-Lyer) The perceived difference in the length of a line depending upon whether arrowheads at either end are pointing toward or away from each other. Both lines are of the same length. Also spelled Mueller-Lyer illusion.

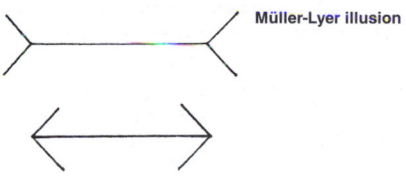
Müller-Lyer illusion

Müller-Lyer rectangles   (F. K. Müller-Lyer) Geometric figures involved in creating a visual illusion, two identical rectangles, one in front of two squares, the other in front of two rectangles of the same length as the squares, appear to be of unequal size.

Müller-Schumann law   (G. E. Müller & F. Schumann) A theory that when two items have been closely associated, it is difficult to form an association between one of the items and a third item. Also known as paradigm of associative inhibition.

Müller's fibers   Glial cells that support all layers of the retina except the rods and cones. Also known as sustentacular fibers. Named after German anatomist Heinrich Müller (1820–1864). See VISUAL PURPLE.

Müller-Urban method   (G. E. Müller & F. M. Urban) In psychophysics, a procedure in which the threshold is set as the median value of the ogive fit to data derived from the constant-stimulus method.

Müller-Urban weighing   (G. E. Müller & F. M. Urban) In psychophysics, a procedure for determining the best value of *h*, the measure of precision, by fitting observations to the normal curve. Also known as Müller-Urban weights, Urban's weights.

MULT   See MULTIPLE SCHEDULE OF REINFORCEMENT.

multa loca tenens principle   A rule that if a drug can substitute for or mimic an action of a natural physiologic agent, it may be able to simulate other natural functions as well. Because of such multiple effects, the administered drug may compete for receptors, enzymes, and other physiological targets.

multiattribute-utility analysis   Using the ratings of judges to quantify the social utility of a given program. Dimensions relevant to program outcomes are weighted in terms of their social importance and the total summated. This analysis allows comparison of different social programs.

multiaxial classification   A system of classifying mental disorders according to several categories of factors; for example, social and cultural influences, plus etiology and clinical symptoms.

multicultural education   1. Programs designed to help people from various backgrounds to appreciate one another and to be able to accept and explain their own culture. 2. Education tailored to and/or respectful of individual needs in terms of language and custom.

multiculturalism   The acceptance of ethnic, racial, religious, linguistic, and cultural plurality; often extended into welcoming such diversity, occasionally to celebrating and encouraging it. Compare cultural pluralism.

multidetermination   Interaction of several different factors in the etiology of a neurosis. Also spelled multi-determination.

multidetermined behavior   Activity determined by multiple past and present influences that interact to produce its current state. Major influences are, in general, genetic, environmental, physiological, and psychological.

multidimensional   Composed of many dimensions and therefore not a pure reflection of any single one. Compare UNIDIMENSIONAL.

multidimensional anxiety   (N. S. Endler) A model of anxiety in which both state and trait anxiety are made up of a number of components. Trait anxiety includes social evaluation, physical danger, ambiguity, and daily routines components, whereas state anxiety includes autonomic-emotional and cognitive-worry components.

Multidimensional Scale for Rating Psychiatric Patients (MSRPP)   (M. Lorr) A grouping of psychiatric symptoms into ten representative manifestations: perceptual distortion, conceptual disorganization, motor disturbance, paranoid projection, disorientation, excitement, hostile belligerence, anxious intropunitiveness, retardation, apathy, grandiose expansiveness. Also known as Lorr Scale.

multidimensional scaling (MDS)   A method for ascertaining the number of factors required to describe a large set of judgments of the form "I is more like j than it is like k," repeating this form of judgment for all possible triplets of the items of the classes represented by i, j, k.

multidimensional variable   An object of study that represents complex behavior that necessitates (a) analysis of its several dimensions and (b) investigation of the ways in which those dimensions fuse and interrelate, as in the study of creative processes.

multidirectional interaction   See FEEDBACK.

multidisciplinary approach   interdisciplinary approach

multifactorial determination hypothesis   A postulate that any attribute of an individual organism may be the resultant of the interaction of many genes.

multifactorial inheritance   The inheritance of a trait or traits governed by a myriad of genetic factors from a large population gene pool. Each of the thousands of possible genes in the total pool may act independently but cumulatively to form an individual phenotype. See MULTIFACTORIAL MODEL (OF INHERITANCE), MULTIPLE-FACTOR INHERITANCE.

multifactorial (MF) model of inheritance   A concept that genetic and environmental causes of a trait constitute a single continuous variable. Genetic defects are assumed due to the adverse effects of many genes. Environmental effects are exerted through many minor events that also have an additive effect. See MULTIFACTORIAL INHERITANCE.

multigenerational transmission process   The passing on of psychological problems over generations as a result of immature persons marrying others with similar levels of separateness from their families.

multigravida   Pertaining to a woman who has had three or more pregnancies (a multipara) whether or not they resulted in live births. Designated Para III, Para IV, etc. See MULTIPAROUS.

multihandicapped   Older term for having more than one mental or physical disability, such as suffering from epileptic seizures and end-stage renal disease, or, as in the case of Helen Keller, being both deaf and blind. See CHALLENGED PEOPLE, PERSON WITH A DISABILITY.

multiinfarct dementia (MID)   A syndrome whose essential feature is a step-wise deterioration of intellectual functions, due to cerebrovascular disease, which has produced a loss of blood supply to patchy areas of the cortex, with onset earlier than in primary degenerative dementia.

Multilevel Academic Survey Tests (MAST)   (K. W. Howell, S. H. Zucker, M. K. Morehead) An examination for use with grades Kindergarten through 12 that provides two methods (Grade Level Tests and Curriculum Level Tests) for measuring academic performance in reading and mathematics.

Multilingual Aphasia Examination (MAE)—Third Edition   (A. L. Benton, K. des. Hamsher, G. J. Rey & A. B. Sivan) A test used to assess the presence, severity, and qualitative aspects of aphasia language disorders in all age groups.

multimodal distribution   A curve of distribution that has more than one peak. See BIMODAL DISTRIBUTION for a typical curve with two peaks.

multimodal theory of intelligence   A point of view that intelligence is a composite of primary abilities.

multimodal therapy (MMT)   According to Arnold Lazarus, a broad-based approach to cognitive-behavior therapy that emphasizes the need to assess seven discrete but interactive modalities. See BASIC ID.

multimonitored   electroconvulsive   treatment (MMECT)   Therapy in which an attempt is made to shorten the time for treatment by inducing four to five seizures in each session and monitoring the patient with an electroencephalograph (EEG) and an electrocardiograph (EKG). Also known as multiple monitored electroconvulsive therapy (MMECT).

multinominal qualitative variable   A variable that can be categorized in several ways; for example, a person by age, religion, income level, gender, education. See DICHOTOMOUS QUALITATIVE VARIABLE .

multiordinal terms   Words that can represent several levels of abstraction, depending on the context in which they are used; for example, love of love is different from love.

multipara   A female who has given birth more than once. See MULTIPAROUS.

multiparous   Pertaining to a mother who has had two or more pregnancies resulting in live births. Pregnancies may be successive or concurrent, as in the case of a birth of twins. Such a woman is identified as a multipara. See MULTIGRAVIDA.

multiphilia   Being sexually aroused by recurrent short-term relations with new partners.

multiple abstract variance analysis (MAVA) design (R. B. Cattell) A system of determining the roles of heredity and environment by solving simultaneous equations representing each of several family groupings.

multiple-aptitude test (MAT)   A battery of separate tests designed to measure a wide range of relatively independent functions, such as the Differential Aptitude Test (DAT).

multiple-baseline design   An experimental design in which several behavior items are assessed before treatment (to get a baseline) and again after experimental manipulation (to determine the effect). See RESEARCH METHODS, RESEARCH TYPES.

multiple causation   Basic assumption that behavior is rarely simple and that a number of interacting elements lead to most complex behaviors.

multiple-choice (M-C) experiment/problem   An experiment in which a participant decides which of several possible choices is correct, usually on the basis of a specific secret code. The participant may be told after a decision whether the guess was correct or incorrect. Most common in cognition and perception. See MASTERMIND.

multiple-choice test   A test requiring the selection of the best answer from a choice of alternatives.

multiple correlation (R)   The multiple correlation between a criterion variable Y and a group of predictor variables $X_1, X_2, \ldots X_p$ is the correlation between Y and the value predicted by the regression equation of Y on the predictors. See COEFFICIENT OF MULTIPLE CORRELATION.

multiple cutoff   A selection strategy in which the applicant must make a specified minimum score on each of several selection criterion (for example, age, education level, work experience) to be considered for acceptance.

multiple delusions   Concurrent delusions, not necessarily interconnected. For instance, persons who simultaneously believe they (a) are in contact with spirits of the dead, (b) are spiritual healers, and (c) can heal any physical or mental disorder.

multiple determination hypothesis   A postulate that most behavior is a product of determinants that vary in their number and potency.

multiple discriminant function analysis   A mathematical procedure based on regression that allows for the classification of subjects into one of several categories (dependent variables) on the bases of their scores on two or more continuous independent or predictor variables.

multiple discriminant technique   A generalization of Fisher's discriminant function technique or the Mahalanobis D^2 method where scores or discriminant criteria are used to assign an individual to one of more than two classifications.

multiple ego states   Many psychological stages relating to different periods of life or to different depths of experience. May be of varying degrees of organization and complexity, and may or may not be capable of being called to awareness consecutively or simultaneously.

multiple-factor   Pertaining to the concept that in a process being studied more than one variable may be responsible for observed results.

multiple-factor inheritance   1. The genetic portion of variability of a trait due to the combined action of several pairs of genes; for example, many genes control color of skin, eyes, hair. 2. The transmission of a genetic trait determined by the combined action of several pairs of genes. See MULTIFACTORIAL INHERITANCE, MULTIFACTORIAL MODEL OF INHERITANCE.

multiple family therapy   A form of group psychotherapy in which two or more family units meet with one or more therapists at once. See MULTIPLE THERAPY.

multiple hurdle (technique)   In job applicant selection, the requiring of satisfactory scores on a number of predictor variables (hurdles), usually increasingly specific and demanding, that are administered over time.

multiple identification   A manifestation of "hysterical" seizures in which a patient identifies with two or more persons and acts out their roles as if in a drama. Also occurs in cases of multiple personality.

multiple-impact therapy   A method of treatment in which an entire set of professionals works with a disturbed family during an intensive, limited period of time.

multiple intelligence   (H. Gardner) Seven established types of intelligence: spatial, logical-mathematical, linguistic-verbal, bodily-kinesthetic, musical, interpersonal, intrapersonal. See BASIC INTELLIGENCE FACTORS, GROUP FACTORS IN INTELLIGENCE, MULTIMODAL THEORY OF INTELLIGENCE.

multiple marital therapy   A form of marital therapy with each marital partner having a personal therapist. Interactions may include: (a) the two therapists meeting independently to discuss their clientsl, (b) a triangular session with two therapists and one client or one therapist and two clients, and (c) all four simultaneously present.

multiple mothering   The use of several warm and caring mother surrogates in a facility for infants. Studies indicate that these infants, when tested after adoption, did not differ materially from home-reared children in school achievement, personal and social development, anxiety level, and response to frustration. See KIBBUTZ, MATERNAL DEPRIVATION.

multiple paired comparisons   Rank-ordering of items by making successive comparisons of pairs and then ranking them.

multiple-personality disorder (MPD)   A diagnosis for a rare pathological condition in which a person apparently has two or more distinct and separate personalities. Renamed dissociative-identity disorder. See ALTERNATING PERSONALITY, ALTERS, DISSOCIATIVE IDENTIFY DISORDER.

multiple psychotherapy   (R. Dreikurs) A technique in which two therapists simultaneously treat a single client; for example, one therapist interviews and tests the client, then with the client present, reports findings to a senior therapist (or a co-therapist) for diagnosis and suggestions about how to proceed, then continues to see the client for individual sessions, returning with the client every x times to report progress, with discussions between the client, the therapist and the senior therapist. See ALTERATIVE PSYCHOTHERAPIES, COOPERATIVE THERAPY, COTHERAPY, DUAL-LEADERSHIP THERAPY, ROLE-DIVIDED THERAPY, THREE-CORNERED THERAPY.

multiple regression   A statistical technique for estimating a best weighing of two or more predictor variables to predict another variable. See MULTIPLE CORRELATION COEFFICIENT, REGRESSION ANALYSIS.

multiple reinforcement schedule   multiple schedule of reinforcement

multiple-response test   A type of test in which the participant must choose more than one of the given choices as correct.

multiple-role playing   The simultaneous reenactment of the same problem, typically by two or more protagonists and two or more assistants, usually for training purpose. For instance, salespeople interact with an obnoxious customer (played by an assistant) under observation by a sales manager who later gives an evaluation, and may have the salespeople role-play until they meet certain standards.

multiple schedule of reinforcement (MULT)   A reinforcement program using multiple schedules which are changed at random. A compound learning schedule useful for analyzing behaviorally active medications. Involves programming of a sequential arrangement of two or more simple schedules, alternating, usually at random, each being accompanied by a distinctive discriminative stimulus as long as the schedule remains in operation. Also known as multiple reinforcement schedule.

multiple sclerosis (MS)   A progressive disease of the central nervous system in which patches of myelin are eroded from white matter. Symptoms include weakness, clumsiness, visual disturbances, apathy, inattention, faulty judgment, depression or euphoria. Onset usually is between the ages of 20 and 40, and, with periods of remission, the disease may continue for as long as 25 years or more. Rapid progression to death with multiple sclerosis is rare. The cause is unknown.

multiple-spike recording   Noting and analyzing of potentials from rapidly firing neurons using microelectrodes connected to high-speed electromechanical oscillographs, spectral analysis filters, and analog-to-digital computer equipment. Such devices may be used for studies in which spike inputs are recorded at rates in excess of 100 per second.

multiple suicides   Joint suicides, usually by a couple but sometimes by a fairly large group. Reasons often relate to expectations of a better life in another world or plane of existence, and, with groups, usually the group is led by a charismatic leader.

multiple T maze   A device for testing learning in laboratory animals, usually consisting of a series of interchangeable units, with junctions as well as one-way doors to prevent retracing in case of error. Pathways contain a number of blind alleys, which the animal learns to bypass as the shortest path to the reward. See FINGER MAZE as an example of a multiple T maze.

multiple trace hypothesis   A postulate that new information interferes with, rather than changes, old information. See CHANGED-TRACE HYPOTHESIS.

multiple transferences   Feelings and attitudes originally held toward family members that become irrationally attached to the therapist and various group members simultaneously. See COLLECTIVE FAMILY TRANSFERENCE NEUROSIS, LATERAL TRANSFERENCE.

multiplex   1. Many networks; a system that permits transmission of multiple messages simultaneously over one circuit (for example telegraphy) or one channel (for example, radio or television). 2. The process of transferring data from many low-transfer rate storage units to one high transfer rate device.

multiplexing in speech   A process of vocal communication whereby several information channels may be functioning independently and simultaneously, using various resonant cavities which are rapidly tuned as needed by neuromuscular control of the tongue, lips, cheeks, and so on. See FORMANTS.

multiplication of personality   A schizophrenic phenomenon in which individual psychic functions of the personality become autonomous and are identified as different people within the person's body. See MULTIPLE PERSONALITY.

multiplication rule In probability, the rule that for two events A and B, p(A and B) = p(A)p(B | A) = p(B) p(A | B). If A and B are independent, this simplifies to p(A and B) = p(A)p(B).

multiplicity-versus-unity dimension Evaluating a work of art in terms of its effects on the viewer. Heightened arousal is achieved by complexity (multiplicity) factors and lowered arousal by elements of harmony (unity). Examples of two such styles are Pablo Picasso (multiplicity) and Piet Mondrian (unity).

multipolarity (S. R. Slavson) Transference in group psychotherapy toward other clients as well as the therapist.

multipolar nerve cell Most common of the three basic varieties of neurons (the other two being unipolar and bipolar) having one axon and three or more dendrites. Multiple neurons may be either principal (or relay) neurons or local circuit (interneurons). Also known as multipolar neuron(e). See RELAY NEURON.

multisensory learning A technique to facilitate acquisition of knowledge that employs a combination of sense modalities at the same time (such as sight, tactile, audition).

multisensory method An approach to teaching reading and spelling that incorporates the visual, auditory, kinesthetic, and tactile modalities, often abbreviated as VAKT.

multiskill(ed) The mastery of varied tasks, procedures, and ways of thinking, leading to flexibility and adaptability. Also known as multiskilling.

multi-stage sampling Samples obtained by steps or stages. Example: To obtain a broad national sample, a person might first select 10 of the states, then select 10% of the counties (or comparable unit) within each of those states, then select the particular elementary schools from which a set number of students would be drawn. See STRATEGIC SAMPLING.

multistage theories Points of view concerned with processes that go through a variety of changes. In some cases, the stages are quite clear, as in information processing. A person receives a unit of information, interprets that information, stores that information, and later may retrieve it, each a discrete step. In other cases, the stages are arbitrarily set as in those of Jean Piaget or Erik Erikson. A person moves from one phase to another generally in a continuous manner although saltatory events do occur.

Multi-State Information System (MSIS) Automated record-keeping system designed to provide comparative statistics for evaluation of programs and treatment procedures in mental hospitals and community mental-health facilities. See MENTAL STATUS EXAMINATION REPORT.

multisynaptic arc A neural pathway that involves the routing of an impulse through several synapses. Also known as polysynaptic arc.

multitrait-multimethod matrix A set of correlations obtained from administering several measures to the same participants. These measures include two or more constructs (traits or characteristics), each of which is measured by two or more methods (such as, self-report, direct observation). The primary purpose of the analysis is to evaluate convergent validity and discriminant validation. See CORRELATION MATRIX.

multivariate Consisting of many variables, especially in experimental design or correlational analysis.

multivariate analysis A statistical method for testing the effects of a number of variables acting simultaneously.

multivariate analysis of variance (MANOVA) A procedure that permits the significance-testing of multiple dependent variables simultaneously. A popular technique following the advent of sophisticated computer-analysis programs. See ANALYSIS OF VARIANCE.

multivariate approaches Ways of studying personality or other phenomena that examine many variables simultaneously.

multivariate data-reducing techniques See CLUSTER ANALYSIS, FACTOR ANALYSIS.

multivariate test In statistics, a test involving several dependent variables.

mummy attitude Describing the immobilized state of a patient in a catatonic stupor.

mu-mu See MICROMICRON.

Münchausen syndrome (R. Asher) A condition characterized by repeated fabrication of clinically convincing symptoms and a false medical and social history. Named after Baron Karl F. H. von Münchhausen, a German soldier-adventurer (1720–1797), famous for telling tall tales. Also spelled Münchhausen syndrome. See IMPOSTOR SYNDROME, MALINGERING, PATHOMIMICRY, TOMOMANIA.

Münchausen syndrome by proxy (MSP) Child abuse in which parents (typically the mother) feign or create illnesses in their children and present them to medical personnel for diagnosis and treatment.

mundane realism Arranging events in an experiment to be as true to life as possible. See EXPERIMENTAL REALISM.

Munich Cooperative Model Hospital group therapy in which typical intrafamilial conflicts are reproduced. The ward staff observes the sessions and applies its observations and interpretations to patient-personnel interactions, while the patients form autonomous groups for emotional support.

Munsell chroma (A. H. Munsell) An expression of the degree of departure of an object color from the nearest grey color on arbitrary scales defined in terms of its Y value (luminous reflectance, or luminous transmittance) and its chromaticity coordinates.

Munsell color system (A. H. Munsell) A method of color notation devised by Albert H. Munsell for use mainly in science, industry, and technology. Introduced in 1905 with numerical designations for hues, tint, and shades of color for accurate identification and specification. Hue is rated by use of a letter and a number, whereas value and chroma by means of numbers. Consequently, every color can be identified by a formula containing these letters and numbers. It has been revised several times.

Munsell hue (A. H. Munsell) Correlate of hue on arbitrary scales defined in terms of luminous reflectance, or luminous transmittance and chromaticity coordinates.

Munsell renotation (A. H. Munsell) Munsell hue, value, and chroma of an object color obtained by reference to the definition of the "ideal" Munsell system.

Munsell value   Expression of the luminous reflectance, or transmittance, of an object on an arbitrary scale giving approximately uniform perceptual steps under usual conditions of observation; correlate of lightness.

murder   See HOMICIDAL BEHAVIOR, LUST MURDER, ORGANIZED SERIAL KILLERS.

Murray's needs   A list of fundamental needs as generated by Henry Murray. A partial list of these terms as used in the Edwards schedule include: achievement, order, deference, autonomy, exhibition, affection, succorance, sympathy, change, endurance, heterosexuality, aggression, intraception, abasement, affiliation. See EDWARDS PERSONAL PREFERENCE SCHEDULE.

Murray's theory   The following items are important for understanding Henry Murray's theory: ACHIEVEMENT MOTIVATION, ACTON(E), AFFILIATIVE DRIVE, AFFILIATIVE NEED, ALPHA PRESS, BETA PRESS, BLAME AVOIDANCE, BLAME ESCAPE, COGNIZANCE NEED, CONJUNCTIVITY, CONSTRUCTION NEED, COUNTERACTION NEED, DEFENDANCE, DEFERENCE, DOMINANCE NEED, DURANCE, ENDOCATHECTION, ENVIRONMENTAL PRESS, ESTABLISHMENT, EXOCATHECTION, EXPOSITION ATTITUDE, EXTRACEPTION, ICARUS COMPLEX, INTRACEPTION, INTRACEPTIVE SIGNALING, INVIOLACY MOTIVE, LIFETIME PERSONALITY, MOTONE, MURRAY'S NEEDS, NEED, NEED INTEGRATE, NEED-PRESS THEORY, NURTURING EXPERIENCES, ORDINATION, PERSONOLOGY, PRESS(ES), PRESS-NEED PATTERN, REGNANCY, SECLUSION NEED, SECONDARY NEEDS, SENTIENCE NEED, SERIAL PROGRAM, SUBSIDIZATION, SUCCORANCE NEED, THEMA, THEMATIC APPERCEPTION TEST, UNITY-THEMA, VERBONE, VISCEROGENIC NEEDS.

muscae volitantes   (flying flies—Latin) Floating particles that are seen in one's own eye. Such particles are remains of an embryologic vascular system in the vitreous humor. Also known as floaters. See FLOATING BODIES, MOUSCAE VOLATES.

muscle contraction   1. The shortening of a muscle. 2. An effect of the pull of muscle fibers on the tissues to which they are attached. The pull is due to an electrochemical action in which alternating filaments of actin and myosin, which form muscle fibers, slide in opposite directions, producing an effect of a myriad of muscle fibers that are shorter but thicker. See ISOMETRIC CONTRACTION, ISOTONIC CONTRACTION, MUSCLE FIBER.

muscle-contraction headache   A common headache due to nervous tension, fatigue, and the like.

muscle dysmorphia   A condition characterized by self-perception of the body as being inadequate and undesirable. Such persons may wear baggy clothing, refuse to be seen in bathing suits, etc. The condition purportedly is common in bodybuilders who, in many cases, have normal or even superior physical features but are still dissatisfied with the reflection in the mirror. See ANOREXIA, BODY-DYSMORPHIC DISORDER.

muscle fiber   A microscopic strand of muscle tissue composed of millions of longitudinally aligned filaments of actin and myosin protein molecules. The actin filaments are attached at intervals to membranes called Z lines; the myosin filaments are arranged in alternate layers with the actin filaments. See MUSCLE CONTRACTION.

muscle-reading   A technique of interpreting slight involuntary muscle actions by one person (percipient) of ideas or willed commands in the mind of another person (agent) from involuntary muscular signals given by the latter and received by the former through physical contact.

muscle sensation   A kinesthetic awareness of movements and tensions in muscles, tendons, and joints.

muscle spindle   (W. Kühne) A collection of muscle fibers enclosed in a fluid-filled capsule of connective tissue that also contains various nerve endings, receptors, and associated tissues.

muscle-tension gradient   A measure of the rate of change of muscle tension during performance of a task, such as taking a test. The muscle-tension gradient is measured on an electromyograph.

muscle tone/tonus   A healthy condition of continual slight contraction or tension in a muscle that keeps it ready to respond instantaneously. Good tone is essential for maintaining posture. Muscles below normal in tone are called flaccid, those with exaggerated tone, spastic. See TONUS.

muscle twitch   Reaction of a muscle to a unitary stimulus, contracting and relaxing.

muscular rigidity   A state of persistent contraction of the skeletal musculature due to disturbance of extrapyramidal pathways of the central nervous system.

muscular type   (L. Rostan) A constitutional type characterized by dominance of the muscular and locomotor systems over other body systems. Similar to Ernst Kretschmer's athletic type.

musculoskeletal system   The combined organ systems of skeletal bones and skeletal muscles, which generally function as a single system in that muscle contractions are required to produce movements of the bones and their associated body tissues.

music(al) therapy   music therapy

musician's cramp   A symptom in which a musician experiences a painful cramp, usually in the arm or hand, which prevents performing. See OCCUPATIONAL NEUROSIS.

musicogenic epilepsy   Epileptic seizures precipitated by music. See REFLEX EPILEPSY.

musicotherapy   Rare name for music therapy.

music therapy   1. Treatment of mental disorders using music. Sometimes known as musicotherapy. 2. The use of music as an adjunct to treatment and rehabilitation. A music therapy program, under the direction of a specially trained therapist, provides a variety of listening and participating experiences adapted to the needs of individuals such as an opportunity for shared experience, emotional expression, relaxation, and nonthreatening enjoyment. Also known as musical therapy.

musophobia   Morbid fear of mice.

mussitation Unintelligible muttering, or lip movements without producing speech.

musturbation Albert Ellis' term characterizing the behavior of clients who are absolutistic and inflexible in their thinking, maintaining that they must not fail, must be exceptional, must be loved, etc.

musty (J. D. Amoore et al.) One of the seven basic stereochemical smell theory qualities having an unpleasant odor, such as is generated in damp environments, by mildewed or decayed materials.

mutagenic Having the power to alter the genetic structure of cells, resulting in the production of new forms. See MUTATION.

mutation Any change in the genetic material of a species that is permanent and transmissible to future generations. May be produced experimentally or accidentally by exposure to external influences (mutagens) such as chemicals or radiation, and also may occur spontaneously. See GENE MUTATION, SPORT.

mutative interpretation In psychoanalytic theory, an interpretation that penetrates the neurotic vicious circle as the therapist allows some of the id energy to be released through the consciousness as an aggressive impulse directed at the therapist.

muteness Deliberate silence on the part of a person in therapy. It may be a sign of resistance to therapy or hostility to the therapist. See MUTISM, RESISTANCE.

mutilation A destructive act with the purpose or result of altering the appearance of something. See GENITAL MUTILATION, SELF-MUTILATION.

mutism Absence of speech whether due to physical defect, voluntary refusal to speak (as in certain religious orders), an expression of anger, or psychogenic inhibition of speech as a hysterical reactions to threats. See AKINETIC MUTISM, ELECTIVE MUTISM.

Mutt and Jeff approach An interrogation strategy used by law enforcement officers in which an apparently gentle, friendly detective (Jeff) is paired with a harsh, ruthless one (Mutt) to increase the suspect's confidence in the former, to whom it is hoped the suspect will confess. Also known as "good-cop/bad-cop approach."

muttering delirium A type of delirium in which the patient's speech is marked by slurring, iteration, dysarthria, and perseveration, and the patient's movements dominated by tossing and trembling.

mutual accommodation A willingness of two or more persons to empathize with each other and modify their own behavior when necessary for cooperation.

mutual contingency interaction A mutually dyadic interaction in which each person contributes to and responds to the other's actions and reactions.

mutualism A relationship between animal and plant organisms by means of which both benefit. There are a number of varieties of mutualism. If the two organisms can live independently of each other, then the relationship is known as facultative; if the mutualism is of such a nature that the organisms cannot survive independently, the relationship is known as obligative. See SYMBIOSIS (meaning 2).

mutuality According to Erik Erikson, the capacity to affirm and strengthen the self and others. It is a hallmark of maturity. Erikson also uses the term to mean "mutuality of genital orgasm with a loved partner . . . with whom one is able and willing to share a mutual trust . . ."

mutually exclusive events Events that are incompatible. Two events A and B are mutually exclusive when if A occurs, B must not occur.

mutual masturbation 1. Refers to two or more individuals masturbating themselves in the same location. 2. Sexual activity in which three or more individuals stimulate each other's genitals and/or their own for sexual gratification. If it involves two individuals, it is dual masturbation. Some authors limit the term masturbation to self-stimulation. Others are not so restrictive.

My. See MYOPIA.

myasthenia Muscular weakness or fatigability observed in certain diseases such as myasthenia gravis but also in chronically depressed people. See MYOPATHIES.

myatonia Physical weakness; deficiency of muscle tone. Also known as amyotonia, amyotony, myatony. See APHORIA.

mydriasis Excessive dilatation of the pupil of the eye caused by sympathetic discharge, such as in states of fear (mediated by endogenous adrenalin), or exogenous drugs, such as cocaine, LSD, amphetamine, or through the anticholinergic drugs (which therefore have the contrary, sympathomimetic effect), the herb and solutions of belladonna, or its associated drugs, atropine or scopolamine.

myelencephalon (marrow brain—Greek) Medulla oblongata. The name medulla oblongata is more frequently used than "myelencephalon." The latter term is used mainly in describing embryonic development and phylogenetic evolution of the brain. The former is used mostly in the context of structural and functional neuroanatomy. In the 1870s, Thomas Huxley suggested the rhombencephalon be descriptively divided into myelencephalon (medulla) and metencephalon (hindbrain).

myelin (R. Virchow) A lipid, or fatty, substance that forms a sheath around nerve fibers. It accounts for the whitish coloration of nervous system tissue as distinguished from gray matter. Myelin is thought to function as an electrical insulator. Increased myelinization is also correlated with increased speed of impulse transmission.

myelinated axon A nerve fiber covered by a myelin (fatty) membrane sheath. The fatty membrane contributes to the coloration of neural tissue sometimes identified as white matter.

myelination The production of myelin around a nerve fiber, a process generally confined to axons of nerves. It develops through a spiral deposition of myelin by glial oligodendrocytes within the central nervous system and by glial Schwann cells outside the central nervous system. These deposits develop along the path of the axons after they have become established. Also known as myelinization.

myelinogenetic law A theory that a nerve is usually not ready to function until its myelin sheath has developed.

myelin sheath An enveloping substance that surrounds some nerve fibers. Myelinated neurons conduct axon spikes more rapidly than nonmyelinated neurons. Also known as medullary sheath.

myelitis Inflammation of the spinal cord.

myeloarchitecture The study of the development and distribution of the fiber processes of the nerve cells of the brain, with special emphasis on the myelinated fibers. See CYTOARCHITECTURE.

myelon Rare term for the spinal cord.

Myers-Briggs Type Indicator (MBTI) (I. B. Myers & K. C. Briggs) A personality questionnaire based on Jungian concepts designed to classify individuals in terms of choices made by respondents who respond to the alternatives provided. Categories include: judgment-perception, thinking-feeling, extraversion-introversion, sensing-intuition. The respondent is assigned a "type" according to the pattern of choices made. Also known as Briggs-Myers Type Indicator. See JUNGIAN TYPOLOGY, PERSONALITY INVENTORY.

myesthesia The muscle sense. Also known as myoesthesis, myoesthesia.

myoclonia 1. Abrupt awakening from the hypnagogic state that sometimes occurs when the sleeper experiences a sense of falling. 2. Any condition characterized by myoclonus, the spasm or twitching of a muscle or muscle group.

myoclonic dementia A condition of dementia accompanied by sudden, brief, jerking muscle contractions. May involve almost any muscles or groups of muscles in nearly any part of the body, including the diaphragm, which produces hiccups as a result of myoclonus. Myoclonic dementia often is associated with Alzheimer-type senile dementia.

myoclonic epilepsy/seizure Repetitive muscle jerking induced by an irritable focus in the brain. Severe petit mal seizure characterized by spasmodic muscular contractions on both sides of the body, usually appearing several years after a series of generalized epileptiform episodes in childhood.

myoclonic movements Spasmodic involuntary muscle contractions that may involve almost any part of the body, depending upon the location of involved neurons.

myoclonus Rapid, involuntary spasms of skeletal muscles. Uncontrolled jerking of limbs. See NOCTURNAL MYOCLONUS.

myoclonus epilepsy A familial type of grand mal epilepsy that begins in childhood and may affect siblings of the affected person. See MYOCLONIC EPILEPSY.

myoelectric arm An artificial arm or prosthesis that can be manipulated by voluntary nerve impulses. The nerve impulses are received by an electronic transducer which converts them into appropriate movements of the prosthesis through tiny electric motors.

myoesthesia myesthesia

myogram A graphic record of the velocity and intensity of muscular contractions.

myograph An instrument for measuring the extent, force, or duration of isotonic muscular contraction, or the tension and duration of isometric contraction. See ISOMETRIC MYOGRAPH, ISOTONIC MYOGRAPH.

myography A diagnostic technique that uses an electrical apparatus to record the effects of muscle activity.

Myokinetic Psychodiagnosis (E. Mira y Lopez) An examination in which the participant makes drawings of patterns using alternately both the left and right hands. Drawings made by the left hand are presumed to reveal information about the genotype; drawings made by the right hand to represent phenotype reactions. See BENDER GESTALT TEST.

myopia (M or My.) Near-sightedness due to distant objects focusing in front of the retina. Also known as shortsightedness. See HYPEROPIA.

myosin A protein important for muscle contraction. See ACTIN.

myosis Obsolete spelling of miosis.

myotatic reflex The simplest muscle stretch reflex based on a synaptic arc; for example, the patellar (knee jerk) reflex. Also known as stretch reflex. See POLYSYNAPTIC REFLEXES.

myotonia 1. Muscular rigidity. 2. The buildup of muscle tone or tension, voluntarily or (especially during sexual arousal) involuntarily.

myotypical response A tendency of transplanted muscle tissue to respond as it would in its normal location in the body. Thus, when a salamander leg bud is transplanted to the opposite side of the body, it continues to move in the same patterns as in the original body connection.

myriachit miryachit

mysophilia (love of dirtiness—Greek) Pathological interest in dirt or filth, often with a desire to be unclean or to be in contact with dirty objects. May be expressed as a paraphilia in which the person is aroused sexually by a dirty partner. See COPROPHILIA.

mysophobia (fear of dirtiness—Greek) 1. Morbid fear of contamination by germs or dirt, usually accompanied by compulsive hand-washing, cleaning, or constantly wearing gloves. 2. Fear of filth. See COPROPHOBIA, DIRT FEAR, MOLYSOPHOBIA, MYSOPHOBIA, RHYPOPHOBIA.

mystical ecstasy A feeling of exaltation following contact with or attempts to get in touch with the infinite, often following long periods of fasting and lack of sleep. In many Eastern religious traditions and in Western monastic traditions, it is one of the goals of spiritual practices.

mystical participation (L. Lèvy-Brühl) Conception that what a person is aware of or thinking about is part of that person's self. See LAW OF PARTICIPATION.

mysticism A doctrine found in most religious traditions that the ultimate spiritual truth is internal and therefore can be reached through meditation, intuition, and contemplation, rather than through external sense experience, priest-mediated rituals, etc.

mysticotranscendence (A. Van Kaam) Going past the usual life form into a new and "higher" state of being.

mystic union   A feeling of spiritual identification with a transcendent reality, be it God, nature, or the universe as a whole. Whereas mystic union is a religious experience, in some cases, patients with schizophrenia relate similar sounding feelings or experiences. Also known as *unio mystica*. See BUDDHISM, COMMUNION, COSMIC CONSCIOUSNESS, COSMIC IDENTIFICATION, COSMIC SENSITIVITY, OCEANIC FEELING, TRANSCENDENTAL MEDITATION, UNITY AND FUSION, ZEN THERAPY.

mystification   1. Distorting another's experience in a variety of ways. 2. A process whereby an individual's oppression is discounted, explained away, and becomes acceptable. 3. Systematic denial by parents of their children's emotions and perceptions, as in saying "Now, that bee-sting doesn't really hurt! You are Daddy's big boy and big boys don't cry." Assumed to cause children to doubt their concepts of reality and to experience fear and confusion as a result.

myth fear   See MYTHOPHOBIA.

mythological themes   Phrase applied to the contents of the collective unconscious. Carl Jung assumed the whole of mythology could be taken as a projection of the collective unconscious. See UNIDENTIFIED FLYING OBJECTS (UFOS).

mythology   The study of myths or sacred stories; or the body of myths themselves. For CarlJung, myths represented basic ideas, or archetypes, stored in the collective unconscious. Sigmund Freud compared myths to dreams that contain hidden meanings, and thought they throw unique light on the cultures from which they stem, and in some instances, as in the Oedipus story, on human nature in general.

mythomania   Abnormal interest in myths, and a tendency to fabricate imaginary experiences and incredible stories. See CONFABULATION.

mythophobia   Morbid fear of hearing myths or stories.

myxedema   (W. W. Gull, W. M. Ord) A condition caused by an advanced state of underactive thyroid leading to hard edema of the subcutaneous tissues, weight gain, dryness and brittleness of the hair, hoarseness, slow reflexes and chronic fatigue, and if the condition exists from birth, leads to mental retardation unless treated. See CRETINISM.

myxophobia   Fear of slime. Also known as blennophobia.

Mz   monozygotic twins (also abbreviated **MZ**).

MZ   1. monozygote, monozygotic. 2. monozygotic twins (also abbreviated **Mz**).

MZa   Abbreviation for monozygotic twins reared or raised apart (also abbreviated **MZA**).

MZt   Abbreviation for monozygotic twins reared or raised together (also abbreviated **MZT**).

n 1. need (also abbreviated **N**). 2. Symbol for the number of (a) variables involved; (b) items or instances in a subcategory or subclass; or (c) responses to extinction. 3. Symbol for the size of a sample or the number of subjects (also abbreviated *n*).

N 1. need (also abbreviated **n**). 2. noun. 3. number. 4. number factor. 5. Symbol for the number of (a) reinforced trials, (b) cases, (c) rewards given, (d) items in a set, or (e) subjects comprising the population. 6. The total number of cases in a sample studied. 7. A sample. 8. Cranial nerve. 9. newton. 10. numerical ability.

NA Narcotics Anonymous

N Ach Abbreviation for David McClelland's need for achievement (also abbreviated **nAch**).

nadir The lowest point, the opposite of zenith.

nadle A gender in the American Indian Navaho culture, neither male nor female. The status of nadle can result from ambiguous genitals at birth, or from the person's decision to take that role. The nadle may assume the privileges, clothing, marriage roles, and responsibilities of males, females, or both, but may not hunt nor participate in war activities. See BERDACHE, TURNIM-MAN.

N Aff See NEED FOR AFFILIATION.

Nagel's anomaloscope (W. Nagel) A screening device for determining color blindness by measuring the amount of two colors an observer must mix to match a different color.

Naglieri Nonverbal Ability Test-Multilevel Form (NNAT-Multilevel Form) (J. A. Naglieri) A group examination of nonverbal reasoning and problem solving for use with levels of kindergarten through grade 12. Said to be independent of educational curricula and cultural or language background.

Naikan (S. Nishimaru) A system of psychotherapy developed in Japan that concentrates the attention of patients on the past, how they were nurtured by others (especially by parents), and how they are the beneficiary of society, all with the intention of increasing social awareness and realization of the importance of past treatment received from others. A client in Naikan therapy is called *Naikansha*. See BUNSAN NAIKAN, ZEN BUDDHISM.

nail-biting The compulsive habit of chewing or shortening own fingernails. Various theories have been advanced for this habit such as general anxiety (nervousness) and fixation at the oral stage of development. Also known as onychophagia, onychophagy.

naive In psychometrics, a person not test-wise. Sometimes spelled naïve.

naive egotistic orientation (L. Kohlberg) Descriptive phrase sometimes applied to the second stage of Lawrence Kohlberg's preconventional level of moral reasoning. See PRECONVENTIONAL LEVEL.

naive misperception Considering that another's reaction to a phenomenon will be identical to the person's own. See PSYCHOLOGISTS' FALLACY.

naive observer An observer or judge who is relatively free of preconceptions. See PHENOMENAL ABSOLUTISM.

naive personality theories Informal, everyday judgments that serve as premature personality assessments; based largely on intuition, common sense, and uncontrolled observation of self and others.

naive realism (J. Piaget) The act of identifying or equating personal perceptions with reality. Piagetian psychology stresses the child's progress away from naive realism toward conceptualization and logical reasoning. As conceptualization and reasoning develop, naive realism diminishes.

naive subjects 1. Research participants assumed to be relatively free of misconceptions. 2. Real research participants, as opposed to confederates or those aiding the researcher. See CONFEDERATES.

nakedness fear See GYMNOPHOBIA.

Nalline Trade name for nalorphine. See NALLINE TEST.

Nalline test The use of this opioid antagonist to diagnose addiction to or determine abstinence from opiates. Injection of small doses precipitates mydriasis (dilatation of the pupil) and other signs of withdrawal such as yawning, sweating, gooseflesh, and tachypnea (rapid breathing). See MYDRIASIS.

nalorphine Generic name for an opioid antagonist that blocks the effects of morphine and other opiates. Thus, it is an excellent, short-acting treatment for opiate overdose. May also be used diagnostically. Similar drugs include naloxone (Narcan), cyclazocine, and naltrexone (ReVia). Trade name is Nalline. See NALLINE TEST.

naloxone Generic name for an opioid antagonist, similar in effects to Nalline. Trade name is Narcan.

naltrexone Generic name for a drug used to control craving of alcohol and, for some users, cocaine. Blocks the effect of opioids. Trade name is ReVia.

name fear See ONOMATOPHOBIA.

nameless crime 1. Obsolete term for sodomy. 2. Any taboo sexual activity, the mere naming of which is considered socially impermissible. 3. In some criminal codes, anal or oral copulation.

NAMH National Association for Mental Health

naming In abnormal psychology, a type of association disturbance observed in schizophrenia in which the patient relates to the world solely by naming objects and actions, such as identifying furniture or other objects in an examining room.

naming area An area of the temporal lobe, lesions of which block the ability to name objects. See SPEECH AREAS.

naming task In learning theory, a task in which participants are presented with a picture of an object and asked to state its name; usually latency as well as accuracy are measured.

Nancy School A clinic and associated group started in Nancy, France by Hippolyte Bernheim and Ambroise-Auguste Liébeault to cure "hysterical disorders" through hypnosis (in that both were due to suggestion), an early recognition of a psychologically caused mental disorder.

nanism Dwarfism, often denoting dwarfism of pituitary insufficiency.

nanogram (ng) One billionth of a gram.

nanometer (nm, NM, or n*u***.)** One-thousand millionth of a meter (10^{-9}). A unit of length of wavelength of light, one billionth (1/1,000,000,000) of a meter, one-thousandth of a micron. Formerly known as millimicron (mu).

nanosecond One-billionth of a second.

nanosomia body type A primordial body type consisting of a dwarfed but well-proportioned body. Sometimes also known as midget. See NANISM, PYGMYISM.

Napalkov phenomenon An unusual conditioned reflex response observed in phobic persons exposed to a fear stimulus. Instead of exhibiting an immediate fear reaction followed by extinction when not reinforced, the fear increases over time.

NAPPH National Association of Private Psychiatric Hospitals

narapoia (R. Cox) The belief that all people are beyond suspicion and represent no harm or threat; antonym of paranoia.

Narcan Trade name for naloxone.

narcissism 1. In general, exaggerated concern with the self, from the mythological Greek Narcissus, who fell in love with his reflection. 2. (S. Ferenczi) Excessive self-love; egocentricity. Seen in some forms of schizophrenia, in persons considered immature, as well as in persons with a neurosis. This pattern of self-interest and concern may start in childhood and persist into adulthood. 3. In psychoanalytic theory, the condition in which sexual self-interest is manifested as the infantile ego instead of part of the phallic stage. See BODY NARCISSISM, DISEASE NARCISSISM, NARCISSISTIC-PERSONALITY DISORDERS, PRIMARY NARCISSISM, SECONDARY NARCISSISM. 4. Sexual self-love; being sexually attracted to or aroused by oneself. Also known as autoerot(ic)ism,

autophilia, autosexualism. 5. (P. Nacke) A form of auto-erotism where excitement occurs through imagery rather than by masturbation. Also known as narcism. See AUTOEROT(IC)ISM (meaning 3).

narcissistic character A personality pattern characterized by excessive self-concern and overvaluation of the self.

narcissistic equilibrium In psychoanalytic theory, a condition of harmonious balance between the ego and the superego.

narcissistic gain In psychoanalytic theory, gratification obtained solely from the functions of organs, as in breathing, walking, and eating.

narcissistic neurosis An inability to form a mature attachment to others because self-love is so prominent that there is no room for anyone else. In psychoanalysis such individuals cannot form a transference to the analyst.

narcissistic object choice In psychoanalytic theory, the investment of the libido in own ego, or in another person similar to the self.

narcissistic oral-fixation A persistent tendency to seek gratification from activities that use the mouth, such as eating, talking, smoking, biting, chewing, sucking. See ORAL EROTICISM, PRIMARY NARCISSISM.

narcissistic personality A self-centered personality pattern characterized by unrealism about the self, personal future, and what can be expected from others.

narcissistic-personality disorder A clinical diagnosis of a disorder characterized by grandiose ideas of self-importance, need for attention and admiration, feeling entitled to special favors, and exploitation of others.

narcissistic problem (H. Kohut) A primary disorder of the self. See NARCISSISTIC PERSONALITY.

narcissistic scar (S. Freud) A long-lasting hurt produced by such experiences as failure, loss of love, and physical deformity. May result in a character disorder manifested by feelings of inadequacy and inferiority.

narcissistic type One of Sigmund Freud's three libidinal types in which the libido is primarily invested in the ego, and the main interest is in self-preservation, with little concern for others or for the dictates of the superego; and if decompensation takes place, mental illness takes the form of psychosis or antisocial disorder. See EROTIC TYPE, LIBIDINAL TYPES, OBSESSIONAL TYPE.

narcoanalysis Brief psychoanalysis using the repeated injection of a narcotic drug to allegedly establish rapport with the therapist, facilitate exploration and ventilation of feelings, uncover significant childhood experiences, and promote the client's insight into unconscious forces that underlie the symptoms. Like similar obsolete procedures such as narcocatharsis, narcohypnosis, narcosuggestion, rarely used. See AMYTAL INTERVIEW, NARCOSYNTHESIS, NARCOTHERAPY.

narcocatharsis A technique of narcotherapy in which the client is asked to ventilate repressed feelings with the expectation of uncovering repressed memories while under the relaxing influence of such drugs as sodium amytal or sodium pentothal usually administered as injections. See NARCOANALYSIS.

narcohypnia   General numbness occasionally experienced upon waking.

narcohypnosis   The rare use of narcotic drugs such as sodium amytal and sodium pentothal as aids in the induction of hypnosis, and as a phase of hypnotherapy. See NARCOANALYSIS.

narcolepsy   (J. B. E. Gélineau) A disorder consisting of a sudden, irresistible urge to fall asleep. Sleep attacks are usually brief and may occur at any time or in the midst of an activity. The episodes often are preceded by hypnagogic illusions similar to rapid-eye-movement (REM)-sleep dreams and brief periods of a form of paralysis in which the person wants to move but is unable to. Also known as paroxysmal sleep. See APNEA, NARCOLEPTIC TRIAD, SLEEP DISORDERS.

narcolepsy-cataplexy syndrome   A symptom pattern consisting of sudden, repeated loss of muscle tone and recurrent sleep attacks. See CATAPLEXY, NARCOLEPSY.

narcoleptic triad   Three symptoms used in the diagnosis of narcolepsy: Falling asleep suddenly and uncontrollably, without obvious cause, and involving abnormality in sleep-stage sequencing. See NARCOLEPSY.

narcomania   Obsolete term for the pathological desire for narcotic drugs, often to relieve pain or discomfort.

narcosis   Obsolete term for a state of stupor induced by narcotic drugs such as barbiturates or heroin. See CONTINUOUS NARCOSIS, RAPTURE-OF-THE-DEEP SYNDROME, STUPOR.

narcosuggestion   A rarely used technique of psychotherapy in which a narcotic drug is administered to facilitate acceptance of suggestions such as reassurance as made by the therapist. See NARCOANALYSIS.

narcosynthesis   (R. R. Grinker & J. P. Spiegel) A treatment technique developed during World War II, in which injected narcotic drugs (sodium amytal, sodium pentothal) stimulate recall of repressed traumas (as a kind of "truth serum"), followed by a "synthesis" of these experiences with the patient's emotional life through discussions in the waking state. Also known as narcotherapy. See NARCOANALYSIS.

narcotherapy   1. Any therapy that employs narcotics. 2. (R. R. Grinker) A 1940s term for the use of the amytal interview as a treatment for "shell shock" or acute traumatic neurosis during the World War II. Also known as narcosynthesis. See NARCOANALYSIS.

narcotic   1. Opioid drug. 2. Any substance that dulls the senses. 3. Any illicit drug (no longer an official term in DSM and many psychiatric texts because of this ambiguity). 4. Opium or one of its derivatives (codeine, morphine, heroin), used to reduce intense pain or induce sleep. Prolonged use can lead to tolerance, physiological addiction and/or psychological dependence. Withdrawal from mild narcotic addiction is marked by perspiration, watery eyes, runny nose, yawning, and sneezing; from heavy addiction by cramps, muscle spasms, vomiting, and diarrhea. Also known as narcotic-analgesic addiction. See OPIOID DEPENDENCE.

narcotic addiction/dependence   Just as "narcotic" has become outmoded due to ambiguity, so has the term "narcotic addiction," as more specific terminologies have evolved in the field of addictions treatment. In the 1940s, opium, morphine, and heroin were the paradigmatic narcotics and drugs of addiction, but since the 1960s, so many other drugs now are abused and receive treatment that narcotics use per se has become largely outmoded. Psychological and physical dependence upon a variety of drugs has been noted, and though opiate addiction differs in quality from barbiturate or benzodiazepine or amphetamine addiction, it has become clear that it's more appropriate to note that a wide range of substances, including nicotine, can generate dependence and abuse. More recent terms include "substance abuse" or "chemical dependency," allowing for treatment without having to first haggle about whether physical withdrawal reactions are part of the problematic substance.

narcotic analgesics   Substances usually derived from opium, administered to relieve pain and discomfort. Common examples are the opium derivatives codeine and morphine, and synthetic opioids such as Dilaudid and Demerol. See OPIUM, SYNTHETIC NARCOTICS.

narcotic antagonists   Drugs that interfere with normal action of narcotics by competing for the same analgesic receptor sites. Narcotic antagonists precipitate immediate severe withdrawal symptoms in narcotic addicts. The prototype narcotic antagonist is nalorphine; others include cyclazocine, levallorphan, and naloxone. See NALLINE.

narcotic blockade   Inhibition of the euphoric effects of opiates such as heroin by administration of a blocking agent, especially methadone, as maintenance treatment for drug abuse. See METHADONE, NARCOTIC ANTAGONISTS.

narcotic dependence   See NARCOTIC ADDICTION.

narcotic hunger   Obsolete phrase for a craving for narcotics, as in opioid dependence, thought to be due to a physiological and psychological need established by long-term use. See NARCOTIC ADDICTION.

Narcotics Anonymous (NA or N.A.)   A mutual-support organization for present and former addicts, modeled after the 12-steps-to-sobriety program of Alcoholics Anonymous.

narcotic stupor   Obsolete phrase for a state of lethargy or limited mobility and decreased responsiveness to stimulation due to the effects of narcotic drugs. May be followed by coma.

narcotism   1. A stupor as the result of a narcotic. 2. Addiction to a narcotic.

narcotization   Obsolete term for the process of becoming dependent upon narcotics. May occur through illicit drug abuse or through the therapeutic administration of narcotic drugs such as morphine. See SOLDIER'S SICKNESS.

narrative literature reviews   (R. J. Baumeister & M. R. Leary) Articles that summarize other writings on a topic. Goals may include theory development, theory evaluation, surveying the state of knowledge, problem identification, and historical accounts. See METAANALYSIS, PAPER.

narrative method   A means of obtaining testimony (or an account of events) by allowing observers to relate the facts in their own ways.

narrotophilia   Dependence on exposure to erotic material to attain sexual arousal or satisfaction. See PARAPHILIA, PORNOGRAPHY.

narrowband   See BROADBAND.

nasal   A sound produced by letting all or most of the air pass through the nose, for example, /ng/ in "sing."

NASA Task Load Index   (S. G. Hart & L. E. Staveland) Workload demands rated by operators on six scales (mental, physical, temporal, performance, effort, and frustration level).

NASH categories of death   (E. Shneidman) The four modes of death stated or implied on a death certificate: Natural, Accident, Suicide, Homicide.

NASPSPA   North American Society for Psychology of Sport and Physical Activity

natal sex   The ascribed gender of a newborn. See PSEUDOHERMAPHRODITISM.

natimortality   The ratio of stillbirths to live births.

national character   Common personality characteristics that differentiate national and ethnic groups. Once a topic of considerable research, often flawed because it measured value-laden traits (perseverance, punctuality), ignored variations within the group, and emphasized description rather than explanation.

National Intelligence Scale (NIS)   A battery of general intelligence tests to be administered to groups.

nationalism   See CHAUVINISM.

National Reference Scale   See ANCHOR TEST.

Native American culture   Elements of American Indian (Amerind) culture that fall within the broad limits of psychology as listed in this dictionary. See BERDACHE, CASSINI LEAVES, CATNIP, COLOR PREFERENCE LAWS, CULTURE COMPLEX, DRUG CULTURE, ECHUL, HELLEBORE, INDIAN HEALTH SERVICE, KIMILUE, PEYOTE, POTLATCH, RH BLOOD-GROUP INCOMPATIBILITY, TOLOA, WINDIGO, YOPO.

native behavior   Any function or action determined by factors present in the organism from the beginning. See INSTINCT.

native lovemap   (J. Money) The pattern of verbal and physical behavior, established by individuals as normal, and which they may expect others to follow in their sexual activity. Lack of trust to express this map to a lover may generate problems of adjustment.

nativism   (H. Helmholtz) A doctrine positing that mental and behavioral factors, as well as physical traits, are inherited. See LAMARCKIANISM, NATURE-NURTURE CONTROVERSY.

nativistic theory   (N. Chomsky) A point of view that humans have an inborn capacity for learning language and that children are born with inherent knowledge. Nicknamed ding-dong theory because it holds that every sensory experience in early humans was like the striking of a bell, producing a corresponding utterance. See DING-DONG THEORY, ORIGIN-OF-LANGUAGE THEORIES.

nativist   A person who accepts nativistic theory.

natural act   In the teachings of some religions, a sex act that can result in procreation, even though considered sinful or illegal, such as incest or rape.

natural aptitude   See APTITUDE.

natural child   1. A child born out of wedlock. 2. A child born to, rather than adopted by, a mother or couple.

natural childbirth   A program for labor and delivery to reduce the need for analgesia. Assumes that the pain results from fear and tension, which can be reduced by understanding the process and by learning exercises that relax (especially breathing exercises) and that develop the muscles used in parturition, plus postures to make the labor more comfortable. Typically the woman and a partner are taught as a team during the last months of pregnancy. First described by British physician Grantly Dick-Read, based on his observations of childbirth in Russia. See LAMAZE METHOD, LEBOYER METHOD.

natural consequences   (R. Dreikurs) A method of training children by giving them information about the probability of consequences of certain undesired behaviors. The parent does not intervene if the child acts incorrectly thus allowing the child to experience the consequences of the behavior, unless the consequences are too painful or harmful. Example: A child does not want to dress appropriately for a cold day. Parent advises child to dress warmly. The child ignores parental warning, and the parent allows the child to venture forth in the expectation that the child will be miserable from the cold and therefore learn from this experience. See ADLERIAN THEORY, FAMILY COUNCIL, LOGICAL CONSEQUENCES.

natural experiment   Real-world (as opposed to experimental or manipulated) phenomena that scientists use to study behaviors. A kind of informal research procedure conducted by making observations, arriving at tentative conclusions (hypotheses) and then testing the validity of these conclusions in some manner. A natural experiment does not involve any manipulation of variables or interventions by the researcher.

natural family planning   Controlling the number of children in a family by the use of natural birth-control techniques, such as the rhythm method, as opposed to the use of condoms, oral contraceptives, diaphragms, and similar devices.

natural fertility   The reproductive rate of an individual or group unaffected by contraception or induced abortion.

natural flow   Being true to the self, being open and spontaneous in the manner of a young child; stripped of all unnatural elements resulting from conditioning from outside influences.

natural group   A relatively stable group based on a common heritage or a deeply ingrained bond, such as a kinship group or religious organization, as contrasted with transient or loose-knit groups such as crowds or audiences.

natural high   1. (W. O'Connell) An optimistic action-oriented approach to living which emphasizes present self-responsibilities. 2. Feelings of exceptional well-being that are not artificially induced.

natural homosexual period   Misleading phrase describing the later middle childhood stage when prepubertal boys seek the company of boys and men, and prepubertal girls often have crushes on each other or on teachers and counselors of the same sex.

naturalism   1. Actions and thoughts based on biological demands. 2. Denial of the influences of supernatural powers.

naturalistic observation   1. A noninteractive empirical process of examining a phenomenon or individual, or groups, without attempting to control or to change the situation. Rather, there is only systematic gathering of data on behavior as it naturally occurs. 2. An unselective observation under uncontrolled conditions. Observers watch and record everyday behavior of subjects in their natural environments, for example, an ethologist studies the behavior of gorillas, an anthropologist observes the eating habits of a tribe, a developmental psychologist studies how parents interact with their children. See OBSERVATIONAL METHOD. 3. Research performed in such a way that the human "participants" or animal subjects are unaware of the researchers. Also known as field study.

natural justice   1. The principle of basic fairness of behavior toward others. See GOLDEN RULE. 2. In law, fundamental principles of legal equity. 3. A legal principle that procedures possibly resulting in harm must be fair; the greater the potential damage, the stricter the standards of fairness. Includes the premise that an accused is entitled to face and answer accusers in a fair hearing. See PROCEDURAL JUSTICE.

natural killer (NK) cells   In the immune system, leukocytes that destroy cells that have been invaded by a foreign substance, including tumors and viruses.

natural language   1. A language spoken or written by humans, as opposed to a programming or machine language. 2. A language such as English that has naturally evolved rather than an artificial language such as Esperanto or Ido.

natural law   1. A general statement of the principles according to which the phenomena of the universe proceed, with special reference to their interrelations. 2. Any sanction of social behavior based on established custom, divine sanction, etc., rather than on legislative enactment.

natural law theory   In theology and philosophy, the primacy of nature in defining the purpose of all natural phenomena. For instance, nonprocreative sexual activity would be considered improper.

natural logarithm   Logarithms to base e, another name for Napierian logarithm.

natural monism   A doctrine positing that all sciences including psychology are ultimately reducible to physics and chemistry, and even chemistry obeys the laws of physics.

natural reasoning   The study of human reasoning in "real" situations involving the estimation of likelihoods.

natural reinforcers   Generally, rewards that occur in the normal occurrence of events, such as friendliness and compliments.

natural selection   (C. Darwin) A theory based on the observation that in nature, organisms able to adapt to changing conditions are more likely to survive whereas individuals or species unable to adjust will fail to survive. The concept sometimes is known as a rule of the survival of the fittest, because of an assumption that physically or intellectually superior individuals are most likely to survive through evolutionary processes. See SURVIVAL OF THE FITTEST.

natural stimulus   A phenomenon in the natural environment, as opposed to artificial (or human-made) environment, that may have some effect on an organism, such as insects, pollen, sunshine.

natural work module   Production of a complete unit by an individual, as in making a complete dress from a bolt of cloth. Compare PIECE-WORK MODULE.

natural work team   A group assigned to complete a meaningful end product by scheduling and apportioning the work as they decide.

nature   1. The universe as a whole. 2. Pertaining to humans, the innate, genetically determined characteristics of individuals, particularly those making up temperament, body type, and personality. See NATURE-NURTURE CONTROVERSY, NURTURE.

nature-nurture controversy/debate   A long-standing dispute over the relative importance of heredity (nature) versus environment (nurture). Nativists and biological determinists emphasize the role of heredity; environmentalists focus on sociocultural and ecological factors including, in the human, family attitudes, child-rearing practices, and economic status. Generally, both are involved with nature governing the behavior of lower species and environment playing a larger role in the more recently-evolved ones within limits set by heredity. See FREE WILL, SOFT DETERMINISM.

nature of man   A component or section usually found in counseling and psychotherapy theories; refers to the biological inclination of people, or the instinctual or natural predisposition of human behavior.

naturism   A health and fitness movement that started mainly in Germany in the early 1900s. It emphasized the health aspects of family-oriented, nonsexual nudism in social clubs.

naturism vs supernaturism   (R. I. Watson) A prescriptive dimension of the philosophical underpinnings of psychology, namely, psychological phenomena are explained only in terms of the resources of the organism versus the need for some other explanatory power. See OPPONENT-PAIRS DIMENSION.

naturopathy   A system of treatment in which only natural (nonmedicinal) agents are used. A person who practices naturopathy is known as a naturopath.

Naturwissenschaftliche Psychologie   (natural science psychology—German) One of two major divisions of psychology as established by early German thinkers. Has been interpreted differently by various psychologists, but essentially views psychology as a biological science, either discounting or not considering the concept of "psyche" or "soul." See GEISTESWISSENSCHAFTLICHE PSYCHOLOGIE.

nausea gravidarum   Latin for morning sickness.

nautilus eye   The eye of a cephalopod (single-footed) mollusk used in studies of vision because the eye consists mainly of a spherical cavity lined with photosensitive cells responding to light that enters through a small hole at the top. The mollusk eye thus is virtually a pinhole camera made of living tissue. This model of the visual system contrasts with the multi-faceted overlapping receptors that are located on the external surface of arthropod (invertebrate animals such as insects) like the Limulus.

nautomania   A nautophobia (morbid fear of ships or water) which affects some sailors, and therefore, is also referred to as seaman's mania.

nautophobia   1. Fear of ships or boats. 2. Morbid fear of water, of being on the water. Compare NAUTOMANIA.

nay-saying   A general immediate tendency on being asked a question, or upon being asked to perform an action, to reply in the negative, such as "I don't know" (to a question) or "No thank you" (to an invitation). Conversely, yea-saying is the opposite general tendency, usually a person readily agrees to almost any question or request.

n_b   The number of scores falling below the lower limit of the interval containing the median.

NCQA   National Committee for Quality Assurance, an external review agency for managed care institutions.

$_nC_r$ The number of combinations (order irrelevant) of *n* items taken *r* at a time.

NE   1. norepinephrine. 2. near effect.

Neandert(h)al man   The best known extinct species of human, first discovered in 1856 at Neanderthal, Germany; later, additional skeletons were found in Belgium, Croatia, France, and elsewhere.

near-death experience   Reports by people who were determined by another, usually a physician, to be clinically dead, and later revived, about their perceptions and sensations of the death experience. These reports may include: an overview of life experiences, a tunnel of light, bright light and feelings of beckoning, peace and serenity. See OUT-OF-BODY EXPERIENCE.

near effect (NE)   (K. Goldstein) The degree of excitation of a neural component as a function of its distance from the point where the stimulus is applied.

nearly-decomposable system   (H. A. Simon) A system composed, in hierarchical fashion, of weakly-linked subsystems (which may, in turn be composed of sub-sub-systems, etc.) so that equilibrium is established rapidly within each subsystem, more slowly among the whole set of subsystems. Near-decomposability has important consequences for system functioning and speed of evolution, and for the computational analysis of system properties. Most natural systems are nearly-decomposable into more or less specialized subsystems. The structure of computer programming languages encourages nearly-decomposable program organizations.

near point   In vision, the closest distance between the eye and a viewed object in which the object can be perceived. As humans grows older, presbyopia (inability to see near objects) occurs, usually adjusted by wearing reading or bifocal lenses. See NEARSIGHTEDNESS.

near-point of convergence   The point nearest the eyes at which an object will be perceived as a single entity, becoming double if brought closer.

nearsightedness   Refers to a person's near point being close to the eye. Results in good focusing for close work, poor vision for long distances. Also known as myopia. Compare FARSIGHTEDNESS. See NEAR POINT.

necessary condition   An absolute requirement for a particular phenomenon to occur. Compare SUFFICIENT CONDITION.

necessary opposition   See ENANTIODRAMA.

Necker('s) cube   A line-drawing of a transparent cube showing all sides, resulting in an ambiguous figure whose three-dimensionality, fluctuates during sustained viewing. First described by Swiss naturalist Louis A. Necker (1786–1841). See BOREDOM, RUBIN'S FIGURE.

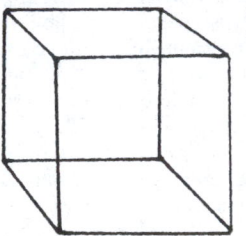

Necker cube   Stare at the cube to see its orientation. Keep staring!

neck stretching   A cosmetic tradition in some natives of Burma in which neck rings are used to increase the neck length.

necromancy   A branch of magic which claims to reveal future events through communication with the dead. See PARAPSYCHOLOGY, PSEUDOSCIENCE.

necromania   Morbid preoccupation with or a pathological desire for sexual relations with corpses, including a morbid interest in funerals, morgues, autopsies, and cemeteries. Seen almost exclusively in males. See NECROPHILIA, TAPHOPHILIA.

necromimesis   A delusion in which people act as if they were dead because they believe they are dead.

necrophile   A person who is sexually aroused by thoughts of death or sexual activity with a dead person. See NECROPHILIA.

necrophilia   (love of corpses—Latin) 1. Being sexually attracted to or aroused by activity with a corpse. 2. Sexual interest in or sexual contact with dead bodies. Necrophiles are almost always men, who often are psychotic. Also known as necrophilism. See ATYPICAL PARAPHILIA, KATASEXUALITY.

necrophilic fantasies   Male (and, rarely, female) fantasies about viewing or having intercourse with a corpse as a means of achieving sexual excitement. Such fantasies are sometimes fulfilled by prostitutes who satisfy necrophilic clients by simulating being dead.

necrophilous character   (E. Fromm) A character orientation characterized by attraction to that which is dead and decaying and seeking to destroy living things.

necrophobia   1. Morbid fear of dead things, especially human corpses. 2. Fear of death or dying. See THANATOPHOBIA.

necropsy   Another name for autopsy, usually "necropsy" is used for animals and "autopsy" for humans.

necrospermia   Immobile or dead spermatozoa in the seminal fluid.

need (n or N) 1. A feeling of unfulfillment or deprivation in the biological system (produced by either physical or environmental imbalances) evidenced by a drive to complete such lack. 2. Loosely, any specific motive, for example, according to Kurt Lewin, a need is "any desire for object possession or any desire to achieve a goal." 3. An internal tension generated by an unsatisfied desire, urge, or wish, or by an organic state of deprivation. Something that if not satisfied will harm the individual. 4. (H. A. Murray) A construct representing a force in the brain that organizes processes such as perception and action so as to change an unsatisfactory condition. See B-REALM, D-REALM, FAILURE TO THRIVE, MARASMUS, MATERNAL DEPRIVATION, NEED VS WANT, NEED-HIERARCHY THEORY, NEED-PRESS THEORY. Kinds of needs include: ABASEMENT, ABUSE, ACHIEVEMENT, AFFILIATIVE, BASIC, BASIC PHYSIOLOGICAL, COGNITIVE, COGNIZANCE, CONSTRUCTION, COUNTERACTION, D-, DEPENDENCY, DOMINANCE, ESTEEM, EXPOSITION, FELT, FRAME-OF-ORIENTATION, HARM-AVOIDANCE, IDENTITY, INFAVOIDANCE, INFRAAVOIDANCE, INSTINCTOID, LATENT, LOVE, MANIFEST, META-, MURRAY'S, NEUROTIC, NURTURANCE, PHYSIOLOGICAL, PRIMARY, PSYCHOLOGICAL, QUASI-, REJECTION, RELATEDNESS, ROOTEDNESS, SAFETY, SECLUSION, SECONDARY, SELF-ACTUALIZATION, SENTIENCE, SOCIAL, STATUS, SUCCORANCE, TISSUE, TOGETHERNESS, TOUCHING, TRANSCENDENCE, VISCEROGENIC.

need-and-drive theories of motivation Theories holding that all motives work in the same way: they are based on biological needs that, when unsatisfied, create tensions called drives.

need arousal A motivational technique used primarily by propagandists, advertisers, and politicians, in which appeals are made to peoples' actual needs and wants, such as the desire for status, health, money-saving, beauty, or security.

need distribution of rewards A situation in which group members who are most in need of rewards receive a disproportional share of them.

need-drive-incentive pattern (theory) A point of view that physiological needs are created by a condition of deprivation that generates a drive to satisfy those needs and creates incentives that in turn lead to consummatory responses to achieve the needs that reduce the drive. In other words, deprivations generate needs which generate drives that control future activity.

need-fear dilemma 1. An approach-avoidance conflict related to the need to experience closeness, coupled with fear of the experience. 2. A conflicting set of conditions facing certain patients with schizophrenia who need structured control of their disorganized psyche yet do not want external influences.

need for achievement (n-Ach, N Ach, nAch or NACH) According to David McClelland, an achievement motive leads the organism to seek high standards of performance, or to compete with a standard of excellence. It is a relatively stable personality trait rooted in the experiences of middle childhood, that motivates individuals to undertake tasks in which there is a reasonable probability of success and to avoid tasks that are too easy and not challenging, or too difficult because of fear of failure.

need for affection A subscale (Hy2) on the Minnesota Multiphasic Personality Inventory, a high score on which indicates a person who expresses optimistic and trusting attitudes toward others; sees others as honest, sensitive, and reasonable; denies having negative feelings about others; avoids confrontations; and needs attention and affection from others.

need for affiliation (N Aff) (H. A. Murray) Desire for association with others of own kind.

need for approval A psychological urge for recognition and acceptance by others, usually an important ingredient of self-worth. One expression of this need is the tendency to portray personal thoughts and attitudes as conforming to socially "correct" or desirable views. See ATTENTION-GETTING.

need for punishment A conscious or unconscious drive to be punished as a means of relieving a sense of real or fancied guilt. Some individuals feel compelled to commit crimes in which apprehension and conviction are certain. Similarly, children frequently persist in naughty behavior until they are punished, after which they appear to be relieved. See ACCIDENT PRONENESS, MASOCHISM.

need gratification The reduction of a need by consummatory behavior. See CONSUMMATORY ACT, NEED REDUCTION.

need-hierarchy theory A point of view that people are motivated by needs such that the first order of needs must be satisfied before the next ones are motivating as arranged in the following hierarchical order: physiological necessities (food, water, oxygen); safety needs (protection against danger); social needs (belonging, friendship); ego needs (self-confidence); self-actualization (developing own potentialities); and beyond this range, some would place spiritual needs (transcendence, the need for higher states of consciousness beyond identity and actualization). Theorists including Abraham Maslow, Douglas McGregor, and Adrian Van Kaam have proposed such hierarchies. Also known as hierarchy-of-needs theory. See MASLOW'S MOTIVATIONAL HIERARCHY, MASLOW'S THEORY OF HUMAN MOTIVATION.

need integrate (H. A. Murray) A need for a certain kind of interaction with a certain kind of object or event. A need integrate with an object or event associated with a childhood press becomes a complex. See COMPLEX, PRESS.

need-integrative therapy Psychotherapy that deals with present problems with the intention of later tackling more fundamental problems.

needle fear See BELONEPHOBIA.

need-persistent response (S. Rosenzweig) A reaction to frustration characterized by focusing on the solution to the problem as contrasted with extrapunitive, ego-defensive, or other responses. See ROSENZWEIG PICTURE-FRUSTRATION STUDY.

need-press method A system of analyzing and scoring each sentence of the stories told by the respondent in the Thematic Apperception Test, as a means of evaluating the needs of the protagonist and the press of environmental factors to which the protagonist is exposed.

need-press theory An explanation of behavior dynamics in terms of fundamental viscerogenic and psychogenic needs, and the stimuli and situations (presses) that arouse these preexistent needs. For instance, a piece of fruit appears desirable only when a person is hungry, and the need for achievement is felt primarily when a person is in a competitive situation.

need reduction The satisfying of a need, and thereby reducing it by some consummatory behavior, for example, if a person is tired, by ceasing activity, the need is diminished.

needs assessment 1. In evaluation research, deciding upon priorities among needs, a need being defined as a condition in which there is a discrepancy between an acceptable state of affairs and an observed state of affairs. 2. Phrase that can be logically applied to individuals and organizations, but in psychology, sociology, and psychiatry usually refers to identification of mental-health needs of a community. Such assessment is difficult. Household surveys and case-finding surveys fail to produce reliable results. More effective are canvassing opinions of local residents and discussions of mental-health-related problems and needs in public forums. Needs assessment leads to the issue of priorities among needs.

need state The unsatisfactory condition of an organism as the result of a deprivation.

need tension An uncomfortable emotional state associated with a need.

need vs want The distinction between "need" and "want"—two terms often confused or treated as equivalent. An unfulfilled need will physically harm the individual; an unsatisfied want causes frustration or disappointment. See NEED.

neencephalon (L. Edinger) The "new brain" or higher levels of the nervous system such as the cortex in contrast to the "old brain" (paleencephalon).

nefesh (the soul—Ancient Hebrew) The seat of feelings and emotions; the total personality. See RUAH.

Neftel's disease (W. Neftel) A condition characterized by paresthesia (abnormal sensations) in the head and trunk, and discomfort when not in a leaning or lying-down position.

negation 1. Denial or refutation of a statement or proposition. 2. In the two-word stage of language development, the use of a negative construction to deny or contradict a statement or suggestion, such as "Don't want."

negation insanity See INSANITY OF NEGATION.

negative acceleration 1. Slowing or decelerating. Compare POSITIVE ACCELERATION. 2. A reduction in the rate of change or development in a given activity or function, for example, a loss of learning as a result of practice.

negative adaptation A gradual loss of sensitivity or weakening of response due to prolonged stimulation.

negative affectivity 1. (D. Watson & L. A. Clark) A personality type characterized by introspection, general dissatisfaction, and concern with personal shortcomings; invites burnout in response to (occupational) stressors. 2. A tendency to respond to one's environment with bad feelings, emotions, reactions.

negative afterimage The visual sensation (usually less bright and in complementary hue) that appears after the initial stimulation has ceased. For instance, after staring at an object and then looking at a neutral surface, what is usually seen is the opposite (complementary) color of the original. See AFTERIMAGE.

negative afterpotential A residual depolarization in the declining phase of the action potential (spike) which decreases the rate of decline. See AFTERPOTENTIAL.

negative ambition (T. Reik) A type of masochistic behavior marked by avoiding competition, missing opportunities for success, and following the line of maximum resistance. Deliberately trying to avoid success. Reasons for such behavior will vary with individuals, but often it is done to spite parents who demand too much from their children.

negative attitudes 1. In general, a pessimistic attitude toward self and others, opportunities, the future, etc. 2. In counseling or psychotherapy, the client's feelings of rejection or disapproval of everything, including the counselor or therapist, and the process. See POSITIVE ATTITUDES.

negative automatic thoughts Cognitions that occur just below the surface of awareness and that include unpleasant, pessimistic predictions often focusing around the negative triad. See NEGATIVE (COGNITIVE) TRIAD.

negative cathexis Repulsion toward an object, person, or idea.

negative (cognitive) triad (A. Beck) Pessimistic thoughts about the self, world, and future.

negative conditioned stimulus In classical conditioning, a stimulus that is presented repeatedly without reinforcement following, tending to inhibit conditioned responses.

negative contrast North American phrase for a video display unit with dark characters on a light background.

negative correlation Inverse connection between variables; as one goes up, the other decreases, such as a negative correlation between children's weight and their running speed, keeping height and age constant.

negative diagnosis The identification of a disorder by excluding possible alternatives. Also known as wastebasket diagnosis.

negative discriminative stimulus A stimulus not associated with a reinforcer and distinct from the discriminative stimulus. If a subject responds to the negative discriminative stimulus as though it were to the discriminative stimulus, reinforcement is not delivered.

negative doubles illusion Mistaking a person for someone else and insisting that that person is not who he or she really is. The patient may believe that the person has undergone changes in appearance for sinister reasons. Also known as Fregoli's phenomenon. See PARANOIA.

negative Electra complex (C. Jung) In psychoanalytic theory, a reversed Electra complex in which the daughter is erotically attached to the mother and regards the father as competition. Freud never accepted the concept.

negative electrode A cathode.

negative electrotaxis See ELECTROTAXIS.

negative feedback A signal from a machine or sensory receptor to reduce or arrest a function.

negative feedback loop   See HORMONAL FEEDBACK.

negative fixation   A generalization about a class of objects or topics that results in avoidance of all items of this group, for example, as a result of being hurt by a small child, a cat may run away from all humans.

negative hallucination   The failure to see an object or person when looking directly at it, as in failing to perceive a certain person in a group in response to hypnotic suggestion.

negative halo (effect)   A tendency to have a negative impression of a person on the basis of a minor aspect of the person, such as stains on the person's shirt. Also known as horns effect.

negative imprinting   An inherited avoidance reaction to particular stimuli, for example, infant monkeys having never before seen a snake will, on seeing one, react with apparent terror and attempt to escape the situation. See IMPRINTING.

negative incentive   An environmental object or condition away from which an organism directs its behavior, as in avoiding extreme heat or cold. Causes affected organisms to engage in avoidance behavior. See BOREDOM, INCENTIVE, POSITIVE INCENTIVE.

negative incentive effect   In social psychology, a greater attitude change under conditions of low reward than high. See COGNITIVE DISSONANCE.

negative induction   (I. Pavlov) An increase in inhibition due to the effects of a preceding excitation.

negative monitoring   Watching for behaviors that are unpleasant, counterproductive, frustrating.

negative nuclear sex   A cell nucleus whose chromosomes contain a single X and no Barr body. All 46,XY males, and most 45,XO females with Turner syndrome, have normal negative nuclear sex. Also known as chromatin negative, negative nuclear gender.

negative Oedipus complex   In psychoanalytic theory, a reversed Oedipus complex in which the son desires the father sexually and regards the mother as a rival. Also known as inverted Oedipus complex. See HOMOSEXUALITY.

negative phase   See FIRST NEGATIVE PHASE, NEGATIVISM.

negative practice   (K. Dunlap) A corrective technique in which an error is intentionally repeated for the purpose of overcoming it. The object is to bring the undesired behavior to the attention of consciousness, for example, purposely typing "hte" repeatedly, after previously typing "hte" when "the" was intended.

negative priming   In learning theory, the effect in which an item ignored on one trial is slower to be processed as an attended-to item on the next trial, relative to a control condition.

negative psychology   reverse psychology

negative recency (effect)   A tendency in prediction to select an event that could have happened but did not, on the argument that it should have, and is consequently more likely to do so in the near future (for example, in gambling on a roulette wheel, red has come up a number of times, so a gambler bets on the black, thinking that black is now due to come up). See GAMBLERS' FALLACY, POSITIVE FREQUENCY.

negative reference group   A standard group against which a person contends, for example, if a certain group is identified as having entirely undesirable characteristics, these unwanted elements can be used as criteria against which a person can assess the self.

negative reinforcement   The cessation of an aversive stimulus after a desired response, that will enhance the strength of the recurrence of the response in the same or a similar situation. See NEGATIVE REINFORCER.

negative reinforcer   An aversive stimulus or stimulus situation that, when discontinued after a desired response, enhances the strength of that response and increases the probability of the recurrence of the response in the same or a similar situation; for example, terminating shock following an animal's correct response is a negative reinforcer. See NEGATIVE REINFORCEMENT, POSITIVE REINFORCEMENT, REINFORCEMENT.

negative resource   An unpleasant surround.

negative response   An abient response. See ABIENCE.

negative reward   A stimulus or stimulus situation that occurs following a response or response sequence that represents a failure to perform at the expected level, for example, a failing grade is a negative reward acting to lessen the probability that the associated behavior will recur. It should not be confused with negative reinforcement.

negative self-verification theory   (W. B. Swann) A point of view that people who hold negative self-views find it uncomfortable to associate with people who see them in a positive way, and therefore have a tendency to seek out people who will confirm their negative self-perceptions. See SELF-VERIFICATION.

negative set   An established pattern of thinking leading to avoidance behavior. Humans who are afraid of certain stimuli will react strongly on presentation of such stimuli. See SET.

negative state relief model   1. An hypothesis that helping-behavior is used by some people in stress situations and periods of boredom and inactivity to avoid or escape dysphoric moods. 2. An assumption that people who are in a bad mood help others in order to improve their mood.

negative stereotype   A biased, oversimplified, inflexible, frequently erroneous conception usually of an ethnic or social group, for example, "All teenagers take drugs and play loud music." Compare POSITIVE STEREOTYPE. See PREJUDICE, RACISM.

negative suggestion   A statement intended to deter or inhibit a feeling, thought, or action on the part of another person.

negative symptom   1. A symptom of schizophrenia characterized by social, motivational, and emotional withdrawal. Compare POSITIVE SYMPTOM. 2. Absence of a behavior ordinarily seen in normal people, indicating a disorder. 3. Absence of a behavior characteristic of a person (for example, a "boisterous" person acts quiet and withdrawn), indicating that all is not well with the person.

negative tele   (J. L. Moreno) A feeling of repulsion projected toward others. A tele is used as the unit of measurement in sociometry. Compare POSITIVE TELE.

negative therapeutic reaction   An increase in neurotic behavior after a period of successful treatment. Usually interpreted as a form of resistance due to a sense of guilt which has established a masochistic need for suffering. See SUPEREGO RESISTANCE.

negative transfer   1. A process in which previous learning obstructs or interferes with present learning, for example, tennis players learning racquet ball must often "unlearn" their tendency to take huge, muscular swings with the shoulder and upper arm. 2. In psychoanalysis, displacement to the therapist of anger or hostility experienced toward the parents or other significant individuals during childhood. Compare POSITIVE TRANSFER.

negative transference   Feelings by either the therapist or the client about the other that are unpleasant, such as anger and disgust.

negative triad   **negative (cognitive) triad**

negative tropism   Automatic movement of an organism away from a source of stimulation. See TAXIS, TROPISM.

negativism   Persistent resistance to the suggestions or requests of others. Considered a healthy expression of self-assertion between the ages of 18 months and four years; also common during adolescence. In catatonic schizophrenia, it may take the form of mutism or refusal of food or care, and is considered an expression of a need to oppose or withdraw from a threatening world. In senility, it is usually a regression to childish ways of expressing anger or gaining attention. Also known as command negativism. See ACTIVE NEGATIVISM.

negativistic response   See NEGATIVISM.

neglect dyslexia   A peripheral dyslexia resulting from impairment in visual processing, rather than impairment of lexical knowledge. Sometimes related to a lesion in the left or right cerebral arteries. Neglect dyslexia is characterized by errors such as omitting areas of text on one side of the page when reading, typically on the side contralateral to the lesion. In right neglect dyslexia, the patient makes errors only with the final letters of words.

neglecting-uninvolved (parenting) style   A form of parenting characterized by lack of warmth, involvement, and control. Children may show attachment disruptions, low self-esteem, conduct problems, poor peer relations, low academic performance.

negligence   In law, generally, the failure to exercise the degree of care that a reasonably prudent person would have shown in similar circumstances.

negotiation with God   In situations perceived as desperate or impossible, some people will "bargain" with God seeking to postpone or eliminate an almost certain consequence by offering to make a dramatic change in behavior. May be personal or interpersonal. Bargains occur as "If you heal my son I will never drink or smoke again" and are testimonies to perceived powerlessness. See WIDOWHOOD CRISIS.

neirophrenia   (L. J. Meduna) A psychosis resembling schizophrenia in certain symptoms such as disturbances of emotion and associations, but distinguished from schizophrenia by a dreamlike state with clouded sensorium. See ATYPICAL PSYCHOSIS.

Nembutal   Trade name for pentobarbital (sodium).

neoanalyst   A person who proclaims to practice psychoanalysis, but who varies the standard psychoanalytic procedures. See NEO-FREUDIAN.

neoassociationism   Any variation of the classical theory of associationism.

neo-associationist theory   (E. R. Hilgard) A systematic account of volition and consciousness that has three main elements: (a) an "executive ego" that controls; (b) subordinate independent subsystems of control; and (c) subsystems that are arranged hierarchically. This theory applies to conscious experience and dissociation as in hypnosis.

neobehavioral counseling/theory   A counseling approach based at least in part on principles of learning. Assumes that the client's behavior is learned and that effective counseling must teach, model, or somehow impart more adaptive interpersonal patterns.

neobehaviorism   (C. L. Hull) A school of psychology that applies the tenets of behaviorism broadly and flexibly, and includes subjective experiences. See BEHAVIORAL ANALYSIS, HULL'S THEORY.

neocerebellum   The dorsal portion of the cerebellum containing fibers that communicate with nuclei of the pons. Phylogenetically, the newest part of the cerebellum.

neocortex   A part of the cerebral cortex assumed to be the most recent evolutionary stage of brain development in mammals. Also known as isocortex, neopallium.

neodissociation   (E. Hilgard) A concept that different components of the mind are dissociated during hypnosis. Also known as neodissociation theory of hypnosis.

neodissociation theory   A point of view that hypnotized individuals enter an altered state of consciousness in which consciousness is divided.

neo-Freudian   A theorist who accepts Sigmund Freud's major doctrines, but with modifications. Includes Melanie Klein, Heinz Kohut, and Heinz Hartmann, among others. Term usually does not apply to Freud's contemporaries who broke away from his school in the early days, such as Carl Jung, Alfred Adler, or Otto Rank. See CULTURALISTS, PSYCHOANALYTICALLY ORIENTED THERAPIES.

neo-Freudian theories   Theoretical modifications of Sigmund Freud's original theory developed by some of his disciples (Erich Fromm, Karen Horney, Harry Stack Sullivan, etc.), which include greater emphasis upon cultural influences rather than instinctual tendencies. See PSYCHOANALYTICALLY ORIENTED THERAPIES.

neogenetic   1. Pertaining to or characterized by neogenesis (regeneration of lost or injured body part). 2. (C. E. Spearman) Pertaining to the creation or generation of new items of knowledge on the basis of sentience.

neographism   The creation of new words in writing. A form of neologism.

neolallism   Abnormal tendency to use neologisms in speech. Such usage may be indicative of a mental condition.

neolocal family   In anthropology, a family system in which a husband and wife live in a new location as opposed to living with either the husband's family (patrilocality) or the wife's family (matrilocality).

neologism   A new word, such as "astronaut," coined for a purpose or for its own sake. In psychology, usually combinations of words or parts of words. Examples of words that were initially neologisms: "acidhead," "appestat." A variation of the Binet or Wechsler Vocabulary List uses neologisms to reduce the advantage of more educated participants. See CONDENSATION, PORTMANTEAU NEOLOGISM.

neologistic jargon/paraphasia   Unintelligible speech containing a mixture of inappropriate words and bizarre expressions coined by the speaker, as in "the criminal is a birth murder because that makes him a double . . . a birth murder is a murder that turns a cut donator extra into a double daughter-son." See MALAPROPISMS, WORD SALAD.

neo-Malthusian   A movement that advocated restricting population growth primarily through voluntary birth control.

neomnesis   1. Memory or recollection of the recent past. 2. Specialized memory for selective events or times, for example, one of a pair of identical twins remembers many early-childhood events whereas the other recalls a great many adolescent events.

neonatal drug dependency syndrome   Behaviors of newborn infants born to mothers who were drug dependent. Such infants are said to be of lower than normal birth weight and to gain weight slowly, and are purportedly restless and irritable.

neonatal period   The period from birth to approximately one month of age.

neonate   The newborn infant. See NEONATAL PERIOD.

neonate differences   Marked differences among newborns in general personality and specific behavior such as excitability, response to noise, and vigor of cries. See TEMPERAMENT.

neopallium   (T. Meynert) The phylogenetically new part of the cerebral cortex, comprising six layers of cells. Also known as the nonolfactory cortex or the pallium (R. A. von Koelliker), or probably better known as the isocortex (the Vogts). See NEOCORTEX.

NEO Personality Inventory   A questionnaire that measures neuroticism, extraversion, openness, agreeableness and conscientiousness. Consists of a self-report form and two observer-report forms to be completed by persons who know the examinee. According to test authors Paul T. Costa and Robert R. McCrae, these five factors constitute the major aspects (domains) of normal adult personality. See FIVE-FACTOR MODEL.

neophasia   A complex language-system with its own vocabulary and rules of grammar invented by certain patients with schizophrenia.

neophenomenology   (D. Snygg & A. Combs) A psychological position whose basic postulate is that behavior is continuously determined by the behavior's phenomenology at each instance of action.

neophilia   A tendency to prefer anything new or different, including clothing, foods, cars, etc.

neophobia   Morbid fear of change or of anything new, unfamiliar, or strange. See CAINOTOPHOBIA, KAINOPHOBIA.

neophrenia   Any childhood mental disorder. See AUTISM.

neoplatonism   A revision of the philosophy of Plato associated with numerous philosophers, but especially with Plotinus (ca. 205–270) in which Platonic, Pythagorean, Aristotelian, and Stoic theories were blended to produce a philosophy congruent with the Christian religious approaches of the time. The most mystical aspects of Plato's philosophy were emphasized. Later revivals occurred in Italy, peaking in the 15th century, and in 17th century England with the Cambridge Platonists.

neopsychic   See ADULT-EGO STATE, EXTEROPSYCHIC.

neopsychoanalysis   Any of several departures from Sigmund Freud's doctrines which nonetheless remain within the general framework. See NEO-FREUDIAN.

neosleep   nonrapid-eye-movement (NREM) sleep

neostriatum   A portion of the corpus striatum that evolved in the relatively recent past and includes the putamen and the caudate nucleus.

neoteny   1. The process of growing young instead of growing old. 2. In zoology, sexual maturation in the larval state. 3. The maintenance of embryonic stages of development in the adult. 4. In evolution, the retention into adulthood of characteristics of the earlier developmental stages characteristic of an ancestral species. As the result of either a general developmental slowing or acceleration of sexual maturation during evolution, the animal tends to become sexually mature while retaining characteristics of the physically immature animal in the ancestral species. Thus, apparently juvenile characteristics are displayed in adulthood.

Neotronics Olfactory Sensing Equipment   See ELECTRONIC NOSES.

nephophobia   nosophobia

nephrogenic diabetes insipidus   Inability of the kidney to concentrate due to an intrinsic renal disease, leading to excretion of extreme amounts of dilute urine, severe thirst, and dehydration. Can be critical for an infant who cannot communicate thirst and therefore suffers water depletion leading to brain damage and mental retardation before the cause is diagnosed. See DIABETES INSIPIDUS.

nepiophilia   1. Sexual attraction toward infants. 2. Being sexually aroused by playing the role of a parent with an infant. See INFANTILISM.

nepotism   Showing favoritism to relatives or significant others, usually regarding appointments to desired positions.

nerve   Thread-like structure of fibers that convey electrochemical signals between organs or body areas and between the external and internal environments of the body. Kinds of nerve include sensory, motor, autonomic, inhibitory, and excitatory. Also known as nerve cell, neuron(e). Types of nerves include: ABDUCENS, ACCELERATOR, ACCESSORY, ACOUSTIC, AUDITORY, AUTONOMIC, CENTRIFUGAL, CENTRIPETAL, CERVICAL, COCCYGEAL, COCHLEAR, CRANIAL, DEPRESSOR, ESODIC, FACIAL, GANGLIATED, GLOSSOPHARYNGEAL, GUSTATORY, HYPOGASTRIC, HYPOGLOSSAL, LINGUAL, MOTOR, OCULOMOTOR, OLFACTORY, OPTIC, PNEUMOGASTRIC, SACRAL, SCIATIC, SENSORY, SEVENTH CRANIAL, SPINAL, SPLANCHNIC, THERMOGENIC, THORACIC, TRIGEMINAL, TROCHLEAR, TROPHIC, ULNAR, VAGUS, VESTIBULAR.

nerve block   The blocking of nerve impulses by anesthetic or other drugs, or by mechanical means.

nerve cell   A basic unit of movement, sensation, and thought/emotion in the body. Simply stated, each nerve cell consists of axon-transmitter, soma, and dendrite-receptor and is innervated by electrochemical transduction across the synapse between neighboring cells. Primary inter-cell transduction chemicals are dopamine, serotonin and norepinephrine. Also known as neuron(e). See CONNECTOR NEURON, MOTOR NEURON, NERVE.

nerve current/impulse   An electrochemical wave (action potential) propagated along a neuron or chain of neurons; the means of receiving and transmitting signals in the nervous system. Also known as nervous current/impulse, neural current/impulse.

nerve deafness   See SENSORINEURAL HEARING LOSS.

nerve ending   Any of a variety of terminals for a nerve fiber, such as annulospiral or flower-spray endings in muscle spindles, basket endings, Krause end bulbs, Meissner corpuscles, and free nerve endings. Also known as end bulb, synaptic knob, terminal button. See TERMINAL END BUTTON.

nerve-energy doctrine   specific-energy doctrine

nerve fiber   1. Long, hairlike projection, for example, an axon, extending from the cell body of a neuron. 2. Loosely, the neuron itself. 3. A polarized cable-like structure such as the axon or dendrite that may be bare or covered with either, or both, a myelin sheath and neurilemma. The nerve fiber transmits potential changes across its boundary membrane.

nerve growth factor (NGF)   A protein that promotes the survival and development of axons in the sympathetic nervous system and some in the brain.

nerve impulse   nerve current

nerve pathway   neural pathway

nerve root   A portion of a sensory or motor nerve connected directly to the brain or spinal cord, for example, cranial or spinal nerves. Dorsal roots are sensory; ventral roots are motor.

nerve spike   The unit of neural activity represented by a temporary change in voltage of about 60 mv. and lasting for about 0.4–2 seconds. The amplitude of the spike potential is constant for any given nerve.

nerve tract   A bundle of axons within the central nervous system. A tract's name indicates its origin, the direction in which the impulses travel, and its destination, for example, the corticospinal tract originates in the cortical area and descends to the gray matter of the spinal cord.

nervism   (I. Pavlov) The Pavlovian concept that all body functions are controlled by the nervous system.

nervosisme   French term for neurasthenia used by French physician Jean Bouchut (1818–1891), similar to George Beard's definition of the construct. See ASTHENIC PERSONALITY, HYPOCHONDRIASIS, TRAUMATIC NEURASTHENIA.

nervous breakdown/prostration   Common but physiologically inaccurate phrase for mental disorder of any type, usually used to label a disorder that has a sudden onset and produces acute distress.

nervous current   nerve impulse

nervous energy   Common phrase for a state of intense activity or drive that suggests nervousness.

nervous exhaustion   Common but physiologically inaccurate phrase for fatigue due to emotional strain. See NEURASTHENIA.

nervous habit   Common phrase for stereotyped tension-reducing behavior, for example, nail-biting or tics.

nervous hunger   The urge to eat as a means of reducing anxiety and gratifying frustrated impulses, derived, according to psychoanalytic theory, from the oral incorporative stage of infantile development.

nervous impulse   nerve current/impulse

nervousness   Common term for a state of restless tension and emotionality with a tendency to tremble and feel apprehensive. The nerves per se may be perfectly normal.

nervous prostration   nervous breakdown

nervous system (NS)   The system of nerve tracts, cells, and receptors, which, with the endocrine organs, coordinates activities of the organism in response to signals from the internal and external environments. Often conceptualized in terms of its structural (central and peripheral) and functional (somatic and autonomic) divisions. See CONCEPTUAL NERVOUS SYSTEM, THIRD NERVOUS SYSTEM.

nervous tissue   The cell bodies and fibrous processes responsible for the various nervous-system functions. The neuroglia is sometimes included.

nervous vomiting   Functional, rather than physiologically-caused emesis ("throwing up"); for psychoanalytical inclined, construed as a rejection of a hated or feared idea or object. Thought to occur most commonly in young women as a physiological symbol of the inability to "stomach this situation." Can also occur on encountering a repulsive sight. See ORGAN LANGUAGE.

nestbuilding   Complex behavior of many birds, as well as some insects, reptiles, fish, amphibians, and mammals (including primates) in building and occupying homes, often to provide for offspring. Forms vary widely, but generally are triggered by hormonal activity in the female, the amount of light, the temperature, and the presence of offspring. In a sense, the human shows the most extensive and complex nestbuilding of all. Also known as nest-building, nesting.

net fertility   The number of offspring of carriers of a specific genetic trait who reach the age category in which the trait is expressed.

network   A sociometric concept employed by Jacob Moreno, who maintained that psychological networks are formed when the parts (individuals or social atoms) form complex chains of interrelations which shape social tradition and public opinion either spontaneously or through propaganda. Types of networks include: COMMUNICATION, FRIENDSHIP, GROUP, KINSHIP, PSYCHOLOGICAL, SEMANTIC, WHEEL. See SOCIAL-NETWORK THERAPY, SOCIOMETRY.

network-analysis evaluation In evaluation research, a method of studying networks of services from the vantage point of agencies within a system or the flow of service recipients through the system. System effectiveness is defined by looking at a person's progress through the network. The application of network evaluation provides a conceptual framework for viewing the institution in the context of the larger system.

network biotaxis 1. A pattern of human or animal stimulation on which the individual's fabric of interrelationships is based. Through the network biotaxis process, individuals influence the behavior of others and are in turn influenced by the same contacts. 2. A process whereby tissue cells arrange themselves in structural patterns within an organ.

network effect (S. H. Foulkes) Refers to interactions and relationships in a patient's environment which play an important part in the production of psychiatric disorders. See NETWORKS, NETWORK THERAPY, SOCIAL-NETWORK THERAPY, PSYCHOLOGICAL NETWORK.

networking 1. Developing or using contacts in an informal group, often career-related. 2. Intercommunication, as through telephone or computer systems.

network-memory model A conceptual framework for memory that consists of complex connections via nodes of concepts to other concepts. These nodes are links such as "belongs to" might connect "house" and "mother."

network therapy A psychological treatment approach in which an attempt is made to involve not only family members but other relatives, friends, and neighbors as sources of emotional support and possible vocational opportunity. Used primarily to prevent rehospitalization of former patients with schizophrenia living in the community. See GROW, RECOVERY INCORPORATED, SOCIAL NETWORK THERAPY.

neural adjustment Action of the central nervous system whereby the incoming impulses are transformed into outgoing impulses.

neural analyzers Peripheral nerve endings that transform stimuli in the central nervous system.

neural arc The nerve pathway usually followed by a nerve impulse from a receptor to an effector. In the reflex arc a sensory neuron or bundle of neurons is connected directly to a motor neuron or neurons; in learned behavior the connections are more complex.

neural circuitry The pathways of nervous impulses from receptor to effector, including connector neurons.

neural conduction The passage of a nerve impulse along nerve fibers from neuron to neuron or muscle.

neural crest A ridge-like area atop the embryonic neural plate that develops into the spinal ganglia and sympathetic nervous system.

neural current nerve current/impulse

Neural Darwinism (G. Edelman) A theory that groups of neurons are selected by experience to form the basis of cognitive operations such as memory and learning. This selectionism is seen as an explanation for the functioning of the brain.

neural discharge The firing of a neuron.

neural disposition A tendency, whether innate or resulting from use, of a neural element, center, or system, to operate in a certain manner.

neural equivalence Ability of one part of the nervous system to take over the functions of another part. See EQUIPOTENTIALITY.

neural excitation A state of activity or irritability, produced in a nerve fiber by stimulation.

neural facilitation Improvement of conduction in a nerve by any of several methods including repeated excitation of the nerve. The greater readiness of a neuron to fire especially through spatial summation.

neural fibril A component of the cytoplasm of a neuron. Composed of ultramicroscopic filaments and tubules. Their true function has not been proved satisfactorily, and earlier theories about their role as conducting elements have not been supported by research. Also known as neurofibril, neurofibrilla(e).

neural fold The tissue layer on either side of the embryonic neural plate that grows over the neural groove to enclose it.

neuralgia Pain that may be recurrent, sharp, and spasmodic, occurring along a nerve or a group of nerves. May be the result of injury or infection, or due to causes that cannot be identified with any organic disorder.

neural groove A fissure in the embryonic neural plate that develops into the neural tube, whose walls evolve into the central nervous system.

neural impulse nerve current/impulse

neural induction The influence of a neuron or group of neurons on another, producing either positive or negative induction effects.

neural integration A process by which inhibitory and excitatory postsynaptic potentials control a neuron's firing rate.

neural irritability A property of nerve tissue that makes it sensitive to stimulation and capable of responding by transmitting electrical impulses. Dependent on polarization of ions on either side of the cell membrane.

neural network model The concept that the brain consists of nerves whose ends eventually either connect to another nerve or a muscle, or connect at an intersection of other nerves that may all work together to convey an original signal in a much more dynamic manner.

neural parenchyma The essential functioning tissue of the nervous system as distinguished from the structural elements.

neural pathway Any route followed by a nerve impulse through the nervous system. May consist of a simple reflex arc or a complex but specific routing such as that apparently required by an impulse transmitting a specific wavelength of sound from the cochlea to the brain. Also known as nerve pathway.

neural plate A primitive region on the back surface of the embryo that will develop into the central nervous system. It is the first structural sign of the human nervous system. The broad front end of the neural plate will eventually become the brain whereas the rear part will develop into the spinal cord. Also known as neuroplate. See NEURULATION.

neural reinforcement The strengthening of a response by the simultaneous activity of a second response.

neural reverberation (D. O. Hebb) See REVERBERATORY CIRCUITS.

neural rivalry **response rivalry**

neural satiation A period of nonreaction to stimuli following considerable stimulation of the area or adjacent areas. See EXTINCTION, INHIBITION.

neural set A (temporary) state of subexcitation of a reflex path; such a path offers a lowered resistance to nerve impulses which can reach it, and appears to attract such impulses. This temporary state is also known as *Bahnung* (S. Exner), and the corresponding permanent state is called canalization. A permanently canalized path is a neurogram or engram.

neural subcenters Parts of the brain that are below the cortex that have specialized functions. An example is the thalamus that is, among other things, a kind of switchboard between input messages and the cortex.

neural substrate That part of the nervous system that affects or is affected by any behavior.

neural trace See ENGRAM, NEUROGRAM.

neural transmission The mechanism whereby a stimulus causes a release of a chemical transmitter substance or change of electrical potential, or both, that propels a nerve signal or impulse along a neural pathway.

neural tube A primitive nervous-system organ that takes shape as a longitudinal ectodermal tube in the middle of the back of a vertebrate embryo during the first days after formation of the zygote (fertilized ovum). Formed from the neural folds which curl over and fuse. The cavity of the neural tube is retained in the ventricles of the brain and the central canal of the spinal cord when they are formed. Many of the congenital defects of the nervous system, for example, spina bifida, originate at this stage of development. See NEURULATION.

neurasthenia A neurotic condition marked by fatigue, debility, insomnia, aches, and pains. Term originated in the 19th century with George Miller Beard, who assumed these symptoms were due to exhaustion from overwork. Term is rarely used today, and the condition is now attributed primarily to emotional conflicts, tensions, frustrations, and other psychological factors. Previously also known as *nervosisme*. See ASTHENIC PERSONALITY, HYPOCHONDRIASIS, TRAUMATIC NEURASTHENIA.

neurasthenic helmet A neurasthenic headache in which patients feel as if their heads were encased in a tightly fitted helmet. See NEURASTHENIA.

neurasthenic neurosis A type of neurosis in which the patient experiences feelings of weakness, is easily fatigued, and otherwise shows signs of neurasthenia.

neuraxis The hypothetical axis formed by a line running through the spinal cord and brainstem.

neurilemma (G. T. Keuffel) A thin membrane that covers the myelin sheath of axons, found mainly on white-matter fibers outside the central nervous system. Composed of Schwann cells, that help in the repair or regeneration of damaged axons. Only axons surrounded by a neurilemma appear capable of regeneration. Also known as neurolemma.

neurin 1. The protein substance of nerve tissue. 2. (W. McDougall) Hypothetical energy involved in nerve excitation.

neuritis Inflammation of a nerve.

neuroanatomy The study of the relationships between the nervous system and the tissues and organs innervated by the nerve fibers.

neurobiotaxis The factors that influence growth of a nerve fiber toward the tissue it will innervate, an action that occurs millions of times during embryological development. The concept has been expanded to explain at least a part of the learning process, as neuron-connecting points grow toward each other in response to a conditioning stimulus.

neuroblast The bud that becomes a neuron emanating from the neural tube.

neurochemistry A branch of neuropharmacology and neurophysiology that deals with the roles of atoms, molecules, and ions in functions of nervous systems. Because chemical substances in a physiological system obey the same laws of nature as in other environments, activities of neurotransmitters, drugs, and other molecules in the nervous system can be explained in terms of basic chemical concepts.

neurocirculatory asthenia **Da Costa's syndrome**

neurocognition The theoretical junction between biological processes of the brain and cognitive effects.

neurocontrol In ergonomics, generally, output directed by the position of the operator's head/helmet, or conceivably by the operator's mental activity. See HEAD-SLAVED.

neurodermatitis Any form of skin inflammation associated with an emotional disorder, for example, urticaria (hives) are marked redness and wheals on the skin that may appear in periods of psychological stress.

neurodevelopmental hypothesis (of schizophrenia) A postulate that schizophrenia is largely due to abnormalities in the prenatal or neonatal development of the nervous system, leading to abnormalities in behavior and brain anatomy.

neuroeffector junction Connecting point between the end of a nerve and the smooth muscle or gland the nerve innervates.

neuroeffector transmission The conduction of nerve impulses to the two general types of effectors, the muscles and glands. May include stimulation through a synaptic connection or through the release of chemical transmitters, acetylcholine, epinephrine, or norepinephrine. Synaptic transmitters are found in skeletal muscles, chemical transmitters in smooth muscles.

neuroendocrinology The study of the relationship between the nervous system, especially the brain, and the endocrine system.

neuroethology A branch of psychology in which the emphasis is on the relationship between neurobiology and behavior. Areas of research include small neural networks, visual discrimination, and the neural control of activity and motivation.

neurofeedback A method of training persons to manage certain behavioral or physiologic disorders, for example, attention deficit/hyperactivity disorder (ADHD), by training them to control the electrical activity of their brains as measured by the surface electroencephalogram (EEG). They are presented a visual or auditory signal that tracks specific features of their spontaneously changing

EEG activity, and are instructed to learn to achieve or increase voluntary control of the signal over a series of sessions. The method has been used successfully for several disorders besides ADHD, including epilepsy, insomnia, and alcoholism, often in conjunction with psychotherapeutic support. Sometimes used as an aid to meditation and attention control. Some recent variations of the method do not require learning to achieve control, using instead audio-visual stimuli known previously to evoke EEG responses as reflexes. Also known as EEG biofeedback, neurotherapy.

neurofibril   A long thin tube found within an axon. See NEURAL FIBRIL.

neurofibrillary degeneration (NFD)   A pathological process of atrophy of nerve fibrils in the fifth and sixth decades of life associated with senile dementia and Alzheimer's disease. A secondary effect of the process, sometimes called Alzheimerization of brain tissue, is reduced blood flow to the cerebrum, resulting in brain hypoxia.

neurogenesis   Formation of the nervous system.

neurogenic   1. Pertaining to a condition or event originating in, starting from, caused by, or produced by, a component of the nervous system. Also known as neurogenous. 2. Pertaining to neurogenesis. Also known as neurogenetic.

neurogenic drive   The automatic functioning of an organ or organ system because of a rhythm or pattern of discharges by nerve tissue. Neurogenic drive rhythms control automatic contractions and relaxations of heart-muscle fibers and the muscles that operate the respiratory system.

neurogenous   neurogenic (meaning 1)

neuroglia   (R. Virchow, O. Dieters, S. Ramon y Cajal) Central nervous system cells that support other tissues. There is inconclusive evidence that neuroglia cells are also directly involved in nervous-system functions, based in part on recordings of electrical potentials in the cells. Also known as glia.

neurogram   1. An automatic or habitual response. 2. The engram or physical register of the mental experience, stimulation of which retrieves and reproduces the original experience, thereby generating memory. Also known as neural trace.

neurohormone   A hormone that stimulates neuronal activity. See NEUROTRANSMITTER.

neurohumor   A substance, such as epinephrine or serotonin, that is liberated at nerve endings to stimulate activity in a neighboring neuron, muscle cell, or gland. The specific chemical agents that transmit neural impulses across synapses and junctions at nerve endings are referred to as neurohumoral.

neurohypophysis   The posterior pituitary gland, the portion of the hypophysis connected by the infundibulum to the hypothalamus. Hormones secreted by the neurohypophysis are vasopressin, also known as antidiuretic hormone, oxytocin. See ADENOHYPOPHYSIS.

neurolemma   neurilemma

neuroleptic drug(s)   (J. de Lay) Major tranquilizers or antipsychotic medications, used mainly to treat manic states and schizophrenias. Also known as neuroleptics. See ANTIPARKINSON DRUGS, ANXIOLYTICS, BUTYROPHENONES, PHENOTHIAZINES, RAUWOLFIA DERIVATIVES, RESERPINE, THIOXANTHENES.

neuroleptic malignant syndrome (NMS)   A potentially fatal condition in which a patient using neuroleptic medication develops severe muscle rigidity, an elevated temperature, and usually at least a few of the following: diaphoresis (sweating), dysphagia (trouble swallowing), tremor, incontinence, clouding of consciousness (ranging from confusion through delirium, stupor and coma), mutism, tachycardia (rapid heartbeat), elevated or labile blood pressure, and abnormal laboratory tests.

neuroleptic syndrome   The series of effects observed in patients who have been administered neuroleptic drugs. Characterized by reduced motor activity and emotionality, indifference to external stimuli, and decreased ability to perform tasks that require good motor coordination. The patient may become cataleptic from high doses. See TARDIVE DYSKINESIA.

neurolinguistic   programming   (A. B. Diltz, R. Bandler, J. Grinder) A vaguely defined system of communication claimed to make neurological changes and to provide five-minute cures for phobias.

neurolinguistics   1. A branch of psychology concerned with brain mechanisms of language and speech. 2. (R. B. Dilts) The study of the structure of subjective experience. Assumes that all external experience is represented in neurological channels that are psychoneurologically preprogrammed to correspond to major sensory channels. 3. The study of neurological mechanisms in the use of language.

neurological amnesia   A loss or impairment of memory due to disease or injury that affects the nervous system. Includes auditory amnesia (and Wernicke's aphasia), tactile amnesia (and astereognosis), verbal amnesia, and visual amnesia. See APHASIA.

neurological evaluation   Analysis of the data gathered of a patient's sensory, motor, and coordination responses. Evaluation includes speech and behavior, muscular strength, gait, deep reflexes, tests of cranial nerves, pain, temperature, discriminative senses, and sensory-organ responses.

neurological examination   A systematic study of the patient's central and peripheral nervous systems covering sensory and motor functions such as reflexes, as well as tests of attention, levels of consciousness, memory, cognitive and related cortical functions, and observation of behavior in general.

neurological impairment   A condition marked by disruption of the nervous system or a part of the system as a result of disease, injury, or effects of a drug or other chemical, for example, parkinsonism, Alzheimer's form of presenile dementia, and Wernicke's encephalopathy.

neurological investigative procedure   A technique used to determine neurological status. Includes (a) Angiography: measures cerebral blood flow to detect obstructions, lesions, aneurisms, leaks; (b) Hemoencephalography: air is introduced into the cerebral spinal fluid to enhance ventricle visualization; (c) Neurometric mapping: variant of EEG to investigate focal epilepsy;

(d) Neuroimaging: structural investigations are the CAT scan and MRI; functional ones are the PET scan and SPECT (nuclear imaging); (e) Electrostimulation; (f) Neurochemical and drug studies; and (g) Electroencephalography and qEEG (quantitative EEG).

neurologist A physician who specializes in the diagnosis and treatment of diseases of the nervous system (neurological disorders).

neurology (T. Willis) A branch of medicine that deals with the normal and diseased nervous system. The diagnosis and treatment of diseases of the nervous system is called clinical neurology.

neuromelanin A dark pigment, similar to the pigment responsible for skin color, that occurs in certain neurons of the nervous system, such as the substantia nigra.

neurometrics (E. R. John) A method of gaining quantitative data about brain functioning using computer techniques in the analysis of electroencephalograms (EEGs) and evoked potentials. Mathematical analysis of data obtained from patients with behavioral symptoms, developmental problems, and neurologic dysfunctions yields objective, operational categories used to identify different types of brain functions in individuals whose behavior manifestations are similar.

neuromodulator Chemical with properties intermediate between those of a neurotransmitter and those of a hormone.

neuromuscular disease Any pathologic condition related to the nerves and muscles. Some of these conditions are Lupus, arteriolateral sclerosis (ALS), and multiple sclerosis (MS).

neuromuscular junction Synapse between a motor neuron's axon and a skeletal muscle fiber. Also known as myoneural junction.

neuromuscular system **motor system**

neuromyal Refers to nerve muscle functions.

neuron (W. von Waldeyer-Hartz) A nerve cell; any conducting cell of the nervous system, consisting of a cell body with nucleus and a varying number of fiber processes extending from the cell body. In addition to conductivity, a common characteristic of neurons is irritability. Also spelled neurone. See two kinds of neurons demonstrated in connector neuron and motor neuron.

neuronal spiking Large electrical discharges from brain or nerve tissue.

neuron doctrine/theory (W. von Waldeyer-Hartz) A point of view by Waldeyer in 1891 that the nervous system consisted of numerous nerve cells (neurons), with nervous energy being relayed by contact only from one neuron to another. Previously, it was assumed that the nervous system consisted of continuous tubelike networks, similar to the vascular system, through which some substance flowed.

neuropathic traits Primary behavior disorders such as nail-biting, enuresis, finger-sucking, sleepwalking, nightmares, fear of darkness, and anxiety.

neuropathology The study of diseases of the nervous system. May include examination of the brain or other relatively large parts of the system for gross defects that may be visible to the naked eye, with neuroimaging techniques, with studies of tissue cells under a microscope, and with laboratory analysis of tissue neurochemistry.

neuropeptides A class of chemicals secreted by the brain and nervous system, also found to affect other systems, such as the immunological system, the skin, various organs. They work both locally and systemically, like hormones. Endorphins, the types that act like an endogenous (generated from within the body) morphine-like substance, are one example. There are scores of others. See PEPTIDE HORMONES.

neuropeptide Y A peptide (a compound of at least two amino acids) found in the brain and gut. When injected into the brain, changes various behaviors including feeding.

neuropharmacology Rare term for the scientific study of the effects of drugs on the nervous system. See PSYCHOPHARMACOLOGY.

neurophrenia Rare term for a behavioral disorder that can be attributed to an impairment of the central nervous system.

neurophysiology A branch of biology and medicine concerned with the normal and abnormal activity of nervous-system functions, including the chemical activity of individual nerve cells.

neuropil(e) A web-like synaptic network of axon and dendrite filaments that forms the bulk of the gray matter of the central nervous system. The cell bodies of the neurons are embedded in the net of fibers.

neuroplasticity A concept that neurons are not necessarily fixed in their functioning but are capable of functional modification as a result of changes of environmental signals.

neuroplate **neural plate**

neuroplexus A network of nerve fibers, particularly autonomic-nervous-system fibers.

neuropsychiatry A branch of medicine that combines the studies of neurology and psychiatry, and thus deals with both organic and functional disorders related to the nervous system.

neuropsychodiagnosis The process of searching for possible organic causes for a mental disorder. May include careful evaluation of heredity, a review of hospital records at the time of birth for clues to a neonatal problem, and changes in auditory or visual abilities, altered states of consciousness, labyrinthine disorders, or lateralization deficiencies in later years.

neuropsychological assessment Evaluation of the localization and extent of possible brain damage to a patient. Evaluations are derived from the results of specialized tests of perceptual, cognitive, and motor abilities that present general and specific challenges to central nervous system functions. See HALSTEAD-REITAN NEUROPSYCHOLOGICAL SCALE, LURIA-NEBRASKA NEUROPSYCHOLOGICAL BATTERY, NEUROLOGY.

neuropsychology A branch of psychology that combines neurology and psychology, concerned primarily with clinical and scientific aspects of the relationship between brain structure and human behavior. See PHYSIOLOGICAL PSYCHOLOGY.

neuropsychosis of defense (S. Freud) Obsolete phrase applied to a group of disorders (hysteria, obsessions, phobias, hallucinatory psychosis, paranoia) that appear to have defense mechanisms (projection, conversion, displacement, etc.) and childhood sexual trauma as common denominators.

neuropsychotropic agents An outmoded name for psychotropic medicines.

neuroreceptor receptor (meaning 2)

neuroscience The study of the structure and function of the nervous system in terms of topics of concern in neurology and related fields, including neuroanatomy, neurophysiology, neuropharmacology, neuroradiology, neuroimmunology, psychology, and psychiatry.

neurosecretion Substance released by the axons of certain nerve cells in the brain that stimulate endocrine glands. See "MIDDLE MAN" HORMONES.

neurosis 1. A neurological disease of unknown etiology. Types of neurosis include: MOTOR, NEURASTHENIC, NUCLEAR, OCCUPATIONAL, ORGAN, PAN-, PSEUDOSCHIZOPHRENIC. 2. Any disorder in which anxiety is the primary feature. Sigmund Freud distinguished between "psycho-neuroses" and "actual neuroses." Types of neurosis include: ACTUAL, AERO-, ANALYTIC, CARDIAC, COLLECTIVE, COUNTERTRANSFERENCE, DECOMPENSATION, MIXED, PENSION. 3. (W. Cullen) A functional (not organic in origin) mental disorder characterized by a high level of anxiety and other distressing emotional symptoms, such as morbid fears, obsessive thoughts, compulsive acts, somatic reactions, dissociative states, and depressive reactions. The symptoms do not include gross personality disorganization, total lack of insight, or loss of contact with reality, and are generally viewed as exaggerated, unconscious methods of coping with internal conflicts and the anxiety they produce. Also known as psychoneurosis. Plural is neuroses. Purported types of neurosis have included: ANXIETY, CHARACTER, COLLECTIVE FAMILY TRANSFERENCE, COMBAT, COMPENSATION, COMPULSIVE, DEATH, DEPERSONALIZATION, DERMATO-, DESTINY, EXISTENTIAL, EXPERIMENTAL, FAMILY, HOMOSEXUAL, HYPOCHONDRIACAL, IATROGENIC, KERAUNO-, MALIGNANT, MONOSYMPTOMATIC, NONCOMBAT MILITARY, OCCLUSAL, PERFORMANCE, PERHAPS, PRISON, PROMOTION, PSYCHO-, RETIREMENT, SITUATION, SUCCESS, SUNDAY, SYMPTOM, TRANSFERENCE, TRAUMATIC, UPROOTING, VEGETATIVE, WAR, WEEKEND. See ARTIFICIAL NEUROSIS, CHRONOPHOBIA, CONVERSION HYSTERIA, DEFENSE PSYCHONEUROSIS, DROMOMANIA, DYSTHYMIC DISORDER, EXISTENTIAL VACUUM, HOUSEWIFE'S SYNDROME, HYPOCHONDRIASIS, INFINITY NEUROSIS, NARCISSISTIC NEUROSIS, OBSESSIVE-COMPULSIVE DISORDER, PANNEUROSIS, PATHONEUROSIS, PHOBIC DISORDERS, REGRESSION NEUROSIS, SEMISTARVATION NEUROSIS, SOCIAL BREAKDOWN SYNDROME, SYMPTOM CHOICE, WERNICKE'S CRAMP.

neurosis vs anxiety See ANXIETY VS NEUROSIS.

neurosyphilis The nervous system symptoms of syphilis, including tabes dorsalis, general paresis.

neurotherapy neurofeedback

neurotic anxiety In psychoanalysis, anxiety that originates in unconscious conflict and is maladaptive in nature, since it has a disturbing effect on emotion and behavior and also intensifies resistance to treatment. See OBJECTIVE ANXIETY.

neurotic arrangement The erroneous organization by persons with a neurosis of ideas and events to justify their behavior.

neurotic character (A. Adler) Personal perceptions leading to consistent dissatisfaction with self, always seeking to move ahead of others, feeling unhappy with the self and unwilling to accept the self "as is." See CHARACTER NEUROSIS.

neurotic claim (K. Horney) A spoiled-child type of thinking, as in "Everyone should be ready to serve me." See NARCISSISM, SPOON-FED.

neurotic conflict 1. In general, an intrapsychic or internal, conflict that leads to persistent maladjustment and emotional disturbance. 2. In Karen Horney's approach, a clash between neurotic needs such as an excessive need for power and independence and the need for love and dependence. See INTRAPSYCHIC CONFLICT.

neurotic defense system In Karen Horney's approach, a pattern of "strategies" adopted to counteract "basic anxiety" arising out of disturbed relations between a child and his or her parents. These strategies generate insatiable neurotic needs grouped into three categories: (a) moving toward people (clinging to others); (b) moving away from people (insisting on independence and self-dependence); and (c) moving against people (seeking power, prestige, and possessions). See HORNEY TRIANGLE, NEUROTIC NEEDS.

neurotic depression A temporary kind of depression precipitated by an intensely distressing event. See REACTIVE DEPRESSION.

neurotic-depressive reaction reactive depression

neurotic disorder Mental pathology characterized by a symptom or syndrome that is distressing to the person and which the person finds unacceptable and alien. Longstanding with no known organic basis and there is no impairment in contact with reality. See AFFECTIVE DISORDERS, ANXIETY DISORDERS, DISSOCIATIVE DISORDERS, NEUROSIS, PSYCHOSEXUAL DISORDERS, SOMATIZATION, SOMATOFORM DISORDERS.

neurotic fiction (A. Adler) A guiding fiction (ambition) that is so unrealistic that its goals cannot be achieved.

neurotic guilt A feeling of guilt due to an actual, fancied, or exaggerated transgression that creates a state of anxiety, loss of self-esteem, and internal conflict. In psychoanalytic theory, the conflict is between the superego and the ego, and the anxiety arises out of a conscious or unconscious fear of punishment or even annihilation. See GUILT FEELINGS.

neurotic hunger strike (A. Adler) Adlerian phrase for a fear of eating that develops in some females soon after puberty, interpreted as an attempt to retard development of a normal adult female body form and thus reject the adult female role. See ANOREXIA NERVOSA.

neurotic insanity panic A form of anxiety produced by a fear of becoming insane.

neuroticism 1. The condition of being neurotic. 2. (H. Eysenck) Proneness to neurosis; also a mild condition of neurosis. One of two major dimensions in Hans Eysenck's factor theory of personality, the other being introversion-extroversion.

neurotic needs (K. Horney) Excessive drives and demands that may arise out of the strategies people use in defending themselves against basic anxiety and in attempts to cope with a threatening world. In cognitive-behavioral theory, "neurotic" needs represent a means of relinquishing control to external sources that are animate, for example a mate and need for love, or inanimate, money and possessions and need for acceptance and esteem. The primary source of discomfort arises in the failure to satisfy the needs and the negative resultant self-evaluation.

neurotic nucleus A personality pattern purportedly associated with persons with neuroses, consisting of high vulnerability to stress and inability to cope with ordinary problems in effective ways. Such individuals are said to lack ego strength, have low frustration tolerance, overreact to minor setbacks, are beset by anxiety, and overwork "favorite" defense mechanisms until they crystallize into symptoms.

neurotic paradox A tendency of persons with a disorder that perpetuates neurotic defenses to which they cling. Presumably, this tendency constitutes a paradox because neurotic defenses prevent maximal functioning and inhibit development in one or more areas. A neurotic pattern such as an inordinate drive for sexual or business success may serve as a defense against anxiety for a time but becomes self-defeating. See ANXIETY, DEFENSE MECHANISM, NEUROSIS.

neurotic personality A pattern of traits and tendencies that increase susceptibility to neurosis of one type or another. The persistently tense, apprehensive, insecure individual may be prone to anxiety neurosis; the overly orderly, cautious, meticulous person is more likely to develop an obsessive-compulsive disorder; a tendency toward fixed irrational fears may develop into a phobic disorder; and a susceptibility to bodily complaints may lead to a hysterical (conversion) disorder.

neurotic process 1. The way an unconscious conflict comes to be expressed by neurotic symptoms and personality disturbances. 2. In Karen Horney's approach, the defensive behavior and strategies employed by a person with a neurosis to maintain an idealized self-image which is in conflict with the real, or actual, self. 3. Conscious or unconscious yielding to demands and expectations of self and others leading to negative self-evaluation upon inevitable failure.

neurotic-process factor (R. B. Cattell) A characterological trait usually significant in discriminating between normal and neurotic behaviors.

neurotic proviso Also known as parapathic proviso, similar to Alfred Adler's junction.

neurotic-regressive debility (R. B. Cattell) A personality dimension marked by such factors as rigidity, incompetence, loss of interests, and inability to mobilize habits to complete a task.

neurotic resignation (K. Horney) A method of escape from situations by withdrawal to avoid any confrontation with the reality of threatening or disturbing factors. See RESIGNATION.

neurotic-sleep attack A psychogenic, uncontrollable urge to sleep, ranging from a few minutes to hours. Cases have been reported of soldiers falling asleep during a bombardment, preachers while delivering a sermon, and patients while having a tooth pulled. See APNEA, NARCOLEPSY.

neurotic sociopath An antisocial person who has a high anxiety level, overdeveloped or misdirected conscience, and feelings of guilt and apprehension which the person appears to ward off by engaging in outward activity that takes the form of stealing, sexual promiscuity, or other antisocial behavior. See PRIMARY SOCIOPATH.

neurotic solution (K. Horney) A method of resolving a neurotic conflict by removing it from awareness.

neurotic syndromes A group of neurotic disorders comprising anxiety disorder, conversion disorder, obsessive-compulsive disorder, dissociative disorder, depressive disorder, neurasthenic disorder, depersonalization disorder, and hypochondriacal disorder. See NEUROSIS.

neurotic-telegraphic speech Verbal communication in which the speaker has difficulty in using more than a minimal number of words (as formerly done in terse telegrams).

neurotic traits A group of adjustment reactions of childhood comprising tics, somnambulism, over-activity, stuttering, specific fears, and school phobia.

neurotic trend (K. Horney) A person's organization of tendencies toward attaining maximum security, primarily by moving toward, away from, or against people.

neurotigenesis The production or induction of a neurosis or neurotic behavior.

neurotransmitter(s) Chemicals that carry the "messages" of the nerves from one nerve cell to another. They are secreted at the ends of the axon, the efferent or outgoing fiber of the nerve cell, enter the synapse, a tiny space between the nerves, some are picked up by the receptor sites on the dendrites, the afferent or ingoing fiber or part of the next nerve cell, and if enough receptor sites are stimulated, this triggers the depolarization or "firing" of that next nerve cell in the network. There have been many different types of neurotransmitters discovered and many variants within each type. Acetylcholine, dopamine, gamma-aminobutyric acid (GABA), norepinephrine, and serotonin are some of the better-known examples.

neurotransmitter receptor A protein embedded in the postsynaptic membrane. When a neurotransmitter attaches to it, the receptor can open a channel for it, or exert other effects.

neurovegetative system Old name for the parasympathetic portion of the autonomic nervous system, which is involved in control of the body's vegetative processes. See VEGETATIVE NERVOUS SYSTEM.

neurovisceral system The parasympathetic portion of the autonomic nervous system, involved in innervation of the internal organs of the body. See NEUROVEGETATIVE SYSTEM.

neurula The early embryonic stage following the morula and blastocyst stages. Plural is neurulae.

neurulation   The process of development of the primitive nervous system in the early stages of embryonic life as the neural plate forms and evolves into the neural tube which eventually becomes the spinal canal and ventricles of the brain. See NEURAL PLATE, NEURAL TUBE.

neustress   Neutral stress that occurs when environmental demands have neither a positive nor a negative effect.

neutral color   A color that lacks hue or saturation, for example, a gray, white, or black.

neutral environment   (S. R. Slavson) 1. An environment in group therapy designed to impose no specific or rigid limitations so that each member can take from the environment whatever is needed. 2. An environment in an institution, such as a mental hospital, in which patients experience no demands or limits.

neutral gray   A shade of gray intermediate between white and black.

neutrality   (S. R. Slavson) Describing the laissez-faire role of the therapist, who remains passive and permissive and does not apply judgments of moral right and wrong or suggest what is proper behavior on the part of patients or clients.

neutralization   1. To make ineffective. 2. (H. Hartmann) In psychoanalytic theory, the use of sexual or aggressive energy in the service of the ego rather than for instinctual gratification, that is, in functions such as problem-solving, creative imagination, scientific inquiry, or decision-making. See DEAGGRESSIVIZATION, DELIBIDINIZATION, SUBLIMATION. 3. (H. Hartmann) In ego psychology, the process by which infantile sexual and aggressive energies are desexualized.

neutralizer   (S. R. Slavson) A member of a therapy group who plays a role of modifying and controlling impulsive, aggressive, or destructive behaviors of other members of the group.

neutral monism   A doctrine positing that originally before mind or matter there was a more fundamental substance that was neither mind nor matter.

neutral stimulus   (I. P. Pavlov) A stimulus that does not produce the expected response, or that does not produce the response elicited after conditioning.

never-married   A single person who has never been married, as opposed to a person who is divorced, widowed, or separated.

new brain   Cerebral cortex and related structures that have appeared relatively late in evolution.

new-father blues   A common expression for temporary feelings of dejection a new father may feel after the birth of his baby, especially if he is unprepared for the change in routine and the complete attention needed by the infant especially by the mother. Also known as paternity blues. See MATERNITY BLUES.

New Hampshire Rule   The pioneer (1871) American test of criminal responsibility. It includes this partial statement: "If the [criminal] act was the offspring of insanity—a criminal intent did not produce it . . ."

new look   The concept of certain social changes being a function of attitudinal-perceptual changes. For various reasons people find certain social aspects no longer aesthetically pleasing, especially styles of clothing, and changes are made to conform to new perceptions.

newness fear   See KAINOPHOBIA, KAINOTOPHOBIA, NEOPHOBIA.

newton (N)   The SI (metric system) unit of force that imparts to a mass of 1 kilogram an acceleration of 1 meter per second. Named after Isaac Newton. See INTERNATIONAL SYSTEM OF UNITS.

Newton's color experiments   (I. Newton) Isaac Newton was first to determine that all colors are found in white light, understanding this from the study of the already well-known spectrum. He demonstrated how different colors could be generated by using a spinning disk, one color on one side, a different one on the other side. In his book, *Optics*, he described a number of experiments including those of afterimages.

Newton's law of color mixture   (I. Newton) A theory that if two color mixtures arouse the same sensation of light or color, a mixture of these mixtures will also arouse that sensation. See NEWTON'S COLOR EXPERIMENTS.

nexus   A connection between two variables which, if causal, makes them interdependent.

NFD   neurofibrillary degeneration

NGF   nerve growth factor

NGRI   See NOT GUILTY BY REASON OF INSANITY.

NHST   null hypothesis significance testing

NIAAA   National Institute on Alcohol Abuse and Alcoholism

niche picking   A tendency of organisms (for example, humans) to select other organisms or environments that are compatible to their level of functioning or expectation. Also known as bird-of-a-feather effect.

nicotine   A prevalent addictive substance, a chemical obtained from the tobacco plant and used for scientific purposes in physiological and pharmacologic studies. A stimulant in small doses, possibly depressive in large doses. Largely responsible for the effects of smoking tobacco. Can be used to mimic the effect of acetylcholine on ACh receptors. Named for French diplomat Jean Nicot, who introduced tobacco into France in the 1560s. See TOBACCO.

nicotine dependence   See TOBACCO DEPENDENCE.

nicotine withdrawal   See TOBACCO WITHDRAWAL SYMPTOMS.

nictophobia   nyctophobia

Niemann-Pick disease   A hereditary disease found predominantly in Jews, characterized by the deposition of lecithin and sphingomyelin in foamy, lipid histiocytes throughout the body, resulting in massive hepatosplenomegaly, nervous system involvement, and compromise of cardiac and respiratory systems. Named after German physicians Albert Niemann (1880–1921) and Ludwig Pick (1868–1935).

night blindness   A visual impairment marked by difficulty or inability to see objects in a dimly lighted environment. May result from Vitamin A deficiency. See HEMERALOPIA.

night-care program   Psychotherapy and supportive activity such as recreational and occupational therapy provided to mental patients during the evening. Patients, in most cases, live in the community and come to the hospital after working hours. Night care makes fuller and more economic use of hospital facilities and enables many patients to be released from full hospitalization sooner than usual. See NIGHT HOSPITAL.

night courting   See BUNDLING, NIGHT CRAWLING.

night crawling   A courtship practice in which a man joins a woman in a bed at night (with or without sexual activity, depending on the culture) in her family home with the knowledge of the family but without disturbing the family. Mainly a South East Asian cultural practice, but reported to occur in some American communities. See BUNDLING.

night-eating syndrome   A disorder experienced by about 10% of obese persons, mostly women, who suffer from insomnia and eat heavily during the night. A form of hyperphagia precipitated by stressful circumstances and occurring every night until the stress is alleviated. See BULIMIA, HYPERPHAGIA.

night fantasy   (S. Freud) A dream that is not a true dream but rather a near-dream fantasy.

night fear   See NYCTOPHOBIA.

night hospital   A type of partial hospitalization that originated in Montreal in 1954. Patients spend the day in the community and receive psychiatric care in the hospital at night. See DAY HOSPITAL, NIGHT-CARE PROGRAM.

nightmare   A vivid dream depicting frightening, disturbing, anxiety-provoking events. The motif is usually helpless terror; typically the dreamer is plunged into a threatening situation, experiences agonizing dread, makes futile attempts to escape, and awakens in a cold sweat. Occurs at all ages, usually in a REM (rapid-eye-movement) period toward the end of the sleep, more common following stressful experiences. Also known as dream anxiety attacks, incubus, oneirodynia gravis. See NIGHT TERRORS, SLEEP-TERROR DISORDER.

nightmare-death syndrome   Phrase similar to *Bangungut.*

night residue   The psychic material of a previous night's dreaming that persists in the person's thoughts after awakening.

nightshade poisoning   Toxic effects of ingestion of the berries of the "deadly nightshade" plant, *Atropa belladonna*, a source of atropine, an anticholinergic drug which paralyzes the parasympathetic nervous system. The symptoms include visual hallucinations, dilated pupils, unresponsiveness, disorientation, and other effects that may mimic an acute schizophrenic reaction. See BELLADONNA.

night terrors   Disturbing dreams, usually during the third or fourth stage (nonrapid-eye-movement) of sleep, from which the sleeper commonly awakes in a terror. Also known as sleep-terror disorder. See NIGHTMARE, PAVOR NOCTURNUS.

nigrostriatal   Refers to the connection between the substantia nigra and the striatum. See SUBSTANTIA NIGRA.

NIH   National Institutes of Health

nihil ex nihilo fit   (nothing comes from nothing— Latin) A scholastic statement of the law of universal causation.

nihilism   A delusion of nonexistence; a fixed belief that mind, body, or the world at large no longer exists ("I am only an empty shell," "This is a dream world," "I died twenty years ago."). Delusions of this kind occur primarily in schizophrenia, severe depression, and occasionally in general paresis, cerebral arteriosclerosis, and senile dementia. Also known as delusion of negation, nihilistic delusion.

nil   Zero.

NIMH   National Institute of Mental Health

ninth cranial nerve   See GLOSSOPHARYNGEAL NERVE.

nirvana   (Sanskrit) A concept originally found in Buddhist thought, the liberation of the individual consciousness, through the extinction of all desire, resentment, and selfishness caused by identification with the ego. Some variation of the concept exists among the different Buddhist schools and Hindu schools of thought.

nirvana principle   (S. Freud) In psychoanalytic theory, a tendency of all instincts and life processes to seek the stability and equilibrium of the inorganic state. The goal of the death instinct, which Sigmund Freud held to be universal. See BUDDHISM.

NIS   National Intelligence Scale

Nissl bodies/granules   (F. Nissl) Granules in the cytoplasm of cell bodies and dendrites of neurons, capable of being stained to identify them from other nuclear tissues. Also known as tigroid bodies. See NEURON, NISSL'S STAIN.

Nissl's stain   A basic dye used to stain Nissl bodies and other granule-like structures in the cytoplasm of neurons. German neurologist Franz Nissl (1860–1919) discovered the technique of staining nerve cells and the substance in the cytoplasm.

nisus   1. (G. Leibnitz) A tendency of any active organism to strive against obstacles. 2. Conscious effort or endeavor.

nit (nt)   A measure of luminance, intended to replace older measurements such as foot-candle. See CANDELA.

nitric oxide (NO)   A gas produced, through nitric oxide synthase, in neurons to facilitate their communication.

nitrogen narcosis   See RAPTURE-OF-THE-DEEP SYNDROME.

nitrous oxide   One of the earliest-known (mid-19th century) recreational substances, this mild anesthetic gas formerly used widely in dentistry sometimes is abused; if not properly used, so as to ensure adequate oxygen supply, can be fatal. Commonly known as laughing gas.

NK cells   See NATURAL KILLER CELLS.

nm   See NANOMETER.

NM   See NANOMETER.

NMRI   nuclear magnetic resonance imaging

NMS   neuroleptic malignant syndrome

NNAT-Multilevel Form   Naglieri Nonverbal Ability Test-Multilevel Form

NO   nitric oxide

nociceptive reflex   A defensive reflexive action evoked by a nocuous or painful stimulus.

nociceptors Pain-sensitive receptors in skin, muscles, joints, and in other tissues. They are tightly packed in the fingertips, which explains why cuts on the finger hurt more than similar cuts would on other parts of the body. Also known as noci-receptors.

noctambulation Walking while asleep. Also known as noctambulism, sleepwalking, somnambulism.

noctiphobia   nyctophobia

nocturia The need to urinate frequently during the night. See NOCTURNAL ENURESIS.

nocturnal emission/orgasm In males, an involuntary ejaculation during sleep, usually as part of an erotosexual dream. Almost all males experience such dreams, 80% experience resulting emission by early 20s, rarer thereafter but more common following orgasmic abstinence. Commonly called wet dream. Orgasm as part of such dreams occurs in about half of women, peaking when in their forties.

nocturnal enuresis Urinary incontinence at night; bed-wetting during sleep. See FUNCTIONAL ENURESIS.

nocturnal hemiplegia/paralysis A form of sleep paralysis in which, during brief periods of falling asleep or awakening, the person is unable to move or speak but can recall the episode. Not considered pathological. Also known as sleep paralysis. See NARCOLEPSY.

nocturnal myoclonus A type of myoclonic (spasmodic or twitching) movement of the limbs that occurs when a person is falling asleep. The involuntary spasms of muscle contractions and relaxations may happen repeatedly and can occur during sleep with sufficient activity to awaken the person. May happen occasionally to any normal individual. See RESTLESS-LEG SYNDROME.

nocturnal penile tumescence (NPT) Erection during sleep, generally during rapid-eye-movement phases in males from infancy to old age. Healthy men typically experience three episodes totalling two to three hours nightly. See NOCTURNAL EMISSION.

nocturnal rhythms Circadian rhythms that occur during the period usually spent in sleeping. Body temperature generally declines during the rest span of a 24-hour period whereas sodium and calcium levels in the blood increase and the level of magnesium in the urine reaches a peak. For nocturnal animals, the nocturnal rhythms are generally the reverse of animals that normally sleep at night.

nocturnal teeth grinding   bruxism

nodal behavior In group therapy, a peak period of great activity, which may be aggressive or disorderly, followed by a period of quietude, the antinode.

nodal point The center of the lens of the eye, the point at which all rays from the visual image pass.

nodding spasm A disorder observed in infants and characterized by head-shaking and nystagmus, which may be continuous or intermittent, but arrhythmic and involuntary and not specifically associated with emotional disturbance.

nodes of Ranvier Short gaps in the myelin sheath surrounding white-matter nerve fibers. The gaps permit an ion exchange at intervals along the axon, resulting in a conductivity effect in which an impulse leaps from one node to the next, a form of nerve-impulse transmission called saltatory conduction. See MYELIN SHEATH.

noegenesis (C. E. Spearman) The production of understanding or knowledge based on observation, realization of relationships, and creation of ideas. See CREATIVITY.

noegenetic A neologism created by Charles Spearman, being a conflation of noetic (intellectual) and genetic (hereditary).

noesis (mind—Greek) 1. An intellectual or cognitive process, particularly when it yields self-evident knowledge. 2. The operation of the intellect alone.

noetic memory (E. Tulving) Semantic memory in which the person is aware of the information stored but not of its point of origin. Compare ANOETIC MEMORY, AUTONOETIC MEMORY.

noetic science The study of intellectual processes such as consciousness, intuition, creativity, and transformation and how they apply to ecology, healing, government, leadership, spirituality, behavior, business, and love.

no excuse (W. Glasser) A concept in reality therapy that there are no excuses for not doing contracted behavior or for irresponsible behavior in general.

noise 1. In general, unwanted and usually unpleasant sound. Nonperiodic sound, in contrast to the periodicity of musical and other sounds. Types of noise include: background, colored, frozen, pink, preferred, random, white. See PREFERRED NOISE CRITERION. 2. As a metaphor, stimuli that mask or distort the desired stimuli. See DIFFERENTIATION THEORY, FALSE ALARM. 3. See EGO NOISE.

noise abatement The application of legislation or technological skills to reduce the level of noise pollution. May require the redesign of automobile or aircraft engines, ordinances that prohibit use of airports at night, or routing of traffic patterns away from residential areas.

noise conditions 1. In industrial psychology, the effects of different types and levels of noise on work performance, hearing, and employee comfort. 2. In environmental psychology, the effects on the public of traffic sounds, subway noise, jet booms, and other sources of noise.

noise effects Physiological and psychological stress produced by noise, especially high levels of unpredictable noise over which the individual can exert no control. Various noise effects include diminished productivity, accuracy, and frustration tolerance, and, possibly, increased aggression. See NOISE CONDITIONS.

noise fear See ACOUSTICOPHOBIA, PHONOPHOBIA.

noise pollution See NOISE ABATEMENT, NOISE CONDITIONS.

nomadism A pathological tendency to wander from place to place, and to repeatedly change residence and occupation. In milder form this tendency may be an attempt to escape from a distressing situation or from responsibility, but in extreme form it may be associated with brain damage, epilepsy, mental deficiency, or psychosis. See PORIOMANIA.

nomatophobia   onomatophobia

nomenclature The systematic classification of technical terms. See TAXONOMY.

nominal 1. Identifying or classifying a phenomenon by giving it a name. 2. That which is of limited or minor importance.

nominal aphasia   1. Knowing a particular word but unable to speak it. Also known as amnestic aphasia. 2. A type of aphasia characterized by an impaired ability to recall the names of objects. Also known as anomia, anomic aphasia, dysnomia.

nominal definition   Arbitrarily assigned definition to a term.

nominal fallacy   A false belief that the causes of a phenomenon have been explained by the naming of it.

nominal group technique (NTG)   In group decision making, a procedure for generating and evaluating ideas, designed to separate the generation from the evaluation. A "paper group" (a group in name only, because no verbal exchange is permitted within it) in a meeting silently generates ideas in writing, gets feedback from the members who record each idea on a flip chart, discusses each recorded idea for clarification and evaluation, and individually votes on priority ideas, with the group decision mathematically derived through rank ordering or rating. See DELPHI TECHNIQUE.

nominalism   1. A philosophical doctrine positing that only concrete particulars are real, whereas concepts and abstractions are merely words. 2. A doctrine positing that scientific theories are never ultimately true or false, but only useful.

nominal leader   A leader in name only, when subordinates no longer obey that person's orders.

nominal realism   Phrase used by Jean Piaget for the young child's conviction that the name of an object, such as a dog, is not just a symbol but an intrinsic part of the object. Shared by many aboriginal peoples who believe they can bless or curse other people by invoking their names. Also known as word realism. See MAGICAL THINKING.

nominal scale   A scale in which numbers are used as labeling devices for identification. Data are simply classified into categories that are mutually exclusive, without indicating order, magnitude, or a true zero point (for example, the numbers on football jerseys). A nominal scale is the lowest form of measurement. See INTERVAL SCALE, ORDINAL SCALE, RATIO SCALE.

nominal stimulus   In information processing, what the researcher "thinks" the participant is encoding. Compare FUNCTIONAL STIMULUS.

nomination technique   A method of studying social structure and personality in which group members are asked to indicate the persons with whom they would like to do a certain thing, or who they feel have certain characteristics. Also known as nominating technique. See SOCIOMETRY.

nominative self   The self as observer of the self. That which is within a person who judges and weighs personal behavior. See CONSCIENCE.

nomograph   A scaled graph (chart) representing values of related variables (organized) along parallel straight lines. The use of a straight-edge enables reading off of a dependent variable when the values of two or more variables is known.

nomological   Conceptual; referring, especially, to lawful properties of a variable. The construct validity of a test is ascertained through a nomological network reflecting research and other experience with the test.

nomology   1. The science of physical or logical law. 2. The science of the laws of the mind. 3. The process of attempting to determine laws by generating hypotheses and testing them. See NOMOTHETIC RESEARCH, NOMOTHETIC SCIENCE, PSYCHOLOGY.

nomothetic   (W. Windelband) Pertaining to the formulation of general laws as the goal of scientific method, as opposed to the study of the individual case; characterizing techniques and methods used to study a single variable or norm in many topics for the purpose of discovering general laws or principles of behavior. The nomothetic approach focuses on the variation found, in many cases, on a specific trait chosen by the researcher as an important dimension of behavior or personality that can be quantified, measured, and used for classification and prediction. Compare IDIOGRAPHIC.

nomothetic approach   See NOMOTHETIC.

nomothetic description   The formulation of the nature and invariant properties of people and things.

nomothetic research   (G. W. Allport) Research that attempts to discover general laws by comparing many individuals. Compare IDIOGRAPHIC RESEARCH.

nomothetic science   A type of science that depends on observations or measurements of groups and comes to generalizations about the group members as a whole. Compare IDIOGRAPHIC SCIENCE.

nomotheticism vs idiographicism   (R. I. Watson) A prescriptive dimension of the philosophical underpinnings of psychology, in which universal principles are established as distinguished from particularities. See OPPONENT-PAIRS DIMENSION.

nonaccidental properties   (I. Biederman) In perception, arrangements of lines or edges that are rarely produced accidentally and consequently are unaffected by minor variations in viewpoint. An aspect of recognition by components theory.

nonage   A person below the legal age for a given activity.

nonaerobic   In the breakdown of phosphagens, glycolysis in which glucose is degraded to lactic acid. Compare AEROBIC.

non compos mentis   (not of sound mind—Latin) In forensic psychology, not mentally capable of handling personal affairs or being responsible for one's own conduct. See COMPOS MENTIS.

noncontinuity hypothesis   In concept formation, a postulate that learning is a discontinuous process of forming and testing hypotheses about what constitutes membership in a given category. Compare CONTINUITY HYPOTHESIS.

nonaffective hallucination   A false perception whose content is apparently unrelated to depression or elation.

nonaggressive conduct disorder   Repetitive, persistent, nonaggressive conduct in which the basic rights of others or major social norms or rules are violated without confrontation with a victim.

nonaggressive erotica   Erotic material that attempts to avoid depictions of violence and aggression (usually toward women), and often depictions of degradation and exploitation.

nonaggressive societies   Communities of people who generally believe in peaceful isolation. Socialization in such is marked by a deemphasis of achievement or power needs, disapproval of aggression, and an affirmation of basic pleasures. The Amish and Mennonites represent such communities in technologically advanced nations.

noncombat military neuroses   Neurotic reactions arising out of the stresses of military life outside of combat situations, among support groups, rear-echelon soldiers, and others who are near combat areas or waiting for combat but do not have the aggressive outlet of soldiers in battle.

noncomplementary role   Patterns of behavior that do not complete or supplement others nor conform with the demands and expectations of others, such as conduct of some adolescents that is contrary to the desires of their parents. See COMPLEMENTARY ROLE, ROLE.

noncompliance   1. Failure to carry out prescribed self-care activities. 2. In medicine, failing to comply with the physician's prescriptions, often not taking prescribed medicines at all or not as directed. See PSYCHOPHARMACOLOGY.

nonconscious   1. A state of unawareness of organisms that ordinarily are capable of consciousness, such as a human who is under general anesthesia. 2. The presumed lack of property of consciousness by some living substance such as plants or viruses.

nonconscious processes   1. Bodily processes that do not reach consciousness, such as the buildup of cholesterol in the blood. 2. In the past, the word "nonconscious" was used to refer to an inanimate object.

nonconsummation   Technically, any failure to complete, but in legal and common use, the absence of penile-vaginal intercourse, usually in a marriage (grounds for annulment or divorce in some jurisdictions).

noncontingent reinforcement   Reactions to certain stimuli not linked to or dependent on a particular stimulus. See NEGATIVE DISCRIMINATIVE STIMULUS.

noncontingent   Unrelated; a control procedure in biofeedback research in which false or random feedback is given regardless of the true physiological response, so that the client will think true biofeedback is taking place.

noncore role   (G. A. Kelly) Roles people play that are peripheral or unimportant in their lives. Compare CORE ROLE.

noncorrection method   See CORRECTION METHOD.

noncuddlers   See CUDDLING BEHAVIOR.

nondeclarative memory   1. Memory not subject to recall. 2. Perceptual, stimulus-response, and motor memory that works independently of the hippocampal formation.

nondecremental conduction   Refers to the all-or-none conduction of nerves.

nondemand(ing) pleasuring   In sex therapy, a behavioral exercise in which one partner "pleasures" the other, gradually increasing from nonintimate to more intimate touching, without expecting or permitting specific responses or activities in the partner, especially performance-related ones.

nondirectional test of hypothesis   A statistical test that specifies only that an effect may be either greater than or less than a criterial comparison, without stating the direction expected. May also state that a relationship may be either positive or negative. See DIRECTIONAL TEST OF HYPOTHESIS.

nondirective counseling/psychotherapy   (C. R. Rogers) Older names for what was later called person-centered therapy, or client-centered therapy or counseling. See PERSON-CENTERED PSYCHOTHERAPY.

nondirective group psychotherapy   (C. R. Rogers) In such groups the therapist refrains from asking questions or making interpretations or judgments, but attempts to encourage individuals to participate. The therapist also tries to generate a feeling of respect for the members, clarifies peoples' statements, shows empathy, and avoids acting as an authority. See NONDIRECTIVE THERAPY.

nondirective play therapy   Psychological treatment of children based on the principle that children have the capacity to revise their own attitudes and behavior. Two major forms: (a) (V. Axline) The therapist provides a variety of play materials and assumes a friendly, interested role without giving direct suggestions. (b) (V. L. Allen) The therapist engages the child in conversation that focuses on present feelings and present situations in the child's life. In either case, the accepting attitude of the therapist encourages the child to try new and more appropriate ways of dealing with problems.

nondirective psychotherapy   Old name for what was later known as person-centered psychotherapy.

nondirective teaching model   (C. R. Rogers) A person-oriented teaching model concerned with developing the capacity for self-instruction as well as emphasizing self-discovery, self-understanding, and the realization of innate potential.

nondisjunction   The failure of pairs of chromosomes to separate during mitotic cell division with the result that both chromosomes move to the nucleus of one daughter cell whereas the other daughter cell fails to receive its normal complement.

nonempirical   Without data, as an opinion or essay.

nonexistence   In the two-word stage of language development, an expression such as "gone cookie" indicating object disappearance or cessation of an activity.

nonexperimental research   Correlational research or descriptive research not designed as a controlled experiment, therefore not justifying causal conclusions. Examples include casual observation, archival research, and surveys. See OBSERVATIONAL METHOD.

nonfalsifiable explanations   Explanations that cannot be revised because they can never be shown to be incorrect by any observable evidence.

nonfluency   Term used to characterize motor, or expressive, aphasia involving such disturbances as dysprosody, dysarthria, and agrammatism.

nonfluent aphasia   **Broca's aphasia**

nongraded class   Generally, a small school class providing special education opportunities for pupils with various disabilities who need individualized learning programs along with group activities; frequently students are grouped according to general chronological age and ability (for example, primary educable, intermediate educable) or by disability (for example, physically challenged, hearing-impaired, learning disabled).

nongraded system Organized, established policies and programs within an educational administrative unit for the delivery of education curricula to pupils emphasizing individualized learning; as opposed to traditional education systems having grades kindergarten through 12.

nonintentional learning The acquiring of knowledge that is not premeditated or deliberate. Similar to incidental learning.

noninvasive procedures Research or therapeutic procedures that minimally interfere with the person. See COMPUTERIZED TOMOGRAPHY, MAGNETIC RESONANCE IMAGING.

nonisomorphic attributions (H. Triandis) When a visitor to a culture attributes the behavior of members of the culture to different causes from the causes used by members of the culture to explain their own behavior. Making nonisomorphic attributions results in misunderstandings and culture shock. It is possible to reduce culture shock by training the visitor to make isomorphic attributions.

nonjudgmental approach A neutral, noncondemning attitude on the part of an interviewer or psychotherapist. See NONDIRECTIVE COUNSELING/PSYCHOTHERAPY.

nonlanguage test An examination that depends minimally on the participant's ability to understand verbal instructions and use words in responding. Also known as nonverbal test, performance test.

nonlinear dynamical systems theory **chaos theory**

nonlinear relationships Two or more sets of data that cannot be described by a straight line of best fit. See CURVILINEAR REGRESSION.

nonliterate Describing cultures or individuals that lack a written language. See ILLITERATE.

nonmanipulated variables Elements in research not under the control of an experimenter that may affect the experiment (for example, the weather). See SUBJECT-SELECTION STUDY.

nonmarital sex Generally, any sexual activity between persons not married to each other.

nonmedullated Unmyelinated. Also known as non-myelinated.

nonmetric Not measurable by an ordinary scale that has regular units such as inches or meters.

nonnormative influences Factors not related to age or history that affect specific individuals during their life cycle. These factors cannot be attributed to the normal process of development or to the impact of environmental, cultural-societal events.

nonoperational goals Future plans that are abstract (often broad and long-term), with unclear steps for accomplishing them.

nonorganic hearing loss An auditory disturbance not due to an impairment of the peripheral hearing mechanism. Deficits may be of psychogenic origin.

nonorganic speech impairment See SPEECH IMPAIRMENT.

nonovert appeals Techniques employed in consumer psychology in which the advertising message is presented by presumably ordinary people who make no overt attempt to persuade. May give the impression to consumers that they are "overhearing" an independent endorsement of a product. Commonly used in "slice of life" television commercials.

nonpara A woman who has not delivered a viable infant. Compare MULTIPARA.

nonparametric statistics A special type of statistics that do not make assumptions about parameters of the population being tested, such as normality of the distribution or the homogeneity of variance. Usually employed with data put in some kind of order. Examples include chi-square and the Mann-Whitney U Test. See DISTRIBUTION-FREE STATISTICS.

nonparametric test A statistical test of the null hypothesis without consideration of the population's distribution or parameters and the assumptions that underlie them.

nonpathological lying Making false statements with conscious intent to deceive in situations that usually involve seeking to avoid punishment or saving others from distress. Such falsehoods are known as "white lies." Compare PATHOLOGICAL LYING.

nonperformers Individuals in a setting who play a passive role, such as members of an audience at a lecture. See PERFORMERS.

nonperson See PERSONALITY DETERIORATION.

nonprobability sampling Selecting a sample without concern for randomness. See CONVENIENCE SAMPLING, JUDGMENT SAMPLE, QUOTA SAMPLE, STRATEGIC SAMPLING.

nonproductiveness (E. Fromm) A negative, life-denying orientation to the world.

nonprojective personality measures Objective group tests that attempt to assess personality such as the Beck Depression Scale and Edwards Personality Inventory.

nonrational Refers to matters such as basic beliefs that are not available for scientific proof, such as the validity of the Golden Rule, whether Adam and Eve actually existed, or whether there are future lives. Not to be confused with irrational; people who accept or reject such points of view may be rational or irrational.

nonrapid-eye-movement (NREM or nREM) sleep Nonrapid-eye movement type of sleep, graded stages I–IV based on electroencephalographic (EEG) criteria. During these periods, which occur most frequently in the first hours of sleep, the electroencephalogram shows gradually decreasing levels of activity, and there is little or no change in pulse, respiration, and blood pressure in the sleeping person. Also known as neosleep, nonREM sleep, telencephalic sleep. See DELTA-WAVE SLEEP, DREAM STATE.

nonreactive measures See UNOBTRUSIVE MEASURES.

nonresponder bias In a questionnaire, the difference in responses between those who returned answers and those who did not.

nonrestraint The management of psychotic patients without the use of restraints, such as a strait-jacket.

nonreversal shift   A form of discrimination learning in which the delivery of reinforcement is suddenly made contingent on another dimension of the task object, such as reinforcement for selecting objects according to size changes to reinforcement for selecting objects according to color. See REVERSAL SHIFT.

nonreward hypothesis   A postulate that an organism that expects a reward upon performing a conditioned situation and does not get the reward is thereby frustrated, leading to greater efforts after subsequent stimuli.

nonsadistic sexual assaulter   A person who uses the minimal force required to succeed in a sexual assault. Predominantly male and typically shy, passive, and inexperienced in sexual activity.

nonsense figure   A figure that appears to have no meaning since it does not correspond to any common or familiar object and is not a recognizable geometric form such as a circle or triangle. They are employed usually in a variety of research problems and for diagnostic purposes. See IMPOSSIBLE FIGURE, NONSENSE SYLLABLE.

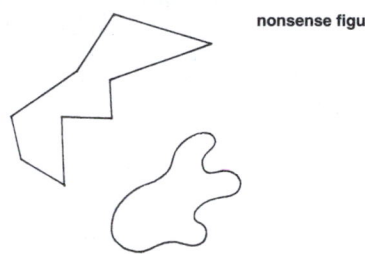

nonsense figures

nonsense syllable   (H. Ebbinghaus) A syllable, usually of three letters (for example, BOH, CAJ, CEG), constructed so as to resemble meaningful English as little as possible. Widely used in rote-learning studies and sometimes as mantras.

nonsense syndrome   Ganser('s) syndrome

nonsomniac   A person who needs little sleep when compared with the average person. Purportedly, some otherwise normal people function well with very little sleep.

nonspecific effects   In research, factors that affect results but that are either difficult or impossible to control, such as in testing drugs, the evident enthusiasm of the drug's developer may affect the judgments of physicians and patients. See NONMANIPULATED VARIABLES.

nonspecific transfer   Transferring A to B on the basis of general rules even though there is nothing in common in A and B. See SPECIFIC TRANSFER.

nonstate theories of hypnosis   A point of view that some people do things automatically by suggestion similar to being under hypnosis, but who are not in a unique state of consciousness, but under the power of social influence. See MOB PSYCHOLOGY, STATE THEORIES OF HYPNOSIS.

nonstatistical evaluation   Data evaluation based on visual inspection criteria. Characteristics of the data (for example, changes in means, trends, and level, as well as the latency of change) are used to infer reliability of the impact of the experimental manipulation.

nonstriate visual cortex   A group of neurons that surrounds the visual sensory area and appears to help evaluate visual sensations as they may relate to previous experiences, thereby serving the functions of identification and recognition of visual images. Associated with eye movements related to visual impressions.

nontraditional marriages   Arrangements between spouses that are at variance with those of the prevailing culture. See SWINGING.

nontraditional student   A person attending school who is different from the other students, typically an older or retired person in a high school or college.

nonverbal auditory perception tests   Tests which measure the recognition, discrimination, and comprehension of sounds such as music, tapping patterns, and the meaning of common sounds. Many use sound recordings, for example, the Seashore Rhythm Test, in which the testee discriminates between like and unlike pairs of musical beats. Others require the identification of familiar tunes, failure on which suggests amusia.

nonverbal behavior   Any action that is not verbal or spoken, for example, when humans communicate with animals they often use hand and body signals rather than spoken language.

nonverbal communication (NVC)   Messages conveyed without the use of words, including eye movements, facial expression, hand and finger movements, body angles, and a variety of sounds. See NONVERBAL BEHAVIOR.

nonverbal intelligence   Mental ability not requiring the use of language, such as mechanical intelligence, knowledge about fishing, social behavior, or emotional intelligence.

nonverbal intelligence tests   Intelligence tests or subtests that require minimal use of language in the administration and responses. See NONLANGUAGE TEST.

nonverbal leakage   See VERBAL LEAKAGE.

nonverbal learning   Acquisition of skill or knowledge that does not necessarily depend on language, such as riding a bicycle.

nonverbal vocabulary tests   Examinations in which the participant signals recognition of a spoken or printed word by pointing to one picture in a set. Permits the evaluation of the recognition vocabulary of many verbally handicapped individuals. Generally simple to administer, often used for screening.

nonzero-sum game   A game in which both opponents can benefit (or lose) according to strategies that often include predicting the other's moves, opposed to a zero-sum game which ends with the winner taking all.

noology   Psychology; the science of the human mind.

noradrenalin(e)   A hormone secreted by the adrenal medulla and released by autonomic-nervous-system neurons. A metabolic precursor to epinephrine, it differs from that hormone in that it is purely vasoconstrictor with minimal effect on glucose metabolism. Excessive levels in the brain have been associated with manic states. Also known as norepinephrine (NE).

norepinephrine(e)   **noradrenaline(e)**

norm   1. A standard or range of values representing the typical performance of a group, or of a child of a certain age, against which comparisons can be made. 2. Any pattern of behavior or performance that is typical of a certain social group. See SOCIAL NORM.

normal   1. A numerical score that represents the usual or average for particular groups. 2. In relation to subjective issues such as mental or physical health, being considered free of abnormalities. 3. In relation to values or attitudes, being considered acceptable. 4. A distribution of data that follows a Gaussian (bell-shaped) curve. See NORMALITY.

normal autism   According to Margaret Mahler, a feature of the first weeks of development, infants are completely within themselves, oblivious to an external world. Also known as autistic phase.

normal curve/distribution   A bell-shaped probability curve showing the expected value of sampling a random variable. Indicates the distribution of random errors of measurement. About 68% of the distribution lies within one standard deviation of the mean, about 95% lies within two standard deviations of the mean, and about 99.7% within three standard deviations. Sometimes known as bell-shaped curve, curve of the normal law of error, Gaussian curve/distribution, normal error curve, normal distribution curve, normal probability curve. See BELL-SHAPED CURVE for a formula.

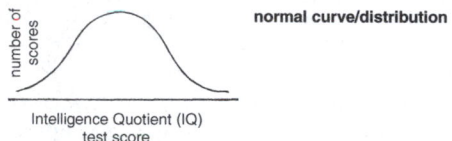

normal curve/distribution

number of scores

Intelligence Quotient (IQ) test score

normal deviance   Behavior, usually sexual, that is defined by law or by certain segments of society as deviant, yet is commonly practiced (and rarely prosecuted, especially against people with otherwise mainstream lifestyles).

normal distribution   See NORMAL CURVE.

normal insanity   1. Refers to bizarre thinking, bizarre behavior, or both, as the result of unusual, stressful, or threatening circumstances with the behavior usually returning to normal when the situation normalizes. 2. Those intermittent instances in life for which (when given a behavioral alternative) a person does not care whether the act is morally right or wrong, or whether it has adverse consequences: it feels good so the person does it; for example, a person may fall in love "at first sight," ride a roller coaster, or drive a car 120 MPH.

normality   Whereas the precise definition of this term is "usualness," its implication is that things are as they should be. For any person normality refers to persons at peace with themselves, not having internal conflicts and in harmony with the environment. See MENTAL HEALTH.

normalization principle   (B. Nirje) The view that persons with mental disabilities, physical disabilities, or both, should not be denied social-sexual relationships because they have disabilities. Such relationships can include a range of emotional and physical contacts from friendship to sexual activity.

normal probability curve   **normal curve/distribution**

normative   Refers to standards or norms of some kind. Social behavior is based on a scale of what is considered normal behavior. Establishing height-weight standards for employment as a fire-fighter is an example of using norms in employment selection.

normative compliance   (A. Etzioni) Effect of perceived social influence on behavior combined with the motivation to comply with the influence.

normative crisis   maturational crisis

normative-reeducative strategy   In social psychology, the idea that societal change should be based on active reeducation of people within the framework of their cultural milieu. Normative-reeducative strategy holds that a program for social change based only on rational appeal is inadequate because behavioral patterns are largely determined by traditional attitudes and cultural norms. See EMPIRICAL-RATIONAL STRATEGY, POWER-COERCIVE STRATEGY.

normative research/survey   Research to obtain data on particular groups and particular topics leading to information such as average performance, such as administering scholastic achievement tests to large samples of same-age children and reporting the mean and standard deviation so that in the future individuals or groups can be compared with these norms.

normative science   A science that sets norms for behavior, education, health, or other cultural or societal aspects.

normative score   A person's score compared with the scores of other individuals, such as a percentile ranking in a particular group. See IPSATIVE SCORE.

normative selection   The choosing of subjects for any particular purpose, such as for polling, based on some pre-established standard (for example, all children in public schools in a particular city in the sixth grade).

normative social influence   Conformity of thinking and behavior as the result of a desire to be socially accepted. See GROUPTHINK, INGROUP, OUTGROUP.

normative survey   See NORMATIVE RESEARCH.

normative unit   (R. B. Cattell) The amount one individual differs or varies from another. Compare IPSATIVE UNIT.

normless suicide   anomic suicide

normophilia   Refers to a sexual response that conforms erotosexually with the norms dictated by custom, religious, or civil authorities. The opposite of paraphilia.

normosplanchnic build/type   (G. Viola) A constitutional body type in Giacinto Viola's system that corresponds roughly to Ernst Kretschmer's athletic type. A physique in which trunk and limbs show average or normal development, that is, an average morphological index.

normotensive individuals   People who have a normal blood pressure for their age and physical condition. See HYPOTENSIVE, HYPERTENSIVE.

normotype   A constitutional body type that is morphologically average. Also known as eumorphic. See NORMOSPLANCHNIC TYPE.

norm-referenced testing   Approach to testing based on comparison of participants' performance with others', for example, of 100 applications from indigenous persons and 100 from immigrants for 10 openings; the 5 top-scoring participants from both groups are selected. See CRITERION-REFERENCED TESTING.

NOS   Not Otherwise Specified

nose rubbing   A greeting or sexual expression used in some cultures where kissing is not common.

nosocomial   A hospital-induced condition unrelated to the patient's primary illness. See IATROGENIC ILLNESS.

nosocomion   A hospital or sanatorium. Also known as nosocomium.

nosocusis   Loss of hearing acuity due to disease. Compare SOCIOCUSIS.

nosogenesis   Rare term for pathogenesis.

nosological approach   The naming and classifying of disorders, as well as the discovery of pathognomonic symptoms and their grouping into syndromes for diagnostic purposes. Contrasts with the dynamic approach which emphasizes causal factors and the inner meaning of symptoms.

nosology   The classification of diseases and disorders, both mental and physical. See PSYCHIATRIC CLASSIFICATION.

nosomania   Hypochondriasis.

nosophilia   Morbid desire to be sick.

nosophobia   Fear of illness. Also known as nephophobia. See PATHOPHOBIA.

nostalgia   A longing to return to a place where a person feels emotionally bound, for example, home or native land. Sometimes related to a feeling of isolation in the present location. Also applied to a longing to return to an earlier period of life that is usually recalled as being pleasant compared with the present. Commonly known as homesickness.

nostophobia   Fear of returning home.

no-suicide contract   An agreement between a client or patient and therapist that the individual will not commit suicide while under treatment. Value of this agreement is unknown.

not-guilty-by-reason-of-insanity (NGRI)   In many jurisdictions the finding that the accused person committed a criminal act, but was not considered "responsible" at the time it was committed. The person was considered to have been mentally compromised due to psychosis, developmental retardation, substance ingestion, debilitating stress, or some other cause. Such individuals generally are sent to a mental hospital or to a specialized prison. See INVOLUNTARY COMMITMENT.

nothingness   (L. Binswanger) A constant threat of losing "one's being," or becoming nothing.

notifiable   Medical condition or behavior that must legally be reported.

notional word   content word

not-me   In Harry Stack Sullivan's personality theory, that part of the personified self based on interpersonal experiences that have evoked overwhelming anxiety, dread, and horror, and which may lead to nightmares, emotional crises, and schizophrenic reactions.

not-me self   (H. S. Sullivan) An aspect of the self-system, a gradually evolving image of the self regarded as dreadful, and that cannot be permitted conscious awareness and acknowledgment.

notochord   Embryonic forerunner of the brain and spinal cord.

notogenesis   A stage of embryonic development in which the notochord (primitive backbone) and mesoderm form in the gastrula.

Not Otherwise Specified (NOS)   Phrase found in DSM vocabulary, referring to conditions that are not or that cannot be precisely identified.

noumena   (I. Kant) That which is apprehended or conceived. Denoting the "thing in itself," an object of purely intellectual intuition that is really unknowable. See NOUMENON, NOUS.

noumenon   (I. Kant) The reality of matter. The actual existence of anything. Contrasts with "phenomenon"— an observation of something.

nous   1. A Greek word for the faculty of reason or intellect which enables people to perceive truth. 2. Spirit. See PLUTARCH.

nouthetic counseling   A form of pastoral counseling based on traditional Christian principles.

novelty   The quality of being new and unusual. One of the major determinants of attention, as in sexual attraction. In consumer psychology, a desire for a change in the absence of dissatisfaction with the present situation.

novelty fear   See NEOPHOBIA.

nPr   The number of permutations (order considered) of n items taken r at a time.

NPT   nocturnal penile tumescence

nREM   Abbreviation for nonrapid eye movement. See NONRAPID-EYE-MOVEMENT SLEEP.

NREM sleep   See NONRAPID-EYE-MOVEMENT SLEEP.

NS   nervous system

Nsec   Symbol for microsecond (also abbreviated μsec, μ-second).

nt   See NIT.

NTD   neural tube defect

NTG   nominal group technique

n, 2n, 3n, 4n   The haploid, diploid, triploid, and tetraploid number of chromosomes in an individual, strain, or (more commonly) cell.

nu   The thirteenth letter of the Greek alphabet. See APPENDIX C.

nubile   1. A sexually mature, fertile woman. 2. An adolescent or young woman of marriageable age. 3. A sexually attractive and desirable woman.

nubilis   In law, someone old enough to marry.

nuclear complex   A central conflict or problem rooted in infancy, such as feelings of inferiority (A. Adler) or an Oedipal situation (S. Freud). See INFERIORITY FEELINGS, OEDIPUS COMPLEX.

nuclear family   A family consisting of a father, mother, and their biological or adopted children. See EXTENDED FAMILY.

nuclear magnetic resonance imaging (NMRI)   Non-invasive imaging technique that produces images based on the responses of the molecular dipole forces of water in the body subjected to an intense magnetic field (via hydrogen-ion spin times T and T2), re-creating a three-dimensional array. Does not require invasive techniques, injections, or radiation exposure and, unlike CAT scans, reveals structure as well as function. See MAGNETIC RESONANCE IMAGING (MRI).

nuclear neurosis/phobia   Common phrase for a pattern of complaints found among some individuals who live or work in the area of nuclear electric power plants. Symptoms include headaches, either anorexia or increased appetite, increased tension, distrust of authority, and worry about radiation exposure. See CHINA SYNDROME.

nuclear phobia   nuclear neurosis/phobia

nuclear problem   The central conflict, the basis of a patient's problems and the one on which therapy should be concentrated. Often a type of maladjustment, for example, sibling rivalry, feelings of inadequacy.

nuclear schizophrenia   A form of schizophrenia that develops gradually but increases in severity. Considered biologically determined, lacks apparent precipitating cause. Social inadequacy is the predominant symptom. Phrase is sometimes considered equivalent to process schizophrenia, but usually process schizophrenia is considered to be a type of nuclear schizophrenia. Compare PERIPHERAL SCHIZOPHRENIA.

nuclei   Plural of nucleus.

nucleic acid   (A. Kossel, F. Hoppe-Seyler) A family of macromolecules found in chromosomes, nucleoli, mitochondria, and cytoplasm of all cells, and in viruses. See DEOXYRIBONUCLEIC ACID (DNA), RIBONUCLEIC ACID (RNA).

nucleoplasm   The protoplasmic substance of the nucleus of a cell. Also known as karyoplasm.

nucleotides   Compounds consisting of a purine or pyrimidine base linked to a ribose sugar molecule and combined with phosphoric acid. The basic unit in deoxyribonucleic acid (DNA) and ribonucleic acid (RNA).

nucleus (n)   (G. G. Valentin) 1. The central portion of a cell and the functional control unit of cellular activity. In most cells, the nucleus contains the deoxyribonucleic acid (DNA) molecules and genetic templates for all anabolic and catabolic functions as well as for reproduction. See CELL NUCLEUS. 2. A mass of nerve-cell bodies with the same or related functions, for example, nucleus cuneatus, nucleus gracilis. Plural is nuclei. Types of nucleus include: AMYGDALOID, ARCUATE, ASSOCIATION, BASAL, BEKHTEREV'S, BRAIN, CAUDATE, CENTRAL TEGMENTAL, COCHLEAR, CORTICOBULBAR, CORTICOPONTINE, CORTICORETICULAR, CUNEATE, DEITER'S, DENTATE, DORSOMEDIAL, EDINGER-WESTPHAL, INTRALAMINAR, LATERAL CERVICAL, LATERAL GENICULATE, LATERAL THALAMIC, LENTICULAR, MESENCEPHALIC, NEUROTIC, OCULOMOTOR, OLIVARY, POSTERIOR, POSTVENTRAL, RAPHE, RED, RELAY, RETICULAR, SPINAL TRIGEMINAL, SUBTHALAMIC, SUPRACHIASMATIC, TECTAL, THALAMIC, TRIGEMINAL, VENTRAL POSTERIOR, VESTIBULAR. See EGO NUCLEI.

nucleus accumbens   A region of the basal forebrain generating dopamine during pleasurable behavior.

nucleus basalis   A small region in the basal forebrain which is the source of the cholinergic system ascending to the neocortex. Damage to the nucleus basalis is associated with Alzheimer's disease.

nucleus cuneatus   A cluster of neurons in the medulla where sensory nerves from the spinal cord terminate.

nucleus of the raphe   central tegmental nucleus

nude-group therapy   (P. Bindrim) A controversial form of group psychotherapy based on the expectation that psychological disclosure will be enhanced by physical disclosure because clothing provides a refuge behind which the clients can hide their feelings, and nudity facilitates breaking through taboos and barriers.

nudism   The public display of the naked human body. Theories offered to explain nudism include (a) rebellion against Victorian modesty, (b) a male's wish to exhibit his masculinity as a reaction against castration anxiety, (c) a female's need to display her body to demonstrate her ability to attract men, and (d) a "back to nature" philosophy, depicting a rejection of prudishness.

nuisance variable   Any variable that is an undesired factor of possible variation in a study. May affect the dependent variable unless it is controlled. Variables may include an undetected disease, temperature variations in different rooms, or different types of cages used for research.

null findings   What occurs when a research hypothesis is not supported by the facts. It is important since knowing what "is not" can be as valuable as knowing what "is"; for example, if research on questionable phenomena frequently produce null results, this is useful information.

null hypothesis (H_o)   A statement that the value of a population parameter is equal to some constant or that the differences between population parameters for different groups is equal to a constant, often zero. In hypothesis testing, the goal is to determine whether the available evidence allows the null hypothesis to be rejected with a given error rate. See STATISTICAL HYPOTHESIS.

null hypothesis significance testing (NHST)   A form of statistical inference in which null and alternative hypotheses are tested. A decision is made to reject the null hypothesis if the probability of obtaining data at least as inconsistent with the null hypothesis as that actually obtained, is lower than some prespecified value.

nulligravida   A woman who has never conceived a child.

nullipara   Not having borne a viable infant.

nulliplex inheritance   Inheritance determined by two recessive genes, one from each parent.

null result   A situation when results are nonsignificant, such as when changes in a dependent variable cannot be judged to reflect changes by changes in the independent variable.

null set (∅)   An empty set with nothing in it. See EMPTY SET.

number (N)   1. Generally, one or more symbols or words indicating quantity. 2. (L. L. Thurstone) The capacity to use numbers rapidly and correctly in calculations, a primary mental ability. See PRIMARY ABILITIES, PRIMARY MENTAL ABILITIES.

number-completion test   An item in some tests in which the participant is asked to supply a missing item in a series of numbers or continue the series, for example, 6, 9, 13, 18, ?. . . (The next number is 24.)

number crunching   Slang for processing large amounts of numeric data.

number factor (N)   An intelligence factor measured by tests of ability to handle numerical problems.

numerical ability (N)   See PRIMARY ABILITIES.

numerology   The study of the occult meaning of numbers, such as dates of birth or figures derived from the letters of a name, as a means of interpreting their influence on a person's life and future. Sometimes considered a type of parapsychology. See ASTROLOGY, PARAPSYCHOLOGY, PSEUDOSCIENCE.

numinous   Awe-inspiring, overwhelming feeling, thought, sensation, or intuition, related to something archetypically experienced as having intense symbolic significance beyond simple everyday personal concerns.

nuptial colors   Special coloration at the beginning of the breeding season in various species, as a signal for mating.

nuptial dance   1. The swimming of some male worms around the female, inducing her to emit a chemical that induces the male to release sperm and the female to shed eggs. 2. Generally, ritualized courtship behavior associated with some birds.

nurse   1. A person trained in dealing with the sick, generally under direction of a physician. See LICENSED PRACTICAL NURSE, NURSE'S AIDE, PSYCHIATRIC NURSE, PUBLIC-HEALTH NURSE, REGISTERED NURSE, REHABILITATION NURSE, VISITING NURSE. 2. To care for, nurture to health, and wait on (as with an ill person). 3. To nourish at the breast.

nurse's aide   A person who works in a hospital or nursing home and shares the responsibility of providing personal care for patients. Usually has minimal background education, a high-school diploma followed by on-the-job training in a hospital or other healthcare facility. Specific requirements vary with the employer institution.

nursing (behavior)   In female mammals, the secretion of milk from the mammary glands and assisting the offspring to suckle until able to obtain food on their own.

nursing home   A long-term care facility designed to provide medical, nursing, social, psychological, recreational, and social-work support to residents afflicted with chronic illnesses or disabilities.

nurturance need   The drive to care for, shield, defend, feed, sustain, and encourage a young child or young animal.

nurture   The totality of environmental factors that influence the development and functioning of an organism throughout life that cannot be attributed to genetics. See NATURE, NATURE-NURTURE CONTROVERSY.

nurturing experiences   1. Experiences that fulfill the need for nurturance. 2. (H. A. Murray) Denoting a fundamental need for protection, support, comfort, healing, and help.

nutmeg   The seed of a peach-like fruit, nutmeg has volatile oils containing alamecin, myristicin, and other active ingredients that when ingested in large quantities can produce intoxicating effects (accompanied by unpleasant side effects) comparable to those produced by cannabis sativa. Generally used as a flavoring agent. Also known as *made shaunda* (Hindi). See MACE.

nutritional disorders   Results of too much of or too little of certain nutrients required for the normal functioning of the organism. Kinds of nutritional disorders include obesity, pellagra, beriberi, kwashiorkor (protein deficiency), vitamin and mineral deficiencies (e.g., magnesium, zinc), or hypervitaminosis. See NUTRITIONAL FACTORS.

nutritional factors   Nutrients required for the normal functioning of the organism, and which, if severely lacking, result in nutritional deficiency disorders.

NVC   See NONVERBAL COMMUNICATION.

NVD   Abbreviation for the triad of symptoms of nausea, vomiting, diarrhea.

n_w   Number of scores within the interval containing the median.

nyctalopia   Inability or decreased ability to see in the dark or in a dimly lighted environment. Also known as hemeralopia, night blindness, nocturnal amblyopia, nyctanopia.

nyctophilia   Preferring night or darkness. Also known as scotophilia.

nyctophonia   A variation of elective mutism in which the person is able to speak at night but is mute during daylight hours.

nyctophobia   Morbid fear of night. Also known as nictophobia, noctiphobia, scotophobia. See ACHLUOPHOBIA.

nymph   1. A sexual young woman. Term derives from Greco-Roman mythology, a goddess personified as a beautiful maiden living in nature. 2. A developmental stage in some arthropods.

nymphae   Labia minora. See LABIA.

nymphette   (V. Nabokov) An adolescent girl.

nympholepsy   Obsolete term for sexual frenzy.

nymphomania   A female disorder consisting of an excessive or insatiable desire for sexual stimulation and gratification. Also known as andromania. The male counterpart is satyriasis. See DON JUANISM, SATYRIASIS.

nymphomaniac   1. A woman exhibiting nymphomania. 2. A woman with high sexual desire and indiscriminate sexual activity. Such women may have strong emotional needs for male companionship, believe that they are unattractive and that the only way to get company is to trade sex for attention. 3. Casually, a term used by men for any woman whose sexual capacity exceeds theirs.

nystagmus   Involuntary rapid movements of the eyeballs. Can be caused by drugs, disorientation, vertigo, motion sickness, damage to the semicircular canals from injury or disease, electrical or thermal stimulation of the ear. The eyeball motion is usually horizontal, but may be rotatory, vertical, or mixed. See POSITIONAL NYSTAGMUS, POSTROTATIONAL NYSTAGMUS.

O   1. observer. 2. organism. 3. Abbreviation for an oscillation or fluctuation in behavior. 4. Ohm. 5. Abbreviation for a subject. 6. See ORIGINAL RESPONSE.

OBE   out-of-body experience

obedience   Compliance, particularly as carried out in response to direct command. Stanley Milgram's pioneering studies measured the extent to which ordinary volunteers in a research setting would obey a minimally coercive authority figure, even if they believed they were hurting, endangering, or killing an innocent person. Types of obedience include: AUTOMATIC, DEFERRED, DESTRUCTIVE. See BEHAVIORAL STUDY OF OBEDIENCE.

obese   Excessively overweight. See OBESITY.

obesity   1. State of being obese, originally based on body weight (20% above age and sex norms), later based more on body fat (from 20% for a 17-year-old male to 37% for a 50-year-old female). Other definitional factors include regional fat distribution, and number and size of fat cells. Generally increases with age. Associated with many disorders. See HYPEROBESITY, HYPERPHAGIA, MORBID OBESITY. 2. A psychogenic condition usually characterized by an excessive drive to eat and always excessive weight (at least 20% above age and sex norms, taking individual constitutions into consideration). See BULIMIA, EATING DISORDERS.

obesity treatments   Efforts employed to produce substantial weight reduction, such as long-term diets, crash diets, group support, hypnotherapy, exercise programs, nutritional education, drug therapy, behavior modification, and dynamic psychotherapy focused on insight into the unconscious purposes served by excessive food intake. Long-term efficacy of such treatments are dubious and some bariatricians (experts on weight control) assume that for some people obesity will be a problem that must be dealt with every day of their lives.

obfuscation   1. To make that which is inherently simple obscure or incomprehensible. 2. A deliberate attempt to confuse.

object   1. Anything, a concrete entity of any kind. Types include: AMBIVALENT, ANXIETY, LOVE, PRIMARY TRANSITIONAL, SECONDARY TRANSITIONAL, SEX, SOCIAL, TRANSITIONAL, UNIDENTIFIED FLYING. 2. In general, an aim or objective of which the person is aware. See MEANS-OBJECT. 3. In psychoanalytic theory, a person, thing, or part of the body through which an instinct can achieve its aim of gratification. Types include: BAD, GOOD, LIBIDINAL, PART-, PRIMARY, WHOLE-.

object addict   A description of some patients with schizophrenia who cling obsessively to objects or ideas perhaps in an effort to prove that they are in contact with reality.

object-assembly test   1. A task of reassembling an object that has been taken apart, such as a simple lock. Used either as a mechanical aptitude test or as a test of ability. 2. Any examination that uses a jigsaw puzzle.

object assimilation   (F. C. Bartlett) A tendency of the memory image of a particular object over time to become more typical of the class to which it belongs.

object attitude   In structural psychology or in studies employing introspection, an attitude displayed by the type of observer who attends closely to the given object or stimulus while directing relatively less attention to the subjective processes as manifested in thoughts, feelings, and perceptions. Compare PROCESS ATTITUDE.

object blindness   1. See APRAXIA (meaning 3). 2. See VISUAL AGNOSIA.

object cathexis/libido   In psychoanalytic theory, the investment of psychic energy, or libido, in objects outside the self, such as another person, a goal, idea, or activity. Compare EGO CATHEXIS.

object choice   In psychoanalytic theory, the selection of an object or person toward which psychic or libidinal energy is directed. See ANACLITIC OBJECT CHOICE, NARCISSISTIC OBJECT CHOICE.

object constancy   1. A tendency for an object to be perceived for what it is despite variations in the conditions of observation. See CONSTANCY. 2. The difference between what is seen and what is perceived; for example, seeing an oval object but knowing that it is a dinner plate results in the plate being perceived or recognized as being round. See NOUMENON. See also PERCEPTUAL CONSTANCY for an illustration.

object display   In ergonomics, an arrangement of the separate pieces of information so as to form a new geometric construct or emergent feature.

object fetish   A sexually arousing inanimate object.

object-finding   In psychoanalytic theory, the process of directing the libido away from the self and toward external objects such as a friend, loved one, interest, or fetish.

object function of a word   A word that has meaning only within itself, for example, a made-up interjection such as "Kazaam."

object identity   Understanding that items remain the same from one encounter to the next.

objectifying attitude   A tendency to react to an object, person, or event while disregarding personal feelings about it.

object-ill   (W. Stekel) Phrase applied by Wilhelm Stekel to the use by patients of objects outside their bodies to symbolize their emotions. See SOMATIZATION DISORDER, SUBJECT-ILL.

objectivation   A defense projection characterized by the recognition in other persons of feelings or impulses failed to be recognized in the self. It is particularly important when it is present in a psychotherapist. See PROJECTIVE IDENTIFICATION.

objective   1. Existing in physical reality outside the self. 2. Characterizing an observation, evaluation, or procedure that is free of personal bias.

objective anxiety   Personal tension and apprehension precipitated by an external object or event, that in some instances may symbolize the original focus of anxiety, as in fear of pointed objects.

objective data   Basic information, such as numbers, not influenced by the bias or interpretation of the observer. In learning studies, such quantitative data as number of responses and time of trial are objective.

objective examination   A test in which subjective evaluation does not play a role in scoring, for example, a multiple-choice test in which scoring standards have been formulated that allow no differences of opinion among different scorers as to the correctness of a response. In contrast, an essay test is a subjective examination.

objective indicator   In a variety of disorders, psychological or physiological, the existence of a single tangible biological factor, common to all individuals with the disorder. Not finding it would imply that the condition is not a unitary illness.

objective orientation   According to Jean Piaget, moral judgment typical of children under age ten, characterized by a nearly exclusive attention to the objective, usually physical, consequences of an act, such as the number of cups broken rather than the child's mischievous behavior. The objective orientation is a kind of literalism manifested by young children before they learn to take a person's motives into account. Compare SUBJECTIVE ORIENTATION.

objective perceivers vs subjective perceivers   Two classifications of persons based on perceptual tendencies: Objective perceivers are more narrow and rigid in focus, and tend to read material accurately but a few letters at a time, whereas subjective perceivers make a broader inspection of the material and interpret what they see.

objective psychology   (V. M. Bekhterev, J. B. Watson) A school of psychology that deals with observations of behavioral processes by competent persons and excludes subjective data. See BEHAVIORISM.

objective psychotherapy   A treatment procedure developed by B. Karpman primarily for use with institutionalized patients and patients with mild-to-moderate emotional disturbances. To reduce the subjectivity resulting from a personal relationship with the therapist, all therapeutic communication is carried out in writing. The patient answers written autobiographical questions, describes and comments on dreams, and reacts to assigned readings. In return, the therapist gives interpretations and points out underlying mechanisms in written memoranda, including a "memorandum as a whole" that summarizes all insights reached in the process.

objective reality   External world of physical objects, events, and forces that can be observed, measured, and tested. See REALITY, VERIDICAL.

objective reference   That characteristic of certain perceptual experiences whereby they are assigned to the external or objective world.

objective scoring   1. Rating based on nonjudgmental factors, for example, on scoring a multiple-choice test, the results will be the same regardless of who performs the scoring. 2. Scoring a test by means of a key or formula, so that different scorers will arrive at the same score, in contrast to subjective scoring in which the score depends on the scorer's opinion or interpretation. Compare SUBJECTIVE SCORING.

objective self-awareness   A reflective state of awareness characterized by regarding the self objectively, acknowledging personal limitations and the existing disparity between the "real" and "ideal" self.

objective set   A tendency to perceive phenomena in a neutral manner without disposition to misinterpret it in any way.

objective sociogram   (J. Moreno) In sociometry, a diagram depicting the interactions and interrelationships between a certain group of people (such as class, team, gang, work group) based on the results of a sociometric test. See SOCIOGRAM.

objective test   Any examination which leads to identical results regardless of who administers it if the administration is correct. The main issue is to eliminate any subjective aspects of the examiner; for example, a multiple-choice test with a time-limit has printed directions to subjects with an answer key and norms available. Any administrator who follows the simple rules should come up with identical scores for any particular person. See OBJECTIVE SCORING.

objective type   The kind of person who tends to view objects and events as existing in themselves rather than in terms of the self.

objectivism   A philosophical doctrine positing that valid knowledge arises gradually in the course of experience through observation and experimentation.

objectivity   1. The state or quality of being neutral or objective; external reality. Opposite of subjectivity. 2. Insistence on use of observations wherein a number of observers can agree that a given event with specified characteristics has occurred. It is based on the demand that knowledge be based on reliable, repeatable observations.

object language   1. In psychology, a language of stimuli and responses adjusted for the organism rather than the experimenter. 2. In computers, the numerical code used by each type of computer. A "language" that is specific to each type of computer, and which the computer obeys directly. See ALGOL, FORTRAN.

object libido   object cathexis

object loss   In psychoanalytic theory, actual loss of a person to whom the patient has been deeply attached, due to death, illness, moving away, rejection, or other cause. A threatened loss of love as the result of any of these reasons.

object love   In psychoanalytic theory, the investment of libidinal energy in an object or person other than the self.

object of instinct   Whatever elicits an instinctual response, for example, the sight of a snake will elicit fear the first time a snake is seen by a monkey.

object-oriented   In computing, a programming language that supports the use of objects.

object permanence   Understanding that an object continues to exist even when it is temporarily out of sight. Jean Piaget assumed that infants did not understand the permanence of objects until Stage 4 of the sensorimotor period. See SENSORIMOTOR PERIOD.

object reflecting relationships   A complicated aspect of reflexion about perceptions of self interacting with perceptions others have of themselves. The minimum number of elements in this complex include: the person veridically (unknowable to humans), the person as self-perceived, the person as seen by others, and the same three positions by interacting persons. See IDIOPANIMA.

object relations   In psychoanalytic theory, (a) the person's relations with other people, who are termed "objects"; (b) relationships to persons, activities, or things that function as sources of libidinal or aggressive gratification. The gratification may occur directly or through sublimation of the psychic energy involved.

object relationship   A parent-child relationship in which the parent is an "object" of admiration and a positive role model for the child.

object relations test   Projective test developed in the 1950s at the Tavistock Clinic in London based on the psychoanalytic theories of Melanie Klein. Consists of 12 pictures with various numbers of ambiguous figures, to which testees make up a story, thereby disclosing conscious and unconscious personality dynamics.

object-relations theory   1. (C. G. Jung) Assumption of a complicated interaction of internal object and archetypical images in psychic reality; emphasizing the mother-infant relationship in the first two years of life. 2. (M. Klein) Melanie Klein's view that the basic human motive is the search for and the attaining of good object (person) relations to maximize personal growth. See ANTILIBIDINAL EGO.

object-reversal test   A learning procedure in which numerous object-discrimination options may be offered, and, as the participant learns to make a correct choice, the problem is reversed so that the participant must make a second choice, and so on, until all objects can be chosen correctly.

objects   In psychoanalytic parlance, other people.

object size   The actual size of an object determined by precise, objective measurements.

object superiority effect   A paradoxical tendency for a stimulus to be more quickly detected if it is enclosed in a larger frame than just by itself. See WORD SUPERIORITY EFFECT.

object symbols   See KEY SYMBOLS.

oblativity   Ability to separate from a mother's influence en route to independence.

obligations fear   See PARALIPOPHOBIA.

obligative homosexuality   A form of sexuality characterized by inability to be emotionally committed to as well as sexually aroused and gratified by members of the other sex. Also known as exclusive homosexuality.

obligative mutualism   See MUTUALISM.

obligatory perception   The visual perception of the neonate characterized by inflexible concentration on configurations and colors of high contrast, such as a tendency to focus on black and white. See PREFERENTIAL PERCEPTION, PRINCIPLE OF MAXIMUM CONTRAST.

obligatory process   A sequence of events that once initiated can neither be controlled or inhibited, for example, a sneeze.

oblique   1. Slanting. 2. Correlated, not independent. Used to describe the relationship between correlated factors in a factor analysis. See ORTHOGONAL.

oblique décalage   (direct discontinuity—French) (J. Piaget) A preliminary function of development that presages the further development of this function in the future. See DÉCALAGE.

oblique rotation   In a factor analysis, a rotation in which the factor axes are allowed to form acute or obtuse angles; the factors are correlated with each other, negative or positive.

oblique solution   In factor analysis, factors not at 90° angles to each other, and consequently not independent of each other. See ORTHOGONAL SOLUTION.

obliviscence   Gradual fading of memories with the passage of time; forgetfulness.

obnubilation   1. Stupor. 2. Clouding of consciousness.

OBS   organic brain syndrome(s)

obscenity   Verbal expressions, drawings, gestures, and written material that violate the norms of good taste and decency in a given society at a given time, in terms of being considered lewd or disgusting. The legal definition of obscene in the United States is based on the 1957 Supreme Court decision in Roth vs United States. See PORNOGRAPHY.

obscenity-purity complex   A rigid set of self-imposed moral standards regarding obscene or "impure" thoughts, feelings, or actions, accompanied by a persistent dread of violating these standards. Also known as puritan complex.

obscurantism   1. Beliefs and actions that are opposed to scientific inquiry, understanding, and the progress of knowledge; deliberate deprecation of established facts and theories, especially if these appear to contradict a given set of political, economic, social, or religious convictions. 2. Intentional obscurity designed to obfuscate. See OBFUSCATION.

observation   The intentional examination of an object or process for the purpose of obtaining facts about it or reporting conclusions based on what was observed. Kinds of observation include: BEHAVIOR(AL), CONTROLLED, MASS, NATURALISTIC, PARTICIPANT-, RANDOM, SELF-, SYSTEMATIC, UNOBTRUSIVE, UNSELECTIVE.

observational errors   Deviations of the reported results from actual values, due either to the observer or to the recording apparatus.

observational learning   1. (A. Bandura) Acquisition of knowledge and competencies through watching the performances of others either directly or in symbolic media. See MODELING, SOCIAL COGNITIVE THEORY. 2. (E. L. Thorndike) The conditioning of an animal to perform an act observed in a member of the same or a different species, for example, the observational learning by a mockingbird that results in an ability to imitate the song patterns of other kinds of birds.

observational-learning theory   social-learning theory

observational method/technique   The scientific method in which observers are trained to watch and record animal or human behavior as precisely and completely as possible without personal bias or interpretation. Tape recorders, cameras, stopwatches, and other devices may be used to increase accuracy. Also known as observation technique.

observation commitment   In forensic psychology, sent to a hospital usually by a court order for a limited period of observation, usually to determine fitness for trial or legal competence.

observation trial   1. Having a trainee observe another person performing an operation. 2. Observing a problem situation without attempting to interfere.

observed self   (W. James) The "me" as seen by the "I." See IDIOPANIMA, LOOKING-GLASS SELF.

observer (O)   A person who watches or perceives. See PARTICIPANT-OBSERVER.

observer drift   A tendency for two behavioral raters working together to begin to agree with each other in a manner that is idiosyncratic to them. Results in apparently high levels of reliability but also yields data different from results produced by another pair of raters assigned to the same project. See CONSTANT ERROR, SIMILAR-TO-ME ERROR.

observer sociogram   (J. Moreno) In sociometry, a diagram depicting the interactions and interrelationships between a certain group of people (such as class, team, work group) based on a co-therapist's impressions. See SOCIOGRAM.

obsession   A thought, image, or impulse that persistently intrudes on consciousness against the person's will. Morbid obsessions, as contrasted with benign perseverations like musical themes or meaningless phrases, have an irrational quality and may dominate consciousness and behavior to the point of interfering with work and social life. Examples are philosophical ruminations (intellectual obsessions), dread of contamination (obsessive fears), thoughts about hurting or killing others (obsessive impulses), and persistent images relating to traumatic events (obsessive fantasies). Kinds of obsession include: CONTAMINATION, COUNTING, HAND-WASHING, MASKED, SOMATIC. See COMPULSION, OBSESSIVE-COMPULSIVE DISORDER.

obsessional brooding   1. Preoccupation with abstract, metaphysical questions concerning life, death, and the universe. See BROODING COMPULSION. 2. A compulsion to worry about relatively trivial matters. Often interpreted as an attempt to escape from emotional problems or forbidden impulses. See INTELLECTUALIZATION.

obsessional character   A personality disorder characterized by such traits as excessive caution and orderliness, worry over slight errors and imperfections, and an overconscientious attitude toward the self and others. See COMPULSIVE-PERSONALITY DISORDER.

obsessionalism   (H.S. Sullivan) Obsessive behavior used as a dynamism or defense measure. See OBSESSIVE BEHAVIOR.

obsessional personality   Trait disturbances characterized by excessive orderliness, perfectionism, indecisiveness, constant worry over trivia, and the imposition of rigid standards on others. Also known as obsessive personality.

obsessional technique   (W. Fairbairn) In psychoanalytic theory, a procedure in which the analysand changes from infantile to mature dependence by internalizing both the accepted and the rejected aspects of the mother.

obsessional thoughts   See OBSESSION, OBSESSIONAL BROODING.

obsessional type   One of Sigmund Freud's three libidinal types in which the libido is largely invested in the superego, and the person is dominated by conscience and may develop an obsessive-compulsive neurosis. See EROTIC TYPE, LIBIDINAL TYPES, NARCISSISTIC TYPE.

obsessive attack   (S. Rado) Major symptoms of obsessive-compulsive psychoneurosis derived from childhood temper tantrums, such as spells of doubting and brooding, alternating with bouts of ritual-making and an urge to injure or kill. See HORRIFIC TEMPTATION.

obsessive behavior   Actions characteristic of an obsessive personality or obsessive-compulsive disorder, such as persistent brooding, doubting, ruminating, worrying over trifles, cleaning up and keeping things in perfect order, or performing rituals.

obsessive-compulsive disorder (OCD)   A diagnosis of patterns of behavior which interfere with the ability to function, characterized by obsessions, compulsions, or both. Obsessions are persistent, recurrent ideas and impulses that appear senseless to the person but cannot be ignored or suppressed. Compulsions are repetitive acts, such as hand-washing, counting, and touching, that must be performed to relieve tension. See OBSESSIVE-COMPULSIVE PERSONALITY.

obsessive-compulsive personality   A persistent personality pattern characterized by an extreme drive for perfection, an excessive orderliness, an inability to compromise, and an exaggerated sense of responsibility.

obsessive-compulsive reaction   A syndrome characterized by a person being driven to repetitive actions in response to persistent thoughts, for example, checking several times that the stove is turned off before leaving the house, then calling the house to ask a person at home to check that the stove is turned off. Adolf Meyer called this an obsessive-ruminative tension state.

obsessive doubt   In obsessive-compulsive disorders, a condition of obsessive brooding, doubt, and uncertainty.

obsessive fantasy   A persistent image or daydream, such as a parent's recurrent mental picture of a child getting lost.

obsessive fear   A persistent, irrational fear, or phobia, such as dread of contamination or fear of thinking immoral thoughts. See OBSESSION, PHOBIA.

obsessive impulse   A morbid, intrusive urge to perform an inappropriate or offensive act, such as shouting an obscene word or stabbing someone.

obsessive-ruminative tension state   Phrase used by Adolf Meyer similar to obsessive-compulsive reaction.

obstacle sense   An ability of the blind to avoid obstacles in their path. See ECHOLOCATION.

obstinate progression   Movements that continue after a patient is restrained, cornered, or otherwise prevented from advancing the body by leg movements. See SYNDROME OF OBSTINATE PROGRESSION.

obstipation   A form of severe constipation usually associated with a functional origin.

obstruction box   A device used in animal studies in which the subject is required to overcome an obstacle or to endure pain to reach a reward; for example, to reach a pedal that can be pressed to deliver pleasurable brain stimulation, a rat may have to walk across a shock grid. Used to help investigators compare the values animal subjects place on different rewards. See OBSTRUCTION METHOD.

obstruction method/technique   A method of determining drive dominance by pitting one drive against another, such as hunger versus thirst, versus sex. By using an obstruction box, the relative strength of various drives can be compared. See OBSTRUCTION BOX.

obtained frequency   The frequency distribution observed in a set of data, and contrasted with the frequency that might be expected from various theoretical assumptions.

obtained score   Raw score, before conversion.

obtrusive idea   An obsessive, unwanted, foreign idea that intrudes on the person's normal flow of thought.

obtrusive (method)   Research in which those studied are at least aware of the researcher's presence, if not disrupted by the data-gathering. Compare UNOBTRUSIVE MEASURES.

obviative   In linguistics, a form used in some languages to refer to an entity (other than the speaker or the addressee) that has not been chosen as the focus of the dialogue.

Occam's razor   (William of Occam) Originally, a form of the more general principle of parsimony stating that "entities should not be multiplied beyond necessity." In this case "entities" refers to demons, spirits, or anything invoked to explain phenomena. Later, mostly used as a synonym for the principle of parsimony. Also spelled Ockham.

occasional cause   Antecedent of a given event incorrectly regarded as directly related to the event.

occasional inversion   (S. Freud) In psychoanalytic theory, sexual activity between persons of the same sex prompted by unavailability of partners of the opposite sex. See FACULTATIVE HOMOSEXUALITY, FAUTE DE MIEUX, SITUATIONAL HOMOSEXUALITY.

occasionalism   A form of parallelism holding that God directly causes the bodily processes that correspond to psychic processes.

occipital cortex of the brain   The back lower or hind portion of the brain. See BRAIN for an illustration.

occipital lobe   The part of the cerebral hemisphere posterior to the rest of the cortex, associated with vision. Compare FRONTAL LOBE. See BRAIN.

occipitopontines   See CORTICOPONTINE NUCLEUS.

occlusal neurosis   The unconscious grinding or setting of teeth when not eating, as in nocturnal bruxism.

occlusion   1. Blockage. 2. An obstruction or closure, as when a cerebral artery is occluded, causing a stroke. 3. A phenomenon of simultaneous firing of two branches of the same neuron which may result in a total output less than the sum of the separate responses.

occult   1. Hidden, not manifest. 2. Mysterious, incomprehensible, secret, especially as applied to a class of phenomena, or presumptive phenomena, that cannot be explained in either everyday or scientific terms, such as premonitory dreams, telepathic awareness, and clairvoyant communications. See EXTRASENSORY PERCEPTION, PARAPSYCHOLOGY, PSI, PSEUDOSCIENCE.

occultism   A belief that natural processes can be controlled by magic or secret methods, or the attempt to control nature or people by such means.

occultism classification   (M. Truzzi) Five categories of research-oriented occultism categories: (a) proto-scientific: scientific attempts made but data not accepted as valid; (b) quasi-scientific: false attempts made to appear scientific as in the case of astrology; (c) pragmatic: belief close to science but no claims are made; (d) shared mystical: similar private experiences; and (e) private mystical: private validation.

occupational ability   The capacity to perform vocational or professional tasks, generally measured by a series of occupational tests.

occupational adjustment   The degree to which a person has compatibly matched abilities, interests, and personality to his or her job or career. Differs from "vocational adjustment" in its emphasis on the interaction between personal characteristics and the objective requirements, conditions, and opportunities associated with the job.

occupational analysis   The systematic collection, processing, and interpretation of information concerning the objective work conditions found in specific occupations.

occupational classification   A way of grouping and ranking jobs and occupations. Systems vary according to the criteria established and the theoretical framework adopted. Used by national census offices for producing employment data, for example the international Standard Classification of Occupations of the International Labour Organization.

occupational commitment   See ORGANIZATIONAL COMMITMENT.

occupational counseling   In an early attempt at vocational counseling, Frank Parsons saw the process as having three steps: (a) relevant knowledge of self, (b) realistic knowledge of occupations, leading to (c) "true reasoning", the making of sensible choices.

occupational cramp   A disability, usually in the hand or arm, that prevents a worker from engaging in occupations, such as writing, driving, sewing, playing an instrument, or firing a weapon. See APHTHONGIA, CARPAL TUNNEL SYNDROME, OCCUPATIONAL NEUROSIS, REPETITIVE STRAIN INJURY, SEAMSTRESS'S CRAMP, TELEGRAPHER'S CRAMP, VIOLINIST'S CRAMP, WERNICKE'S CRAMP, WRITER'S CRAMP.

occupational cultures   The social groups that arise from intense occupational ties. Also known as occupational communities/subcultures.

occupational disease   Common term for a disease or illness caused by work. Some, such as asbestosis, black lung disease, hearing loss, and silicosis, are clearly work-related; others, such as repetitive strain injury, back pain, and headache, have etiologies that may be harder to establish. Historically, the attributed causes have been more affected by social and economic factors than by medical science. See OCCUPATIONAL CRAMP.

occupational drinking   A pattern of consumption of above-average amounts of alcohol due in part to the nature of the imbiber's occupation, such as in advertising or public relations where attendance is expected at cocktail parties and similar forms of entertainment of clients or customers.

occupational ergonomics   The science of designing workplaces to be safe, efficient, and satisfactory.

occupational family   A group of jobs or vocations with similar ability requirements.

occupational hierarchy   An organization of occupations in order of increasing requirements of ability or competence, and, in some cases, according to prestige.

occupational inhibition   Inability to perform to expectation which may be expressed as poor work performance or reactive symptoms of illness such as fatigue or vertigo. See OCCUPATIONAL NEUROSIS.

occupational level   An occupation or class of occupations that requires a given degree of education or other training and competence.

occupational mobility   The movement of an occupational group or individual member of an occupation through the social stratification system.

occupational neurosis   Term suggested by W.R. Gowers in 1888, when "neurosis" meant a neurological disease of unknown etiology. Later, with Sigmund Freud's distinction between "psycho-neuroses" and "actual neuroses," occupational neurosis was given (especially by physicians hired by employers) the former meaning, and taken as a (psycho-)neurotic reaction to employment, usually in the form of tension and anxiety, with symptoms such as cramps that interfered with work. The symptoms were often interpreted as conversion (hysterical) reactions produced by such psychogenic factors as emotional conflict, resentment against working conditions, near accidents, fear of failure, or by the inherent susceptibility of that class or type of employee. Symptoms are increasingly likely to receive a medical diagnosis, as Gowers originally suspected.

occupational norm   The average or typical scores obtained from tests of abilities for a given occupational category.

occupational psychiatry   The application of psychiatric theory and practice to the workplace, such as in the occupational rehabilitation of psychiatric patients.

occupational rehabilitation   A phase of rehabilitation, or reestablishment of prior skills, in which the ability to work is restored or improved through vocational counseling and evaluation, job-finding, or work in a sheltered setting.

Occupational Safety and Health Act (OSHA)   An American statute passed in 1970 to raise occupational health standards.

occupational segregation   The restriction, whether by custom, educational opportunities, or legislation, of certain categories of workers to specific jobs. As an example of horizontal segregation, workers in heavy industry tend to be male; those in retail trade and consumer services are mostly female. That most higher status occupations are held by men, even in largely female occupations, is an example of vertical segregation.

occupational stability   1. A characteristic behavior trait of a person who rarely changes jobs. 2. A measure of the proportion of employees in a given group or organization who have held the same post for one, two, three, or more years.

occupational stress   Tension and strain experienced by workers and executives on the job, arising out of such factors as pressure to produce, resentment against superiors, disagreeable working conditions, fatigue, occupational hazards, excessive competition, or anxiety over possible unemployment.

occupational test   An examination designed to measure potential ability or actual proficiency in a given occupation.

occupational therapist   See OCCUPATIONAL THERAPY.

occupational therapy (OT or O.T.)   A form of rehabilitative therapy consisting of useful tasks and activities that use minor skills, such as basket-weaving, clay-modeling or gardening. Aimed at helping patients to develop constructive interests, focus attention outside themselves, reestablish self-esteem, bring them into contact with others, and keep them from lapsing into inertia. In some countries occupational therapy is the treatment of choice for mental disorders. Such a therapist is known as an occupational therapist (OT or O.T.).

occurrence rate   The frequency of occurrence of any event per unit of time, for example, number of errors made by every employee on the same job task on a daily basis. Also known as rate of occurrence/of response, response rate. See INCIDENCE, PREVALENCE.

OCD   obsessive-compulsive disorder

oceanic feeling   1. Phrase sent to Sigmund Freud by R. Rolland to describe mystical, religious emotion. 2. (S. Freud) A regression to an early phase of ego-feeling, reviving the experience of nursing infants before they learn to distinguish their own ego from the nonego or external world. 3. In later psychoanalytic theory, a sense of unlimited power associated with identification with the universe as a whole, originating in infancy, accompanied by a feeling of omnipotence arising from the infant's control over movement and the immediate satisfaction of own narcissistic needs. May surface in adulthood as a schizophrenic delusion or religious experience. See COSMIC IDENTIFICATION, MEGALOMANIA, OMNIPOTENCE OF THOUGHT.

Oceanic kiss   A traditional greeting in Polynesia in which one person sniffs the cheek of another.

Oceanic position   A coital position reported by Pacific island anthropologists in which the woman lies on her back while the man kneels or squats between her parted legs. See COITUS.

ochlophobia   Fear of crowded places, or crowds, especially mobs. See AGORAPHOBIA, DEMOPHOBIA.

ochophobia   See AMAXOPHOBIA.

Ockham's razor   See OCCAM'S RAZOR.

O'Connor Finger Dexterity Test   (J. O'Connor) A timed performance test to measure fine motor dexterity; requires the placing of pins in each hole on a board.

O'Connor vs Donaldson   A 1975 proceeding in which the United States Supreme Court ruled that no nondangerous person can be custodially confined if that person can survive successfully in freedom.

O'Connor Wiggly Block   A psychomotor aptitude test designed by Johnson O'Connor in the 1940s, using a block of wood the size of a breadloaf. After its nine pieces are disassembled in sight of the participant with some items reversed, the participant is asked to reassemble the block. Data are both impressionistic (how the participant tackled the block, comments made, attitudes demonstrated) and objective (time to reassemble). See WIGGLY BLOCK TEST for an illustration of a Wiggly Block.

octave effect (in stimulus generalization)   (L. G. Humphreys) The finding that when an organism is conditioned to respond to a tone, the response generalizes more to a pitch that is an octave higher or lower than to one that is closer to the original.

ocular dominance   eye dominance

ocularmotor accommodation   Focusing the image on the retina by the process of flattening or thickening the lens.

ocular pursuit (movements)   Successive fixations of an eye in following a moving object. Eye movements elicited by a target's velocity, rather than its position, are necessary for following that moving target. After an initial overshoot, a higher velocity saccadic movement is superimposed to reacquire the target. As target velocity increases, the slower velocity pursuit movements must rely on additional reacquiring saccades, especially at speeds of greater than 20 degrees-per-second. Also known as visual pursuit/tracking.

oculi   Plural of oculus.

oculogravic illusion   A false sensation of movement, generally seen in two contexts: (a) when being whirled around or tilted (such as on a fast carousel), the feeling of being pulled away from the center of the movement. See SLOW ROTATION ROOM. (b) When a vehicle's forward velocity is suddenly and substantially increased (decreased), the acceleration force vector combines with the gravity force vector to "fool" the otoliths into signaling that the body is pitched upward (or downward). Compounded by the eyes rolling up (or down).

oculogyral illusion/movement   The apparent movement of faint light due to nystagmus produced by body movements. It is slight body movements that make it appear that the light has moved. See NYSTAGMUS, SLOW ROTATION ROOM.

oculogyric crisis/spasm   A symptom of parkinsonism (or a side effect of certain antipsychotic drugs) in which there is prolonged and uncontrollable rotation of the eyeballs, accompanied by tics and contraction of the cervical muscles resulting in a bizarre twisting of the neck. The patient may maintain the position for minutes to hours. See TARDIVE DYSKINESIA.

oculomotor changes   Pertaining to three eye reactions: Eyeball movements to see at different locations; lens changes leading to accommodation; pupil changes to adjust to light.

oculomotor nerve   Cranial nerve III. It innervates upper eyelid and most of the muscles associated with movement and accommodation of the eye and constriction of the pupil (all eye muscles except the external rectus and superior oblique).

oculomotor nuclei   The terminal point for most of the ascending fibers of the vestibular nerves.

oculus   The eye; the eyeball and the optic nerve. Plural is oculi.

OD   1. See OVERDOSE. 2. Abbreviation for the Latin *omni die*, meaning "every day" (also abbreviated **o.d.**). 3. Abbreviation for *oculus dexter*, meaning "right eye" (also abbreviated **O.D.**).

odalisque   Female slave or concubine in an Oriental harem.

ODD   oppositional defiant disorder

odd-even reliability   A method of assessing the reliability of a test by correlating scores on the odd-numbered items with scores on the even-numbered items. A special case of split-half reliability.

oddity problem/task   A learning or perception discrimination task of identifying which object is different (usually in size, color, or shape) from the others (generally two) presented. The purpose is to test the ability to perceive relationships and differences among a number of similar objects. Performed well by adult nonhuman primates and children above the age of six. See ANIMAL INTELLIGENCE, INTELLIGENCE TESTING, WGTA.

odds   An estimation of the ratio of success to failure.

odds ratio   The ratio of two odds. Unlike other measures of association, 1.0 represents a complete absence of relationship.

odic force   A hypothetical force thought to surround natural things. See REICHENBACH PHENOMENON.

odontophobia 1. Morbid fear of teeth and of being bitten by teeth. 2. Fear of going to the dentist, also known as dental phobia.

odor A scent, a sensory experience produced by stimulation of the olfactory nerve organ by volatile substances. See HENNING SMELL THEORY, INFRARED THEORY OF SMELL, OLFACTION, SMELL, SMELL MECHANISM, STEREOCHEMICAL SMELL THEORY, ZWAARDEMAKER SMELL SYSTEM.

odorant stimuli Airborne molecules of volatile substances that are soluble in water or fat.

odor display See OLFACTORY DISPLAY.

odor fear See OLFACTOPHOBIA, OSMOPHOBIA, OSPHRESIOPHOBIA.

odorimetry 1. The measurement of odors. 2. See OLFACTOMETRY.

odorivector (J. F. Mateson) A quality of odor; the odor's vapor. See MATESON MULTISTIMULUS OLFACTOMETER.

odor prism A prism-shaped graphic representation of the six primary odors (putrid, burned, spicy, resinous, ethereal, fragrant) and their relationships. Also known as smell prism. See HENNING ODOR PRISM for an illustration.

odynophobia algophobia

Oedipus complex In psychoanalytic theory, the erotic feelings of a son (ages 3–5) toward his mother, accompanied by rivalry, fear, and hostility toward the father. Also applied to the corresponding relationship between the daughter and father, sometimes called the female Oedipus complex or the Electra complex. Sigmund Freud claimed this conflict becomes the basis for a neurosis if not adequately resolved. Karen Horney felt it was neither normal nor universal, and that when it does occur, it is a neurotic relationship fostered by provocative behavior on the part of the parent. Anthropologists question the universality of the Oedipus complex, since there are many cultures in which it does not appear. Named for the Greek myth and play about King Oedipus who killed his father, unknowingly married his mother, and then blinded himself. Also known as Edipus complex, Oedipal complex/conflict/situation. See CASTRATION COMPLEX, COMPLETE OEDIPUS, ELECTRA COMPLEX, NEGATIVE OEDIPUS COMPLEX, NUCLEAR COMPLEX, OEDIPISM.

Oedipal phase/stage In psychoanalytic theory, the phallic stage of psychosexual development, usually between ages three and seven, during which the Oedipus complex is stated to manifest itself.

Oedipism 1. Self-injury to eyes. Some children punch their own eyes, sometimes until they go blind. Causes vary, but apparently sometimes done to gain attention. Hidden observers have noted that some children start this behavior when a parent is approaching, probably expecting that the parent will then give them attention by asking them to stop. It is related to children's rocking and head-banging. Name is derived from the mythical King Oedipus, who blinded himself after killing his father and unknowingly marrying his mother. Also spelled Edipism. 2. Having an Oedipus complex.

oenomania Alcoholism.

O factor The internal state of an organism. Also known as O element.

OFD See OROFACIAL DYSKINESIA.

office landscaping Generally, the design of a large workplace to make it more psychologically and esthetically pleasing, and, by extension, more productive. Typically features a large open expanse in which workspaces are partitioned by movable furniture, screens, plants, or accessories. (Some workers find this noisy, distracting, and lacking in privacy; others enjoy the contact and solidarity.) See OPEN OFFICE.

Office of Strategic Services (OSS) Assessment An intensive, three-day series of evaluations conducted by the OSS in the United States during World War II to select for assignments related to military intelligence. Included paper-and-pencil tests, stress interviews, problem-solving exercises, and various innovative situational tests.

office romance A liaison between co-workers, a common occurrence due to the influence of proximity and shared similarities.

offspring See CHILDREN, PROGENY.

off-the-job training Vocational training provided by an employer outside of regular working hours. Examples include presentations in lecture or printed form, or on videotape or computers. Compare ON-THE-JOB TRAINING.

ogival curve A graphic representation of a cumulative distribution; an S-shaped or sigmoid curve with a point of inflexion in the middle and the slope positive (or negative) throughout its length. Also known as ogive (curve).

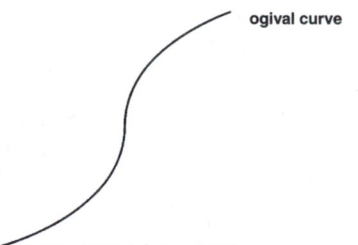

ogival curve

Ohio State Leadership Studies (R. M. Stogdill) Research to uncover effects of specific supervisory behaviors on subordinates. Based on responses to questionnaires using critical incident technique.

Ohm (O or ω) (G. S. Ohm) The SI unit of electrical resistance, an Ohm is the electrical resistance between two points of a conductor in which one volt of potential difference produces a current of one ampere.

Ohm's (acoustic) law (G. S. Ohm) In audition, the principle that the ear can reduce complex tones into a series of simple sine waves. Formula: $I = V/R$, where I is the current in amperes, V is the potential difference in volts, and R is the resistance in ohms.

O-H scale See OVERCONTROLLED-HOSTILITY SCALE.

oikofugic Pertaining to an urge to travel or wander from home.

oikophobia Morbid fear of houses. Also known as ecophobia, oikiophobia. See DOMATOPHOBIA.

oikotropic A tendency to be homesick when away from friends and family.

O_{jk} Observed frequency for the *jk*th cell.

old boys' network Slang for men who know each other, who purposefully or inadvertently discriminate against nontraditional employees, particularly women.

old brain Usually the brain stem (the first part of the brain to develop in evolution) but sometimes taken as the thalamus as well, or all parts of the human brain except the neocortex. Also known as archipallium.

old jobs Describing jobs normally held by older employees. These jobs are characterized by requiring more experience and skill and less physical strength than jobs held by younger people.

old-sightedness Far-sightedness characteristic of old age and typically increasing beyond the age of forty. See PRESBYOPIA.

olfactie A unit measurement of smell intensity on the Zwaardemaker scale. See OLFACTOMETER.

olfaction 1. The act of smelling. 2. The sense of smell, activated by stimulation of spindle-shaped receptor cells in the olfactory epithelium located in the nasal passages leading from the nostrils to the throat. See SMELL, VIBRATIONAL THEORY.

olfactometer A research instrument used to regulate the amount and intensity of olfactory stimuli. See MATESON MULTISTIMULUS OLFACTOMETER.

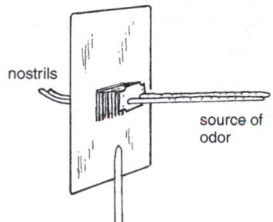

nostrils

source of odor

olfactometer A device for evaluating smells. The two tube endings at the left are inserted into the nostrils, while the other end is positioned near the source of the odor.

olfactometry Determining the sensitivity of the olfactory organ. Also known as odorimetry.

olfactophilia 1. The enjoyment or love of smells. 2. A paraphilia based on odors; being sexually aroused by odors, typically odors of the genital areas.

olfactophobia Morbid fear of odors. Also known as osmophobia, osphresiophobia.

olfactorium A specially designed room free of all odors except those introduced in measured quantities by a researcher in the study of smell.

olfactory areas Brain structures associated with the sense of smell. Research evidence has been compiled by excision or ablation of tissues in and about the rhinencephalon with varied and often conflicting results. Only lesions of the olfactory bulb seem to produce a consistent disruption of olfactory functions.

olfactory brain Refers to all those parts of the brain once regarded to have olfactory functions. They include many structures such as the olfactory bulb and tract, the uncus, hippocampus, dentate gyrus, habenula, fornix, and amygdala. Also known as the rhinencephalon. See OLFACTORY AREAS.

olfactory bulb A bulb-like ending on the olfactory nerve in the anterior lobe of each cerebral hemisphere. See AMACRINE CELL.

olfactory cells Cells that detect smell. Humans have about 5–6 million; cats, 75 million; and bloodhounds, 100 million of these cells.

olfactory cortex piriform area/cortex

olfactory display A display that uses olfaction as the sensory medium, as in the addition of a distinctive "leak tracer" to an odorless gas.

olfactory epithelium An area of olfactory receptors or nerve endings in the lining of the nose. See OLFACTORY RECEPTORS.

olfactory eroticism Pleasurable sensations, particularly of an erotic nature, associated with the sense of smell. See OLFACTOPHILIA.

olfactory hallucination A false perception of odors, which are usually experienced as unpleasant or repulsive, such as onions or decaying flesh. Such hallucinations, if persistent, may indicate the presence of a serious mental disorder.

olfactory nerve (Archillini, J. Hunter) Cranial nerve I. Sensory nerve of smell originating in the olfactory epithelium and then distributed to the nasal mucous membrane and from there to the olfactory bulb.

olfactory prism See HENNING'S ODOR PRISM, STEREOCHEMICAL SMELL THEORY.

olfactory receptors Specialized spindle-shaped cells having cilia at their ends, located on the cribriform plate in the roof of the nasal cavity, affected by odors, thereby transmitting olfactory sensations (smells).

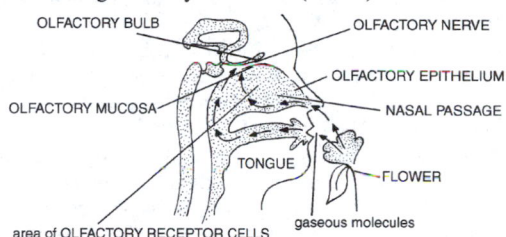

OLFACTORY BULB — OLFACTORY NERVE

OLFACTORY EPITHELIUM

OLFACTORY MUCOSA — NASAL PASSAGE

TONGUE — FLOWER

area of OLFACTORY RECEPTOR CELLS — gaseous molecules

olfactory receptors

olfactory sense organ A receptor for the fibers of the olfactory nerve lying almost hidden in the mucosa of the roof of the nasal cavity. Also known as olfactory rods. See OLFACTORY EPITHELIUM.

olfactory stimulation The excitation of the spindle-shaped cells in the nasal cavity by inhalation of volatile substances called odors.

olfactory sulcus A small groove or furrow on the surface of each of the cerebral hemispheres located on the inferior side of the frontal lobes. Separates the gyrus rectus from the medial orbital gyrus.

olfactory tract A band of nerve fibers that originates in the olfactory bulb and extends backward along the bottom side of the frontal lobe to a point called the olfactory trigone, at which point the tract divides into three strands leading to the medial and lateral olfactory gyri and the olfactory tubercle. See LATERAL OLFACTORY TRACT.

olfactory trigone See OLFACTORY TRACT.

olfactory tubercle A small oval elevation near the base of the olfactory tract leading from the olfactory bulb to the brain. Occurs rarely in humans but is a common structure in animals that depend upon the sense of smell to survive. The olfactory tubercle contains auxiliary olfactory-nerve fibers and cells.

oligarchic style (R. J. Sternberg) In the theory of mental self-government, a preference for dealing with multiple, competing goals of equal perceived importance; individuals with this style often fail to complete tasks because of their inability to assign priorities.

oligarchy A form of government in which a few rule the many.

oligergasia Adolf Meyer's term for mental deficiency.

oligocephaly Mental deficiency caused by inadequate brain development.

oligodactyly A congenital anomaly marked by a fewer-than-normal number of fingers or toes.

oligodendroglia A satellite structure or support cells that are associated with neurons in the central nervous system. Also known as oligodendria. See NEUROGLIA.

oligoencephaly (C. E. Benda) A form of mental deficiency associated with asymmetrical physical development, often marked by an abnormally small brain, nervous-system irregularities, and low resistance to disease.

oligologia Lack of terms wherewith to make fine distinctions; for example, Eskimos have many terms for different kinds of snow, whereas people in temperate climates may have two or three, and people in tropical areas may have only a single term.

oligophrenia (I. A. Fölling) Mental deficiency or mental retardation. Term is used primarily in Great Britain and Russia. Oligophrenia sometimes is used with a modifying term, as in phenylpyruvic oligophrenia. See PHENYLKETONURIA.

oligophrenic response In Rorschach testing, seeing only parts of a human being, whereas people who are considered normal tend to see a whole human being. Considered a sign of mental retardation.

oligophrenopsychology 1. A study of cognitive impairment based on brain deficiencies as a result of trauma or disease. 2. (E. Burr) The study of the potential abilities of persons with severe mental deficiency to aid in the development of programs for teaching such children vocational skills to help them to become self-sufficient.

oligopoly Competition among only a few.

oligospermia An abnormally low content of spermatozoa in male semen samples. It is one of several factors responsible for male infertility. The usually accepted minimum level of sperm needed to insure fertility is 20 million sperms per milliliter (one-thousandth of a liter—a bit less than a teaspoonful). Also known as oligospermatism, oligozoospermatism, oligozoospermia. See AZOOSPERMIA.

olivary nucleus An olive-shaped mass of gray matter in the medulla, containing nuclei of fibers that connect the cerebral cortex with other parts of the brain.

olivocochlear bundle A group of auditory-nerve fibers extending from the superior olive through the descending neural pathways to the area of the cochlear hair cells.

ololiuqui The seed of the Mexican morning-glory or Latin American snake plant vine *Rivea corymbosa*, which contains substances chemically related to lysergic acid diethylamide (LSD), but is less potent. Described in the 16th-century reports of the explorer Francisco Hernandez as a plant eaten by Aztec priests when they "wanted to commune with their gods and to receive a message from them."

olophonia Defective speech due to malformed vocal organs.

OLSAT Otis-Lennon School Ability Test. The seventh edition of this test (1995) is abbreviated **OLSAT7**.

Olympian view (of rationality) (H. A. Simon) A theory that pictures "a heroic man making comprehensive choices in an integrated world."

ombrophobia Morbid fear of rain or of rainstorms.

ombudsman 1. An impartial person appointed by an organization or legislature to hear and investigate complaints and grievances of private citizens, including patients, against government agencies, hospitals, or other facilities. 2. Often used as the equivalent of a mediator between an individual and any large organization.

OMD organic mental disorder

omega 1. The twenty-fourth and last letter of the Greek alphabet. See APPENDIX C. 2. The square of a correlation that serves as an estimate of the degree of the effect of A (the independent variable) on B (the dependent variable). Thus a correlation of 0.90 becomes omega 0.81 and represents about 81% of the effect of A on B. See OMEGA SQUARED.

omega squared The square of omega. A population index indicating the proportional reduction in the variance of Y given the value of X.

omen An occurrence supposed to portend or foreshadow a future event, but not causally connected with it. See PSYCHICS.

omicron The fifteenth letter of the Greek alphabet. See APPENDIX C.

omission training The scheduled delivery of a positive reinforcer if a particular behavior does not appear.

ommatidium A unit of a compound eye of an arthropod. Each element is a complete structure capable of responding to light, even when other elements are destroyed or covered. The combination of the elongated ommatidia forms a mosaic image on the animal's retina.

ommetophobia Morbid fear of eyes. Also known as ommatophobia.

omnibus test A quiz or examination in which test items fall into several different categories; however, the items are not grouped by category but are mixed together in a kind of a spiral within the test to yield a single score.

omnipotence (of the id) In psychoanalytic theory, an infant's feeling of being all-powerful and that all wishes must and will be fulfilled. Later, adults who have lost contact with reality may experience delusions of infinite power, wealth, or potency, which may be a regression to infantile omnipotence. See MEGALOMANIA, SPOILED CHILD.

omnipotence of thought A subjective feeling that personal wishes can be gratified and reality changed by deliberation alone. See GRANDIOSE IDEAS, MAGICAL THINKING, OCEANIC FEELING.

omnipotent therapist See PRESTIGE SUGGESTION.

OMS Abbreviation for organic mental syndrome. See ORGANIC SYNDROME.

onanism 1. *Coitus interruptus* (penile withdrawal with sperm not deposited in the vagina.) Term derives from the biblical passage in which "Onan went to his brother's wife" and "spilled it (his seed) on the ground" (Genesis 38:9). Authorities in the 18th century interpreted the story as a condemnation of both withdrawal and masturbation. 2. Mistakenly defined as masturbation.

Ondine' curse sleep apnea

Oneida Community A self-sufficient Methodist community founded in the 1830s in Vermont, growing to 350 members by the 1870s. It practiced group marriage and the eugenic selection of parents. See COITUS RESERVATUS, GROUP MARRIAGE.

oneirism A dream-like state in a condition of wakefulness. A waking dream state.

oneirodynia An unpleasant or painful dream, such as a nightmare. See ONEIRONOSUS.

oneirogmus Nocturnal seminal emission, or ejaculation, usually occurring during an erotic (or "wet") dream. See WET DREAM.

oneirology The scientific study of dreams and their interpretation. Sometimes known as oneiromancy. See DREAM INTERPRETATION.

oneiromancy The divination of future events by analysis of dreams. See PRODROMIC DREAMS.

oneironosus A morbid form of dreaming. Distinguished from oneirodynia (nightmare) in that a nightmare's essence is helpless terror and the sleeper awakens, whereas in oneironosus the dream continues.

oneirophrenia 1. A hallucinatory state that can be caused by lack of sleep, overuse of drugs, and sensory deprivation. 2. (L. Meduna) A psychosis resembling schizophrenia in certain symptoms, such as disturbances of emotion and associations, but distinguished from schizophrenia by a dreamlike state with clouded sensorium. See ATYPICAL PSYCHOSIS.

oneiroscopy Rare term for evaluation of a person's mental condition through dream analysis.

one-night stands Meeting people for sexual purposes without the intention of forming interpersonal bonds.

one-shot case study The simplest and the least useful of research designs consisting of X (an event) and O (observations) in the pattern X O. It is usually employed under extraordinary situations such as following a disaster (X) and then would be observations (O) following the disaster. There are no controls.

one-tailed probability See ONE-TAILED TEST, TWO-TAILED TEST.

one-tailed test A statistical hypothesis test in which a directional alternative hypothesis is considered; that is, only evidence of a difference in the expected direction is considered as evidence leading to the rejection of the null hypothesis.

one-trial learning The mastery of a skill or an increment of learning on the first trial, for example, a cat that jumps onto a hot stove will most likely never do it again.

one-way analysis of variance A statistical test of the null hypothesis that the means of the populations corresponding to the levels of the independent variable are equal. The test statistic is the ratio of the variance estimates based on the group means ("between") and the pooled within-group variance ("within") which is distributed as F under the null hypothesis, given that certain assumptions are satisfied. This procedure is typically employed when the researcher has interval or ratio data and one independent variable with three or more levels. See T-TEST.

one-way mirror/screen A pane of glass that in a well-lit room appears to be a conventional mirror, but through which researchers on the other side, if in darkness, can see what is going on in the well-lit room. See ONE-WAY VISION SCREEN.

one-way vision screen An observation screen made of wire netting or thin cloth brightly illuminated on one side and dark on the other, permitting vision from the dark side toward the light but not vice versa. See ONE-WAY MIRROR/SCREEN.

one-word stage (of language development) The first stage of child language, in which the maximum sentence length is one word.

oniomania An uncontrollable impulse to spend money, and to buy without regard to need or use.

onion-garlic personality dichotomy According to Nicholas Cummings, psychotherapy patients may be divided for treatment purposes into those who suffer (onion personality) and those who make everyone else suffer (garlic personality). The name is based on the observation that eating onions creates an unpleasant after-taste for the eater; whereas eating garlic creates an unpleasant breath or environment for others.

on-line In computers, connected electronically and ready for, or actually, data-processing.

onomatomania 1. Obsessive preoccupation with words or names, including persistent intrusion of certain words and sentences into thoughts. 2. Obsessive preoccupation with a particular word, an attempt to recall a particular word, or fixation on the word's possible significance.

onomatophobia 1. Morbid fear of names, naming, or being named. 2. Fear of a particular word or name because of its supposed significance. Also known as nomatophobia.

onomatopoeia Formation of words that seem to imitate the sound of the thing or action they represent, such as "hiss" or "sizzle." May be characteristic of certain types of schizophrenia, in which case the "onomatopoiesis" is occasionally preferred. See ONOMATOPOEIC WORDS.

onomatopoeic theory A point of view about linguistic origins stating that early humans imitated the sounds of animals, infants, and natural phenomena, and used these imitations as symbols representing the phenomena. Sometimes also spelled onomatopoetic theory. See BOW-WOW THEORY, ONOMATOPOEIC WORDS, ORIGIN-OF-LANGUAGE THEORIES.

onomatopoeic word A word that sounds like the object represented, such as an infant's "maa" for mother or "daa" for daddy. See ONOMATOPOEIC THEORY.

onset   In linguistics, the portion of a syllable that precedes the nucleus, such as "spl" in the word spleen.

onset insomnia   Difficulty falling asleep.

on-the-job training   Vocational training provided by an employer during regular working hours for the purpose of supplying the worker with the required knowledge or skills for satisfactory production. Compare OFF-THE-JOB TRAINING.

On the Origin of Species   The title of Charles Darwin's 1859 book that systematized the argument for the evolution of speciation through natural selection. See NATURAL SELECTION.

on (or off) the wagon   Slang for abstention from alcoholic beverages, or a fall from grace when "off," meaning drinking again.

ontoanalysis   A form of analysis that probes the ultimate nature of being; existential analysis.

ontogenesis   ontogeny (meaning 1)

ontogenetic   Relating to the biological development of an individual organism. Also known as ontogenic.

ontogenetic psychology   The systematic study of the origin and growth of mental life and behavior in the individual organism.

ontogenetic zero   The instance of the creation of certain organisms when the zygote is formed. See DEVELOPMENTAL ZERO.

ontogenic   1. Characterizing not only the biological development of the individual but also psychological growth in terms of the stages of life and their relation to developmental processes such as learning, thinking, and expression of needs and purposes. 2. See ONTOGENETIC.

ontogeny   1. Development of an individual organism's internal and external features, such as the changes of a person's nose from birth to old age. It is the biological and developmental history of a single organism, as distinguished from phylogeny, the development of the species. Also known as ontogenesis. 2. The statement of G. Stanley Hall that "ontogeny recapitulates phylogeny" described a theory that emphasized the developmental course of a single organism progresses, from its inception, through the successive stages of all of the organisms from which it evolved. Hall emphasized that human and animal zygotes were practically indistinguishable and that human infants had tails at one stage of their intra-uterine development. Compare PHYLOGENY.

ontology   1. Philosophical study of the nature of being or reality. 2. The branch of philosophy that deals with the abstract nature of "being" (present status) and "becoming" (dynamic process of growth and development). 3. Science of existence or of being. Term was introduced into psychology by Christian Wolff. See METAPHYSICS.

onychophagy   Nail-biting. Also known as onychophagia.

onychophagist   A person who habitually bites own fingernails.

oocyte   An immature ovum, produced by the division of an oogonium into two daughter cells; the larger daughter cell becomes an oocyte and the smaller cell becomes a polar body. The first maturation division produces a primary oocyte; the second maturation division generates a secondary oocyte and a first polar body at ovulation. The latter degenerates; fertilization causes the oocyte to complete phase 2 of meiosis, forming a haploid ovum, secondary polar body, and a diploid zygote. See MEIOSIS, POLAR BODY, PRIMARY OOCYTE.

oogenesis   The formation and development of an egg. See POLAR BODY.

oogonium   An immature egg cell of the female before it begins dividing in the ovary into a primary oocyte and a polar body. Plural is oogonia.

oosperm   (The fertilized ovum) zygote.

open adoption   An adoption in which the biological parents and the adoptive parents know each other and may agree to allow the biological parents to have information about, or even contact with, the adopted child.

open book exam/test   An examination in which the examinee can bring and refer to books or notes while answering.

open call system   A communication system in which a single sound may have different meanings depending on context or accompanying signals, as in human speech. See CLOSED CALL SYSTEM.

open classroom   A classroom with minimal restrictions, usually with tables rather than desks, giving students freedom of movement. See OPEN CLASSROOM DESIGN.

open classroom design   A concept of classroom planning that provides a study environment based on results of behavioral-mapping techniques. The open classroom may have movable chairs and desks rather than fixed rows of desks in parallel patterns. Consequently, the class can sit in a circle so that each person can see all others. See OPEN CLASSROOM.

open class society   A social structure in which upward and downward social mobility is possible. Compare CASTE SYSTEM.

open consultation   In industrial psychology, generally, managers treating subordinates as equals.

open-cue situation/test   A learning situation in which all the cues required to arrive at a goal are visible to the participant who must comprehend the relationships that link cues to goal.

open-door policy   1. A policy of maintaining an open hospital or hospital unit, usually associated with the concept of a therapeutic community. 2. The availability of any political, managerial, or other official to be visited by a subordinate rather than going through a chain of command.

open-ended question   In an examination, survey, or interview, a question that students, participants, or respondents answer in their own words. Example of an open-ended question: "What did you do yesterday?" can be responded to in many different ways. However, a closed-ended question, such as "Feeling OK?", is usually answered with "No" or "Yes." Also known as open question. See CLOSED-ENDED QUESTION.

open group 1. A counseling or therapy group that new members may join at specified times or at any stage during the course of therapy. Compare CLOSED GROUP. 2. In group therapy, a group in which new members can enter or leave at any time. Also known as continuous group.

open hospital A psychiatric hospital without locked doors or physical restraints. Also known as open-door hospital.

opening techniques Methods used by a counselor or therapist at the beginning of the relationship to establish rapport and trust.

opening-up meditation A meditation technique characterized by achieving a clear mind by eliminating all thought, thus becoming receptive to new experiences.

open instinct The ability of certain animals to adjust to environmental conditions, when what is usually needed, to effect certain behavior is not available, and possibly to carry this new information to further generations. This is in contrast to the usual idea of instinct as immutable behavior. See CLOSED INSTINCT, LAMARCKIAN THEORY.

open lewdness Legal phrase for unacceptable public sexual behavior.

open loop model of stress See CLOSED LOOP MODEL OF STRESS.

open loop system In ergonomics, a system that when activated, needs or does not allow any further control, as in firing a rocket that has no guidance system. Compare CLOSED LOOP SYSTEM.

open marriage 1. An arrangement in which both partners agree that one or both of them can engage in extramarital sexual activity. Also known as sexually open marriage (SOM). See NONTRADITIONAL MARRIAGE, SWINGING. 2. A marriage that is adaptable and flexible, especially regarding roles and personal identity, with an emphasis on honesty and trust.

open-mindedness Readiness to consider different points of view. See OPEN-CLOSED MINDS.

open minds vs closed minds (M. Rokeach) Refers to attitudes held on topics usually considered to arouse emotion, such as positions on political, social, economic views. Persons with "open minds" will tend to weigh evidence critically; those with "closed minds" will tend to refuse to consider dissenting evidence. Topics such as religion, political ideology, sex/gender differences, racial differences, or status quo, may be more likely to result in closed-mindedness. See AUTHORITARIAN PERSONALITY.

open shop In labor relations, a workplace in which there are no requirements for union membership or dues payment. Compare CLOSED SHOP.

open skills vs closed skills (C. E. Poulton) Two types of task ability: Open skills are those performed in, and externally paced by, dynamic environments; closed skills are performed in static environments and require less adaptions. Driving a car requires both.

open societies vs closed societies (K. Popper) Describing two types of social structures: Open ones are liberal, democratic, and based on the creativity of many individuals, whereas closed ones are authoritarian and inhumane.

open study A preliminary or pilot trial of a therapeutic technique in which researcher and participants know all the relevant details of the research. Compare BLIND STUDY, DOUBLE BLIND STUDY.

open system 1. A concept of personality that conceives of it as having a dynamic potential for growth, reconstitution, and change through extensive transactions within itself and the environment. 2. Any system with permeable boundaries permitting exchange of information between its elements and with the outside environment. 3. A biological system in which growth can occur without conforming to laws of thermodynamics or a demonstrated constancy of energy relations. 4. A system that accepts inputs from the external environment, transforms them, and sends them back to the environment as outputs.

open system theory (D. Katz & R. L. Kahn) In organizational psychology, using a metaphor from biology, an organization is viewed as an open system; for instance, an organization "imports energy" (by hiring), and "transforms energy" (in making products).

open ward A hospital ward or unit in which the entrance/exit doors are not locked.

operandum 1. That which is operated upon. 2. Any observable response in a conditioning study that presumably was reinforced by the stimulus presented. 3. In mathematics, the quantity or symbol upon which a mathematical operation is performed. 4. (B. F. Skinner) In operant-conditioning research, the environmental segment upon which the participant or subject produces an effect to obtain reinforcement, for example, a lever that an animal presses is an operandum. Term was coined by B. F. Skinner as a substitute for the anthropomorphic term "manipulandum."

operant 1. Work or that which works. 2. (B. F. Skinner) An event that can be objectively measured, consisting of responses with which the organism operates on the environment to produce consequences such as reinforcing stimuli. According to Skinner who introduced the term, "operant" distinguishes between reflexes and responses, with emphasis on behavior operating on the environment generating consequences. 3. An emitted response that is strengthened by a contingent reinforcement. Compare RESPONDENT.

operant avoidance/escape The escape from unpleasant circumstances by employing behavior previously learned during operant conditioning.

operant behavior Any action produced and maintained by its consequences, for example, an animal presses a lever that delivers food; a voluntarily emitted response already within an organism's repertoire that serves to have an effect on its environment (for example, a bird may peck the grass for food).

operant chamber 1. A box in which an animal is put for research purposes, especially for reinforcement studies. 2. A compartment in which animals can be placed for operant or classical conditioning. Sometimes known as "Skinner box." See SKINNER BOX for an illustration.

operant conditioning   Phrase applied by Burrhus Skinner to a process in which behavioral change (and presumably learning) occurs due to reinforcing (rewarding) certain desired behavior and withholding rewards or punishing undesired behavior. Examples are teaching a dog to do tricks by giving it a treat when it does what is wanted; rewarding behavioral change in psychiatric patients by giving them candy or cigarettes when they act as the therapist wants. Also known as instrumental conditioning. See BEHAVIOR MODIFICATION, LOGICAL CONSEQUENCES, NATURAL CONSEQUENCES, SHAPING.

operant conditioning chamber   See SKINNER BOX.

operant learning   A form of learning that takes place as a result of presentation of a reward following the response to be strengthened. See OPERANT CONDITIONING.

operant level   Baseline of behavior as it occurs naturally prior to reinforcement, such as the amount of lever-pressing (if any) that occurs before a study begins.

operant paradigm   A learning model that assumes most relevant human behavior is controlled by the consequences.

operant reserve   The number of responses made in an operant-conditioning program after the reinforcement has been withdrawn. It is a measure of the strength of conditioning.

operant response   Any action by an organism that has an effect upon the environment, for example, a pigeon in a training box pecks a button which in turn provides food for the bird.

operant score   (H. B. English) A measurement of the alteration in the physical and social environment caused by a participant or animal subject's behavior. See INTERACTIVE SCORE.

operant therapy   A form of psychotherapy based on rewards given by the therapist to the client when the client shows improvement of thinking or behaving.

operating characteristic   A curve showing the probability of accepting the null hypothesis at different levels of a parameter.

operation   1. Any surgical procedure. See SHAM OPERATION. 2. The act, or process of functioning. 3. As used by Jean Piaget, a mental act; the derivation of logical relationships in the process of manipulating either physical objects or symbols, as in the manipulation of symbols to solve an equation. The process of performing operations, according to Piaget, is central in the building of intellect. See CONCRETE OPERATIONAL STAGE, FORMAL OPERATIONAL STAGE. Other kinds of operation include: COMBINATORIAL, CONVERGENT, CONVERGING, DIALECTICAL, SECURITY.

operational analysis   The process of evaluating the relationship between input and output in a system.

operational definition   1. A concept introduced by Percy Bridgman of a definition that specifies the precise operations (methods) by which any phenomenon or construct is created, determined, or measured, as in stating the operational definition of "intelligence" is "the score on the intelligence test." 2. A definition that depends on exact facts and directs exact conditions to attain a desired result.

operational evaluation   process evaluation

operationalism   A doctrine positing that a concept's meaning and validity depend upon the procedures used to define or establish it, that each concept must take as its meaning a single observable and measurable operation. Operationalism might define an emotional disorder as a score on a diagnostic test. Sometimes known as operationism. See OPERATIONAL DEFINITION.

operational research   Application of scientific methods to the study of complex organizations and to the solution of complex problems involving conflicting goals, concepts, and decisions. Also known as operations research (OR).

operationism   1. (P. Bridgman) A system or doctrine of developing definitions from the way things work (operation). 2. Scientific movement, the major assumption of which is that the adequate (operational) definition of variables is critical for progress. Sometimes known as operationalism. See OPERATIONAL DEFINITION.

operations research (OR)   1. Generally, an approach to analyzing a complex system (an individual, group, organization, or machine) to determine its overall functioning and to maximize its effectiveness. 2. (R. L. Ackoff) An approach to problem solving that includes: (a) The formulation of a problem; (b) Developing a mathematical model to represent the system; (c) Deriving a solution from the model; (d) Testing the model and the solution from the model; (e) Establishing controls over the solution; and (f) Implementation of the solution.

operative knowledge   (J. Piaget) Knowledge acquired in the process of cognitive-based behavior. According to Piagetians, operative knowledge should be more strongly emphasized in intelligence tests and schools as it is central to the development of intellect. See FIGURATIVE KNOWLEDGE, OPERATION.

operators   (R. Gelman) Mental processes involved in comprehending the effect of different numerical manipulations, for example, knowing that adding an orange to a bowl of oranges changes the number, but rearranging the oranges does not. See ESTIMATORS.

ophidiophilia   Abnormal fascination with snakes. See SNAKE SYMBOL.

ophidiophobia   Morbid fear of snakes. Also known as ophiciophobia, ophiophobia. See HERPETOPHOBIA, SNAKE SYMBOL.

ophthalmic artery   A branch of the internal carotid artery that arises near the point where it enters the skull. The numerous small branches of the ophthalmic artery supply blood to the various tissues of the ocular orbit, the eyeball, and the muscles of the eye, internal and external. It also supplies the eyelids and lacrimal glands.

ophthalmic nerve   (T. Willis) A division of the trigeminal nerve that passes forward from the trigeminal ganglion of the cavernous sinus through the superior orbital fissure. Supplies sensation to the orbit, the anterior part of the nasal cavity, and skin of the nose and forehead. Also known as nervus ophthalmicus.

ophthalmometer   An instrument for detecting and measuring the amount of astigmatism in the eye.

ophthalmoscope   An optical instrument for the examination of the eye's fundus and refractive errors. May be direct permitting examination of the eye at close range so as to observe an erect image, or indirect by use of a lens that produces an inverted image of the fundus. Also known as funduscope.

opiate(s) 1. Dried, powdered opium-poppy products with analgesic, relaxation, euphoric, and addictive properties. 2. In a more general sense, substances that act in many ways like opiates, more precisely called opioids. Whereas morphine and codeine are natural derivatives (even though they can be synthesized), and heroin and hydromorphone (Dilaudid) are semi-synthetic forms, other chemicals are unrelated to opium, but have an opiate-like effect, for example, meperidine (Demerol), methadone, and codeine, oxycodone, and fentanyl. Historically, opiates have had many medical uses, including their use as aids in anesthesia, postoperative pain relief, anti-diarrheal agents, and cough suppressants. See OPIOIDS.

opiate antagonist/blockers Medicines that block the effect of opiate drugs.

opinionaire A questionnaire that measures opinions.

opinion-giver role In a group, contributing relevant information to help reach a decision. Compare OPINION-SEEKER ROLE.

opinion leader In consumer psychology, someone who influences the purchase choices of others. Once thought to be community social leaders, now seen as considered knowledgeable and trusted in specific areas by neighbors, or as celebrities in some domain.

opinion poll Determining the opinions of a particular group of people. May be as simple as asking people in a room to raise their hands if they agree or disagree on any topic, or as complicated as attempting to predict a national election. See PUBLIC-OPINION POLL.

opinion-seeker role In a group, soliciting information, attitudes, opinions, to help reach a decision. Compare OPINION-GIVER ROLE.

opioid Denoting a drug, synthetic or semi-synthetic, that produces effects similar to those of morphine, but is not derived from opium. See NARCOTIC ANALGESICS, SYNTHETIC NARCOTICS.

opioid-related disorders A general category of mainly psychosocial problems that can be associated with the use of opiates and their associated substances, such as dependence, abuse, intoxication, sexual dysfunction, sleep disorder, poor health, psychosis, delirium, and withdrawal.

opioid withdrawal symptoms Interruption of a supply of morphine or heroin to a person who has developed dependence on the narcotic. Withdrawal symptoms begin with restlessness and yawning, followed by complaints of feeling cold and difficult jerky breathing. After prolonged sleep, the patient's symptoms intensify, accompanied by abdominal cramps, vomiting, diarrhea, excessive sweating, and muscle twitching. The symptoms begin to subside after about ten days. See SUBSTANCE WITHDRAWAL SYMPTOMS, WITHDRAWAL REACTION.

opisthotonos (Hippocrates, A. Littré) Tetanic spasm or increased tone of the muscles of the back, resulting in retraction of the head and lower limbs. Purportedly associated with hysteria. Also spelled opisthotonus.

opium (Theophrastus) A narcotic drug produced from the resin of the unripe seed pod of the opium poppy, *Papaver somniferum*. Opium and its derivatives are eaten, smoked, injected, sniffed, and drunk. It is the source of morphine, codeine, heroin, and other narcotic drugs. The action of opium is due mainly to its morphine content which is analgesic and euphoric, capable of producing a deep sleep from which the user can be easily aroused.

Oppel Kündt illusion (J. J. Oppel & A. A. Kundt) The apparent perception that given two equal spaces seen at the same time, the one that is filled appears longer than the unfilled one. German physicist Johann J. Oppel (1815–1894) originally presented the illusion under the name "geometricoptical illusion."

Oppel Kündt illusion The distances between lines a and b, and lines b and c are the same, but one distance seems longer than the other.

Oppenheim reflex (H. Oppenheim) An extension of the great toe when the examiner strokes downward on the inside of the tibia of the lower leg. Named after German neurologist Hermann Oppenheim (1858–1919), who first described the reflex.

opponent cells Cells in the lateral geniculate nucleus that subtract one type of cone's output from another cone's output, thus making color vision possible. See OPPONENT PROCESS THEORY OF COLOR VISION.

opponent pair dimension See PRESCRIPTIVE ANALYSIS.

opponent process theory of color vision 1. (E. Hering) An explanation of color vision based on the assumption of three receptor systems, black–white, red–green, yellow–blue, in the retina of the eyes. In color vision, certain cells in the second retinal layer of the eyes are stimulated by green and inhibited by red, others are stimulated to yellow and inhibited by blue, a third group affected by gradations of grey from light to dark. Overstimulation of one of the modes leads to a compensatory reaction to the opposing modality. Also known as Hering theory of color vision. 2. (L. M. Hurvich & D. Jameson) A revision of the Hering theory stating that the receptors are like switches so that affecting any receptor means dampening the opposite receptor. Consequently, stimulating the blue will dampen the yellow. Since the pairs oppose one another only one pair-member can be effective at a time. See COLOR VISION, LADD-FRANKLIN THEORY, YOUNG-HELMHOLTZ THEORY.

opponent-process theory of emotion (R. L. Solomon) A point of view that every emotion generates an opposing emotion that acts to control it, existing after the original emotion has dissipated (for example, pain is reversed into pleasure for the masochist). Proposed originally to augment stimulus-response learning theory, later applied to paraphilic addiction by John Money. Also known as opponent-process theory (of acquired motivation). See DIALECTICAL MATERIALISM.

opportunistic rape Unplanned sexual assault, usually in the course of an argument or a crime such as burglary. Also known as impulse rape, situational rape.

opportunistic sex Spontaneous sexual activity, characteristically without protection from potential consequences such as pregnancy or disease.

opportunity class A class for pupils of any age or grade who are not considered suitable or do who not adapt to ordinary classroom procedures.

opportunity structure (R. Cloward & L. B. Ohin) The pathways to success in American culture (such as schooling) which, when blocked, may lead to delinquency.

opposites test An examination in which the participant is instructed to give the opposite of the stimulus word, for example, being given "Always" and replying "Never".

oppositional defiant disorder (ODD) A diagnosis of a persistent pattern of disobedient, negativistic, and provocative opposition to authority figures occurring between three and 18 years of age, manifested by temper tantrums, violation of minor rules, dawdling, argumentativeness, and stubbornness.

oppositional thinking Janusian thinking

opsin The protein portion of the rhodopsin molecule. In the retinal rod cells (light sensitive receptors in the first neuron level of the retinal layers of the eye), when rhodopsin is activated by photons (light particles), it breaks down into retinene and opsin. Usually, retinene and opsin rejoin almost immediately as new molecules of rhodopsin. See RETINA, RETINENE, RHODOPSIN, RODS.

opsoclonus An ophthalmological disorder, sometimes called "dancing eyes," marked by quick, irregular bursts of ocular movement, vertically and horizontally. Sometimes associated with myoclonic jerking of the limbs. See NYSTAGMUS.

Optacon An electronic tactile display for those who are visually impaired or blind. An optical "camera" picks up the visual images and translates them to vibrations conveyed to the fingertips. Compared with Braille, takes longer to learn, but can be applied to any printed matter without Braille's restrictions, bulkiness, and production problems. Optacon is an abbreviation of optical-to-tactile converter. See VISATONER.

optical axis A theoretical line that passes through the center of both the cornea and the lens; the center of vision.

optical defect A condition of the eye that prevents light rays from focusing properly on the retina.

optical flow pattern The dynamic changes in the retinal image that occur as the observer or the object seen moves.

optical illusion A false visual image produced by physical factors, psychological factors, or both.

optical projection 1. The formation of a visual image by means of a slide projector or similar device. 2. The location of objects in space which correspond to the image on the retina.

optical scanner A device for (a) detecting small or isolated areas by means of reflected or projected light, usually read into a computer; (b) used in questionnaire and exam marking; (c) able to translate directly from printed material to a computer.

optical-to-tactile converter Optacon

optic chiasm(a) (Rufus of Ephesus) A flat quadrangular body in the area of the hypothalamus where tracts of optic-nerve fibers from the left and right eyes meet and separate again. Lateral fibers from each eye cross over to the cortex on the opposite side of the brain so that each hemisphere receives fibers from both eyes. See DECUSSATION HEMIANOPIA.

optic disk An area of the retina where optic-nerve fibers gather before leaving the retina. Because the area is relatively insensitive to light, it is called the blind spot. See SCOTOMA.

optic-fiber regeneration A process demonstrated in lower organisms such as amphibia, when nerve tracts grow together again after they have been cut and frayed, for example, functional optic-fiber regeneration has been established in the newt even when the tract was inverted so that dorsal fibers faced ventral fibers, and vice versa.

optic lobes An uncommon name for inferior colliculi. A pair of elevations on the midbrain that contain visual reflex centers, that is, the upper part of the corpora quadrigemina.

optic nerve Cranial nerve II. The sensory nerve of vision originating in the receptor cells of the retina and distributed to the occipital cortex. Discovered by Alcmaeon in the 6th century BC. See OPTIC TRACT.

optic radiation Visual-nerve tracts that run between the lateral geniculate body of the hypothalamus and the internal capsule. Most of the fibers of the human optic tract travel this route, via the geniculate-body-internal-capsule radiation, on their way to the visual cortex in the occipital lobe. Some visual-tract fibers pass through the superior brachium and superior colliculus to the pretectal region.

optic tract (B. Panizza) A bundle of nerve fibers leading from the optic chiasma to termination in the lateral geniculate body (LGB) in the thalamus, where a new relay of fibers then take off to the visual area of the occipital lobe cortex. On the other side of the optic chiasma, the optic tract is known as the optic nerve.

optimal adjustment The ultimate goal of living for many people: achieving a balance between needs/wants and attainments, being satisfied and happy. See OPTIMAL FUNCTIONING.

optimal apparent motion The maximum effect of the phi phenomenon due to proper combination of timing, space, and brightness. Also known as beta motion. See APPARENT MOTION, KORTE'S LAW.

optimal functioning (M. Jahoda) A point at which an individual achieves the individual's utmost potential. See SELF-ACTUALIZATION.

optimal group size (J. B. Calhoun) A group size (number of members) that results in a comfortable level of interaction for members of a given species, that is, a group size not small enough to produce isolation, not large enough to cause undesirable interactions. Crowding has shown negative responses in animals.

optimal interpersonal distance The physical distance between two or more people that they judge to be comfortable while interacting. Comfortable distance varies with the type of relationship, interaction, and setting, and with national, personality, and social-class differences. See BUBBLE THEORY, CIGARETTE-SMOKE REACTIONS, PROXEMICS.

optimal level of arousal (C. Leuba) The degree to which an organism acts in ways to achieve homeostasis. Organisms learn which responses are necessary to achieve the desired level of status whether excitement or tranquility.

optimal level theories Points of view that the best methods of arousal are those that are pleasurable, and the best way to motivate an organism is through stimuli that are naturally motivating.

optimal man (G. A. Kelly) Refers to the highest level of functioning achieved when a person is constantly open to validations of personal constructs, and is willing to examine and validate new experiences in an ever-changing world.

optimal personality Based on factor-analytic investigations, core elements (efficiency, creativity, inner harmony, relatedness, transcendency) represent ideal self-actualization according to Richard Coan. See FULLY FUNCTIONING PERSON, HUMANISTIC PSYCHOLOGY, OPTIMAL MAN.

optimal viewing position (for words) The best location of the point of initial gaze fixation, generally near a word's center.

optimism A positive attitude that everything happens for the best, or that wishes will ultimately be fulfilled. If these feelings are persistent in the face of adversity, they may be defenses against anxiety and disappointed expectations. Also known as Panglossianism after a character in Voltaire's novel Candide. See ORAL OPTIMISM. Compare PESSIMISM.

optimize To modify circumstances to achieve greater or the best results for the purpose in hand.

optimum 1. Best value for a given purpose in a series. 2. Best value in a given series (often neither the maximum nor the minimum), for example, when traveling in a car with a capacity to go to 100 miles an hour, a speed of 60 miles an hour may be optimal for the average driver.

optimum duration In reaction studies, denoting the most favorable duration of time between signal and stimulus for producing prompt response in a given situation. Both shorter and longer stimulus durations tend to produce slower response.

optional stopping (of research) Terminating a study at the whim or careful decision of the researcher, often on the basis of initial favorable results.

optogram The image of a light-reflecting object on the retina of the eye.

optokinetic effect Apparent movement of an object, such as a light in a dark background. Caused by eye movement or neural activity.

OR operations research

oracle A prophet, sibyl, or other person with the purported power of foreseeing the future and through whom a diety is believed to speak. See PSYCHICS.

oral-aggressive character In psychoanalytic theory, a personality type resulting from sublimation of the oral-biting stage and marked by aggressiveness, envy, and exploitation. See ORAL CHARACTER.

oral-aggressive type (S. Freud) A personality type that features social hostility and assertiveness. See TYPOLOGY.

oral-anal sex Sexual stimulation of the anal area with the mouth or tongue. Also called anilingus.

oral anxiety In psychoanalytic theory, signs of nervousness, tension, apprehension, expressed at the oral stage of childhood by images of chewing and swallowing a loved or feared object, such as a parent.

oral behavior Activities that use the mouth, such as thumb-sucking, smoking, eating, kissing, nail-biting, talking, and oral sex.

oral-biting period In psychoanalytic theory, the second phase of the oral stage of psychosexual development, from about the eighth to the 18th month, during which children begin to feel that they are independent persons, express anger by biting their mothers' breasts or the nipples of bottles, and derive satisfaction from chewing on whatever they can put in their mouths. Also known as oral-sadistic phase.

oral character In psychoanalytic theory, a pattern of personality traits derived from the oral stage of psychosexual development. A person who has experienced sufficient sucking satisfaction and adequate attention from the mother figure during the oral-sucking period will develop an oral receptive character marked by friendliness, optimism, generosity, and dependence on others. If there is not satisfaction during the sucking and biting stage, the person, it is hypothesized, will develop an oral-aggressive character, with tendencies to be hostile, critical, envious, exploitative, and overcompetitive. See ORAL-AGGRESSIVE CHARACTER, ORAL-RECEPTIVE CHARACTER.

oral coitus Fellatio.

oral-contraceptive (OC) pill A combination of synthetic estrogen and progesterone, the female sex hormones responsible for the menstrual cycle, formulated in dosages that can be taken by mouth. The synthetic hormones in the pill alter the normal menstrual activities so that ovulation and related functions are prevented. It was introduced as a contraceptive in 1960 and has been 99% effective in preventing pregnancies. Also known as "the pill."

oral dependency In psychoanalytic theory, a tendency to be dependent on other people and to seek from them the same type of satisfaction originally experienced during the oral stage when the mother figure protected, nursed, and showered love and attention on the child.

Oral Directions Test A subtest of Otis' Personnel Tests for Industry for screening lower-level job applicants.

oral drive An urge to get pleasure from mouth activities such as sucking, kissing, tasting.

oral erot(ic)ism/gratification In psychoanalytic theory, the pleasure derived from oral activities such as smoking, chewing, biting, talking, kissing, and oral-genital contact. See ORAL-INCORPORATIVE PHASE.

oral-eroticism phase In psychoanalytic theory, the first phase of psychosexual development when the mouth is the principal erogenous zone and sucking is the most important source of gratification. Also known as oral-sucking period.

oral fixation   In psychoanalytic theory, persistence of immature gratifications associated with the oral phase of psychosexual development. Examples are nail-biting, thumb-sucking, baby talk, and excessive dependence on the mother or mother surrogate.

oral genital contact   The application of the mouth to the genitalia as a form of sexual stimulation. Application of the mouth to the male genitals is called fellatio; application of the mouth to the female genitals is called cunnilingus. Also known as buccal intercourse, orogenital activity.

oral herpes   Common name for herpes simplex I.

oral history   A history that relies on interviews, usually with older persons.

oral impregnation   A myth that fertilization can occur from mouth contact. Circulated in many variations, primarily as a warning that pregnancy can result from kissing or fellatio.

oral-incorporative phase   In psychoanalytic theory, the earliest phase of psychosexual development in which the infant unconsciously feels he or she is ingesting, or incorporating, the mother's being, along with the milk swallowed. This phase is also thought by some psychoanalysts to lay the foundation for feelings of closeness and dependence, as well as for possessiveness, greed, and voraciousness. See INCORPORATION, ORAL-EROTICISM PHASE.

oralism   A method of teaching the deaf auditory communication skills such as lipreading and speaking. Also known as oral method.

orality   The oral factor in eroticism or neurosis, ranging from pleasure in biting, sucking, smoking, or oral sex to speech-making, addictions, overeating, and excessive generosity.

oral libido   A psychoanalytic phrase for the linking of sexual energy with erotic pleasure associated with the mouth.

oral-lingual dyskinesia   **buccolingual masticatory syndrome**

oral optimism   Phrase applied to optimism as an oral-character trait, which psychoanalysts assume stems from full oral satisfaction in infancy. Theorized to give a child a lasting sense of self-confidence and a positive outlook on life. See ORAL CHARACTER.

oral orientation   The process of interacting with the environment in terms of oral needs, for example, an infant uses his or her mouth not only as a prime source of gratification but as a primary orientation organ to the external world, since he or she learns to identify objects by placing them in his or her mouth.

oral-passive type   (S. Freud) A personality type characterized by dependency, lack of initiative, and retreat into fantasies. See RECEPTIVE CHARACTER, TYPOLOGY.

oral personality   In psychoanalytic theory, refers to a type of person "centered" around the mouth, characterized by emphasizing mouth functions such as speaking, eating, or smoking. Because of unsatisfactory oral-stage experience such persons are thought by psychoanalysts to "devour" others and their time, energy, and affection. See ORAL CHARACTER.

oral pessimism   In psychoanalytic theory, a pessimistic, depressive pattern assumed to originate in frustration and deprivation experienced by the infant during the oral stage of psychosexual development, particularly at the hands of a cold, disinterested mother or primary caretaker.

oral phase/stage   In psychoanalytic theory, the first stage of psychosexual development, occupying the first year of life, when the mouth is the principal erotic zone and gratification is achieved by sucking the nipple during feeding and, toward the end of the period, by biting. See ORAL EROTICISM, ORAL SADISM.

oral primacy   Refers to an infant's first contact with the postnatal world, which is primarily with the mouth.

oral progesterone test   An obsolete test for pregnancy. When a woman missed a menstrual period, a dose of progesterone would cause menstruation if not pregnant.

oral reading   Moving the lips while reading silently.

oral-receptive character   In psychoanalytic theory, a personality pattern characterized by dependence, optimism, and expectation of nourishment and care from external sources, just as the mother figure provided these satisfactions during the oral-sucking period.

oral-receptive personality   A personality type demonstrated by the seeking of satisfaction primarily by oral means, such as by eating, chewing, smoking and other mouthing behavior.

oral regression   In psychoanalytic theory, returning to an earlier stage of development when orality was primary in pleasure seeking. See ORAL PRIMACY, ORAL STAGE.

oral sadism   In psychoanalytic theory, the primitive urge to use the mouth, lips, and teeth as instruments of aggression, mastery, or sadistic sexual gratification.

oral-sadistic cathexis   1. The concentration of psychic energy on oral-sadistic activities and aggressive urges, such as biting during early infancy. 2. The persistence of this type of activity in adult life in the form of sexual foreplay, aggressive character traits.

oral sex   General phrase for the stimulation of a sexual partner other than on the mouth, by kissing, licking, biting, or sucking. See ANILINGUS, CUNNILINGUS, FELLATIO.

oral (sound)   In linguistics, a sound produced with a raised velum, allowing airflow only through the oral cavity.

oral test   An examination in which the questions are posed and answered by speech.

oral triad   (K. Lewin) The major desires of the infant in the early oral phase are to devour, to be devoured, and to go to sleep.

Orbison illusion   Given a square superimposed on a series of equally spaced concentric circles with its center coinciding with the center of the circles, the sides of the square will appear concave. The illusion also takes another form involving two circles. Named after American psychologist William D. Orbison (1912–1952).

orbital gyri   A group of four gyri located about an H-shaped orbital sulcus of the ventral region of the frontal lobe. They are identified as medial, anterior, lateral, and posterior orbital gyri.

orbit method   In early time-and-motion research, Frank Gilbreth used a lighted ring on the hand of small-parts assemblers and a time exposure to photograph the movements, modifying the work layout and procedures to maximize orbital instead of jerky motion.

orbitofrontal cortex   The ventral area of the frontal lobes having strong connections with the hypothalamus. Lesions or ablation of the orbitofrontal cortex can result in abnormal repetition of responses, loss of inhibitions, and hypersexuality.

orch(i)ectomy   The surgical removal of one or both testes. Does not necessarily eliminate coital ability but may reduce desire. Orch(i)ectomy before puberty can affect the development of male secondary sex characteristics. Also known as orchidectomy. See CASTRATION.

orchis   Testis.

order   1. In biological taxonomy, the division immediately below class and above family. 2. (H. A. Murray) Neatness, tidiness, precision; one of Murray's catalog of needs. 3. Sequence. Kinds of order include: ABAB, ABBA, HIERARCHICAL, HOOK, PECKING, RANK, SOCIAL, TIME, ZERO.

order effect   1. An influence operating over time or causing a progressive change. If the order in which two experimental treatments are administered makes a difference, this shows an order effect. 2. Effects on behavior of presenting two or more experimental treatments to the same participant. 3. In multiple-treatment designs, the impact of a treatment may depend on whether it appears first (or in some other place) in the treatments presented to participants or subjects. If the position of the treatments influences the results, this is an order effect. See COUNTERBALANCING, SEQUENCE EFFECTS.

orderliness   An adaptive tendency to be neat and tidy and keep everything in place. In excess it may express a need for security, and when extreme may be an obsessive-compulsive characteristic or a symptom of organic brain disease. See COMPULSIVE ORDERLINESS.

order of a matrix   The number of rows and columns in a matrix, for example, a 5 × 7 matrix means 5 rows by 7 columns.

order of magnitude   An ordering of data, scores, or objects from lowest to highest so that every item but the last is followed by an item of greater value.

order of merit (comparisons)   A rating by ranking, comparing, or classifying people. Also known as merit ranking.

ordinal measurement   Measurement in order of magnitude of scores where the intervals are not necessarily of equal distance from each other.

ordinal position   Any place or rank as indicated by number, specifically the child's position or birth order in the family, for example, the second child. Many relationships have been suggested between birth order and personality development. See BIRTH ORDER.

ordinal scale   A scale that deals only with rankings. This scale shows only that an item is larger than another, but not how much larger. It lacks a true zero point. See INTERVAL SCALE, NOMINAL SCALE, RATIO SCALE.

ordinary chorea   Sydenham's chorea

ordinate   The vertical Y axis on a two-dimensional chart. See ABSCISSA, CARTESIAN COORDINATE SYSTEM.

ordination   1. (H. A. Murray) Higher mental processes by which a person selects and puts into operation a plan of action that has a desired end state. See SERIAL PROGRAM. 2. To invest officially with ministerial or priestly authority.

Orestes complex   A son's repressed impulse to kill his mother, or the actual act of matricide. Derived from the myth of Orestes who killed his mother, Clytemnestra, and her lover.

orectic   Affective or appetitive aspects of behavior. In psychoanalytic theory, contrasts with the cognitive aspects.

orexia   (appetite—Greek) The affective and conative aspects of behavior, excluding its cognitive aspect.

organ   Any part of the body with a specific function, such as vision, digestion, respiration. Also known as organon (meaning 1), organum.

organelle   A little organ or body; a specialized structure (for example, mitochondrion, cell nucleus, cell membrane) that serves specific functions (for example, cell metabolism, cell respiration, the synthesis of new chemicals).

organ erot(ic)ism   Sexual arousal or sexual attachment associated with a particular organ of the body.

organic   1. Relating to an organ. 2. Pertaining to or formed by an organism. 3. In psychology, refers to a problem with a physical bodily origin having to do with behavior, for example, an organic sleep dysfunction, due to hormonal imbalance or circulatory inadequacy. 4. In psychiatry, refers to a condition or disorder that is basically somatic or physical as contrasted with functional or psychogenic. 5. In chemistry, a carbon compound. 6. In casual usage, especially applying to foods, those grown or raised "naturally." 7. In law, fundamental.

organic-affective syndrome   A disturbance of mood resembling a manic or depressive episode, resulting from a specific organic cause.

organic amnesia   1. Failure to register or retain experiences due to organic causes, such as a stroke or traumatic brain injury. 2. A failure to register or retain experiences due to physiological changes in the nerve cells resulting from toxic conditions, such as: (a) lead poisoning, barbiturate poisoning, or acute alcoholic intoxication; (b) damage or destruction of nerve cells associated with head injury or brain tumors; and (c) degeneration of brain tissue caused by cerebral arteriosclerosis or senile brain disease. Loss of memory may be fragmentary or diffuse; recovery is usually gradual and incomplete if at all. See ALCOHOL-AMNESTIC DISORDER, AMNESTIC SYNDROME, MULTI-INFARCT DEMENTIA, PRIMARY DEGENERATIVE DEMENTIA.

organic anxiety   An anxiety linked to a painful organic disorder and attenuated in dream processes that represent efforts to cure the ailment through wish-fulfillment.

organic approach/viewpoint   A theory that all disorders, mental and physical, have a physiological basis. In psychiatry, adherents hold that all psychotic disorders, including those usually classified as functional, such as schizophrenia and manic-depressive disorder, and possibly the more severe neurotic disorders, result from structural brain changes or biochemical disturbances of the nervous or glandular system. First advocated by Hippocrates and Galen, but not systematically developed until Wilhelm Griesinger and Emil Kraepelin launched the organic era in the latter part of the 19th century. Also known as organicism.

organic brain syndromes (OBS)   Acute or chronic syndromes of impairment of brain-tissue function due to such factors as head injury, toxic conditions, encephalitis, systemic infection, brain tumor, or cerebral arteriosclerosis. Refers to a pattern of organic psychological and behavior symptoms without reference to etiology. Distinguished from "organic mental disorders" (in which the etiology is known). See AMNESTIC SYNDROME, ATYPICAL OR MIXED ORGANIC BRAIN SYNDROMES, DELIRIUM, DEMENTIA, INTOXICATION, ORGANIC DELUSIONAL SYNDROME, ORGANIC HALLUCINOSIS, ORGANIC PERSONALITY SYNDROME, ORGANIC-AFFECTIVE SYNDROME, WITHDRAWAL.

organic defect   A congenital disorder not the result of a genetic anomaly but caused by conditions in the womb; for example, if the mother were a tobacco smoker, alcoholic, or substance abuser, this could generate defects in the infant.

organic-delusional syndrome   A complex of symptoms including delusions, typically persecutory, produced by some toxic substances, or by temporal-lobe epilepsy or cerebral lesions. Such persons may appear perplexed or disheveled, speech may be rambling, but there is no clouding of consciousness, loss of general intellectual ability, or prominent hallucinations.

organic dementia   An irreversible intellectual deterioration due to chronic brain disorder, as in advanced cerebral arteriosclerosis and Korsakoff's syndrome.

organic disease/disorder   1. Mental or emotional impairment concluded to be physiological in origin. 2. An illness resulting from a demonstrable abnormality in the structure or biochemistry of body tissue or organs. 3. A condition of abnormality, mental or physical, based on somatic causes as opposed to functional or psychogenic causes. See PSYCHOGENIC DISORDERS.

organic drivenness   A state of hyperactivity resulting from brain damage that involves brainstem disorganization.

organic hallucinations   False perceptions associated with a specific organic factor. Stimulation or irritation of a cerebral site or sensory pathway may be a factor; precipitating causes can be an aneurysm or tumor, an adverse reaction to a medication such as ephedrine or propranolol, or abuse of alcohol, cocaine, or mescaline.

organic headache   Pain felt in the head caused by a brain disease.

organicism   organic approach

organicity   Denoting organic cerebral impairment, or brain damage.

organicity assessment   An evaluation of the functional effects of brain damage. Because single tests generally are inadequate, organicity assessment considers a broad range of possible general and specific factors, covering deterioration of various aspects of functioning, specific effects, and differential damage information based on evidence of location and extent of the disorder. See CEREBRAL-DYSFUNCTION TESTS.

organicity tests   See CEREBRAL-DYSFUNCTION TESTS.

organic mental disorder (OMD)   1. A heterogeneous group of mental disturbances resulting from transient or permanent brain dysfunction due to specific organic factors having been affected by alcohol, opiates, cocaine, as well as infections, traumas, metabolic disorders, and aging. 2. Old name for cognitive disorders.

organic paralysis   Loss of ability to move muscles due to injury to nerves. Compare HYSTERICAL PARALYSIS.

organic personality syndrome   A disorder characterized by a noticeable change in behavior or personality due to an identified organic factor that damages the brain, such as head trauma, vascular disease and Huntington's chorea. The change includes at least one of the following: displays of temper, unprovoked crying, loss of impulse control (for example, shoplifting, sexual indiscretions), apathy and disinterest, and suspiciousness or paranoia.

organic problem-solving   (K. Duncker) Analysis from above. In Gestalt psychology, a problem-solving strategy that is governed by insight and productive thinking. Compare MECHANICAL PROBLEM-SOLVING.

organic psychosis   1. A psychotic condition caused by a disorder of the organs or parts of the body. 2. A mental disorder of impairment of brain tissue function, particularly of the cerebral cortex. Such psychoses are characterized by gross disorganization of mental capacity and mood, as well as inability to interact socially or to cope with ordinary demands of everyday life. Examples include: alcoholic psychoses (such as delirium tremens, Korsakoff's psychosis), senile psychoses (such as Alzheimer's disease, Pick's disease), and psychoses resulting from various other conditions (such as poisoning, intracranial infection, brain trauma). See some entries beginning with ORGANIC.

organic repression   Retroactive amnesia associated with a head injury. Patients may be unable to recall events prior to the injury, and the amnesia is clearly different from the kind people who have psychogenic amnesia. See FUGUE.

organic retardation   Failure of an organ or organ system to develop normally because of a genetic defect, dietary deficiency, or hormonal disorder.

organic sensations   Visceral sensations which arise from deep within the body (for example, a rumbling stomach).

organic set   The proper placement of any given bodily organ into a definite and relatively permanent form.

organic speech impairment   See SPEECH IMPAIRMENT.

organic syndrome   A pattern of symptoms that characterize a particular organic mental disorder. Caused by a developmental, structural or physiological abnormality in the brain, as contrasted to a functional syndrome wherein the brain appears to be normal. Typical symptoms are memory loss, impaired intellectual functions, disorientation, defective judgment, and perceptual deficit. Sometimes known as organic mental syndrome (OMS).

organic therapies   Somatic treatments in psychiatry, including electroconvulsive treatment, electronarcosis, electrosleep therapy, faradic shock treatment, psychopharmacology, and psychosurgery. Clinical psychologists often advise clients to follow advice given by the clients' physicians, or they themselves give clients general advice such as to limit smoking, drinking, or taking of illicit drugs, to exercise and to follow a sensible diet, and may suggest to their clients specific questions to ask their physicians.

organic variable (OV)   A process within the organism that collaborates with an immediate stimulus to produce a particular response. A headache may be an organic variable due to an irritating noise in the neighborhood. Also known as O variable.

organigram   In organizational psychology, a diagram of an organization's hierarchy, especially in regard to communication. Similar to an organizational chart.

organ inferiority   Any type of perceived or actual congenital defects in organ systems thought by Alfred Adler to result in compensatory strivings to overcome the deficiencies.

organism (O)   Any living entity from a microbe to a whale, including humans and plants.

organismic   (G. Fechner) Pertaining to the organism as a whole rather than to particular parts. Organismic theories hold that behavior is an interrelated and interactive function of the entire integrated organism, also a metaphorical framework for understanding relationships and interactions as having "living" qualities for dynamic growth and developmental change. See HOLISTIC APPROACH.

organismic model   A broad approach to developmental psychology research, holding that the cognitive organization of the child is affected by the same adaptive forces that account for the evolution of body forms.

Organismic Personality Theory I   Kurt Goldstein, who first published his theory in the 1930s, assumed a holistic position about personality, stressing the need to understand the individual both intensively and as a whole. He assumed a Gestalt view that individuals had a need to become whole, which meant achieving full accomplishment of their potentialities. He was a forerunner in the human potential movement. See ABSTRACT ATTITUDE, ABSTRACT BEHAVIOR, HOLISTIC THEORIES.

Organismic Personality Theory II   Apparently developed independently of Kurt Goldstein's theory that had been published seven years earlier in German, Andras Angyal stressed the importance of two aspects of personality: (a) the need for mastery (growth) and (b) the need for acceptance (love). See HETERONOMY, UNITAS MULTIPLEX.

organismic psychology   1. An approach to psychology that emphasizes the total organism and rejects distinctions between mind and body. It embraces a molar, holistic approach and the interbehavior between organism and environment. 2. (R. Wheeler) An Americanized version of Gestalt psychology that emphasized embryological principles.

organismic theories   See ORGANISMIC.

organismic valuing process   1. The making of individual judgments or assessments of the desirability of any action or decision on the basis of personal sensory evidence and life experience. 2. (C.R. Rogers) A process by which the self-actualization tendency evaluates experiences as maintaining or enhancing the person.

organismic variable (OV)   1. Any property of the organism, such as age, sex, or name. 2. One of the four behavioral assessment factors of the SORC system and the factor that refers to physiological and psychological influences, for example, the effect of alcohol or drugs of abuse. See SORC VARIABLES. 3. An element in a body that varies across individuals, for example, two similarly sized organisms of the same species may have different size hearts, lungs, kidneys. 4. An organismic element, such as a nerve, that differs between and within individuals. The efferent and afferent nerves may differ in speed of carrying their messages. Such variations can affect individual responses to specific stimuli and complex situations.

organization   1. A social and often a legal entity designed to accomplish stated goals. Types of organization include: CENTRALIZED, CHILD FIND, HEALTH-MAINTENANCE, MATRIX, SOCIAL. 2. Coordinated biological activities of the organism as determined by genetic factors, interactions with the environment, and level of maturation. Types include: SENSORY, SOMATOTOPIC, TONOTOPIC, TOPOGRAPHICAL, TRAIT. 3. (M. Wertheimer, K. Koffka, W. Köhler, & G. Katona) In Gestalt psychology: (a) In perception, the active recognition of meaningful patterns and whole-relations. (b) In thinking, an insight into the structure or central features of a problem. A productive solution may entail a structural reorganization of the problem such that irrelevant details have been stripped away, that central features have become salient, and that the situation or problem is seen more veridically. See SUBJECTIVE ORGANIZATION, VISUAL ORGANIZATION. See also LIBIDO ORGANIZATION, PREGENITAL ORGANIZATION.

organizational behavior modification   Application of learning theory principles to effect organizational changes.

organizational chart   See ORGANIZATIONAL STRUCTURE.

organizational citizenship behavior   Activity that goes beyond the formal job requirements to benefit the organization.

organizational climate   The sum of shared opinions of individuals in any organization about the status of the organization as a place to work in, or otherwise participate in the organization.

organizational commitment   Acceptance of the organization's goals, willingness to extend the self for the organization, desire to remain with it, and a feeling of loyalty, dedication, and emotional attachment to it. Usually measured with self-report scales.

organizational culture   The generally unwritten but shared assumptions, beliefs, and values that characterize an organization.

organizational culture profile   (C. A. O'Reilly, J. Chatman, & D. Caldwell) A Q-sort test to measure organizational culture with 54 "value statements."

organizational delinquency   (T. Hogan & R. Hogan) Counterproductive behavior such as theft.

organizational development   A planned, often ongoing effort to alter an organization to be more effective and pleasant to work in.

organizational effectiveness   Ability of an organization to meet the needs of the organization and of its members.

organizational humanism   An extension of the humanistic movement of the 1950s and 1960s into an organizational context. An extension of the human relations movement that, for instance, warns against continued hierarchical and manipulative control in the guise of valuing individuality and diversity.

organizational identification   (H. A. Simon) Attachment to a social group (family, organization, ethnic group, nation, or other) that leads individuals to make decisions wholly or partly in terms of their advancement of the group goals. Identification has its roots both in emotion and in cognition (bounded rationality). See BOUNDED RATIONALITY.

organizational justice   The applications of principles of distributive and procedural justice within an organization.

organizational politics   The enhancement or protection of personal interests though using power, influence, or other actions that are not officially sanctioned by the organization, often one that lacks clear policies. Techniques include blaming and attacking others, controlling access to information, image building, cultivating supporters, and aligning with powerful others.

organizational reach   (M. Mann) The influences of corporations over many people in diverse locations.

organizational structure   The formal interrelationships that define the hierarchy and often communication channels within an organization, generally depicted on an organizational chart.

organized play   Structured play supervised by a teacher, group leader, or therapist, conducted along lines established by the leader in contrast to free play. See PLAY.

organized serial-killer   A type of serial killer who meticulously plans and carries out murders, often using his or her, own weapon, then removing it from the scene. Compare DISORGANIZED SERIAL-KILLER.

organizing   In labor relations, forming a union.

organizing effect   The long-lasting effect of hormones during a critical period in early development.

organ jargon   (A. Adler) Somatic symptoms, such as gastro-intestinal disorders, considered a weakness wrongly attributed to women, being weak. Also known as body language, organ language.

organ language/speech   Somatic expressions of emotional conflict or disturbance, for example, difficulty in swallowing may represent an unpalatable situation; an asthmatic episode may symbolize a load on the chest; itching may symbolize irritation or that "something has gotten under the person's skin." Often used interchangeably with body language. Also known as hypochondriac language. See BODY LANGUAGE.

organ neurosis   A psychoanalytic phrase for a functional disorder in which a physiological change occurs, that is, for what has been called a psychosomatic or psychophysiologic disorder, a somatoform disorder. Phrase is not usually applied to conversion (hysterical) disorders but may include such conditions as migraine, peptic ulcer, hyperthyroidism, essential hypertension, bronchial asthma, and ulcerative colitis. See ORGAN JARGON.

organ of Corti   (A. C. Corti) A ridge of specialized cells on the floor of the spiral bony cavity of the cochlea. Contains four rows of internal and external auditory-hair cells that respond to different sound frequencies, and fire neural impulses that produce auditory sensations. The hair cells communicate with the vestibulocochlear (eighth cranial) nerve. Also known as acoustic papilla, spiral organ.

organogenesis   1. Formation of organs during development. Also known as organogeny. 2. A beginning in organic or somatic tissue. How bodily tissues begin to have a behavioral effect, for example, aphasia may originate in a cortical lesion in the parolfactory area. Also known as somatogenesis.

organogenetic period   The first six to eight weeks of human pregnancy, during which the embryo develops from a (fertilized egg) zygote into a complex organism. See ORGANOKINETIC PERIOD, SOMATOGENESIS.

organogeny   **organogenesis** (meaning 1)

organokinetic period   The last seven months of human pregnancy, following the organogenetic period.

organoleptic analysis   Phrase used by the American Food and Drug Administration for smelling.

organon   1. See ORGAN. 2. A body of principles by means of which knowledge may be acquired or produced, for example, the Bible.

organotherapy   Treatment that uses substances normally produced by body organs, such as the administration of insulin in the treatment of diabetes, or of hormones in hormone replacement therapy.

organ pleasure   In psychoanalytic theory, the pleasure and arousal associated with stimulation of the erogenous zones and organs (oral, anal, urethral, skin, muscle, breast, genital areas).

organ specificity hypothesis   A postulate that the patient suffering from psychosomatic disorders unconsciously selects a particular organ or part of the body (such as stomach for ulcers, skin for hives) to be the physical manifestation of the patient's stress or tension that has not been otherwise discharged.

orgasm Sexual climax characterized by experiencing paroxysmal reactions that release sexual tension. Can occur in masturbation or any other kind of sexual activity. The peak period of sexual excitement lasts less than one minute in most males and females. Males ordinarily eject semen. An orgasm is also characterized by increased blood pressure and heart rate, and a mild diminition of lucidity. Orgasmic potential is highest in men around the age of 18 and in women at around 35. Also known as climax, coming. Types of orgasm include: A-FRAME, ALIMENTARY, DRY, INHIBITED, INHIBITED FEMALE, INHIBITED MALE, PHARMACOGENIC, REICHIAN, VAGINAL, VULVAL. See ACME, EJACULATION, EJACULATION PHYSIOLOGY, SEXUAL-RESPONSE CYCLE.

orgasm disclosure ratio In sex therapy, the number of people who have witnessed a person experience an orgasm in a given time period divided by the total number of people with whom the person is sexually interacting within that time frame.

orgasmic Pertaining to an orgasm. Also known as orgastic.

orgasmic dysfunction See INHIBITED FEMALE ORGASM, INHIBITED MALE ORGASM.

orgasmic phase See SEXUAL-RESPONSE CYCLE.

orgasmic platform In sexual arousal of the human female, the thickening of the walls and the tightening and elevation of the outer third of the vagina due to vasocongestion of the vestibular bulbs.

orgasmic reconditioning/reorientation A behavior-modification technique used in sex therapy, in which the usual unsuitable and undesirable fantasies or pictorial representations are employed to arouse the patient (such as pictures of young naked children) who then masturbates. These stimuli are gradually replaced by more conventional sexual representations, at first just before orgasm, and later at progressively earlier points, to develop normal patterns of arousal.

orgasmic reorientation orgasmic reconditioning

orgasmic stage (W. Masters & V. Johnson) The third phase of the four-phase sexual response cycle, during which orgasm occurs, followed by the fourth stage, resolution. See ORGASM, SEXUAL-RESPONSE CYCLE.

orgastic orgasmic

orgastic impotence Inability of the male to achieve orgasm in spite of normal erection. Thought to be due to anxiety, such as the unconscious fear of "letting go," or of losing an important product of the body; considered a difficult-to-treat disorder. See IMPOTENCE.

orgastic potency The ability of the male or female to achieve full orgasm during the sex act. Considered by Wilhelm Reich as a sign of mental health. See ORGONE THERAPY, IMPOTENCY.

orgiastic Pertaining to a situation characterized by indulgence, revelry, frenzy, and indiscriminate sexual behavior.

orgone (energy) A "life energy" or supposed force that permeates the universe, present in healthy bodies and concentrated in the sexual organs during sexual activity. The orgone, Wilhelm Reich held, was related to cosmic radiation, and he speculated that it might be responsible for the origin of life from earth and water (biogenesis), as well as the formation of hurricanes, tornadoes, and galaxies. See BION.

orgone accumulator/box A box resembling a telephone booth designed by Wilhelm Reich, in which the patient sits or lies in for the purpose of capturing vital "orgone" energy, concentrating its power on the sex organs as a means of restoring full orgastic potency as well as curing several diseases.

orgone box orgone accumulator

orgone therapy A therapeutic approach of Wilhelm Reich based on the concept that the achievement of "full orgastic potency" is the key to psychological well-being. The orgasm, he assumed, is the emotional-energy regulator of the body, whose purpose is to dissipate sexual tensions that would otherwise be transformed into neuroses. Also known as vegetotherapy. See CHARACTER-ANALYTIC VEGETOTHERAPY.

orgonomy 1. The natural science of orgone energy and its functions. 2. Name of a new "science" based on Wilhelm Reich's theory of life energy. Two aspects of this approach were the psychological or psychiatric orgone therapy (originally called character analytic vegetotherapy and orgone therapy), that employed the orgone accumulator/box. See CHARACTER-ANALYTIC VEGETOTHERAPY.

orgy 1. A social gathering marked by revelry, including unrestrained sexual indulgence. 2. Wild indiscriminate destructive activity. Derived from a term originally employed to identify ceremonies held by the ancient Greek and Roman populations to honor their deities. See APOLLONIAN, DIONYSIAN.

Oriental nightmare-death syndrome *Bangungut*

Oriental psychology Asian psychology

orientation 1. Awareness of the self and of outer reality; the ability to identify the self and to recognize the time, the place, and the person spoken with. Types include: AUTOPSYCHIC, DIS-, DOUBLE, REALITY. 2. In industrial psychology, the process of introducing an applicant or employee to the job situation. See INSTRUMENTAL ORIENTATION. 3. In environmental psychology, the process of adaptation to a setting, such as a home, neighborhood, or community. Established by familiarization with details of the setting so that movement and use do not depend upon the use of memory cues, such as maps. See ADAPTIVE BEHAVIOR. 4. An organism's position in space. See SPACE ORIENTATION. 5. A tendency to move toward a source of stimulation. See GOAL ORIENTATION(meaning 1). 6. A person's general approach, ideology, or point of view. Types include: CONTROL, DEFECT, EXPLOITATIVE, GOAL, GOOD-BOY-NICE-GIRL, HEDONISTIC, HOARDING, INSTRUMENTAL, LAW-AND-ORDER, LEGALISTIC, MARKETING, NAIVE EGOTISTIC, OBJECTIVE, ORAL, PRODUCTIVE, REALITY, RECEPTIVE, SEXUAL, SPATIAL, SUBJECTIVE.

orientation disorders Confusion as to time, place, personal identity, or situation. See DISORIENTATION.

orienting reaction Behavior, often fight or flight, following the orienting reflex, involving heightened alertness and behavioral orientation to the total environment.

orienting reflex An unconscious tendency of the body to adjust itself in certain directions to maximize and assimilate stimuli seen, heard, or smelled. See TAXIS.

orienting response A behavioral and physiological reaction to a novel, unexpected, or threatening stimulus. Also known as general arousal.

origence   A personality trait found in creative people emphasizing individuality and rejection of conventionality.

original cause   The initial or "first" cause in a sequence of events that leads to some causal effect.

original nature   The sum-total of characters or traits inherited by an organism.

original position   A hypothetical situation: How would people in a new society (for example, on a deserted island) begin to establish a moral code?

original response (O)   In Rorschach test scoring, any response that occurs fewer than once in 100 participants, regardless of the goodness of its form. Original responses of good quality are stated to indicate superior intelligence or creativity but those of poor quality are considered an indication of mental disorders. Quality is, of course, a subjective judgment of the examiner who may decide it is of good quality if the examiner can see what the participant sees.

original score   Raw score.

original sin   In Christian theology, the sin of disobedience, committed by Adam; the consequence was the loss of innocence and expulsion from paradise. In Catholic and some other Christian theologies, the state in which all humans are born.

origin-of-language theories   Attempts to explain how humans developed language. Examples are the pooh-pooh (or exclamation or interjectional) theory (L. H. Gray), which sees the beginnings of language in interjections that express emotions; ding-dong (or nativistic) theory (M. Maller), which holds that speech began with vocal expressions that were given to the encounter of objects; yo-he-ho theory (L. Noird), according to which speech began as outcries under the strain of work; ta-ta theory (R. Paget), which sees the origin of language in combinations of gestures and tongue movements; and sing-song theory (O. Jespersen), holding that language evolved from inarticulate chants of ritualistic nature. Among numerous other theories, most deal with human imitation of animal and other natural sounds, including the animal-cry, onomatopoeic, cuckoo, bow-wow, and the hey-nonny-nonny theories. All are speculative, as the earliest written records are about 4,000 years old, whereas language probably originated a million years ago. See ANIMAL CRY, ATAVISM, BOW WOW, CUCKOO, DING DONG, EXCLAMATION, HEY-NONNY-NONNY, ONOMATOPOEIC, POOH-POOH, SING-SONG, TA-TA, YO-HE-HO.

Orleans-Hanna Algebra Prognosis Test   Work-sample tests in which students are provided with sample material to learn and are immediately tested on it. Similar to Orleans-Hanna Geometry Prognosis Test.

Orne effect   Martin Orne demonstrated that if participants know what a researcher is looking for, they will often behave accordingly. Also known as good subject effect. See DEMAND CHARACTERISTICS.

ornithophobia   Morbid fear of birds. Also known as bird fear.

orofacial dyskinesia (OFD)   A behavior pattern observed in aging patients who make chewing, mouthing, and tongue movements that resemble symptoms of tardive dyskinesia. The patients usually are toothless and suffer from chronic institutionalization and dementia.

Ortgeist   Influence of a given culture upon theories and research, as compared with Zeitgeist, influence of a given historical era on theories and research. See ZEITGEIST.

orthergasia   (A. Meyer) Synonym for euergasia. Adolf Meyer used both terms to denote normal psychobiological, or mental, functioning.

orthobiosis   Correct living, both hygienically and morally.

orthodox analysis   psychoanalysis (meaning 3)

orthodox psychoanalysis   Psychoanalytic treatment that adheres, without modification, to Sigmund Freud's basic procedures (such as free association, dream interpretation, analysis of resistance, and transference) as well as to his basic aim of developing insight into unconscious sources of emotional problems to help patients restructure their personality. See PSYCHOANALYSIS (meaning 3).

orthodox sleep   nonrapid-eye-movement (NREM) sleep

orthodromic activation of nerve impulses   Refers to the normal direction of conduction of nerve impulses from the cell body to the end of the nerve fiber. See ANTIDROMIC ACTIVATION OF NERVE IMPULSES.

orthogenesis   A theory that evolution has an intrinsic direction and successive generations follow the same plan regardless of natural selection. See EVOLUTION, EVOLUTIONARY THEORY.

orthogenetic principle   A theory that the perception of shapes, forms, objects, and stimuli follows a specific and predictable life-span trend. Early in life, children perceive the world in a diffuse or global manner; as they get older, they learn to integrate the parts of the stimulus pattern with the whole stimulus pattern simultaneously in relation to each other.

orthogenital   Sexually normal.

orthognathic   Pertaining to a facial profile angle of 85° to 93° with the forehead and upper and lower jaws forming an approximately vertical line. Also known as orthognathous.

orthogonal   At 90° angles to each other; independent; unrelated. In factor analysis, axes may be either oblique (correlated) or orthogonal (uncorrelated). See OBLIQUE.

orthogonal Latin square   See GRECO-LATIN SQUARE DESIGN.

orthogonal polynomial   Relating to an algebraic expression that has many terms whose axes are at 90° angles with one another. Used in the analysis of data for trend.

orthogonal rotation   In a factor analysis, a rotation that maintains the independence of factors; that is, the angles between factors are kept at 0°.

orthogonal solution   1. Factors at 90° angles to each other, and consequently not correlated. 2. (E. Oetting) Eugene Oetting's orthogonal model of identity, indicating that each individual can maintain multiple cultural identities at the same time and need not be limited to a single cultural identity. See FACTOR ANALYSIS.

orthographic dysgraphia   A disorder characterized by ability to correctly spell only words that have a regular spelling.

ortho-kinesis Movement regulated by the amount of stimulation.

orthology The study of the use of language concentrating on the meaning of words and the proper way of connecting words to words to generate meaning.

orthomolecular psychiatry The treatment of personality problems by administering combinations of chemicals. A controversial approach to psychiatric treatment based on the theory that mental disorders are due to biochemical abnormalities that result in an increased need for specific substances. This need is determined by medical tests; treatment consists of the administration of large doses of vitamins (megavitamin therapy), trace elements, or other substances. It has not been proven or conclusively shown to be effective in the long run. See MEGAVITAMIN THERAPY.

orthonasia (K. R. Eissler) Term applied to a program in which children are taught about death as a part of life, to enable them to incorporate healthy attitudes toward death in their coping repertoire. See ANTICIPATORY MOURNING, DEATH NEUROSIS.

orthopedic disorder Any anatomical or functional abnormality of the musculoskeletal system, either congenital or acquired. Examples are torticollis, clubfoot, and scoliosis. See CONGENITAL ORTHOPEDIC CONDITION.

orthopsychiatry An interdisciplinary approach to mental health, in which psychiatrists, psychologists, social workers, pediatricians, sociologists, nurses, and educators collaborate on the study and treatment of emotional and behavioral problems before these problems become severe and disabling. The approach is basically prophylactic, emphasizing child development, family life, and mental hygiene.

orthoptics An eye-exercise program designed to train patients with extraocular muscle imbalance to coordinate the vision in the left and right eyes.

Ortho-Rater An instrument used for testing visual functioning.

orthostatic epileptoid Obsolete phrase referring to children who experience fainting spells and occasional convulsions after arising in the morning or maintaining a standing posture for a long period.

orthostatic hypotension Lowered blood pressure when standing up, often accompanied by lightheadedness or even fainting, an occasional side effect of certain psychotropic and other types of medicine.

orthotics-prosthetics The design, manufacture, and tailoring of prostheses or orthopedic appliances for persons with physical disabilities, such as a heart pacemaker or an artificial hand controlled by voluntary nerve impulses.

orthotist A technician who makes and fits braces for orthopedic patients. See PROSTHETIST.

orthriogenesis (P. Federn) Full restoration of the ego at the moment of awakening as the cathexis, which vanished during deep sleep, has its function restored.

oscillograph An instrument that graphically records wave forms of electrical energy.

oscillometer An instrument used in measuring oscillation, or changes in arterial pulsation, primarily of the extremities.

oscilloscope An electric device that displays visually an electrical or sound wave on a fluorescent screen.

Oseretsky Tests of Motor Abilities (N. I. Oseretsky) Tests that measure motor abilities in children.

OSHA See OCCUPATIONAL SAFETY AND HEALTH ACT.

osmolagnia Sexual arousal from odors. See OLFACTOPHILIA.

osmometer 1. A device that measures osmosis, the flow of a solute from an area of higher to lower density across a semipermeable membrane. 2. A device that measures the sense of smell, in this case it is also known as an osphresiometer.

osmophobia olfactophobia

osmoreceptor A receptor presumed to exist in the brain for the purpose of measuring the concentration of various substances, notably salt in the body's extracellular fluid. Considered to account for thirst motivation.

osmotic thirst A need to drink resulting from loss of cellular fluids affecting osmotic pressure levels resulting in dehydration. Also known as osmometric thirst.

OSPE Ohio State Psychological Examination

osphresiolagnia Morbid or fetishistic interest in odors. Frequently associated with infantile sexuality. See RENIFLEUR.

osphresiometer See OSMOMETER (meaning 2).

osphresiophilia Abnormal attraction to odors and smells.

osphresiophobia olfactophobia

osphresis Olfaction.

OSS See OFFICE OF STRATEGIC SERVICES ASSESSMENT.

ossicles (Empedocles of Agrigentum) Any small bones but particularly the chain of three tiny bones in the middle ear that transmit sound-wave vibrations from the tympanic membrane facing the external environment to the oval window of the inner ear, where the organ of Corti is located. The middle-ear ossicles are the incus, malleus, and stapes.

osteopathy A recognized, scientific system of medical practice based on the concept that disorders of body and mind are a function of body malfunctions or distortions of structure that can be returned to health chiefly by manipulation of the body, although medications and surgery may be used. Compare ALLOPATHY, HOMEOPATHY.

Ostwald color system (F. W. Ostwald) The organization of chromatic and achromatic samples, consisting of 24 hues arranged around the outside of a circle with the complementary colors for each hue located along the circle's diameters. By combining adjacent colors, any color on the Ostwald scale can be produced. Also known as Ostwald Color Atlas. See COLOR CIRCLE.

OT occupational therapy or occupational therapist (also abbreviated **O.T.**)

OTA Office of Technology Assessment (U.S. Congress)

OTC See OVER-THE-COUNTER DRUG.

Othello syndrome Paranoid jealousy in which a spouse, usually the wife, is suspected of sexual infidelity, triggering rage and violence. Derived from Shakespeare's Othello, who killed his wife Desdemona, who was actually faithful to him. See CONJUGAL DELUSION.

other-directed (D. Riesman) Refers to persons whose values, goals, and behavior stem primarily from identification with group or collective standards in contrast to individually defined standards. According to David Riesman, other-directedness is increasing in contemporary society. Also known as outer-directed. See INNER-DIRECTED, TRADITION-DIRECTED.

other-enhancement See IMPRESSION MANAGEMENT.

other-race face perception effect The finding that recognition memory is better for faces of the "race" the person belongs to than for people of other races. Also known as own-race bias.

others See SIGNIFICANT OTHERS.

other-total ratio (OTR) (B. Mullen) In group dynamics, a formula that assumes that self-awareness depends upon the ratio of the total number of group members (T) to the number of people in the majority (O) on some issue.

Otis-Lennon School Ability Test (OLSAT) (A. S. Otis & R. T. Lennon) A test designed to measure reasoning ability using verbal and nonverbal materials. Items are of the pictorial, verbal, figural and quantitative type.

Otis Quick-Scoring Mental Ability Tests (A. S. Otis) A series of group intelligence tests, designed to measure intelligence in grades one through four, four through nine, and nine through sixteen (college). The tests served as the model for the Army Alpha and Beta tests.

otogenic tone 1. A sound generated within the ear. 2. A tone that arises from within the auditory mechanism rather than from an external stimulus. Also known as subjective tone. See ACOUSMA, TINNITUS.

otohemineurasthenia A unilateral deafness for which no organic cause can be found.

otoliths (G. Breschet) Tiny calcium particles in the gelatinous membrane of the acoustic macula of the inner ear. The force of gravity on the otoliths stimulates neighboring nerve receptors which translate the stimuli into information about the position of the animal in space, or in water. Also known as otoconia, statoconia.

otology The science of the mechanisms of hearing.

otosclerosis A formation of spongy bone that develops in the middle ear and immobilizes the stapes at the point of attachment to the oval window facing the inner ear. Causes progressive deafness as the ossicles fail to transmit vibrations from the tympanic membrane to the inner ear. It is considered hereditary.

OTR other-total ratio

Ouija board (From the French and German words for "yes," *oui* and *ja*.) A trademark for a board painted with numbers and letters. A movable pointer, allegedly influenced by supernatural forces, spells out messages through the hands of the person holding the pointer. Often seen as a form of automatic writing.

outbreeding 1. Introduction of new ideas or customs into a social group. 2. Mating outside one's own group. See HYBRID VIGOR.

outcome 1. The end result. 2. In game theory, outcome determines a particular set of payments, one set being paid to each participant. 3. In experimental psychology, the dependent variable in the research indicating the degree of response basic to experimental prediction. Outcomes of an experiment are also known as elementary events, simple events.

outcome criteria Establishment of standards to determine the effectiveness of any method of treatment.

outcome dependence In negotiation, reliance on others to agree to a person's proposals. Since both sides commit to an agreement, each depends on the others to reach it.

outcome evaluation In evaluation research, a process to decide whether the program achieved its stated goals. A randomized, controlled experimental model is the ideal model generally agreed upon for evaluating the effectiveness of a program outcome. (In realistic evaluation situations, the degree of rigidity needed to apply these statistical methods with confidence is rarely achieved.)

outcome expectations (A. Bandura) People's beliefs that given courses of action will lead to particular outcomes. The outcomes may be material, social, or self-evaluative. See SOCIAL COGNITIVE THEORY.

outcome interdependence In negotiation, the positive correlation between group goals and the rewards directing an individual's actions; everyone's goals are furthered when an individual's goals are reached or rewarded.

outcome-referenced scores The expression of performance in terms of a predicted outcome or behavior. For instance, when interpreting scores on an interest inventory, it might be said that the respondent's interests were similar to those of architects.

outcome research/study A systematic investigation of the efficacy of a therapeutic technique, or of the comparative efficacy of different techniques, with one or more disorders.

outdoor training programs Controversial exercises designed to provide managers, management teams, and work groups with experiential training in leadership and teamwork skills through structured outdoor activities.

outer boundary (P. Federn) A flexible boundary that exists between the ego and the outside world. If the outer boundary is blurred, the person experiences a feeling of unreality. See EGO BOUNDARY, INNER BOUNDARY.

outercourse Sexual behavior other than sexual intercourse. Term was coined in the late 1980s to counter the phallocentrism of the American culture and to promote noncoital forms of pleasuring. See FOREPLAY, PETTING BEHAVIOR.

outer-directed (D. Riesman) Being strongly affected by the social environment. A conformist. Also known as other-directed. Compare INNER-DIRECTED.

outer-directed (person) An individual who is readily influenced and guided by the attitudes and values of other people. Compare INNER-DIRECTED (PERSON).

outer ear External ear.

outer granular layer The fifth layer in the retina of the human eye.

outer hair cells external hair cells (of ear)

outer plexiform layer   The outer synaptic layer of the retina where rods and cones make contact with bipolar cells.

outgroup   A group to which a person does not belong. Compare INGROUP.

out-group   Persons or groups outside or excluded from membership in a specified in-group. Use of the term implies that the person has or is temporarily adopting the perspective of the in-group member. Also known as they-group. Compare IN-GROUP.

outgroup extremity effect   A situation in which a person's evaluations of outgroup members are more extreme than their evaluations of members of their own group. Compare INGROUP EXTREMITY EFFECT.

outgroup homogeneity bias   A tendency of members of a group to assume more similarity of members of an outgroup than there is.

outing   1. Self-revelation of being gay or lesbian to one's own family or the public. 2. Disclosing the sexual orientation of a closet homosexual. 3. The campaign of the AIDS Coalition to Unleash Power (ACT-UP) to threaten to publicly reveal gay and lesbian politicians in order to force more governmental AIDS (acquired immunodeficiency syndrome) research funding.

outlier   Data that are outside normal extremes or not representative.

out-of-body experience (OBE)   1. In parapsychology, a dissociative experience characterized by imagining that the soul or spirit has left the body and is acting or perceiving on its own. It is a neurologic phenomenon that may occur when death is imminent, and in some cases can be induced by the suggestion of a medium, or "sensitive," or by the use of hallucinogens, notably phencyclidine. 2. Awareness of being outside of one's own body.

out-of-the-box   Slang for basic or original; by extension, simple or unadorned.

outpatient   An ambulatory patient whose physical or mental disorder can be treated without the need for confinement in a hospital, clinic, or other facility.

outpatient commitment   Placement in a hospital via a legal decision that an out patient/in patient needs psychiatric or psychological care. In the United States, every state has a law for doing so, usually involves a complaint that is approved by a judge and usually one or more physicians. See INVOLUNTARY COMMITMENT.

outpatient services   Services performed for ambulatory patients in hospital units, clinics, and mental-health centers. Include group and individual therapy, family therapy, psychological evaluation, emergency psychiatric diagnosis and treatment, home treatment, and social case work.

outplacement counseling   (P. Pedersen) The providing of psychological support, assistance, and advice to persons voluntarily or involuntarily leaving their position of employment.

output   1. That which is produced. 2. The level or degree of work performance completed, often within a given amount of time. 3. A communication that conveys a signal to another person or another part of the communications system. 4. In cybernetics, the response of an organism or mechanism.

output interference   In learning theory, the lower likelihood of recalling additional items after recalling the initial ones, because the recalled items interfere with the ability to recall others.

outreach counseling   Professional advice provided outside of a traditional office, such as going in the field and interviewing and counseling people in the street, in clubs, or playgrounds.

outreach services   Services for the mentally ill, including aftercare for discharged mental patients living in the community, provided by a mental hospital or community mental-health center. Include medication maintenance, home visits, emergency treatment, supportive psychotherapy, and social services provided by case workers and case managers.

outshining hypothesis   In recognition tasks, a postulate for why context effects are not reliably observed; if an item is a strong cue it will overpower the context cue.

outside density   The number of persons per acre; population density within a community. A relationship has been found between outside density and social pathology. Compare INSIDE DENSITY.

outsider   An isolate.

outsight   (K. Rigney) Understanding another or others in depth, comprehending their background, thoughts, motives. It is more intellectual than empathic. See INSIGHT.

Outward Bound   An organization that organizes wilderness survival training exercises to foster teamwork, communication, and trust. See OUTDOOR TRAINING PROGRAMS.

outwork   Work performed outside the normal main workplace. Includes any work contracted to be performed in small shops, other factories, or the home. See HOMEWORK.

OV   1. organic variable. 2. organismic variable.

ova   Plural of ovum.

oval window   (Fallopius) A membrane on the surface of the cochlea which receives sound vibrations transmitted through the middle ear. The stapes, the third bone in the chain of ossicles, is attached to the oval window. The cochlea is fluid-filled, and movements by the stapes are translated from air-pressure to water-pressure changes by the oval window. Also known as fenestra ovalis, fenestra vestibuli.

O variable   organic variable

ovarian cycle   The pattern of physiological functions in the ovary associated with the menstrual cycle. The major physiological change during the ovarian cycle is the development of the egg follicle which evolves into a temporary endocrine gland, the corpus luteum, after ovulation.

ovarian hormone   See ESTROGEN.

ovarian pregnancy   Ectopic pregnancy in which the embryo implants in the ovary.

ovary   An almond-shaped female gonad located on either side of the uterus in the lower abdomen. The ovaries of the prepubertal female contain about 350,000 immature ova, of which fewer than 400 will develop into mature ova to be released at a rate of about one per month between menarche and menopause.

overachiever   A person, usually a student, who achieves above the capacity calculated by aptitude and general-intelligence tests. Overachievement appears to be mainly a phenomenon of the middle classes, and has been noted more frequently in females than in males. See UNDERACHIEVER.

overactivity   Excessive, restless activity especially as a defense against anxiety or as an expression of a manic state. Usually less extreme than hyperactivity. See FLIGHT INTO REALITY.

overage   Characterizing a person beyond the average or usual age associated with a given behavior or trait. Usually, applies to a child or student who is chronologically older than the others in the grade. Underage in this context refers to a student who is younger than the other classmates.

overambition   Wanting to be much more than a person really is or could be. A basic reason for neurosis, according to Alfred Adler. See CENTRAL CONFLICT.

overanxious disorder   A diagnosis for a condition of persistent and generalized anxiety, tension, and apprehension of childhood, often manifested as being fearful of making mistakes, possibly due to over-critical and over-demanding parents.

overattribution   (E. E. Jones) In social psychology, a tendency for observers to make biased attributions about an individual even though the person's actions are constrained by the situation. See FUNDAMENTAL ATTRIBUTION ERROR.

overbreathing   See HYPERVENTILATION.

overcharged idea   A conflict that continually manifests itself in a person's dreams in the form of various symbols and identifications because it is, in effect, overcharged with repressed psychic energy.

overcompensation   1. More than balancing a deficiency. 2. An excessive reaction to any situation or condition; more activity than necessary to meet a deficiency. 3. Denoting a pathological need for dominance. 4. (A. Adler) An extreme, neurotic striving for power and self-aggrandizement motivated by an inferiority complex; overcompetitive, overaggressive behavior in response to feelings of inadequacy. A key concept of Adlerian psychology. See INFERIORITY COMPLEX, MASCULINE PROTEST. 5. See COMPENSATION.

overconfidence   (B. Fischoff et al.) A tendency to be more certain than called for that own predictions or answers to questions are accurate.

overcontrolled   1. Identifying a cluster of childhood behavior symptoms or behavior deficits resulting from strict parental supervision. Overcontrolled children are usually internalizers with feelings of shyness and being unloved, and may complain of fears and tenseness. 2. Refers to adults who are extremely concerned with being proper in all respects.

Overcontrolled-Hostility scale   A scale on the Minnesota Multiphasic Personality Inventory, high scores on which are associated with aggression and violence. Also known as O-H scale.

overcorrection   In therapy, a technique used when a person displays inappropriate behavior, the person is asked to repeat the behavior in a more appropriate, but exaggerated, manner.

overcrowding   A higher concentration of organisms per unit of space than is customary for a given species. Experimental overcrowding conditions significantly increase abnormal behavior and aggression in rats even when enough resources preclude the need for competition. In humans, overcrowding is associated with stress patterns, for example, stimulus overload.

over-determination   1. In psychoanalytic theory, a concept that several factors may collaborate to produce a single symptom, dream, disorder, or aspect of behavior. 2. Sigmund Freud's theory that all events have more than one meaning or explanation. 3. The ascribing of many meanings to the elements of a dream or neurotic symptom.

overdose (OD or **O.D.)**   1. Taking a greater dosage of a drug than is recommended or prescribed. 2. Taking too much of a drug such that, without medical intervention, doing so usually results in death. Phrase used particularly in cases of death by illicit substance use, whether accidental or suicidal.

overeating   See HYPERPHAGIA.

overexclusion   Attitude of a personality type with a narrow focus on what is morally right and proper, a person who has little "give": a martinet.

overextension   1. Hyperextension. 2. A tendency of young children, as they begin to relate concepts to words, to extend a word beyond its specific meaning, for example, to refer to all animals as "doggie."

overgeneralization   1. Constructing a general rule from isolated incidents and applying it too broadly. 2. The pattern seen in the language of young children in which they apply a standard rule to all instances, even when an exception is required. 3. In language using few words to cover a multitude of items, such as all females are girls, all acquaintances are Bill, all animals are cute. Found in the extremely young and the extremely old. Also known as overregularization. See OVEREXTENSION (meaning 2).

overhabituation   (L. E. Gardner) A type of overtraining due to the continuation of habituation training after the response stabilizes or disappears, resulting in slower spontaneous recovery.

overhelping   Unneeded help given to others, often to make them appear incompetent.

overinclusion   (N. Cameron) Inability of a person to stop a certain unnecessary or inefficient action from a sequence of actions following a particular stimulus.

overjustification effect   Disregarding the intrinsic motivation for a behavior by providing an extrinsic rationale; a tendency, on being promised a reward for doing what the person already likes doing, to see the reward, rather than intrinsic interest, as the motivation for performing the task.

overlap   Monocular cue for perceiving distance; nearby objects partially block the view of more distant objects. Also known as interposition, because nearby objects are interposed between the eyes and more distant objects.

overlap hypothesis   (J. E. Anderson) In psychometrics, explains the increasing consistency of intelligence quotient (IQ) scores as participants become older, on the basis that knowledge and skills remain constant and therefore increasingly overlap with time.

overlapping membership See COMMUNICATION IN-TERLOCKS.

overlapping psychological situation Two (or more than two) events that occur at the same time, each demanding attention. Reactions can vary from a simple decision to complete frustration, depending on the character of the events.

overlearning (H. Ebbinghaus) 1. Learning past the point of just learning. 2. A result of constant repetition leading to memorization; for example, after not reciting the alphabet for many years a person can probably recite it quickly since it was overlearned in early childhood. 3. Continued rehearsal after the material has been learned. Can improve later retrieval.

overlearning reversal effect (A. J. North & D. T. Stimmel) An experimental result of a discrimination-learning-task experiment in which rats that had learned that a primary cue was to be avoided found it easier to shift to a new primary cue than did rats who had not undergone the former conditioning.

overloading Subjecting an organism to excessive stress, such as forcing it to handle or process an excessive amount of information in too short a period of time. See STIMULATION OVERLOAD.

overload principle In exercise physiology, a theory that a specific exercise overload in terms of some combination of training frequency, intensity, mode, and duration must be applied to effect physiologic improvement.

overmanning **overstaffing**

overorganization Redundancy in organization, as when there are too many rules, too many options for reaching goals, too much "red tape." See BUREAU-CRACY.

overpayment inequity Employees' perception that their compensation is worth more than their input.

overprotection Nontechnical term for parental behavior that is excessive but done under the guise of being a "good parent." This tends to harm a child's normal development.

overregulation A transient error in linguistic development in which the child attempts to make language more regular than it actually is, for example, by using "breaked" instead of "broken."

overresponse An abnormally strong reaction to a stimulus.

oversexed See NYMPHOMANIA, SATYRIASIS.

overshadowing Interference with the conditioning of a stimulus because of the simultaneous presence of another stimulus that is easier to condition. See MEMORY ILLUSIONS.

overshooting 1. In game theory, overestimating the likeliest event. 2. In perceptual-motor activity, passing beyond the intended or normal limit or position.

oversimplification Typified by rudimentary generalizations, arguing by anecdote, and "either-or" thinking.

overstaffing A condition in which the number of persons available for a program or function is well above the maintenance minimum. Once known as overmanning. Compare UNDERSTAFFING.

oversubmissiveness See COMPLIANCE.

overt behavior Actions directly observable by others.

over-the-counter (OTC) drug A drug available for sale without prescription.

overt homosexuality Gay or lesbian tendencies that are consciously recognized and openly expressed, in contrast to latent or unconscious homosexuality. See COMING OUT (OF THE CLOSET).

overt integrity test 1. Assessing the likelihood of dishonesty based on job applicants' thoughts, feelings, admissions of past dishonesty, and attitudes toward honesty and punishment. 2. An assessment of the likelihood of dishonesty, such as theft, by assessing the participant's thoughts, feelings, and expectations.

overt response Any observable or external reaction, for example, a response that can be seen or heard. The study of overt behavior is the province of behaviorists. Compare COVERT RESPONSE.

overt self How a person appears to others; generalizations that others would make about the individual's personality. See IDEAL SELF, OVERT SELF.

overtone A partial in a complex tone; any tone, other than the fundamental tone, of which a sound is composed. When the frequency of an overtone is an exact multiple of the fundamental tone, it is called a harmonic. See FOURIER SERIES.

overvalued idea A false or exaggerated belief maintained with less rigidity or duration than a delusion, for example, the conviction of being indispensable in an organization.

overwork Generally, working beyond the point of fatigue.

ovulation The release of a mature ovum from its ovarian follicle.

own control design An experimental design in which repeated measures are taken on the same subjects so that each serves as its own control. See REPEATED-MEASURES DESIGN, WITHIN-SUBJECTS DESIGN.

own race bias **other-race face perception effect**

Oxford index A weighting of wet-bulb (W) and dry-bulb (D) temperatures, also known as wet-dry (WD) index, in which $WD = 0.8W + 0.15D$.

oximeter A filter photometer attached to the ear and used for monitoring or measuring changes in arterial oxygen saturation without extracting blood.

oxycephaly A congenital syndrome characterized by a high, pointed shape of the skull. Also known as acrocephalia, acrocephaly.

oxygen debt The amount of oxygen required by the muscles after the beginning of work, above that which is supplied to them by the circulatory system.

P

p   1. probability (also abbreviated **P**). 2. percentile. See STATISTICAL SIGNIFICANCE. 3. percentage. 4. See PRACTICAL INTELLIGENCE. 5. proportion.

P   1. See PROBABILITY RATIO. 2. psychometrist. 3. Symbol indicating the degree of personality organization and ability. 4. See DRIVE STATE. 5. In Rorschach test scoring, a symbol for popular response. 6. See PERCEPTUAL SPEED. 7. Pharmacop(o)eia. 8. person.

P(A)   Symbol indicating the probability of event A. See PROBABILITY.

PA   See PSYCHOANALYSIS.

p(A/B)   Symbol indicating the conditional probability of A given B. See PROBABILITY.

PAC   professional advisory committee

pacemakers   Medical devices that help establish and maintain certain biological rhythms. Term usually is applied to cardiac pacemakers. Other pacemakers control uterine contractions or the rhythm of the movements of cilia. See THALAMIC PACEMAKER.

pacer stimulus   (W. N. Dember & R. W. Earl) A stimulus that becomes the ideal. See THEORY OF CHOICE.

Pacian corpuscle   (A. Vater, F. Pacini, F. G. Henle) One of the encapsulated sensory endings, it is one of the largest sensory receptors and will frequently have a diameter of 1 mm. Found subcutaneously in both hairy and nonhairy (glabrous) skin as well as in deep musculoskeletal tissue. They are especially prevalent below the skin of the digits. The Pacian corpuscle is sensitive to pressure and is rapidly adapting, that is, it responds to changes in pressure. The nonneural portion of the capsule is made of layered fibroblast-like cells surrounding an axon terminal. Other encapsulated skin receptors include Meissner's corpuscles, and Ruffini endings. Also known as Pacinian corpuscle, and Vater's corpuscles after German anatomist Abraham Vater (1684–1751).

Pacinian   Pertaining to Filippo Pacini.

Pacinian corpuscle   Pacian corpuscle

pacing   See EDUCATIONAL PACING.

PAD   primary affective disorder

pain   A common, unpleasant sensation evoked by a harmful stimulus. Pain is similar for everyone physiologically but widely varied in terms of behavioral response, interpretation, and, presumably, subjective experience. Acute pain is usually externally caused; chronic pain is more diffuse, generally endogenous, and long-lasting. See ENDORPHINS, GATE THEORY, PHANTOM PAIN, PSYCHIC PAIN, SUBSTANCE P.

pain pathways   Various (depending on the type of pain) afferent nerve conduits from the receptors to the central nervous system.

pain-pleasure principle   See PLEASURE-PAIN PRINCIPLE.

pain sense   A special sense found in virtually every part of the periphery and in many internal regions.

paint-sniffing   A form of substance abuse in which the fumes of paint, especially spray-paint, are persistently inhaled to produce a "high." See GLUE-SNIFFING, HUFFING, INHALANT-RELATED DISORDERS.

pain spot   A point on the skin peculiarly sensitive to hurtful stimuli, which has a much lower limen for pain than adjacent regions.

pain tolerance   The highest intensity of a pain stimulus that an organism will voluntarily endure. See DOLORIMETER.

pain threshold   The lowest intensity of a stimulus that a participant perceives as painful. See DOLORIMETER.

pair bonds   Strong, lifelong attachments that occur between two animals; it includes "love" when speaking of humans.

paired-associate learning (PAL)   A rote method used in verbal learning and retention studies whereby a participant must learn stimulus-response pairs of words or nonsense syllables. In a retention test, the participant attempts to recall the second item (response) when presented with the first item (stimulus); for example, upon hearing the word "brown" the participant is to respond "zebra." Also known as paired associate task. See ANTICIPATION LEARNING METHOD.

paired associates   1. Items paired in some manner so that one is the stimulus and the other the response. See JOST'S LAW (OF ASSOCIATES). 2. A common test of memory in which stimulus items (usually words) are presented in pairs, after which one becomes the stimulus and the other the response. See PAIRED-ASSOCIATE LEARNING.

paired associations   A method of research developed by Mary Calkins in which words are associated with other words in a procedure used to study human learning. See PRIMACY EFFECT.

paired comparisons (L. L. Thurstone) In psychophysics, a method that scales or places items based on psychological judgments, in terms of psychological distance. Mathematical assumptions are made from comparisons obtained from participants who must, of two stimuli, choose one over the other, such as the more preferred one, the more intense one.

paired comparisons (method) In consumer product testing, jury members choose the preferred of two products, then compare the preferred one with a third, continuing until all have been compared, yielding an overall rank order of preference.

pairing hypothesis A postulate that the mere presence of a stimulus when a response is reinforced is sufficient for that stimulus to gain control over the behavior.

pairmates Among animals (for example, titi monkeys), a male and a female that mate exclusively with each other and will generally remain together. Also known as established pair.

PAL 1. paired-associate learning. 2. Police Athletic League.

palatine reflex swallowing reflex

paleencephalon (L. Edinger) Old brain; evolutionarily-ancient part of the brain in certain organisms including humans, such as the cerebellum and other areas not related to the cerebrum. Also known as metameric nervous system. Compare NEENCEPHALON.

paleocerebellum (L. Edinger) From an evolutionary standpoint, an ancient part of the cerebellum (consisting of portions of both the anterior and posterior lobes) which regulates postural tone. Also known as spinocerebellum because of its close relationship to the spinal cord.

paleocortex The evolutionarily ancient cortex of the brain, primitive in structure, with approximately four layers, and located mainly on the brain's ventral surface. Sometimes known as archipallium, olfactory cortex.

paleontology A branch of biology which investigates organisms that existed in the past.

paleopallium The olfactory cortex. See PALEOCORTEX, PIRIFORM AREA.

paleopsychology 1. The study of unconscious psychological processes in contemporary people assumed to have originated in earlier stages of human evolution. 2. A reconstruction of the psychological reactions of prehistoric humans, for example, embalming the dead may have been done due to the belief that the dead might regain life. See COLLECTIVE UNCONSCIOUS.

paleospinothalamic tract A group of somatosensory fibers in the ventrolateral tracts that run directly into the intralaminar nuclei of the thalamus. Involved in both crude touch and pain sensations.

paleosymbols A symptom of schizophrenia characterized by a reversion to self-created idiosyncratic words or phrases, which appear to represent a return to the level of autistic expression of the young child. Remnants of common verbal symbols can frequently be detected, especially in the neologisms used by these patients.

paligraphia The obsessive repetition of letters, words, or phrases in writing. See PALINPHRASIA.

palilalia 1. A speech disorder characterized by repetition of words and phrases with increasing speed and loss of meaning. Frequently observed in Parkinson's and Alzheimer's diseases. 2. See PALIPHRASIA.

palilexia Abnormal frequent re-reading of words or phrases.

palilogia An obsessive repetition of utterances or spoken phrases. See PALIPHRASIA.

palimony A concept similar to alimony, the payment of money or other valuables to a member of a long-term romantic relationship, upon separation. Term originated as a contraction of pal and alimony.

palindexia A form of dyslexia in which words or sentences are read backwards. See STREPHOSYMBOLIA.

palingenesis Development of an individual organism, in so far as it epitomizes the separate stages in the evolution of its race or species.

palingraphia Backward writing. See MIRROR WRITING.

palinlexia A type of dyslexia characterized by backward reading, for example, "nip" for "pin," or "house my is this" for "this is my house." See STREPHOSYMBOLIA.

palinopsia Recurring visual hallucinations.

paliphrasia Involuntary repetition of words or phrases in speaking. Also known as palilalia, palinphrasia. See PALILOGIA.

paliopsy The brief persistence of a visual image of objects no longer in the patient's visual field. It is a diagnostic sign of a lesion in the occipital lobe.

pallesthesia Sensitivity to vibration, frequently tested by placing a tuning fork in contact with a bony surface of the skin. Also known as palmesthesia, palmesthesis. See VIBRATION EXPERIENCE.

palliative Easing or reducing pain or discomfort without removing the cause.

pallidohypothalamic tract A group of nerve fibers that links the globus pallidus to the hypothalamus. It is associated with the eating behavior of animals.

pallidum globus pallidus

palmar 1. In humans, refers to the palms of the hands. 2. In primates, refers to the four palms, the skin of which is hairless, ridged, and supplied with sweat glands driven by sympathetic nervous system arousal.

palmar conductance Skin of the ventral surface of the hand as a conductor of electricity. Palmar sweating is used in some lie-detector systems as an indication of anxiety. See GALVANIC SKIN RESPONSE.

palmar reflex/response Flexion of the fingers when the palm is scratched; the grasping response of the newborn.

palm-chin reflex See PALMOMENTAL REFLEX.

palmesthesia See PALLESTHESIA, VIBRATION EXPERIENCE.

palmistry A pseudoscience that interprets lines and other skin surface features of the palm as signs of personality traits or for predictions of the individual's future. An old occult concept, it is accepted as valid in many places and by many people. Also known as ch(e)iromancy, chirognomy, chirosophy. See ASTROLOGY.

palmomandibular sign   A reflex present in the neonate until about the tenth day of life, consisting of automatic opening of the mouth in response to pressure on the palms or forearm.

palmomental reflex   Contraction of the muscles of the chin, in a twitching motion, usually unilateral, although occasionally bilateral, produced by scratching the ipsilateral palm. Observed in some patients with toxic brain damage or frontal lobe organic lesions, but rarely occurs in normal persons after infancy. Also known as palm-chin reflex, pollicomental reflex.

palpebral fissure   A hypothetical line between the upper and lower eyelids. When the eyelids are open, the palpebral fissure forms an elliptical space. Also known as rima palpebrarum.

palpitation   Rapid, sometimes irregular heart beat associated with anxiety, stress, physical exertion and certain cardiac valvular abnormalities.

palsy   Obsolete term for paralysis. Term is still used in compound expressions such as cerebral palsy.

PAM   See PRECATEGORICAL ACOUSTIC STORAGE.

pamper   Providing extra special attention and care. Generally considered undesirable parental behavior. See MONKEY LOVE.

pampered style (of life)   A pattern of living characterized by doing little or nothing for others and either manipulating or forcing others into satisfying one's own needs. Alfred Adler stated that pampered children became hated children.

pampering   Raising children who will likely be unable to adjust to the normal stresses and strains of life by having everything done for them and being given whatever they want. This apparently loving behavior is thought by some psychologists to mask anger, hatred, or both, on the part of the adults who do the spoiling. See PAMPERED STYLE OF LIFE, SPOONFED.

PAN   positional alcohol nystagmus

pan(o)phobia   **pantophobia**

panacea   A remedy for all diseases and difficulties. A cure-all.

pan-anxiety   An all-pervading anxiety condition. Compare FREE-FLOATING ANXIETY.

pancreas   (Herophilus, C. Bernard) An endocrine (ductless) gland located along the lower wall of the stomach, between the duodenum and spleen. Contains alpha and beta cells, which release glucagon and insulin, controlling blood-sugar levels.

pandemic   Occurring universally or over a large area, as in several countries. Pandemic is more general than epidemic. See ENDEMIC.

pandemic child abuse   (D. Finkelhor) Common abuse of children by adults, physically and psychologically, usually by their parents, not severe enough to come to the attention of authorities and generally considered inconsequential by the parents.

pandemonium model   (O. Selfridge) In pattern recognition, a feature analysis model in which "demons" perform various information-processing tasks. It assesses the degree to which stimulus features are present and uses the information to determine the nature of the target stimuli.

panderer   **pimp**

panerotic   The potential for sexual arousal to arise from virtually any experience.

pangenesis   A theory of heredity proposed by Charles Darwin who held that traits were transmitted from parents by particles of each body organ or part concealed in the ovum and spermatozoon of the parents to the next generation. Holds that mental traits also were inherited by pangenesis.

panglossia   A type of abnormal garrulousness observed in psychotic patients, especially those in a manic state.

Panglossianism   A general personality feature relating to misplaced optimism, viewing life through rosy glasses regardless of reality. Based on Dr. Pangloss, a character in Voltaire's novel, *Candide*, who often stated "This is the best of all possible worlds." See FUNDAMENTAL POSTULATE, POLLYANNA ATTITUDE.

panic   An acute reaction characterized by terror, confusion, and irrational behavior, precipitated by a threatening situation such as an earthquake, fire, or being caught in a stalled elevator. Terror is increased by such factors as uncertainty, exhaustion, suggestion, frustration, and the hysterical behavior of other people. Types of panic include: HOMOSEXUAL, NEUROTIC INSANITY, PREPSYCHOTIC, PRIMORDIAL.

panic attack   An episode of acute anxiety and disorganization. See MAJOR DEPRESSION, PANIC DISORDER, SCHIZOPHRENIC DISORDERS, SOMATIZATION DISORDER.

panic disorder (PD)   A pathological condition marked by repeated panic attacks consisting of sudden apprehension or terror, and including such symptoms as dizziness, sweating, palpitations, shortness of breath, choking sensations, fear of dying or of going "crazy." See MAJOR DEPRESSION, PANIC, SCHIZOPHRENIC DISORDERS, SOMATIZATION DISORDER.

panmixis   In genetics, random breeding, or mating throughout a population without regard for genotype. Also known as panmixia.

pan-neurosis   A condition found in neurotic schizophrenia in which all types of neurotic symptoms are present at once or within a short period, including phobias, obsessions, compulsions, depression, and a wide variety of hysterical and psychophysiologic disturbances.

pan-normalization   (R. B. Cattell) The simultaneous bringing of related scales to comparable units that provide maximum normalization to all scales.

panoramic memory   A form of hypermnesia characterized by vivid recollection of long stretches of life (for example, "My whole life flashed before my eyes") when facing a possible death situation, as in nearly drowning.

panphobia   Fear of everything.

panpsychism   A monistic doctrine that assumes reality is ultimately psychic in nature.

pansexualism   A doctrine positing that all human behavior can be explained in terms of sexuality, a theory associated with Schopenhauer and Freud, who stressed the importance of sexuality more than any of the earlier students of the workings of the mind.

pantagamy   Group marriage.

pantomime 1. The expression of feelings and attitudes through gestures rather than words. 2. A nonverbal therapeutic technique sometimes employed when verbal expression is blocked.

pantophobia Fear of anything and everything. Also known as pamphobia, pan(o)phobia.

pantry-check technique In consumer psychology, an inspection of the kitchen shelves or cabinets of households to determine whether advertising-research participants actually use the products they claim to prefer. Interviews alone often prove inadequate as evidenced by market-research control studies which show that as many as 15% of respondents may claim to use, prefer, or at least be acquainted with a particular product that has never been marketed or advertised. See RECOGNITION TECHNIQUE.

Panum phenomenon A visual illusion produced by binocular fusion of separate images presented to the left and right eyes, the fusion image appearing closer to the eyes than the stimuli. Named after Danish physiologist Peter L. Panum (1820–1885).

Papaver somniferum Botanical name of the opium poppy. See OPIOID DRUGS.

paper-and-pencil test General term for the common type of test in which the questions are presented on paper and the answers are written, in distinction from one in which the participant responds otherwise. (A maze test in which the participant traces the maze with a pencil would be considered a performance test, because the emphasis is on maze learning, not drawing the path.) Compare PERFORMANCE TEST.

paper chromatography See CHROMATOGRAPHY.

paperless office A workplace in which information is entirely stored, manipulated, and transferred electronically.

Papez circle (J. W. Papez) A network of nerve centers and fibers associated with emotions. Includes the hippocampus, fornix, mammillary body, thalamus, and cingulate cortex, completing the circle through the hippocampus. See PAPEZ'S THEORY OF EMOTIONS.

Papez-Maclean theory of emotion Papez's theory of emotions

Papez's theory of emotions (J. W. Papez) A point of view that emotional experience is controlled by the Papez circle of central nervous system structures, a modification of the Cannon-Bard theory of the emotions. As Papez's 1937 proposal for a mechanism of emotion was generally ignored until Paul MacLean expanded it and named the structure the limbic system, it is also known as the Papez-Maclean theory of emotion.

papillae Clusters of taste buds on the tongue. Singular is papilla.

Pappenheim See ANNA O, TALKING CURE.

parabiosis 1. Obsolete term for the temporary loss of conductivity or excitability in a nerve. 2. See PARABIOTIC PREPARATION.

parabiotic preparation (A. Forel) The surgical joining together of two animals or genetically similar organisms for research purposes. Also known as parabiosis.

parablepsia Abnormal or distorted vision, as in visual hallucination or illusion.

parabulia (E. Kraepelin) A distortion of volition, or will, in which an intended action is interrupted, or "derailed," by a "cross impulse"; for example, reaching for an object, then suddenly flinging it away. It is an example of ambivalence, frequently found in patients with schizophrenia. See ABULIA.

paracentral lobule The extension of the precentral and postcentral gyri onto the medial portion of each hemisphere, it is notched by the central sulcus.

paracentral sulcus A fissure on the medial side of the cerebral hemisphere, extending upward from the cingulate sulcus between the precuneus and the paracentral lobule.

paracentral vision A form of vision that uses the retinal area immediately surrounding the fovea.

parachromatism A type of color blindness characterized by seeing colors with a distorted perception.

parachromatopsia Partial color blindness. Also known as parachromopsia.

paraconditioning Situations in conditioning experiments that appear to be conditioning but are not truly such.

paracusia 1. Partial deafness, especially to deeper tones. 2. Any abnormality of hearing other than simple deafness, for example, impairment in determining the direction from which a sound comes. Also known as paracusis. 3. Auditory hallucinations or illusions.

paracyesis Old term for a pregnancy that develops outside the uterine wall. Later known as ectopic pregnancy.

paradigm 1. A model, pattern, or diagram of the functions and interrelationships of a process. 2. In psychological research, an experimental design of the various steps of an experiment, or a model of the process or behavior under study. 3. A schematic representation of a sequence of activities or operations embodied in an experiment or field study. 4. (T. Kuhn) A systematic pattern to organize and conduct research within any sphere of knowledge; paradigmatic shifts occurred in psychology as a science of introspection to psychology as behaviorism. 5. A set of assumptions limiting an area to be investigated scientifically and specifying the methods to be used for collecting and interpreting the data to be obtained.

paradigm clash A controversy or conflict produced when a new set of assumptions threatens to replace an established set of assumptions.

paradigm of associative inhibition Müller-Schumann law

paradigm shift 1. A system-wide alteration in thinking, procedures, orientation. 2. (T. S. Kuhn) A fundamental reorganization of how people think about an entire topic. For instance, Copernicus' evidence that the earth revolved around the sun caused a paradigm shift in astronomy.

paradox Evidence that appears to be inconsistent with or contradictory to the known facts of a particular phenomenon. Types of paradox include: ARPEGGIO, AUBERT-FLEISHEL, COMTE'S, CONSISTENCY, DISTANCE, FECHNER'S, LEONARDO'S, NEUROTIC, REINFORCEMENT RETROACTIVE, SIMILARITY.

paradoxia sexualis Sexual thoughts and behavior not consistent with the age of a person.

paradoxical cold   An effect produced in thermal-nerve endings sensitive to both cold and hot temperatures. The fibers have double peaks, including one for heat that is above the threshold of pain. Touching an object that fires a warm and a cold receptor can produce an illusion of cold. See HEAT GRILL for an illustration.

paradoxical command   A request that cannot be carried out such as asking a person not to think about giraffes.

paradoxical directives   Suggestions by anyone to anyone else, but usually the phrase refers to instructions by a therapist to do exactly the opposite of what common sense would indicate. One purpose is to show how ridiculous the original intention is. See LEANING TOWER OF PISA, PARADOXICAL INTENTION.

paradoxical intention (PI)   (V. E. Frankl) A method developed by Viktor Frankl for the treatment of phobias. Phobic persons are instructed to magnify their fear reactions such as sweating or accelerated heart rate in an actual phobic situation. Enables such persons to achieve distance from their symptoms, especially if they are able to laugh at themselves in the situation.

paradoxical intervention   A technique used in psychotherapy in which patients are directed to continue undesired symptomatic behavior and even to increase it to show the patients that they have voluntary control over their symptoms. See PARADOXICAL COMMAND.

paradoxical reaction   An unexpected response to a drug that is contrary to the expected effect, for example, some children experience excitement rather than sedation after being administered phenobarbital, which notably disinhibits and therefore seemingly excites children.

paradoxical sleep (PS)   (M. Jouvet) A state of sleep from which the individual cannot easily be awakened in spite of the fact that it appears to be light, according to the EEG (electroencephalographic) pattern. The paradoxical sleep stage lasts for about six or seven minutes in a cycle that follows an initial 25-minute period of light sleep.

paradoxical thinking   Perverted or contrary cognitive processes.

paradoxical warmth   A sensation of warmth produced when a cold object of approximately 30°C (86°F) stimulates a cold receptor. Compare PARADOXICAL COLD.

paradox of freedom   The realization that individuals perceive themselves to be inwardly free to choose the way they act, despite the fact that their lives are shaped by outside forces. See SOFT DETERMINISM.

paragasia   An unintended action.

parageusia   A distorted sense of taste or a taste hallucination.

paragrammatism   paraphasia

paragraphia   1. A psychological distortion in written material consisting, for example, of transposed or omitted letters and words, or insertion of incorrect and irrelevant words. 2. Loss of ability to write from dictation, although the words are heard and comprehended.

parahypnosis   1. Abnormal sleep, such as evident in nightmare or somnambulism. 2. An abnormal type of sleep that may be induced by anesthetics or hypnosis. Such persons may sleepwalk, be suggestible, or, when under a general anesthetic, be aware of comments made by doctors or nurses in the operating room.

parakinesia   1. Movement executed in an awkward, clumsy, or grotesque manner. See DYSKINESIA. 2. Any motor abnormality. Also known as paracinesia, paracinesis, parakinesis.

parakinesis   1. See PARAKINESIA. 2. See PSYCHOKINESIS (PK).

paralalia   1. Any speech defect, especially the substitution of one speech sound for another. 2. Speech disturbance in which intelligibility is affected, as in saying "wabbit" for "rabbit" or "lello" for "yellow." See LALLATION.

paralalia literalis   1. Stammering or stuttering. 2. A difficulty in forming certain sounds correctly, sometimes accompanied by stammering.

paralanguage   Communication sounds that are not words, such as tone, inflection, grunts, whistles.

paraldehyde   An unpleasant-smelling liquid formerly used as a relatively safe sedative in the 1930s through 1950s.

paralexia   A reading disorder characterized by the transposition of word order and the inclusion of additional words.

paralinguistic   Those aspects of communication available in retirement homes as well as in cribs for expressing intended meaning, such as facial expressions, gestures, and the prosodic patterns of vocalization (for example, intonation and stress).

paralinguistic cues   Nonverbal cues in communications that qualify how a word or verbal message is sent or received; cues such as tone of voice, emphasis, spacing of words, pauses, uttered sounds (other than words), and inflection (pitch/loudness).

paralinguistic features   The formal patterns of speech that characterize an individual, including intonation and voice quality, such as, "plaintive," "husky," or "falsetto." A paralinguistic feature is also known as a paralanguage. See PSYCHOLINGUISTIC FEATURES.

paralinguistics   The study of vocal qualifiers. See PARALINGUISTIC FEATURES.

paralipophobia   Excessive fear of neglecting personal duty or obligations. See HYPENGYOPHOBIA.

parallax   An illusion of movement of objects in the visual field when there is a change in position from which they are viewed, as when the head is moved from side to side. Objects beyond a point of visual fixation appear to move in the same direction as the eye shift, those closer seem to move in the opposite direction. 2. See PHI PHENOMENON.

parallax threshold   See PARALLAX.

parallel conduction   Transfer of electricity through a circuit that is divided into branches and arranged in such a way that the current flows through all of its parts at the same time (in contrast to serial conduction).

parallel distributed processing (PDP) hypothesis   In cognitive psychology, a postulate that in thinking or searching memory a number of nodes or units are working at the same time, each with different connections of different strengths in a massively parallel and interactive network, leading to several streams of information coming into play simultaneously.

parallel dream   (C. G. Jung) Jungian phrase for a dream that parallels a conscious wish or attitude.

parallel forms   Alternate, equivalent versions, usually of tests. Used to avoid a practice effect on successive or readministrations, and to assess alternate-forms reliability. See ALTERNATE-FORMS RELIABILITY.

parallelism   1. In psychology, a doctrine positing that the mind and body are different, and cannot affect each other, even though events in the two realms occur in parallel (for every conscious process there is a corresponding organic process). See MIND-BODY PROBLEM, PHYSICALISM, PSYCHOPHYSICAL PARALLELISM. 2. In anatomy, being structurally parallel.

parallel law   (G. Fechner) A theory that if two stimuli of different intensities are presented to a receptor for a given time, absolute sensory intensities will diminish but the difference ratio remains unchanged.

parallel play   1. Activity of at least two children who are playing next to but not with each other. 2. Autonomous play without direct interaction. It is characteristic of children between 18 months and three years. See COOPERATIVE STAGE, SOLITARY STAGE.

parallel processing   A theory of information-processing stating that two separate sets of stimuli (information sources) can be attended to simultaneously, thus accounting for the apparent ability to carry on different cognitive functions at the same time. One information source may be processed consciously whereas another source is attended to subconsciously. Compare SERIAL PROCESSING.

paralog   A nonsense word of two syllables, such as bugzip. See NONSENSE SYLLABLE.

paralogia   Illogical thinking and verbal expression, observed primarily in patients with schizophrenia. The condition takes many forms, such as drawing false inferences, talking beside the point, or giving incorrect answers to questions. Eugen Bleuler cited the example of a patient who justified his insistence that he was Switzerland by saying "Switzerland loves freedom. I love freedom. I am Switzerland." Also known as paralogical thinking, perverted thinking, perverted logic. See EVASION, GANSER SYNDROME, PALEOLOGICAL THINKING, PRELOGICAL THINKING.

paralogical thinking   paralogia

paralogism   An unintentional or unnoticed fallacy.

paralysis   1. Loss of voluntary movement in a muscle through injury to or disease of the nerves supplying the muscle. Also known as palsy. 2. Loss of any function. 3. A symptom of various physical and psychological disorders characterized by a partial or complete loss of motor function in a body part. Kinds include sensory paralysis, in which the sensory function is impaired although movement is not necessarily lost; paralysis agitans (a misnomer as it suggests a combination of paralysis and movement, although the term sometimes is used interchangeably with parkinsonism); and flaccid paralysis, a form of the disorder associated with a loss of tendon reflexes). Other kinds of paralysis include: CONVERSION, GENERAL, HYSTERICAL, IMMOBILIZATION, NOCTURNAL, ORGANIC, PSEUDO-, SLEEP.

paralysis agitans   Obsolete phrase for parkinsonism. See PARALYSIS.

paralysis of the insane   See GENERAL PARALYSIS/PARESIS.

paralytic dementia   Obsolete phrase for general paralysis/paresis.

parameter   1. In general, a standard limiting or determining factor. 2. A descriptive property of scores for a population such as the population mean or population standard deviation. 3. In statistics, a value of a population or of a statistical universe, usually unknown. 4. In mathematics, a quantity that may have various values, each fixed within the limits of a stated case or discussion. 5. A measure ascertained from all possible observations in a population or universe, for example, a population mean (μ) distinguished from a sample mean. 6. In psychoanalysis, a technique that departs from the classical method of interpretation, such as advice, suggestion, or reassurance. 7. In colloquial usage, a limit. 8. A constant in an equation.

parametric statistics   Statistical techniques (based on the normality assumption) used to test hypotheses concerning population parameters or to establish confidence limits for parameters. They require a number of restrictive assumptions about the population(s) under investigation.

parametric test   A test of the null hypothesis that calls for certain information about the distribution and parameters of the measures and the assumptions that underlie them.

paramimia   A form of apraxia characterized by inability to express feelings with appropriate gestures.

paramimism   A gesture or other movement that has a meaning to the patient although others may not understand its significance.

paramnesia   A falsification or distortion of memory, as in the conviction that events heard about have actually been witnessed, or the illusion of having seen a scene that is actually new. Also known as false memory. See CONFABULATION, DÉJÀ RACONTÉ, DÉJÀ VU, JAMAIS VU, RETROSPECTIVE FALSIFICATION.

paranoia   1. (S. Sergeivich) A delusional system characterized by having incorrect ideas about suffering persecution. Such ideas may be broad, or limited to a particular topic, and may be patently nonsense, or quite sensible and logical. In some cases, paranoia is part of a larger and more encompassing mental disorder such as schizophrenia. 2. (R. A. Vogel) Refers to disorders of thinking. 3. (R. von Krafft-Ebbing) Any systematized form of delusional insanity. 4. (E. Kraepelin) A special form of insanity. Types of paranoia include: ALCOHOLIC, AMOROUS, CLASSICAL, CONJUGAL, EROTIC, EXALTED, LITIGIOUS, PROJECTIONAL, REFORMATORY. See ACUTE PARANOID DISORDER, ALCOHOL-PARANOID STATE, ATYPICAL PARANOID DISORDER, CONJUGAL PARANOID TYPE, INVOLUTIONAL PARANOID STATE.

paranoia querulansi   Obsolete phrase for litigious paranoia. See PARANOID LITIGIOUSNESS.

paranoia senilis   A type of paranoia associated with senility and marked by delusions of being spied upon by neighbors, robbed by family members, and similar persecution fantasies.

paranoiac   A person suffering from paranoia.

paranoiac character   Obsolete phrase for a personality type whose primary symptom is a tendency to blame the environment, including other persons, for personal difficulties.

paranoid 1. Pertaining to or characterized by paranoia. 2. Having systematized or transient delusions, usually grandiose or persecutory, with few other signs of personality disorganization or deterioration. See PARANOIA.

paranoid disorders Pathological conditions characterized by thought disturbances of a persecutory form but without gross personality disturbance. Includes paranoia and paranoid states.

paranoid litigiousness A delusional state that leads to continuous legal procedures against presumed enemies.

paranoid personality A hypothetical personality type characterized by an attitude of general suspiciousness or overwariness of other people; the attitude that other people are most likely to be dangerous, or looking to take advantage of the paranoid person. See PARANOIA.

paranoid pseudocommunity (N. Cameron) The extensive delusional systems in which the paranoid person may live.

paranoid schizophrenia A disorder in which delusions are not so classically systematized as in paranoia, but personality deterioration is more evident, with gross affective (emotional) disturbances and adaptive and intellectual malfunctioning. See PARANOID TYPE SCHIZOPHRENIC DISORDER.

paranoid state A pathological condition characterized by hallucinations but with less systematized and less complex delusions than in paranoia, and without bizarre dissociation and deterioration of paranoid type schizophrenic disorder.

paranoid tendency Refers to suspicious people with feelings of superiority that makes them appear to be likely candidates for full-blown paranoia.

paranoid type general paresis A psychosis occurring in advanced general paresis, in which the most prominent symptom is delusion of persecution. See PARESIS.

paranoid type schizophrenic disorder A form of schizophrenia characterized by late onset, with one or more of the following manifestations: delusions of persecution or grandeur, delusional jealousy, and persecutory or grandiose hallucinations, but without gross disorganization of behavior. Also known as paranoid schizophrenia.

paranomia A form of aphasia characterized by calling objects by incorrect names.

paranormal 1. Pertaining to any phenomenon that cannot be explained by existing knowledge. 2. (C. D. Broad) Alternative term for psychic or parapsychological.

paraphasia 1. A pathological condition characterized by habitual introduction of incorrect, distorted or inappropriate words during speech. 2. A form of aphasia characterized by loss of ability to speak correctly, with disturbances such as substitutions, reversals, or omission of sounds or syllables within words, or reversals of words within sentences. Speech may be quite unintelligible if the disturbance is severe. Also known as paragrammatism, paraphrasia.

paraphemia 1. A speech disorder marked by habitual introduction of inappropriate words. 2. Distorted speech.

paraphia A distortion of the sense of touch. Also known as parapsia, pseudaphia.

paraphilia 1. Sexual deviation. 2. A group of psychosexual disorders in which deviant forms of sexual behavior with atypical functions, objects, or frequencies are necessary for sexual excitement. 3. Refers to recurrent responsiveness to and obsessive dependence on an unusual or socially unacceptable stimulus to experience sexual arousal and achieve orgasm. A person with this condition is a paraphiliac. Below are a list of philias or paraphilias:

sexually attracted to or aroused by:	Name of Parahilia:
adolescent (imitating an)	adolescentilism
amputee partner (being or fantasizing being an amputee)	acrotomophilia, apotemnophilia
andromimetic female or preoperative female-to-male transsexual	andromimetophilia
animals	zoophilia
animals (inflicting pain on)	zoosadism
animals (oral contact with or the smell of)	zoolagnia
arson	erotic pyromania
baby (impersonating or being treated as one)	infantilism, autopedophilia, autonepiophilia, diaperism, nepiophilia
bisexual orientation	amphiphilia, androgynophilia
cemeteries	taphophilia
corpses and death	necromania
corpse (imagining self as one)	autonecrophilia
cross-dressing	transvestism, transvestophilia
cross-dressing (male as a female)	eonism
death (anything to do with)	necromania
deformity, filth, or ugliness	saliromania
disaster (arranging for one and watching it happen)	symphorophilia
enema (being administered one)	klismaphilia, klismophilia
exhibitionism	apodysophilia
exaggeration of or preoccupation with sexual matters	erotomania
feces (creating graffiti about)	coprography
feces (thinking about, seeing, smelling, or handling)	coprolagnia
feces (eating)	coprophagia
feces (smelling, tasting, or seeing their production)	coprophilia
filth, ugliness, or deformity	saliromania
genitals (exposing in public)	exhibitionism
genitals (having others view own)	passive scoptophilia
genitals (looking at own)	autoscopophilia
graffiti (creating about excrement)	coprography
humiliating, punishing, torturing someone	sadism
impersonating or being treated as a baby	infantilism, autonepiophilia, autopedophilia, diaperism, nepiophilia
impersonating or being treated as a juvenile by a sexual partner	juvenilism

intruding on and fondling a sleeping stranger	somnophilia
juvenile (impersonating or being treated as one by a sexual partner)	juvenilism
listening (to sexual encounters or accounts of them)	ecouteurism
looking (at own body and genitalia)	autoscopophilia
lust murder	erotophonophilia, homocidophilia
male(s)	androphilia
murder (of lustful nature)	erotophonophilia, homocidophilia
nonsexual inanimate object or nongenital body part	fetishism
obscene talk	erotolalia
being observed while engaged in sexual activity	autoagonistophilia
odors (esp. from sexual areas)	olfactophilia, osmolagnia
odors (particular)	renifleurism
partner with body characteristics prominent/different from one's own	morphophilia
partner or self tattooed/pierced for jewelry, esp. in genital region	stigmatophilia
playing the role of a parent with an infant	nepiophilia
postpubertal or adolescent partner	ephebophilia
prepubertal or early pubertal child	pedophilia, pedomania
prostitutes	pornolagnia
punishing, humiliating, or torturing someone	sadism
punishment (receiving discipline, humiliation, forced servitude)	masochism, algophilia
recurrent short-term relations with new partners	multiphilia
repeating the same activity with many partners	polyiterophilia
rubbing against someone, usually a stranger in public	frottage
sadism and masochism (combined, usually in role-playing)	sadomasochism
secretly watching others	voyeurism
self-inflicted pain	automasochism
self-inflicted whipping	autoflagellation
self-inflicted mutilation	automutilation
self-strangulation	asphixophilia, autoerotic asphyxiation
sex (secretly watching others having sex)	voyeurism
sex (listening to sexual encounters or accounts of them)	ecouteurism
sex partner (a woman)	gynophilia
sex partner (of the opposite sex)	heterophilia
sex partner (of the same sex)	homophilia
sex partner (one-legged)	monopediomania
sex partner (a criminal)	hybristophilia
sex partner (much older)	gerontophilia
sex partner (transvestite/ gynemimetic/ preoperative male-to-female transsexual)	gynemimetophilia
sexual activity with a corpse	necrophilia
sexual love of self	autophilia
sexual services (charged or forced to pay for)	chrematisophilia
small creatures, for example, ants, crawling on the genitalia	formicophilia
soiled or filthy items	mysophilia
spiritual beings, or having sex with such	spectophilia
staging one's own masochistic death	autoassassinatophilia
stealing	kleptophilia
strangers (intruding on and fondling a sleeping stranger)	somnophilia
surprise assault on a nonconsenting stranger	biastophilia
surreptitiously touching a stranger on an erotic body part	toucherism
talking about sexual or obscene matters to a stranger	scatophilia
telephone sexual/obscene talk to an unknown listener	telephone scatophilia, telephonicophilia
terrified resistance of a nonconsenting victim to sex assault/degradation	rapism, raptophilia
touching/feeling skin, fur, hair, leather, or fabric	hyphenophilia
torturing, punishing, or humiliating someone	sadism
ugliness, deformity, or filth	saliromania
undressing (secretly watching someone)	voyeurism
upsetting a stranger by exhibiting the penis (erect or not)	peodeiktophilia
urine (the smell or taste of)	urolagnia
urine/urination	undinism, urophilia
using/hearing obscene words or reading/listening to erotic narratives in partner's presence	narratophilia
viewing erotic material alone or with a partner	pictophilia
viewing sexual acts, others' genitalia, or both	active scoptophilia
watching partner have sex with an animal	mixoscopia bestialis
watching partner have sex with another person	mixoscopia
women's shoes	retifism
writing sexually obscene material, graffiti, letters	pornographomania

paraphobia   A mild form of phobia, the kind many people may suffer from, as opposed to an unusual phobia, such as a fear of pancakes.

paraphonia   1. Inadequate voice capacity. 2. An abnormal or pathological change in voice quality, especially of its tone.

paraphora   A minor emotional disturbance.

paraphrasia   **paraphasia**

paraphrenia   1. (J. Guislain) Folly. 2. Paranoid psychosis in old age. 3. Term given to schizophrenia when it appears for the first time in later life. 4. Obsolete term occasionally used by Sigmund Freud in place of dementia praecox and schizophrenia, and later to include both schizophrenia and paranoia. 5. (E. Kraepelin) A group of paranoid states, including paraphrenia confabulans (falsification of memory with delusions of grandeur and persecution) and paraphrenia fantastica (auditory hallucinations and unsystematized delusions about fantastic adventures).

paraplegia A form of paralysis that usually affects the legs and lower part of the trunk. See HYSTERICAL PARALYSIS.

parapraxia A condition characterized by loss of ability to perform purposive acts. See PARAPRAXIS.

parapraxis In psychoanalytic theory, behavioral errors or unintentional mistakes, usually of words but also of actions, that purportedly reveal a person's wishes, attitudes, impulses, or all three. Sigmund Freud brought these phenomena to general attention. See FREUDIAN SLIP, SLIPS OF THE TONGUE.

paraprofessionals in psychology Assistants with minimal training, not specified, who under the direction and control of the psychologist do specified tasks, such as interviewing from a form, scoring tests, administering group tests, etc.

paraprosexia A fixed idea that does not change or advance.

parapsychology (Boirac) 1. A branch of psychology that investigates areas beyond the ordinary concern of academic psychology such as whether it is possible to communicate with others alive or dead solely using mental processes. 2. The systematic study of anomalous psychological phenomena, such as extrasensory perception and psychokinesis, that appear to intrinsically defy any explanation in terms of sensory-motor processes.

parasexuality Any abnormal or perverted form of sexual behavior. See PARAPHILIA, SEXUAL PERVERSION.

parasitism In biology, the living together of two dissimilar organisms, a relationship that is beneficial to one and detrimental to the other. See SYMBIOSIS.

parasitophobia Excessive fear of parasites. See ACAROPHOBIA, PEDICULOPHOBIA.

parasomnia Abnormal behavior associated with sleep disorders including nightmares, sleep terrors, sleep walking.

parasuicide An attempted but unsuccessful suicide, or suicidal gesture.

parasympathetic division (J. N. Langley) A major subdivision of the autonomic nervous system (ANS), the other major subdivision being the sympathetic division. See PARASYMPATHETIC NERVOUS SYSTEM.

parasympathetic drugs **cholinergic drugs**

parasympathetic nervous system The part of the autonomic nervous system, primarily involving cholinergic responses, tending to evoke bodily functions that are more of a quieting nature, including salivation, drying of the skin and usually the opposite of the sympathetic nervous system.

parataxia A state of mind or repository of attitudes, ideas, and experiences gathered during personality development not effectively integrated into the growing collection and residue of other attitudes, ideas, and experiences of the individual's personality. Also known as parataxis. See LIFETIME PERSONALITY, PERSONALITY PROBLEMS.

parataxic distortion 1. The poor integration of thoughts, feelings, and attitudes. 2. (H. S. Sullivan) Misinterpretation of present perceptions, judgments, events, and relationships due to the influence of earlier experiences. See CONSENSUAL VALIDATION.

parataxic experience (H. S. Sullivan) A cognitive process characterized by perceiving causal relations but not on the basis of reality or logic, but rather in response to preestablished concepts.

parataxic mode (H. S. Sullivan) Denoting the subjective, autistic interpretation and communication of experience and events characteristic of young children who have not yet reached the stage of reasoning and logic.

parataxic thinking (H. S. Sullivan) A form of thinking that is beside the orderly way of thinking, or beside the point. In Harry Sullivan's theory of three hierarchical forms of thinking (protaxic, parataxic, and syntaxic), parataxic refers to a false belief that one of two associated events must be causative, or that correlation means causation.

parataxis In linguistics, joining phrases or sentences without conjunctions.

parateresiomania An abnormal desire to observe, particularly sexual activities. In Freudian terms, it is the counterpart of exhibitionism. See EXHIBITIONISM, VOYEURISM.

parathymia A distortion of mood, a schizophrenic disturbance characterized by reacting in a completely inappropriate manner, as in laughing when told that parents have died.

parathyroid glands (I. V. Sandström, G. Moussu, W. G. MacCollum, C. Voegtlin) One of four (sometimes more) pea-sized endocrine (ductless) glands, two on each side of and embedded in the thyroid glands. Secretes a hormone necessary for regulating calcium and phosphate metabolism.

paratype The totality of environmental influences that act upon an organism to produce individual expression of a genetic trait or character.

paratypic Relating to environmental pressures and influences on the development of an organism.

paraverbal therapy (E. Heimlich) A therapeutic technique developed for children who have difficulty communicating verbally and who have such disorders as hyperactivity, autism, withdrawal, or language disturbances. A nonthreatening, nonverbal approach is employed using music, movement, and art.

para-world A world of quantified, logical, and mathematical imaginary constructs used by the scientist to draw conclusions about the everyday world.

parcelled factor analysis In personology, finding that better simple structure is obtained when small parcels of items are used instead of simple items. The factor spaces remain essentially the same.

parenchyma Functioning tissues of a body organ or gland, as distinguished from supporting or connecting tissues. Also known as parenchyme, parencyme.

parens patriae The constitutional power of the state to involuntarily commit mentally ill persons who are considered to be in need of care and treatment.

parent   See the following kinds of parent(s): AU-THORITARIAN, AUTHORITATIVE, DEMOCRATIC, DEPRESSED, LAISSEZ-FAIRE, PERMISSIVE, REFRIGERATOR, REJECTING-NEGLECTING, SCHIZOPHRENOGENIC, SINGLE, WEEKEND.

parental behavior   1. In mammals, actions that generally include providing a suitable "nursery" before or around the time the offspring are born, retrieving the offspring that stray from the "nursery" or place of birth, feeding, weaning, and "teaching" of the offspring. 2. In birds, behavior similar to that of mammals except that nest-building may begin before ovulation, followed by incubation of the eggs and care of the offspring. 3. In humans, such behavior is less dependent on hormonal changes and more dependent on cultural factors and upbringing than among other animals, but most parents want to see that their infants are well nourished, comfortable, loved, and properly trained for success in life.

parental care   Bringing up, feeding, cleaning, caring for, and raising of the offspring or young animal by its father and mother.

parental imperative (hypothesis)   A postulate that biological and cultural factors cause humans to suppress certain behaviors or characteristics during parenthood. When the demands of parenthood cease, these suppressed characteristics can surface. Many marriages tend to disintegrate and couples often tend to return to earlier forms of behavior when their children leave the home. See EMPTY-NEST, MID-LIFE CRISES.

parental intercourse   See PRIMAL SCENE.

parental investment (PI)   (R. Trivers) An evolutionary concept referring to the total amount of time and resources parents must invest in offspring to assure their viability. Species vary in degree of parental investment; some, such as sea turtles, offer little beyond the bearing of young; others, such as many birds and humans, provide a great deal. In most sexually reproducing species, sexes are asymmetrical with respect to parental investment; usually the female invests more than the male, though there are exceptions such as the stickleback fish in which the involvement is greater in males.

parental perplexity   A relationship of parents to children marked by a lack of parental spontaneity, indecisiveness, and an inability to sense and satisfy a child's needs. Such children are likely to be confused and to respond in a random and unpredictable manner. Parental perplexity may be a causative factor in some mental disorders of children. See DOUBLE BIND.

parental preferences (of children)   A tendency for a parent to love or cherish one child more than the other(s). Whereas many parents declare that they love their children equally, most parents do have "favorites" usually known by the children. Such preferences can affect children in various ways, some favorably and some unfavorably. See BIRTH ORDER THEORY.

parental rejection   Persistent denial of approval, affection, or care by one or both parents, sometimes concealed beneath a cover of overindulgence or overprotection. Purportedly results in corrosion of self-esteem and self-confidence, a poor self-image, inability to form attachments to others, tantrums, generalized hostility, and development of psychophysical and emotional disturbances. See REACTION FORMATION.

parental styles   Based on prior work by Karen Horney on social relationships, Nira Kefir developed an isosceles triangle to serve as a kind of map with an infinite number of positions on child-rearing styles. The three points of the triangle read from the top (in a clockwise direction) "Equality," "Escape," "Conflict," with the center of the triangle indicating a "Laissez-faire" attitude. Any single incident or summation of overall attitudes may be diagrammed for various research or counseling purposes. See HORNEY TRIANGLE.

parental suit   A legal action in which a court of law usually determines paternity. See PATERNITY SUIT.

parent counseling   Professional guidance of parents of problems related to raising their children, including their roles in this process. See FAMILY COUNCIL, FAMILY EDUCATION.

Parent-effectiveness Training (PET)   (T. Gordon) A client-centered parenting education model centering around discussions of principles, practices, and problems of child-rearing conducted on an individual or group basis. A balance is maintained between the child's feelings and needs, and those of the parents.

parent figures   Imagined substitute parent or parents based on real persons who are known to children (such as relatives or friends) or unknown (such as movie actors); they subjectively take the place of the living or lost parent or parents, who serve as model parents and become the object of emulation and attachment. See FATHER SURROGATE, SURROGATE FATHER, SURROGATE PARENTS.

parent image   1. A parent that exists in the mind of a person, but not necessarily as an accurate image in general or in particulars. See IMAGE, MENTAL IMAGE. 2. A surrogate parent.

parenting   The process of bringing up children. Different ways in which to accomplish this process can be visualized on a graphic representation of an isosceles triangle. At the top, represented by two arrows one above the other, both aiming in the same direction, is democratic parenting; at the lower left, with two arrows one above the other facing each other is autocratic parenting; at the lower right with two arrows facing away from each other is rejecting parenting; and in the middle with no arrows is permissive parenting, other variations can be mapped out. See AUTHORITARIAN-REJECTING PARENTS, NONAUTHORITARIAN REJECTING PARENTS, PARENTING STYLE, PARENTAL REJECTION, REJECTING-NEGLECTING PARENTS. See HORNEY TRIANGLE for an illustration.

Parenting Stress Index (PSI)   (R. R. Abidin) A screening and diagnostic instrument designed to identify stressful areas in parent-child interactions.

parenting training   Any system for teaching parents how to deal with undesirable behavior by their children. Some such procedures work with children until about the age of ten. Among common problems are sibling rivalries, cleanliness of room, cooperation in doing chores, obedience of family rules, etc. See DEMOCRATIC PARENTING, FAMILY RELATIONSHIP INDEX.

Parents Anonymous   A self-help group for parents concerned about abusing their children.

Parent-Teachers Association (PTA)   An organization found in most American elementary schools, organized for various purposes, including lecturing on education, discussion of children's progress or of persistent problems that can be handled by either participants or through community action.

parergasia   1. Literally, perverted functioning. 2. Adolf Meyer used the term to replace "dementia praecox," since he thought this disorder is best described in terms of disorganized behavior and distorted thought processes. See DEMENTIA PRAECOX. 3. (E. Kraepelin) Performing an unintended action, as in opening the mouth when asked to close the eyes. Considered a symptom of schizophrenia. See PARABULIA, DERAILMENT OF VOLITION. 4. Obsolete term for schizophrenia.

parerogis   (A. Meyer) Psychotic manifestations such as delusions and hallucinations.

paresis   Generally, partial paralysis of organic origin. Originally called general paralysis of the insane; identified as a distinct disorder by French physician A. L. Bayle in 1825; associated with syphilis in 1857 and confirmed in 1897 by R. von Krafft-Ebbing; syphilitic spirochetes found by Noguchi and Moore in 1913 in the brains of patients who had died with paresis; first successfully treated with malarial fever treatment by Wagner-Jauregg in 1917. See GENERAL PARALYSIS/PARESIS, SYPHILIS.

paresthesia   Abnormal cutaneous, or skin, sensations, such as tingling, tickling, itching, or burning when no stimulus can be perceived generating the feeling. Can be due to a variety of causes, including neurological disorders, reactions to drugs. Also spelled paraesthesia.

paretic psychosis   general paralysis/paresis

Pareto chart   A vertical bar chart that displays the frequency and relative importance of problems or conditions. It is designed to suggest a starting point for process improvement by helping groups separate the few vital problems from the many trivial ones. Also known as Pareto analysis. Named after Italian mathematical economist turned sociologist Vilfredo Pareto (1848–1923).

Pareto optimality   A situation occurring when the distribution of economic welfare cannot be improved for one person without reducing that of another. See PARETO CHART.

Pareto principle   A theory that a legitimate welfare improvement occurs when any change improves the lot of at least one person. See PARETO CHART.

pareunia   coitus

parietal association cortex   The cortex in the parietal area of the brain that is not purely sensory motor, but is involved in multi-modal associations, sensory information processing, and sensory-motor integration.

parietal cortex   An area of the cortex in the parietal area (upper posterior wall) of the brain. See BRAIN for an illustration.

parietal lobe   That part of the brain directly behind the frontal lobe, above the temporal lobe, and in front of the occipital lobe. It is responsible for the sense of touch, multimodal associations, and aspects of language functioning. See BRAIN for illustration.

Paris school   A group of doctors working at the Salpêtrière Hospital in Paris who accepted the views of Philippe Pinel (humanistic treatment of the mentally ill) and of Jean Charcot (in his neurological studies of hypnotism) during the 1860s.

parity   A woman's status regarding having delivered live children.

Parkinsonian   Pertaining to or suffering from Parkinson's disease.

parkinsonism   1. See PARKINSON'S DISEASE. 2. Any disorder that presents symptoms resembling those of Parkinson's disease. Symptoms may occur in association with neurosyphilis, encephalitis, cerebral arteriosclerosis, or poisoning by carbon-monoxide gas or manganese products. Some medications such as Haloperidol, reserpine, and phenothiazines may cause drug-induced parkinsonism. "Paralysis agitans" is sometimes used synonymously with parkinsonism. Also known as pseudoparkinsonism. See DYSKINESIA, PARALYSIS, PARKINSON'S DISEASE.

Parkinson's disease   (J. Parkinson) A degenerative neurological disease, not uncommon in older people, characterized by tremors, stiffness in the joints, and a general decline in the animation of the musculature. Relevant because neuroleptic medicines can have side effects that in some ways mimic this condition. The disease especially involves a complex of nerve cells in the brain and their associated tracts of nerves called the "extrapyramidal" system, and so these side effects are also known as extrapyramidal symptoms or parkinsonian symptoms. Part of the cause of Parkinson's disease seems to be a deficiency of dopamine in the brain. Also known as shaking palsy, trembling palsy, spasmus agitans. See PARKINSONISM.

Parkinson's law   The ironic principle by British political scientist C. Northcote Parkinson that "work expands so as to fill the time available for its completion."

parmia   (R. B. Cattell) A personality characteristic consisting of boldness, venturesomeness, and imperviousness to threats.

parole   1. In psychiatry, a method of maintaining supervision of a patient who has not been discharged from a mental hospital, but who is away from the confines of a hospital, such as at a halfway house. A patient on parole typically may be returned to the hospital at any time without formal action by a court. 2. In penology, release of a person from a correctional institution, prison or reformatory prior to the conclusion of a maximum sentence, usually determined by a parole board of three to five people. Such individuals are to check in with their parole supervisors periodically, and are liable to spot checks to determine whether they are working, and are subject to return to the institution if they violate the terms of their parole such as by excessive drinking, substance abuse, not working, and associating with undesirable companions. See RECIDIVISM.

parolfactory area   A site of the cerebral cortex near the olfactory tract.

parorexia   1. A morbid compulsion to consume unusual foods or other substances. 2. A disorder of perverted appetite or desire for unusual food, such as the craving of some pregnant women for unusual dishes. See CISSA, PICA.

parosmia   Any disorder of the sense of smell, either organic or psychogenic, particularly subjective perception of nonexistent odors. A perverted sense of smell is sometimes seen in children or psychotics who perceive odors differently from others. Also known as parosphresia, parosphresis.

parosphresia   parosmia

paroxysm   1. The sudden intensification or recurrence of a disorder or an emotional state. 2. A spasm or seizure. 3. A sudden violent spasmodic convulsion.

paroxysmal drinking   Phrase similar to E. M. Jellinek's epsilon alcoholism.

paroxysmal sleep   1. See NARCOLEPSY. 2. Disturbed sleep with brain patterns similar to waking states.

parricide   1. The killing of one's own parent, either patricide (father) or matricide (mother). 2. A person who commits such an act.

parsimony   1. Economy or thriftiness. 2. (C. L. Morgan) In research, explaining a phenomenon in the simplest manner and with the fewest terms. Scientific theories observe a principle of parsimony in keeping hypotheses and explanations simple. See LAW OF PARSIMONY.

parsing   The process used to assign words in a sentence to their syntactic categories.

parthenogenesis   A form of nonsexual reproduction (or agamogenesis) in which an unfertilized ovum develops into an offspring, as occurs in some lower animals, such as bedbugs and bees. Also known as apogamia, apogamy, apomixia, virgin generation.

parthenophobia   Excessive fear of girls or of virgins.

partial adjustments   (H. S. Sullivan) Techniques used by some patients with schizophrenia to reduce environmental stress during the period immediately before an acute psychotic episode, for example, compensatory or sublimatory activities or defense reactions such as negativism and rationalization.

partial agraphia   Ability to write single letters but not words or phrases.

partial aim   A pregenital form of libido satisfaction, for example, oral eroticism.

partial correlation   An estimate of a correlation between two variables with one or more other variables held constant. See COEFFICIENT OF PARTIAL CORRELATION.

partial hospitalization   In psychiatry, hospital treatment of mental patients on a part-time basis. See DAY HOSPITAL, NIGHT HOSPITAL, WEEKEND HOSPITAL.

partial insanity   In forensic psychiatry, describing a borderline condition in which mental impairment is not sufficiently severe to render the individual completely non-responsible for criminal acts. See LIMITED RESPONSIBILITY, M'NAGHTEN RULES.

partial instinct   component instinct

partialism   1. Fetishism or sexual perversion in which a person only obtains sexual arousal from observing parts of a human body or sexual satisfaction from contact with body parts, such as feet, breasts, or buttocks. See FETISHISM, PARAPHILIA. 2. Sexual responsiveness to and gratification from only a partner with some specific attribute. See FETISHISM, PHILIA.

partial null hypothesis   A null hypothesis that there is no difference between any pair of group means on the dependent variable in a multigroup experiment.

partial reinforcement (PR)   1. The presentation of reinforcement subsequent to some but not all occurrences of the correct response. See PARTIAL REINFORCEMENT EFFECT. 2. Any reinforcement schedule that is not continuous, for example, a fixed-ratio or variable-ratio schedule. It is the type of reinforcement most often found in nature. See PARTIAL SCHEDULE OF REINFORCEMENT. 3. See PARTIAL REWARD.

partial reinforcement effect (PRE)   A tendency for partial reinforcement to increase resistance to extinction more than continuous reinforcement. See OPERANT CONDITIONING, REINFORCEMENT.

partial report   (G. Sperling) A technique to estimate the amount of information a person can absorb from a briefly presented stimulus; cues are presented as to which subsets of the displayed items are to be reported. Compare WHOLE REPORT.

partial reward (PR)   The delivery of part of a reward or reinforcement, similar to intermittent reinforcement. Rarely known as partial reinforcement.

partial schedule of reinforcement   Reinforcing an organism on a certain percentage of trials less than 100%, or one of the operant schedules such as fixed-ratio or variable interval. Also known as partial reinforcement schedule. See OPERANT CONDITIONING, PARTIAL REINFORCEMENT EFFECT.

partial sight   A seriously defective visual condition, often defined as acuity of less than 20/70.

partial tone   A simple component of a musical tone, for example, a first partial or fundamental. Partial tones are responsible for the characteristic sounds of musical instruments.

participant   A person who knowingly and willingly participates in an experiment, test, survey, etc. Distinguished from "subject," which implies participation without knowledge or consent, such as with animal studies. The concept is similar to informed consent. See MILGRAM'S OBEDIENCE EXPERIMENTS, THORNDIKE'S PUZZLE BOX.

participant modeling   (A. Bandura) A procedure for changing behavior in which effective styles of behavior are modeled for people and then they are helped with various mastery performance aids. See SOCIAL COGNITIVE THEORY.

participant-observation   A type of observational method in which an observer enters a group as a member while avoiding a conspicuous role that would alter group processes and bias data. Cultural anthropologists are participant-observers when they enter the life of a given culture to study its structure and processes. See PARTICIPANT-OBSERVER (meaning 1).

participant-observer   1. A person who acts like a group member while, at the same time, functions as an observer of group processes. Ordinarily, the members of therapeutic groups are informed of the special status of such a person. See PARTICIPANT-OBSERVATION. 2. (H. S. Sullivan) A therapist who plays an active part in the therapeutic process by identifying with patients' reactions, and uses their own feelings as clues to their faulty patterns.

participant vs subject See SUBJECT VS PARTICIPANT.

participation 1. Taking part in an activity; joining with others in some activity. 2. The interfacing of two or more systems that mutually influence each other. 3. (J. Piaget) A tendency of children to confuse their wishes, fantasies, or dreams with reality. 4. A primitive tendency to perceive similar things as the same.

participation chart A chart expressing the quantity and quality of each individual's contributions to a group endeavor or discussion.

participation interdependence In negotiation, the realization that it takes two sides to bargain.

participative decision making Problem-solving in which all relevant individuals (including, in the industrial context, lower-level employees) contribute to solutions.

participative leadership A democratic type of supervision wherein those affected by decisions have a voice in formulating policy.

participative management 1. Generally, consultation by administrators with subordinates. 2. A type of management in which the leader consults with those led before making decisions. Or, the decision-making is shared with followers are delegated who the power to implement their decisions.

particular complex A complex derived from a specific event in the person's life; for example, a child mistakenly fed only ice cream for a week following a tonsillectomy developed a life-long aversion to ice cream.

particular friendship A euphemism for an emotional connection (presumably sexual or potentially so) between persons of the same sex.

particularism A philosophical doctrine that any human behavior must be understood in the context of that individual's total history (heredity and environment). In a sense, this position of particularism explains and perhaps excuses all misbehavior. See BEHAVIORISM, DETERMINISM, FREE WILL, SOFT DETERMINISM, UNIVERSALISM.

particularist tradition Viewing persons as comprising sets of independent traits or elements, some in apparent contradiction with each other, rather than the holistic point of view of the unity of the personality. See HOLISM.

particulate inheritance (F. Galton) A transfer of genetic material such that offspring present a mosaic of paternal and maternal characters based on Mendel's laws. See BLENDING INHERITANCE.

partile An equal part. See PARTILISM.

partilism The division into equal parts, any series of numbers, such as into four parts (quartiles) or into ten parts (deciles), or one hundred parts (centiles).

part-instinct   component instinct

partisan zealotry An attitude toward inquiry in which an existing point of view is regarded as true, and championed energetically, regardless of plausible arguments and disagreements to the contrary. See BENEVOLENT ECLECTICISM, COMPARATIVE ANALYSIS, PARANOIA.

partition measure Any statistic that sets off one part of a frequency distribution from another. Refers primarily to partial measures, such as the median, upper quartile, third decile.

partitive behavior Reacting only to the intellectual implications of a situation, neglecting any feelings or motives. Processes at odds with a person's natural motivations, considered by Trigant Burrow to be due to innately incorrect pressures of social forces: the essential cause of neuroses and maladjustment in society. See DISSIPATIVE BEHAVIOR, PHYLOANALYSIS, PHYLOBIOLOGY.

part method of learning A learning technique in which the material is divided into sections, each part to be mastered separately in a successive order. Compare WHOLE METHOD OF LEARNING.

partner swapping See SWINGING.

part object An expression of libido in which a part of the body is the love object, for example, the female breast or bare feet. See FETISHISM.

part-object In psychoanalytic theory, refers to some anatomical part of a person which is viewed as a love object. Compare WHOLE-OBJECT.

part-set cuing In learning theory, asking for recall of a list of items under the condition that some of the items from the list are supplied as a cue. (Paradoxically, the part-set cuing seems to deter recall.) Also spelled part set cuing.

partunate period The hours following birth, when the neonate adapts to its existence as an independent being in a environment totally different from the uterine one.

parturiphobia Excessive fear of the birthing process. See MAIEUSIOPHOBIA.

parturition The act of giving birth; childbirth.

part-whole problem A fundamental issue in psychology as to whether the proper way to study any particular issue is by subdividing the concern to its basic parts or whether to view the whole as an entity with the parts subserving the whole. See LEARNING, MEMORY AID, MEMORY SYSTEM, MEMORIZING, STUDY.

PAS precategorical acoustic storage

Pascal's triangle A triangle of numbers based on the binomial coefficient. Name derives from Blaise Pascal, who did not invent the triangle but popularized it. See BRANCHED FORMAT PROGRAM for a vocabulary test based on this concept.

passage A sequence of steps involved in social movement, a kind of expected protocol of operations regulating how a person changes situations. See RITES DE PASSAGE.

passing stranger effect   ancient mariner effect

passion flower The flower and fruit of a climbing herb, *Passiflora incarnate*, that grows in the southern United States. Passion flower has been used for a variety of medicinal purposes ranging from treatment of burns and hemorrhoids to neuralgia and insomnia. Passion flower tea has long been a folk remedy for the relief of nervous tension.

passionate love (E. Hatfield) A state of intense longing for union with another.

passive Submissive; being acted upon rather than acting. Term was once used to characterize the feminine role, as in Sigmund Freud's early writings.

passive-aggressive behavior   The actions of a hostile person demonstrating aggression in a passive way; for example, an unhappy employee performs a task slowly, slovenly, with a scowl, not enough to justify dismissal, but enough to cause a supervisor to feel angry and powerless.

passive-aggressive personality disorder   A diagnosis of a chronic disturbance in personality characterized by the use of various means to resist normal social and occupational behavior, such as procrastination, stubbornness, inefficiency, or misplacing important materials.

passive algolagnia   (A. Schrenck-Notzing) A sexual disorder characterized by a desire to inflict pain or humiliation or receive it from others. See MASOCHISM.

passive analysis   A type of psychoanalysis in which interpretations or suggestions by the analyst are minimal. See NONDIRECTIVE APPROACH.

passive avoidance   A personality pattern characterized by a tendency to "coast along" in life, showing little initiative and no ambition, and apparently content to follow directions. Assumed to begin early in life, such individuals show neither enthusiasm nor concern for their own situation. See AFFECT-ENERGY, AUTISM, DEFERENCE BEHAVIOR.

passive-avoidance learning   Training a subject to avoid an aversive stimulus by not making a particular response, such as not stepping down from a small platform.

passive castration complex   See ACTIVE CASTRATION COMPLEX, CASTRATION COMPLEX.

passive-dependent personality   A hypothetical personality type characterized by helplessness, timidity, lack of self-confidence, and extreme dependence. See DEPENDENT-PERSONALITY DISORDER.

passive euthanasia   1. Doing nothing to sustain life for an organism in mortal pain or suffering. See EUTHANASIA. 2. Not seeking aid, which will result in death, such as when a person realizes death is imminent but does not call for help.

passive expectation   (J. Piaget) The behavior of an infant who apparently knows that a desired hidden object still exists but does not attempt to retrieve it.

passive forgetting   A fading away of certain memories due to lack of interest or exercise.

passive immunization   A process of acquiring immunity that occurs commonly during pregnancy when the mother's antibodies pass through the placenta to provide temporary protection for the fetus. When passive effects wane, active immunization (the injection of a specific antigen into the body) may be required. See IMMUNITY, IMMUNIZATION.

passive introversion   A psychoanalytic concept of a type of introversion, or inward direction of the libido, caused by an inability to turn it outward.

passive learning   **incidental learning**

passive listening   In counseling, attentive listening by the counselor without intruding upon or interrupting the client in any way. Compare ACTIVE LISTENING. See ATTENTIVENESS, NONDIRECTIVE APPROACH.

passive management by exception   (J. J. Hater & B. Bass) A corrective transaction between the leader and the led in which the leader waits for deviations, errors, and mistakes to occur before taking corrective action. See LAISSEZ-FAIRE LEADERSHIP, TRANSFORMATIONAL LEADERSHIP.

passive masturbation   Obsolete phrase for being masturbated or receiving oral sex.

passive mode of consciousness   See CONSCIOUS PROCESSES.

passive neurograms   (M. Prince) Hypothetical memories in the brain that are quiescent but nevertheless serve to direct behavior without awareness on the part of the person. See UNCONSCIOUS CEREBRATION.

passive-observational study   A research design in which the relations among variables are observed but not manipulated. Typically, the focus is on characteristics of different subjects or the relations among nonmanipulated variables. See SUBJECT-SELECTION STUDY.

passive performance   See ACTIVE PERFORMANCE.

passive-receptive longing   The desire to return to the infantile state where narcissistic needs are gratified without striving or reciprocation.

passive recreation   Recreational therapy in which the emphasis is on amusement or entertainment, as in listening to a musical concert, as opposed to recreation that requires physical or mental exertion.

passive registration theory   **copy theory**

passive resistance   A tactic for opposing authority pioneered by Mahatma Ghandi in his dispute with the British government in India, since adopted by many movements. Typically consists of protesters occupying a public or off-limits location and allowing themselves to be arrested without resisting. Effect is mainly on swaying public opinion.

passive scoptophilia   Being sexually aroused by having others view one's own genitals. Compare ACTIVE SCOPTOPHILIA.

passive sexual trauma   A psychological trauma from observing sexual activity and associating it with some negative event. Compare ACTIVE SEXUAL TRAUMA.

passive therapist   A nondirective therapist who plays the role of a catalyst rather than a director or interpreter in group or individual psychotherapy. See ACTIVE THERAPIST, CLIENT-CENTERED PSYCHOTHERAPY, NONDIRECTIVE APPROACH.

passive transport   The movement of substances across a semipermeable membrane by simple osmotic pressure, or without the assistance of enzymes or other energy systems. Compare ACTIVE TRANSPORT.

passive vocabulary   1. The vocabulary used in reading and listening, as opposed to vocabulary used in writing and speaking (active vocabulary). 2. The quantity of words a person can understand when read or heard in context. Sometimes known as recognition vocabulary. Compare ACTIVE VOCABULARY.

passivism   An attitude of submissiveness, especially in sexual relations, for example, male passivism.

passivity   A form of adaptation, or maladaptation, in which the individual adopts a pattern of submissiveness, dependence, and retreat into inaction.

PASS model (J. P. Das) A theory that individual intelligence should be measured in terms of the basic cognitive mechanisms that underlie intelligent behavior, specifically, the three interdependent components of processing, attention, and planning.

pastimes In transactional analysis, complementary transactions employed to fill in time or to pass time; social maneuvers that both defend and gratify.

past lives–future lives A concept of continuous reincarnation, or the continuance of an aspect of the self from death to birth that has been repeated in the past and will continue in the future.

pastoral counseling The application of psychotherapeutic principles and techniques by clergy to parishioners who come to them with problems of various kinds including emotional difficulties. A pastoral counselor receives psychological training intended to harmonize with religious orientations. Usually, pastoral counseling uses the techniques of supportive therapy while avoiding intensive exploration of unconscious motivation. See SUPPORTIVE PSYCHOTHERAPY.

pastoral psychiatry/psychology A branch of psychiatry/psychology associated with religion, with the objective of offering relief from anxiety, guilt, and other emotional disorders. Phrase usually is extended to include the role of the clergy in providing psychological relief through marriage and family counseling.

pastoral stage That form of culture in which herds of sheep, cattle, etc., are maintained for livelihood.

past-pointing Failure of pointing (a test for vestibular function).

past projection Looking backward in history in an attempt to understand events that shaped personal or another person's views, attitudes and behaviors.

PAT Progressive Achievement Tests

patched-up control group A group not randomly selected from the pool of subjects in the study. The group membership is selected in some manner to help rule out specific rival hypotheses and decrease the plausibility of specific threats to internal validity. See SAMPLE OF CONVENIENCE, SAMPLE OF OPPORTUNITY, SAMPLING.

patellar reflex The reflexive tendency of the lower leg to extend when the knee joint is struck, usually by a rubber hammer. Also known as knee-jerk reflex.

paternal behavior In some social cohorts, there are various expectations of the proper role of the father, and such expectations challenge many such groups in countries like the United States where there is a considerable amount of cultural diversity. Experts on parenting disagree on what are the best roles of both fathers and mothers.

paternalism Protective control over behavior of individuals by an authority figure representing a political entity, business, union, or other organization. Connotation may be favorable or critical.

paternity blues New-father blues; a period of undesirable feelings, such as depression, frustration, experienced by some men on recently becoming a father. Compare MATERNITY BLUES, POSTPARTUM DEPRESSION.

paternity suit In law, a civil legal action brought by a woman against a man charged with impregnating her out of marriage and who is therefore liable for support. See PATERNITY TEST.

paternity test An analysis usually of blood to establish biological paternity.

path analysis See STRUCTURAL EQUATION MODELING.

path coefficient A measure that expresses the degree of relationship between two variables.

pathema Obsolete term for a disease.

pathemia (R. B. Cattell) A personality characteristic marked by emotional immaturity and inappropriately focused feelings, as opposed to realistic and objective attitudes.

pathergasia (A. Meyer) Obsolete term for emotional or psychological maladjustment due to a physical defect or malfunction.

path-goal theory (of leadership) (R. J. House) A point of view that an effective leader clarifies the transactional exchange and the path the subordinate needs to follow for goal attainment. Contingencies include the motivation and expectancies of the subordinate and the structure of the situation.

pathic A person who assumes a passive role in any sexual act, especially when the act is considered a perversion. See PASSIVISM.

pathicism Male homosexual activity in which the passive partner simulates female behavior and garb.

pathoclisis 1. Sensitivity to injury or disease. 2. A series of subclinical conditions, such as viral infections, arteriosclerosis, overuse of alcohol, or minor head traumas that cumulatively affect nervous-system functioning.

pathocure The displacement of a neurosis by an organic disease. The opposite of pathoneurosis.

pathogenesis 1. The origination of a disorder. 2. Any mechanism resulting in the development of a disease or morbid process. Rarely also known as pathogeny.

pathogenic Causing or leading to pathology. Also known as morbific, morbigenous, nosogenic, nosopoietic, pathogenetic.

pathogenic family pattern Family attitudes, standards, and behavior that lay the groundwork for mental disorder, for example, parental rejection, overprotection, overindulgence, perfectionism, encouragement of sibling rivalry, marital conflict, double-bind situations, and excessively harsh, lenient, or inconsistent discipline. See DOUBLE-BIND.

pathogenic secret Knowledge of personal, shameful, and reprehensible actions that have not been disclosed to others, such that the pathogenic dynamics of guilt and the feelings that it generates overwhelm the constructive activities in which the person would otherwise engage. Can eventuate in depression, anxiety, and other crippling symptoms. This concept has long been familiar to religious institutions, but a secularization of the assumption can be credited to Moritz Benedikt who used it in his psychotherapy. Full disclosure to a therapist serves as a cleansing confession. Its implications for religious practice and for psychotherapy are self-evident.

pathogeny   1. The cause and course of a mental or physical disease. Also known as nosogenesis, pathogenesy. See PSYCHOLOGICAL AUTOPSY. 2. See PATHOGENESIS (meaning 2).

pathognomic   1. Characterizing a sign or symptom specifically diagnostic of a particular disease or disorder. 2. A group of symptoms suggestive of a disorder. Also known as pathognomonic.

pathognomic signs   1. A constellation of symptoms indicative of a particular physical or mental disorder. 2. Rorschach signs that point toward maladjustment.

pathognomonic   pathognomic

pathognomy   The recognition of feelings, emotions, and character traits, particularly when they are signs or symptoms of disease.

pathography   The study of pathology. See MÖBIUS.

pathokinesis   The dynamics, course, or development of an illness.

pathological doubts   A distressing condition characterized by exaggerated concerns about topics such as health, finances, and love. Generally the person is acutely sensitive to signs of possible trouble or deviation in the areas of concern. For example, a pimple is a sign of cancer, and a friend who fails to say hello hates the person. See ABULIA, ANXIETY, HYPOCHONDRIA, WORST CASE SCENARIO.

pathological drowsiness   somnolence

pathological fallacy   A mistake of overgeneralization in which pathological characteristics observed in a single or a few abnormal individuals are attributed to the general population. Critics claim that Sigmund Freud was guilty of perpetuating this fallacy because Freud based his theories on clinical cases.

pathological gambling   Compulsive wagering. An undesirable behavioral condition that drives many otherwise normal people to poverty, despair, ruination of careers and family, and criminal behavior. Such gamblers often base their gambling on invalid logic; for example, a gambler lost the money needed to support the family on the assumption that by betting at the race track enough money would be made to retire. See GAMBLER'S FALLACY, GAMBLER'S ANONYMOUS.

pathological grief reaction   An extreme or inappropriate response to bereavement, such as failure to recognize that a person has died (denial), irrational feelings of responsibility for the death, extreme guilt feelings over previous death fantasies, persistent depression and hopelessness, and excessive apathy or inertia. See GRIEF.

pathological guilt   See GUILT FEELINGS.

pathological lying   A persistent, compulsive tendency to falsify or tell "tall tales" out of proportion to any personal advantage that can be achieved. The condition is found among alcoholics and patients of brain syndromes, but is most common among swindlers, impostors, con artists, and other antisocial individuals who in some cases do not seem to feel or understand the nature of a falsehood. See CONFABULATION.

pathological mendicancy   A morbid compulsion to beg even when there is no real need for financial help.

pathological sleepiness   somnolence

pathology   1. The scientific study of the structural and functional changes involved in physical and mental diseases. See GENIUS AND PATHOLOGY, SOCIAL STRESS THEORIES OF PATHOLOGY. 2. A disordered condition, or disease. Kinds of pathology include: BRAIN, ECO-, FOCAL, GRAPHO-, LANGUAGE, META-, NEURO-, PHYSIO-, PSYCHO-, RETARDATION PSYCHO-, SOCIAL, SPEECH.

pathology and genius   See GENIUS AND PATHOLOGY.

patholysis   (J. Kevorkian) Physician-assisted suicide. See ALTRUISTIC SUICIDE, LIVING WILL, SUICIDE.

pathometry   The study of the number of individuals in a population affected with a certain disease at a given time, and of the conditions leading to increase or decrease in this number.

pathomimeses   pathomimicry

pathomimicry   Conscious or unconscious feigning of disease symptoms, usually to escape punishment or other unpleasant consequences, such as avoiding going to school (for children) or to work (for adults). Also known as pathomimeses. See CHRONIC FACTITIOUS DISORDER, MALINGERING, MUNCHAUSEN'S SYNDROME, MUNCHAUSEN'S SYNDROME BY PROXY.

pathomiosis   Minimization by people of their diseases. See DENIAL.

pathomorphism   Any abnormal or extreme body build.

pathoneurosis   A neurotic reaction to a physical disease and the limitations it imposes, as in denial of incapacity, or the idea that a disease was inflicted as punishment.

pathophobia   Inordinate dread and fear of disease. Also known as nephophobia. See MONOPATHOPHOBIA, NOSOPHOBIA.

pathophysiological pattern   A differential diagnostic schema employed to determine whether a set of signs and symptoms for a particular complaint (for example, dizziness, headaches, or epileptic seizures) may be psychological or biochemical in origin. May be translated into a computer program for future retrieval. See COMPUTER ASSISTED INSTRUCTION, COMPUTERIZED DIAGNOSIS.

pathophysiology   The study of diseases caused by biochemical abnormalities. Many such disorders involve sensory- or motor-nerve dysfunctions that result from chemical-messenger defects, metabolic errors, or adverse effects of drugs or environmental chemicals.

pathopsychosis   A psychotic condition that evolves from an organic disorder, such as general paresis or brain tumor.

pathways to goals   Perceptions of alternative ways to achieve particular goals.

patient (Pt or PT)   A person who is ill and under treatment by a physician, chiropractor, or other health provider for physiological disorders or problems such as pneumonia. Kinds of patients include: ANALYTIC, BAD-, GOOD, IDENTIFIED, OUT-, TARGET. See CLIENT VS PATIENT ISSUE, PATIENT-CLIENT ISSUE.

patient-centered services   Mental-health services directly available to workers, such as emergency psychiatric treatment, diagnosis, case-finding, and referral to clinics and social agencies. See ENVIRONMENT-CENTERED SERVICES.

patient-client issue   A dilemma of whether to label those who see a therapist for assistance as clients or patients. There are at least three views: (a) all are patients in that they suffer and they need help; (b) all are clients, people with problems who need understanding, information, and clarification; (c) people in the community are clients, those in institutions are patients. Psychiatrists usually take view (a), psychologists, view (b).

patient government   An organization of patients in a mental hospital who meet for such purposes as making recommendations on rules and regulations, providing assistance with ward administration, planning social events, improving hospital decor, and orienting new patients. See THERAPEUTIC COMMUNITY.

patient in noncompliance   A patient who does not follow the recommended dosages of prescribed drugs. Also known as defaulter, drug defaulter.

patient medication instruction (PMI)   Directions on taking prescribed or recommended medication.

patient-oriented consultation   See PSYCHIATRIC CONSULTATION.

patients' rights   See BILL OF RIGHTS, RIGHTS OF PATIENTS.

patriarchal family   A family in which the father is the final authority, decision-maker, and main or sole provider, while the mother plays subservient roles as full-time housewife. See PARENTING, PARENTING STYLES.

patriarchy   1. In anthropology, refers to rule by males. 2. An attitude, expressed in various ways in different cultures and in individual situations, of males being in control of their families, including the females. Compare MATRIARCHY. See MEN'S LIBERATION MOVEMENT, MOMMY TRACK.

patricide   1. The killing of one's own father. 2. A person who commits such an act. See MATRICIDE, PARRICIDE.

patrilineage   Familial descent considered through the male members. See GENS, MATRILINEAGE.

patrilineal   Pertaining to inheritance through the male line. See PATRILINEAGE.

patrilineal clan   A group of people organized in terms of common ancestry through males, or terms of interests of males. Also known as gens.

patrilineality   In anthropology, refers to ancestry being traced through the father.

patrilocal family   In anthropology, a family system in which a wife goes to live with her husband's family. Compare MATRILOCAL FAMILY, NEOLOCAL FAMILY.

patrilocality   See MATRILOCAL FAMILY, NEOLOCAL FAMILY.

patriophobia   Morbid fear of inheriting unpleasant traits, especially of having a hereditary disease. Also spelled patroiophobia.

pattern   A design. A configuration of elements that form a whole. Kinds include: ACTION, ACTIVATION, AFFECTOMOTOR, BEHAVIOR(AL), CAREER, DEMOGRAPHIC, DISSOCIATIVE, EMOTIONAL, FAMILY, FIXED ACTION, INNATE, LIFE-ORGANIZATION, MITTEN, PATHOGENIC FAMILY, PATHOPHYSIOLOGICAL, POSITIVE SPIKE, PRESS-NEED, REACTION, REPETITIVE, RESPONSE, ROLE ACTION, SCALLOP, SLEEP, SPECIFIC DYNAMIC, STARTLE, STIMULUS, TONAL, WAVE-INTERFERENCE.

pattern analysis   A method of organizing items into clusters as a step in measuring a common variable such as an interest in an outdoor occupation or clerical work.

pattern discrimination   1. An ability of organisms to distinguish differences in patterns such as sound frequencies and the order in which the differences occur, as in bird calls and other communicating sounds of various species. 2. Responding to the visual pattern projected by a painting as opposed to responding separately to each color, texture, and shape. Also known as temporal-frequency discrimination.

patterned interview   In industrial psychology, a semistructured personnel interview predesigned to cover certain specific areas (such as work history, education, home situation), but at the same time to give the interviewer an opportunity to guide the dialogue into side channels and ask questions on points that need to be clarified.

patterning   Establishing a system or pattern of responses to stimuli, or a pattern of stimuli that will evoke a new or different set of responses. Used to retrain people who have suffered brain damage that disrupts normal sensory-motor activities.

patterning exercises   (R. J. Dolman & C. H. Delgato) A controversial treatment in which brain-injured children are given special exercises designed to retrace the step-by-step organization of the central nervous system through the various developmental stages, such as moving the arms and legs, or creeping and crawling. The object of the process is to overcome the effects of brain dysfunction by developing missing abilities that have inhibited motor, perceptual, and cognitive development.

pattern learning   A complex type of learning characterized by predicting certain consequences by a pattern of prior events, for example, guessing in advance that the weather is going to change and in what way based on clues. Also, in families, members can tell when a parent is about to commence a drinking binge or hysterical furor. See PREDICTION, PREDICTION VALIDITY.

pattern matching theory   A point of view that people can recognize similarities and differences between certain patterns presented and certain patterns in their memory. This ability varies considerably between people.

pattern recognition   The recognition of a specific pattern from a group of different patterns or displays.

pattern variable   (T. Parsons, E. Shils) Five dimensions suggested to categorize any action with precision: specificity-diffusion, affectivity-neutrality, universality-particularism, quality-quantity, and self orientation-collective orientation.

pattern vision   Ability to discriminate among shapes, sizes, and other features of objects in the environment by visual patterns. Pattern vision is lost following a lesion or excision of the striate cortex.

pausimenia   Obsolete term for menopause.

Pavlovian conditioning   classical conditioning

Pavlovian   Refers to the work of others who follow the line of research of Ivan Pavlov on classical conditioning. Frequently a synonym for classical when conditioning is referred to. Pavlov's classic work on the digestion of dogs and the psychological consequences of classical association ushered in tens of thousands of experiments on animal and human learning.

Pavlovianism　　Ivan Pavlov's view that mental processes and physiological processes are identical and that the former may be studied via the latter. Includes the experimental procedures of conditioning introduced by him.

Pavlov's theory　　The following items are important for understanding Ivan Pavlov's theory: CLASSICAL CONDITIONING, CONCENTRATION, DELAYED RESPONSE, DIFFERENTIAL INHIBITION, DISINHIBITION, EXCITATORY-INHIBITORY PROCESSES, EXTERNAL INHIBITION, FIRST SIGNALING SYSTEM, INHIBITION OF DELAY, INTERNAL INHIBITION, INVESTIGATORY REFLEX, LAW OF EXTINCTION, NEGATIVE INDUCTION, NERVISM, NEUTRAL STIMULUS, POSITIVE INDUCTION, PSYCHIC SECRETION, SECOND SIGNALING SYSTEM, SIGNALLING SYSTEMS, TRANSCORTICAL PATHWAYS, UNCONDITIONED REFLEX/RESPONSE.

pavor　　(terror—Latin) A terrifying nightmare that upon awakening continues to appear to be real with the terror continuing while awake, the dreamer refusing to accept that this was a nightmare. Day time incidents are known as *pavor diurnas* and night terrors are called *pavor nocturnus*.

pavor diurnus　　(day terror—Latin) A terror or fear reaction that may occur in a small child during his or her afternoon nap.

pavor nocturnus　　(night terror—Latin) Night-terrors; an extreme form of nightmare, most likely to occur between the ages of 3 and 12, in which children suffer from panic reactions and have great difficulty in reorienting themselves to reality. Usually, after a later sleep, they remember nothing about the terrifying experience. See SLEEP-TERROR DISORDER.

pavor sceleris　　(crime terror—Latin) Fear of "bad" people, such as thieves and murderers. See SCELEROPHOBIA.

pay-and-don't-go　　(E. Berne) Colloquial label used in Transactional Analysis for self-defeating patterns of behavior which, according to Eric Berne, "can be stopped just by stopping."

pay compensation　　**wage compensation**

payoff　　1. Benefit (including money) associated with making a certain type of response to a stimulus. 2. (E. Berne) A colloquial label used in Transactional Analysis for rewards for playing a social "game" in which a reward of some kind is promised or bestowed, usually undeservedly. See PAY-AND-DON'T-GO. 3. See PAYOFF MATRIX.

payoff matrix　　A pattern of limitations (including rewards, punishments, or both) explained to players in a game as a phase of the rules. The payoff is dependent upon the choice made between alternatives. See PAYOFF.

P(B/A)　　Symbol indicating conditional probability of B, given A has already occurred.

PCL-R　　See PSYCHOPATHY CHECKLIST-REVISED.

PCP　　See PHENCYCLIDINE.

Pcs　　See PRECONSCIOUS.

PD　　1. panic disorder. 2. Prisoner's Dilemma. 3. personal disposition.

PDD　　primary degenerative dementia

PDP　　1. See PARALLEL DISTRIBUTED PROCESSING HYPOTHESIS. 2. Psychopharmacology Demonstration Project.

p.e.　　probable error (also abbreviated **PE, P.E.**)

PE　　1. pneumoencephalogram. 2. Probable error (also abbreviated **P.E., p.e.**).

Peabody Picture Vocabulary Test-Revised (**PPVT-R**)　　(M. Dunn & L. Dunn) An examination in which sets of four pictures are presented to the participant, who selects the one that corresponds to a word uttered by the examiner. Purportedly yields an estimate of the participant's vocabulary, grade level and IQ (intelligence quotient). Used with ages 2½ years to adult.

PeaCe Pill (PCP)　　Slang for phencyclidine.

peak clipping　　The elimination of a high amplitude portion of speech waves by electronic means, causing some loss of naturalness but little if any loss of intelligibility. Makes it possible to reduce high-intensity noise and enable a hearing aid or public address system to use its power to the best advantage.

peak experience　　A moment of awe or ecstasy common to all, but which may be experienced more frequently by self-actualizers. According to Abraham Maslow, peak experiences are sudden insights into life as a powerful unity transcending space, time, and the self, such as at the birth of one's children or upon the climber reaching the long awaited mountain top. They may be associated with and elicited by experiences connected to mysticism, love, and the arts. See MASLOW'S THEORY OF HUMAN MOTIVATION, SELF-ACTUALIZATION.

Pearson chi square　　See CHI SQUARE.

Pearson product-moment correlation (r)　　(K. Pearson) Measure of the degree of linear relationship between two quantitative variables, ranging from 1.00 (for a perfect linear relationship) to 0 for no overall linear relationship) to −1.00 (for a perfect negative linear relationship). Also known as Pearson's r, product-moment correlation.

peccatiphobia　　Morbid fear of committing a sin. Also known as peccatophobia. See ENOSIOPHOBIA, HAMARTOPHOBIA.

pecking order　　(T. Schjelderup-Ebbe) A hierarchy of prestige in any group, but named for chickens, where it is easily observed that one hen at the top of the social order can peck any others; the one at the bottom can be pecked by any. A related hierarchy in cows is known as horn order.

pederast　　See PEDERASTY.

pederasty　　Sexual relations between a man (a pederast) and a boy. Formerly termed pedicatio(n).

pederosis　　Obsolete term for pedophilia.

pedestrian movement　　Generally regular and predictable flow of pedestrian traffic in a public area, such as a shopping mall, plaza, or street intersection.

pediatric psychology　　(L. Wright) Any psychological intervention in a nonpsychiatric medical setting dealing primarily with children.

pedicatio(n)　　Obsolete term for pederasty or bestiality.

pediculophobia　　Morbid fear of lice. Also known as phthiriophobia.

pedigree Family tree; an ancestral line of descent. See CLAN, FAMILY, KINSHIP, PEDIGREE METHOD.

pedigree method 1. The study of family history and genealogy as a means of tracing traits that might be inherited. Applied with dubious results by Francis Galton in his studies of genius and by Henry Goddard in his studies of mental defect. See GENETIC COUNSELING. 2. In animals, the purity of the background of any animal in terms of standards established by various groups. A relevant example is that of laboratory rats used so often by psychologists in research on learning.

pediophobia 1. Morbid fear of dolls. 2. Rare term for fear of children, usually called pedophobia.

pedolalia Baby talk.

pedology A branch of biology and of sociology concerned with the child in its physical, mental, and social development. Also known as paidology.

pedomania See PEDOPHILIA.

pedomorphism 1. Attributing childish attributes to human adults. 2. Describing adult behavior in relation to child behavior.

pedomorphosis A process characterized by adults retaining juvenile characteristics.

pedophile A person with pedophilia. An adult who is sexually attracted to children.

pedophilia 1. Literally and originally, love of children. 2. Sexual desire by adults (usually men) for children. 3. In law, a sexual offense by an adult upon a child. May take the form of voyeurism, exhibitionism, touching/being touched, and intercourse. Commonly known as child molestation. Spelled paedophilia in Britain.

pedophobia Morbid fear or strong dislike for children. Sometimes known as pediophobia.

pedophthoria In ancient Greece, the seduction of a boy by a man.

peduncle A stalk-like bundle of nerve fibers.

peeping Tom Common phrase for a voyeur. Derived from the name of a tailor who, according to the 11th-century legend, peeked at the virtuous Lady Godiva as she was riding naked through the streets of Coventry, her husband's town, to protest his unjust taxation policies. See HYSTERICAL BLINDNESS.

peep show (booth) In an "adult" store, a cubicle or small room that can be rented to watch pornography or live sexual performances.

peer counseling A formal group therapy arrangement in which no one in the group is recognized as the therapist, with the group's activities structured to attempt to achieve positive therapeutic effects.

peer group An assemblage of persons, all of whom are similar in terms of the purpose of the group.

peer-group pressure Impact or influence of children's social groups on individual members, usually the power of the peer group to engender conformity.

peer pressure A tendency for an individual in a group to conform to group ideals and behavior; to think and act in ways similar to others in the group in an attempt to be accepted. See CONFORMITY, GROUPTHINK, PEER-GROUP PRESSURE.

peer rating Evaluation of an individual's behavior by associates. See PEER REVIEW.

peer review 1. Evaluation of effort or work, such as the summary of a research done by peers. 2. Professional evaluation of performance with the objective of maintaining or improving the quality of care and of promoting professional growth and development. 3. A common procedure of scientific journals: articles submitted for publication are sent (usually "blind") to one or more editors considered knowledgeable in the area for examination, leading to a recommendation to accept it for publication, reject it, or revise it. See PROFESSIONAL STANDARDS REVIEW ORGANIZATION.

peer review organization (PRO) A group of people, usually elected by members of the organization, who become gatekeepers and have authority to accept and reject members, usually for infractions of rules. In psychology, an example is the American Board of Professional Psychology, whose members must be members of the American Psychological Association, and who must conform to its rules of professional behavior. See PROFESSIONAL STANDARDS REVIEW ORGANIZATION.

peer tutoring Students teaching other students.

pegboard test An examination that calls for pegs to be put into boards. Some pegs are identical, and the task for such test is to see how fast pegs can be inserted. In some cases, the pegs are small and are to be picked up with tweezers. The most common kind of pegboards, especially for young children, have pegs of different shapes. The test is intended to measure intelligence, manual dexterity, and mechanical aptitude.

Peggy Lee syndrome (D. Weis) In young women, the disappointment with their first sexual experience. Derived from the song "Is That All There Is?"

peg-word mnemonic system A method of memorizing lists of items by associating new items to be remembered with an already-learned list; for example, a telephone pole, pants, and a three-legged stool are paired with bread, eggs, and lettuce, by visualizing a loaf of bread nailed to the telephone pole, eggs broken on the pants, and lettuce under the stool. Later, by visualizing pole, pants, stool, the person also recalls bread, eggs, lettuce. Also known as peg system of memory, pegword method.

pejorism A pessimistic attitude; a tendency to view everything in the worst possible way. See PESSIMISM.

pellagra (F. Frapolli) A niacin-vitamin-deficiency disease, found sometimes in people who are alcoholic or who live on a corn-based diet with insufficient vegetables, dairy products, and proteins containing tryptophan. Causes psychiatric symptoms of dementia and irritability, along with many bodily symptoms, such as chronic diarrhea, dermatitis, weakness.

pellet A bit of food used in instrumental and operant learning studies with rats and other experimental animals. Pellets are available in standard weights and sizes with standard contents.

pendulum chronoscope An instrument used in the early years of psychological research to measure short time intervals with exactitude. Two pendulums of different lengths were released simultaneously, the shorter pendulum swung faster than the longer pendulum but the elapsed time between the simultaneous release of the two pendulums and the eventual synchrony of the two was known. See CHRONOSCOPE for a later instrument.

penetrance   1. The percentage of cases in which a particular gene manifests a particular characteristic trait or disease in the developed organism, or phenotype. 2. In ergonomics, the conspicuity of a signal.

penetration   1. Entering. 2. Entrance of the penis into the vagina. Legal interpretation of penetration in cases of rape or illicit intercourse vary but generally regard penetration to have occurred if the glans of the penis passes beyond the labia majora. Also known as *immissio penis*. 3. Mental sharpness. 4. In vision, focal depth.

penetration response   A projective test response that contains a suggestion of weakness or penetrability, for example, a "hole in the wall." Persons with schizophrenia purportedly mention more penetration responses in Rorschach testing than those with a neurosis or those considered normal.

peniaphobia   Morbid fear of poverty.

penile   Referring to the penis.

penile clamp   1. A ring for wearing on the distal end of the penis to control urinary incontinence. 2. A proximal-end band to aid in maintaining an erection.

penile implant   A rigid rod or inflatable device surgically implanted to permit men with erectile dysfunction to copulate. See PENILE PROSTHESIS.

penile plethysmograph   A device placed around the penis and connected to a recording device that measures the degree of expansion of the penis when erect. Used for a variety of purposes, in psychology primarily to determine which stimuli sexually excite a male. Compare VAGINAL PLETHYSMOGRAPH.

penile prosthesis   Various devices, from a simple sheath to a self-contained inflatable implant, to assist a male with erectile dysfunction to copulate. See PENILE IMPLANT.

penilingus   **fellatio**

penis   The male organ of coitus and urinary excretion.

penis captivus   Literally, captured penis, held by vaginal muscles during intercourse, unable to be withdrawn until flaccid. Occurs in many animals, including dogs. See VAGINA DENTATA.

penis display   See PHALLIC AGGRESSION/DISPLAY.

penis envy   (S. Freud) A psychoanalytic theory that girls envy boys because they have penises. According to Sigmund Freud, between the ages of three and six, when girls discover they lack this organ, they feel "handicapped and ill-treated," blame their mothers for the loss, and want their penis back. Criticized by many, including Margaret Mead and Karen Horney. Also known as phallus envy. See CASTRATION COMPLEX, PHALLOCENTRIC CULTURE.

penis fear   See PHALLOPHOBIA.

penis feminis   The clitoris.

penis holding   A greeting or oath-swearing custom in some tribal cultures. See PHALLIC OATH.

penis pride   A male feeling of superiority and power associated with the possession of a phallus.

penis ring   See PENILE CLAMP.

penis symbol   See PHALLIC SYMBOL.

penis-vagina fixation   The reduction of all sexual activity to penile penetration of the vagina.

penoclitoris   A sexually ambiguous phallus of a neonate.

penology   The scientific investigation of punishment for crime, both as a deterrent and as a means of reformation.

Penrose triangle   An example of an impossible figure that generates the impression of three dimensions. See DEVIL'S PITCHFORK.

Penrose triangle   A demonstration of why seeing is not always believing, as it is impossible to build such a figure.

pension neurosis   Neurotic behavior induced by anxiety over obtaining a pension, the intense desire to obtain one, and concern over being able to obtain one. See RETIREMENT NEUROSIS.

pentobarbital   Generic name of an intermediate-acting barbiturate used commonly mainly in the 1960s and 1970s as a sleep medication. Acts by depressing neural thresholds and reducing nervous activity. May be used in psychotherapy to make the person less inhibited and therefore facilitate self-expression. Can also be abused as a "downer." A trade name is Nembutal. See BARBITURATE, TRUTH SERUM, TWILIGHT SLEEP.

pentylenetetrazol   Generic name for a synthetic compound that stimulates the cardiovascular and central nervous systems. Trade names include Cardiazol (Europe) and Metrazol (U.S.). See METRAZOL SHOCK THERAPY.

peodeiktophilia   Being sexually aroused by upsetting a stranger by exhibiting the penis (erect or not).

peonage   See INSTITUTIONAL PEONAGE.

peotillomania   Rare term for a nervous tic characterized by tugging or pulling on the penis. Also known as false masturbation, pseudomasturbation.

PEP   1. See PSYCHOEDUCATIONAL PROFILE. 2. See PSYCHOEPISTOEMOLOGICAL PROFILE.

pep pills   Common name for stimulant drugs, usually containing amphetamine or caffeine as the principal ingredient. See KEEP-AWAKE PILLS.

PEPS   Productivity Environmental Preference Survey

peptic ulcer disease (PUD)   The erosion of a tissue surface of the stomach, duodenum, or both, associated with increased secretion of hydrochloric acid (HCL) and pepsin (a digestive enzyme), during periods of emotional stress. See ULCER.

PER   Periodic Evaluation Record

perceived collective efficacy   (A. Bandura) A groups' shared belief in their capabilities to organize and execute the courses of action required to produce given levels of attainment. See SOCIAL COGNITIVE THEORY.

perceived reality   A person's experience of reality; subjective experience in contrast to objective, external reality.

perceived self   A person's perception of the self. See IDIOPANIMA, SELF-ESTEEM, SELF-REGARD.

perceived self-efficacy (A. Bandura) People's beliefs in their capabilities to produce given levels of attainment and to exercise control over events that affect their lives. Beliefs of personal efficacy affect how people think, feel, motivate themselves and what they accomplish. See SOCIAL COGNITIVE THEORY.

perceivers See OBJECTIVE PERCEIVERS VS SUBJECTIVE PERCEIVERS.

percentile (p) The hundredth part of a statistical distribution. One-fifth of cases fall below the 21st percentile. Also known as centile.

percentile norm A norm expressed as a percentile rank rather than as a variation from the mean or other ways of evaluating a person in relation to others.

percentile rank (PR)/score A score that represents the percentage of cases that fall below the value of any given test score or result; for example, a percentile rank of 80 indicates that in 80% of cases tested a lower score was recorded.

percentile scale A simple scale based on 100% of the population of any group with which an individual is being compared. See PERCENTILE RANK (PR)/SCORE.

percept 1. That which is perceived, a perceptual experience. 2. A phenomenological experience.

percept image A concrete image which may appear as a fantasy or memory image, and which represents a primitive level of intellectual life, commonly found in patients with schizophrenia.

perceptanalysis (Z.A. Piotrowski) A process of inferring personality characteristics from a participant's responses to the Rorschach inkblots. See PIOTROWSKI RORSCHACH SYSTEM.

perception 1. In vision, the ability to see in three dimensions, objects in the distance, and also to be aware of the amount of the distance from the self. 2. The awareness of (having) the senses being stimulated by external objects, qualities, or relations. Immediate experiences, as opposed to memory; ability to select, organize, and interpret various sensory experiences into recognizable patterns. The interpretation placed upon a stimulus or experience, determined by general organization principles. Types of perception include: ABSTRACT, ANORTHOSCOPIC VISUAL, AUDITORY DISTANCE, AUDITORY, AUDITORY SPACE, AUTOMORPHIC, BINOCULAR, CATEGORICAL, CONSTRUCTIVIST, CROSS-MODAL, CUTANEOUS, DEPTH, DERMO-OPTICAL, DYS-, ECOLOGICAL, EGO, ENDOPSYCHIC, EXTRASENSORY, FIGURE-GROUND, GLOBAL, HAPTIC, INTERPERSONAL, MIRROR-IMAGE, OBLIGATORY, PHENOMENAL, PHYSIOGNOMIC, PREFERENTIAL, PRE-, REGULARITY, REMOTE, ROTATION, SELECTIVE, SELF-, SENSE, SIZE, SOCIAL, SPACE, SPECTATOR, STEREOSCOPIC DEPTH, SUBLIMINAL, TACTILE, TIME, VERIDICAL, VISUAL.

perception deafness Inability to analyze or perceive sounds normally due to some impairment of the inner ear or auditory-nerve pathways leading to the brain. Also known as sensorineural impairment.

perception of equilibrium An experience which affords data with respect to the center of gravity of the organism, enabling it to establish and maintain an upright posture. Also known as static sensation. See EQUILIBRIUM.

perception of motion pictures See PHENOMENAL MOTION (meaning 2).

perception of spatial relations An awareness of the relative position of objects in space. See SPATIAL RELATIONS.

perception of television See PHENOMENAL MOTION (meaning 2).

perception time The amount of time which elapses from the presentation of an object to its recognition by the observer minus (a) the time spent in overcoming inertia of the receptor and (b) the time of transmission of the nerve impulse from receptor to brain centers.

perceptive 1. Pertaining to or having the power of perception. 2. Describing a sensitive and discriminating person, especially in the judgment of other people.

perceptive impairment and nerve loss See SENSORINEURAL HEARING LOSS.

perceptron (F. Rosenblatt) In information processing, a device comprising photocells and a simple logical device, which can recognize letters and other visual patterns.

perceptual closure Perceiving items as an organized whole that were previously seen separately. See GESTALT.

perceptual consciousness (S. Freud) Rare phrase denoting the "psychic system" that receives stimuli from the external world, as distinguished from the system that records these stimuli in the form of memory traces.

perceptual constancy (H. von Helmholtz) A tendency for a percept to remain constant despite changes in the stimulus, for example, a white cloth continues to appear white whether viewed in bright sunlight or in deep shade.

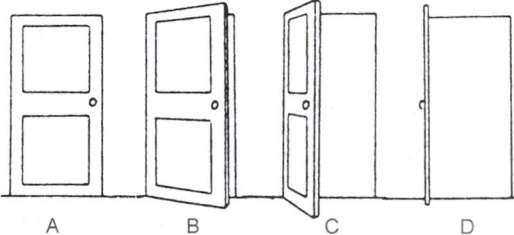

A   B   C   D

perceptual constancy b, c, and d are perceived as rectangular due to the "set" provided by a.

perceptual cues See DEMAND CHARACTERISTICS.

perceptual cycle (hypothesis) (U. Neisser) A postulate that perception has a three-part cycle: (a) an anticipatory schema, (b) a sampling of the stimulus field, and (c) the stimuli of the environment. The cycle continues as perception goes on.

perceptual decentering (J. Piaget) The developing abilities of children to consider a variety of relevant features when asked to solve a problem or when asked to make judgments about invariant features of phenomena; for example, young children often concentrate or center on a single perceptual feature (such as height) in making judgments about quantity. Older children achieve a more balanced view of the quantity problem by considering the width of the container as well as the height, thus decentering from individual perceptual features. See DECENTER.

perceptual defect/deficit   An impaired ability to organize and interpret sensory experience; difficulty in observing, recognizing, and understanding people, situations, words, numbers, concepts, or images.

perceptual defense   1. A perceptually selective process whereby a person defensively blocks or distorts (hesitates, misidentifies, adds material that is not there, or acts ignorant of) perceptions considered threatening or disagreeable to that person. 2. An unconscious self-protective process in avoiding unpleasant stimuli. See DENIAL for a related process.

perceptual deficit   perceptual defect

perceptual disorder/disturbance   A disorder of perception, such as (a) recognizing letters but not words, (b) an inability to judge size or direction, (c) confusing background with foreground, (d) an inability to filter out irrelevant sounds or sights, (e) body-image distortions, and (f) difficulty with spatial relationships, for example, perceiving the difference between a straight and a curved line.

perceptual distortion   Inaccurate interpretation of perceptual experience, as in the distorted images produced by dreams or hallucinogenic drugs, geometrical illusions (for example, the Müller-Lyer illusion), visions occurring in states of sensory deprivation or dehydration, and distortions produced by expectation or suggestion. See MÜLLER-LYER ILLUSION for an illustration.

perceptual disturbance   perceptual disorder

perceptual expansion   1. The development of the ability to recognize, interpret, and organize intellectual, emotional, and sensory data in a meaningful way. 2. The enriched understanding of personal experience that takes place in psychotherapy when defenses are relaxed.

perceptual extinction   An effect of certain unilateral cortical lesions in which a stimulus, usually tactual or visual, is not detected. If a single stimulus is presented on either side of the midline, it is detected by the subject, but when two similar stimuli are presented at the same time, one on each side of the midline, the stimulus on the side contralateral to the lesion is not detected. See REPRESSION, SUPPRESSION.

perceptual field   All elements and aspects of the environment of which the individual is aware at any given point in time.

perceptual filtering   The process of focusing attention on a selected few of the myriad sensory stimuli that constantly bombard the body's various nerve receptors. It is a necessary function for the survival of the organism, which is physically incapable of responding to all of the simultaneous neural inputs.

perceptual fluency   The ability to recognize a particular stimulus under impoverished presentation conditions.

perceptual illusion   A mistaken perception due primarily to some characteristic of the sensory mechanism, or to conditions inherent in the objective relations present. Also incorrectly known as sense illusion, sensory illusion. Some illusions include: ARISTOTLE'S, DEL BOEUF'S, GEOMETRICAL, HIGH HAT, LINEAR PERSPECTIVE, MÜLLER-LYER.

perceptualization   1. The process of organizing sensory inputs into a realistic and meaningful whole. 2. Awareness of reality as it appears to the senses.

perceptual learning   1. Training of an organism to perceive relationships between stimuli and objects in the environment. 2. Being able to see or hear differently than previously, for example, a person originally repelled by Picasso's paintings learns to understand and appreciate the value of Picasso's work. Or, a person who hated the complexity of a symphony begins to appreciate the coordination of the various instruments in an orchestra.

perceptually handicapped   Refers to a person who is learning-impaired because of deficits in the perception of sensory stimuli.

perceptual maintenance   In environmental design, the construction of an environment to facilitate sensory functions, such as vision and hearing, and to provide an appropriate level of perceptual stimulation for the activity carried out, as in designing a classroom to ensure good light, comfortable seating, adequate ventilation, and proper acoustics.

perceptual masking   Interference of one stimulus with another, preventing proper perception, for example, of an object or space.

perceptual-motor disabilities   Combinations of challenges (handicaps) that include one or more sensory and motor functions, as in a person who is deaf and has cerebral palsy.

perceptual-motor learning   The mastering of a skill that requires both perceptual and motor responses, for example, driving an automobile.

perceptual-motor match   The ability to correlate perceptual data with a previously learned body of motor information. Children with brain damage may have to touch everything they see because they cannot make the perceptual-motor match automatically.

perceptual norm   In social psychology, the socially approved and usually well-established, well-defined, traditional way of perceiving the environment; norms which members of a given social group are expected to observe.

perceptual organization   A concept that elements in a perception are integrated and coordinated thereby providing meaning to an organism with the various elements of the perception having differential values in eliciting a response. See GESTALT PSYCHOLOGY.

perceptual restructuring   The process of modifying a perception to accommodate new information.

perceptual rivalry   sensory inattention

perceptual schema   A person's cognitive patterns that form a frame of reference for responding to environmental stimuli.

perceptual segregation   The separation of one part of a perceptual field from the whole, by physical boundaries or attention-diverting methods.

perceptual sensitization   The increased likelihood of perception due to expectation; for example, stating "I smell smoke" may result in other people sniffing the air, alert to any hint of smoke. See PERCEPTUAL DEFENSE, PERCEPTUAL VIGILANCE.

perceptual set   A tendency to perceive objects, people, or events according to a certain frame of reference (for example, on learning that a person is a member of a group that is generally disliked, a first impression of that person will be less favorable than if this group membership was not known).

perceptual sociogram   (J. L. Moreno) In sociometry, a diagram depicting the interactions and interrelationships between members of a class, gang, team, or work group that is based on the results of each member indicating which other members appear to accept or reject that person. See SOCIOGRAM.

perceptual speed (P)   A primary mental ability, according to research by L. L. Thurstone and supported by other studies, that involves the ability to make rapid and accurate identification of visual elements, seeing similarities and differences. Can be tested by number or word-comparison tests. See PRIMARY ABILITIES, PRIMARY MENTAL ABILITIES.

perceptual structure   The total combination of cognition and perception of a complex stimulus, the elements meshing to a single unit of sensation.

perceptual style   The characteristic way a person attends to, alters, and interprets sensory stimuli.

perceptual synthesis   The integration of experience from all the senses to establish sensory information and eliminate unessential information with respect to similarities and differences. This includes touch and perception of one's own movements.

perceptual training   A method of enhancing the ability to interpret perceived objects or events in concrete terms. May be employed, for example, in accelerating the ability of a child to recognize letters of the alphabet by having the child trace the outlines of the letters.

perceptual transformation   1. A change in the way a problem, event, or person is perceived by the inclusion of new information or a different perspective. 2. Reacting differently to usual perceptions due to changes either in the field or in the person, consequently due to objective or subjective changes.

perceptual vigilance (effect)   A phenomenon whereby experimental participants require shorter tachistoscopic exposure durations to recognize threatening as opposed to nonthreatening stimuli. See PERCEPTUAL DEFENSE, PERCEPTUAL SENSITIZATION, TACHISTOSCOPE.

perch   See FIXATION POINT.

percipient   1. A person who perceives. 2. In parapsychology, the alleged recipient of parapsychological messages. 3. In parapsychology, the person experiencing, demonstrating, or being tested for extrasensory perception (ESP).

perennial dream   A childhood dream that recurs repeatedly during adult life.

perfectionism   1. A compulsive tendency to demand of others or of the self a higher level of performance than required by the situation. 2. Demand of self, of others, or both, for a higher level of performance than reasonable. Considered by some theorists to be the basic cause of personal misery because nothing that the person does (or others do) is good enough. Striving for perfection may be viewed as a favorable trait but perfectionism is seen as a neurotic disability. See FEELINGS OF INFERIORITY.

perfect negative relationship   See COEFFICIENT OF CORRELATION.

perfect pitch   An ability to correctly identify the pitch of a sound on hearing it. For some it appears to be an inherited facility, but other people may learn to distinguish relative pitch or have a well-developed memory for pitches.

perfect positive relationship   See COEFFICIENT OF CORRELATION.

performance   Activity or behavior that leads to a result, such as a change in the environment. See ACTIVE PERFORMANCE, AS-IF PERFORMANCE, GUIDED PERFORMANCE, JOB PERFORMANCE.

performance anxiety   1. Anxiety associated with fear of being unable to perform a task, which often is a sexual activity, as in cases of impotence caused by a fear of failure. 2. A tendency to become anxious during a complex performance due to factors in the surround, for example, an acrobat who has performed a particular routine many times before, is nervous because a role model is in the audience. See HUMPHREY'S LAW, PERFORMANCE NEUROSIS, TESTOPHOBIA.

performance assessment   An appraisal of the growth or deterioration in learning and performance through the administration of ability and achievement tests. See PERFORMANCE REVIEW.

performance contract   A formal agreement that a person will receive remuneration based on performance. In industry this is sometimes known as piece work. See ACCOUNTABILITY, PIECE-RATE PAYMENT.

performance-cue effect   Knowledge of how a group performed can influence a rater's judgments of the performance.

performance curve   See LEARNING CURVE.

performance neurosis   An alteration of personality in the direction of a disorder as a result of performing an undesired or hated task, such as being forced to move a corpse, or being raped.

performance operating characteristic (POC)   The simultaneous performance of two different tasks compared with each other, such as patting the belly with one hand and rubbing the head with the other hand. Generally, if a person does one task well, the other will be done poorly.

performance phase   In John Dollard's and Neal E. Miller's conceptions, a state of being during which a person acquires new, more adaptive responses and habits.

performance review   A formal evaluation of how a person is progressing in training or working. Such information helps morale and may favorably affect performance. Sometimes known as knowledge of results. See PERFORMANCE APPRAISAL.

performance test   A type of test requiring nonverbal or nonlanguage responses, typically using blocks and formboards. See NONLANGUAGE TEST.

performative   A verbal utterance that performs an action, such as "I make a motion" or "I offer you a job."

performers   Individuals in a psychodrama who have central or dominant roles.

perhaps neurosis   An obsessive neurosis in which the person is preoccupied with what might have been if the person had taken an alternative course of action regarding a past event.

periamygdaloid cortex   A part of the cortex associated with the sense of smell. Also known as pyriform cortex, pyriform lobe.

periblepsis   The wild stare of a delirious person: an expression of terror, bewilderment, and consternation.

perikaryon 1. The cytoplasm of the cell surrounding the nucleus. 2. The cell body of a neuron as distinct from its axon and dendrites.

perilymph A cushion of fluid that separates the bony labyrinth and the membranous labyrinth of the inner ear.

perimacular vision A type of vision that uses the retinal area surrounding the macula.

perimeter 1. The boundaries of a two-dimensional figure. 2. An instrument for mapping the zones of the retina. With one eye covered, the participant fixates straight ahead and discerns the stimulus "out of the corner" of the eye. See PERIMETRY.

perimetry The measurement of the peripheral visual field. See PERIMETER (meaning 2).

period 1. A duration or division of time. Types of period include: ABSOLUTE-REFRACTORY, ADAPTATION, ANALOGY, CONSOLIDATION, CRITICAL, EMBRYONIC, ENACTIVE, FANTASY, FETAL, FORE-, GERMINAL, GESTATION, INTUITIVE, JUVENILE, LATENT ADDITION, NATURAL HOMOSEXUAL, NEONATAL, ORAL-BITING, ORGANOGENETIC, ORGANOKINETIC, PARTUNATE, POSTPARTUM, PRACTICE, PRELINGUISTIC, PRENATAL, PRESOLUTION, RECESS, REFRACTORY, RELATIVE REFRACTORY, SENSITIVE, SENSITIZATION, SEXUAL LATENCY, SOLUTION, STORM-AND-STRESS, SUPERNORMAL, TRANSITIONAL, WARM-UP, YOUTH. 2. A stage of a disease. See INCUBATION PERIOD, LATENCY PERIOD. 3. Slang for menstrual period.

Periodic Evaluation Record (PER) See MENTAL STATUS EXAMINATION REPORT.

periodicity See RHYTHM AND PERIODICITY.

periodicity theory An explanation for the ability of a person to make pitch discriminations. Maintains that the cue for pitch perception is the frequency of the impulse in the auditory system. See TELEPHONE THEORY.

periodic leg movements in sleep (PLMS) Movements of the legs that occur about every 20 to 40 seconds during sleep, and are most often found in people who have restless leg syndrome (RLS).

periodic reinforcement Any reinforcement that operates on a regular schedule.

period prevalence A time period during which the frequency of occurrence of a disease or disorder in a defined group is assessed, for a period of time as short as a month or as long as a decade. Phrase is commonly used in epidemiology.

period rage The experience of participants in historical re-enactments (especially of battles) feeling that they actually are the people they have been playing. See PSYCHODRAMA, RAGE.

peripatologist An instructor of the blind or partially sighted who specializes in teaching visually-impaired persons to orient themselves to their surroundings and to move about independently, safely, and confidently.

peripheral 1. Located at the outside, on the surface, or away from the center. 2. Incidental rather than essential. 3. Equipment such as a printer or scanner that increases the versatility of a computer.

peripheral androgen blocker A steroid drug that blocks the virilizing effects (such as hirsutism) of androgens in females.

peripheralism 1. Behavior explained in terms of overt events rather than based on the central nervous system. 2. A doctrine positing that behavior is a function of stimuli that reach the organism from the immediate environment. 3. A view of behaviorists that emphasizes events at the periphery of an organism, such as skeletal muscles and sex organs, rather than the functions of the central nervous system. Also known as peripheralist psychology. Compare CENTRALISM.

peripheralism vs centralism (R. I. Watson) A prescriptive dimension of the philosophical underpinnings of psychology, namely, focusing on psychological events occurring away from the presumed center of the organism (such as sensory processes) versus at the center (such as thinking). See OPPONENT-PAIRS DIMENSION.

peripheral nerve fiber classification Peripheral nerve fibers are classified according to size into types C, B, and A. Type C are slow unmyelinated fibers, and include postganglionic autonomic and some visceral and somatic sensory fibers. Type B fibers are of the preganglionic autonomic system. Type A can be further broken down into three afferent (AI, AII, AIII) and three efferent (Aα, Aβ, Aγ) groups. See A FIBER.

peripheral nervous system (PNS) 1. A network of motor and sensory nerves that control muscles and glands. 2. Nerves that connect the central nervous system (CNS) to muscles, sense organs and glands. 3. That part of the nervous system besides the brain and the spinal cord: the somatic nervous system and the autonomic nervous system (ANS). See CENTRAL NERVOUS SYSTEM.

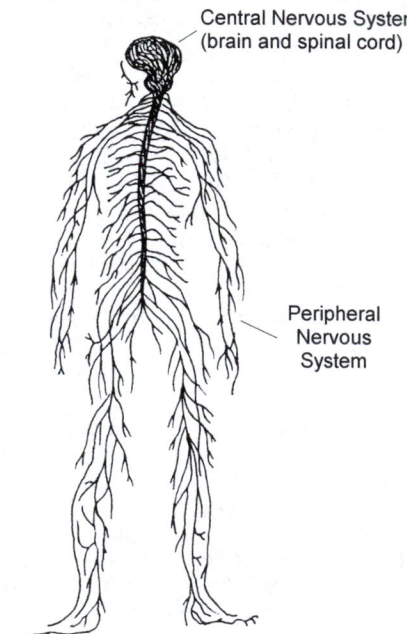

peripheral nervous system

peripheral vision Visual experiences due to stimulation of the outlying portions of the retina.

periphery (S. Maddi) An aspect of personality that is situational and behavioral rather than central and phenomenological.

Perky effect (C. W. Perky) A tendency to falsely believe that an actual experience is due to imagination; for example, a research participant is asked to imagine a star and to try to "project" the star onto a screen. Meanwhile, the experimenter actually does project a faint image of a star on the screen. The participant is likely to believe that the star seen and described regarding size and position is due to imagination and not reality.

perlocutionary effect The response and reaction of a speech on auditors, such as pleasure, anger, inspiration, fear.

permanence concept Recognition that objects have an independent existence, "detached from the self" (Jean Piaget). During the first few months of life, an object out of sight is out of mind, for example, a toy covered with a cloth ceases to exist. This idea is superseded by awareness of the permanence of things, which gives rise to the concept of objective reality.

permanent planning A system of establishing a permanent home for children, ideally with their original families, to avoid the condition in which they might be shifted continually from one foster home to another.

permastore (H. P. Bahrick) The storage of material studied many years ago, such as foreign languages, that were never subsequently used. See MEMORY STORAGE.

permeable family (D. Elkind) The postmodern successor to the modern nuclear family, such as a new family consisting of a couple, each with children from a previous relationship and also children they have produced in the present relationship. See BLENDED FAMILY.

permissive belief A view that allows a person to participate in behavior that the person knows should not be done, such as when on a strict reducing diet, thinking "This one little piece of chocolate can't have that many calories," so that the person can eat the chocolate. See RATIONALIZATION.

permissive doll play See DOLL PLAY.

permissive environment An environment in which acting out and free expression of opinion and emotion are allowed though not necessarily approved or encouraged.

permissiveness An approach to child-rearing in which the children are given wide latitude in expressing feelings and opinions and even in acting-out behavior. The object is to encourage children to assume responsibility for their own behavior; but some parents go to the extreme and refrain from giving the children the positive guidance they need.

permissiveness with affection A value system holding that sexual activity between unmarried persons is acceptable if the couple is in love or engaged.

permissive parent (D. Baumrind) A parent who disavows punitive restrictions and tries to cultivate a positive, affirmative, accepting environment in the home. Rules are explained, and the children participate in decision-making. See AUTHORITARIAN PARENT, AUTHORITATIVE PARENT, DEMOCRATIC PARENTING, REJECTING-NEGLECTING PARENT.

permissive parenting (B. Spock) A child-rearing style characterized by minimal demands being made on children, lax enforcement of rules, and the failure to provide guidance or restrictions even if they are desired by the children. See AUTHORITARIAN, AUTHORITATIVE, DEMOCRATIC PARENTING, PERMISSIVE PARENT.

permutation The number of possible arrangements of n (n stands for any number). The formula is $n! = (1)(2)(3) \ldots (n-1)(n)$, Where: $0! = 1$, where n is any number. Example: The letters "r," "a," and "y" can be arranged as six permutations (ray, rya, ayr, ary, yar, yra). The formula for determining permutation in advance n-factorial (n!), calls for multiplying the number of objects or items (in this case 3) by all numbers preceding it down to 1 (in this case $3 \times 2 \times 1 = 6$). Five items gives 120 permutations. Ten items, such as ABCDEFGHIJ, yields 3,628,800 permutations.

pernicious anemia A Vitamin B-12 deficiency disease that can sometimes present as dementia in older persons and should be considered before assuming the patient is "senile," as it is largely reversible with proper nutritional supplements.

perplexity state A form of confusion in which patients are bewildered and uncertain about their own thoughts. It is most frequently found in schizophrenia, but a similar disorder sometimes occurs in toxic or infectious conditions, or in patients with head injuries.

persecution complex A set of symptoms associated with persons who feel they are the ongoing target of persecution, often stemming from prior life experiences in concentration camps, or persecution in flight. Symptoms may include anxiety, heightened reactivity, irritability, depression, psychophysiological disorders, phobic reactions, and unconscious identity with the aggressor. Should not be confused with the Stockholm syndrome. See SURVIVAL GUILT.

perseveration 1. Continuing some action to an unusual degree. 2. The pathological repetition of anything (for example, the same act, idea, word, or phrase) long past a normal amount. 3. (R. B. Cattell) Persistent repetition of behavior even when it is not successful. 4. Inability to interrupt a task or shift from one task or procedure to another. Extreme perseveration is frequently observed in patients with brain damage or schizophrenia.

perseveration factor A unitarily functioning factor varying in degree from one individual to another, showing itself as a tendency for mental processes to have a certain lag or inertia, and, also when activated, to perseverate. Also known as p factor.

perseveration set A tendency or predisposition acquired in a previous situation which is transferred to another situation where it may facilitate or interfere with the task at hand.

perseverative error 1. The continuing recurrence of an error, for example, the consistent misspelling of a word. 2. In neuropsychology, repetition of an incorrect response, frequently noted in patients with frontal lobe damage. 3. An error made by a subject usually at the same point in a series; for example, in a two-choice (either go right or go left) maze, a subject can complete the first seven of ten steps perfectly but at the eighth step frequently or constantly goes left rather than right and does not seem able to learn this particular required response to success. See FUNCTIONAL PLATEAU, NEGATIVE PRACTICE, PLATEAU.

perseverative functional autonomy Behavior that seems to have no purpose except possibly the pleasure of activity. See FUNKTIONSLUST, PROPRIATE FUNCTIONAL AUTONOMY.

perseverative speech　A speech disorder characterized by persistent, inappropriate repetition of the same word or phrase.

persistence of vision　A tendency of visual excitation to outlast the stimulus.

persona　1. A mask worn by an actor in ancient times (for example, Roman antiquity) to indicate a role played, a possible origin of the term "personality." 2. (C. G. Jung) Carl Jung used the term to refer to the "face" or "mask" or way of appearing appropriate to a specific role or social setting. It both shields an individual and reveals suitable aspects of the personality, but is often at variance with the personality as a whole. See HYPOCRISY THEORY.

personal adjustment　A person's adaptation to living and working conditions in family and community, with emphasis on interfacing of the personality with that of others with whom regular personal contacts are necessary.

personal attribution　dispositional attribution

personal audit　An oral or written interview or questionnaire designed to encourage respondents to assess their own personal strengths and liabilities.

personal causation　A belief that personal intentions and motives play a significant role in determining personal behavior.

personal commitment　Stage six of Lawrence Kohlberg's stages of moral development, representing concern with individual principles, conscience, and consistent, universal, ethical standards. See GURU STAGE, MORAL DEVELOPMENT, MORAL REASONING, POST-CONVENTIONAL LEVEL.

personal constant　Heinis constant

personal construct　(G. A. Kelly) 1. Primarily cognitive means by which people construe or interpret the events of their worlds. It is dichotomous and bipolar; it has a range of convenience, applying to some phenomena and not to others; and it may have greater or less permeability, or flexibility. 2. A concept of self based on bipolar elements such as "good-bad," "strong-weak," "kind-cruel," that people generate unknowingly. See PERSONAL CONSTRUCT THERAPY.

personal construct theory　(G. A. Kelly) Perhaps the most psychological of all personality theories, it consists primarily of a number of postulates, based on the central idea that a person's processes are psychologically channeled by the way in which he or she anticipates events. See FIXED-ROLE THERAPY, REPERTORY GRID.

personal construct therapy　(G. A. Kelly) A form of therapy in which clients are viewed as scientists who have developed theories about themselves and others, known as personal constructs. The essence of the therapy is to help clients see what their constructs are and to evaluate them, and if found faulty to revise them, thereby changing ways of thinking. See FIXED ROLE THERAPY.

personal data sheet　A questionnaire designed to elicit biographical facts about a person, including age, sex (gender), education, occupation, interests, and health history. Also known as demographic inventory questionnaire.

personal disjunction　A person's acknowledgement of the difference between what that person wants to achieve and what that person is likely to achieve.

personal disposition (PD)　(G. W. Allport) The individual trait pattern unique to a particular person. Most people can be described by 5 to 10 central, highly characteristic dispositions or traits. Of more limited occurrence, secondary dispositions are aroused by a narrow range of stimulus situations. See CARDINAL DISPOSITION, COMMON TRAIT, TRAIT.

personal-distance zone　The physical distance comfortable for interactions with friends and acquaintances. In North American the zone is ½ to 1¼ meters (1½ to 4 ft.). See BUBBLE CONCEPT OF PERSONAL SPACE, OPTIMAL INTERPERSONAL DISTANCE, PERSONAL SPACE, PROXEMICS.

personal document　A person's creative endeavors or productions, especially writings, such as diaries, short stories, but also including inventions, art works, that provide objective evidence of the individuality of the person who produced them. Such documents can serve a variety of purposes, including evaluation of sanity, assessment for employment or for a biography.

personal-document analysis　Examination of a person's letters, diaries, and other personal documents as a key to his or her personality. A case-study technique advocated by Gordon Allport.

personal equation　(F. Bessel) Phrase used in the early days of reaction-time studies to represent a difference in the rapidity of response of equally competent observers. Based on the discrepancy in time taken for astronomer Nevil Maskelyne and assistant D. Kinnebrook to estimate the exact transit time of a star over a line as viewed through a telescope (about one second). Maskelyne fired Kinnebrook over the discrepancy. Astronomer Friedrich Bessel concluded that there were consistent differences between people. See REACTION TIME.

Personal Experience and Attitude Questionnaire　A screening test for psychopathic behavior, containing 150 items on emotional instability, sexual psychopathy, nomadism, criminalism, and other psychopathic traits.

personal fable　1. (D. Elkind) The strong belief among early adolescents that they are unique and invulnerable (for example, other people will grow old and die but not them). 2. Adolescent egocentrism characterized by an exaggerated sense of personal uniqueness and indestructibility, which may be the basis of risk-taking behavior common during adolescence.

personal-growth group　A small group that uses encounter methods for self-discovery and the development of members' potential. See ENCOUNTER GROUP, HUMAN-POTENTIAL MOVEMENT.

personal-growth laboratory　A sensitivity-training institute that seeks to develop the participants' capabilities for constructive relationships, creative effort, leadership, and understanding of others through various modalities of experience and expression, such as art activities, intellectual discussions, sensory stimulation, and interactions on an emotional level. See GROWTH GROUPS, SENSITIVITY GROUPS.

personal-history questionnaire　A questionnaire that records information about a person's (usually a student's) special abilities, interests, extracurricular activities, family life, and any unusual medical, emotional, or other problem relating to scholastic performance or social adjustment.

personal identity   **identity** (meaning 2)

personal idiom   Distinguishing behavior characteristics or mannerisms of an individual.

personal image   An unconscious manifestation of personal experience, as distinguished by Carl Jung from the collective unconscious (the division of the unconscious comprising psychic contents common to all humankind, for example, general concepts of right and wrong), and the racial unconscious (the division of the unconscious comprising psychic contents continued from one generation to another, for example, motives and images that recur in an age and cline, without historical tradition or migration).

personalism   A variation of the statement "Man is the measure of all things," with the implication that behavior of anyone else is interpreted in terms of a personal set of values and goals.

personalistic approach   A view of history that celebrates the influence of individuals on events. Considers the effect of people such as Albert Einstein, Sigmund Freud, and Charles Darwin and asks if someone else would have come up with their concepts had they not done so?). See ZEITGEIST.

personalistic psychology   (J. M. Cattell) A school of psychology aimed at understanding individuals as living, dynamic, goal-oriented, feeling entities in contrast to generalizations about humans in general. A number of psychologists have taken this approach, including Wilhelm Dilthey, Eduard Spranger, and Franz Brentano. Among the 20th century psychologists, Alfred Adler, Gordon Allport, and Carl Rogers stressed an individualistic approach. See IDIOGRAPHIC PSYCHOLOGY, NOMOTHETIC PSYCHOLOGY, ZEITGEIST.

personality   1. A complex psychological construct that serves as an heuristic for understanding how an individual or a collectivity of persons typically behaves in situations that present to them differing affordances and demands. Dozens of theoretical models of personality have been developed, as well as paradigms for understanding the developmental processes that shape healthy and diseased personalities. 2. Persons' self-appraisal that leads to their conviction, "my personality is how I typically think, feel, and act. Only I can fully understand that. And my social behavior is not always truly representative of who I know myself to be." 3. The characterization of a person by observing others. This classical view was articulated by William James, who wrote, "Properly speaking, a man has as many social selves as there are individuals who recognize him and carry an image of him in their mind. But as the individuals who carry the images fall naturally into classes, we may practically say that he has as many different social selves as there are distinct groups of persons about whose opinion he cares." 4. An interior constellation of traits disposing individuals to act and experience themselves in generally consistent, enduring ways. This view was articulated by the renowned trait theorist, Gordon W. Allport, who wrote as follows: Personality is "... the dynamic organization within the individual of those psychophysical systems that determine his unique adjustment to the world." Innumerable personality types have been described that take their designation from a salient (usually pathognomonic) characteristic. Such categories are overlapping and allow multiple membership. Most are of limited scientific value. The principal limitation of such a taxonomy is that it largely refers to diseased rather than healthy personalities. Examples are: ACCIDENT-PRONE(NESS), ACROMEGALOID, ADDICTIVE, ALTER, ALTERNATING, ANAL, ANAL RETENTIVE, ANAL-EXPULSIVE, ANANCASTIC, ANDROGYNOUS, AS-IF, ASTHENIC, AUTHORITARIAN, BASIC, CHOLERIC, CO-CONSCIOUS, COMMON, COMPULSIVE, CYCLOTHYMIC, DR. JEKYLL-MR. HYDE, DUAL, DYSSOCIAL, EMOTIONALLY UNSTABLE, EPILEPTIC, EXPANDED, EXPLOSIVE, EXTRAPUNITIVE, HYPOMANIC, IMMATURE, INADEQUATE, INFANTILE, INTRACONSCIOUS, LIFETIME, LOKIAN, MALEVOLENT, MANIFEST, MELANCHOLIC, MIGRAINE, MULTIPLE, NARCISSISTIC, NEUROTIC, OBSESSIONAL, OBSESSIVE-COMPULSIVE, OPTIMAL, ORAL, ORAL-RECEPTIVE, PASSIVE-DEPENDENT, PREMORBID, PREPSYCHOTIC, PRETRAUMATIC, PRIMARY, PRIVATE, PSEUDOINDEPENDENT, PSEUDO-, PSYCHOPATHIC, SCHIZOID, SCHIZOTHYMIC, SCHIZOTYPAL, SECONDARY, SHUT-IN, SOCIOPATHIC, SPLIT, STORMY, SUBCONSCIOUS, TYPE A, TYPE B, ULCER. See PERSONALITY CHANGES.

personality assessment   The evaluation of such factors as intelligence, skills, interests, aptitudes, creative abilities, attitudes, and facets of psychological development by a variety of techniques including: (a) observational methods that use behavior sampling, interviews, and rating scales; (b) personality inventories such as the Minnesota Multiphasic Personality Inventory (MMPI); (c) projective techniques such as the Rorschach and Thematic Apperception Tests (TAT); and (d) information from other sources such as interviews with people who know the individual or materials that the individual in question has written or done. Sometimes, apparently contradictory information is found among various assessments of an individual. See COMREY PERSONALITY SCALE, EYSENCK PERSONALITY INVENTORY, MINNESOTA MULTIPHASIC PERSONALITY INVENTORY, PERSONALITY INVENTORY/TEST, Q-SORTS.

personality breakdown   Disintegration of the sense of self, leading to an inability to function normally. See ANOMIE.

personality changes   A tendency for people's basic personality characteristics to alter over time; for example, shy people become outgoing; aggressive people become passive; friendly people become hermits. May be abrupt or gradual, unintentional or intentional (such as due to counseling or therapy), or a function of aging or trauma or disease. See CONVERSION, PERSONALITY, ROLE TRANSITIONS, SHIFTING ROLES, TRANSFORMATION.

personality cult   See CULT OF PERSONALITY.

personality deterioration/disintegration   A progressive decline in a person's sense of personal identity, self-worth, motivational forces, and emotional life to the point where the person appears to be a "changed person" or even a "nonperson." See DETERIORATION.

personality development   The gradual development of characteristic emotional responses or temperament, a recognizable style of life, personal roles and role behaviors, a set of values and goals, typical patterns of adjustment, characteristic interpersonal relations and sexual relationships, characteristic traits, and a relatively fixed self-image. For more information, see these kinds of personality development: ATYPICAL, CHARACTER, COGNITIVE, EGO, MORAL, SEX.

personality disorder   1. A group of behavioral anomalies characterized by pervasive, maladaptive patterns of perceiving, relating to, and thinking about the environment, others, and the self, when these patterns interfere with long-term functioning of the individual and are not limited to isolated episodes. Such patterns of behavior are distinguished from psychotic and neurotic symptoms. 2. Loose phrase for any pervasive personality pattern not in accord with the equally nonspecific phrase "normal personality." Can be characterized as being of three types: (a) covert: the person experiences such feelings as loneliness, worthlessness, inadequacy, doubt, terror, guilt, but appears normal to others; (b) overt: the person's behavior such as pathological repetitive behavior, talking aloud to the self, unresponsiveness to others, disclosing paranoid ideas, is observed by others; and (c) mixed: the person has covert and overt signs of abnormal or pathological behavior. In the field of nosology (classifications of disorders), there are hundreds of terms to describe personality disorders, many of which are found in this volume. See DIAGNOSTIC AND STATISTICAL MANUAL OF MENTAL DISORDERS, INTERNATIONAL CLASSIFICATION OF DISEASE.

personality dynamics   The totality of covert elements that combine to make the individual move toward goals. An explanation for behavior based on the combination of that person's thoughts, wants, and feelings. See PERSONALITY INTEGRATION.

personality formation   The organization or structure of the components of an individual's character or personality.

personality-formation theories   Many theories of personality formation exist, some biologically based, some based on social circumstances, some that combine biological and social circumstances, still others that add the element of individual responsibility. Alfred Adler saw personality as an interaction of heredity, environment and the individual's creativity. Gordon Allport saw personality as a dynamic organization of traits. Sigmund Freud saw personality as the result of a conflict between heredity (id) and society (superego) for control of the ego. See BEHAVIORISM, EXISTENTIALISM, FIELD THEORY, INTERACTIONISM, NATIVISM, PSYCHODYNAMIC THEORIES, SITUATIONISM, SOCIAL LEARNING THEORIES, SPONTANEITY THEORY, TRAIT THEORIES, TRANSCENDENCE, TYPE THEORIES.

personality integration   1. The unification of an individual's personality dynamics to minimize inner conflicts and achieve effective adjustment. 2. The synergistic working of various elements of the inner self, such as memories, values, self-regard, attitudes toward others, goals, that enables a person to maintain a stable self and operate effectively.

Personality Inventory for Children (PIC)   (R. Wirr & D. Lachar) A questionnaire consisting of true-false items filled out by a knowledgeable adult, usually the mother. Based on the principles of the Minnesota Multiphasic Personality Inventory (MMPI), it contains a Lie scale, an overall Adjustment scale and 12 clinical scales. Designed for children ages 3 to 16.

personality inventory/test   1. Any instrument used to help evaluate personality or measure personality traits. 2. A standardized scale that assesses various aspects of the personality by having a participant respond to a listing of characteristics or situations. There are no correct and incorrect answers. It is mainly a self-appraisal inventory about certain traits and their application to the participant and practically all can be manipulated by participants. See BERNREUTER PERSONALITY ADJUSTMENT INVENTORY, COMREY PERSONALITY SCALE, EYSENCK PERSONALITY INVENTORY (EPI), MILLON CLINICAL MULTIAXIAL INVENTORY, MINNESOTA MULTIPHASIC PERSONALITY INVENTORY (MMPI), PERSONALITY ASSESSMENT.

personality model   (N. S. Endler) An analogical representation of a set of phenomena, without as much explanatory power as a theory, which attempts to approximate the "real world." Personality research and theorizing has been guided by four such basic models: See TRAIT MODEL, PSYCHODYNAMICS, SITUATIONISM, INTERACTIONISM.

personality problem   A psychological maladjustment that interferes with personal or social life but lacks the severity of a neurosis or psychosis.

personality psychology   The systematic study of the human personality, including: (a) its nature and definition, (b) its maturation and development, (c) the structure of the self, (d) key theories (trait theories, psychoanalytic theories, role theories, learning theories, type theories), (e) personality disorders, (f) individual differences, and (g) personality tests and measurements.

personality sphere   The complete range of definable personality traits. See SOURCE TRAITS, SURFACE TRAITS.

personality structure   The organization of the personality in terms of basic components and their relationship to each other. An arbitrary division of elements of personality as per theorists: lifestyles—Alfred Adler; trait clusters (cardinal, central, secondary)—Gordon W. Allport; ego, id, superego—Sigmund Freud; hierarchy of needs—Abraham Maslow; individual phenomenology—Soren Kierkegaard; constitutional types—William Sheldon.

personality test   An exam, verbal or written, that intends to assess persistent characteristics or patterns of behavior in a given individual. Such tests tend to be either questionnaires to which participants check the answers that apply to them, or projective tests in which replies are subject to interpretation by an examiner. Examples include: A STUDY OF VALUES, ALIENATION TEST, BECK DEPRESSION INVENTORY, BEHN-RORSCHACH TEST, BEM SEX-ROLE INVENTORY, BENDER VISUAL-MOTOR GESTALT TEST, BERNREUTER PERSONAL ADJUSTMENT INVENTORY, BLACKY TEST, BRAZELTON NEONATAL BEHAVIORAL ADJUSTMENT SCALE, BRIEF PSYCHIATRIC RATING SCALE, CALIFORNIA PERSONALITY INVENTORY, CALIFORNIA TESTS OF PERSONALITY, CHILDRENS' APPERCEPTION TEST, CHILDRENS' PERSONALITY QUESTIONNAIRE, CHILDRENS' DEPRESSION INVENTORY, CLINICAL ANALYSIS QUESTIONNAIRE, COMREY PERSONALITY SCALES, GENERAL ANXIETY SCALE FOR CHILDREN, HAND TEST, HARROWER-ERIKSON GROUP RORSCHACH, INCOMPLETE SENTENCES BLANK, JUNG ASSOCIATION TEST, LEVY DRAW AND TELL A

STORY TECHNIQUE, MAKE A PICTURE STORY TEST, MANIFEST ANXIETY SCALE, MAUDSLEY PERSONALITY INVENTORY, MILLON TESTS, MOONEY PROBLEM CHECKLIST, MYERS-BRIGGS TYPE INDICATOR, PERSONAL ORIENTATION INVENTORY, ROSENZWEIG PICTURE FRUSTRATION TEST, ROTTER INCOMPLETE SENTENCE FORM, SIXTEEN PF TEST, THEMATIC APPERCEPTION TEST, WORLD TEST.

personality theories   Systematic views of how the personality develops, matures, and changes. There are a number of such theories mentioned in this book such as Sigmund Freud's Psychoanalysis, Carl Jung's Analytical Psychology and Alfred Adler's Individual Psychology. There are many such theories, many of them partial rather than comprehensive. See BEHAVIOR THEORY, BIOSOCIAL THEORY, COGNITIVE-BEHAVIOR THEORY, CONSTITUTIONAL THEORY OF PERSONALITY, EXISTENTIAL-HUMANISM THEORY, LOGOTHERAPY, ORGANISMIC THEORY I AND II, PERSON-CENTERED THEORY, PERSONAL CONSTRUCTS THEORY, PSYCHOBIOLOGICAL THEORY, PSYCHOSYNTHESIS.

personality trait   A relatively stable and consistent behavior pattern which is considered to be a characteristic component of an individual's personality.

personality-trait theory   See ALLPORT'S PERSONALITY-TRAIT THEORY, CATTELL'S FACTORIAL THEORY OF PERSONALITY.

personality type   1. Simplistic classifications of people into categories usually described by a single term, such as brilliant, stingy, cruel, lazy, sweet. See PERSONALITY. 2. A classification of humans into specific categories determined by physique or other outstanding characteristics. Examples include Carl Jung's division into introvert and extrovert; Eduard Spranger's value types (theoretical, esthetic, social, religious, active, etc.); Erich Fromm's character types (exploiting, marketing, hoarding, etc.); and William Sheldon's constitutional types (ectomorphic, mesomorphic, endomorphic). See NOMOTHETIC APPROACH.

personal man   Carl Jung's phrase for persons who identify more with the persona or "mask" adopted for the outside world than with deeper layers of their own personality. Contrasts with individual man, who identify with deeper aspects of the self.

personal motives   Drives, urges, goals, originating in unique individual experience as contrasted with inborn drives (physiological) and those common to members of a particular culture (cenotropes).

personal myth   (E. Kris) Distorted autobiographical memories that serve to keep threatening experiences out of consciousness.

Personal Orientation Inventory (POI)   (E. Shostrom) A test developed by Everett Shostrom to measure self-actualization.

personal plan   1. A conception of any person about his or her personal future, whether or not known to others, that may have general goals, specific goals, or both. 2. A written plan of intervention and action developed by an agency with participation of all concerned which identifies a growth continua of development outlining progressive growth steps of direction from where the individual is at entry; usually based on diagnostic or relevant data that assist understanding of the individual situation.

personal relationship   See CONTACT BEHAVIOR.

personal-social inventory   An instrument that measures various personal traits associated with emotional and social patterns and overall adjustment. The rater may be the individual in question or an outside observer such as a teacher or counselor. See VINELAND SOCIAL MATURITY SCALE.

personal-social motive   See SOCIAL MOTIVE.

personal space   1. A physical area surrounding a person that a person will defend. 2. The area immediately around the body considered to be part of the self or part of personal territory. It is analogous to a country's territorial waters, into which intruders may not come. 2. The preferred amount of linear distance that people prefer to keep from other people, strangers and others. Research shows that in different cultures, different personal space limits occur. See BUBBLE CONCEPT OF PERSONAL SPACE, ENVIRONMENT, OPTIMAL INTERPERSONAL DISTANCE, PERSONAL-DISTANCE ZONE, PERSONAL-SPACE INVASION, PROXEMICS, SURROUND.

personal-space invasion   In social psychology, the intrusion by one person in the personal space of another. In the personal-space invasion one person inappropriately and uncomfortably crowds another without apparent motive. See PERSONAL SPACE, OPTIMAL INTERPERSONAL DISTANCE, PERSONAL-DISTANCE ZONE, PROXEMICS.

personal standing   A rating that people make of themselves and others on the basis of appearance, dress, deportment, and behavior, that serves to indicate to others whether to approach or not approach another person on the basis of potential friendship or intimacy (for example, whether a person has a perpetual smile or frown in neutral situations).

personal unconscious   (C. G. Jung) The part of the unconscious unique to the individual, including repressed or forgotten experiences as well as creative potentials. Differentiated from the collective unconscious pertaining to race or culture.

person-centered therapy   (C. R. Rogers) Originally called nondirective counseling and client-centered therapy, it is an approach to psychotherapy in which clients express their thoughts and feelings while the therapist sets up an accepting atmosphere and clarifies the clients' ideas rather than directing the treatment process. In this system the therapist asks no questions, gives no advice, and makes no diagnoses. The three major concepts are that therapists should (a) be genuine; (b) have unconditional positive regard for the client; and (c) demonstrate empathic understanding. See AUTOCHTHONOUS, CLIENT/PATIENT, NONDIRECTIVE APPROACH, NONDIRECTIVE PLAY THERAPY.

person factor/variables   (W. Williams, S. Cecil) Old phrase for the biological basis of psychological behavior.

personification   1. The attribution of personal or human characteristics to an object or abstraction. 2. (H. S. Sullivan) The pattern of feelings and attitudes toward others arising out of interpersonal relations with them. 3. The image a person has of someone else. 4. See ANTHROPOMORPHISM.

personified self (H. S. Sullivan) The organization of interpersonal experiences that make up self-representation, or self-image. Based on the acceptable and approved "good-me," the unacceptable and disapproved "bad-me," and the anxiety-provoking "not-me." The personified self becomes a source of security and a defense against anxiety. See various entries beginning with SELF-.

person-machine system Equipment, often electronic, that is designed to be operated by people. Ranges in complexity from a surgeon's scalpel to the computer/internet system. Once known as man-machine system.

personnel data Information about employees or job applicants derived from personnel tests, application forms, interviews, physical examinations, and letters of reference, used in matching individuals and jobs.

personnel placement The assignment of an existing or newly-hired employee to the particular job for which the employee is considered best qualified.

personnel psychology The art or science of (a) making desired choices in the hiring of people; (b) managing people to cooperate with others to generate an effective operating team; and (c) dealing with individuals' aspirations and development. Increasingly being called human resource management.

personnel selection The matching of job applicants and present employees to job requirements, usually relying on tests, interviews, and demographics.

personnel specifications The criteria (or predictors) for effective performance of a particular job, including such factors as education, training, work experience, physical characteristics, abilities, and interests. Also known as job specifications.

personnel tests Individual or group tests used in employee selection and assessment of job performance, comprised of (a) aptitude tests, measuring basic abilities and skills; (b) achievement tests, measuring job specific abilities such as computer skills; and (c) personality and interest inventories, used as "predictors" of job performance.

personnel training An industrial training program designed to achieve such goals as development of knowledge and skills, orientation to the company, and modification of supervisor or employee attitudes, through such learning procedures as audiovisual aids, lectures, simulated devices, conference method, role playing, laboratory training, case discussions, behavior modeling, business games, and programmed instruction.

personology 1. The study of personality. 2. The study of individual personality from the holistic point of view, on the assumption that actions and reactions, thoughts and feelings, and personal and social functioning can be understood only in terms of the whole person. 3. (H. A. Murray) Term applied by H. A. Murray to his theory of personality as a set of enduring tendencies that enable humans to adapt to life. Holds that personality is also a mediator between an individual's fundamental needs (viscerogenic and psychogenic) and the demands of the environment.

Personology Theory A biosocial theory that overlaps with many others including the ideas of Alfred Adler, Adolf Meyer, and Kurt Goldstein, by whom Gardner Murphy was certainly affected; nevertheless, he introduced a number of specific concepts such as teleological movement toward perfection, the canalization of thinking and acting, the individual as a thinking reactor to stimuli, and even Kurt Lewin's view of individuals in context. The following are important for understanding Gardner Murphy's theory: BIOSOCIAL THEORY, CONFLICT, NEED, INTERORGAN GENERALITY, NEURON DOCTRINE, SELF-MAINTENANCE MORES, SHARED AUTISM.

person-situation controversy The debate concerning the primacy of an individual's characteristics over the specificity of a situation in determining behavior.

Persons of Opposite Sex Sharing Living Quarters (POSSLQ) A habitation category to join "single" and "married," as an alternative classification to "common-law married."

person with a disability Phrase replacing older terms such as "crippled," "handicapped," and "retarded," that carry negative connotations. Focuses on what the person can rather than cannot do. Reflects the fact that some disabilities may be due to societal attitudes or environmental barriers rather than to the perceived disability. See CHALLENGED, LABELING, ROSENTHAL EFFECT, SELF-FULFILLING PROPHECY, SPECIAL-NEEDS PEOPLE.

perspective 1. An ability to view objects, events, and ideas in realistic proportions and relationships. 2. The delineation of the relative position, size, and distance of objects in a plane surface as if they were three-dimensional. 3. The ability of a person to be able to understand another person from more than one point of view. 4. Point of view. See EMPATHY, OUT-SIGHT, PERSPECTIVE TAKING.

perspective taking Attempting to understand and value the beliefs and feelings of others. See EMPATHY, PERSPECTIVE.

persuasion Attempts to get another person to change a thought or behavior. To succeed, such factors are the logic of the message, the credibility of the source of the message, the attending circumstances of the communication, and relevant historical factors, plus history of those who receive the communication with some open to new ideas and others who are closed to them.

persuasion therapy Supportive psychotherapy to attempt to induce clients to modify faulty attitudes and behavior patterns by appealing to logic and good sense. Alfred Adler and others (notably P. C. Dubois and Joseph Déjérine) advocated this technique as a brief alternative to reconstructive methods. See PASTORAL COUNSELING.

persuasive-arguments theory (E. Burnstein & A. Vinokur) In group dynamics, an explanation of polarization following discussion. Assumes that members shift toward the more valued pole or the one that generates more persuasive arguments. Compare SOCIAL COMPARISON THEORY.

persuasive communication   Human interactions to attempt to influence the thinking and behavior of others whether for the good of the persuader, the persuadee or both.

pertinence model   (D. Norman) In perception, a quality related to the personal relevance of a stimulus; a weak stimulus with high pertinence value can attract attention.

perturbation   (E. S. Shneidman) A measure of how mentally upset, disturbed, perturbed a person is; a component of the suicidal scenario; to be distinguished from lethality.

perturbation theory   1. A means of disposing of varieties of extraneous factors among true psychological factors, such as these causes of errors: instruments, observers, subject sampling, observation. 2. An approach that sets aside artificial factors, from scoring methods, scaling, etc., that encumber the true psychological factors emerging from a research. See CHANCE ERROR, CONSTANT ERROR, DESIGN OF RESEARCH, ERROR VARIANCE, EVALUATION OF RESEARCH, TRUTH, VALIDITY.

pervasive developmental disorders   A group of disorders that have severe distortions of many physical and mental functions, such as language, social skills, attention, perception, reality testing, and movement. Some may be due to neurological anomalies and some due to faulty factors during development such as inadequate or incorrect information by parents, failure to develop social skills, lack of attention, or critical attitudes by those in a child's surround.

perversion   1. Behavior considered unnatural to the group of which the person is a member. 2. A culturally unacceptable or prohibited form of behavior, particularly in the sexual sphere (a paraphilia). See CANNIBALISM, COPROPHILIA, FETISHISM, SADISM, MASOCHISM, NECROPHILIA, PEDOPHILIA, ZOOPHILIA.

perverted logic/thinking   **paralogia**

pessimism   A personality trait characterized by negative thinking and discouragement, and an inclination to emphasize the worst rather than the best, believing in failure rather than success. See ORAL PESSIMISM.

PET   1. Parent-effectiveness training. 2. Positron-emission tomography.

Peter Panism   Refusal to acknowledge growing older, expressed in such ways as ignoring birthdays, dying the hair, undergoing cosmetic surgery, and proving personal prowess. Derives from the ever-young protagonist of Sir James Barrie's 1904 play *The Boy Who Never Grew Up.* Also known as Peter Pan syndrome.

Peter principle   (L. J. Peter) A satirical comment that in an organization, people often rise to their level of incompetence.

petit mal   (small sickness—French) A form of epilepsy characterized by sudden, brief lapses of consciousness during which the patient sits motionless with a dazed, expressionless face, but does not have a convulsion or fall. Also known as absence, minor epilepsy. See GRAND MAL.

petite absence   See SHORT-STARE EPILEPSY.

petitio principii   **begging the question**

petrifaction   1. Turned into stone. In mythology this fantasy represents punishment for voyeuristic behavior. 2. (R. D. Laing) Metaphorically turning into a stone when under threat, being unresponsive to certain stimuli, such as a person interviewed under threat of torture generating a state of immobility and insensitivity. See DEATH-FEIGNING, TONIC IMMOBILITY.

PET scan   See POSITRON EMISSION TOMOGRAPHY.

pet therapy   See ANIMAL-ASSISTED THERAPY.

petting (behavior)   Sexual activity that may lead to sexual stimulation and orgasm without coitus. Often classified as "light petting" (mostly kissing and touching) and "heavy petting" in which participants may go as far as possible without actually engaging in sexual intercourse. See TECHNICAL VIRGIN.

petty commodity production   (K. Marx) Production in which the producer owns the means of production and the scale of production is small.

peyote   The source of the hallucinogen mescaline, a small Mexican cactus of the species *Lophophora williamsii.* The entire cactus is psychoactive, but only the portion above the ground is eaten, being sliced into disks called "mescal buttons." Peyote is the only American plant that has been used continuously in religious ceremonies from prerecorded times. Also known as pellote, peyotl.

p factor   See PERSEVERATION FACTOR.

PFQ   See SIXTEEN (16)-PERSONALITY FACTOR QUESTIONNAIRE.

Pfropfschizophrenia   A form of schizophrenia superimposed on mental retardation, usually with paranoid episodes with delusions and hallucinations, which may be followed by gradual regression to infantile, deteriorated behavior. Inaccurately spelled propfschizophrenia.

PF Study   See PICTURE-FRUSTRATION STUDY.

PGO   See PONTINE GENICULATE OCCIPITAL SPIKES/WAVES.

PGR   See PSYCHOGALVANIC REFLEX/RESPONSE.

PGSR   See PSYCHOGALVANIC SKIN-RESISTANCE AUDIOMETER.

pH   Hydrogen ion concentration, acidity-alkalinity being rated on a scale from 0 to 14. 7 is neutral, 0–6 indicates increasing acidity and numbers 8–14 increasing alkalinity.

Ph.D.   doctor of philosophy, written PhD on occasion.

Phaedra complex   Incestuous love of the mother for her son. In mythology, when Phaedra's stepson rejected her overtures, Phaedra accused him of rape, then hanged herself. See MOTHER-SON INCEST.

phagomania   Insatiable desire to consume food. See BULIMIA.

phagophobia   Morbid fear of eating, or swallowing. See ANOREXIA NERVOSA, CIBOPHOBIA.

phakoscope   (H. von Helmholtz) A viewing instrument that uses reflected images from the surface of the lens of the eye for observation of size changes during the accommodation process of the lens.

phallic aggression/display   Posturing by the male to show the penis, often erect. Seen in various animals as a dominance message. Also known as penis display.

phallic character In psychoanalytic theory, a person who displays patterns of behavior arising out of a reaction formation to castration fear such as boastfulness, excessive self-assurance, narcissistic vanity, and in some cases aggressive or exhibitionistic behavior. In women, the reaction to penis envy is thought to be in the form of masculine behavior or antagonism toward males. Also known as phallic-narcissistic character.

phallic display phallic aggression

phall(ic)ism Reverence for the creative forces of nature as symbolized by the phallus; phallic worship.

phallic love 1. Love characteristic of the phallic period. 2. A strong emotional feeling for genitals (of one's own or of others), whether of the same or other gender (sex), individual or generalized. See LOVE.

phallic mother In psychoanalytic theory, the fantasy among male children that the mother has a penis.

phallic-narcissistic character In psychoanalytic theory, a personality pattern of Don Juan behavior as a defense mechanism against castration anxiety. Caused by an unresolved Oedipus complex. See DON JUANISM.

phallic oath Based on some anthropological evidence and an unclear biblical allusion, the swearing of an oath with one's own hand on own penis or testicles, possibly as a gesture of solemnity, or on someone else's organs as a sign of respect. See PENIS HOLDING.

phallic phase/stage (S. Freud) In psychoanalytic theory, the stage of psychosexual development starting around age 4, when sexual feeling is first focused on the genitalia, and masturbation becomes a major source of pleasure. See OEDIPUS COMPLEX.

phallic pride In psychoanalytic theory, the sense of superiority and even omnipotence experienced by boys when they discover that they have a penis and girls do not.

phallic primacy In psychoanalytic theory, the stage of psychosexual development which follows the pregenital period (oral and anal), beginning in the third year of life, when the penis and the clitoris gradually become the central erotogenic zones. See PHALLIC PHASE/STAGE.

phallic sadism Aggression associated with the child's phallic stage of psychosexual development. Children interpret sexual intercourse as a violent, aggressive activity on the part of the male. See ORAL SADISM.

phallic symbol In psychoanalytic theory, any pointed or upright object that resembles or represents the penis, such as cigars, pencils, trees, skyscrapers. (Sigmund Freud is rumored to have said, "Sometimes a cigar is. . .just a good smoke.") See LINGAM, SYMBOLISM.

phallic woman In psychoanalytic theory, a woman who is fixated at the phallic stage, and as a result consciously seeks to deny that she lacks a penis, or unconsciously wishes to castrate all men so that they will also be deprived of a penis.

phallic worship Religious ceremonies that honor the penis, as in the Greek cults of Dionysus and Priapus, and in ancient and modern Hindu, Shinto, and Buddhist rites.

phallo-centric (E. Jones) A tendency of psychoanalytic theory to attach extreme importance to the penis and to explain the psychology of women as a reaction to the discovery that they lack a penis.

phallocentric culture A culture which views the penis as a sacred giver of life, source of power or symbol of fertility.

phallophobia Morbid fear of the penis, especially of the erect penis.

phallus 1. The penis or an object that resembles the form of the penis, for example, the clitoris or the undifferentiated primordial tissue that eventually develops into either the clitoris or the penis. 2. In psychoanalytic theory, the penis during the period of infantile sexuality. Also spelled phallos.

phallus girl The fantasy of some transvestites of being a girl with a hidden penis.

phaner(o)mania A persistent impulse to touch or stroke part of one's own body, such as the nose or the breasts.

phanerothyme Obsolete term introduced by Aldous Huxley in 1956 for what was vaguely called psychotomimetic. See HALLUCINOGENS, PSYCHEDELICS.

phantasm An illusion or pseudohallucination, usually of an absent person appearing in the form of a spirit or ghost, but recognized by the observer as being imaginary or illusory, as opposed to a true hallucination.

phantasmagoria The imagined process of raising or recalling the spirits of the dead.

phantasticum Old term suggested by toxicologist Louis Lewin to identify a category of drugs capable of producing hallucinatory experiences. The same drugs were later called hallucinogens or psychedelics.

phantom A stimulus perceived that does not exist in reality.

phantom breast See BREAST-PHANTOM PHENOMENON.

phantom color In the Kanizsa figure, if the inducing elements have a particular color, the triangle will tend to have a weak desaturated hue. See KANIZSA FIGURE.

phantom limb phenomenon A feeling that an amputated limb (or other body part) is still there. Usually temporary and accompanied by paresthesias such as tingling, burning, or itching; may be due to stimulation of the nerve ends or psychological reactions. Also known as phantom extremity. See BREAST-PHANTOM PHENOMENON, PSEUDOESTHESIA.

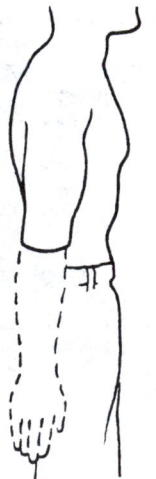

phantom limb

phantom-lover syndrome   A type of delusional loving included in the category of erotomania. Patients, usually with schizophrenia, believe a distinguished person, whom they do not know, is in love with them.

phantom reaction   See BREAST-PHANTOM PHENOMENON, PHANTOM LIMB.

phantom sound   A single sound heard when two qualitatively similar sounds with slight differences in intensity are brought to the two ears separately.

pharmacodynamics   1. How drugs affect the body, what the positive (or negative) effects are, drug-drug interactions (how more than one drug modifies the effects of another drug), how much it takes to be effective, and how much it takes to become toxic. 2. The cellular and tissue response to the relative concentration at the active site of a drug, that is, how a medicine acts on the body. Compare PHARMACOKINETIC(S).

pharmacogenetics   The study of genetic factors that can influence the response of individuals to different drugs, and at different dosages.

pharmacogenic orgasm   A pleasurable sensation sometimes obtained by using drugs of abuse.

pharmacokinetic(s)   The attainment and maintenance of the appropriate contrast of a drug. Includes consideration of factors that affect absorption, distribution, metabolism, and elimination of the substance or its metabolites. Competing drugs, levels of binding proteins in the blood, amount of fat or water in the body, levels of liver or kidney function, and dose and time dependence are examples of more specific factors. These account in part for differences in appropriate prescription for different ages. In psychiatry, a special pharmacokinetic feature involves whether or not a drug can penetrate the membranes and vessels which seem to protect the brain in a special way (the "blood-brain barrier").

pharmacokinetic interactions   How the body handles a drug, how it's absorbed, where it's distributed, what organs it reaches, how it is neutralized or metabolized (taken apart or combined with other chemicals by enzymes in the liver or elsewhere, or excreted by the kidneys); how the drug competes with other drugs in the system.

pharmacological antagonism   Drug antagonism that is competitive between a receptor stimulator and a receptor blocker, such as between morphine and naloxone. Phrase is used to distinguish the interaction from physiological antagonism between drugs that have opposing actions.

pharmacology   The study of the preparation, qualities, uses, and effects of drugs.

pharmacomania   Obsolete term for an abnormal desire to take or administer drugs.

Pharmacop(o)eia (P)   A listing of drugs starting with their purposes, chemical structures, properties, dangers, recommended doses, side effects and research history.

pharmacophobia   Rare term for a morbid fear of medicine. See NONCOMPLIANCE.

pharmacopsychosis   Rare term for a psychosis causally related to taking a drug.

pharmacotherapeutic regimen   The plan for the use of medicines.

pharmacotherapy   The treatment of mental disorders with medicines, as contrasted to psychotherapy, or somatic therapy such as using electroconvulsive treatments, and wet packs. See CHEMOTHERAPY, HOMEOPATHY.

pharmacothymia   Obsolete term for a compelling, neurotic desire to take drugs.

phase   1. A stage in the development of life, such as puberty or adulthood. 2. A recurrent state of any cyclical process such as a sound wave or a phase of the moon. Types of phases include: ABSOLUTE-REFRACTORY, ANAL, ANAL-SADISTIC, ANA-, AROUSAL, AUTISTIC, CANNIBALISTIC, CATABOLIC, CLONIC, DEUTEROPHALLIC, EXCITEMENT, FIRST NEGATIVE, GENITAL, INTER-, LIBIDINAL, LUTEAL, MAGIC, META-, NEGATIVE, OEDIPAL, ORAL, ORAL-EROTICISM, ORGASMIC, PERFORMANCE, PHALLIC, PLATEAU, POSTAMBIVALENT, PREGENITAL, PRESUPEREGO, PRODROMAL, PROLIFERATIVE, PROTOPHALLIC, REFRACTORY, RELATIVE REFRACTORY, RESOLUTION, REVERSAL, SECOND NEGATIVE, SENSITIVE, SHOCK, SUPERNORMAL RECOVERY, TELO-, URETHRAL, VAGINAL. See also STAGES.

phase cue   A sound localization cue in binaural hearing. At frequencies below 800 Hertz (cycles per second), the time of arrival of sound waves reaching the ears on opposite sides of the head is often sufficiently different to indicate from which direction the sound is coming from.

phase difference   A difference in phase sequence of two sound waves, resulting in beats or alternating intensities.

phase locking   Synchronization of neurons to fire in a regulated manner with certain other repetitive stimuli, a phenomenon especially noted in auditory fibers of the ear.

phase sequence   (D. O. Hebb) A series of nerve-cell assemblies linked in a functional relationship, for example, a conscious thought process.

phase shift   A sleep disorder caused by a disruption of the normal sleep-wake cycle, resulting in alertness during a usual sleeping period and sleepiness during a usual waking period.

phasic activation   1. Attentional mechanisms related to the diffuse thalamic projection system that are transitory rather than tonic or persistent in nature. 2. Mechanisms that are transitory rather than tonic or persistent in nature.

phasic functions   Transient increases of attention and arousal associated with the diffuse thalamic projection system. Longer tonic effects are associated with the reticular activating system.

phasmophobia   Morbid fear of ghosts. See DAEMONOPHOBIA.

phatic communication   Talk for the sake of talk, without meaningful communication.

phenakistoscope   (J. A. Plateau) A viewing device that causes a deceptive image. Used in the first effort to show motion pictorially. See STROBOSCOPE.

phencyclidine (PCP)   A street drug used since the late 1960s which provokes a giddy euphoria in small doses, and a variety of problematic symptoms, anxiety, violent rage and surprisingly destructive strength, catatonia, confusion, mood shifts, and in overdose, high blood pressure, coma, and rarely, death. At first considered a type of hallucinogen PCP was later no longer classified with those drugs. May be sprinkled on marijuana and smoked, taken as pills or injected. Street names include: angel dust, hog, PeaCe Pill, rocket fuel, superjoint, tranq, zombie.

phenelzine   Generic name of an antidepressant of the less-frequently used class of monoamine oxidase inhibitors (MAOIs). Trades include Nardil.

phengophobia   Morbid fear of daylight or, generally, of any time other than night time. See FEAR OF DARKNESS.

phenmetrazine   Generic name for an anorexic drug. See ADRENERGIC DRUGS.

phenobarbital   Generic name for a widely used sedative-hypnotic medicine in the 1920s through the 1950s, as a sleep aid, in small doses as an antispasmodic (to treat the "spasms" of an irritable bowel), as an anti-epileptic drug, and as a mild tranquilizer (before that term became common, the general term before that was "sedative"). However, it had a low therapeutic/toxic ration, meaning that relatively little past the therapeutic dose could be fatal. A long-acting drug, it left people who used it as a sleep-aid with a hangover, and made children who took it for "febrile seizures" a bit sluggish and slowed their learning. Has been superseded by the mild tranquilizers. Trade name is Luminal. See BARBITURATES.

phenobarbitone   British name for phenobarbital.

phenocopy   Imitation of a phenotype resulting from the interaction of an environmental effect and a genotype, such as the effect of sunlight on skin or hair, resulting in variations that mimic the natural coloring or texture of other phenotypes, thus a pale white skin may tan to look dark.

phenomenal absolutism   1. Uncritical certainty of naive observers that they are perceiving in a direct, un-mediated way the attributes of various objects. 2. Belief that personal perceptions may be taken as objective reality.

phenomenal field   1. The totality of a person's experiences, both conscious and unconscious. 2. The private world of experience, that makes up a person's unique frame of reference. 3. Subjective reality including everything within the personal field of awareness. 4. In Gestalt psychology, the immediate experience-world in which all organisms live. Also known as phenomenological field. See PHENOMENAL SELF.

phenomenalism   1. A doctrine positing that sequential events can be causally related even if they occur in different places, without direct contact. 2. A philosophical doctrine that appearances, or experienced phenomena, are the only real accessible entities and therefore only they provide the true objects of knowledge.

phenomenalistic introspection   A process used by Sigmund Freud in which people are asked to report their thoughts in a natural free-flowing manner without restraints or interruptions. See FREE ASSOCIATION.

phenomenal motion   1. Movement that is not real but is experienced as real, such as continuing to feel the rocking movement of the ocean after leaving a boat. 2. The illusion or appearance of motion as on film; for example, the picture perceived on a television screen is actually a single point of light that moves so rapidly that the whole scene changes about 30 times a second, giving the impression of continuous movement; "Movies" generate their effect of apparent movement by a rapid success of static pictures that occur about 80 times a second. See APPARENT MOVEMENT, PHENOMENOLOGICAL FIELD.

phenomenal perception   That which a person uniquely perceives. For example, in viewing the illustration at AMBIGUOUS FACES, one person may see a face looking to the left and another face looking to the right. Both see the same circle, a curving line and two dots, but interpret it differently.

phenomenal regression   In perception, people often do not see what actually exists but rather what they expect to see. Without conscious intention, the imagination is used to some extent to create the final impression. See CONSTANCY for an example of this phenomenon.

phenomenal report   1. An account of everything within a personal field of awareness. 2. An account of personal responses to a specific stimulus. 3. A summary account of personal thoughts and feelings about participating in an experiment. See PHENOMENOLOGICAL FIELD, PHENOMENOLOGY.

phenomenal self   The "self" as experienced by an individual at a given time. See PHENOMENOLOGICAL FIELD.

phenomenistic causality   (J. Piaget) A type of childish logic in which coincidences are viewed as causal relationships, such as believing the sun hides at night because it is afraid of the dark. See ANIMISM.

phenomenological analysis   A method of radical empiricism in which overt behavior and immediate experience are observed and studied without concern for biographical data or reliance on assumptions of unconscious mental activity.

phenomenological method   The unbiased description of natural mental experience as it occurs to the experiencer. See PHENOMENALISTIC INTROSPECTION.

phenomenological therapy   An approach to therapy, exemplified best by Carl Rogers's approach of person-centered therapy, that attempts to see matters from the client's frame of reference.

phenomenologists   Psychologists and philosophers who approach the study of human nature by seeking to understand consciousness. In contrast to the "behaviorists," they are interested in making use of individual subjective experience, introspective reports, and mental processes, to derive their understanding of the world from the individual's point of view. For theories of this type, see EXISTENTIALISM, HUMANISM, INDIVIDUAL PSYCHOLOGY, PERSON-CENTERED THERAPY, PERSONAL CONSTRUCTS, PERSONALISM.

phenomenology 1. The systematic study of immediate experience, or of the world as it appears to the observer; contrasted with an analytic approach of Wilhelm Wundt and his followers. 2. The theory that knowledge of humans, including psychology and psychiatry, should be based on immediate, ongoing experience, attending to phenomena as they are directly presented. Observation must come before analysis and interpretation. The phenomenology movement was initiated at the beginning of the 20th century by the German philosopher Edmund Husserl; it has greatly influenced Gestalt psychology and modern Existentialism. See EXISTENTIAL PHENOMENOLOGY.

phenomenon 1. Any information available through the senses. 2. Any experienced extraordinary event. Types of phenomena include: ADAPTATION-LEVEL, ANTIDROMIC, AUBERT, AUBERT-FORSTER, AUTOKINETIC, AUTOSCOPIC, BEZOLD-BRÜCKE, BIRDS OF A FEATHER, BLUE-ARC, BREAK, BREAST-PHANTOM, CHROMATIC DIMMING, CLASP-KNIFE, CLEVER HANS, COCKTAIL-PARTY, COLORED-SHADOW, DOPPELGANGER, DOPPLER, ECHO, EMMERT'S, ENTOPTIC, EPI-, ERROR, FÉRÉ, FREGOLI'S, FUCHS, GAMMA, HOLMES, HONI, I-KNEW-IT-ALL-ALONG, INDEPENDENT, ISAKOWER, JET-LAG, JUST-WORLD, NAPALKOV, OVERCONFIDENCE, PANUM, PHI, POLTERGEIST, PÖTZL, PROUST, PULFRICH, PURKINJE, REICHENBACH, RELEASE, REVOLVING-DOOR, RIDDANCE, SECURE BASE, SOCIAL, STAIRCASE, STATE-DEPENDENT, TARCHANOFF, TIP-OF-THE-TONGUE, TRANSFERENCE, TWO PLUS TWO, WOLF PACK, ZEIGARNIK.

phenomotive (W. Stern) A motive that can be revealed and observed introspectively. See VISUALIZATION.

phenothiazines General name for the most widespread class of antipsychotic drugs, especially during the 1950s and 1960s. See ANTIMANICS, CHLORPROMAZINE, NEUROLEPTICS, NEUROLEPTIC SYNDROME, TARDIVE DYSKINESIA.

phenotype (W. L. Johannsen) All the visible and physical characteristics of an organism. The phenotype (what an organism looks like) is the manifestation of the genotype (genetic constitution) during the developmental history of the organism. What a person sees in the mirror is his or her phenotype based on the genotype that exists as a particularized human genome.

phenylketonuria (PKU) (A. Fölling) A syndrome characterized by congenital deficiency of phenylalanine 4-mono-oxygenase associated with the inability to metabolize phenylalanine to tyrosine. The deficiency is routinely tested for in infants at birth and dietary elimination of phenylalanine can be instituted as a preventive measure. If untreated PKU can lead to severe mental retardation called phenylpyruvic oligophrenia.

phenylpyruvic oligophrenia See PHENYLKETONURIA.

pheromones (P. Karlson) Glandular odoriferous secretions by a male or female used for identification of territory or for communication purposes. Especially important for survival of the species since a female's pheromones lead males to her during mating time. Most evident among insects such as butterflies, but seen among domestic animals if not spayed or castrated. Despite a concerted search, only minor and indirect evidence has surfaced for pheromones in humans. For instance, women living together tend to synchronize their menstrual cycles, and women in intimate relations tend to have more regular cycles as if caused by pheromones from the partner, as do sexually inactive women exposed to male odors. See EXTERNAL CHEMICAL MESSENGER, VOMERONASAL SYSTEM.

phi (ϕ, Φ) The twenty-first letter of the Greek alphabet. See APPENDIX C.

phi coefficient (r_ϕ or Φ) A computational approach to obtaining a correlation estimate when both variables are dichotomous, such as YES/NO rather than continuous. Used primarily to express the degree of association between two discrete dichotomous variables. From a four-fold table phi is calculated by: $\Phi = (|bc-ad|) \div [(a+b)(a+c)(b+d)(c+d)]^{1/2}$, Where: r_ϕ or Φ is the Φ coefficient, bc is the product of entries in cells b and c, ad is the product of entries in cells a and d, and the denominator are the marginal sums of 2×2 table. (Or: Where the letters refer to the cell and marginal frequencies of a table.) When the variables are true dichotomies, phi ranges only from zero to +1.00 and Φ_{max} is rarely unity; it is interpreted by Φ/Φ_{max}. When the category of the variables is ordered by scaling each dichotomous variable 0 or 1, phi ranges as do correlation coefficients from −1.00 to +1.00. Also known as fourfold coefficient, fourfold-point correlation.

Phi-gamma function ($\phi(\gamma)$) A psychophysical function for measuring the intensity of stimuli observed by judges in relation to a threshold. Empirically, the distribution of judgmental responses takes the shape of an ogive—a cumulative normal distribution.

phi-gamma hypothesis A postulate that data obtained by the constant stimulus method will fit the phi-gamma function and generate a normal curve. Also known as the phi-gamma assumption.

philia 1. Craving, affinity, or love for specific objects or situations. The near-opposite of phobia, except that only a few phobias have a specifically sexual context whereas most philias (called paraphilias) are erotic attachments experienced almost exclusively by men, often termed fetishes. Virtually anything can form the basis for such an attachment, due to the effects of simple classical conditioning, cultural teaching, and the human imagination. See MANIA, PARAPHILIA, PHOBIA. 2. Nonsexual attachment between friends.

Phillips Scale (L. Phillips) A method of analyzing the premorbid social and sexual adjustment of patients with schizophrenia as part of a prediction of the chances for early recovery by the patient.

Phillips 66 method/technique (C. Phillips) A procedure used especially for lecture-type sessions in which groups of six individuals meet for six minutes. Members are asked to form subgroups of six people; one person in each group volunteers to act as the spokesperson for that group; the groups discuss a given topic for six minutes; the various spokespersons call out to the whole group questions generated by each of their groups and the lecturer responds to these.

philoprogenitive   A trait of loving children that, according to Franz Gall, is demonstrated by a prominent bump or feature of the cranium. See GALL'S PERSONALITY AREAS, PHRENOLOGY.

philosophical psychology   1. The study of philosophical issues related to psychology, including the body-mind problem, the nature of consciousness, the place of values in human life, the meaning of existence, and the nature and limits of scientific method. 2. See RATIONAL PSYCHOLOGY.

philosophy   A discipline that attempts to understand the first principles of all knowledge based primarily on reason and logic, and covering such topics as theology, metaphysics, epistemology, ethics, politics, history, and aesthetics. Academic psychology developed out of philosophy, and many people who studied psychology in colleges up to about 1940 took their courses in philosophy departments. In the history of psychology, prior to the modern age that began about 1880, many of the people now regarded as precursors of psychology were philosophers, such as Aristotle and Plato.

philter   A drug that allegedly provides magical power to the person taking it. Also spelled philtre. See OCCULTISM.

phi motion   (Max Wertheimer) In Gestalt psychology, the perception of what appears to be a continuous smooth motion of a single object from one place to another when physically two separate objects are successively displayed in two distinct locations. Compare PHI PHENOMENON.

Phineas Gage (1823–1861)   A railroad worker who, while packing gunpowder with a tamping rod, ignited the gunpowder, driving the tamping rod into his cheek and through his skull, doing massive damage to his left frontal lobe. He survived the accident and whereas apparently his memory and intelligence were not changed, his personality after this event was drastically different. Previous to the accident he was considered a "nice" congenial person, but after the accident he was so ill-tempered, irritable, and vulgar, that he was no longer "Gage." The first unpremeditated frontal lobotomy. See BRAIN INJURIES, FRONTAL LOBE DAMAGE, PRETRAUMATIC PERSONALITY.

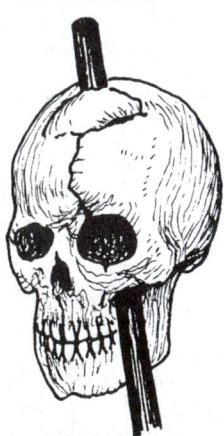

Phineas Gage   An illustration depicting how the skull of Phineas Gage might have looked with the tamping rod through it.

Phineas Gage syndrome   (A. R. Damasio) Undesirable personality changes as the result of a frontal lobotomy or similar frontal lobe damage.

phi phenomenon   An illusion of apparent motion, generated by stationary stimuli, which occurs, for example, when two lights flashed in brief succession are perceived as continuous motion from one to the other. Commonly seen in the apparent movement of lights around a theatre marquee or in lighted road signs which appear to have a moving arrow. Also known as pure phi phenomenon. See APPARENT MOVEMENT, GESTALT.

phlegm   Mucus.

phlegmatic (type)   (Hippocrates, Galen) One of the original constitutional personality types described by Hippocrates and revised by Galen who attributed an apathetic individual to the dominance of phlegma (mucus) over other humors (body fluids). See HUMORAL THEORY, TYPOLOGY.

phlogiston theory   A view that when something burned, some material called phlogiston, was lost. A number of scientists, such as Lavoisier, apparently independently showed that this was not so, and that matter can neither be created nor destroyed but only changed.

phobia(s)   Excessive, unrealistic, uncontrollable, morbid fears of specific persons, places, and situations, including some that few other people have. The most usual explanation for a specific phobia is that early in life, before conscious memory, people were frightened at a certain time, certain place, or by a certain event, and that subsequently a fear was associated with that particular situation or event. List of phobias follow.

Fear of	Name of Phobia
air	aerophobia
alcoholism	alcoholophobia
aloneness (being alone)	autophobia, eremi(to)ophobia, eremophobia, monophobia.
aloneness (being left alone)	monophobia
angina attack	anginophobia
animal skin(s) or fur	doraphobia
animals	zoophobia
bacilli	bacillophobia
bacteria	bacteriophobia
barren space	cenophobia, kenophobia
beards	pogonophobia
beating (of being beaten/flogged)	mastigophobia, rhabdophobia
bed (going to)	clinophobia
bees	apiphobia, melissophobia
birds	ornithophobia
birth of malformed fetus or of giving birth to a monster	teratophobia
blood or bleeding	hemaphobia, hematophobia, hemophobia
blushing	ereuth(r)ophobia, erythrophobia
bodily odor	bromidrophobia, bromidrosiphobia
books	bibliophobia
brain disease	meningitophobia
breaking a mirror or mirrors in general	catotrophobia, eisoptrophobia, spectrophobia

bridges (crossing a river bridge)	gephrophobia	deserted place(s)	eremophobia
		diabetes	diabetophobia
bullets, thrown objects, or missiles	ballistophobia	dirt	coprophobia, mysophobia, rhypophobia, rupophobia
burial (of graves or of being buried alive)	taphephobia, taphophobia	dirt (being dirty)	automysophobia
bulls	taurophobia	disease (specific)	monopathophobia
burglars, bad, or evil people	scelerophobia	disease (in general)	nephophobia, nosophobia, pathophobia
cancer	cancer(o)phobia, carcinophobia	disorder	ataxiophobia
		dog(s)	cynophobia
carriages	amaxophobia	dolls	pediophobia
cats	ailurophobia, galeophobia, gatophobia, geleophobia	double vision	diplopiaphobia
		draft(s)	aerophobia, anemophobia
		drink	potophobia
change	kaino(to)phobia, neophobia	drugs or medicine	pharmacophobia
childbirth	parturiphobia, tocophobia, maieusiophobia, ped(i)ophobia	duration or time	chronophobia
		dust	amathophobia, koniophobia
children		duty (neglect or omission of)	paralipophobia
choking	angi(o)nophobia, pnigophobia	duty (responsibility)	hypengyophobia, ergasiophobia, ergophobia, hypegiaphobia
cholera	cholerophobia		
church(es)	ecclesiophobia, euclosephobia	eating (food)	cibophobia, phagophobia, sitophobia
climbing	climacophobia		
clouds	nephophobia	electricity	electrophobia
coitus	coitophobia	emptiness or empty spaces	kenophobia
cold	cheimaphobia, cheimatophobia, psychro(po)phobia	enclosure (being enclosed)	clithrophobia
		error(s)	harmatophobia
		everything	pamphobia, pan(o)phobia, pantophobia
color(s)	chrom(at)ophobia		
comet(s)	cometophobia	excrement	coprophobia, scatophobia
computers (using them)	computerphobia, cyberphobia	eyes	ommatophobia, ommetaphobia
confinement (being confined or locked in)	claustrophobia, clithrophobia	failure	kakorrhap(h)iophobia, kakorraphiaphobia
constipation	coprostasophobia	falling asleep or sleeping	hypnophobia
contamination (especially by feces)	coprophobia, molysmophobia, mysophobia, scatophobia.	fatigue	kopophobia, ponophobia
		fear or fearing	phobophobia
		feathers	pteronophobia
corpse(s)	necrophobia	feces (contamination by)	coprophobia, molysmo-phobia, mysophobia, scato-phobia.
criticism (in general)	enissophobia		
criticism (by a group)	homilophobia		
crossing a street	agyrophobia, dromophobia	fever	febriphobia, pyrexiophobia
crowds or crowded places	agoraphobia, demophobia, ochlophobia	filth (personal)	automysophobia
		filth (in general)	coprophobia, mysophobia, rhypophobia, rupophobia
crystals	crystallophobia		
dampness or moisture	hygrophobia	fire	pyrophobia
darkness	scotophobia, achluophobia, nyctophobia	fish	ichthyophobia
		flash of light or lightning	selaphobia
		floods	antlophobia
dawn	eosophobia	flowers	anthophobia
daylight	phengophobia	flutes or phallic-shaped instruments	aulophobia
death or dead things (especially humans)	necrophobia, thanatophobia		
		flying	aviophobia
death (impending death)	meditatio mortis, thanatophobia	fog	homichlophobia
		food or eating food	cibophobia, phagophobia, sit(i)ophobia
defecation (process or product)	rhypophobia		
		foreign languages	xenoglossophobia
deformity	dysmorphophobia	forest(s) or woods	hylephobia, hylophobia
demons or (the) devil	demon(ophob)ia, satanophobia, entheomania	freedom	eleutherophobia
		frogs	batrachophobia
		fun	cherophobia
dental procedures or teeth	odontophobia	functioning	ergasiophobia
depth(s) or deep place(s)	bathophobia	fur or animal skin(s)	doraphobia

genitals (female)	eurotophobia
germs	microphobia, spermophobia, spermatophobia
ghosts	phasmophobia
glare of light	photaugiaphobia
glass	crystallophobia, hyalophobia, hyelophobia
God	theophobia
gold	aurophobia
graves or being buried alive	taphephobia, taphophobia
gravity	barophobia
hair or hair disease	chaetophobia, tricho(patho)phobia
hair (proliferating on body)	hypertrichophobia
heart disease	cardiophobia
heat	thermophobia
heaven	ouranophobia, siderophobia, uranophobia
heights, high places or objects	acrophobia, altophobia, batophobia, hyp(o)sophobia,
hell	hadephobia, stygiophobia
heredity	patroiophobia
home or returning home	nostophobia, ecophobia, oecephobia, oikophobia
homosexuality or homosexuals	homophobia
horses	equinophobia, hippophobia
houses	domatophobia, oikophobia
human companionship	anthropophobia, phobanthropy
humidity or moisture	hygrophobia
humiliation	catagelophobia
ice or frost	cryophobia
ideas	ideophobia
idleness or sitting still	thaasophobia
illness	nosophobia
imagined deformities in appearance	dysmorphophobia
imperfection	atelophobia
infection	molysmophobia
infinity	apeirophobia
injury	traumatophobia
innovation or newness	neophobia
inoculation(s)	trypanophobia, vaccinophobia
insanity	lyssophobia, maniaphobia
insects	acarophobia, entomophobia
itch or itching	acarophobia
jealousy	zelophobia
justice	dikephobia
knives	aichmophobia
knowledge	epistemophobia
lakes	limnophobia
large objects	macrophobia, megalophobia
laughter (being laughed at)	catagelophobia
left side (things to own left)	levophobia, sinistrophobia
lice	pediculophobia, phthiriophobia
light	photophobia
lightning	astra(po)phobia, keraunophobia
locked up (being confined or locked in)	claustrophobia, clithrophobia

loneliness	erem(i)ophobia, monophobia
looks (being looked at or stared at)	scophophobia, scopophobia
losing one's mind	phrenophobia
machinery	mechanophobia
magic	rhabdophobia
man or men	anthrophobia, androphobia
many things	polyphobia
marriage	gametephobia, gametophobia, gam(o)phobia
materialism	hylephobia
medicine(s)	pharmacophobia
men or males	androphobia
meningitis	meningitophobia
meteors	meteorophobia
mice	musophobia
microbes	bacillophobia, microbiophobia
microorganisms	microphobia
mind	psychophobia
minute objects	microphobia
mirrors or breaking a mirror	catotrophobia, eisoptrophobia, spectrophobia
mites	acarophobia
mobs	ochlophobia
moisture or dampness	hygrophobia
money	chrematophobia, chrometophobia, chronmetophobia
monsters or giving birth to a monster	teratophobia
motion	dromophobia, kinesophobia, kinetophobia
movement(s)	kinesophobia
nakedness or naked body	gymnophobia
names, naming, or being named	nomatophobia, onomatophobia
needles or sharp objects	belonephobia
neglect or omission of duty	paralipophobia
night	noctiphobia, nyctophobia
northern lights	auroraphobia
novelty	kainophobia, kaino(to)phobia, neophobia
nudity	gymnophobia, nudophobia
odor (personal)	bromidrosiphobia
odor (of bodies)	bromidrophobia, bromidrosiphobia
odor (in general)	olfactophobia, osmophobia, osphresiophobia
one thing	monophobia
open places or public places	agoraphobia
overwork (being overworked)	ponophobia
pain	algophobia, odynophobia, ponophobia
particular word or name	onomatophobia
passing high buildings	batophobia
people (in general)	anthrophobia, anthropophobia, phobanthropy
people (bad or evil people, especially burglars)	scelerophobia

phobia(s)	phobophobia	small objects or animals	micro(bio)phobia
pins	enetophobia	smell(s)	olfactophobia, osmophobia,
places (in general)	topophobia		osphresiophobia
places (deserted ones)	eremophobia	smothering	pnig(er)ophobia
pleasure	hedenophobia, hedonophobia	snakes	herpetophobia,
points, pointed items	aichmophobia		ophidiophobia,
poison	iophobia, toxi(co)phobia,		ophi(ci)ophobia
	toxophobia	snow	chionophobia
poison (being poisoned)	toxophobia, iophobia	society	anthrophobia
poverty	peniaphobia	solitude	eremophobia, eremiophobia,
precipice(s)	cremnophobia		autophobia, monophobia
pregnancy	maieusiophobia	sound(s)	acousticophobia,
priests	hierophobia		phonophobia
public places or open	agoraphobia	sourness	acer(b)ophobia, aerophobia
places		specific illness	nosophobia
punishment	poinephobia	speech or speaking in	lal(i)ophobia, gloss(o)-
rabies	cynophobia,	public	phobia, phonophobia
	hydrophobiaphobia,	speed (going fast)	tachophobia
	hydro(phobo)phobia	spiders	arachnophobia,
railroads or trains	siderodromophobia		arachnaphobia,
rain or rainstorms	ombrophobia		arachne(o)phobia
rectum or rectal disease	proctophobia, rectophobia	spirits	pneumatophobia
red (the color) or of	erythrophobia	stairs	climacophobia
blushing		standing up	stasiphobia, stasophobia
religion, rites, or sacred	hierophobia	standing erect and walking	stasibasiphobia, basiphobia
objects		stares (being stared at)	scophophobia, scopophobia
reptiles	herpetophobia	stars	siderophobia
responsibility	hypengyophobia,	stealing	kleptophobia
	ergasiophobia, ergophobia,	stillness	eremiophobia
	hypegiaphobia	stings (from an insect)	cnidophobia
retribution from God for	theophobia	stories	mythophobia
sinning		strangers, foreign people	xenophobia
ridicule	catagelophobia,	and cultures	
	katagelophobia	street (crossing the)	agyrophobia, dromophobia
right (things to own right)	dextrophobia	string	linonophobia
river(s)	potamophobia	stuttering or stammering	lal(i)ophobia
robbers	harpaxophobia	success	polycratism
rods	rhabdophobia	suffocation	anginophobia
ruin	atephobia	sun or sunlight	heliophobia
rusty objects	iophobia	swallowing	phagophobia
sacred religious objects	hierophobia	symbolic representation	symbolophobia
saints	hag(io)phobia	or symbolism	
Satan or the devil	Satanophobia	symmetry	symmetrophobia
scabies	scabiophobia	talking	lal(i)ophobia
scratch (of being scratched)	amychophobia	tapeworms	taeniophobia
sermons	homilophobia	taste	geumaphobia,
sex	aeratephobia, erotophobia,		geumatophobia
	gen(o)phobia	teeth or dental procedures	odontophobia
sexual intercourse or	coitophobia,	thinking (of having to	phrenophobia
activity	cypri(do)phobia	think)	
sexual love	erotophobia	thinking	phronemophobia
shadows	sciophobia	thirteen (the number)	triskaidekaphobia,
ships	nautophobia		tredecaphobia
shock	hormephobia	thunder or thunderstorms	brontophobia, tonitrophobia,
sin or sinning	hamartophobia,		keraunophobia,
	peccatophobia,		astra(po)phobia
	peccat(t)iphobia,	time	chronophobia
	enosiophobia	touch (any kind)	haptophobia, haphophobia,
sitting down	kathisophobia, thaasophobia		thixophobia
skin	dermatosiophobia	touching or being touched	(h)aphephobia, haptephobia
skin disease(s)	dermatopathophobia,	travel	hodophobia
	dermatosiophobia,	trembling	tremophobia
	dermatophobia	trichinosis	trichinophobia
sleep or of going to sleep	hypnophobia	tuberculosis	phthisiophobia,
slime	blennophobia, myxophobia		tuberculophobia

tyrants	tyrannophobia
urine	urophobia
vehicles or riding in them	amaxophobia, hamaxophobia, ochophobia
venereal disease	cyprido(o)phobia, cypriphobia, venereophobia
voices	phonophobia
void(s)	kenophobia
vomiting	emetophobia
vulvas	aeratephobia
walking	basiphobia
water	aquaphobia, hydrophobia, nautophobia
waves	cymophobia
weakness	asthenophobia
wind or drafts	ancraophobia, anemophobia
women or females	gynophobia, genephobia, gynephobia, horror feminae
words	lexophobia, logophobia
work	ergasiophobia, ergophobia, ponophobia
worms or infestation by worms	helminthophobia, verminiphobia, vermiphobia
wound or injury	traumatophobia
writing	graphophobia, graphaphobia
young girls	parthenophobia

phobic anxiety   (S. Freud) A type of anxiety that stems from unconscious sources but is displaced to objects or situations (insects, telephone booths, open areas) that represent the real fear but pose little if any actual danger in themselves. See FLOATING ANXIETY, PANIC.

phobic attitude   (F. Perls) A behavior pattern apparently characterized by disruptions in the awareness of and attention to experience in the present (for example, engaging in a fantasy of the future to escape a painful present reality). See GESTALT THERAPY.

phobic character   Phrase applied by Otto Fenichel to extremely inhibited, fearful persons. When faced with internal conflicts, such individuals resort to the defense mechanisms employed in phobic reactions, namely, projection, displacement, and avoidance.

phobic disorders   A group of disorders in which the essential feature is a persistent, irrational fear and avoidance of a specific object, activity, or situation. The person may know that the fear is unreasonable, but it is nevertheless so intense that it interferes with everyday functioning and is often a significant source of distress. See PHOBIA.

phobic reaction   Neurosis characterized by persistent irrational fears of such an intense and dominating character that they interfere with everyday life. In facing a phobic situation, such as walking through a tunnel, the person experiences not only acute distress, but autonomic symptoms such as stomach upset. If the person continues to walk into the tunnel, these feelings may increase to panic proportions. See PHOBIC DISORDERS.

phobophobia   Morbid fear of acquiring a phobia, or of being afraid.

phoenix   A legendary bird that lives about 500 years and upon death burns up and is reborn from its ashes, thus a symbol of psychological regeneration or rebirth of people who suddenly change for the better, sometimes seen in people who have divorced or lost a life-partner.

phon   1. A word element or speech sound. 2. A measure of subjective loudness, equal to 40 sones, a frequency of 1000 Hertz (cycles per second). The phon offers an arbitrary benchmark for measuring sound intensity, whereas the decibel scale has no threshold or zero but represents a ratio in loudness between two sounds of different intensities. Compare DECIBEL.

phonantograph   A device that changes sounds into graphical waves.

phonasthenia   1. Abnormal voice production characterized by articulation being too high, too loud, etc. 2. See BREATHY VOICE.

phonation   The production of voiced sounds by means of vocal-cord vibration.

phonatory theory   A fundamental concept related to voice production: the movements of the vocal cords, caused by the breath pressure, determine the intensity, the pitch, and some of the voice qualities, such as different types of hoarseness.

phone   A unit of speech sound that can be discriminated from other sounds. Contrast PHONEME. See INTERNATIONAL PHONETIC ALPHABET.

phoneidoscope   An apparatus that permits visual recording of sound waves that can be used for various purposes, including identifying a person whose voice was recorded. Also known as phonelescope.

phonelescope   **phoneidoscope**

phoneme   A fundamental structural unit of sound, audible speech, or group of speech sounds combined into syllables and words, each language having a limited number and each phoneme having relevance only for that language. English has 45 to 50 phonemes, depending on who generates them. They are usually displayed as follows /p/ /t/.

phoneme-grapheme correspondence   A relationship between the graphic elements of a language (such as letters and signs) and the phonological-grammatical units for which they stand (such as phonemes, syllables, and words). In most writing systems, as in English, the "fit" is far from being perfect, which is the main reason for difficulties in spelling.

phonemic disorders   Disturbances of speech sounds that distinguish words from one another; for example, in aphasic speech disorders, the patient loses those phonemes first that were most recently acquired, the opposite of the way phonemes are learned.

phonemic restoration effect   A tendency to perceive a speech sound that was purposefully omitted from a spoken statement.

phonemics   The study of sounds in any language. See PHONETICS.

phonetic method   Training people with vocal disabilities (such as those who are deaf) to speak by a variety of methods.

phonetic reading   Reading by decoding the phonetic significance of letter strings. Also known as sound reading.

phonetics   The study of speech processes, that is, the production of perceptions and transcriptions of phones (speech sounds) including the anatomy, neurology and pathology of speech. See PHONEMICS.

phonetic symbolism   (R. Brown) A word may, in any of a number of ways (including onomatopoeia but not limited to onomatopoeia) suggest its meaning to a person who has not yet learned its meaning.

phoniatrics   The study of speech habits, the science of speech.

phonic method   A procedure for teaching reading by emphasizing the sound of letters or groups of letters. Also known as phonics, sounding.

phonics   1. The science of sound. 2. See PHONIC METHOD.

phonism   1. Auditory synesthesia; a form of synesthesia in which a sound generates a sensation in another sense, such as taste or smell. 2. Experiencing a particular sound when a nonauditory stimulus occurs, such as hearing a tinkling sound when tasting salt. See PHONOPSIA, PHOTISM, SYNESTHESIA.

phonogram   A graphic or symbolic representation of speech sounds.

phonological dysgraphia   A writing disorder characterized by inability to sound out words, write them phonetically, or both.

phonological dyslexia   A reading disorder in which a person can easily read familiar words, but not unfamiliar words or pronounceable nonwords. See ACQUIRED DYSLEXIA, DEVELOPMENTAL DYSLEXIA.

phonological loop   (A. Baddeley) A memory store that can briefly retain speech-based information. It comprises the articulatory control process and the phonological store. See WORKING MEMORY.

phonological loop model   In working memory, a storage system for speech-related input. Information is held in a phonological loop for up to two seconds and is then lost unless maintained by subvocal rehearsal.

phonology   1. The study of sounds in a language. 2. The sound system of a language (phonemes and their phonetic description). 3. The history of sound changes in a language. See LINGUISTICS.

phonopathy   Any vocal disorder.

phonophobia   1. Exaggerated fear of sounds. 2. Fear of voices or the sound of one's own voice; fear of speaking aloud. See ACOUSTICOPHOBIA, GLOSSOPHOBIA, LALIOPHOBIA.

phonopsia   A condition in which certain sound stimuli elicit the subjective sensation of color. See PHONISM, SYNESTHESIA.

phonoscope   Obsolete term for a device that changes sounds into visual waves, such as a spectrograph.

phoria   Directions assumed by the eyes in binocular fixation when there is no adequate stimulus to produce fusion of gaze.

phosphenes   Visual images perceived through stimuli other than light on the retina. May result from pressure on the eyes (as in pressing against the closed lids), a blow to the back of the head ("seeing stars"), and electrostimulation of the occipital cortex. See PHOTOPSY.

phot   A light unit, the centimeter-gram-second (cgs) unit of illumination equal to about 929 footcandles (10,000 luxes). See LUMEN, MILLIPHOT.

photerythrosity   Increase in sensitivity to light near the red end of the spectrum. See DEUTERANOPE.

photic driving   A technique used to stimulate epileptic activity in cortical neurons of patients suspected of having epilepsy.

photic sensitivity   **photosensitivity**

photism   1. A false perception or hallucination of light. 2. Experiencing colors when a particular nonvisual stimulus occurs, for example, hearing a bell ring and perceiving a bright light. See PHONISM, PHOTOPSY, SYNESTHESIA.

photobiology   1. The study of the effects of color on organisms, for example, experiments indicate that a pink room tends to have a calming effect on violent children. 2. The study of the effects of light, including color, on behavior.

photochromatic interval   Visual stimuli sufficient to affect the rods but not enough to affect the cones, so that the sensation of light is produced but not the sensation of color.

photochronograph   A recording device for determining sequential phases of movement by photographing minute intervals of time from a series of pictures of a moving object.

photocounseling   The use of photographs or videotape about the client's life to obtain insight into the client's behavior and needs, and to facilitate rapport, communication, and behavior change.

photoelectric oximeter   A type of oximeter that measures or monitors changes in the blood's volume in the optical path without extracting blood. Compare REFLECTANCE OXIMETER.

photogenic epilepsy   A form of reflex epilepsy in which seizures are precipitated by a particular kind of visual aberration, such as a flickering light. See EPILEPSY, PHOTIC DRIVING.

photographic memory   A common name for eidetic imagery occurring in adults. See EIDETIC IMAGERY.

photokinesis   The action of light on organisms that incites them to action, as in a cockroach scurrying away from a light source.

photokymograph   A recording device for photographing waves of movement, such as the saccadic movement of the eyes during reading.

photoma   A visual hallucination in which sparks or light flashes are seen without external stimuli. See PHOTOPSY.

photomania   1. An abnormal craving for light. 2. Sun worship. See SEASONAL AFFECTIVE DISORDER (SAD).

photometer   A light meter. An instrument designed to measure the intensity of light or to determine the light threshold. Generally, photometers measure candlepower, illuminance, and luminance by adjusting two unequal lights until they appear equal, and equating them with a known brightness. See WEDGE PHOTOMETER.

photometry   The measurement of the intensity of light.

photon 1. A particle of light. 2. A unit of visual stimulation defined as that illumination upon the retina which results when a surface brightness of 1 candle per square meter is seen through a pupil of 1 square millimeter area.

photoperiodism Reactions of certain animals and plants to changes in the lengths of days or intensity of light in the environment, affecting seasonal migration, reproductive cycles, and changes in pelts and plumages as well as changes in colors of leaves and their shedding.

photophobia Fear of light or a strong negative reaction to light.

photopia 1. (J. H. Parsons) Extreme sensitivity to light. 2. See PHOTOPIC VISION.

photopic luminosity The relative effectiveness of various wavelengths of light on visual acuity under light-adapted conditions.

photopic-sensitivity curve A graphic representation of data obtained as a participant adjusts the brightness of light at various wavelengths until the test light appears as bright as a standard patch of white light.

photopic vision 1. Vision as it occurs under illumination sufficient to permit the discrimination of colors. 2. Cone-based vision, associated with daylight activity during which the rods are relatively ineffective due to bleaching of the their rhodopsin content.

photopigment A protein dye bonded to a substance derived from vitamin A; when struck by light it bleaches and stimulates the membrane of the photoreceptor in which it resides.

photopsin A protein in the cones of the retina. Along with retinene, a product of the breakdown of iodopsin upon exposure to light.

photopsy The sensation of light flashes in the absence of actual light stimulation probably caused by mechanical stimulation of visual nerve tissue. Sometimes known as photoma, photopsia. See PHOSPHENE.

photoreceptor 1. A receptor stimulated by energy of the band of wave lengths that make up the visible spectrum. 2. A visual receptor; a rod or cone cell of the retina.

photosensitivity 1. Sensitivity to light, especially sunlight, experienced by albinos. 2. Susceptibility to seizures precipitated by light in persons with photogenic epilepsy. 3. Intolerance of light in response to certain illnesses or chlorpromazine and neuroleptic drugs. Also known as photic sensitivity.

phototaxis Behavior expressed by movement toward or away from a light source. See PHOTOKINESIS, TAXIS, TROPISM.

phototherapy 1. The use of environmental light for psychotherapeutic purposes, such as daily exposure to bright light to treat seasonal affective disorder (SAD). 2. The use of nonultraviolet, full-spectrum SAD fluorescent light (known as a sun box) for treating SAD. Persons with SAD are exposed to such light for two hours daily during winter months. Based on the idea that the SAD results from inadequate stimulation by light.

phototropism 1. An orienting response, either positive or negative, to light. 2. Automatic movement of an organism toward or away from a light source, for example, cockroaches move away from light (negative phototropism). See PHOTOTAXIS, TAXIS, TROPISM.

PHR point-hour ratio

phrase-structure grammar A theory that structural aspects of language can best be reduced to phrase components, as meaningful units. In recall experiments, participants made the highest number of mistakes between phrases while making fewer mistakes within phrases, indicating the tendency to remember phrases as units.

phratry (L. H. Morgan) In anthropology, extended kinship grouping; phratries are often organized around a division of labor.

phrenasthenia Obsolete term for mental deficiency.

phrenology A pseudoscientific approach contending that psychological attributes correspond to swellings and hollows in the skull, reflecting the development of particular areas of the brain. Called craniology by Franz Gall, renamed phrenology by Johann Spurzheim. Also known as Gall's craniology. See GALL'S PERSONALITY AREAS for an illustration of a human head with various sections mapped out. Note where the occipital area where a bump allegedly indicates love of children.

phrenophobia 1. Morbid fear of losing one's mind, of "going crazy." 2. Morbid fear of having to think. See PHRONEMOPHOBIA.

phrenopraxic Obsolete term for drugs that have an altering effect on the psyche. See PSYCHOTOMIMETICS, PSYCHOTROPIC DRUGS.

phrictopathic sensation An indefinite unpleasant, tingling sensation of touch that is not clearly identified as to location. See EPICRITIC SENSATION.

phronemophobia Morbid fear of thinking or making a mental effort. See PSYCHOPHOBIA.

PHS Public Health Service (DHHS)

phthinoid Ernst Kretschmer's term for an asthenic (narrow, underdeveloped) body type. Such a physique has the flat, narrow chest associated with the stereotype of the tuberculous patient.

phthiriophobia See PEDICULOPHOBIA.

phthisic type (Hippocrates) A body type described as thin and flat-chested, as were people suffering from tuberculosis. See TYPOLOGY.

phthisiomania tuberculomania

phthisiophobia Morbid fear of tuberculosis. Also known as tuberculophobia.

phylesis 1. Natural course of evolutionary development. 2. Relating to a biological line of descent.

phyletic status An organism's position within a single line of evolutionary descent.

phyloanalysis A means of investigating disorders of human behavior, both individual and collective, resulting from impaired tensional processes that affect the organism's internal reaction as a whole. Trigant Burrow adopted this term to replace his earlier term, "group analysis," which was first used to describe the social participation of many persons in their common analysis. See GROUP THERAPY. Also see DISSIPATIVE BEHAVIOR, I-PERSONA, PARTITIVE BEHAVIOR, PHYLOBIOLOGY, SEMIOPATHIC, SOCIAL IMAGE.

phylobiology (T. Burrow) 1. A personality theory that attempts to unite biological and social factors to form a total view not only of individuals but of human societies. 2. A type of behavioral science that emphasizes biological rapport with the environment as a governing, unitary force that motivates the organism.

phylogenesis The origin and evolution of species, or of any organ or function in a given species.

phylogenetic Hereditary elements common to all members of that species.

phylogenetic functions The functions common to all members of a species, as contrasted with ontogenetic (or individual) characteristics.

phylogenetic mneme The racial ancestral memory assumed to exist in a person's deep unconscious. See RACIAL MEMORY, UNCONSCIOUS.

phylogenetic principle (G. S. Hall) A doctrine positing that ontology recapitulates phylogeny or individuals from embryo to adulthood repeat the stages of human evolution.

phylogeny (E. Haeckel) The evolutionary development of a species, as opposed to ontology, the development of a single individual. For Carl Jung, the phylogenetic origins of personality lay in the individual's inheritance, through primordial images, the past experience of the human race. See COLLECTIVE UNCONSCIOUS.

physiatrics Physical therapy.

physical adjustment Harmonizing of the human organism with its physical environment.

physical anthropology The study of the physical attributes, as distinguished from the mental or cultural attributes, of the human. See ANTHROPOLOGY.

physical determinism A doctrine that developed out of the physical sciences, emphasizing that physical facts are absolutely dependent upon and conditioned by their causes.

physical education In rehabilitation, the use of physical exercise to correct defects, improve the patient's physical condition, encourage socialization, and build morale.

physicalism 1. A doctrine positing that all of reality, including the mind, can be reduced to physical reality. 2. A doctrine positing that all aspects of psychology can eventually be explained by physical science; all psychological matters are essentially explainable in physical terms. 3. A general point of view that the only reality is physical elements, things that can be seen and touched and that other facets in the universe including thoughts are based on these physical elements. See EMPIRICISM, IDEALISTIC MONISM, OPERATIONALISM, POSITIVISM.

physically correct In describing dolls, complete with external genitals.

physical stimulus 1. A stimulus that can be described fairly exactly for other experimentalists; for example, a bell-sound can be duplicated fairly closely by knowing all its physical properties, and the same for a light, etc. 2. A stimulus that can in some manner be measured in terms of its effect on the surface of the body, such as the power of a blow, the loudness of a sound, or the brightness of a light.

physical strain See STRESS.

physical symbol system hypothesis (A. Newell & H. A. Simon) The postulate that the necessary and sufficient condition for a physical system, living or artificial, to be capable of displaying intelligence is that it be a physical symbol system. See PHYSICAL SYMBOL SYSTEM.

physical symbol system (A. Newell & H. A. Simon) An operative system (brain, computer) capable of inputting, outputting, storing, transforming and comparing symbols (simple or complex patterns capable of denoting other internal or external patterns or stimuli). See ARTIFICIAL INTELLIGENCE, COGNITIVE SIMULATION.

physical therapy (PT) 1. Treatment of pain, disease, or injury using physical means. Also called physiotherapy. 2. A branch of medicine concerned with promotion of health and prevention of physical disability, usually from musculo-skeletal disorders. Includes evaluation and rehabilitation of persons with temporary or permanent disabilities due to pain, injury, or disease, using therapeutic (as opposed to medical or surgical) means. 3. The treatment of bodily disorders using, for example, cold, heat, exercise, rest, water, and massage, to relieve pain and improve muscle function. See MEDICAL TREATMENT.

physician-originated disorder See IATROGENESIS, IATROGENIC ILLNESS.

physiodrama See PSYCHODRAMA FORMS.

physiodynamic therapies Treatments of mental disorders that involve affecting the body to generate cognitive-emotional reactions to bring psychotic people back to their senses, such as the use of cold-water high-pressure hoses, and chairs that fall suddenly through the floor, lowering people into pits filled with snakes. More modern methods include the use of wet packs, metrazol injections, and electroconvulsive shocks. See DISJUNCTIVE THERAPIES, MEDICAL TREATMENT.

physiogenic Pertaining to a disorder organic in origin.

physiognomic perception (H. Werner) Denoting the tendency of children to view the world in light of emotional and motor qualities. The same tendency is frequently found in persons under the influence of hallucinogenic drugs who attribute human attributes such as motivations and emotions to inanimate objects.

physiognomic thinking The first stage in the process of thought development of children. Characterized by the child's tendency to animate objects and project his or her self into them ("This block is my dog"), a step called syncretic thought by Jean Piaget.

physiognomy (Aristotle, J. Lavater, C. Lombroso) The assessment of personality from facial features, holding, for instance that a receding chin indicates weakness, a high forehead, intelligence. Also known as physiognomics. See CONSTITUTIONAL TYPOLOGY, PHRENOLOGY, SOCIAL STEREOTYPE, STIGMATA OF DEGENERACY.

physiological age A measurement of the level of development or deterioration of an individual in terms of functional norms for various systems.

physiological antagonism A form of drug antagonism in which two substances have opposing actions. A stimulant such as caffeine would show physiological antagonism in combination with a barbiturate drug. Also known as pharmacological antagonism.

physiological basis (of personality)   Patterns of reaction that may have a biochemical or genetic basis. A pattern may be associated, for example, with amounts of endocrine secretions, or it may be genetic, as in familial incidences of schizophrenia or certain inborn errors of metabolism.

physiological cycles   Bodily activities that change regularly, usually in terms of inherent elements such as sleeping patterns.

physiological dependence (to drugs)   The need to use a drug, accompanied by tolerance and, if discontinued, severe withdrawal effects.

physiological feedback   The instrumental conditioning of autonomic responses by central reinforcement (electrical stimulation of the brain) in a paralyzed organism, thereby ruling out mediation by skeletal movements. The phenomenon is considered controversial. Sometimes known as internal feedback. See BIOFEEDBACK.

physiological gradient   See PHYSIOLOGICAL PRESSURE.

physiological limit   A theoretical maximum ability. Such limits are hard to define with certainty. For instance, the winning Olympic long jump in meters by year was 6.35 in 1896, 7.185 in 1900, 7.34 in 1904, 7.445 in 1924, 8.06 in 1936, 8.24 in 1972, 8.54 in 1980, 8.72 in 1992, and 8.5 in 1996.

physiological maintenance   The design and construction of an environment so that it proves safe and comfortable with respect to such variables as safety hazards, ventilation, temperature, and noise level.

physiological memory   1. A memory for somatic experiences outside conscious awareness, for example, the memory of a conditioned-automatic-system response. 2. The storage of memory traces by means of ribonucleic acid (RNA).

physiological motive   Behaviors based on physiological needs such as thirst, hunger, sexual drives.

physiological needs   The most basic level of Abraham Maslow's hierarchy of needs; survival needs such as for food, air, water, and sleep.

physiological paradigm   The concept that mental disorders are caused by abnormalities of brain anatomy and physiology. The physiological paradigm includes the point of view that mental disorders can be treated with drugs, surgery, or other techniques ordinarily used to correct bodily malfunctioning.

physiological psychology   1. (W. Wundt) The study of the physiology of behavior. 2. Original name for the study of physiological aspects of behavior, particularly regarding the nervous and hormonal systems. An integrative specialty that draws from disciplines such as physiology, pharmacology, biology, anatomy, and neurology, its electro-chemical techniques tend to be highly instrumented. See BIOPSYCHOLOGY, NEUROSCIENCE, PSYCHOBIOLOGY, PSYCHOPHYSIOLOGY.

physiological response specificity   (J. Lacey) A principle that an individual who physiologically responds to a stimulus in a particular manner will respond similarly to other stimuli. For example, the physiological response of increased heart rate by one person can also be initiated by excitement, fear, tension, or stress, whereas another person might experience only a dry mouth under similar conditions.

physiological self-regulation   An ability of people to learn to control their internal organs and vital functions such as blood pressure, dilation of the arteries of the brain, and brain-wave activity through the use of biofeedback or operant reinforcement.

physiological time   The amount of time taken by the nervous system in processing information, starting with the stimulus striking the surface of the body (such as light on the retina) and the movement of the electrical circuitry of the body to the moment of the beginning of the reaction of the muscles, as in pressing a button.

physiological zero   The temperature at which an object in contact with the skin feels neither warm nor cold, usually about 90°F (32°C) for the hands and feet. Compare PSYCHOLOGICAL ZERO.

physiology   The science of the chemical and physical activities of the cells and organs of plants and animals, as opposed to static anatomical or structural factors. Kinds of physiology include: EJACULATION, ELECTRO-, MICROPSYCHO-, NEURO-, PATHO-, PSYCHO-, SENSORY PSYCHO-.

physiopathology   The study of disorders of physiology, both functional and organic, including their causes and how they may affect the total personality and the various activities of the individual.

physiotherapy (PT)   See PHYSICAL THERAPY (meaning 1).

physique type   The basic physical structure, build, and body type as related to various constitutional types. See BODY TYPE, BODY-TYPE THEORIES.

pi   The sixteenth letter of the Greek alphabet. See APPENDIX C.

PI   1. proactive inhibition. 2. proactive interference. 3. paradoxical intention. 4. parental investment.

pia-arachnoid   The pia mater and arachnoid coverings of the cerebrum, considered as a single organ.

Piagetian tasks   (J. Piaget) Simple hands-on problems used to assess the level of development of certain basic concepts (such as the concept of conservation) in children.

Piagetian theory   The study of cognitive development, showing how the child gradually abandons animistic explanations; acquires such concepts as cause and effect, space and time, and number; and gradually learns to apply them in thinking logically, using imagination, and forming hypotheses. The following are important for understanding the theory of Jean Piaget and his collaborators: ADAPTATION MECHANISM, ANIMISTIC THINKING, ARTIFICIALISM, AUTONOMOUS STAGE, CATEGORICAL THOUGHT, CENTRATION, CIRCULAR REACTION, CLASS INCLUSION, CODIFICATION-OF-RULES STAGE, COGNITIVE DEVELOPMENT, COGNITIVE PSYCHOLOGY, COGNITIVIST, CONCRETE OPERATIONAL STAGE, CONCRETE OPERATIONS, CONSERVATION (THEORY), CONSTRUCTIONISM, CONSTRUCTIVISM, COORDINATION OF SECONDARY SCHEMES, DÉCALAGE, DECENTER, DECENTRATION, DEFERRED IMITATION, DEVELOPMENTAL TEACHING MODEL, DISCOVERY METHOD, DISEMBODIED THOUGHT, DISEQUILIBRIUM, DISTRIBUTIVE JUSTICE, EGOCENTRIC, EGOCENTRIC SPEECH, EQUILIBRIUM, EXPIATORY PUNISHMENT, FIGURATIVE KNOWLEDGE, FORMAL OPERATIONAL STAGE, FUNCTIONAL INVARIANTS, GENERALIZING ASSIMILATION, GENETIC EPISTEMOLOGY,

GENEVA SCHOOL OF GENETIC PSYCHOLOGY, HETERONOMOUS STAGE, HETERONOMY, HORIZONTAL DÉCALAGE, HYPOTHETICO-DEDUCTIVE REASONING, IMMANENT JUSTICE, INDISSOCIATION, INRC, INTENTIONAL BEHAVIOR, INTERNALIZED SPEECH, INTERIORIZED IMITATION, INTUITIVE STAGE, INVARIANT SEQUENCE, LOGO, MAKE-BELIEVE, MORAL INDEPENDENCE, MORALITY OF CONSTRAINT, MORALITY OF COOPERATION, MORAL JUDGMENT, MORAL REALISM, MORAL RELATIVISM, NAIVE REALISM, NOMINAL REALISM, OBJECTIVE ORIENTATION, OBJECT PERMANENCE, OBLIQUE DÉCALAGE, OPERATION, OPERATIVE KNOWLEDGE, ORGANIZATION, PARTICIPATION, PASSIVE EXPECTATION, PERCEPTUAL DECENTERING, PERMANENCE CONCEPT, PHENOMENISTIC CAUSALITY, PHYSIOGNOMIC THINKING, PIAGETIAN TASKS, PRECAUSAL THINKING, PREOPERATIONAL STAGE, PREOPERATIONAL THOUGHT, PREPARATORY THOUGHT, PRIMARY CIRCULAR REACTIONS, PUBERTAL STAGE, QUANTITATIVE CONSERVATION, RECIPROCAL PUNISHMENT, RECOGNITORY ASSIMILATION, REPRESENTATIONAL SKILLS, REPRESENTATIONAL STAGE, REPRESENTATIONAL THOUGHT, REPRESENTATIVE INTELLIGENCE, REVERSIBILITY, RULES OF THE GAME, SCHEMAS, SCHEMES, SECONDARY CIRCULAR REACTION, SENSORIMOTOR INTELLIGENCE, SENSORIMOTOR STAGE, SENSORIMOTOR THEORY, STAGES OF HUMAN COGNITIVE DEVELOPMENT, STRANGER ANXIETY, SYMBOL, SYMBOLIC FUNCTION, SYMBOLIC PLAY, SYNCRETIC THOUGHT, SYNCRETISM, TERTIARY CIRCULAR REACTION, TOPOLOGY, TRANSDUCTIVE REASONING, VERBAL PROPOSITION, VERTICAL DÉCALAGE.

pia mater   A membrane covering the brain and spinal cord, being itself covered in turn by the arachnoid and (outermost) the dura mater.

piano theory (of hearing)   place theory (of hearing/ of pitch)

piblokto   A culture-specific syndrome observed among Eskimos, usually women. The afflicted person tears off clothing, runs naked in subzero weather and emits sounds of wild animals or birds, with the period of activity lasting about two hours. Also known as *pibloktog, pibloktoq, piloktoq.*

PIC   See PERSONALITY INVENTORY FOR CHILDREN.

pica   An eating disorder manifested as a craving for unnatural nonnutritive substances such as hair, clay, paint, or dirt. Compare CISSA. See DYSGEUSIA.

Pick's disease   (A. Pick) A rare degenerative disease of the brain involving atrophy of the higher associative areas of the cortex. The disorder is progressive and includes increasing difficulty in thinking, concentrating, and abstracting, followed by bewilderment, rambling talk, inability to read, write, or speak, as well as paralysis, incontinence, debility, and death. See PRIMARY DEGENERATIVE DEMENTIA.

Pickwickian syndrome   Extreme obesity marked by grotesque body shape and associated physiological factors, such as shortness of breath, hypersomnia (constant sleepiness), and general weakness. Name is based on a character in Charles Dickens' novel *The Pickwick Papers.*

picometer (pm)   One-millionth of a micrometer; one trillionth of a meter. Also known as bicron. Formerly known as micromicron.

pictograph   A means of describing statistical facts by means of pictures such as pie charts.

pictophilia   A condition that requires looking at erotic or pornographic pictures or films to get sexually aroused and to be able to function sexually. See VOYEURISM.

pictorial imagery   See IMAGERY.

picture   See the following kinds of pictures: CLOUD, CONCRETE, INWARD, RETINAL, STEREOSCOPIC MOTION.

picture-anomalies test   A nonverbal task of social intelligence that depends upon the ability of a person to detect absurdities in cartoon pictures. Aids in the diagnosis of right temporal-lobe lesions, since patients with such disorders are likely to find the absurd figures logical and the logical figures ridiculous.

picture-arrangement test   1. A task attempting to measure intelligence, in which a number of pictures are to be put in a logical sequence. Separate illustrations depicting behavior (for example: (a) picking up a package, (b) untying the cords, (c) opening the box, and (d) taking a toy out of the box) may be presented to a participant in four elements in "bdac" order with instructions to put them in the proper or logical order. 2. (S. S. Tomkins) A projective examination of 25 plates, each with three drawings of a person performing various activities. The participant must arrange the plates in a sequence and tell a story about what is happening.

picture-completion test   An examination designed to assess intelligence based on the completion of a picture, such as a teapot without a handle. The task is either to point out that the handle is missing or, in a group test, to draw the handle.

picture-frustration test   See ROSENZWEIG PICTURE-FRUSTRATION STUDY.

picture-interpretation test   An examination in which the participant must interpret a pictorial situation. Usually considered a test of intelligence.

picture superiority effect   In memory research, the ability to recall or recognize previously-shown pictures better than shown words.

picture-world test   A children's projective examination in which participants compose a story about realistic scenes, adding objects or figures as they wish. The child is instructed to picture either a world that actually exists or one that the child would like to exist. See WORLD TEST.

Piderit drawings   Simplified drawings of parts of the human face. The drawings are in interchangeable pieces (brow, nose, eye, mouth) that can be rearranged in various alternative composite forms to show a variety of possible facial expressions, illustrating the effect of how small changes in one part of the face can create major changes on overall expression. Described by Theodor Piderit, the Piderit drawings were later used by E. G. Boring and E. B. Titchener as models for the demonstration of emotional expression.

pidgin English A type of creolized language, used often by natives of any locale where two or more languages are spoken, having elements of both languages. "Wea yu wen?" is an expression that might be heard in Hawaii derived from "Where you went?" and in English "Where did you go?" The Hawaiian pidgin is a truncated and simplified use of English. Also spelled pigeon English. See CREOLE, EBONICS.

piece-rate payment In industry, payment per "piece" produced. First championed by F. W. Taylor.

piece-work module Production of individual parts of a unit by more than one person, each person handling, in sequence, part of a job. Example: In making clothing, someone cuts a pattern, another sews the pieces together, a third makes button holes, etc.

pie chart A circle divided by radii into sectors of different sizes, representing proportional magnitudes. Compare BAR GRAPH.

Pigem's question A question designed to elicit projective responses by a patient usually undergoing a mental status examination or prior to psychotherapy. The question usually is a variation of "What would you like most to change in your life?"

pigeon English Variant spelling of pidgin English.

pig Latin Popular children's secret language, which is normal English to which two extra rules have been added to confuse others. The initial consonant cluster is moved to the end of a word, followed by the diphthong *ay*, so that the name of the language becomes *igpay Atinlay*.

PIL Purpose in Life

(the) pill Common name for an oral-contraceptive pill.

piloerection Goose flesh, goose pimples, goose skin, or chicken skin; a temporary roughness of the skin as a reaction to cold, fear, or sexual or other excitation. See PILOMOTOR EFFECT/RESPONSE.

piloktoq piblokto

pilomotor effect/response The stimulation of the smooth piloerector muscles which control movement of the hair, causing it to become erect or "stand on end." An example of this effect is seen in angry or frightened cats with hair erect. See PILOERECTION.

pilomotor effect/response

pilot study Preliminary research to prepare for a subsequent research. It reveals potential problems, gives an estimate of the amount of time the research will need, and may generate enough information so that either the area of research will be pursued or cancelled.

Piltdown man Originally considered one of the earliest types of primitive humans, represented by a skull found in 1912 near Piltdown, England, later found to be a hoax.

Piltz's reflex A reflexive change in the size of the pupil when attention is suddenly fixed on a phenomenon. Jan Piltz held that the reflex is mediated by emotional arousal; for example, positive arousal results in an enlarged pupil and negative arousal results in a contracted pupil.

pimp A person who procures prostitutes for customers and appropriates a portion of their fee. Also known as panderer.

pincer technique Grasping an object between finger and thumb. Its appearance is a measure of fine motor development in infants.

pincushion distortion A departure of optical images from truthful representation of their objects, such that a square is represented in the image with its sides bending inward.

pineal body/gland A gland found near the center of the brain assumed by René Descartes to connect the soul to the body. Its function in humans is not certain—possibly the source of melatonin, a substance that inhibits estrus and ovarian growth. In certain animals it appears to function as a kind of third eye. Also known as epiphysis (cerebri).

pineal eye See THIRD EYE.

Pinel's classifications/system (P. Pinel) A classification of mental disorders into four types by Philippe Pinel in the 18th century: Melancholia (depression), Mania with delirium, Mania without delirium, Dementia (mental deterioration). In contrast, see APPENDIX B for a list of DSM-IV classifications.

pink-collar ghetto Slang for the concentration of women in low-paying jobs.

pink noise A mixture of white noise, which is a mixture of all audible wavelengths, with a sound signal. "White noise" takes its name metaphorically from white light which is composed of all visible wavelengths of light. White light added to red yields pink light, thus providing the basis for another metaphor.

pinna (wing—Latin) Part of the external ear other than the auricle, auricula, concha, and meatus.

pinocytosis The recycling of portions of the presynaptic membrane into synaptic vesicles.

Pintner Manikin Test **Manikin Test**

Pintner-Paterson Scale of Performance Tests (R. Pintner & D. G. Paterson) A series of 15 performance tasks for participants ranging in most instances from 4 to 15 years of age. Particularly applicable to participants who do not speak English or who have hearing and speech defects.

Piotrowski Rorschach system Zygmunt Piotrowski's method for interpreting the Rorschach, differs considerably from other approaches of other interpreters. See PERCEPTANALYSIS, RORSCHACH TEST.

Piper's law (H. E. Piper) Hans Piper's principle that for a uniformly stimulated retinal area, the threshold for luminance is inversely proportional to the square root of the area stimulated. Formula: $B = L(A^{1/2})$ Where: L stands for luminance, A is the retinal area, and B is the brightness. (Brightness for large areas of the retina, for small areas see Ricco's law.)

piriform area/cortex A pear-shaped region of the rhinencephalon containing clumps of stellate and pyramidal cells. Receives olfactory tracts of the second order and relays impulses to the hippocampal formation. Also spelled pyriform area. See ALLOCORTEX.

pitch The sound quality of highness or lowness mainly dependent on the frequency of vibration, identified in Hertz (cycles per second).

pitch discrimination   An ability to detect changes in sound frequencies. In humans, because of the design of the cochlea, higher frequencies can be analyzed with less difficulty than lower frequencies.

pithiatism   1. Term coined by Joseph Babinski for removal of hysterical symptoms by persuasion, on the theory that these symptoms are produced by suggestion and can therefore be eliminated by suggestion. 2. (P. Dubois) Curing nervous and mental disorders by persuasion. Paul Dubois may be considered the founder of modern psychotherapy.

Pitres' rule   (A. Pitres) A postulate that when a multilingual person recovers from aphasia, most likely the language in which that person was most fluent is recovered first.

pituitarism   A disorder of pituitary-gland functioning. Overactivity is identified as either pituitarism or hyperpituitarism, and deficient activity as hypopituitarism.

pituitary (gland)   "Master gland" located in the base of the brain connected to the hypothalamus by the pituitary stalk. The anterior portion of the pituitary is called the adenohypophysis and the posterior, the neurohypophysis. The anterior produces seven hormones, six of which control other endocrine glands. The posterior lobe secretes two hormones. The pituitary's role of releasing hormones that stimulate the production of other hormones resulted in its identification as the master gland of the endocrine system. Also known as hypophysis.

pivot words   A small set of words a child uses in most sentences at the earliest stage of grammatical development. Can be attached to a large number of other words to form a meaningful two-word sentence; used by children between 18 and 24 months of age.

pixel   In computer graphics, one spot in a rectilinear grid of thousands of such spots that are individually "painted" to form a screen or printer image. Term derives from picture/pix element.

Pk   See PSYCHOKINESIS.

PK   See PSYCHOKINESIS.

placebo   (I shall please—Latin) 1. In medicine, inert substances given to patients in place of bona fide medications. 2. In psychotherapy, placebos are most often sham treatments used in research to control for the effects of attention. See PLACEBO EFFECT.

placebo effect   A tendency for a beneficial effect to occur if a person is expecting that a treatment will be therapeutic. A placebo is a neutral treatment (such as an inactive pill) that may nevertheless promote healing because of the hope and confidence placed in it. Compare TOMATO EFFECT. See PLACEBO.

placebo reactor   A person who tends to react to a placebo as if the inert substance actually had a pharmacologic effect. Various studies indicate that such individuals are suggestible, or possess other traits that account for their responses. However, a placebo reactor generally does not react to all placebos. Sometimes known as placebo-responder. See PLACEBO EFFECT.

place code   The system that codes information about sound frequencies in different locations on the basilar membrane.

place conditioning   Pairing of an object with a location.

place learning   Gaining familiarity with a location or site, such as where food is located, where to go to escape. See RESPONSE LEARNING.

placement   The assignment of a student to a level of learning or of a job applicant to a position of employment.

placement counseling   A vocational-placement service that provides advice to persons (with or without disabilities) about job opportunities for which they may be qualified. Such counseling may include coaching or training persons for job interviews, procedures for filling out applications properly, and other details that may be psychological obstacles for job hunters. Additional services are usually available for people with physical or psychological disabilities.

placement test   1. An examination to aid a placement officer working in a school, in industry, or the military, to assign persons to suitable positions. 2. In parapsychology, a psychokinesis technique in which the participant tries to influence falling objects to land in a designated area of the throwing surface.

placenta   An organ formed in the lining of the uterus that unites a fetus to the maternal uterus.

placental immunity   Refers to the placenta's ability to protect the unborn and the newborn child from many infectious and toxic agents in the mother. Syphilis is an example of an exception.

placentaphagia   A postnatal behavior of some placental mammals: eating the placenta, membranes, and umbilical cord. Purposes may include: for hygiene, to benefit from placental hormones, and to hide evidence of the birth from predators.

place theory (of hearing/of pitch)   An explanation for pitch perception, proposed by Hermann von Helmholtz, based on the assumption that the place of stimulation on the basilar membrane determines the sound frequency perceived by a person, since this membrane was assumed to consist of a series of resonating fibers, each tuned to a different frequency. Also known as harp theory (of hearing), piano theory (of hearing). See FREQUENCY THEORY (OF HEARING), HEARING THEORIES, HELMHOLTZ THEORY, RESONANCE THEORY (OF HEARING), VOLLEY THEORY (OF HEARING).

Placido's disk   A device used in detecting irregularities on the surface of the cornea, consisting of a disk with concentric black rings and a hole in the middle through which reflections of the rings on the cornea may be viewed. Named after Portuguese ophthalmologist Antonio Placido da Costa (1848–1916).

placing   In humans, a reflex movement characterized by lifting the feet onto a surface during the first three months of life.

placing reaction   A postural reaction of an animal held in such a manner so that its feet hang free. The animal will attempt to place its feet on any solid surface it can see. Placing reaction is one of several possible limb adjustments directed toward firm support of the body.

PLAN   See PROGRAM FOR LEARNING IN ACCORDANCE WITH NEEDS.

planaria   A flatworm with the ability to regenerate parts of itself even if cut into two pieces, used by James McConnell in controversial experiments on the transfer of memory.

planchette   A device consisting of a smooth board on which are usually printed the words "Yes" and "No" as well as the letters of the alphabet. A small movable triangular device held gently by the fingers will purportedly point to the letters of the alphabet to spell words or point to "Yes" or "No" in response to questions. The concept is that the device will spell out messages from persons deceased. See AUTOMATIC WRITING, OUIJA BOARD.

Planck's principle   A theory that new scientific facts triumph not by convincing opponents, but because opponents die and newer generations accept the principle. Named after German physicist Max Planck (1858–1947).

planned parenthood   1. Decision by sexually active person to have or not have children, usually by discontinuing or continuing birth control procedures. 2. A philosophical tenet that every child should be wanted and that couples should have information on and access to effective birth control. 3. An international organization dedicated to providing education and resources regarding family planning and health services. Founded by Margaret Sanger as the American Birth Control League, renamed Planned Parenthood in 1942.

planning space   (A. Newell & H. A. Simon) A problem space that is abstracted from an initial problem space to simplify the search for solutions, usually by abstraction of the important features and operators and omission of detail. See PROBLEM SPACE.

planophrasia   Obsolete term for a flight of ideas as manifested in cases of manic-depressive (bipolar) psychoses.

plantar reflex   A flexion of the toes, in newborns caused by stroking of the sole.

plastic-arts therapy   The use of media such as clay that can be manipulated, used in play therapy and physical rehabilitation.

plasticity   1. Flexibility and adaptability, as opposed to rigidity. 2. The modifiability of the nervous system which makes it possible to learn and register new experiences. 3. The capacity of some organisms with particular genotypes to vary in their developments depending on the environment; for example, axolotls (a type of salamander) develop differently in Mexico than in the northern United States due to variations of nutrients in the water they inhabit. 4. Refers to the great diversity of stimuli for consummatory behavior, especially for exploring and manipulating novel stimuli which increases the diversity of learned instrumental behavior. See FUNCTIONAL RIGIDITY, RIGIDITY.

plasticity of the brain   The ability of the brain to make adjustments following damage, recovering abilities lost as a result of trauma or disease over time.

plastic surgery   A branch of surgery that specializes in the removal, transfer, and repair of damaged or diseased tissue so that a body area can be restored to a normal or near-normal form. From the point of view of psychology, people who have either inherited conditions, such as hemangioma (port-wine stains) on the face, or developmental anomalies, such as cleft palate, are socially handicapped by their appearance and plastic surgery may help them to establish a better self-image as well as other-image. See BODY-DYSMORPHIC DISORDER, DISFIGUREMENT.

plastic tonus   Nonbehavior noted in some patients with catatonia. If a limb is put in a position by someone else, it will tend to remain in that position. See FLEXIBILITAS CEREA, WAXY FLEXIBILITY.

plateau   1. A flat place. 2. (W. L. Bryan) A period in learning when no apparent learning takes place. The plateau can be due to boredom, fatigue, disinterest, etc., but often is a period of consolidation and a new period of learning will follow. See illustration at LEARNING CURVE, the top right side of the curve appears to be reaching asymptotic limits (generating a plateau).

plateau phase   (W. Masters & V. Johnson) A phase of human sexual response in which sustained sexual tension precedes orgasm. See SEXUAL-RESPONSE CYCLE.

plateau speech   Monotonous verbal expression found in some central nervous system disorders such as epilepsy and multiple sclerosis. The effect results from a loss of normal pitch characteristics of vowel sounds.

Plateau's spiral   (J. A. Plateau) A spiral with equally spaced arms that may be rotated to produce various phenomena, including: the sensation of color (if the spiral is white on black), seeming expansion or contraction (depending on the direction of rotation), and apparent movement when the spiral is stopped. The spiral is sometimes attributed to Ernst Mach who used a wider black spiral on white background. See TALBOT-PLATEAU LAW.

Platonic   Pertaining to Plato; to resemble Plato in terms of thinking and feeling.

Platonic friendship   A social relationship between two individuals of opposite or same sex, in which sexual relations or strong emotions are not evident.

Platonic ideal(ism)   A concept that real understanding of phenomena, including objects, depends on cognitive comprehension of the essential idea of a class of objects.

Platonic love   1. A type of love in which there is no overt sexual behavior or desire. 2. A favorable attitude toward a person outside a family consisting of caring and concern without any element of erotic desire. See LOVE.

platycephaly   A condition in which the crown of the head is abnormally flat.

platykurtic   A distribution of scores flatter than a normal distribution, that is, having more scores at the extremes and fewer in the center than in a normal distribution. See KURTOSIS for an illustration of three classes of distributions.

play   Activities freely sought and pursued for the sake of enjoyment. Group play can be of the parallel type, the competitive type, or of the cooperative type, or any combination of these three. Play is important to children, giving them various kinds of physical and social skills. It is also a prime means of exploring the self and the world, as well as a means of maintaining mental health and achieving a balanced life. Also known as ludic activity. See PLAY THERAPY, PARALLEL PLAY.

play acting   Dramatic play in which children, teenagers, or adults (including group-therapy patients) take different roles, and in the process test out relationships, rehearse different ways of dealing with situations, identify with important figures, realize their wishes in imagination, and play out feelings of anger, jealousy, or fear within the safe realm of make-believe. See PSYCHODRAMA.

players   See GAME THEORY.

play-group psychotherapy (S. R. Slavson) A therapeutic technique on the preschool level introduced in 1943. Materials of many kinds (clay, toys, blocks, figurines) are used to stimulate the expression of conflicts and fantasies, and to give the therapist an opportunity to ask questions and help the children in a group understand their feelings, behavior, and relationships. See GROUP PSYCHOTHERAPY.

playing dead See DEATH-FEIGNING.

playing possum Death-feigning, or nonbehavior as a form of self-defense. Named for the opossum's tendency toward immobility when threatened.

play therapy The use of play activities and materials (clay, water, blocks, dolls, puppets, drawing, finger paint) in child psychotherapy and mental hygiene. Play techniques are based on the theory that such activities mirror the child's emotional life and fantasies, enable the child to "play out" feelings, and to test out new approaches and relationships in actions rather than words. This form of therapy is usually nondirective and nonpsychoanalytic, but may be conducted on a more directive or on a more analytical level. It is occasionally termed ludotherapy. See DIRECTIVE PLAY THERAPY.

pleasantness-unpleasantness See WUNDT'S TRIDIMENSIONAL THEORY OF EMOTION.

pleaser One of four basic lifestyles according to Nira Kefir. The pleaser is most concerned about being insignificant and so attempts to achieve acceptance and significance by being agreeable at all costs in all situations. See MAJOR PRIORITIES.

pleasure center (J. Olds) Sites in the brain that when electrically stimulated possibly result in pleasurable feelings. The areas appear to be primarily in the lateral hypothalamus, limbic system ending in the frontal lobes.

pleasure ego (S. Freud) Early phrase used by Sigmund Freud to distinguish between two ego processes: a pleasure ego which acts on behalf of unconscious mental processes, and a reality ego, which uses consciousness, reality-testing, judgment, and activity to "strive for what is useful and guard itself against damage." The distinction later crystallized into the structural distinction between the id, ego, and superego.

pleasure fear See HEDONOPHOBIA.

pleasure-pain principle (S. Freud) A psychoanalytic point of view that humans are governed by the two-pronged desire for gratification of instincts (pleasure) and discharge of tension (pain). Also known as pain-pleasure principle, pleasure principle.

pleniloquence A compulsion to talk incessantly.

pleonasm Redundancy in language, the use of excess of words to express an idea.

pleonexia 1. An abnormal greediness or desire for the acquisition of objects. 2. Describing a symptom of air hunger or abnormal intake of oxygen.

plethysmograph An instrument that measures and records changes in volume in a part or an organ of the body. See PENILE PLETHYSMOGRAPH, VAGINAL PLETHYSMOGRAPH.

plexiform layer 1. One of two layers of nerve cells in the retina. 2. The outermost layer (layer I) of the neocortex comprised mainly of axons and dendrites.

plexus A network of nerves, blood vessels or lymphatic nodes, such as the solar plexus that is located in the abdomen behind the stomach.

PLISSIT Acronym used in counseling for sexual problems, meaning Permission (to do various things the person might ordinarily think are not allowed), Limited Information (as much information as the therapist thinks is proper), Specific Suggestions (told exactly what and how to do it, and sometimes shown how), Intensive Therapy (usually with another therapist).

PLMS See PERIODIC LEG MOVEMENTS IN SLEEP.

plosive A speech sound made by building pressure in the air tract and suddenly releasing it. May be voiced, such as, /b/, /d/, /g/, or voiceless, for example, /p/, /t/, /k/. Also known as explosive, obstructive, occlusive, opening sound, stop.

plural 1. In social sciences, generic term for any unsystematized collection of people grouped together for convenience in describing their specialized attributes. 2. Refers to a class of organisms greater than one in number. Sometimes also spelled plurel.

pluralism A doctrine positing that ultimate reality consists of more than one sort of entity, such as electrons, monads, persons. Compare MONISM.

pluralistic behavior (F. H. Giddings) Any action, or any response to a specific stimulus, which is performed universally, or almost universally, by individuals of a given group or region.

pluralistic ignorance (F. Allport) A false belief when meeting new people that an aspect of the person's world view differs from those of the others and to "fit in" the person must play a role in accordance with this false belief. Example: A person meets a group of people perceived by the person to be Republicans, so the person proceeds to express Republican views to be part of their conversation. Other members of this group, although they are also not Republicans, express views consonant with those of this person for the same reason. See ALLPORT A-S REACTION STUDY, EVENT SYSTEM, GROUPTHINK, J-CURVE, MASK, STEREOTYPE, TELIC CONTINUUM.

plural marriage See GROUP MARRIAGE.

plurel Irregular form of plural.

plus-minus situation (A. Adler) The value or usefulness of a person as perceived by others on a hypothetical scale ranging from low to high. The score is based on the degree to which that person gives or has given to others, rather than where that person actually is in terms of factors such as popularity, financial status, or creativity. See ALLOCENTRIC THEORY, ALTRUISM, ALTRUISTIC SUICIDE.

plus-sum game A kind of game that a player will eventually win because a winning strategy exists, for example, professional poker players familiar with the odds for certain hands will tend to beat players who bet solely on hunches.

plutomania An inordinate striving for money and possessions.

PM primary memory

PMA 1. primary mental abilities. 2. positive mental attitude.

PMA Test See PRIMARY MENTAL ABILITIES TEST.

PMI   patient medication instruction

PMS   See PREMENSTRUAL (TENSION) SYNDROME.

PMT   Porteus Maze Test

P$_n$ Symbol for the *n*th percentile point.

p-n   See PRESS-NEED PATTERN.

PNAvQ   See POSITIVE-NEGATIVE AMBIVALENT QUOTIENT.

PNC   preferred noise criterion

P-   Symbol indicating a poorly organized unstable person or unstable personality.

pneumatism   (Erasistratus) The semi-mystical belief that breathing is due to a holy spirit, the vital principle.

pneumatograph   pneumograph

pneumatophobia   Morbid fear of spirits. See DE-MONOPHOBIA.

pneumogastric nerve   vagus nerve

pneumograph   A flexible tube filled with air that can be placed around the chest. Connected to a tambour, it activates a stylus on a kymograph to record subtle volume changes in respiration. Also known as pneumatograph.

pneumographic analysis   Examination of the records of thoracic movements or volume changes during respiration.

pneumophonia   A voice disorder characterized by excessive breathiness.

pneumotaxic center   A mechanism in the central nervous system that controls breathing. Also known as autonomous respiratory center.

pnigerophobia   Morbid fear of smothering. Also sometimes called pnigophobia.

pnigophobia   Morbid fear of choking. Also sometimes called pnigerophobia. See ANGINOPHOBIA.

PNP   psychogenic nocturnal polydipsia

PNS   peripheral nervous system

PO   1. See POSTOPERATIVE. 2. In prescriptions, an abbreviation meaning "By mouth."

POC   performance operating characteristic

poetry therapy   (A. Lerner) A technique that uses poetry for the purpose of facilitating the expression and resolution of client feelings; also getting clients to express themselves through the writing of poetry for their own therapy. Poetry is used as a vehicle or adjunctive healing agent to complement other systems of therapy. Also known as psychopoetry. See BIBLIOTHERAPY, METAPHOR THERAPY.

Poggendorf illusion   (J. C. Poggendorff, F. Zöllner) A visual illusion in which a straight diagonal line looks jagged when it appears to pass behind parallel lines or figures.

pogonophobia   A fear of beards.

POI   Personal Orientation Inventory

poikilotherm   An organism, for example, a reptile, whose body heat or temperature varies according to the temperature of the surrounding medium. Commonly known as cold-blooded animal. Compare HOMOIO-THERM.

poinephobia   Morbid fear of punishment.

point-biserial correlation   A product moment correlation when one of two traits is measured on a continuous scale and the other is dichotomous. See BISERIAL CORRELATION.

point estimation   A single numerical value used to estimate any element of a parameter, without allowing for the band of uncertainty around the number. See INTERVAL ESTIMATE.

point fear   See AICHMOPHOBIA.

point-for-point correspondence   A relationship in which for every point in one variable there is a corresponding point in a second variable.

point-hour ratio (PHR)   A grade given by teachers transformed into numbers where A, B, C, D = 4, 3, 2, 1, respectively. Numbers are multiplied by the number of credit hours, that is, for any student, all numbers are added and then divided by the total credit hours. Thus, a person with all A's has a 4.0 point-hour ratio. See GRADE POINTS, GRADE-POINT AVERAGE.

pointing   A test for vestibular function in which a person, first with eyes open and again with the eyes closed, touches an extended index finger to the closely-held index finger of the examiner as the two stand facing each other. Knowing the location of the examiner's fingers, people with normal function should be able to touch them again with eyes closed. Failure is called past-pointing.

pointing the bone   See VOODOO DEATH.

point-localization test   A somatosensory examination in which a skin area, usually on the hand, is touched twice with an intervening period of one second. The participant is required to determine whether the points touched were in the same place.

point mutation   The mutation of a single gene.

point of extinction   The point at which a conditioned response ceases to occur, as a result of the elimination of the reinforcer.

point of regard   A visual fixation point on a line of sight that terminates on the retinal fovea.

point of subjective equality (PSE)   The value of a comparison stimulus that, for a given observer, is equally likely to be judged as higher or lower than a standard stimulus.

point prevalence   In epidemiology, the total number of cases of a disease existing in a given population at a given point in time, as opposed to during a specified time frame, or period prevalence. See INCIDENCE.

point ratio   A measure of a student's school grades by transferring letter grades into numbers: A = 4, B = 3, C = 2, D = 1. These numbers are multiplied by course credit hours (usually 3-2-1) and the resulting sum is divided by credit hours. Example: If a student's grades are A, B, C, D for four courses, the first two having 3 credit hours each and the second two courses having 2 credit hours each, the formula would then be (A) $3 \times 4 +$ (B)$3 \times 3 +$ (C)$2 \times 2 +$ (D)$2 \times 1 = 27/10 = 2.7$ (or B minus average).

point scale   A method of generating a final score on certain tests in which each item gotten correct receives various point values. Item 7 may have a point value of 1 and item 8, a point value of 3. The total points are then added and then that number is changed to some other score such as mental age, percentile, Z score. For instance, suppose two children, each chronological age 12 years, 3 months, take the same test based on points: Child A gets a score of 37 and Child B, a score of 54; Child A's mental age becomes 11 years, 4 months and Child B's mental age is 13 years, 9 months.

Poiseuille's law   (J. L. M. Poiseuille) A mathematical relationship among blood pressure, resistance, and flow. Named after French physiologist and physicist Jean L. M. Poiseuille (1797–1869).

poisoning the well   A variation of the *ad hominem* argument in which the integrity of a supporter of a point of view is attacked.

poison-pen (psycho)therapy   (J. Watkins) A technique that allows a client to release hostility via the writing of angry letters that are then discussed in psychotherapy but are not mailed to the addressee.

Poisson Distribution   (S-D. Poisson) A statistical distribution that shows the probability of occurrence of rare events randomly distributed in time and space. This statistic is used for estimating number of such events as infrequent accidents. Known as the law of small numbers or rare events.

polar body   A small, incomplete ovum produced during the process of oogenesis, or egg formation, in the human ovary. Normally, as the oocyte is being formed during the meiosis stage of gamete-cell division, the division occurs unequally. One small cell, the polar body, is pinched off and allowed to degenerate, while the larger cell proceeds to yield the oocyte, or regular ovum. The polar body contains the haploid set of 23 chromosomes.

polar continuum   Usually represented by a line, the middle of which is considered neutral, with the distances leading away from the middle (in opposite directions and representing opposite concepts) indicating increasing strength or amount. Used for estimations, for example, a list of terms for levels of intelligence are presented on a horizontal line. Terms range from the extreme left, "vegetative idiot," through the midpoint of the line, "average intelligence," to the extreme right, "genius." Phrases such as "mentally retarded," "borderline intelligence," and "superior intelligence" are placed in relation to their meanings and strength of the other concepts.

polarities   In psychoanalytic theory, the opposing forces that govern all mental life: (a) subject (ego) versus object (external world); (b) pleasure versus unpleasure, or pain; (c) active versus passive. In neuroses, the balance between some or all of these antitheses is disturbed. One of the major aims of psychoanalysis is to restore this balance.

polarization   The separation of electrical charges across the semipermeable membrane of a cell caused by segregation of ion species into the intracellular and extracellular compartments.

polarized membrane   A membrane with an electrical potential gradient from the inside to the outside. At rest, the outside of the membrane is positive compared to the inside, due to an excess of positive ions outside and an excess of negative ions inside the membrane.

polarized synaptic transmission   Conductance of nerve impulses across synapses in one direction only (from axon to dendrite or to cell body).

polar opposites   Extremes of a continuum, for example, sweet-sour, strong-weak, light-heavy, dominant-submissive. Such opposites were used in G. A. Kelly's repertory grid and C. E. Osgood's semantic differential method.

polar profiles   (G. A. Kelly) A method of describing concept, attitudes, personalities, by generating a series of scales with contrasting terms such as "fearful versus courageous" or contrasting values such as "completely against versus absolutely for." In such scales, a respondent indicates where on the scale he or she belongs. Ordinarily these profiles have from five to seven positions. See RATING SCALES, SEMANTIC DIFFERENTIAL.

Police Athletic League (PAL)   Community associations operated by off-duty, volunteer law enforcement personnel who meet with young people at risk for delinquency. The officers serve as role models and attempt to divert the young people's energies into athletics.

policy analysis   In evaluation research, a collection of techniques of synthesizing information (a) to specify alternative policy and program choices in cost-benefit terms, (b) to assess organizational goals in terms of inputs and outcome performance, and (c) to provide additional information as a guide for future decisions concerning research activities.

policy research   Generally, the application of social scientific findings to a problem identified by a client. Usually multi-disciplinary; may be descriptive, analytical, or evaluative. Also known as consultancy, especially in the commercial sector.

political correctness   1. Choosing words that do not exclude, belittle, limit, demean, or hurt. Sometimes used pejoratively, especially by traditionalists. 2. An ideology in the 1990s in the United States that rejects many traditional values and promotes special status for certain contemporary beliefs and certain groups of people who have historically been mistreated and are in need of protection and special treatment. 3. Derogatory term for excessive concern over special-interest groups.

political genetics   Incorporation of genetic principles and practices into politics and government policy.

political psychiatry/psychology   The application of psychiatric and psychological principles and knowledge to the formation of public policy, especially as it relates to mental-health services, treatment of the mentally ill, questions of medical ethics, prosecution and rehabilitation of criminals, and attempts at thought or behavior control. See PSYCHOPOLITICS.

political socialization   The induction of political attitudes by socialization through parents, relatives, friends, and schools.

political sociology   A branch of sociology that studies the social causes and consequences of power distributions, and the socio-political conflicts that lead to changes in authority.

political system   An institution concerned with the regulation of people. Among the more major general concepts are: (a) anarchy: no diminution of power of individuals or of families, each unit operates on its own without necessary cooperation with any others; (b) democracy: power theoretically lies primarily at the bottom of the population pyramid; and (c) autocracy: rule by one person, such as an absolute autocrat distributing (bestowing) lesser powers to others. Historical examples of autocracy include monarchies, and more recently, facism in Europe. See DIVINE RIGHT OF KINGS.

political type   (E. Spranger) A personality characterized by concern with power over other people and being in charge of events. See TYPOLOGY.

politics of recognition   identity politics

Politzer's acoumeter   (A. Politzer) An older device for measuring sound intensity thresholds. Sound was produced by a hammer striking a surface, the sound's intensity varied by changing the distance of the device from the ear.

poll   See PUBLIC-OPINION POLL.

pollution   In environmental psychology, the presence of toxins.

Pollyanna attitude   1. A general personality feature characterized by eternal optimism and refusal to accept evil or failure despite evidence of such. Named after a character in Eleanor Porter's novel, *Pollyanna*. 2. A defense mechanism characterized by blind optimism; maintaining the conviction that "all is well." Also known as a Pollyanna mechanism. See FUNDAMENTAL POSTULATE, PANGLOSSIANISM.

poltergeist phenomena   Unexplainable occurrences such as movement of objects, breakage of objects, or both, traditionally attributed to ghostly and discarnate interventions but often associated with the presence of an adolescent person.

poltergeists   Purported spirits, ghosts, usually of the noisy and mischievous variety. Such ghosts are heard but not usually seen, as opposed to a silent apparition.

polyandry   Marriage of a woman to more than one husband at any time, a situation accepted historically and currently in some cultures. See POLYGAMY, POLYGYNY.

polychromatic theory   A point of view that there are many kinds of retinal cones, each sensitive to a particular band of frequencies of light waves.

polychronic task   (E. T. Hall) Work that involves doing all parts of a job, for example, in a garment factory, a worker who sews the whole garment from pattern to finish. Compare MONOCHRONIC TASK.

Polycrates complex   In psychoanalytic theory, an unconscious need for punishment, demonstrated by feelings of guilt, anxiety, etc., found occasionally in successful people. Based on the mythology of Polycrates who believed that his success aroused the envy of the gods. "Polycratism," is sometimes used for the fear of success. See SAMSON COMPLEX, SUPERSTITION, SUCCESS NEUROSIS.

Polycratism   1. (S. Ferenczi) Unfounded fear that God will punish the person for being successful. 2. See POLYCRATES COMPLEX.

polycyesis   A multiple pregnancy.

polydactyly   Additional digits on the extremities (hands, feet, paws). Also known as polydactylia, polydactylism.

polydipsia   Excessive thirst. See PSYCHOGENIC POLYDIPSIA.

polydrug abuse   Dependence on two or more drugs of abuse. Sometimes known as polydrug addiction.

polydystrophic oligophrenia   Technical name for Sanfilippo's syndrome.

polyestrous   Pertaining to animals (including humans) that have multiple estrus cycles annually. Some birds ovulate once every 24 hours until a nest of eggs is filled. See ESTROUS BEHAVIOR, ESTRUS.

polygamy   Marriage to more than one spouse at the same time. See POLYANDRY, POLYGYNY.

polygenetic   Having many sources, being controlled by many different genes.

polygenic trait   A trait determined by numerous sets of genes rather than only one set, for example, normal intelligence. The majority of human traits are polygenic.

polyglot   A person conversant in many languages.

polyglot amnesia   A tendency to forget how to speak a current language and speak a language spoken at a much earlier period, after a severely traumatic experience of an organic or functional nature.

polyglot neophasia   A variation of neologism in which a patient, usually in a manic or paranoiac state, creates one or more languages which may be structured with their own vocabulary, grammar, and syntax.

polyglot reaction   Recovery from aphasia in which a multilingual person first uses another language rather than the mother tongue, which would be the most usual recovery in such cases. See PITRES' RULE.

polygraph   An apparatus for recording several responses concurrently, as in a lie detector, where changes in respiration, blood pressure, and the galvanic skin response (GSR) are recorded on a moving tape. Scottish-English cardiologist James Mackenzie (1853–1925) produced the forerunner of the modern polygraph. See KEELER POLYGRAPH.

polygyny   Marriage to more than one wife at any time, a situation accepted historically and currently in some cultures. See POLYANDRY, POLYGAMY.

polyideic somnambulism   Ideational content related to more than one idea that occurs in a state of sleepwalking. Compare MONOIDEIC SOMNAMBULISM.

polyiterophilia   Being sexually aroused by repeating the same sexual activity many times with many partners.

polylogia   Continuous and usually incoherent speech. See LOGORRHEA.

polymath   A person of encyclopedic learning.

polymatric   Having many mothers. Term pertains to a family or household in which the child-rearing responsibilities are shared by two or more persons. Compare MONOMATRIC.

polymorphism   Ability to assume different forms, used by some animals for camouflage and mate attraction. See CRYPSIS, HETEROSIS, SPORT.

polymorphous   Having a variety of forms or shapes.

polymorphous perverse/perversity In psychoanalytic theory, a capability of responding to many kinds of sexual excitation, such as touching, smelling, masturbating, defecating, hurting, viewing. According to Sigmund Freud, this capacity stems from early infancy, is expressed in some degree in normal sexual activity, and takes pathological form in practices often characterized as perversions. See FOREPLAY, PARAPHILIAS.

polyneuritis Inflammation of a large number of spinal nerves. See BERIBERI, THIAMINE DEFICIENCY.

polyonomy Having many variations, for example, a person who is obviously mentally disturbed may be referred to generally as "mad," "neurotic," or "unstable."

polyop(s)ia Having more than one image on the retina of a single stimulus, as in double vision. See ANORTHOPIA, DIPLOPIA.

polyorchid A male having one or more supernumerary testes.

polyphagia Pathological overeating. See BULIMIA.

polypharmacy Pejorative term relating to the use of more than one medicine at a time. Term is used in two different senses: (a) Patients (especially older persons) who have several different medical conditions may get prescriptions for each of them, and the resulting drug interactions can be problematical; (b) In the psychiatric treatment of a patient, sometimes several medicines are prescribed. As comorbidity has become increasingly recognized, it is appropriate that different conditions might require more than one medication, such as treating a patient with Tourette's Disorder and comorbid obsessive-compulsive disorder (OCD) with a low dose neuroleptic for the tics, but also adding a serotonin-reuptake inhibitor (SRI) such as fluoxetine for the OCD symptoms. On the other hand, if one medicine could be found that would be effective, it is better to avoid polypharmacy.

polyphasic activity Behavior characterized by attempting to perform more than one activity simultaneously, for example, eating while reading a newspaper or making business telephone calls. See TYPE A BEHAVIOR.

polyphasic sleep rhythm A sleep pattern of several relatively short naps, such as shown by a human infant who will ordinarily have about six sleep periods daily.

polyphobia Morbid fear of many things.

polyphrasia logorrhea

polypnea 1. Abnormal increase in the rate and depth of breathing, which may be deep, labored, and rapid. Also known as hyperpnea. 2. See TACHYPNEA.

polysensory units Neurons that respond to more than one type of stimulus.

polysomnography (PSG) A recording of various physiological processes (such as eye movements, brain waves, heart rate, or penile tumescence) throughout the night, often for the diagnosis of sleep-related disorders.

polysurgical addiction A compulsion to undergo surgical operations, often unnecessary, as in a patient undergoing one surgical procedure after another even when organic pathology cannot be found. See CHRONIC FACTITIOUS DISORDER WITH PHYSICAL SYMPTOMS, HYPOCHONDRIASIS, SOMATIZATION DISORDER.

polysynaptic arc multisynaptic arc

polysynaptic reflexes Complex reflexes that involve two or more synapses. See GOLGI REFLEX, MYOTATIC REFLEX.

polythetic taxonomy A categorization of species on the basis of overall similarity. Compare MONOTHETIC SIMILARITY.

polytoxicomanic Obsolete term for a person with an abnormal desire to consume various toxic substances, including narcotics or other drugs of abuse.

polyvitamin therapy The administration, frequently self-prescribed, of a combination of vitamins, usually including the B complex, in large doses. It is commonly necessary in the treatment of alcoholism and other nutritional disorders. The vitamin-B deficiency associated with chronic alcoholism contributes to central nervous system symptoms (for example, Korsakoff's psychosis).

POMC See PROOPIOMELANOCORTIN.

Pompadour fantasy A variation of the hetaeral fantasy characterized by a woman daydreaming of being the lover, mistress, or wife of a man who is immensely powerful, rich, and accomplished (for example, a king or emperor), thereby making her the envy of all other women. Name is based on Madame Pompadour, the publicly acknowledged mistress of King Louis XV.

POMS See PROFILE OF MOOD STATES.

ponderal index (W. Sheldon) The ratio of a person's height to the cube root of that person's weight.

P_1 In genetics, indicates the parental generation.

ponophobia Morbid fear of being overworked. See KOPOPHOBIA.

pons (varolii) (bridge—Latin) (C. Varolio) A part of the central nervous system between the midbrain and the medulla oblongata, appearing as a swelling on the ventral (inner) side of the brainstem. Serves as a bridge between different areas of the nervous system and helps in coordinating voluntary movements. See METENCEPHALON.

pontine geniculate occipital (PGO) spikes/waves Electroencephalographic (EEG) peaks that occur during sleep and indicate neural activity in the pons, lateral geniculate, and occipital cortex. See PARADOXICAL SLEEP.

pontine sleep A phase of sleep during which dreaming takes place. Name is based on the pons' involvement in this phase of sleep. Also known as dream state.

pontocerebellar pathway Nerve structures through which an impulse passes while moving from the pons to the cerebellum.

Ponzo illusion (M. Ponzo) A tendency that if two objects of identical size are placed between a pair of converging lines, the objects will appear to be of different sizes, the one closer to the point of convergence appearing larger than the other. Sometimes known as the railroad illusion.

pooh-pooh theory A point of view about the origin of language, that it began by vocal interjections such as "Ah," "Ugh," "OW." See ORIGIN-OF-LANGUAGE THEORIES.

pooled interdependence   The situation in which each unit of an organization is somewhat dependent on the resources generated by other units. For instance, the success of a bank depends on the performance of all its branches, each of which operates rather independently.

pooled variance   The weighted average of two sample variances, each randomly selected from a population with unknown variance.

pooling   The combining of data, scores, or test results and treating them as a single variable.

poor mouth   A compulsion to deny being financially stable, characterized by acting as though one is about to be dispossessed from the home, living on a small portion of income, and denying any possession of wealth.

popular psychology   Colloquial phrase for the simplification and overuse of psychological principles and terminology. Also known as pop psych. See PSEUDO-SCIENCE, PSYCHOBABBLE.

popular response (P)   In Rorschach test scoring, responses given most frequently by normal participants, identified as P, as opposed to original or unique responses, identified as O that occur rarely.

population   1. Total number of individuals, humans or other organisms, in a given geographical area. 2. In statistics, population is a universe with certain unknown characteristics; a population is sampled statistically for the purpose of describing its parameters. See SAMPLE.

population density   Number of individuals per acre or other measure. In many countries, high population density is significantly related to various forms of social pathology; this is apparently not true in all countries, for example, Japan. See OVERCROWDING, OVERPOPULATION, POPULATION RESEARCH.

population genetics   The discipline dealing with the biochemistry of inheritance.

population research findings   Studies of population-related issues and problems. See FAMILY PLANNING, POPULATION DENSITY.

population standard deviation   See STANDARD DEVIATION.

poriomania   An irresistible, apparently aimless impulse to run away or wander off, either consciously or in a state of amnesia during which an irresponsible act or a crime may be committed. Occurs in epileptic and senile patients. Also known as poriomanic fugue. See FUGUE, NOMADISM.

poriomanic fugue   **poriomania**

pornographomania   1. Morbid impulse to write obscene letters. 2. Being sexually aroused by writing sexually obscene material, graffiti, and letters.

pornography   Writings or illustrations likely or designed to cause sexual arousal in some individuals; the creation or the study of such works. Legal interpretations of this term vary. Also known as psychological aphrodisiacs. See EROTICA.

pornolagnia   An attraction to prostitutes as sexual objects.

porropsia   A visual disorder in which objects appear to be more distant than they actually are, though their size is unchanged.

Portable Fatigue Meter   (T. Hosokawa) An apparatus to measure critical flicker fusion frequency, used to measure workplace fatigue.

Porter-Lawler model of motivation   (L. Porter & E. Lawler) A comprehensive chart that interrelates process theory variables and performance, rewards, and job satisfaction.

Porter's law   A theory that the critical flicker frequency increases with the logarithm of the brightness of the stimulus independent of the stimulus wavelength. Also known as Ferry-Porter law. Named after British scientist Thomas C. Porter (1860–1933).

Porteus Maze Test (PMT)   (S. Porteus) One of the original paper-and-pencil intelligence tests designed to assess ability to plan ahead and apply reasoning to the solution of a problem. In its various forms, a Porteus maze consists of a complex set of straight pathways that turn abruptly at 90° angles and run into numerous blind alleys. Only one pathway leads directly through the maze. This nonverbal, culture-fair test was originally developed by Stanley D. Porteus for use in anthropological research, but was also used to evaluate people with verbal disabilities and to assess brain damage. Porteus presented the first version of the test in 1913. It later became part of the Arthur Point Scale. Also known as Porteus Mazes. See ARTHUR POINT SCALE OF PERFORMANCE TESTS, CULTURE-FREE INTELLIGENCE TEST.

portfolio test   In consumer psychology, consumers are presented with a portfolio of advertisements, then tested for recall.

portmanteau neologism   An artificial word formed by condensing several other words, for example, "Stagflation," from "stagnation" and "inflation." See NEOLOGISM.

position   1. The location in space of an object in relation to a reference point or other objects. See INTERPOSITION, SECONDARY POSITION, SERIAL-POSITION EFFECT. 2. A social standing or rank of a person in a social group. See ORDINAL POSITION, ORIGINAL POSITION. 3. A person's stand on an issue. See DEPRESSIVE POSITION, FALSIFIABILITY POSITION, INFORMATION-OPTIMIZATION POSITION, MENTALIST POSITION. 4. A technique. See CABBIE POSITION, COITAL POSITION, MISSIONARY POSITION, OCEANIC POSITION, SEXUAL POSITION, SLEEPING POSITION. 5. See POSITIONS.

positional alcohol nystagmus (PAN)   Nystagmic (flip/drift-back) eye movements when the head is turned following alcohol consumption in the past ten or more hours. Starts as PAN1 (the flip is in the direction of head rotation) and converts midway to PAN2 (flip is in opposite direction to head turn). See NYSTAGMUS.

positional economy   All the goods, services, occupations, etc., that are either scarce or subject to congestion through more use. Examples: high-level jobs, desirable residential locations, good tickets to a theatrical event.

position defense   In consumer psychology, the maintenance of a company's or a brand's success through promotion or expansion. Compare PREEMPTIVE DEFENSE.

position effect   In extrasensory perception (ESP) or psychokinesis (PK) tests, a tendency to systematically hit or miss a trial due to its position in the sequence of the trials.

positioning   A technique in psychotherapy in which the therapist operates in a manner different from usual, as in giving information or directions contrary to what a client expects. See LEANING TOWER OF PISA APPROACH, PARADOXICAL COMMAND.

position-negative ambivalent quotient (PNAvQ) (V. C. Rainy) A ratio of remarks showing a positive or favorable self-evaluation to negative and ambivalent remarks in a given statement by a counselee. Research has indicated that the percentage of negative remarks about the self decrease as therapy continues.

position power   Formal authority granted by an organization, as in high military rank.

position preference   Essentially, the tendency of an organism, whether innate or learned, to turn (jump) consistently to the right or left or to alternate as in learning discrimination problems, or the slight preference to turn right or left in a T- or Y-maze at the start of learning.

positions   In transactional analysis, refers to the four positions that can be adopted or held about self and others: (a) "I am O.K. and you are O.K."; (b) "I am O.K. and you are not O.K."; (c) "I am not O.K. and you are O.K."; and (d) "I am not O.K. and you are not O.K."

positive acceleration   1. Generally, going increasingly faster, commonly known as acceleration. 2. An improvement in the rate of change or development in a given activity or function as a result of practice, for example, a gain in learning. Compare NEGATIVE ACCELERATION.

positive addiction (concept)   An assumption that some life activities a person feels a need or urge to participate in, such as meditating and jogging, are "positive" even though the person feels compelled to do so. Deemed a healthy therapeutic alternative to a negative addiction such as drug dependence.

positive affectivity   A tendency to respond to one's environment with good feelings, emotions, reactions. Opposite of negative affectivity.

positive afterimage   An image that remains after a visual stimulus ceases. It is similar to the original image, occurs rarely, lasts a few seconds, and is caused by a continuation of receptor and neural processes following cessation of the stimulus; it is approximately the color and brightness of the original stimulus. Compare NEGATIVE AFTERIMAGE.

positive afterpotential   Beginning after the negative afterpotential, a shift to a potential that is more positive than the resting potential. See AFTERPOTENTIAL.

positive aftersensation   1. A sensation of the original hue that persists after stimulation ceases. 2. Phrase sometimes used interchangeably with positive afterimage.

positive attitude   1. In general, describing a person's reaction to a situation, event, or outlook on life that is upbeat and optimistic. 2. In counseling or psychotherapy, a client's feelings of self-approval, acceptance and approval of the counselor or therapist, another person, object, and the treatment process. Compare NEGATIVE ATTITUDE.

positive cathexis   In psychoanalytic theory, the investment of positive emotions such as love or approval in an object, idea, or activity. Compare NEGATIVE CATHEXIS.

positive conditioned reflex   A phase of a differential conditioning system in which an organism is trained to respond in different ways to two different stimuli, for example, an animal may be conditioned to lift a leg on one cue, a positive conditioned stimulus, and fail to lift the leg on a second cue, a negative conditioned stimulus. See INHIBITORY REFLEX.

positive correlation   When high scores on one factor predict high scores on another, for example, many hours spent studying will probably be reflected in higher school grades.

positive discrimination   Policies and practices favoring groups that have been historically disadvantaged.

Positive Disintegration   (D. Dabrowski) A system of psychotherapy based on the concept that an individual must be analyzed to the point of disintegration before the pieces can be put together to become whole again.

positive electrotaxis   See ELECTROTAXIS.

positive eugenics   Denoting practices and policies (for example, mate selection) that attempt to "better" the qualities of humans, to develop them to the "highest" degree. Compare NEGATIVE EUGENICS. See EUGENICS.

positive feedback   1. A signal to a machine that its speed or output should be increased, or from a receptor that a reaction or activity should be enhanced. 2. An external signal that will increase, enhance or continue some behavior, for example, a good grade on a particular test; the smile of a parent when a child earns parental approval; the applause of an audience to a particular statement in a speech. See ROSENTHAL EFFECT.

positive findings bias (in research)   1. The greater likelihood of positive or confirming results being published than negative or disconfirming ones. 2. The interpretation of ambiguous results in favor of the construct being tested. 3. The attribution of chance results to the variable of interest.

positive frequency   In attempting to predict an event that is only as likely to occur as some other event, selecting the event that has occurred most often in the recent past, for example, in tossing a coin, betting that the coin will next show "heads" if "heads" have come up in the few tosses immediately before. See GAMBLER'S FALLACY, NEGATIVE RECENCY, POSITIVE RECENCY EFFECTS.

positive hallucination   The perception of an object not actually present; can be induced by hypnotic suggestion. Can be a symptom of psychosis.

positive hit ratio   An index of decision-making effectiveness; the number of successful applicants divided by the number of those selected by the procedure.

positive incentive   An environmental object or condition that constitutes a goal toward which an organism directs its behavior, for example, food or warmth. It elicits approaching behavior. See INCENTIVE, NEGATIVE INCENTIVE.

positive induction   (I. P. Pavlov) Increased neural activity in a stimulated area due to preceding inhibition in neighboring areas.

positive interdependence   The realization that effort must be coordinated between the individual and the group to attain a goal.

positive motivations See RESPONSE-HOLD MECHANISM.

positive-negative ambivalent quotient (PNAvQ) (V. Raimy) The ratio of positive to negative self-statements made by a person, typically obtained in counseling and psychotherapy with the expectation that the ratio will change over the course of therapy in the direction of greater positive self-statements. See VALUE ANALYSIS.

positive punishment A procedure in which the presentation of an aversive stimulus immediately following the occurrence of a particular behavior results in a decrease in the rate of responding of that behavior.

positive recency effect A tendency to expect that a succeeding event will be similar to prior ones, for example, if red had come up X number of times on a roulette wheel, the expectation that red will again come up. Compare NEGATIVE RECENCY EFFECT. See GAMBLER'S FALLACY.

positive regard A parent's warm, caring, accepting feelings for a child. Considered necessary for the child to develop a consistent sense of self-worth. Carl Rogers also used the phrase to refer to a counselor's feelings for a client as a separate individual whom the counselor cares for and values. See CONDITIONAL POSITIVE REGARD, UNCONDITIONAL POSITIVE REGARD.

positive reinforcement/reinforcer (B. F. Skinner) A stimulus presented after a response that increases the probability that the response will appear again, given the same or similar stimulus situation (for example, presenting food to a hungry animal after it has pressed a bar). More commonly known as reward. See NEGATIVE REINFORCEMENT, REINFORCEMENT.

positive resource A pleasant surround (for example, soft music).

positive retroaction **retroactive facilitation**

positive reward A reinforcer. (The word "reward" is always considered positive and so the word "positive" is redundant.) Compare NEGATIVE REWARD.

positive schizophrenia (T. J. Crow) A form of schizophrenia characterized by delusional and hallucinatory symptoms considered produced by excessive dopamine activity. See NEGATIVE SCHIZOPHRENIA, SCHIZOPHRENIA.

positive self-regard (S. Standal) Favorable regard of self that has been internalized and thus comes primarily from the person's conclusions and not from others. See POSITIVE REGARD.

positive spike pattern An electroencephalograph (EEG) pattern observed in examination of epilepsy patients, marked by spikes that occur at frequencies of 14 to 16 per second. Such patterns may be associated with behavioral changes that may range from hostility and rage to complaints of aches and pains which might appear to be psychosomatic in nature except for verification by EEG analysis.

positive stereotype A biased, oversimplified, inflexible, frequently erroneous conception usually of persons in certain social groups or professions of higher status for example, "All doctors are smart, kind, and want to help people." A positive stereotype ignores the unique, individual qualities of persons belonging to the stereotyped group, and may reflect a desire to emulate such people.

Involves the false attribution of many qualities such as happiness, honesty, and general life satisfaction, seen as belonging with wealth or status, to such people. Compare NEGATIVE STEREOTYPE. See ROLE MODEL.

positive symptom A symptom of schizophrenia shown by the presence of, for instance, delusions, hallucinations, and thought disorders. Compare NEGATIVE SYMPTOM.

positive tele See TELE.

positive transfer The enhancement of learning one task due to learning another. In proactive facilitation, learning task A helps learn task B; in retroactive facilitation, learning task B helps learn task A. Also known as learning set. Compare NEGATIVE TRANSFER.

positive transference In psychoanalytic theory, displacement to the therapist of attachment, love, idealization, or other positive emotions originally experienced toward parents or other significant individuals. Compare NEGATIVE TRANSFERENCE. See TRANSFERENCE.

positive tropism Obsolete name for automatic orientation of an organism toward a source of stimulation, for example, the attraction of a moth to a flame or of a plant to the sun. See TAXIS, TROPISM.

positivism (A. Comte) 1. A philosophical doctrine that knowledge is limited to observed facts and what can be deduced from those facts; an approach that underlies empiricism and behaviorism and rejects metaphysical speculation. See COMTE'S PARADOX. 2. (E. Mach) A position that immediate experience is the basis of science. Secondary means of information such as graphs, dials, scales must be interpreted by human sense organs. See LOGICAL POSITIVISM, VIENNA CIRCLE.

positivist criminology The study of the social causes of illegal behavior.

positron emission tomography (PET) A diagnostic procedure of tracking radioactive glucose in the functioning brain. Also known as PET scan.

possession 1. In the two-word stage of language development, an expression of ownership, as in "Mommy dress." 2. Belief of being taken over by some spirit or person. See DEMONIC POSSESSION, POSSESSION TRANCE DISORDER.

possession trance disorder A dissociative trance disorder characterized by the replacement of the person's typical identity with that of one attributed to a spirit, power, deity, or another person. Often associated with stereotyped "involuntary" movements and amnesia. Examples of this disorder include *amok* and *bebainan* (Indonesia), *ataque de nervios* (Latin America), *latah* (Malaysia), *pibloktoq* (Arctic), and possession (India). See entries.

possessiveness A tendency to view certain other living organisms, especially people, as belonging to the person with this attitude. May be marked by not wanting, or even preventing, other people from speaking with the coveted person. See JEALOUSY.

POSSLQ See PERSONS OF OPPOSITE SEX SHARING LIVING QUARTERS.

postal Slang for going berserk. Term is based on incidents of disgruntled or dismissed postal employees going on a deadly shooting rampage at the workplace, sometimes ending in suicide. Also known as "going postal." See INTERMITTENT EXPLOSIVE DISORDER.

postambivalent phase/stage   In psychoanalytic theory, the ultimate phase leading to pure love. Also known as real love.

postcentral area   The primary sensory area of the parietal lobe with fibers involved in touch and taste sensations.

postcompetition anxiety   In sport psychology, residual anxiety experienced by athletes in regard to a past event. See PRECOMPETITION ANXIETY.

postconcussion(al) syndrome   The consequence of head injuries. The brain strikes against the hard inside of the skull, generating various damages, some minor, some major. Short-term results may be "seeing stars," feelings of faintness, giddiness; long-term results, especially after repeated blows, as suffered by certain athletes, especially boxers, who become "punchdrunk" are slowness of speech, and cognitive deficits. See POSTTRAUMATIC PERSONALITY DISORDER.

postconstructionism   (J. Derrida) A philosophical doctrine that all theories, scientific principles, and concepts are but linguistic constructions lacking actual existence or being.

postconventional level   (L. Kohlberg) The third and highest level of moral reasoning according to Lawrence Kohlberg, characterized by commitment to valid moral principles sustained independently of any identification with family, group, or country. At this stage moral values are no longer determined by tradition or social groups but are defined in terms of their application to situations as well as the individual's conscience and ethical principles. Stage 5 of this level reflects legalistic, utilitarian concerns with individual rights in relation to the needs of society. Stage 6 is concerned with the application of self-determined, rational principles that have universal validity. Also known as postconventional stage of moral development. See CONVENTIONAL LEVEL, KOHLBERG'S THEORY OF MORAL DEVELOPMENT, MORAL CODE, MORAL DEVELOPMENT, MORALITY, PRECONVENTIONAL LEVEL.

postcopulatory behavior   Integral components of the sexual behavior repertoire following copulation, particularly in birds and mammals. Possibly designed to avoid agonistic behavior or to disengage the reproductive activity, permitting other activity.

postdental   alveolar

postdisaster adaptation   The range of responses following the crisis phase of a disaster. In addition to the constructive responses involved in rebuilding and reconstruction, long-term negative psychological consequences may ensue or preexisting disorders may be aggravated. Common psychological problems associated with disasters include grief, anxiety, and psychosomatic complaints. See DISASTER SYNDROME, PREDISASTER ADAPTATION.

postemotive schizophrenia   A type of schizophrenia in which symptoms are triggered by an emotional crisis. The patient in such cases usually is predisposed to the disorder because of an existing condition, such as schizoidism. The emotional crisis may be such that it threatens sex life, self-preservation, or a similar basic psychological aspect of personal life.

postemployment services   In vocational rehabilitation, follow-up services provided by an appropriate agency to help a recently employed person with a disability adjust to the new job situation.

postencephalitic amnesia   A form of severe memory disorder that occurs in some patients who have recovered from an episode of viral encephalitis. Symptoms may include a gross defect of recent memory, partial retrograde amnesia, and difficulty in following ongoing events. However, the brain infection causes no other significant intellectual deficits in patients experiencing the memory disorder.

postepileptic twilight state   A mental state characterized by uncertainty that follows an epileptic episode. May last for a variable period of time during which the patient may perform activities that cannot be recalled later. See TWILIGHT STATE.

posterior commissure   A large bundle of nerve fibers that crosses from one side of the cerebrum to the other, composed mainly of myelinated tracts connecting oculomotor and related cells of the midbrain.

posterior diencephalon   An area of the forebrain that contains the thalamus and epithalamus along with the pineal body. Lesions in the posterior diencephalon of laboratory animals result in changes in sleep patterns.

posterior nucleus   The most caudal portion of the thalamus, it is a poorly differentiated area that receives input primarily from the pain and somesthetic systems.

posterior orbital gyrus   See ORBITAL GYRI.

posterior parietal lobe   An area of the cerebral cortex generally posterior to the postcentral sulcus. Contains the superior parietal lobule and the angular and supramarginal gyri. Lesions in this area often results in various types of agnosias.

posterior rhizotomy   A procedure in which a posterior spinal nerve root (as opposed to an anterior one) is severed within the spinal canal. Performed for the relief of pain or to control a disorder. See RHIZOTOMY.

posterior subarachnoidean space   cisterna magna

postexertional myalgia   Technical name for a "Charley horse."

postexperimental inquiry/interview   A meeting with the goal of debriefing research participants after the study. Specific purposes may include determining whether demand characteristics may account for the results (asking participants about their perceptions of the purpose of the study and how they thought they were supposed to respond), acknowledging any deception, requesting confidentiality, answering questions, and offering thanks. See DEBRIEFING.

postfigurative culture   (M. Mead) A society or culture in which children learn chiefly from their parents, grandparents, and other adults rather than from formal teachers. See CONFIGURATIVE CULTURE, PREFIGURATIVE CULTURE.

postganglionic autonomic neurons   Nerve cells of the autonomic system that innervate certain target organs such as the kidneys, ovaries, and salivary glands. See PREGANGLIONIC AUTONOMIC NEURONS.

post hoc ergo proper hoc   A false cause. Wrongfully attributing as the cause of an event something that preceded the event.

post hoc fallacy   Faulty causal inference from correlational data.

posthypnotic amnesia   A person's incapacity to remember what transpired during his or her hypnotic trance. Typically, the person is instructed to forget the hypnotic experience until receiving a prearranged cue from the hypnotist; at that point, memory of the experience returns. See HYPNOSIS.

posthypnotic suggestion   A suggestion given to a hypnotized person to carry out at a time after the termination of the hypnotic experience in response to a given cue. See HYPNOSIS.

postictal depression   A state of depression that follows a seizure, as in cases of epileptic episodes. The postictal depression phase of an epileptic episode appears as a distinctive phase of the seizure pattern on electroencephalographic (EEG) records.

postjudice   (N. Pinckney) The development of prejudice on the part of previously neutral people following exposure to one or more people of a particular group, coming to dislike the offending person or group and then generalizing that the disliked behavior is symptomatic for all others of that category. See PREJUDICE.

postmodernism   An intellectual movement in the humanities and the social sciences maintaining that claims about social and psychological knowledge cannot be objective. Knowledge claims are influenced by the personal circumstances of the theories and researchers making those claims, and by the social structures within which intellectuals operate. On the contrary, postmodernists assert that institutional inequalities, personal interests, subjective motives, and social power play an important role in the type of knowledge generated by intellectuals. Theories and findings cannot transcend the time and the place where they were produced. Unlike positivism, which sought to create universal and generalizable theories, postmodernism maintains that knowledge claims should be limited to the context where the research takes place. Furthermore, postmodernism states that intellectuals should not pretend to be value-free, but should disclose their values so that others may scrutinize their research in light of these values. Postmodernists claim that much of the social and psychological knowledge produced in the last 100 years was used to support social structures of inequality from which academics benefit. Postmodernists seek to elucidate the role played by values, subjectivity, and politics in social knowledge.

postmortem examination   Autopsy.

postmulticulturalism   1. The recognition that celebrating cultural differences is out of date, having been replaced by commitments to inclusiveness. 2. The appearance of diverse approaches to accommodating diversity.

postnatal sensorineural lesions   An impairment of the inner ear, or auditory-nerve pathways, acquired sometime during life. Results in loss of hearing. May be due to such agents as injury, drug toxicity, viral infections, diseases such as mumps, measles, or scarlet fever, and simply old age.

postOedipal   In psychoanalytic theory, a rare term pertaining to the period following the resolution of the Oedipus complex, approximately between ages six and 12. Suggested by L. E. Peller to replace "latency," which implied falsely that sexual interest is completely latent or missing during these ages.

postoperative (PO)   Following an operation.

postoperative disorders   Neurotic or psychotic reactions following surgery. Neurotic reactions include anxiety, hysterical symptoms and even panic. Children who have not been properly prepared for an operation may become phobic, negativistic, and extremely dependent. Psychotic reactions include disorientation, hallucinations, delusions, and acute manic, depressive, or schizophrenic episodes in predisposed patients.

postpartum blues   postpartum depression

postpartum depression   Transient depression starting days or weeks after childbirth in a woman who was not depressed during pregnancy. Attributed to hormone fluctuations as well as to social and psychological factors. Affects one-third of new mothers (one-half, when including a mild version sometimes termed baby blues). Also known as maternity blues, postpartum blues. See POSTPARTUM PSYCHOSIS.

postpartum emotional disturbances   Transient emotional disorders following childbirth, including depression ("maternity blues"), indifference or hostility toward the child or father, feelings of anxiety and apprehensiveness, and disturbed sleep patterns. For more extreme reactions, see POSTPARTUM DEPRESSION, POSTPARTUM PSYCHOSIS, PUERPERAL DISORDERS.

postpartum period   The period of time following childbirth during which the mother's reproductive system gradually returns to its prepregnancy state. Sometimes known as postpartal period.

postpartum psychosis   A psychotic episode associated with childbirth that may include severe depression, withdrawal from reality, delusions, hallucinations, and physical attacks on the baby. May be caused by a combination of hormone fluctuations, inadequate parenting knowledge and family support, preexisting personality defects and maladjustments, marital instability, inability to assume responsibility, lack of desire for the infant, and financial burdens. Also known as puerperal psychosis.

postreconstructive surgery   Surgical operations performed on an arm, leg, or other body part subsequent to the original reconstructive procedure. Often required to achieve optimum functioning, and may involve the transfer of muscle or tendon fibers between body areas, or redirecting nerve fibers.

postremity principle   1. (V. W. Vocks) A theory that the most recent response learned by an organism is the one most likely to be made when the stimulus situation is repeated. 2. (E. R. Guthrie) An organism faced with making a decision is likely to repeat the prior successful decision. See CONTIGUITY THEORY.

postrotational nystagmus   The nystagmus (eyes moving back and forth) that occurs when rapid rotation of the body ceases.

postschizophrenic depression   A period of depression that may follow an acute schizophrenic episode. Viewed by some authors as a routine event in recovery from schizophrenic decompensation, as a mood disturbance that existed previously and was masked by the schizophrenic episode, or as a side effect to drug treatment for schizophrenia.

poststructuralism (J. Derrida) A leftist philosophical doctrine, which is a development beyond the structuralism of Levi-Strauss. It is closely related to (or the same thing as) "social constructionism," which is the doctrine that all perceptions, theories, scientific principles, concepts, and attempts to determine truth are nothing but cognitive and linguistic constructions shaped by the society in which the individual lives; they have no independent ontological status. See POSTMODERNISM.

postsynaptic 1. In reference to a neuron that obtains a charge from other neuron over the synapse. 2. The cell on the receiving side of a synapse. See PRESYNAPTIC, SYNAPSE.

postsynaptic potential (PSP) A graded electric potential at a dendrite or other receptive portion of a neuron generated as a result of afferent (incoming) synaptic activation.

posttest An examination given at the end of any procedure, usually to check against the pretest, for example, students registering for a course in basic economics were given a pretest; after completing the course they were given a posttest to measure whether they had gained any knowledge and, if so, how much per group and per individual.

posttetanic potentiation (PTP) A condition in which an overabundance of transmitter substance accumulates at the synaptic knobs of a spinal motor network following a period of rapid firing of impulses through the synapses. The posttetanic potentiation may continue for about 60 seconds after the build-up of transmitter substance.

posttraumatic amnesia (PTA) A period of amnesia following a blow to the head or an acute psychological trauma. The traumatic event may be forgotten (retrograde amnesia), or events following the trauma may be forgotten (anterograde amnesia). Or both retrograde and anterograde amnesia may occur.

posttraumatic communicating hydrocephalus A form of hydrocephalus (a condition of fluid in the brain) involving the frontal lobes after a head injury. There may or may not be a lesion, and diagnosis usually is based on a CAT scan or radioisotope scan or pneumoencephalography. The disorder occurs most commonly in older individuals and is characterized by dementia, an abnormal gait, and incontinence.

posttraumatic constitution A number of syndromes that are varied in character, often with both neurotic and psychotic manifestations. One of the more common types, Friedmann's complex, is possibly due to cerebral vasomotor disturbance resulting in headache, irritability, fatigability, and insomnia.

posttraumatic disorders Emotional or other disturbances whose symptoms appear after a patient has endured a traumatic experience, such as symptoms of amnesia, personality disorders, epileptic episodes, headaches, and gastrointestinal effects such as constipation. See POSTTRAUMATIC STRESS DISORDER, TRAUMATIC NEUROSIS.

posttraumatic epilepsy Epileptic seizures precipitated by a blow to the head severe enough to cause brain damage. Seizures may occur soon after the injury, or in some cases months or years later.

posttraumatic headache A headache following a severe trauma, often accompanied by vivid, terrifying nightmares and startle reactions that symbolize the threat to survival experienced during the event.

posttraumatic neurosis See POSTTRAUMATIC STRESS DISORDER, TRAUMATIC NEUROSIS.

posttraumatic personality disorder A diagnosis of a personality disturbance occasionally observed after a severe head injury. Some patients become indifferent and withdrawn, but they are more likely to be irritable, impulsive, petulant, extremely selfish, and irresponsible. Older patients and those suffering from frontal-lobe damage may show impaired memory with confabulation. See POSTCONCUSSION(AL) SYNDROME.

posttraumatic stress disorder (PTSD) A mental and emotional condition resulting from exposure to severe stressors whereby a person has experienced or witnessed an event or events involving actual death or threat of death to self or others. Can be acute or chronic and is often misdiagnosed due to the prevalence of other conditions with similar or overlapping symptoms marked by severe anxiety and depression. PTSD is thought to resemble shell shock in World War I and traumatic neurosis later. It can evolve individually or in a group, frequently developing as part of a dual diagnosis in conjunction with other disturbances. Common events evoking the disorder are: military combat, Prisoners-of-War experiences, natural and human-induced disasters, physical assault, hostage-taking, and sexual abuse. A combination of psychotropic medications and psychological deconditioning procedures is frequently needed in its amelioration.

posttraumatic syndrome A reaction pattern that may develop days or weeks after a catastrophe. Major features arc mild-to-acute anxiety attacks, recurrent nightmares, irritability, and persistent tension with tremors, restlessness, and insomnia. If persistent, it is identified as posttraumatic stress disorder (PTSD).

posttreatment followup Periodically checking to see how people who have received some kind of treatment are doing.

postulate 1. A fundamental assumption that does not require proof. See AXIOM. 2. To make a statement; to generate a claim without proof.

postural aftereffect An observation that after a body part is held in an unusual position and returned to normal, the body part appears to be held in the opposite location to the originally-held unusual position.

postural alignment A phase of orthopedic rehabilitation in which emphasis is given to symmetrical alignment of muscles, bones, and joints so that physical stresses of sitting or standing will not result in pain, discomfort, or added wear and tear during the lifetime of the patient. See ALEXANDER TECHNIQUE, ROLFING, TRAGER MENTASTICS.

postural communication Conveying information by bodily movement, orientation, attitude, or all three. An important means of communication between most motile organisms is by postural changes. Animals with limited communication skills clearly indicate certain information by bodily changes. The pilomotor effect in cats is an example. Humans also communicate feelings and attitudes by postural changes.

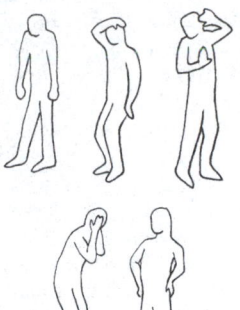

postural communication Five different postures. Most people can identify what such postures are conveying; for example, top row, from left to right: Anger, Surprise, Avoidance; bottom row, Grief and Defiance.

postural control A landmark behavior in development when, at about three weeks of age, infants lying on their stomachs are first able to lift their heads and raise their chins. Within a few weeks, further steps in postural control are achieved, such as holding the head erect, turning it, and sitting with and then without support. These abilities, in which there is wide variability, expand the child's psychological field immeasurably.

postural echo The movement of parts of the bodies in imitation of others, usually done unconsciously. Also known as synchrony.

postural echo

postural hypotension An abnormal drop in blood pressure that may occur when an erect posture is abruptly assumed. Involves a complex rerouting of blood flow through arteries and veins but is basically the result of a sudden pull of gravity on blood to lower body areas with a resultant impaired blood flow to the brain, producing a brief dizziness or even loss of consciousness. Also known as orthostatic hypotension.

posturality The study of postures, used mostly by directors of theatricals in training actors how to demonstrate and portray various emotional states. See PILOMOTOR RESPONSE, POSTURE COMMUNICATION.

postural reflex Any of a variety of tonic reactions or complex limb movements needed to support the body, shift weight, grasp objects, or maintain balance in a variety of situations, such as slipping on a floor.

postural set A positioning of the body with increased muscle tonus in readiness for a response, such as when a batter is getting set for the next pitch of a baseball.

posture The position or bearing of the body. Kinds of posture may include the body being erect, recumbent, prone, or supine. Like gesture and facial expression, posture can be expressive of underlying attitudes toward the self or external world, for example, a rigid posture is

said to be frequently observed in obsessive-compulsive individuals, and a bent, in-drawn posture in schizoids.

posturing Maintaining a bizarre body position or attitude for an extended period of time. Commonly observed in certain patients with schizophrenia.

postvention (E. S. Shneidman) To make therapeutic "ventions" after a dire event has occurred, such as working with survivors of suicide, murder, cancer, or with persons who have directly experienced personal trauma or natural catastrophe.

postventral nucleus See VENTRAL POSTERIOR NUCLEUS.

pot Slang for marijuana.

potamophobia Morbid fear of rivers. See AQUAPHOBIA.

potassium deprivation Lack of potassium in the diet, a situation that can disrupt sodium metabolism, causing muscular weakness, respiratory paralysis, and damage to the heart and kidneys.

potency 1. In general, power. 2. The ability of the male to copulate, with an implication of maintaining an erection, ejaculation, and sometimes impregnation. Compare IMPOTENCE. 2. In embryology, the developmental potential of a cell or structure.

potential (E or V) An electrochemical charge that builds up between the inner and outer sides of a neural membrane. Generally, there is an excess of negative charge inside and an excess of positive charge on the outside when the inner and outer ions are in equilibrium. The potential difference has been measured as a range of 50 to 100 millivolts. For some kinds of potentials, see ABUSE, ACTION, AFTER-, BEHAVIOR, BIOELECTRIC(AL), BRAIN, COMPOUND ACTION, CORTICAL, DC, EFFECTIVE-REACTION, END-PLATE, ENDOLYMPHATIC, GRADED, POSTSYNAPTIC, RESTING, SPIKE.

potential difference In psychophysiology, a relative difference between the electrical charges on the outer and inner surfaces of the neuronal membrane.

potential-stress score See LIFE-CHANGE UNITS.

potentiometer An electronic device for measuring potential difference (EMF) by comparison with a known voltage.

potlatch A ceremony among Native Americans of the Northwest (especially the Kwakiutl nation) that consists in establishing prestige by giving away or destroying personal possessions, usually with the goal of outdoing others in being able to make such sacrifices.

potophobia Fear of drink.

Pötzl effect/phenomenon Dreaming of something not consciously "seen," as when a participant dreams of tachistoscopic images not consciously apprehended during a trial. Named after Austrian psychiatrist Otto Pötzl (b. 1877). See SUBCEPTION.

Pötzl's syndrome (O. Pötzl) A form of pure alexia associated with visual-field defects and disturbances of the color sense. Purportedly due to a lesion in the medullary layer of the lingual gyrus of the dominant hemisphere, with damage to the corpus callosum. See PÖTZL EFFECT/PHENOMENON.

poverty fear See PENIAPHOBIA.

poverty of content (of speech)   Refers to verbal communication adequate in quantity but repetitious and lacking in content to be qualitatively adequate, frequently observed in patients with schizophrenia.

poverty of ideas   1. A thought disturbance found in schizophrenic, senile, and severely depressed patients who are limited to repeating a few simple or meaningless phrases. See LACONIC SPEECH. 2. Phrase sometimes used interchangeably with intellectual impoverishment.

poverty of speech   laconic speech

poverty trap   The situation of low income people who are deterred from working by the taxation and benefits systems.

POW   See PRISONER OF WAR REACTION/ SYNDROME.

power   1. Brute physical strength. See POWER TEST (meaning 2). 2. In human relations, the ability to control, persuade, coerce, force, or manipulate others. Types of power include authority or legitimate, coercive, expert, referent, and reward. See POWER COMPLEX, POWER FIELD, POWER PLAY. 3. In psychometrics, the ability of an inferential statistical procedure to detect existing differences between groups. See POWER FUNCTION, POWER (OF A TEST). 4. The amount of work a machine can perform. 5. In optical viewing instruments (such as telescope, microscope), the degree of magnification. 6. In mathematics, the product of a number multiplied by itself, or an exponent. 7. In physics, the rate of performing work.

power analysis   Determination of the probability that a statistical test will result in the rejection of a null hypothesis that is false and should be rejected.

power-assertion   Discipline based on the physical or material superiority of the parents (spanking, withdrawal of privileges, etc.) or of the authority of position as in the case of military officers. Excessive use may lead to aggressive, rebellious children in families and revenge-seeking subordinates.

power-coercive strategy   In social psychology, a strategy based on the uses of economic, social, and political power to effect societal change, usually through nonviolent measures, for example, organized boycotts, strikes, demonstrations, and lobbying. See COERCIVE STRATEGY, EMPIRICAL RATIONAL STRATEGY, NORMATIVE REEDUCATIVE STRATEGY.

power complex   (C. G. Jung) An overwhelming desire to control other people, making them subservient to personal wishes. People who batter others who are weaker than themselves, such as some parents of their children, and some males of females, demonstrate this condition. When a person has political or economic power and has this condition, results may be damaging, dangerous, and deadly. See BATTERED CHILDREN, BATTERED WOMEN, BATTERED-CHILD SYNDROME, BATTERING MEN'S EXCUSES.

power distance   (G. Hofstede) The extent to which members of a culture accept an unequal distribution of power. In small-power-distance societies such as Denmark, inequality is minimized, superiors are accessible, and differences in power are downplayed; in large-power-distance ones such as Mexico, inequality is accepted as natural.

power elite   A relatively small group of people in any government, democratic or autocratic, who are believed to decide fundamental governmental policies.

power factor   A general intellectual factor that energizes other mental functions and determines the general efficiency of the brain.

power field   (K. Lewin) In a life-space situation, the presses (influences on the individual from the environment) and pushes (influences on the environment from the individual). See PRESS.

power figure   A person who represents power or authority.

power function   1. Theoretical relationships between the strength of physical stimuli and of subjective experiences. 2. The power of a statistical test at preestablished levels of risk to reject a false hypothesis.

power law   A theory that there is a positive correlation between the number of times a task has been practiced and increase of skill in that area.

power (of a test)   The power of a hypothesis test with respect to a particular alternative hypothesis is the probability that the null hypothesis will be rejected given that the alternative hypothesis is true.

power play   A transaction designed to coerce others into doing what they would not otherwise do.

power test   1. A test requiring the solution of difficult items without time pressure. Compare SPEED TEST. 2. In exercise physiology, a measurement of the maximal activation of the energy system, as in stair-sprinting, jumping, sprint running, arm cranking.

power therapies   (J. Davison) Systems of therapies that make incredible claims for curing all kinds of problems ranging from posttraumatic stress disorder to multiple sclerosis.

PQ4R   A suggested method for studying: Preview the subject; Question it; then Read, Reflect, Recite, and Review. See SQ3R.

PPVT-R   Peabody Picture Vocabulary Test-Revised

Pr   See PRESBYOPIA.

PR   1. partial reinforcement. 2. partial reward. 3. percentile rank. 4. public relations.

practic (functioning)   Purposeful coordination.

practical intelligence (p)   Common sense.

practical intelligence tasks   In ordinary life, problems usually faced at work that are poorly defined, have personal involvement, partial information available for solution, with numerous possible answers.

practice   See MASSED PRACTICE, DISTRIBUTED PRACTICE.

practice curve   A graphic representation of progress in learning with trials plotted on the horizontal axis and successes or errors on the vertical axis. See LEARNING CURVE.

practice effect   In learning, any change or improvement that results from practice or repetition of task items. It is a potentially invalidating factor in certain tests if some participants receive coaching. However, the practice effect is more pronounced in specific areas such as vocabulary; and through systematic control measures it can be minimized.

practice limit   In any learning situation, the point at which continued practice yields no more results; the optimal level that can be achieved by practice on a given task by a given participant at a given time. See CUMULATIVE (FREQUENCY) DISTRIBUTION for an example of this. Note that learning results rise until a certain point (curve at the top right-hand corner) then learning results decrease (where the practice limit begins).

practice material   In experiments or tests, the introductory items or examples that illustrate test procedure and acquaint the participant with the nature of the problems. Practice material is not scored.

practice period   1. A learning session. 2. In experiments or tests, the introductory period in which the participant or participant is provided with relevant practice material and allowed time to become acquainted with the nature of the problems.

practice theory of play   A point of view that children's play prepares them for adult roles. See PSYCHODRAMA, ROLEPLAYING.

practicum   1. A short-term training experience to learn skills, such as counseling, by practicing them under supervision. 2. A school course that emphasizes hands-on experience.

practicum supervision   Observation, instruction, and formative evaluations of trainees by skilled practitioners in fields such as psychological testing, counseling, psychotherapy, and similar professions.

pragmatic   An equivalent of "practical" rather than "theoretical," concerned with results regardless of other considerations.

pragmatics   A branch of semiotics; the theory that deals with the relation between signs and their users, both senders and receivers.

pragmatism   (J. Dewey, W. James) A philosophical doctrine that the truth of an idea depends upon its practical consequences, and that the main purpose of thinking is to achieve a better adjustment to the environment. See FUNCTIONALISM.

Prägnanz   (simplicity, precision—German) 1. In Gestalt psychology, tendency for the organization of any whole to be as good as the prevailing conditions allow. 2. (M. Wertheimer) Denoting the most characteristic shape which a form or structure can assume, and toward which, according to Wolfgang Köhler, every form or structure tends. Often referred to as the law of Pragnanz. Also spelled Praegnanz. See LAW OF PRECISION, PRINCIPLE OF PRÄGNANZ.

prana   (life breath—Sanskrit) 1. A concept found in various forms of Yoga. Various breathing practices ("pranayama") meant to control the prana comprise one of the eight limbs of the yogic system. 2. The Life energy that flows throughout the body being directed by the breath. Wilhelm Reich termed this energy "orgone" and indicated that its flow was blocked by the presence of body armor. See CHI, ELAN VITAL, KI, ORGONE BOX.

prandial drinking   Ingesting of water or other fluids with meals.

praxernia   (R. B. Cattell) A quality of personality marked by practical, conforming behavior.

praxiology   (K. Dunlap) Knight Dunlap's term for the science of psychology dealing mainly with actions and overt behavior, to the exclusion of consciousness and metaphysical concepts. See BEHAVIORISM.

praxis   In philosophy, the transformational nature of human action and the priority of action over thought. Sometimes associated with Marxism.

prayer   Communication with a spiritual entity, usually in the form of praise, petition, or gratitude.

PRE   partial reinforcement effect

preadolescence   The developmental period preceding puberty, comprising approximately the two years between the ages of ten and 12 in females and 11 and 13 in males. Also known as prepuberty, prepubescence, prepubertal stage.

preanimistic   See PRIMITIVE.

preattentive analysis   An examination of stimuli that may extract information about sound, speech, and meaning prior to the material's entry into awareness.

precategorical acoustic storage (PAS)   1. Echoic memory, the phrase specifies that material in such storage has not yet been categorized. Also known as precategorical acoustic memory (PAM). 2. (R. G. Crowder) In learning theory, a theory of echoic memory holding that auditory to-be-remembered items are stored in a relatively uncategorized code for around two seconds in a modality-specific sensory memory system. Termed precategorical because it contains unanalyzed information.

precausal thinking   (J. Piaget) A tendency of the young child (below age eight) to perceive natural events such as rain, wind, and clouds in terms of intentions and willful acts, in anthropomorphic (having human characteristics) rather than in mechanical terms.

precentral area   motor area

precipice fear   See CREMNOPHOBIA.

precipitating cause   The particular factor, usually a traumatic or stressful experience, that is the immediate cause of a mental disorder. The onset of a behavioral disturbance is usually associated with more than one stressor that predisposes the patient to a mental disorder, but one precipitating event turns a latent condition into the manifest form of the disorder. See CAUSALITY, PROXIMATE CAUSE.

precision index   An indicator of how close measures are to the mean.

precision law   See LAW OF PRECISION.

precision of process (h)   Reciprocal of the variance. h indicates extent of certainty. Related to the phi-gamma function and the phi-gamma hypothesis.

preclinical psychopharmacology   The area of psychopharmacology that precedes the actual clinical application of a new drug on an individual patient or patient population. Usually includes laboratory studies of the pharmacological mechanisms of the drug, extrapolation of research data into human-use terms, and evaluation of possible interactions with drugs in use or with patient idiosyncrasies. Similar to the concept of beta-testing for computer software.

precocial animals   Animals (such as ducks, horses, and some species of deer) able to walk soon after birth.

precocious puberty In humans, abnormally early sexual maturity, usually before the age of eight in a female and ten in a male. Usually caused by an endocrine-gland tumor that results only in premature development of secondary sex characteristics. True precocious puberty is marked by mature gonads capable of ovulation or spermatogenesis, adult levels of female or male sex hormones, and secondary sex characteristics. There are recorded cases of females below the age of ten giving birth. Also known as pubertas praecox.

precocity An early, often premature, development in a child of physical, mental, or artistic functions and characteristics, such as Wolfgang Amadeus Mozart's precocity in music.

precognition Extrasensory awareness of a future event, that is, noninferential foreknowledge, knowledge of events that could not have been predicted by any rational means or observations. See EXTRASENSORY PERCEPTION, PARAPSYCHOLOGY.

precompetition anxiety In sports psychology, anticipatory anxiety experienced by athletes prior to an event. See POSTCOMPETITION ANXIETY.

preconception A conclusion reached before the facts are known and evaluated.

preconditioning The presentation of two stimuli consecutively without reinforcement to determine if the participating organism will respond to both stimuli when conditioned to respond only to the first.

preconscious (Pcs) 1. (E. Claparède, J. Breuer, S. Freud) In psychoanalytic theory, the division of the personality that contains thoughts, feelings, and impulses not presently in awareness, but which can be readily called into consciousness (for example, a friend's face, a verbal cliché, and the memory of a recent event). 2. Characterizing the mental contents themselves. 3. A period in the existence of any organism before it gains any aspect of consciousness; for example, in humans, some assume there is no consciousness in the zygote (the united sperm and egg), but that as development proceeds in utero, and following birth, somewhere along the line preconsciousness ends and consciousness takes over. Also known as foreconscious.

preconscious thinking (O. Fenichel) Identifying the pictorial, magical, fantasy thinking of children that precedes the development of logical thinking. Later, types of preconscious thinking can be found in the daydreaming of patients with hysteria, the concepts of patients with a compulsive neurosis, and the thinking processes of patients with schizophrenia.

preconventional level (of moral development) The first level of moral reasoning in children, according to Lawrence Kohlberg, marked by obedience, unquestioning acceptance of parents' moral definitions, and evaluation of an act's material consequences only. Stage 1 of this level reflects concern with punishment and reward. In Stage 2, an act is appraised for its potential for self-gratification although awareness of others' needs does exist. See CONVENTIONAL LEVEL, MORAL DEVELOPMENT, POSTCONVENTIONAL LEVEL.

precuneus An area of the parietal lobe located between the parieto-occipital fissure and the cingulate sulcus. Immediately behind the precuneus is the wedge-shaped cuneus lobule of the occipital lobe. Also known as quadrate lobule.

precursor That which comes before another, with the implication that the precursor is in some manner logically related to what follows, for example, DSM-III was a precursor of DSM-IV.

predation The act of preying upon other animals. Behavior characterized by the stalking, capturing, and killing of other animals for food. Such behavior is exhibited by predatory, or predacious animals. See PREDATORY BEHAVIOR.

predator pressure The effect of predators upon their prey, tending to affect number and geographical distribution of prey which become less apt to serve as food over time. See DARWINISM.

predatory aggression See ANIMAL AGGRESSION.

predatory behavior Activity in which one animal preys on another. Has been described in terms of food deprivation and eating, but some animals will hunt and kill without eating the prey, for example, a cat may hunt and kill a mouse, but then not eat the mouse.

predatory paraphilias A category of paraphilias characterized by the ability to indulge in the perceived "sinful act of lust" only if it is stolen or taken from an innocent person by force or stealth. Includes biastophilia (assaulting unsuspecting strangers), rapism, or raptophilia (terrifying, degrading, and sexually assaulting a victim), somnophilia, or the "sleeping princess syndrome" (intruding on and fondling a sleeping stranger), kleptophilia (in which stealing results in sexual arousal).

predelay reinforcement A delayed-response test in which an animal is rewarded at a certain place, but prevented for a time from returning to the place, to determine whether it will return to the original location after the delay.

predelinquent youths Children considered at high risk for delinquency because of certain signs (such as truancy, involvement with gangs) and disadvantaged sociocultural background.

predementia praecox An early stage of schizophrenia when the patient becomes preoccupied with fantasies and daydreams and loses the capacity for coping with difficulties. Overt symptoms of schizophrenia may appear when the predementia praecox patient encounters a stress that a normal person would handle without great difficulty.

predestination A theory that everything is preordained; human behavior has already been determined by an omniscient and omnipotent being. Humans are nevertheless responsible for their actions. Also known as predeterminationism.

predetermination See PREDESTINATION.

predicate thinking A thought process in which objects are considered identical only because they bear some resemblance to each other.

prediction The determination in advance of certain other events, a basic attribute of any science. Psychology predicts the behavior of single individuals (idiographics) and of groups (nomothetics) to various statistical levels. See PRECOGNITION.

predictive efficiency 1. The number or proportion of correct predictions that a test can or does make. 2. (G. A. Kelly) How well a construct anticipates events; the measure of the validity of a construct.

predictive validity   The degree of relationship between a test or instrument that is used to predict performance and the performance itself.

predictive value   The validity of a test as a predictor of accurate information.

predictor-cell assemblies   A theoretical model of motoneurons in a network that allows for evaluation of inputs so that an appropriate response is predictable. The mechanism resembles an electronic computer flow chart.

predictor display   In ergonomics, an augmented display that depicts not only the current status of the system but also likely impending changes, showing, for instance (usually in fast time), a submarine, aircraft, or spacecraft operator how the vehicle will move if the controls are held constant. Used in high-order systems, especially large vehicles, where the operator must be "ahead of the system" by making anticipatory control inputs.

predictors   See FRAMINGHAM STUDY, PERSONNEL SPECIFICATIONS, PERSONNEL TESTS.

predisaster adaptation   The range of responses to disaster warnings. Most people appear to be passive when confronted with warnings of a disaster, such as an earthquake. Includes making emergency stores of food; engaging in alarmist activities, such as buying expensive insurance policies. See CRISIS EFFECT, LEVEE EFFECT, POSTDISASTER ADAPTATION.

predisposing cause   1. Cause relatively remote in time from its effects. 2. A factor that increases the probability that a mental disorder or hereditary characteristic will develop.

predisposition   1. A risk factor. A person is said to have a predisposition for a behavioral deficit or problem when the probability of the behavior occurring in that person is greater than for the average person. Similar to "vulnerability." Predispositions may be conditional or unconditional. 2. In genetics, any hereditary factor that, given the necessary conditions, will lead to the development of a certain trait, characteristic, or disease.

preemie   Slang for a premature infant.

preemptive construct   (G. A. Kelly) A biased point of view about other individuals, seeing only a single aspect of others with the implication that the aspect tells all pertinent information about them. See CONSTELLATORY CONSTRUCT, PROPOSITIONAL CONSTRUCT.

preemptive defense   In consumer psychology, the launching of a marketing or other program before the competition starts one. Compare POSITION DEFENSE.

preening   Behavior of one animal toward another, usually of the same species, as in licking or otherwise grooming it. Can be self-directed.

preestablished harmony   (G. W. Leibnitz) A doctrine positing that psychological and physiological processes follow parallel harmonious paths without interaction between them in contrast to René Descartes' position. See ISOMORPHISM, PINEAL BODY.

preference behavior   Moving toward or away from an object when the choice has been induced by conditioning. The organism may have been conditioned with or without rewards for making the "correct" decision.

preference method   A research technique in which a subject chooses one of several possible stimuli, such as a food choice by animals, or various choices by human participants, such as paintings, activities, or vocations.

preference reversals   A change in the preferred order of the choices as a function of change in the context in which the changes are presented.

preference test   The presentation of product samples, to a consumer jury, for preference determinations.

preferential effect   (K. R. Rao) In extrasensory perception (ESP) research, a class of the differential effect where the positive scoring (hitting) on one of the two contrasting conditions is related to the participant's preference for that condition.

preferential matching   In parapsychology, a method of scoring responses to free material in which a judge ranks stimuli, responses, or both, in terms of their similarity to each stimulus object.

preferential perception   In infants, the visual perception characterized by a certain flexibility as the child no longer appears fixated on high contrast areas but begins to focus on, differentiate, and favor certain colors and configurations. See OBLIGATORY PERCEPTION which precedes preferential perception.

preferred noise   Background sound, as of music or rain, that is optimal for a given task environment such as studying or performing surgery.

preferred noise criterion (PNC)   (L. L. Beranek) In ergonomics, curves that show the relationship between sound intensity and frequency to achieve a given PNC level for different tasks.

preferred-octave speech interference level   (A. Peterson & E. Gross) An index to estimate the effects of noise on speech intelligibility.

prefigurative culture   A society or culture in which children have a knowledge superior to their parents. Because of the extremely rapid rate of social change and the resulting isolation of many adults, Margaret Mead has proposed that contemporary society may be moving toward a prefigurative culture in which children will possess a keener intuition of the present and thus will have to "navigate the future." For example, in the computer age many children have superior knowledge of computers to their parents or teachers. See CONFIGURATIVE CULTURE, POSTFIGURATIVE CULTURE.

preformism   A doctrine positing that development consists of the emerging into adult form of the traits and capacities that exist in prototypical form in the germ cell, such as the 16th and 17th-century concept of the "homunculus," a minute but completely formed human body in the spermatozoon. Preformism contrasts with the epigenetic principle of successive differentiation in complex and cumulative stages of development. See EPIGENESIS, EPIGENETIC THEORY.

prefrontal areas   Parts of the cerebral cortex anterior to the frontal lobes. Contain association areas involved in integrating problem-solving and related activities. See FRONTAL ASSOCIATION AREA.

prefrontal lobotomy   Psychosurgery characterized by severing the nerve fibers primarily connecting the dorsomedial and anterior nuclei of the thalamus with the prefrontal lobes of the neocortex, once performed to reduce psychotic reactions. Also known as leucotomy.

preganglionic autonomic neurons   Neurons of the autonomic nervous system located in the central nervous system. Their impulses are relayed to internal organs such as the bladder, heart and arteries by postganglionic autonomic neurons located in the autonomic ganglia.

pregenital love   In psychoanalytic theory, the phase before dominance of the genital zone, when the libido is directed toward anal, urethral, and oral satisfactions.

pregenital organization   Freudian phrase for libido functions in the developmental phase preceding genital primacy.

pregenital phase   In psychoanalytic theory, the stages of psychosexual development that precede the stages of phallic primacy, when the penis and clitoris become central erogenous zones, and genital primacy, when the sex organs begin to exert a dominant influence. Comprises the first stages of sexuality, when the libido is concentrated on the mouth, anus, and urethra rather than the genital organs.

pregenital stages   A psychoanalytic concept of the three early stages of psychosexual development in terms of the focus of gratification: oral (the mouth or eating), anal (excretion), and phallic (genitals). See CHARACTER TYPES.

pregnancy   The gestational process between conception and delivery; in the human, 280 days from the first day of the last menstrual period. Also known as cyesis, cyophoria, gravidity. See ABORTION, ADOLESCENT PREGNANCY, ARTIFICIAL INSEMINATION, ECTOPIC PREGNANCY, EMBRYO, FALLOPIAN TUBES, FALLOPIAN-TUBE PREGNANCY, FERTILIZATION, FETUS, GESTATION, INFERTILITY, MENSTRUATION, OVUM, PREGNANCY FANTASY, PRENATAL CARE, SEX, SPERM, TOXEMIA OF PREGNANCY, TRIMESTER, ZYGOTE.

pregnancy fantasy   Incorrect ideas about pregnancy on the part of those who do not know the biological facts of life, such as that the infant will be a gift from the father, or that it will be born through the anus, mouth, or umbilicus. Underlying them all, according to psychoanalytic theory, is the identification of the infant with the breast, the feces, or the penis, all of which are highly desired objects that have been viewed as part of the self, but then taken away. Neurotic symptoms, such as fear of mutilation, vomiting, or fear of being devoured by the fetus, may develop during pregnancy due to revival of pregenital fantasies. See FALSE PREGNANCY.

pregnancy rate   The ratio of pregnancies per 100 woman-years.

prehension   The act of grasping, clasping, or seizing, usually with an appendage adapted for that purpose. The hands of humans and primates and the tails and toes of certain species of monkeys are prehensile, or adapted for prehension.

preinquiry   A method of evaluating whether demand characteristics may account for research results by conveying information to the participants about the experiment without actually running them through the conditions. Participants are also asked to complete the dependent measures to determine whether their performance yields the expected results.

prejudice   In social psychology, a persistently held attitude toward a certain group or individuals, more often negative than positive, formed in advance of sufficient evidence (literally, prejudgment). Typically, prejudicial attitudes are thought to be mostly acquired from parents, friends, and social groups, and are frequently perpetuated for psychological reasons, such as deriving a sense of power from lording it over others, or using minority groups as scapegoats. See POSTJUDICE, RACISM, STEREOTYPE.

p-relation   rho-relation

prelinguistic period   The stage preceding the development of actual speech, roughly the first year of life. Comprises the earliest infant vocalizations as well as the babbling stage characteristic of the second half of the first year. Holophrases (single-word expressions) usually emerge near the beginning of the second year.

preliterate   Refers to a culture that has not acquired a written language.

preloading   An experimental procedure used in the study of thirst in which an animal subject's stomach is injected with a large quantity of water.

prelogical thinking   In psychoanalytic theory, primitive or primary thought processes characteristic of early childhood, when thought is under the control of the pleasure principle rather than the reality principle, as in daydreaming. See PARALOGIA, PALEOLOGIC THINKING, PRIMARY PROCESS.

Premack's principle/rule   David Premack's contention that given two behaviors with differing likelihoods of occurring, the behavior more likely to occur may be used to reinforce the less likely behavior.

premarital counseling   Educational and supportive guidance provided to individuals planning marriage. May be offered by a member of the clergy, sex-education specialist, or therapist, who is prepared to provide advice and answers to questions covering a wide range of matters, such as rights and responsibilities of each partner, birth-control methods, and sexual compatibility.

Pre-Marital Counseling Inventory   (R. B. Stuart) Paper-and-pencil test that measures a couples' attitudes, expectations, and understanding of the partner.

premarital sex   Sexual relations before marriage. Also known as premarital relations. See FORNICATION.

premature ejaculation   1. Penile ejaculation that occurs either before, immediately or soon after penetration into the vagina. 2. In marital counseling, any ejaculation, regardless of how long it takes, if it occurs before either partner wishes it to occur. 3. A psychosexual disorder in which ejaculation occurs before the person wishes it, due to recurrent and persistent absence of reasonable voluntary control. Phrase is used only if the disturbance is not due to a mental disorder. Also known as ejaculatio praecox. See SQUEEZE TECHNIQUE.

premature infant   An infant born prior to 37 weeks of gestation, weighing under 5.5 pounds, or both.

prematurity   A state of underdevelopment.

premeditation   1. In general, the process of thinking about or planning to perform a particular action prior to its actual performance. 2. Legal term applied to crimes, that are planned rather than the result of circumstances or spontaneous behavior; first degree murder is thus distinguished from manslaughter.

premenstrual disorders Transient emotional disturbances associated with glandular imbalance preceding menstrual flow, especially tension, irritability, anxiety, and general upset. More severe disturbances, such as depression, disgust, guilt feelings, self-depreciation, and migraine may be experienced; some religions view menses as defiling, necessitating purification rites. See PREMENSTRUAL (TENSION) SYNDROME (PMS).

premenstrual-stress syndrome See PREMENSTRUAL DISORDERS, PREMENSTRUAL (TENSION) SYNDROME (PMS).

premenstrual (tension) syndrome (PMS) In some women of reproductive age, the regular monthly experience of physiological and emotional distress, usually during the several days preceding menses. Symptoms may include fatigue, edema, irritability, tension, anxiety, and depression, and usually diminish with the onset of the menstrual period. Cause is uncertain. The condition is commonly known as PMS. See PREMENSTRUAL DISORDERS.

premise 1. A statement from which a conclusion is drawn or which contributes in part to a conclusion. 2. In logic, a proposition that is part of an argument either to be accepted or to be proved. Also known as premiss.

premonitory dreams Dreams that predict events correctly. See CLAIRVOYANT DREAM, PRODROMAL DREAM, TELEPATHIC DREAM.

premoral stage Stage zero of Lawrence Kohlberg's stages of moral reasoning, corresponding to infancy (birth to roughly 18 months) and is followed by stage 1 of Kohlberg's preconventional level. See CONVENTIONAL LEVEL, MORAL DEVELOPMENT, POSTCONVENTIONAL LEVEL.

premorbid Characterizing a person's condition before the onset of disease or disorder.

premorbid adjustment A measure of the ability of a patient with schizophrenia to have made adequate social and sexual adjustments before the onset of symptoms of the disorder. Premorbid adjustment, as used in the *Phillips Scale*, has been found to be valuable in predicting the rate of recovery from schizophrenia.

premorbid personality Previously existing personality defects that predispose a person to one or another mental disorder, determining, for example, that the person would become depressive rather than schizophrenic.

premotor area/cortex An area of the frontal lobes of the brain containing cells concerned with the organization of motor impulses. Premotor cortex cells contribute to coordinated movements of body parts. After suffering a lesion in the premotor cortex, a patient may have difficulty in manipulating the fingers, as in fastening buttons on clothes, or playing a musical instrument. Also known as intermediate precentral area.

premsia (R. B. Cattell) A personality characteristic consisting of emotional sensitivity, absence of aggressiveness, and dependence.

prenatal care Medical and psychological services rendered to pregnant females.

prenatal counseling Giving information and advice for planning a successful pregnancy, including consideration of the future of the child, or advice pertaining to the termination of a pregnancy. For those who wish to deliver the infant, planning for the future of the child at home, or the child's future if given up for adoption; dealing with friends and relatives, especially parents, and with society; and the effects the event will have on a person's life as a whole.

prenatal developmental anomaly Congenital abnormality that originates in the course of prenatal development, for example, a cleft palate.

prenatal influences Any influence on the developing organism between conception and birth. Early theories cited such "old wives' tales" as the concept that strawberry-colored birthmarks may be acquired by the child if the mother watches a fire. More recent theories emphasize the effects of maternal conditions, diseases, and behaviors such as rubella, toxoplasmosis, sexually-transmitted diseases, AIDS, barbiturate poisoning, substance abuse, lead poisoning, blood incompatibility, nutritional deficiency, excessive smoking, maternal vitamin deficiency, as well as the effects of maternal emotional stress.

prenatal masculinization The masculinizing effect of androgenic hormones on fetal sexual anatomy and behavioral pathways in the brain prior to birth.

prenatal period The developmental period between conception and birth, commonly and roughly divided into the germinal period (approximately the first two weeks), the embryonic period (the first two months), and the fetal period (from two months to birth). See GESTATION PERIOD.

prenatal sensorineural lesions A congenital abnormality of the inner ear, or of the auditory nerve, resulting in loss of hearing associated with damage to the embryo in utero, or maternal illness during the first three months of pregnancy, for example, rubella.

prenatal stress Psychological and physical tension on the part of pregnant women; adverse conditions with the potential to negatively affect the unborn child, for example, if a pregnant woman does not get proper nutrition, the fetus also lacks nourishment; if constantly under emotional stress, in an extremely noisy or polluted environment, excessive production of adreno-cortical (stress) hormones can adversely effect the embryo or fetus.

prenotion Term once used to mean narrowing the ranges of memory by processing information in several different ways rather than by repeating it in rote fashion.

prenubile Pertaining to the time before a female is able to conceive. See NUBILE.

prenuptial agreement A verbal or written agreement of a couple prior to marriage, usually stipulating disposition of property in the case of divorce. Also known as a prenup.

preoccupation (with thought) A state of being self-absorbed and "lost in thought," ranging from transient absentmindedness to a symptom of autistic schizophrenia in which the patient withdraws from external reality and turns inward upon the self.

preOedipal   In psychoanalytic theory, refers to the first stages of psychosexual development when the mother is the exclusive love object of both sexes and the father is not yet considered either a rival or a love object.

preoperational stage   (J. Piaget) The period of cognitive development between ages two and seven when the ability to record experiences symbolically emerges along with the ability to represent an object, event, or feeling in speech, movement, drawing, and the like. During the later two years of the preoperational stage, egocentrism diminishes noticeably with the emerging ability to adopt the point of view of others. Also known as symbolic stage. See CONCRETE OPERATIONAL STAGE, FORMAL OPERATIONS, REPRESENTATIONAL STAGE, SENSORIMOTOR STAGE.

preoperational thought   (J. Piaget) The type of thinking manifested by a child during the preoperational stage.

preorgasmic state   Physiological status during sexual intercourse following intromission and before orgasm, a period that usually lasts from 30 seconds to three minutes, characterized by increased breathing, heart rate, blood pressure, semispastic muscle contractions, and maximum increase in the size of the penile glans and upper vaginal walls.

preorgasmic status   1. Refers to a person not yet capable of being orgasmic, such as a child. 2. Refers to a person capable of being orgasmic but who has not as yet achieved orgasm. See FRIGIDITY, SEXUAL DYSFUNCTION.

preparation   1. The state or process of increasing readiness for an activity, for example, compiling data needed to solve a problem. 2. A step in the creative process that involves making an intensive study of the problem.

preparatory adjustment   Being set to react, especially to a specific stimulus. See SET.

preparatory interval   The time period between a warning signal and actual stimulus presentation.

preparatory research   Preparation that ordinarily occurs before the actual research.

preparatory response   Any or all of a chain of responses leading to the final response.

preparatory set   A special alertness or preparedness to respond in a particular manner to an expected stimulus, action, or event. May be manifested physically and mentally prepares; for example, a tennis player set to receive a serve physically demonstrates a preparatory set, while a chess player anticipating an opponent's next move experiences a preparatory set mentally. Postural set and motor set are narrower terms, referring mainly to physiological responses. See MENTAL SET, MOTOR SET, POSTURAL SET, SET.

preparatory thought   (J. Piaget) Cognitive abilities shown by children during the formal operational stage.

preparedness   A conditioning predisposition in which the individual has a biological sensitivity to certain stimuli which are associated in turn with an unconditioned stimulus. For instance, primates may have an inherent preparedness to associate objects such as snakes, spiders, and enclosed spaces, with aversive events.

preperception   A readiness state before a stimulus is received, possibly including imagery, for example, anticipating what it will be like to make a deep sea dive or parachute out of an airplane.

prephallic masturbation equivalents   In psychoanalytic theory, autoerotic activities occurring before sexuality is centered in the genital organs; autoerotic pleasure derived from the mouth, anus, urethra, skin, musculature, or from motor activity, sensation, and perception.

prephallic (stage)   A stage of psychosexual development preceding the phallic stage. Includes the oral and anal phases of development.

prepartal eclamptic symptoms   A classification of eclamptic symptoms (convulsions) occurring in pregnant women before the delivery of a child. See ECLAMPTIC SYMPTOMS.

prepossession   A favorable bias or prejudice toward a theory, etc.

prepotence   (A. A. Ukhtomski) Power exhibited by certain reflexes to inhibit other reflex action, in the area in which they manifest themselves.

prepotency   Characteristic of certain specific biological phenomena, such that they tend to prevail as compared with other possible phenomena.

prepotent habit   A recurring behavior so well-established that it tends to prevail over other, less well established behaviors.

prepotent   response   A response that has higher priority than other responses, for example, a pain response.

prepotent stimulus   Given an array of stimuli that impinge on an organism, the stimulus that achieves first response; for example, a stimulus that produces pain is likely to be the first noted of several competing stimuli.

preprogramming   Innate potentiality of any organism to respond to any new stimulus.

prepsychotic panic   A stage in the development of schizophrenia in which the patient's self-image is disordered and the patient feels guilty, unlovable, humiliated, or otherwise different, but has not yet acquired symptoms of delusions and hallucinations.

prepsychotic personality   A marginally adjusted individual displaying characteristics and behavior that may later develop into psychosis, for example, eccentricities, withdrawal, litigiousness, apathy, hypersensitivity, or grimacing.

prepsychotic psychosis   latent psychosis

prepuberty   Prepubertal stage, prepubescence, preadolescence.

prepyriform area   Olfactory projection area of the inferior temporal lobe.

prerecognition hypothesis   1. A postulate that an expectation of an event comes as the result of previous experiences in similar situations. 2. A point of view that future events cast their shadow before they happen, and that some people have special psychic abilities to predict catastrophes.

prerelease anxiety state   A type of anxiety experienced by prison inmates who fear being released and having to compete in the outside world again. See FURLOUGH PSYCHOSIS.

presbycusis   The gradual diminution of hearing acuity associated with aging. Involves raising of the absolute threshold for sounds.

presbyophrenia   A senile psychosis characterized by confusion, disorientation, defective memory, confabulation, misidentification, agitation, poverty of ideas, and puerile but generally amiable behavior. Also known as Kahlbaum-Wernicke syndrome, Wernicke's dementia.

presbyopia (Pr)   A visual impairment of aging due to decreased lens elasticity and accommodation that causes the near point of distinct vision to become farther removed from the eye. Normally occurs when people reach their forties and usually is correctable with bifocal lenses.

preschizophrenic ego   A condition of impaired ego synthesis observed in the prepsychotic personality of the schizophrenic patient, who lacks the normal characteristic of an integrated person. Typical symptoms are withdrawal into fantasies, dreams of one's own death, aimless over-aggressiveness, and bizarre somatic sensations.

preschool programs   Educational curriculums for children who are below the required minimum age for participation in regular classroom work. Preschool programs for special-needs children are designed to help develop social skills and provide stimulation at levels appropriate for the individual children.

prescient   Ability to predict events before they occur.

pre-scientific psychotherapies   Procedures used historically to treat mental disorders, such as the use of sleep, dancing, music, and drawing by the Egyptian physician Inhotep (born 2050 BC); the use of sleep, dreaming, and suggestion by the Cult of Asclepias, Greek god of medicine; the exorcism by Israelites and Christians of demons, presumed causes of mental disorders.

prescribing   In psychology or counseling, giving clients clear and explicit directions as to what to do in certain instances, for example, prescribing a particular regimen.

prescription privilege   Legal entitlement to administer or prescribe pharmaceuticals restricted to prescription use. Commonly possessed by physicians and dentists, and in some jurisdictions by nurses and physicians' assistants. Whether this should be extended to specially trained clinical psychologists, particularly for psychoactive drugs, is a matter of debate; some have been so trained by the United States Department of Defense to do so.

prescriptive analysis   A set of eighteen opponent-pair dimensions such as consciousness-unconsciousness, staticism-dynamicism, established by Robert Watson to be applied to any theoretical view to determine whether the theory is related to these issues.

presenile degeneration   **senium praecox**

presenile dementia   See PRIMARY DEGENERATIVE DEMENTIA.

presenility   Premature old age; the condition of an individual, not old in years, who displays the physical and mental characteristics of old age.

presentation   1. The act of exposing a subject or participant to stimuli or learning materials during an experiment. 2. In psychoanalytic theory, the means or vehicle through which an instinctual drive is expressed. 3. In childbirth, the position of the neonate at the cervix.

presentation rituals   (E. Goffman) Social preparatory procedures including salutations, compliments, invitations, etc., intended to generate favorable interactions with others. See AVOIDANCE RITUALS, DEFERENCE BEHAVIOR.

presenting   Posturing and other behavior of animals to conspecifics (members of own species), typically includes lowering the front end of the body. Used to communicate submission, invitation to copulate, or both. See LORDOSIS.

presenting problem/symptom   The physical symptoms, psychological problem, or both, that caused the patient to seek professional attention. Often, but not always, the most urgent problem, especially in the case of psychological problems.

Present State Examination (PSE)   (J. Wing) A structured interview comprising about 400 items, including a wide range of symptoms likely to be manifested during an acute episode of one of the functional neuroses or psychoses. Developed by psychiatrist J. Wing in the 1960s at the Maudsley Hospital in England.

presolution period   In solving a problem, the time during which no progress is made. See SOLUTION PERIOD.

presolution variability   Describing behavior, whether overt or covert, of an organism attempting to solve some kind of a problem, prior to finding the solution. Such behavior may appear random.

prespeech development   The earliest forms of perceptual experience, learning, and communication that precede actual speech and are requisite for its development, for example, an infant's attention to sound, perceptual discriminations, and limitation and production of sounds. Infants attend to sound at birth and can differentiate the human voice from other sounds within the first month. Cross-cultural studies reveal that mothers routinely use techniques that help their infants acquire language; for example, they shorten their expressions, stress important words, simplify syntax, and speak in higher registers and with exaggerated distinctness. For prespeech sounds, see BABBLING, BABY TALK, INFANTILE SPEECH.

press   (H. A. Murray) An environmental stimulus, person, or situation that arouses a psychogenic or viscerogenic (basic physiological) need. Examples are the birth of a sibling, parental discord, feelings of social inferiority, or the sight of food when hungry.

Pressey X-O Test   (S. L. Pressey) One of the first tests of attitudes and interests, on which the respondent crosses out or circles preferences.

press-need (p-n) pattern   (H. A. Murray) The relationship between "needs" and "presses" (environmental situations), for example, sexual desires and activities necessary to get a mate, hunger in an animal and activities necessary to capture a meal.

pressure In abnormal psychology, excessive or stressful demands made on an individual. Psychological pressure may vary with different persons depending upon their educational, occupational, family, and other demands, such as parental pressure for achievement. For different meanings of the term, see the following types of pressure: ACOUSTIC, ACU-, BLOOD, DIASTOLIC BLOOD, DISGENIC, GRANULAR, GROUP, HIGH BLOOD, MINIMAL AUDIBLE, PEER, PEER-GROUP, SELECTION, SOCIAL, SYSTOLIC BLOOD.

pressure gradient A gradual reduction in pressure extending in all directions when a stimulus is applied to the skin.

pressure of activity Compulsive hyperactivity characteristic of the manic phase of bipolar disorder. Patients talk "a mile a minute," move restlessly about, pour forth an endless flow of unrealistic ideas, and, in cases of hypermania, may also decorate themselves with badges, break up furniture, and make indiscriminate sexual advances. See DEPRESSION, MANIA.

pressure of ideas See THOUGHT PRESSURE.

pressure of speech Accelerated, uncontrollable talking which includes, in some cases, ordering other people about or declaiming in theatrical tones. A symptom of mania and some cases of schizophrenia and organic brain syndromes. Also known as pressured speech. See HAPLOLOGY, LOGORRHEA.

pressure sense The sensation of stress or strain, compression, expansion, pull, or shear, usually caused by a force in the external environment. Receptors for the pressure sense may interlock or overlap with the pain receptors so that one sensation is accompanied by the other. See PRESSURE.

pressure-sensitive spot Extra sensitive spots on the skin, usually located near body hairs.

pressure spot Any of the points on the body surface particularly sensitive to pressure stimuli.

pressure-threshold test A sensory examination in which pressure sensitivity is measured with a series of hairs of graded stiffness. See HAIR ESTHESIOMETER for an illustration of an instrument used in such a test. The hand is pressing a fine hair on the participant's arm; if the participant does not feel the hair bend, another instrument with a stiffer hair will be used; when a participant states that the hair is felt, this is the pressure threshold.

prestidigitation **magic** (meaning 1)

prestige A state of being held in high esteem by peers or the whole community, particularly when others are influenced by the person's position.

prestige motive The drive to acquire favorable opinions of others.

prestige suggestion Supportive, symptomatic psychotherapy that depends upon the prestige of the therapist in the eyes of the patient. The "omnipotent" therapist may abolish the symptoms, at least temporarily, by suggestion.

prestriate area/cortex 1. An area of the cerebral cortex lying near the primary visual area, concerned with visual memory. 2. A visual-association center in the occipital portion of the cerebral cortex. Also known as Brodmann's areas 18 and 19.

presuperego phase The early stage of life according to psychoanalysis before the superego is formed. Includes the oral, anal, and phallic stages of development of approximately the first five years of life, at which time the superego replaces the Oedipus complex, according to psychoanalysts.

presynaptic 1. Refers to a neuron that provides input to another neuron. 2. The cell on the sending side of a synapse. See POSTSYNAPTIC.

presynaptic heteroreceptor A receptor on a terminal button membrane that receives input from another button via an axoaxonic synapse and binds with the neurotransmitter.

presynaptic inhibition A mechanism whereby an impulse is blocked at a synapse by reduced release of a transmitter substance associated with a partial depolarization. The effect is most likely to occur at an axo-axonal synapse. See HYPERPOLARIZATION.

pretend situations See DIRECTIVE-PLAY THERAPY.

preterm viability The development of the fetus sufficient for it to survive outside the uterus, usually beginning roughly around the 24th week after conception.

pretest See BEFORE-AFTER DESIGN, PRETEST-POSTTEST CONTROL GROUP DESIGN, PRETEST-POST-TEST.

pretest-posttest Testing before and after treatment of experimental participants with the differences attributed to the experimental treatment.

pretest-posttest control group design An experimental design with a minimum of two groups. Usually, one group receives the experimental condition and the other does not. The essential feature of the design is that experimental participants are tested before and after the intervention. Any differences are then attributed to the experimental treatment.

pretraumatic personality The personality traits of a person before an injury that may have resulted in a mental disorder. The pretraumatic personality is important for the proper diagnosis and prognosis of a posttraumatic personality disorder and for administration of the appropriate therapy. Compare POSTTRAUMATIC PERSONALITY. See FRONTAL LOBE DAMAGE, PHINEAS GAGE.

prevalence In epidemiology, the total number of cases of a disease existing in a given population at a given point in time (point prevalence) or during a specified time (period prevalence). See INCIDENCE.

prevention Efforts to control the occurrence or reduce the severity of undesirable phenomena such as mental disorders, birth defects, delinquency and crime, environmental disasters, drug addiction, accidents, and physical disease. See PRIMARY PREVENTION, SECONDARY PREVENTION, TERTIARY PREVENTION.

preventive intervention Active, immediate efforts undertaken by mental health experts to deal with emergencies, such as suicidal threats or attempts, psychotic breaks, cyclothymic crises, or dyscontrol episodes. See EMERGENCY PSYCHOTHERAPY.

preventive psychiatry   A branch of preventive medicine concerned with forestalling mental disorders (primary prevention), limiting the severity of illness through early detection and treatment (secondary prevention), and reducing disability resulting from disorder (tertiary prevention). Overlaps with the fields of psychology, social work and related professions.

preverbal   Pertaining to the period in a child's life prior to acquiring language ability.

preverbal construct   (G. A. Kelly) A concept that may have developed during the pre-speaking stage and which is still maintained, but without it having a verbal symbol.

prevocational training   Rehabilitation programs that emphasize basic work skills, usually offered to adolescents and adults with disabilities who have not had actual work experience in a competitive job market. Usually takes place in sheltered workshops.

prexis   1. Motor activity. 2. Performance of an action.

priapism   A rare, pathological, persistent penile erection, usually painful and without sexual arousal. Named for Priapus, the Greco-Roman god of procreation, and the basis of a cult that worshiped the phallus. Incorrectly called satyriasis, which is a psychological process rather than a physical problem.

price-quality relationship   A general assumption that the costlier products are superior to less costly ones.

prick experience   A sensation produced when a pin, needle, or small electrical stimulus is applied to a receptor area of the skin. May appear as a variation of other somatic sensations, such as itch, tickle, pain, or pressure, depending upon how the stimulus is applied.

pride   A feeling of self-esteem which may be exaggerated or unfounded (conceit, false pride) or a reflection of admirable self-assurance and determination (as in setting high standards and doing one's personal best). Sandor Rado applied the term domesticated pride (also known as moral pride) to overvaluation of the self in obsessive patients, interpreted as a reaction to guilt, fear, and repressed feelings of humiliation. Distinguished from real pride or brute pride based on self-assertive rage.

pride system   (K. Horney) A self-concept based on some standard the person sets up about what qualities are "good" and what are "bad" about the self.

prima facie   Self-evident, at first glance (such as during a test, having partially concealed notes on the topic of the test would be prima facie evidence of attempting to cheat on the test).

primacy   In general, the status of being first, most important, most potent.

primacy effect   A tendency for facts, impressions, or items that are presented first in formal learning situations to be learned or remembered better than others. Applies especially to information of high interest and familiarity. In psychodiagnostic known as anchoring. Also known as primacy law/principle, principle of primacy. See PAIRED ASSOCIATIONS, RECENCY EFFECT, SERIAL-POSITION EFFECT.

primacy-recency   Two terms given to two effects observed in serial rote learning, namely, that the recall of the first and last portions of the serial list is superior to that of the middle portion. See SERIAL POSITION CURVE and its illustration for an example.

primacy zone   In psychoanalytic theory, the erotogenic area that dominates others in the libido organization. According to Sigmund Freud, one primacy zone succeeds another in the order of oral, anal, phallic, and, finally, genital.

primal   1. First, such as early feelings. 2. Primitive or savage.

primal anxiety   (O. Rank) In psychoanalytic theory, the most basic form of anxiety, first experienced when the infant is separated from the mother at birth and suddenly has to cope with the flood of new stimuli. See BIRTH TRAUMA, SEPARATION ANXIETY.

primal depression   A depression experienced in early childhood, due primarily to disappointment stemming from lack of "emotional supplies" of security and love that children need to maintain self-esteem. Otto Fenichel, among others, traced cases of adult depression to this type of childhood experience.

primal fantasies   In psychoanalytic theory, presumed fantasies often employed by children to fill gaps in their knowledge of sexual experience, especially fantasies about conception, birth, parental intercourse, and castration. Such fantasies are most clearly revealed in dreams and daydreams, and are also known as unconscious fantasies.

primal father   (S. Freud) A hypothetical head of a "primitive" tribe whom Sigmund Freud pictured as slain and devoured by his sons, and later revered as a god. The crime has a tragic effect on the son who killed him, and becomes enshrined in the culture of the tribe. See PRIMAL-HORDE THEORY.

primal-horde theory   (S. Freud) A speculative reconstruction of the original human family comprised of a dominant male holding sway over a subordinate group of females and probably younger men. Sigmund Freud used the theory to account for the origin of exogamy (marrying outside the social group belonged to), the incest taboo, guilt, and totemism.

primal ictal automatism   A form of psychomotor epilepsy in which semipurposeful activities are automatically performed without preceding aura and followed by amnesia.

primal repression   In psychoanalytic theory, the screening out of unconscious material of a primordial type. Also known as primary repression. Compare SECONDARY REPRESSION. See REPRESSION.

primal sadism   (S. Freud) Freudian phrase for a part of the death instinct identical to masochism that remains within the person, partly as a component of the libido and partly with the self as an object.

primal scene   1. Generally, a child's real or imagined observation of parents engaged in coitus, with assumed violence and pain. 2. In psychoanalytic theory, the child's first observation or memory (whether due to reality or fantasy) of parental intercourse or seduction.

primal scream   (A. Janov) Powerful utterance due to abreaction, most commonly associated with patients in primal therapy. See PRIMAL THERAPY.

primal-scream therapy   primal therapy

primal therapy (A. Janov) System of psychotherapy that features the expression of blocked feelings. The treatment technique includes getting patients to relive basic traumatic events and to discharge painful emotions associated with them. The events frequently involve feelings of abandonment or rejection experienced in infancy or early childhood, and during the therapeutic session, the patient may sob, cry, scream, or writhe in agony. Afterwards a sense of release and rebirth and freedom from "primal pain" is said to occur, and the person is purportedly divested of the defenses used to escape or anesthetize the pain.

primal trauma An original painful situation experienced in early life that is presumed to be the basis of a neurosis in later life.

primary abilities The unitary factors revealed by factor analysis said to be essential components of intelligence. Seven primary abilities identified by L. L. Thurstone: verbal meaning (V), word fluency (W), numerical ability (N), spatial relations (S), memory (M), perceptual speed (P), and reasoning (R). These factors are measured by the Primary Mental Abilities Test.

primary affective disorder (PAD) An affective disorder occurring not as the result of another condition. Other diagnoses may exist independent of the PAD.

primary aging In humans, the normal growth and development up to about age 25 when a person is at the peak of physical and mental ability before the slow decline of such abilities with losses and deficits governed by inborn and time-related processes but also affected by stress, trauma and the environment. Differing abilities have differing growth and decline curves. Also known as biological aging. Compare SECONDARY AGING.

primary amentia Mental retardation caused by hereditary factors.

primary anxiety (S. Freud) A fundamental anxiety of neonates, usually due to overstimulation.

primary appraisal An immediate judgment of the situation in terms of threats, personal goals, well-being, and affordances for personal growth.

primary attention Attention that does not require conscious effort, for example, attention to an intense, powerful, or arresting stimulus. Compare SECONDARY ATTENTION.

primary behavior disorders General phrase applied to behavioral disorders in children and adolescents, including habit disturbances (nail-biting, temper tantrums, enuresis), conduct disorders (vandalism, fire-setting, alcohol or drug use, sex offenses, stealing, glue-sniffing), certain evident neurotic symptoms (tics, somnambulism, stuttering, overactivity), and school-centered difficulties (truancy, school phobia, disruptive behavior). See PARENTING TRAINING.

primary cause Identifying a condition or event that predisposes to a disorder which probably would not have occurred in the absence of the primary cause, for example, sexual contact is a common primary cause of a venereal disease.

primary circular reactions A second substage of sensorimotor development. Repetitive action that, according to Jean Piaget, represents the earliest nonreflexive infantile behavior; for example, in the first months of life, hungry infants may repeatedly attempt to put their hands in their mouths. A primary circular reaction indicates a primitive link between goal (easing hunger) and action (attempting to suck on hand). See SECONDARY CIRCULAR REACTION, TERTIARY CIRCULAR REACTION.

primary cognition The manner of perceiving the world in infancy when there are no ways of distinguishing between the self and the nonself. Psychoanalysts, among others, have assumed schizophrenia represents a regression to a state of primary cognition.

primary color/hue A group of basic colors from which all the various hues can be produced by mixing in different combinations. Some investigators assume human color perception involves combinations of three primary colors, blue, green, and red; others contend that yellow, violet, or both, should be included because of findings of visual color sensitivity peaks at those wavelengths. See LADD-FRANKLIN THEORY, YOUNG-HELMHOLTZ THEORY.

primary correlation A measure of the relationship of two variables when no other variables are considered. Also known as simple correlation.

primary cortical zone One of the three types of cortical regions behind the central sulcus, it consists of specific-sense primary projection areas. See SECONDARY CORTICAL ZONE, TERTIARY CORTICAL ZONE.

primary data The original experimental or observational data prior to statistical treatment and analysis. See RAW DATA.

primary degenerative dementia (PDD) senile dementia

primary dementia See SIMPLE SCHIZOPHRENIA.

primary deviance 1. Generally, violation of rules, laws, or mores of a group. 2. (E. Lemert) Marginal deviance, compared to secondary deviance, which is pivotal and engulfing.

primary drive A species-specific drive that is unlearned, universal, and having an organic basis. See INSTINCT, SECONDARY DRIVE.

primary emotion (W. McDougall) Certain emotions (anger, fear, grief, or joy) judged to be primitive in nature, from which other more complex emotions develop.

primary empathy An approach in the Carl Rogers system of client-centered therapy in which the therapist tries to restate to clients their thoughts, feelings, and experiences from the client's point of view in an attempt to demonstrate to the client that the therapist knows how the client is thinking and feeling. See PERSON-CENTERED THERAPY.

primary environment An environment central in a person's life and in which personal or family interactions can be sustained, such as a home or the work place. Similar in concept to primary territory. Compare SECONDARY ENVIRONMENT.

primary erectile dysfunction A form of male sexual impotence characterized by never having been able to achieve penile erection rigidity sufficient for sexual intercourse. Also known as primary impotence. See MALE SEXUAL DISORDERS.

primary factor   See TERMINAL FACTOR.

primary gains   Basic psychological benefits derived from neurotic symptoms such as the relief from anxiety generated by conflicting impulses or threatening experiences. Also known as paranosis, paranosic gains. Compare SECONDARY GAINS, TERTIARY GAINS.

primary group   1. The group that has greatest relevance to a person's values, interests, concerns. For most people in their youth, this is the family. Later, it may be other groups, such as those relating to religion, politics, economics. 2. A face-to-face group characterized by relatively strong, enduring, intimate, and complex relationships, such as a family, a partnership, or long-term therapy group. Primary groups are associated with mutual cooperation, problem solving, protection, and companionship. In contrast to secondary groups, they tend to be smaller, more cohesive, and more meaningful to the individual.

primary homosexuality   Homosexual feelings experienced at some level in childhood, but not acted upon until later in life.

primary hue   **primary color**

primary identification   In psychoanalytic theory, the first form of identification, occurring in the oral stage of development when infants regard their mother's breasts as parts of themselves. After weaning they begin to differentiate between their selves and external reality. Also known as primary narcissistic identification.

primary impotence   **primary erectile dysfunction**

primary integration   The realization by children that their own bodies are separate from the environment presumed to occur in the early narcissistic stage before the libido is directed to objects of the external world. Later it becomes a "lust of pain" as a condition for sexual gratification. Also known as erotogenic masochism.

primary line of sight   An imaginary line going from a point looked at to the center of the pupil. See CHIEF RAY.

primary memory (PM)   1. William James in 1890 proposed that a "primary" memory system was closely related to consciousness and differed from memory for general knowledge. 2. (N. C. Waugh & D. A. Norman) Name given in 1965 by Waugh and Norman to what was later known as short-term or working memory. See SHORT-TERM MEMORY. 3. (A. Adler) The first memory a person can recall from childhood. See EARLY RECOLLECTIONS.

primary memory image   **eidetic image**

primary mental abilities (PMA)   A theory of intelligence hypothesizing seven major abilities, the focus of Schaie's work on the aging of intelligence. Essentially Schaie supported L. L. Thurstone's earlier findings of these factors: verbal comprehension, spatial orientation, inductive reasoning, numeracy, word fluency, associative memory, perceptual speed. See PRIMARY ABILITIES.

Primary Mental Abilities Test (**PMA Test**)   (L. L. Thurstone & T. Thurstone) The examination often employed when both fluid and crystallized intellectual performances are to be evaluated. See PRIMARY ABILITIES.

primary mental deficiency   Subnormal intelligence due to genetic factors.

primary microcephaly   A congenital disorder in which microcephaly (having an abnormally small head) is the primary, and usually the only, evidence of an anomaly of fetal development. The most common characteristic is a normal-size face combined with a small cranium. The forehead is low and narrow but recedes sharply. The back of the head is flat, and the vertex often is pointed. Mental retardation and spasticity of limbs are neurologic deficits.

primary motivation   The drives related to unlearned body needs, for example, hunger, thirst, or sex.

primary narcissism   In psychoanalytic theory, the earliest type of self-love, in which the infant's libido is directed toward its body and its satisfaction rather than toward others in its environment. At this stage the child forms a narcissistic ego ideal stemming from feelings of omnipotence arising partially out of the fact that its slightest gesture leads to satisfaction of needs and partially out of increasing abilities, and partially as a reaction formation to feelings of helplessness and anxiety. Compare SECONDARY NARCISSISM.

primary narcissistic identification   **primary identification**

primary need   An unlearned need that arises out of biological processes and leads to physical satisfaction, such as the need for air, water, food, rest, sleep, urination, defecation, and sex. Similar to H. A. Murray's viscerogenic needs. See DRIVE, PHYSIOLOGICAL NEEDS, PRIMARY MOTIVATION, SECONDARY NEEDS.

primary object   The first object an infant attaches to psychologically and usually physically, the mother's breast.

primary odors   Irreducible odors, from which the other odors can be produced by mixture. The nature of these is still speculative. See HENNING ODOR PRISM, ZWAARDEMAKER ODOR SYSTEM.

primary oocyte   The first stage in the development of an ovum from a cell of germinal epithelium in the ovary. The process is similar to that of the development of spermatozoa from a primordial germ cell in the male, except that instead of dividing equally, the female germ cell divides into one large primary oocyte and one small polar body. In the next stage, the step is repeated to produce a secondary oocyte and secondary polar body.

primary orgasmic dysfunction   Inability to experience orgasm under any condition of stimulation. See IMPOTENCE, PRIMARY ERECTILE DYSFUNCTION, SEXUAL AROUSAL, SEXUAL DISORDERS, SEXUAL DRIVE, SEXUAL INHIBITION.

primary personality   1. The original personality, as opposed to a secondary personality or secondary personalities, of a multiple-personality (dissociative identity) individual. 2. A hypothetical entity, a personality originating in the zygote; for example, the personality that would exist if there were no environmental influences, as opposed to a secondary personality developed in a social context.

primary prevention   Efforts directed to laying a firm foundation for mental health so that mental disorders will not develop. In general, three types of preventive measures are used: (a) biological measures, including measures to prevent birth defects, prenatal care of the mother, obstetrical techniques designed to prevent birth injury, and health, safety, and nutritional measures during childhood; (b) psychological measures, including adequate parenting, approval and encouragement, firm but kind discipline, freedom to explore, experiment, and express feelings, emotional support during periods of stress, and promotion of constructive interpersonal relations; and (c) sociological measures, including reduction of social stresses that lead to personality distortion, creation of a healthy social environment, and development of community resources that help to maintain mental health. See MENTAL HEALTH, PARENTING TRAINING.

primary process   In psychoanalytic theory, the primitive cognitive mode, characteristic of infants and children, not based on rules of organization or logic. It is illogical, entirely pleasure-oriented, has no sense of time or order, and does not discriminate between reality and fantasy, as in the dreams, fantasies, and magical thinking of young children, and the distorted logic, neologisms, and bizarre gestures of regressed patients with schizophrenia. See PRELOGICAL THINKING.

primary-process thinking/thought   Thought processes dominated by the mechanisms of the primary process, especially condensation, symbolism, and displacement, and exemplified by the daydreaming and fragmented irrational thinking of a patient with schizophrenia. See PRIMARY PROCESS.

primary quality   A fundamental and indispensable property of an object, such as its weight.

primary-reaction tendencies   Characteristic ways individuals react to stress. Appear to be constitutional since they are observed in infants, such as reacting to a change in routine by developing a fever, experiencing sleep disturbances, or showing signs of digestive distress.

Primary Reading Profiles   (J. B. Stroud) A paper-and-pencil test measuring primary reading skills of children in grades 1-3.

primary reinforcer   1. That which is naturally desired by organisms, especially food and water, which in classical conditioning is usually identified as the US (unconditioned stimulus). 2. In operant conditioning, a stimulus that increases the probability of a response without a need to learn the value of the reinforcer; a stimulus that possesses inherent, or rewarding, characteristics, such as food. See REINFORCEMENT.

primary reinforcement   1. In classical conditioning, the presentation of the reward or unconditioned stimulus (US) immediately following the conditioned stimulus (CS). 2. In instrumental conditioning, the presentation of the reward immediately following the instrumental response. Compare SECONDARY REINFORCEMENT.

primary relationship   A long-lasting, emotional relationship, such as a life-long friendship, more firmly established than other relationships (friendships).

primary relationship therapy   (R. Postel) A re-parenting form of psychotherapy for adults who feel they had been rejected by one or both parents. Treatment may include being cuddled and spoon-fed by the therapist as well as a variety of other procedures, playing games such as patty-cake, being told stories, expressing fantasies. See PSYCHODRAMA.

primary repression   In psychoanalytic theory, the mental process that screens out unconscious material, such as infantile wishes and impulses that have never become conscious, as contrasted with "repression proper" in which the repressed material has already been in the realm of consciousness. Considered the earliest and strongest of the various repression modalities, due to the urgent need to avoid guilt, anxiety, insecurity and concerned with id-oriented wishes such as those related to the Oedipal situation. Also known as primal repression. See REPRESSION, SECONDARY REPRESSION.

primary reward   Any stimulus inherently rewarding to an organism; for example, food is a primary reward to a hungry animal. See PRIMARY REINFORCEMENT/ REINFORCER.

primary self   The basic psychosomatic unit existing in the infant at birth.

primary sensory areas   Areas of the cerebral cortex that receive input from the sensory nuclei of the thalamus, or the olfactory stria. There are primary sensory areas for each of the senses except pain, the vestibular sense, and smell.

primary sex characteristics   See SEX CHARACTERISTICS.

primary sexual dysfunction   A sexual dysfunction that has always existed, for example, a man has never been able to have an erection or a woman has never been able to experience an orgasm. See PRIMARY ORGASMIC DYSFUNCTION, SECONDARY SEXUAL DYSFUNCTION.

primary signal(ing) system   first signaling system

primary skin senses   The senses (pressure, pain, warm, and cold) which fuse to arouse cutaneous experiences of greater complexity.

primary sociopath   Antisocial individuals who exhibit a low anxiety level and an undeveloped conscience, and who engage in criminal activities as a way of life or as a form of rebellious, antisocial, egocentric behavior. See NEUROTIC SOCIOPATH.

primary source   The basic or first origin of information, such as a handwritten draft of a speech. Compare SECONDARY SOURCE.

primary stuttering   The neuromuscular spasms and dysfluencies in the speech of young children without accompanying irrelevant movements of the face or body, and with absence of awareness or anxiety related to speaking. Compare SECONDARY STUTTERING.

primary symptoms   (E. Bleuler) Symptoms demonstrated by people afflicted with serious mental disorders, such as schizophrenia, in their natural environment, in their home, school, workplace, society, as distinguished from the secondary symptoms displayed in an institution. See FUNDAMENTAL SYMPTOMS, SECONDARY SYMPTOMS.

primary tastes   Irreducible taste experiences of salty, sour, sweet, and bitter.

primary territory 1. In social psychology, a space controlled by and identified with a person or group who uses it exclusively and to whom it is essential, for example, an apartment or house. Similar to primary environment. See PROXEMICS, SECONDARY TERRITORY. 2. "Home" of certain individual animals or groups of animals; their usual area of residence. Usually marked in some way, often by urination at the boundaries of the area they consider theirs to warn others to keep away from their territory. See SECONDARY TERRITORY, TERRITORIAL AGGRESSION, TERRITORIAL DOMINANCE.

primary thinking See PRELOGICAL THINKING.

primary thought disorder A pathological disturbance in cognition primarily observed in schizophrenia and characterized by incoherent and irrelevant intellectual functions and peculiar language patterns that include bizarre syntax, neologisms, and word salad.

primary transitional object An object selectively acquired by an infant because of its anxiety-reducing value, such as a "teething device" that helps induce sleep, acquired during the first year of life. Compare SECONDARY TRANSITIONAL OBJECT. See TRANSITIONAL OBJECT.

primary visual system That part of the visual system that begins with the visual receptors of the retina and continues through the optic nerve and tract to the lateral geniculate nucleus of the thalamus and from the thalamus via the visual radiations to end in the primary visual cortex of the occipital lobe.

primary zone During various stages of psychosexual development, the limited area of maximal erotic satisfaction, such as looking, touching, listening, being touched.

primed errors Mistakes made due to the influence of a prior response.

prime(s) Single (′), double (″), triple (‴) primes are used to distinguish between different values of the same variable, for example, a′, a″, a‴, or to show the derivatives of a function, for example, f′(a); f″(a).

primigravida A woman in her first pregnancy. Also known as gravida I.

priming A process of increasing the availability of various types of information in an individual's mind by exposure to stimuli that activate such information.

priming effect An increase in learning efficiency that is attributable to instruction meant to facilitate a learning task.

priming the pump technique See DOUBLE TECHNIQUE.

primipara A female that has given birth once. See PRIMIPAROUS.

primiparous Bearing or having borne a child only once. Thus, a woman who has had only a single pregnancy resulting in a child, regardless of whether it was a single or multiple birth, is identified as a primipara. Also known as uniparous.

primitivation A loss of all higher ego functions such as objective thinking, reality testing, and purposeful behavior, together with regression to the primitive stage of development characterized by magical thinking, helplessness, and emotional dependence. Also known as primitivization.

primitive 1. In anthropology, pertaining to the earliest stage of human development, before the advent of social organization, as humans now know it, and many times characterized (from a Western perspective) as savage or uncivilized. More recently known as "primary," as in primary culture. 2. (S. Freud) In psychoanalytic theory, the two earliest stages in the development of the psyche: the preanimistic, in which human life is at the mercy of the external world, and the animistic, in which the world is populated by demons and souls which have power over external events and human life. See ANIMISM.

primitive credulity A tendency to believe, as most children do, what a person is told until there is reason for doubt.

primitive superego 1. According to some psychoanalysts, such as G. Bychowski, the primary image of the self, which at an early age instilled narcissism and grandiosity in the ego and thus compensates for the infant's feelings of weakness and passivity. 2. According to other psychoanalysts, a superego that antedates parental influences and is responsible for organizing and differentiating the cells of the fetus in accordance with hereditary factors.

primitive thinking See PRELOGICAL THINKING.

primitivization **primitivation**

PRIMO (M. Diamond) Acronym to represent the five cardinal aspects of an individual's sexual profile according to Milton Diamond. (P = gender Patterns; R = Reproduction; I = sexual Identity; M = sexual Mechanisms; O = sexual Orientation).

primogeniture A tradition dating from biblical times in which the eldest son inherits the family property upon the death of the father.

primordial Earliest formed, primitive, existing from the beginning, original.

primordial image Early phrase for archetypal image. As used by Carl Jung, an archetypal idea, such as the original, unconscious mother image in the mind of the child, which Jung concluded to be ultimately derived from the racial, or collective, unconscious. See ARCHETYPE.

primordial image of hero birth (C. G. Jung) A concept that the unconscious contains a pregnancy dream in which the hero to be born represents and molds the individuality, or soul, of the dreamer.

primordial impulse First drives, manifested in life, such as sucking and biting.

primordial nanosomia A hereditary type of dwarfism characterized by normal mental development, normal reproductive ability, and a well-proportioned dwarf body. See MIDGET.

primordial panic A reaction observed in some children with schizophrenia who express fright and anger with disorganized motor responses similar to the startle responses of infants. Also known as elementary anxiety.

primrose path courtship (R. Libby) An early, exclusive, and structured relationship followed by a role-rigid marriage.

principal-axis factor analysis A method of factor analysis developed by Karl Pearson which later was called the principal factor method. It is designed so that the factors account for the maximum amount of the total commonality among the variables.

principal component factor analysis   A widely-used form of factor analysis in which factors are extracted using the principle of least squares fit.

principal component method   In factor analysis, the extraction of a factor that accounts for most of the variance, with additional factors extracted in terms of descending importance.

principal neuron   Golgi Type I neuron

principle   1. A basic truth. 2. A fundamental value. 3. A universal law. See LAW OF..., METHOD OF...

principled moral reasoning   The third level of moral reasoning proposed by Lawrence Kohlberg, based on personal standards of behavior. See MORAL DEVELOPMENT, PRINCIPLED STAGE.

principled negotiation   (R. Fisher & W. Ury) Bargaining by (a) removing people issues from the problem issues, (b) focusing on interests rather than on positions, (c) inventing options leading to mutual gains, and (d) insisting on objective criteria rather than dealing with stubbornly-held positions. See INTEGRATIVE BARGAINING/NEGOTIATION.

principled stage   Stage six of Lawrence Kohlberg's seven stages of moral development, representing concern with individual principles, conscience, and consistent, universal, ethical standards. See GURU STAGE, MORAL DEVELOPMENT, POSTCONVENTIONAL LEVEL.

principle-learning   Mastering the nature of the relationships that bind concepts, facts, and principles together; acquiring knowledge about meaningful links or associations between facts within a larger conceptual framework.

principle of advantage   See LAW OF ADVANTAGE.

principle of anticipatory maturation   A theory that nearly all functions of organisms can be evoked experimentally at some time prior to the normal appearance of the function, since structures develop before they are actually needed for interaction with the environment. Also known as anticipatory maturation principle.

principle of belongingness   Edward Thorndike's principle of learning which states that connections between items are more readily formed if the items are closely related in some way, so that one may elicit the other, for example, "Coney" and "Island."

principle of closure   See LAW OF CLOSURE.

principle of constancy   See LAW OF CONSTANCY.

principle of creative results   A gestalt-like concept of the whole being more than the sum of its individual parts. Wilhelm Wundt claimed that the totality of mental processes was more than the sum of individual processes. See GESTALT.

principle of distributed repetitions   A theory of the learning process, according to which an ability is acquired with a smaller number of repetitions if these repetitions are distributed over a longer period of time than if they are crowded together. In practice these repetitions are often spaced gradually farther and farther apart (progressively distributed practice).

principle of economy   See LAW OF CONSTANCY.

principle of equipotentiality   See LAW OF EQUIPOTENTIALITY.

principle of good shape   A Gestalt theory that the organization of structures or figures will be as "good" (that is, symmetrical, uniform, stable and complete) as the prevailing conditions permit.

principle of independent assortment   See MENDELIAN LAWS OF INHERITANCE.

principle of independent segregation   See MENDELIAN LAWS OF INHERITANCE.

principle of inertia   1. A tendency of a body to resist change from rest to motion. 2. (C. E. Spearman) A theory that those people who start slow tend to take a long time to finish. 3. (F. Alexander) A form of repetition-compulsion but with a greater emphasis on automatic action. Also known as inertia principle.

principle of intimacy   A Gestalt concept that there is interdependence of elements, that parts taken out or added change the whole.

principle of least interest   (W. Waller) A theory that given a social situation in which two people are involved, the person who has the least amount of interest in maintaining the relationship will be the one to control the relationship.

principle of least effort   (G. Zipf) A theory that there is an inverse relation between frequency of use and effort, for example, short words in any language are used more often than long words. Also known as Zipf's law. See LAW OF LEAST EFFORT.

principle of mass action   See LAW OF MASS ACTION.

principle of maximum contrast   A theory that there is a tendency of infants and young children to attend to obvious perceptual opposites and striking contrasts rather than to subtle differences. See OBLIGATORY PERCEPTION.

principle of optimal stimulation   (C. Leuba) A theory that organisms tend to learn those responses that lead to optimal stimulation or excitation. Also known as optimal-stimulation principle.

principle of parsimony   See LAW OF PARSIMONY.

principle of Prägnanz   See LAW OF PRÄGNANZ.

principle of primacy   See PRIMACY EFFECT.

principle of proximity   See LAW OF PROXIMITY.

principle of rationality   In decision making, a theory that if the objective and subjective knowledge used to form a judgement are understood, and the goals of the person making it are understood, then the outcome of the decision or judgement can be accurately predicted.

principle of recency   See RECENCY EFFECT.

principle of reciprocity   1. In social psychology, a theory that persons tend to like others who like them. 2. Generally, the "golden rule": Do unto others as you would have them do unto you. Known as the norm of reciprocity in social psychology.

principle of similarity   See LAW OF SIMILARITY.

principle of the irresistible impulse   See IRRESISTIBLE IMPULSE.

principle of universal rationality   principle of sufficient reason

principles transfer   See TRANSFER BY GENERALIZATION.

prior entry   (W. Tchisch) Hearing a sound before it occurs. A famous example of a mistake in an experiment. Tchisch thought this was due to a miracle. William James pointed out that it was due to poor experimental procedure.

prior-entry law   See LAW OF PRIOR ENTRY.

priority types   See MAJOR PRIORITIES.

prism   (I. Newton) A triangular lens with the property of bending light waves passing through it so that they are broken down into their component wave lengths in spectral order.

prismatic stimulation   The use of special lenses to distort normal vision, used for special purposes in perceptual researches. See VISUAL INVERSION.

prisoner's dilemma (PD)   (R. D. Luce & H. Raiffa) A game used in social-psychological studies in which participants must choose between competition and cooperation. It derives from a standard detective ploy (used when incriminating evidence is lacking) in which two suspects are first separated and then told that the one who confesses will go free or receive a light sentence. The prisoner may choose silence, hoping that the other suspect does the same (a cooperative motive) or that the other prisoner may confess, hoping to improve his or her own situation (a competitive motive). The game is used in studies investigating the motives associated with competition and cooperation. Also known as Prisoner's Dilemma Game (PDG). See PAYOFF MATRIX.

prison neurosis   Negative reactions to imprisonment considered to be abnormal when compared with reactions by other prisoners, most of whom soon adjust to the reality of their situation. May include fearfulness of routine procedures such as the noisy closing of all cell doors simultaneously, difficulty in eating and sleeping. See DEPERSONALIZATION DISORDER, MALADJUSTMENT, SOCIAL MALADJUSTMENT, NEUROSIS.

prisoner-of-war reactions/syndrome   Situational personality disturbances occurring in individuals subjected to the physical and psychological strains of prisoner-of-war (P.O.W.) experience. Reactions vary greatly from individual to individual, but include depression due to loss of freedom and identity; personality changes such as sudden withdrawal and suspiciousness; inertia and loss of interest due to confinement and debilitating conditions; loss of ego strength; and, occasionally, death. The disturbance has been compared by psychoanalytically oriented therapists to the anaclitic depression observed in hospitalized and deprived children. Varying degrees of posttraumatic stress disorder follow in the majority of cases.

prison psychologist   See CORRECTIONAL PSYCHOLOGY.

prison psychosis   An emotional disturbance precipitated by actual or anticipated incarceration. Types of disturbances vary, and in many cases are due to long-standing tendencies toward schizophrenia or paranoid reactions released by the stress of imprisonment. Symptoms include delusions of innocence, pardon, ill treatment, or persecution; periods of excitement; or rage and destructiveness. See GANSER SYNDROME.

privacy   (J. Altman) Selective control of access to the self and a group by regulation of input from others through use of barriers and regulation of personal output in the form of communication with others. Term refers to the right of patients in institutions to control the amount and disposition of the information divulged to others.

private acceptance   1. Change of opinion that occurs when the targets of social influence personally accept the influencer's position. Also known as conversion. 2. A positive reaction to a new statement, regulation, order, etc., though not necessarily stated or acted upon. See PLURALISTIC IGNORANCE.

private logic   (A. Adler) Unconscious central views about self and others that direct the person. Adlerian psychotherapy aims to find a patient's erroneous private logic to expose to the patient and then neutralize, as in discovering that a patient believes "I can never succeed and there is no use in trying."

private mental hospital   A hospital for patients with mental disorders, usually organized and run by a corporation (profit or not for profit). Typically smaller than public mental institutions, usually have a far higher doctor-patient ratio, and generally offer specialized, intensive treatment rather than chronic care limiting their service to those who can afford to pay.

private parts   Common phrase for genitals. Also known as privates.

private personality   An inner sense of continuity resulting from a person generally feeling and responding similarly across situations.

private practice   Offering one's professional service to the general public for a fee. A psychologist in private practice may work alone or in a small group, and may specialize in testing, counseling, psychotherapy, clinical areas, as well as servicing businesses and industry.

privation   1. A lack of the necessities of life; absence of the means required to satisfy needs. 2. In psychoanalytic theory, the rule which prescribes sexual abstinence on the theory that the energy of the dammed-up libido will be used to release early emotional experiences and thereby contribute to the therapeutic process. See ABSTINENCE RULES.

privilege   The legal right of a person to prevent professionals, such as physicians, from testifying about information obtained in the course of treatment. Recognized in most American states. See PRIVILEGED COMMUNICATION.

privileged communication   1. Confidential information regarding a patient, obtained by psychologists, psychiatrists, or social workers, etc., and that cannot be divulged to certain others without the patient's consent. 2. Laws of evidence in some jurisdictions and ethical guidelines of the profession provide that certain kinds of communications between persons who have a special confidential or fiduciary relationship need not be divulged. There are exceptions, subject to changes over time in any jurisdiction. See PRIVILEGE.

PrL   See PROLACTIN.

p.r.n.   *pro re nata*

PRO   peer review organization

pro-abortion movement   Former name for the pro-choice movement.

proactive　Describing a self-starter rather than a reactor.

proactive facilitation　In learning theory, the easier learning of one task due to experience with a previous one; for instance, experience riding a tricycle helps learning to drive a car. See RETROACTIVE FACILITATION.

proactive inhibition (PI)　Interference with recall of newly learned materials created by memories from prior learning, for example, the study of French may (for some people) interfere with learning Spanish. See NEGATIVE TRANSFER, PROACTIVE INTERFERENCE, RETROACTIVE INHIBITION.

proactive interference (PI)　An effect similar to proactive inhibition that occurs in tests having two or more types of stimuli, such as color discrimination and nonsense figures. During new trials the participant tends to confuse the new stimuli with those in previous trials. Compare RETROACTIVE INHIBITION.

proactive psychology　An outlook that is forward-looking in terms of choice, aspirations, goals, and striving. The psychology in which a person is, in some part, responsible for his or her own fate. Contrasted to "reactive psychology" in which personal action is in response to external stimuli. See THIRD-FORCE PSYCHOLOGY.

probabilism　A doctrine positing that events or sequences of events can be predicted with a high, though not perfect, degree of probability and validity on the basis of rational and empirical data. Holds that psychology is a probabilistic science, a science of generalities rather than universalities. See STOCHASTIC.

probabilistic category　In concept formation, a category in which stimulus features usually belong to one category but may sometimes belong to an alternative one. Compare DETERMINISTIC CATEGORY.

probabilistic functionalism　1. A program of research developed by Egon Brunswik which dealt with questions related to how well the perceptual system could deal with stimuli in a natural environment. 2. A doctrine positing that behavior is best understood in terms of its probable success in attaining goals.

probabilistic hypotheses　(E. Brunswik) A postulate that a perception and the behavior related to the perception will probably be harmonious, correct, and meaningful.

probability (p or *P*)　The degree to which an event is likely to occur as compared with alternatives. Formula: $P = p \div (p + q)$, Where: P is the probability that the event will occur, p is the number of chances that a specified event will occur, and q is the number of chances that some other event(s) will occur. See TRANSITIONAL PROBABILITY.

probability curve　A graphic representation of the expected frequency of occurrence of a variable. See NORMAL CURVE.

probability density function　The continuous analogue to the probability distribution; used to assign probabilities to continuous events such as time.

probability forecasting/judgment　Anticipation of future events or behavior based on knowledge of past experiences. See PROBABILITY THEORY.

probability judgment　**probability forecasting**

probability learning　Refers to a class of experiments which typically have a long series of discrete trials on each of which the experimental participant is supposed to indicate which of two cues will be presented. The cues are presented randomly with a fixed probability.

probability matching　In a probability learning experiment, probability matching is said to occur if the probability with which the participant indicates that a cue will occur matches the probability that it does occur.

probability measure　A statement of the relative frequency with which a given element in an ensemble will be found in state x- of classification x. The probability measure is variously symbolized: $p(x)$ or $p(i)$ or p-.

probability of response　The probability of an occurrence when chance is involved, such as the probability of getting one hundred "heads" when one hundred coins are tossed at one time or in sequence. The implication is that certain events can be compared to the chance probabilities.

probability ratio (P)　1. Number of circumstances under which a given event will occur (p), divided by the total number of circumstances in a certain defined set (q); written p/q. 2. The expectation of the percentages of occurrence of a certain event within a particular set, such as the ratio of male human infants to total number of infants born in any particular year in any special location.

probability sample　A sample in which each member of the population has a known chance greater than zero of being selected. Compare CONVENIENCE SAMPLE, JUDGMENT SAMPLE, QUOTA SAMPLE, RANDOM SAMPLE.

probability sampling　A sampling process in which members of subgroups are selected in relation to the percentage of members of a larger group, for example, sampling opinions of psychologists; if nationally there were one psychologist in every 200,000 people, then in a state that had a population of 10,000,000, the desired sample size would be 50 psychologists for that state. Also known as stratified sampling.

probability table　A chart or table showing the relative frequency of an occurrence under specified conditions.

probability theory　(J. Cardanos, P. Simon de Laplace) An essential element of science that relates to the concepts of chance and prediction. In most experiments, the probability of chance occurrences is known and deviations from chance represent the probable validity of a concept.

probable error (PE, P.E. or p.e.)　In statistics, a phrase historically used as a measure of dispersion equivalent to half the interquartile range (the middle 50% of a normal distribution). Supplanted by the standard deviation.

probable error of the mean　A statistic showing the range within which 50% of sample means will fall. This statistic has now been supplanted by the standard error of the mean.

proband　An individual with an apparent inherited disorder, who forms the baseline for the construction of a pedigree. By tracing the same or similar traits in other members of the family, the inheritance factor may be determined. Also known as index case.

probation   Following conviction for a crime, suspension of the sentence for a specified period of time dependent on fulfillment of a contract as determined by a judge. Usually includes reporting regularly to a probation officer, remaining employed, and refraining from engaging in certain activities. Failure to act in accordance with the terms of probation may result in the person going to prison to fulfill the original sentence.

probe   1. To investigate or explore in depth. 2. In psychology, a follow-up question in an interview or survey. See PROBING (TECHNIQUE).

probe technique   probing technique

probing response   (C. R. Rogers) A response from either the counselor or counselee that seeks further information.

probing (technique)   1. A means of checking for short-term memory retention by asking a person who has memorized a list of items to respond to a single item. 2. In Rorschach testing, after the first administration, asking the participant detailed questions about how the blot was perceived. 3. In surveys or interviews, asking the respondent questions that follow-up recent responses. 4. In clinical practice, asking direct questions to stimulate additional discussion to uncover relevant information or help the client come to a particular realization. Also known as probe technique.

probit   In statistical analysis, an arbitrary probability unit that forms the scale into which percentages may be transformed so that data evenly distributed between zero and 100% change into a normal distribution with a standard deviation of one probit.

probit analysis   (D. J. Finney) The use of probits in statistical analysis, particularly quantal assay data, as in assessing the potency of hormones and drugs. Specifically, the probit of the proportion P is the abscissa that corresponds to a probability P in a normal distribution with a mean and variance of 5 and 1 respectively. Derived from the constant process method of G. E. Müller & F. M. Urban. Also known as method of probits.

problematic   Characterizing a situation or problem in which the outcome is uncertain.

problem behavior   1. Any conduct that is maladjustive, destructive, or antisocial. 2. Behavior that is perplexing to the individual or others.

problem box   In animal research, a problem-solving test consisting of a box with latches, strings, or other fastenings that the subject must learn to manipulate in such a way as to get out of or, in some cases, get into. See THORNDIKE PUZZLE BOX.

problem checklist   A type of self-inventory listing various personal, social, educational, or vocational problems. The respondent indicates the items that apply to his or her situation. See MOONEY PROBLEM CHECKLIST.

problem child   Generally, a child whose behavior either brings the child into an unusual degree of conflict with others or who in some way deviates from expected behavior. (It sometimes turns out that the problem is with the caretakers.)

problem drinking   See ALPHA ALCOHOLISM.

problem isomorphs   (J. R. Hayes & H. A. Simon) Alternative representations of a single problem that can be matched, one on another, so that problem states are matched with problem states and operators with operators. Isomorphic problems can vary enormously in difficulty, hence provide a means for research on the sources of problem difficulty. See PROBLEM SPACE.

problem representation   (A. Newell & H. A. Simon) A problem space or a task representation. See PROBLEM SPACE.

problem space   (A. Newell & H. A. Simon) A representation of a problem in terms of (a) starting and goal positions, (b) other positions (possible states of the world) that the problem solver may traverse in search of a solution, and (c) the processes, including actions and tests, used in making the search.

problem-solving   Procedures, overt or covert, in the solution of problems. See GENERAL PROBLEM SOLVER, INDUCTIVE PROBLEM-SOLVING, INTRAGROUP PROBLEM-SOLVING, MECHANICAL PROBLEM-SOLVING, ORGANIC PROBLEM-SOLVING, TRIAL AND ERROR.

problem-solving behavior   1. A step-by-step process through which people attempt to overcome difficulties and reach a conclusion, usually through trial and error behavior. The use of reasoning or creative thinking. 2. John Dewey's four-stage outline of such behavior: (a) motivation, reasons for trying to solve the problem; (b) delimitation, defining the problem; (c) hypotheses, or tentative solutions; and (d) testing, for verification; still holds. This process seems to apply, though in simpler form, to the behavior of apes in stacking boxes or putting sticks together to obtain a lure.

problem-solving interview   In industrial psychology, a technique used on both the employee and supervisory level, in which an interview is focused on specific issues, usually of a human-relations nature, with the aim of encouraging the worker to become more sensitive to the needs and aims of fellow workers.

problem that has no name   Sexism (phrase defined by Simone de Beauvoir in 1953 and popularized in the United States by Betty Friedan in 1963).

procaine   A local anesthetic used in studies of neural activity to suppress electrical excitability of an axon without affecting depolarizing processes.

procedural justice   1. The perceived fairness in the process used to reach a decision. See NATURAL JUSTICE. 2. Responses to perceived inequities that depend on the judged fairness of the process used to arrive at the outcome.

procedural knowledge   Knowing how to perform a task, such as pilot an airplane, as opposed to knowing how an airplane is able to fly (declarative knowledge). Also known as functional knowledge.

procedural language   A structured language that tells how a task is performed or that presents a step-by-step process for solving a problem.

procedural memory   1. Memory of how to go about certain activities, such as driving a car. 2. Capacity to deal with skills without conscious attention or effort. See DECLARATIVE MEMORY.

procedural rationality (H. A. Simon) Goal-oriented decision making using processes designed to reach correct choices, in the light of the limits of human bounded capabilities for rationality. See BOUNDED RATIONALITY, SUBSTANTIVE RATIONALITY.

procedural reinstatement hypothesis See ENCODING SPECIFICITY PRINCIPLE.

proceptive (S. Rosenzweig) Pertaining to planned conception with a specific goal preference instead of social regulation for improving a breed. See EUGENICS, EUTHENICS.

proceptivity Female behavior patterns designed to sexually solicit the male.

process analysis 1. In evaluation research, an analytic procedure that focuses on the internal elements of an evaluation program; a qualitative approach with emphasis on identifying ways of improving program operations and designs. 2. In psychometrics, an examination of the processes, skills, and reaction tendencies that participants use when responding to test items. Methods include probing, observing, and statistical analysis.

process attitude In structural psychology or in studies employing introspection, an attitude displayed by the type of observer who attends closely to subjective experience as manifested in perceptions, feelings, and thoughts while directing relatively less attention to a specific object or stimulus. See OBJECT ATTITUDE.

process evaluation In evaluation research, an in-house function in which the evaluator quickly moves into the situation to be evaluated, conducts the evaluation, feeds back findings to the program administrator for immediate program modification (if necessary), then repeats the process. Also known as operational evaluation.

processing error An error that takes place during the measuring, recording, computation, or interpretation of data.

process loss 1. Reduction in individual members' performance as a result of their participation in a group. 2. Time spent by group members in "maintenance activities" not related to productive work or task accomplishment.

process observer In certain groups, such as in sensitivity training, the member whose role is to observe and later report on the group's functioning, such as a co-therapist in a therapy group who is designated to summarize the group's processes either internally to all members or externally to the therapist at the end of the session. Usually concentrates on the quality of goal-oriented behavior (such as decision-making, debate, voting) and on the actions of any group member, noting the interrelations of all members and subgroups. Also called neutral observer.

processomania Term introduced by Leonardo Bianchi to describe a mania for litigation. See LITIGIOUSNESS.

processor In information theory, any device or system that can perform specific operations on data that have been presented to it in proper quantified format.

process psychosis A chronic, progressive form of schizophrenia that tends to terminate in permanent dementia. See PROCESS SCHIZOPHRENIA.

process-reactive dimension (of schizophrenia) Categorizing patients with schizophrenia according to the suddenness of onset of psychotic symptoms. Patients with process schizophrenia have a history of psychological disorder, and hospitalization is the result of gradual deterioration. Patients with reactive schizophrenia have a normal prepsychotic history, and the onset of psychotic symptoms is sudden. Process schizophrenia is marked by a long-term gradual deterioration before the disease is manifest whereas reactive schizophrenia is associated with a rapid onset of symptoms after a relatively normal premorbid period. See PROCESS SCHIZOPHRENIA, REACTIVE SCHIZOPHRENIA.

process research The study of various psychological mechanisms or processes of psychotherapy that produce a positive prognosis.

process schizophrenia (G. Langfeldt) 1. A diagnosis of long-term schizophrenia attributed to heredity or to other physiological causes rather than to environmental or other psychological reasons. 2. Phrase sometimes applied to schizophrenic cases that begin early in life, develop gradually, and are thought to be due to endogenous factors, possibly of a constitutional nature. These patients are often withdrawn (into an "inner world"), socially inadequate, and they indulge in excessive fantasies, even though they have never been subjected to any special situations of stress. Also known as nuclear schizophrenia. Compare REACTIVE SCHIZOPHRENIA. See PROCESS-REACTIVE DIMENSION (OF SCHIZOPHRENIA).

process studies Investigations of any activity for reasons for success or failure, for example, in group psychotherapy focusing on the characteristics of the therapeutic interaction that appear to be responsible for positive changes. In one study of group therapy, nine major factors were found in three areas: emotions (acceptance, altruism, transference); cognition (spectator therapy, universalization, intellectualization); action (reality testing, ventilation, interaction). See CLINICAL FACTOR ANALYSIS.

process theories of motivation Theories that deal with how various factors motivate. Contrasts with need theories that are concerned with what motivates. For instance, a need theory might contend that money is a motivator for employees, and a process theory would explain the mechanism by which remuneration affects motivation.

process variables 1. Those interpersonal factors that are operative during the course of counseling and psychotherapy and determine their evolution. 2. Any sets of psychological acts that influence the evolution of a process over time.

prochlorperazine Generic name for an early antipsychotic used in the 1960s. Used in the 1970s primarily (in low doses) as an anti-emetic (anti-nausea agent). Trade name is Compazine.

pro-choice movement Generally, individuals and organizations favoring freedom of reproductive choice for women, including their entitlement to undergo an abortion without jurisdictional interference. Once also known as pro-abortion movement, a phrase now rejected because the movement has broader concerns and does not advocate abortion for those who oppose it.

procreational behavior Any behavior pattern normally associated with sexual reproduction.

procreation fantasy   An imagined participation in sexual reproduction. Observed occasionally in women who experience a false pregnancy. A male procreation fantasy may manifest itself as playing the role of a father who begets a famous offspring.

procreative sex   Coitus engaged in for the purpose of achieving pregnancy. The only form of morally acceptable sex in some religions and traditions.

Procrustes rotation   (R. B. Cattell) Deliberate rotation of a factor matrix to best possible agreement with a hypothetical target matrix.

proctophobia   Morbid, obsessive fear of anything having to do with the anus or rectum, such as defecation, enemas, rectal examinations, anal intercourse, and rectal disease. Also known as rectophobia.

procuring   Colloquial and sometimes legal term for obtaining customers for a prostitute. See PIMP.

procursive epilepsy   dromolepsy

prodigy   A rare individual who shows an extraordinary talent in one or more areas, usually at an early age, and quite often in mathematics or music, for example, Blaise Pascal and Wolfgang Amadeus Mozart. If superior endowment is the cause of their exceptional abilities, prodigies still require the opportunities to train and develop their gifts. See PRECOCITY.

prodromal   (running before—Greek) An early symptom of a mental or physical disorder that serves as a warning or premonitory sign (such as the aura that often occurs before epileptic seizures) which may, in some cases, lead to preventive measures. Also known as prodromic phase. See PRODROME.

prodromal dream   A dream that contains a warning of impending disorder. In the fourth century, Hippocrates suggested that the symptoms of illness may appear in dream symbolism long before they manifest themselves in waking life. Later, Carl Jung revived this concept and cited dreams he concluded to be prodromic. Alfred Adler explained that dreams could be considered preparatory planning that anticipates future behavior. Also known as prodromic dream. See PROPHETIC DREAMS, PRODROMAL MYOPIA.

prodrome   1. A sensory warning of an impending physiological or mental disorder. Especially notable in epilepsy. Patients with epilepsy who experience such warnings may have time to sit down, or put themselves in safer positions, so as to minimize injury to themselves or others during an epileptic seizure. 2. The early stage of a disease.

prodromic   Tending to predict, an early sign or warning.

product appeals   Advertising appeals directed toward a specific type of consumer personality.

product image   (E. Dichter) The unique identity of a product, or special brand of product, intended to create a receptive feeling for the product in the mind of the consumer.

production   In learning theory, the connecting of declarative knowledge to procedural knowledge; a production specifies a rule for taking an action.

production deficiency   1. Generally, failure to achieve a desired goal due to lack of use of some potential, such as not using all available resources. 2. In cognitive development, the tendency to not come up with the right strategy to perform a task.

production method   In experimental psychophysics, a task set to the participant who is to respond to a particular stimulus in a prescribed manner, such as to press a red key as soon as possible if a word is a noun and a blue key if a word is verb.

production system   Application to cognitive psychology of a phrase introduced in logic by Emil L. Post, and later in computer science by Robert Floyd and others. An information processing system whose actions (resembling S-R pairs of associationism) consist of a set of conditions followed by a set of one or more actions ($C \rightarrow A$), such that whenever the conditions are satisfied, the actions are executed. Typically, the conditions are knowledge elements in short-term memory, whereas the actions may be motor actions or operations on the internal symbol system.

productive love   Love without dependency on others. Knowledge and respect for the other person as well as caring are considered essential elements of this type of love. According to Erich Fromm, productive love is accomplished through active effort and is an aspect of the productive orientation. See LOVE.

productive memory (theory)   A point of view that most remembering involves reconstruction, in contrast to the idea that memory is chiefly a retrieval process. In the process of reconstruction, it is assumed that alterations of memory occur that reflect the individual's personal and cultural background and current needs. See RECONSTRUCTION.

productive orientation   (E. Fromm) A personality pattern characterized by developing and applying personal potentialities without being unduly dependent on outside control. Such an individual is highly active in feeling, thinking, and relating to others, and at the same time retains the separateness and integrity of the self. See PRODUCTIVE LOVE.

productive thinking   (E. Fromm) A form or style of thinking in which a given question or issue is considered with objectivity as well as respect and concern for the problem as a whole. A feature of productive orientation.

productivity   1. The capacity to produce goods and services having exchange value. Vocational rehabilitation programs use the productivity of persons with disabilities as a major measure of the effectiveness of their programs. 2. (R. W. Brown) One of the three formal properties of language, consisting of the ability to combine individual words to produce an unlimited number of sentences. See SEMANTICITY. 3. In psychometrics, the extent or quantity of the participant's responses. 4. In linguistics, the relative freedom with which an affix combines with stems of the appropriate category; for instance, in English the plural suffix "s" is highly productive.

Productivity Environmental Preference Survey (PEPS)   (R. Dunn) Likert-scale test to determine how adults like to learn, concentrate, and work. Used for placement, counseling, office design.

product-moment correlation (K. Pearson) The most often used correlation between two variables that vary on a straight line. Also known as Pearson product-moment correlation. See CURVILINEAR CORRELATION for an example of a correlation of a curved rather than straight relationship.

product scale A scale of products or performance samples assigned numbered or lettered merit values.

product structure In organizational psychology, divisions according to the products dealt with, rather than around the usual functional activities such as production, marketing, and finance.

product-testing 1. The testing of consumer response to a new product before or after it has been offered for sale. Usually is conducted on a limited scale in certain test markets, such as Canton, Ohio and Elmira, New York, both of which have been studied intensively as populations with known consumer characteristics. Large-scale advertising campaigns are based on results of the localized product-testing which also may influence changes in product or package design. 2. Evaluating products comparatively, with a consumer jury, or in a beta-testing trial.

proestrous The period immediately preceding estrus, a phase of cyclic sexual behavior in female mammals.

professional advisory committee (PAC) A group, usually composed of senior members of a professional organization, whose task it is to set policy and to publish its determinations to the general membership.

professional-aptitude tests Any tests designed for use in selecting candidates for professional training by measuring mental capacities, types of information, skill, and approaches needed for higher education and for effectiveness in such areas as accounting, dentistry, engineering, law, medicine, nursing, psychology, social work, teaching, and theology.

professional-client sexual relations rules In psychology, the *Ethical Principles of Psychologists and Code of Conduct* (1992) states: (4.5) "Psychologists do not engage in sexual intimacies with current patients or clients." (4.06) "Psychologists do not accept as therapy patients or clients persons with whom they have engaged in sexual intimacies." (4.07) (a) "Psychologists do not engage in sexual intimacies with a former therapy patient or client for at least two years after cessation of or termination of professional services." Part (b) goes into further details.

professional development The increasing of qualifications and competencies through training and experience.

professionalization The process in which guidelines and rules of conduct are established and enforced in a given profession. Specific concerns focus on criteria for professional training, minimal qualifications for entrance into practice, and guidelines for fees, general business practices, and ethical relations between professional members, colleagues, and clients or patients.

professional neurasthenia A form of occupational neurosis characterized by feeling so debilitated that the organ or body parts normally required for performing the work cannot be used. Completing work to normal standards seems impossible. See BURNT OUT.

professional review Continuing education as a means of learning about improving methods of practice, quality of care as well as professional growth and development in any profession.

Professional Standards Review Organization (PSRO) In the United States, an organization of physicians authorized by federal law in a given region as a means of reviewing the quality of health-care services, and determining whether the in-patient services rendered are medically necessary. See PEER REVIEW.

profile 1. A graphic representation of scores or other data by means of curves or histograms. 2. A verbal summary of a person, a critical diagnostic biographical review.

profile analysis A method of evaluating a person in terms of that person's traits judged against a set of norms or standards.

profile chart A curve uniting points that represent an individual's scores on various tests. See illustrations at ASYMMETRICAL DISTRIBUTION and LEARNING CURVE.

profile matching system In business, industry, the military, etc., the establishment of a series of desired traits, abilities, for particular positions, or for emergency situations, and then checking individual applicants against these desired traits; for example, during World War II, an American was needed who was fluent in Chinese and Russian, and a search of the whole country turned up one such person.

Profile of Mood States (POMS) (D. M. McNair) A short paper-and-pencil test that measures six dimensions of affect: tension/anxiety, depression/dejection, anger/hostility, vigor/activity, fatigue/inertia, and confusion/bewilderment.

profile similarity coefficient (rp) (R. B. Cattell) A coefficient to substitute for a correlation coefficient in determining the similarity of two profiles. Used in finding types.

profile test An examination that gives several separate measures of different variables of an individual's characteristics across several areas.

profiling The process of studying behavior patterns of certain individuals usually for the purpose of identifying and locating criminals who operate according to set patterns. See MODUS OPERANDI, ORGANIZED SERIAL KILLERS, RITUALISTIC KILLING.

profound mental retardation A diagnostic category applying to persons with intelligence quotients (IQs) below 20, comprising about 1% of the retarded population. Due to sensorimotor abnormalities as well as intellectual deficit, they do not achieve more than rudimentary speech and limited self-care, and require a highly structured environment with constant aid and supervision throughout life. Formerly called vegetative idiots.

progerism A premature state of resignation to old age even though the person may be relatively young, expressed by the idea that someone has "grown old overnight."

progesterone (W. M. Allen, G. W. Corner) The hormone of pregnancy, secreted by the corpus luteum of the ovary and carried to the uterus where it stimulates tissue changes needed for implantation of the embryo after fertilization of the ovum. Protects the embryo and enhances development of the placenta. Progesterone also aids in the function of prolactin in preparing the mammary glands for the nursing the offspring.

progestin 1. Any of a group of natural or synthetic progestational agents. 2. Term originally was used to identify progesterone, a hormone produced by the corpus luteum.

prognathy Anatomical conformation of a jutting jaw.

prognosis A prediction of the future course, duration, severity, and outcome of a disease or mental disorder.

prognostic test Instruments that forecast future abilities, skills, attitudes, etc. Such tests will vary considerably in their predictive abilities between fields. Typing may be predicted quite well, musical ability somewhat, and clinical psychology not well at all.

program evaluation In evaluation research, a process whose purpose it is to: (a) contribute to decisions on installing, certifying, and modifying programs; (b) obtain evidence to support or oppose a program; and (c) contribute to basic knowledge.

Program for Learning in Accordance with Needs (PLAN) (J. C. Flanagan) An elementary and high school planning/teaching system; a method of schooling based on evaluation of students in terms of their actual knowledge of academic subjects and then assigning further academic units. See KELLER PLAN.

program-impact evaluation In evaluation research, determining the effects of a program designed to produce some type of goods or service, measured in terms of success or failure in achieving the goals or objectives established before the program was implemented.

programmed instruction The presentation of material in a series of sequential, graduated steps or frames by book or computer for self-instruction. The learner makes a response at each step; if it is correct, it leads to the next step, if incorrect, it leads to further review. Used in academic, industrial, and government settings. See TEACHING MACHINES.

programmed learning See PROGRAMMED INSTRUCTION.

programming 1. Preparation of a sequential operation in such areas as social organization or experimental research. 2. The process of feeding coded instructions into a computer that will direct it to perform a specific set of operations in language that it can read and understand. Once the computer is programmed, it can repeat the same operations indefinitely.

progression law The theory that successive increments of sensation increase in arithmetic progression while stimulus increments increase in geometric progression.

Progressive Achievement Tests (PAT) (W. Elley) A five-part paper-and-pencil, New Zealand educational assessment instrument for ages 7–15.

progressive assimilation In linguistics, the modification of a sound due to the influence of a preceding segment.

progressive education (J. Dewey) A broad educational approach that includes an emphasis on experimentalism (as opposed to dogmatism) in teaching, learning by doing, recognition of individual differences in the rate of learning, latitude in choosing areas of study according to interest, and a closer relationship between academic learning and experience in the world outside the classroom.

progressively distributed process A method of memorization that calls for a person to go over certain materials to be learned a number of times, but the time period between repetitions is increased every time. See PRINCIPLE OF DISTRIBUTED REPETITIONS.

Progressive Matrices Test See RAVEN'S PROGRESSIVE MATRICES TEST.

progressive myopia Denoting a gradual loss of accommodation for distant vision associated with aging. See MYOPIA.

progressive part training In learning, any procedure with a number of movements or steps, beginning either with the first or the easiest and moving forward in iterations until the whole process has been learned (for example, in learning to drive an automobile, learning how to adjust the mirrors and seat, start the motor, steer, put the car in gear, step on the brake, and so on).

progressive relaxation 1. A process of training to relax the skeletal musculature consciously. 2. (E. Jacobson) A technique in which a person learns to relax the entire body by becoming aware of tensions in various muscle groups, and then relaxing them one at a time. 3. A stress reduction technique in which people learn to relax by alternately flexing and relaxing their muscles in a particular muscle group and then progressively relaxing other muscles throughout their body. See AUTOGENIC TRAINING, RELAXATION PRINCIPLE, RELAXATION TRAINING.

progressive teleologic regression (S. Arieti) A patient with schizophrenia's purposive return to the primary-process level, in an attempt to cope with the world and a self-image that are bizarre, threatening, and frightening. The regression, however, is progressive, since it fails to accomplish its purpose and becomes more extreme and may lead to total dilapidation. See TELEOLOGIC REGRESSION.

progressive total A cumulative or running total; the sum of all scores or values that have been gathered or computed up to a particular point.

prohibited behavior Activity that usually is not allowed in any of a wide range of cultures, for example, incest, murder, treason, stealing, laziness, deceiving others, adultery, and assuming wrongful prerogatives. See COMPELLED BEHAVIOR, FREE WILL, MALUM IN SE, MALUM IN RES, TABOO.

project To perceive or attribute to another person what is disowned in the self. See PROJECTION.

Project Head Start A federal program in the United States intended to help young children from low income families gain the benefits of children of middle and upper income families through educational efforts such as learning to speak good English.

projection   1. (S. Freud) In psychoanalytic theory, (a) a defense mechanism of attributing to others what is actually true of the self, often used to justify prejudice or evade responsibility, possibly developing into paranoid delusions, as in "I am not against you; you are against me"; (b) the misinterpretation of mental activity as actual events; (c) the process by which impulses, wishes, or aspects of the self are imagined to be located in some external object. 2. Viewing a mental image as objective reality. 3. (M. Klein) A normal developmental process in which infants attribute to objects their own impulses. 4. Prediction.

projection areas   Areas of the cerebral cortex associated with particular sensory systems. Each sense has two or more cortical areas where its inputs are projected. Each projection area is identified with a Roman numeral, such as Visual I, Visual II. See LOCALIZATION OF FUNCTION. See BRAIN for an illustration.

projection fibers   Nerve fibers that terminate in areas of the central nervous system away from the region of their cell body.

projection neuron   Golgi Type I neuron

projection therapy   A form of psychotherapy in which children play out their problems, anxieties, and fantasies with toys of their own choosing. Some therapists participate and make interpretations, others remain on the sidelines as observers. See MAKE-A-PICTURE STORY, PLAY THERAPY.

projectional paranoia   A classical form of paranoia in which unacceptable feelings and impulses are projected onto others, for example, attributing to someone else a personal hostility or tendency to cheat. See PROJECTED JEALOUSY.

projective device   (E. Dichter) In consumer psychology, a word-association technique employed in motivation research. Key words are mixed with neutral background words and participants are asked to make associations without being aware of which terms are the key words. Such projective devices enable advertisers to learn which words are likely to be most attractive to consumers when used in advertising copy.

projective doll play   See DOLL PLAY, PROJECTIVE PLAY.

projective identification   An interactional form of projection, used both normally and as a defense, through which a person invests inner states and defenses into another person. That is, while remaining aware of impulses, the person misattributes them as being appropriate reactions to the behavior of the other person.

projective method   projective test

projective play   A variation of play therapy in which dolls and other toys are used by children to express their unconscious feelings, which can be helpful in diagnosing their mental disturbances. See MAKE-A-PICTURE STORY TEST.

projective psychotherapy   (M. R. Harrower-Erikson) A treatment procedure in which selected responses on various projective tests are "fed back" to the patient, who associates with them in much the same way that analytic patients make free associations to dreams.

projective test   A procedure in which a person reveals characteristic traits, feelings, attitudes, and behavior patterns through responses to relatively unstructured stimuli such as ambiguous pictures, inkblots, or play materials. The method is based on the unconscious tendency of the participant to attribute personal thoughts, meanings, and feelings to others or to objects, and to impose a personal interpretation on what is seen. Also known as projective method/technique.

projectivity   A personality trait marked by the disavowal of unacceptable and feared impulses projected onto other persons and groups, especially weaker minority groups outside the conventional social milieu. Projectivity was identified by Teodor Adorno and Else Frenkel-Brunswik as a trait associated with the authoritarian personality. See AUTHORITARIANISM, PROJECTION.

project method   A teaching method in which students work either along or in groups to initiate, develop, and carry through a project with minimal guidance from the teacher.

projected jealousy   Behavior in which sex partners who are unfaithful, or those who repress impulses to be unfaithful, accuse their sex-partners of being unfaithful, thereby projecting their own impulses onto their partner. See PROJECTION.

projicient   Relating the organism to its environment.

prolactin (PrL)   A hormone secreted by the anterior pituitary gland to stimulate the development and production of milk by the mammary glands. Also known as lactogenic hormone, luteotrophic hormone.

proliferative phase   A portion of the menstrual cycle when the endometrium thickens and becomes enriched with a blood supply in anticipation of the arrival of a fertilized ovum (zygote) to be implanted in the tissue. If the next ovum is not fertilized, the enriched endometrial layer is shed, resulting in menstruation.

prolonged sleep treatment   The treatment of certain mental disorders by means of prolonged sleep. Also known as *Dauerschlaf*. See CONTINUOUS-SLEEP THERAPY, SLEEP TREATMENT.

Promethean will   A personality factor trait expressed as irreverence, aggressiveness, determination, resourcefulness, and egotism.

promiscuity   1. In humans, a pejorative term for a behavior pattern of transient, casual sexual relations with a variety of partners. See DON JUANISM, DOUBLE STANDARD, NYMPHOMANIA. 2. (J. L. Brown) In animals, a mating system in which there are multiple copulations with no pair bonding.

promise of marriage   In law, a commitment to wed, the violation of which may be held to be a breach of contract.

promotion neurosis   A condition occasionally associated with obsessional neurosis characterized by an inability to function when given added responsibility or authority (for example, a career soldier is promoted to sergeant; the soldier thereupon resigns, due to fear of leading a squad).

promotive interaction   The encouragement and facilitation of members' efforts for the group to reach a goal.

promotive interdependence (M. Deutsch) When the linkages between the goals of two or more people are such that if one person obtains his or her goal, the others will also.

promotive tension A reaction related to another person's goal attainment. Feelings of defeat and anger or pride and happiness, depending on basic relationships between the two people; for example, another person has won the lottery a person wished to win; the latter may react with pleasure if the winner is a relative, or with disappointment if it is a rival. Known as BIRG-ing (basking in reflected glory) in social psychology.

prompt 1. A cue given in the material being studied or by a teacher that signals the learner to make the expected response. 2. A nudge, hint, suggestion, or other help, especially in memory testing. 3. In behavior therapy, reminders of what to do. 4. A signal from a computer or other machine indicating that the operator is to make a response.

prompting A procedure often used in psychodrama, in which the therapist mimes visual instructions (as opposed to giving verbal instructions) to the assistants who are interacting with the hero, usually out of sight of the hero.

prompting method See ANTICIPATION METHOD.

prone Lying face downward. Compare SUPINE.

pronoun reversal A speech phenomenon observed often in cases of infantile autism in which children refer to themselves in the second or third person while identifying others by first-person pronouns, as in a child self-referring as "she" or "he" and to another person as "me."

proof 1. In psychology, a term better replaced by words such as conclusion or evidence. Novice researchers sometimes expect to "prove" a hypothesis or theory, whereas experienced ones speak of evidence for/against, confirming/disconfirming, or support at a specific confidence level of the hypothesis or theory. 2. In law, a conclusion or judgment based on facts and other evidence. 3. In publishing, an initial printing (originally an engraving term for a trial impression to prove the acceptability of a plate). 4. Short for proofreading. 5. Sufficient information to convince a skeptic that a premise is true. Examples of three kinds of proof: (a) logical (if X is larger than Y and Y is larger than Z, then Z is larger than X); (b) empirical (one person finds the evidence for the existence of ESP inconclusive whereas another is satisfied with the same evidence); and (c) authority (two people argue whether a phrase in the poem *In Flanders Fields* is "the poppies blow" or "the poppies grow," and the criterion, the published poem, shows that the latter is correct).

proofreader's illusion In reading, not noticing errors such as misspellings, omissions, extra letters, transpositions, and faulty syntax or grammar, especially when they are minor and embedded in a familiar and interesting context, and when reading for pleasure. See STREPHOSYMBOLIA.

proopiomelanocortin (POMC) A large molecule secreted by the pituitary. A precursor for adrenocorticotropic hormone and opiates such as beta-endorphin.

prop Originally a support that "props up" a structure, hence, any device or procedure that facilitates some action. For instance, smoking a pipe and wearing glasses can be props to imply thoughtful competence; office decor can be props to create visitors' expectations.

propaedeutic Preparatory instruction. The introduction to a topic.

propaedeutic task A task used as a teaching aid, particularly in teaching persons with mental challenges. Such a task usually is a simpler form of another task.

propaganda Intentional effort to influence the beliefs and actions of others. Deliberate persuasion is primarily accomplished through an appeal to emotions designed to win support for an idea or course of action, often to belittle or disparage the ideas or programs of others. Propaganda may be hidden or open. If hidden it hides behind a facade of "rational" arguments. See BANDWAGON EFFECT, BRAINWASHING, CARD-STACKING, FEAR APPEAL, FLOGGING A DEAD HORSE, GLITTERING GENERALITIES, INDOCTRINATION, SUGGESTION.

propaganda analysis The study of the techniques, appeals, content, and effectiveness of propaganda.

propaganda inoculation The success of Nazi propaganda, based on Adolf Hitler's conviction that a Big Lie repeated endlessly will eventually be accepted, led William McGuire to suggest that a type of inoculation against propaganda is necessary. Calls for efforts to be made by responsible agencies, to provide counterpresentations of what are clearly incorrect beliefs being disseminated, partly by presenting both sides of potentially explosive issues.

propagated error An error that inputs to another operation, thus producing another error.

propagation Transmission of information or energy.

propensity A strong tendency or inclination toward a certain action or type of behavior, arising out of habit or hereditary predisposition.

propfhebephrenic psychosis Psychotic behavior pattern superimposed upon or concomitant with mental retardation. Also known as *propfschizophrenia*. See OLIGOPHRENIA.

prophase The first phase in cell division. See MEIOSIS, MITOSIS.

prophecy formula Any formula (usually a regression equation) employed for estimating the scores to be expected on some future measurement. Prophecy formulae are used to assess the reliability coefficients of altered tests such as those with double or half the number of items upon which the original test reliability was established.

prophetic dreams Dreams alleged to predict future events, as in warning of a natural catastrophe or invasion by an enemy. Prophetic dreams are found in the religious writings of the Egyptians, Assyrians, Hebrews, Muslims, and Greeks. Carl Jung felt that dreams can throw light on the influence of the collective unconscious on the future behavior of the individual; Alfred Adler held that dreams represented future intentions whereas Wilhelm Stekel used symbolic-dream material in forecasting the wishes of the dreamer. See PRODROMIC DREAM.

prophylactic maintenance   Administration of drugs that tend to prevent or reduce the risk of recurrence of symptoms of a disorder, such as Methysergide used in prophylactic maintenance of migraine headaches; lithium administered as part of the prophylactic maintenance regimen for manic-depressive (bipolar) disorders.

prophylaxis   The use of systematic preventive methods in avoiding disease or disorder, either mental or physical.

propinquity   1. Closeness in place and time considered an important factor in the development of friendships and romance. It is associated with group territorial behavior. See PROXEMICS. 2. In learning theory, closeness in place and time increases learning.

proposita   A female proband or index case. Compare PROPOSITUS.

proposition   1. A statement put forward for acceptance or rejection; a proposal or scheme to be acted upon. 2. In grammar, a sentence or part of a sentence that contains an assertion or declaration about the subject. See VERBAL PROPOSITION.

propositional analysis   Reducing complex remarks into propositions which are the smallest units of knowledge possible for individual analysis.

propositional construct   (G. A. Kelly) A statement about a single aspect of a person among other aspects of the person. See CONSTELLATORY CONSTRUCT, PREEMPTIVE CONSTRUCT.

propositus   A male proband or index case. Compare PROPOSITA.

propriate functional autonomy   (G. W. Allport) Mental and physical operations at the highest level of philosophical and moral discourse. Attempts to achieve transcendence beyond mere existence, to discover the true self, to understand life and to come to grips with eternal issues. Projection of long-term purposes and goals and development of a plan to attain them. See FUNCTIONAL AUTONOMY, PROPRIUM.

propriate striving   (G. W. Allport) The final stage in the development of the proprium (Gordon Allport's term for "self"), emerging in adolescence with the search for identity. It includes experimentation common to adolescents before making long-range commitments. Because Allport believed in the independence of adult motivation, in contrast to childhood motivation, adolescence is considered especially significant as the time when conscious intentions and future-oriented planning begin to motivate the personality. See FUNCTIONAL AUTONOMY, PROPRIUM.

proprietary drug   Any chemical used for medicinal purposes that is formulated or manufactured under a name protected from competition by trademark, also through patent or secret process. The ingredients, however, may be components of generic drugs that have the same or similar effects.

proprioception   The sense of body movement and position; the reception of stimuli from nerve endings or organs located in the muscles, tendons, and joints and the labyrinth of the ear. Sensations are mediated by the fifth cranial nerve and enable the body without visual clues to determine its spatial orientation through effects of changes in muscle tension or muscle stretching as body positions change, coupled with the labyrinthine stimuli which react to gravitational changes. The two proprioceptive senses are the static and kinesthetic. Proprioception is an important basis for feedback within the organism. Also known as proprioceptive sensation. See FEEDBACK, KINESTHESIS.

proprioceptive   An ability to know the positions of parts of one's own body or their movement when the eyes are closed.

proprioceptive sensation   proprioception

proprioceptive stimuli   Body parts that generate proprioceptive sensation through their positioning or movement.

proprioceptor   (C. S. Sherrington) A receptor sensitive to body and position movement including motion of the limbs. Compare EXTEROCEPTOR, INTEROCEPTOR, PROPRIOCEPTOR. See PROPRIOCEPTION.

proprium   Gordon Allport's term for the self; that which is consistent, unique, and central for an individual. The proprium incorporates body sense, self-identity, self-esteem, self-extension, rational thinking, self-image, propriate striving, and knowing. It develops from infancy through adolescence and has seven cumulative stages. Development at each stage rests on the achievements of earlier stages. However, the mature proprium is far more than an echo of the past; it is an integrated biosocial entity with its own aims and motives. See PERSONALITY.

propulsion gait   A gait observed in parkinsonism patients, marked by short, shuffling steps that begin slowly but increase in rapidity while the body leans forward to maintain balance.

***pro re nata* (p.r.n.)**   Latin for "as occasion arises," "as needed," used in prescriptions.

prosencephalon   (F. Chaussier) Forebrain. The most anterior part of the three primary embryological divisions of the vertebrate brain (encephalon), or the part of the adult brain derived from this tissue.

prosocial   Behaviors considered to be socially valuable. See SOCIAL INTEREST.

prosocial aggression   Any act of aggression that has socially constructive and desirable consequences, as in intervening to prevent a holdup or rape, or demonstrating against social injustice. See ANTISOCIAL AGGRESSION.

prosocial behavior   Any act, deed, or behavioral pattern that is socially constructive or in some way beneficial to another person or group. Phrase applies to a broad range of behavior including simple everyday acts, for example, providing assistance to a person crossing the street. See ALLOPATHIC THEORY, ANTISOCIAL BEHAVIOR, GEMEINSCHAFTGEFÜHL, SOCIAL INTEREST.

prosody   Pattern of rhythm, inflection, pitch, tempo, and loudness in sounds, particularly speech, occasionally in machine auditory displays.

prosopagnosia   Visual agnosia characterized by difficulty in recognizing people's faces.

prosopolethy Rare condition characterized by an inability to recognize faces. Such patients cannot recognize their own faces whether in a photograph or in a mirror.

prospective research Research planned in advance, and measuring aspects of certain behavior as time goes on, often making use of controls and other features of good experimental design. See RETROSPECTIVE RESEARCH, EX POST FACTO RESEARCH.

prospective study A longitudinal study that begins at the beginning time-wise, identifying an individual or group and following that individual or the group over time. Compare RETROSPECTIVE STUDY.

prospect theory In decision theory, stating that outcomes of decisions are changes in relation to a reference point, and distinguishes between losses and gains.

prostasia Social dominance; being first in line.

prosternation **camptocormia**

prosthetist A technician who makes and fits artificial limbs for amputees. See ORTHOTIST.

Prostitutes Anonymous A self-help support group, modeled after the 12-step format of Alcoholics Anonymous, for men and women who are or were in the sex industry who are trying to quit, seek recovery, or find an alternative employment. See GAMBLERS ANONYMOUS, GROW, RECOVERY INC.

prostitution Sex services based on the payment of money or exchange of other property or valuables. Term applies to any sexual service (coitus, oral sex, gratification of paraphilias), performed as a commodity. See MALE HOMOSEXUAL PROSTITUTION.

protagonist In psychodrama, the 'hero' or central character of any roleplaying situation.

protanomaly Red-color blindness in which the red-sensitive retinal receptors do not function normally although some red sensitivity may be present.

protanope One of the three groups of dichromats. A person who cannot recognize or see the first primary color red. Also spelled protonope. Compare DEUTERANOPE, TRITANOPE.

protanopia Complete color-blindness due to loss of color perception in the red area of the spectrum. Term distinguishes a complete lack of red-color vision from a deficient red-color vision (protanomaly).

protasis A premise as found in an hypothesis, usually introduced by the word "if" or an equivalent term.

protaxic experience (H. S. Sullivan) A cognitive process in which the infant does not distinguish between the self and the external world.

protean career (D. Hall) A career that is independent and directed by the needs and values of the individual.

protected classes Historically disadvantaged groups that have been given special protection by law, usually relating to the workforce. In the United States they include women, people with disabilities, African Americans, Hispanics, and Native Americans; in Canada, women, people with disabilities, visible minorities, and aboriginals.

protective armamentarium Temporary anatomy for the protection and nourishment of the embryo, instructions for formation being contained in the DNA (deoxyribonucleic acid) coding.

protective exclusion In industry, the barring of employees or applicants for their safety, as in fertile women being excluded from a workplace where they may absorb teratogens.

protective reflex/response Withdrawal by an organism of its whole body or some part of its anatomy in response to painful or annoying stimulation.

protein deficiency Lack of a normal quantity of proteins, particularly complete proteins, in the diet or body tissues. Complete proteins contain essential amino acids, which must be acquired from meals since they cannot be synthesized by the body's chemistry. In addition to the need for certain amino acids for basic structural and functional processes, several amino acids are required for learning and other mental activities. These include glutamic acid, lysine, and cystine. Protein deficiency also may occur as a result of a lack of carbohydrates or fats in the diet, a condition that causes the body to consume its own proteins as a source of energy. If the self-digestion process of protein-burning is not controlled, irreversible damage to vital organs results. See KWASHIORKOR.

protein hunger A preference for protein or other amino-acid sources exhibited in experimental animals on various deficiency diets. When an amino-acid solution in a rat's diet is diluted, the animal increases its intake of the diluted protein source until the deficiency is compensated. Even when the amino acids are made less palatable by the addition of quinine (that has an unpleasant taste), animals consume the needed amount.

protein-synthesis inhibitors Substances that interfere with the normal production of proteins and thus presumably retard learning ability if long-term memory involves storage of learning experiences in protein molecules. Protein-synthesis inhibitors may include sedative-hypnotic and tranquilizing drugs, which appear to cause learning deficits.

protension (R. B. Cattell) A personality trait consisting of jealousy, suspicion, and rigidity in defense.

protensity (E. B. Titchener) The experience of the duration of a mental process. See DIMENSIONS OF CONSCIOUSNESS.

Protestant (work) ethic See WORK ETHIC.

prothetic Relating to changes in quantity of a stimulus and perception of the stimulus, changes are subjectively identical in terms of the quality of the sensation but quantitatively different. Thus, if pinching the skin is painful; pinching the skin harder is more painful. But in both cases the pinching causes pain, such that the harder the pinch the stronger the pain. See METATHIC.

protocol 1. The original notes of a case or research study, recorded on the spot. 2. The verbatim record of what was said by a client or participant. 3. Research method. 4. Conventions of conduct. 5. Technical standards for electronic intercommunication.

protocol analysis (K. A. Ericsson, A. Newell & H. A. Simon) The process of using think-aloud protocols as data for understanding and explaining the cognitive processes used in task performance.

protopathic (H. Head) Denoting primary sensitivity to pain and temperature.

protopathic sensation   (H. Head) Relating to basic or first pain or suffering. Responsive only to the basic or gross and poorly localized sensations such as pain, heat, and cold. See EPICRITIC.

protopathic system   A subsystem of the somatosensory system, it carries fibers from receptors for cold, warmth, pain, and crude applications of touch. See EPICRITIC SENSATION, EPICRITIC SYSTEM.

protophallic phase   (E. Jones) A presumptive first phallic stage in which children assume that all other people are built like themselves regarding external sexual organs. See DEUTEROPHALLIC PHASE.

protoplasm   A complex semifluid substance which is the living matter of all plant and animal cells and tissues. See CYTOPLASM, NUCLEOPLASM.

protopsyche   (S. Ferenczi) A primitive stage of development to which the psyche regresses when it makes the leap from the mental to the somatic that occurs when conversion symptoms develop.

prototaxic experience   (H. S. Sullivan) A response, either negative or positive, that occurs in the first year of life, in which the infant characteristically seems unaware of time, space, or self. See PROTOTAXIC MODE.

prototaxic mode   (H. S. Sullivan) A chaotic, undifferentiated, fleeting, and uncommunicable mental state that occurs in the infantile period when self-awareness and concepts of time and space are lacking. See PROTOTAXIC EXPERIENCE.

prototheory   1. An incomplete, untested theory or initial working hypothesis. 2. Term is sometimes used to characterize an explanation offered as a justification of a clinical strategy.

prototypal approach (to classification)   Classifying abnormal behavior with the assumption that there are prototypes of behavior disorders that, rather than being mutually exclusive, can blend into others that share similar characteristics.

prototype   1. Original version. 2. A typical member of a class; for example, a terrier may be considered more of a prototype of a dog than either a Chihuahua or a St. Bernard.

prototype model   In information processing, holds that as exemplars of categories are presented, the cognitive system creates a prototype or "running average" of the category members. On the presentation of a new item, its similarities to various categories is determined, and the category it most resembles is chosen.

protovitamins   Food components, for example, carotenes, that activate vitamins such as A and D.

Proust phenomenon   Based on Marcel Proust's novel in which the main character recalls past events evoked by smells; research has indicated that of the various senses including vision, taste, and audition, smells are most likely to bring past memories into recall.

proverb test   A verbal task in which the participant attempts to explain the meaning of proverbs, such as "A poor workman blames his tools."

provisional try   The trial-and-error behavior of an animal engaged in a problem situation such as a maze in which alternative pathways are tried out in the process of finding the correct course. Humans often engage in similar behavior when faced with new problems.

provocation   Inciting to action, the first step of a violent interaction; interpersonal aggression is often initiated by mutual provocation.

proxemics   (T. E. Hall) 1. Nonverbal expression involving spatial distance between interacting people and their orientation toward each other as reflected in distance separating them. Touch and eye contact in some cultures (for example South America) is more comfortable than in others (for example Finland). 2. In social psychology, the study of interpersonal spatial behavior including territoriality, interpersonal distance, spatial arrangements, crowding, and other aspects of physical environment that affect human behavior, such as an inquiry as to whether areas with high population density have a greater incidence of mental illness than other areas. See BODY BUFFER ZONE, BUBBLE CONCEPT OF PERSONAL SPACE, CIGARETTE-SMOKE POLLUTION, CROWDING, DISTANCE ZONES, ETHOLOGICAL MODELS OF PERSONAL SPACE, GROUP SPACE, INSIDE DENSITY, INTERACTION TERRITORY, INTERPERSONAL DISTANCE, INTIMATE ZONE, OPTIMAL INTERPERSONAL DISTANCE, OUTSIDE DENSITY, PERSONAL-DISTANCE ZONE, PERSONAL SPACE, PERSONAL-SPACE INVASION, PRIMARY TERRITORY, PROPINQUITY, PUBLIC-DISTANCE ZONE, PUBLIC TERRITORY, SECONDARY TERRITORY, SOCIAL DISTANCE, SOCIAL ZONE, SOCIOFUGAL SPACE, SOCIOMETRIC DISTANCE, SOCIOPETAL SPACE, TERRITORIALITY.

proximal   Nearer the main part; for example, the shoulder is the proximal end of the arm, the hand is the distal end.

proximal criteria   In judgment formation, standards used to make short-term decisions. Compare DISTAL CRITERIA.

proximal-distal sequence/trend   In physical development, the progressive tendency for organs and functions close to an organism's center (proximal) to develop sooner than those more peripheral or distant (distal). Also spelled proximo-distal trend. See CEPHALOCAUDAL DEVELOPMENT.

proximal receptors   Sense-organ receptors that detect stimuli in direct or near-direct contact with the body, such as those of taste and touch.

proximal response   A response that occurs in organisms, specifically glandular reactions or muscular activity. Compare DISTAL RESPONSE.

proximal stimulus   (E. Brunswik) A stimulus that directly affects a receptor. Contrasts with distal stimulus, for example, an insect landing on a person is a proximal stimulus whereas an insect seen flying in the environment is a distal one.

proximate cause   In a sequence of events, the final one that has the direct effect. For instance, an insurance policy may protect against lightning but not from fuse failure. If lightning blows a fuse that in turn causes damage, the insurer may deny coverage on the basis that the proximate cause was the blown fuse. Compare REMOTE CAUSE.

proximity law/principle   See LAW OF PROXIMITY.

proximo-distal trend   proximal-distal sequence/trend

proximodistal development　　A progression of physical and motor development from the center of the organism toward the periphery, for example, children learn to control shoulder movements before arm and finger movements.

proxy variable　　A stand-in variable. For instance, the correlates of work absenteeism may be complex physiological, psychological, economic, geographical, and social processes, but the proxy variables that first surface may be age or sex.

prudery　　Excessive modesty, particularly in sexual matters.

prurient interest　　A longing for something considered immoral or lewd. In American law, "shameful and morbid interest in nudity, sex, or excretion." An appeal to prurient interest is one of the characteristics of obscenity as determined by the Supreme Court.

pruritus　　An itching dermatitis due to sensory-nerve irritation and resulting from organic or functional conditions. See PSYCHOGENIC PRURITUS.

Psa　　See PSYCHOANALYSIS.

PSE　　1. Point of subjective equality. 2. Present State Examination.

psellism　　Stammering, stuttering, or other speech defects, for example, indistinct or faulty pronunciation. See BALBUTIES. (Many speech pathologists no longer distinguish between stammering and stuttering, since they are both assumed to emanate from the same learned anxiety laden conflicts or neurological disorders.)

pseudesthesia　　pseudoesthesia

pseudoachondroplastic spondyloepiphysial dysplasia (PAD)　　A type of dwarfism characterized by a normal shape and size of the head, a relatively normal trunk, and abnormally short arms and legs. See ACHONDROPLASIA, BONE DISEASE, DWARFISM, NANISM.

pseudoaffective　　Sham emotion. Simulating reactions indicative of feeling or emotion.

pseudoaffective behavior　　A response to a stimulus in which the reaction is influenced or controlled by experimental lesions of the cortex, and therefore may not represent a true, natural reaction. See SHAM RAGE.

pseudoaggression　　A neurotic reaction in which masochistic tendencies are denied by transforming them into aggression toward others. See REVERSAL.

pseudoamok syndrome　　Behavior, probably hysterical in nature, in which all the symptoms observed in *amok* are simulated, such as withdrawal, brooding, sudden emotional outburst, except that the people do not hurt anyone, and meekly give themselves up when cornered. See AMOK.

pseudoangina　　Subjective feelings of a heart attack when the heart is actually in good shape. See HYPOCHONDRIASIS.

pseudoanhedonia　　A common abnormal reaction among older persons, characterized by denial of pleasure, especially those suffering from chronic brain syndrome. These patients act as if "Nothing matters; just leave me alone," whereas they are actually acting out of a variety of motives such as resistance to pressure, punishment of others for their own deficiencies, self-punishment, and a bid for sympathy.

pseudoasthma　　A sensation of dyspnea due to psychological factors such as excitement, emotionalism, tension. Also known as nervous emotionalism.

pseudoauthenticity　　False or copied expression of thoughts and feelings.

pseudochondroplasia　　A false conviction of having a disorder or other pathology of the bones.

pseudocollusion　　A temporary sense of closeness to others based on transient events such as being in an accident or natural disaster, or in a therapy group.

pseudocommunication　　Distorted or unsuccessful attempts at communication, or vestiges of communication in the form of fragments of words, apparently meaningless sounds, and unfathomable gestures. It is characteristic of disorganized (hebephrenic) schizophrenia.

pseudocommunity　　1. A delusional social environment developed by a paranoiac. 2. (N. Cameron) A paranoid delusion in which a group of real or imagined persons are believed to be organized for the purpose of conspiring against the patient.

pseudoconditioning　　Excitation of a response to a previously neutral stimulus when it is presented following a series of conditioned stimuli, for example, if a fire siren sounds three times in one day, the first two sounds may not produce a reaction, but the third has an effect. The response is probably a form of sensitization and not conditioning, because there is no pairing of a new stimulus with an old stimulus. Also known as false conditioning. See PSEUDOCONDITIONING PROCEDURE.

pseudoconditioning procedure　　The same number of conditioned stimulus (CS) and unconditioned stimulus (US) presentations are administered as in instrumental conditioning, but the CSs and USs are presented randomly and singly (never paired). Following such training, extinction or test trials are held to determine if the response to the CS differs from that obtained under normal (double stimulation) conditioning trials.

pseudoconversation　　A form of egocentric, unsocialized speech (sometimes called a "collective monologue") in which two- or three-year-old children talk without endeavoring to communicate with others or to share or exchange ideas with them.

pseudoconvulsion　　A type of seizure associated with hysteria, in which the patient may collapse and experience muscular contractions, although other signs, such as pupillary signs, loss of consciousness, and amnesia, are not observed. May be a conscious or unconscious act intended to gain sympathy.

pseudocopulation　　1. Bodily contact between a male and female with liberation of sperm but without actual sexual union. 2. Body contact between two persons for sexual gratification, simulating coitus but without penetration. See FROTTAGE, INTERFEMORAL SEX, LAP DANCING, VESTURED GENITAL APPOSITION.

pseudocyesis　　False pregnancy; whereby the female experiences pregnancy symptoms (for example, morning sickness, tender breasts, abdominal distension) but is not pregnant.

pseudodementia   1. A pathological condition usually based on some transient situation (such as a tragedy, depression, or extreme fear) characterized by behavior indicative of some organic mental disorder. Purportedly under the control of the person affected to some extent. 2. A condition in which the patient develops cognitive capacities to a normal degree but suddenly appears to deteriorate, without physical impairment, and acts as though mentally impaired. Such patients are usually unable to answer the simplest questions or give a coherent account of themselves. May occur, reversibly, in depression, or manifest itself in hysterical form. See GANSER SYNDROME, HYSTERICAL PSEUDODEMENTIA, HYSTERICAL PUERILISM.

pseudoepilepsy   A seizure that has the outward appearance of an epileptic episode but lacks the clinical characteristics of a true epileptic seizure, such as electroencephalographic (EEG) dysrhythmia. The person can suddenly end the seizure on command or when it is ignored by observers. Also known as pseudoseizure. See TEMPER TANTRUM.

pseudoesthesia   An illusionary sensation, for example, a feeling of irritation in a limb that has been amputated. Also known as pseudesthesia. See PHANTOM LIMB.

pseudoexhibitionism   Behavior shown invariably by a male, especially when under stress, characterized by displaying his genitals in public as a substitute for regular sexual activity. Distinguished from true exhibitionism, which is a more pervasive paraphilia.

pseudofamily   A foster family or other substitute for a biological family, which tends to the needs of an infant or child.

pseudogeusia   A taste sensation not appropriate to a stimulus or a taste sensation that occurs without a stimulus, that is, a false perception of taste.

pseudogiftedness   An apparent talent in a child that develops not from any inborn ability or motivation but rather from an ability to imitate others.

pseudogroup   A group whose members have been assigned to work cooperatively but who have no intention or interest in so doing.

pseudohallucination   A vivid hallucination, usually visual, which the person recognizes as hallucinatory and pathological. Observed primarily in schizophrenia and organic psychosis, and is considered a step toward a true hallucination.

pseudohermaphrodite   An individual whose gonads are of one sex but whose superficial sexual characteristics and external genitalia resemble those of both sexes. See HERMAPHRODITE.

pseudohermaphroditism   A form of hermaphroditism caused by a hormonal disturbance, such as adrenal virilism in females resulting in a large hooded clitoris, fusion of the labia, and changes in the voice and hair distribution. The same hormonal abnormality in males results in precocious puberty. Another form of pseudohermaphroditism may occur in animals after injecting pregnant females with male hormones in an effort to produce female offspring with male characteristics. Also known as pseudohermaphratism.

pseudohomosexuality   1. Aspects of behavior that appear to others to be evidence of homosexuality but are not specifically sex-oriented, such as voice, gestures, mannerisms, and clothing preference that falsely give observers "evidence" that a particular person is a lesbian or gay man. 2. A relationship of a same-sex couple based not on sexual activity but on dependence or power, as in prisons. See SITUATIONAL HOMOSEXUALITY.

pseudohostility   Superficial negative interactions, such as quarreling initiated by one person to permit avoidance of deeper, more genuine and more intimate expressions of anger that could lead to open hostilities and even violence.

pseudohydrophobia   See CYNOPHOBIA.

pseudoidentification   A defense mechanism characterized by adopting the opinions of others to protect the self against attack or criticism. (Because the person only pretends to agree with other people, the identification is false.) Compare IDENTIFICATION WITH THE AGGRESSOR.

pseudoimbecility   Consciously or unconsciously simulating mental defect, as opposed to actual mental retardation; a pattern in which a person (young or old) uses the appearance of stupidity as a defense or escape (because a stupid person is not punished as much as a normal person). Also known as pseudodebility, pseudofeeblemindedness. See PSEUDORETARDATION.

pseudoindependent personality   A behavioral pattern characterized by presenting a facade of extreme independence, self-reliance, and aggressive self-assertion, but harboring, and denying, strong underlying dependent needs such as the need to be cared for and supported by others.

pseudoinsomnia   A complaint of insomnia by a patient who actually sleeps an adequate number of hours. Reasons for such complaints are often obscure, and may involve a subtle misperception of the amount of sleep, the complaint may be a symptom of anxiety or depression or the sleep may be troubled and the person does not feel rested when awake.

pseudoisochromatic charts/plates   Sheets consisting of colored dots so arranged that a color blind person sees either no pattern at all or a different pattern of dots from the normal person. They are used as a test for color blindness. See ISHIHARA COLOR TEST.

pseudolalia   The production of meaningless speech sounds. See ULULATION.

pseudologia fantastica   A clinical syndrome characterized by elaborate fabrications usually concocted to impress others, escape an undesirable situation, or boost the ego. Unlike confabulations, these fantasies are believed only momentarily and are dropped as soon as they are contradicted by evidence. Typical examples are the "tall tales" told by sociopaths, though the symptom is also found in neuroses and psychoses.

pseudologica   Pathological lying, whether in speech or in writing.

pseudomania   A pathological condition characterized by confessing to committing a crime when actually innocent. After crimes are announced by the media, law-enforcement agencies often receive "confessions" by persons with this condition.

pseudomature syndrome   A pattern occasionally found in children who behave in a mature manner by taking over some of the responsibilities of the home. Appears in children of alcoholic or psychotic parents, and in children with disabled siblings. Phrase is unfortunate, because often such children really are mature beyond their years, and there is nothing pseudo or false about such children.

pseudomemory   A false memory, such as a spurious recollection of events that never took place. Once also known as pseudomnesia. See AMNESIA, PARAMNESIA.

pseudomental deficiency   pseudoretardation

pseudomnesia   Rare term for a disorder of false memory. See PSEUDOMEMORY.

pseudomotivations   (E. Bleuler) The explanations or reasons some patients create to justify earlier behavior. Such patients may not be aware of the inconsistencies in the excuses, or may be indifferent to them.

pseudomutuality   A facade of harmony in any group, such as a family or a work team that appears open and friendly but in reality hides anger and resentment.

pseudomutual relationship   A social situation that on the surface appears satisfying but in reality is not, such as a marriage when both spouses pretend to be happy and compatible to each other and to outsiders, even though both are dissatisfied with the situation.

pseudoneurotic schizophrenia   A type of schizophrenia characterized by all-pervasive anxiety and a wide variety of neurotic symptoms but with underlying psychotic tendencies (autistic withdrawal, inappropriate emotional responses, anhedonia, subtle thought disturbances) which at times develop into brief psychotic episodes termed micropsychoses.

pseudonomania   An abnormal urge to lie or falsify information

pseudoparalysis   Apparent inability to move any or all parts of the body, when actually there is no medical reason for such immobility, but rather it is due to an hysterical situation.

pseudoparkinsonism   See PARKINSONISM.

pseudopersonality   A fictitious characterization contrived by persons in efforts to hide facts about their true selves from others, for example, a prostitute may contrive a pseudopersonality for business or social reasons or to maintain a certain amount of anonymity. The pseudopersonality usually evolves into a character defense.

pseudophone   (S. P. Thompson, P. T. Young) An instrument used in studying the localization of sound. It diverts to the left ear those sounds that would normally enter the right ear, and vice versa.

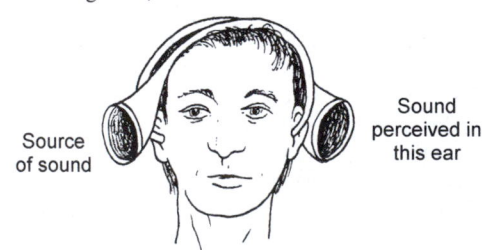

Source of sound

Sound perceived in this ear

pseudophone

pseudoprecocious puberty   See PRECOCIOUS PUBERTY.

pseudopregnancy   In mammals, a condition in which a female exhibits signs and symptoms resembling pregnancy when not pregnant. Seen in species in which copulation induces ovulation, also in dogs. Also known as false pregnancy.

pseudoprodigy   A person who develops an exceptionally high degree of skill or knowledge usually at an early age, and often in a limited area, primarily as a result of overtraining by overzealous parents or teachers. See PRODIGY.

pseudopsychology   An approach to psychology that uses unscientific or fraudulent methods, for example, astrology, numerology, palmistry, phrenology, physiognomy. See PSEUDOSCIENCE.

pseudopsychopathic schizophrenia   A type of schizophrenia in which psychotic tendencies are masked or overlaid by antisocial tendencies such as pathological lying, sexual deviations, and violent or other uninhibited behavior.

pseudoreminiscence   See CONFABULATION.

pseudoretardation   Delayed intellectual development due to adverse cultural or psychological conditions rather than congenital ones. Among these conditions are maternal deprivation, inadequate schooling, intellectual impoverishment due to social factors, severe emotional disturbance, and perceptual deficits. Also known as pseudomental deficiency, pseudofeeblemindedness. See CANAL BOAT CHILDREN, PSEUDODEMENTIA, SIX-HOUR RETARDED CHILD.

pseudoschizophrenias   See ACUTE DELUSIONAL PSYCHOSIS.

pseudoschizophrenic neurosis   (M. Roth) A phobic anxiety depersonalization neurosis, a form of mixed neurosis, which some consider an endogenous depression and others a temporal-lobe or limbic-system disorder.

pseudoscience   A system of theories and methods that claims falsely to be scientific or that is falsely regarded as scientific. For examples and related entries, see ASTROLOGY, BIORHYTHMS, CHARACTEROLOGY, CLAIRVOYANCE, DIANETICS, DOWSING, EXORCISM, EXTRASENSORY PERCEPTION, MEDIUM, NUMEROLOGY, OBSCURANTISM, OCCULT, ORGONOMY, OUIJA BOARD, OUT-OF-BODY EXPERIENCE, PALMISTRY, PARAPSYCHOLOGY, PHRENOLOGY, PHYSIOGNOMY, POLTERGEIST, PRECOGNITION, PSEUDOPSYCHOLOGY, PSI, PSYCHOKINESIS, PSYCHICS, SEANCE, SUPERSTITION, TELEPATHY.

pseudoscope   (C. Wheatstone) An optical instrument designed to create visual illusions by transposing images between the left and right eyes and inverting distance relations so that solid objects appear hollow and hollow objects solid.

pseudoseizure   pseudoepilepsy

pseudosenility   An acute, reversible confusional state or depression in older persons resulting from such factors as drug effects, malnutrition, diminished cardiac output, fever, alcoholism, intracranial tumor, an unreported fall, or a metabolic disturbance.

pseudosexual precocity   In a young female, premature development of breasts, lactation, and menstruation without pubic hair and pubertal growth spurt. Caused by pituitary tumor or inadequate thyroid activity.

pseudotrisomy 18   A congenital disorder, assumed due to an autosomal-recessive trait, marked by the same general anomalies found in chromosome-18-trisomy patients. However, chromosome studies of such people fail to show signs of chromosome-18 trisomy, translocation, or other abnormalities. All of the patients observed have had mental retardation. See CHROMOSOME-18 TRISOMY.

pseudovoyeur   A person who views pornography, strip shows, etc., as a substitute for sexual relations but for whom voyeurism is not a true paraphilia.

PSG   See POLYSOMNOGRAPHY.

PSI   Parenting Stress Index

psi   1. The twenty-third letter of the Greek alphabet, commonly used to represent psychology. 2. (R. H. Thouless) General term that includes extrasensory perception (ESP) and psychokinesis (PK) and refers to all parapsychological abilities. 3. Denoting unspecified mental functions purportedly involved in telepathy and other parapsychological processes which presently challenge scientific explanation. Term is usually explained as an abbreviation of psychic. See APPENDIX C.

psi abilities   Alleged abilities to transcend natural laws. They can be classified as three general types: (a) extrasensory perception (ESP), the ability to communicate or to see things in ways normal people cannot; (b) precognition (PC), the ability to forecast the future; and (c) psychokinesis (PK), the ability to move things by power of the mind. None has withstood scientific scrutiny despite much research; in a controversy with Gardner Murphy, Edwin Boring stated that no person ever has shown a reliable (consistent) ability to do any of these things.

PSI Basic Skills Tests for Business, Industry, and Government   (W. W. Ruch) A series of some 20 short, paper-and-pencil tests to assess the ability to perform various clerical and office work. Published by Psychological Services, Inc.

psi function (ψ function)   See PSYCHOMETRIC FUNCTION.

psilocybin   (A. Hofmann) A hallucinogenic substance obtained from the Mexican mushroom *Psilocybe mexicana.*

psi-missing   (J. B. Rhine) A tendency to miss the target when attempting to hit, for example, a participant in an extrasensory perception test obtains significantly fewer hits than expected by chance.

psi process   Any paranormal ability.

psi system   (S. Freud) Any part of psychic mechanism: the perception, memory, the unconscious system, etc.

psittacism   Automatic speech without content.

psopholalia   1. Infantile babbling. 2. Incomprehensible speech.

PSP   See POSTSYNAPTIC POTENTIAL.

PSR   Physicians for Social Responsibility

PSRO   Professional Standards Review Organization

PSY   In the Minnesota Multiphasic Personality Inventory, the psychoticism scale.

psychache   (E. Shneidman) Mental suffering: hurt, anquish. Psychological pain in the mind. See SUICIDE.

psychagogy   A method of reeducational psychotherapy that emphasizes the relationship of the patient to the environment, particularly the social environment.

psychalgalia   Mind or soul pain. Also known as algopsychalia, phrenalgia, psychalgia.

psychalgia   1. See PSYCHALGALIA. 2. See PSYCHIC PAIN. 2. Pain experienced as the result of psychological, behavioral, or emotional factors. Also known as psychogenic pain.

psychasthenia   Literally, weakness of the mind; an obsolete term applied to neurosis characterized by anxiety states, phobias, obsessions, and compulsions, all of which Pierre Janet attributed to lack of conscious control which he assumed occurs when "psychic tension" or energy is diminished by constitutional deficiency, fatigue, stress, or internal conflict.

psychataxia   A form of mental confusion in which the patient is unable to make a sustained mental effort or maintain attention.

psyche   (breath, life, spirit, human soul, mind—Greek) 1. The mind in its totality, as distinguished from the physical organism. 2. The self, or soul.

psycheclampsia   Emotional convulsion; acute mania.

psychedelic (drugs)   A class of drugs that generate altered states of "expanded consciousness." They have been used experimentally for therapy, by other cultures for religious rituals, and by the counterculture as mind-expanding agents in the late 1960s. Since then, classified as drugs of abuse. Whereas LSD (lysergic acid diethylamide) is the paradigmatic drug in this class, mescaline, psilocybin, and psychedelic amphetamines such as MDMA ("Ecstasy") are also notable. Marijuana is a mild psychedelic and various other substances generate a mixture of psychedelic effects and simple delirium (for example, PCP, nitrous oxide, volatile fumes). The phrase "psychedelic" was coined in 1956 by Humphrey Osmond, meaning mind-revealing or mind-manifesting. These drugs have also been called "psychotomimetics" because in the mid-1960s some of their effects were not differentiated from psychosis. However, this is misleading, as is the term "hallucinogens," also used for this class, because some do not cause significant hallucinations, and this is a relatively minor aspect of their actual effect. See HALLUCINOGENS, PSYCHOTOMIMETICS.

psychedelic experience   Reactions to hallucinogenic or other mind-altering drugs, including bizarre images, distorted perceptions, visual hallucinations, terrifying visions, time expansion or contraction, synesthesias, alternating with periods of envisioning kaleidoscopic colors, feelings of oneness with the universe, and transcendental ecstasy. Similar experiences have been known to occur without the use of drugs. See EUPHORIA, EUTHYMIC MOOD.

psychedelic therapy   An approach used experimentally in the 1960s that used the mind-altering qualities of LSD as an adjunct to the psychotherapeutic process. See PSYCHIC DRIVING (meaning 2).

psychelytic   psycholytic

psychergograph   An apparatus that presents a stimulus for discrimination as soon as the subject makes a correct response to a preceding stimulus. Also known as serial discriminator.

psycherhexic   Infrequent term to describe drugs that are "psychotropic" or "psychedelic."

psycherograph   serial discriminator

psychiatric aide   A trained person who tends to the personal needs of psychiatric patients, providing physical care (dressing, bathing, feeding) as required, psychological care, companionship, understanding, and encouragement. Since psychiatric aides are in more direct and continuous contact with the patients than other members of the psychiatric team, aides play a crucial part in the "therapeutic community" of the hospital, and can often contribute information and insight of great value to other staff members. Their role is therefore more professional than that of the old-time attendant.

psychiatric anaphylaxis   Broad phrase applied to reactivation of earlier symptoms, such as hives, by an activating event which is emotionally similar to the one that produced the original sensitivity. See ANAPHYLAXIS.

psychiatric classification/nosology   The grouping of mental disorders into diagnostic categories. The *Diagnostic and Statistical Manual of Mental Disorders* (DSM) and the *International Classification of Diseases* (ICD) represent attempts to generate a unified and logical nosology.

psychiatric consultation   A process in which a professional acting as a diagnostician or psychotherapist gives advice, information, or guidance to one or more colleagues (colleague-centered consultation), to members of an organization, such as a clinic, professional group or hospital (agency-centered consultation), or to members of the client's family. Similar to psychological consultation.

psychiatric diagnosis   See CLINICAL DIAGNOSIS.

psychiatric disability   Chronic loss or impairment of function due to a mental disorder, resulting in a severe handicap in meeting the demands of life.

psychiatric disorder   A mental disorder.

psychiatric emergency   A situation in which immediate medical or custodial care is required, as in a suicidal attempt, an acute psychotic break, a panic attack, a state of furor, an amnesic episode, a natural or man-made disaster, or a sudden loss of control (explosive disorder).

psychiatric epidemic   Instances of mass hysteria or behavioral outbursts in groups, such as dancing mania and biting mania, which may sweep through entire populations.

psychiatric epidemiology   The study of the incidence, distribution, and techniques for controlling mental disorders in a given population. See EPIDEMIOLOGY.

psychiatric examination   A comprehensive medical and psychological evaluation or diagnostic formulation for such purposes as clarification of the symptom picture, a tentative understanding of the development and dynamics of the patient's disorder, classification for treatment purposes, formulation of a tentative treatment plan, and prognosis. May include clinical interview, history-taking, medical examination, and psychological testing.

psychiatric history   Information gathered by a mental health care worker from members of the patient's family or directly from the patient. May include such data as age, sex, marital status; an account of the general nature and development of the disorder; the patient's conception of the illness, family history of hereditary conditions, child-rearing methods, family relationships, and environmental factors; the developmental history of the patient; and a description of personality tendencies, attitudes, interests, and interpersonal relationships. Sometimes known as patient history. See ANAMNESIS.

psychiatric hospital/institution   A mental hospital.

psychiatric illness   A mental disorder.

psychiatric institution   psychiatric hospital

psychiatric interview   1. General phrase for any one-on-one session with a psychiatrist for diagnostic or therapeutic purposes. 2. (H. S. Sullivan) A four-stage therapeutic interview consisting of: (a) formal inception, in which the therapist observes the patient during the first nondirective contact; (b) reconnaissance, in which the therapist questions the patient; (c) detailed inquiry, in which periods of acute anxiety in the patient's life are examined to formulate and test hypotheses regarding his problems; and (d) termination, in which the whole process is summarized in terms of the patient's past and future interpersonal relationships. 3. A formal procedure in which a psychiatrist performs a mental status evaluation of a patient, including orientation, affect, cognition, abstract thinking.

psychiatric nosology   psychiatric classification

psychiatric screening   See SCREENING.

psychiatric services   Diagnostic, therapeutic, and prophylactic services offered in a variety of settings, including general hospitals, colleges, adult homes, health-related facilities, skilled-nursing facilities, intermediate-care facilities, halfway houses, residential facilities, and community-health centers.

psychiatric social treatment   Therapy directed to the adjustment of a patient to social life in the community. Treatment may require increased insight, emotional retraining, and modification of the environment so that the patient can adapt more easily to it. Also known as psychological social treatment.

psychiatric social work   A field of specialized social work concerned primarily with psychiatric patients and their families. Psychiatric case work is performed all on an outpatient basis, and consists primarily of: (a) evaluation of family, environmental, and social factors in the patient's illness; (b) collaboration on intake, orientation, and development of a treatment plan; (c) conducting group and family counseling; (d) planning for discharge and follow-up care; and (e) maintaining relationships with community agencies.

psychiatric team   A multidisciplinary group of professionals and paraprofessionals who work together under the leadership of a psychiatrist in a mental hospital, psychiatric unit, mental-health center, or clinic. The team usually consists of psychiatrists, clinical psychologists, psychiatric social workers, psychiatric nurses, and adjunctive therapists such as dance, music, art, and recreation specialists.

psychiatric unit   A unit of a general hospital organized for treatment of acutely disturbed psychiatric patients on an in-patient basis. Usually includes provision for emergency coverage and admission, treatment with psychotropic drugs or electroshock therapy, group therapy, psychological examinations where indicated; and use of adjunctive modalities such as social work services, occupational therapy, art therapy, movement therapy, and music therapy, as well as discussion groups.

psychiatrist   A physician who specializes in the diagnosis, treatment, prevention, and study of mental and emotional disorders. In the United States, educational requirements consist of premedical training in a four-year college, a four-year program in medical school, a one-year hospital internship, a three-year residency in an American Medical Association approved hospital or agency, and at least two additional years of experience followed by an examination for certification by the American Board of Psychiatry and Neurology. See PSYCHIATRY.

psychiatry   (J. C. Reil, J. C. Heinroth, E. von Feuchtersleben) A medical specialty concerned with the study, diagnosis, treatment, and prevention of mental and emotional disorders. Training for psychiatry includes the study of psychopathology, biochemistry, psychopharmacology, neurology, neuropathology, psychology, psychoanalysis, genetics, social science, and community mental health, as well as the many theories and approaches advanced in the field itself.

psychic   1. General term for all phenomena associated with the mind. 2. A medium, a fortuneteller. A person credited with or who professes to have parapsychological abilities. See EXTRASENSORY PERCEPTION.

psychical research   Old name for parapsychology.

psychic apparatus   (S. Freud) Mental structures and mechanisms including the unconscious, preconscious, conscious and id, ego, and superego. Also known as mental apparatus. See STRUCTURAL MODEL, SYSTEMATIC APPROACH.

psychic blindness   Inability to see due to some psychological rather than physiological condition.

psychic death   Extreme withdrawal from others or activities, often characterized by giving up.

psychic determinism   A doctrine positing that all mental, or psychic, events obey the law of cause and effect and are not subject to free will or pure chance. See DETERMINISM, DYNAMIC APPROACH.

psychic driving   1. The replaying of recorded psychodynamically significant material by clients and their therapists after agreeing to be recorded. The client is given the recorded material to listen to at home. 2. (E. Cameron) Term used in Canada in the 1950s for the administration of high doses of LSD followed by sedation to patients in mental hospitals.

psychic dynamism   See DYNAMIC THEORY.

psychic energizer   (N. S. Kline) Outmoded phrase used to describe the earliest antidepressant drugs, which were derived from anti-tuberculosis medicines. See MONOAMINE OXIDASE INHIBITORS (MAOIs).

psychic energy   In psychoanalytic theory, the dynamic force behind all mental processes. According to Sigmund Freud, the basic source of this energy is the id, or instinctual needs of the individual, which seek immediate gratification. Carl Jung also believed in a reservoir of psychic energy, termed libido, but placed primary emphasis on channeling this energy into the development of the personality and the expression of cultural and spiritual values rather than pleasurable gratification of biological instincts. Also known as mental energy. See ID, LIBIDO.

psychic equivalent   psychomotor epilepsy

psychic helplessness   A state of helpless anxiety which Sigmund Freud thought to be first experienced during the birth process due to respiratory and other physiological changes occurring at that time. Freud held the psychic helplessness state to be the prototype of all later anxiety states.

psychic impotence   A functional inability of the male to perform sexual intercourse despite intact genitalia and sexual desire. May be manifested in many forms including premature ejaculation, inability to achieve erection, or the need for certain unusual conditions to perform coitus.

psychic inertia   In psychoanalytic theory, fixation at an infantile stage, which acts as a form of resistance and impedes therapeutic progress. Both Sigmund Freud and Carl Jung recognized such inertia as a basic characteristic of neurosis.

psychic isolation   1. (C. Jung) Phrase introduced by Carl Jung to identify withdrawal from social contacts to prevent unconscious material from being revealed. 2. A feeling of estrangement when material from the collective unconscious erupts into consciousness.

psychic link   Alleged ability of some people to be aware of a phenomenon without direct sensory experience, such as the alleged ability of a twin, especially an identical twin, to sense the mood, or physical condition of an absent twin, even if the other twin is thousands of miles away. See PSYCHICS, PSYCHICAL RESEARCH.

psychic masturbation   The achievement of sexual arousal, possibly including orgasm, through sexual fantasies without physical manipulation of any part of the body. See WET DREAM.

psychic mobility   A social psychological phenomenon characterized by the changing of a population from previously established social norms, concepts, or attitudes toward new ones. An expression of the freedom of humans to manifest desires that may have been previously dormant, in new or novel ways, as in dressing styles, home furnishings, choice of music. Psychic mobility is more active when people have greater discretionary income.

psychic norm   A standard for mental health, described as being in harmony with self and others, happy to be in conformance with cultural mores, and suffering no impairment of reasoning, judgment, or intellectual abilities.

psychic pain   Emotional discomfort associated especially with feelings of acute anxiety and in some cases with hallucinations, obsessions, or depressive thoughts. It is usually localized in the head. Sometimes known as psychalgia. See ALGOPSYCHALIA, GUILT FEELINGS.

psychic reality 1. In psychoanalytic theory, the inner, or internal reality of fantasies, wishes, fears, dreams, memories, and anticipations, as distinguished from the external reality of actual events and experiences. 2. Experience of an inner world including the dynamic relations between complexes, unconscious fantasies and archetypal images.

psychic reflex The psychic reflex (more properly the "psychical reflex") is an early phrase used by Ivan Pavlov to characterize the indirect nature of elicitation of the gastric reflex. Rather than being elicited by a stimulus operating directly in the stomach, the psychical reflex was mediated in a higher center of the nervous system, hence "psychical." Phrase is not obsolete because of revivals of interest in Pavlovian conditioning manifested, for example, in the work of Rescorla.

psychic reflex arc (S. Ferenczi) Phrase used by Sandor Ferenczi for the Freudian autoplastic (adjustment to reality) stage of development when adaptation is achieved by simple motor discharge, such as the whimpering of an infant which modifies himself or herself rather than the environment.

psychic research The investigation of paranormal events. Also known as parapsychology.

psychic resilience An ability to withstand a great deal of psychological trauma, such as results from the death of a loved one.

psychic satiation See SATIATION.

psychic scar The residual symptoms of a mental disorder that may remain after completion of appropriate therapy; for example, a delusion may remain after delirium.

psychic secretion (I. P. Pavlov) A secretion elicited by a previously neutral stimulus. See SALIVATION.

psychic seizure A seizure occurring in psychomotor epilepsy, during which the patient experiences psychological disturbances such as vivid panoramic memories or a "twilight state" during which the patient is disoriented and utters unintelligible sounds or performs automatic activities. See PSYCHOMOTOR EPILEPSY.

psychic suicide A form of self-destruction characterized by a "decision" to die that results in death without resorting to a physical agency. There is only anecdotal evidence of the reality of this phenomenon. See VOODOO DEATH.

psychic system Any part of the total personality having distinct dynamic properties; responding in expected manners to aspects of the psychic field.

psychic tension A sense of emotional strain experienced in emergency situations or situations that generate inner conflict or anxiety. See STRESS, TENSION.

psychic tone See ATONIA.

psychic trauma (C. Frederick) An experience that inflicts damage to the personality, often of a lasting nature, such as sexual assault, discovery of one's own adoption under adverse circumstances, child abuse, abandonment by a parent, or being in a natural catastrophic event. See ACUTE TRAUMATIC DISORDER, TRAUMATIC DISORDERS, RECOVERED MEMORY.

psychic triumvirate (S. Freud) In psychoanalytic theory, the three-part governing system of the personality (id, ego, superego).

psychic vaginismus A painful vaginal spasm due to repugnance toward the sexual act that prevents normal sexual intercourse.

psyching-up 1. Casually, getting mentally prepared for an important or demanding event such as giving a speech or entering a boxing ring. 2. In sports psychology, preparing for an event by increasing the arousal level, narrowing the focus, and planning the activities. Also called "getting psyched."

psychism A doctrine positing that a principle of life pervades all nature.

psychoacoustics An interdisciplinary study of sound and hearing with contributions from physics, psychology, and physiology.

psychoactive Mind-altering; a term once used to describe a drug that changed perception, mood, or thought processes. Term is no longer used with such specificity, now simply a synonym for psychotropic. See PSYCHEDELIC.

psychoactive drug A chemical substance that affects normal mental functioning, altering either mood, thought processes, or both. May be a tranquilizer as well as psychedelic, stimulant, or sedative. Divisions (with an example) include: depressants (Miltown), hallucinogens (hashish, LSD), narcotics (morphine), stimulants (amphetamine, cocaine). Other classifications are anti-anxiety drugs (Valium), antipsychotics (Haldol), antidepressants (Prozac) and others (such as Inderal).

psychoanaleptica See PSYCHOLEPTICA.

psychoanalysis (PA or Psa) 1. General term for any form of dynamic psychology stressing the importance of drives. In this sense "psychoanalysis" is spelled with a lower case p. 2. Any of a number of variant systems of personality theory based originally on Sigmund Freud's system that was changed by others such as by Carl Jung and Karen Horney. 3. A theory of human behavior, especially relating to the functions of the mind as well as an associated method of psychological treatment. Also known as classical analysis, orthodox analysis. See PSYCHOANALYSIS.

Psychoanalysis (J. Breuer, S. Freud) A theory of dynamic psychology and a therapeutic technique based upon a complex theory by Sigmund Freud. Focuses on unconscious forces such as repressed impulses, internal conflicts, and childhood traumas. Its main concepts are infantile sexuality, instincts, pleasure and reality principles, the three-fold division of the psyche into id, ego, and superego, and the central importance of defenses against anxiety. As a form of therapy, Psychoanalysis is directed primarily to psychoneuroses, which it seeks to eliminate by the patient establishing a constructive therapeutic relationship (transference) with a psychoanalyst. Specific methods of therapy are free association, dream interpretation, analysis of resistances and defenses, and working through the feelings and experiences revealed in the transference process. See PERSONALITY FORMATION THEORIES, PERSONALITY THEORIES. See also some items attributed to Sigmund Freud: ABSTINENCE RULE, ACTIVE CASTRATION COMPLEX, ACTUAL NEUROSIS, ANACLISIS, ANACLITIC OBJECT CHOICE, ANAL BIRTH, ANAL TRIAD, ANAL-SADISTIC PHASE, ANATOMY IS

DESTINY, ANTICATHEXIS, CATHARSIS, CENSOR, CONTROL, CRITICIZING FACULTY, DEFERRED OBEDIENCE, DETERMINING QUALITY, DISCHARGE OF AFFECT, DRIVE ATTRIBUTES, DUAL-INSTINCT THEORY, EGO CATHEXIS, EROTIC LOVE, ESTHETIC PLEASURE, ETHICAL APPROACH, FORE-UNPLEASURE, INSTINCTUAL ANXIETY, INTRAPSYCHIC CENTER, LIBIDINOUS TYPES, NIGHT FANTASY, NIRVANA PRINCIPLE, OEDIPAL COMPLEX, OVERDETERMINATION, PHOBIC ANXIETY, PLEASURE EGO, PRECONSCIOUSNESS, PRIMAL FATHER, PRIMAL SADISM, PSYCHIC APPARATUS, RETENTION HYSTERIA, SECONDARY ELABORATION, UNCONSCIOUS GUILT, VAGINAL PHASE, WIT WORK.

psychoanalyst   A practitioner of the personality theory and procedures of Sigmund Freud, and variants of those procedures in the treatment of mental disorders.

psychoanalytically-oriented   A designation of people who practice psychotherapy, who have not been trained and graduated by standard psychoanalytic institutes, who practice or use some variation or part of Sigmund Freud's theory and therapeutic techniques.

psychoanalytic anthropology   The application of principles and insights gained from the treatment of persons with neuroses to the understanding of unconscious factors responsible for behavior in aboriginal societies. Among the topics dealt with are the psychic function of taboos, the handling of aggression, the importance of the leader, the study of myths and rituals, and the interpretation of customs and mores found in different cultures.

psychoanalytic development psychology   A description of the internalization of interpersonal relations in psychoanalytic terms; also, the effect of human object relationships on the organization and structure of the psyche.

psychoanalytic group psychotherapy   Group therapy in which basic psychoanalytic concepts and methods, such as free association, analysis of resistances and defenses, and dream interpretation, are used in modified form. Some specific types include: (a) (A. Wolf) an approach in which the group members act as cotherapists and freely associate with each other; (b) (W. R. Bion) an approach in which the focus is on the emotional states of the group in relation to a central problem; (c) (H. Thelen) an approach in which the emphasis is on the emotional and cognitive relations between the individual and the group culture.

psychoanalytic perspective   A point of view about personality based generally on the dynamic theory of Sigmund Freud that considers personality to be dependent on the conflict between basic drives (id) and the dictates of society (superego) as mediated by the mind (ego).

psychoanalytic setting   An environment designed to encourage the patient to attend to the inward world of feeling, fantasy, and early experience, and to voice whatever comes to mind. Sessions are held in a private study free from distracting influences. Clients generally recline on a couch, while therapists sit out of sight to take notes, observe significant gestures, facial expressions, and postural changes.

psychoarchaeology   (S. Rosenzweig) A method by means of which levels of communication are unraveled to reveal the meanings that inhabit the idioverse (Saul Rosenzweig's term for personality).

psychobabble   Jocular and mildly pejorative term for the excessive use of psychological terminology.

psychobioanalysis   bioanalysis

psychobiogram   (E. Kretschmer) A type of personality profile developed by Ernst Kretschmer that includes data concerning a patient's heredity and history, plus information about intelligence, temperament, and attitudes, combined with somatotype evaluation.

psychobiography   A biography stressing the psychological factors that raised that person to eminence. Among better-known psychobiographies are Sigmund Freud's study of Dostoevski, Erik Erikson's biography of Mohandas Gandhi, Phyllis Bottome's biography of Alfred Adler, and Henry Murray's analysis of Herman Melville.

psychobiological factors   The multiple determinants of personality and biobehavioral, psychological, and sociological factors that Adolf Meyer cited in his holistic, multidisciplinary approach. See PSYCHOBIOLOGICAL THEORY, PSYCHOBIOLOGY.

psychobiology   1. (F. E. Beneke, F. Groos, H-M. Bernheim) The study of mental functions in other life processes and activities. 2. (A. Meyer) A holistic approach developed by Adolf Meyer, in which the individual is viewed as an integrated unit, and both normal and abnormal behavior are explained in terms of biological, sociological, and psychological determinants. Symptoms are seen as real but distorted attempts at adjustment which can be understood by observing the patient in concrete, everyday activity and by compiling an anamnesis (biographical report) based on all phases of a patient's history, physical and mental, conscious and unconscious. Meyer assumed that this study, which he termed "distributive analysis and synthesis," would reveal assets out of which a more effective personality could be developed. Psychobiology is a field of biology as opposed to biopsychology which is a field of psychology. See ERGASIA, ERGASIOLOGY, MULTIMODAL THERAPY, SYNTROPHY.

psychochemistry   A field of chemistry concerned with the relationships between chemicals and behavior, including genetic or metabolic aspects of behavior (for example, different individuals may react in different ways to the same stimulant, because of inherited traits that affect metabolism of drugs). See PSYCHOACTIVE DRUGS.

psychochemistry intelligence   The effects of biochemical factors such as drugs, hormones, and nutritional factors on intelligence, learning, or performance; for example, caffeine may improve mental performance temporarily, whereas a dietary deficiency of niacin can result in lowered performance of mental tasks.

psycho-clarity   (R. L. Powers) Adlerian diagnosis as psychotherapy. A client, in explaining, learns symptoms' context and workings, discovering purpose (meaning) as substitution for problem-solving. Based on the idea that individuals cannot change their minds until they know (can speak) their minds. Common language shapes common sense of difficulties. See ALDERIAN PSYCHOLOGY, FICTION, GUIDING FICTION, PRIVATE LOGIC.

psycho-imagination therapy (J. E. Shorr) Psychotherapy that calls for the client or patient to imagine certain situations in the time dimensions of past, present, and future, with the imagination being directed and catalyzed by the therapist. See COVERT CONDITIONING, MEDITATION, NAIKAN PSYCHOTHERAPY.

psychocultural stress (E. D. Wittkower) Cultural factors that generate significant psychological tension or anxiety, and, in many cases, mental illness. Wittkower classified these factors under (a) cultural content, including frustrating rules and taboos, values such as vain pursuit of success and racial discrimination; (b) social organization, including anomie and rigidity that demands adherence to prescribed social norms; and (c) sociocultural change, as in rapid technological development or migration from a rural to an urban area.

psychodance See PSYCHODRAMA FORMS.

psychodiagnostics Detection and assessment of specific psychological disorders through examinations of a client's behavior, speech, and test results.

psychodietetics Application of nutritional principles and nutritional supplements in the treatment of mental and neurologic disorders, for example, pellagra, beriberi, phenylketonuria (PKU).

psychodometer An instrument that uses a tuning fork in the measurement of response time.

psychodrama A technique of psychotherapy developed by Jacob Moreno, in which patients achieve new insight and alter faulty patterns of behavior through spontaneous enactment of life situations. The process involves: (a) a protagonist, or patient, who presents and acts out emotional problems and interpersonal relationships; (b) trained "auxiliary egos" who play supportive roles representing significant individuals in the dramatized situations; and (c) a director or therapist who guides this process and leads an interpretive session when it is completed. Various special techniques are used to advance the therapy, among them, exchanging roles, soliloquy, the mirror, enactment of dreams, and hypnotic dramatizations. See ALTER EGO, AUXILIARY EGO, DIRECTOR, HYPNODRAMA, MIRROR TECHNIQUE, PROTAGONIST, ROLEPLAYING, SWITCHING.

psychodrama forms (J. L. Moreno) The various types of psychodrama developed to explore the private worlds of patients and provide them with therapeutic experiences, including: (a) sociodrama, which deals with the active structuring of social worlds and collective ideologies; (b) physiodrama, which blends physical conditioning with psychodrama; (c) axiodrama, which deals with ethics and the eternal verities such as truth, justice, and beauty; (d) hypnodrama, which combines psychodrama with hypnosis; (e) psychomusic, in which spontaneous music is a part of psychodrama; and (f) psychodance, which uses spontaneous dance.

psychodramatic shock A form of psychotherapy in which a patient is encouraged to relive a traumatic event to achieve a cathartic effect, for example, a patient may be asked to revive a hallucinatory experience by acting it out, using members of the staff to recreate the situation as a psychodrama.

psychodynamic fallacy The viewing of others' motivation in terms of personality factors.

psychodynamic psychotherapy A view of psychotherapy emphasizing causes and drives within the individual, but stressing ongoing intense psychological processes rather than physical deficits, excesses, or imbalances as set forth in the biological or somatic view.

psychodynamics 1. Interpretation of behavior in terms of mental and emotional processes. 2. The pattern of motivational forces, conscious or unconscious, that gives rise to a particular psychological event or state, such as an attitude, action, symptom, or mental disorder. These forces include drives, wishes, emotions, and defense mechanisms, as well as biological needs such as hunger and sex. Also known as dynamics. See DYNAMIC APPROACH.

psychodynamic theory See DYNAMIC APPROACH, PSYCHODYNAMICS.

psychodysleptica See PSYCHOLEPTICA.

psychoeducational diagnostician A specialist trained in the diagnosis and remediation of children with learning disabilities.

psychoeducational problems See SCHOOL PSYCHOLOGY.

Psychoeducational Profile (PEP) (E. Schopler) A test that measures the educational potential of children who are autistic, who have developmental disorders, or both, usually regarded as untestable.

psychoendocrinology The study of the hormonal system to discover sites for the manifestation of biochemical abnormalities that play a significant role in the production of mental disorders.

Psychoepistemological Profile (PEP) (J. R. Royce) A Canadian paper-and-pencil test to evaluate the participant's approach to reality. Quantifies three epistemic styles: rationalism, empiricism, metaphorism.

psychoexploration Any of a group of psychotherapeutic techniques used for diagnostic or treatment purposes that include catharsis, hypnosis, abreaction, interviews, fantasizing, narcoanalysis, and narcosynthesis.

psychogalvanic reflex/response (PGR) (A. Vigouroux, I. R. Tarchanoff) Involuntary, physiological changes in the electrical conductance of the skin resulting from reactions to psychologic stimuli such as emotional stressors, and measurable by the psychogalvanometer. Also known as galvanic skin response (GSR). See FERE PHENOMENON, TARCHANOFF METHOD.

psychogalvanic skin-resistance audiometer (PGSR) A procedure adapted for testing the auditory acuity of young children and suspected malingerers using lie-detector-type procedures. Dermal-sweating responses to controlled test tones are graphically recorded. See GALVANIC SKIN RESPONSE (GSR), KEELER POLYGRAPH, LIE DETECTOR.

psychogalvanometer An ultrasensitive galvanometer used in measuring electrical changes in the skin surface. See PSYCHOGALVANIC SKIN-RESISTANCE AUDIOMETRY.

psychogender Term used in the treatment of intersexed patients to distinguish between psychological sex identification and biological sex.

psychogenesis The origin and development of mental or psychic processes. See PSYCHOGENIC.

psychogenetic factors See ENDOGENESIS.

psychogenetics   The study of inherited mental disorders.

psychogenic   Conditions resulting from psychological, mental, or emotional factors, as contrasted with organic or somatic factors. Also known as functional.

psychogenic amnesia   A temporary inability to recall important personal information that is too extensive to be explained by ordinary forgetfulness. See MOTIVATED FORGETTING.

psychogenic aspermia   A form of psychogenic impotence in which emission of semen does not occur.

psychogenic constipation   A condition observed in obsessive-compulsive persons who assign so much importance to "regularity" that abnormal amounts of time and effort are devoted to daily bowel movements.

psychogenic disorders   Functional disorders (disorders that do not have an organic basis) thought to be due to such psychological factors as emotional conflicts or stress. Phrase applies to all types of psychoneuroses, psychophysiologic and somatoform disorders, personality disorders, and functional psychoses. See FUNCTIONAL DISORDER.

psychogenic fugue   A dissociative disorder in which people may forget their identity. See FUGUE.

psychogenic hallucination   A false perception arising from psychological factors, such as a need to enhance self-esteem, or relief from a sense of guilt, as opposed to hallucinations produced primarily by physiological conditions such as intoxication.

psychogenic hypersomnia   Sleep attacks or sleep of excessive duration, precipitated by psychological factors such as a wish to escape from a threatening or other anxiety-provoking situation. Also known as somnolent detachment. See NARCOLEPSY.

psychogenic mutism   See MUTISM.

psychogenic needs   See NEED-PRESS THEORY.

psychogenic nocturnal polydipsia (PNP)   Feeling thirsty throughout the night in spite of presumably adequate fluid intake.

psychogenic pain   psychalg(al)ia (meaning 3)

psychogenic pain disorder   A somatoform illness characterized by severe, prolonged pain for which there is no evidence of physical basis, but there is evidence of psychological involvement. See FLIGHT INTO DISEASE, HYPOCHONDRIASIS.

psychogenic polydipsia   Excessive fluid ingestion for no observable physiological reason.

psychogenic pruritus   A psychosomatic dermatological disorder characterized by a functional itching that resists treatment. See PRURITUS.

psychogenic stupor   A state of extreme unresponsiveness without loss of consciousness, associated with functional rather than organic syndromes, as in catatonic and depressive states, combat exhaustion, and extreme panic. See BENIGN STUPOR, MALIGNANT STUPOR, STUPOR.

psychogenic torticollis   Spasmodic contractions of the neck muscles due to psychosomatic origins. See SPASMODIC TORTICOLLIS.

psychograph   A graph that represents the degree to which various traits differ within the individual. Also known as trait profile. See PSYCHOLOGICAL PROFILE.

psychographics   (E. Demby) 1. A branch of psychology that deals with the study of lifestyles of a population in quantitative and visually descriptive terms. Term describes an extended form of demographics that surveys activities, interests, and opinions of the population, in addition to such factors as income, education, and place of residence. 2. See PSYCHOGRAPHIC SEGMENTATION.

psychographic segmentation   (E. Demby) In consumer psychology, the division of buyers into groups on the basis of variables such as social class, age, income, family status, lifestyle, and personality. Also known as psychographics.

psychography   The natural history and description of mental phenomena, as in psychoanalysis and psychobiology.

psychohistory   The interpretation of historical events, trends, and personalities in psychological terms. See APPLIED PSYCHOANALYSIS.

psychoinfantilism   The appearance in an adult of psychic qualities normally associated with a child. It is not regarded as a disease state but a reaction to a severe crisis or a difficult decision characterized by uncertainty, mental weakness, dependence on stronger persons, and inability to cope alone.

psychokinesis (PK or **Pk)**   1. The alleged ability to influence external objects or processes without the intervention of any known physical energies or forces. 2. In parapsychology, the alleged ability to control external events and move or change the shape of objects through the power of thought, for example, to influence the roll of dice or bend a piece of metal by exerting "mind over matter." Also known as telekinesis. See EXTRASENSORY PERCEPTION (ESP).

psycholagny   Sexual self-stimulation through fantasy.

psycholepsy   A sudden depressive state, marked by a dramatic decline in the level of mental tension, and generally associated with persons lacking emotional stability. The abrupt psycholeptic crisis usually follows an experience of ecstasy or triumph during which psychic tension is at a peak.

psycholeptics   Old term for psychotropic drugs that were perceived to have their primary effect on the mind rather than on the nervous system. Include minor tranquilizers, antidepressant drugs, and the hallucinogens that cause a disintegration of psychic functions.

psycholinguistic approach   A theory of language acquisition advocated by Noam Chomsky stating that children naturally learn a system of language rules by which they generate sentences, rather than learning strings of words.

psycholinguistics   The study of the psychological functions of language and of the effects of language on individual and group relationships. Primary functions are to promote communication, to enable people to use concepts as tools of thought, to study language as a medium for the expression of feelings and emotions, and to enable humans to build a body of literature that enriches human life. It is the study of language from a psychological rather than from a linguistic perspective. See DEVELOPMENTAL PSYCHOLINGUISTICS, ILLINOIS TEST OF PSYCHOLINGUISTIC ABILITIES, LINGUISTICS, PHONOLOGY, PSYCHOLOGICAL LINGUISTICS.

psychological anaphylaxis   Physical anaphylaxis is an extreme and sometimes life-threatening hypersensitivity to ingested substances such as peanuts. Psychological anaphylaxis extends the same concept to psychological factors, such as objects or persons that are reminders of traumatic experiences. See ANAPHYLAXIS, PSYCHIATRIC ANAPHYLAXIS.

psychological aphrodisiacs   Any environmental or experiential condition not involving drugs or ingestion that increases sexual desires or interests. See PORNOGRAPHY.

psychological assessment   See PSYCHOLOGICAL EXAMINATION.

psychological atomism   A doctrine of mind that assumes experiences are composed of elementary psychic units or atoms. Also known as composition theory.

psychological autopsy   1. An investigative technique for gathering data related to the thoughts and activities of persons who commit suicide and to the conditions surrounding death. 2. (E. S. Shneidman) A psychological procedure to clarify the cause of death in cases where the mode of death is equivocal (usually either accident or suicide) done by interviewing relevant survivors. The focus is on reconstructing the entire event together with the decedent's intention at the time of death.

psychological color solid   color solid

psychological deficit   1. The performance of any significant psychological process at a level below that of a "normal" person. 2. Vague phrase for insufficiencies of capacities or abilities in specific functions, whether real or imagined.

psychological dependence   1. A feeling of behavior, pattern of behavior, or both, characterized by being somewhat compulsively attached to a situation, person, or substance in spite of significant problems arising out of this relationship. See CODEPENDENCE. 2. A dependence on chemical substances without physiological dependence, meaning that there is no evidence of tolerance or withdrawal. It is associated with marijuana, amphetamines, and caffeine. Tolerance is likely to occur but not in significant degree, and withdrawal symptoms are usually mild compared with those associated with alcohol and narcotic drugs. Compare PHYSIOLOGICAL DEPENDENCE.

psychological determinism   A doctrine stressing the importance of biologically determined forces that dictate the direction of a person's subjective life (such as ideas, fantasies). Assumes that there is no action without a preceding cause. Sometimes known as empirical determinism.

psychological differentiation   A tendency to discriminate a stimulus embedded in a complex context from its environment. Related to cognitive style.

psychological dimension   (E. Titchener) A cognitive mode with respect to which conscious data may vary.

psychological distance   1. A degree of feeling for a person involving such factors as caring, empathy, sympathy, interest, and concern. 2. Behavior ranging from complete avoidance to physical and social intimacy such as might be found in a honeymooning couple. 3. The existence of and maintenance of an attitude of alienation from either specific individuals or specific

classes of people, for any of many reasons, such as feeling superior or inferior to others, having been hurt or fearing to be hurt, or fearing being contaminated. See DISCRIMINATION, FEELINGS OF INFERIORITY, EQUITY, PREJUDICE, PROXEMICS.

psychological dynamics   (J. Bentham) The concept of hedonism based on the human tendency to avoid pain and to seek pleasure as well as on the principle of self-interest.

psychological environment   The surround at any time for any individual as it is perceived or as the individual is acted upon by external forces. See PROXEMICS.

psychological esthetics   A branch of psychology that deals with the psychological effects of different art forms, patterns, colors, composition, and other aspects of visual stimuli contained in paintings, sculpture, photographs, architecture, natural landscapes, and the like. Certain colors or patterns may excite viewers whereas others may have a calming effect. Psychological esthetics also may be applied to the study of political, social, economic, or other influences on the work of artists.

psychological examination   The examination of a person, such as a counselee, by means of interviews, observations of behavior, and administration of psychological tests, with the purpose of evaluating personality adjustment, abilities, interests, and functioning in important phases of life. The purpose of the psychological examination may be to determine needs, identify difficulties and problems, and contribute to the diagnosis of mental disorder and determination of the type of treatment required. Also known as mental examination. See PSYCHOLOGICAL ASSESSMENT.

psychological factors affecting physical condition Refers to psychological conditions and situations that may cause or exacerbate physical symptoms, such as having a heated argument with a spouse, or the death of a child; examples of physical conditions and symptoms are tension headaches, compulsive overeating, angina pectoris, asthma, rheumatoid arthritis, gastric ulcer, ulcerative colitis, nausea, and vomiting. See CONVERSION DISORDER, PSYCHOSOMATIC DISORDER, SOMATOFORM DISORDER.

psychological factors   Functional factors, as opposed to organic (constitutional, hereditary) factors, that contribute to the development of personality and the etiology of mental disorder. Psychological factors include, among others, childhood experiences, faulty role models, rejection or overprotection, and traumatic experiences, as well as individual creativity.

psychological field   (K. Lewin) The life space or environment as perceived by the person at any given moment.

psychological geography   (J. L. Moreno) The pattern of an entire community showing the location and interrelations of groups within it, with emphasis on the "psychological currents" flowing between them.

psychological homeostasis   (R. Stagner) Extension of Walter Cannon's notion of biological homeostasis to include the idea that people develop a self-concept, self-percept, and perceptual structures to insure the maintenance of biological and social steady states.

psychological invalidism   An attitude of patients characterized by refusal to accept that they have been cured of or never really had a physical disorder. An insistence on living as though ill in an attempt to get the benefits (attention, concern, care) that accompany invalidism. See SECONDARY GAIN.

psychological linguistics   General phrase for different approaches to language from the point of view of psychology. By observation and experiment, psychological linguistics explores how humans acquire language, how humans behave in producing and perceiving speech, how humans use language to learn other skills, how the use of language is related to memory, and how language interrelates with thinking. See LINGUISTICS, ORIGIN-OF-LANGUAGE THEORIES, PSYCHOLINGUISTICS.

psychological masquerade   (R. Taylor) Apparent psychological symptoms actually caused by physical or organic conditions. See PSYCHOSOMATIC DISORDER.

psychological me   The self; the totality of the personality as experienced by the person. See ME.

psychological measures   See PRIMARY PREVENTION. (Not to be confused with psychological assessment or psychometrics.)

psychological model   1. In systems-analysis evaluation, an approach dealing empirically with the interrelatedness of all the factors that may affect performance, meanwhile monitoring possible side effects of the treatment. 2. A theory as to how some psychological process occurs, subject to empirical verification or refutation.

psychological moment   The instant of "now." The period of time of immediate awareness, the meeting point between past and future. Also known as specious present.

psychological motive   1. Any motive not assumed to arise from purely physiological need, that is, a learned motive or a motive that has a mental, emotional, or cultural origin. 2. A motive, such as competition, that arises from interactions with others. May be universal, culture-specific, or individual.

psychological need   A need fostered by environmental interactions with the individual, such as a social-approval need.

psychological network   Loose but cohesive interrelationship of individuals, families, and social groups that helps form social traditions and emotional support for the participants.

psychological rapport   Carl Jung's phrase for transference, which he described as "the intensified tie to the physician which is a compensation symptom for the defective relationship to present reality," and "inevitable in every fundamental analysis."

psychological reactance   Dissatisfaction with an activity especially when outside influences exert pressure to continue it.

psychological rehabilitation   The development or restoration of an effective identity in a client with a disability through psychological approaches such as counseling, individual or group therapy, ability assessment, and medications. The object is to help the clients improve their self-image, cope with emotional problems, and to become a more competent, autonomous person.

psychological scale   A measuring device for a psychological function, such as intelligence and attitudes.

psychological social treatment   See PSYCHIATRIC SOCIAL TREATMENT.

psychological statistics   Mathematical methods that describe, summarize, or lead to inferences about data dealing with the behavior or cognition of individuals or groups. These methods include measures of central tendency, variability, correlation, significance, probability, and the like. See STATISTICAL PSYCHOLOGY.

psychological stress   See STRESS.

psychological test   A standardized instrument (test, inventory, scale) used in measuring intelligence, general and specific mental abilities (such as reasoning, comprehension, abstract thinking), specific aptitudes (such as mechanical aptitude, manual coordination, dexterity), achievement (such as reading, spelling, arithmetic), attitudes, values, interests, personality, and personality disorders. See APPENDIX F.

psychological testing   The use of objective or projective tests to assess behavior, attitudes, motives, or traits, for purposes such as psychodiagnosis, research, or personnel and educational assessment. Makes use of questionnaires, interpretation of ambiguous stimuli, ratings of self and others, intellectual problems, and the like. Psychological testing also comprises the development and construction of tests, and their validity, reliability, and standardization. See GENERAL ABILITY TESTS, INFANT AND PRESCHOOL TESTS, INTELLIGENCE TESTS, INTEREST INVENTORIES, MECHANICAL APTITUDE TESTS, MOTOR TESTS, PROFESSIONAL APTITUDE TESTS, SCHOLASTIC APTITUDE TESTS, SPECIAL ABILITY TESTS. See also APPENDIX F.

psychological time   Subjective estimation of time based on such factors as the occurrence and nature of events, experience with the time taken by regularly-occurring events, and physiological rhythms. See TIME SENSE.

psychological tremor   A trembling of the body or a part of the body, for example, the hands due to psychological causes (as opposed to organic causes).

psychological type   A category of individuals classified according to certain characteristics, whether overt (such as behavioral type) or covert (such as inherited type). See BIOTYPOLOGY, CONSTITUTIONAL TYPES, JUNGIAN TYPOLOGY.

psychological warfare   A type of warfare in which propaganda and other techniques are used to lower the morale of the enemy and to heighten the support of the war effort by a country's or other group's own population.

psychological weaning   The process of breaking away from anyone or any organization or group on which a person may be dependent. Examples include: children who move out of their parents' homes and out from under their control, spouses who divorce each other, patients separating from their therapists, persons leaving cults or religions, etc.

psychological zero   The level at which a sensation (temperature, pressure, sound) is not experienced, for example, the psychological zero for the temperature of the skin is approximately 90°F (32°C) for most of the body, but 82°F for the ear and 98°F for the armpit. See PHYSIOLOGICAL ZERO.

psychologism   1. A doctrine positing that everything should be viewed from the point of view of the psychology of individuals, based on the classical (Hellenistic) expression "Man is the measure of all things." 2. Pejorative term deriding the importance of psychology. 3. Pejorative term for the reduction of philosophical and theological reflection to psychological processes. 4. A doctrine positing that the problem of the validity of human knowledge can be solved by the study of mental processes. John Locke's *Essay Concerning Human Understanding* is considered a classic in this area. See EPISTEMOLOGY.

psychologist   A professionally trained person who spends working time in researching, teaching, writing, or practicing clinically in one or more branches of behavioral science. Training includes a wide variety of courses leading to a doctorate obtained at a university or school of professional psychology. In most jurisdictions certification or licensing is required for participation in the profession. Psychologist's activities are carried out in a variety of settings: schools, colleges, social agencies, hospitals, clinics, the military, industry and business, prisons, government agencies, and in private practice.

psychologistic   A critical term used by positivists to characterize subjective psychologists and used by behaviorists to characterize cognitive psychologists.

psychologistics   (P. M. Carman) The study of the functions of a psychologist; also relates to the logistics employed by psychologists in carrying out their varied responsibilities.

psychologist's fallacy   1. The projection by a psychologists of what they assume to be appropriate thoughts or behaviors into the mind of the client. 2. Erroneous conjecture by one person about the thoughts and feelings of others.

psychology (Ψ)   1. (H. B. English & A. C. English) A branch of science dealing with behavior, acts, or mental processes, as well as the mind, self, or person who behaves or acts or who has the mental processes. 2. The science of human and animal behavior as part of the total life process, including those bodily systems associated with behavior, sensory and motor functions, social interactions; the sequence of development, hereditary and environmental forces, conscious and unconscious mental processes, mental health and disorder, the dynamics of behavior, the observation, testing, and experimental study of behavior, and the application of psychological knowledge to such fields as employment, education, psychotherapy, and consumer behavior. 3. From an eclectic point of view, the science of the overt and covert behavior of living organisms. 4. From a behavioral point of view, the science of overt behavior. 5. Historically, the study of the mind and its functions. 6. In psychoanalytic theory, the study of the conscious and unconscious mind. 7. The science of the nature, functions, and phenomena of the human mind (formerly also of the soul). 8. In later and broader usage, includes: (a) the scientific study of the mind as an entity and its relationship to the physical body, based on observations of behavior and activity aroused by specific stimuli, and (b) the study of behavior of individuals or of selected groups of individuals in interaction with the environment. 9. (W. James) The science of Mental Life both of its "phenomena" and "conditions." 10. In 1874, Herbert Spenser divided psychol-

ogy into two types: "objective" (behavior) and "subjective" (mind). Types of psychology include: ABNORMAL, ACT, ADLERIAN, ADVERTISING, AEROSPACE, ANALYTIC, ANIMAL, APPLIED, ARCHITECTURAL, ARMCHAIR, ASSOCIATION, ATOMISTIC, AVIATION, BEHAVIOR(AL), BIO-, BUSINESS, CHILD, CLINICAL, COGNITIVE, COGNITIVE-BEHAVIORAL, COLLECTIVE, COLLEGE, COMMUNITY, COMPARATIVE, COMPARATIVE NEURO-, CONSTITUTIONAL, CONSULTING, CONSUMER, CONTENT, CORRECTIONAL, COURTROOM, CRIMINAL, CROSS-CULTURAL, CROWD, CULTURAL SCIENCE, DEPTH, DEVELOPMENTAL, DIALECTICAL, DIFFERENTIAL, DYNAMIC, ECOLOGICAL, EDUCATIONAL, EGO, EMPIRICAL, EMPLOYMENT, EMPTY ORGANISM, ENGENDERING, ENGINEERING, ENVIRONMENTAL, ETHNO-, EVOLUTIONARY, EXISTENTIAL, EXPERIMENTAL, EXPERIMENTAL SOCIAL, FACULTY, FOLK, FORENSIC, GANZHEIT, GENERAL, GENETIC, GENEVA SCHOOL OF GENETIC, GERO-, GESTALT, HEALTH, HERBARTIAN, HORMIC, HUMAN-FACTORS, HUMANISTIC, ID, IDIOGRAPHIC, IDIOTHETIC, INDIVIDUAL, INDUSTRIAL-ORGANIZATIONAL, INFORMATION PROCESSING, INTERBEHAVIORAL, INTROSPECTIVE, LEIPZIG SCHOOL OF GESTALT, LIBERATION, MANAGERIAL, MASS, MATHEMATICAL, MEDICAL, META-, MILITARY, MOB, NEGATIVE, NEURO-, NOMOTHETIC, OBJECTIVE, OLIGOPHRENO-, ONTOGENETIC, ORGANISMIC, PALEO-, PARA-, PEDIATRIC, PERSONALISTIC, PERSONALITY, PERSONNEL, PHILOSOPHICAL, PHYSIOLOGICAL, PROACTIVE, PSEUDO-, PSYCHOANALYTIC DEVELOPMENT, PUBLIC-SERVICE, RACE, RATIONAL, REACTION, REFLECTIVE, RESPONSE, S-R, SAFETY, SCHOOL, SCIENTIFIC, SELF-, SOCIAL, SOMATO-, SPECULATIVE, SPORTS, STIMULUS-RESPONSE (S-R), STRUCTURE, SUBJECTIVE, SUBJECTIVE-OBJECTIVE, THOMISTIC, TONE, TOPOGRAPHICAL, TOPOLOGICAL, TRANSPERSONAL, TYPHLO-, UNDERSTANDING, UR-, VARIATIONAL, VECTOR, VICTIMIZATION, WAR. See ANTHROPONOMY, PSYCHOLOGY DEFINITIONS.

psychology definitions   An overview of some historical definitions in chronological order to illustrate different views of this term:

1884 "The science of the soul." (J. McCosh)

1890 "The science of mental life, both of its phenomena and their conditions." (W. James)

1902 "The science of mental phenomena." (Collier's Encyclopedia)

1904 "The science of the mind, neither more nor less." (E. B. Titchener)

1913 "The positive science of the behavior of living things." (W. McDougall)

1929 "The science, which studies and explains the working of the mind." (C. E. Seashore & C. L. Hull)

1934 "The branch of science which investigates mental phenomena or mental operations." (H. Warren)

1940 "The science which deals with the mind and mental processes–consciousness, sensation, ideation, memory, etc." (L. E. Hinsie & R. J. Campbell)

1958 "A branch of science dealing with behavior, acts or mental processes. . ." (H. B. English)

1961 "The science that studies the behavior of animals and human beings." (C. Morgan)

1974 "The scientific discipline that deal with behavior

of man and other animals." (Encyclopedia Britannica)

1987 "The science of mind and behavior." (Merriam-Webster's Collegiate Dictionary)

1989 "The scientific study of behavior and conscious experience." (D. Coon)

1994 "The scientific study of mental processes, conscious and unconscious, as well as the behavior of living organisms." (*Encyclopedia of Psychology*)

The above definitions demonstrate that in most cases, the only thing that all commentators agreed on is that psychology is a science. Many early definitions mention only the "mind," whereas most subsequent definitions include "behavior." Apparently, the early psychologists viewed psychology as strictly covert operations whereas later ones, following John B. Watson, recognized overt behavior. Later attitudes assume a holistic combination of mind and body into a unitary conception of psychology. Note that only one definition explicitly mentions the unconscious.

psychology of religion   (W. James) The branch of psychology which investigates the phenomena of religion in the individual or in different human groups.

psycholytic   Literally, mind-releasing or mind-loosening; obsolete term once used to identify certain substances, such as psychedelic drugs, that have an effect on mental and emotional processes. Also spelled psychelytic.

psycholytic therapy   (H. Leuner) Outmoded technique of LSD therapy developed by H. Leuner, but almost completely discarded because of difficulty in controlling the drug reactions. Out-patients were given small doses of the drug in groups or individually, and psychological material elicited under its influence was analytically interpreted. See LSD PSYCHOTHERAPY.

psychometric approach   An assumption that understanding a person in depth can be obtained by an examination of that person's psychometric tests, especially those derived by factor analysis. See IDIOGRAPHIC APPROACH, NOMOTHETIC APPROACH.

psychometric examination   A series of psychological tests administered to determine intelligence, manual skills, personality characteristics, interests, or other mental factors.

psychometric function   psychophysical function

psychometrician   1. A specialist in the science of mental tests and in the evaluation of results. 2. A person who specializes in psychological measurements, either as a test constructor or as a test examiner. Also known as psychometrist (P).

psychometrics   1. Quantitative measurement of psychological characteristics through statistical techniques. See PSYCHOPHYSICS (meaning 2). 2. See PSYCHOMETRY (meaning 1).

psychometrist (P)   psychometrician

psychometrizing   psychometry (meaning 2)

psychometry   1. (C. Wolff) The science, fields, or process of measuring abilities and personality through psychological tests and statistics. Also known as psychometrics. 2. (J. Buchanan) In parapsychology, a practice in which a psychic uses an object to obtain paranormal information about it or about persons associated with it. Also known as psychometrizing. See PARAPSYCHOLOGY.

psychomimetics   psychotomimetic drugs

psychomimic syndrome   A condition in which a person develops symptoms of an illness actually suffered by another person, who may have died of the disorder. The mimicking person lacks any organic evidence of the illness, and the person who experienced the actual disease was usually ambivalently related to the patient. The symptoms usually occur around the anniversary of the death of the other person. See ANNIVERSARY REACTION, VOODOO DEATH.

psychomotility   A motor action or habit influenced or controlled by a mental process, for example, tics, handwriting, gait, stammering, or dysarthria, which may be signs of psychomotor disturbance.

psychomotor   Pertaining to mind combined with movement; motor activity induced by psychic action.

psychomotor action   1. Physical movement without intention based on a cognitive event, for example, thinking about an enemy and without being aware of it, making a fist. 2. An action or reaction that is the result of an idea or perception.

psychomotor agitation   A state of tense, restless physical and mental overactivity, as in agitated depression, may include wringing of hands, pacing the floor, bemoaning personal fate.

psychomotor attack   1. A brief temporal-lobe seizure characterized by extreme, sometimes violent, activity, for which there is complete amnesia. 2. See PSYCHOMOTOR EPILEPSY.

psychomotor disorder   A disturbance in the psychological control of movement; a motor disorder precipitated by psychological factors, such as epileptic seizures brought on by stress, temporal-lobe seizures (psychomotor epilepsy), psychomotor retardation associated with depression, and hyperactivity exhibited during a manic episode.

psychomotor epilepsy   A type of epilepsy characterized by a brief, trancelike, "dreamy" state accompanied by paramnesias (déjà vu, *jamais vu*), ill-defined hallucinations, chewing and swallowing movements, repetitive automatic activities, and in some cases feelings of rage or terror which may lead to violent behavior. Such patients although appearing to remain conscious, are unaware of their behavior during such episodes. The electroencephalogram (EEG) reveals characteristic spike discharges in the temporal lobe, hence the condition is also known as psychic equivalent, psychomotor attack, temporal-lobe epilepsy. See FUROR.

psychomotor excitement   A state of physical and mental overactivity characterized by extreme restlessness, flight of ideas, and pressure of speech. Most frequently found in the manic phase of bipolar disorder.

psychomotor hallucination   The false sensation that parts of the body are moving or being moved to different areas of the body.

psychomotor retardation   A general slowing (motor inhibition) of mental and physical activity most frequently observed in major depressions and catatonic schizophrenia. Patients sit for hours with folded hands, speak haltingly if at all, find it hard to concentrate and think, and feel that an enormous burden is holding them back.

psychomotor seizure A small seizure with loss of consciousness that lasts a minute or two. See PSYCHOMOTOR EPILEPSY.

psychomotor stimulants Old phrase similar to psychostimulants.

psychomotor tests 1. Tests which, although based on other psychological processes (for example, sensory, perceptual), require a motor reaction such as copying designs, building blocks, or manipulating controls. 2. Skill tests requiring a coordination of sensory processes with motor activities as in the Crawford Small Parts Dexterity Test, and the Minnesota Rate of Manipulation Test.

psychomusic See PSYCHODRAMA FORMS.

psychoneural parallelism psychophysical parallelism

psychoneuroendocrinology The study of the interactions of the nervous system, the endocrine system (the various glands that secrete hormones), and behavior. The interactions of the hypothalamus, the pituitary, and the adrenals have been of special interest in considering reactions to stress.

psychoneuroimmunology The study of the relation of the nervous system, psychological factors, and the immune system.

psychoneuromuscular theory A point of view that imagery facilitates subsequent performance by innervating the muscles similarly to the innervation that will be needed for the actual performance.

psychoneurosis (P. C. Dubois) Neurosis.

psychonomic Denoting an approach to psychology that emphasizes quantitative measurement, experimental control, and operational definitions.

psychonomics The science of the laws governing the mind, also of the environmental factors that influence development.

Psychonomic Society An organization whose object is "to promote the communication of scientific research in psychology and related sciences."

psychonosology The systematic classification of mental disorders. See NOSOLOGY.

psychonoxious (A. Hess) A person or condition that such a person induces which creates adverse feelings of distress odium, anxiety and dysfunction. See PSYCHOTOXIC.

psychopath (D. T. Lykken) An unsocialized person whose failure of socialization resulted largely from innate temperamental or "characteralized" peculiarities. Such persons are considered prone to antisocial tendencies such as lying, stealing, and cheating. See PSYCHOPATHY, SOCIOPATH.

Psychopathia Sexualis Phrase used by Richard von Krafft-Ebing for psychosexual abnormalities, and the title of his 1886 text that described and classified varieties of sexual behavior (and that used Latin for terms that were considered too distasteful for the public to read).

psychopathic drive (A. Hess) A putative drive observed when the psychopath is drawn to wreaking destruction even if it is clear the psychopath will be caught; a need to cause distress, also seen in the "Lokian personality" named after, Loki, the Norse god of turmoil, mischief and destruction. See LOKIAN PERSONALITY.

psychopathic personality See ANTISOCIAL REACTION.

psychopathic schizophrenia A form of schizophrenia in which psychotic tendencies are masked or overlaid by antisocial tendencies such as pathological lying, sexual deviations, and violent or other uninhibited behavior.

psychopathologist A medical or psychological professional person who studies the causes of mental disorders. See PSYCHOLOGICAL AUTOPSY, PSYCHOPATHOLOGY.

psychopathology (E. von Feuchtersleben) 1. The study of mental disorders. May involve biochemistry, pharmacology, psychiatry, neurology, cytology, experimental psychology, and other related subjects (topics). 2. The intrapsychic dynamics of a given condition, refers especially to the cognitive-affective realm, and including less centrally both the somatic or neurophysiological dynamics and family and cultural dynamics. 3. (J. Bentham) Psychological pathology.

psychopathy 1. Refers to behavior disorders such as character disorders, narcissism. 2. Broad term for any psychological disorder or mental disease, usually of an unspecified nature. 3. Obsolete term for the pathological condition of a person whose failure of socialization resulted largely from innate temperamental and "characteralized" peculiarities. Originally known as "moral insanity" by J. C. Pritchard until Adolf Meyer renamed this syndrome "constitutional psychopathic inferior," generating the impression of a hereditary basis. Later known as "antisocial personality disorder." See AUTISTIC PSYCHOPATH, CONSTITUTIONAL PSYCHOPATH.

Psychopathy Checklist-Revised (PCL-R) (R. Hare) A symptom-based scale used to rate psychopathy, often in forensic populations.

psychopedics Outmoded term for a branch of psychology that specializes in the psychological treatment and guidance of children. Similar to later phrases such as behavioral pediatrics, child psychiatry, child psychology.

psychopenetration test An outmoded examination of emotional flexibility or rigidity of a patient based on reactions to five questions during carbon-dioxide inhalation therapy. The questions are designed to elicit evidence of the degree of unconscious resistance to the concepts of sex, killing, attention, deceiving, and showing feelings. The reactions are used as a guide to therapeutic procedures. See CARBON-DIOXIDE INHALATION THERAPY.

psychopharmacological drugs Any medications used in the treatment of mental disorders. See PSYCHOPHARMACOLOGY.

psychopharmacology (D. I. Macht, N. W. Thorner) 1. The study of how medicines can affect experience and behavior. One of the most rapidly evolving areas in psychiatry as new agents are introduced and new indications (applications) are found for existing medicines. 2. Occasionally, the term is less precisely used to refer also to the treatment of psychiatric problems with medicines, though psychopharmacotherapy is more correct.

Psychopharmacology Demonstration Project (PDP) A project in the United States Department of Defense in which certain psychologists were given training in the administration of psychotropic medications.

psychopharmacotherapy   The use of pharmacologic agents in the treatment of mental disorders, for example, an acute psychotic reaction might warrant antipsychotic drugs and major tranquilizers, which will not cure the disorder but will provide significant relief from symptoms so that social rehabilitation and psychotherapeutic techniques may be employed with greater effectiveness.

psychophobia   Morbid fear of the mind, of thinking about the mind, or simply of thinking. See PHRONEMO-PHOBIA.

psychophysical dualism   A doctrine positing that mental processes have parallel organic and psychic aspects but that there is no interaction or causal relation between them. See PSYCHOPHYSICAL PARALLELISM.

psychophysical function   1. A psychometric relationship between a stimulus and judgments about the stimulus, as expressed in a mathematical formula. 2. The relationship of a physical entity to a psychological perception, such as the varying amount of light from a source, based on a meter versus the degree of illumination reported by an experimental participant. Also known as psychometric function.

psychophysical law/relationship   A mathematical relationship between the strength of a sensation and the intensity of the stimulus. The relationship is such that the sensation is generally at least roughly proportional to the logarithm of the stimulus.

psychophysical methods   Standard techniques used in investigating psychophysical problems, such as average error, equal-appearing intervals, and limits. See PSYCHOPHYSICS.

psychophysical parallelism   1. A doctrine positing that for every mental event there is a corresponding event in the nervous system. A variation of psychophysical dualism. An old philosophical position suggested by among others David Hartley and Gottfried Leibnitz. 2. An aspect of the mind-body issue in which the psyche and the physical aspects are considered to be in tandem perfectly correlated. Also known as psychoneural parallelism. See BODY-MIND DICHOTOMY, MIND-BODY PROBLEM, PSYCHOPHYSICAL DUALISM.

psychophysical relationship   psychophysical law

psychophysical scaling method   A procedure for establishing a subjective difference scale along some dimension such as loudness, pleasantness, pitch. See DIRECT SCALING, INDIRECT SCALING.

psychophysics   (G. T. Fechner, E. H. Weber) 1. The study of sensation as a function of the physical properties of stimulants. 2. A branch of psychology that deals with relationships between stimulus magnitudes, stimulus differences, and corresponding sensory processes. Quantitative measurement of the relation between experienced aspects of stimulation (such as brightness, loudness) and the characteristics of the stimulus, usually its intensity. See FECHNER'S LAW, WEBER'S LAW.

psychophysiologic(al) disorders   1. A somatic disorder with significant emotional or psychological origins. 2. See PSYCHOSOMATIC DISORDERS.

psychophysiology   The study of physiological relationships in normal and abnormal behavior. See PHYSIO-LOGICAL PSYCHOLOGY, PSYCHOSOMATIC MEDICINE.

psychopoetry   (A. Lerner) A technique that uses published poetry for the purpose of facilitating the expression and resolution of client feelings; also getting clients to express themselves through the writing of poetry for their own therapy. Also known as poetry therapy.

psychopolitics   (B. Wedge) 1. Research and action on the psychological aspects of political behavior, such as the effects on society of different types of leadership (democratic, fascist, socialist). 2. The use of psychological tactics or strategies by politicians. See POLITICAL PSYCHIATRY.

psychorelaxation   (E. Jacobson) A method of treating anxiety and tension by practicing general bodily relaxation, as in systematic desensitization. See AUTOGENIC TRAINING, RELAXATION THERAPY.

psychorrhea   A symptom of hebephrenic (disorganized) schizophrenia consisting of a stream of vague, bizarre, and usually incoherent theories of philosophy.

psychorrhexis   A war-time variation of anxiety neurosis in which the patient expresses anguish and perplexity rather than fear or excitement. Symptoms include a rapid pulse and slow breathing rate, fever, jaundice, restlessness, facial spasms, and automatic movements. The condition tends to affect persons with a previous labile sympathetic system who experience severe mental trauma while physically exhausted. Death may occur within a few days in some cases.

psychosciences   Sciences that deal with the mind and mental behavior, with mental diseases and disorders, and with their treatment and cure-in particular, psychology and psychiatry.

psychose passionnelle   French phrase similar to de Clérambault's syndrome.

psychosensory   Perception and interpretation of sensory stimuli.

psychosexual   The interaction of the physiosexual and psychological dimensions of human behavior.

psychosexual development   In psychoanalytic theory, the step-by-step growth of sexual life as it affects personality development. Different stages purportedly leave their mark on people's personality, especially if sexual development is fixated at a single stage. Also known as libidinal development.

psychosexual disorders   A group of disorders of sexual functioning that have a psychological rather than a physiological basis. Including sexual attitudes perceived as abnormal by individuals about their own sexuality and the sexuality of others. What is considered normal or abnormal at any time and place will differ in other times and places. See EGO-DYSTONIC HOMOSEXUALITY, GENDER-IDENTITY DISORDERS, PARAPHILIAS, PSYCHOSEXUAL DISORDERS NOT ELSEWHERE CLASSIFIED, PSYCHOSEXUAL DYSFUNCTIONS.

psychosexual dysfunctions   A group of sexual disorders characterized by an inability to complete any or all phases of the sexual-response cycle. May include inhibited sexual desire, inhibited sexual excitement, inhibited female orgasm, inhibited male orgasm, premature ejaculation, functional dyspareunia, functional vaginismus, and atypical psychosexual dysfunction.

psychosexual incongruity   Inconsistency among gender role, gender identity, and sexual anatomy.

psychosexual neutrality theory   A point of view that a human infant is born lacking a gender identity.

psychosexual stages   See PSYCHOSEXUAL DEVELOPMENT.

psychosexual trauma   A frightening, degrading, or otherwise traumatic sexual experience in earlier life (for example, incest or molestation) that is related to a current psychosexual dysfunction.

psychosis   1. A severe mental disorder of organic, psychological, functional cause, or the combination, that leads to bizarre mental states and behavior. Signs may include confusion, delusions, hallucinations, incoherence, phobias, mood swings, mutism, violence. 2. Loose term for various "insanities," such as the schizophrenias. 3. A severe emotional illness. Kinds of psychoses include: ACUTE DELUSIONAL, ACUTE PSYCHOTIC BREAK, ACUTE SHOCK, AFFECTIVE, AKINETIC, ALCOHOLIC PARANOIA, ALCOHOLIC PSYCHOSES, ALLOPSYCHOSIS, ALTERNATING, ANTIPSYCHOTICS, ATYPICAL, AUTISTIC, AUTOPSYCHOSIS, BARBEDWIRE, BIOGENIC, BORDERLINE, BRIEF REACTIVE, BROMIDE INTOXICATION, BUFFOONERY, CANNABIS, CARDIAC, CIRCULAR, CIRCULATORY, COLLECTIVE, DEGENERATIVE PSYCHOSES, DEPRESSIVE, DETERIORATIVE, DRUG-INDUCED, EXHAUSTIVE, EXOTIC, FAMILIAL, FOLIE A DEUX, FUNCTIONAL, FURLOUGH, GENERAL PARESIS, GERIOPSYCHOSIS, GOVERNESS, HYPOPSYCHOSIS, HYSTERICAL, IATROGENIC, INDUCED, INFECTIVE, INTERMITTENT, INVOCATIONAL, INVOLUTIONAL PSYCHOTIC REACTION, LATENT, MALIGNANT, MANIC-DEPRESSIVE ILLNESS, MODEL, MONOSYMPTOMATIC, MOOD-CONGRUENT PSYCHOTIC FEATURES, MOOD-INCONGRUENT PSYCHOTIC FEATURES, NEUROPSYCHOSIS OF DEFENSE, PARANOID PSYCHOSIS, PATHOS, POSTPARTUM, PRISON, PROTEST, PSEUDONEUROTIC SCHIZOPHRENIA, SCHIZOAFFECTIVE, SEMANTIC, SENILE PSYCHOSES, SEPTICEMIA, SHOCK, SITUATIONAL, SOMATOPSYCHOSIS, SYMBIOTIC, SYMPTOMATIC, TABETIC, TOXIC-INFECTIOUS, TOXIC, UNIPOLAR MANIC-DEPRESSIVE, UNIPOLAR. See ATYPICAL PSYCHOSIS, BRIEF REACTIVE PSYCHOSIS, SCHIZOAFFECTIVE DISORDER, SCHIZOPHRENIFORM DISORDER.

psychosis with cerebral arteriosclerosis   See MULTI-INFARCT DEMENTIA.

psychosis with mental retardation   The episodes of excitement, depression, hallucinations, or paranoia that occur occasionally in persons with mental impairment but are usually temporary.

psychosocial deprivation   Lack of adequate opportunity for social and intellectual stimulation, a significant factor in emotional disturbance and delayed mental development in children. See PSEUDORETARDATION.

psychosocial development   Recognition of the existence of others as total individuals that occurs in late infancy, evolving into independent interaction with others on the basis of reciprocity about age three into sophisticated relational patterns in adolescents and adulthood.

psychosocial dwarfism   Reversible retardation of bodily growth associated with behavioral symptoms that are also reversible upon change from an adverse living situation to a benign, salutary, therapeutic environment.

psychosocial effect   In research, an experimenter bias effect dependent on affecting experimental participants through moods and attitudes of data collectors. See EXPERIMENTER BIAS.

psychosocial factors   Social situations, relationships, and pressures that have psychological effects, such as business competition, rapid technological change, work deadlines, and changes in roles and status.

psychosocial mental developmental delay   Apparent slowing of mental development due to abnormal social conditions, such as being ignored or being prohibited from participating in activities considered normal for age. May be reversed.

Psychosocial Pain Inventory   (R. K. Heaton) Paper-and-pencil test that attempts to measure factors related to chronic pain; high scores imply less suitability for medical management.

psychosocial rehabilitation   Programs for people with injuries, disorders, or diseases with treatment for regaining their prior abilities at home or in benign communitarian settings.

psychosocial-sexual system   The complex of social, psychological, and cultural attitudes toward sexuality in all its forms that varies from society to society.

psychosocial stages   See ERIKSON'S STAGES OF PSYCHOSOCIAL DEVELOPMENT.

psychosocial stressor   A life situation that creates such severe stress (such as divorce, the death of a child, prolonged illness, change of residence, a natural catastrophe, or a highly competitive work situation) that it may contribute to the development or aggravation of a mental or social disorder.

psychosocial therapy   Psychological treatment techniques designed to help persons with emotional or behavioral disturbances to adjust to situations that require social interfacing with other members of the community. Psychosocial therapy generally is more important in city settings where the individual encounters more persons with different backgrounds and personalities than in a rural or village setting.

psychosomatic   (J. C. Heinroth, H. F. Dunbar) Characterizing a type of disorder that involves both the mind (psyche) and the body (soma), especially illnesses that are primarily physical with a psychological etiology.

psychosomatic disorder/illness   1. A disorder characterized by physical symptoms resulting from psychological factors, usually involving one system of the body, such as the gastrointestinal, respiratory, or genito-urinary. 2. Physical or structural changes in the body, presumably psychogenic in nature, that involve a single organ system usually under autonomic nervous system innervation characterized by backache, tension headache, insomia, bronchial asthma, paroxysmal tachycardia, migraine, peptic ulcer, heartburn, constipation, impotence, menstrual disorders.

psychosomatic illness (hypothesis)   (F. Alexander) A postulate that various major psychosomatic illnesses are due to specific psychological states. For instance, asthma (unresolved dependency); constipation (lack of social interest); duodenal ulcer (frustration); hives (dependency longing); essential hypertension (feelings of inferiority); migraine (repressed hostility); rheumatoid arthritis (repressed rebellion).

psychosomatic medicine (F. Alexander) A branch of medicine that evaluates an illness in terms of organic and psychological components. As most illnesses incorporate both organic and psychological factors, each case must be considered on the basis of the specific nature and relative importance of these factors.

psychosomatic suicide A self-destructive impulse occasionally observed in patients with ulcerative colitis and bronchial asthma, purportedly caused by intense frustration. Repression of this impulse may lead to a powerful attack that resists medical treatment.

psychosome An organism seen as having psychic and somatic aspects.

psychostimulants Drugs that stimulate the nervous system. In addition to cocaine and amphetamine, various street drugs, caffeine, over-the-counter sleep aids or appetite suppressants (containing ephedrine) and the medicines used to treat hyperactivity or ADHD in children and adults are for the most part psychostimulants.

psychosurgery 1. Surgery on the brain, with the intention of altering brain tissue to change the patient's thinking, behavior, or both, for example, prefrontal lobotomy and the use of supercold temperature to freeze certain brain tissues (cryogenics). 2. Removal or the cutting apart of specific areas of the brain to alleviate pain or arrest severe behavioral disorders such as epileptic seizures. See HEMISPHERECTOMY, LOBECTOMY, LOBOTOMY.

psychosynthesis 1. (S. Potter) As a general movement, an attempt to unify and harmonize various components of the unconscious, such as dreams, fantasies, and instinctual strivings with the rest of the personality. This principle was advocated by Carl Jung and termed constructive approach, in contrast to Sigmund Freud's reductive approach. 2. (R. Assagioli) As a psychotherapy, a system that builds on psychoanalysis but, according to Roberto Assagioli, tries to complete what psychoanalysis started. An essential aspect of this system is its philosophic emphasis on values. It aimed for "up" as well as "down" as Sigmund Freud had tried. It has close ties to the theories of Alfred Adler, and to Freudian revisionists such as Karen Horney and also to existentialists and humanists.

psychotechnics 1. The application of psychological principles to alter or control behavior. 2. The practical application of psychological principles in economics, sociology, and business. 3. Hugo Munsterberg's term for applied psychology.

psychotechnology A body of psychological facts and principles involved in the practical applications of psychology.

psychotherapeutic processes See PSYCHOTHERAPIES.

psychotherapies See APPENDIX E.

psychotherapist A person professionally trained to treat mental, emotional, and behavioral disorders.

psychotherapy Any systematic methodology based on some theory of personality intended to achieve desirable changes in thinking feeling and behavior. More than 400 different systems of psychotherapy have been identified. See APPENDIX E for a list of types of (psycho)therapy. See INTEGRITY GROUPS, MAINSTREAMING, MEDITATION, MULTIPLE IMPACT TRAINING.

psychotherapy by reciprocal inhibition See RECIPROCAL INHIBITION.

psychotic 1. Pertaining to a psychosis or psychoses. 2. As a noun, a person afflicted with a psychosis.

psychotic character A borderline psychotic disorder in which the pathological individual is able to maintain a relationship with others who remain unaware of the disorder due to the fact that the individual gratifies their repressed wishes (for example, a group may elevate a megalomanic individual to a position of leadership because of their need for hero worship).

psychotic-depressive reaction A psychosis of depressed mood, generally precipitated by situational factors in a person without a history of recurrent depression. See MAJOR DEPRESSION.

psychotic disorder psychosis

psychotic disorders not elsewhere classified See ATYPICAL PSYCHOSIS, BRIEF REACTIVE PSYCHOSIS, SCHIZOAFFECTIVE DISORDER, SCHIZOPHRENIFORM DISORDER.

Psychotic Inpatient Profile (M. Lorr) Test that attempts to measure 12 syndromes of adult psychiatric patients. Paper-and-pencil, it is answered by a trained attendant.

psychoticism A factor developed by Hans Eysenck as a means of assessing the dimensions of personality that includes a disposition toward psychosis and psychopathy, distinguishing persons considered normal, schizophrenic, or manic-depressive from each other. The system uses tests of judgment of spatial distance, reading speed, level of proficiency in mirror drawing, and adding rows of numbers.

psychotic mannerisms Behavior that indicates to others that the person is mentally ill. Evident lack of responses or inappropriate reactions (for example, mutism, repetition of silly statements, facial contortions, nonresponding to questions, strange body movements).

psychotogenic 1. An agent that induces psychosis or signs and symptoms that resemble manifestations of psychoses. Hallucinogenic drugs are capable of producing psychotogenic states marked by sensory illusions, distortions, and hallucinations, accompanied by a loss of control, paranoid delusions, intense depression, or an overwhelming flood of anxiety. 2. Pertaining to the action of a psychotomimetic drug. See PSYCHEDELICS.

psychotogens Obsolete term for psychotomimetic drugs.

psychotomimetic drug (J. Gerard) Drugs now classed as psychedelics or hallucinogens but originally used in laboratory experiments to determine if they could induce psychoses, or states mimicking psychoses, on the basis of their psychogenic effects. The group includes LSD. Psychomimetics also include amphetamine drugs which in cases of chronic abuse can lead to compulsive behavior patterns, violence, paranoia, and other psychotic symptoms. Also known as psychomimetics, psychotomimetics. See PHANEROTHYME, PSYCHEDELICS.

psychotoxic (A. Hess) A person, compound, object, or condition that induces a person to experience distress, dysfunction, anger, odium, dislike, and anxiety. See PSYCHONOXIOUS.

psychotropic drug   Any medicine that has a primary effect on mood, behavior, thought, or other mental processes. Major classes of psychotropics include antipsychotic drugs, anti-anxiety drugs, stimulants, sedative-hypnotics, and antidepressants. Drugs of abuse such as the opioids and hallucinogens are also psychotropic. Generally excluded are substances that may have mind-altering effects although that is not their primary function. See PSYCHOACTIVE.

psychrophobia   Morbid fear of the cold or a cold object. Also known as cheima(to)phobia, cheimophobia, cryophobia, psychropophobia.

Psy.D.   See DOCTOR OF PSYCHOLOGY.

Pt   See PATIENT.

PT   1. physical therapy. 2. See PHYSIOTHERAPY. 3. See PATIENT.

PTA   1. See POSTTRAUMATIC AMNESIA. 2. parent-teachers' association.

P-technique   1. (R. B. Cattell) A factor analytic technique that compares a person's scores on several measures in different situations and at various times. See FACTOR ANALYSIS. 2. Factor analysis for data varying over time. See Q METHODOLOGY, R METHODOLOGY.

pteronophobia   Morbid fear of feathers. See ORNITHOPHOBIA.

ptosis   A sinking or drooping of an organ or part of the body. Term is usually applied to a drooping eyelid associated with paralysis of the third cranial nerve. The condition may also occur in persons who are anemic or those with a neurosis on awakening. Plural is ptoses. See PROLAPSE.

PTP   posttetanic potentiation

PTSD   See POSTTRAUMATIC STRESS DISORDER.

puberism puberty

pubertal sexual recapitulation theory   A point of view that the beginning of adult sexuality development at puberty involves a recapitulation of the stages of infantile sexuality. Assumes that sexuality at puberty first must regress toward the infantile state to recapitulate.

pubertal stage   (J. Piaget) A period of development during which instinctual forces move a person toward the choice of a love object, usually a member of the opposite sex.

puberty   Attainment of sexual maturity, the developmental stage when hormones trigger the maturation of the genital organs and the appearance of secondary sexual characteristics. Occurs from about 11 to 13 years of age in females and 12 to 14 years of age in males, and is marked by ejaculation of sperm in the male, onset of menstruation and development of breasts in the female, and growth of pubic hair; also an increasing interest in the opposite sex in both genders. Also known as puberism. See PERSISTENT PUBERISM, PRECOCIOUS PUBERTY.

puberty praecox   Puberty occurring at an early age. Also known as pubertas precox.

puberty rites   Initiation into adult life of a pubescent member of a community through ceremonies, cultural-lore indoctrination, and similar customs. In some societies, part of such ceremonies may involve mutilation or scarification of the genitalia. See CIRCUMCISION, CLITORIDECTOMY, GENITAL MUTILATION, PUBIC RITE.

pubescence   The period or process of reaching puberty. Also known as pubescency.

pubescent growth spurt   The rapid development of bone and muscle in response to a surge in somatotropin (growth hormone). See PUBERTY.

pubic rite   A puberty rite in which a part of the ceremony may involve mutilation or scarification of the genitalia. See PUBERTY RITES.

public-criticism fear   See HOMILOPHOBIA.

public-distance zone   In social psychology, the area of physical distance between persons in formal, official, or ceremonial interactions. The public-distance zone is defined from 3½ to 7½ m (11½ to 24½ ft.). See PERSONAL-DISTANCE ZONE, PROXEMICS.

public-health approach   Mental and physical health revolving around three prime concepts: (a) the host, or vulnerable individual (in terms of general health, past history, genetic makeup, etc.); (b) the relevant environment (including its stressful aspects, both physical and psychological); and (c) the agent (the specific modality or sequence of environmental events that results in an identifiable disease or disorder such as syphilitic infection producing general paresis). The approach also focuses on levels of prevention (primary, secondary, tertiary), the prevalence of different diseases, and identification of high-risk groups.

public-health nurse   A graduate of a professional nursing school who has received additional special training in public-health services. A public-health nurse is concerned with the health of individuals or populations in their own environment, such as home, work, or school. Such a nurse often has a graduate degree in public-health science.

public micturition dysfunction   See BASHFUL BLADDER SYNDROME.

public opinion   A general attitude of a population toward a specific issue or group of issues, whether correct or incorrect (for example, in tenth-century Europe, the general belief was that the sun rose in the morning and set in the evening and that the earth did not move).

public-opinion poll/survey   An attitude survey administered to a representative sample of a given population to discover the distribution of beliefs on particular issues. The validity of polls is affected by such factors as sampling techniques, wording of questions, interviewer effects, and respondents' needs for answers that reflect social desirability.

public relations (PR)   Generally, the use of publicity to represent a corporation or individual in a favorable light.

public self   An aspect of self as known to others. See JOHARI WINDOW.

public-service psychology   An area of psychology that focuses on problems encountered by psychologists employed full-time in federal, state, and local government agencies.

public-speaking anxiety   Feelings of tension, fear, and apprehension when speaking, especially in a formal presentation, to a group. Probably affects most people; commonly known as stage fright.

public territory   In social psychology, a public space temporarily used by a person or group, for example, a park bench or bus seat. See PROXEMICS.

pudendum   1. External genital organs, especially of females. 2. See VULVA.

pubescence   The period or process of reaching puberty. Also known as pubescency.

PUD   peptic ulcer disease

puer aeternus   (eternal boy—Latin) (C. G. Jung) Jungian phrase for the archetype of eternal youth.

puerilism   Immature, childish behavior characteristic of the stage between the infantile and puberty phases of development; a behavior pattern observed frequently in immature personalities. See HYSTERICAL PUERILISM, IMMATURE PERSONALITY.

puerperal disorders   Pathological conditions occurring during the giving of birth that extends from the termination of labor to the return of the uterus to its normal condition. Puerperal disorders of personality include schizophrenic and depressive reactions and, occasionally, manic episodes or delirious states precipitated by infection, hemorrhage, exhaustion, or toxemia. See POSTPARTUM EMOTIONAL DISTURBANCES, POSTPARTUM PSYCHOSIS.

puerperal psychosis   Rare name for postpartum psychosis.

Puerto Rican syndrome   A culture-specific syndrome occurring in Puerto Rico under the name of *mal de pelea* (fighting sickness—Spanish). As in *amok*, the individual goes off by himself and broods, then suddenly and apparently without provocation becomes violent and strikes out at anyone nearby. Unlike *amok*, the episode usually subsides before anyone is killed.

Pulfrich effect/phenomenon   (C. P. Pulfrich) A visual illusion of seeing a pendulum swinging in an elliptical pattern when viewed through a visual filter.

pull-out program   The process in which a student with a disability is removed from the general classroom into a special teaching environment for at least part of the school day.

pulse reactor   A person whose reaction to a stressful situation is manifested by changes in the circulatory system, as indicated by altered pulse strength and rate. Some pulse reactions are a normal fight-or-flight type of autonomic response.

pulvinar   A large nucleus that forms the dorsal posterior region of the thalamus. It is an association nucleus. The input of the pulvinar is derived from other thalamic nuclei, particularly from the lateral (visual) and medial (auditory) geniculate nuclei as well as the ventral posterior (touch) nuclei. The pulvinar projects to the posterior parietal and posterior temporal lobes.

pun   A play on words based on a double meaning (double entendre). Puns range from the lowest form of humor ("Upun my word") to an incisive and creative form of wit, as in Benjamin Franklin's statement "We must all hang together, or assuredly we shall all hang separately." From a pathological point of view, puns are a common product of the flight of ideas that occurs in manic episodes. Like other forms of humor, puns frequently release latent hostilities or sexual impulses. See JOKE.

punch-drunk   Casual phrase describing a person who has suffered cerebral injury due to repeated blows to the head, usually said in reference to veteran pugilists. See BOXER'S DEMENTIA.

punctate   Marked with dots or points, pertaining to parts of the skin that contains points sensitive to a tactile stimulus. See ESTHESIOMETRY to see how punctate spots are found on the surface of the skin.

punctate sensitivity   In the study of skin senses, greater sensitivity in certain spots of the skin than in others. The phenomenon distinguishes four primary senses among the skin senses: pain, touch, cold, and warmth. See SKIN MAPPING for an illustration.

punding   Compulsive, stereotyped, purposeless searching and grooming behavior of a person who overuses amphetamines.

pungent   (J. D. Amoore et al.) One of the seven basic smell qualities in the stereochemical smell theory; vinegar is a typical example.

punishment   1. In general, the administration of pain or loss as retribution for wrongful deeds. 2. In operant conditioning, a stimulus that inflicts discomfort for failure to make the proper response, resulting in a decreased probability that the improper response will recur. Kinds of punishment include: EXPIATORY, MIDAS, POSITIVE, RECIPROCAL, SELF-, SOCIAL, VICARIOUS. See BEHAVIOR MODIFICATION, EFFECTS OF PUNISHMENT ON EXTINCTION, NEED FOR PUNISHMENT, REINFORCEMENT, SELF-PUNISHMENT.

punishment fear   See POINEPHOBIA.

punishment oriented   See MORAL REASONING.

punk   1. Slang for a young man who allows older men to use him sexually, often for money. See WOLF. 2. A male prostitute.

pupillary reflex   (R. Whytt) The automatic change in size of the pupil in response to light changes or a change of fixation point. Also known as light reflex.

pupillometer   An optical device for measuring the diameter of the pupil.

pupillometrics   (E. Hess) The measurement of changes in the size of the pupils of the eyes as a function of sympathetic nervous system arousal.

pupillometry   The photographic recording and measurement of pupil diameters, usually as they change due to emotions or intensity of stimuli.

pupilloscope   retinoscope

pupil of eye   An aperture in the eye through which light passes to the retina. Located in front of the lens but at the back of the anterior chamber containing aqueous humor. The size of the opening is controlled by a circle of muscle innervated by fibers of the autonomic nervous system.

puppetry therapy   The use of puppets as a projective form of play therapy.

puppy love   Casual phrase for romantic feelings an adolescent has toward another, usually of a different gender. It is usually highly idealized, intense and transient, but nevertheless a sign of growing emotional maturity. See CALF LOVE, LOVE.

Purdue tests   (J. Tiffin) A series of tests used in vocational guidance and the selection of industrial personnel. Include both paper-and-pencil and performance tests. The latter measure perceptual-motor skills, mechanical adaptability, and hand-finger-arm dexterity; a well-known example is the Purdue Pegboard Test. See PEGBOARD.

pure alexia   An inability to read, without the ability, to write. Caused by brain damage.

pure color   The appearance of a color when fully saturated.

pure erotomania   See DE CLÉRAMBAULT'S SYNDROME.

pure line   A genetic line of organisms descended from a common ancestor through self-fertilization, which continue to breed true regardless of environmental differences. Some laboratory rats are an example of a pure line.

pure meaning   (L. Vygotsky) The final union of language and thought in adult reasoning. According to Lev Vygotsky, language and thought begin as independent processes but coalesce around age two, leading to the development of egocentric speech, inner speech, verbal thought, concept development, and eventually pure meaning.

pure phi phenomenon   Phrase sometimes used for the more specific meaning of phi phenomenon to distinguish it from the more general concept of phi motion.

pure research   Research designed to answer a theoretical or academic question, or to develop a theory, not intended or expected to have any social or economic value. Compare APPLIED RESEARCH.

pure science   Research for the sake of knowledge. Compare APPLIED SCIENCE.

pure speed test   See SPEED TEST.

pure-stimulus act   1. (C. L. Hull) An act that does not move an organism toward its goal although it does activate proprioceptive stimuli that initiate the appropriate operant response. 2. An act preparatory and intermediate to the achievement of a response. See HULL'S THEORY.

pure strategy   In game theory, a set of directions to be followed according to a pregame plan, in which one of the competitors makes a decision to play the game in the same way each time, as in playing for the "least loss" on each play.

pure tone   A tone produced by a simple vibration, for example, a tuning-fork tone. See TUNING FORK for an illustration of this instrument.

pure-tone audiometer   An instrument that produces and transmits sounds to the ear, controlled on pitch and decibel scales.

pure-tone audiometry   A technique of measuring hearing loss using an instrument with electronically generated tones whose intensity is controlled by an attenuator. Hearing loss is expressed as the number of decibels in excess of the lowest intensity at which the normal ear can detect the tone. The tones are presented to each ear via head phones, at controlled frequencies.

purism vs utilitarianism   (R. I. Watson) A prescriptive dimension of the philosophical underpinnings of psychology, namely, focusing on knowledge for its own sake versus emphasis on the usefulness of knowledge. See OPPONENT-PAIRS DIMENSION.

Puritan complex   obscenity-purity complex

puritanical attitude   Inflexible adherence to a rigid moral code, including the tendency to hold others to perfectionistic standards. Characteristic of individuals with compulsive personalities. See OBSCENITY-PURITY COMPLEX.

Purkinjé afterimage   (J. E. Purkinjé) A second positive visual aftersensation that appears most plainly in the hue complementary to that of the primary sensation. Obtained by first fixating on a bright light and then closing the eyes, an afterimage of the same color as the original stimulus image will be seen, followed by a second brief afterimage of a complimentary color of the original stimulus. Also known as Bidwell's ghost. See AFTERIMAGE.

Purkinjé cell   (J. E. Purkinjé) The principal neuron of the cerebellar cortex. It has an extensive dendritic arborization and sends its axon to the deep nuclei of the cerebellum or, less frequently, to the vestibular nuclei. Purkinjé cell degeneration is associated with impaired coordination, tremors when movement is initiated, and reduced speed of movement.

Purkinjé figures   (J. E. Purkinjé) Shadowy images on the retina created by its blood-vessel network.

Purkinjé phenomenon/shift   (J. E. Purkinjé) 1. A shift in peak sensitivity from the red end of the spectrum during intense light to the blue end of the spectrum with dim light. 2. A visual phenomenon in which colors appear to change with the level of illumination; for example, a rose may appear to be a bright red and its leaves a bright green at the beginning of twilight, then gradually the red color may appear to change to black and the green to gray as the level of daylight declines, affecting the brilliance of the red end of the spectrum before the blue end.

Purkinjé-Sanson images   (J. E. Purkinjé, L. J. Sanson) Three reflected images of a fixated object produced by the surface of the cornea and the front and back of the lens.

Purkyne   See PURKINJÉ.

puromycin   An antibiotic. Because it is a protein synthesis inhibitor, puromycin has been used in some learning experiments to determine a possible molecular basis for memory.

purposeful accident   An "accident" that a person causes deliberately, such as dropping and breaking a dish because the person does not want to wash dishes. Compare PURPOSIVE ACCIDENT.

purposeful behavior   Actions aimed at achieving a consciously intended goal.

Purpose in Life (PIL)   (J. C. Crumbaugh) A short paper-and-pencil test that attempts to measure the degree to which an adult has life goals, based on "will to meaning."

purposeless hyperactivity   A symptom of certain forms of organic brain disease characterized by exaggerated emotional responses or prolonged periods of excessive activity that has no purpose. Also known as occupational delirium.

purposive accident   A mishap assumed to be motivated by unacknowledged wishes or needs such as to express resentment, punish the self, and cause self-injury to obtain sympathy. Also known as intentional accident. Compare PURPOSEFUL ACCIDENT. See PARAPRAXIS.

purposive behaviorism   (E. C. Tolman) A combination of gestalt (field) concepts with behaviorism applied primarily to the study of animal learning. In maze-running, the animal creates a cognitive map out of sign gestalts from environmental cues and goal expectations. This involves place-learning (learning to go to a particular place rather than learning a particular movement, starting from the same place), reward expectancy, and latent learning (incidental learning, without reward). The total process involves a combination of variables: physiological drive, environmental stimuli, heredity, previous training, and maturity or age. See HORMIC PSYCHOLOGY, LATENT LEARNING, PLACE-LEARNING, REWARD EXPECTANCY.

purposive manipulation   The systematic control of an independent variable in an experiment. Contrasted with selection of independent variable values. See INDEPENDENT VARIABLE CONTROL.

purposive(ness)   1. In general, the view that purposes are effective determiners of behavior; that behavior can be explained by its being directed toward specific goals. 2. (E. C. Tolman) An important principle of Edward Tolman's theory of behavior stating that learning is rationally directed and involves hypotheses, expectations, explicit goals, etc. 3. (A. Adler) In personality theory, the view that a main motivator is expectancy. Also known as purposivism. See HORMIC PSYCHOLOGY, INDIVIDUAL PSYCHOLOGY, TELEOLOGY.

purposive psychology   Hormic psychology

purposive sampling   A sampling procedure in which the investigator seeks to obtain representative samples by selecting individuals according to the investigator's judgment rather than by random methods.

purposive view (of motivation)   A theory that people imagine the future in terms of available alternatives, and choose the one whose anticipated outcomes are the most desirable.

purposivism   Any type of psychological system which holds that purposes in some sense are, in addition to stimuli, effective determinants of behavior. See PURPOSIVE(NESS).

pursuitmeter   A moving target that a participant is to follow. Also spelled pursuit meter.

pursuit pendulum   A swinging pendulum whose movement a participant is to follow.

pursuit rotor   A dish-sized disk with a contact spot (target) near the edge. The participant attempts to keep a hand-held stylus touching the target as the disk rotates at an increasing, controlled rate; the total time out of contact is recorded. Other versions require following a moving light around a square, circular, or triangular pattern. Used to test hand and arm control for vocational evaluation, research, and demonstration of learning principles. Also known as pursuitmeter.

pursuit rotor

putamen   (K. F. Burdach) A subcortical structure of the forebrain. A part of the lenticular nucleus lateral to the globus pallidus; with the caudate nucleus it forms the neostriatal portion of the basal ganglia. Receives input from the neocortex and is involved in control of movement.

putative   1. Accepted as real or true. 2. Hypothesized or inferred. An explanation usually of errant behavior in terms of internal states that impel the individual to usual actions. An example would be the behavior of persons diagnosed with antisocial personality disorder. See LOKIAN PERSONALITY, PSYCHOPATHIC DRIVE.

putrid   1. (H. Henning) A quality of olfactory sensation of which rotten meat is a typical example. A foul odor found in Henning's odor prism. 2. (J. D. Amoore et al.) One of the seven primary qualities of smell in the stereochemical smell theory. Usually described as an unpleasant stink, due to putrefaction of organic matter. Also known as rotten.

puzzle box   (E. L. Thorndike) A box in which an animal can be confined and from which an escape is possible by performing some arbitrary response, originally used by Thorndike in studying animal learning. See THORNDIKE PUZZLE BOX.

puzzling leap   See PROTOPSYCHE.

pycnodysostosis   An autosomal-recessive syndrome characterized by dense but defective bones, open skull sutures, and short stature. The patients rarely reach an adult height of five feet, and about 20% are likely to have mental retardation. Also known as pyknodysostosis.

Pygmalion effect   Rosenthal effect

pygmalionism   Falling in love with a personal creation. Name derives from Pygmalion in Greek mythology who fell in love with the statue he carved of Aphrodite. See ROSENTHAL EFFECT.

pygmyism   A constitutional anomaly consisting of a dwarfed but well-proportioned body, roughly equivalent to the primordial nanosomia body type. It is a typical body build for certain groups of people known as "pygmies," particularly in central Africa. Communities of similar small people have been described in myths and ancient literatures of Europe.

pyknic (body) type   (E. Kretschmer) A short, thickset, stocky type of person who, according to Ernst Kretschmer, tends to be jovial, extroversive, and subject to mood swings (manic-depressive behavior or cyclothymic temperament). See CONSTITUTIONAL TYPE.

pyknodysostosis   pycnodysostosis

pyknoepilepsy   Short-stare epilepsy. See PYKNOLEPSY, SHORT-TERM EPILEPSY.

pyknolepsy   A form of petit mal epilepsy, or a condition related to it, in which children below the age of seven experience frequent, brief clouding or interruption of consciousness, with the eyes turning upwards and the arms and trunk suddenly stiffening. The condition usually clears up spontaneously.

pyramidal cell   1. Principal neuron of the cerebral neocortex and of the hippocampus. The cell body is pyramidal in shape. Typically a single long dendrite with multiple branches arises from the apex of the pyramid and several dendrites arise from the base. The axon leaves the area of the cell body to terminate in another region of the central nervous system. 2. A neuronal cell so named because of its pyramidal shape. Pyramidal cells in the motor cortex of the frontal lobes give rise to voluntary motor impulses. Impulses travel downward in pyramidal tracts. See PYRAMIDAL SYSTEM.

pyramidal system/tract   (P. E. Flechsig) Axons of cortical neurons that originate in the motor area of the cortex, the premotor area, somatosensory area, and the frontal and parietal lobes and extend through the internal capsule, the crus cerebri, the pons and the pyramids of the medulla. The pyramidal tract crosses on the ventral surface of the posterior medulla and continues in the lateral part of the contralateral spinal cord. The pyramidal tract fibers communicate with neurons that innervate the peripheral muscles. See EXTRAPYRAMIDAL MOTOR SYSTEM.

pyramids   Bulges on the front of the medulla in which the dorsolateral tract crosses from one side of the brain to the opposite side of the spinal cord. See DORSOLATERAL TRACT.

pyrexiophobia   Fear of fever. Also known as febriphobia.

pyrolagnia   The arousal of sexual excitement by large fires or conflagrations. Also known as erotic pyromania.

pyromania   1. A morbid love of fire. 2. Compulsive fire-setting behavior. See FIRE-SETTING BEHAVIOR, INCENDIARISM, PYROLAGNIA.

pyrophobia   Morbid fear of fire.

q 1. proportion in a sample. 2. space error. 3. proportion not in the class in question.

Q 1. question. 2. questionnaire. 3. quotient. 4. semi-quartile range or quartile deviation. 5. coefficient of association. 6. luminous energy. 7. in Rorschach test scoring, a symbol for self-doubt or subject. 8. quantitative test. See ACE TEST. 9. See COULOMB.

QALYs See QUALITY ADJUSTED LIFE YEARS.

QD *quaque die*, Latin for every day.

Q-data (R. B. Cattell) Information about a person gathered from responses to questionnaires and interviews. Compare T-DATA.

QEB Quantitative Electrophysiological Battery

qEEG See QUANTITATIVE ELECTROENCEPHALOGRAPH.

QID *quater in die*, Latin for four times a day (also abbreviated **q.i.d., Q.I.D.**)

Q method The use of questionnaires to obtain information.

Q methodology Factor analysis across individuals rather than across tests. Q methodology will show how individuals cluster together in their ratings or responses, but does not show how traits, abilities, or other test patterns cluster together. Also known as inverted factor analysis, Q-technique. See FACTOR ANALYSIS, INVERTED FACTOR ANALYSIS, R METHODOLOGY.

QNF quadruple neuromuscular facilitation

QNST Quick Neurological Screening Test, also the QNST-2 or Quick Neurological Screening Test-2.

QRS complex The "high blip" on a cardiogram following the P wave.

Q sort (W. Stephenson) A self-reporting technique used primarily in personality assessment. The person is asked to sort a series of statements or trait names into categories, ranging, for example, from "least characteristic of —," to "most characteristic of —." The number of categories is determined by the examiner. Q sorts can be used to make comparisons between different factors, such as a person's opinion of the "real" and "ideal" selves, or the difference between a person's self-view and a spouse's view of the person. Q sorts can be correlated to yield a mathematical indicator of degree of agreement of the sorts. Also known as Q-sort.

QT Quick Test

Q-technique (W. Stephenson) Factoring of correlations between persons rather than tests. Originally called inverse factor analysis.

Quaalude Trade name for methaqualone. Also known in slang as 'lude. See 'LUDE, METHAQUALONE.

quack Slang for an unqualified or incompetent practitioner, particularly medical. Also known as charlatan.

quadrangular therapy Marital therapy with four people present, usually both spouses and the therapists of each.

quadrigeminum One of the corpora quadrigemina, the colliculus superior or the colliculus inferior.

quadriplegia Paralysis of all four limbs, a condition usually associated with severe cerebral palsy or spinal injury that results in loss of sensation and of voluntary motion from the neck down. Also known as tetraplegia. See PERSON WITH A DISABILITY.

quadroon Obsolete racist term associated with the southern United States for a person with one African American and three non-African American grandparents.

quadruple neuromuscular facilitation (QNF) In exercise physiology, the facilitatory effects during bidirectional double concentric contractions.

quadruped A four-footed animal (such as a cat), as opposed to a biped, or two-footed animal (such as a human).

quale (what kind—Latin) A sense datum or item of experience observed without reference to its context or significance. The unique quality of an experience for any person, for example, when two people see a certain color and they both identify it as "red" they may both have subjective experiences of different qualities but both identify the phenomenon as red. Plural is qualia.

qualia Plural of quale. Structuralists felt that qualia constitute the basic data of psychology, whereas Gestaltists doubted their existence.

qualitative data 1. Information about differences not expressed as quantities; characteristics determining different kinds rather than sizes, such as distinctions between males and females, animals and humans. 2. Used in experiential or phenomenological research to refer to a specific type of data collection and analysis reflecting the fact that human experience cannot be quantified. This research is often done in ecologically natural settings.

qualitative development   The emergence or appearance of a new form of behavior (for example, the development of object permanence) that cannot be measured with a previous standard of measurement. Compare QUANTITATIVE DEVELOPMENT.

qualitative judgment   See VALUE JUDGMENT.

qualitative variable   A variable described in terms of its quality or qualities rather than its quantity. Statistically, a variable not measurable by hard, fast rules of a number system. The chi-square statistic and its related C^2, indicating a strength of relationship or index of association, can be used to advantage with qualitative variables. See CHI-SQUARE.

quality   The character or characteristics of a sensation or other entity that makes it unique; a difference in kind rather than quantity, as between various sounds of the same note played on different instruments. Types of quality include: DEPENDENT-PART, DETERMINING, FORM, PRIMARY, SECONDARY, SENSE, VOICE. See DIMENSIONS OF CONSCIOUSNESS.

quality adjusted life years (QALYs)   In health economics, a measure that incorporates an assessment of quality of life (usually defined in terms of physical mobility and comfort) into life expectancies.

quality assessment/assurance   Evaluation of the quality of a service in terms of effectiveness, appropriateness, acceptability, efficacy, adequacy of diagnostic evaluation, length of stay, and measures of outcome.

quality circle   A group, usually in business or industry, that meets to plan how to improve a process or product. Originated in Japan, where managers and employees would sit in a circle at weekly meetings. Led to the development of Theory Z and the use of "Z teams." See THEORY X, THEORY Y, THEORY Z.

quality complex   A concoction of ideas, memories, dreams, adding up to uncertainty of reality.

quality control   A general term referring to improving the quality of manufactured goods in particular.

quality of worklife (QWL) movement/program   Started in the United States in the 1970s as a loose network of academics, by the 1980s had grown into an international grouping of trade unionists, managers, and social scientists into a cooperative program of employees and managers to enhance job satisfaction and morale by improving the physical and especially the psychological aspects of the job. Emphasizes worker participation in job design, improved communication, job security, reducing stressors, and providing job enrichment. See INDUSTRIAL DEMOCRACY, JOB ENRICHMENT.

quanta   Plural of quantum.

quantal   Refers to a variable that varies in predictable discrete steps.

quantal hypothesis   A postulate that sensations occur in discrete steps, and not in a smooth continuum. See QUANTUM THEORY.

quantitative approach   Based on Edward Thorndike's concept that if a phenomenon exists it can be measured. The doctrine, advanced by Sigmund Freud, that mental processes such as tensions, obsessions, pleasure, and unpleasure, differ in quantity as well as quality. Even though the amounts cannot be measured as exactly as in the physical sciences, they nevertheless exist, for example, the level of tension existing in the psyche today can be compared with the amount last week through subjective judgment, and also objective measurement by using such instruments as a psychogalvanometer. See BIOFEEDBACK, BIOFEEDBACK TRAINING.

quantitative conservation   (J. Piaget) The awareness that changing the arrangement of elements does not change the number of elements.

quantitative data   Events assigned certain well-defined, discrete, numerical values for the purpose of data processing.

quantitative development   A change that can be measured with a common metric over the course of time, as in measuring height changes in centimeters. Compare QUALITATIVE DEVELOPMENT.

quantitative electroencephalograph (qEEG)   A technique for neuromapping multiple analytic variables, usually from 20 electrode placements. Yields a multicolored, spectral-activity, topographic map that reflects activity pattern, coherence, and phase. See ELECTROENCEPHALOGRAM, ELECTROENCEPHALOGRAPH.

Quantitative Electrophysiological Battery (QEB)   In neurometrics, a computer analysis of evoked brain potentials recorded as the participant is confronted with a series of changes in the environment, called challenges. See NEUROMETRICS.

quantitative genetics   The branch of genetics that is concerned with differences in genetically influenced traits that are of degree, rather than of kind. Whereas individuals can be sorted into discrete categories for some genetic analyses, quantitative genetic principles are used where there are continuously distributed gradations. Usually such traits are influenced by many genes, each with a small effect, rather than by a few major genes, each with a large effect.

quantitative inheritance   See MULTIFACTORIAL INHERITANCE.

quantitative semantics   (H. D. Lasswell) A systematic, quantitative procedure for coding the themes in qualitative material; a systematic study of verbally communicated material by determining the frequency of specific ideas, concepts, or terms. Also known as content analysis.

quantitative variable   A variable that relates to a specific amount. Statistically, a variable that can be subjected to mathematical treatment, such as using an index or coefficient to represent its numerical equivalent.

quantitativism vs qualitativism   (R. I. Watson) A prescriptive dimension of the philosophical underpinnings of psychology, namely, psychological data in measurable form versus data that differ in type. See OPPONENT-PAIRS DIMENSION.

quantity objection   (W. James) An argument against the claims of structuralists who held reductionist concepts of perception and sensation, such as that mauve was a subpart of purple. Functionalists held that these were holistic sensations, not divisible in terms of magnitude. See GESTALT, HOLISM.

quantum   1. The least possible amount of energy. 2. A definite amount. 3. The fixed quantity of neurotransmitter released by the presynaptic terminal. It is the minimum amount that a terminal can release at a time; larger amounts are generally integral multiples of the quantum. Plural is quanta.

quantum jump/leap   An abrupt, often dramatic change.

quantum theory   In psychology, a point of view that changes in sensation occur in discrete steps and not along a continuum, based upon the all-or-none neural activity law. Sometimes known as quantal hypothesis.

quartile   Each of the four quarters of a distribution of scores. The first quartile would be the highest quarter, the fourth quartile the lowest.

quartile deviation   One-half the difference between the 75th and the 25th percentiles in a frequency distribution of measures. Twice the quartile deviation (Q) gives the range of the middle 50 percent of the measures of a series. Can be used as a rough estimate of variability, especially when the median is taken as the measure of central tendency.

quasi-experimental design   Experimentation in which full control of standard procedures is not possible, for example, when random assignments to groups cannot be made so as to ensure their comparability.

quasi-experimental research   Research with intact groups or samples of convenience in which random assignments to experimental and control conditions, to obviate the systematic influence of contaminants, may not be possible.

quasi-father   (D. A. Schulz) A man, not the biological father, who provides financial support and child care, and is regarded by relatives as a family member.

quasi-group   A number of associated people, not quite yet a group but with potential to become one (for example, the members of a seminar).

Quasimodo complex   A personality disorder arising out of concern over a defect in personal physical appearance. Derived from the name of the protagonist in Victor Hugo's novel *The Hunchback of Notre Dame*.

quasi-need   1. (K. Lewin) A tension state that initiates goal-directed activity with an origin in intent or purpose rather than a biological deficit. 2. Any nonbiological need.

quat   khat

quaternity   A unit of four components, a term sometimes applied to Carl Jung's four-fold concept of personality (feeling, thinking, intuiting, sensing). For Jung the quaternity is an archetype exemplified in myriad ways, such as the four points of the compass, four-dimensional thinking, and the four points of the cross.

queen   Slang for an effeminate, older homosexual (gay) man.

Queens College Step Test   A test of aerobic fitness in which the pulse rate is measured in groups who complete a given number of step-ups per minute on a 16.5-inch bleacher step for three minutes.

queer   Pejorative term for a homosexual, usually male. Term is used as a noun or adjective.

querulent   A quarrelsome, complaining, irritable, suspicious person. Characteristic of paranoid personalities. See LITIGIOUS PARANOIA.

question-begging   An error in logical processes of assuming the truth of a proposition that is trying to be proven. Also known as circular reasoning. Compare THEORY-BEGGING.

question command   In linguistics, an order phrased as a question, as in "Would you mind keeping quiet?"

questionnaire (Q)   A survey in which the questions and responses are written (printed), providing an efficient means of collecting data from respondents.

question stage   1. In the two-word stage of language development, the transformation of all types of sentences into questions through rising intonation on question words, as in "When go?" 2. In general, the "questioning age," in which frequent questions are asked from about age three and peaking around age six. "What" and "Who" questions usually precede "Why" and "How" questions.

queue   A line of people usually in order of first arrival such as those waiting for a bus or entering a theatre.

quick-and-dirty   Slang for procedures such as research that are efficient or hurried, yielding results that are approximations.

quickened display   See QUICKENING (meaning 2).

quickening   1. The movements (sometimes the first movement) of a fetus as perceived by the mother. Usually occurs in weeks 16 to 20 of gestation. In the 1600s, thought to mark the infusion of the human soul. 2. In tracking tasks, an operator's quick learning the consequences of a control action (resulting in faster performance) by using a quickened display, one that provides immediate information about the position of the control and usually reduces the lag in system response.

quickie   Slang for a brief, usually spontaneous, act of copulation.

Quick Neurological Screening Test (QNST)   (M. Mutti, H. M. Sterling, & N. V. Spalding) An individually-administered examination to evaluate a person's maturity of motor development, skill in controlling large and small muscles, motor planning and sequencing, sense of rate and rhythm, spatial organization, visual and auditory perceptual skills, balance, and attention. Revised as the Quick Neurological Screening Test-2 (QNST-2), it assesses areas of neurological integration as they relate to learning. Used in the screening of individuals with learning difficulties, disabilities, or both.

Quick Test (QT)   A brief intelligence examination used for screening purposes and for use with persons with severe disabilities, since the participant may respond by pointing or nodding without using words.

quiet biting (attack)   Behavior that has been elicited in cats by electrical stimulation of the brain, mirroring normal predatory attacks.

quiet breathing   In linguistics, breathing that is more rapid, shallow, even, and restful than speech breathing.

Quincke tubes   A set of glass tubes that produce high-pitched sounds when air is blown across the open ends. Formerly used in the study of hearing thresholds. Named after German physician Heinrich I. Quincke (1842–1922).

quintile   One-fifth of any extended quantity, just as a quartile is one-fourth of any set of data and a stenion one-ninth. See PERCENTILE.

quota control   A survey-sample technique in which the quota of certain elements is proportional to the distribution in the general population. See QUOTA SAMPLING.

quota sample   A sample comprising a prescribed number in each of several categories. See NONPROBABILITY SAMPLING.

quota sampling   1. A common method of selecting survey respondents in public-opinion research as an economical alternative to random sampling. Respondents with specific demographics, usually age, sex, and socioe-conomic class, are chosen. 2. A type of sampling that preestablishes the number of individuals to be taken from various levels of the population, such as x% from low-income levels, y% from medium, and z% from upper income levels. See PROBABILITY SAMPLING.

quotidian   Daily.

quotient hypothesis   An interpretation of Weber's Law according to which the quotients or ratios of any two successive just-noticeable differences in a given sensory series are always equal. See WEBER'S LAW.

QWERTY (keyboard)   The standard arrangement of alphanumeric keyboards, named after the first six letters of the letter-keys at the upper left. Designed by C. L. Sholes in the 1870s to curtail typing speed (by separating letters often used sequentially) and thus to reduce key jamming.

QWL   See QUALITY OF WORKLIFE MOVEMENT/PROGRAM.

r 1. The product-moment correlation coefficient. 2. A symbol for the Pearson product-moment coefficient of correlation.

R 1. The original response prior to conditioning. 2. A response. 3. The multiple correlation coefficient. 4. A general reasoning factor or ability. 5. In Rorschach test scoring, a symbol for total responses. 6. Spearman's footrule correlation. 7. A stimulus, from the German *Reiz*. 8. Primary abilities. 9. Primary reasoning.

rabbit-duck figure (L. Wittgenstein) A line-drawing that can look like the head of a rabbit facing in one direction or the head of a duck facing in the other direction.

rabdomancy An alleged method of finding objects, underground water, etc., by means of divining rod or stick. Also spelled rhabdomancy. See DOWSING.

rabies encephalitis Viral inflammation of the central nervous system transmitted by the bite of a rabid animal, and characterized by fever, chills, nausea, vomiting, headache, vertigo, hydrophobia, and, in most cases, death.

rabies fear See CYNOPHOBIA, HYDROPHOBO-PHOBIA.

race 1. A controverted classification of people according to real or imagined biological characteristics such as skin color and blood-group membership, and occasionally according to sociological variables. Humans have been thus categorized into between 2 and 160 groups. Race is generally regarded as a construct without sufficient empirical validity. See ETHNICITY. 2. Within one species, a set of common physical characteristics that appear to distinguish one group from another.

race differences Variations in physiological qualities, mental qualities, or both, allegedly associated with "race." Research indicates that any differences in intelligence quotient (IQ) between such groups decrease in size when both groups have approximately the same socioeconomic status and educational opportunities.

race experience The accumulated experiences, habits, knowledge, traditions of members of successive generations in a community.

race prejudice A point of view (usually negative) about a particular group concerning their special characteristics in terms of their "race" or ethnic background. See RACE, RACE DIFFERENCES.

race psychology A subfield of comparative psychology that attempts to determine the psychological characteristics of various "races." See ETHNICITY.

racial discrimination The unfavorable treatment of individuals of particular racial groups as compared with the general treatment of other racial groups including the person's own. Prejudice does not necessarily lead to discrimination, but discrimination is probably based on prejudice. See RACIAL PREJUDICE, RACIALISM, STEREOTYPE.

racialism 1. A doctrine positing that, though races may be identical in all respects except appearance, they nonetheless should be kept separate. See ETHNOCENTRISM, PREJUDICE, RACE DIFFERENCES, STEREOTYPE. 2. See RACISM.

racial memory A proposition by Carl Jung that people have inherited the common body of experiences or memories of all humans; not personal and idiosyncratic, but present in everyone as generic memories. See COLLECTIVE UNCONSCIOUS, RACIAL UNCONSCIOUS.

racial prejudice An attitude, generally unfavorable, directed toward the members of a particular "race." See POSTJUDICE, RACIALISM.

racial unconscious (C. G. Jung) A theory that in the human unconscious, elements continue from generation to generation. Therefore humans would not only inherit their physical attributes from their ancestors but also their memories. See COLLECTIVE UNCONSCIOUS, RACIAL MEMORY.

racism 1. The belief, often supported by actions, that some "races," particularly the person's own, are superior to others in psychological as well as other matters. 2. Prejudice and possibly discrimination on the basis of race. 3. Sometimes used as a synonym for racialism. See AVERSIVE RACISM, ETHNOCENTRISM, PREJUDICE, RACE DIFFERENCES, STEREOTYPE.

racket feelings In transactional analysis, habitual patterns of emotions that people purposefully and repeatedly engage in to achieve social goals.

rad See RADIAN.

radial maze An apparatus for measuring learning in animals (such as a rat), consisting of a central platform from which arms radiate to feeding boxes; the animal must remember which boxes have been visited and which not.

radial reflex Flexion of the forearm when the lower end of the radius is tapped. If the fingers also flex, it is a sign of hyperflexia.

radian (rad) The part or arc of a circle equal to the radius of the circle, an SI (metric system) unit of a plane angle.

radiance The degree of radiant energy deposited on a surface based on the rate of emission of the energy and the extent of the deposit. See LUMINANCE.

radiant flux A measure of the amount of emission of radiant energy (light) expressed in watts or ergs per second. See LUMINOUS FLUX.

radiation 1. Distribution of energy from its source. 2. The distribution of pain outward from its source. 3. Electromagnetic energy being absorbed. 4. The transmission of electromagnetic waves (for example, short radio waves) or nuclear particles for diagnostic, therapeutic, or experimental purposes. 5. Spreading of excitation to adjacent neurons.

radical 1. Characterizing behavior directed toward sudden, extreme, and fundamental changes. 2. Pertaining to fundamental changes. 3. A person who advocates fundamental changes.

radical behaviorism (B. F. Skinner) A version of behaviorism that denies the usefulness of mental activity as explanations of behavior and therefore restricts itself to the study of how an organism's environment, including the environment of its body, controls its overt and covert behavior. See BEHAVIOR ANALYSIS, DESCRIPTIVE BEHAVIORISM, PHENOMENOLOGY.

radical empiricism 1. A psychological-philosophical doctrine of William James, based on the concept that psychology should be the study of the total human imbedded in society, rather than the study of isolated elements as in structuralism, and that only immediate experience exists. 2. A version of idealism proposed by William James, proposing that only immediate experience, not objects (*pace* materialism), or extra-human ideas (*pace* postKantian idealism) exists, and that there is a rich plurality of experiencing agents. See FUNCTIONALISM.

Radical Feminism 1. An outgrowth of revolutionary ideas of the 1960s as part of the women's liberation movement; the advocacy of an extreme attitude that all men were the enemies of all women. 2. A kind of feminism stemming from the North American civil rights and peace movements of the late 1960s, views the oppression of women as a fundamental form of servitude; intent on significant and rapid social change; questions why women must accept inequality of opportunity and rights relative to men.

radicalism The urgent proposal of radical changes. In this sense radical means "going to the root" of problems.

Radical Psychiatry (C. Steiner) A point of view that people who are disturbed psychologically are victims of the social-economic-political system and it is the system that should be changed, not the individuals.

radical therapy Any system of psychotherapy that concentrates on the ills of society rather than on the ills of individuals. Advocates that the focus of treatment be on the social, political, and economic system rather than on individuals who simply reflect social pathology, for example, Claude Steiner's Radical Psychiatry.

radiculitis Inflammation of a spinal-nerve root, particularly the portion between the spinal cord and the intervertebral canal.

radioactive isotopes Variations of chemical elements that have the same number of nuclear protons but different numbers of neutrons, that emit radiation in the form of alpha particles or beta or gamma rays.

radioactive tracers Chemical compounds prepared with a radioactive isotope, such as calcium (^{45}Ca) or carbon (^{14}C), so that their metabolic paths can be traced through body tissues. See TRACERS.

radiograph 1. An X-ray picture. 2. An apparatus for making a radiogram, or photographic image produced by X-rays or radioactive isotopes. See PROTON-BEAM RADIOGRAPHY.

radioimmunoassay A procedure used to detect a substance in the body, such as insulin, by means of radioactivity. Useful in determining abnormal hormone levels, allergies, infections, and drug overdoses.

radioisotope A radioactive isotope. May be used in diagnosis, therapy, or research because of its radioactive properties, for example, in encephalography (radioisotopic encephalography).

radiometer An instrument that measures radiant energy. Also known as Roentgenometer.

radiometry The measurement of radiant energy.

radix (root—Latin) 1. In physiology, a bundle of nerves at the point of entry or departure from the central nervous system. Plural is radices. 2. (M. Wertheimer) In Gestalt psychology, the structural core or root of a problem or situation.

RAE rotational aftereffect

rage Intense anger during which the body mobilizes itself for attack. A combination of feeling and behavior, usually demonstrated by threatening words, rapid breathing, hostile facial expressions, and threatening bodily postures. It is a primitive response to frustration and a person in a rage is likely to be violent upon provocation. See SHAM RAGE.

raging hormones Nontechnical name for adjustment reaction of adolescence.

Ragona Scinà contrast/experiment A demonstration of simultaneous contrast.

railroad fear See SIDERODROMOPHOBIA.

railroad illusion See RAILWAY ILLUSION.

railway illusion A misperception wherein two equal-sized horizontal lines look different in size because of converging angled vertical lines. Also known as Ponzo illusion, railroad illusion. See LINEAR PERSPECTIVE for an illustration.

rain fear See OMBROPHOBIA.

Raman effect/shift (C. V. Raman) A shift in the frequency of light caused by the interaction of a photon with the energy level changes of an atom or molecule exposed to the photon.

rami Plural of ramus.

rami communicantes Groups of nerve fibers connecting sympathetic ganglions to spinal nerves.

ramifying linkage method A procedure for locating all groups and subgroups in factor analysis.

ramus (branch, bough—Latin) A branch of a nerve or vein, or a neural tract linking the sympathetic ganglia to the spinal cord and visceral or peripheral organs. Plural is rami. See PLEXUS.

rana pipens A type of frog often used in experiments.

Rand formula   In Canadian labor relations, provides that employees do not have to join the union but must, if they are members of the bargaining unit, pay dues to the union. Named after Justice Ivan Rand. Also known as agency shop in the United States.

random   1. Occurring without volition. 2. Haphazard, by chance. 3. Not predictable.

random activity/movement   Diffuse movement. Behavior or activity without any apparent purpose or direction, such as an infant's movements.

random assignment   The process of assigning subjects to experimental and control groups on the basis of some chance method such as tossing a coin or using a table of random numbers to eliminate bias in assignment of subjects to the groups. See RANDOMIZED-GROUP DESIGN.

random effects model   A paradigm for an experimental design that assumes the experimental subjects to be randomly selected; an attempt to ensure that all units of the population have an equal chance of being selected.

random error   An error due to chance alone, randomly distributed around a true score. May be contrasted to constant error or systematic bias. Also known as chance error, variable error.

random factor   A determinant that emerges in factor analysis, that correlates with some of the measures but not all of them.

random group   A sample of a population in which every person in the population is equally likely to have been chosen, and the choice of a person is independent of the choice of all others. See RANDOM SAMPLE.

random group design   An experimental design based on subjects being assigned by chance to a condition in a between-subjects design. See BETWEEN-SUBJECT DESIGN.

randomization (of groups)   Establishing two or more equivalent sub-groups in such manner that every person in the larger group has an equal chance to be in any of the groups to be formed. Many apparently reasonable methods, such as alphabetizing last names, may be biased rather than random.

randomization test   1. A procedure used after the selection of subjects to determine whether in fact the selection was truly random. 2. A nonparametric statistical test to determine how likely it is that differences in two matched samples are a function of chance.

randomize   To make selections by pure chance or to distribute items in a completely haphazard fashion.

randomized clinical trial (RCT or rCT)   An experimental design used in determining the value of some clinical technique or drug by using two essentially equal groups (a control group and an experimental group). In some cases, the double blind procedure is used in which neither the experimenters nor the participants know which is the experimental group (receives the treatment) or the control group (receives a placebo). Only the experimenter knows which treatment is active, but never sees the participants. See BLIND EXPERIMENT.

randomized-group design   An experimental design in which members of available sample groups are randomly assigned to various treatment conditions without controlling for background variables. See MATCHED-GROUP DESIGN.

randomizer   An electronic device to produce random numbers.

random mating   Chance mating. Mating without any kind of selection on the part of either individual.

random model   An experimental paradigm used in the analysis of variance, in which the experimenter randomly samples the independent variables. Also known as components of variance model. See FIXED MODEL, MIXED MODEL.

random movement   random activity

random noise   Sound consisting of a random mixture of different frequencies which are not multiples or harmonics of each other. See WHITE NOISE.

random numbers   A set of numbers between lower and upper limits selected by chance alone, generally done through computers. Books of tables of random numbers exist.

random observation   Any observation that occurs spontaneously or by chance, is uncontrolled, and is not part of a schedule of organized observation.

random sample   A selection of members of a population governed solely by chance, such that every member and any combination of members has an equal chance of being selected. May be contrasted with a casual, haphazard, or convenience sample in which no systematic means is used to insure that chance governs selection. Also known as probability sample. See HAPHAZARD SAMPLING, RANDOM GROUP, SELECTED GROUP.

random sampling   Any procedure for drawing samples so that every individual in the population has an equal change of being selected, and every combination of members has an equal chance of being chosen, the selection of each individual being independent of any other member's selection. See AREA SAMPLING, CLUSTER SAMPLING, STRATIFIED SAMPLING, SYSTEMATIC SAMPLING.

random variable   A variable whose value depends upon chance. For example, if two unbiased dice are thrown properly, the numbers 2 and 12 should each theoretically come up an equal 2.77% number of times thrown, the theoretical limit is achieved with an infinite number of throws.

range   The interval between the highest and the lowest scores of a distribution, obtained by simple subtraction. Also known as crude range. See MEASURE OF VARIATION.

range effect   In pursuit or tracking, a tendency to make movements too large when the target motion is small and too small when the target motion is large.

range-of-affect hypothesis   (E. A. Locke) In predicting job satisfaction, a postulate for explaining how have-want discrepancies and the importance of job facets determine the potential range of satisfaction that can be elicited by a given job facet.

range of attention   The number of objects that can be perceived or correctly apprehended during an exposure so short as to exclude eye-movements and counting. Also known as span of attention.

range of audibility   The difference between the lowest and the highest tones that an individual organism can hear. Differs among species and individuals. A typical human young adult can hear frequencies from 20 to 20,000 Hertz (cycles per second).

range of convenience (G. A. Kelly) Events predictable by a construct.

range of hearing See RANGE OF AUDIBILITY.

range of minus judgments In experiments on perceptual judgments, the difference between lowest and highest estimates. See BALANCE OF MINUS JUDGMENTS.

range of reaction reaction range

range restriction The selection of a limited portion of a sample, for example, studying persons with intelligence quotients (IQs) between 90 and 100. In practice, this often leads to lower correlations with other measures.

range scale A series of numbers based on some logical premise about the magnitude of skills and abilities, often used to rate individuals as compared with others or to some standard.

rank As a verb, putting things in order by size. As a noun, it refers to the position where any particular item of a set is to be found. By itself, knowing rank often means little. To be ranked third may be the same as being last, and to be ranked 100th may mean being in the top 1% of a group. For rank to be meaningful the size of the set, as well as other relevant factors, must be known.

rank correlation (P) 1. Refers to any of a number of measures of the correlation between ranked variables, such as the Spearman rho coefficient, based on the numerical differences between the corresponding ranks, or Kendall's tau coefficient, based on the proportion of disagreements in rank ordering. 2. A procedure for determining the degree of relationship between two variables each placed in their rank order. Also known as rank-difference correlation, rank-order correlation, Spearman's rho, Spearman rank-order correlation.

rank correlation coefficient See COEFFICIENT OF RANK CORRELATION, RHO, SPEARMAN RANK-DIFFERENCE METHOD.

rank-difference correlation Rare name for rank correlation.

rank-difference method See RANK-ORDER (CORRELATION) COEFFICIENT.

ranked distribution A method of distributing scores or values in an order from highest to lowest or lowest to highest.

Rankian psychoanalysis Rankian therapy

Rankian therapy A variation of psychoanalysis proposed by Otto Rank that stressed short-term therapy and the importance of birth trauma. Rank's original contribution to psychoanalysis emerged in the 1920s. Also known as Rankian psychoanalysis. See BIRTH EXPERIENCE, BIRTH TRAUMA, TRUE SYMBOLISM, WILL THERAPY.

Rankine An absolute scale of temperature in which the degree intervals are equal to those of Fahrenheit scales, X° Rankine equalling $(X - 459.7)$° Fahrenheit. Named after Scottish engineer and physicist William J. M. Rankine (1820–1872). Also known as degree Rankine.

ranking method A research procedure employed for a variety of purposes in which a person is asked to put in rank order a number of stimuli. Can be used either for judgments that cannot be compared against a standard (such as beauty of paintings) or against objective standards such as objects with known weights.

rank order An arrangement of a series of items, for example, scores or individuals, in an order of their magnitude or value. See RANKING METHOD.

rank-order correlation rank correlation

rank-order (correlation) coefficient coefficient of rank correlation See COEFFICIENT OF CORRELATION.

rank-order method A technique of arranging a series of items (scores, individual cases) according to an order of merit.

Ranschburg effect/inhibition An experimental demonstration of retroactive inhibition. An example of inhibition of similarity of materials. Paul Ranschburg found that people tend to remember more numbers if they are presented in different sized font than if they are identical in size when a group of numbers are shown briefly by some method such as the use of a tachistoscope.

Ranvier's node Periodic gaps in the myelin sheath of a myelinated nerve fiber. The gaps permit ion exchanges only at intervals along the axon, resulting in a form of nerve-impulse transmission known as saltatory conduction which increases speed of conduction of the action potential. Named after French pathologist Louis A. Ranvier (1835–1922).

rape 1. Sexual relations by force, intimidation, or threat against the will of the target, usually a woman; but in homosexual rape, the rapist and target are of the same sex. In psychology, rape is sometimes interpreted as a means of gratifying sexual impulses, aggressive impulses, or both, as well as a need to humiliate the victim. Local laws define specific variations, such as the absence or presence of genital penetration, the married or unmarried status of the parties, or the interpretation of the term "consent." See ACQUAINTANCE RAPE, DATE RAPE. 2. The unwanted sexual penetration of a person (of either sex) by a finger or other object. 3. Sexual activity with an unduly young partner. See STATUTORY RAPE.

rape counseling The provision of guidance and support for victims of rape. Rape crisis centers are located in many communities to offer counseling soon after a sexual attack. See RAPE-TRAUMA SYNDROME.

rape-trauma syndrome A complex set of thoughts, feelings, and behavior including confusion, fear, anger, guilt, humiliation, rage, and shame often experienced by a rape victim. May include fear of being alone, phobic attitudes toward sex, vaginismus, fear of all males, repeated washing of the body, and such symptoms may persist for a year or more after the rape. The rape-trauma syndrome may be aggravated by an attitude of others that the victim must have "invited" rape by provocative clothing or behavior. See POSTTRAUMATIC-STRESS DISORDER (PTSD), VICTIM BLAMING.

rap group/session A group interaction in which the members engage in informal dialogue about their current problems usually without a professional leader present. The purpose of such groups is often described as consciousness-raising.

raphe The demarcation of the joining of two halves of an organ. Also spelled rhaphe. See RAPHE NUCLEUS.

raphe nucleus (F. Chaussier) A brain stem nucleus containing serotonin and is thought to control sleep.

rapid-change theory 1. A point of view that the status of older persons in previously static societies declines if there are sudden social changes. 2. A concept related to insight and to Gestalt theory, based on the assumption that cognitive, emotional, and behavioral changes can be instantaneous or abrupt and permanent. See CONVERSION, EPIPHANY, INSIGHT, ONE-TRIAL LEARNING.

rapid-eye-movement behavior disorder See REM BEHAVIOR DISORDER.

rapid-eye-movement latency See REM LATENCY.

rapid-eye-movement rebound See REM REBOUND.

rapid-eye-movement sleep (REM sleep) (E. Aserinsky & N. Kleitman) A stage of sleeping during which dreaming occurs, characterized by an active "awake" EEG (electroencephalographic) pattern, appearing approximately every 90 minutes. Called REM because during this period, the eyes move more rapidly, as in scanning, than during other stages of sleep. See DREAM STATE, RHOMBENCEPHALIC SLEEP, SLEEP CHARACTERISTICS, SLEEP RHYTHM.

rapid-eye-movement sleep deficiency See REM SLEEP EFFICIENCY.

rapid sequential visual presentation (RSVP) In research on reading, the display of text at a quick rate, normally one word at a time in a fixed location on a screen. Designed to avoid eye movements.

rapid-smoking treatment A behavior-modification method for people who desire to stop smoking tobacco products by having them smoke much more than usual under controlled circumstances in the expectation that negative effects of excessive smoking will lead the person to stop smoking.

rapism A perpetrator being sexually aroused by the terrified resistance of a nonconsenting victim to sexual assault, degradation, or both.

rapport (F. A. Mesmer) A comfortable and relaxed relationship between two people such as a tutor and a student, or a doctor and a patient. It implies that the confidence inspired by the person with the higher social status produces trust and willing cooperation in the other. Rapport between a client and the therapist is considered important by many therapists as necessary for the success of treatment.

rapprochement 1. The establishment of cordial relations between conflicting individuals or groups. Attempts to establish rapprochements of large entities, including whole governments, have been suggested; for example, the GRIT system proposed by Charles E. Osgood is a strategy to prevent wars by a system of graduated compromises. See MARRIAGE COUNSELING. 2. (M. Mahler) In a theory of separation-individuation, a phase of the process in which the child, after about 18 months of age, makes active approaches to the mother, as contrasted with the preceding stage in which the child was relatively oblivious of her.

raptophilia See RAPISM.

rapture 1. Delight in the awareness of experience. 2. A subjective state of extreme joy or ecstasy, often identified with mystical or spiritual ecstasy. 3. In some mystical traditions, an ecstatic state in which the soul is lifted out of itself by divine power, allowing it to see beyond ordinary human vision.

rapture of the deep syndrome An acute, transient psychosis experienced by scuba and deep-sea divers, assumed to be precipitated by an excessively high blood-nitrogen level (nitrogen narcosis), in combination with sensory deprivation.

raptus (seized—Latin) Excited agitation.

raptus action A reaction to extreme, unbearable tension characterized by being suddenly seized by a destructive impulse, such as to commit suicide, set a fire, commit a violent crime. See AMOK, ISOLATED EXPLOSIVE DISORDER.

raptus melancholicus A rare sudden and unexpected violence-oriented reaction as a result of depression.

rare detail (dr) A judgment made by a Rorschach interpreter that a certain detail seen on an inkblot is of good quality and reported less than once in 100 examinations.

RAS reticular activating system

Rasch model A technique that describes test items in terms of the parameter of item difficulty. See LATENT TRAIT THEORY.

rate 1. Any amount of change per unit of time. 2. To assign a rank or a score to individual or grouped persons, productions, objects, etc.

rate conditioning A type of conditioning in which reinforcement is dependent upon the rate of responding. Reinforcement occurs when the number of responses per unit of time is either higher or lower than a previously established rate.

ratee The person being rated.

rate law A theory that the strength of a stimulus is indicated by the rate of firing of the affected axon(s).

rate of change A measurement of acceleration, plus or minus, that results from dividing one function by another, for example, the number of times a rat will continue pressing a bar in 10-minute intervals after the bar has been deactivated compared with how often it had been pressed when it had been effective in providing food for the rat.

rate of first admissions A ratio of the number of first admissions to a hospital for treatment during a year to the population of the area, such as a city, county, or state. The figure may be expressed as the number per 100,000 population, a percentage, or both.

rate of manipulation tests Any of a variety of several tests that call for a participant to move objects, turn and move them, etc., usually employed to determine mechanical aptitude, for example, the Minnesota Rate of Manipulation Test.

rate of occurrence/response See RESPONSE RATE.

rater The person who does the rating.

rater consistency A tendency of judges to agree in evaluating the same person, product, process.

rater reliability See INTERRATER AGREEMENT.

rate score The number of items finished in a test per unit of time.

rate test A trial based on time limits, usually containing many items. The score is the number of items gotten correct. Typically, such tests are made with enough difficulty so that even the best performers will answer some items incorrectly.

rating   1. The process of assigning numeric grade values according to some criterion of judgment, opinion, or feeling. 2. A number or grade, such as A, B, etc., assigned to a person, test result, etc., in terms of comparative value.

rating error   A tendency of judges to rate most people at the top (most favorable rating) of a scale. The man-to-man rating scale was devised to defeat the leniency error by demanding that raters rank-order people they are evaluating.

rating of behavior   Assigning scores to individuals, based on their behavior, in terms of an established standard or scale, as in observing and rating each child on a playground using preestablished behavior categories such as timidity and aggressiveness.

rating scale   A systematic method or procedure (usually employing a printed form) for evaluating a phenomenon in a standard fashion. Often a rating scale consists of short phrases describing the variables to be evaluated; for example, graduate-school applicants are rated by former professors on dimensions reflecting intellectual and social development.

rating scale checklist   A list of characteristics to be marked by a rater about the phenomena being rated.

rating technique   A procedure in which judges put various attributes in some sequence along a subjective continuum.

ratio   1. A relationship between the numerator and the denominator of a fraction expressed as a decimal number. Thus, the ratio of "one to two" is 0.50; the ratio of one to four is 0.25, etc. 2. Any relationship between two quantities expressed as a quotient or the product of a mathematical division. For example, the original Binet intelligence quotient (IQ) is the ratio of the mental age (MA) divided by the chronological age (CA).

ratio IQ   The ratio between a person's mental age and chronological age.

ratio of association-sensation   A numerical quotient of the association cortex to the sensory cortex in terms of their weight or volume. See ASSOCIATION-SENSATION RATIO.

ratio reinforcement/schedule   See RATIO SCHEDULE OF REINFORCEMENT.

ratio scale   1. A class of scales that is completely specified except for its unit size. Its zero point is fixed (for example, size, length, duration). 2. A scale with a true zero point, in which unit sizes are equal, so that, by way of example, the 2 is twice as big as 1, and 9 is three times bigger than 3. See INTERVAL SCALE, NOMINAL SCALE, ORDINAL SCALE.

ratio schedule of reinforcement   A pattern of reinforcement in which receipt of a reinforcer is determined by a constant or changing number or responses that need to be emitted for reinforcement to occur. When the number is one, the reinforcement schedule is called continuous. In contrast to reinforcement delivered on the basis of a time schedule only. Also known as ratio reinforcement schedule. See FIXED-RATIO SCHEDULE OF REINFORCE-MENT, INTERVAL SCHEDULE OF REINFORCEMENT, VARIABLE-RATIO SCHEDULE OF REINFORCEMENT.

ratiocination   (E. A. Poe) The mental process of reasoning and coming to conclusions based on the mental arrangement of facts and hypotheses. Detective work is essentially based on ratiocination, putting into logical order all information gathered about a crime in an attempt to discover the culprit.

rational   1. The reasoning process. 2. Being capable of reasoning. 3. Proceeding in a reasonable fashion. 4. Descriptive of a sensible or reasonable person.

rational coinage   The creation of new terms with clarity and a rationale. Coining a new term when an old word does not exist or will not suffice, for example, when new objects, theories, or events occur. See NEOGRAPHISM, NEOLOGISM.

rationale   The basic reason or logic behind a decision of some kind.

rational-economic man   A concept based on Adam Smith's *Wealth of Nations* that people act in a sensible and rational manner in terms of their general interests, well-being, and economic affairs.

rational ego/self   A facet of personality that functions more on cognitive (thinking) than affective (emotions) or conative (desire) levels.

rational elaboration of ideas   1. Analyzing inferences mentally before rejecting or accepting them. 2. The process of evaluating one's own ideas.

Rational Emotive Behavior Therapy (REBT) (A. Ellis) A system of therapy which emphasizes that people largely upset themselves by their irrational and self-defeating thinking. REBT uses a large number of cognitive, emotive, and behavioral methods to help people understand how they are upsetting themselves and what to do about changing their self-defeating and dysfunctional beliefs into rational philosophies. Formerly known as Rational Emotive Therapy (RET). Also known as Rational Psychotherapy. See COGNITIVE BEHAVIOR MODIFICATION.

Rational Emotive Therapy (RET)   The name used by Albert Ellis from 1961 to 1993 for what he later called Rational Emotive Behavior Therapy.

rational equation   A procedure for establishing a meaningful number in a psychological process, based on data and assumptions regarding the process.

rationalism   A doctrine positing that reasoning is superior to perception in the search for truth.

rationalism vs irrationalism   (R. I. Watson) A prescriptive dimension of the philosophical underpinnings of psychology, namely, focusing on intellectual or common-sense determinants versus emotional or nonintellectual dominance. See OPPONENT-PAIRS DIMENSION.

rationality   Reasonableness, good sense of equity and proportion.

rationalization   1. (E. Jones) An explanation that others would deem an excuse. A socially acceptable reason is substituted for an unacceptable one when a person wants something or wants to do something. People may be unaware that they are rationalizing, or they may do so deliberately, hiding the real reason for their intended behavior or past behavior. Such excuses reduce guilt or the chances of being criticized, losing face, or losing self-respect. 2. A defense mechanism in which questionable reasons are given to justify unacceptable behavior or personal shortcomings, for example, "If I don't do it someone else will"; "Doesn't everybody cheat?"; "An expensive car saves money in the end"; "You have to spank children to toughen them up." Excuses of this kind are used to ward off feelings of guilt, maintain self-respect, and protect the self from criticism. See FACE-SAVING BEHAVIOR.

rationalization appeal　　In advertising, appeals based on apparently reasonable means of meeting goals of intended readers, listeners, or both. See CONSUMER PSYCHOLOGY.

rational knowledge　　Conclusions deduced from a set of assumptions by the careful, reflective use of logic, rather than knowledge obtained from any other source or method. See A PRIORI, EMPIRICAL KNOWLEDGE, INTUITIVE KNOWLEDGE, LOGIC.

rational learning　　Acquiring meaningful knowledge, a form of learning based on comprehension, including a clear understanding of learned material and the relationship among its components. See ROTE LEARNING, BLIND LEARNING.

rationally suicidal　　Describing people who provide explanations for suicide that appear to make sense to other people. Examples of such explanations are being terminally ill, in unbearable pain, and wishing to save dependents the enormous costs of the dying process.

rational number　　A number based on the ratio of two whole numbers.

rational principle　　A mind set for how the person intends to solve a problem or determine a fact, such as deciding to use inductive versus deductive reasoning.

rational problem-solving　　Working on solutions to problems in a logical and systematic fashion.

rational psychology　　The understanding of psychological matters based on theoretical or theological bases rather than on experience. Also known as philosophical psychology. See EMPIRICAL PSYCHOLOGY.

rational reinforcement　　A reward for certain behaviors that correspond to normal expectation. See LOGICAL CONSEQUENCES.

rational self　　See SELF.

rational type　　According to Carl Jung, a personality type stressing cognition and perception rather than emotions and intuition. Compare IRRATIONAL TYPE.

Rat Man　　The name given to a patient of Sigmund Freud who had an obsessive-compulsive personality from which Freud developed his theory of obsessional neuroses.

rattus norvegicus　　A strain of white laboratory rats often used in psychological research on learning.

rauwolfia　　(L. Rauwolf, R. W. Wilkins) A tropical tree or shrub of the genus *Rauwolfia*; an extract from the roots of *Rauwolfia Serpentina* of India, containing substances such as Reserpine.

Raven's Progressive Matrices (RPM)　　A nonverbal intelligence examination intended to be culture-fair, frequently given to groups of people who might have a language disability. Based on a series of grids or matrices forming eight patterns from which the ninth is to be determined on the basis of logic. John Raven introduced the Progressive Matrices in the 1930s and then revised and extended them several times. Also known as Raven Progressive Matrices Test. See CULTURE FAIR, CULTURE FREE, MILL HILL VOCABULARY SCALES.

raves　　Slang for (typically) late-night dance parties geared to teenagers, in warehouse-type buildings, with their own subculture of garb, talk, music, and drugs. See ECSTASY.

raving madness　　Obsolete term for insanity, especially the manic phase of bipolar disorders.

raw data　　Information that has not been transformed into a more meaningful form.

raw score　　The original score on a test before it has been transformed for comparison to others' scores. For example, a raw score of 68 out of 100 on a history test may be the 40th percentile, whereas a raw score of 32 out of 100 on a mathematics test may be at the 80th percentile. Although the raw score in history is higher, the percentiles indicate that the mathematics score is actually a better performance. Also known as crude score, gross score. Compare STANDARD SCORE. See PERCENTILES, Z SCORE.

ray　　A line indicating the presence and direction of travel of light or radiant energy.

Rayleigh equation　　(J. W. Rayleigh) An equation for color mixture showing the proportion of red and green stimuli necessary for a normal human eye to perceive yellow. Persons who are red-weak or green-weak require different proportions.

Rayleigh test　　(J. W. Rayleigh) A means of determining red-green color blindness using the Rayleigh equation.

RB　　reactional biography

RBC　　See RECOGNITION BY COMPONENTS THEORY.

RBD　　REM behavior disorder

RBMT　　Rivermead Behavioral Memory Test

R_c　　Old abbreviation for conditioned response (also abbreviated **CR**).

RCAF Classification Test　　An intelligence instrument used for World War II air-crew selection by the Royal Canadian Air Force (RCAF). Also known as C Test.

rCBF　　regional cerebral blood flow

R class　　See RESPONSE CLASS.

R correlation　　(R. B. Cattell) A process in factor analysis that determines how closely two functions are related via obtaining data from a number of subjects and correlating the data.

RCRT　　Infrequent abbreviation for Role Construct Repertory Test.

RCT　　randomized clinical trial (also abbreviated **rCT**)

RdA　　See READING AGE.

RDC　　Research Diagnostic Criteria

Rdq　　See READING QUOTIENT.

reach envelope   In operating controls of a mechanism, the physical area that an operator can reach with ease (for example, in an airplane, pilots need to touch or examine many items, some below them, some in front of them, and some above them).

reactance   1. A theory that restrictions on any type of object or behavior add to its desirability. 2. A positive response to a forbidden, difficult-to-obtain or denied goal. 3. A negative reaction in response to another person who interferes with freedom of action, resulting in an increased desire to overcome the person. 4. Impedance to an electric current.

reactance theory   (J. Brehm) The proposed explanation for reactance (a person reacting negatively to outside forces attempting to control or restrict that individual). Such forces may lead to increased desirability of the object or action that is wanted but is denied. Operationally, some people use "reverse psychology" to enhance the desirability of something by implying that an object or purpose cannot be obtained.

reaction   1. Response to a stimulus. 2. The results of a particular therapeutic method or medication. 3. Socially, the overall attitude of a person or a group to some new concept or event, if favorable, a positive reaction; if unfavorable, a negative reaction. Types of reaction include: ABANDONMENT, ACQUIRED, ACUTE STRESS, ADAPTIVE, ADJUSTMENT, ADOLESCENT ADJUSTMENT, ADRENERGIC, ADULT SITUATIONAL, ADVERSE DRUG, AGGRESSIVE UNDERSOCIALIZED, AHA EXPERIENCE/, ALARM, ANNIVERSARY, ANTICIPATORY, ANTIGEN-ANTIBODY, ANTISOCIAL, ANXIETY, ARREST, ASTHENIC, AVERSION, AVOIDANCE, BALANCING, CANCER, CARDIAC, CATASTROPHIC, CHOICE, CIVILIAN-CATASTROPHE, COMBAT, COMPLEX, COMPOUND, COMPROMISE, CONFIRMING, CONTINUOUS-DISCRIMINATION, CONVERSION, CONVULSIVE, DEFENSE, DEFENSE-ORIENTED, DEFENSIVE AVOIDANCE, DEFENSIVE EMOTIONAL, DEFENSIVE, DEFERRED, DEHYDRATION, DELAYED, DENTAL-PATIENT, DIABETIC, DIFFERENTIAL, DISCRIMINATION, DISSOCIATIVE, DUPLICATIVE, DYSSOCIAL, EMERGENCY, FIGHT-OR-FLIGHT, FOLLOWING, GROSS STRESS, HAND-TO-MOUTH, HOPPING, HYPERSENSITIVITY, IDIOSYNCRATIC, IMPLICIT, INFANT ADJUSTMENT, INVOLUTIONAL PSYCHOTIC, LOCAL STATIC, MOBILIZATION, MOTOR CONVERSION, NEGATIVE THERAPEUTIC, NEUROTIC-DEPRESSIVE, OBSESSIVE-COMPULSIVE, PARADOXICAL, PATHOLOGICAL GRIEF, PHOBIC, PLACING, POLYGLOT, PRIMARY CIRCULAR, PRISONER-OF-WAR, PSYCHOTIC-DEPRESSIVE, RUNAWAY, SCHIZOPHRENIC, SECONDARY CIRCULAR, SELECTIVE, SENSORY, SERIAL, SHOCK, SITUATIONAL, SPECIAL-SYMPTOM, SPOILED-CHILD, STARTLE, STARVATION, STRESS, TASK-ORIENTED, TERTIARY CIRCULAR REACTION, VISCERAL, WITHDRAWAL. See ALLPORT A-S REACTION STUDY, CIRCULAR BEHAVIOR, DELAYED-REACTION EXPERIMENT, MOTOR-REACTION TYPE, PRIMARY-REACTION TENDENCIES, REACTION VS DISORDER, REPETITION-COMPULSION, SPECIFIC-REACTION THEORY.

reactional biography (RB)   (A. Anastasi) An individual's response to any environmental stimulus, that may vary widely among persons for the identical stimulus and whose influence on the person's subsequent development may cover an almost unlimited range.

reaction arc   The path taken by a neural impulse from a receptor through connector neurons, to an effector.

reaction chain   See CHAIN BEHAVIOR.

reaction formation   A defense mechanism in which unacceptable-to-the person impulses are denied and switched to the opposite. For example, initially a new parent has a negative reaction to the newborn infant, but later becomes extremely loving and protective of the infant in reaction to the original dislike.

reaction index   (C. Frederick) A brief pencil-and-paper measurement scale assessing the presence and severity of psychic trauma (PTSD), encompassing a wide variety of catastrophic situations with separate standardized forms for adults and children.

reaction key   A device resembling a telegraph key to be pressed down with a finger upon obtaining a preestablished signal. The reaction key ordinarily drives another device that measures the speed of reaction to the stimulus signal. Also known as response key.

reaction latency ($_StR$)   (C. L. Hull) The time period between the start of the stimulus to the start of the reaction. See HULL'S THEORY.

reaction levels   Several levels of functioning of the nervous system from simple (calling for relatively few neurons) to complex (calling for many neurons interacting).

reaction mechanisms   Sensory and muscular elements that control and permit responses to stimuli.

reaction pattern   Typical behaviors of any organism or groups of similar organisms to specific stimuli.

reaction potential ($_SE_R$)   In Clark Hull's theory, the momentary strength of the tendency of S to evoke R. The function of habit strength ($_SH_R$) multiplied by drive strength (D). See HULL'S THEORY.

reaction process   The totality of the steps in reaction-time experiments.

reaction psychology   Old name supplanted by behavioral psychology. Previously called response psychology.

reaction psychosis   Mental illness caused by environmental conditions, such as long-term solitary confinement, torture, or extreme and continued violence.

reaction range   The extent of an individual organism's reactions as determined by genetic factors. Genetic conditions define the maximal mental and physical boundaries of an individual but environment, experience and self-control determine whether those boundaries are reached. In child development, it is more commonly referred to as "range of reaction."

reaction threshold ($_SL_R$)   (C. L. Hull) The magnitude of the momentary reaction potential needed to generate a response. See HULL'S THEORY.

reaction time (RT)   (H. Helmholtz, F. Donders, W. Wundt, E. B. Titchener, J. Baldwin) The speed of a response following a stimulus. Depends upon a variety of factors such as age, sex, state of mind, or drugs. Also known as response time and latency.

reaction time apparatus   A chronoscope-equipped apparatus for testing elapsed time (latency) between the stimulus application and the organism's immediate reaction to it. Often used with a reaction (tapping) key or with just two switches, one each controlled by the experimenter and by the participant. See LATENCY OF A RESPONSE, REACTION TIMER.

reaction time experiment Research on the time taken (latency) between the stimulus and the response. Also known as response experiment.

reaction timer Any instrument intended to measure the time difference between the appearance of a stimulus and the beginning of the response to the stimulus. See CHRONOSCOPE for an example of an instrument that was used early in psychological experiments. A key was pressed by the examiner when a stimulus was presented and another key when the participant responded, thus measuring the time. More sophisticated time-measurements have supplanted this relatively simple system. See REACTION TIME APPARATUS.

reaction-time test Any task designed to measure the interval between the application of a stimulus and the start of the participant's response. See LATENCY OF A RESPONSE.

reaction type A manner of responding in a reaction-time experiment, in terms of how a participant appears to concentrate. Some people appear to focus on the appearance of a stimulus; others concentrate on having their fingers press the key as soon as possible; others appear to try to pay equal attention to the sensory and the motor modalities. Also known as response type. See MOTOR REACTION TYPE, SENSORY REACTION TYPE.

reaction variables (N. S. Endler & D. Magnusson) Behavioral variables which can be classified in terms of overt behavior, covert reactions, physiological reactions, and "artificial" behavior ("test" behavior, role playing, and other reactions to artificial situations constructed to elicit individual differences in behavior for a specified variable).

reactivation The process of achieving fuller memory for an event through recalling a portion of the event.

reactivation of memory (hypothesis) A postulate that lost or forgotten memories can be recalled by "triggers." It was hypothesized (but later proven false) that every experience that has occurred to an individual was still stored somewhere in that individual's brain and that appropriate measures (for example hypnosis) would result in having these memories come to consciousness. See RECOVERED MEMORIES.

reactivation process (H. Kohut) The process of mirror transference that helps to restore self-esteem in a patient diagnosed with narcissistic-personality disorder. See MIRROR TRANSFERENCE.

reactive alcoholism A form of alcoholism similar to E. M. Jellinek's alpha alcoholism.

reactive attachment disorder A diagnosis of a personality disorder noted in young children who appear unable to make appropriate social relations. Children who have been kept in isolation a long time or grossly neglected tend to have this particular disorder. See HOSPITALISM, MARASMUS.

reactive attachment disorder of infancy A pathological condition found in infants who have been neglected, not picked up, not handled, nor otherwise stimulated by others, characterized by the infants' indifference and apathy. See MARASMUS.

reactive confusion Term used in ICD-8 for an acute psychotic episode characterized by a state of personal devastation and disorientation especially in older persons. It is generally precipitated by a sudden and unwelcome change in their circumstances such as a death in the family or movement to a nursing home. "Reactive excitation" is used in a similar sense. See INTERNATIONAL CLASSIFICATION OF DISEASES.

reactive depression Depressive behavior due to reaction to environmental changes, such as situational stressors, but not due to inner pathology. A transient, nonrecurrent depression precipitated by an intensely distressing event such as loss of a loved one, loss of a job, or a financial setback. Also known as depressive reaction, exogenous depression, neurotic-depressive reaction, reactive depressive disorder. See ENDOGENOUS DEPRESSION, REACTIVE DISORDER.

reactive disorder A pathological mental condition (for example reactive depression, and reactive schizophrenia) which is apparently precipitated by severe environmental pressures or a traumatic event. See SITUATIONAL PSYCHOSIS.

reactive ego alteration The expenditure of energy in repressing libidinal or aggressive impulses in which the ego is altered by a reaction-formation effect against the impulses.

reactive epilepsy Epileptic seizures apparently due to specific causes, such as injuries or psychological situations.

reactive excitation See REACTIVE CONFUSION.

reactive hyperemia The marked increase in blood flow that follows restoration of arterial inflow to a previously ischemic (local anemia due to blocked blood supply) limb.

reactive inhibition (I_R) In Clark Hull's theory, a tendency for response magnitude to decrease with increasing practice or fatigue. See HULL'S THEORY.

reactive mania Strong aggressive uncontrolled behavior as a reaction to an external event.

reactive measure 1. A measurement that alters the variable under investigation. 2. An unstable measure because the very process of measurement affects it; for example, a person who is conscious of being observed may react both to the observer and the knowledge of being observed as well as to the ostensible stimulus or situation. Compare UNOBTRUSIVE MEASURES.

reactive-process dimension (of schizophrenia) See PROCESS-REACTIVE DIMENSION (OF SCHIZOPHRENIA).

reactive psychosis situational psychosis

reactive reinforcement In psychoanalytic theory, a conception that conscious attempts to elicit and reinforce emotions generate at an unconscious level the opposite tendency regarding the emotions. Related to the concept of reactance at an unconscious level. See REACTANCE THEORY.

reactive schizophrenia　An acute form of schizophrenia that develops in response to predisposing or precipitating environmental factors such as extreme stress. Considered due to a tendency to react negatively to certain environmental situations, for example, an emotionally unstable person has a child and then reacts in a schizophrenic manner due to the additional responsibility of taking care of that child. See PROCESS-REACTIVE DIMENSION (OF SCHIZOPHRENIA), PROCESS SCHIZOPHRENIA, REACTIVE DISORDER.

reactive states　Mental conditions resulting from physical or psychological trauma, for example, depression following a serious operation. See various entries beginning with REACTIVE.

reactive symptoms　Secondary effects of organic brain syndromes demonstrating deterioration of cognitive functions.

reactive tendency　An instinctive or unlearned reaction to some new stimulus. For example, many animals will avoid a confrontation with a snake, even if they have never seen a snake before.

reactive type　Descriptive of a person who does not take initiative but tends to depend on stimulations from others.

reactivity　1. The potentiality of readily responding to certain stimuli automatically and without thought. 2. The process of reacting.

readability level　The level of difficulty of reading determined by aspects of reading material, such as general intelligibility, difficulty of vocabulary, sentence length and structure, legibility of the printed material, and human interest in the topic.

readership-survey technique　Any of several advertising-research methods of determining how thoroughly a consumer may have read specified copy in a print-media advertisement. The consumer is shown a list of products, brand names, or company names. If the consumer claims to have seen an ad for any of them in a particular magazine or newspaper, that person is asked to recall information about the content of the advertising copy.

readiness　1. Being prepared or set for action or reaction. 2. Having developed or prepared to learn or achieve some specific task or skill based on the individual's physical, intellectual, and social development. 3. A concept in education that assumes that children pass through the same sequence of stages but at different rates. If instruction is tied to individual rates of growth, a child is not presented with material before being "ready" to learn the material.

readiness law　law of readiness

readiness test　Any of several means to determine whether a person has the present potential to learn something. Most such tests are in the field of education.

reading age (RdA)　1. The score on a reading test that has been calibrated to ages of normal school children. See INDIVIDUAL DIFFERENCES. 2. The ability to read at a certain level of difficulty, established by being the level of difficulty at which most persons of that age can read, not necessarily the person's chronological age; for example, a 4-year-old may have a reading age of 15. Compare READING READINESS (meaning 2).

reading delay　Inability to read at the typical ability level for age, refers to elementary school-age children whose reading-achievement level is two or more years below their age peers. Once known as reading retardation. See READING DISABILITY, READING DISORDERS.

reading disability　Poor reading skills associated with such conditions as perceptual deficit, faulty habit patterns, poor comprehension, deficient vocabulary, minimal brain dysfunction, and environmental deprivation. See PARALEXIA, STREPHOSYMBOLIA.

reading disorders　See ALEXIA, DEVELOPMENTAL READING DISORDER, DYSLEXIA.

reading epilepsy　A form of reflex epilepsy in which reading precipitates myoclonic jaw movements. If reading continues after the initial symptom, a general convulsion may occur.

reading fear　See BIBLIOPHOBIA.

reading habit　A tendency on opening a book to look at the upper left hand corner of the left page for those who read English, or to the top right of the right hand page for those who read Hebrew or Chinese, etc.

reading ladder　A method of evaluating or teaching reading by establishing various "rungs" of ability. Can be used in evaluation, referring to the number of the rung the reader is on, or in teaching, moving from a present rung to the next higher rung.

reading machine　Any of several devices that can change printed material into sound or vibrations that can be understood by people with visual-impairments, or vibrations alone for those with hearing- and visual-impairments.

reading quotient (RdQ or Rdq)　The relationship between a person's reading age divided by either chronological age (in the case of a child) or mental age (in the case of an adult). See READING AGE.

reading readiness　1. The development of early language skills, auditory and visual discrimination, cognitive abilities, and fine motor coordination. 2. A point in time for any individual child's ability to learn to read.

reading retardation　See READING DELAY.

reading span　The average number of words perceived while reading as measured by eye fixations. Can be estimated by a person looking at another person's eye movements as he or she reads. Good readers will have relatively few eye movements (thus large reading spans) per line. See RECOGNITION SPAN.

readmission　Re-entry of a client to a mental hospital or other institution. See RECIDIVISM.

reafference　The perception of movements of stimuli when the stimuli have not changed, due to movements in the sensory organs, as when looking at a point of light in a dark room, the dot may appear to move (due to the movement of the eye) even though the dot itself is stable.

reafference principle　A theory that changes of sensory events can be caused by the movements of the sense organs themselves, for example, the quantity and quality of hearing can be changed by moving the external ear toward or away from the origin of the sound. In contrast ex-afferences are changes of consequences of sensory events dependent on real changes in the environment (for example, changes in perceived tone of a sound due to the source itself changing). See BIOFEEDBACK.

reagent   1. In early psychology, an occasional name for an introspective observer, based on analogy to the chemical term. 2. In chemistry, a substance that causes chemical changes or reactions in another substance.

reagin   Old term for the Wassermann antibody. An antibody that can cause strong allergic reactions.

real   Having actual rather than theoretical or probable existence.

Realangst   (real anxiety—German) Anxiety based on natural or suitable causes, such as anxious feelings just before a major operation. Similar to objective anxiety. Also known as real(ity) anxiety. See ANXIETY.

real anxiety   English phrase similar to the German *Realangst*.

real-based factor analysis   (R. B. Cattell) A variation of factor analysis in which the factors retain their unit size. This design permits establishing a true zero.

real base factoring   (R. B. Cattell) A basic system of factor analysis which allows factors to assume different sizes and to be measured from true zeros.

real-ideal self congruence   (C. R. Rogers) The achievement by a person of that person's ideal self, for example, a person takes a Q-sort for ideal self and for present self. If the two distributions correlate positively with each other, there is congruence between that person's ideal and real self.

realism   1. A philosophical doctrine that objects have an existence independent of the observer (in contrast to idealism). 2. A philosophical doctrine enunciated by Plato that abstract concepts have a greater genuine reality than the physical objects to which they refer (in contrast to nominalism). 3. Pragmatically accepting the world as it is rather than maintaining an idealistic view. 4. In research, a situation when research findings match those of the real world. 5. In education, a movement that schooling should teach practical rather than academic subjects. 6. A philosophical and psychological doctrine about cognition, holding that perception makes direct contact with objects in the world, as opposed to representational theories holding that perception is of mental copies of objects, not objects themselves. Advanced by the Scottish common sense philosophers of the eighteenth century and revived c. 1910 by American neorealists. Influential on E. C. Tolman, J. Gibson, and B. F. Skinner. 7. (J. Piaget) In Piagetian theory, an inability of young children to separate objective and subjective aspects of experience.

realism factor   In psychological esthetics, objective measurements of artistic items in contrast to judgments dominated by subjective or idealistic factors.

realism of confidence   An indication of a person's ability to make good predictions.

realistic job preview   job preview

realistic thinking   Cognition based or focused on the objective qualities and requirements in different situations. Realistic thinking permits adjustment of thoughts and behavior to the demands of a situation; it is predicated on the ability to interpret external situations in a fairly consistent, accurate manner. This, in turn, is based on the capacity to distinguish fantasy and subjective experience from external reality. See REALITY TESTING.

reality   1. That which is measurable, tangible, reliable and valid versus what is fanciful, false, illusory, and meaningless. 2. The environment, or external world, as contrasted to the internal world of thoughts, feelings, and fantasies. See OBJECTIVE REALITY, PSYCHIC REALITY, RELATIVITY OF REALITY, SOCIAL REALITY.

reality adaptation   1. The gradual adjustment of infants to external reality. Includes changing from being self-centered and relatively oblivious to the environment to gradually understanding, reacting, and dealing with people and things in a successful manner. 2. The capacity of a person to adjust to life's realities.

reality anxiety   Real anxiety. See REALANGST.

reality assumption   A perception of things as they really are, including insights about self-perception that are fundamental to the functioning of the self-structure.

reality awareness/contact   The degree to which people note and react to their environment, especially to other people, in terms of accuracy and objectivity.

reality confrontation   A situation occurring when new and correct information is presented that differs from prior beliefs or opinions, as in a child learning that the couple thought to be biological parents actually adopted the child.

reality denial   See DENIAL.

reality ego   See PLEASURE EGO.

reality feeling   An attitude characterized by acceptance of the reality of the physical world as experienced.

reality life of the ego   In psychoanalytic theory, the practical everyday life of a patient and its real problems, which the therapist may help to improve indirectly in carrying out the main task of treating the patient's conflicts by analyzing impulses and resistances.

reality monitoring   See MEMORY ILLUSIONS.

reality monitoring hypothesis   (M. K. Johnson) A postulate that most people are constantly observing themselves, their social and physical environment, and are alert to making decisions about their goals.

reality orientation   1. An attempt to comprehend the relationships that link environmental events and interactions between persons so that outcomes may be predicted and the person's own behavior can be molded to existing conditions. 2. A regulatory mechanism that represents the demands of the external world and requires an individual to forego, modify, or postpone gratification. See ATTRIBUTION THEORY.

reality principle   A theory of the awareness of, acceptance of, and adjustment to the reality of people and things in the environment.

reality roleplaying   Acting in some stereotyped appropriate manner for the social situation, for example, students play the role of student when in class.

reality testing   The checking of a hypothesis by behavior. For example, a person believes another will decline an invitation to a movie; if the former invites the latter to a movie, this is reality testing. See PSYCHODRAMA.

reality therapy   (W. Glasser) A system that focuses on a therapist helping clients to understand reality and to operate accordingly. Includes an examination of the client's daily behavior and suggestions for adaptive behaviors.

real-life test A probationary period of usually 1–2 years, generally imposed as a standard needed prior to sex-change surgery. A male is expected to live as a woman and a female is required to live as a man. The person thus comes to see what life would be like in the other sex (gender).

real limits Points on a scale located a half-unit on either side of a given point representing the interval on the scale to which the number refers, for example, the number 5 refers to the interval from 4.5 to 5.5.

real love Affection and support given another for a long period of time without thought of any return. See POSTAMBIVALENT PHASE.

real pride See PRIDE.

real self According to Karen Horney, what a person actually is, in theory not known to anyone including the person.

real-simulator model (M. Orne) An experimental design in which some people are instructed to simulate hypnosis, or some other psychological state, while other people are genuinely experiencing them.

real-world setting See FIELD EXPERIMENT, MUNDANE REALISM, STRESS TEST.

rearrangement test A task that calls for parts to be put together in some logical manner, such as a jigsaw puzzle.

reason 1. An intellectual process involved in considering the totality of a situation. 2. An explanation or motive for a behavior.

reasonable Apparent property of a proposition that, without further evidence, seems to be logical and possibly true and correct.

reasoning 1. A type of thinking that depends upon logical processes of an inductive or deductive character. 2. A process of thinking or the solving of problems. See RATIOCINATION.

reasoning development The process of clear thinking as it grows from infancy through adulthood. See REALITY ADAPTION.

reasoning insanity See PARANOIA, PSYCHASTHENIA.

reasoning mania An extreme form of doubting reality, related to paranoia. See ABULIA.

reasoning test A type of test that provides problems for people that can be solved through the use of logic, knowledge, or both. An example of a test item: "fish is to water as bird is to _____?" (air).

reassociation A process of renewing or reviewing a forgotten or repressed traumatic event as in hypnoanalysis, so that the experience will be integrated with the person's normal personality and consciousness. See MULTIPLE PERSONALITY.

reassurance 1. An attempt to reduce another person's anxiety or fears by the use of words. Used in supportive counseling to encourage people to express their ideas and feelings and to consider more positive views presented by the counselor. 2. (C. R. Rogers) A response that attempts to soothe or pacify feelings. Also known as reassuring response.

reattribution 1. Assigning alternative causes to events. See ATTRIBUTION, CAUSAL ATTRIBUTION. 2. Reinterpreting the nature and purpose of psychological symptoms. 3. Reinterpreting personal behavior in a positive manner. See REFRAMING.

rebelliousness 1. Resistance to authority, especially parental authority. 2. In adolescence, an expression of the need for independence.

Reber's law (A. S. Reber) A conclusion that the more closely a phenomenon is examined, the more complex it appears.

rebirth fantasy Dreams of being symbolically reborn, usually expressed in dreams about emergence from water. Variously interpreted as: (a) a desire to return to the tranquillity of the womb and start life over; (b) an unconscious incestuous wish for the mother; (c) an attempt to deny death; or (d) an expression of the religious belief in resurrection.

Rebirthing (L. Orr) A holistic healing method based on breathing rhythms that sometimes includes ablution (dipping of the individual in water) as a symbol of spiritual cleansing and reemergence from the fluid environment of the womb.

rebound A reaction of a person following a rejection, such as seeking to attain a similar although possibly inferior goal.

rebound contraction Spontaneous contraction of a muscle upon release from brief inhibition.

rebound effect 1. A tendency to overcompensate following deprivation. 2. A sudden increase of behavior following a period of inhibition. The analogy is of a rubber ball being dropped and bouncing up again, for example, eating more high-calorie and high-fat foods than is normal after refraining from eating such foods while on a restricted diet. See DIETING, YO-YO DIETING.

rebound illusion In watching a moving object that stops abruptly, a tendency to falsely perceive that the object bounced back.

rebound insomnia A tendency for people who have been on hypnotic medication to have more trouble falling asleep for a period of time after they have stopped the medicine, when they are rebounding from the sedative effect.

rebound phenomenon (of Gordon Holmes) 1. The forcible motion of a limb towards the source of pressure when that pressure is suddenly removed. Considered a sign of cerebellar lesions. Also known as Gordon Holmes Rebound phenomenon. 2. A reaction measured by the test for ataxia determining whether cerebellar ability to control coordinated movement has been lost. Also known as Holmes' phenomenon/sign.

REBT Rational Emotive Behavior Therapy

rebus writing A graphic expression, intermediate between picture-ideographs and phonetic characters, consisting of symbols and pictures of objects, the names of which resemble in sound the words or word-elements for which they are substituted (for example, a picture of a hand and another of a shirt cuff to mean "handcuff").

recalibration The adjustment of any instrument of measurement toward greater accuracy.

recall   The process of remembering elements (such as thoughts, words, actions) of a past event to reconstruct what actually happened. See FREE RECALL.

recall item   An item in a memory test to which people are to supply the correct answer from their memory, in contrast to a recognition item where people identify the correct answer from a number of choices. Test examples: (Recall) "Who developed the Wiggly Block Test? _____." (Recognition) "The Wiggly Block Test was developed by (a) Anthony Marsella, (b) Johnson O'Connor, (c) Alan Auerbach, (d) Frank Dumont. Choose one."

recall memory   The retrieval of information in the absence of specific cues, as in reciting the alphabet. See RECOGNITION MEMORY.

recall method/test   immediate recall test

recall score method   Measuring the degree of retention (or rate of forgetting) by computing the percentage of items once learned that a person can name or otherwise reproduce after any given interval or intervals from the learning period. See EBBINGHAUS' FORGETTING CURVE for an example of how recall tends to drop over time. Also see EBBINGHAUS'S SAVINGS METHOD.

recapitulation doctrine   1. A theory proposed by Ernst Haeckel that species growing to maturity pass through all stages of evolutionary development characteristic of the species, that is, ontogeny recapitulates (or repeats) phylogeny. During early development, an individual repeats certain stages through which its species passed in its evolution from lower forms of animal life. The human embryo, for example, has gill slits at a stage of its development and a tail at another. 2. (G. S. Hall) Influenced by Ernst Haeckel's theory, Granville Hall asserted that a child's mental development is determined primarily by phylogenesis (the historical development of the organism). This position asserts that a child's mind goes through stages representative of human evolution. See items attributed to Erik Erikson, Jean Piaget, and Lawrence Kohlberg in this dictionary for variant views. Also known as biogenetic law, recapitulation principle/theory. See BIOGENIC LAW, FORMAL PARALLELISM.

recasts   Feedback from adults that helps to shape a child's speech into a more mature form.

recathexis   In psychoanalytic theory, an attempt by a patient with schizophrenia to restore, or "reconstitute" the lost object world; to regain contact with reality.

received view   See LOGICAL POSITIVISM.

receiver   1. Any entity that accepts any kind of information in a variety of forms. 2. In communication theory, a device or process that translates a signal into a message, for example, the sensory apparatus of vision or hearing, or a radio receiver.

receiver-operating characteristic curve (ROC curve)   A measure of hits versus misses in signal-detection experiments that can be displayed on a chart in terms of proportions of hits and misses.

receiving type   See RECEPTIVE CHARACTER.

recency   See PRIMACY-RECENCY.

recency effect/law   A tendency in memorizing a list of items for the last item to be most easily recalled. See PRIMACY EFFECT, SERIAL-POSITION EFFECT.

recenter   Colloquial term meaning to come back to a "center," after being "off-center" or having lost focus but now returning to a better status or situation.

receptive amimia   See AMIMIA.

receptive aphasia   A communication disability usually due to brain damage, characterized by an inability to understand either spoken words or writings. Such persons once were identified as word-deaf or word-blind. The condition, however, concerns all forms of language, not just words. Also known as impressive aphasia, logamnesia, sensory aphasia. See EXPRESSIVE APHASIA, RECEPTIVE DYSPHASIA.

receptive character   Erich Fromm's phrase for an adult behavior pattern resulting from growing up in an environment that encouraged an attitude of "expecting to receive." A passive, dependent, and compliant personality type, roughly equivalent to the oral-passive or passive-dependent types as described by others. "The world owes me a living" is such a person's philosophy. See EXPLOITATIVE CHARACTER, FROMM'S TYPOLOGY, PASSIVE PERSONALITY, RECEPTIVE ORIENTATION.

receptive dysphasia   Developmental difficulty in understanding language. See RECEPTIVE APHASIA.

receptive field   1. An area of the surface of a sensory organ served by a nerve fiber. 2. An area of the brain that receives projections from a sensory organ system. 3. An area where stimulations lead to specific responses. For example, the area just below and in front of the knee will elicit the patellar reflex (knee jerk) when tapped. Also known as receptor field.

receptive language   A form of language received and understood through gestures or spoken or written symbols. A disturbance in the central nervous system may disrupt the normal receptive language process. Compare PRODUCTIVE LANGUAGE.

receptive orientation   (E. Fromm) A personality pattern characterized by passivity and dependency with unwillingness to take responsibility for self or personal actions. May involve the search for a "magic helper," and a need to conform. See MAGIC HELPER, RECEPTIVE CHARACTER.

receptivity   The state of an organism ready to receive particular stimuli. For example, female animals in heat (estrous) are receptive to mates at that time.

receptor   1. A specialized area on a nerve membrane, a blood vessel, or a muscle that receives the chemical stimulation that activates or inhibits the nerve, blood vessel, or muscle. 2. The parts of cells that respond to certain chemicals but not others. In psychopharmacology, the neuroreceptors in the brain are becoming recognized as particularly important structures. Some medicines act by stimulating certain receptor sites whereas other drugs inhibit or block them. Also known as neuroreceptor.

receptor adaptation   The slowing of the firing rate of the sensory system in relation to a constant stimulus, with the result that the stimulus appears less intense.

receptor field   receptive field

receptor potential   1. The innate capacity of an organ to receive stimuli. 2. An electrical potential across the membrane of a receptor cell of a sense organ. May vary with the intensity of a stimulus. Potentials in the retina, for example, change with the light falling upon the eye.

receptor set   The readiness of a sense organ to receive stimulation.

receptor site   See RECEPTOR.

receptor test   The readiness of a sense organ, like the eye or ear, to receive stimulation, as in turning the head or eyes in a particular direction to see or hear stimuli.

recess   1. A small hollow. 2. A period of rest, particularly between work or study periods.

recessive   Suppressed, unless paired with a similar recessive on the homologous chromosome. See RECESSIVE GENE.

recessive character   In genetics, a member of a pair of Mendelian characters which, when crossed with the other member of the pair, may not appear in individuals of the first generation of offspring, but is latent and may appear in subsequent generations.

recessive gene   A gene which will only be expressed in the offspring if it is present on two homologous chromosomes or on a hemizygous chromosome. Recessive genes are located within every cell of a body but will not be evident in the phenotypes when a dominant gene overrides it. Fortunately, most lethal or harmful genes are recessive. See DOMINANT GENE, GENE.

recessive inheritance   The transmission of a recessive genetic trait. A recessive inheritance is expressed as a physical trait only when it is contributed at conception by gametes of both parents.

recessive trait   A trait in the genes that gives way to a dominant trait in the case of pairing. However, if both parents have the same recessive gene in their genotypes, the trait may appear in the phenotype of their offspring. Also known as recessiveness.

recidivation   Relapse of some pathological or undesirable condition, such as a disease, a symptom, a criminal behavioral pattern. See RECIDIVISM.

recidivism   1. A tendency toward recidivation. 2. Repetition of delinquent or criminal offenses by a person previously found guilty of committing crimes. See RECIDIVISM RATE. 3. A tendency for mental patients to have many relapses. Also known as recidivation. See RECIDIVISTIC SCHIZOPHRENIA.

recidivism in schizophrenia   **recidivistic schizophrenia**

recidivism rate   The percentage of previously convicted criminals reconvicted in any jurisdiction, institution, or group. Same for return of discharged mental patients who return to a hospital.

recidivist   A person who tends toward recidivation, such as a repeat offender or a reinstitutionalized mental patient.

recidivistic schizophrenia   A form of schizophrenia in which there are intermittent, recurring, acute episodes after a long period of remission. The episodes usually duplicate past episodes, but with new features. Also known as recidivism in schizophrenia.

recipathy   Reciprocity of two people who share thoughts and feelings.

reciprocal altruism   1. Exchange of aid between animals, generally of different species. See ANIMAL SPECIES COOPERATION, MUTUALISM, SYMBIOSIS. 2. (R. L. Trivers) Aid given by one organism to another nonrelated organism in which the reason for such aid is not readily apparent nor is there an indication that the aid will be reciprocated.

reciprocal determination   (A. Bandura) The causal model on which social learning theory is founded. This approach reflects one-sided causation in which behavior is either shaped and controlled by the environment or driven by internal dispositions. Rather, human functioning is the result of the interplay between personal, behavioral and environmental influences. See SOCIAL COGNITIVE THEORY.

reciprocal inhibition   1. Interference of two items with one another, leading to lack of memory of either. 2. Blocking of a memory owing to the interference of another memory or related activity. 3. (C. S. Sherrington) Cessation of passage of a nerve impulse when another is elicited. See AUTOGENIC TRAINING, SYSTEMATIC DESENSITIZATION.

reciprocal inhibition psychotherapy   (J. Wolpe) A behavior modification technique that attempts to substitute a more adaptive behavior for a symptom by learning an alternative means of reducing anxiety. The inhibiting of a response by the substitution of an antagonistic response. See DESENSITIZATION, PSYCHOTHERAPY BY RECIPROCAL INHIBITION, SYSTEMATIC DESENSITIZATION.

reciprocal innervation   (C. S. Sherrington) Interaction between nerves that permits a muscle to relax while another contracts. See RECIPROCAL INHIBITION.

reciprocal interference   The negative effect of two learned tasks on each other.

reciprocal liking   The essence of friendship when two individuals find each other compatible.

reciprocal overlap   A situation whereby afferent nerve fibers branch at every synapse level and communicate with several neighboring higher order cells.

reciprocal punishment   According to Jean Piaget, a type of punishment advocated by children age eight and older in which the punishment is made to fit the crime. For example, a child who consistently neglects to feed a pet rabbit after agreeing to do so, would not be fed until the rabbit is fed. In this way, children gain insights into the consequences of their neglect. See EXPIATORY PUNISHMENT, LOGICAL CONSEQUENCES.

reciprocal regulation   The pathological interaction between a child and an overprotective parent who dominates and distorts the child's psychological apprehension of reality, and the child in turn controls the parents' self-esteem by being subservient.

reciprocal roles   Human roles established by law, tradition, or experience as in marriage or partnerships, in which the various individuals know their own and others' rights, privileges, and obligations (for example, in a marriage, one spouse feeds the dog while the other spouse prepares breakfast).

reciprocal teaching procedures 1. A process of instruction by means of which students are separated into two sections (for example, A and B), section A learns about topic X and section B learns about topic Y. Next the students become tutors. Section A teaches topic X to section B, and section B teaches topic Y to section A. See TUTORING EFFECT. 2. (M. & S. Cole) An approach to reading instruction in which a teacher and a small group of students read the same material silently to themselves and then take turns discussing its meaning.

reciprocity 1. A mutual exchange. See GOLDEN RULE, RECIPROCAL ALTRUISM. 2. A concept of developing as much concern for the welfare of others as for the self. Thought to develop during Jean Piaget's autonomous morality stage. See RECIPROCAL PUNISHMENT, RECIPROCITY NORM.

reciprocity law/principle A theory that a response is a joint function of both the duration and the intensity of a brief stimulus. In, for example, visual and other physiological events, increased intensity can compensate for reduced duration, and vice versa. Also known as Bunsen-Roscoe law.

reciprocity norm A social standard that persons should assist and not harm those who help them. The statement attributed to Ambrose Bierce that "No good deed goes unpunished" indicates the possibility of negative reactions to assistance. See GOLDEN RULE.

reciprocity principle reciprocity law

recitation (method) A technique for memorization in which a person spends time mentally, audibly, or both, repeating the material to be learned. Also known as recitation procedure. See REREADING METHOD.

recitation theory A point of view that memory will be maximized if material is rehearsed.

reclining position of client The use of the couch as originally employed by Sigmund Freud in psychoanalysis. The client lies down, with the therapist seated close to the back of the client's head, while the client free-associates.

recoding Revision of the symbolic structure of information when the structure proves inadequate for further processing. See INFORMATION PROCESSING, INFORMATION PROCESSING PSYCHOLOGY.

recognition by components (RBC) theory (I. Biederman) In perception, a view that people recognize objects by identifying a relatively small number of basic components (starting with edges) and then specifying the relations among them. See NONACCIDENTAL PROPERTIES.

recognition item In a memory or knowledge test, selecting a correct item from a series of items. See RECALL ITEM.

recognition (memory) A sense of awareness and familiarity experienced when encountering people, events, or objects that have been encountered before, or when experiencing material learned in the past. See RECALL MEMORY, VISUAL PERCEPTION.

recognition method A means of measuring memory by presenting a series of items to be remembered and then testing the individual in some manner to learn how many of these items are identified as having been seen previously. Also known as recognition procedure/test.

recognition span The number of items, such as words, numbers, or objects, that can be apprehended by a single visual fixation, (in about 1/20th of a second.) Also known as reading span.

recognition technique A method of measuring any kind of learning by asking people to identify material previously learned. For instance, in consumer-psychology research, a participant is asked to recall information about a product based on previous exposure to its advertisements. The participant also may be asked questions about ads that have never appeared, to determine false recognitions. See PANTRY-CHECK TECHNIQUE.

recognition test See RECOGNITION METHOD, RECOGNITION TECHNIQUE.

recognition vocabulary A person's fund of understood words, whether read or heard, used or not. If never used, known as passive vocabulary.

recognitory assimilation (J. Piaget) 1. An ability of children to detect and report differences between similar stimuli. 2. A behavioral response by infants indicating that an object is recognized as familiar.

recollection Remembering a specific past event or person usually in the context of time and place. Occurs spontaneously in ordinary life and during free association, but it can also be stimulated by hypnosis. See EARLY RECOLLECTIONS.

recombinant DNA Artificial genetic material created by removing pieces of genes from a species and implanting them in the chromosomes of another species. See DEOXYRIBONUCLEIC ACID (DNA), GENE SPLICING.

recombination 1. A process of reuniting parts that somehow got separated. 2. A natural occurrence in genetic reproduction in which material contained in homologous chromosomes is exchanged during the first meiotic division, resulting in new gene combinations. See CROSSOVER.

recompensation A theory that individuals who successfully deal with stressful situations improve themselves, related to Friedrich Nietzsche's dictum: "What does not kill me, strengthens me." See DECOMPENSATION, OVERCOMPENSATION.

reconditioning Reestablishing a conditioned response that has weakened or been extinguished. May be brought about by additional reinforcement or by additional presentation of the unconditioned stimulus.

reconditioning therapy A form of behavior therapy in which a client is conditioned to replace undesirable responses with desirable responses. See AVERSIVE THERAPY, RECIPROCAL INHIBITION THERAPY.

reconnaissance (H. S. Sullivan) The second phase of a therapeutic interview during which, while obtaining a case history, the therapist formulates tentative hypotheses about the client.

reconstituted family A new nuclear family arrangement formed following marriages or remarriages, such as when two people, each already with children from previous relationships, marry, or when a person without a child forms a domestic partnership with a person who has a child. Also known as blended families.

reconstitution   1. Revision of personal attitudes or goals. 2. The final stage of the grieving process experienced by people with catastrophic illnesses with no possibility of improvement. After going through the stages of denial, ventilation, and defensiveness, patients generally accept the inevitable. See STAGES OF DYING. 3. See RECONSTRUCTION.

reconstruction   1. A form of recollection marked by the imaginative or logical recreation of an experience or event that has been only partially stored in memory. 2. In psychotherapy, the process of readjustment of the self following a successful understanding of the causes of prior attitudes the person held.

reconstruction dream   A dream that has the effect of solving a personal puzzle, putting things together, and making sense of disparate elements, especially about the self and in terms of earlier life experiences and relations with others. See DREAM FUNCTION, INCORPORATION DREAM, PRODROMAL DREAM, PROPHETIC DREAM.

reconstruction method   1. A form of recollection generated by re-creation of an experience or event that has been only partially stored in memory, or fully stored but partially unrecoverable. See RECONSTRUCTIVE MEMORY. 2. In psychotherapy, revival of memories significantly related to the cause of an emotional problem. May be highly nonveridical. 3. (E. A. McCamble) A method of testing memory, in which the participant is required to restore to the original order, a series of items that was previously studied in one order and then disarranged. 4. In memory research, having the participant restore a disrupted stimulus sequence to the original sequence. See MEMORY, MEMORY AIDS, MEMORY RETRIEVAL.

reconstructive memory   Combining of actual details from long-term memory with items that seem to fit the occasion.

reconstructive psychotherapy   An attempt to change people in therapy by enhancing insight into personality development, unconscious conflicts, and adaptive responses, by bringing into consciousness an awareness of and insight into forgotten memories, illogical conclusions, conflicts, fears, inhibitions, and similar manifestations. See ABREACTION, DEPTH THERAPY.

reconstructive surgery   A branch of surgery that specializes in the repair of damaged or diseased tissue (for example, breasts after mastectomy, congenital harelip) so that a body can be restored to normal or near-normal form. See PLASTIC SURGERY, STIGMA.

recording camera   See PHOTOKYMOGRAPH.

recovered memory   A memory, usually of a painful type, especially of sexual abuse by a trusted adult, that emerges into consciousness years after the event or events. The topic is controversial, with skeptics questioning whether such memories are real or false, whether they emerged spontaneously or were suggested or enhanced by the therapist.

recovery   1. Recuperation. 2. The return of an injured, damaged, or otherwise incapacitated person or organism to normal functioning.

Recovery, Inc.   An organization of patients recovering from schizophrenia, founded by Abraham Low, who took the position that patients with schizophrenia talk crazy because they think crazy, but if they talked normally they would think normally. Patients listen to Low via auditory recordings, counseling them essentially on how to communicate properly. Low's emphasis is on tension avoidance, free will, bibliotherapy via reading of Recovery's organizational principles, and mutual support of group members. See DIDACTIC GROUP THERAPY, SELF-HELP GROUPS.

recovery of function   The regaining of normal functioning of a lost ability.

recovery quotient (RQ)   A ratio of the number of patients discharged during any period, to the total number in the original group. Also known as recovery ratio.

recovery ratio   1. A ratio between neurological arousal and discharge, a measure of recovery of function. 2. See RECOVERY QUOTIENT.

recovery stage   1. A period during which an organism is returning to a formerly normal level of functioning. 2. The last of the three stages of the disaster syndrome observed in civilian catastrophes wherein persons gradually regain control of themselves, but remain apprehensive, talking incessantly about the disaster. The experience may be later relived in nightmares. The other two stages are the shock stage and the suggestible stage. See POSTDISASTER ADAPTATION, POSTTRAUMATIC DISORDER.

recovery time   1. The time needed by a neuron to recover from its refractory period to be able to fire again. 2. The time required for a physiological process to return to a normal state after it has been altered by a response to a stimulus. For example, in humans the refractory interval required after a male orgasm before the reproductive organ can respond again to sexual stimulation.

recovery wish   In psychotherapy, the wish, and will, to get well, considered by many to be an important element in determining prognosis. Many factors tend to perpetuate neurotic illness and nullify the recovery wish, such as an unconscious need for punishment (moral masochism), secondary gains derived from the disorder, lack of self-esteem, and narcissistic gratification derived from talking about personal problems.

recreation   Pleasurable or enjoyable activity.

recreational drugs   Substances, whether legal such as alcohol, or illegal such as marijuana, consumed for the purpose of enjoyment of the effects. See DESIGNER DRUGS.

recreational therapy   Employing recreational activities in a therapeutic program. The purpose is to increase enjoyment of life, stimulate activity and self-expression, enhance socialization, and counterbalance self-concern. See ARTS AND CRAFTS, ART THERAPY, DANCE THERAPY, MUSIC THERAPY.

recreation specialist   A playground director or anyone who specializes in recreational activities for people, including those with psychological or physical problems.

recruiting system   1. Part of the thalamic area of the brain associated with wakefulness and sleep. 2. See INTRALAMINAR SYSTEM.

recruitment   1. An effect of continued applications of a steady stimulus on the strength of response of an organism. 2. A rapid increase in the sensation of loudness once the threshold of hearing has been reached. It is characteristic of sensorineural impairment due to inner-ear problems. 3. The hiring of people for selected purposes. See EXCITATORY RECRUITMENT, INHIBITORY RECRUITMENT.

recruitment of loudness   A phenomenon that as the loudness of a tone increases, the perception of loudness is greater for partially deaf people than those with normal hearing.

rectal reflex   Defecation urge due to fecal matter in the rectum.

rectal sex   anal sex

rectangular distribution   A bar graph that has a flat top due to having the same number of units (people, test scores, etc.) in each of the categories of the distribution. For example, if the horizontal divisions of the graph are hat sizes, and there are exactly the same number of hats of each size in a store this would lead to a rectangular distribution. Also known as rectilinear distribution.

rectilinear   Linear. See LINEAR CORRELATION, LINEAR REGRESSION.

rectophobia   Fear of anything having to do with the rectum. Also known as proctophobia.

rectus   Any straight muscle. There are rectus muscles in the abdominal wall and in the extremities. See EYE MUSCLES, RECTUS OCULI.

rectus oculi   Four straight muscles that control the movements of the eyeballs. They are the superior, inferior, medial, and lateral recti. See EYE MOVEMENTS.

recuperative theory   A point of view that a purpose of sleep is for the brain to repair and recover from the day's activities.

recurrence   1. In the two-word stage of language development, an expression indicating presence, absence, and repetition, as in "More cookie." 2. Periodic appearance of some stimulus or sensation, conditions, etc.

recurrent   Reappearing or repeated after an interval of time.

recurrent circuits   A network of neurons and synapses which make it possible for a nerve impulse to make a complete circular path back to its starting point.

recurrent collateral inhibition   A negative-feedback system in the sensory or motoneuron system that prevents rapid repeated firing of the same neuron. The mechanism depends upon one branch of a motoneuron axon that loops back toward the cell body and excites an inhibitory Renshaw cell. The Renshaw cell in turn inhibits the motoneurons, including the cell with the feedback loop.

recurrent conation   A tendency of an organism to attempt to achieve satisfaction by an instinctive reaction after prior failure to succeed.

recurrent depression   A depression that has the tendency to reappear periodically, often according to the same pattern whether it is of the unipolar or bipolar type. See MAJOR DEPRESSION.

recurrent dreams   Repeated dreams. Sigmund Freud thought they arose from a masochist's need for self-criticism. Carl Jung regarded them as more revealing than single dreams, and found that, in a dream series, later dreams often throw light on the earlier ones. Alfred Adler considered recurrent dreams as an attempt to come to terms with disturbing experiences.

recurrent images   Auditory, visual, or other images that persistently reoccur.

recurrent inhibition   The phenomenon of a neuron, on firing, becoming unable to fire again due to a postsynaptic reaction.

recurrent mania/psychoses   Mental disorders that come and go, with the implication that they are biologically rather than socially dependent.

recurrent vision   Succession of positive and negative afterimages.

recurring-figures test   A memory task in which people are shown a series of cards featuring generally nonsensical figures or geometric forms. Some figures appear on more than one card, and the participant must try to recall whether a figure has appeared on a previous card. See NONSENSE FIGURES for examples of such figures.

recurring-phase theories   Points of view that specific identified issues repeatedly dominate group interaction.

recursion   1. In mathematics, a function defined in terms of itself. 2. Complete linguistic structures embedded within others. Important in estimating the sophistication of a child's language capability.

recursive   A process in mathematics that continues until a specified condition is met. Recursiveness also occurs in psychology, for example, in self-referencing statements, in music, and in pictorial art. See FACTORIAL.

recursive thought   Cognitive activity characterized by wondering, considering, or thinking about what another person is thinking about. See EMPATHY, PERSPECTIVE TAKING.

recuse   Refusing to participate in an activity, usually for ethical reasons.

recusants   Persons who refuse to participate or exercise their authority, usually on the basis of some ethical principle. For example, in an evaluation of subordinates, a supervisor recuses (excuses himself or herself) from the evaluation process because of a personal relation with the person being evaluated. See CONFLICT OF INTEREST.

redbird   Slang for Seconal.

red-color fear   See ERYTHROPHOBIA.

Red Cross nurse   Derogatory name for a person that appears to search for others who are in trouble and who tries to console and aid them. Phrase is used mostly in group psychotherapy of those members who come to the rescue of persons who they perceive as being mistreated. Such persons often negatively affect the attempts of therapists to get clients to see themselves clearly. See HELP-REJECTING COMPLAINER, RED-CROSS NURSING.

red-cross nursing   (G. Bach) Satiric term applied to therapists that spend a lot of time reassuring clients that there is nothing wrong with them, that time will cure all problems, and other platitudes. See RED CROSS NURSE, TRANSFERENCE CURE.

Red Dye No. 3   A synthetic food coloring associated with hyperactivity because of its presumed effects on brain-cell structure and function.

red-green blindness   The most common form of color blindness in which a visual defect causes certain shades of red and green to be confused.

red-green responses   A form of color vision in which responses of certain retinal receptors are excited while others are inhibited by the same wavelength. Since red and green are at opposite ends of the spectrum, it is assumed that a red excitatory response is accompanied by a green inhibitory response, each representing a different receptor process. See OPPONENT PROCESS.

red herring   A logical fallacy based on an irrelevant issue, for example, "Why should we explore outer space when there are homeless people in our country?" Also known as ignoring the question.

redintegration   (W. Hamilton) 1. Restoration to health. 2. Generally, a return to a normal condition, as in restoration of injured parts. See REINTEGRATION (meaning 2). 3. The revival of a complete mental state, such as a memory, upon being exposed to a small part of that state. For example, the smell of baking bread reminds a person of a happy childhood event. See REDINTEGRATIVE MEMORY.

redintegrative memory   The placement of pieces of memory to form a unity. A kind of mental detective work in which a series of early memories are pieced together to generate a whole connected memory. See MEMORY.

redirective activity   Behavior elicited by two different stimuli but resulting behavior is directed by only one of the stimuli.

red nucleus   (C. von Monakow) A nucleus of the extrapyramidal motor system in the ventral tegmentum of the midbrain. Receives input from the dentate nucleus of the cerebellum and the neocortex and gives rise to the contralateral (crossed) rubrospinal tract. The most important function of the red nucleus and the rubrospinal tract is to control muscle tone in flexors. Also known as nucleus ruber.

red reflex   The appearance of redness of the pupil of the eye that occurs when light shines into the retina directly in line of sight. This phenomenon is sometimes seen in photographs if the light came from the same direction as the camera.

red-sighted   Increased sensitivity to the color red, tending to see a red tinge to objects. Compare YELLOW-SIGHTED.

red tape   A metaphor for undue delays caused by formalities within an organization. For example, a transaction that should in theory take five minutes, takes several hours of visiting different offices, standing in lines, filling out forms, waiting and being redirected elsewhere. See BUREAUCRACY.

reduced cue (hypothesis)   A postulate that upon further repetitions of conditioning, less and less of the original stimulus is needed to get the response. See CUE REDUCTION, MINIMAL CUE.

reduced eye   A device intended to be a simplified schema of an eye and its functions. See EYE for an example of a reduced eye.

reduced score   A score from which a constant has been subtracted to make computation easier, the constant is added later on.

reductio ad absurdum   A procedure in logic to disprove a proposition by showing that it leads to an absurd conclusion. See LEANING TOWER OF PISA CONCEPT for an example.

reduction   Lessening of tension or the tendency of moving forward toward the achievement of a goal.

reduction-division   The process of meiosis (gamete production), in which a cell containing the full complement of chromosomes divides into two cells each of which has half of the normal number of the chromosomes.

reductionism   1. An approach for understanding complex processes and phenomena through the study of their simpler units and their interrelations with other simple units. Often used by physiological psychologists to understand human behavior and the functioning of the brain, glands, and muscles as they study discrete neurological and biochemical events and substances of the nervous system. 2. The attempt of Structuralists to discover irreducible mental contents. 3. In philosophy of science, refers to explanation on one theory by a deeper theory; for example the reduction of Mendelian to molecular genetics. Also known as reductionist analysis, reductionist explanation. See ATOMISM, GESTALT THEORY, PSYCHOSYNTHESIS, STRUCTURALISM.

reduction of data   The simplification of raw data through the use of, for instance, averages and totals.

reduction screen   (D. Katz) 1. A device for reducing or limiting visual perception used in experiments. 2. Any object interposed between the eye and most objects in the environment to make only the target object visible.

reductive approach   See PSYCHOSYNTHESIS.

reductive interpretation/method   (C. G. Jung) A process of carefully studying behavior to locate sources of unconscious elements in the psyche. Professional psychoanalysts and nonprofessionals (for example, detectives) make such interpretations. See PSYCHOTHERAPY, UNCONSCIOUS.

redundancy   1. In ordinary usage, this means more of anything than necessary. See REDUNDANCY PRINCIPLE. 2. Duplication of cells that perform specialized functions. Thus, vital functions may be continued even if some cells are damaged, destroyed, or removed. 3. Having two organs when only one is necessary, for example, two kidneys. 4. See REDUNDANCY IN LANGUAGE. See also DISTRIBUTIONAL REDUNDANCY.

redundancy in language   In information theory, the concept that a person usually communicates more information than necessary to be understood, refers to parts of a message that can be deleted without loss of meaning. Redundancy is built into grammatical rules and syntactic conventions, constituting roughly 50% of most spoken and written language. Duplication reinforces the intended meaning of a communication by enhancing the probability of correct interpretation. For example, a message that begins: "I am pleased to inform you. . ." generates an understanding that a favorable reply is forthcoming. See INFORMATION THEORY, REDUNDANCY.

redundancy principle   A theory that there are established, frequent, repetitive behavioral sequences between participants. For example, saying "Good morning" and "How are you?" hundreds of times a week, especially by those people in certain jobs and professions that call for contact with many people daily. See HABIT.

reduplicated babbling   Verbal behavior of infants at about 18 months of age during which time they utter a series of identical sounds, typically a single vowel and consonant, such as "pu-pu-pu."

reduplication   1. A redoubling. 2. A duplication, existence in an organism of two similar organs or body parts, for example, two eyes, ears, breasts, kidneys, ovaries, testicles. See REDUNDANCY (meaning 3).

reduplicative memory deception   False memory observed in people who insist they already have experienced an event, such as breakfast, when in fact the event has not yet occurred.

reduplicative paramnesia   A conviction that the person has an exact duplicate somewhere in existence. Also known as Doppelganger phenomenon.

re-education   1. The process of retraining or restoring a previously held function. 2. A concept that if maladjustment is a combination of learned attitudes and resulting behavior, then treatment calls for the afflicted person to be taught new and better ways of coping with life. This is attempted through relationship therapy, behavior therapy, hypnotic suggestion, counseling, persuasion therapy, nonanalytic group therapy, and reality therapy. Also known as re-educative therapy.

reefers   Slang for marijuana cigarettes. Also known as doobies, joints.

reenactment   1. Refers to mental processes, as in going over a particular thought in a compulsive manner. 2. In psychodrama, a client playing a certain part in therapy that the client had played in real life with the intention of receiving comments and criticisms from others. 3. Reliving traumatic events, repressed experiences, and past relationships while reviving the original emotions associated with them. This technique is used in psychodrama, scream therapy, and primal therapy. See ABREACTION.

reentry   The return to normal society from a restrictive environment such as a prison, mental hospital, or even the environment of an intensive encounter group.

reentry students   People returning to the classroom or other learning environment after a period of absence.

Re-evaluation Co-counseling   (H. Jackins) A peer counseling method which posits that optimal human intelligence, normally limited by psychological distress, can be recovered through cathartic release of that distress. Co-counselors alternate as counselor and client, and learn the needed theory and skills in counseling classes.

reference axes   The establishment of two fundamental axes in factor analysis against which other factors are charted.

reference group   Any group with which an individual identifies, accepting its values and attempting to achieve its goals for self. May be a family, a group of classmates, a religious organization, a professional associations, a trade union, or a political organization each serving as a point of reference for lifestyle and behavior. See REFERENCE-GROUP THEORY.

reference group power   Social power held because of membership in a group that exercises power in certain domains. See REFERENT POWER.

reference-group theory   A point of view that attitudes, including prejudices, are largely determined by the normative, or reference, group from which people derive their social and interpersonal standards. See REFERENCE GROUP.

reference man/woman   (A. R. Behnke) A theoretical model for an average 20–24 year-old man and woman based on anthropometric studies of thousands of individuals. Gives mean values for stature, mass, head circumferences, skeletal diameters (including proportionality constants), fat calculations, etc., in various groups. See HUMAN BODY SIZE.

reference memory   semantic memory

reference vector   A set of coordinates in factor analysis that indicates the degree of intercorrelation of coefficients of correlation.

reference woman   See REFERENCE MAN/WOMAN.

referent   1. A person, object, or concept pointed out by a symbol of some sort. 2. Suggested transfer of an individual from one professional person to another. See REFERRAL.

referential   Using words to refer to objects or to events with no attempt to communicate any further.

referential attitude   An attitude of expectancy observed in certain patients with schizophrenia who believe they are targets of hostility and are seeking justification for their belief.

referential communication   The gathering of additional information by a listener to clarify a meaning previously produced by a speaker.

referential communication skill   Ability to produce unambiguous verbal messages as well as to recognize the ambiguity or unclearness of verbal messages made by another.

referentiality   Dependence on some person or group, real or imagined, with whom or with which the individual establishes values. For example, never telling a lie because the person admires U.S. President George Washington, who was rumored to have always been truthful.

referential meaning   The direct object of a message, for example what can be pointed at, such as "that person."

referential style   Pertaining to the use of language, mostly nouns, to talk about things. Seen in early language learning in children. Contrasts with expressive style, in which language is used to talk about feelings and actions.

referent power   Social power held because of association with a more powerful person; for example, the presumed authority that the personal secretary of the president of a corporation has. See REFERENCE GROUP POWER.

referral   1. A suggestion to see a professional person, agency, or institution for evaluation, consultation, or treatment. May be either general or specific, for example, "See a dentist" or "See Dr. Miura, who is an orthodontist." See REFERENT. 2. Sending of a sensation from a part of the body to another. For example, irritation of the gall bladder may produce a referral of pain to the shoulderblade.

referred pain/sensation　A sensation or pain in a part of the body even though another part has been stimulated. For example, a headache behind the eye may be caused by a taut neck muscle.

refixation　In reading, the eye jumps from one fixation point to another when it settles, it is a refixation. See SACCADIC MOVEMENTS.

reflect　1. To bend or to throw back. See REFLECTANCE. 2. To meditate; to ponder. 3. In psychotherapy, to repeat the client's last spoken phrase to continue the discussion. See REFLECTION OF FEELING.

reflectance　The portion of total light that strikes a surface and then is reflected by a particular surface. Reflectance would be higher if light bounced off a mirror than off a dark cloth. See REFLEXION COEFFICIENT.

reflectance oximeter　A type of oximeter with photodetectors located on either side of the light source, usually the forehead, that measures or monitors changes continuously in arterial oxygen saturation without extracting blood. Compare PHOTOELECTRIC OXIMETER.

reflected color　The color of an object as seen as a reflection from another object rather than seeing it directly.

reflection　1. Cognitive functioning, especially introspection. Contemplative thinking directed to the analysis or the understanding of some personal event or consideration of the probable results of some form of behavior. See INTROSPECTION. 2. Considering either the meaning of a single phenomenon or attempting to integrate and understand a complex of phenomena. 3. Meditation. 4. In optics, return of light from a surface. See REFLECTION ANGLE. 5. (R. Descartes) Self-awareness of mental processes; the realization that mind exists apart from body, that the person has control over the self, responsibility for thoughts and actions, awareness of "who" he or she is as well as of who others are, and ability to judge the moral rightness and wrongness of behavior. See IDIOPANIMA, OBJECT REFLECTING RELATIONSHIPS.

reflection angle　The angle between the path of a ray of light and the line perpendicular to the surface from which the light is reflected.

reflection coefficient　A measure of the degree of luminosity based on the amount of light reflected from a surface in relation to the original light source. See REFLECTANCE.

reflection-impulsivity　(J. Kagan) Degree of hesitation by a child when considering the possible proper responses to a question or problem.

reflection of feeling　(C. R. Rogers) A therapist's response to a client's comment, in which the therapist (in the tradition of Carl Rogers) attempts to indicate both an understanding of what the client is saying and how the client feels. It is an example of empathy, expressing in effect: "I know how you think and how you feel." By communicating the essence of the client's experience from the client's point, hidden or obscured feelings can be brought to light for clarification. Also known as reflection response, reflective listening.

reflection response　1. In Carl Rogers's system of person-centered therapy, a remark made by the therapist reflecting the client's thoughts and feelings. See REFLECTION OF FEELING. 2. In Rorschach test scoring, a participant commenting that the inkblot represents a bilateral reflection of one half of the card.

reflective listening　**reflection of feeling**

reflective psychology　(K. Buhler) Consideration of one's own intended action, divided into experience, behavior, and effects. Involves consideration of past history and potential results of any behavioral act. See PHENOMENOLOGY.

reflex　1. An inborn reaction to a particular stimulus. 2. An unlearned automatic species-specific physiological reaction to a particular stimulus. Reflexes often involve a faster response to a stimulus than might be possible if a conscious evaluation of the input was required. 3. (J. F. Fernel, M. Hall) An automatic physiological reaction to a particular stimulus, for example, blinking of the eyes if an object suddenly comes near them. Also known as reflex action. Various reflexes include: ACCOMMODATION, ACHILLES (TENDON), ACOUSTIC, ACUTE AFFECTIVE, ALLIED, ALTERNATING RESPONSE, ANKLE JERK, ANTAGONISTIC, ATTENTION, ATTITUDINAL, AUDITORY-OCULOGYRIC, AXON, BABINSKI, BICEPS, BEKHTEREV-MENTAL, BLADDER, BLINKING, BULBAR RETRACTION, CEREBRAL CORTEX, CHADDOCK, CHAIN, CHEMICAL, CIRCULAR, CLASP-KNIFE, COMPENSATORY, COMPOUND, CONDITIONED, CONJUNCTIVAL, CONSENSUAL EYE, CORNEAL, CRANIAL, CREMASTERIC, CROSSED, CUTANEOUS-PUPILLARY, CUTANEOUS-SECRETORY, DARWINIAN, DEEP, DEFECATION, DEFENSE, DELAYED, DETERMINATE, DIRECT, DORSAL, EAR, ELBOW, EMPTYING, EPIGASTRIC, EXTENSION, EXTENSOR THRUST, EYE-WINK, FIXATION, FLEXATION, FLEXION, GASTROCOLIC, GLUTEAL, GOLGI, GORDON, GRASPING, GRASPING AND GROPING, HAAB'S PUPIL, HERING-BREUER, HETERONYMOUS, HOMONYMOUS, HUMORAL, INCREMENTAL, INHIBITORY, INITIAL, INTERSEGMENTAL ARC, INVESTIGATORY, IRITIC, KNEE-JERK, LACRIMAL, LANDAU, LARYNGEAL, LIGHT, MAGNET, MASS, McCARTHY'S, MICTURITION, MORO, MYOTATIC, MYXEDEMA, NEGATIVE MOVEMENT, NOCICEPTIVE, OCULOCARDIAC, OCULOCEPHALOGYRIC, OPPENHEIM, ORIENTING, PALM-CHIN, PALMER, PALMOMENTAL, PATELLAR, PLANTAR, POLICOMENTAL, POLIGALVANIC, POLYSYNAPTIC, POSITIVE CONDITIONED, POSITIVE MOVEMENT, POSTURAL, PROTECTIVE, PSYCHIC, PSYCHOGALVANIC, PUPILLARY, QUADRUPEDAL, RADIAL, RECTAL, RED, REINFORCED, RESPIRATORY OCCLUSION, RIDDANCE, RIGHTING, ROOTING, ROSSOLIMO, SALIVARY, SCAPULAR, SCHAEFFER, SCRATCH, SCROTAL, SEGMENTAL, SEXUAL, SKIN, SOLE, SPINAL, STANCE, STARTLE, STATIC, STEPPING, STRETCH, STRUGGLE, SUCKING, SUPERFICIAL, SUPRAORBITAL, SUPRASEGMENTAL, SWALLOWING, SWIMMING, TENDON, THUMB-CHIN, TONIC-LABYRINTH, TONIC NECK, TONIC NECK-EYE, TONIC, TRICEPS, TROT, TYMPANIC, ULNAR, UNCONDITIONED, VIRILE, VISUAL-PLACING, VISUAL-RIGHTING, WINK, WITHDRAWAL, WRIST, ZYGOMATIC. See COCHLEOPALPEBRAL REFLEX TEST, CONDITIONED-REFLEX THERAPY, DAZZLE REFLEX OF PEIPER.

reflex act hypothesis　A postulate that psychological acts follow the same general pattern as neurological reflexes. Like the reflex arc, they begin with stimulation from an external or internal source, proceed to a central regulatory system (the mind–psyche), and discharge through efferent channels.

reflex action   **reflex**

reflex after-discharge   The continuing of a reflex response after the original eliciting stimulus no longer is active.

reflex arc/circuit   (M. Hall) 1. The essential neural mechanism involved in a reflex, that is, the sensory, motor, and association neurons which provide a link between the stimulus and the response. 2. A generalized concept of a reflex consisting of its three basic elements: A stimulus affecting an afferent (sensory) neuron, that in turn affects an efferent or motor neuron, that in turn triggers a muscular or glandular reaction. See PSYCHIC REFLEX ARC.

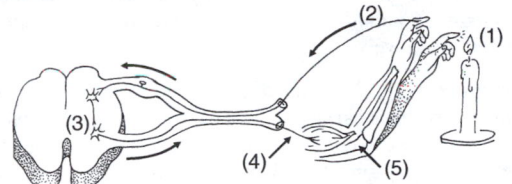

reflex arc/circuit   The hand touches candle (1) and information goes through the sensory neuron (2) to the interneuron (3) in the spinal cord, which then conveys a message through the motor neuron (4) in the area to the muscle (5) and the hand is moved away from the flame even before the brain receives the information.

reflex association   (V. Bekhterev) A conditioned response.

reflex center   A group of cells that act in concert to produce a reaction.

reflex chain   See CHAIN REFLEX.

reflex circle   1. A tendency for muscle contractions to activate proprioceptive reflex loops, thereby strengthening the muscle contraction. 2. A tendency of a muscle reaction to stimulate proprioceptors that then restimulate the muscle. 3. Feedback that occurs when contraction of a muscle, through stimulation of kinesthetic receptors in that muscle, provides stimulation for a further contraction. Purportedly plays a part in babbling and the grasping reflex of infants.

reflex circuit   **reflex arc**

reflex conduction   Transmission of nerve impulses through reflex arcs.

reflex epilepsy   A type of epilepsy marked by convulsions triggered by sensory input, such as sound, touch, or light. The episode often is controlled by reflexive inhibition caused by another strong compensating stimulus. See REFLEX INHIBITION.

reflex excitability   Gradations of reflex thresholds during periods of sleep versus wakefulness. During sleep, tendon reflexes, such as the knee jerk, have an increased threshold whereas cutaneous stimuli (touching the skin) produce a normal reaction of brushing away the stimulus or perhaps scratching the area.

reflex facilitation   Helping to enhance a reflex though not participating in the reflex. The concept is similar to that of a catalyst in chemistry.

reflex figure   A pattern of reflexes involved in a complex action such as walking or running. Some four-legged animals extend the right forelimb while the right hind limb undergoes a flexion reflex and the left hind limb undergoes a crossed extension reaction, the pattern alternating with each step of the reflex figure.

reflex inhibition   A reduction or even elimination of a reflex because an incompatible reflex has occurred.

reflex integration   Combining of two reflexes into a single more complex reflex.

reflexion   British spelling of reflection.

reflex latency/time   The elapsed time between the start of the stimulus and the reflex response. Also known as central reflex time.

reflexogenous zones   Areas of the surface of the body that on being stimulated by particular stimuli elicit reflexes.

reflexology   1. (V. Bekhterev) A system of psychological thought developed by Russian psychologists, that human behavior can be explained on the basis of the reflex as the fundamental behavioral unit, with other processes building on these units. 2. The study of involuntary automatic responses to stimuli, particularly as they affect the behavior of humans and other animals. 3. The view, supported by the work of Charles S. Sherrington and later Ivan Pavlov, that psychological processes can be explained by the biologically-based associations among sensorimotor relationships. 4. A system of mental and physical treatment by pressing various areas of the soles of the feet that allegedly correspond to various areas of the body. The area along the inner side of either foot is said to contain early memories. See UNCONVENTIONAL THERAPIES.

reflex principle   See REFLEX-SENSITIZATION PRINCIPLE.

reflex reserve   (B. F. Skinner) Amount of useless or inappropriate behavior continuing during extinction; for example, a rat was conditioned on hearing a particular tone to press a bar and receive food. Now, the researcher no longer rewards the bar pressing behavior subsequent to the tone. The amount of continuing useless bar-pressings is the reflex reserve. Phrase is a misnomer because the behavior is really an operant rather than a reflex. The phrase was coined and abandoned by Skinner.

reflex schema   Innate mental organization that becomes stabilized with repeated activations brought about by motor response to sensory stimulation.

reflex sensitization   See REFLEX-SENSITIZATION PRINCIPLE.

reflex-sensitization principle   A theory that after a response has been repeatedly elicited by a stimulus, it can be elicited by a neutral stimulus. Sometimes known as reflex principle/sensitization.

reflex summation   Fusion and mutual reinforcement of two or more afferent nerve impulses in the production of a reflex response.

reflex theory of thinking   See SPEECH MECHANISMS OF THINKING.

reflex time   **reflex latency**

reformatory paranoia   A form of megalomania (delusions of importance and capability) characterized by concocting plans to reform the world and trying to convince others to follow such ideas. See REFORMISM AS DELUSION.

reformism   A doctrine positing that some behavior is considered to be morally wrong or evil, and that measures should be taken to change the attitudes and behavior of such violators. See PROJECTION.

reformism as delusion   Concept that has distinctly political implications where protesters of various types have been considered mentally ill throughout history. In Russia, during the Stalinist era, some political reformers were institutionalized and "treated" for their delusions. See REFORMISM.

refraction   Changing the direction of something, such as light. As when the lens of the eye bends light deposited on the retina.

refraction error   error of refraction

refractive index   A numerical expression indicating the degree of deviation made by a path of light in going through various media or being reflected from one medium to another.

refractoriness   1. Inability or unwillingness to conform to social standards. Rebellion against legitimate authority. 2. The state of a neuron during its refractory period. 3. Refractory to treatment indicating persistence of condition despite efforts to cure.

refractory   1. Unresponsive, not reacting to a stimulus. 2. Unwilling to bend, accommodate, yield, or otherwise accommodate. Term is usually employed in a superior-inferior situation with the inferior person (such as a child) refusing to give in to a superior person (such as a parent). 3. A stubborn condition, such as disease that does not respond to any kind of treatment.

refractory mental illness   Mental disorders that resist all efforts of treatment including medications and electroconvulsive methods. See LEUCOTOMY, LOBOTOMY, TOPECTOMY.

refractory period   A rest period after a nerve or muscle cell has discharged. These periods are divided into: (a) an absolute refractory period (during which time no response can be elicited), (b) a relative refractory period (during which they may respond to a strong stimulus), and (c) a return to normal. The whole process is measured in milliseconds.

refractory phase   The rest period following orgasm, during which time a male cannot have an erection. See SEXUAL-RESPONSE CYCLE (SRC).

reframing   1. Changing of a prior attitude when considered from a different perspective. See RELABELING. 2. Reconceptualization. 3. Changing the conceptual point of view, emotional point of view, or both, of a situation and placing in a different frame that fits the "facts" of the concrete situation equally well, but thereby changes its entire meaning.

refrangible   Capable of being reflected, as light rays.

refrigerator parents   1. Parents who provide for their children but who are cold and unloving. 2. (L. Kanner) Obsolete theory describing parents of autistic children as cold, intellectual, and relatively uninterested in their children.

refutation   A decisive argument against a proposition either by an exercise in logic or by presenting incontrovertible evidence.

regard field/line   A straight line which connects the objective fixation point (or regard point) with the center of rotation of the eye. Also known as line of regard.

regard plane   A theoretical plane which passes through the center of rotation of the two eyeballs and the fixation point in the objective field. Also known as plane of regard.

regard point   The point in the objective field toward which the center of the eye is directed. Also known as fixation point, point of regard.

regeneration   1. Restoration of a lost physical element. For example, after losing its tail, a lizard regrows it. 2. Renewal of thoughts, feelings, and desires.

regeneration of nerves   Ability of certain nerve cells to repair themselves after injury or to have new cells grow in their place. Nerves of the central nervous system of amphibia are able to perform this function, but warm-blooded animals do not have this ability. Some myelinated nerves, those beyond the central nervous system of humans, are able to perform a self-repair function, however.

regimen   1. A planned program toward a goal of mental or physical health. 2. An overall treatment plan including a schedule of therapeutic measures that usually extends for a long period of time until the final goal is achieved.

region   1. A specific area or demarcated place. 2. In psychology, an area or section of life space. See FIELD THEORY.

regional cerebral blood flow (rCBF or RCBF)   The rate of flow of blood through a given area of the brain.

regional-localization theory   A point of view that the brain has special areas that control special functions. See BRAIN CENTERS.

regional static reaction   See SEGMENTAL STATIC REACTION.

region of acceptance/retention   In statistical hypothesis testing, the set of outcomes of a statistical test for which the null hypothesis would be retained.

region of rejection   In statistical hypothesis testing, the set of values of the test statistic for which the null hypothesis would be rejected.

regions of life space   In Kurt Lewin's theory, the assumption that in any moment of time there are various possibilities of action, varying in attractiveness, with various boundaries for some. See SPACE OF FREE MOVEMENTS.

register   Ranges of sound frequencies that musical instruments, or human voices, are capable of producing.

registration   1. The first step in learning and memory, in which stimuli make an impression or record on the central nervous system. 2. Ability to understand. 3. The capacity to notice elements in the real world. 4. Comprehension of the nature of things and events.

regnancy   (H. A. Murray) A concept that specific brain processes control psychological phenomena. The briefest unit of experience that integrates many physiological and psychological activities. See REGIONAL-LOCALIZATION THEORY.

regnant construct   (G. A. Kelly) A supervisory mental construct that affects all other constructs.

regression   1. A return of symptoms; a relapse. See CREATIVE REGRESSION. 2. Moving backward; a retrograde movement or action. Types of regression include: ACT, AGE, FILIAL, HYPNOTIC, SPONTANEOUS. 3. Returning to a more primitive mode of behavior due to inability to function at the current more advanced level. See FRUSTRATION-REGRESSION HYPOTHESIS, HABIT REGRESSION, MOBILIZATION VS REGRESSION, PROGRESSIVE-TELEOLOGICAL REGRESSION. 4. (A. Magnus) In Freudian theory, a defense mechanism characterized by a return to an earlier life stage of attitude and behavior in a threatening situation. It is sometimes an unconscious attempt to gain control or special attention and sympathy, or to force others to solve one's problems. See EGO REGRESSION. 5. In statistics, a method for deriving equations for predicting variables. Types of regression include: CURVILINEAR, LINEAR, MULTIPLE, STATISTICAL. See LAW OF FILIAL REGRESSION, MULTIPLE REGRESSION EQUATION, PHENOMENAL REGRESSION.

regression analysis   A statistical technique for predicting one score from another. For example, a linear regression equation of the form $Y = a + bX$ might be used to predict students' college grades from their high school grades, with Y the estimate of college grade, X the high school grade, and a and b constants that lead to optimal prediction.

regression artifacts   Measurements on individuals who when first measured were at the extremes, but on remeasurement come closer to the mean. See REGRESSION TO THE MEAN.

regression coefficient   A value in the regression equation that indicates the slope of the regression line. See BETA COEFFICIENT.

regression curve   In establishing relationships of two correlated variables, the graphic result is generally either a straight line or a smooth curve.

regression effect   A tendency for individuals who get extremely high or low scores on any performance test to come closer to the generalized mean of that test upon subsequent performances, as a function of the unreliability of the test. See REGRESSION ARTIFACTS.

regression in the service of the ego   (E. Kris) Returning to an earlier and more suitable level of functioning, especially of creativity. See REGRESSION NEUROSIS.

regression line   A straight or curved line fitting a set of points. Usually on coordinates that best describe the fit between two sets of variable data based on the correlation between the data.

regression neurosis   Return to an earlier, more primitive, inadequate, and inappropriate mode of functioning. Return to an earlier stage of life when responsibilities could be avoided and wishes could be easily fulfilled. See REGRESSION IN THE SERVICE OF THE EGO.

regression of libido   A psychoanalytic concept that the libido at any time may go to a lower or earlier channel of expression.

regression saccade   In reading, a type of saccade (jerky eye movement) characterized by the reader casting a rhythmic eye motion leftward.

regression time   The amount of time expended by a reader in returning to preceding words and rereading them.

regression to the mean   1. In general, if Y is predicted from X, the best prediction of Y is less extreme than the value of X used to make the prediction, when the correlation between X and Y is not perfect. 2. In genetics, a tendency of offspring of parents with unusual characteristics (such as height) or abilities (such as musical talent) to tend to have less of the characteristics than their parents, that is, to be closer to the mean in the characteristic that was extreme in the parents. Also known as regression toward the mean, statistical regression. See REGRESSION EFFECT.

regression to the real object   phenomenal regression to the real object

regression weight   Rare name for regression coefficient.

regressive alcoholism   Phrase similar to E. M. Jellinek's gamma alcoholism.

regressive behavior   Describing activity characterized by going "backward" rather than "forward," particularly in relation to maturity or health.

regressive development   Behavior gained and then lost, as when an infant seems to possess a skill such as walking and then loses it, only to show it again later.

regressive-inspirational group psychotherapy   (E. W. Lazell) A form of group therapy usually conducted in mental hospitals in which group discussion and interaction is used to help seriously regressed group members to bolster their morale.

regressive-reconstructive approach   A psychotherapeutic technique in which the client is encouraged to regress to an earlier stage of life and to revive and reproduce a traumatic situation that occurred at that time, as a means of bringing about personality change and achieving greater emotional maturity. See REPARENTING.

regressive substitute   See REGRESSION.

regressive transmission   See SEGREGATION.

regret   A form of guilt usually related to an action that was either taken or not taken (including an action considered wrongful), but the person wishes the reverse had been done.

regularity perception   In viewing an ambiguous figure such as the one below, a tendency to perceive white stripes on a black background due to the white stripes being more regular; otherwise the black would be foreground and the white would be background. See FIGURE-GROUND PERCEPTION, GESTALT.

regularity perception   A tendency to see white bands on a black background because the white bands are more regular in shape.

regulation   1. Control of how and how quickly a phenomenon progresses or is formed. 2. Maintenance of normal structure or functions.

regulator   See SOCIAL REGULATOR CUE.

regulatory behavior   1. Physiological control of the current status of the individual. 2. An effect of society in general, and the laws in particular, in controlling social behavior. See SOCIAL REGULATOR. 3. Any behavior that helps keep an organism in balance by fulfilling primary needs.

regulatory drive (theory)   A point of view that organisms have needs, organic or social, that generate restlessness and a search for sources of need-fulfillment. See REGULATORY BEHAVIOR.

regulatory system   Any system that helps maintain homeostasis, or balance, in an organ or organism.

rehabilitation   1. Correction of some kind of maladjustment, mental or physical, toward a prior superior level of functioning. 2. The restoration of persons with physical or mental disabilities to their fullest possible functioning in all aspects of life. It is described as the fourth phase of medical practice, the others being prevention, diagnosis, and treatment. In psychotherapy, it is recognized that residuals of mental disorder may remain after treatment, and the rehabilitation process is designed to keep these residuals from interfering with social and occupational activities. See HABILITATION, PSYCHIATRIC REHABILITATION, PSYCHOLOGICAL REHABILITATION, SEXUAL REHABILITATION, SOCIAL REHABILITATION.

Rehabilitation Award of APA Division 22   Psychological Aspects of Disability award, granted occasionally to those who have made outstanding professional contributions in the field of rehabilitation.

rehabilitation center   An organization devoted to the restoration of persons with mental or physical disorders and disabilities, to an adequate level of functioning. Techniques may include vocational training, work in a sheltered situation, occupational therapy, physical therapy, educational therapy, social therapy, recreational therapy, and psychological counseling as well as living in a halfway house or other group residence during the readjustment period.

rehabilitation counselor   A professional worker trained to evaluate and guide persons with physical, mental, and/or emotional challenges or disabilities in all major phases of the rehabilitation process. See CHALLENGED, DISABLED, DISABILITY, PERSON WITH A DISABILITY.

rehabilitation program   An overall system of rehabilitation services provided in support of medical-surgical therapy for persons with physical disabilities and psychotherapy therapy for persons with mental disabilities. The total rehabilitation program includes subdivisions of physical, recreational, and occupational-therapy, psychological, social-service, educational, and vocational programs, as well as appropriate special areas such as speech and hearing or mobility training for the blind.

rehabilitation psychologist   A person who devotes professional time to the emotional and behavioral therapy needs of clients, regardless of the cause of their disability. See CLINICAL PSYCHOLOGIST.

rehabilitation team   A group of various health professionals who coordinate their efforts at rehabilitating individuals. May include plastic surgeons, orthopedic surgeons, neurologists, psychiatrists, physical therapists, occupational therapists, social workers and psychologists, among others, depending upon the needs of patients.

rehearsal (in memory)   In memory, "maintenance rehearsal" refers to repetition for short-term memory without intention of storing that knowledge permanently, as in repeating a phone number just obtained from a phone book to dial it on a nearby telephone. "Elaborative rehearsal" refers to adding information from long-term memory to the to-be-recalled information (hence, elaborating on it), for example, in trying to remember to buy spaghetti at the grocery store, recalling the last time it was eaten at a restaurant with a particular person.

Reichenbach phenomenon   (K. L. von Reichenbach) The alleged energy (od, odic force, odylic force) experienced by sensitive people to emanations from physical matter as sensations of various kinds such as colors or variations in temperature.

Reicher-Wheeler effect   (G. M. Reicher & D. D. Wheeler) A tendency for letters briefly presented for recognition to be recognized more easily when presented in the context of a word than when presented alone. Also known as the word-superiority effect.

Reicher-Wheeler task   (G. M. Reicher & D. D. Wheeler) In research on reading, participants see a short target display of a word or nonword, followed by two test alternatives for one letter position. For instance, on one trial the target might be WORD. If the, for example, fourth letter position is then tested, the alternatives could be D and K.

Reichian analysis   A system of psychotherapy developed by Wilhelm Reich, who stressed full orgastic potency as the criterion of mental health and who, among other concepts in his system generated the concepts of bioenergetics, character analysis, character armor, life energy, orgone accumulator. See entries and also BION, BODY ARMOR, CHARACTER-ANALYTIC VEGETOTHERAPY, ORGONE (ENERGY), ORGONE THERAPY, ORGONOMY, PRANA, REICHIAN ORGASM, SOMATIC ARMOR.

Reichian orgasm   According to Wilhelm Reich, an involuntary, pleasurable movement throughout the entire body that accompanies sexual climax in persons relatively free of what Reich called "body armor." The orgasm is followed by a sense of rebirth and renewal.

Reid's movement illusion   (T. Reid) If a person is asked to move an object horizontally a certain distance and then asked to move the same object vertically the same distance, the horizonal distance will usually be less than the vertical distance.

reification   1. The error of regarding an abstraction as concrete, and attributing causal powers to it. Also known as fallacy of misplaced concreteness. 2. Regarding an abstract concept as a tangible object. For example, considering an intelligence quotient (IQ) to be as real as a person's brain. (Naming a phenomenon does not make it real.) 3. A form of thinking frequently observed in patients with schizophrenia, characterized by confusing the abstract with the real.

reincarnation   A concept of the rebirth of the essence of an individual (soul, identity, personality) after death into one or more successive existences, the actual form (spirit, human, or animal) being dependent on the individual's conduct in the previous existence. There are variations to the concept in different religious and philosophical traditions, especially Eastern.

reindoctrination   See DEPROGRAMMING.

reinforce   1. To increase the probability of a response to a given situation. 2. Refers to the capacity of certain stimuli to accomplish the former. For example, training a dog by saying "roll-over" and rewarding it with food whenever it does so is an example of the animal's behavior being reinforced. Throughout life, a person's behaviors are constantly being reinforced in subtle ways by others. See REINFORCEMENT.

reinforced reflex   A response whose manifestation has been so greatly accentuated by frequent rewards that the particular stimulus produces immediate appropriate reactions as though they were physiological reflexes.

reinforcement   1. Any consequence of an event that tends to increase the probability of the event being repeated. 2. In psychoanalytic theory, a dream in which the primary motive of the dreamer is expressed by a dream within a dream. 3. In neurology, the action of one neural excitatory process on another thus increasing the intensity or efficiency of the second process. 4. In conditioning, the process by which the conditioned stimulus (CS) is followed by presentation of the unconditioned stimulus (US). Types of reinforcement include: ACCIDENTAL, ADVENTITIOUS, ALTERNATIVE, APERIODIC, AUTOGENIC, CHAINED, CONCURRENT, CONDITIONED, CONJUNCTIVE, CONTINGENCY, CONTINGENT, CONTINUOUS, COVERT BEHAVIORAL, COVERT NEGATIVE, COVERT POSITIVE, COVERT, DELAYED, DIFFERENTIAL, DIFFERENTIAL RATE, FIXED-INTERVAL, HIGHER ORDER, HOMOGENEOUS, INTERLOCKING, INTERMITTENT, INTERNAL, INTERPOLATED, INTERVAL, JENDRASSIK, MIXED, MULTIPLE, NEGATIVE, NEURAL, NONCONTINGENT, PARTIAL, PERIODIC, POSITIVE, PREDELAY, PRIMARY, RATIO, RATIONAL, REACTIVE, SECONDARY, SELF-MANAGED, SELF-, SERIAL, SUCCESSIVE DIFFERENTIAL, SUPERSTITIOUS, SYSTEMATIC, TANDEM, TERMINAL, VICARIOUS, WITHDRAWAL. See AVERSIVE REINFORCEMENT CONDITIONING, DELAY OF REINFORCEMENT, GRADIENT OF REINFORCEMENT, REINFORCEMENT SCHEDULES, TIME OUT FROM REINFORCEMENT.

reinforcement An example of a pigeon being reinforced: In the past, this bird confined in a box accidentally touched the black object and a seed was dispensed into the food box. Over time, the bird learned to peck the black object to obtain seeds.

reinforcement analysis   Evaluation of the strength of various kinds of reinforcements. Also known as functional analysis of environments.

reinforcement contingencies   Circumstances when reinforcement will be given in shaping behavior. For example, to teach a dog to sit on command, the dog should be rewarded with a treat when the dog sits voluntarily.

reinforcement counseling   A behavioral approach to counseling based on the idea that behavior is learned and can be predictably modified by various reinforcement techniques that strengthen or weaken specific types of behavior through schedules of positive or negative reinforcement. See REINFORCEMENT SCHEDULES.

reinforcement delay   The time period after a conditioned reflex and before administration of an operant consequence. See INTERSTIMULUS INTERVAL.

reinforcement-expectancy model   (J. Rotter) A paradigm of personality status based on principles of expectancy.

reinforcement gradient   A concept of "closeness" (in time, space, etc.) and the effectiveness of reinforcement: the closer the reinforcement is to the response, the more effective it is. B. F. Skinner found practically instantaneous reinforcement preferable in teaching animals certain skills. See GRADIENT OF REINFORCEMENT.

reinforcement hypothesis   A postulate that learning requires reinforcement of a response above and beyond the contiguity of stimulus and response. A concept not in as much vogue as it once was since reinforcement can be negative as well as positive, though B. F. Skinner emphasized the positive.

reinforcement mechanisms   Processes in the brain that react positively or negatively to various stimuli. See SELF-STIMULATION for an illustration of reinforcement.

reinforcement retroactive paradox   The contradictory idea that a reinforcement after an activity can strengthen that activity, thus having a backward effect. Also known as reinforcement retroactive hypothesis.

reinforcement schedule   In operant theory, the exact description of the contingency between a response and the consequences that follow it. For example, a response might be reinforced according to the number of responses needed to "buy" the reinforcer (ratio schedules), or the time since the last reinforcement (interval schedules). Types of schedules of reinforcement include: ADJUSTING, ALTERNATE, CHAINED, CONCURRENT, CONJUGATE, CONTINUOUS, DIFFERENTIAL OF LOW RATES, DIFFERENTIAL OF HIGH RATES, EXTINCTION, FIXED-INTERVAL, FIXED RATIO, INTERLOCKING, INTERMITTENT, INTERPOLATED, LOW RATES, MIXED, MULTIPLE, NONINTERMITTENT, SECOND ORDER, TANDEM, VARIABLE-INTERVAL, VARIABLE RATIO. See MATCHING LAW, REINFORCEMENT.

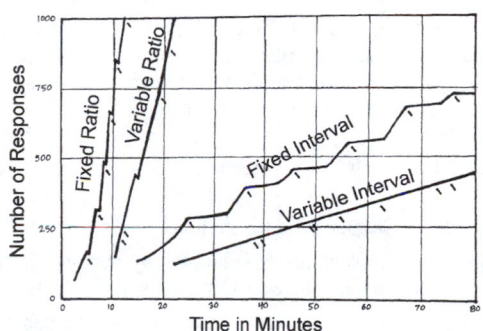

Time in Minutes

reinforcement schedule In operant conditioning research, four basic schedules of reinforcment have been studied. They are placed in this order from left to right: fixed ratio (*FR*)—every *nth* response is reinforced; variable ratio (*VR*)—responses are based on a particular ratio but they occur without any regularity; fixed interval (*FI*)—reinforcement intervals remain constant; variable interval (*VI*)—average intervals vary randomly. In this graph, the most effective reinforcement schedule is the fixed ratio and the least effective is the variable interval.

reinforcement survey schedule   A self-report inventory which seeks to discover reinforcing experiences in a respondent's life.

reinforcement theories   Any of several theories of reinforcement such as those proposed by E. L. Thorndike, E. B. Guthrie, B. F. Skinner, or C. L. Hull.

reinforcement therapy   Therapeutic techniques (operant conditioning using positive reinforcement) applied to initiating, maintaining, or modifying behavior.

reinforcement value   (J. Rotter) A variable that indicates the preference by a person for a particular reinforcement.

reinforcer   1. Reward; a thing having the property of strengthening a response. 2. In classical conditioning, the reinforcer is repetition of the pairing of the unconditioned to the conditioned stimulus. 3. In operant conditioning, the reinforcer is the effect following the behavioral act. Positive reinforcement occurs with the presentation of a pleasant stimulus contingent on a response; negative reinforcement occurs with the withdrawal of a noxious stimulus contingent on a response. See REINFORCEMENT.

reinforcing cause   A condition that tends to maintain maladaptive behavior in a patient. For example, the special attention given a person who is ill, which can in fact contribute to a delayed recovery. See ADVANTAGE BY ILLNESS, SECONDARY GAINS.

reinforcing stimulus (RS)   Any event that acts to maintain a response or enhance its strength. For instance, in classical conditioning, it is the unconditioned stimulus; in operant conditioning, it is the reward stimulus presented after a person or other animal has made the desired response, such as a bit of food after a child says "please" or after a dog begs. See NEGATIVE REINFORCEMENT, POSITIVE REINFORCEMENT, REINFORCEMENT.

reinstatement   Re-enactment of any previously learned material.

reintegration   1. A classical conditioning process in which a sensory stimulus associated with a second stimulus becomes capable of arousing the same response that the second stimulus arouses. 2. In psychiatry, a process of reorganizing mental processes after they have been disorganized by a mental disorder. Sometimes known as redintegration.

Reissner's membrane   A membrane in the cochlea separating the scala vestibuli and the scala media. Named after German anatomist Ernst Reissner (1824–1878). Also known as vestibular membrane. See BASILAR MEMBRANE.

Reix limen (RL)   German phrase for absolute threshold.

Reiz (R)   German term for stimulus.

rejected   In sociometry, refers to any person who is not accepted by anyone else. Compare STAR.

rejected child   A child who is not accepted by parents or other supervisory adults or by peers. Rejection may be due to passive factors, such as the appearance of a child who looks unusual, or to active factors, based on the child's behavior.

rejecting-neglecting parent   A parent who ignores a child, shows little concern, gives little attention, and who generally fails to enrich the child's environment. Diana Baumrind distinguishes between a nonauthoritarian rejecting-neglecting parent who may minimally encourage independence, and the authoritarian rejecting-neglecting parent who exercises excessive control and demands obedience. See AUTHORITARIAN PARENT, AUTHORITATIVE PARENT, PERMISSIVE PARENT.

rejection   1. Denial of love, attention, interest, or approval. 2. Nonacceptance of persons or of their behavior. 3. A discriminatory attitude toward a minority group. 4. Denial of gratification of an impulse or instinct. 5. Inability to assimilate something, such as food.

rejection need   A desire, most often unconscious, to be rejected, frequently based on feelings of mixed superiority-inferiority or of guilt. Few people consciously want to be rejected, however the concept implies that a person may operate in such a way as to invite rejection, possibly due to unconscious wants. See MASOCHISM, NEED FOR PUNISHMENT.

rejuvenants   Substances claimed to have the effect of restoring strength, vigor, or youthful qualities to a cell, tissue, or organism. In some cultures, exotic substances such as rhinoceros's horns are believed to have rejuvenating powers. See ETHNOBOTANY.

rejuvenation   1. A process of restoring youth to an organism. 2. In physiology, any treatment intended to achieve prior vitality to an individual. 3. In psychology, parallel attempts to have a person return to an earlier psychological state, having greater joy of living, interest in other people, etc.

Rel.ƒ   Abbreviation for relative frequency.

relabeling   Giving something a different name that is a euphemism, often because the former name had negative connotations or consequences. Relabeling can occur for reasons of fashion, politics, evolving language. See REFRAMING.

relapse   Reoccurrence of symptoms of a disease or disorder after a period of improvement.

relapse rate   Incidence of clients or patients who have recovered or improved who later suffer a recurrence of their disorder.

related measures design   A quasiexperimental design that employs the same participants as controls and as subjects. Scores are obtained from subjects before and after the treatment, and the changes can be measured for individuals and for the group (for example, a group of supervisors take a test on leadership before and then a parallel test after training, to see whether the group as a whole has done better and how much change has occurred for specific individuals). See REPEATED MEASURES DESIGN.

related model   **segregated model**

relatedness   (R. Coan) Reciprocal relations with another or with others of a mutually gratifying nature, with empathy, understanding, and an ability to communicate in depth.

relatedness needs   A desire to be with and to have interactions with certain kinds of other people. See EXISTENTIAL ISOLATION.

related to recall score method   See RECALL METHOD.

relation   1. In general, any kind of cause and effect between two organisms. 2. Mutuality between two organisms, what they have in common. See SYMBIOSIS. 3. A noncausative relationship between two variables such that variation in one variable results in variation in the other. See CORRELATION. 4. A relative; a person who is related through blood or marriage (for example, cousin, uncle, brother-in-law). See KINSHIP SYSTEM.

relational aggression   Behavior that interferes with someone else's friendships or relationships, or behavior that denies the person inclusion in a group. See LOKI PERSONALITY.

relational determination   In Gestalt psychology, the qualities or properties of parts of a whole depend upon their relation to each other and to the whole of which they are parts.

relational problem   A set of difficulties generated by socially inept or misunderstood behavior.

relational research   A type of research characterized by "if this, then that." Does not necessarily represent causation. For example, studying incarcerated criminals raised in either one- or two-parent households to establish the possible causal relationship between early family structure and later criminal behavior.

relational simplex scaling   (R. B. Cattell) A theory that different scales in different variables will have reached an equal interval, true zero nature when rescaling results in the highest intercorrelations. See INTERVAL SCALE, RATIO SCALE.

relation learning   Learning to respond to two stimuli based on the relation between them (for example, pick the darker stimulus) rather than responding to the absolute features of either, or both, stimuli.

relation measure   Any mathematical procedure, such as the correlation coefficient, that demonstrates the degree of change in one function in relation to another.

relationship   1. In general, a connection or relation between two or more phenomena (for example, objects, events, persons). 2. More specifically, a social arrangement consisting of two people who are "committed" to each other, such as lovers. See RELATIONSHIP SYSTEM.

relationship system   Any of several systems of defining familial connections, kinship connections, or both, between people.

relationship therapy   1. (J. Levy, J. Taft) Any form of psychotherapy in which the personal relationship between client and therapist is a key factor, serving such purposes as providing emotional support, creating an accepting atmosphere that fosters personality growth. In group therapy, the relation between other people can be a factor as well. 2. (F. H. Allen) Warm friendly contact by caring adults with troubled children as a means of accelerating their capacity to change.

relative accommodation   The working of two eyes or ears in harmony with one another, leading to greater information than with either alone, resulting in being able to recognize the distance of objects from the viewer or the source of a sound.

relative deprivation   (S. Stouffer) The sense, judgment, or feeling of not attaining what was expected; of being worse off than those with whom persons compare themselves. Compare RELATIVE GRATIFICATION.

relative effect law   law of relative effect

relative error   In statistics, the absolute error divided by the true value.

relative fatigue   Decrease in output of responses to stimuli as compared with prior behavior.

relative frequency (Rel. *f*)   The ratio of the occurrence of a specific event to the total frequency.

relative gratification   (S. Stouffer) The sense, judgment, or feeling of attaining more than what was expected; of feeling blessed with having more than others. See RELATIVE DEPRIVATION.

relative height   A monocular cue to perceiving distance. Humans have a tendency to see taller items as further away than similar items of shorter height.

relative limen   See RELATIVE THRESHOLD.

relative motion/movement   A monocular depth cue for estimating the relative distances of two or more stationary objects when the viewer is in motion, due to objects changing position on the retina differently, with nearer ones appearing to change the most.

relative pitch   The pitch of a tone as compared with some standard.

relative position   interposition

relative refractory period   Following the absolute refractory period of either a nerve or a muscle fiber, an intermediate period during which a nerve or muscle fiber can be excited but only by strong impulses. Also known as relative refractory phase. See ABSOLUTE REFRACTORY PERIOD, REFRACTORY PERIOD.

relative risk   A concept in epidemiology of the ratio of the incidence of a disorder among individuals who have been exposed to a risk factor divided by the incidence among individuals known not to have been exposed to that risk factor.

relative sensitivity   Incremental degrees of awareness of a difference between experiences. Two individuals may differ for example, in sensitivity to changes in tone or to differences in degrees of weight of objects with one being more able to judge smaller differences.

relative size   A monocular depth cue used in estimating distances of objects of familiar size when viewed from far away. For example, a horse viewed from 100 m away would be estimated to be the size of an average horse. See SIZE CONSTANCY.

relative variability   The relationship between the size of the mean and variations from the mean. The formula is $r.v. = 100\ Mw \div M$, where MV equals the mean variation and M equals the mean.

relativism   A doctrine positing that any social behavior, value, or principle cannot be understood outside of its context of the whole of the society from which it springs. Holds, for example, that *malum in res* (evil in the law) contradicts the principle of universality of ethics and laws, for example, *malum in se* (evil in itself).

relativity attitude   The assumption that values, such as truth or honor, are dependent on historical and social contexts.

relativity law   1. A theory that every phase of experience is influenced by every other simultaneous phase of experience. Any experience is understood only in terms of other experiences. 2. A theory that the amount that a stimulus must be changed for an observer to be able to notice that the stimulus has changed is a constant fraction of the stimulus intensity (for example, a small change in a weak stimulus might be noticeable, but a larger change must be made in a strong stimulus if that change is to be noticeable). Also known as Weber's law.

relativity of reality   Variations in human concepts of the external world. Each person has their own interpretation of reality, each distorting it to different degrees through wishful thinking, various defense maneuvers, and pathological defenses against internal conflicts and repressed impulses. See REALITY.

relaxation   1. The reduction of physical or mental tension by resting. 2. The return of a muscle to its normal state after being stretched or contracted. 3. A tension-free state in which internal conflicts and disturbing feelings of anxiety, anger, and fear are eased and a state of tranquility prevails.

relaxation principle (in therapy)   1. A technique in psychotherapy wherein therapists adjust themselves to the presumed mood of the client to get in greater harmony with the client. 2. (S. Ferenczi) A psychotherapeutic technique, based on the idea that a loving, tender, permissive approach to clients was more effective in releasing their repressed impulses and making them accessible to analysis than a strict application of Sigmund Freud's privation philosophy. See PRIVATION.

relaxation response   A protective mechanism against stress through the body reducing tension; the opposite of the fight-flight reaction.

relaxation techniques   Any of a variety of procedures used to relieve stress and tension.

relaxation therapy   (S. Ferenczi) 1. A type of therapy based on the idea that clients learning how to relax can be therapy in an of itself. The speculation that in classical psychoanalysis, the lying on the couch for the traditional fifty-minute hour was in itself conducive to wellness. 2. The use of muscle-relaxation techniques as an aid in the treatment of emotional tension. 3. (E. Jacobson) The use of suggestions aimed at increasing stages of relaxation. For example, suggesting that the client's muscles are relaxing in various body parts, breathing is becoming slower and more regular, that the heart is beating more slowly. A state of tranquility is desired in the hopes that attitudes will change about an existing physiological condition, such as a move toward greater acceptance. Various degrees of this system are used in a number of specific systems of psychotherapy such as, Autogenic Training, Ego-state Therapy, EST. Compare ACTIVE THERAPY. See DIFFERENTIAL RELAXATION, MUSCLE RELAXANTS.

relaxation training   Behavior processes of different types intended to achieve harmony and equilibrium in people, physically and mentally. See AUTOGENIC TRAINING, PROGRESSIVE RELAXATION.

relay neuron   **Golgi Type I neuron**

relay nuclei   Nuclei in the thalamus that transmit information from sensory tracts or subcortical structures to the neocortex, for example, the lateral geniculate nucleus. The optic tract terminates in the lateral geniculate nucleus and neurons in the lateral geniculate neuron send axons through the visual radiations to the visual cortex of the occipital lobe.

relearning   1. In common parlance, learning something again that was previously learned and then forgotten. 2. The process of regaining ability that was lost. See RELEARNING METHOD/PROCEDURE.

relearning method/procedure   A process used in memory research to measure how much time or how many repetitions it will take to relearn something to the same standard as earlier (for example, a person learns 20 nonsense terms in 50 trials, a month later the same person relearns the same material to the same criterion in only 30 trials, the difference of 20 trials indicates the amount of retention). Also known as relearning savings, savings method.

relearning savings   **relearning method/procedure**

release   1. The experience of freeing the self from constriction, as may occur as a result of a confession or acceptance of the reality of an event or submission to the logic of circumstances. 2. Removal of inhibitory effects of higher neural levels on lower levels. 3. A hypothetical structure to explain why a particular stimulus releases a particular response.

release phenomenon   The unrestricted activity of a lower brain center when a higher center with inhibitory control is damaged or excised.

releaser   1. Any stimulus that will trigger a pre-established response. For example, certain male fish will only show sexual interest in female fish if they have a particular shape. 2. A specific stimulus for a young member of a particular species that enables a potential reaction of individual animals to respond in a species-specific manner. For example, a particular cry or movement of a mother will result in a specific reaction on the part of her brood (whelps, cubs, fledglings, etc.) to react simultaneously in the same manner, perhaps crouching, or returning to their den or nest. Also known as sign stimulus. See IMPRINTING, INNATE RELEASING MECHANISM.

release theory of humor   A point of view that humor first tends to raise and then lower anxiety.

release therapy   1. (D. Levy) A form of therapy in which young children "play out" anxieties, frightening experiences, and traumatic events with such materials as figurines, toy animals, and water guns. 2. Psychotherapy that calls for clients to express themselves as fully and as forcefully as possible. See PSYCHODRAMA, AQUA-ENERGETICS, CREATIVE AGGRESSION, PRIMAL THERAPY.

release zone   The location in the interior of the postsynaptic membrane of a synapse where synaptic vesicles release their neurotransmitter.

Rel. *f*   See RELATIVE FREQUENCY.

reliability   A measure of the degree of consistency of sets of variables, such as tests given to the same people more than once. A perfectly reliable test would give exactly the same scores time after time and thus would have a test-retest reliability coefficient of +1.00 whereas a completely unreliable test would have a coefficient of 0.00 (zero). Most published tests have reliability correlations from 0.70 to about 0.95. There are a variety of methods for obtaining measures of consistency such as Coefficient Alpha, various Kuder-Richardson formulas, the Hoyt ANOVA approach. See INDEX OF RELIABILITY, SPLIT HALF METHOD OF RELIABILITY, TEST CONSTRUCTION, VALIDITY.

reliability index   See INDEX OF RELIABILITY.

reliability sampling   A statistical measure or assessment of the extent of correspondence or agreement between at least two samples drawn from the same population.

reliable   Stable or consistent. A test is reliable if it gives the same result on further measurements or repeatedly measures with precision the construct it is purported to measure. See ODD-EVEN RELIABILITY, RELIABILITY, RELIABILITY COEFFICIENT, SPLIT-HALF RELIABILITY.

relief   A feeling characterized by pleasantness due to the removal of tension, strain, or boredom.

relief-distress quotient   See DISTRESS-RELIEF QUOTIENT.

relief-oriented belief   A personal idea that has the purpose of alleviating some kind of discomfort characterized by thinking that performing a certain action will benefit the person, such as "If I think happy thoughts, my leg will get better."

religiocentrism   The conviction that a person's own religion is more important than or superior to other religions. See ETHNOCENTRISM.

religion   An organized system of values and beliefs that serve as moral and social guides. Many religions have "leaders" (teachers, priests, etc.) to instruct others and conduct rituals. Many cultures have developed their own unique religious systems. Most religions may have developed concepts dealing with the origins of life, moral right and wrong behavior, and assumptions about afterlife.

religiosity   The denotation of religiosity refers to a person excessively or pretentiously concerned with religion; however, the contemporary connotation is of a person excessively concerned about religion.

religious conduct   1. A system of beliefs, ceremonies, and practices relating to the supernatural, God or gods, and to other humans. 2. Any behavior that helps humans accept the fact of their mortality.

religious consciousness   1. Awareness of religious precepts especially during institutional services. 2. An elevated state of consciousness resulting from various religious beliefs and practices. 3. An altered state of consciousness induced through ritual or religious introspection.

religious delusions   Abnormal personal convictions associated with religious beliefs, such as grandiose ideas in which self-chosen people view themselves as saints, messiahs, or religious authorities who can cure illness or save humankind, or in which a person claims to be the incarnation or reincarnation of a recognized historical religious figure.

religious experience   Any event of importance to an individual that has spiritual aspects connected with it. For instance, a person feels transported to a state of tranquility.

religious faith   Belief in a supreme being or a spiritual force that sets standards of conduct, responds to prayer, and often assures the ultimate triumph of good over evil. Usually, but not always associated with an organized religious system accompanied by rituals and doctrines. Sigmund Freud regarded religion as a collective neurosis, which mankind would eventually outgrow. O. Hobart Mowrer viewed mental illnesses as the result of sins. See FAITH HEALING, MAGICAL THINKING, RELIGIOUS THERAPY.

religious healers   See FAITH HEALING.

religious instinct hypothesis   A postulate that all humans have a tendency to want to believe in a religion, to practice certain rituals, and to act according to the principles of the religion.

religious mania   A state of acute hyperactivity, agitation, and restlessness related to religion, sometimes accompanied by hallucinations. See STIGMATA.

religious-objects fear   See HIEROPHOBIA (meaning 3).

religious resignation   An attitude of passively accepting unpleasant or disastrous events in terms of believing that such is foreordained by a higher power and that a person should submit to such events without any attempt to improve matters.

religious therapy   Counseling or psychotherapy provided or planned by a cleric or other religious authority oriented toward psychological relief or improvement, including such activities as counseling, the confessional, classes.

religious trance   A state of ecstasy or transformation due to deep personal involvement in religion, usually precipitated by a specific religious practice, such as meditation, breathing practices, chanting, or even ritual dancing. May involve religious revelations.

religious type   One of Edward Spranger's six classifications of people, those who seek to understand the universe as a whole and are concerned with spiritual truth and with the unity of all experience.

REM   See RAPID-EYE-MOVEMENT SLEEP.

REM behavior disorder (RBD)   A sleep disorder that occurs during rapid-eye-movement (REM) sleep that may include nightmares and violent behavior.

REM latency   The time period between falling asleep and the first rapid-eye-movement (REM) manifestation.

REM rebound   A tendency of a person deprived of rapid-eye-movement (REM) sleep, usually by being awakened during REM sleep to catch up on REM on further sleeping.

REM sleep efficiency   A percentage of total sleep spent in the rapid-eye-movement (REM) state.

REM sleep   A stage of sleep characterized by rapid conjugate eye movements (coordinated movements of the two eyes functioning together) during D-state sleep. Also known as activated sleep, active sleep, desynchronized sleep (D sleep).

Remak's band   (R. Remak) The core of the axon (axis cylinder). Once known as the primitive band.

remake memory   **long-term memory (LTM)**

remedial education   See REMEDIAL INSTRUCTION/TEACHING.

remedial instruction/teaching   1. Training in an attempt to achieve normality or to obtain a higher level of functioning when functioning below expectation. 2. The treatment of learning disorders through audiovisual devices, programmed learning, study in a resource room, or individual tutoring.

remedial loop   In a branching type choice situation, as progress is made, the possibility exists of coming eventually closer to the true position on a continuum by correcting for errors and for chance successes. See PASCAL'S TRIANGLE.

remedial reading   The training of people, usually children, who are well below normal expectation, in their ability to read. There are a number of different systems intended to help different types of reading deficiencies.

remedial teaching   **remedial instruction**

remember   To reinstate a memory or to be able to visualize a previously learned image or to repeat a previous learned experience or action, especially after a period of unawareness of the event or person or action.

remembering   The process of consciously reviving or bringing to awareness previous events, experiences, or information. Remembering is also the process of retaining such material, which is essential to learning, since without it humans would not profit from training, practice, or past experience. See RECALL, RECOGNITION, RECOLLECTION, RELEARNING METHOD.

remembrance   1. In general, refers to various aspects of memory such as retention and recollection. 2. (R. L. Moreland & J. M. Levine) In group dynamics, a period of time during which remaining group members reminisce about a former member, who appraises the past experiences in the group.

reminiscence   1. A recalling of a past event. 2. Telling about past events. 3. In the psychology of learning, a temporary rise in memory (the retention curve) after learning a task, higher than the score immediately after the learning. 4. The recollection of previous experiences, especially those of a pleasant nature, dwelling on the past.

reminiscence therapy   The encouragement of discussion of life history, the writing of one's own life story, or both, to improve psychological well-being. Often used with older people.

remission   1. Improvement of a condition, physical or mental, that may or may not be permanent. 2. The cessation or stopping of symptoms of any kind of disorder. In most cases the term implies that the disease or condition is still present, but that there is a temporary improvement in the situation. See SPONTANEOUS REMISSION.

remission of schizophrenia   A situation of a person previously diagnosed with schizophrenia who is now declared free of the disorder.

remorse   1. A feeling of regret for past misdeeds. 2. Anguish caused by a sense of guilt, which may have a real or fancied basis. Various methods are used to relieve (or "undo") feelings of guilt, ranging from bestowing gifts to doing penance. See UNDOING.

remote association   1. In a free association test, a response to the stimulus word that is less common or would involve intermediate steps to see the connection between the stimulus and the response. 2. Any kind of association between an item and another item not logically related to or associated with it. 2. Sensation obtained indirectly. For example, sensing the hardness of a fruit by pressing it with an eraser rather than with a finger. See RESIDENT SENSATION.

remote-association test   (S. A. Mednick) A task to determine creativity. A person is given three words that have no evident association between them such as "music," "food," "cow" and asked to find a fourth word that relates to the other three.

remote conditioning   See TRACE CONDITIONING.

remote cause   In any chain of causes, an event distant from the effect that to some extent influenced the effect.

remote dependency   The effect of an element upon another element in a series when the two elements are separated by other intervening elements. For example, learning a series of nonsense syllables, remembering syllable number 8 might depend on remembering syllable number 3.

remote effects   The effects resulting from an intervention in a part of the system other than that being specifically studied.

remote masking   The suppression of low-frequency tones by high-frequency tones. See MASKING.

remote memory   Recall or recognition of experiences or information dating from the distant past. Older person have this ability, although they may be forgetful of more recent events. See LONG-TERM MEMORY.

remote perception   Knowledge about an object by some indirect method of perceiving it. For example, persons wearing blindfolds recognizing the existence of a wall by the sound of their footsteps or their speech bouncing back from the wall.

remotivation   Efforts directed toward stimulating discouraged, withdrawn persons by various individual or group activities.

Ren   A concept from Confucian philosophy meaning human-heartedness of which kindness is a component. May be similar to Alfred Adler's *Gemeinschaftesgefühl*, relating to the primary responsibility to consider and look to the needs of others. "Ren" is the Pinyin romanization used in mainland China; "jen" is the Wade-Giles romanization used in Taiwan.

renal rap   (E. A. Corsini) A support group for renal disease patients who interact while on dialysis. See GROUP THERAPY.

Renard Diagnostic Interview   (L. Robins) A standard structured interview developed by Robins and collaborators, it attempts to obtain sufficient information for the diagnosis of certain personality disorders.

renifleur   1. A person who obtains sexual interest and excitement from smelling bodily odors. Sometimes known as a sniffer. 2. A person with a morbid interest in body odors, especially as a means of sexual excitement. See OSPHRESIOLAGNIA.

renin   An enzyme secreted by the brain and kidney, which stimulates the formation of angiotensin I, a hormone involved with vasoconstriction of arteries and fluid retention in the regulation of blood pressure. Also known as angiotensinogenase.

Renpenning's syndrome   A condition of mental retardation inherited as X-linked recessive and lacking any associated physical abnormality. Named after 20th century Canadian physician H. Renpenning.

Renshaw cell   1. A neuron that functions to inhibit the actions of motor neurons. 2. An inhibitory cell that communicates with motoneuron axons near the spinal cord. It is a part of the negative-feedback system that prevents rapid repeated firing of motoneurons. Named after American neurophysiologist B. Renshaw.

renunciation   1. Surrender of self, possessions, etc. 2. In psychoanalytic theory, a refusal of the ego to follow impulses of the id or unrealistic demands of the superego. 3. In religion, the surrender of one's will to a deity.

reorganization   (W. Wertheimer) An operation of "dividing into sub-wholes and still seeing these sub-wholes together, with clear reference to the whole figure and in view of the specific problem at issue... The realization of how parts (sub-wholes) fit together and complete the whole; the realization of the inner relatedness between their fitting together and the whole-features of the figure." An important part of Gestalt theory asserting that learning involves mental restructuring not just addition of knowledge as in Associationism theory.

reorganization principle/theory   A principle of Gestalt theory that new learning or perception requires a reorganization of understanding or perception, such that what seemed arbitrary or made no sense before, is reorganized into a structure that does make sense. See INSIGHT.

REP Test   See ROLE CONSTRUCT REPERTORY TEST.

repair mechanism/process   A method of teaching by stopping or interrupting an error in progress, informing the person of the error.

repair theory   A point of view that sleep has a recuperative function for mental as well as physical tasks.

reparation   1. Amends, compensation. 2. Repairing, restoration. 3. In psychoanalytic theory, the defense mechanism of reducing guilt by doing good works. 4. (M. Klein) All creative activity, used to resolve one's inherent ambivalence to objects.

reparative therapy   (J. Nicolosi) A controversial psychological treatment aimed at changing the sexual orientation of lesbians and gay men. Based on the argument that such people engage in an unnatural and dangerous lifestyle and thus are in need of such therapy.

re-parenting   General procedure used in a variety of therapeutic systems to provide a client with presumably missed childhood experiences. The process calls for the client to be treated as an infant or young child, fed with a spoon, hugged, cradled, sung to, and otherwise provided with what that person (or the therapist) feels the person was deprived of. See PRIMARY RELATIONSHIP THERAPY.

repeatability   1. The possibility of performing a particular behavior or set of behaviors exactly as before to elicit the same responses or results as before. 2. In research, an experimenter observes certain phenomena, using the same methods, the same experimenter or other experimenters re-perform the experiment to determine whether the same phenomena are observed each time. See REPLICATION.

repeated measures designs   1. Experimental designs in which all participants receive two or more values on the independent variable. 2. A research design in which all subjects receive the same treatment. See BETWEEN-GROUPS DESIGNS.

repeated measures   Remeasuring a second or additional times in an attempt to be more certain of the accuracy of measurement. See RELIABILITY.

repeated treatment designs   See REPEATED MEASURES DESIGN.

repeaters   See RECIDIVISM, RECIDIVISTS, REVOLVING-DOOR PHENOMENON.

repellent   1. Capable of driving away or repelling. 2. A substance emitted by an organism to keep others away. Whereas a skunk's odiferous emission is well-known, other organisms, including trees, have also developed repellents against invaders. Also spelled repellant. See PHEROMONE.

repersonalization   See HYPNOSIS.

repertoire   All behaviors available or possible for a person or group under given environmental conditions.

repertory grid   (G. A. Kelly) A diagnostic procedure for determining how people see other people. Based on polar opposites. See ROLE CONSTRUCT REPERTORY TEST.

repetition   1. Recurrent behavior. 2. Learning by rehearsing.

repetition-compulsion   1. In psychoanalytic theory, a term used by Sigmund Freud to describe the unconscious need to reenact early traumas in the attempt to overcome or master them. 2. Irrational tendency to repeat any maladjustive behavior over and over. 3. An unconscious tendency to reenact early traumas in nightmares, rumination, etc., in the attempt to overcome or master them. Also known as repetition-reaction. See ZEIGARNIK EFFECT.

repetition compulsion/pattern   (P. Janet) Obsessive-compulsive behavior in which a person feels compelled to repeat simple operations, as in checking a door many times before being certain that it has been locked properly. See REPETITION-COMPULSION.

repetition law   See LAW OF FREQUENCY.

repetition pattern   repetition-compulsion

repetition priming   Increase in the frequency of a word being identified or understood via recent exposures to that word but without awareness.

repetition-reaction   repetition-compulsion (meaning 3)

repetitive pattern/schema   1. A persistent attitude or form of behavior repeated automatically and unconsciously, for example, deliberateness, or use of a particular gesture. 2. (J. Piaget) Patterns of behavior endlessly repeated by children for no evident reason, except perhaps for the apparent pleasure of the activity. See FUNCTIONLUST, MANNERISM, TIC.

repetitive strain injury (RSI)   1. Pain or damage to a part of the body that has been subjected to frequent and repetitious motion. See CARPAL-TUNNEL SYNDROME. 2. Painful spasm of the muscles used in writing or typing, once considered a conversion or hysterical symptom due to unconscious conflicts, especially if the same muscles may be used without pain in other activities such as shuffling cards. See WRITER'S CRAMP.

replacement formation   The substitution of an idea or a set of ideas for others.

replacement memory   The substitution of one memory for another, as in a screen memory (a recollection of an event that a person is uncertain actually happened). See SCREEN MEMORY.

replacement sample   A sampling process in which an item or person is selected and measured, and then that item or person is returned to the pool from which the original sampling was done.

replacement therapy   The substitution of healthy ideations for unhealthy ones through any or a combinations of methods, by focusing on constructive activities and interests.

replacement treatment   In medicine, a treatment technique in which a natural or synthetic substance is substituted for one that is deficient in the body of the patient. See PSYCHOPHARMACOLOGY.

replication (study)   The exact repetition of a research, generally by a new experimenter with new participants to determine whether the same results will be obtained as before.

replication therapy   1. A behavior therapy technique that concentrates on reinforcing a person's successful everyday behavior. 2. A psychodrama procedure in which an artificial situation is constructed to enact or reenact a repetition of a past situation by a new one or an imagined future one.

report   1. The protocol or account of observations by an observer or an actor in a situation. 2. An oral or written statement by a psychologist or other professional about a case.

report method   Asking participants questions about an experiment in which they took part, for example, after a study on frustration, asking the participants to tell how they felt during the process.

report program generator (RPG)   Symbolic language designed to simplify a programmer's problem in writing computer programs that produce reports, adapted particularly for handling a large volume of preprinted forms. RPG eliminates the task of developing some of the processing steps.

repose   A period of rest, relaxation.

re-present   To present once more.

represent   1. To stand for and in some respects take the place of another thing. 2. Symbolic substitution.

representation   1. The process of using a symbol or image to stand for an object, act, or unconscious impulse. 2. Re-experiencing a previous event occurring in the absence of any relationship to associated stimuli via memory or mental imagery.

representationalism   A doctrine positing that what is perceived is a true copy of the outside world.

representational skills   (J. Piaget) In Piagetian theory, the cognitive skills involved in understanding the world of people, objects, and events, including the ability to use images, words, and at least rudimentary concepts and elementary logic.

representational stage   (J. Piaget) In Piagetian theory, a period of cognitive development that encompasses the preoperational and concrete operational periods.

representational thought   (J. Piaget) Internalized thought including memories of prior experiences.

representation factors   See REPRESENTATIVE FACTORS.

representation problem   The degree of difficulty involved in constructing an internal representation to solve an unfamiliar problem.

representative   Standing for something else, such as a symbol for an object, or a single score for an array of scores.

representative conclusion   A prediction about a whole population, including mean and range, based on a random sample of the population. Usually, the more representative the sample, the more accurate the conclusion.

representative design   1. A research design that includes all relevant variables (experimental and statistical) that will affect the dependent variable. 2. (E. Brunswick) An experimental arrangement that attempts to use all variations of factors in stimulus-response research including stratified samples of subjects. See MULTIVARIATE APPROACHES, REPRESENTATIVE SAMPLE.

representative factors   1. Activities that permit an organism to continue or renew a response when the original stimulus is discontinued. 2. Verbal symbols and imagery that serve as mediators of ideation.

representative heuristic   1. Refers to a single item taken by chance from an array of similar items that will represent the class of items. Thus, if an explorer finds a previously unknown form of life, it will most probably tell a great deal about other similar forms of life. 2. A generalization about organisms on the basis of partial information, for example, that animals with cloven hooves are herbivorous (eat grass), even though pigs are omnivorous (eat anything). 3. Classifying a phenomenon in terms of how closely it resembles a particular prototype. See REPRESENTATIVENESS BIAS.

representative intelligence   (J. Piaget) In Piagetian theory, a developmental period that children from about ages 2 to 8 experience in which symbols represent concrete objects and events.

representative measure   1. A number that stands for a particular set of other numbers, such as the average, the median, or the mode. 2. A score that gives general information about a certain population. For example, the mean intelligence quotient (IQ) of high school students in the United States is 104. 3. A number that substitutes for another number for the sake of convenience in calculating. For example, the number 1 may be used to represent one million. Also known as representative score/value.

representativeness   Close correspondence between a sample and the population from which it is drawn so that the character of the sample accurately reflects the population from which it is drawn. A representative sample reproduces the essential characteristics and constitution of a population in correct number and proportions. Representativeness is the foundation of scientific sampling. See REPRESENTATIVENESS BIAS, REPRESENTATIVENESS HEURISTIC.

representativeness bias   An error in judgment that occurs as a result of the use of the representativeness heuristic as described by D. Kahneman & A. Tversky. A person would demonstrate the representativeness bias by guessing that given the two choices a slender person carrying books of poetry is more likely a university professor than a truck driver. This judgment would likely be in error because of the "base rate"; there are substantially more truck drivers than university professors, and the odds are with the truck drivers. The judgment was based upon a perceived similarity between characteristics of the person judged and a stereotype of professors.

representativeness heuristic   1. In general, inferring the cause of an event or a condition by the resemblance of the latter to a salient feature of the former. Emphasis is on establishing a positive relationship. Although a valuable cognitive device, it can, when crudely used, result in failure to include other relevant information. Example: Turmeric has a billiant yellow color, which indicates that it has the power to cure the jaundice (cited by John Stuart Mill). 2. In statistics, a reasoning heuristic (stated by D. Kahneman & A. Tversky) that can lead to systematic errors in estimating probabilities. Emphasis is on sources of error, that is, the negative aspects of the heuristic. A person who uses this heuristic evaluates the probability of an uncertain event, or a sample, by the degree to which it (a) resembles essential properties of its presumed parent population; and (b) reflects a salient feature of the process by which another known event or sample was generated.

representativeness test   An examination that contains all necessary items to measure the function it is intended to evaluate. For example, a test that measures social, academic, and mechanical intelligence, if these three factors represent what intelligence is. See OMNIBUS TEST.

representative sample   1. A sample of a particular population that has characteristics similar to the larger population. 2. A sample that is a close representation of the intended population. The *Literary Digest* that mis-predicted the 1936 presidential elections claiming that Alfred Landon would beat Franklin D. Roosevelt was based on a sample taken from telephone books and consequently was not representative since only relatively wealthy people had telephones at that time. See BIASED SAMPLE, REPRESENTATIVE SAMPLING, REPRESENTATIVENESS.

representative sampling   The selection of a sample that will insure a valid representation of the total population. See REPRESENTATIVE SAMPLE.

representative score   representative measure

representative theory   A philosophical concept that reality can only be known through ideas.

representative value   representative measure

repress   An unconscious attempt to hold back, to reduce, or to prevent something from happening. "Repress" has the concept of unintentionality whereas "suppress" includes the concept of intentionality.

repressed complex   1. A group of emotional factors or ideas hidden from consciousness, thereby becoming the source of abnormal behavior. 2. In psychoanalytic theory, refers to the inhibition of gratification due to repressive forces in the id or superego. See REPRESSION, SUPPRESSION.

repressed memory   1. In Freudian terms, these are infantile memories of impulses and thoughts unacceptable to the ego that are pushed into the unconscious. 2. Traumatic memories or recollections of trauma that are psychologically pushed into the unconscious.

repressed wish   An unconscious desire that may emerge in dreams, hypnosis, when angry, or while in psychotherapy. See ABREACTION.

repression   A tendency to unintentionally forget unhappy, unpleasant, or traumatic events as part of a defense mechanism, but memories of the events are still in the unconscious. Sigmund Freud considered repression the most important of the defense mechanisms. Three major kinds of repression have been distinguished: primal, primary, and secondary. Wilhelm Griesinger called this concept *Verdrängung*. See ABREACTION, AFTER EXPULSION, ORGANIC REPRESSION, STRANGULATED AFFECT, SUPPRESSION.

repression-resistance   ego resistance

repression sensitization   Heightened reactions on a continuum of denial and worry to perceived threats to well-being.

repression-sensitization scale   A scale on the <u>Minnesota Multiphasic Personality Inventory</u> (MMPI) used in estimating a person's tendency to be careful in meeting anxiety-provoking situations.

repressive approach   An attempt to eliminate symptoms by command, persuasion, or suggestion, without exploring their unconscious sources or attempting to bring about basic personality changes. See SUPPRESSIVE APPROACH.

repressive-inspirational group psychotherapy (L. Cody Marsh) An approach, actually suppressive rather than repressive in the sense of attempting to strengthen an individual's defenses instead of breaking through them to elicit unconscious material; inspirational in the sense of using various measures to encourage participants in groups to generate enthusiasm and convictions through testimonials, socializing, sharing of experiences, reassurance, and esprit de corps. See ALCOHOLICS ANONYMOUS for an example.

reproducibility coefficient   coefficient of reproducibility

reproduction   1. The process of generating of similar or identical elements, as in procreation. See REPRODUCTIVE BEHAVIOR. 2. Generating a copy of something from memory, such as the drawing of a design. 3. In learning, the repetition of a task in the manner in which it was learned originally.

reproduction method/procedure   A means of testing a participant's accuracy of memory by asking for a reproduction of given material, either orally or graphically. Also known as method of reproduction.

reproductive behavior   Activity that leads to propagation of the species. The mechanism varies with the type of organism, ranging from simple cell division in a unicellular organism to in higher species a merger of chromosomes contributed by male and female parents and supervision of the offspring until they are able to survive in the external environment. See ASEXUAL REPRODUCTION, SEXUAL REPRODUCTION.

reproductive effort   Attempts, whether successful or not, of an organism to reproduce itself.

reproductive facilitation   1. In learning, refers to that which assists memory. 2. In sexuality, refers to events or structures that enable organisms to mate. It has been noted that many animals kept in artificial settings such as zoos will not reproduce, but in some instances when the zoo environment is made to look as much as possible like their natural one, reproduction has been facilitated and offspring produced. 3. Later improvement in reproducing a formerly learned response or behavioral sequence.

reproductive failure   Inability to conceive or to deliver a normal offspring that will grow to maturity.

reproductive function   1. All processes involved in the conception and birth of offspring. 2. Alternately, solely the sexual functions.

reproductive functioning   A series of behaviors that lead to the creation of new members of the species, as seen in the spawning of salmon.

reproductive imagination   Noncreative type of imagination, generating images based on previously experienced patterns.

reproductive instinct   1. Innate drive of organisms to proceed to reproduce themselves. 2. A behavioral drive or impulse as expressed in courtship, nest-building, and parental activity.

reproductive interference   1. In learning, factors that interfere with perfect reproduction of learned material. For example, in studying mathematics and chemistry together, each may negatively affect memory of the other topic. 2. In sexual reproduction, refers to the effect of factors that inhibit mating or factors that prevent conception or gestation including psychological ones (such as fear) or physiological (such as improper diet of the mother).

reproductive memory   A reliable memory, one that can be trusted even though everything that was originally learned or experienced may not be recalled.

reproductive ritual   A formal pattern of behavior for sexual activity, pregnancy, birth, or attaining biological maturity. See PUBERTY RITES.

reproductive selection   A tendency in some classes of animals for males to compete with each other for reproductive rights to the females. Consequently, the genetic traits of the successful males are passed on to their offspring.

reproductive strength   1. The summation of all factors that contribute to a given response. 2. In learning, all factors affecting the production of a suitable response in any situation. 3. The relative capacity of any organism or classes of organisms to reproduce themselves.

reproductive success   Ability of a species to produce viable offspring.

reproductive tendency   See ASSOCIATIVE TENDENCY.

reproductive type   (L. Rostan) A constitutional type in the Rostan system, characterized by a dominance of the reproductive system over other body systems. Roughly comparable to Nicola Pende's hypergenital type. See CONSTITUTIONAL TYPES, TYPES.

repulsion   1. In general, a strong feeling of dislike, aversion, or repugnance leading to rejection or escape. 2. In genetics, a process whereby genes of different parents show an aversion to entering the same gametes, resulting in an excess of some parental gene combinations and a deficiency of new combinations as might be expected according to the Mendelian principle of independent assortment.

repulsive   (H. Zwaardemaker) In Zwaardemaker's smell system, a classification of unpleasant odors, characterized by the smells of bedbugs and belladonna.

reputation   An estimate of a person's character by society at large or of the members of the social group to which the person belongs.

reputation rating   Any of several procedures for determining how a person is viewed by others.

required behavior/relationship   Behavior deemed proper for any person in terms of social expectation for time and place, age and situation. Behavior strongly reinforced either by law or social convention.

requiredness   (W. Köhler, M. Wertheimer, K. Koffka) In Gestalt psychology, parts of a whole form a configuration which places specific demands upon those parts and upon all of the remaining parts that constitute the whole. What is missing to complete a Gestalt figure.

re-reading (method)   A procedure for checking memory of some material after it has been read a required number of times. Also known as re-reading procedure/test.

RES   See RETICULOENDOTHELIAL SYSTEM.

resampling   Using given sample data to repeatedly simulate (usually via a computer) hypothetical samples and to recalculate the statistic of interest.

res cogitans   (thinking thing—Latin) Refers to the mind as contrasted to the body, which Descartes saw as operating mechanically. See CARTESIAN DUALISM, CONARIUM.

Rescorla-Wagner theory   (R. Rescorla & A. Wagner) A point of view that conditioning does not only depend on mere co-occurrence of the unconditioned stimulus and the conditioned stimulus, but whether the conditioned stimulus actually predicts the unconditioned stimulus. For example, if a bell is ringing all of the time and a whistle is sounded directly preceding the presentation of the unconditioned stimulus (food), the bell that co-occurred would not signal the coming of the food but the whistle would.

rescue fantasy   A daydream characterized by imagining saving the life of a parent or another important person.

rescuer   In transactional analysis, a person who seeks out people in need of some kind of help with the intention of saving them. Also known as "nebbish chaser." See RED CROSS NURSE.

research   1. Systematic effort to discover or confirm facts by scientific methods of observation and experiment, usually including investigation of previous research in libraries or computerized sources. 2. Any logical procedure for uncovering the essence of any phenomenon based on logical conceptualizations. Types of research include: APPLIED, BASIC, DESCRIPTIVE, EXPERIMENTAL, EXPLORATORY, FIELD, ISSUE BASED,

LIBRARY, MARKET, NONEXPERIMENTAL, OBSERVA-TIONAL, PERSONNEL, PURE, RELATIONAL, THEORY BASED.

research design 1. The overall strategy of the research, such as correlational, or experimental, or ethnomethodological. 2. A proposal for research detailing the rationale and method. See CRUCIAL EXPERIMENT, DESIGN OF RESEARCH, RESEARCH METHODS, RESEARCH TYPES.

Research Diagnostic Criteria (RDC) A formal method of evaluating past or present mental states to lead to new diagnoses. See RENARD DIAGNOSTIC INTERVIEW.

researcher bias Attitudes, negative or positive, of researchers, about the participants or subject matter of the study. Any attitude not aimed at finding the "truth" may cause problems and affect the validity of a research. Many people are unaware of their biases, including the enthusiasm to find positive results that may warp their findings.

research ethics A corpus or doctrine bearing on the rights of individuals and the societies of which they are members, as well as of other sentient experimental subjects that need to be treated with compassion. Research projects are adjudicated relative to ethical acceptability by institutional review boards of those institutes, academies, and laboratories that conduct psychological research. Among the operative principles are safeguarding privacy of information obtained, ensuring minimal risk (physical or psychological) to the participants, insuring informed consent of adults or of children's legal guardians, and appropriate use of research findings for advancing the welfare of the populations at issue.

research for action Studies undertaken not only for the sake of theoretical learning but for finding something immediately practical, as in studying various kinds of animal behavior that can be used for commercial purposes. See APPLIED RESEARCH.

research method Any standard procedure, such as controlled observation or the hypothetico-deductive method for determining the truth of hypotheses or the discovery of facts. See RESEARCH DESIGN.

research question A tentative assumption, interpretation, or hypothesis concerning a particular phenomenon that is explicitly stated so that it may be accepted or rejected at a particular level of satisfaction. It is the first step in any research study.

research system A formal process of conducting a research, be it as simple as observation or as complex as a study that may take years and hundreds of individual experiments. See RESEARCH DESIGN.

research types According to Mary Allen, research can be categorized into these major types: (a) applied, to obtain useful information; (b) basic, to prove a theory; (c) descriptive, to accurately portray a situation; (d) explanatory, to find reasons; (e) exploratory, to make initial efforts at knowing something; (f) relational, to find connections between events. Also, studies can be classified as either field research or laboratory research. See RESEARCH DESIGN.

resentment A feeling of anger and antipathy because of perceived injustices done to the person by others.

reserpine An important psychotropic medication, an early anti-psychotic drug, not related to the phenothiazines. Also used as an anti-hypertensive agent and occasionally for intractable dyskinesia. Its side effect of depression was common and severe enough that it fell out of favor as soon as other drugs with less severe side effects became available. Reserpine was a refined form of a sedative, *Rauwolfia Serpentin*, used in ancient India and may thus be one of the earliest known psychotropic agents. Trade names include Serpasil.

reservation Not being completely open and honest, having misgivings or second thoughts; not disclosing everything in a communication, such as a significant detail. See RESERVED.

reserve capacity An ability of the body to demonstrate unusual potentials of behavior under emergency conditions.

reserved 1. Holding back from social participation. 2. An attitude or style of life that is not forthcoming. Voluntarily restrained.

res extensa (tangible thing—Latin) A thing that has substance, is tangible, can be seen, felt, and measured. See CARTESIAN DUALISM, CONARIUM.

residence rate A ratio of the number of patients residing in institutions of a given type on a given date to the total population of the city, county, state, or another area.

residential care Services provided to persons with disabilities in a foster home or group home, as opposed to a large institution.

residential center/facility Domiciles for certain types of people, such as those who are emotionally disturbed, disadvantaged, or older. The facility usually has a program that includes group therapy or counseling, social and recreational activities, work experiences, and provides assisted living situations.

residential schools 1. Special educational facilities for delayed-development or disadvantaged children. 2. Boarding schools, where children live usually throughout the school year.

residential treatment facility Small institutions, such as large private homes in which disturbed children, adolescents, and in some cases adults reside. Programs usually includes counseling, social and recreational activities, and work experiences.

resident sensation The sensation on the skin's surface; stimuli perceived directly rather than indirectly through an intermediary. See REMOTE ASSOCIATION.

residual 1. The difference between the entire and the computed value of an experiment. 2. What remains after a loss of some kind, such as the amount of vision left in a person after an accident. 3. A condition in which acute symptoms have subsided, but chronic or less severe symptoms remain. See RESIDUUM.

residual attention-deficit disorder The condition of children who were once diagnosed as having attention-deficit hyperactivity disorder (ADHD), after the hyperactivity component has disappeared. Inattention and impulsivity usually remain in most of such children that will negatively affect their social and occupational behavior into adulthood, even though the hyperactivity has disappeared. See ATTENTION DEFICIT HYPERACTIVITY DISORDER (ADHD).

residual delusion   (C. Neisser) False beliefs originally developed in an acute state of mental disorder but now retained while in a chronic state.

residual deviance (hypothesis)   (T. Scheff) A postulate that behavioral disorders are due to the person's intention to break the rules after all other reasons have been excluded.

residual epilepsy   See MYOCLONIC EPILEPSY.

residual matrix   In factor analysis, what remains after all factors have been removed from the matrix. See RESIDUUM.

residual rules   Norms of social behavior that are not usually considered, and usually only noticed when they are broken such as being caught staring too long at another person.

residual schizophrenic   A person who fluctuates between evident schizophrenia and apparent improvement, but who during the improvement phase still demonstrates some schizoid tendencies.

residual schizophrenic disorder   A diagnosis for a person who has experienced at least one episode of schizophrenia, but at the present time is functioning normally. Also known as residual schizophrenia.

residual state infantile autism   The status of a person once diagnosed as having infantile autism and now showing some signs of the illness, such as poor communication and social peculiarities.

residue method   (J. S. Mill) An approach for determining causation by subtracting known causes of part of the phenomenon and then concluding that the remaining antecedents must have caused the remainder of the phenomenon.

residuum   1. In factor analysis, what remains of the original correlations when all factors have been extracted. 2. A trace memory that cannot be recalled but which is assumed to exist because relearning is easier. See SAVINGS.

resignation   1. Giving in or accepting things as they are, with no intention to contend against opposing forces. 2. An attitude of apathetic surrender to the situation or symptoms, frequently occurring in institutionalized patients. 3. (K. Horney) One of Karen Horney's three basic orientations, representing the desire to be free of others. Horney differentiated between two kinds: dynamic resignation while looking for opportunities for change, and neurotic resignation or withdrawal to avoid any conflict. See INSTITUTIONALIZATION, NEUROTIC DEFENSE SYSTEM.

resilient children   Children able to deal successfully with stresses and traumas that would devastate most other children. Less accurately known as "invulnerables."

resinous   1. In general, relating to resin. 2. In Hans Henning's odor system, an odor obtained from natural resinous materials such as solidified tree sap or resin used on violin bows. See HENNING ODOR PRISM.

resistance   1. Action against an opposing force. 2. In psychotherapy, a decision, conscious or unconscious, not to cooperate in some respects with the therapist. Conscious resistance is the withholding of information due to embarrassment or fear. In psychoanalysis, unconscious resistance is stated to emerge in the ego's struggle to maintain repression of the anxiety-evoking unconscious material as it gradually rises to consciousness in the course of treatment. See ANALYSIS OF RESISTANCE, ANALYTICAL INSIGHT, CONSCIOUS RESEARCH, EPINOSIC RESEARCH, ID RESEARCH, REPRESSION RESEARCH, SUPEREGO RESEARCH, TRANSFERENCE RESEARCH. 3. The ability of an organism to withstand harmful effects of antagonistic agents (for example, toxins, drugs, pathological environmental conditions).

resistance sensation   Fusion of kinesthetic and cutaneous sensations evoked by pressure and muscular tension, when the muscle or muscles concerned are contracting against an opposing external force. Also known as sensation of resistance.

resistance stage   (H. Selye) The second stage of the general adaptation syndrome, in which the body combats or defends itself against the stressor. Adaptation is manifested, in part, by the increased secretions of the adrenal glands. Also known as stage of resistance. See ALARM REACTION, EXHAUSTION STAGE, GENERAL ADAPTATION SYSTEM, RESISTANCE TO STRESS.

resistance to extinction   A measure of the strength of conditioning based on the endurance or persistence of a conditioned response during extinction trials. The number of trials required to cause extinction provides a standard for judging the strength of conditioning.

resistance to stress   1. The degree of capacity to endure physical or psychological pressure. 2. (H. Selye) The second stage of the general adaptation syndrome (GAS). It follows the alarm reaction which is marked by psychosomatic or physiological changes related to emotional stress. The organism attempts to adjust to the stressful situation to endure and survive. See RESISTANCE STAGE.

resistant attachment   Behavior of infants who, after showing distress when separated from their mother figures on reunion with them, display anger and indifference. Distinguished from avoidant, disorganized, and secure attachments. See ATTACHMENT DISORDER.

resocialization   In group dynamics, the processes in which members who have failed to fulfil their role within the group renegotiate their roles in it.

resolution   1. Solving a problem or situation by examining its specific parts in a logical order. 2. In vision, ability to distinguish detail. See RESOLVING POWER.

resolution law   (H. Jennings) A partial explanation of behavior modification stating that the changing of one physiological state into another becomes easier and more rapid after it has taken place a number of times.

resolution of anxiety   The process of locating the cause of anxiety which often results in obtaining peace and calm as may occur in successful psychotherapy.

resolution phase   (W. Masters & V. Johnson) The final stage of the human sexual-response cycle (SRC) during which the male cannot have an erection nor the female an orgasm. See SEXUAL-RESPONSE CYCLE.

resolving power The capacity to perceive two identical items (such as dots or lines) that are close or next to each other as separate rather than as a single item.

resonance 1. In acoustics, a vibration of some object from the sound of another object. 2. In personality theory, an emotional reaction of sympathy and empathy with another person.

resonance box A wooden box for amplifying/changing the intensity of the pitch of a tone by means of a mounted tuning fork to amplify the intensity of the sound when the tuning fork vibrates. Also known as resonator (box). See TUNING FORK for illustration of such a box.

resonance place theory (of hearing) (H. Helmholtz) A point of view that different portions of the basilar membrane are tuned to specific frequencies of sound. Also known as harp theory of hearing, piano theory of hearing, place theory of hearing, resonance theory of hearing. See THEORIES OF HEARING.

resonance volley theory A theory of hearing that combines theories of resonance and of frequency.

resonator (box) resonance box

resource attractor An attribute such as ability, training, or power that attracts other resources because the holder of these resources has a competitive advantage in gaining more such resources.

resource awareness A counselor's awareness of various community resources for client referrals; generally a knowledge of persons and agencies that can meet clients' needs (such as information, financial assistance, and professional services).

resource depletion theory A point of view that there will be a reduction of resources (financial, affective, intellectual) in families dependent on the number of children that could lead among other things to lower intelligence test scores for children in large families. There seems to be no firm evidence for this theory. See BIRTH ORDER THEORY.

resource person A person known to be of specific assistance to people with questions, problems, etc. Often acts as an advisor or consultant to a group, such as a high school guidance counselor.

resource-reduction hypothesis A postulate that reduction in the quality of cognitive functions is a result of a reduced quantity of cognitive elements available to the person. See DIALECTICAL MATERIALISM.

resource teacher A specialist who works with children with learning disabilities and acts as a consultant to other teachers for special problems.

resource theory (U. G. Foa) A model of the nature of transactions of items or actions as part of social exchanges. Holds that exchanges are generally similar in kind and of comparable value. See EQUITY THEORY, SOCIAL EXCHANGE THEORY.

respect An attitude indicating valuing of another person and treating the person accordingly.

respectability An attitude toward an individual or a group of people, such as a family, indicating social approval.

respiration (R) Breathing. Restriction in breathing may result from anxiety and also cause anxiety.

respiration rate The rate of breathing, an index of emotionality, used in some "lie-detector" tests. See INSPIRATION-EXPIRATION RATIO.

respiratory depression Reduced rate of oxygen intake produced by narcotic drugs such as morphine. Narcotics raise the threshold level of the respiratory center that normally would react to increased carbon dioxide in the tissues by increasing the rate and depth of breathing. Respiratory depression is a primary hazard of morphine use.

respiratory distress syndrome A pathological condition affecting preterm infants characterized by underdeveloped lungs with air sacs that collapse, resulting in serious breathing difficulty and sometimes death by suffocation. Also known as hyaline membrane disease.

respiratory eroticism In psychoanalytic theory, the gratification of libidinal drives through use of the respiratory apparatus, as in smoking cigarettes.

respiratory occlusion reflex Any panicky reaction to the threat of loss of oxygen, or smothering.

respiratory type (L. Rostan) A body type considered to have a predominance of circulatory and respiratory system in relation to other types. See CONSTITUTIONAL TYPES.

respirograph A graphic recording of breathing including number of breaths per unit of time, strength and duration.

respite care 1. The relocation and care of a person who has various difficulties such as physical illnesses, psychiatric conditions, or old age, in an intermediate location, not the person's home or the home of friends or family, nor in an institution. Generally, in a shelter of some kind. See HALFWAY HOUSE, SHELTERED CARE. 2. The providing of temporary caregivers to relieve the normal attendant, usually a family member, of a person with a disability.

respondent 1. A response identified as a behavior elicited by a specific stimulus. 2. An organism that reacts to the stimulus. 3. Whoever responds to a questionnaire. 4. A reflex elicited by a specific evolutionarily significant stimulus event such as salivation to food on the tongue. Compare OPERANT. See RESPONDENT TOPOGRAPHY.

respondent aggression See AGGRESSION.

respondent behavior (B. F. Skinner) The response of an organism to a specific stimulus. A response is "elicited" by specific stimuli, such as in a person trying to catch a ball. Also known as elicited behavior. (Opposed to operant behavior in which a response is "emitted" by an organism in the absence of specific stimuli.) See EMITTED BEHAVIOR, RESPONDENT.

respondent conditioning B. F. Skinner's terminology for classical conditioning.

respondent topography Phrase used by followers of B. F. Skinner to connote the array of behaviors that are conditionable by Ivan Pavlov's classical conditioning procedures as opposed to the responses ("operants") that are conditioned by the instrumental procedures used by Skinner and other behaviorists. "Respondents" are reflexes that are elicited by a specific evolutionarily significant stimulus event such as salivation to food on the tongue. "Operants" are emitted responses that are strengthened by a contingent reinforcement.

response (R) 1. Respondent behavior; overt or covert reaction of the body or any part of the body, including muscles and glands, as the result of stimulation, such as a knee jerk when the patella is struck, jerking a hand away as a result of touching a hot object, or the reaction of the body to a drug. 2. Operant behavior; any act or behavior that an organism is capable of emitting. 3. Psychological behavior; any psychological reaction to information or observation or memory. 4. Social behavior; in a relationship, reactions of each to the other. Types of response include: ABIENT, ACHROMATIC, ACQUIRED, ADAPTIVE, ALPHA BLOCK, ALPHA, ALTERNATION, ANALOGY PRINCIPLE, ANATOMY, ANTEDATING, ANTICIPATORY, ANXIETY-RELIEF, APPROACHING, ARBITRARY, AUTOCLITIC, AUTONOMIC, AUTOPHONIC, AVERSION, AVOIDANCE, BALANCING, BARRIER, BETA, BLINK(ING), CHAINED, CHROMATIC, CIRCULAR, CIRCULAR CONDITIONED, CIRCULAR-PATTERN, COLOR, CONDITIONED AVOIDANCE, CONDITIONED ESCAPE, CONDITIONED, CONFABULATED, CONSUMMATORY, CONTAMINATED, CONTINUOUS-DISCRIMINATION, CORTICAL-EVOKED, COVERT, DEFENSE, DELAYED CONDITIONED, DELAYED, DERMAL-SWEATING, DETAIL, DIFFERENTIAL, DIFFUSED, DIFFUSION, DIRECT CORTICAL, DISCRIMINATION, DISCRIMINATIVE, DISTAL, EGOCENTRIC, ELECTRIC SKIN, ELECTRODERMAL, EMOTIONAL, EVOKED, EXPLICIT, FEAR, FETAL, FIGHT-OR-FLIGHT, FIXATED, FIXATION, FLOATING-LIMB, FRACTIONAL ANTEDATING GOAL, FRUSTRATION, GALVANIC SKIN, GLANDULAR, IMPLICIT, IMPLICIT SPEECH, IMPUNITIVE, INCOMPATIBLE, INDIVIDUAL, INSTRUMENTAL, INTENTIONAL, INTERPRETIVE, INTROPUNITIVE, INTRUSION, INVOLUNTARY, KINESTHETIC, LOCAL, LOCATION, MIMETIC, MORO, MOVEMENT, MYOTYPICAL, NEED-PERSISTENT, NEGATIVE, OLIGOPHRENIC, OPERANT, ORIENTING, ORIGINAL, PALMAR, PENETRATION, PILOMOTOR, POPULAR, PREPARATORY, PREPOTENT, PROBING, PROTECTIVE, PROXIMAL, PSYCHOGALVANIC, REASSURING, RED-GREEN, REFLECTION, RELAXATION, RIGHTING, SELECTIVE, SENSORY, SERIAL, SEXUAL, SKIN CONDUCTANCE, SMETS-PATTERN, SPECIES-SPECIFIC, STARTLE, STATIC, STEREOTYPED, TARGET, TEXTURE, TRIAL, UNCONDITIONED, VACUUM, VIRILE, VISTA, VOLUNTARY, W, WITHDRAWING, YELLOW-BLUE.

response acquiescence A tendency to agree with statements on a personality test or survey questionnaire regardless of content.

response adequacy The degree to which a reaction to a stimulation either satisfies the person, or the person's reaction is positive in terms of achieving an intended goal.

response amplitude (A) 1. The degree or amount of specific behavior in reacting to a specific stimulus in a classically conditioned situation. 2. The degree of a response measured in some manner from zero (no response) to maximum response. See HULL'S THEORY.

response attitude A set or tendency to respond in a particular manner to a specific stimulus or categories of stimuli.

response bias 1. A tendency for a person to operate in a predictable manner to various situations. Multiple choice and other tests have been developed to attempt to defeat such tendencies. 2. A tendency to make various kinds of responses due to expectation unique for the responding individual. 3. The unusual interpretation of a stimulus due to unique interpretation of the meaning of the question. Also known as test-taking attitude. See NAY-SAYING, YEA-SAYING.

response by analogy principle (E. L. Thorndike) A law of transfer of training that any organism, animal or human, in a new and unfamiliar situation who has to respond to the demands of the environment, will respond in a manner similar to the way it had previously responded in a familiar and similar situation. See RESPONSE ATTITUDE, RESPONSE BIAS.

response circuit Movement, simple or complex, of neuron changes from receptors to effectors, such as what occurs between a bright light being flashed on the eye and the eyelids closing.

response class A variety of common behavior patterns due to environmental factors. Also known as R class. See HABIT.

response competition A situation characterized by an inability to determine which of several associations is correct.

response complexity As the number of participating factors leading to a desired response increases, so do the potential behaviors necessary to achieve the desired goal.

response comprehension The effect of a stimulus increases as the stimulus energy increases until it reaches a certain point, then the effect of a stimulus decreases.

response cost 1. A procedure in operant conditioning in which a participant who misbehaves is punished by a loss of previously earned reinforcers. See TOKEN ECONOMY. 2. The removal (or the result thereof) of a positive stimulus to decrease undesired behavior.

response-cost contingencies Rewards or punishments for specific desirable or undesirable behaviors in particular situations—for example, rewards for completing homework assignments.

response criterion (β) The strength of a stimulus that determines a response. Any stimulus below this point does not elicit a response. See SIGNAL-DETECTION THEORY.

response detail In Rorschach testing, reporting on a particular part of the whole blot as a unique entity.

response deviation A tendency toward inconsistence in responding to particular stimuli, such as test items.

response differentiation The situation where an organism can make two or more different kinds of responses to the same stimulus.

response direction/sense The spatial orientation of a response in relation to the source of the stimulation.

response dispersion Reactions which appear to be irregular, random and aimless.

response duration The length of time that an individual response lasts.

response equivalence   Similarity between two or more responses elicited by the same or similar stimuli. It is related to "response generalization," the chief difference being that generalization refers to quite similar or nearly identical responses made to similar stimuli whereas response equivalence usually refers to responses that are less similar but still closely allied.

response-executing function   See DUAL-AROUSAL MODEL.

response experiment   **reaction experiment**

response frequency   The number of responses per unit of time.

response function   The purpose that a response serves.

response generalization   A tendency for an organism to respond not only to a specific stimuli but over time to respond to similar conditioned stimuli. For example, if an organism is trained to respond to an isosceles triangle, after being conditioned, it may later respond similarly to any triangle. Compare RESPONSE EQUIVALENCE.

response generalization gradient   If an organism has been conditioned to respond to a particular stimulus, the more other stimuli appear to the organism to be like the conditioned stimulus, the more likely the organism is to respond, and conversely, the more a stimulus departs from an original value the weaker the responsivity of the organism to it. A gradient is a regular rate of change between two variables. In this case, the variables would be the characteristics of stimulus 1 and stimulus 2, and as their similarity increased so would the rate of response. Also known as gradient of response generalization. See RESPONSE-GENERALIZATION PRINCIPLE.

response-generalization principle   A theory that when a conditioned stimulus regularly elicits a specific response, that stimulus will also evoke other related responses. For example, if a rat is conditioned to press a bar at the sound of a buzzer, the buzzer will be able to evoke similar responses in associated situations such as pressing a trap door to obtain reinforcement. See STIMULUS GENERALIZATION.

response hierarchy   A ranking of behavior patterns in an organism's repertoire according to the probability that they will occur in a given situation.

response-hold mechanism   A drive-gate filter system that restricts the flow of stimuli to those compatible with a certain response pattern, such as those for positive motivations, considered necessary for survival of individuals and the species.

response inferred organismic value   An organismic variable not directly measurable but that can be inferred from behavior. For example, a person considered to be normal and a person with advanced dementia are presented. Their physical appearance gives no evidence of the mental differences between them. However if they move, talk, or interact, an observer will be able to indicate which person has dementia. In other words, not until responses are viewed can inferences be made about another person's internal states.

response inhibition   (O. H. Mowrer) Refers to existing factors in a participant that generate inhibition of response to certain stimuli.

response instance   A single predictable unit of response to a stimulation.

response integration   (G. Mandler) The mutual strengthening/activation of the constituent features of a response as a consequence of its exercise.

response intensity   A measure of the strength of a response. See RESPONSE RATE.

response key   **reaction key**

response latency   A difference in time (usually milliseconds) between receiving a stimulus and responding, such as the interval between seeing a light and pressing a key. Also known as latency of reply. See LATENCY OF RESPONSE.

response learning   The mastering of a physical response, rather than understanding of the response.

response learning process   In some situations, a response calls for complicated steps, and there can be more than one way of learning the proper responses, such as solving a finger-maze while blindfolded. One participant may memorize movements such as "Left, Left, Right, Left," whereas another may learn the proper response by relying on muscle tensions.

response magnitude/strength   The size or degree of response to a stimulus measured in terms of amplitude, duration, frequency, or intensity. See RESPONSE MEASUREMENT.

response measurement   Any measurement of responses such as their speed, intensity, duration, latency, strength.

response operating characteristic (ROC)   1. In psychophysics, a characteristic noticed in the tendency of a judge or subject to be either cautious or careless. 2. In signal detection research, individual variations in reporting hits, misses, and false alarms. See RESPONSE OPERATING CHARACTERISTIC CURVE, SIGNAL DETECTION THEORY.

response-oriented psychologies   1. Theories or systems in psychology that favor and focus on S-B (Stimulus-Behavior) or S-O-R (Stimulus-Organism-Response) as a primary means of understanding behavior. See STIMULUS-RESPONSE PSYCHOLOGY. 2. Points of view in psychology that focus on the essential nature of responses such as act psychology, behaviorism, functional psychology, or reaction psychology. These contrast with content psychologies oriented to static aspects of the self, such as structural psychology. Sometimes known as response-oriented systems/theories. See BEHAVIORISM.

response-oriented systems/theories   **response-oriented psychologies** (meaning 2)

response pattern   Discernible arrangement of responses to form a kind of unity of behavior in various situations. Thus, for example, some organisms will move toward an unfamiliar stimulus and others will move away.

response prevention   In behavior therapy, treatment intended to stop ritualistic behavior of people with obsessive-compulsive symptoms. See DELAY THERAPY.

response probability   An estimate of the chances of a particular response being made.

response psychology   Old name for what was next called reaction psychology and later behavioral psychology.

response rate   Responses per unit of time. Response rate, response intensity, and response time can be used to measure degree of learning as well as for other purposes. Also known as occurrence rate, R-occurrence.

response reference   The location of the response on the body of the responder, varying from touching the body (proximal) to far away from the body (distal). For example, an unseen person is talking, the unseen person is the distal stimulus but the vibrations of the voice felt by the ear drums are the proximal stimuli.

response-reinforcement contingency   The essential relation between a response and the rewarding effect derived therefrom.

response-response conditioning   A type of conditioning in which one response is a prerequisite for a second response. Also known as R-R conditioning.

response-response (R-R) laws   Theories concerning the relationships of one type of response to another type. See R-R LAWS AND RESPONSE-ORGANISM-RESPONSE LAWS.

response rivalry   A situation that occurs when opposing neural impulses are triggered simultaneously. Also known as neural rivalry.

response schema   See SCHEMA.

response selection   Choosing an appropriate response from alternatives, based on information gleaned from previous experience.

response sense   response direction

response set   1. A tendency to respond in a particular style regardless of the question; a readiness to respond or a state of concentration as the person prepares to react to a stimulus. See RESPONSE STYLE. 2. In social psychology, a tendency to respond to questionnaire items in a way that is influenced more by the social implications of a person's answers than by the question content. For example, the tendency to give answers that do not reflect true attitudes but seem socially acceptable. Also, some individuals show response set by tending to answer "Yes" to the items on any questionnaire. See RESPONSE SETS. 3. Readiness in a response situation to concentrate on one of several possible cues.

response sets   According to Mary Allen, tendencies to respond to personality questionnaires or survey interviews in a stereotyped manner. Examples of response sets: (a) acquiescent, Yes/No replies; (b) cop-out, selecting neutral alternatives; (c) extremity, giving extreme answers; (d) fabrication, making-up answers, lying; (e) faking bad, saying what is socially unacceptable; (f) inconsistent, giving careless answers; (g) nay-saying, a tendency to respond in the negative, saying "No"; (h) faking good, social desirability, saying what is socially acceptable; and (i) yea-saying, a tendency to respond in the affirmative, saying "Yes." See RESPONSE BIAS.

response shock (R-S or R/S) interval   The time between the last undesired response and the initiation of shock that is to be an aversive stimulus to achieve avoidance conditioning to accomplish extinction of the response.

response strength   response magnitude

response style   A person's usual way of responding to any test. For example, on a multiple choice test always selecting the shortest alternative or accepting the first choice or the most unlikely choice. A response "style" refers to general, habitual ways of responding, "set" includes ways of responding to particular kinds of questions. See RESPONSE SET, RESPONSE SETS.

response suppression   Inhibition of a conditioned response by conditioned fear.

response-switch mechanism   A variation of the response-hold mechanism that deals with potentially noxious or damaging stimuli. Noxious or damaging stimuli might include alcoholism and illicit drug use and they could eventually become accepted as positive in helping the organism survive in a stressful environment. See ADDICTIVE PERSONALITY, IATROGENIC ADDICTION.

response system   All elements of an organism's body involved in making a response. Includes sensory elements, neural connectors, glandular and muscle systems to various degrees and extents depending on the complexity of the organism's structure.

response threshold   The limen (the minimum amount of external and internal stimuli) required to activate a particular response.

response time   The elapsed time between the onset of a stimulus (for example, a red traffic light) and the beginning of the perceiver's response (for example, depressing the car's brake). Measures the speed of response, which differs in different sense modalities, and is affected by such factors as intensity of stimulus, motivation, drugs, age, sex, and set. Also known as reaction time. See RESPONSE DURATION, RESPONSE LATENCY.

response type   reaction type

response topography   Consideration of the nature of responses, especially in operant conditioning, such as with which part of its body does an experimental animal press a response bar and with how much force?

response variable   1. The dependent variable in any research. 2. Changes in reaction of the subject to an experimental stimulus, or stimulus variable.

responsibility fear   See ERGASIOPHOBIA, ERGOPHOBIA, HYPEGIAPHOBIA, HYPENGYOPHOBIA.

responsive(ness)   1. Ready to react to a physiological or psychological stimulus. 2. Concern for others.

REST   See RESTRICTED ENVIRONMENTAL STIMULATION TECHNIQUE/THERAPY.

rest   1. A state of relaxation, immobility, recuperation. 2. A period of recuperation after completion of a specific task. 3. In music, a period of silence.

restatement (of content)   (C. R. Rogers) Paraphrase, reflection of feeling, perception-checking techniques in psychotherapy, in which therapists rephrase statements made by clients to demonstrate that the statements have been understood and that the client's feelings are noted. This method provides a mirror in which clients can "see" their feelings and ideas more clearly. See CLARIFICATION, INTERPRETATION, MIRRORING.

rest-cure   An old method to "cure" both mind and body by going to a spa or a monastery to relax, contemplate, meditate, for example, the healing temple of Epidaurus that existed from 600 BC to 200 AD was for such a purpose.

rest-cure technique (S. W. Mitchell) A treatment approach developed for persons with nervous disorders that Silas Mitchell attributed to the hectic pace of life in the "railroad age." His regimen consisted of extended rest, physical therapy, massage, environmental change, mild exercise, and a nutritious diet. Also known as Mitchell Rest Cure, Mitchell('s) Rest Therapy, rest cure/technique. See MORITA THERAPY, NAIKAN THERAPY.

rest home A facility for people diagnosed as needing an environment free from stress to recuperate from physical or psychological disorders. Also known as adult home.

resting potential The electrical difference between the outside and the inside of an inactive polarized membrane. It is usually about 50 to 100 millivolts, representing an excess of negatively charged ions on the inside of the membrane. The charge outside a neural membrane normally is positive. The resting potential is temporarily lost in an active nerve impulse and during hyper- and depolarizations insufficiently large to produce a nerve impulse.

rest(ing) tremor A localized tremor that occurs when the affected area is at rest. For example, if a person types for a long period of time, after stopping, the person's hands might shake for a short period of time.

restitution Making amends for damage done, actual or imagined, usually arises from a long-term deep sense of guilt.

restitutional schizophrenia A condition observed in patients with schizophrenia characterized by regaining touch with reality and normality in mental processes lost by regression. Symptoms may include delusions or hallucinations, social and speech characteristics typical of schizophrenia, and some symptoms of catatonic behavior. See SCHIZOPHRENIC SURRENDER.

restitution of psychological function A return to normality after having lost some function due to brain damage, not because the brain cells regenerate (they do not), but because other parts of the brain take over some of the nonfunctioning or missing portions of the brain.

restitutive therapies Short-term therapies based on the induction of altered states of consciousness. Pharmacologic agents are used in most of these therapies, either to enable the patient to achieve a peak or transcendental experience, which purportedly has a beneficial effect in itself; or to render the patient more amenable to other techniques. See PSYCHEDELIC THERAPY.

restless-leg syndrome (RLS) An overwhelming need to move the legs, general uneasiness similar to the need to scratch or to sneeze, usually occurring soon after going to bed, often leading to insomnia. Also known as Ekbom's syndrome.

restlessness 1. In objective behavior, a state of erratic movements and aimless activity. 2. In subjective feelings, a state of discontent and disorientation, including inability to think logically. See LOCOMOTOR ACTIVITY.

restoration Replacement of any lost structure, function, or material in an organism. Also known as regeneration.

restoration therapy 1. In a person who has lost certain mental and emotional functions, attempts to reestablish prior levels of functioning, usually through counseling and psychotherapy. 2. Treatment directed toward the establishment of normal or near-normal structure and function in a body part or system that has suffered a damaging loss or deficiency whether due to disease, injury or psychological trauma. Also known as restorative therapy.

restorative ritual An action performed to feel better, to achieve a feeling of normality, usually to feel clean, such as taking a bath or a shower to resume tranquility.

Restorff phenomenon (H. von Restorff) 1. In experiments with paired-associates learning, items are recalled better when a pair is presented for learning by itself as opposed to when presented with others in a series. 2. A memory-process theory predicted on observations that in a series of items those that contrast with most of the others in the series will be retained better than items that are similar. Sometimes known as isolation effect, Köhler-Restorff phenomenon, Restorff effect, von Restorff effect. See KÖHLER-RESTORFF PHENOMENON.

rest pause/period Cessation of activity taken on a regularly scheduled or discretionary basis for purposes of rest, relaxation, refreshment, and avoidance of overfatigue or boredom.

restrain To hold back or prevent some action, usually by one person of another, but also of the self. See RESTRAINT.

restrained-eating hypothesis (S. Schachter) A postulate that people who are obese are oversensitive to external food cues, and are more likely to eat foods that are easily available even when they are not hungry, in contrast to people who are not obese who can ignore tempting food cues and generally eat only when hungry.

restraining forces Elements that keep psychological perceptual phenomena apart from each other, preventing them from forming a total Gestalt.

restraining therapy A paradoxical technique in psychotherapy in which the therapist takes the position that the client is fine and that there is no need for change, in the expectation that the client will disagree and due to reactivity take steps to improve to prove the therapist wrong. See PARADOXICAL THERAPY, REACTANCE THEORY.

restraint 1. In psychiatry, preventing a patient from causing harm to self or others through use of an intervention such as straightjacket or medication. 2. Inhibition of an organism's activity by an overwhelming outside force. 3. Self-inhibition of certain undesirable behaviors by self-control (such as counting to ten until calm) or by various other means such as prayers, exercises, tearing up or breaking things, getting drunk or even self-mutilation. See ABSTINENCE.

restricted affect A tendency to have emotional expressions reduced in range and intensity from normality, showing apathy, lack of comprehension, lack of importance. A common symptom in depression, inhibited personalities, and schizophrenia. See FLAT AFFECT.

restricted codes of language Spoken language with a limited vocabulary, many personal pronouns, and expectations that the listener already knows certain elements in the communication.

restricted environmental stimulation technique/ therapy (REST)   Reduction of ambient information and stimulation, usually as a research technique in the work context.

restricted learning   A species-specific phenomenon relating to an organism's reaction to certain stimuli that results in meaningful adaptations in that organism's behavior.

restructure   To view the self, others, or events (in the past or currently) in a new manner depending on a shift in attitudes or values. See CONVERSION.

restructure-members method   relearning method

rest tremor   rest(ing) tremor

resultant   The effect of the combination of two or more forces at the same time.

resultant note/tone   A tone produced when two tones are sounded together and a tone of an entirely new nature is produced.

resumption of interrupted action   Zeigarnik effect

resymbolization   Redefining by a recovering patient of conceptions, especially those related to conflicts.

RET   Rational Emotive Therapy

retained-members method   relearning method

retaliation   See TALION, TALION PRINCIPLE.

retardation   1. Reduction of the normal rate of development or growth. Types of retardation include: BORDERLINE MENTAL, CULTURAL-FAMILIAL MENTAL, DEVELOPMENTAL, EDUCATIONAL, ENDOGENOUS MENTAL, EXOGENOUS MENTAL, FAMILIAL, LANGUAGE, MENTAL, MILD MENTAL, MODERATE MENTAL, ORGANIC, PROFOUND MENTAL, PSEUDO-, PSYCHOMOTOR, READING, SEVERE MENTAL, UNSPECIFIED MENTAL. 2. Delay in the appearance of a conditioned response due to presentation of the unconditioned stimulus too late after the start of the conditioned stimulus.

retardation psychopathology   Disorders of various types that often accompany mental retardation. May be a direct result of the retardation, such as difficulty in learning, or due to social factors, such as attitudes of others to the person with retardation, differential treatment in the home in relation to other children, or lack of privileges.

retarded   Old term for being below normal expectation for some function, particularly maturation and intellectual capacity. Replaced by "challenged" to reduce the stigma carried by words such as "retarded" and "retardation" as well as to indicate that such disabilities may be overcome.

retarded children classification   Categories for different mental capacities, historically with terms having negative connotations, such as feebleminded, idiot, imbecile, moron, vegetative idiot. Replaced by terms, such as "educable" (mentally challenged), "trainable" (mentally deficient), and "custodial" (of such low intelligence as to require constant care). See CLASSIFICATION OF MENTAL DISEASES, MENTAL RETARDATION.

retarded depression   A symptom of depression demonstrated by lethargy, slowness, and generally subnormal activity.

retarded ejaculation   Difficulty of males to achieve ejaculation in normal sexual intercourse. See EJACULATORY INCOMPETENCE.

retarded schizophrenia   A form of schizophrenia in which the patient speaks, moves, and responds slowly and with great difficulty, if at all. See PSYCHOMOTOR RETARDATION.

rete   1. A network. 2. A network of blood vessels or nerves. Plural is retia.

rete mirabile   (Galen) A network of blood vessels located at the base of the brain. A cranial rete mirabile is found in the brains of certain domestic animals and as a congenital lesion in humans.

retention   1. The amount remembered after learning a task. Can be measured in a number of ways such as how much can be recalled, or how much less time and effort it will take to relearn the task after a period of time following the learning. See RELEARNING METHOD. 2. Persistent maintenance of a learned response or information. 3. The persistence of learned behavior when it is not being practiced. 4. Inability or refusal to urinate or defecate.

retention curve   A graphic representation of a participant's retention of material over a period of time. Also known as memory curve. See EBBINGHAUS' CURVE OF RETENTION.

retention hysteria   Phrase used by Sigmund Freud in 1895, but later discarded. Denoted a type of hysteria in which a traumatic experience is suppressed, or "retained," resulting in conversion of the emotion associated with it into somatic symptoms. Freud attempted to cure this condition by getting the patient to "abreact," or relive, the experience.

retention of affect   See STRANGULATED AFFECT.

retentiveness   Properties of any organism that makes it possible to retain material. Also known as retentivity. See LEARNING.

retentivity   retentiveness

retest   The second administration of a test. In developing psychological tests, the test-retest procedure is generally employed to determine the reliability of the test.

retest consistency   A desirable attribute of a test, when it produces the same or similar scores for a person over repeated trials the test has high consistency. See RELIABILITY, TEST-RETEST RELIABILITY.

retest reliability   A mathematical indicator of the degree of consistency of measurement based on the same test being taken more than once. See RELIABILITY.

retia   Plural of rete.

reticular   Consisting of clumps or networks of body tissues.

reticular activating system (RAS)   (V. Bekhterev, G. Moruzzi & H .W. Magoun) A complex of brain neurons found in the brain stem from the medulla to the midbrain. This control center of the brain regulates such functions as arousal, attention, muscle tone, alertness, and sleep. The RAS serves as an indirect route for sensory impulses transmitted to the cerebral cortex. Its main function appears to be alerting the cerebral cortex for incoming information. The RAS is a nonspecific projection system. Also known as reticular formation (rf or RF).

reticular formation (rf or **RF)**   A complex of neurons located in the center of the brainstem, containing ascending and descending neurons that end in the cerebral cortex. Involved in attention, arousal, posture and sleep. See BRAIN for an illustration.

reticular membrane   A netlike membrane in the cochlea of the inner ear.

reticular nucleus   A nucleus conveying information between the inner ear and the brain.

reticular stratum   See CORIUM.

reticuloendothelial system (RES)   (K. A. Aschoff, F. J. Kallman) A macrophage system made up of the true macrophages (mononuclear phagocytic system) as well as cells lining the sinusoids of the spleen, lymph nodes, and bone marrow. Kallman assumed that the RES played a role in protecting persons against schizophrenia.

retifism   Sexual fetishism when sexual excitement is achieved through contact or masturbation with a shoe or foot. Purportedly shoes represent female genitals to the fetishist. Term derives from an 18th century French educator, Rétif de la Bretonne.

retina   Embryonically, part of the brain that has pushed out toward the front of the human skull. The retina is the photosensitive portion of the eye. There are three layers of cells in the retina, those at the posterior wall of the eye are known as the rods and the cones. The layers also contain bipolar cells (in layer two), and ganglia (in layer three) whose fibers extend to a collecting point at the back of the eyeball where they form the optic nerve. See DETACHED RETINA, DIABETIC RETINOPATHY.

retinal bipolar cells   Neurons in the second layer of the retina that collect inputs from rod and cone cells near the surface and relay the impulses to the ganglion cells in the third layer of the retina. They have multiple dendrites that may communicate with several different rod or cone cells.

retinal color mixture   A process within the retina of the eye when it is simultaneously or in rapid succession stimulated by various colors.

retinal color zones   The retina reacts to colors in terms of various zones, for example, the center of the retina is sensitive to most colors, whereas areas away from the center react to specific colors only, such as yellow and blue.

retinal cones   Receptors in the first layer of the retinal neurons containing photo-sensitive chemicals that react to certain colors. Retinal cones are concentrated near the center of the retina and are involved in space perception and visual acuity, in addition to color perception. Although originally named for their shape, cone cells now are identified by function since some cone cells resemble rod cells, and vice versa. See CONES.

retinaldehyde   retinene

retinal densitometry   A method for measuring the amount of light absorbed by the retina.

retinal disparity   The difference between the right and left retinal images that gives the viewer two perceptions of the same object. The fusion of these two images results in the sense of a third dimension of the object, as well as helping to estimate the distance between the viewer and the object. Also known as binocular disparity.

retinal elements   A seldom-used term for the various parts of the retina including the rods and the cones and their accessory nerves. See RETINENE.

retinal field   That portion of the retina available for vision. The distribution of retinal receptors (rods and cones) that hyperpolarize in light and depolarize in darkness. The retinal fields generally increase in power and number in the peripheral areas as illumination diminishes and decrease as illumination increases.

retinal fusion   A process of convergence of vision that occurs whenever the retina of each eye sees the same thing and presents the brain with a single image. Also known as binocular fusion, binocular integration. See BINOCULAR VISION, FUSION.

retinal ganglion cells   Cells in the third, or inner, neuron layer of the retina that collect inputs from bipolar cells and transmit them along fibers that form the optic nerve. Retinal ganglion cells may communicate with more than one bipolar cell so that they may collect inputs from a number of different rod or cone cells.

retinal horizon   The horizontal meridian of the retina when the terrestrial horizon is perceived when the eyes are in a primary position, that is, looking straight forward.

retinal horizontal cells   Association cells in the retina that collect inputs from some receptor cells and feed impulses back to others.

retinal illuminance   The amount of light hitting the surface of the retina. See LUX, TROLAND.

retinal image/picture   An image formed on the retina of an eye when it is focused on an external object. The resolution of the image varies with the diameter of the pupil, the focus becoming sharper as illumination of the object increases and the aperture of the pupil decreases.

retinal layers   Strata of the retina. See RETINA.

retinal light   A condition of sensing, or "seeing" a grayish color in a situation of complete blackness, apparently due to intrinsic activity within the visual system. See CORTICAL GREY, IDIORETINAL LIGHT.

retinal macula   A yellowish depressed area on the retina at a point lateral to and below the optic disk. At its center is the fovea centralis, the area of maximum visual acuity containing only cones. Also known as macula lutea.

retinal mixture   See COLOR MIXTURE, RETINAL COLOR MIXTURE.

retinal oscillations   The excitation effect of a brief visual stimulus experienced in persistent aftersensations or alternating dark and light bands.

retinal picture   retinal image

retinal rivalry   An effect of alternating visual images in the left and right eyes when each is focused on a different field and the images cannot be fused to produce a single interpretation. A fluctuation of sensations then occurs from one eye to the other. Also known as binocular rivalry.

retinal rods   See RODS.

retinal size   The size a viewed object casts on the retina. Sizes of viewed objects are not in direct proportion to their actual sizes as well as not in the same plane (they are inverted), but the brain interprets the actual size correctly, a phenomenon called size constancy. See CONSTANCY.

retinal zones   See COLOR ZONES, RETINAL COLOR ZONES.

retinene   A form of vitamin A, a chemical constituent of the retinal pigment rhodopsin. Produced by the photochemical reaction in rods of the eye when rhodopsin is exposed to light (rhodopsin breaks down into retinene and opsin). Also known as retinaldehyde.

retinitis   Inflammation of the retina.

retinitis pigmentosa   Pathology of the pigment of the retina leading to diminished color sensitivity.

retinoblastoma   An eye tumor that develops from cells of the retina. It is a rare disorder that apparently is hereditary and unusual in that it generally occurs in persons of above-average intelligence, as opposed to the frequent association of below-normal intelligence with many other inherited neurological disorders.

retinoptic representation   **retinopty**

retinopty   The isomorphic (one-to-one) representation of the retina on the visual cortex of the brain. Also known as retinoptic representation.

retinoscope   An instrument designed to determine whether light going through the cornea and lens focuses properly on the retina. Also known as skiascope.

retirement counseling   Individual or group counseling of employees for the purpose of helping them prepare for retirement. Discussions usually include such topics as mental and physical health, recreational activities, part-time or consultant work, finances, insurance, government programs, and deciding where to reside.

retirement neurosis   A persistent state of maladjustment among retirees, characterized primarily by feelings of emptiness, uselessness, and meaninglessness, as well as general apathy and loss of initiative. Persons most susceptible to this neurosis have depended upon work as their major source of satisfaction and self-esteem, and have not developed absorbing interests or productive activities to pursue during the later years of life. See DISENGAGEMENT THEORY, PENSION NEUROSIS, ROLE DEPRIVATION.

retirement village   A social living community limited to retired, usually older, adults.

retraction   1. Withdrawal of a limb or appendage. 2. Admitting an error and no longer maintaining the truth of some proposition.

retreat from reality (hypothesis)   A postulate that a person with a mental illness is unable to cope with the undesirable aspects of life, and has "escaped" by losing touch with reality. Holds that such persons avoid getting well because a return to reality and sanity would require them to confront their problems. See DEFENSE MECHANISM, DENIAL, FLIGHT FROM REALITY.

retrieval   A process of searching for a memory, as in trying to remember the name of an acquaintance. It is the third stage in the memory process, following encoding and storage. See RETRIEVAL CUE.

retrieval cue   An aid used in recall. For example, in trying to remember an elementary school teacher's name, recalling the topic taught in the expectation that this will lead to the forgotten name.

retrieving behavior   Animal activity characterized by picking up and carrying to the nest, or lair, young offspring that may have wandered away. See PARENTAL BEHAVIOR.

retroaction   Effect of new learning upon past learning. If positive, it is called retroactive facilitation; if negative retroactive inhibition.

retroactive   1. Having a backward effect. 2. Affecting the past, refers to the effect of Y (a later element) on X (something that occurred before).

retroactive amnesia   1. Memory loss going back in time from the occurrence of a major trauma, with loss being greatest for events closest to the time of the trauma. 2. Inability to recall or remember any event which occurred during a certain period of time prior to a shock or functional disturbance, with relatively unimpaired memory for earlier events.

retroactive association   A connection between an item in a series and one preceding it.

retroactive facilitation   1. The strengthening of previously learned material by subsequent learning. 2. A tendency for a later formed association to strengthen a previously formed association. Also known as positive retroaction.

retroactive inhibition/interference (RI)   Negative or disrupting effect of new learning on old learning, especially if the two sets of material are similar. It is one of the processes to blame for forgetting. Compare PROACTIVE INHIBITION.

retroactive therapy   A procedure intended to undo the harmful effects of a particular cause, especially if the disorder was experimentally induced. See SECTOR THERAPY.

retrobulbar   Located in the brain behind the eyeball.

retrocognition   A concept in extrasensory perception (ESP) having to do with a person having knowledge of past events without direct or indirect information from normal sources.

retroflection   1. Bent backward. 2. (S. Rado) A psychoanalytic term to characterize rage turned back on the self. 3. In Gestalt theory, a contact boundary disturbance in which a person substitutes self for environment, considered a chief reason for social isolation. Also known as retroflexion.

retrogenesis   A concept that growth processes develop out of undifferentiated structures rather than from developed structures.

retrograde   1. Retreating, going backward. 2. In physiology, meaning degenerating or deteriorating.

retrograde amnesia   Loss of memory for events prior to a precipitating event such as a major injury, psychological or physiological trauma. Amnesia is greatest for events that took place closest to the time of injury. See ANTEROGRADE AMNESIA, MEMORY LOSS, RETROACTIVE AMNESIA.

retrograde degeneration technique An old method of determining connections from one area of the brain to another, especially the thalamus to the neocortex, based on the fact that the neuron cell body loses its ability to stain deeply with Nissl stains when the target of its axons is destroyed. For example, after damage to the visual cortex it is possible to map out the areas of the thalamus that send axons to this area of the cortex because the thalamic neurons will not stain as darkly as neurons that send axons to intact areas of the cortex. As an experimental technique this has been replaced by the use of substances such as horseradish peroxidase that are transported from the terminals of the axon to the cell body and subsequently visualized.

retrograde ejaculation The ejaculation of semen in a reverse direction. The effect is sometimes the result of surgery of the prostate gland. The semen is ejaculated into the urinary bladder, from which it is excreted later. Also may happen when the penis is squeezed just before ejaculation.

retrograde transportation Movement of substances in a nerve away from the axon and toward the cell body.

retrography The act or process of writing backward. Also known as mirror writing.

retrogression Reversion to an earlier level of functioning.

retropulsion Running backwards in short steps, behavior that may occur as a result of Parkinson's disease. See RETROPULSIVE EPILEPSY.

retropulsive epilepsy A form of epilepsy in which a major symptom is an impulse to run backward.

retrospection Review of, or reconsideration of, an experience. It pertains to the recent past, whereas "introspection" is a reflection on the present.

retrospective audit A method of evaluation of the effectiveness of diagnostic and therapeutic procedures that includes a review of patients after they have been discharged. See TREATMENT AUDITS.

retrospective falsification 1. A process of modifying memories without conscious intent to do so with the result that the memory will serve unconscious needs. May generate interesting conflicts between memories of people who earlier shared the same experience, each of whom believes to have recalled a particular incident exactly and who both may have experienced this kind of falsification. 2. In paranoid schizophrenia, the addition of false details about past experiences to support delusional systems. See PARAMNESIA.

retrospective reference Associating a memory with a point in time, for example, recalling that a friend was last seen during an Olympic year in South Korea, then remembering the year was 1988.

retrospective report A report based on memory of past events.

retrospective research/study 1. A technique for investigating an event that occurred at a prior time, generally through interviews of either a person or group, or by interviews of observers or through examination of available records. 2. Research that starts with the present and tries to explain it in terms of past events. Retrospective research cannot manipulate variables or make use of a true experimental design. See EX POST FACTO RESEARCH, PROSPECTIVE RESEARCH.

return of the repressed Surfacing to the conscious level of ideas or impulses that had been repressed into the unconscious level.

return sweep The return of the eye from the end of a line to the beginning of the next line while reading. See SACCADIC MOVEMENT.

re-uptake 1. Reabsorption of a substance. 2. Neurotransmitters being reabsorbed by neuronal endings following release after firing. 3. A mechanism by means of which a neurotransmitter is drawn back into the presynaptic terminal that released it. Re-uptake is controlled by a pumping action of the presynaptic neuron utilizing a force powered by cellular energy. See ACTIVE TRANSPORT.

revealed-differences technique A method of studying the behavior of members of a family in a laboratory setting by posing a question and observing how the members reach agreement on an answer.

revenge Retaliation for real or fancied injustices, which may in turn lead to a fear of retaliation from the target of aggression.

reverberating circuits A neural circuit that recycles signals almost continuously so that retrieval on demand is possible. Also known as reverberatory circuits.

reverberating circuit theory A point of view that a cell assembly can function as an independent unit within the brain, and can continue to respond to a stimulus even after the stimulus has been discontinued.

reverberation Repeated reflection of sound within an enclosure.

reverberatory circuits reverberating circuits

reverence An attitude of solemn regard for a person, object, or concept.

reverie A pleasant, ruminative, dreamlike state characterized by wandering thoughts. Differentiated from daydreaming in that the associations have no recognized goal. Also known as revery.

reversal 1. In general, any change in an opposite direction. 2. See REVERSAL OF AFFECT.

reversal design An ABA type of research design: (A1)—Subjects' behavior studied and measured under certain baseline conditions; (B)—An experimental condition is imposed; (A2)—The original A baseline conditions are reestablished to see whether the B condition affected changes in the final conditions. See CROSSOVER DESIGN.

reversal errors Mistakes made in reading in which letters are twisted backwards, for instance, seeing the word BAT and reading TAB. An example of dyslexia. See STREPHOSYMBOLIA.

reversal formation Roughly equivalent to "reaction formation," the preferred term.

reversal learning 1. Knowledge based on the changing of the meaning of symbols so that what meant one thing at a former time now means something else. 2. A conditioning technique in which an animal must adapt to making correct selections that previously were the incorrect choices.

reversal of affect An attitude or emotion taking a new direction, such as aggression toward others being turned to aggression against the self. Also known as reversal, inversion of affect. See PSEUDOAGGRESSION.

reversal phase   A phase in single-case designs consisting of the reintroduction of a nonintervention condition (baseline) to see whether performance returns to or approximates the level of the original baseline.

reversal shift (learning)   A form of discrimination learning in which the delivery of reinforcement is made contingent on the opposite value of the original dimension, with a second dimension continuing to be irrelevant. Compare NONREVERSAL SHIFT.

reverse causality   In attempting to understand relationships between cause and effect, a tendency to attribute what is actually the cause to the effect. For example, does the ingestion of lead paint cause a lower intelligence quotient (IQ) or is it that children with lower IQs tend to eat lead paint?

reverse discrimination   Preferential treatment accorded individuals or groups who have been unfairly treated in the past.

reverse psychology   Casual terminology for tactics to manipulate another to perform an action when it is believed the person will respond "negatively" to a suggestion. Often used by parents and caretakers who may say to a child "This fruit is too delicious. I am sure that you don't want any," expecting that the child will then want some. Also known as negative psychology. See REACTANCE THEORY.

reverse tolerance   A paradoxical event in that there is an increase of the sensitivity of the body to certain drugs due to prior taking of the drug, so that now smaller amounts of the drug can have the same effect as larger amounts did originally.

reversibility   1. Capable of being modified, for example a person's perception or judgment of a visual illusion changing upon examination. 2. A basic assumption that different behaviors of different species are fundamentally based on the same underlying processes. Thus, studying the learning patterns of animals can shed light on the learning patterns of humans. See GENERALITY, UNIVERSALITY. 3. Operant-based behavior responding to a prior learned stimulus after being reinforced by a subsequent stimulus. 4. (J. Piaget) A cognitive structure which develops during the concrete operational period characterized by ability to reason backward and forward in relation to cause and effect. In part, this accounts for the child's increasing ability to understand problems of conservation.

reversible   Capable of being reversed.

reversible figure   A drawing that initially gives one impression but upon further examination appears to give another. For example, what appeared to be foreground is now distant; what appeared to be the figure is now ground; and vice versa. Also known as alternating perspective, ambiguous figure, reversible configuration. See NECKER CUBE, RUBIN'S FIGURE, SCHROEDER'S STAIRCASE ILLUSION for examples of reversible figure illusions.

reversible figure-ground   (E. Rubin) A tendency of a part of a complex perceptual input (figure) to stand out as separate from and in front of its field (ground). See FIGURE-GROUND EFFECT, RUBIN'S FIGURE for illustrations.

reversing lenses/prisms   Lenses on eyeglass-like apparatuses that reverse the visual field. George Stratton used such lenses in a classic experiment on vision.

reversion   1. Return to a prior level of development. 2. A recessive gene re-appearing in a phenotype after having been dormant for several generations. The offspring may resemble a remote ancestor more closely than a member of the immediate family. For example, two short, dark-haired parents may produce a tall, red-haired child if both had ancestors with these traits. 3. See REGRESSION.

ReVia   Trade name for naltrexone.

review   1. Re-examination of completed work or material studied. 2. A periodical study of the state of the art of any profession concentrating on new materials and techniques. 3. A study of effectiveness of any person, group, organization or procedure to see whether it is effective, cost-effective, time-effective. See ADMISSION CERTIFICATION, CONTINUED-STAY REVIEW, PROFESSIONAL REVIEW, UTILIZATION REVIEW.

revival   1. Obsolete term for recall. 2. The reappearance of a lost memory.

Revised Beta Examination, Second Edition (Beta-II)   (C. E. Kellogg, N. W. Morton) A revision of the Beta Examination intended for persons who cannot read and those with limited English proficiency. Six separately timed tests (Mazes, Coding, Paper Form Boards, Picture Completion, Clerical Checking, Picture Absurdities) are intended to measure different aspects of nonverbal ability. See BETA EXAMINATION/TEST.

revivification   1. In general, renewal of life and strength. 2. In hypnosis, a technique in which suggestion is used to induce the participant to revive and relive forgotten or repressed memories.

revolving-door phenomenon   1. A tendency for the same patients to be repeatedly admitted, discharged and readmitted to various clinics, mental hospitals, for substance abuse, mental disorders, etc. See READMISSION, RECIDIVISM. 2. See RECIDIVISM RATE.

revolving drum   A device, common in the early years of the 20th century, to measure various kinds of activity, such as the activity of animals. See ACTIVITY CAGE for a similar apparatus. Not to be confused with a "memory drum."

reward   1. A satisfying stimulus obtained after successful performance. Rewards are of two basic types: intrinsic and extrinsic. 2. See POSITIVE REINFORCEMENT. 3. A positive motivating stimulus. For example, in an experiment, a reward is given to a participant or animal subject upon successful termination of a desired (by the experimenter) response. Types of reward include: CONTINGENT, DELAYED, EXTRINSIC, INTRINSIC, NEGATIVE, POSITIVE, PRIMARY, SECONDARY, TOKEN, TRANSACTIONAL CONTINGENT. See LOGICAL CONSEQUENCES, NATURAL CONSEQUENCES, REINFORCEMENT.

reward by the superego   In psychoanalytic theory, a feeling of satisfaction for attitudes or behavior which unconsciously elicit the approval of the superego, for example, for renouncing unsocial or aggressive impulses.

reward centers   (J. Olds & M. Olds) Areas in the brain that may produce the experience of pleasure in an organism. For example, the medial nucleus of the hypothalamus.

reward conditioning   See OPERANT CONDITIONING.

reward-cost stage   A phase in development occurring around the age of two years, characterized by children sharing common expectations about friendship and activities.

reward delay   See DELAY-OF-REWARD GRADIENT, DELAYED REWARD.

rewarded alternative method   A forgetting and relearning technique characterized by eliminating the reward of an undesired response and rewarding a new desired one.

reward expectancy   1. (E. C. Tolman) A response-readiness set that develops when animals expect to be rewarded for a current action as they were in a similar situation in the recent past. 2. A state of mind for humans that directs certain behavior in the expectation that certain desirable consequences will occur following this particular behavior.

reward learning   See OPERANT CONDITIONING.

reward situation   Expecting to receive some kind of external payment or compensation for some activity or behavior, rather than performing it for its own sake. For example, a rat repeatedly presses a bar in a Skinner box to obtain food or a child performs yard work to be allowed to drive the family car.

reward system   A set of interrelated factors that link a particular stimulus with some form of tangible or intangible satisfaction. In animal self-stimulation experiments, a reward system may consist of the animal pressing a lever that allows an electric current to flow to electrodes implanted in cells of its limbic system, apparently giving the animal a pleasurable sensation since the animal will repeatedly press the lever sometimes to exhaustion. See SELF-STIMULATION MECHANISM for an illustration.

reward training   Reinforcing a desired response by giving the organism being studied, be it an earthworm or a human, positive reinforcement following the desired response. See BEHAVIOR MODIFICATION, REWARD SITUATION.

RF   reticular formation (also abbreviated **rf**)

RFT   See ROD-AND-FRAME TEST.

rG   1. See CONSUMMATORY RESPONSE. 2. See GOAL RESPONSE.

r$_G$ See FRACTIONAL ANTEDATING GOAL RESPONSE.

R$_g$ Symbol for any goal-attaining response.

RGB system   A method of classifying colors in terms of the degrees of Red, Green, and Blue in them.

rg-sg   See FRACTIONAL ANTEDATING GOAL RESPONSE.

rhabdomancy   **rabdomancy**

Rh blood-group incompatibility   An immunoreaction disorder caused by genetically determined antigens called Rh factors (for rhesus monkeys used in early studies). If a Rh-negative mother bears a child with Rh-positive antigens, and if the next child also has Rh-positive antigens, if any of the fetus' blood enters the mother's circulation (through the placenta), the fetus will be negatively affected and among consequences are jaundice, anemia, and mental retardation. Also known as Rhesus incompatibility. See RH FACTOR, RH REACTION.

Rh factor   Any of at least eight different kinds of antigens, each determined genetically. A person whose blood cells carry an Rh factor is said to be Rh-positive; a person whose blood cells lack an Rh factor is Rh-negative. See RH BLOOD GROUP INCOMPATIBILITY, RH REACTION.

Rh reaction   An adverse effect that can occur in blood transfusions and pregnancies when an Rh-negative person's blood is mixed with Rh-positive blood from another. It is similar to an immune reaction to an invasion of the body tissues by a foreign agent. In pregnancy, an Rh-negative mother may carry an Rh-positive fetus, her body forming anti-Rh antibodies that destroy the red blood cells of the fetus. See RH BLOOD-GROUP INCOMPATIBILITY.

rhabdophobia   1. Morbid fear of being punished or beaten with a rod, or of rods in general. See MASTIGOPHOBIA. 2. Fear of magic.

rhaphe   **raphe**

rhathymia   A carefree attitude.

rhembasmus   Obsolete term for indecision. See ABULIA.

rheobase   A threshold of neural tissue excitability, the minimum level of electric current needed for contraction of a muscle, or excitation of a nerve. Also known as rheobasis. See CHRONAXIE.

rheoscopic   Methods of viewing rapidly moving objects, such as the flywheel of an automobile by various methods such as by stroboscopes, or fast movie cameras.

rheostat   An instrument that can be used to regulate the amount of electric current.

rheotaxis   A tendency of fish and other organisms to orient themselves toward the source of the flow (against the current) in a stream of water. See TAXIS, TROPISM.

rheotropism   A tendency of parts of organisms (such as leaves, roots, stems of a plant) to move against the direction of a current. See TAXIS, TROPISM.

rhesus   Generic name for the primate, *Macaca mulatta*.

Rhesus incompatibility   See RH BLOOD GROUP INCOMPATIBILITY.

Rhine cards/deck   (J. B. Rhine) A set of five stimulus cards, similar to a deck of playing cards, devised by J. B. Rhine for the experimental study of telepathy or thought transmission. See ZENER CARDS.

rhinencephalon   (G. St. Hilaire, R. von Kölliker) 1. Historically, a collective term for parts of the brain related to the sense of smell. Once (but no longer) including the gyrus fornicatus, hippocampus, and amygdala. 2. Collective term for parts of the cerebral hemisphere directly related to olfaction (sense of smell) including the olfactory bulb, olfactory peduncle, olfactory tubercle, olfactory cortex, cortical nucleus of the amygdala. 3. A section of the brain including the olfactory bulb plus other tracts including the hippocampus and the fornix. Sometimes known as smell brain. See ARCHIPALLIUM, LIMBIC SYSTEM.

rhinolalia   A speech disorder characterized by abnormal nasal resonance. Also known as rhinism, rhinophonia.

rhinophonia   1. Dysphonia (difficulty or pain in speaking) characterized by a nasal voice. 2. See RHINOLALIA.

rho   1. The seventeenth letter of the Greek alphabet. See APPENDIX C. 2. (P) A Greek letter used to signify the coefficient of rank correlation.

rho correlation   1. A measurement of degree of consistency of two series of scores by comparing their rank order positions. 2. A computational approach for obtaining the product-moment correlation with ranked scores on both variables. The Spearman rho correlation coefficient is a measure of the relationship between two variables that may be obtained by first ranking the variables then finding the Pearson correlation coefficient between the ranks.

rhodopsin   (G. Wald) Reddish photochemical visual pigment, found in the rods of the retina, which is bleached by light to visual orange, visual yellow, and then to white. Necessary in twilight or night vision. Light causes rhodopsin to separate into opsin and retinene, whereas darkness causes rhodopsin to be formed by the combination of retinene and opsin. Also known as visual purple. See ADAPTATION, DARK AND LIGHT ADAPTATION, DUPLICITY, RETINENE.

rhombencephalon   Inclusive term for the pons, cerebellum, and medulla oblongata. In embryology, that part of the brain developed from the caudal end of the three primary vesicles of the embryonic neural tube; further divided into metencephalon and myelencephalon. Also known as hindbrain, hindbrain vesicle.

rhombencephalic sleep   The second phase of sleep during which there are distinctive, measurable brain-wave activities while dreaming, and rapid eye movements occur. See DEEP SLEEP, TELENCEPHALIC SLEEP.

rho-relation   (M. Wertheimer) In Gestalt psychology, a relation that is "sensible with regard to the inner structure of the given situation"; rho-relations involve meaningful whole qualities or dependent part qualities as opposed to blind connections within an entire structure. Also known as P-relation. See PART QUALITIES.

rhyme (in mnemonics)   The use of rhyme (and sometimes rhythm) to aid memory, as in "Thirty days hath September/April, June, and November." See MNEMONICS.

rhyming delirium   An unusual mental disorder characterized by speaking in rhymes, for example, "I am free, as you can see; you are wrong, that's my song." An occasional symptom of the manic phase of a manic-depressive (bipolar) reaction.

rhypophagy   scatophagy (meaning 1)

rhypophobia   1. Extreme negative reaction to feces or the act of defecation. 2. Fear of filth. Also known as rupophobia, rypophobia.

rhythm   1. A uniform pattern of beats, as in a heart. 2. The regular alternation of two different states. 3. In electroencephalography, a regular occurrence of an electrical event.

rhythm disorders   Pathological conditions of speech production in terms of timing of syllables and words, including repetitions, prolongations, and stammering. Speech therapists use a variety of techniques to assist people with such problems including rewards and encouragement. See BEHAVIOR THERAPY, TIME AND RHYTHM DISORDERS.

rhythm method   A technique of contraception in which the woman abstains from coitus during the days of the month in which she is most likely to become pregnant, usually just before and after ovulation.

rhythm-periodicity   Regular repetition that characterizes not only biological processes such as pulse, respiration, hunger, menstruation, urination, and metabolic changes, but behavioral phenomena as well, such as thumb-sucking, nursing, masturbation, mood changes, and rhythmic games, dances, and songs. Many pathological manifestations are also rhythmic or periodic: the manic-depressive (bipolar) cycle, the tendency to repeat traumatic experiences in recurrent dreams, and the repetitive activities of obsessive-compulsives. See REPETITION-COMPULSION.

rhythmic sensory-bombardment therapy   A form of sensory-overloading treatment in which certain types of patients with psychoses or neuroses are bombarded with sound, light, or touches applied intermittently and rhythmically for a particular period of time, usually one hour.

rhythmic stimulation   An automatic effect of a flickering light characterized by synchronization of the electroencephalographic (EEG) pattern to the frequency of the flicker. The effect of light flicker on brain waves may vary with different species of animals. Flickering lights may precipitate seizures in predisposed individuals.

RI   retroactive inhibition/interference

ribonuclease   An enzyme that breaks down ribonucleic-acid molecules into smaller units.

ribonucleic acid (RNA)   A complex nucleic acid molecule containing ribose, phosphoric acid, adenine, cytosine, guanine, and uracil. RNA is found in intracellular nucleoprotein particles, or ribosomes, where it plays a role in linking amino acids into protein molecules. Controls cellular activities, and purportedly plays a role in memory.

ribosomal RNA   A kind of RNA (ribonucleic acid) located in ribosomes within the endoplasmic reticulum (ER) of living cells, involved in protein synthesis. Also known as template RNA. See RIBONUCLEIC ACID (RNA).

ribosome   Granular structures that occur in the cytoplasm of living cells where they function as protein factories. They may be found singly or in clusters, bound to the endoplasmic reticulum or floating freely in the cytoplasm.

Ribot's law   (T. A. Ribot) A theory that in cases of recovery from loss of language (aphasia), the first language to be recalled will be the first originally learned.

Ricco's law   (A. Riccò) A theory that the perceived brightness of vision of small images depends on the amount of light delivered and not on how it is distributed on the retina. The formula is L (light intensity) × A (area) equals K (a constant for the threshold). The law is for brightness for small areas of the retina, for large areas, see PIPER'S LAW.

rickets   A disease usually occurring in infants and young children caused by a dietary deficiency of vitamin D and calcium. Characterized by softening of the bones and skeletal deformities such as bowed legs. See OSTEOMALACIA.

riddance phenomenon/reflex　(S. Rado) Various reflexes that help to eliminate annoying or painful agents from the body, including scratching, spitting, vomiting, sneezing, and the shedding of tears.

Ridgway color system　A method of categorizing, 1,115 hues based on the colors of bird feathers. Named after American ornithologist Robert Ridgway (1850–1929).

ridicule fear　See CATAGELOPHOBIA.

right-and-wrong cases method/procedure　(G. T. Fechner) A common psychophysical procedure for determining accuracy of perceptions. A standard stimulus is displayed as a constant in comparison with other similar stimuli. The participant is asked to distinguish between them (such as which is the louder, the longer, the heavier) with the percentage of correct answers determining the degree of discrimination. Also known as method of constant stimuli. See MAGNITUDE ESTIMATION, METHOD OF LIMITS.

right-and-wrong test　A measure of criminal responsibility that asks whether the person under legal consideration was able to distinguish between moral right and wrong (at the time of the crime). See CRIMINAL RESPONSIBILITY, M'NAGHTEN RULES.

right-associates method/procedure　(G. Müller) A memory method for use when materials to be memorized are presented in pairs. After memorization, one member of a pair is produced and the participant is expected to reproduce its associate.

righteousness　Conformity to ethical or moral standards of conduct conceived to be the commands of a deity or the formulation of some divinely established plan of way of living.

right-handedness　The preferential use of the right hand for major activities, such as eating, writing, and throwing; a component of dextrality that applies to about 90% of the population. See CEREBRAL DOMINANCE, DEXTRALITY, DEXTRALITY-SINISTRALITY, HANDEDNESS, LATERALITY.

right hemisphere　The right half of the cerebrum. Compared with the left hemisphere, the right hemisphere plays only a minor role in language functions in most people, and therefore, is called the nondominant hemisphere. The right hemisphere plays an important role in visuospatial and emotional functions as well as in the control of the left half of the body and the right side of the retina of each eye. See HANDEDNESS.

righting reflex　An automatic tendency for an organism, such as a turtle, to return to an upright position when it has been thrown off balance or placed on its back. Also known as righting reaction/response. See VISUAL-RIGHTING REFLEXES.

right lateral ventricle (of the brain)　See BRAIN VENTRICLES, LEFT LATERAL VENTRICLE (OF THE BRAIN).

right-left disorientation　A disorder characterized by general difficulty in distinguishing between the right and left sides.

right neglect dyslexia　See NEGLECT DYSLEXIA.

right of the first night　Phrase similar to *Jus primae noctis* (Latin).

right-or-wrong test　See RIGHT-AND-WRONG TEST.

right-side fear　See DEXTROPHOBIA.

rights of disabled　In the United States, a basic constitutional right guaranteed all persons in the United States and reinforced by special legislation and court rulings to protect people in mental institutions and in society. For instance, children with mental retardation are protected against corporal punishment and inadequate medical care, mental patients are allowed to refuse treatment administered primarily for the benefit of the hospital staff, and confidentiality of records is assured. Later, various disabilities rights legislation mandated that public facilities must have ramps and bathrooms accessible to persons using wheelchairs, etc. See BILL OF RIGHTS, INSTITUTIONAL PEONAGE, UNITED NATIONS DECLARATION ON RIGHTS OF THE MENTALLY RETARDED.

rights of patients　In the United States, a doctrine positing that patients who are involuntarily hospitalized (legally committed) have the right to communicate with persons outside the facility, to keep clothing and personal effects, to vote, to follow a religion of their choice, to be employed if possible, to execute wills or other legal instruments, to enter into contractual relationships, to make purchases, to be educated, to marry, to retain licenses and permits, to sue or be sued, and not to be subjected to unnecessary restraint.

rights of the mentally retarded　In the United States, rights of persons who are mentally challenged as stated by the *United Nations Declaration on the Rights of Mentally Retarded Persons* (1971): Persons who are mentally challenged have the same rights to the maximum degree of feasibility as other humans including the right to receive proper medical care, physical therapy, education, training, rehabilitation, and guidance; the right to economic security; the right to work; the right to live with one's own family or foster parents or, if this is not feasible, to live in an institution under circumstances as close as possible to family life; and protection from abuse and exploitation.

right tail of a distribution　See TAILS OF A DISTRIBUTION.

right temporal lobectomy　See TEMPORAL LOBECTOMY.

right to refuse treatment　The basic prerogative of a person to reject any kind of treatment, medical or psychological, even when in a hospital or a prison. Among the various legal cases that established this right are *Wyatt v Stickney* (325 F. Supp. 781, 1972) that allows Americans the right to refuse treatment of such procedures as lobotomy until after the patient has a consulted with an attorney or others. See FORCED TREATMENT.

right to treatment　The principle that a facility that has assumed the responsibility to provide treatment for a patient is legally obligated to provide adequate treatment.

rigid control　The use of inner restraints, such as inhibitions, repression, suppression in coping with environmental stressors.

rigid family　A family situation based on possessive, dominating parental control. See CHAOTIC FAMILIES.

rigidity   1. In physiology, strong and persistent muscular contraction as in certain neuromuscular disorders. 2. Inability or unwillingness to change views, attitudes, or values. 3. A personality trait characterized by inability or strong resistance to changing personal behavior, or to altering opinions and attitudes. See AFFECTIVE RIGIDITY, DECEREBRATION, INTELLECTUAL RIGIDITY, OPISTHOTONOS.

rimming   Slang for licking the area between the scrotum or vagina to around the anus.

ring chromosome   A defective chromosome that results from breakage in both arms of a chromatid which then fuses at the ends to form a circle. Such abnormalities tend to involve an X chromosome.

ring chromosome 18   A congenital disorder characterized by microcephaly, ear and eye abnormalities, and severe mental deficiency.

ring D syndrome   See CHROMOSOME 13, DELETION OF LONG ARM.

Ringelmann effect   (M. Ringelmann) A tendency for group members to become less productive as their group size increases.

ring-finger dermatitis   A cutaneous disease of an area of a finger where a ring is worn. May be marked by itching, redness, eruption of small blisters, or similar effects. Caused by either a cutaneous reaction to an emotional problem, or a chemical irritation from substances in or on the ring, such as soap beneath the ring.

Rinné test   A tuning-fork test used to aid in differentiating between a conductive and sensorineural hearing loss. Named after German otologist Friedrich Heinrich A. Rinné (1819–1868).

ripen   To approach maturity. Term is properly limited to plants and applied to the fruit and seed.

risk   See AT RISK, HIGH-RISK STUDIES, MORBIDITY RISK, RISK FACTOR.

risk aversion   A tendency to "play it safe" under most conditions, even when only minimal risk is involved and a favorable outcome is highly likely.

risk factor   1. Some element, tangible or intangible, assumed to be causally associated with some kind of disease or abnormality. 2. Any variable statistically associated with a behavior disorder. 3. Like marker variables, a risk factor is any variable whose value is statistically associated with a parameter of a behavior disorder. Although the phrase is not used consistently in the literature, a risk factor, but not a marker variable, implies the operation of a causal variable. Driving without a seat belt may be considered a risk factor for bodily injury in an accident. See MARKER VARIABLE.

risk hypothesis   See ETHICAL-RISK HYPOTHESIS.

risk level   Establishment of a particular level of expectation about possible failure on the basis of predicted percentages of successes and failures. In some cases, a failure rate of 10% may be acceptable (for example, school testing of any class) but in other cases a failure rate of even 0.0001% may be considered unacceptable (for example, the performance of part of a helicopter motor). See CONFIDENCE LEVEL.

risk metrics   A numerical system of indicating chances of developing some kind of abnormal condition. See INCIDENCE, PREVALENCE.

risk recreation model   A theory that describes risk-taking recreational activities according to a five-phase, transactional cycle.

risk-rescue rating   (A. Weismann) A rating system for suicide attempts, considering A (risk score—severity of the attempt) and B (rescue score—degree of danger) in the formula $(A \times 100) \times (A–B)$. See SUICIDOLOGY.

risk-taking   A pattern of taking unnecessary risks, possibly motivated, usually unconsciously, by masochistic needs, bravado, and the desire to prove the self or tempt fate. See PATHOLOGICAL GAMBLING.

risky predictions   To determine whether a hypothesis is true or whether a field, such as psychology, is a science is to make risky predictions, testing the limits of the theory. Karl Popper pointed out that different therapists could make diagnostic statements with great assurance of correctness, but unless they generate disconfirmable hypotheses, there was no way to determine their validity. See FALSIFYING HYPOTHESIS.

risky shift   A tendency for the average of individual decisions, after discussion of a problem, to be more risky than before the discussion. A change in opinion of an individual to a more risky decision following a group discussion. See CAUTIOUS SHIFT, CHOICE SHIFT.

risky-shift effect research   Studies on the purported tendency of groups to make riskier decisions on most problems than the average group member who decides alone. Experimental procedures can be of three major types: (a) initial individual decisions by a person who is or who becomes a leader; (b) individual decisions after group discussion and decisions; and (c) individual decisions following group discussion but no group decision.

Ritalin   A trade name for methylphenidate.

rite   **ritual** (meaning 2)

rites de passage   (rites of passage—French) (A. van Gennep) The formal acknowledgements of transitions of a person's life course from one level of status to another by formal ceremonies. Examples include baptism, citizenship, bar mitzvah, graduation, marriage.

rites of passage   *rites de passage*

ritual   1. An elaborate formal process usually part of a celebration. 2. A ceremonial procedure, repeated in the same way over a long period of time, usually conducted during religious and fraternal services, the military, and other settings. Also known as rite. 3. An established formal ceremony, often used to mark an important occasion, for example, baptism, bar mitzvah, burials, citizenship-granting, indoctrination, marriage. See RITES OF PASSAGE.

ritual abuse   (G. Rhoades) A method of control of people of all ages consisting of physical, sexual, and psychological mistreatment through the use of rituals. See SATANISM.

ritualistic killing   Sacrificing a life in a specific manner, often done as part of a religious ritual. See MODUS OPERANDI, ORGANIZED SERIAL KILLERS.

ritual-making   (S. Rado) A form of obsessive behavior by means of which a person operates in a highly stereotyped manner day after day until exhaustion.

rituals   1. A series of acts, religious and profane, repeatedly and, occasionally, compulsively carried out as a defense against anxiety, or for release of tension. 2. Repetitive stereotyped behavior patterns seen in obsessive-compulsive people. 3. See RITUAL.

rivalry   The pursuit of the same indivisible goal by two or more individuals or groups. See COMPETITION.

river fear   See POTAMOPHOBIA.

Rivermead Behavioral Memory Test   (RBMT) (B. Wilson) An examination that measures separately the capacities to remember names, recognize faces, recall named objects, learn a route, indicate orientation in time and space, and carry out instructions in the future.

r-K scale   See DIFFERENTIAL K THEORY.

RL   Abbreviation for *Reizlimen* (German), the absolute stimulus limen or threshold.

R-methodology   A factor analysis across tests rather than across individuals. Shows how traits, abilities, etc., fall into patterns called factors, but it does not show how individuals cluster together. Compare Q METHODOLOGY.

RMS   root-mean-square

RNA   See RIBONUCLEIC ACID.

road rage   Slang for a driver's loss of temper and inappropriate aggressive behavior in response to a real or imagined misdeed by another driver.

road warrior   Slang for a person who drives a car aggressively; it is asserted that such a person is not ordinarily so overtly aggressive.

robber fear   See HARPAXOPHOBIA.

Robinson Crusoe age   Phrase similar to Erik Erikson's industry versus inferiority stage.

robot   1. A machine that simulates a human. 2. An insensitive, unfeeling, unintelligent, mechanical imitation of a human.

robotics   An aspect of artificial intelligence by means of which a robot is made to act in the manner of an intelligent person in making limited choices or performing various simple actions, such as playing chess.

robustness   In statistics, the degree of sensitivity of a statistical test to determine violations of crucial assumptions.

robust statistic   A statistic relatively insensitive to the presence of outliers and violations of assumptions such as normal distribution of data.

ROC   1. See RECEIVER-OPERATING CHARACTERISTIC CURVE. 2. Response operating characteristic.

R-occurrence   See RESPONSE RATE.

ROC curve   See RECEIVER-OPERATING CHARACTERISTIC CURVE.

rocking   The stereotyped back-and-forth motion observed in some people including those with severe retardation, senility, autism, and psychoses.

rocking and headbanging   Peculiar behavior noted in some otherwise normal children, typically, seated by a wall, who rock and bang the back of their heads. Purportedly, most such children have been ignored or neglected and have learned that this is one way to get attention. Related in dynamics to Oedipism (self-inflicted eye injuries).

rod   See RODS.

rod-and-frame test (RFT)   (H. Witkin) A way of measuring field independence. A participant is asked to indicate the true vertical by manipulating a rod within a frame when the frame in which the person is seated is tilted at various degrees from the vertical. Field-independent people are not so affected to the same degree as field-dependent people by the angle of the frame. See FIELD DEPENDENCE, FIELD INDEPENDENCE.

rod fear   See RHABDOPHOBIA.

rods   (A. von Leeuwenhoek) Low-threshold, achromatic, rod-shaped receptors for twilight or night vision. In the human eye, 120 million visual receptors in the retina transduce gray values of light images into neural impulses (thereby coding information about light and dark). Rods are located, for the most part, in the periphery of the eye and are important for scoptic (night) vision, as they detect variations in light levels rather than color. Also known as retinal rods, rod cells. Compare CONE(S) (meaning 2).

rods and cones layer   Jacob's membrane

rods of Corti   (A. Corti) Elongated structures forming an arch in the organ of Corti in the inner ear. They are based on the basilar membrane, whose upper ends lie between the inner and outer hair cells.

rod vision   The ability to see in twilight or in the near dark based solely on the action of the rods of the retina.

Roentgen (rays)   Röntgen (rays)

Rogerian   A follower of the concepts, philosophy, and methods of Carl Rogers. See ADLERIAN, FREUDIAN, JUNGIAN.

Rogerian   counseling/therapy   person-centered psychotherapy

Rogerian theory   The psychotherapeutic system of Carl Rogers that posits that clients have the capacity to achieve most psychotherapeutic goals in a situation where they feel they are completely accepted and understood without the therapist asking questions, making suggestions, or giving information, advice or analysis. Important therapeutic methods are reflection of feeling and paraphrasing, thereby helping the person gain clearer self-perception. The following items are important for understanding Carl Rogers' theory: ACTIVE LISTENING, CLIENT-CENTERED THERAPY, CONDITIONAL POSITIVE REGARD, CONDITIONS OF WORTH, CONGRUENCE, EXISTENTIAL LIVING, FULLY FUNCTIONING PERSON, GROWTH PRINCIPLE, HELPING RELATIONSHIP, INCONGRUENCE, INTERPRETIVE RESPONSE, NONDIRECTIVE COUNSELING/PSYCHOTHERAPY, NONDIRECTIVE GROUP PSYCHOTHERAPY, NONDIRECTIVE TEACHING MODEL, ORGANISMIC VALUING PROCESS, PASSIVE LISTENING, PERSON-CENTERED THERAPY, POSITIVE REGARD, PRIMARY EMPATHY, PROBING RESPONSE, REASSURING RESPONSE, REFLECTION OF FEELING, REFLECTIVE RESPONSE, RESTATEMENT (OF CONTENT), ROGERIAN, ROGERS' THERAPEUTIC CONCEPTS, SELF-ACTUALIZATION, THREAT, UNCONDITIONAL POSITIVE REGARD, UNCRITICALNESS.

Rogers' therapeutic concepts   Three basic necessities for a successful psychotherapeutic experience according to Carl Rogers: congruence, empathic understanding, unconditional positive regard.

Rohypnol   A trade name for flunitrazepam. See DATE-RAPE DRUGS.

rok-joo   Thai name for *koro*, a mental disorder observed in the Phillipines. See KORO.

Rokeach Value Survey   (M. Rokeach) A form with 36 items used for value clarification and therapy that compares the rankings of a respondent's value statements against those of a reference group.

Rolandic cortex   (L. Rolando) A part of the brain where sensorimotor rhythm is recorded.

Rolandic fissure   sulcus centralis

Rolando's sulcus   sulcus centralis

role   1. The functions assigned or adopted by an individual in a social structure. 2. The set of behaviors expected of a person possessing a certain social status. 3. A pattern of behavior appropriate for a particular situation or status. A person may play a variety of roles, such as supervisor or subordinate. 4. The part played by an actor in a play; the theater is the metaphor from which the social-psychological concept is taken. See SOCIAL ROLE. ("Role" and "personality" are sometimes incorrectly used interchangeably; role focuses on position or status in a social structure rather than on shifts in personality, as going from being shy to outgoing.)

role action pattern   The structured invariant set of behaviors that people exhibit in certain social roles.

role ambiguity   A stressful situation in which a person does not know the proper or desired response to make usually to a new or unexpected event.

role behavior   The conduct considered proper for a person's social or vocational role. See SOCIAL ROLE.

role category   See SOCIAL ROLE.

role changes   A change from usual patterns of behavior, function, or position of an individual in particular situations or status in a social structure. See CONVERSION, PERSONALITY, ROLE TRANSITIONS, SHIFTING ROLES, TRANSFORMATION.

role clarification   Information provided for how to behave in a particular role.

role conflict/strain   1. Tension that arises when a person fills two or more roles that clash. Intrarole conflict means that the source of tension can be located within a single role, for example, the parental role when two children have incompatible needs. Interrole conflict arises in the clash between two different roles, for example that of parent and that of employee. 2. The tension a person may experience when there are two competing ways to behave in any particular situation, for example, pacifists being physically attacked and having to choose between passivity or responding by counterviolence.

role confusion   1. According to Eric Erikson, a situation that may arise when a person who belongs at a particular stage of life does not have a clear understanding of what social role to play. Pampered children are likely to have role confusion. 2. Masculine behavior in a female or feminine behavior in a male. Also known as identity confusion/diffusion. See GENDER IDENTITY, GENDER-IDENTITY DISORDER OF CHILDHOOD, IDENTITY VERSUS ROLE CONFUSION, TRANSGENDERISM.

Role Construct Repertory Test (REP Test)   (G. A. Kelly) A procedure intended to determine people's perception of the world by examining their constructs of reality (based on the idea that constructs determine behavior). Designed to help clinicians identify clients' constructs, such as what behavior is desirable or undesirable in a given situation. Sometimes also abbreviated RCRT.

role-construct theory   (G. A. Kelly) A cognitive theory of human behavior stating that people attempt to select constructs or concepts that can make their environments understandable and predictable while providing clues for constructive behavior. Holds that a person seeks to sustain and substantiate a construct system once it has been developed.

role count   The number of roles that a person plays in society.

role deprivation   A loss of cultural and psychological contact for certain classes of individuals, such as children who are not allowed to play with other children, institutionalized persons, people prevented, for any of various reasons, from entering the life of the community, generally leading to decreased ability to interact normally with others or some degree of psychopathology. Seen when people institutionalized for many years and then released do not know how to adjust to the complexity of normal society.

role-divided psychotherapy   (G. Bach) A therapy group that meets for part of a session without the therapist present and also for a time with the therapist present. See MULTIPLE THERAPY.

role diffusion   (E. Erickson) Denoting those who have not as yet resolved their role identity. See IDENTITY, ROLE CONFUSION.

role discontinuity   The sudden change of a role, for example, a law-abiding citizen is arrested and must shift to the role of defendant or prisoner.

role distance   An increase of objectivity about anything or anyone important in the past, present, or future. Being able to view such phenomena from a new perspective, for example, no longer being concerned about social situations that previously generated negative emotions.

role distortion   1. An inappropriate form of social behavior. 2. A change in role behavior from what is expected to an undesirable form.

role-enactment theory   A point of view that people who are hypnotized and asked to act in ways they may not ordinarily operate may be cooperating without conscious intent with the hypnotist rather than being in a trance. See HYPNOSIS.

role expectation   How other members of a society believe a person in a given situation should behave. For example, a technician who makes a housecall is expected to play a somewhat different role from the one played were the technician to have been visited at the shop. There are different expectations for the behavior of people in and out of various uniforms, be they nurses, physicians, postal workers, or police officers. See SOCIAL ROLE.

role-expectations hypothesis   A postulate that confirmation of employees' prior expectations about the nature of their jobs leads to lower turnover and higher levels of job satisfaction and organizational commitment.

role experimentation   The assumption of a different behavioral role, usually in the expectation of being more successful by acting in a different manner, often based on behavior of another who is admired. See FIXED ROLE THERAPY, PSYCHODRAMA.

role model   Anyone who serves, knowingly or unknowingly, as a model for others.

role obsolescence   A situation in which the social role of an individual or type of individual has diminished importance within the group or population.

role overload   Strain on an individual resulting from too many directions or expectations for a particular role. It may mean that one role has too many components or that one person has too many roles.

roleplay   1. People playing a role different from their usual one in a real situation, perhaps to impress others. 2. Playing an anticipated role, for example, preparing how to act if suddenly promoted into an executive position. 3. Acting a make-believe role in a psychodrama.

roleplaying   1. Theatrical acting. 2. Social role taking. 3. Dissembling (putting on a false act). 4. Acting a part of another person for either educational (sociodrama) or therapeutic purposes (psychodrama), for example, training employees to handle problems with customers or rehearsing ways to cope with stress in family conflicts. 5. In psychodrama, any of several forms of spontaneous action techniques, for example role-reversal, used for instruction or therapy. The essence of roleplaying is making believe that a contrived situation is real. See REALITY ROLEPLAYING, SWITCHING, VISUALIZATION.

role rehearsal   1. The imitation of adult roles by children, such as playing "house." 2. Acting or speaking in an artificial situation (such as alone in front of a mirror), in preparation for some event (such as delivering a speech).

role-relaxed consumers   People who are relatively immune to influence, especially interpersonal, valuing economic and quality aspects of products more than style and fashion.

role reversal   In psychodrama, taking on the role of another with whom the person has been interacting, especially a person with whom there has been conflict. For example, a person complains about another to others in group therapy. Under the therapist's direction, the complainer roleplays with another member pretending to be the latter. Next, they reverse roles. This process is supposed to give the complainer a new perspective after being in the latter's "shoes." Also known as switching.

role set   In organizations, roles established for specific individuals. For example, a treasurer records and handles financial matters.

role shift   In any two-person relationship, a shift by each partner to the prior behavior of the other. See ROLE REVERSAL.

role specialization   1. The assumption of various roles of individuals in any group, large or small, such as being dominant or submissive, taking responsibility for certain functions or areas, making certain kinds of decisions, joining with specified others for various purposes, or acting as an equal with others in certain decision modalities. 2. The relative decision-making influences of X and Y, whose role structure may be classified in four categories: (a) X = dominant, (b) Y = dominant, (c) X and Y acting independently of each other, and (d) X and Y in a syncretic relationship (decisions made jointly).

role strain   role conflict

role taking   1. Assuming a particular attitudinal role, behavioral role, or both, to be more popular, to gain attention, to get along, etc. 2. Assuming the role or point of view of another person. An essential process in cognitive and social development.

role theory of personality   A theory that describes personality development as the gradual acquisition of roles prescribed by a particular culture, in some cases having a variety of roles for any person, depending on social situations, in effect acting as others consider proper for the various situations. See TRAIT.

role therapy   A system of psychotherapy introduced by George Kelly that uses real-life psychodrama. The basic concept of this system is that a person decides on a role model and works out the aspects of the model with the therapist and then role-plays the model not only in the office of the therapist but in social life, returning to the therapist periodically for reevaluation. See PSYCHODRAMA.

role training   Rehearsing an anticipated situation so that the response is appropriate in the actual situation.

role transitions   Movement in life from one role to another, for example, a student becomes an employee and then a retiree. Each of these events represents a new social role for that person. See ROLE CHANGES, SHIFTING ROLES.

Rolfing   (I. P. Rolf) A massage treatment known formally as "structural integration" characterized by deep penetration of the fingers and hands into the muscles to realign the body with the field of gravity. The theory suggests that the body assumes certain characteristic postures due to muscle arrangements, and if the arrangements can be changed (for example, if a stooped person were to stand upright), that personality changes will also occur. Developed in the 1930s, it did not become widely known until the 1960s.

rolling (of eyes)   See TORSION.

romance   See FAMILY ROMANCE.

Roman charity   Breast-feeding an adult. (Based on a Roman legend that an older man falsely imprisoned and not fed, is suckled by his lactating daughter who is allowed to visit but not to bring food, sustaining him until his release. The subject of many paintings, and echoed in John Steinbeck's *The Grapes of Wrath*.)

romantic love   A passionate state of physical and emotional attraction felt for another person with a tendency toward idealization.

romanticism   An attitude toward life that emphasizes artistic elements, freedom, spontaneity, loving, freedom from constraints.

Romberg('s) sign/symptom   (M. H. von Romberg) A sign of hysteria or neurological damage indicated by the swaying motion of people who try to stand upright when their feet are close together and eyes are closed.

Romeo and Juliet effect   A tendency for restrictions placed on a set of people (for example, young lovers) by others (for example, parents) to increase their desire to be together. An example of reactance.

$R_{1.23...n}$ Symbol for a multiple correlation coefficient.

$r_{12.34}$ Symbol for a partial correlation.

Röntgen (rays)   Obsolete name for X-rays.

rooming-in   Mother and newborn in the same hospital room after birth, permitting touching and looking at the child by the mother, with the expectation that this procedure will, among other benefits, help establish bonding between the two. Rooming-in is an alternative to the more common practice of having newborns stay in a separate nursery.

root conflict/problem   1. In psychotherapy, the assumed basic or ultimate reason for maladjustment presumably not known either to the client or patient and also not by the therapist at the beginning of therapy: the ultimate reason for maladjustment. 2. A nuclear problem stemming from early life which affects the personality of an older person. See BASIC MISTAKE.

rootedness (need)   According to Erich Fromm, a wish to belong and identify with others, including ancestors and ancestry. To know "roots" is considered to be a basic human requirement for normality because it provides emotional security and reduces the isolation and insignificance thought to lie at the heart of human existence. See BROTHERLINESS, INCESTUOUS TIES.

rooting reflex   A "primitive" feeding-related response characterized by turning toward the source of a touch on the cheek, as in an infant touched on the cheek opening the mouth and searching for a nipple.

root-mean-square (RMS)   The square root of the mean of the squares of numbers in question. If the numbers involved are deviations from the mean, the result is the standard deviation of the distribution. See STANDARD DEVIATION.

root-mean-square deviation (RMS)   The square root of the sum of values squared divided by the number of values. When values are deviations from the mean, the RMS equals the standard deviation. See STANDARD DEVIATION.

Rorschach categories   A variety of categories established by a number of experimenters for scoring the Rorschach. Major ones are R, the total number of responses; W, seeing an inkblot as a whole; M, whether action is implied in the perception of the inkblot; A whether the perception is of an animal; P whether the perception is popular (frequently seen) or unusual, and determination of the quality of the perception.

Rorschach determinant(s)   Any element of a participant's responses, verbally or physically, that the examiner regards as meaningful. There are a number of systems of Rorschach determinants as by Bruno Klopfer, Samuel Beck, John Exner. The statement "All the blots look like rocks" would be considered a normal response for a young child or person with mental retardation, but as abnormal for a normal adult. Among the determinants suggested by Hermann Rorschach and others are the form of the percepts, whether there is movement, shading, seeing tiny details, reactions to color, and the viewing of the entire blot as a whole.

Rorschach Ranking Test   A variation of the Rorschach in which participants rank various possible replies in terms of their likelihood of appearance.

Rorschach (Test)   (H. Rorschach) A projective technique in which the participant is presented with ten unstructured inkblots, 5 achromatic (black and white) and 5 chromatic (in colors), in sequence and asked "What might this be?" or "What do you see?" The examiner classifies the responses according to such factors as color (C), movement (M), detail (D), whole (W), popular or common (P), animal (A), form (F), human (H), original (O), small detail (d). The intention of giving such a test is to interpret the participant's personality structure in terms of such factors as emotionality, cognitive style, creativity, bizarreness, and various defensive patterns. Interpretations are based on objective and subjective determinants. Psychologists' views differ as to the psychometric quality of the Rorschach (its reliability and validity), some asserting it has little or none. Also known as Rorschach Inkblot Test, Rorschach Technique, the Rorschach. See PROJECTIVE TESTS.

Rorschach Inkblot Test   A version of an inkblot of the Rorschach type.

Rosanoff association list/test   See KENT-ROSANOFF TEST.

Rosenbach's sign   An inability to close the eyes immediately and completely on command, considered a diagnostic sign of neurasthenia. Also, rapid fluttering motion of the eyelids in hyperthyroidism, absence of the abdominal skin reflex in the presence of inflammatory bowel disease. Named after German physician Ottomar Rosenbach (1851–1907).

Rosenberg Draw-a-Person Technique   A projective test in which a child draws a human figure and is asked what the person is like, after which the child is asked to redraw the figure; and if there are any changes, the examiner asks questions designed to reveal the reasons for the changes.

Rosenthal effect   (R. Rosenthal) 1. A form of self-fulfilling prophecy or expectancy effect, in which, for example, the expectation that a student will succeed or fail leads to that result, or in which an experimenter unconsciously biases the data. 2. A tendency for people considered significant in a person's life (for example, parents, teachers) to affect the person's future depending on whether the person is told by them that he or she is superior (for example, more intelligent, capable), or inferior (for example, stupid, clumsy) to others. In other words, the expectations by people that another will succeed or fail leads to that result. Also known as behavior confirmation, experimenter effects, expectancy, expectancy effects, Pygmalion effect, pygmalionism. See PYGMALIONISM, SELF-FULFILLING PROPHECY.

Rosenzweig Picture Frustration Study (**P-F Study**) (S. Rosenzweig) A series of cartoon type drawings of people in various situations with cartoon "balloons" over their heads. Participants write in the "balloons" what they believe the cartoon persons are saying or thinking. A projective test, the examiner interprets the responses in terms of frustration. Also known as Rosenzweig Picture Frustration Test.

Rosetta Stone Matrix According to Raymond Cattell, the matrix ending research on primary-second-order relations. Named from analogue with the Rosetta stone which revealed the relation of Egyptian hieroglyphics to Greek script.

Rossolimo method A collection of tests designed to provide a psychological profile of mental capacity. Named after Russian neurologist Grigoriy I. Rossolimo (1860–1928).

Rossolimo reflex (G. I. Rossolimo) A sign of brain pathology when there is a flexion of the toes of the foot following tapping the balls of the toes. See ROSSOLIMO METHOD.

Rostan types (L. Rostan) A unique system of body types (out of dozens that have been suggested) included because of the unique nature of the classification, namely concern with aspects of the inner structure of the body. See CEREBRAL TYPE, CONSTITUTIONAL TYPES, DIGESTIVE TYPE, MUSCULAR TYPE, REPRODUCTIVE TYPE, RESPIRATORY TYPE.

rostral Pertaining to the anterior or front end of an organism.

rostrum A beak-shaped structure, such as the rostrum of the corpus callosum in the area where it curves backward under the frontal lobe. Plural is rostrums, rostra.

rotary-pursuit procedure A method of testing for sensorimotor ability or learning by use of a rotating horizontal disk on which there is a constantly changing and moving target that the participant must follow with a pointer. Also known as rotary-pursuit task/test.

rotation 1. A turning about around a central axis. 2. In factor analysis, refers to a movement of axes to achieve maximal loading.

rotational aftereffect (RAE) A type of figural aftereffect in which illusions of movement are created after actual rotation has stopped.

rotation(al) nystagmus Involuntary, jerky, horizontal movement of the eyes induced by rotation of the head around an axis. See AFTER-NYSTAGMUS, NYSTAGMUS.

rotation chair A chair that can revolve around a vertical axis.

rotation nystagmus **rotation(al) nystagmus**

rotation perception Sensitivity to motion produced by rotation of the body, due to fluid in the semicircular canals, followed by the sensation of rotating in the opposite direction when the actual rotation is stopped.

rotation system A technique of group psychotherapy in which the therapist works with each individual member in sequence in the presence of other group members.

rotation table A horizontal board on a vertical pivot that can rotate in the horizontal plane. Used in perceptual-motor research. See ROTARY-PURSUIT PROCEDURE.

rotation tachistoscope A device in which a rotating disk provides a series of visual impressions to a participant at preset intervals.

rotation treatment See GYRATOR TREATMENT.

rote learning A form of learning by means of repetition, such as "2 times 1 equals 2, and 2 times 2 equals 4." Students can answer correctly but may lack comprehension of the concept.

rote memorization See ROTE LEARNING.

rote memory See MEMORY.

rote recall The precise recollection of information that has been stored in its entirety, for example, an address, chemical formula, color pattern, or piece of music. Also known as verbatim recall.

rotoplot program (R. B. Cattell) A program to facilitate rotation for simple structure by immediately showing the effect of a shift in factor analysis.

rotoscope An apparatus that can provide brief exposures in rapid succession. The participant can control the rate of exposures. Can be used to examine rapidly moving machinery when exposures are timed precisely to the movements of the machinery, generating an impression of no movement of moving machinery. See STROBOSCOPIC ILLUSION.

Rotter Incomplete Sentences Blank (**ISB**) (J. Rotter) A questionnaire of forty incomplete sentences that a respondent is to complete. Examining the endings of the sentences gives the clinician a perspective of the client, including attitudes to self and others; for example, the statement "When I am angry, I..." may elicit responses, such as "eat," "cry," "smash stuff." "want to make others miserable," "kill myself." Also known as Rotter Incomplete Sentence Form. See PROJECTIVE TECHNIQUES.

roughness discrimination A test of somesthetic sensitivity in which a participant is expected to determine by touch which of a choice of surfaces has a greater roughness. The surfaces may be grades of sandpaper. The ability is sometimes lost following a lesion in a brain area related to the sense of touch.

round dance A communicative dance performed by a honey bee when a food source is found close to the hive. Contains information about the direction and the distance of the food source. See BEE COMMUNICATION for an illustration of such a dance. See also ANIMAL COMMUNICATION, DANCING LANGUAGE.

rounding off In mathematics, if a decimal number has too many digits on the right side of the decimal point (for example, 3.57494) for practical purposes, a procedure may be used to decrease the number of digits and thereby make the number easier to multiply, divide, etc., without significantly affecting the outcome.

round table technique   A system of group psychotherapy pioneered by Willis McCann. Three connecting rooms are used. In room A are the therapist and others who, through a one-way window, can see the therapy room. Room B is the therapy room where eight patients are seated around a round table, a microphone in the center. In room C are other patients selected from various wards who also can see and hear what is going on in the therapy room B. Those in the therapy group can neither hear nor see anyone besides themselves. They have two tasks: (a) To recommend a member of their group to go to a staff meeting for possible discharge, and (b) if a member is discharged from their group, to agree on a member from group C to join them. No patient can be considered for discharge unless there is a majority vote of the people in the round table. There are a considerable number of theoretical considerations and practical implications of this unusual method of group therapy. See MILIEU THERAPY.

round window   A circular membrane in the cochlea dividing the inner and middle ear, located below the oval window. Its function is to reduce the fluid pressure in the middle ear generated by the oval window. When the stapes of the middle ear vibrates the oval window in transmitting sound impulses, the displaced cochlear fluid might damage delicate inner-ear structures if they were not protected by the round window. Also known as fenestra cochleae/rotunda.

Rouse vs Cameron   See LEAST-RESTRICTIVE ALTERNATIVE.

routine   A set of coordinated behaviors usually conducted without conscious intention, such as always putting shoes first on the left rather than on the right foot. See HABIT.

RPM   1. <u>Raven's Progressive Matrices</u>. 2. Revolutions per minute (also abbreviated **rpm**).

RPS   Revolutions per second (also abbreviated **rps**).

RQ   recovery quotient

R-R conditioning   See RESPONSE-RESPONSE CONDITIONING.

R-R laws   In classical behaviorism (for example, K. Spence), laws concerning associations between responses, in contrast with S-R laws, which concern associations between stimuli and responses. The former tend to be correlational, the latter causal.

rr laws   Laws based on covert responses.

r_s A symbol for the sample Spearman rank-order correlation coefficient.

RS   reinforcing stimulus

R/S   See RESPONSE SHOCK INTERVAL.

RSI   repetitive strain injury

R→S relationship   Characterizing consequence learning, the relationship that expresses the effect of a response on stimulus events (the physical and social environment).

r_{st} Symbol for stability coefficient.

RSVP   rapid sequential visual presentation

RT   reaction time

R-technique   A factor analytic technique that compares many people on several specific measures. The use of factor analysis to locate common traits in personality.

r_{tet} 1. Tetrachoric coefficient of correlation. 2. The tetrachoric correlation coefficient (also abbreviated R_t, r_t.)

$r_{1I, 2II, 3III}$ Symbols for the reliability coefficients of 1, 2, 3, etc.

Ru   Rare designation for unconditioned response (also abbreviated **UCR, UR**).

RU 486   An abortifacient drug.

ruah   (spirit—Ancient Hebrew) The mind; the center of understanding.

rubber   1. Slang for a condom. 2. A person who deliberately and persistently seeks sexual excitement by rubbing against other people. Also known as frotteur. See FROTTEURISM.

Rubella   A viral disease that produces eruptions similar to those of measles. It is usually not serious except when it occurs during pregnancy, when it may cause birth defects that include blindness, deafness, cerebral palsy, and/or mental retardation. Also known as German measles, three-day measles. See CONGENITAL-RUBELLA SYNDROME.

Rubenfeld Synergy Method   A form of psychotherapy devised by Ilana Rubenfeld that uses words, imagery, sound, and touch to access the emotions and memories that are purportedly causing bodily energy blockage, tension, and imbalance.

Rubin('s) Figure   (E. Rubin) A figure that will alternately look like a goblet or the profiles of two people facing each other, an example of a reversible figure. Viewers may see two faces in black facing each other against a white background or a goblet in white against a black background. Also known as goblet figure, Rubin's goblet-profile figure. See NECKER CUBE, REVERSIBLE FIGURE, REVERSIBLE FIGURE GROUND.

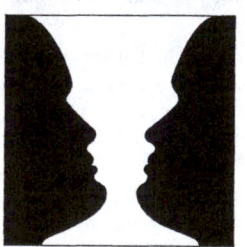

Rubin's figure   Two profiles or one vase? Keep looking!

Rubinstein-Taybi syndrome   (J. H. Rubinstein & H. Taybi) A familial disorder marked by facial abnormalities, including microcephaly and hypertelorism, broad thumbs and toes, and mental retardation. Hypotonia and a stiff gait are common. One study of intelligence of the patients found more than 80% had intelligence quotients (IQs) of less than 50. Also known as broadthumb-hallux syndrome.

rubrospinal tract   The efferent bundle of neurons originating in the red nucleus of the midbrain and extending the entire length of the spinal cord. See CORTICOSPINAL TRACT.

Rucker plan   See GAINSHARING.

rudiment   1. The basic or fundamental element of a more complex organ. 2. An element in the body, such as the vermiform appendix which may have had a function in ancestral beings, but no longer serves any apparent purpose.

Ruffini corpuscles   **Ruffini's endings**

Ruffini papillary endings   Nerve endings in the papillary layer of the skin associated with pressure sensations. Also known as Ruffini end organ, Ruffini papillary plumes.

Ruffini's endings   One of the most common forms of pressure receptors, they are found in hairy and smooth skin and in joint capsules and are the most lightly covered of all encapsulated sensory endings. They adapt to pressure changes (mechanical distortion) slowly and their nerve fibers usually maintain sustained production of action potentials in response to pressure. Also known as Ruffini corpuscles.

rule   A conceptualization of a way to operate, especially in how to learn, for example, in mathematics, always calculating a term within parentheses first; or "if your teacher and the book say contradictory things, give more weight to your teacher."

rule learning   A type of concept learning characterized by understanding of the "why" of a rule versus learning the rule without knowing its basis or logic. For example, a person can learn to use logarithms without understanding what they mean, but if the person understands the meaning then this is an example of rule learning.

rule modeling   Imitative processes by which people learn to control their behavior by the same underlying rules that they have watched a model follow, even when confronted with superficially different situations.

rule of abstinence   abstinence rule

rule of thumb   A heuristic assumption or an estimate based on logic, experience, and common sense, intended to be an approximation to the exact measure.

rulers   According to Alfred Adler, one of four main types of people, those who dominate others socially. See ADLER'S PERSONALITY TYPES.

rules of inference   Rules that permit valid inferences from statements of premises. For example, the statement "Dogs are mammals" may be considered equivalent to "Dogs are animals" if all mammals are animals.

rules of the game   (J. Piaget) Refers to a changing attitude toward rules. Children accept rules of games as inviolable. With the coming of adolescence, they no longer accept the rules as unbreakable, but that they can be changed on mutual consent, and are but conventions rather than absolute.

rum fits   alcoholic epilepsy

rumination   1. Short for rumination disorder (of infancy). 2. Obsessive concern about a topic, constantly going over it in the mind for an extended period of time. A common symptom of obsessive-compulsive disorder (OCD).

rumination disorder (of infancy)   Persistent behavior of infants characterized by bringing up food or drink without vomiting. Such behavior can lead to death of the infant. Squirting the nostrils of children with lemon juice while they are in the process of rumination is a preferred method of getting infants to discontinue this dangerous process. Also known as rumination (syndrome).

rumor   A connected account of some event that is supposed to have happened but for which there is no substantiation. Rumors abound in certain situations when there is uncertainty about the future, such as for a military group waiting for offensive action. Also spelled rumour.

rumor-intensity formula   A formula to predict the amount and the strength of rumors based on the relationship between the importance and the ambiguity of a concern. When the importance and the ambiguity of a rumor are multiplied this leads to many rumors but if a matter is completely either unimportant or completely nonambiguous, then there are no or few rumors.

Rumpf('s) sign   A reaction in cases of neurasthenia in which pressure over a point of pain increases the pulse rate by as much as 20 beats per minute. Named after German physician Theodor Rumpf (1851–1923).

run   1. The carrying out of an experiment. 2. A sequence of symbols such as a set of numbers in some pattern. 3. A single, continuous performance of a computer routine. 4. To leave an institution, such as a prison, school, or group home, without permission. See PAROLE.

run amok   To go into a wild frenzy with intention to kill. See AMOK.

runaway reaction   Leaving home to escape or avoid undesired situations, particularly during childhood or adolescence.

runner's high   exercise high

running rate   1. A constant rate, one that does not vary. 2. Speed that an organism achieves in an attempt to gain a particular goal or to escape from a threatening situation.

running wheel   Drum-like wheel mounted on a horizontal axis in which an animal can run, usually found inside a cage and attached to a counter that indicates numbers of revolutions made by an animal within a particular time period. A measure of body activity. See ACTIVITY CAGE for an illustration of such a wheel.

runs test   A statistical procedure to determine whether a particular sequence is within or outside of normal expectation, for example, checking whether a deck of cards is in a random order. Research indicates that seven or eight shuffles are needed to achieve random distribution of cards in a new deck.

runway   1. A pathway, generally straight and without obstacles, used often in observing the learning behavior of small animals, generally, laboratory rats. 2. An alley in a maze. 3. The pathway that leads from a starting box to a goal box or to the main part of a maze. See Y-MAZE for an example.

rupophobia   rhypophobia

rural environment   An environment characterized by open land and a relatively sparse population that depends full- or part-time on agricultural activities as a means of livelihood. In environmental psychology, rural environment often is used as a basis for comparison with physical and social conditions that produce stressors, for example, air-pollution levels, crowding, and crime rates. See URBAN ENVIRONMENT.

rush   The effect and sensation of alertness and euphoria experienced by taking certain drugs such as amphetamines. See FLASH.

Russian fly   Spanish fly

Russmethode   A process (no longer used) of depositing smoke particles upon a continuously passing ribbon of paper for tracing by means of needles, as might be used for lie detection reactions.

rut   A seasonal period of sexual excitement in animals. Sometimes restricted to male animals only. See ESTROUS BEHAVIOR.

Rutherford theory   telephone theory (of hearing)

Rutz typology   A system of categorizing individuals' personalities developed by Oscar Rutz on the basis of bodily shape, including these three types: spherical, parabolic, and pyramidal.

R_v   Correlation of percentage of unlike signed pairs.

Rybakoff's figures   (T. Rybakoff) Square figures that have been cut into irregular patterns, the task of participants being to assemble them to form a square. See WIGGLY BLOCK.

s 1. sensation. 2. See SPECIFIC FACTOR. 3. Symbol for the standard deviation for sample data, standard deviation of a sample. 4. See VARIABLE STIMULUS.

s See SPECIFIC ABILITY FACTOR.

S 1. stimulus. 2. Sensation or sensory intensity when R (*Reiz*) stands for the stimulus, from *Sinneseindrück*. 3. The subject in a study (use proscribed as of the 2nd ed., 1974, of the *Publication Manual of the American Psychological Association*). 4. Spatial ability, spatial relations, or spatial relationships. 5. In Rorschach test scoring, symbol for white space. 6. See STANDARD STIMULUS. 7. As referred to by Luria, Sherashevski.

S.A. social age

SA 1. Schizophrenics Anonymous. 2. Self-assessment. See SELF-APPRAISAL.

saboteur See INTERNAL SABOTEUR.

SAC stimulus as coded

saccade One saccadic movement.

saccadic movement Rapid, jerky eye movements (saccades), from one fixation point to another as in reading or visual exploration. During eye movement, there is little or no seeing.

saccadic speed The rate of velocity of eye movements that separate successive visual fixations as in ordinary reading.

saccadic time The sum of the time of intervals during which the eye is in motion when reading, contrasted with the fixation time.

saccule Part of the vestibular mechanism of the inner ear which along with the utricle and the three semicircular canals maintains the mechanism of balance. Also known as sacculus.

sacral division That part of the parasympathetic portion of the autonomic nervous system located in the sacral area of the spinal cord.

sacral nerves Spinal nerves in the neighborhood of the sacrum (last lumbar vertebra).

sacred Something to be revered, to be treated with the greatest respect, such as a religious statue, the name of a deity.

sacred disease An early name for epilepsy as used by the ancient Greeks, based on the belief that seizures were evidence of divine visitation. Hippocrates, however, rejected this view, saying "Surely it, too, has its nature and causes whence it originates, just like other diseases, and is curable by means comparable to their cure."

sacrifice In psychoanalytic theory, a tendency of patients to deprive themselves of things they really need, as an unconscious attempt to bribe the superego or to make restitution for guilty thoughts or actions. Sigmund Freud interpreted sacrifice of humans in primitive societies in Oedipal terms, claiming that it was a form of symbolic parricide. See UNDOING.

sacrificial paraphilias A category of paraphilias in which one or both of the partners must atone, usually through acts of penance, suffering, or sacrifice, for their lust. Masochism or self-sacrifice, and sadism or partner sacrifice are the most common type of this paraphilia. This category also includes symphorophilia (or being excited by disasters), asphyxiophilia (self-strangulation), and erotophonophilia (lust murder).

SAD seasonal affective disorder

sadism (R. von Krafft-Ebing) 1. Denoting cruelty in general. 2. Preference during erotic activity to punish, humiliate, or hurt the sexual partner; sometimes extended to include animals. Although technically a deviation, some degree of sadism is an accepted part of sexual foreplay in some cultures. Also known as active algolagnia. Compare MASOCHISM. 3. A form of perversion in which the person derives pleasure from inflicting pain, abuse, and maltreatment.

sadness 1. An emotional attitude characterized by an unpleasant feeling tone and expressing itself in sighing, weeping, as well as passivity and diminished tone of the voluntary muscles. 2. In psychoanalytic theory, a quiet mood resembling sorrow and grief, due to accepting that some loss has occurred or that satisfaction is elusive. A feeling state characteristic of depression.

sadomasochism (S-M) Being sexually aroused by combined sadism and masochism, usually in role-playing.

sadomasochistic A combination of sadism and masochism in the same person. A sadomasochist is a person who gets sexual pleasure by hurting and being hurt. See SADOMASOCHISTIC RELATIONSHIP.

sadomasochistic (S-M or S & M) relationship A complementary interaction, usually sexual in nature, based on the enjoyment of suffering by one partner and the enjoyment of inflicting pain by the other. Also known as sadomasochism.

SADS See SEASONAL AFFECTIVE DISORDER (SYNDROME).

safe compartment   The compartment of a one-way avoidance apparatus in which shock is never delivered. Organisms have to enter this compartment to avoid or escape shock.

safeguarding tendency   (A. Adler) A defense mechanism that wards off feelings of inferiority, used to preserve self-esteem, through such processes as distortion, repression, and regression. See DEFENSE MECHANISMS.

safe sex   Practices that attempt to reduce the risk of unwanted pregnancy or of contracting sexually-transmitted diseases during sexual activity. Includes prudent selection of partners, avoidance of high-risk activities, and using appropriate barriers against transmission.

safety device   (K. Horney) Any psychological means used in protecting the self from threats, particularly from the hostile elements of the environment. See DEFENSE MECHANISMS, SAFEGUARDING TENDENCY.

safety motive   (K. Horney) Indirect neurotic behavior whereby a person tries to protect the self from external or environmental threats, as by avoiding competition.

safety needs   The second level in Abraham Maslow's hierarchy of needs (after physiological needs) consisting of needs for freedom from illness or danger and the need for a secure, familiar, predictable environment. Safety needs take precedence over needs for belonging, esteem, and self-actualization. See NEED-HIERARCHY THEORY.

safety psychology   The study of the human and environmental factors involved in accidents and accident prevention. Environmental measures include such factors as safe highway construction, safe working conditions, noise abatement, and improved design of kitchens and bathrooms. See ACCIDENT PRONENESS, ACCIDENT REDUCTION.

sagittal axis   In vision, a straight line extending from the center of the retina through the center of the lens and pupil to the center of the object viewed.

sagittal fissure   A longitudinal fissure that divides the cerebrum into left and right hemispheres.

sagittal (plane)   A slice of a body that would divide the left and right sides from top to bottom. Term may be modified by a directional adjective, as in medial sagittal, for a vertical slice at the center of an organ. See HORIZONTAL SECTION.

Saint Anthony's dance   Historic name for a kind of chorea. Other historic choreas include Saint John's dance, Saint With's dance, Saint Vitus' dance.

Saint Anthony's fire   Name given in the Middle Ages to the ergotism which causes agonizing burning sensations of the limbs. Relief reportedly was obtained by a trip to the shrine of Saint Anthony, where those afflicted were fed meals free of the disease agent, ergot fungus. See ERGOTISM.

Saint Dymphna's disease   Early name for mental disease based on the name of the patron saint of the insane, a medieval Irish princess who, according to legend, fled to the Continent to escape the incestuous advances of her father. See GHEEL COLONY.

Saint Hubert's disease   **hydrophobia**

Saint John's dance/evil   See CHOREA, SAINT ANTHONY'S DANCE.

Saint Mathurin's disease   Phrase sometimes used to identify epileptic psychosis and also severe mental retardation. Phrase derives from Saint Mathurin (also known as St. John of Matha), the patron saint of idiots and fools.

Saint Modestus' disease   **chorea**

Saint Valentine's disease   **epilepsy**

Saint Vitus' dance   Obsolete name for an infective or toxic form of chorea associated with rheumatism. Later known as Sydenham's chorea. See CHOREA.

Saint With's dance   See CHOREA, SAINT ANTHONY'S DANCE.

sales-aptitude tests   Examinations developed as an aid in sales-personnel selection, by measuring understanding of sales principles or by appraising interests and drives related to salesmanship.

sales-survey technique   A method of testing the effectiveness of advertising appeals by analyzing sales of a product after it has been advertised in one or several communities, and comparing the results with sales of the same product in areas where it was not advertised. See CONSUMER PSYCHOLOGY, SPLIT RUN.

salience   Distinctness. A property of certain items in the environment that draws attention of people. Also known as saliency.

salience hypothesis   A postulate that emotionally arousing dreams are more easily recalled.

salient   That which "stands out" or forces attention to it. Everything else in the perception becomes the ground to the salient object. See FIGURE-GROUND.

saline   A quality of gustatory sensation of which the taste of common salt (sodium chloride) is a typical example. Also known as salty. See SALT TASTE.

saliromania   Being sexually attracted to or aroused by filth, ugliness, or deformity.

salivary glands   A system or group of glands with ducts opening into the mouth cavity whereby they discharge saliva, which assists in mastication.

salivary reflex   A process involving any increase, decrease, or change in the specific secretory activity of one or more salivary glands, due to excitation or inhibition of their efferent nerves resulting from stimulation of an afferent nerve.

salivation   The secretion of saliva by the salivary glands.

Salpêtrière   An institution for females in Paris in 1656, transformed by Philippe Pinel from an asylum for the infirm, criminal, mentally retarded, aged, and insane to a hospital when he was appointed director in 1795. Treatment there had been proverbially brutal.

Salpêtrière school   (J. Charcot) The term "school" in this sense refers to the philosophical, theoretical, and operational views of Jean Martin Charcot accepted by the professional staff at La Salpêtrière hospital in Paris during Charcot's tenure. He stressed treatment of hysteria by means of hypnosis. Notable students include P. Pinel and S. Freud. See NANCY SCHOOL.

salpingectomy   The surgical removal of a Fallopian tube. Psychosexual conflicts often are sequelae of the procedure.

salpinx   1. The oviduct. Also known as fallopian tube. 2. The eustachian tube.

saltation   1. A dancing or leaping, as in pathology (for example, chorea) or physiology (for example, saltatory conduction). 2. An abrupt genetic mutation or variation in a species.

saltatory   Proceeding by jumps or leaps rather than moving in a steady progression.

saltatory conduction   1. Transmission of action potentials in myelinated axons by jumping from one node of Ranvier to the next. 2. A nerve-impulse transmission that occurs in myelinated fibers. A saltatory conduction theory contends that impulses along a myelinated fiber get a boost at the nodes of Ranvier along the fiber after losing momentum between the nodes. See RANVIER'S NODE.

saltatory spasm   1. A muscle spasm of the lower extremities, manifested by jumping or skipping movements. The condition is usually of hysterical origin. 2. An irregular movement, jumping about in unexpected manners and time.

salt balance   A system in which the body's homeostatic mechanisms maintain a favorable relationship between the amounts of fluid and sodium ions in the body tissues.

salt taste   A gustatory sensation stimulated in the taste buds at the edge of the tongue by ions of certain chemical compounds. Although the sensation is associated with table salt, similar sensations can be produced by a number of other chemical salts.

salty   Saline.

salutogenesis   (A. Antonovsky) A concept of how people manage to cope with pathological conditions, physical and social. The study of how a person is able to thrive in spite of myriad pathogenics in the environment based on sociopsychological factors such as having a sense of coherence.

SAM   See SEARCH OF ASSOCIATIVE MEMORY.

samadhi   (Sanskrit) The ultimate yogic goal and state of consciousness marked by deep calm and concentration. In it, all dualistic thinking is merged into a unified realization of reality. See NIRVANA.

same-different theory   (M. Diamond) A point of view that all individuals undergo a developmental self-analysis of how they compare with their peers. From this they come to see themselves as belonging to certain categories and not others. In regard to sexual development it leads a person to see himself or herself as male, female, or intersex, androphilic, gynecophilic, or ambiphilic, transsexual or not and so forth.

same group procedure   In research, a plan by which a group serves as its own control. See ABBA DESIGN.

same-opposite test   See SYNONYM-ANTONYM TEST.

same-sex marriage   An arrangement similar to traditional marriages but engaging two people of the same gender. See DOMESTIC PARTNERSHIPS.

sample   In statistics, a portion of a population of elements or subjects studied. A sample is drawn in an attempt to generalize about or to describe the population as a whole. Types of sample or sampling include: ACCIDENTAL, ADEQUATE, AREA, BEHAVIOR, BIASED, BLOCK, CONTROLLED, CONVENIENCE, DELAYED MATCHING, DOMAL, DOUBLE, HORIZONTAL, MATCHED, NONPROBABILITY, PROBABILITY, QUOTA, RANDOM, REPLACEMENT, REPRESENTATIVE, SELECTED, SNOWBALL, STANDARDIZATION, STRATIFIED, STRATIFIED RANDOM, SYSTEMATIC, TIME, VERTICAL, WITH REPLACEMENT, WITHOUT REPLACEMENT. See JOB-SAMPLE EXPERIENCES, MATCHING TO SAMPLE, POPULATION, SAMPLING STRATEGIES, SMALL-SAMPLE THEORY, WORK SAMPLE TEST.

sample bias   Any factor or method of sampling that makes the sample nonrepresentative and is therefore likely to distort results.

sample of convenience/of opportunity   1. Participants included in an investigation selected merely because they are available, whether or not they are suitable for test of the hypotheses or conditions of interest. 2. In some situations, for any of a variety of reasons, taking whoever or whatever is immediately available as a sample, as in a professor using students as a sample for some research. Rarely also known as accidental sample.

sample overlap   When individuals are included in two samples.

sample space   The set of all sample points possible in a sampling experiment; the space, made up of all possible samples.

sampling   In surveys and experimental studies, the process of selecting a limited number of units (for example, respondents or subjects) that are presumed to be representative in relevant ways of the population as a whole. Types of sampling include: ACCIDENTAL, AREA, BEHAVIOR(AL), BIASED, BLOCK, CLUSTER, COHORT, CONTROLLED, CONVENIENCE, CROSS-SECTIONAL, DOMAL, DOUBLE, HAPHAZARD, LONGITUDINAL, MATCHED, MULTI-STAGE, NONPROBABILITY, PROBABILITY, PURPOSIVE, QUOTA, RANDOM, RELIABILITY, REPRESENTATIVE, SELECTED, SELECTIVE, SITUATIONAL, SNOWBALL, STANDARDIZATION, STRATIFIED, STRATIFIED RANDOM, SYSTEMATIC, SYSTEMATIC RANDOM, UNRESTRICTED, VERTICAL, WITH REPLACEMENT, WITHOUT REPLACEMENT.

sampling area/block   In sampling, the selection of a particular sector or area of a geographical tract to represent the whole tract.

sampling distribution   The sampling distribution of a statistic for samples of size n is the distribution of the values of that statistic for all possible samples of size n selected from the population.

sampling error   Deviations of the summary values yielded by samples, from the values yielded by the entire population. See REPRESENTATIVE SAMPLING, SAMPLING.

sampling population   In experimental studies or surveys, the population from which a sample is selected. The sample consists only of those cases actually studied whereas the population is the entire group of cases within a specified area from which the sample is taken. If the sample is truly representative, the experimental findings should apply within a prescribed confidence band that depends upon, among other things, the method of sampling and the sample size relative to the population size.

sampling reliability   Any means of measuring the consistency of data from two or more samples of the same population.

sampling servo   A device that measures errors in sampling and provides corrections.

sampling stability   When repeated samplings from the same population yield consistent results.

sampling strategies   The method by which a researcher samples from a population. According to Mary Allen there are fifteen major sampling strategies. Types of sampling include: COHORT, CONVENIENCE, CROSS-SECTIONAL, LONGITUDINAL, MULTI-STAGE, NON-PROBABILITY, PROBABILITY, PURPOSIVE, QUOTA, RANDOM, STRATIFIED RANDOM, STRATIFIED, SYSTEMATIC RANDOM, SYSTEMATIC, TREND.

sampling theory   Principles of drawing samples to represent the population.

sampling variability   The variability of repeated samples with regard to the distribution of summary statistics.

sampling with or without replacement   In sequentially sampling a particular population, when each item selected is replaced in the population before the next selection, and therefore can be re-selected, it is called sampling with replacement. If items selected cannot be reselected, it is called sampling without replacement.

Samson complex   (R. J. Corsini) The willingness to destroy one's enemies even if one has to die in the process, seen in people who commit murder and then suicide.

sanction   1. The ground or reason for approval of a person's action. 2. In sociology, any means by which officials or other agents of a social group induce or compel an individual to act in conformity with the standards commonly accepted in the group, for example, legal, moral, religious.

Sandler's A-statistic (A)   A parametric statistic for testing the null hypothesis concerning two population means. Formula: $A = (\Sigma D^2) \div (\Sigma D)^2$, where ΣD^2 is the sum of the squares of the differences, and $(\Sigma D)^2$ is the square of the sum of the differences.

S & M   See SADOMASOCHISTIC RELATIONSHIP.

sand therapy   The use of sand as a means of psychotherapy, usually with young children. Therapists use sand or similar materials to create images which are then discussed, or they may ask the children to create the images.

Sanfilippo syndrome   (S. I. Sanfilippo) Several types of severe mental retardation due to enzyme deficiencies. Also known as polydystrophic oligophrenia. See AUTOSOMAL RECESSIVE INHERITANCE.

Sanford envelopes   (E. C. Sanford) A set of envelopes, similar in visual appearance but weighted so as to form a progressive series, used to test the discrimination of lifted weights.

S-anger   See STATE ANGER.

sanguine (type)   One of the four constitutional and temperamental types originally established by Hippocrates, and later developed by Galen, who thought that the good humor, positive attitudes, optimism, and enthusiasm displayed by such individuals was due to the predominance of the blood over other body fluids. See HUMORAL THEORY, TYPOLOGY.

sanitarium   An institution for the treatment and convalescence of persons with chronic diseases such as rheumatism, tuberculosis, neurological disorders, or mental disorders. Also known as sanitoriom.

sanity   Legal term for the perceived normal mental condition of the human individual. Compare INSANITY.

Sanson images   See PURKINJE-SANSON IMAGES.

Sapir-Whorf hypothesis   Whorfian hypothesis

Sapphism   Rare term for lesbianism. Name is based on a Greek poetess, Sappho, purported to be a lesbian who lived on the island of Lesbos.

SAR   See SEXUAL ATTITUDE REASSESSMENT WORKSHOP.

sarcasm   A caustic, derisive remark. It is often a form of verbal aggression or criticism.

SAT   1. Scholastic Aptitude Test renamed Scholastic Assessment Test in 1994. 2. Stanford Achievement Test.

S-A-T   1. school ability test. 2. school achievement test.

Satanism   1. In the Dark Ages, the belief that witches had been possessed by the devil. 2. In modern times, the worship of Satan in the form of rituals, including the alleged abuse of animals and people.

Satanophobia   Morbid fear of the devil. See DEMONOPHOBIA.

satellite clinic   A facility operated on an outreach basis by a hospital. Located in the inner city, in suburbs, and in rural areas, and usually provide crisis services, outpatient treatment, precare, and aftercare.

satellite housing   Apartments or single-family homes where patients can live without direct supervisory care but with access to emergency treatment.

satellitosis   An accumulation of neuroglia cells that forms around a damaged neuron in the central nervous system.

satiation   Satisfaction or gratification in terms of a need (for food, fluid, sexual stimulation, etc.) or a psychic goal (such as disposable income). See SATIETY.

satiety   (O. J. Schwartz) A subjective feeling of satisfaction that enough food has been eaten. This signal comes to the brain from the tenth cranial nerve, the vagus, via gut wall contractions in the duodenum (the first part of the small intestine). See SATIETY CENTER.

satiety center   A hypothetical location, presumably located in the hypothalamus of the brain that regulates appetite. Also known as the appestat. See APPETITE, FOOD-SATIATION THEORY, HUNGER DRIVE, VENTROMEDIAL NUCLEUS OF THE HYPOTHALAMUS (VMH).

satire   Sustained sarcasm or ridicule in oral or literary form.

satisfaction of instincts   Gratification of innate needs such as hunger, thirst, sex, which tends to discharge tension and restore the organism to a balanced state. Also known as gratification of instincts. See HOMEOSTASIS.

satisfice (H. A. Simon) To choose an alternative that is "good enough," that is, that satisfies certain goals and constraints, without necessarily being optimal. See BOUNDED RATIONALITY.

satisficing hypothesis (H. A. Simon) A postulate that people act so as to gain only a certain satisfactory level of utility. Compare MAXIMIZING HYPOTHESIS. See BOUNDED RATIONALITY, RATIONALITY, UTILITY THEORY.

satisfier 1. (E. L. Thorndike) A reward or circumstance that an organism does nothing to avoid, often doing things to attain or preserve it. 2. A reward or circumstance that leads to satisfaction; or under bounded rationality to an alternative that is "good enough."

satori Enlightenment according to Zen Buddhism. A state or moment of illumination in which reality is perceived "as it is."

saturated test In factor analysis, a test shown to have a high degree of correlation with a given factor.

saturation 1. In color theory, the degree of color intensity, or vividness; hue intensity; the degree to which a hue is weakened by white light. Highly saturated colors have little if any whiteness and appear to be pure hue, but colors of low saturation are "washed out" or "pastels." See MUNSELL COLOR SYSTEM, SATURATION SCALE. 2. Denoting the extent to which a test is correlated with a factor.

saturation scale Numbers applied to a series of color-stimuli alike in hue and brilliance but different in saturation, parallel to a similar scale of desaturate stimuli, and such that adjacent numbers represent just-noticeably different stimuli.

satyriasis A male psychosexual disorder that features insatiable desire for sexual conquests. Also known as Don Juan syndrome, satyromania. It is the counterpart of nymphomania in the female. See DON JUAN, EROTOMANIA.

sauce Béarnaise effect Casual phrase for a learning response characterized by an association to a highly specific stimulus, with learning after a single trial, and a delayed negative consequence. It represents an analogy to becoming ill some hours after a meal that included sauce Béarnaise. Regardless of the cause of the illness, the sauce will be identified with it.

savant (knowledgeable—French) 1. A person with a rare gift, often a person with a mental or social disability, for example, a blind self-taught pianist could repeat complicated musical pieces after hearing them once; some persons diagnosed with autism can calculate complex mathematical problems such as cubing roots of six digit numbers mentally; some persons can tell on what day of the week any date occurred. When such persons appear to have mental challenges they are known as idiot(s) savants. 2. A polymath; a learned person.

Savart's wheel (F. Savart) A device for producing sounds of high frequency used to measure limits of hearing.

savings (method) (H. Ebbinghaus) A technique for measuring retention in which the participant relearns something. "Savings" are measured by the difference between the number of trials or errors originally required to learn and the number required in relearning. Also known as relearning method, saving procedure.

savings score The difference between the time or the number of trials taken to learn something the first time, and the time or the number of trials taken to relearn the same thing at a later time (for example, to memorize a long poem it may take a total of 4 hours the first time, and to relearn it a year later it may take 3 hours. The savings score would then be 1 hour, more commonly expressed as 25%).

savor The relatively recent consideration of taste and smell to be a single sense.

saw-toothed theory (F. Fiedler) A contingent theory of leadership. Task-oriented leaders are most effective when faced with highly unfavorable or highly favorable situations. Relations-oriented leaders do best when situations are in between in favorableness. Esteem and power of the leader and structure of the situation contribute to the favorableness of the situation to the leader.

saw-tooth waves A wave form that has roughly the appearance of the teeth of a saw, for example, bursts of sharp electroencephalographic (EEG) waves occurring during rapid-eye-movement (REM) sleep.

S-B See STANFORD-BINET INTELLIGENCE SCALE.

SB-IV See STANFORD-BINET IV.

scab A dysphemism for workers who replace those on strike.

scabiophobia Morbid fear of scabies or skin disease. See ACAROPHOBIA.

scaffolding Arranging a child's external reality to make it easier for the child to progress and advance cognitively and also socially or physically. Adults affect or modify the environment for such purposes.

scalability 1. A characteristic of an item that allows it to be assigned a position in a quantitative progression. 2. (L. Guttman) A characteristic of items that permits them to form a Guttman scale, such that if a person responds to a given item in the keyed direction, that person will also answer in the keyed direction all items that represent lesser degrees of the measured variable, assuming no errors are made.

scala media The middle of three liquid-filled scalae, into which the cochlea of the inner ear is partitioned. Contains the organ of Corti, regarded as the true organ of hearing. See SCALA TYMPANI, SCALA VESTIBULI.

scalar analysis The process of determining where an item fits or is located on a scale, for example, to determine the strength of a motive.

scala tympani (A. M. Valsalva) One of the three liquid-filled scalae, or canals, in the cochlea of the inner ear. At basal end contains the round window of the cochlea, which relieves fluid pressure on cochlear structures resulting from vibrations transmitted by the middle-ear bones to the oval window of the cochlea. Joined to scala vestibuli at apex by small opening called the helicotrema. See SCALA MEDIA, SCALA VESTIBULI.

scala vestibuli (A. M. Valsalva) One of the three liquid-filled scalae, or canals, in the cochlea of the inner ear. It opens at the basal end of the cochlea into the vestibule of the labyrinth, where the oval window receives sound vibrations transmitted by the stapes, one of the middle-ear bones. The air vibrations are converted here to fluid vibrations. See SCALA MEDIA, SCALA TYMPANI, VESTIBULAR CANAL.

scale (ladder, staircase—Latin) 1. A system of arranging items in a progressive series according to their magnitude or value. 2. In measurement theory, either a structure preserving mapping of an attribute or, sometimes, the set of all such mappings. See SCALE TYPE.

scale attenuation effects Some reduction in the range of scale values used by participants. Can arise from difficulties in interpreting results when performance on the dependent variable for all participants is either nearly perfect (a "ceiling effect") or nearly lacking altogether (a "floor effect").

scaled test 1. A type of test in which the items are arranged in order of increasing difficulty. 2. An examination in which the items are assigned a value, or score, according to some ordering principle.

scale points The possible values that a scale is allowed to have, or all used for the scale.

scale reproducibility (L. Guttman) Refers to a test indicating which test items were answered correctly and incorrectly by the final score. Items are ordered by increasing difficulty, a participant's score is such that every item below that score has been passed and every item above that score is considered failed. See GUTTMAN SCALING.

scales of measurement See SCALE TYPE.

scale type (S. S. Stevens) A classification of the transformation group that characterizes all possible representations from an attribute structure into a particular numerical structure. The most common scale types are nominal, ordinal, interval, and ratio.

scale types See these kinds of scales: ABSOLUTE, ACHROMATIC-DICHROMATIC, ADAPTIVE BEHAVIOR, ADDICTIVE, AGE-EQUIVALENT, AMERICAN HOME, ANTI-SEMITIC, ANOMIE, ANXIETY, APGAR, ARITHMETIC, ATTITUDE, ATTITUDES TOWARD DISABLED PERSONS, BALANCED, BARRON-WELSH ART, BEAUFORT WIND, BINET-SIMON, BIPOLAR RATING, BOGARDUS SOCIAL-DISTANCE, BRAZELTON NEONATAL BEHAVIORAL ASSESSMENT, BRIEF PSYCHIATRIC RATING, CAIN-LEVINE SOCIAL COMPETENCY, CALIFORNIA INFANT, CATEGORICAL, CATTELL INFANT INTELLIGENCE, CELSIUS, CHROMATIC, COLUMBIA MENTAL MATURITY, COMFORTABLE INTERPERSONAL DISTANCE, CONTINUOUS, CONTINUOUS RATING, CUMULATIVE, DESIGNATORY, DEVELOPMENTAL, DIFFICULTY, DISTANCE, DOGMATISM, E, E-F, EQUAL-INTERVAL, FAHRENHEIT, FASCISM (F), GALGARY GENERAL HOSPITAL AGGRESSION, GRADE, GRAPHIC RATING, GRIFFITHS MENTAL DEVELOPMENT, HALSTEAD-REITAN, HANDWRITING, I-E, INTERNALIZATION, IOWA STUTTERING, IPSATIVE, KELLEY DESEGREGATION, LEAST-PREFERRED COWORKER, LETHALITY, LIFE-CHANGE RATING, LIKERT PROCEDURE, LINCOLN-OSERETSKY MOTOR DEVELOPMENT, LOVE, MACH, MANAGERIAL GRID, MASCULINITY-FEMININITY, MENTAL, MERRILL-PALMER, MICKEY FINN, ORDINAL, PHILLIPS, PINTNER-PATERSON, POINT, PRODUCT, PSYCHOLOGICAL, RANGE, RATING, RATIO, REPRESSION-SENSITIZATION, SATURATION, VALUE, SHIPLEY-INSTITUTE FOR LIVING, SOCIAL MIND, SOCIAL READJUSTMENT, SOCIAL-DISTANCE, SPECTRAL, SUSCEPTIBILITY, SOCIAL READJUSTMENT, SOCIAL-DISTANCE, SPECTRAL, SUSCEPTIBILITY, STANFORD-BINET, TAYLOR MANIFEST ANXIETY, TEST ANXIETY, THORNDIKE'S HANDWRITING, TONAL, VINELAND SOCIAL MATURITY, WARD ATMOSPHERE, WECHSLER'S, WRITTEN COMPOSITION.

scale value A particular (usually numerical) value that an experimenter using a scale of an attribute assigns to a particular member of a sample.

scaling The process of designing or constructing a scale to represent an attribute of the population or to show the ordered distribution of scores or other items, for example, psychological test results.

scaling technique The procedure for forming a particular type of scale, such as a Guttman scale, a Likert type scale. Usually a mathematical or computer-based algorithm to go from qualitative data to some numerical scale, such as multidimensional scaling.

scalloping See SCALLOP PATTERN.

scallop pattern A response pattern characteristically associated with fixed-interval (FI) reinforcement schedules in which appropriate or meaningful responses diminish sharply or stop altogether after reinforcement but dramatically increase directly before the next reinforcement is scheduled to occur. Scalloping gets its name from the wavy, "scalloped" appearance of the fixed-interval curve.

scalogram Also known as Guttman scale, the preferred name is cumulative Guttman scale.

scalogram analysis See GUTTMAN SCALING.

scam A set of deceptive behaviors intended to cheat people of valuables, usually money, as in a confidence game.

Scanlon plan/way A method of rewarding employees by asking for suggestions to make profits rise by cutting down on steps, etc., and then giving bonuses or other benefits to the workers as a group rather than to individuals. (Named after Joe Scanlon, an American union leader in the 1930s.) See GAINSHARING.

scanning 1. Rapidly examining a situation before making a response. 2. Skimming written material to identify the main ideas or to search for specific information. 3. In medicine, a brain-scan or CAT-scan procedure in diagnosing a patient. 4. An anxious feeling of "being on edge" characterized by impatience, irritability, and difficulty concentrating and sleeping. See VIGILANCE. 5. An automated procedure for entering written or printed material into a computer.

scanning hypothesis (W. Dement) A postulate that eye movement during dreaming is due to the dreamer "watching" the actions of the dream.

scanning speech 1. Drawling, slurred, monotonous, or singsong verbal expression, such as occurs in some cases of multiple sclerosis. 2. Syllables separated by long pauses.

scan path A pattern of eye movements used to examine an object. The scan path varies from one object to another (for example, in one study, results indicated that when women look at men, they typically look at the men's ties first).

scapegoating   A process whereby anger and aggression are displaced onto other, usually less powerful, groups or persons not responsible for the aggressor's frustration. The true source of frustration lies in a person or entity that cannot be directly confronted, or in the psychological deficiencies of the attacker. In the latter case, the defense mechanism of projection is at work. Also known as scapegoatism, scapegoat mechanism. See DISPLACEMENT, PROJECTION.

scapegoat mechanism   **scapegoating**

scapegoat theory   A point of view that people with prejudices seek innocent people as outlets for their anger due to frustration. See SCAPEGOATING.

scaphocephalic   Describing a keel-shaped head, long and narrow.

scapular reflex   Contraction of the scapular muscle elicited by scratching the skin over the scapula (shoulder blade), or between the scapulae. Also known as interscapular reflex.

Scarpa's ganglion   (A. Scarpa) A vestibular ganglion which is the source of the fibers of the vestibular nerve that supplies the utricle, the saccule, and the ampullae of the semicircular ducts. The axons of Scarpa's ganglion form a part of the eighth cranial nerve.

SCAT   See SCHOOL AND COLLEGE ABILITY TEST.

scat   1. Slang for heroin. 2. Dung or excrement. 3. Style of singing with meaningless but onomatopic syllables. 4. Rare slang for whiskey.

scatology   (dung—Greek) Preoccupation with obscenities, lewdness, and filth, mainly of an excremental nature. Term is usually associated with anal eroticism. Also known as scatologia. See COPROPHEMIA, TELEPHONE SCATOLOGIA.

scatophagy   1. The eating of excrement; eating of filth. Also known as coprophagy, rhypophagy. See PICA. 2. Being sexually aroused by eating excrement or other filth.

scatophilia   Being sexually aroused by talking about sexual or obscene matters, usually to an unknown person.

scatophobia   1. Abnormal repugnance to the excreta. 2. Morbid fear of excrement, or of being contaminated by dirt and feces. 3. Fear of filth. Also known as coprophobia, koprophobia.

scatter   A tendency for an individual's test profile to show a pattern of high and low points rather than a single level for all subscores.

scatter analysis   The study and evaluation of the relationships among subtest scores.

scatter diagram   (F. C. Mills) A scatter diagram shows the relationship between two quantitative variables. The values of one variable appear on the horizontal axis, and values of the other variable are on the vertical axis. Each is represented by a point determined by the values on the two axes. Also known as scattergram, scatterplot. See SCEDASTICITY for two examples of scatter plots.

scattergram   **scatter diagram**

scattering   A form of thinking observed in patients with schizophrenia who make tangential or irrelevant associations that may be expressed in incomprehensible speech.

scatterplot   **scatter diagram**

scavenging behavior   In animal psychology, feeding on dead organic matter, such as carrion or scraps left by other animals, a type of behavior found in many species such as vultures, hyenas, jackals, and chimpanzees.

scedastic error of measurement   (J. B. Carroll) A random, unsystematic error or variance arising from various sources such as sampling errors in the choice of test items, or variation in psychophysical response criteria. Also known as scedastic error of variance.

scedasticity   The extent to which amount of variability remains constant across successive rows or columns within a scatter diagram. Homoscedasticity (when variability remains constant) and heteroscedasticity (when variability fluctuates markedly from one row or column to another). Many inferential statistics assume homoscedasticity.

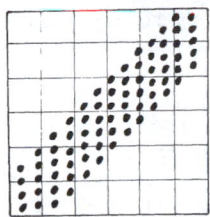 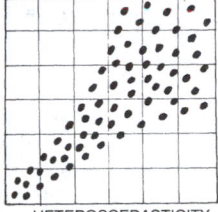

HOMOSCEDASTICITY   HETEROSCEDASTICITY

scedasticity

scelerophobia   Morbid fear of "bad people" or criminals, such as burglars, swindlers, or kidnappers. Also known as pavor sceleris.

scent marking   In animal behavior, placement of odors (through urine or pheromones) in particular areas to either warn other animals, such as rivals to keep away or to attract others for mating purposes. Many antelopes, for example, have marking glands between the cloven hoofs, around the eyes, or both. See PHEROMONES.

Schadenfreude   (damage/joy—German) Malicious enjoyment of someone else's misfortunes.

Schaeffer reflex   The dorsal flexion of the great toe induced by pinching the Achilles tendon. The effect is observed in cases of pyramidal tract lesions when the lower motor centers are released from normal inhibition controls. Named after German neurologist Max Schaeffer (1852–1923).

schedule   1. A questionnaire. 2. An operational plan for a series of tests, experiments, or other activities, usually designed to include a time frame for various stages. 3. A planned program, used mostly for behavior modification experiments or therapy, in which predetermined intervals or rates of rewards or punishments are given contingent upon various behaviors.

scheduled drugs   Certain medicines have a greater potential for being abused, and so these have been categorized by the United States Federal government, and their use is contained by variably increased degrees of legal requirements. For instance, Schedule 2 drugs, such as Ritalin or morphine, cannot be refilled by physicians over the phone or without a separate (and in many states, a special) prescription form. Schedule 1 drugs, such as LSD or heroin, cannot legally be used at all except by being part of an officially approved scientific study. Schedules 3 and 4 drugs, such as Valium, have less abuse potential and there are slight restrictions, such as having to be represcribed every six months.

schedule maintenance   See   MAINTENANCE SCHEDULE.

Schedule of Recent Experience   A self-report questionnaire concerned with recent events in a person's life. Scores on this test are purported to help predict forthcoming illnesses.

schedule of reinforcement/of reward   (B. F. Skinner) In operant conditioning, the rate or time interval in which desired responses are followed by consequences in learning experiments. See CONTINUOUS REINFORCEMENT, FIXED-RATIO REINFORCEMENT SCHEDULE, FIXED-INTERVAL REINFORCEMENT SCHEDULE, INTERMITTENT REINFORCEMENT, REINFORCEMENT, VARIABLE-INTERVAL REINFORCEMENT SCHEDULE, VARIABLE-RATIO REINFORCEMENT SCHEDULE.

scheduling theory   In industrial psychology, the optimization of arrangement of steps in production to achieve maximum efficiency and minimum cost (for example, in assembling automobiles, all parts arriving just in time for placement).

Scheiner's experiment   (C. Scheiner) A demonstration of ocular accommodation, in which the eye is covered with a card, provided with two pinholes separated by a distance less than the pupillary diameter; objects at a distance either less or greater than that of the focus of accommodation, are seen double. The other eye is closed during testing.

schema   1. A conceptual model of how to operate in terms of a future project or how to organize something already in existence. 2. (J. Piaget) An organized pattern of behavior. Early schemas are sensorimotor in nature (seeing, handling, sucking, etc.), and the child fits more and more new things into them through the processes of assimilation and accommodation. Alternative plural forms include schemas, schemata. See CIRCULAR REACTIONS, SENSORIMOTOR PERIOD.

schematic eye   See REDUCED EYE.

schematic image   A mental picture or representation of a given object composed of that object's most conspicuous features. Once formed, the schematic image is the model against which similar perceptual configurations are judged. According to Jerome Kagan, the ability to construct schematic images is fundamental once the infant is able to perceive complete forms.

schematization   A compression of complex data or information in an easy to understand manner (for example, an outline).

scheme   1. A plan, device, outline, or systematic project. 2. In lay usage it usually has a connotation of deviousness.

Schicksalsanalyse   German term similar to analysis of fate. Diagnostic and therapeutic system developed in 1930s by Lipot Szondi based on heredopsychiatry and psychoanalysis.

schismatic family   A noncohesive family with members in disagreement with each other.

schismogenesis   The generation of a schism or cleavage in any group.

schizencephalic   Pertaining to structural abnormalities of the brain manifested as divisions or clefts in the brain tissues. Structural deformities may appear as cavities that result from maldevelopment during fetal life or early infancy or from destructive lesions of the brain area.

schizmatic family   (T. Litz) A divided family featuring disharmony and conflicts between the parents, and also with children in conflict with parents and other siblings.

schizoaffective disorder   A controversial category sometimes used when a differential diagnosis between affective disorders, schizophreniform disorder or schizophrenic disorders cannot be made.

schizoaffective psychosis   A form of schizophrenia in which the initial symptoms are those of mania or depression, sometimes leading to a misdiagnosis of the true nature of the disorder. As the disease progresses, the schizophrenic factors become dominant.

schizocaria   Obsolete term for an acute, malignant form of schizophrenia in which the patient's personality rapidly deteriorates. Also known as catastrophic schizophrenia.

schizogenic family   A hypothetical type of family with parents that are not themselves schizophrenic but who operate in such a way that the children are likely to become schizophrenic. Humorists turn the concept around and say that it is the children who drive the parents "mad." See SCHIZOPHRENOGENIC MOTHERS.

schizoid   A shut-in or introverted personality, unsocial, given to fantasy, whose emotional life may be dissociated from ideational content, due to abnormal mental development. See SYNTONIC.

schizoid character   See SCHIZOID PERSONALITY, SCHIZOID-PERSONALITY DISORDER.

schizoid disorder of childhood and adolescence   A diagnosis for a persistent pattern (of at least three months) manifested by young people who lack close friends other than relatives, have no apparent interest in making friends, find no pleasure in being with peers, avoid contact with others and show no interest in participating in team sports and other activities. Also known as schizoid disorder of youths.

schizoidism   A complex of behavioral factors that includes seclusiveness, quietness, and other introversion traits indicating a separation by the person from the surroundings, the confining of psychic interests to the self, and in many cases a tendency toward schizophrenia. Also known as schizoidia.

schizokinesis   1. Differential susceptibility for learning, retention, and recall in various systems in the body, so that with a given stimulus, one system may overreact and the other underreact. 2. A drug effect characterized by dissociation of visceral and motor functions.

schizomania   **schizoid-manic state**

schizoid-manic state   A psychotic state cited by Adolf Meyer, A. A. Brill, and Eugen Bleuler, combining features of both manic and schizophrenic excitement. Also known as schizomania.

schizoid personality   Describing a person's characteristics that resemble the behavior observed in schizophrenia but in a milder form. A character disorder distinguished by withdrawal, diminution of affect, protracted introspection, and sometimes a breaking away from reality, but without evident intellectual or emotional deterioration. See PERSONALITY DISORDERS.

schizoid-personality disorder   A diagnosis of a personality disorder similar to schizoid disorders of childhood or adolescence but seen in adults, characterized by long-term emotional coldness, absence of tender feelings for others, indifference to praise or criticism and to the feelings of others, friendships with no more than two persons; but there are no eccentricities of speech, behavior, or thought as found in schizotypal disorder.

schizophasia   Jumbled speech observed in some patients with advanced schizophrenia. See WORD SALAD.

schizophrenia   Term introduced by Eugen Bleuler to replace "dementia praecox," a functional psychotic disorder characterized by disturbances of thinking often with delusions, bizarre behavior, and inappropriate moods such as apparent lack of emotional feelings. Categorizations of schizophrenia including: AMBULATORY, BORDERLINE, BURNED-OUT, CATATONIC, CHILDHOOD, CHRONIC, CHRONIC UNDIFFERENTIATED, DISORGANIZED, HEBEPHRENIC, LARVAL, LATENT, MIXED, PARANOID, POSTEMOTIVE, PROCESS, PSEUDONEUROTIC, PSEUDOPSYCHOPATHIC, REACTIVE, REGRESSIVE, RESIDUAL, RESTITUTIONAL, RETARDED, SIMPLE, SYMPTOMATIC, THREE-DAY, UNDIFFERENTIATED. See ACUTE SCHIZOPHRENIC EPISODE, HEBEPHRENIA, PARANOID-SCHIZOID POSITION, PFROPFSCHIZOPHRENIA, RECIDIVISM IN SCHIZOPHRENIA, SCHIZOCARIA, SCHIZOPHRENIC DISORDERS.

schizophrenic disorder   A complex group of psychotic conditions associated with such symptoms as disorganized speech, inappropriate behavior, delusions, hallucinations, emotional flatness, and lack of motivation. See SCHIZOPHRENIA.

schizophrenic excitement   A state of acute hyperactivity, impulsivity, and in some cases elation, occurring most frequently in the catatonic form of schizophrenia. See SCHIZOPHRENIC DISORDER, CATATONIC TYPE.

schizophrenic personality   See SCHIZOID-PERSONALITY DISORDER, SCHIZOTYPAL-PERSONALITY DISORDER.

schizophrenic reactions   A group of psychotic reactions in which the person's sense of reality is distorted or lost; associated with autism, ambivalence, and dissociations.

schizophrenic spectrum   (S. Kety) A hypothetical range of schizophrenic states that appear to have a genetic etiology similar to classic schizophrenia. There are wide differences in intensity in these states, due, it is thought, to environmental or genetic modification of the common genetic diathesis.

schizophrenic states   See ACUTE DELUSIONAL PSYCHOSIS.

schizophrenic surrender   A phrase first applied by C. M. Campbell to regressive symptoms characteristic of the breakdown of the ego in patients with schizophrenia who are no longer able to make efforts at restoration or "restitution." These patients withdraw further and further from reality and may experience feelings of depersonalization, fantasies of world destruction, and delusions of grandeur. The regressive pattern reaches its most extreme form in hebephrenia (disorganized schizophrenia). See DISORGANIZED TYPE SCHIZOPHRENIC DISORDER, RESTITUTIONAL SCHIZOPHRENIA.

schizophreniform disorder/state   A relatively short-term period (less than six months) of what appears to be schizophrenia that generally has a good prognosis after the episode is over. See SCHIZOPHRENIC DISORDER.

schizophreniform state   (G. Langfeldt) A condition resembling schizophrenia. See SCHIZOID.

schizophrenogenic   Denoting a factor or influence causing or contributing to the onset of schizophrenia. See SCHIZOPHRENOGENIC MOTHER.

schizophrenogenic mother   (F. Fromm-Reichmann) A mother assumed to contribute to the development of schizophrenia, particularly in male children. Purportedly, she tends to be cold, rejecting, dominating, perfectionistic, insensitive, overprotective, seductive, and rigidly moralistic. Newer data tend not to support the construct. See DOUBLE-BIND.

schizophrenogenic parents   (Y. Alanen) Relating to parents who produce or cause schizophrenia in their children.

schizotaxia   1. A genetic predisposition to schizophrenia which may become overt if environmental stresses are severe. 2. (P. Meehl) A basic neurological deficit in the ability to integrate thought and emotions resulting in decreased capacity to cope with life stress; characterized by anhedonia and thought disorder; possibly inherited.

schizothemia   In communication such as a conversation, repeated interruption by the speaker abruptly changing topics or subject matter in mid-sentence. See FLIGHT OF IDEAS.

schizothymia   A personality pattern characterized by schizoid behavior such as introversion and seclusiveness, but within the limits of normality. Also known as schizothymic personality.

schizothymic personality   schizothymia

schizothymic type   A personality type associated with a tendency toward schizophrenia. The body type is generally, according to Ernst Kretschmer, of the mixed asthenic-athletic type. See TYPOLOGY.

schizotypal personality   Sandor Rado's name for what was previously called ambulatory schizophrenia.

schizotypal-personality disorder   A diagnosis of a personality disorder characterized by various oddities of thought, perception, speech, and behavior not severe enough to warrant a diagnosis of schizophrenia. Symptoms include at least four of the following: magical thinking, ideas of reference, social isolation, recurrent illusions or depersonalization; vague or metaphorical speech; inadequate rapport with others; suspicious or paranoid thoughts; and undue sensitivity to real or imagined criticism.

Schlaftiefenmesser   German term for an apparatus intended to measure the depth of sleep; at fixed temporal intervals it automatically releases a series of balls of constant weight, from increasing heights, which fall upon sound-boards and disturb the sleeper, who is instructed to stop the apparatus at the instant of awaking. See SOUND PENDULUM for an example of such an instrument

Schlemm's canal   A small, ring-shaped channel in the sclera of the eye, close to its junction with the cornea, forming the outlet through which the aqueous fluid finds its way back into the general circulation.

Schnauzkrampf (snout cramp—German) Term used by Karl Kahlbaum to describe the snoutlike protrusion of lips observed in some catatonic patients.

scholastic 1. Pertaining to school. 2. Pertaining to a particular approach in medieval philosophy.

scholastic acceleration educational acceleration

scholastic achievement test Any examination that measures knowledge and ability in a specific area of academic study, such as chemistry, history, mathematics, Spanish, or literature. Also known as school achievement test (S-A-T).

scholastic aptitude tests A group of tests usually validated against measures of academic achievement. See INTELLIGENCE TESTS.

Scholastic Aptitude Test (SAT) A set of verbal and mathematical questions with heavy emphasis on abstract intelligence, used in selecting candidates for college admission. Published by the Educational Testing Service on behalf of the College Entrance Examination Board.

Scholastic Assessment Test (SAT) Formal name of the Scholastic Aptitude Test since 1994.

school 1. An institution of instruction and learning of any grade. In the United States, when used without qualification this term generally denotes an institution of primary or secondary level. 2. A body of adherents to some specific theory, doctrine, method, or leader; a school of thought. 3. A major subdivision of a university.

school ability tests (S-A-T) 1. Scholastic tests used to assess how much of a topic is known, often determines the student's placement. 2. A general examination of intelligence used to assess aptitude, for example, of whether a student is likely to benefit from an accelerated course. Sometimes known as school aptitude tests.

school achievement test (S-A-T) scholastic achievement test

school activity record Written or recorded data detailing a student's extracurricular involvement in school activities, clubs, or special projects. See ACTIVITY LOG.

School and College Ability Test (SCAT) An academic aptitude examination extending, in three levels, from the end of grade 3 through grade 12 plus a form for college juniors and seniors. All levels yield a verbal score based on a verbal analogies test; a quantitative score based on comparison of fundamental number operations; and a total score. Published by the Educational Testing Service.

school grades Teachers' evaluations generally based on subjective impressions and/or test scores representing the child's achievement given on A-B-C-D scale or a numerical scale of 0 to 100.

schooling Systematic instruction.

school integration Generally, the incorporation of different ethnic and racial groups in the same classes in school. Following a U.S. Supreme Court ruling, there was the federally-enforced racial integration of Little Rock (Arkansas) Central High School in 1957 and the University of Mississippi in 1962. At other times and places the term refers to incorporation within a single education system of different genders ("coeducation"), native language speakers, religious groups, cultural groups, and basic approaches to education. Also applied by some to mainstreaming children with exceptional needs.

school phobia An apparently irrational fear of school. Considered a form of separation anxiety. See SCHOOL REFUSAL, SEPARATION-ANXIETY DISORDER.

school psychology A field of psychology concerned with psychoeducational problems arising in primary and secondary schools.

school readiness The ability of a child to adjust to the demands of a school in terms of control of self and ability to profit from instruction. Sometimes assessed by instruments, such as the Orleans-Hanna Algebra Prognosis Test; sometimes in a one-on-one session with a professional who serves as instructor, examiner, and clinician.

school refusal Children refusing to go to school, frequently due to separation anxiety. See SCHOOL PHOBIA, SEPARATION ANXIETY.

schools of psychology In the history of psychology as a science rather than a philosophy, a number of assumptions about behavior, known (for the lack of a better term) as "schools," have been put forth. Some schools include: ACT PSYCHOLOGY, ATOMISM, BEHAVIORISM, COGNITIVISM, CONNECTIONISM, CREATIVE SYNTHESISM, CYBERNETICS, DYNAMIC PSYCHOLOGY, ECLECTICISM, EMERGENTISM, EMPIRICISM, ENVIRONMENTALISM, EPIPHENOMENALISM, EXISTENTIALISM, FIELD THEORY, FINALISM, FORMALISM, FUNCTIONALISM, GESTALT, HEREDITARIANISM, IDEALISM, INDETERMINISM, INTERACTIONISM, INTERBEHAVIORALISM, MATERIALISM, MECHANISM, MOLECULARISM, MONOIDEISM, NATIVISM, NEOBEHAVIORISM, NEOPHENOMENOLOGY, OPERATIONALISM, ORGANISMIC, ORTHOGENESIS, PANPSYCHISM, PARALLELISM, PERIPHERALISM, PERSONALISM, PHENOMENALISTIC, PHENOMENOLOGY, PHILOSOPHICAL PSYCHOLOGY, PROBABILISM, PURPOSIVISM, RATIONAL PSYCHOLOGY, S-O-R, S-R, SENSATIONALISM, SITUATIONALISM, SOCIAL-LEARNING THEORY, STRUCTURALISM, TELEOLOGY, VITALISM, VOLUNTARISM.

Schreber case A landmark case of Sigmund Freud's based on his analysis of Memoirs of a Neurotic by Daniel P. Schreber. His notes on this case, published in 1911, contained an interpretation of paranoid processes and ideas and their relation to repressed homosexuality. What Freud either did not know, or did not mention, was that Schreber's father, a physician, had, in effect, tortured his son by forcing him to wear uncomfortable body braces day and night to correct the son's posture.

Schröder staircase (H. Schröder) An optical illusion, a line drawing of a staircase in which the stairs alternately appear as correct-side-up or upside-down. Also spelled Schroeder's staircase.

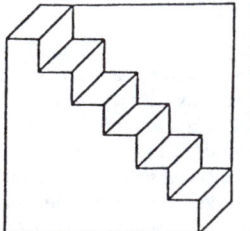

Schröder staircase Is the staircase rightside up or upside down? There is a tendency to initially perceive a staircase ascending in the normal manner; later, the impression may shift to that of one that is upside down.

schuldig (guilty or indebted—German) In existential psychology, a characterization of human relations to the natural world, other persons, and the self.

Schwann cells/sheath Neurilemma, or satellite cells, which form a sheath over most of the length of a peripheral nerve (relative of oligodendroglia in the brain which produce myelin sheaths). Named for Theodor Schwann, who founded the cell theory of animal structure. Also known as neurilemma. See MYELIN SHEATH.

sciatic nerve A large peripheral nerve which connects the receptor and effector organs in the leg with the spinal cord.

science Organized or systematic knowledge based on an accumulating body of empirical observations.

scientific attitude An attitude characterized by an objective and impartial approach and the use of empirical methods in the search for knowledge.

scientific explanation An account of some fact, phenomenon, or event based on a combination of fact, observation, and logic subject to further proof.

scientific management A system created by Frederick Taylor to improve industrial efficiency through the use of rest periods, productivity-based incentives, and time-and-motion studies. Also known as Taylor system, Taylorism.

scientific method The use of carefully planned naturalistic observation and experimentation in obtaining and verifying data and in discovering laws and principles that govern phenomena.

scientific psychology Knowledge about behavior based on the scientific method in contrast to knowledge based solely on theories, opinions, random observation, or on authority, such as from Aristotle.

scientific rationality (A. Staats) A concept that psychology can never be a science if it is fragmented. See BRIDGING, FRAGMENTATION, UNIFIED POSITIVISM.

scientific theories (in psychology) According to Melvin Marx, theories in psychology are of three types: (a) deductive, based on derivations of propositions to be tested by logical premises; (b) inductive, based on accumulation of evidence without deliberate attempt to achieve it; and (c) functional, based on small frequently modified hypotheses used as tools to permit more meaningful theoretical propositions. See GENERAL-SYSTEMS THEORY.

scientism Exclusive reliance on a narrow conception of science.

scientist-practitioner model (V. Raimy) A paradigm based on a decision made at a 1949 USPHS conference in Boulder, Colorado that practitioners of psychology should be trained as scientists. Also known as the Boulder Model. See PSY. D.

Scientology A controversial human-potential development system with a spiritual and religious dimension developed by L. Ron Hubbard. Central to the system is the hypothetical "engram," alleged to influence behavior and regarded as the cause of mental and psychosomatic illness. Engrams are the result of painful past experiences and psychological shocks suffered in the present and previous incarnations. Scientology training is aimed at healing illness by "clearing" and erasing the engrams. See DIANETICS.

scierneuropsia See SCIEROPIA.

scieropia A visual anomaly in which objects appear to be in a shadow. May be due to an emotional or psychological disorder, in which case the condition is identified as scierneuropsia.

SCII Strong-Campbell Interest Inventory

scintillating scotoma Transient localized blindness that may follow the autochthonous "perception" of bright colored lights; usually a prodromal symptom of a migraine headache. Also known as flittering scotoma, teichopsia.

sciophobia Fear of shadows.

sciosophy Any system of thought not supported by scientific methods, such as astrology, phrenology, numerology.

scissors gait A walk observed in some cerebral palsy patients who must cross their legs in scissors fashion in taking steps.

sclera The tough, white outer coat of the eyeball which is continuous with the cornea at the front and the optic-nerve sheath at the back of the eyeball. Also known as sclerotic coat/layer.

sclerosis Hardening of the neural or other tissues of the body. See DIFFUSE SCLEROSIS.

sclerotic coat/layer sclera

SCN See SUPRACHIASMATIC NUCLEUS.

scofflaw Literally, a person who scoffs at the law; does not obey the laws.

scope The entire group of phenomena, events, or general data which properly fall within the limits of a given inquiry.

SCOPE Acronym for Systematic, Complete, Objective, Practical, and Empirical, a set of diagnostic procedures.

scophophobia scopophobia

scopic method A technique of measuring scores or data by direct observation rather than by graphic representation in which instruments are used.

scopolamine A psychotomimetic, anticholinergic substance derived from *Hyoscyamus*, a poisonous Eurasian herb of the nightshade family. An anticholinergic drug that can produce electroencephalographic (EEG) synchronization and apparently can inhibit the stimulatory effect of acetylcholine. Depresses the central nervous system causing feelings of fatigue and sleep. Sometimes employed during the birth process to produce twilight sleep in the mother. Also known as hyoscine. In the 1940s thought to function as a "truth serum." See ANTICHOLINERGICS, ANTIHISTAMINES.

scopophilia Sexual pleasure derived from watching others in a state of nudity, disrobing, or engaging in sexual activity. If scopophilia is persistent, term is equivalent to voyeurism. Also known as scoptophilia, scotophilia.

scopophobia Fear of being seen or looked at by others, especially fear of being stared at. May be a sign of extreme shyness or self-consciousness. Also known as scophophobia.

score A quantitative value assigned to test results, or other measurable responses or judgments.

score equating Adjusting scores on different tests or different kinds of tests to make their interpretation meaningful. For example, SAT scores are available for most applicants, but only ACT for some; a system of score equating may permit estimation of ACT scores from the SAT.

scoterythrous vision A type of color blindness in which long wavelength stimuli (reds) are lessened in effectiveness or appear darkened because of a deficiency in perceiving the red end of the spectrum.

scotom(at)ization 1. A process of psychic depreciation, by means of which a person attempts to deny everything positive about self that affects self-esteem. 2. A tendency to ignore or be blind to impulses or memories that would threaten the ego. Considered to be a defense mechanism and may also be a form of resistance. See BLIND SPOT.

scotoma 1. An isolated area of absent or depressed vision within the visual field. An absolute scotoma is an area in which perception of light is lost completely. Other kinds of scotoma include: annular, central, color, peripheral, scintillating. Commonly known as a "blind spot." Plural is scotomata. See OPTIC DISK.

scotomata Plural of scotoma.

scotometer A measuring instrument for locating and mapping scotomata (the blind or partially blind areas of the retina). See SCOTOMA.

scotophilia Nyctophilia. Also known as scopophilia.

scotophobia Nyctophobia, morbid fear of night or of darkness. See ACHLUOPHOBIA, FEAR OF DARKNESS, NICTOPHOBIA.

scotopia Term introduced by J. Parsons for what was later known as scotopic vision.

scotopic Dark adapted. Also, vision in relative darkness, after adjustment or adaptation.

scotopic adaptation   dark adaptation

scotopic vision Visual perception in dim light that uses rod-cell function. Also known as twilight vision.

scotopsin A protein substance in the rod cells of the retina that combines with retinene to form rhodopsin, the light-sensitive visual pigment.

SCR skin conductance response

scratch fear See AMYCHOPHOBIA.

scratch reflex Repetitive scratching in response to skin irritation, for example, scratching a dog's shoulder sends an impulse to the spinal cord where an interneuron connection must be made with a motor nerve of another spinal segment so that a hind leg muscle group will get the message to scratch the shoulder.

scree test Raymond Cattell's name for a test to determine the number of factors to extract in factor analysis.

screen defense A defensive device in which a memory, fantasy, or dream image is unconsciously employed to conceal the real but disturbing object of personal feelings.

screened touch matching In parapsychology, an extrasensory perception (ESP) card-testing technique in which the participant guesses in each trial the top card in a pack held out of sight by the researcher.

screening 1. Initial patient evaluation to determine a person's suitability for a particular type of treatment. 2. Process of selecting items for psychological testing. 3. Determining, through a preliminary test, whether or not a person requires a more thorough evaluation. See MULTIMODAL THERAPY.

screening audiometry A technique for testing hearing by rapidly presenting low and high frequencies at a controlled, fixed intensity, usually 20 to 25 decibels, to determine if the participant is responding at each frequency for each ear being tested.

screening programs Organized systematic efforts to identify persons with certain disorders such as hypertension, diabetes mellitus, or phenylketonuria through the use of tests and other diagnostic and evaluative procedures.

screening test A short quiz used for preliminary assessment.

Screening Tests for Young Children and Retardates (STYCAR) A series of tests to screen children for deficiencies in hearing, language use, and vision.

screen memory The recollection of an event that the person is uncertain truly happened. May be a form of unconscious resistance occurring in psychotherapy. Also known as cover memory.

script 1. (E. Berne) An unconscious life plan usually based on early experiences that guide a person toward general or specific life goals. See LIFESTYLE ANALYSIS, SCRIPT ANALYSIS. 2. Cursive writing. 3. The characters which constitute handwriting. See HANDWRITING ANALYSIS. 4. In child development, a basic way for children to organize and interpret their world through a schema that provides descriptive information as to what and when an event can be expected to occur in a familiar situation. 5. See SEXUAL SCRIPT.

script analysis (E. Berne) In transactional psychotherapy, the analysis of the patient's unconscious life plan in its totality. The script is based on fantasies, attitudes, and "games" derived from the patient's early experiences. See GAMES, LIFE SCRIPT, SEXUAL SCRIPT.

script theory 1. (E. Berne) In transactional analysis, a point of view that people early in life develop various methods of how to deal with social situations, that have become an established sequence. 2. A point of view that some social interactions follow learned "scripts," for instance, sexual scripts (J. Gagnon & W. Simon) that teach children how to behave in dating. See LIFESTYLE ANALYSIS.

Scripture weights (E. W. Scripture) A set of small elder-pith disks, 3 mm. in diameter, suspended by a fine fiber, each from a separate handle; they form a graded series of weights, 1 mg, 2 mg, 3 mg...to any desired magnitude, employed in research experiments.

scriveners' palsy   writer's cramp (meaning 1)

scrotal reflex The relatively slow (for a reflex) contraction of the dartos tunic, a thin layer of nonstriped muscle fibers immediately under the skin of the scrotal pouch. The effective stimulus is either stroking or applying cold to the perineum.

scrupulosity Overconcern with questions of right and wrong and meticulous attention to detail. A common characteristic of the obsessive-compulsive personality.

scrying   See CRYSTAL GAZING.

SCT   sentence-completion test

sculpting   A family therapy technique in which members of a family and a therapist first discuss the "functioning position of each member," then create a "living sculpture" in which the members of the family assume various positions as decided, such as submissive, bossy, clinging, detached. The object is to help them become more aware of themselves and their relationships to each other.

S-curve   See S-SHAPED CURVE.

SD   1. See DISCRIMINATIVE STIMULUS. 2. systematic desensitization.

S^D   Symbol for a stimulus in the presence of which the main response will be rewarded (that is, operant conditioning). See DISCRIMINATIVE STIMULUS, STIMULUS DISCRIMINATION (meaning 2).

S_D   See DRIVE STIMULI.

S^Δ   Symbol for a stimulus in the presence of which the main response will not be rewarded (that is, operant extinction). Compare S^D. See DISCRIMINATIVE STIMULUS, STIMULUS DISCRIMINATION (meaning 2).

SD   standard deviation (also abbreviated **S.D.**)

SDAT   Abbreviation for senile dementia of the Alzheimer type. See ALZHEIMER'S DISEASE.

S-delta   See S^Δ.

SDMT   Stanford Diagnostic Mathematics Test

SDRT   Stanford Diagnostic Reading Test

SDT   signal-detection theory

SE   standard error

seaman's mania   nautomania

seamstress' cramp   A neurotic symptom consisting of an inability to perform such manual operations as threading a needle and using scissors in cutting cloth. See CONVERSION DISORDER, OCCUPATIONAL NEUROSIS.

séance   (session—French) A parapsychological practice characterized by a group of persons sitting in a darkened room to observe psychic phenomena, such as communications from deceased persons.

search for glory   (K. Horney) Attempting to fulfill an idealized self-image.

search guide   A structured, functional guide to the solution of certain classes of problems. See ALGORITHM.

search of associative memory (SAM)   (R. M. Shiffrin) A memory model holding that short-term memory is a limited-capacity buffer that affects which items are stored in the long-term memory and assembles retrieval cues that access information in it.

Seashore('s) audiometer   (C. E. Seashore) A device used to measure sound-intensity thresholds. An electronic buzzer or tuning fork produces a sound whose intensity is varied by means of a potentiometer and conducted to a sort of telephone system. See AUDIOMETER.

Seashore Tests of Musical Ability   (C. E. Seashore) The oldest of musical aptitude tests. A phonograph record contains the stimuli used to measure the ability to discriminate small differences in pitch, loudness, time, rhythm, timbre, and tonal pattern. Also known as Seashore Measures of Musical Talents.

sea-sickness   A form of motion sickness (nausea) experienced on moving platforms on water. See MOTION SICKNESS.

seasonal   Pertaining to or influenced by the seasons. See CYCLIC.

seasonal affective disorder (syndrome) (SAD or SADS)   Depression-like status resulting from lack of sunlight, experienced by some people during the dark seasons of the year (late fall, winter, and early spring) alleviated by light, natural or artificial.

seasonality effect   The greater prevalence of schizophrenia in those born in the late winter or early spring; recent data suggest no such relationship.

seasonal variation   Different mood reactions to seasonal changes. See SEASONAL AFFECTIVE DISORDER.

seat of mind   An old idea that in the brain there had to be a single point where the unitary soul affected the body. René Descartes thought it might be the pineal gland or conarium.

seclusion need   (H. A. Murray) A wish for privacy, the drive or urge to be alone.

seclusiveness   A tendency to isolate the self from social contacts or human relationships.

secobarbital sodium   sodium secobarbital

Seconal   Trade name for sodium secobarbital.

secondary advantage   secondary gain

secondary affective disorder   A chronic disturbance of mood occurring simultaneously with other disorders.

secondary aging   1. Physical or biological changes related to disease, injury or abuse of the body. 2. Aging processes accelerated by disabilities resulting from disease. Compare PRIMARY AGING.

secondary amentia   Mental retardation due to environmental or external factors. See AMENTIA.

secondary appraisal   A person's evaluation of personal ability to cope with a particular event. Compare PRIMARY APPRAISAL.

secondary attention   Active attention that requires conscious effort, for example, the close examination needed to analyze a painting or sculpture. Compare PRIMARY ATTENTION.

secondary autoerotism   Erotic pleasure produced by indirect association with the erogenous zones, such as stroking one's own thighs.

secondary automatic   Characterizing certain types of response, which become automatic only after repetition or practice.

secondary cause   A contributing factor to the onset of mental-disorder symptoms although the factor in itself would not be sufficient to cause the disorder.

secondary circular reaction   According to Jean Piaget, repetitive action, usually emerging around the age of four to five months, that signifies the infant's aim of making things happen. The behavior involves objects outside the infant's body (such as banging with a spoon, banging feet on mattress to move a toy dangling from crib), whereas in primary circular reactions, infants use their own bodies (such as banging with a fist, thumbsucking, toe-biting). This forward step occurs during the sensorimotor period. See COORDINATION OF SECONDARY SCHEMES, PRIMARY CIRCULAR REACTION, TERTIARY CIRCULAR REACTION.

secondary control A method of coping with problems by going along with them, accepting reality instead of trying to change it.

secondary correlation An apparent correlation between two items or events due to a third variable. If two items correlate with each other to a significant degree and a third variable correlates with both, it may be that the third variable invalidates the original correlation; for example, if the activity level of birds correlates with the activity level of mammals throughout the year, it may be that weather affects them both. Researchers attempt to remove the influence of weather by partialing out the effects of the common underlying variables. The original high correlation is erroneously regarded as spurious. See PARTIAL CORRELATION, SPURIOUS CORRELATION.

secondary cortical zone A cortical region behind the central sulcus that is concerned with perception. (A zone is labeled primary, secondary, or tertiary depending on its function). See PRIMARY CORTICAL ZONE, TERTIARY CORTICAL ZONE.

secondary defense symptoms A set of defensive measures employed by obsessional neurosis patients when primary defenses against repressed memories no longer offer protection, such as obsessional thinking, phobias, ceremonials, superstitions, or pedantry.

secondary deviance Maladjustment or emotional disturbance experienced by those whom society labels "deviant" that stem from such attributions, as in emotional difficulties experienced by some normally functioning young African American males who are stereotyped as aggressive and violent by a white racist society. Compare PRIMARY DEVIANCE.

secondary disposition In Gordon Allport's theory, a specific tendency to behave in a particular way in a particular situation.

secondary drive A learned urge or motive such as the desire for a particular kind of food or drink. Compare ACQUIRED DRIVE, PRIMARY DRIVE.

secondary elaboration (S. Freud) The process of altering the memory and description of a dream to make it more coherent and less fragmentary or distorted. Also known as secondary elaboration of dreams.

secondary emotions The result of two emotions blending so that for example, the primary emotions of surprise and fear can be combined into shock.

secondary environment An environment incidental or marginally important in a person's life in which interactions with others are comparatively brief and impersonal, for example, a bank or shop. See PRIMARY ENVIRONMENT.

secondary erectile dysfunction Loss of ability to produce or maintain an erection as needed for successful intercourse, in comparison to never having been able to have an erection (primary erectile dysfunction). Sometimes known as secondary impotence. See IMPOTENCE, PRIMARY ERECTILE DYSFUNCTION, SECONDARY IMPOTENCE.

secondary evaluation (S. Anderson) A critical review of the data, the reports, or both, of an evaluation, studied and reported upon by another evaluator. Sometimes referred to as metaevaluation because it occurs "above and beyond" the primary evaluation.

secondary extinction Cessation or weakening in rate or intensity of a conditioned response as a result of its association with another response that has been or is in the process of being extinguished; generalization of extinction.

secondary factors (R. B. Cattell) Factors found by performing a factor analysis on the intercorrelations of primary factors. Sometimes loosely designated higher order or global factors.

secondary function When a behavior has two purposes or selective values, the one of lesser importance. For example, allogrooming among zebras has the primary function of establishing and maintaining social ties with its secondary function as a stress reducer.

secondary function type A person dominated by the secondary function, showing signs of a narrow but deep consciousness, and possessing such characteristics as persistence, stubbornness, introversion, intensiveness, or inflexibility. See SECONDARY FUNCTION.

secondary gains Advantages derived from a neurosis, other than the primary gain of relieving anxiety or internal conflict, such as extra attention, sympathy, avoidance of work, personal service, and domination of others. Also known as epinosic gains. Compare PRIMARY GAINS, TERTIARY GAINS.

secondary groups Aggregates of people characterized by relatively weak, superficial interpersonal relationships, for example, large lecture classes. Compare PRIMARY GROUPS.

secondary identification A pathological form of identification consisting of incorporating the traits of another person into the self for defensive purposes, for example, unconsciously attempting to restore a deceased person to life by adopting his or her characteristics.

secondary impotence Inability of a male to perform sexually about one-quarter of the time that sexual intercourse is attempted under normal conditions, or inability to perform under certain circumstances. In the latter case it is also known as secondary erectile dysfunction. See IMPOTENCE, PRIMARY ERECTILE DYSFUNCTION.

secondary integration In psychoanalytic theory, the normal evolution of pregenital psychic components into an integrated psychosexual unit on an adult, genital level.

secondary memory (SM) Recall for material whose span exceeds the capacity of primary memory. Various authorities differ, some claim 5–7 chunks, others 5–9 chunks. Often referred to as long-term memory.

secondary mental deficiency A type of subnormal intelligence due to disease or brain injury rather than congenital factors.

secondary motivation Acquired or learned drives that lack a bodily basis, for example, an urge to learn classical music or to become a movie star. Such motives are of lower rank (intensity) than primary motives. These can be viewed from an idiographic (individual) point of view for individuals and from a nomothetic (group) point of view for people in general. See MOTIVES.

secondary narcissism Self-love that develops later in life, after the original infantile primary narcissism, such as narcissism in the form of a delusion of grandeur. Compare PRIMARY NARCISSISM.

secondary needs (H. A. Murray) Needs that have been learned. See SECONDARY MOTIVATION.

secondary oocyte See OOCYTE, PRIMARY OOCYTE.

secondary personality A second self that has its own behavior patterns, attitudes, name, and way of speaking and dressing, all of which are usually in sharp contrast to the original, or primary, personality. See DISSOCIATIVE-IDENTITY DISORDER, MULTIPLE PERSONALITY.

secondary position Any position of binocular fixation other than the primary position.

secondary posttraumatic stress disorder **vicarious traumatization**

secondary prevention 1. The prevention of mental disturbances through an early identification of persons at risk and the correction of maladaptive patterns of behavior and thought within the life sphere of those individuals. 2. Early case finding, prompt care and treatment, with the aim of arresting disorders, mental and physical, in their incipient stages. See PREVENTIVE PSYCHIATRY.

secondary process (thinking) Psychoanalytic term denoting thought processes, resting on realistic perception, including problem-solving, judgment, and systematic thinking that enable people to meet the external demands of the environment, and the internal demands of instincts, in rational, effective ways. Compare PRIMARY PROCESS.

secondary quality A nonessential characteristic of an object, not necessary for its identification, for example, the color of a toy.

secondary reinforcement The process of conditioning by the use of a learned reinforcer, as in teaching a participant the value of a token needed to obtain a reward. See PRIMARY REINFORCEMENT, REINFORCEMENT.

secondary reinforcer A reinforcer, originally neutral that acquires reward value on the basis of association with a primary reinforcer. See SECONDARY REWARD.

secondary relationship A time-limited, event-specific relationship between individuals or groups, for example, two people have a business connection and interact with each other each day from 9am–5pm, each performing specified operations according to general rules until the task they are working on has been achieved.

secondary repression In psychoanalytic theory, the repression of material that might remind the person of what was originally repressed. See PRIMAL REPRESSION, PRIMARY REPRESSION, REPRESSION.

secondary reward Something of value needed to retrieve a primary reward. A secondary reward could be a map showing the location of buried treasure, the primary reward. See SECONDARY REINFORCER, TOKENS.

secondary sensation **synesthesia**

secondary service system An array of service components which apply to certain extraordinary needs of certain primary clients but do so within the context of a target clientele composed of persons most of whom are identified as challenged or disabled.

secondary sex(ual) characteristics The differentiating characteristics of males and females apart from their genitalia; for example, the colors of (male) peacocks differ considerably from (female) peahens, and the breast-sizes and occurrence of facial hair of men and women usually differentiate them. See SEX CHARACTERISTICS.

secondary sexual dysfunction A sexual dysfunction that has not always existed, follows a period of satisfactory functioning, and is not due to satiation. Compare PRIMARY SEXUAL DYSFUNCTION.

secondary source A published work that reports (often summarizes) data, research conclusions, and/or theories that have previously appeared in print. The initial publication by the original researcher or theorist is known as a primary source. Scholarly publications cite primary rather than secondary sources whenever possible.

secondary stuttering Neuromuscular spasms and speech dysfluencies accompanied by anxiety and habitual movements to conceal or alter speech blockages. Compare PRIMARY STUTTERING.

secondary symptoms 1. (E. Bleuler) Pathological symptoms, such as apathy and loss of initiative, that stem from the hospital environment rather than from the disease itself. See ACCESSORY SYMPTOMS, FUNDAMENTAL SYMPTOMS, IATROGENESIS, SOCIAL-BREAK-DOWN SYNDROME. 2. Pathological symptoms that are ancillary to the main diagnosis, such as the poor self-concept of a child with dyslexia.

secondary tension In group dynamics, feelings of discord, friction, and discomfort that occur in groups that have passed through an earlier period of primary tension.

secondary territory A space routinely used by a person or group who do not control or use it exclusively, for example, the local tennis court. Habitués may harbor feelings of possession but will acknowledge others' primary claims. See PRIMARY TERRITORY, PROXEMICS.

secondary trait (G. W. Allport) A personal characteristic that appears occasionally in a person, but not sufficiently to be considered a primary trait.

secondary transitional object A psychoanalytic term for some object selectively acquired by an infant because of its anxiety-reducing value, adopted around the age of two, such as a security blanket (as opposed to a primary transitional object such as the thumb). See INDIVIDUATION, SYMBIOSIS, TRANSITIONAL OBJECT.

secondary tympanic membrane A thin membrane which covers the round or cochlear window at the basal end of the scala tympani. Oscillates in accordance with the alternating pressures exerted on the perilymph by movements of the stapes at the oval window.

second childhood 1. Lay phrase for the hypothetical tendency of the aged to regress to a childish state of mind. 2. Sometimes used as a synonym for senility.

second-messenger hormonal accessories See CYCLIC NUCLEOTIDES.

second nature Common name for the ability to do something without thought as though it were instinctive.

second negative phase A resurgence of resistance on the part of children usually in an attempt to achieve autonomy. Follows the first negative phase that was altered usually by parental action, and represents another attempt of children to get their way. See EXTINCTION.

second-order autonomous nervous system neurons Unmyelinated postganglionic neurons whose cell bodies lie in the ganglia outside the central nervous system. Their axons (postganglionic fibers) terminate in the heart, smooth muscles, or glandular tissue. See SECOND-ORDER NEURON.

second-order BASIC I.D. Arnold Lazarus' method of re-examining a specific problem that is not responding to treatment, by reassessing it across its seven modalities. See BASIC I.D., MULTI-MODAL THERAPY.

second-order conditioning Using a conditioned stimulus for further conditioning, as a secondary reinforcement.

second-order factors The factors found by extraction from intercorrelations of primary factors. See FACTOR ANALYSIS, HIGHER-ORDER FACTORS.

second-order isomorphism Identity or similarity between icons or images rather than between physical objects.

second-order language   metalanguage

second-order neuron The second neuron in any neuronal pathway, such as the neurons of the dorsal horn of the spinal cord that give rise to the lateral spinal thalamic pathway that carries pain impulses to the brain or the unmyelinated postganglionic neuron whose cell body lies in the ganglia outside the central nervous system. Their axons (postganglionic fibers) terminate in the heart, smooth muscles, or glandular tissue.

second order thinking In children's development, the ability to develop rules about rules, as well as keeping competing thoughts in mind while processing them.

second sight Common or slang phrase for clairvoyance.

second signaling system Refers to human language and symbolic knowledge based, according to Ivan Pavlov, on the first signaling system (first order classical conditioning to external stimuli). Derives from individual experience within a culture and depends on language, abstraction, generalization, analysis, and synthesis. Also known as secondary signal system. See FIRST SIGNALING SYSTEM, LANGUAGE, SIGNALING SYSTEM.

second visual system A proposed visual system, governed by midbrain rather than the cortex, and involving identification of the location of objects.

secret control See DELUSION OF INFLUENCE.

secretion 1. A specific chemical substance produced by the activity of a gland or other tissue. 2. The process by which gland cells, by expending energy, form and discharge a secretion.

sect A group whose members actively follow a leader or adhere to a set of doctrines, beliefs, and rituals. It is generally a dissenting faction that breaks away from a larger religious, political, or other social organization. See CULT.

section A thin slice, usually transversely, cut from the brain, spinal cord or muscle, usually for histological (microscopic) examination.

sectional sensitivity In perception, a value of sensitivity measured by equating and differentiating two supraliminal sense distances or sections cut from the whole sense continuum.

sectioning 1. The division of students in classes into smaller groups for separate instruction with the intention of maximizing learning. 2. In physiology, refers to the act of creating sections of tissue, often for the purpose of microscopy.

sector therapy (F. Deutsch) A goal-limited adjustment therapy, it focuses on specific "sectors" revealed by clients' autobiographical accounts. The procedure enables clients (or patients) to understand their faulty thinking patterns and gradually establish better patterns with the aid of the therapist. See ASSOCIATIONISM, ASSOCIATIVE ANAMNESIS.

secular 1. Pertaining to what is not religious in nature; civil or temporal. In secular societies, many religions may exist independently of the laws and governing institutions over which they ostensibly exert no influence. 2. Refers to long periods of time as the secular Roman games that took place once every 120 years.

secular humanism A nontheistic philosophy that: (a) rejects supernaturalism, (b) embraces idea of individual's capacity for self-realization through reason, (c) may be antagonistic to traditional religion while often expressing many of the ethical foundations of religion, and (d) holds respect for the human being as a core value. See GOLDEN RULE, HUMANISM.

secular trend 1. The main pattern or direction of a time series, as distinguished from temporary or seasonal variations. 2. A generality based on sequences, especially in families with children, for example, in large families, feelings of children toward their parents may generally go from the strongest held by the oldest child, with strength of such feelings waning sequentially with each child, with the youngest child feeling the least amount of attachment to the parents. 3. A drop in the average age of when puberty starts across generations. Over successive generations, a tendency for physical or behavioral milestones to be achieved at increasingly younger ages (for example, puberty occurring on the average at age 14, then age 13, age 12, age 10).

secundigravida A woman in her second pregnancy. Also known as Gravida II.

secundines Structures expelled from the uterus after a birth, particularly the placenta and umbilical cord.

secure attachment A child's ability to use the parent as a safe base, and to be consoled after separation, when fearful, or when otherwise stressed. See AVOIDANT ATTACHMENT, DISORGANIZED ATTACHMENT, RESISTANT ATTACHMENT.

secure base phenomenon A tendency of infants, human and animal, to explore areas but always remain close to their mothers.

security A sense of safety, emotional well-being, self-confidence, and optimism with no painful feelings or emotions.

security blanket 1. A transitional object that serves to calm young children, apparently reducing their anxiety. Some children will refuse to go to sleep if they are not holding their preferred object. 2. Nontechnical phrase for any object, person, or idea, that helps an adult cope with difficult aspects of life. See TRANSITIONAL OBJECT.

security operations   (H. S. Sullivan) A variety of defensive measures, such as arrogance, boredom, or anger, used as a protection against anxiety or loss of self-esteem, usually at the expense of harmonious interpersonal relationships.

sedative   1. Any substance that relieves excitement or irritability by depressing the central nervous system. 2. Any substance that soothes or allays excitement.

sedative amnestic disorder   Temporary impairment in long-term and short-term memory without clouding of consciousness, following prolonged heavy use of a barbiturate or similarly acting sedative or hypnotic. Also known as hypnotic amnestic disorder. See AMNESTIC SYNDROME.

sedative occupation   Work activity that has a sedating effect because of its monotonous repetition. Examples such as weaving and basket making have been used in mental hospitals for therapeutic purposes especially in foreign countries. See OCCUPATIONAL THERAPY.

sedative-hypnotics   A general category of medicines which tend to act as a sedative in smaller doses and to put people to sleep in larger doses. Can intoxicate patients, generate tolerance, withdrawal, and delirium when withheld, and in some patients, cause anxiety, amnestic syndromes, sexual dysfunctions, as well as sleep, mood, and psychotic disorders.

seduction   1. Inducement of a person to participate in sexual intercourse. Common law does not recognize seduction as a crime. Some jurisdictions regard seduction as a crime if it involves a promise by a man to marry a woman in the near future if she will submit to intercourse before marriage. See CASANOVA. 2. To be led astray, allured to err in conduct or belief.

seduction theory (of neuroses)   In psychoanalytic theory, Sigmund Freud originally (1896) held that all neuroses resulted from sexual abuse in childhood, usually by the father.

seed psychosurgery   **stereotactic tractotomy**

seeing-eye dog   A guide dog used by persons who are blind. See ANIMAL-ASSISTED THERAPY.

SEG   sonoencephalogram

Séglas type   A psychomotor type of paranoia identified by Jules Séglas in the 1890s.

segmental reactions   See SPINAL REFLEXES, SUPRA-SEGMENTAL REFLEXES.

segmental reflex   A response mediated by a single region of the spinal cord.

segmental theory of the nervous system   A point of view that each segment of the nervous system, in segmented animals, regulates and controls primarily (or exclusively) the activities of the corresponding segment of the body.

segmentation   1. Progressive division of the original germ cell into many cells. 2. Division (usually in embryonic stages) of the body of higher animals into a series of segments or metameres. 3. In behavior modification, division of a complex sequence of behaviors into parts, with one or two components learned at a time.

segregated model   In evaluation research, a relationship between the program director, the production unit, and the evaluation unit, in which the production unit and the evaluation unit share equal importance and easy access to the program director. Also known as related model. See INTEGRATED MODEL.

segregation   Isolation of items with a minimum of interfacing between them. The items may be mental processes, ethnic groups, or a pair of gametes. Some segregated entities, such as genes, can give rise to new combinations.

Seguin Form Board   An apparatus created by Edouard Seguin in the mid-1800s as one of the earliest performance tests used in assessing intelligence and training persons with mental challenges. Wooden geometric figures must be matched with recesses of the same shape in the form board. Included in some performance tests of intelligence, such as the Grace Arthur Point Scale.

Seguin's signal   Obsolete name for aura, the warning symptoms of epileptic attack, especially muscle contractions.

seiza   (quiet sitting—Japanese) Meditative sitting in which a person achieves inner peace.

seizure   1. Sudden onset of symptoms of a disease condition, including convulsions, palpitations, dizziness, or other disagreeable sensations. 2. The specific pattern of signs or symptoms of an epileptic disorder, for example, grand mal epilepsy, in which the seizure is interpreted in terms of neural discharges within a certain area of brain tissues. See CONVULSION, EPILEPSY.

seizure disorders   Also known as epileptic disorders, but the preferred phrase is convulsive disorders.

seizure dyscontrol   Extreme lack-of-control behavior occasionally occurring immediately after a grand mal seizure, characterized by indiscriminate acts of aggression such as assaulting the nearest person or terrorizing other patients.

sejunction   A separation; a breaking of continuity in the mental processes.

selaphobia   Morbid fear of a flash of light. See ASTROPHOBIA.

selected group   An experimental group selected with respect to specified criteria related to the purpose of the experiment, such as a sample of persons age 65 and over for a study of attitudinal patterns in older persons. See RANDOM SAMPLE, SELECTED SAMPLE.

selected sample   A technique for establishing in advance, certain criteria for selection of a sample; for example, from a prison population the selection of all prisoners who are from 25 to 50 years of age, have a high school education, and are in for forgery. See SELECTED GROUP.

selection   The process of choosing an individual or object or procedure, for a practical purpose, such as studying, testing, classifying, or working. Usually a two-step process in research. First, the participants available for the project are determined relative to the population to which the results will be generalized; for example, a researcher desiring to demonstrate an intervention procedure with depressed out-patients arranges to study clients at four university clinics in three states who are diagnosed with depression during a two-year period. Second, the actual participants are selected from the panel of available individuals; for example, the researcher may choose 10 pairs of clients at each location with the pairs matched for gender, family living situation, and severity of the depression.

selection abstraction   Coming to a conclusion on the basis of a detail out of context and ignoring other information. Overemphasizing one element, while ignoring other important elements in studying or evaluating a complex issue. Also known as selective abstraction.

selection bias   Selecting participants for experimentation in a nonrandom (biased) manner, as in selecting specially motivated persons or those in preferred groups when selection is supposed to be unbiased.

selection index (D)   (H. J. Eysenck) A mathematical formula used to determine the discriminatory power of a test or test item. Formula: $D = A \div (A+B+C)$, where **B** is the proportion of persons who belong in a category and whose scores are appropriate for that category, **A** is the proportion of individuals who belong in a category but whose scores did not put them there, and **C** is the proportion of individuals not belonging in a category in which their scores put them. Occasionally known as index of selection.

selectionist   A person who assumes that natural selection explains the process of organic evolution.

selection method   See METHOD OF SELECTION.

selection pressure   That which has the effect of altering the genetic composition of a population in favor of survival. See DARWINISM, EVOLUTION.

selection ratio   1. The percentage of individuals selected based on some criterion, such as all students whose SAT scores are at least 1200. 2. In I/O psychology, the number of job applicants devided by the number accepted.

selection test   An examination to determine various aptitudes and abilities, used for predicting job performance and thus for employing people. A common such test is a speed-typing test.

selective abstraction   selection abstraction

selective action   1. Behavior which is multiply determined, and not singly as in impulsive action. 2. See SELECTIVE REACTION/RESPONSE.

selective adaptation   Responses to stimuli not identical but close to the original stimulus; stimulus generalization.

selective agency/agent   Any factor or combination of factors in the environment, through whose operation the process of natural selection is brought about.

selective amnesia   A localized inability to recall certain events. The usual explanation is that such events were so horrible or devastating for the person that they are blocked out of consciousness. See PSYCHOGENIC AMNESIA, RECOVERED MEMORIES.

selective analysis   An approach in psychotherapy in which aspects chosen for interpretation reflect the therapist's own interests and problems rather than the patient's needs and conflicts.

selective-answer test   An examination in which a question or problem is presented together with several answers presented for the participant's choice. See MULTIPLE-CHOICE TEST.

selective attention   A tendency of people to notice matters of interest to them and ignore others. Also known as controlled attention.

selective breeding   Attempting to achieve certain physical structure and temperament of living organisms by picking certain desired characteristics from samples of the organisms and permitting their reproduction, as in the breeding of cows for milk, horses for endurance, and plants for insect-resistance.

selective dropout   A situation when certain participants cease to be available or choose not to continue participating in a research because of illness, schedule conflicts, lack of interest, etc., thus producing a biased sample of participants. See ATTRITION.

selective exposure   Observing only some instances of a phenomenon, not observing all possible instances, resulting in a limited amount of information from which to draw conclusions or form opinions. See BIAS.

selective inattention   (H. S. Sullivan) A form of perceptual defense in which anxiety-provoking or threatening experiences are ignored or forgotten. The failure to notice what the self does not want to, or cannot cope with. See SENSORY OVERLOAD.

selective learning   A situation in which an organism exposed to a variety of stimuli, some similar to each other, has learned to ignore some stimuli but to respond to others.

selective listening   Attending to some stimuli while neglecting other stimuli.

selective migration   Movement of a nonrepresentative sample from a population, such as only the poorest or only those of a certain religion. A concept used in reference to possible reasons for the superior scores of Asian-American children on intelligence tests: the speculation that Asian emigrants to the United States may have been an intellectually superior group, a nonrepresentative sample of their native populations.

selective perception   A tendency to see what a person wants to see, for example, in a number of people examining a complex painting, some tend to focus on the women in the painting, some the men, and some the animals.

selective permeability (in the nervous system)   The property of the cell membrane of a neuron that allows certain ions to pass through it more easily than other ions. Both the resting membrane potential and the action potential depend on this property.

selective placement   1. Assignment of a phenomenon to a category. 2. In industry, assignment of an applicant to one of several job openings based on test results and other information.

selective reaction/response   A reaction that has been differentiated from a group of possible alternative reactions. Sometimes known as selective action.

selective retention   1. A preference or tendency to remember some information over other information. Varies greatly from person to person with respect to accuracy and quantity, and dependent on such factors as interest, experience, motivation, and emotional factors. In short, people remember what they are interested in. See REPRESSION. 2. In industry, continued employment of individuals usually based on announced and objective performance criteria.

selective sampling effect   1. A tendency for not all persons who are contacted for a study to choose to volunteer, often producing a biased sample of individuals that may not permit generalization to nonvolunteers. See BIASED SAMPLING. 2. The panel (experimentally accessible population) differs in major aspects from the target population of the research.

selective silence   Purposive silence, remaining quiet or not speaking for some period of time. In psychotherapy, a therapist may decide at a particular time that it would be best to remain silent, thus generating a tension that may lead the client or patient to speak up.

selective survival   1. A principle that not all members of a given cohort survive over time, yielding a sample that is no longer representative of its original cohort. 2. Natural selection.

selective synthesis   A connection or association between successive thoughts in a stream of thoughts.

selective thinking   A succession of thoughts, each chosen through a process of selective association, or synthesis. See FREE ASSOCIATION.

selective value   The relative importance of any given factor or combination of factors in determining the progress or rate of change in the evolution of organs, or of species, through natural selection.

self   The totality of all characteristic attributes, conscious and unconscious, mental and physical, of a person. William James thought humans have many selves, as they adapt differentially to different situations. Carl Jung conceived of the self as an archetypal image of unity and as the true center of the total personality, including both its conscious and its unconscious parts. Karen Horney held that the real self has the capacity for growth and development. Gordon Allport conceived of self as consisting of a gradually developing body sense, identity, self-estimate, and set of personal values, attitudes, and intentions. Types of self include: BAD, BODILY, CREATIVE, EMPIRICAL, IDEAL, IDEALIZED, LOOKING-GLASS, NOT-ME, OBSERVED, OVERT, PERSONIFIED, PHENOMENAL, PUBLIC, RATIONAL, REAL, SENSE OF, SENSORY, SOCIAL, TRANSPARENT, TRUE. See DEFORMATION OF THE SELF, DISORDERS OF THE SELF, SELF AS DOER.

self-abasement   1. Act of degrading or demeaning the self. 2. Extreme submission to the will of another person. Also known as self-debasement.

self-absorption   Being so concerned with self as to preclude concern for others. See GENERATIVITY VS SELF-ABSORPTION.

self-abuse   Archaic euphemism for masturbation. Phrase is without scientific foundation and apparently evolved from an 8th century attempt to identify masturbation as "the sin of Onan" (Onan actually engaged in coitus interruptus) and to substantiate unscientific claims that a number of diseases were produced by masturbation, including blindness and mental retardation.

self-acceptance   Recognition of personal abilities and achievements, together with acknowledgment and acceptance of personal limitations. Lack of self-acceptance is generally considered a major characteristic of emotional disturbance.

self-accusation   A process or habit of blaming the self, usually unjustifiably and out of a false sense of guilt. Often a factor in depression. Also known as intropunitiveness. See ANGER-IN, INTROPUNITIVE RESPONSE, SELF-ABASEMENT.

self-activity   Behavior consciously intended by a person that is not the result of external conditioning factors but is based on personal reflection, consideration and other phenomenological processes. See SELF-CONTROL.

self-actualization   (K. Goldstein, A. Maslow) According to Abraham Maslow, the full exploitation of personal potentialities so as to develop maximum self-realization, and ideally to integrate physical, social, intellectual, and emotional needs. According to Heinz Ansbacher, a follower of Adler, self-actualization is the only true drive. See HUMANISTIC PERSPECTIVE, NEED-HIERARCHY THEORY, TELEOLOGY.

self-administered test   A quiz in which the instructions are sufficiently self-evident not to require further clarification by the examiner. Also known as self-administering test.

self-alienation   1. An unpleasant state characterized by feeling unknown or estranged from the self. 2. A feeling that the self is not real. 3. A feeling of being unworthy.

self-analysis   An attempt by a person for formal self-understanding. Ranges from temporary analysis of a single incident to in-depth analysis as practiced by Sigmund Freud, and as recommended by Karen Horney and Theodor Reik. See DIDACTIC ANALYSIS.

self-appraisal   A person's conception and evaluation of the self, including values, abilities, goals, and personal worth. Also known as self-assessment/-concept/-evaluation/-rating. See SELF-IMAGE, SELF-PERCEPTION.

self as doer   Summary phrase for the whole person acting as a purposive, causal agent, including such processes as thinking, remembering, and intending.

self-assertion   A characteristic endeavor to stand up for the self and to avoid submission to others. Assertion avoids both the errors of aggression and of obsequity.

self-assessment (SA)   self-appraisal

self-attention theory   (B. Mullen) In group dynamics, a model arguing that self-awareness increases as the number of people in the majority increases and the individual's subgroup becomes smaller.

self-awareness   An attainment of insight into personal attitudes, motives, reactions, defenses, strengths, and weaknesses; a major goal of psychotherapy. Sometimes known as self-understanding.

self-blaming depression   An unpleasant state of mind characterized by self-derogation and self-accusation for faults or misdeeds, usually to an unwarranted degree. See SELF-ACCUSATION, SELF-CENSURE.

self-care   Daily activity such as eating, dressing, grooming, (ordinarily) managed alone for the purpose of personal maintenance.

self-censure   A person's conscious self-blame, condemnation, or guilt in judging own behavior to be inconsistent with personal standards of moral conduct. See SELF-ACCUSATION, SELF-BLAMING DEPRESSION.

self-concept   self-appraisal

self-concept tests   Personality tests designed to determine how individuals view aspects of themselves: attitudes, values, goals, body concepts, personal worth, and abilities. Three frequently used techniques are: (a) checking adjectives, (b) responding "Yes" or "No" to questions, (c) sorting Q-sort cards. See ADJECTIVE CHECKLIST, MINNESOTA MULTIPHASIC PERSONALITY INVENTORY, Q-SORT.

self-confidence   Self-assurance; trust in personal abilities, capacities, and judgment.

self-confrontation   Directly facing one's own attitudes or shortcomings, as in evaluating the way that the self is perceived by others and noting the possible negative consequences of self-behavior.

self-congruence   Degree of agreement between what a person would like to be and what the person actually is. Also, in Rogerian developmental theory, the correspondence dictated by the organismic valuing process and the conditions of self-worth. Can be tested by a q-sort of the ideal self.

self-consciousness   Extreme sensitivity about personal behavior, appearance, or other attributes; overconcern about the impression the person makes on others.

self-consensus bias   A tendency to believe that other people think and have values similar to the person's own. See PSYCHOLOGIST'S FALLACY.

self-consistency   1. A behavior or personality characterized by a high degree of internal stability and cohesiveness. 2. Compatibility of all aspects of a theory or system.

self-contradiction   A logical fallacy depending on two premises that cannot both be true, for example, "We must destroy this village to save it."

self-control   Ability to be in command of personal behavior, and to restrain or inhibit personal impulses.

self-control techniques   A behavior-therapy approach in which clients are trained to evaluate their own behavior, and reinforce desired behavior with appropriate material or social rewards. Sometimes involves placing the self in situations that lead to the desired behavior.

self-correlation   The correlation of any test or measuring instrument with aspects of itself. The correlation may be between separate administrations of the test or between different sections of the test. See RELIABILITY.

self-criticism   Ability to scrutinize and evaluate own behavior, and to recognize personal weaknesses, errors, and shortcomings.

self-cutting   Self-mutilation consisting of repeatedly cutting the wrists or body. Some "slashers," as they are called, ordinarily report feeling little pain. Self-cutting is purported to be a strategy employed by persons from severely abusive backgrounds to keep painful feelings at bay by replacing emotional pain with physical pain, to gain attention from people, to stop dissociative episodes of derealization or depersonalization, or to confirm self-existence.

self-debasement   self-abasement

self-deception   A failure to recognize personal limitations. The development of a false or unrealistic self-concept.

self-defeating behavior   An action that blocks a person's own goals and wishes; for example, the tendency to compete so aggressively that the person cannot hold a job.

self-demand feeding/schedule   Providing food to an infant or animal when the individual shows signs of wanting to eat; for example, leaving food out all day a day for house pets, or feeding infants when they begin to cry. Also known as demand feeding.

self-denial   An act of suppressing desires and foregoing satisfactions. Often a form of self-punishment for real or fancied guilt.

self-derogation   A tendency to disparage the self, often as a result of false expectations or aspirations, or an exaggerated sense of self-blame. Frequently found in depression. Milder forms often follow receipt of a compliment. See SELF-ACCUSATION, SELF-HATE.

self-desensitization   A behavior-therapy procedure in which the person, when confronted with fear-eliciting objects or situations, engages in coping strategies designed to reduce anxiety, such as rehearsal strategies, muscle relaxation. See SYSTEMATIC DESENSITIZATION.

self-destructiveness   See DEATH INSTINCT, DESTRUCTIVE BEHAVIOR.

self-determination   Control of personal behavior by internal convictions and decisions rather than external demands. Also known as self-direction. See INTERNAL LOCUS OF CONTROL.

self-development   Growth or improvement of own qualities and abilities.

self-differentiation   A measure of the uniqueness of an individual with respect to other members of a particular group.

self-direction   **self-determination**

self-discipline   The control of personal impulses and desires; foregoing immediate satisfaction in favor of long-term goals. The earliest meaning of discipline; but as discipline came to mean external control, at least in some contexts, the self- was added for clarity.

self-disclosure   Revealing innermost feelings, fantasies, experiences, and aspirations. Under proper conditions, as in group therapy, self-disclosure is assumed by many to be a requisite for therapeutic change and personal growth.

self-discovery   1. In existentialism, the process of finding the unique self; the "quest for identity." 2. In psychoanalytic theory, the freeing of the repressed ego, including personal aims and goals, from limitations imposed by submission to others.

self-display/-exhibition   A tendency to make the self unduly conspicuous in social situations via physical, intellectual, or moral excellences and/or excesses.

self-distribution   In Gestalt theory, the potentiality of the human mind to perceive a complex set of stimuli and to organize them in a meaningful gestalt.

self-dynamism   (H. S. Sullivan) A pattern of motivations or drives that comprise a person's self-system, particularly the pursuit of biological satisfaction, security and freedom from anxiety.

self-effacement   (K. Horney) Neurotic idealization of compliancy, dependency, and self-less love as a reaction to identification with the hated self.

self-effacing solution   One of Karen Horney's three basic orientations toward life, representing an appeal to be loved by others. See SELF-EXPANSIVE SOLUTION.

self-efficacy   1. Judgements about one's own capabilities to organize and execute courses of action required to attain designated types of performances. 2. (A. Bandura) Convictions that a person can successfully execute the behavior required to produce a desired outcome in a particular situation. A comprehensive sense of the person's own capability, effectiveness, strength, or power to attain desired results.

self-embedded sentence   A sentence that has a clause within the main frame of the sentence, for example, in "The boy who brings our paper is here," the clause "who brings our paper" is embedded in the sentence "the boy is here."

self-employment   Conducting own business or profession, as opposed to working for others.

self-encystment   Withdrawal within the self when the environment is perceived as exceedingly hostile.

self-esteem   An attitude of self-acceptance, self-approval, and self-respect.

self-estrangement   See ALIENATION.

self-evaluation   self-appraisal

self-evaluation maintenance model   (B. Mullen) In group dynamics, holds that individuals seek group membership provided that (a) they feel superior to other members in areas that are central to their self-concept, and (b) the other members excel in areas that are not central to their self-concept.

self-evident   Characterizing certain fundamental truths which are held to be indisputable, and to be worthy of acceptance as soon as they are stated, without need for evidence or proof.

self-excitation   The stimulation of an organ by its own activity, as in the case of muscular contractions producing stimuli which cause the muscle to contract again. See FEEDBACK, REVERBERATING CIRCUITS.

self-exciting circuit   A self-sustaining circuit of interneurons that occurs when a nerve impulse is transmitted from the main axon to a collateral then to a second neuron and back again to the original cell, exciting it a second time. This process may happen repeatedly without the instigation of a new external stimulus.

self-expansive solution   One of Karen Horney's three basic orientations toward life, which represents a striving for mastery. See SELF-EFFACEMENT SOLUTION.

self-expression   The free expression of personal feelings, thoughts, talents, attitudes, or impulses through such means as verbal communication, poetry, arts and crafts, dancing, and dramatic activities.

self-extension   (G. W. Allport) A characteristic of an early stage in the development of the proprium (self), beginning roughly at age four, marked by the child's emerging ability to incorporate people, objects, and abstractions into the self-concept.

self-extinction   A phrase used by Karen Horney for an inability or unwillingness to stand up for the self characterized by not fully living life, following others blindly.

self-feeding   1. Ability to eat by oneself, without direct assistance of others. See DAILY-LIVING AIDS. 2. In child development, refers to infants learning the skill of feeding themselves.

self-feeling   (W. McDougall) A person's conception of the self in terms of own standards.

self-focus   Ability, that may be unique for humans, to think about the self, a kind of self-reflection.

self-fulfilling prophecy   1. A tendency of a person's behavior to conform to expectations of others. Robert Rosenthal found that teachers' preconceptions about their students' abilities influenced the children's achievements. See ROSENTHAL EFFECT. 2. A tendency to perceive what the person expects to observe. See PERCEPTUAL SET.

self-fulfillment   The process of developing and expressing personal basic capacities and aspirations. See SELF-ACTUALIZATION, SELF-REALIZATION.

self-gratification   Satisfaction of personal needs, particularly needs associated with appetites and drive for self-enhancement.

self-handicapping   Any behavior or choice in performance-setting that enhances personal opportunity to excuse failure and accept credit for success.

self-handicapping strategy   A psychological ploy by means of which a person provides an excuse for failing a task by purposefully neglecting to prepare, as in neglecting to rehearse before an audition. The purpose is to create an acceptable excuse for an anticipated poor showing so that shortcomings can be attributed to circumstances and not to lack of ability. See SELF-FULFILLING PROPHESY.

self-hate   An extreme loss of self-esteem in which patients despise and derogate themselves, as in a self-blaming depression. See SELF-ACCUSATION.

self-help   Taking responsibility for the self in coping with various problems and difficulties. See SELF-ACTUALIZATION.

self-help group (SHG)   A group or program for persons with a disorder, and in some cases members of their families, banding together for purposes of emotional support, morale-boosting, and practical assistance. See ALCOHOLICS ANONYMOUS, NARCOTICS ANONYMOUS, GAMBLERS ANONYMOUS, WEIGHT WATCHERS, RECOVERY, INC..

self-hypnorelaxation   A form of self-hypnosis in which patients are trained to respond to their own relaxation suggestions.

self-hypnosis   The process of putting the self in a trance or trance-like state through autosuggestion. See AUTOHYPNOSIS.

self-ideal   ego ideal

Self-Ideal Q Sort   (W. Stephenson) A personality test designed to measure the discrepancy (or degree of correlation) between a person's self-concept and self-ideal. See Q-SORT TECHNIQUE.

self-identification   1. Loving a person similar to the self. 2. The admiration of one's own qualities when these qualities are present in another.

self-identity   Gordon Allport's theory of self that entails an awareness of inner sameness and continuity.

self-image (K. Horney) A personal picture or concept of self, including a self-evaluation of ability, personal worth, goals, and potential.

self-inflicted wounds See SELF-MUTILATION.

self-injurious behavior (SIB) Repetitive behaviors that harm the self, such as biting own arms, hands, lips, as well as head-banging or hitting the self. Seen in children with mental deficiency, children with autism, patients with schizophrenia, persons with substance abuse problems, compulsive gamblers, and masochistic adolescents and adults. SIB is the target of behavioral and pharmacological treatments.

self-insight The understanding of the self in depth, sometimes associated with successful psychotherapy. See DERIVATIVE INSIGHT, INSIGHT, OUTSIGHT.

self-instructional training (SET) 1. (D. Meichenbaum) An intervention aimed at self-regulation that teaches a person how to develop a variety of self-control behaviors (for example, how to self-monitor, plan and evaluate own performance). 2. (D. Meichenbaum) A cognitive-behavioral therapy procedure that teaches clients mental restructuring through modeling and cognitive-behavioral rehearsal (example of the latter: periodically expressing: "I am a worthwhile person and people should respect me"). See AFFIRMATION, COUÉ METHOD, INNER DIALOGUE.

self-inventory A questionnaire or series of statements on which the respondent checks characteristics or traits that apply to himself or herself. Goes beyond a checklist by summarizing the performance by scores on several scales.

selfish gene hypothesis A postulate that a living organism is merely the effect of the genes of that individual desiring to replicate themselves. In the famous question: Which came first, the chicken or the egg, the egg is "selfish" in producing chickens to perpetuate its existence.

selfishness Exaggerated regard for personal advantage, accompanied by a disregard for the welfare or happiness of others.

self-love 1. Love and respect for the self. According to Erich Fromm, a love of self is a prerequisite for love of others. 2. Excessive self-regard; a narcissistic attitude toward own body, abilities, or personality. See EGOTISM, NARCISSISM.

self-maintenance mores (G. Murphy) Unstated rules which sustain and preserve the life of the individual and the group.

self-managed reinforcement A personal plan to reward the self for maintaining a particular regimen of either doing something or not doing something (for example, if a person on a restricting diet loses a pound each week, the person will self-reward by buying himself or herself something nice). See BEHAVIOR MODIFICATION, SELF-CONTROL TECHNIQUES.

self-management A behavior therapy program in which clients learn to apply techniques to help modify their undesired behavior, such as smoking, excessive eating, or aggression. Based on personal decisions, books, lectures, group instructions, etc. A client learns to pinpoint the problem, set realistic goals, and use various contingencies (consequences for the self) to increase, decrease, or change the circumstances of occurrence of the desired behavior, and monitors personal progress. Sometimes known as self-management reinforcement.

self-marking test An examination that automatically scores a person's responses as correct or incorrect. Feedback may occur after each item or, more commonly, at the end of the test.

self-maximization The drive to maintain feelings of personal adequacy through competitive situations, such as striving for accomplishing more, perhaps to achieve higher status at home, at school, or at work.

self-misconceptions (V. Raimy) Major misconceptions about the self likely to lead to major problems; for example, phrenophophobia (I am going insane); special person (I deserve special consideration); obsessions (life is full of "musts" and "shoulds").

self-mutilation A destructive act resulting in own disfiguration. In some cases the person appears to be inflicting self-punishment to relieve intense and (usually exaggerated) feelings of guilt. See LESCH-NYHAN SYNDROME, SELF-INJURIOUS BEHAVIOR.

self-objectification (G. W. Allport) Objective knowledge about the self; self-understanding.

self-observation Self-scrutiny, either of the body and its functioning or of the psyche and its functioning. See INTROSPECTION.

self-perception Awareness of the various components that constitute the self, such as personal unique feelings, impulses, aspirations, and personality characteristics. Phrase is often used interchangeably with self-percept and self-concept.

self-perception theory (D. Bem) A point of view that self-evaluation is based on personal judgments of the quality of one's own behavior.

self-presentation See IMPRESSION MANAGEMENT.

self-preservation instinct Colloquially dubbed the first law of nature, an almost universal impulse of all organisms to survive. See ALTRUISM.

self-psychology (M. Calkins) A system of psychology that interprets all behavior in reference to the self. See PERSONALISTIC PSYCHOLOGY.

self-punishment Inflicting harm on the self for real or fancied misdeeds, usually to relieve a sense of guilt. Particularly common in depression and taking many forms, such as verbal self-castigation, extreme self-denial, masochistic infliction of pain, and, in extreme cases, self-mutilation and suicide. See EGO SUFFERING, EXPIATION, ILLNESS AS SELF-PUNISHMENT, SELF-ACCUSATION.

self-punishment mechanism In psychoanalytic theory, a process which gives rise to moral and ethical over-severity of the superego in its conflict with the primitive impulses of the id, and results in neurotic symptoms.

self-rating scale Any questionnaire, inventory, or other instrument used by a person to rate or assess own characteristics, attitudes, interests, or performance.

self-rating **self-appraisal**

self-realization A process or goal of fulfilling personal potentialities, including aptitudes, goals, and capacities. A major objective in many therapeutic approaches, such as psychodrama, client-centered counseling, organismic theory, and humanistic psychology. Roberto Assagioli speaks of self-realization as the experience and awareness of the "higher self," the synthesizing spiritual center of the personality as a whole. Carl Jung considered self-knowledge, particularly the understanding and acceptance of the archetypal ideas in the collective unconscious, as the path to self-realization. This ultimate goal of everyone (but reached by virtually no one) is a difficult, lengthy process that only begins in middle age with the manifestation of the self archetype. See SELF-ACTUALIZATION.

self-recitation A learning technique in which study time is at least partially spent in reciting or recalling learned material.

self-reference 1. A persistent tendency to direct a discussion or the attention of others back to the self. 2. In logic, a thing referring to itself, for example, "this sentence is false."

self-referral 1. Taking responsibility for oneself by applying to a professional person or agency for assistance when such is needed. Contrasted with referral by another, professional or lay including own family. 2. Voluntary admission to a mental health facility, even under strong pressure from others, in contrast with formal commitment by a court or mental health professional. While details vary from state to state, a self-referred patient is, in theory, entitled to discharge upon request during normal business hours.

self-reflexivity A process whereby a person defines and directs personal behavior rather than simply responding to stimuli.

self-regard That aspect of the self concept which develops from the esteem or respect accorded the self.

self-regulation (A. Bandura) A human capacity to exercise control over personal thoughts, feelings and actions. In this form of self-directedness, people monitor their behavior, judge it according to personal standards and guide and regulate their behavior through self-evaluative reactions. See SOCIAL COGNITIVE THEORY.

self-reinforcement The rewarding of the self for appropriate or desired behavior, a part of cognitive-behavioral therapy (for example, a person has abstained from smoking, and buys him- or herself a treat).

self-report checklist A questionnaire on which respondents indicate personality characteristics and behavior that apply or do not apply to them, sometimes with indication of degree. The clinician reads the responses and notes pertinent information. Differs from a self-report inventory in that it does not summarize the responses as scores on several scales. See MOONEY PROBLEM CHECKLIST, WOODWORTH-MATTHEWS PERSONAL DATA SHEET.

self-report inventory A questionnaire on which respondents indicate personality characteristics and behavior that apply or do not apply to them, sometimes with indication of degree. Replies are categorized into such dimensions as "aggressive/timid" usually on the basis of

the test developer's theoretical constructs about personality. See ALLPORT A-S REACTION STUDY, BELL ADJUSTMENT INVENTORY, GUILFORD-ZIMMERMANN TEMPERAMENT SURVEY, MINNESOTA MULTIPHASIC PERSONALITY INVENTORY.

self-repudiation Self-disparagement or self-depreciation. See SELF-ACCUSATION.

self-respect A feeling of self-worth and self-esteem, especially a proper regard for self values, character, and dignity. Phrase is similar to self-esteem.

self-schema A cognitive framework comprising organized information about the self in a specific realm of experience; a component of identity that is organized and well-defined, as in a clear conception of the self as parent or worker.

self-selection bias In research, if a number of people are asked to participate in an experiment, those likely to volunteer are probably not representative of the population or total group. In addition to being a bias of volunteers rather than nonvolunteers, it also arises when the phenomenon to be studied cannot be randomly assigned to participants; for example, in studying children who are in daycare versus homecare, a researcher cannot randomly assign children to these conditions. See SAMPLE BIAS, SAMPLING.

self-selection of diet The assumption that animals and humans, given choice, will tend to select foods that maintain them in good health. See APPETITE CONTROL, CAFETERIA FEEDING, FOOD PREFERENCES, SPECIFIC HUNGER, SUGAR SELF-SELECTION.

self-sentiment 1. (W. McDougall) A subjective feeling for the self. 2. (R. B. Cattell) The factor Q_3 in the 16PF which represents the person's attachment to own self-concept. See INFERIORITY FEELINGS.

self-serving bias A tendency of people to blame others or the situation for personal failure and to take credit for personal successes.

self-statement training (SST) In self-instructional training, cognitive-behavioral rehearsal such as periodically thinking or saying "I am a worthwhile person and people should respect me." See AFFIRMATION, COUÉ METHOD, INNER DIALOGUE.

self-stimulation 1. In persons with autism, any repetitive behavior that absorbs attention, such as rocking, arm flapping. 2. Attempts made by people to become more active, to get additional inputs from personal behavior. These can be subjective, such as day dreams or active such as talking out loud when alone. Young children will babble to break monotony.

self-stimulation mechanism (J. Olds) A system of electrodes inserted in certain brain areas so that the organism can stimulate neurons associated with possibly pleasurable sensations. Rats with electrodes implanted in the septal area have pressed a bar as many as 5,000 times an hour to administer a brief, mild electric shock to this "pleasure center." See LIMBIC SYSTEM, REWARD SYSTEM, SENSORY SELF-STIMULATION.

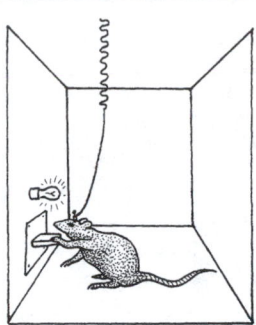

self-stimulation mechanism   The rat presses a lever continously to receive a light jolt of electricity in the limbic area of the brain that apparently is pleasurable enough to motivate the rat to continue doing so. One rat was reported to have stimulated itself more than 2,000 times per hour for a period of 26 hours—over 50,000 times.

self-sustaining neurotic interaction cycle   A feedback cycle in which the pathology of one person contributes to the pathology of a second, which then cycles back to strengthen the pathology of the first. See FOLIE À DEUX.

self-synchrony   In dance therapy, movement in relation to own speech. See SYNCHRONY.

self-system   (H. S. Sullivan) A stable personality resulting from relationships with parents and other significant adults, in which approved attitudes and behavior patterns tend to be retained, and disapproved actions and attitudes tend to be blocked out. See ADAPTIVE DELINQUENCY, AUTHORITARIAN PARENTS, PARENTAL REJECTION, PARENTAL TRAINING.

self-talk   (A. Ellis) Internal dialogue characterized by repeatedly uttering "internalized sentences" to the self. The sentences often confirm and reinforce beliefs and attitudes. Such dialogue is usually pejorative, in which self-criticism is prominent and frequently based on illogic, for example, "She does not like me and therefore I am worthless and there is nothing I can do about it." A task of the therapist is to encourage clients to replace self-defeating self-talk with more constructive self-talk. See INTERNAL DIALOGUE, INTERNALIZED SPEECH, RATIONAL-EMOTIVE-BEHAVIOR THERAPY.

self-test   As used by Milton Diamond, a challenge a person gives to the self. Especially as seen among transsexuals where he (or she) is trying to convince himself he really is a male or female and should live life as a man or woman.

self-theory   1. A point of view that a personal sense of identity, worth and capacity is the key factor in personality organization and function. 2. (V. Raimy) The aspects of the total personality, such as concepts, ideas, values, kinks and quirks of any person accepted as being part of that person.

self-transcendence   A change in personal focus from preoccupation with self to attention to another person, worthy cause or other activity. Viktor Frankl maintains that deep commitment to something beyond the self is a central feature of the healthy individual. See SOCIAL INTEREST.

self-understanding   Knowing what motivates the self, awareness of why the person behaves in particular ways, etc. Sometimes known as self-awareness.

self-verbalization   (A. Ellis) Self-statements, often irrational, oral or implicit, made by people about themselves and others, that help to establish illogical self-defeating points of view. See RATIONAL-EMOTIVE BEHAVIOR THERAPY.

self-verification hypothesis   (W. B. Swann) A postulate that each person has a self-concept that he or she wishes would be accepted and validated by others, thereby confirming what he or she already knows. See PHENOMENOLOGY, SELF-CONCEPT.

self-worth   A subjective judgment or appraisal of being a worthwhile human. A person who recognizes own worth tends to also have a high degree of self-acceptance and self-esteem.

sem   (R. B. Cattell) A simple structure factor found in dynamic attitude measures: The core of the replicable "sentiment."

SEM   See STANDARD ERROR OF THE MEAN.

semanteme   A content word or phrase that expresses a single clear-cut or obvious meaning. In contrast, a morpheme is a unit used to measure linguistic connections. The phrase "can open-er-s" consists of the four indicated morphemes but only a single semanteme (idea). In contrast, a phoneme is a unit used to measure basic speech sounds of which there are approximately 32 in English. Each term, semanteme, morpheme and phoneme, refers to the smallest possible unit of its type; one person cannot speak of a "part of a semanteme."

semantic aphasia   Memory loss in which the person is unable to comprehend the meaning of words even though able to utter them. See LOGICOGRAMMATICAL DISORDERS.

semantic barrier   1. A problem in communication due to misinterpretation of the meaning of words especially if two people are angry with each other. 2. A problem in communication due to people being unaware of subtle local meanings of terms, for example, the word *fille* in French means "girl," however, can also mean "whore." A tourist calling a French girl *"fille"* in France may find that the appellation is resented. See CAUSAL ATTRIBUTION.

semantic code   The encoding of an object, idea, or impression in terms of its conceptual or abstract components; for example, if a typewriter is remembered in terms of a machine for producing printed letters on paper, a semantic code is used. Whereas if typewriter is remembered as a mental picture of its shape, an imagery code would be used. See IMAGERY CODE.

semantic component   In communication, the meaning of words, in contrast to their sounds or grammatical aspects. People make judgments about other people in terms of words used as well as sentence structure.

semantic conditioning   A form of classical conditioning in which a word, phrase, or sentence functions as a conditioned stimulus as a result of pairing with an unconditioned stimulus. For example, using young children, the Russian psychologist Volkova in 1953 pronounced the Russian word for "good" and then a second later delivered cranberry puree to the children's mouths via a chute. After a number of pairings of the word and the puree, the children salivated to the word alone. Volkova then pronounced some sentences that could be construed as possessing a "good" meaning and some that could not. She found that the children would salivate to those that implied "good" but not to those that did not.

semantic confusion Formation of unconscious bridges between words and concepts resulting in an incorrect memory, for example, saying "house" when meaning to say "hotel," or addressing "Ms. White" as "Ms. Brown." See SEMANTIC PARAPHASIA.

semantic counseling Advice in which emphasis is placed on interpretations of meanings, particularly those related to adjustment and maladjustment. See RECOVERY, INC., SEMANTIC THERAPY.

semantic dementia Inability to feel or appreciate the full meaning of emotional concepts such as love, grief, and shame. According to Harvey Cleckley, this is a major feature of the psychopathic personality.

semantic differential (test) A measure of attitudes in which a concept is rated on a series of dimensions. A technique developed by Charles Osgood for measuring the connotation of any given concept by a respondent for any given concept by rating it on a seven-point scale with reference to pairs of opposites such as strong/weak, cruel/kind, good/bad.

semantic dispersion See SEMANTIC DISSOCIATION.

semantic dissociation Confusion between symbol and meaning that results in an inability to communicate, often found in patients with schizophrenia. The three elements in such failed attempts to communicate are: (a) semantic dissolution, complete loss of meaning; (b) semantic dispersion, meaning and syntax are lost or reduced; and (c) semantic halo, coherent but ambiguous language. Sometimes known as semantic dissolution.

semantic dissolution See SEMANTIC DISSOCIATION.

semantic encoding The encoding of meaning, including the meaning of words.

semantic field Groups of words related along some dimension that gives them related meanings; for example, the words red, blue, purple, comprise a semantic field of color. Such words can only be described using other words within the same field; for example, the word "purple" can only be explained by referring to other colors.

semantic generalization Making a connection between an object (such as a bell) and a word or phrase (such as "clang" or "ting-a-ling") that symbolizes the object. See ONOMATOPOEIA, SEMANTIC CONDITIONING.

semantic halo See SEMANTIC DISSOCIATION.

semantic jargon (C. Wernicke) Receptive, or sensory aphasia. The patient utters actual words and sentences, but with defective meaning, for example, a patient said "My wires don't hire right," when asked about poor vision.

semantic memory 1. A type of long-term memory having to do with the storage of meanings. 2. A type of long-term memory for generalizations of meaning and conceptions. The organized store of all experiences on the basis of which people make immediate decisions. Also known as reference memory. See EMPIRICAL KNOWLEDGE, LEXICAL MEMORY, LONG-TERM MEMORY.

semantic network Hypothetical neural connections in the brain between words and related elements, seen as being close to each other, interconnecting with each other, or both. See ENGRAM, LONG-TERM MEMORY, NEURAL-NETWORK MODEL.

semantic paraphasia A semantic disorder in which conversational speech is fairly fluent but objects are misnamed, though some association connection may exist. A pipe may be called a "smoker," and glasses a "telescope." The condition occurs in cases of diffuse disease, confusion, drowsiness, and Korsakoff's syndrome. See PARAPHASIA, SEMANTIC CONFUSION.

semantic priming A tendency of one word to suggest another, for example, in a word-association test, "bread" is more likely to elicit the response "butter" than the response "oil." See ASSOCIATION TEST.

semantic primitive The concept that any word that involves content can be reduced to more basic terms. Thus, "bicycle" can be reduced to more primitive or basic meanings including possibly effort, moving, wheels, work.

semantic psychosis (H. Cleckley) A tendency of the antisocial person to distort the meaning of words. See PATHOLOGICAL LYING.

semantic reorganization In eclectic counseling, a technique that helps the client to express and understand feelings more effectively; it sometimes involves clarification and reflection of client statements.

semantic satiation A phenomenon, well known to lexicographers, of a common word losing its meaning or its spelling being suspected, upon being reviewed a number of times.

semantic therapy (A. A. Low) A form of psychotherapy, usually with patients with schizophrenia in remission, that focuses on the meanings or reinterpretations of words; for example, a therapist focuses on "I can't bear the pain" to show that all pains can be borne. See GENERAL SEMANTICS, RECOVERY INC.

semantically rich domains (H. A. Simon) Task domains to which belong a large amount of empirical knowledge that is potentially useful (or essential) to the solution of problems in the domain. Synonymous with knowledge-rich domains. See STRONG METHODS.

semanticity The learning of meanings of words and the process of communicating meaning through language. According to Roger Brown, it is one of the three formal properties of language. See DISPLACEMENT, PRODUCTIVITY.

semantics (M. Bréal) The study of the meanings of words and their historical development. Term replaced "semasiology." See GENERAL SEMANTICS, SEMASIOLOGY.

semantogenic disorder A chronic mental disturbance originating in a misinterpretation of the meanings of emotion-colored words.

semasiography Graphic symbols, such as the outline of a man with trouser legs spread apart or a woman wearing a dress, found on the doors of public restrooms.

semasiology The study of development and changes in the meanings of words, a branch of philology. Also known as historical semantics. See SEMANTICS.

sem(e)iology 1. The art of using and interpreting signs or sign language. 2. In medicine, the study of the meaning of symptoms of diseases. 3. In philosophy, the theory of signs and symbols; comprising syntactics, semantics, pragmatics. Also known as sem(e)iotics.

sem(e)iosis A mental or symbolic process in which something functions as a sign for the organism.

semen The fluid discharged through the penis during ejaculation, containing spermatozoa and secretions needed to sustain the viability of the spermatozoa within the female reproductive tract. The secretions originate in the prostate gland, the seminal vesicles, and other glands of the male reproductive system.

semenarche A male's first ejaculation. See SPERMARCHE.

semicircular canals Three hollow, tubular cavities located within the base of the skull, housing the vestibular apparatus of the inner ear. Each canal connects at 90° angles to the other two and is filled with fluid endolymph, allowing changes in body position to alter pressures within the system, thus imparting a sensation of spatial orientation to vestibular receptors located in the ampullae (junction points) of the three canals.

semicircular ducts Membranous tubes contained within the semicircular canals of the inner ears. They are the superior (anterior); the posterior (vertical), and the horizontal (lateral) ducts, corresponding to the bony semicircular canals. Each duct presents a dilation at one end, called the ampulla.

semiconscious Loose term applied either to an extremely low degree of attention or to subconscious or subliminal experiences. Also known as half conscious.

semi-experimental designs Research designs that are not true experimental designs because subjects cannot be, or are not, randomly assigned to groups (self-selection bias or the focus of study is a subject or organismic variable). See QUASI-EXPERIMENTS.

semi-interquartile range See INTERQUARTILE RANGE.

seminal 1. Original, the beginning of something important, such as a theory that spawns other theories or strikes out in a new direction. Term comes from the word "semen" which in Latin meant "seed." 2. Less commonly, pertaining to the seed of men, animals, or plants.

semiology 1. The study of signs and symbols and their meanings. Also spelled semeiology. See SEMIOTICS.

semiopathic (T. Burrow) Pathological use of symbols.

semiosis **sem(e)iosis**

semiotic movement A trend toward formalization of systems of visual communication by the use of signs or symbols, such as mathematical formulas, or other symbolic systems. Examples include: + (plus), < (is less than), Ψ (psychology), ☺ (have a nice day). See SEMEIOSIS.

semiotics The study and application of codes of communication that fall into two natural groups: information provided by physical behavior and information provided through the use of symbols, especially words. Animals generally either have instinctual or learned methods of communication with other animals and humans that involve noise or change in behavior. The sounds and appearance of an angry dog with the change of its body conformation and growls give clear indication of intent to attack. At a higher level, humans use signs, such as shaking the head sideways to indicate "negation" and up and down to express "affirmation" (differing in cultures) but chiefly words (differing in cultures) such as poetry to express emotions and thoughts. Also known as semeiotics. See PILOERECTION, SEMEIOSIS, SEMIOLOGY, SEMIOTIC MOVEMENT.

semipermeability Refers to the state of something, especially a membrane, that allows the passage of certain substances on a selective basis, for example, the flow of nutrients through a cell membrane. See PERMEABILITY.

semiplosive affricate

semistarvation neurosis Reactions such as those experienced by experimental participants who volunteered to live for six months on a diet typical of the famine areas during World War II. The symptom pattern consisted primarily of apathy, dejection, withdrawal, irritation, and preoccupation with food.

senescence 1. The process of growing old. 2. The period during which a person grows old. See SENILITY.

senile brain disease Degeneration of the brain in old age. See SENILE PSYCHOSES.

senile chorea Severe, progressive dyskinesia in older persons, characterized by stereotyped or disorganized movements of an involuntary nature.

senile delirium A form of senile psychosis in which the patient experiences clouding of consciousness, hallucinations, insomnia, restlessness, and wandering. The symptoms often follow a head injury, infection, or exposure to surgical anesthesia.

senile dementia A chronic brain disorder characterized by irreversible degeneration of the brain's blood vessels and generalized brain atrophy (especially frontal lobe). A syndrome of subtle onset and no specific cause, usually starting after age 65. Its principal features include gradual, progressive loss of intellectual ability, including memory, judgment, and abstract thought, together with changes in personality and behavior, such as apathy, withdrawal, and irritability. Also known as primary degenerative dementia (PDD). See ALZHEIMER'S DISEASE, DEMENTIA, PICK'S DISEASE.

senile dementia of the Alzheimer type (SDAT) Alzheimer's disease

senile deterioration A syndrome associated with the effects of aging on the brain such as due to cerebral atherosclerosis, characterized by such symptoms as memory gaps and confabulation, apathy, irritability, suspiciousness, hoarding, disorientation, attention deficits, and a tendency to wander from home.

senile plaques Areas of brain-tissue degeneration found in older persons. The plaques are composed of granular material and filaments that can be identified pathologically with a silver stain. Senile plaques are associated with symptoms of Alzheimer's disease.

senile psychoses A group of psychoses resulting primarily from degeneration of the brain in old age (senile dementia, or senile brain disease). They comprise, in order of prevalence, the simple-deterioration, paranoid, depressed and agitated, delirious and confused, and presbyophrenic types.

senilism The appearance of symptoms of senility in old age or before.

senility   Moderate-to-severe loss of physical strength and decline in mental functions such as memory, alertness, and flexible thought processes due to advanced old age. See PRIMARY DEGENERATIVE DEMENTIA, PSEUDOSENILITY.

senior citizen   Common phrase for a person who has reached the age of retirement, which, in the West, is usually 65, whether the person is retired or employed. For some purposes, such as store discounts, as young as 55.

senium praecox   Rare phrase for premature senility (usually before age 55), associated primarily with the two major forms of presenile dementia, Alzheimer's disease and Pick's disease. Also known as presenile degeneration.

senium   The period of old age.

senopia   A change in visual acuity in which the visual power of older persons returns to that of their youth.

sensate focus(ing)   Usually part of a series of exercises in sex therapy designed to train clients in receiving and giving sensual pleasure. Concentration is on feelings while touching parts of one's own body or being touched by someone else. The intent is to permit a person with sexual dysfunctions to accept and enjoy such touching as preparatory for normal sexual relations.

sensate-focus-oriented therapy   (W. H. Masters & V. Johnson) A form of therapy conducted by male-female teams in joint interviews with sexual partners. Treatment steps include a detailed history of relevant factors; a contract specifying behavior during treatment; communication improvements; prescribed body-massage exercises between the couple, first at non-erotic areas, then at erotic areas. See SENSATE FOCUS(ING).

sensate sociocultural systems   (P. Sorokin) In social systems thinking, beliefs based empiricism, encouraging social science. See IDEATIONAL SOCIOCULTURAL SYSTEMS.

sensation(s)   An irreducible unit of experience produced by stimulation of a receptor, or sense organ, and the resultant activation of a specific brain center leading to awareness of a sound, odor, color, shape, taste, temperature, pressure, pain, muscular tension, position of the body, or changes in the internal organs.

sensationalism   1. (T. Hobbes, T. Locke) A doctrine positing that all knowledge originates in sensations, that even reflective ideas and intuitions can be traced back to elementary sense impressions. Holds that there are no innate ideas. Sometimes known as sensationism. 2. Aiming for startling or exciting effects in selection or creation of works of art and literature.

sensation attributes   In structuralism, the separable aspects of sensations according to Edward Titchener: quality, intensity, clarity, duration. See STRUCTURALISM.

sensation elements   The conscious and distinct components of feelings. Edward Titchener identified 32,820 visual and 11,600 auditory sensations in his *An Outline of Psychology* (1896). See STRUCTURALISM.

sensation increment   In psychophysics, a just barely detectable increase in the intensity of a sensory experience. See DIFFERENCE LIMEN, JUST-NOTICEABLE DIFFERENCE.

sensation level (SL)   The intensity level of a particular stimulus or sensation, such as the degree of electric shock as measured in volts, or the loudness of auditory stimuli, in which case sensation level is measured in number of decibels. See BEL.

sensation level of sound (SL)   A level of sound intensity in decibels where the reference pressure is the absolute threshold for that frequency for the ideal observer.

sensation-seeking   Common phrase for the tendency of people to seek various kinds of stimulations, from simple touching and looking, to the "rush" acquired by such activities as skydiving.

sensation type   (C. G. Jung) A personality category characterized by behavior dominated by sense perception, as contrasted with thinking, feeling, and intuition. This type of person attends primarily to sensory experience or to the objects that elicit sensations for obtaining information.

sensation unit   1. A discriminable sensory experience. 2. See JUST-NOTICEABLE DIFFERENCE (J.N.D.).

sense   1. A neural organ or system. 2. A perception based on a sense-organ function. 3. A special kind of awareness; intuition, such as sixth sense. 4. A personality trait. 5. Good judgment or intelligence. 6. A consensus ("the sense of the meeting"). 7. A specific class of experiences, dependent upon a special type of receptor, or upon a specific manner of application of stimuli. Sometimes known as modality, mode. 8. Meaning ("to make sense of the dream").

sense characterizations   The senses can be separated in many ways: (a) visual (light-dark); (b) chemical (smell-gases and taste); (c) cutaneous (touch, pull, warmth, cold, pain); (d) common chemical (sensitivity to acids, alkalies, and salts); (e) hearing (sound); (f) deep senses (kinesthetic-muscle/sense-muscle contractions, movements of body parts, organic-hunger, thirst, and sex). Classifications of senses vary among experts.

sense datum/impression   A sensation or unit of information conveyed by a receptor organ. Also known as sensum.

sensed difference   A clearly perceived difference between two stimuli that are introduced simultaneously or consecutively. Above the difference limen. See DIFFERENCE LIMEN.

sense discrimination   An ability to differentiate stimuli; particularly, the degree to which a person can distinguish closely related sensory stimuli, as in differentiating among similar shades of green. Also known as sensory discrimination.

sense distance   The interval between two distinct sensations along a given dimension, such as the distance between C and G on the musical scale.

sensei   1. Japanese term for an instructor or mentor. 2. A person who supervises Morita and Naikan therapy. These kinds of therapy are philosophically oriented and senseis are not viewed as therapists but as guides or teachers.

sense experience   Awareness produced by stimulation of a sense receptor. See SPECIFIC NERVE ENERGIES.

sense feeling   Pleasant or unpleasant affect associated with a sense experience.

sense illusion   See PERCEPTUAL ILLUSION.

sense impression   See SENSE DATUM.

sense intuition   The final synthesis of sensory data in the act of perception, which results in the apprehension of external objects.

senseless learning   (G. Katona) A form of intellectual acquirement based upon rote memorization, often without understanding what is acquired; for example, a child memorized which states bounded New York, but when asked what "bounded" meant, said this was not important. It was important to know only the names of the states.

sense of coherence   (A. Antonovsky) Recognition by a person considered "normal" and "well-adjusted" of being a part of society, of having control over own destiny, of knowing "who" he or she is. A global orientation of confidence that life is meaningful, and of being capable of meeting worthwhile challenges. See SALUTOGENESIS.

sense of direction   An ability of organisms to orient themselves in relation to the points on the compass (for example in homing and migration) without the use of known receptors. Theories attempting to explain such abilities include, for example, that organisms orient themselves using certain environmental landmarks such as the sun, moon, stars, or using prevailing winds, magnetic or electrical currents. Also known as direction sense, location response.

sense of equilibrium   A sensation of and ability to maintain balance while motionless or moving, controlled by cells in the semicircular canals of the inner ear where endolymph detects motions because of the effect of gravity. Also known as labyrinthine sense, static sense, vestibular sense.

sense of guilt   Painful feelings of culpability associated with a violation of the person's moral, social, or religious code. Similar to guilt feelings.

sense of identity   Awareness of being a separate and distinct person. The first signs of a sense of identity are thought to appear when the infant experiences separation from the primary caregiver and begins to be aware of the ability to move and perceive the environment. Similar to identity. See SELF, SEPARATION-INDIVIDUATION.

sense of presence   Awareness of an invisible spirit or divine being. Typically vivid, overwhelming, and precisely localized.

sense of self   A person's feeling of identity, uniqueness, and self-direction. See SELF-IMAGE, SENSE OF IDENTITY.

sense organ   A sensory receptor and the specialized cells and associated structures that support its functions.

sense perception   The process of assimilating inputs from sense organs and interpreting the information as knowledge about objects or events.

sense process   A psychophysical operation involved in sensation. Also known as sensory process.

sense quality   A particular sensation that persists through quantitative changes such as hue or putridness.

sense-ratios method   A system of scaling sensory magnitudes by selecting stimuli that form equal ratios along the scale.

senses   Categories of sensation: audition, kinesthetic, pain, pressure, smell, taste (sometimes combined with smell and called savor), temperature (sometimes divided into cold and heat), vestibular, visual. Each sense modality has its own receptors, responds to characteristic stimuli, and has its own pathways to a special part of the brain. Notice that the senses of antiquity (hearing, sight, smell, taste, touch) have been increased to nine; the number of sense modalities depends on the precise definition of "separate receptor" and "own pathway to brain" used. Also note that a variety of other names of senses have been suggested, such as balance, direction, equilibrium, hunger, joint, light, muscular, posture, space, thirst, time, or viscera, most of which can be subsumed under the others. As in the case of instincts, more sensation-types may be suggested. Also known as sense modality. See SENSE CHARACTERIZATION.

sensibilia   (B. Russell) Summation of all sense data, evident or not evident to the individual. The plural of sensibile.

sensibility   1. A capacity to be stimulated by sensory inputs. 2. A capacity for intense feeling in contrast with cognition. T. S. Eliot claimed the first separation of feeling and thought is found in late 17th century poetry.

sensibilometer   Touch-key, in which the application of body (usually finger or hand) pressure makes the circuit.

sensible   1. Reasonable, marked by good sense or practicality. 2. Any object, or any part or aspect of an object, apprehendable directly through sensory receptors. See SENSIBILITY. 3. Conscious, free from delirium particularly following an illness.

sensible discrimination   See SENSE DISCRIMINATION.

sensing   1. Awareness of a sensation either from the environment such as an insect on the skin or from within the body such as a feeling of hunger. 2. One of Carl Jung's four basic functions of conscious experience. Sensing (that is, sense-perception) tells the person that something exists; thinking tells what it is; feeling tells whether it is agreeable or not; and intuition tells whence it comes and where it is going.

sensitive   1. Easily affected or hurt, "touchy." 2. Refers to a person who is alert to signals of various sorts from other people. 3. In parapsychology, a person who allegedly is capable of receiving supernormal messages or knowledge, that is, has extrasensory perception. See PSYCHIC.

sensitive dependence (phenomenon)   (S. Barton) A tendency for two sets of initial conditions that differ by an arbitrarily small amount at the outset, to diverge dramatically over the long range. Also known as butterfly effect. See CHAOS THEORY, NONLINEAR DYNAMICAL SYSTEMS THEORY.

sensitiveness   A psychophysical disposition marked by a low threshold for various stimuli or situations.

sensitive period/phase   The stage in development when an organism can most advantageously form specific attachments or acquire necessary skills. In humans, the first year of life is considered important for the development of a secure attachment bond or basic trust. See CRITICAL PERIOD, IMPRINTING.

sensitive soul   To the medieval Scholastic School, the kind of soul concerned with sensation. Plants have only a vegetative soul; animals also have a sensitive soul; rational animals (humans) also have an intellective soul.

sensitive zone   Any point on the body highly responsive to a particular type of stimulus, such as touch or pain.

sensitivity   1. The capacity to be receptive to stimuli. 2. Emotional and esthetic awareness; and responsiveness to the feelings of others.

sensitivity training   (K. Lewin) Activities within a training group in which participants seek to develop understanding of themselves and others in group situations. They participate as normal equals. See ACTION RE-SEARCH, ENCOUNTER GROUP, GROUP THERAPY, HU-MAN-RELATIONS TRAINING, LABORATORY TRAINING, PERSONAL-GROWTH LABORATORY, TRAINING GROUP.

sensitization   The process of becoming susceptible to a given stimulus. See SYSTEMATIC DESENSITIZATION.

sensitization period   The interval of time required for an end organ (sensory receptor) to become sensitive to a given stimulus. See REFRACTORY PERIOD.

sensitization theory   A point of view that a synapse that has been fired repeatedly eventually becomes more active or more effective in exciting the postsynaptic cell. See COVERT SENSITIZATION, NEUROBIOTAXIS.

sensor   A sense organ, or a sensitive device that responds to a particular type of energy changes.

sensorial reaction   sensory reaction

sensorimotor   Refers to a mixed nerve with both afferent and efferent fibers.

sensorimotor activity/behavior   Responses which follow directly after sensory stimulation.

sensorimotor aphasia   A combination of receptive and expressive aphasia characterized by an impairment or loss of ability to perceive and understand as well as to use language. May be acoustic, tactile, or visual, or some combination. Also known as global aphasia, total aphasia.

sensorimotor arc   A path in the conduction of neural impulses from receptor to effector. Also known as neural arc, nervous arc, reflex arc.

sensorimotor behavior   sensorimotor activity

sensorimotor cortex   Areas of the brain separated by the central fissure. The motor cortex is anterior and the somatosensory cortex is posterior to the central fissure. See BRAIN.

sensorimotor egocentrism   A form of egocentrism characteristic of Jean Piaget's sensorimotor stage, incorporating a lack of understanding that objects exist independently of personal actions and that the self is just one entity among many. See SENSORIMOTOR STAGE.

sensorimotor intelligence   1. (J. Piaget) Cognitive capacities of children during the sensorimotor stage of the first two years of life relating to the integration of sensations and motor behavior. 2. Knowledge obtained from sensory perception and motor actions about objects in the environment.

sensorimotor rhythm (SMR)   The rhythm generated by the sensorimotor area of the brain's cortex of about 12–14 Hertz (cycles per second). Also known as sensory motor rhythm.

sensorimotor stage   According to Jean Piaget, the first major stage of cognitive development, extending from birth through 18–24 months of life, characterized by development of sensory and motor processes, and by the infant's first knowledge of the world. Some rudimentary awareness of the reality of time, space, and cause and effect is present. This stage has six substages: (a) innate reflexes; (b) repetitive reflexes; (c) reproduction of events; (d) coordination of procedures; (e) discovery of new ways to achieve results; and (f) the ability to represent absent events by symbols. See CONCRETE OPERATIONAL STAGE, FORMAL OPERATIONAL STAGE, PREOPERATIONAL STAGE, SENSORIMOTOR THEORY.

sensorimotor theory   The proposal by Jean Piaget that from birth to 18–24 months of life there occurs a transformation of action into thought; at first there is a gradual shift from inborn to acquired behavior, then from body-centered to object-centered activity, ultimately permitting intentional behavior and inventive thinking. See SENSORIMOTOR STAGE.

sensorineural deafness   Absence or loss of hearing function due to pathology in the inner ear, or along the nerve pathway from the inner ear to the brainstem. Also known as hearing loss, sensorineural hearing loss. See NERVE DEAFNESS, PERCEPTIVE IMPAIRMENT AND NERVE LOSS.

sensorineural impairment   perception deafness

sensorium   1. The sensory and perceptual mechanism as a whole, involving afferent and efferent nerves as well as the brain. See CLEAR SENSORIUM, CLOUDED SENSORIUM. 2. Prior to the mid-19th century, the seat of the sense impressions in animals including humans: the brain.

sensorium commune   (Aristotle, G. Prochaska) A hypothetical seat of sensation in the central nervous system. (Aristotle as well as Juan de Vives thought this "rendezvous of sensation" was the heart.)

sensory   Pertaining to a part or all of the neural apparatus, including supporting structures, involved in the experience of sensation.

sensory acuity   An ability to react to stimuli of minimal intensity or duration, and to discriminate minimal differences among stimuli. A measure of the minimal difference for discrimination. See DIFFERENCE THRESHOLD.

sensory adaptation   1. Reduced responsiveness as a result of adaptation or modification of the receptors or fatigue of the muscles rather than to habituation. 2. The loss of a sensation due to the stimulus being continued, for example, in entering a room that has a distinctive smell; if the odor continues, after a period of time adaptation occurs and the person is no longer conscious of the smell.

sensory amimia   A communication disorder characterized by inability to interpret the gestures of others. See AMIMIA.

sensory amusia   Impairment or loss of the ability to perceive and comprehend musical tones and sequences. See AMUSIA.

sensory aphasia   Disturbance in the ability to comprehend language as a result of brain damage. Also known as receptive aphasia. See WERNICKE'S APHASIA.

sensory area/region   Any part of the cortex that receives information from the various sensory nerves. Kinds of sensory areas include auditory, somatic, olfactory, visual. See SOMATIC AREA.

sensory ataxia   An inadequate conductive capacity of the sensory nerves leading to loss of motor control.

sensory automatism   Misperceptions that may occur if a phenomenon is studied or examined for a long time, as in looking through a microscope at an inanimate item that eventually appears to move or change shape or size.

sensory awareness   An ability to perceive sense data, or stimuli, received through the sense organs, such as sights, sounds, and cutaneous sensations.

sensory-awareness   group   A human-potential group primarily concerned with increasing the members' awareness of their own feelings and the feelings of others through a variety of procedures and then reporting their feelings and bodily sensations at a given moment. See ENCOUNTER GROUP, GESTALT THERAPY, SENSORY-AWARENESS PROCEDURES.

sensory-awareness procedures   Methods used in sensate-focus and similar therapies to help people become more aware of their feelings and to accept new ways of experiencing sensations (for example, a trust exercise of closing one's eyes and falling backwards into the outstretched arms of others).

sensory capacity   An ability to receive and evaluate inputs from sense organs. Usually depends upon freedom from any impairments along the sensory pathways and proper functioning of the sense organs. An example is the visual system that depends on the eye, neural pathways and the optical centers in the brain plus those in the rest of the brain that operate top-down to restructure the primary systems.

sensory circle   The area of the skin within which two or more points of touching are felt as a single touch.

sensory conditioning   A method of developing stimuli that can be substituted for each other by repeating them as paired stimuli until either will elicit the same response.

sensory-conditioning system   A concept similar to what Ivan Pavlov called "first signaling system."

sensory conformance   In environmental psychology, a criterion of design of a living or working area, such as lighting designed to meet the optimum needs for specific visual tasks. See BEHAVIORAL FACILITATION, CONFORMANCE.

sensory conversion symptoms   One of two major categories of conversion symptoms that includes tunnel vision, anesthesias, impairment of taste or smell. The other major category is motor conversion symptoms.

sensory cortex   Parts of the cerebrum that are terminal areas for sensory pathways. See SENSORY AREA.

sensory cues   Stimuli that evoke a response or a behavior pattern.

sensory deficit   Loss, absence, or marked impairment of a normal sensory function, such as vision, hearing, or the sense of taste or touch.

sensory deprivation   1. A condition in which an organism, usually early in life, is deprived of normal sensory stimulation, which results in temporary or permanent sensory dysfunction. 2. Experimental deprivations of humans achieved by eliminating as much visual/auditory/factual stimulation as possible, usually done by placing a person in light-proof and sound-proof cubicles for extended periods. See SENSORY DEPRIVATION CHAMBER, SENSORY DEPRIVATION EFFECTS.

sensory deprivation chamber   An isolated "room" used to determine reactions of participants in complete isolation, as in underwater chambers or in light-proof and sound-proof cubicles mimicking real-life situations such as occurs in solitary confinement, deep-sea diving, or loss of eyesight.

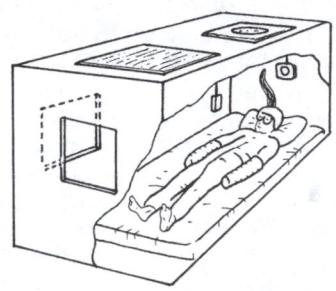

sensory-deprivation chamber   An example of one form of sensory-deprivation chamber, usually located underground. The participant is monitored by a microphone device, and is padded usually with cuffs over the arms and sometimes the legs.

sensory deprivation effects   Experiments on early sensory deprivations with animals have demonstrated strong and lasting negative effects on their later behavior. Children so deprived show serious intellectual and social deficiencies even though the explanation is uncertain. In experimental deprivations with adult humans, hallucinations, delusions, panic, hypersuggestibility, and incoherent fantasies often occur, although there is some evidence that these phenomena occur due to the artifact of suggestions by the researcher or the context (for example, visible emergency equipment in the room). Deficiency of sensory stimuli can adversely affect an organism's ability to thrive, and may also affect the organism's mental ability. See SENSORY DEPRIVATION CHAMBER for an illustration of a sensory deprivation apparatus.

sensory discrimination   sense discrimination

sensory disorder/disturbance   Anatomical or physiological abnormality that interferes with optimum transmission of information from a sense organ to its appropriate reception point in the brain or spinal cord. The abnormality may be at any point from the receptor organ to the final location in the brain for organic or psychogenic disorders of sensory functions, such as anesthesias, paresthesias, or blindness.

sensory drive   Urgent desire for a particular sensation.

sensory enrichment   Providing an organism, such as a child, with an environment filled with different elements such as music, lights, or people, considered an improvement over ordinary sensory stimulation. Among results noted is increased brain development.

sensory epilepsy   A form of psychomotor epilepsy usually caused by a temporal-lobe lesion, manifested by paresthesias of all or a part of the opposite side of the body. The seizures are manifested by hallucinations of sight, smell, or taste, and may occur without loss of consciousness.

sensory evaluations   Ratings of products such as foods or cosmetics or perfumes by their taste, color or smell.

sensory-evoked potential   An electrical potential that can be detected in the central nervous system when a sensory organ of an anesthetized animal is stimulated. The mapping of sensory-evoked potentials in the cortex helps locate sensory-projection areas for the various sense organs.

sensory exploration   A kind of behavior that appears spontaneously in animals and young children who feel, taste, or smell practically everything in their immediate environment. See CURIOSITY, MOTOR MANIPULATION.

sensory extinction   Failure to report sensory stimuli from one region when two regions are stimulated simultaneously on the same modality, even though when the region in question is stimulated by itself the stimulus is correctly reported. A defect likely to occur in occipital-parietal brain lesions.

sensory feedback   See BIOFEEDBACK.

sensory field   The totality of the stimuli that impinge on a receptor or participant at a given time.

sensory gating   Blocking one or more sensory stimuli from consciousness while focusing on one or more other stimuli, often purposefully. See GATING.

sensory homunculus   An imaginary organism drawn to the proportional scale of its tactile areas to body surface. A human would be shown with a huge nose and a small torso.

sensory homunculus hypothesis   A postulate that the behavior of an organism is determined by a cognitive agent, called the homunculus, located within the brain proper whose behavior is just as complex as is the organism's behavior that is to be explained. In sardonic drawings, the homunculus is usually a caricature of a person.

sensory illusion   See PERCEPTUAL ILLUSION.

sensory inattention   An observation used in neurological examinations: Inability to perceive a stimulus applied to one part of the body when an identical stimulus is applied to a corresponding part of the body on the opposite side. Such failure occurs for the side of the body opposite a brain lesion. Also known as perceptual rivalry. See SENSORY EXTINCTION.

sensory-information store (SIS)   An extremely short period of "seeing," "hearing," or "feeling" a no-longer-active stimulus, as though it were still there. Also known as sensory memory.

sensory information tasks   Laboratory activities yielding information about the status of an individual's sensory system, such as measures of vision, smell, and taste.

sensory input   Stimulation of a sensory organ, causing an impulse to travel to its appropriate destination in the brain or the spinal cord.

sensory integration   (H. Birch, M. Bitterman) A concept that simultaneous or contiguous stimulation of two different sensory modalities may result in the activation of one of them when the other is activated.

sensory-integrative functioning   Normal neural processes involved in perceiving and evaluating sensory inputs from the environment before responsive impulses are transmitted through the motor nerves. Most bodily activities require a combination of motor and sensory-integrative functioning.

sensory interaction   Integration of sensory processes in performing a task, as in listening to a lecture while looking at the blackboard's illustrations.

sensory isolation   A situation in which sensory stimulation is reduced greatly. Animals so isolated as infants do not recover full abilities. Humans under such conditions, as in long-term prison, tend to experience a variety of sensory deficits, hallucinations, etc. See SENSORY DEPRIVATION, SOCIAL-ISOLATION SYNDROME.

sensory limen/threshold   See ABSOLUTE THRESHOLD, DIFFERENCE THRESHOLD.

sensory memory   A memory that lasts about a half second for vision and about two seconds for audition. Permits humans not to recognize that movies or television are a series of still pictures but get the impression of continuous movement and this kind of memory makes sounds such as speech or music seem seamless. See SENSORY-INFORMATION STORE, SHORT-TERM MEMORY.

sensory modalities   1. In reaction-time experiments, the phrase applies to a particular reaction-response type of motor set or readiness. The other two types are mixed and motor. See REACTION TYPE, RESPONSE TYPE. 2. More generally, the specific senses involved such as visual and auditory in a warning to yield to a police car.

sensory-motor memory   1. Fragments of physical and emotional experiences that cannot be accounted for by organic illness, current situations, thought patterns, or all three. These recollections may be seen as a dissociated aspect or representation of a traumatic experience. Also known as body memories, somatic memories. 2. Memory of what some motor activity felt like, for example, remembering riding a bicycle as the muscle movements in the legs.

sensory nerve/neuron   A nerve or bundle of neurons that carry impulses from a receptor to the central nervous system. See AFFERENT FIBERS, NEURON.

sensory organization   The process of organizing nerve impulses from receptors into a meaningful perception.

sensory overloading   A situation or experience in which many diverse stimuli (for example, verbal, visual, tactile) are simultaneously impinging on an organism, more than the organism can deal with. See DISPLAY, SENSORY DEPRIVATION, STRESS.

sensory pathway   A route followed by nerve impulses traveling from sense-organ receptors to sensory areas of the brain or other points in the body.

sensory polyneuropathy   Nervous-system disorder that occurs almost exclusively in cases of bronchogenic (of bronchial origin) cancer. Eventually, the patient loses all sensation.

sensory preconditioning   An unintended situation when a particular stimulus that was associated with the intended conditioned stimulus generates the same response as the conditioned stimulus. See SENSORY INTEGRATION.

sensory-projection area   A region of the cerebral cortex where afferent fibers from sense organs terminate.

sensory psychophysiology   The study of the functioning of the sensory system.

sensory reaction/response   A reaction in which the participant's attention during the preparatory period is directed to the stimulus rather than to the response. Also known as sensorial reaction/response.

sensory reaction type   See REACTION TYPE, SENSORY MODALITIES, SENSORY REACTION/RESPONSE.

sensory reactor   (A. A. Lazarus) A person who responds to the world mostly in terms of the basic senses, thereby reducing (but sometimes triggering accentuated responses in) imagination and feelings.

sensory region   sensory area

sensory register   A storage location that briefly retains a fairly complete representation of sensory stimulation.

sensory response type   See REACTION TYPE, SENSORY MODALITIES, SENSORY REACTION/RESPONSE.

sensory root   An area of the spinal cord where sensory-nerve fibers enter the cord on either side of the vertebral column, between the vertebrae. As the fibers approach the cord, they come together as a single nerve representing all the sensory receptors for one body segment.

sensory-seeking motive   In search for an emotional "high" (a combination of excitement and fear) people do dangerous things such as skydive, scale cliffs, race motorcycles, and other evidently dangerous behaviors. See THRILL.

sensory self-stimulation   Stimulating sensory areas of the cortex by a device controlled by the subject that completes an electrical circuit with electrodes implanted in the brain. See SELF-STIMULATION MECHANISM.

sensory spots   Skin spots or locations of high sensitivity to tactile, thermal, or pain stimuli.

sensory stimulation   Arousal of a sense organ by physical energy, such as light waves, sound waves or odors.

sensory stimuli   Stimuli that produce responses directly without the mediation of cognitive elements such as ideas.

sensory summation   Increased experience of sensation by either spatial or temporal neural combinations leading to experiencing sensations to a greater degree than otherwise would be the case.

sensory system   The total structure involved in sensation, including sense organs, afferent nerves, and sensory areas in the cerebral cortex in which these tracts terminate.

sensory tests   Means of measuring various sensory abilities, such as visual acuity, depth perception, color discrimination, and auditory acuity. See COLOR WHEEL, HOWARD-DOLMAN APPARATUS, SNELLEN CHART.

sensory threshold   See ABSOLUTE THRESHOLD, DIFFERENCE THRESHOLD.

sensory transduction   The process by which physical energy (for example, sound waves) is transformed into sensory experiences. See INFORMATION PROCESSING.

sensual   Refers to satisfaction obtained from indulging or overindulging in activities that involve the appropriate senses, for example, sex or food.

sensual pleasure   A pleasant affective experience due directly to sensory stimuli, for example, smelling a fragrant flower.

sensum   sense-datum

sensuous   Refers to the sensory aspect of an experience or something capable of arousing and enhancing the senses. Coined by John Milton to avoid the overindulgent implication of the word sensual.

sensus communis   (binding of senses—Latin) Phrase used by Aristotle for an aspect of functioning which integrates the various sense modalities and enables a person to perceive such complex interacting qualities as unity, motion, rest, time, and shape. Aristotle thought the integrating organ was the heart. See COMMON SENSE.

sentence-completion test (SCT)   (A. F. Payne, A. D. Tendler) A projective technique in which the person is to complete an unfinished sentence by filling in the missing word or phrase, for example, "Late at night I usually feel_____." Also known as incomplete-sentence test. See ROTTER INCOMPLETE SENTENCE BLANK.

sentence-repetition test   An examination in which the participant must repeat sentences of increasing difficulty and complexity directly after the examiner reads them, found in some intelligence tests, such as the Stanford-Binet.

sentience   1. A state of mind ready to receive sensations. 2. The simplest or most primitive form of cognition, or pure sensing without thinking.

sentience need   (H. A. Murray) The desire, urge, motivation, to enjoy sights, sounds, and other sensuous experiences.

sentiendum   Any elementary qualitative feature of perceptible objects.

sentient   The awareness capacity of an organism: ability to sense a stimulus or to know that the organism has responded to a stimulus. Whereas humans are considered to be sentient, animals, especially mammals are also considered to be sentient. However, the distinction becomes increasingly less clear if organisms such as plants, earthworms, and amoebas have such ability.

sentiment   Attitude or expression of soft, gentle, subdued emotions.

sentimentality   Overindulgence in emotional display especially that connected with love or pity.

separate ova   Two or more gametes released from the ovary, or ovaries, at the same time. Fertilization of the separate ova results in multiple births of nonidentical individuals. See DIZYGOTIC TWINS.

separation anxiety 1. The normal alarm or fear in a young child separated or facing the prospect of separation from the primary caregiver. Usually first noted at six months and is most active between six and ten months. 2. Fear or concern about being removed from an object or person of emotional attachment or fear that such will leave. If excessive fear exists, neurotic attachment is indicated. See SEPARATION DISTRESS, SEPARATION-ANXIETY DISORDER.

separation distress Discomfort and anxiety felt by infants when they lose contact with their attachment figure, usually the mother or mother surrogate. See SEPARATION ANXIETY.

separation-anxiety disorder A pathological condition demonstrated by excessive dependency on either persons or places, with fear of moving away from what is considered to be a safe place. See SCHOOL PHOBIA, SCHOOL REFUSAL.

separation-individuation Phrase used by Margaret Mahler for the process in which the infant gradually differentiates self from the mother and attains the relatively autonomous status of a toddler.

seppuko Japanese term for ritual suicide. Also known as hara-kari.

sept A subdivision of a clan or a segment of a larger family unit. A clan may be composed of several septs affiliated through a common interest rather than a common ancestor.

septal area Forebrain nuclei of the limbic system that separate the lateral ventricles of the brain. In humans and other primates they are a ventral continuation of the septum pellucidum. Neurons of the medial septal nuclei provide cholinergic input to the hippocampus. The lateral septal nuclei receive input from the hippocampus. The septal nuclei also interconnect with the hypothalamus and other subcortical sites via the medial forebrain bundle. Damage to the septal area results in a temporary display of aggressive behavior and impairments in some types of learning. See BRAIN for an illustration.

septal region of the brain See SEPTAL AREA.

septicaemia psychosis Toxic psychosis associated with a severe infection and characterized primarily by delirium.

septum Partition or wall.

septum lucidum Old name for septum pellucidum.

septum pellucidum A triangular two-layer membrane separating the two lateral ventricles. Communicates with the corpus callosum (above) and the body of the fornix (below). Also known as pellucid septum, septum lucidum. See SEPTAL AREA.

septum transversum A ridge in the wall of the ampullae of the semicircular canals, which contains the nerve endings.

sequelae Residual effects of an illness or injury, particularly effects in the form of impairment, such as paralysis that is the sequela of an episode of poliomyelitis. Singular is sequela.

sequence The temporal order in which a series of events occurs. See DEVELOPMENTAL SEQUENCE.

sequence effects In multiple-treatment research designs, several treatments may be presented to participants, for example, treatments A-B-C for some participants, B-C-A for other participants, and so on for other combinations. If different sequences yield different outcomes, this is known as a sequence effect. See ORDER EFFECTS.

sequence preference A tendency to respond in a particular direction or distinctive manner, for example, the initial tendency of an experimental animal to make right turns first and then to alternate left and right turns; on entering a large room, always walking on the left side.

sequential analysis 1. Decisions made in sequences or separate steps, usually at each step of a procedure, to determine the acceptability of the data. 2. A group of statistical procedures including stepwise regression, stepwise discriminant analysis, and hierarchical analysis. 3. Research strategies designed to investigate cause-and-effect relations in social behavior by noting the behavior, as well as the temporal sequencing of the behaviors. Also known as sequential sampling.

sequential design(s) (K. W. Schaie) The simultaneous analysis of two or more cross-sectional, longitudinal, or time-lag sequences, in developmental psychology. A research design in which persons of different but overlapping ages are observed and tested usually for a number of years. By studying several individuals of overlapping ages, this design reduces the amount of time required by a longitudinal study while improving generalizability. In addition, the design provides greater depth than a cross-section approach.

sequential development See GENERAL-TO-SPECIFIC SEQUENCE, INDIVIDUATION.

sequential learning 1. Acquisition of knowledge or skill which calls for information to be acquired stepwise in a specified order, each increment of information must be mastered in its entirety before the next increment may be attempted. For example, the Keller Plan for college courses. 2. Occasional synonym for chaining or chained responses. 3. Particularly in pre-1950 use, a synonym for serial anticipation learning.

sequential marriage Having a number of legal mates, one at a time. In many societies, this is permitted if the mate is dead; in some it is not permitted if the mate is still alive, and in some, a series of marriages is permitted given interposed divorces.

sequential memory Remembrances of the proper order of things or concepts. Also known as serial memory.

sequential processing In information processing theory, a capacity to solve problems in a stepwise fashion. See SIMULTANEOUS PROCESSING.

sequential sampling sequential analysis

sequential test An examination to determine when the point has been reached where the addition of further data is probably unnecessary for a given level of statistical significance.

sequestration A process of separating the unacceptable or pathological aspects of a personality from the normal parts, as when patients unable to control impulses isolate themselves from such impulses and eventually become unaware of them; convicted criminals who admitted guilt to a crime may later convince themselves of their innocence.

serendipitous findings   (W. B. Cannon) In research, while looking for evidence of a particular hypothesis, finding evidence for something else. See NORMATIVE SURVEY.

serendipity   (H. Walpole) The faculty for making fortunate discoveries by accident; the knack of finding something valuable while looking for something else. Often considered a characteristic of a creative scientist.

serial act   A set of actions that occur in sequence, each being cues for the following action.

serial anticipation   A learning method in which items are arranged in a series and the participant must anticipate the next item in the series. See ANTICIPATION LEARNING METHOD, SERIAL LEARNING METHOD.

serial anticipation (learning) method   anticipation method

serial association   A learning technique in which verbal items are teamed in a specific order.

serial behavior/response   An integrated sequence of responses that elicit the next in fixed order, as in playing music. The individual responses that comprise the sequence are referred to as serial responses.

serial conduction   See PARALLEL CONDUCTION.

serial discrimeter   An apparatus that presents a new stimulus for a discrimination response when a desired response to the preceding stimulus is made. See MEMORY DRUM for a machine of this general type.

serial discriminator   psychoergograph

serial exhaustive search   A complete search of the elements in working memory, presumably one item at a time.

serial-exploration method   A psychophysical method used in determining the smallest difference that can be perceived. Synonym for the method of limits.

serial interpretation   A technique in which an analyst studies a series of consecutive dreams, which may provide clues that would be overlooked in interpreting a single, isolated dream.

serialization   The process of organizing objects along a quantified dimension, for example, by weight, size, or volume.

serial-killer   (R. Ressler) A person with a pattern of murdering others in specific and often unusual manners. See DISORGANIZED SERIAL-KILLER, ORGANIZED SERIAL-KILLER.

serial learning   A technique for measuring associative learning in which a participant is given the first item in a previously learned list of items (digits, syllables, or words) and asked to produce each successive item of the serial learning list on the basis of the item immediately preceding it. Each response elicits (becomes a stimulus for) the next response in the series. Also known as serial-order learning. See SERIAL ANTICIPATION.

serial learning list   See SERIAL LEARNING.

serial-learning task   (H. Ebbinghaus) Asking a participant to memorize a list of items in a particular order. Research in memory is often based on serial learning tasks, usually by having a participant memorize a series of nonsense syllables to some particular level, such as repeating the whole list without error three consecutive times; later checking to determine how many trials are needed to relearn the whole list to the prior extent. See SAVINGS SCORE, SERIAL-POSITION EFFECT.

serial lists   See SERIAL LEARNING.

serial memorization   See ANTICIPATION LEARNING METHOD.

serial memorization list   A serial learning list. See SERIAL LEARNING.

serial memory task   (H. Ebbinghaus) The ability of a person to recall a list of information in the order in which it was originally presented. Also known as sequential memory. See MEMORY DRUM.

serial-memory search   A retrieval process in which each item in short-term memory is examined by the retriever in the order in which it was encoded.

serial method   In experimental research, the method of presenting stimuli successively, as distinguished from simultaneous presentation. See SERIAL LEARNING, SERIAL MEMORY, SERIAL-POSITION CURVE.

serial polygamy   Sequential marriage.

serial position   See SERIAL-POSITION EFFECT.

serial-position curve   In memory research, in which a list of items is presented and then an attempt is made to recall them, the plot of percent recalled against the serial position in which the item was presented in the list. See NONSENSE SYLLABLES, SERIAL-POSITION EFFECT.

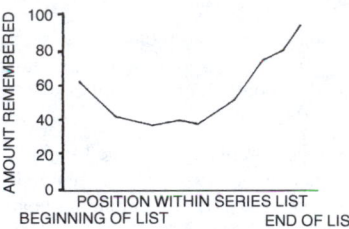

serial-position curve   This general U-shaped curve indicates that on studying a series of items and trying to remember them, both the last and the first items are best remembered, with those in the middle least remembered.

serial-position effect   In serial learning tasks, the effect of an item's position on how well or how fast it is learned, for example, usually the first and last items are best recalled with the last a bit better than the first, the greatest number of errors occur just after the mid-point when all items are equally difficult.

serial processing (theory)   A theory of information processing stating that rapid shifting between different information sources accounts for the apparent ability to carry on separate cognitive functions simultaneously. Holds that two sets of stimuli cannot be processed simultaneously. Also known as intermittent processing, sequential processing. See PARALLEL PROCESSING.

serial program   (H. A. Murray) A set of planned subgoals leading to the final goal.

serial reaction   continuous-discrimination reaction

serial recall   In memory research, presenting a series of items, such as nonsense syllables, and asking participants to recall them in the same order that they were presented. See FREE RECALL, SERIAL MEMORY, SERIAL-POSITION EFFECT.

serial reinforcement   1. The process of reinforcing selected responses during serial learning. 2. A technique used to test memory in which each correct response increases the probability of the next correct response occurring.

serial response   See SERIAL BEHAVIOR.

seriation   Arrangement of unorganized material or information into an orderly series that aids in the understanding of relationships between events; useful for analysis and interpretation.

series   An arrangement of items in some logical manner, such as children by age or books by content, magazines by date of publication so that identifying numbers can be assigned to them.

sermon fear   See HOMILOPHOBIA.

serotonergic neuron   A nerve that contains serotonin or is activated by the substance. While these neurons number only in a few hundred thousand (less than one-millionth of all neurons), they project fibers to virtually all parts of the central nervous system with each neuron influencing as many as 500,000 target neurons. They are involved in regulation of body temperature, respiration, eating and sleeping. Also spelled serotoninergic neuron. See SEROTONIN.

serotonin (5HT)   A neurotransmitter with a more specific chemical name of 5-hydroxy-tryptamine, and often abbreviated as 5HT; this substance has become focus of a great deal of attention following the introduction of the new antidepressants such as Prozac. Brain levels of serotonin have been associated with psychiatric symptoms such as depression, bulimia, aggressiveness, obsessions and compulsions. Serotonin is derived from the essential amino acid tryptophan and found in the blood, nerve cells, and other tissues. Serotonin functions as a smooth-muscle stimulator, a constrictor of blood vessels, and inducer of nightly sleep.

serotoninergic neuron   **serotonergic neuron**

serotonin receptors   Receptors for serotonin found in the brain and in peripheral areas. Some brain serotonin receptors are blocked by lysergic acid diethylamide and some are not. One type of brain serotonin receptor also mediates postsynaptic potentials whereas the other kind does not. Different types of serotonin receptors also are found in the smooth muscles of the intestine.

serotonin reuptake inhibitors (SRIs)   A class of medicines that is widely prescribed as antidepressants. Prozac was the first, introduced in the mid-1980s; several others have followed. Used for treating depression, and also in the treatment of obsessive-compulsive disorder (OCD), bulimia, and other conditions. Also known as selective serotonin reuptake inhibitors (SSRIs).

Serpasil   Trade name for reserpine, one of the oldest major tranquilizers.

serviceable duration   **useful duration**

servomechanism   A goal-directed, error-sensitive, self-correcting machine with four basic processes: Input, throughput, output, feedback (for example, a torpedo that uses stimuli from the target as well as information from its own output to stay on course). Also known as servo system.

SES   See SOCIOECONOMIC STATUS.

SES levels   Refers to the socio-economic status of a person or sample, and is usually measured by obtaining the prestige of the occupations, levels of education, and income levels in a given society.

sessile   Characterizing organisms fixed in location, that is, which lack active or adequate locomotor organs (for example, trees and clams).

SET   1. See SELF-INSTRUCTIONAL TRAINING. 2. See STUDENTS' EVALUATION OF TEACHING.

set   1. A fixed pattern of behavior or responses, such as a predictable sequence of motor-neuron activity. 2. Temporary readiness to respond in a certain way to a specific situation or stimulus, for example, a motorist gets set to move ahead when the traffic light changes; a sleeping parent is set to awaken when the baby cries; a tennis player is set to respond to the movement of a ball. 3. A temporary tendency to respond in a certain way due to recent experiences, labeled *Einstellung* by the Gestaltists, and summarized by the statement "practice makes blindness" (for example, persons shown a sequence of letters such as D, P, and E, tend to perceive an ambiguous figure as a B, whereas persons shown a sequence of numbers such as 38, 52, and 74, tend to perceive the figure as a 13; participants who have used a particular pattern to solve a series of similar problems do not see a simpler solution on a later problem). 4. In statistics, a group or series of objects or ideas. See EINSTELLUNG EFFECT, WATER-JUG PROBLEMS.

set point   The point at which an individual organism's weight "thermostat" is set. When the body falls below this weight, changes in hunger and metabolic rate usually act to restore the lost weight. See APPESTAT.

set-up   Slang for the configuration of instruments or apparatus as arranged and adjusted for the investigation of a given experimental problem.

set weight   For any organism, a hypothetical ideal weight established via heredity. See APPETITIVE CENTER.

SEU   subjective expected utility

seven plus or minus two   (G. Miller) The limits of short-term memory chunks that the mind can hold at any time. The preferred name of this concept is magical number seven plus or minus two.

seventh cranial nerve   See FACIAL NERVE.

severe mental retardation   A category of mental retardation characterized by having a mental age of three or less (adult intelligence quotient—IQ below 20). Such persons cannot dress themselves nor control their bowels and were once known as vegetative idiots.

sex   1. Physical and mental traits that distinguish between male and female. 2. Physiological and psychological processes related to procreation and erotic pleasure. See SEX VS GENDER.

sex adjustive gender coding   See SEX CODING.

sex adventitious gender coding   See SEX CODING.

sex-appropriate behavior   See SEX-TYPING.

sex assignment   **gender assignment**

sex change   The surgical alteration of external gender characteristics to make them resemble as closely as possible the physical traits of the preferred gender (other sex), usually accompanied by hormone treatments. The changes are limited to external appearances (secondary sexual characteristics) and do not affect the person's inherent reproductive role or genotype. See ASSIGNED GENDER, CROSS-GENDER BEHAVIOR, PSEUDOHERMAPHRODISM, TRANSGENDERISM TRANSSEXUALISM.

sex characteristics   Primary sexual characteristics include structures directly involved in reproduction of the species, for example, gonads. Secondary sexual characteristics are overt physical features not directly concerned with reproduction, such as the presence or absence of facial hair, voice quality, and size of breasts.

sex chromatin   A mass observed in the nucleus of tissue cells of females during interkinesis. The substance represents X—chromosome material not involved in tissue-cell metabolism. The presence of sex chromatin in tissue cells is generally regarded as proof of the sexuality of females. Also known as Barr body.

sex-chromosomal aberrations   Structural or functional disorders, or both, associated with the complete or partial absence of a sex chromosome or with extra sex chromosomes. Examples: pseudohermaphroditism with XX and XY mosaicism; Klinefelter's syndrome (XXY); Turner's syndrome (XO, missing the second chromosome); and males with XYY sex-chromosome combinations rather than a normal XY complement.

sex chromosomes   The X and Y chromosomes that carry traits identifying males and females. See SEX DETERMINATION.

sex counseling   A form of guidance provided to sex partners about matters such as impotence, frigidity, birth control, infertility, and general feelings of inadequate sexual performance.

sex derivative gender coding   See SEX CODING.

sex determination   A genetic mechanism that determines the gender of offspring. In humans, a fertilized egg (zygote) with two X chromosomes becomes a female, and such an egg with one X and one Y becomes a male. The XX or XY constitute one of 23 pairs of human chromosomes.

sex differentiation   The process of acquiring sex-distinctive features (internal gonads, external genitals, brain structure) during development in the womb, which is largely controlled by hormones. Anatomical differences do not begin to appear until the seventh week of fetal development. See SEX HORMONES.

sex discrimination   **gender discrimination**

sex distribution/ratio   The proportion of male and female persons in a sample, such as infants born in a given population. The average gender distribution is about 106 males per 100 females at birth; because of higher mortality ratio of males, the proportion becomes reversed in later life.

sex drive   The primary impulse directed to sexual gratification. See SEXUAL DRIVE.

sex education   A formal course of instruction in reproductive processes that often includes psychological and social aspects in addition to the physiological.

sex fear   See COITOPHOBIA, CYPRIDOPHOBIA, EROTOPHOBIA, GENOPHOBIA.

sex feeling   A pleasurable feeling associated with coitus or other erotic contact.

sex flush   A rash-like redness of the skin that appears on the chest, breasts, or both, during sexual arousal; more common in women.

sex hormones   The hormones (chemical messengers) that stimulate various reproductive functions. Primary sources of the sex hormones are the pituitary gland and the male and female gonads. Sex hormones include: androgens (including androsterone), crystalline androgenic steroids (including testosterone), crystalline steroids (including progesterone), estrogenic steroids (estrone, estriol, estradiol), and proteohormones (including prolactin).

sex hygiene   Health-maintenance procedures, including prevention of getting venereal diseases.

sex identification   The gradual adoption of the attitudes and behavior patterns associated with one or the other gender. Confusion about sexual identity may give rise to psychological problems. There has been dispute (for example, between Laurence Kohlberg and Sandra Bem) about whether physical sex differences are noticed before psychological or social gender differences. See SEX ROLES, SISSY, TOMBOYISM.

sex identity   1. An individual's biologically determined sexual state. 2. The internal sense of maleness or femaleness. See GENDER IDENTITY, SEXUAL IDENTITY.

sex-influenced character/gene   An inherited trait dominant in one gender but recessive in the other (for example, male pattern baldness).

Sex Information and Education Council of the United States (SIECUS)   A nonprofit health organization whose aim is to establish human sexuality as a health entity, identifying the special characteristics that distinguish human sexuality from human reproduction, as well as to promote responsible sex as a creative and recreative force.

sex instincts   Erotic drives and, in psychoanalytic theory, sublimations of these drives; manifestations may involve the channeling of erotic, or libidinal, energy into artistic and scientific pursuits. Also known as sexual instincts.

sex interest   Readiness to engage or participate in sexual discussions, viewing, or other activities related to or leading to sexual contact.

sex irreducible gender coding   See SEX CODING.

sexism   Prejudicial beliefs and practices directed against women; only rarely refers to prejudice against men. A primary factor in sex discrimination.

sex-limited   Characteristic of a trait or anomaly that affects one sex only.

sex-linked characteristic/trait   An inherited trait (for example, hemophilia, red-green color blindness) carried in the sex chromosomes (Y and X chromosomes) and thus is linked with the gene that determines sex.

sex-negative   Describing cultures that take a restrictive view of sexual matters outside of procreative marital coitus.

sex object   A person, animal, or inanimate object toward which sexual energy is directed.

sex offender (S.O.)   A person who has been convicted of committing a sex act prohibited by law. Not necessarily a sexual deviate or psychologically disturbed individual since local laws may ban fornication, obscenity, foreplay, or discussing the "facts of life" with children, which in different cultures or communities may considered noncriminal events.

sex offenses   Erotic acts prohibited by laws, for example, in most countries of the western world, forcible and statutory rape, incest, adultery, prostitution, pimping, bestiality, and forcible sexual assault without coitus. See MOLESTATION.

sexological examination   The scientific study of a person's sexual behavior in terms of physiological, psychological, sociological factors and influences.

sexology   The study of human and animal sexual behavior in all aspects, overt and covert. See AMERICAN ACADEMY OF CLINICAL SEXOLOGY, SEX INFORMATION AND EDUCATION COUNCIL OF THE UNITED STATES.

sex perversion   Any sexual practice regarded by the community or subculture as an abnormal means of achieving orgasm or sexual arousal. In some cultures, sexual perversion is applied to any practice other than penile-vaginal intercourse. See PARAPHILIAS.

sexploitation   Slang for the exploitation of sex by advertising, the media, television and movies.

sex preselection   Predetermination of the gender of offspring through sex-control technology.

sex ratio   **sex distribution**

sex reassignment   **gender reassignment**

sex rehabilitation   Restoration of ability to perform sexual activity following correction of a dysfunction, such as impotence or rape-trauma syndrome.

sex reversal   1. A procedure in which the physical features of one gender are established in a pseudohermaphrodite, usually by surgery supported by hormones and other techniques. 2. Any sex change; any surgical, chemical, psychological program of changing apparent males to females or vice versa. See SEX CHANGE.

sex rivalry   1. Any behavior that results from favoring one gender as superior to the other. 2. The competition between a parent and child of the same gender for the affections of the other parent.

sex roles   Behavior and attitudinal patterns characteristically associated with masculinity and femininity as defined in a given society. See GENDER IDENTITY.

sex-role inversion   An abnormal behavior pattern marked by females acting masculinely and males acting femininely. See SISSY BEHAVIOR, TOMBOYISM.

sex-role stereotypes   Fixed, simplified concepts of the traits and behavior patterns thought within a culture to be typical of each gender. See BERDACHE.

sex selection   1. Choosing a mate for the purpose of producing offspring to continue the survival of the species. Among animals and many humans, the process tends to favor selection of mates with traits attractive to members of the other gender. 2. Selecting the sex of offspring, as through selective abortions.

sex sensations   Visual, auditory, tactile, taste, odor (or pheromone) stimulation that leads to heightened sex interest.

sex service   See PROSTITUTION.

sex-shared gender coding   See SEX CODING.

sex therapy   The treatment of psychosexual disorders with techniques that vary with the problem and its severity. Generally requires psychological treatment, often including behavior-therapy methods, as well as correction of misinformation and teaching the patient the basic facts about sex anatomy, physiology, and sexual techniques. See SENSATE-FOCUS-ORIENTED THERAPY.

sex trauma   Any disturbing experience associated with sexual activity. Rape, incest, and other sexual offenses may be a cause of trauma for people of both genders and all ages. Some research speculates that the reactions of adults, such as parents, to what has occurred to their children, can sometimes harm the children as much as the actual sexual event.

sex-typing   1. Any form of behavior or any attitude regarding appropriate male and female behavior. 2. The labeling process whereby certain characteristics or responses are categorized as masculine or feminine in accordance with prevailing gender-role stereotypes. See FEMALENESS, FEMININE ATTITUDE, FEMININE IDENTIFICATION, FEMININITY, MALENESS, MASCULINE ATTITUDE, MASCULINE-FEMININE SCALE, MASCULINE-FEMININE TESTS, MASCULINE IDENTITY, MASCULINITY.

sexual abuse   1. Biased behavior toward anyone based on sex or gender. 2. Mutilations, such as clitoral ("female") circumcision. 3. Rape and other violent or degrading behaviors, such as sexual harassment, usually by men directed toward women, children, or both. 4. Improper behavior toward a child in terms of sexual subject matter that would be considered (a) behavior suitable only between consenting adults or (b) behavior illegal for adults. What constitutes sexual abuse differs between (and among) societies and also in historical context; for example, currently, female clitoridectomy is performed in various parts of the world as part of the culture's tradition. Historically, boys were sodomized with general approval in certain cultures.

sexual abusers   People who abuse others sexually. See FREE WILL, PEDOPHILIA.

sexual adjustment   The establishment of a satisfactory relationship with sexual partner or partners.

sexual anesthesia   Absence of normal sensation associated with coitus. Usually psychogenic and associated with earlier unpleasant sexual experiences. Evidence of the functional nature of sexual anesthesia is noted in the fact that most such people report they obtain pleasure by masturbation. See FRIGIDITY.

sexual anomaly   A congenital or developmental abnormality of the reproductive system, such as the presence of both male and female gonads in an infant. See PSEUDOHERMAPHRODISM.

sexual arousal   Stimulation and arousal of the reproductive organs by mental influences such as dreams or fantasies, or by environmental factors such as erotic odors, pornographic art or movies, or by physical contact. See SEXUAL-RESPONSE CYCLE.

sexual assault   Forced participation of an unwilling person in sexual activity by the use of physical violence or by threats. May involve actual physical contact, such as rape, undesired touching, or menacing words, or action such as indecent exposure.

sexual attitude reassessment (SAR) workshop   A workshop designed to reduce sexual inhibition, facilitate communication, and provide basic information. Typically intensive, multimedia, and lasting a day to a week. Also known as sexual attitude restructuring.

sexual attitudes   Beliefs about sexual activities and roles.

sexual aversion disorder   Persistent or recurrent aversion to and avoidance of all or almost all genital contact with a partner, and sometimes of all sexual activity.

sexual battery   Sexual assault with actual physical contact.

sexual behavior   A pattern of activity related to reproduction of the species or to sensual stimulation for pleasurable satisfaction with or without the objective of reproduction. May include some form of courtship, postural accommodations for intercourse, and genital reflexes. In some species, sexual behavior may occur only at certain seasons in certain locations or at specific stages of estrus cycles. The onset of sexual behavior in humans usually occurs during puberty.

sexual bimaturism   In animals, differences between ages for males and females when sexual maturation occurs.

sexual burnout   Boredom with the same sexual routine, marked by a sense of physical depletion and emotional emptiness, a negative self-concept, and no or little interest in the sexual partner.

sexual curiosity   Typical interest about sexual matters. See PARAPHILIA.

sexual delusion   A false belief or interpretation maintained despite evidence to the contrary regarding personal sexual identity, appearance, practices, or attitudes.

sexual development   Progressive steps toward sexuality, including attitudes and behavior as well as physical characteristics, usually from infancy through puberty. See PSYCHOSEXUAL DEVELOPMENT.

sexual deviancy/deviation   Any sexual behavior regarded as significantly different from the standards of acceptability established by a local culture or subculture. Deviant forms of sexual behavior involve atypical functions, objects, or frequencies, including voyeurism, fetishism, bestiality, necrophilia, transvestism, sadism, and exhibitionism. In the Shaker subculture, all sexual activity was considered deviant. See NYMPHOMANIA, PARAPHILIAS, PERVERSION, SATYRIASIS.

sexual dimorphism   The relative differences between males and females of any species. In some cases, males and females are of equal size and appearance; in others, males and females differ in size and appearance, for example, in peafowl, the (male) peacock is large and colorful, whereas the (female) peahen is small and plainly colored.

sexual disorders   Any physical or psychological impairment of the ability to perform coitus. Phrase usually is applied to functional disorders, such as impotence or frigidity, but not to behaviors such as rape, incest, sadism, or sodomy.

sexual drive   Primary impulse directed to sexual gratification and, ultimately, to reproduction. Unlike other drives described as primary, such as hunger and thirst, an individual organism's survival does not depend on sex, though survival of the species does. Sexual drive is affected by early experiences, instructions by others, and external stimulation. In humans this drive is less seasonal, less dependent on the estrous cycle, more varied in expression, more subject to cortical control, and aroused by a wider variety of stimuli than in the "lower" species. Sometimes known as sex drive. See INSTINCTS.

sexual dysfunction   Lack or loss of ability to participate in typical sexual activity, such as coitus. Causes of sexual dysfunction may be psychological or physiological, or both.

sexual end-pleasure   A sensation complex associated with the climax of sexual intercourse at the stage of orgasm.

sexual erethism   An abnormal state of heightened sexual excitement. Sometimes known as hyperhedonia.

sexual fantasy   An erotic fantasy that may precede or accompany sexual behavior. Also known as copulation fantasy.

sexual functioning   1. Performance of intercourse. 2. Capability of performing intercourse.

sexual function of smell   The smell mechanism is an instinctual component in sexual foreplay. In some societies genital odors are considered a potent sexual stimulant; in the United States and some other cultures, body odors of all kinds are taboo, as indicated by the wide use of deodorants and perfumes. See COMPONENT INSTINCT, COPROPHILIA, SMELL.

sexual harassment   Unwelcome sexual advances. Can range from a person whistling at a stranger to demands for sexual favors from people in authority put on those below them, such as employer to an employee. Historically, persons of higher rank harassed those beneath them, for example, kings and queens expected their subjects to submit to sexual advances. See DROIT DU SEIGNEUR, RAPE, SEX OFFENDERS, SEX OBJECT, SEX TRAUMA, SEXUAL ABUSERS, SEXUAL ASSAULT.

sexual history   1. A collection of information relating to a person's sexual behavior as a part of developing a case history. Because many cases of mental disorder involve a disturbed sexual relationship, the sexual history often leads to an understanding of a patient's conflicts. 2. Interview technique developed by Alfred Kinsey in the 1940s to gather a detailed profile of the respondent's sexual experiences.

sexual identity   (R. J. Stoller) The way a person views the self as male or female. Usually this inner conviction of identification coincides with society's and parental impressions and mirrors outward physical gender appearance. Most usually coincides with the gender role and "gender identity" held and presented in society. In the case of transsexuals and some others, however, sexual identity does not coincide with gender identity. See CORE IDENTITY, GENDER IDENTITY, SEX IDENTITY.

sexual infantilism   A tendency of a mature person to engage in sexual behavior characteristic of a small child. May be manifested in certain forms of psychosexual disorders such as voyeurism, fetishism, or lovemaking limited to foreplay acts of kissing, biting, or stroking.

sexual inhibition   Unconscious suppression of the sexual impulse; especially the inability to feel sexual desire, to perform sexually, or to experience sexual gratification, due to such factors as fear of inadequacy or feelings of guilt and thoughts that sex is sinful. See INHIBITED FEMALE ORGASM, INHIBITED MALE ORGASM, INHIBITED DESIRE, INHIBITED SEXUAL EXCITEMENT.

sexual instincts   Innate erotic impulses. Also known as sex instincts.

sexual inversion   Obsolete phrase for homosexuality.

sexual involution   Generally refers to degeneration. Has been used as a pejorative phrase for sexual deviancy.

sexuality   The capacity to derive pleasure from sexual flirtation and stimulation, and particularly from sexual intercourse. Includes all types of behavior into which sexual energy is channeled, including sublimation into creative art and scientific investigation.

sexualization   In psychoanalytic theory, the process of investing sexual energy in an organ or function. In the course of development, different parts of the body (mouth, nipples, hands) and different activities (dancing, joking) may become sexualized. The process may occur on an unconscious level.

sexual latency period   In psychoanalytic theory, the period in childhood from about the fifth or sixth year to puberty, during which both sexual and aggressive drives are relatively suppressed; an abandoned notion.

sexual latency   Retardation in sexual matters.

sexual liberation   The social trend away from repressive mores toward tolerance or acceptance of all forms of consensual sexuality.

sexual lifestyle   Individual patterns of sexual behavior.

sexually dimorphic nucleus   A preoptic nucleus that is larger in male than in female rats and that affects their sexual behavior.

sexually transmitted disease (STD)   A broader phrase than venereal disease (VD), that may include gonorrhea, herpes, syphilis, HIV, and AIDS as well as other diseases. Transmitted through various modes of sexual contact. The phrase STD does not usually carry the same stigma as venereal disease. See VENEREAL DISEASE.

sexual masochism   A psychosexual disorder in which people apparently prefer to be mistreated before, during, and after sex. Purportedly, more men prefer this sort of sex than do women. The man is usually humiliated by a woman, known as a mistress or dominatrix, and may be blindfolded, bound, spanked, whipped, punished, usually leading to the desired sexual climax. Generally known as masochism, which is a broader term. The reciprocal paraphilia is sexual sadism.

sexual maturation   A stage of development of the reproductive system at which coitus and reproduction can be achieved.

sexual mosaicism   Refers to an organism having body tissues that contain cells with two karyotypes, male (46,XY) and female (46,XX), or variants thereof.

sexual negativism   (M. Hirschfeld) Lack of interest in sex that could be attributed to a deficit of sexual hormones.

sexual orientation   1. The dominant sexual behavior pattern of an individual; specifically, a preference for sexual activities with persons of the same or opposite sex, or both, or some paraphilia. 2. Refers to the gender, male or female, of the erotic-love-affectional partners a person prefers. Usually referred to as heterosexual, homosexual, bisexual, or ambisexual. Sometimes the expression "sexual preference" is used. This implies that there is choice involved. See AMBIPHILIC, ANDROPHILIC, GYNECOPHILIC.

sexual-orientation disturbance (SOD)   Obsolete diagnostic category replaced in DSM-III by egodystonic homosexuality.

sexual orientation grid   (F. Klein) A two-dimensional scale to describe sexuality in terms of seven factors (attraction, behavior, fantasies, emotional preference, social preference, life-style, self-identification) and three time frames (five years ago, the current year, future goal). Individuals can rate themselves in each of the 21 cells, using the 0–6 criteria of the Kinsey Six Scale. The sum of the ratings is divided by the number of ratings to yield a sexual orientation rating from 0 to 6.

sexual positions   The physical postures of individuals during sexual activity. See COITAL POSITIONS.

sexual preference   1. Choice of types of mates. 2. Choice of methods of sexual expression. Compare SEXUAL ORIENTATION.

sexual reflexes   1. Penile erection and elevation of testes usually produced by stimulation of the male genitalia. 2. Clitoral, vaginal, and secretion responses usually produced by stimulation of the female genitalia. 3. Components of sexual behavior, such as the cremasteric reflex, that are not under direct control of the higher brain levels and may be stimulated through spinal or bulbar neural connections. 4. Reflex activity involved in orgasm. See SEX FLUSH, SEXUAL REFLEXES.

sexual reproduction   That mode of generation or reproduction of new organisms that involves and follows the union of two sex cells (male and female gametes) to form a zygote. Also known as gamogenesis, syngenesis. Compare ASEXUAL REPRODUCTION.

sexual response   1. Reaction to sexual stimulation. Initial visible response in a female is usually marked by erection of the nipples. In the male, the most noticeable sexual response is penile erection. 2. Many mammals, such as cats of both genders, will often demonstrate a sexual response by raising their rumps.

sexual-response cycle (SRC)   According to William Masters and Virginia Johnson, men and women exhibit a four-stage sexual response cycle, differing mainly in manifestations characteristic of the gender. The stages include (a) appetitive or excitement phase (sexual desire), lasting several minutes to hours; (b) plateau phase (erection in male, vaginal lubrication in female), lasting about 30 seconds to three minutes; (c) orgasmic phase (ejaculation in male, orgasm in female), lasting about 15 seconds; and (d) resolution phase (a feeling of relaxation, of well-being, inability to have further erection or orgasm), lasting from 15 minutes to one day, the shorter period being associated with absence of orgasm. Men generally go through these cycles five times faster than do women. See SEXUAL AROUSAL.

sexual sadism   A psychosexual disorder in which sexual excitement is achieved by acting in such manner to generate physical or psychological pain on another person. See SADISM.

sexual script   (W. Simon & J. H. Gagnon) Expectations a person has about sexual feelings, roles, behavior, and relationships; the associated attitudes that define a person's general orientation to sexuality. Sex expectations are learned or acquired in the process of socialization and thus reflect the influences of culture, family, and individual experience.

sexual sensations   Effects of stimulation of the genitalia and other erogenous zones.

sexual stimulation   See GENITAL STIMULATION, MASTURBATION.

sexual surrogate   A person, typically a woman, who usually under the direction of a psychotherapist, acts as a friend and lover to someone who has problems with sexuality, including psychic impotence, premature ejaculation, excessive shyness, etc., and will operate in a variety of ways, including engaging in sexual intercourse to achieve satisfaction.

sexual synergism   Sexual arousal that results from a combination of stimuli experienced simultaneously. Combinations of various stimuli such as the environment, clothing, odors, lighting, and sounds can have differential effects from each stimulus occurring singly. Phrase may be applied to situations in which the stimuli might appear to be somewhat contradictory, such as love and hate, excitement and fear, pleasure and pain.

sexual tension   Anxiety and restlessness associated with the sex drive and a normal desire for release of sexual energy. May be complicated by fear of inadequate performance, fear of an unwanted pregnancy, fear of discovery, fear of contracting a sexually transmitted disease (STD) or other concerns.

sexual trauma   The harmful resultant of an unpleasant sexual experience that occurred usually early in life.

sexual-value system   1. Needs of stimulation and response that a person feels are necessary for a satisfactory sexual relationship. 2. Opinions concerning what is appropriate sexual behavior.

sexual vandalism   Morbid acts to destroy the erogenous zones of figures portrayed in illustrations, and other forms of art.

sex variance   Sexual behavior considered as not normal by any particular group or society. Concepts of what is normal or abnormal change over time and vary from place to place. See BERDACHE, HOMOSEXUALITY, INVERSION, MASOCHISM, SEX OFFENSES, SEX PERVERSION, SEX-ROLE INVERSION, SEXUAL DISORDERS, SEXUAL DEVIANCY, SEXUAL INVERSION, SEXUAL POSITIONS, SEXUAL ORIENTATION, SEXUAL POSITIONS, SEXUAL PREFERENCE, SEXUAL SADISM.

sex vs gender   Although some psychologists use the terms sex and gender interchangeably, others use "gender" to emphasize social, psychological, and cultural factors, and use "sex" to refer to physiological factors. In addition, the words "sex" and "sexual" are usually equivalent. In this dictionary, if a concept is not found under "sex" it may be under "gender" or "sexual."

s factor   See SPECIFIC FACTOR.

sG   See FRACTIONAL ANTEDATING GOAL STIMULUS.

shade   1. Any color darker (that is, of a lower brightness) than medium gray. 2. Specific brightness of any gray.

shading   1. A depth perception (concave/convex) cue, sometimes called shadow or light and shadow. A monocular cue since it requires only one eye. See MONOCULAR DEPTH CUES. 2. (L. Berk) A conversational strategy characterized by changing from one topic to another by modifying the focus of the conversation gradually.

shading shock   In Rorschach testing, manifesting unusual responses to the shading of the inkblot pattern. Considered an indication of emotionality.

shadow   An archetype that encompasses a person's animalistic side. Represents instincts inherited from lower organisms, mainly sexual and aggressive, which tend to be unacceptable to the conscious ego and are repressed into the personal unconscious where they may form complexes. According to Carl Jung, it includes tyrannical, brutal, aggressive, and selfish impulses that are largely not in awareness. See ID.

shadowed message   A message used in experiments studying focus of attention that is presented to one ear which the participant is required to repeat aloud, "shadowing," as it progresses. A different message that is to be ignored, the unshadowed message, is presented to the other ear. The method was invented by E. Colin Cherry and was extensively used by D. E. Broadbent and others.

shadowing   1. In industrial psychology, a technique characterized by an observer following a particular individual, usually an executive, usually for several days with the intention of later reporting to that executive (or to a committee) areas of behavior that could use improvement. 2. Repeating a message immediately after hearing it. 3. Following an employee for the purpose of seeing what the job entails, a form of job analysis.

shadowing technique   A method for studying the selectivity of the auditory system in which people wearing earphones are asked to repeat a message as they hear it. See DICHOTIC LISTENING.

Shafer-Murphy effect   A tendency for a person rewarded in some manner for making a particular selection of a reversible figure to tend to see the same aspect of that figure in the future. See SHAFER-MURPHY FACES for an illustration of two faces. If a person reported seeing the face on the left and was consequently rewarded, and the same figure was re-shown at a later time, the tendency would be for the person to report seeing the left face more often than a person who saw the left face the first time but was not rewarded for doing so.

Shafer-Murphy faces   Circles with wavy lines forming contours separating the circles into halves. Dots are placed in the left and the right halves to represent eyes. Examination of the two faces will generate fluctuation of figure and ground, with the observer sometimes seeing the left face and sometimes the right face. See BRUNSWIK FACES.

Shafer-Murphy faces
Shafer-Murphy faces. Used in research about personality.

shaken baby   An infant that has been abused by being shaken, often by parents attempting to make the child stop crying. Infants can be permanently damaged or killed by such treatment. Injuries resulting from shaking are referred to as Shaken-baby syndrome. See BATTERED BABY.

Shaker subculture   A religious organization whose members' bodies shook during religious ecstasy, from which the name derives. The Shakers stressed complete separation of the sexes and absolute celibacy. See SEXUAL DEVIANCY.

Shakespeare's seven ages of man   From Jaques' soliloquy in *As You Like It*. "And one man in his time plays many parts, His acts being seven ages. . .": Infancy, school boy, lover, soldier, justice (middle-age), old age, and senility.

shaking palsy   (J. Parkinson) Original name for Parkinson's disease.

Shakow formboards   See KENT-SHAKOW INDUSTRIAL FORMBOARDS.

shallow processing   (E. Tulving, K. Craik) The cognitive encoding of a stimulus based on its superficial characteristics such as its shape. Generally leads to poorer memory of the stimulus than deep processing. See DEEP PROCESSING.

shallow side   See VISUAL CLIFF.

shallowness of affect   An impaired ability to react emotionally; extreme apathy and indifference even in situations that usually arouse intense feeling. A common symptom of schizophrenia. See FLATNESS OF AFFECT.

shaman   (Mongolian) "Medicine man" or priest, who uses allegedly supernatural or magical powers, especially trance or possession, to communicate with the spirit world. The primary purposes include the curing of mental or physical illness, or to gain guidance in the solving of various problems, be they physical, emotional, social, economic, or political. Also known as witch doctor in some locations.

sham disorders   Persistent conditions that simulate physical or psychological symptoms are produced by the person and are under voluntary control. See FICTITIOUS DISORDERS, MALINGERING.

shame   A painful feeling of humiliation associated with guilt, immodesty, dishonorable behavior, or not living up to personal expectations; disgrace. In psychoanalytic theory, Sigmund Freud (1896) interpreted shame as fear of ridicule; G. Piers, as the response to the failure to live up to one's ego ideal.

shame-aversion therapy   A form of behavior therapy in which the undesired behavior, usually a sexual deviation, is demonstrated before a neutral audience with the assumption that the patient will feel shame and thereby discontinue such practice.

shame culture   A culture in which the avoidance of shame is a preoccupation.

shamelessness   Gross immodesty or impudence, frequently observed in mania and general paresis, disorders in which normal cortical control is suspended.

sham feeding   An experimental procedure used in the study of the metering of food intake; it involves a surgical operation so that food entering an experimental animal's mouth is chewed and swallowed, but passes through an opening in the esophagus and never reaches the stomach. See SHAM OPERATION.

shamming   1. Deceptive behavior intended to give an incorrect impression to other organisms. 2. An attitude, posture, or activity manifested by a human or subhuman organism, which simulates or resembles the responsive posture or attitude ordinarily due to some quite different stimuli or situations. See DEATH-FEIGNING, MALINGERING.

sham operation   1. In animal research, a control surgical procedure similar to an operation performed on other experimental animals in the same study, but leaving intact a structure removed by the experimental operation. Surgery on two animals will be identical to a point but then one of them will be treated differently to see whether different results will occur. This procedure controls for the stress of the experimental operation. See SHAM FEEDING. 2. A procedure in which all elements except a specific end-point are performed. Used for experimental control or for placebo purposes. In this sense it is also known as sham surgery.

sham rage   A quasi-emotional state, characterized by manifestations of fear and anger upon trifling provocation; produced in animals by lesions in the septum, electrical stimulation of or lesions in the hypothalamus, and the removal of the cerebral cortex (decortication). It is assumed that higher central nervous system influence is required for true rage. See PSEUDOAFFECTIVE BEHAVIOR.

sham surgery   A surgical procedure with a different goal from what the patient is led to believe. See SHAM OPERATION (meaning 2).

shape   The spatial form of an object as it stands out from its background.

shape coding   Easily distinguished shapes of controls that can be identified by touch, as might be found on airplanes. See CONTROL-DEVICES RESEARCH for examples.

shape constancy   A tendency to perceive the "true" shape of an object even when the image on the retina is distorted, for example, an object known to be circular is seen as a circle even when viewed at an acute angle and it therefore casts an ellipse on the retina. See PERCEPTUAL CONSTANCY for an illustration of this phenomenon.

shaping (of behavior)   An operant-conditioning procedure in which behavior is modified by the step-by-step reinforcement of closer and closer approximations to the desired response. A behavior-therapy technique devised by B. F. Skinner. Sometimes known as approximation conditioning, behavior-shaping, or response differentiation. See BEHAVIOR THERAPY, METHOD OF APPROXIMATION, METHOD OF SUCCESSIVE APPROXIMATION.

shaping therapy   A form of behavior therapy that uses shaping techniques to develop more acceptable forms of behavior in the patient. See SUCCESSIVE APPROXIMATION.

shardism   Coming to conclusions from shards (small bits of information).

shared autism (theory)   (G. Murphy) A point of view that members of groups can have shared beliefs that have no validity or basis in reality. See DELUSIONS, FOLIE À DEUX.

shared field   A psychological field in which two or more persons have common feelings and attitudes.

shared paranoid disorder   A type of *folie à deux* in which two people living together, typically spouses, have the same false ideas about having enemies or of being mistreated.

shared psychotic disorder   A type of *folie à deux* in which two people living together, typically spouses or family members, have the same delusion or hallucination.

sharp   1. Mentally acute. 2. Something insistent to the senses, such as (a) an acid taste, a pungent smell, localized pain; (b) a high pitched shriek; (c) intense cold. 3. Irritable, harsh in temperament, prone to pungent retorts.

sharpening   1. (F. Bartlett) A phenomenon in which some details of a memory are omitted while others are more sharply defined and accentuated than in the original experience. 2. In communication, a tendency to distort a story so that, while overall details drop out (leveling), certain others are brought into prominence, making the story more pointed. See ASSIMILATION, LEVELING, LEVELING-SHARPENING, RUMOR.

sheep-goat effect   (G. Schmeidler) A tendency for those who believe in the possibility of extrasensory perception (sheep) to obtain scores above mean chance expectation in contrast to those not believing in such a possibility (goats) who tend to score below the expected mean in extrasensory perception tests.

Sheldon's Constitutional Theory of Personality A point of view by William Sheldon that every person possesses some degree of three primary temperamental components that relate to three basic body builds, or somatotypes, measured along a seven-point scale. The three main body types—ectomorphy, endomorphy, and mesomorphy—are correlated respectively with the three components of temperament, termed cerebrotonia, viscerotonia, somatotonia.

shell shock   (N. Fenton) A World War I (1914–1918) phrase describing soldiers' adverse reactions to battle conditions, including having to be relieved of military duty. Symptoms included irritability, anxiety, and sleeplessness. These reactions have subsequently been given various names such as battle fatigue, combat fatigue, war neurosis. See POSTTRAUMATIC STRESS DISORDER.

shelter care   A placement unit for the custody, care, and management of children considered unmanageable in the community, or who may be involved in court and child-welfare services.

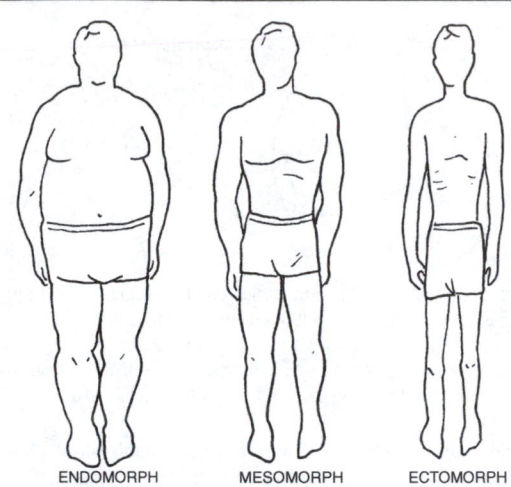

ENDOMORPH   MESOMORPH   ECTOMORPH

Sheldon's Constitutional Theory of Personality   The three basic body types, according to William Sheldon in the 1950s.

sheltered employment   Provision of a structured program of activities involving work evaluation, work adjustment, occupational skill training, and short-term remunerative employment designed to effect placement in the competitive labor market. The Salvation Army and Goodwill Industries are examples of such organizations.

sheltered workshop   A work-oriented rehabilitation facility for persons with disabilities having a controlled working environment utilizing work experience and related services for assisting such persons to progress toward normal living and a productive vocational status.

shenjin shuairuo   *shinekeishitsu*

Sherashevski   The person with a photographic memory described by A. R. Luria in *Mind of a Mnemonist.* (Spelling of name varies.)

SHG   self-help group

shiatsu   Japanese term for a form of massage based primarily on use of fingers to apply pressure to those specific parts of the body used in acupuncture. See ACUPUNCTURE.

shifting roles   As people progress along the life span timewise they change social roles, for example, a student becomes a teacher (role transitions) or a shy person becomes outgoing (role changes).

shift in the direction of original inclination A phrase used by Roger Brown for the observation that the mean of individual decisions before discussion of certain kinds of problems shifts, after group discussion of the problems, in the direction of the position implicit in the cumulative arguments concerning the problem.

shift work   Employment scheduled during the swing shift (usually 4 p.m. to midnight) or night shift (midnight to 8 a.m.). Studies show wide variations in the attitudes of employees and their abilities to adjust their circadian rhythms and adapt to changes in sleep, meals, digestion, and social patterns during these work shifts, no doubt complicated by the practice in many companies of changing the shift worked by each employee either weekly or monthly.

shikata ganai   (can't be helped—Japanese) Phrase used in industry for any unmanageable situation.

shinekeishitsu   A syndrome reported of Asian males, especially Chinese and Japanese, with a variety of symptoms of the general neurasthenic type including somatic complaints, insomnia, impotence, and general malaise. Also known as *shenjin shuairuo, shenkui*. See NEURASTHENIC NEUROSIS.

shingles   A painful condition that appears in some adults who have been exposed to the herpes zoster virus (chicken pox) characterized by intense pain and a rash on the backs of the upper arms and thighs or buttocks. May recur and may be precipitated by emotional stress. See HERPES ZOSTER.

Shipley-Institute for Living Scale for Measuring Intellectual Impairment   (W. C. Shipley) A scale used for determining pathological deterioration of intelligence. A conceptual quotient is obtained and scores below 100 are purported to indicate mental impairment due to age, disease or injury. Initially published as the Shipley-Hartford Retreat Scale for Measuring Intellectual Impairment, the Retreat was later renamed the Institute for Living, and the scale was also renamed.

shock   1. Sudden depression of the nervous system produced by accident, operation, or strong emotion. 2. A condition of lowered excitability in nerve centers following section of their connections with other centers. 3. Direct physical effects of the impact of one mass upon another. 4. Electrical current applied to a person. See ELECTROSHOCK THERAPY.

shock fear   See HORMEPHOBIA.

shock phase   See GENERAL ADAPTATION CONDITIONING.

shock probation   The short-term imprisonment of certain individuals to "teach them a lesson" and then putting them on probation in the community.

shock psychosis   A war-time reaction of combat soldiers who are overcome by shock or fright and experience delusions in which everything and everybody in the environment is regarded as hostile. Wild motor activity, mutism, sleep disturbances, depression, and immobility were among the effects observed after hospitalization. Rehabilitation included relearning sphincter control and recovering the ability to speak and feed themselves. See BATTLE FATIGUE, COMBAT FATIGUE, COMBAT REACTIONS, WAR NEUROSIS.

shock reaction   An acute emotional disturbance occurring immediately after a traumatic event, such as a car accident or natural catastrophe. During this "shock stage," the person is usually so dazed and stunned as to be unaware of the extent of injuries suffered, and in extreme cases may become stuporous, disorganized, and amnesic for the precipitating event. See DISASTER SYNDROME.

shock stage   The first of the three stages of the disaster syndrome observed in civilian catastrophes wherein persons are so stunned by overpowering anxiety that they do little to help themselves or others. The other two stages are the recovery stage and the suggestible stage. See SHOCK REACTION.

shock therapy/treatment   A form of psychiatric treatment in which electric current or various chemicals such as insulin or Metrazol are administered to patients resulting in unconsciousness, convulsions, or both, intended to improve the mental status of the patient. See ELECTROCONVULSIVE TREATMENT, INSULIN-COMA THERAPY.

shook yong   koro

short-answer examination/test   An objective test using such techniques as multiple choice, fill-in, true-false, and matching alternatives instead of requiring lengthy or complex answers.

short-circuit appeal   The use of emotional rather than intellectual appeals to arouse an audience.

short-circuiting   1. Development of a shorter neural pathway as a result of practice which lowers its excitability threshold. 2. A process in the operant learning of a behavior sequence or chain where the individual discriminative stimuli for each step gradually drop out or are ignored, permitting the responses to be performed more rapidly. 3. An attempt to achieve something directly rather than going the usual (longer) route. See HABIT, HABIT FORMATION.

short-circuit theory   (M. Wertheimer) A provisional hypothesis according to which phenomenal movement (phi-phenomenon) is due to a short-circuit between the regions of the brain excited by each stimulus, thereby giving rise to a new, structured unity.

short-sample technique   A method of reporting behavior by preestablishing periods of observations, for example, watching a particular child's behavior in a particular environment for a 10 minute interval, every half hour.

short-stare epilepsy   One of three subdivisions of petit mal epilepsy, the others being myoclonic and akinetic epilepsy. The patient stops and stares uncomprehendingly for a moment or two. Also known as petite absence, pyknoepilepsy.

short-term memory (STM)   Reproduction, recognition, or recall of a limited amount of material after a period of up to about ten seconds. Frequently tested in intelligence or organicity evaluations. See IMMEDIATE MEMORY, LONG-TERM MEMORY.

short-term storage theory   An information-processing theory of memory maintaining that short-term storage is organized through sound, has a limited capacity, and loses material through decay. Compare LONG-TERM STORAGE THEORY.

short-term therapy   A form of brief psychotherapy aimed at assistance with emotional problems and maladjustments during a period of weeks rather than months. Short-term approaches may be applied on a deeper level, as in hypnoanalysis and narcosynthesis, on a level of emotional reeducation, or on a more symptomatic level, as in reconditioning and other forms of behavior therapy. Also known as brief psychotherapy. See BEHAVIOR THERAPY, DIRECTIVE COUNSELING, GOAL-LIMITED THERAPY, HYPNOTHERAPY, NARCOTHERAPY, REALITY THERAPY, SECTOR THERAPY.

short-term vs long-term (memory) store   (R. C. Atkinson & R. M. Shiffrin) The theoretical underlying memory systems that account for short- and long-term memory performance. See SHORT-TERM MEMORY, LONG-TERM MEMORY.

shotgunning   A hit and miss process rather than a clearly focused procedure. Trying with little or no rationale: shoot and perhaps you'll hit something since the shot scatters so widely.

shoulds   (K. Horney) Rigid and excessively difficult demands on the self, created to support the idealized self-image.

showing off   Slang for display behavior performed by humans intended to attract attention. In young children, daredevil stunts, for example, riding a bicycle without holding on to the handlebars are attention-getting devices. With increasing maturity, such displays become more sophisticated. Also, various kinds of clothing worn in different ways may be seen as attempts to gain coveted attention. See DISPLAY BEHAVIOR.

shrink   Slang for a psychotherapist, psychiatrist, or psychoanalyst.

SHRM   Society for Human Resource Management

shunning   Total withdrawal of social interaction from an individual who has violated the group mores; the term most properly applies to the "Pennsylvania Dutch" (Amish, Mennonites, Dunkards) but similar techniques are found under other names in behavior modification (loosely, time-out), English labor unions (sending someone to Coventry), and the 6th century B.C. Pythagorean cult at Croton. If only the majority of the group withhold attention the procedure often fails as the individual and the "dissenters" form a strong social bond. See SOCIAL PUNISHMENT.

shut-in personality   Withdrawn, isolated, asocial character, common among persons who become schizophrenic. This type is also described as schizoid.

shuttle box   In avoidance-conditioning research, a box with two compartments usually employed with animals with each compartment wired so that they can alternately be safe and deliver shock. The animal must learn to shuttle on signal to avoid shock. See SHUTTLE-RESPONSE METHOD.

shuttle-response method   A form of avoidance conditioning in which the animal must shuttle from one compartment of a cage or box to another to avoid, or barring that, escape shock. The compartments are separated by a swinging door, hurdle, or some other obvious dividing line. See SHUTTLE BOX.

shuttle technique   In Gestalt therapy, a method whereby the client's attention is shuttled back and forth between two topics or two activities for the purpose of facilitating awareness.

shyness disorder   Persistent behavior characterized by excessive avoidance of other people, or excessive discomfort, embarrassment, and inhibition in the presence of others. Called avoidant-personality disorder in DSM-IV. See AVOIDANT DISORDER OF CHILDHOOD OR ADOLESCENCE.

SI   Abbreviation for the *Système International d'Unités* the French phrase for International System of Units.

sialometer   Saliva meter. Originally, a rather simple apparatus for collecting and measuring saliva flow for experimental analyses and studies. Oscillographs, Teflon tubing, and electronic recording devices have largely superseded the less sophisticated equipment. See CLASSICAL CONDITIONING for an illustration of how saliva was obtained from the mouth of a dog by Ivan Pavlov.

SIAM   speech interface assessment method

Siamese twins   Monozygotic twins whose bodies fail to separate completely during embryonic life, resulting in two conjoined bodies, sometimes sharing vital organs. In some cases, the twins may be safely separated by surgery. Also known as conjoined (symmetrical) twins.

sib   1. In anthropology, a social group, larger than the family, which reckons descent through either parent. 2. In biology, a synonym for sibling.

sibilant   A fricative sound produced by forcing the air through an opening between the tongue and roof of the mouth, for example, /s/, /Z/, or /sh/.

sibling   1. One of two or more children born of the same parents. 2. In strict usage, the term applies only to full brothers and sisters and excludes children born simultaneously, for example, twins.

sibling rivalry   Competition among siblings for the attention, approval, or affection of one or both parents, or for other recognition or rewards, as in sports or school grades. Sibling rivalry can cause family problems due to quarrels and fights between competing siblings. Also known as sibling jealousy.

sibship   All children in a family. See SIBLING.

sibship method   A technique used in genetics, particularly in determining inherited personality factors, in which the incidence of a mental disorder among blood relatives is compared with the distribution of the disorder in the general population. Such studies have found a higher incidence of schizophrenia in twins and close family members than in the general population.

sibyl   An oracle; a female prophetess. See PSYCHIC.

sick headache   Usually a migraine headache.

sickle-cell anemia   A recessively-inherited blood disorder resulting in the production of defective red blood cells that clog blood vessels and interrupt the flow of oxygen to body tissues.

sickle dance   A communicative dance performed by certain species of bees to indicate the presence of a food source 10 to 15 or more meters away. May contain some directional information concerning the food source. See ANIMAL COMMUNICATION, BEE COMMUNICATION for an illustration of such a dance.

sick role   A protective role provided as a matter of common social custom to people who are injured or physically or mentally ill.

SID   *semel in die*, a Latin phrase used in prescription writing, meaning "once daily" (also abbreviated **S.I.D.**, **s.i.d.**, **sid**).

side effects   Additional undesirable reactions that occur following administration of a drug. Side effects can occur (a) as a result of an interaction between drugs with opposing effects, because of an additive or synergistic effect of drugs with the same or similar effects; (b) as an allergic reaction or extreme sensitivity of a patient due to genetic or other factors; or (c) in some cases, as an emotional effect. Also called adverse effects, untoward effects, unwanted effects.

siderodromophobia   Morbid fear of railroads or of traveling by train.

siderophobia   Morbid fear of the stars or any evil that might come down from them. See URANOPHOBIA.

Sidman avoidance conditioning   (M. Sidman) A free-operant avoidance procedure in which a brief shock comes on if the animal has not responded within, for example, 20 seconds of the previous response (lever-press, wheel-turn, etc.). There is no warning signal, just the passage of time. A lever-press resets the clock to zero. Sidman avoidance is understood (by Skinnerians) to be an example of punishment: Over time, every possible behavior is punished and thereby suppressed, leaving only the lever-press response. Sometimes known as free-operant shock-delay procedure, Sidman avoidance schedule/technique.

SIDS   Sudden Infant Death Syndrome

SIECUS   Abbreviation for Sex Information and Education Council of the United States.

sight   A sense whose receptive organ is the eye, and whose usual stimulus is radiant energy of wave-lengths approximately 380 to 760 nanometers.

sighting line   A visual axis that extends along a line from a point of fixation to the point of clearest vision on the retina.

sight method (of reading)   A reading-learning technique in which a student is taught to recognize entire words rather than parts of words that represent sounds. See PHONICS.

sight vocabulary/words   In reading, words that are recognized instantly without additional analysis. See SIGHT METHOD.

sigma (Σ, σ)   The eighteenth letter of the Greek alphabet. See APPENDIX C.

sigma score   See Z SCORE.

sigmatism   lisping

sign   1. An expression that stands for a known thing created from known associations. 2. Objective, observable indication of a disorder or disease. See SOFT SIGN. 3. In psychoanalytic theory, indicating the presence of some process or thing. For instance, a patient's facial expression could be a sign of anxiety. Compare SYMBOL, SYMPTOM.

signal   1. A stimulus pattern leading to a response. 2. A sign communicated from one individual or electromagnetic device to another.

signal anxiety   1. A reaction in which a combination of feelings of tension, apprehension, dread, is a sign or anticipation of impending threat from internal or external sources. Serves the purpose of warning the individual to mobilize resources to deal with danger through fight, flight, or surrender. 2. In psychoanalytic theory, the response of the ego to internal danger, and the stimulus to the formation and use of defense mechanisms.

signal-detection task   1. An experimental task consisting of many trials in which the participant attempts to detect a signal embedded in noise as opposed to a proportion of trials that are only noise. Outcomes possible are reject, hit, false alarm, miss. All sorts of stimuli may be tested and the detection criterion of the participant can be manipulated. See DETECTION THEORY. 2. An experimental task in which the participant attempts to detect a signal's absolute threshold. See JUST-NOTICEABLE DIFFERENCE.

signal-detection theory (SDT)   1. A body of concepts relating to the perception of signals on a background of noise—an outgrowth of studies on the detection of targets by radar in World War II. Two factors operate: detection (d') and bias (β) which can be readily distinguished by the technique. 2. A point of view that sensory thresholds are dependent on environmental, physical and motivational factors. Also known as detection theory.

signal learning   Learning that a certain signal indicates the forthcoming arrival of a particular stimulus.

signalling systems   Ivan Pavlov distinguished between the first signaling system (first-order conditioning to external stimuli) and a second signaling system in which words are higher-order conditioned stimuli that have been paired with external conditioned stimuli (thought and language), which makes it possible for the individual to think before acting and to generalize from experience. See FIRST SIGNALING SYSTEM, SECOND SIGNALING SYSTEM.

signal to noise ratio (s/n)   The ratio between intensity of a signal and the noise in the background. See SIGNAL-DETECTION THEORY.

signal words   In ergonomics, words, usually on signs, that convey an important message, such as DANGER.

signation   A form of lisping characterized by the substitution of /th/ for /s/ and /z/. Also known as interdental sigmatism.

sign gestalt   Edward Tolman's phrase for a cognitive process consisting of a learned relationship between an environmental cue and a participant's expectations. See SIGN LEARNING.

significance   In statistics, a measure of the probability that a result is due to chance. Statistical significance at the 1% or 0.01 level means that there is only one chance in one hundred that the result can be ascribed to sampling or measurement error. It does not imply importance or meaningfulness of the result. See PROBABILITY RATIO, SIGNIFICANT DIFFERENCE, TEST OF SIGNIFICANCE, TYPE I ERROR, TYPE II ERROR.

significance level (p)   In hypothesis testing, the null hypothesis is rejected if data at least as extreme as that actually obtained is sufficiently unlikely to have occurred if the null hypothesis was true. The significance level, conventionally set at .05 or .01, is the probability that is considered small enough to reject the null hypothesis.

significance testing   A means of evaluating statements based on a sample made about a population, particularly in terms of either retaining or rejecting the null hypothesis (H_o).

significant difference   A difference between population parameters for different groups for which the null hypothesis, that there is no difference can be rejected. Also known as statistical significance. See SIGNIFICANCE.

significant other (S.O.)   1. A person considered important in one's life, such as parent, spouse, or close friend. 2. A person with whom another has an enduring sexual relationship but without marriage. 3. (H. S. Sullivan) A person who represents to another person an authority, a mentor.

significate (E. C. Tolman) An object or event that generates expectancy of a particular desired goal, for example, in Ivan Pavlov's classical experiment with dogs, the sound of a bell signified that food was forthcoming.

signifier A symbol that represents something that does not resemble the thing it represents. Infants are not capable of understanding signifiers, such as the word "danger."

signing A method of communication for people who are deaf, hearing-impaired, or both, consisting of finger spelling and sign language. Also known as manualism, manual method. See BRAILLE, SIGN LANGUAGE.

sign language Communication with and among the deaf or hearing-impaired by means of hand or body movements representing ideas, actions, or objects. The most common sign language in the United States is Ameslan (American Sign Language). See FINGER SPELLING, HOME SIGNS, SIGNING.

sign learning (E. C. Tolman, O. H. Mowrer) An organism's learned expectation that one stimulus (the sign) will be succeeded by another (sign-significate) as long as a familiar behavioral pattern is followed. In this sense the organism does not form habits, only learning a series of movements. Also known as sign gestalt learning. See MAZE LEARNING, SIGN LEARNING.

sign-significance relation Expectancy of a given phenomenon.

sign stimulus   releaser

sign system (P. Schilder) A characterization of psychotherapy since it depends upon language as the major tool for exploring and understanding the hidden causes of a patient's problems, and gaining access to a person's inner personality. Certain statements, and how a person acts gives signals for understanding problems and potential solutions. See LISTENING WITH THE THIRD EAR.

sign test A statistical test in which cases are classified into two groups (for example, present versus absent, or above versus below the mean), and then this classification is tested for deviation from a chance distribution.

SII Strong Interest Inventory

sildenafil Generic name for a pharmaceutical that blocks an erection-inhibiting enzyme, approved in the United States in 1998 for the treatment of impotence. Trade name is Viagra.

silent monitor A concept of Robert Owen, an idealistic social reformer, author of *Principle of the Foundation of Human Character*, who argued for the importance of the social environment in the formation of human personality. See BEHAVIORISM.

silent pause A tactic in communication that can lead people to listen intently, that permits a speaker to plan a surprise for listeners, controlled by the length of the pause as well as prior behavior, intended to have various effects on listeners from tears to laughter, evoking a feeling of peace or anger, etc.

silent thinking stage A thought period with no communications. See INNER DIALOG.

Silva Mind Control (J. Silva) A system of self-hypnotism, relaxation, meditation, and mental imagery aimed at improving memory, controlling pain, stimulating healing and creativity. Can be learned individually or in groups. Based on the assumption that cognitive abilities become enhanced in the "alpha" state, the mental state characterized by increased alpha component of the electroencephalogram. See ERHARD SEMINAR TRAINING, SCIENTOLOGY.

silver-cord syndrome A parental relationship in which the mother is domineering over her children. See SCHIZOPHRENOGENIC MOTHER.

similar-to-me error A common mistake occurring when raters assume a ratee is similar to themselves. See PSYCHOLOGISTS' FALLACY.

similarities test A task in which the participant must either state the likenesses between items or arrange items in categories according to their similarities.

similarity 1. Correspondence between any objects. 2. The capacity of two different stimuli to produce the same effect. See AUTOCHTHONOUS LAWS OF COGNITIVE ORDER, DISCRIMINATION.

similarity and attraction See BIRDS-OF-A-FEATHER PHENOMENON.

similarity paradox   Skaggs-Robinson hypothesis

simpatia A focus on enhancing smooth interpersonal relationships and minimizing conflict, a cultural value particularly associated with the Hispanic workplace.

simple aggressive type (S. Arieti) A subgroup of the antisocial personality characterized by acting on pure impulse. Compare COMPLEX AGGRESSIVE TYPE.

simple causation A view that one event causes another in an observable and direct way. An analogy is of a billiard ball that moves only if struck by another ball. See MULTIPLE CAUSATION.

simple correlation   primary correlation

simple event   elementary event

simple eye An eye which contains only a single focusing system. Characteristic of vertebrates and certain invertebrates. Contrasted with compound eye, which contains more than one focusing system.

simple phobia An anxiety condition characterized by a persistent, irrational fear of a specific object (such as a knife, needle, hair) or of a specific organism (such as a cat, bee, snake) or of a specific situation (such as, heights, closed spaces, being stared at), together with an urge to avoid these sources of fear, and awareness that the fear is excessive, unreasonable, or unfounded. Among the more unusual phobias found listed in various sources are fears of bearing a monster, riding in carriages, comets, flutes, gravity, dust, left, moisture, sitting down, standing up, walking. See PHOBIA.

simple reaction time (SRT or RT) The time taken when there is only one stimulus applied and only one response; for example, a person must press a button as fast as possible whenever a light goes on—the time taken between the appearance of the light and the pressing of the button is the simple reaction time (SRT). See REACTION TIME LIMITS, REACTION TIME RANGE.

simple schizophrenia   One of the four major types of schizophrenia described by Emil Kraepelin, characterized primarily by gradual withdrawal from social contact, lack of initiative, and emotional apathy.

simple stepfamily   A stepfamily in which only one of the two parents brings children to live in the reconstituted family.

simple structure   (L. L. Thurstone) A set of criteria for adequacy of a rotated factor-analytic solution. These criteria call for each factor to show a pattern of high loadings on some variables, and near-zero loadings on others, with each factor showing a different pattern. This arrangement makes each factor as clear-cut as possible.

simple tone   See PURE TONE.

simple type general paresis   demented type general paresis

simple universal   (W. J. Lonner) A nomothetic idea, concept, or behavior that transfers across cultures and organizations; for example, when General Norman Schwartzkoff declared that "Anytime a group of humans comes together, there is always a leader," he was stating a simple universal.

simplex inheritance   The inheritance of a given character through a single gamete, that is, from one parent only.

simulate   1. To copy: many animals simulate the appearance of other animals to keep predators away. 2. To fake: to pretend a condition is different from what it truly is, such as to malinger being sick when actually well; to feign being well when actually sick; to dissemble liking a person who is really disliked. 3. To emulate the behavior by means of a model, particularly a computer model.

simulated environment   A research method used to investigate the psychological mechanisms and processes of participants in real social environments by "simulating" those environments in a realistic way, usually through role-playing by using furniture similar to that in the participant's home or office environment and by using persons informed about the purposes of the research. Also known as simulation.

simulated family   A teaching technique in which hypothetical family situations are enacted by clinicians or other professional persons. The method is also used in family therapy, with one or more members of the family participating along with others who play the roles of other family members. See ROLE-PLAYING.

simulator   A training device that resembles as much as possible the actual equipment to be used. See LINK TRAINER.

simulators   Individuals who are asked to comply with a request to act as if they had actually received a treatment or intervention, when in fact they had not. The procedure is designed to determine whether the demand characteristic of a situation and the properties of subjective rating system need refinement in order to judge whether the simulation appears authentic. The judgement is made by an experimenter who is "blind" as to who the simulators are.

simultanagnosia   1. Impairment in the ability to perceive or integrate certain visual stimuli possibly due to a lesion in the anterior portion of the left occipital lobe, for example, ability to name the objects represented in a picture but not the action that is taking place. 2. Inability to comprehend more than one element of a visual scene at the same time or inability to integrate the parts into a whole.

simultaneity   (R. J. Corsini) An explanation for the powerful effects of psychodrama as a therapeutic technique in that the hero of the drama simultaneously must think, act, and feel in reaction to verbal and actional stimuli and is not in control of the situation as in conventional therapy.

simultaneous conditioning   A classical-conditioning technique in which the conditioned stimulus and the unconditioned stimulus are presented together or in which the conditioned stimulus is presented a second or two before the unconditioned stimulus and continues until the unconditioned stimulus is presented.

simultaneous contrast   1. Under certain circumstances a particular hue causes nearby objects to take on the hue of its complementary—as when yellow footlights make shadows on the stage appear bluish, or make light blue shadows appear to be dark blue. See COLOR CONTRAST, CONTRAST, CONTRAST EFFECT. 2. The apparent brightness of an object can be changed by its context, for example, a particular shade of gray will appear brighter (lighter) when surrounded by a ring of dark gray than it will when surrounded by a ring of medium or light gray. See BRIGHTNESS CONTRAST.

simultaneous fertilization   The fertilization of two or more ova at approximately the same time by the spermatozoa of one or more males. Women have been known to give birth to fraternal twins of different "races." See SUPERFECUNDATION.

simultaneous masking   See MASKING.

simultaneous pairing   See FORWARD PAIRING.

simultaneous processing   An ability of the information processing system to understand the overall relationship among several elements and to meaningfully integrate a variety of stimuli at the same time. See SEQUENTIAL PROCESSING.

simultaneous scanning   (J. Bruner) One of four strategies used in formulating concepts, involving testing different hypotheses. See CONCEPT-FORMATION STRATEGIES.

sin   An offense against moral or religious laws. See DELUSION OF SIN AND GUILT.

sine wave   The theoretical shape of a sound wave or electromagnetic wave as plotted on a graph with rectangular coordinates. See WAVE for an example of a sine wave.

sing-song theory   A point of view that language came about due to ritualistic incantations. See ORIGIN-OF-LANGUAGE THEORIES.

single blind   See SINGLE-BLIND (PROCEDURE/TECHNIQUE).

single-blind (procedure/technique) An experimental condition in which the participant or patient, but not the experimenter or physician, is unaware of the experimental treatment, manipulation, or drug administered. See BLIND EXPERIMENTAL SUBJECTS, DOUBLE-BLIND, DOUBLE-BLIND CROSSOVER, TRIPLE-BLIND.

single-case experimental design A method of investigating treatment techniques and their effects by focusing on changes in the behavior of individual clients, as contrasted with group research and average change among many clients. Individuals serve as their own control. Usually involves a number of observations obtained at different times and depends on the judgment of the therapist and the client. Also known as intrasubject replication design, single-subject design.

single cell recording Measuring the electrical activity of a single cell with microelectrodes.

single channel model A theory that at any one time there can only be one cognitive element going for any person. It is impossible to have two thoughts simultaneously, although transitions can be fast enough so that a person believes he or she is thinking of many things simultaneously. See SERIAL PROCESSING.

single-gene defect See GENETIC DEFECT.

single-major-locus model (SML) The mode of inheritance in which only two alleles are assumed to be involved in manifestation of the trait in question, that is, the normal allele and abnormal allele are responsible for the trait.

single parent A person who takes on the responsibilities for protecting and raising any offspring or adopted children alone.

single photon emission computerized tomography (SPECT) An emerging technique that shows brain function by measuring blood perfusion reflected by brain metabolism. Useful for detecting anoxia/hypoxia.

singles test In parapsychology, a psychokinesis technique in which the participant tries to influence dice to fall with a specified face up.

single-subject design single-case experimental design

singleton 1. An only child. 2. With animals for any breeding period, having a single offspring.

singleton sib(ling) of twins A child who has at least one set of twins as siblings. In research, the test score of one of the twins (selected at random) is correlated with the test score of the singleton (sibling that is not a twin). See TWIN STUDIES.

single variable rule A research principle that only a single factor should be varied at any time and any changes are to be attributed to that factor.

singularism A doctrine positing that the entire universe may be explained in terms of a single principle. See PLURALISM.

sinistrad writing Handwriting in which the line of progress is from right to left.

sinistral(ity) A tendency or preference to be left-handed or to use the left side of the body in motor activities. See ANATOMICAL DIRECTIONS, DEXTRAL, LEFT-HANDEDNESS.

sinistration Toward the left; sometimes used to refer to the direction in which mirror writing proceeds. See ANATOMICAL DIRECTIONS.

sinistrophobia levophobia

sinning-fear See ENOSIOPHOBIA, PECCATIPHOBIA.

Sinsteden's windmill (W. J. Sinsteden) A reversible figure of a windmill, the vanes appear to change direction of rotation depending upon the perception of the observer, for example, whether the observer believes he or she is looking at the "front" or the "back."

sinusoidal Describing the shape of sine wave. See SINE WAVE for an illustration.

SIR 1. See AGGREGATE INHIBITORY POTENTIAL. 2. See GENERALIZED INHIBITORY POTENTIAL.

SIS sensory-information store

sissy behavior 1. Pejorative slang for conduct in a male considered to be more like that of the concept of traditional female rather than traditional male behavior. Compare TOMBOYISM. 2. Especially denoting a person who demonstrates cowardice.

Sisyphus dream A frustration dream. Named after the king in Greek mythology who was condemned in Hades to roll a large stone up a hill, a stone that always rolled back down on him.

SIT 1. Slosson Intelligence Test. 2. stress-inoculation training.

sitophobia Fear of food, also known as cibophobia. See PHAGOPHOBIA.

sitting-fear See KATHISOPHOBIA, THAASSOPHOBIA.

situated identities Refers to a tendency to take on different social roles in different social settings; that is, a person's appropriate role or behavior pattern shifts according to the situation. See EXTRAINDIVIDUAL BEHAVIOR.

situated knowledge (D. Haraway) A social constructivist position that grew out of cultural studies and feminist critiques of science as a challenge to the objectivity of scientific knowledge, on the one hand, but designed to avoid complete relativism, on the other. The approach is one of positioned rationality, according to which, knowledge can properly emerge only from multiple, partial, positioned perspectives. It is opposed to the concept of transcendence, which makes knowledge universal. Knowledge must be viewed from the position of the knower, power relationships among knowers, and the relationship between the knower and the object of knowledge.

situational analysis A method of studying behavior in a natural setting, as opposed to a laboratory.

situational approach A concept in selecting leaders that each situation may need a different kind of person as a leader. See SITUATIONAL LEADERSHIP.

situational attribution The assignment of external causes to one's own or another's behavior. Also known as environmental attribution. See ATTRIBUTION ERROR, ATTRIBUTION THEORY, DISPOSITIONAL ATTRIBUTION.

situational conditions In educational psychology, all relevant external variables within the classroom setting that influence student's learning and achievement, such as physical environment, social relationships, goals, organization of material, teaching methods, time factors, methods of testing, consequences of performance, and type of reinforcement.

situational crisis   A stressful and unpredictable life experience such as the death of a family member, illness, accident, surgery, loss or change of job, or marital disruption. Sometimes known as unanticipated crisis. See ACCIDENTAL CRISIS, MATURATIONAL CRISIS.

situational determinants   Environmental conditions that exist before and after a behavioral activity, the conditions then serving as the basis of assessment of results; for example, in School A, children are made to do homework; in School B, which is comparable in all other respects, no homework is given. All students in both schools then take final examinations. Any significant changes would then be attributed to the homework. If no significant difference, the conclusion might be that homework made no difference in amount of learning attained. See ANTECEDENT-CONSEQUENCE RESEARCH.

situational effect   An experimenter bias situation that results when participants are in varying situations, such as a bare room or a well-furnished office, in a quiet situation or a noisy room. For instance, research indicates that interviewers who see interviewees in well-furnished offices tend to give them higher ratings than when they see the same interviewees in bare offices. See EXPERIMENTER BIAS.

situation(al) ethics   A way of making decisions based on the considerations of the particular people involved and the specific context in which behavior takes place. Also known as contextual ethics. See MORAL RELATIVISM.

situational homosexuality   Male-male or female-female sexual activity that develops from a transient situation or environment. May be more likely to occur in a prison, school, or military setting where persons are segregated according to gender (sex). See FAUTE DE MIEUX, OCCASIONAL INVERSION, PSEUDOHOMOSEXUALITY.

situation(al)ism   A doctrine positing that the environment and immediate situational factors are of primary importance as determinants of behavior.

situational leadership   1. A management style based on the premise that each situation requires a different leadership style. See SITUATIONAL APPROACH. 2. (P. Hersey & K. Blanchard) Telling, selling, participating, or delegating by the leader contingent on the follower's maturity.

situational neurosis   Neurotic symptoms that occur only in certain situations, as in returning to a home where the person had been mistreated as a child, and developing neurotic symptoms.

situational orgasmic dysfunction   (W. Masters, V. Johnson, & R. C. Kolodny) The inability of a woman to experience orgasm with a particular sex partner or in a particular situation. A major subcategory is coital anorgasmia, when a woman is orgasmic by a variety of means but not during intercourse. See PERFORMANCE ANXIETY.

situational psychosis   A severe but temporary disturbance with such symptoms as delusions and hallucinations, resulting from a traumatic situation such as imprisonment. Also known as reactive psychosis.

situational reaction   A disturbance precipitated by severe, disrupting conditions of life as opposed to unconscious conflicts or other internal sources of maladjustment. See TRANSIENT SITUATIONAL DISTURBANCE.

situational restraint   A form of behavior control dependent upon environmental arrangements (screens on windows, immovable furniture) so that the risk of dangerous or destructive acts by patients or prisoners will be minimized, as opposed to physical restraints such as handcuffs or strait-jackets.

situational sampling   Observation of an individual in several significant and real situations as part of the study of behavior.

situational semantics   The assumption that the truth or falsity of a statement can only be determined in terms of its context. The totality of events surrounding the statement must be known to judge its validity.

situational test   1. A task in which a person is observed in some real-life situation, for example, pairing a sales applicant with an experienced salesperson, the latter remaining silent while watching the applicant deal with a customer. 2. Research that places a participant in a natural setting or in an experimental setting that approximates a natural one to test either the participant's ability to solve a problem that requires adaptive behavior under stressful conditions or to test reactions to what is thought to be a stressful experience. See PSYCHODRAMA, ROLE-PLAYING.

situational therapy   environmental therapy

situational unit   In Kurt Lewin's theory, an aspect of a psychological field that determines the direction and speed of behavior. See FIELD THEORY.

situational-stress test   A situation task with emotional stress as an integral component. See SITUATION TEST.

situationally-independent activeness   An ability to stick to a goal rather than to be affected by outside events, to maintain momentum necessary to achieve the initial task. Such a person overrides obstacles, defeats barriers, suffers setbacks, and in other ways conquers difficulties in pursuit of an established intention.

situation awareness   In ergonomics, attentiveness to all aspects of a complex, demanding, and changing situation (as in military aviation or emergency medicine) that point to the appropriate response.

situation neurosis   A form of neurosis induced by a situation, usually highly stressful, such as rape or combat, as opposed to a character neurosis with roots in a childhood personality disturbance.

situation set   A state of readiness for a situation, such as preparation for an expected thunderstorm.

six-hour retarded child   A child mistakenly judged to be retarded or a slow learner in school (for about six hours a day) while functioning well outside in a complex social world without any signs of exceptionality. This mistake, often leading to a lifelong programming for failure, is made by adults who fail to realize that the child lacks habits such as sitting still and following instructions. Also known as six-hour retardates. See ALTERNATIVE EDUCATIONAL SYSTEMS, EDUCATIONAL RETARDATION, MENTAL RETARDATION, SYSTEM OF MULTICULTURAL PLURALISTIC ASSESSMENT.

Sixteen Personality Factor Questionnaire (16PF) (R. B. Cattell) The test of personality source traits derived from factoring the personality sphere of 16 variables.

sixth cranial nerve   See ABDUCENS NERVE.

sixth sense   1. Vague phrase, similar to the concept of intuition, for "knowing" about something without evidence from any of the five traditional senses. 2. More specifically, having paranormal psychic abilities, a phenomenon that has not been established to scientific satisfaction. See ACTUAL SENSE, IDEALIZED SENSE, INNER SENSE, SENSES.

sixty-nine (69)   Slang for an oral-sex position of two people, lying down, head to foot, with each mouthing the sex organs of the other simultaneously. Also known as *soixante-neuf* (French).

size-age confusion   A tendency to assume that children who are larger than normal for their age also will be more mature.

size constancy   The awareness that objects do not change apparent size when the retinal image changes as they move closer or farther away. Has been demonstrated in infants as young as two months, and also in fish, ducklings, kittens, and monkeys. See PERCEPTUAL CONSTANCY.

size discrimination   Ability to distinguish differences in the sizes of objects based on visual or tactile exploration.

size distance illusion   **corridor illusion**

size of reinforcement (*K*)   In Clark Hull's theory, the symbol for the size of an objective reward in incentive motivation, the energizer of learned behavior. See HULL'S THEORY.

size perception   See RETINAL SIZE.

size-weight illusion   A tendency to equate weight with size; the tendency to perceive an object of larger dimensions as having greater weight than an equally heavy but smaller object. Also known as Charpentier's illusion.

Sk   See SKEWNESS.

Skaggs-Robinson hypothesis   (E. Skaggs, E. Robinson) A postulate that in learning identical materials, one set enhances the retention of the other, but as the materials become dissimilar, one interferes with the retention of the other. However, when the materials are completely dissimilar, retention increases again, but not to the level achieved when the materials were identical. Also known as similarity paradox.

skeletal age   The state of physical maturation based on skeletal maturation. See CARPAL AGE.

skeletal muscles   The muscles that provide the force to move a part of the skeleton. Also known as voluntary muscles.

skelic index   In anthropometry, the ratio between length of the legs and length of the trunk.

Skene's glands   **distal urethra**

skeptical postmodernism   (P. M. Rosenau) A movement within postmodernism that doubts the credibility of any moral or epistemological claims. Adherents of this school of thought are reluctant to endorse new theories of knowledge because of fear that they may become just as dogmatic as many positivist theories of the past. This strand of postmodernism has been criticized for its lack of moral vision and political action.

skewed distribution   An asymmetrical distribution in which the scores cluster around one end of the distribution. See SKEWNESS.

skewed family   (T. Litz) A kind of family in which one member dominates all others in the family.

skewness (Sk)   A measure of the deviation from normality of a distribution of scores, in which cases pile up at one extreme of the distribution and are reduced at the other extreme. If the distribution tends to the right side (larger values have more cases) it is known as positive skewness; and if to the left side, negative skewness.

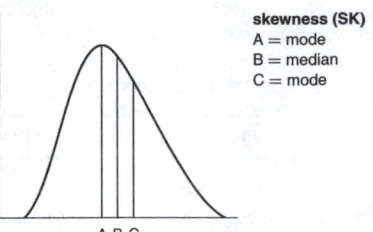

skewness (SK)
A = mode
B = median
C = mode

A B C

skiascope   An instrument for measuring the refractive condition of the eye. Also known as retinoscope, sciascope.

skid row   A deteriorated area usually found in big cities comprising of shoddy bars, shabby hotels, and cheap luncheonettes frequented by alcoholics and vagrants.

skill   1. An acquired high-order ability to perform complex motor acts smoothly and precisely. 2. Outside psychology sometimes includes knowledge or keen cognitions.

skill theory   (K. W. Fischer) A point of view reinterpreting Jean Piaget's stages in information processing terms, so that each stage is an extended period of skill acquisition characterized by children acquiring new competencies, integrating them with others, and transforming them into more efficient, generalizable, higher-order skills.

skimming   A rapid, somewhat superficial, reading of material to get the general idea of the content.

skin conductance response (SCR)   **galvanic skin response**

skin-disease fear   See DERMATOSIOPHOBIA.

skin disorders in psychiatry   Skin conditions exacerbated by or resulting from internal conflicts and emotional situations. Attempts have been made to explain these conditions in terms of such concepts as self-punishment (for example, scratching the self), expressions of hostility, acute stress, threatening situations, conflicts. See STIGMATA.

skin electrical properties   See GALVANIC SKIN RESPONSE.

skin erot(ic)ism   Sexual pleasure derived from stroking, rubbing, or licking the skin, especially during the forepleasure stage of sexual excitement. Painful stimulation of the skin is basic in masochism.

skin-injury fear   See DERMATOPHOBIA.

skin mapping   A way of demonstrating skin perceptions, such as pain spots and pressure spots, on different parts of the body, by generating a grid pattern on the skin, usually on the inner arm or the back, and then using a fine pin pressing on the various boxes on the grid while participants report their sensations.

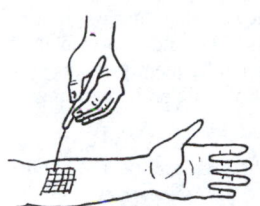

skin mapping   Detection of skin sensitivity using a hair esthesiometer.

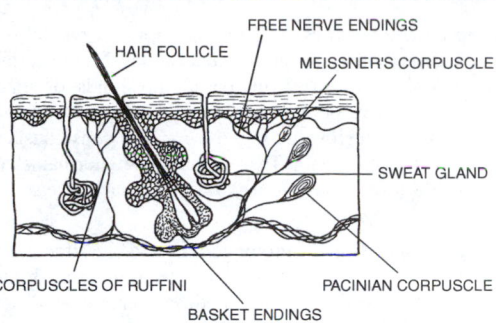

skin receptors

Skinner box   A chamber for operant-conditioning experiments that has (a) a manipulandum appropriate to the organism, as a bar or lever to be depressed by a rat or a key to be pecked by a pigeon; (b) a means of delivering a consequence, usually a food reward but possibly an aversive stimulus such as electric shock; (c) a highly restricted environment, that is, no additional objects beyond the four walls. There often is, in addition, a provision for presenting antecedent stimuli in the form of lights and sounds. B. F. Skinner abhorred the phrase, preferring operant conditioning chamber.

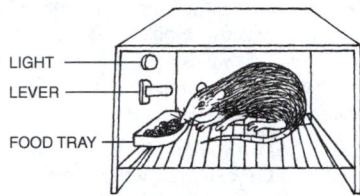

Skinner box   A version of a box as devised by B. F. Skinner used in research on the learning of animals. Includes a light or a buzzer, a rod to be pressed, and a box to which food is dispensed from an automatic feeder outside the box.

Skinnerian conditioning   Operant conditioning, named after the American psychologist Burrhus Frederic Skinner.

Skinner's theory   The following items are important for understanding B. F. Skinner's theory: BEHAVIOR(AL) ANALYSIS, DELAY OF REINFORCEMENT, DESCRIPTIVE BEHAVIORISM, DISCRIMINATED OPERANT, DRL, EFFECTS OF PUNISHMENT ON EXTINCTION, EXPERIMENTAL ANALYSIS OF BEHAVIOR, GENERALIZED CONDITIONED REINFORCERS, IMMEDIATE REINFORCER, MAND FUNCTION, OPERANT, OPERANT CONDITIONING, POSITIVE REINFORCEMENT, RADICAL BEHAVIORISM, RESPONDENT CONDITIONING, SUPERSTITIOUS BEHAVIOR, SUPERSTITIOUS REINFORCEMENT, TACT, TEXTUAL, WALDEN II.

skin-popping   Slang for injection of narcotics under the skin, as opposed to mainlining (injecting into a vein).

skin potential   The electrical potential of the surface of the skin.

skin pupillary reflex   The pupil dilates when the skin on the neck is stimulated.

skin receptors   Nerve endings in the skin that respond to pain, pressure, temperature, or other stimuli.

skin reflex   See SUPERFICIAL REFLEX.

skin sensation   **dermal sensation**

skin senses   See SKIN RECEPTORS, SKIN STIMULATION, SKIN-SENSORY SPOTS.

skin-sensory spots   Areas of the skin that contain nerve endings for stimuli such as heat, cold, pain, and touch. Some areas of the skin have a greater concentration of skin-sensory spots than others, for example, the fingertips have more skin-sensory spots per square centimeter than the skin of the back.

skin stimulation   A cutaneous sensation experienced as pain, pressure, cold, warmth, tickle, or itch through nerve receptors in the skin.

Skoptsism   A religious sect whose members practice a castration ritual based on a passage in Matthew (19:12) of the King James edition, regarding eunuchs. In their first degree of castration, called the small seal, the scrotum and testicles are removed. The second stage, or grand seal, requires removal of the penis. Women members of the sect, which originated in Russia in the 15th century, also participate in ceremonies that include removal of breasts and genital excisions. Term derives from the Russian term *skopets* meaning eunuch.

skull trephining   See TREPHINATION.

skyscraper fear   See BATOPHOBIA.

SL   1. sensation level. 2. See SENSATION LEVEL OF SOUND.

slap in the face treatment   See TORPILLAGE.

slashers   Nontechnical term for persons who self-mutilate by cutting their wrists. See CUTTING.

SLD   specific learning disability

sleep   The state of the organism characterized by partial or total suspension of consciousness, muscular relaxation and inactivity, reduced metabolism, and relative insensitivity to stimulation. See ACTIVATED SLEEP, CONTINUOUS SLEEP THERAPY, DELTA-WAVE SLEEP, DESYNCHRONIZED SLEEP, DREAM STATE, HYPOSOMNIA, MONOPHASIC SLEEP RHYTHM, NEUROTIC SLEEP ATTACKS, NREM SLEEP, ORTHODOX SLEEP, PARADOXICAL SLEEP, PARASOMNIA, POLYPHASIC SLEEP RHYTHM, SLEEP STAGES, SYNCHRONIZED SLEEP, TEMPLE SLEEP, TWILIGHT SLEEP.

sleep apnea   The cessation of breathing during sleep. May be caused by obstruction of the airway by mucus or excessive tissue, or possibly by reduction of stimulation of the respiratory center. Although associated with many disorders such as major epilepsy and concussion, it is also observed in healthy and otherwise normal individuals. Also known as Ondine's curse. See SUDDEN INFANT DEATH SYNDROME.

sleep center   A nucleus in the hypothalamus which, when stimulated, induces sleep.

sleep characteristics   The conditions of mental and somatic rest that include reduced levels of certain physiological activities, increased thresholds of many reflexes and responses to stimulation, and amnesia for events occurring during the loss of consciousness associated with sleep. These distinguish normal sleep from a loss of consciousness due to injury, disease, or drugs.

sleep deprivation   Prolonged period of time without sleep may result in fatigue, disorientation, brainwave abnormalities, paranoid ideas, perceptual distortions, and behavioral abnormalities. Many psychotic-like symptoms, such as disorientation, detachment from reality, and paranoid reactions, appear after six or seven days without sleep.

sleep disorders   Sleep problems occurring either before sleep such as insomnia or during sleep such as nocturnal enuresis. See APNEA, ENURESIS, EKBOM'S SYNDROME, HYPERSOMNIA, INSOMNIA, NARCOLEPSY, NIGHTMARE, NOCTURNAL ENURESIS, NOCTURNAL MYOCLONUS, PHASE SHIFT, REM BEHAVIOR DISORDER, RESTLESS-LEG SYNDROME, SLEEP APNEA, SLEEP-TERROR DISORDER, SLEEPWALKING DISORDER, SOMNAMBULISM.

sleep drive   The basic physiological urge to sleep appears to be governed by sleep and waking centers in the hypothalamus, and by deactivation of the reticular activating system (RAS). Sleep duration for human adults averages about eight hours per night with the most restorative sleep occurring in the first four hours. Light sleep that occurs in the last four hours, features dreaming approximately every 90 minutes.

sleep drunkenness   A state of being half-awake and half-asleep, with normal orientation absent while the mind is under the influence of nightmarish thoughts. Some persons become dangerously violent during this state and may inflict injury on persons nearby. Also known as somnolentia.

sleep epilepsy   Obsolete phrase for narcolepsy.

sleeper effect   (C. Hovland) A tendency to be affected by a message, especially a persuasive communication, after a time delay rather than immediately after the message has been received.

sleep fear   See HYPNOPHOBIA.

sleepiness   Drowsiness or tiredness. See SOMNOLENCE.

sleeping positions   While serving as a military physician in World War I, Alfred Adler observed that people while sleeping tended to assume certain postures and he noted that these positions correlated with evident personality factors. According to Adler, some people who slept with their heads under pillows were shy, those who spread out their arms and legs tended to be outgoing and friendly, etc. See CLINICAL DIAGNOSIS, DIFFERENTIAL DIAGNOSIS.

sleeping sickness   Common phrase for Economo's disease or encephalitis lethargica, characterized by excessive sleepiness or sleep of excessive duration. See HYPERSOMNIA.

sleep inversion   A tendency to sleep during the day and to remain awake at night when not required by a work schedule. Sleep inversion is frequently observed in patients with schizophrenia or organic brain damage.

sleep jerks   See NOCTURNAL MYOCLONUS.

sleep learning   A hypothetical ability to acquire knowledge while asleep.

sleeplessness   Wakefulness, the inability to fall asleep. See INSOMNIA.

sleep numbness/paralysis   nocturnal hemiplegia

sleep patterns   Habitual, individual patterns of sleep such as two four-hour periods, daytime napping, various forms of insomnia (initial, intermittent, matutinal), or excessive sleep as a means of evading reality or regressing to an infantile state.

sleep rhythm   sleep-wake(fullness) cycle

sleep spindles   An electroencephalographic (EEG) pattern observed during the first few minutes of sleep when the relatively slow alpha-wave pattern changes suddenly to bursts of waves with a frequency of about 15 spikes per second. The bursts of rapid EEG waves are the spindles, indicating a state of light sleep.

sleep stages   During normal sleep the electroencephalograph (EEG) exhibits waveforms of progressively slower frequencies and larger amplitudes from stage 1 to stage 4 and then the progression reverses until stage 1 is regained. (Stage 1 emergent or rapid-eye-movement sleep.) The process then repeats itself throughout the night with time spent in stage 1 and stage 2 increasing and the amount of time spent in stages 3 and 4 decreasing as the night continues. Virtually all of stage-4 sleep appears during the first half of the night. Stage 1, occurring as sleep is entered, is characterized in the EEG by relatively fast waves (greater than 13 cps) of reduced amplitude interspersed with slower waves (4 to 7 cps) of larger amplitude. Stage 2 is characterized by low voltage fast activity broken by 3 to 6 cps waves of larger activity and also by "sleep spindles" which are regular 14–15 cps waves lasting only a few seconds. Stage-3 sleep is characterized by a dominance of delta rhythm (1 to 3 cps) with some spindle activity. Stage 4 is characterized by the delta rhythm. Collectively, stages 1 through 4 are referred to as slow-wave sleep or nonREM sleep. About 90 minutes after first entering sleep, an EEG state resembling stage 1 is regained, but the eyes move rapidly from side-to-side, hence the designation REM. REM is also associated with complete relaxation of the large postural muscles.

sleep state   The five-step progression of the sleep stages from stage zero (ten Hertz or cycles per second brain wave rhythm) to stage 4 (delta sleep). Also known as S-state. See DREAM STATE, WAKING STATE.

sleep talking   Verbalization during sleep, either in the form of mumbling or an approximation of waking speech. Usually but not always occurs during nonrapid-eye-movement (NREM) sleep, and the sleeper is sometimes responsive to questions or commands. Sleep talking is not considered pathological in most cases, and occurs at one time or another in the majority of persons.

sleep-terror disorder   A pathological sleep disturbance characterized by high arousal and an appearance of being terrified. Unlike nightmares, the "night terrors" of sleep-terror disorder occur during Stage 4 sleep, within 2 or 3 hours of falling asleep, and are seldom remembered. Also known by the Latin phrase *pavor nocturnus.* Not uncommon in early childhood and usually passes without any complications or residues. Also known as night terrors. See NIGHTMARE.

sleep treatment   (J. Klaesi) The use of prolonged sleep as a treatment modality, usually in cases of agitated depression, manic excitement, and acute anxiety neurosis. Jacob Klaesi used barbiturates and other drugs to keep such disturbed people asleep for eight to ten days, calling the technique prolonged narcosis. Also known as continuous-sleep therapy/treatment, prolonged-sleep treatment. See CONTINUOUS NARCOSIS, DAUERSCHLAF.

sleep-wake(fulness) cycle   The natural process of brain-controlled bodily rhythms that results in alternate periods of sleep and wakefulness. Humans tend to have monophasic sleep-wake cycles, with one long period of sleep and one long period of wakefulness each day. Periods of stress or extreme boredom, as well as manic and depressive episodes, may disrupt the cycle. Also known as sleep rhythm. See MONOPHASIC SLEEP RHYTHM, POLYPHASIC SLEEP RHYTHM.

sleepwalking disorder   A disorder that occurs repeatedly during delta wave or nonrapid-eye-movement (NREM) sleep in which the person gets out of bed and performs tasks such as opening doors, or eating. The "sleepwalker" is unresponsive if disturbed, can only be awakened with great difficulty, and will ordinarily not remember the episode the next morning. See NOCTAMBULATION, SOMNAMBULISM.

SLI   specific language impairment

slice-of-life commercials   See NONOVERT APPEALS.

slippage   1. The difference between what is predicted and what is attained. See COGNITIVE SLIPPAGE. 2. In industry, failure to meet a deadline for shipment of goods or for completion of a project or report.

slip of speech   slips of tongue

slips of tongue   1. Irrelevant words inserted in a sentence, due not to ignorance or mispronunciation but to some confusion of association. 2. (S. Freud) A concept that some "mistakes" are directed by repressed wishes, that persons say or do what they really want to, whether aware of it or not, as in saying "I hope she's sick" instead of, "I hope she's well," the statement made is what is really meant. This concept has been popularized to mean that there are really no accidents. Also known as lapsus linguae, slip of speech. See FREUDIAN SLIP, PARAPRAXIS, SPOONERISM.

slogans   In consumer psychology, catchy phrases developed as attention-getting advertising devices associated with product images. Slogans help the consumer recall the name of a product brand and may be revised periodically as a result of continuing studies of consumer psychology. See PROPAGANDA.

slope   A coefficient of rate and direction of one variable in relation to another. Often refers to the rate and direction of change of a variable over time. The formula for linear slope given two points, (X_1, Y_1) and (X_2, Y_2) is: **slope** $= (Y_2 - Y_1) \div (X_2 - X_1)$.

Slosson Intelligence Test (SIT)   (R. L. Slosson, Jr.) An oral examination intended to measure intelligence, its 195 items are arranged in a chronological scale from fifteen days to twenty-seven years. Yields an estimate of mental age and intelligence quotient (IQ).

slowdown   In labor relations, a reduction of productivity or work effort by employees, usually as a tactic to pressure management into making concessions. See WORK-TO-RULE.

slow learner   A child of somewhat lower-than-average academic intelligence, usually measured at 80 to 95 intelligence quotient (IQ) on intelligence tests. Slow learners constitute 15% to 17% of the typical school population. Phrase is often imprecisely applied to the educable mentally retarded as well as children of normal capacity whose scholastic progress is none-the-less slow. See ACADEMIC INHIBITION, ACADEMIC UNDERACHIEVEMENT DISORDER, MENTAL RETARDATION.

slow-release forms   Refers to some medicines that are prepared in such a way that they deliver their medications over many more hours than the ordinary formulation. Also called time-release or timed-release.

slow rotation room   A circular, enclosed experimental room designed to assess rotation effects upon humans. The room rotates its vertical centerline: to participants, visually the room appears to be at rest, but vestibularly it is not. Fully furnished, participants live in the room for up to several weeks. See CANAL SICKNESS.

slow-to-warm-up child   A child whose temperament is inactive, is somewhat negative, and who exhibits mild, low-key reactions to stimuli. Compare EASY CHILD, DIFFICULT CHILD.

slow wave   A delta wave. See SLOW-WAVE SLEEP.

slow-wave sleep (SWS)   A stage of deep sleep characterized by slow, synchronous delta waves. It is controlled by serotonin-rich cells in the brainstem; increased levels of serotonin stimulate slow-wave sleep while abnormally low levels of the substance result in insomnia. Slow-wave sleep has a restorative function that helps eliminate feelings of fatigue. See DEEP SLEEP, DELTA-WAVE SLEEP, SEROTONIN.

$_sL_R$ See REACTION THRESHOLD.

slychology   Pejorative slang describing a prostitution of psychology when used to manipulate people for advantage or profit. See ETHICS.

S-M   See SADOMASOCHISM, SADOMASOCHISTIC RELATIONSHIP.

SM   secondary memory

smallest space analysis (SSA)   A statistical model that represents similarity coefficients among sets of objects by distances in a multidimensional space. On a correlation matrix of test items, it represents items as points in a Euclidean plane such that the higher the items are correlated, the closer together are the two points. The resulting map is easier to interpret and to see data patterns in than a table of coefficients.

small-for-dates   Phrase indicating that a baby is underweight for its gestational age.

small group   For research purposes, about ten people. In group psychotherapy the optimal number is considered to be eight clients.

small-object fear   See MICROPHOBIA.

small-penis complex   An emotional concern of some males that their penis is too small to give a female partner adequate satisfaction. Often is given impetus by the visual distortion that results when the male looks downward toward his genitals, a perspective that can make an average penis appear smaller than average.

small-sample theory   A point of view that population characteristics can be extrapolated to a satisfactory degree from a small number of cases if certain mathematical techniques are used. See SAMPLING ERROR.

smell   1. The olfactory sensation that enables an organism to detect particles of substances in inhaled air. 2. The odors themselves. See OLFACTION, SMELL MECHANISM.

smell brain   A part of the brain (rhinencephalon) which mediates olfactory sensitivity and which, in some animals, is large in proportion to the rest of the brain. See OLFACTION, OLFACTORY BULBS, SMELL MECHANISM. See also BRAIN for an illustration.

smell compensation   (H. Zwaardemaker) The hypothetical obliteration of two odors, each by the other. Hans Henning and others have failed to verify this phenomenon.

smell mechanism   The sense of smell originates in olfactory receptors which extend numerous cilia into the mucosal layer in the roof of the nasal cavity. Ions of molecules of substances carried to the olfactory mucosa stimulate the receptors, which carry impulses in axonal bundles to the olfactory bulb, which receives the impulses and sends them on to the telencephalon through the olfactory nerve. See INFRARED-THEORY OF SMELL, STERIC THEORY OF ODOR, RAMAN SHIFT.

smell prism   A graphic representation of the six primary odors. See ODOR PRISM.

Smets-pattern responses   (G. Smets) Responses by test participants to Smets patterns, or checkerboard patterns in which the checkered elements have been rearranged. The various patterns contain from 64 to 900 elements. The participants are asked to judge the patterns for beauty, visual discomfort, or other factors.

smiles report   Colloquial phrase for any all-too-typical evaluation form completed at the end of conferences to attempt to measure the effectiveness of the conference. Such a method usually generates information on what the participants thought of the program and instructor but do not measure its effectiveness.

SML   See SINGLE-MAJOR-LOCUS MODEL.

smoked drum   A recording device, no longer used, that consists of a cylinder overlaid with glazed smoked paper so as to receive tracings from a stylus, which moves to and fro at 90° angles to the direction of the drum's rotation.

smoking motives   Reasons for drawing the smoke of tobacco or other substances into the mouth or lungs range widely: relaxation of tension, keeping the hands occupied, habit, behavior intended to impress others, a means of curbing appetite, as well as dependence on nicotine. Freudian interpretations include oral gratification and the death wish. See TOBACCO DEPENDENCE, TOBACCO WITHDRAWAL.

smoky   A quality of olfactory sensation, of which tar and tobacco smoke are typical examples. Also known as burned, burnt, empyreumatic.

smoothed curve   A graphic representation of a curving line that has been adjusted to eliminate erratic or sudden changes in slope so that its fundamental shape and direction will be evident. See MOVING AVERAGE.

smooth muscles   Short-fibered muscles under control of the autonomic nervous system. Function primarily for involuntary processes and are able to remain in a contracted state for long periods of time or maintain a pattern of rhythmic contractions indefinitely without fatigue. Smooth-muscle tissues are found in the digestive organs and the muscles of the eyes. Unlike skeletal muscles, they do not require exercise. Also known as involuntary muscles.

smooth-pursuit eye movements (SPEM)   Normal eye movements of following a moving target smoothly. Rates of disordered patterns (jerky movements) occur only 6% in otherwise normal persons, but 70% to 80% in persons with schizophrenia, and 45% to 50% in first-degree relatives of persons with schizophrenia. The schizophrenic patterns are purportedly due to dysfunction in the area of the reticular activating system.

smothering-fear   See PNIGEROPHOBIA, PNIGOPHOBIA.

SMP   See SURVEY OF MANAGEMENT PRACTICES.

SMR   See SENSORIMOTOR RHYTHM.

s/n   See SIGNAL TO NOISE RATIO.

snake fear   See OPHIDIOPHOBIA.

snake symbol   (C. G. Jung) In psychoanalytic theory, the penis. The symbol is frequently found in dreams as well as in primitive rites and art productions in which it probably represents life. Also found in the medical caduceus. See OPHIDIOPHILIA.

S-   1. A discriminative stimulus that suppresses instrumental behavior because it signals the nonavailability of reinforcement. See S-DELTA. 2. An aversive stimulus.

Snellen (Test) Chart   (H. Snellen) A device for testing visual acuity, consisting of printed letters ranging in size from tiny to huge and read by the participant at a given distance. Also known as Snellen letters/test. See LANDOLT CIRCLES.

sniffing of chemicals   See GLUE SNIFFING, HUFFING, INHALANT-RELATED DISORDERS, VOLATILE-CHEMICAL INHALATION.

sniff sign   Identifying a type of breathing experienced by persons with tracheal tumors who inhale with small, sharp, sniffing breaths. An example of an organic disorder often mistaken as a symptom of a psychological condition.

snow   Slang for cocaine.

snowball sampling   Any of the varieties of sample selection in which each person interviewed or otherwise encountered is asked for names of other people who then will also be included in a sample.

snowbirds   1. Refers to people who live in the north country except during the winter when they live in moderate climates, for example, Canadians who winter in Florida. 2. Slang for cocaine addicts.

snow blindness   A visual distortion caused by exposure to extreme intensities of white light, either marked by photophobia, an illusion that all objects are red, or by a temporary loss of vision.

snow fear   See CHIONOPHOBIA.

S.O.   1. significant other. 2. sex offender.

SOAP   Acronym for subjective report (or symptoms), objective findings, assessment of patient's response, plan for what is to be done about the problem. See PROBLEM-ORIENTED RECORD.

soar   (J. Laird, A. Newell & P. Rosenbloom) A computer program design for computer simulation of cognitive processing that operates in an arbitrary set of problem spaces, and learns by chunking procedures on the basis of experience, and is capable of performing a wide range of tasks. See ARTIFICIAL INTELLIGENCE.

sociability index/rating   An evaluation of a person's degree of sociability based on the amount of time devoted to social activities.

sociability   The need or tendency to seek out companions, friends, and social relationships. See AFFILIATION.

sociable type   (E. Spranger) A person who is friendly, compassionate, considerate, and congenial. Sometimes known as social type.

social   Pertaining to the specific relationship of individual organisms to other members of the species, or to habits, characteristics, etc., likely to be acquired through experience with other individuals.

social acceptance   A continuous variable defined by the extent to which one or more persons willingly associates with another in various domains of public and private interaction.

social action   A group action directed to achieve benefits for the community or a segment of the population. See SOCIAL-ACTION PROGRAM.

social-action program   A planned and organized effort to change some phase of society, such as enactment of gun-control legislation or initiating improvements in community services.

social activities   Events that bring individuals together in a pleasurable environment, such as concerts, games, or parties. Frequently a part of the rehabilitation process for persons with mental or physical disabilities because of their need to experience contact with others of their community to gain self-confidence, self-acceptance, and self-esteem.

social adaptation/adjustment   An adequate adjustment to the demands, restrictions, and mores of a particular society, including the ability to live and work with others in a reasonably harmonious manner, and to carry on social interactions and relationships that are satisfying to self as well as others.

social adaptiveness   Ability of some people to adjust to a variety of social situations.

social adjustment   social adaptation

social-adjustment theory   A theoretical approach to social adaptiveness based on the processes involved in adaptation to social norms. See ASSIMILATION CONTRAST CHANGE THEORY, ADAPTATION PERIOD, ADAPTATION-LEVEL THEORY.

social age (S.A.)   An estimate of a person's social capacities that can be done in a number of ways. Often in clinical situations with young children, this age is assigned by interviewing parents and other adults using scores on the Vineland Social Maturity Scale. The social age when divided by the chronological age yields a social quotient.

social agency   An organization, private or governmental, that supervises or provides personal services, especially in the fields of health, welfare, and rehabilitation. The general objective of a social agency is to improve the quality of life of its clients.

social aggregate   All the individuals inhabiting a designated geographical area.

social anchoring   Reliance on group trends or on an interpretation of group attitudes to make decisions.

social animal   See SOCIAL BEING, SOCIAL INSTINCT, ZOON POLITIKON.

social animism   A concept of the world fashioned to fit the thinking and emotions of a person, as observed in patients with schizophrenia who believe, if they feel inferior, that everyone views them as inferior people.

social anthropology   The study of societies, especially ways of life, mores, taboos, and values. See ANTHROPOLOGY.

social anxiety   Feelings of apprehensiveness about one's own social status, social role, and social behavior.

social ascendancy   Upward mobility in prestige, power, or influence, for either individuals or groups.

social assimilation   1. The process by which two or more cultures or cultural groups become fused, although one is likely to remain dominant. 2. The assimilation of individuals into a majority culture.

social atom   (J. Moreno) A reference to a single person (the atom) in a social group (the molecule) represented by the interactions of the person with others to whom the person is attracted or by whom the person is repelled.

social attitude   An opinion shared by many people, at least within a social group.

social behavior   Conduct under the control of or influenced by society or a social group.

social being   An organism that, to survive and propagate, lives with other members of a species in a social setting where patterns are established for nurturance of the young, food-gathering or cultivation, and mutual aid or defense. See SOCIAL INSTINCT, ZOON POLITIKON.

social bond   A link that unites members of a social group such as a club or gang. Usually established by such factors as similar interests, goals, or attitudes.

social-breakdown (syndrome)   A symptom pattern observed primarily in chronic mental patients, and long-term prisoners. Consists of such reactions as withdrawal, loss of interest and initiative, submissiveness and passivity, and progressive social and vocational incompetence due to lack of stimulation, overcrowded conditions, unchanging routine, and disinterest on the part of the staff. Also known as chronicity, institutionalism, institutional neurosis, social-disability.

social case-work   A type of social work concerned with the personal needs, social relationships, and environmental pressures of individual clients. Also known as case-work.

social category   A categorization or division of people by the social rank or class they are in, for example, the self-employed, the retired, the military, professors.

social censorship   See CENSORSHIP.

social change   The process of altering the general character of a society, as in the Industrial Revolution of the 19th century, and the introduction of nuclear technology and freer expression in the 20th century. Rapid social change increases stress and may create some psychological problems. See FUTURE SHOCK.

social class   A large group or division of society that shares a common level of education, occupation, and income as well as many common values and, in some cases, similar religious and social patterns. Child-rearing practices, physical setting, social environment, educational opportunities, emotional adjustment, and occupational opportunities may all be affected by social class.

social climate   The character of the milieu in which individuals and groups live, that is, prevailing customs, mores, and social attitudes that influence their behavior and adjustment. See SOCIAL ENVIRONMENT.

social climbing   An attempt to improve personal social standing through being accepted in a higher class. Phrase implies an attempt to cater to or "hobnob" with selected members of the higher class through manipulation.

social clock   1. Predictable events in the physical and social history of an individual from birth through death. 2. Culturally preferred timing of social events dictating when a person should, for example, leave home, marry, have children, and retire.

social code   General phrase for laws and other social rules and standards accepted by a specific community or society.

social-cognitive theory   (A. Bandura) A theory that assigns a central role to cognitive, vicarious, self-regulatory, and self-reflective processes in human adaptation and change. In this approach, behavior; cognitive, biological, and other personal factors; and environmental events all operate as interacting determinants of human functioning. This is an expanded version of social learning theory. See MODELING, OBSERVATIONAL LEARNING, RECIPROCAL DETERMINATION, SELF-EFFICACY, SELF-REGULATION.

social cohesion   A tendency of individuals with similar interests to be integrated into a meaningful group. It is an effective force in group therapy.

social comparisons   See SOCIAL-COMPARISON THEORY.

social-comparison theory   A point of view that success and happiness do not depend on personal reality circumstances, but rather on being in a superior situation compared to others. People partially or primarily assess their accomplishments and values through comparison with others. See ETHNOCENTRISM, SELF-CONCEPT.

social competence   Ability to handle a variety of social situations effectively; skill in interpersonal relations.

social compliance   (H. Hartmann) The result of the influence of the social structure on the behavior of individuals leading them to conform to behavioral expectations. Hartmann held that a study of interactions with the social surround would be a major contribution to understanding people.

social consciousness   An awareness of the needs of others and of the fact that personal experiences are shared by others.

social-consequence theory   A point of view that behavioral, emotional, and mental disorders proceed from social as well as physiological causes.

social constructionism   See POSTSTRUCTURALISM.

social contact   1. In general, relationships with others, typically includes sharing of thoughts, frequent visits, attending parties or social events together. 2. In mental institutions, arranged or encouraged communications or relationships between patients and other individuals, particularly persons who are not members of the immediate family or health-care team, all done to overcome the tendency of some patients to isolate themselves.

social contagion   The effect of peoples' opinions on other people. The result of contact among and between people in the spread of ideas, feelings, concepts, rumors and overall values.

social context   The specific circumstances or general environment that serve as a backdrop for social status or interpersonal behavior.

social continuity   The transmission of social standards by others, usually parents and most often mothers, to children.

social contract   (J. J. Rousseau) An early theory, advanced to explain the origin of social relations, according to which humankind at first lived in isolated families or as isolated individuals, and upon recognizing the advantages of cooperation, met together and voluntarily agreed to forego certain individual privileges to secure the benefits of united action.

social control   The power of institutions, organizations, and laws to influence or regulate the behavior of individuals and groups; the impact of religion, the economic system, education, the communications industry, and other social forces on individual or group behavior.

social conventions   Rules for proper behavior in any social group. Unfamiliarity with such conventions may generate problems for the foreigner in a new place because what may be acceptable actions, signals, words, or sounds in one culture may be highly offensive in another culture.

social Darwinism   1. (H. Spencer) A theory that the fittest in human society do and should dominate those who are inferior. 2. The extension of Charles Darwin's theory of evolution into social movements or theory, such as the eugenics movement that advocated sterilization of the "unfit" and the encouragement of propagation in the "genetically superior." See EUGENICS.

social decrement   Loss of performance when people are in the presence of others. Usually occurs when they are in the process of learning. Compare SOCIAL INCREMENT. See SOCIAL SUPERVALENT.

social deficit   Inability or unwillingness to perform social activities commensurate with chronological age, intelligence, or physical condition.

social degeneracy   A social condition in which the circumstances and habits of individuals have become so ill-adapted to healthy living that the members of the group can no longer function together and tend to regress to more primitive forms of institutions and customs.

social density   1. The number of individuals per given unit of space. 2. The number of interpersonal interactions likely to occur in a particular geographic area. See SPATIAL DENSITY.

social deprivation   Lack of adequate opportunity for social experience. During development, some persons do not interact with others similar to themselves and as a result are usually disadvantaged in many respects. Frequently due to parental overprotection or to an isolated environment.

social desirability   A tendency on self-report instruments (personality, attitudes, interests) to respond according to what is perceived as being socially desirable rather than on personal "true characteristics." Research suggests that any social cohort is likely to establish a class system in relation to other people. As a general rule, those persons considered inferior are avoided, usually on the basis of race, nationality, religion, occupation, or a combinations of these. See FAKING GOOD, SOCIAL CLASS, SOCIAL COMPARISONS, SOCIAL DESIRABILITY PYRAMID, SOCIAL DESIRABILITY THEORY.

social-desirability bias   A tendency of respondents to questionnaires to shift their answers to personal questions in the direction of perceived majority opinion or social consensus. Such biases necessitate control measures in research situations. See FAKING GOOD, RESPONSE SET.

social-desirability factor   A tendency to modify speech and behavior to elicit approval from others. See ASCH CONFORMITY EXPERIMENT.

social desirability pyramid   A hierarchy of perceived social worth; at the top of the pyramid are few persons having qualities deemed fit to admire or emulate, such as gentility, grace, proper manners, whereas at the bottom of the pyramid are many people with qualities considered undesirable, unrefined, vulgar, and coarse. See ISOLATE, SOCIAL PYRAMID, STAR.

social desirability theory   A point of view that some people possess certain characteristics that make them more popular, depending on the social situation, than others.

social determinism   A doctrine positing that history is primarily influenced by broad social forces rather than by individuals. See CULTURAL DETERMINISM, SOFT DETERMINISM, ZEITGEIST.

social development   The gradual acquisition of attitudes, relationships, and behaviors that enable the individual to function as a member of society. See VINELAND SOCIAL MATURITY SCALE.

social diagnosis   In social work, identifying environmental conditions related to or causing a patient's disorder.

social differentiation   In any close-knit society, a hierarchy develops in social status levels for any individual accepted within that society; for example, in a small town where everyone knows each other, the hierarchy may be based on length of residency, wealth, education level, or occupation. See SOCIAL.

social-disability   **social-breakdown (syndrome)**

social disapproval   Unfavorable, overt, or indirect judgment passed by a significant portion of a given social group upon certain people (members), based upon their conduct, general behavior, or physical makeup.

social discrimination   1. Prejudicial treatment on the basis of apparent physical factors, such as race or ethnicity. 2. Discriminatory treatment on the basis of behavioral factors (such as rudeness, etiquette, felony records, filthiness) that elicit discomfort in others. Making such people feel unwelcome. See SOCIAL DESIRABILITY.

social disintegration   The disruption and fragmentation of a social group or community, with legal and institutional breakdowns and individual demoralization and emotional disturbances. See ANOMIE.

social disorganization   Change or modification of the institutional habits of individuals, as when the children of a family become adults and no longer obey a parent, or the members of a church cease to attend services, or there is lack of commitment to any group, as small as a family or as large as a nation. See ANOMIE.

social distance   The degree of separateness maintained between individuals, groups, or both, often because of lack of knowledge, sometimes because of prejudices. See PROXEMICS.

social-distance scale   A rating scale on which the respondent indicates the degree of intimacy he or she would accept in association with a member of a specific social group. May ask a question, such as "Would you want a person of type X as a neighbor?" Type X might refer to older people, people with young children, people of specific nationalities, religions, "races," etc. The Bogardus Social Distance Scale is used to indicate the degree of intimacy acceptable in association with individuals of specific ethnic groups. See SOCIAL-DISTANCE THEORY.

social dominance   1. Being in a position of power, authority, or status in a particular social setting. Can change with the situation (for example, a parent may dominate the children at home but is subordinate at the office). 2. A hierarchy of relationships among organisms of a similar type or species with some organisms behaving in a dominating or superior manner, and others behaving in a submissive manner; for example, some animals such as chickens, wolves, cows, and monkeys establish a hierarchy. See ALPHA MALE, HOOK ORDER, PECKING ORDER.

social drift   A hypothesis that persons unable to function adequately in society, for example certain mentally ill and deviant persons, tend to collect in the lower socio-economic strata as a result of their inability to achieve a more effective mode of adaptation.

social drift theory   A point of view concerning the relation between social class and mental illness suggesting that the greater incidence of severe pathology among individuals in lower socio-economic classes is due to various kinds of inadequacy. People with poor or inadequate social and other skills drift into the segments of society where deficits do not preclude social acceptance. Also known as social selection theory of pathology.

social drive   The urge to establish social relationships and to be gregarious.

social dyad   A set of two interacting persons or groups in which varied social relationships take place between them, such as in the rivalry between two brothers, transference between therapist and client, harmony or hostility between business owners and their employees.

social dynamics   1. The processes and effects of social and cultural changes. 2. A branch of social psychology that focuses on such processes.

social ecology   The study of organisms, human or animal, in relation to their social and physical environments.

social elimination   Selective action, of animals and humans, who in a variety of ways avoid or remove from the society undesired individuals for a variety of reasons: for being different, considered inferior, maladjusted to the prevailing type of social organization, or otherwise subject to social disapproval.

social-emotional leader   A type of leader who stresses creating and maintaining good psychological conditions within groups; concerned more with process than with product.

social engineer   A person engaged in social policy planning and in organizing community action programs dealing with such problems as crime, drug abuse, and urban decay.

social environment   The contact that any person experiences in dealing with others in terms of exposure to ideas, values, ways of operating, etc.

social evolution   Series of progressive changes in the organization of a society that take place over time.

social-exchange theory   A point of view that in social relations, persons operate to maximize gains and minimize costs. Behavior is primarily motivated by reciprocity and expectation of reward; the idea that social interaction is based on the exchange of various emotional, social, and material benefits. Social-exchange theory derives from a stimulus-response orientation. See GAMES PEOPLE PLAY.

social facilitation   1. A tendency to work faster and more accurately in the presence of others. Such behavior usually only occurs on uncomplicated tasks or tasks previously mastered through practice. 2. To note the effect on performance when in the presence of others. See SOCIAL DECREMENT, SOCIAL INCREMENT, SOCIAL SUPERVALENT.

social factors   In rehabilitation psychology, social influences such as the attitudes of members of the community toward a disability and the resultant effect on the patient's self-image and morale.

social feedback   A direct report of the effect of personal behavior or verbal communications on other people. Such feedback could take the form of laughter after telling a joke, or a warm handclasp in response to a compliment.

social feeling   Recognition of the needs of others and willingness to cooperate with them. See GOLDEN RULE, SOCIAL INTEREST.

social field   See SOCIAL ENVIRONMENT.

social fission   Division of a social group into smaller groups owing to internal dissension or environmental conditions that endanger the survival of the group as originally constituted. See SOCIOMETRY.

social fixity/immobility   A feature of rigid class systems (for example, the traditional caste system of India) such that a person's or a group's movement from one social class to another is impossible or only possible in rare cases. Compare SOCIAL MOBILITY.

social flexibility   **social mobility**

social force   Any power, energy, or stimulating value supposedly inherent in the group, as distinguished from the powers of individuals.

social gerontology   The study of old age from the point of view of society, including the contributions of older persons to the community, health problems of the aged, provision of appropriate medical care, residences, and communities for retirees.

social group   A cluster of two or more persons with a common interest or a common goal.

social growth   Improvement of individuals and of groups in knowledge and ability in dealing with other individuals and groups. See SOCIAL INTEREST.

social habit   A common form of social behavior deeply ingrained and often appearing to have an automatic quality, such as saying "Thank you" or "How are you?"

social heredity   Inaccurate synonym for social transmission.

social heritage   Culturally learned social behaviors that remain unchanged across generations, such as shaking hands or bowing when introduced to a new person.

social hunger   A desire to be accepted by a group; a primary incentive for improvement in a therapy group.

social identity   (K. E. Scheibe) A person's "birthright" (assigned membership in terms of physical self: gender, race, and social level) that is psychologically important for adjustment and survival. See BELONGINGNESS, SOCIAL DETERMINISM, SOCIAL NEEDS, SOCIAL HUNGER, SOCIAL POWER.

social identity theory   (H. Tajfel) A point of view that people when formed into groups even on arbitrary bases, tend to view their group as superior to other groups. See BELONGINESS, CHAUVINISM, PREJUDICE.

social image   (T. Burrow) Strongly held ideas by particular social groups and whole societies that prevail despite lacking objective evidence, for example, that males and females have innate differences in intelligence, ability, character; that people of different ethnic origins somehow differ greatly from others. See CHAUVINISM, ETHNOCENTRISM, PREJUDICE, STEREOTYPE.

social immobility   1. The limitation of the ability to change one's social station, usually on the basis of birth. 2. See SOCIAL FIXITY.

social-impact assessment   Evaluation of the social effect of a proposed project while in the planning stage concerning predicted benefits to the environment and people.

social impact theory   A point of view that the social potency of any source of influence depends on the strength, immediacy, and number of influencers involved.

social incentive   Conditions in any social group that lead to the increase of specific behaviors to satisfy social needs of individuals.

social increment   Increase in performance when people are in the presence of others as compared with when they are alone. Usually occurs when they have accomplished skills. Compare SOCIAL DECREMENT. See SOCIAL DEFICIT, SOCIAL FACILITATION.

social indicators   Variables by which the quality of life of a society can be assessed. Many social indicators have been suggested by different authorities—among them, poverty, unemployment, mental health, public safety, leisure and recreation, life expectancy, labor conditions, and status of older persons.

social influence   General phrase to indicate that in any community of people, each individual to a various extent affects the others.

social-inquiry model   A teaching model concerned with methods of resolving social issues through logical reasoning and academic inquiry.

social insects   Species of insects who live together in a community, with various individuals having special tasks, biologically determined. Ants and bees are among such insects. See BEE COMMUNICATION.

social instinct   A basic craving for social contact, which first manifests itself in a feeling of belonging to a family, eventually encompassing relatives, friends, associates and, for some people, all of humankind. See GREGARIOUSNESS, HERD INSTINCT, SOCIAL ANIMAL.

social integration   1. The process by which an individual is assimilated into a group. 2. The process of bringing together different groups to form a unified society.

social intelligence   (E. L. Thorndike) A basic intelligence factor characterized by potential to get along with people. The degree of ease and effectiveness displayed by a person in social relationships. See COGNITIVE INTELLIGENCE, SOCIAL INTELLIGENCE.

social interaction   Any process that involves reciprocal stimulation and response between two or more individuals, ranging from the first encounters between parent and offspring to complex business interactions.

social interest   (A. Adler) In Individual Psychology, the sense of caring and concern for the welfare of others that, ideally, continues to guide behavior throughout life. It is considered essential for mental health. See GEMEINSCHAFTSGEFÜHL.

social interference   In learning certain skills, such as music, the tendency to make more mistakes in the presence of others than when alone. Especially occurs if the person present is considered superior in the skill being practiced by the learner. See PERFORMANCE ANXIETY, SOCIAL FACILITATION.

social intervention   Social action programs designed to produce an increased level of some type of social good or services.

social introversion   A behavioral trait manifested by shy, inhibited, and withdrawn people who avoid contact with others. See MINNESOTA MULTIPHASIC PERSONALITY INVENTORY.

social island/isolate   A person who avoids interactions with others, or who maintains limited relations. Also known as loners, the prime examples are hermits.

social isolation   Loss of contact with other people, whether voluntary or involuntary. See HERMITISM.

social-isolation syndrome   In animal experiments, a condition produced in rhesus monkeys by raising them in total isolation, resulting in abnormal behavior of an apparently autistic nature such as rocking, huddling, self-clasping, self-mouthing, retreating into corners, as well as impaired behavior.

Socialist Feminism   Marxist Feminism

sociality   Willingness to cooperate with and adapt to the demands of a group; gregariousness; sociability.

socialization (of individuals)   1. In psychology, the process by which individuals acquire socially desirable attitudes and behaviors as members of a social group. 2. The process of becoming aware of and learning various value-system behavior patterns. 3. The internalization of the norms and values of the person's culture. 4. In economics, the control of industries by the state. See DISCIPLINE, PARENTING, SOCIALIZATION PROCESS.

socialization process   Acquisition of roles, behavior, and attitudes expected of the individual in society. According to John Bowlby, the socialization process starts as soon as the child (a) orients toward people; (b) makes differential responses to the mothering one; (c) approaches and clings to the mothering one; and (d) at the age of four begins to manipulate and establish reciprocal relationships with others. See SOCIALIZATION OF INDIVIDUALS.

socialized conduct disorders   Illegal activities engaged in by individuals in groups who otherwise appear socialized (without a strong undercurrent of hostility).

socialized delinquency   Refers to juveniles committing criminal and near-criminal acts because they follow sanctioned modes of behavior of a deviant subgroup of which they are members.

socialized drive   A primary drive modified to conform to acceptable social behavior, for example, eating without gorging.

socializing activity   Behavior that helps a person interact with other members of a group, such as movement therapy or participating in a party.

social judgment theory   A point of view that persuasive messages are subject to the receiver's perception and evaluation of them; attitude change is more affected by communications that fall within the latitude of acceptance than by those falling in the latitude of rejection.

social lag   The failure of social institutions to keep up with advances in science.

social latitude   In social relations, the various degrees of deviance from conventional behavior that are observed in any specific group; for example, in a military academy, cadets behave uniformly in the presence of superiors, but when unsupervised, cadets relax and individuals freely express themselves in ways unacceptable when in the presence of superiors.

social-learning theory   1. (A. Bandura) A point of view that people learn acceptable social behavior by watching and imitating others. 2. Broadly, describing personality theories that rely on social learning principles to explain human development. 3. More specifically, a theory developed by Julian Rotter that describes the potential for a specific behavior to occur as a function of expectancy and reinforcement value. See MEDIATED GENERALIZATION, MODELING, SOCIAL COGNITIVE THEORY.

social loafing   A tendency to "take it easy" and perform less when working on a group project in comparison with how a person works if held individually accountable (for example, if members of a group were tested individually on their pulling power, the sum might be 5000 pounds, but if the group as a whole were pulling simultaneously, the result would be less than 5000 pounds because of some not pulling their full weight).

social maladjustment 1. Inability to develop relationships that satisfy affiliation needs. 2. The lack of social finesse or tact. 3. A breakdown in the process of maintaining constructive social relationships. See SOCIAL INTROVERSION.

social man Refers to humans, and some animals, being essentially social creatures needing and wanting interactions with others. See SOCIAL BEING, ZOON POLITIKON.

social masochism 1. (T. Reik) Identifying the attitude of giving up, as when a patient becomes submissive and passive in tolerating defeat and misfortune. 2. Behavior that tends to invite mistreatment by others. See LEARNED HELPLESSNESS, MASOCHISM.

social maturity The development of social standards and behavior that are the norm for adults or for the particular age of the individual.

social maturity scale A questionnaire containing items usually answered by someone else rather than the person being evaluated, with the questions asking for factual information, such as: "Does this person read and understand comic strips?" "Does this person take public transportation on his or her own?" Ordinarily, items answered "Yes" are summed to generate a score that is translated to a social maturity age-level. See VINELAND SOCIAL MATURITY SCALE.

social mind A hypothetical concept that a group mind exists that cannot be explained in terms of the traits of the individual members of the group. See GROUP MIND.

social-mindedness (O. Sperling) Altruism directed toward the search for the causes and solutions of social problems. See SOCIAL INTEREST, SOCIAL-MINDFULNESS.

social mobility 1. Social flexibility; the capacity of a society or social group to allow for changes in individuals' and groups' social status and social roles, and to permit or encourage free interactions among its members. 2. Ability of individuals, usually through their own efforts, to move upward or downward in social status. See DOWNWARD MOBILITY, HORIZONTAL GROUP, SOCIAL FIXITY, UPWARD MOBILITY, VERTICAL GROUP.

social mores Customs and codes of behavior established by social groups usually not supported by legal sanction, but which may be as powerful in their effect in controlling behavior. See SOCIAL NORMS.

social motive/needs Any motive that depends for its fulfillment upon interaction with others. May be universal as in the need for affiliation, or it may be culture-specific as in the achievement drive. See NEED-HIERARCHY THEORY.

social movement A collective effort of individuals and groups to resolve a major social problem or in some way to alter the existing social structure. Compare SOCIAL MOBILITY.

social needs social motives

social-network therapy A form of psychotherapy in which various persons who maintain significant relationships with the patient in different aspects of life (relatives, friends, coworkers) are assembled in small or larger group sessions to interact with the patient. An unusual kind of reality therapy. See GROUP THERAPY, NETWORK THERAPY, SOCIAL THERAPY.

social neuter A group member who has little or no influence on people. See ISOLATE, SOCIOMETRY.

social norms Standards of correct, acceptable behavior established by a specific group. Social norms set forth the attitudes and behavior expected of group members. Also known as group norms.

social object Any person, group, or animal with whom a person establishes a social relationship in actuality or fantasy, including imaginary companions and inanimate objects. Dolls and teddy bears may fall into this category.

social order Presumption that in any community of people some kind of organizing principle exists that permits the group to operate as an harmonious whole. The larger and the more diverse the population, the more complex the social order; Many layers of regulations exist, with violations leading to conflicts with others who obey the regulations, and serious violations leading to police actions. See SOCIAL PROBLEM.

social organism Refers to a social group as though it were a living entity in emphasizing its dynamic qualities.

social organization A system that links individual humans into groups through kinship, areas of residence, or common interests.

social ossification Social behavior so ingrained that it is difficult to change, a problem that becomes evident when a person moves to a new environment with different social codes.

social pathology The study of patterns of social organization, attitudes, and behaviors that tend to influence the mental health of individuals negatively.

social perception An impression, sense, or both, of personalities and social traits of others, based on their behavior.

social phenomenon Any behavioral process, event, or accomplishment that results from the interaction of two or more individuals.

social phobia Excessive fear of other people, especially of being in groups. More extreme than shyness. See FEELINGS OF INFERIORITY.

social planning Decisions to put into effect various measures intended to achieve desired social goals such as improve education, or reduce delinquency.

social power 1. Refers to the assumption that people are controlled by their expectations of what they think that others expect of them. 2. A formal power invested in officials, especially the police, or other forces such as the national guard or the military under special situations, to control behavior identified as unlawful. 3. See SOCIAL INFLUENCE.

social pressure 1. Any social force that has the effect of encouraging or inducing conformity. See PEER PRESSURE. 2. An excessive or stressful demand made on an individual by other individuals. The degree of pressure of any situation will depend upon educational, occupational, familial, and other personal histories.

social progress Any changes in social habits, culture, institutions, or other social organizations, regarded as evidence of improvement, especially of moral betterment.

social psychiatry   A broad area of psychiatric research and practice covering the relation between mental disorder and the environment. The social point of view is an outgrowth of three major forces: (a) recognition of sociological, anthropological, ecological, and epidemiological factors in the etiology of mental illness; (b) the social emphasis of Alfred Adler, Karen Horney, Harry Sullivan, Erich Fromm, and others; and (c) development of the public-health approach and the field of community psychiatry. Social psychiatry focuses on such matters as cross-cultural concepts of normality, social patterns of drug abuse and behavior, social attitudes toward illness, community mental-health centers, and social treatment and prevention. Also known as sociocultural psychiatry. See CROSS-CULTURAL PSYCHIATRY.

social psychology   (W. McDougall) A branch of psychology that studies the psychological (cognitive, affective, behavioral) processes of individuals as influenced by group membership, group interactions, and other factors that affect social life, such as status, role, and class. Examines the effects of social contacts on the development of attitudes, stereotypes, etc. See SOCIOLOGY.

social punishment   A reaction of some people to the misbehavior of others that includes withdrawing or moving away from the offenders rather than any kind of active or physical punishment toward them. Ignoring, avoiding, or shunning others are powerful methods for indicating disapproval and thereby promoting the change of behavior. See NATURAL CONSEQUENCES, SHUNNING.

social pyramid   Refers to power distribution in social structures having the shape of a pyramid; characterized by absolute power, or rulers, at the top, with various layers of persons with diminishing power as the base of the pyramid is approached, the final layer being those with little or no power.

social quotient (SQ or S.Q.)   The result of a person's estimated social age divided by chronological age multiplied by 100. Given two 10-year old children, one child is estimated to behave as a five-year-old—the ratio is therefore 5/10 with a resulting SQ of 50; the second child is estimated to behave as a typical ten-year-old—the ratio is 10/10 with a resulting SQ of 100. See VINELAND SOCIAL MATURITY SCALE.

Social Readjustment Scale   (T. Holmes, R. Rahe) A list of 43 items compiled from a sample of raters by Holmes and Rahe deemed the most traumatic social events that may be experienced in life with the first five being: Death of Spouse (100), Divorce (75), Marital Separation (65), Jail Term (63), Death of Close Family Member (63), and the last five being Change in number of family get-togethers (15), Change in Eating Habits (15), Vacations (13), Christmas (12), Minor violations of the law (12). The numbers in parentheses refer to the mean values with Death of Spouse set at one hundred.

social reality   The shared attitudes and opinions held by members of groups in societies; the network of information, interpretations, and commonly held beliefs that affect individuals.

social recovery   (H. S. Sullivan) Restoration of a normal or near-normal mental state through social therapy and improvement in social skills. See SOCIAL THERAPY.

social referencing   Examination of other people's expressions and their behavior to know how to react to an unusual event or in an unusual situation. Seen in infants with caregivers. See IMITATION, NONVERBAL BEHAVIOR.

social-reform programs   Intervention programs developed to counter deleterious aspects of social systems. Their primary objective is to reduce the effects of malfunctions in the particular social system. Also known as countermeasure-intervention programs.

social regulator cue   In social situations, a signal usually of sound, sight, or both, that gives people information as to what is about to happen or what can be expected to happen; for example, clearing of a throat may indicate a speech is about to be made; others stop what they are doing to listen.

social rehabilitation   The achievement of a higher level of social functioning of persons with mental or physical challenges through social and recreational activities and/or participation in clubs and other organizations.

social relational moral perspective   Moral judgment according to the belief that shared feelings and agreements, especially between close associates, are more important than self-interest.

social relationships   See NORMALIZATION PRINCIPLE.

social repair mechanisms   Strategies that allow friends to remain so even when serious differences cause a rift. See FACE-SAVING BEHAVIOR.

social repression   Methods adopted by various agencies, ranging from parents to the legal system, to prevent behavior considered improper.

social resistance   Group opposition to changes that may clash with traditional values in response to any of a variety of reforms, such as new programs in schools, or destruction of buildings.

social responsibility norm   A societal standard that prescribes socially commendable behavior. A social ideal that a person should help those in need of assistance. See GEMEINSHAFTSGEFUEHL, INDIFFERENCE.

social retrogression   Social changes characterized by deterioration, that is, by less effective organization and specifically a return to older and less effective organizations.

social role   The functional position and the part played by the individual in a group situation, such as parent, squadron leader, teacher, or vice-president of an organization. Positions of this kind are "role categories," and the attitudes and behavior that people associate with each category are "role expectations" or "role behaviors."

social sanction   A method of social control that enforces a group's standards by authorizing punishment for violation of the group's rules. Punishment is usually of the subtle informal type, not speaking to people, not inviting them to desired functions, not acknowledging them, and sometimes, of the overt type, telling violators what they have done wrong. See SOCIAL PUNISHMENT.

social scale   A system of assigning individuals to various social classes or categories. In some cultures a person remains at the social level born into until death. See CASTE SYSTEM.

social science　　Generic phrase that covers all sciences dealing with human relations and including psychology, sociology, economics, political science, ethnology, history, and other related disciplines.

social selection　　A tendency to make choices based on external characteristics such as gender, age, "race," attractiveness, resulting in advantages for certain individuals that gives them greater opportunities in the struggle for existence.

social selection theory of pathology　　**social drift theory**

social self　　The role exhibited during contact and interaction with other people, often contrasted with the real self. See IDIOPANIMA, IMPRESSION MANAGEMENT.

social services　　Services arranged or provided by professionals, usually social workers, including visiting-nurse service, homemaking assistance, mental-health counseling, housing for needy citizens and other government benefits.

social situation　　The configuration of social factors that influences the behavior of an individual in particular circumstances.

social-skills training (SST)　　A procedure or treatment for overcoming social inhibition or ineffectiveness. Behavior rehearsal, cognitive rehearsal, and assertiveness training are applied to essentially normal and functioning persons as well as certain people with poor social skills who may be taught, for example, to substitute direct verbal expression for violence, withdrawal, or other maladaptive patterns. See SOCIAL THERAPY.

social smile theory　　A point of view that a smile on the face of an infant or an adult will affect others favorably and therefore smiling has a survival value.

social space　　Behavior space. A person in any situation has a range of behavioral options that will be considered appropriate or acceptable by others. According to Kurt Lewin, the space is empirical, as opposed to one that is hypothetical. See FIELD THEORY.

social statics　　A branch of sociology which investigates the social forces as they effect the organization of society at any given time; that is, the study of social forces in equilibrium. See SOCIAL DYNAMICS.

social statistics　　(L. A. Quetelet) The application of statistics to the study of social data, particularly to the development of physical and intellectual qualities of humans. Sometimes known as demography.

social status　　The position or rank of an individual in a social group or class in relation to other members. See PECKING ORDER.

social stimulus　　1. Any nonphysical stimulus that elicits a social response. 2. An individual or group that elicits a social response.

social stimulus value　　An independent variable of social significance that influences others' behaviors; may be directly emitted or may be indirect; stimuli previously associated with others, or social norms, etc.

social stratification　　Differentiated socioeconomic levels in a society. See SOCIAL CLASS.

social stress theories of pathology　　Views concerning the relation between social class and mental illness stating that the greater factors of environmental stress facing the poor lead to their greater incidence of social and personal pathology. See DIATHESES-STRESS CONCEPTION, SOCIAL DRIFT THEORY.

social-stress theory　　A point of view that effects of certain glandular responses are changed in some members of animal groups as the sizes of the groups increase beyond an optimal number. Social competition may lead to adrenal and other glandular stresses which may in turn produce physiological and behavioral deficits. See CROWDING.

social structure　　Organization of a group in terms of interpersonal relationships, objectives, and stratification of members.

social studies　　Subjects or topics usually studied in formal education including history, economics, civics, sociology, politics, etc.

social subordination　　(G. Simmel) The control of behavior (individual or group) through the actions of others or by impersonal principles or laws, as in the control of a family by a dominant parent; motorists driving at a constant speed limit prescribed by law.

social subvalent　　Loss in quality of work done by an individual working in a group, as compared with the performance of the same individual working alone. Compare SOCIAL SUPERVALENT.

social supervalent　　Gain in quality of work done by an individual working in a group, as compared with the performance of the same individual working alone. Compare SOCIAL SUBVALENT. See SOCIAL INCREMENT.

social-systems analysis　　A method of understanding patterns of individual responses as interdependent with larger social systems, rather than searching for simple causal relations to isolated stimuli.

social technology　　The use of the principles and methodology of the social sciences (for example, economics, sociology, psychology) to develop practical strategies for confronting and resolving conflicts and problems of society.

social therapy　　(G. Gazda) Therapeutic and rehabilitative approaches focused on improved social functioning of people through such means as milieu therapy, recreational therapy, occupational therapy, patient government, work therapy, remotivation, and the therapeutic community.

social-therapy club　　See MENTAL-PATIENT ORGANIZATION.

social transmission　　The transfer from one generation to the next of its customs, language, values, knowledge and other aspects of the cultural heritage of a group.

social trap　　1. A situation in which two parties, by each rationally pursuing their own self-interests, become caught in mutually destructive behavior. 2. A situation that prompts individuals to act in their immediate self-interest to the detriment of other group members' needs or long-term outcomes.

social type   A person whose goals and values are primarily socially determined, a person who is essentially altruistic in dealing with other people. Similar to Edward Spranger's sociable type. See ALLPORT-VERNON-LINDZEY STUDY OF VALUES.

social will   The dominating desire and decision of the members of a social group, regarded figuratively as an individual phenomenon. Also known as general will.

social withdrawal   Retreat from society and interpersonal relationships, usually accompanied by an attitude of indifference, detachment, and aloofness. Social withdrawal is a common expression of schizophrenic autism. See AUTISM, WITHDRAWAL, WITHDRAWAL REACTION.

social-work aide   A nonprofessional social worker who performs limited social-work duties, such as interviewing clients and providing practical services to patients and families under the supervision of professional social workers.

social worker   A person trained in an accredited graduate school to help individuals and families deal with personal and practical problems, including problems related to mental or physical disorder, poverty, living arrangements, social life, marital relationships, child care, occupational stress, and unemployment. Social workers are major members of treatment and rehabilitation teams in clinics, social agencies, mental-health centers, psychiatric units, and general hospitals. See COMMUNITY SOCIAL WORKER, FAMILY SOCIAL WORK, MEDICAL SOCIAL WORKER, PSYCHIATRIC SOCIAL WORK.

social zero   Refers to a person belonging to a social group but who lacks an important role in the group as determined by the attitudes of other members. Similar to J. L. Moreno's concept of "isolate." Compare STAR. See SOCIOGRAM.

social zone   In social psychology, the area of comfortable physical distance between persons engaged in relationships of a relatively formal nature, such as business interactions or relationships between attorneys and clients. The social zone is defined as a distance of from 1¼ to 3½ meters (4 to 11½ feet). See PROXEMICS.

sociatry   (J. L. Moreno) The assumption that in any group, the more different the members and possibilities for interaction, the more likely the group will move toward optimal functioning since opposing elements will balance the group toward normality. See SOCIOGRAM, SOCIOMETRY, TELE.

societal   1. Pertaining to a society or to social groups. 2. Having the character of a society.

societal-reaction theory   labeling theory

Société Canadienne de Psychologie   Canadian Psychological Association

society   1. A large group of individual organisms of a species, particularly humans, whose members are typically formally organized and mutually interdependent. 2. Social organization within a society as a whole.

Society for Psychical Research   Formed in London in 1882 to investigate spiritualism and related phenomena. Sigmund Freud and William James were members.

sociobiology   (E. O. Wilson) The systematic study of the biological basis for social behavior. A theoretical point of view that stresses how natural selection can influence complicated patterns of social behavior that often appear to be incongruous with natural selection, as in altruism. Also known as Darwinian psychology. See CROWDING.

sociocenter   A person who is the most popular or preferred member in a group, with many others being affected by that person. Similar to "star" in sociometry. See STAR.

sociocentrism   A tendency to identify with one's own social group to the extent that its group norms and prescriptions form a standard against which other people are judged. Usually refers to smaller social groups whereas ethnocentrism refers to larger ethnic, religious, racial, or national groups. See ETHNOCENTRISM.

sociocognitive biases   In evaluation research, the realization that evaluators may be susceptible to subtle biases due to inaccurate judgments that result from shortcomings in cognitive processing. Such biases appear to be universals that intrude regardless of values or ethics.

sociocultural change   See PSYCHOCULTURAL STRESS.

sociocultural factors   In psychology and psychiatry, environmental conditions that play a part in normal behavior but also in the etiology of mental disorder, mental retardation, or social pathology. Examples of negative sociocultural factors are slums, poor job opportunities, inadequate medical care and education. See CULTURE-SPECIFIC SYNDROMES.

sociocusis   The loss of hearing acuity due to noise generated in modern society, for example, from machines, loud music, traffic. Also spelled socioacusis.

sociodrama   (J. L. Moreno) Roleplaying for instruction or information rather than for therapy, as in an experienced salesperson demonstrating to trainees how to handle a particular selling situation. See PSYCHODRAMA.

sociodramatic play   Make-believe games characterized by children enacting various social roles, such as playing "house." Typically appears around age 2½ years. See LUDIC BEHAVIOR.

socioeconomic status (SES)   The hierarchical grouping of people on a scale of prestige and privilege, determined by such factors as family background, wealth, occupation, education as well as what schools have been attended, race, nationality, or religious background.

socioempathy   In social or interpersonal interactions, the awareness or intuitive recognition of the roles or status of others in relation to the self.

sociofugal   The features of a surround that have the effect of driving certain organisms under certain conditions away from the source of the effect, for example, bright lighting and uncomfortable seating in fast-food establishments that discourage lingering over meals. See SOCIOPETAL.

sociofugal space   1. A seating arrangement that discourages or prevents interactions among group members. 2. A physical environment designed to discourage interpersonal interaction, for example, the design of church pews and of solitary-confinement cells. See PROXEMICS, SOCIOPETAL SPACE.

sociogenesis   A process by which an individual's ideas or development are affected or influenced by social experience.

sociogenetics   The study of the genetic influences on the origin and development of societies.

sociogenic   Characterizing an idea, attitude, or other mental process generated by sociocultural influences.

sociogenic hypothesis   A postulate that sociological factors, such as living in impoverished circumstances, contribute to the cause of mental or behavioral disorders, for example in schizophrenia or criminality.

sociogram   (J. L. Moreno) A diagram or chart demonstrating the nature of preferences in a group. In a group, each member is asked to choose three others to work with one person might be chosen more often than any other person (a star) and some might not be chosen at all (an isolate). Arrow heads in the diagram indicate who is picked by whom. A solid line means a pair who select each other. See SOCIOGRAM ANALYSIS, SOCIOMETRIC CLEAVAGE.

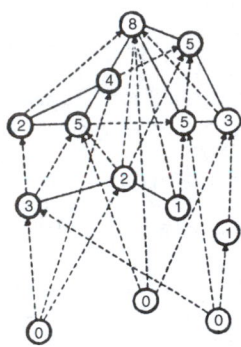

sociogram   In this diagram, 14 individuals (each represented by a circle) were asked to choose three others from a group of associates. Their choices are represented by lines, with arrows indicating their target choices. If an unbroken line with no arrows is shown, this means mutual choice. In this example, eight people chose the individual at the top of the chart (the star), and none of the bottom three were selected by anyone (isolates).

sociogram analysis   Evaluating the interactions and interrelationships between members of a class, gang, team, or work group. Jacob Moreno employed four types of sociogram analyses: (a) intuitive, based on relationships noted by the therapist; (b) observer, consisting of another person's impressions; (c) objective, based on a sociometric test; and (d) perceptual, in which each member indicates which other members appear to accept or reject him or her. See SOCIOMETRY, STAR. See SOCIOGRAM for an illustration of an objective analysis.

socio-group star   (J. L. Moreno) In sociometry, a person who is preferred or most frequently chosen by other members of a group. Also known as star.

sociolect   In linguistics, within any social group using a dialect somewhat different from other dialects. See CREOLE, PIDGIN, SOCIOLINGUISTICS.

sociolinguistics   The study of language in societies, applying techniques and findings from linguistics and various social sciences. Mainly concerned with the individual's language in the context of the community or culture.

sociological factors   Social conditions that affect human behavior. They determine, in part at least, the types and incidence of mental disorder, for example, socioeconomic and educational levels, urban decay, the customs and mores of particular groups.

sociological measures   See PRIMARY PREVENTION.

sociology   (A. Comte) The scientific study of the formation, structure, and functioning of organizations, groups, societies, and institutions. See CLINICAL SOCIOLOGY.

sociometric analysis   sociometry

sociometric cleavage   The separation of a formerly united group into two or more parts as determined by the use of sociometric methods (for example, in examining a sociometric diagram it may be evident that there are two or more cliques within any group). See SOCIOGRAM, SOCIOMETRY.

sociometric clique   On a sociometric test, a group of individuals who nominate each other by the same criterion while infrequently selecting persons outside the group. See SOCIOMETRY.

sociometric distance   1. The degree of closeness or acceptance between individuals or groups as measured on a social-distance scale. 2. In sociometry, an individual's standing in a specified group as determined using a sociogram. Those frequently chosen are close to the center and those not chosen are on the periphery. See PROXEMICS, SOCIAL DISTANCE, SOCIAL-DISTANCE SCALE, SOCIOMETRY.

sociometrics   sociometry

sociometry   (J. L. Moreno) A method of evaluating both a group and individuals in a group essentially by asking group members to choose one or more individuals to work with or be with. Reveals significant information, such as which members are considered most popular ("stars"), which tend to be rejected or asocial ("isolates"), and which are the best leaders. It also brings to light the existence of cliques, pairs, triangles, and other patterns of group structure. Also known as sociometric analysis, sociometrics. See SOCIOGRAM.

socionomic force   A force which, though not itself social in character, modifies the action of social forces and is therefore a factor in determining social organization and progress.

socionomics   The study of nonsocial influences on social groups, that is, the ways in which physical environment modifies society (for example, the effects of different terrains and climactic conditions or ratio of females to males on economic and social organization).

sociopath   1. (D. Lykken) A person who remained unsocialized largely because of parental malfeasance or nonfeasance. Such a person tends to act in a crude and violent manner. 2. A person with an antisocial-personality disorder. Term supplanted "psychopath." See NEUROTIC SOCIOPATH, PRIMARY SOCIOPATH, PSYCHOPATH.

sociopathic behavior   Socially pathological actions such as stealing, rape, child molestation, embezzlement, prostitution, burglary, murder, drug abuse, and sadism. See DYSSOCIAL BEHAVIOR.

sociopathic disorder   Relating to a social illness or disorder; a lack of social responsibility occasioned by inability or unwillingness to conform to prevailing social norms. See CHARACTER DISORDER.

sociopathic personality   A class of people who have difficulty in accepting or adapting to normal ethical and social standards. See ANTISOCIAL PERSONALITY DISORDER, ANTISOCIAL REACTIONS, SEXUAL DEVIANCY, SOCIOPATHIC DISTURBANCE.

sociopathic-personality disturbance   Behavior characterized primarily by failure to adapt to prevailing ethical and social standards, and lack of social responsibility. Includes addiction, antisocial reaction, dyssocial reaction, sexual deviancy.

sociopathy   A destructive attitude of indifference toward the feelings of others, an active dislike of social conformance, a tendency to exploit or take what is wanted from others. Also known as antisocial personality disorder. See ANTISOCIAL REACTION, MORAL IMBECILITY, PSYCHOPATHY.

sociopetal   The features of a surround that have the effect of drawing people together, for example, a group entering a restaurant will prefer to go to a self-contained, dimly lit area. See SOCIOFUGAL.

sociopetal space   1. A seating arrangement that promotes interaction among group members. 2. A physical environment designed to encourage interpersonal interaction, as in a classroom seating arrangement forming a circle. See PROXEMICS, SOCIOFUGAL SPACE.

sociotaxis   A change in behavior due to contact from other individuals or social groups that is in accord with their social network, for example, a person attends a social gathering, unknowingly dressed in an unconventional manner, thus experiencing feelings of discomfort and consequently adjusts dressing habits to conform with the group's standard. See TAXIS, TROPISM.

sociotechnical systems approach   A blending of the technical and social systems of an organization.

sociotherapy   A supportive approach based on modification of the person's environment, intended to lead to improvement in interpersonal adjustment, for example, foster-home placement for a child abused by parents.

sociotrope   (E. Boring) A person sensitive to social issues, or a person who allows social factors to influence judgment and decisions. Compare BIOTROPE.

sociotrophy   A personality dimension characterized by dependency on interpersonal relationships and needs for closeness and nurturance.

socius   1. An individual as a member of society. He or she is the primary social unit. 2. A colleague or comrade.

Socratic dialog(ue)/method   1. In counseling, a carefully constructed series of questions designed to arrive at logical responses to a problem and proper conclusions about future actions. 2. Inductive dialectic procedure leading a person to accept or admit the desired conclusion by means of a progressive series of leading questions that are answered in turn.

SOD   sexual-orientation disturbance

sodium-Amytal interview   A diagnostic or therapeutic interview conducted with a patient who has been injected intravenously with sodium Amytal, or amobarbital, a short-acting hypnotic and sedative drug which relaxes the patient and facilitates the expression of repressed feelings and memories. Also known as Amytal interview. See AMYTAL, NARCOTHERAPY, TWILIGHT SLEEP.

sodium secobarbital   A barbiturate commonly used in the 1950s and 1960s as a sleep medicine (hypnotic). This medium-duration chemical was also abused as a "downer." May also be referred to as secobarbital sodium. Trade name is Seconal. See DOWNER.

sodomy   1. In many jurisdictions, any "unnatural" sex act, that is, other than penovaginal coitus between lawfully married male and female. Critics observe that such "crimes against nature" include what many adults consider normal foreplay. 2. Anal intercourse between any two humans, presumably derived from the town of Sodom described in Genesis 18–19 in which anal intercourse between homosexual males was among the sins. See PEDERASTY. 3. Oral sex between humans of different sexes. 4. A human achieving sexual gratification through contact with animals. See BESTIALITY, ZOOERASTY, ZOOPHILIA.

soft data   Subjective impressions, data not gathered by quantitative and objective means (for example, notes on behavior observed, psychiatric diagnoses). See EPISTEMOLOGY, HARD DATA, RESEARCH METHODOLOGY.

soft determinism   1. A doctrine regarding the attempts to reconcile determinism and indeterminism (free will). Alfred Adler posited that whereas heredity and environment are important in determining personality and behavior of an individual, the individual also has control over own life. Adler concluded that from an idiographic point of view, indeterminism was correct, but from a nomothetic point of view, determinism was correct, and that the proper point of view was to consider both as true. 2. An existentialist point of view that within the limitations of personal constitution and past experience, it is possible to determine one's own goals, type of life, and future. See DETERMINISM, HARD DETERMINISM, SCHOOLS OF PSYCHOLOGY.

soft-headed   See HARD-NOSED.

soft palate   Fibromuscular tissue attached to the posterior portion of the hard palate near the uvula. Separates the oral cavity from the pharynx and, when elevated, closes off the nasopharynx to produce normal speech sounds. Also known as velum palatinum.

soft psychology   Slang for the social/clinical, rather than the laboratory and natural-based, side of psychology.

soft signs   (S. Coren) Any of a number of clinical or behavioral symptoms that may indicate the presence of neurological damage. Left-handedness, sleep disturbances, slowed physical maturation and minor sensory deficits sometimes are considered soft signs of damage due to such factors as birth stress or birth trauma. This is in contrast to recognizable, consensually agreed upon signs of neurological deficits. See ALINORMAL SYNDROME.

soft spots   Spaces (fontanelles) between the bones of the neonate's skull that have not yet changed from cartilage to bone.

soldier's heart   Da Costa's syndrome

Soldiers' sickness   A phrase coined during World War I for morphine dependence caused by the administration of large and frequent injections of morphine to wounded soldiers. See IATROGENIC ADDICTION, NARCOTIZATION.

sole reflex   See PLANTAR REFLEX.

solipsism   (I alone—Latin) 1. A philosophical doctrine that there can be no proof that phenomena exist outside of the mind because everything is dependent upon personal perception. 2. A view that "only I exist, everything and everyone else is due to my imagination." See EGOISM.

solitary play   Playing alone. Typical play pattern of children below the age of two, but can occur at any age.

solitude fear   See AUTOPHOBIA.

Solomon four-group design   (R. L. Solomon) An experimental design used to evaluate the effect of pretesting. The design can be considered as a combination of the pretest-posttest control group design and a posttest-only design in which pretest (provided vs not provided) and the experimental intervention (treatment vs no treatment) are combined.

solution learning   (O. H. Mowrer) Trial-and-error efforts in addition to memory search efforts to find answers to problems.

solution period   The time in which progress is made while trying to solve something. See PRESOLUTION PERIOD.

solvent inhalation   The practice of inhaling fumes of industrial solvents and aerosol sprays capable of producing intoxication. The fumes may contain alcohol, ether, chloroform, or trichloroethylene. May be followed by tolerance to the solvents, tissue damage to the brain, liver, and kidneys, and death. A far more common and pervasive effect is mild dementia. Also called huffing.

SOM   Abbreviation for sexually open marriage. See OPEN MARRIAGE (meaning 1).

soma   (body—Greek) 1. The body as a whole; all organic tissue; the body as distinguished from the mind or psyche. 2. A drug that produces euphoria and hallucinations, from Aldous Huxley's novel *Brave New World* where it was a control technique used by the state.

som(a)esthesia   Body senses (somatic senses): kinesthetic, tactile, and organic or internal sensitivity. Also known as som(a)esthesis, somatesthesia, somnesthesia.

somasthenia   Old term for a neurosis of which the main symptom is chronic physical weakness. Also known as somatasthenia. See CHRONIC FATIGUE IMMUNE DYSFUNCTION SYNDROME.

somatesthetic perception   **somesthetic perception**

somatic   Pertaining to the body. See SOMA.

somatic areas   Two main areas of the cortex mapped with evoked potentials to locate projection points associated with the various somatic senses. Also known as somatic sensory areas, somatosensory cortex. See SENSORY-PROJECTION AREA.

somatic armor   (W. Reich) A means of affecting character armor neurosis by the process of evoking and discharging repressed emotions. See CHARACTER ARMOR.

somatic cell   1. Any cell that is not a germ cell (reproductive cell). Also known as a body cell. 2. A body cell with the diploid set of chromosomes as distinguished from a haploid gamete cell produced by the gonads.

somatic compliance   1. (A. Adler) The expression of psychological disturbances through bodily malfunctions. The reasons why a person with a conversion neurosis becomes blind rather than paralyzed are often conjectural. One theory is that the affected organ is constitutionally predisposed to breakdown; another, that it symbolizes or otherwise represents the person's unconscious impulses or conflicts. 2. (L. Salk) A point of view that the body does what the mind tells it to, including becoming ill. See CONVERSION, HYSTERIA, SOMATIC WEAKNESS, SYMPTOM CHOICE.

somatic concern   Anxious preoccupation with bodily processes such as digestion and elimination. See HYPOCHONDRIASIS.

somatic delusion   A false belief that individual bodily organs, or the body as a whole, are disturbed or disordered, for example, that the stomach or heart is missing, or that the legs are two yards long. Most frequently observed in psychotic states such as schizophrenia. Also known as somatopsychic delusion.

somatic depression   A type of depression characterized by poor appetite, sleep disturbances, weight changes and vague somatic complaints.

somatic disorder   1. Any organic disorder, as distinguished from a functional or psychogenic disorder. 2. Persistent behavioral disturbances resulting from organic factors such as hereditary conditions, infections, or drugs such as heroin or alcohol.

somatic function   Any function of sensation and muscular contraction in which the somatic nervous system is concerned. Contrasted with visceral functions controlled by the autonomic nervous system.

somatic hallucination   The false perception of a physical occurrence, such as electric currents or a cancerous growth, within the body. Frequently observed in patients with paranoid schizophrenia.

somaticizer   1. (N. Cummings) A person who translates emotional stress into physical symptoms. 2. Historically, the replacement term for hypochondriac. See CONVERSION, HYPOCHONDRIA, HYSTERIA.

somatic memories   **sensory-motor memory**

somatic nervous system   Part of the nervous system that involves sensory and motor neurons innervating the skeletal muscles and related skin receptors.

somatic obsession   Preoccupation of people with their bodies or parts of their bodies. Some mental patients have a monosymptomatic neurosis and may spend much time studying their bodies and comparing their physical features with those of others.

somatic posture   Position of the body and its parts. May convey information about personality, current mood, etc., for example, some people slouch, others stand up straight. According to Alfred Adler, people demonstrate by their sleeping postures, something of their waking personalities. See SLEEPING POSITIONS.

somatic receptors   Sensory organs located in the skin including the deeper kinesthetic sense organs. Kinds of somatic receptors include free nerve endings, Merkel's cells, Meissner corpuscles, Krause end bulbs, Golgi tendon organs, kin(a)esthetic receptors, and hair-follicle basket nerve endings.

somatic senses   Senses of pressure (or touch), pain, heat, coldness, and movement (kinesthetic sense), mediated by receptors in the skin, visceral organs, muscles, tendons, and joints.

somatic sensory areas   **somatic areas**

somatic sensory system   Areas of the cerebral cortex (primarily in back of the fissure of Rolando) concerned with kinesthesis and the cutaneous senses.

somatic therapy   The medical treatment of mental disorders by organic methods such as electroshock therapy, psychotropic drugs, or megavitamins.

somatic weakness   The vulnerability of an organ or organ system to psychological stress.

somatist   A person who considers that neuroses and psychoses are manifestations of organic disease. Original focus was on bodily lesions.

somatization   1. Psychophysiologic disorders as psychogenic conditions. 2. (W. Stekel) The organic expression of neurotic disturbance. Term was used by Wilhelm Stekel for what was later called "conversion." See ORGAN NEUROSIS, PSYCHOLOGICAL FACTORS AFFECTING PHYSICAL CONDITION.

somatization disorder   Constant complaints about physical symptoms of illnesses with no objective evidence of any reasonable biological cause. See CONVERSION DISORDERS, HYSTERIA, HYPOCHONDRIA.

somatization reaction   Rare phrase for the bodily symptoms that occur in almost every neurosis, and also as a separate category that includes such psychophysiologic disorders as psychogenic asthma and peptic ulcers. See ORGANIC NEUROSIS, PSYCHOLOGICAL FACTORS IN PHYSICAL CONDITION, SOMATIZATION.

somatoform disorder(s)   1. Mental disorder characterized by physical symptoms for which no physical basis can be found. 2. Conversion disorders of a physiological type. See ATYPICAL SOMATOFORM DISORDER, CONVERSION HYSTERIA, HYSTERIA, HYPOCHONDRIASIS, PSYCHOGENIC PAIN DISORDER, SOMATIZATION DISORDER.

somatogenesis   1. Transformation of germ-cell material into somatic or body cells. 2. Generation of any organismic phenomenon within body tissues. 3. The origin of behavioral or personality traits or disorders in organic factors, such as anatomical or physiological changes. See ORGANOGENESIS.

somatogenic factors   See ENDOGENESIS.

somatognosia   Awareness of own body as a functioning entity, especially false perceptions of own body. See MACROSOMATOGNOSIA, MICROSOMATOGNOSIA.

somatology   1. The investigation of the general bodily constitution and physiology of humans. Also known as physical anthropology. 2. The scientific study of the human body, subdivided into anatomy and physiology.

somatometry   The classification of persons according to body form, and relation of the types to physiologic and psychologic characteristics. See BODY TYPE.

somatopathic drinking   The chronic consumption of alcoholic beverages to the point of physical complications such as adverse effects on the stomach, liver, pancreas, or kidneys, but without physical or psychological dependence. Such people often exhibit nutritional-deficiency symptoms and diminished job efficiency. Similar to E. M. Jellinek's beta alcoholism.

somatophrenia   A mental condition that exaggerates or imagines body ills; less frequently used than hypochondria.

somatoplasm   Tissue cells of the body as distinguished from the gametes, or germ cells. See GERM PLASM.

somatopsychic delusion   1. One of three classifications of delusions suggested by Karl Wernicke, characterized by a patient's body being the subject of the delusion. Wernicke's other two classifications are autopsychic (a patient's personality is the subject of the delusion) and allopsychic (the external world is the subject of the delusion). 2. See SOMATIC DELUSION.

somatopsychic disorders   Psychological disturbances resulting from organic factors, as in the effects of opiates on behavior, or the postencephalitic syndrome consisting of impulsivity and overactivity, resulting from epidemic encephalitis.

somatopsychological factors   Elements of the body and physique that affect the behavior of persons; the influence of body shape and body health upon individual behavior and attitudes.

somatopsychology   The study of psychological consequences of somatic changes such as suddenly gaining or losing weight, being disfigured by an accident, loss of a limb, blindness.

somatopsychosis   1. A mental disorder due to physiological causes. 2. Delusions about own body, such as being certain of smelling like onions even though no one else thinks so. 3. A psychosis in which the patient's delusions involve the body or body parts. See BODY-DYSMORPHIC DISORDER.

somatosenses   The "touch" sensory systems: the cutaneous, kinesthetic, and visceral systems.

somatosensory cortex   somatic sensory areas

somatosensory systems   Sensory nerve systems that transmit impulses to and from the skin, muscles, joints, and certain parts of the viscera. The receptors in all those areas are similar in appearance and function, and their fibers follow the same general pathways through the central nervous system.

somatotherapy   1. Therapy directed at bodily or physical disorders. 2. In psychiatry, a variety of therapeutic interventions employing chemical or physical (as opposed to psychological) methods.

somatotonia   (W. Sheldon) A personality type allegedly associated with a mesomorphic (muscular, athletic) physique. Characterized by a tendency toward energetic activity, physical courage, action-mindedness, assertiveness, and love of power. Also known as somatotonic temperament/type. See SHELDON'S CONSTITUTIONAL THEORY OF PERSONALITY.

somatotopagnosia   Inability to identify any part of own or another's body. Also known as somatagnosia, somatotopagnosis. See AUTOTOPAGNOSIA.

somatotopic organization   Distribution of motor areas of the cortex relating to specific activities of skeletal muscles. The hemispheres can be mapped to locate somatotopic organization areas by electrical stimulation of a point in the cortex. See SOMATIC SENSORY AREAS.

somatotopy   Indications on the cerebral cortex where sensory aspects are to be found. See SENSORY HOMUNCULUS.

somatotropin   A protein hormone of the anterior lobe of the pituitary that promotes body growth among other things. Also known as growth hormone, pituitary growth hormone, somatotrop(h)ic hormone, somatotrophin.

somatotype The body build or physique of a person. Often assumed to be related to temperamental or behavioral characteristics. Numerous categories of somatotypes have been proposed by various investigators since ancient times. See HUMAN BODY TYPE.

somatotype theory A point of view that body types are related to personality types. Hippocrates concluded that human body types (specifically, humors) and personalities were related. See SOMATOTYPOLOGY, TYPOLOGY.

somatotypology The classification of individuals according to body builds, usually correlated with personality characteristics. Also known as somatotyping. See CONSTITUTIONAL TYPES.

somber-bright dimension In psychological esthetics, a system of classifying artistic styles on the basis of emotional effects. Research evidence shows that intense brightness, high saturation, and hues that correspond to long wavelengths of light tend to excite a participant.

somesthesia A sense of the position of the body and its condition, which is derived from sensory information from receptors in the skin, joints, muscles and other areas of the body. Also known as somatesthesia, somesthesis. See KINESTHESIA (KINESTHESIS).

somesthetic area A region of the parietal lobe of the brain in which sensory impulses from somatic receptors are received. Studies indicate that the body surface is projected in the postcentral gyrus area in the same relationship as the dermatomes represented by the nerve fibers.

somesthetic disorders Dysfunctions involving the somatic senses, such as visual-spatial or body image disturbances, difficulty in maintaining postural awareness, or lack of sensitivity to pain, touch, or temperature. Usually are related to brain damage in the parietal lobe, as from gunshot wounds.

somesthetic perception Awareness of the bodily condition including all perceptions and kinesthetic states. Also known as somatesthetic perception.

somesthetic senses Touch sensations, from the outside or internally, as detected by the skin, joints and muscles.

somesthetic stimulation The stimulation of kinesthetic, tactile, or visceral receptors which constitute human bodily senses.

somnarium An institution for the treatment of psychological disorders, particularly neuroses, by sleep. See SLEEP TREATMENT.

Sommer Tridimensional Movement Analyzer (R. Sommer) A device for demonstrating three spatial components of hand and figure movements on a single dimension as on a moving tape. Used to record involuntary movements in research on physiological responses to stimuli.

somnambulism Walking while asleep. A disorder of sleep, involving complex motor acts, that occurs primarily during the first third of the night but not during REM (rapid eye movement) sleep. Also known as noctambulation, oneirodynia, somnambulance, sleepwalking. See DELTA WAVES, MONOIDEIC SOMNAMBULISM, NON-RAPID-EYE-MOVEMENT SLEEP.

somnambulistic state 1. A state of mind in which walking or talking or other complex acts occur during sleep. 2. A hypnotic phase in which a person in a deep trance, may appear to be awake and in control of behavior but is actually under the control of the hypnotist.

somnifacients Obsolete term for agents capable of inducing sleep. Term is sometimes applied to sedative-hypnotic drugs, and is similar to soporifics.

somniferous Sleep-inducing; soporific.

somniloquy Talking in one's sleep. Also known as somniloquence, somniloquism.

somnium dream A type of dream that arises from deep and obscure sources. Carl Jung distinguished this type of dream from insomnium dreams, or those that reflect the current state of a person's body and psyche.

somnolence Pathological sleepiness or drowsiness, sometimes prolonged for days. The condition may be due to overmedication, brain injury (somnolence is a warning sign after head trauma to have the person evaluated for a possible expanding intracranial blood clot), narcotic drugs, epidemic encephalitis, conversion disorder, or other conditions. See TWILIGHT SLEEP.

somnolent detachment Harry Sullivan's phrase for psychogenic hypersomnia. In infants, a means of escape from anxiety through sleep. See NARCOLEPSY.

somnolentia Obsolete term for sleep drunkenness.

somnology The study of sleep. See HYPNOLOGY.

somnophilia Being sexually aroused by intruding on and fondling a sleeping stranger.

SOMPA System of Multicultural Pluralistic Assessment

sonance Fusion of successive pitches, distinguished from timbre, which involves fusion of simultaneous pitches.

sonant 1. In phonetics, a voiced sound produced by means of vocal-cord vibrations (for example, /b/, /v/, /z/), as opposed to a voiceless sound (for example, /p/, /t/, /f/). 2. In phonology, a semivowel, that is, a speech sound that can have features of both a vowel and a consonant, for example, /r/ as in "read," /w/ as in "well," or /y/ as in "yellow."

sone A unit of the ratio scale of loudness; a 1,000-hertz (cycles per second) tone 40 decibels above its mean absolute threshold is defined as one sone.

Sonicguide Headworn electronic device that provides an auditory signal about the walking environment for the visually impaired.

sonoencephalogram (SEG) Echoencephalogram. See ECHOENCEPHALOGRAPH.

sonogram A graphic of a complex sound showing the relative energy among different sound frequencies, usually over time. See BIOMEDICAL ENGINEERING, ECHOENCEPHALOGRAM, ULTRASOUND TECHNIQUE.

sonometer 1. An instrument for auditory experiments and demonstrations made by stretching one or more strings over a resonating box. See AUDIOMETER. 2. An instrument for measuring the sound vibration of an object.

sonomotor Pertaining to movements caused by sound.

sophistry The use of fallacious or ambiguous arguments often with the intention to confuse or deceive others.

Sophistry Therapy (T. D. Evans) A group technique used to expose false arguments that protect personal hidden reasons (the elements in thinking used to justify inappropriate behavior). Once exposed, a new structure of thinking is built and put into action. Sophistry therapy assumes behavior follows in the wake of thought.

sophomania The delusion of having great wisdom.

sophrosyne The quality of having a sound mind. State of being prudent, logical, reasonable, self-controlling. See HUBRIS.

soporifics 1. Sleep inducing drugs or situations. 2. Agents capable of producing sleep, particularly a deep sleep. See SEDATIVE-HYPNOTICS, SOMNIFACIENTS.

SOR stimulus-organism-response (also abbreviated S-O-R)

SORC variables Four types of variables employed in behavioral evaluations: situational determinants (S), organismic variables (O), overt responses (R), and reinforcement contingencies (C).

sorcery The use of supernatural knowledge or power gained in any manner, especially through the connivance of evil spirits. Also known as enchantment, magic, necromancy, witchcraft.

sorcery drugs A group of plant substances including belladonna, opium, mandrake, aconite, and hemlock. The substances have been chewed, smoked, or brewed into potions throughout human history for therapeutic and intoxicating purposes. See ETHNOBOTANY, ETHNOPSYCHOPHARMACOLOGY.

Sörge (worry, care—German) Caring. *Sörge*, for Martin Heidegger, was the basis of all being and he assumed that humans can overcome everything because of their capacity for caring. See SOCIAL INTEREST.

sororate Marriage to a deceased wife's (unmarried) sister. Marriage to a deceased husband's (married or unmarried) brother is termed levirate. Culturally-based situations sometimes encountered in family therapy.

S-O-R learning (model) 1. An approach to learning theory in which intervening variables, sometimes called hypothetical constructs and only used after careful operational definition, play a major role. Typically the notion of trial-and-error as the basis of problem solving is rejected. Contrast with S-R learning and S-S learning. For examples of S-O-R see Clark Hull's HYPOTHETICO-DEDUCTIVE THEORY OF LEARNING and the CELL-ASSEMBLY THEORY of Donald O. Hebb. 2. A tripartite model of consumer information processing proposed by M. J. Houston and M. L. Rothschild. Involvement of the consumer with a given product is analyzed as situational (S), enduring (O), or a simple learned response (R).

S-O-R psychology 1. Combining notions of the British empiricist philosophers with the introspective approaches of Wilhelm Wundt and Hermann Ebbinghaus led to the focus on association between subjective sensory impressions exemplified by the writings of E. C. Tolman. In some regards the approach of Wolfgang Köhler belongs here, although he considered learning and perceiving to be essentially the same thing. The perceived importance of the S-R, S-O-R and S-S distinctions lessened considerably in the late 20th century. See S-R PSYCHOLOGY, S-S PSYCHOLOGY. 2. In the latter half of the 20th century computer models of behavior developed. They distinguished between input (S), processing (O—by the neutral system sometimes referred to as a "wet computer"), and output (R).

S-O-R theory emphasizing organism One of the three groupings used by M. H. Marx and W. A. Hillix for contemporary theories, which includes most of those customarily labeled personality theories. The focus of these psychological theories is decidedly upon the organism and its characteristics. Marx and Hillix note that the notion of three categories cannot be pushed too far, as few theories deal exclusively with S or O or R. S-O-R includes Gordon Allport's personality-trait theory, Raymond B. Cattell's factor theory of personality, the typology theory of Hans J. Eysenck, the neoanalytic theory of Erich Fromm, the organismic psychology of Kurt Goldstein, the neoanalytic theory of Karen Horney, the biosocial theory of Gardner Murphy, the personology theory of Henry A. Murray, the person-centered therapy approach of Carl R. Rogers, William H. Sheldon's constitutional theory of personality, and the interpersonal theory of Harry Stack Sullivan. Compare S-O-R THEORY EMPHASIZING PERCEPTION, S-R THEORY.

S-O-R theory emphasizing perception One of the three groupings used by M. H. Marx and W. A. Hillix for contemporary theories, which includes most "field" theories, particularly those that are heavily influenced by Gestalt psychology. The focus of these psychological theories is decidedly upon the context of behavior, often with emphasis on a holistic approach. It includes the probabilistic functionalism of Egon Brunswick, the neuropsychology approach of Karl S. Lashley, the topological psychology approach of Kurt Lewin, and Edward C. Tolman's purposive behaviorism. Compare S-O-R THEORY EMPHASIZING ORGANISM, S-R THEORY.

sorting test A technique for assessing the ability to conceptualize. The participant is asked to arrange an assortment of common objects by categories. A young child might group random objects by size or shape, whereas an older person will more likely categorize objects on the basis of functional relationships. See CLASS INCLUSION, GOLDSTEIN-SCHEERER TESTS.

soteria 1. A nonhospital, residential therapeutic community for patients with acute schizophrenia operated by a specially trained, indigenous, nonprofessional staff with no or very low use of medication. Intervention is variously described as milieu therapy, sociotherapy and psychotherapy. 2. The possessions or other objects, including collections, acquired for a feeling of security. Distinguished from accumulation, which refers to the continued possession of unclassified, useless, or meaningless objects. See HOARDING CHARACTER.

soteriological (R. Walsh) One of three views of the purpose of psychotherapy: transcendence of the problems confronted at the existential level. The other two are (a) traditional, reducing pathology, and (b) existential, confronting the problems of existence.

soul   1. A metaphysical entity hypothesized to have a permanent existence; the immortal spiritual part of humans. Humanists, who do not accept the concept of soul, take the position that "mind" is the equivalent of "soul." The same word serves for both the mind and the soul in German (*Geist*) and in French (*esprit*). See CREATIVE SELF. 2. The whole of one's energies, the emotional aspects of a human, the animating principle, as seen in the phrase "with all one's heart and soul."

soul image   In Jungian psychology, the deeply unconscious portion of the psyche composed of the animus (male) and anima (female) archetypes.

soul kiss   French kiss

soul theory   A point of view that mental phenomena are the manifestations of a specific nonmaterial substance, usually assumed to be distinct from material substance (the body).

sound   1. In physics, the vibration of molecules (that is, pressure propagation) through an elastic medium. The velocity of sound is a function of both density and elasticity, about 340 m/sec in air at 15°C (1100 ft/sec at 59°F), about 1370 m/sec (4500 ft/sec) in the liquid of the human inner ear, and about 1510 m/sec at 30°C (4950 ft/sec at 86°F) for pure water. 2. In psychology, the frequency range detectable by the organism's ear, about 20 to 20,000 Hertz (cycles per second) for normal, young humans; 1,000 to 150,000 Hz for bats; 100 to 32,000 Hz for cats; 40 to 40,000 Hz for dogs; 30 to 40,000 Hz for horses (approximate values for animals). 3. Free from disease, as in "sound of mind." 4. Free from logical error or bias, as in "sound advice." 5. Deep, undisturbed, as in "sound sleep."

sound-air conduction   The path that sound waves travel to result in their perception. Originating sound compresses and decompresses air that travels to the eardrums. Resulting vibrations move the bones of the inner ear causing the oval window of the cochlea to vibrate, generating waves that bend hairs in the Organ of Corti and send neural signals to the brain. See BONE CONDUCTION, HEARING.

sound cage   A device for measuring sound localization.

sound direction/distance   See AUDITORY SPACE PERCEPTION.

sound energy flux   The average over one period in ergs per second of the rate of flow of acoustic energy through a given area.

sound fear   See ACOUSTICOPHOBIA, PHONOPHOBIA.

sound frequency   The number of cycles (vibrations) per second, measured in hertz (Hz). The range of vibrations per second of the human ear is 20 to 20,000 Hz, of the human speaking voice (fundamental tones) is 75–150 Hz for a bass with a soprano extending to 4,000 Hz. The lowest sung note (fundamental frequency) in the classic literature is the Bb of 58 Hz with the highest the f^3 of almost 1,400 Hz; overtones produced extend to around 12,000 Hz. See FREQUENCY OF SOUND.

sound hammer   A device (used in reaction-time experiments) consisting of a piece of metal whose fall upon a metal plate produces a sound signal. For an illustration see SOUND PENDULUM.

sounding   phonic method

sounding out   See PHONIC METHOD.

sound intensity (*I*)   The strength of the particle vibration, or the rate of sound-energy transmission through a medium; related to the square of the amplitude and the square of the frequency of a sound wave. Sound intensity (*I*) is related to sound pressure by the formula: $I = p^2 \div dc$, where: p is the root-mean-square (RMS) of sound pressure, d is the density of the medium, c is the speed of sound in the medium.

sound level meter   An instrument used to measure levels of sound at different frequencies.

sound localization   The determination of the direction of the source of a sound. Experienced (usually) unconsciously by intensity, phase differences, and differences in the time of arrival of the sound waves at the right and left ears.

sound pendulum   A device constructed to generate a standard sound. The one below was developed by Lehmann and was known as the acoumeter. See WUNDT SOUND PENDULUM for another version.

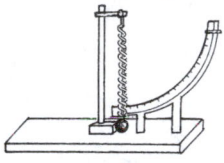

sound pendulum   A primitive system used in assessing how soundly people slept. The ball is raised to a predetermined height and dropped to strike against a block.

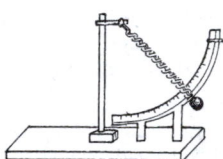

sound perimetry   A method of measuring the ability of a participant to localize sounds in space.

sound-pressure level (SPL)   A common reference level (0.0002 dyne per square centimeter, the absolute threshold for a 1,000 Hz tone) used in specifying sound intensity in decibels. See BEL

sound profile   A graphic representation of sounds uttered in speech, usually of vowels and consonants. May be done for a single person or for a group's linguistic system. See VOICEPRINT.

soundproof room   A cubical so constructed as to be relatively impervious to outside sounds.

sound shadow   An area in which sound is blocked by a nontransmitting object, such as a person's body particularly the head and pinna (external ear).

sound spectrogram   An image of a pattern made by sounds.

sound spectrograph   A graph which shows an analysis of a succession of complex tones, often speech. The horizontal axis of the graph is the time during which the auditory stimulus exists, with the nature of that stimulus identified; the vertical axis is sound frequency in Hertz; and the body of the graph shows which frequencies are identified as contributing to the tone. See FOURIER ANALYSIS.

sound spectrum   An analysis of complex tones into their component frequencies and intensities. Also known as acoustic spectrum, tonal spectrum.

sound symbolism (phenomenon)   (W. Köhler) When people were shown abstract drawings and given options for what to name them, Wolfgang Köhler discovered that soft and rounded figures tended to be given "soft-sounding" names whereas straight and pointed figures tended to be given "hard-sounding" names (names with consonants), for example, the word "Kleona" is likely to be linked to the drawing at the right whereas the word "Pinckney" the drawing at the left.

sound symbolism

sound wave   Periodic pressure fluctuation in a medium, such as air or water, that may be perceived as a sound by a human if the frequency is between 20 and 20,000 hertz (cycles per second). See SOUND.

sour   1. (H. Henning) One of the four principal qualities of taste, a quality of gustatory sensation of which the taste of citric acid (lemon juice) and acetic acid (vinegar) are typical examples. Also known as acid. See BITTER, SALINE, SWEET. 2. In music, out of tune.

source amnesia   1. A tendency sometimes shown in patients with amnesia to be more impaired in their ability to recall "where" they have acquired new information than "what" they remembered. 2. A phenomenon of knowing something but not remembering where that knowledge came from, as in being introduced to a person for the second time but not recalling where the initial introduction took place.

source confusion   1. Memory distortion important in criminal cases, in which a witness may recall the original incident and postevent information but may confuse the postevent information as part of the original event. 2. Memory distortion characterized by misrecalling who provided the information, such as forgetting whether it was from Person A or Person B.

source language   1. The original language or native language of the learner of a foreign language or of an artificial (for example, computer) language system. 2. The language from which a translation is made. See TARGET LANGUAGE.

source memory   A remembrance of the origin of any memory such as where an event occurred or who made a certain statement. See EPISODIC MEMORY.

source trait   (R. B. Cattell) A trait discovered and defined by simple structure. See FACTOR ANALYSIS.

sour-grapes mechanism   A rationalization process characterized by expressing satisfaction at not doing what was desired, or claiming that things desirable but not obtainable are not worth the getting. Also known as sour-grapes attitude/reaction. Compare SWEET-LEMON MECHANISM.

SPA   State Psychological Association

spaced learning   A learning procedure in which practice periods are separated by time intervals at other activities or rest periods. Generally considered more effective than massed learning/practice, with the most data available for verbal material and motor skills. Also known as distributed practice, spaced practice/repetition. Compare MASSED LEARNING/PRACTICE.

space-eikonometer   An instrument for measuring space or depth cues of images or figures. Used for studying stereoscopic vision and aniseikonia.

space error   1. A constant error found in simultaneous presentation of (visual) stimuli in the psychophysical methods, for example in measuring the difference threshold the light stimulus on the left is consistently judged by an observer to be slightly brighter than the light on the right. Controlled by placing the constant stimulus on the left during half of the trials (counterbalancing); analogous to the time error in presentation of successive stimuli, as in hearing where an observer may consistently report the first tone as slightly softer. 2. An error in judging the position of a stimulus due to its spatial relationship to the observer.

space factor   An ability, identified by factor analysis, which accounts for individual differences in the capacity to perceive spatial relations.

space of free movements   A subjective perception of the number of possible choices for behavior.

space orientation   An ability to locate or adjust own position in space.

space perception   An awareness derived from sensory inputs of the spatial properties of objects in the environment, including their shape, dimension, and distances.

space relations   Direction and distances of objects from one another or from the observer.

spandrel   (S. J. Gould) Features that presently enhance an organism's fitness, but in the past did not. For example, the "friendly," submissive, approaching greeting most dogs give humans increases the likelihood of biological success today when dogs are either pets or working companions, whereas such behavior would have decreased biological success centuries ago when dogs were both a competitor for scarce food and a major food source for humans. See ADAPTATION, DARWINISM, EMERGENT EVOLUTION, EVOLUTION, EXAPTATION.

Spanish fly   An insect, *Cantharis vesicatoria*, employed in dried form primarily in the topical (on skin) treatment of warts but on occasion internally as a diuretic. Previously incorrectly considered an aphrodisiac. Ingestion of the substance can be deadly. Also known as Russian fly. See CANTHARIDES.

span of apprehension/of attention   See ATTENTION SPAN.

spasm   A sudden involuntary muscle contraction, which may vary from a twitch to a convulsion. A continuous spasm is called a tonic spasm. A spasm that alternates between contraction and relaxation is known as a clonic spasm. Spasms may also be identified with body parts, such as vasospasms (of blood vessels). A common form of clonic spasm is known as hiccups. See BRISSAUD'S DISEASE, HABIT SPASM, TONIC.

spasmodic laughter   Periods of laughter without any apparent cause, found in schizophrenia, hysteria, and organic and pseudobulbar diseases of the brain, as well as in dancing mania. Also known as gelasmus. See COMPULSIVE LAUGHTER.

spasmodic torticollis   Spasms of the neck muscles causing a tipping of the head, the direction of the head depending on which neck muscles are involved. Ordinarily associated with psychological disorders and usually responds to psychotherapy in lieu of surgery. Also known as wryneck syndrome.

spasmophemia   Disturbance in the rhythm of speech; a blocking or hesitation in speech production, frequently called stuttering.

spastic   In process of having spasms. See MUSCLE TONE, SPASM.

spastic colitis   Spasms of the colon; often thought to be of a psychosomatic nature. See COLITIS, STOMACH REACTOR.

spastic dysphonia   A functional voice disorder characterized by intermittent laryngeal spasms which interfere with normal speech.

spastic hemiparesis   Partial paralysis on one side of the body complicated by muscle spasms of the limbs on the affected side. The muscle contractions may be quite painful. Treatment may include biofeedback training in addition to medications and braces.

spasticity   A motoneuron disorder marked by rigidity and clonus, which in turn is due to involuntary resistance to stretching of a muscle by increased tension. Involves deep tendon reflexes and results in a jerking action of the limbs.

spastic speech   Difficult, labored verbal communication associated with spastic paralysis.

spatial ability (S)   Ability to orient, or visualize own body in space, or to detect spatial relationships. A deficit in spatial ability may be observed in persons with brain injuries who are unable to perform effectively in map-reading tests or who have difficulties in recognizing shapes tactually. Also known as spatial orientation.

spatial density   The amount of space per individual in a given area. Phrase is sometimes used in experiments on the effects of crowding in which a same-size group is observed interacting in different-size areas. See SOCIAL DENSITY.

spatial disorders   Pervasive disruptions of space perception, usually associated with parietal-lobe lesions and including impaired memory for locations, route-finding difficulties and poor judgment of the localization of stimuli. Patients may underestimate the distance of far objects and overestimate the distance of near objects, or may be unable to align objects according to instructions.

spatial frequency   In perception research, the number of cycles (one dark plus one light bar) per degree of visual angle. High spatial frequency carries information about stimulus detail; low conveys information about the general shape.

spatial intelligence   Ability to visualize and mentally rotate figures in two- and three-dimensional space. One of Louis Thurstone's primary factors of intelligence, it is measured on the 1986 Stanford-Binet by the Paper Folding and Cutting test. Sometimes known as spatial orientation. See PRIMARY ABILITIES, PRIMARY MENTAL ABILITIES, SPATIAL ABILITY, THURSTONE PRIMARY MENTAL ABILITIES.

spatial limen/threshold   The smallest distance on the skin at which two stimuli are perceived as two stimuli rather than a single stimulus. Also known as two-point discrimination/threshold. See ESTHESIOMETER for an illustration of how this is done.

spatial orientation   spatial ability

spatial relations (S)   The three-dimensional relationship of objects in space, such as their distance apart and their position to each other. Also known as spatial relationships. See DEPTH PERCEPTION, PRIMARY ABILITIES, SPACE RELATIONS.

spatial summation   A neural mechanism present in the spinal-motor system in which a neuron is fired by the summation of several synaptic inputs being discharged simultaneously. Spatial summation firings occur at points where the discharge of a single synapse would not be sufficient to produce the energy needed to activate the neuron.

spatial threshold   See SPATIAL LIMEN.

spatial vision   Perception of patterns and details in images observed through the visual sense.

spaying   The surgical removal of the ovaries of a female mammal as a sterilization procedure. Such a female, and also one that has otherwise been rendered incapable of reproducing, is referred to as "spayed."

speaking-fear   See GLOSSOPHOBIA, LALIOPHOBIA.

speaking in tongues   Speaking what appears to be gibberish to the average observer, usually observed in cases of religious ecstasy (see the gospel of Mark 16:17), but sometimes heard in particular mental disorders, as well as in people who are under severe stress, especially fear. See GLOSSOLALIA, XENOGLOSSIA.

Spearman-Brown (prophecy) formula   (C. E. Spearman & W. Brown) A formula used to estimate the reliability of an assessment measure if it were to be lengthened and shortened. Also known as step-up/step-down formula. Formula: $r_{nn} = nr_{xx} \div [1 + (n-1)r_{xx}]$, where: n is an integer, r_{xx} is the original reliability estimate. Most often used with split-half methods for calculating internal reliability, doubling the length of a test: $r_{22} = 2r_{1/21/2} \div (1 + r_{1/21/2})$, where r_{22} is the reliability of original test (signifies doubling the length of the test), and $r_{1/21/2}$ is the reliability coefficient obtained by correlating scores on ½ of the test with scores obtained from the other ½.

Spearman footrule correlation (R)   (C. E. Spearman) A formula for computing a correlation based on gain in ranks from the first to the second variable by the equation: $R = 1 - (6\Sigma G) \div (N^2 - 1)$, where: G is the positive difference in ranks, N is the number of cases involved in the ranking, and R is the Spearman footrule correlation. Used for rough rank correlation. Also known as Spearman's footrule.

Spearman rank-difference method   A coefficient of rank correlation (rho) based on the differences between paired ranks. See COEFFICIENT OF RANK CORRELATION.

Spearman rank-order correlation   See COEFFICIENT OF RANK CORRELATION.

Spearman rho coefficient   **coefficient of rank correlation**

Spearman's *g*   (C. E. Spearman) General intelligence. See SPEARMAN'S TWO-FACTOR THEORY.

Spearman's hypothesis   (C. E. Spearman) A postulate that the difference in cognitive abilities is essentially a difference in *g*, the general factor common to all cognitive tests. See INTELLIGENCE TESTS.

Spearman's method   See COEFFICIENT OF RANK CORRELATION.

Spearman's *s*   (C. E. Spearman) Specific factors in intelligence. See SPEARMAN'S TWO-FACTOR THEORY.

Spearman's theory   The following items are important for understanding Charles Spearman's theory: CORRELATES, FOOTRULE CORRELATION, FUNDAMENT, GENERAL FACTOR, GROUP FACTORS IN INTELLIGENCE, LAW OF DIMINISHING RETURNS, LAW OF SPAN, NEOGENETIC, PRINCIPLE OF INERTIA, SPEARMAN-BROWN (PROPHECY) FORMULA, SPEARMAN FOOTRULE CORRELATION, SPEARMAN RANK-DIFFERENCE METHOD, SPEARMAN'S HYPOTHESIS, SPEARMAN'S TWO-FACTOR THEORY, SPECIAL FACTOR, SPECIFIC ABILITY, TETRAD DIFFERENCE METHOD, TETRAD DIFFERENCES, THEOREM OF INDIFFERENCE OF THE INDICATOR, TWO-FACTOR THEORY (OF INTELLIGENCE).

Spearman's two-factor theory   (C. E. Spearman) A point of view that two basic factors comprise intelligence: a general factor known as *g* complemented by several specific ability factors labeled as *s*. See GENERAL FACTOR, SPECIAL FACTOR.

special abilities   A vague expression suggesting a set of nonoverlapping abilities, each of which may vary independently of any general ability or average level of ability. See SPEARMAN'S TWO-FACTOR THEORY.

special ability test   An examination designed to measure some special ability or restricted group of capacities, as distinguished from a general ability test.

special aptitude   See SPECIFIC ABILITY.

special child   1. A child with special problems who needs special education and training. Includes children who are slower to learn the same material as peers, children with physical disabilities, emotional disabilities, or both. Similar to "exceptional child." 2. (V. Raimy) A child who has been mentally abused by parents and relatives by having been given incorrect information about himself or herself that is accepted as true, such as about intelligence, appearance, abilities. Such children, if they continue to believe such false designations, are purported to become problem children and problem adults. See ATYPICAL CHILD, EXCEPTIONAL CHILD, SPECIAL CLASSES, SPECIAL EDUCATION, SPECIAL SCHOOL, SPOILING.

special classes   Educational programs designed specifically for students with particular intellectual, behavioral, or physical disabilities, for example, blindness, deafness, or speech impairment. See SPECIAL CHILD, SPECIAL EDUCATION.

special education   School services and instruction provided to children with learning disabilities such as perceptual deficit, minimal brain dysfunction, blindness, deafness, and neurological disorders, as well as to children with intellectual ability so far above or below the norm that they require special curricula or special classes. See SPECIAL CHILD, SPECIAL CLASSES.

special educational programs   School services for children with disabilities that may adapt standard teaching materials and methods to the type of disability to achieve the optimum level of training for such children. Kinds of programs include diagnostic-descriptive approach, cross-categorical approach, and individually prescribed curriculum.

special factor (*s*)   (C. E. Spearman) A specialized ability which comes into play in particular kinds of cognitive tasks. A special factor such as mathematical ability, is contrasted with the general intelligence factor, *g*, which underlies every cognitive performance. See GENERAL FACTOR, SPEARMAN TWO-FACTOR THEORY.

Special K   Slang for ketamine hydrochloride.

special-needs child   **educable-mentally-retarded (EMR) child**

special needs people   Persons with physical or psychological disorders or disabilities. See CHALLENGED, PERSON WITH A DISABILITY.

special process (hypothesis)   (N. P. Spanos) A postulate that a person's behavior while under hypnosis is qualitatively different from nonhypnotic behavior. See STATE THEORIES OF HYPNOSIS.

special school   A facility that provides education for disadvantaged or disabled children who are not prepared to cope with the intellectual and social skills demanded of children in regular schools.

special senses   Refers to the four cranial senses of vision, audition, gustation, olfaction.

special-symptom reaction   A personality disorder comprising such behavior dysfunctions or conditions as stuttering, nail-biting, enuresis, tics, and compulsive gambling.

special visceral efferent fibers   See ACCESSORY NERVE.

special vulnerability   Particularly low tolerance for certain kinds of stress.

speciation   The development of new species.

species   A subgroup of a genus. A class of organisms having common appearances that are capable of reproduction resulting in (theoretically) viable offspring during natural mating behavior (without laboratory or experimental manipulation).

species fitness   Ability of various species to survive under changing environmental conditions.

species-specific/-typical   Phrase replacing for some scientists the concept of instinct, referring to the common occurrence of certain behaviors of individuals of certain species in similar environmental circumstances.

specific ability factor (s)   (C. E. Spearman) A special ability or aptitude that does not correlate with other abilities, as opposed to general ability, which correlates at least moderately with other abilities. (A general ability is an ability used for all cognitive tests; a specific ability is an ability used for a particular test.) Also known as special aptitude. See SPEARMAN'S HYPOTHESIS, TALENT.

specification   1. The act of making a full, detailed, and definite statement or classification. 2. Citation of definite examples to illustrate a classification or argument.

specific-attitudes theory   The point of view that certain psychosomatic disorders are associated with particular attitudes, such as the feeling of being mistreated and the occurrence of hives. A similar concept is the specific-reaction theory.

specific determiners   Key words such as "sometimes," "never," "always," "occasionally" which may give away the answer to a true-false item to participants who do not really know the answer.

specific developmental disorders   Conditions or disorders of specific areas of functioning, but not due to any other disorder. See ATYPICAL SPECIFIC DEVELOPMENTAL DISORDER, DEVELOPMENTAL ARITHMETIC DISORDER, DEVELOPMENTAL ARTICULATION DISORDER, DEVELOPMENTAL LANGUAGE DISORDER, DEVELOPMENTAL READING DISORDER, MIXED SPECIFIC DEVELOPMENTAL DISORDER.

specific dynamic pattern   (F. Alexander) The specific nuclear conflict or dynamic configuration of a particular psychosomatic disorder.

specific-energy doctrine   Originally advanced by Johannes Müller in the 1830s as specific energy of nerves, a theory that the quality of a sensory experience is determined by the type of receptor. Still considered valid and there is agreement that the sense of pain, for example, originates with pain receptors. Also known as nerve energy doctrine, specific energy of the senses. See LAW OF SPECIFIC NERVE ENERGY.

specific energy of nerves   Phrase used by Johannes Müller for specific nerve energies.

specific energy of the senses   (A. J. McKeage) Phrase considered by some neurophysiologists to be preferable to Johannes Müller's specific energy of nerves. See SPECIFIC NERVE ENERGIES.

specific excitant   A special kind of stimulus required to fire an impulse in a particular receptor. A sensory receptor may be sensitive only to the specific stimulus for which it was designed by nature, for example, a specific excitant for the retinal cells is light, rather than sound or temperature.

specific factor (s)   1. A factor found only in one test, or a limited number of tests. Compare GENERAL FACTOR. 2. A designated special factor found in factor analysis of ability tests that for a particular test represents the specific ability required to do well in that area. Also known as s factor. See SPECIFIC ABILITY.

specific hunger   An urge to eat foods required by the body to maintain constant weight, adequate energy, and normal health. An animal may have a specific hunger for protein and by self-selection seek protein-rich foods even though palatable but protein-deficient foods are available. See SELF-SELECTION OF DIET.

specific inhibition   Ego function inhibition, for example anorexia or impotence.

specificity   1. The quality of being unique, of a particular kind, or limited to a single phenomenon, for example, a stimulus that elicits a specific response, or a psychosomatic symptom localized in a particular organ such as the stomach. 2. (I. P. Pavlov) Refers to distinctions between stimuli.

specificity doctrine of traits   A theory that human traits are situation specific, contrasted with the view that they can be categorized into general traits such as honesty, dishonesty, cleanliness, or suggestibility, that are transsituational. Holds that, for example, a person who is honest in one situation may be dishonest in another.

specificity of behavior   Restricted response to a particular stimulus, as when withdrawing a limb when it is touched instead of responding with the whole body.

specificity of evaluation   See WORK-FLOW INTEGRATION.

specific language impairment (SLI)   A genetic factor responsible for difficulties in understanding grammatical rules regardless of intelligence levels or brain integrity. Identical twins purportedly have more SLI than fraternal twins. See DEVELOPMENTAL DYSPHASIA.

specific learning disability (SLD)   A learning disorder such as reading or arithmetic difficulty that cannot be associated with a specific physical or mental defect such as mental retardation or cerebral palsy.

specific nerve energies   A doctrine positing that sensation depends upon which nerve is stimulated rather than upon how the nerve is stimulated. Visual sensations occur not only from stimulation of light but also from electric shock to the optic nerve or eye-ball pressure. Called "specific energy of nerves" by Johannes Müller. Some neurophysiologists prefer the phrase specific energy of the senses. Also known as nerve-energy doctrine, specific-energy doctrine.

specific phobia   Excessive, unrealistic, uncontrollable fear elicited by a particular object or situation that in humans does not normally produce fear, for example, cats. Compare UNIVERSAL PHOBIA. See PHOBIA.

specific-reaction theory   A point of view that psychosomatic symptoms result from an innate tendency of the autonomic nervous system to react in a particular way to a stressful situation.

specific serotonin reuptake inhibitor (SSRI)   A chemical that inhibits the reuptake of serotonin but not other neurotransmitters. See SEROTONIN REUPTAKE INHIBITORS.

specific thalamic projection system   Direct sensory pathways via the thalamus for visual, auditory, and somesthetic impulses.

specific transfer   The application of specific skills and knowledge acquired in one field to another field. See GENERAL TRANSFER.

specimen description   A type of observation in which a single subject is observed over a specified period of time with detailed, objective records taken of behaviors and settings. See CASE STUDY.

specimen record   In observational studies, a written, chronological account of a subject's behavior during a given observational session. A specimen record should be as complete a description as possible, ideally including all behavioral details.

specious present   Now. The present moment, as opposed to past or future. An absolute instance of time too small to be measured. Sometimes known as psychological moment, timeless moment.

SPECT   single photon emission computerized tomography

spectator effect   (R. B. Zajonc) An effect on the quality of performance when persons know that they are being observed. See PERFORMANCE ANXIETY.

spectator perception   Personal observation of self-effectiveness and self-efficiency by a person lacking self-confidence, usually leading to impaired performance. See PERFORMANCE ANXIETY.

spectator role   (W. Masters & V. Johnson) A behavior pattern in which natural sexual responses are blocked because the person is observing himself or herself closely and worrying about how well or poorly he or she is performing, rather than participating freely. See PERFORMANCE ANXIETY.

spectator therapy   A tendency of group-therapy members to benefit from observing other patients with similar problems.

spectophilia   Attraction to or obsession with spirits. More common in cultures where humans are believed to be able to copulate with demons, as in Europe of the Middle Ages. See INCUBUS, SUCCUBUS.

spectral absorption   The ability of chemicals to absorb light of specific wavelengths, determined by passing lights of nearly pure wavelengths through chemical solutions and measuring the amount of light absorbed. In visual spectral absorption, the principle is applied by measuring the degree to which wavelengths of light decompose retinal pigment molecules.

spectral color   One of the colors of the spectrum produced when white light is refracted by a prism. See SPECTRUM.

spectral hue   Hues produced by monochromatic light. The following approximate wavelengths (in nanometers) give rise to the following hues: violet 380–450, blue 450–480, blue-green 480–510, green 510–550, yellow-green 550–570, yellow 570–590, orange 590–630, red 630–750 nm. See COLOR CIRCLE, EXTRASPECTRAL HUE.

spectral scale   A set of colors formed by arranging the spectrum as a series of equal units according to just-noticeable chromatic differences, when differences in brilliance are eliminated. Also known as chroma scale.

spectral sensitivity curve   A measurement of the relative degree of absorption by retinal pigments at various wavelengths of light, recorded on a graph of rectangular coordinates. See LUMINANCE.

spectrocolorimeter   (A. W. Volkmann) An instrument that measures colors to designate them numerically; it matches a sample by partial reflection with a mixture of spectral light of a single wave-length and a standard white.

spectrogram   A spectral record; such as a photograph, map, or chart. See SOUND SPECTROGRAPH.

spectrograph   1. Visual plotting of certain characteristics of sound, primarily the human voice, demonstrating time, frequency, and intensity. Spectrograph patterns may be used to identify people by their voice, as in identifying people by voice for entrance into secure locations. Not generally accepted by courts of law as a means of identifying voices. More commonly known as voiceprint. See LIE DETECTOR, SOUND SPECTROGRAPH. 2. A plot of the characteristics of light reflected or transmitted by an object, the results of using a spectroscope. A typical forensic use would compare paint samples from two sources to determine if they came from the same batch made by a particular manufacturer.

spectrograph(ic) analysis   voiceprint

spectrometer   A device that measures the wavelengths of colors in a spectrum. See SPECTROSCOPE.

spectrophobia   See EISOPTROPHOBIA.

spectrophotometer   An instrument that measures the spectral transmission characteristics of an object such as a filter. A very narrow band of wavelengths is produced, often by use of a prism, and passed through a sample container to a device such a a phototube that measures light intensity. By comparing, for each wavelength in turn, the amount of light at the terminus when the object is and is not in the sample container a light spectrograph may be drawn.

spectroscope   An instrument designed to measure the spectrum or spectral characteristics of an object. Contrast with spectrometer, which operates on light rays.

spectroscopy   The observation and analysis of the spectrum of light from any source.

spectrum   1. The series of visible colors produced when white light, for example, sunlight, is refracted through a prism. 2. The range of colors visible to a given species of organisms. 3. Radiant energy that can be projected after refraction. See SPECTRAL COLORS.

spectrums of consciousness   (K. Wilber) A comparison of Western and Eastern views of consciousness as shown by psychotherapeutic systems. Western views stress healing the split between conscious and unconscious processes or of being versus nonbeing. Eastern approaches that Kenneth Wilber labels "level-of-mind therapies" address nondualistic consciousness.

speculation   Conjectural thinking not supported by scientifically determined evidence.

speculative psychology   Viewing aspects of human and animal behavior and then jumping to conclusions. If the conclusions are formally studied, they become science; if not, they remain speculations. See ARMCHAIR PSYCHOLOGY.

speech   Communication through conventional vocal and oral symbols.

speech act   See VOICE SOUNDS.

speech-and-hearing centers   See COMMUNITY SPEECH-AND-HEARING CENTERS.

speech aphasia   (H. Head) Inability to express language orally. Henry Head listed four types of speech aphasia: (a) verbal, difficulty in forming words; (b) syntactical, in which certain parts of speech (usually articles and prepositions) are slurred or dropped out; (c) nominal, inability to name names; and (d) semantic, difficulty in forming sequential language.

speech areas (of the brain)   Locations of the cerebral cortex areas associated with voice communications. These areas are generally located on the left hemisphere. Many of these areas were discovered by studying lesions found on patients with specific speech deficits such as Broca's area in the third convolution of the frontal lobe. See WERNICKE'S AREA.

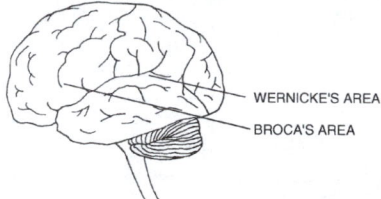

speech areas (of the brain)

speech audiometry   The measurement of hearing in terms of the reception of spoken words presented at controlled levels of intensity.

speech block   A temporary inability or a delay in producing the proper speech sounds, as in stuttering.

speech conservation   Phrase coined by the military during World War II referring to preventive speech therapy given to newly deafened persons to keep their speech and voice disturbance to a minimum.

speech correction   The professional field which deals with eliminating speech defects and improving intelligibility of speaking. See SPEECH PATHOLOGY.

speech delayed child   A person who is late in learning to speak. Whereas in some cases this is due to mental deficiency and in some cases to autism, many otherwise normal children who were speech retarded, gain normal use over time. Once known as speech retarded child.

speech derailment   A type of paraphasia, or perverted speech, seen primarily in schizophrenia, characterized by disconnected and apparently meaningless sounds.

speech development   The process of a human, usually an infant, acquiring speech skills in sequential stages varying in length. The prelanguage stage typically lasts about a year and consists of the infant making cooing and then babbling sounds. The uttering of first actual words occurs beginning about 12 months, during this holophrastic stage of single words can have the meaning of sentences. At about 18 months of age, the telegraphic stage of two-word units appears. See ORIGIN-OF-LANGUAGE THEORIES.

speech disorders   Verbal communication troublesome for the speaker, interfering with communication, creating a problem for the listener. Speech disorders are classified as: (a) disorders of articulation, for example, lisping and baby talk; (b) disorders of phonation or voice, for example, falsettos, some cerebral palsied and cleft palate speech; and (c) disorders of rhythm, for example, stuttering and cluttering, any one or more of which may be present. See LANGUAGE DISORDER, SPEECH DISTURBANCE, SPEECH IMPAIRMENT.

speech functions   Verbal communication as it is used to communicate ideas, maintain social relationships, express feeling and emotion, or all the above. Style of speech, and choice of words may give cues as to personality and level of a person's mental development. Speech disorders such as verbigeration, circumstantiality, and paralogia are symptoms of mental or emotional disturbance.

speech impairment   Any difficulty in communicating by voice due to organic or nonorganic causes. Nonorganic types include neurotic-telegraphic speech, aphonia, and elective mutism. Organic types include global aphasia, Broca's aphasia, Wernicke's aphasia, conduction aphasia, and anomic aphasia.

speech impediment   Loose phrase applied to stuttering and other slight disturbances of the free flow of speech.

speech interface assessment method (SIAM)   A technique for studying speech transmission.

speech lateralization   The role of hemispheric asymmetry in the control of verbal communication. For most individuals, speech centers are located in the left hemisphere, which is relatively dominant for the speech function. See LANGUAGE LOCALIZATION, WADE DOMINANCE TEST.

speech mechanisms of thinking   (I. P. Pavlov) A concept that the speech mechanisms involved in thinking are a central brain process. Reflects the highest integration of stimuli to the cortex by means of second-signal associations.

speech pathology   The diagnosis and treatment of functional and organic speech defects. See SPEECH CORRECTION.

speech reaction time   vocal reaction time

speech-reading   lip-reading

speech-reception threshold (SRT)   Measurement of a person's threshold for speech for individual frequencies to determine the level at which that person can repeat simple words, or understand simple connected speech.

speech reeducation/rehabilitation   Training to restore a lost or disabled speech function. See SPEECH CORRECTION.

speech registers   Verbal communication variations adapted to changes in social expectations, as in the vocabulary children use on the playground as opposed to in their homes or classrooms, or college students use with peers versus that with parents.

speech retarded child   speech delayed child

speech synthesizer   A mechanical-electronic device that can produce noises that sound like human speech. Although many such devices sound artificial, some are close to normal human speech.

speech theories   See ORIGIN-OF-LANGUAGE THEORIES.

speech therapy   The application of remedies, treatment, and counseling for the improvement of speech functions.

speech tolerance level (TL)   1. The hearing level at which speech becomes uncomfortably loud. 2. A level of maximum amplification the person can tolerate in a hearing aid.

speech-to-noise ratio   Signal-to-noise ratio when the signal is speech.

speed   1. Time-rate of motion, change, or progress. 2. An inverse measure of the time required to perform a given act. 3. Slang for amphetamine compounds. See METHAMPHETAMINE. 4. Quickness of performance, as "with speed" or "full speed."

speed-accuracy tradeoff   A tendency for people to lose accuracy when instructed to speed up or to lose speed when instructed to focus on accuracy. Whereas this may be true for any single individual, as a whole, "fast workers" make fewer errors than do "slow workers." See IDIOGRAPHIC PSYCHOLOGY, NOMOTHETIC PSYCHOLOGY to understand the apparent contradiction in this definition.

speedball   1. Slang for an intravenous dose of cocaine and heroin or, sometimes, cocaine and morphine. 2. Slang for a glass of wine to which grain alcohol or similar has been added.

speed counter   See TACHOMETER.

speeding up   The exerting of pressure on workers, either through wage incentives or by other means, to increase the quantity of output or to reduce labor costs.

speed reading   Reading at a faster rate than normal for that person. Whether the person can retain as much material at the faster speed is unknown.

speed score   See RATE SCORE.

speed test   An examination consisting of a large number of easy items but having a short time limit designed so that virtually no one completes the test. Many tests of clerical, mechanical, or psychomotor abilities are of this type. On a pure speed test any item attempted by an appropriate respondent will be answered correctly. See POWER TEST.

spell   1. A state of mind and body, different from the usual or typical, that can be caused by a variety of methods, such as by hypnosis. 2. A psychological means of putting a person into a trance or other mental state by means of suggestion. See HYPNOSIS. 3. A supposed ability of some people capable of generating miraculous events by reciting certain words in special ways or with special ornaments or equipment thus controlling the actions of humans, deities, or forces of nature for good or for evil. See WITCHCRAFT. 4. The ability to know the letters that comprise a word and in what sequence they are used in that word. Important in educational and developmental psychology. 5. An interval of rest, as "stop for a spell" or, at an onerous task, "we agreed to spell each other." 6. Reading letter-by-letter at the first stages of acquiring the skill.

spelling demons   Words that people have trouble spelling correctly or such words persistently misspelled by many persons, including a word in this sentence.

SPEM   smooth-pursuit eye movements

sperm   (seed—Latin) General term for the male gamete (sex cell), or for the semen containing male gametes (spermatozoa). Occasionally spelled sperma.

spermacrasia   Deficiency of spermatozoa in semen. See SPERM ANALYSIS.

sperm analysis   Part of the evaluation of male fertility based on the sperm count per milliliter of ejaculate and the degree of spermatozoa motility. The average male ejaculate after three days of continence is at least three milliliters of semen with approximately 100,000,000 spermatozoa per milliliter of which at least 60% show adequate motility for movement from the vagina to the fallopian tubes. See SPERMATOZOON.

spermarche   A male's first spontaneous ejaculation of seminal fluid. See WET DREAM.

spermatogenesis   The formation of mature sperm. The process of production of spermatozoa in the seminiferous tubules of the male testis. Spermatogenesis is continuous in humans after the onset of puberty and seasonal in some animal species.

spermatophobia   Morbid fear of semen or the loss of semen.

spermatorrhea   Involuntary discharge of semen, in the absence of orgasm.

spermatorrhea ring   Historically, an infibulation device for men promoted in the late 19th century as a method of preventing masturbation or unlawful intercourse. Consisted of a small belt or ring lined with teeth or spikes that made painful contact with the penile shaft during erection. See CHASTITY BELT.

spermatozoon   A mature or viable male gamete or sex cell. The normal human spermatozoon, contains 23 chromosomes. Enzymes in the head of the spermatozoon enable the male gamete to dissolve the protective barriers on the surface of the female ovum. One thousand human sperms head-to-tail will be approximately a half-inch in length. Plural is spermatozoa. See SPERM ANALYSIS.

spermicide   Any agent that kills spermatozoa. Some contraceptive jellies and foams contain spermicides.

spermophobia   Fear of germs. See BACILLOPHOBIA, MICROBIOPHOBIA, MICROPHOBIA.

spheresthesia globus   **globus hystericus**

spherical aberration/error   Failure of light rays to converge at the same focal point because of the curvature of a lens. Rays at the center of the lens are bent more than those refracted at the periphery of the lens. To avoid the typical aberration at the periphery of both the cornea and the lens, human vision research commonly uses either a very small artificial pupil or a Maxwellian view (light stimulus narrowed to a pinpoint as it reaches the lens). See CHROMATIC ABERRATION.

spherical lens   A lens whose surfaces are either spherical, or spherical and plane, and which consequently refract equally in all meridians.

sphincter   A ring-shaped muscle which, on contracting, partly or wholly closes a natural orifice, for example, closes the iris (makes the pupil smaller) of the eye.

sphincter control   An ability to control the muscles that open and close certain openings of the body, particularly anal and urinary sphincters. See ANAL CHARACTER, DEFECATION REFLEX, TOILET TRAINING.

sphincter cunni   In women, another name for the bulbospongiosus muscle; in men it is called ejaculator seminis.

sphincter morality   (S. Ferenczi) According to psychoanalytical theory, some personality characteristics such as obstinacy, extreme orderliness, and parsimony result from overly strict toilet training. See ANAL CHARACTER, TOILET TRAINING.

sphygmograph   (K. Vierordt) An instrument for measuring the strength and rapidity of the pulse.

sphygmomanometer   (O. H. Rogers, S. Riva-Rocci) An instrument used for studying blood-pressure changes, also used in some lie detector systems. Also known as sphygmometer.

spicy   (H. Henning) The quality of olfactory sensation of which nutmeg is a typical example, one of the six principal classes of odor.

spider fantasy   Spider images or stories that occur in dreams, phobias, and folklore. These fantasies are so prevalent that psychoanalysts conclude this insect has special significance.

spider fear   See ARACHNEOPHOBIA.

Spielmeyer-Vogt disease   (W. Spielmeyer & O. Vogt) A variety of Tay-Sachs disease beginning between the ages of six and twelve and resulting in death within two years. Characterized by cerebroretinal degeneration. See AMAUROTIC FAMILIAL IDIOCY, TAY-SACHS DISEASE.

spike-and-dome discharge   See DART AND DOME.

spike potential   A change in electrical potential produced by the transmission of a nerve impulse. Marked by a rapid swing of perhaps 100 millivolts from a negative charge through a positive charge and back to a resting potential stage, all within 1/1,000 of a second. See ACTION POTENTIAL.

spike-wave activity   A seizure pattern that may be seen in the electroencephalogram during an epileptic episode. The spike-wave pattern involves a rapid large voltage fluctuation (spike) followed by a slower large voltage fluctuation (wave). The pattern of spike-wave discharge is repeated in a regular rhythm (usually 3 to 3.5 Hz) and are characteristic of the absence type (or *petit mal* type) of seizure.

Spillman's illusion   (L. A. Spillman) An illustration of a grid of white squares and dark alleys and dark squares and light alleys, with a gradient of lightness in the alleys running from top to bottom and left to right of the grid. The light regions are seen in the intersections of dark alleys on light background and dark regions at the intersections of light alleys on dark background. It is a variant of the Hermann grid.

Spillman-Redies effect   (L. A. Spillman & C. Redies) A tendency for the Ehrenstein illusion when placed on a background of random dots (instead of brightness enhancement in the illusory areas) to result in the dots appearing to be less densely packed, and the seemingly circular illusory areas appearing to lie in front of the background.

spinal animal   A laboratory animal whose spinal cord has been separated from the brain so that nerve processes of the body are spinal only. Also known as spinal preparation.

spinal canal   A canal in which the spinal cord is enclosed, formed by openings in the vertebrae of the spinal column, that runs from the brain down to the coccyx.

spinal center   Any group of nerve cells in the spinal cord which act as an integrated unit in the performance of some relatively specific sensorimotor function.

spinal column   The backbone enclosing the spinal canal in which is found the spinal cord.

spinal conditioning hypothesis   A postulate that conditioned reflexes might be established through circuits in the spinal cord that lack interconnections to central nervous system structures above the cord. Experiments have failed to demonstrate such conditioning.

spinal cord   Part of the central nervous system that extends from the lower end of the medulla, at the base of the brain, down to the lumbar area of the vertebral column. The spinal cord is enclosed in a spinal canal formed by openings in the vertebrae of the spinal column.

spinal ganglia   Clumps of sensory-neuron cell bodies that form the dorsal roots of the spinal cord.

spinal gate   A mechanism in cells of the substantia gelatinosa that transmits excitatory and inhibitory signals to the brain, that modifies pain signals in accordance with messages from higher centers which reflect previous experience and the influence of emotional factors and personality on pain perception. Also known as gating mechanism. See GATING.

spinal nerves   (T. Willis) The 31 pairs of nerves that originate in the spinal cord and extend into the body's dermatomes (skin areas) through openings between the vertebrae of the spinal column. The spinal nerves include in decreasing order eight cervical, 12 thoracic, five lumbar, five sacral, and one coccygeal nerve. See CERVICAL NERVES.

spinal reflexes   The set of reflexes involved in functions such as posture or locomotion. They are sometimes classed as segmental spinal reflexes, if the circuit involves only one segment of the spine; or intersegmental spinal reflexes, if the impulses must travel through more than one spinal segment. Reflexes that require brain activity are suprasegmental spinal reflexes.

spinal root   The junction of the spinal nerve and the spinal cord; the sensory roots on the dorsal side of the cord and motor roots on the ventral side.

spinal tonus   A continuous degree of spinal-cord contractility maintained after connections to the brain have been severed.

spinal trigeminal nucleus   A nucleus of the descending spinal branch of the fifth cranial (trigeminal) nerve with extensions into the spinal cord. Sometimes described as part of the medulla and a continuation of the substantia gelatinosa of Rolando in the spinal cord.

spindle waves   Electroencephalogram patterns associated with light sleep characterized by delta-waves that occur at a frequency of about 14 Hertz (cycles per second).

spindles   Muscle or tendon fibers that have sensory and motor fibers that provide information to the brain about muscle movements.

spindling in EEG   Bursts of EEG (electroencephalographic) activity that follow positive reinforcement during conditioning. The effect indicates a state of attention or excitement.

spinocerebellar tract   A major nerve tract that carries impulses from the muscles and other proprioceptors through the spinal cord to the cerebellum.

spinothalamic tract   A bundle of nerves that ascends from the spinal cord to the thalamus and to the brain stem, carrying somatic sensory impulses. The spinothalamic tract contains two groups of fibers. The central spinothalamic tract carries pressure sensations, and the lateral spinothalamic tract carries pain and temperature information.

spiral ganglion   Site of the cell bodies for the hair cells of the auditory nerve. Located in the inner wall of the cochlea, near the organ of Corti.

spiral omnibus test   A type of test consisting of a variety of items from more than one discipline (mathematics, English, geography) arranged in order of difficulty. Items of a given type or content appear throughout the test, intermingled with other types of similar difficulty, in a spiral of increasing difficulty. Contrasts with the spiral test which has items only within a single subject. See OMNIBUS TEST, OTIS-LENNON MENTAL ABILITY TEST, POWER TEST, SPIRAL TEST.

spiral organ   The organ of Corti.

spiral test   A printed examination that has an equal number of different types of items within a single domain, such as mathematics, presented in recurring order (for example, the first item may be addition, the second subtraction, the third multiplication, the fourth division, and then continuing with more difficult items in the order of addition, subtraction, multiplication, division, etc). Compare SPIRAL OMNIBUS TEST.

spirit   1. The vital principle of life in a living entity, which is said to enter the body sometime between conception and birth and exit the body at death. Most religious cultures believe that, in the unembodied state, the spirit can be a source of either benefit or harm to the living. Thus, prayers to and communication with such spirits are integral in many religious traditions. Also known as soul. 2. A present mood or temper, such as being in low or high spirits. 3. Attitude, such as school spirit, or the spirit of the law. 4. In pharmacy, any liquid that has alcohol as part of its solution, an essence, a distilled extract.

spiritism   Belief in communication with nonincarnate personalities or spirits. See SPIRITUALISM (meaning 2).

spirit photography   The production of photography of persons, upon which appear superimposed images, assumed to be of spirits, allegedly produced by supernormal means.

spiritual   1. Pertaining to spirit. 2. Concerned with more elevating aspects of life, which may or may not be connected with a specific religion or religious practice.

spiritual factors   Moral and religious influences on behavior; transcendental forces and values.

spiritualism   1. A metaphysical doctrine that the universe is basically nonmaterial, or incorporeal. 2. A belief that it is possible to communicate with the deceased through mediums. Sometimes known as spiritism.

spirituality   1. A quality of personality characterized by a tendency to be preoccupied with moral and religious issues rather than with affairs of the material world or intellectual pursuits. 2. The subjective experience of something sacred, numinous, or greater than self. Awareness of spirituality may be associated with religion or it may occur spontaneously anywhere, as in nature or in a deeply moving experience such as falling in love, or in a close encounter with death. Spiritual awareness is often characterized by feelings of awe, reverence, and love.

spirograph   An instrument for measuring and recording respiratory movements (the rate and amount of breathing). See INSPIRATION-EXPIRATION (I/E) RATIO.

spirometer   An instrument used for measuring the air capacity in the lungs. Can provide information regarding the amount of inhaled and exhaled air during speech production.

SPL   sound-pressure level

splanchnic   Refers to the viscera (abdominal organs), employed in the definitions of various body types in which the abdomen is a prominent feature. See ENDOMORPH, MEGALOSPLANCHNIC, MICROSPLANCHNIC, NORMOSPLANCHNIC.

splanchnic nerves   A type of nerve that enables communication both ways between the spinal cord and digestive organs.

splenium   A blunt enlargement at the posterior end of the corpus callosum where it overlaps a portion of the third ventricle of the brain.

splinter skill   An ability developed by a child that is not an integral part of the typical developmental sequence.

split brain   The cerebral hemispheres of the brain functioning independently. Split brains are produced by surgery as well as naturally as a result of injury or by a disease. Also known as divided brain. See CEREBRAL DOMINANCE, FUNCTIONAL PLASTICITY, LATERALITY.

split-brain experiments   (R. W. Sperry) Research on the behavioral and cognitive capacity of animals or humans after the corpus callosum has been severed and the two hemispheres are separated from each other, to see how the post-operative individual perceives, learns, reacts to stimuli, etc.

split-brain treatment   (R. W. Sperry) Brains that have been surgically split in half at the corpus callosum to end serious epileptic episodes. Roger Sperry demonstrated with such people postoperatively, that the right and left hemispheres of the brain do not communicate with each other.

split-field method   (E. A. Bott) In research, a procedure sometimes adopted in examining the subject-matter of a field of inquiry whereby the subject-matter is divided and each part is dealt with as a different entity. See SPLIT-LITTER METHOD.

split-half correlation   A method for estimating the reliability (consistency of measurement) of a test. The instrument is given in the usual way to a group but is scored as if the odd-numbered items are one test and the even-numbered items are a second test. The correlation between the two parts provides an estimate of the full test's reliability, with the Spearman-Brown correction often used to adjust the reliability coefficient for test length. Also known as split-half reliability.

split-half reliability technique   A measure of the internal consistency of a test, obtained by correlating responses on half the test with responses on the other half. See ODD-EVEN RELIABILITY, SPLIT-HALF CORRELATION.

split-litter method/technique   Randomly assigning animals from the same litter to different groups; a type of matched-groups design. See SPLIT-FIELD METHOD.

split-off consciousness/experience   (W. James) A partly organized set of experiences that are independent of a person's organized consciousness. Used to designate the subordinate phases of dual and multiple personality.

split personality Common phrase for multiple personality (dissociative identity disorder). Sometimes confused with schizophrenia (which literally means a splitting or shattering of the mind but does not involve the formation of a second personality; in schizophrenia the mind is split from reality).

split run In advertising research, running two advertisements in a magazine in two similar localities, with the intention of determining which one produces the greater result, that then may lead to national advertising using the one that appears superior. Also done with cable T.V. systems where different parts of town view different versions of a commercial.

split-span tests (D. Broadbent) Examinations using dichotic hearing, for example, presenting different numbers simultaneously in different ears. Participants generally repeat the information from just one ear, giving evidence that the brain's attention span includes only one of two competing messages.

splitting 1. Dichotomizing, as in distinguishing between good self and bad self. 2. Viewing people and situations as either all good or all bad. 3. Failure to integrate the positive and negative qualities of the self.

splitting situation A process used in co-therapy whereby the client (or patient) can appeal to one of the therapists about the other. The situation is analogous to a child dealing with both parents.

S+ 1. A discriminative stimulus that evokes instrumental behavior because it signals the availability of reinforcement. 2. A positive stimulus or reward.

spoiled-child reaction A behavior pattern in children marked by a lack of self-care, independence, and responsibility, attributed to parental overindulgence and oversolicitude. Alfred Adler stated that a pampered child becomes a hated child. See SPECIAL CHILD, SPOON FEEDING.

spontaneity 1. Activity initiated by an organism or object without apparent immediate external stimulation. 2. A quality of being able to make rapid decisions with little thought; to be lively, acting naturally; to get and act upon new ideas. Also known as being spontaneous.

spontaneity test (J. L. Moreno) A sociometric test in which the participant is encouraged to improvise freely by roleplaying in typical life situations with members of a group who have been judged to be emotionally related to the participant. The goal is to elicit insight into interpersonal relationships not revealed by standard sociometric tests that deal only with attraction and repulsion.

spontaneity therapy/training (J. L. Moreno) A personality training program in which the patient (or client) learns to act naturally and spontaneously in real life situations by practicing such behavior in a group situation through graduated sessions.

spontaneous abortion Interruption of pregnancy with loss of the fetus as a result of natural biological causes. Emotional disturbances also may be causative factors. See MISCARRIAGE.

spontaneous alternation In research, the mouse, rat, or other subject, without being trained to do so, tends to alternate between left- and right-choices in a Y-maze or T-maze on successive trials. This factor is often considered in determining the effects of brain lesions and drugs.

spontaneous behavior An action not the result of any apparent external stimulus. See AUTOCHTHONOUS.

spontaneous deflections Galvanic skin reflexes that occur without known stimulation or cause.

spontaneous discharge 1. The firing of a neuron without stimulation. 2. The firing of neural impulses or spike potentials without direct influence of an external stimulus. See SPONTANEOUS NEURAL ACTIVITY.

spontaneous generation The long-discredited theory that living organisms can develop from nonliving matter. Purported evidence included the development of maggots on decaying meat, but inadequate controls for flies laying eggs accounted for the data. Also known as abiogenesis.

spontaneous human combustion The alleged bursting into flames of a person without being set on fire. Purportedly, such combustion results from some internal reaction rather than from an external source.

spontaneous movement Motion occurring in the absence of any particular stimulus.

spontaneous neural activity Automatic firing of neurons in the absence of observable stimuli. The effect has been attributed to an excessive buildup of neurotransmitter chemicals at the synapses.

spontaneous recovery 1. In research, reappearance of a conditioned response after it has been experimentally extinguished. 2. In learning research, reappearance of a (classically or instrumentally) conditioned response when the organism is returned to the apparatus after (a) the response has been experimentally extinguished, and (b) the organism has been outside the learning situation for a period of hours to days. 3. See SPONTANEOUS REMISSION.

spontaneous regression A purported phenomenon of hypnosis in which a participant suddenly relives an event from an earlier age, for example, during childhood, and may exhibit appropriate behavior for that age.

spontaneous remission Recovery or partial recovery from a disorder independent of formal treatment. Also known as spontaneous recovery.

spontaneous thought An idea, concept, memory, etc., that comes to mind suddenly without any prior apparent reason. See AUTOCHTHONY.

spontaneous variation Variation, or heritable alteration in type of the organism, due to factors within the germ cell itself and not to crossing or to environmental factors. See SPORT.

spoon feeding 1. Literally, conveying food to the mouth of a person who is unable to self-feed (for example, spoon feeding an infant). 2. Metaphorically, making life easy for a person who gets unwarranted assistance. See PAMPERING.

spoonerism To mispronounce or transpose certain consonants in speech. Named after the English clergyman W. A. Spooner (1844–1930), who was probably slightly aphasic. Spooner allegedly habitually made such mistakes as referring to "our queer old dean" when he meant "our dear old queen."

s population See STIMULUS POPULATION.

sport 1. A mutation; an organism that deviates at birth considerably from normal variation. 2. In genetics, an organism that has undergone mutation and is distinctly different from its parents. See FREAK.

sport psychology   The study of behavioral, affective, and cognitive aspects of sport settings (sometimes including the behavior of spectators as well as participants), and the use of psychological principles to optimize the performance and well-being of athletes. Exercise and Sport Psychology became Division 47 of the American Psychological Association (APA) in 1987.

sport socialization   In sport psychology, the process of learning to live in and understand a sport culture or subculture by internalizing its beliefs, values, attitudes, and norms.

sports psychologist   A psychologist who helps athletes by predicting their potentialities, instilling positive attitudes, arranging effective training schedules, watching for possible emotional crises, and acting as a source of emotional support. See SPORT PSYCHOLOGY.

spot-pattern test   A type of test in which the task is to reproduce, after brief exposure, a pattern or design consisting of spots or dots.

spouse   Either a husband or a wife, each person of a married couple.

Spranger's typology   The classification by Eduard Spranger of humans according to six cultural values (theoretical, economic, political, esthetic, social, and religious). Used in the Allport-Vernon-Lindzey Study of Values. See CHARACTER TYPES, IMPLICIT PERSONALITY THEORIES, NAIVE PERSONALITY THEORIES.

spreading activation   In cognitive psychology, refers to the fact that the arousal of the potential for making one response spreads to associated responses. See SPREADING ACTIVATION MODEL/THEORY.

spreading activation model/theory   A point of view of semantic memory suggesting that the activation of a concept or idea can activate others to the extent to which the concepts or ideas have shared meanings.

spreading depression   1. The observation that, if the cortex of the brain is touched, surrounding areas are affected in an inhibitory manner. 2. Describing the Pavlovian phenomenon of negative induction. See NEGATIVE INDUCTION.

spread of effect   1. A generalization that satisfaction or dissatisfaction associated with a response will spread to other aspects of the situation. 2. (E. L. Thorndike) The concept that later became reinforcement. Edward Thorndike noted that certain successful or "satisfying" results of behavior patterns of cats tended to be repeated. See THORNDIKE PUZZLE BOX. 3. A tendency for subjects to repeat reinforced responses to neighboring stimuli in a list.

spurious correlation   A correlation between two variables that does not result from any causal influence of one variable on the other but rather from the influence of a third variable on both of them; for example, in elementary schools there is a positive correlation between verbal skills and shoe size because of the influence of age on both variables.

spurt   The sudden sharp increase in the rate of a process, such as a growth spurt around the time of puberty. See END SPURT, INITIAL SPURT.

S.Q.   social quotient

SQ3R   A technique for effective study consisting of Survey, Question, Read, Recite, and Review. See PQ4R.

squeaky wheel   In general, refers to people who demand more loudly than others a disproportional amount of attention.

squeeze technique   (J. H. Semans) A technique for overcoming premature ejaculation. The partner squeezes the head of the penis until the urge to ejaculate and some of the erection disappears. By repeating this maneuver, the frustrated male becomes conditioned to last longer before ejaculation.

SQUID   superconducting quantum interference device

squiggle game   (D. W. Winnicott) A technique in which a child and a therapist take turns in drawing lines that gradually evolve into a significant object. The drawing elicits comments or stories from the child and paves the way toward dealing with anxiety-laden situations. See ART THERAPY.

squint   See CROSS-EYE, STRABISMUS.

squint glasses   Eyeglasses composed of prismatic lenses, used for the study of color vision. See STENOPEIC SPECTACLES.

S-R   Stimulus-response or stimulus elicits response (also abbreviated **S → R, SR**).

SRA Mechanical Aptitude Test   A type of task that measures mechanical aptitude in three ways: by identification of different tools; by fitting pieces together as a test of space relations, and by solving problems in shop arithmetic. (SRA stands for Science Research Associates.)

SRC   sexual response cycle

SRIs   serotonin reuptake inhibitors

S-R learning (model)   A point of view introduced by Edward Thorndike holding that learning is primarily a trial-and-error process (some prefer the phrase trial-and-success to focus on the importance of reward) in which associative connections, or S-R bonds, are established between stimuli (S) and responses (R). The use of intervening variables and cognitive structures as explanations is rejected along with the notion that insight plays a role in problem solving. A highly developed form follows the work of B. F. Skinner, but S-R also includes the social learning theory of John Dollard and Neal Miller. Compare S-O-R LEARNING, S-S LEARNING.

S-R psychology   1. Following the lead of the British empiricist philosophers but also rejecting as poor science the concepts of instinct and will as explanations for association, led to the focus on association between observable stimuli and responses notable in the writings of Edwin R. Guthrie, Clark L. Hull, Edward L. Thorndike, and John B. Watson. The advances in technique in physiological psychology (following on the work of Ivan Pavlov), accompanied by fewer attempts at the all-encompassing theory reduced importance of the S-R, S-O-R and S-S distinctions in the late 20th century. See S-O-R PSYCHOLOGY, S-S PSYCHOLOGY. 2. An approach that focuses on the stimulus-response (S-R) connection as the unit for studying an organism's overt behavior, usually with the assumption that the consequences of the behavior determine the future probability of the response. Minimal attention is given to the characteristics of the organism, hence the sobriquet "black-box psychology." See ASSOCIATIONISM, BEHAVIORISM.

SRR   systematic rational restructuring

SRT   1. simple reaction time. 2. speech-reception threshold.

S-R theory   One of the three groupings used by M. H. Marx and W. A. Hillix for contemporary theories, which includes most of the traditional learning theories. The focus of these psychological theories is decidedly upon the response (and often the immediate consequence of that response). It includes the social learning theory of John Dollard and Neal Miller, the stimulus sampling theory of William K. Estes, Edwin R. Guthrie's contiguous conditioning theory, Clark L. Hull's hypothetico-deductive theory of learning, and the learning approach of B. F. Skinner. Compare S-O-R THEORY EMPHASIZING ORGANISM, S-O-R THEORY EMPHASIZING PERCEPTION.

SS   1. See STANDARDIZED SCORE. 2. See SUM OF SQUARES.

SSA   1. Social Services Administration. 2. smallest space analysis.

S-shaped curve   Any plot of one variable against another that is monotonic increasing, and is at first convex and then becomes concave. Examples include: A graphic design that shows the learning process: (a) a period of increasing returns from practice during early trials; (b) a period during which the rate of improvement remains constant; and (c) a period of decreasing improvement over time if not reinforced. Also known as S-curve. See LEARNING CURVE, OGIVE, RATES OF RETURN.

S-S interval   Periods between successive presentations of two stimuli.

S-S learning (model)   In this approach that focuses on the association between stimuli not only are intervening variables used but also, typically, some form of cognitive structures. A clear example is the stimulus sampling theory of William K. Estes that postulates underlying stochastic processes. Also included is the expectancy theory of Edward C. Tolman's purposive behaviorism, which postulates association of the sign (S_1) and the significate (S_2). The approach of Ivan Pavlov and the social learning theory of Albert Bandura are sometimes placed here although they have some S-O-R characteristics. Compare S-O-R LEARNING, S-R LEARNING.

S sleep   See NONRAPID-EYE-MOVEMENT SLEEP.

S-S psychology   An approach to psychology holding that associations develop full strength on a single trial. The stimulus sampling theory of E. R. Guthrie is often referred to as an S-S approach. Some would label Ivan Pavlov's cognitive learning theory S-S. See S-O-R PSYCHOLOGY, S-R PSYCHOLOGY.

s^2   The sample variance.

S-S relationship   A connection between two stimulus events in the environment.

SSRI   specific serotonin reuptake inhibitor

SST   1. social skills training. 2. Self-Statement Training. 3. stimulus-sampling theory.

S-state   The sleeping state, as contrasted with the D-state (dream state) and W-state (waking state). See CONSCIOUSNESS, DREAM STATE, RAPID-EYE-MOVEMENT SLEEP, SLEEP, WAKEFULNESS, W-STATE.

St   See STANDARD STIMULUS, STIMULUS.

ST   standardized test

stabilimeter   An instrument for measuring postural stability and body sway when the participant is standing erect and blindfolded and asked to remain immobile.

stability   1. Absence of variation or motion, as applied to genetics (invariance in characteristics), personality (few mood changes), or body position (absence of body sway). 2. Unchanging rank position over time of a specific group in terms of some factor, such as intelligence test performance, traits, personality characteristics. See INSTABILITY.

stability coefficient (r_{st})   retest reliability

stability-instability   One of the two dimensions of psychological functioning according to Hans Eysenck. The other dimension is extraversion-introversion. Also known as neuroticism-stability. See EYSENCK'S TYPOLOGY.

stability-lability   A dimension of sensitivity to stimuli due to individual variations in autonomic nervous systems. Thus, a labile person would be expected to react to a wider range of stimuli than a stable person.

stabilized retinal image   A stimulus so arranged by a complex mirror system and contact lens that it affects the same point on the retina every time, regardless of eye movements.

stabilizing selection   An evolutionary circumstance that occurs when a population tends to maintain its dominant characteristics due to the tendencies of individuals preferring the typical characteristics in mates and therefore shunning characteristic-deviant individuals for reproductive purposes.

stable rate   Performance in which there is little or no variability over time, as in single-case experiments.

stage   1. A natural division in a changing process, usually characterized by biological or other qualities. 2. In development, a period of little change in ability (like a plateau) that is preceded and followed by accelerated change. 3. An arbitrarily selected period of time in which a particular behavior or feature seems to distinguish the time from periods before and after, for example, the "terrible twos" is distinguished by toddlers' increased negativity and difficulty for adults to control.

stage fright   An anxiety reaction associated with speaking or performing before an audience or being otherwise subjected to public scrutiny. May involve becoming tense and apprehensive, perspiring profusely, stuttering, forgetting the speech, or fleeing the situation. See PUBLIC SPEAKING ANXIETY, SOCIAL PHOBIA.

stage of exhaustion   See EXHAUSTION.

stage of resistance   See RESISTANCE STAGE.

stage theories (of development)   Theories of the evolution of personality that view individuals as developing through a series of stages. Sigmund Freud posited five, Jean Piaget four, Lawrence Kohlberg three, Erik Erikson eight, Carl Jung four, Harry Sullivan seven stages, and Ken Wilber nine. Some theorists, such as Alfred Adler, Albert Bandura, and B. F. Skinner, either did not posit stages or directly criticized the concept of stages. See INCREMENTAL THEORY OF DEVELOPMENT.

stage theory (of mate selection)   A point of view regarding the process by which individuals are attracted to one another, fall in love, and marry (in cultures where such behavior is encouraged or expected). This process is defined in terms of discrete stages corresponding to the deepening and stabilizing of the relationship, and in part by stimulus variables and social role expectations.

stages of change theory   (J. O. Prochaska) Steps suggested to gain the self-control necessary to change behavior, such as to stop-smoking or to eat sensibly: (a) precontemplation, keeping in mind the advantages and consequences, negative and positive, of the change; (b) contemplation, period of thinking about benefits while preparing to change; (c) preparation, getting ready to make the change; (d) action, beginning the new program; and (e) maintenance, staying on the program.

stages of dying   According to Elizabeth Kübler-Ross, five major attitudes experienced by a person after being informed of having a terminal illness or condition with poor prognosis: (a) Denial Stage; rejection of the information, "It can't be true!"; (b) Anger Stage; bitterness, resentment, hostility at having to die, "Why me?"; (c) Bargaining Stage; being amiable and cooperative, "If I do this...I should be allowed to live a little longer"; (d) Depression Stage; nonreactive to loss of body parts or preparatory thoughts for ultimate loss of life, "Why try?"; and (e) Acceptance Stage; taking a passive attitude with increasing detachment "I might as well enjoy what time I have left." Hope of survival, however, persists through all these phases.

stages of human cognitive development   Four discernible phases of human cognitive development moving from simple sensations to complicated thinking according to Jean Piaget. The stages are: sensorimotor, preoperational, concrete, and formal operations. See entries for further information.

stages of man   See ERIKSON'S STAGES OF PSYCHO-SOCIAL DEVELOPMENT.

STAI   State-Trait Anxiety Inventory

stair fear   See CLIMACOPHOBIA.

staircase illusion   Schroeder's staircase illusion

staircase method   In psychophysical research, an up-and-down procedure in which a participant is first given a low stimulus that the participant cannot perceive, and then gradually the stimulus is increased in power until the participant senses it. Later, the participant is shown a strong stimulus that is gradually reduced in power until the participant can no longer perceive it. Also known as up-and-down method. See METHOD OF LIMITS.

staircase phenomenon   (H. Bowditch) A graduated sequence of increasingly stronger muscle contractions that occur when a corresponding sequence of identical stimuli is applied to a rested muscle. May be explained as a warm-up effect. In German it is called *Treppe*.

stalking behavior   See PREDATION.

stammer   To hesitate in speech, halt, repeat, and mispronounce, by reason of embarrassment, agitation, or unfamiliarity with the subject; distinguished from stutter. "Stuttering" and "stammering" are used interchangeably since both originate from learned anxieties about speech. See STUTTERING.

stance reflex   Postural movements of anyone standing up to relieve pressure on feet, joints, neck, etc, but always to maintain stability of stance.

standard   1. A criterion model against which performances are judged or evaluated; may be arbitrarily set or based on prior performance such as the best ever. 2. A fixed unit such as the nautical mile.

standard deviation (SD, S.D., s, or σ)   (K. Pearson) A measure of the spread or deviations of scores about the mean of a distribution. In a normal distribution, about two-thirds of the cases fall within the limits of one SD above and below the mean. It is the square root of the variance. The standard deviation for a sample set of scores may be obtained by finding the sum of the squared deviations of the score around the sample mean, dividing by the degrees of freedom, n − 1, and taking the square root. Formula: $SD = [\sum (X_i - X)^2 \div N]^{1/2}$, where: X_i is the ith value, X is the mean, N is the number of values, and SD is the standard deviation. (The standard deviation of a sample is usually noted by s, that of a population mean by σ.) Descriptively called the root-mean-squared deviation. See VARIANCE.

standard difference   **standard ratio**

standard English   A mode of communication accepted by lexicographers as being free of regional variations and having a generally accepted grammar. Linguists can rate speakers for spoken standard English from 0 (perfect English) to 10 (sounds almost like another language). Linguists can easily identify people who come from India, Canada, Australia, and different regions of the United States and England, as well as countries where English is the preferred second language. See BLACK ENGLISH, EBONICS.

standard error (S.E. or SE)   The standard deviation of a sampling distribution. Every statistic (for example, the mean) varies from sample to sample, and the standard error indicates how much spread a particular statistic will show around its central value.

standard error of difference   See CRITICAL RATIO.

standard error of measurement   The extent of variation in test scores expected on retests because of the unreliability of the measuring instrument. Formula: $S_e = S_x (1 - r_{xx})^{1/2}$, where: S_e is the standard error, and r_{xx} is the original reliability estimate.

standard error of the mean (SEM, σ_x, or σ_M)   The standard deviation of a sampling distribution of means, showing how much the means of an infinite number of samples will vary. A large standard error of the mean indicates that there is considerable variation in successive samples of the mean. Formula: $\sigma_M = (\sigma_M^2)^{1/2} = \sigma \div (N)^{1/2}$, where, σ_M is the standard error of estimate, and N is the size of the sample.

standard error of estimate (σ_{est})   A measure of the degree to which a regression line fits a set of data; the error in estimating one variable from another on the basis of a linear correlation coefficient. Formula: $\sigma_{est} = \sigma_0 (1 - r^2)^{1/2}$, where σ_0 is the standard deviation of the dependent variable, r is the correlation coefficient, and σ_{est} is the standard error of estimate.

standardization of testing   Establishing standard procedures for administration and scoring of testings to achieve uniformity for diverse groups.

standardized interview (schedule)   A structured interview with preestablished questions and procedures designed to collect data uniformly, to provide a basis for objective scoring, and eliminate interviewer bias and other sources of variability.

standardized measuring device   A test or instrument that has been administered to a large representative sample of the population for which it is to provide reliable norms with regard to the subject matter assessed.

standardized score   1. To bring a group of data into relation with a given standard. 2. To devise a standard for treatment of certain data. 3. The response of a known group having known characteristics. Also known as standard score (SS). See NORMS, STANDARD SCORE.

standardized test (ST)   An examination whose validity and reliability have been established by thorough cumulative empirical applications and analysis and which has clearly defined characteristics and instructions for administration and scoring.

standard observer   1. In research, a person who is expected to remember or to make notes of everything observed. 2. An ideal observer in certain types of research to whose level all experimenters should attempt to achieve.

standard ratio   The difference between two means divided by the standard error of the difference between the two means. Also known as standard difference.

standard score   A set of scores may be standardized by taking each score, subtracting the mean, then dividing the difference by the standard deviation. The resultant score, known as a standard, standardized, or z score, gives the number of standard deviations the original score was above or below the mean. The entire set of standard scores has a mean of 0 and standard deviation of 1. In a normal distribution, over 99% of the cases lie between $z = -3.00$ and $z = +3.00$. Also known as standardized score, z score, Z score, Z-score. See STANINE, T SCORES.

standard stimulus (S or St)   The stimulus used as the basis of comparison for other stimuli applied in a psychophysical experiment, for example, in comparing loud sounds to a sound of a given intensity. Also known as standardized stimulus. See PSYCHOPHYSICAL EXPERIMENT, PSYCHOPHYSICAL METHODS.

standing wave   A wave such as one found on the string of a musical instrument. The wave movement is upward and downward but does not radiate outward from its origin. The part that does not move is called the node (in the center of the wave) and the part that travels the most is called the antinode (the top and bottom of the wave). See WAVE for an illustration.

Stanford Achievement Tests (SAT)   (T. L. Kelley, R. Madden, E. F. Gardner, H. C. Rudman) A standard achievement test battery for grades one through nine. Test has been revised many times since it was first published in 1923. Norms are based on hundreds of thousands of students from hundreds of communities across the United States.

Stanford-Binet IV (SB-IV)   An examination applicable from age two to adult, this version (1987) differs markedly from previous version in that it contains 15 tests measuring respectively Verbal Memory, Quantitative Reasoning, Abstract-Verbal Reasoning, and Short-term Memory presented by test question type rather than the spiral omnibus test format previously used. Administration begins with Vocabulary which determines where to begin with the other items. No single participant takes all of the 15 tests and usually the complete test has 8 to 15 items. Results are converted to Standard Age Scores and intelligence quotients (IQ) are not available.

Stanford-Binet Intelligence Scale (S-B)   An individual test designed primarily to assess the intelligence of school children, developed originally in 1905 by Alfred Binet and Théodore Simon in French. The scale was revised by Lewis Terman in 1916 in English at Stanford University, revised again in 1937 by Lewis Terman and Maud Merrill, and subsequently revised again in 1960 with the prior L and M forms combined into a single form. In addition, a deviation intelligence quotient (IQ) was used rather than the prior system of dividing mental age (on the test) by chronological age. This test had a range from mental age two to superior adult. At the early ages, items included building a bridge with three blocks and at the upper ages, it depended mostly on vocabulary-type items. Also known as Stanford-Binet Scale/Test. See INTELLIGENCE TESTS.

Stanford diagnostic tests   A series of tests used to determine deficits in language and mathematics, for example, the Stanford Diagnostic Reading Test attempts to identify specific areas of difficulty in the reading process; the Stanford Diagnostic Mathematics Test attempts to identify problem-solving difficulties. See DIAGNOSTIC EDUCATIONAL TESTS.

Stanford Diagnostic Reading Test (SDRT)   See STANFORD DIAGNOSTIC TESTS.

Stanford Diagnostic Mathematics Test (SDMT)   See STANFORD DIAGNOSTIC TESTS.

Stanford Hypnotic Susceptibility Scale   (E. Hilgard) A standardized 12-item scale used to measure hypnotizability by means of a participant's response to suggestions.

stanine (score)   A 9-point scale of normalized scores, with the mean being 5, and 2 for its standard deviation. Stanines were first used to describe a participant's performance on a battery of tests constructed for the Army Air Force during World War II. See STANDARD SCORE.

stapedius   A muscle that controls the movement of the stapes in the middle ear, innervated by the facial nerve. The stapedius has a modulating control on the stapes, reducing vibrations caused by intense noises which might otherwise damage delicate inner-ear structures.

stapes   (G. F. Ingrassia) A stirrup-shaped ossicle; the innermost of the three bones of the middle ear. The flat side of the stapes is attached to the oval window on the side of the cochlea, allowing vibrations received from the ear drum, to be relayed by the chain of ossicles to the oval window which converts sound vibrations to changes in fluid pressure. The plural is stapes or stapedes. Also known as stirrup. See EAR.

star   In sociometry, the person chosen by all (or by most) of the group. The group member most frequently designated as the person with whom other members would wish to work or spend time in some way. Also known as sociocenter. See ISOLATE, SOCIOMETRIC ANALYSIS, SOCIOMETRIC CLIQUE, SOCIOMETRY. See also SOCIOGRAM for an illustration.

star cells   See STELLATE CELLS.

star fear   See SIDEROPHOBIA.

startle   1. An overall bodily reaction immediately following onset of sudden unexpected stimulation, for example, a response to a pistol shot. 2. To cause a violent or sudden motor response, and resembling a momentary fear; as by an unexpected noise or flash of light. 3. Rapid, pervasive response to a sudden, powerful unexpected stimulus. Usually includes closing of the eyes, widening of the mouth, increased heartbeat and respiration, flexion of the trunk and extremities, and increased alertness. This pattern is so uniform across individuals that many psychologists consider it an inborn, primitive self-preservation mechanism. Occurs in normal persons as well as in acute anxiety disorders. Also known as startle pattern/reaction/reflex/response.

starvation reactions   The common effects, physiological and psychological, as a result of an extreme lack of food, nutrients, etc. Physiological effects may include general weakness, hunger pangs, sluggishness, and susceptibility to disease. Psychological effects may include the slowing down of thought processes, difficulty in concentration, apathy, irritability, reduced sexual desire, and loss of pride in appearance. See HUNGER PAINS, SEMI-STARVATION NEUROSES, STARVATION REACTIONS.

stasibasiphobia   Morbid fear of standing upright and walking. Also known as basiphobia, stasobasophobia.

stasiphobia   Morbid fear of standing or getting up, sometimes resulting in a psychogenic inability to do so. Also known as stasophobia. See ASTASIA-ABASIA.

stasis   1. Stagnation. 2. A state of inactivity and stagnation in an organism, a person, or a society; equilibrium in which change and growth do not occur.

stasobasophobia   stasibasiphobia

stasophobia   stasiphobia

STAT   Sternberg Triarchic Abilities Test

state   1. Any momentary experience or mental process. 2. A condition which shows no progressive change for the time and in the respect considered, for example, a state of anxiety.

state anger   (C. Spielberger) A psychobiological state consisting of feelings accompanied by muscular tensions, activated by the autonomic nervous system, evoked by being attacked, being treated unfairly, and by perceived injustice, and frustrations. Also known as S-anger. Compare TRAIT ANGER.

state anxiety   (N. S. Endler) Within the interaction model of anxiety, state anxiety refers to a temporary emotional state (encompassing cognitive-worry components and autonomic arousal) resulting from situational stress, specific and congruent with trait anxiety.

state-dependent behavior   Activity affected by emotional conditions, for example, an angry person says something hurtful to another that the person would not have said otherwise.

state-dependent learning   An act of learning that occurs during a particular biological or psychological state. Will not readily transfer to or cannot be retrieved in states unrelated to the state in which learning originally occurred, for example, an animal trained to run a maze while under the influence of a certain drug may not run it successfully without the drug. Also known as dissociated learning.

state-dependent memory   Recall that is better when the attempt is made under the same conditions as the original learning than when the recall state and the original state do not match. See STATE-DEPENDENT LEARNING.

state-dependent phenomenon   Behavior triggered by the affective state of a person.

statement validity analysis   In forensic psychology, the assessment of the accuracy of a statement (usually in regard to a crime) based on characteristics of the statement itself as opposed to nonverbal aspects of its expression. Usually based on the transcript of a video/audio taped interview. Also known as criterion-based content analysis.

state of consciousness   The totality of experience at any given moment, with emphasis on the actual contents of awareness and their interrelation. See FIELD OF CONSCIOUSNESS, LEVELS OF CONSCIOUSNESS, PHENOMENOLOGY.

state system   Neural structures that determine the general level of responsiveness, or readiness to respond, of the organism.

state theories of hypnosis   A point of view that for hypnosis to be real, that a trance must be established first. See NONSTATE THEORIES OF HYPNOSIS.

State-Trait Anxiety Inventory (STAI)   (C. D. Spielberger) A questionnaire of 20 items using four-point scales of frequency and intensity for measuring anxiety. See ANXIETY.

static anthropometry   See ANTHROPOMETRY.

staticism vs developmentalism   (R. I. Watson) A prescriptive dimension of the philosophical underpinnings of psychology, namely, a cross-sectional view versus a longitudinal one. See OPPONENT-PAIRS DIMENSION.

static reflex/response   A postural reflex that orients the body against a force, such as gravity.

static sense   sense of equilibrium

statistical ant/rat   See STATRAT.

statistical artifact   An anomaly of data that may lead to an incorrect conclusion.

statistical attenuation   1. The reduction of the accuracy of statistical findings by any kind of error. 2. A reduction in variability of a statistical measure. For example, the standard deviation (SD) of scores on intelligence measures decrease as one moves from high school to college to graduate school due to more of those with lower scores dropping out; with other factors kept constant this attenuation of s.d. will cause a reduction in the validity correlation of this test scores with school grades. Psychometricians have developed a correction for attenuation based on theoretical models to somewhat deal with the problem.

statistical control The use of statistical methods to reduce the effect of factors that could not be eliminated or controlled during an experiment, such as the use of analysis of covariance to correct effects of extraneous variables.

statistical decision theory The branch of mathematics dealing with uncertainty, in which the decision-making process is studied and particular decision-rules are established. Treats the decision-making process as one in which a signal is conceived as occurring in a background of noise. The signal and noise both vary in strength. An observer reports the presence of a signal whenever its strength exceeds the background noise by an amount that exceeds a criterion for the making of a positive response. See SIGNAL-DETECTION THEORY.

statistical dependence Two variables associated with one another because of overlapping elements. This does not necessarily mean that one causes the other, but rather that the relationship is due to the common basis in two samples. See STATISTICAL ARTIFACT.

statistical difference significant difference

statistical error Contrary to general use outside mathematics and science, error in this sense does not necessarily indicate a mistake or that an erroneous conclusion will be drawn, otherwise "law of error" would be an oxymoron. E. F. Lindquist points out that error (the impact of extraneous variables) constant for all replications throughout an experiment cannot be adequately handled; to the extent that if it is present the conclusion will, indeed, be incorrect, most likely with problems of external validity. But the three types of variable error can be handled by appropriate research procedures found in standard texts. For Lindquist Type S Error is due to the effects of random sampling on a single occasion, for example, it is possible that brighter students are assigned to one experimental group than to another. Type G errors have the same effect on all members of a single treatment group but differ from that on another group, as might happen when there is a better room or better teacher. Type R error is more complex: Lindquist suggests that a particular treatment may be more effective in certain settings, say a school that has heavy parental involvement but less effective in other settings, a lack of transituational generality.

statistical expectation A probability based upon mathematical calculation. Sometimes known as the expected value.

statistical hypothesis A direct statement made about a population and never about a sample. Null and alternative hypotheses are two kinds of statistical hypotheses.

statistical inference The process of drawing conclusions about population parameters from sample data. See INFERENTIAL STATISTICS.

statistical-learning theories A theory of learning modeled on statistical sampling theory, such as W. K. Estes' theory that assumed that the stimuli present on any learning trial are a sample of a population of stimuli and that responses are conditioned to those stimuli fully on that trial. With succeeding trials, the stimulus sample includes more and more of those in the stimulus population. Although conditioning happens in a single trial, learning takes place gradually as the response is conditioned to increasingly large numbers of these stimuli. See CONCAVE LEARNING CURVE, HULL'S THEORY OF LEARNING, LAWS OF LEARNING, LEARNING THEORY, STOCHASTIC LEARNING MODEL.

statistical prediction Knowing that a variable, X, predicts within an acceptable band of error, a variable, Y, allows one to use X to estimate the value of Y more accurately than by chance or sheer guessing; the higher the correlation between the variables the more likely the estimate will be correct.

statistical psychology A branch of psychology that uses statistical models and methods in attempts to provide explanations for phenomena.

statistical regression See REGRESSION TOWARD THE MEAN.

statistical sequential test A procedure to determine whether a sequence of events is statistically biased or unbiased; for example, research has shown that seven shuffles of a new set of playing cards are needed to bring them to random positioning.

statistical series A set of values, quantitative or qualitative, which may vary among themselves, but which have some common characteristic or origin.

statistical significance A measure of the probability that a result is due to chance. A difference between population parameters for different groups for which the null hypothesis, usually that the difference is 0, can be rejected with a given probability of being correct. See SIGNIFICANCE, SIGNIFICANT DIFFERENCE, TYPE I ERROR, TYPE II ERROR.

statistical stability 1. A tendency of a particular statistic to be dependable, that is, measure the same thing repeatedly. Similar to reliability. See RELIABILITY. 2. A tendency of a particular statistic to be accurate, that is, measure what it intends to measure. Similar to validity. See STATISTICAL SIGNIFICANCE.

statistical tables Organized lists of numbers that are used with statistical procedures. Range from simple lists of squares of numbers (in older texts) to the area under a normal curve for various z-scores to critical values for various distributions (t, χ^2, F) used in inferential statistics.

statistical weighting The assignment of a mathematical constant to a statistic to represent its relative value to the total statistic. It is generally agreed that some observations of behavior are more trustworthy than others; one assumption is that unusual scores, often called outliers, are among the least trustworthy. While some will simply eliminate observations that are extremely far from the mean (outliers are at least two standard deviations from the mean), others prefer statistical weighting where, although no data are thrown away, observations close to the mean count more, are more heavily weighted by perhaps a factor of 2 or 3, than observations that are one or two standard deviations from the mean. See WEIGHT, WEIGHT DISCRIMINATION.

statistics 1. The branch of mathematics that uses data to find or support answers for quantifiable questions. 2. A numerical datum; or a mathematical summary or description of a body of data. 3. An estimate of a parameter, obtained by sampling. See DESCRIPTIVE STATISTIC, INFERENTIAL STATISTIC, NONPARAMETRIC STATISTIC.

statoconia Otoliths.

statocyst A sac containing small solid particles, called otoliths, which shift with the force of gravity when the animal moves its head. Found mainly in lower animals, it functions as a receptor for the sense of balance. The movements of the otoliths (literally, ear stones) indicate to the animal which countermovements are needed to maintain balance. See GEOTAXIS.

statokinetic reflexes/responses Postural reflexes and other muscular reactions that enable a person to maintain balance and orientation while walking, running, or jumping.

statrat A computer program of probable behavior for an animal such as a rat. The question is where would the "rat" (or a drunken sailor) go when placed on a certain spot and given freedom to move in any direction. Used for research purposes such as checking the behavior of drunken people, those with Korsakoff's disorder, the senile. Also known as drunken sailor's walk.

statue of Condillac (E. B. Condillac) A hypothetical model used to explain the gradual acquisition of human senses, using an imaginary statue that first develops an olfactory apparatus, and then the other senses, one by one. See CONSTANCY HYPOTHESIS, LAW OF CONSTANCY.

status 1. The state or position of an individual or group, for example, a person's standing in a social group. 2. A persistent condition, as in status epilepticus.

status comparison Comparison of personal abilities and shortcomings with the same or similar qualities in other people. See FEELINGS OF INFERIORITY.

status dilemma Not knowing how to behave in a particular social situation (such as being invited to an employer's home) because norms for behavior have not been established or are unknown.

status dysraphicus A hereditary disorder marked by a number of developmental anomalies resulting from faulty development of the spine or spinal cord during the embryonic stage.

status epilepticus Continuous, prolonged, uninterrupted series of grand mal seizures, sometimes resulting in death. See VALIUM.

status grouping The grouping of individuals according to their social standing.

status liability The condition prevailing when the deviancy of high-status individuals is so extreme that they are not protected against sanction, and they are especially accountable for any negative outcomes.

status need An urge or desire to attain a high degree of social recognition, prestige, or power.

status offenses Conduct considered illegal based on status; for example, a juvenile but not an adult is liable for violating curfew laws, smoking cigarettes, drinking alcoholic beverages, and only a married individual can commit adultery.

status passage Regulated behavior in accordance with strict protocol of a particular social position.

status role The function fulfilled by an individual who, through membership in a group, lends status to the group as a whole because of reputation, special abilities, or achievements; for example, a Nobel prize-winning professor fulfills a status role in a university.

status sequence Steps in achieving status, for example, in politics winning an election as a county chairman, then as a mayor, then as a senator and then as president.

status symbol An object that indicates a person's status, for example, an expensive car is taken by many as a symbol of high status. Wearing shabby clothing to work may symbolize low or high status.

statutory rape 1. Legal phrase applied in cases in which a person (male or female) consents to sexual intercourse although not qualified because of age to give lawful consent. 2. Sexual relations with anyone below a certain age of consent. See RAPE.

staves (R. B. Cattell) Units of five equal steps covering the normal distribution curve. See STANINE.

STD sexually transmitted disease

steadiness apparatus A device used to measure the amount of involuntary movement made when the finger or arm is held as nearly motionless as possible.

steady state See HOMEOSTASIS.

stealing-fear See KLEPTOPHOBIA.

steatopygia Large quantities of fat in the buttocks. In some cultures this attribute is considered a sign of female beauty. Also known as Hottentot bustle.

Stegreiftheater (theater of spontaneity—German) An early version of what was later to become J. L. Moreno's "psychodrama" in which actors given a brief synopsis of a plot acted it out based on spontaneous words and actions.

Steinzor effect (B. Steinzor) In group dynamics, a tendency for group members to comment immediately after the person sitting opposite them comments.

stellate cells Any of a number of the larger pyramidal cells below the plexiform layer of the cortex. Some of them have a star-like shape. At the bottom of the outer pyramidal layer, most cells are of the stellate type.

stem See BRAIN STEM.

stem of an item The part of an objective test item that poses the question or sets the task. A multiple-choice item consists of a stem and two or more response-options, one of which is the correct answer.

stenin A protein coating the synaptic vesicles.

stenometer A device, such as the hand dynamometer for measuring strength of muscles.

stenopeic spectacles/visors (Paul of Aegina, A. Paré, F. Donders) Spectacles with a narrow opening or slit, used to protect the eyes against snow-blindness.

stenosis Abnormal narrowing of a body conduit or passageway. A spinal stenosis is a narrowing of the opening in the spinal column that restricts the space needed for the spinal cord.

stens (R. B. Cattell) Units of ten equal steps covering the normal distribution curve, having a mean of 5.5 and a sigma of 2. See STANINE, STAVES.

step-down test A method of passive avoidance learning in which an animal receives a shock if it steps down from a central platform onto a grid floor. Latency of response is used to evaluate a variety of treatments like central nervous system lesions and drugs.

step functions   Movement in terms of discrete intervals rather than continuous movement, for example, on a digital watch, the face will read 10:10 for a full minute before it will move to the next interval 10:11, whereas in an hour-glass, sand continuously trickles to a lower chamber in an analogical mode.

step interval   Also known as class, class interval, class size, interval. See CLASS INTERVAL.

steppage gait   Infrequently used phrase for a gait seen in certain types of neuromuscular disorders or as the result of a severed tendon that controls the foot or toes. Characterized by the affected foot slapping against the floor or ground when the person is walking. See FOOT DROP.

stepping reflex   A reflex movement that gives the appearance of stepping, elicited during the first two weeks of life by holding infants with their feet touching a surface, and moving the infants gently forward.

stepwise phenomenon   In Gestalt theory, the tendency for the steps in a continuum to appear smoothly progressive, for example, a descending series of sounds, or the bodily growth of an infant to maturity.

stepwise transformation   Abrupt changes rather than smooth changes. Sudden insights or rapid emotional changes are examples.

steradian   A unit of measure for a solid angle subtended by $1m^2$ of the surface of a sphere 1 meter in radius. See LUMINOUS FLUX.

stereo-agnosis   See ASTEREOGNOSIS.

stereochemical smell theory   (J. D. Amoore, J. W. Johnston & M. Rubin) A chemical smell theory based upon the spatial arrangement of atoms in molecules. Lists seven primary odor qualities, each odor supposedly being associated with a typical change or shape of odorous molecules: (a) Camphoraceous (spherical-shaped)—mothballs and camphor; (b) Ethereal (small, flat, thin)—dry-cleaning fluid; (c) Floral (key-shaped)—roses; (c) Musky (disk-shaped)—angelica root oil; (e) Pepperminty or Minty (wedge-shaped)—peppermint candy; (f) Pungent (shape undetermined)—vinegar; and (g) Putrid (shape undetermined)—rotten eggs. See CROCKER-HENDERSON (ODOR) SYSTEM, HENNING SMELL SYSTEM, SMELL, SMELL MECHANISM, STERIC THEORY OF ODOR, ZWAARDEMAKER SMELL SYSTEM.

stereocilia   Short immobile cilia (hairs) on the surface of cells such as the semicircular canals of the inner ear. See BALANCE RECEPTORS.

stereognosis   Ability to recognize an object by touch.

stereogram   A three-dimensional picture. Two flat photographs, each differing slightly from the other so arranged that when viewed binocularly through a stereoscope, gives the tridimensional effect of a solid object in relief. See STEREOSCOPE.

stereopsis   Stereoscopic vision, capacity for depth perception.

stereopsyche   Peculiar motor activities of patients with schizophrenia, such as catatonic postures and fetal positions. Their movements and postures appear to be isolated from the rest of the psychic structure of the patient.

stereoreceptor   Any receptor of an organism by means of which responses to three-dimensional objects are initiated.

stereoscope   (C. Wheatstone) A device that presents two slightly disparate pictures of the same scene, one to each eye, the separate retinal images fusing to produce a binocular, three-dimensional image. Used for vision-testing and training. See STEREOGRAM.

stereoscopic acuity   The ability to locate visually an object in three-dimensional space, often a Howard-Dolman apparatus is used.

stereoscopic depth perception   A capacity to determine distances better by viewing distant stimuli with two rather than with one eye due to each eye seeing what is viewed from a different angle than the other.

stereoscopic motion pictures   Motion pictures that give the impression of third dimension or depth. Usually viewers wear special glasses with polarized lenses, one vertically and one horizontally.

stereoscopic vision   Awareness of three-dimensionality, solidity, and the distance between observer and objects observed. Due to the two eyes, being set apart, seeing the object(s) from slightly different angles. More commonly known as depth perception.

stereotactic instrument   A device that holds an animal's head in a position which, when coordinated with information from the coordinates of brain atlases, allows an electrode to be inserted into a precise area or structure of the brain. Designed to permit experimental work on the brains of animals without doing much damage to neighboring tissues. Also known as stereotaxic instrument. See BRAIN, BRAIN IMAGING TECHNIQUES, BRAIN MAPPING, BRAIN RESEARCH.

stereotactic tractotomy   A form of psychosurgery in which radioactive 'seeds' are implanted below the head of the caudate nucleus to relieve symptoms of anxiety, severe depression, and obsessional states. Also known as seed psychosurgery.

stereotaxic instrument   stereotactic instrument

stereotaxis   An orienting response toward or away from contact with solid objects, resulting in a tendency to crawl into corners or holes. Also known as stereotropism, thigmotaxis. See TAXIS, TROPISM.

stereotaxy   The precise positioning of a point in three-dimensional areas, such as finding the exact location of a nerve center in the brain. Also known as stereotaxic technique. See STEREOTACTIC INSTRUMENT.

stereotropism   An orienting response toward solid objects. An older term for stereotaxis. Also known as thigmotaxis. See TAXIS, TROPISM.

stereotype   (H. Didot) 1. A common concept or heuristic. 2. A generalized perception ascribing particular traits, characteristics, values, aspect, appearance or behavior to a group or a member of a group without regard to accuracy or applicability. 3. The act of making such a judgment with an unwillingness or inability to alter personal point of view. See NEGATIVE STEREOTYPE, POSITIVE STEREOTYPE, PREJUDICE, RACISM. See also STEREOTYPED MOVEMENT, STEREOTYPED-MOVEMENT DISORDERS.

stereotype accuracy   The ability to determine accurately in what way an individual's traits correspond to a stereotype associated with an age group, ethnic group, professional group, or some other group. See DIFFERENTIAL ACCURACY.

stereotype threat   (C. M. Steele) A social-psychological disadvantage for a person in a situation where a negative stereotype exists for the person as a member of a group or person with a particular characteristic.

stereotyped movement   Sudden movement of various body parts that occur at odd times and have no apparent stimulus. See PSYCHOMOTOR EPILEPSY, HABIT, TIC, TOURETTE'S DISORDER.

stereotyped responses   Characterizing certain responses which are always performed in substantially the same manner.

stereotypic-movement disorders   Repetitive actions that are purposeless or even dangerous to self and others. Also known as stereotyped-movement disorders. See ATYPICAL TIC DISORDER, ATYPICAL STEREOTYPED-MOVEMENT DISORDER, CHRONIC MOTOR-TIC DISORDER, STEREOTYPY, TOURETTE'S DISORDER, TRANSIENT-TIC DISORDER.

stereotypy   Persistent pathological repetition of the seemingly senseless words, phrases, or movements. A common symptom in autistic children and in patients with obsessive-compulsive disorder or catatonic schizophrenia. In psychoanalytic theory, the condition is frequently interpreted as an unconscious effort to allay anxiety and gain a feeling of security. For autism and in Harlow's monkey studies, the symptoms are sometimes attributed to cerebellar damage, and persons with autism might engage in them to screen out overstimulation from other senses. Also known as stereotyped behavior.

steric theory of odor   A point of view that certain odors are perceived because they are produced by chemical molecules of certain shapes. The molecules that fit a receptor in a lock-and-key manner cause the neural membrane to become depolarized or hyperpolarized, an effect which in turn signals the cue that identifies the odor. See SMELL MECHANISM, STEREOCHEMICAL SMELL THEORY.

sterile   1. Unable to have progeny whether due to physiological defect, disease or surgery. 2. Free of contaminations of living organisms. 3. Being intellectually or emotionally vacant.

sterility   Infertility, being incapable of reproducing. See FECUNDITY, INFERTILITY.

sterilization   The process of rendering an organism incapable of sexual reproduction. May be performed surgically or may result from injury or from exposure to radiation, heat, infectious agents such as mumps virus, or chemicals.

Sternberg Task/Test   A method of testing memory developed by Saul Sternberg. Participants are shown a set of diverse items, for example a comb, knife, paper clip, key and a chain. Later, a variety of other items plus these five are shown, and the participants must reply immediately whether each item shown is one of the set seen before or a different one.

Sternberg Triarchic Abilities Test (STAT)   (R. J. Sternberg) An examination intending to measure analytical and creative abilities in the verbal, quantitative, figural and essay domains.

Stern's disease   (W. L. Stern) Presenile psychosis associated with thalamic degeneration. See COGNITIVE DISORDER, DEMENTIA.

Stern variator   (W. L. Stern) An apparatus used to produce pure tones of variable frequency by varying the length of the resonating air column. An attached scale gives readings of the frequency of vibrations.

steroid(s)   Complex organic molecules that have in common four interconnected hydrocarbon rings, three with six carbon atoms and one with five. The molecules are the basic form of male and female sex hormones, adrenal-cortical hormones, and other natural substances such as vitamin D and cholesterol.

Stevens' power law   (S. S. Stevens) A psychophysiological law asserting that equal stimulus ratios produce equal subjective ratios. Also known as power law, Stevens' law, Stevens' power function.

sthenic feeling   An affect of heightened energy, activity, or excessive excitement such as anger or pronounced joy.

sthenic type   A constitutional type characterized by strength and vigor and roughly equivalent to Ernst Kretschmer's athletic type.

sthenometer   A gauge for measuring strength of muscles. See HAND DYNOMETER.

stick shaker   In ergonomics, a control that vibrates as a tactile signal to the operator, mainly confined to aircraft control yokes to warn the pilot of an impending stall.

stiff-man syndrome   A disorder of the voluntary-muscles characterized by severe intermittent painful spasms of the muscles of the trunk, neck, and upper arms and legs. Occurs in cases of hyperthyroidism and certain other diseases and may resemble catatonia.

stigma   1. A mark of shame. 2. A blemish on the skin. 3. Overt evidence of a disease. 4. A personal trait that clearly distinguishes the individual from others and which constitutes or is assumed to constitute a physical, psychological, or social disadvantage, for example, a physical deformity, a known history of criminal conduct or psychiatric illness, a different sexual preference. Term signifies social disapproval and may lead to discrimination or social isolation. See STIGMATA, STIGMATA OF DEGENERACY.

stigmata   (marks—Greek) Spontaneous development of sores or wounds on the head, hands, feet, and side corresponding to the location of wounds suffered by Jesus Christ during the crucifixion. At least 300 cases of stigmata have been reported, chiefly among deeply religious women, although the first recorded case was St. Francis of Assisi. Stigmata have been viewed as a conversion reaction. Another opinion is the that stigmatics generate their own wounds either consciously or unconsciously. Also known as stigmatization. See CONVERSION HYSTERIA, SKIN DISORDERS.

stigmata of degeneracy   Describing certain physical characteristics which, in Cesare Lombroso's view, indicated a hereditary tendency to criminal behavior. Among them were small, pointed ears, a low forehead, and close-set eyes. This theory was decisively disproved by research by Charles Goring in his book *The English Criminal*. See DEGENERACY THEORY, PHYSIOGNOMY, STIGMA.

stigmatophilia   Being sexually attracted to or aroused by the partner or self being tattooed, scarified, or pierced for wearing jewelry, especially in the genital region.

Stiles-Crawford effect   (W. S. Stiles & B. H. Crawford) A tendency for light beams that pass through the middle of the pupil to be stronger than those that enter along the edges of the pupil; applies primarily to cone vision.

Stiller's sign   (B. Stiller) A floating tenth rib, which is associated with a tendency to neurasthenia. Also known as costal stigma, Stiller's rib.

Stilling Test   (J. Stilling) A chart composed of dots of different colors. Some of the dots form numbers visible to the normal eye but not to the color-blind or color-weak eye. The first color vision test to use isochromatic plates, it was later adapted and modified by Shinobu Ishihara in his test. Also known as Stilling's Color Table. See COLOR BLINDNESS, ISHIHARA CHART.

stilted speech   When not a cultural phenomenon, a defensive manner consisting of formal, affected, or pompous speech, characteristic of a self-conscious, arrogant, or rigid personality. When observed in some patients with schizophrenia it may represent a delusional identity.

stimulants   1. Agents that excite functional activity in an organism or in a part of an organism. May be classified according to the body system or function excited, for example, cardiac, central nervous system, genital stimulants, and by the type of drug or other agent producing the stimulation, such as amphetamine, methylxanthine, convulsant, analeptic stimulants. 2. Medicines chiefly used to promote a focusing of attention and thereby a decrease in hyperactivity, especially in the condition of Attention deficit hyperactivity disorder, both in children and adults. Most common forms, methylphenidate (Ritalin), dextroamphetamine (Dexedrine), and pemoline (Cylert). Occasionally some of these have been used in other conditions such as low-grade depression associated with physical illness.

stimulate   1. To apply a stimulus to a receptor. 2. To start a nerve impulse. 3. To arouse a high degree of organic activity. 4. To arouse, excite, enhance, or motivate a normal response physically, emotionally or intellectually, including any appetitive function such as sex or food.

stimulating occupation   An occupational activity that has an arousing and stimulating effect.

stimulation   1. Any observable change (typical or atypical, and including inhibition) in the metabolism or other function of a living tissue, produced by applying some external agency. 2. Act of applying such an external agency (that is, a stimulus).

stimulation effects   Physiologic changes produced when a stimulus alters the electrical potential of a neuron by producing an irritating effect on the cell membrane, which in turn disrupts the ionic balance on either side of the membrane. The potential change travels along the nerve fiber to a terminus or synapse, which can pass the impulse along to a neighboring fiber. In vitro (test-tube) experiments show increased temperature, increased oxygen consumption, and other metabolic effects when neurons are exposed to electrical stimulation.

stimulation method   An approach to the treatment of speech disorders in which the emphasis is placed on the development of auditory concepts; the learning of speech sounds by listening to them.

stimulation motive   A desire for new and different experiences, seen even in infants who prefer to look at complex rather then simple visual stimuli and in adults who seek to experience novelties.

stimulation time   (F. C. Donders) The interval between the application of a stimulus and the arousal of the afferent nerve impulse, that is, the time taken to overcome the inertia of a receptor by a given stimulus. See REACTION TIME.

stimulator   A device used to excite or stimulate a receptor. An early type of stimulator was an induction coil wired to a vibrator that would convert direct current electricity into pulsations. An important part of later stimulators was a device for controlling the rate of change in the electric current since a steady current flow loses its stimulus effect.

stimulogeneous fibrillation   (S. Bok) The observation that nerve axons grow (galvanotropically) away from other active neurons, that is, away from a cathode pole.

stimulus (S)   (goad—Latin) In general, any event or situation, internal or external, that elicits a response from the organism; or, more specifically, any change in the physical-energy level that activates a sense organ, or receptor. The activity of the sense organ is termed the proximal stimulus, and the physical energy that excites it is termed the distal stimulus. Human receptors are limited to a relatively small range of energy changes (in hearing, 20 to 20,000 Hz, or cycles per second), and are also limited to only six types of stimuli: photic (eyes), acoustic (ears), chemical (nose, tongue), thermal (skin), mechanical (pressure, touch), and destruction of tissue (pain). Electrical energy has the unique ability of exciting all sense channels. See CONDITIONED STIMULUS, HULL'S THEORY, SUBLIMINAL STIMULUS, UNCONDITIONED STIMULUS.

stimulus as coded (SAC)   Any particular stimulus cannot be considered constant because although an experimenter presents an unvarying stimulus, two perceivers do not necessarily interpret the stimulus in the same manner. Whether the stimulus works depends to a great extent on how a participant understands or interprets the stimulus. See EFFECTIVE STIMULUS, FUNCTIONAL STIMULUS.

stimulus attitude   An expectant set in which the participant is ready to respond to a particular stimulus.

stimulus barrier   A process by means of which organisms protect themselves from overstimulation. Based on an innate ability to perceive and differentiate painful and pleasurable states.

stimulus-bound   1. Pertaining to a perception dependent upon the qualities of the stimulation. 2. Characterizing behavior that tends to be inflexible and determined primarily by the stimulus situation.

stimulus continuum   Series of stimuli related to each other along a specific dimension, such as a series of tones in the diatonic scale, or an unbroken series of shades of blue.

stimulus control   Arranging the environment in such a way that a given response is either more likely or less likely to occur, for example, buying only one pack of cigarettes weekly to decrease the likelihood of smoking.

stimulus differentiation   1. A process whereby an organism learns to differentiate between similar stimuli. See STIMULUS DISCRIMINATIONthe preferred term for this meaning. 2. A Gestalt phrase for distinguishing different parts or patterns in a visual field.

stimulus discrimination   1. Ability to distinguish between similar stimuli, as in distinguishing a circle from an ellipse. 2. In operant learning, a process by which an organism comes to distinguish between situations in which a response is or is not reinforced (S^D and S^Δ, respectively), learning to make the response only in certain situations. When the organism responds more frequently (at a higher rate, with a shorter latency) to S^D than to S^Δ then it is said that a discrimination has been formed. Requires both the differential reward conditions and the correspondingly appropriate differential behavior. See S^D, S^Δ.

stimulus equivalence   Two or more related stimuli eliciting the same response or allied responses. Equivalence implies less similarity between the stimuli than occurs in generalization. See STIMULUS GENERALIZATION.

stimulus error   In Titchener's introspective method, the error involved in responding to a stimulus in terms of its purpose or meaning (for example, "chair") instead of its properties as a stimulus (size, shape, etc.). See STRUCTURALISM.

stimulus function   (J. R. Kantor) What occurs psychologically in response to a stimulus. In the interbehavioral field a psychologist can seriously err by limiting analysis to the formal properties of a stimulus (an object is only a stimulus for Kantor if it is associated with a response). "X is a pill" has very different meanings, different stimulus functions, when X is replaced by "Sue" and, alternatively, by "Aspirin." Similarly, a teen upon walking into a kitchen and saying "That's a beautiful cake," may be complimenting the baker or may be asking to eat a piece. What occurs physically is the stimulus, what occurs psychologically is the stimulus function. For Kantor it is impossible to separate stimulus function and response function, they are two sides of the same coin. Related to stimulus-function evolution.

stimulus-function evolution   The change in stimulus function that occurs with experience, for example an apple goes from something to place one's tongue on as an infant, then something to be rolled on the floor, then something to take to parent with request that it be cut up, then something to be made into a pie.

stimulus generalization   A tendency for a conditioned response to be evoked by a range of stimuli similar (but not identical) to the conditioned stimulus; for example, if a dog is conditioned to bark when a particular bell is sounded, the dog tends to make the same response to a wide range of bells. A child who nearly drowns in the bathtub may develop a fear of wading and swimming. In research, alternative stimuli are employed to determine the extent of stimulus generalization, by noting which stimuli produce the same response as a target response. See RESPONSE-GENERALIZATION PRINCIPLE.

stimulus-generalization gradient   Expression of the functional relationship between stimulus similarity and response strength; as the stimulus becomes less similar to the original conditioned stimulus, the response probability decreases proportionately.

stimulus gradient   A means of determining distance in terms of variations of the quality of the perceptual field, for example, near items are clearly seen and farther items are vaguely seen.

stimulus hunger   A need to receive new and varied stimulation from the environment. Satisfaction of this need is assumed to be essential to normal functioning. See SENSORY DEPRIVATION.

stimulus intensity dynamism (V)   In Clark Hull's theory, the concept that the stronger the stimulus, the stronger the response of the organism. See HULL'S THEORY.

stimulus method   In speech training, the correction of speech defects by exposing the student repeatedly to sounds that he or she must discriminate between and then try to reproduce.

stimulus object   (J. R. Kantor) Any object or person that elicits a response from an organism. See INTERBEHAVIORAL PSYCHOLOGY.

stimulus-organism-response (S-O-R)   A model of behavior. A stimulus touches the periphery of the body at a sensory organ (exteroceptive) or an internal stimulus occurs (interoceptive, proprioceptive), the organism routes the sensation through the nervous system (often including the brain) to the muscles where some kind of overt or covert response occurs. See S-O-R LEARNING, S-O-R THEORY.

stimulus-organism-response learning (model)   S-O-R learning (model)

stimulus-organism-response theory   See S-O-R THEORY EMPHASIZING ORGANISM, S-O-R THEORY EMPHASIZING PERCEPTION.

stimulus overload   (S. Milgram) Exposure to too many environmental stimuli to be comfortably processed, resulting in stress and behavior designed to restore equilibrium. According to Stanley Milgram, the "unfriendliness" of urbanites may represent a necessary strategy for screening out environment stimuli in the effort to maintain psychological balance. See HOMEOSTATIC MODEL.

stimulus pattern   The grouping of stimuli into an organized configuration, as in a painting or sonata.

stimulus population   A measurable number of independent events in the environment, of which only a single event is effective at a given time.

stimulus-response (S-R)   General phrase for stimuli above the absolute threshold that produce a response, for example, a blow by a rubber hammer on a knee that elicits the patellar response. In the early years of psychology as a scientific enterprise, this was virtually the sole view. In later years the S-O-R and S-S views also attained respectability, possibly surpassing S-R in prominence. See S-O-R THEORY, S-R THEORY, S-S LEARNING.

stimulus-response correlation   A conclusion that there is a predictive relationship between a particular stimulus and a particular response due to the stimulus being followed by the response beyond an established level of chance.

stimulus-response learning (model)   S-R learning (model)

stimulus-response psychology   A point of view that psychology is based on the fact that live organisms responsed to stimuli, either exteroceptive (from outside, such as falling rain that leads a person to seek shelter) interoceptive (internal cues such as a belly ache that leads to taking medicine) or proprioceptive (feedback from muscles). Also known as S-R psychology. See S-O-R LEARNING, S-R LEARNING, S-S LEARNING.

stimulus-response relationship   1. The view that stimulus-response association is best understood as the reinforcement strengthening the responding, as put forth by the radical functional behaviorism of John Watson. See S-R LEARNING. 2. The view that stimulus-response association is best understood as the reinforcement strengthening the environmental (S) control of responding. See S-O-R LEARNING, S-S LEARNING.

stimulus-response theory   S-R theory

stimulus sampling theory (SST)   (W. K. Estes) Based to some extent on E. R. Guthrie's and B. F. Skinner's views about learning, Estes considered learning to occur in an all-or-none fashion by association of stimulus elements with a particular response. When a response is made it is associated with a number of stimulus elements that are present at that exact moment (contiguity); as a response occurs several times in the same general setting it will become associated with more and more stimulus elements of that complex stimulus; the probability that the response will occur in the future due to the presence of that particular complex stimulus depends on the number of stimulus elements of that complex that have been associated with, been present during, the particular response.

stimulus set   In reaction-time experiments, the expectancy or readiness associated with concentration on the stimulus rather than the response.

stimulus situation   All the components of an occurrence or experience that, taken as a whole, comprise a stimulus to which an organism responds. Phrase is used to accentuate the complexity of behavior-arousing events. That is, a stimulus may be perceived as a unitary pattern but may be composed of many elements, as in a concert, or championship boxing bout.

stimulus-stimulus association   1. Conditioning such that the presentation of one stimulus (the sign in E. C. Tolman's terminology) comes to activate a representation or mental image (the significate in Tolman's terminology) of the other stimulus. See S-S LEARNING. 2. A form of mediated learning based on the association of one stimulus with another, for example, a dog is trained to salivate on hearing a bell and later after an associative connection is made between hearing a bell and seeing a triangle, the sight of the triangle will produce salivation. Also known as higher order conditioning, mediated generalization.

stimulus-stimulus learning (model)   S-S learning (model)

stimulus strength ($_S L_R$)   (C. L. Hull) Effectiveness of any stimulus in eliciting a response or series of responses. See HULL'S THEORY, STIMULUS VALUE.

stimulus tension   A subjective reaction to a stimulus; any tension induced by a stimulus. According to Sigmund Freud, pain increases the stimulus tension and pleasure lowers it. See HOMEOSTASIS.

stimulus trace   (C. L. Hull) The presumed continued activity in a nerve after stimulation has ended. See HULL'S THEORY.

stimulus value   1. Strength of a given stimulus as measured in standard units, such as a shock of 40 volts. 2. The perceived importance of a person's identity either by the person or by another; the perceived importance may differ depending on the perceiver. 3. See STIMULUS STRENGTH. 4. See STIMULUS FUNCTION.

stimulus variable   The stimulus as one of a group of variables; a possible independent variable in a psychological experiment.

stimulus word   A word presented to a participant to elicit a response. Many tests and procedures employ oral presentation of stimulus words, for example, learning experiments or projective techniques such as the word-association test.

stinginess   Miserliness; lack of generosity. In psychoanalytic theory, this trait is thought to stem from the anal-retention stage of psychosexual development. See ANAL CHARACTER.

stinkin' thinkin'   Slang for a defective way of thinking that leads people to begin to experiment with addictive substances, phrase is used by people in various addictive recovery groups such as Alcoholics Anonymous, Synanon.

stirp   1. The sum-total of the genes or determiners present in a given zygote (fertilized ovum). 2. Family or stock. 3. Descendant.

stirpiculture   The breeding of animals for special purposes.

stirrup   1. See STAPES. 2. A stirrup-shaped attachment to a medical examination or surgical table in which the feet are placed in an elevated and extended width position so that they and the legs may be kept in a particular attitude to allow certain procedures, such as gynecological examination.

STM   short-term memory

stochastic Refers to a system of events whose probability of occurrence changes constantly, although the probability of a predictable occurrence increases with the number of events. A stochastic model is opposed to a strictly deterministic one. See PROBABILISM.

stochastic learning theory A probabilistic model that uses chance and random considerations in attempting to predict behavioral irregularities and individual differences.

Stockholm syndrome The formation of an emotional bond between captors and hostages if the two parties are in close relationships under stressful conditions for a long time. This phenomenon was first identified in a bank robbery situation that lasted five days in Stockholm. Psychologically, its meaning extends beyond simply identifying with the aggressor. It encompasses being profoundly grateful to the captor(s) for allowing the captive(s) to live and being spared great bodily harm. See IDENTIFICATION WITH THE AGGRESSOR.

stocking anesthesia See GLOVE ANESTHESIA.

stomach activity and emotion The gastrointestinal effects that intense emotions have on the stomach, including inhibition of muscular contractions, and the flow of gastric juices, under the control of the autonomic nervous system. See STOMACH REACTOR.

stomach loading (W. B. Cannon) The effect of a distended stomach on appetite. In animal experiments, expanding a balloon in the animal's stomach or filling the stomach with water or an inert substance decreases the amount of food eaten. Distention of the stomach walls triggers nerve impulses to the hypothalamus, which results in inhibition of the urge to eat.

stomach reactor A person who responds to stress through symptoms of gastrointestinal distress, for example, colitis or peptic ulcers. See STOMACH ACTIVITY AND EMOTION.

stooge A person who participates in research in a misleading role, most often in social psychology, who appears to participants to be either a researcher or another participant, but who, instead follows the secret directions of the researcher. Also known as a confederate. See AUSSAGE TEST, OBEDIENCE.

stop consonant In speaking, making a sound that ends with the mouth closed, as in saying "come." See PHONEME, PHONETICS, PHONOLOGY.

storage-and-transfer model of memory (R. C. Atkinson) A multistore model of memory which holds that there are three types of memory: sensory, short-term, and long-term.

storage capacity 1. The ability to remember, either on a short-term or long-term basis. Short-term memory is sometimes tested by having participants repeat a sequence of numbers they have just heard. Long-term memory is sometimes tested in schools by final examinations. 2. Utmost capacity of information possible for a person to retain in memory. There have been individual cases, such as of Talmudic scholars, whose memory capacity is extraordinary. See IDIOT SAVANT, LONG-TERM MEMORY, SHORT-TERM MEMORY.

storage (memory) Refers to a hypothetical location where memory resides when not in use. Information is stored permanently in long-term memory.

store image In consumer psychology, a generalized perception that customers have of retail stores. According to John Guaspari, it is composed of macro-expectations (what customer knows of chain department stores) and micro-expectations (what customer knows of a particular store through experiences there, advertising, etc.).

storm-and-stress period A period of emotional turmoil. G. Stanley Hall used the phrase to characterize adolescence, which he thought corresponded to the turbulent transition from savagery to civilization. See STURM UND DRANG PERIOD.

stormy personality (S. Arieti) A personality pattern in which life is punctuated by an unending series of crises and abrupt changes in occupation and relationships.

story-book counseling A group technique with children wherein a story is read for the purpose of getting pupils to identify with characters and to discuss characters and symbols in the story as related to their own life concerns.

story fear See MYTHOPHOBIA.

story-recall test An examination which requires participants to recall details of a story told or read to them.

strabismometer An instrument for measuring the deviation of the eyes in strabismus (cross-eyes). Also known as strabometer.

strabismus Any abnormal alignment of the eyes; squint. Also known as heterotropia. See BRAID'S STRABISMUS, CROSS-EYE, DOUBLE VISION, GRIEG'S DISEASE.

straight line learning curve A theoretical curve depicting learning occurring at a steady rate. See graph A of CUMULATIVE RECORD for an example.

straight line processing Thinking that proceeds in a logical linear sequence, from A to B to the end, rather than jumping around from A to M to F, etc.

straight-line sensory system Afferent nerves that go directly from the site on the body to the brain, thus bringing sensations directly to the brain without other connections.

strain Indicating excessive tension in a muscle or nerve unit, usually due to an activity overload, or in psychological adjustment, usually due to an emotional overload, intellectual overload, or both.

strait-jacket A restraining device consisting of a tough canvas shirt with long sleeves that contain a person's extended arms and hands, allow the sleeves to be crossed diagonally across the chest extending around the waist and fastened behind the back with leather straps. Used sometimes as an immediate control measure with violent, assaultive, self-injuring, or physically dangerous and uncooperative patients. Also known as camisole.

strange-hand sign A tactile perceptual disorder characterized by an inability of patients to recognize their own left hand. When clasping their two hands, they may be unable to acknowledge without visual clues that the left hand is their own. Due to a corpus callosum defect. Also known as *la main étrangère* (the unknown hand).

strangeness fear An irrational fear of the unfamiliar; neophobia.

stranger anxiety/distress (J. Piaget) In developmental psychology, a wariness or tension in the presence of unfamiliar persons, commonly shown by infants between age 8 and 12 months, but also found in later years. Considered less the result of insecurity, anxiety, and/or threat and more a reflection of the infant's developing ability to compare unfamiliar persons with stored schemas of familiar persons.

stranger fear 1. A fear of strangers that infants commonly display for a few months beginning at about 8 or 9 months of age. See SEPARATION-ANXIETY DISORDER, STRANGER ANXIETY. 2. See XENOPHOBIA.

Strange Situation (test) (M. Ainsworth) A test that determines the nature of a child's attachment to a caregiver. In her studies of attachment, Mary Ainsworth described a series of episodes wherein a child is with the mother, then with a stranger, then left alone, and then reunited with stranger and mother in a specific sequence, with the child's reactions noted in the various situations.

strangulated affect (S. Freud) Inhibition or retention of the normal discharge of emotion, which leads to a substitute discharge in the form of physical symptoms. This theory was advanced to explain the dynamics of conversion hysteria. Later supplanted by the concept of repression.

strategic intervention therapy An approach to family therapy employing specific strategies, plans, and tactics to force changes in behavior.

strategy 1. (A. Newell & H. A. Simon) A component of an information processing system that (a) influences the directions of search, and (b) is not a fixed (physiological) component of the system, but is subject to learning and modification. 2. In game theory, a set of directions (pure or mixed) selected for a special course of action. See HEURISTIC SEARCH.

stratification Horizontal layering or organization. Term is usually applied to such divisions of a social group or society as a whole.

stratificational grammar A linguistic, theoretical model designed to explain the processes of acquisition and comprehension of a language, including a conceptual framework explaining the storage of information in cortical neurons and the subsequent outputting of such information to other receptors (including humans and animals) for communication purposes.

stratified random sampling Dividing a population in sub-groups on some logical basis, for example, people who are homeless, those renting apartments, those renting houses, and those owning their own homes, and then taking random samples from each of these groups in proportion to the total number in each sub-group.

stratified sample A sample drawn in such a way as to include representation of particular groups in proportions dictated by research objectives, for example, oversampling minorities in a study to permit detailed analysis of that group. See STRATIFIED RANDOM SAMPLE.

Stratton's experiment A classic experiment on visual distortion in which George M. Stratton wore special glasses for 87 hours, distributed over 8 days, that inverted images 180 degrees from normal. The experiment answered questions about perceptual and behavioral changes that take place during prolonged exposure to an inverted world. Stratton adapted to the new situation by eventually operating in a normal manner to what he perceived; he had to readapt when the glasses were removed.

Strauss syndrome (A. A. Strauss) A pervasive pattern of hyperactivity, perseveration, and perceptual disorders manifested by some children with learning disabilities. Also known as minimal brain dysfunction syndrome.

streaming The separation of individuals in an ongoing process, such as schooling, or any kind of learning or operation, on the basis of differential abilities. Also known as tracking. See TRACKING IN EDUCATION, TRACKING IN INDUSTRY, TRACKING IN PSYCHOTHERAPY.

stream of action The continuous activities of an organism.

stream of consciousness Phrase introduced by William James, a functionalist, to describe consciousness as a continuous, dynamic flow of ideas and images rather than a static series of discrete components. Phrase differentiates between the functionalist and structuralist approaches. Also known as stream of thought.

street fear See AGYIOPHOBIA.

Street figures (R. Street) Illustrations or graphics of everyday objects that have been treated in such a manner that they look like haphazard mosaics but that may be seen as a totality by some people. It is an example of the Gestalt principle of Prägnanz.

Street figures At initial glance the series of blobs may appear to be a random pattern, but, on further examination, are organized via the gestalt principle of perception into a form that is meaningful, in this case a dog.

street hustlers People who conduct illegal businesses from the streets, rather than from store-fronts (for example, some people sell imitation brand name merchandise for "bargain" prices, others, such as prostitutes, sell themselves). See MALE HOMOSEXUAL PROSTITUTION.

street names (of drugs) The various slang names of illicit substances or legal medicines obtained illegally, usually used by substance-addicted persons and "drug dealers." Such names may change from year to year, vary depending on location, and a particular drug may have simultaneously a number of different slang names. See ECSTASY, ICE, LYSERGIC ACID, PHENCYCLIDINE.

street smarts See EVERYDAY INTELLIGENCE.

stren   (W. Hollister) Denoting an experience that strengthens personality by producing greater maturity, sensitivity, self-confidence, or depth. Strens are contrasted with traumas, but are often initially viewed as traumatic events, for example, experiences described by Nietzsche: "What does not kill me strengthens me."

strength-duration curve   The progressive decrease in muscular strength due to work over a period of time until complete exhaustion of the muscle is reached.

strephosymbolia   (S. Orton) A condition characterized by a tendency to reverse letters or numbers, as in reading "Dog" as "God," or "619" as "916." Attributed to a failure to establish the left-hemisphere dominance, the speech area of the brain, it is also an aspect of dyslexia. Also known as twisted symbols.

strepographia   Reversed writing. Also known as mirror-writing. See ALEXIA, DYSLEXIA, STREPHOSYMBOLIA.

stress   1. Forces on an organism of a deleterious nature that disturb its normal equilibrium (homeostasis). If excessive or prolonged, stress may overtax the organism's resources and lead to a breakdown of organized functioning, or decompensation. Types of situations that produce stress include frustrations, deprivations, conflicts, and pressures. 2. A state of physical or psychological strain which imposes demands for adjustment upon the individual. See STRESS THEORY. 3. Emphasis put on a word or thought in speaking or writing.

stress-adaptation theory   A point of view that stress depletes the reserve capacity of individuals, thereby placing them in a vulnerable position for illnesses, mental and behavioral dysfunction, or both. Also known as general adaptation syndrome (GAS).

stress-decompensation model   The concept that abnormal behavior develops as a result of stress that leads to decompensation, or to gradual progressive deterioration of normal behavior.

stress immunity   Highly developed capacity to tolerate emotional or intellectual strain; failure to react to stressful situations or events.

stress-inoculation training (SIT)   (D. Meichenbaum) The treatment of stress reactions on a preventative basis in a similar fashion to the concept of a medical inoculation. A type of cognitive-behavioral therapy that prepares clients to deal with stress-inducing events by teaching them self-control coping skills and then having them rehearse these skills while gradually being exposed to stressors.

stress interview   1. Usually a job-related interview for positions that call for great self-control, such as serving as a spy or as an administrator of a difficult group in which the interviewer(s) attempt to provoke or unsettle the applicant. 2. A lengthy interview, intended to try a participant's endurance. The participant is subjected to conditions of emotional strain; for example, under glaring lights, police in alternating pairs interrogate a suspected criminal. See STRESS TEST (meaning 1).

stressor   A stimulus, event, or situation that taxes the adaptive capacity of an organism, either physically or psychologically. The event may be potentially injurious to the organism. See STRESS.

stress reactions   Faulty, maladaptive, pathological behavior resulting from external conditions of pressure or strain, as well as physiological reactions leading to a breakdown of organized functioning. May include behavioral symptoms, such as poor motor control, disorganized speech patterns, accidents incurred; physiological symptoms, such as increase of glucose levels in the blood leading to accelerated heart rate; and/or subjective symptoms, such as feelings of loss of control. Continued stress leads to the general adaptation syndrome (GAS) and if continued may lead to decompensation and even death.

stress situation   Any condition that puts an extra burden on an individual organism's capacity to adapt (for example, extreme hunger, an overcompetitive environment, combat conditions, marital conflicts, constant criticism, a taxing job). Stress is also on a continuum from small to large, and the time interval of exposure is also a factor. In humans, reactions to stress situations vary considerably across individuals because each has a characteristic reaction to perceived stress along a continuum, for example, from a look of disdain from another, to being fired. Some people view stress situations as challenging, whereas others view them as sources of frustration. How a person views and copes with such situations determines whether it is stressful (and to what extent) or not.

stress test   1. An examination or task conducted in a natural "real-world" setting designed to ascertain the participant's capacity to perform a relatively complex task under purposefully stressful conditions. 2. A medical test in which a person runs on a treadmill while being monitored for cardiac problems. 3. The cold-pressor test, submerging a person's hand in a bucket of ice and water, used to measure psychological and physiological reactions to stress.

stress theory   A point of view that certain stimuli perceived as noxious or threatening cause adverse emotional, behavioral, and physiological reactions. See GENERAL ADAPTATION SYNDROME, STRESS.

stress tolerance   1. Capacity to withstand pressures and strains; the ability to function effectively under conditions of stress. 2. The quality and quantity of stress that an organism can endure (for example, his stress tolerance is low). Also known as frustration tolerance. See STRESS, STRESS SITUATION.

stretch receptor   An effector neuron or neuron complex in the kinesthetic system that conveys information about muscle effort, such as stretching, to the brain.

stretch reflexes   Spinal reflexes that involve increased tension or contraction in extensor muscles which support the body against the pull of gravity. Also known as myotatic reflexes. See EXTENSOR THRUST.

stria atrophica   Technical name for "stripes" on the skin that may result from rapid growth or rapid weight gain and loss, usually acquired during pregnancy. Commonly called stretch marks. Also known as lineae albicantes.

stria terminalis   A tract of fibers running between the amygdala and hypothalamus. The fibers carry impulses from the amygdaloid nuclei to the septal, hypothalamic, and thalamic areas. Experimental stimulation of this area may evoke escape or defense behavior in animals.

striae acusticae/medullares A band of transverse nerve fibers passing across the floor of the 4th ventricle of the brain, which connect with the cochlear division of the auditory nerve.

striate Having stripes. See CORPUS STRIATUM.

striate body See CORPUS STRIATUM.

striate cortex An area of the occipital lobes of the cortex where the visual functions are centered. The entering fibers are so concentrated in this region that they form a white band, the stripe of Gennari, and suggest the name striate.

striated muscle Phrase generally applied to the tissue of skeletal, or voluntary, muscles. It is striated ("striped") in appearance under a microscope because of the alternation of muscle fibers that permit the muscle to shorten and thicken during contraction. An exception is cardiac-muscle tissue which is striated but involuntary. Also known as striped muscle.

striatum The portion of the developing forebrain that becomes the basal ganglia. The striatum tissues are forced back over the thalamus during the forebrain growth, leaving the cell bodies as basal ganglia nuclei.

stridor A shrill, high-pitched sound.

stridor dentium bruxism

string A series of connected items, such as pearls on a necklace or alphabet letters comprising a word.

string fear See LINONOPHOBIA.

string galvanometer (W. Einthoven) A galvanometer that used deflection of a cord to increase sensitivity to electric current. Originally used to record cardiac currents ("*electrokardiograms*").

strip (E. Goffman) In psychology, in any large series of events, those to which special attention is paid, for example, on examining a bank's videotape, looking for a small part of the recording during which period the bank was being robbed.

stripe of Gennari A collection of optic-nerve fibers in the striate cortex. The bundle forms a white band visible to the naked eye. Also known as stripe of Vicq d'Azyr.

striped muscle striated muscle

stripe of Vicq d'Azyr stripe of Gennari

strip key A test-scoring key in the form of a long strip of paper that aligns with the test answers.

strith (H. A. Toops) A unitary trait-group within a population, for example, all children between the ages of 10 and 12 might be a strith. See ULSRITH.

striving for superiority A basic concept of Alfred Adler's Individual Psychology, which holds that humans are motivated by an innate, sovereign drive for self-realization. This drive is defined as the urge for completion and perfection rather than for superiority in the sense of social status or domination over others.

stroboscope (S. Stumpfer) A device that emits bursts of light on a moving object, such as a wheel, that appears to stand still, or to reverse its direction, depending upon the speed of movement and the rate at which the light with which the moving object is viewed, flashes on and off. Also known as stroboscopic disk.

stroboscopic effect An illusion of apparent motion in which individual objects which are slightly different, such as a series of photographs or line drawings, appear to move continuously when seen in rapid succession. This effect occurs, for example, when the individual frames of a motion picture are shown rapidly. See PHI PHENOMENON, STROBOSCOPIC ILLUSION.

stroboscopic illusion Making a moving object such as a rotating fan appear motionless, or move in reverse, by illuminating it with a series of intermittent light flashes. See ROTOSCOPE, STROBOSCOPE.

stroboscopic movement The apparent motion of a series of separate stimuli occurring in close consecutive order; for example, in motion pictures, people may appear to be moving slowly if many pictures were made per second, or the same people to be moving rapidly if fewer pictures were taken per second.

stroke 1. In transactional analysis, the basic unit of social interaction, the acknowledgement or recognition of another person. 2. An interruption of arterial blood flow to an area of the brain. If it lasts more than a few seconds, it often results in the death of brain tissue and ensuing neurological damage. May be due to a hemorrhage of a blood vessel in the brain, or an embolism or thrombosis. Can deprive the brain of oxygen and nutrients, causing loss of function. Sometimes known as apoplexy, cerebral-vascular accident, cerebrovascular accident, vascular accident. See ARTERIOSCLEROTIC BRAIN DISORDER, CEREBRAL INFARCT.

stroking A metaphor referring to doing something pleasant for another person, such as paying a compliment. The analogy is petting a cat.

Strong-Campbell Interest Inventory (SCII) Title of 1981 edition of what is now the Strong Interest Inventory (SII).

Strong-Campbell Interest Inventory form of the Strong Vocational Interest Blank (SVIB-SCII) Title of the 1974 edition of what is now the Strong Interest Inventory (SII).

Strong Interest Inventory (SII) (E. K. Strong, Jr.) An interest inventory consisting of 317 items to which possible responses are either Like-Indifferent-Dislike or Yes-No-?. Items include occupations, school subjects, activities and types of people. The first version was published in 1927 as the Strong Vocational Interest Blank (SVIB) for Men with the SVIB for Women appearing in 1938. Responses were empirically (criterion) keyed for different occupations, that is, responses of participants were compared with typical patterns of persons successfully engaged in various occupations. Major revisions, including a unified form for both genders, began with the 1974 SVIB-SCII.

strong law of effect Edward Thorndike posited that learning depended on reinforcement. The strong law emphasizes this point of view by stating that reinforcement is both necessary and sufficient for learning to occur.

strong methods (A. Newell & H. A. Simon) Problem-solving heuristics that make use of information about the structure of a particular problem domain, hence are limited in application but may be powerful in well-structured domains. See KNOWLEDGE-RICH DOMAINS.

Strong Vocational Interest Blank (SVIB) for Men Title of 1927 edition of what has become the Strong Interest Inventory.

Strong Vocational Interest Blank (SVIB) for Women Title of 1938 edition of what has become the Strong Interest Inventory.

Strong Vocational Test Infrequent name for the Strong Interest Inventory.

Stroop effect (J. R. Stroop) A tendency for color names printed in black to be more easily called off than color names printed in different colors. For example, if the word "red" is printed in green ink, and the word "blue" in yellow ink, it is much more difficult to correctly call off the names ("red" and "blue") due to the interference of the (green and yellow) colors.

Stroop Test (C. Golden) A three-part examination in which (a) color names are read as fast as possible, (b) the colors of rows of dots are rapidly named, and (c) cards are presented on which color names are printed over the incorrect colors to test the ability of the participant to name the color in spite of the conflict. Considered to measure cognitive control, based on the work of J. R. Stroop. See STROOP EFFECT.

structural analysis 1. The study of words through the analysis of word units, such as prefixes, suffixes, and root words. 2. In transactional analysis, the step preceding actual treatment, the segregation and analysis of ego states (parent, adult, and child). See EGO STATES. 3. The analysis of the more permanent aspects of an individual's personality—the personality structure as differentiated from functions.

structural disorder An organic dysfunction or impairment caused by a defect in a physiological structure, for example, memory impairment due to structural damage to the brain. See BEHAVIORAL DISORDERS, FUNCTIONAL DISORDERS.

structural eidetics One of two types of eidetic images occurring either from memory or from imaging. The other type is known as typographic eidetics. See EIDETIC IMAGERY.

structural equation modeling The systematic analysis of causal relations commonly used in the analysis of nonexperimental data.

structural family therapy (S. Minuchin) Systemic therapy that provides a method for the rational solution of family problems, based on the theory that these problems are the result of a poorly structured family life. To modify this structure, the entire relationship system of the family and the part each person plays in that system must be modified. Parents are guided to become the executives in the family system. See EXPERIENTIAL PSYCHOTHERAPY, FAMILY THERAPY.

structural group (J. L. Moreno) People of different types, temperaments, personalities, educational levels, brought together in a group, based on the concept that their interaction will maximize each other's benefits in the therapeutic process. See STRUCTURED GROUP.

structural hypothesis In psychoanalytic theory, A postulate that total personality is divided into three divisions, or functions: (a) the id, which represents instinctual drives; (b) the ego, which controls id drives and mediates between them and external reality; and (c) the superego, which comprises moral precepts and ideals. Sigmund Freud proposed this hypothesis to replace the "topographic" division of the mind into three regions: the unconscious, preconscious, and conscious. Also known as structural model/theory. See PSYCHIC APPARATUS.

structural integration See ROLFING.

structuralism (W. Wundt) The dominant school of psychology in Germany and the United States between 1879 and 1920, led by Wilhelm Wundt in Germany and E. B. Titchener in the United States. The school based its approach on the introspective analysis of the components of consciousness, namely sensations, images, and affective or emotional states. It sought to describe these irreducible mental contents in terms of the "What" (quality, intensity, clearness, duration), the "How" (interrelationships), and the "Why" (investigation of physiological correlates on the principle that mental and physiological events run a parallel course). Also known as structural psychology. See ATOMISM, BEHAVIORISM, FUNCTIONALISM, GESTALT PSYCHOLOGY REDUCTIONISM.

structuralists Therapists who emphasize changing or realigning a family's organizational structure to improve its transactional patterns.

structural profile (A. A. Lazarus) A quantitative assessment of how active behaviorally, deeply emotional, etc, a person is across the BASIC ID.

structural psychology structuralism

structural rules of language The rules governing how semantic, syntactic, morphological, and phonological units are nested into each other; how sounds are transformed into words, words into phrases, phrases into utterances, and utterances into discourse, to create meaning in a language. See CONNECTED DISCOURSE, PRAGMATIC RULES, SEMANTICS.

structural theories See BODY-TYPE THEORIES, CONSTITUTIONAL TYPE (THEORIES).

structural therapy A system of treatment for autistic children who are provided a structured environment that emphasizes physical and verbal stimulation in a gamelike setting. The purpose is to increase the amount and variety of stimuli received by the patients, thereby helping them to relate to their environment in a more realistic manner.

structural variables (N. S. Endler & D. Magnusson) Within the context of the interactional model of personality, a type of mediating variable that resides within the person (such as abilities, competence, cognitive complexity and intelligence) and is assumed to influence behavior.

structuration (A. Giddens) A social structure constantly reproduced as a result of continous sociocultural processes.

structure   1. The composition, spatial interrelations, and character of material parts in an organism. 2. Arrangement of materials or of parts in any complex aggregate, for example, in a sentence, a house, consciousness, etc. 3. In Gestalt psychology, the inherent character of a Gestalt. The alteration of one part in a Gestalt structure almost inevitably produces changes in other parts. Contrasted with "constellation," a group of units having no functional relations. See CONFIGURATION, GESTALT.

structured exercises   Techniques used in personal-change groups, in which members engage in leader-arranged exercises, including games and experiments, such as (a) staging a fantasy fight between perceived weak and strong selves, (b) describing joyous moments of life, or (c) pretending to shrink to take an imaginary journey to a troublesome part of one's own body.

structured group   1. A therapy group in which members are selected on the basis of their potential for effecting therapeutic changes in each other. Also known as structural group. 2. Directed activities in a group designed to achieve specific purposes.

structured interactional group psychotherapy (H. Kaplan) A form of group therapy in which the therapist provides a "structural matrix" for the group's interactions, particularly by selecting a different member of the group to be the focus of the interaction in each session.

structured interview   An interview based on a predetermined set of questions or topics. Used in market research to determine consumer reactions to ads or products, or the reasons for purchasing a particular product or service. This type of interview is also used in personnel departments for employment and by child developmentalists, for example, in parent and child interviews. See PATTERNED INTERVIEW, STANDARDIZED INTERVIEW (SCHEDULE).

Structured Learning   (A. P. Goldstein, R. P. Sprafkin, J. J. Gershow) A relatively complex system of psychotherapy that employs a wide variety of procedures including modeling, psychodrama, performance feedback and transfer of training. It was developed to be suitable for people not served by verbal-oriented therapies, and depended on observations of others as well as others evaluation of them, all directed by the therapist or therapists. See ACTUALIZING THERAPY, FIXED ROLE THERAPY, FUNCTIONAL THERAPY, IMPASSE/PRIORITY THERAPY, MULTIPLE IMPACT THERAPY for other systems of this general type.

structured learning theory   (R. B. Cattell) A dynamic learning point of view which predicts learning from the dynamic structure of the individual, in terms of the stimulus and the ambient situations.

structured observation   A procedure characterized by a researcher establishing a cue for some behavior and observing it, usually in a laboratory.

structured personality test   A questionnaire, inventory or self-rating device consisting of a rather objective, standardized items for personality measurement (for example, a True-False test compared to the less-structured or projective Rorschach test).

structured stimulus   A stimulus that is clear and simple and does not require much if any interpretation (for example, in an experiment, when a red light flickers a participant presses a button on the left and when a green light flickers, the participant presses a button on the right). Compare UNSTRUCTURED STIMULUS.

structured written interview technique (SWIT)   A method of quickly gathering information, typically from widely dispersed employees or from witnesses to an incident. The questionnaire comprises questions that go to the heart of who, what, when, where, how, and why details, and are worded so as to elicit more than yes-or-no answers. See INCOMPLETE SENTENCE BLANK.

structure-function   Relation, property, or response activity resulting from a totality regarded as a unit rather than from its parts as such or their interconnections; that is, a configurational pattern or response.

structure of intellect model   Joy Paul Guilford viewed intelligence as a three-dimensional model composed of 120 small blocks which, when assembled would generate a $4 \times 5 \times 6$ larger block. One side (4 across) dealt with contents (figural, symbols, semantics, behavioral), one side (5 across) had to do with operations (cognition, memory, divergent production, convergent production, evaluation) and the longest (6 across) related to products (units, classes, relations, systems, transformations, implications). Also known as structure of intellect (theory). See BASIC INTELLIGENCE FACTORS, CONTEXTUAL INTELLIGENCE, FACTOR THEORY OF INTELLIGENCE.

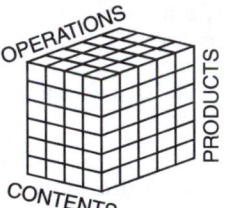

structure of intellect model

structure psychology   A school of psychology that attempts to relate body types and traits. See CONSTITUTIONAL TYPOLOGY.

structures   A Piagetian concept regarding organized properties of intelligence that change with age. See OPERATIONS, SCHEMES.

structuring   1. A common practice in psychotherapy, usually done in the first session in which the therapist explains to the new patient about important aspects of the therapy, for example, the therapist promises confidentiality, indicates how the process works, and answers any questions the patient has. Mundane issues such as number of sessions, or fees, are usually discussed at this time. 2. Presenting a frame of reference, a set of specific instructions, guidelines or directions.

struggle for existence   (C. Darwin) Designating biological competition, emphasizing the fact that the securing of nutriment and mates, and the avoidance of climatic dangers and of enemies involve a competitive contest between members of the same or allied species. See NATURAL SELECTION, SURVIVAL OF THE FITTEST.

struggle reflex   A response consisting of violent, usually uncoordinated movements if suddenly restrained by anyone; a pseudo-reflex.

Struktur Psychologie German name for structure psychology.

stub factors (R. B. Cattell) In factor analysis, smaller factors left as orthogonal remnants of higher order factors in lower orders.

stuck-togetherness A situation common in dysfunctional families in which roles and boundaries are blurred to such a degree that no family member has a distinct identity.

Student Pseudonym of William Gosset. See GOSSET.

student's disease Phrase applied to persons, typically students who believe they have the symptoms of a disease or mental disorder that they have been studying, or which they have read or heard about. Also known as intern's disease.

students' evaluation of teaching (SET) An anonymous multiple-choice evaluation by pupils of a teacher's perceived effectiveness, usually at the end of a course and usually divulged before final grades are assigned.

Student's t test A statistical method analogous to the calculation of the normal deviate, both of which are used for tests of significance. William Gosset's paper on the t statistic was published under the name of Student. Also known as t test. See T-DISTRIBUTIONS.

study 1. Systematic observation. 2. Research, detailed examination, analysis of some phenomenon. 3. A review of literature. 4. A research project less formal than a controlled experiment and without independent and dependent variables. See RESEARCH DESIGN. 5. See EXPERIMENT. 6. See RESEARCH. (Some researchers use "study" and "experiment" interchangeably, and some researchers distinguish between an experiment having independent and dependent variables, while a "study" has only correlative variables.)

study skills Any method used to facilitate the process of studying, such as outlining, taking notes, underlining, or silent recitation. See SQ3R.

Study of Values See THE ALLPORT-VERNON STUDY OF VALUES.

stump hallucination **phantom limb**

stupidity-misery syndrome (J. Dollard & N. Miller) These authors' suggested phrase for a neurosis.

stupor A mental state characterized by unresponsiveness and immobility. In organic cases, such as toxic states, brain disease, and epileptic seizure, stupor may involve complete suspension of conscious thought processes and unawareness of the surroundings. In functional conditions, such as catatonic and depressive stupors, the patient is mute and motionless, but there is no loss of consciousness or sensation; mental activity may be intense, and the patient may be well aware of the surroundings.

Sturm und Drang **period** German phrase for the storm-and-stress period of adolescence.

stuttering 1. Spasmodic halting or hesitation in speaking, which is unintended and uncontrollable, resulting in reiteration of the same phoneme, for example, "B- b- b- b- baby..." 2. A speech disorder characterized by repetitions and prolongations of the initial part of a word. Primary stuttering occurs in young children who are not fully aware of their speech patterns and stutter rather effortlessly. Secondary stuttering develops in older children and adults and is marked by tension, anxiety and struggling to avoid speech blocks which have become incorporated into the stuttering pattern. The disorder is difficult to overcome and usually requires a combination of skilled psychotherapy and speech therapy in its treatment. See DYSPHEMIA, PRIMARY STUTTERING, PSELLISM, SECONDARY STUTTERING. (Speech pathologists no longer distinguish between stammering and stuttering, since both are assumed to have an etiology that is neurological as well as environmental and learned.)

stuttering gait A gait characterized by hesitancy in taking steps, a walking pattern observed in certain schizophrenic or somatization patients. In some cases it is organic in origin. Also known as gait stuttering.

STYCAR See SCREENING TESTS FOR YOUNG CHILDREN AND RETARDATES.

stygiophobia Fear of hell. See HADEPHOBIA.

style of life (M. Weber, A. Adler) According to Alfred Adler, the unique pattern of a person's total behavior including thoughts, feelings, and actions. See LIFESTYLE, LIFE SCRIPT, PERSONALITY.

stylistic ratings A system of evaluating works of art in terms of technical attributes, as opposed to reactions or moods of participants who view the art. Based on such factors as importance of shapes, lines, composition, surface textures, and reproduction of objects or people portrayed. Stylistic dimensions may include classicism, subjectivism, and expressionism.

stylus A pencil-like device, with or without a metal tip, for maze tracing, tapping, or coordination test.

stylus maze A type of maze that consists of grooves, usually employed with blindfolded people. The blindfolded person uses a pencil-like device (the stylus) to trace the maze. The experimenter will pick up the stylus and restart the person when the person's stylus enters a dead end. See FINGER MAZE.

S-type In the perceptual typology of Erich Jaensch, the "disintegrated," person, whose perceptions are unstable, irregular, not firmly tied to reality. Compare J-TYPE.

S_u Rare abbreviation for unconditioned stimulus (also abbreviated **UCS, US**).

SU 1. See AUDITORY SENSATION UNIT. 2. A logarithmic unit of loudness.

sub 1. Submissive, usually in the context of sadomasochism. 2. Substitute. 3. Rare slang for a marginal or derelict person.

subarachnoid space The space beneath the delicate arachnoid membrane surrounding the brain and spinal cord. It is occupied by cerebrospinal fluid, which drains into the superior sagittal sinus.

subcallosal gyrus   A portion of the medial limbic system behind the cingulate gyrus but with functions reciprocal to those of the cingulate gyrus. The subcallosal gyrus has functions inhibitory to motoneuron activity, whereas the cingulate gyrus enhances the motoneuron functions.

subception   (R. Lazarus & R. A. McCleary) Discrimination without awareness, distinguished from perception, which implies awareness. Having some cognitive or emotional reaction that can be noted by careful electronic testing but not noticeable to the individual being tested, for example, a person may hear various spoken words and be unaffected. Yet certain words will produce a special reaction reliably of which the person is unaware. See LIE DETECTION, SUBLIMINAL PERCEPTION.

subcoma insulin treatment   The obsolete treatment of severe anxiety and tension states by intramuscular injection of small doses of insulin that induce drowsiness and hypoglycemia but not coma. Since the patient can walk about during the treatment period it is also known as ambulatory insulin treatment, subshock insulin treatment.

subconscious   (R. Lotze) An aspect of the mind not in immediate awareness, but which affects behavior, and is available to consciousness under a variety of circumstances. See PRECONSCIOUS, UNCONSCIOUS.

subconscious personality   A personality of a multiple-personality (dissociative identity) patient that is not dominant at the time. When a subconscious personality becomes dominant, the previously dominant personality becomes the subconscious personality. See MULTIPLE PERSONALITY.

subcortical   Relating to a nervous-system structure or process below the level of the cortex (for example, spinal reflexes).

subcortical centers   Any of the central nervous system nuclei located at levels below the cerebral cortex, including such structures as the thalamus, hypothalamus, and basal ganglia. Within each structure may be several special subcortical centers, such as nuclei of the hypothalamus that regulate sleep, water balance, protein metabolism, and sexual activity. Sensory relay nuclei within the thalamus link skin, muscle, and other body tissues with the cortex.

subcortical dementia   A disorder marked by excessive slowness in making intellectual responses. The cause is an abnormality of the subcortical structure resulting in a malfunction of the activating mechanisms. Diagnosis is based in part on the length of time considered to be normal for responding to a question.

subcortical learning   A type of learning that occurs under certain conditions during cortical spreading depression produced by a temporary lesion, for example, induced by an injection of potassium chloride into the cortex. The technique is used to study interhemispheric transfer when one hemisphere is affected by the temporary chemical lesion.

subcultural delinquent   A person who breaks laws of the state and who is part of a culture that does not accept the legitimacy of such laws. See SOCIALIZED DELINQUENT.

subculture   A secondary set of customs including religious, social, ethnic, that serve to characterize and distinguish a subgroup from the larger one in which the members live. Subcultural groups usually share with the larger society a common language as well as certain basic values and behavioral traits, but they retain their separate group identity.

subculture of violence   Customs or beliefs, common in some social groups, that physical violence is the proper method of dealing with insults and affronts.

subcutaneous sensibility   A sensory capacity allied to the touch senses, that exists in the deeper portion of the true skin (tela subcutanea), and of which the Pacinian corpuscles are assumed to be a representative receptor.

subdelirious state   The precursor of a full delirium, marked by restlessness, headache, irritability, hypersensitivity to sound and visual stimuli, as well as emotional instability. A subacute delirious state may also appear independently or after an episode of delirium and may persist for months. In these cases the typical symptoms are clouding of consciousness, perplexity, and incoherent thinking. Also known as subdelirium.

subdural   Beneath or within the dura, the outer covering of the brain.

subfecundity   The below-average ability to reproduce an adequate number of offspring needed for survival of the species. See FECUNDITY.

subgoal   A component of a large or complex goal. Many problems can be solved by identifying the subgoals and working to achieve each of them, for example, if a major goal is retirement, the prospective retiree may establish a series of financial subgoals, expecting annually to achieve certain levels of savings.

subhuman   Pertaining to organisms or organic phenomena below the human level of organization.

subictal epilepsy   A type of epilepsy marked by muscle twitchings or uncoordinated involuntary movements, depression, anxiety, or somatization behavior. Difficult to diagnose because no convulsions occur and electroencephalographic findings are negative. However, the patient responds to antiepileptic drugs.

subintentioned death   (E. S. Shneidman) Any death (other than suicide) in which the decedent has played a significant albeit an unconscious, indirect, or covert role in hastening the death-date.

subitizing   (E. L. Kaufman, M. W. Lord, T. W. Reese, & J. Volkmann) Perceiving at a glance how many objects are presented, without estimating or counting. The limit appears to be seven, for humans, trained birds, and wild crows. Also known as subitization. See APPREHENSION SPAN, MAGICAL NUMBER SEVEN PLUS OR MINUS TWO.

subject (O or S)   1. An organism used in an experiment without its permission. The subject may be further identified as an experimental subject or control subject. 2. A person whose experiences are being reported or evaluated. 3. Term used for all individuals in experiments until the 1994 edition of the *Publication Manual of the American Psychological Association*. Humans are now called "participants" to acknowledge their role. 4. A person participating in a social psychology experiment. Such a person may be unaware that an experiment is underway or unaware of the nature of the experiment.

Since the person does not give explicit permission regarding participation, he or she is a "subject." See SUBJECT VS PARTICIPANT. The symbol S has been limited to mean stimulus since the 1974 edition of the APA *Publication Manual.*

subject analogues   Research studies using animals as substitutes for humans, often to establish something that will later be tried on humans.

subject bias   A tendency of participants in an experiment to operate differently from normal because of their prior beliefs, attitudes, and preferences. See HAWTHORNE EFFECT.

subject complex   (M. Prince) An unusual reaction to a certain topic (such as God, sex, animals), usually negative and avoiding.

subject-ill   Refers to the use by patients of their own bodies to symbolize their emotions in a kind of organic language. Wilhelm Stekel distinguished between subject-ill patients and object-ill patients who express their emotions through symbolization of objects outside their bodies. See SOMATIZATION DISORDER.

subjection   The state of being under the control of another individual or an organization.

subjective   Characterizing an internal state of a person inaccessible to other persons.

subjective attributes   Those perceptual qualities uniquely dependent on the persons who experience their perceptions, such as a particular taste or color.

subjective colors   Pastel colors perceived when viewing interwoven black and white disks rotating on a color wheel.

subjective contour   The perception of a contour when a contour does not actually exist as affected by the properties of the whole perception. Also known as illusionary contour. See KANISZA FIGURE for an illustration.

subjective culture   (H. C. Triandis) A cultural group's characteristic way of viewing (perceiving, evaluating, judging) the social environment. Includes the way experience is categorized and labeled, the attitudes, beliefs, self- and role-definitions, norms, and values shared with those who speak a language dialect, during a historical period, in a narrow geographic location.

subjective error   1. In experimental psychology, an error caused by prejudice, bias, or unsystematic procedures. 2. An error attributable to individual variations in perception and interpretation of experience.

subjective examination   A test, such as an essay or an oral exam, whose scoring depends upon the interpretation of the examiner. Compare OBJECTIVE EXAMINATION.

subjective expected utility (SEU)   A guide to human decision making in which people, usually without any great amount of thinking, decide whether to do or not do something. In effect, people think of the positive and the negative consequences of certain decisions as well as the possibility of the percentages of what may go wrong, and many decisions are made almost instantly. People who take chances and who are optimistic are considered "radicals" and those who do not take chances and who are pessimistic are labeled "conservatives."

subjective-objective psychology   (H. Spencer) A division of psychology into two parts: subjective (of self) and objective (of others).

subjective organization   A collection of objects, such as books or photographs, or abstract concepts that are organized according to personal preference, by their size, for example, or in terms of the quality of the items, or the nature of the contents of the books and the pictures. The organizer follows no rules, except personal preference. A strategy of encoding information for retention, mnemonic effeciency.

subjective orientation   Moral reasoning typical of children over age ten, characterized by the ability to take a person's motives into account when judging an act. See OBJECTIVE ORIENTATION.

subjective-outcome value   Behavior influenced by personal or subjective values placed by on a specific act or outcome.

subjective perceivers   See OBJECTIVE PERCEIVERS VS SUBJECTIVE PERCEIVERS.

subjective probability   A personal and intuitive estimate regarding the probability of events occurring, that may or may not be realistic.

subjective psychology   The psychological approach that focuses on introspective or phenomenological data.

subjective-quality point   See POINT OF SUBJECTIVE QUALITY.

subjective reasoning   Believing that feelings are the same as or equivalent to facts.

subjective scoring   Rating based on the judgment of the scorers. Compare OBJECTIVE SCORING.

subjective selection   Any type of decision that leaves room for a person's choice beyond objective factors and therefore may lack intersubject validity.

subjective sensation   A sensation produced without sufficient external stimulation, for example, an illusion.

subjective test   An examination scored according to personal judgment or nonobjective, unsystematic standards such as the Rorschach test. See PROJECTIVE TESTS.

subjective trait   A trait not accessible to measurement in terms of any standard test (for example, cheerfulness).

subjective types   People who tend to judge events solely in relation to themselves.

subjective units of distress (SUD)   A subjective differential scale of emotional pain and suffering.

subjective visual field   The spatial aspect of conscious experience between successive visual presentations.

subjectivism factor   1. Possible bias contributed to data because of the intrusion of the conscious or unconscious point of view of the participant. See SUBJECT BIAS. 2. Impressionistic or surrealistic types of paintings due to artists' personal values and points of view.

subjectivity   Focusing on personal feelings and thoughts, and interpretation and evaluation of events or ideas in the light of personal experience. Also known as subjectivism.

subject of consciousness   The self considered as currently undergoing reportable cognitive experiences.

subject-selection study　A passive-observational study in which the investigator varies the independent variable by selecting participants with different characteristics (for example, persons who have experienced trauma vs those who have not) or with varying degrees of that characteristic (for example, people with high, medium, or low scores on a measure of risk taking, depression, or helplessness). Groups are formed based on personological selection criteria. Also known as quasi-experiment.

subject variable　A variable of individual differences in an experiment, for example, the participant's sex or occupation. The subject variable is neither manipulated by the experimenter, as is an independent variable, nor does it usually change in the experiment, as is a dependent variable. Differences that occur in subject variables may be controlled in the statistical analysis. Also known as organismic variable.

subject vs participant　In research, the difference between these two terms has to do with the degree of understanding, willingness and agreement on the part of individuals in an experiment. Research animals (such as rodents, monkeys) that lack apparent understanding about, or choice in, participation are termed "subjects," as well as humans who are the focus of such observation or manipulation without declaring their willingness to participate (such as the infant, J. B. Watson's Little Albert, and persons in social psychology research). However, humans who volunteer for, or agree to participate in, an experiment are considered "participants." Some psychologists use the terms interchangeably; some consider participant to be an example of political correctness at its worst.

sublimation　(S. Freud) Satisfying an unacceptable desire indirectly in a socially acceptable manner, for example, an aggressive drive may be expressed on the football field.

subliminal　Below the limit of sensory perception; below the limit or threshold of consciousness. See SUBCEPTION.

subliminal consciousness　The level of consciousness in which a stimulus may affect behavior even though the person is not aware of it.

subliminal learning　Mastered material or habits whose origins cannot be directly recalled because they were acquired without awareness, that is, subliminally.

subliminal perception　Subconscious perception of stimuli that are too weak or too rapid to be consciously perceived but that nevertheless can be discriminated or can affect behavior. (Research does not support the idea that subliminal messages significantly affect behavior, and there is no evidence that subliminal messages from advertisers can influence buying habits.) See SUBCEPTION.

subliminal processes　Relating to processes occurring below the perceptual threshold, or too weak to be identified clearly.

subliminal stimulus　Pertaining to a stimulus of lower intensity than required by the established threshold, or to a stimulus so faint or brief that an observer is not aware of it. Energy or change in energy is insufficient to fire a nerve impulse in a receptor.

submission　A mode of behavior in a person's relations with others, characterized by the tendency to yield to others, or to adjust self-behavior to the domination of others.

submissiveness　A tendency to yield and comply with the orders of others. See COMPLIANCE.

subnormal　Inferior, or significantly below the normal level by a given standard.

subnormal period (of neuron)　The period of time, measured in milliseconds, when neuron excitability is below normal. It follows a supernormal period of excitability. Compare SUPERNORMAL PERIOD (OF NEURON).

subordination　In classification, the placing of a given species, or class of data, as a lower group.

subpotency　Lesser degree of power, in comparison to the average of similar organisms, in some aspect of either reception of information or expression of action, due to certain biological factors, either acquired or inherited.

subservience　Willingness to subordinate personal behavior to the purpose or interests of others. See LOVE.

subshock insulin treatment　**subcoma insulin treatment**

subshock therapy　A form of shock treatment that does not involve convulsions, such as electroconvulsive therapy (ECT) administered at a mild level.

subsidiation　1. The overcoming of obstacles on the path to success, moving from goal to goal. 2. The relationship of means to an end, for example, the achievement of a series of subgoals necessary to reach an ultimate objective.

substance abuse　Overuse of a drug, usually addictive, or product (for example, tobacco, volatile fumes). Although many substances can be abused, this phrase usually refers to the illicit use of drugs. See SUBSTANCE DEPENDENCE.

substance-abuse delirium　A disorder that occurs within a week of cessation or reduction in the heavy use of certain addictive substances. Characteristics are clouding of consciousness, disorientation, and other symptoms of delirium, with rapid heartbeat, sweating, and elevated blood pressure.

substance abuse indicators　Signs of substance abuse: (a) at least one psychological sign (mood shifts, uninhibited impulses, irritability, loquacity); (b) at least one neurological sign (slurred speech, uncoordinated movements, unsteady gait, impaired attention or memory); (c) maladaptive behavior (impaired judgment, defective social or occupational functioning, and failure to meet responsibilities).

substance dependence　A compelling urge for and physiological dependence on an addictive substance to the degree that acquiring and using the substance becomes a priority in the person's life. See SUBSTANCE ABUSE, SUBSTANCE WITHDRAWAL, SUBSTANCE WITHDRAWAL SYMPTOMS.

substance sniffing　A method of getting intoxicated by inhaling various substances including paint and gasoline. Also called huffing.

substance-use disorders   Diagnosis of people with pathological behavior associated with regular and detrimental use of substances that affect the central nervous system.

substance withdrawal   The cessation or reduction of intake of a substance previously used regularly to induce a state of intoxication. See ALCOHOL WITHDRAWAL, AMPHETAMINE OR SIMILARLY ACTING SYMPATHOMIMETIC WITHDRAWAL, BARBITURATE OR SIMILARLY ACTING SEDATIVE OR HYPNOTIC WITHDRAWAL, OPIOID WITHDRAWAL, TOBACCO WITHDRAWAL, WITHDRAWAL.

substance withdrawal symptoms   Unpleasant symptoms following the cessation or reduction of drugs that produce at least three of the following reactions: nausea and vomiting, malaise or weakness, rapid heartbeat, sweating, elevated blood pressure, anxiety, depressed mood or irritability, drop in blood pressure when standing; and coarse tremors.

substantia gelatinosa   Lamina II of the spinal cord. It is traversed by many large axons of the dorsal columns. The neurons of the substantia gelatinosa are extensively interconnected small neurons at the tip of the dorsal horn of the spinal cord. They receive synapses from collaterals of branches of peripheral fibers of the extralemniscal somatosensory systems such as those involved in pain. The substantia gelatinosa cells appear to affect only neighboring cells in the dorsal horn and through this effect act as part of the "gating" mechanism whereby touch input can reduce pain. See GATING.

substantia nigra   (black substance—Latin) (S. von Soemmering, J. B. Luys) Part of the extrapyramidal motor system composed of gray matter, lying between the tegmentum of the midbrain and the crus cerebri. Cells of the compact portion of the substantia nigra produce the neurotransmitter dopamine. The axons of these cells terminate in the neostriatum (caudate and putamen). Loss of these neurons results in Parkinson's disease.

substantive complexity   The degree to which the nature of a project or work requires thought and independent judgment.

substantive equality   In social and industrial psychology, the concept that sometimes differences must be considered to achieve genuine rather than formal, treat-everyone-the-same fairness. Also known as equality of outcome rather than equality of process. See AFFIRMATIVE ACTION.

substantive rationality   (H. A. Simon) Human goal-oriented decision making that is best designed to achieve its goals, as judged from outside, objectively. See BOUNDED RATIONALITY, PROCEDURAL RATIONALITY.

substantive states   (W. James) The parts of an experience which have sufficient definiteness and sufficient duration to be observed and denoted by nouns, verbs, and adjectives.

substitutability   In Morton Deutsch's theory of interdependence, one person's actions replacing the actions of another.

substitute formation   symptom formation

substituting   Providing some social support, especially in a therapy group, by actual behavior rather than words, such as a smile, a nod, a pat on the back, or even holding the person in a hug. See RE-PARENTING.

substitution   Replacement of blocked or unattainable goals with alternative satisfactions, as in adopting a child when a person cannot have a biological child, or raiding the refrigerator after a disappointment in love.

substitution hypothesis   A postulate that if a person has a particular neurotic problem and manages to stop it such as by self-control, drugs, or social influence, the cause of the problem will probably remain in the person and will demonstrate itself in another way. See SYMPTOM SUBSTITUTION.

substitution learning   A form of learning in which a symbol is substituted for another, as in deciphering a code.

substitution of goals   Choosing a new goal if a desired goal is considered not attainable.

substitution test   Any task or quiz in which the participant exchanges one set of symbols for another, for example, a code test in which symbols or letters are substituted for numbers.

subsume   To assign an object, datum, or type of phenomena, to its logical position under a more general class.

subsystem   An organized component within an overall system, such as a family within a society.

subtest   A separate component of a test or test battery.

subthalamic nuclei   Nuclei linked by reciprocal pathways to the basal ganglia. They are found in the transitional zone between the midbrain and the diencephalon. Destruction, usually by hemorrhage and usually limited to one subthalamic nucleus, results in ballismus (hemiballismus), an uncontrollable flailing of the limbs contralateral to the side damaged.

subthalamus   The transitional zone of tissue between the thalamus and the mesencephalic tegmentum. Contains portions of the red nucleus and the substantia nigra, as well as groups of fibers known as fields of Forel.

subtherapeutic dose   An amount of medicine which is insufficient to provoke an optimal response or perhaps any response at all. See INCOMPLETE TRIAL.

subthreshold potential   A graded potential resulting from a stimulus not of sufficient intensity to produce a spike potential. Because of its below-threshold intensity, the impulse does not travel beyond the immediate region of its own fiber. See LOCAL POTENTIAL.

subtraction method   A technique for determining a subject's reaction time to make a choice, as in subtracting sensory time and motor time from total time to calculate the time used to decide on a response. See DISCRIMINATION-REACTION TIME.

subtractive color mixture   In the mixture of "surface color," such as paints or pigments, when one component cancels out certain effects, for example, if yellow and blue paints are mixed, green results. Compare ADDITIVE COLOR MIXTURE in which "film color," such as lights are mixed. See COLOR MIXTURE.

subtractive principle   In color mixture, a principle depending upon the fact that the apparent color of a pigment, or any body which selectively absorbs light of different wave-lengths, is complementary to the color of the light which is absorbed.

subvocal speech   1. Faint movements of the lips, tongue, and larynx. These movements resemble speech movements but are inaudible. John B. Watson considered this the equivalent of thinking. 2. Talking silently to the self, as in thinking with words. Also known as inarticulate speech.

subvocalization   1. Internal representation of speaking such as in rehearsing an imaginary two-way conversation. An observer might note that such a person's lips are moving. 2. The same phenomenon noticeable while either reading or watching a movie. Also known as covert speech, implicit speech response, internal speech.

success   Accomplishing desired goals. See FAILURE THROUGH SUCCESS, SUCCESS NEUROSIS.

successive   Characterizing two or more experiences in contiguous segments of time.

successive approximation (method)   method of successive approximations (meaning 2)

successive contrast   Negative afterimagery, removal of the color red after its perception, is for example, followed by an image of its complementary color, blue-green. Compare simultaneous contrast where the complementary color is evident (in the surrounding area) during original stimulation. See COLOR CONTRAST, CONTRAST EFFECT.

successive induction   The succession of movements of limbs or other body parts in a pattern of antagonistic reflex actions. In walking, for example, successive induction requires alternate flexion and extension of muscles of the lower limbs.

successive-intervals method   A variation of the equal-appearing intervals method in which intervals are defined verbally or by the use of samples. Also known as method of successive intervals.

successive-practice method   method of successive practice

successive reproduction   (F. Bartlett) A technique used to study the way in which information in long-term memory is altered by reconstruction. Participants are asked to reproduce or recall the same material at successive time intervals, and the variations in their reproductions are recorded.

successive scanning   (J. Bruner) One of four strategies people use in formulating concepts, involving testing one hypothesis at a time. See CONCEPT-FORMATION STRATEGIES.

successive-stage theory   1. In group dynamics, any theory that specifies the usual order of the phases through which a developing group typically progresses. 2. In personality, any theory such as psychoanalysis that specifies a necessary sequence of developmental stages.

success neurosis   Disturbing and possibly disabling feelings that may include guilt, unworthiness, fear of failure, experienced by some persons who have accumulated fame and wealth (especially if both were attained quickly). According to Eugene Landy, movie actors, rock stars, etc., are prone to experience this neurosis. See POLYCRATES COMPLEX.

succinylcholine   A short-acting muscle-paralyzing drug which is used in electroconvulsive treatments (ECT) for depression, so that the patient does not have violent muscle contractions.

succorance need   (H. A. Murray) The desire for protection, aid, and support. See URPSYCHOLOGY.

succubus   Medieval term for a demon or evil spirit in female form who was purported to have intercourse with a sleeping man. Occasionally a demon with no gender implied. Also known as succuba. Compare INCUBUS.

sucker   Slang for a person who is extremely gullible, a greenhorn. See BARNUM EFFECT.

sucker effect   A tendency of a group member to undertake a disproportionate amount of the work. Compare SOCIAL LOAFING.

sucking evaluations   The use of pacifier-type apparatus to test children's mental and physical statuses.

sucking reflex   1. A basic reflexive action in which some mammalian young grasp the mother's nipple using the mouth, drawing milk into the mouth by suction. 2. In psychoanalytic theory, sucking is considered the earliest autoerotic gratification and a prime activity of the oral stage of psychosexual development. See THUMB-SUCKING.

suckling   1. The act of breastfeeding. Instinctive behavior of mammals to feed themselves by sucking the nipple. See ETERNAL SUCKLING. 2. An unweaned infant. Also called a nurseling.

SUD   See SUBJECTIVE UNITS OF DISTRESS.

Sudden Infant Death Syndrome (SIDS)   The sudden, unanticipated death of an infant for no apparent reason. The deceased usually is a child between the ages of one and 12 months who dies quietly during sleep with no signs of a struggle or sounds of distress. Also known as cot death, crib death. See SLEEP APNEA.

sudden insight   See AHA EXPERIENCE, DISCONTINUITY HYPOTHESIS.

suffering   Experiencing pain or acute distress, either psychological or physical. Suffering may be proportionate to the situation, or it may be grossly exaggerated or coldly minimized to satisfy a need for sympathy, attention, or control over others. May also be self-induced, as in self-mutilation and martyrdom. See MASOCHISM, SADISM, SEXUAL MASOCHISM, SEXUAL SADISM, UNPLEASURE.

suffering-hero daydream   A waking fantasy in which the wish for pity and compassion is fulfilled in the imagination. See CONQUERING-HERO DAYDREAM, FANTASY.

sufficient condition   A requirement fulfilled so that something else can occur or happen. Compare NECESSARY CONDITION.

sufficient reason law   See LAW OF SUFFICIENT REASON.

sufficient statistics   The application of enough statistical procedures to a set of data to evaluate all possibilities needed to come to a conclusion. An estimator θ_{est} is a sufficient estimator of θ if the conditional joint probability function of the sample observations, given θ_{est}, does not depend on the parameter θ.

suffix effect   (R. G. Crowder) In learning theory, the effect of a redundant item (the suffix) on immediate serial recall.

suffocation fear   A conversion symptom associated with acute anxiety that interferes with respiration. See SMOTHERING FEAR.

suffragette   Historical term for a woman active in various countries in campaigning for the right for women to vote. See FEMINISM.

sugar self-selection   A food-preference effect observed in rats that have been allowed to choose between sugar and a protein. Normally, animals will select food required by the body. But rats will develop a fondness for sugar and continue to choose it rather than protein even when the body needs the protein. See BLOOD SUGAR, CAFETERIA FEEDING.

suggestibility   A state in which the ideas, beliefs, or attitudes of others are uncritically adopted. Seen in persons with somatization personalities or persons under hypnosis.

suggestible stage   The second of the three stages of the disaster syndrome observed in civilian catastrophes wherein persons regress to a state of dependence and passively accept directions from others. The other two stages are the recovery stage and the shock stage.

suggestion   1. An idea or course of action. Usually expressed in words, as in hypnotic commands, "pep talks," or testimonials, but it may also be pictorial, as in advertisements for beauty creams. For different types of suggestion, see AUTOSUGGESTION, PRESTIGE SUGGESTION, PROPAGANDA, SUGGESTION THERAPY. 2. The process of an idea causing the recollection of another idea, an association.

suggestion therapy   A form of psychotherapy in which distressing symptoms are alleviated through direct suggestion and reassurance. The technique, sometimes coupled with a hypnotic trance, has been found to be effective in relieving the effects of stress and superficial conversion symptoms. Therapy may be accompanied by an explanation of the meaning and the purpose of the symptoms, but no attempt is usually made to modify the patient's basic personality.

suggestive psychotherapy   A type of therapy that uses the influence and authority of the therapist. See DIRECTIVE PSYCHOTHERAPY.

suicidal crisis   An emergency situation in which suicide is threatened or attempted. Among the factors that most frequently precipitate such a situation are: (a) Severe depression, including involutional psychosis and the depressive phase of bipolar disorder; (b) schizophrenic disorders; and, less frequently (c) alcoholism, ill health, marital conflict, loss of a loved one, and business failure.

suicidal gesture   See PARASUICIDE.

suicidal ideation   Thoughts of suicide, or preoccupation with suicide.

Suicidal Intent Scale   A three-point, fifteen-item measurement instrument that attempts to assess the seriousness of suicide intent in terms of the objective circumstances related to the attempt.

suicidality   1. (E. S. Shneidman) An assessment of how likely a person is to commit suicide in the near future. See LETHALITY. 2. Suicidal intention, ideation, or behavior, as in "The assessment focused on suicidality."

suicide   The intentional, overt act of killing oneself. Types of suicide include: ALTRUISTIC, ANOMIC, COLLECTIVE, EGOISTIC, PARA-, PSYCHIC, PSYCHOSOMATIC.

suicide-prevention center   An emergency or crisis-intervention facility dealing primarily with persons having suicidal thoughts, or who have made suicidal threats or attempts. Such centers are usually staffed by social workers with mental health preparation, trained to deal with such emergencies either in person or over a telephone hotline.

suicidology   (E. S. Shneidman) The scientific study of suicide and suicide prevention, as in The American Association of Suicidology.

suigenderism   A nonsexual relationship between children of the same gender (sex), as during the period of childhood when boys prefer to play with boys and girls prefer to be with girls. Common until preodolesence.

sui juris   Legally entitled to manage one's own affairs, competent in the legal sense.

suk-yeong   koro

sulcus   A shallow groove on the surface of the brain, less deep than a fissure.

sulcus centralis   (L. Rolando, V. d'Azyr) A prominent fissure that makes a double-S-shaped pattern along the lateral surface of the hemisphere from a point beginning near the top of the medial surface. It marks the border between the frontal and parietal lobes. Also known as central fissure/sulcus, fissure of Rolando, Rolandic fissure, Rolando's sulcus, sulcus of Rolando. See BRAIN.

sulcus lateralis cerebri   (F. Sylvius) A well-defined fissure that runs along the lateral surface of the cerebral cortex, separating the frontal and parietal areas from the temporal region, it is the most prominent fissure on the surface of the cortex and isolates much of the temporal lobe. Also known as fissure of Sylvius, lateral fissure/sulcus, Sylvian fissure. See BRAIN.

sulcus of Rolando   sulcus centralis

sulcus principalis   A groove in the contours of the cerebral-cortex frontal lobe of certain infrahuman primate species such as the rhesus monkey. The cortex surrounding it is involved in delayed response learning.

Sullivan's theory   The following items are important for understanding Harry Stack Sullivan's theory: CONSENSUAL VALIDATION, CONSTRUCTIVE REVERIE, DETAILED INQUIRY, DYNAMISM, FORMAL INCEPTION, GOOD-ME, INCEPTION, INTERPERSONAL PSYCHIATRY, INTERPERSONAL RELATIONS, INTERPERSONAL THEORY, INTERPERSONAL THERAPY, ISOPHILIA, LATE ADOLESCENCE, LUST DYNAMISM, MALEVOLENT TRANSFORMATION, MOTHERING, NOT-ME, OBSESSIONALISM, PARATAXIC DISTORTION, PARATAXIC EXPERIENCE, PARATAXIC MODE, PARATAXIC THINKING, PARTIAL ADJUSTMENTS, PERSONIFIED SELF, PROTAXIC EXPERIENCE, PROTOTAXIC EXPERIENCE, PROTOTAXIC MODE, RECONNAISSANCE, SECURITY OPERATIONS, SELECTIVE INATTENTION, SELF-DYNAMISM, SELF-SYSTEM, SIGNIFICANT OTHER, SOCIAL RECOVERY, SOMNOLENT DETACHMENT, SYNTAXIC EXPERIENCE/MODE, SYNTAXIS, TERMINATION, UNCANNY EMOTIONS.

summa libido   The highest point of sexual pleasure. Also known as acme.

summarizing symbols   See KEY SYMBOLS.

summated rating scale   See LIKERT SUMMATED SCALE.

summating potential   An electrical potential detected in the cochlea that builds up slowly and persists beyond the instant of stimulation.

summation   1. (Σ) Addition of a set of numbers, sum of a series. Symbol Σ (Σx indicates the sum of all the values of **x** in the set). 2. The increased intensity experienced in a sensation when two stimuli are presented to a receptor in rapid succession (temporal summation) or to adjacent areas (spatial summation). See SPATIAL SUMMATION, TEMPORAL SUMMATION.

summation effect   A tendency for the same stimulus simultaneously striking two different receptors to generate a single sensory quality, for example, being touched on the skin of the back at two separate points results in perception of a single touch as the two point threshold on the human back is large. Also, if the same stimulus is simultaneously seen by the two different retinas of the eyes only a single object is perceived. See BINOCULAR CELLS.

summation of stimuli   The process of superimposing or adding other stimuli to an originally given stimulus; depending on the precise process the combined stimuli may be perceived as more intense, of longer duration, as larger, etc., than the original stimulus.

summation time   The longest interval between the presentation of two similar, brief stimuli such that they are perceived as a single stimulus. For example, two lights each 25 milliseconds in duration presented 50 milliseconds apart in approximately the same location will just barely be perceived as a single light since the total elapsed time is close to the critical value of approximately one tenth of a second. The same two lights with a 100 millisecond gap between them will be perceived as two successive lights.

summation tone   A third tone heard when two pure tones (usually must differ by at least 50 hertz, or cycles per second) are simultaneously sounded. For example, when a 900 Hz and a 1,000 Hz tone are sounded the observer also hears a 1,900 Hz tone that exists only psychologically, that is, is not detected in the air by the techniques of physics. First reported by Helmholtz in the mid-19th century; much more difficult to hear than the difference tone (in the example, a 100 Hz tone would also be heard) reported by Tartini in the early 18th century. The 100 and 1,900 Hz tones constitute the first-order combination tones for 900 Hz and 1,000 Hz; higher-order tones of both subtypes can be detected under ideal conditions. Compare BEAT.

summative evaluation   An appraisal of a student's achievement at the conclusion of an educational program. Also known as terminal assessment.

summator (technique)   A little used projective test in which the participant responds to low-intensity sounds and reports what he or she heard. See VERBAL SUMMATOR.

summer depression   A mood disorder characterized by depression, sleep disturbances, and anorexia.

sum of cross products   A cross-product is the multiplication of an element with its paired elements, so for N pairs of elements (x_i, y_i), the sum of the cross-products is the sum for $i = 1$ to N of all multiplied $(x_i)(y_i)$ pairs. The notation is $\sum_{i=1}^{N}(x_i)(y_i)$. The sum of cross-products is used in the calculation of a number of statistics including the Pearson product-moment correlation coefficient (r), simple and multiple linear regression, analysis of covariance, discriminant analysis, cluster analysis, and factor analysis.

sum of squares (SS)   A square is the multiplication of an element with itself, so for N elements (x_i), the sum of squares is the sum for $i = 1$ to N of all squared (x_i). The notation is $\sum_{i=1}^{N}(x_i)$. The sum of squares is a concept primarily used in analysis of variance and analysis of covariance. These statistics reveal how much of the variance (the SS) is due to various treatment variables and variable combinations.

Sunday neurosis   Aggravation of neurotic symptoms such as anxiety attacks, on Sundays or during weekends and holidays. Also known as weekend neurosis. See HOLIDAY SYNDROME.

Sunday night insomnia   Difficulty in falling asleep on Sunday nights because of irregular weekend sleeping patterns and possibly irregular weekend activity patterns, among other reasons.

sundowner   1. Characterizing an older person whose intellectual and emotional adjustments are satisfactory during the day, but who becomes confused and agitated at night. 2. An alcoholic drink consumed in early evening, or an evening party featuring same. 3. Colloquial term for someone holding a second job outside of typical working hours; a moonlighter.

sundown syndrome   A tendency for cognitive ability to diminish in the late afternoon or early evening. Probably found most in "morning persons."

sunk costs   (D. F. Halpern) An aspect of critical thinking, believing that an object's or service's value is a function of time spent on doing it (as well as other resources invested) rather than its value on the open market. For example, management (invested 8 employees for 3 months plus $400,000 in overhead and supplies) may view a project in a rather different way than an individual employeed (invested 3 months labor) due to differing sunk costs.

sunlight fear   See HELIOPHOBIA.

sunrise fear   See EOSOPHOBIA.

sunrise syndrome   A tendency toward unstable cognitive ability upon rising in the morning. Probably found most in "evening persons."

suo yang   Chinese name for *koro*.

superconducting quantum interference device (SQUID)   An imaging apparatus that captures images of the brain by detecting minute changes in magnetic fields.

superconscious   1. (K. Stanislavsky) Intuition that enables mental "leaps" to new understandings, ability to generate absolutely new solutions. Considered by Stanislavsky as responsible for works of genius, it explains such breakthroughs as Albert Einstein's theory of relativity, the art of Pablo Picasso and the music of the young Mozart. 2. A higher level of consciousness thought by some as the next stage in human evolution. See GENIUS, INEFFABILITY, INTUITION.

superego In psychoanalytic theory, the ethical component of the personality, representing the internalization of society's standards, determining personal standards of moral right and wrong as well as aims and aspirations. Two subsystems, the ego-ideal and the conscience. See DOUBLE SUPEREGO, GROUP SUPEREGO, HETERONOMOUS SUPEREGO, LAW AND ORDER ORIENTATION, MORAL JUDGMENT, PARASITIC SUPEREGO, PRESUPEREGO PHASE, PRIMITIVE SUPEREGO, PRINCIPLED STAGE, REWARD BY THE SUPEREGO.

superego anxiety In psychoanalytic theory, anxiety caused by unconscious superego activity that produces feelings of guilt and demands for atonement, fear that one is not living up to one's own standards.

superego lacunae In psychoanalytic theory, superego defects in psychopathic persons purportedly acquired from parents with similar defects, indicating that antisocial behavior may represent an acting-out of the unconscious impulses of the parents.

superego resistance Opposition to the psychoanalytic process created by the superego, which generates a sense of guilt that gives rise to the need for punishment. Observed in people with obsessions and cases of masochistic behavior. Also known as negative therapeutic reaction.

superego sadism In psychoanalytic theory, the aggressive, rigid, punitive aspect of conscience, with energy derived from the destructive forces of the id, its intensity and strength dependent upon the violent and sadistic fantasies of the child's primordial strivings.

superfecundation Nearly simultaneous fertilization of two separate ova by two different spermatozoa, usually but not necessarily by the same male. See SUPERFETATION, TWINS.

superfemale A female born with more than the normal XX complement of female chromosomes. The additional X chromosomes often are associated with mental retardation, sterility, and, despite the term superfemale, underdeveloped female sexual characteristics. See SUPERSEX.

superfetation Obsolete concept that two fetuses of different ages and that are not twins can be present in the uterus, due to impregnation of two ova liberated in successive periods of ovulation. Also known as hypercyesis, multifetation, superimpregnation. See SUPERFECUNDATION.

superficial 1. Shallow in thinking or behavior. 2. Pertaining to or located on the surface of the body or of an organ. 3. In reference to matters of little importance.

superficial reflex A contraction of muscles elicited by scratching or pinching the skin immediately over or near them. Also known as skin reflex.

superhuman Beyond human knowledge or ability.

superior colliculus One of a pair of rounded prominences on the dorsal surface of the midbrain and immediately beneath the pineal gland. Receives fibers from the optic tract through the brachium of the superior colliculus brachium. The superior colliculus is involved in visual reflexes (eye movement); the four adjoining colliculi, two superior and two inferior, form the corpora quadrigemina.

superior function The dominant element among Carl Jung's four basic psychological functions that dominates the others, which then become auxiliary functions.

superior intelligence An arbitrary category of general intelligence attained by 15% of the population. Includes persons with an intelligence quotient (IQ) of 116 or more on either or both the Wechsler and Stanford-Binet scales.

superiority Striving to better the self according to Alfred Adler. The superiority drive powers the person's motive to become strong, competent, achieving, creative. Adler's use of the term does not include striving to be better than someone else but to overcome one's own (normal or abnormal) feelings of inferiority. See INFERIORITY COMPLEX.

superiority complex (A. Adler) An apparent belief in being personally superior to everyone else purportedly hides feelings of inferiority. See INFERIORITY COMPLEX, SUPERIORITY FEELINGS.

superiority feelings An attitude characterized by an exaggerated idea of one's personal physical or mental abilities, or both, in comparison with the abilities of others. Usually considered a defense against inferiority feelings. Compare STRIVING FOR SUPERIORITY.

superior longitudinal fasciculus Bundle of nerve fibers that runs from front to back, extending from the frontal lobe to the occipital lobe, with fibers that also communicate with the temporal lobe via the arcuate fasciculus.

superior oblique One of the six muscles used in controlling eye movements, for looking downward and inward. The superior and inferior oblique muscles also control rotation movements of the eyeball. Controlled by the fourth cranial nerve. See INFERIOR OBLIQUE, INFERIOR RECTUS, LATERAL RECTUS, MEDIAL RECTUS, SUPERIOR RECTUS.

superior olivary complex A collection of nuclei appearing as small masses of gray matter in the pons. The cells receive terminals and collaterals from the cochlear nuclei on the same and opposite sides through the trapezoid body, a concentration of transverse nerve fibers in the pons. Neurons in this complex provide fibers to the ascending auditory system and cholinergic fibers to the efferent olivocochlear bundle. The olivocochlear bundle is involved in enhancing signal-to-noise ratio at the level of the receptive hair cells of the cochlea.

superior olive A structure in the medulla that receives fibers from auditory nerves of both ears. Consists of two or three small masses of gray matter in the tegmentum of the pons.

superior rectus One of the six muscles used in controlling eye movements, for looking upward. Controlled by the third cranial nerve. See INFERIOR OBLIQUE, INFERIOR RECTUS, LATERAL RECTUS, MEDIAL RECTUS, SUPERIOR OBLIQUE.

supermale A man born with more than the usual complement of male chromosomes. Early findings suggested that men with XYY chromosome sets were large, aggressive, and generally lower than average intelligence. However, the first cases were discovered in prison inmates, and further study showed that normal, average men in the general population also may have an extra Y chromosome. See SUPERFEMALE, SUPERSEX.

superman (F. Nietzsche) A hypothetical being, superior to the human type but evolved therefrom, who is assumed to possess all the intellectual and other mental characters of humans, without limits. An individual who would emerge suddenly with superior ability to control himself or herself, rejecting conventional "herd morality."

supernatural Belonging to a higher order or system than that of nature, transcending the ordinary course of nature.

supernormal 1. Characterizing certain occurrences which are not open to explanation in terms of any known principles of science, but which are thought to be consistent with natural law, and destined with the advance of science to be reduced to natural law. 2. Distinctly above the norm or median, for example, in intelligence or other ability.

supernormal period (of neuron) A brief time span, of between 15 and 100 milliseconds, that may occur immediately after the refractory period of a neuron-firing cycle. During the supernormal period, excitability is greater than normal. A cause may be the overshooting of the resting potential. Compare SUBNORMAL PERIOD (OF NEURON).

supernormal recovery phase A phase (following the total and partial refractory periods) in the recovery of conductivity in nerve fibers after the transmission of a nerve impulse, during which excitability and the intensity of the nerve impulse are increased above the normal. See SUPERNORMAL PERIOD.

superordinate goal 1. A common goal, individuals put aside subgoals that generate competition to cooperate for a "greater good." 2. A goal that is more important to a group or to two negotiating sides than to the individuals, and that requires mutual dependence to achieve.

superordinate identity Group identity that transcends the individual identities (personal, gender, ethnic, etc.) of members.

superordinate stimulus In a learning situation, the stimulus to be responded to is defined by two or more elements, for example, out of a variety of flashing lights of different shapes and colors, the superordinate stimulus would be a particular combination, such as a yellow oval.

superordination Being classified as higher or better than most others in some special manner, for example, being considered the most intelligent (having the highest IQ) in the school. The effects of such information on people can vary from making some people shyer and more concerned, to making others bolder and less concerned about themselves and others. In general, authorities think that such information to the person is detrimental in the long run.

supersensitivity In physiological psychology, heightened responses of neurotransmitter receptors caused by damage to afferent axons or past blockage of neurotransmitter release.

supersex Refers to having an excess of either male or female sex chromosomes. A supersex organism may be sterile or fertile, depending upon factors other than the number of sex chromosomes in their gametes. See SUPERFEMALE, SUPERMALE.

supersonic sounds Sound waves whose frequency is so high (over 20,000 hertz, or cycles per second) that humans cannot hear them, but many animals, such as dogs, can.

superstition 1. A belief or practice based on the operation of supernatural or magical forces, such as charms, omens, or exorcism. 2. Denoting any unscientific belief accepted without question, groundless or unfounded notion. See ANIMISM, FAITH HEALING, MAGICAL THINKING, SUPERSTITIOUS CONTROL.

superstitious behavior (B. F. Skinner) The result of an "accidental" conditioning in which a response happened to occur just prior to a reinforcement that was really contingent on time elapsing or other noncontingent factor. The response rate nonetheless increases in that environment.

superstitious control The illusion that a person can influence outcomes through various practices (such as a rain dance, prayers and incantations, a chant) designed to protect the self or alter the environment. Certain writers maintain that superstitious control serves a positive psychological function in averting the development of learned helplessness. See FAITH HEALING, MAGICAL THINKING.

superstitious reinforcement (B. F. Skinner) Reinforcing stimuli that follow a response by happenstance but appear to the individual as the natural consequences of that response.

supersummativity (C. Ehrenfels) A Gestalt-like assumption that the elements of a perception, when they form a whole, are more than the elements themselves, possess emergent qualities. Similar to the concept that the whole is more than the sum of its parts. See GESTALT, GESTALT LAWS OF ORGANIZATION.

supervalent Characterizing an idea that takes on excessive intensity and cannot be eliminated by personal efforts, for example, extreme jealousy stemming from a source concealed in the unconscious.

supervalent thought An obsession; thinking devoted almost exclusively to a single topic; for example, after losing money in a foolish investment, a person constantly reviews the steps made in such a bad decision, wonders why the mistake was made, and dwells on the consequences. See RUMINATION.

supervision 1. Guidance, direction, and correction of a trainee in some field (for example, psychotherapy, education) provided by a person experienced in the field. 2. In the world of work such oversight may well continue beyond the trainee stage.

superwoman syndrome The belief system and behavior of a woman who feels impelled to do and "have it all"; usually the woman lives with a partner, holds down a job, assumes the major responsibility for child care, and performs all the "traditional" women's role functions at home, for example, cleaning, cooking, and entertaining.

supination Act of assuming a supine position, as in lying on the back or turning palms upward.

supine (position) 1. In a horizontal position, face up, lying on the back. See PRONE. 2. The arm or hand in a position with the palm upward.

supplementary motor area An area of the cortex located on the medial surface of the superior frontal gyrus in front of the primary motor cortex from which electrical stimulation can elicit movement. In humans the movements are of three types: assumption of postures, complex coordinated movement of limbs, and rapid incoordinated movements. Movements of limbs are on the side opposite to the stimulation while postural changes are bilateral. This region has a somatotopic organization, with neurons distributed in a pattern that resembles the general design of the body. Cells relating to eye function, for example, occur near motoneurons associated with face muscles.

supply item An objective test item requiring the participant to supply the correct answer (for example, name a furry animal that flies, in contrast to a recognition item in which the participant selects an answer from a list of possibilities. Also known as a completion test item. See RECALL ITEM.

supportive ego (S. R. Slavson) A member of an activity-therapy group who helps a fellow member work out intrapsychic difficulties.

supportive leadership A management style wherein employees are valued, listened to, treated fairly, paid appropriately and otherwise dealt with in a caring manner.

supportiveness In counseling, an attitude or response of acceptance, encouragement, or reassurance displayed by the counselor. See REASSURANCE, SUPPORTIVE PSYCHOTHERAPY.

supportive personnel Health professionals who function in special areas of diagnosis, therapy, and rehabilitation in support of activities of medical-surgical personnel. They include occupational, recreational, and physical therapists. Also known as support personnel.

supportive psychotherapy Psychological treatment directed at relieving current emotional distress and symptoms without probing into the sources of conflicts or attempting to alter basic personality structure, applied to clients with minor or limited problems or when there is no time for more fundamental treatment.

supportive services Various mental health organizations provide for the needs of clients, for example, employment counseling, psychologic or psychiatric service, medical supervision, and general wellness programs, to permit the clients to cope with job and other life demands outside the sheltered-workshop, half-way house, or hospital environment. Also known as support services.

supportive therapy Treatment aimed at providing encouragement, suggestions, reframing and advice, intended to ease a person's psychic pain. "Supportive" indicates brief therapy for transitory, situational problems, such as the loss of a partner or the failure to attain an important goal.

support personnel supportive personnel

support services supportive services

supposition 1. A hypothesis, theory, or guess related to a theory or a prognosis, based usually on little evidence. 2. A statement considered sufficiently probable that it is assumed to be true at least for the present discussion.

suppression To consciously keep something a secret. Suppression differs from repression which represents unconscious censoring.

suppressive approach An attempt to eliminate symptoms by command, persuasion, or suggestion, without exploring their unconscious sources or attempting to bring about basic personality changes.

suppressive therapy A form of psychotherapy directed to the reinforcement of the patient's or client's defense mechanisms and the suppression rather than the expression of distressing experiences and feelings. See EXPRESSIVE THERAPY.

suppressor area An area of the cortex which, when stimulated, inhibits cortical activity of other areas. May be an artifact of stimulating blood vessels.

suppressor variable A measure that is useful primarily due to its relationships with other variables, that "suppresses" irrelevant variance and thereby permits the relationship between two other measures to be detected. For example, there is only a modest relationship between a test of geography aptitude and grades in a geography course until a test of reading achievement is added; by removing variance due to reading ability, which affects both the aptitude test score and the course grade, a much stronger correlation is obtained. If the correlation between the two variables does not change or decreases appreciably with the addition of the third variable, then that third measure is not a suppressor variable. See MULTIPLE CORRELATION, PARTIAL CORRELATION.

suprachiasmatic nucleus (SCN) A group of cells of the anterior hypothalamus that influence circadian rhythmicity and are thus related to the biological clock. Receives direct projections from the retina and may be affected by the melatonin from the pineal gland.

supraconscious (F. von Hayek) Refers to intuitive feeling or knowledge about the correct thing to do, it involves the making of "good decisions" without understanding or being able to explain why such decisions were made (for example, "it just felt right"). See INTUITION, SUBCEPTION.

supraliminal Above the difference threshold or absolute threshold.

supraliminal difference The difference between various stimuli that are above the difference threshold, a rare term for difference threshold.

supraliminal differences method See MEAN GRADATIONS METHOD, METHOD OF MEAN GRADATIONS.

supramarginal gyrus See POSTERIOR PARIETAL LOBE.

supraorbital reflex Contraction of the eyelid muscle elicited by a tap over the supraorbital foramen. Sometimes known as McCarthy's reflex.

supraordinate stimulus A stimulus element in operant conditioning that indicates to the organism the element of the surround to which it is supposed to pay attention.

suprasegmental In linguistics, phonemic elements added to spoken sounds including stress and pitch to provide voice with distinctiveness of speech.

suprasegmental reflex An automatic or mechanical response that requires some control by brain areas as well as the spinal cord and the various neuromuscular connections of the limbs and trunk.

surd   A sound produced without vibration of the vocal cords, for example, /p/, /t/, /f/. See VOICELESS SOUND.

surdimutism   Deaf-mutism.

surdity   Deafness.

surdomute   Both deaf and dumb.

surface color   A color perceived as localized on the surface, as opposed to a color that permeates an object, such as a red book or a green leaf. See FILM COLOR.

surface dyslexia   Acquired dyslexia. Persons with this disorder can read words out loud, but have difficulty understanding what they read. See ACQUIRED DYSLEXIA, DEVELOPMENTAL DYSLEXIA.

surface realism   Refers to whether information about human behavior obtained in laboratory conditions is meaningful since they are not real-life situations. In some cases, such as studying basic sensory effects, realism is of no importance.

surface structure   (N. Chomsky) A linear relationship between the words of a sentence, that is, the relationship that is merely formal or grammatically consistent. The surface structure may or may not contain real meaning, and may not reveal the underlying grammatical deep structure. See DEEP PHASE STRUCTURE.

surface therapy   A pejorative term for nondepth therapy carried out on a conscious level and directed toward relieving the patient's symptoms and emotional stress through such measures as explanations, reassurance, suggestion, reinforcement of present defenses, and direct attempts to modify attitudes and behavior patterns. "Surface" implies a focus on symptoms, with minimal deep probing. Compare DEPTH THERAPY.

surface traits   (R. B. Cattell) Clusters of overt behavior that seem to go together, but do not necessarily have a common cause. See PERSONALITY SPHERE, SOURCE TRAITS.

surgency   (R. B. Cattell) A personality trait marked by cheerfulness, responsiveness, and sociability. One of the source traits.

surplusage   The assumption that most organisms, including humans, have more potentials, mental and physical, than necessary to survive.

surplus energy theory   A point of view that play activities of human and animal young are due to the superabundance of energy in growing organisms, this extra energy manifesting itself in inherited modes of behavior typical of the species.

surplus meaning   A connotation or implication that goes well beyond the observable. Explanatory concepts that refer to vague or undetectable internal processes are said to contain surplus meaning. Contributes to lack of genuine communication, which may or may not be realized by the discussants.

surplus powerlessness   (M. Lerner) A feeling of personal lack of self-efficacy, as opposed to that resulting from, for instance, oppression, economic disadvantage, and denial of resources and a political voice.

surplus reality   Psychological experiences of other than physical reality; experiences that seem valid to the person experiencing them although they may not be real, such as spiritual revelations or visions, consultation with the ghosts of people deceased, dreams reported as meaningful.

surprisal   In information theory, the surprise value of a message. The greater the surprisal, the more information the message relates; for example, "Man gives birth to twins" would have more surprisal than "Woman gives birth to twins."

surprise   An attitude aroused by some unexpected situation which manifests itself in certain characteristic gestures, facial expression, etc. Surprise is not as strong in the impression made as the terms "astonishment" and "alarm."

surprisingness   A measure of the degree to which personal expectations are disconfirmed. Term is used mostly in psychological esthetics and in environmental psychology. See COGNITIVE DISSONANCE.

surreptitious   Characterizing something suspect or underhanded, such as an unwarranted insertion of data, premise, or argument in a report or discussion, usually done intentionally and always in an obscure way, designed to deceive the reader or listener.

surrogate   A person or object that substitutes for the role of an individual who has a significant position in a family or group. A surrogate may substitute for an absent parent, child, or mate. Young animals may use softcloth material as a surrogate mother, and young humans may use stuffed toys as surrogate companions. See IMAGINARY COMPANION, MOTHER SURROGATE, SECURITY BLANKET, SURROGATE PARTNER.

surrogate parent image   See PARENT IMAGE.

surrogate partner   In sex therapy, a person, usually a woman, trained to help a patient overcome sexual inhibitions and resistances so that satisfactory sexual relations can be achieved. Also called sexual surrogate.

surround   All elements of a person's environment that can be immediately apprehended, that can be perceived with any of the senses.

survey   1. An overall inspection for any particular purpose, such as to determine whether everything in an office is where it should be. 2. A method of gaining certain information by asking specific people specific questions. See SURVEY TEST. 3. A comprehensive overview of an idea, person, or group.

survey errors   Some errors that may occur in doing surveys: (a) not enough people surveyed, (b) poor selection of sites or individuals at the sites, (c) wrong type of interviewers, (d) interview biases in the survey questions, (e) questions posed incorrectly.

survey method/research   A research technique utilizing written questionnaires or personal interviews to discover the attitudes and beliefs of a given population, as in a public-opinion poll. Many variables must be controlled including experimenter bias, sampling procedures, interview format, and question-wording. In general, external validity tends to be stronger than internal validity.

Survey of Management Practices (SMP)   (C. L. Wilson) A comprehensive questionnaire for measuring managerial skills. Each item, using anchors, focuses on competency, not just frequency of behaviors.

survey test   A test designed to yield accurate information about a large group of individuals.

survival   The innate need, drive and source of animal behavior. Leads humans to seek health, nutrition and protection from physical danger. See SURVIVAL BEHAVIOR, SURVIVAL OF THE FITTEST.

survival behavior 1. Actions that enhance the survival of an organism and/or its species. 2. Activity that was useful at some earlier stage of evolution, but which has become without significance to an organism through change in its body structure, or mode of life.

survival of the fittest (H. Spencer, C. Darwin) A concept that individual organisms or species whose structural organization is such as to best meet the general conditions of life, will, on the average, live or endure the longest and propagate the most extensively. See DARWIN, EVOLUTION THEORY, NATURAL SELECTION.

survival value The capacity of an attitude or physical quality to contribute to the survival of individuals or populations.

survivor guilt Feelings of guilt for having survived a catastrophic situation when others did not, as in concentration-camp syndrome. Based on such thoughts as "I should have done something" or "Maybe my mom died because I did something bad." Also known as survival guilt. See CONCENTRATION-CAMP SYNDROME, PERSECUTION SYNDROME, SURVIVOR SYNDROME.

survivor syndrome A constellation of symptoms observed in survivors of a disaster such as a flood, earthquake, or hurricane. May include symptoms of indelible images of death, continuing anxiety, guilt over having lived while others died, numbing, depression, withdrawal, loss of interest and enjoyment in activities, and increased smoking and drinking (of alcoholic beverages). See CONCENTRATION-CAMP SYNDROME, SURVIVAL GUILT.

susceptibility 1. Vulnerability to disorders, physical or mental, due to genetic factors, environmental factors, or both. See DIATHESIS-STRESS MODEL. 2. Amenability to change or alteration, whether socially valenced as positive or negative. 3. Capable of emotions and strong feelings, particularly of being offended.

susceptibility rhythms Cyclical variations in sensitivity to infections or allergic responses.

suspense An attitude resulting from the balance of conflicting motives, or from the absence of certain data requisite to the formation of a decision or judgment, characterized by the inhibition of responsive activity or vacillation.

suspiciousness An attitude of mistrust toward the motives or sincerity of others. Extreme, pervasive suspiciousness is a common characteristic of the paranoid personality.

sustained attention The maintenance of a high state of attention over a long period of time.

sustentacular cells Cells that provide structural support for other cells or tissues, for example, cells that surround the olfactory neurons.

susto (fright—Spanish) A culture-specific syndrome seen mostly among Hispanic Americans manifested by "loss of soul," anorexia, asthenia and anxiety. See CULTURE-BOUND DISORDERS.

SVIB See STRONG VOCATIONAL INTEREST BLANK FOR MEN/FOR WOMEN.

swallow-belch method The technique of speaking without a larynx by swallowing air, then belching while the lips, teeth, and tongue are manipulated to form word sounds as the air is expelled. See LARYNGECTOMY.

swallowing reflex The simultaneous and chained activity of certain muscles in the mouth and throat, whereby liquid or solid food is passed from the mouth into the esophagus. Also known as palatine reflex.

sweet-lemons mechanism A rationalization in which a disappointment is justified by giving reasons for being satisfied with the status quo, for example, a person just rejected by a new acquaintance may find that the present lover has sterling qualities that were overlooked. Sometimes known as sweet-persimmons mechanism. Compare SOUR-GRAPES MECHANISM.

sweet taste A gustatory sensation associated with a sugary effect on the taste buds. One of the four principal qualities of taste according to Hans Henning. Sometimes is described as the opposite of sour or bitter. Small concentrations of table salt (sodium chloride) produce a sweet taste on the tongues of some individuals. Sweet-sensitive taste buds are concentrated at the tip of the tongue.

swimming reflex A pseudo-reflex of the healthy newborn infant consisting of "paddle-like" motions of the limbs when the baby is placed in water.

Swindle's ghost (P. F. Swindle) A positive afterimage that appears after a lengthy delay. Following the primary stimulus, the observer's eye was illuminated for 40 minutes and then remained in the dark for 10 minutes; the afterimage appeared when the eye was briefly illuminated through the closed lids.

swinging 1. Common term for uninhibited sexual expression, including such activities as "one-night stands," group sex, male-male sexual encounters, female-female sexual encounters, and experimentation with such deviations as sadism and masochism. 2. The two-couple practice of exchanging marital partners for sex. See OPEN MARRIAGE, WIFE-SWAPPING.

SWIT structured written interview technique

switching See ROLE REVERSAL.

switch process The transition from depression to mania and mania to depression in some cases of bipolar disorder. The switch to depression goes mania to hypomania, then to a period characterized by a labile mood and activity, and finally to psychomotor retardation and then to deep depression.

SWS slow-wave sleep

sybian A saddle-like device with a vertical phallus, designed for female masturbation, typically in pornography. See DILDO, VIBRATOR.

sycophant A servile self-serving flatterer.

Sydenham's chorea (T. Sydenham) An acute disorder of the nervous system usually occurring together with rheumatic fever, occurring mostly in young people. Symptoms are jerky irregular movements that disappear while sleeping. Also known as chorea minor, ordinary chorea.

syllabic synthesis The process of forming bizarre new words or neologisms from parts of other words, as occurs in dreams and in the language of certain patients with schizophrenia.

syllabism The use of syllabic characters instead of letters as adopted in certain written languages, such as Ancient Egyptian, Chinese and Japanese.

syllable-span test   A mental test similar to the digit-span test, except that syllables are used instead of digits.

syllogism   Formalized reasoning in which acceptance of two premises as true seem to compel acceptance of a third judgment, the conclusion (for example, all men are mortal, Socrates is a man, therefore Socrates is mortal).

Sylvian fissure   A deep groove or fissure on the lateral surface of each cerebral hemisphere, which extends horizontally from the gyrus frontalis inferior to the gyrus supramarginalis and demarcates the temporal from the frontal and parietal lobes. Also known as fissure of Sylvius.

symbiosis   1. Literally, living together. 2. In biology, the living together of two dissimilar organisms, usually each being helpful to the other. Also known as symbiotic relationship. Sometimes known as mutualism. Other forms include amensalism, commensalism, parasitism, synnecrosis. 3. Mutual cooperation between two persons, such as parent and child, client and therapist. 4. An unhealthy social relationship between two people characterized by excessive mutual dependency as well as mutual exploitation. See CODEPENDENCY, SYMBIOTIC PSYCHOSIS. 4. Mutually interdependent relationship between a mother and infant during the infant's earliest months of life. See SYMBIOTIC INFANTILE PSYCHOSIS.

symbiotic infantile psychosis   (M. Mahler) A mental disorder occurring between 2–5 years of age characterized by excessive emotional dependence on the mother, inability to tolerate separation from her, reactions of anger and panic if separation is threatened, and developmental lag. Also known as symbiotic infantile psychotic syndrome. See PERVASIVE DEVELOPMENTAL DISORDER, SEPARATION-ANXIETY DISORDER.

symbiotic marriage   A partnership of two individuals, each dependent upon the other for the gratification of certain psychological needs. Both partners may have neurotic or otherwise unusual needs that could not be satisfied easily outside the marriage or with a healthy partner. See CODEPENDENCY, SYNERGIC MARRIAGE.

symbiotic psychosis   A disorder characterized by excessive emotional dependence on someone else. See CODEPENDENCY, SEPARATION-ANXIETY DISORDER, SYMBIOTIC INFANTILE PSYCHOSIS.

symbiotic relatedness   (E. Fromm) Attachment of one individual to another characterized by the former lacking psychological autonomy due to the development of a style of relating based on merging with the latter. See CODEPENDENCY.

symbol   1. Any object, figure, or image that represents something else such as a musical notation, letter, word, pictograph, or activity. Some symbols such as → (an arrow) are widely recognized as indicating movement or attention to the direction indicated. See INDIVIDUAL SYMBOL, UNIVERSAL SYMBOL. 2. In psychoanalytic theory, a symbol is something other than itself from which it derives its significance.

symbol-arrangement test   See KAHN TEST OF SYMBOL ARRANGEMENT.

symbol-digit test   A test that requires the participant to translate a set of symbols into a set of digits. See CODE TEST.

symbolic act(ion)   A simple or complex action, unconscious and automatic expressing an underlying meaning, for example, pulling the earlobe might indicate irritation; licking of lips while looking at food may indicate a desire to eat. See SYMPTOMATIC ACT.

symbolic construct   A symbol, generally a word, that stands for a set of relationships among empirical data.

symbolic displacement   Transferring a response, usually emotional, from its original stimulus to one that represents it, for example, a person harboring homicidal impulses might develop a morbid fear of knives or guns.

symbolic display   A symbol that conveys another meaning besides the obvious one, the other meaning being sometimes only understood by a certain group of people, for example, wearing a bandanna of a certain color may signify that the person is in a street gang. See DISPLAY.

symbolic function   (J. Piaget) Ability to learn by using mental representations (symbols or signs) to which a child has attached meaning; this ability, characteristic of preoperational and higher thought, is shown in deferred imitation, symbolic play, and language.

symbolic interactionism   A theory of the way symbolic meanings of social acts (including roles and social structures) influence social interaction.

symbolic logic   (B. Russell) Applying symbols to formal logic, thereby establishing an artificial language or symbolic calculus so precise as to avoid the ambiguities and logical inadequacies of ordinary languages. Also known as mathematical logic.

symbolic loss   In psychoanalytic theory, an unconscious ego interpretation of a rejection as a complete loss equivalent to a death in the family.

symbolic masturbation   In psychoanalytic theory, the handling of body parts that are symbolic substitutes for the penis or clitoris, for example, the nose, ear lobe, mouth, or fingertips. Also may be expressed in the twisting or pulling of garments or hair strands.

symbolic mode   Jerome Bruner's third stage of cognitive development, following the enactive and iconic periods. Enables the young child to depict and convey ideas through the use of words, sounds, and play. See ENACTIVE MODE, ICONIC MODE.

symbolic parricide   In psychoanalytic theory, the tendency for people to act in such a manner as to punish themselves, as a result of their guilt, for having death wishes against their parents or close relatives. See SACRIFICE.

symbolic play   (J. Piaget) Creative behavior during which a child makes an object stand for something else. See MAKE-BELIEVE.

symbolic process/thinking   A cognitive activity that uses symbols, such as words or formulae, as in thinking, remembering a theory, or problem-solving.

symbolic realization   The fulfillment of a blocked desire through a substitute, for example; a person unable to rebel against an authoritarian parent, may rebel against all symbols of authority, such as the laws or customs of society.

symbolic representation (J. Bruner) A means of recording information in memory by storing symbols such as words or numbers, which permits a person to be efficient in recovering stored material. See ENACTIVE REPRESENTATION, ICONIC REPRESENTATION.

symbolic rewards Words or objects that have no intrinsic value but nevertheless are valued by the person, such as being listed in *Who's Who in America*. See TOKEN REWARD.

symbolic stage **preoperational stage**

symbolic synthesis Abstract reasoning used in solving problems of logic and mathematics. It is said that both quantum mechanics and the special theory of relativity are examples. Another example is the German chemist August Kekule dreaming about a snake biting its tail during the period in which he was perplexed about the structure of the benzene molecule; the dream symbols assisted him in synthesizing his knowledge of the chemical and thus in proposing the benzene ring model.

symbolism 1. In psychoanalytic theory, the substitution of a representation, or symbol, for a repressed impulse or threatening object to avoid censorship by the superego, for example, dreaming of a steeple instead of a penis. 2. In analytical psychology, Carl Jung maintained that mythological and religious symbols throw special light on the collective unconscious. See PHALLIC SYMBOL, THRESHOLD SYMBOLISM.

symbolization Unconscious mental states in which images, objects, or gestures represent repressed thoughts, feelings, or impulses (for example, a person always communicated with an ex-spouse in red ink, which symbolized that the ex had taken all the money and left the person "in the red"). Symbolization is found in many mental disorders, such as the body language of conversion disorder and the gestures and grimaces of patients with schizophrenia.

symbolophobia 1. Morbid fear of symbolism, especially that others might see something symbolic in own words or actions. 2. Fear of symbols or symbolic representation.

symmetrical distribution A distribution in which the values above the mean are a mirror image of those below the mean. In such a distribution the mean, median and mode have identical values. See NORMAL CURVE and KURTOSIS for illustrations of this phenomenon. Compare ASYMMETRICAL DISTRIBUTION.

symmetry 1. Balance and harmony in the proportions of objects or works of art, an esthetically pleasing quality. 2. In a narrower sense, the mirror-like correspondence of parts on opposite sides of a center.

symmetry compulsion 1. The obsessive need to balance one behavior with another to compensate for it. 2. Habitual behavior of moving objects so their position is in some respects symmetrical.

Symonds Picture-Study Test (P. M. Symonds) A projective examination for adolescents, consisting of 20 pictures of interpersonal situations. The participant tells a story about each of the pictures, and the interpreter analyzes these productions in terms of their dynamics. Also known as Symonds' Picture-Story Test.

sympathectomy 1. Severing of sympathetic nerves. 2. The destruction of one or more sympathetic nerves or excision of one or more sympathetic ganglia to relieve a disorder of function of the sympathetic division of the autonomic nervous system.

sympathetic chain Interconnections among the ganglia of the sympathetic nervous system.

sympathetic division (J. N. Langley) Refers to a subdivision of the autonomic nervous system, the other major subdivision being the parasympathetic division. See AUTONOMIC NERVOUS SYSTEM, SYMPATHETIC NERVOUS SYSTEM.

sympathetic dyspraxia A form of apraxia (loss of ability to perform purposeful movements) affecting the left limbs in patients afflicted with a right hemiplegia and aphasia due to lesions in Broca's area.

sympathetic ganglion Any of the nerve clusters of the sympathetic division of the autonomic nervous system that form a beadlike chain on either side of the spinal cord.

sympathetic induction The transfer of one person's emotions to another, for example, a child finds a dead rat and picks it up to show another child. The second child screams and runs away, the first child drops the rat and also screams and runs away.

sympathetic nervous system Part of the autonomic nervous system (ANS), primarily involving adrenergic responses, tends to evoke bodily functions that are more of an emotional nature, including dry mouth, perspiration, etc.; usually the opposite of the parasympathetic nervous system. Sometimes known as visceral nervous system.

sympathetic vibration 1. In physics, a particular object moving in the same cycles as something else as a result of transmission of energy, usually through the air. See RESONANCE. 2. In psychology, something of the same kind, of two or more people being in harmony of feelings and of thoughts.

sympathin A neurohormonal nerve-impulse mediator secreted at sympathetic-nerve synapses. Term usually is applied only when the mediator cannot be identified as epinephrine or norepinephrine.

sympathism **sympathy-seeking**

sympathomimetic Evoking the action of the sympathetic nervous system (a "mimetic" is a drug which "mimics" another action; at one point, psychedelic agents were misleadingly termed "psychotomimetics.") The phrase sympathomimetic drugs (or sympathomimetics) refers to drugs that stimulate the sympathetic nervous system, especially stimulants, but also cocaine.

sympathomimetic drug See SYMPATHOMIMETIC.

sympathy Sensitive appreciation or emotional concern for, and the sharing of the mental and emotional state of another person or animal or of a group. See EMPATHY.

sympathy-seeking A tendency to seek emotional support by arousing sympathy; the habit of eliciting the concern and assistance of others by dwelling on personal misfortune which is usually ascribed to an unkind fate or the faults of others. Sometimes known as sympathism.

sympatric species Those species that occupy the same habitat or overlapping habitats. Compare ALLOPATRIC SPECIES.

symphorophilia   Being sexually aroused by arranging a disaster and watching it happen.

symptom (sym)   1. In medicine, any deviation from normal functioning considered indicative of physical or mental disorder. 2. An event indicative of another event, for example, a series of strikes in a particular company is symptomatic of unrest in the organization. 3. In theories of psychotherapy, some feature that causes the patient distress (and that may or may not be linked to other symptoms or causes). See SIGN.

symptomatic act   An action that appears to be meaningless (such as playing with own necklace) but which may indicate a hidden motivation. These are sometimes called symbolic actions, since they may represent repressed impulses, such as an urge to masturbate. See PARAPRAXIS, SYMBOLIC ACTION.

symptomatic alcoholism   Obsolete name for a concept similar to E. M. Jellinek's alpha alcoholism.

symptomatic autoscopy   Rare delusional disorder that has an organic basis in which a patient sees a "double" who looks, talks, acts, and dresses like the patient. Compare IDIOPATHIC AUTOSCOPY.

symptomatic epilepsy   A type of epilepsy due to known conditions such as brain inflammation, high fever, brain tumor, vascular disturbances, structural abnormality, brain injury, or degenerative disease. See IDIOPATHIC EPILEPSY.

symptomatic psychosis   A severe mental disorder associated with impairment of brain-tissue functions. See COGNITIVE DISORDERS, ORGANIC BRAIN SYNDROMES, ORGANIC MENTAL DISORDERS.

symptomatic schizophrenia   (E. Rodin) Recurrent episodic schizophrenic reactions characterized by clouded sensorium, and partial memory loss. See ONEIROPHRENIA.

symptomatic treatment   (H. Eysenck) Treatment directed toward the relief of distressing symptoms as opposed to treatment focused on underlying causes and conditions and the reconstruction of the patient's personality. Major techniques used in symptom removal are behavior therapy (many of whose practitioners doubt the existence of underlying causes), hypnotherapy, suggestion therapy, and narcotherapy. See SYMPTOM SUBSTITUTION.

symptom bearer/wearer   A person in a group (for example a family) who appears to have the overt characteristics of a mental disorder while the other group members do not. Such a person may be a scapegoat blamed for misbehavior that only reflects the family's pathology. Sometimes known as identified patient. See FAMILY THERAPY THEORY, IDENTIFIED PATIENT.

symptom choice   The unconscious "selection" of a particular symptom as an expression of underlying pathology. It is difficult to explain why a given person develops a compulsion rather than a phobia, or becomes somatization-blind rather than paralyzed. Explanations include: constitutional predispositions, parental behavior patterns, retained infantile behavior patterns, fixation at an early psychosexual stage, and specific traumatic experiences. Also known as choice of a neurosis. See LOCALIZATION OF SYMPTOMS, SOMATIC COMPLIANCE.

symptom cluster   A group of related symptoms that usually occur together, as in a syndrome.

symptom complex   A syndrome.

symptom formation   In psychoanalytic theory, the process of developing a somatic or behavioral substitute for an unconscious impulse or conflict that provokes anxiety, for example, conversion symptoms such as glove anesthesia, or phobias such as fearful avoidance of crowds. Also known as substitute formation.

symptom localization   See LOCALIZATION OF SYMPTOMS.

symptom neurosis   Loose phrase for a psychoneurotic disorder with a specific pattern of symptoms (such as obsessive-compulsive, phobic, dissociative, anxiety), as opposed to individual neurotic traits and tendencies such as meticulousness, apprehensiveness, or irrational fears. See NEUROTIC PERSONALITY.

symptom removal   The elimination of various overt and covert symptoms by direct treatment without consideration of underlying dynamics. See BEHAVIORISM, BEHAVIOR PSYCHOTHERAPY, PSYCHOTHERAPY.

symptom specificity   A group of symptoms involving an organ that is the focus of a psychosomatic disorder. A person whose psychosomatic problem is the heart is likely to have an unusually large variety of complaints expressed as cardiovascular symptoms, rather than complaints about other possible organs or disorders.

symptom substitution   In psychoanalytic theory, a tendency for one neurotic symptom to be replaced by another when the first is removed. Thought to be eradicated only by removing the underlying conflict. Researchers from other perspectives often question the validity of the concept.

symptom-symbol hypothesis   A postulate that it is possible to determine the underlying causes of mental disorders by understanding symptoms.

symptom wearer   **symptom bearer**

Synanon   (C. E. Dederich) A self-help organization begun by former drug addicts to help rehabilitate active drug addicts through residential treatment and group encounters. Originated in 1958 in Santa Monica, California.

synapse   (C. Sherrington & M. Foster) The space between the synaptic knob of a neuron and the membrane of a neighboring dendrite, cell body or axon. The synaptic cleft may actually be no larger than 1/150th of a micron in width. Usually measured in angstrom units. (A micron is 1/10,000 part of a millimeter; an angstrom is 1/10,000 part of a micron, one ten-billionth of a meter.) Most psychotropic medicines operate by stimulating the secretion of a neurotransmitter from the axon, modifying the receptors of the dendrite, or altering other functions or enzymatic reactions relating to the process of neurotransmission. Also known as synaptic cleft/gap/junction, except that "synapse" is more general, and can refer to the process as well as the structure. See AXOAXONALS.

synapse time   (C. Sherrington) That part of the time (latency to response) between stimulus and response in a reflex which is attributable to the time consumed by transmission of the nerve impulse across synapses.

synaptic cleft/gap   **synapse**

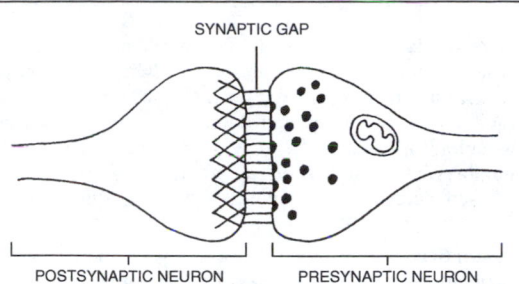

SYNAPTIC GAP

POSTSYNAPTIC NEURON   PRESYNAPTIC NEURON

synapse   The juncture point of two neurons. The neurons do not touch each other, separated by a millionth of an inch. Chemical neurotransmitters cross over at the speed of 1/10,000 of a second. More than 50 different neurotransmitters have been identified.

synaptic depression   A mechanism of habituation; a condition of the nervous pathways that occurs at synapses. Also known as intrinsic fatigue.

synaptic junction   **synapse**

synaptic knob/swelling   A small bulb at the end of a neuron. A nerve impulse reaching the bouton leads it to release neurotransmitters to the synaptic cleft. Also known as bouton (terminal), boutons terminaux, end button/foot, terminal (bouton/bulbs/button).

synaptic resistance   Interference with the transmission of a nerve impulse across a synapse, for reasons other than competing inhibitory synapses.

synaptic transmission   The passing on of electric energy from presynaptic to postsynaptic neuron.

synaptic vesicles   Small granules in the cytoplasm of synaptic knobs. Synaptic vesicles are the sources of the transmitter substance released by the synaptic knobs when a nerve impulse arrives at the terminus of an axon branch. See SYNAPTIC KNOBS.

synchronicity   1. Events that occur simultaneously, that are not known to be causally related. 2. (C. G. Jung) Events that occur simultaneously and whose coincidence is meaningful but not known to be causally related.

synchronism   The occurrence of several developmental disorders at about the same time of embryonic or fetal life.

synchronization   1. A pattern of brain waves that appears to be coordinated with mental or physical activity. Alpha-wave synchronization may be observed during periods of relaxed mental states in one hemisphere during split-brain verbal and spatial tasks whereas theta-wave synchronization can be recorded during slow-wave sleep, in which the electroencephalographic rhythm may be coordinated with the heartbeat. 2. The coordination of the menstrual cycles of women who live together.

synchronized sleep   The type of sleep associated primarily with stages 2, 3, and 4 sleep, or deep-sleep states, when electroencephalographic recordings show slow synchronous (Delta) waves. The waves appear to follow a rhythm of cell activity; brain-cell metabolism is at a minimum level; and the brain is in a resting state. Also known as slow-wave sleep.

synchrony   1. In dance therapy, people moving together in harmony, which tends to bring people closer together. 2. Self-synchrony, or movement in relation to own speech. 3. Interactional synchrony, in which the movement of a listener is synchronous with the speech and movements of the speaker. 4. See POSTURAL ECHO.

syncope   (cutting short—Greek) A transient fainting spell resulting from cerebral anemia, due to sudden reduction in the blood supply to the brain (for example, feeling faint after standing up quickly after lying down or squatting).

syncretic thought   (J. Piaget) A prelogical stage of thinking in a child's life, characterized by egocentric and animistic thought processes; for example, if the sun shines brightly on a child's birthday, the child may think this is because it is the child's birthday. See PHYSIOGNOMIC THINKING, PRIMARY PROCESS, SYNCRETISM.

syncretism   The integration of diverse elements from two or more systems, theories, or concepts into a new system, theory, or concept.

syndrome   1. See DISEASE. 2. A constellation of symptoms and signs which together constitute a recognizable illness, physical or mental. Also known as symptom complex. Syndromes defined in this dictionary include: ABSTINENCE, ACQUIRED IMMUNE DEFICIENCY, ACROMEGALOID-HYPERTELORISM-PECTUS CARINATUM, ADAPTATION, AKINETIC-ABULIC, ALCOHOLIC BRAIN, ALINORMAL, AMNESIC DISORDER, AMNESIC-CONFABULATORY, AMOTIVATIONAL, ANDROGENITAL, ANGRY-WOMAN, ANTIMOTIVATIONAL, ANTON'S, ANTON-BABINSKI, APALLIC, APATHY, APERT'S, AROUSAL, AUTOSCOPIC PHENOMENON, BABINSKI'S, BATTERED-CHILD, BINGE-EATING, BLOCQ'S, BONNET'S, BORDERLINE DISORDERS, BRIQUET'S, BROWN-SÉQUARD, BUCCOLINGUAL MASTICATORY, CANNON'S EMERGENCY, CAPGRAS', CARPAL TUNNEL, CARPENTER'S, CAT-CRY, CAT'S-EYE, CHARLES BONNET'S, CHINA, CHRONIC BRAIN, CHRONIC FATIGUE, CHRONIC FATIGUE IMMUNE DYSFUNCTION, CINDERELLA, CLÉRAMBAULT'S, CLUMSY-CHILD, CONCENTRATION-CAMP, CONGENITAL-RUBELLA, COTARD'S, CRI DU CHAT, CRYING-CAT, CULTURAL, CULTURE-SPECIFIC, CUSHING'S, CYANOTIC SYNDROME OF SCHEI, DA COSTA'S, DE CLÉRAMBAULT, DELETION, DELILAH, DEPENDENCY, DEPERSONALIZATION, DISABILITY, DISASTER, DISCONNECTION, DISPLACED-CHILD, DON JUANISM/DON JUAN, DONAHUE'S, DONALD GREEN, DOWN'S, DYSMNESIC, EFFORT, EKBOM'S, EPISODIC DYSCONTROL, FAILURE-TO-GROW, FAILURE TO THRIVE, FEMINIZING-TESTES, FETAL-ALCOHOL, FETAL-TOBACCO, FRAGILE X, FRÖHLICH'S, FRONTAL-LOBE, GANSER('S), GENERAL-ADAPTATION, GILLES DE LA TOURETTE'S, GOITZ', GRAY-OUT, HAPPY-PUPPET, HOLIDAY, HOUSEWIFE'S/HOUSEBOUND HOUSEWIFE'S, HUGHLING JACKSON'S, HURRIED CHILD, HYPERACTIVE-CHILD, HYPERKINETIC, IMPOSTOR, INTENSIVE-CARE, JUMPING FRENCHMEN OF MAINE, KLINEFELTER'S, KLÜVER-BUCY, KORSAKOFF'S, LATERAL HYPOTHALAMIC, LESCH-NYHAN, MAIN'S, MALIN, MARFAN'S, MIDAS PUNISHMENT, MIDDLE-CHILD, MIXED ORGANIC BRAIN, MÜNCHAUSEN BY PROXY, MÜNCHHAUSEN, NARCOLEPSY-CATAPLEXY, NEONATAL DRUG DEPENDENCY, NEUROLEPTIC, NEUROLEPTIC MALIGNANT, NEUROTIC, NIGHT-EATING, NIGHTMARE-DEATH, NONSENSE, ORGANIC-AFFECTIVE, ORGANIC, ORGANIC BRAIN, ORGANIC-DELUSIONAL, ORGANIC

PERSONALITY, ORIENTAL NIGHTMARE-DEATH, OTH-ELLO, PERSECUTION, PHANTOM-LOVER, PICK-WICKIAN, POSTCONCUSSION, POSTCONCUSSIONAL, POSTTRAUMATIC, PÖTZL'S, PREMENSTRUAL (TEN-SION), PREMENSTRUAL-STRESS, PRISONER-OF-WAR REACTIONS, PSEUDOAMOK, PSEUDOMATURE, PSY-CHOMIMIC, PUERTO RICAN, RAMSAY HUNT'S, RAPE-TRAUMA, RAPTURE OF THE DEEP, RENPENNING'S, RESTLESS-LEG, RING D, RUBINSTEIN-TAYBI, SAN-FILIPO, SEASONAL AFFECTIVE DISORDER, SILVER-CORD, SOCIAL-ISOLATION, STOCKHOLM, STUPIDITY-MISERY, SUDDEN INFANT DEATH (SIDS), SUNDOWN, SUNRISE, SUPERWOMAN, SURVIVOR, TEMPORAL-LOBE, TESTICULAR-FEMINIZATION, TOURETTE'S, TURNER'S, VULNERABLE-CHILD, WERNER'S, WHITE-OUT, WRYNECK, XO, XXXX, XXXXX, XXXXY, XXXY, XY, XXYY, XYY.

synecdoche　A metaphor in which part of something is used for the whole or vice versa, such as "The fleet had fifty sails" (sails stands for boats), "All men are created equal" (men meaning humans), "ink flowed" (for a message).

synectics model　An educational approach that emphasizes creative problem-solving and the development of teaching methods that enhance student creativity, for example, encouraging metaphorical thinking. See AL-TERNATIVE EDUCATIONAL SYSTEMS, MONTESSORI SYSTEM.

synergic autonomy　A psychological balance of dependence and independence, with the ability to function effectively in either manner under appropriate conditions.

synergic marriage　A marriage enhanced by the contributions the partners make in satisfying each other's needs in a positive manner. See SYMBIOTIC MARRIAGE.

synergism　1. Interdependent relationship; working together. 2. A concept that ideas and reactions are the product of combinations of factors working together, reinforcing each other.

synergistic muscles　Muscles that work together to produce a specific action, such as flexion or extension of a limb. Synergistic muscles are classed according to homonymous reflex action, in which stimulation of a muscle causes contraction of that muscle, and heteronymous reflex action, in which stimulation begins in one muscle but causes another member of the synergistic-muscle group to contract.

synergistic　Pertaining to synergy.

synergogy　(J. S. Mouton, R. R. Blake) A combination of learner- and teacher-centered instruction based on self-responsibility, clear measures of performance, and a spirit of competition in a context of teamwork.

synergy　1. Coordination of forces or efforts to achieve a goal, for example, a group of muscles working together to move a limb. 2. (R. B. Cattell) The descriptive component in group syntality (total "personality" profile of a group) which expresses the total amount of a member's interest in the group.

synergy theory　(R. S. Woodworth) A point of view that mental synthesis is a unitary response, whether perceptual or motor, aroused by the aggregate of sensory or other elements, conceived as stimuli converging upon a single response mechanism.

synesthesia　(F. Galton, G. Fechner) An experience in which stimulation of one sensory modality also arouses sensations in another; for example, words or sounds (and sometimes tastes and odors) may be experienced as colors. Musical notes may yield specific colors. Or numbers are experienced as sounds. Also known as crossed perception, secondary sensation, synaesthesia. See CHROMESTHESIA.

synidetics　(F. B. Jones) The study of conscious experience relating to awareness of events that are simultaneously observable within the organism and its environment. The purpose is to determine the physiological and psychological factors that affect and are affected by awareness.

synkinesia　Involuntary movement that accompanies a voluntary action. Often a sign of neurologic damage, as in movement of paralyzed muscles when other muscles are contracted. Also known as synkinesis.

synnecrosis　In biology, the living together of two dissimilar organisms, a relationship detrimental to both. See SYMBIOSIS.

synomorphy　(R. G. Barker) The quality of the fit between the physical situation and the persons occupying it.

synonym-antonym test　A type of test in which the participant is given word pairs to be identified as equal or opposite in meaning.

synonyms　Two different words or terms with essentially the same meaning.

synopsia　A form of synesthesia in which visual sensations are closely associated with auditory sensations and appear regularly whenever the latter are stimulated, for example, hearing the middle C of a musical instrument and visualizing the color green. See SYNESTHESIA.

synoptic　1. Describing a brief sketch, or synopsis. 2. Refers to a form of synesthesia in which sounds are perceived as colors. See SYNOPSIA.

syntactical aphasia　Loss of ability to correctly communicate using grammar. A form of aphasia characterized by grammatical errors, particularly in the combinations or sequences of words in sentences.

syntactics　(C. W. Morris) The branch of semiotics that deals with the formal relations between signs, their signification (meaning), and the reaction to them by observers acting as interpreters of the signs.

syntality　(R. B. Cattell) The "personality" profile of a group.

syntax　One of the two major aspects of grammar having to do with the arrangement of word combinations to convey meaning, for example, the same five words in two combinations: "John threw Mary the ball." Or "Mary threw John the ball." The other major aspect of grammar is morphology.

syntaxic thinking　(H. S. Sullivan) Refers to the highest level of cognition, which includes logical, goal-directed, reality-oriented mentation; entails the use of symbols; and relies on consensual validation. Also known as syntaxic experience/mode/thought.

syntaxis　(H. S. Sullivan) Communications that are unmistakable, for example, (pointing to a cat) "That is a cat."

synthesis 1. A process of combining elements to form a whole. 2. The integration of personality factors such as attitudes, impulses, and traits into a coherent unified totality. This process requires a perception of own personality as a whole, reconciliation of conflicting values and tendencies, and the achievement of a balance among all aspects and levels of the psyche, both conscious and unconscious. See PERSONALITY DYNAMICS, PERSONALITY INTEGRATION, PSYCHOSYNTHESIS. 3. In problem-solving, deductive reasoning; adding up parts to gain a whole; reasoning from cause to effect. See COGNITIVE STYLE (meaning 1).

synthetic approach A perceptual method in which the observer tends to make judgments based on an integrated whole, as opposed to analysis of the parts. Experimental evidence indicates that individual personality factors are associated with synthetic and analytic perceivers.

synthetic causal model A multivariate causal model which depicts various causal weights and paths, the directionality of causal relationships, and interactions among causal variables. In this sense, "synthetic" means "integrative."

synthetic language A language developed for the purpose of its becoming a universal communication system, usually based on a simple grammatical system. Esperanto is an example of such a language, and it has been simplified by a revision called Ido.

synthetic narcotic Any compound created in a laboratory that provides pain relief. See MORPHINE, OPIOIDS, OPIUM.

synthetic speech Sounds that resemble speech but are made by machines.

synthetic trainer A device used to train persons under conditions that closely resemble actual operating situations. See LINK TRAINER, SIMULATOR.

synthetic validity An indicator of the validity of test sections to predict suitability to jobs. Such a test contains a number of items, each attempting to predict overall success for a specific job based on particular abilities or skills (for example, in the selection of salespeople, a high degree of verbal skills may be posited, but whether the skill is actually needed depends on first finding that successful and unsuccessful salespeople actually differ in verbal skills). See J-COEFFICIENT.

synthetism (P. Gauguin) An abstract painting style developed in the 1880s, characterized by brilliant colors separated by black lines. The art form was explained as an expression of ideas, moods, and emotions synthesized into an abstract illustration. Also known as cloisonnism.

synthonia 1. A personality trait characterized by emotional reactions to all kinds of stimuli, though such a person appears to be "normal." 2. Refers to a person apparently out of control, over-reacting to external stimuli, and who appears pre-manic on the bipolar continuum. See HYSTEROSYNTONIC.

syntone A "normal" person who is in emotional harmony with the social and physical environment. See HYSTEROSYNTONIC, SYNTONIA.

syntonia A personality trait of people who demonstrate considerable sensitivity to the environment.

syntonic Being in harmonious responsiveness to the social and physical environment. The condition of being syntonic is called syntony. The reverse of syntonic is dystonic.

syntropy (A. Meyer) Literally, turning together; a term used to characterize healthy, harmonious, mutually beneficial relationships and associations. See SYNTHESIS.

syphilis (lover of swine—Greek) A contagious venereal disease caused by infection with *treponema pallidum*. Term derives from the infected hero of a 16th-century poem by Fracastorius, a shepherd named Syphilus. Also known as lues. See BAYLE'S DISEASE, CEREBRAL SYPHILIS, CONGENITAL SYPHILIS, GENERAL PARESIS, INTRACRANIAL GUMMA, MENINGEAL SYPHILIS, WASSERMANN TEST.

syphilophobia Morbid fear of either contracting syphilis or having contact with syphilitics.

syringomyelia A disorder in which the pain and temperature senses are absent or defective in a particular part of the body due to disruption of the crossed ascending fibers of the spinal cord. See STATUS DYSRAPHICUS.

system 1. A set of elements organized to work together to perform a function. 2. A method of classification or procedure. 3. A set of facts and concepts that serve as the framework of a service or program.

system analysis The discovery and identification of sources of error or variability in a system, the measurement of these errors, and the arrangement of elements to improve system performance.

systematically biased sampling A sampling procedure not representative of the major traits of a population and which errs in a consistent manner, for example, drawing a sample from the dean's list of the senior class (top rated students) when the entire senior class is the population under study.

systematic approach Sigmund Freud's original division of the psyche (1913) into three "systems": The unconscious (Ucs), the conscious (Cs), and the preconscious (Pcs), which stands between the conscious and unconscious systems. Also known as descriptive approach, qualitative approach, topographic model. See DYNAMIC APPROACH, PSYCHIC APPARATUS.

systematic behavior theory See HULL'S BEHAVIOR SYSTEM, HULL'S THEORY.

systematic behavioral universal (W. J. Lonner) A theory about relationships that explains "if then outcomes" across cultures and organizations. The model and theory are universal, although when exceptions occur, they usually can be situations explained by the peculiarities of the culture or organization.

systematic desensitization (SD) 1. (M. C. Jones) A method of getting organisms (animals and humans) to lose an irrational fear, by gradually exposing the organism to what is feared. 2. (J. Wolpe) In behavior therapy, a counterconditioning procedure in which during a pleasant and relaxed state, a client is introduced to gradually unpleasant stimuli with the intention of reducing the anxiety associated with the unpleasant stimuli. See RECIPROCAL INHIBITION.

systematic determination The serial flow or progress of thought, which proceeds according to the principles of association.

systematic distortion   The process by which memory traces show gradual, progressive changes with time in an orderly pattern but differing from the reality. See LEVELING-SHARPENING.

systematic error   An error in data or conclusions that is regular and repeatable (unlike a chance error) due to improper collection or statistical treatment of the data. The error may be in calculation, in observation, in equipment, etc. See COMPENSATING ERROR.

systematic errors of observation   Alterations in the data collected in an investigation which occur persistently due to some general bias of the observer or to the method of conducting the investigation. A special case of this is constant error in which the alterations are all in one direction. See ACCIDENTAL ERRORS, PERSONAL EQUATION.

systematic evaluation   Operating "by the book" by routinely following a particular procedure in mental examinations, interviewing, etc.

systematic experimental introspection   The main method for the study of psychology started by Wilhelm Wundt about 1860–1970 in Germany under the general heading of structuralism, brought to America in the last years of the 19th century by E. B. Titchener, a student of Wundt. It was a method of inquiry of the contents of the conscious mind in which people were trained to be sensitive to their phenomenology and to report immediate sensory experiences to the psychologist who provided them with questions. Introspection and consequently structuralism was criticized simultaneously by Gestaltists, functionalists and behaviorists but is still used in a modified way by both experimentalists in inquiries about personal thinking during various experimental conditions and by psychotherapists. See STRUCTURALISM.

systematic experimental method   The gathering of data according to an objective, organized method that will yield reliable information about some aspect of behavior.

systematic observation   1. The intentional study of a phenomenon that constitutes the initial stage of a study, preceding the formation of hypotheses. 2. A procedure employed in research of naturally occurring events of looking at them and making exact reports, as in observing a child through a one-way window and speaking into a tape recorder to record every movement the child makes.

systematic random sampling   A planned sample based on both systematic selection processes and random selections.

systematic rational restructuring (SRR)   A system of psychotherapy in which the patients are encouraged to imagine anxiety-provoking situations while discussing them in a realistic manner with the expectation that this will allay their anxieties.

systematic reinforcement   Broad phrase denoting some form of consciously planned reinforcement. Phrase is nonspecific as to particular schedules of reinforcement.

systematics   biological taxonomy

systematic sampling   A type of probability sampling in which all population members can be accounted for and listed. The sample is systematically selected without bias, for example, listing all members alphabetically and then selecting every fifth name. See DOMAL SAMPLING.

systematized delusion   A false, irrational belief that is highly developed, superficially coherent and convincing, and resistant to change. Delusions characteristically found in paranoid states stand in sharp contrast to transient, fragmentary delusions that occur in delirium. Most delusions fall between these two extremes. See PARANOIA.

Système International (SI) d' Unités   French phrase for the International System of Units, an extension and refinement of the metric system.

system equation   A mathematical description of the characteristics of a system based on the relation of input to output.

systemic   1. Pertaining to a system. 2. Relating to a somatic condition of the entire organism or organ system rather than individual areas or parts.

systemic counseling (theory)   (T. Gunnings) An approach of counseling that emphasizes changing the social environment derived from the dominant racial group to meet the needs of minorities and to resolve racial conflicts that interfere with the adjustment and growth of minority individuals; it views the counselor as an advocate and agent of change.

systemic sense   Part of the nervous system that receives signals from receptors in the body's internal organs. Also known as interoceptive sense.

system justification   A tendency to support the present hierarchy of a social group or the status quo.

system model   See FAMILY MODEL.

system model of evaluation   In evaluation research, a method of assessing organizational effectiveness in terms of a working model of a social unit capable of achieving a goal, concerned with assessing the allocation of resources by the organization to reach an optimum level of operation.

System of Multicultural Pluralistic Assessment (SOMPA)   (J. R. Mercer & J. F. Lewis) A test designed to provide a fair method of evaluating children (ages 5–11 years) for their academic learning ability based on a combination of (a) physiological factors, (b) scores on a standard intelligence test as well as sociability, and (c) comparisons with other children of the same status. See SIX-HOUR RETARDATES.

system research   A discovery process of general principles applicable to the design and development of new systems, including instruments and machines.

systems analysis   An examination of any kind of system with interconnecting elements as to cost and efficiency.

systems theory   See GENERAL-SYSTEMS THEORY.

systole   The contractile phase of the cardiac cycle. Coinciding with the period between the first and second heart sounds. Compare DIASTOLE.

systolic blood pressure   The pressure of the blood against the arterial walls produced by the contraction of the heart ventricular muscles, as the blood is forced into the aorta and the pulmonary artery. See BLOOD PRESSURE.

s**yx**   Symbol for the sample standard error of estimate in regression.

syzygy   In analytical psychology, the melding of a male and female, often in the form of a divine couple. (From the Latin *syzygia* meaning "conjunction.")

Szondi Test   An unsubstantiated projective examination consisting of 48 photographs of psychiatric patients divided into six sets of eight types (sadistic, homosexual, epileptic, hysteric, catatonic, paranoiac, depressive, manic). One set is presented at a time, and the patient is instructed to select the two pictures liked best and the two disliked most. According to Lipot Szondi, these choices are determined by recessive hereditary factors and therefore reveal the patient's true personality. See FAMILIAL UNCONSCIOUS, FATE ANALYSIS, GENOTROPHISM.

T 1. In Rorschach test scoring, symbol for response time or time taken to complete. 2. Abbreviation for temperature, especially in Celsius degrees. See TEMPERATURE SCALES, TEMPERATURE SENSE. 3. Abbreviation for Time. 4. In psychophysics, a transition point. 5. Transmittance of radiant power, or radiant power transmission. 6. A point of change. 7. Abbreviation for total. 8. A Wilcoxon test statistic.

TA transactional analysis

tabes (dorsalis) (J. G. Brendel, R. Remak, J. A. Fournier, G. V. D. de Boulogne) A wasting disease of the posterior columns of the spinal cord marked by loss of muscular sensations and inability to make coordinated movements. M. H. von Romberg gave the first classical description of tabes dorsalis, but Jean Fournier reported syphilis as the cause. Also known as locomotor ataxia.

tabetic psychosis A psychotic state that occasionally occurs in cases of locomotor ataxia due to syphilis.

table A figure, usually of boxes made by horizontal and vertical lines, designed to organize, classify, or summarize information, usually numerical, in a visual form.

table of random numbers Generally a collection of numbers from zero to 9 arranged in a matrix, as in a 10 × 10 or other square distribution, with each space in the matrix having a digit there by pure chance, for example, the top left (or right bottom, etc.) corner for five up and down might be:

```
4 3 8 9 9
7 2 4 6 8
4 1 6 5 1
1 3 0 5 2
9 0 7 7 3
```

From such a list a person could select in advance any of the rows or columns for selecting odds and evens or other various combinations. Such tables are usually computer-generated and are considered to approach but not achieve perfection in being random.

table-tipping/turning In parapsychology, the levitation or other movements of tables during seances. See LEVITATION, SEANCE.

taboo (set apart—Tongan) 1. An object, person, word, or act that is at once sacred, dangerous, uncanny, and surrounded by religious prohibitions. 2. A conventional ban placed by tradition or custom upon certain acts, modes of dress, topics, or words in conversation, etc., the infringement of such convention being a matter not of legal prosecution but of social reproval and persecution.

Also known as *kapu, tabu, tapu*. See INCEST TABOO, VIRGINITY TABOO.

tabula rasa concept (blank slate—Latin) A view advanced by John Locke, that at birth the mind is a blank slate or tablet devoid of ideas, and that all knowledge is therefore derived from sensory experience. See EMPIRICISM.

tabulation An arrangement of a collection of data or results in tabular form, that is, in two or more columns (or rows).

tachisme (blot, stain—French) A form of painting in which fortuitous abstract patterns are sought by unconventional techniques. Allowing paint to be splashed, dribbled, trickled, or slapped randomly onto the canvas. The procedure is used in art therapy. Also known as action painting.

tachistoscope (A. W. Volkmann) An apparatus that exposes visual material on a screen for specified brief periods. Words, numbers, pictures, and symbols can be presented in the right, left, or both visual fields. Has experimental, diagnostic, and other practical uses; for example, it is sometimes used in training persons in speed-reading and remedial reading programs. Also known as tach, T-scope. See MEMORY DRUM for an example.

tachometer 1. A device that measures/indicates the rotary speed of a shaft, or sometimes the linear velocity of a liquid. 2. A device for measuring linear or angular velocity or change in velocity; most commonly applied to a manual instrument which, through the operation of centrifugal force and a hand on a dial, is used to measure the revolutions per minute of shafting. Also known as hematachometer, speedometer, speed counter.

tachophobia Fear of speed.

tachyathetosis A sense of uneasiness, twitching, or restlessness that occurs in the legs after retiring for the night. Also known as Ekbom's syndrome, restless-leg syndrome.

tachycardia Pathologically rapid heartbeat, often associated with drugs or anxiety. See ARRHYTHMIA.

tachylalia **tachylogia**

tachylogia 1. Rapid speech. Also known as tachylalia, tachyphasia, tachyphemia, tachyphrasia. 2. Abnormally rapid or fast excited speech. See PRESSURE OF SPEECH. 3. See TACHYPHEMIA (meaning 1).

tachyphagia   A morbid form of rapid eating observed in regressed patients with schizophrenia. Patients may place any object, food or inedible substances, in their mouths and then swallow it. See CISSA, PICA.

tachyphasia   tachylogia

tachyphemia   1. See TACHYLOGIA. 2. Speech characterized by persistent volubility and rapidity. May interfere with educational and emotional growth if left untreated. Similar to logorrhea. See PRESSURE OF SPEECH.

tachyphrasia   tachylogia

tachyphrenia   Rapid mental processes.

tachyphylaxis   An acute tolerance for a substance as indicated by progressively decreasing response to repeated administration. In a case of tachyphylaxis, the blood pressure of a patient might continue to rise despite repeated injections of a drug that normally would lower the blood pressure.

tachypnea   Rapid breathing. Also known as polypnea.

tachypsychia   Abnormally rapid action of psychological processes.

tacit   Assumed or agreed upon implicitly, that is, without being actually stated in words, and often without being recognized, such as a tacit assumption.

tacit knowledge   Knowing how rather than knowing what. Ability to understand a concept or perform a skill even though a person may be unable to explain the fundamentals to someone else. Compare FORMAL ACADEMIC KNOWLEDGE.

tact   1. A social convention in which a concept is phrased so as not to upset or hurt the feelings of others. May involve the use of euphemistic terms such as "passed away" (for death), "erratic" or "eccentric" (for mentally ill). 2. (B. F. Skinner) Relating to verbalizations which name, symbolize, or otherwise represent aspects of the person's world. See MAND, SOCIAL RULES AND STANDARDS.

tactic   Pertaining to taxis.

tactile   Pertaining or relating to the sense of touch. Also known as tactual.

tactile agnosia   Inability to recognize objects or forms by touch. Also known as astereognosis, finger agnosia. See AMORPHOSYNTHESIS, APHASIA, ASYMBOLIA.

tactile amnesia   A loss of the ability to judge the shape of objects by touch, due to brain injury or disease. A form of astereognosis.

tactile circle   An area of the skin where two tactile stimuli presented simultaneously are perceived as a single stimuli.

tactile hallucination   A false perception of touch, as in feeling an electric shock, being masturbated by an invisible hand, or being bitten by fleas, all in the absence of any observable stimuli. Also known as haptic hallucination, tactual hallucination.

tactile illusion   An illusion in the field of cutaneous sensation. Also known as tactual illusions. See ARISTOTLE'S ILLUSION.

tactile perception   An ability to perceive sensations from nerve receptors that react to touch stimuli. Touch stimuli generally involve contact with the skin or mucous membranes. Other cutaneous sensations, for example, itch and tickle, are due to mild stimulation of pain receptors. Cold and warmth also are cutaneous sensory qualities.

tactile-perceptual disorder   A condition due to brain damage resulting in difficulty in discrimination of sensations that involve touch receptors. People with this disorder may be unable to determine the shape, size, texture, or other physical aspects of an object merely by touching it.

tactile receptors   See MEISSNER'S CORPUSCLES, MERKEL'S DISKS.

tactile sensation/sense   See TOUCH SENSATION.

tactile stimulation   Activation of a sensory receptor by a touch stimulus. Compare TACTUAL STIMULATION.

tactile tests   Any of a variety of performance, memory, or discrimination tests in which the participant uses touch only. For instance, in B. Milner's test of immediate memory, blindfolded participants are handed (left and right separately) wires formed into nonsense shapes, and required to match them with the same or opposite hand.

tactual   1. Pertaining to or caused by touch. 2. See TACTILE.

tactual localization   The indication of points on the skin that have been touched by an experimenter when the participant is blindfolded. See LOCAL SIGNS.

tactual sensation   See TOUCH SENSATION.

tactual shape discrimination   Ability to determine shapes of objects by touch alone, such as differentiating between a cylinder and a sphere when unable to see the objects.

tactual size discrimination   Ability to judge the comparative size of two objects that cannot be seen and may be evaluated through the sense of touch. Used as a test for the possible presence of a cortical lesion that would interfere with this ability.

tactual stimulation   The identification of material by means of touch. Compare TACTILE STIMULATION.

Tadoma method   (S. Alcorn) A technique of communicating with people who are both hearing- and vision-impaired; they place their fingers on the cheek and neck, and their thumbs on the mouth, of a speaker and translate the vibrations and muscle movements into words. The name is derived from Tad Chapman and Oma Simpson, the first students of Sophia Alcorn (who originated the technique in the 1930s) to be instructed by this method.

taeniophobia   Morbid fear of tapeworms, of having tapeworms.

Taft-Hartley Act   In American labor relations, restrictions legislated in 1947 against unfair practices of unions such as illegal picketing and refusing to bargain. Set the pattern for North American labor legislation for the next 25 years.

TAG   talented and gifted

tagging   Attaching a radioactive isotope to a molecule for the purpose of tracing the molecule's pathway through body tissues. For example, if nicotine is tagged with a radioactive isotope the path of the nicotine may be traced through the lungs and bloodstream of the smoker. See RADIOACTIVE ISOTOPES, RADIOACTIVE TRACERS.

tag question 1. In linguistics, a question requesting confirmation at the end of an otherwise declarative sentence. In English, if the statement is positive, the tag is negative; if the statement is negative, the tag is positive, for example, "It's cold, isn't it?" and "She won't do that, will she?" During the fourth year, most children develop the ability to ask a tag question correctly. 2. In interviewing, a follow-up question.

T'ai Chi Ch'uan Ancient Chinese martial art meditation used for centering, grounding, and balancing the body. A form of *Ch'uan* (indicative of a person's power to control thoughts and actions) in which specific mind-exercises are used to implement and complement the body's activities. The physical system of exercise is comprised of a number of slow, repetitive, circular movements, done while standing-up; the whole exercise takes about 20 minutes. Also known as circular gymnastics. Also called T'ai chi.

tails of a distribution Upper and lower extremes of a sample distribution that together or separately may be used as limits for rejection in hypothesis testing. One-tailed tests are used when the hypothesis is directional (when it states that a population mean is greater than or equal to, or that it is less than or equal to, another population mean). A two-tailed test is used to explore whether there is a difference without specifying direction. Rejection of a null hypothesis in either the one-tailed or two-tailed test is commonly described in terms of either the 1% or 5% level of significance.

takt time 1. Japanese-English phrase for the time between products coming off an assembly line. 2. The time allowed or taken to perform one set of tasks assigned to each employee.

Talbot (Q) A unit of radiant light energy. Named after English inventor William Talbot (1800–1877). See TALBOT-PLATEAU LAW.

Talbot-Plateau law (W. Talbot) A theory that if a light flickers so rapidly that it is perceived as continuous, its brightness will be reduced by the ratio between the period when the light actually is on and reaches the eye and the whole period.

talent A high level of inborn ability in a special area, for example, music, which can be enhanced by training or practice to a greater level of proficiency. See ABILITY, GENIUS.

talented and gifted (TAG) Phrase used in schools primarily to identify children believed to be particularly apt for advanced programs.

talion Retaliation; especially in kind, according to the biblical injunction "an eye for an eye, a tooth for a tooth." The talion law/principle plays an important part in psychoanalytic theory, since it includes the general idea of retribution for defying the superego, and the specific fear (talion dread) that all injury, accidental or intentional, will be punished in kind, such as a voyeur being afflicted with a visual disturbance. See LOGICAL CONSEQUENCES, NATURAL CONSEQUENCES.

talion dread Symbolic anxieties that represent the unconscious fear of penalties or retribution for an act. See TALION.

talion law/principle See TALION.

talisman A figure, inscription, or object of any sort that is believed to possess magical properties favorable to the possessor.

talking books Audio recordings of persons (often with professional speaking experience) reading print material, once produced mainly for the benefit of persons with visual or physical challenges. Typically, copies of these books were mailed to such individuals who were provided with special audio equipment. Nowadays, books-on-tape, as they are more commonly called, are widely available and are popular with a broad mainstream "readership."

talking cure 1. Phrase coined by Sigmund Freud, but the method was devised and used by Joseph Breuer in his treatment of a patient (Anna O). 2. A derogatory characterization of psychoanalysis based on the idea that the technique involves only the verbal expression of feelings and recollections. See VERBALIZATION.

talking-fear See LALOPHOBIA.

talking (it) out Common phrase for freely ventilating personal conscious problems and immediate feelings. Anxious, upset individuals may gain temporary relief through verbally unburdening themselves and "letting off steam," but in effective therapy patients give voice to what is innermost in their minds, not what is uppermost.

talking typewriter An archaic machine (replaced by the computer) designed for use by persons with visual challenges. When the key for a letter or number is pressed, an electronic device emits the sound of the symbol.

tall tales See CONFABULATION, PATHOLOGICAL LYING, PSEUDOLOGIA FANTASTICA.

tambo(u)r A membrane, usually flexible, used on certain recording devices. It is sensitive to pressure changes and moves a stylus to produce a written record. See KYMOGRAPH.

tambour-mounted cage A research device which indicates its occupant's activity by wobbling as the caged animal moves.

taming See NEUTRALIZATION.

TAND See TANDEM SCHEDULE OF REINFORCEMENT.

tandem In psychotherapy of a couple, the seeing of each partner successively. Compare CONJOINT.

tandem schedule of reinforcement (TAND) An intermittent-reinforcement schedule in which a single reinforcement is contingent upon successful completion of two units of behavior. Also known as tandem reinforcement schedule.

tandem therapy In marriage therapy, the practice of the therapist seeing the partners separately. Compare CONJOINT THERAPY.

T and V (R. W. Brown & A. Dolman) Symbols used generally for familiar and formal second-person pronouns of address (for example, *Tu* and *Vous* in French, Thou and You).

tangential speech A mode of speaking in which a speaker does not keep on the topic but keeps on generating asides and often is not able to remember what was originally the topic; constantly "going of on tangents."

tangential thinking   A thought disturbance in the associative thought process in which the patient tends to "jump" from the topic under discussion to other topics which arise in the course of associations. In extreme form it is a manifestation of loosening of associations, a symptom most frequently found in certain types or organic brain disorders. Also known as tangentiality. See CIRCUMSTANTIALITY.

tangent screen   A black screen, which may be a sheet of black felt material, used for testing or plotting the area a participant can see while looking straight ahead as the examiner moves a light or small white object about the periphery of the participant's field of view. The participant reports whether or not the light or object can be seen, and the point on the tangent screen is marked.

T-anger   (C. Spielberger) Abbreviation of trait anger.

tantra   (to weave together—Sanskrit) In North America, a catchall word for various spiritual/metaphysical practices, often with an erotic component.

tantric fusion   The first phase in tantric union during which a couple meditates while having sexual intercourse. The two supposedly surrender their egos and merge into one being while lying completely motionless and relaxed and experiencing the flow of life energy (prana) between them. The individual selves transcend time and death and share in the immortal being of the Divine Self.

tantric sex   A sexual practice as part of the Hindu system of tantra yoga. After the insertion of the penis into the vagina, neither party moves, each sublimating their sexual desires while meditating. Ideally, there is no release of semen by the male. The union is believed to represent the merging of Shiva and Shakti (*kundalini*) in the state of enlightenment. See KAREZZA.

Tantrism   See HINDU TANTRISM.

tantrum   A temper tantrum.

tanyphonia   An abnormally thin, weak, and metallic voice caused by excessive tension in the vocal apparatus. Also known as thin voice.

Taoism   A Chinese philosophy that emphasizes harmony with the course of nature. See YIN AND YANG.

tap   In linguistics, the sound made by rapidly touching the tip of the tongue to the back of the teeth. In English, taps are always voiced, and usually spelled with a t or d.

tape feed   In computers, a mechanism that feeds tape to be read or used by a machine.

tapering   Decreasing the amount of medicine used gradually, over days, weeks, or even months, rather than just stopping abruptly.

tapetum   1. In general, any membranous layer. 2. A light-reflecting layer in the retina of many animals. Kinds of tapetum include *tapetum lucidum* in elasmobranchs (rays, sharks), *tapetum fibrosum* in ungulates (hoofed animals), and *tapetum cellulosum*, in carnivores and lower primates. Absent in humans. Plural is tapeta.

tapeworm fear   See TAENIOPHOBIA.

taphophobia   taphephobia

taphophilia   Morbid attraction for cemeteries. See NECROMANIA, NECROPHILIA.

taphophobia   Morbid fear of graves or of being buried alive. Also spelled taphephobia.

tapping board   An apparatus for measuring manual tapping performance; it usually consists of a metal plate on which the participant taps with a metal stylus, the taps being registered.

tapping test   A task in which the participant is directed to make (usually with a pencil or metal stylus) as many taps as possible within a given time limit. A test with high reliability and unknown validity with anything useful. See DOTTING TEST.

tarant(ul)ism   1. Any mental disorder that leads people to hop about in what may appear to be a kind of dance. 2. (G. Baglivi) A hysterical dancing mania in epidemic form that occurred primarily in Italy during the 15–17th centuries then believed due to being bitten by the spider *Lycosa tarantula*. See CHOREOMANIA, MASS HYSTERIA.

Tarasoff decision   A legal decision by the California Supreme Court (in the case of a patient who confided to his therapist an intention to kill a friend and later did so) that a therapist who knows or reasonably believes that a patient poses a threat to a third party must warn or otherwise protect the latter from violence and the threat of violence. Similar cases have been decided variously in other jurisdictions, which in some cases have enacted statutes covering such a situation. The American Psychological Association ethics guidelines endorse the Tarasoff decision in clinical practice. See CONFIDENTIALITY.

taraxein   (R. G. Heath, S. Martens, B. E. Leach, M. Cohen & C. Angel) A protein substance obtained from blood samples of patients with schizophrenia. Investigators have claimed that the substance produces symptoms of schizophrenia when injected into normal persons. Analysis of taraxein indicates it contains a copper compound. See ANTIBRAIN ANTIBODY.

Tarchanoff phenomenon   (I. R. Tarchanoff) A form of galvanic skin response, a reaction to certain stimuli by a change in electrical resistance of the skin, particularly on the palms. The effect is produced by activity of the sweat glands and may occur as a reaction to certain stimuli especially those that generate emotional arousal. Sometimes known as electrodermal response (EDR), Féré phenomenon, galvanic skin response (GSR), psychogalvanic reflex (PGR). Compare FÉRÉ PHENOMENON. See GALVANIC SKIN RESPONSE, LIE DETECTOR, PSYCHOGALVANIC SKIN-RESISTANCE AUDIOMETRY.

tardive   1. Late. 2. A condition related to an illness or disorder of some kind, that shows up long after the beginning of the pathological condition.

tardive (oral) dyskinesia (TD or TOD)   A syndrome consisting of potentially irreversible, involuntary, spasmodic movements, mainly thrusting or chewing movements of the tongue and mouth, lip pursing, cheek puffing, writhing movements of hands and trunk. Tends to occur as a side effect of the use of neuroleptic drugs, usually after use for a long time and in older people, but occasionally with smaller doses in certain patients who are apparently more susceptible to this effect. Dyskinesia means dysfunctional movement. See DYSTONIA.

target 1. That which is aimed for. 2. Refers to a search or a resultant "hit," as in a malicious statement although made to a group of people, is directed at only one person, the target. 3. In medicine, a particular pill is aimed at (targeted) at a specific organ or to other specific part of the body.

target behaviors In behavior therapy, the selected behaviors that client and therapist are trying to encourage, eliminate, or modify.

target language 1. A foreign language being taught, or the artificial (for example, computer) language system that is being acquired. 2. The language into which a translation is made. Compare SOURCE LANGUAGE.

target patient In structured interactional group psychotherapy, the member who becomes the focus of special attention and discussion. In some cases, the person targeted is critically assessed (may feel verbally attacked) by all other members.

target population In making selections of subjects or participants from a larger population, deciding which types of people are to be studied, for example, Asians, females, ages 15 to 19.

target range 1. On a project, the established minimal standards for acceptance. 2. In research, the outcome variation that is expected, acceptable, or desirable.

target response The designated response, response sequence, or behavior that constitutes the goal of shaping. It is the desired result of the shaping process. See SHAPING.

target stimulus In a test or experimental procedure, a specific stimulus to which subjects must attend. For example, in tests of hearing, a specific tone that must be identified.

target test **aiming test**

Tartar type Obsolete phrase referring to people with Down syndrome, whose facial features have been likened to those of Mongols or Tartars. See MONGOLOIDISM, TRISOMY 21 SYNDROME.

Tartini('s) tone (G. Tartini) A third tone heard if two notes are sounded hard; a difference tone, or a third tone generated by two original tones of different frequencies, with a frequency equal to the difference between the two original frequencies. Also known as difference tone.

task According to J. B. Carroll, any activity in which a person engages, given an appropriate setting to achieve a specifiable class of objectives, final results, or terminal states of affairs. See AUFGABE. Types of task include: ACADEMIC INTELLIGENCE, CARD-SORTING, COGNITIVE, CONJUNCTIVE, DELAYED MATCHING-TO-SAMPLE, DETECTION, DEVELOPMENTAL, DISTRACTING, DOUBLE-ALTERNATION, FALSE BELIEF, INTERPOLATED, LEXICAL-DECISION, LIFE, MONOCHRONIC, PAIRED ASSOCIATE, POLYCHRONIC, PRACTICAL INTELLIGENCE, PROPAEDEUTIC, ROTARY-PURSUIT, SENSORY INFORMATION, SERIAL-LEARNING, SIGNAL-DETECTION, WORD-FRAGMENT COMPLETION.

task analysis 1. The breakdown of a topic into its component skills, required knowledge, and specific operations to identify what skills and knowledge must be possessed to master the topic. 2. (A. Newell & H. A. Simon) Task analysis undertakes to provide a complete characterization of a task environment and the various problem spaces that can be used to seek problem solutions in the environment. See PROBLEM SPACE, TASK ENVIRONMENT, TASK INVENTORY.

task cycle theory (C. L. Wilson) In organizational psychology, a view that there is a sequence of skills that, when displayed by a leader, provides signs and meaning to the group members regarding the task set for them. Derived form E. C. Tolman's cognitive learning paradigm.

task demands A set of established procedures for accomplishing a particular task that may be as simple as how to change a tire on a car to how to do a heart transplant. See JOB DESCRIPTION.

task environment (A. Newell & H. A. Simon) An objective characterization of the task confronting an individual, as distinguished from the problem spaces (problem representations and actions) that the individual generates while seeking to accomplish the task. See PROBLEM SPACE.

task force An ad hoc group established for an emergency special purpose, such as a committee formed to help people who have been rendered homeless due to a hurricane.

task inventory In industrial psychology, a list of the specific tasks required by a job or position. Also known as job inventory. See TASK ANALYSIS.

task-oriented Descriptive of a person who concentrates entirely on a project of some kind, is oblivious to anyone talking, music playing, people passing by, or any other usual distractors.

task-oriented approach/reaction A realistic manner of coping with stressors as opposed to dependence on an ego-defensive approach.

task-oriented dialogue understanding system (TDUS) A communication system for person-machine dialogue designed to aid repair operations on electromechanical equipment.

task-oriented group An aggregate of persons primarily devoted to solving a problem, creating or producing a product, or other goal-directed behavior.

task significance In work activities, feeling that what is being done is meaningful. For example, during a war, employees in Company X, that have been induced to assume the mindset that they are making airplanes, had lower morale, motivation, and efficiency than employees of Company Y, who had been indoctrinated to say that they were helping to win the war.

task structure The clarity or ambiguity of a task. If there is only one obvious way to perform it and the correctness can be seen easily, there would be high task structure.

task substitution (K. Lewin) A research procedure for studying the relationships of personality tension-systems which involve the replacement of one task by another.

task synergy See SYNERGY.

taste   1. To perceive with the gustatory nerves. 2. A sensation produced by stimulation of the taste buds in the mouth. It depends upon molecules of food substances entering pores or other openings in and around taste buds where they react chemically with receptors to trigger nerve impulses. The taste experienced is influenced by the type of receptor and the concentration of flavor substance. See GUSTATION, HENNING'S TASTE TETRAHEDRON, SWEET TASTE, SALT TASTE, TONGUE, WATER AS TASTE.

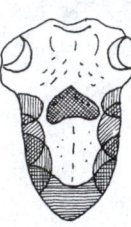

taste   Four different taste areas found on the tongue.

taste adaptation   Continued ingestion of a particular substance, such as mustard, tends to gradually lead to a general loss of sensation for that substance. Seen in some people who habitually eat (and actually enjoy) hot peppers, whereas other people may experience extreme pain in their mouths when tasting the same kinds of peppers for the first time. Were they to continue eating these peppers, the burning sensation would eventually lessen for most people.

taste aversion   Learned avoidance of foods or any particular food, for any reason. See LEARNED TASTE AVERSION.

taste blindness   An inability to taste certain substances at normal concentrations but usually able to taste the substance at high concentrations. For example, unable to taste sugar when a tablespoon of sugar is in a pint of water, but able to taste sugar when a teaspoon of sugar is in a tablespoon of water.

taste bud   A sensory receptor containing gustatory cells, located primarily on the tongue but occasionally present in other areas of the mouth in different species. Some catfish have 100,000 taste buds over their whole bodies, whereas chickens have only 24 taste buds. A human adult has approximately 10,000.

taste cell   A cell found mostly in the tongue that conveys information to the brain about what has been put in the mouth. See GUSTATORY NERVE.

taste fear   See GEUMAPHOBIA.

taste solitary tract   A neural pathway that receives impulses from a receptor that is differentially sensitive to only a single kind of taste stimuli.

taste tetrahedron   A graphic representation in the shape of a tetrahedron showing the relationships of the four basic tastes: sweet, sour, salty, bitter.

TAT   Thematic Apperception Test

ta-ta theory   See ORIGIN-OF-LANGUAGE THEORIES.

tau   The nineteenth letter of the Greek alphabet. See APPENDIX C.

tau coefficient of correlation   Kendall's Tau

tau effect   (H. Helson) A phenomenon by which timing of stimulation of sensory organs (skin surfaces, eyes, or ears) influences perception of the distance between the stimuli. For instance, if the time between the first and second stimulus is shorter than that between the second and third, the first two stimuli are perceived as being closer together spatially. Such phenomena exist even when a participant knows that stimuli are equally distant.

taurophobia   Morbid fear of bulls.

tautology   Repetition of the same word or phrase, or of a literal equivalent in the same sentence.

tautophone   A projective device consisting of a recording of random indistinct vocal sounds which the participant is asked to interpret.

Tavistock Institute   In England an organization that propounds humanistic, as well as psychoanalytic, approach to organizational theory as found, for example, in therapy groups.

taxa   Plural of taxon.

taxes   Plural of taxis.

taxinomy   **taxonomy** (meaning 1)

taxis   1. Systematic classification by arrangement of phenomena in an orderly fashion. See TAXONOMY. 2. The movement of motile organisms in response to a stimulus. Considered to be an instinctive, directed reaction to a stimulus; it can be positive as when the organism is drawn toward the stimulus or negative when the organism is repelled. Kinds of taxes include chemotaxis (movement influenced or directed by chemicals in the environment), geotaxis (movement toward the earth), klinotaxis (movement interrupted by pauses to evaluate stimuli sources), phototaxis (movement toward a light source), tropotaxis (movement in a direct path toward a source, such as a food smell). Different types of taxes involve different mechanisms. Taxis differs somewhat from tropism, which tends to be an involuntary reaction to a natural force such as light or gravity and usually refers to plants. 3. The involuntary movement or orientation of an organism (usually a type of fauna) toward (positive taxis) or away (negative taxis) from a source of stimulation. See KINESIS, TROPISM.

taxometric analysis   (P. Meehl) The application of cluster and latent class methods to the investigation of taxa (that is, nonarbitrary classes).

taxometrics   Any formal mechanical, mathematical, or algorithmic method for identifying taxa (that is, nonarbitrary classes) and for classifying individual entities into or out of the taxa.

taxon   A taxonomic group. Plural is taxa.

Taxonome Program   According to Raymond Cattell, a program which operates on a matrix of interpersonal pattern similarity coefficients to reveal statistical and trait types. Also known as Taxonomy Program.

taxonomy   1. A system of classifying items according to their natural relationships. Once spelled taxinomy. 2. The systematic ordering and identifying of groups. See BIOLOGICAL TAXONOMY. 3. The classification of plants and animals based on commonalities of structures and functions. For instance the classification of humans is Kingdom Animal (separated from plants); Phylum Chordata (having a spine); Class Mammals (nourishing their young with milk); Order Primates (having relatively large and complex brain); Family Hominidae (tool-makers); Genus Homo (walks upright); and Species (subdivisions from *homo habilis* to modern *homo sapiens*).

taxonomy of educational objectives (B. S. Bloom) The general aims or goals of formal education which are: knowledge (of facts), comprehension, application, analysis, synthesis and evaluation.

Taylor's manifest anxiety scale See MANIFEST ANXIETY SCALE.

Taylor-Russell Tables (H. C. Taylor & J. T. Russell) These tables, rarely used, are intended to assist people in making decisions about which tests to use in making selections in industrial employment.

Taylor system **Taylorism**

Taylorism The prototype system of scientific management, improving industrial efficiency through the use time-and-motion and similar studies. Frederick Taylor first applied his rational, engineering approach to the industrial workplace in 1881. Also known as scientific management, Taylor system.

Tay-Sachs disease (TSD) An autosomal-recessive disorder affecting primarily Ashkenazi Jews of central and eastern European origin. A neurological disease marked by progressive degeneration of the cortical neurons. Possibly due to a deficiency of hexosaminidase A enzyme. Motor-nerve development is normal until the sixth month of infancy, followed by a loss of acquired skills. Symptoms include loss of vision, increasing muscular weakness and paralysis, and mental retardation. Children who survive beyond the age of two tend to be bedridden and fail to respond to stimulation; death often occurs before the age of five. Named after British physician Warren Tay (1843–1927), and American neurologist Bernard P. Sachs (1858–1944). Also known as familial amaurotic idiocy, GM2 gangliosidosis, infantile amaurotic idiocy.

TBR See TO-BE-REMEMBERED ITEMS.

TC therapeutic community

TCA See TRICYCLIC ANTIDEPRESSANTS.

T-cells Immune system cells that directly attack intruder cells or stimulate added response by other immune system cells.

TCP Slang for analog of phencyclidine.

TD Abbreviation for tardive dyskinesia. See TARDIVE (ORAL) DYSKINESIA.

T-data (R. B. Cattell) 1. Information gathered from test situations in which a person taking an objective test is not told which aspects of behavior are being observed or evaluated. 2. Objective test data in individual personality description. Contrasted with Q-data from questionnaires.

TDD system See TELECOMMUNICATION DEVICES FOR THE DEAF.

t-distributions An important family of symmetrical distributions, which vary from the normal distributions and are used as the basis for exact tests of significance when working with small samples. When samples are large, t-distributions approximate the normal distribution. See STUDENT'S T.

TDUS See TASK-ORIENTED DIALOGUE UNDERSTANDING SYSTEM.

TE 1. time error. 2. See TRIAL-AND-ERROR LEARNING.

teachable language comprehender (TLC) (M. R. Quillian) A computer program designed to "extract and somehow retain meaning from natural language text." It assumes a hierarchical network of links between concepts, which are represented as nodes in the network.

teacher effectiveness evaluation Methods of deciding the usefulness of teachers. Subjective methods include asking others, principally students themselves. Objective methods include testing students for the amount of learning they display.

teaching games Classroom instruction in the form of games designed to engage students' active interest as they work on specific skills, for example, vocabulary or mathematics games. Teaching games provide incentives to students in the form of rewards or the pleasure of winning.

teaching machine An instrument that (a) automatically presents programmed material to the learner; (b) provides an opportunity to check understanding at each step through problems or questions; (c) feeds back information to the learning whether the response is correct or incorrect; and (d) directs the person to another suitable item. Some of these "machines" are books that keep the student moving from page to page depending on whether answers are correct or incorrect. Also known as learning machines. See BRANCHING PROGRAM, COMPUTER-AIDED INSTRUCTION.

teaching model See DEVELOPMENTAL TEACHING MODEL.

teaching style Those personal attributes that define a teacher's classroom methods and behavior. Some qualities associated with teacher effectiveness are mastery of subject matter, pedagogical thinking, organizational ability, enthusiasm, warmth, calmness, and the establishment of rapport with students.

teaching styles (K. T. Henson & P. Borthwick) According to these authors, there are six different specific styles of teaching: child-centered, cooperative planner, emotionally exciting, learning-centered, subject-centered, task-oriented.

team approach A multidisciplinary approach to diagnosis and therapy combining the services of psychiatrists, clinical psychologists, psychiatric social workers, and other specialized personnel such as movement, occupational, and recreational therapists.

teamwork 1. Working together toward a common goal or on a common project. In developmental psychology, a six-year-old child may participate in loosely organized games with several children; in first grade, a class is divided into small groups; by fourth grade children are capable of acting as a group. Thereafter, teams and clubs with complex rules develop rapidly. 2. In industrial psychology, the cooperative effort of formal or informal groups.

tearoom trade British slang for homosexual interactions in public places.

tears Fluid secreted by the lacrimal glands to keep the conjunctiva and cornea of the eyes moist. See BOGORAD'S SYNDROME, CROCODILE TEARS, CRYING.

teasing   Social behavior by which an individual, though adopting a playful attitude, intentionally induces in another a feeling of annoyance.

tectorial membrane   In the cochlea of the ear, a rigid flap of tissue that extends over the hair cells like a porch roof and contains a gelatinous substance in which the hair cells are embedded. Comprises, along with the basilar membrane and hair cells, the organ of Corti. Also known as Corti's membrane, techtorial membrane, tectorium.

technical   Pertaining to some branch of science or art especially to the practical details rather than to principle or theory.

technical term   A word or phrase used in any science in a specialized way, to denote some datum, method, or other subject-matter comprised within the given field.

technique   1. A characteristic way of achieving a given end by specially skilled manual activity or other bodily activities as distinguished from mere verbalization. 2. A manner of performance or the details of performance of a specific phenomenon or act (such as experimentation, testing).

technological gatekeeper   A person more informed than others in the relevant literature, a person who has better contacts with experts, or both.

technological illiteracy   Refers to the inability of some people to function in an increasingly technical society. See COMPUTER ILLITERACY.

techtorial membrane   **tectorial membrane**

tectal nuclei   Nerve cells located in the superior and inferior colliculi of the corpora quadrigemina. They receive fibers from the upper neurons of the lateral lemniscal system, inherited from the afferent-nerve system of primitive ancestors.

tectum   (roof—Latin) 1. In general, any rooflike structure. Plural is tecta. 2. In the midbrain, a part that is the "roof" to distinguish the structure from the "floor" of the midbrain. It contains the superior colliculi sensory centers for visual impulses and the inferior colliculi sensory centers for auditory impulses.

teeter-totter effect   (H. H. Mosak) A tendency for two siblings, especially those who have been in competition as children, that if one is successful the other becomes a failure.

tegmentum   (covering structure—Latin) 1. In general, a covering structure. Plural is tegmenta. 2. In the midbrain, a part of the cerebral peduncle above the substantia nigra and a structure associated with sensory and motor tracts passing through the midbrain. Also known as tegmentum mesencephali.

teichopsia   **scintillating scotoma**

telalgia   Pain experienced in a different place from where the source of the pain is located.

tele   (J. L. Moreno) A feeling projected toward others. Described as a psychic force leading to relationships between people, such that "there is a chemistry between them." Positive tele equals attraction for and negative tele means repulsion. Tele is the unit of measurement in sociometry. See FRIENDSHIP, LOVE.

tele(o)stereoscope   A device for viewing distant objects, useful for studying convergence and disparity in depth perception. A series of mirrors are placed so that distant objects or pictures appear to be closer to the viewer than they actually are.

telebinocular   A type of stereoscope used in visual tests.

teleceptor   A receptor for distant stimuli, for example, the eye or ear. Also known as teleoceptor. See DISTANT RECEPTOR.

telecommunication devices for the deaf (TDD)   Apparatus that sends, receives, and prints messages. Sometimes known as TDD systems.

telecommuting   White-collar employment that the worker performs at home, typically linked to the employer by computer.

telegnosis   In parapsychology, alleged knowledge of distant events without direct communication, as a form of clairvoyance.

telegony   Supposed influence of an earlier impregnation upon the character of the same mother's later offspring by another male.

telegrammatism   The reduction of a spoken message to words conveying basic meaning, analogous to a telegram message of old.

telegrapher's cramp   A painful spasm in the fingers making it impossible to operate a telegraphic key. See CARPAL-TUNNEL SYNDROME, OCCUPATIONAL NEUROSIS.

telegraphic speech   1. Language that gets the point across although many parts of the message have been omitted. 2. (R. W. Brown) Descriptive phrase for the speech of young children in the "duo-stage," roughly between the ages of 18 and 30 months when most speech is in the form of two-word expressions known as duos. Such speech uses only the most germane and prominent features of language while by-passing articles, prepositions, and other ancillary words. See DUOS, PIDGIN ENGLISH.

telekinesis   1. Motion of objects allegedly produced from afar by force of will. 2. Levitation or movement of objects attributed to occult forces. Such incidents are purported to occur mostly in homes where adolescent males reside. Also known as psychokinesis.

telelic change   Voluntarily accepting new information related to achieving a personal goal. For example, a student registered for a course in Latin after being told that to become a lawyer, Latin was necessary; informed by a vocational counselor that Latin was no longer necessary to become a lawyer, the student withdrew registration.

telemetry   1. The science of measuring a quantity. 2. The transmission of information about an organism, whether of physiological variables or simply its location, over distances. 3. A method of obtaining information about organisms using electric impulses that can travel over great distances. For example, in marine biology research, small radio transmitters are implanted in sharks and whales. Humans are also sometimes tracked using radio transmitters locked to an ankle, especially those who have been put under house arrest.

telencephalic   Pertaining to the telencephalon or endbrain.

telencephalic sleep   **nonrapid-eye movement sleep**

telencephalic vesicles   Paired diverticula that develop from the prosencephalic brain vesicle at the anterior end of the neural tube about the end of the fifth week of gestation and give rise to the cerebral cortex, the subcortical white matter, the olfactory bulb and tract, the basal ganglia (including the amygdala) and the hippocampus. See FOREBRAIN.

telencephalon   The anterior end of the brain considered from the developmental standpoint, consisting chiefly of the cerebral hemispheres. Also known as cerebrum, end-brain.

teleoceptor   teleceptor

teleologic hallucination   A false perception in which people believe they receive advice, usually from a disembodied spirit, as to the course they should follow.

teleologic regression   See PROGRESSIVE TELEOLOGIC REGRESSION.

teleology   1. A doctrine positing that the existence of everything in nature can be explained in terms of purpose. 2. In the purposive view, the concept that behavior is best understood in terms of the organism's life goals and orientation to the future. 3. A doctrine positing that behavior is best explained in terms of ends and purposes rather than instincts and childhood experiences. 4. The emphasis in Alfred Adler's Individual Psychology on goals and ideals chosen by individuals to fulfill themselves. See HORMIC, HORMIC PSYCHOLOGY.

teleonomy   1. A doctrine positing that life has purpose, and behaviors, structures, functions exhibited by the organism are seen as having evolutionary survival value. 2. The study of behavior patterns that appear to be a function of a concealed purpose. A child or a pet dog may behave in an antisocial manner that actually is a teleonomic method of obtaining a display of attention or affection from the parent or pet owner.

teleoperator   A machine that extends the operator's manipulating (and sometimes sensing) capability, generally to a remote or hostile location.

teleopsia   A visual anomaly that leads people to judge objects to be much further away from where they really are. Due to lesions in the parietal temporal region. See DISTANCE SENSE.

teleostereoscope   telestereoscope

teleotaxis   Being pulled in two directions. If an organism is attracted to two or more sources of stimulation, it will go to one of them, rather than to an intermediate point. See TAXIS, TROPISM.

teleotherapeutics   Treatment at a distance, as in a person living thousands of miles away blessing a glass of water to purportedly cure an ailing person who drinks it. See ALTERNATIVE THERAPIES, EXTRASENSORY PERCEPTION, FAITH CURE, HEALING GROUPS, HYPNOANALYSIS, MENTAL HEALING.

telepathic dream   (W. Stekel) A dream allegedly stimulated or influenced by the dream of another person sleeping elsewhere, often next to the dreamer, or in an adjoining bed or room.

telepathy   In extrasensory perception, the alleged thought transference from one person to another. Mind reading; extrasensory awareness of another person's thoughts or mental states.

telephone scatologia/scatophilia   1. A form of psychosexual disorder characterized by obtaining sexual arousal from making obscene telephone calls. 2. Being sexually attracted to or aroused by saying obscene things on the telephone to an unknown listener. See SCATOPHILIA.

telephone sex   Engaging in sexual conversation over the telephone, such as for pay by calling a phone number whereupon a person at the other end uses sexually explicit language while the caller masturbates.

telephone support service   A service provided by mental-health clinics, community mental-health centers, and drug-treatment centers in which a trained individual gives emotional support and practical guidance over the telephone to persons undergoing emergencies. See HOTLINE.

telephone theory (of hearing)   (W. Rutherford) A theory of pitch that assumes that the rate of impulse frequencies in the auditory nerve is the same as the frequencies of the sound stimulus. Because a nerve fiber would be unable to transmit sounds above 1,000 Hertz (cycles per second), the telephone theory has been modified to propose that nerve fibers fire in groups to carry higher sound-frequency impulses; this is called the volley theory. Similar to frequency theory. See HEARING THEORIES.

telephonicophilia   See TELEPHONE SCATOLOGIA/SCATOPHILIA.

teleplasm   In parapsychology, a hypothetical substance that emanates from a psychic medium in the form of a human, presumably capable of telekinetic activities.

telergy   1. Automatism. 2. The purported direct influence of the mind of a person or spirit upon the brain of another person. A process resulting in telepathy.

telesis   1. A goal to be attained through planned conduct. 2. The realization, or accomplishment, of an end, or purpose. 3. The attainment of certain intangible goals (such as security) by the pursuit of tangible goals (such as by learning a trade).

telestereoscope   (H. Helmholtz) A binocular stereoscope for viewing distant objects, consisting of a series of mirrors so placed that distant objects or pictures appear to be closer to the viewer than they actually are. Useful for studying convergence and disparity in depth perception. Also spelled teleostereoscope.

telesthesia   In parapsychology, alleged ability to perceive objects or events beyond the normal range of human perception.

telesthetic taste   (L. Morgan) A chemical or food sense in aquatic animals, corresponding to the taste sense of terrestrial animals, but includes distant reception of stimuli.

teletactor   A device that amplifies and transmits sounds to the skin, for use in teaching speech to the hearing-impaired.

teleworker   1. Telecommunications employee. 2. Worker who telecommutes, usually from home.

telic   Characterizing a final end or purpose, that is, with intention. Contrasted with ecbatic, the result or behavior without aim or intention.

telic continuum   (F. H. Allport) A curve representing the frequency with which a purpose, or an institutional or customary prescription, is carried out in overt behavior. See J CURVE.

tell-tale eye   (E. Hess) A concept that a person's eyes reveal hidden thoughts and emotions by dilations and contractions of the pupils. See PUPILLOMETRY.

telodendria   The terminal fibrils of an axon, with further branchings of the synaptic knobs. Usually wind through dendrites and other structures of neighboring neurons, making synaptic associations with them.

telodendron   The branching terminal of the axon of a neuron. Also known as endbrush, end-brush.

telophase   The end or final phase of mitosis, in which new nuclei are formed.

telos   A goal or purpose.

temper   A display of anger, or an undue readiness to become angry.

temperament   1. An individual organism's constitutional pattern of reactions, including characteristics such as general energy level, emotional make-up, and intensity and tempo of response. Though such a pattern purportedly has an inherent basis, and is manifested early in life, it may be modified in some degree by life experiences, for example, a placid person may become more vigorous, and a volatile person may become more controlled. 2. Considered a physiological constitutional trait, it refers to the general mood of a person.

temperature comfort variations   Differences in levels of ambient temperature comfort. For example, a person may be comfortable in an environment of 55° to 105° Fahrenheit, but another person's range of comfort may be within 20° of difference, such as from 65° to 85°. People living together may find such differences a source of controversy as to what to wear and whether to turn on the heater or the air conditioner. See INDIVIDUAL DIFFERENCE.

temperature drive   A form of behavior observed in both cold-blooded and warm-blooded animals characterized by activities designed to achieve an optimum temperature in their environment. Fish and rats, for example, can learn to press a bar that adjusts the temperature of the water or air around them; humans adjust thermostats or change their clothing. The anterior part of the hypothalamus contains a center for temperature regulation, which appears to produce circulatory changes throughout the body.

temperature effects   Stress effects, both psychological and physical, to wide variations from optimal environmental temperatures. The effects on comfort are also dependent upon such influences as humidity, wind, and personal acclimatization. See COLD EFFECTS, HEAT EFFECTS.

temperature eroticism   In psychoanalytic theory, the erotic pleasure of feeling warm, assumed to stem from the oral stage of psychosexual development when the child was cuddled by the mother or mother figure. In later stages the sensation of heat is a normal accompaniment of sexual excitation, and may also be experienced when desiring or fantasizing about sexual activity.

temperature illusion   Overestimation of a warm or cold environment when the body or some part of the body has been recently stimulated by a less warm or a less cold environment, respectively.

temperature scales   A system of arranging degrees of warmth in a progressive series according to objective measurements. Scientists since 1960 have agreed to use the Celsius scale (formerly called the centigrade scale) that begins with 0° (the temperature at which water freezes) and 100° (the temperature at which water boils). Another scale is the Kelvin scale (also known as the absolute scale) that begins with 0° which is known as absolute zero and is equivalent to −273° (Celsius) and −459° (Fahrenheit). Fahrenheit's freezing point is set at 32° and boiling at 212°. See CELSIUS SCALE, FAHRENHEIT SCALE, KELVIN SCALE.

temperature sensation   Generic phrase applied to both cold and warmth sensations.

temperature sense   1. Senses of warmth and cold. Part of the sense of touch, the ability to recognize differences in temperature. 2. A part of the somatosensory system with receptors at various depths in the skin and other body surfaces that may be exposed to the environment, such as the tongue. Temperatures generally above 33°C (91°F) on the skin produce a sensation of warmth whereas those below cause a feeling of coolness. The impulses generated are carried by slow A fibers to the thalamus.

temperature sensitivity   Ability of an organism to distinguish degrees of warmth (or cold) by means of specific receptors.

temperature spots   Areas of the skin that contain temperature-sensitive receptors.

temper tantrum   A violent outburst of anger commonly occurring between the ages of two and four and characterized by such behaviors as screaming, kicking, biting, breath-holding, hitting, and head-banging. The episodes are usually out of proportion to immediate provocation and are regarded as an expression of accumulated tensions and frustrations. Also known as tantrum. See BREATH-HOLDING, OPPOSITIONAL DISORDER.

template   1. A standard item that serves as a mold or pattern against which other items are matched or compared. 2. The original or standard form on which additional items are to be made conforming in all important respects to the original. A template can be used for checking identity or correct replies (for example, a sheet with holes can be placed exactly over a multiple-choice test paper to show which items were marked correctly if through the hole a pencil mark can be seen).

template matching theory   A point of view about the common task of judging whether two similar items are identical or not identical. The theory states that first one item, then the other item, is etched on the brain and the two can be compared by transient memories. The first memory image serves as a template for the second one.

template RNA   ribosomal RNA

temple sleep   A forerunner of modern sleep treatment popular in ancient Egypt, Babylonia, and Greece in which people with various disorders slept on a temple floor to learn through dreams what treatments would be most effective. In the cult of Aesculapius, sleep was apparently induced by drugs, potions, hypnosis, or ventriloquism. The dreams were interpreted by a priest or oracle. In some cases, it was claimed, Aesculapius himself would appear in a dream to heal the patient outright. See SLEEP TREATMENT, THEURGIC APPROACH.

temporal   1. Refers to the side of the head (the temple), as in temporal lobe. 2. Refers to time (for example, temporal consistency).

temporal avoidance conditioning   In operant conditioning, a procedure in which an aversive stimulus (for example, an electric shock) is applied at regular intervals (for example, every 20 seconds) unless a correct response by the experimental organism (for example, the pushing of a lever) delays the aversive stimulus for a set amount of time. No warning stimulus is used. Because M. Sidman worked with this procedure it is sometimes also known as Sidman avoidance conditioning. Also known as avoidance without warning signal.

temporal bone   A bone at the side and base of the skull, which contains the mechanisms of hearing.

temporal conditioning   A learning procedure similar to that of trace conditioning except that an unconditioned stimulus is offered at regular intervals but in the absence of an accompanying conditioned stimulus.

temporal consistency   (W. Mischel) Behavior that remains consistent over time in similar situations.

temporal contiguity   A situation of various events occurring in direct succession, one directly after the other. Two events are contiguous when there is no gap between the ending of the first and the beginning of the second.

temporal cortex of the brain   See TEMPORAL LOBE.

temporal-frequency discrimination   pattern discrimination

temporal hallucinations   temporal-lobe illusions

temporal lobe   An area of the cerebral hemisphere immediately behind the lateral fissure, on the lower outside surface of the hemisphere, containing the auditory projection and auditory association areas, and an area for visual processing. Lesions of the temporal lobe result in visual deficits and memory loss. The degree of memory loss depends in part on the size and location of the lesion. Lost learning skills can be restored in most cases. See BRAIN for an illustration.

temporal lobectomy   The surgical excision of a temporal lobe or a portion of the lobe. Temporal lobectomy is sometimes used in treating temporal-lobe epilepsy. Verbal deficits may be observed after left temporal lobectomy and performance deficits after right temporal lobectomy, but in many cases functional disturbances existed before the surgery. See PARAPHASIS, VERBAL ABILITY, VERBAL PARAPHASIA.

temporal-lobe epilepsy (TLE)   psychomotor epilepsy

temporal-lobe hallucination/illusion   Distorted perceptions associated with temporal-lobe epilepsy seizures. These illusions often include distortions of the sizes or shapes of objects, recurring dreamlike thoughts, sensations of *déjà vu* or *jamais vu*, and of the head separating from the body or the sound of threatening voices. Also known as temporal hallucinations. See AUDITORY HALLUCINATION, HALLUCINATION.

temporal-lobe syndrome   A complex of personality traits associated with temporal-lobe epilepsy. The traits include a profound sense of righteousness, preoccupation with details, compulsive writing or drawing, religiosity, and changes in sexual attitudes. See TEMPORAL-LOBE HALLUCINATION.

temporal maze   A maze used in the double-alternation test of memory and reasoning ability. The participant is required to make different turns in the same place, such as two to the left (LL) followed by two to the right (RR). Sometimes known as T-maze.

temporal-perceptual disorder   A pathological condition observed in some people with lesions in the left hemisphere who have difficulty in the temporal perception of visual and auditory stimuli. Patients with this disorder may be unable to identify the sequences of vowels repeated at measured time intervals.

temporal resolution   In interpreting PET (positron emission tomography) scans, the time span over which the technique is appropriate.

temporal sign   Any characteristic of a memory experience which serves as a cue to locate the original experience at a certain point in the time series.

temporal summation   An effect sometimes produced as a motoneuron response to two successive impulses, neither of which is of sufficient intensity to cause the response. The partial depolarization of the first firing continues for a few milliseconds and is able, with the additive effect of the second, to produce the energy to complete the neuronal discharge.

temporary commitment   Involuntary emergency hospitalization of a mental patient for a limited period of observation or treatment. See COMMITMENT, VOLUNTARY COMMITMENT.

temporary threshold shift (TTS)   A temporary condition in which the normal level of perception is altered or disrupted. For example, after relatively prolonged exposure to loud noise, the absolute threshold may shift so that minimal sound intensities that could normally be detected are temporarily inaudible. A similar shift can occur in other sense modalities.

temporizers   In child psychology, parents who have not worked out a consistent pattern of parental and authoritative behavior. Drifting from one situation to the next, they seem unsure how to resolve conflicts with their children. They are not consistently authoritarian nor do they consistently emphasize reason and cooperation). See APPEASERS, COOPERATORS, DICTATORS.

temporomandibular joint (TMJ)   The point of attachment of the upper and lower jaws. The joint is susceptible to arthritis, congenital and developmental anomalies, muscular problems, and neoplasms (new growth). See TMJ SYNDROME.

temporomandibular joint (TMJ) syndrome A degenerative arthritic disease of the point of attachment of the upper and lower jaws (temporomandibular joint). Symptoms may include headaches, deafness, tinnitus, or pain in the ear. TMJ frequently is associated with bruxism and may respond to biofeedback training. See TEMPOROMANDIBULAR JOINT.

temptation A stimulus or motive which tends to change the direction of attention and activity from a well-considered or dominant course of behavior to some action that is seen as temporarily pleasurable.

tendency The characteristic of certain movements, changes, courses of events, or masses of data of any sort, such that they indicate a definite line or direction of progression or an approach to some point or goal.

tendency wit A type of wit that has some deep meaning or that serves some purpose, as opposed to abstract or harmless wit. According to Sigmund Freud, tendency wit is a means of gratifying a craving that may be crude or hostile.

tendentious apperception A tendency to perceive what the person wishes to perceive in an event or object, for example, Alfred Adler's tendency to interpret human experience in terms of the drive for personal superiority.

tender-minded (W. James) Denoting a personality trait characterized by intellectualism, idealism, optimism, dogmatism, religiosity, and monism. Compare TOUGH-MINDED.

tendo calcaneus Achilles heel.

tendon A band of tough fibrous tissue that links a muscle to a bone.

tendon reflexes The reflexes that involve the muscle-spindle feedback circuit so that when a tendon to an extensor muscle is tapped, the muscle is suddenly stretched. Tendon reflexes can be demonstrated by the knee-jerk reflex action.

tendon sensation The kinesthetic sensation produced by stimulation of receptors in a tendon, for example, by stretching it. Also known as tendinous sensation.

tenet A statement of faith accepted by people belonging to a particular theoretical, philosophical, or religious group. In psychology, theories are based on certain central beliefs, for example the following summaries from a textbook on personality, with statements presented by the authors:
    Analytical Psychology: (C. G. Jung) Personality is influenced by the existence and potential activation of a collective transpersonal unconscious.
    Asian Personality Theories: (Many contributors) A newborn infant, as a result of its previous lives, has certain personality and character traits which, after this present life, are transmitted to its next existence.
    Behaviorism: (Many contributors) The basic aim of psychology and the study of personality is the prediction and control of behavior.
    Constitutional Theories of Personality: (W. Sheldon) The somatotype provides a universal frame of reference for how humans grow and develop, independent of culture.
    Existential Personality Theory: (Many contributors) Personality is primarily constructed through the person's attribution of meaning.
    Individual Psychology: (A. Adler) Man, like all forms of life, is a unified organism.
    Person-Centered Theory: (C. R. Rogers) Each person has an inherent tendency to actualize unique potential.
    Personal Constructs Theory: (G. Kelly) All human interpretations of the universe are subject to revision.
    Psychoanalysis: (S. Freud) The mind is composed of the id, ego, and superego.
    Sociological Theories of Personality: (Several major proponents) Biological variables do not determine but only influence behavior.
    Soviet Personality Theory: (Marx et al.) Psyche processes are a function of the brain, the highest form of organic matter.

Tenon's capsule (J. R. Tenon) A fibrous sheath which envelops the back of the eyeball the tendons of its extrinsic muscles, and to a certain extent the muscles themselves. Named after French pathologist and oculist Jacques R. Tenon (1724–1816).

TENS transcutaneous electrical nerve stimulation

tensiometry Measurement of muscular force.

tension 1. A feeling of physical and psychological strain accompanied by discomfort, uneasiness, and pressure to seek relief through talk, action or rest. 2. The strain resulting from contraction or stretching of a muscle or tendon. See PSYCHIC TENSION.

tension headache Persistent head pain produced by acute or prolonged emotional tension, and usually accompanied by insomnia, irritability, and painful contraction of the neck muscles. See HEADACHE.

tension law (J. Delboeuf) A principle that an organism is normally adjusted to a certain optimal level of external stimuli (temperature, atmospheric pressure, illumination, sound), and that any change (increase or decrease) in these stimuli produces a condition of disequilibrium or tension in the organism. Compare HOMEOSTASIS.

tension reduction Alleviation of feelings of tension through such means as relaxation therapy, tranquilizing drugs, muscle relaxants, hypnotic suggestion, periods of meditation, verbal catharsis, movement therapy, sex therapy.

tension-relaxation Dimensions or attributes of Wilhelm Wundt's tridimensional theory of emotion characterized by alternating between feeling calm and feeling tense. Also known as feeling of tension-relaxation. See EXCITEMENT-DEPRESSION, PLEASANTNESS-UNPLEASANTNESS.

tensor tympani One of the two muscles involved in movements of the middle-ear ossicles. It reacts automatically to help disengage the ossicles briefly when loud noises are received as air vibrations at the eardrum. The person hears a distorted sound but the tensor tympani-reflex action protects the inner ear structures from damage.

tenth cranial nerve See VAGUS NERVE.

tenting (effect) Elevation of the uterus from the pelvic cavity into the abdominal cavity during sexual arousal.

tentorium cerebelli A fold of dura mater that separates the surface of the cerebellum from the basal surfaces of the occipital and temporal lobes of the cerebral cortex.

tenure　　1. Length of employment. See TURNOVER. 2. In academia, a privilege granted to faculty: not having to apply for renewals of their teaching contract. 3. Especially in unionized jobs, security of employment once the probationary period is completed.

teonanacatl　　A Mexican mushroom, *Psilocybe mexicana*, that is the source of the psychedelic drugs psilocybin and psilocin. Also known as God's flesh, magic mushroom.

teratogen　　From the Greek, meaning "monster-producing." Any drug or other agent (such as a virus) that causes abnormal fetal development. Teratogens have the most damaging effects from the first three weeks of pregnancy (embryo stage) to eight weeks, often before the pregnancy is detected. See FETAL ALCOHOLIC SYNDROME, TERATOLOGICAL DEFECTS, THALIDOMIDE.

teratogenesis　　A process by which a teratogen causes developmental abnormalities in a fetus. Also known as teratogeny.

teratological defects　　Fetal structural or functional abnormalities caused by genetic factors or by environmental influences such as exposure to drugs during pregnancy. See TERATOGEN.

teratology　　Literally, "the study of monsters." The study of agents that disturb prenatal development and produce abnormalities. Also, the study of the production, development, anatomy, and classification of malformed fetuses. See DYSMORPHOLOGY.

teratomorph　　A fetus or offspring with developmental abnormalities as the result of teratogens. See MONSTER, TERATOGENIC.

teratophobia　　1. Morbid fear of monsters. 2. Fear of bearing and giving birth to a monstrously deformed child.

term　　1. A limited or definite period, such as the human gestational period of 266 days from conception, usually marking the end of pregnancy. See GESTATION PERIOD. 2. A descriptive word or phrase.

Terman Group Test of Mental Ability　　(L. M. Terman) A battery of ten verbal tests used to measure the general mental ability of students in grades 7 to 12.

Terman-McNemar Test of Mental Ability　　(L. M. Terman & Q. McNemar) A group-intelligence scale designed for grades 7 through 12, consisting of seven types of verbal tests: synonyms, classification, logical selection, information, analogies, opposites, and best-answer.

Terman-Merrill Revision　　The 1937 revision (translation and adaptation) by Lewis Terman and Maud Merrill of the 1916 Binet-Simon Scale. Usually referred to as the Stanford-Binet.

terminal　　1. Final; pertaining to the end of a process. 2. Pertaining to the end of an object, organ, body.

terminal age　　See TERMINAL MENTAL AGE.

terminal assessment　　The appraisal of a student's achievement at the conclusion of an educational program. Also known as terminal assessment.

terminal behavior　　The expected and final behavior as shaped by the use of operant conditioning.

terminal bulb/knob　　The swollen ending of the axon of a neuron, from which neurotransmitters are released into the synapse. Also known as synaptic bouton/bulb/button/knob/swelling, terminal bouton/button.

terminal care (project)　　Service for the terminally ill, provided by hospices, which are usually free-standing units or associated with a hospital, nursing home, or extended-care facility. The emphasis is on palliative care, pain control, supportive psychological services, and involvement in family and social activities, to enable these individuals to live out their lives in comfort, peace, and dignity.

terminal drop　　A sudden decrease in intellectual performance shortly before death.

terminal factor　　Any factor obtained during factor analysis at the point where it is no longer worth while trying to add more factors.

terminal insomnia　　**termination insomnia**

terminal knob　　See TERMINAL BULB.

terminal limen (TL)　　**terminal threshold**

terminal mental age　　(A. Binet) On certain tests, such as the Stanford Binet, that have test items established by age levels, the level below the age level on which all test items are failed. Also known as maximal age, terminal (mental) level, terminal (mental) year. See INTELLIGENCE, INTELLIGENCE QUOTIENT, INTELLIGENCE TEST.

terminal organ　　A special organ connected with either of the two terminals of the neural arc, called receptor and effector respectively.

terminal reinforcement　　A reward delivered at a goal or after the organism performs the correct response or response sequence.

terminal sensitivity　　The extreme degree of sensitivity potential of an organism.

terminal stimulus (TR)　　The maximum stimulus to which an organism can respond. Also known as *terminalischer Reiz* (German).

terminal threshold　　The maximum stimulus intensity that will produce a sensation. Also known as terminal limen (TL).

termination　　1. In general, an end or ending. 2. In therapy, a technical term referring to how therapy ends. In some cases, the client will suggest termination, in some cases the therapist. Termination can be either immediate or drawn out. In drawn out termination, instead of a sudden ending, sessions are first scheduled further apart, for example, sessions on a weekly basis might be set bi-weekly or monthly for several more sessions. 3. H. S. Sullivan's final phase of an interview. See FOLLOW-UP COUNSELING, PSYCHIATRIC INTERVIEW.

termination insomnia　　A form of insomnia characterized by habitually awakening at an unreasonably early hour, feeling unrefreshed, and inability to go back to sleep. Common in older persons, in people with cerebral arteriosclerosis, and those suffering from chronic anxiety, depression, and severe daytime fatigue. Also known as matutinal insomnia, terminal insomnia.

terminology　　The systematic treatment of terms in any branch of science. See NOMENCLATURE, TERM.

territorial aggression　　The act of defending or enlarging territory by fighting or threatening intruders. Characteristic of rats, chimpanzees, wolves, and other animals, but also observed in children laying claim to a sandbox, and street gangs defending their turf.

territorial dominance   1. A phenomenon in which individuals control interactions with others when a meeting occurs in what the former consider their own territory. 2. By extension, the tendency for people to dominate interpersonal interactions to a greater extent when in their own homes or offices as opposed to when in neutral places.

territoriality   1. A tendency of groups or individuals to defend a particular domain or area of interest. 2. An individual animal's tendency to define a certain space as its habitat in which it will fight trespassing animals regardless of their species. 3. By extension, territoriality refers to similar characteristic human attitudes toward their dwellings and other essential spaces. Human aggression is considered by some theorists to be related to human territoriality. See GROUP TERRITORIAL BEHAVIOR, PROXEMICS.

territorial marking   The marking by an animal of its home territory with an olfactory signal.

terror   The extreme emotional manifestation of fear.

terror dream   See SLEEP-TERROR DISORDER.

tertiary circular reaction   In developmental psychology, according to Jean Piaget, an infant's action, usually emerging near the beginning of the second year, that creatively alters former schemes to fit the requirements of new situations. It differs from earlier behavior in that the child can, for the first time, develop new schemes to achieve a desired goal. This occurs at sensorimotor stage 5. See COORDINATION OF SECONDARY SCHEMES, PRIMARY CIRCULAR REACTION, SCHEMES, SECONDARY CIRCULAR REACTION.

tertiary cortex   A region of the cytoarchitecture of the cerebral cortex in which zones of overlapping parietal, temporal, and occipital sensory activities are located. The cells are mainly from the upper layers of the cortex and are involved in integration of auditory, somatosensory, and visual impulses.

tertiary cortical zone   One of the three types of cortical regions behind the central sulcus, it is concerned with cells that integrate information areas. See PRIMARY CORTICAL ZONE, SECONDARY CORTICAL ZONE.

tertiary gains   Describing benefits obtained by someone other than the patient as a result of the patient's illness or injury. See PRIMARY GAINS, SECONDARY GAINS.

tertiary memory   Long-term, unlimited-capacity memory for overlearned, meaningful material.

tertiary prevention   The application of rehabilitative measures designed to prevent relapse and to forestall or reduce disabilities arising out of mental disorder, such as difficulty in finding and adjusting to work, and problems of participating in family, social, and community life.

tertiary-process thinking   (S. Arieti) Innovative, imaginative, creative thought processes that transcend both primary- and secondary-process thinking. See CREATIVE THINKING, DIVERGENT THINKING, PRIMARY PROCESS, SECONDARY PROCESS.

tertiary sex characteristics   Sex differences that are mostly learned.

tessellated   1. Checkered; made up of small squares. 2. Characterizing inherited structural patterns in which two different colors or textures alternate in checker-board fashion on the body covering of a creature.

test   1. A method of examination to determine whether a particular phenomenon (such as disease, disorder, substance) exists in an organism. See PSYCHOLOGICAL TEST. 2. A standardized set of questions or other criteria designed to assess knowledge, skills, interests, or other characteristics of a subject. 3. A set of operations designed to assess the validity of a hypothesis. See APPENDIX F for a list of tests.

testability   1. Ability of a scientific proposition to withstand challenges to the data, design, or other aspects of the premise on which it is based. 2. Any statement or belief capable of being tested. Also known as testable.

test administration   The process of conducting tests, particularly psychometric instruments, and often including test selection, administration, scoring and interpretation, and reporting. See STANDARDIZED TESTING.

test age   A score obtained on a test standardized in age units or age equivalents.

testamentary capacity   The legal ability to make a will, based on mental competency.

test anxiety   A type of anxiety associated with fear of being unable to perform a task. An example of PERFORMANCE ANXIETY.

Test Anxiety Inventory   (C. D. Spielberger et al.) An inventory of 20 statements describing subjective reactions to taking tests, indicating the degree of worry and emotionality the participant experiences.

test anxiety scale   (G. Mandler & S. B. Sarason) A scale designed to measure the extent of anxiety experienced in anticipation of and during the taking of an intellectually challenging test.

testaria   A feminist wordplay on "hysteria" to describe males who remain detached and cannot express emotion.

test battery   1. A collection of tests used together to predict a single criterion. 2. A group or series of related tests administered at one time, with scores recorded separately or combined to yield a single score. 3. A number of tests used for checking whatever is being measured at least twice in an attempt to be more sure of the outcome of the evaluation. For example, in evaluating the intelligence of school children, a psychometrician may use two or more tests of different types (such as a test that centers on language and another that centers on nonverbal functions). 4. A combination of tests, selected so as to elicit a variety of meaningful measures, and balanced with respect to the total scores as to provide maximal efficiency as a measuring instrument. 5. A series of different tests, as for intelligence, scholastic abilities, vocational interests, personality attributes to provide an overall assessment of an individual. Rarely also known as battery of tests. See these batteries: ACHIEVEMENT, ARMED SERVICES VOCATIONAL APTITUDE, FROSTIG MOVEMENT SKILLS TEST, GENERAL APTITUDE TEST, LURIA-NEBRASKA NEUROPSYCHOLOGICAL, QUANTITATIVE ELECTROPHYSIOLOGICAL, TEST.

test bias   A situation that occurs whenever anyone takes a test whose norms are based on a population different from the one to which the participant belongs.

test construction   Developing tests, usually so that they have both validity (does the test measure what it claims to?) and reliability (how consistently does the test measure what it claims to measure?). Some tests have face validity (appear to measure what they claim to measure) and can also be valid and reliable, such as a typing test that measures how well a person types, but some tests that do not have face-validity, such as projective tests, are sometimes based on logic sufficient to justify their existence as well as objective evidence of their validity and reliability. See PROJECTIVE TESTS, SUBJECTIVE TESTS.

test cutoff   The test score used to separate pass/failure, accept/reject.

test discrimination index   A measure of the discrimination power of a test. If the correlation between a test's scores and prediction of an effect correlates with r = .60, its discriminating power is about 36%, r squared. Or, another way is to divide the number of successful predictions by unsuccessful predictions. If the two numbers are equal, the score is 1 or pure chance; if there were 90 successes and 10 failures, the test discrimination index would be 9.

testes   Plural of testis.

testicle   The male gonad or reproductive gland. Term is commonly used to describe the testis and its surrounding structures, including the scrotum.

testicular-feminization syndrome   A form of pseudo-hermaphroditism in which an individual who is genetically a male is born with external genitalia and secondary sexual characteristics of a female but also has male testes. The internal female reproductive organs, the uterus and Fallopian tubes, are absent in such an individual. Such a person is sometimes known as an XY female.

testimony   1. Oral or written statements of a witness used as evidence of certain facts and events. 2. (Figuratively) any evidence produced to substantiate a hypothesis.

testing   See PSYCHOLOGICAL TESTING.

testing effect   A variety of consequences of taking tests, such as developing an intractable attitude toward tests (positive or negative) or learning how to take tests in the future to achieve unwarranted positive results.

testing method   See CLINICAL METHODS OF PSYCHOLOGY.

testing of limits   (B. Klopfer) A procedure in administering the Rorschach, used when the examiner is not satisfied that the results obtained conventionally are sufficient. The examiner re-administers the test, asking direct questions, such as, "Some people see this as a bird or a bat. Does it look like that to you?"

test interpretation   The evaluation of the meaning of a test. The process requires skill, including knowing the details about the test, on whom the test was standardized, whether the participant falls within the group originally tested, how and when it was administered, whether the participant wanted to take the test and what the test means to the participant.

testis   One of the male gonads, or reproductive glands, normally located in the scrotum. Plural is testes. Also known as orchis. See ARRESTED TESTIS, ECTOPIC TESTIS, HYPERMOBILE TESTIS, TESTICLE.

test item   A single question or problem, a separate scorable element of a test.

test marketing   In consumer psychology, the marketing of a new product in a few representative locations prior to a full-scale launching, usually to forecast sales or evaluate marketing techniques.

test of hypothesis   See DIRECTIONAL TEST OF HYPOTHESIS, NONDIRECTIONAL TEST OF HYPOTHESIS.

test of significance   A measure of the probability that a result can be attributed to chance.

Test-Operate-Test-Exit (TOTE)   A fundamental cognitive unit of behavior, designed to replace the reflex arc or S-R associationism.

testophobia   Casual term for a fear of taking tests or of being tested. May account for test results that do not accurately reflect the normal standard of physical or mental performance by a participant, for example, blood pressure frequently shows a much higher reading when tested by a psychologist than it would be during a typical day at home or at work. See PERFORMANCE ANXIETY.

testosterone   (E. Laquer, A. F. J. Butenandt) A male sex hormone and one of the most active of the androgens produced by the testes. Stimulates the development of male reproductive organs, including the prostate, and secondary features such as the beard and bone and muscle growth. Women normally secrete small amounts of testosterone, but above-normal levels can result in traits of masculinity. The main function of the Y sex chromosome is the production of enzymes that build testosterone molecules.

test power   The ability of a statistical test to detect effects of a given size. See POWER OF A TEST.

test profile   1. A chart or similar graphic representation depicting a participant's relative standing on a series of tests. 2. See PSYCHOGRAPH.

test-retest coefficient/reliability   The degree of correlation between scores of the same subjects on an identical test administered two separate times. The resulting test-retest coefficient is the value that expresses the correlation and helps to indicate the test's reliability. A coefficient of 0.70 or higher is an acceptable indication of reliability. See COEFFICIENT OF STABILITY, COEFFICIENT OF STABILITY, CORRELATION.

test scaling   Scoring a test to secure a series of quantitative values in which (ideally) each unit shall be equal to every other unit.

test score   A numerical value assigned as a measure of performance on a test.

test selection   The choice of a test or set of tests that can be the most useful in providing accurate diagnostic or other psychological information. Test selection is made on the basis of medical or psychological history, interviews, or other pretest knowledge of the individual or group to be tested.

test sensitization   Alteration of participant performance due to administration of a test before (pretest) or after (posttest) the experimental condition or intervention. The test may influence (for example, augment) the effect of the experimental condition. A potential threat to external validity if the effect of the experimental condition does not generalize to different testing conditions.

tests of significance   See HYPOTHESIS TESTING.

test sophistication   Familiarity with a particular test or type of test, which might enhance or otherwise distort performance in ways different from what could be expected were there no familiarity. See TEST-WISE.

test standardization   See STANDARDIZATION OF TESTS.

test statistic   A statistic designed to provide a test of a statistical hypothesis. Some test statistics (such as *z*- and *t*-ratios, with known sampling distributions) are not used for estimating population parameters. However, as a probability statement they enable an experimenter to decide whether or not to reject a null hypothesis.

test-study-test method   1. An approach to teaching that measures a student's knowledge before teaching or study and after that, as in administering a test at the beginning and then at the ending of the school year. 2. Specifically, an approach to the teaching of spelling that uses a pretest to determine the words a child knows, followed by study of the words that are failed, then by a retest.

test-taking strategies   In responding to multiple-choice items on a test, having a preestablished pattern when the correct answer is not known, as in always selecting the next-to-last choice.

test value   (E. B. Titchener) A tentative result, obtained with a relatively few observations, designed primarily to determine the limits of the stimuli to be employed in psychophysical experimentation.

test-wise   Describing an individual who has taken a number of tests, and who is presumably less naive about tests and consequently more adept at taking them than a person who is relatively new to the testing process. See TEST SOPHISTICATION.

tetanic contraction   Sustained contraction of a muscle.

tetany   Muscle spasms. Also known as tetania. See CALCIUM-DEFICIENCY DISORDERS, HYPOPARATHY-ROIDISM.

tetany type   The T-type of the Marburg school. See EIDETIC IMAGERY.

tetartanopia   **tetartanopsia**

tetartanopsia   A rare form of color blindness marked by difficulty in discriminating between yellow and blue. Luminosity function is normal, but yellow and blue processes have confused or possibly merged connections. Also known as tetartanopia.

tetrachoric correlation   A correlation estimated from a 2×2 table, assuming that both variables are continuous and normally distributed.

tetrachromatism   A type of vision which requires a minimum of four light wavelengths to combine (in varying amounts or magnitudes) to achieve a metameric match with any arbitrary color seen.

tetrad difference criterion/method   (C. E. Spearman) A difference method for determining whether the correlations among four tests can be accounted for by a single factor. See FACTOR ANALYSIS.

tetrad differences   (C. E. Spearman) In a correlation matrix any combination of four adjacent correlations such that $r_{ac}r_{bd} - r_{bc}r_{ad} \rightarrow 0$. When this condition is reached or approached it has become the accepted criterion for a two-factor pattern; a general factor (g) with an associated specific factor (s). (The symbol $\rightarrow$ means "approaching.")

tetrahydrocannabinol (THC)   The psychedelic element in marijuana and hashish. See CANNABIS, HASHISH, ORGANIC MENTAL DISORDERS, PSYCHEDELICS.

tetraplegia   **quadriplegia**

tetraploid   Having four haploid sets of chromosomes.

text-blindness   See ALEXIA.

textual   (B. F. Skinner) A relationship between viewing something and reacting to what was viewed. The idea that a person will react verbally to a nonverbal stimulus, for example, a participant sees an and replies "arrow" or sees the word "mother" and replies "mother." See CONTEXT.

textural aspect   (W. Sheldon) A measurement of the coarseness or fineness of body characteristics. See SHELDON'S CONSTITUTIONAL TYPES.

texture gradient   A monocular cue for perceiving distance. A texture gradient consists of changes to less distinct textures which indicate increasing distance. See GRADIENT OF TEXTURE.

texture response   In Rorschach testing, any mention of the texture quality of a blot, indicative of sensitivity.

texture segregation task   A task in which participants are presented with displays containing many elements and asked to identify which part of the display is different from the rest.

T₄   Symbol for thyroxin.

T function   A measure of the reduction of information required to locate an element in a given classification if it has already been located in one or more other classification. See REDUNDANCY.

TG   See TRANSFORMATIONAL GRAMMAR.

TGA   transient global amnesia

TGG   See TRANSFORMATIONAL GRAMMAR.

T-group   Based on group research by Kurt Lewin and various associates, training (hence the T) groups devised primarily to train professionals, directed by the National Training Laboratory, intended to be at the same time an environment to learn how groups work and to learn about the self in group interactions. Also known as training group. See ENCOUNTER GROUP, ENCOUNTER MOVEMENT, GROUP THERAPY, SENSITIVITY TRAINING.

thaassophobia   Excessive fear of idleness, of sitting, of being seated. See KATHISOPHOBIA.

thalamic   Relating to the thalamus.

thalamic lesion   A loss of structure or function of a part of the thalamus resulting in such effects as avoidance-learning deficits. Animals that have experienced a thalamic lesion take much longer to learn to avoid an electric shock, although they learn eventually. Effects vary somewhat with the amount or part of the thalamus affected.

thalamic nuclei   Large masses of cell bodies on the thalamus which relay incoming sensory impulses (except olfactory) to cortical areas. See DORSOMEDIAL NUCLEUS, LATERAL GENICULATE BODIES, LATERAL THALAMIC NUCLEUS, MEDIAL GENICULATE BODIES, MIDLINE NUCLEUS, RETICULAR NUCLEUS.

thalamic pacemaker   Groups of nuclei in the thalamus that trigger waves of electrical activity in the cerebral cortex. Several nuclei have been found to initiate cortical discharges, including the intralaminar, midline, reticular, and ventralis anterior nuclei.

thalamic theory of Cannon   Also known as hypothalamic theory of Cannon, another name for the Cannon-Bard theory (of emotions) due to both the thalamus and the hypothalamus' involvement in emotion when external stimulation occurs. See PAPEZ'S THEORY OF EMOTIONS.

thalamic theory of emotion   (W. B. Cannon) A point of view that the thalamus acts directly and in interaction with the cortex in adding a particular quality to simple sensory processes. Also known as thalamic theory of the emotions. See CANNON-BARD THEORY (OF EMOTIONS).

thalamus   A cerebral relay center situated at the bottom of the cerebral hemispheres in the forebrain. The thalamus receives sensory information, which it sends to sensory areas of the cortex, serving as a relay point for nerve impulses traveling between the spinal cord and brainstem and the cerebral cortex. The thalamus is structured so that specific areas of the body surface and cerebral cortex are related to specific parts of the thalamus. The plural is thalami. See CANNON-BARD THEORY (OF EMOTION), EXTRINSIC THALAMUS, POSTERIOR THALAMUS.

thalassophobia   Morbid fear of the sea. Also known as nautophobia.

thalectomy   A psychosurgical procedure in which lesions are made in the thalamus by electrocoagulation. Also known as Grantham lobotomy, thalamotomy.

thalidomide   A tranquilizing drug used especially in Europe in 1960–1961, until it was discovered to be a human teratogen. When taken during pregnancy the drug produced undeveloped arms and legs, but it also had neurologic effects that included deafness, sixth- and seventh-cranial-nerve palsies, microcephaly, meningoencephalocele, and a greater-than-average incidence of mental retardation. See PIPERIDINEDIONES.

thanatology   (R. Park) The study of death and dying, including grief and mourning, psychological preparation for death, attitudes toward dying, and techniques of counseling and psychotherapy appropriate for the dying individual and family.

thanatomania   Obsolete term for an uncontrollable impulse to commit suicide.

thanatophobia   1. Morbid fear of death or dying. 2. Fear of impending death. Also known as *meditatio mortis*. See NECROPHOBIA.

thanatopsy   Autopsy.

Thanatos   (death—Greek) (S. Freud) In psychoanalytic theory, the purported death instinct directed toward destruction of life and a return to the inorganic state. The aggressive drive in all its forms, such as violence, hostility, or sadism, is regarded as an expression of Thanatos. See DESTRUDO, MORTIDO.

thank-you test   Casual term for a criterion for involuntary commitment: it is justified if it is predicted that the individual, after recovery, will thank those who carried out the commitment.

that's-not-all approach/technique   A method of gaining compliance in which a small extra incentive is offered before the target person has agreed to, or rejected, a request or offer.

THC   See TETRAHYDROCANNABINOL.

The Allport-Vernon Study of Values   A paper-pencil test developed by G. W. Allport, P. E. Vernon and G. Lindzey designed to measure the relative prominence of the following six values: theoretical, economic, aesthetic, social, political and religious. Also known as Allport-Vernon-Lindzey Study of Values, Study of Values.

Theater of Spontaneity   An experimental theater established in Vienna in 1921, in which the process of playing unrehearsed, improvised parts proved to be not only effective training for actors, but frequently had a salutary effect on their interpersonal relationships. This technique evolved into the psychotherapeutic approach which Jacob Moreno named psychodrama and brought to America in 1925. The original German name for this theatre was *Stegreiftheater*.

theft   See KLEPTOMANIA.

The Hand Test   (E. E. Wagner) A projective technique designed to elicit prototypal action tendencies, consisting of ten cards portraying line drawings of hands in ambiguous poses, requiring the participant to "Tell what the hand is doing." Replies can be scored according to Wagner's four dimensions of interpersonal, environmental, maladjustive, withdrawal or interpreted in terms of an examiner's personality theory. Used with individuals 6 years of age and older.

theism   A belief in the existence of a god or gods. See AGNOSTICISM, ATHEISM, INTRINSIC RELIGION, PSYCHOLOGY OF RELIGION, RELIGIONS, RELIGION.

thelarche   Beginning of development of breasts in females.

thema   The unit of interplay between an individual and the environment in which a need and a press interact to yield satisfaction. A unifying "plot" behind behavior in Henry Murray's system.

Thematic Apperception Test (TAT)   (C. D. Morgan & H. A. Murray) A projective technique based on drawings depicting people in various situations, such as a person seated at a piano with eyes closed. Participants make up a story about the past of the person, present situation and what will happen in the future. Introduced in the 1930s, still widely used. See PROJECTIVE TECHNIQUE, RORSCHACH TEST.

Thematic Apperception Test (TAT)
An example of a Thematic Apperception Test stimulus card.

thematic organization points (TOPs)   (R. C. Schank) In learning theory, high-level analogies between situations that are different in detail but related in structure.

thematic paralogia   A speech characteristic marked by the incessant, distorted dwelling of the mind on a single theme or topic.

thematic paraphrasia   Incoherent speech that wanders from the theme or topic.

thematic test   Any examination in which a participant is required to tell a story. See THEMATIC APPERCEPTION TEST, THOMPSON THEMATIC APPERCEPTION TEST.

theme interference   A cognitive conflict in the preconscious mind of the patient that is emotionally charged and related to an actual life experience or fantasies of the patient without being adequately resolved. The therapist must identify the themes and reduce or eliminate them because they interfere with the therapy.

theomania   A delusion of being God or believing that God directs personal thoughts and behavior.

theophagy   The sacramental eating of a god in the form of some food or a sacrificed animal or human.

theophobia   1. Morbid fear of gods. 2. Morbid fear of God. 3. A fear of retribution from God for personal sins. 4. Fear of God, gods, and heavenly beings.

theorem   1. A scientific proposition or premise that can be proved in a series of logical steps. 2. A statement generally accepted as true. See HYPOTHESIS, THEORY.

theorem of indifference of the indicator   (C. E. Spearman) For the purpose of indicating the level of general cognitive ability (G) possessed by a person, any test will do as well as any other, provided that their correlations with G are equally high.

theoretical construct   hypothetical construct

theoretical orientation   The basic philosophical position of the original developer of a system. Example: Carl Rogers' abiding belief that a person could in effect do self-therapy under the conditions of being accepted and listened to with empathy.

theoretical type   (E. Spranger) A personality type featuring rationality and inquisitiveness, being logical and sensible. See THINKING TYPE, TYPOLOGY.

theories of color vision   Hypotheses about the physiological mechanisms underlying color phenomena, used to explain or coordinate the visual phenomena in question. Also known as color theories, color-vision theories. Theories of color vision include: DOMINATOR-MODULATOR, DUPLEX, DUPLICITY, GRANIT, HECHT, HERING, LADD-FRANKLIN, LAND, OPPONENT-PROCESS, THREE-COLOR, TRIRECEPTOR, YOUNG-HELMHOLTZ. See COLOR VISION THEORIES.

theory   1. A body of interrelated principles and hypotheses that explain or predict a group of phenomena and have been largely verified by facts or data. Kurt Lewin said "Nothing is as important as a good theory." 2. In common usage, a guess, opinion, conjecture, or supposition.

theory-begging   1. Intellectual dishonesty of making some unproved or unprovable statement and then associating it with some fact to generate in the listener belief in the original statement. 2. (G. Razran) Fallacy of labeling of a theoretical assumption as a behavioral fact. See QUESTION-BEGGING.

theory-laden   1. A concept that can only be understood once the underlying theories are understood. For example, the concept that people benefit by donating time to the community is found in numerous philosophical and religious writings, as well as the Individual Psychology theory of Alfred Adler via the concept of *Gemeinschaftsgefühl* as necessary behavior for the treatment of mental disorder. See GEMEINSCHAFTSGEFÜHL. 2. A set of writings that are bound up in singular theories, such as Sigmund Freud's.

theory of aging   See CYBERNETIC THEORY OF AGING, EVERSION THEORY OF AGING.

theory of choice   (W. N. Dember & R. W. Earl) A point of view that perception is affected by stimuli and behavior is determined by perception. Individuals have ideal choices with preferred levels of complexity. Purportedly, an individual will not select a stimulus that is less complex than the individual's ideal (pacer stimulus), but may select stimuli that are more complex.

theory of complexes   According to Carl Jung, complexes are themes around which material in the (personal) unconscious is organized, are the most important part of the unconscious, and have the purpose of making that part of the unconscious conscious. The word association method that Jung employed was an example of the use of this procedure to locate complexes. See COMPLEX.

theory of distributed associative memory (TODAM)   (B. B. Murdock) A model of memory that explains memory for serial order and recognition.

theory of mental self-government   A model devised by R. J. Sternberg as a bridge between intelligence and personality; it proposes a set of intellectual styles that are framed in terms of the various functions (for example, legislative or executive), forms (for example, monarchic, or anarchic), levels (that is, global/local), and other aspects of governments.

theory of misapplied constancy   A point of view that in an illusion, the inappropriate interpretation of cues is the result of having learned cues for maintaining size constancy.

theory of omnipotence   A point of view held by some young people that they have mental control over other people, making others do as they wish. See OMNIPOTENCY OF THOUGHT.

theory of reasoned action   See AJZEN-FISHBEIN MODEL.

theory of situated identities   A point of view that a person will take on different social roles in different social settings. See EXTRAINDIVIDUAL BEHAVIOR.

theory theory   (S. Gelman, A. N. Meltzoff) A point of view about the mental development of children that challenges views proposed by Jean Piaget. Similar in some respects to views held by George Kelly, this theory assumes that children attempt, at much earlier ages than Piaget has suggested, to try to make sense out of life by establishing their own theories and then testing them. See FUNDAMENTAL POSTULATE, PERSONAL CONSTRUCTS, PIAGETIAN THEORY.

theory verification   Procedures governed by canons of scientific method for establishing the acceptability of theory.

Theory X   See THEORY X AND Y.

Theory X and Y   (D. McGregor) Contrasting approaches to management based on assumptions about workers. Theory X views employees as passive, unconcerned, and lazy, thus requiring strong positive directions for them to operate efficiently; Theory Y assumes that employees are potentially capable, creative, and responsible and calls for managers to treat them with respect. Compare THEORY Z.

Theory Y   See THEORY X AND Y.

Theory Z   (W. Ouchi) A combination of Japanese and American management and organizational structures to achieve superior results. Compare THEORY X AND Y.

theotherapy   Usage of prayer or religious exercises to treat physical or mental conditions.

The Question   (R. Dreikurs) A query posed to determine whether a person's problem is medical (physiologically determined) or whether it is psychological (based on hidden goals). A therapist asks, for example, "If you did not have this symptom (problem, disease, condition, etc.) what would you do?" A reply such as "I would go to work to support my family" may indicate that the condition is functional (psychological) but a reply such as "I would not be in such pain (or so weak, etc.)" may indicate that the condition is physiological. See INDIVIDUAL PSYCHOLOGY.

therapeutic   1. Pertaining to the treatment of disease. 2. In reference to successful therapy. "Therapy" is treatment of an illness; "therapeutic" refers only to therapies that work (as many therapies have potential to cause mental and physical harm). See IATROGENIC.

therapeutic abortion   An abortion performed for medically indicated reasons such as mother's health or a severe, genetic anomaly of the fetus.

therapeutic agent   Any instrumentality used to advance the treatment process, such as a drug, the therapist, a therapeutic group, electroshock, occupational therapy, or a therapeutic community.

therapeutic alliance   A cooperative relationship between client and therapist. Considered by many to be a necessary aspect of successful psychotherapy in that both the therapist and the patient have a meeting of the minds and desire to work together to achieve certain agreed-upon goals. This concept questions whether forced or induced counseling or therapy is effective. See HELPING RELATION.

therapeutic atmosphere   A climate of genuineness, empathetic warmth, and "unconditional positive regard" (Carl Rogers) in which the patient feels free to verbalize feelings and emotions, and make constructive changes in attitudes and reactions.

therapeutic bond   A therapeutic alliance sometimes involving transference, countertransference, or both.

therapeutic coitus   A Taoist and tantric belief that specific positions and rituals have health benefits by rectifying energy imbalances.

therapeutic communication   Any comment or observation by the therapist that increases the patient's awareness or self-understanding.

therapeutic community (TC)   (T. F. Maine, M. Jones) The use of patients' social environment to provide them with a therapeutic experience by allowing them active participation in their own care and the daily problems of the community as defined by Maxwell Jones, including: (a) the standard treatment processes; (b) interactions between the patient and all members of the staff; (c) the development of constructive social relationships among the patients; (d) the esthetic character of the architecture, grounds, and furnishings; (e) participation in patient government and community meetings; (f) all types of supportive therapy, recreational, occupational, industrial, and educational. See MILIEU THERAPY, SOCIAL-BREAKDOWN SYNDROME.

therapeutic crisis   A turning point in a treatment process (especially in psychotherapy), usually due to sudden insight, acting out, or a significant revelation on the part of the client or patient. The crisis may have positive or negative implications, and may lead to a change for the better or the worse, depending on how it is handled.

therapeutic group   A group of people who meet under the leadership of a therapist for the express purpose of working together toward improvement in the mental and emotional health of the members.

therapeutic group analysis   group-analytic psychotherapy

therapeutic impasse   A situation in which progress in the treatment process has ceased, and failure is likely. This situation occurs when further insight is not forthcoming, or when the process is blocked by extreme resistance or severe transference and countertransference conflicts.

therapeutic matrix   In marital therapy, the specific combination of therapist and persons used in the sessions, for example, a different therapist for each spouse in collaborative therapy, or seeing the couple together in conjoint therapy.

therapeutic recreation   A rehabilitation program of community recreation activities, such as art, theater, music, sports, and hobby and craft projects for persons with disabilities. It is designed to provide opportunities to interact with others in the community, thereby gaining experience and confidence in independent living.

therapeutic relaxation   See RELAXATION THERAPY.

therapeutic role   The functions of the therapist or other therapeutic agent in treating disorders or alleviating a distressing condition.

therapeutics   A branch of medicine concerned with the treatment of disease.

therapeutic social clubs   (J. Bierer) Groups established in a mental hospital that are not to be attended by hospital personnel. Based on Adlerian theory and philosophy, such groups are expected to have social and therapeutic value.

therapeutic soliloquy   A procedure pioneered by Jacob Moreno in which patients are asked to discuss themselves in front of others without interruption and to demonstrate also by physical behavior their thoughts, past, present and even future behavior.

therapeutic stalemate   In therapy, a situation of the progress between a client and a therapist coming to a halt. Causes may not be apparent, but may include, the reluctance of the client to venture past a certain point, or the clumsiness of the therapist. Also known as analytic impasse.

therapeutic touch   1. A procedure in which the therapist moves the hands over a patient's body to heal by generating electric activity around the "aura" surrounding the body. See GREATRAKES, TOUCH THERAPY, UNCONVENTIONAL THERAPIES. 2. Massage therapy. 3. TOUCH THERAPY (meaning 1).

therapeutic window   The range of plasma (not dosage) levels of a drug within which optimal therapeutic effects occur. With psychotropic drugs the range may be different for different patients depending on such factors as age, sex, constitutional characteristics, and concurrent medications.

therapist   A person who has been trained and given some kind of license or approval to treat mental or physical disorders or diseases in a professional manner. See PSYCHOTHERAPIST.

therapist obligations   See CONTRACT.

therapist's assistant   Somewhat mocking phrase for a person in a therapy group who self-appoints to act as the therapist or who echoes the therapist. See GROUP BEHAVIOR.

therapy   (service, waiting on—Greek) A system of treatment designed to cure a pathological mental or physical condition or relieve the symptoms of the condition. See APPENDIX E for a list of therapies.

therapy group climate   In contrast to work or social groups, the boundaries of acceptable behavior in therapeutic groups are much greater, and in many cases what would be considered completely unacceptable behavior in other groups is permitted and even expected in such groups, including intimate self-revelations and critical remarks directed toward other members. See GROUP BEHAVIOR.

therapy supervision   Psychotherapy conducted by a trainee under the supervision of a qualified therapist.

Therblig   (F. Gilbreth & L. Gilbreth) Separate units of a repeated work activity, such as grasp, transport or search, isolated for observation or measurement in a time-and-motion study. (Therblig is Gilbreth spelled backwards, almost.)

there-and-then approach   A historical approach to therapy focusing on the roots of the client's (or patient's) difficulties in past experience. See HERE-AND-NOW APPROACH.

theriomorphic   Having the form of an animal.

theriomorphism   The assignment or attribution of animal characteristics to humans. Also known as zoomorphism. See ANTHROPOMORPHISM.

thermaesthesia   **thermoesthesia**

thermal discrimination   An ability to detect changes in temperatures. Although some animals, for example, snakes, are able to locate prey by differences of a fraction of a degree between the environment and body heat, efforts to locate their cortical centers of thermal discrimination have failed.

thermalgesia   1. A state in which a warm stimulus produces pain. 2. Pain caused by warmth. Also known as thermoalgesia. See CAUSALGIA.

thermalgia   Burning pain. A form of neuralgia whose objective sign is reddening of the skin, with people feeling painful sensations of being burnt. See CAUSALGIA.

thermal illusion   The sensation of extreme heat produced by simultaneous sensations of warmth and cold, as from holding a set of adjoining multiple hot and cold pipes.

thermal sense/sensitivity   See TEMPERATURE SENSE, TEMPERATURE SENSITIVITY, VASCULAR THEORY OF THERMAL SENSITIVITY.

thermal stimulation   Application or withdrawal of physical heat, by either convection or radiation, to excite a receptor.

therman(a)esthesia   **thermoanesthesia**

thermanalgesia   **thermoanesthesia**

thermesthesia   **thermoesthesia**

thermesthesiometer   A meter sensitive to heat variation. A temperature-controlling instrument that can be regulated to provide continuous warm or cold stimuli (such as in tactile or skin experiments).

thermistor   A device used to measure temperatures according to their effects on the electrical resistance of semiconducting materials. Tiny thermistors can be implanted in neurons to measure such data as the energy of metabolic activity during nervous-system functions.

thermoalgesia   **thermalgesia**

thermoanalgesia   **thermoanesthesia**

thermoanesthesia   1. Loss of the temperature sense; inability to distinguish between heat and cold by touch. Also known as ardanesthesia, thermanalgesia, therman-(a)esthesia, thermoanalgesia. 2. Absence of the heat sense. 3. Inability to note heat or temperature changes.

thermode   A copper device through which water can be circulated at a controlled temperature. Can be implanted in an organ of an animal to determine the effects of temperature changes on surrounding tissues. Much information about thermal receptors has been obtained in this manner.

thermoesthesia   Sensitivity to warmth and cold, that is, the ability to distinguish changes in temperature. Also spelled therm(a)esthesia.

thermogenic nerves   Nerves which control heat production.

thermography   A diagnostic technique using thermally sensitive liquid crystals, infra-red photography, or other technology to measure temperature changes in the body, usually to detect tumors (cool) or inflammation (warm).

thermohyperesthesia   Abnormal reactions to temperature changes; excessive sensitivity to warmth and cold.

thermohypesthesia   Diminished sensitivity to warmth and cold. Also known as hypothermesthesia, thermohypoesthesia.

thermophobia   Morbid fear of heat.

thermophore   A device for applying thermal, or temperature stimulation to the skin and registering the time of application; a rounded metal cap is applied to the skin, the contact making an electric circuit; water of the required temperature flows through this metal stimulus-cap.

thermoreceptor   1. A receptor or sense organ which may be adequately activated by appropriate temperature stimuli. 2. A part of the nervous system that has the function of monitoring and maintaining the temperature of the body core and its vital organs. Purportedly separate from the temperature-sensitivity network of receptors and fibers located in the skin. In some animals, the thermoreceptor is presumed to be located in areas of the hypothalamus that have a blood temperature approximating that of the heart and that are sensitive to cooling effects.

thermoregulation   Behavioral characteristics associated with voluntary adjustments of an organism to less-than-optimum temperatures in the environment. Thermoregulation behavior may be involved in moving closer to or farther away from hot or cold areas of space such as a room.

thermostatic theory   A proposal relating to stabilizing body heat; a centralist position, in which the brain is considered to monitor the homeostatic balancing of the body with particular regard to body heat (an animal eats to keep warm and stops eating when too hot). Compare GLUCOSTATIC THEORY.

thermotaxis   1. A tendency for an organism such as an animal to orient itself toward or away from heat or cold. The term thermotropism is seldom used and usually refers to this tendency in plants. See TAXIS, TROPISM. 2. Regulation of the temperature of the body.

thermotropism   1. Motion by a part of an organism, such as leaves of a plant, toward or away from a heat source. 2. See THERMOTAXIS (meaning 1).

thesis   1. A proposition formally offered for proof or disproof. 2. A systematic treatise required for an advanced academic degree.

theta   The eighth letter of the Greek alphabet. See APPENDIX C.

theta effect   Illusion of movement.

theta feedback   Rhythms associated with decreased tension in somatic musculature.

theta rhythm   Sine-wave patterns, recorded with electroencephalography equipment, that are regular, occurring at a rate of 4–7 hertz (cycles per second). Theta waves are observed in paradoxical sleep of animals, light (stage-2) sleep in humans, and in the drowsiness state of newborn infants.

theta wave   Brain waves having a slow rate of 4 to 7 hertz (cycles per second).

theurgic approach   (divine work—Greek) An ancient Egyptian system of magic based on a belief in divine intervention in human affairs, and in beneficent deities who may come to the aid of the mentally or physically ill. See TEMPLE SLEEP.

they-group   out-group

thiamin(e)   The B_1, component of the B-vitamin complex present in various foods and also normally present in blood plasma and cerebrospinal fluid. Deficiency of thiamin(e) results in neurological symptoms, as in beriberi and alcoholic peripheral neuropathy.

thiamine deficiency   A disorder caused by a lack of vitamin B_1, and marked by anorexia, neuritis, and, in severe cases, beriberi, which can result in damage to the heart and central nervous system. See WERNICKE'S DISEASE.

thiazides   Abbreviated name for benzothiadiazides.

thigmesthesia   Sensitivity to pressure-type stimuli, such as the uncomfortable feeling sometimes experienced while wearing finger rings. See THIGMOHYPERESTHESIA.

thigmohyperesthesia   A disorder that may have physiological or psychological origins manifested by abnormal sensitivity to pressure-type items. People with this disorder cannot tolerate for example, wearing a wedding ring, and may complain about the feel of clothing or of bedcovers. See THIGMESTHESIA.

thigmotaxis   A form of barotaxis in which an organism orients in relation to a solid body. See TAXIS, TROPISM.

thigmotropism   1. A simple orienting response, either positive or negative, to external contact. 2. Motion by a part of an organism, such as leaves of a plant, toward or away from a touch stimulus. See TAXIS, TROPISM.

thin voice   tanyphonia

thing   Loose term applied to unitary objects, generally exclusive of living organisms.

thing constancy   (E. Brunswik) A tendency of perceptions to remain unchanged despite variations in the external conditions of observation. See CONSERVATION.

think-aloud protocols   (K. A. Ericsson, A. Newell & H. A. Simon) Recordings of verbalizations concurrently with or subsequent to the problem-solving activities of a human participant. Such protocols are obtained by request that the participant "think aloud" while working on a problem. They are interpreted as behavioral data, frequently useful in understanding the problem-solving process, and are to be distinguished from verbalizations obtained when a participant is asked to introspect.

thinking   Cognitive behavior in which images or ideas that represent objects and events are experienced or manipulated; symbolic or implicit mental processes. These processes include imagining, remembering, problem solving, daydreaming, free association, concept formation, and creative thought. Types of thinking include: ABSTRACT, ALLUSIVE, ANIMISTIC, ASSOCIATIVE, ASYNDETIC, AUTISTIC, CONCRETE, CONVERGENT, CREATIVE, CRITICAL, DICHOTOMOUS, DIRECTED, DIVERGENT, JANUSIAN, MAGICAL, PALEOLOGIC, PHYSIOGNOMIC, PRECAUSAL, PRECONSCIOUS, PREDICATE, PRELOGICAL, PRIMARY-PROCESS, PRODUCTIVE, REALISTIC, TANGENTIAL, TERTIARY-PROCESS, WISHFUL. See ARCHAIC THOUGHT, ARTIFICIAL INTELLIGENCE, AUDIBLE THOUGHT, CATEGORICAL THOUGHT, CONSTRAINT OF THOUGHT, CONTENT-THOUGHT DISORDER, FORMAL-THOUGHT DISORDER, FRAGMENTATION OF THINKING, GROUPTHINK, IMAGELESS THOUGHT, MOTOR THEORY OF THOUGHT, OMNIPOTENCE OF THOUGHT, PARALOGIA, PRIMARY

THOUGHT DISORDER, SECONDARY PROCESS, SPONTANEOUS THOUGHT, STREAM OF CONSCIOUSNESS, SYMBOLIC PROCESS, SYNCRETIC THOUGHT, SYNTAXIC THOUGHT, TREND OF THOUGHT, UNEMOTIONAL THOUGHT, VERBAL THOUGHT.

thinking aside A form of asyndesis (inability to join separate ideas into a coherent concept) observed in patients with schizophrenia whose thinking patterns tend to drift into insignificant side associations so that their thoughts appear lacking in unity of ideas.

thinking-fear See PHRONEMOPHOBIA, PSYCHOPHOBIA.

thinking horse See CLEVER HANS.

thinking-opinion-belief See THOBBING.

thinking stream A succession of ideational experiences uninterrupted by significant experiences of any other type. Also known as stream of thinking, stream of thought.

thinking styles Typology proposed by R. J. Sternberg in his theory of mental self-government, as a bridge between intelligence and personality and as a way to refine and expand the assessment of abilities and achievement.

thinking through In psychotherapy, attempting to achieve insight into one's personal behaviors by examining one's motivations and objectives, their etiology, their probable interpretation by others, and their most likely, possibly unanticipated, consequences.

thinking type One of Carl Jung's rational-functional-psychological types, exemplified by the person whose life is ruled by reasoning and reflection. See THEORETICAL TYPE, TYPOLOGY.

thinning A process of changing the reaction of organisms from their acceptance of many stimuli of a certain type to their acceptance of but a few stimuli. For example, a dolphin is being conditioned to respond to the sight of a circle, but the dolphin responds to almost anything that has curves and a single perimeter, such as ovals. Thinning involves exposing the dolphin to circles that are reinforced and to ovals that are not, until it distinguishes between the two shapes. See DISCRIMINATION LEARNING.

thiopental (sodium) An ultrashort-acting barbiturate that when administered intravenously produces almost immediate loss of consciousness. See BARBITURATES, PENTOTHAL SODIUM.

thioxanthene A class of tricyclic drugs that resemble the phenothiazines in pharmacologic activity and molecular structure, used mainly in the treatment of schizophrenias.

third cranial nerve See OCULOMOTOR NERVE.

third ear (T. Reik) Ability of some people, especially therapists, who on hearing an account are able to understand it in depth. This intuitive talent may be assisted by understanding human nature. An experienced therapist listening to a patient talk might arrive at quite different conclusions from those which the patient intended, or that might be concluded by someone not so well-attuned to the implications of the statements. See LISTENING WITH THE THIRD EAR, SENSORY-AWARENESS GROUPS.

third eye Refers to a small, cone-shaped structure (the pineal body) in the epithalamus, between the superior colliculi. In certain animals (for example, lampreys, lizards, tadpoles) the anterior portion of the pineal body contains photosensitive neurons and has been regarded as a possible third eye, the pineal eye. See PINEAL GLAND.

third force in psychology Abraham Maslow's optimistic, growth-oriented psychology, different from both psychoanalysis and behaviorism but not necessarily competitive with them. See HUMANISTIC PSYCHOLOGY.

third-force therapy A relatively new trend in psychotherapy contrasting with both the psychoanalytic and behavior-therapy approaches, comprising various humanistic, existential, and experiential therapies. In general, third-force therapy revolves around direct experience; the here-and-now; concrete, immediate personality change; responsibility for self; group interactions; trust in natural processes and spontaneous feeling rather than reason; emphasis on personal growth rather than cure or adjustment; and self-exploration and self-discovery. Also known as humanistic therapy. Examples of third-force therapy include: BIOENERGETICS, CLIENT-CENTERED PSYCHOTHERAPY, EXISTENTIAL PSYCHOTHERAPY, EXPERIENTIAL PSYCHOTHERAPY, GESTALT THERAPY, IMAGERY THERAPY, PRIMAL THERAPY, RATIONAL PSYCHOTHERAPY, REALITY THERAPY, TRANSACTIONAL ANALYSIS. See THIRD FORCE IN PSYCHOLOGY.

third moment See MOMENT.

third nervous system According to Trigant Burrow, neural processes involved in communication through the use of symbols. Burrow held that misuse of these processes is responsible for behavior disorders.

third party facilitation The use of a mediator to help resolve a dispute between two parties.

third party payers Financial intermediaries that control the flow of money from clients to therapists. In therapy, third party payers are usually insurance companies or government agencies (for example, the Health Care Financing Administration).

third sex 1. A designation by Magnus Hirschfeld (1868–1935) of gay men (male homosexuals). Later research has indicated that there may be hereditary, gender-linked characteristics of gay men. 2. Infrequently used and inaccurate phrase for gay men or lesbians.

third-variable problem An effect posed by the correlation of two variables which do not cause each other, but rather another (third) variable may account for both variables. See DIRECTIONALITY PROBLEM.

third ventricle A cerebrospinal-fluid-filled cavity of the brain, appearing as a cleft between the two thalami of the hemispheres. Communicates with the lateral ventricles at the anterior end and with the fourth ventricle through the aqueduct of Sylvius. See BRAIN VENTRICLES.

Third World Phrase used since the 1940s as an analogy to the "third estate" in the French Revolution, referring to states outside the two main opponents in the Cold War, and since the 1960s to mean countries of the developing world, as opposed to the capitalist and communist ones.

thirst   A sensation caused by a need for increased fluid intake to maintain an optimum balance of water and electrolytes in the body tissues. Stimulation of the lateral hypothalamus with crystals of carbachol, a cholinergic drug, for example, is followed by a greatly increased urge to drink water. See ELECTROLYTE IMBALANCE, HEMORRHAGE AND THIRST, LOCAL THEORY OF THIRST, WATER REGULATION.

thirteen fear   See TRISKAIDEKAPHOBIA.

thixophobia   Morbid fear of touching another person. Also known as haphophobia, haptophobia.

thobbing   Thinking distorted by emotions, prejudice, or bias. Term is derived from thinking, opinion, belief.

Thomistic psychology   A form of psychological philosophy based on the teachings of Saint Thomas Aquinas. It is an interpretation and supplementation of the work of Aristotle as it relates to Christian theology. Became the official philosophy of the Roman Catholic Church in 1897.

Thompson Thematic Apperception Test (**T-TAT**) (C. E. Thompson) A projective technique for use with African Americans. Participants are shown pictures of African Americans in various situations and asked to generate stories. It is a variant of the Thematic Apperception Test. See THEMATIC APPERCEPTION TEST.

thoracic nerves   Twelve pairs of nerves that originate in the spinal cord. See SPINAL NERVES.

thoracicolumbar system   A portion of the spinal cord that extends along the 12 thoracic and three lumbar sections of the spine, including roots of the autonomic nervous system's sympathetic fibers. Fibers of the thoracicolumbar system innervate structures of the head, such as the eye and salivary glands, well beyond the usual range of nerves from the thoracic region of the spinal cord. Also known as thoracolumbar system.

Thorazine   Trade name for the hydrochloride form of chlorpromazine, a sedative, antiemetic, and tranquilizer.

Thorndike Handwriting Scale (E. L. Thorndike) A method of evaluating a person's handwriting by having a person write a standard sentence in cursive writing and then comparing it with a number of other handwritings varying in quality until a match is found.

Thorndike-Lorge List (E. L. Thorndike & D. I. Lorge) The first (1944) tabulation of the frequencies of 30,000 English words occurring in a variety of printed sources. Since then, superseded by others.

Thorndike Puzzle Box (E. L. Thorndike) A wooden box with sides made of slats used to study learning through animal escape behavior. The door of the box could be opened from the inside by the imprisoned animal. The incentive to escape was food, placed outside the box, that the animal could see through the slats. Thorndike described the puzzle box in 1898.

Thorndike Puzzle Box   A box constructed so that a cat placed inside can escape easily if it knows how: by moving either of the two small horizontal bars on the door of the cage. Edward Thorndike observed that most cats learn, by trial and error, how to escape from the box. When returned to the cage, over repeated trials, the cat escapes in increasingly less time.

Thorndike's basic intelligence factors   According to E. L. Thorndike, three basic factors of intelligence are: (a) cognitive, the ability to learn symbols; (b) mechanical, the aptitude to deal with things; and (c) social, the potential to get along with people.

Thorndike's Laws of Learning   Three laws of learning proposed by Edward Thorndike, namely the laws of exercise, effect, and readiness.

Thorndike's theory   The following are important in understanding Edward Lee Thorndike's theory: ANIMAL INTELLIGENCE, ANNOYER, ASSOCIATIONISM, BELONGINGNESS, COGNITIVE INTELLIGENCE, CONDUCTION UNIT, CONNECTIONISM, DRIVE-REDUCTION THEORY, EMPIRICAL LAW OF EFFECT, IDENTICAL-COMPONENTS THEORY, LAW OF ASSOCIATIVE SHIFTING, LAW OF BELONGINGNESS, LAW OF DISUSE, LAW OF EFFECT, LAW OF EXERCISE, LAW OF PIECEMEAL ACTIVITY, LAW OF READINESS, LAW OF UNREADINESS, LORGE-THORNDIKE INTELLIGENCE TESTS, MECHANICAL INTELLIGENCE, OBSERVATIONAL LEARNING, PUZZLE BOX, RESPONSE BY ANALOGY PRINCIPLE, SATISFIER, SOCIAL INTELLIGENCE, STIMULUS-RESPONSE THEORY, THORNDIKE-LORGE TEST, THORNDIKE PUZZLE BOX, THORNDIKE'S BASIC INTELLIGENCE FACTORS, THORNDIKE'S HANDWRITING SCALE, THORNDIKE'S LAWS OF LEARNING, THORNDIKE'S TRIAL-AND-ERROR LEARNING.

Thorndike's Trial-and-Error Learning   (E. L. Thorndike) A theory that learning involves an S-R (stimulus-response) process in which neural connections are established when a response to a stimulus results in satisfaction or pleasure.

thought broadcasting   A symptom of some forms of schizophrenia characterized by the abnormal belief or experience that personal thoughts are being expressed or "broadcast" out loud so that they can be heard by others.

thought deprivation/obstruction   An abrupt, involuntary interruption in the flow of thought or speech. Also known as blocking, emotional blocking.

thought derailment/disorganization   A disorder characterized by disorganized, disconnected thought processes. Similar to cognitive derailment, cognitive slippage.

thought disorder/disturbance   Any disturbance in the thinking processes that affects communication, language, or thought content, including such disorders as blocking, poverty of ideas, loosening of associations, verbigeration, circumstantiality, neologisms, paralogia, concrete thinking, incoherence, word salad, and delusions. Thought disorder is considered one of the most important signs of schizophrenia. See CONTENT DISORDER, FORMAL-THOUGHT DISORDER.

thought disorganization   thought derailment

thought disturbance   Refers to any bizarre, inconsistent, disconnected thinking. Sometimes known as thought disorder.

thought-echoing   An auditory hallucination in which patients hear their own thoughts repeated in spoken form. Also known as *echo des pensées* (French).

thought experiment   1. In early experimental psychology, a type of experiment designed to discover the nature of thought. See IMAGELESS THOUGHT. 2. An experiment that is not executed in vivo but only mentally.

thought impulses   A poorly named concept relating to dreams that originate from ordinary life situations, such as having to take an examination, in contrast to dreams that originate from deep hidden unconscious forces. See DREAM ANALYSIS, DREAM MATERIAL.

thought insertion   The abnormal belief or experience that personal thoughts do not belong to a person but have been put or "inserted" into the mind by someone else. A symptom of some forms of schizophrenia. See THOUGHT BROADCASTING, THOUGHT TRANSFERENCE.

thought obstruction   See BLOCKING, THOUGHT DEPRIVATION.

thought processes   General phrase for any type of thinking or symbolic process involved in such activities as judgments, imagination, planning, problem-solving, and drawing inferences.

thought-reading   See MIND-READING.

thought stopping   1. Eliminating negative cognitions and images, and refocusing on relevant cues. 2. A behavior therapy technique in which the therapist shouts "Stop!" to interrupt a trend toward undesirable thoughts, and teaches clients to apply this technique to themselves. See RECOVERY, INC.

thought transference   Alleged mental telepathy in which the mental activities of one person are thought to be transmitted without physical means to the mind of another person. See TELEPATHY.

thought withdrawal   A delusion that thoughts have been stolen from the person, resulting in fewer thoughts.

Thouless ratio   (R. H. Thouless) A modified version of the Brunswik ratio in which the logarithmic transforms of the values of the stimulus S, albedo A (the light reflected by a surface), and response R are used. The ratio is: $(\log R - \log S)/(\log A - \log S)$.

threat   1. Any real or imagined danger to an individual or group, or an indication of an impending disaster. 2. Suggesting a degree of coercion. 3. (C. R. Rogers) Feelings resulting from the awareness of incongruities between personal experiences and self-concept. 4. (G. A. Kelly) Impending awareness of a change in a person's basic construct.

threats to external experimental validity   (D. T. Campbell & J. C. Stanley) Eleven design deficiencies that can markedly reduce a study's generality and hurt the applicability of the conclusions of a research project: (a) target population is not the experimentally accessible population; (b) interaction of personological variables and treatment effects (some types of participants respond differently to the experimental manipulation); (c) multiple-treatment interference (impact of specific components cannot be determined); (d) Hawthorne effect (change due to participants knowing they are in a study); (e) novelty effect (any change produces an increment in behavior); (f) experimenter effect (includes researcher expectation effects, recording errors, intentional errors, impact of biosocial and psychosocial attributes on participants); (g) pretest sensitization (results only apply to those who have had the pretest experience); (h) posttest sensitization (treatment effects may not appear for a period of time); (i) measurement of the dependent variable (includes jingle fallacy, jangle fallacy); (j) interaction of treatments with time; and (k) ambiguous independent variable. See THREATS TO INTERNAL EXPERIMENTAL VALIDITY.

threats to internal experimental validity   (D. T. Campbell & J. C. Stanley) Seven design deficiencies that can make the conclusions of a research project tenuous: (a) history (an uncontrolled variable occurring between the pre- and post-measure, a hidden treatment); (b) maturation (of subjects over the course of the study); (c) testing (the pre-measure itself has some cognitive or affective impact); (d) instrumentation (changes in the measuring devices, including judges, over the course of the study); (e) statistical regression (probable tendency of persons whose scores are extreme at initial measuring to be closer to the population mean on the second measurement); (f) selection (participant groups unequal prior to treatment application); and (g) experimental mortality (differential loss of subjects from the groups). See THREATS TO EXTERNAL EXPERIMENTAL VALIDITY.

threctia   (R. B. Cattell) The source trait H(-) in the 16PF. A temperamental trait of extreme lack of boldness, expressed as a genetic timidity.

three-color theory   Any doctrine to the effect that color vision can be explained on the basis of three elementary chromatic processes which combine in varying degrees of activity to yield the various colors, including grays. Also known as three-component theory, trichromatic theory.

three-component theory   See THREE-COLOR THEORY.

three-cornered therapy   (P. Pedersen) A general form of psychotherapy in which three persons are involved. Most often the pattern includes two clients and a single therapist. However, other variations include one client and two therapists, or a client and a therapist in addition to someone who represents the client, as in the case when the client and the therapist do not speak the same language. See MULTIPLE THERAPY.

three-day schizophrenia   A brief psychotic episode with schizophrenia-like symptoms such as agitation, incoherence, hallucinations, and poorly organized delusions. Precipitated by extreme external stress, as from natural disasters, fires, or combat.

3-D   Abbreviation for three dimensional. See TRIDIMENSIONAL VISION.

three-dimensionality   See DEPTH PERCEPTION.

360-degree feedback system   In industrial psychology, a term originating in the early 1990s for employee ratings from various sources, such as managers and subordinates. In "true" or "full" 360-degree feedback, the sources include at least the employee's self-ratings, the supervisor, and peers. Sometimes known as 360-systems.

Three Paper Test   (P. Marie) An intelligence and memory task using three sheets of paper. An examiner points to the three papers and tells the participant, for example, "Please pick up the three papers. Put one paper on that chair, put one under the door, and put one on the window sill." Whether the participant completes all three directions, and also how they are completed, yields information to the examiner.

three-pedal apparatus   A device for measuring the "intelligence" of animals. The animal may obtain food at the center of the device but only after it makes a certain number of stops, touching pedals in a particular sequence, established by the experimenter. For example, a chicken must touch the first and then the second pedal (1-2 sequence) for food to appear. But a pig must learn a 2-3-1-3 sequence. "Intelligence" is in quotes because these animals are being compared with humans and not with qualities that are necessarily meaningful for animals. See TEMPORAL MAZE.

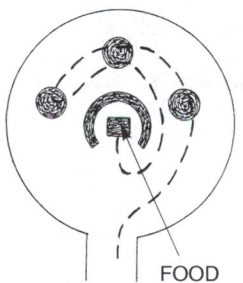

three-pedal apparatus   Shown from above, the dotted line is the path the animal must take to reach the food.

three-pronged clevis   Devil's pitchfork

three-term contingency   (B. F. Skinner) A situation in which a discriminative stimulus sets an occasion on which a probability response produces consequences.

threshold   A point along a continuum of strength or amount sufficient to just detect or identify a stimulus (absolute threshold), or to discriminate between two stimuli (differential threshold). The threshold usually is set at 50% success either for an individual or for a group. Also known as limen. Types of threshold include: ABSOLUTE, AUDITORY, BEHAVIORAL, BLACKOUT, BRIGHTNESS, DETECTION, DIFFERENCE, DUAL, RESPONSE, SENSORY, SPATIAL, SPEECH-RECEPTION, TERMINAL, TWO-POINT, WAVELENGTH.

threshold difference   That value of a stimulus judged to be different from an adjacent stimulus with an arbitrarily chosen probability (usually 0.5 in psychophysical experimentation), statistically determined from a set of observations. Also known as just-noticeable difference.

threshold for a neuron   The amount of excitation required for a neuron to initiate action.

threshold for bodily motion   The minimum rate of rotation, or the minimum rate of positive and negative acceleration in rotary and rectilinear (forward) motion, necessary for organic sensibility for the perception of bodily motion.

threshold logic unit (TLU)   (F. Rosenblatt) In learning theory, a basic unit in the "perceptron" neural model to explain pattern discrimination.

threshold of consciousness   The psychic level at which the nonconscious becomes conscious experience.

threshold of differences   just-noticeable difference

threshold shift   A change in the threshold for any sense, whether temporary or permanent. For example, a person who had 20-20 vision may suddenly have poorer vision either temporarily due to minor injury to the eyes or permanently if increasing age changed vision sharpness.

threshold symbolism   A dream image that symbolizes the desire to wake up. Images of this kind are thought to occur during the hypnagogic state between sleep and waking. See HYPNAGOGIC HALLUCINATION.

threshold theory   (E. G. Bormann) In group dynamics, a conflict model holding that conflict serves a useful function for groups as long as it does not exceed the tolerance threshold for too long.

threshold traits analysis   (F. M. Lopez, G. A. Kesselman & F. E. Lopez) A procedure for performing a job analysis that examines the job functions performed and the personnel attributes required. See JOB ANALYSIS.

thrill   A sudden, intense, emotional condition, either pleasant or unpleasant, such as the thrill of joy or of horror. There are often confused dermal sensations, such as of tingling, perception of temperature change, with these sensations changing rapidly in location and intensity.

thrombosis   The presence or formation of a blood clot (a thrombus) in a blood vessel or the heart. A thrombosis in the brain tissues can cause a stroke. Plural is thromboses.

thrombus   A clot in the cardiovascular system formed from constituents of blood. Plural is thrombi. See THROMBOSIS.

throughput   In a dynamic system, the processing or transformation of inputs into the intended goals (outputs).

throwback   atavus

thrownness   In existential psychology, a person's starting point in life characterized by feelings of fear and anxiety at being in the world without a meaning or set direction, feeling lost or at odds in life; related to existential angst.

thumb opposition   Ability to coordinate the thumb and index finger in pincer-like movements. It begins to develop around the third or fourth month, although it is not fully achieved until the second half of the first year, as eye-hand coordination grows more skillful.

thumb-sucking   A common, though not universal, phenomenon among infants and young children, formerly classified as a habit disturbance if it persists beyond three or four years. The common explanation is in terms of a basic sucking impulse from which the child derives pleasure as well as comfort and relaxation.

Thurstone Attitude Scales   (L. L. Thurstone) A series of statements, each selected according to the method of equal-appearing intervals, assigned a scale value on the basis of the judgment of at least 100 participants, on such topics as capital punishment, communism, the church, and censorship. See LIKERT SCALE.

Thurstone Primary Mental Abilities   Based on early factor analysis, Lewis L. Thurstone declared that intelligence consisted of seven independent factors: Word fluency, Memory, Numerical, Perception, Reasoning, Space, Verbal. See BASIC INTELLIGENCE FACTORS, GUILFORD FACTORS OF INTELLIGENCE, INTELLIGENCE, MENTAL ABILITIES.

Thurstone-type attitude scales   Scales which measure attitude by requiring the respondent to place statements such as "Do you like to eat fruits?" and "Do you like to eat oysters?" in rank order. Louis Thurstone used the method of equal-appearing intervals. A panel of judges were given one hundred 3 × 5 cards on each of which was printed a statement mentioning a different food. Judges put each card in one of five piles ranging from "absolutely no" to "absolutely yes" with a middle one of "not sure." Replies were tallied from low preference (like to eat rattlesnake?) to high preference (like to eat ice cream?). See ATTITUDE SCALE, LIKERT SCALE.

thwart   In research, to prevent a subject from achieving a goal or completing an SOR (stimulus-organism-response) sequence. See THWARTING.

thwarting   Placing barriers in an individual's way so that some goal cannot be satisfied, or so that there is unusual difficulty in satisfying it, leading to feelings of frustration and anger. See THWART.

thymergasia   One of Adolf Meyer's "ergasias" established to describe forms of human behavior, this term was applied to the category of manic-depressive (bipolar) disorders.

thymine   (A. Kossel) A pyrimidine base with one carbon ring found in deoxyribonucleic acid (DNA) but not ribonucleic acid (RNA). Forms a complementary pair across each strand of the double helix of the DNA molecule by joining with adenine. See ADENINE, CYTOSINE, DEOXYRIBONUCLEIC ACID (DNA), GUANINE, URACIL.

thymogenic drinking   The undisciplined consumption and dependence on the effects of alcohol, but without losing control or being unable to abstain. Similar to Elvin M. Jellinek's alpha alcoholism.

thymoleptics   Agents that have a mood-changing effect, particularly drugs that can relieve the symptoms of severe depression.

thymopathic   Term introduced by Eugen Bleuler to describe an abnormal disruption of mood that he concluded was evidence of a genetic susceptibility to manic-depressive (bipolar) psychosis.

thymus   (B. da Carpa, R. Bright, A. Paltauf) A ductless, gland-like body in the lower neck region that reaches a maximum size at puberty, then undergoes involution (reduction). Associated with the body's immune-response system. Plural is thymi, thymuses. See THYMECTOMY.

thyroid-stimulating hormone (TSH)   thyrotropic hormone

thyroid (gland)   (Vesalius, T. Wharton) The largest of human's endocrine (ductless) glands, located on the front and sides of the throat. Produces the hormones that stimulate a number of organs and systems involved in skeletal growth and sexual development, including controlling calcium levels in the blood.

thyrotrop(h)ic hormone (TTH)   The hormone thyrotropin, produced by the anterior pituitary gland to control the growth and function of the thyroid gland. Thyrotropic hormone is used in the differential diagnosis of thyroid-gland disorders. Also known as thyroid-stimulating hormone (TSH).

thyroxin (T$_4$)   (E. C. Kendall, C. R. Harington) A hormone of the thyroid gland that catalyzes a number of metabolic activities and influences growth and development. Vitamin requirements, defense against infection, and metabolism of fats, carbohydrates, and proteins depend upon thyroxine levels in the body. Also spelled thyroxine.

TIA   transient ischemic attack

tic   Involuntary contraction of muscles, for example, continually clearing the throat, or grimacing. See TOURETTE'S DISORDER/SYNDROME.

tic disorder   A persistent condition characterized by a repeated, involuntary contraction of a small group of muscles, causing significant impairment of day-to-day functioning. Lasting a period of weeks to years. See TOURETTE'S DISORDER/SYNDROME.

tic douloureux   (painful tic—French) Trigeminal neuralgia.

ticket-of-leave   British phrase roughly equivalent to "parole" during which period a convict under general supervision may work outside of the correctional institution.

tickle (experience)   A sensory experience resulting from a complication of contact sensations, such as being touched on certain areas of the body (for example soles of feet, underarms) resulting in a strong feeling tone, marked by convulsive movements of escape and laughter. It is assumed that the involved receptors also are those for itch and pain and the method of stimulation accounts for the different sensation. See HYPERGARGALESTHESIA.

tickling paradox   A paradox that persons cannot experience the effect of being tickled by tickling themselves.

TID   *ter in die*, Latin for three times a day (also abbreviated **t.i.d, T.I.D.**). See APPENDIX D.

tidal air   Refers to the normal exchange of gases (oxygen, carbon dioxide) inhaled and exhaled by a person while at rest or asleep.

tidal volume (TV)   The volume of air moved during either the inspiratory or expiratory phase of each breath.

tie-in   In negotiation, an issue introduced by one side that must be agreed to by the other side, who considers it irrelevant.

tied image   The correlation of an experienced sensation with an imagined sensation, as in tasting something and imagining what it looks like.

tight cultures   (H. Triandis) A cultural syndrome organized around the theme of criticism or punishment for even minor deviations from the norms of the collective. Compare LOOSE CULTURES.

tight-rope test   A measure of the ability of animals, especially laboratory rats, to maintain balance while climbing a sloping cord or wire to obtain food. Has been employed in learning experiments. See ANIMAL INTELLIGENCE.

tigroid bodies   Particles observed in the protoplasm of neurons, including their dendrites. They can be identified by the way in which they absorb certain histological stains. Also known as chromophil substance, Nissl bodies/granules.

tilde (∼) 1. A symbol for negation when it appears in front of something, such as ∼ X means "Not X." Used in mathematical and logical formulas. 2. A mark used over some letters of words to indicate a variant pronunciation of the letter. 3. In mathematics, "similar to."

tilt-board See TILTING BOARD.

tilting board An apparatus used for vestibular stimulation; it consists essentially of a flat board with dimensions of approximately 6 ft. by 2 ft. which swings freely about a horizontal axis; the person lies upon the board. The apparatus resembles a children's teeter-totter. Also known as tilt-board.

timbre A tonal quality or character, as determined by the complexity of the sound waves that impinge on auditory receptors. Pure tones are rarely heard; most tones are "colored" since they result from composite sound waves. Timbre accounts for the different sound qualities of the same note played by different musical instruments, since the fundamental tone is accompanied by different harmonics and overtones generated by each instrument's individual structure.

time agnosia Inability to perceive the passage of time, usually due to a disorder of the temporal area of the brain. Causes may include a stroke or alcoholic coma, as well as a head injury; soldiers have experienced time agnosia after a combat trauma. Patients are unable to estimate short time intervals and long periods of time appear much shorter than they actually are.

time and motion evaluation (F. Gilbreth & L. Gilbreth) Studies of various ways to do things as efficiently as possible to reduce the time taken for repetitive motions. For instance, Frank Gilbreth found that it took 4 seconds less to button his shirt from the bottom up than from the top down. See EFFICIENCY, METHODS ANALYSIS, MOTION ECONOMY, THERBLIG.

time-and-motion study Analysis of industrial operations into their component movements, noting the time required for each, for the purpose of increasing productivity, setting pay rates, reducing fatigue, and preventing accidents. See EQUIPMENT DESIGN, THERBLIG.

time and rhythm disorders Speech and language problems related to the timing of sounds and syllables, including repetitions and prolongations and stuttering. The disorders often are functional, and complicated by guilt feelings of the afflicted person. The condition may be treated with a combination of psychotherapy and speech therapy, using such techniques as cancellation (interrupted stuttering), voluntary stuttering, or rewarding or reinforcing fluent speech efforts.

time cluster The pattern of occurrence of a causal or other variable across time. May be regular, cyclic, bursts, random, multiharmonic, chaotic, etc.

time consciousness The condition of one who suffers agenda anxiety and the pervasive concern that one's goals may not all be achieved. See HURRY SICKNESS, TYPE A PERSONALITY.

time course 1. The values of a variable dimension as a function of time. 2. The temporally related dimensions of a variable, such as cyclicity, latency, duration, and rate. The time-courses of variables are frequently presented in graphical form with time on the horizontal axis and the value of the variable on the vertical axis.

timed tests Examinations with time limits.

time discounting Preferring to obtain something immediately rather than later, usually despite knowledge that waiting will result in something of greater value. See IMMEDIATE GRATIFICATION.

time disorientation Loss of the ability to keep track of time or the passage of time. This inability to identify the day or month is a common mental-disorder symptom. See DISORIENTATION, TIME AGNOSIA.

time distortion Perceptual distortion of the passage of time. For example, during altered states of consciousness an hour may seem like a minute, or a minute seem like an hour. Can be due to ingestion of psychedelic substances such as magic mushroom (teonanacatl).

time error (TE) In psychophysics, a tendency to misjudge items that are dependent upon their relative position in time; for example, the first of two identical tones sounded consecutively tends to be judged as louder.

time-extended therapy (I. Yalom) A form of group psychotherapy in which prolonged sessions can last continuously for many hours. The experience is sometimes highly emotional and revealing since "there's no place to hide" and, due to fatigue, participants do not have the energy to play defensive games. See ACCELERATED INTERACTION, MARATHON GROUP.

time fear See CHRONOPHOBIA.

time judgments An observation that intervals of up to five or six seconds are judged most accurately. Boring events such as an uninteresting lecture are judged much longer than equal periods of time spent doing enjoyable things. See PSYCHOLOGICAL TIME.

time-lag study (K. Warner Schaie) The comparison of two or more samples of the same chronological age, but measured at different calendar times.

time-lagged correlations Correlating serial data points at time point 1 with those at a subsequent or prior time period. The time lag of the correlations may vary.

timeless moment An absolute instance of time, not measurable because it is infinitesimally small. There is only past and future in this technical sense. Also known as specious present, as the instant that we reflect on it, it is past.

time-limited psychotherapy (TLP) Psychotherapy, typically brief, that is limited to a predetermined number of sessions. Theoretical, monetary, political, and organizational considerations have provided impetus for growth in this genre of psychotherapy.

time-limit method/procedure A method of arranging test material and instructions such that each participant works for the same length of time. Efficiency is measured by the amount (or amount and quality) of work done in this established constant time.

time localization (K. Rigney) A tendency of humans at various stages of life to be cognitively in the past, present or future. Infants presumably are always in the present and perhaps those in senile states are mostly in the past. Adults probably differ considerably in the proportion of time spent in reminiscing about the past, being in the present, or speculating about the future.

time order The sequence in which stimuli are presented in psychophysical experiment.

time-out (TO) In behavior therapy, a technique that removes people (usually children) from an area when misbehaving to teach them to discontinue the undesired behavior. Used in schools to decrease the frequency of undesirable behavior by isolating children for a period of time. See BEHAVIOR MODIFICATION.

time-out from reinforcement A behavior-therapy technique in which undesirable behavior is weakened by moving the patient into a nonreinforcing area.

time-out procedures 1. In operant conditioning, a time interval during which a reinforcement does not occur. A time-out procedure may be used to eliminate stimulus effects of earlier behaviors or as a marker in a series of events. 2. In education, a behavior modification procedure in which pupils are asked to leave the classroom for exhibiting undesired behavior.

time perception Awareness of the passage of time, including the ability to estimate time intervals, to tell time accurately by clocks or approximately by the position of the sun, as well as the ability to judge time duration by circadian rhythms. See PSYCHOLOGICAL TIME, TIME PERCEPTION.

timers See INTERVAL TIMERS.

time samples In testing or research procedures, those samples in which cases are drawn or observed in a sequence of relatively brief, specific time frames. For example, the observation of covert smoking in high-school stairwells between 2 p.m. and 3 p.m. over a period of one month.

time sampling The determination of when to make observations so that the maximal representative behaviors are included within the minimum total period of observation.

time score A score based on the amount of time used to complete a particular task, sequence, or series of problems. For example, the number of minutes a three-year-old child requires to solve a simple jigsaw puzzle.

time sense 1. The direct experience of the passage of time. 2. Ability to judge an interval of time. Time subjectively slows when bored or inactive and speeds when the person is active and interested. Drugs, temperature, and hypnosis may speed or slow subjective passages of time. See PSYCHOLOGICAL TIME, TIME PERCEPTION.

time-sense apparatus An instrument for determining the accuracy of time estimation.

time-sequential design (K. Warner Schaie) Samples are drawn to represent two or more chronological age levels at two or more equivalent times of measurement. All samples are assessed only once. Design permits simultaneous estimation of time-of-measurement and chronological age differences, assuming cohort effects are trivial or of no interest.

time series A statistical series ordered sequentially in time, for example, a learning curve, accident rates over a number of years, or monthly rates of admission to mental hospitals. See PSYCHOLOGICAL TIME.

time-series assessment (J. Gottman) A diverse set of assessment strategies to describe and analyze the time-courses and interrelationships of multiple variables. With time-series assessment, behavior problems or hypothesized causal variables are measured frequently (for example, 30 or more measurements) across time.

time study A measurement of the time required to perform certain tasks (usually combined with motion study). See THERBLIG.

timidity 1. A tendency to experience anxiety when meeting new persons or situations. 2. Shyness and avoidance of other people. 3. Inability to assert the self. 4. An emotional attitude marked by hesitation, and by a tendency to experience fear in situations which do not justify the fear attitude.

timing-of-events model (B. Newgarten) A theoretical model, that describes adult social and emotional development as a response to whether the occurrence and timing of important life events is expected or unexpected. See NORMATIVE-CRISIS MODEL.

tingling Experience characterized by short, intermittent, tactual sensations localized at some point or region of the periphery of the body.

tinnitus Noises in one or both ears, including ringing, buzzing, or clicking sounds due to acute ear ailments and in disturbances in the receptor mechanism, drug side effects, and epileptic aura.

TIP treatment improvement protocol

tip-of-the-tongue phenomenon/state (TOT) 1. (R. Brown & D. McNeill) A temporary inability to recall a known word in memory with definite ability to recall phonologically and semantically related words while rejecting them as not the sought-after target. 2. The experience of attempting to retrieve from memory a specific fact, often a name or word, that eludes such attempts while hovering tantalizingly on the rim of consciousness. Illustrates a preconscious process in that the given fact is ordinarily accessible and is only temporarily unavailable to consciousness. 3. When given a definition and told to recall the corresponding word, the inability always to do so, especially with target words that are rare and unique in sound, such as "fallow."

tissue An organic structure composed of identical or similar cells with the same or similar function. The four basic tissues of the body are: (a) epithelium, the cellular layer covering all free surfaces, such as cutaneous, mucous, and serous; (b) connective tissues, such as blood, bone, and cartilage; (c) muscle tissue; and (d) nerve tissue.

tissue need The requirements of cells of an organism for oxygen, water, and appropriate nutrients, as well as a suitable environment for growth.

tissue rejection The natural resistance of the body tissues to transplants or grafts of cells or organs from the body of a genetically different individual. See IMMUNITY FACTORS, ORGAN TRANSPLANTS.

Titchener's theory The following items are important in understanding Edward Titchener's theory: AMPLITUDE OF LIGHT WAVE, ATTENSITY, COMPOUND TONES, CONTEXT THEORY OF MEANING, FOCAL ATTENTION, INTROSPECTIONIST, INTROSPECTIVE METHOD, PSYCHOLOGICAL DIMENSION, SENSATION ATTRIBUTES, SENSATION ELEMENTS, STIMULUS ERROR, TONAL PENCIL, TOUCH PYRAMID.

titration   A technique employed in the determination of an optimum dose of a drug needed to produce a desired effect in a particular individual. The dosage may be gradually increased until a noticeable improvement is observed in a patient or adjusted downward because of overdose or other adverse effects. Many people self-titrate optimum levels of caffeine, nicotine, or alcoholic beverages in this manner.

TL   1. terminal limen. 2. tolerance level.

TLC   1. tender loving care. 2. teachable language comprehender.

TLE   Abbreviation for temporal-lobe epilepsy. See PSYCHOMOTOR EPILEPSY.

TLP   time-limited psychotherapy

TLU   threshold logic unit

T-lymphocyte   A leucocyte originating in the thymus and having immune system functions.

TM   transcendental meditation

TMA   1. transcortical motor aphasia. 2. Slang for analog of amphetamine/methamphetamine.

T-maze   A simple type of maze shaped like the letter T consisting of a single choice point and two paths, one of which is incorrect whereas the other leads to the goal box. More complicated structures are designed by joining several T-maze components. See FINGER MAZE for an example. See also TEMPORAL MAZE.

TMD   trainable mental defective

TMJ syndrome   See TEMPOROMANDIBULAR JOINT SYNDROME.

TMR   trainable mentally retarded

TMT   trail-making test

TO   time-out

tobacco   The dried leaf of *Nicotiana* plants; it is smoked, chewed, or sniffed for its stimulant effects. Tobacco has no known therapeutic value but is of interest because its dried, processed leaves are universally smoked, sniffed, or chewed. Tobacco is addictive.

tobacco addiction   An addiction to the nicotine in tobacco. See TOBACCO DEPENDENCE.

tobacco dependence   An inability to stop smoking even when this dependency is evidently life-threatening, as in Raynaud's disease (when the capillaries of the body are affected and amputation of limbs appears necessary). See TOBACCO ADDICTION.

tobacco withdrawal symptoms   Physical and psychological symptoms that may occur as the result of ceasing to use tobacco products. Physical symptoms may include an inability to sit still, chewing of lips or fingernails, weight gain, and upper-respiratory cold-like symptoms. Psychological symptoms may include an intense desire for tobacco, irritability, tension, headaches, anxiety, uneasiness, and insomnia. The withdrawal symptoms may last for days, months, or years and recur temporarily (for example, every 100 days). Symptoms allegedly last longer in people who regret that they quit. Nicotine appears to be the addictive agent.

to-be-remembered (TBR) items   In learning and memory tasks, material that the participant is to learn.

tocophobia   Fear of pregnancy, of being pregnant. See MAIEUSIOPHOBIA.

TOD   See TARDIVE (ORAL) DYSKINESIA.

TODAM   theory of distributed associative memory

toe shaker   Slang for a tactile aircraft display that vibrates the pedals to warn the pilot to not push them so hard. See STICK SHAKER.

Tofranil   Trade name for imipramine hydrochloride.

togetherness need   1. The infant's need for psychic union with the mother or care-giver. 2. A general need for close attachments to other persons. See ATTACHMENT BEHAVIOR, BONDING.

toggle (switch)   A control with two (occasionally three) positions, usually up-down or left-right. Hence, to toggle is to change from one of two control positions to the other.

toilet training   The process of teaching a child to control the emptying of the bowel or urinary bladder by learned inhibition of natural reflexes; and to excrete in the "proper" place and manner. The toilet-training period of a child's life is a period assumed by some to be important because of its influence on mental health in later years. See DEFECATION REFLEX, MICTURITION REFLEXES.

token   An object that stands for, or represents something else (for example, a poker chip). Chimpanzees have been trained to work for objects that have no value in and of themselves but can be exchanged for true rewards or reinforcers (token rewards). In some behaviorist-oriented institutions, residents are given tokens of different colors for desired behavior that can later be redeemed for desired commodities or privileges. See TOKEN ECONOMY, TOKEN REWARD.

token economy   An operant conditioning procedure used in a controlled environment such as a school, jail, or mental hospital. The tokens, which can be exchanged for rewards or privileges, are given for behaving as specified by the staff, and can also be charged or taken away for infringement of rules. See BEHAVIOR MODIFICATION.

token reward   See TOKEN, TOKEN ECONOMY.

tolerance   1. A tendency to be less responsive to a stimulus, especially over a period of continued exposure. 2. In social relationships, an attitude of indulgence or acceptance, especially for ideas or behavior that differ from personal ones or the society at large. 3. Adjustment of the chemistry of the brain to the presence of a chemical which, in turn, then diminishes or even loses its capacity for modifying brain activity. It is associated with the use of all sedative-hypnotic drugs, such as barbiturates, and is followed by withdrawal symptoms when regular doses of the drug are interrupted, thus indicating physiological dependence on that drug. Also known as drug tolerance. See SUBSTANCE DEPENDENCE.

tolerance level (TL)   The hearing level at which speech becomes uncomfortably loud. It also represents the level of maximum amplification the person can tolerate in a hearing aid. See SPEECH TOLERANCE LEVEL.

Tolman's purposive behaviorism   (E. C. Tolman) A combination of Gestalt concepts with behaviorism applied primarily to the study of animal learning. In maze-running, the animal creates a cognitive map out of sign gestalts which consist of environmental cues and subjective expectations. Other influential factors are place-learning (starting from the same place), reward expectancy, and latent learning (incidental learning, without reward). The total process involves a combination of variables: physiological drive, environmental stimuli, heredity, previous training, and maturity or age. The following items are important in understanding E. C. Tolman's theory: DETERMINANT, BELIEF-VALUE MATRIX, CAUSAL TEXTURE, COGNITIVE MAP, COGNITIVE PLAN, CONFIRMATION, DISCRIMINANDA, DOCILITY, EQUIVALENCE BELIEF, EXPECTANCY THEORY, FIELD COGNITION MODE, MANIPULANDUM, MEANS-END CAPACITY, PURPOSIVE BEHAVIORISM, REWARD EXPECTANCY, SIGN LEARNING, VALENCE.

toloa An herb used by the Algonquin, the Zufii, and other Native American nations in rituals that included an adolescent search for identity. Also known as *wysocean*.

tomato effect (A. Scheuer) Being negatively affected by something because the person believes it to be harmful although it is not. Name derives from when tomatoes were first introduced to Europe when they had this reputation, thus "causing" many illnesses. Compare PLACEBO EFFECT.

tomboyism A tendency of girls to manifest or adopt behavior associated with boys in Western society. Such behavior is more acceptable than "feminine" behavior in the boy in many cultures. Ordinarily, tomboyism diminishes as the girl grows older. However, females with congenital adrenogenital syndrome and a high androgen level may remain masculine in their interests and behavior. See ROLE CONFUSION.

Tomkins-Horn Picture Arrangement Test A projective examination in which the participant arranges sets of three sketches of the same interpersonal scene in the sequence "which makes the best sense," after which a sentence is to be written that tells the story depicted.

tomography A system of radiological examination using a series of X-rays, each of which shows a section of the body or an organ that is adjacent to the next section. See COMPUTERIZED AXIAL TOMOGRAPHY.

tomomania Compulsive urge to be operated on. See MUNCHAUSEN SYNDROME.

tonal See TONE.

tonal attribute A measurable characteristic of a tone: pitch, volume, timbre, loudness. Sometimes known as auditory attributes/dimensions, tonal dimensions.

tonal bell (C. E. Ruckmick) A bell-shaped model used to demonstrate the relationships of the various tonal attributes.

tonal brightness An aspect of sound that generates the impression of "liveliness" rather than "dullness". Brightness is felt in music, varying in loudness, at a fast tempo, whereas dullness is heard in music that has little variations and is generally slow.

tonal character See TIMBRE.

tonal chroma tonality

tonal color See TIMBRE.

tonal dimension See TONAL ATTRIBUTE.

tonal dullness See TONAL BRIGHTNESS.

tonal fusion The blending of two or more tones into a single tonal experience.

tonal gap A range of pitches to which a person may be partially insensitive or totally insensitive (known as island deafness), although able to perceive tones on either side of the gap.

tonal interaction In humans, refers to how the cochlea of the inner ear manages to hear two or more tones occurring simultaneously.

tonal island A region of normal pitch acuity surrounded by tonal gaps. See TONAL GAP.

tonality A pitch attribute by which a tone sounds more closely related to its octave than to the adjacent tone on the scale; also, the sum of the relationships between the tones of a musical scale. Also known as tonal chroma. See TONAL ATTRIBUTE.

tonal patterns The sequence of tones or musical notes that forms a tune. Tonal-pattern discrimination requires a cortical mechanism for storing tonal information. Lesions in the temporal lobe can result in tonal-pattern deficits, particularly when there is a long time span between two notes in a usual sequence.

tonal pencil A graphic representation of the relationship between pitch and volume.

tonal scale In humans, the normal range of sound frequencies perceived by a young adult, from about 20 to about 20,000 Hertz (cycles per second). Also known as tonal range.

tonal sensation An experience produced by stimulation of the ear by relatively simple periodic sound-waves. Also known as tone sensation.

tonal spectrum See ACOUSTIC SPECTRUM, SOUND SPECTRUM.

tonal volume The extensity or space-filling quality of a tone. For example, a pipe organ has greater tonal volume than a flute.

tonaphasia Loss of ability to remember tunes due to cerebral lesion.

tone 1. A sound caused by a periodic vibration or sound wave in an elastic medium. 2. A unit of measure of the musical interval. 3. The characteristic timbre of an instrument or voice. 4. A state of normal muscle tension, especially when the muscles are firm and strong. Types of tones include: AFFECTIVE, BEAT-, COLOR, COMBINATION, COMPLEX, COMPOUND, DIFFERENCE, FEELING, FUNDAMENTAL, GENERATING, HEDONIC, HIGHEST AUDIBLE, INTERMITTENCE, INTERRUPTION, MUSCLE, OTOGENIC, PARTIAL, PURE, SUMMATION, TARTINI'S, WHOLE.

tone character See TIMBRE.

tone color The quality of sound of an instrument, such as the same note played on two pianos, an inexpensive instrument and a symphony instrument, the tones will differ in subjective richness.

tone deafness Inability to discriminate differences in pitch, and hence to distinguish one tune from another. Also known as asonia.

tone psychology See TONPSYCHOLOGIE.

tone sensation tonal sensation

tone variator A device that can produce pure tones of variable pitch.

tone-color See TIMBRE.

tongue   An organ located in the mouth that is particularly well innervated for touch sensitivity and musculature, is somewhat sensitive to taste through taste buds on the tip, back, and sides, and in the human is the prime organ of speech articulation.

tongue kiss   French kiss

tongue-showing   1. (J. Smith, J. Chase, A. Lieblich) A form of nonverbal expression in which a person's tongue is partially exposed. An unconscious act, often performed during a task and may include showing a limp tongue, tongue-flicking, lip-licking. Signals that the person is concentrating and does not want to be interrupted. 2. A childish act in which the tongue is extended out of an otherwise closed mouth as a sign of rebellion or disrespect.

tongue thrust   A reflexive extension of the tongue, especially during the feeding process, a symptom occurring in some cases of cerebral palsy and other musculoskeletal disorders.

tongue-tie   A speech impairment due to the membrane on the underside of the tongue being abnormally short and inflexible. See ANKYLOGLOSSIA.

tonic   1. Continuous, as opposed to alternating, intermittent, or transitory. 2. See TONIC SPASM.

tonic activation   Persistent arousal as opposed to intermittent or transitory arousal. Compare PHASIC ACTIVATION.

tonic conduction   A type of nerve-impulse transmission that may occur in some nerve and muscle fibers over short distances. Tonic conduction is caused by electrical energy leaking through the insulating sheath of a nerve fiber. Also known as electrotonic conduction.

tonic contraction   The contraction of groups of muscles whose fibers maintain muscular tonus.

tonic epilepsy   A type of epilepsy in which tonic, but not clonic, muscle contractions occur.

tonic immobility (response)   Complete stillness of the body (except for an occasional muscle twitch) due to contraction of muscle groups. Usually the result of a sudden fear or emotion-provoking stimulus. Sometimes known as death feigning, freezing.

tonicity   1. The normal state of tension of a muscle or other organ. May be eutonic (normal), hypertonic (strongly tensed), or hypotonic (weakly tensed). 2. A degree of mental tension, which is high in a manic episode. See entries that begin with TONIC.

tonic labyrinth reflexes   Straightening of limbs when an animal is placed on its back, elicited by a stimulation of the vestibular organ.

tonic neck reflex   An automatic postural response of early infancy characterized by the infant's head turning to one side, as the arm and leg on the opposite side flex and the arm and leg on the same side extend. See TONIC REFLEX.

tonic neck-eye reflexes   Compensatory eye movements in response to changes of position of the head with reference to any plane, including the horizontal, mediated by the VIII cranial to 4th cervical and oculomotor nerves.

tonic phase of a convulsion   A part of the pattern of grand-mal epilepsy that involves muscular contractions, usually followed by a clonic phase.

tonic pupil of Adie   An unilateral eye defect in which the pupil responds poorly to light and slowly to convergence.

tonic reflex   1. Occurrence of a long delay after a reflex before the muscles relax. 2. A complex set of automatic responses that may involve muscle groups throughout the body as muscle tonus is increased in preparation for an activity, such as the general head- and body-postural changes observed when a boxer or a football player prepares to meet an opponent in bodily contact.

tonic spasm   A sudden involuntary muscle contraction that is continuous. Contrasts with a clonic spasm that alternates between contraction and relaxation of a muscle. See SPASM, TONUS.

tonitrophobia   Abnormal or excessive fear of thunder. Also known as brontophobia, keraunophobia. See ASTRAPHOBIA.

tonoclonic   Describing simultaneous or apparently simultaneous tonic and clonic muscle spasms.

tonometer   1. A device that can produce a tone of a given pitch or can measure the pitch of other tones. 2. A device that can measure tension or pressure. The second instrument is also known as a tenonometer.

tonometry   A method of measuring intraocular pressure (IOP) in the diagnosis of glaucoma and ocular hypertension.

tonoscope   An instrument for the visual analysis of complex sounds by the principle of the stroboscope.

tonotopic organization   The arrangement of centers and pathways of neural sensations in the cochlea and auditory areas of the cortex with respect to different sound frequencies. The orderly relationship of responsiveness to different frequencies can be projected as a cochlear map in the cortical auditory areas I and II.

Tonpsychologie   (tone psychology—German) Refers to the psychological study of music and is the title of a two-volume work on the topic published in 1883 and 1890 by German psychologist Carl Stumpf.

tonus   Tension in muscles when they are not shortening or lengthening, as in flexing of biceps. Tonus serves to keep the muscles ready for action. See TONIC.

tool design   In industrial psychology, design of instruments and tools in terms of such human factors as efficiency and avoidance of muscle fatigue or injury. See EQUIPMENT DESIGN.

tool subjects   Academic subjects, for example, reading or arithmetic, regarded as basic tools for gaining advanced knowledge.

tool-using behavior   In comparative psychology, the ability of animals including humans to use objects as tools. For example, a finch may use a cactus spine to probe for insects and chimpanzees frequently use sticks to push into ant nests, and leaves for cleaning themselves. In a laboratory situation, chimpanzees have been known to pile up five boxes to reach hanging food. The use of tools requires a capacity to generalize relationships between the presence, for example, of a stick lying randomly in the environment, and its perceived usefulness in extending the animal's reach. Said to distinguish primitive humans from modern humans.

toot   Slang for cocaine.

tooth fear   See DENTIST FEAR, ODONTOPHOBIA.

topagnosis   Inability to determine the location of tactile stimuli. Also known as topagnosia, topoanesthesia. Compare TOPOGNOSIA.

topalgia   A pain localized in a single small area or spot. Often a symptom occurring in hysteria or neurasthenia whereby localized pain, without evident organic basis, is experienced.

topastic error of measurement   (J. B. Carroll) The partly random, partly systematic error or variance which results when a participant in a multiple-choice psychological test has the opportunity to get some of the answers correct by guessing. Also known as topastic error of variance.

topdog   In Gestalt therapy, internal moral codes that cause anxiety and conflict in an individual when deviated from. Frederick Perls term for the part of the personality that stands for the "should nots" and "shoulds" of behavior. Similar to Sigmund Freud's "superego" or to Eric Berne's "parent." Compare UNDERDOG.

top-down analysis   Critical thinking, beginning with general principles and working "down" to details; deductive thinking. Compare BOTTOM-UP ANALYSIS.

top-down approach   (C. A. Boneau) In cognitive psychology, an aspect of information processing in which the recognition of the input is based, at least in part, upon an expectancy or a hypothesis about what the stimulus might be. This hypothesis is checked against the analyzed elements of the input and accepted or rejected, in which case a new hypothesis is formed. Compare BOTTOM-UP APPROACH.

top-down processing   1. Generally, a procedure that starts at the highest level of a concept such as a theory, with each step influenced by the one(s) above. 2. Deductive reasoning from a general premise or hypothesis to particulars. 3. In information processing, particularly pattern recognition, the assumption that expectancies shape perceptions; initial steps of perception and cognition are influenced by subsequent steps, where superordinate goals, intentions, and knowledge, can dominate lower psychological functions (as in overlooking misspelled words). 4. In linguistics, the process of communicating something verbally by starting with a meaningful thought, selecting phrases to express it, and uttering the corresponding sounds, usually as sentences. 5. In computer programming, identifying basic program functions and dividing them into smaller subfunctions (modules) of more manageable size. 6. In physiological psychology, a postulate that cortical functions govern certain caudal and distal functions. See BOTTOM-UP PROCESSING.

topectomy   A psychosurgical procedure in which selected areas of the frontal cortex are excised in cases of refractory mental illness that have not responded to electroconvulsive or other types of treatment. Both procedures are dated.

topesthesia   An ability to identify where a light touch is applied to any part of the skin.

topical   Pertaining to something applied to the surface of the body, such as sunscreen lotion.

topical flight   A disturbance in thinking consisting of a rapid succession of superficially related ideas; a constant series of digressions in the flow of thought observed primarily in acute manic states, and more occasionally in schizophrenia. Also known as flight of ideas. See PRESSURE OF ACTIVITY, PRESSURE OF SPEECH.

topoanesthesia   Inability to localize tactile sensations. Also known as topagnosis.

topognosia   An ability to recognize the location of a sensation. Also known as topognosis. Compare TOPAGNOSIS. See TOPESTHESIA.

topographagnosia   Topographical disorientation.

topographic   Characterizing mental processes interpreted from the standpoint of their localization in the mental apparatus.

topographical disorientation   A disorder of spatial visualization exemplified by difficulty or inability to recall or describe the arrangement of rooms in a house or the furniture in a room of a house in which the person lives. Also known as topographagnosia.

topographical memory   Recall of the location of objects or familiar routes. Defects in this memory may be manifested in disorientation or getting lost in one's own neighborhood or home.

topographical organization   The arrangement of structures in an organism, as in the orderly relationship between distribution of neural receptors in an area of the body and a similar distribution of neurons representing the same functions in cortical cells. Auditory and visual receptors occur several times in the cortex in patterns representing their positions in respective sense organs.

topographical psychology   (C. G. Carus) The process of mapping the mind, or locating the various mental processes in different regions of the mind. Carl Jung located the archetypes in the deeper regions of the unconscious, whereas Sigmund Freud divided the mind into three strata, or layers (conscious, preconscious, unconscious). Also known as mental topography.

topographic hypothesis/model   Carl Gustav Carus' original model of the mind in which access to awareness of contents and functions was divided into four systems: conscious, preconscious, general absolute, and partial absolute. The model had interactional elements; later adopted by Sigmund Freud, but was eventually replaced by Freud's structural model. See SYSTEMATIC APPROACH, UNCONSCIOUS PROCESSES.

topographic mapping of the brain   Description of the different parts of the brain in terms of their physical relation to each other and the skull. See BROCA'S AREA, BRODMANN'S AREA, CEREBRAL CORTEX, PHRENOLOGY.

topographic model   topographic hypothesis

topography   1. In anatomy, a description of a part of the body, particularly in relation to a definite area of the surface. 2. Theories so arranged that clearly defined stages can be displayed on a chart in an ascending order (such as Abraham Maslow's Theory of Motivation) or in a descending order (such as Eric Erikson's Stages of Life). 3. (K. Lewin) A view of personality that can be demonstrated on a chart in terms of pulls and pushes to explain behavior at any instant of time.

topological psychology   Kurt Lewin's system of psychology in which the behavior of the individual at any moment is classified in terms of the function of the attracting and repelling forces (positive and negative valences) in the psychological environment (or life space). The result is a geometric map, or topology, of needs, purposes, and goals. See SOCIAL FIELD, VALENCES, VECTOR ANALYSIS, VECTORS.

topology   1. In general, the study of geometric forms and their transformation in space. 2. A branch of mathematics that focuses on the connections and relations among things. Kurt Lewin used topological concepts in describing behavior in the life space. 3. A study of the facets of personality. See TOPOLOGICAL PSYCHOLOGY.

topophobia   Morbid fear of a particular place, or of the place where the person happens to be. Also known as angiophobia.

toposcope   (G. Walter & H. W. Shipton) An elaborate electroencephalographic (EEG) viewing device with cathode ray tubes corresponding to various cranial electrode positions. Used for making detailed studies of EEG relationships. The apparatus, developed in 1951, projects the electrical activity of the cerebral cortex as a visual system.

TOPs   See THEMATIC ORGANIZATION POINTS.

torpedoing   See TORPILLAGE.

torpillage   1. A form of aversion therapy in which a strong electric current is applied to a person in a state of hysteria. The practice, sometimes used in wartime conditions, produces a painful shock that is more aversive than the situation the person tries unconsciously to escape. Also known as torpedoing. 2. A sudden slap in the face applied to a person considered hysterical.

torpor   Sluggishness, inactivity, particularly occurring in a case of severely disordered consciousness. Only a strong stimulus can arouse a patient from the stupefaction of torpor.

Torque Test   (T. H. Blau) A simple test of cerebral dominance based on the directions of a person's hand-drawn circles (clockwise or counterclockwise).

Torrance Tests of Creative Thinking   (E. P. Torrance) Three batteries of test items that attempt to measure creative thinking. Including thinking creatively with words, with pictures, with sounds and words, applicable from kindergarten to graduate school. The object is to test for three characteristics identified by J. P. Guilford: fluency, flexibility, and originality. See ARP TESTS, CREATIVITY TEST.

torsion   Rotation of the eyeballs about their sagittal or antero-posterior axes. Also known as rolling, torsional movement/rotation, wheel-movement.

torsional movement/rotation   See TORSION.

torsion dystonia/spasm   An extrapyramidal side effect, a spasm, usually of the neck, drawing it to one side. Also known as dystonic musculorum deformans. See EX-TRAPYRAMIDAL SIDE EFFECTS, TORTICOLLIS.

torticollis   A continuous or spasmodic contraction of the neck muscles, resulting in rotation of the chin and twisting of the head to one side. May be neurological or psychogenic, and it may symbolize avoidance of a feared or guilt-laden sight. Also known as wryneck syndrome.

torture   The infliction of pain (usually physical and extreme) to extract information or confession, intimidate, exact revenge, or achieve perverse sexual or psychological pleasure. See SADISM.

TOT   See TIP-OF-THE-TONGUE PHENOMENON.

Total Battery Composite   The total score on the Bruininks-Oseretsky Test of Motor Proficiency. See FINE MOTOR COMPOSITE, GROSS MOTOR COMPOSITE.

total color blindness   A severe congenital deficiency in color vision, hereditary or acquired, in which all colors appear as grays. Also known as achromatism.

total institution   (E. Goffman) A place where whole blocks of people are bureaucratically processed, such as prisons and monasteries.

totalism   (E. Erikson) The organization of the self-concept that has rigid, arbitrary boundaries.

total-push therapy   (A. Meyerson) 1. A supportive approach originated by Meyerson primarily for the treatment of chronic institutionalized patients with schizophrenia. He advocated the wearing of attractive clothing, and the use of a stimulating environment and constant activities to keep up the patients' morale and to prevent further deterioration. 2. An eclectic system of psychotherapy vigorously applied to achieve immediate goals in the changing of the behavior of clients, including children. 3. A supportive approach that applies a variety of vigorous therapeutic techniques to the overall treatment of the client. See MILIEU THERAPY, THERAPEUTIC COMMUNITY.

total package arbitration   A situation in which the arbitrator must select the proposal of one side or the other. Also known as final-offer arbitration.

total quality management (TQM)   An integrated, pervasive approach to maximizing the quality of products or services.

total recall   The ability to remember and describe an experience in its entirety. Generally common for short-term memories of a simple kind, for example, a person paying close attention to a simple phenomenon can probably describe it almost perfectly. However, complex, long-term total recall is difficult and doubtful even when recounters may be certain that they have delivered a complete and accurate account. In some cases, mnemonics may help, for example, in recalling extremely long strings of numbers. See ASSUAGE TEST.

total-time hypothesis   (B. R. Bugelski) A postulate that the more time a person spends rehearsing an item, the better will be the memory for that item.

TOTE   Test-Operate-Test-Exit

totem   1. In anthropology, a revered animal, plant, natural force, or inanimate object conceived as a tribal ancestor, symbol, protector, or tutelary spirit of the clan in preliterate society. Usually associated with prohibitions against harming it. See TOTEMISM. 2. (S. Freud) A symbol of the primal father who was murdered when his sons rebelled against his mastery of the primal hoarde. See OEDIPUS COMPLEX.

totemism   The practice of using nonhuman objects, such as animals, plants, or inanimate objects, to represent individuals or groups as a refuge for the soul. In several nonWestern cultures, the person or group believes the totem symbol offers protection for those who adhere to certain rules of the tribe or clan whose members are forbidden to harm the totem animal, plant, or object.

touch   The sensation produced by contact of an object with the surface of the skin. Sensitivity to touch varies in different parts of the body; the lips and fingers are far more sensitive than the trunk or back. Neurologists distinguish between deep touch (pressure) and light touch (cotton wisp) appreciation. These sensations follow diverse neural paths.

touch blends   An ability to simultaneously determine multiple properties of materials when applied to the skin. For example, if a mustard plaster is placed on a person's back, the person can feel simultaneously its weight, dampness, and temperature.

toucherism   Being sexually aroused by surreptitiously touching a stranger on an erotic body part.

touch fear   See HAPTEPHOBIA, HAPTOPHOBIA.

touch fibers   Nerve fibers that are receptors for mechanical stimuli, such as stroking or light contact.

touching (in therapy)   1. Two types of touching: (a) formal (part of the therapy) as in bioenergetic analysis, Trager mentastics, and dance therapy, and (b) informal, as in spontaneous reaching out by either the client or the therapist, such as a handshake on meeting or a hug at the end of the final session. Some counselors and therapists never touch clients whereas others are much more likely to do so as part of their procedures. 2. Refers to the practice of sensitivity-group members who use physical contact with others as a means of breaking down barriers in interpersonal communication.

touching (need)   Characterizing a disorder of association in which people must touch an object to be able to recognize the object. A disturbance similar to naming.

touch pyramid   (E. Titchener) Geometrical representation of the relations between the principal pressure-pain sensations.

touch sensation   A sensation aroused by stimulation of certain receptors in the skin, through contact with some object, that is, either a pressure or a contact sensation.

touch sense   1. An ability to perceive a stimulus applied in the form of cutaneous stroking, pressure, or light contact with a hair or similar object. 2. A sense whose receptors lie in the skin or immediately beneath it, including pressure, warmth, cold, pain, and possibly others. Also known as cutaneous sense, dermal sense, skin sense, tactile sense. See HAPTIC PERCEPTION.

touch spot   Any of the small areas of the skin particularly sensitive to contact.

touch therapy   1. (D. Krieger, L. Rosa) A technique used mostly by nurses, which consists of touching a patient's body to aid in the therapeutic process. Also known as Therapeutic Touch. See MESMERISM. 2. Physical contact with another for the purpose of comforting or helping that person. 3. A form of therapy based on the concept that most people find it pleasant to be touched in an appropriate context, especially when in physical or psychological distress. Historically, the "laying on of hands" for comforting and curing is found in many cultures. It includes informal contact, as in a parent holding an upset child; formal contact, as in a massage; and psychotherapeutic, by a professional such as a psychologist as part of the theory of the system rather than as a handshake on meeting or a hug on separation. In addition, there are numerous specialized techniques, some

founded in science (such as applied kinesiology, physical therapy, physiatry, and sports massage); and others combining science with constructs such as "adjusting," "auras," "balancing," "energy fields," "moxibustion," and "polarity," purporting to prevent, relieve, or cure many ills known to humankind. Types of touch therapy include: acupressure, Alexander technique, body wraps, chiropractic, Esalen massage, Feldenkrais method, friction rubs, Hellerwork, hydrotherapy, Lomilomi (Hawaiian massage), Mesendieck system, myotherapy, naprapathy, oriental massage, osteopathy, polarity therapy, reflexology, Reichian therapy, Rolfing, shiatsu, Swedish massage, Therapeutic Touch, and the Trager mentastics approach. Some adherents have programs for infants and pets; others focus on a body area, such as craniosacral therapy, deep muscle therapy, and facial massage. See BIOENERGETIC ANALYSIS, MASSAGE, THERAPEUTIC TOUCH, TOUCH.

tough-minded   (W. James) Denoting a personality trait characterized by empiricism, materialism, skepticism, and fatalism. Compare TENDER-MINDED.

tough-mindedness   According to Hans Eysenck, a factor in attitude measurement orthogonal to such attitudes as conservative-radicalism, contrasting communist and fascist (tough-minded) attitudes with liberal (tender-minded) attitudes.

Tourette   See GILLES DE LA TOURETTE, TOURETTE'S DISORDER/SYNDROME.

Tourette's disorder/syndrome (TS)   (G. de la Tourette) A neurologic disorder characterized by both motor and vocal tics (for example, repeatedly shrugging the shoulders, grimacing, or clearing the throat), often comorbid with attention-deficit hyperactivity disorder (ADHD) or obsessive-compulsive disorder (OCD). In many cases there is an irresistible impulse to utter obscenities. The condition is more prevalent than originally thought. Sometimes known as coprolalia, Gilles de la Tourette's syndrome (after Georges Gilles de la Tourette who originally called it coprolalia), maladie des tics, multiple tics with coprolalia, tic, tic convulsif with coprolalia, tic disorder, Tourette's.

TOWER   Acronym used in rehabilitation institutes that stands for Testing, Orientation, Work Evaluation in Rehabilitation.

Towers of Hanoi   (J. R. Hayes & H. A. Simon) A traditional problem much used in problem-solving research that involves moving disks among three pegs under certain restrictions so as to reach a specified assignment of disks to pegs. The Towers of Hanoi have given rise to many isomorphic problems that have been used in research on problem difficulty. The puzzle, sometimes known as the Burmese pyramid, was invented in 1883 by French mathematician Edouard Lucas and sold as a toy. See PROBLEM ISOMORPHS.

toxic   Poisonous. See TOXICITY.

toxic delirium   A kind of delirium resulting from infectious diseases such as pneumonia or malaria in their acute or convalescent stage.

toxic disorders   Brain syndromes due to acute or chronic intoxication, including mercury, manganese, lead, bromide, alcohol, and barbiturate poisoning.

toxic-infectious psychosis A severe mental disorder occurring during or after an infectious disease or poisoning by an exogenous toxin. Major symptoms are delirium, stupor, epileptiform attacks, hallucinosis, confusion, and incoherence. See TOXIC DELIRIUM, TOXIC DISORDERS.

toxicity The capacity of a substance to produce poisonous effects in an organism. The toxicity of a substance is related to the size of the dose per body weight of the individual or in terms of the minimum dose needed to affect 50% of an animal population. See BEHAVIORAL TOXICITY.

toxicomania A morbid desire to consume poisons, or a severe dependency on drugs.

toxicophobia A morbid fear of being poisoned or of poison. Also known as iophobia, toxiphobia, toxophobia.

toxic psychosis An acute or chronic brain disorder resulting from ingestion of poisons or drugs, infectious diseases, or exhaustion.

toxin A poisonous substance.

toxoplasmosis A disease caused by the infection of a warm-blooded animal by the protozoan parasite *Toxoplasma gondii*. When acquired by a pregnant woman, toxoplasmosis can be transmitted to the fetus, causing hydrocephalus, blindness, mental retardation, and other nervous-system disorders. See CONGENITAL TOXOPLASMOSIS.

toy demonstrator A person who instructs low-education and low-income parents in their own homes in effective ways to interact with their infants and preschool children.

toys See MARITAL AIDS.

toy tests The use of toys for projective purposes, such as the use of dolls. The general procedure is to demonstrate to young children that certain dolls represent parents, siblings, and other people of importance in the child's life. One of the dolls represents the child being tested, and when this is well-established, the child is asked to place the various dolls in certain arrangements, such as where everyone would sit at dinner time, who are best friends, who is it that nobody likes, or who is nice to everyone. The procedure attempts to gain insight into the child's thinking and feeling by how the child responds. See BLACKY TEST, MAKE A PICTURE STORY TEST.

TPAL A pregnancy classification system (total number, number of premature deliveries, number of abortions, and number of living children).

tpmo (H. A. Murray) Abbreviation for the allowable time, place, mode and object for need satisfaction.

TQM total quality management

TR Abbreviation for terminal stimulus, from the German *terminalischer Reiz*.

trace A hypothetical construct of memories supposed to exist in the brain. See MNEME, ENGRAM.

trace conditioning A learning procedure in which a conditioned stimulus and an unconditioned stimulus are separated by a constant interval. The effectiveness of the method can be measured in terms of alpha-wave blocking to a previously neutral stimulus.

trace decay theory A point of view that material learned leaves a trace in the brain that eventually disappears unless practiced and used. Also known as decay theory. See ENGRAM, MNEME.

trace perseverative (C. L. Hull) The lingering impulse following cessation of a stimulus. See HULL'S THEORY.

trachyphonia An abnormal hoarseness of the voice.

tracing 1. Any graphic display of electrical or mechanical cardiovascular events. See ELECTROCARDIOGRAM. 2. See also RADIOACTIVE TRACERS, TAGGING.

tracking 1. Following or pursuing, usually for observing individuals for purposes such as learning more about them as individuals or as members of a group, or for providing the individuals with certain opportunities or for maximizing their potentials. See IDIOGRAPHIC PSYCHOLOGY. 2. In formal academic education, following the progress of students in various subjects (topics) and providing material to keep them occupied at the correct level of functioning. 3. In education practice, keeping children at the growing edge of their abilities, for example, a child of ten is allowed to study language arts at the sixth grade level and mathematics at the third grade level if these are the levels of the child's abilities. This is in opposition to a traditional system that would force the child to study both English and math at the fourth grade level. See STREAMING. 4. In industry, a follow-up investigation of a new employee or of an employee in a new position to determine how the employee is progressing, usually with periodic reports either to the person in question or to higher management. 5. Literally, the following or shadowing of a person to observe and evaluate how that person operates. Usually done when it is suspected that the person is not functioning properly, for example, a consulting industrial psychologist follows an executive, later making a report with conclusions and a recommendation to the proper authority (for example, an other executive, the president, or the executive board of the company). See SHADOWING. 6. See also PREDATION.

tracking behavior A kind of behavior controlled by a moving target. In compensatory tracking, the person attempts to keep the "target" stationary, as when the speedometer is kept as close as possible to 50 miles per hour. In pursuit tracking, the aim is to keep on the target (as in the pursuitmeter test). A sniper trying to hit a moving target is pursuit tracking.

tracking in education See TRACKING (meanings 2 and 3).

tracking in industry See TRACKING (meanings 4 and 5).

tracking in psychotherapy (A. A. Lazarus) Assessing the "firing orders" that clients employ when upsetting themselves, for example, a CIS Sequence (cognition-imagery-sensation) versus an ISC pattern (imagery-sensation-cognition) to understand the client better and suggest suitable alternate processes of operating. See TRACKING.

tract A bundle or group of nerve fibers. Term usually is applied to groups of fibers within the central nervous system. A bundle of nerve fibers outside the central nervous system often is identified as a nerve. See AXON.

tractable Yielding, easily influenced. See DOCILITY.

traction sensation A cutaneous sensation aroused by pulling the skin away from the body. Also known as pull sensation.

trademark Any word, symbol, or device used to identify products. Trademarks are an important part of a product image, especially after they have been established for a number of years in association with acceptable and reliable products.

trade test A task designed to measure competence in a skilled trade, based on either information questions or job-skill items usually of the work-sample variety.

trade union union (meaning 4)

tradition The set of social customs or other ethnic or family practices handed down from generation to generation.

traditional marriage 1. A formal relationship of a man and woman, joined in wedlock for the primary purpose of establishing a family which may or may not include children. 2. A traditional marriage generally follows a period of courtship approved by both families, public announcement of wedding plans, and a wedding ceremony. In some cultures, a traditional marriage requires that the bride and groom be forbidden to meet before the wedding ceremony. 3. A marriage wherein the husband is the head of the family and decision maker. The wife's role centers around child care and household matters. Compare NONTRADITIONAL MARRIAGES, SAME-SEX MARRIAGE.

traditional psychotherapies The treatment of personality problems, maladjustments, and mental disorders by psychological means, especially those established by Carl Jung (analytic psychology), Sigmund Freud (psychoanalysis) and Alfred Adler (individual psychology). Traditional therapies are distinguished from other types of psychotherapies such as COGNITIVE-BEHAVIORAL THERAPIES, GROUP THERAPIES, HUMAN-POTENTIAL THERAPIES. See entries.

tradition-directed (D. Riesman) Describing persons whose values, goals, and behavior are largely determined by traditional cultural heritage, social norms usually transmitted by their parents. Compare INNER-DIRECTED, OTHER-DIRECTED.

tragedy of the commons (G. Hardin) An example of a social trap in which actions that benefit individuals can damage society as a whole. Illustrated by the story of settlers who successfully grazed their small flocks on a common pasture, whereupon some increased the numbers of sheep and goats until the pasture was ruined for all.

Trager mentastics (M. Trager) A psychotherapeutic technique used to free a patient of tensions and aberrations through shaking movements and massage-like movements, usually to a prone patient, while the therapist talks to the patient. See ALTERNATIVE PSYCHOTHERAPIES, BIOENERGETIC ANALYSIS, BODY THERAPIES.

trailer test In consumer psychology, pretesting, usually of advertisements, in a trailer at a shopping center. Typically, shoppers participate in a simulated shopping situation, then view commercials, and are given various coupons, the redemption of which indicates the commercials' influence.

trail-making test (TMT) 1. A neuropsychological task used in attempting to assess a person's capacity to scan and integrate information when pressed for time. 2. An easily administered test of visual conceptual and visuomotor tracking. A two-part subtest of the 1944 Army Individual Test Battery in which the participant draws lines connecting consecutively numbered/lettered circles. Because it requires attention functions, also used to detect brain injury.

train 1. In general, to guide or direct the learning process in a human, or in an animal, so as to induce certain habitual responses, complex habits, or attitudes desired by the trainer. See TRAINING. 2. In electrostimulation of the brain, a series of impulses.

trainability Capacity to benefit from training in a particular skill.

trainable See INTELLIGENCE QUOTIENT, TRAINABLE MENTALLY RETARDED.

trainable mental defective (TMD) trainable mentally retarded

trainable mentally retarded (TMR) Phrase applied to persons with mental retardation, usually in the moderate category (intelligence quotient of 35 to 49), who cannot profit from academic education even in special classes, but who are capable of achieving a degree of self-care and social adjustment at home, and vocational usefulness in a closely supervised setting such as a sheltered workshop. Once known as trainable mental defective (TMD). See MENTAL RETARDATION.

trainer 1. A professional leader or facilitator of a sensitivity-training group, or T-group. 2. A teacher or supervisor of individuals learning to practice psychotherapy. 3. A practice device that is a simple and inexpensive substitute for the real thing.

train fear See SIDERODROMOPHOBIA.

training Systematic instruction and practice by which an individual acquires competence in a vocational or recreational skill or activity. See PRACTICE.

training aids The use of devices that simulate or resemble equipment used on the job to train personnel, especially when the actual equipment may be impractical due to cost or possible injury.

training analysis Didactic analysis and psychoanalytic treatment, conducted by senior analysts on students training to become psychoanalysts.

training evaluation See EVALUATION OF TRAINING.

training group (K. Lewin) An experiential group concerned with fostering the development of leadership skills, communication skills, and attitude change. Training groups grew out of Kurt Lewin's work in the area of small-group dynamics. Also known as T-group. See INTENSIVE GROUP EXPERIENCE.

training school A rehabilitation facility for children with mental difficulties using interdisciplinary teams of therapists in a homelike setting. The children are given medical and psychological care while being carefully evaluated and trained in vocational areas in which they show the greatest promise of success. The training school also provides full social and recreational experiences.

training supervision   In some systems of psychotherapy, especially psychoanalysis, after a therapist has been certified as competent and begins independent practice, a contact is still maintained with a training supervisor who will meet periodically with the therapist to review procedures, attempt to solve problems, and otherwise be of help to the therapist. See TRAINING ANALYSIS.

training transfer   See TRANSFER OF TRAINING.

training validity   The extent to which (a) the trainees match the criteria established for them in the training program and (b) they mastered the training.

train of ideas   A sequence or succession of associated ideational processes or functions. Also known as train of thought.

trait   1. An enduring personality characteristic that determines a person's behavior. 2. In genetics, an attribute resulting from a hereditary predisposition, for example, hair color or facial features or a behavioral tendency. Types of trait include: ABILITY, ANAL-EROTIC, BASIC PERSONALITY, CARDINAL, CENTRAL ORGANIZING, CENTRAL, CHARACTER, COMMON, COMPENSATORY, CULTURE, DOMINANT, ENVIRONMENTAL MOLD, ERIC, FACTOR, NEUROPATHIC, NEUROTIC, PERSONALITY, POLYGENIC, RECESSIVE, SECONDARY, SEX-LINKED, SOURCE, SUBJECTIVE, SURFACE, UNIQUE.

trait-and-factor counseling   (E. Williamson) A theory of counseling that focuses on assessing behavioral traits of the client in relationship to educational and career placement as well as social adjustment. Also known as directive counseling, counselor-centered therapy, trait-factor.

trait anger   (C. Spielberger) A psychobiological state that represents a personality factor of anger proneness. Individuals with strong Trait-anger dispositions are much more likely to experience State-anger (S-anger) than those with low Trait-anger dispositions. Also known as T-anger. See ANGER, HOSTILITY, AGGRESSION.

trait anxiety   (N. S. Endler) Within the interactional model of anxiety, trait anxiety is the predisposition to respond to specific types of threat, such as social evaluation, physical danger, ambiguity, or daily routines.

trait-behavior correspondence   The extent to which an observed behavior, such as cutting in front of a line of people waiting to enter a theatre, is attributed to a personality trait, such as rudeness or aggressiveness.

trait difference   The difference between the relative strength of one trait and another trait in any individual. A person who is average in responsibility and low in tension shows a greater trait difference than a person who is high in both. See IPSATIVE SCALING.

trait level tests   Inventories to measure chronic, stable, and persistent behaviors and/or characteristics.

trait organization   The way in which personal traits are related and comprise a unique, integrated whole.

trait profile   A diagram that charts test scores that represent individual traits. These scores or ratings are arranged on a common scale to depict the pattern of traits visually. Also known as psychograph.

trait-rating   An observation technique in which a given behavioral trait or feature is observed, rated, and recorded, for example, a character trait such as industriousness in a school child.

trait theory   A point of view that personality is a collection of traits. See PERSONALITY-TRAIT THEORY (ALLPORT), FACTORIAL THEORY OF PERSONALITY (CATTELL).

trait theory of leadership   A point of view that management style or leadership is a function of individual traits, some physical (for example, height), some cognitive (for example, knowledge), some emotional (for example, self-control), etc.

trait variability   A scattering or dispersion of various trait measures shown by the individual.

trance   1. A sleep-like state characterized by markedly diminished consciousness and responsiveness to stimuli. 2. Being in a dissociated state, not responsive to normal stimuli. 3. In psychoanalytic theory, a state of dissociation occuring in hypnosis, hysteria, and dream-states in which the ego is not functioning. 4. The purported mental state of mediums when in contact with the spirit world.

trance disorders   Disorders listed under the category of Dissociative Disorder Not Otherwise Specified, in the DSM-IV. These disorders are seen as location or culture bound and are single or episodic disturbances in the person's state of consciousness, identity, or memory. Typically there is a narrowing of awareness for the person of their immediate surroundings or "involuntary" stereotyped behaviors or movements. Also known as dissociative trance disorders.

trance logic   Describing a tendency of hypnotized individuals to engage simultaneously in logically contradictory or paradoxical trains of thought. It has been suggested that trance logic may be viewed as evidence for the parallel-processing theory in that there appears to be simultaneous registration of information at different levels of awareness. That is, incoming information appears to be processed by separate systems, some information being recorded consciously whereas other information does not reach consciousness.

trance state   A hypnotic state of dissociation and diminished response to external stimuli, induced by hypnosis, occurring in catalepsy, or found in groups undergoing religious excitement, as in revivalist meetings. In shamanic traditions, it is during the trance state that the soul of the shaman travels to the spirit world to communicate with spirits, deities, etc. See TRANCE.

tranquilizer   A drug used to relieve tension or combat psychotic symptoms without significant sedation. A tranquilizer that reduces agitation is a minor tranquilizer whereas one that reduces psychosis is a major tranquilizer (also known as a neuroleptic agent, neuroleptics). Tranquilizers generally cause gross behavioral changes such as reducing motor activity, decreasing emotionality, and producing an indifference to external stimuli. See ATARACTICS, RESERPINE.

tranquilizer chair   A heavy wooden chair in which patients of Benjamin Rush, the first American psychiatrist, were strapped at the chest, abdomen, ankles, and knees, with the patient's head inserted in a wooden box. Rush preferred this method of restraint to the straitjacket for "maniacal" patients because it reduced the flow of blood to the head and did not interfere with bloodletting, a standard medical treatment of the time.

transaction   1. A relationship event depending on the transfer of forces between participating parties. 2. Any interaction between the individual and the social or physical environment, especially during encounters between two or more persons. 3. (R. S. Lazarus) The dynamics of an ongoing and changing interaction between an individual and the environment in some given context, expressed at a higher level of abstraction so that its relational meaning is conveyed for that individual.

Transactional Analysis (TA)   A form of dynamic group or individual psychotherapy originated by Eric Berne, that focuses on interactions that reveal internal "ego states," and the games people play in social situations. Involves: (a) a study of three ego states (parent, child, adult) and determination of which is dominant in the transaction in question; (b) identification of the tricks and expedients, or games, habitually used in the patient's transactions (called by common names such as "payoff," "con," and "Ain't it awful?"); and (c) analysis of the total "script," or unconscious plan of the patient's life, to uncover the sources of emotional problems. Also see ADULT-EGO STATE, ANTITHESIS, EGO STATE, GAMES PEOPLE PLAY, LIFE SCRIPT, PAY-AND-DON'T-GO, SCRIPT, SCRIPT ANALYSIS, SCRIPT THEORY.

transactional contingent reward   A component of transactional leadership in which the leader grants a specific reward to a subordinate in exchange for a specified task. See TRANSACTIONAL LEADERSHIP.

transactional evaluation   The application of systems-theory principles to program innovations. Designed to minimize the disruption of the reallocation process occurring when changes are introduced in an organization and thereby minimizes personal threat and defensiveness felt by the system participants.

transactionalism   A doctrine positing that people can make a difference by perceiving needs and by making changes in the environment. Compare TRANSACTION-ALISMEMPIRICISM, NATIVISM, RATIONALISM.

transactional leadership   1. (J. M. Burns) A management style in which leaders and followers enter into an exchange beginning with a process of negotiation to establish what is being exchanged and whether it is satisfactory. Such leadership depends on the leader's power to reinforce subordinates for their successful completion of the bargain. 2. The style of leadership that emphasizes what rewards an individual can expect for different levels of effort and performance. See ACTIVE MANAGEMENT BY EXCEPTION, CONTINGENT REWARD, PASSIVE MANAGEMENT BY EXCEPTION, TRANSFORMATIONAL LEADERSHIP.

transactional psychotherapy   A form of psychotherapy that places special emphasis on the actual transactions between the client and the other people in the client's life. See TRANSACTIONAL ANALYSIS.

transactional theory of perception   (A. Ames) A point of view that fundamental perceptions are learned reactions based on interactions with the environment. These reactions generate expectancies to which new experiences tend to conform.

transactional-transformational leadership paradigm (B. M. Bass) A type of leadership generated by a charismatic person, based not only on contingent reinforcement (reward-punishment consequences) but also on attitudes beyond self-interests such as the advancement of society or some other high-minded goal; in addition, followers of such leadership are asserted to develop desirable personal qualities such as greater maturity and self-esteem. See LEADERSHIP, TRANSFORMATIONAL LEADERSHIP.

transadulthood   The period of life beginning with the ending of the teen years to the beginning of the 30s, during which time considerable changes generally occur before full maturation.

transcend   To rise above or to go beyond.

transcendence   1. "Rising above" basic biological potentials, becoming more spiritual, having "higher" goals, attaining a superior level of understanding. The highest level in Abraham Maslow's hierarchy of needs. 2. The process of "going beyond" a current life form that has been congenial and congruent in a specific life period. See TRANSCENDENCE CRISIS, TRANSCENDENCE LIFE FORM, TRANSCENDENCE THEORIES OF PERSONALITY.

transcendence crisis   According to Adrian Van Kaam, a period of basic insecurity that arises when people are about ready to move to a higher level of being. See IDENTITY CRISIS, TRANSCENDENCE, TRANSCENDENCE LIFE FORM, THEORIES OF PERSONALITY.

transcendence life form   Adrian Van Kaam's phrase for an aspect of life that liberates, modulates and regulates the determinants of the historical, vital, and functional dimensions of a person's life. See TRANSCENDENCE THEORIES OF PERSONALITY, TRANSCENDENCE CRISIS, TRANSCENDENCE LIFE FORM.

transcendence need   According to Erich Fromm, the desire to create so as to rise above passivity and attain a sense of meaning and purpose in an impermanent and seemingly random or accidental universe. Both creativity and destructiveness are considered by Erich Fromm to be manifestations of transcendence needs.

transcendence theories of personality   Points of view that call for people transcending (going above and beyond) determinative-formative conditions, whether biological or social, to higher states of being. See TRANSCENDENCE, TRANSCENDENCE CRISIS, TRANSCENDENCE LIFE FORM.

transcendence therapy   A spiritually oriented form of psychotherapy that employs metaphysical terminology. As defined by Adrian Van Kaam, the developer of this system, "Transcendence therapy is intended to help people surpass past ways of life wholesomely and is based on the discipline of holistic formation called Formative Spirituality."

transcendency   Potentiality to move forwards or upwards from present status to a more desirable status.

transcendental   Going beyond normal human understanding and potentials.

transcendent(al) function   (C. G. Jung) A cognitive process by means of which opposite aspects of the personality, including conscious and unconscious portions, are united into an effectively functioning complex of symbolic awareness, attitude, and integration. See INDIVIDUATION.

transcendental meditation (TM)   Technique for achieving a transcendental state of consciousness, introduced by Maharishi Mahesh Yogi, based upon ancient Hindu writings. The modernized version of the discipline consists of a series of six steps that culminate in sitting with eyes closed for two 20-minute periods a day, while repeating a mantra to block distracting thoughts and to induce a state of relaxation in which images and ideas can arise from deeper levels of the mind and from the cosmic source of all thought and being. Objective is a greater sense of well-being, more harmonious interpersonal relations, and a state of "absolute bliss." See MYSTIC UNION.

transcendental state   A level of consciousness held to reach beyond waking, sleeping, and hypnotic states, characterized physically by lowered metabolism and reduced adrenergic functions, and psychologically by alleviation of tension, anxiety, and frustration, and a high level of tranquillity.

transcendent counseling   (F. Harper) A form of counseling that deals with changing the lifestyle of the client. Uses interpersonal counseling as well as treatment through training activities involving relaxation, meditation, exercise, and nutrition.

transcendent goals   Goals which go beyond self-interest. See TRANSFORMATIONAL LEADERSHIP.

transcortical   Passage of an impulse from one part of a cortex to another.

transcortical aphasia   A type of aphasia due to a lesion that may be extensive without damaging the Broca or Wernicke areas. Those areas, however, may become isolated from the rest of the brain, and as a result such people can repeat spoken words even though they may have difficulty in producing or understanding speech. See TRANSCENDENTAL MEDITATION.

transcortical motor aphasia (TMA)   A form of aphasia resulting from lesions in the anterior speech areas. See COMBINED TRANSCORTICAL APHASIA, TRANSCORTICAL SENSORY APHASIA.

transcortical pathways   A concept associated with Ivan Pavlov's experiments of the 1920s indicating the presence in the neocortex of direct links between sensory and motor areas. Pavlov argued that conditioning was not possible in decorticated animals, but other researchers demonstrated that conditioning was difficult but possible in the absence of transcortical pathways.

transcortical sensory aphasia (TSA)   1. A form of aphasia resulting from lesions in the posterior speech areas. 2. A speech disorder showing difficulty in speech comprehension but the ability to repeat words. Caused by brain damage, usually posterior to Wernicke's area. See COMBINED TRANSCORTICAL APHASIA, TRANSCORTICAL MOTOR APHASIA.

transcription   1. Translating something in form A to form B, for example, a stenographer changing spoken words to pencil marks. 2. The transfer of genetic code information from one form of nucleic acid (for example, ribonucleic acid) to another (for example, deoxyribonucleic acid).

transcultural psychiatry   Cross-cultural psychiatry.

transcutaneous electrical nerve stimulation (TENS)   A procedure to relieve pain by applying prolonged, mild, electrical stimulation to the areas afflicted.

transcutaneous electrical stimulation   Electrical stimulation in acupuncture.

transdermal patch   A treated patch of fabric that when adhered to the skin with an adhesive allows for the diffusion of chemicals (for example, nicotine) through the skin over a period of hours or days.

transduce   To convert from one form into another, such as a physical touch on the surface of the body to electric energy in the nerves.

transducer   Extremely sensitive amplifying resistor that transfers energy from one form to another.

transducing   The neurological process of converting information within the brain from one sensory modality to another, such as auditory-to-visual-to-motor.

transduction   1. The conversion of one form of energy into another. 2. In sensation, the transformation of stimulus energies into neural firings thereby giving the organism information about the intensity of the stimulus. 3. The neurological process of converting information within the brain from one sensory modality to another, such as auditory-to-visual-to-motor.

transductive reasoning   (J. Piaget) Reasoning in which a child compares specifics and concludes that specifics similar in one respect are similar in all respects. See CORRELATIONAL LOGIC.

transection   1. The severing or cutting across a nerve tract, fiber, axon, or the spinal cord. 2. A cross section.

transfer   1. The process of transferral. 2. The carryover of information or skill from one process to another. See TRANSFER OF TRAINING. 3. In Gestalt psychology, a crucial test of genuine understanding or insight: Can a solution to a problem be successfully applied to other problems that are structurally similar but differ in superficial detail?

transfer appropriate learning   (J. Bransford) Learning that respects the expected retrieval conditions; for example, to teach phonetics, it would be better to emphasize the position of the lips and tongue and the consequent sound rather than the meaning of the words.

transfer by generalization   The transfer from one situation to another of general principles rather than behavior patterns. Also known as transfer of principles.

transference   1. Shifting of symptoms from one side of the body to another. 2. In psychotherapy, projections onto others of schemas deriving from one's personal history. 3. In psychoanalytic theory, the projection upon the analyst of unconscious feelings and wishes originally directed toward important individuals, such as parents, in the patient's childhood. See ANALYSIS OF TRANSFERENCE, COUNTERTRANSFERENCE, DISTORTION BY TRANSFERENCE, DUAL-TRANSFERENCE THERAPY, INSTITUTIONAL TRANSFERENCE, IDENTIFICATION TRANSFERENCE, LIBIDINAL TRANSFERENCE, NEGATIVE TRANSFERENCE, POSITIVE TRANSFERENCE.

transference analysis   An analysis in which the therapist calls attention to the feelings of clients toward the therapist in an attempt to help clients better understand themselves.

transference cure/remission   flight into health

transference improvement   The alleviation of neurotic symptoms through a transference relationship with the therapist who is unconsciously perceived as a parent-figure.

transference-love   In psychoanalytic theory, feelings of affection and attachment transferred from the original love objects, such as parents, to the analyst. It is an artifact of the analysis, not the "real thing," since it is a reenactment of infantile feelings and is not related to the character or even sex of the analyst as a person. See POSITIVE TRANSFERENCE, TRANSFERENCE.

transference neurosis   In psychoanalysis, neurotic reactions released by the transference process, because the patient's early conflicts and traumas are revived and relived. These reactions are an artificial illness which replaces the original neurosis and helps the patient become aware that his or her attitudes and behavior are actually repetitions of infantile drives. The transference neurosis must be resolved if the patient is to be free from the harmful effects of past experiences, and adopt more appropriate attitudes and responses.

transference phenomenon   The identification of a figure in the present with significant figures in the past.

transference remission   See FLIGHT INTO HEALTH, TRANSFERENCE CURE.

transference resistance   In psychoanalysis, a form of resistance to the disclosure of unconscious material, in which the patient maintains silence or attempts to act out feelings of love or hate, transferred from past relationships, to the analyst. See ANALYSIS OF TRANSFERENCE, NEGATIVE TRANSFERENCE, POSITIVE TRANSFERENCE.

transfer of learning   (J. V. McConnell) A theory associated with experiments with ribonucleic acid (RNA) molecules as possible units of stored information or engrams. Presumes that RNA molecules from a trained animal can be ingested by or be injected into a naive animal that will then have the memory trace of the trained animal. Experiments have involved the feeding of minced trained flatworms to naive flatworms or injecting naive rats with RNA extracted from the brains of trained rats. Evidence of transfer was inconclusive. Sometimes known as transfer of memory.

transfer of memory   transfer of learning

transfer of principles   transfer by generalization

transfer of training   The influence of prior learning on new learning, either to enhance it (positive transfer) or to hamper it (negative transfer), for example, knowing how to drive an automobile will help in learning to drive a tractor. See FACULTY PSYCHOLOGY, FORMAL DISCIPLINE.

transfer RNA (tRNA)   A ribonucleic-acid (RNA) molecule that has the ability to transfer specific amino acids to protein molecules during the synthesis of proteins. Each amino acid has a corresponding transfer RNA molecule. See REVERSE TRANSFERASE.

transfer validity   The extent to which one process applies to another.

transfiguration   A change of form, appearance, or essence. For example, on a physical level, a change of appearance of the body as the result of a disease process, accident or plastic surgery; on a psychological level, a change of attitudes, or personality traits. See CONVERSION, IMMEDIATE THERAPY.

transformation   1. Metamorphosis. 2. In psychoanalytic theory, the change in feelings or impulses as a means of disguising them to gain admittance to consciousness.

transformational grammar (TG)   1. An approach to the study of language that assumes that each surface structure of a sentence has a deep structure associated with it. 2. Grammar that describes a language by laying down procedures for transforming one grammatical pattern into another, for example, changing sentence types and adding or deleting elements or modifying their order. The most advanced transformational grammar is Noam Chomsky's transformational-generative grammar.

transformational leadership   1. (B. Bass) A management style in which followers are motivated to work for transcendental goals and for higher-level self-actualizing needs instead of immediate self-interests. 2. A leadership style characterized by a leader's concern for the performance of the subordinates and a leader's efforts to develop the potential of the subordinates. 3. A style of leadership that inspires and transforms the followers. Found among leaders with much charisma. See CHARISMATIC LEADERSHIP.

transformational rules   In linguistics, rules of grammar that are applied to strings of symbols.

transformation of affect   The changing of a feeling, or affect, into its opposite in dreams; for instance, a feeling of love may be obscured in the dream as a feeling of hatred.

transformation of knowledge   Applying knowledge from prior learning to the successful solution of a new problem.

transformation stage   A stage in Carl Jung's analytic psychology wherein clients understand themselves and begin to make positive changes.

transformation theory   1. A point of view that one biological species becomes changed in the course of time into another radically different species. 2. (C. Darwin) The argument that, over time, various species change their form. For example, a small four-toed animal called eohippus that lived in the Eocene period eventually transformed itself into the horse. Also known as evolution, evolutionism, transformism. See CREATIONISM.

transformed score   1. Any score that has been changed from its original raw form in terms of rank order, for example, percentile or standard score. 2. Any score that derives from the gross or raw score, transformed to be meaningful, for example, a student takes a test in science (score 47) and a test in social studies (score 91). These raw scores if transposed to percentiles for a particular population might be transformed as follows: 47th–93rd percentile and 91st–64th percentile. Consequently in relation to others, the raw score 47 is better than the raw score 91.

transgendered persons   1. Cross-dressers, transvestites, transsexuals, or others who noticeably mix and match in their person significant aspects of male and female cultural life and living. Whereas some of this is not unusual in anyone, when it gets readily noticeable, the term transgendered may be used. See TRANSGENDERISM. 2. Persons, usually male, who enact the social role of the other gender. 3. Transsexuals who do not have sex-change surgery. 4. Gynecomimetic or andromimetic persons who do not want surgery. 5. See TRANSGENDERIST.

transgenderism   A psychosexual state marked by a mixing of sex roles. The cause of transsexualism or transgender behavior is not known and there probably are several varieties. See ROLE CONFUSION.

transgenderist   A person who manifests chronic partial transposition of the gender-identity role. Also known as transgendered person. See TRANSGENDERISM.

transgenerational hypothesis   A postulate that explains deviant behavior on the basis of its having been learned from earlier generations.

transgenerational patterns   Patterns of behavior that appear in several generations.

transhumance   The seasonal movement of herd animals.

transience   A feeling of impermanence combined with an anticipation of loss. The idea that everything is transitory may interfere with enjoyment of life and preclude the establishment of deep or lasting relationships. The normal individual, on the other hand, focuses primarily on the here and now and is presumably not frightened by the idea of eventual or possible losses.

transient ego ideal   (S. Lorand) A temporary state of mind a patient experiences as the result of a therapist serving as a source of temporary love and acceptance.

transient global amnesia (TGA)   A sudden, temporary loss of memory ability. Other functions may continue normally during the memory disruption.

transient group   A group that forms and dissolves easily. See NATURAL GROUP.

transient ischemic attack (TIA)   A mild stroke that may last for a few minutes and in some cases a few hours, the symptoms then receding without loss of consciousness or functional brain tissue by the patient. May be caused by a sudden brief interruption in blood supply to the vertebral-basilar or carotid-middle cerebral artery. See CEREBRAL ISCHEMIA.

transient situational disturbance   An acute, temporary reaction to an overwhelmingly stressful situation, experienced by an individual who does not have an underlying personality disorder. May occur at any period of life, and is due, for example, to separation from the mother in infancy, rejection or frightening experiences during childhood, parental conflict or natural catastrophe in adulthood, or menopause and forced retirement in later life. Also known as transient situational personality disorder. See ADJUSTMENT DISORDER, ADULT SITUATIONAL REACTION, ADJUSTMENT REACTION OF INFANCY, ADJUSTMENT REACTION OF CHILDHOOD, ADJUSTMENT REACTION OF ADOLESCENCE, AND ADJUSTMENT REACTION OF LATER LIFE, GROSS STRESS REACTION.

transient tremor   A tremor that appears and disappears without treatment. See TREMOR.

transient variation   See MUTATION.

transitional cortex   A portion of the cortex that lies between the primitive cortex, or archipallium, and the neocortex, thought to represent the newest phase of animal-brain development in terms of evolution.

transitional employment workshop   A sheltered workshop, or similar rehabilitation facility, specifically designed to advance a person with a disability toward the open job market. The transitional period may be extended as needed for those people unable to cope with a rapid change from sheltered workshop to competitive employment situations.

transitional object   1. Usually a toy employed by children as means of having fun but which has a future purpose. For example, playing with a doll may help a child learn to later care for an infant. 2. An object that serves as a link between infant and mother, the infant's first separate "not me" possession containing qualities of both mother and child, such as a babyblanket or stuffed animal, and that provides comfort to the child in times of separation from mother and home.

transitional period   The interval between two states such as between one equilibrium state and another.

transitional probability   The likelihood of a given event being followed by a second event.

transitional program   A rehabilitation project in which persons with a disability live with members of their own family on the hospital grounds for several days before being transferred to home-care treatment. During the transitional period, the person with the disability and family members occupy a cottage where nurses, dietitians, psychotherapists, and other hospital staff members instruct the family members in the methods of medical care and rehabilitation required for the person's disability.

transitive inference task   To test the ability of children to think in relative terms, a child is asked to infer a third relation from two others (for example, told that a blue line is longer than a green one and that a green one is longer than a yellow, and asked if the blue is longer than the yellow).

transitivism   The illusory transfer of symptoms or other characteristics to other people, for example, a patient's belief that other persons are also experiencing the same hallucinations, are also being persecuted, or are also lacking a stomach or another internal organ. Sometimes known as transitivity.

transitivity   1. A concept in which a relationship between two entities is transferred to a third. The principle that if A is smaller than B, and B is smaller than C, then A is smaller than C. 2. See TRANSITIVISM.

transitory problems   Conditions of concern that come and go, often in unpredictable patterns, perhaps occurring ten times in twenty years and lasting from a short period of time, such as several hours, or lasting days to as much as weeks at other times.

transituational   Pertaining to a behavioral pattern that demonstrates itself in a variety of situations; for instance, shyness may be seen in a person across a number of different places, but not in some others, such as in a family.

translation   1. A change into another form. 2. In communications, a change from one language to another, difficult to do since some concepts and words in language Alpha do not exist in language Beta. 3. In genetics, information from one cell to another, such as deoxyribonucleic acid (DNA) to ribonucleic acid (RNA) and from RNA to a ribosome.

translocation   In genetics, the change in location of one chromosome to another, both chromosomes usually becoming fused in the transfer. See AUTOSOMAL ABERRATIONS, DOWN'S DISEASE, TURNER'S SYNDROME.

transmarginal inhibition   (I. P. Pavlov) A protective reaction of the nervous system to overstimulation.

transmethylation hypothesis   A postulate that certain normal body chemicals are turned into LSD-like chemicals in the brain due to some metabolic defect.

transmigration   1. To change from one state of existence (essence) to another. 2. A belief that the soul of a person leaves the body at death and goes into another body. See REINCARNATION, RESURRECTION.

transmission   1. Transfer. 2. Sending or dispatching of objects, words, symbols, or neural impulses. 3. Spreading of a disease. See HORIZONTAL TRANSMISSION, VERTICAL TRANSMISSION. 4. Passing hereditary traits on from one generation to the next. 5. Handing down customs and mores from generation to generation. See CULTURAL PROCESS, CULTURAL TRANSMISSION.

transmission deafness   Loss of hearing due to failure of the eardrum or ossicles (three bones of the inner ear) to convey information of sound to the brain.

transmission unit (TU)   A logarithmic unit of sound intensity. See DECIBEL.

transmitter   An instrument or device that encodes and sends a message or impulse to a receiver or aids in its transmission, for example, a synaptic transmitter.

transmitter substance   (T. R. Elliott) A chemical that facilitates the passage of a nerve impulse from one nerve cell to another. Released by a nerve impulse as it arrives at a synapse of a neuron (neuronal terminal) the chemical diffuses across the synaptic gap to excite or inhibit the neurons of the postsynaptic membrane. See ACETYLCHOLINE.

transmutation   1. A change. 2. To change the appearance of things. See TRANSFORMISM, TRANSMUTATION OF MEASURES, TRANSMUTED SCORES.

transmutation of measures   Changing scores of one type into an equivalent system, as in changing raw scores into percentiles.

transmuted scores   A set of scores or values that have been converted from one scale to another.

transneuronal degeneration   See TRANSSYNAPTIC DEGENERATION.

transorbital lobotomy   A rare psychosurgical procedure in which a narrow rotating blade is introduced through the socket above the eyes to sever connections between the frontal lobe and the thalamus. The technique has a lower incidence of several side effects frequently observed in prefrontal lobotomy, such as incontinence and apathy.

transparency   An attempt to become invisible, not to be noticed in certain social situations, (such as when asked to volunteer for a task) by avoiding eye-contact, remaining still, or hiding behind another person.

transparent plane color   Two-dimensional color that presents a clear, unclouded mode of appearance and permits objects to be seen beyond and behind it in visual space, for example, colors in clear glass panes.

transparent self   (S. Jourard) Describing a personality that is real, open, revealing of inner self, genuine, and authentic.

transpersonal   1. Beyond the personal. Pertaining to individual or collective experiences of self-transcendence and nonordinary states of consciousness. 2. Archetypal, symbolic meanings that cannot be explained in terms of individual or personal life experiences alone. Collective psychic contents that are nearly universal.

transpersonal psychology   1. An area in humanistic psychology concerned with the exploration of "higher" states of consciousness and transcendental experiences. "Transpersonal" refers to the concern with ends that transcend personal identity and individual, immediate desires. 2. Studies transpersonal experiences and their correlates, and expands the field of inquiry to include body, mind, emotions, and spirit.

transplacental   Crossing the placenta. See HORIZONTAL TRANSMISSION, PLACENTAL BARRIER.

transplantation   1. Removal of something from one place to another, as in the transplantation of a body organ or skin graft. 2. Removal of a person from a permanent home to a transient residence or nursing home, a situation that may result in emotional disturbances such as anxiety, depression, and other effects.

transplantation shock   The mental distress experienced by a person as the result of transplantation. See TRANSPLANTATION (meaning 2).

transposability   (C. Ehrenfels) An aspect of form quality seen in music in that a melody is the same regardless of the notes played if in proper sequence.

transposition   1. The interchange of positions of two or more elements in a system. 2. In a learning situation, a reaction of the subject to a relationship of the elements rather than the elements per se. 3. In music, the change from one key to another. 4. (W. Köhler & M. Wertheimer) In Gestalt psychology, the application or transfer of a principle or relationship learned in one situation to other related situations. See TRANSFER.

transposition experiment   A learning situation in which the subject responds to relationships among stimuli rather than to particular stimuli.

transposition of affect   The transfer of the affective component of an unconscious idea to an unrelated idea or object, as frequently occurs in obsessive-compulsive disorder (OCD). Also known as displacement of affect.

transsexual   1. A person who has changed from living in his or her original gender to living in the other. Usually, after sexual reassignment surgery, living as either a male or a female rather than the original gender. 2. A person of one sex who thinks and acts as though of the other sex. Some such individuals desire to actually procure the surgical alteration and effect the removal of their secondary sexual characteristics by hormonal treatment. 3. A person with the external genitalia and secondary sexual characteristics of one sex, but whose personal identification is that of the other biological sex. Transsexuals, pre-surgery, view themselves as members of the other biological sex. See GENDER IDENTITY, SEXUAL IDENTITY.

transsexualism 1. The state of being a transsexual. 2. A conscious desire to change the anatomic sexual characteristics, stemming from the personal conviction of being a member of the opposite sex. Such persons often desire or actually attain surgery to bring their anatomy into conformity with their self-concept. See AMBISEXUALITY, CROSS DRESSING, GENDER, GENDER IDENTITY, SEX, SEXUAL IDENTITY, TRANSSEXUAL, VAGINAL ENVY.

transsynaptic degeneration Deterioration of any connecting neuron to a neuron that follows it via synapsis thereby having an effect somewhere up the line to the final point.

transsynaptic filament A filament that extends between the membranes of an axon and a neighboring dendrite. Purportedly the structure, observable only with an electron microscope, is involved in an exchange of materials during the growth period when axons and dendrites are moving toward each other as part of the development of an organism's nervous system.

transverse orientation compass reactions

transverse plane The horizontal plane in humans, such as a crosswise (transverse) cut through the body at 90° angles to the cephalocaudal axis, dividing the body or any part of it into upper and lower parts.

transvestism transvestitism

transvestite (TV) A person who dresses as a member of the opposite gender. A cross-dresser. This might be full-time or occasional. See CROSS-DRESS, DRAG QUEEN, GYNEMIMETOPHILIA, TRANSVES(TI)TISM.

transves(ti)tism 1. Cross-dressing (wearing clothes of the opposite gender), usually by males, often lifelong, not generally related to homosexuality. 2. Being sexually attracted to or aroused by cross-dressing. 3. Cross-dressing, or thus inclined to with associated feelings of sexuality and excitement, sometimes with uncomfortable feelings when dressed in garments of one's own gender. Spelled transvestitism in early literature. 4. (O. Fenichel) In psychoanalytic theory, a male's belief that donning women's clothes enhances his virility by enabling him to identify with a phallic woman.

transvestophilia See TRANSVESTISM.

Transylvania effect Phrase applied to abnormal behavior correlated with the phases of the moon. See LUNACY, LUNATISMUS.

trapezoid body A configuration made when transverse nerve fibers in the pons with origins in the cochlear nucleus, (related to the auditory system) pass fibers of the medial lemniscus (related to the proprioceptive system.)

Traube-Hering waves (L. Traube & H. E. Hering) Rhythmic and relatively slow oscillations in blood pressure not correlated with the heartbeat or respiration.

trauma 1. The result of a painful event, physical or mental, causing immediate damage to the body or shock to the mind. Psychological traumas include emotional shocks that have an enduring effect on the personality, such as rejection, divorce, combat experiences, civilian catastrophes, and racial or religious discrimination. 2. Continuing result of such an event to body or mind or both. Plural is traumata, traumas.

traumatic anxiety A state of apprehensiveness or an anxiety attack precipitated by a physical or psychological trauma such as a natural catastrophe, combat experience, business loss, or marital failure.

traumatic delirium An acute delirium following a head or brain injury. In some patients the delirium may become chronic, with symptoms of confabulation, disorientation, and memory deficit.

traumatic disorders Brain damage resulting from physical injury.

traumatic encephalopathy Diffuse brain disease caused by an injury to the brain. Among various symptoms are headaches, dizziness, poor concentration, personality changes, drowsiness, and insomnia.

traumatic event/experience Physical or psychic injury stressful or shocking, that may be the original cause of some emotional or mental disorder. Some such events early in life may be the foundations for adult neuroses or psychoses. See TRAUMA.

traumatic neurasthenia A type of neurasthenia (physical and mental weakness) that follows a physical injury experienced in an accident. The neurasthenia may have been an underlying neurosis aggravated by the trauma. See SECONDARY GAINS.

traumatic neurosis An emotional disorder precipitated by an acutely disturbing situation or experience, characterized by such symptoms as preoccupation with the trauma, at least partial amnesia for the event, reduced efficiency, nightmares, irritability, and autonomic dysfunction. See COMBAT FATIGUE, PSYCHORRHEXIS.

traumatic pseudocatatonia A catatonic-like reaction that is the result of an injury, usually of short duration. See SHOCK, TRAUMA.

traumatic psychosis Mental disorder brought on by physical injury, usually to the brain.

traumatophilia Unconscious wish for, or tendency toward, injury. See MASOCHISM.

traumatophilic Person who seems to experience an undue amount or level of traumatic experiences, who seems to enjoy collecting or discussing them, or both.

traumatophilic diathesis Accident proneness, predisposition to accidents. See VICTIM RECIDIVISM.

traumatophobia Morbid fear of sustaining an injury.

travel phobia See HODOPHOBIA.

traveling wave A wave of pressure that follows a course, affecting objects in its path that may in turn continue the effect in different physical media. For example, a sound wave of pressure is converted in the middle ear to a mechanical vibration that in turn is translated into a fluid pressure wave in the cochlea and finally into nerve impulses tuned to the sound wave's frequency. See WAVE.

traveling wave theory of hearing A modification of the place theory of hearing developed by Georg von Békésy. See HEARING THEORIES.

treatment (TX or Tx)　　1. Administration of appropriate measures, for example, drugs or psychotherapy, designed to relieve a pathological condition. Types of treatment include: ADJUVANT, AMBULATORY, BIOLOGICAL, BIOMEDICAL, COERCIVE, COLD-PACK, COMBINED, CONTINUOUS-BATH, CONTINUOUS-SLEEP, CROSS-CULTURAL, DEPLETIVE, ELECTROCONVULSIVE, EXPERIMENTAL, FORCED, INTRUSIVE, MORAL, MULTIMONITORED ELECTROCONVULSIVE, PROLONGED SLEEP, PSYCHIATRIC SOCIAL, PSYCHOLOGICAL SOCIAL, RAPID-SMOKING, REPLACEMENT, SHOCK, SLEEP, SPLIT-BRAIN, SUBCOMA INSULIN, SUBSHOCK INSULIN, SYMPTOMATIC. See RIGHT TO TREATMENT, RIGHT TO REFUSE TREATMENT, THERAPY, THERAPEUTICS. 2. The manner in which experimental procedures are applied and the resulting data evaluated. See EXPERIMENT, RESEARCH, STUDY.

treatment audit　　An evaluation of the effectiveness of diagnostic and therapeutic procedures. They may take the form of analyses of individual cases or of a patient population. Retrospective audits include a review of patients after they have been discharged. Concurrent audits are conducted while patients are still under treatment. Such evaluations are usually used to target the effectiveness of individual practitioners as well as overall evaluations of the treatment personnel.

treatment bias　　A tendency for treatment of any kind, including mental, to be affected by the social class or cultural background of the patient.

treatment combination　　The combining of various independent variables within a well-constructed experimental design.

treatment duration　　The length of time for any treatment, physical or mental. As a general rule, the more damaged the person is the longer the treatment.

treatment-evaluation strategies　　The determination of the effects of a particular treatment through application of different evaluation research procedures. See DISMANTLING-TREATMENT STRATEGY, TREATMENT-PACKAGE STRATEGY.

treatment improvement protocol (TIP)　　A systematic model to evaluate improvement toward a goal; for example, during a rehabilitation process, dates and signs of improvement are noted in a structured format.

treatment integrity　　The fidelity with which treatment is rendered. In evaluating psychotherapy systems it is important to know whether the therapists assigned to use any particular method did, in fact, stick to their assigned or preferred systems.

treatment levels　　Appropriate, randomly-selected levels of the different kinds of the independent variable used in an experiment. They should cover as wide a range as necessary for detecting any real effects of the independent variable. The spacing and number of the levels should sufficiently define the shape of the function relating the independent and dependent variables. Distinctions should be made between qualitative and quantitative treatments, although some studies combine both. See RESEARCH DESIGNS, RESEARCH METHODOLOGY.

treatment-package strategy　　The application of several therapeutic components as a means of determining whether specialized treatment alters the problem for which they were designed.

treatment protocol　　The formal way to proceed in various systems of psychotherapy. In some psychotherapies, such as Alfred Adler's Individual Psychology, no explicit rules exist, whereas in others systems such as Carl Rogers' Person-Centered Therapy, strict adherence to its rules are expected.

treatment resistance　　1. In therapy, refers to clients who do not respond in a positive manner to the more commonly-used techniques, and therefore may require different strategies of treatment (such as a change in procedure or therapist). 2. In medicine, a certain percentage of patients tend not to respond to the first line or more commonly-used medicines, and a more complex strategy is then required. Some examples include: (a) higher doses; (b) another medicine of a different type; (c) combining with another medicine (polypharmacy); (d) adjunctive use of a hormone or nutrient.

tredecaphobia　　triskaidekaphobia

tremolo　　Rapid periodic variation in pitch, loudness, or both of a tone, usually considered an unpleasant sound.

tremograph　　(A. R. Luria) An instrument for measuring body tremors. Also known as tremometer, tremorgraph.

tremometer　　See TREMOGRAPH.

tremophobia　　Morbid fear of trembling.

tremor　　1. A slight involuntary quaking or shaking movement. 2. Any trembling of the body or a part of the body. Psychologic tremors may be mild or violent and uncontrolled. A coarse tremor involves a large muscle group in slow movements whereas a fibrillary tremor is caused by a small bundle of muscle fibers that produce a fine tremor. A senile tremor is associated with aging. Some tremors occur only during voluntary movements. See INTENTION TREMOR, PARKINSONISM.

tremorgraph　　tremograph

trend analysis　　The analysis of a set of variable measurements, taken at different intervals, to determine if there is evidence of a trend.

trend correlation　　The correlation of time series to identify leading and lagging indicators that can be used for forecasting.

trend extrapolation　　The fitting of curves (linear, quadratic, or S-shaped) through past time series to predict future results.

trend of thought　　A tendency to think in terms of a particular pattern of ideas with an affective tone. See AUTISTIC FANTASY, DELUSIONAL SYSTEM.

trend sampling　　Samples taken at different times so that the effect of time can be ascertained. See LONGITUDINAL SAMPLING, STRATEGIC SAMPLING.

trend test　　Analysis of data early in a study to determine the direction of the results.

trepanation　　trephination

trephination　　A surgical procedure in which a disk of bone is removed from the skull, purportedly one of the oldest types of surgery, based on evidence found in skulls of prehistoric humans with round holes that apparently had healed, possibly done in an attempt to cure mental disorders. Also known as skull trephining, and, especially in England, trepanation.

Treppe (stairs, staircase—German) The response of a muscle, particularly cardiac muscle, to repeated single induction shocks of equal strength, by progressively increasing the strength of muscle contractions up to a maximum. Henry Bowditch called this the staircase phenomenon.

triad 1. Assortment of three things having a common element. 2. A set of three persons involved in a dynamic relationship, such as three partners in a business. See DYAD. 3. In group psychotherapy, the father, mother, and child relationship.

triadic theory of intelligence **triarchic theory of intelligence**

triadic therapy The treatment typically of two people in a relationship, usually a marriage, meeting with a therapist not for counseling but rather for simultaneous treatment, for example, one partner cannot quit smoking and the other cannot manage money. Unable to quit these behaviors alone, they both decide to go to therapy. Sometimes known as triangular therapy. See CONJOINT MARITAL THERAPY.

Triad Training Model (P. Pedersen) An innovative method of psychotherapy involving three persons in interaction: (a) the therapist; (b) the therapee, a person who is hostile either to the therapist, therapy, culture, etc.; and (c) a catalyst, a person who represents the therapee's ethnic group, "race," religion or other affiliation. The catalyst is to serve as a kind of bridge of communication and support to therapee and therapist to achieve the usual goals of counseling. See CROSS-CULTURAL TREATMENT.

triage Sorting people into (a) those beyond help, (b) those who can be helped, (c) those who can function with minimal help. See TRIAGE SITUATIONS.

triage (situations) 1. In emergency situations in which immediate treatment cannot be applied to all, the sorting of people into three categories: those requiring immediate treatment, those who can wait for treatment, and those who do not need treatment or who are beyond help. 2. A method of allocating scarce resources among social programs only to those most likely to benefit from them.

trial In tests or experiments, a practice session or performance of a given task, for example, one pass through a maze.

trial analysis/therapy In psychotherapy, especially psychoanalysis, a provisional period during which the therapist, with or without consultation with others, determines if a client is appropriate to the particular treatment, or the treatment appropriate to the client.

trial-and-error (TE) learning Learning by experimenting and gaining knowledge and skills through a succession of trials. Successes are used to retain effective, failures to discard ineffective, approaches and strategies.

trial-and-error method In animal learning, a sporadic set of movements to achieve an objective in a novel situation, such as escaping from an imprisoned situation. Movements that succeed are more frequently repeated in subsequent trials, and movements that fail gradually disappear. When animals repeat the same successful movements over several trials, it is said that they have learned. See VICARIOUS TRIAL AND ERROR.

trial-and-success Phrase preferred by some to trial-and-error, focuses on the importance of reward.

trial identification (R. Fliess) A process in which therapists try to put themselves "in the clients' shoes" in an attempt to empathize with the client regarding the best mode of treatment. See EMPATHY, PERSON-CENTERED METHOD.

trial lesson A diagnostic technique providing information about a child's learning style and most appropriate teaching approaches for that child.

trial marriage The open living together by two people with the expressed intent of determining how well they get along, and with the further intention, if they are in good accord, to eventually formalize the relationship by a conventional marriage. See EXPERIMENTAL MARRIAGE.

trial response A tentative response made to see whether that particular response will work (achieve desired results). See TRIAL-AND-ERROR METHOD.

trial therapy **trial analysis**

triangular counseling See TRIAD TRAINING MODEL.

triangular theory of love (R. J. Sternberg) The proposal that love has three components: (a) intimacy (the emotional component), (b) passion (the motivational component), and (c) commitment (the cognitive component). According to Robert Sternberg, the components singly or in combinations produce different kinds of love. See LOVE.

triangular therapy A type of marriage therapy in which the two partners meet with the therapist as a group. Sometimes known as triadic therapy. See CONJOINT MARITAL THERAPY.

triangulate A means of determining the validity of a hypothesis if two researches using different methods draw the same conclusion about the particular hypothesis. For example, if two different types of studies both indicate that male infants are more aggressive than female infants, the hypothesis of greater male aggression is supported.

triarchic theory of intelligence (R. J. Sternberg) A proposal that intelligence comprises three types of abilities: (a) componental, analytical; (b) experiential, insight and creativity; and (c) contextual, practical knowledge. According to Robert Sternberg, the components singly or in combinations produce different kinds of intelligence. Also known as triadic theory of intelligence. See BASIC FACTORS OF INTELLIGENCE, FACTOR THEORY OF INTELLIGENCE, GROUP FACTORS IN INTELLIGENCE, GUILFORD DIMENSIONS OF INTELLIGENCE, INTELLIGENCE.

tribade (to rub—Greek) 1. A woman who rubs her genitals against those of another woman for sexual pleasure. 2. A lesbian. 3. Rarely, a male who practices equivalent behavior.

tribadism Orgasm by friction without penetration. Also known as tribady. See TRIBADE.

triceps reflex Extension of the forearm by tapping the triceps tendon at the elbow when the forearm is partly flexed.

triceptor theory A point of view that the retina contains three types of receptors, one for each of the primary colors of trichromatism. See TRICHROMATIC THEORY.

trichesthesia   A sensation of the scalp when pulling on a hair.

trichinophobia   Morbid fear of acquiring trichinosis.

trichopathophobia   Morbid fear of growing excessive facial hair (in women). See HYPERTRICHOPHOBIA, TRICHOPHOBIA.

trichophagy   Persistently biting and eating one's own hair.

trichophobia   Morbid fear of hair. Also known as chaetophobia. See TRICHOPATHOPHOBIA.

trichorrhexomania   The compulsion to break off one's own hair with the fingernails.

trichotillomania   Compulsive hair pulling; an irresistible impulse to pull out one's own hair.

trichotomy   Separating any thing into three parts, they not being necessarily equal.

trichromat   A person possessing normal color vision. See TRICHROMATISM.

trichromatic theory   A point of view that normal color perception depends upon retinal pigments sensitive to three primary wavelengths, blue, green, red. Some investigators have argued that the retina also may have special sensitivity to yellow or violet, or both. Also known as three-component theory. See TRICEPTOR THEORY, TRIRECEPTOR THEORY.

trichromatism   Normal color vision; the capacity to distinguish the three primary color systems of black-white, red-green, and blue-yellow. Also known as trichromatopsia.

trick   A psychic mechanism used to conceal from the self, knowledge of self-weakness. See DENIAL, REPRESSION.

tricomponent theory of attitudes   A point of view that an attitude is (a) an affective feeling of liking/disliking, based on (b) beliefs/cognitions about an object, which leads to (c) a readiness to behave in a certain manner.

tricyclic antidepressants (TCA)   A class of antidepressant drugs, some other classes being the serotonin-reuptake inhibitors (SRIs) and the monoamine oxidase inhibitors (MAOIs). Used mainly in the 1970s and 1980s. Some TCAs are also useful in the treatment of nighttime enuresis, night terrors, some forms of attention-deficit hyperactivity disorder (ADHD), school phobia, social phobia, and separation anxiety disorders. See CLOMIPRAMINE.

tridimensional theory of emotion   A point of view of Wilhelm Wundt that all feelings or emotions have three dimensions: excitement-calmness, pleasantness-unpleasantness, tension-relaxation. These can be visualized in three-dimensional (3-D) space.

tridimensional vision   Vision involving discernment of depth or distance. Can be determined artificially by a stereoscope or by 3-D motion picture.

trifacial nerve   The name given by French physician Francois Chaussier (1746–1828) for the trigeminal nerve.

trifactorial designs   (K. W. Schaie) A three-factor scheme (age, cohort, time of measurement) for measuring and explaining developmental changes.

trigeminal nerve   (Fallopius, J. F. Meckel, J. B. Winslow) Cranial nerve V. Largest of the cranial nerves, it carries both sensory and motor fibers. The motor fibers are primarily involved with the muscles used in chewing, tongue movements, and swallowing. The sensory fibers innervate the same areas, including the teeth and most of the tongue in addition to the jaws. Some trigeminal nerve fibers innervate the cornea, face, scalp, and the dura mater membrane of the brain.

trigeminal neuralgia   A facial neuralgia involving the trigeminal nerve, characterized by paroxysms of excruciating pain. Also known as *tic douloureux* (French).

trigeminal nucleus   Either of two nuclei associated with the three main roots of the trigeminal nerve. One, the spinal trigeminal nucleus, extends downward in the medulla to the upper region of the spinal cord and receives fibers from pain and temperature receptors. The other, the main sensory trigeminal nucleus, receives large myelinated fibers from pressure receptors in the skin and relays impulses upward to the thalamus. See SPINAL TRIGEMINAL NUCLEUS.

trigger   1. Emotionally-charged stimuli that lead to both conscious and unconscious responses. 2. An environmental event or word that activates a spontaneous abreaction or the recovery of a memory. Triggers can be sensory or affective, involving sounds, smells, touches, or words. 3. See TRIGGERING CAUSE.

trigger action   The case in which one train of energy serves to release another train of (latent) energy.

triggered causal variable   A causal variable that does not act, appear, or is not measurable until preceded by another variable. Compare LATENT CAUSAL VARIABLE.

trigger features   Patterns of sensory stimulation that initiate responding in particular sensory neurons.

triggering cause   A stimulus or phenomenon that initiates the immediate onset of a behavior problem. Sometimes known as trigger.

triggering event   In group dynamics, an event that introduces a conflict.

trigram   Three letters consisting of two consonants with a vowel in between (for example, NAZ, BOJ, ROF). Used for research purposes, they were previously called nonsense syllables.

trigraph   A cluster of three letters having a single sound (for example, the "ing" in "playing"). See DIGRAPH.

triiodothyronine   An iodine-containing amino acid, one of the active principles of the thyroid gland. Similar to but more potent than thyroxine, once thought to be the primary thyroid hormone.

trill   In linguistics, the sound made by passing air over the raised tongue tip and vibrating it for a time.

trimester   A period of approximately three months, as in referring to the first, second or third trimester of pregnancy.

triolist   A person who, in a three-way sexual relationship, enjoys both a female-male sexual relationship with a partner and observing the partner in male-male (or female-female) sexual activities with a third person. The male-female sexual relationship may be maintained with either or both of the other partners.

triorchid   Pertaining to a male having three testes.

trip   See ACID TRIP.

triple alternation   A learning situation in which a subject is required to, for example, turn right three times (RRR), then left three times (LLL) to reach a goal or receive a reward. See ALTERNATION METHOD.

triple blind control   See TRIPLE BLIND (STUDY).

triple blind (study)   (A. Auerbach) Ethically questionable research design in which not only do neither the administrators nor the participants know the identity of the treatment (double blind), but neither knows that any research is being conducted. For instance, to measure malingering or the placebo effect of analgesics, a military commander might replace injectable morphine with weaker or placebo doses without the knowledge of either the practitioners or the patients (triple-blind control). See BLIND EXPERIMENT.

triple insanity   A rare psychotic disorder or psychosis of association in which three intimately related persons simultaneously share identical delusions. Also known as *folie à trois* (French).

triple-receptor theory   A proposal that cones of the retina are of three types, some sensitive only to red, blue, or green. See THEORIES OF COLOR VISION, THREE COLOR THEORY.

triploid   Having three complete sets of chromosomes, instead of two. See CHROMOSOMAL ABERRATION.

triploid karyotype   A chromosome combination in a cell nucleus that consists of three copies instead of the normal diploid (or two copies) for a tissue cell, or haploid (or one copy) for a germinal cell or gamete, for example, an XXX sex-chromosome combination. See CHROMOSOMAL ABERRATION.

trireceptor theory   A hypothesis that color vision depends upon the operation of three kinds of receptors in the retina; each of these, with its nerve connections, being assumed to mediate a fixed fundamental or primary hue-quality, all gradations of color being dependent upon the proportions of activity of the three. See COLOR THEORIES.

trisexuality   In psychoanalytic theory, the representation in dreams of three aspects of sexuality, man, woman, and child, at the same time. The concept of the patient's desire to play the three roles symbolically and simultaneously is regarded as a manifestation of a tripartition of the mind.

triskaidekaphobia   Superstitious fear of the number thirteen. Also known as tredecaphobia.

trisome   A three-bodied chromosome. See TRISOMY.

trisomy   Having three instead of the usual two chromosomes in each cell nucleus. It is the cause of several disorders.

trisomy 21   A condition associated with 85% of Down-syndrome cases, characterized by the presence of three No. 21 chromosomes in the body cells rather than the normal pair. The extra chromosome may be contributed by either parent. Also known as 47,XX + 21, 21 trisomy, chromosome-21 trisomy. This condition is often treated as synonymous with Down disease.

tristimulus value   A hue as defined in terms of the percentage of the trichromatic primaries (red, green, blue) needed to match it.

tritanope   The rarest of the three groups of dichromats. A person who cannot recognize or see the third primary color blue. Compare DEUTERANOPE, PROTANOPE.

tritanopia   A form of color blindness in which the person has some loss of luminosity in the blue portion of the visual spectrum, apparently as a result of a blue-pigment deficiency. The condition differs from tetartanopia marked by a confusion of yellow and blue without loss of blue luminosity.

triune brain   (P. MacLean) An argument that the human brain originally was simple and later developed an addition to the first stage, a second level, and finally a third and present stage.

tRNA   See TRANSFER RNA.

trochlear nerve   Cranial nerve IV. It contains the motor components of the superior oblique muscle of the eyeball. Also known as pathetic nerve.

Troland   (L. T. Troland) A measure of the amount of illumination on the retina; equal to the illumination per square millimeter of pupil received from a surface of 1 lux brightness.

tromophonia   Dysphonia (difficulty or pain in speaking) characterized by tremulous voice.

Tropenkoller   (tropic rage—German) A culture-specific syndrome occurring among young males in Africa. Affected individuals, as well as those affected by a similar disorder "*misala*," start quarrels and rapidly work themselves up to a frenzy of speech and wild gesticulation without apparent purpose or cause. The episode lasts from a few minutes to a few hours, after which the person collapses in exhaustion.

trophic function   Activities associated with the ingestion of food substances and metabolism of the nutrient components.

trophic nerve   A nerve that aids or regulates the nutrition of a tissue.

trophotropic   (W. R. Hess) Relating to trophotropism.

trophotropic function   Relating to nutritive functions (for example, digestion, cell maintenance) that are largely controlled by the parasympathetic nervous system centers of the hypothalamus. Appetite is apparently a trophotropic function when associated with relaxation.

trophotropic process   (W. Hess) Central nervous system functions associated with arousal of the organism to nutrition. This process was an outgrowth of the theory proposed earlier by Walter Cannon to explain the sympathetic and parasympathetic networks involved in food seeking. See ERGOTROPIC PROCESS.

trophotropism   A form of chemotaxis characterized by movement of living cells in relation to nutritive material. Also known as trophotaxis. See TAXIS, TROPISM.

tropism   1. The movement of plants and animals away from or toward a stimulus that often exists as a natural force, such as sunlight or gravity. For instance, a morning glory plant turns to face the sun as it moves (heliotropism) while its roots follow magnetic lines of force and gravity. Although "tropism" and "taxis" were once considered synonyms, the modern tendency is to use "tropism" to refer to plants and "taxis" to refer to animals; also taxis may be used in the general sense and tropism to refer to a specific type of taxis. 2. Obsolete term for the involuntary movement of an organism (usually a type of flora) toward (positive tropism) or away from (negative tropism) a source of stimulation. Closely associated with Loeb's muscle tension hypothesis. See GEOTROPISM, HELIOTROPISM, NEGATIVE TROPISM, POSITIVE TROPISM, RHEOTROPISM, TAXIS, THERMOTROPISM.

tropostereoscope A stereoscope that turns or adjusts, usually consisting of two adjustable, adjoining tubes provided with a mechanism to hold observed images in place. Designed to demonstrate the influence of double images in depth perception.

tropotaxis A kind of taxis in which movement indicates a direct path orientation toward a source or a particular stimulus, such as a food smell, rather than interrupted or zig-zagging movement as seen in klinotaxis. See TAXIS, TROPISM.

trot reflex A diagonal reflexive response that typically appears in about the fifth month of human fetal life. Stimulation of a foot may produce a response not only of the stimulated member but of the opposite hand. Thought to be a precursor of postnatal locomotion, as in crawling and walking.

Troxler effect (I. P. Troxler) A tendency for visual objects to fade in the periphery of the visual field when a point in its center is steadily attended to. Due to the organization of the peripheral retina, which requires larger eye movements than the fovea, to break the adaptation brought about by steady fixation.

Trp See TRYPTOPHAN.

truancy Absence from school without permission. See CONDUCT DISORDER.

true Valid. Corresponding to reality, conforming to fact, being coherent, or consistent with logical relations. Compare FALSE.

true anxiety See INSTINCTUAL ANXIETY, REALISTIC ANXIETY.

true experiment Research in which the arrangement permits maximum control over the independent variables or conditions of interest. The investigator is able to assign subjects to different conditions on a systematic (usually random) basis, to include alternative conditions (for example, treatment and control conditions) as required by the design, and to control possible sources of bias within the experiment.

true-false test A questionnaire or task in which a person is asked to react to statements as "True" (T) or "False" (F). See SELECTIVE-ANSWER TEST.

true memory Recollection of an event that did take place.

true score 1. A measure that would be obtained by taking the average of an infinitely large number of measurements of (a) a given individual on similar tests taken under similar conditions or of (b) a variable expressed in the behavior of a universe of individuals. 2. A score, "assumed" to be true, based, for example, on a very large and representative sample of a national population.

true self 1. Who a person really is, something that may be impossible to determine. 2. (E. Fromm) The total of an individual's potentialities that could be developed under ideal social and cultural conditions. Phrase is used in the context of Erich Fromm's approach to neurosis as a reaction to cultural pressures and repressed potentialities. The realization of the total self is a major goal of therapy.

true symbolism Symbolism that meets the following standards suggested by Ernest Jones, Otto Rank, and Hans Sachs: (a) representation of unconscious material; (b) constant or limited meaning; (c) evolutionary basis with regard to individual and "race"; (d) nondependence on individual factors only; (e) phylogenetic parallels with the symbolism found in myths, cults, and religions; (f) a linguistic link between the symbol and the symbolized idea.

true variance The actual variance of a total population rather than the obtained variance from a sampling.

true zero In a measurement scale, a zero that does not represent what is being measured.

true zero factoring (R. B. Cattell) A basic system of factor analysis which allows factors to assume different sizes and to be measured from true zeros.

truism A statement or proposition whose truth is so obvious to both speaker and audience that it need not be formulated or need not be supported by argument or fact.

truncated distribution A distribution of cases that in which one end of the distribution of values is attenuated. See CHANCE.

trust Belief in the honesty and integrity of another. See BASIC TRUST, INTERPERSONAL TRUST.

trust exercises Procedures commonly used in group therapy and in growth groups, with variations intended to help people learn to trust others. See BEHIND-THE-BACK TECHNIQUE, BLIND WALK.

trust vs mistrust The first of Erik Erikson's stages of psychosocial development, in the first year of life and occurring roughly during Sigmund Freud's oral stage, during which infants either develop an attitude of trust or an attitude of mistrust of other people and themselves. Influenced by the kind of care received. See BASIC MISTRUST, BASIC TRUST, ERIKSON'S STAGES OF PSYCHOSOCIAL DEVELOPMENT.

truth The correspondence of a judgment or thought with an actual occurrence.

truth-sayers People who are inclined to tell the truth even under situations when most other people would, to protect others' feelings, tell a lie. Such people are often accused of being tactless, for example, after eating at a dinner party, on being asked if the meal was enjoyed, replying in the negative.

truth serum A common name for sedative, barbiturate drugs such as Amytal or Pentothal when used to evoke suppressed or repressed memories. Name derives from the reported use of drugs by police to extract confessions from criminals. See AMYTAL INTERVIEW.

tryptamines A group of drugs that bear a chemical relationship to serotonin (5-hydroxytryptamine) and include a number of agents with psychedelic effects similar to those of LSD. The prototype of the series is dimethyltryptamine (DMT) that occurs naturally in a variety of plants in many areas of the world. Also known as tryptamine derivatives. See PSYCHEDELICS, SEROTONIN.

tryptophan (Trp)   (R. Neumeister, F. G. Hopkins) An essential amino acid of the human diet, a precursor of the neurotransmitter serotonin, and therefore of increasing interest to neuropharmacologists. It is also a precursor of the B vitamin niacin, needed to prevent the neurologic and other effects of pellagra. See SEROTONIN.

tryptophan depletion   The administration of a diet designed to lower both tryptophan and the synthesis of 5-HT in the brain.

TS   1. See TOURETTE'S DISORDER/SYNDROME. 2. Terminal sensation or greater sensation. See TERMINAL SENSITIVITY.

TSA   transcortical sensory aphasia

T-scale   A scale used in interpreting scores obtained on a test; it ordinarily ranges from 0 to 100 with 50 being the mean (or from -5σ to $+5\sigma$), the unit of measurement being one-tenth of the standard deviation. The scores on this scale are called T-scores.

T-scope   See TACHISTOSCOPE.

T-score   A set of scores with mean equal to 50 and standard deviation equal to 10. See T-SCALE.

T-score transformation   A standard score transformed to a scale with a mean of 50 and a standard deviation of 10.

TSD   Tay-Sachs disease

TSH   thyroid-stimulating hormone

T statistic   See WILCOXON T STATISTIC.

T-TAT   Thompson Thematic Apperception Test

t-**test for independent groups**   A *t*-test comparing two separate groups, each measured once, such as comparing hypnotizability of college students and high-school students. See *T*-TEST FOR MATCHED GROUPS.

t-**test for matched groups**   A *t*-test for the difference between two means obtained on a single group of subjects, or for the difference between two means in which the scores are significantly correlated. See *T*-TEST FOR INDEPENDENT GROUPS.

TTH   See THYROTROP(H)IC HORMONE.

T₃RU   Abbreviation for T_3resin uptake.

TTR   type-token ratio

TTS   temporary threshold shift

T type   (E. R. Jaensch) A personality type classified in terms of eidetic imagery that persists after adolescence and is associated with tetany on the basis of blood mineral tests. In the T type the imagery resembles the afterimage rather than the memory image (as in the other type classified, the B type). Also known as tetany type. See B TYPE, MARBURG SCHOOL, WÜRZBURG SCHOOL.

TU   transmission unit

tubal ligation   A surgical procedure to block or sever the fallopian-tube passageway between the ovaries and the uterus for female sterilization. Does not affect sex drive, ability for coitus, or menstrual cycles, and often can be surgically reversed. See VASECTOMY.

tubal pregnancy   A fallopian-tube pregnancy.

tubectomy   The excision or tying of one or both of the Fallopian tubes.

tuberculomania   Unfounded obsession of having developed tuberculosis. Also known as phthisiomania.

tuberculophobia   Morbid fear of acquiring tuberculosis. Also known as phthisiophobia.

tuberculous meningitis   A complication of tuberculosis with infection of the meninges and brain itself that may cause deafness, mental deficiency, convulsions, or a form of hydrocephalus.

tuberous sclerosis   (D. M. Bourneville & E. Brissaud) A congenital disorder, transmitted as an autosomal-dominant trait, characterized by nodular lesions on the face and in the brain, mental deficiency and seizures. Many such people have average intelligence, but the intelligence quotient (IQ) tends to decline as they grow older. Also known as Bourneville's disease, epiloia.

tufted cell   A special type of cell for the sense of smell. Axons of the tufted cells pass through the anterior commissure to the olfactory bulb on the other side of the head.

tuitional analysis   A treatment and training program that people in training in some systems of psychotherapy are required to participate in as clients or patients before being qualified in that system. See DIDACTIC ANALYSIS, TRAINING ANALYSIS.

Tukey's Honestly Significant Difference Test (HSD) (J. W. Tukey) A multiple comparison test designed for controlling Type 1 error when post hoc pairwise comparisons between means are made.

tumescence   Tumefaction, or condition of swelling or being swollen. Term sometimes is applied to the swelling of the cavernosum bodies of the penis or clitoris as a result of sexual stimulation or a similar tumefacient. Compare DETUMESCENCE.

tuning   Definite maximum of sensory intensity that can be aroused in each specific pressure, warm, or cold spot, and that cannot be increased by any excessive degree of stimulation.

tuning fork   A fork-shaped device with two tines, made of specially tempered steel, that emits a specific pure tone when struck.

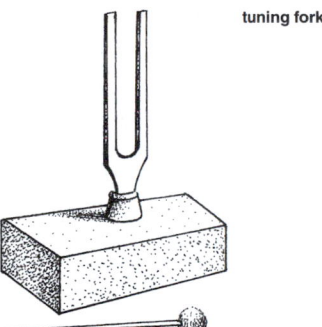

tuning fork

tunnel of Corti   A triangular space enclosed within the arch of Corti in the internal ear.

tunnel vision   1. Restriction in the field of vision that produces the effect of perceiving the world through a long tunnel or tube. Peripheral vision may be entirely lost. Tunnel vision may be a hysterical (conversion) symptom. 2. Metaphorically, taking a narrow view, behaving as if wearing blinders.

turbinate   A raised, conch-like structure within the nasal cavity that deflects currents of inhaled air. The turbinates provide a blood-warmed surface that helps humidify and raise the temperature of inhaled air before it continues into the pharynx and lungs. They also direct an increased flow of air over olfactory receptors when sniffing an aroma.

turf   The geographical or psychological area claimed as personal space. See TERRITORIAL AGGRESSION.

Turing machine   (A. M. Turing) Essentially, the basis of modern computers, developed in the 1930s, that has many similarities to the functioning of the human brain, intended to demonstrate among other things, that this machine can substitute for humans in replying to questions put to it.

Turing test   (A. M. Turing) A misnomer as it is not a test, but rather the question of whether computers can think. The "test" is whether machines can duplicate human thinking precisely.

Turner's syndrome   A chromosomal disorder marked by the absence of all or a part of one of the two X chromosomes in a female karyotype. The effects include absence of menstrualonset, webbing of the neck, short stature, and aortic coarction. The karyotype in most cases is 45,XO, resulting in infertility (more than 99%), but the syndrome may occur in a very small percentage of females who are fertile because of a gene mosaicism in which some cells contain two X chromosomes and others contain one or none. Named after American endocrinologist Henry H. Turner (1892–1970). Also known as XO syndrome, gonadal dysgenesis. See TRANSLOCATION.

turnim-man   Phrase used by natives of the Sambia tribe in Papua, New Guinea for what they considered to be a third sex (male pseudohermaphrodites found to have a deficiency in the enzyme 5-alpha-reductase). See PSEUDOHERMAPHRODITE.

turning against the self   In psychoanalytic theory, directing sadism toward the self. Considered one of four instinctual vicissitudes, along with reversal into its opposite, repression, and sublimation by Sigmund Freud. Considered a defense mechanism by Anna Freud.

turning inward   A process of self-scrutiny, examining "who," "what," and "why," questions about the self. Considered to be both a positive process if a person is attempting self-enlightenment, or a negative process if a person is attempting escape from reality or contact with others. See ENTROPY and also terms beginning with SELF-.

turnover   In industrial psychology, the leaving of a job whether voluntarily or involuntary. Turnover records are frequently used to measure job tenure (how long workers remain on the job) as well as job satisfaction or dissatisfaction. See LABOR TURNOVER.

tutorial counseling   (F. Thorne) 1. A process whose focus is on teaching clients to understand themselves in the functioning environment and to acquire skills for improving situational adjustment. 2. A form of directive counseling during which the therapist acts as a teacher and the counselee behaves like a student. A more sophisticated variation of father-son or mother-daughter talks.

tutoring effect   A tendency for people to learn most what they themselves teach, even more than those who are taught.

TV   1. tidal volume. 2. See TRANSVESTITE.

twelfth cranial nerve   See HYPOGLOSSAL NERVE.

Twenty-Four Hour Therapy   (A. Landy) A psychotherapeutic regime in which the patient is supervised 24-hours a day by the therapist's assistants who take complete control over the patient, directed by the therapist who has control (including legal, medical, and financial) over the patient, getting ongoing information from the assistants and directing them by mobile telephone. Usually, someone other than the patient, such as parents or partners, generates this process for those in desperate situations when no other method seems possible or profitable.

twenty-minute hour   A form of brief, supportive "psychotherapy" administered by a general physician. Suggestion, exhortation, advice, environmental manipulation, and prescription of drugs are among the techniques used in this type of therapy.

Twenty Statements Test   (M. Kuhn) A self-attitude measure in which respondents are to give 20 answers to the question "Who Am I?"

twilight attacks   Psychomotor seizure characterized by sudden changes in consciousness accompanied by meaningless speech and automatic movements.

twilight sleep   1. A state of dim awareness, usually induced by drugs. 2. A state of somnolence, or prolonged drowsiness, observed in cases of sleep drunkenness and sometimes maintained by hypnotic drugs for therapeutic purposes. See SCOPOLAMINE, SLEEP DRUNKENNESS, SLEEP TREATMENT, SOMNOLENCE.

twilight state   A clouded state of consciousness characterized by being temporarily unaware of surroundings, experiencing fleeting auditory or visual hallucinations, and responding to them by performing irrational acts such as undressing in public, running away, or becoming violent. The disturbance occurs primarily in psychomotor epilepsy, dissociative reactions, and alcoholic intoxication. On regaining normal consciousness, patients usually report they felt they were dreaming, but have has little or no recollection of their behavior. See DREAM STATE, POSTEPILEPTIC TWILIGHT STATE.

twilight vision   scotopic vision

twin   One member of a pair of children produced at a single birthing incident. Those born from one egg are known as monozygotic (identical) twins and essentially are physical replicas of each other. Those born of two eggs are known as dizygotic (fraternal) twins.

twin control   In studying siblings, there are several possibilities in comparing (A1 and A2) monozygotic twins (one egg), (B1 and B2) dizygotic twins (two eggs), and (C) monozygotic individuals (one egg). Each of these five possibilities can be compared with any other, or in various combinations of questions about heredity and environmental effects on siblings of different kinds. See CO-TWIN CONTROL, METHOD OF CO-TWIN CONTROL.

twinning   1. The simultaneous production of two or more embryos within a single uterus. See TWINS. 2. Production of two symmetrical objects from a single object by division.

twin studies of concordance Research regarding family members may include: (a) siblings of different sexes or (b) of the same sex, (c) fraternal twins, and (d) identical twins. The degree of concordance in research studies of diseases and disorders generally go from a low to high in the order shown from (a) to (d).

twin study (F. Galton) Research on identical twins, fraternal twins, or both, that attempts to assess genetic influence on personality by studying their resemblances and differences when reared either together or apart. The purpose is to gather data on the issue of heredity versus environment with respect to intelligence, personality, and mental disorders. Also known as twin-study method. See CO-TWIN CONTROL, CONCORDANCE, DIZYGOTIC TWINS, KALLMANN, MONOZYGOTIC TWINS, SIAMESE TWINS, SIBLING.

twin-study method The process of comparing twins, either fraternal or identical, for similarities and differences either during development or later in life. The more unusual and important studies are of identical twins that were separated in infancy, reared apart, and then evaluated in adulthood. See TWIN STUDY.

twisted symbols The reversal of letters or numbers, for example, the word "bat" read as "tab." Also known as strephosymbolia.

Twitchell-Allen Three-Dimensional Personality Test (D. A. Twitchell-Allen) A projective examination intended for children that consists of 28 statuettes. The child first selects two statuettes and is asked to tell two stories about the selected pieces, then to tell a story about three of the statuettes. Various counts are made by the examiner of the number of people mentioned, words and parts of speech, etc., used in telling the stories. Results are tabulated to give various results, and the examiner arrives at a conclusion about the child's personality. See PROJECTIVE TESTS, THEMATIC APPERCEPTION TEST.

twitching Sudden, local, convulsive movement, or a series of such movements.

two-aspect theory See DOUBLE-ASPECT THEORY, MIND-BODY PROBLEM.

two-dimensional leader-behavior space managerial grid

two-factor design A factorial design in which two independent variables are manipulated.

two-factor theory (of intelligence) A point of view by Charles Spearman that intelligence consists of two kinds of factors: A general global intelligence factor (g) considered to be an inherited intellectual capacity that influences all-around performance and several specific factors (s), assumed to account for the differences between scores on different tasks.

two-factor theory of emotions (S. Schachter) A point of view that emotions are due to physiological arousal and cognitive interpretations of that arousal. See EMOTIONS, JAMES-LANGE THEORY (OF EMOTION).

two-factor theory of avoidance (O. H. Mowrer) The argument that there are two stages to avoidance learning. In the first stage the subject learns to fear a neutral stimulus that was paired with an unpleasant stimulus, and in the second stage the subject learns to avoid the fear of the conditioned stimulus and is rewarded by disappearance of the warning stimuli.

two-neuron arc A polysynaptic nerve circuit in which an impulse must pass through an interneuron before firing a motoneuron. Each synapse adds about 8/10 of a millisecond to the travel time of a nerve impulse, thus responses that pass through multiple neurons and synapses usually require more time compared with more direct routing of impulses.

two-phase movement An act in which the initial movements are preparatory and may even be contradictory to the ultimately desired movement.

two-plus-two phenomenon Erroneous conclusions from facts; for example, if people who were athletic in youth live longer than those who were not athletic, coming to the conclusion that engaging in athletics promotes longevity may be an error. It may be that the youths who were athletic were healthier than those who were not athletic to begin with, and therefore lived longer. Also known as 2+2 phenomenon.

two-point discrimination/threshold 1. The smallest discernible distance between two stimulated points on the skin. The difference is measured with an esthesiometer and differs depending upon the region stimulated. The two-point discrimination test has been employed in studies of the effects of parietal lesions of the brain, particularly people who have suffered missile wounds in the head. 2. The smallest degree of distance of two points touching the skin perceived as two separate sensations. A caliper is usually employed. Two-point thresholds are fairly large on the backs of people, and smaller in other areas, such as on the tip of a finger. See ESTHESIOMETER, SPATIAL THRESHOLD.

two-point finger test (M. Kinsbourne & E. K. Warrington) One of several tests to diagnose defects of touch perception, especially finger agnosia. The examiner touches two places on the same or different fingers; the patient reports whether one or two fingers were touched.

two-process model (of recall/of retrieval) (E. Tulving & D. M. Thomson) An approach comprising a stage of generating candidate items, followed by a recognition test performed on each of the candidates.

two-rod test A task used to assess ability to judge distances as one of several skills indicating an aptitude for flying airplanes. The test consists of one rod set at a distance (such as 30 feet) away from the participant and another rod set at a distance further away than that. The second rod can be remotely moved forward and backward by a seated participant. The goal is to place the two rods as close together as possible.

two-sided message A consumer-psychology technique in which an attempt is made to change the attitude of a person by presenting both favorable and unfavorable arguments, rather than one side of an issue. Studies indicate the two-sided message has a greater effect on persons with higher education and those who believe that a source that presents both sides has greater credibility.

two-stage-memory theory A point of view that information acquired by learning processes is stored first in an immediate-memory mechanism from which items are transferred into a permanent memory. The transfer priority may be based on the frequency of repetition in the immediate memory, as in the example of ability to store in the permanent memory telephone numbers that are repeated in the immediate memory.

two-tailed probability   See ONE-TAILED TEST, TWO-TAILED TEST.

two-tailed test   A statistical test of an experimental hypothesis that does not specify the expected direction of an effect or a relationship.

two-way analysis of variance   A statistical test analyzing the joint and separate influences of two independent variables on a dependent variable.

two-way table   A scatter diagram or matrix showing the distribution of two variables.

two-word stage (of language development)   The period in a child's verbal development when two-word utterances occur, usually about age two. This period indicates the beginning of syntactical knowledge. See DUOS, TELEGRAPHIC SPEECH.

TX   See TREATMENT.

tympanic canal   See SCALA TYMPANI.

tympanic cavity   A membrane-lined cavity in the bone of the skull, adjacent to the mastoid cells. See MIDDLE EAR, TYMPANUM.

tympanic membrane   A diaphragm that separates the external ear from the middle ear and serves as a device for transferring the pressure waves of sounds to a mechanical device in the form of the bony ossicles. Also known as eardrum, tympanum.

tympanic reflex   A reaction of the muscles of the middle-ear ossicles to loud sounds. The stapedius muscle and to a lesser extent the tensor tympani attenuate the sound intensity by deflecting the ossicles. Studies show the tympanic reflex can reduce sound intensities transmitted through the middle ear by the equivalent of as much as 20 decibels.

tympanometry   The measurement of mobility, or changes in pressure of the external and middle ear. Negative pressure would be an index of congestion and possible transitory hearing loss.

tympanum   1. The middle ear, or tympanic cavity. 2. The eardrum, or tympanic membrane.

type   1. Establishment of some criterion for classifying phenomena, such as classifying humans on the basis of gender (sex), age, size. 2. Establishing a standard of some sort for any of various purposes, for example, breeders of animals may decide that a certain conformation of body, color of fur, is ideal for dogs of a certain breed, thus such dogs will be judged as to how close they are to the ideal. See entries beginning with TYPE and TYPES.

type A behavior   A lifestyle pattern associated with increased risk of coronary heart disease marked by a tendency toward three specific factors of (a) speed and impatience (hostility), (b) hard-drivingness, and (c) job-involvement, as well as clenching of teeth and fists, rapid body movements, and polyphasic activity such as shaving or eating while reading a newspaper or making business telephone calls. Some research also indicates an obsession with numbers. See TYPE A PERSONALITY.

type A personality   (M. Friedman) Descriptive phrase for a personality pattern with a lifestyle that predisposes an individual to coronary heart disease. Type A individuals are considered highly competitive in all aspects of life, such as work, recreation, friendship, and love, and they tend to be hostile when frustrated. See TYPE B BEHAVIOR, TYPE B PERSONALITY.

type α thinking   (M. Wertheimer) In Gestalt psychology, productive or active thinking based on structural insight, structural mastery, and reorganization of a problem to find a meaningful solution; thinking oriented toward looking for closure of gaps, centering, grouping and transition from poor structures to good structures.

type B behavior   Behavior patterns free of aggression and hostility, marked by an absence of time urgency and lack of a compulsive need to display or discuss personal accomplishments and achievements. See TYPE B PERSONALITY.

type B personality   (R. Rosenman) A personality pattern outlined to distinguish people from the Type A personality. Type B individuals are considered to take a less-stressed approach to life, such as being able to relax without feeling guilty, work without being easily frustrated, and participate in sports or other recreational activities without feeling a need to prove their superiority. They are generally nonaggressive and easy-going and less prone to coronary disease than type A personalities.

type fallacy   A generalization that individuals can be classified as distinct types, although evidence shows that human characteristics form a continuum.

type γ thinking   (M. Wertheimer) In Gestalt psychology, blind, premature conclusions with no real sense of direction; forged by methods of drill, by external associations, by external conditioning, by memorizing, by blind trial and error.

Type I conditioning   Classical conditioning (I. P. Pavlov). See CLASSICAL CONDITIONING, PAVLOVIAN CONDITIONING, TYPE S CONDITIONING.

Type I error   Rejection of the null hypothesis when it is in fact true. An experimenter makes this error when concluding there is a significant effect or relationship, although neither is present in reality.

Type-R conditioning   The R refers to a response being correlated to the controlling stimulus and not to a stimulus as in Type S. See INSTRUMENTAL CONDITIONING.

types   See the following entries for types: ACTIVE AGGRESSIVE REACTION, ADENOID, ADLER'S PERSONALITY, ANTHRO-, APOPLECTIC, ARCHE-, ASTHENIC, ATHLETIC, ATTITUDINAL, AUDITORY, AUTOSTEREO-, B, BEHAVIOR(AL), BIO-, BODY, CEREBROTONIC, CHARACTER, CHOLERIC, CLINICAL, CONSTITUTIONAL, DIGESTIVE, DYSPLASTIC BODY, ECTOMORPHIC BODY, EIDETIC, ENDOMORPHIC BODY, EROTIC, EXPERIENCE, EXPRESSIVE VOCABULARY, EXTRAVERTED, FEELING, FUNCTIONAL, GENO-, HOMO-, HYPERCOMPENSATORY, HYPERGENITAL, HYPERTONIC, HYPERVEGETATIVE, HYPOAFFECTIVE, HYPOGENITAL, IMAGERY, INTEGRATE, INTELLIGENT TEST ITEM, INTROVERTED, INTUITIVE, IRRATIONAL, JUNG'S FUNCTIONAL, KARYO-, KRETSCHMER'S CONSTITUTIONAL, LEARNING, LEPTOSOME, LIBIDINAL, LINEAR, MACROSPLANCHNIC, MELANCHOLIC, MESOMORPHIC, MICROSPLANCHNIC, MOBILE, MORPHOGENO-, MOTOR-REACTION, MURRAY'S, MUSCULAR, NANOSOMIA, NARCISSISTIC, NORMOSPLANCHNIC, NORMO-, OBJECTIVE, OBSESSIONAL, ORAL-PASSIVE, PARA-, PERSONALITY, PHENO-, PHLEGMATIC, PHYSIQUE, PROTO-, PSYCHOLOGICAL, PYKNIC, RATIONAL, REACTION RESPONSE, REACTION, REACTIVE, RECEIVING, RELIGIOUS, REPRODUCTIVE, RESEARCH, RESPONSE, SANGUINE, SCALE, SECONDARY FUNCTION,

SENILE DEMENTIA OF THE ALZHEIMER, SENSATION, SENSORY REACTION, SENSORY RESPONSE, SOCIAL, SOMATO-, STHENIC, SUBJECTIVE, T, TARTAR, TETANY, THINKING, UNITARY, VISUAL. See TYPOLOGY.

Type-S conditioning   The S refers to a stimulus being correlated to the controlling stimulus and not to a response as in Type R. See PAVLOVIAN CONDITIONING.

Type T (personality)   (F. Farley) A thrill- or excitement-seeking personality, associated with a fondness for activities such as racing or riding on rollercoasters.

type theories of personality   Assumptions that people fall into personality classes. There have been many such points of view starting with that of Hippocrates' concept of personality being based on the balance of bodily fluids (humors), with the most complex being William Sheldon's somatotypes and the more recent, Nira Kefir's dispositional sets. The underlying rationale of type theories is that they are constitutional in origin beginning with the ideas of Aristotle, who in his book *Physiognomica* starts by discussing several theories held by the ancients.

type-token distinction   An argument that semantic memory consists of general categories (types) and specific examples of those categories (tokens).

type-token ratio (TTR)   A ratio of the number of different words to the total number of words in a person's sample of written or verbal communication. The greater the variety of words compared with the repetition of words the higher the index of verbal diversification. See FLESCH INDEX.

Type II conditioning   Instrumental conditioning (B. F. Skinner). See INSTRUMENTAL CONDITIONING, INSTRUMENTAL LEARNING, OPERANT CONDITIONING, TYPE-R CONDITIONING.

Type II error   Acceptance of the null hypothesis when it is false. An experimenter makes this error in concluding that a particular effect or relationship is not present, whereas in fact it is. Also known as beta error.

typewriter for the blind   See TALKING TYPEWRITER.

typewriter maze   (F. Lumley) A kind of maze in which the participant must continually press a series of letters on a typewriter when a signal sounds until the correct letter is hit by trial and error. Errors are related to sequential position. It was devised to investigate serial phenomena in sequential learning of motor tasks, utilizing different elements throughout the series.

typhlopsychology   The study of mental development of the blind or visually impaired with ways of correcting vision or in educating such individuals to compensate for their challenges.

typicality effect   A tendency for certain category members to typify a category better than others; for instance, canary represents the bird category better than chicken.

typing   1. The process of classifying an organism or other entity. 2. Operating a typewriter or similar equipment. Perhaps the most common perceptual-motor task in which humans interact with machines, comprising four stages: input (converting text into chunks), parsing (decomposing chunks into ordinal character strings), translation (converting characters into movement specifications), and execution (implementing movement in ballistic fashion).

typographic eidetics   One of two types of eidetic images characterized by being prolonged afterimages, not necessarily being accurate representations being either hue-positive or hue-negative. The other type is known as structural eidetics. See EIDETIC IMAGERY.

typology   1. Any systematic scheme used for classification of phenomena. 2. A dimension of personality. Gordon Allport viewed a type as a combination of certain traits, habits, and attitudes that can be seen in a variety of people but fits no one person exactly. A kind of single word caricature. Examples of types:

Hippocrates/Galen:
sanguine   choleric   melancholy   phlegmatic
Jung:
thinking   feeling   sensing   intuiting
Adler:
useful   ruling   avoiding   getting
Kefir:
pleasers   superiors   comforters   controllers
Dreikurs:
attention   power   defeat   revenge (of children).
Also known as types. See CONSTITUTIONAL TYPE, PERSONALITY TYPES.

U

U 1. A test statistic in the Mann-Whitney U test. 2. In psychophysics, abbreviation for upper. 3. unit (meaning 2).

UCR See UNCONDITIONED REFLEX, UNCONDITIONED RESPONSE.

UCs Abbreviation for unconscious mind (also abbreviated **Ucs.**). See UNCONSCIOUS (meaning 2).

UCS See UNCONDITIONED STIMULUS.

Ucs. See UNCONSCIOUS (meaning 2).

UCV See UNCONTROLLED VARIABLE.

U fibers Nerve pathways that run through pyramidal-cell white matter from one cortical neuron to another. Thought to be the fastest route of impulses in cortical transmission.

UFO unidentified flying object

ufology The study of unidentified flying objects (UFOs), assumed by some to be real sightings and by others to be misperceptions or fabrications. Many people have reported seeing UFOs or being abducted by "aliens." See UNIDENTIFIED FLYING OBJECT.

UG universal grammar

ulcer An erosion of a tissue surface, such as the mucosal lining of the digestive tract. See GASTRODUODENAL ULCERATION.

ulcer personality (F. Alexander) A hypothetical personality pattern associated with proneness to the formation of peptic ulcers (usually of stomach or duodenum) characterized by an appearance of being tense, driven, and aggressive, but actually being passive and dependent.

ulnar nerve The sensory and motor nerve which supplies the shoulder, wrist, palm, and little finger.

ulstrith (H. A. Toops) A group composed of individuals in a given population who fall in the same class or category in each of the traits involved in the study.

ultimate attribution error Using internal attributions to explain socially desirable actions by members of the person's own group, and undesirable actions by members of an opposing group, and external attributions for undesirable actions of the person's own group and desirable ones of others.

ultimate causation How a characteristic contributes to the fitness of a species, as opposed to proximate causation (how a characteristic occurs in an individual).

ultimate value A measure toward which a series tends as more terms are included.

ultradian rhythm A periodic change in physiological processes, psychological processes, or both, that is thought to have a cycle shorter than one day. See CIRCADIAN RHYTHM, INFRADIAN RHYTHM.

ultraertia In mating behavior, excessive intensity, responsiveness, urgency, or incessancy.

ultrashort-acting barbiturates Barbiturates rapidly absorbed from the stomach that usually produce an immediate effect.

ultrasonic Refers to energy waves, similar to sound waves but of higher frequencies. Ultrasonic waves are above 30,000 Hertz (cycles per second) and are not audible to humans. See SOUND WAVE.

ultrasound technique The measuring and recording of deep bodily structures through the reflection of ultrasonic (above 30,000 Hertz, usually 1.6 to 10 MHz) sound waves for medical (especially fetal) diagnosis and occasionally therapy. Also known as ultrasonography technique.

ultraviolet Describing electromagnetic rays beyond the violet end of the visible spectrum; light wavelengths below 400 nanometers, and also below human capacity to see them.

ultraviolet absorption The absorption of ultraviolet wavelengths of light by substances. Such activity by olfactory receptors is necessary for the perception of odors, according to one theory.

ululation (to cry out, yell—Latin) 1. Incoherent wailing. 2. High-pitched vocalization in which some mid-Eastern women rapidly tongue the upper lip to cause a distinctive sound, to communicate emotion. 3. Inarticulate or animal-like cries made by some persons who are mentally challenged or psychotic. Sometimes known as pseudolalia.

umbrella General metaphoric term for overarching; for instance, an umbrella model of memory might include recall and recognition.

Umweg (roundabout—German) A detour problem/test.

Umwelt (environment—German) 1. Relating to the world in terms of its physical and biological aspects. 2. Perceptual world in which an organism lives. 3. In the existential philosophy of Martin Heidegger, the nearest world of the body and its attributes. See EIGENWELT, MITWELT.

unaccomplished action effect (B. Zeigarnik) A tendency for interrupted tasks to be better remembered than completed tasks; for example, if a person hears a joke but not the punch line, the person is more likely to remember the joke than if it had been completed. See GESTALT, ZEIGARNIK EFFECT.

unaided recall An ability to remember without any assistance of any kind.

unambivalent In psychoanalytic theory, paired motives or affects that are not mutually inconsistent or in conflict with one another.

unanticipated crisis A situational or accidental crisis.

unanticipated transition An event that occurs without warning, such as being fired from a job.

unaspirated sound In linguistics, a sound made without movement of air. For instance the "t" sound in "top" is aspirated, but in "stop" it is unaspirated.

unbiased error A random error, one that is due purely to chance.

unbiased estimate 1. An estimate formulated on the basis of a representative sample. See UNBIASED ESTIMATE OF VARIANCE. 2. An estimate of the value of the parameter. If a sample statistic is an unbiased estimate of a parameter, the mean of the distribution of a huge number of sample values (obtained by repeated sampling) drawn from a given population, converges on the corresponding value of the parameter.

unbiased estimate of variance A variance estimate that has been shown to be unbiased. The correction is made by using $N-1$ in place of N in the denominator. The sample variance, $s^2 = \sum(X-\bar{X})^2 \div (N-1)$. Population variance, $\sigma^2 = \sum(X-\bar{X})^2 \div N$.

unbiased estimator Given a sample statistic that estimates a population parameter, the statistic is an unbiased estimator if the mean of its sampling distribution equals the value of the parameter.

uncanny emotions (H. S. Sullivan) The sense of weirdness and unreality that sometimes accompanies dreams, nightmares, states of intoxication, and some mental disorders. These feelings inspire dread, horror, and a feeling of uncertainty. See NOT-ME, PAVOR.

uncertainty 1. In general, absence of belief, due to insufficient information. 2. ($\hat{H}$) In statistics, a condition described with mathematical precision under the laws of probability. Probability is the quantification of uncertainty. Denote the probability of an event with the symbol P, $0 \leqslant P \leqslant 1$. Where $P(1)$ indicates complete certainty. Formula: $\hat{H} = \log_2 A$, where A is the number of equally likely alternatives, H is the measure of uncertainty.

uncertainty-arousal factor In psychological esthetics, responses that reflect autonomic (as opposed to cortical) arousal reactions to a stimulus such as a work of art. The uncertainty may be due to simple-complex, clear-indefinite, or disorderly-orderly components.

uncertainty avoidance (G. Hofstede) The extent to which people in a given culture feel threatened by or uncomfortable with ambiguous situations, and the degree to which they try to avoid them by seeking greater career stability, establishing more formal rules, rejecting deviant ideas and behavior, and accepting absolutisms and the attainment of expertise.

uncertainty factor In psychological esthetics, describing a participant's responses to a work of art that include high positive ratings on simple-complex and clear-indefinite scales, and high negative ratings on a disorderly-orderly scale. See UNCERTAINTY-AROUSAL FACTOR.

uncertainty level In psychological esthetics, the interval between the upper and lower levels of differences in judgments.

uncertainty principle A theory that it is impossible to measure simultaneously the location and the velocity (momentum) of an atomic particle. Also known as Heisenberg indeterminacy principle after the physicist, Werne Heisenberg, who originated it.

uncinate fasciculus A bundle of nerve fibers connecting the anterior and inferior portions of the frontal lobe, appearing as a compact bundle as the fasciculus bends around the lateral sulcus while spreading into a fan shape at either end.

uncinate gyrus See UNCUS (meaning 2).

uncivilized Pertaining to something that, from a Western perspective, is savage or has not yet been tamed or "civilized." See PRIMITIVE.

unconcernedness An attitude characterized by a lack of interest in almost everything, or little interest in specific things.

unconditional love (E. Fromm) A love similar to agape.

unconditional positive regard (C. R. Rogers, S. Standal) An attitude of concern, acceptance, and warmth on the part of therapists, as well as others, primarily parents, considered conducive to positive self-esteem and personality growth. See CONDITIONAL POSITIVE REGARD, FREE, PERSON-CENTERED THERAPY, UNCRITICALNESS.

unconditioned primary reinforcer A reinforcer (such as a stimulus) that operates as an operant without prior conditioning, for example, food is an unconditioned stimulus for hungry animals. See UNCONDITIONED STIMULUS.

unconditioned reflex (UCR, UR, Ru) An innate, unlearned, reflexive response to a stimulus, as in salivation at the sight or smell of food. See UNCONDITIONED RESPONSE.

unconditioned response (UCR, UnCR, UnR, or UR) In classical conditioning, the unlearned reaction to an unconditioned stimulus; any original reaction that occurs naturally and in the absence of conditioning, for example, in Ivan Pavlov's experiment, the dog's salivation. The UCR serves as the basis for establishment of the conditioned response, and it is frequently reflexive in nature. Also rarely abbreviated R_u. Compare CONDITIONED RESPONSE.

unconditioned stimulus (UCS, UnCS, UnS, or US) In classical conditioning, a stimulus that is not learned, one that elicits a natural or unconditioned response, as in withdrawal from a hot object, contraction of the pupil to light, or salivation when food is smelled. Rarely abbreviated Su, S_u. Compare CONDITIONED STIMULUS.

unconscious 1. Absence of awareness, as in a coma or sleep, or in phrases like "unconscious prejudice." Dreams, fantasies, slips of the tongue, and neurotic symptoms are often considered manifestations of unconscious processes. 2. (**UCs, Ucs.**) In psychoanalytic theory, a division or region of the psyche that contains memories, emotional conflicts, wishes, and repressed impulses not directly accessible to awareness, but which have dynamic effects on thought and behavior. See COLLECTIVE UNCONSCIOUS, FAMILIAL UNCONSCIOUS, ID, PERSONAL UNCONSCIOUS, RACIAL UNCONSCIOUS.

unconscious cerebration Thinking that occurs in the absence of awareness. See INCUBATION.

unconscious cognitive process Refers to the workings of the unconscious mind, the basic concept of the unconscious as being real despite lack of proof of its existence. Humans learn, think, remember, and have ideas, feelings, or desires that remain in "a hidden vault" and that may emerge quite suddenly and completely without any prior awareness. See HYPNOSIS, PERCEPTUAL CUES, PERCEPTUAL VIGILANCE, SUBLIMINAL PERCEPTION.

unconscious factors 1. Influences operating below the level of consciousness, such as repressed experiences, latent impulses, defense mechanisms, buried feelings, memories. 2. (C. G. Jung) In Jungian theory, the contents of the racial or collective unconscious.

unconscious fantasies In psychoanalytic theory, fantasies about sex that are most clearly revealed in dreams and daydreams. Also known as primal fantasies.

unconscious guilt A sense of having done wrong, or as Sigmund Freud preferred to say, an unconscious need for punishment, produced by hidden impulses or behavior that conflict with the precepts of the superego.

unconscious homosexuality Homosexual tendencies not consciously recognized by the person having them. See LATENT HOMOSEXUALITY.

unconscious identification with the aggressor Behavior by a person being mistreated that appears, both to an unbiased observer and to the aggressor, as indicating that the victim actually desires the mistreatment, even though the victim may not be aware of it. See STOCKHOLM SYNDROME.

unconscious impulse An urge of which a person is not aware. See UNCONSCIOUS MOTIVATION.

unconscious inference theory A point of view that some guesses or instances of intuition are really based on knowledge that has been forgotten.

unconscious knowledge Ideas, feelings, desires, etc., that are unknown to a person until they surface, usually suddenly. The statement "I didn't even know that I knew that" is an example of this concept. See UNCONSCIOUS COGNITIVE PROCESS.

unconscious memory In several schools of psychology, memory that has moved from the conscious to the unconscious level of the mind. See REPRESSION.

unconscious motivation Wishes, impulses, aims, and drives of which a person is not aware. Resulting behaviors may include purposive accidents, slips of the tongue, and dreams that express unfulfilled wishes. See FREUDIAN SLIP.

unconscious process A psychic activity that takes place without a person's conscious awareness, for example, the dynamics of repression or denial.

unconscious resistance The evident resistance or negative reaction to something (for example, a certain topic or memory) of which the person is consciously unaware. In depth psychology, it is not uncommon for a client to avoid discussion of certain topics, to minimize their importance, or refuse to discuss them, thus defeating the purpose of psychotherapy and sabotaging one's progress. See ANALYTICAL STALEMATE, DENIAL, REPRESSION.

unconscious transfer Correctly identifying something, such as a person or object as familiar, but incorrectly identifying the location or time. Thus, an eyewitness to a crime may identify the suspect as familiar but err recalling the location or time of having seen that person.

uncontrolled variable (UCV) In research, an extraneous factor in an experiment that operates outside of the investigator's design of measurement or procedures of control.

unconventional behavior Actions which depart from the correct or traditional patterns of behavior common to the members of a given group.

unconventional therapies Those methods of treating mind, body, or both, that are not considered mainstream. Each of the treatment forms listed below, as examples, has a contingency of strong supporters. Critics of such therapies hold that the placebo effect explains any beneficial results. See ACUPRESSURE, ACUPUNCTURE, AROMATHERAPY, CRYSTAL HEALING, HOMEOPATHY, REFLEXOLOGY, THERAPEUTIC TOUCH.

uncorrelated axes In factor analysis, axes at right angles to each other, meaning that they are independent of (not correlated with) other factors. See OBLIQUE, ORTHOGONAL.

uncovering techniques In psychotherapy, techniques directed to break through persons' repressions to bring latent conflicts and traumatic experiences to the surface where they can be studied.

uncriticalness (C. R. Rogers) A nonjudgmental attitude on the part of the therapist, considered essential in Carl Rogers' nondirective approach as well as in other forms of psychotherapy, since criticism tends to inhibit the client's efforts to recognize and revise self-defeating patterns.

uncrossed transactions (E. Berne) Interactions that result in expected responses that are appropriate to the situation. Also termed complementary reactions. See TRANSACTIONAL ANALYSIS.

UnCS See UNCONDITIONED STIMULUS.

uncus 1. Any hook-shaped structure. Plural is unci. 2. Area near the base of the brain that receives olfactory sense impulses. Also known as parahippocampalis, uncinate gyrus, uncinate gyri.

underachievement 1. Accomplishing less than a person is able or desires to. 2. Accomplishing less than what is predicted or expected. Underachievement may be specific to an area of study or it may be general. Purportedly more prevalent among males than females and is common in bright and even gifted children. It also occurs among average students and the educable mentally retarded. See ACADEMIC-UNDERACHIEVEMENT DISORDER, DISCOURAGEMENT. Compare OVERACHIEVER.

underachiever 1. In general, any person manifesting underachievement. 2. More specifically, a person, usually a student, who achieves far below demonstrated capacity, especially if aptitude or general-intelligence scores exceed achievement scores by 30%.

underage In educational circles, refers to a student who is younger than the other classmates. Compare OVERAGE.

underarousal A physiological response to a stimulus that is inadequate to initiate an expected action.

underclass A group that is outside the mainstream of society.

undercontrolled A type of behavior marked by a lack of sufficient self-control expected for a person of a particular age and in a particular setting, such as hyperactivity of a child of six while in a church.

underdog 1. (E. Berne) Verbal representation of primitive urges of the basic self. 2. (F. Perls) Descriptive term for rationalizations and self-justifications employed to allay feelings of guilt or shame arising from an inability to meet personal moral standards of behavior. See GESTALT THERAPY, ID, TOPDOG.

underestimation Acceptance (in the statistical treatment of experimental work) of a value below that which the data warrant. An underestimate is generally used deliberately to avoid the possibility of the quantitative conclusions being invalidated by unnoted factors. See CAUTION.

underextension In cognitive development, an early language error in which children use a particular word to refer to only one event or object rather than applying it to other similar ones.

underload In industrial psychology, insufficient stimulation on the job, leading to stress.

underlying form In linguistics, a form from which phonetic forms are derived by rule.

undermanning   understaffing

underpayment A form of inequity, such as inadequate compensation, that can lead to job dissatisfaction, lack of motivation, and in some cases lowered productivity, either internally (within the same firm) or externally.

undersexed Lay term for low sexual motivation. See HYPOSEXUALITY, INHIBITED SEXUAL DESIRE, INHIBITED SEXUAL EXCITEMENT.

undersocialized 1. Characterizing a person who has not developed adequate social feelings or good social relationships, and who tends to be egocentric and unconcerned about others. See AGGRESSIVE UNDERSOCIALIZED CONDUCT DISORDER, CONDUCT DISORDER, NONAGGRESSIVE UNDERSOCIALIZED CONDUCT DISORDER. 2. Characterizing an animal that was exposed to too few other animals, humans, or novel situations during a critical socialization period and therefore exhibits undesirable or antisocial behavior, such as aggressiveness or fearfulness in later encounters or situations.

understaffing The situation in which the number of persons available for a program or function falls below the maintenance minimum. Once known as overmanning. Compare OVERSTAFFING.

UNDERSTAND (J. R. Hayes & H. A. Simon) A theory, in the form of a computer program, to explain how problem instructions in natural language can be understood and transformed into a symbolic problem representation suitable as an input to a problem-solving simulation like the General Problem Solver.

understanding 1. Generally, insight into or comprehension of information acquired from unrelated or related observations and organized through a flexible framework of personal knowledge. 2. In counseling and psychotherapy, the process of discerning the network of relationships existing between a client's behavior and the environment, history, aptitudes, motivation, ideas, feelings, relationships, and modes of expression. 3. (H. A. Simon, J. R. Hayes) Understanding information means the ability to use the information whenever it is relevant, for example, a description of a problem is understood by a computer or person who can convert the description into a problem space in which a search for a solution can be conducted. Understanding is a matter of degree. See PROBLEM SPACE, UNDERSTAND. 4. (M. Wertheimer, K. Duncker, G. Katona, C. Stern) In Gestalt psychology, the product of insight, centering and organizing of rho-relations; the goal of learning and thinking. 5. An agreement.

understanding psychology (W. Dilthey) A concept that the task of psychology is to understand what the natural sciences can explain. Psychology is seen as the first of the human sciences including politics and economics, since all behavior depends on the workings of the mind.

understatement A report concerning some value obtained partly from empirical data and partly by estimate, in which liberal allowance is made for possible error, so that the value reported is reasonably assumed to be less than the true value. See UNDERESTIMATION.

understimulation theory A point of view, based on studies of sensory-deprivation effects, that severe anxiety and other psychological disturbances can be caused by insufficient stimulation. It has been used to explain vandalism and other crimes that occur in urban settings where young people lack exposure to a great variety of environmental stimuli. See DIVERSIVE EXPLORATION, SENSATION-SEEKING.

undescended testicle A testicle that has not descended into the scrotum. Also known as arrested testis. See CRYPTORCHIDISM.

undeveloped potential Personal aspects or aptitudes unknown to or unrecognized by the individual. See JOHARI WINDOW.

undifferentiated 1. In anatomy or physiology, not differentiated; having no special structure or function. 2. Describing complex assemblages that might be characterized or ordered in some form of logical arrangement; for instance, the alphabet may be categorized into vowels and consonants or into 26 categories. 3. Immature, as in a child presented with Rorschach cards seeing vague meaningless shapes and colors, and reporting they all look like "rocks," whereas the same person 20 years later sees dozens of well-differentiated perceptions.

undifferentiated marketing Selecting the entire marketplace, focusing on common needs rather than on differences. Relies on mass distribution and advertising.

undifferentiated schizophrenic A person exhibiting clear symptoms from more than one of the major types of schizophrenia (simple, catatonic, paranoid, disorganized), divided into acute undifferentiated type schizophrenia, chronic undifferentiated type schizophrenia. Considered by some to be a meaningless catch-all category in terms of explaining or predicting behavior.

undifferentiated-type schizophrenic disorder A disorder that does not meet the criteria for other types of schizophrenia, or meets the criteria for more than one type. There are usually, however, prominent psychotic features, such as delusions, hallucinations, incoherence, or grossly disorganized behavior. See UNDIFFERENTIATED SCHIZOPHRENIC.

undinism An abnormal condition in which sexual thoughts are aroused by water or urination. Sometimes known as urophilia. See URETHRAL EROTICISM, UROLAGNIA.

undoing (A. Freud) In psychoanalytic theory, an unconscious ego defense mechanism in which attempts are made to counteract guilty impulses or behavior through acts of atonement and expiation. A person considered healthy or normal may try to make amends by apologizing or making restitution, whereas an obsessive-compulsive person may seek to rid the self of guilt by continuously washing hands or the repetitive recitation of a prayer. See SACRIFICE.

undue entitlement An unreasonable claim to special consideration by a person who thinks he or she is somehow entitled to such privileges. See ENTITLEMENT PROGRAMS, SPOONFEEDING.

undulatio reflexa (reflex waves—Latin) (R. Descartes) A notion that the body has unconscious motives that keep the body going in absence of volition. See REFLEX ACTION.

unemotional thought (S. Rado) The highest evolutionary level of integration, at which action and self-control are based on reason, logic, science, and common sense.

unequal twins Fraternal twins, one of whom is born less developed than the sibling.

unequivocal Having but one meaning. Admitting only a single interpretation. Also known as univocal. Compare AMBIGUOUS.

unfair labor practices In law, typically actions by an employer that inhibit freedom of choice regarding union membership, or by a union inhibiting the employer's business or not properly representing members.

unfilled pause In speech, a gap of silence before the speaker continues. Such periods may be done consciously to achieve a desired effect or may be accidental such as the speaker being unable to formulate the next thought. See SILENT PAUSE.

unfilled-time interval A time period during which a person is unoccupied; waiting, neither thinking nor doing. Such time subjectively goes much slower than its counterpart, filled-time. Compare FILLED-TIME INTERVAL.

unfinished business In therapy, the discussion of: (a) unresolved conflict and feelings; (b) insufficient disclosure of relevant past experiences; and (c) incomplete feelings and thoughts.

unfinished story An unfinished tale to be completed via role playing, discussion, or writing. It is a projective technique meant to stimulate identification, personal information about the participant's concerns, and dialogue.

unfitness Inferiority of an organism in structure or behavior, due to its inability to cope successfully with environmental conditions.

unfreezing The emancipation from rigid beliefs and stereotypes of self, others, and the world, often a goal of psychotherapy.

uniaural Pertaining to one ear alone. Also known as monaural.

unidentified flying objects (UFOs) Refers to unusual objects seen moving in the sky, usually shaped like disks. Purported to be vehicles used by extraterrestrial beings. See UFOLOGY.

unidextrality The preferred use of one side of the body rather than the other, such as being strictly right-handed. See AMBIDEXTRALITY.

unidimensional Containing a single dimension, composed of a pure factor. Compare MULTIDIMENSIONAL.

unifamilial Occurring in a single family.

unified positivism (A. Staats) An approach positing how psychology could avoid fragmentation. See BRIDGING, SCIENTIFIC RATIONALITY.

unified theory of cognition (A. Newell) A computer simulation of cognitive processes that seeks to incorporate in a single program the whole range of human cognitive functions. See COGNITIVE SIMULATION, SOAR.

uniform 1. Having only one form. 2. Of the same form as another. See UNIFORMITY.

uniformism A concept applied to total adherence to the standards and behavior of the person's peer group.

uniformity Similarity of events or processes, such that their essential characteristics, components, or relations can be described in a single statement or law that applies to all instances.

uniformity of nature (theory) A final summary of all laws formulated for natural phenomena in a given branch of science (such as chemistry and physics) that states: Given the same or similar antecedents, the same or similar consequents will always follow.

unilateral 1. Pertaining to or confined to one side of the body. 2. In human relations, refers to the making of decisions without consideration for others who should be involved in the decision-making.

unilateral couple counseling Advising only one member of a domestic or other partnership, usually because the other is unaware of or unwilling to join the counseling.

unilateral descent In anthropology, refers to ancestry being traced through only one parent. Compare BILATERAL DESCENT. See MATRILINEAL, PATRILINEAL.

unilateral lesion An injury or change in tissue of an area of one hemisphere of the brain with effects that vary according to the dominance of the hemisphere and the function affected. The unilateral lesion effect generally occurs on the contralateral (opposite) side of the body to the part of the brain affected.

unilateral neglect   A visual-spatial disorder associated with lesions of the parietal lobe, characterized by a tendency of people with this condition to neglect the space on the side of the body opposite the side of the lesion.

unilateral sensorimotor cortex lesion   Any interruption of function caused by destruction of normal tissue in the sensorimotor area of a single hemisphere of the brain. May affect certain tactual functions such as roughness discrimination without altering the ability of an individual to make size judgments through the sense of touch.

unilateral sexual precocity   Premature development of sexual structures on only one side of the body.

unimodal   1. Describing a phenomenon that has only one dimension. 2. Describing a frequency distribution having a single mode, that is, one peak.

unintegrated   (B. Neugarten) A personality pattern in late adulthood of people who show disorganized behavior patterns and have gross defects in psychological functioning, poor emotional control, intellectual deterioration, low activity levels, and low life satisfaction.

unintegrated motivation component   According to Raymond Cattell, one of the two main second-order factors found in the pattern of intercorrelations among objective tests of motivation strength. Represents an unconscious, unintegrated source of motivation. The other main second-order factor is the integrated motivation component.

uniocular   Pertaining to a single eye.

union   1. A coalition of parts or members, such as the joining of two people in marriage. 2. The physical joining of two or more bodies or objects. 3. A subjective emotional state characterized by feeling joined with God in mystical ecstasy. 4. In labor relations, a collectivization of employees, usually sanctioned by statute, that formally negotiates the terms and conditions of work. Also known as trade union.

union shop   In labor relations, a business arrangement in which all members of the bargaining unit must become and remain union members.

uniovular twin   monozygotic twin

uniparous   Refers to a female who has borne only once. Also known as primiparous.

unipolar depression   An affective disorder distinguished from bipolar disorder in that it features only recurrent episodes of depression. See BIPOLAR DISORDER, UNIPOLAR DISORDER.

unipolar disorder   A severe affective disorder characterized by recurrent depressive episodes or, far more rarely, recurrent manic episodes.

unipolar mania   A form of manic-depressive (bipolar) illness featuring recurrent episodes of mania without episodes of depression. See BIPOLAR DISORDER, UNIPOLAR DISORDER.

unipolar manic-depressive psychosis   A manic-depressive (bipolar) illness characterized by one type of episode, usually recurrent depression. See BIPOLAR DISORDER, UNIPOLAR DISORDER.

unipolar neuron   A nerve cell which has an axon but no dendrite. Phrase may be misleading since a unipolar neuron has a dendritic zone at the end opposite from the synaptic terminals, as does a normal bipolar cell. However, the cell body, or perikaryon, of a unipolar neuron is outside the fibrous process rather than inside as is the case with other types of neurons. True unipolar neurons are found only as receptor cells in peripheral sensory organs, for example, the rods and cones of the retina. Dorsal root neurons are referred to as pseudounipolar neurons. Also known as unipolar cell.

unipolar stimulation   A method of stimulation in which an electric current is passed between one electrode on or in the tissue, and another outside the tissue.

uniprocess learning theory   A point of view that learning is a single process, rather than a combination of, for instance, short-term, long-term, declarative, and iconic learning.

uniqueness   In factor analysis, the square root of that part of the total variance of a given variable entered into the factor analysis that is unique to that variable and which it does not have in common with any other variable in the analysis. Uniqueness is composed of the variable's specificity and random measurement error (unreliability).

unique trait   A personality trait observed in only one individual or one member of a population; never found replicated in other members of that group. See SUI GENERIS.

unisex   1. Behavior, appearance, or items used by both sexes. 2. A lifestyle marked by an interchange of sex roles in clothing choices, work assignments, and other environmental factors. 3. Refers to public toilets in some societies used by both sexes.

unit   1. A single person or thing. 2. (U) A magnitude used as a common denominator in measurement. 3. Any datum considered without regard to its internal partitions or complexities.

unit-alike maze   A maze in which all units, goalboxes, and choice-points are essentially identical.

unitary illness   A disorder clearly dependent on a clear cut causative factor, for example, a toothache.

unitary-resource model   In cognition, a model that views attention as a single pool of resources reserved for mental activities.

unitary type   In eidetic theory, the type of person whose afterimages, eidetic images, and memory images show marked similarity. See B TYPE, MARBURG SCHOOL, T TYPE.

unitas multiplex   1. (A. Angyal) The argument that an integrated personality is characterized by numerous components in harmony with each other. This means connectedness between subsystems of the personality. 2. (W. Stern) A complex of elements that has the appearance and function of an entity, such as the human body. See HOLISM.

unit character   An inherited characteristic transmitted in its entirety to an offspring.

United Nations Declaration on the Rights of Mentally Retarded Persons   A 1971 declaration that persons with mental retardation have the same rights to the maximum degree feasible. See RIGHTS OF THE MENTALLY RETARDED.

United States Employment Service (USES) <u>Basic Oc-cupational Literacy Test</u> (BOLT)   An examination provided by the United States Employment Service for assessing the literacy skills of educationally deficient adults in terms of occupational literacy requirements. The examination covers vocabulary, reading comprehension, arithmetic computation, arithmetic reasoning. Aimed at establishing the degree of minimum reading capacity needed by people for various jobs. Also known as USES Basic Occupational Literacy Test (BOLT), USES BOLT.

unitization of services   The administrative division of a hospital (obstetrics, surgery, etc.) and of social agencies (counseling, home services, etc.) into semi-autonomous units, usually on the basis of function.

unit normal distribution   A normal distribution of measures or magnitudes whose standard deviation is equal to 1 and whose total area is equal to 1.

unity   Mind and body functioning harmoniously with each supporting the other, with imbalances in one being corrected by the other.

unity and fusion   In altered states of consciousness, an affective state in which the normal differentiation between self and environment may seem to recede or disappear while the person experiences a sense of merging, fusing, or uniting with other persons, objects, nature, or the universe. See MYSTIC UNION.

unity of command   Accountability to a single superior.

unitypic   Differentiation of homologous male and female structures (usually applied to sexual anatomy, sometimes to brain and behavior).

unity-thema   (H. A. Murray) An unconscious assortment of interrelated needs linked to early childhood press that may dominate many areas of functioning in present life.

univariate   Characterized by a single variable.

univariate research method   A basic standard research procedure that has two elements, an independent variable and a dependent variable. See MULTIVARIATE APPROACH.

universal   Anything considered to be always true, such as "Pi times the diameter of a circle equals the circumference."

universal complex   An emotional experience or complex, based upon one of the fundamental instincts. Sigmund Freud theorized that two such tendencies or instincts were Eros and Thanatos.

universal grammar (UG)   (N. Chomsky) A theory that in human communications there is a fundamental built-in set of principles that apply to language structures.

universalism   A philosophical doctrine positing that some aspects of the human mind are universal, for example, the abstract concept of *malum in se*, the concept that humans recognize some behaviors as intrinsically evil such as killing others against their will. See FREE WILL, MALUM IN RES, PARTICULARISM.

universality   Any characteristic present in all normal members of the species.

universalization   Affirming a nomothetic principle considered to be true for all time and in all cultures, however, what appears to be universal at one point may later be found not to be so.

universal motives   Desires, urges, and goals held by all living organisms, seen as an upward movement toward perfection or a forward movement toward completion. The following goals have been considered universal: ACHIEVEMENT, COMPETENCY, COMPETITIVE, GROWTH, INTRINSIC, MASTERY, SAFETY, SUPERIORITY.

universal phobia   Phrase used by Sigmund Freud for "common phobias," which consist of an exaggerated, intensified fear of situations and objects which many humans detest or fear to some extent, such as death, illness, solitude, or snakes. Compare SPECIFIC PHOBIA. See PHOBIA.

universal phonetic sensitivity   (J. F. Werker) The ability of infants to discriminate the contrasts between sounds that are necessary for learning any language.

universal sociolinguistic norm   (R. W. Brown) In a language with two forms of address such that one (T) is used reciprocally between status-equal familiars, and another (V) is used reciprocally between status-equal strangers, the T form will always be used downwards socially and the V form upwards socially. (From the French, *tu* which is used between familiars whereas *vous* is used in more formal situations.) See T AND V.

universal symbol   1. A sign that has the same significance for all humans, regardless of their culture, such as rubbing the belly to indicate hunger, smiling to show pleasure. 2. A psychoanalytic concept that certain objects dreamed about have symbolic meanings, such as an upright object like a pencil representing the penis and a pocketbook representing the vagina. See INDIVIDUAL SYMBOL.

universal tendency   In linguistics, structural patterns or traits found in most languages.

universe   1. In statistics, the total group under consideration in a study or experiment from which samples are drawn. See POPULATION (meaning 2). 2. The totality of existing things or phenomena, considered as constituting a single system.

universe of discourse   The field in which the topic or subject under discussion or investigation is situated.

unlearned behavior   Acts not a consequence of any training or teaching. For example, most children master the act of walking without any guidance; neonates (newborn infants) are able to suckle. See INSTINCT.

unlearned factor (in forgetting)   (A. W. Melton & J. M. Irwin) The unlearning of original responses; when the original responses intruded during the learning of an interpolated list, they were not reinforced since they were incorrect (in that context), leading to their being extinguished. Also known as Factor X.

unlearning   In classical conditioning, a situation in which new stimulus-response associations impede the maintenance of previously-learned associations. See DECONDITIONING.

unmedullated   **unmyelinated**

unmoral   Relating to a person to whom moral considerations do not apply, such as one with profound retardation.

unmyelinated   Refers to axons lacking a myelin sheath. Also known as amyelinated, amyelinic, nonmedullated, nonmyelinated, unmedullated.

unnatural   Legal, religious, and lay term often referring to deviant sexual behavior.

unobtrusive measures   Quantifiable information obtained without the awareness of the organism(s) being studied (such behavior is thus assumed to be unaffected by the investigative process).

unobtrusive observation   Any research procedure in which experimental participants (human or animal) do not know they are being studied.

unpleasure   In psychoanalytic theory, the feelings of tension, psychic pain, and "ego suffering" consciously felt when "instinctual" needs and wishes (the pleasure drive of the id particularly for food and sex) are denied gratification. Term is from the German *Unlust*, meaning listlessness.

unprepared learning   Learning that is neither predisposed nor precluded by evolution.

unproductive mania   manic stupor

unreality   See DEPERSONALIZATION, FEELING OF UNREALITY.

unreleased sound   In linguistics, a sound made with closure between the tongue tip and the alveolar ridge with articulation stopped before the sound is released; in English, common in syllables that end a word.

unresolved   1. In science, issues not yet understood but presumably solvable. 2. In therapy, conflicts not yet solved or understood. 3. In perception, stimuli that are not separable by the observer.

unrest   A state of mind and body characterized by a feeling of uneasiness and a tendency toward acts that have no particular relation to comprehensive goals; movement without purpose.

unrestrained eaters   Persons who eat as much as they want.

unrestricted sampling   A kind of sampling drawn from a population in which all members have the same chance of being selected.

UnS   See UNCONDITIONED STIMULUS.

unselected sample   An ambiguous term for the selection of participants (usually for research purposes), frequently those who happen to be easily available, such as students in a particular class. Also known as sample of convenience, sample of opportunity.

unselective observation   Random observation; not paying attention to any elements in particular. See NATURALISTIC OBSERVATION.

unsexed by failure   (M. Mead) Male's loss of sexual interest following a challenge to their masculine self-identity, such as posed by unemployment, rejection, or feeling old. It has been confirmed by William Masters and Virginia Johnson and others, who have documented the diminution of testosterone in males under stress.

unsociable   Inclined to shun, or being disagreeable in the company of other persons.

unsocial   1. An individual who does not "fit" into the current social system. 2. An act at variance with accepted behavior.

unsocialized   Lacking in social training or habits, or in qualities of sympathy and social cooperation.

unsocialized disturbance of conduct   A childhood behavioral disorder marked by disobedience, hostility, and aggressiveness.

unspaced learning   Massed learning. Compare SPACED LEARNING.

unspaced practice   A learning method in which no intervals or rest periods are allowed between trials.

unspaced repetition   A procedure in the learning of a verbal series, or of a complicated motor act performed at first with errors and malcoordinations. Repetitions succeed one another without interruption or intervening rest periods until the learning standard is achieved.

unspecified mental retardation   A diagnostic category comprising persons of any age presumed to be retarded, but who are too impaired or uncooperative to be evaluated by standard intelligence tests.

unspecified substance dependence   A substance-abuse disorder in which the drugs vary or are not known.

unstable   Likely to change without warning. See BIPOLAR DISORDER, INTERMITTENT EXPLOSIVE DISORDER.

unstressed   In linguistics, a syllable that is minimally stressed or not stressed in pronunciation.

unstructured   Characterizing an object, stimulus, or procedure that does not have a definite pattern, such as stimuli used in projective techniques (inkblots, ambiguous pictures). See RORSCHACH INKBLOTS.

unstructured interview   1. A kind of interview in which the person being interviewed is given little direction. Questions or instructions may be vague, such as "Tell me about yourself," in contrast to specifics such as "Tell me about your schooling, (family life, occupation, hobbies)." 2. An interview in which the interviewer is free to modify the questions and to follow up on the answers.

unstructured stimulus   1. An unforeseen and generally unwanted event. 2. A complex or uncompleted stimulus that calls for the person experiencing it to use imagination and creativity to understand or to complete it; for example, a Rorschach inkblot is an unstructured stimulus, both vague and imprecise. Compare STRUCTURED STIMULUS.

unstructured tests   See PROJECTIVE TESTS.

unusual paraphilia   A rare psychosexual disorder in which unusual images or acts are necessary for sexual excitement. Some examples are coprophilia, frottage, klismaphilia, mysophilia, necrophilia, telephone scatologia, urophilia. See entries.

Unusual Uses Test   A test of creativity in which participants are asked to think of, for instance, all the things they could do with a paperclip and an ice cube.

unwell   Euphemism for premenstrual tension or especially menstruation.

unweighted model   In social psychology, a concept that a person forms impressions of others by combining all information about them with equal weight. Compare WEIGHTED MODEL.

unweighted test   An examination (for example, a multiple-choice test) in which each question is worth the same score (for example, one point). Compare WEIGHTED TEST.

unwillingness to examine the dark side   A tendency of people who consistently misbehave to refuse to consider implications of their general attitude toward other people and the consequences of their behavior. See DENIAL, REPRESSION.

up-and-down method   **staircase method (in psychophysics)**

upgrading   In employment, preparation for or the promotion to a better job.

upper ceiling   The highest level or score possible.

upper motor neuron   A neuron issuing from the brain that conducts impulses to cranial and spinal nerves, serving independent voluntary behavior.

uppers   Slang for stimulant drugs. Compare DOWNERS.

up-regulation   In physiological psychology, the dynamic state in which target cells form more receptors in response to increasing hormone levels.

uprooting neurosis   Phrase used by Hans Strauss for neurotic reactions precipitated by relocating to an environment where people speak a different language and have different lifestyles. See MIGRATION ADAPTATION.

upset   A condition of emotional disturbance evident to others.

upsilon   The twentieth letter of the Greek alphabet. See APPENDIX C.

upward communication   The transmission of messages from lower- to higher-status individuals.

upward mobility   The movement of a person or group from one social class to a higher one. Associated with relaxed class systems operating within expanding economies. See DOWNWARD MOBILITY, SOCIAL MOBILITY.

upward Pygmalion effect   The influence that a person's behavior has on superiors.

upward appraisal   The evaluation of people who are at a higher level than the rater.

UR   1. utilization review. 2. See UNCONDITIONED REFLEX, UNCONDITIONED RESPONSE.

uracil   A nucleoid component of ribonucleic acid (RNA) but not of deoxyribonucleic acid (DNA). Uracil is a pyrimidine base, that is, uracil has only one carbon ring. See ADENINE, CYTOSINE, DEOXYRIBONUCLEIC ACID, GUANINE, RIBONUCLEIC ACID, THYMINE.

uraniscolalia   A speech difficulty due to a cleft palate (uranoschisis).

uranism   Obsolete term for a variant of homosexuality or transsexualism in which a man has the orientation of a woman, and therefore finds men more attractive sexually than women. Term derives from Aphrodite Urania, the Greek goddess of love. Karl H. Ulrich coined two related terms in the 1860s: urning and urninde. See entries.

uranophobia   Morbid fear of heaven or the sky. See SIDEROPHOBIA.

uranoschisis   Cleft palate. Also known as uraniscochasm.

urban ecology   The application of biological principles to explain spatial distributions in urban populations. Pioneered by Chicago sociologists in the 1920s.

urbanism   In sociology, patterns of social life typical of urban populations.

urbanization   1. The trend toward living in cities (defined by the United States Bureau of the Census as all populations centers of 500,000 or more people). 2. City formation.

Urban's tables   A set of tables for use with Urban's modifications of the constant process (phi-function of gamma). Named after American 20th century psychophysicist Frank Urban. See INDEX OF PRECISION.

Urban's weights   **Müller-Urban weights**

UR-defenses   Three fundamental beliefs that Jules Masserman assumed help to protect humans from anxiety: (a) the delusion of invulnerability and immortality; (b) the delusion of an omnipotent servant available to individuals in dire trouble; and (c) the conviction of others' ultimate goodness and kindness toward the person who has these ideas. Term is from the German *Ur-* "primeval."

urethral anxiety   A type of anxiety and tension associated with urination (often preventing voiding), particularly urination in a public place.

urethral character   In psychoanalytic theory, a personality type characterized by a long-term history of bed-wetting and a pattern of traits acquired as a reaction formation to the shame and humiliation associated with enuresis, such as excessive ambition, lack of perseverance, and boastfulness.

urethral complex   A concept introduced by Henry A. Murray to describe a psychological state between the Freudian oral and anal stages of development. The complex is manifested by an overly ambitious, strongly narcissistic adult with an obsession for immortality. Also known as Icarus complex.

urethral erot(ic)ism   1. See UROLAGNIA (meaning 1). 2. In psychoanalytic theory, a tendency to derive pleasure or sexual excitement from watching others urinate, from being urinated on during sexual relations, or from drinking urine. Sometimes known as urinism, urolagnia.

urethral phase   (S. Freud) A stage of psychological development that represents a transition from the anal to the phallic stage with some characteristics of both stages. Characterized by conflicts about urethral control, resolution of which leads to pride, self-competence, and gender identity.

URI   Abbreviation for upper respiratory infection; the common cold.

urine test   1. Common term for pregnancy test. 2. Slang name for a drug test.

urinogenital   Pertaining to the combined urinary and genital systems. Also known as urogenital. See URNING.

urninde   (K. H. Ulrich) Obsolete term for a lesbian who plays the passive role in sexual contacts with other females. See URANISM, URNING.

urning   (K. H. Ulrich) Obsolete term for a gay man (male homosexual) who takes the passive role in sexual contacts with other males. See URANISM, URNINDE.

uroclepsia   A pathological condition of involuntary urination.

urogenital floor muscles   Five muscles covering the floor of the pelvic cavity. In the male, they facilitate ejaculation contractions.

urolagnia   1. A morbid preoccupation with urine and urination. Also known as urethral erot(ic)ism. 2. Being sexually aroused by watching a person urinating. See UNDINISM, URETHRAL EROTICISM, UROPHILIA.

urolagnic   A person who is sexually stimulated from acts involving urine (for example, watching other urinate, from being urinated on, or drinking urine). See URETHRAL EROT(IC)ISM.

urophilia   1. A psychosexual disorder marked by a pathologic interest in urine. See UROLAGNIA, URETHRAL EROTICISM. 2. See UNDINISM.

urophobia   Morbid fear of urine.

URpsychology   (J. Masserman) A concept that humans are being observed and protected by "someone" or some "higher power" that will intervene to save those in danger. Also spelled URpsychologie, from the German prefix ur, for primitive or original. See UR-DEFENSES.

urticaria   Temporary raised wheals in the skin which itch considerably. Among causes are psychic stimuli. Also known as cnidosis, hives, nettle rash, uredo.

US   See UNCONDITIONED STIMULUS.

use and disuse theory   (J. Lamarck) A point of view that structural or functional changes in organs, brought about by their use or disuse, are passed on to progeny. Also known as use-inheritance. See DARWINISM, LAMARCKIANISM.

use law   In learning theory (E. L. Thorndike), the more a connection between a given stimulus and a given response is exercised, the more readily will the stimulus bring about this response. Also known as law of exercise. See FREQUENCY LAW.

useful duration   The temporal portion of the initial passage of electric current instrumental in producing a response in nerves or muscles, with additional stimulus duration having no additional effect. Also known as serviceable duration.

useful field of view   Phrase describing a vision test administered mainly to older drivers, which measures ability to perceive relevant detail in complex, machine-displayed pictures.

usefuls   Refers to one of four main types of people according to Alfred Adler, those who are socially cooperative. See ADLER'S PERSONALITY TYPES.

useless movements   Movements in a complex response that do not assist in attaining an adaptive result, and which often impede its attainment.

useless studying   Studying without learning. A common problem for children ranked at the bottom 25% of school children, who go to classes, listen and apply themselves but who are not yet able to learn or to understand what they are being taught. The situation worsers the older children get, as they fall further behind their cohorts. See FORCED RESTUDYING, XYZ GROUPING.

user-friendly   Originally a computer phrase meaning that the software is intuitive and easy to understand, now broadened to mean any system designed for easy, simple, intuitively-obvious operation. Also spelled without the hyphen and sometimes as a single word.

USES BOLT   See UNITED STATES EMPLOYMENT SERVICE (USES) BASIC OCCUPATIONAL LITERACY TEST (BOLT).

USES Basic Occupational Literacy Test (BOLT)   Another and perhaps the preferred name for the United States Employment Service (USES) Basic Occupational Literacy Test (BOLT).

U-shaped curve   A graphic representation of a distribution shaped like the letter U. See CATENARY CURVE.

us-them thinking   Perceptions of others as different from self, that ensue especially in the face of competition. See ETHNOCENTRISM.

us-versus-them effect   (J. C. Turner) In social psychology, a tendency to view others as belonging to either the person's own group or to an outgroup.

uterine theory   (Hippocrates) A discredited point of view that hysteria is solely a feminine disturbance, caused by displacement of the uterus.

uteromania   Obsolete term for nymphomania.

uterus   A hollow muscular organ in female mammals in which the offspring develops from a zygote. Also known as metra, womb. Plural is uteri. See WANDERING UTERUS.

U test   Mann-Whitney U test

utilitarianism   1. A social or economic theory which regards the practical usefulness of any object or plan as the proper criterion for judging its value. See FUNCTIONALISM. 2. In British political/moral philosophy and social theory of the 1700s–1800s, economic liberalism.

utility   1. The fitness or usefulness of a character, organ, mechanism, function, or operation, to preserve the life of an organism, continue the species, or bring to completion some biological process. Also known as usefulness. 2. In economic theory, the benefit or satisfaction derived from the consumption of a commodity. 3. In 18th-century moral philosophy, the "greatest happiness" principle: Actions are right if they promote well-being.

utility function   In consumer psychology, a buyer's satisfaction with different levels of product attributes.

utility index (of a test)   1. The importance of a test in general "applied" work. 2. Where the benefits of hiring a successful employee and the costs of hiring one who proves to be unsuccessful can be determined, the utility is given by $B(N_s) - C(N_u) = S$, where B is the average benefit accrued from a successful hire, N_s and N_u are the numbers of successful and unsuccessful ones, and S is the cost of the selection program.

utility (of a test)   In decision theory, the usefulness of a test, especially in terms of its costs and benefits. See UTILITY INDEX (OF A TEST).

utility theory   In decision making, a point of view that the rational choice is that which is indicated by logical analysis.

utilization review (UR)   1. A periodic review by an appointed committee of the quality of services and the use of facilities, typically in an institution such as a hospital. 2. Evaluation of the cost and effectiveness of an organization to determine whether or not it should maintain services.

Utopia   (Sir Thomas More) A perfect society. Usually refers to utopian, utopianism; spelled utopia.

utriculus   The larger of the two membranous sacs in the labyrinth of the inner ear. Communicates with the semicircular canals associated with the sense of balance and also receives the utricular filaments of the acoustic nerve. Also known as utricle. Plural is utriculi.

utterance generator   (V. A. Fromkin) In linguistics, a theory that includes several stages of representation of an utterance and considers how and when speech errors are produced.

uvea   The iris, ciliary body, and choroid coat of the eye, considered as a unit and constituting the pigmentary layers of the eyeball.

uveal tract   The middle layer of the three-layer structure of the eye which includes the iris. See EYE STRUCTURE.

uvular (sound)   A sound made with the tongue touching or near the uvula.

uxoricide   The murder of a wife by her husband.

Uznadze illusion   (D. N. Uznadze) A printed figure of two identical, adjacent circles, one enclosed in a larger concentric circle. When viewing the smaller circles alternately with the larger circle, the enclosed circle appears smaller than the other small circle. Similar to the Delboeuf illusion.

V

v   volt (also abbreviated **V**)

V   1. verb. 2. volt (also abbreviated **v**). 3. volume. 4. stimulus intensity dynamism. 5. variable stimulus. 6. verbal ability. 7. coefficient of variability. 8. variance. 9. Vision. 10. visual acuity (also abbreviated **VA**).

VA   1. Veteran's Administration. 2. visual acuity.

V-A   See VENTRICULOATRIAL SHUNT.

VABS   Vineland Adaptive Behavior Scales

vaccinophobia   Morbid fear of being vaccinated or inoculated. Also known as trypanophobia.

vacuum activity   1. Highly motivated behavior that occurs in response to no apparent external stimulus. 2. A distorted or incomplete response that may be observed when motivational energy accumulates in a neural center but an appropriate releasing stimulus does not occur. The motivational energy forces its way past the inhibitory blocking system to cause the vacuum activity.

vacuum aspiration   Abortion procedure commonly used in the first trimester of pregnancy by suction of the contents of the uterus.

vacuum response   Behavior that appears in the absence of its usual releasing stimulus, possibly due to a high drive state.

VAD   See VASCULAR DEMENTIA.

vagabond neurosis   **dromomania**

vagina   (sheath, husk, scabbard—Latin) 1. The tubular passage in female mammals from the uterus to the vulva. Normally collapsed but expandable. Serves as an exit passage for the menstrual flow, receives the penis during copulation, and is the birth canal in normal deliveries. 2. Sometimes used (incorrectly) to mean any or all of the vulva.

vagina dentata   (toothed vagina—Latin) In psychoanalytic theory, the fantasy that the vagina has "teeth" that can castrate the male partner during coitus. Rooted in men's castration anxiety and in women's penis envy and subsequent desire to castrate men. See PENIS CAPTIVES.

vaginal code   (M. Diamond) A coital sequence which enhances the likelihood that pregnancy will ensue. Each species has its own patterns of copulation that help enhance fertility among conspecifics and thwart it among nonconspecifics.

vaginal envy   A desire in males to become pregnant and bear children. May be expressed by male transsexuals and transvestites in Western cultures and has been observed in rituals and ceremonies of societies that regard menstruation and childbirth as sacred functions. See FEMININITY COMPLEX, WOMB ENVY.

vaginal father   In psychoanalytic theory, a male who dreams or fantasizes that he has a vagina. Originates from strong identification with the mother and is associated with feminine, nonaggressive behavior, an intense rivalry with women, and the performance by men of traditionally "wifely" duties in marriage.

vaginal hypoesthesia   Insufficient vaginal sensation or sexual response.

vaginal lubrication   The movement of plasma fluid from vaginal blood vessels into the vaginal canal. Occurs as a primary sexual response as well as during the dreaming phase of sleep. See SEXUAL-RESPONSE CYCLE.

vaginal orgasm   An orgasm experienced through vaginal stimulation. Sigmund Freud theorized a distinction between this "mature" type and the "immature" one resulting from clitoral stimulation, since refuted by the research of William Masters and Virginia Johnson. Other studies of the Graefenberg spot (G spot) suggest three types: clitoral, vaginal, and blended.

vaginal phase   (S. Freud) The phase in girls that corresponds to a boy's phallic phase from ages 3 to 5, during which vaginal sensations and incorporative imagery predominate.

vaginal plethysmograph   A device placed in the vagina and connected to a recording device to measure the degree of sexual arousal as changes in the vagina's size, volume, and vasocongestion. See PLETHYSMOGRAPH.

vaginal sex   Sexual intercourse via insertion of a penis in a vagina.

vaginal spasms   **vaginismus**

vaginismus   Involuntary contractions of the perineal and paravaginal muscles in response to attempts at a sexual or medical examination insertion. May cause pain and prevent the insertion. A rare and distressing condition, not generally related to capacity for sexual arousal. Usually responds to psychological, medical (dilation), or behavioral therapies. Also known as vaginism, vaginal spasms. See DYSPAREUNIA, FUNCTIONAL VAGINISMUS, PSYCHIC VAGINISMUS.

vagus nerve (Marinus, D. de Marchetti) Cranial nerve X. It constitutes an important part of the parasympathetic system. As a mixed nerve with sensory and motor fibers it innervates the external ear, vocal organs, thoracic and abdominal viscera as well as the tongue. Also known as pneumogastric nerve.

VAKT See FERNALD METHOD.

valence (E. C. Tolman & K. Lewin) In field theory, a quality of objects that affects their attractiveness to organisms. An object that attracts has positive valence, whereas one that repels has negative valence.

valence-instrumentality-expectancy theory (V. H. Vroom) In industrial psychology, a point of view that behavior is influenced by (a) degree of certainty that some outcome will follow the behavior, and (b) how much that outcome is valued. Also known as expectancy theory, valence-expectancy theory.

valid 1. That which is true, correct, proper. 2. Producing the desired result. See VALIDITY (meaning 2).

validation 1. The process of measuring validity. 2. Loosely, in social and therapeutic interactions, reaffirmation.

validity 1. The characteristic of being founded on truth, accuracy, fact, or law. 2. In statistics and testing, the ability of a test to measure what it is supposed to measure. Validity is often confused with reliability which means consistency of measurement. A test can be highly reliable, but not valid, but highly valid tests are also highly reliable. Types of validity include: A PRIORI, CONCURRENT, CONGRUENT, CONSENSUAL, CONSTRUCT, CONTENT, CONVERGENT, CRITERION, DEFINITIONAL, DIFFERENTIAL, DISCRIMINANT, EMPIRICAL, ETIOLOGICAL, EXTERNAL, FACE, FACTORIAL, INCREMENTAL, INTERNAL, INTRINSIC, NOMOLOGICAL, PREDICTIVE, SAMPLING, SYNTHETIC, TRAIT.

validity coefficient See COEFFICIENT OF VALIDITY.

validity criterion An independent and external measure of what a test is designed or presumed to measure.

validity effect A tendency to believe that something is true because affirmations of its truth have been constantly repeated.

validity generalization The application of validity evidence to situations in addition to those from which the evidence was obtained.

Valium Trade name for the benzodiazepine drug diazepam. It followed Librium as an even more widely-used mild tranquilizer or anti-anxiety drug, especially in the 1970s and 1980s. Also used as a muscle relaxant and intravenous or rectal suppository treatment for status epilepticus.

VALS See VALUES LIFESTYLE GROUPS.

Valsalva maneuver Forced exhalation against a closed glottis, commonly occurring in activities that require rapid, extreme, brief application of force, such as weight lifting, straining to expel stool, or a child's temper tantrum.

value 1. A goal or standard considered especially worthy by an individual or a society. In Rogerian and psychoanalytic theory, the moral values of society are incorporated into the psyche through identification with the parents. 2. Denoting the degree of excellence assigned to an object or activity. 3. The mathematical magnitude, or quantity, of an object. 4. The market price of an item or service.

value analysis In evaluating content of written material, establishing in advance some sort of standard to be judged, such as terms reflecting positive attitudes, and counting them to obtain a numerical index such as the number of positive terms per one thousand words. See POSITIVE-NEGATIVE AMBIVALENT QUOTIENT.

value judgment 1. A qualitative judgment, in contradistinction to a quantitative judgment. 2. An assessment of persons, objects, or events in terms of their value or worth rather than of their objective characteristics.

values clarification 1. In therapy, step-by-step exercises to help a client become more aware of plural values and how these values affect daily living and decision making. 2. In general, attempts by certain groups of people (such as teachers, preachers), to get others (such as students, a congregation) to prioritize what is important to them in such matters as lifestyle, personal philosophy, or goals.

values education An attempt to raise the moral levels of students, as either (a) an independent aspect of total education or (b) a specific course. In the first method, students are treated in a respectful manner and given responsibility, thereby generating higher ethical standards on the part of the students; and in the second method, the curriculum contains lectures, readings and visual material intended to achieve the same results as the first method.

Values Lifestyle Groups (VALS) In consumer psychology, target markets segmented by demographics and lifestyle, as established by questionnaire responses.

value system 1. The hierarchical ordered system in which a person ranks, consciously or unconsciously, one value or ideal over another (for example, a person may believe that democracy is "better" than autocracy). 2. The moral, social, esthetic, economic, and religious concepts accepted either explicitly or implicitly by an individual or a particular society.

vampirism 1. A belief in fictional blood-sucking creatures. 2. In literature, often portrayed in a manner suggesting sexual pleasure associated with sucking blood from a person of the opposite sex, a representation of the "love bite." 3. Interpreted by some clinicians as oral sadism, Oedipal strivings, fear of castration, or aggressive hostile feelings.

vandalism Willful defacement or destruction of property. A persistent pattern of vandalism is a common symptom of aggressive conduct disorders. See SEXUAL VANDALISM.

vandalized lovemap The substitution of a paraphilia for normal psychosexual development, purportedly due to an early (usually traumatic) sexual experience. See LOVEMAP.

Vandenbergh effect The early onset of sexual maturity in female mice that are housed with males. Caused by a pheromone in the male's urine.

vanity Excessive self-appreciation, and often a marked desire for the notice and praise by others of personal appearance, attainments, etc. See NARCISSISM.

variability 1. The ability of an individual, situation, or species to change. 2. A characteristic of being subject to modification in value, quality, form, etc., from time to time. 3. In statistics, the degree to which scores differ from each other or from their central tendency. See AVERAGE DEVIATION, DISPERSION MEASURE, RANGE, STANDARD DEVIATION, VARIANCE.

variable 1. (S-F. Lacroix) An element in an experiment or test that varies, that is, takes on different values, while other conditions remain constant. A general and widely used term, especially in a research context, for any element whose value can or does change. Types of variables include: AUTOCHTHONOUS, CATALYTIC, CATEGORICAL, CONFOUNDING, CONTENT, CONTINUOUS, CONTROL, CONTROLLED, CRITICAL, DEMOGRAPHIC, DEPENDENT, DISCONTINUOUS, DISCRETE, DISTAL, E/C INTERVENING, EXTRANEOUS, FUNCTIONAL, HIDDEN, INDEPENDENT, INDEX, INTERVENING, LURKING, MARKER, MEDIATING, MODERATOR, MOTIVATIONAL, MULTIDIMENSIONAL, NONMANIPULATED, NUISANCE, ORGANIC, ORGANISMIC, QUALITATIVE, QUANTITATIVE, RANDOM, REACTION, RESPONSE, SORC, STIMULUS, STRUCTURAL, SUBJECT, SUPPRESSOR, UNCONTROLLED. 2. Deviating from the type in some way, such as structure, form, physiology, or behavior.

variable chorea of Brissaud (E. Brissaud) A condition characterized by highly variable choreiform movements that come and go, increase and decrease, and appear to be quick at one time and slow at another. May be a form of Tourette's disorder/syndrome.

variable-interval schedule of reinforcement (VI) In operant conditioning, a type of interval reinforcement in which the reinforcement or reward is presented after unpredictable periods of time. Reinforcement is not contingent on the number of correct responses emitted during the intervals. Also known as variable-interval reinforcement schedule. Compare FIXED-INTERVAL SCHEDULE OF REINFORCEMENT, INTERVAL SCHEDULE OF REINFORCEMENT.

variable-ratio schedule of reinforcement (VR) In operant conditioning, an intermittent reinforcement schedule in which a response is reinforced after an unpredictable number of responses, determined by a random series of values having a certain mean and lying within a certain range. Also known as variable-ratio reinforcement schedule. Compare FIXED-RATIO SCHEDULE OF REINFORCEMENT.

variable stimulus (V or s) 1. The independent variable. 2. Any one of a set of experimental stimuli that vary from a constant stimulus.

variance 1. The state of being variable or different. 2. (V) A measure of dispersion in a frequency distribution. It is the second moment of the curve calculated by the squared deviations about the mean. Variance may be obtained for either a sample or a population. Formulas: for sample variance, $S^2 = \sum[x^2 \div (n-1)]$, for population variance, $\sigma^2 = \sum(x^2 \div N)$, where: $x = (X - M)$. Types of variance include: BETWEEN GROUPS, BETWEEN-GROUPS, CO-, ERROR, INTERACTION, SEX, TRUE, UNBIASED, WITHIN-GROUPS. See ANALYSIS OF VARIANCE, HOMOGENEITY OF VARIANCE, ONE-WAY ANALYSIS OF VARIANCE, TWO-WAY ANALYSIS OF VARIANCE.

variance ratio (F) A ratio between two estimates of variance in the same population reached by different methods. See F DISTRIBUTION.

variate The magnitude of a particular observation or measurement.

variation 1. Generic term used to characterize any differences between organisms, whether due to heredity or environment. 2. A change or alteration of any datum in some specific respect.

variational psychology A branch of psychology that studies the nature, magnitude, cause, and consequences of psychological differences among individuals of the same type. See DIFFERENTIAL PSYCHOLOGY.

variation coefficient (V) See COEFFICIENT OF VARIATION.

variations of aging (D. O. Cowgill) Twenty-two variations of aging across cultures, for instance, how old-age is defined, status of the aged, and retirement practices.

variator See TONE VARIATOR.

varied mapping condition (W. Schneider & R. M. Shiffrin) In human information processing studies, a research condition in which the targets and distracters in a visual search task are mixed across trials; for instance, an item that distracts on one trial might be a target on another. Compare CONSISTENT MAPPING CONDITION.

variform universal (W. J. Lonner) A convention influenced to some extent by culture or organizations; for example, single parenting is common in some cultures, and in others uncles are as important as fathers. But the simple universal, the parenting, per se, must occur in some way in all cultures, and is likely to influence leader-follower relations that emerge.

varimax 1. A particular kind of factor analytic rotation, that approximates simple structure, and results in factors that are orthogonal to each other. See VARIMAX ROTATION. 2. (H. F. Kaiser) In exploratory factor analysis, a (computerized) method for the orthogonal rotation of the axes of either principal components or principal factors to achieve an approximation to Louis Thurstone's criterion of simple structure, whereby each test is maximally loaded on only one factor and each factor has a maximum number of near-zero loadings. The varimax criterion approximates simple structure by maximizing the variance of the squared loadings on each factor. Varimax militates against the appearance of a general factor. See VARIMAX ROTATED PRINCIPAL COMPONENTS, VARIMAX ROTATION.

varimax rotated principal components A varimax rotation of the factors extracted by the method of principal components.

varimax rotation A method of factor rotation in factor analysis, that results in orthogonal factors that approximate simple structure, and maximize the variance accounted by each factor.

vas deferens In males, the excretory testis duct and a continuation of the epididymis canal. Spermatozoa travel through the duct from the epididymis to a junction with the seminal-vesicle duct emptying into the urethra. Also known as ductus deferens, seminal duct, spermatic duct.

vascular dementia (VAD)   A brain disorder in which a series of cerebral infarcts destroy neurons, causing brain atrophy and behavioral impairments. Formerly known as multi-infarct dementia; easily confused with dementia of the Alzheimer's type (DAT). See ALZHEIMER'S DISEASE.

vascular headache   **migraine headache**

vascular insufficiency   A failure of the cardiovascular system to deliver adequate blood flow to body tissues.

vascular sensation   A complex of sensations (temperature, and a mingled tension, tickling and mixed pain) which attends abrupt and extreme constriction or dilation of blood vessel changes in the skin, as in blushing.

vascular theory (of thermal sensitivity)   A point of view that cold and warm sensations are related, respectively, to the constriction or dilation of blood vessels.

vasectomy   A surgical procedure leading to male sterilization by blocking spermatozoa from the testes from being discharged from the penis by cutting the vas deferens, then blocking the openings. After the procedure, spermatozoa should be absent from ejaculated fluids. Also known as deferentectomy.

vasoconstriction   The constriction or narrowing of a blood vessel. It is controlled by the fibers of the sympathetic nervous system or by agents such as amphetamine or epinephrine. See ERGOT DERIVATIVES.

vasoconstrictor   1. Causing constriction of blood vessels. Also known as vasoconstrictive. 2. A substance, such as the hormone vasopressin, that causes constriction of the blood vessels so that the size of the bore of the arterioles is reduced. 3. A nerve that when stimulated causes constriction of blood vessels.

vasodilation   The dilation of blood vessels. Term commonly is applied to the size of the bore of the arterioles. Also known as vasodilatation.

vasodilator   1. Causing dilation of blood vessels. Also known as vasodilative. 2. A substance that causes dilation of the blood vessels so that the size of the bore of the arterioles is increased. 3. A nerve that when stimulated causes dilation of blood vessels.

vasomotor   A nerve, drug, or other agent that can affect the diameter of a blood vessel.

vasopressin (VP)   Posterior pituitary hormone that raises blood pressure and permits the kidneys to reabsorb water, thereby concentrating the urine. Also known as antidiuretic hormone (ADH).

vasopressor   That which compresses blood vessels. See PRESSOR SUBSTANCE.

vasospasm   A sudden involuntary contraction or hypertonia of blood vessels. Also known as angiohypertonia, angiospasm. See SPASM.

Vater's corpuscles   **Pacinian corpuscles**

VD   venereal disease

VD.RL test   Venereal Disease Research Laboratory test; a blood serum test for syphilis.

vector   (bearer, carrier—Latin) 1. In physics and mathematics, a force that has both specific magnitude and specific direction, often represented by a line of specific length with an arrow indicating the point of application of the force. 2. (K. Lewin) In field theory, a method of indicating forces involved in "psychological locomotion" within a person's life space. A psychological force that impinges on a person, resulting in the person moving in one direction or another. 3. (H. A. Murray) An action tendency, based on a particular need. 4. In factor analysis, a row of numerical values (a row vector) or a column of numerical values (a column vector).

vector analysis/psychology   Mathematics phrase applied by Kurt Lewin to a technique for studying a person's relationships within the "life space," and for depicting the forces, or vectors, that act upon any person at any given moment. The vectors, such as conflicting goals, are represented diagrammatically by lines of different length and direction. See FIELD THEORY, TOPOLOGICAL PSYCHOLOGY, VALENCE, VECTOR.

vector psychology   See VECTOR ANALYSIS.

vectors   In topological (or vector) psychology, the direction of psychological forces resulting from the interplay of attracting and repelling factors (positive and negative valences) in a person's psychological environment. See TOPOLOGICAL PSYCHOLOGY.

vegan   A complete vegetarian who abstains from all animal product, including dairy products and eggs. Vegans are also likely to abstain from the wearing of leather and animal fur.

vegetative   1. Describing behavior that has deteriorated to a point where the individual appears to lead an almost vegetable-like existence. 2. Pertaining to basic physiological functions of the autonomic nervous system such as those involved in growth, respiration, sleep, digestion, elimination, and homeostasis. Many of these functions, such as respiration and digestion, become disturbed when the individual faces extreme stress, and many of the characteristic symptoms of depression, such as decreased appetite, insomnia, and diminished sexual response, are vegetative in nature.

vegetative function   Any one of the biological processes relating to nutrition and growth in organisms.

vegetative idiot   Obsolete phrase for a person with severe mental retardation. See AMENTIA.

vegetative level/state   A passive, "dilapidated," state of deterioration in which the patient is immobile, out of contact with the environment, and unresponsive to questioning, and ultimately has to be fed and toileted. See CEREBRAL ARTERIOSCLEROSIS, CHRONIC SCHIZOPHRENIA, SENILE BRAIN DISEASE.

vegetative nervous system   Obsolete phrase for the autonomic nervous system based on the fact that it controls the internal functions of the organism but not movement, sensation, or thought. Also known as sympathetic nervous system.

vegetative neurosis   A neurosis in which chronic internal conflicts and repressed emotions produce disturbances in the internal organs, resulting in such symptoms as duodenal ulcer and essential hypertension. Also known as visceral neurosis.

vegetative retreat A tendency to regress to infantile behavior marked by visceral reactions when facing a dangerous reality situation (for example, adults who express a need for help by developing diarrhea or turning to thumb-sucking instead of taking an appropriate action).

vegetative soul See SENSITIVE SOUL.

vegetative state   vegetative level

vegetative system (E. Hess) The nervous system that controls internal-to-the-body functioning. See VEGETATIVE NERVOUS SYSTEM.

vegetotherapy   orgone therapy

vehicle fear See AMAXOPHOBIA.

veiling field See VISUAL TASK EVALUATOR.

veiling glare A quality of intense brightness reflected off a transparent screen that impedes the view through it. Common in cars, where reflections of the top of the dashboard seen in the windshield can result in disability glare.

velar In speech, a pharyngeal sound made behind the hard palate. Also commonly known as guttural.

velleity A low or weak degree of desire.

velocity of nerves Measurement by an electromyograph indicates that nerves go at a speed of 40 to 60 meters a second or about 44 yards to 66 yards per second.

velum 1. Any structure resembling a curtain. 2. A veil of white matter, such as the superior and inferior medullar vela that form a part of the cerebellar-medullary roof over the fourth ventricle. Plural is vela. See SOFT PALATE.

velum palatinum Fibromuscular tissue attached to the posterior portion of the hard palate. Also known as soft palate.

venereal Refers to sexual intercourse and consequences thereof, especially diseases.

venereal disease (VD) Outmoded phrase for a subset of sexually transmitted diseases (STDs).

venereal-disease fear See CYPRIDOPHOBIA, VENEREOPHOBIA.

venereophobia Morbid fear of contracting a venereal disease. Also known as cypridoophobia, cypridophobia.

venery Obsolete term for excessive sexual activity, especially of the illicit nature. Also known as licentiousness, promiscuity.

Venn diagrams Charts of partially overlapping circles that indicate logical relations between sets (each circle represents one set) or proposition terms, and operations on sets or proposition terms. The relations or operations are expressed by exclusion, inclusion, or intersection of the circles and by different kinds of shading for empty areas, areas that are not empty, and areas that may be either. Named after English logician John Venn (1834–1923), the diagrams were based on the similar work of the Swiss mathematician Leonhard Euler (Euler diagrams). Many variations of Euler diagrams and Venn diagrams are used in psychology.

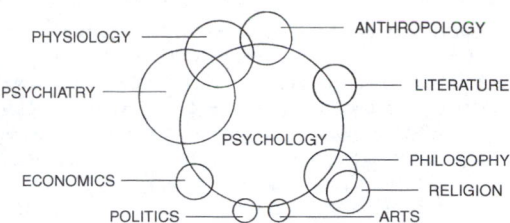

Venn diagrams

ventilation The free expression of feelings or emotions, especially in a therapy session.

ventral Pertaining to the abdomen, belly, or anterior surface or side of an organism. Now generally substituted for anterior. Compare DORSAL.

ventral posterior nucleus The thalamic nucleus that receives primary somatosensory information and relays that information to the neocortex, particularly to the postcentral gyrus. It is divided into a medial and a lateral component.

ventral tegmental area of Tsai An area below the medial lemniscus that appears to be one of the structures in the rat brain that is a source of rewarding effects when self-stimulated through implanted electrodes.

ventricle 1. The stomach. 2. A normal body cavity, as of the heart. 3. Any small cavity in the body, as of the brain that has several ventricles that serve as reservoirs of cerebrospinal fluid. They include the two lateral ventricles, the third ventricle, and the fourth ventricle, which communicate with each other and with the spinal cord and subarachnoid spaces. See BRAIN VENTRICLES.

ventricle puncture A surgical procedure in which an opening from the outside is made to the lateral ventricle areas of the brain.

ventricular system A network of ventricles and passageways to the spinal cord and subarachnoid spaces of the brain through which the cerebrospinal fluid circulates as a possible source of nutrients for central nervous system (CNS) tissues.

ventriculoatrial (V-A) shunt A surgically created passage for draining cerebrospinal fluid from the ventricles of the brain to the external jugular vein, as in the treatment of hydrocephalus.

ventriloquism A mode of speaking characterized by keeping the lips closed, so that the listener mislocates the source of sound and is often subject to the illusion that inanimate objects are talking.

ventrodorsal Proceeding from the front to the back, anterior to posterior. Opposite of dorsoventral (back to front, posterior to anterior).

ventromedial nucleus of the hypothalamus (VMH) A pea-sized structure in the brain that controls appetite. An area of the hypothalamus that is associated with the inhibition of eating after certain nutritional requirements of the body have been met. If the ventromedial nucleus suffers loss of structure or function, a condition of hyperphagia, or overeating, results. Also known as appestat, satiety center.

VEP visual evoked potential

verb-adjective ratio As an index of verbal diversification, it is the ratio of the number of verbs to the number of adjectives used in a sample of speech or writing. Varies with conditions of measurements and with personality characteristics.

verbal ability (V) A demonstrated capacity to communicate effectively by speech. Brain areas necessary for normal speech appear to be distributed over a broad region of the cerebral cortex and can be mapped by electrical stimulation. However, stimulation of a specific area will produce only phonemes or vocalizations; complete words apparently require simultaneous stimulation of combinations of speech areas. See PRIMARY ABILITIES.

verbal alexia A form of agnosia in which individual letters may be recognized but not whole words or combinations of letters, such as APA.

verbal amnesia A loss of the ability to remember words due to neurological disorder or disease. See NEUROLOGICAL AMNESIA.

verbal aphasia Inability to produce speech. Due to a cortical lesion, usually due to damage to Broca's area. See APHASIA, BROCA'S AREA, CORTICAL MOTOR APHASIA, EXPRESSIVE APHASIA, SPEECH APHASIA, WORD DUMBNESS.

verbal automatism Refers to common speech mannerisms in a fugue state. See AUTOMATISM.

Verbal Behavior A 1957 book by B. F. Skinner in which he generalized from studies of animal learning to language, concluding that people speak as they do because they have been reinforced for doing so.

Verbal Behavior Therapy (A. Bandura) A combination of conditioning and social learning theory, this system of behavior therapy emphasizes selection of carefully delineated problems and goals with follow-up of results. The general process calls for an analysis of a specific problem, getting a measure of its frequency and severity and then designing a means to reduce it and then working on another specific problem. See BEHAVIOR THERAPY.

verbal comprehension A primary mental ability according to research by L. L. Thurstone, supported by other studies, that amounts to a person's passive vocabulary, that is to say, the number of words that a person can recognize. See PRIMARY ABILITIES, PRIMARY MENTAL ABILITIES.

verbal conditioning A procedure in which special verbal responses are reinforced so as to increase the participant's facility in responding to a verbal stimulus.

verbal context effect In communication, the probability of a particular word following another word (for example, what would be the most likely next word? "Hello, how have you. . .?")

verbal deprivation hypothesis (B. Bernstein) A postulate that the form of language learned by a child could possibly hinder the child when it comes time to learn abstract forms of information. See ELABORATIVE CODES, RESTRICTED CODES OF LEARNING.

verbal generalization A statement of a universal principle or general judgment.

verbal intelligence An ability to use words and symbols effectively in communication and problem-solving.

verbalism 1. Reliance, in thinking, upon associations between words instead of upon relations between things. 2. Uncritical acceptance of definitions as if they were explanations, or statements of causal relations.

verbalization 1. The expression of thoughts, feelings, and fantasies in words. In psychoanalysis, which has been commonly described as "the talking cure," the client is encouraged to freely associate in words rather than to act out or rely on gestures. It is a major procedure in other forms of psychotherapy as well, such as the nondirective approach. 2. Pathological and extreme expression of thoughts, feelings, and fantasies, as in the pressured speech of people in a manic state.

verbal leakage Phrase sometimes applied to slips of the tongue and dreams that reveal information about a person's motives and behavior that the person has attempted to conceal. Body language that tries to conceal information is described by some psychologists as nonverbal leakage. See FREUDIAN SLIP, LAPSUS CALAMI, LAPSUS LINGUAE, LAPSUS MEMORIAE, PARAPRAXIS.

verbal learning The process of learning to respond verbally to verbal stimuli, which may include symbols, nonsense syllables, lists, or words, and the solution of complex problems stated in words.

verbal loop hypothesis A postulate that understanding and remembering is based on the brain translating into words what is brought to it by the senses.

verbal masochism A psychosexual disorder in which a person enjoys hearing words that are humiliating and insulting, and derives sexual excitement from the abuse. According to Theodore Reik, the sexual excitement may depend upon the choice and emphasis of words or sentences used.

verbal memory 1. Memory for words; the capacity to remember written or spoken material that was previously learned, such as a poem. 2. The storing of imagery using words as a means of coding the information. See MOTOR MEMORY, SYMBOLIC REPRESENTATION, VISUAL MEMORY.

verbal overshadowing The influence of a verbal label on memory for pictorial stimuli.

verbal paraphasia Inclusion of inappropriate words and phrases in speech. See PARAPHASIA.

verbal proposition (J. Piaget) A construct or abstraction that represents a given fact or phenomenon, such as, an algebraic formula or a concept in sociology. The capacity to manipulate verbal propositions in reasoning signals the adolescent's arrival at the stage of FORMAL OPERATIONS.

verbal protocol analysis A technique for studying cognitive processes in which the participant is asked to talk aloud while making a decision or solving a problem.

verbal suggestion (E. Jones) Describing the method of influencing, or molding, a person's mind by hypnotic suggestion. See IDEOPLASTY.

verbal summator A projective method in which an instrument produces low-intensity vowel sounds that the participant is asked to translate into words.

verbal test 1. Any examination, task, or scale in which performance depends upon the ability to deal with words. 2. Any test that measures verbal ability.

verbal thought (L. Vygotsky) A reasoning process that requires language and thus represents the merging of language and thought. See INNER LANGUAGE, PURE MEANING.

verbatim recall **rote recall**

verbiage The use of a superabundance of words in sentences.

verbigeration 1. The constant repetition of meaningless words or phrases. Also known as catalogia. 2. (K. Kahlbaum) A symptom of mental disorders characterized by utterance of meaningless and highly stereotyped repetitions of words for extended periods of time. Also known as cataphasia. See HALLUCINATORY VERBIGERATION.

verbochromia A form of synesthesia in which a person experiences color sensations at the sound of certain words.

verbomania 1. A rush of rapid, uncontrollable, and incoherent talking. Also known as logorrhea. 2. Loosely, a morbid preoccupation with words.

verbone (H. A. Murray) A verbal-action pattern, or a unit of verbal action. See ACTON(E), MOTONE.

Verdrängung German phrase used by Wilhelm Griesinger for repression in mental illness. Similar to Sigmund Freud's repression.

vergence A turning movement of the eyes. If they turn inward, the movement is convergence; if outward, divergence.

veridical (true—Latin) Truthfully spoken, what is real, genuine. Corresponding to truth or objective fact.

veridical hallucinations Purported states and dreams that correspond to a real situation (as when the apparition of a distant person coincides temporally with that person's death reported at a later time).

veridical perception Relating to a perception said to be true and confirmed as a result of continued exposure to the perceived subjects, especially when reinforced by precise descriptions and measurements.

verification The use of objective empirical data to test or support the truth of a statement, conclusion, or hypothesis.

verificationism **Vienna Circle** (meaning 1)

vermi(ni)phobia Fear of worms. Also known as herminthophobia.

vermis (cerebelli) The median lobe of the cerebellum that lies between the two hemispheres.

Vernier (pendulum) chronoscope (P. Vernier, E. Sanford) An early type of chronoscope used to measure reaction times, consisting of pendulums that were able to swing at different intervals.

vernix (caseosa) The pasty substance that covers and protects the skin of the fetus.

Veronal (E. Fischer & J. von Mehring) Trade name for the first clinically useful barbiturate. Known as barbital in the United States and barbitone in England.

Verstehen (understanding—German) 1. In evaluation research, a precondition to research involving understanding of language, cultural-symbol systems, and behavior, usually by participant observation. 2. An understanding of mental constructs, as well as behavior, in the studies of programs and cultures.

Verstehende psychologie (psychology of understanding—German) (W. Dilthey) A point of view about psychology in the late 19th and early 20th centuries in which the main objective of psychological research was not to be causal explanations but rather its understanding. This point of view championed by Wilhelm Dilthey was rejected by most experimentalists of the era.

vertex The top of anything that has a vertical dimension. Plural is vertices.

vertex potential A potential recorded by electrodes placed at the vertex (top) of the skull. Seems to be evoked by a variety of stimuli but is closely associated with attention.

vertical axis 1. A direction perpendicular to the horizon, or head-to-toe in a human body; comparable to the cephalocaudal axis in quadruped (four-legged) animals. 2. The ordinate (y-axis).

vertical décalage (J. Piaget) A change in a child's functioning during movement from one developmental stage to another. See DÉCALAGE.

vertical group A group composed of individuals from different social classes. See HORIZONTAL GROUP, SOCIAL MOBILITY, VERTICAL MOBILITY.

vertical-horizontal illusion (W. Helmholtz) If parallel lines of equal length are in a vertical position there is a tendency to view them as longer or taller than the same parallel lines placed in a horizontal position. For this reason, people who are on the shorter side are advised by tailors to wear clothing that emphasizes the vertical, such as up-and-down stripes to generate the illusion of being taller, and people who consider themselves too tall are asked to do the opposite. See the illustration of two squares below.

vertical-horizontal illusion
Helmholtz square.

vertical job enlargement The expansion of responsibilities associated with a particular job, by requiring the employee to perform more complex tasks and undertake increased responsibility and autonomy. Compare HORIZONTAL JOB ENLARGEMENT.

vertical loading In industrial psychology, job enlargement in which higher-level jobs are reclassified to be performed by lower-level employees. Compare HORIZONTAL LOADING.

vertical location In placement of a student in a school or an applicant in a job, the level of the hierarchy in which the person is placed. In a school, ordinarily it would be at a grade level. See HORIZONTAL LOCATION, PLACEMENT.

vertical mobility Progress or displacement from one class to another. The movement from class to class in a social system. See VERTICAL GROUP.

vertical (occupational) segregation See OCCUPATIONAL SEGREGATION.

vertical sample A sample of people who are from different categories, such as people living in big cities, rural areas, towns, villages. See VERTICAL SAMPLING.

vertical sampling   A method that preestablishes the number of individuals to be taken from various levels of the population, for example, three annual income levels are established with a certain number of individuals in each. The quotas would depend on the proportion of each level; in percentage terms the first level might be 8%, the second level 68%, and the third 24%. See PROBABILITY SAMPLING, QUOTA SAMPLING.

vertical transmission   Mother-to-fetus transmission of infection; transplacental transmission. Compare HORIZONTAL TRANSMISSION.

vertigo (dizziness)   A sensation of whirling and dizziness, attributable usually to over-stimulation of the semicircular canal receptors. Can be due to organic disorder (such as Ménière's disease or brain tumor), psychological stress (conflicts, tensions, anxieties), or activities that disturb the labyrinthine mechanism in the inner ear (as in a roller coaster ride or flying in a small airplane).

very large scale integrated circuit (VLSIC)   A 1-megabit computer chip with a large number of circuits that work together.

very short-term memory   Memory storage that lasts only a few seconds.

vesania   (B. de Sauvages, K. Kahlbaum) Obsolete term for insanity, or mental disorders, especially those not known to be organic in origin, such as mania, melancholia, and paranoia.

vesical   Pertaining to or located in the bladder.

vesicle   A small, fluid-filled, saclike, internal structure, such as synaptic vesicles containing transmitter fluid.

vestibular adaptation   An effect of repeated suppression of the vestibular function observed in persons whose routine activities include frequent or repeated head movements, such as dancers and figure skaters. Thus, a skater who routinely performs rapid vertical spins to the left without dizziness may become disoriented trying a horizontal spin to the right.

vestibular apparatus   A set of three fluid-containing half-circle tubes located at the vestibule of each inner ear. Each canal is oriented longitudinal to one of the three planes of movement. The displacement of the fluid upon movement informs the brain as to the velocity and direction of the motion.

vestibular canal   See SCALA VESTIBULI.

vestibular hallucination   A false visual or cutaneous sensation due to an irritation or disorder of the vestibular apparatus.

vestibular membrane   **Reissner's membrane**

vestibular nerve   A part of the eighth cranial nerve that carries cochlear nerve fibers associated with the sense of balance or orientation in space. Most of the ascending fibers terminate in the oculomotor nuclei, although some probably communicate with neurons in the thalamus.

vestibular nuclei   The cell bodies of the neurons associated with the sense of balance located in the posterior part of the fourth ventricle. Fibers of the vestibular nuclei may join the eighth cranial nerve, the statoacoustic nerve, that enters the brainstem below the pons.

vestibular nystagmus   A nystagmus (rhythmic oscillation of the eyeballs) caused by stimulation of the vestibular apparatus.

vestibular-ocular fixation   Gaze fixation while the body or the surround moves, to deter dizziness. Used by spinning dancers (figure-skaters can rotate too fast to permit this).

vestibular proprioception   Awareness of position and movement of the body as mediated by structures of the inner ear.

vestibular receptors   Nerve cells associated with the sense of balance located in the cristae (crests) of the semicircular canals and the maculae (small different colored spots on tissues) of the utricle and saccule of the cochlea. They occur in two similar forms, a hair cell enclosed in a chalice-like nerve ending, and a cylindrical hair cell that synapses at its base with a nerve ending.

vestibular sacs   A pair of structures in the inner ear that contribute to a sense of upright body position.

vestibular sensations   The sense of balance as well as body movements mediated by movements of semicircular canals of the inner ear.

vestibular sense   Another name for labyrinthine sense, sense of equilibrium, static sense. See SENSE OF EQUILIBRIUM.

vestibular system   A network of receptors and nerve fibers that comprise the sense of balance. Sensory hair cells in compartments of the cochlea detect movements of the head through the shifting of fluid, granules, or other substances (depending upon the species) due to the force of inertia. The resulting impulses are transmitted to the cerebellum, spinal cord, and other structures. The response to stimulation of the vestibular receptors may require complex reflex actions intended to compensate for a loss of balance. The vestibular system may involve the ocular system (by nystagmus) and the digestive tract, (motion sicknesses such as sea sickness).

vestibule   1. A body cavity serving as the entrance to another body cavity. 2. A central cavity of the bony labyrinth of the middle ear, and the anatomical parts (utricle and saccule) of the membranous labyrinth containing receptors for the equilibrium sense.

vestibule school   Vocational phrase for the short-term intensive training program provided to new workers in a building or area separate from the area of production.

vestibulocochlear nerve   **acoustic nerve**

vestibulospinal system   One of the suprasegmental routes of reflex action, involving one or more segments of the spinal cord and connections of the sensory and motor nerves in brain areas. The vestibulospinal system has a facilitating effect on stretch reflexes. A lesion that decerebrates will affect the vestibulospinal system and result in a form of muscular rigidity.

vestige   1. A trace of something that once existed. 2. In biology, a degenerated, atrophied, or rudimentary structure that was more developed in earlier stages of the individual or species.

vestured genital apposition   Mutual genital-area pressing or rubbing between two clothed persons. See FROTTAGE, LAP DANCING.

vesuvius   Time-limited, cathartic, ritualized verbal hostility outburst by permission of attending spouse, friend, co-worker, or family member done under the direction of a counselor or therapist. Named for the Italian volcano that erupted.

V4 An area of the fringe of Brodmann's area 19 of the cortex. See BRODMANN'S AREA/CONVOLUTION.

VI See VARIABLE INTERVAL SCHEDULE OF REINFORCEMENT.

viable Capable of living. See VIABILITY.

viability 1. A medical determination that a fetus can survive outside the uterus. 2. See VIABLE. 3. By extension, a concept that seems promising or worth pursuing.

Viagra Trade name for sildenafil.

vibration The periodic motion of an object, such as a tuning fork, with a frequency usually measured in Hertz (Hz) once identified as cycles per second (cps).

vibration experience/sensation A sensation produced by contact with a pulsating, or rapidly vibrating, object that stimulates somatic receptors in the skin. Can be measured with a mechanical vibrator that can be adjusted for threshold frequencies of the effect. Also known as pallesthesia, palmesthesia, palmesthesis, vibration sense, vibratory sensation.

vibration rate The number of vibrations per second, once identified as cycles per second (cps) now called Hertz (Hz).

vibration receptors Nerve endings that respond to various ranges of vibration frequencies. Have been identified through histological studies as Pacinian corpuscles. They have been located at depths ranging from the skin surface to as deep as the membranes covering bones. Some receptors seem most sensitive to vibrations between 100 and 600 Hertz (cycles per second) while others react only to those below 100 Hertz.

vibration sensation/sense vibration experience

vibrational theory One of several explanations for the phenomenon of odor discrimination, based on a concept that variations in the structure and movement (vibrations) of molecules of aroma particles enable olfactory receptors to distinguish between substances. Other theories of odor discrimination relate to infrared, ultraviolet, or Raman-shift optical properties of odor particles.

vibrator 1. A device that makes vibrations. 2. An electrical hand-held device, often phallic shaped, used for sexual stimulation. See DILDO.

vibratory sensitivity Responsiveness to contact with a vibrating stimulus.

vibrotactile threshold Generally the fingertips' ability to detect a vibrating stimulus. Used to determine limits for occupational exposure to, and to quantify neuropathy resulting from, hand-transmitted vibration.

VIBS Abbreviation for Vocabulary, Information, Block-Design, Similarities. Subtests on the Wechsler-Bellevue Scale, scores on which supposedly did not decline as rapidly for age compared with other items.

vicarious Describing the substitution of one object or function for another, as in obtaining substitutive satisfaction by viewing the experiences of others in television programs.

vicarious brain process (hypothesis) A postulate that if there is damage to a part of the brain, another part of the brain will assume the function of the damaged part. Also known as alternative brain process.

vicarious conditioning A conditioned response occurring sympathetically by observing another's reaction to a particular stimulus (for example, a child finds a dead rat and screams, another child, witnessing the first child finding the dead rat and screaming, is vicariously conditioned).

vicarious enjoyment/pleasure Individuals finding pleasure indirectly by sharing feelings of success, etc., of others, from people close to them, especially their own children, and of anyone, including strangers, with whom they identify in some manner.

vicarious experiences Indirect wisdom gained through symbols. Knowledge obtained second-hand from books, television, word-of-mouth, observation, etc., rather than from personal experiences.

vicarious function A theory intended to explain the ability of humans and other animals to recover from effects of brain damage. However, many functions are not well localized in the brain, and many brain areas can assume a function previously performed by a brain area that has been damaged. See LOCALIZATION.

vicarious learning Any learning that is wholly a result of indirect experience and observation, as contrasted with learning based on direct experience and practice. A common context is children learning what to do by seeing the consequences of others' actions.

vicarious living A lifestyle in which personal behavior is identified with some hero or ideal, thereby avoiding a need for self-fulfillment through developing one's own personality.

vicarious punishment (A. Bandura) The observed punishment of the behavior of a model that decreases the probability of similar behavior in observers.

vicarious reinforcement (A. Bandura) The observed outcomes of the behavior of a model that increases the probability of similar behavior in observers.

vicarious traumatization Psychological stress associated with emergency rescue and medical workers. Also known as secondary posttraumatic stress disorder.

vicarious trial and error (VTE) (K. Muenzinger) 1. Mental trial and error; the mental testing-out of several possible responses before making a decision or committing to overt action, as in playing chess. 2. Behavior in which the organism substitutes partial responses, correct or incorrect, for completed, reinforced responses.

vice A significant or minor habitual mode of behavior at variance with social standards. A euphemism for illicit sexual behavior, as in vice squad.

vicious circle 1. (K. Horney) A behavioral loop in which basic anxiety and basic hostility serve to increase anxiety and hostility rather than to reduce them. 2. A chain reaction situation in which a person "solves" problems through unhealthy defensive reactions which serve to complicate the earlier problems, making them harder to solve. See INTERACTIONISM.

vicious circularity Fallacious reasoning that occurs when an answer is based on a question and the question is based on the answer, with no appeal to outside, independent information.

vicious habit (A. Meyer) Denoting persistent actions or behaviors resembling functional psychoses.

victim   1. A person who has been wronged feels powerless. 2. A person who is the subject of a rescue effort. 3. A person being persecuted.

victim blaming   (W. Ryan) A tendency to blame people for their misfortune. It emphasizes internal problems and locates the source of suffering within individuals, in large disregard for the role of social factors in the creation and perpetuation of human suffering and oppression.

victimization psychology   The study of victims. See VICTIM RECIDIVISM.

victimless crime   Behaviors considered criminal at various times and places even though there may be no victims, such as gambling or deviant sexual behavior (according to the law) between consenting adults (such as prostitution).

victim precipitation (hypothesis)   A postulate that a victim, usually of rape or incest, is partially responsible for it. See VICTIM BLAMING.

victim recidivism   A tendency of a victim of a crime to be involved repeatedly in the same type of situation. According to some surveys, at least 25% of such victims had previous experiences of the same general kind. Purportedly, reasons may include: masochistic tendencies, defiant or thoughtless behavior (such as walking alone at night), living in a risky environment, a timid manner that may attract criminals, a recording artifact, or possibly accident proneness. See ACCIDENT-PRONE PERSONALITY, TRAUMATOPHILIC DIATHESIS.

Victorianism   A set of cultural values associated with conservatism, politeness, and especially prudery, named for the reign of England's Queen Victoria from 1837–1901, in which these values prevailed.

video-related euphoria   (A. Dagher) Apparently pleasant feelings seen mainly in male adolescents after the extended playing of sophisticated video games, possibly due to the release of dopamine in the brain, yielding the same kind of pleasure as the use of addictive substances.

videotape methods   The use of videotaped recordings of persons' behavior in individual or group-therapy sessions for therapeutic, research, or teaching purposes. Among the areas of application are dance therapy, speech therapy, family therapy, group therapy, behavior therapy, mental-retardation programs, psychiatric-nursing instruction, and psychodrama.

Vienna Circle   1. A group of scientists and philosophers in the 1920s and early 1930s, such as Rudolf Carnap, Herbert Feigl, Philip Frank, and Otto Neurath, who took the position of logical positivism, namely, that all possible concepts should be translated into numerical terms. Sometimes known as verificationism. 2. A group in Vienna whose work influenced the operational definition concept of Percy Bridgman. Also known as Viennese Circle. See OPERATIONAL DEFINITION.

Vienna Psychoanalytic Society   See WEDNESDAY EVENING SOCIETY.

Vienna School   A group of practitioners of psychoanalysis who followed the theories of Sigmund Freud. Also known as Viennese School. See WEDNESDAY EVENING SOCIETY, WIENER SCHULE.

Vierordt's law   (K. von Vierordt) A principle that the more mobile a body part is, the smaller is the cutaneous two-point threshold, for example, the lips have a far greater ability to move than the skin of the back; hence the lips can discriminate a smaller two-point separation than the back.

VIE theory   valence-instrumentality-expectancy theory

Vieth-Müller circle   (G. U. Vieth & J. P. Müller) A hypothetical circle that passes through the fixation point and the optical centers of the lenses of the eyes and lies in the plane of regard.

vigilambulism   A form of unconsciousness that resembles somnambulism but occurs in the waking state with automatism.

vigilance   1. The alerting function of the nervous system. In conditioning studies, vigilance is represented by a sudden sharp spike of alertness or arousal following a positive or negative conditioned stimulus. The spike of alertness is sometimes identified as a stimulus-vigilance spike. 2. See GENERALIZED-ANXIETY DISORDER. 3. See SUSTAINED ATTENTION.

Vigotsky   See VYGOTSKY.

Vincent Curve/Method   A procedure to make learning curves of different individuals comparable. The total number of trials for each participant is divided into an equal number of fractional parts and performance is plotted within each part, permitting the learning curves to be averaged over a number of participants who took unequal numbers of trials to learn. Named after American psychologist Stella B. Vincent (1862–1951). Also known as Vincent Learning Curve.

Vineland Adaptive Behavior Scales (VABS)   (P. Harrison, S. Sparrow, D. Balla, & D. Cicchetti) Instruments used to evaluate children. Scales come in three versions: Two are administered through interviews of parents or car-givers, and the third is to be filled out by a classroom teacher. Results fall into four categories: Communication, Daily living skills, Socialization, and Motor Skills.

Vineland Social Maturity Scale   A test used in assessing the development of individuals, including possible mental deficiency, from infancy to 30 years of age. Persons acquainted with participants rate them on self-help, locomotion, communication, self-direction, socialization, and occupation. Named after the Vineland Training School for the mentally retarded by Edgar A. Doll, the author of the scale. See SOCIAL AGE, SOCIAL QUOTIENT.

violence   1. The expression of hostility and rage through physical force directed against persons or property. It is aggression in its most extreme and unacceptable form, and most investigators conclude it has no therapeutic justification, since there are more constructive and humane ways of expressing anger. It is usually socially justified in defensive wars or in combatting terrorism. 2. Harmful behavior without hostility or rage, as in a saying from ancient Greece "The boys throw stones and shout with glee and the frogs die in agony."

violinist's cramp   1. A symptom of occupational neurosis in which a musician experiences a psychogenic spasm of the arm or hand muscles and is unable to play an instrument. 2. A result of repetitive-strain injury (RSI). See WRITERS' CRAMP.

viraginity (female warrior—Latin) 1. In women, having pronounced masculine psychological qualities. 2. A tendency of a woman to act with socially prescribed manners of a man and to possess masculine qualities, including sexuality. Once used to describe a vituperative or scolding woman. Also known as virago.

viral hypothesis of schizophrenia The speculation that schizophrenia may be caused by a viral infection.

viral RNA (vRNA) Transferable nucleic acids presumably ancestral to the viruses.

virgin New, untouched. Usually indicating a female who has never had sexual intercourse. See VIRGINITY.

virginal anxiety Tension or uncertainty associated with a person's first sexual encounter.

virginal tribute See JUS PRIMAE NOCTIS.

virgin birth 1. A pregnancy from an unfertilized ovum. 2. The religious belief that a prophet was conceived without coitus and through the intervention of a god. 3. Parthenogenesis (common in some insect species). 4. Birth following pregnancy from artificial insemination.

virgin fear See PARTHENOPHOBIA.

virginity The state of a female who has not participated in sexual intercourse. Traditionally, a woman was assumed to possess virginity if the hymen was intact, but a non-intact hymen is not *prima facie* evidence of loss of virginity. Virginity was regarded as a sign of magical qualities in several cultures, for example, by the ancient Romans who assigned virgins to guard sacred objects and to deal with the gods. See DEFLORATION, WEDDING NIGHT.

virginity taboo A social prohibition against "defloration" of the woman (elimination of the intact hymen) before marriage. This common taboo may have various psychological and socioeconomic motivations, for instance, as a means of keeping women under the control of their father and husband, restricting their sexual activity, and insuring that they have not been impregnated.

virgo intacta Latin for virgin.

virile 1. Pertaining to males. 2. Masculine, manly, or macho. 3. Possessing masculine traits.

virile reflex/response Obsolete phrase for the erection of the penis elicited by visual, remote tactual, olfactory, or other stimuli.

virilism 1. A condition in which females develop masculine secondary sexual characteristics such as facial hair due to hyperactivity of the adrenal cortex. 2. The presence in a woman of sexual characteristics peculiar to men, such as absence of breasts and of menstruation. Also known as masculinization.

virility 1. The quality of being virile. 2. The composite features of normal primary male sexual characteristics. See MASCULINITY.

Virola A genus of South American trees used in Colombia, Brazil, and Venezuela as a source of hallucinogenic snuffs. An effect of the snuff is microscopia and an "ability to talk with the little people."

virtual reality The experience created by computer-generated, interactive, multimedia displays and clothing-like apparatus that give the impression of being in a real situation.

vis a tergo (a force from behind—Latin) 1. Extrinsic motivating factors. 2. The idea that the present is determined by the past.

Visatoner An electronic device that enables a blind person to read printed material. Moving the Visatoner over a line of print results in a series of tones that can be translated after extensive training by the user into patterns of letters of the alphabet. See OPTACON.

viscera Organs in any great body cavity, particularly the abdominal and thoracic cavities. See SPLANCHNIC.

visceral 1. Relating to the viscera. 2. Pertaining to feelings felt in the viscera (belly) known usually as "gut feelings" characterized by knowing that something is correct without necessarily knowing why. 3. Specific feelings such as dread, terror, fear, felt in the viscera, experienced while, for example, looking down from a high place and feeling "butterflies" in the stomach. 4. Relating to feelings of hunger that actually start in the ventral lateral nucleus of the hypothalamus (appestat).

visceral afferent fibers Sensory nerves that carry impulses from the viscera to the central nervous system.

visceral brain (P. D. MacLean) Refers to the concept of the limbic system serving as a kind of brain, where experiences are recorded and expressed as feelings. See PAPEZ-MACLEAN THEORY (OF EMOTION).

visceral drive A motive derived from a physiological need.

visceral epilepsy A type of epilepsy in which the symptoms are expressed through a visceral organ disturbance, such as in the gastrointestinal organs. The association purportedly involves lesions in brain areas from which visceral sensations arise.

visceral learning Mastering the regulation of personal visceral functions such as blood pressure or temperature, typically through the use of biofeedback techniques. Sometimes known as learned autonomic control.

visceral nervous system Rare phrase for the sympathetic nervous system.

visceral neurosis vegetative neurosis

visceral reactions Responses of visceral organs. These include stomach contractions, secretion of adrenaline, nausea and "butterflies."

visceral sensations organic sensations

visceral sense/sensitivity 1. A sense or sensation associated with functions of the viscera. 2. Susceptibility of the internal organs to stimulation. Parts of the alimentary canal are sensitive to pressure and pain, the esophagus and stomach to variations in temperature. See ORGANIC SENSE.

viscero(re)ceptor A nerve-receptor organ in one of the visceral organs.

viscerogenic ergs (R. B. Cattell) Instances in which an ergic factor can be shown to be due to physiological pressures.

viscerogenic need (H. A. Murray) A primary, physiological need that arises from organic processes and leads to physical gratification. Includes the need for air, water, food, sex, urination, and defecation.

viscerotonia In William Sheldon's constitutional theory of personality, the temperament or psychological component of the endomorph, being easy-going and fun-loving. A tendency toward love of comfort, love of food, relaxation and sociability. Also known as viscerotonic temperament. See ENDOMORPHIC (BODY) TYPE, SHELDON'S CONSTITUTIONAL THEORY OF PERSONALITY.

viscosity of libido In psychoanalytic theory, the fluidity of the libido, which moves slowly through phase after phase from infancy to maturity, and can remain fixed at, or return to, an earlier phase at slight provocation.

viscus Singular of viscera.

visibility coefficient See COEFFICIENT OF VISIBILITY.

visibility curve 1. A graphic representation of the relative visibility, or brilliance, of various wavelengths of radiant energy. 2. A graphic representation of the relative visibility of light of different hues, contrasts, luminance, or other properties. Also known as visibility-level curve.

visible 1. Able to be seen. 2. On hand, available, as in visible resources. 3. Constructed or depicted so as to show aspects that are normally hidden, as in a visible brain.

visible spectrum The range of that part of the electromagnetic spectrum whose radiations are usually visible, having wavelengths extending from about 3800 angstroms (one ten-billionth of a meter) for violet light to about 7800 angstroms for red light. Also known as visual spectrum.

visible speech A representation of vocal sound produced by converting sound waves into visible light patterns that can be photographed.

visile 1. Visual. 2. Relating to the type of mental imagery recalled most readily (that which a person has seen) in comparison to audile and motile imagery. 3. A class of individuals who use mainly the sense of sight, or whose imagery is mainly visual. Also known as visual type.

vision (V) 1. The sense of sight in which the eye is the receptor and the stimulus is radiant energy in wavelengths ranging from approximately 400 to 760 millimicrons. 2. That which is seen. 3. A visual hallucination. Types of vision include: ACHROMATIC, ALTERNATING, ANOMALOUS COLOR, BINOCULAR, CENTRAL, CHROMATIC, DISTANCE, DOUBLE, FACIAL, FOVEAL, INDIRECT, MESOPIC, MONOCULAR, PARACENTRAL, PATTERN, PERIMACULAR, PERIPHERAL, PHOTOPIC, RECURRENT, ROD, SCOTERYTHROUS, SCOTOPIC, SPATIAL, STEREOSCOPIC, SUPER-, TRIDIMENSIONAL, TUNNEL, TWILIGHT. See VISUAL PERCEPTION, VISUAL SYSTEM.

visionary rituals Refers to a group meeting of indigenous people usually directed by a shaman during which process there are ingestions of various roots or other substances such as henbane or epena that tend to generate hallucinatory episodes. See PEYOTE.

vision logic (K. Wilber) A postformal operational stage in which the relationship among multiple ideas is seen simultaneously, allowing a kind of network logic rather than only linear logic.

vision-test card/chart A series of letters, numerals, arbitrary characters, lines, or pictures, used to determine visual acuity and the range of distinct vision.

vision theory A systematic attempt to account for the various phenomena of visual perception in the known structure and functions of the visual organs. Also known as theory of vision. See COLOR VISION THEORIES.

Vipassana meditation A self-reflective East Indian practice, also referred to as mindfulness meditation. Said to reduce recidivism in prisoners.

vista response (V) In Rorschach test scoring, an inkblot response interpreting shading as depth.

visual Relating to vision.

visual accommodation See ACCOMMODATION (OF THE EYE).

visual acuity (V or VA) The degree of clarity, or sharpness, of visual perception. May be measured in one or more of several ways, such as the ability to detect tiny gaps between two parts of a figure, called the minimum separable method, or the ability to discern a fine dark line on a light background or a fine light line on a dark background. See ACUITY GRATING.

visual adaptation 1. An ability of the retina to adjust to either continued stimulation or a lack of stimulation. 2. Changes in the eye (primarily in the photoreceptors, partly in the iris) to adjust to light of high or low intensity.

visual agnosia An inability to recognize visual stimuli, such as objects. Observed in humans with brain lesions. A similar effect has been noted in experimental animals, who must touch objects to identify them. Also known as object blindness.

visual agraphia An impaired ability to write due to failure to recognize letters, numbers, or words. The condition results from lesions in the occipitoparietal areas.

visual allachesthesia A symptom of a parietal lobe lesion manifested as a transposition of visual images to an opposite point in space.

visual amnesia A loss of the ability to recognize familiar objects, printed words, or handwriting by sight, due to neurological disease or injury. See APHASIA.

visual angle An angle subtended by any object of vision at the nodal point of the eye.

visual aphasia An inability or difficulty in understanding written language. See ALEXIA.

visual apperception test A projective technique used with individuals 12 years of age and older. The participant is presented with plates of randomly drawn lines and is asked to color in the patterns or objects seen, and finish and title the drawing.

visual area In humans, a vision-specialized cortex located at the occipital pole of the brain, although other areas of the brain also participate in visual perception.

visual aura A type of sensory seizure in which flashes of light precede a grand mal seizure. The aura also may occur without the seizure.

visual axis A straight line that extends from the external fixation point through the nodal point of the eye to the area of the fovea.

visual capture/domination   A phenomenon by which visual information is more influential than information from the other senses. See VISILE.

visual cliff   (E. J. Gibson) A research apparatus for testing depth perception in human and animal infants. It is a structure topped by heavy glass. One-half of the surface below the glass is a short drop (the shallow side); the other half is a drop of several feet (the deep side). The infant subject is placed on a board in the middle of the structure and must crawl to one of the two sides to get off. Most children and animal participants refuse to crawl over to the "deep side," indicating the presence of depth perception at an early age.

visual closure   Ability to identify a familiar object from an incomplete visual presentation.

visual comfort probability   (S. K. Guth) In ergonomics, the percentage of people who would find a given level of glare acceptable.

visual constancies   Tendencies for visual perceptions, particularly regarding size, shape, and brightness, to stay constant even as visual sensations change.

visual convergence   Binocular cue in depth perception, effective at distances less than about 60 feet, that arise from inward turning (convergence) of both eyes for near objects and the divergence of the eyes for far objects, so that the axes meet at the point of fixation. See VERGENCE.

visual cortex   A region of the cerebral cortex in which retinal images are projected by impulses carried from the eyes by the optic nerves. Located in the occipital area of the brain. See BRAIN.

visual cycle   The system of metabolic phases of visual pigments, particularly rhodopsin, which during periods of vision goes through simultaneous and continuous cycles of breaking down into opsin and retinene and being reformed from the same substances. An equilibrium between the processes depends upon the intensity of the light stimulus, which energizes the breakdown of rhodopsin, and upon the oxidation energy for the reverse action.

visual depth   The distance of an object from the eye.

visual discrimination   An ability to distinguish shapes, patterns, hidden figures, or other images from similar objects that differ in subtle ways. Some species suffer a loss of this function after brain lesions and bump into objects that normally would be avoided.

visual-distortion test   An examination of a participant's psychological reaction to the visual distortion produced by wearing a pair of glasses with lenses of +6.00 or −6.00 diopters for several minutes. The distortion is assumed to cause a temporary breakdown of the synthetic and integrative functions of the ego, and is therefore a measure of ego strength.

visual dominance   If messages arrive simultaneously to the various senses, the visual message usually predominates.

visual domination   visual capture

visual evoked potential (VEP)   The potential evoked by a visual stimulus.

visual field   1. The total amount of the external world that is visible to the immobile eye at a given time. 2. The subjective, three-dimensional space in which objects, distances, and movements are perceived.

visual-field defect   Any of a number of types of partial or total blindness due to an interruption in the flow of visual impulses between the retina and the visual cortex. The interruption may be caused by a lesion before, after, or in the optic chiasm, in all or a part of the optic-radiation fibers, and involving tracts of one or both eyes. Each possible lesion produces a different visual-field defect.

visual fixation   The orientation of the eyes so that images fall on the foveas, in the central part of the retinas.

visual form   The total impression produced by the arrangement of the contour lines of an object or drawing.

visual hallucination   The false perception of visual images in the absence of external stimulation, such as seeing visions of angels, large animals, or insects crawling on the walls or on the skin. Most common in delirium tremens (alcohol-withdrawal delirium) and ingestion of hallucinogenic drugs. See FORMICATION, LILLIPUTIAN HALLUCINATION for examples.

visual hearing   Comprehension of another's speech, done especially by people with auditory deficits, by examination of the speaker's body movements, especially the face and most particularly the lips. See LIP-READING.

visual imagery   Francis Galton, the first psychologist to study images (contents of the "mind's eye") found a considerable variation in the visualizing ability of people. See BETTS' TEST OF VISUAL IMAGERY.

visual impairment   The partial or complete loss or absence of vision, due to disease, injury, or congenital defect. Visual impairment also may result from degenerative disorders, such as cataracts, glaucoma, refractive errors, and certain cases of astigmatism.

visual induction   The effect on the perception of one area of a visual field of stimulation of a different area, for example, a small yellow square may cause surrounding gray areas to appear blue.

visual inversion   Turning vision upside down (180 degrees) by use of special lenses. George Stratton wore such glasses for 8 days on one eye, the other being blindfolded, and by the end of the demonstration he was quite capable of visual-motor coordination in that condition. See PRISMATIC STIMULATION.

visualization   1. An ability to create a visual image in the mind. 2. In consumer psychology, a motivation-research technique that uses imaginary or fictitious situations or conditions to induce consumers to reveal the true reasons for their choice of products. Participants are asked what kind of person they think would buy the product.

visualization technique   A hypnotic method in which participants imagine a situation or activity other than their present one. Participants focus on details of the imagined scene either for the purpose of anxiety- or stress-reduction, or rehearsal for new behaviors, bringing into play all the senses.

visual learning   Training or conditioning that depends upon visual cues. The brain center for visual learning is concluded to be in the inferotemporal area where experiments indicate cortical cells are highly active in analyzing visual inputs. However, lesions in the center reduce but do not eliminate performance of this function, indicating that other cortical areas also are involved.

visual line   See VISUAL AXIS.

visually guided reaching   Attempts to touch or grasp as a response to seeing something, demonstrating coordination of the visual-motor systems.

visual masking   Negatively affecting a perception of a short visual stimulus by presenting another visual stimulus at the same time and place. See MASKING.

visual memory   The capacity to remember in the form of visual images what has previously been seen. See MOTOR MEMORY, VERBAL MEMORY.

visual memory span   The number of items (for example, letters, words, numbers, syllables) that can be recalled immediately after a visual presentation. See AUDITORY MEMORY SPAN.

visual-motor coordination   The ability to synchronize visual information with the movements of different parts of the body, as in learning to play volleyball.

visual motor gestalt test   See BENDER VISUAL MOTOR GESTALT TEST.

visual organization   Gestalt phrase for a visual field that appears to be organized and meaningful.

visual organization tests   A variety of instruments for measuring perceptual functioning, often based on ambiguous-figure tests originally designed for personality assessment. They include hidden figures, hidden words, optical illusions, masked stimuli, visual searching, and tracking.

visual perception   The visual observation and recognition of objects. The process is initiated by light reflected from the objects onto nerve receptors in the retina that transduce (to convert to another form) the nerve impulses and project them onto cortical cells, which in turn transmute (to change in form) them into images. Recognition is achieved by relating the viewed object to similar images stored in memory.

visual persistence   The hypothesized continuation of a particular pattern of neural activity in response to a visual stimulus.

visual phosphene   A visual sensation produced by a stimulus other than visual light. May occur with the eyes closed, and the stimulus may be pressure on the eyeball or an electrical current in the occipital or other visual area of the brain. The sensation appears as a flicker, and in the case of the electrical stimulation, the response varies with the frequency of the current. Electrical stimulation of the brain (ESB) usually uses direct current.

visual-placing reflex   The act of animals in placing their legs so as to reach a surface they can see. Animals that have undergone surgical decortication may lose their normally automatic response and fail to stretch their legs toward a visible surface.

visual process   Any change or operation which occurs in vision, or (in certain contexts) the operation of vision in general.

visual projection   The act of attributing a spatial object location to a visually perceived object.

visual purple   (H. Müller, F. Boll, W. F. Kühne) A substance found in the rods of the vertebrate retina, especially of the dark-adapted eye, which bleaches rapidly on exposure to light, and is assumed to be the substance underlying scotopic (twilight) vision. Also known as rhodopsin.

visual pursuit   ocular pursuit (movements)

visual recognition tests   A variety of instruments that measure perceptual functioning. They include tests for the recognition of faces, pictures, and figure and design.

visual-righting reflexes   The reflexes that automatically orient the head to the visual fixation point of the moment.

visual search   A type of test sometimes employed in diagnosis of visual-perception disorders. The participant is asked to seek a number or other item from a random display distributed over areas of both the left and right visual fields. Results are based on the relative amount of time required to find the items on the left and right sides of a midline.

visual search behavior   The way an individual scans or processes a visual scene.

visual-search perceptual disorder   A pathological condition exemplified by difficulty in locating a specific number from a random array on a board as a result of a lesion in one of the hemispheres. Normal persons perform better when the number sought is to the left of the midline. Patients with left hemisphere damage also do better when the number is on the left of the midline, whereas those with right-hemisphere damage perform better in the search when the number is to the right of the midline.

visual sequential memory   An ability to recall a sequence of visual stimuli such as letters, words, or pictures. See EIDETIC VISION.

visual space   The three-dimensional perspective of the visual field.

visual-spatial ability   The capacity and ability to comprehend and conceptualize visual representations and spatial relationships in learning and in the performance of such tasks as reading maps, navigating mazes, conceptualizing objects in space from different perspectives, and various geometric operations. Beginning in adolescence, males, on the average, show a definite superiority in visual-spatial ability; females, on the average, display superiority in verbal ability. See FROSTIG DEVELOPMENTAL TEST OF VISUAL PERCEPTION.

visual spectrum   Wavelengths of light accessible to humans, from about 380 millimicrons for violet light to 740 millimicrons for red light. Also known as visible spectrum.

visual stimulation   The stimulation by light of a frequency and intensity that will trigger a response by receptor cells in the retina. The stimulus is measured in photons (units of radiant energy) that are capable of altering the composition of visual pigments in the retinal cells.

visual system   A general name given to the network of receptors and nerve cells and fibers that enable organisms to perceive the external environment through the medium of electromagnetic energy. The system includes nerve cells and fibers in the retina, between the retina and the visual cortex, and within the visual cortex where images from the eyes are projected and analyzed. See EYE STRUCTURE for an illustration.

visual task evaluator (H. Blackwell) A contrast-reducing visibility meter; it superimposes a field of uniform, variable luminance (the veiling field) over the view of the target to measure its visibility as its luminance is decreased and that of the veiling field is increased.

visual texture Organized detail in the visual field, the fine detail diminishing with distance and larger objects becoming smaller.

visual thresholds The minimal level of stimulation of light that will alert a person to the change in illumination.

visual tracking ocular pursuit (movements)

visual type A person who tends to think in visual terms and whose imagery is predominantly visual. Compare AUDILE TYPE.

visual yellow A yellow substance formed in the retina under certain circumstances when visual purple is bleached by the action of light. See VISUAL PURPLE.

visuoconstruction defect A disorder associated with a parietal-lobe dysfunction. Characterized by difficulty in assembling the various parts of an object into a complete structure. See CONSTRUCTIONAL APRAXIA.

visuographic tests Instruments that assess perceptual processes and motor responses, mainly by measuring copying and free drawing ability. Most common examples are the Bender-Gestalt and the Draw-a-Person Tests.

visuo-motor behavior rehearsal In sport psychology, a motor-performance enhancement program that integrates relaxation training and imagery.

visuomotor theory A model of the development of the motor system and its interaction with learning. The theory focuses on the dependence of each successive state of development upon an earlier level.

visuospatial agnosia A disorder of spatial orientation, which may be tested by such techniques as having the participant point to objects or other stimuli located in different parts of the participant's visual fields.

visuo-spatial scratchpad A major system in the working memory model, assumed to be responsible for establishing and manipulating visuo-spatial images. Also known as visuo-spatial sketchpad. See IMMEDIATE MEMORY.

vital 1. Pertaining to life. 2. Of essential importance.

vital capacity The total volume of air that can be voluntarily moved in one breath, from full inspiration to maximum expiration, or vice versa. Also known as forced vital capacity.

vital energy A creative vital force. See VITALISM.

vital fluids (theory) Refers to the belief that the loss of seminal fluid drains vital fluids from the body, the brain, or both, depriving a man of strength.

vital index 1. Vital capacity divided by weight, both taken in metrics. 2. The ratio of births to deaths during a given time period for a given population.

vitalism 1. The vital dimension of the life form, in the formation theory of personality, representing the formative influence of the organism and its impulses on the life form of the person. 2. A doctrine positing that the functions of living organisms are determined, at least in part, by an inorganic force or principle. The biologist Hans Driesch was the chief exponent of this view, holding that life processes are autonomous and purposive, and that potentialities for growth and development are realized through an agent to which he applied Aristotle's "entelechy" which means full reality in Greek. The philosopher Henri Bergson called this creative, vital force the *elan vital*. See FORMATION, FORMATIVE ATTACHMENT.

vitality 1. The property or characteristic of being alive or of exercising the organic functions. 2. Ability of an organism to maintain its organic existence.

vital signs The usual preliminary testing made during medical attention of a person's temperature, pulse rate and blood pressure.

vital statistics Data, usually compiled by a government agency or insurance firm, on the rates of births, deaths, and disease in a population. See BIOSTATISTICS.

vitamin (C. Funk) An organic substance generally found in food sources and essential in minute quantities for normal growth and health maintenance. A vitamin may function as a coenzyme, aiding in the various metabolic steps of utilization of carbohydrates, fats, and proteins. Lack of certain foods in the diet can result in diseases due to a deficiency of such substances. See BERI-BERI, PELLAGRA, PERNICIOUS ANEMIA.

vitamin-A toxicity A rare pathologic condition caused by excessive intake of vitamin A. Usually characterized by drowsiness, irritability, headache, and vomiting, followed by skin peeling and hair loss. Children may suffer from intracranial pressure. See HYPERVITAMINOSES.

vitamin deficiency Lack of a vitamin needed for normal body-system functions. Several B vitamins, including thiamine and niacin, are important for normal metabolism of neurons. A deficiency of niacin may result in severe disorders including pellagra and a form of dementia; a deficiency of thiamine (associated with excessive alcohol consumption) may result in beriberi. Other vitamins, such as A and D, may affect mental functions indirectly through a debilitating effect that makes it difficult to perform learning tasks. See BERIBERI, PELLAGRA, PERNICIOUS ANEMIA.

vitamin-D toxicity A rare pathologic condition caused by excessive intake of vitamin D characterized by nervousness, weakness, anorexia, nausea, and kidney disorders. See HYPERVITAMINOSES.

vitamin model (of employee satisfaction) (P. B. Warr) Specifies different attributes of work that need to be present in at least minimal amounts to produce a satisfied employee.

vivid data Novel, arresting, and/or unexpected perceptual stimuli that dominate a person's perceptual attention.

vitreous (humor) A transparent, jelly-like mass that fills the eyeball from the concave surface of the retina as far forward as the lens. Also known as vitreous body. See EYE STRUCTURE, HUMOR.

vivisection In general, refers to any form of animal experimentation, particularly if it causes distress or suffering to the animal subject. More specifically, the cutting or dissection of a live animal for research purposes. See ANIMAL RIGHTS.

VLSIC very large scale integrated circuit(s)

VMH See VENTROMEDIAL NUCLEUS OF THE HYPOTHALAMUS.

VNA Visiting Nurse Association

vocabulary growth Linguistic development as measured by the increase in the child's vocabulary. Recognition vocabulary increases from about 20 words at 15 months to 270 at two years, 900 at three, 1,500 at four, 2,000 at five. By the end of elementary school, the child recognizes up to 20,000 words; by the end of high school, a few students recognize up to 80,000; and by the end of four-year college, some students recognize 250,000 or more. The Old Testament has about 6,000 different words; and Shakespeare's vocabulary, which is considered huge, is "limited" to 20,000. See ACTIVE VOCABULARY, PASSIVE VOCABULARY.

vocabulary test 1. An examination designed to determine the number and level of words that a participant can use (active vocabulary) or understand (passive vocabulary). 2. A trial in which a standard list of words is presented to a participant, who is asked to define them or indicate which words of a limited choice are either synonyms or antonyms to the key word, for example, "leap" means: fall, drop, jump, tree?

vocabulary word A word that has a full lexical or semantic meaning, such as a noun, verb, or adjective. Also known as content word, contentive, full word, lexical word, notional word, open-class word, semanteme.

vocal cords A set of ligaments in the larynx that produce sounds by vibrating when respiratory air passes through them.

vocal-image voice The audible speech patterns that have been electronically transformed into visual patterns which may be read by the hearing impaired.

vocalization The use of the voice in uttering sounds without words, as in babbling, screaming, barking, and singing arpeggios or scales in music practice.

vocal reaction time Response latency, or period from the presentation of a stimulus to the beginning of a vocalized response. Also known as speech reaction time, speech response time, vocal response time.

vocal register The tonal or pitch range of an individual's voice.

vocation That form of productive activity in which a person engages as a means of subsistence. See CAREER.

vocational adjustment The degree to which individuals make use of their abilities in obtaining the kind of work or career best suited to their desires, opportunities, and talents. Phrase emphasizes the relations between personal aptitudes, interests, and achievement, whereas occupational adjustment focuses on the relationship between the individual and objective work conditions. See OCCUPATIONAL ADJUSTMENT, VOCATIONAL CHOICE.

vocational appraisal The prediction by a vocational counselor of a client's potential for success and fulfillment in a particular occupation. Based on the counselor's understanding of occupational opportunities considered in terms of the client's personality, intelligence, abilities, and interests as revealed in interviews and tests.

vocational-aptitude test A task designed to assess the ability, interest, personality, and other factors deemed essential for success in a particular occupation.

vocational choice A process that may begin in adolescence or even before, with an examination of individual interests, strengths, and limitations in light of their meaning within a given vocational context. A mature vocational choice involves sufficient self-understanding to correctly match up personal interests and resources to the perceived requirements and conditions that obtain in a specific vocation or profession. See VOCATIONAL ADJUSTMENT.

vocational counseling The process of counseling an individual on job selection, where and how to seek employment, adjustment to the job, and human relations or other personal problems affecting job satisfaction and job performance.

vocational education A training program designed to help a person meet the necessary qualifications for a particular job or profession.

vocational evaluation work evaluation

vocational guidance (F. Parsons) The process of assisting a person, by certain systematized procedures, to choose a vocation, prepare for it, enter it, and make progress in it. The process of helping a person choose an appropriate vocation through such means as: (a) depth interviews; (b) administration of aptitude, interest, and personality tests; and (c) discussion of the nature and requirements of specific types of work in which the person expresses an interest.

vocational maladjustment Broad phrase referring to inadequate job performance or a lack of personal satisfaction with or fulfillment in a job or profession. May result if a person's ability level is not matched to the job or if a variety of social or psychological factors inhibit harmonious functioning on the job, for example, insufficient compensation or benefits, or friction with superiors or fellow workers.

vocational maturity (D. Super) An index of the congruence between personal vocational behaviors and societal expectations. Varies by stage of the occupational life cycle.

vocational rehabilitation The process of developing or restoring the productivity of persons with mental or physical disabilities through vocational guidance, testing, training, and adjustment to the work situation. Includes development of skills that have been lost or neglected, and helps a person find employment either in the business or industrial world or in a sheltered workshop. An effective program enables the person with the disability to become a contributing member of society and promotes psychological adjustment by enhancing self-esteem and morale.

vocational selection 1. The process of choosing from a group of applicants for a vocation those most likely to succeed in that vocation. 2. The process of selecting the people best fitted to do a job in terms of probability for success. Selection of such people is done through aptitude tests and interviews.

vocational services Vocational testing, guidance, counseling, training, and assistance in finding employment, as provided by a school, hospital, clinic, or rehabilitation center.

vocational training An organized program of instruction designed to equip a person with the requisite skills for placement in specific jobs or trades. See VOCATIONAL REHABILITATION.

Vogt's German neurologist, Oskar Vogt (1870–1959), and wife, French psychiatrist, Cécile Vogt (1875–1962). They extensively mapped cortical areas, using one of their student's (Korbidian Brodmanns) divisions of the brain as a guide. See ALLOCORTEX, AUTOGENIC THERAPY, CYTOARCHITECTONICS, ISOCORTEX, JUXTALLOCORTEX, SPIELMEYER-VOGT DISEASE.

voice The sound made by passing air out through the larynx and tensing the vocal cords.

voice box A common name for the larynx.

voice change Deepening of a boy's voice due to enlargement of the larynx associated with puberty.

voice disorders Phonatory voice deviations affecting pitch, loudness, and quality of voice.

voiced or voiceless stop Two kinds of plosives (speech sounds made by building pressure in the air tract and suddenly releasing it). A voiced stop, for example, /b/, /d/, /g/, or voiceless stop, for example, /p/, /t/, /k/. See ALVEOLAR, LABIAL, PLOSIVE.

voiced sound In phonetics, a sound produced by means of vocal-cord vibrations (for example, /b/, /v/, /z/), as opposed to a voiceless sound. Also known as sonant.

voice-key A response key operated by sound waves of the human voice.

voiceless sound In phonetics, a sound produced without vocal-cord vibrations (for example, /p/, /t/, /f/), as opposed to a voiced sound. Also known as surd.

voice-onset time (VOT) In linguistics, the time between the release of air in voicing a consonant and the onset of the vibrations of the vocal cords in the voicing of the following vowel.

voiceprint As true of a fingerprint, the distinctive pattern of voice characteristics of a person as portrayed on the screen of a spectrograph (an instrument that converts sound waves into visible patterns). The visual plot is used to demonstrate errors in speech, identify people, etc. Voice printings have been used in some courts of law to identify criminals, but its acceptance as a forensic tool seems to lie between fingerprinting or DNA (deoxyribonucleic acid) analysis (both well accepted), and polygraphing (not well accepted). Also known as spectrograph analysis. See SPECTROGRAPH.

voice quality A characteristic of a person's speech for example, plaintive, husky, falsetto. See PARALINGUISTIC FEATURES.

voice-recognition systems Computer systems used to analyze distinctive features of a human voice. See ARTIFICIAL INTELLIGENCE, EXPERT SYSTEMS, VOICEPRINT.

voices Hallucination of talk, especially of derogatory or accusatory or other remarks concerning the person. Usually a sign of mental disorder. Also known as hearing voices.

voice sounds Noises made by the mouth and adjoining structures, generated by some organisms such as humans and other mammals. In humans, messages may be conveyed via various sounds other than speech especially if combined with various facial expressions and gestures.

voice-stress analyzer An instrument that records alterations in the voice undetectable to the human ear and that occur automatically when a person is under stress. Used in lie detection.

voice therapist A specialist who is knowledgeable in the areas of physiology and pathology of voice production and concerned with diagnosis and remediation of voice disorders. The specialist is often part of a team including an otolaryngologist (ear and throat specialist), internist, neuropsychiatrist, psychologist, and audiologist.

voice timbre See TIMBRE.

void-fear See KENOPHOBIA.

vol A unit of subjective loudness, the apparent volume of a 1000-Hz, 40-dB tone. See DECIBEL.

volar Pertaining to or located in the palm of the hand or the sole of the foot.

volatile-chemical inhalation The sniffing of volatile chemicals for their intoxicating effects. Substances include paint thinners, methyl alcohol, spray-can freons, lacquer thinners, plastic-glue solvents, gasoline, and kerosene. The fumes are absorbed directly into the bloodstream through the lungs and can produce immediate euphoria. Most volatile solvents are fat soluble and are retained in body tissues for long periods of time instead of being rapidly metabolized. They damage parts of the cell membranes of various relatively fatty tissues, leading to liver, nerve, and brain damage. Also called huffing. See INHALANT-RELATED DISORDERS.

volition 1. Will, or the act of willing. 2. Process of choosing a course of action voluntarily or without direct external influence. See DERAILMENT OF VOLITION.

volitional tremor Any trembling of the body or a part of the body, for example, the hands that occurs during voluntary movements. See TREMOR.

Volkerpsychologie Wilhelm Wundt's German term for Folk Psychology. See CULTURAL PSYCHOLOGY.

volley (fire) 1. Synchronous discharge, especially the case in which rhythmic series of pulsations of like frequency and in phase with one another are transmitted simultaneously along the different fibers of a nerve. 2. Brief succession of nerve pulsations, of muscular twitches, etc.

volley principle/theory A variant of the alternation-of-response theory in which individual nerve fibers respond to one stimulus in a burst of stimuli whereas others in the group respond to the second, third, or Nth stimulus. The result is that successive volleys of impulses are fired to match the frequency of the stimulus input and yet no single fiber is required to respond to each of the individual stimuli in the group. See HEARING THEORIES, TELEPHONE THEORY.

volley theory of hearing (E. G. Wever & C. W. Bray) An explanation of hearing based on the concept that fibers in the basilar membrane of the inner ear react in synchronized volleys to permit the brain to appreciate complex sounds since individual fibers cannot achieve the results singly.

volometer An early instrument reputed to measure "will, determination, persistence." Participants tried to stand as long as possible with their heels raised one-quarter inch off the floor. When their heels touched the floor a buzzer sounded and the time was noted.

volt (v or V) (A. Volta) The SI (metric system) unit of electromotive force necessary to produce a current of one ampere through a resistance of one ohm.

voltage-activated gate Barrier in the neuronal membrane that opens as it depolarizes.

voltmeter An instrument for measuring electromotive force in volts.

volubility Excessive, uncontrollable talkativeness. See LOGORRHEA.

volume (V) 1. Space occupied by matter, normally expressed in science in metric units. See CAPACITY (meaning 2). 2. Generally, loudness. See DECIBEL. 3. In psychophysics, the quantity of "space" a stimulus is judged to occupy. For example, in auditory stimuli high-pitched tones are perceived as "small" or "thin"; low-pitched tones as "large" or "full." The unit for volume is the vol. See DECIBEL, VOL.

volume hypothesis A postulate that auditory experiences possess a metaphorical attribute called volume, measured in terms of loudness (see DECIBEL) or fullness of sensory experience which varies from large to small.

volumetric thirst A need to drink that occurs because of the depletion of extracellular fluid such as caused by vomiting, diarrhea or bleeding.

voluntarism A doctrine positing that volition is the fundamental mental process and only voluntary actions can change the course of events. Usually contrasted with determinism. See FREE WILL.

voluntary Pertaining to the will or its activity.

voluntary activity Action preceded by the idea and desire of accomplishing a certain result.

voluntary admission In psychiatry, the admission of a person to a mental hospital or unit at the person's request. Also known as voluntary commitment/hospitalization.

voluntary agencies and organizations Nonprofit groups supported in whole or in part by public contributions and devoted to the amelioration of public-health or social-welfare problems.

voluntary ataxia An effect of damage to the nerve tracts carrying kinesthetic impulses to the brain and marked by a lack of control over movement of the limbs. Because of ineffective restraint on the movements, through absence of feedback signals, such people tend to make overextended actions such as reaching far beyond an object they are attempting to grasp.

voluntary behavior Any act, conduct, or function in which a deliberate action is performed by an individual. Determined by the interaction of sensory and central processes. Compare INVOLUNTARY BEHAVIOR, REFLEXIVE BEHAVIOR.

voluntary commitment voluntary admission

voluntary control The regulation of activities such as movements, impulses, or affects by conscious intention.

voluntary movement A motion made by choice or intention, in contrast to an automatic one such as a reflex.

voluntary muscle A muscle over which an organism has control, such as one in the tongue, in contrast to an involuntary muscle, such as the heart. Also known as skeletal muscle.

voluntary process Activity marked by intention and volition, that is, consciously desired, chosen, planned, regulated, and under cortical control, in contrast to a reflex action or involuntary behavior. See VOLUNTARY RESPONSE.

voluntary response A deliberately chosen reaction to a stimulus that may have required a complex coordination of excitatory and inhibitory impulses with feedback signals from visual and other systems.

voluntary simplicity In Asian philosophy, the deliberate decision to live simply and to deemphasize material goods.

volunteer In the health field, a person who contributes services without compensation, to a hospital, social agency, rehabilitation center, or nursing home.

volunteer bias Error resulting from differences between volunteers and nonvolunteers participanting in attitudes or personality in any kind of research. Volunteers may have stronger motivation, may want more excitement, may be seeking self-understanding, etc., and these attributes may in part account for their differential responses.

vomeronasal system A set of sensory receptors located near the olfactory receptors and particularly sensitive to pheromones. Prominent in most mammals. See JACOBSON'S ORGAN, PHEROMONES, HUMAN PHEROMONES.

vomiting Ejecting the contents of the stomach through the mouth. See NERVOUS VOMITING.

vomiting center The lower central region in the medulla oblongata which mediates the vomiting reflex.

von Baer See BAER.

von Bekesy See BÉKÉSY.

von Bertalanffy See BERTALANFFY.

von Domarus principle An explanation of schizophrenic thinking developed by Eilhard von Domarus which proposes that patients with schizophrenia perceive two things as identical merely because they have identical predicates or properties. This principle appears to be contradicted by the paranoid delusion, in which individuals are perceived as impostors of themselves, such as in Cotard's syndrome.

von Ehrenfels　　See EHRENFELS.

von Frey　　See FREY.

von Frisch　　See FRISCH.

von Gerlach　　See GERLACH.

von Goethe　　See GOETHE.

von Gudden　　See GUDDEN.

von Haller　　See HALLER.

von Hartmann　　See HARTMANN.

von Helmholtz　　See HELMHOLTZ.

von Kölliker　　See KÖLLIKER.

von Krafft-Ebing　　See KRAFFT-EBING.

von Kries　　See KRIES.

von Leibniz　　See LEIBNIZ.

von Marxow　　See MARXOW.

von Meduna　　See MEDUNA.

von Meinong　　See MEINONG.

von Neumann　　See NEUMANN.

von Recklinghausen　　See RECKLINGHAUSEN.

von Restorff　　See RESTORFF.

von Vierordt　　See VIERORDT.

voodoo death　　A culture-specific syndrome observed in societies in many parts of the world, especially Haiti. A person, usually one who has transgressed a taboo, is cursed by a medicine man. The person withdraws to a hut, refuses to speak or eat, and dies within a few days. Death is thought to occur due to wound shock, heart arrhythmia, adrenaline shock, vagal-nerve overstimulation, anorexia, poisoning, and increased susceptibility to serious disease due to "giving up." See CURSING MAGIC, MAGICAL THINKING, PSYCHIC SUICIDE.

voodoo(ism)　　A polytheistic religion, practiced chiefly in the West Indies, in which the tradition of African cults and magic is intermingled with rites derived from Catholicism. Also known as *vodun*. See FAITH HEALING, VOODOO DEATH.

Vorstellung　　German term similar to idea.

VOT　　voice-onset time

voyeur　　A person who obtains sexual gratification from watching nudes or others engaged in sexual acts. Also known as a peeping Tom. See VOYEURISM.

voyeurism　　A psychosexual disorder characterized by secretly watching others undressing or having sex and being sexually aroused by doing so. Sometimes known as scopophilia. See INSPECTIONISM, PEEPING TOMISM.

voyeuse　　A female voyeur.

VR　　See VARIABLE RATIO SCHEDULE OF REINFORCEMENT.

vRNA　　See VIRAL RNA.

Vroom-Yeton model (of leadership)　　(V. H. Vroom & P. W. Yetton) A prescriptive, cognitive model that indicates the best supervisory technique to use in a given situation. Uses a decision tree, focuses on group decision-making, covers techniques from autocratic through consultative to democratic. Also known as normative model.

VTE　　See VICARIOUS TRIAL AND ERROR.

vulnerability　　1. Generally, susceptibility to being hurt. 2. (S. Haynes) The degree to which an individual is susceptible to developing a behavior disorder given the occurrence of particular causal events. A "vulnerable" person is one with a relatively high probability of developing a disorder when exposed to specific conditions.

vulnerability factor　　A variable that affects the probability of a behavior disorder, given the occurrence of triggering variables. A risk factor.

vulnerable-child syndrome　　A disturbance in psychosocial development observed in children who have recovered from a serious illness but are still overly protected by their parents.

vulva　　External female genitals, comprising mons veneris, labia majora and minora, clitoris, Bartholin's glands, and urethral and vaginal orifices. Plural is vulvae. Also known as pudendum, vestibule. (Named for a Scandinavian goddess.)

vulval orgasm　　Sexual climax in which certain pelvic muscles contract, elevating the uterus so as to increase the area for the seminal pool ("tenting"), thus facilitating fertilization.

Vvedenskii　　See WEDENSKY.

Vygotsky blocks　　Thirty-two wooden blocks of varying colors, sizes, weights, and shapes with one of four nonsense words (sometimes a number) on the underside. Used by Lev Vygotsky (who credited their invention to L. S. Sakharov) and other Russian psychologists in research on cognition through block-sorting tasks in the Vygotsky Test. See HANFMANN-KASANIN CONCEPT FORMATION TEST.

Vygotsky-Sakharov method　　(L. S. Vygotsky & L. S. Sakharov) A technique for the practical investigation of concept formation.

Vygotsky's theory　　The following concepts are important for understanding Lev Vygotsky's theory: See HIGHER MENTAL PROCESSES, INNER LANGUAGE/SPEECH, PURE MEANING, VERBAL THOUGHT, VYGOTSKY BLOCKS, VYGOTSKY-SAKHAROV METHOD, VYGOTSKY TEST.

Vygotsky Test　　(L. S. Vygotsky) A measuring instrument devised to study the process of thinking and concept formation and to detect thought disturbances and impaired ability to think abstractly. The participant is asked to sort and classify blocks of different sizes, shapes, and colors, into categories, such as green-flat-circular. See HANFMANN-KASANIN CONCEPT FORMATION TEST, VYGOTSKY BLOCKS.

W

w   1. A weight in statistics. 2. In Rorschach test scoring, a symbol for a response that uses almost all the card. 3. weight (also abbreviated **W**). 4. Symbol for weight of food incentive. 5. See WILL FACTOR.

W   1. Weber fraction. 2. weight (also abbreviated **w**). 3. See WILL FACTOR. 4. See COEFFICIENT OF CONCORDANCE. 5. In Rorschach test scoring, a symbol for the whole blot seen as a single unit. 6. See WORD FLUENCY. 7. Watt. 8. Symbol for work involved in response.

WAB   Western Aphasia Battery

Wada test   (J. Wada) A test of speech lateralization in which sodium Amytal is injected into the carotid artery on one side to anesthetize the hemisphere on the injected side. Evidence of dysphasia is shown if the side injected is dominant for language. Both sides are sometimes tested on different days. (Speech representation generally is in the left hemisphere for right-handed persons.)

wage compression   A narrowing of the ratios of the compensation paid across positions. Also known as pay compression.

wage-labor   Salaried employment. Term is sometimes used to emphasize the weak bargaining position of employees who have nothing to offer except their labor.

WAIS   Wechsler Adult Intelligence Scale, see WECHSLER ADULT INTELLIGENCE SCALE-REVISED.

WAIS-R   Wechsler Adult Intelligence Scale-Revised

WAIS-III   See WECHSLER ADULT INTELLIGENT SCALE-THIRD EDITION.

waist-to-hip ratio   A measure of obesity in the human; ratios above 0.9 are associated with increased risk of death from various illnesses.

waiting-list control group   In research, a group designed to control for threats to internal validity of an experiment. After experimental participants (human or animal) receive the intervention, this control group receives the intervention.

waitress's dilemma   The memory problem faced by servers who have to recall (from large group of customers ordering multi-course meals) who ordered what, without making full or any notes. The solution includes meaningful encoding of the orders based on existing knowledge, attaching retrieval cues to some specified structure, and practice.

wakanda   (the mysterious one—Sioux) Denoting an impersonal, all-pervading supreme power in the universe.

wakefulness   1. Awareness of surroundings coupled with an ability to communicate with others or to understand what is being communicated by others. See CONSCIOUSNESS. 2. A relaxed state characterized by electroencephalographic (EEG) alpha waves that border on signs of drowsiness. See SLEEP CHARACTERISTICS. 3. Inability to sleep. See INSOMNIA.

wakefulness of choice   In a sleep cycle, the pattern of waking that results from training or learning.

wakefulness of necessity   In a sleep cycle, the pattern of waking that results from physical needs or discomfort.

waking center   An area of the posterior hypothalamus which may extend through the system to the brainstem. Laboratory animals with lesions of the posterior hypothalamus, and humans suffering tumors or inflammations in that structure, develop abnormal tendencies to sleep. A similar effect results from lesions in the reticular activating system.

waking dream   A clear hallucinatory state that occurs either just before falling asleep, or more likely on awakening. Also known as hypnogogic imagery.

waking hypnosis   (H. Wells) Hypnosis induced without reference to sleep by having the participants fix their attention on an object and close their eyes tightly. Wells found that the waking method has a distinct advantage over the sleeping method; it is easier to learn, easier to apply, appears less occult, and a higher percentage of participants can be hypnotized.

waking state   See W-STATE.

Walden II   (B. F. Skinner) A fictional description of an ideal society based on the principles of operant conditioning. See HUMANISTIC COMMUNITARIAN SOCIALISM, UTOPIA.

Wald-Wolfowitz runs test   (A. Wald & J. Wolfowitz) A large-sample nonparametric test of randomness based upon serial covariance. Measures whether two data samples were derived from a single population by analyzing the pattern of runs. See RUNS TEST.

walk-in clinic   A hospital or stand-alone clinic in which diagnostic or therapeutic service is available without an appointment.

walk-through performance testing (WTPT)   (J. W. Hedge & M. S. Teachout) In employment interviewing, job applicants describe in detail how they would perform the job sought, after which the description is checked against a checklist of actions, standards, and other correlates of successful job performance.

Wallerian degeneration (A. Waller) Deterioration of the myelin sheath and axis cylinder from the point of injury of a peripheral sensory or motor nerve toward the cell body, regenerating if the Schwann cell neurilemma is left intact. See WALLER'S LAW.

Waller's law A theory that if posterior roots of the spinal cord are cut on the central side of the ganglia, those portions of the (cut) nerves which lie within the spinal cord degenerate, whereas the peripheral portions of the same nerves (not being severed from the ganglia) do not degenerate. Named after British physiologist Augustus V. Waller (1816–1870).

wall-eye 1. See EXOTROPIA. 2. Lack of parallelism of the visual axes of the eyes, in which they are turned away from each other. Having the eyes point outward (toward the temples), rather than pointing in parallel, the opposite of cross-eyed. See DIVERGENCE, GRIEG'S DISEASE. Sometimes spelled as one word or without the hyphen.

waltzers dancing mouse

wandering attention A condition of being easily distracted by almost any external stimulus. See DRIFTING ATTENTION.

wandering behavior Walking aimlessly about as in a fugue, with no destination or purpose, usually due to impairment of some kind, such as alcohol abuse, psychological trauma, or brain damage.

wandering impulse 1. A love to wander, or roam. 2. The propensity to leave home and travel or change surroundings, or to move frequently from one locality to another. See DROMOMANIA, NOMADISM. 3. A phenomenon noted in people suffering from senility, moving without direction in a state of disorientation. Also known as wanderlust. See FUGUE, NOMADISM.

wandering speech Inability to keep to the topic when speaking. Seen in some mental disorders.

wandering uterus Pseudomedical phrase for a uterus in an allegedly abnormal position, causing dysmenorrhea, dyspareunia, backache, etc. Possibly related to folklore of a wandering uterus from the time of Plato and Hippocrates. Also called tipped uterus.

Wandervogel movement A 1920s German youth naturalism movement.

want 1. A desire for something that if denied will not harm the person who desires it. See NEED VS WANT. 2. In cognitive psychology, the subjective experience of desire, a major motivational force for humans and animals. See CONATION.

Ward Atmosphere Scale (R. Moos) A scale used in the assessment of hospital ward circumstances including evaluation of staff support, patient autonomy, and patient involvement in hospital affairs.

warehousing Common term for confining patients with mental disorders to large institutions for long-term, often lifetime, custodial care.

warlock A male who practices sorcery. Also known as a wizard. See WITCHCRAFT.

warm-blooded animals Common name for homeotherms.

warm fuzzy Slang for a feeling of support, nurturing, and caring.

warming up (period) warm-up period

warm sensation Warmth.

warm spot Any of the minute, pointlike spots on the skin or mucous membrane that are particularly sensitive to warm stimuli. Also known as warmth spot. Compare COLD SPOT.

warm stimulus A stimulus that gives rise to a sensation of warmth, usually an object touching the skin that is warmer than the skin itself.

warmth (sensation) The quality of sensation due normally to stimulation by some object whose temperature is higher than the temperature of the skin or other part stimulated. Also known as warm sensation.

warmth spot warm spot

warm-up 1. In a group situation, a procedure or process that induces individuals or groups to relax so that they become more receptive and ready to participate in the group's activity. Important in group psychotherapy and psychodrama. 2. Preparation for physical and vocal activities.

warm-up effects In learning theory, the influence of preparation or "set" upon transfer (introduced by Mosso in 1906) and retention (reported by R. B. Ammons and by A. L. Irion in the 1940s).

warm-up period The beginning of certain series of behaviors characterized by attempts that are irregular, slow, or inexact, but lead at length with practice to a succession of fairly uniform results. Preliminary trials are termed a "warming-up period" or "warm-up process." Also known as warming up (period).

war neurosis A traumatic neurosis precipitated by war-related experiences, including not only catastrophic events such as bombings but long exposure to combat conditions, and internal conflicts over killing or the expression of fear. Symptoms may include persistent anxiety and tension, nightmares, irritability, exhaustion, depression, and in some cases phobias and conversion symptoms such as paralysis or bent back (camptocormia). See COMBAT FATIGUE, COMBAT REACTIONS, POSTTRAUMATIC STRESS DISORDER, SHELL SHOCK.

warning signal The preliminary stimulus or signal commonly used in response experiments to prepare the participant for prompt intentional response.

war psychology The practical application of psychological principles to gain advantages over the enemy. May include techniques to motivate own forces, such as martial music for the purpose of inciting feelings of patriotism and unity; designing basic training to subjugate individuality and develop the acceptance of authority; deliberate circulation of misinformation, as in tales of the enemy's barbarism and stereotyped images to dehumanize the perception of an enemy and to harden soldiers to kill. Other techniques intended to influence an enemy range from the design of tall helmets to intimidate to the use of camouflage to make detection more difficult.

Wartegg Drawing Completion Form (E. Wartegg) A projective test designed for children aged five and above. Requires participants to connect lines and dots to make pictures, title them, and tell the examiner which pictures they like the most and which least.

Washoe (A. Gardner & B. Gardner) A chimpanzee (named after the Washoe Valley) taught to communicate in sign language in the 1960s by the Gardners.

Wassermann test   One of several types of blood tests for the detection of syphilis. Named after German bacteriologist August P. von Wassermann (1866–1925).

wastebasket classification   A diagnostic category into which all kinds of conditions are "dumped," such as "psychopath" for any kind of social disorder, and "schizophrenia" for various types of psychoses. Not to be confused with wastebasket diagnosis.

wastebasket diagnosis   The identification of a disorder by excluding possible alternatives. Also known as negative diagnosis. Not to be confused with wastebasket classification.

wat   (C. L. Hull) A unit for measuring reaction potential, named for J. B. Watson. See HULL'S THEORY.

WAT   word-association test

watch test   A crude examination of auditory acuity based on determining the distance from which the participant can hear a watch ticking.

water (as taste)   To the traditional basic tastes of antiquity (sweet, sour, salty), L. M. Bartoshuk suggested a fifth taste: Water. See HENNING'S TASTE TETRAHEDRON.

waterfall illusion   An example of a negative aftereffect. It is an illusion of apparent movement that occurs as a result of steady visual fixation on any portion of a waterfall. When the observer's gaze is shifted to the surrounding scenery, it appears to move in an upward direction. May be demonstrated in the laboratory with a waterfall illusion device such as one described by William James in his *Principles of Psychology* (1890). See AFTEREFFECT, AFTERIMAGE, APPARENT MOTION, ILLUSION.

water fear   Morbid fear of water. See AQUAPHOBIA, HYDROPHOBIA, NAUTOPHOBIA, THALASSOPHOBIA.

water-jug problems   (A. S. Luchins) A set of problems to be solved mentally using sets of water jugs (for example, imagining being given a full ten-pint jug, and being asked to measure out one pint using only an empty two-pint and three-pint jug to measure with). May be used to demonstrate the effects of prior experience and set on problem-solving.

water-jug problems   A mental set apparatus.

water on the brain   Common phrase for cerebral edema (abnormal accumulation of fluid in the intercellular spaces of brain tissue).

water regulation   A complex mechanism for maintaining optimum balance between those fluids contained within the boundaries of body cells and those fluids that are extracellular. See THIRST.

water-seeking behavior   Actions demonstrated by those animals that have been deprived of water. Animals usually follow visual and olfactory clues toward possible water sources.

Watson-Glaser Critical Thinking Appraisal   (G. B. Watson & E. Glaser) A test intended to measure a participant's ability to recognize assumptions, infer, deduct, interpret, and evaluate arguments.

Watson's behaviorism   See BEHAVIORISM.

watt (W)   The standard unit used in measuring electrical power; an SI (metric system) unit equivalent to the amount of energy expended while doing one joule of work for one second. Named after Scottish engineer and inventor James Watt (1736–1819).

wave   1. The regular alternating motion of particles which is communicated to adjacent particles, so that the undulating motion advances continuously. 2. An undulatory movement or a series of such movements along a surface or through the air. 3. A data collection point, especially in a longitudinal study.

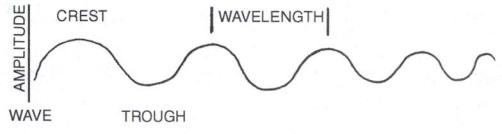

wave

wave amplitude   The height of a wave from its tip to its trough. May be used in describing or measuring a variety of waves, including sound waves and electromagnetic waves. See WAVE for an illustration.

wave frequency   1. The temporal wave frequency is calculated as the number of times the tip of a wave passes a particular point in space in a set period of time. 2. The spatial wave frequency is calculated as the distance between peaks of a wave form. See WAVE for an illustration.

wave-interference patterns   A principle of holographic photography in which a three-dimensional image can be projected in space by light waves that converge from different angles at the site of the image. The principle has been proposed as an explanation for the ability to store spatial and temporal information and reconstruct the image of the original by recall processes.

wavelength (λ)   The distance between two successive wave crests, mid-points, or troughs. It is the length of one complete wave. Formula: $\lambda = v \div f$, where v is the velocity, f is the frequency, and λ (lambda) is the wavelength. See WAVE for an illustration.

wavelength thresholds   Minimum and maximum light or sound wavelengths that can be perceived. In the visual system, wavelength thresholds vary somewhat with intensity but are generally around a minimum of 380 and a maximum of 760 millimicrons. Species differ in their wavelength thresholds for both vision and audition.

wave of excitation   Continuous chemical or electrochemical change in a localized region of the nervous system (especially cortex) capable of arousing responses from effectors.

waxy flexibility   Patients with catatonia assume and maintain unusual postures and offer little resistance to others moving the patient's arms or legs. Also known as *cerea flexibilitas*. See CATALEPSY.

WAY technique   See WHO AM I?, WHO ARE YOU?

Wb   See WEBER.

WB   See WECHSLER-BELLEVUE INTELLIGENCE SCALE(S).

WB scale   The Wechsler-Bellevue Scale; a test battery designed to measure intelligence in adults. See WECHSLER ADULT INTELLIGENCE SCALE-REVISED, WECHSLER INTELLIGENCE SCALE FOR CHILDREN.

W chromosome   The sex-determining chromosome in some insects, birds, and fishes, comparable to the Y chromosome in mammals.

WCST   Wisconsin Card Sorting Test

weak ego   An ego subject to unconscious impulses that may disintegrate under strain, developing mental symptoms or character defects.

weakening   In linguistics, a decrease in the time or degree of a consonant's closure, often due to a neighboring vowel. Also known as lenition.

weak kidneys   A neologism, understood to mean enuresis even though enuresis has little to do with the kidneys.

weak methods   (A. Newell, H. A. Simon) Problem-solving heuristics that require little knowledge for application to any particular task domain, hence are very general, but correspondingly inefficient. See EXPERT-NOVICE DIFFERENCES, HEURISTIC SEARCH.

weakness fear   See ASTHENOPHOBIA.

weakness sensation   An experience characterized by an abnormal intensity of the kinesthetic sensations accompanying slight muscular exertion.

weaning   1. The process, optimally gradual but often sudden, of withholding from a young mammal, especially a human infant, its mother's milk (or bottle-fed formula), and substituting nourishment with alternate milks, solid food, and other forms of emotional nourishment. Also known as ablactation. 2. The breaking up or dissolving of the transference situation, applied especially to the end phases of psychotherapy.

weapons effect   (L. Berkowitz) A tendency for the presence of a weapon to be a cue for aggression.

wear-and-tear theory of aging   A point of view that bodies age because of continuous use and accumulated "insults." See PROGRAMMED-AGING THEORY.

Weber (Wb)   The SI (metric system) unit of magnetic flux, equal to a flux that produces an electromotive force of one volt in a single turn of wire as the flux is uniformly reduced to zero in 1 second. Named after German physicist (and brother to Ernst) Wilhelm Eduard Weber (1804–1891).

Weber-Fechner law   (E. H. Weber, G. T. Fechner) A theory proposed by Gustav Fechner that as the physical intensity of any given stimulus is decreased or increased by a constant ratio, the magnitudes of sensations also decrease or increase by equal increments. Formula: $S = k \log R$, where S is the magnitude of a sensation (measured in number of jnd's above threshold), R is the magnitude of stimulus intensity (measured in terms of detection threshold), and k is some arbitrary constant. Fechner published this reformulation of Ernst Weber's law in 1860. See FECHNER'S LAW, WEBER'S LAW.

Weber fraction/ratio   See WEBER'S LAW.

Weber's experiment   Declared by E. G. Titchener as a classic experiment, Ernst Weber discovered that discriminations of weight was a constant fraction of 1/40 or a 2.5% difference between two weights. Also known as weight-lifting experiment. See WEBER'S LAW.

Weber's law   The name suggested by Gustav Fechner for the psychophysical phenomenon originally explored by Ernst Weber (1834) in which the smallest difference between the magnitudes of two stimuli that can be detected (the "just noticeable difference" or JND) is a constant proportion of the magnitude of the standard stimulus. Formula: $\Delta I \div I = k$, where I is the intensity of the comparison stimulus, ΔI is the increment in intensity that is just detectable, and k is a constant. Sometimes known as the relativity law. [$\Delta I/I$ is known as the Weber fraction/ratio.] See FECHNER'S LAW, JUST-NOTICEABLE DIFFERENCE, PSYCHOPHYSICS, STEVENS' LAW.

Wechsler Adult Intelligence Scale-Revised (WAIS-R)   (D. Wechsler) An intelligence test (1981) that provides both an overall measure of intelligence as well as separate verbal and nonverbal scores. Possibly the most widely used and researched intelligence scale for adults. The test was revised (1997) as the Wechsler Adult Intelligence Scale-Third Edition (WAIS-III). See CULTURE-FAIR TESTS, INTELLIGENCE QUOTIENT.

Wechsler Adult Intelligence Scale-Third Edition (WAIS-III)   (D. Wechsler) The 1997 revision of the Wechsler Adult Intelligence Scale-Revised (WAIS-R).

Wechsler-Bellevue Intelligence Scale(s)   (D. Wechsler) An individual intelligence scale for adults and older children developed in 1939, consisting of six verbal and five performance subtests which yield separate verbal and performance intelligence quotients (IQs) as well as an overall IQ. Also known as WB, WB scales. Supplanted by the WAIS in 1958.

Wechsler Individual Achievement Test (WIAT)   (D. Wechsler) An achievement battery intended to determine academic difficulties and learning disabilities. Standardized with the Wechsler Intelligence Scale for Children-Third Edition (WISC-III).

Wechsler Intelligence Scale for Children (WISC)   (D. Wechsler) The original WISC comprised a series of twelve tests for children from ages five to sixteen. A verbal, performance and a full-scale intelligence quotient (IQ) can be derived from computation of the subtest scales. See WECHSLER INTELLIGENCE SCALE FOR CHILDREN.

Wechsler Intelligence Scale for Children-Third Edition (WISC-III)   (D. Wechsler) A widely used, individually administered intellectual ability test for children from 6 to 17 years of age, in its third (1991) edition. Verbal subtests are information, similarities, arithmetic, vocabulary, comprehension, and, as a supplement, digit span. Nonverbal are picture completion, coding, picture arrangement, block designs, object assembly (symbol search and mazes are supplementary). Norms derived from 2,200 American children.

Wechsler Memory Scale-Third Edition (WMS-III)   (D. Wechsler) A 1997 revision of the Wechsler Memory Scale (WMS) for use in assessing the relationship between memory and intellectual functions in ages 16 to 89 years. The original WMS was first revised in 1987 as Wechsler Memory Scale-Revised (WMS-R).

Wechsler Preschool and Primary Scale of Intelligence (WPPSI)   (D. Wechster) A series of eleven tests for children age four to six and a half years providing intelligence quotient (IQ) for verbal, performance and full scale IQ. First published in 1967, the test has been revised. See WECHSLER PRESCHOOL AND PRIMARY SCALE OF INTELLIGENCE-REVISED (WPSSI-R).

Wechsler Preschool and Primary Scale of Intelligence-Revised (WPSSI-R)   (D. Wechster) A 1989 revision of the Wechsler Preschool and Primary Scale of Intelligence (WPPSI), it is designed for children from ages 3 to 7 years, 3 months. Norms are based on 1,700 children.

wedding night   The night of the wedding ceremony and traditional time for a couple to begin sexual relations. Some cultures condone a couple being sexually intimate before marriage, others do not.

Wedensky effect   (N. I. Wedensky) A finding that following application of a maximal stimulus to a neuromuscular preparation, a subthreshold stimulus (otherwise too small to evoke a response) will evoke a response.

Wedensky facilitation   (N. I. Wedensky) Enhancement of excitability of a nerve due to the arrival of an impulse at a blocked zone although the impulse is not conducted through the blocked zone.

Wedensky inhibition   (N. I. Wedensky) 1. Depression of muscular response due to rapid stimulation of the motor nerve when slower stimulation of the motor nerve results in muscular response. 2. A principle that with a nerve-muscle preparation a critical frequency for stimulating the nerve can be found, at which rate the muscle responds with a very rapid series of twitches (for example 200 per second), whereas if the rate of stimulation be somewhat increased the muscle responds with a single contraction followed by complete relaxation. Relates to the theory of neuromuscular inhibition by interference of overcrowding of nerve pulsations.

wedge photometer   An instrument for measuring differential sensitivity to brightness changes. An optical wedge has one side illuminated by a constant source of light while the other side's source of light is finely adjusted. Enables the participant to differentiate between small differences in light stimulation.

Wednesday Evening Society   The original name given to the group that met in Sigmund Freud's home in 1902 to discuss what then was called psycho-analysis. Alfred Adler, Paul Federn, Otto Rank, and Wilhelm Stekel were members of this group. It became the Vienna Psychoanalytic Society in 1910. See VIENNA SCHOOL.

weekend hospital   Partial hospitalization in which psychiatric patients function in the community during the week but spend the weekend in the hospital. See DAY HOSPITAL, PARTIAL HOSPITALIZATION.

weekend neurosis   **Sunday neurosis**

weekend parents   A derogatory term for those parents who tend to devote only their weekends to personal contact with their children because both parents work full-time outside the home. Children of such parents, as a result, acquire a higher degree of lifestyle and behavioral influences from other caregivers (babysitters, day-care-center personnel), schools, and media, particularly television.

we group   1. The group to which the person belongs. 2. See IN-GROUP.

weighing   See ITEM WEIGHT, WEIGHT, WEIGHTING.

weight (w or W)   1. In physics, the force of gravity multiplied by the mass of the body. 2. Numerical coefficient used as a multiplier of an item to reflect its relative importance, such as in selecting an employee, the weights for education, special training, and recent relative experience may be 1, 1.5, and 3 respectively.

weight comparison instruments   Apparatus devised for the presentation of stimuli in lifted weight experiments. Gustav Fechner's version was a number of identical square-bottomed receptacles covered with a lid and lifted by a handle. Alfred Binet's version was a number of identical shotgun shells that were to be put in rank order by weight.

weight cycling   A common experience of many people who have gone on reducing diets, characterized by repeatedly losing and gaining weight. See YO-YO DIETING.

weight discrimination   An ability to distinguish weight differences of identical or similar objects.

weighted checklist   A checklist on which some or all items are multiplied by a factor, making them more or less important than others.

weighted item   A test item multiplied by numbers that reflect the relative importance or usefulness of the item in predicting a criterion.

weighted model   In social psychology, a concept that a person forms impressions of others by differentially weighting the information about them. Compare UNWEIGHTED MODEL.

weighted score   A special value or weight given to particular items of a test because of their significance or relative importance as compared with the other items scored. See WEIGH, WEIGHING.

weighted test   1. A test in which individual questions or items may be differentially weighted (multiplied by a factor other than 1). For instance, a question that turned out to be hard might be weighted by 0.7, an item that everybody got right could be weighted by 0.4, and a discriminative question (answered correctly by most of the top overall scorers and wrong by the low scorers) might be weighted by 1.5 or more. 2. In a test battery or group of tests, a test that is statistically emphasized or deemphasized. 3. Increasing the value, decreasing the value, or both, of parts of a test (to make it to make it work better or appear to). 4. An examination (for example, an essay test) in which some questions may be assumed to be more difficult and therefore are assigned more weight, that is, a greater number of points. Compare UNWEIGHTED TEST.

weight experiment   A psychophysical experiment originated by E. H. Weber in which the participant judges small differences between freely lifted weights. Also known as weight-lifting experiment. See FECHNER'S LAW, PSYCHOPHYSICS, WEBER'S EXPERIMENT, WEBER'S LAW.

weighting   The assignment of proportional values to the various data, results, etc., in a set of experiments, tests, or statistics, in accordance with their assumed or determined value in the set or group. Also known as weighing. See ITEM WEIGHT, WEIGHT.

weightlessness   Being in a zero-gravity environment, as in a free-fall or in outer space, and thus deprived of normal cues about body position and orientation.

weight-lifting experiment   **weight experiment**

weight regulation   A process of body-energy homeostasis under control of the appetitive center in the hypothalamus. The weight regulation mechanism seeks an optimum balance between food intake and energy expenditure by the organism after a certain body weight is achieved. Experimental evidence indicates that obese animals usually reduce food intake after reaching a certain weight level and eat only enough to maintain the much-higher-than-average weight. Research also indicates that in humans, weight regulation may be influenced by a variety of additional factors including environmental cues. See APPETITE CONTROL, MORBID OBESITY.

weight sense   See KINESTHESIA.

Weight Watchers   An organization devoted to helping individuals attain and maintain optimal weight, for a fee, using a trade marked dieting plan, and assisting the dieter in reaching set goals by providing weekly support-group meetings and weigh-ins. See SELF-HELP GROUPS.

Weigl-Goldstein-Scheerer Test   (E. Weigl, K. Goldstein & M. Scheerer) A concept-formation task requiring the participant to sort geometric figures according to shape and color, and to shift from one category to another. Has been used for a variety of purposes, especially in studying brain injury or brain damage.

Weingarten rule   A United States Supreme Court ruling that employees who belong to unions are entitled to union representation, if requested, during questioning by an employer or an agent thereof.

Weismannism   A theory of evolution, advocated as a result of studies by German biologist August F. Weismann (1834–1914), which denied the heritability of acquired characters, and assumed the continuity of the germ-plasm through successive generations. Weismann rejected the Lamarckian theory of acquired characteristics. See DARWINISM, HEREDITY.

well-being   A subjective state of being well. Includes happiness, self-esteem, and life satisfaction.

well-defined problem   A problem having a goal that is clearly stated, a readily identified starting point, and a comparatively simple way to tell when a solution has been obtained.

wellness   (J. Matarazzo) The emphasis in health and medical counseling toward healthy lifestyles, preventative measures, and self-treatment.

wellness programs   Programs designed to encourage regular exercise, proper nutrition, weight control, stress management, and avoidance of harmful substances.

Weltanschauung   (world view—German) The total body of an individual's or a societal group's philosophic beliefs and observations about human life, society, and the world at large.

Weltschmerz   (world pain—German) Sentimental melancholy and pessimism over the state of the world, accompanied by a romantic acceptance of this sadness as a natural aspect of human life.

Wepman Test of Auditory Discrimination   (G. P. Wepman) An examination used in demonstrating an ability to discriminate between spoken signals. Among the items, two words are spoken and the participant must decide whether the words spoken were alike or different. See SIGNAL-DETECTION THEORY.

wer(e)wolf   "Man-wolf," from the Old English *wer* or "man." According to ancient superstition, a person who had been changed into a wolf, or who was capable of changing into a wolf at will. See LYCANTHROPY, MASS HYSTERIA, TRANSYLVANIA EFFECT.

Werner's disease/syndrome   A rare hereditary disorder affecting both sexes and characterized by signs of premature aging that may appear before the age of 20. Individuals usually are of short stature. Symptoms include graying and loss of hair, skin atrophy, hypofunction of the endocrine glands, accumulation of calcium deposits in the tissues, and a form of arthritis. Also known as progeria adultorum. Named after German physician Otto Werner (b. 1879). See PROGERIA.

Wernicke-Geschwind theory   An explanation of how the brain processes information related to speech and other verbal behavior.

Wernicke's aphasia   (C. Wernicke) Loss of the ability to comprehend sounds or speech, and in particular, to understand or repeat spoken language (word deafness) and to name objects or qualities (anomia). The condition is due to brain damage. Also known as Bastian's aphasia, cortical sensory aphasia. See APHASIA, AUDITORY AMNESIA.

Wernicke's area/center   An area of the left cerebral cortex which lies immediately behind and below the primary receptive area for hearing and which is essential to the comprehension of meaning in language. Damage to Wernicke's area results in an inability to comprehend spoken language and often affects the comprehension of written language as well. The area is named for Carl Wernicke who first reported a lack of comprehension of speech in patients who had suffered a brain lesion in that part of the brain. See BROCA'S AREA.

Wernicke's cramp   (C. Wernicke) A muscle cramp due to psychogenic factors, such as fear or anxiety. Also known as cramp neurosis. See OCCUPATIONAL NEUROSIS.

Wernicke's dementia/syndrome   (C. Wernicke) A senile psychosis characterized by confusion, disorientation, defective memory, confabulation, misidentification, agitation, poverty of ideas, and puerile but generally amiable behavior. Also known as Kahlbaum-Wernicke syndrome, presbyophrenia.

Wernicke's disease   (C. Wernicke) A symptom triad of ocular palsy, ataxia, and polyneuropathy associated with a thiamine, or vitamin-B1, deficiency. Individuals may exhibit signs of mental confusion and aphonia. Cerebral blood flow is usually reduced significantly. The condition is observed in chronic alcoholism. Also known as cerebral beriberi.

Wernicke's theory   The following items are important for understanding Carl Wernicke's theory: DELUSION CLASSIFICATION, HYSTERICAL PSEUDODEMENTIA, SEMANTIC JARGON, WERNICKE-GESCHWIND THEORY, WERNICKE'S APHASIA, WERNICKE'S AREA/CENTER, WERNICKE'S CRAMP, WERNICKE'S DEMENTIA/SYNDROME, WERNICKE'S DISEASE.

Wertheimer's theory The following items are important for understanding Max Wertheimer's theory: CENTERING, GAP, GESTALT LOGIC, HOMOTYPE, LAW OF PREGNANCE, LAW OF PROXIMITY, LAW OF SIMILARITY, LAW OF GOOD CONTINUATION, ORGANIZATION, PHI PHENOMENON, REQUIREDNESS, RHO-RELATION, SHORT-CIRCUITING THEORY, TYPE-ALPHA THINKING, TYPE-GAMMA THINKING.

Werther syndrome (J. W. Goethe) Cluster suicide.

Western Aphasia Battery (WAB) (A. Kertesz) A battery used in identifying aphasia syndromes and in determining the degree of their severity. Evaluates clinical aspects of language function, as well as reading, writing, calculation ability, and nonverbal skills. Also used with persons with brain injury who do not have aphasia.

Western perspective Attitudes, assumptions and thought processes adopted by those acculturated to the American and Western European cultures of the world.

wet brain 1. Slang for an alcoholic. 2. See CEREBRAL EDEMA.

wet dream 1. A true physiologic orgasm that occurs during sleep. 2. Common expression for nocturnal emission of semen, frequently occurring during an erotic dream. See ONEIROGMUS.

wet nurse A woman who breastfeeds another woman's infant often for pay.

wet pack Wet sheets wrapped around the body of delirious or agitated patients to calm them. See HYDROTHERAPY.

Wetzel grid A visual device for plotting interrelations of height, weight, and age over a period of years. Usually used for children and adolescents. Named after American pediatrician Norman C. Wetzel (b. 1897).

Wever-Bray theory of hearing (E. G. Wever & C. W. Bray) A point of view that the electrical activity generated in the cochlea is a response to external stimuli. It is not identical with the electrical nerve impulse carried by the auditory nerve, but may be due to conversion of sound energy to the electrical energy of the nerve impulse. Also known as aural microphonics, Wever-Bray effect. See VOLLEY THEORY (OF HEARING).

WF word fluency (also abbreviated **W**)

W factor See WILL FACTOR (meaning 2).

WFMH World Federation for Mental Health

WGTA Wisconsin General Test Apparatus

Wh questions Queries that begin with WH such as Who, When, Where, Why, commonly asked by young children either to learn more about matters important to them or to question the legitimacy of behaviors and requests of others.

What If technique (A. Adler) A procedure used to encourage clients to imagine or explore what it would be like if their wishes or feelings were realized. See THE QUESTION.

Wheatstone bridge (C. Wheatstone) An electrical circuit for the equating of resistance, used in measures of galvanic skin response or other similar measurements of electrical resistance.

Wheatstone chronoscope (C. Wheatstone) A chronoscope originally designed for measuring the velocity of cannon balls, later used to measure reaction time in psychological research.

Wheatstone-Hipp chronoscope (M. Hipp) An improved version of the Wheatstone chronoscope, developed by Mathias Hipp. Used in modified form in psychological laboratories, commonly known as Hipp chronoscope.

Wheatstone stereoscope (C. Wheatstone) The first stereoscope; based on two mirrors placed side-by-side at an angle.

wheelchair sports Recreational and rehabilitative activities in which persons confined to wheelchairs participate in individual and team sports. They include basketball, bowling, archery, table tennis, and standard track and field events such as shotput, discus, javelin, sprints, and relays.

wheel network 1. A communication and information pattern in which a person in the center (usually an administrator) gives information and instructions to one person at a time. 2. An organizational system for group problem solving. In a group of five members, the centrally-located one is the "hub," the only one with which the others can communicate. Designed to centralize information and delegate responsibility. See COMMUNICATION NETWORK, COMPLETELY CONNECTED NETWORK, GROUP NETWORK.

wheel of life A graphic technique in which program participants plot the degree of time/energy they invest in each of six life tasks: occupation, friendship, intimacy, leisure, spiritual, self.

whipping Common form of sexual sadism and masochism in which some people derive sexual excitement from watching others being whipped, being whipped themselves, or from fantasies of whipping or being whipped. See FLAGELLATION.

whipping boy 1. Historically, a companion to the son of royalty, who, if the young aristocrat misbehaved, was punished instead. 2. By extension, a person unjustly punished.

Whipple tachistoscope (G. M. Whipple) A rotary disk tachistoscope activated by a pendulum.

whipsawing A metaphor for the technique in which one group gains an advantage, followed by others demanding the same concessions in sequence. Also known as leapfrogging.

whirl sensation A sense of circular movement of the head, or of rotation of the entire objective world about the head, due to stimulation of the semicircular canals by, for example, drugs, nystagmus, or head rotation. Also known as whirling. See DIZZINESS, VERTIGO.

whisper aphonia Oral communication without complete vocal-cord function, a physiological laryngeal sound phenomenon.

whisper test A crude or screening examination of auditory acuity in which the examiner whispers test words from a distance of 20 feet while the participant, with one ear plugged, responds without watching the examiner. See SIGNAL DETECTION THEORY, WATCH TEST.

whistleblowing The reporting of wrongdoing, generally by an employee of a company to an enforcement agency or the public. (Derives from sports, where a referee blows a whistle to deal with a rule infraction.) Some jurisdictions prohibit an employer from retaliating against a whistleblower. See ALTRUISM.

white collar crime (E. Sutherland) Refers to the misdeeds of those in the upper levels of society. Used broadly to refer to, for instance, crime by employees against their employers, and the skirting of moral or statutory laws by corporate executives.

white collar work Colloquial term for nonmanual labor.

white commissure A bundle of myelinated fibers that crosses from one side of the spinal cord to the other. Neurons that receive input from the periphery concerned with pain, temperature, light touch, and some proprioceptive information send their axons through the white commissure to form pathways on the opposite side of the spinal cord that carry this information to the brain. Located between the ventral gray commissure and the ventral median fissure of the spinal cord. Also known as anterior or ventral white commissure.

white lies False statements that are made with a conscious intent to deceive, usually to save others from distress rather than for any personal gain. See LYING, NONPATHOLOGICAL LYING, PATHOLOGICAL LYING.

white matter 1. A portion of the nervous system composed of nerve fibers enclosed in myelin sheaths which contribute a white coloration to otherwise grayish structures. The sheaths cover only the fibers, however, so the cell bodies of the myelinated nerves are gray. 2. Those parts of the brain or spinal cord which appear whitish or pale gray due to the color of the myelin surrounding the axons of neurons. Compare GRAY MATTER.

whiteness constancy Perceiving items as having consistent whiteness even when their illumination varies. See BRIGHTNESS CONSTANCY, PERCEPTUAL CONSTANCY.

white noise The sound ("whoosh," "hiss") heard when many sound waves of different lengths are combined so that they reinforce or cancel one another haphazardly. Used for masking purposes. Analogous to white light, a mixture of all wavelengths of light. See COLORED NOISE, NOISE.

white-out syndrome A feeling of anxiety, isolation, and detachment sometimes extending into a psychotic state, associated with Arctic explorers, mountaineers, and others exposed to prolonged stimulus deprivation. See SENSORY DEPRIVATION.

white rami communicantes Myelinated fibers of the preganglionic branches of the sympathetic-nervous-system ganglia. Located along the thoracic and upper lumbar segments of the sympathetic tract, and function as input fibers from the spinal nerves.

white slave A woman who has been forced into prostitution. The phrase, coined in a 19th century drama, *The White Slave*, is an extension of the concept of the Black slave.

White Slave Act The Mann Act, passed by the United States in 1910, defining as a felon a person who aids in the transport of a female across a state line for any "immoral purpose."

white space response (S) In Rorschach test scoring, a response to open, clear areas within the blots.

whitiko A culture-specific syndrome purportedly seen among Algonquin Indians, demonstrated by a compulsive desire to eat human flesh. Also spelled *wihtigo, wihtiko, windigo, witigo*. See CULTURE-SPECIFIC SYNDROMES.

Whitten effect Estrous synchronization in a group of female rats due to a pheromone in the males' urine.

WHO World Health Organization

Who Am I? A projective test that explores self-concept by examining a participant's responses to the question "Who am I?"

Who Are You? A projective test in which a person is asked to write three short answers to the question "Who are you?" The answers are analyzed for the information they reveal about the person's identity or self-concept. Also known as WAY technique.

whole and part learning Two ways of memorizing information of considerable length. In the whole method, the person tries to learn the material (poem, list, etc.) all at once, beginning-to-end. In the part method, the person tries to learns small increments (such as lines of a poem) to perfection and then attempts to assemble them. Also known as part and whole learning, whole-part method of learning. See DISTRIBUTED LEARNING, PART METHOD OF LEARNING, WHOLE LEARNING, WHOLE-LEARNING METHOD.

whole-channel (view) In consumer psychology, a concept usually applied to international marketing comprising three channels: the seller, the channels between nations, and channels within foreign countries.

whole-object (M. Klein) In psychoanalytic theory, refers to a person viewed as a love object when that love is for the whole person. Compare PART-OBJECT.

whole-part method of learning whole and part learning

whole report In learning theory, a technique used in attention-span studies in which the participant is to report all of the items from a display. Compare PARTIAL REPORT.

whole-report technique (O. Sperling) A method that involved asking participants to report as much information as they could following the brief presentation of visual stimuli.

whole tone One of the larger steps in a musical scale, roughly equivalent to two semitones.

whole word method The teaching of reading by asking children to learn the whole word as a unit rather than breaking it down into sounds.

wholism Less frequent spelling of holism.

whore 1. A prostitute. 2. By extension, a person who sells sexual or other services in a questionable or unethical manner.

Whorfian hypothesis A linguistic relativity postulate that language directly influences perception. What is perceived depends on the availability of appropriate linguistic categories. Benjamin Whorf presented the linguistic relativity hypothesis in the early 1940s. Also known as Sapir-Whorf hypothesis, Whorf's hypothesis.

WIAT Wechsler Individual Achievement Test

wideband procedures Evaluation methods considered lacking in accuracy, for example, making judgments about people from photographs. They can nonetheless provide useful information.

Wide Range Achievement Test (WRAT) (G. S. Wilkinson) An individual achievement test used primarily for remedial and vocational as well as general educational purposes, measuring the participant's level of skill in reading, spelling, and arithmetic computation, with an adjustable range from ages 5 to 75 years of age.

Wide Range Assessment of Visual Motor Abilities (WRAVMA) (W. Adams & D. Sheslow) A measure that attempts to provide an evaluation of visual-motor, visual-spatial, and fine motor skills of individuals 3–7 years of age.

wide-range test Generally, a test that is designed for use on people over a wide age range.

widowhood crisis A period, often lasting at least a year because of anniversaries and fresh memories, in which a widow must adjust to the loss of her husband and readjust her life accordingly. Typically, she experiences a loss of status and loss of identity as well as going through the mourning process based on the stages of dying delineated by Elizabeth Kübler-Ross: denial, anger, negotiation with God (bargaining), depression, and finally acceptance. Group therapy and the Widow-to-Widow Program have been found particularly effective in helping to meet this crisis. See MOURNING, WIDOW-TO-WIDOW PROGRAM.

Widow-to-Widow Program An organization established for mental health purposes that includes the visiting of women who have recently become widows by other widows or mental-health teams who offer them support of various kinds. See DEATH NEUROSIS, WIDOWHOOD CRISIS.

wife-beating See BATTERED WIVES.

wife-swapping A practice in which two or more couples agree to swap spouses for sexual purposes. May include watching the husband or wife participate in sexual activity with another's spouse. Use of the phrase "wife-swapping" rather than "husband-swapping" reflects a bias toward viewing wives as objects or property. Also known as partner-swapping. See OPEN-MARRIAGE, SWINGING.

Wiggly Block Test (J. O'Connor) A manual-dexterity task in which nine wavy blocks are reassembled into a single rectangular block from which they have been cut. See O'CONNOR WIGGLY BLOCK.

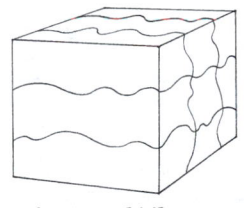

Wiggly Block Test After showing this completed block to a participant, it is disassembled into separate blocks and mixed up and the participant must reassemble it. Both the objective time taken to complete the task and the subjective judgment of the examiner are involved in the final evaluation.

wihtigo whitiko

Wilcoxon Matched-Pairs Signed-Ranks Test (F. Wilcoxon) A nonparametric test for two related samples of ordinal data, useful to test the difference between sets of ranked data that come in pairs when both the direction and the magnitude of the difference in pairs of elements are known. Named after Irish-American chemist and statistician Frank Wilcoxon (1892–1963). Also known as Wilcoxon test.

wild boy of Aveyron A supposed feral child, unsocialized and nonliterate, found living in the woods in the Aveyron around 1800 and studied by French physician Jean Itard. It has been suggested that the boy actually was a subnormal child abandoned in the woods by his parents. Itard's attempts to teach the boy inspired his pupil Edouard Seguin to develop materials and methods for training persons with mental retardation. See FERAL CHILDREN, WOLF CHILDREN.

wildcat strike In labor relations, a spontaneous strike not sanctioned by the union.

wild children See FERAL CHILD, WILD BOY OF AVEYRON, WOLF CHILDREN.

wild ducks In industrial psychology, slang for employees who are creative, but independent and abrasive. Also known as mavericks.

Wilder's law of initial values law of initial values

wilding Slang for antisocial behavior, especially of adolescents, often when they are affected by alcohol or drugs, during which time they experience high emotionality, destroy property, and injure or kill people as part of a group process.

wild psychoanalysis (S. Freud) Sigmund Freud's characterization of procedures that depart from the technical process of psychoanalysis, for example, offering direct advice to a patient, or making dynamic interpretations before the patient is ready for them.

Wilks Lambda In multivariate analysis of variance, a criterion for linear hypothesis testing based on all eigenvalues. Named after American mathematician Samuel Stanley Wilks (1906–1964). See LAMBDA INDEX.

will 1. A function or group of functions concerned in delayed conscious response. 2. A conscious decision to act or undertake a course of action. See DYSBULIA, VOLITION. 3. The self in action. 4. As employed by Arthur Schopenhauer and many others, the totality of irrational and emotional impulses, usually regarded as having primacy over intellect. See FREE WILL, FREEDOM OF WILL.

will disturbances Deficiency or lack of will power identified by Karl Bleuler as a basic symptom of schizophrenia. Such patients may appear lazy and lacking in objectives and motivation. Another form of will disturbance observed in patients with schizophrenia is characterized by a high degree of activity that is bizarre, trivial, inappropriate, or purposeless.

will-do factors In industrial psychology, employee or applicant variables such as motivation, interests, and personality characteristics, as opposed to "can-do" factors comprising knowledge, skills, and specific aptitudes.

Wille zur Macht (will to power—German) (F. Nietzsche, A. Adler) Strivings for superiority which in many personality theories are considered a basic part of human nature. Striving to better personal abilities is viewed as a healthy process (Adler); striving to dominate others is considered an unhealthy process (Nietzsche). See SUPERIORITY.

will factor (w or W) 1. Conation: the intensity of a desire to achieve. 2. In factor analysis, the factor correlated with persistence, purpose, striving, and effort. Also known as W FACTOR.

Williamsburg Asylum   The first public-supported (as opposed to private) mental hospital in the United States of America. Opened in 1773, it was dedicated to the care and treatment of patients with mental disorders. Later renamed the Eastern (Virginia) State Hospital.

Willowbrook Consent Judgment   A landmark legal decision pertaining to the rights of person with mental retardation and referring to conditions in living-out arrangements including education, food, medical and psychological services and other factors in their treatment. See RIGHTS OF THE MENTALLY RETARDED.

will power   The capacity to make difficult decisions and to implement them. For this phrase to have meaning it needs an anchor or base for comparison and consequently would not be used by psychologists casually. Sometimes spelled willpower. See ABULIA.

Will-Temperament Tests   (J. E. Downey) An early attempt to measure personality and temperamental differences primarily through controlled handwriting tasks. Also known as Downey's Will-Temperament Tests.

will therapy   (O. Rank) A form of psychotherapy that claimed that neuroses can be avoided or overcome by asserting the will (or "counterwill"), and by achieving independence. According to Otto Rank's theory, life is a long struggle to separate the self from the mother psychologically (similar to separating the self from the mother physically during birth). Also known as Rankian therapy. See BIRTH TRAUMA, LIFE FEAR.

will to live   The determination to live in spite of an adverse, life-threatening situation such as a severe illness. There is considerable evidence, mostly anecdotal, that a strong will to live can enhance the chances for recovery, or at least prolong the life of the individual, and can enable many persons to endure deprivation, incarceration, and both physical and mental punishment. Also known as will to survive.

will to meaning   (V. Frankl) The need to find a suitable meaning and purpose in life. The basis and fundamental motivation of logotherapy, developed by Viktor Frankl as a technique for addressing problems related to the contemporary experience of meaninglessness. See EXISTENTIAL VACUUM.

will-to-power   Alfred Adler's phrase for what he thought to be the dominant human motive, holding that frustrations of this motive lead to compensatory reactions or to a feeling of inferiority. See WILLE ZUR MACHT.

Wilson-Patterson Attitude Inventory   (G. D. Wilson & C. H. Patterson) A social attitude scale used to assess conservatism-liberalism, realism-idealism, militarism, antihedonism, ethnocentrism and puritanism.

wimmin   A spelling used by some feminists for woman/women, to avoid the man/men ending.

wind-chill index   (P. A. Siple & C. F. Passel) An index on which the subjective effects of different wind velocities and temperatures can be compared. For instance, at an air temperature of 32°F (0°C) and a wind speed of five miles an hour, the wind-chill is 29°F (−.7°C). The original index was a scale of subjective reactions that included 80 for hot, 200 for pleasant, 400 for cool, and 800 for cold.

wind effects   Examples: a light wind can have a refreshing effect, particularly on a hot or humid day; a strong, howling wind can cause feelings of fear and anxiety; tornadoes and hurricanes generate feelings of terror and helplessness. See ANEMOMANIA, BEAUFORT WIND SCALE, CHANGE OF ENVIRONMENT, ENVIRONMENTAL PSYCHOLOGY.

wind fear   See ANEMOPHOBIA.

windigo   whitiko

windmill illusion   An illusion of apparent motion in which the direction of rotating blades or spokes is intermittently perceived to reverse directions. (This illusion is not the same as the seeming reversal in the direction of rotation of a wheel, as occasionally seen in motion pictures. Stagecoach wheels that appear to rotate backwards in a Western movie results from the stroboscopic effect in combination with limitations resulting from the number of frames per second photographed by the motion picture camera.) See STROBOSCOPIC EFFECT (ILLUSION).

window   1. Fenestra. See OVAL WINDOW, ROUND WINDOW. 2. An opening. See THERAPEUTIC WINDOW.

wind tunnel   A corridor through which air can be blown to test the performance of aircraft or other objects in a simulated outdoor environment. Also used to study effects of wind or changing air pressures on behavior. See AIR-PRESSURE EFFECTS.

Wingate test   A test of physical performance involving 30 seconds of maximal exertion on either an arm-crank or a leg-cycle ergometer, the resistance of which is based on body mass.

winking   1. Involuntary or voluntary rapid closing and opening of the eyes to spread tears over the conjunctiva to keep the eyes moist. More frequently called blinking. 2. A form of nonverbal behavior characterized by voluntary closing and opening of an eyelid to convey a message.

wink reflex   1. Closure of the eyelid, stimulated by drying of the cornea. See WINKING (meaning 1). 2. See CORNEAL REFLEX.

win-lose   In games theory, a zero-sum strategy in which, for every gain on one side, there is a corresponding loss on the other.

win-lose (dynamic)   In negotiation, the perception of every action of the other side as an attempt to prevail or dominate.

win-stay/lose-change (rule)   In organizational psychology, the practice of organizations to stay with a winning course of action, and to change in response to failure.

win-stay/lose-shift (strategy)   A procedure in two-alternative choices in which the participant stays with the same response when correct but changes response when wrong.

win-win   In games theory, a situation wherein a negotiation permits both sides to benefit.

wiring   Slang for a procedure practiced by individuals in various governmental departments and large corporations of establishing standards for promotions in jobs or in assignment of contracts, written so as to favor special individuals or corporations. See GLASS CEILING, JOB DISCRIMINATION.

WISC See WECHSLER INTELLIGENCE SCALE FOR CHILDREN.

Wisconsin Card Sorting Test (WCST) (D. A. Grant & E. A. Berg) An examination for detecting perseverative thinking and assessing abstract reasoning ability. Used by clinicians in discriminating frontal from nonfrontal lesions.

Wisconsin General Test Apparatus (WGTA) A device designed at the University of Wisconsin for learning and perceptual research with rhesus monkeys. A moveable screen and presentation tray allows stimuli to be presented to or hidden from the monkey, and for it to manipulate them.

wisdom Reflective knowledge, especially concerning the practical conduct of life.

wisdom factor The use of knowledge and life experience to help the self adapt to the aging process.

wish Denoting ordinarily a desire or longing, but more broadly used in psychoanalytic theory to denote any urge, striving, tendency, or impulse that operates on a conscious or unconscious level.

wish-fulfillment 1. In general, the gratification or realization of desire. 2. In psychoanalytic theory, the drive to free the self from the tension created by instinctual needs such as sex and hostility.

wishful thinking Thought processes governed by inner wishes and desires rather than by logic or reality; believing what one wants to believe.

wit 1. Mental function consisting of the ability to make amusing, incisive comments that throw light on a subject (topic) or person. 2. In psychoanalytic theory, a verbal retort, jibe, or pun that suddenly and strikingly releases a repressed or hidden feeling or attitude. See EXAGGERATION IN WIT, TENDENCY WIT.

witch A person, usually female, who practices wicca. See WITCHCRAFT.

witchcraft 1. Sorcery practiced by a person reputed to possess supernatural powers, usually deriving from a compact with the devil. A woman who practices such sorcery is called a "witch," whereas a man who does so is a "wizard" or "warlock." See CURSING MAGIC, DEMONOLOGY, HEX DOCTORS, INCUBUS, SHAMANISM, SORCERY DRUGS, SUCCUBUS. 2. A form of feminist, earth-based religion. Also known as wicca or white witchcraft.

witch doctor Sometimes used as a synonym for Shaman. See ALTERNATIVE THERAPIES, FAITH HEALING.

witch's milk Colloquial for a milky secretion from breasts of newborn children of both genders. Also known as hexenmilch.

witch's Sabbath A ceremony observed by some groups during the Middle Ages in defiance of the church. Included drinking of wine spiked with henbane or belladonna, which reportedly produced sexual arousal accompanied by hallucinations. Participants who were caught were usually tortured into confessing, then burned alive.

withdrawal 1. Removal. 2. Leaving or cancelling participation. See RECUSE. 3. A state of depression or lack of normal social or work interaction. See SOCIAL WITHDRAWAL. 4. Ceasing participation in an activity, such as leaving an experimental treatment group. See ATTRITION. 5. An unpleasant state of deprivation after ceasing the use of an addictive substance or involvement in a pseudoaddictive behavior. See WITHDRAWAL SYMPTOMS. 6. Voluntarily discontinuing a drug or prescribed medication to avoid withdrawal (meaning 5).

withdrawal-destructiveness (E. Fromm) According to Erich Fromm, a style of relating based on withdrawal and isolation from others as well as destructive behavior directed toward others.

withdrawal dyskinesia A condition of generally temporary tardive dyskinesia-like symptoms which occur following the cessation of treatment with neuroleptic medications.

withdrawal method In sexual intercourse, removal of the penis from the vagina prior to ejaculation, usually for the purpose of contraception. See COITUS INTERRUPTUS.

withdrawal reaction 1. A tendency to remove the self from active involvement in the environment, which can be mild, as in times of grief, or extreme, as in catatonic schizophrenia. See ADJUSTMENT DISORDER WITH WITHDRAWAL, SOCIAL WITHDRAWAL. 2. The physical retraction of a body part from a painful stimulus. See REFLEX, WITHDRAWAL REFLEX. 3. See WITHDRAWAL SYMPTOMS.

withdrawal reflex A response stimulated by any unexpected threat to the well-being of the individual, characterized by sudden movement away from the potentially damaging stimulus as a natural survival procedure.

withdrawal symptoms Unpleasant reactions experienced when people who have habitually taken addictive substances such as tobacco, alcohol, and narcotic drugs, cease to do so. Symptoms include an intense craving and preoccupation with the addictive substance, restlessness, anxiety, tenseness, perspiration and other physiological symptoms. Possibly some of the reported discomforts are exaggerated to justify the continued use of the substances; conversely, the discomfort of withdrawal from some substances, such as heroin, is intensely painful to the point of requiring hospitalization. See PHYSIOLOGICAL DEPENDENCE, PSYCHOLOGICAL DEPENDENCE.

withdrawing response A reaction of retraction of a body part or the entire organism from the stimulus or situation that induced it. Also known as abient response, avoiding response, defense reaction, negative response, nociceptive reflex.

within-family differences Common differences of opinions and values between family members. Conflicts between parents can be traumatic for children; conflicts between parents and children can be difficult if the parents come from a different environment and have "old-fashioned" ideas of correct behavior. See GENERATION GAP.

within-groups variance A variation in scores occurring among the participants in an experiment not resulting from an experimental treatment. See BETWEEN-GROUPS VARIANCE.

within-subjects design   An experimental design in which all participants receive every treatment, and consequently serve as their own control. See BETWEEN-SUBJECTS DESIGN.

witigo   whitiko

witness   1. To observe an occurrence of any sort. Usually, but not necessarily, limited to visual observation. 2. A person who can reliably report memory of an occurrence seen or heard. See EXPERT WITNESS.

wit work   Freudian phrase used to describe the psychic processes involved in producing witticisms.

Witzelsucht   (compulsive wisecracking—German) A type of joking mania, a symptom occurring in lesions in the frontal association areas, often resulting from tumors or cerebral arteriosclerosis. See MORIA.

wizard   warlock

WMS   See WECHSLER MEMORY SCALE-THIRD EDITION.

WMS-III   See WECHSLER MEMORY SCALE-THIRD EDITION.

WMS-R   Wechsler Memory Scale-Revised

wolf   1. Slang for a man who is constantly on the prowl for women for sexual purposes. See DON JUAN. 2. Prison slang for an aggressive man who looks for sexual relations with younger men ("punks").

wolf children   Refers usually to two girls who were apparently raised by wolves in India, and who adopted their major life patterns, such as bolting their food, night howling, and running on all fours. When captured, they were approximately 18 months and eight years old, respectively; the younger girl died within a year of capture. The older lived until about age 17 and learned to walk in a half-crouch, acquired a 50-word vocabulary, and learned to wear clothes and run errands. See FERAL CHILDREN, WILD BOY OF AVEYRON.

Wolfenden Report   A 1957 report of a British committee chaired by J. F. Wolfenden recommending that homosexual activity between consenting adults in private no longer be illegal.

Wolf Man   Landmark case reported by Sigmund Freud in 1918, involving a conversion symptom (constipation), a phobia (for certain animals), a religious obsession (piety alternating with blasphemous thoughts), and an appetite disturbance (anorexia), diagnosed as reactions to early experiences. The case strengthened Freud's theory of infantile sexuality.

wolf pack phenomenon   In group therapy, a situation when some or all members attack one of the members, sometimes under the control of the therapist, sometimes spontaneously. See GROUP THERAPY, TARGET PATIENT.

womb   uterus

womb envy   (K. Horney) A man's jealousy over a woman's ability to bear and nurse children. May sometimes be a psychological characteristic of a transsexual or transvestite male whose gender identity is female. See PENIS ENVY, VAGINAL ENVY.

womb fantasy/phantasy   1. (O. Rank) An unconscious wish to return to the peaceful security of the womb to escape the traumatic conditions of life. 2. In Freudian dream analysis, a wish to return to the security of fetal life by returning to the womb, usually expressed in symbolic form such as living under water, or being alone in a cavern.

women in psychology   1. The National Council of Women Psychologists was founded in 1941, and later renamed the International Council of Women Psychologists. In 1959, membership was extended to men when it was renamed the International Council of Psychologists. 2. In the early days of psychology, with a few notable exceptions, psychologist were male, but the proportion of women and their status within the profession has been steadily increasing. In some countries, such as Colombia, women psychologists have long outnumbered men; in Norway, educational psychology was pioneered by women; in England, women graduates have outnumbered men since 1970. In the United States, the proportion of women receiving doctorates is steadily rising.

Women's Bureau   Generally, a government agency that deals with problems, legislation, and statistics relating to women. The largest is that of the U.S. Department of Labor.

women's lib   women's liberation movement

women's liberation movement   A name given by American women to feminism in the 1960s with the objective to free themselves from (a) the sexual double standard, or the idea that young males need to experience early sexual relations but that young women should retain their virginity until marriage; (b) being relegated to inferior positions in business; (c) receiving lower pay than men for the same work; (d) the total responsibility for child-rearing and homemaking; (e) the dominance of the male not only in the home and in business but in the arts and sciences as well; and (f) the traditional stereotype of women as fragile, passive, dependent individuals who are governed by emotion rather than reason. Also known as women's lib. See CONSCIOUSNESS-RAISING, DOUBLE STANDARD, FEMINISM, FEMININITY, GENDER ROLE, HOUSEWIFE SYNDROME, JUS PRIMAE NOCTIS, PIBLOKTO, RADICAL THERAPY, RAP GROUP, RAPE COUNSELING, RAPE-TRAUMA SYNDROME, SEX DISCRIMINATION, SEXISM, SEX ROLES, SEX-TYPING, TOMBOYISM, UNISEX, WORKING MOTHERS.

women's roles   The functions and status of women in society. In some cultures, a woman's role is limited to domestic duties; elsewhere she may actively participate in industry, armed forces, government, often in addition to "traditional" roles of homemaking, child-rearing, and volunteer service. See FEMINIST MOVEMENT, SUFFRAGETTE, WOMEN'S LIBERATION MOVEMENT.

Women's Studies   An interdisciplinary academic area in which issues relating to women are explored through theory, research, and practice. The general rubric of Women's Studies encompasses the study of women from the perspectives of psychology, sociology, literature, history, and biology, among others.

women with penis   In psychoanalytic theory, some children between ages 2 and 5 believe that all women once possessed or will grow a penis; and the discovery by boys that girls lack a penis may cause castration anxiety.

woman-year   A year of exposure to pregnancy in a sexually-active, fertile woman; a measure for comparing the effectiveness of contraception methods.

wonder   An emotional condition elicited usually by objects that are novel, seemingly important, and intellectually baffling. See CURIOSITY.

Woodworth-Mathews Personal Data Sheet (R. S. Woodworth & J. Mathews) A personality inventory containing 116 yes-no items designed for use in educational institutions as a screening device for neurosis in children and adolescents.

woolly mammoth (P. Wachtel) Repressed conflicts encapsulated in the unconscious for many years, like prehistoric mammoths that were frozen and preserved for millennia.

word In linguistics, a minimal free form; the smallest unit that is normally able to function as a sentence. See FREE FORM.

word approximation A speech disturbance of schizophrenia in which conventional words are used in unconventional or inappropriate ways (as in metonymy), or new but understandable words are constructed out of ordinary words, for example, "easify" for "simplify."

word-association test (WAT) A common projective examination in which the participant responds to a stimulus word with the first word that comes to mind. Invented by Francis Galton for use in exploring individual differences; Emil Kraepelin was the first to apply it to the study of abnormality; Carl Jung compiled a list of 100 words designed to uncover complexes; others such as G. R. Kent & A. J. Rosanoff, and D. Rapaport et al., have devised other lists. See ASSOCIATION, ASSOCIATIONISM, JUNG ASSOCIATION TEST.

word-blindness (H. C. Bastian, A. Kussmaul) An inability to understand written language or a difficulty in reading words. Often associated with brain injuries. Rudolf Berlin renamed this condition dyslexia. The preferred term is alexia.

word-building test A task in which the person constructs as many words as possible out of a given group of letters.

word configuration The general visual pattern of a word as produced by the combination of shapes or particular typeface or script.

word counts The examination of a designated sample of spoken or written speech for the purpose of determining the rate of occurrence or the prevalence of specific words. Such word counts are useful for a variety of purposes such as in teaching vocabulary or writing books for children. See WORD-FREQUENCY STUDY.

word deafness auditory aphasia

word dumbness An inability to communicate well in speech or writing usually due to brain damage. See APHASIA, BROCA'S AREA, EXPRESSIVE APHASIA.

word fluency (WF or W) Ability to list words rapidly in certain designated categories, such as words that begin with a particular letter. Associated with a part of the brain anterior to the Broca's area of the dominant frontal lobe. Persons with lesions in that part of the brain are likely to suffer word fluency deficits in verbal tests and tasks. See BROCA'S AREA, PRIMARY ABILITIES.

word-form dyslexia An inability to read except by spelling out the letters.

word-fragment completion task A test of implicit memory in which the participant, when given a fragmented word, has to fill in the missing letters (for example, fill in the missing vowels of the following word: M-M-RY). See IMPLICIT MEMORY.

word-frequency study The study of the rate of occurrence or the prevalence of specific words in a designated sample of spoken or written speech. See WORD COUNTS.

word-length effect A major determinant of immediate memory; lists of short words are more easily remembered than those of long words. The variable is the time needed to speak/hear the word, rather than the number of letters.

word-of-mouth Informal social channels of communication.

word-reaction time The interval between the presentation of a stimulus word and the moment of beginning the utterance of the response word. Also known as word-response time.

word-recognition skills A cluster of word-recognition strategies used in reading, such as use of sight words, context clues, phonics, and structural analysis.

word-recognition threshold Usually measured as the minimum time for the presentation of a word that can be read by the observer. See TACHISTOSCOPE.

word salad/hash 1. A jumble of incoherent words, meaningless words, phrases and neologisms that may occur as a result of the disorganized thought processes characteristic of some forms of schizophrenia. See HEBEPHRENIA. 2. The utterings of individuals disoriented through intoxication by alcohol or drugs. Also known as jargon aphasia, paraphrasia.

word sentence A single word being a sentence, for example "Coming?" Sometimes known as holophrase (meaning 1).

word-span test A mental examination, essentially similar to the digit-span test, except that words are used instead of digits. The participant hears a series of individual words and is asked to repeat them in the same order.

word superiority effect (WSE) (J. M. Cattell) A paradoxical ability of people to respond quicker to some whole words that have a particular letter than to the letter itself, for example, in a reaction test responding faster on seeing "axe" than seeing "x."

work 1. In various fields of psychology, a noun and verb generally referring to human behavior that is goal-directed, disciplined, structured by task and time, requiring some combination of physical and mental capabilities, and required rather than voluntary. 2. In physics, the application of force over distance. 3. Production through muscular or psychological activity of physical or psychological results; for example a weight lifted, a problem solved.

work addiction A compulsive dependence on work as the primary means of maintaining self-esteem and self-worth.

workaholic Common term for a person who has a craving for work beyond the normal amounts, or whose self-imposed pressure to work interferes with other aspects of life. See FLIGHT INTO REALITY, WORK ETHIC.

work curve A plotted record of the amount of muscular or mental performance in successive time periods.

work decrement   1. A decline in the size or rate of output of a task per unit of time. 2. In research, a decline in the magnitude of responses as a function of frequency of the response. 3. A decrease of efficiency of any activity as a result of its continuous exercise.

worker characteristics   Attributes associated with a worker's ability to accomplish job objectives. They may be psychological, as in tolerance for heights in construction workers, or physical, as in small stature to work in confined places. See JOB DESCRIPTION, JOB PLACEMENT, JOB REQUIREMENTS.

work ethic   Valuing hard work as a goal in life and seeking success as the expression of self-worth and justification for personal existence. Following Max Weber, known as the Protestant work ethic, as the concept is a product of Western European culture. See ACHIEVEMENT ETHIC, DELAY OF GRATIFICATION.

work evaluation   Assessment of an employee's job performance in terms of specific job objectives, which vary according to the type of work performed. An assembly-line worker may be evaluated according to factors such as safe operation of machines and number of operations performed in a given time; a manager may be evaluated on planning and executing long-term assignments and ability to motivate others. Also known as vocational evaluation.

work fear   See ERGASIOPHOBIA, ERGOPHOBIA, PONOPHOBIA.

work-flow integration   In industrial psychology, a scale that combines equipment automation (the extent to which tasks are performed by machines), work-flow rigidity (the extent to which the sequence of work activities are inflexible), and specificity of evaluation (the extent to which work activities can be assessed by specific, quantitative methods).

work-flow rigidity   See WORK-FLOW INTEGRATION.

workforce   General term referring to employees.

work-for-pay unit   Found in in-patient or aftercare work facilities, a component of a comprehensive rehabilitation program for mental patients. Such units usually offer prevocational screening and evaluation, and vocational training in addition to compensating patients for their work. See SHELTERED WORKSHOP.

work function scale   In industrial psychology, an inventory of the task activities, usually divided into tasks involving data, people, and things. See JOB ANALYSIS.

work groups   Formal and informal workplace groups that collaborate as a team for short or extended periods.

working alliance   Two or more people with different interests, abilities, or both, cooperating toward a particular common end, such as in counseling, where a person with a problem meets with a counselor who shares the same goal of arriving at a desirable solution.

working backward   A heuristic strategy in which a person discovers the steps needed to solve a problem by initially defining the desired goal and then moving backwards toward the beginning point to determine how the final goal can be reached. Compare WORKING FORWARD.

working conditions   Work-place arrangements under which employees carry out their jobs, including variables such as illumination, atmospheric conditions, noise, work schedule, and rest periods.

working forward   Starting with the initial state and transforming it, in the hope of approaching the goal state. Compare WORKING BACKWARD.

working hypothesis   A preliminary (possibly temporary) prediction to guide the design of a research study.

working mean   Seldom used phrase for assumed mean.

working memory   1. (A. Baddeley) An influential view of immediate memory that emphasizes both processing and storage. It includes a "central executive" (a controlling attentional mechanism) and a number of subsidiary systems that include the phonological loop and the visuo-spatial sketch pad. 2. A component of the memory process, usually referred to as "short-term memory," that holds a few items briefly before the information is either stored in long-term memory or forgotten. Information that has been stored in long-term memory but which is then retrieved to carry out some specific purpose (or mental "work"), such as recalling a telephone number, is also held in working memory as it is used.

working model   In developmental psychology, a child's image of a parent as a productive and successful member of the workforce.

working mothers   Mothers who are employed, whether home-based or outside the home. See WORKING PARENTS.

working out   1. In psychoanalytic theory, the stage in the treatment process characterized by identification of the patient's personal history and psychodynamics. 2. Exercising.

working over   Describing the psychic processes involved in reorganizing, adjusting, and otherwise modifying excitations to prevent the harmful effects of discharging outward undesirable responses. See MEDIATIONAL LEARNING.

working parent   A primary caretaker of young children who works outside the home. Such a person is assumed to have additional stresses and role conflicts, counterbalanced in varying degrees by feelings of self-fulfillment, economic advantages, and availability of day-care facilities.

working through   In psychotherapy, the process of self-confrontation, dealing repeatedly with repressed feelings, threatening impulses, and internal conflicts until they are satisfactorily solved.

working vocabulary   active vocabulary

work inhibition   Performing below capacity. See ACADEMIC UNDER-ACHIEVEMENT DISORDER, ADJUSTMENT DISORDER IN RELATION TO TASKS.

work involved in response (*W*)   In Clark Hull's theory, the assumption that responses are accompanied by effort (work) which generates reactive inhibition. See HULL'S THEORY.

work-limit method   Arranging materials and instructions, so that every participant performs the same task, that is, covers the same material.

work-limit test   An examination in which all participants perform the same task but scores are based on the time required for the performance. Also known as unit-task tests.

work rehabilitation center A facility, such as a sheltered workshop, in which efforts are made to habilitate or rehabilitate the persons with physical or mental disabilities through a paid work program geared to their abilities and interests.

work sample (performance) test   work sample test

work sample test 1. A procedure for selecting or sometimes evaluating employees, in which they are asked to perform tasks that represent a given job (for example, prospective typists type a letter, teachers give a lecture). Standardized tests have been devised for a variety of jobs. Also known as job sample test, work-sample performance test. 2. A work performance task based on the analysis of how a specific job element is performed under standardized conditions.

work satisfaction See JOB SATISFACTION.

workspace The physical area within which one performs most or all job tasks. Examples are desks, aircraft cockpits, assembly-line stations.

workspace design Work stations designed for effective, comfortable, and safe performance of tasks, for example, the placement of materials, tools, and controls within easy reach, and a comfortable, adjustable seat adapted to the particular job. See THERBLIG.

workspace envelope The area within which a person can reach and operate; often global.

work-study program Any of a variety of educational programs combining classroom study with job experience to provide students with money, practical work experience, and work-related contacts.

work-team counselor In industrial psychology, a member of a work team elected by the members to serve as leader.

work therapy The use of paid work activities, for example, weaving, packaging, or assembly as a therapeutic agent for persons with mental or physical disabilities. The rationale is that productive work keeps people from lapsing into inertia, focuses their attention outside themselves, provides healthy physical activity, develops their skills, and helps to maintain their sense of self-esteem. See CHALLENGED.

work-to-rule In labor relations, a work slowdown in which employees do only what they are told or required, and typically observe all precautions whether or not warranted. See SLOWDOWN.

work-up The compilation of relevant information about a patient or client in advance of treatment; may refer to such advance preparation performed during the practice of social work, psychology, or psychiatry, as well as to portions of the patient's history obtained during the practice of medicine.

Work Values Inventory (D. Super) A test administered in the 1960s to study career choices in school children.

world design (L. Binswanger) How, according to existentialists, people fit into the world, their total personalities including their phenomenology and behavior.

world-destruction fantasies/phantasies Daydreams that feature mental images of the world coming to an end. See NIHILISM, NUCLEAR NEUROSIS, SCHIZOPHRENIC SURRENDER.

world-regions According to Ludwig Binswanger, three kinds of surroundings in which being-in-the-world finds expression: *Umwelt*, the biological and physical surroundings; *Mitwelt*, the human environment; and *Eigenwelt*, the psychological and physical self.

world-system (theory) A historical description of the growth of the capitalist economic system, and its effects on capitalist and pre-capitalist cultures.

World Test   Bolgar-Fischer World Test

world-view Any theory regarding the nature of the universe, or of phenomena in general and their interrelatedness. See WELTANSCHAUUNG.

World War I army tests (A. Otis, L. M. Terman et al.) A series of paper-and-pencil tests used for screening the general intelligence of military personnel during World War I administered in groups. The Alpha form was used with persons who could read; the Beta with those who could not, consisting of pictures and administered with vocal instructions. See INTELLIGENCE TESTS, GROUP TEST, NONVERBAL INTELLIGENCE TESTS.

worm fear See HELMINTHOPHOBIA, TAENIOPHOBIA.

worry A state of mental distress or agitation due to concern for an impending or anticipated event, threat, or danger.

worship 1. The act of offering honor and adoration to a deity. 2. A system of practices that constitute people's relation with their god or gods.

worst scenario 1. Generally, imagining the most undesirable results and consequences possible of an action that a person is considering doing. May help in making a decision and preparing for the "worst case scenario." 2. In counseling, a situation in which the counselor considers the effects of various strategies and advises the client of the possibility of failure and the worst results that might occur, often to demonstrate that it might be worthwhile for the client to take a chance with some new behavior. See AWFULIZING, DEVIL'S ADVOCATE.

worth A subjective appreciation, or measure, of the importance of a given datum or factor of any sort, in relation to other data or factors of the same class. See SELF-WORTH.

WPA World Psychiatric Association

W% (H. Rorschach) In Rorschach test scoring, the percentage of whole responses in relation to total responses. A whole response is seeing the whole blot as a single unit.

WPPSI See WECHSLER PRESCHOOL AND PRIMARY SCALE OF INTELLIGENCE.

WPPSI-R See WECHSLER PRESCHOOL AND PRIMARY SCALE OF INTELLIGENCE-REVISED.

WRAT   Wide Range Achievement Test

WRAVMA See WIDE RANGE ASSESSMENT OF VISUAL MOTOR ABILITIES.

W response In Rorschach test scoring, a response that takes in the whole inkblot.

writer's block Inhibited creativity in a writer, mostly due to unconscious factors.

writer's cramp   An occupational disorder caused by excessive use of a writing instrument and affecting the muscles of the thumb and adjacent two fingers of that hand. Forms include: neuralgic, paralytic, spastic, tremulous. Also known as dysgraphia, graphospasm, mogigraphia, scrivener's palsy. See CARPAL TUNNEL SYNDROME, OCCUPATIONAL NEUROSIS, REPETITIVE STRAIN INJURY.

writing accent   Peculiar characteristics of an individual's handwriting that purportedly appear in the handwriting of others of the same nationality. See GRAPHOLOGY.

writing angle   The angle between the downstroke and the base-line of writing. The angle in slanting writing is under 45°, normal slanting writing about 60°, vertical writing about 90°, backhand writing over 90°. Also known as angle of writing.

writing fear   See GRAPHOPHOBIA.

writing test   A test to measure skills such as word fluency (for example, writing as many words as possible beginning with the letter S in five minutes) and writing speed (for instance, the speed of writing dictated sentences).

written aphasia   An inability to communicate well by writing, usually due to brain damage. See APHASIA, BROCA'S AREA, EXPRESSIVE APHASIA.

written composition scale   A scale used in evaluating the quality of writing, consisting of samples of literature each assigned a numerical score value by experts. The composition to be evaluated receives the score of that extract which it most nearly equals in excellence. See HANDWRITING SCALE.

wrongful dismissal   In law, termination of employment (particularly without prior notice) without valid or just cause.

wrong number technique   (S. Gaertner & L. Bickman) A social psychology procedure originally used to see if people are more likely to help members of their own "race" or skin color. Researchers, who imitated stereotypical speech patterns of African American or Caucasian persons, reported in a phone call, ostensibly to a garage, but actually to randomly selected subjects that their car had broken down. When the respondents from a population that includes various minorities understood that the call had been misdialed, they were asked to phone the "garage" (a research confederate) because the caller was out of coins. Depending on the subject's response, the results then showed the tendency to assist other members or either the same or another race.

wryneck syndrome   Intermittent or continuous spasms of the neck muscles, causing a turning and tipping of the head. The direction of head movement depends upon which of the several neck muscles are involved. The condition is commonly associated with psychological disorders, and usually responds to psychological treatment. Also known as spasmodic torticollis. See CAMPTOCORMIA, TORTICOLLIS.

WSE   word-superiority effect

W-state   The waking state, as contrasted with the S-state (sleep state) and D-state (dream state). See CONSCIOUSNESS, SLEEP, WAKEFULNESS.

WTPT   walk-through performance testing

Wundt curve/illusion   (W. Wundt) A misperception in which straight lines appear to curve in a certain direction when viewed through a prism and seem to curve in the opposite direction when the prism is removed.

Wundt gravity phonometer   (W. Wundt) An apparatus for determining the difference limens for intensity of sound. A steel ball is held in an electromagnetic device which can be fixed at any height above a plate of hard wood (ebony); when released, the ball produces a sound whose objective intensity is roughly proportional to "height of fall" multiplied by the "weight of ball." Used for purposes such as determining the soundness of sleep and auditory acuity. See SOUND PENDULUM for an example of a similar instrument.

Wundt illusion   **Wundt curve**

Wundt sound pendulum   (W. Wundt) An apparatus for determining the difference threshold for sound. Two pendulums are supported so that their bobs, when at rest, just touch the opposite faces of an ebony block; when raised through any desired arc and released, each bob strikes the block with a force proportional to its height of fall. See WUNDT GRAVITY PHONOMETER.

Wundt's principles of emotional expression   Three principles formulated by Wilhelm Wundt as a reformulation of Charles Darwin's principles about animals demonstrating emotion. Wundt attributed such show of emotion to direct innervation, association of analogous sensations, and relation of movements to images. See TRIDIMENSIONAL THEORY OF EMOTION.

Wundt's theory   The following items are important for understanding Wilhelm Wundt's theory. See BLICKFELD, CREATIVE SYNTHESIS, ESTIMATION DIFFERENCE, EXCITEMENT-CALMNESS, INTROSPECTIONISM, INTROSPECTION METHOD, LAW OF PSYCHIC RESULTANTS, PLEASANTNESS-UNPLEASANTNESS, STRUCTURALISM, SYSTEMATIC EXPERIMENTAL INTROSPECTION, TENSION-RELAXATION, TRIDIMENSIONAL THEORY OF EMOTION, WUNDT CURVE/ILLUSION, WUNDT GRAVITY PHONOMETER, WUNDT SOUND PENDULUM, WUNDT'S PRINCIPLES OF EMOTIONAL EXPRESSION.

Wundt's tridimensional theory of emotion   See TRIDIMENSIONAL THEORY OF EMOTION.

Würzburg School   (O. Külpe) A school of psychology developed in Germany, largely as a reaction to the structuralist approach of Wilhelm Wundt. Instead of reducing experience to its basic elements (sensations, images, feelings), the Würzburg School focused on intangible mental activities such as judgments, meanings, determining tendencies (or sets), all of which were termed conscious attitudes or *Bewusstseinslage* (states of consciousness). See AUFGABE, DETERMINING TENDENCY, EINSTELLUNG, IMAGELESS THOUGHT, SET.

W^x   (H. Rorschach) In Rorschach test scoring, the code used to score a response to only a part of the inkblot.

Wyatt vs Stickney decision   A 1972 American legal decision about the use of such hazardous treatments as lobotomy, electroconvulsive therapy, and aversive-reinforcement conditioning. It recognized a patient's right to full information regarding the treatment, and the right to refuse it. See CONSUMERISM, FORCED TREATMENT, RIGHT TO REFUSE TREATMENT.

X

x 1. Deviation of a class from mean value of the variable. 2. In Rorschach test scoring, a symbol for rare reply seeing only part of a usual total. 3. Standardized score (Z preferable). 4. Value on the abscissa (horizontal on a graph). 5. An unknown score. 6. Elements from a first set of data. 7. Any difference or deviation. 8. Deviation of a class interval from a mean.

x′ x prime

X 1. Dependent variable. 2. A raw score. 3. The range of possible scores. 4. Reference to an X chromosome.

Xanax Trade name for the benzodiazepine tranquilizer alprazolam.

xanthines A group of stimulants related chemically to the xanthine bodies in urine and animal tissues. See CAFFEINE EFFECTS, THEOBROMINE.

xanthocyanop(s)ia A form of color blindness in which red and green are not perceived and objects are seen in shades of yellow or blue. See DEUTERANOMALY, PROTANOMALY, TRITANOMALY.

xanthogenic radiations Light stimuli which normally give rise to the experience of yellow.

xanthopsia Yellow-sightedness; a condition characterized by objects appearing yellow. May occur in certain types of poisoning and jaundice.

X axis See ABSCISSA, AXIS, X, X VALUE.

X chromosome (R. Henking, C. E. McClung) In humans and most animals, the sex chromosome found in both males and females. Such females normally have two X chromosomes, one contributed by each parent, whereas such males normally have an X chromosome contributed by the mother and a Y chromosome contributed by the father. Also known as McClung's chromosome. See CHROMOSOME, FRAGILE X CHROMOSOME, Y CHROMOSOME.

xenoglossophilia A tendency to use strange or foreign words, particularly in a pretentious manner.

xenoglossophobia Fear of foreign languages, and of learning a foreign language.

xenoglossy (C. Richet) The paranormal skill of speaking in an unfamiliar language. The understanding, reading, writing, and pronunciation by a purported "sensitive" of a real language which allegedly was never learned. Also known as xenoglossia, xenoglossis. See CLAIRVOYANCE, SPEAKING IN TONGUES.

xenophobia 1. Morbid fear or dislike of strangers. 2. Fear or dislike of foreign cultures and places. 3. Fear of unfamiliar people; suspicious, hostile attitudes or aggressive behavior toward people of other nationalities or minority groups. 4. See STRANGER ANXIETY.

xenophonia A speech defect characterized by alteration in accent and intonation.

xenorexia The swallowing of foreign objects, as in a mental hospital patient undergoing repeated surgery to remove such objects as spoons and pens from the stomach.

xerodermic idiocy A syndrome acquired as an autosomal-recessive trait marked by microcephaly and mental retardation combined with dwarfism and xeroderma pigmentosum (a genetic syndrome of hypersensitivity to sunlight resulting in pigment abnormalities and skin cancer).

xerophthalmia Night blindness, usually caused by keratinization of ocular tissue. Also known as conjunctivitis arida, xeroma, xerophthalmus.

xi 1. The point of apparent subjective equality. 2. The fourteenth letter of the Greek alphabet. See APPENDIX C.

X-linked trait An inherited characteristic controlled by a gene on the X chromosome. Examples are hemophilia and color-blindness.

Xo A variable whose value depends on another variable.

X1 Predicted raw score, goes up to X2, X3, etc.

XO syndrome Turner's syndrome

X-O Test Any task of this type in which the participant crosses out (negative) or circles (positive) preferences of a number of items having to do with choice. See PRESSEY X-O TEST.

x prime (x′) Deviation from an assumed mean.

Xq28 A genetic marker region at the end of the long arm of the X chromosome. Research in the 1990s suggests that it is associated with male homosexuals within the maternal line.

X-ray A short-wavelength electromagnetic emission produced by passing a high-voltage current through a vacuum tube. Used to visualize internal body-tissue structures and to destroy malignant cells. Also known as Roentgen ray. Usually known as a radiograph in medical practice.

XTC Slang for a compound resembling (meth)amphetamine.

X theory   See THEORY X AND Y.

X value   For points located in a plane defined by the horizontal X-axis (abscissa) and the vertical Y-axis (ordinate), the X value of a point is the shortest distance between that point in the plane and the Y-axis. Compare Y VALUE.

XX   In humans and most animals, the notation for sex chromosomes for biological females. In humans, it is also written 46,XX, indicating 46 chromosomes (44 autosomes and two X sex chromosomes).

XXX   A human chromosomal abnormality marked by three (instead of two) X chromosomes and two (instead of one) Barr bodies. Incidence is 0.001 live female births. Some mental retardation is possible. Also known as X trisomy and 47,XXX.

XXXX syndrome   In humans, a chromosomal disorder in which a female received four X chromosomes (double the usual amount for a female). Most such individuals have minor physical anomalies and mental retardation. Also known as 47,XXXX.

XXXXX syndrome   In humans, a rare disorder in which a female acquires five X chromosomes rather than the normal two. Such individuals have mental retardation and also a series of physical anomalies of various kinds including visual difficulties and microcephaly. Also known as 49,XXXXX.

XXXXY syndrome   In humans, a rare disorder in which a male inherits three extra X chromosomes (for a total of four). Individuals have a number of anomalies that may include a short broad neck, and muscular hypotonia as well as abnormally small genitalia. Most have mental retardation. Also known as 49,XXXXY.

XXXY syndrome   In humans, a rare disorder in which a male has one Y chromosome (normal for a male) and three X chromosomes (when one is usual for a male). Such individuals have small genitalia and half have feminized breasts. Almost all have mental retardation and show Klinefelter's syndrome.

XXY syndrome   In humans, a chromosomal disorder affecting males born with a karyotype of 47,XXY, resulting in small testes, absence of sperm, enlarged breasts, and excretion of follicle-stimulating hormone (FSH). The preferred name is Klinefelter's syndrome.

XXYY syndrome   In humans, a disorder in which the recipient has double the number of normal chromosomes. Deformity of the skeleton, genital anomalies, and mental retardation are common. Also known as 48,XXYY.

XY   In humans and most animals, the notation for sex chromosomes for biological males.

XY female   See TESTICULAR FEMINIZATION SYNDROME.

xylotherapy   Medical treatment by the application of certain woods to the body.

XYY syndrome   In humans, a chromosomal anomaly in which a male has one X chromosome and two Y chromosomes. Erroneously associated with males who were aggressive, violent and more likely to commit crimes than the general population. It was originally assumed that the extra Y chromosome predisposes males to such behavior, but the theory was modified as XYY anomalies were later found among normal males. Also known as 47,XYY.

xyz grouping   In education, grouping pupils according to ability into three sections for separate instruction. To conceal the basis of grouping, those considered to be the "slow learners" are usually made the Y rather than the Z group. See ABILITY GROUPING for discussion.

XYZ system   An artificial system, based on mathematics, for identification and specification of colors. See RGB SYSTEM.

y 1. Derivation from the ordinate value. 2. The value of an ordinate or the vertical axis. 3. The deviation of an item from the mean ordinate value. 4. The value of an ordinate relative to the abscissa. 5. Items from a second set of data.

Y 1. In Rorschach test scoring, a symbol for perception based on the surface of a card. 2. Whatever is predicted by other variables. 3. The name of a variable; the value of a score on that variable.

Yale studies Usually refers to the work of Yale University researchers led by Carl Hovland in the 1950s on persuasion and communication, later contradicted by the elaboration likelihood model.

yantra A visual pattern on which attention is focused during some forms of Buddhist and Hindu meditation. See MANTRA, MANDALA.

yaqona A Fijian drink made from the powdered root of *piper methysticum*. Also known as *yanggona*. See KAVA.

Yates correction (F. Yates) A statistical adjustment in computing chi-square (χ^2) from small samples, in which the differences between observed and expected frequencies are decreased by 0.5 depending on whether the observed values are less or greater than expected, respectively. It helps bring the distribution (based on a discontinuous frequency) nearer to the continuous chi-square distribution from which published tables for testing chi-square are derived. Formula: $\chi^2 = \Sigma[(|o-e| - 0.5)^2 \div e]$, where o is observed frequency, e is expected frequency, and χ^2 is chi-square. Also known as correction for continuity. See CHI-SQUARE, CHI-SQUARE DISTRIBUTION.

YAVIS Acronym for Young, Adaptable (or Attractive or Affluent), Verbal, Intelligent, Successful. Refers to the group of people for whom psychoanalysis is said to work best. Compare HOUND.

Y axis See ORDINATE, Y, Y VALUE.

Y chromosome In humans and most animals, the sex chromosome found only in males. A male results when a Y chromosome contributed by the father is paired with an X chromosome contributed by the mother. In early stages of prenatal development, a major function of the Y chromosome appears to be the activation of a series of events that lead to the development of male genital organs.

yea-saying A general tendency on being asked a question, or being asked to do something, to automatically reply in a positive manner. Conversely, nay-saying is the general tendency to automatically deny or reply in a negative manner to almost any question or request.

yellow-blue response A graded potential reaction correlated with the spectral sensitivity of the retinal receptors. The response at the blue end of the spectrum is negative, or hyperpolarized, and the response at the yellow end is positive, or depolarized. Thus, blue may have an inhibitory, and yellow an excitatory influence on retinal receptors and ganglia in producing color vision.

yellow-dog contract In labor relations, slang for contracts forbidding unions or stipulating as a condition of employment that the applicant is not, and will not become, a union member. Initially used by railroads in the American West, named for Asians who worked for substandard wages.

yellow-sighted 1. Heightened color sensitivity for yellow, or a tendency to see all objects tinged with yellow. 2. See XANTHOPSIA.

Yerkes-Dodson law (R. Yerkes & J. D. Dodson) The theory that task performance is an inverted U-shaped function of emotional arousal. Performance is enhanced by moderate (presumedly anxious) arousal conditions and is reduced at low and high levels of arousal. As task difficulty increases, the optimal level of arousal for its performance decreases. A simple task requires moderate to high arousal for optimal performance, whereas performance on a hard task is enhanced by a lower level of arousal. Derived from their 1908 study in which mice learned a visual discrimination task with three levels of difficulty under three intensities of shock motivation.

Yerkes multiple-choice apparatus (R. Yerkes) An early (1916) apparatus for the presentation of multiple rather than two stimuli as in the Yerkes-Watson discrimination apparatus. In a fan-shaped layout, a rat placed at the "handle" end would choose one of nine or more stimulus compartments, one of which (for instance, "the second on the right") always provided a food reward.

Yerkes-Watson discrimination apparatus (R. Yerkes & J. B. Watson) An early (1911) device to measure visual discrimination. A rat chooses the left or right side (each marked with a different geometric shape) of a barrier; an incorrect choice results in an electric shock from the floor grid. The apparatus was modified by P. E. Fields in 1928 and K. S. Lashley in 1930.

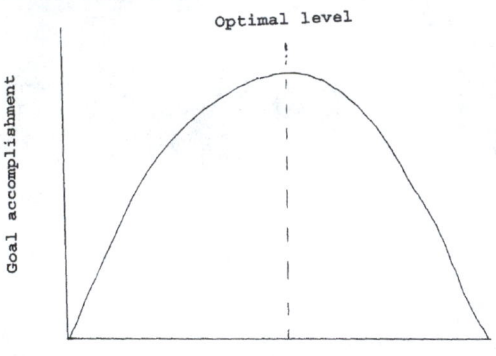

Yerkes-Dodson law   A graph reflecting the Yerkes-Dodson law. Those with little arousal (motivation, energy, drive, etc.) at the left end of the drawing and those who have extreme degrees (at the right end) are less successful in accomplishing tasks than those with a moderate degree of arousal.

Yerkish   (R. & D. M. Rumbaugh) An artificial language named for primatologist Robert Yerkes, in which symbols stand for words. Chimpanzees would press keys showing arbitrary geometric shapes to communicate, such as asking for specific food. The shapes (lexigrams) are moved to different keys in different trials.

yes man/woman   Nontechnical name for a person who uncritically and sycophantically supports a superior. See GROUPTHINK.

yes-no question   A query that must be answered either in the affirmative or the negative. On many applications and other forms, a respondent is given only two alternatives ("Yes" and "No") as responses to various questions. By circling or underlining the alternatives, the person gives information. See FORCED-CHOICE FORMAT.

yield management   In business psychology, a form of variable pricing, as in an airline that charges different amounts for the same trip as a function of the seating class; the passenger's travel record, status, or demographics; and the time of day, week, or year.

yield ratio   In industrial psychology, the percentage of applicants who proceed to the next stage in the selection process. If 16 interviews result from 200 résumés obtained from one source (recruitment advertisement, employment agency, etc.), the yield ratio is 8%.

Yin and Yang   In Chinese Tao philosophy, two complementary and opposing forces or principles by which Tao manifests itself. The interaction of Yin and Yang determine the fate of individuals as well as the universe. Yin is seen as negative, passive, and feminine, complementary to Yang, which is seen as positive, active, and masculine. See DUALISM, T'AI CHI CH'UAN.

Y-maze   1. A maze in the shape of the letter Y. The learner must choose either the left or right arm. 2. A box-like laboratory device consisting of a walled-in series of pathways in the general shape of a Y. Used in measuring comparative strengths of different drives.

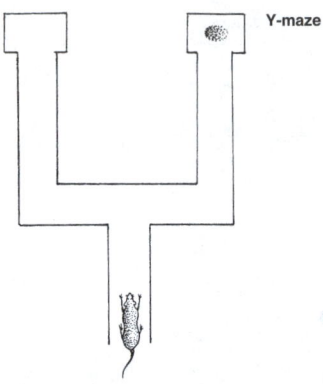

Yoga   (union, yoke—Sanskrit) A school of Hindu philosophy that seeks to achieve union with the Supreme Being or supreme principle through a prescribed, eight-limbed system, which includes moral disciplines, physical postures, breath-control practices, and meditation. In some forms of yoga, postures are used as aids in releasing tension and achieving a state of contemplation, self-control, and mental relaxation.

yo-he-ho theory   A point of view that speech originated because of the strained cries of workers as they struggled in groups against the environment. See ORIGIN-OF-LANGUAGE THEORIES.

yohimbine   A mild stimulant derived from the bark or leaves of the west central African tree *Pausinystalia yohimba* or the *Corynanthe yohimbi* plant, marketed as a mild aid in the treatment of erectile dysfunction, but of uncertain effectiveness. See APHRODISIAC.

yoked control   In operant conditioning, a procedure to insure that both a control and an experimental animal receive the same stimuli at the same time, but in which only one animal may respond (for example, the experimental animal may be able to postpone electric shocks by making a required response, while the control animal receives the same shocks without being able to postpone them).

yoked-control group   A group of animals that is equal with respect to potentially important but conceptually and procedurally irrelevant factors that might account for group differences. Yoking refers to equalizing the experimental and control groups on a particular variable that might systematically vary across conditions.

yoking   See YOKED-CONTROL GROUP.

yopo   A stimulant drink made from the bark of the *Paullinia yopo* tree having about 2½ percent caffeine, used by some natives of Colombia.

young adulthood   1. A period in which men or women who have recently passed through adolescence, reach the height of physical and mental vigor, attain basic independence from their families, and are ready to achieve an intimate, meaningful relationship with someone else. During this period, choice of an occupation and choice of a partner usually take place, both of which are tests of adaptability and maturity. 2. (E. Erikson) The first of the three stages of adulthood, one that presents the crisis of intimacy versus isolation. "The ego strength of young adulthood is love—a mutual, mature devotion."

Young-Helmholtz theory (of color vision) A point of view to explain color vision in terms of retinal cones sensitive to three different wavelengths of light (red, green, blue). Other colors are perceived by stimulation of two of the three kinds of cones, for example, yellow from simultaneous stimulation of red and green cones. Explains color blindness as due to partial or total absence of certain cones. In 1802, Thomas Young explained color sensation in relation to the presence in the retina of structures sensitive to red, green, and violet; in 1852, Hermann von Helmholtz rediscovered the theory. Also known as Young-Helmholtz trichromatic (three-color) theory.

young jobs Vocations usually held by younger employees. Such jobs usually require more physical energy and strength but less experience and skill than jobs held by older workers. Compare OLD JOBS.

youth culture A society that places a high premium on youth, youth values, and perpetuation of youth, and usually tends to derogate the values and needs of mature and older persons. See COUNTERCULTURE.

youth period A stage of life between childhood and adulthood. See ADOLESCENCE.

yo-yo effect Slang for recurrent changes and reversions to the original. Usually applied to losing weight and regaining it, a common experience partly because weight gain occurs more easily with repeated cycles of weight loss. See LIFESTYLE.

Y theory See THEORY X AND Y.

yuppie disease/flu Common name for chronic fatigue immune dysfunction syndrome (CFIDS) or chronic fatigue syndrome. See MONONUCLEOSIS.

Y value For points located in a plane defined by the horizontal Y-axis (ordinate) and the vertical X-axis (abscissa), the Y value of a point is the shortest distance between that point in the plane and the X-axis. Compare X VALUE.

z The ordinate in a normal distribution.

Z 1. A standardized score based on the normal distribution. 2. Translation of r to the Z transformation. 3. A statistic used to transform correlation coefficients, often for the purpose of averaging them. 4. A statistic used to transform correlation coefficients, usually for the purpose of comparing them with other correlations. 5. In Rorschach test scoring, a symbol denoting the capacity for organizing the inkblots into meaningful patterns.

zazen In Zen Buddhism, a method to attain deep meditation; meditators sit with spine and head straight, legs crossed, hands folded with palms up, eyes open, breathing rhythmically, with mind in a state of relaxed attention.

z chart A graphic representation of time consisting of three curves: (a) the original amount per each successive unit of time; (b) a cumulative curve that gives the sum of the ordinates of the preceding curve; (c) a total curve, each point of which gives the total amount for a preceding interval of time, the same interval as that covered by the original curve, for example 52 weeks, 24 hours, or some other natural period. Also known as zee chart.

zee chart   z chart

Zeigarnik effect/phenomenon A tendency for interrupted, uncompleted tasks to be better remembered than completed tasks if the tasks are performed under non-stressful conditions. Blyuma Zeigarnik and Kurt Lewin claimed that the phenomenon is due to the operation of a persistent kind of tension (a quasi-need or *Spannung*) that dissipates when the task is completed, for example, a joke is more likely to be remembered if the punch-line is not heard. Under conditions of stress, the Zeigarnik effect may be reversed. Also known as resumption of interrupted action. See UNACCOMPLISHED ACTION EFFECT.

Zeitgeber (time giver—German) Term sometimes used in research of biological rhythms, referring to phenomena in the environment to which an organism's innate rhythms may be matched, such as the alternation of day and night, changing of the seasons, or temperature. See BIORHYTHM, CIRCADIAN RHYTHM.

Zeitgeist (spirit of the time—German) (M. Arnold) A prevailing cultural climate that affects people's thinking and acting, such as politically correct thinking. See PUBLIC OPINION.

zelophobia Morbid fear of jealousy or having reason to be jealous.

zelotypia Excessive zeal, almost to the point of insanity in the advocacy of any cause.

Zen Buddhism A Japanese form of Buddhism in which spiritual unity and illumination, or *satori*, is achieved through direct, intuitive experience as contrasted with the scientific, intellectual approach. One method of preparing the way for such insight is to devote the self to the solution of an insoluble problem, such as "What is the sound of one hand clapping?" See BUDDHISM.

Zener cards (K. E. Zener) A deck of five cards, each of which has different symbols (cross, circle, rectangle, star, and wavy lines) used in research on extrasensory perception and other paranormal phenomena.

   Zener cards

Zen telegrams (P. Reps) A warm-up procedure used in poetry therapy. Using a brush and paint, a person draws a nonsense figure and nonsense words and later all in the group examine and discuss these productions.

Zen therapy A form of psychotherapy which, like existentialism, is concerned with the unique meaning of the person's life rather than improvement of adjustment or removal of symptoms. The goal is sought through contemplation of self-existence, and grappling with the nature of humankind. This process helps to release inner tension and, if effective, leads to a climactic experience of oneness with the universe and a feeling of being transformed. See EXISTENTIALISM, MYSTIC UNION, ZEN BUDDHISM.

zeppia (R. B. Cattell) A factor trait described as a flexible superego.

zero-base budgeting An approach to budgeting in which each item proposed is evaluated on its own current merits, regardless of its merits in any previous budget. Helps to identify unnecessary allocations of resources, investments, and personnel.

zero correlation Ideally a correlation that is exactly 0.00 but in practice any correlation that is not significant based on prior standards of required statistical significance. See SIGNIFICANCE, SIGNIFICANCE LEVEL.

zero efficiency Inability to perform any scorable amount of a given task or test graded according to various difficulty levels.

zero-intercept   The y-intercept (y-value corresponding to x = 0) when reaction times are plotted on the Y axis and the number of items is plotted on the X axis.

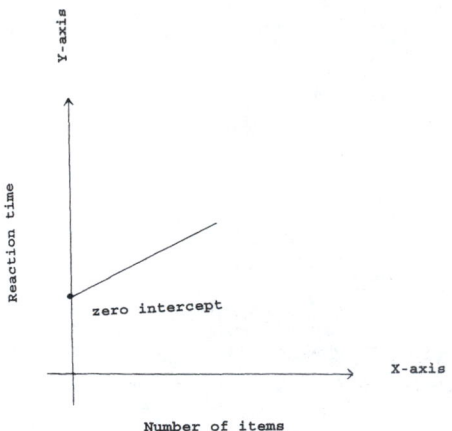

zero-intercept

zero-level channel   In consumer psychology, sales from a manufacturer directly to the final customer with no intermediaries. Also known as direct marketing.

zero order   In reference to a correlation between two variables that are not in any way changed from their original value, as by some elements being held constant. See CORRELATION, MULTIPLE CORRELATIONS, PARTIAL CORRELATION.

zero-order correlation   A degree of correlation between two variables without partialing out, or allowing for, the influence of other related variables. A zero-order correlation may have any value between +1.00 through 0.00 to −1.00.

zero population growth (ZPG)   A condition in which the number of births and deaths is balanced and there is no increase or decrease in population, or little change.

zero-sum (game)   1. Generally, a game that only one player can win. 2. In game theory, a game of chance in which all participants are likely (probabilistically speaking) to win as much as they lose (for example, two people toss coins, one person wins on "heads" and the other person wins the coins on "tails," and theoretically each ends with the same number of coins each started with). Compare MINUS-SUM GAME, PLUS-SUM GAME. See EXPECTED VALUE.

zeta   The sixth letter of the Greek alphabet. See APPENDIX C.

Zeus jealousy   (I. D. Suttie) A man's jealousy of a woman's capacity to bear and nurse children.

Zidovudine   Trade name for azidothymidine (AZT).

Zipf's law   (G. K. Zipf) In linguistics, a theory that a relationship exists between effort and accomplishment, a kind of least effort principle. The observation that in any language, the words used most frequently tend to be short, whereas the words used less frequently tend to be long, or in mathematical terms there is a negative correlation between the length of words and number of times it is uttered.

zipper clause   In labor relations, slang for provisions that unfairly extend management rights.

z-line   In the microscopic structure of a muscle, a narrow dark line of myofibrils that bisects the I band and adheres to the sarcolemma to give stability to the structure. The repeating unit between two Z lines is the sarcomere, the functional unit of the muscle.

zoanthropy   The delusion of being an animal. See LYCANTHROPY.

zoetrope   zootrope

Zöllner('s) illusion/lines   (J. K. F. Zöllner) When short bars cross long vertical bars at 45° the direction of slant alternating from one vertical bar to the next, the latter are perceived as no longer vertical but slanted in the direction opposite to the slant of the cross bars. Since the overall pattern of the illusion is that of a herringbone-patterned fabric, the illusion is also known as the herringbone illusion.

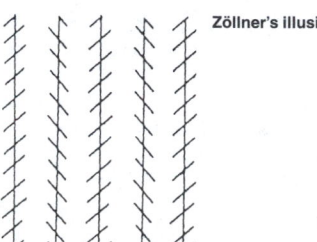

Zöllner's illusion/lines

zombie   1. A person who has allegedly been deeply drugged with native poisonous compounds, subsequently buried and then resuscitated, thereby generating a person without will, indifferent and highly suggestible. 2. Slang for anyone who appears to be strange, slow-moving and apparently not in touch with reality.

zone of comfort   An area around an organism, usually circular, within which the organism feels safe and secure, relative to other organisms (for example, zebras accept lions a certain distance away but if a lion crosses an invisible line, the zebras will run). Humans have individually different zones of comfort that vary across cultures and societies. See ATTACK BEHAVIOR, PROXEMICS, TERRITORIAL BEHAVIOR.

zone of optimal functioning   In sport psychology, the level of anxiety associated with maximal performance.

zone of potentiality   A range of readiness for learning a concept or skill not yet achieved, for example, students who have learned how to add, may now be considered ready to learn how to subtract or how to multiply.

zone of proximal development   (L. S. Vygotsky) The conceptual space between what a child is capable of doing independently and with assistance.

zone out   Slang for letting the mind wander as, for example, a response to repetitive, boring work.

zooerastia   Rare term for bestiality. Also known as zooerasty.

zoöid   1. Resembling an animal. 2. A motile stage in those species which have alternation of generations, as true of caterpillar and medusa.

zoolagnia   1. A sexual attraction toward animals. 2. Being sexually aroused by oral contact with or by the smell of animals. See ZOOERASTIA, ZOOERASTY, ZOOPHILIA.

zoological classification   The designation for the hierarchy of animal types arranged from most to least inclusive as follows: kingdom, phylum, class, order, family, genus, species, variety. See TAXONOMY.

zoology   The branch of biology which deals with animals. See COMPARATIVE PSYCHOLOGY.

zoomania   Excessive, abnormal love for animals. More severe than zoophilia.

zoomorphism   1. Attribution of animal traits to humans, deities, or inanimate objects. 2. The use of animal psychology or physiology to explain human behavior. Compare ANTHROPOMORPHISM.

zoomythic   Mythology in which deities have animal forms.

zoon politikon   (social animal—Greek) See SOCIAL INSTINCT.

zoophile   1. A person opposed to any animal experimentation. 2. A person who loves animals, especially if the person likes animals more than humans, such as in preferring the company of animals to the company of people.

zoophilia   1. See ZOOPHILISM. 2. A disorder characterized by an extreme degree of attraction to animals by a human. 3. Being sexually attracted to or aroused by animals. 4. Legally, term is sometimes considered synonymous with sodomy (anal intercourse, oral intercourse, or both, with a human or animal). 5. See BESTIALITY, ZOOERASTY.

zoophilism   Love of animals, particularly an abnormal fondness or devotion to animals. Not as severe as zoomania.

zoophobia   Morbid fear of animals in general. See ANIMAL FEAR.

zoopsia   A visual hallucination in which the patient sees insects or other animals, as in cases of delirium tremens.

zoosadism   Sadistic satisfaction obtained from torturing an animal, with or without sexual contact with the victim.

zootrope   An optical device, shaped like a tube, that may be rotated while a person looks into one end. The cylinder is divided into separate figures that, when rotated while looking into the tube, give the impression of movement. Used before the invention of the cinema to demonstrate that the illusion of movement could be created by showing unit pictures in close sequence. Also spelled zoetrope. See STROBOSCOPE.

Zoth's acoumeter   (O. Zoth) An older form of audiometer that measured the threshold of hearing as the lowest height from which a ball dropped on a sounding board was heard. See WUNDT GRAVITY PHONOMETER.

ZPG   zero population growth

Z-Process (Therapy)   (R. Zaslow) A controversial treatment, first used for autistic children, then with disturbed adolescents and psychotic adults. Included confining or holding persons against their will while demanding that they respond to a therapist's questions, such as "Tell me your name", before permitting the client to be released. Children were kept immobile and even tickled until they responded as the therapist wanted.

Remarkable claims have been made about the efficacy of this method, but evidence is inconclusive. Also known as Z technique.

z_r   Transformed value of the correlation coefficient r.

Z score   In the statistical treatment of data, a standard score in which the difference between an individual score and the mean is expressed in terms of units of standard deviations. Formula: $z = (X - M) \div SD$, where X is the score, M is the mean, and **SD** is the standard deviation. [Their sum = 0, their standard deviation = 1.0]. Also known as standard(ized) score, z score, Z-score. See STANDARD DEVIATION.

Z technique   **Z-Process (Therapy)**

Z-transformation   In statistics, another name for the Fisher r-to-Z transformation.

Zugenruhe   Increased activity in birds as the time for migration approaches.

Zürich School   A group of psychoanalysts who were followers of Carl Jung, as opposed to the Viennese School of Sigmund Freud's followers. The school is named after Zurich, Switzerland, where Carl Jung practiced psychiatry for many years.

Zwaardemaker olfactometer   (H. Zwaardemaker) An apparatus for the control and measurement of odorous stimuli. See ODOR PRISM, SMELL, SMELL MECHANISM.

Zwaardemaker smell system   (H. Zwaardemaker) A classification of odors in separate groups based on Carolus Linnaeus's seven-class system. Hendrick Zwaardemaker added two more classes (ethereal and empyreumatic) to Linnaeus' original seven, thus proposing nine: (a) ethereal—fruits, wine; (b) aromatic—camphor, spices; (c) fragrant—flowers, vanilla; (d) ambrosiac—musk, sandalwood; (e) alliaceous—garlic, chlorine; (f) empyreumatic—coffee, creosote; (g) hircine or caprylic—cheese, rancid fat; (h) foul or repulsive—bedbugs, belladonna; and (i) nauseous or nauseating—feces, rotten meat. A number of other odor-classification systems proposed different numbers of classes, such as Crocker-Henderson (four) and Amoore (seven). Hans Henning, in contrast to Zwaardemaker, reduced Linnaeus' classes to six, arranging them into a prism. See HENNING SMELL PRISM, STEREOCHEMICAL SMELL THEORY.

zygomaticus   A set of muscles innervated by the facial nerve (the seventh cranial nerve) which activate the movement of the upper lip outward, upward, and backward.

zygosis   The union of two gametes.

zygote   (yoked—Greek) In reproduction, the fertilized egg produced through union of the female's egg and the male's sperm. Since the egg and the sperm each provide one-half of the total complement of chromosomes, the fertilized egg (zygote) constitutes the first complete cell of the developing organism from which all other cells develop. Following a two-week period (in humans) of rapid cell division, the zygote develops into an embryo. See EMBRYO, FETUS, GAMETE, PREGNANCY.

Zyve test   A test of scientific aptitude.

zyz   (H. B. English) A bogus nonsense syllable suggested by Horace B. English, which he thought was suitable to end his dictionary, and this editor concurs.

PREFIXES, SUFFIXES, AFFIXES

Psychologists should be able to discern the meanings of a many new words that begin with, end with, or contain certain prefixes, suffixes, etc. For instance the term **bradykinesis**, if **brady** means "slow" and **kinesis** means "movement" it can probably be guessed that the term means *slow movement*.

Some of the following are prefixes, some are suffixes and some are combining forms that can be prefixes, suffixes or can occur within a word. Most are of Latin or Greek origin. Examples of words in which the combining forms occur are given in parentheses.

a-/an- away, lacking, without (ACHROMATIC)

-ab- away from (ABNORMAL)

-aceous- in the nature of, characteristic of (CAMPHO-RACEOUS)

-acusia hearing (PARACUSIA)

-ad pertaining to (MONAD)

-ad- increase, toward, adjacent to (ADDITIVE, ADDUCTOR)

af-/ag- toward (AFFERENT, AGGRESSION)

agog(ue)- leading to (HYPNAGOGIC)

agor(a)- open, public place (AGORAPHOBIA)

-akine- absence of or impaired motion (AKINETIC APRAXIA)

alg(es)-/-alg(ia)-/-algesia/-algy pain (ALGOLAGNIA)

-all(o)- other, another (ALLOCENTERED)

-allach-/-alak- elsewhere (ALLACHESTHESIA)

-allotrio- perverted, offensive, strange (ALLOTRIOGEUSTIA)

-alt(er)- other, another, second (ALTER EGO)

amaur(o)- dark (AMAUROTIC)

ambi- both, around (AMBIDEXTROUS)

ambly- dim (AMBLYOPIA)

-amnes- loss, impairment of memory (AMNESIA)

amphi- around, all about, on both sides or ends (AMPHIGENOUS)

ampli- spacious, maximum (AMPLITUDE)

an- up, back, against, upon, without (ANABOLISM, ANOSMIA)

ana- away from, back, up, upper (ANACLISIS)

-andr(o)- male, maleness (ANDROGEN)

anomal(o)- irregular (ANOMALOUS)

-ant(e)- prior to, in front of (ANTEDATING RESPONSE)

ant(i)- opposed to, counteracting, relieving (ANTIPATHY)

-ante(ro)- prior to, before (in front of) (ANTEROGRADE AMNESIA)

-anthrop(o)- male, human (ANTHROPOLOGY)

apti- fitness (APTITUDE)

arche- primitive (ARCHETYPE)

-atel(o)- defective development (ATELIOSIS)

-ation process (FIXATION)

-audi(o)- sound, hearing (AUDILE, AUDITION)

-aur- ear (AURICLE)

aut(o)- self, itself (AUTOEROTIC)

-bary- heavy, difficult (BARYLALIA)

bi(n)-/bi(s)- two, two-fold, twice, double (BINOCULAR)

-bio- life, living organisms (BIOCHEMISTRY)

-bis- both, twice (BISECT)

-brachy- short (BRACHYCEPHALY)

brady- slow (BRADYACUSIA)

-bulia will (ABULIA)

-cac(o)- bad, unpleasant (CACOPHONY)

cen(o)/coen(o)- common, frequent (COENOCYTE)

centi- hundred, hundredth (CENTIMETER)

-cept- received (PERCEPTION)

-cerebr(o)-/-cerebri- brain (CEREBRAL)

-cheir(o)-/-chir(o)- hand (CHEROMANCY, CHIROPRACTIC)

chrom(a)-/chromat(o)- color (CHROMAESTHESIA)

-chron(o)- time (CHRONOLOGY)

-cide destroying, killing (HOMOCIDE, SUICIDE)

-cip(a)- receive, take (ANTICIPATORY)

circum- around (CIRCUMFERENCE)

-claustr(o)- barrier, cage, enclosing (CLAUSTROPHOBIA)

-climac-/-climax- stairs, ladder, step, high point (CLIMAX)

co- together, equal (CO-VARY)

-coen(e)-/-cene-/coeno- common, general, sharing (COENOCYTE)

cogn- know (COGNITION)

com- with, together (COMBINATION)

con- **(col-/cor-/com-/co-)** with, affiliated (CONCURRENT)

-contr(a)-/-counter- opposite, against (CONTRACEPTION, COUNTERCONDITIONING)

-crypt(o)- concealed, hidden (CRYPTOGRAM)

-cumul- a heap (ACCUMULATOR)

cycl- circular (CYCLIC)

de- away from, reversal of a process (DEANALIZE)

deci- one-tenth (DECIMETER, DECIMAL)

-demo- people, population (DEMOGRAPHIC)

-deuter(o)-/-deuto- two, second, secondary (DEUTERANOPE)

-dextr(o)-/-dexter- right, right-hand side (DEXTRALITY)

di(a)- between (DIENCEPHALON)

di(s)-/-di- two, double, two-foldness (DICHOTOMY, DIPLOID)

-dia- through, apart, completely (DIACHRONIC)

-dipl(o)- double (DIPLOID)

dis- apart, separation, opposite of, absence of (DIS-INHIBITION)

dis-/-dys- abnormal, bad, faulty, difficult, painful, impaired, morbid (DISPLASIA, DYSFUNCTION)

-dolich(o)- long (DOLICOCEPHALIC)

du(o)- two (DUALISM)

dy- two (DYAD)

dynam(o)- power, energy, force, strength (DYNAMICS)

-dys- bad, abnormal, difficult, painful, morbid, incomplete (DYSFUNCTION)

-ec-/-ect(o)- outer, external, outside, out of (ECTO-CHONDRAL)

eco- home (ECOLOGICAL)

ef- outside (EFFERENT)

-em-/-en- in (EMPATHY, ENZYME)

-ence process, quality of (TRANSFERENCE)

-end(o)- within (ENDODERM)

ent(o)- internal, within (ENTEROCEPTOR)

ep(i)- upon, above, over (EPIBLAST)

equi- equal (EQUIDISTANT)

-erg(o)-/-ergas- activity, work (ERGONOMICS)

-esis process (AMNIOCENTESIS)

-esthesia/esthes(io)- feeling, sensitivity (ANESTHESIA)

eth- custom, behavior (ETHOLOGY)

ethno- ethnic race, people, cultural group (ETHNO-CENTRISM)

-eu- agreeable, easy, good, healthy, normal, well (EUGENICS)

eury- broad, wide (EURYMORPH)

ex(o)-/-ex(tra])- external, outer, outside (EXOCRINE, EXTRASENSORY)

-exo-/-exter-/-extra- outer, outside (EXOGAMY, EXTEROCEPTIVE, EXTRAPYRAMIDAL)

extro- directed outward (EXTROPUNITIVE)

-fili(a)- son, daughter, relation (FILIAL)

-gam(o)-/-gamy/-gamous marriage, union for reproduction (GAMETE, MONOGAMY)

-gen(e)-/-genes-/-genet-/-jen- generation, production (IATROGENESIS, GENETICS)

gen(o)- ancestry (GENOTYPE)

-genesis creation, origin, development (ABIOGENESIS)

-genic genus or kind, produced by, producing (PATHO-GENIC)

-ger(o)-/-geront- old age (GERONTOLOGY)

-geus/-geusia sense of taste (GUSTATION, PARAGEU-SIA)

-gloss(o)- tongue, speech, language (GLOSSALALIA, GLOSSARY)

gno(s) knowledge (AGNOSIA)

gon(o)- genitals, offspring (GONADS)

gonad- testis, ovary (GONADOTROPHIC)

-gram- record, tracing of (ELECTROENCEPHALOGRAM)

-graph- writing, writer, recording, recording instrument (GRAPHOLOGY)

-gymn(o)- nude (GYMNASIUM)

gyn-/-gyno/-gynec- women (GYNECOLOGY, GYNO-SPERM)

-gyr(o)- circle, circular, rotation (GYROSCOPE)

-hapl(o)- single, simple (HAPLOID)

-hapt(o)- touch, contact, combination (HAPTOMETER)

heb(e)- youth, puberty (HEBEPHRENIA)

-hedon- pleasure (HEDONISM)

-hemi- half, unilateral condition (HEMISPHERE)

-heter(o)- other, different, unlike (HETERODOX)

-hol(o)- complete, entire, whole (HOLISM)

-homeo-/-homoeo- resembling, similar, like (HOMEO-STASIS)

homo- [Greek] identical, uniform, same (HOMO-ZYGOUS)

homo- [Latin] man, mankind (HOMUNCULUS)

-hum-/-hom- earth, soil, on the ground (HUMAN, HUMBLE)

-hyp(o)- under, below, less than normal, to a low degree, inferior, deficient (HYPOCHONDRIA, HYPOTHALAMUS)

-hyper- excess, above, over, superiority, abnormality (HYPERACTIVE)

-hypn(o)- sleep (HYPNAGOGIC)

-hyster(o)- uterus, womb (HYSTERECTOMY)

-ia(sis) disorder, pathological condition (HYPOCHON-DRIASIS)

-iatr(o)-/-iatrist/-iatry medicine, healing, physician (IATROGENIC)

-ic(al) relating to, pertaining to the word of (PSYCHO-GENIC, RADICAL)

-ics study, practice (DYNAMICS)

-id particle of, body structure (CHROMATID)

ideo- thought, idea (IDEOLOGY)

-idio- peculiarity, personal, private (IDIOSYNCRASY)

infra- below (INFRAHUMAN)

inter- between (INTERVIEW)

intero- from the inside (INTEROCEPTOR)

intra-/intr(o)- within (INTROJECTION)

intro- directed inward (INTROJECTION)

-ion act, process (REGRESSION)

ipse- sameness (IPSILATERAL)

-ism doctrine, condition (ANIMISM)

-iso- same, alike, equal (ISOCHRONAL)

-kat(a)-/-kato-/-kath- downward, going down, beneath, against (KATASEXUALITY)

kin(es)-/-kine-/kines(i)-/-kinet(o)- action, movement (KINESIMETER, KINESTHESIS)

-klepto- steal (KLEPTOMANIA)

kurt- curved (KURTOSIS)

-labi(o)- lips (LABIAL)

-lagn(ia)- lust (ALGOLAGNIA)

-lal(ia)- speak, speech (GLOSSOLALIA)

-later- side (BILATERAL)

lept(o)- weak, peaked, thin, slender, slight, small, fine, delicate (LEPTOKURTOSIS, LEPTOSOME, LEPTOMORPH)

-lev(o)-/-laevo-/levu- left side (LEVOPHOBIA)

-lex- word, speech (ALEXIA)

limin- threshold (SUBLIMINAL)

-log(o)- speech, reasoning, words (LOGAMNESIA, LOGISTICS, LOGORRHEA)

-logy/-ology knowledge, science, study of, field of study (PSYCHOLOGY)

lumin- Light (LUMINANCE)

-mace-/-macr(o)- large, long, enlarged (MACROPSIA)

-mal- bad, wrong, ill, diseased, abnormal, defect (MALADAPTIVE)

-mate- act, move (AUTOMATED)

-meg(al)-/-mega(lo)- large, enlarged (ACROMEGALY, MEGALOMANIA)

-ment act, result (ASSESSMENT)

-ment- about the mind (AMENTIA)

-mes(o)- middle position, medium, median size (MESOKURTIC, MESODERM)

-met(a)- among, between, with, beyond, change (METAANALYSIS, METABOLISM)

-meter measure, measurement, measuring device (KILOMETER)

-metr(y) measurement (PSYCHOMETRY)

-micr(o)- small, enlarging what is small (MICROELECTRODE)

mid- middle, median (MIDBRAIN)

-mis(o)- wrong, bad, hatred (MISNOMER, MISOGYNY)

-mne(m or s)- memory (AMNESIA)

-mod- measure, manner (BIMODAL)

-mon(o)- one, single, alone (MONOCULAR)

mono- one (MONOAMINE, MONOGAMY)

-morph form, shape (ECTOMORPH)

-morph(o)-/-morphous sleep, form, shape, structure (MORPHINE, MORPHOLOGY)

multi- many (MULTIPHASIC)

-nat(e) born (NEONATE)

ne(o)- new, recent (NEONATE)

-necr(o)- death, dissolution (NECROPSY)

-noct(i)- night (NOCTURNAL)

-noi- mind, thought (PARANOIA)

-nom(i])- name, term (BINOMIAL)

-nom- custom, law (AUTONOMIC)

non- not (NONAGGRESSIVE)

-nos(o])- disease (NOSOLOGY)

-nyct(o)- darkness, night (NYCTOPHOBIA)

-nymph(o)- nymph, female (NYMPHOMANIA)

ob- **(oc-/of-/og-/op-)** toward, opposite to (OBJECTION)

-odyn-/-odynia pain (ANODYNE)

-oid resembling (SCHIZOID)

-olig(o)- few, scant, deficient (OLIGARCHY)

-ology/-logy science of, field of study (PSYCHOLOGY)

omni- all, total (OMNIPOTENT)

-oneir(a)- dream (ONEIROLOGY)

-onto- existence, being, individual (ONTOGENETIC)

-opisth(o)- posterior, backward, behind (OPISTHION)

-opsia/-opsy/-opsin/-posy condition of vision (OPSIS)

-opt(o)- vision, eyes (OPTICAL)

-orth(o)- straight, correct, normal (ORTHODOX, ORTHOPSYCHIATRY)

-osis/-asis condition, esp. diseased, abnormal (PSYCHOSIS, HYPNOSIS)

-osm(ia) smell, sense of smell, olfaction (ANOSMIA)

-ot(o)- ear, hearing (OTOLITH, OTOSCOPE)

-otic similar to, relating to, disease, pathological condition (NEUROTIC)

paed(o)-/paid(o)- child (PEDIATRICS)

palaeo-/paleo- ancient, primitive (PALEOCEREBELLUM)

-pali(n)- repetition, reversal of direction (PALINDROME)

-pan-/-pant(o)- all, every, generalized (PANDEMIC)

-par(a)- resembling, perversion, abnormal, beyond, beside, near, distorted (PARADOX, PARANOIA, PARALLEL, PARALYSIS)

-parthen(o)- girl, virgin(al), unspoiled, early stage (PARTHENOGENESIS)

-parv(i)- small (PARVITUDE)

-path(o)- suffering, disease (PSYCHOPATH, PATHOLOGY)

-pathy disease, feeling, suffering, therapy, remedy (PSYCHOPATHY)

ped(ia)- infants, children, boys (PEDAGOGY)

-per(i)- around, near, enclosing (PERIPHERAL, PERIMETER)

-phag-/-phagia-/-phago-/-phagy eat, hunger, eating (APHAGIA, PHAGOPHOBIA)

-phasia speech (DYSPHASIA)

-phemia speech (TACHYPHEMIA)

-phil(o)- love, fondness, interest (PHILOSOPHY)

-philia craving, attraction (PEDOPHILIA)

-phob(o)-/-phobia fear (PHOBIA)

-phon(o)-/-phone/-phony voice, speech, sound (TELEPHONE)

-phot(o)- light (PHOTISM)

-phren(o)-/-phrenia mind (PHRENOLOGY)

phyl(o)- race, species (PHYLOGENY)

physi(o)- growth, nature (PHYSIOLOGICAL)

-platy- broad, flat (PLATYKURTIC)

-pleio-/-pleo- multiple, excessive, or greedy (PLEONEXIA)

-poiesis production, formation (HEMOPOIETIC)

poly- many, manifold (POLYGAMY)

post- behind, after, later (POSTSYNAPTIC)

-prax- performance (APRAXIA)

pre-/prae- before (place or time) (PREMORBID)

-presby(o)- old age, elder (PRESBYOPIA)

prim- first (PRIMITIVATION)

pro- favorable, in place of, before, forward, in front of (PROCLIVITY, PROJECTION)

-prot(o)- first, primary, preceding, primitive, earliest (PROTOTYPE, PROTANOPIA)

proxim- near (PROXIMAL)

-pseud(o)- erroneous, false, spurious, falsely imitating (PSEUDOSCIENCE)

-psych(o)- mind, mental, personality (PSYCHOLOGY)

quasi- approximately (QUASI-EXPERIMENTAL)

-quis(i)- get, gain (ACQUISITION)

-rad-   root, rod, ray (RADICAL, RADIAL)
re-   back, again (REACTION, REITERATE)
-ret-   net, net-like (RETICULAR)
retro-   backward, behind (RETROACTIVE, RETRO-GRADE)

-scat(o)-   feces, filth (SCATOLOGY)
-schisis/-schisto-/schiz(o)-   split, fissure (SCHIZO-PHRENIA)
-scop(e)   viewer (STROBOSCOPE)
scopia/scopic/-scopo-/-scopy   visual observation (device), watching, inspection (MICROSCOPE)
-scot(o)-   darkness, blindness (SCOTOPIC)
-sem-   signs, meaning (SEMANTICS)
sema-   sign (SEMANTICS)
semi-   half (SEMICIRCULAR)
-sen(il)-   old, aging (SENILITY)
-sinistr(o)-   left side (SINISTRAD)
-soci-   companion (ASSOCIATION)
socio-   social, to join, be a companion (SOCIODRAMA)
-som(at)-/somato-   body (SOMATOTONIA)
somno-   sleep (SOMNOLENCE)
-spect-   look, view (INTROSPECTION)
-stasis-   stable, fixed, standing (HOMEOSTASIS, STASI-MORPHY)
-steno-   narrow (STENOSIS)
stere(o)-   solid, hard, firm, three-dimensional (STEREOSCOPE)
-sthen-   strength, force (PSYCHASTHENIA, STENIC TYPE)
-stra(ct)-   draw (ABSTRACTION)
strepho-   twisted (STREPHOSYMBOLIA)
sub-   below, lower order, beneath, less than, under (SUBVOCAL, SUBCEPTION)
super-   higher (order, quality, quantity, or degree), above (SUPEREGO)
supra-   above, higher than, on top of, lying above or upon (SUPRALIMINAL)
-surd-   deaf, silent (SURDITY)
-sym-/-syn-   union, fusion, together (SYMBIOSIS, SYNDROME, SYNAPSE)

tach(isto)-/-tachy-   quick, fast (TACHISTOSCOPE, TACHYCARDIA)
-tact-   touch (TACTILE)
-tax-   arrangement (ATAXIA)
-tel(e)-/-telo-/tele(o)-   far, distance, end, consumation, purpose (TELEPATHY, TELEOLOGY)
temp(o)-   time (TEMPORARY, TEMPORAL AVOID-ANCE CONDITIONING)
-tempor-   temple (TEMPORAL LOBE)
-terat(o)-   deformed, monstrous (TERATOGENESIS)
-thanat(o)-   death (THANATOS)
-therapy   treatment, cure, healing (PSYCHOTHERAPY)
-tion   condition (REACTION)
-ton(o)-   sound, tone (TONAL GAP)
-top(o)-   place, location, position, region (TOPOGRA-PHY, TOPECTOMY)
trans-   across, surpassing, through, beyond, from one to another (TRANSDUCER, TRANSACTION)
-troph(o)/-trophy   nourish, nurse, develop (HYPER-TROPHY)
-tropic-/-trop-/-tropy/trop(o)-   turning toward, influencing, deviating, turn, bend (TROPOMETER, TRO-POSTEREOSCOPE)

un-   not, lack, absence (UNBIASED)
uni-   single, one, unitary (UNILATERAL)

val-   worth, strength (VALENCE)
veri-   truth (VERIDICAL)
vir-   man, adult male (VIRILE)

-xen(o)-   different, strange, alien (XENOPHOBIA)
-xer(o)-   dry (XEROMENIA)

-y   condition, sickness (ACROMEGALY)

-zoo-   animals (ZOOERASTY)

DSM-IV TERMS

Diagnostic and Statistical Manual of Mental Disorders (DSM). Originally based on the *International Classification of Diseases* issued by the World Health Organization, the American Psychiatric Association published the first edition of this manual in 1952, and revisions in 1968, 1980, 1987, and 1994. Terms such as *Bipolar I Disorder, Most Recent Episode Mixed, Severe Without Psychotic Features (296.63)* go beyond the scope of this dictionary. This dictionary includes our definitions of about one hundred of the diagnostic categories of the DSM-IV, as listed below with their code numbers.

academic problem (V62.3)
acculturation problem (V62.4)
acute stress disorder (308.3)
adjustment disorder with depressed mood (309.0)
alcohol intoxication (303.00)
alcohol abuse (305.00)
amphetamine dependence (304.40)
anorexia nervosa (307.1)
antisocial behavior (V71.01)
antisocial-personality disorder (301.7)
anxiety disorder (300.00)
attention-deficit/hyperactivity disorder NOS (314.9)
autistic disorder (299.00)
avoidant personality disorder (301.82)
bereavement (V62.82)
bipolar disorder (296.80)
body dysmorphic disorder (300.7)
borderline personality disorder (301.83)
borderline personality disorder (301.83)
borderline intellectual functioning (V62.89)
bulimia nervosa (307.51)
cannabis intoxication (292.89)
communication disorder (307.9)
conduct disorder (312.8)
conversion disorder (300.11)
cyclothymic disorder (301.13)
dementia (294.8)
dependent personality disorder (301.6)
depersonalization disorder (300.6)
disorder of infancy, childhood, or adolescence (313.9)
disruptive behavior disorder (312.9)
dyspareunia (302.76)
dysthymic disorder (300.4)
eating disorder NOS (307.50)
encopresis (307.7)
enuresis (307.6)
exhibitionism (302.4)
factitious disorder (300.19)
female orgasmic disorder (302.73)
fetishism (302.81)
hallucinogen-induced mood disorder (292.84)
histrionic personality disorder (301.50)
hypochondriasis (300.7)
intermittent explosive disorder (312.34)
kleptomania (312.32)
learning disorder (315.9)
male orgasmic disorder (302.74)

malingering (V65.2)
medication-induced movement disorder (333.90)
mental disorder (293.9)
mental retardation, severity unspecified (319)
moderate mental retardation (318.0)
mood disorder (296.90)
narcissistic personality disorder (301.81)
narcolepsy (347)
neuroleptic malignant syndrome (333.92)
obsessive-compulsive disorder (300.3)
paranoid personality disorder (301.0)
paraphilia (302.9)
pathological gambling (312.31)
pedophilia (302.2)
personality disorder (301.9)
pica (307.52)
posttraumatic stress disorder (309.81)
premature ejaculation (302.75)
profound mental retardation (318.2)
psychotic disorder NOS (298.9)
pyromania (312.33)
reactive attachment disorder of infancy/childhood (313.89)
reading disorder (315.00)
rumination disorder (of infancy) (307.53)
schizoaffective disorder (295.70)
schizoid personality disorder (301.20)
schizophreniform disorder (295.40)
schizotypal personality disorder (301.22)
separation anxiety disorder (309.21)
severe mental retardation (318.1)
sexual dysfunction (302.70)
sexual sadism (302.84)
sexual masochism (302.83)
sexual abuse of a child (V61.21)
sexual aversion disorder (302.79)
shared psychotic disorder (297.3)
sleepwalking disorder (307.46)
social phobia (300.23)
somatization disorder (300.81)
specific phobia (300.29)
stereotypic movement disorders (307.3)
stuttering (307.0)
Tourette's Syndrome (TS) (307.23)
trichotillomania (312.39)
vaginismus (306.51)
voyeurism (302.82)

THE GREEK ALPHABET

These letters of the Greek alphabet are arranged alphabetically in terms of their English names, but their proper order within the Greek alphabet is indicated in the definitions. Often, especially in statistical material, these symbols are presented without explanation. Some definitions include references to entries defined in the dictionary's glossary. For example, in **alpha**, TYPE I ERROR is referred to and defined in this dictionary.

alpha (α, **A**)   The first letter of the Greek alphabet. Lowercase refers to the probability of rejecting a true hypothesis, making a TYPE I ERROR.

beta (β, **B**)   The second letter of the Greek alphabet. Uppercase refers to the probability of accepting an hypothesis when it is actually false, making a TYPE II ERROR.

chi (χ, **X**)   The twenty-second letter of the Greek alphabet. The square of the Uppercase refers to the statistic CHI SQUARE.

delta (δ, Δ)   The fourth letter of the Greek alphabet. Uppercase refers to the absolute difference between two population means; also an increment increase. Lowercase tells the number of degrees of freedom associated with the chi square value. Also, the difference between two quantities.

epsilon (ϵ, **E**)   The fifth letter of the Greek alphabet. Lowercase means a member of as "a epsilon A" or "a is a member of A."

eta (η, **H**)   The seventh letter of the Greek alphabet. Lowercase is a symbol for the CORRELATION RATIO.

gamma (γ, Γ)   The third letter of the Greek alphabet. Lowercase refers to the coefficient of predictive association between sets of ordered classes. Also in psychophysics the difference between a perception and the THRESHOLD.

iota (ι, **I**)   The ninth letter of the Greek alphabet.

kappa (κ, **K**)   The tenth letter of the Greek alphabet. Lowercase is a curve criterion.

lambda (λ, Λ)   The eleventh letter of the Greek alphabet. Lowercase is a symbol for wavelength of light.

mu (μ, **M**)   The twelfth letter of the Greek alphabet. Lowercase refers to the population mean.

nu (ν, **N**)   The thirteenth letter of the Greek alphabet. Lowercase is the number of degrees of freedom for a t or CHI SQUARE variable.

omega (ω, Ω)   The twenty-fourth and last letter of the Greek alphabet. Lowercase is the population index showing the relative reduction in the variance of Y given the X value for an observation.

omicron (o, **O**)   The fifteenth letter of the Greek alphabet.

phi (ϕ, Φ)   The twenty-first letter of the Greek alphabet. Uppercase is the symbol for PHI COEFFICIENT.

pi (π, Π)   The sixteenth letter of the Greek alphabet. Lowercase is a mathematical constant equal to 3.1416.

psi (, Ψ)   The twenty-third letter of the Greek alphabet. Uppercase is used to represent psychology. Lowercase refers to the value of a particular unit among a set of units.

rho (ρ, **P**)   The seventeenth letter of the Greek alphabet. Lowercase is the symbol for RANK ORDER CORRELATION.

sigma (σ, Σ)   The eighteenth letter of the Greek alphabet. Uppercase is a symbol for a series of values. Lowercase is a symbol for standard deviation and for millisecond. Lowercase squared is symbol for VARIANCE.

tau (τ, **T**)   The nineteenth letter of the Greek alphabet. Lowercase refers to KENDALL'S TAU.

theta (θ, Θ)   The eighth letter of the Greek alphabet. Uppercase is a symbol for the population value of a proportion.

upsilon (υ, Υ)   The twentieth letter of the Greek alphabet. Lowercase refers to the so-called "true" score of an individual on Y.

xi (ξ, Ξ)   The fourteenth letter of the Greek alphabet. Lowercase is a symbol for subjective equality in psychophysics (threshold). Also, it is used to stand for the median of a population.

zeta (ζ, **Z**)   The sixth letter of the Greek alphabet. Lowercase refers to the difference between the squares of the CORRELATION RATIO and the CORRELATION COEFFICIENT.

MEDICAL PRESCRIPTION TERMS

Many terms used in prescriptions come from the Latin, such as the letter **c** = con (meaning with) and from Greek such as **collyr** = collyrium (meaning poultice, eye wash). These terms are included for those few psychologists who already have permission to write prescriptions, for psychiatrists, for psychologists who are also physicians, and for psychologists in medical settings who may need to understand the meaning of such abbreviations.

a.c.   before meals
āā   of each
ad lib.   freely, as desired
anti.   antidote
aq. dest.   distilled water
bid/b.i.d./BID/B.I.D.   twice a day
c/c̄   with
caps.   capsule
contra.   contraindication
d.   daily
dc/DC   discontinue
fl.   fluid
ft. puiv.   make a powder
ft.   make
gtt.   a drop
h   hour
h.s.   just before sleep
hor. som.   just before sleep
int.   internal or interior
liq.   solution
m.   a fluid measure, about one drop
M.   mix
noct.   at night

non rep.   do not repeat
o.h.   every hour
o.m.   every morning
o.n.   every night
p.c.   after meals
p.r.n. or prn   as occasion arises, as needed, as required
q. 2h   every two hours
q. 4h   every 4 hours
q.d.   once a day
q.h.   every hour
qid/q.i.d./Q.I.D./QID   four times daily
q.o.d.   every other day
q.s. or qs   a sufficient quantity
s   without
sem.   half
s.i.d./S.I.D./SID   once a day
sig.   write on label
ss   half
stat   immediately
syr   syrup
tid/t.i.d./T.I.D./TID   three times a day
ut dict.   as directed

SYSTEMS OF TREATMENT

The list of titles below are systems of "treatments" that fall for the most part in (psycho)therapies, but also include counseling and physiological treatments. Endings of most of the systems are diverse including *analysis, counseling, healing, psychiatry, psychotherapy, storage, therapy, treatment* but some such as psychoanalysis and psychodrama are complete.

Action-oriented
Activity-group
Activity-play
Actualizing
Adjustment
Adjuvant
Ahistoric
Allocentered
Ambulatory
Anaclitic Psychoanalytic Group
Analytic Psychology
Analytical
Animal Assisted
Antiandrogen
Aqua-energetics
art
Assertion-structured
Assignment
Attitude
Autogenic Training
Autonomous
Autosymbolism
bath
Behavior(al)
Behavior modification
Bibliotherapy
Bioenergetic analysis
Biofeedback
Biofunctional
Biogenetics
biological
Blue-collar
Body
Brain-wave
Brief
Brief Group
Brief-stimuli
Carbon-dioxide
Character-analytic
Client-centered
Co-counseling
Cognitive
Cognitive Behavior
Collaborative
Combined
Computerized
Concurrent
Conditioned-reflex
Conditioning
Conjoint

Conjoint Family
Continous-Bath
Continuous-sleep
Contractual
Controlled-drinking
Corticoid
Co-therapy
Covert Modeling
Creative Aggression
creative arts
Crisis
Crisis-intervention group
Dance
Deep Psychobiology
Delay
Depth
Deterrent
Dialogical
Didactic
Didactic Group
Direct Psychoanalysis
Directive
Directive-play Drama
Divided Self
Drug
Dyadic
Eclectic
Ego
Ego-state
Eidetic
Electro-sleep
Electroconvulsive shock
Emotive
Encouragement
Environmental
Ericksonian
Evocative
Existential
Existential-Humanistic
Experiential
Expressive
Extended-family
Eye Movement Desensitization and Reprocessing (EMDR)
Family
Family Group
Feminist
Fixed Role
Focal
Focusing
Forced Counseling

Functional
General
Gestalt
Goal-limited
Graphic-arts
Group
Group Analysis
Group-analytic
Group Bibliotherapy
Heteronomous
Holistic
Hydrotherapy
Hypnoanalysis
Hypnodelic
Hypnotherapy
Imagery
Imago Relationship
Immediate
Impasse-priority
Implosion
Indirect Method Of
Individual
Insight
Inspirational Group
Instigation
Insulin-coma
Integrated
Integrative
Integrity
Intensive
Interactional
Interpersonal
Interpretive
Interview
Interview Group
Leaderless-group
Light
Limited-Term
Logotherapy
Long-Term
LSD
Major-role
Marathon Group
Marital
Marriage
Mechanical Group
Medical
Metaphor
Metrazol Shock
Milieu
Minimum-change
Mitchell Rest
Modeling
Morita
movement
Multimodal
Multiple
Multiple Marital
Multiple Family
Multiple-impact
Music(al)
Naikan
Narrative
Nondirective
Nondirective Group

Nondirective Play
Nude
Objective
Object-Relations
Occupational
Operant
Orgone
Paraverbal
Person-centered
Personal Construct
Persuasion
pet
pharmacotherapy
Phenomenological
Physical
Plastic-arts
Play
Play-group
Poetry
Poison-pen
Primal
Primal-scream
Primary Relationship
Problem-solving Group
Prgrammed Success
Projection
Projective
Provocative
Psychedelic
Psycho-imaginative
Psychoanalysis
Psychoanalytic Group
Psychodrama
Psychodynamic
Psycholytic
Psychomaterialism
Psychopharmacotherapy
Psychosocial
Psychosynthesis
puppetry
Radical
Rankian
Rational
Rational-Emotive-Behavior
Re-education/Re-educative
Re-evaluation Co-counseling
Reality
Reciprocal Inhibition
Relationship
Relaxation
Release
Religious
Replacement
Replication
Repressive-inspirational Group
Responsive
Restoration/Restorative
Restraining
Retroactive
Rhythmic Sensory-Bombardment
Role-divided
Rolfing
Rubenfield Synergy
Sector
Self-image
Semantic

Sensate-focus-oriented
Sensory-bombardment
Sex
Shame-aversion
Shaping
Shock Treatment
Short-term Storage
Short-term
Situational
Social
Social Therapy
Social Network
Solution-focused
Somatic
Spontaneity Training
Strategic Family
Strategic Intervention
Strategic Solution-focused
Structural
Structural Family
Structured Interactional Group

Subcoma Insulin
Suggestion
Suggestive
Suppressive
Surface
Thought-field
Three-cornered
Third-force
Time-extended
Total-push
Touch
Trager mentastics
Transactional Analysis
Transendence
Twenty-four Hour
Vegetotherapy
Verbal Behavior
Will
Work
Z-process Attachment
Zen

MEASURING INSTRUMENTS

This is a list of "measuring instruments" defined or mentioned in this dictionary. They are of varying types: paper and pencil, performance, projective. Some are carefully researched and have norms, and some are projective instruments. Some were written by individuals; some were done by committees, some are of historical value, and some were in use as of the time of compilation. They attempt to measure many kinds of attributes including vocational aptitudes, attitudes of various kinds, intelligence, and aspects of personality. And some have more than one name.

A Test
ACE test
Adaptive Behavior Scale
Adult Basic Learning Examination
Alienation Test
Allport A-S Reaction Study
Alpha Examination/Test
American College Testing Program
American Home Scale
American Council on Education Test
Anti-Semitic scale
Apgar scale
Armed Services Vocational Aptitude Battery
Army tests
Army General Classification Test
ARP tests
Arthur Point of Performance Tests Scale
AS scales
Attitude Toward Disabled Persons Scale
Auditory Apperception Test
Assuage test
Bárány test
Barron-Welsh Art Scale
Basic Occupational Literacy Test
Bayley Scales of Infant Development
Beck Depression Inventory
Behn-Rorschach Test
Bell Adjustment Inventory
Bem Sex-Role Inventory
Bender Visual-Motor Gestalt Test
Bennett Differential Aptitude test
Bennett Test of Mechanical Comprehension
Benton Visual Retention Test
Bernreuter Personal Adjustment Inventory
Beta Examination/Test
Betts' test of visual imagery
Binet-Simon Scale /Binet Scale/Test
Black Intelligence Test of Cultural Homogeneity
Blacky Test
Boehm Test of Basic Concepts
Bogardus Social-Distance Scale
Bolgar-Fischer World Test
Brazelton Neonatal Behavioral Assessment Scale
Brief Psychiatric Rating Scale
Bruininks-Oseretsky Test of Motor Proficiency
Bühler baby tests
Buss-Durkee Inventory

Caine-Levine Social Competency Scale
Calgary General Hospital Aggression Scale
California Tests of Mental Maturity
California Tests of Personality
California Infant Scale for Motor Development
California Psychological Inventory Test
California Achievement Tests
California F scale
California Infant Scale
California Verbal Learning Test-Children's
California Achievement Tests
California Personality Inventory
California Verbal Learning Test-Adult Version
Career Maturity Inventory
Category Test
Cattell Infant Intelligence Scale
Cattell inventories
Chicago Q-Sort
Child Find
Child Behavior Checklist
Children's Personality Questionnaire
Children's Apperception Test
Children's Category Test
Children's Depression Inventory
Children's Problems Checklist
Children's State-Trait Anxiety Inventory
Children's Memory Scale
Children's Embedded Figures
Classroom Environment Scale
Clinical Analysis Questionnaire
Clinical Evaluation of Language Fundamentals-Revised
Cognitive Abilities Tests
College Entrance Examination Board Advanced Placement Program
Columbia Mental Maturity Scale
Comfortable Interpersonal Distance Scale
Compass Diagnostic Test of Arithmetic
Completion, Arithmetic, Vocabulary and Directions Test
Comrey Personality Scales
Concept Mastery Test
Conflict Resolution Inventory
Cooper-Harper Scale
Coping Strategies Questionnaire
Cornell Word Form
Cornell Selective Index
Crawford Small Parts Dexterity Test

Culture Fair Test
Cut down, Annoyed, Guilt Feelings, Eye-opener
DAH test
Despert fables
Diagnostic Interview Schedule
Doerfler-Stewart test
Draw-a-person test
Draw-a-Man Test
Edwards Personal Preference Schedule
EGY test
Elgin checklist
Elizur s test
Embedded Figures Test
ESP forced-choice test
ESP free-response test
Experience Inventory
Eysenck Personality Inventory
Fear Survey Schedule II
Fels Parent Behavior Rating Scales
Finger Oscillation Test
Fink-Green-Bender Test
Forer Structured Sentence Completion
Franck Drawing Completion Test
Frostig Developmental Test of Visual Perception
Frostig Movement Skills Test Battery
Gates-MacGinitie Reading Tests
Geist Picture Interest Inventory
General Aptitude Test Battery
General Anxiety Scale for Children
Gesell Development Scales
Goldstein-Scheerer Tests
Goodenough-Harris Drawing Test
Goodenough Draw-a-Man Test
Gordon Occupational Check List
Graduate Record Examination
Graves Design Judgment Test
Griffiths Mental Development Scale
Guilford-Zimmerman Temperament Survey
Halstead-Reitan Neuropsychological Battery
Hampstead Index
Hand Test
Hanfmann-Kasanin Concept Formation Test
Harris Tests of Lateral Dominance
Harrower-Erikson Group Rorschach
Healy Completion Test
Heidbreder test
Hejna test
Hering-Binet test
Hiskey-Nebraska Test of Learning Aptitude
Holland Vocational Preference Inventory
Holmgren test
Hopkins Symptoms Checklist
Horn-Hellersberg Drawing Completion Test
HSD test
Hunt-Minnesota Organic Brain Damage Test
I-E Scale
Illinois Test of Psycholinguistic Abilities
Immediate Test
Incomplete-pictures test
Incomplete Sentences Blank
Index of Adjustment and Values
Infant Behavior Record
Interest Inventory
Iowa Scale of Stuttering Severity
Iowa Tests of Basic Skills

IPAT Anxiety Scale
Ishihara Color test
Janet's test
Jung association test
Kahn Test of Symbol Arrangement
Kaufman Adolescent and Adult Intelligence Test
Kelley desegregation scale
Kent E-G-Y Test
Kent-Rosanoff Free Association Test
Kent Series of Emergency Skills
Knox Cube Test
Kohnstamm maneuver/test
Kohs' Block Design Test
Kuder Occupational Interest Survey
Kuder Preference Record-Vocational
Kuhlmann-Anderson Tests
Kuhlmann-Binet Test
Kwalwasser-Dykema Music Test
Least-Preferred Coworker Scale
Leiter International Performance Scale/Test
Levy Draw-and-Tell-a-Story Technique
Lichtheim Test
Lincoln-Oseretsky Motor Development Scale
Lowenfeld Mosaic Test
Luescher Color Test
Luria-Nebraska Neuropsychological Battery
Mach Scale
Machover Draw-a-Person Test
Macquarrie Test for Mechanical Ability
Maddox rod test
Make-a-Picture-Story Test
Manifest Anxiety Scale
Manikin test
Marie Three-Paper Test
Marston deception test
Masculine-Feminine Scale
Maslach Burnout Inventory
Mathematics Usage Test
Maturity Inventory
Maudsley Personality Inventory
McAdory Art Test
McCarthy Scales of Children's Abilities
McCarthy Screening Test
Meier Art Judgment Test
Memory-for-Designs Test
Mental Status Examination
Merrill-Palmer Scale of Mental Tests
Metropolitan Achievement Tests
Miller Analogies Test
Millon Clinical Multiaxial Inventory
Millon Index of Personality Styles
Millon Behavioral Health Inventory
Millon Adolescent Clinical Inventory
Minnesota Spatial Relations Test
Minnesota Rate of Manipulation Test
Minnesota Paper Form Board Test
Minnesota Mechanical Assembly Test
Minnesota Clerical Aptitude Test
Minnesota Multiphasic Personality Inventory
Minnesota Vocational Interest Inventory
Monroe Diagnostic Reading test
Mooney Problem Checklist
Mosher Forced-Choice Guilt Inventory
Multidimensional Scale for Rating Psychiatric Patients
Myers-Briggs Type Indicator

Myokinetic Personality Test
Myokinetic Psychodiagnosis Test
National Intelligence Scale
National Reference Scale
Nelson-Denny Reading Test
Oseretsky test
Otis Quick Scoring Mental Ability Test
Otis-Lennon School Ability Test
Parenting Stress Index
Peabody Picture Vocabulary test
Personal Orientation Inventory
Phillips Scale
picture-arrangement test
Picture-interpretation test
Picture World Test
Picture-anomalies test
Picture-completion test
Pintner-Paterson Scale of Performance Tests
Porteus Mazes
Position Analysis Questionnaire
Pre-Marital Counseling Inventory
Present State Examination
Press test
Pressey X-O Test
Primary Mental Abilities Battery
Primary Reading Profiles
Productivity Environmental Preference Survey
Profile of Mood States
Progressive Matrices Test
Progressive Achievement Tests
PSI Basic Skills Tests for Business, Industry, and
    Government
Psychoeducational Profile
Psychoepistemological Profile
Psychosocial Pain Inventory
Psychotic Inpatient Profile
Purdue Pegboard Test
Purpose in Life
Quick Test
Raven's Progressive Matrices Test
Readjustment Scale
Renard Diagnostic Interview
Research Diagnostic Criteria
Rinné test
Rokeach Value Survey
Role Construct Repertory Test
Rorschach Ranking Test
Rorschach Projective test
Rosanoff Association Test

Rosenberg Draw-a-Person Technique
Rosenzweig Picture Frustration Study/Test
Rotter Incomplete Sentence Form
Sargent Insight test
Scholastic Aptitude Test
School and College Ability Test
Seashore tests of musical ability/talents
Shipley-Institute for Living Scale
Sixteen PF test
Stanford Hypnotic Susceptibility Scale
Stanford-Binet Intelligence Scale
Sternberg Triarchic Abilities
Stilling Test
Strategies Questionnaire
Strong Vocational Interest Blank
Strong-Campbell Interest Inventory
Stroop Test
Symonds Picture-Study Test
Szondi test
Taylor Manifest Anxiety Scale
Terman Group Test of Mental Ability
The Allport-Vernon Study of Values
The Hand Test
Thematic Apperception Test
Three-paper test
Thurstone Attitude Scales
Tomkins-Horn Picture Arrangement Test
Trail-Making Test
U.S. Employment Service Basic Occupational
    Literacy test
Vineland Adaptive Behavior Scales
Vineland Social Maturity Scale
Vygotsky test
Ward Atmosphere Scale
Wechsler Adult Intelligence Scales
Wechsler-Bellevue Scales
Wechsler Intelligence Scales for Children
Weigl-Goldstein-Scheerer Test
Wepman Test of Auditory Discrimination
Who am I?
Who are you?
Wide Range Achievement Test
Wiggly Block Test
Wilcoxon matched-pairs signed ranks test
Will-Temperament Tests
Wilson-Patterson Attitude Inventory
Wisconsin General Test Apparatus
Woodworth-Matthews Personal Data Sheet
Work Values Inventory

SYMBOLS

α alpha, coefficient alpha; probability of rejecting an actually true (correct) null hypothesis when it is true; risk of making a type I error; alpha risk.

A Alpha.

α_j The population treatment effect for the jth level of factor A; alternatively, the estimated treatment effect for the jth level of factor A, where A is a fixed (versus random) effect.

$\alpha\beta_{jk}$ Treatment effect in the population for the jkth cell in two-factor analysis of variance.

β beta, response criterion; probability of accepting the null hypothesis when it is actually false (risk of type II error); regression weight in a multiple regression equation applied to an independent variable or predictor in standard score form. The critical likelihood ratio.

β_k Subscripted beta is a treatment effect in the population for the kth level of Factor B.

B Beta.

$\beta_1, \beta_2, \ldots, \beta_{J-1} \ldots$ Population regression coefficients for linear and curvilinear trends between Y and X.

β_1 Measure of relative skewness.

$\beta_{12\cdot3}, \beta_{12\cdot34}$ Beta coefficients.

$\beta_{13\cdot24}, \beta_{24\cdot23}$ Beta coefficients.

β_2 Measure of relative kurtosis.

β_y Population regression coefficient.

$\beta_{Y\cdot X}$ Regression coefficient for prediction of **Y** from **X** in the population.

γ gamma, coefficient of predictive association between sets of ordered classes.

γ_1 Measure of relative skewness (see β_1).

γ_2 Measure of relative kurtosis (see β_2).

Γ Gamma.

δ delta, the number of degrees of freedom associated with a chi-square value; a determinant; also difference between two population means, $\mu_1\mu_2$. Noncentrality parameter for noncentral t or noncentral F.

$\Delta = |\mu_1 - \mu_2| \div (\sigma \mathbf{Y} \div \mathbf{X})$ Population effect size: Absolute difference between two population means, relative to the standard deviation for either population. Mean square successive difference.

Δ Delta, in statistics in interpolation, denotes a finite difference; a major determinant (without a subscript); a minor determinant (with subscript). In calculus, an increment, as $\Delta y = $ an increment of y.

$\Delta^2 (\mathbf{D}^2)$ Mean square successive difference.

ϵ epsilon, a member of, as "a ϵ A" reads as "a is a member of A"; an acceptable limiting false positive rate.

ϵ^2 epsilon-squared, differentiation ratio without bias.

E Epsilon.

ζ zeta, test for linearity of regression, value in the Fisher r to Z transformation corresponding to the population correlation.

ζ_r Population value corresponding to the statistic z_r.

Z Zeta.

η eta, the correlation coefficient; coefficient of curvilinear correlation; the population value of the correlation ratio, measuring the fit of the observations to the means of the vertical or horizontal arrays.

H Eta.

$\acute{\eta}$ eta (variant).

$\eta^2_{Y\cdot X}$ Sample index showing the relative or proportional reduction in the variance of Y given the X value for an observation: the percent of variance in Y explained by X.

η_{xy}, η_{yx} Correlation ratio in the population.

η_{yx} Correlation ratio.

θ theta, population value of a proportion; any statistic.

Θ Theta.

θ_0 Value of θ specified by the null hypothesis.

ι iota.

I Iota.

$\acute{\iota}$ iota (variant).

κ kappa, a curve criterion; Cohen's coefficient of agreement.

K Kappa.

λ lambda, wavelength.

λ_1 A constant appearing in the ith orthogonal polynomial.

λ_{AB} Symmetric measure of predictive association in a contingency table.

Λ Lambda.

λ_B Asymmetric measure of predictive association for a contingency table.

μ mu, mean of a population; assumed value of (used in null hypothesis testing); moment; micron; used with subscript to indicate variable: μ_x.

M   Mu.

$\mu\mu$ mu-mu, micromicron.

μ_0 Value of population mean under the null hypothesis.

μ_1 Value of population mean under the alternative hypothesis.

μ_D Mean of the difference between paired scores.

μf Microfarad.

μsec Microsecond.

ν nu, number of degrees of freedom; $\nu_1\nu_2\nu_3$ (nu$_1$, nu$_2$, nu$_3$); moments about arbitrary origin; the true score of an individual on Y.

N   Nu.

ν_1, ν_2 Number of degrees of freedom for numerator and denominator, respectively, for an F ratio; the parameters of the F distribution.

ξ xi.

Ξ Xi.

o   omicron.

O   Omicron.

π pi, a mathematical constant (3.1415926+), the ratio of the circumference of a circle to its diameter; Scott's coefficient of agreement.

Π Pi, the continued product of.

ρ rho, correlation coefficient in a population; the Spearman rho or rank-order variable, being a variant of the product moment correlation P = [COV (x,y)] ÷ $(\sigma_x\sigma_y)$; rank-difference correlation; coefficient of intraclass correlation.

P   Rho.

ρ_I Coefficient of intraclass correlation.

σ^2 Population variance [E $(x - \mu)^2$] on a complete enumeration of all items, with subscripts as for σ.

ς sigma (variant).

σ sigma, standard deviation for ungrouped data, also symbolized SD, s; in physics, a millisecond or one-thousandth of a second, also symbolized msec; standard deviation of a population; the population standard deviation of a random variable of measures; standard error of a statistic (followed by a subscript indicating the statistic); maximum likelihood estimate of σ.

Σ Sigma, summation sign for a series of values: add values to the right of it.

$\sigma^2(\ldots)$ Variance of.

σ^2_σ Standard error of variance.

σ_σ Standard error of standard deviation.

σ_D The standard deviation of the distribution of the differences between the central effects of two stimuli.

σ_{diff} Standard error of difference.

σ_{est} Standard error of estimate.

σ_m Standard error of the mean, also symbolized σ_x.

σ_M Standard error of the mean; the true standard error of the mean, given samples of size N from some population; standard error of measurement

σ_{med} Standard error of the median.

σ_p Standard deviation of a proportion.

σ_P Standard error of percentage.

σ_r Standard error of Pearson correlation; standard error of coefficient of correlation.

σ_u Standard deviation of regression.

σ_v Standard error of coefficient of variation.

σ_x Standard error of the mean, also symbolized σ_m.

σ_X Standard deviation of scores on **X**.

σ_{x-y} Standard error of difference between two statistics X and Y.

Σ_{XY} The sum of paired products of X and Y measures, each in deviation form.

τ tau, Kendall's tau, a measure of relationship between pairs of ranks. Not actually a coefficient of correlation, but primarily an index that shows rank-order agreement, or the tendency of two rank-orders to be alike; Kendall's rank-correlation coefficient.

$\sigma_{x \cdot y}$ True standard error of estimate for predictions of X from Y.

σ_Y Standard deviation of scores on **Y**.

$\sigma_{y \cdot x}$ True standard error of estimate for predictions of Y from X.

$\sigma_{y \backslash x=2}$ Population standard deviation of the Y's at X = 2.

σ_Z The standard error of the **Z** transformation of r or σ.

T   Tau

υ upsilon, the so-called "true" score of an individual (score) on Y.

Υ Upsilon.

ϕ/ϕ_{max} phi-coefficient.

ϕ phi, the phi coefficient, a product moment r based on two dichotomous variables; the null (empty) set; measure of fourfold point correlation; transformation of percents to angles.

ϕ^2 phi-square, index of mean square contingency for a population or a sample contingency table.

Φ Phi, phi-coefficient.

$\phi\gamma$ phi-function of gamma.

χ chi.

χ^2 chi-square, the usual usage for chi; a variable with a chi square distribution; used to determine probability that a distribution of frequencies within categories is in accordance with a stated hypothesis; the Pearson chi-square statistic; value used in test for goodness of fit; variable distributed as probability distribution.

X Chi

ψ psi, value of a particular comparison among population means.

Ψ Psi, Psychology.

ω omega, ohm, a unit of electric resistance, also symbolized by O, Ω.

ω^2 Population index showing the relative or proportional reduction in the variance of Y given the X value for an observation; the percent of variance in Y explained by X.

Ω Omega, ohm, also symbolized by O, ω.

$\acute{\omega}$ omega (variant).

$1 - \beta$ Power of a statistical test against some given true alternative to the null hypothesis.

12^r34 Partial correlation coefficient for X_1 and X_2 and expected X_3 and X_4.

a_j The estimated treatment effect for the jth level of factor A; alternatively, the estimated treatment effect for the jth level of factor A, where A is a random (versus fixed) effect.

A Ampere; Sandler's A statistic.

A/m^{-1} Ampere per meter, a unit of magnetic field strength.

AD Average deviation.

$\mathbf{b_1, b_2, \ldots, b_{j-1} \ldots}$ Alternate form for $\beta_1, \beta_2, \ldots, \beta_{j-1} \ldots$ regression coefficients for linear and curvolinear trends between x and y.

$\mathbf{b_{12:34}}$ Regression coefficient of variable X_2 on X_1 excluding X_3 and X_4.

C Coefficient of mean square contingency; coefficient of contingency; coulomb, a unit of electric charge.

C_A Coefficient of association.

cd/m^{-2} Candela per square meter, a unit of luminance.

CR Critical ratio, also symbolized by C.R.

cum % Cumulative percent.

cum f Cumulative frequency.

df Degrees of freedom, also symbolized d.f.

/ Diagonal or shilling bar means divided by, also symbolized $\div$.

d' d-prime; the deviation of the midpoint of a class from an arbitrary origin in class interval units.

E An efficiency ratio, expected frequency or theoretical value in the calculation of chi-square (χ^2); an event; index of forecasting efficiency; potential, also symbolized V.

EQ Educational quotient, also symbolized E.Q.

E.S. Sample Effect Size: the absolute difference between two means expressed relative to the standard deviation $(\overline{X}_1 - \overline{X}_2)/\text{SD}$.

F Farad, a unit of electric capitance; the F-test, a ratio between two variables; variance ratio.

$f(\mathbf{X})$ Density function; frequency function of the random variable X.

$\mathbf{F(X)}$ Distribution function; cumulative distribution function.

$\mathbf{f_1, f_2, f_3, f_n}$ First generation in genetics.

$\mathbf{F_{max}}$ A test of homogeneity of variance equal to the ratio of the largest to the smallest variance.

$_f\mathbf{X}$ A score multiplied by its corresponding frequency.

F' F-prime, F-ratio; one of several corrected F ratios.

$\mathbf{f^e}$ Expected frequency, as in a χ^2.

$\mathbf{f^o}$ Observed frequency, as in a χ^2; also O, Ω, ω.

G Geometric mean, also symbolized G_m; grand total of observations.

G.M. Guessed mean.

$\mathbf{g_1}$ A measure of skewness.

$\mathbf{g_2}$ A measure of kurtosis.

$\mathbf{G_m}$ Geometric mean, also symbolized G.

$\mathbf{h^2}$ Communality; heritability.

h The hypothetical frequency in the chi-square test of goodness of fit or the chi-square test of independence; a variable subscript; size of a class interval; length of a vector in cosine model of correlation.

H Bit; Henry, a unit of inductance; indicator of a statistical hypothesis.

$\mathbf{H_1}$ The alternative hypothesis.

$\mathbf{h_i^2}$ Common variance of an observed variable.

$\mathbf{H_m}$ The harmonic mean, also symbolized HM.

HM The harmonic mean, also symbolized H_m.

$\mathbf{H_0}$ The null hypothesis.

HSD Honestly Significant Difference Test, Tukey's multiple comparison test.

Hz Hertz, a unit of frequency; a cycle per second.

I Identity matrix, item identity; a physical dimension of intensity or magnitude, such as luminance, weight, or temporal duration.

$\mathbf{I_0}$ The absolute threshold: $I_0 = I_{0.50}$, $I_N = 0$.

$\mathbf{I_M}$ The mean of the productions or reproductions of a standard stimulus.

$\mathbf{i_{md}}$ Class interval in which the median falls.

$\mathbf{i_{mo}}$ Class interval in which the mode falls.

j Variable subscript often denoting the jth treatment group or factor level, or denoting columns.

J Joule, a unit of energy; the number of different experimental treatments or groups in an experiment.

k A constant; number of samples or treatments or times a test is lengthened in an experiment; number or size of groups, classes, variables, strata, etc., or subgroups in a sample; number of arrays in correlation table; an arbitrary positive number; coefficient of alienation.

$\mathbf{k^2}$ Coefficient of nondetermination.

K Kendall's coefficient of consistency; in a two-factor experiment, number of treatment groups or levels of the second factor; number of "blocks" of observations in an experiment; Kelvin; the number observations in the Kolmogorov-Smirnoff Test which are equal to or less than X.

K-S Test Kolmogorov-Smirnoff Test.

kg/m^{-3} Kilogram per cubic meter, a unit of density.

l A linear function of random variables; lower limit of a class interval.

L Lower confidence limit; in defining range, lowest score of a sample.

LL Lower limit of the class in which the median falls; lower limit of a group of numbers.

l$_m$ Lower limit of a modal group.

lm Lumen, a unit of luminous flux.

L$_{Md}$ Lower limit of the class interval containing the median, also symbolized L$_{me}$.

L$_{me}$ Lower limit of the class interval containing the median, also symbolized L$_{Md}$.

L$_{mo}$ Lower limit of modal group or class.

Log^{-1}a Number whose log is a.

log$_e$m Logarithm to the base e for the value m.

LRL Lower real limit of a group of numbers.

lx Lux, a unit of illumination.

m Moment about the mean (value of nth moment is $\sum x^n/N$); number of items in a test; value of the midpoint of a class of a population distribution; in the sign test, the frequency of the less frequent sign.

m^2/s^{-1} Square meter per second, a unit of kinematic viscosity, diffusion coefficient.

m/s^{-1} Meter per second, a unit of velocity.

m/s^2 Meter per second squared, a unit of acceleration.

m^2 Square meter, a unit of area.

M Is measured by; sample arithmetic mean; mean of a sample, also symbolized by $\overline{X}$.

M' M-prime, arbitrary origin.

M.D. Mean deviation.

Mdn Median, also symbolized Md.

mμ Millimicron, also symbolized mu, μ.

M$_2$ Second moment about the mean (variance).

m^3 Cubic meter, a unit of volume.

M$_3$ Third moment about the mean.

M$_4$ Fourth moment about the mean.

Md The median, also symbolized Mdn.

M$_D$ Mean difference between N matched pairs.

M$_G$ Geometric mean.

MS Mean square in the analysis of variance.

msec Millisecond, also symbolized σ.

MS$_{error}$ Unbiased estimate of the population error variance.

M$_w$ Weighted mean.

M' M-prime, assumed mean.

n Number of cases (values) of a variable in a sample from a universe of size N; number of items in a test; number of times a test is lengthened; number of degrees of freedom; number of pairs; number (size) of any one of several samples containing the same number of observations; number of participants in a group.

N/m^{-2} Newton per square meter, a unit of pressure.

N The total number of independently drawn cases, observations or elements in a population when n is the number in a sample; alternative symbol to n$_N$; total number of participants in a research study; Newton, a unit of force.

N s/m^{-2} Newton second per square meter, a unit of dynamic viscosity.

(N$_r$) Number of unordered combinations of N things taken r at a time.

N.S. Not significant, in a statistical test.

N$_p$ Number of cases in one of two categories, the other being N$_q$.

nPn Number of permutations of n things taken altogether.

N$_q$ Number of cases in one of two categories, the other being N$_p$.

O Observed frequency as in the calculation of chi-square (χ^2); ohm, also symbolized by Ω, ω, f^o.

p Sample proportion or probability estimate in one of two mutually exclusive classes; parameter of a binomial; number of independent variables in the multiple regression; probability of a given event size; probability of "success" in a single Bernoulli trial; as subscript: of the proportion; significance level.

p ⊃ q Conditional.

P.E. Probable error of a statistic.

P(...) Same as P().

P() The probability of event(s) within parentheses, also symbolized p(A), P(...).

p(A) Same as P().

P(A < X < B) Probability of X falling between the fixed values A and B.

P(A\B) Conditional probability; probability of A occurring given that B occurs.

P(R) The probability of the response R.

P(R\I$_j$) The probability of the response R on trials on which I$_j$ is presented.

P(R\R) The probability of R given the response R was made on the preceding trial.

P$_1$ Intraclass correlation coefficient for a population.

p_i Sample proportion in the ith class; estimate of the probability of the occurrence of the ith event; parameter of a binomial population.

P_i Percentile point (subscript denotes particular percentile point, as P_{10}, P_{40}, etc.).

p_k The proportion of scores in a set that belong to a subset, k.

P Percentile (subscripts indicate which percentile is meant); probability level of occurrence of an event; proportion (percentage or fraction) of elements in one class of a dichotomous population; sample proportion of "successes" in sampling from a Bernoulli distribution.

$pq^r xy$ Estimate of correlation between two sets (x and y)when one is lengthened p times and the other q times.

$p^r xx$ Spearman-Brown reliability coefficient for a test whose length is increased p times.

P_r^n Number of permutations of n things taken r at a time.

p' p-prime, sample proportion or percentage.

q Probability of failure; proportion of nonoccurrences; $1 - p$; proportion of cases in a category; arbitrary symbol designating one or more variables partialed out of the primary variable(s).

Q Quartile deviation or semi-interquartile range, defined as $(Q_3 - Q_1) \div 2$; percentage where $Q = 100 - P$ or fraction where $Q = 1.00$; probability of nonoccurrence of an event; proportion of cases in the other class of a dichotomous population (the other being P).

q_α Tabled value for degrees of freedom and α level of significance.

Q_1 The first quartile, equivalent to the 25th percentile.

Q_2 The second quartile, equivalent to the median and 50th percentile.

Q_3 The third quartile, equivalent to the 75th percentile.

QD Quartile deviation or semi-interquartile range (Q).

Q_I Interquartile range equals $Q_3 - Q_1$.

Q_m Quadratic mean.

r^2 Coefficient of determination; percent of variance of one variable explained by the other.

r Coefficient of correlation; Pearson product moment coefficient of (linear) correlation; Pearson product-moment correlation; used with subscripts to denote variables correlated, for example, r_{xy}, r_{21}, etc.; designates the number of steps separating ordered means; number of rows in a contingency table; as subscripts of the correlation; of rows; of ranks.

R The range of values of a set of measurements; a matrix of correlations; a given response which may be defined; number of runs in a sequence associated with the runs test; rank-order coefficient of correlation; multiple correlation (product moment r between unmodified variable(s) and the weighted sum of two or more variables; in a scoring formula the number of right answers; in two-way analysis of variance experimental

design, the numer of rows in the data table for a two-factor experiment.

R^2 Value of a multiple correlation coefficient; in a multiple correlation, the percent of variance in the criterion (dependent) variable explained by the entire set of predictor (independent) variables.

$r!$ r factorial; product of the integers from r to 1.

R'_N The number of elements in R'.

R_1 and R_2 The sum of ranks for the group having a sample size of n_1 or n_2. R_1 and R_2 are used in a wide variety of nonparametric tests involving ranks, for example Mann-Whitney U-formula, Wilcoxon matched Pairs Signed Ranks Test, Kruskal-Wallis one-way anova, Friedman Two-Way anova, etc.

r_{11} Reliability coefficient.

$R_{1 \cdot 234}$ Multiple correlation coefficient for variable X_1 as predicted by variables X_2, X_3, and X_4.

$(R_{1 \cdot 23 \ldots n})$ Coefficient of multiple correlation between dependent variable X, and the independent variables X_2, X_3 ... X_n.

rad/s^{-1} Radian per second, a unit of angular velocity.

$:$ Ratio of; ratio; is to.

r_{bis} Biserial coefficient of correlation, also symbolized r_b, r_{bi}.

r_c Intraclass correlation coefficient.

r_{hh} Reliability coefficient for half a test.

$r_{pb}(r_{pt\,bis})$ Point biserial correlation; the product moment r between a dichotomous variable and a continuous variable.

r_{pR} Reliability coefficient for a test lengthened R times.

r_{rho} Spearman rank-order correlation coefficient.

r_s Serial correlation coefficient; Spearman rank correlation, this symbol r_s used in preference to ρ (rho) to avoid confusion with the population correlation.

r_S Spearman rank coefficient of (linear) correlation.

r_t Tetrachoric correlation coefficient, also symbolized r_{tet}.

r_{tet} Same as r_t.

r_{tt} Reliability coefficient.

r_{xx} See r_{tt}.

r_{xy} Pearson product-moment correlation coefficient between the variables x and y, often symbolized simply as r.

$r_{xy \cdot z}$, $r_{12 \cdot 3}$ Partial correlation coefficient for X_1 and X_2, excluding X_3.

$r_{x \cdot yz}$, $r_{1 \cdot 23}$ Multiple correlation coefficient.

r^n r to the power of n.

r' r-prime, coefficient of rank correlation.

R' R-prime, the set of responses allowed in a given experimental design.

s   Standard deviation for ungrouped data, also symbolized SD; standard deviation of a sample; estimate of the standard error of a population; number of subjects in a repeated measurements design.

s^2 Variance of a sample.

S   Sample space of an experiment; set of all possible outcomes of an experiment; sum of squares used in anova and covariance; sample standard deviation; number of subjects in a repeated measurements design; a statistic in the Kendall (tau) test maximum likelihood estimator.

S^2yx Variance of y residuals from regression line.

S.D.   Standard deviation.

s_b^2 Between-group variance estimate.

S_D Standard deviation of the difference scores.

SD   Standard deviation, also symbolized σ, s.

SE   Standard error.

S_{err} Standard error of measurement.

$S_{est\,x}$ Standard error of estimate when predictions are made from Y to X.

$S_{est\,y}$ Standard error of estimate when predictions are made from X to Y.

S_{est} Standard error of estimate.

S_k Skewness, also symbolized Sk.

Sk   Same as S_k.

s_p Standard error of the proportion.

$^s p_1 - p_2$ Standard error of the difference in proportions.

s_r Standard error of the correlation.

SS   Sum of squares in anova; standard score.

SS_{BG} Sum of squares between groups.

SS_{WG} Sum of squares within groups.

s_w^2 Within-group variance estimate.

s_y Sample standard deviation; standard error of estimate of Y variable.

s_y', s_x' Standard deviation of predicted values of Y and X.

$s_{y\cdot x}$ Standard error of estimate for a sample.

$s_{y\cdot x}$, $s_{x\cdot y}$ Standard error of estimate.

s_z Standard error of z.

s' s-prime, stimulus trace.

S' S-prime, the set of stimulus values used in a given experimental design.

t   Student's *t*-test: the ratio of any statistic to an unbiased estimate of its standard error; a random variable following the distribution of t with v degrees of freedom; number of trials in a repeated measurements design; statistic for testing a null hypothesis or estimating confidence limits when σ is unknown; as subscript: total. Value of t that cuts off the upper portion of the sampling distribution of t.

T   Wilcoxon Test statistic; Smaller sum of ranks with the least frequent sign; in Wilcoxon matched pairs signed-ranks test and in the Mann-Whitney test the sum of scores T within a set (or sum of ranks in groups with smaller sums); McCall's T score, a standard score with arbitrary mean of 50 and arbitrary standard deviation of 10; a correction factor for ties. Tesla, a unit of magnetic flux density.

T_i The sum of all scores in group *i*; a true score of an observation.

Ts   True score on a test for an individual subject.

u   The upper limit of a class interval; ordinate of unit normal curve.

U   Upper confidence limit; symbol for the Mann-Whitney U nonparametric test statistic; the universal set.

UL   The upper limen.

URL   Upper real limit of a group of numbers.

U' Mann-Whitney U test statistic.

v   Number of runs in a sample; degrees of freedom.

V/m   Volt per meter, a unit of electric field strength.

V   Potential, also symbolized E; variance of a population; variation coefficient. Volt, a unit of electric potential.

w   Width of a confidence interval; weight assigned each value of a variable; as subscript: within.

W   Coefficient of stability; Kendall coefficient of concordance; width of a confidence interval; universal set; number of wrong answers on a test; weight used in obtaining a weighted mean; the Weber fraction: $W = \Delta I / I_N$. Watt, a unit of power.

Wb   Weber, a unit of magnetic flux.

W_r The difference that a comparison must exceed in order to be declared significant in Newman-Keuls and Duncan's tests.

x   A column matrix or vector; number of objects in one category or the number of successes; midpoint of a class interval; multiplied by, also symbolized by ·, as in $6 \cdot 7 = 42$.

x   The small italicized x stands for a deviation of individual X value from its arithmetic mean $\overline{X}$, $(X - \overline{X})$.

X_0 Assumed origin.

X_1 Value of the dependent variable in multiple correlation and partial correlation.

$X_2, X_3 \ldots X_m$ Values of independent variables in multiple correlation and partial correlation.

X_p Percentile, a score X that exceeds the proportion p of a set of ordered scores.

X_{ul} Score at upper limit of interval containing X.

x' x-prime, deviation from an assumed mean.

X   The boldfaced capital symbolizes set of scores on the dimension.

X The unboldfaced capital is the most common symbol for a variable or score dimension; a matrix value of an independent variable in a correlation matrix; the horizontal axis or dimension in a scatter diagram.

X′ X-prime, score predicted by a regression equation; a coded variable; a transformed score; a regressed score in the original scale units.

X′, Y′ Predicted scores, as from a regression equation.

(X,Y) A joint event, consisting of a value for variable X paired with a value for variable Y.

X$_{\ell\ell}$ Score at lower limit of interval containing X.

y The dependent variable; an observation; height of the ordinate of the normal distribution.

y The small italicized y stands for the deviation of individual Y value from its arithmetic mean $\overline{Y}$, $(Y - \overline{Y})$.

Y A random variable; the vertical axis in a scatter diagram; the value of a dependent variable in a correlation matrix.

Y$_c$ Y value determined from trend or regression line.

Y′ Y-prime, Y score predicted from X; a coded score.

z Standard score with a mean of zero and a standard deviation of unity; the ratio of a normally distributed statistic to its standard error; the abscissa of a normal curve; deviation of a sample mean or of a specific score from the population mean expressed in standard deviation units; a standard normal variable; a statistic for testing the null hypothesis when σ is known; as subscript: refers to transformations of r; the standardized normal deviate cutting on a tail of the normal distribution equal in area to, ϵ.

Z Standard score; Fisher's logarithmic transformation of r (value corresponding to r_{xy} in Fisher's r to Z transformation), which varies without limit and is approximately normally distributed.

Z$_r$ Fisher's logarithmic transformation used in testing significance of a correlation coefficient.

z′$_y$ Y′ expressed in terms of a z-score.

$^2\sqrt{}$ Square root; $^3\sqrt{}$ cube root.

$\sqrt{}$ Root; radical sign; square root. The square root, with superscript numeral: extract that root, without superscript: square root.

! Factorial, such as N!, the factorial of integer N.

() Parentheses, subjects terms enclosed to the same operation.

(∠) Angle.

+ Plus, positive.

= Equal to.

{} Braces. Encloses elements of a set, as in {a b}, set of all a such that the statement b is true.

[] Brackets; sum of, subjects terms enclosed to the same operation.

≈ Approximately equal.

× Multiplication, also symbolized ·, as in 5 · 2 = 10.

· Multiplication, multiplied by, also symbolized by ×.

∑ Algebraic sum.

^ And (logic).

Å Angstrom, also symbolized Du for angstrom unit.

∅ Arbitrary circle.

→ Arrow, approaches limit: (variable at left) approaches as limit (variable at right).

∏ Continued product of all terms.

∮ Contour integral.

° Degrees.

÷ Divided by, also symbolized by /.

/ Divided by, also symbolized by ÷.

″ Double prime; second.

≡ Identical, is identical with; identity, also symbolized : :.

∞ Infinity.

∫ Integration. Shows that the expression following is to be integrated, such as $\int f(x)dx$ means the indefinite integral of f(x) with respect to x.

∩ Intersection, indicating both; as in: A∩B, the intersection of A and B.

∩ Intersection, indicating both; as in: A∩B = both A and B occur.

≥ Is greater than or equal to.

≤ Is less than or equal to.

< Is less than, for example a < b indicating that a is less than b.

> Is greater than, for example a > b indicating that a is greater than b.

⊆ Is a subset of.

⊂ Is a proper subset of.

∇² Laplacian.

∨ Logical exclusive or.

− Minus.

∓ Minus or plus, either subtract or add.

≪ Much less than.

≫ Much greater than.

‖ Parallel to.

∂ Partial derivative.

⊥ Perpendicular to.

± Plus or minus, either add or subtract.

′ Prime; minute.

~ Similar to.

∅ The empty set.

˜ Tilde, varies in a fixed relation with the difference between.

∮   Union; indicating either or both; as in A∮B, the union of A and B.

ϕ   Zero vector.

|| Absolute value of deviations disregarding signs, for example, $|-6| = 6$.

$\propto^3$ Measure of skewness

∠s   Angles.

ˆ   Circumflex; an estimator; uncertainty in a sample, such as $\hat{H}$.

⊥ s   Perpendiculars.

⊙   Circle.

|z| Absolute value of a standardized score.

→ ∞   Approaches infinity.

⋯   Ellipsis.

$\hat{H}$ Uncertainty.

°C   Degrees Celsius, a measure of customary temperature: $t/°C = T/°K -273.15$.

°F   Degrees Fahrenheit.

°K   Degrees Kelvin.

≮   Not less than.

≠   inequalities.

≢   Not equal to, also symbolized ≠.

≯   Not greater than.

≈   approximately equal.

∵   Because; since.

⟊   between

≅   congruent.

~   cycle, one complete wave vibration.

∝   Directly proportionate to; varies directly as; varies with infinity.

∨   disjunction

⩾   Equal to or greater than, also symbolized ≧.

⩽   Equal to or less than, also symbolized ≦.

≈   Estimated by.

⇔   Identical, also symbolized ≡.

≐   Approximately equal to, also symbolized ≈, ≊, ≃.

~   isomorphic.

≁   not isomorphic.

$\hat{p}$ Estimator of p, the paramter of a binomial population.

$\hat{s}$ Sample standard deviation based on unbiased variance estimate, expressed as $s = [\sum x^2 \div (N-1)]^{1/2}$.

$\hat{s}^2$ Unbiased estimate of the population variance, expressed as $s^2 = \sum x^2 \div (N-1)$.

$\overline{S}$ S-bar, arithmetic mean of two or more standard deviations.

$S_{\overline{D}}$ The symbol for standard error of the difference.

$^s D$ Estimated standard error of the difference between means, direct-difference method. Also symbolized $^s\hat{D}$.

≃   Similar or equal to.

$\overline{S}_X$ Standard error of the mean; estimated standard error of a sample mean.

$S_{\overline{X}_1 - \overline{X}_2}$ Estimated standard error of the difference between means. Standard error of two independent means.

$\hat{X}$ Predicted value of X; also X', $\tilde{X}$.

$\tilde{X}$ Predicted value of X, also X', $\hat{X}$.

$\tilde{X}, \tilde{x}$ Sample estimate computed from a regression equation.

$\overline{Y}$ Y-bar, mean of a sample.

$\tilde{Y}$ Predicted value of Y; also Y', $\hat{Y}$.

$\hat{Y}$ Predicted value of Y; also Y', $\tilde{Y}$.

$\tilde{y}$ Deviation of Y from $\overline{Y}$.

$\overline{y}$ Same as $\overline{Y}$.

∃   There exists.

∴   Therefore; hence.

$\overline{X}$ X-bar, arithmetic mean of a sample, also symbolized by M.

LEARNING THEORY SYMBOLS

A   Reaction or response amplitude (C. L. Hull).

a   An incentive substance.

Asn   Strength of association.

B   Mean number of responses in a response cycle (C. L. Hull).

β   Response criterion.

C   1. An activity, condition, state of an animal's neurons (E. L. Thorndike). 2. Larger habit strength or larger reaction potential in behavior withdrawal (C. L. Hull).

C_D Drive condition.

CER   Conditioned emotional response.

CR   Conditioned (or conditional) response (I. P. Pavlov), also rarely symbolized $\mathbf{R_c}$.

CS   Conditioned (or conditional) stimulus (I. P. Pavlov), also rarely symbolized $\mathbf{S_c}$.

ΔR   Same as **DR**.

d   Drive.

d′   According to Clark Hull: $d' = \dot{D} - D$.

D   1. Drive, drive strength. 2. Selection index. 3. Distance or difference in logarithmic units between the stimulus on which a subject is tested and one on which the subject is trained (K. Spence). 4. Strength of primary drive after formation of the specific habit (C. L. Hull).

$\overline{D}$ According to Clark Hull: $\overline{D} = 100 \times [(D + D) \div (\dot{D} + Md)]$.

$\dot{D}$ Strength of all nondominant drives that are operating at a given moment in time (C. L. Hull).

D′   The strength of the primary drive during the formation of a habit (C. L. Hull)

DR   Increment of response, also symbolized as **ΔR**.

E   1. Experimenter. 2. Hypothetical excitatory process (I. P. Pavlov).

f   An incentive substance (C. L. Hull).

F   The constant amount by which potential habit strength is lessened by each reinforcement (C. L. Hull).

FIx   Fixed interval schedule of reinforcement: x indicates the number of (usually) minutes before reinforcement (B. F. Skinner).

FRx   Fixed ratio schedule of reinforcement; x indicates the number of responses required before reinforcement (B. F. Skinner).

g   1. General intelligence factor (C. E. Spearman). 2. A fractional part of a goal reaction that may break off from a behavior sequence as a FAGR or fractional antedating goal reaction (C. L. Hull).

G   1. General ability. 2. A primary goal reaction, goal, or goal object (C. L. Hull).

GG   Goal gradient.

G.O.   Goal-orientation index (C. L. Hull).

h   In animal research, number of hours of food deprivation of subjects.

H   Habit strength (C. L. Hull), also symbolized as $_SH_R$.

I   Hypothetical inhibitory process (I. P. Pavlov).

I_R Reactive inhibition (C. L. Hull).

I_S The stimulus intensity serving as "signal + noise" in a given experiment.

J   Delay in reinforcement (C. L. Hull).

K   Incentive motivation, a component of reaction potential (C. L. Hull).

K′   K-prime, size of reinforcement; the physical incentive in motivation (C. L. Hull).

M   Learning maximum (C. L. Hull).

n   1. Number of variables. 2. Number of responses to extinction (C. L. Hull).

N   1. Number of reinforced trials (C. L. Hull). 2. Number of instances of a given phenomenon in a total population.

N′   Total number of cases in a second group.

O   1. Organism experimented on, also symbolized *S*. 2. Observer. 3. Oscillation, the degree of variability in response strength of a given response system (C. L. Hull).

Os   Observers.

P   1. Person. 2. Physiological drive state.

r   A pure-stimulus act (C. L. Hull).

R   1. Response. 2. Stimulus, a rarely used symbol from the German term *Reiz*, seen in older writings.

R/S   Response shock interval, also symbolized **R-S**.

$\mathbf{R_c}$ Rare symbol for conditioned response (I. P. Pavlov), usually symbolized **CR**.

R_G A goal attaining response; a consummatory response (C. L. Hull).

r_G Goal response, an instance of a pure-stimulus act (C. L. Hull).

RL   *Reiz-Limen*, German phrase for stimulus threshold.

Ro   The original response to the indifferent stimulus before it was conditioned.

RS   Reinforcing stimulus.

R/S   A ratio between magnitude of response (R) and intensity of stimulus (S) (B. F. Skinner).

RT   Reaction time.

$\mathbf{R_u}$ Rare symbol for unconditioned response (I. P. Pavlov), usually symbolized **UR**.

s   1. Specific ability factor (C. E. Spearman). 2. The afferent impulse evoked by the stimulus (C. L. Hull).

s′   Stimulus trace (C. L. Hull).

ss   Sensations.

S   Stimulus.

S   Subject (in an experiment).

S^+ Positive discriminative stimulus (B. F. Skinner).

S^- Negative discriminative stimulus (B. F. Skinner).

SΔ   Discriminative stimulus, also symbolized S^D.

S_c Rare symbol for conditioned stimulus (I. P. Pavlov), usually symbolized **CS**.

S_d Drive stimuli (C. L. Hull).

S^D Discriminative stimulus, also symbolized **SΔ**.

S_D Drive stimulus, a hypothetical afferent impulse that results from a drive (C. L. Hull), also symbolized $\boldsymbol{D}$.

$_sE_R$ Excitatory or reaction potential (C. L. Hull).

$_s\underline{E}_R$ Reaction potential resulting from stimulus generalization; generalized reaction potential (C. L. Hull).

$_s\dot{\overline{E}}_R$ Momentary reaction potential, the net reaction potential as affected by oscillation (C. L. Hull).

$_s\overline{E}_R$ Effective reaction potential; net reaction potential (C. L. Hull).

S_g Fractional goal stimulus (C. L. Hull).

S_G Fractional antedating goal stimulus; goal stimulus (C. L. Hull). A stimulus resulting from goal-directed behavior ($\boldsymbol{R}_G$).

$_sH_R$ Habit strength (C. L. Hull), also symbolized as $\overline{\boldsymbol{H}}$.

$_s\overline{H}_R$ Effective habit strength; habit strength resulting from stimulus generalization (C. L. Hull).

$_{s'}H_R$ Strength of a habit based on the same response being conditioned to another stimulus (C. L. Hull).

$_sI_R$ Conditioned reactive inhibition or amount of conditioned inhibitory potential (C. L. Hull).

$_s\underline{I}_R$ Generalized inhibitory potential (C. L. Hull).

$_s\overline{I}_R$ Aggregate inhibitory potential (C. L. Hull).

$_sL_R$ Reaction threshold, stimulus strength that will barely evoke a response (C. L. Hull).

$_sO_R$ Behavioral oscillation, change from moment to moment of reaction potential (C. L. Hull).

S-O-R   Stimulus-Organism-Response, also symbolized **SOR**.

S⇔R   Stimulus-Response interaction.

S-R   Stimulus-Response (relationship), also symbolized **SR**, **S→R**.

S→R   Stimulus-response or stimulus-response relationship; the symbol is read as "S leads to R".

S↔R   Stimulus-response interaction or interbehavior (J. R. Kantor).

S-R-S   Stimulus-response sequence: a stimulus leads to a response that leads to another stimulus.

$_{ss}\mathbf{H_R}$ Summation of habit strengths associated with at least two stimulus elements that lead to a given R (C. L. Hull).

St.   Stimulus.

$_{st_R}$ Median reaction latency (C. L. Hull).

$_sT_R$ 1. Reaction latency. 2. Reaction time (C. L. Hull).

$\mathbf{S_u}$ Rare symbol for unconditioned stimulus (I. P. Pavlov), usually symbolized **US**.

$_sU_R$ Unlearned stimulus-response connections; hypothetical innate receptor-effector connections that make possible unlearned responses (C. L. Hull).

TE   1. Trial-and-error learning. 2. Time error.

TR   *Terminalischer Reiz*, German phrase for terminal threshold.

UCR   Unconditioned (or unconditional) response (I. P. Pavlov), also **UR**.

UCS   Unconditioned (or unconditional) stimulus (I. P. Pavlov), also **US**.

UnCS   Infrequently used abbreviation for the unconditioned stimulus, **US** is preferred.

UR   Unconditioned (or unconditional) response (I. P. Pavlov), also **UCR**.

US   Unconditioned (or unconditional) stimulus (I. P. Pavlov), also **UCS**.

V   Stimulus intensity dynamism, the magnitude of the intensity component of a reaction potential (C. L. Hull).

VIx   Variable interval schedule of reinforcement; x indicates the average number of (usually) minutes before reinforcement (B. F. Skinner).

VRx   Variable ratio schedule of reinforcement; x indicates the average number of responses required before reinforcement (B. F. Skinner).

VTE   Vicarious trial and error.

w   Weight of food incentive (C. L. Hull).

W   Work involved in response (C. L. Hull).

Y   The response YES, in sensory discrimination experiments.

YNP   YES-NO-procedure in sensory discrimination experiments.

RORSCHACH DESCRIPTORS

The symbols below come from various sources including Samuel Beck, Marguerite Hertz, Bruno Klopfer, and Zygmunt Piotrowski as well as unknown others. The diagnostic meanings of the terms are not indicated, since they vary. For example, an excess of A responses on the part of adults is considered by Klopfer to be a sign of immaturity but other authorities might not agree. In addition, some Rorschach examiners accept certain symbols but reject others.

A few symbols may be universal including A (animal), At (anatomy), C (color), D (large detail), d (small detail), F (form), F+/F- (good form/poor form), H (human), M (movement), O (original), O+/O- (good original/poor original), P (popular response), S (white space), and W (whole).

If a symbol cross-references to another symbol, the second symbol is the preferred one. Thus, **An** See **At**. means that **At** is the preferred symbol.

Some symbols used in administration of the Rorschach:

A Animal response.

a% Proportion of animal content responses.

a Animal content (Also **Aobj**).

Aobj See **a**.

Ad A response that mentions parts of living animals.

Adx A response that mentions a part or detail of an animal when ordinarily the whole animal would be reported.

An See **At**.

At Anatomy response (Also **An**).

c A response that mentions shading.

c′ A response determined by shading.

C Color response.

C′ A response determined by black, white, or gray.

Cd Color denial, a response that denies that the color had anything to do with the image or object reported or that the color of the inkblot is incorrect.

C_{des} Color description, a response that mentions color incidentally.

CF A response that mentions color and form together, with color dominant and form secondary.

Cn Color naming, a response in which the participant names or lists the colors as a direct response.

Cp Color projection, a response that mentions color in an area of an inkblot that is in reality, gray.

C_{sum} The sum of weights for the color response.

C_{sym} Color symbolism, a response in which symbolic meaning is attributed to a color.

D Large detail.

d Small detail.

Dd Unusual detail.

dd Tiny detail.

dD A confabulated detail.

Dds A detail response to a minor white space.

DdW A response that mentions minor details of an unusual detail (Dd).

dc Edge detail, a response based on the contour of the edge of the inkblot.

di Inside detail, of an object inside of an inkblot area.

Do Detail response as given by mental retardates or small children.

dr Rare detail.

Dr A rare response of a large detail.

Ds A response elicited by a major white space on the test card.

DW A response relative to a major detail determining the whole inkblot.

F Form response.

F- Poor form response.

F+ Good form response.

F+% The proportion of "good" form responses in relation to total number of form responses.

FC A form response influenced by the colored areas of the test card.

Fc A response primarily in terms of form, shading and color described as giving texture to the form.

Fc′ A response in terms of shading in light gray areas of the form, somehow influenced by the shape of the given area.

FK See **V**.

FM Animal movements.

FV See **V**.

FY A form determined by flat gray.

h See **H**.

H A response that mentions human figures (Also **h**).

Hd Responses that include parts of human figures.

k Shadow response.

K Diffused response.

L Lambda index/ratio, the ratio of all nonF (An, dd, G, K, etc.) scorings to all F (F, F+, F-) scorings.

m Movement of objects.

M Human movement or of an animal described as human-like.

O Original response, one that appears less often than once in a hundred records.

0+ An original response of good quality.

0- An original response of poor quality.

P Popular response, one that occurs frequently to a given inkblot.

Po Position response, one determined or elicited by the location of the inkblot area of the card.

Q Doubt expressed by participant.

R   Total number of responses.

S   White space response of card beyond the inkblot.

T   1. Total time required to respond to all the Rorschach Inkblot cards. 2. Texture response.

V   Vista response (Also **FK, FV**).

V   Vista response involving depth.

W   Whole response.

W%   The percentage of whole responses.

W^r   A response to the whole, leaving out a small part. Usually called "cut-off whole."

W^x   A response to part of the card.

Y   A response in which gray is the determinant.

Z   A response involving interactions of parts of the inkblots.

Biographies

This is to acknowledge the people who devoted much of their time to help develop and refine the material contained with in these pages. After due consideration. I decided to establish a separate appendix of biographies, to include only deceased people who had contributed to psychology: to give dates of birth and death if known, place of birth, major profession, and other information. I searched through dictionaries, histories of psychology, specialized texts, as well as general and specialized encyclopedias to find items. Allo of this to be limited to three lines on my computer. I called on Florence Denmark to supply some of the women in psychology. Finally, I asked Josef Brozek, Frank Denmark, Anthony Marsella and Joseph Matarazzo to examine, modify and approve the list.

Note: After due consideration, it was decided to establish a separate appendix of biographies, and to include only deceased people who had contributed to psychology; to give dates of birth and death if known, place of birth, major profession, and other information. To find items, research was completed via dictionaries, histories of psychology, specialized texts, as well as general and specialized encyclopedias. In addition, Florence Denmark supplied some names of women in psychology and Josef Brozek, Frank Dumont, Anthony Marsella, and Joseph Matarazzo examined and approved this Appendix.

> Fechner... was for seven years a physiologist; for fifteen years a physicist; for a dozen years an invalid; for fourteen years a psychophysicist; for eleven years an experimental estheticist; for at least two score years throughout this period recurrently and persistently, a philosopher and finally during his last eleven years, an old man whose attention had been brought back by public acclaim and criticism to psychophysics.
>
> From Edwin Boring's *A History of Experimental Psychology* (Appleton-Century-Crofts, 1957).

Abelard, Peter (1079–1142) French theologian. Declared that logic was superior to faith. Focused on intention of acts, held that *why* an act was done was more important than *what* was done.

Abraham, Karl (1877–1925) German psychoanalyst. Contributed to Freudian theory of psychosexual development especially as it bears on the aims of the libido.

Abu Yusuf Al-Sabbah (803–873) Arabian philosopher. Assumed that there is only one intellect shared by all humans, and that every soul is directed by this intellect.

Ach, Narziss (1871–1946) German psychologist. Associated with the Würzburg School. Championed systematic experimental introspection.

Achillini, Alesandro (1463–1512) Italian physician. Student of William of Ocham, asserted the supremacy of reason over faith. Studied the ear and identified the malleus, incus, and labyrinth.

Ackerman, Nathan W. (1909–1971) Russian-American physician. Regarded the family as a unit of diagnosis and related children's problems to patterns of parenting.

Adkins, Dorothy (1912–1975) American psychologist. Made contributions to statistical theory and test construction, with specific attention to factor analytic techniques.

Adler, Alexandra (1901–?) Austrian-American physician. Followed in her father's (Alfred's) footsteps, refining his theoretical concepts in the Individual Psychology movement.

Adler, Alfred (1870–1937) Austrian physician. Founder of Individual Psychology and pioneer in group counseling. His pragmatic theories have been incorporated in current theory and practice.

Adorno, Theodor (1903–1969) German-American psychologist. Interested in the sociology of music. Collaborated in the study of the authoritarian personality.

Adrian, Edgar D. (1889–1977) English physiologist. Recorded electrical activity in a single afferent nerve fiber, providing experimental proof of the "all-or-nothing law of nerves."

Agassiz, Louis (1807–1873) Swiss physician. Considered the most famous biologist of his day, he opposed Charles Darwin's conclusions bearing on a theistic explanation of different species.

Agrippa von Nettesheim, Cornelius (1486–1535) German physician. Held that "Opinions clash; nothing is self-evident, perceptions are relative, theories are unprovable."

Albertus Magnus (1193–1280) German theologian. Wrote commentaries of the works of Aristotle that influenced generations of scholars.

Alcmaeon (of Croton) (ca 500 B.C.)   Greek philosopher. Recognized the brain as the organ for sensation and thought.

Alexander, Franz (1891–1964)   Hungarian-American physician. Analytic revisionist. Related psychoanalysis to learning theory. Specialized in deviant and criminal behavior and psychological illnesses.

Alexander of Tralles (ca 525)   Byzantine physician. Wrote 12 books on pathology, suggested that hallucinations could be cured by tricking patients.

Al-Farabi (870–950)   Arabian philosopher. Brought together Greek philosophy and Islamic thought. Stated urge to power was a main human motive.

Al-Ghazzali (1058–1111)   Arabian philosopher. Held that ultimate truth was not attainable through reasoning. Influenced, among others, Thomas Aquinas and Blaise Pascal.

Al-Kindi (803–873)   Arabian philosopher. Combined the philosophy of Plato and Aristotle. Viewed the world as a unity. Thought there was a universal intelligence.

Allport, Floyd H. (1890–1978)   American psychologist. Called the founder of experimental social psychology. Developed the J-curve of social behavior.

Allport, Gordon W. (1897–1967)   American psychologist. Conducted research on personality theory, expressive movement, rumor, and prejudice.

Alzheimer, Alois (1864–1915)   German neurologist. Studied and researched neurological deficits and first described the disease that bears his name.

Ames, Adelbert Jr. (1880–1955)   American psychologist. Developed the Ames Distortion Room.

Ames, Louise Bates (1908–1996)   American psychologist. Student of child growth and development. Did research at the Gesell Institute on school failures. Expert in Rorschach testing.

Anderson, Rose Gustava (1893–1978)   American psychologist. Researched in the area of child clinical psychology and test construction. Developed a number of intelligence tests.

Angell, Frank (1857–1939)   American psychologist. Conducted experiments in psychophysics, especially audition. Established a psychological laboratory at Stanford University.

Angell, James (1869–1949)   American psychologist. A founder of the Chicago school of functionalism. Opposed Edward Titchener's structuralism.

Angyal, Andras (1902–1960)   Hungarian psychologist. Championed holistic psychology. Held that the two basic human motivations are mastery and love.

Anokhin, Peter (1898–1974)   Soviet neurophysiologist. A holistic critic of Russian reflexologists. Developed a functional theory.

Antonovsky, Aaron (1923–1994)   American-Israeli sociologist. Concerned with public health issues, developed the concept of salutogenesis and conducted research in that area.

Apgar, Virginia (1909–1974)   American physician. Developed the Apgar Scale that evaluates newborns for five factors of physical normality.

Aquinas   Thomas Aquinas

Aragón, Enrique (1880–1942)   Mexican physician. Founded the first psychology laboratory in Mexico in 1906.

Aretaeus (of Cappadocia) (1st century AD)   Physician of Asia Minor. Considered in his time to be the most astute physician since Hippocrates. Described frenzy, epilepsy, mania, and melancholia.

Aristippus (435–366 B.C.)   Greek philosopher. Disciple of Socrates, founder of a school of hedonism. Stressed value of pleasure able feelings and avoidance giving pain to others.

Aristotle (384–322 B.C.)   Greek philosopher. An empiricist who posited a blank view of the mind. His works on a theory of the mind, of logic, of ethics, and ontology are still influential.

Arnold, Magda B. (1903–?)   Austrian psychologist. Contributed to physiological, clinical and experimental psychology and to motivation theory. Formulated a comprehensive theory of emotion.

Arouet, Francois   Voltaire

Arps, George (1874–1939)   American psychologist. The last American student of Wilhelm Wundt. Conducted research on touch and visual perception.

Artemidorus (Daidianus) (ca. 170 A.D.)   Greek philosopher. Authored books on dreams and ancient rites.

Asch, Solomon E. (1907–1996)   American psychologist. Designed conformity experiments demonstrating how individuals are affected by majority opinion even when such opinions are evidently wrong.

Asclepiades of Bithynia (ca. 124 B.C.)   Greek physician. Called the founder of music therapy. Opposed humoral doctrine of diseases. Classified psychoses as febrile and nonfebrile.

Asratyan, Ezra (1903–?)   Russian psychologist. Specialized in research on traumatic shock effects and reflex activity.

Attar, Fariduddin (1142–1230)   Persian chemist. Known as "The Druggist." Stated that the collective human soul is part of the divine soul, and not ascertainable to humans.

Aubert, Hermann (1826–1892)   German psychologist. Known for his research on visual adaptation and indirect vision, cutaneous space perception and body orientation.

Augustine of Hippo (354–430)   North African theologian. Established three divisions of the mind and is considered a precursor of psychoanalysis and existentialism.

Avempace   Ibn Bajjah

Avenerius, Richard H. (1843–1896)   German philosopher. Advocated the view that conscious experience can be studied as well as objective data.

Averroës Ns (1126–1198) Arab philosopher; born in Spain. His commentaries on Aristotle's work eventually gave rise to the philosophical school in Western Europe known as Averroism.

Avicenna (980–1037) Arabian physician. A polymath in whose philosophy one finds definitions of the practical and the contemplative intellect. Also known as Ibn Sina.

Azam, Eugène (1822–1899) French physician. Studied multiple personalities. Considered hypnosis and hysteria to be similar phenomena.

Babbage, Charles (1792–1871) British mathematician. Developed the first programmable computing machine that had the main elements of the modern computer.

Babinski, Joseph (1857–1932) Polish-French physician. The Babinski reflex, normal in infants, is for adults a sign of pyramidal cord lesion.

Babkin, Boris P. (1877–1950) Russian physiologist. Researched neonatal behavior and identified a reflex in infants.

Bacon, Francis (1561–1626) English philosopher. Analyzed sources of error in perception and reasoning: developed a taxonomy of prejudices and promoted experimental science.

Bacon, Roger (1220–1292) English philosopher. An inductivist, promoted the use of mathematics and experimentation in science. Primary field of interest was optics.

Baer, Karl E. von (1792–1876) Russian-German physician. Studied the haptic system (sense of touch) and touch sensations. Also developed tools for such research.

Baillarger, Jean (1806–1890) French physician. Studied hallucinations and aphasia. Established that the cerebral cortex has six layers. Supported Gall's phrenology.

Bain, Alexander (1818–1903) Scottish psychologist. Identified "organic sense" of movement in muscles, (kinesthesis). Discussed mental life in relation to physiology.

Baird, John W. (1869–1919) Canadian psychologist. Studied accommodation and convergence in depth perception.

Baldwin, James M. (1861–1934) American psychologist. Studied the evolutionary development of children, individual differences. Compiled first dictionary of philosophy and psychology.

Ball, Rachel Stutsman (1894–1980) American psychologist. Known for her work in child development and test construction. Wrote *Mental Measurement of Preschool Children*.

Bárány, Robert (1876–1936) Hungarian-Swedish physician. Nobel prize winner in 1914 for physiology of the vestibular apparatus. Invented the Bárány chair.

Bard, Philip (1898–1977) American psychologist. Helped to revise the James-Lange theory of emotion.

Bardon, Jack I. (1925–1993) American psychologist. Initiated reforms in schools stressing the importance of mental health aspects started ecological psychology.

Barker, Roger G. (1903–1990) American psychologist. Studied environmental social conditions at a research field station in Kansas.

Bartlett, Frederic C. (1886–1969) British psychologist. A student of memory and author of *Remembering*.

Bartley, S. Howard (1910–1988) American psychologist. Researched physiology of perception, especially vision, as well as fatigue.

Basedow, Johann (1730–1790) German educator. Founded a school where children were regarded and treated as children, not as small adults.

Basov, Mikhail (1892–1931) Russian psychologist. Stressed the importance of objectivity of observation and cautioned against subjectivity in interpretation.

Bateson, Gregory (1904–1980) English-American anthropologist-philosopher. Began the Bateson project in communications. Proposed double bind as a cause for schizophrenia.

Bateson, William (1861–1926) English zoologist. Established the Mendelian concept of heredity. Coined the term genetics. Experimented with hybridization.

Bayes, Thomas (1702–1761) British theologian. Developed Bayes' theory, mathematical basis for inferential probability that predicts probability of future events from past events.

Bayle, Antoine L. (1799–1858) French physician. Discovered that general paralysis as mental disorder had three stages: monomania, mania, and dementia.

Bayle, François (1622–1709) French physician. Declared that mental disorders were due to natural causes, and not the result of demonic possession.

Bayley, Nancy (1898–1995) American psychologist. A pioneer in the measurement of intellectual and psychomotor functions in infants and young children.

Beach, Frank (1911–1988) American psychologist. Studied differences in the sexual and parental behavior of various animals.

Beard, George M. (1839–1883) American physician. Researched animal magnetism, clairvoyance, and spiritualism. A pioneer in medical uses of electricity.

Beaunis, Henri (1830–1921) French psychologist. Collaborated with Alfred Binet in establishing a psychological laboratory at the Sorbonne. Founded the first French psychological journal.

Beccaria, Cesare (1738–1794) Italian attorney. Author of *Crimes and Punishment* which changed the barbarous penal system of his time to a more humane modern system.

Bechtereff, Vladimir   Bekhterev, Vladimir

Beck, Samuel J. (1896–1980) American psychologist. First to attempt to develop a rational system for using the Rorschach as a clinical diagnostic instrument.

Beebe-Center, John (1897–1958) American psychologist. Concerned with hedonistic reactions to odors and tastes. Devised the Gust Scale of Taste.

Beers, Clifford (1876–1943) American social activist. Author of *A Mind that Found Itself*, started the first Society for Mental Hygiene. He helped reform institutes for the mentally ill.

Békésy, Georg von (1899–1972) Hungarian-born American biophysicist. Contributed to the neuroanatomy of the inner ear and the theory of hearing.

Bekhterev, Vladimir M. (1857–1927) Russian physician. Known for his work on conditioned motor withdrawal reflexes.

Bell, Charles (1774–1842) British physician. Discovered that sensory nerves enter the dorsal side and motor nerves leave the ventral side of spinal cord.

Bender, Lauretta (1897–1987) American physician. Conducted research on sexually traumatized children and developed The Bender Visual-Moto Gestalt Test.

Benedickt, Moritz (1835–1920) Austrian physician. Innovator in criminology and electrotherapy, developed principle of pathogenic scent.

Benedict, Ruth Fulton (1887–1948) American anthropologist. Studied American Indian cultures. Held that "Cultures have human personalities."

Beneke, Friedrich (1798–1854) German philosopher. Regarded the mind and the body as interacting; a pioneer of psychobiology.

Benes, Edvard (1884–1948) Czechoslovakian sociologist. Student of Thomas Masaryk, wrote many articles in political science and in psychology.

Benham, Charles E. (1860–1929) English amateur scientist. Invented a child's toy called "the artificial spectrum top" which later became known as Benham's Top.

Benjamin, Harry (1885–1986) German-American physician. Pioneered studies in gerontology and especially sexology, including transsexualism.

Bentham, Jeremy (1748–1832) English philosopher. Held that "Pain and pleasure are the primary human motives" and that "All men are hedonists." A founder of utilitarianism.

Bentley, Arthur (1870–1957) American philosopher. Developed a methodology of behavioral science research. He was concerned with the social nature of language.

Benussi, Vittorio (1878–1927) Italian-Austrian psychologist. A follower of the Act School of Brentano, experimented on space perception and optical illusions.

Berengario da Carpi, Giacomo (1460–1530) Italian physician. Raised doubts about rete mirabile. Described the thymus, corpus striatum, the pituitary gland. Also known as Berengarius.

Berengarius Berengario da Carpi

Berger, Johannes or Hans (1873–1941) German physician. Considered to be the founder of psychophysiology. A pioneer of electroencephalography.

Bergson, Henri (1859–1941) French philosopher. Concluded that evolution depends on the principle of élan vital.

Beritashvili, Ivan S. (1885–1975) Georgian physiologist. Specialized in experimentation of neurophysiological aspects of human behavior as well as conditioned reflexes.

Berkeley, George (1685–1753) Irish-English philosopher. Concluded that nothing exists but the mind and that constancy of perception is an attribute of the mind.

Berlyne, Daniel E. (1924–1976) Scottish-Canadian psychologist. Main interests were sensory experiences as well as esthetics.

Bernard, Claude (1813–1878) French physiologist. Demonstrated that emotions and moods were affected by hormones. Introduced the phrase "internal secretion." A founder of experimental psychology.

Berne, Eric (1910–1970) Canadian-American physician. Devised a system of psychotherapy called Transactional Analysis (TA).

Bernheim, Hippolyte (1840–1919) French neurologist. Co-founder with Liébeault of the Nancy School of mental treatment that specialized in using hypnosis on patients.

Bernoulli, Jacob or Jacques (1654–1705) and John or Jean (1667–1745) Swiss brothers, mathematicians and scientists. Developed eponymic terms in theorems and systems.

Bernshtein, Nikolai (1896–1966) Russian physiologist. Emphasized the active nature of behavior. Also known as Nicholas Bernstein.

Bernstein, Julius (1839–1917) German physiologist. Did fundamental research on nerves, found a correspondence of body area sensations and areas of the brain.

Bernstein, Nicholas Bernshtein, Nikolai

Bertalanffy, Ludwig von (1901–1972) Austrian-Canadian professor. The creator of general-systems theory. Concerned with theories of human development.

Berthold, A. A. (1813–1861) German physiologist. Published first article on gonadal transplantation that showed a direct link between the testes and secondary sexual characteristics.

Berzelius, Jons Jakob (1779–1848) Swedish chemist. Introduced system of chemical symbols. Named amino acids, organic and inorganic chemistry, and coined many other chemical terms.

Bessel, Friedrich W. (1784–1846) German astronomer. Learning of the dismissal of an astronomer (Kinnebrook) for inaccurate observations, he discovered the personal equation in perception.

Bethe, Albrecht (1872–1954) German physiologist. A precursor of behaviorism, recommended that in dealing with animals, only behavioral terms should be employed.

Bettelheim, Bruno (1903–1990) Austrian-American psychologist. Concerned with psychotic children. Declared autism was due to cold and aloof parents.

Bibring, Grete (1899–1977) Austrian physician. Taught and practiced psychiatry and psychoanalysis at the Harvard Medical School.

Bichat, Marie Francois (1771–1802) French physician. Founded the science of histology. Viewed mental disorders as due to abnormalities of anatomy and histological structures.

Biervliet, J. J. (1859–1945) Belgian psychologist. Developed an educational psychology on the basis of experimental methods.

Binet, Alfred (1857–1911) French psychologist. Studied individual differences, hypnosis, intelligence. With Théodore Simon developed Binet-Simon Scale.

Bingham, Walter V. (1880–1952) American psychologist. A pioneer in applied psychology. Helped develop World War I intelligence tests.

Binswanger, Ludwig (1881–1966) Swiss physician. Developed existential analysis that aimed to reconstruct the inner worlds of people with mental disorders.

Bleuler, Eugen (1857–1939) Swiss physician. Studied mental disorders in depth. Substituted the term schizophrenia for the older phrase dementia praecox.

Blix, Magnus (1882–?) Swedish physiologist. Discovered that the sensations of pressure, pain, cold and warmth are separate cutaneous sensations.

Block, Jeanne H. (1923–1981) American psychologist. Made significant contributions in several areas including delayed gratification in children, cognitive styles and creativity.

Blondel, Charles (1876–1939) French physician. Concerned with group psychology. Declared that individuals in groups tend to lose their individuality and become part of the group.

Blonskii, Pavel (1884–1941) Soviet psychologist. Held that "Psychology is a...biological science." Concerned with the cognitive development of children.

Boas, Franz (1858–1942) German-American anthropologist. A prime contributor to the study of cultures. Held that "Social traditions are molding forces in behavior."

Boder, David (1886–1961) Russian-American oral historian. Established the first psychological museum. Conducted psychological research in prisons.

Bodin, Jean (1530–1596) French political philosopher. Established a legal differentiation between bodily and mental disorders.

Boerhaave, Hermann (1668–1738) Dutch physician. The author of an influential text on diagnosing and caring for people with mental disorders.

Bogardus, Emory S. (1882–1973) American sociologist. A prolific writer in the field of sociology and developer of a social distance scale.

Boiko, Evgenii (1909–1972) Russian psychologist, a follower of Ivan Sechenov and Ivan Pavlov. Researched in the area of human communications.

Bonnet, Charles (1720–1793) Swiss naturalist. Anticipated Brentano's act psychology. Considered memory to be a function of activities in nerve fibers.

Boole, George (1815–1864) English mathematician. Interested in symbolic logic which he declared belonged to mathematics rather than to philosophy.

Bordin, Edward (1913–1992) American psychologist. A student of counseling and psychotherapy. Performed studies on personality and vocational choice.

Boring, Edwin G. (1886–1968) American psychologist. Wrote the *History of Experimental Psychology*, stressing interaction of individual creativity and the zeitgeist.

Bosquillon, Édouard (1744–1816) French physician. Advocated the then common medical treatment of blood-letting for people with mental disorders.

Bòss, Medard (1903–?) Swiss physician. Trained originally in psychoanalysis, became an existentialist, stressing freedom of choice in human behavior.

Bourdon, Benjamin B. (1869–1943) French psychologist. Started an early experimental laboratory in France. Experimented on perception and sensation.

Bowditch, Henry P. (1840–1911) American physiologist. First to demonstrate the all-or-none law of nerve impulse transmission in heart muscles.

Bowlby, John (1907–1990) English physician. Developed a comprehensive theory of maternal-infant bonding based on contemporary psychology and Darwinian evolutionary theory. Studied maternal deprivation on infants.

Bradley, Francis (1846–1924) Scottish philosopher. The last exponent of the Scottish school of psychology.

Braid, James (1795–1860) British physician. Developed a theory of hypnosis and helped to make hypnosis respectable.

Braille, Louis (1809–1852) French educator. Adapted the method of reading military messages in the dark by raised letters for use by the blind.

Bray, Charles (1904–1982) American physician. Researched electrical potentials in cochlea and auditory nerves.

Brentano, Franz (1838–1917) German philosopher. Pioneered act psychology, opposing Wilhelm Wundt's emphasis on content.

Brett, George S. (1879–1944) English-Canadian psychologist. A historian of psychology. Wrote a three-volume work on the topic.

Breuer, Joseph (1842–1925) Austrian physician. Informed Sigmund Freud of his treatment of Anna O by the "talking cure." Discovered the function of the semicircular canals in the ears.

Brewster, David (1781–1868) Scottish physicist. Main interest was in optics. Invented the kaleidoscope and improved Charles Wheatstone's stereoscope.

Bridgman, Percy W. (1882–1961) American physicist. A logical positivist who introduced the concept of operational definition. Wrote *Logic of Modern Physics*.

Brill, Abraham (1874–1948) Austrian-American physician. An early psychoanalyst, translated the works of Sigmund Freud, as well as of Carl Jung and Eugen Bleuler, into English.

Broad, Charlie Dunbar (1887–1971) English philosopher. Student of paranormal behavior. Suggested that some phenomena cannot be studied scientifically due to unspecified limiting principles.

Broadbent, Donald (1926–1993) English psychologist. Specialized in communication theory, seeing humans as information processing systems. Also researched decision-making.

Broca, Pierre Paul (1824–1880) French physician. Known for locating the speech center in the brain, now known as Broca's area.

Brodmann, Korbinian (1868–1918) German physician. Described 52 occipital and pre-occipital areas of cerebral cortex. Named is variously spelled.

Brown, John (1735–1788) Scottish physician. Named neurasthenia, a term used by George Beard and Pierre Janet.

Brown-Séquard, Charles E. (1818–1894) French physiologist. Demonstrated the crossing over of sensory fibers in the spinal cord.

Brown, Thomas (1778–1820) Scottish physician. Held a common sense philosophy of psychology, supported by J.S. Mill and Alexander Bain.

Brown, Warner (1882–1956) American psychologist. An experimentalist, conducted research in the areas of memory, perception and learning.

Brown, William (1881–1952) English psychologist. Concentrated on testing theory. The Spearman-Brown Prophecy formula was developed in collaboration with Charles Spearman.

Bruch, Hilde (1904–1984) German-American physician. Studied eating disorders (obesity and anorexia nervosa) in relation to mental disorders, primarily schizophrenia.

Brücke, Ernst von (1819–1892) German psychologist. An opponent of vitalistic explanation of causation and a mentor to Sigmund Freud.

Bruno, Giordano (1548–1600) Italian theologian. A humanist reformer, denied the validity of Aristotle's dualism and proposed a monist doctrine; suggested a united universe.

Brunswik, Egon (1903–1955) Hungarian American psychologist. Conceptualized probabalistic functionalism, and also researched shape and form constancy.

Bryan, William L. (1860–1955) American psychologist. Conducted classical telegraph studies on learning.

Buber, Martin (1878–1965) German philosopher. Emphasized the Importance of I-Thou existentialist relationship. Wrote *Knowledge and Man*.

Buffon, Georges (1707–1788) French naturalist. Anticipated Darwin's theories. Researched color vision as well as afterimages.

Bühler, Charlotte B. (1893–1974) Austrian-American psychologist. Regarded as humanist psychologist, emphasized the principle that heathy humans are active and purposeful.

Bühler, Karl Ludwig (1879–1963) Austrian-American psychologist. Opposed the views of Sigmund Freud, Wilhelm Wundt and E. B. Titchener.

Bujas, Zoran (1910–?) Croatian psychologist. Specialized in sensory psychophysiology, especially the sense of taste. Investigated fatigue, motivation and energy expenditure.

Buridan, Jean (ca 1300–1385) French philosopher. Concerned with behavior when there are two equal goals. Buridan's ass named after him.

Burnham, William H. (1855–1941) American psychologist. A founder of the mental hygiene movement, took a dynamic, goal-oriented point of view of normal personality adjustment.

Buros, Oscar K. (1905–1978) American psychologist. A cataloger and historian of mental measurement instruments.

Burrow, Trigant (1875–1950) American physician. The first American to be a psychoanalyst. Was an independent founder of therapy groups and created a theory he called Phyloanalysis.

Burt, Cyril L. (1883–1971) British psychologist. Centered his interests in child development, delinquency, mental tests and statistics.

Burton, Robert (1577–1640) English author. His *Anatomy of Melancholy* is a useful compendium of the thinking of his times on many issues, including psychological ones.

Burtt, Harold (1890–1991) American psychologist. Helped to establish standards for selecting pilots during World War I, did early research on lie detector tests.

Butler, Samuel (1835–1902) English novelist. In *Erewhon* he discussed original views on criminology, and the effect of machines on humans.

Bykov, Konstantin M. (1886–1959) Russian physiologist. Worked under Ivan Pavlov, and conducted numerous conditioning experiments.

Cabanis, Pierre Jean Georges (1757–1808) French physician. Stated that the brain was the organ of consciousness. Held that body and soul were two aspects of one faculty.

Calkins, Mary American Psychologist. Established one of the first psychological laboratories in the United States. Developed a system of self-psychology.

Calmeil, Jean (1798–1895) French physician. Concluded that gross pathologies of the brain caused mental symptoms.

Campbell, Angus A. (1910–1980) American psychologist. Conducted research in voting behavior, racial attitudes; researched measures of quality of life.

Campbell, Donald T. (1916–1996) American psychologist. Known for groundbreaking studies of scientific inquiry, quasi-experimental designs, and his views on evolutionary epistemology.

Cannon, Walter B. (1871–1945)   American physiologist. Researched emotion and digestion. Held that "adaptive physiological changes occur under stress."

Cantril, A. Hadley (1906–1969)   American psychologist. Main contribution was the development of accurate measures of public opinion.

Capgras, Jean Marie J. (1873–1950)   French physician. Co-discoverer of a psychotic delusion known as the Capgras symptom.

Carlson, Anton (1875–1956)   Swedish-American psychologist. Researched in the area of physiological sensations with emphasis on experiences of hunger.

Carmichael, Leonard (1898–1973)   American psychologist. A student of linguistics, did research on reading and edited a handbook on child psychology.

Carnap, Rudolf (1891–1970)   German philosopher. A member of the Vienna Circle and a founder of logical positivism. Wrote on the philosophy of science.

Carpenter, William P. (1813–1885)   English physician. Doubted the theory of evolution applied to human mental activities. Stressed a free will theory of human behavior.

Carr, Harvey (1873–1954)   American behaviorist. Doubted whether psychology was really a hard science. His main contribution was his concept of adaptive acts.

Cartesius   Descartes

Cattell, James McKeen (1860–1944)   American psychologist. Studied reaction time, perception, etc., in the interest of determining individual differences.

Cattell, Psyche (1893–1989)   American psychologist. Her main interest was in mental and physical development of children. Created the Cattell Infant Intelligence Scale.

Cattell, Raymond B. (1905–1998)   British-American psychologist. Promoted a factor analytic approach to theories of personality. Authored influential works in trait psychology and personality.

Charcot, Jean-Martin (1825–1893)   French physician. Most eminent neurologist of the late 19th century. Investigated the unconscious through hypnosis. Freud and Janet were his students.

Chavez, Ezequiel (1868–1946)   Mexican psychologist. An educational reformer, researched Mexican character and helped to develop psychology in Mexico.

Chelpanov, Georgii (1862–1936)   Russian psychologist. Prime founder of experimental psychology in Russia.

Chen, Li (1902–?)   Chinese psychologist. Studied with Charles Spearman, specialized in industrial psychology as well as the development of children.

Claparède, Édouard (1873–1940)   Swiss psychologist. Stressed biological bases of psychology. Defined experimental pedagogy.

Clark, Mamie Phipps (1917–1983)   American psychologist. With husband Kenneth Clark conducted groundbreaking work on the self-identity of Black children.

Claudius Galenus   Full name of Galen (of Pergamun).

Cleanthes (330–231 B.C.)   Greek philosopher. Viewed the soul as devoid of initial impressions. As did Aristotle asserted the view that the mind at origin is a tabula rasa.

Clérambault, G. G. de (1872–1934)   French physician. Studied erotic disorders, especially erotomania.

Coghill, George E. (1872–1941)   American physician. His research on salamanders reinforced Gestalt theory. He observed that molar movements appeared first, then specialized movements.

Cohen, Jacob (1923–1998)   American psychologist. Wrote influential and widely used books on multiple regression and statistical power.

Coleridge, Samuel Taylor (1772–1834)   English poet, critic, philosopher. His speculative psychology describes three types of imagination (primary, secondary, fancy).

Combe, George (1788–1858)   Scottish phrenologist. Originally an opponent of phrenology, ended as a major spokesman for it after conversion by Johann Spurzheim.

Comenius, John Amos (1592–1670)   Moravian theologian. Divided early development into four educational age groups: birth to 6, 6 to 12, 12 to 18, and 18 to 24 years of age.

Comrey, Andrew Laurence (1923–?)   American psychologist. A psychometrician, specialized in factor analysis and related techniques.

Comte, I. Auguste (1798–1857)   French philosopher, social reformer and behaviorist. Rejected introspection. Founded positivism. Held that only objective knowledge can be valid.

Condillac, Etienne Bonnot de (1714–1780)   French philosopher. A sensationist, wrote treatises on sensation, biology and reasoning. Averred, It is always our thought we perceive.

Condorcet, Antoine (1743–1794)   French philosopher. A rationalist, assumed that if people assumed scientific attitude, social problems would be solved.

Confucius (551–479 B.C.)   Chinese philosopher. Discussed human nature and how it could be modified through education. Teachings are recorded in the *Analects of Confucius*.

Conolly, John (1794–1866)   English physician. Took a then unpopular position that the insane could be dealt with humanely and without restraints.

Cooley, Charles H. (1864–1929)   American sociologist. Was concerned with the importance of a self-concept. Formulated the concept of the "looking-glass self".

Coombs, Clyde H. (1912–1988) American psychologist. Made significant contributions to quantification of subjective values. Was primarily interested in statistical measures.

Copernicus, Nicolas (1473–1543) Polish astronomer. Had a profound influence in science by his theory that the earth turned daily on its axis.

Coriat, Isadore (1875–1943) American physician. Interested in mental disorders, disputed Sigmund Freud's assumption that neuroses had sexual etiologies.

Cornelius, Hans (1863–1910) Austrian psychologist. Maintained that form quality was an attribute of experience and must be perceived as a whole.

Cotyloid, Adolph (1796–1874) Belgian mathematician. Considered a founder of modern statistics. Demonstrated that human behavior followed mathematical logic.

Coué, Emile (1857–1926) French pharmacist. Proponent of autosuggestion. Claimed many cures through this means.

Craik, Kenneth (1914–1945) British experimental psychologist. Specialized in the study of eye adaptation to illumination changes and, generally, of visual efficiency.

Crissey, Marie Skodak (1910–?) American psychologist. Contributed to knowledge of mental retardation. Discussed the critical influence of environment on intellectual development.

Croce, Benedetto (1866–1952) Italian philosopher. An ethicist who valorized intuition. Held that "The self-creating mind is the only reality."

Cronbach, Lee J. (1916–?) American psychologist. A specialist in mental measurement, held that scientists are construers of nature besides being discoverers.

Crosby, Elizabeth (1888–1983) American neuroanatomist. An authority on animal nervous systems. Showed the reptilian brain to be the precursor of aspects of brains of higher animals.

Crozier, William (1892–1955) American physiologist. Studied animal behavior especially tropisms. Experimented with flicker fusion and other sensory processes.

Crutchfield, Richard (1912–1977) American psychologist. Pioneered the use of analysis of variance and covariance in research as well as new methodologies of opinion surveys.

Cullen, William (1710–1790) Scottish physician. Attributed mental disorders to physiological disturbances and treated a variety of disorders with diet, purging, and bloodletting.

Cuvier, Georges (1769–1832) French zoologist. Established comparative anatomy and paleontology. Improved Linnaeus's system of classification. Anticipated Darwin.

Dabrowski, Kazimierz (1902–1980) Polish-Canadian psychologist. Organized the Institute of Mental Health in Warsaw, and in Canada promoted his system of positive disintegration.

Dale, Henry (1875–1968) English physician. Isolated acetylcholine. Coined the terms cholinergic, adrenergic.

d'Alembert, Jean le Rond (1717–1783) French scientist. Postulated d'Alembert's principle, that the sum of external influences on the body is equal to the body's kinetic reaction.

Dallenbach, Karl M. (1887–1971) American psychologist. Did research on attention, memory, perception and forgetting. Supported Titchener's views on structural psychology.

Dalton, John (1766–1844) English chemist. Suggested that dichromasy was caused by missing optic receptors.

Darley, John (1910–1991) American psychologist. Specialized in counseling, especially as pertained to research and practice.

Darwin, Charles R. (1809–1882) English naturalist. Provided data for the theory of evolution, researched animal behavior and expressions of emotions.

Darwin, Erasmus (1721–1802) English physician. Developed his own concept of evolution, similar to that of Lamarck. Grandfather of both Charles Darwin and Francis Galton.

Dashiell, John (1888–1975) American psychologist. An early behaviorist, author of *Fundamentals of Objective Psychology*, generated a psychology combining biology and behavior.

da Vinci, Leonardo (1452–1519) Italian artist. Discussed binocular visions. Demonstrated three ventricles of the brain by injecting molten wax into the brain of an ox.

Davy, Humphery (1778–1829) English chemist. One of the first to experience the effects of nitrous oxide. Held that "Nothing exists but thoughts. The universe is composed of. . .ideas. . ."

d'Azyr, Vicq (1748–1794) French physician. Discovered that the convolutions of the brains of monkeys were few in number, and in humans they were neither symmetrical or structurally consistent.

Dearborn, Walter (1878–1955) American psychologist. Determined that reading skills depend on a complex of cognitive, emotional, and motivational factors.

De Condillac, Etienne Bonnot Condillac

Decroly, Ovide (1871–1932) Belgian psychologist. Mainly interested in children's mental processes, found that variable social class partially explained intelligence quotient (IQ).

Déjerine, Joseph Jules (1849–1917) Swiss-born French physician. Conducted a variety of experiments with split brains. With wife, Augusta Klumpke, identified and described cortical lesions.

Delabarre, Edmund (1863–1945) American psychologist. Studied muscle movements. Invented the kymograph and other research devices. A founder of the American Psychological Association.

de La Mettrie, Julien Offray La Mettrie, Julien Offray de

Delboeuf, Joseph Jean (1831–1896) Belgian psychologist. Researched sensation differences. His work influenced Edward Titchener. In later life experimented with hypnotism.

de le Boë, François (1614–1672) German physician. First noted and named the fissure of Sylvius after his alternate name, Franciscus Sylvius.

De los Rio, Francisco (1840–1915) Spanish philosopher. A student of Wilhelm Wundt, published a handbook that covered the works of Wundt, Gustav Fechner and Hermann von Helmholtz.

Dembo, Tamara (1902–1993) Russian-American psychologist. Conducted research on frustration and worked to improve conditions for persons with disabilities.

Deming, W. E. (1900–1993) American management theorist. Struggled to improve American manufacturing quality. In post World War II, the Japanese corporate world was affected by his ideas.

Democritus (of Abdera) (ca. 450–380 B.C.) Greek philosopher. Was an exponent of materialism. Held that the "Brain is the center of thinking. All matter is composed of atoms."

Dennis, Wayne (1905–1976) American psychologist. His main professional concern was the effect of the environment during early life on later maturation.

de Paul, Vincent (1580–1660) French priest. Established a hospital for the mentally ill stressing humane treatment. Took the position that mental and physical illnesses were comparable.

de Sade, Marquis Sade, Marquis de

De Sanctis, Sante (1862–1935) Italian physician. A researcher who established a laboratory in Italy, pioneered in the education of mentally handicapped children.

Descartes, René (1596–1650) French scientist. Initiated modern philosophy. In the Platonic tradition discussed theory that mind and body affect each other though they are distinct.

Destutt de Tracy, Antoine (1754–1836) French philosopher. Follower of Condillac, he stressed that human thought is a complex product of sensations.

Deutsch, Helene (1884–1982) Polish-born American psychologist. Probably Sigmund Freud's last student. Focused on the areas of the psychology of women, bereavement and female sexuality.

Dewey, John (1859–1952) American psychologist. His reflex arc concept in psychology reinforced school of functionalism. Held that people are proactive. Was an educational innovator.

Dichter, Ernest (1907–1992) Austrian-American psychologist. Called the founder of motivational research. Applied psychology techniques to business and advertising.

Diderot, Denis (1713–1784) French philosopher. Noted encyclopedist, he developed his own method of philosophical inquiry. He presaged Charles Darwin.

Digman, John (1924–1998) American psychologist. Pioneered in the development of the theory of so-called the Big Five Personality factors.

Dilthey, Wilhelm (1833–1911) German philosopher. Maintained that human psychology is a teleological dynamic.

Dix, Dorothea (1802–1887) American educator. A reformer of prisons and mental hospitals, she campaigned to convince legislators to institute humane treatments of "lunatics".

Dodge, Raymond (1871–1942) American psychologist. His main concern was motor performance and visual perception. The first to classify eye movements.

Dogiel, Alexander Stanislavovich (1852–1922) Russian histologist. The most distinguished Russian neurohistologist. Studied the histological structure of nerve fibers.

Dollard, John (1900–1980) American psychologist. Defined how life histories could contribute to unified understanding of humans.

Donders, Franciscus (1818–1889) Dutch physician. Conducted reaction-time research. Precisely measured Bessel's personal equation.

Doppler, Johann (1803–1853) Austrian physicist. Discovered the mathematical relationship between the pitch of sound and a steady sound source.

Downey, June E. (1875–1932) American psychologist. Divided temperament traits into mercurial-speedy, dynamic-aggressive and slow-deliberative.

Dreikurs, Rudolf (1897–1972) Austrian-American student and colleague of Alfred Adler. A proponent of music therapy, group therapy, and parent training.

Drever, James, Sr. (1873–1950) Scottish psychologist. Developed a system of psychology that stressed the importance of goals rather than history for understanding people's behavior.

Driesch, Hans (1867–1941) German biologist. Claimed vital energy, a teleological force, provided direction and order to organisms.

Dr. Mises Pseudonym of Gustav Fechner.

Dubois, Paul-Charles (1848–1918) Swiss-French physician. First psychotherapist in the modern tradition. Coined the term psychoneurosis.

Du Bois-Reymond, Emil (1818–1986) German physiologist. Broke with ancient concepts of nerve function. Declared no other force exists in humans besides common physical-chemical ones.

Duchenne, Guillaume (1806–1875) French physician. Described locomotor ataxia. He was the first person to use electricity for therapy.

Duffy, Elizabeth (1902–1959) American psychologist. Contributed the "activation theory," a theory of motivation, which integrated experimental physiological data.

Duijker, Hubert (1912–1983) Dutch psychologist. Interested in communication and cooperation between various areas of psychology, wrote on national stereotypes.

Dumas, Georges (1886–1946) French physician. An experimentalist, researched in the area of the emotions, attempting to locate their physiological origins.

Dunbar, Helen Flanders (1902–1959) American physician. Researched psychosomatic disorders, aging and accident-prone personalities. Founder of psychosomatic medicine.

Duncan, David Beattie (1916–?) Australian-American mathematician. Conducted major research in biostatistics. Developed linear theory and methods, time series analyses.

Duncker, Karl (1903–1940) German psychologist. Was interested in the dynamics of problem-solving. Author of *Psychology of Productive Thought*.

Dunlap, Knight (1873–1949) American psychologist. Known best for his development of the Dunlap chronoscope. Researched in diverse areas including religion and vision.

Dunne, John William (1875–1949) British philosopher. Researched the area of prodromic (predictive) dreaming believing that time was the unfolding of pre-ordained events.

Duns Scotus, John (?1250–1292) Scottish philosopher. In contrast to Thomas Aquinas, affirmed the priority of will over intellect.

Durkheim, Emile (1858–1917) French sociologist. Wrote classic essay on suicide. Suggested the existence of a group mind.

Dvorak, Vinko (1848–1922) Czech physicist. Ernst Mach's assistant. It was his work that Ernst Mach presented on the stereoillusion in 1872.

Dymphna, Saint (7th century) Irish princess. A Christian martyr; became the patron saint of the insane.

Ebbinghaus, Hermann (1850–1909) German psychologist. Produced nonsense syllables to study memory using himself as the subject.

Edwards, Allen L. (1914–1994) American psychologist. Specialized in personalty measurement and statistics and research design.

Edwards, Jonathan (1703–1758) American theologian. Declared that humans did not have free will. Wrote on psychological issues and anticipated some of Sigmund Freud's ideas.

Eells, Kenneth Walter (1913–?) American psychologist. Researched student counseling, psychological testing and student use of drugs.

Ehrenfels, Christian von (1859–1932) Austrian psychologist. Anticipated Gestalt psychology. Opposed Wilhelm Wundt's elementarism.

Ehrlich, Paul (1854–1915) German physician. Contributed to neuron theory. Developed a method of staining nerve tissue with methylene blue. The founder of modern-day chemotherapy.

Elliotson, John (1791–1868) English physician. Used hypnosis for cure of diseases and as an anesthetic for surgery. Founded a journal to perpetuate his theories.

Ellis, Henry Havelock (1859–1939) English physician. Specialist in sex. Concluded that homosexuality was congenital. Objected to Sigmund Freud's views on children's sexuality.

Empedocles (ca 490–430 B.C.) Greek philosopher and statesman. Discussed the values of good and evil and the concept that change (flux) was eternal.

English, Horace B. (1892–1961) American psychologist. Concerned with the area of child psychology, wrote one of the earliest dictionaries of psychology.

Epictetus (50–138) Greek philosopher. Held that the world was rational and good. Believed that life was pre-planned and individuals should accept their fate.

Epicurus (341–270 B.C.) Greek philosopher. Advocated hedonism. Counseled a life of contemplation. Believed in existence of atoms and did not believed in predestination.

Erasistratus (ca 310–250 B.C.) Greek physician. Held that "The soul resides in the brain." First to distinguish between sensory and motor nerves.

Erasmus, Desiderius (1466–1536) Dutch theologian. Departed from the scholastic tradition to humanism. Believed there was no absolute truth.

Erdmann, Benno (1851–1921) German psychologist. His main interest was cognitive processes. Distinguished between imagination, thinking and fantasy.

Erickson, Milton H. (1901–1980) American physician. Interested in color blindness and time distortion. Developed Ericksonian therapy that involved hypnosis.

Erickson, Molly **Harrower-Erickson, Molly**

Erikson, Erik (1902–1980) Austrian-American lay psychoanalyst. Believed psychoanalysis helped cope with problems of life. Developed a life cycle of eight stages.

Esdaile, James (1809–1859) British-Indian physician. A follower of Mesmer and of Elliotson, performed surgery using hypnosis as an anesthetic.

Esquirol, Jean E. (1772–1840) French physician. One of first to apply statistical methods for mental disorders. Looked for psychological, rather than biological, reasons, for disorders.

Euler, Leonhard (1707–1783) Swiss physicist. Contributed to mathematical logic employed up to the present time by scientists in all fields including psychology.

Ewald, Julius (1855–1921) German psychologist. Developed the pressure-pattern theory of hearing, challenging Helmholtz.

Exner, Sigmund (1846–1926) German psychologist. Known for his work on adaption to hue, and studies of apparent visual movement. Gave reaction experiment its name.

Eysenck, Hans J. (1916–1998) German-British psychologist. A personality psychologist and test constructor. A persistent critic of psychoanalysis, defended behaviorism.

Fabre, Jean Henri (1823–1915) French entomologist. In a ten-volume work, *Souvenirs entomologiques*, described aspects of insect behavior.

Fairbairn, Ronald W. (1889–1964) British physician. Evolved a systematic theory of object relations with radical modifications of Freudian theory.

Fallopius, Gabriele F. (1523–1563) Italian physician. Introduced the terms cochlea and labyrinth in his study of the human ear. Fallopian tubes (human oviducts) are named after him.

Falret, Jean-Pierre (1794–1870) French physician. Was able to convince French lawmakers to view mental alienation as a meaningful legal concept.

Fantz, Robert L. (1925–1981) American psychologist. A researcher who used visual perception as a procedure to study animals and infant humans.

Faraday, Michael (1791–1867) English physicist. Introduced electrical terms used in research on bodies and bodily functions including anion, anode, ion, cathode, and electrode.

Fechner, Gustav T. (1801–1887) German psychologist. Was the principal developer of psychophysics by connecting and systematizing relationships between psychology and physics. Used the pseudonym "Dr. Mises."

Federn, Paul (1871–1950) Austrian physician. Saved minutes of the Wednesday Evening Society (Freud's group) for publication. Introduced the concept of the meaning of flying dreams.

Fenichel, Otto (1899–1946) Austrian psychoanalyst. A disciple of Freud. Emphasized disturbing emotional experiences in childhood as the primary causal factor in neuroses.

Féré, Charles S. (1852–1907) French physician. A collaborator of Alfred Binet, discovered the psychogalvanic reflex and constructed the first ergograph.

Ferenczi, Sandor (1873–1933) Hungarian psychoanalyst. Favored a more active and interactive mode of treatment in contrast to Sigmund Freud.

Fernald, Grace (1879–1950) American psychologist. First psychologist to work at the Chicago Psychopathic Institute. With William Healy she developed the Healy-Fernald test series.

Ferree, Clarence E. (1877–1942) American psychologist. Conducted considerable research in the area of vision.

Ferrier, David (1843–1928) British physician. Noted for localization of brain functions. Mapped the cerebral cortex of the monkey. Improved advances in brain operations.

Ferster, Charles (1922–1981) American psychologist. Applied behaviorism to education and clinical psychology.

Festinger, Leon (1919–1989) American psychologist, theorist and experimenter in social psychology. Operating from a Gestalt point of view, developed the theory of cognitive dissonance.

Feuerbach, Ludwig (1804–1872) German philosopher. Criticized the idea of personal immortality, thought that human bodies are given back to nature. Influenced Karl Marx.

Fichte, Johann Gottlieb (1762–1814) German philosopher. Stressed free will, "The mind can reflect upon itself."

Fisher, Ronald A. (1890–1962) English statistician. Innovator of statistical concepts such as analysis-of-variance (ANOVA) and null hypothesis.

Fitts, Paul M. (1912–1965) American psychologist. Applied theoretical concepts to practical human/engineering problems, such as aviation cockpit design.

Flanagan, John (1906–1996) American psychologist. Evaluated performance, aptitudes and vocational interests. Helped select aviators during World War II.

Flechsig, Paul (1847–1929) German physician. His myelogenic studies led to many discoveries in the brain and spinal cord.

Flesch, Rudolf (1911–1986) Austrian-American psychologist. Specialized in the study of language and reading. Developed a scale for measuring difficulty of reading.

Fliess, Wilhelm (1858–1928) German physician. A nose and throat specialist, close friend of Sigmund Freud, shared interest in sexual research and influenced Freud's theory of bisexuality.

Flourens, Marie-Pierre Jean (1794–1867) French physician. Pioneer of brain ablation. Established a holistic theory of brain functioning.

Flournoy, Théodore (1854–1920) Swiss psychologist. Researched reaction time, imaging, sensation and hypnosis.

Flügel, John (1884–1955) British psychologist. Author of *A Hundred Years of Psychology*, reflecting broad historical scholarship.

Foerster Förster

Fontana, Gasparo (1730–1803) Austrian-Italian physician. Noted that nerve electricity produced muscle contractions. His wax models of the brain are still in view in an Austrian museum.

Forbes, Alexander (1882–1965) American physiologist. A researcher, developed electronic amplifier of physiological reactions and measured spinal reflexes.

Forel, August-Henri (1848–1931) Swiss neurologist. Studied both human and animal anatomy and behavior. Later specialized in insect behavior. Was a prison reformer.

Foster, Vilem (1882–1932) Czech psychologist. Professor at Charles University. Developed instruments for attention and known for his dynamic theory of color vision.

Fourier, Francois Charles Marie (1772–1837) French reformer. Assumed that repression of passions was responsible for human discontent, crime, immorality. "Society corrupts humans".

Fourier, Jean-Baptiste (1768–1830) French mathematician. Developed the Fourier theorem. Researched properties of heat. Classified personality types.

Frankl, Victor (1905–1998) Austrian physician-psychologist. Founder of Logotherapy, based primarily on his experiences in surviving a Nazi concentration camp. Championed "Will to Meaning."

Franklin, Benjamin (1706–1790) American statesman. Served on a committee in Paris to evaluate hypnotic cures of Franz Anton Mesmer. Researched visual aftersensation.

Franz, Shepherd Ivery (1874–1933) American psychologist. Pioneered extirpation experiments on animals. Localized some brain functions.

Frazer, James (1854–1941) British anthropologist (who never travelled). Foremost student of mythology of many countries, author of *The Golden Bough*.

Freeman, Frank N. (1880–1961) American psychologist. Specialized in the study of twins and in hand movements in writing. Developer of the Freeman time unit (FTU).

Frenkel-Brunswick, Else (1908–1958) Polish-American psychologist. Investigated prejudice and developed innovative methods of assessing personality.

Freud, Anna (1895–1982) Austrian-British psychologist. Specialized in the treatment of children, advanced theories of her father based on her direct observation of children.

Freud, Sigmund (1856–1939) Austrian physician. Founded psychoanalysis, stressing conflicts between aggressive impulses and conscience as prime causes of mental and behavioral disorders.

Frey, Maximilian von (1852–1932) German physiologist. Investigated skin sensations. Found skin spots for pain, warmth, and cold. Invented "von Frey's hairs" for such research.

Frisch, Karl von (1886–1982) Austrian ethologist. Researched animal behavior. Discovered that bees used "dances" based on sun orientation and distance to inform other bees of food sources.

Fritsch, Gustav (1838–1927) German naturalist-physician. With E. Hitzig conducted early studies of brain localization by electrically stimulating the brains of dogs.

Fröbel, Friedrich (1782–1852) German educator. Held that "The goal of education is to develop innate potentials." Founded and named the first kindergarten.

Fröbes, Joseph (1866–1947) German-Dutch psychologist. Attempted to integrate philosophical and empirical psychology.

Fröhlich, Alfred (1871–1953) Austrian neurologist. Discovered the disorder known as Fröhlich's syndrome, due to malfunction of the pituitary's frontal lobe.

Fromm, Erich (1900–1980) German-American physician. Opposed Sigmund Freud's strictly sexual theory and emphasized the importance of social factors in human behavior.

Fromm, Erika (1910–?) German born psychologist. Trained in Gestalt theory, she conducted pioneering clinical and research work with hypnoanalysis in the area of ego functioning.

Fromm-Reichmann, Frieda (1889–1957) German-American physician. Stressed the importance in psychotherapy of abreaction and insight.

Frostig, Marianne B. (1906–?) Austrian psychologist. Conducted research and wrote on the etiology of learning disabilities. Developed Frostig Developmental Test of Visual Perception.

Fullerton, George S. (1859–1925) American philosopher. Collaborated with James McKeen Cattell in psychophysical experiments.

Galen (of Pergamum) (ca 130–200) Greek-Roman physician. Applied Hippocrates' four-humors theory to pathology. Used pulse rate as a "lie detector."

Galileo (1564–1642) Italian physicist. Founded modern research logic and procedures. His objective experiments revolutionized current physics and overthrew long-held Ptolemaic conceptions.

Gall, Franz J. (1757–1828) German physician and anatomist. Studied skulls in an attempt to find a relationship between mental faculties and head conformations. Began phrenology.

Gal'perin, Pyotr (1902–1988) Russian psychologist. Developed a theory of stage-by-stage formation of mental operations.

Galton, Francis (1822–1911) English scientist and researcher. Studied hereditary traits in families. Researched in a number of areas including measurement.

Galvani, Luigi (1737–1798) Italian physician. Discovered that animal tissues generate electricity. The Galvanic skin response (GSR) was named after him.

Ganser, Sigbert J. (1853–1931) German physician. Studied brain anatomy. Identified Ganser('s) syndrome, absurd behavior and verbalizations found chiefly in prisoners.

Garcia, Guillermo (1902–1969) Mexican physician. Interested in psychopathology. Brought psychology as a science to Mexico, invited major American psychologists to Mexico.

Garner, Richard (1843–1920) American psychologist. Doubted Charles Darwin's theory, studied the brains of apes and compared them to brains of humans and found essential dissimilarities.

Garth, Thomas (1872–1939) American psychologist. Studied race differences and concluded that the concept of race was meaningless in psychological areas.

Gassendi, Pierre (1592–1655) French theologian. Attempted to reconcile mechanical atomism with Christian concepts. Rejected the ideas of Descartes, saw proof of God in nature.

Gauss, Johann Karl F. (1777–1855)   German mathematician. Discovered many mathematical concepts such as the Gaussian curve often used by researchers.

Gemelli, Agostino (1878–1959)   Italian psychologist-physician. An important theoretician and an innovator in applications of psychology.

Gerlach, Joseph von (1820–1896)   German physician. Developed the concept that the gray matter of the brain was composed of a network (rete mirabile) of dendrites.

Geschwind, Norman (1926–1984)   American physician. Reintroduced the concept of disconnection syndrome. Speech dysfunctions were due to damage to various points in the nervous system.

Gesell, Arnold (1880–1961)   American physician. Authority on child development. Stressed importance of heredity over environment.

Geulinex, Arnold (1624–1669)   Dutch philosopher. A follower of Descartes, he started occasionalism which included an ethical theory. Affirmed the role of the will in making decisions.

Ghiselli, Edwin (1907–1980)   American psychologist. Was interested in personnel psychology and measurement theory. Researched the reliability of vocational measures.

Gibson, Eleanor Jack (1910–?)   American psychologist. Known for research of perceptual development in infants and young children, using the visual cliff.

Gibson, James J. (1904–1979)   American psychologist. Researched form and motion perception. His "ecological optics" challenged Hermann von Helmholtz's procedures.

Gilbreth, Frank (1868–1924)   American engineer. With wife Lillian studied work movements in the interest of improving work conditions and productivity.

Gilbreth, Lillian Moller (1878–1972)   American psychologist. Specialized in studies of industrial efficiency. With husband Frank developed "Therblig," a measurement unit.

Gilles de la Tourette, Georges (1857–1904)   French physician. Identified the disorder named after him, which he originally labeled coprolalia.

Giraldès, Joachim (1808–1875)   Portuguese physician. Anatomist who studied the brains of hydrocephalic mental defectives.

Glover, Edward (1888–1972)   British physician. A psychoanalyst, who founded an institute to study delinquency and criminality; classified mental disorders.

Glueck, Eleanor Touroff (1898–1972)   American sociologist. After careful research studies of delinquent youths she concluded that the social environment was the primary cause of delinquency.

Glueck, Sheldon (1896–1972)   American sociologist. With his wife, Eleanor, researched causes of delinquency. Found the answer to be the social environment.

Goclenius, Rudolphus   Goeckel, Rudolf

Goddard, Henry (1866–1957)   American psychologist. Championed eugenics in the United States of America. Held that heredity was the main cause of mental retardation.

Gödel, Kurt (1906–1977)   Austrian-Hungarian mathematician. Known for his Gödel's Proof based on logic and mathematics.

Goeckel, Rudolf (1547–1628)   German philosopher. The word "*psychologie*" was first seen in print in his *Psychologie: Hominemo Perfectionest*. Also known as Rudolphus Goclenius.

Goethe, Johann Wolfgang von (1749–1832)   German writer, scientist, statesman, experimenter. Wrote a two volume book on color vision. His writings influenced Sigmund Freud and Carl Jung.

Goffman, Erving (1922–1982)   American microsociologist. Pioneered the dramaturgical perspective in sociology.

Goldstein, Kurt (1878–1965)   German-American physician. Developed a holistic theory of personality that emphasized that the main human motive was self-actualization.

Golgi, Camillo (1843–1926)   Italian physician. Invented silver staining method for studying nerve cells. Identified eponyms such as Golgi apparatus.

Goltz, Friedreich (1834–1902)   German physiologist. Developed the hydrostatic concept that the weight of the fluid in the semicircular canals varies with the position of the head.

Gompertz, Benjamin (1779–1865)   English mathematician. Self-educated, worked on mathematical problems, especially those of astronomy and statistics. A pioneer in actuarial science.

Goodenough, Florence L. (1886–1959)   American psychologist. A historian of mental testing; creator of the Draw-a-Man Test, for testing for intelligence, later for assessing personality.

Gosset, William S. (1876–1937)   British statistician. Developed modern statistical thinking, the concepts of the probable error of the mean and Student's t. Wrote under the pen name Student.

Gratiolet, Louis Pierre (1815–1865)   French physician. Noted that convolutions of the surface of the brain had a functional order and that development differed by race, age, and gender (sex).

Greatrakes, Valentine (1629–1683)   Irish soldier. After serving with Cromwell, announced he had the "king's touch" and cured thousands. The king's touch was supposed to cure scrofula.

Greenacre, Phyllis (1894–?)   American psychologist. Clinician and teacher. Authority in child psychoanalysis. Author of *Trauma, Growth, and Personality*.

Griesinger, Wilhelm (1817–1868)   German physician. Worked toward a "physiological medicine." Considered all mental disorders to be diseases of the brain.

Groos, Karl (1861–1946)   German psychologist. Specialized in the study of the playing of children, seeing it as a preparation for later life.

Grosseteste, Robert (1175–1253) English theologian. His studies of Aristotle and Plato set the stage for harmonizing supernatural ideas.

Guilford, Joy Paul (1897–1987) American psychologist. Did factor analytic studies of personality. Viewed intelligence as a complex of different abilities.

Guillaume, Paul (1878–1962) French psychologist. Researched behavior analysis, Gestalt psychology, habit formation and psycholinguistics.

Gumplowicz, Ludwig (1838–1909) Polish sociologist and social Darwinist. Argued that social evolution is a struggle for economic resources resulting in the survival of the fittest.

Guthrie, Edwin R. (1886–1959) American psychologist. Created a contiguity theory of learning that asserts learning develops primarily by association in time rather than by reinforcement.

Guttman, Louis (1916–1987) American psychologist. His main interest was in psychometrics, nonparametric analysis and social psychology. Developed the Guttman scaling method.

Haeckel, Ernst H. (1834–1919) German biologist. His formula: "Ontology recapitulates phylogeny" influenced a generation of developmentalists. G. S. Hall elaborated on it.

Hall, Calvin (1909–1985) American psychologist. An investigator of dreams and personality theories. With Robert Tryon researched the intelligence inheritance of rats.

Hall, Granville Stanley (1844–1924) American psychologist. A developmentalist, founded the first formal psychological laboratory in America. First president of the APA.

Hall, Marshall (1790–1857) Scottish physician. Stated that behaviors fall into four categories: voluntary, involuntary-medulla, involuntary-muscular and involuntary-spinal.

Haller, Albrecht von (1708–1777) Swiss biologist. A founder of the science of experimental physiology, assembled all then-known knowledge of physiology in an eight-volume text.

Halstead, Ward (1908–1969) American psychologist. Developed tests to measure brain functioning, later revised as the Halstead-Reitan Neuropsychological Test Battery.

Hamilton, Max (1912–1988) German-British physician. Conducted double-blind studies on psychotropic drugs. Created a scale to measure depression.

Hamilton, William (1788–1856) Scottish philosopher. Asserted that the basic principle of psychology is the unity and activity of the mind.

Hammurabi (1792–1750 B.C.) Babylonian king. Established Code of Hammurabi, recommended olive oil and opium for the treatment of mental disorders produced by demonic possession.

Hanfmann, Eugenia (1905–1983) Russian-American psychologist. Primarily interested in the thinking and personality development of children. Co-author with Jacob Kasanin a concept formation test.

Harlow, Harry F. (1905–1981) American psychologist. Demonstrated utilizing artificial surrogate mothers, that infant monkeys required comforting tactile stimulation.

Harlow, Margaret Cain (1918–1971) American psychologist. Collaborated with husband, Harry Harlow, in research in child development and comparative psychology.

Hartley, David (1705–1757) English physician. Founder of British associationism. Concluded that contiguity was the unique determinant of association.

Hartley, Hermann O. (1912–1980) American statistician. Advanced statistical methodology, sample survey theory, and estimation theory of mathematical techniques.

Hartley, Ruth (1905–?) American psychologist. Prominent in child development, clinical, educational, and social psychology, personality development and early childhood education.

Hartmann, Eduard von (1842–1906) German philosopher. Established the importance of the unconscious mind in human behavior, followed by Charcot, Janet, Freud, and Jung.

Hartmann, Heinz (1894–1970) German physician. Departed from Freud to some extent, emphasizing the importance and the independence of the ego, and in doing so started ego psychology.

Harvey, William (1578–1675) English physician. His work marked the beginning of modern physiology. He is credited with discovering circulation of blood.

Havighurst, Robert J. (1900–1991) American psychologist. Advanced understanding of personality and moral development in children and adolescents using research designs.

Hayashi, Rasran (1583–1657) Japanese Confucian. Held that principle was prior and material force was posterior; they were two and yet one.

Head, Henry (1861–1940) English neurologist. Noted for his studies on cerebral cortex and aphasia. Performed research on pain.

Healy, William (1869–1963) British-American physician. Pioneered guidance clinics for disadvantaged and problem children. Developed intelligence tests.

Hearnshaw, Leslie (1907–1991) English psychologist. A historian, started as an industrial psychologist investigating effects of aging, also biographed Cyril Burt.

Hebb, Donald Olding (1904–1985) Canadian psychologist. Sought an explanation for the high intelligence quotients (IQs) of some brain-damaged people; this lead to his cell-assembly theory.

Hecht, Selig (1892–1947) American physiologist. Provided the first careful measurements of most basic visual phenomena, including the least amount of light detectable by the human eye.

Hegel, Georg Wilhelm F. (1770–1831) German philosopher. Proposed a dialectical logic of thesis, antithesis, and synthesis. Anticipated Karl Marx, Sigmund Freud, and Jean Piaget.

Heidbreder, Edna (1890–1985) American psychologist. Author of *Seven Psychologies*, a summary of major theories of psychology. Studied concept attainment, systematic psychology.

Heidegger, Martin (1889–1976) German philosopher. An existentialist in the Kierkegaardian tradition, stated that freedom comes from acceptance the human condition.

Heider, Fritz (1896–1988) Austrian-American psychologist. Originated attribution approaches and balance theory in social psychology. Researched interpersonal perception.

Heinroth, Johann (1773–1843) German physician. Classified in hierarchical fashion psychological process from instincts at lower level to highest level.

Hellpach, Willy (1877–1955) German psychologist. Stated that people must be understood as summations of multiple factors, biological, social, personal.

Helmholtz, Hermann von (1821–1894) German physician. Founder of physiological psychology, researched speed of nerve conduction, and reaction times, lens accommodation and acoustics.

Helmont, J. B. *van Helmont, J. B.*

Helson, Harold (1898–1977) American psychologist. Studied perception and sensory phenomena. Received the Warren Medal in 1959 for developing the concept of adaptation-level.

Helvétius, Claude-Adrien (1715–1771) French philosopher. Asserted that sensations were the primary source of intellectual activity. His work was condemned by the Sorbonne.

Henle, Mary (1913–?) American psychologist. Often identified as a "psychologist's psychologist," she was known as an interpreter of Gestalt psychology.

Henmon, Vivian (1877–1950) American psychologist. Researched individual differences. Co-author of a test of mental ability.

Henning, Hans (1885–1946) German psychologist. Known for his research in taste and smell, attempted a structural classification of odors in the mode of a geometric solid.

Heraclitus of Ephesus (ca 540–480 B.C.) Greek philosopher. Argued that though there is unity of change, flux is constant, and permanence is an illusion. "Everything comes out of fire."

Herbart, Johann Friedrich (1776–1841) German philosopher Assumed psychology should be based on experience, metaphysics, and mathematics. Was also an educational theorist.

Herder, Johann (1744–1803) German philosopher. Rejected the Enlightenment's exaltation of universal truth through science, stressed organic development and plurality of truths.

Hering, Karl Ewald (1834–1918) German physiologist and psychologist. Proposed a theory of color vision that called for substances in the retina that reacted to colors.

Hermann, Imre (1889–1984) Hungarian physician. A psychoanalyst who developed a theory of instincts in infants, conducted research in choice behavior.

Hernández-Peón, Raúl (1924–1968) Mexican psychophysiologist. Studied habituation, attention, facilitation and sleep.

Herophilus (ca 335–280 B.C.) Greek physician. Held that the brain was the main organ of the nervous system and the seat of intelligence.

Herrick, C. Judson (1868–1960) American neurologist. Did extensive exploration of the brain and declared that brains of higher orders of mammals developed from simpler brains.

Herskovits, Melville (1895–1963) American anthropologist. His major contribution involved cultural factors in perception, especially about engineered environments.

Hertz, Marguerite (1899–?) American psychologist. Contributor to the understanding of child development, psychopathology, personality measurement and interpretation of the Rorschach.

Hess, Walter Rudolf (1881–1973) Swiss physiologist. Pioneered electric stimulation of the brain and studied resulting organic and behavioral reactions.

Heymans, Corneille (1892–1968) Belgian physiologist. Working with anesthetized dogs, demonstrated sensory organs in the carotid artery help breathing. Studied blood pressure.

Hilgard, Josephine Rohrs (1906–1989) American physician. A practicing therapist, she conducted research in sibling rivalry and affiliation as well as anniversary reactions.

Hippocrates (ca 460–377 B.C.) Greek physician. Considered to be the founder of Western medicine. Denounced religious explanations for physical and mental illnesses. Posited the humoral theory of four constitutional types based on humors in bodily fluids.

His, Wilhelm (1831–1904) Swiss physician. His observations of axons laid the groundwork for the neuron doctrine.

Hitzig, Julius (1838–1907) German physician. Working with anesthetized dogs, discovered that certain brain functions were localized in the motor area.

Hobbes, Thomas (1588–1679) English philosopher. Proclaimed humans to be self-seeking and hostile and that the social contract is supported because it protects people from enemies.

Hobhouse, Leonard (1864–1929) English sociologist. Concerned with evolution. Claimed that the "Mind and body have evolved simultaneously."

Höffding, Harald (1843–1931) Danish psychologist. Author of the first Danish psychology text. Conducted experimental investigations of phenomenology.

Hollingworth, Harry L. (1880–1956)   American psychologist. Held that redintegration is the foundation of a systematic general association psychology.

Hollingworth, Leta Stetter (1886–1939)   American psychologist. Studied cognitively handicapped children. Advanced understanding why they frequently became problem children.

Holmes, Gordon M. (1878–1965)   Irish neurologist. Improved the accuracy of neurological examinations, investigated neurophysiology of sensory perception in the cerebral cortex.

Holmgren, Frithiof Alarik (1831–1897)   Swedish physiologist. Established first physiological laboratory. Studied color vision and color blindness. Developed the Holmgren color test.

Holt, Edwin (1873–1946)   American psychologist. Viewed psychology as mostly concerned with specific response patterns and with relationships stressing meaning and preferences.

Holzinger, Karl J. (1892–1954)   American psychologist. Researched the area of twin development and pioneered variations of factor analytic methodology in psychological research.

Hooker, Evelyn (1907–1996)   American psychologist. Concluded homosexual men and women were essentially normal and were wrongly classified as perverse by psychologists and psychiatrists.

Horney, Karen (1885–1952)   German-born physician. Stressed that social rather than biological factors explained mental illness. Expressed feminist principles. Recommended self-analysis.

Horsley, Victor Alexander (1857–1916)   English physician. Co-invented stereotaxic device used for destruction or electrostimulation of brain tissue.

Hovland, Carl I. (1912–1961)   American psychologist. Studied communicator credibility, and order effects of data presented in the form of propaganda. Did research on memory.

Hsün-Tzu (3rd C.B.C.)   Chinese philosopher. Held that humans are evil by nature and goodness comes from training. Contradicted the ideas of Ming Tzu.

Huarte, de San Juan (1530–1592)   Spanish physician. Held that it was possible to evaluate people for physical and mental abilities with the intention to suggest best occupations.

Hull, Clark L. (1884–1952)   American psychologist. Established a rigorous behavioral system with complex notational system to explain and predict behavior.

Humboldt, Wilhelm (1767–1835)   German philosopher. A forerunner of psycholinguistics, declared that language determined a person's view of the world. Presaged Nietzchean philosophy in that regard.

Hume, David (1711–1776)   Scottish philosopher. A skeptic, denied any ultimate verification of facts. Was even critical of his own skepticism. Inspired Immanuel Kant.

Humphrey, George (1889–1966)   English psychologist. A learning theorist, saw learning as the central point in adjustment of individuals, balancing needs with reality factors.

Hunt, J. McVicker (1906–1991)   American psychologist. Studied the long-term effects of early experience using food-deprived rats in their infancy and their later hoarding behavior.

Hunt, Thelma (1903–1992)   American psychologist. Specialized in the psychometric selection of professionals including physicians.

Hunter, Walter (1889–1954)   American psychologist and Behaviorist. Invented apparatus to study animal behavior, such as the figure-8 maze.

Huntington, George (1850–1916)   American neurologist. Described Huntington's chorea (also called Huntington's disease) a hereditary disorder that results in severe physical and mental deficits.

Husserl, Edmund (1859–1938)   German philosopher. The founder and prime exponent of modern phenomenology, concerned with importance of studying immediate experience.

Hutt, Max (1908–1985)   American psychologist. Established child evaluation at the City College of New York. Pioneered in diagnosis of perceptual-motor phenomena for psychotherapy.

Huxley, Aldous (1894–1963)   English novelist. Championed the use of psychedelic drugs to achieve mystical religious experiences. Authored *Brave New World*.

Huxley, Thomas H. (1825–1895)   British biologist. Endorsed Darwinian theory of evolution; advanced the sciences of anatomy and human physiology.

Huygens, Christian (1629–1695)   Dutch mathematician. Formulated a wave theory of light. Invented pendulum clock that permitted exact time measurements and wrote an early book on probability.

Ibn Bajjah (ca 1095–1138)   Islamic scientist. Held that "The soul returns to reality by escaping from possessions." Also known as Avenpace.

Ibn Al-'Arabi (1165–1240)   Arabian philosopher. Developed a version of pantheism known as Unity of Being. Affected Western philosophers' interest in Sufi concepts.

Ibn Khaldun (1332–1406)   Arabian historian. Claimed that analyzing the past enables humans to understand the present and predict the future.

Ibn Sina   Avicenna

Ingenieros, Jose (1886–1925)   Argentinean psychologist. Helped to introduce Auguste Comte's positivism to Argentina which he called genetic psychology.

Ishihara, Shinobu (1879–1963)   Japanese physician. Known for the Ishihara Plates, a convenient and often-used test of color blindness.

Itard, Jean-Marc-Gastard (1775–1838)   French physician. A pioneer in mental deficiency; trained a feral child (wild boy allegedly brought up by animals) of Aveyron. Studied deaf-mutes.

Ivanov-Smolensky, Anatolii G. (1885–1983)   Russian pathophysiologist. Reorganized Soviet psychiatry on the basis of Ivan Pavlov's teachings. Also spelled Ivanov-Smolenskii.

Jackson, John Hughlings (1835–1911) British neurologist. Adopted principle of psychological dissolution to aphasia. Stated that epileptic movements were due to foci in motor cortex.

Jacobi, Maximilian (1775–1858) French physician. Emphasized nonmaterial (purely psychic) concepts and procedures in the treatment of mental disorders.

Jaensch, Erich Rudolf (1883–1940) German psychologist. Studied (with his brother Walter) eidetic imagery. Proposed two bio-types of imagery.

Jaensch, Walter (1889–?) German psychologist. Identified constitutional factors in eidetic types, especially hyperfunctions of the thyroid.

Jalota, Shyam (1904–?) Indian psychologist. Conducted field assessment of mental abilities. Modified a number of statistical techniques.

James, William (1842–1910) American physician. Argued that physiological changes generated emotions. Considered to be America's premier psychologist. Wrote *Principles of Psychology*.

Jami (1414–1492) Persian Sufi mystic. Held that "God is absolute truth and humans can reach this truth only through love."

Janet, Pierre (1859–1947) French physician. Published first cathartic cure. Studied hysteria, dissociation, and described psychasthenia (Janet's disease).

Janis, Irving L. (1918–1990) American psychologist. Suggested that appropriate preparations known as stress inoculation would prevent maladaptive behavior.

Jaspers, Karl (1883–1969) Swiss-German physician. Distinguished three modes of living: being there, being one's self, and being-in-itself.

Jastrow, Joseph (1863–1944) American psychologist. A popularizer of psychology. Attacked Freudian theory. Drew the rabbit-duck ambiguous figure.

Jennings, Herbert S. (1868–1947) American geneticist. Studied mutations and advanced the knowledge of tropistic behavior.

Jersild, Arthur (1902–1994) American psychologist. Specialized in developmental psychology. Described development in terms of changes in hidden phenomena of thoughts and feelings.

Johnson, Charles (1893–1956) American sociologist. Founded and edited *Opportunity*, intended to raise African American awareness. Gathered sociological data on different "races."

Jones, Edward E. (1926–1993) American psychologist. Contributed to attribution theory and theories of interpersonal perception.

Jones, Ernest A. (1879–1958) Welsh physician. An early disciple of Sigmund Freud. Author of adulatory and uncritical three volume biography of Freud.

Jones, Mary C. (1896–1987) American psychologist. Early behaviorist. First to research removal of fears of

children. Conducted longitudinal studies of child development.

Jordan, Camille (1838–1921) French mathematician. Applied the function of bounded variation to the topological version of the circle, or Jordan curve.

Jost, Adolph (1874–1920) German psychologist. An associate of Georg Müller, his doctoral dissertation led to the exposition of what is known as Jost's law of association.

Judd, Charles H. (1873–1946) American psychologist. Studied reading problems by photographing saccadic eye movements. Held that "Children need to learn to do abstract thinking."

Jung, Carl G. (1875–1961) Swiss physician. A former Sigmund Freud associate who developed Analytical Psychology that emphasized the importance of evolutionary history and teleology for understanding human behavior.

Kafka, Franz (1883–1924) Austrian author. A novelist who is widely thought to have expressed best the anxieties of a person in the 20th century with his novels *The Trial* and *The Castle*.

Kahlbaum, Karl (1828–1899) German physician. Introduced a number of terms in the field of mental disorders including catatonia, cyclothymia, hebephrenia, verbigeration.

Kallmann, Franz Josef (1897–1965) German-American psychologist. Conducted twin studies of patients with schizophrenia and declared that a genetic factor existed to explain this disorder.

Kandinsky, Viktor (1825–1890) Russian physician. Proposed a personality classification system. Wrote a book on pseudohallucinations.

Kant, Immanuel (1724–1804) German philosopher. A disciple of David Hume. Declared that psychology could never be a science and that mental processes could not be measured.

Kantor, Jacob R. (1888–1984) American psychologist. An interbehaviorist. Held that "The stimulus and the responding agent are of equal importance."

Kardiner, Abram (1891–1981) American physician. Co-founded the New York Psychiatric Institute, the first psychoanalytic training center in the United States.

Kasanin, Jacob Sergi (1897–1946) American physician. Wrote books and papers on schizophrenia. Co-authored with Eugenia Hanfmann a concept formation test.

Katona, George (1901–1981) American psychologist. A pioneer in behavioral economics and efficiency measures. Researched consumers' expectations and behavior.

Katz, David (1884–1953) German psychologist. One of the first people to combine experimental and phenomenological methods in studying psychological topics.

Keeler, Leonarde (1903–1949) American criminologist. Improved on an earlier version of a polygraph developed by William Marston. Started a private practice of lie detection.

Keller, Fred S. (1899–1996)   American psychologist. A behaviorist who developed a reinforcement theory of learning. Planned a personalized system of school instruction.

Kelley, Truman Lee (1884–1961)   American psychologist. Developed new methods for the use of statistics in experimental psychology. Constructed aptitude tests using factor analysis.

Kellogg, Winthrop N. (1898–1972)   American psychologist. He and his wife raised their son and a chimpanzee as siblings for a nine-month period to compare their mental and physical development.

Kelly, E. Lowell (1905–1986)   American psychologist. An innovator, whose research focused on longitudinal studies of adult personality and personnel selection.

Kelly, George A. (1905–1967)   American psychologist. Originated a unique cognitive personality theory and therapy based on personal constructs.

Kendall, Maurice G. (1907–1983)   English statistician. Developed a number of different statistical procedures, including the Kendall Rank-order correlation coefficient.

Kent, Grace H. (1875–1973)   American psychologist. A clinician with a strong interest in measuring. Known for developing the Kent E-G-Y Test and the Kent-Rosanoff Free Association Test.

Kepler, Johannes (1571–1630)   German astronomer. Posited his three laws of planetary motion in a fanciful work, Somnium (A dream) to avoid being accused of heresy.

Kierkegaard, Soren A. (1813–1855)   Danish theologian. Developed an existential philosophy which affirmed the primacy of existence over essence. Anticipated depth psychology and wrote on "angst."

Kiesow, Federico (1858–1940)   German-Italian psychologist. Founded Psychological Institute in Turin. Researched taste, illusions, imagery, dreams.

Kinsey, Alfred C. (1894–1956)   American zoologist. Studied human sexual behavior based on quantified self-reported data acquired through interviews.

Kinsky, Francis (1739–1805)   Czechoslovakian educator. Affirmed that teaching should be based on a student's aptitudes, and that they should learn principles rather than memorizations.

Kirchhoff, Theodor (1853–1922)   German physician. Proposed that mental disorders were personality rather than somatic disorders.

Kirkbride, Thomas (1809–1883)   American physician. Opposed blood letting and restraints in treating the insane. Urged reform of the design of institutions for people with mental disorders.

Kjerstad, Conrad Lund (1883–1967)   American psychologist. Main interests included the psychology of learning, personality, and character and the philosophy of education.

Klages, Ludwig (1872–1956)   German psychologist. Created a characterologic system based on expressive movements, especially handwriting.

Klein, Melanie (1882–1960)   Vienna-born English psychoanalyst. Researched children. Held that "Emotions are present in infants, and one can analyze children by watching them play."

Kleitman, Nathaniel (1895–?)   American psychologist. Researcher on sleep. He and students slept in a cave to see whether they could establish different diurnal patterns.

Klemm, Gustav (1884–1939)   German psychologist. Was interested in hypnosis. Suggested a mechanistic explanation for phenomenon of animal hypnosis.

Klineberg, Otto (1899–1992)   Canadian-American psychologist. Researched ethnic issues. Asserted that "Racial differences are mostly due to cultural factors."

Klopfer, Bruno (1900–1971)   German-American psychologist. A Jungian therapist who specialized in the administration and interpretation of the Rorschach Technique.

Kluckhohn, Clyde (1905–1960)   American anthropologist. Concerned with social adjustment, emphasized the important role of goal attainment of individuals in a social environment.

Kluckhohn, Florence R. (1905–?)   American sociologist. Analyzed problems faced by dual-career women. Suggested that patterns of values of "subcultures" differed from middle mainstream groups.

Klüver, Heinrich (1897–1979)   German-born American physician. Co-discoverer of the Klüver-Bucy syndrome.

Koch, Helen Lois (1895–1977)   American psychologist. Contributed to child development research, and practical work in child welfare. Authored *Twins and Twin Relations*.

Koch, Sigmund (1917–1996)   American psychologist. Edited *Psychology: A Study of a Science*, which helped to define status of mid-century psychology.

Koelliker   **Kölliker**

Koffka, Kurt (1886–1941)   German-American psychologist. A co-founder of the Gestalt movement, applied Gestalt principles in studying psychological development.

Kohlberg, Lawrence (1927–1987)   American psychologist. In a Piagetian tradition, developed a psychology of moral development. Affirmed that development proceeded in sequences of stages.

Köhler, Wolfgang (1887–1967)   Estonian-American psychologist. A Gestaltist. Discovered that some animals, especially chimpanzees, solved problems by insight.

Kohs, Samuel C. (1890–1984)   American psychologist. His main interest was psychology applied to social problems and the measurement of intelligence.

Kohut, Heinz (1913–1981)   Austrian-American physician. Developed a "self" theory which challenged the ideas of Sigmund Freud. Emphasized narcissistic lines of development.

Kölliker, Rudolf von (1817–1905) Swiss biologist. Published the first book on comparative anatomy. Gave evidence that spinal nerves went to the brain. Also spelled Koelliker.

König, Arthur (1856–1901) German physicist. Postulated that curves of brightness are a function of wavelength. Added 8,000 items to the second edition of Helmholtz's *Physiological Optics*.

Konorski, Jerzy (1903–1973) Polish psychologist. Described what later became known as operant behavior. Rejected Ivan Pavlov's theory in favor of Charles Sherrington's views.

Korchin, Sheldon (1921–1989) American social psychologist. Performed fundamental research primarily in the areas of stress and anxiety.

Kornilov, Konstantin (1879–1957) Russian psychologist. Student of pedology (child psychology) and of reaction psychology (reflexology). His theories were based on Marxist principles.

Korsakoff, Sergei S. (1853–1900) Russian physician. Identified an amnestic syndrome as well as a psychosis affecting alcoholics. Also spelled Korsakov.

Korzybski, Alfred H. (1879–1950) Polish-born American scientist. Known for his research and writings in semantics.

Kraepelin, Emil (1856–1926) German physician. Classified mental disorders; his major divisions include: dementia praecox and manic-depressive psychosis.

Krafft-Ebing, Richard von (1840–1902) German neurologist specializing in forensic psychiatry. His major work *Psychopathia Sexualis* was a clinical report of deviant sexual behaviors.

Krech, David (1909–1977) Russian-American psychologist. Known primarily for fundamental researches in animal (rat) studies involving comprehension of biological factors in learning.

Kretschmer, Ernst (1888–1964) German physician. He concluded that psychopathology type was determined by body types: asthenic, athletic, dysplastic, and pyknic.

Kries, Johannes von (1853–1928) German physiologist. Specialized in vision studies, determining the detection thresholds for hue; indicated the role of retinal rods and cones.

Kris, Ernst (1900–1957) Austrian-American psychologist. A psychoanalyst who stressed the importance of ego psychology. Was interested in the creative processes of artists.

Krishnan, B. (1917–1980) Indian psychologist. Advanced psychology in India. His main research interests were in clinical, counseling, and Indian psychology.

Krüger, Felix (1874–1948) German psychologist. Established the Leipzig Gestalt school of psychology, stressing the totality of the individual. Also spelled Krueger.

Kubie, Lawrence (1896–1973) American physician. Attempted to reconcile psychoanalytic theory and neurology to establish a comprehensive personality system.

Kuhlmann, Frederick (1876–1941) American psychologist. Worked with the mentally retarded. Published the Kuhlmann-Binet Test and was co-author of the Kuhlmann-Anderson Test.

Külpe, Oswald (1862–1915) German psychologist. Author of the first experimental psychology text. Opposed Wilhelm Wundt's theories. Founded the Würzburg school.

Kulpe, Peter (1862–1915) Russian psychologist. Wrote first psychology text on research. Wrote against Wilhelm Wundt's structuralism resulting in many studies on thought processes.

Kuo, Zing-Yang (?–1970) Chinese psychologist. Concerned with examination of the organism interacting over time with its environment. Author of The *Dynamics of Behavior Development*.

Kwalwasser, Jacob (1894–1977) American educator. A pioneer in the study of the psychology of music, co-developed the Kwalwasser-Dykema Music Test.

Ladd, George T. (1842–1921) American psychologist. Studied relationships between the mind and nervous system. "The function of the mind is to adapt."

Ladd-Franklin, Christine (1847–1930) American psychologist and logician. Developed the Ladd-Franklin color-sensation theory and theory of color vision. Criticized Freudianism.

Laing, Ronald D. (1927–1992) English physician. Took the position that schizophrenia was not an illness, but a creative way to deal with impossible family and social situations.

Lamarck, Jean-Baptiste de (1744–1829) French zoologist. Espoused the theory of genetic transfer of acquired biological characteristics.

Lambert, Johann H. (1728–1777) German astronomer. Developed the Lambert method of color mixing. Devised methods for accurately measuring light.

La Mettrie, Julien Offray de (1709–1751) French priest. Concluded "Thought and soul are identical" and "humans are machines." Repudiated dualistic concept of a person.

Land, Edwin H. (1909–1991) American inventor. Presented a new theory of color vision. Presented a new method of generating instant black-and-white photographs. Invented the Polaroid camera.

Landis, Carney (1897–1962) American psychologist. A clinical psychologist interested in psychopathology. Known for work on the startle phenomenon.

Lange, Carl G. (1834–1900) Danish physiologist. Concluded that emotions are the result and not the cause, of bodily reactions. Co-developed with William James a theory of emotion.

Lange, Ludwig (1863–1936) German physicist. Provided an explanation for personal equation differences. Some people react to the stimulus and others focus on the response.

Langer, Susanne K. (1895–?) American psychologist. Considered in early 1900s American's premier female psychologist. Focused on linguistics and esthetics. Wrote *Philosophy in a New Key*.

Langfeld, Herbert (1879–1958) American psychologist. Asserted that emotions are conveyed via art. Was a broad-based experimenter in the German tradition.

Langfeldt, Gabriel (1895–?) Scandinavian physician and psychologist. Developed the concept of the schizophreniform state and process schizophrenia.

Langley, John (1766–1832) English physiologist. Researched the nervous system, differentiated between voluntary and involuntary muscles.

Lapicque, Louis (1866–1952) French physiologist. His speciality within neurophysiology was nervous excitability. Studied chronaxie of motor fibers.

Laplace, Pierre Simon de (1749–1827) French mathematician. Advanced statistical and personality theory, especially in formulating the normal curve distribution.

Lashley, Karl S. (1890–1958) American psychologist. Discovered that brain loci can be co-opted in service of different functions in rats and that humans learn simple habits at the same rate.

Lavaggi, Ugo (1889–1944) Italian philosopher. Held that struggles are not necessary and that life should be a series of compromises with stronger forces. The big fault is ambition.

Lavatar, Casper (1741–1801) Swiss pastor. Studied physiognomy. Analyzed and described individual characters.

Lavoisier, Antoine (1743–1794) French scientist. Considered the founder of modern chemistry. Instituted social improvements in France and finally ended the phlogiston theory.

Lazarus, Moritz (1824–1903) German psychologist. Argued that truth is to be determined by psychological means. Held that research must consider ethical values of a society.

Le Bon, Gustave (1841–1931) French sociologist. Wrote groundbreaking treatise on the psychology of crowds, which varies significantly from that of individuals.

Leeper, Robert W. (1904–1986) American psychologist. Trained in behaviorism, was critical of it. Affirmed that rats could modify their behavior due to presumed altered motivation.

Leeuwenhoek, Antoni (1632–1723) Dutch scientist. Specialized in microscopic observation. Helped refute the theory of spontaneous generation, first to observe bacteria.

Lehmann, Alfred Georg L. (1858–1921) Danish psychologist. Started the first Danish psychological laboratory. Studied brightness contrast and breathing curves.

Leibnitz, Gottfried Wilhelm von (1646–1716) German philosopher. Declared synchronicity exists between mind and body; each operates parallel to the other but does not affect the other.

Leighton, Dorothea (1908–?) American anthropologist. Trained in social psychiatry, psychological testing, and natural sciences. Honored for research on Southest Native Americans.

Lenneberg, Eric (1921–1975) German-American psychologist. A student of language, especially as language relates to its biological foundations.

Leonardo da Vinci da Vinci, Leonardo

Leont'ev, Aleksei Nikolaevich (1903–1979) Russian psychologist. With Lev Vygotsky, was the first to apply the historical method to the study of mental processes.

Lepois, Charles (1563–1633) French physician. Denied a well-established belief originated by Hippocrates that hysteria is caused by a "wandering" uterus.

Lerner, Arthur (1915–1998) American psychologist and poet. Held Ph.D.s in psychology and in English, indicating his love for language. Developed and maintained poetry therapy.

Leuba, James Henry (1868–1946) American psychologist. Concentrated on the psychology of religion. Criticized Sigmund Freud's psychoanalysis. An innovator in educational methods.

Leuret, Francois (1797–1851) French physician. Proposed that variations in convolutional patterns be used as a criterion for differentiation. Named fissure of Rolando.

Levy-Bruhl, Lucien (1857–1939) French anthropologist. Concentrated his attention on the mind of aboriginal people. Viewed the people as "primitive" as their environment.

Lewes, George (1817–1878) English philosopher. Took the position that humans used their minds to control both their heredity and environment, and had free will to deal with both.

Lewin, Kurt (1890–1947) German-American psychologist. Established field theory. Held that "People are constantly interacting with many psychological forces."

Liapounoff, I. (1857–1918) Russian mathematician. Coined phrase central-limit theorem.

Lichtheim, Ludwig (1845–1928) German physician. A pioneer in modern neurology. Developed Lichtheim Test for persons with serious speech defects.

Liébeault, Ambroise (1823–1904) French physician. Co-founded with Bernheim, the Nancy School that held divergent views on hypnosis from those held in Paris by Jean-Martin Charcot.

Likert, Rensis (1903–1981) American psychologist. Interested in determining social attitudes, developed a scaling technique for reporting results of surveys.

Lindsley, Donald B. (1907–?) American psychologist. Showed the importance of the reticular activating system in linking emotion to a general arousal process.

Link, Edwin A. (1904–1981) American psychologist. Developed the Link trainer to teach people to pilot a plane without leaving the ground.

Linke, Felix (1849–1970) German physiologist. The first person to state that the human body had a cybernetic character in its functions.

Linnaeus, Carolus (1707–1778) Swedish biologist. A founder of systematic biology. His nomenclature and system for classifying plants and animals proved robust and is used to this day.

Linton, Ralph (1893–1953) American anthropologist. Was a synthesizer, attempting to understand humans simultaneously from cultural, anthropological, and phenomenological point of views.

Lippitt, Ronald O. (1914–1986) American psychologist. An associate of Kurt Lewin, participated in research on democratic, authoritarian, and laissez-faire styles of leadership.

Lipps, Theodor (1851–1914) German psychologist. Advocated act psychology, introduced the concept of empathy.

Lissauer, Heinrich (1861–1891) German neurologist. Researched the pharmacology, anatomy, and pathology of the central nervous system.

Listing, Johann B. (1808–1882) German physicist and physiologist. Published papers on vision, optics, and optical apparatus.

Locke, John (1632–1704) British philosopher. Founder of British empiricism. Endorsed and popularized Aristotelian view that there were no innate ideas in the mind (tabula rasa).

Loeb, Jacques (1859–1924) German-American biologist. Held that "Tropism explains animal behavior due to local action theory. Animals are living machines."

Lombroso, Cesare (1835–1909) Italian physician. Started scientific research on criminals by his concept of atavistic criminal types, still accepted by some criminologists.

Lord Avebury   Lubbock, John

Lord Kelvin   Thomson, William

Lorenz, Konrad Z. (1903–1989) Austrian naturalist and ethologist. Held that "Animal behavior is a product of adaptive evolution." Conceptualized doctrine of imprinting.

Lorge, Irving D. (1905–1961) American psychologist. Studied reading and intelligence. Developed scales for both. With E. L. Thorndike generated a scale of frequency of words in English.

Lotze, R. Hermann (1817–1881) German physician. Helped establish physiological psychology. Conceptualized the doctrine of local signs. Affirmed depth perception is learned, not innate.

Louttit, Chauncey (1901–1956) American psychologist. Proponent and trainer in clinical psychology, especially in relation to the psychological development of children.

Lubbock, John (1834–1913) British naturalist. Studied insects, declared that instincts determined their complex behavior. Pioneered studies of animal behavior. Also known as Lord Avebury.

Lucretius (95–55 B.C.) Greek philosopher. Took the monistic point of view that both mind and spirit were manifestations of the body.

Luria, Alexander R. (1902–1977) Russian psychologist. Researched the effects of stress on human reactions. Designed tests for brain deficits. Also spelled Aleksandr Luriya.

Lu Xingsham (1138–1191) Chinese philosopher. An idealistic philosopher who said that "Space and time are in my mind, and it is my mind that generates space and time."

Lysenko, Trofim (1898–?) Russian biologist. Adopted Lamarckianism for all aspects of science including psychology during the Stalin regime.

MacCorquodale, Kenneth (1919–1986) American psychologist. Rebutted Noam Chomsky's attack on B. F. Skinner's theories.

MacFarlane, Jean Walker (1894–1989) American psychologist. Helped to establish and advance research on clinical and developmental psychology.

Mach, Ernst (1838–1916) Austrian philosopher. Concluded that sensations were the essence of science. Established the basic principles of modern scientific positivism.

Machiavelli, Niccolo (1469–1527) Florentine statesman. Wrote a treatise on how to gain and maintain political control.

Machover, Karen Alper (1902–1996) American psychologist. Developed the projective Machover('s) Draw-A-Person Test, that calls for telling a story about the person drawn.

MacKinnon, Donald W. (1903–1987) American psychologist. Collaborated with H. A. Murray in personality research. Participated in OSS assessment program in World War II.

Magendie, François (1783–1855) French physiologist. Demonstrated how spinal nerves function. Introduced morphine into medicine. Discovered the separate functions of nerves.

Mahalanobis, Prasanta Chandra (1893–1972) Indian statistician. Proposed an economic theory that became India's economic strategy for 20 years. Founded the Indian Statistical Institute in 1931.

Mahler, Margaret S. (1897–1985) Hungarian-American psychoanalyst. A psychoanalytic pioneer of the social development of infants and children.

Maier, Norman R.F. (1900–1977) American psychologist. Researched problem solving and reasoning in animals as well as executive and leadership development in humans.

Maimonides, Moses (1135–1204) Spanish philosopher. Reconciled Greek science and Jewish faith. Concluded existence of a divine creator impossible to prove.

Maine de Biran, Pierre (1766–1824) French philosopher. Explored his own mind and concluded willed actions were the prime facts of psychology.

Makarenko, Anton (1888–1939) Russian educator. Rehabilitated homeless and delinquent children in Russia after World War I through using collectives.

Malacarne, Michele V. G. (1744–1816) Italian physician. Contributed to knowledge of cretinism. Published the first book on the cerebellum.

Malebranche, Nicolas de (1638–1715) French philosopher. A follower of René Descartes, held "Mind can not have knowledge external to itself." Soul has understanding and will.

Malinowski, Bronislaw (1884–1942) Polish-British anthropologist. The founder of social anthropology, pioneered studies of the aboriginal people of New Guinea and the Trobriand Islands.

Malpighi, Marcello (1628–1694) Italian physician. Published a study of the cerebral cortex at the microscopic level also discovered the capillaries.

Malthus, Thomas R. (1766–1834) English political economist. Wrote *Essay on the Principle of Population*, which affirmed that population growth can outstrip food supplies.

Marbe, Karl (1869–1953) German psychologist. Known for research on introspections in the making of judgments that led to formulation of the law that bears his name.

Marcel, Gabriel (1889–1973) French philosopher. Based on experiences in WW I, constructed a philosophy concerned with personal experience. Known as the first French existentialist.

Marcus Aurelius Antonius (26–121) Roman emperor. A follower of the stoic philosophy of Epictetus. Analyzed virtue and value of self-sacrifice. Viewed the soul as devoid of impressions.

Marey, Etienne J. (1830–1904) French physiologist. Invented the sphygmograph and the cardiograph. First scientific studies of avian flight inspired pioneers of aeronautics.

Marie, Pierre (1853–1940) French physician. Devised the Marie Three-Paper Test (an intelligence test). Participants were given three pieces of paper and instructions regarding what to do with them.

Mariotte, Edmé (1620–1684) French physicist. A founder of experimental physics in France. Discovered a blind spot in the retina of the eyes.

Markoff, Andrei A. (1856–1922) Russian mathematician and statistician. Offered proof of the central limit theorem. Worked on the concept of mutually dependent variables. Also spelled Markov.

Marquis, Donald G. (1908–1973) American psychologist. Specialized in industrial/organizational matters relating to social psychology, including group decision-making.

Marr, David C. (1945–1980) British psychologist. Developed the first of complex computer models to learn the details of human vision.

Marshall, Henry (1852–1927) American philosopher. Was interested in esthetics. Asserted that conscious experience was superior to introspection for understanding psychology.

Marston, William Moulton (1893–1947) American psychologist. Investigated the relationship between blood pressure and lying and thereby developed a primitive type of lie detector.

Martin, Lillien Jane (1859–?) American psychologist. Founded the first mental hygiene clinic for "normal" children and first counseling center for senior citizens.

Marx, Karl H. (1818–1883) German philosopher. Thorough materialist proposed that economic factors were primary and affected aspects of human thinking and institutional functioning.

Masaryk, Thomas G. (1850–1937) Czechoslovakian statesman. Wrote on a variety of issues including hypnotism, child psychology, and psychology as a science.

Mashburn, Neely C. (1886–1974) American physician. Developed an apparatus for measuring physiological coordination used for pilot selection.

Maskelyne, Nevil (1732–1811) English astronomer. Known for having dismissed his assistant because of difference in timing that led to discovery of the personal equation.

Maslow, Abraham (1908–1970) American psychologist. Generated a hierarchical theory of motivation. A co-founder of humanism, the "third force" in psychology and of transpersonal psychology.

Masson, Antoine-Philibert (1806–1860) French physicist. Invented the electrical telegraph. Studied the production of sounds, vision, and other phenomena.

Matteucci, Carlo (1811–1868) Italian physicist. Studied tetanized muscles and animal electricity with fishes.

Matsumoto, Joji (1877–1954) Japanese psychologist. After the surrender of Japan to allied forces, when sweeping changes were made in Japan, he participated in revising Japan's constitution.

Maxwell, James Clerk (1831–1879) Scottish physicist. In addition to work in electromagnetism, studied color-mixtures theories, invented color disks and lenses.

Maxwell, William (1581–1641) English physician. One of the first to use hypnosis (which he called "animal magnetism") as treatment, a century before Franz Mesmer.

May, Rollo (1909–1994) American psychologist. A leader in humanistic psychology, was an existential therapist, and an influential writer in these areas.

Mayo, Clara (1931–1981) Austrian-born psychologist. A social psychologist who conducted important research on how nonverbal communication and behaviors influence gender and race relations.

Mayo, George Elton (1880–1949) Australian-American psychologist. Was a founder of industrial sociology. Instituted classic research on Hawthorn Effect.

McAdory, Margaret (1890–?) American educator. Published an early test to measure artistic appreciation known as the McAdory Art Test.

McCallie, Joseph M. (1863–1942) American psychologist. Researched acuteness of hearing and vision and educational statistics.

McCarthy, Dorothea Agnes (1906–1974) American psychologist. Main interest was in child development, particularly language usage and language disorders.

McClelland, David C. (1917–1998) American psychologist. A specialist in personality theory and for innovation in measurements and research in achievement motivation.

McConnell, James V. (1925–1990) American psychologist. Performed controversial "memory transfer" research with flatworms that suggested that memories may be stored biochemically.

McCosh, James (1811–1895) Scottish psychologist. Played a major role in the presentation of the then-new psychology of Wilhelm Wundt. Attempted to reconcile religion and evolution.

McCulloch, Warren (1899–1969) American physician. Proposed principle of redundancy of potential command to explain complex behavior. Researched neural networks.

McDougall, William (1871–1938) British-American psychologist. Conceived Hormic psychology. Held that "Behavior is best understood in terms of purpose."

McGeoch, John A. (1897–1942) American psychologist. A functionalist who specialized in research on human and animal learning. Suggested that interference affected memory loss.

McGraw, Myrtle (1899–1988) American psychologist. Contributed information about the capacities of human infants. Co-twin research led to *Growth: A Study of Johnny and Jimmy.*

McNaghten   M'Naghten

McNemar, Quinn (1900–1986) American psychologist. A psychometrician, specialized in individual differences. Developed the McNemar test, revised the Stanford Binet test.

McTaggart, John (1866–1925) English philosopher. Demanded criteria for scientific meaning which became *logical positivism*. Said a statement cannot be made unless it can be tested.

Mead, George Herbert (1865–1931) American sociologist. A self-theorist. Held that "Self is object of awareness, at birth there is no self. We acquire many selves."

Mead, Margaret (1901–1978) American anthropologist. Pioneered research methods in cultural anthropology. Held that "Sex roles are a function of cultures."

Meduna, Ladislas von (1896–1964) Hungarian-American physician. Developed somatic treatments of mental disorders of the convulsive type, especially metrazol treatment.

Meinong, Alexius von (1853–1920) Austrian psychologist. A leader of the Austrian school of psychology at Graz. Established theories of assumptions, evidence, objects and values.

Meissner, Georg (1829–1905) German physician. Discovered receptor corpuscles in the skin of hands and feet.

Melton, Arthur W. (1906–1978) American psychologist. In the debate whether short-term memory was an independent or continuous process, declared it was continuous.

Mencius (371–289 B.C.) Chinese philosopher. Author of *Four Books*, claimed that filial piety was the basis of Chinese society. Held that humans were naturally good.

Mendel, Gregor J. (1822–1884) Austrian monk. Arrived at laws of genetic inheritance by crossbreeding garden peas. His concepts are still generally accepted.

Mendeleev, Dmitri (1834–1907) Russian chemist. Invented periodic table of elements. Contrary to Ernst Mach, affirmed one could that scientifically hold to existence of things unseen: for example, atoms.

Meng-tzu   Ming Tzu

Menninger, Karl (1893–1990) American physician. Author of a number of popular books in psychology and psychiatry, and head of the Menninger Clinic, a center for psychoanalytic training.

Mercier, Désiré (1851–1926) French priest. Tried to reconcile neothomistic philosophy and scientific psychology.

Merei, Ferenc (1909–1986) Hungarian psychologist. Principally concerned with group functions and leadership power, especially as it pertained to participation in wars.

Merleau-Ponty, Maurice (1908–1961) French philosopher. An existential phenomenologist, was concerned about relation of human consciousness and the physical world.

Merrill, Maud A. (1888–1978) American psychologist. Established a psychological clinic for children. Revised the Stanford-Binet Scale with Lewis Terman.

Mersenne, Marin (1588–1648) French philosopher. A Catholic monk, friend, and supporter of René Descartes, investigated the properties of sound and estimated its velocity.

Meschieri, Luigi (1919–1985) Italian psychologist. A strong exponent of scientific rigor in research in individual differences and psychometry.

Mesmer, Franz A. (1734–1815) German physician. Considered by some scholars the Columbus of dynamic psychiatry. "Magnetized" (hypnotized) his patients to cure afflictions.

Messer, August (1867–1937) German psychologist. Attempted a theoretical reconciliation of Wilhelm Wundt's content and Franz Brentano's act psychology.

Mettrie, Julien Offray de La   La Mettrie, Julien Offray de

Meyer, Adolf (1866–1950) Swiss-American physician. Established psychobiology, emphasizing the need for physicians to take full life histories.

Meyer, Max (1873–1967)   American psychologist. An uncompromising neurophysiological reductionist, presaged modern cognitive neuropsychology.

Meynert, Theodore (1833–1892)   Austrian physician. A pioneer in cytoarchitectonics. Detailed a description of the cerebral cortex. Introduced association and projection in neurology.

Michotte, Albert E. (1881–1965)   Belgian psychologist. Investigated mental processes, perception-learning and causality.

Miles, Catherine Cox (1890–?)   American psychologist. Conducted biographical studies on intelligence and assigned intelligence quotients to deceased on the basis of biographies.

Miles, Walter (1885–1978)   American psychologist. Devised practical training applications, for example, prescribed red goggles for army pilots so they would be dark-adapted.

Milgram, Stanley (1933–1984)   American psychologist. Noted for innovative social research findings, especially on obedience.

Mill, James (1773–1836)   British philosopher. Concluded that mental activity consists of sensations and ideas. Consciousness is due to association of ideas.

Mill, John Stuart (1806–1873)   British philosopher and economist. Conceptualized laws governing association of ideas. Coined many terms applicable to psychology and promoted utilitarianism.

Mills, Wesley (1847–1915)   American psychology. A senior animal psychologist, attacked E. L. Thorndike's findings, asserted that animals should be studied in the field, not laboratories.

Ming Tzu (371–189? B.C.)   Chinese philosopher. A confucianist who declared that goodness is natural to people and declared sense of right and wrong was inherent in people. Also known as Meng-tzu.

Minkowski, Oscar (1858–1931)   German physician. Reported psychological experiments with human fetuses.

Mira y Lopez, Emilio (1896–1964)   Spanish physician. Founder of applied psychology in Spain. Developed the Myokinetic Personality Test (MKP), a culture-free personality test.

Mises, Dr.   A pseudonym used by Gustav Fechner.

Misiak, Henryk (1911–1992)   Polish-American psychologist. An experimental perception researcher. Discovered that critical flicker fusion decreases with age.

Mitchell, Silas W. (1829–1914)   American physician. While a surgeon in the Civil War, developed Mitchell Rest Cure to treat "nervous problems."

M'Naghten, Daniel (1813–1865)   English murderer. The first individual found not guilty of murder by reason of insanity.

Möbius, Paul J. (1853–1907)   German physician. Studied pathology in superior men, especially sexual deviations. Also spelled Moebius.

Moede, Walter, (1888–1958)   German psychologist. An early social and industrial psychologist.

Moll, Albert (1862–1939)   German physician. Introduced hypnosis to Germany and studied spiritualism, sexual pathology, and criminology. First to scientifically study sexual development.

Molyneux, William (1656–1698)   Irish astronomer. Posed the question of whether a person born blind who regained sight could identify shapes by sight alone that had only been known by touch.

Moniz, Egas (1874–1955)   Portuguese physician. Performed the first frontal leucotomy (lobotomy) on a psychiatric patient.

Montaigne, Michel de (1533–1592)   French philosopher. Affirmed common experience and aspirations of humans. Held that reason alone could not be trusted but experience was best teacher.

Montesquieu, Charles (1689–1735)   French philosopher. Author of *The Spirit of Laws*, which analyzed political and social structures and helped initiate the Enlightenment (Age of Reason).

Montessori, Maria (1870–1952)   Italian physician. Established and directed a state orthophrenic school in Rome for handicapped children.

Moore, Kate Gordon (1878–1961)   American psychologist. Researched in the areas of memory, attention, vision, and esthetics. Published textbooks on educational psychology and esthetics.

Morel, Benedict A. (1809–1873)   French physician. Held that "Mental diseases are hereditary and are evident by their obvious physical signs."

Moreno, Jacob L. (1892–1974)   Austrian-American physician. A group therapist, developed psychodrama, sociodrama, and methods for analysis of groups.

Morgagni, Giovanni (1682–1771)   Italian physician. Discovered a link between lesions in the brain and clinical abnormalities of speech.

Morgan, Clifford T. (1915–1976)   American psychologist. A physiological psychologist, studied effects of hunger on the brain and contributed to human engineering research.

Morgan, Conway Lloyd (1852–1936)   British-American psychologist. Held that animal behavior is best explained by the simplest alternative.

Morita, Shoma (1874–1938)   Japanese physician. Originated Morita therapy, stressing rest.

Moro, Ernst (1874–1951)   Austrian pediatrician. Researched digestive problems of children.

Mosso, Angelo (1846–1910)   Italian physician. Demonstrated that toxic substances in blood caused fatigue. Considered to be the founder of sports psychology. Created Mosso ergograph.

Mouchet, Enrique (1886–1977)   Argentinean psychologist. Did important research on perception and started the first journal of psychology in Latin America.

Mowrer, O. Hobart (1907–1982)   American psychologist. Known for the two-factor theory of learning as well as a device controlling nocturnal enuresis. Stressed sin that had not been confessed caused neuroses.

Mudd, Emily Hartshorne (1898–?)   American psychologist. Expert and authority on marriage counseling, and family and marital therapy.

Muenzinger, Karl (1885–1958)   American psychologist. An animal experimentalist, worked with Edward Tolman, performing experiments with rats.

Müller-Freienfels, Richard (1882–1949)   German psychologist. A prolific and popular author, generated a dynamic "Life Psychology" system based on philosophic tenets.

Müller, Georg Elias (1850–1934)   German experimental psychologist. Studied psychophysics, invented the first memory drum.

Müller, Johannes Peter (1801–1858)   German physiologist, anatomist, pathologist. Established the doctrine of specific energies of nerves. A founder of modern experimental physiology.

Müller-Lyer, Franz K. (1857–1916)   German physician. A social reformer. Probably best remembered for two illusions that bear his name.

Munck, Hermann (1839–1912)   German physician. Removed a dog's occipital cortex and the dog could see but could not recognize objects, which Munck called psychic blindness.

Munsell, Albert H. (1858–1918)   American painter. Devised the Munsell color system based on a wheel with hues equally spaced along its rim.

Münsterberg, Hugo (1863–1916)   German-American psychologist. Considered the founder of applied psychology. Pioneered studies in forensics, economics, aesthetics, and social problems.

Murchison, Carl A. (1887–1961)   American psychologist. A prolific author, editor, and publisher, edited a number of psychological journals and books. A biographer-historian.

Murphy, Gardner (1895–1979)   American psychologist. Researched parapsychology, social psychology, personality, and history of psychology.

Murphy, Lois (1902–?)   American psychologist. An early student of projective techniques, she researched the social development of children.

Murray, Henry A. (1893–1988)   American psychologist. Devised a motivational theory based on needs and presses. Co-devised the TAT technique.

Murrell, Kenneth (1908–1984)   British psychologist. Founder of the Ergonomics Research Society, conducted research in ergonomics generating practical solutions in various applications.

Myasishchev, Vladimir (1893–1973)   Russian psychologist. Rejected Russian reflexology theory. United physiological and clinical psychology.

Myers, Charles Roger (1906–1985)   Canadian psychologist. Author of a seminal article on the identification of scientific eminence in psychology. The prime Canadian psychologist of his era.

Myers, Charles Samuel (1873–1946)   British psychologist. Founded Cambridge Psychological Laboratory, author of standard influential textbooks.

Myers, Frederick (1843–1901)   English author. Interested in occult concepts and unusual unmeasurable mental phenomena, such as hallucinations. Formulated a theory of the unconscious.

Myers, Isabel Briggs (1897–1980)   American personologist. Influenced by her mother's (Katharine Cook Briggs) opinions on personality: co-author of Meyers-Briggs Type Indicator test.

Neill, Alexander (1883–1973)   English educator. Developed an extremely permissive school system known as the Summerhill method, intended for use with disturbed children.

Neumann, Heinrich (1814–1884)   German physician. Decried attempt to classify mental disorders and suggested a single classification for all disorders.

Neumann, John von (1903–1957)   Hungarian-American mathematician. In psychology, known for discussions of similarities and differences of brains and computers.

Newcomb, Theodore (1903–1984)   American psychologist. Showed interpersonal and intrapersonal events were dependent, each affecting the other; social class affects social attitudes.

Newton, Isaac (1642–1727)   English scientist. Experimented with optics. Proposed the first two laws of color mixture. Noted persistence of sensations after stimuli ceased.

Neyman, Jerzy (1894–?)   Rumanian-American statistician. Devised and named confidence limits. With Egon Pearson developed further R. A. Fisher's likelihood ratio test.

Nicholas of Autrecourt (1300–1356?)   French theologian. A humanist and follower of William of Ockham. Espoused Thomistic doctrine that all that humans can know comes through the senses.

Nietzsche, Friedrich Wilhelm (1844–1900)   German philosopher. Developed notion of sublimation, the id, repression, unconscious motivation, and other constructs adopted in later psychoanalysis.

Nissen, Henry (1901–1958)   American psychologist. Worked mostly with chimpanzees, studying their complex behavior in perception and learning.

Nuttin, Joseph (1909–1988)   Belgian psychologist. Held that "Motives are processed as plans, projects, tasks. Future prospects are behaviorally important."

Obonai, Tarao (1899–1968)   Japanese psychologist. An eclectic researcher, specialized in perception based on the concepts of Ivan Pavlov, Ewald Hering, and Wolfgang Köhler.

Occam, William of (1280–1349)   English philosopher. Stated that explanatory entities must not be multiplied beyond necessity—the law of parsimony. Also spelled Ocham, Ockham.

Ochorowicz, Julian (1850–1917) Polish psychologist. The first to lecture in Poland on psychophysics. Established an International Congress which met in Paris in 1889.

Ockham, William of Occam, William of

O'Connor, Johnson (1891–1973) American psychologist. Specialized in psychometry, particularly in industry, ran a general testing service in New York, and developed tests.

Oersted, Hans Christian (1777–1851) Danish physicist. Co-inventor with Johann Schweiger of the galvanometer used in studying animal electricity.

Ogden, Charles (1889–1957) English linguist. Originated *Basic English*, intended to be a logical, simple, standard means of communication. He was a follower of Jeremy Bentham.

Ohm, Georg S. (1787–1854) German physicist. Developed, with Hermann Helmholtz, the resonance theory of hearing.

Okonji, Michael (1936–1975) Nigerian psychologist. Researched Piagetian intellectual development and child-rearing.

Olds, James (1922–1976) American psychologist. Pioneer in brain recording and brain manipulation in freely behaving animals. Mapped pleasure centers in rats' brains.

Origen (185–254) Egyptian theologist. Differentiated between rational soul (cognitive—higher senses) and animal soul (physiological reactions).

Ortega y Gasset, José (1883–1955) Spanish philosopher. Humanist who influenced Spanish thinking. Held that a person's life here and now is the basic reality.

Osgood, Charles E. (1916–1991) American psychologist. Studied meaning, his research on semantic space provided a new technique for understanding words and concepts: the semantic differential.

Ostwald, Friedrich Wilhelm (1853–1932) German chemist. Generated a color system by means of which any color can be produced. Received Nobel Prize in 1909 for work with catalysts.

Otis, Arthur S. (1886–1963) American psychologist. Developed a model for tests that was later adapted by the Robert Yerkes group into the Army Alpha and Army Beta tests used during World War I.

Panizza, Barthelmeo (1785–1867) Italian physician. Discovered the pathway from the eyes to the brain. Showed that fibers crossed, and lesions on brain affected the eye on other side.

Papez, James W. (1883–1958) American physician. Proposed a physiological mechanism for emotion that was further developed by Paul MacLean. Wrote *Comparative Neurology*.

Paracelsus, Philippus Aureolus (1493–1541) Swiss-German physician. Opposed witch hunting. Used pharmaceuticals in treating mental disorders.

Pareto, Vilfredo (1848–1923) Italian sociologist. Declared that all societies eventually must change by revolutions because they tend to be run by a minority of the rich and powerful.

Parkinson, James (1755–1824) English physician. Identified paralysis agitans, then called "shaking palsy."

Parsons, John (1868–1957) English physician. An experimenter in optics and vision. Introduced terms such as photopia (daylight vision) and scotopia (twilight vision).

Pascal, Blaise (1623–1662) French mathematician. Developed a calculating machine. With Fermat, invented theories of probability. Was an experimentalist of the first rank.

Paterson, Donald G. (1892–1961) American psychologist. leader in applied psychology, especially student counseling and the measurement of intelligence.

Pavlov, Ivan P. (1849–1936) Russian physiologist. Demonstrated that a neutral stimulus (a bell) could activate responses (salivation) that reacted to a natural stimulus (food) to experimental dogs.

Pearson, Karl (1857–1936) English statistician. Invented statistical methods among which was correlation. Coined the phrase standard deviation.

Peckham, George (1845–1914) American biologist. A pioneer observer of animal behavior. His main interest was insects, particularly spiders and wasps.

Peirce, Charles S. (1839–1914) American philosopher and logician. Held that "Pragmatism is a theory of meaning, not truth. Concepts must have practical effects."

Penfield, Wilder (1891–1976) Canadian physician. Developed a treatment for some forms of epilepsy. Discovered that stimulation of cortex evoked flashback memories.

Penrose, Lionel (1898–1972) British physician. Concentrated on the study of mental deficits, especially Down syndrome.

Perls, (Fritz) Fredrick R. (1893–1970) German-American physician. Established Gestalt Therapy that stressed here-and-now processes to achieve emotional growth and maturity.

Perry, Ralph (1876–1957) American psychologist. Held that introspection could be predicted from observation. Argued the mind within was similar to the mind outside.

Pestalozzi, Johann (1746–1827) Swiss educator. A theorist who started a number of schools based on the concept that children should be taught according to their basic character and aptitudes.

Peter of Spain (1225–1277) Spanish-Italian philosopher. Wrote a health manual suggesting steps to determine the efficacy of medications. Also known as Petrus Hispanus. Became Pope John XXI.

Peterson, Joseph (1878–1935) American psychologist. Investigated learning and individual differences. Did research on acoustics.

Petrus Hispanus   Peter of Spain

Pfaffman, Carl (1913–1994)   American psychologist. His main interest was in the areas of taste and smell; explored the relationship of their physiological and psychological aspects.

Pflüger, Eduard (1829–1910)   German physiologist. Employed electric stimulation of motor nerves. Coined the terms anelectrotonus, catelectrotonus.

Pfungst, Oskar (1874–1932)   German psychologist. Discovered that Clever Hans (a horse) was responding to inadvertent signals given by his trainer and was not able to understand words.

Phillips, E. Lakin (1915–1994)   American psychologist. A psychotherapist whose motto was "Change the environment and you change behavior."

Piaget, Jean (1896–1980)   Swiss psychologist. Conducted extensive observational studies of his own children. Formulated influential stage theory of cognitive development.

Piderit, Theodor (1826–1912)   German anatomist. Developed a theory of expressive movements, especially facial expressions. Showed with drawings how combinations changed facial features.

Piéron, Henri (1881–1964)   French psychologist. A behaviorist concerned with activities of organism and their sensory-motor relations to the environment.

Pillsbury, Walter Bowers (1872–1960)   American psychologist. Known as an eclectic researcher and historian of psychology. Was also an educational reformer.

Piltz, Jan (1870–1931)   Polish physician. Researched the cortical control of pupils and the symptomatology of nervous disorders, especially pupillary symptoms.

Pilzecker, Alfons (1865–1920)   German psychologist. Assistant to and collaborator with Georg Muller. Co-formulator of the consolidation theory of memory.

Pinel, Philippe (1745–1826)   French physician. Opposed the then popular doctrine of phrenology. Established a humanistic regimen in mental hospitals.

Pintner, Rudolf (1884–1942)   American psychologist. A pioneer in mental testing, collaborated on the Pintner-Paterson Performance tests as well as other intelligence tests.

Piotrowski, Zygmunt A. (1904–1985)   Polish-American psychologist. Researched personality and described a unique system for interpreting the Rorschach inkblots.

Piper, Hans E. (1877–1915)   German physiologist. Conducted physiological studies. Formulated a law of luminance.

Plateau, Joseph A. (1801–1883)   Belgian physicist. Studied color vision, color mixing and stroboscope viewing. Wrote a book on visual perception.

Plater, Felix (1536–1614)   German physician. Thought that some mental disorders were due to brain lesions and some to demonic possession.

Plato (ca 428–347 B.C.)   Greek philosopher. Pupil of Socrates, teacher of Aristotle. Thought brain the site of the mind. Three aspects of the psyche or soul were reason, feeling and appetite.

Plotinus (204–270)   Greek philosopher. An introspectionist, Established a neo-Platonic school of thought. Discussed nature of the soul-body interaction. Conceptualized the subconscious.

Plutarch (?48–?119)   Greek philosopher. Wrote biographies of Greek and Roman personages and distinguished between rational spirit (nous) and soul (psyche) which was the basis of life.

Poggendorff, Johann Ca. (1796–1877)   German physicist. Known as the editor of a journal of chemistry and physics for 52 years. Concentrated on the history of science.

Poincaré, Jules (1854–1912)   French philosopher. Assumed that "Creativity is due to unconscious selection of opportunities due to prior experiences and learning."

Poisson, Siméon (1781–1840)   French mathematician. Described a mathematical distribution, called the Poisson distribution, that was lost for sixty years.

Polanyi, Michael (1891–1976)   Hungarian physician. Made contributions to physiology and was concerned with the concept of tacit knowledge and religion.

Polyak, Stephan (1889–1955)   Yugoslav-American physician. An expert on the anatomy of the visual system of vertebrates.

Ponzo, Mario (1882–1960)   Italian psychologist. Originally was interested in the touch sensations, later pioneered applied psychology in Italy. Researched breathing activity.

Popper, Karl (1902–?)   Austrian philosopher. Exponent of rationalism, attacked assumptions of logical positivism. Advocated tests of falsifiability to test theories.

Porter, Noah (1811–1894)   American philosopher. Author of the *Science of Man* and *Human Intellect*. Compared the psychology of Wilhelm Wundt and others with philosophic doctrines.

Porteus, Stanley D. (1883–1972)   Australian-American psychologist. Devised maze tests to be culture free intelligence tests. Pioneered cross-cultural intelligence research.

Pratt, Joseph (1872–1956)   American physician. Considered the founder of group psychotherapy because of his creation of the "class method" for the treatment of tuberculosis.

Pressey, Sidney L. (1888–1979)   American psychologist. Inventor of the first teaching machine in 1925, was a researcher and innovator in the field of education.

Preyer, Wilhelm T. (1841–1897)   German physiologist. Researched color vision, hearing and hypnosis. Wrote about his own child's development in *The Mind of a Child*.

Priestley, Joseph (1733–1804)   English chemist. A follower of David Hartley, was an associationist. Investigated color vision.

Prince, Morton (1854–1929) American physician. Investigated unusual aspects of personality such as hysteria and multiple personalities.

Pritchard, James (1786–1848) English physician. Developed the concept of "moral insanity," a term that later became "psychopathic inferiority" and then "sociopathy."

Prochaska, Georg or Jiri (1749–1820) Czech-Austrian physiologist. An early investigator of reflexes, thought that reflexes involved brain action.

Proshansky, Harold (1920–1990) American psychologist. An experimental social psychologist, was concerned with topics such asocial conflict, later interested in environmental issues.

Protagoras (ca 485 B.C.) Greek philosopher. Most famous of the sophists, he intended to teach virtue in people. Known for the statement "Man is the measure of all things."

Pulfrich, Carl P. (1858–1927) German physicist. Was interested in perception and optics. Researched photometry.

Purkinje, Johannes Evangelista (1787–1869) Czech physiologist. Inspired by Goethe's work, he specialized in vision. Also spelled Jan Purkyne/Purkinje.

Pyrrho of Elis (360–270? B.C.) Greek philosopher. Founded the skeptical school. Denied the validity of the senses. They held that any concepts might be overturned by further events.

Pythagoras (ca 580 B.C.) Greek philosopher. Held that "Reasoning is centered in the brain." His teachings influenced Plato and Aristotle.

Quetelet, Lambert A. (1796–1874) Belgian mathematician. Held that "The average is ideal form. Distributions around average are nature's errors."

Quimby, Phineas (1802–1866) American religious leader. Used hypnosis to cure Mary Baker Eddy of "hysterical paralysis." He labeled the technique "animal magnetism."

Radecki, Waclaw (1887–1953) Polish-Brazilian psychologist. Founded and organized the first Congress of Psychology in Latin America.

Radö, Sandor (1890–1972) Hungarian-American psychoanalyst. Coined the term "schizotypal personality" that had been known earlier as ambulatory schizophrenia.

Raimy, Victor (1913–1987) American psychologist. Helped to establish the scientist-practitioner model. Held that "Self-concept changes reflect psychotherapy advances."

Raman, Chandrasekhara V. (1888–1970) Indian physicist. Specialized in acoustics and optics. Received Nobel Prize. Discovered what is known as the Raman shift.

Ramón y Cajal, Santiago (1852–1934) Spanish histologist and neurologist. Held that "Neurons are the basic structure of the nervous system." Developed a gold stain to study nervous tissue.

Rand, Gertrude (1886–1970) American psychologist. Co-developer with her husband of the Ferree rotary campimeter. Invented a number of other instruments to measure vision.

Rank, Otto (1884–1939) Austrian lay psychoanalyst. Generated a version of psychoanalysis that centered on birth trauma and separation. Influenced Carl Rogers' theory of therapy.

Ranschburg, Paul (1870–1945) Hungarian physician. Studied memory. Demonstrated retroactive inhibition.

Rapaport, David (1911–1960) Hungarian-American psychologist. Attempted to unite psychoanalysis to scientific psychology.

Raven, John (1902–1970) English psychologist. Interested in measuring intelligence by culture-fair methods. Developed several tests.

Ray, Isaac (1807–1881) American physician. Influential in early development of psychiatry. Developed an eclectic system of psychotherapy.

Rayleigh, John W. (1842–1919) English physicist. Invented a formula for color mixtures as well as a method for identifying people who were color blind. Also researched audition.

Razran, Gregory (1901–1973) Russian-American psychologist. Conducted fundamental research on classical conditioning. Was a leading authority on Russian psychology.

Redl, Fritz (1902–1988) Austrian-American psychologist. Specialized in disturbed adolescents and stressed the importance of the social environment in causation and treatment.

Refi, Francesco (1626–1697) Italian biologist. Produced experiment evidence that Aristotle's theory of spontaneous generation was incorrect. Held that "Life comes from life."

Reich, Wilhelm (1897–1957) Austrian-American psychoanalyst. A psychoanalyst who developed a form of character analysis practiced in the Orgone Institute which he founded.

Reichenbach, Hans (1891–1953) German-American philosopher. A founder of the Berlin school of logical positivism. Wrote *The Rise of Scientific Philosophy*.

Reid, Thomas (1710–1796) Scottish clergyman. Held that "Minds know more than what they possess." Proposed what eventually became faculty psychology.

Reik, Theodor (1888–1969) Austrian-American psychologist. A lay psychoanalyst who inspired Sigmund Freud's *Question of Lay Analysis*.

Reil, Johann C. (1759–1813) German physician. Pioneer in dissociated personality, dream analysis, and ideas adopted by later theorists, wrote a text for psychotherapy.

Renatus Cartesius **Descartes, Rene**

Retzius, Amders Adolf (1796–1860) Swedish anatomist. Coined terms brachycephalic, dolichocephalic, mesocephalic.

Révész, Géza (1878–1955) Hungarian-Dutch psychologist. Researched a wide variety of topics in psychology including genius, music, vision, thought, and language.

Reymert, Martin (1883–1953) Norwegian-American psychologist. Established a library for research about children, later another to study aging. Researched feelings and emotions.

Rhazes (860–930) Arabian physician. Experimented with diverse methods of treating mental disorders.

Rhine, Joseph B. (1895–1980) American psychologist. Popularized extrasensory perception (ESP) and researched it for 60 years.

Ribot, Théodule A. (1839–1916) French psychologist. Thought that mental disorders are due to faulty brain functioning. Introduced dynamic psychology in France.

Riccò, Annibale (1844–1919) Italian astrophysicist. Developed a theory of vision in terms of available light.

Richet, Charles (1850–1935) French physiologist. Researched both hypnosis and parapsychology and declared both were genuine.

Richter, Curt (1894–1988) American psychologist. Concerns included the biological clock, self-selected diets, and rat poison avoidance.

Riggs, Lorrin A. (1912–?) American psychologist. Studied eye movements, visual acuity, and developed an improved electroretinogram.

Rignano, Eugenio (1870–1930) Italian philosopher. Held that memory was the master explanatory element in psychology.

Rivers, William H. (1864–1922) British psychologist and anthropologist. Did anthropological work in New Guinea. Among first to recognize shell shock during World War I.

Roback, Abraham A. (1890–1965) American psychologist. An influential writer of close to 2000 articles and books in psychology, was a major exponent of psychology of his era.

Robinson, Edward S. (1893–1937) American psychologist. Researched learning, especially retroactive inhibition.

Roe, Ann (1904–1991) American psychologist. Main efforts were in understanding people with superior abilities in various fields of science, the arts, and the professions.

Rogers, Carl R. (1902–1987) American psychologist. Developed a nondirective psychotherapy that became a dominant force in post-World War II America.

Rohracher, Hubert (1907–1972) Austrian psychologist. A personality theorist. Rejected the concept of an unconscious. Stressed importance of introspection in research.

Rokeach, (Mendel) Milton (1918–1988) American psychologist. Held that "There are three central concepts in social psychology: Self, Values, Attitudes—in that order of importance."

Rolando, Luigi (1770–1831) Italian physician. Mapped out areas of the brain. Rejected Franz Gall's phrenological assumptions as invalid.

Rolf, Ida P. (1896–1979) American physical therapist. Developed a system of deep muscle massage that she claimed had psychological benefits.

Romanes, George J. (1848–1894) English naturalist. Wrote the first book on comparative psychology, used anecdotal method to explain complex animal behavior.

Romberg, Moritz H. von (1795–1873) German neurologist. Wrote the first systematic book on neurology. Reported that patients with locomotor ataxia swayed with eyes closed and heels together.

Rorschach, Hermann (1884–1922) Swiss physician. Developed an inkblot test for the study of personality.

Rosanoff, Aaron J. (1878–1943) Russian-American psychologist. Worked with shell-shocked cases in World War I. Co-developer of the <u>Kent-Rosanoff Free Association Test</u>.

Rosenberg, Bina (1899–1971) Russian-American physician. An Adlerian who conducted research in personality theory in the area of group psychotherapy.

Ross, Edward (1866–1951) American sociologist. Created a comprehensive sociological theory; wrote *Social Psychology*, the first book in that field, as well as *Social Control*.

Rousseau, Jean-Jacques (1712–1778) French philosopher. Proclaimed people were essentially good, developed a theory of education that children were to learn but not be taught.

Royce, Joseph (1921–1989) Canadian psychologist. Concerned with correlates of emotion and with individual differences.

Royce, Josiah (1855–1916) American philosopher. A practical idealist concerned with logic, religion, ethics, values, good and evil. Stressed the concept of the unity of human thought.

Rubin, Edgar (1886–1951) Danish phenomenologist. Researched visual perception, especially figure/ground distinction.

Rubinstein, Sergei (1889–1960) Russian psychologist. Concerned with the unity of consciousness.

Ruckmick, Christian (1886–1961) American psychologist. Popularizer of psychology, he also researched physiological topics. Developed a number of scientific instruments.

Rumi, Jalaluddin (1207–1273) Persian philosopher. Proposed that the "Ultimate truth is reached by love."

Rush, Benjamin (1745–1813) American physician. Reformed treatment of the mentally ill in colonial times, thought insanity was based on blood imbalances.

Russell, Bertrand (1872–1970) British scientist. Attempted to base physics on sensory experiences. Wrote in many fundamental areas of knowledge.

Rutherford, William (1839–1899) British physician. Developed the telephone theory of hearing; postulated that the organ of Corti vibrates in phase with eardrum.

Ryle, Gilbert (1900–1976) British philosopher. Concerned with linguistic aspects of the mind and behavior, attacked the concept of the "ghost in the machine" (mind controlling behavior).

Sacher-Masoch, Leopold von (1836–1895) Austrian lawyer. In his real life and novels, pain was associated with sexual pleasure. Richard Kraft-Ebing coined the term masochism after him.

Sachs, Hans (1881–1947) Austrian physician. An early psychoanalyst, first training analyst. Concerned with Freudian interpretation of dreams, as well as art.

Sade, Marquis de (1740–1814) French philosopher. People, like animals, should only be concerned with their pleasure. Established drama therapy at the Charenton Insane Asylum.

Sahakian, William S. (1921–1986) Armenian-American psychologist. A historian of psychology. Developed an innovative system of philosophical psychotherapy called infection theory.

Sakel, Manfred (1900–1957) Polish-Austrian-American physician. Developed insulin coma therapy, a presumed treatment for schizophrenia, later discredited.

Sanai, Hakim (ca 1046–1141) Persian philosopher. Assumed that what he considered to be lower vices, such as lust, interfered with perceived higher levels of truth.

Sander, Friedrich (1889–1971) German psychologist. Demonstrated that related parts may form a total gestalt.

Sanford, Edmund C. (1869–1924) American psychologist. Invented the pendulum chronoscope. Wrote the first American experimental psychology manual.

Sanford, Nevitt (1909–1995) American psychologist. A personality theorist, the author of The *Explorations in Personality*, and co-author of *The Authoritarian Personality*.

Sapir, Edward (1884–1939) American anthropologist. Held the Nietzschean view, "Understanding its language is necessary to understand a culture." Endorsed by Benjamin Whorf.

Sartre, Jean-Paul (1905–1980) French philosopher. Considered to be one of the outstanding existentialists of the twentieth century and a strong defender of human dignity.

Sato, Koji (1905–1971) Japanese psychologist. Researched the concepts of transposition, psychopathology. Promoted the use of Zen.

Saucerotte, Nicholas (1741–1814) French physician. A neurologist who observed various anomalies due to cerebral disorders (nystagmus, etc.) Described acromegaly.

Saudek, Robert (1881–1935) English graphologist. Assumed that handwriting was not only an indicator of basic personality but also of associated social factors.

Sauvages, Boissier de (1706–1767) French physician. One of the earliest people to attempt a nosology of mental disorders.

Savart, Felix (1791–1841) French physician. Became a professor of experimental physics and conducted many experiments in the area of acoustics.

Schachter, Stanley (1922–?) American social psychologist. Developed a theory that affirmed that emotional reactions are based on cognitions.

Scheerer, Martin (1900–1961) German-American psychologist. With Kurt Goldstein, developed a number of concept formation tests.

Scheiner, Cristoph (1573–1650) German astronomer. Experimenter on vision. Discovered the visual phenomenon that bears his name.

Scheler, Max (1874–1928) German philosopher. A proponent of Edmund Husserl, he was a phenomenologist who concentrated on the importance of moral values. Inspired theories of Victor Frankl.

Schelling, Friedrich (1775–1854) German philosopher. Asserted that the physical and the spiritual were two aspects of the same entity; his ideas influenced Carl Jung.

Schilder, Paul (1886–1940) Austrian-American physician. Began a systematic analysis of Sigmund Freud's work.

Schiller, Johann (1759–1805) German writer. Known as a poet, developed a character typology that influenced a number of later psychologists including William James and Carl Jung.

Schlosberg, Harold (1904–1964) American psychologist. Concerned with a variety of research areas such as scaling of facial expressions and visual perception.

Schneirla, Theodore (1902–1968) American psychologist. Primarily interested in animal psychology, stressed impossibility of separating learning from instincts.

Schopenhauer, Arthur (1788–1860) German philosopher. His pansexual, pessimistic, irrationalist, instinctual, and predetermist philosophy was mirrored by Freud.

Schröder, Heinrich (1810–1885) German bacteriologist and educator. Designed a reversible figure of a staircase.

Schumann, Friedrich (1863–1940) German psychologist. Collaborated with G. E. Müller. Gave evidence against the concept of form-quality. Was a precursor of Gestalt psychology.

Schwann, Theodor (1810–1882) German physician. An anatomist, described the medullary sheath that surrounds most nerve fibers.

Schweiger, Johann (1779–1859) Danish physicist. Co-inventor with Hans Oersted of the galvanometer used in studying animal electricity.

Scott, Walter D. (1869–1955) American psychologist. A pioneer of personnel and consumer psychology. Spearheaded World War I classification system.

Scotus, John   Duns Scotus, John

Scripture, Edward W. (1864–1945)   American psychologist. Wrote *The New Psychology*, a manual for experimentation. Coined the term "armchair psychology."

Sears, Pauline Snedden (1908–1993)   American psychologist. Followed the careers of women who had been in the Terman study of gifted individuals.

Sears, Robert (1908–1989)   American psychologist. Conducted child rearing research and investigated effects of punishment as an inducer of aggression.

Seashore, Carl Emil (1866–1949)   American psychologist. Researched psychology of music, developed tests to predict artistic and musical talent.

Sechenov, Ivan M. (1829–1905)   Russian physiologist. Showed that mental activity had a physiological basis. Called by Ivan Pavlov, "the Father of Russian physiology."

Séguin, Edouard F. (1812–1880)   French-American psychologist and physician. Started a number of schools for retarded children.

Selye, Hans (1907–1982)   Austrian-Canadian physician. Developed the concept of the general adaptation syndrome resulting from any kind of stress.

Selz, Otto (1881–1944)   German psychologist. Researched in the area of cognition: productive thinking. Stressed the importance of the process rather than the content.

Seneca (4 B.C.–A.D. 65)   Roman philosopher. A stoic philosopher who argued the dualistic position that the soul and the body were in tension.

Shakow, David (1901–1981)   American psychologist. A clinical psychologist, he pioneered in the development of the experimental psychopathology of schizophrenia.

Sheldon, William H. (1899–1977)   American physician. A psychologist who attempted to correlate personalities with physiques (body types).

Sherif, Carolyn Wood (1922–1982)   American social psychologist. Contributed to understanding inter-group relations. Studied the relationships among social power, gender, and the self system.

Sherif, Muzafer (1906–1988)   Turkish-American psychologist. His Robbers' Cave experiment showed the effects of cooperation and competition between groups as well as rivalry.

Sherrington, Charles S. (1857–1952)   English physiologist. Studied color vision, tactual and muscular senses. Discovered reciprocal innervation.

Shock, Nathan (1906–1989)   American psychologist. A physiologically based scientist who researched basic developmental factors throughout the life span.

Sidis, Boris (1867–1923)   American psychologist. Pioneered the study of unconscious motivation. Experimented on his son, pushing him when young to extraordinary cognitive activities.

Sighele, Scipio (1868–1913)   Italian physician. One of the first to consider suggestion and hypnosis as part of social psychology.

Simon, Theodore (1873–1961)   French physician. Collaborated with Alfred Binet on the first intelligence test.

Singh, Sheo (1932–1979)   Indian psychologist. Studied the impact of urban conditions on the social, emotional, and cognitive functions of rhesus monkeys.

Skinner, Burrhus F. (1904–1990)   American psychologist. An experimenter, personality theorist, and prime exponent of objective behaviorism. Architect of operant conditioning.

Skodak, Marie Crissey   Crissey, Marie Skodak

Small, Willard (1870–1943)   American psychologist. Developed the maze as a convenient method of studying the learning of animals.

Smith, Adam (1723–1790)   English philosopher. Proposed that humans were driven by passion and regulated by ability to reason. His influence in economics has resonated among psychologists

Smith, Philip (1884–1970)   American psychologist. Experimented with the removal of the pituitary gland (hypophysectomy) on animals and demonstrated that it is a growth gland.

Smuts, Jan C. (1870–1950)   South African statesman. Developed a philosophy that is holistic, integrative, counter-reductionist, and individual. Greatly influenced Alfred Adler.

Snellen, Herman (1834–1908)   Dutch physician. An ophthalmologist who devised the Snellen Test Chart, a quick test for central visual acuity.

Snezhnevsky, Andrei (1904–?)   Russian physician. Specialized in psychopharmacology. Classified schizophrenia in terms of progression of the disorder.

Socrates (469–399 B.C.)   Greek philosopher. A seminal thinker whose impact on Western Civilization is incalculable. Condemned to death or exile (his choice) for unorthodox teaching, he chose death.

Soemmering, Samuel T. von (1755–1830)   Prussian physician. An atomist who described and named cranial nerves in his work: *The Brain and the Origin of the Cranial Nerves.*

Solomon, Richard L. (1919–1992)   American psychologist. Did basic research on avoidance reactions of animals as a function of traumatic experiences.

Sommer, Robert (1864–1937)   German physician. Tried to apply psychological methodology to psychiatry. A developer of research apparatus.

Sorokin, Pitirim (1889–1968)   Russian-American sociologist. Main concern was with the importance of love and altruism. He distinguished between sensate and ideational cultural systems.

Spearman, Charles E. (1863–1945)   English psychologist. Recognized for his use of statistical procedures to isolate and quantify elements of intelligence.

Spence, Kenneth (1907–1967)   American psychologist. Formulated and tested theories of discrimination, instrumental and classical learning.

Spencer, Herbert (1830–1903)   English philosopher. Developed a theory of evolutional associationism. Held that association integrates the differentiation process.

Sperry, Roger W. (1913–1994)   American neurobiologist. His split-brain experimentation opened a new door to the understanding of perception and organization of behavior.

Spinoza, Baruch (1632–1677)   Dutch philosopher. Developed the double-aspect theory that mind and body are in parallel interactions. Rationalist-deductive philosopher. Wrote *Ethics*.

Spitz, René (1887–1974)   Austrian-American psychologist. A psychoanalyst with strong interest in socialization of children, researched maternal deprivation and marasmus.

Spock, Benjamin (1903–1998)   American physician. Was the voice of sanity in raising infants, advised mothers to follow their instincts in terms of baby care.

Spranger, Eduard (1882–1963)   German psychologist. Classified people into six types. In addition to the physical and mental, there was the realm of the spirit.

Spurzheim, Johann C. (1776–1832)   Austrian phrenologist, philosopher, and anatomist. Identified 37 faculties of the mind, each with a cortical location.

Stagner, Ross (1909–1997)   American psychologist. Researched fascist attitudes and international relations. Developed the concept of psychological homeostasis.

Starbuck, Edwin (1866–1947)   American psychologist. Concerned with character training, did fundamental research on religious issues such as conversion.

Saint Dymphna   Dymphna, Saint

Steiner, Rudolf (1861–1925)   Austrian philosopher. An idealistic reformer who founded the Anthroposophical Society and the Waldorf School System.

Steinthal, Heymann (1823–1899)   German philosopher. In collaboration with Moritz Lazarus, established ethnopsychology. Generated the concept of the group mind.

Stekel, Wilhelm (1868–1940)   Austrian physician. Suggested the Wednesday Evening Society later to become the Vienna Psychoanalytic Society. Introduced the concept of Thanatos.

Steno, Nicolus (1638–1686)   Danish physiologist. Criticized René Descartes for his blind acceptance of the pineal gland as the seat of the soul. Steno suggested other means to resolve the question of its function.

Stephenson, William (1902–1989)   English-American psychologist. A psychometrician, developed the Q-sort technique. Interested in advertising research and communication theory.

Stern, William L. (1871–1938)   German psychologist. Studied individual differences. Introduced and named the concepts of mental quotient and applied psychology.

Stevens, Stanley S. (1906–1973)   American psychophysicist. Known for his power law. Conceived aural quantum theory. Was concerned with exact measurements in psychophysics.

Stewart, Dugald (1753–1828)   Scottish philosopher. Popularized Thomas Reid's faculty psychology. Franz Gall and Johann Spurzheim used the concepts in their work with phrenology.

Stilling, Jacob (1842–1915)   German ophthalmologist. Researched vision. Developed the first color blindness test using colored dots, later improved by Shinobu Ishihara.

Stitny, Thomas (ca 1325–ca 1405)   Czechoslovakian minister. Considered the first Czech psychologist by Josef Brozek and Jiri Hoskaveca. Wrote on humanist attitudes and ethical issues.

Stoelting, Christian (1864–1943)   American businessman. Stoelting collaborated with psychologists in the design of instruments of precision for use in laboratory research.

Stogdill, Ralph M. (1904–1978)   American psychologist. Specialized in leadership, identified physical, intellectual, personality and social factors of prominent leaders.

Stolz, Lois Hayden Meek (1891–1984)   American psychologist. Made important research and practical contributions to child development and welfare and parent-child relations.

Stone, Calvin (1892–1954)   American psychologist. Was primarily interested in comparative psychology, studied instincts, reaction to shock and reproductive behavior of animals.

Störring, Gustav E. (1903–1946)   German psychologist. Primarily interested in psychopathology. Held that experimental psychology encompassed logic and epistemology.

Stouffer, Samuel (1900–1960)   American sociologist. Known for his surveys. Senior author of a study of the American soldier, emphasizing the theory of relative deprivation.

Stout, George F. (1860–1944)   English psychologist. Philosophical speculations on psychology in the Scottish School tradition. Anticipated Gestalt psychology.

Strang, Ruth Mary (1895–?)   American psychologist. Pioneer educator in school guidance movement. Published books including *Introduction to Child Study* and *Psychology of Adolescence*.

Stratton, George M. (1865–1957)   American psychologist. Was a pioneer in the investigation of visual distortion and performed a classic study on inverted vision.

Strong, Edward K., Jr. (1884–1963)   American psychologist. Specialized in studies on vocational interests. Created the Strong Vocational Interest Blank (SVIB).

Stroop, John R. (1897–?)   American psychologist. An educator, with a strong interest in religion. Established the Stroop color-word test.

Student   Gosset, William

Stumpf, Carl (1848–1936)   German psychologist. Formulated a theory of music. Opposed Wilhelm Wundt's theories in favor of Brentano's psychology.

Stutsman, Rachel   Ball, Rachel Stutsman

Sullivan, Harry Stack (1892–1949)   American physician. Devised a cross-disciplinary psychotherapy that stresses the contextual and social dimensions of life labeled Interpersonal Theory of psychiatry.

Sully, James (1842–1923)   English psychologist. Interested in the study of children, founded a society for this purpose. Spread information to England of German psychology.

Super, Donald (1910–1964)   American psychologist. His interests lay in the area of vocational development and adjustment. A dominant voice in 20th century career psychology.

Swedenborg, Emmanuel (1688–1772)   Swedish theologian. Studied the functions of the cortex of the brain. Earliest writer about cerebrospinal fluid. Held that blood mixed with "spirits".

Sydenham, Thomas (1624–1689)   English physician. Contributed to medical classification. Insisted hysteria was not only a woman's disease. Described Sydenham's chorea (St. Vitus' Dance).

Sylvius, Franciscus   de la Boë, François

Symonds, Percival M. (1893–1960)   American psychologist. A prolific author and editor, as well as author and developer of tests and inventories.

Szondi, Leopold or Lipot (1893–1986)   Hungarian-Swiss physician. Originated a therapy system: *Schicksalanalyse* (analysis of destiny), and developed a projective test that bears his name.

Taine, Hippolyte (1828–1893)   French philosopher. A strong proponent of the scientific method being applied in ways that were at the time innovative, such as to the study of literature.

Tajfel, Henri (1919–1982)   Polish-British psychologist. Formulated social bases for social conflict based on social identity theory.

Takamine, Jokichi (1854–1922)   Japanese-American chemist. First to isolate the adrenal medulla's active principle, adrenaline.

Tarchanoff, Ivan R. (1846–1908)   Russian physiologist. Researched various areas of human physiology including X-ray effects on organisms, nervous system functions, and sleep.

Tarde, Gabriel (1843–1904)   French sociologist. A criminologist who emphasized the importance of instinctive social imitation.

Tartini, Giuseppe (1692–1770)   Italian musician. Discovered what is known as the Tartini tone or difference tone.

Tawney, Guy (1870–1947)   American psychologist. A doctoral student of Wilhelm Wundt, conducted early research on behaviorism, consciousness and religious conversion.

Taylor, Frederick W. (1856–1915)   American engineer. Founder of scientific management principles in industry. Increased efficiency by the use of rest periods.

Taylor, James G. (1897–1973)   Scottish psychologist. Mainly concerned with the paradoxical issue of a stable perceptual world in view of variable organismic and environmental factors.

Teplov, Boris (1896–1965)   Russian psychologist. Was concerned with visual processes and interrelationship between sensory modalities as well as individual differences.

Terman, Lewis M. (1877–1956)   American psychologist. Studied gifted children. Adapted the Binet-Simon Test as the Stanford-Binet Test. Researched marriages.

Tetens, Johann Nikolas (1736–1807)   German-Danish philosopher. Stressed self-observation as basis of empirical psychology. Concerned with emotional states.

Teuber, Hans-Lukas (1916–1977)   German-American psychologist. Studied psychological effects of brain damage caused in battle, using quantitative methods.

Thales (ca 620–550 B.C.)   Greek philosopher. One of the seven elders of ancient Greece. Affirmed that water was the basis of all matter. Used geometry to predict an eclipse of the sun.

Theophrastus (372–287 B.C.)   Greek philosopher. As one of the first to attempt to describe different personality types he is considered the founder of literary characterology.

Theophrastus Bombastus von Hohenheim   Paracelsus, Philippus Auredeus

Thibault, John W. (1917–1986)   American social psychologist. Interested in groups and conflict resolution as well as the evolution of group norms.

Thomas Aquinas (ca. 1225–1274)   Italian theologian. Developed a rational psychology grounded in Aristotelian principles. Strove to make faith and human reason compatible.

Thomasius, Christian (1655–1728)   German philosopher. Probably the first to do psychological research. Rated people interviewed on a four-point scale. Interested in individual differences.

Thompson, Clara Mabel (1893–1953)   American physician. Historian of psychiatry. Repudiated Freudian myths about women. Took a position between Harry S. Sullivan and Sandor Ferenczi's views.

Thomson, William (1824–1907)   British physicist. The developer of the many "brass instruments" that early psychologists used in their experiments and of the Kelvin scale. Also known as Lord Kelvin.

Thomson, Godfrey (1881–1955)   British psychologist. Regarded the mind as being made up of a series of "bonds" similar to Edward Thorndike's "connections."

Thorndike, Edward L. (1874–1949)   American psychologist. Studied animal intelligence, developed three laws of learning.

Thorndike, Robert (1910–1990) American psychologist. Had a special interest in careers, including under- and over-achievement.

Thouless, Robert H. (1894–1984) English psychologist. Attempted to reconcile religion and psychology as science. Researched extrasensory perception in psychokinesis.

Thudichum, Wilhelm (1829–1901) German physician. Isolated chemical elements from the brain. Suggested that insanity is due to poisons manufactured by the body.

Thurstone, Louis L. (1887–1955) American psychologist. Conducted research on mental measurements and attitude scaling. He made fundamental contributions to factor analysis.

Thurstone, Thelma Gwinn (1897–?) American psychologist. Contributed with her husband, L. L. Thurstone, to the development of the Primary Mental Abilities Battery.

Tiffin, Joseph (1905–1989) American psychologist. A leading writer on industrial psychology, responsible for the Purdue vocational aptitude tests.

Tillich, Paul (1886–1965) German-American theologian. Believed that "Religious questions arise out of human situations and are practical, not theoretical."

Tinbergen, Nikolaas (1907–1988) Dutch-English ethologist and experimental zoologist. Conducted research on instincts and social behavior of animals.

Tissot, Simon A. (1728–1797) Swiss physician. Popularized the "degeneracy theory," holding that the loss of "vital fluid" through masturbation caused insanity.

Titchener, Edward B. (1867–1927) British-American psychologist and systematist. Carried on Wilhelm Wundt's experiments of introspective analysis of feeling states and attention.

Tizard, Jack (1919–1989) New Zealand-English psychologist. Was a social activist who put basic psychological principles to work in dealing with children with disabilities.

Tolman, Edward Chase (1886–1959) American psychologist. A learning theorist and experimenter. Originated a Gestalt concept of purposeful behavior. Stressed a molar approach.

Traube, Ludwig (1818–1876) German physician. Introduced auscultation, percussion, and animal experimentation in medical curricula in Germany. Published papers on medical topics.

Troland, Leonard T. (1889–1932) American psychologist. His main interest was visual perception. Co-inventor of colored movies. The retinal illuminance unit is named for him.

Troxler, Ignaz Paul (1780–1866) Swiss physician. Wrote on physiological optics. Described the fading of steadily fixated visual objects.

Tryon, Robert (1901–1967) American psychologist. Known for his study of the inheritance of intelligence in rats. Developed cluster analysis, a simpler form of factor analysis.

Tuke, David (1827–1895) British physician. Was the compiler of *Dictionary of Psychological Medicine*, the first dictionary in its particular field.

Tuke, William (1732–1822) British humanist. Founded a retreat for mental patients in York, England that became the model for other hospitals; a contemporary of Pinel in France.

Turing, Alan M. (1912–1954) British mathematician. Key figure in computer design and artificial intelligence. Conceptualized the Turing machine.

Turró, Ramón (1854–1926) Spanish psychologist. Intrigued by Ivan Pavlov's work, he studied newborn animals to learn their early responses, declared early learning was based on hunger.

Tversky, Amos (1937–1996) Israeli-American psychologist. Research efforts were in similarity, judgment under uncertainty, decision making and support theory.

Twitmeyer, Edwin (1873–1943) American psychologist. Worked on the conditioning of the patellar reflex independently of Ivan Pavlov.

Tyler, Leona (1906–1993) American psychologist. Assumed a philosophical-theoretical synthesis in understanding behavior.

Tylor, Edward (1832–1917) English anthropologist. Assumed that the best way to understand primitive people is to use psychological principles.

Uexküll, Jacob Johann von (1864–1944) German biologist. Early student of animal behavior. Suggested that psychology avoid mentalistic terminology.

Ukhtomski, Alexei A. (1875–1942) Russian physiologist. A theoretician of central nervous systems.

Underweight, Bounden (1915–1944) American psychologist. Major student of learning and forgetting; author of *Psychological Research*.

Underwood, Benton J. (1915–1994) American psychologist. An experimentalist, he concentrated on the dynamics of interference and forgetting in memory research

Unzer, Johann August (1727–1799) German physician. Helped popularize concept of reflex, using verb "to reflect" in reference to reflex action.

Urban, Wilbur (1873–1952) American psychologist. A student of Wilhelm Wundt, he studied the philosophical concepts of values as well as emotions.

Uznadze, Dmitrii (1886–1933) Georgian psychologist. He established theory of set as an objective approach to the unconscious.

Vaihinger, Hans (1852–1933) German philosopher. Developed the philosophy of "as-if." Provided a conceptual framework for Alfred Adler who incorporated this concept into his fictional goals.

Valentine, Charles (1879–1964) English psychologist. Main work was in the field of educational psychology. Later wrote on the topic of an experimental psychology of beauty.

van Helmont, J. B. (1577–1683) Flemish physician. Introduced the concept of animal magnetism. Influenced Mary Baker Eddy and Franz Anton Mesmer.

Varolio, Constanzio (1543–1575) Italian physician and anatomist. Described the pons, known as pons Varolii.

Vernon, Magdalen D. (1901–1991) English psychologist. Specialized in visual perception and conducted research in the area of reading.

Vernon, Philip E. (1905–1987) British psychologist. Studied the effects of environmental and cultural factors on intellectual development. Concerned with measurement of mental factors.

Vervorn, Max (1863–1921) German biologist. An early behaviorist. Advocated the avoidance of mentalistic and vitalistic concepts.

Vesalius, Andreas (1514–1564) Flemish physician. Author of the first comprehensive work on human anatomy. Overthrew certain long-held views of Galen.

Vico, Giambattista (1668–1744) Italian philosopher. Regarded as a founder of historiography and of constructivist psychology. A precursor of contemporary hermeneutics and modern epistemology.

Vierordt, Karl von (1818–1884) German physiologist. Known for his work on time-sense. He apparently initiated work on right-wrong cases before Gustav Fechner.

Vieth, Gerhard U. A. (1763–1836) German educator. Introduced physical education to the educational curriculum and developed a theory of physical exercise.

Vieussens, Raymond de (1641–1716) French physician. His *Neurographia Universalis* (1685), was the most complete text on the central nervous system up to that time.

Vigotsky, Lev S. Vygotsky, Lev S.

Viola, Giacinto (1870–1943) Italian physician. Established physiological personality types similar to those of Hippocrates, based on a morphological index using several body measurements.

Virchow, Rudolph (1821–1902) German physician. An anatomist, he developed a modern theory of disease. The first person to describe and name neuralgia.

Viteles, Morris S. (1898–1988) American psychologist. Researched individual differences. Specialized in employee selection and accident prevention.

Vives, Luis Juan de (1492–1540) Spanish educator. Held that knowledge is of value only if put to use. Treated the mentally ill with kindness.

Vogt, Karl (1817–1895) German philosopher. An early behaviorist, who decried the use of mentalistic terms in psychology. Did extensive examinations of human brains.

Volta, Alessandro (1745–1827) Italian physicist. Developed instrumentation later used by others in electricity-based neurological experiments.

Voltaire (1694–1778) French writer. Author of the novel *Candide*, a satire on optimism. A leader of the Enlightenment, satirist, and political polemicist. His name was François Arouet.

von Baer See BAER.

von Békésy See BÉKÉSY.

von Bertalanffy See BERTALANFFY.

von Ehrenfels See EHRENFELS.

von Frey See FREY.

von Frisch See FRISCH.

von Gerlach See GERLACH.

von Goethe See GOETHE.

von Gudden See GUDDEN.

von Haller See HALLER.

von Hartmann See HARTMANN.

von Helmholtz See HELMHOLTZ.

von Hohenheim See PARACELSUS.

von Kölliker See KÖLLIKER.

von Krafft-Ebing See KRAFFT-EBING.

von Kries See KRIES.

von Leibniz See LEIBNIZ.

von Marxow See MARXOW.

von Meduna See MEDUNA.

von Meinong See MEINONG.

von Neumann See NEUMANN.

von Recklinghausen See RECKLINGHAUSEN.

von Restorff See RESTORFF.

von Romberg See ROMBERG.

von Sacher-Masoch See SACHER-MASOCH.

von Soemmering See SOEMMERING.

von Vierordt See VIERORDT.

Vvedenskii See WEDENSKY.

Vygotsky, Lev S. (1896–1934) Russian psychologist. Showed the importance of speech in human behavioral patterns. Made significant advances in educational psychology.

Wagner-Jauregg, Julius (1857–1940) Austrian physician. Initiated fever treatments (malaria) for general paresis. Contemporary opponent of Sigmund Freud's theories.

Waldeyer-Hartz, Heinrich Wilhelm von (1836–1921) German physician. Known for his work on histology of the nervous system. Coined the terms "chromosome" and "neuron."

Wallace, Alfred (1823–1913) British naturalist. Independently came to the same conclusions about evolution as Charles Darwin.

Wallon, Henri (1879–1962) French psychologist. Stressed the importance of biological maturation.

Walter, William G. (1910–1976) British-American physiologist. Brain researcher, using electroencephalography (EEG) and electroconvulsant therapy (ECT).

Wang, Yangming (1472–1528) Chinese philosopher. Held that all people should regard all things as interconnected be bound by ethical principles, and strive to be sages.

Ward, James (1841–1924) English philosopher. Subdivided psychology into three parts, cognition, feeling (affection) and conation.

Warner, Lucien (1900–1963) American psychologist. Studied animal drives, learning and discrimination. Helped develop a system to train seeing-eye dogs.

Warner, William Lloyd (1898–1970) American sociologist. Applied his field techniques as one of the researchers of the Hawthorne experiment.

Warren, Howard C. (1867–1934) American psychologist. Accepted Baruch Spinoza's double aspect theory of psychology. Edited the first American general psychology dictionary.

Washburn, Margaret Floy (1871–1939) American psychologist. Concluded that conscious processes and overt behavior were two distinct phenomena. The author of *Animal Mind*.

Watson, Goodwin B. (1899–1976) American psychologist. Studied personality, group psychotherapy, and management training. He was skeptical of the validity of intelligence tests.

Watson, John B. (1878–1958) American psychologist. Founded behaviorism, denied the value of introspection and held that "Thought is subvocal speech."

Watson, Robert I. (1909–1980) American psychologist. In later life, Watson became a historian of psychology. Developed opponent-pairs dimensions.

Watt, Henry J. (1879–1925) English psychologist. Studied experiences during acts of word association.

Weber, Ernst Heinrich (1795–1878) German physiologist. Studied sensory physiology of skin-touch and temperature, as well as muscle effort.

Weber, Max (1864–1970) German sociologist. Developed methodology for the social sciences stressing plurality of causes. Renowned for his "Protestant ethic" concept.

Wechsler, David (1896–1981) Romanian-American psychologist. Devisor of the Wechsler-Bellevue Intelligence Scales and other tests that bear his name.

Wedensky, Nikolai I. (1852–1922) Russian neurophysiologist. Studied the physiology of the nervous system, especially the role of inhibitory processes. Also spelled Vvedenskii, Vvedensky.

Weiss, Albert P. (1879–1931) American psychologist. An early protagonist of radical behaviorism. Argued that both biophysical and biosocial properties must be studied.

Weisskopf-Joelson, Julia (1885–?) Austrian psychologist. Humanist-existential philosopher. Known for her

clinical research on the TAT and her research on transcendental experience.

Wellman, Beth Lucy (1885–?) American psychologist. Researched child development, with contributions in language development, sex differences, and measures of intelligence.

Wells, Frederick (1884–1964) American psychologist. Pioneered in research in experimental psychopathology. Revised the Army Alpha test.

Werner, Heinz (1890–1964) German-American psychologist. Known for his work on the origins of metaphor and lyrics. Author of *Comparative Psychology of Mental Development*.

Wernicke, Carl or Karl (1848–1905) German neurologist. Described sensory aphasia, now known as Wernicke's aphasia. Many other disorders bear his name.

Wertheimer, Max (1880–1943) Czechoslovakian-American psychologist. Rejected associationism in favor of Gestalt psychology. Explained and researched the Phi phenomenon.

Wever, Ernest Glen (1902–?) American psychologist. Researched the experimental psychology of hearing. Co-authored text on the aural microphonic Wever-Bray theory of hearing.

Weyer, Johann (1515–1588) Dutch physician. Founder of modern psychiatry. Revived rational explanations for maladaptive behavior and mental disorders.

Wheatstone, Charles (1802–1875) English physicist-inventor. Researched light, vision, sound. Invented the chronoscope, stereoscope and the Wheatstone bridge.

Wheeler, Raymond H. (1892–1961) American psychologist. Accepted but modified Gestalt psychology; called his version "organismic psychology."

Wherry, Robert James, Sr. (1904–1981) American psychologist. Developed statistical models for prediction; known for work on factor analysis and hierarchical factor rotation.

Whipple, Guy M. (1876–1941) American psychologist. A leader in the testing movement in the United States of America. Designed a number of instruments for laboratory research.

White, William Alanson (1870–1937) American physician. Became the superintendent of St. Elizabeth's Hospital in Washington, which became a leading center for psychiatric training.

Whitehead, Alfred North (1861–1947) English-American philosopher. Asserted that intuition is the basis of knowledge. Believed people can best be understood by their emotions and goals.

Whiton-Calkins, Mary Calkins, Mary

Whorf, Benjamin L. (1897–1941) American linguist. Developed a linguistic relativity theory known as the Whorfian hypothesis, which was highly dependent on Sapir and Nietzsche.

Whytt, Robert (1714–1766)   Scottish physician. A vitalist, he played a major role in clarifying the concept of spinal reflexes.

Wickens, Delos D. (1909–1988)   American psychologist. Conducted research on animals and humans. Known for introducing concepts of proactive and retroactive inhibition in the conditioned response.

Wiener, Norbert (1894–1964)   American mathematician. The developer of the concept of cybernetics. Also proposed a method known as the Shannon-Weiner measure of information.

Wiersma, Enno (1858–1940)   Dutch psychologist. Studied mental disorders and attempted to find the biological explanations of causation.

Wilkening, Howard (?–1995)   American psychologist. Wrote The *Psychological Almanac* which in one volume contained a glossary of terms and an array of information about mathematical tables.

Wirth, Wilhelm (1876–1952)   German-Dutch psychologist. An experimenter primarily in the area of perception. Searched for connection between perceptions and illusions.

Wissler, Clark (1870–1947)   American anthropologist. Found no significant correlations between physiological measurements (such as perception of weights) and intelligence, undermining Francis Galton's theories.

Witasek, Stephan (1870–1915)   Austrian psychologist. Mainly concerned with esthetics. Was a leader in the Austrian school of act psychology and a disciple of Franz Brentano.

Witkin, Herman A. (1916–1979)   American psychologist. Researcher of body and visual cues. Described field-dependent and field-independent people. Developed the rod-and-frame test.

Witmer, Lightner (1861–1956)   American psychologist. Established the first psychological clinic at the University of Pennsylvania in 1896.

Wittgenstein, Ludwig (1889–1951)   Austrian philosopher. His major concerns were related to the issues of understanding and communication.

Wohlwill, Joachim (1928–1987)   German-American psychologist. Concerned with development and environmental psychology, he developed objective descriptions of the environment.

Wolfe, Harry (1858–1918)   American psychologist. The second American to get a Ph.D. with Wilhelm Wundt. Founded the first psychological laboratory in Nebraska.

Wolff, Christian von (1679–1754)   German philosopher. Made a distinction between rational and empirical psychology, preferring the former.

Wolff, Kaspar Friedrich (1733–1794)   German-Russian scientist. A founder of modern embryology, after whom the Wolffian body, ducts, and ridge are named.

Wollstonecraft, Mary (1759–1797)   English writer. Published the first feminist manifesto, *A Vindication of the Rights of Woman*.

Wolpe, Joseph (1915–1998)   South African-American physician. Developed a procedure of systematic desenitization as a means of reducing anxiety.

Woodworth, Robert S. (1869–1962)   American psychologist. An exponent of dynamic functional psychology. Studied personality, learning.

Worcester, Elwood (1862–1940)   American psychologist. A student of Wilhelm Wundt, he became a minister and started the Emmanuel Church movement, a religiomental health effort.

Wundt, Wilhelm or William (1832–1920)   German psychologist and physiologist. Established the first psychology laboratory in 1879. Researched experience and sensation.

Xenophanes (ca 530 B.C.)   Greek poet from Colophon. Theorized about the nature of the gods, covering the struggle between scientific naturalism and religion.

Xun Zi (313–238 B.C.)   Chinese philosopher. Theorized that the mind is the product of the body and can be modified by external sources. Held that thought is superior to the senses.

Yela-Granizo, Mariano (1921–1994)   Spanish psychologist. Specialized in epistemology and history of biological and personal behaviorism. Developed a theory of, continuum of intelligence.

Yerkes, Robert M. (1876–1956)   American psychobiologist. A pioneer with Edward Thorndike in studies of animal behavior. Established the Yerkes-Dodson law.

Young, Paul T. (1892–1978)   American psychologist. A pioneer in the study of hedonic factors as well as sound localization.

Young, Thomas (1773–1829)   British physiologist. First to describe and measure astigmatism. Discovered interference of light.

Yule, George (1871–1951)   English statistician. Developed a number of statistical procedures that have been used in psychological research.

Zachary, Caroline B. (1894–1980)   American psychologist. Early advocate of progressive education of children. Believed that schools should promote social adjustment and mental health.

Zangwill, Oliver (1913–1987)   English psychologist. Conducted research on memory, emphasizing patterns of cerebral processes.

Zaporozhets, Alexander (1905–1981)   Russian psychologist. Studied the role of active participation in children's learning.

Zeigarnik, Blyuma (1900–1988)   Russian psychologist. Discovered that interrupted tasks were remembered better than noninterrupted tasks (the Zeigarnik effect).

Zener, Karl E. (1903–1964)   American psychologist. Studied conditioning and motivation. Modified conditioning procedures. Conducted phenomenological analyses of perception.

Zeno of Citium (333–262 B.C.)   Greek philosopher. Founder of the theory of stoicism. The world as he saw it was governed by a divine intelligence. Life was to be accepted in a happy spirit.

Ziehen, Georg Theodor (1862–1950) German physician. Helped to popularize psychology, took the position that behavior could be studied in its own right without tracing its origins.

Zilboorg, Gregory (1890–1959) Russian-American physician. Psychoanalyst concerned with criminology and schizophrenia. Wrote a history of psychiatry.

Zipf, George K. (1903–1950) American psychologist. Concentrated on the study of language. Developed the principle of least effort.

Zöllner, Johann Karl Friedrich (1834–1882) German astrophysicist. The founder of astrophotometry, described the Zöllner illusion.

Zoth, Oscar (1864–1933) German physiologist. Researched basic sensations and physiological optics. Constructed instruments in physiology.

Zubin, Joseph (1900–1990) American psychologist. Specialized in research of mental disorders, principally schizophrenia, emphasizing statistical methodology.

Zwaardemaker, Hendrik (1857–1930) Dutch physiologist. Devised the double olfactometer, classified odors in nine categories.

3